2014

WRITER'S MARKET

DELUXE EDITION

includes a 1-year online subscription to

WritersMarket.com

Where & How to Sell What You Write

THE ULTIMATE MARKET RESEARCH TOOL FOR WRITERS

To register your *2014 Writer's Market Deluxe Edition* book and **start your 1-year online subscription**, scratch off the block below to reveal your activation code*, then go to www.WritersMarket.com. Find the box that says "Have an Activation Code?" then click on "Sign Up Now" and enter your contact information and activation code. It's that easy!

WM-X73NR233

UPDATED MARKET LISTINGS FOR YOUR INTEREST AREA
EASY-TO-USE SEARCHABLE DATABASE • RECORD-KEEPING TOOLS
PROFESSIONAL TIPS & ADVICE • INDUSTRY NEWS

*valid through 12/31/14

WritersMarket.com
Where & How to Sell What You Write

Activate your WritersMarket.com subscription to get instant access to:

- **UPDATED LISTINGS IN YOUR WRITING GENRE:** Find additional listings that didn't make it into the book, updated contact information, and more. WritersMarket.com provides the most comprehensive database of verified markets available anywhere.

- **EASY-TO-USE SEARCHABLE DATABASE:** Looking for a specific magazine or book publisher? Just type in its name. Or widen your prospects with the Advanced Search. You can also search for listings that have been recently updated!

- **PERSONALIZED TOOLS:** Store your best-bet markets, and use our popular recording-keeping tools to track your submissions. Plus, get new and updated market listings, query reminders, and more—every time you log in!

- **PROFESSIONAL TIPS & ADVICE:** From pay rate charts to sample query letters, and from how-to articles to Q&A's with literary agents, we have the resources writers need.

YOU'LL GET ALL OF THIS WITH YOUR INCLUDED SUBSCRIPTION TO

WritersMarket.com

Where & How to Sell What You Write

14TH ANNUAL EDITION

2014 WRITER'S MARKET

DELUXE EDITION

Robert Lee Brewer, Editor

WD
WRITER'S DIGEST
BOOKS
WritersDigest.com
Cincinnati, Ohio

2014 Writer's Market. Copyright © 2013 F + W Media, Inc. Published by Writer's Digest Books, an imprint of F+W Media, Inc., 10151 Carver Road, Suite 200, Blue Ash, Ohio 45242. Printed and bound in the United States of America. All rights reserved. No part of this book may be reproduced in any form or by any electronic or mechanical means including information storage and retrieval systems without permission in writing from the publisher, except by a reviewer, who may quote brief passages in a review.

Publisher: Phil Sexton

Writer's Market website: www.writersmarket.com
Writer's Digest website: www.writersdigest.com

Distributed in Canada by Fraser Direct
100 Armstrong Avenue
Georgetown, Ontario, Canada L7G 5S4
Tel: (905) 877-4411

Distributed in the U.K. and Europe by F&W Media International
Brunel House, Newton Abbot, Devon, TQ12 4PU, England
Tel: (+44) 1626-323200, Fax: (+44) 1626-323319
E-mail: postmaster@davidandcharles.co.uk

Distributed in Australia by Capricorn Link
P.O. Box 704, Windsor, NSW 2756 Australia
Tel: (02) 4577-3555

Library of Congress Catalog Number 31-20772
ISSN: 0084-2729
ISBN-13: 978-1-59963-732-7
ISBN-13: 978-1-59963-733-4 (*Writer's Market Deluxe Edition*)
ISBN-10: 1-59963-732-4
ISBN-10: 1-59963-733-2 (*Writer's Market Deluxe Edition*)

Attention Booksellers: This is an annual directory of F + W Media, Inc. Return deadline for this edition is December 31, 2014.

Edited by: Robert Lee Brewer
Cover designed by: Claudean Wheeler
Interior designed by: Geoff Raker
Production coordinated by: Greg Nock

CONTENTS

PROMOTING WORK

MARKETS

CONSUMER MAGAZINES 431

TRADE JOURNALS 702

CONTESTS & AWARDS 807

RESOURCES

INDEX

FROM THE EDITOR

For years, I've been working toward this moment, the moment when I get to share that I've found success as a writer using the advice from *Writer's Market* to get my first book of poems published (*Solving the World's Problems*, from Press 53). I'm very excited, but I'm not completely surprised. After all, I get an infusion of new publishing advice every year in this book.

For instance, successful writers are always quick to point out that perseverance is one of the key qualities to finally "making it." In his interview, bestselling author Wiley Cash advises writers, "Don't see rejection as a reason to stop trying." Echoing those thoughts, mega-blogger Jeff Goins says, "Don't quit. Outlast those who are lucky and outwork those who are lazy."

That work includes honing your craft, making connections, submitting your work for publication, and managing your business as a freelance writer. While there are plenty of great books that cover the craft, the *Writer's Market* team works every year to provide writers with the essential information needed to complete the other three tasks.

And now I can honestly say that I'm not only the editor of this book, but I'm also a very satisfied reader. You can find the same success as I have by working through the high points and the low, and always keeping your eye on improving your writing career.

Until next we meet, keep writing and marketing what you write.

Robert Lee Brewer
Senior Content Editor
Writer's Market and WritersMarket.com
http://writersdigest.com/editor-blogs/poetic-asides
http://blog.writersmarket.com
http://twitter.com/robertleebrewer

HOW TO USE
WRITER'S MARKET

Writer's Market is here to help you decide where and how to submit your writing to appropriate markets. Each listing contains information about the editorial focus of the market, how it prefers material to be submitted, payment information, and other helpful tips.

WHAT'S INSIDE?

Since 1921, *Writer's Market* has been giving you the information you need to knowledgeably approach a market. We've continued to develop improvements to help you access that information more efficiently.

NAVIGATIONAL TOOLS. We've designed the pages of *Writer's Market* with you, the writer, in mind. Within the pages you will find **readable market listings** and **accessible charts and graphs**. One such chart can be found in the ever-popular "How Much Should I Charge?" article.

Since 1921, *Writer's Market* has been giving you the information you need to knowledgeably approach a market. We've designed it with you, the writer, in mind.

We've taken all of the updated information in this feature and put it into an easy-to-read and navigate chart, making it convenient for you to find the rates that accompany the free-lance jobs you're seeking.

ICONS. There are a variety of icons that appear before each listing. A complete Key to Icons & Abbreviations appears on the right. Icons let you know whether a listing is new to the book (⊕), a book publisher accepts only agented writers (Ⓐ), comparative pay rates for a magazine (Ⓢ-ⓈⓈⓈⓈ), and more.

ACQUISITION NAMES, ROYALTY RATES AND ADVANCES. In the Book Publishers section, we identify acquisition editors with the boldface word **Contact** to help you get your manuscript to the right person. Royalty rates and advances are also highlighted in boldface, as is other important information on the percentage of first-time writers and unagented writers the company publishes, the number of books published, and the number of manuscripts received each year.

EDITORS, PAY RATES, AND PERCENTAGE OF MATERIAL WRITTEN BY FREELANCE WRITERS. In the Consumer Magazines and Trade Journals sections, we identify to whom you should send your query or article with the boldface word **Contact**. The amount (percentage) of material accepted from freelance writers, and the pay rates for features, columns and departments, and fillers are also highlighted in boldface to help you quickly identify the information you need to know when considering whether to submit your work.

QUERY FORMATS. We asked editors how they prefer to receive queries and have indicated in the listings whether they prefer them by mail, e-mail, fax or phone. Be sure to check an editor's individual preference before sending your query.

ARTICLES. Many of the articles are new to this edition. Writers who want to improve their submission techniques should read the articles in the **Finding Work** section. The **Managing Work** section is geared more toward post-acceptance topics, such as contract negotiation and organization. With self-promotion a

KEY TO ICONS & ABBREVIATIONS

⊕ market new to this edition

Ⓐ market accepts agented submissions only

⊘ market does not accept unsolicited submissions

☻ award-winning market

☿ Canadian market

◐ market located outside of the U.S. and Canada

◖ online opportunity

Ⓢ market pays 0-9¢/word or $0-$150/article

ⓈⓈ market pays 10-49¢/word or $151-$750/article

ⓈⓈⓈ market pays 50-99¢/word or $751-$1,500/article

ⓈⓈⓈⓈ market pays $1/word or over $1,500/article

☞ comment from the editor of *Writer's Market*

⛏ tips to break into a specific market

ms, mss manuscript(s)

b&w black & white (photo)

SASE self-addressed, stamped envelope

SAE self-addressed envelope

IRC International Reply Coupon, for use when mailing to countries other than your own big key in freelance success, there is a section of articles dedicated to this topic too: **Promoting Work**.

IMPORTANT LISTING INFORMATION

1) Listings are based on editorial questionnaires and interviews. They are not advertisements; publishers do not pay for their listings. The markets are not endorsed by *Writer's Market* editors. F + W Media, Inc., Writer's Digest Books, and its employees go to great effort to ascertain the validity of information in this book. However, transactions between users of the information and individuals and/or companies are strictly between those parties.

2) All listings have been verified before publication of this book. If a listing has not changed from last year, then the editor said the market's needs have not changed and the previous listing continues to accurately reflect its policies.

3) *Writer's Market* reserves the right to exclude any listing.

4) When looking for a specific market, check the index. A market may not be listed for one of these reasons:

   - It doesn't solicit freelance material.
   - It doesn't pay for material.
   - It has gone out of business.
   - It has failed to verify or update its listing for this edition.
   - It hasn't answered *Writer's Market* inquiries satisfactorily. (To the best of our ability, and with our readers' help, we try to screen fradulent listings.)

IF WRITER'S MARKET IS NEW TO YOU . . .

A quick look at the **Contents** pages will familiarize you with the arrangement of *Writer's Market*. The three largest sections of the book are the market listings of Book Publishers; Consumer Magazines; and Trade Journals. You will also find other sections of market listings for Literary Agents and Contests & Awards. More opportunities can be found on the WritersMarket.com website.

Narrowing your search

After you've identified the market categories that interest you, you can begin researching specific markets within each section.

Consumer Magazines and Trade Journals are categorized by subject within their respective sections to make it easier for you to identify markets for your work. If you want to publish an article dealing with parenting, you could look under the Child Care & Parental Guidance category of Consumer Magazines to find an appropriate market. You would want to keep in mind, however, that magazines in other categories might also be interested in your article. (For example, women's magazines publish such material.)

Contests & Awards are categorized by genre of writing. If you want to find journalism contests, you would search the Journalism category; if you have an unpublished novel, check the Fiction category.

Interpreting the markets

Once you've identified companies or publications that cover the subjects in which you're interested, you can begin evaluating specific listings to pinpoint the markets most receptive to your work and most beneficial to you.

In evaluating individual listings, check the location of the company, the types of material it is interested in seeing, submission requirements, and rights and payment policies. Depending on your personal concerns, any of these items could be a deciding factor as you determine which markets you plan to approach. Many listings also include a reporting time.

Check the Glossary for unfamiliar words. Specific symbols and abbreviations are explained in the Key to Icons & Abbreviations appearing on the back inside cover. The most important abbreviation is SASE—self-addressed, stamped envelope.

A careful reading of the listings will reveal that many editors are very specific about their needs. Your chances of success increase if you follow directions to the letter. Often companies do not accept unsolicited manuscripts and return them unread. If a company does not accept unsolicited manuscripts, it is indicated in the listing with a (⊘) icon. (Note: You may still be able to query a market that does not accept unsolicited manuscripts.)

Whenever possible, obtain submission guidelines before submitting material. You can usually obtain guidelines by sending a SASE to the address in the listing. Magazines often post their guidelines on their websites, and many book publishers do so as well. Most of the listings indicate how writer's guidelines are made available. You should also familiarize yourself with the company's publications. Many of the listings contain instructions on how to obtain sample copies, catalogs or market lists. The more research you do upfront, the better your chances of acceptance, publication and payment.

Guide to listing features

Following is an example of the market listings you'll find in each section of *Writer's Market*. Note the callouts that identify various format features of the listing.

EASY-TO-USE REFERENCE ICONS

DIRECT E-MAIL ADDRESSES

SPECIFIC CONTACT NAMES

DETAILED SUBMISSION GUIDELINES

SPECIFIC PAY RATES

$ THE GEORGIA REVIEW

The University of Georgia, Athens GA 30602-9009. (706)542-3481. Fax: (706)542-0047. E-mail: garev@uga.edu. Website: www.uga.edu/garev. **Contact:** Stephen Corey, editor. **99% freelance written**. Quarterly journal. Our readers are educated, inquisitive people who read a lot of work in the areas we feature, so they expect only the best in our pages. All work submitted should show evidence that the writer is at least as well-educated and well-read as our readers. Essays should be authoritative but accessible to a range of readers. Estab. 1947. Circ. 3,500. Byline given. Pays on publication. No kill fee. Publishes ms an average of 6 months after acceptance. Accepts queries by mail. Responds in 2 weeks to queries. Responds in 2-3 months to mss. Sample copy for $10. Guidelines available online.

- No simultaneous or electronic submissions.

NONFICTION Needs essays. For the most part we are not interested in scholarly articles that are narrow in focus and/or overly burdened with footnotes. The ideal essay for *The Georgia Review* is a provocative, thesis-oriented work that can engage both the intelligent general reader and the specialist. **Buys 12-20 mss/year.** Send complete ms. **Pays $40/published page.**

PHOTOS Send photos. Reviews 5x7 prints or larger. Offers no additional payment for photos accepted with ms.

FICTION "We seek original, excellent writing not bound by type. Ordinarily we do not publish novel excerpts or works translated into English, and we strongly discourage authors from submitting these." **Buys 12-20 mss/year.** Send complete ms. **Pays $40/published page.**

POETRY "We seek original, excellent poetry. We do not accept submissions via fax or e-mail. If a submission is known to be included in a book already accepted by a publisher, please notify us of this fact (and of the anticipated date of book publication) in a cover letter." Reads year-round, but submissions postmarked May 15-August 15 will be returned unread. Guidelines available for SASE or on website. Responds in 2-3 months. Always sends prepublication galleys. Acquires first North American serial rights. Reviews books of poetry. "Our poetry reviews range from 500-word 'Book Briefs' on single volumes to 5,000-word essay reviews on multiple volumes." Buys 60-75 poems/year. Submit maximum 5 poems. **Pays $3/line.**

TIPS "Unsolicited manuscripts will not be considered from May 15-August 15 (annually); all such submissions received during that period will be returned unread. Check website for submission guidelines."

BEFORE YOUR FIRST SALE

Everything in life has to start somewhere and that somewhere is always at the beginning. Stephen King, Stephenie Meyer, John Grisham, Nora Roberts—they all had to start at the beginning. It would be great to say becoming a writer is as easy as waving a magic wand over your manuscript and "Poof!" you're published, but that's not how it happens. While there's no one true "key" to becoming successful, a long, well-paid writing career *can* happen when you combine four elements:

- Good writing
- Knowledge of writing markets
- Professionalism
- Persistence

Good writing is useless if you don't know which markets will buy your work or how to pitch and sell your writing. If you aren't professional and persistent in your contact with editors, your writing is just that—your writing. But if you are a writer who embraces the above four elements, you have a good chance at becoming a paid, published writer who will reap the benefits of a long and successful career.

As you become more involved with writing, you may read articles or talk to editors and authors with conflicting opinions about the right way to submit your work. The truth is, there are many different routes a writer can follow to get published, but no matter which route you choose, the end is always the same—becoming a published writer.

The following information on submissions has worked for many writers, but it is by no means the be-all-end-all of proper submission guidelines. It's very easy to get wrapped up in the specifics of submitting (Should I put my last name on every page of my manuscript?) and ignore the more important issues (Will this idea on ice fishing in Alaska be appropriate for a regional magazine in Seattle?). Don't allow yourself to become so blinded by submission procedures that you forget common sense. If you use your common sense and develop professional, courteous relations with editors, you will eventually find your own submission style.

DEVELOP YOUR IDEAS, THEN TARGET THE MARKETS

Writers often think of an interesting story, complete the manuscript, and then begin the search for a suitable publisher or magazine. While this approach is common for fiction, poetry and screenwriting, it reduces your chances of success in many nonfiction writing areas. Instead, try choosing categories that interest you and study those sections in *Writer's Market*. Select several listings you consider good prospects for your type of writing. Sometimes the individual listings will even help you generate ideas.

Next, make a list of the potential markets for each idea. Make the initial contact with markets using the method stated in the market listings. If you exhaust your list of possibilities, don't give up. Instead, reevaluate the idea or try another angle. Continue developing ideas and approaching markets. Identify and rank potential markets for an idea and continue the process.

As you submit to the various publications listed in *Writer's Market*, it's important to remember that every magazine is published with a particular audience and slant in mind. Probably the number one complaint we receive from editors is the submissions they receive are completely wrong for their magazines or book line. The first mark of professionalism is to know your market well. Gaining that knowledge starts with *Writer's Market*, but you should also do your own detective work. Search out back issues of the magazines you wish to write for, pick up recent issues at your local newsstand, or visit magazines' websites—anything that will help you figure out what subjects specific magazines publish. This research is also helpful in learning what topics have been covered ad nauseum—the topics you should stay away from or approach in a fresh way. Magazines' websites are invaluable as most post the current issue of the magazine, as well as back issues, and most offer writer's guidelines.

The same advice is true for submitting to book publishers. Research publisher websites for their submission guidelines, recently published titles and their backlist. You can use this information to target your book proposal in a way that fits with a publisher's other titles while not directly competing for sales.

Prepare for rejection and the sometimes lengthy wait. When a submission is returned, check your file folder of potential markets for that idea. Cross off the market that rejected the idea. If the editor has given you suggestions or reasons why the manuscript was not accepted, you might want to incorporate these suggestions when revising your manuscript.

After revising your manuscript mail it to the next market on your list.

Take rejection with a grain of salt

Rejection is a way of life in the publishing world. It's inevitable in a business that deals with such an overwhelming number of applicants for such a limited number of positions. Anyone who has published has lived through many rejections, and writers with thin skin are at a distinct disadvantage. A rejection letter is not a personal attack. It simply indicates your submission is not appropriate for that market. Writers who let rejection dissuade them from pursuing their dream or who react to an editor's "No" with indignation or fury do themselves a disservice. Writers who let rejection stop them do not get published. Resign yourself to facing rejection now. You will live through it, and you'll eventually overcome it.

QUERY AND COVER LETTERS

A query letter is a brief, one-page letter used as a tool to hook an editor and get him interested in your idea. When you send a query letter to a magazine, you are trying to get an editor to buy your idea or article. When you query a book publisher, you are attempting to get an editor interested enough in your idea to request your book proposal or your entire manuscript. (Note: Some book editors prefer to receive book proposals on first contact. Check individual listings for which method editors prefer.)

Here are some basic guidelines to help you create a query that's polished and well-organized. For more tips see "Query Letter Clinic" article.

- **LIMIT IT TO ONE PAGE, SINGLE-SPACED,** and address the editor by name (Mr. or Ms. and the surname). *Note*: Do not assume that a person is a Mr. or Ms. unless it is obvious from the name listed. For example, if you are contacting a D.J. Smith, do not assume that D.J. should be preceded by Mr. or Ms. Instead, address the letter to D.J. Smith.
- **GRAB THE EDITOR'S ATTENTION WITH A STRONG OPENING.** Some magazine queries, for example, begin with a paragraph meant to approximate the lead of the intended article.
- **INDICATE HOW YOU INTEND TO DEVELOP THE ARTICLE OR BOOK.** Give the editor some idea of the work's structure and content.
- **LET THE EDITOR KNOW IF YOU HAVE PHOTOS** or illustrations available to accompany your magazine article.
- **MENTION ANY EXPERTISE OR TRAINING THAT QUALIFIES YOU** to write the article or book. If you've been published before, mention it; if not, don't.
- **END WITH A DIRECT REQUEST TO WRITE THE ARTICLE.** Or, if you're pitching a book, ask for the go-ahead to send in a full proposal or the entire manuscript. Give the editor an idea of the expected length and delivery date of your manuscript.

A common question that arises is: If I don't hear from an editor in the reported response time, how do I know when I can safely send the query to another market? Many writers find it helpful to indicate in their queries that if they don't receive a response from the editor (slightly after the listed reporting time), they will assume the editor is not interested. It's best to take this approach, particularly if your topic is timely.

A brief, single-spaced cover letter is helpful when sending a manuscript as it helps personalize the submission. However, if you have previously queried the editor, use the cover letter to politely and briefly remind the editor of that query—when it was sent, what it contained, etc. "Here is the piece on low-fat cooking that I queried you about on December 12. I look forward to hearing from you at your earliest convenience." Do not use the cover letter as a sales pitch.

If you are submitting to a market that accepts unsolicited manuscripts, a cover letter is useful because it personalizes your submission. You can, and should, include information about the manuscript, yourself, your publishing history, and your qualifications.

In addition to tips on writing queries, the "Query Letter Clinic" article offers eight example query letters, some that work and some that don't, as well as comments on why the letters were either successful or failed to garner an assignment or contract.

Querying for fiction

Fiction is sometimes queried, but more often editors prefer receiving material. Many fiction editors won't decide on a submission until they have seen the complete manuscript. When submitting a fiction book idea, most editors prefer to see at least a synopsis and sample chapters (usually the first three). For fiction published in magazines, most editors want to see the complete short story manuscript. If an editor does request a query for fiction, it should include a description of the main theme and story line, including the conflict and resolution. Take a look at individual listings to see what editors prefer to receive.

QUERY LETTER RESOURCES

The following list of books provide you with more detailed information on writing query letters, cover letters, and book proposals. All titles are published by Writer's Digest Books.

- *Formatting & Submitting Your Manuscript*, 3rd Edition, by Chuck Sambuchino
- *How to Write Attention-Grabbing Query & Cover Letters*, by John Wood
- *How to Write a Book Proposal*, 4th Edition, by Michael Larsen
- *Writer's Market Companion*, 2nd Edition, by Joe Feiertag and Mary Cupito

---

THE SYNOPSIS

Most fiction books are sold by a complete manuscript, but most editors and agents don't have the time to read a complete manuscript of every wannabe writer. As a result, publishing decision makers use the synopsis and sample chapters to help the screening process of fiction. The synopsis, on its most basic level, communicates what the book is about.

The length and depth of a synopsis can change from agent to agent or publisher to publisher. Some will want a synopsis that is 1-2 single-spaced pages; others will want a synopsis that can run up to 25 double-spaced pages. Checking your listings in *Writer's Market*, as well as double-checking with the listing's website, will help guide you in this respect.

The content should cover all the essential points of the novel from beginning to end and in the correct order. The essential points include main characters, main plot points, and, yes, the ending. Of course, your essential points will vary from the editor who wants a 1-page synopsis to the editor who wants a 25-page synopsis.

NONFICTION BOOK PROPOSALS

Most nonfiction books are sold by a book proposal—a package of materials that details what your book is about, who its intended audience is, and how you intend to write the book. It includes some combination of a cover or query letter, an overview, an outline, author's information sheet, and sample chapters. Editors also want to see information about the audience for your book and about titles that compete with your proposed book.

Submitting a nonfiction book proposal

A proposal package should include the following items:

- **A COVER OR QUERY LETTER.** This letter should be a short introduction to the material you include in the proposal.
- **AN OVERVIEW.** This is a brief summary of your book. It should detail your book's subject and give an idea of how that subject will be developed.
- **AN OUTLINE.** The outline covers your book chapter by chapter and should include all major points covered in each chapter. Some outlines are done in traditional outline form, but most are written in paragraph form.
- **AN AUTHOR'S INFORMATION SHEET.** This information should acquaint the editor with your writing background and convince him of your qualifications regarding the subject of your book.
- **SAMPLE CHAPTERS.** Many editors like to see sample chapters, especially for a first book. Sample chapters show the editor how you write and develop ideas from your outline.
- **MARKETING INFORMATION.** Facts about how and to whom your book can be successfully marketed are now expected to accompany every book proposal. If you can provide information about the audience for your book and suggest ways the book publisher can reach those people, you will increase your chances of acceptance.

- **COMPETITIVE TITLE ANALYSIS.** Check the *Subject Guide to Books in Print* for other titles on your topic. Write a one- or two-sentence synopsis of each. Point out how your book differs and improves upon existing topics.

For more information on nonfiction book proposals, read Michael Larsen's *How to Write a Book Proposal* (Writer's Digest Books).

A WORD ABOUT AGENTS

An agent represents a writer's work to publishers, negotiates contracts, follows up to see that contracts are fulfilled, and generally handles a writer's business affairs, leaving the writer free to write. Effective agents are valued for their contacts in the publishing industry, their knowledge about who to approach with certain ideas, their ability to guide an author's career, and their business sense.

While most book publishers listed in *Writer's Market* publish books by unagented writers, some of the larger houses are reluctant to consider submissions that have not reached them through a literary agent. Companies with such a policy are noted by an (Ⓐ) icon at the beginning of the listing, as well as in the submission information within the listing.

Writer's Market includes a list of literary agents who are all members of the Association of Authors' Representatives and who are also actively seeking new and established writers.

MANUSCRIPT FORMAT

You can increase your chances of publication by following a few standard guidelines regarding the physical format of your manuscript. It should be your goal to make your manuscript readable. Follow these suggestions as you would any other suggestions: Use what works for you and discard what doesn't.

In general, when submitting a manuscript, you should use white, 8½×11, 20 lb. paper, and you should also choose a legible, professional looking font (i.e., Times New Roman)—no all-italic or artsy fonts. Your entire manuscript should be double-spaced with a 1½-inch margin on all sides of the page. Once you are ready to print your manuscript, you should print either on a laser printer or an ink-jet printer.

MANUSCRIPT FORMATTING SAMPLE

(1) Your Name
Your Street Address
City State ZIP Code
Day and Evening Phone Numbers
E-mail Address

Website (if applicable)
(2)

50,000 Words **(3)**

TITLE

by

(4) Your Name

(5) You can increase your chances of publication by following a few standard guidelines regarding the physical format of your article or manuscript. It should be your goal to make your manuscript readable. Use these suggestions as you would any other suggestions: Use what works for you and discard what doesn't.

In general, when submitting a manuscript, you should use white, 8½×11, 20-lb. bond paper, and you should also choose a legible, professional-looking font (i.e., Times New Roman)—no all-italic or artsy fonts. Your entire manuscript should be double-spaced with a 1½-inch margin on all sides of the page. Once you are ready to print your article or manuscript, you should print either on a laser printer or an inkjet printer.

Remember, articles should be written after you send a one-page query letter to an editor, and the editor then asks you to write the article. If, however, you are sending an article "on spec" to an editor, you should send both a query letter and the complete article.

Fiction and poetry is a little different from nonfiction articles, in that it is rarely queried. More often than not, poetry and fiction editors want to review the complete manuscript before making a final decision.

(1) Type your real name (even if you use a pseudonym) and contact information **(2)** Double-space twice **(3)** Estimated word count **(4)** Type your title in capital letters, double-space and type "by," double-space again, and type your name (or pseudonym if you're using one) **(5)** Double-space twice, then indent first paragraph and start text of your manuscript **(6)** On subsequent pages, type your name, a dash, and the page number in the upper left or right corner

ESTIMATING WORD COUNT

Many computers will provide you with a word count of your manuscript. Your editor will count again after editing the manuscript. Although your computer is counting characters, an editor or production editor is more concerned about the amount of space the text will occupy on a page. Several small headlines or subheads, for instance, will be counted the same by your computer as any other word of text. However, headlines and subheads usually employ a different font size than the body text, so an editor may count them differently to be sure enough space has been estimated for larger type.

For short manuscripts, it's often quickest to count each word on a representative page and multiply by the number of pages. You can get a very rough count by multiplying the number of pages in your manuscript by 250 (the average number of words on a double-spaced typewritten page).

PHOTOGRAPHS AND SLIDES

In some cases, the availability of photographs and slides can be the deciding factor as to whether an editor will accept your submission. This is especially true when querying a publication that relies heavily on photographs, illustrations or artwork to enhance the article (i.e., craft magazines, hobby magazines, etc.). In some instances, the publication may offer additional payment for photographs or illustrations.

Check the individual listings to find out which magazines review photographs and what their submission guidelines are. Most publications prefer you do not send photographs with your submission. However, if photographs or illustrations are available, you should indicate that in your query. As with manuscripts, never send the originals of your photographs or illustrations. Instead, send digital images, which is what most magazine and book publishers prefer to use.

SEND PHOTOCOPIES

If there is one hard-and-fast rule in publishing, it's this: *Never* send the original (or only) copy of your manuscript. Most editors cringe when they find out a writer has sent the only copy of their manuscript. You should always send copies of your manuscript.

Some writers choose to send a self-addressed, stamped postcard with a photocopied submission. In their cover letter they suggest if the editor is not interested in their manuscript, it may be tossed out and a reply sent on the postcard. This method is particularly helpful when sending your submissions to international markets.

MAILING SUBMISSIONS

No matter what size manuscript you're mailing, always include a self-addressed, stamped envelope (SASE) with sufficient return postage. The website for the U.S. Postal Service (www.

usps.com) and the website for the Canadian Post (www.canadapost.ca) both have postage calculators if you are unsure how much postage to affix.

A book manuscript should be mailed in a sturdy, well-wrapped box. Enclose a self-addressed mailing label and paper clip your return postage to the label. However, be aware that some book publishers do not return unsolicited manuscripts, so make sure you know the practice of the publisher before sending any unsolicited material.

Types of mail service

There are many different mailing service options available to you whether you are sending a query letter or a complete manuscript. You can work with the U.S. Postal Service, United Parcel Service, Federal Express, or any number of private mailing companies. The following are the five most common types of mailing services offered by the U.S. Postal Service.

- **FIRST CLASS** is a fairly expensive way to mail a manuscript, but many writers prefer it. First-Class mail generally receives better handling and is delivered more quickly than Standard mail.
- **PRIORITY MAIL** reaches its destination within two or three days.
- **STANDARD MAIL** rates are available for packages, but be sure to pack your materials carefully because they will be handled roughly. To make sure your package will be returned to you if it is undeliverable, print "Return Postage Guaranteed" under your address.
- **CERTIFIED MAIL** must be signed for when it reaches its destination.
- **REGISTERED MAIL** is a high-security method of mailing where the contents are insured. The package is signed in and out of every office it passes through, and a receipt is returned to the sender when the package reaches its destination.

MAILING MANUSCRIPTS

- Fold manuscripts under five pages into thirds, and send in a #10 SASE.
- Mail manuscripts five pages or more unfolded in a 9×12 or 10×13 SASE.
- For return envelope, fold the envelope in half, address it to yourself, and add a stamp, or, if going to Canada or another international destination, International Reply Coupons (available at most post office branches).
- Don't send by Certified Mail—this is a sign of an amateur.

QUERY LETTER CLINIC

Many great writers ask year after year, "Why is it so hard to get published?" In many cases, these writers have spent years—and possibly thousands of dollars on books and courses—developing their craft. They submit to the appropriate markets, yet rejection is always the end result. The culprit? A weak query letter.

The query letter is often the most important piece of the publishing puzzle. In many cases, it determines whether an editor or agent will even read your manuscript. A good query letter makes a good first impression; a bad query letter earns a swift rejection.

THE ELEMENTS OF A QUERY LETTER

A query letter should sell editors or agents on your idea or convince them to request your finished manuscript. The most effective query letters get into the specifics from the very first line. It's important to remember that the query is a call to action, not a listing of features and benefits.

In addition to selling your idea or manuscript, a query letter can include information on the availability of photographs or artwork. You can include a working title and projected word count. Depending on the piece, you might also mention whether a sidebar might be appropriate and the type of research you plan to conduct. If appropriate, include a tentative deadline and indicate whether the query is being simultaneously submitted.

Biographical information should be included as well, but don't overdo it unless your background actually helps sell the article or proves that you're the only person who could write your proposed piece.

THINGS TO AVOID IN A QUERY LETTER

The query letter is not a place to discuss pay rates. This step comes after an editor has agreed to take on your article or book. Besides making an unprofessional impression on an editor, it can also work to your disadvantage in negotiating your fee. If you ask for too much, an editor may not even contact you to see if a lower rate might work. If you ask for too little, you may start an editorial relationship where you are making far less than the normal rate.

You should also avoid rookie mistakes, such as mentioning that your work is copyrighted or including the copyright symbol on your work. While you want to make it clear that you've researched the market, avoid using flattery as a technique for selling your work. It often has the opposite effect of what you intend. In addition, don't hint that you can rewrite the piece, as this only leads the editor to think there will be a lot of work involved in shaping up your writing.

Also, never admit several other editors or agents have rejected the query. Always treat your new audience as if they are the first place on your list of submission possibilities.

HOW TO FORMAT YOUR QUERY LETTER

It's OK to break writing rules in a short story or article, but you should follow the rules when it comes to crafting an effective query. Here are guidelines for query writing.

- Use a normal font and typeface, such as Times New Roman and 10- or 12-point type.
- Include your name, address, phone number, e-mail address and website, if possible.
- Use a one-inch margin on paper queries.
- Address a specific editor or agent. (Note: The listings in *Writer's Market* provide a contact name for most submissions. It's wise to double-check contact names online or by calling.)
- Limit query letter to one single-spaced page.
- Include self-addressed, stamped envelope or postcard for response with post submissions. Use block paragraph format (no indentations). Thank the editor for considering your query.

WHEN AND HOW TO FOLLOW UP

Accidents do happen. Queries may not reach your intended reader. Staff changes or interoffice mail snafus may end up with your query letter thrown away. Or the editor may have set your query off to the side for further consideration and forgotten it. Whatever the case may be, there are some basic guidelines you should use for your follow-up communication.

Most importantly, wait until the reported response time, as indicated in *Writer's Market* or their submission guidelines, has elapsed before contacting an editor or agent. Then, you should send a short and polite e-mail describing the original query sent, the date it was sent, and asking if they received it or made a decision regarding its fate.

The importance of remaining polite and businesslike when following up cannot be stressed enough. Making a bad impression on an editor can often have a ripple effect—as that editor may share his or her bad experience with other editors at the magazine or publishing company. Also, don't call.

HOW THE CLINIC WORKS

As mentioned earlier, the query letter is the most important weapon for getting an assignment or a request for your full manuscript. Published writers know how to craft a well-written, hard-hitting query. What follows are eight queries: four are strong; four are not. Detailed comments show what worked and what did not. As you'll see, there is no cut-and-dried "good" query format; every strong query works on its own merit.

Jimmy Boaz, editor
American Organic Farmer's Digest
8336 Old Dirt Road
Macon GA 00000

Dear Mr. Boaz, **1**

There are 87 varieties of organic crops grown in the United States, but there's only one farm producing 12 of these—Morganic Corporation. **2**

Located in the heart of Arkansas, this company spent the past decade providing great organic crops at a competitive price helping them grow into the ninth leading organic farming operation in the country. Along the way, they developed the most unique organic offering in North America.

As a seasoned writer with access to Richard Banks, the founder and president of Morganic, I propose writing a profile piece on Banks for your Organic Shakers department. After years of reading this riveting column, I believe the time has come to cover Morganic's rise in the organic farming industry. **3**

This piece would run in the normal 800–1,200 word range with photographs available of Banks and Morganic's operation.

I've been published in *Arkansas Farmer's Deluxe, Organic Farming Today* and in several newspapers. **4**

Thank you for your consideration of this article. I hope to hear from you soon.

Sincerely,

Jackie Service
34 Good St.
Little Rock AR 00000
jackie.service9867@email.com

1 My name is only available on our magazine's website and on the masthead. This writer has done her research. **2** Here's a story that hasn't been pitched before. I didn't know Morganic was so unique in the market. I want to know more. **3** The writer has access to her interview subject, and she displays knowledge of the magazine by pointing out the correct section in which her piece would run. **4** While I probably would've assigned this article based off the idea alone, her past credits do help solidify my decision.

BAD NONFICTION MAGAZINE QUERY

Dear Gentlemen, 1

I'd like to write the next great article you'll ever publish. My writing credits include amazing pieces I've done for local and community newspapers and for my college English classes. I've been writing for years and years. 2

Your magazine may not be a big one like *Rolling Stone or Sports Illustrated,* but I'm willing to write an interview for you anyway. I know you need material, and I need money. (Don't worry. I won't charge you too much.) 3

Just give me some people to interview, and I'll do the best job you've ever read. It will be amazing, and I can re-write the piece for you if you don't agree. I'm willing to re-write 20 times if needed. 4

You better hurry up and assign me an article though, because I've sent out letters to lots of other magazines, and I'm sure to be filled up to capacity very soon. 5

Later gents,

Carl Bighead
76 Bad Query Lane
Big City NY 00000

1 This is sexist, and it doesn't address any contact specifically. 2 An over-the-top claim by a writer who does not impress me with his publishing background. 3 Insults the magazine and then reassures me he won't charge too much? 4 While I do assign material from time to time, I prefer writers pitch me their own ideas after studying the magazine. 5 I'm sure people aren't going to be knocking down his door anytime soon.

Marcus West
88 Piano Drive
Lexington KY 00000

August 8, 2011 **①**

Jeanette Curic, editor
Wonder Stories
45 Noodle Street
Portland OR 00000

Dear Ms. Curic,

Please consider the following 1,200-word story, "Turning to the Melon," a quirky coming-of-age story with a little magical realism thrown in the mix. **②**

After reading *Wonder Stories* for years, I think I've finally written something that would fit with your audience. My previous short story credits include *Stunned Fiction Quarterly* and *Faulty Mindbomb*. **③**

Thank you in advance for considering "Turning to Melon."

Sincerely,

Marcus West
(123) 456-7890
marcusw87452@email.com

Encl: Manuscript and SASE **④**

① Follows the format we established in our guidelines. Being able to follow directions is more important than many writers realize. **②** Story is in our word count, and the description sounds like the type of story we would consider publishing. **③** It's flattering to know he reads our magazine. While it won't guarantee publication, it does make me a little more hopeful that the story I'm reading will be a good fit. Also, good to know he's been published before. **④** I can figure it out, but it's nice to know what other materials were included in the envelope. This letter is not flashy, but it gives me the basics and puts me in the right frame of mind to read the actual story.

BAD FICTION MAGAZINE QUERY

To: curic@wonderstories808.com **1**
Subject: A Towering Epic Fantasy

Hello there. **2**

I've written a great fantasy epic novel short story of about 25,000 words that may be included in your magazine if you so desire. **3**

More than 20 years, I've spent chained to my desk in a basement writing out the greatest story of our modern time. And it can be yours if you so desire to have it. **4**

Just say the word, and I'll ship it over to you. We can talk money and movie rights after your acceptance. I have big plans for this story, and you can be part of that success. **5**

Yours forever (if you so desire), **6**

Harold
(or Harry for friends)

1 We do not consider e-mail queries or submissions. **2** This is a little too informal. **3** First off, what did he write? An epic novel or short story? Second, 25,000 words is way over our 1,500-word max. **4** I'm lost for words. **5** Money and movie rights? We pay moderate rates and definitely don't get involved in movies. **6** I'm sure the writer was just trying to be nice, but this is a little bizarre and kind of creepy. I do not so desire more contact with "Harry."

GOOD NONFICTION BOOK QUERY

To: corey@bigbookspublishing.com
Subject: Query: Become a Better Parent in 30 Days **1**

Dear Mr. Corey,

2 As a parent of six and a high school teacher for more than 20 years, I know first hand that being a parent is difficult work. Even harder is being a good parent. My proposed title **3** *Taking Care of Yourself and Your Kids: A 30-day Program to Become a Better Parent While Still Living Your Life* would show how to handle real-life situations and still be a good parent.

This book has been years in the making, as it follows the outline I've used successfully in my summer seminars I give on the topic to thousands of parents every year. It really works, because past participants contact me constantly to let me know what a difference my classes have made in their lives. **4**

In addition to marketing and selling *Taking Care of Yourself and Your Kids* at my summer seminars, I would also be able to sell it through my website and promote it through my weekly e-newsletter with over 25,000 subscribers. Of course, it would also make a very nice trade title that I think would sell well in bookstores and possibly retail outlets, such as Wal-Mart and Target. **5**

Please contact me for a copy of my full book proposal today. **6**

Thank you for your consideration.

Marilyn Parent
8647 Query St.
Norman OK 00000
mparent8647@email.com
www.marilynsbetterparents.com

1 Effective subject line. Lets me know exactly what to expect when I open the e-mail. **2** Good lead. Six kids and teaches high school. I already trust her as an expert. **3** Nice title that would fit well with others we currently offer. **4** Her platform as a speaker definitely gets my attention. **5** 25,000 e-mail subscribers? She must have a very good voice to gather that many readers. **6** I was interested after the first paragraph, but every paragraph after made it impossible to not request her proposal.

BAD NONFICTION BOOK QUERY

To: info@bigbookspublishing.com
Subject: a question for you ❶

I really liked this book by Mega Book Publishers called *Build Better Trains in Your Own Backyard*. It was a great book that covered all the basics of model train building. My father and I would read from it together and assemble all the pieces, and it was magical like Christmas all through the year. Why wouldn't you want to publish such a book? ❷

Well, here it is. I've already copyrighted the material for 2006 and can help you promote it if you want to send me on a worldwide book tour. As you can see from my attached digital photo, I'm not the prettiest person, but I am passionate. ❸

There are at least 1,000 model train builders in the United States alone, and there might be even more than that. I haven't done enough research yet, because I don't know if this is an idea that appeals to you. If you give me maybe $500, I could do that research in a day and get back to you on it. ❹

Anyway, this idea is a good one that brings back lots of memories for me.

Jacob ❺

❶ The subject line is so vague I almost deleted this e-mail as spam without even opening it. ❷ The reason we don't publish such a book is easy—we don't do hobby titles. ❸ I'm not going to open an attachment from an unknown sender via e-mail. Also, copyrighting your work years before pitching is the sign of an amateur. ❹ 1,000 possible buyers is a small market, and I'm not going to pay a writer to do research on a proposal. ❺ Not even a last name? Or contact information? At least I won't feel guilty for not responding.

GOOD FICTION BOOK QUERY

Jeremy Mansfield, editor
Novels R Us Publishing
8787 Big Time Street
New York NY 00000

Dear Mr. Mansfield,

My 62,000-word novel, *The Cat Walk,* is a psychologically complex thriller in the same mold as James Patterson's Alex Cross novels, but with a touch of the supernatural a la Stephenie Meyer. **1**

Rebecca Frank is at the top of the modeling world, posing for magazines in exotic locales all over the world and living life to its fullest. Despite all her success, she feels something is missing in her life. Then she runs into Marcus Hunt, a wealthy bachelor with cold blue eyes and an ambiguous past.

Within 24 hours of meeting Marcus, Rebecca's understanding of the world turns upside down, and she finds herself fighting for her life and the love of a man who may not have the ability to return her the favor.

Filled with demons, serial killers, trolls, maniacal clowns and more, *The Cat Walk* follows Rebecca through a gauntlet of trouble and turmoil, leading up to a final climactic realization that may lead to her own unraveling. **2**

The Cat Walk should fit in well with your other titles, such as *Bone Dead* and *Carry Me Home*, though it is a unique story. Your website mentioned supernatural suspense as a current interest, so I hope this is a good match. **3**

My short fiction has appeared in many mystery magazines, including a prize-winning story in *The Mysterious Oregon Quarterly*. This novel is the first in a series that I'm working on (already half-way through the second). **4**

As stated in your guidelines, I've included the first 30 pages. Thank you for considering *The Cat Walk*.

Sincerely,

Merry Plentiful
54 Willow Road
East Lansing MI 00000
merry865423@email.com

1 Novel is correct length and has the suspense and supernatural elements we're seeking. **2** The quick summary sounds like something we would write on the back cover of our paperbacks. That's a good thing, because it identifies the triggers that draw a response out of our readers. **3** She mentions similar titles we've done and that she's done research on our website. She's not afraid to put in a little extra effort. **4** At the moment, I'm not terribly concerned that this book could become a series, but it is something good to file away in the back of my mind for future use.

BAD FICTION BOOK QUERY

Jeremy Mansfield
Novels R Us Publishing
8787 Big Time Street
New York NY 00000

Dear Editor,

My novel has an amazing twist ending that could make it a worldwide phenomenon overnight while you are sleeping. It has spectacular special effects that will probably lead to a multi-million dollar movie deal that will also spawn action figures, lunch boxes, and several other crazy subsidiary rights. I mean, we're talking big-time money here. **1**

I'm not going to share the twist until I have a signed contract that authorizes me to a big bank account, because I don't want to have my idea stolen and used to promote whatever new initiative "The Man" has in mind for media nowadays. Let it be known that you will be rewarded handsomely for taking a chance on me. **2**

Did you know that George Lucas once took a chance on an actor named Harrison Ford by casting him as Han Solo in Star Wars? Look at how that panned out. Ford went on to become a big actor in the Indiana Jones series, *The Fugitive, Blade Runner*, and more. It's obvious that you taking a risk on me could play out in the same dramatic way. **3**

I realize that you've got to make money, and guess what? I want to make money too. So we're on the same page, you and I. We both want to make money, and we'll stop at nothing to do so.

If you want me to start work on this amazing novel with an incredible twist ending, just send a one-page contract agreeing to pay me a lot of money if we hit it big. No other obligations will apply. If it's a bust, I won't sue you for millions. **4**

Sincerely,

Kenzel Pain
92 Bad Writer Road
Austin TX 00000

1 While I love to hear enthusiasm from a writer about his or her work, this kind of unchecked excitement is worrisome for an editor. **2** I need to know the twist to make a decision on whether to accept the manuscript. Plus, I'm troubled by the paranoia and emphasis on making a lot of money. **3** I'm confused. Does he think he's Harrison Ford? **4** So that's the twist: He hasn't even written the novel yet. There's no way I'm going to offer a contract for a novel that hasn't been written by someone with no experience or idea of how the publishing industry works.

PERFECT PITCH:

Pitches That Never Fail

....

by Marc Acito

"A first-time novelist sets the record at a writers conference for the most pitches, leading to a multiple-book deal, awards, translations, excellent reviews and a movie option. An inspiring true success story, a literary version of Seabiscuit, except the horse is a writer."

As pitches go, this one's devoid of conflict, but that's the point. This scenario actually happened to me. Hence my qualification for writing this article.

My writing students get nervous when I ask them to pitch their works-in-progress on the first day of class, particularly if they're just starting. "I wouldn't know how to describe it," they say. "I don't know what it's about."

....

A pitch is simply another story that you're telling. A very, very short one.

....

And therein lies the problem. To some degree, we can't know what our novel/memoir/screenplay/play/nonfiction book is entirely about until we've gotten it down. But I contend that thinking about the pitch ahead of time helps focus a writer's goals for a piece. It's not just a commercial concern, it's an artistic one.

Writers are storytellers and a pitch is simply another story that you're telling. A very, very short one. Rather than view pitching as if you were a salesman in a bad suit hawking used cars, imagine that you're a pitcher for the Yankees and that the agent or editor is the catcher: They're on your team, so they really want to catch the ball.

Or, put another way, you're a different kind of pitcher, this one full of cool, refreshing water that will fill their empty glass.

But first you've got to get their attention.

THE HOOK

"I need something to grab me right away that tells me exactly why I should want to read this submission (of all the submissions on my desk)," says Christina Pride, senior editor at Hyperion.

A hook is exactly what it sounds like—a way to grab a reader like a mackerel and reel them in. It's not a plot summary, but more like the ad campaign you'd see on a movie poster. Veteran Hollywood screenwriter Cynthia Whitcomb, who teaches the pitching workshop at the Willamette Writers Conference in Portland, Oregon, recommends that writers of all genres start with a hooky tagline like this one from *Raiders of the Lost Ark:*

> *"If adventure had a name, it'd be Indiana Jones."*

That's not just first-rate marketing, it's excellent storytelling.

Here are some of my other favorite taglines for movies based on books, so you can see how easily the concept works for novels:

- "Help is coming from above." (*Charlotte's Web*)
- "From the moment they met it was murder." (*Double Indemnity*)
- "The last man on earth is not alone." (*I am Legend*)
- "Love means never having to say you're sorry." (*Love Story*)

The last one actually isn't true; love means always saying you're sorry, even when you're not, but the thought is provocative and provocation is exactly what you want to do.

When I pitched my first novel, *How I Paid for College,* I always started the same way. First, I looked the catcher right in the eye (this is very important—how else are they going to catch the ball?). Then I said,

> *"Embezzlement. Blackmail. Fraud...High School."*

I began my query letters the same way.

"I always begin my proposals with a question," says Jennifer Basye Sander, co-author of *The Complete Idiots Guide to Getting Published.* "I want to get an editor nodding their head in agreement right away."

No, you're not asking something like, "Are you ready to rock 'n roll?" but instead an open-ended conversation starter like, "Can you be forgiven for sending an innocent man to jail?" (Ian McEwan's *Atonement*) or "What does it take to climb Mount Everest?" (Jon Krakauer's *Into Thin Air).* Particularly useful are "what if?" questions like "What if an amnesiac didn't know he was the world's most wanted assassin?" (Robert Ludlum's *The Bourne Identity*) or "What if Franklin Delano Roosevelt had been defeated by Charles Lindbergh in 1940?" (*The Plot Against America*, Philip Roth).

Acito employs humor in his novels, but there's nothing funny about the effectiveness of his pitches.

The same also holds true for nonfiction. If you sat down in front of an agent and asked, "What if you could trim your belly fat and use it to fuel your car?" trust me, they'd listen. Questions like that make the catcher want to know more. Which is exactly what you do by creating…

THE LOG LINE

No, it's not a country western dance done in a timber mill. And without realizing it, you're already a connoisseur of the genre, having read thousands of log lines in *TV Guide* or imdb.com or the *New York Times* Bestseller List. A log line is a one-sentence summary that states the central conflict of your story. For example:

> "A teen runaway kills the first person she encounters, then is pursued by the dead woman's sister as she teams up with three strangers to kill again."

Recognize it? That's *The Wizard of Oz.*
Here's another:

> "The son of a carpenter leaves on an adventure of self-discovery, rejects sin, dies and rises again transformed."

Obviously, that's *Pinocchio.*
Okay, seriously, here's the one I did for *How I Paid for College*:

> "A talented but irresponsible teenager schemes to steal his college tuition money when his wealthy father refuses to pay for him to study acting at Juilliard."

It's not genius, but it captured the story succinctly by identifying the protagonist, the antagonist, and the conflict between them. In other words, the essential element for any compelling story.

AND HERE'S THE PITCH...

Pitches are often referred to as "elevator pitches" because they should last the length of your average elevator ride—anywhere from 30 seconds to two minutes. Or, for a query letter, one page single-spaced. That's about 350 words, including "Dear Mr. William Morris" and "Your humble servant, Desperate Writer."

Essentially, the pitch is identical to a book jacket blurb: it elaborates on the set-up, offers a few further complications on the central conflict, then gives an indication of how it wraps up. When it comes to the ending, "don't be coy," says Erin Harris, a literary agent at the Irene Skolnick Agency in Manhattan. "Spoil the secrets, and let me know what really happens." Agents and editors want a clear idea of what kind of ride they're getting on before investing hours in your manuscript. Make it easy for them to do their jobs selling it.

> Agents and editors want a clear idea of what kind of ride they're getting on before investing hours in your manuscript.

Nowhere was this clearer to me than when I read the jacket copy of my first novel and saw that it was virtually identical to my query letter.

Indeed, your best practice for learning how to pitch is to read jacket descriptions (leaving out the part about the author being a "bold, original new voice"—that's for others to say).

Or think of it as a very short story, following the structure attributed to writer Alice Adams: Action, Backstory, Development, Climax, End.

It's as easy as ABDCE.

"The best queries convey the feeling that the author understands what the scope, structure, voice, and audience of the book really are," says Rakesh Satyal, senior editor at HarperCollins to authors such as Paul Coelho, Armistead Maupin and Clive Barker. "To misunderstand or miscommunicate any of these things can be truly detrimental."

That's the reason we often resort to the Hollywoody jargon of it's "This meets that," as in "It's *No Country for Old Men* meets *Little Women*." Or it's...

- ...*Die Hard* on a bus (*Speed*)
- ...*Die Hard* in a plane (*Con Air*)
- ...*Die Hard* in a phone booth (*Phone Booth*)
- ...*Die Hard* in a skyscraper (no, wait, that's *Die Hard*).

HOW I PAID FOR COLLEGE

A Tale of Sex, Theft, Friendship and Musical Theater

A novel by Marc Acito

Embezzlement...Blackmail...Fraud...High School.

How I Paid for College is a 97,000-word comic novel about a talented but irresponsible teenager who schemes to steal his college tuition money when his wealthy father refuses to pay for acting school. The story is just true enough to embarrass my family.

It's 1983 in Wallingford, New Jersey, a sleepy bedroom community outside of Manhattan. Seventeen-year-old Edward Zanni, a feckless Ferris Bueller type, is Peter Panning his way through a carefree summer of magic and mischief, sending underwear up flagpoles and re-arranging lawn animals in compromising positions. The fun comes to a screeching halt, however, when Edward's father remarries and refuses to pay for Edward to study acting at Juilliard.

In a word, Edward's screwed. He's ineligible for scholarships because his father earns too much. He's unable to contact his mother because she's off somewhere in Peru trying to commune with the Incan spirits. And, in a sure sign he's destined for a life in the arts, Edward's incapable of holding down a job. ("One little flesh wound is all it takes to get fired as a dog groomer, even if you artfully arrange its hair so the scar doesn't show.")

So Edward turns to his loyal (but immoral) misfit friends to help him steal the tuition money from his father. Disguising themselves as nuns and priests (because who's going to question the motives of a bunch of nuns and priests?) they merrily scheme their way through embezzlement, money laundering, identity theft, forgery and blackmail.

But along the way Edward also learns the value of friendship, hard work and how you're not really a man until you can beat up your father. (Metaphorically, that is.)

How I Paid for College is a farcical coming-of-age story that combines the first-person-smart-ass tone of David Sedaris with the byzantine plot twists of Armistead Maupin. I've written it with the HBO-watching, NPR-listening, Vanity Fair-reading audience in mind.

As a syndicated humor columnist, I'm familiar with this audience. For the past three years, my bi-weekly column, "The Gospel According to Marc," has appeared in 18 alternative newspapers in major markets, including Los Angeles, Chicago and Washington, DC. During that time I've amassed a personal mailing list of over 1,000 faithful readers.

How I Paid for College is a story for anyone who's ever had a dream...and a scheme.

www.MarcAcito.com
(503) 246-2208
Marc@MarcAcito.com
5423 SW Cameron Road, Portland, OR 97221

"I appreciate when agents and authors offer good comp titles," confirms Hyperion's Christina Pride. "It's good shorthand to help me begin to position the book in my mind right from the outset in terms of sensibility and potential audience."

Agent Erin Harris agrees. "For example," she says, "the premise of one book meets the milieu of another book." As in *Pride and Prejudice and Zombies*, an idea I will forever regret not thinking of myself.

When citing comp titles, be certain to invoke the most commercially successful and well-known works to which you can honestly liken yourself. No agent wants to earn 15 percent of *Obscure Literary Title* meets *Total Downer by Author Who Committed Suicide*.

So I steered clear of my lesser-known influences and focused on the big names, saying, "*How I Paid for College* is a farcical coming-of-age story that combines the first-person-smart-ass tone of David Sedaris with the byzantine plot twists of Armistead Maupin."

That line also made it onto the jacket copy.

My book hasn't changed, but I continue to update the pitch as I develop the movie. What started as "*Ferris Bueller* meets *High School Musical*," turned into "A mash-up of *Ocean's 11* and *Glee*." By the time the movie actually gets made it'll be "*iTunes Implant Musical Experience* meets *Scheming Sentient Robots*."

"A word of caution," Harris adds. "Please do not liken your protagonist to Holden Caulfield or your prose style to that of Proust. Truly, it's best to steer clear of the inimitable."

Speaking of the inimitable, while the titles of *Catcher in the Rye* and *Remembrance of Things Past* are poetically evocative, they wouldn't distinguish themselves from the pack in the Too-Much-Information Age. Nowadays, your project is competing for attention with a video of a toddler trapped behind a couch. (I'm serious, Google it, it's got all the makings of great drama: a sympathetic protagonist, conflict, complications, laughter, tears and an uplifting ending. All in two minutes and 27 seconds.)

So while it's not a dictum of the publishing industry (though, given the nosedive the industry has taken, what do *they* know?), I think 21st century writers would do well to title their works in ways that accommodate the searchable keyword culture of the Internet.

In other words, *To Kill a Mockingbird* was fine for 1960, but if you tried promoting it today, you'd end up at the PETA website.

Like the logline, the catchiest titles actually describe what the book is about. Consider:

- *Eat, Pray, Love*
- *Diary of a Wimpy Kid*
- *Sh*t My Dad Says*
- *A Portrait of the Artist as a Young Man*

In those cases, the title is the synopsis. Similarly, some titles, while less clear, include an inherent mystery or question:

- *Sophie's Choice*

- *The Hunger Games*
- *And Then There Were None*
- *The Hitchhiker's Guide to the Galaxy*

Lastly, even if the reader can't know automatically what the title means, it helps if it's simple and memorable, like:

- *Twilight*
- *Valley of the Dolls*
- *The Thorn Birds*
- *Captain Underpants*

One way to tell if you've got an effective title is to submit it to the "Have you read…?" test. If it feels natural coming at the end of that sentence, you're on the right track.

Granted, straightforward titles are easier if you're writing nonfiction like *Trim Your Belly Fat and Use it to Fuel Your Car*. As is the final part of the pitch.

BUILDING A PLATFORM

Along with branding, platform is one of the most overused buzz words of the last decade. "If you are writing nonfiction," Erin Harris says, "it's important to describe your platform and to be a qualified expert on the subject about which you're writing"

In other words, if you're going to write *Teach Your Cat to Tap Dance* you better deliver a tap-dancing cat, along with research about the market for such a book.

For first-time novelists this can prove challenging. But Harris says that every credit truly helps: "If you have pieces published in literary magazines, if you have won awards, or if you have an MFA, my interest is piqued."

That last advice should also pique the interest of every fledgling writer out there. In my case, what actually got me an agent wasn't just the pitch, it was the fact that I met best-selling novelist Chuck Palahniuk at a workshop and he'd read a column of mine in a small alternative newspaper. Ultimately, it's not about who you know, it's about who knows you. So publish wherever you can. You never know who's reading.

Write on.

MARC ACITO is the award-winning author of the comic novels *How I Paid for College* and *Attack of the Theater People*. *How I Paid for College* won the Ken Kesey Award for Fiction, was a Top Teen Pick by the American Library Association and is translated into five languages the author cannot read. A regular contributor to NPR's *All Things Considered*, he teaches story structure online and at NYU. www.MarcAcito.com

LANDING THE SIX-FIGURE DEAL

What Makes Your Proposal Hot

by SJ Hodges

It's the question every first-time author wants to ask:

"If I sell my book, will the advance even cover my rent?"

Authors, I am happy to tell you that, yes, the six-figure book deal for a newbie still exists—even if you're not a celebrity with your own television show! As a ghostwriter, I work with numerous authors and personalities to develop both nonfiction and fiction proposals and I've seen unknown first-timers land life-changing deals even in a down economy. Is platform the ultimate key to their success? You better believe it's a huge consideration for publishers but here's the good news, having a killer platform is only one element that transforms a "nice deal" into a "major deal."

You still have to ensure the eight additional elements of your proposal qualify as major attractions. Daniela Rapp, editor at St. Martin's Press explains, "In addition to platform, authors need to have a fantastic, original idea. They have to truly be an expert in their field and they must be able to write." So how do you craft a proposal that conveys your brilliance, your credentials, your talent and puts a couple extra zeroes on your check?

ONE: THE NARRATIVE OVERVIEW

Before you've even written word one of your manuscript, you are expected to, miraculously, summarize the entirety of your book in such a compelling and visceral way that a publisher or agent will feel as if they are reading the *New York Times* review. Sound impossible? That's because it is.

That's why I'm going to offer two unorthodox suggestions. First, consider writing the first draft of your overview after you've created your table of contents and your chapter outlines. You'll know much more about the content and scope of your material even if you're not 100% certain about the voice and tone. That's why you'll take another pass after you complete your sample chapters. Because then, you'll be better acquainted with the voice of your book which brings me to unorthodox suggestion number two… treat your overview as literature.

I believe every proposal component needs to be written "in voice" especially because your overview is the first page the editor sees after the title page. By establishing your voice on the page immediately, your proposal becomes less of a sales document and more of a page-turner. Remember, not everyone deciding your fate works in marketing and sales. Editors still have some buying power and they are readers, first and foremost.

TWO: THE TABLE OF CONTENTS AND CHAPTER OUTLINES

Television writers call this "breaking" a script. This is where you break your book or it breaks you. This is where you discover if what you plan to share with the world actually merits 80,000 words and international distribution.

Regardless of whether you're writing fiction or nonfiction, this element of your proposal must take your buyer on a journey (especially if it's nonfiction) and once more, I'm a big fan of approaching this component with creativity particularly if you're exploring a specific historical time period, plan to write using a regional dialect, rely heavily on "slan-guage" and especially if the material is highly-technical and dry.

This means you'll need to style your chapter summaries and your chapter titles as a form of dramatic writing. Think about the arc of the chapters, illuminating the escalating conflict, the progression towards a resolution, in a cinematic fashion. Each chapter summary should end with an "emotional bumper," a statement that simultaneously summarizes and entices in the same way a television show punches you in the gut before they cut to a commercial.

Is it risky to commit to a more creative approach? Absolutely. Will it be perfect the first time you write it? No. The fifth time you write it? No. The tenth time? Maybe. But the contents and chapter summary portion of your proposal is where you really get a chance to show off your skills as an architect of plot and structure and how you make an editor's job much, much easier. According to Lara Asher, Acquisitions Editor at Globe Pequot Press, it is the single most important component of your proposal. "If I can't easily understand what a book is trying to achieve then I can't present it to my colleagues. It won't make it through the acquisitions process."

THREE: YOUR AUTHOR BIO

Your author bio page must prove that you are more than just a pro, you are recognized by the world at large as THE DEFINITIVE EXPERT on your topic and you have first-hand experience tackling the problems, implementing your solutions and you've seen positive results not only in your personal life but in the lives of others. You have to have walked the walk and talked the talk. You come equipped with a built-in audience, mass media attention, and a strong social network. Your bio assures your buyer that you are the right writer exploring the right topic at the right time.

FOUR: YOUR PLATFORM

Platform, platform, platform. Sit through any writing conference, query any agent, lunch with any editor and you'll hear the "P" word over and over again. What you won't hear is hard and fast numbers about just how large this platform has to be in order to secure a serious offer. Is there an audience to dollar amount ratio that seems to be in play? Are publishers paying per head?

"I haven't found this to be the case," says Julia Pastore, former editor for Random House. "It's easier to compel someone to 'Like' you on Facebook or follow you on Twitter than it is to compel them to plunk down money to buy your book. Audience engagement is more important than the sheer number of social media followers."

With that said, if you're shooting for six-figures, publishers expect you'll have big numbers and big plans. Your platform will need to include:

Cross Promotional Partnerships

These are organizations or individuals that already support you, are already promoting your brand, your products or your persona. If you host a show on HGTV or Nike designed a tennis racket in your honor, they definitely qualify. If, however, you're not rolling like an A-lister just yet, you need to brainstorm any and every possible connection you have to organizations with reach in the 20,000 + range. Maybe your home church is only 200 people but the larger association serves 40,000 and you often write for their newsletter. Think big. Then think bigger.

Specific, Verifiable Numbers Proving the Loyalty of Your Audience

"Publishers want to see that you have direct contact with a loyal audience," says Maura Teitelbaum, agent Folio Literary Management. Meaning a calendar full of face-to-face speaking engagements, a personal mailing list, extensive database and verifiable traffic to your author website.

But how much traffic does there need to be? How many public appearances? How many e-mails in your Constant Contact newsletter? Publishers are loathe to quote concrete numbers for "Likes" and "Followers" so I'll stick my neck out and do it instead. At a minimum, to land a basic book deal, meaning a low five-figure sum, you'll need to prove that you've got 15 - 20,000 fans willing to follow you into hell and through high water.

For a big six-figure deal, you'll need a solid base of 100,000 rabid fans plus access to hundreds of thousands more. If not millions. Depressed yet? Don't be. Because we live in a time when things as trivial as angry oranges or as important as scientific TED talks can go viral and propel a writer out of obscurity in a matter of seconds. It is only your job to become part of the conversation. And once your foot is in the door, you'll be able to gather…

Considerable Media Exposure

Publishers are risk averse. They want to see that you're a media darling achieving pundit status. Organize and present all your clips, put together a DVD demo reel of your on-air appearances and be able to quote subscriber numbers and demographics about the publications running your articles or features about you.

Advance Praise from People Who Matter

Will blurbs really make a difference in the size of your check? "I would include as many in a proposal as possible," says Teitelbaum. "Especially if those people are willing to write letters of commitment saying they will promote the book via their platform. That shows your efforts will grow exponentially."

FIVE: YOUR PROMOTIONAL PLANS

So what is the difference between your platform and your promotional plan? Your promotional plan must demonstrate specifically how you will activate your current platform and the expected sales results of that activation. These are projections starting three to six months before your book release date and continuing for one year after its hardcover publication. They want your guarantee to sell 15,000 books within that first year.

In addition, your promotional plan also issues promises about the commitments you are willing to make in order to promote the book to an even wider market. This is your expansion plan. How will you broaden your reach and who will help you do it? Publishers want to see that your goals are ambitious but doable.

Think about it this way. If you own a nail salon and you apply for a loan to shoot a movie, you're likely to be rejected. But ask for a loan to open your second salon and your odds get much better. In other words, keep your promotional plans in your wheelhouse while still managing to include:

- Television and Radio Appearances
- Access to Print Media
- A Massive Social Media Campaign
- Direct E-mail Solicitations

- E-Commerce and Back of Room Merchandising
- New Joint Partnerships
- Your Upcoming Touring & Speaking Schedule with Expected Audience

You'll notice that I did not include hiring a book publicist as a requirement. Gone are the days when an advance-sucking, three-month contract with a book publicist makes any difference. For a six-figure author, publishers expect there is a team in place: a powerful agent, a herd of assistants and a more generalized media publicist already managing the day-to-day affairs of building your brand, growing your audience. Hiring a book publicist at the last minute is useless.

SIX: YOUR MARKET ANALYSIS

It would seem the odds against a first-time author hitting the jackpot are slim but that's where market analysis provides a glimmer of hope. There are actually markets considered more desirable to publishers. "Broader is generally better for us," says Rapp. "Niche generally implies small. Not something we [St. Martin's Press] can afford to do these days. Current affairs books, if they are explosive and timely, can work. Neuroscience is hot. Animal books (not so much animal memoirs) still work. Military books sell."

"The health and diet category will always be huge," says Asher. "But in a category like parenting which is so crowded, we look for an author tackling a niche topic that hasn't yet been covered."

Niche or broad, your market analysis must position your book within a larger context, addressing the needs of the publishing industry, the relevant cultural conversations happening in the zeitgeist, your potential audience and their buying power and the potential for both domestic and international sales.

SEVEN: YOUR C.T.A.

Choose the books for your competitive title analysis not only for their topical similarities but also because the author has a comparable profile and platform to your own. Says Pastore, "It can be editorially helpful to compare your book to *Unbroken* by Hillenbrand, but unless your previous book was also a bestseller, this comparison won't be helpful to our sales force."

Limit your C.T.A. to five or six solid offerings then get on BookScan and make sure none of the books sold fewer than 10,000 copies. "Higher sales are preferable," says Rapp. "And you should leave it to the publisher to decide if the market can hold one more title or not. We always do our own research anyway, so just because the book is not mentioned in your line-up doesn't mean we won't know about it."

EIGHT: YOUR SAMPLE CHAPTERS

Finally, you have to/get to prove you can…write. Oh yeah, that!

This is the fun part, the pages of your proposal where you really get to shine. It is of upmost importance that these chapters, in harmony with your overview and chapter summaries, allow the beauty, wisdom and/or quirkiness of your voice to be heard. Loud and clear.

"Writing absolutely matters and strong sample chapters are crucial." Pastore explains, "An author must be able to turn their brilliant idea into engaging prose on the page."

Approach the presentation of these chapters creatively. Consider including excerpts from several different chapters and not just offering the standard Introduction, Chapter One and Two. Consider the inclusion of photographs to support the narrative, helping your editor put faces to names. Consider using sidebar or box quotes from the narrative throughout your proposal to build anticipation for the actual read.

NINE: YOUR ONE-PAGER

Lastly, you'll need a one-pager, which is a relatively new addition to the book proposal format. Publishers now expect an author to squeeze a 50- or 60-page proposal down to a one-page summary they can hand to their marketing and sales teams. In its brevity, the one-pager must provide your buyer with "a clear vision of what the book is, why it's unique, why you are the best person to write it, and how we can reach the audience," says Pastore. And it must do that in less than 1,000 words. There is no room to be anything but impressive.

And if you're shooting for that six-figure deal, impressive is what each component of your book proposal must be. Easy? No. But still possible? Yes.

SJ Hodges is an 11-time published playwright, ghostwriter and editor. Her most recent book, a memoir co-authored with Animal Planet's "Pit Boss" Shorty Rossi was purchased by Random House/Crown, hit #36 on the Amazon bestseller list and went into its 3rd printing less than six weeks after its release date. As a developmental editor, SJ has worked on books published by Vanguard Press, Perseus Book Group and St. Martin's Press. SJ is a tireless advocate for artists offering a free listing for jobs, grants and fellowships at her Facebook page: facebook.com/constantcreator. She can be reached through her website: sjhodges.com.

HOW TO FIND SUCCESS IN THE MAGAZINE WORLD

··

by Kerrie Flanagan

Contrary to popular belief, magazines are still going strong. According to the latest study by the Magazine Publishers of America there are over 20,000 magazines in print. This is good news if you are looking to write for magazines. But before you jump in, there are a few things you should know that will increase your chances of getting an acceptance letter.

KNOW THE READER

Every magazine has a certain readership; teenage girl, mother of young children, budget traveler and so on. It is imperative you know as much about that reader as you can before submitting a query to the editor, because the more you know about who reads the magazine, the more you can tailor your query, article or essay to best reach that audience.

Geoff Van Dyke, Deputy Editor of the Denver magazine, *5280* said, "I wish people would truly read the magazine, like cover to cover, and understand our readership and voice and mission before sending queries. Sometimes—more often than not—writers submit queries that make it clear that they don't really understand *5280*, don't understand our readers or our mission, and, thus, the query is a bad fit. If they just spend a little more time on the front end, it would make all the difference." So how can you find out who is the target audience for a specific magazine? The key is in the advertising. Companies spend thousands of dollars getting their messages out to their consumers. They are only going to invest their money in a magazine directed at their target market. By paying attention to the ads in a publication (and this goes for online too) you can learn a lot about the reader. What are the ages of the people in the ads? Are they families? Singles? What types of products are highlighted? Expensive clothes? Organic foods? Luxury cars and world travel or family cars and domestic travel?

Another way to find out the demographics of the reader is to locate the media kit on the magazine's website. This is a document intended to provide information to potential advertisers about their readership, but is a gold mine for freelance writers. The media kit provides information like the average age, income, gender, hobbies, home ownership, education and marital status.

This becomes invaluable when looking at ideas and topics to pitch to a magazine. For instance, in the media kit for *5280* magazine, 71% of the readers are married, 93% own their own home and 78% have lived in Colorado for more than 10 years or are natives of the state. With this little bit of information, pitching an article on where to find the best deals on apartments in Denver, is definitely not a good fit since most of their readers own their own home. An article on the best bars in Denver to meet other singles is also not a good idea for this publication, but one on the most romantic weekend getaways in Colorado to take your spouse is a possibility. It is also clear that when writing the article, time does not have to be spent explaining to the reader things about Colorado that people who live in the state already know since 78% of the readers have been there for more than a decade.

KNOW THE MAGAZINE

Once you understand the reader, then you need to familiarize yourself with the actual magazine. Take the time to explore who are the writers, the length of the articles and the departments.

Tom Hess, editor with *Encompass Magazine* wishes more writers would take the time to know his magazine, in all its forms, before querying. "Too few writers make the effort, and those who do, get my immediate attention."

One way to do this with print magazines is to literally take apart the magazine. To see who writes for the magazine, find the masthead, the page in the front of the magazine that lists the editors and contributing writers. Tear it out so you have it as a reference. Now, go through the magazine, page by page and make a note by each article with a byline to find out who wrote the piece. Was it an editor? A contributing editor? If you can't find their name on the masthead, then they are a typically a freelance writer. A contributing editor is usually not on staff, but writes frequently for the magazine.

Now go through and pay attention to the length of articles and the various departments. How many feature stories are there? Is there a back page essay? Are there short department pieces in the front?

By knowing all of this information, you can better direct your query to the areas of the magazine that are more open to freelance writers and tailor your idea to better fit the type of articles they publish.

KNOW THE STYLE

Each magazine has its own style and tone. It's what makes the difference between *The New Yorker* and *Time Magazine*. Some magazines are very literary, others are more informational, so it is important to study the magazines to have a good understanding of their style.

Below are two travel writing examples portraying Ketchikan, Alaska, but with very different styles. As you read over each selection, pay attention to the style by looking at the use of quotes, the point of view (first person, third person…), the descriptions and the overall tone of the article.

Example 1

In Ketchikan, there are many great things to see and do. The roots of the three Native Alaskan tribes, the Tlingit, Haida, and Tsimshian run deep on this island where you can find the world's largest collection of totem poles. In a beautiful cove, eight miles north of downtown is Totem Bight State Park where 14 historic totems are found along with a native clanhouse. Totems can also be viewed at the Totem Heritage Center and the Southest Discovery Center. At the Saxman Tribal house and at the Metlakatla Long House, skilled groups bring Native dance to life with regular performances.

Example 2

The rest of the world disappeared when I entered this lush, green rainforest. Stillness and peace embraced me while I strolled on the wooden walkway, in awe of the surrounding beauty: moss hung from trees, foliage so dense it provided shelter from the rain and beautiful rivers flowed, in search of the ocean. Ketchikan, Alaska, is in the heart of the Tongass National Forest, and an unlikely place to find the Earth's largest remaining temperate rainforest.

The first article provides information and facts about traveling to Ketchikan to see the totem poles. This article would be a good fit for a magazine liek *Family Motor Coaching*. The second article definitely has a different style; one that is more poetic and descriptive and more likely to be found in *National Geographic Traveler*.

Both pieces are good, but are unique in their style and tone. By understanding this aspect of a magazine, your query or article can better reflect the voice of the publication and increase your chances of an assignment and well-received article.

KNOW THE GUIDELINES

Most magazines put together submission guidelines, spelling out exactly what they are looking for with articles and how to submit your idea to them.

"I wish writers would understand exactly what kind of material we are looking for," said Russ Lumpkin, managing editor of *Gray's Sporting Journal*, "and that they would adhere strictly to our submission guidelines. We publish fly fishing and hunting stories and accept only digtal submissions via e-mail. A poem about watching butterflies submitted through the mail creates work that falls out of my ordinary work flow. And that's aggravating."

The submission guidelines are usually found in the "About Us" or "Contact Us" section on a magazine's website as well as in great resources like *Writer's Market*. Read the guidelines carefully and follow them when submitting your query or article.

KNOW HOW TO WRITE AN EFFECTIVE QUERY LETTER

Once you have done all your upfront research and have found a magazine that is a good fit for your idea, it is time to write a good query letter. The letter should be professional and written in a style and tone similar to the article you are pitching.

Robbin Gould, editor of *Family Motor Coaching* believes a writer needs to submit as comprehensive a query as possible and be fully aware of the magazine's focus, particularly when dealing with a niche publication. "A writer who misuses terms or makes erroneous statements about the subject he or she proposes to cover indicates a lack of knowledge to the editor," says Gould. "Or a query that simply states, 'Would you be interested in an article about XXX?' with minimal explanation wastes everyone's time and suggests the writer is looking for any publication to take the article. If the writer doesn't show much attention to detail up front, the editor probably won't spend much time considering the idea."

There are basic components that should be included in every query letter.

- **Salutation (Dear Mr. Smith).** Find out who the correct editor is to direct your query. You should be able to find this information online. If not make a quick phone call to the publishing company and ask, "Who would I direct a travel query to?" Ask for spelling and the editor's e-mail. Unless you know the editor, use a formal salutation with Mr., Mrs., or Ms. If you are not sure if the editor is a man or woman, put their full name.
- **Good Hook.** You have about 10 seconds to catch the attention of an editor. The opening should be about one to three sentences in length and needs to lure the editor in right away.
- **Article Content.** This is the bulk of your query and should be about one paragraph. It will focus on the main points of the article and the topics you plan to cover.
- **Specifics.** Here you will include the specifics of the article: word count, department where you think it will fit, possible experts you are going to interview and other information pertinent to the piece.
- **Purpose.** In one sentence, share the purpose of your article. Will your article inform, educate, inspire, or entertain?

- **Qualifications.** This is not the place to be shy. You need to convince the editor that you are the perfect person to write this article. If you do not have any published clips, then really expand more on your experiences that relate to your article. If you are pitching a parenting article and you have six kids, mention that. It clearly positions you as an expert in the parenting field.
- **Sending.** Most magazines accept and want queries by e-mail. When sending a query via e-mail, include your information in the body of the message, not in an attachment. Make sure your contact information is at the bottom of the e-mail. Put something noticeable in the subject line. For example: QUERY: The Benefits of Chocolate and the Creative Process.

By following all the steps in this article you will be ready set off on a magazine-writing journey equipped with the necessary tools and confidence to get your queries noticed, and in the end, see your articles in print.

Kerrie Flanagan has 130+ published articles and essays to her credit. In addition she is the director of Northern Colorado Writers, a group she founded in 2007 that supports and encourages writers of all levels and genres through classes, networking events, retreats and an annual writer's conference. Kerrie is also available for writing coaching. Visit her website for more information about her and NCW. www.KerrieFlanagan.com

EARN A FULL-TIME INCOME FROM BLOGGING

by Carol Tice

It sounds like a dream. Instead of sending query letters and relying on editors to give you paying assignments, you start your own blog and turn it into a money-maker. No matter where in the world you want to live, you're able to earn a good living.

For a growing number of writers, it's not a dream. I know because I'm among the writers who now earn more from their own blogs than they do from freelance assignments.

But it's not easy, by any means. The vast majority of blogs never find an audience and their authors never earn a dime. It's hard to stand out—at the end of 2011, pollster Nielsen reported there were over 181 million blogs, up from 36 million in 2006.

In this vast sea of blogs, how can you write one that stands out and becomes the basis for a money-earning business? It begins with setting up the blog to attract a loyal readership. Once you build an audience, there are a limited number of ways you can earn income from your blog audience—I spotlight the five of the most popular methods below.

SETTING IT UP TO EARN

Many blogs don't attract readers because they lack basic elements of design and usability that make blogs appealing, says Seattle WordPress trainer Bob Dunn (www.bobwp.com). Dunn's own blog, BobWP, is the platform on which he's built his business.

How do you create an attractive blog?

Use a professional platform
Free blog platforms such as Blogger and Moveable Type have limitations that make it hard to look professional (and some free platforms prohibit commerce). If you're serious about

blogging, pay for a host and use WordPress—it's now the dominant blogging platform, Technorati reports.

Offer contact information

Many bloggers cultivate an air of mystery, using a pen name and providing no contact info. But readers want to know who you are and be able to e-mail you questions, says Dunn.

Have an About page

With a million scams on the Internet, the About page has become a vital blog component—it's usually the most-visited page after the Home page, Dunn says. This is the place where readers get to know you and learn why you write your blog.

"I can't tell you how many times I go on a blog and there's no About page," says, Dunn. "It should be more than a resume, too—tell a story."

Clean up the design

No matter how wonderful your writing is, if your blog is a clutter of tiny type, dark backgrounds, multiple sidebars, and flashing ads, readers will leave, Dunn says. Begin with a simple, graphical header, title, and tagline that quickly communicate what your blog is about. You have just a few seconds in which to convey what you write about before readers leave, so be clear.

Make navigation simple

Many bloggers end up with multiple rows of tabs or long drop-down menus. Try to simplify—for every additional click you require, you will lose some readers, Dunn says.

Pick a niche topic

While most blogs ramble about whatever the author feels like discussing that day, business-focused blogs stick to a subject or a few related topics, notes Dunn. This allows you to attract and keep readers interested in your subject.

Create useful content

Write with your readers' needs in mind, rather than about your own interests, says Mexico-based Jon Morrow. His year-old blog Boost Blog Traffic (boostblogtraffic.com) earned $500,000 in 2012. If you don't know what readers want, Morrow says, take polls and ask questions to find out.

Write strong headlines

If you want readers to find your posts online, your headlines need key words and phrases that relate to your topic, to help them rank well in Google searches for your topic. You can do keyword research free using Google's tool (https://adwords.google.com/o/KeywordTool). Headlines also need to be lively and interesting to draw readers—Morrow offers a Headline Hacks report on his blog that dissects effective headline styles.

Use blog style

Blog posts are different from magazine articles because of how people read—make that skim—online, says Dunn. Good blog-post paragraphs are short, often just one or two sentences. Posts with bold subheads or bulleted or numbered lists are easy to scan and often enjoy higher readership.

Make sharing easy

To grow your audience, you'll need readers to spread the word, says Dunn. Make that easy with one-click sharing buttons for Twitter, Facebook and other popular social-media platforms. You should be active in these platforms, too, building relationships with influential people who might send you readers.

Start guest posting

One of the fastest ways to build your blog audience is by guest posting on popular blogs with lots of traffic. Your guest post will give you a link back to your own blog and allow new readers to find you. This is usually not paid work, but think of it as a marketing cost for your blog-based business. Many top blogs do accept guest posts—look for writer's guidelines on their sites.

"The big secret to making money from blogging is to get serious about marketing," Morrow says.

Build an e-mail list

The best way to stay in touch with readers is via an e-mail list visitors are encouraged to join, says Dunn. Subscribers who sign up through real simple syndication, or RSS, don't reveal their e-mail address, so it's hard to sell them anything.

START EARNING

Once your blog is set up to entice readers, you're ready to experiment with ways to generate income off your blog. Among the common approaches:

1. Freelance Gigs

Add a "Hire Me" tab to your site to begin attracting freelance blogging gigs from online businesses and publications. That's the approach U.K.-based writer Tom Ewer took when he quit his job and launched his blog Leaving Work Behind (www.leavingworkbehind.com) in 2011.

A brand-new writer at the time, Ewer quickly got a couple of freelance blogging clients by applying to online job ads. More clients approached him after seeing his guest posts on big blogs and finding his blog from there. Ewer was soon blogging for pay about topics including WordPress and government contracting. By late 2012, he was earning $4,000 a month as a paid blogger at $100 a post and up, working part-time hours.

A similar strategy worked for Nigerian blogger Bamidele Onibalusi, who began his online-earning themed blog YoungPrePro (www.youngprepro.com) in 2010, when he was just 16. By 2012, he was making $50,000 a year writing for blog owners who learned of him from his dozens of guest posts on top blogs including DailyBlogTips and ProBlogger.

He's blogged for paying clients in the U.S., U.K., Greece, and elsewhere about real estate, accounting, and weight loss, among other topics. Onibalusi says he impresses prospects with long, highly useful posts with strong key words that attract an ongoing stream of readers.

"Google has sent me most of my business," he says.

2. Books & eBooks

Build a major following on your blog, and you can earn well writing and selling your own books and e-books. That strategy has been successful for Jeff Goins of the writing and social-change blog GoinsWriter (goinswriter.com), who has two Kindle e-books and a traditionally published print book under his belt.

Launched in 2010 and now boasting 25,000 subscribers, GoinsWriter has loyal fans who help drive more than $3,500 a month in sales of his two low-priced e-books, including his co-authored *You Are a Writer (So Start Acting Like One)*, which goes for just $2.99.

Goins first creates excitement around his e-books by blogging about the upcoming release first. Then, as the publication date nears, he gives more than 100 diehard fans a free PDF of the e-book in exchange for Amazon reviews. When he officially publishes a few days later on Amazon and elsewhere, the glowing reviews help encourage thousands of purchases. The reviews and frequent downloads keep his e-books ranking highly for the writing category, which drives more sales. Links in the e-book also help bring more blog readers.

E-book sales also kicked off the blog-earning career of Pat Flynn, a southern Californian who first had modest blog-monetizing success with an e-book he wrote on how to pass an architectural exam. He started the Smart Passive Income (www.smartpassiveincome.com) blog in 2008 to dissect that success. This second blog went on to greatly surpass the original project, bringing in over $200,000 its first year alone.

3. Affiliate Sales

Flynn earns primarily through affiliate sales, a strategy in which a blogger receives a commission for selling someone else's product or service. It's an approach that works best with a large audience—Smart Passive Income has 57,000 subscribers and gets 100,000 visitors a month.

His audience includes many bloggers who need to set up their websites, so many of his affiliate products are tools or services that enable bloggers. Flynn's top-selling affiliate product in 2012 was website host Bluehost, from which he now typically earns $20,000 or more monthly. He receives a commission every time someone signs up for website hosting through his unique affiliate links.

"I find products that help them get from A to Z," he says. "They're recommended products I've actually used. You want to be sort of an expert in it."

Flynn builds loyalty by creating free blog posts that offer "high value content that would usually require payment." Rather than slapping up ads that might annoy readers, he simply states that site links earn him a commission. Fans are happy to click, and even send him thank-you notes about the products he sells.

Like many top-earning bloggers, Flynn uses videos and podcasts to help promote his blogs. Flynn's Smart Passive Income Podcast has brought many new readers—it's one of the top business-related podcasts on iTunes and has seen more than 2 million downloads.

4. Courses & Coaching

When you've built your reputation through delivering useful blog posts, you can sell your fans more advanced information on your topic. Courses and coaching are the main earners for Boost Blog Traffic's Morrow, who teaches a guest-blogging class and takes just 10 students at a time in his $10,000-a-head, five-month coaching course. The secret sauce in the guest-blogging class includes personal introductions by Morrow to top blog editors.

Build your authority enough, and customers pay just for the opportunity to learn from someone they respect, says Morrow.

"I'm not really selling products," he says. "I'm selling me."

Morrow attributes part of his earning success to hard work to improve the marketing campaigns for his paid programs. He says he's spent hundreds of hours testing and tinkering with marketing e-mails and promotional videos that help sell the courses. Now that he's refined his process, he says he needs to spend only five hours a week on his guest-blogging course. Affiliates do much of the selling of his blogging course for him.

An extension of this teaching niche is public speaking, for which top presenters can earn tens of thousands of dollars per appearance. Morrow recently presented at the New Media Expo (formerly known as BlogWorld), for instance.

5. Membership Community

Once you're publishing, teaching, speaking, and creating audio and video materials on a topic, bloggers can leverage all that content to earn even more through a paid membership community. Inside the community, members can access large amounts of training materials and their favorite expert's advice via chat forums for one low monthly rate, instead of paying for it piecemeal. The community model allows bloggers to earn more as additional members join without having to do much more work, as members mostly access existing content.

Large communities can be major money generators—for instance, A-List Blogger Club (www.alistbloggingbootcamps.com/alist-blogger-club-join), a blog-building training community started by top blogger Leo Babauta of Zen Habits that I used to learn how to build my own blog, had roughly 900 members in 2012 paying $20 apiece per month. The blog Write to Done (writetodone.com) serves as the main platform that introduces writers to the club.

Blogging is not for every writer. It's a lot of work coming up with post ideas and writing several posts a month or even a week. It can be many months until a blog starts to earn money, and there are no guarantees it will ever catch on. But for writers with the drive to stick with it and a willingness to learn about blog marketing, the rewards can be rich.

Carol Tice writes the Make a Living Writing (www.makealivingwriting.com) blog and runs the writers learning community Freelance Writers Den (freelancewritersden.com). She has written two nonfiction business books and co-authored the Kindle e-book *13 Ways to Get the Writing Done Faster* (www.amazon.com/Ways-Writing-Done-Faster-ebook/dp/B009XM03SK).

FINDING FREELANCE OPPORTUNITIES ONLINE:

How to Start Making Money Online

by Carol Tice

Print markets have been hard-hit by the economic downturn, especially newspapers. But there's another part of the freelance-writing marketplace that's still growing—and it's as close as your computer.

Demand for writers is strong online, and expected to keep growing as readers increasingly consume news and read magazines via the Internet. To make their online product stand out, many print publications assign online-exclusive features. There are also a growing number of former print magazines that are now only published online, including *U.S. News & World Report*, *eWeek* and *PC Magazine*. Though the *Writers Market* only recently began tracking online publications, there are already over 100 online consumer and trade publication markets included in this guide.

Publications aren't the only digital writing opportunity, either. Increasingly, businesses use website content including blog posts as an affordable way to find new customers and keep existing customers loyal. Changes to how Google ranks websites have brought lower search rankings for sites using duplicate content—and that means more businesses need writers to create unique material for their site.

"Google's 2011 algorithm update has created an even stronger demand from clients for richer, original, and better-quality content," says Ed Gandia, co-author of *The Wealthy Freelancer*. "It's definitely good news."

AVOIDING SCAMS

Many writers have already discovered the dark underbelly of the online writing markets: writing "opportunities" at appallingly low rates—$10 per written piece or even less—and outright scams. Fly-by-night startups promise only exposure and a link to your website, or possibly a few pennies if readers click on your page's ads.

Some website editors may request several sample articles on a specific topic before deciding to make a hire. Often, the work is then simply published without payment or permission.

Avoid ripoffs with a few simple steps:

- **RESEARCH YOUR MARKET.** Remember that anyone can put up a website. Find the business name and then do Internet searches to see what's being said. The best on-line markets are usually long-established publications and businesses. Try to get a sense of the organization's size, too, as bigger markets often pay better. Don't take claims about "big traffic" on a site at face value, either—check web-traffic ranking sites such as Alexa (http://www.alexa.com/) to get a more reliable measure of a site's readership.

- **GET FULL CONTACT INFORMATION.** Would you write for a print magazine that provided no street address or phone number, where the editor didn't give you her last name? I hope not. Don't treat online markets any differently.

- **ASK AROUND.** Before you write for an online market, tap your writer networks to see if anyone has written for the site previously. Other writers may be able to give you a reality check on whether it's a legitimate market.

- **SIGN ON THE DOTTED LINE.** If a website wants you to start writing to meet a short deadline and says a contract will follow later, be wary. Get a contract that spells out payment, payment terms, deadlines, and ownership rights before you start work.

SPECIAL SKILLS FOR BLOGGERS

With some online markets, writing can be as simple as e-mailing your editor a Word document with your article. But writers with other skills—social-media savvy, experience using key words to get search rankings, and knowledge of blogging software such as WordPress—have a definite edge, especially in landing blogging assignments.

For instance, at AOL's community-news network Patch.com, editors favor writers who understand how to promote their pieces on Twitter and other social-media platforms, says editor-in-chief Brian Farnham.

"Social media is part of our DNA," says Farnham. "If you know how to do it, it doesn't just benefit us—it benefits your personal brand."

Writing a personal niche blog and promoting it in social media is a great way to gain experience and create a writing sample to show editors. Your blog can also be a showcase that demonstrates you understand online writing style.

Online readers tend to be skimmers and scanners, preferring articles with bulleted or numbered lists or bolded subheads, notes Christina Hoffmann, editor of the National Association of Realtors' HouseLogic (http://www.houselogic.com/) website for homeowners.

Launched in early 2010, the site aims to publish one new story each business day, assigns $1-a-word features, and also pays bloggers at competitive rates.

BREAK-IN OPPORTUNITY: ONLINE LOCAL NEWS

Community or "hyperlocal" sites offer decent pay to new writers with an interest in reporting on local events. These sites feature neighborhood news stories that are off the radar of big-city papers. The big gorilla of this niche is AOL's Patch.com (http://www.patch.com/), but your region may also have independent sites that do well and offer writer pay. One example is the popular West Seattle Blog, which gets more than 1 million monthly pageviews.

Launched in 2009, Patch has since grown to over 860 sites in communities across the U.S. Editor-in-chief Brian Farnham says Patch continues to expand where it sees a community need or a big news story. For instance, Patch added sites in New Hampshire, Iowa and South Carolina in late 2011 to get a ringside seat for presidential-primary coverage.

Most Patch sites have relationships with at least two regular freelance writers, says Farnham. Good story pitches have a new slant on a local issue, and writers should be ready to turn stories around quickly.

"We love people with a reporter's soul and the motivation to get out there," he says. "Not everyone wants to cover a city council meeting for three hours."

Rates vary, depending on length and whether fieldwork is required, but generally run $50-100 per story—similar to what you might get at a local alternative city paper. Editors are accessible, with email addresses listed at the top of their Patch's home page.

The best time to break in is when a new Patch starts up, Farnham says. As the sites mature, they have fewer paid assignments and rely more on feeds from unpaid community bloggers. On the plus side, if you get accepted to freelance at one local Patch, it's easy to pitch other area Patches for additional assignments.

Shorter sentences and shorter paragraphs are typical online compared with print markets, says Hoffmann. Additionally, online assignments often require writers to include links to relevant related materials and mentioned resources. "Internal" links that send readers back to older content on the same website are also important.

Pay tends to be lower for blogging work than for articles—$50 to $100 a post is considered a good blog-post rate. Major corporations and established media companies tend to be good payers, says longtime financial writer Lydia Dishman, who has blogged for websites owned by *Forbes* magazine, CBS, and American Express, among others. Dishman says her experience in social media definitely helped her land her blogging gigs. Writers with a journalism background such as Dishman are well-positioned for blogging, as many have deadline-writing experience and understand libel issues, which are a prime concern for website owners.

Paid blogging may call for posting as often as every business day, so you'll need to know how to scan relevant news sources online to develop a constant supply of story ideas on your topic. One quick method is to set up Google alerts (http://www.google.com/alerts) on key industry phrases.

"You need to be tapped into everywhere there might be news on your industry," she says.

FINDING YOUR FIRST ONLINE MARKETS

If you haven't written for online markets and are looking to break in, start with websites of local businesses you frequent, or an industry where you have experience. For instance, when copywriter Sean Platt broke into writing online, targeting local florists to write web copy made sense, as he'd previously owned a flower shop. He's since branched out to other industries, writing for companies in the legal, tax, and health insurance fields. One of his specialties is creating white papers for companies to use as free downloads to build customer interest.

"I wouldn't even leave your city," says Platt, who writes the GhostwriterDad blog. "Just look for the people who are making money online. Those are the people who can afford to pay you."

To discover good online markets, scan news sites for announcements about new websites or editor changes at online publications. For business clients, read the business pages of your local paper or press-release sites to find local companies that are promoting their success, says Platt. Then, study their website along with competitors' to spot missing elements you could pitch as a writing project. A blog that hasn't been updated in months is always a good entry point.

One challenge to cracking online markets is locating contact names. Where most print publications have a masthead page that lists editor contact information, finding out who to contact at an online magazine or information portal can take a bit more sleuthing.

If the "About" or "Contact" pages aren't helpful, try searching Google for "editor <publication name>." Alternatively, try searching for the company on LinkedIn to see if you can turn up editor names. Another social-media resource for finding editors is MuckRack (http://muckrack.com/), which tracks media players' activity on Twitter. If the site lists a phone number, simply call to ask who you could send a pitch. Most online markets prefer e-mail submissions.

ONLINE ARTICLE MARKETS

If you are currently writing for any print publications, begin your online-market search with a look at their website. Compare it with the magazine to see if they are creating unique content or "online exclusives." If so, try to learn their needs from your current editor or get an introduction to the online features editor. This is how I crossed over from writing for *Entrepreneur*'s print magazine to blogging for their website.

Online publications have a bad reputation for offering low pay compared with print. But ad dollars have gravitated away from print and to the Internet in the past few years—for instance, digital-ad revenue at *The Atlantic* topped print-ad revenue for the first time in fall 2011. That growing online revenue is helping to lift online writing rates.

Increasingly stiff competition for Internet readers in many topic niches is also inspiring rate hikes. For instance, after several years of commissioning only $100 short how-to business articles, in 2009 the portal Allbusiness.com (http://www.allbusiness.com/) looked to differentiate the site by assigning in-depth, reported features to experienced business writers at much higher rates, notes former senior editor David Hennessy. (The site ceased making assignments completely in early 2012 as owner Dun & Bradstreet contemplated its sale—an example of the rapid change that characterizes today's online media markets.)

Where most print publications have a masthead page that lists editor contact information, finding out who to contact at an online magazine or information portal can take a bit more sleuthing.

At base, querying online article markets is a similar process to querying in print. Study your target website carefully—"Follow the brand on Facebook and Twitter too," Hoffmann says—then, query editors with fresh ideas that haven't been covered on the site before. HouseLogic's Hoffmann likes to see "buzzy, engaging ideas."

Writers' most common mistake? "I don't get a sense the writer looked at our site to see if we already have content on that angle," she says.

As with most online sites, Hoffmann would like to see article pitches for HouseLogic that are both newsy and could use relevant industry key words and phrases that receive a high volume of online searches, says Hoffmann.

To prep an online query, you can discover popular search terms using Google's free Keyword Tool (https://adwords.google.com/select/KeywordToolExternal).

BUSINESS WEBSITES

To stay competitive, businesses are spending more to keep their websites fresh, says copywriter-author Ed Gandia. One of his favorite copywriting assignments is a "website refresh," where a medium-to-large business's website of 50 pages or more is revamped with fresh content. Gandia recommends targeting companies selling high-margin products such as software that are frequently updated. That creates a need for regular rewrites.

Writing web content can be a great initial project, as it allows you to learn a lot about a business, notes Gandia. You can then propose additional projects such as white papers, case studies, virtual brochures or updated brand messaging. Rates can range from $50 an hour and up to $200 an hour or more, as you acquire expertise in a company or industry.

Think you won't know what to write? Ask lots of questions of the business owner. Then study competitors' sites and ask the client which ones they think do the best job.

"Your swipe file," he says, "is right there online."

Carol Tice has more than a decade of freelance-writing experience, for publications including *Entrepreneur, Seattle Times, Seattle Magazine,* and *Alaska Airlines* magazine, and clients including Costco, American Express, and Dun & Bradstreet. She writes the Make a Living Writing blog (http://www.makealivingwriting.com) and serves as Den Mother of the writers' learning and support community, Freelance Writers Den (http://freelancewritersden.com).

REPRINTS AND RESLANTS

More Money in the Bank

by Sue Bradford Edwards

Your goals this year include making more money with your writing, and it should be doable. After all, you've been selling your work for some time now and have a solid resume. Deadlines pepper your calendar.

To increase your income, you can take on more assignments, but look at your calendar. You're working close to capacity now. If you take on much more, the quality of your work will suffer.

Fortunately, there is another solution. Maximize your efforts by selling both your research and your writing multiple times.

SELLING ONE PIECE REPEATEDLY

The easiest way to do this is by selling a piece of writing more than once. Selling a reprint is, in short, re-selling a piece of writing that has already been published. To make this work, you have to plan ahead in terms of what rights you sell.

"I sell a lot of reprints, so I always try to retain reprint rights, or nonexclusive reprint rights," says Kelly James-Enger, a long time freelancer and author of books including *Writer for Hire: 101 Secrets to Freelance Success*. "Sometimes markets will buy first N.A. serial rights and then I can reprint the story after the story first runs. In other cases, I'll sell all rights but see if I can negotiate retaining nonexclusive reprint rights. Markets don't always agree but it doesn't hurt to ask."

Jennifer Brown Banks, a freelancer who writes for blogs and magazines, agrees. "I typically extend 'one-time' rights or 'reprint' rights; thus I retain authorship to my pieces to place them as I wish in the future."

If you have kept the necessary rights, the next step is to find receptive markets. "Sometimes I Google 'reprint markets,'" Banks says. "Other times I simply check the writer's guidelines of popular publications to assess the possibilities. Checking by themes is another way."

While more smaller than larger publications accept reprints, some niche markets are also more receptive. "I look for smaller, regional, and/or specialty mags that need content about subjects I cover," James-Enger says. "I've had the most success selling to parenting, fitness/health, and bridal magazines."

Another possible market for reprints is anthologies. This is where Abigail Green, author of over 200 individual pieces, resells her essays.

If you are already making sales, an editor may contact you. "*Writer's Digest* once asked for a reprint of a piece I did for their magazine, for inclusion in a special edition annual publication, and I simply sold it for 25% of the original price," says C. Hope Clark, editor of Funds for Writers and author of the mystery *Lowcountry Bribe*. "We both recognized that as a fair price and didn't dicker on the payment. Very simple arrangement."

When an editor wants to reprint something that has appeared in another family of magazines, arrangements become more complicated. "Sometimes the editor has seen a particular story and wants to run it in her own magazine," says James-Enger. "If I own the rights, we negotiate from there. In others, an editor I've worked with before, or who knows I have hundreds of articles available, will contact me and ask for a story on a specific subject. If I have something that will work, I'll ask what they usually pay for reprints or ask for a specific amount to reprint it."

Banks has also been contacted by an editor. "I have been approached somewhat informally by a regular editor with whom I've worked for many years," says Banks. "Since she manages a print publication, she will sometimes request to use articles I have posted online for a similar niche."

Selling reprints takes very little work, but some writers wonder if the check you will receive is too small to bother. "I've actually made more money from my reprints in some cases than the original article," says Banks. "I've been paid $50 for a feature piece that I've later resold for $150."

The downside is that, because you are selling the same article, you will only be able to sell it so many times before you are looking at competing magazines. No editor wants to run content that a competitor has already published. Fortunately, you can also increase your income by reselling your research and basic knowledge on a topic.

COMING AT THE TOPIC IN A DIFFERENT WAY

Reslants offer more opportunities than reprints because, you are selling similar, not identical, pieces of writing. Explains Green, "Let's say you see a movie. You can write a movie review, or you can write a piece for writers on what they can learn from actors, or you can write an opinion piece on how shows like Glee and The Voice have influenced popular culture," she says. "You aren't taking the same article and selling it to *Parents* and *Parenting*. You're taking the same topic and reslanting it to different audiences. In most cases, the article will vary so much because you are writing for different audiences, different markets, and a different word count, that they are completely different articles."

Many writers worry that reslanting a topic will be just as much work as writing a whole new piece. "I usually end up with five times as much material as I can use in the finished piece," Green says. "Why let it go to waste? With practice, you go into an assignment thinking 'How else can I approach this topic for a different market?' It becomes second nature."

Banks agrees, "It is a means of 'working smarter, not harder,'" she says. "I typically do this with my relationship articles, as well as 'how-to' writing pieces. These are always popular reads."

THE DOWNSIDE TO RESLANTING

Do you dread writing two articles on the same topic, let alone four or five? You aren't alone.

"I'm not the normal voice of authority on this," says Clark. "I abhor having to take old material and reshape it. I'd much prefer to maybe take resources or research and write an entirely new piece. My voice is fresher, and I never have to worry about anyone saying they've seen it someplace before."

Says Clark, "My feelings about this go back to a fiasco that occurred years ago with two competing magazines. I took the same topic and wrote entirely different pieces for these two magazines. While the topic was similar, the pieces were original. However, these competing magazines just happened to decide to publish the pieces in the same month. I received my writer's copies in the mail the same day, and while I should've been ecstatic to see my name in print, I was devastated that they'd chosen the same month. Even though they were unique pieces, the editors were not happy. My name was the same. The topic was the same."

"I've never pitched competing magazines since. And if I ever decide to, it'll be with entirely different topics. One of the magazines wouldn't speak to me for five years. I totally get it. Magazine editors have their hands full trying to keep subscribers through novel and unique material, and situations like mine don't make their jobs easier. My advice to others is to avoid reslanting and refocusing pieces to competing publications. They watch each other like a hawk."

The moral of the story? Make sure no two stories appear the same. Change your approach. Change your audience. A humorous essay for a women's magazine doesn't duplicate a journalistic article for a men's fitness site. The editors won't feel cheated and you won't be bored writing two pieces that are too similar.

Change the market and the audience and you will have a piece that is only vaguely related to the others you have written on the same topic. "I wrote a piece for *Fit* on using heart rate monitors to lose weight," James-Enger says. "Then I did a story for *Experience Life* on using them to get more out of your workout. Several months later, I wrote a piece for a men's fitness magazine on using heart rate monitors to get more out of your cardio workout. Typically men prefer to lift weights and hate doing cardio. Then I wrote a piece for *Family Circle* on using your heart rate to get more out of your walks. What I do is come up with a specific angle for the story for a particular market, and see how many times I can reslant the topic—in this case, how heart rate monitors can help you get more from your workout." In this way, James-Enger wrote four unique articles using the same basic idea.

Green often reslants her work by changing her approach, penning both essays and articles. "I could write a first person essay about growing up in a TV-limited household," she says. "That's just a straight essay, but I have also reslanted that into a reported piece where I interviewed experts and included reports on the effects of screen time."

A new tone can also reslant a piece. "Even within just the essay genre, you can reslant," Green says. "You can take a more humorous slant and do a humor piece. I've written some essays in the style of a letter to my younger self. It's the same material but you alter how you approach it."

Using different sources for different markets is another way to reslant a piece. "If I'm writing for an online magazine and want to later submit a piece to a print publication, I may change the links that I provide as 'resources' to book recommendations," Banks says. "Additionally, I will sometimes lessen word counts for online readers and give shorter paragraphs and bullet points for easier skimming of material."

These authors aren't reslanting and then looking for a market. "Usually when I'm reslanting I'm doing it for a specific market such as one looking for letters to your younger self," says Green. Having a market in mind can help you find the new slant.

Once you know a topic, each subsequent piece comes together with less effort. "I think the best advice is to avoid what I call 'one-shots,' where you write about a subject only once," James-Enger says. "Come up with different angles and look for noncompeting markets that you can pitch the story to. You'll still have do additional research, typically interviewing more or different sources, but you already know a lot about the subject matter so the second, third, etc. stories take less time to write and make you more efficient. Even if you don't think of a second angle when you first come up with the initial idea, be open to finding more as you research and write the piece. That happens to me frequently. Or I will see something in the news or a recent study that makes me think of a new way to approach a story I have written in the past."

One final piece of advice. Periodically go through your files and take a look at what hasn't sold. "One example that I give in my class I had a work related anecdote that I reslanted 5 different ways over the course of several years before I finally sold it," Green says. "I tried a women's magazine, a business magazines, tweaking it slightly for the market. It finally sold to the career section of a newspaper when I slanted it to be about finding personal space at work. That wasn't the approach I took in the original but I eventually found a home for it." Reslanting your work opens up a variety of markets and increases sales.

You've heard the advice—work smarter, not harder. Apply this to your writing life by selling your research and your writing as many times as possible. If you do, you will find your by-lines and bank deposits adding up as you build a name for yourself as the go-to author on a variety of topics.

SUE BRADFORD EDWARDS works from her home in St. Louis, MIssouri. Her articles have appeared in *Writer's Digest, Children's Writer* newsletter, the *Writer's Guide,* and more publications. Find out more about her and her work at One Writer's Journey (suebe.wordpress.com).

FUNDS FOR WRITERS 101:

Find Money You Didn't Know Existed

....

by C. Hope Clark

When I completed writing my novel over a decade ago, I imagined the next step was simply to find a publisher and watch the book sell. Like most writers, my goal was to earn a living doing what I loved so I could walk away from the day job. No such luck. Between rejection and newfound knowledge that a novel can take years to sell enough for a single house payment, I opened my mind to other writing avenues. After researching in depth, I learned that there's no *one* way to find funds to support your writing; instead there are *many*. So many, in fact, that I felt the need to share the volume of knowledge I collected, and I called it FundsforWriters.com.

Funds are money. But obtaining those funds isn't necessarily a linear process, or a one-dimensional path. As a serious writer, you study all options at your fingertips, entertaining financial resources that initially don't make sense as well as the obvious. In the end, it's about publishing. In the interim, it's about identifying the fiscal resources to get you there.

GRANTS

Grants come from government agencies, nonprofits, businesses and even generous individuals. They do not have to be repaid, as long as you use the grant as intended. No two are alike. Therefore, you must do your homework to find the right match between your grant need and the grant provider's mission. Grantors like being successful at their mission just as you like excelling at yours. So they screen applicants, ensuring they fit the rules and show promise to follow through.

Don't fear grants. Sure, you're judged by a panel, and rejection is part of the game, but you already know that as a writer. Gigi Rosenberg, author of *The Artist's Guide to Grant Writing*, states, "If one funder doesn't want to invest in your project, find another who does.

And if nobody does, then begin it any way you can. Once you've started, that momentum will help your project find its audience and its financial support."

TYPES OF GRANTS

Grants can send you to retreats, handle emergencies, provide mentors, pay for conferences, or cover travel. They also can be called awards, fellowships, residencies, or scholarships. But like any aspect of your writing journey, define how any tool, even a grant, fits into your plans. Your mission must parallel a grantor's mission.

The cream-of-the-crop grants have no strings attached. Winning recipients are based upon portfolios and an application that defines a work-in-progress. You don't have to be a Pulitzer winner, but you must prove your establishment as a writer.

You find most of these opportunities in state arts commissions. Find them at www.nasaa-arts.org or as a partner listed at the National Endowment for the Arts website, www.nea.gov. Not only does your state's arts commission provide funding, but the players can direct you to other grant opportunities, as well as to artists who've gone before you. Speaking to grant winners gives you a wealth of information and a leg up in designing the best application.

Foundations and nonprofits fund the majority of grants. Most writers' organizations are nonprofits. Both the Mystery Writers of America (www.mysterywriters.org) and Society of Children's Book Writers and Illustrators (www.scbwi.org) offer scholarships and grants.

Many retreats are nonprofits. Journalist and freelancer Alexis Grant, (http://alexis-grant.com/) tries to attend a retreat a year. Some ask her to pay, usually on a sliding scale based upon income, and others provide scholarships. Each time, she applies with a clear definition of what she hopes to gain from the two to five-week trips. "It's a great way to get away from the noise of everyday responsibilities, focus on writing well and meet other people who prioritize writing. I always return home with a new perspective." A marvelous resource to find writing retreats is the Alliance of Artists Communities (http://www.artist-communities.org/).

Laura Lee Perkins won four Artist-in-Residence slots with the National Park Service (http://nps.gov). The federal agency has 43 locations throughout the United States where writers and artists live for two to four weeks. From Acadia National Park in Maine to Sleeping Bear Dunes National Lakeshore in Michigan, Laura spoke to tourists about her goals to write a book about Native American music. "Memories of the US National Parks' beauty and profound serenity will continue to enrich my work. Writers find unparalleled inspiration, quietude, housing, interesting staff, and a feeling of being in the root of your artistic desires."

Don't forget writers' conferences. While they may not advertise financial aid, many have funds available in times of need. Always ask as to the availability of a scholarship or work-share program that might enable your attendance.

Grants come in all sizes. FundsforWriters posts most emergency grants on its grants page (www.fundsforwriters.com/grants.htm) as well as periodic new grant opportunities such as the Sustainable Arts Foundation (www.sustainableartsfoundation.org) that offers grants twice a year to writers and artists with children under the age of 18, or the Awesome Foundation (www.awecomefoundation.org), which gives $1,000 grants to "awesome" creative projects.

Novelist Joan Dempsey won an Elizabeth George Foundation grant (http://www.elizabethgeorgeonline.com/foundation/index.htm) in early 2012. "I applied to the Foundation for a research grant that included three trips to places relevant to my novel-in-progress, trips I otherwise could not have afforded. Not only does the grant provide travel funds, but it also provides validation that I'm a serious writer worthy of investment, which is great for my psyche and my resume."

FISCAL SPONSORSHIP

Nonprofits have access to an incredibly large number of grants that individuals do not, and have the ability to offer their tax-exempt status to groups and individuals involved in activities related to their mission. By allowing a nonprofit to serve as your grant overseer, you may acquire funds for your project.

Deborah Marshall is President of the Missouri Writers Guild (www.missouriwritersguild.org) and founder of the Missouri Warrior Writers Project, with ample experience with grants in the arts. "Although grant dollars are available for individual writers, writing the grant proposal becomes difficult without significant publication credits. Partnering with a nonprofit organization, whether it is a writing group, service, community organization, or any 501(c)3, can fill in those gaps to make a grant application competitive. Partnering not only helps a writer's name become known, but it also assists in building that all-important platform."

Two excellent groups that offer fiscal sponsorship for writers are The Fractured Atlas (www.fracturedatlas.org) and Artspire (www.artspire.org) sponsored by the New York Foundation for the Arts and open to all US citizens. Visit The Foundation Center (www.foundationcenter.org) for an excellent tutorial guide to fiscal sponsorship.

CROWD SOURCING

Crowd sourcing is a co-op arrangement where people support artists directly, much like the agricultural co-op movement where individuals fund farming operations in exchange for fresh food. Kickstarter (www.kickstarter.com) has made huge strides in making this funding method successful in the arts.

Basically, the writer proposes his project, and for a financial endorsement as low as $1, donors receive some token in return, like an autographed book, artwork, or bookmark.

The higher the donation, the bigger the *wow* factor in the gift. Donors do not receive ownership in the project.

Meagan Adele Lopez (www.ladywholunches.net) presented her debut self-published book *Three Questions* to Kickstarter readers, requesting $4,400 to take her book on tour, create a book trailer, pre-order books, and redesign the cover. Eighty-eight backers pledged a total of $5,202. She was able to hire an editor and a company that designed film trailers. For every $750 she received over her plan, she added a new city to her book tour.

Other crowd sourcing companies are up and coming to include Culture 360 (www.culture360.org) that serves Asia and Europe, and Indie GoGo (www.indiegogo.com), as well as Rocket Hub (www.rockethub.com). And nothing stops you from simply asking those you know to support your project. The concept is elementary.

CONTESTS

Contests offer financial opportunity, too. Of course you must win, place or show, but many writers overlook the importance that contests have on a career. These days, contests not only open doors to publishing, name recognition, and money, but listing such achievements in a query letter might make an agent or publisher take a second glance. Noting your wins on a magazine pitch might land a feature assignment. Mentioning your accolades to potential clients could clinch a freelance deal.

I used contests as a barometer when fleshing out my first mystery novel, *A Lowcountry Bribe*, Bell Bridge Books. After I placed in several contests, earned a total of $750, and reached the semi-finals of the Amazon Breakthrough Novel Award (www.createspace.com/abna), my confidence grew strong enough to pitch agents. My current agent admits that the contest wins drew her in.

Contests can assist in sales of existing books, not only aiding sales but also enticing more deals for future books . . . or the rest of your writing profession.

Whether writing short stories, poetry, novels or nonfiction, contests abound. As with any call for submission, study the rules. Double checking with entities that screen, like FundsforWriters.com and WinningWriters.com, will help alleviate concerns when selecting where to enter.

FREELANCING

A thick collection of freelancing clips can make an editor sit up and take notice. You've been vetted and accepted by others in the business, and possibly established a following. The more well known the publications, the brighter your aura.

Sooner or later in your career, you'll write an article. In the beginning, articles are a great way to gain your footing. As your career develops, you become more of an expert, and are expected to enlighten and educate about your journey and the knowledge you've acquired. Articles are, unarguably, one of the best means to income and branding for writers.

Trade magazines, national periodicals, literary journals, newsletters, newspapers and blogs all offer you a chance to present yourself, earn money, and gain readers for a platform. Do not discount them as income earners.

Linda Formichelli, of Renegade Writer fame (www.therenegadewriter.com) leaped into freelance magazine writing because she simply loved to write, and that love turned her into an expert. "I never loved working to line someone else's pockets." A full-time freelancer since 1997, with credits like *Family Circle*, *Redbook*, and *Writer's Digest*, she also writes articles, books, e-courses, and e-books about her profession as a magazine writer.

JOBS

Part-time, full-time, temporary or permanent, writing jobs hone your skills, pad your resume, and present avenues to movers and shakers you wouldn't necessarily meet on your own. Government and corporate managers hire writers under all sorts of guises like Social Media Specialist and Communications Specialist, as well as the expected Reporter and Copywriter.

Alexis Grant considers her prior jobs as catapults. "Working at a newspaper (*Houston Chronicle*) and a news magazine (*US News & World Report*) for six years provided the foundation for what I'm doing now as a freelancer. Producing stories regularly on tight deadlines will always make you a better writer."

Joan Dempsey chose to return to full-time work and write her novel on the side, removing worries about her livelihood. "My creative writing was suffering trying to freelance. So, I have a day job that supports me now." She still maintains her Facebook presence to continue building her platform for her pending novel.

DIVERSIFICATION

Most importantly, however, is learning how to collect all your funding options and incorporate them into your plan. The successful writer doesn't perform in one arena. Instead, he thrives in more of a three-ring circus.

Grant states it well. "For a long while I thought of myself as only a journalist, but there are so many other ways to use my skills. Today my income comes from three streams: helping small companies with social media and blogging (the biggest source), writing and selling e-guides and courses (my favorite), and taking freelance writing or editing assignments."

Formichelli is proud of being flexible. "When I've had it with magazine writing, I put more energy into my e-courses, and vice versa. Heck, I'm even a certified personal trainer, so if I get really sick of writing I can work out. But a definite side benefit to diversifying is that I'm more protected from the feast-or-famine nature of writing."

Sometimes pursuing the more common sense or lucrative income opportunity can open doors for the dream. When my novel didn't sell, I began writing freelance articles. Then I established FundsforWriters, using all the grant, contest, publisher and market research I did for myself. A decade later, once the site thrived with over 45,000 readers, I used the very research I'd gleaned for my readers to find an agent and sign a publishing contract . . . for the original novel started so long ago.

You can fight to fund one project or study all resources and fund a career. Opportunity is there. Just don't get so wrapped up in one angle that you miss the chance to invest more fully in your future.

C. HOPE CLARK manages FundsforWriters.com, a site selected for *Writer's Digest's* 101 Best Websites for Writers for the past twelve years. She is also author of *A Lowcountry Bribe*, the first in The Palmetto State Mystery Series published by Bell Bridge Books . She lives on the banks of Lake Murray, South Carolina and presents to several writers conferences each year.

GHOSTWRITING 101

by *Eva Shaw*

What do *Jersey Shore*'s Snooki, B.B. King, Hillary Clinton, Richard Petty and Michelle Obama in common? They're friendly with ghosts. These people and countless others have hired ghostwriters to write for them.

Celebrities, entrepreneurs, academics, sports stars, business movers and shakers, media darlings, scientists, politicians, reality-wannabe flashes in the pan, even kids who have seen heaven, along with regular people who have a story to tell or information to share routinely engage ghostwriters to capture their words for print. It's estimated that 60 to perhaps 80 percent of published nonfiction books are ghosted. Among those in the know, it's said that some of the big names in fiction work with or have hired ghosts.

IT'S REWARDING

Curious how you can boost your writing career by ghostwriting? Let's walk through the process and then decide. Ghosts write a multitude of projects including novels, nonfiction books, essays, articles, blogs, reports, speeches and columns. To make it simple for your crash course in ghosting, let's refer to projects as "books."

Ghostwriting is rewarding on countless career levels but novices often have misconceptions about it. Once in a while I'll even meet a hopeful writer who sneers and says, "It's immoral to be a ghostwriter." Not so. Actually so way not so.

Sure it's not for every writer, but becoming a ghost can skyrocket a career regardless of the genre. Imagine collecting outstanding clips, have "your" work appear in a multitude of publications, able to give knock-out references, and build a rock-solid platform? Think about how having those perks would help when you're ready to sell that novel or submit a nonfiction book proposal. Exactly. You'd have credibility to spare and your own writing business.

In our service-oriented society, ghostwriting is a field with growth potential. When I began ghosting years back, ghosts were hush-hush. Today ghostwriters, sometimes called collaborators, editors or even "great helpers," are part of the publishing team that brings a multitude of projects to market.

....

I make it clear to my clients that their agent, editor or publisher must be aware of our relationship.

....

Agents, editors and publishers appreciate working with a professional writer and there's no need for a ghost to stay in the closet. I make it clear to my clients that their agent, editor or publisher must be aware of our relationship.

Why do clients hire a ghost? The reasons include:

- The client may be an adequate writer, but doesn't want to write the book.
- The client realizes that good writing requires expertise; it's more efficient when performed by a professional.
- The client may not have the skills or talent to write.
- The client may not have the time to write.

Why don't more writers ghost? Perhaps it is the fear of the unknown or not being quite as sure of their craft as they would like others to believe. Ghostwriting requires you to be a better-than-average writer and have first-rate people skills.

THE GHOSTING PROCESS

The process for all ghosting is similar whether you're writing a book or an article although the steps might be in a different order.

- The client approaches you or you find the client.
- You send or provide samples of your writing and give references.
- You meet, review the project, and work out the project.
- You discuss all the financial details. (FYI: I talked with other ghosts and we have much in common when it comes to money. We usually split our fees into two to four parts, with half of the fee due on the contract's signing.)
- If needed, an attorney or agent might look over the contract to make sure it outlines exactly what your role will be.
- A timeline for completion of the project is developed and agreed upon.
- You write the book. You work on as many drafts as necessary until you're satisfied and know your client will be, too.
- You give the draft to the client. The client reviews it, makes changes or comments, and you go back to work.

- You rewrite the book and present the final draft.
- You're paid the final installment and the client says, "Good bye."

SIMPLE AS 1, 2, 3

Clients are everywhere. Really.

1. Tell everyone you know that you are a ghostwriter. Go ahead. Whether you live in a hamlet or a metropolis, there are people who need your writing services, but they won't know until you explain how and what you do. While plenty of ghosts advertise their services, that's expensive. Instead, I ask for referrals—that's been working extremely well for 20 years.
2. Pitch the publishing industry. Publishers (big and small), agents, editors and book packagers seek out ghostwriters. Why not write some sizzling queries and offer your services? Too few ghosts do this.
3. Keep your eyes out for clients. Did you just read an article or meet someone who has an amazing story or a fascinating career? You're looking at a potential ghosting client. Approach this person for an article interview, place the article, and then consider if she or he just might want to write a book (using you as a ghost).

THE UNVARNISHED TRUTH

When the project is completed, some clients will bid you farewell especially if you've been hired as a contractor. Most of mine stay with me for the long run. How so? I provide a service that's fast, on deadline, efficient and cost effective. I'm honorable, confidential, and competitive in pricing, provide references and always go the extra distance.

Ghosting isn't always rosy. Sometimes there's a bad match between the ghost and the client.

Why bother? Clients go out of their way to recommend me to others. I've written for doctors, lawyers, movie stars, high-profile CEOs, artists, entrepreneurs, fitness and health experts and others with stories to share. I call my clients the "authors" of the material and keep their names and our projects private unless the client permits me to share the info. I'm often privy to a lifestyle or opinions unknown to the public; my clients trust me with their work and lives.

Ghostwriting isn't always rosy. Sometimes there's a bad match between the ghost and client or the client decides to write the material themselves. With corporate clients, budgets are snatched away or the corporation goes in another direction. Once I was fired when

I confronted a client because she asked me to plagiarize, hotly claimed the writing as her own. It stings. If it does happen to you, dust off your britches and try again.

IT'S THE VOICE

There is an art to capturing your client and it starts with listening. You not only must know how to write, but be able to listen and then translate the voice of your client into words that reflect the flair, style, phrases, unusual slang, witticisms, and elements that make the client sound unique. Clients talk about soft markets, bottom lines, team play, cosmic consciousness, and billions of expressions. Some use elongated, complex sentences interspersed with statistics; others prefer short, snappy, slightly whimsical phrases. Duplicating word patterns is the essence of ghostwriting. Here's a secret: All ghostwriting clients want to have their written material sound intelligent and smooth, even if their speaking patterns and words are not.

There is an art to capturing clients and it starts with listening.

If you haven't done so already, start listening to how people speak. How do their speech patterns differ? Next time you're watching the evening news, why not practice "ghosting" with the anchors? In addition to words, watch how they use their hands, change their expressions, move their eyes, and even hesitate when thinking. This info conveys the distinct persona of clients.

INTERVIEWING CLIENTS

Yes, you should interview clients although you don't have to tell them you're doing so. At your first meeting, most clients want to know: Do you like the project's idea? What is your background? What's your experience? Are you available? What's this going to cost? Be ready with answers and you'll be considered a pro.

What should you look for in a client? That depends, however, at your meeting, if the client's comments or behavior checks any items below, proceed with eyes wide open.

- The client is late more than once for a meeting and without a reasonable excuse.
- The client is overbearing.
- The client doesn't let you ask questions.
- The client has trouble staying on the topic.
- The client forgets your name or that your time is valuable.
- The client insists you agree right then to write the book, without knowing all the details.
- The client balks or pales when you discuss money.
- The client wants you to write for free.

Before you decide to accept a ghosting gig, ponder the project and ask yourself some questions about this potential client and their book.

- Can the client afford my services?
- Will I be able to sleep if I disagree with the book's ideas or topics?
- What's my gut-level feeling about the client and the book?
- How committed is the client to the book?
- Can I be totally at ease with the client?
- Will the client allow me to be truthful?

Be sure to ask your potential clients questions. I do. The following questions give insight into a client's motivation and help me decide if a client is right. There are no wrong answers.

- Why are you hiring a ghost? Most will say they don't have the time or talent to write.
- What is your goal for the project? If money is the goal, that's okay.
- What working arrangement do you visualize with the ghost?
- Where are you in the writing process?
- Who else have you worked with? Ugly comments? Could be a red flag.
- Who will buy your book and why? You might have to educate a client on this because, as you know, there has to be a market for the book.
- What is the budget for a ghostwriter?
- What do you want from a ghost?

MONEY FOR WORDS

As a ghost, you'll set your own prices and determine your worth. There are no absolutes when it comes to the fees ghosts charge and the fees can fluctuate depending on your location, the client and your experience. If you already have an hourly fee for writing, then estimate how long this book (or whatever) project will take you to complete.

Most ghosts calculate how much to charge by the amount of work required and the time it will take to complete the work. If you're offered $5,000 to ghost a book that might sound great, but if it will take you a year with countless meetings and revisions, you might be working for less than minimum wage.

> Most ghosts calculate how much to charge by the amount of work required and the time it will take to complete the work.

Since it will be up to you to decide on the fee, how is that approached? Here's what I say: "Dr. Jones, what is your budget for a ghostwriter?" By calling the fee "the budget" it eliminates personal involvement and returns it all to the business of writing.

What can you expect? It's been my experience that ghostwriting articles or columns, the fees are between $25 and $100/hour. Ghosting an article for a popular magazine, rates are $1/word or from $300-3,000 per project. If you're writing continuing columns for a local publication, the fees may be $50-300. When ghostwriting a book the rates range from $5,000 to many zeros over that.

ON YOUR MARK...

If you can put your ego aside and think of ghostwriting as a business, you will succeed. There are clients everywhere, from a local tax attorney who needs a workbook for her seminar to a neighbor who wants you to write a memoir just for her family. After scores of ghosting projects, my best advice is: Give it a try. Be friendly and sincere. Have a good contract. Have fun.

Ghosting isn't for every writer. That's good. It means there's more lucrative work for you and me.

Eva Shaw, Ph.D. (www.evashaw.com) is the ghostwriter/author of 70 books, many best sellers and award winners. Under her byline, they include: *Ghostwriting for Fun & Profit, Writeriffic 2: Creativity Training for Writers, Write Your Book in 20 Minutes, Shovel It: Nature's Health Plan, What to Do When a Loved One Dies, For the Love of Children, There's No Business Like Show Business, Insider's Guide to San Diego, The Sun Never Sets*, and more. Eva's work has been featured in publications such as *USA Today, Shape, Country Living, San Diego Union Tribune, Los Angeles Times, Costco Connection, Publisher's Weekly, Washington Post, the Wall Street Journal* plus she has ghosted more than 1000 columns, articles and short stories. She's a regular presenter at writing conferences and teaches six different online writing courses (with Education to Go, www.ed2go.com) that are available worldwide. She lives and writes in Carlsbad CA with husband Joseph and their rambunctious Welsh terrier, Miss Rosy Geranium.

SELF-PUBLISHING CHECKLIST

Below is a checklist of essential hurdles to clear when self-publishing your book. This list makes the assumption that you've already completed and polished your manuscript. For more information on self-publishing, check out *The Complete Guide to Self-Publishing*, by Tom and Marilyn Ross (Writer's Digest).

❏ **CREATE PRODUCTION SCHEDULE.** Put a deadline for every step of the process of self-publishing your book. A good rule of thumb is to double your estimates on how long each step will take. It's better to have too much time and hit your dates than constantly have to extend deadlines.

❏ **FIND EDITOR.** Don't skimp on your project and do all the editing yourself. Even editors need editors. Try to find an editor you trust, whether through a recommendation or a search online. Ask for references if the editor is new to you.

❏ **FIND DESIGNER.** Same goes here. Find a good designer to at least handle the cover. If you can have a designer lay out the interior pages too, that's even better.

❏ **DEFINE THE TARGET AUDIENCE.** In nonfiction this is an important step, because knowing the needs of the audience can help with the editing process. Even if you're writing fiction or poetry, it's a good idea to figure out who your audience is, because this will help you with the next few steps.

❏ **FIGURE OUT A PRINT AND DISTRIBUTION PLAN.** This plan should first figure out what the end product will be: printed book, e-book, app, or a combination of options. Then, the plan will define how the products will be created and distributed to readers.

- [ ] **SET PUBLICATION DATE.** The publication date should be set on your production schedule above. Respect this deadline more than all the others, because the marketing and distribution plans will most likely hinge on this deadline being met.

- [ ] **PLOT OUT YOUR MARKETING PLAN.** The smartest plan is to have a soft launch date of a week or two (just in case). Then, hard launch into your marketing campaign, which could be as simple as a book release party and social networking mentions, or as involved as a guest blog tour and paid advertising. With self-publishing, it's usually more prudent to spend energy and ideas than money on marketing—at least in the beginning.

- [ ] **HAVE AN EXCELLENT TITLE.** For nonfiction, titles are easy. Describe what your book is covering in a way that is interesting to your target audience. For fiction and poetry, titles can be a little trickier, but attempt to make your title easy to remember and refer.

- [ ] **GET ENDORSEMENT.** Time for this should be factored into the production schedule. Contact some authors or experts in a field related to your title and send them a copy of your manuscript to review. Ask them to consider endorsing your book, and if they do, put that endorsement on the cover. Loop in your designer to make this look good.

- [ ] **REGISTER COPYRIGHT.** Protect your work. Go to http://copyright.gov for more information on how to register your book.

- [ ] **SECURE ISBN.** An ISBN code helps booksellers track and sell your book. To learn more about securing an ISBN, go to www.isbn.org.

- [ ] **CREATE TABLE OF CONTENTS AND INDEX (FOR NONFICTION).** The table of contents (TOC) helps organize a nonfiction title and give structure for both the author and the reader. An index serves a similar function for readers, making it easier for them to find the information they want to find. While an index is usually not necessary for fiction or poetry, most poetry collections do use a table of contents to make it easy to locate individual poems.

- [ ] **INCLUDE AUTHOR BIO.** Readers want to know about the authors of the books they read. Make this information easy to find in the back of the book.

- [ ] **INCLUDE CONTACT INFORMATION.** In the front of the book, preferably on the copyright and ISBN page, include all contact information, including mailing address and website. E-mail address is optional, but the more options you give the better chance you'll be contacted.

❏ **EXECUTE MARKETING PLAN.** Planning is important, but execution is critical to achieving success. If you're guest posting, finish posts on time and participate in comments section of your blog post. If you're making bookstore appearances, confirm dates and show up a little early—plus invite friends and family to attend.

❏ **KEEP DETAILED ACCOUNTING RECORDS.** For tax purposes, you'll need to keep records of how much money you invest in your project, as well as how much you receive back. Keep accurate and comprehensive records from day one, and you'll be a much happier self-published author.

PUBLISHERS & THEIR IMPRINTS

The publishing world is in constant transition. With all the buying, selling, reorganizing, consolidating, and dissolving, it's hard to keep publishers and their imprints straight. To help make sense of these changes, here's a breakdown of major publishers (and their divisions). Keep in mind that this information changes frequently. For instance, Random House and Penguin are currently in the process of merging. The website of each publisher is provided to help you keep an eye on this ever-evolving business.

HACHETTE BOOK GROUP USA

www.hachettebookgroup.com

CENTER STREET

FAITHWORDS

GRAND CENTRAL PUBLISHING

Business Plus

5 Spot

Forever

Forever Yours

GCP African American

Grand Central Life & Style

Twelve

Vision

HACHETTE BOOK GROUP DIGITAL MEDIA

Hachette Audio

LITTLE, BROWN AND COMPANY

Back Bay Books

Bulfinch

Mulholland Books

Reagan Arthur Books

LITTLE, BROWN BOOKS FOR YOUNG READERS

LB Kids

Poppy

ORBIT

YEN PRESS

HARLEQUIN ENTERPRISES

www.harlequin.com

HARLEQUIN

Harlequin American Romance

Harlequin Bianca

Harlequin Blaze

Harlequin Deseo

Harlequin Historical

Harlequin Intrigue

Harlequin Tiffany

Harlequin Teen

Harlequin Medical Romance

Harlequin NASCAR

Harlequin Presents

Harlequin Romance

Harlequin Superromance

Harlequin eBooks

Harlequin Special Releases

Harlequin Nonfiction

Harlequin Historical Undone

HQN BOOKS

LUNA

MIRA

KIMANI PRESS

Kimani Press Arabesque

Kimani Press Kimani Romance

Kimani Press Kimani TRU

Kimani Press New Spirit

Kimani Press Sepia

Kimani Press Special Releases

Kimani Press eBooks

RED DRESS INK

SILHOUETTE

Silhouette Desire

Silhouette Nocturne

Silhouette Nocturne Bites

Silhouette Romantic Suspense

Silhouette Special Edition

Silhouette eBooks

SPICE

SPICE Books

SPICE Briefs

STEEPLE HILL

Steeple Hill Café©

Steeple Hill Love Inspired

Steeple Hill Love Inspired Historical

Steeple Hill Love Inspired Suspense

Steeple Hill Women's Fiction

Steeple Hill eBooks

WORLDWIDE LIBRARY

Rogue Angel

Worldwide Mystery

Worldwilde Library eBooks

HARLEQUIN CANADA

HARLEQUIN U.K.

Mills & Boon

HARPERCOLLINS

www.harpercollins.com

HARPERCOLLINS GENERAL BOOKS GROUP

Amistad

Avon

Avon Inspire

Avon Red

Broadside Books

Caedmon

Collins Design

Ecco

Harper

Harper Business

Harper Design

Harper Luxe

Harper paperbacks

Harper Perennial

Harper Perennial Modern Classics

Harper Voyager

HarperAudio

HarperBibles

HarperCollins e-Books

HarperOne

ItBooks

Rayo

William Morrow

HARPERCOLLINS CHILDREN'S BOOKS

Amistad

Balzer + Bray

Collins

Greenwillow Books

HarperCollins Children's Audio

HarperFestival

HarperTeen

Rayo

Katherine Tegen Books

Walden Pond Press

HARPERCOLLINS U.K.

Fourth Estate

HarperPress

HarperPerennial

The Friday Project

HarperThorsons/Element

HarperNonFiction

HarperTrue

HarperSport

HarperFiction

   Voyager

   Blue Door

   Angry Robot

   Avon U.K.

HarperCollins Childrens Books

Collins

   Collins Geo

   Collins Education

   Collins Language

HARPERCOLLINS CANADA

HarperCollinsPublishers

Collins Canada

HarperPerennial Canada

HarperTrophyCanada

Phyllis Bruce Books

HARPERCOLLINS AUSTRALIA

HarperCollins

Angus & Robertson

HarperSports

Fourth Estate

Harper Perennial

Collins

Voyager

HARPERCOLLINS INDIA

HARPERCOLLINS NEW ZEALAND

HarperCollins

HarperSports

Flamingo

Voyager

Perennial

ZONDERVAN

Zonderkids

Editorial Vida

Youth Specialties

MACMILLAN US (HOLTZBRINCK)

http://us.macmillan.com

MACMILLAN

Farrar, Straus & Giroux

Faber and Faber, Inc

Farrar, Straus

Hill & Wang

HENRY HOLT & CO.

Henry Holt Books for Young Readers

Holt Paperbacks

Metropolitan

Times

MACMILLAN CHILDREN'S

Feiwel & Friends

Farrar, Straus and Giroux Books
    for Young Readers

Kingfisher

Holt Books for Young Readers

Priddy Books

Roaring Brook Press

First Second

Square Fish

PICADOR

PALGRAVE MACMILLAN

TOR/FORGE BOOKS

Tor

Forge

Orb

Tor/Seven Seas

ST. MARTIN'S PRESS

Minotaur Press

Thomas Dunne Books

BEDFORD, FREEMAN & WORTH
PUBLISHING GROUP

BEDFORD/ST. MARTIN'S

HAYDEN-MCNEIL

W.H. FREEMAN

WORTH PUBLISHERS

MACMILLAN KIDS

YOUNG LISTENERS

MACMILLAN AUDIO

PENGUIN GROUP (USA), INC.

www.penguingroup.com

PENGUIN ADULT DIVISION

Ace

Alpha

Amy Einhorn Books/Putnam

Avery

Berkley

Blue Rider Press

Current

Dutton

G.P. Putnam's Sons

Gotham

HP Books

Hudson Street Press

Jove

NAL

Pamela Dorman Books

Penguin

Penguin Press

Perigree

Plume

Portfolio

Prentice Hall Press

RIVERHEAD

Sentinel

Tarcher

Viking Press

Price Stern Sloan

YOUNG READERS DIVISION

Dial Books for Young Readers

Dutton Children's Books

Firebird

Frederick Warne

G.P. Putnam's Sons Books for Young Readers

Grosset & Dunlap

Philomel

PUFFIN BOOKS

Razorbill

Speak

Viking Books for Young Readers

RANDOM HOUSE, INC. (BERTELSMANN)

www.randomhouse.com

CROWN PUBLISHING GROUP

Amphoto Books

Backstage Books

Billboard Books

Broadway Business

Clarkson Potter

Crown

Crown Archetype

Crown Business

Crown Forum

Doubleday Religion

Harmony

Image Books

Potter Craft

Potter Style

Ten Speed Press

Three Rivers Press

Waterbrook Multnomah

Watson-Guptill

KNOPF DOUBLEDAY PUBLISHING GROUP

Alfred A. Knopf

Anchor Books

Doubleday

Everyman's Library

Nan A. Talese

Pantheon Books

Schocken Books

Vintage

RANDOM HOUSE PUBLISHING GROUP

Ballantine Books

Bantam

Del Rey

Del Rey/Lucas Books

Del Rey/Manga

Delacorte

Dell

The Dial Press

The Modern Library

One World

Presidio Press

Random House Trade Group

Random House Trade Paperbacks

Spectra

Spiegel and Grau

Triumph Books

Villard Books

RANDOM HOUSE AUDIO PUBLISHING GROUP

Listening Library

Random House Audio

RANDOM HOUSE CHILDREN'S BOOKS

Kids@Random

Golden Books

Princeton Review

Sylvan Learning

RANDOM HOUSE DIGITAL PUBLISHING GROUP

Books on Tape

Fodor's Travel

Living Language

Listening Library

Random House Audio

RH Large Print

RANDOM HOUSE INTERNATIONAL

RH Australia

RH of Canada Limited

RH India

RH Mondadori

RH New Zealand

RH South America

RH Group (UK)

Transworld Ireland

Verlagsgruppe RH

SIMON & SCHUSTER

www.simonandschuster.com

SIMON & SCHUSTER ADULT PUBLISHING

Atria Books/Beyond Words

Folger Shakespeare Library

Free Press

Gallery Books

Howard Books

Pocket Books

Scribner

Simon & Schuster

Threshold Editions

The Touchstone & Fireside Group

Pimsleur

Simon & Schuster Audioworks

SIMON & SCHUSTER CHILDREN'S PUBLISHING

Aladdin Paperbacks

Atheneum Books for Young Readers

Bench Lane Books

Little Simon®

Margaret K. McElderry Books

Paula Wiseman Books

Simon & Schuster Books for Young Readers

Simon Pulse

Simon Spotlight®

SIMON & SCHUSTER INTERNATIONAL

Simon & Schuster Australia

Simon & Schuster Canada

Simon & Schuster UK

THE WRITING ENTREPRENEUR

....

by J.M. Lacey

If you are writing full time, or even part time, and you claim the business on your taxes, you are an entrepreneur. Running a business comes with unique challenges and perks. If you are a sole proprietorship, or LLC, and you have no staff, you are marketing your own business, managing contracts and filing your own taxes. So how do you enjoy writing while simultaneously running a business? How can social networking ease your burden? Do your business cards scream amateur? How can you get a client to sign a contract—on your terms? And what really is considered tax deductible for a writer?

THE HAPPY WRITER

Before you even begin your writing business, there are some things to consider to help you build your career.

Kelly James-Enger, author of *Six Figure Freelancing–The Writer's Guide to Making More Money* and freelancer for the last 14 years, says that finding a niche, something you're good at, will help stem the tide of financial insecurity. "Specializing helps set you apart from everyone else and it's easier to get assignments."

To maintain a happy, balanced writing life, she also offers some tips for writers:

- **CHOOSE A MARKET YOU'D LIKE TO WRITE FOR MORE THAN ONCE,** then focus on building relationships.
- **HAVE A DAILY PRODUCTION GOAL,** such as how many queries you plan to send.
- **THINK LONG TERM.** Make sure what you do is leading you in the direction you want to reach.
- **CONSIDER WHAT THE MARKET WILL BEAR,** not just what you want to do. "Don't have all your money come from one source," she adds. "Diversify what you can do."

- **BE CAREFUL ABOUT WORKING NON-STOP.** Have a set time to turn off the e-mail and computer. Avoid working weekends and nights.

GETTING CLIENTS

Things that seem small to you—business cards, websites, stationery—can make a big impression. Prospects will never know how well you write if they can't get past a non-professional set-up.

Get simple, classy, clean and sophisticated cards professionally printed. Include your phone number, mailing, web and e-mail addresses, if you want paying clients to contact you. Your stationery should be the same.

Your website is going to be your most important marketing tool. Make sure your site is personalized, professional and provides the information your prospect will need, such as articles, client list, and portfolio.

. . . .

Your website is going to be your most important marketing tool.

. . . .

There are many books and articles that will tell you to save money and go ahead and design your own site. I disagree 100 percent. Unless you have had training in marketing, design, SEO and html construction, your site will look homemade. Plus, you are too intimate with your own business to have an objective outlook.

Websites aren't as expensive as they used to be, but you will have to dish out a few to several hundred dollars, depending on your needs. To run a business, you have to spend money, and if you pour your investment into anything, it should be your website. Write your own content and save money, but hand the rest over to the professionals. To keep more dollars in your wallet, offer to do a trade with your designer—materials for them and a website for you.

"But I'm a writer," you say, "what does design matter?" If your site looks thrown together, prospects will think your writing is treated the same. And frankly, if your site is difficult to navigate—too much scrolling, tiny fonts, unorganized, dark background—they'll give up looking. No one has that much time or patience.

You also need a professional e-mail address, so get rid of your Yahoo, Gmail and Hotmail, and use your real name. JMLacey@jmlacey.com sounds a lot better than trixie_partygirl@hotmail.com. Save that for your personal accounts.

Next, find work by writing letters, making cold calls, sending e-mails and getting out there. Target businesses (or magazines) for whom you'd like to write. My first major client came via a cold call to another prospect. After I met with the initial contact, she referred me to someone else. I contacted that business immediately, and within three days, I had snagged that client and am still with them over two years later working on multiple projects.

Can social networking help? Yes, if you use it wisely. Join groups like LinkedIn, Facebook and Twitter, but make sure anytime you type a comment or message, it's with the purpose of building your business. You can direct people to your site and blog, but don't ask for their business. Try to type messages and/or guide them to helpful articles and information. Remember the WIIFM—What's In It For Me? It's about *them,* not you. Eventually, your readers will gain confidence in your expert abilities. Be cautious that your networking habits do not become time suckers. Try to have a set time each day, and a set amount of time, to check in with all your networks and forums.

CONTRACTS

Once you have a client, how do you get paid on your terms?

As you establish your business and writing credentials, try to have a solid, though not inflexible idea, of how much you will be paid. Understand what to charge for your level of expertise and geographical area. Most clients, especially corporate clients, prefer project fees instead of hourly rates. So have a base in your head, if you can, of how long something will take you, and come up with a reasonable fee.

Figure out how much you're willing to go down if the client tries to negotiate. Be confident in your figure, but be agreeable with the client. Before I type the contract, I usually state the estimate then ask: "Will that work within your budget?" You want to avoid going too low just to get that project, but don't quote so high you quote yourself out of a job. It takes trial and error, but after a while, you'll learn and gain confidence.

Make sure your contract covers everything unexpected because once you quote a price you can't retract and ask for more. For example, my contracts outline the project and everything that goes with it—three edits, one additional meeting (even via phone), conception, content and design. If the project goes over what was agreed upon—additional edits, meetings, pages, etc.—I charge the additional fee stated in the contract. I also charge extra for commercial photos and anything that might crop up as I go along. But I have to have it covered or I lose money. And don't forget to include the deadline.

Most important, be certain the contract states what you will be paid and when. For my new clients, especially for large projects, I always ask for one-third to one-half down payment. If I'm hiring outside contractors, such as a web designer, I will ask for my contractor's fee in full, if I can, just in case the project flops. All my clients know they will receive an invoice when they've approved the final draft, and my invoice states "payment due upon receipt."

Some commercial clients have their own contracts written by lawyers who really should use writers. If you don't understand something, ask. Contracts are for negotiating. Include your requirements, like the additional charges for extra work. You want to be comfortable signing that contract.

Do not do the work or research until you have it in writing. People will try to get you to "look" at their stuff so you can get a handle on what they want. That's fine, but either wait until you have the contract, or tell them you charge for your research. The reason? You want people to respect you as a professional from the start. Otherwise, they will expect more for nothing.

> Do not do the work or research until you have it in writing.

Target clients that will pay you what you are worth. Again, use your discretion, but be firm. If they start out by saying, "I don't have much money," run, because they don't and you have a business to operate. If they tell you, "We can market you," then unless they are a marketing agency, they can't do anything to help you that you can't do. To run your business effectively, establish yourself as a professional by not catering to the low-paying, time-sucking gigs that will get you nowhere except homeless.

TAX DEDUCTIONS

If you claim your writing on your taxes, then it isn't a hobby. This means that almost everything you do and buy for your business is tax deductible.

So what can you deduct? Pretty much anything office-related (computer, pens), books, magazine subscriptions and conferences are among your deductions. And anything you need that will help you in your research, such as travel expenses. In my case, CDs and concert tickets are included in my write-offs as a classical music writer.

Building your writing business takes time. It can take several months to a few years, but it will happen. The more effort you put into it, the sooner it will thrive. But above all, your professional habits will only increase your chances of being successful.

NEGOTIATING TIPS FOR WRITERS FROM AN EDITOR

While being an editor pays the bills around here, I always see a writer when I look in the mirror. And just to show you how much I care about my fellow writers, I'm going to make my life as an editor potentially more difficult by sharing my negotiating tips for writers.

Different editors surely approach negotiation in their own unique ways, but these are my tips for handling editors like myself.

- **ALWAYS TRY TO NEGOTIATE.** I loathe negotiating. Judging by the lack of negotiation from most of my freelancers, I've concluded that most of them loathe negotiating too. But I think it's important for writers to at least try to negotiate from the beginning, because I take those writers a little more seriously, especially if they...

- **DELIVER THE GOODS ON EACH ASSIGNMENT.** Write an amazing article with great sources and examples, and I'm more likely to offer you a better contract the next time around. If I don't, I may be trying to maintain the status quo, but you should try to nudge me again. And I emphasize nudging.

- **DON'T MAKE YOUR DEMANDS A "MY-WAY-OR-THE-HIGHWAY" SITUATION.** That is, don't make it that kind of situation unless you're willing to take the highway. There have been situations, especially when I'm working with a new freelancer, in which I'm not able or willing to go over my initial offer. There have been very good pitches that I let walk, because I couldn't (or wouldn't) go higher. Believe me, I always wish I could offer more, but I have to fill my pages with great content (not squander it all on a handful of articles). That said...

- **PITCH ME WITH AN IDEA THAT IS UNIQUE AND TRULY HELPFUL FOR MY AUDIENCE.** If you pitch me on an interview or list of query tips, I'm less likely to get excited than if you pitch me on an article that tells writers how to make a living off Twitter in 30 days (and actually have the track record to back up that claim). For instance, Lynn Wasnak, who puts together our "How Much Should I Charge?" piece, is far and away my top paid freelancer, because she has to survey professionals in several different fields of writing. It's a unique piece that is truly helpful for my audience. As such, she has greater negotiating power. Still...

- **CHOOSE YOUR BATTLES.** I advise negotiating each time you get a new assignment. Maybe I'll give a little, maybe I won't. But please pick your battles about what you want to negotiate. Don't fight over every single clause in your contract. That gets annoying on my end, and I'm just too busy to enjoy being annoyed. Related to that...

- **DON'T BE A PEST.** I'm more willing to negotiate with writers who complete their assignments on time and don't contact me every couple days with a revision of an already turned in piece or who try to re-negotiate the fee on an article after I've already assigned the piece. I like it when writers ask questions and want to make sure they understand an assignment, but I don't like to have to constantly haggle over things after we've come to an agreement. That's a good way to not receive any more assignments in the future.

- **THINK OF CREATIVE WAYS TO NEGOTIATE.** Offer to write a sidebar for an extra fee—or a series of blog posts. If the editor is unable to offer more money, ask for more complimentary copies. Or some other related comp that the editor may be able to send your way. Editors like to make writers happy (especially if they do a great job), so help them help you get more out of your relationship.

—ROBERT LEE BREWER

J.M. LACEY (http://jmlacey.com) is an independent writer, marketing and public relations professional. She has over 14 years worth of experience in journalism, marketing, public relations, and sales, working for both the corporate and non-profit sectors. She maintains a classical music blog (http://seasonkt.com) and works with small to large businesses creating websites, advertisements, biographies and other marketing and publicity needs. She is also a public speaker and teaches workshops on writing for businesses and on marketing at writing and corporate conferences.

CONTRACTS 101

······························

by Cindy Ferraino

After you do a victory dance about getting the book deal you always dreamed about or your article hitting the top of the content list of a popular magazine, the celebration quickly comes to a halt when you realize you are not at the finish line yet. Your heart begins to beat faster because you know the next possible hurdle is just around the corner—the contract. For many, the idea of reviewing a contract is like being back in first grade. You know you have to listen to the teacher when you could be playing outside. You know you have to read this contract but why because there are terms in there that look like an excerpt from a foreign language syllabus.

Before I changed my status to self-employed writer, I was working as a grants and contracts administrator at a large medical university in Philadelphia. I helped shepherd the MD and PhD researchers through the channels of grants and contracts administration. While the researchers provided the technical and scientific pieces that could potentially be the next cure for diabetes, heart disease or cancer, I was there to make sure they did their magic within the confines of a budget and imposed contractual regulations. The budget process was easy but when it came to contract regulations—oh well, that was a different story. I became familiar with the terms such as indemnifications, property and intellectual rights and conditions of payments. In addition to the budget process, I was an integral part of reviewing and negotiating a grant or contract that had the best interests for every party involved.

After my son was born, I left the university and my contracts background went on a brief hiatus. Once my son went off to school, I began freelance writing. After a few writing gigs sprinkled with a few too many rejection slips, I landed an assignment for *Dog Fancy* magazine. I was thrilled and eagerly anticipated the arrival of a contract in my inbox. As

I opened the document, the hiatus had lifted. I read through the contract and was able to send it back within a few hours.

For many new freelancers or writers who have been around the block, contract administration is not something that they can list as a perk on their resume. Instead of searching through the Yellow Pages for a contract lawyer or trying to call in a special favor to a writer friend, there are some easy ways for a newbie writer or even a seasoned writer to review a contract before putting a smiley face next to the dotted line.

TAKE A DEEP BREATH, THEN READ ON

Remember breaking those seals on test booklets and the voice in the background telling you "Please read the directions slowly." As you tried to drown out the voice because your stomach was in knots, little did you know that those imparting words of wisdom would come in handy as you perspired profusely over the legal jargon that unfolded before your eyes. The same words go for contracts.

Many writers, including myself, are anxious to get an assignment under way but the contract carrot continues to loom over our creative minds. "I'm surprised by writers who just skim a contract and then sign it without understanding what it means, "says Kelly James-Enger. James-Enger is the author of books including *Six Figure Freelancing: The Writer's Guide to Making More* (Random House, 2005) and blog Dollarsanddeadlines.blogspot.com. "Most of the language in magazine contracts isn't that complicated, but it can be confusing when you're new to the business."

When I receive a contract from a new publisher or editor, I make a second copy. My children call it "my sloppy copy." I take out a highlighter and begin to mark up the key points of the contract: beginning and end date, conditions of payment, how my relationship is defined by the publisher and what the outline of the article should look like.

The beginning and end date of a contract is crucial. After I recently negotiated a contract, the editor changed the due date of the article in an e-mail. I made sure the contract was changed to reflect the new due date. The conditions of the payments are important because it will describe when the writer will be paid and by what method. Most publishers have turned to incremental payment schedules or payments to be made online like Pay-Pal. How the publisher considers your contractor status is important. If you're a freelance contract writer, the contract should reflect that as well as identify you as an independent contractor for IRS tax purposes. Finally, the contract will highlight an outline of what your article or proposal should look like.

After I recently negotiated a contract, the editor changed the due date of the article in an e-mail. I made sure the contract was changed to reflect the new due date.

As you slowly digest the terms you are about to agree to for your assignment or book project, you gain a better understanding of what an editor or publisher expects from you and when.

CUTTING TO THE LEGAL CHASE

Once you have had a chance to review a contract, you may be scratching your head and saying, "Okay, now what does this all mean to me as a writer?" James-Enger describes three key areas where writers should keep sharp on when it comes to contracts—Indemnification, Pay and Exclusivity provisions.

INDEMNIFICATION is a publisher's way of saying if something goes wrong, we are not responsible. If a claim is brought against another writer's work, a publisher does not want to be responsible for the legal aftermath but you could be the one receiving a notice in the mail. James-Enger warns writers to be on the lookout for indemnification clauses. "In the U.S., anyone can sue anyone over just about anything," she says. "I'm okay with agreeing to indemnification clauses that specify breaches of contract because I know I'm not going to plagiarize, libel or misquote anyone. But I can't promise that the publication will never be sued by anyone whether or not I actually breached the contract."

CONTRACT TIPS

Even seasoned freelancers can find themselves intimidated by contracts. Here are a few things to consider with your contract:

- **KEEP COPY ON RECORD.** If the contract is sent via e-mail, keep a digital copy, but also print up a hard copy and keep it in an easy-to-find file folder.

- **CHECK FOR RIGHTS.** It's almost never a good idea to sell all rights. But you should also pay attention to whether you're selling any subsidiary or reprint rights. The more rights you release the more payment you should expect (and demand).
- **WHEN PAYMENT.** Make sure you understand when you are to be paid and have it specified in your contract. You may think that payment will come when the article is accepted or published, but different publishers have different policies. Get it in writing.
- **HOW MUCH PAYMENT.** The contract should specify exactly how much you are going to be paid. If there is no payment listed on the contract, the publisher could use your work for free.
- **TURN IN CONTRACT BEFORE ASSIGNMENT.** Don't start working until the contract is signed, and everything is official. As a freelancer, time is as important as money. Don't waste any of your time and effort on any project that is not yet contracted.

PAY is where you want the publisher "to show you the money." Writers need to be aware of how publishers will discuss the terms of payment in the contract. James-Enger advises to have "payment on acceptance." This means you will be paid when the editor agrees to accept your manuscript or article. If there is "no payment on acceptance," some publishers will pay when the article is published. "Push for payment whenever you can," she says.

EXCLUSIVITY PROVISIONS are where a particular publisher will not allow the writer to publish an article or manuscript that is "about the same or similar subject" during the time the publisher runs the piece. Because of the nature of the writing business, James-Enger feels writers need to negotiate this part of the contract. "I specialize in health, fitness and nutrition, and I'm always writing about a similar subject," she says.

WHEN TO HEAD TO THE BARGAINING TABLE

Recently, I became an independent contractor for the American Composites Manufacturing Association (ACMA). When I reviewed the terms of the contract, I was concerned how my independent contractor status was identified. Although I am not an ACMA employee, I wanted to know if I could include my ACMA publications on my resume. Before I signed the contract, I questioned this issue with my editor. My editor told me I may use this opportunity to put on my resume. I signed the contract and finished my assignment.

Writers should be able to talk to an editor or a publisher if there is a question about a term or clause in a contract. "Don't be afraid to talk to the editor about the changes you'd like to make to a contract," James-Enger says. "You don't know what you'll get or if an editor is willing to negotiate it, until you ask."

When writers have to approach an editor for changes to a contract, James-Enger advises writers to act professionally when it comes to the negotiations. "I start out with saying—I am really excited to be working with you on this story and I appreciate the assignment, but I have a couple of issues with the contract that I'd like to talk to you about," she says. "Sure I want a better contract but I also want to maintain a good working relationship with my editor. A scorched-earth policy doesn't benefit any freelancer in the long run."

In today's economy, writers are a little more reluctant to ask for a higher rate for an article.

Negotiating payment terms is a tricky subject for some writers. Writers want to get the most bang for their buck but they don't want to lose a great writing assignment. Do your research first before you decide to ask an editor for more money to complete the assignment. Double check the publisher's website or look to see if the pay scale is equivalent to other publishers in the particular industry. Some publishers have a set publishing fee whereas others may have a little more wiggle room depending on the type of the assignment given. In today's economy, writers are a little more reluctant to ask for a higher rate for an article. If the publisher seems to be open to discussion about the pay scale, just make sure you approach the situation in a professional manner so as to not turn the publisher away from giving you another assignment.

WHO WILL OWN YOUR WRITING?

Besides payment terms, another area that writers may find themselves on the other end of the negotiation table is with ownership rights. We all want to take credit for the work that we have poured our heart and soul into. Unfortunately, the business of publishing has different ways of saying how a writer can classify their work. Ownership rights vary but the biggest one that writers have a hard time trying to build up a good case against is "all rights." "All rights" is exactly what it means: *hope you are not in love with what you have just written because you will not be able to use it again.*

RIGHTS AND WHAT THEY MEAN

A creative work can be used in many different ways. As the author of the work, you hold all rights to the work in question. When you agree to have your work published, you are granting a publisher the right to use your work in any number of ways. Whether that right is to publish the manuscript for the first time in a publication, or to publish it as many times and in as many ways as a publisher wishes, is up to you—it all depends on the agreed-upon terms. As a general rule, the more rights you license away, the less control

---

you have over your work and the money you're paid. You should strive to keep as many rights to your work as you can.

Writers and editors sometimes define rights in a number of different ways. Below you will find a classification of terms as they relate to rights.

- **FIRST SERIAL RIGHTS.** Rights that the writer offers a newspaper or magazine to publish the manuscript for the first time in any periodical. All other rights remain with the writer. Sometimes the qualifier "North American" is added to these rights to specify a geographical limitation to the license. When content is excerpted from a book scheduled to be published, and it appears in a magazine or newspaper prior to book publication, this is also called first serial rights.

- **ONE-TIME RIGHTS.** Nonexclusive rights (rights that can be licensed to more than one market) purchased by a periodical to publish the work once (also known as simultaneous rights). That is, there is nothing to stop the author from selling the work to other publications at the same time.

- **SECOND SERIAL (REPRINT) RIGHTS.** Nonexclusive rights given to a newspaper or magazine to publish a manuscript after it has already appeared in another newspaper or magazine.

- **ALL RIGHTS.** This is exactly what it sounds like. "All rights" means an author is selling every right he has to a work. If you license all rights to your work, you forfeit the right to ever use the work again. If you think you may want to use the article again, you should avoid submitting to such markets or refuse payment and withdraw your material.

- **ELECTRONIC RIGHTS.** Rights that cover a broad range of electronic media, including websites, CD/DVDs, video games, smart phone apps, and more. The contract should specify if—and which—electronic rights are included. The presumption is unspecified rights remain with the writer.

- **SUBSIDIARY RIGHTS.** Rights, other than book publication rights, that should be covered in a book contract. These may include various serial rights; movie, TV, audio, and other electronic rights; translation rights, etc. The book contract should specify who controls the rights (author or publisher) and what percentage of sales from the licensing of these rights goes to the author.

- **DRAMATIC, TV, AND MOTION PICTURE RIGHTS.** Rights for use of material on the stage, on TV, or in the movies. Often a one-year option to buy such rights is offered (generally for 10 percent of the total price). The party interested in the rights then tries to sell the idea to other people—actors, directors, studios, or TV networks. Some properties are optioned numerous times, but most fail to become full productions. In those cases, the writer can sell the rights again and again.

Sometimes editors don't take the time to specify the rights they are buying. If you sense that an editor is interested in getting stories, but doesn't seem to know what his and the writer's responsibilities are, be wary. In such a case, you'll want to explain what rights you're offering (preferably one-time or first serial rights only) and that you expect additional payment for subsequent use of your work.

The Copyright Law that went into effect January 1, 1978, states writers are primarily selling one-time rights to their work unless they—and the publisher—agree otherwise in writing. Book rights are covered fully by contract between the writer and the book publisher.

In recent months, I have written for two publications that I had given "all rights" to the company. My rationale is that I knew I would never need to use those articles again but I did make sure I was able to include those articles for my byline to show that I have publishing experience.

If you feel that you want to reuse or recycle an article that you had written a few years ago, you might want to consider negotiating an "all rights" clause or maybe going to another publisher. "We don't take all rights so there is no reason for authors to request we change the rights clause," says Angela Hoy, author and owner of WritersWeekly.com and Booklocker. com. "Our contracts were rated 'Outstanding' by Mark Levine (author of *The Fine Print of Self-Publishing*) and has also been called the clearest and fairest in the industry."

James-Enger is also an advocate of negotiating contracts that include an "all rights" clause. "I hate 'all rights' contracts, and try to avoid signing them as they preclude me from ever reselling the piece as a reprint to other markets," she says. "I explain that to editors, and I have been able to get editors to agree to let me retain nonexclusive reprint rights even when they buy all rights—which still lets me market the piece as a reprint." James-Enger also advises that "if the publisher demands all rights, then negotiate if the payment is sub-standard."

So if you are just receiving a contract in the mail for the first time or you are working with a new publisher, you should not be afraid of the legal lingo that blankets the message "we want to work with you." Contracts are meant to protect both the interests of the publishers and writers. Publishers want the commitment from writers that he or she will provide their best work and writers want to be recognized for their best work. But between those contracts lines, the legal lingo can cause writers to feel they need a law degree to review the contract. No, just sit back and relax and enjoy the prose that will take your writing to the next level.

CINDY FERRAINO has been blessed with a variety of assignments, including newspaper articles, magazine articles, ghost-written articles, stories for books, and most recently authoring a book on accounting and bookkeeping terminology, *The Complete Dictionary of Accounting & Bookkeeping Terms Explained Simply* (Atlantic Publishing Group).

RECORDKEEPING 101

Keep Records to Save on Your Taxes

....

by Joanne E. McFadden

Few people enjoy preparing their tax returns. For the self-employed, which many writers are, this means extra work, namely the Schedule C, Profit or Loss From Business. The extra work, though, results in tax savings, making it worth the time and effort.

I didn't get really serious about my record keeping until a few years ago when I decided to give myself the gift of thorough, stress-free tax preparation. I set up a system that made everything all ready to go at tax time, thus saving me valuable time that I could be writing or researching. I eliminated tax time procrastination and the anxiety of collecting, organizing and adding up my business expenses the night before meeting with my accountant.

In addition to eliminating the stress of filing my tax return, developing a system that made me already prepared at tax time with minimal effort also reduced the amount of taxes I paid because I maintained an extremely thorough accounting of the expenses I could deduct from the amount of my freelance income.

GET MOTIVATED

Being self-employed means that one pays the employer's share as well as the employee's of Social Security and Medicare, which is 7.65 percent twice, for a total of 15.3 percent. Like a regular employer, you get a deduction for the employer's half, points out Internal Revenue Service (IRS) spokesperson Eric Smith. Nevertheless, the better a person keeps track of legitimate, tax-deductible business expenses, the less self-employment *and* federal taxes he pays, legally. This seems to be reason enough to take the time to set up a system that allows you to do just that, without a last-minute scramble before April 15.

Yet, the most common mistake that people make is simply failing to keep adequate records or any records at all, according to Ronald R. Mueller, author of *Home Business Tax*

Savings, Made Easy! who has dedicated a whole career to helping and instructing people with home-based businesses about their taxes. "Paperwork is part of running a business," Mueller said. "People don't recognize the importance of it until they're audited," he said. If a person doesn't have adequate records to prove his expenses at an audit, he could end up having to pay up, with interest.

For me, tax time used to mean facing a hanging file folder full of crumpled up, disorganized receipts that I had to spend hours organizing and tallying. It also meant finding caches of receipts that I had failed to throw in the file folder long after I had filed my tax return, so I paid more taxes than I owed because of my sloppy record-keeping. (If the amount of excluded expenses is significant enough, one can file an amended return, but keeping good records in the first place is far more efficient.)

If this sounds familiar, read on to find out how to keep complete, organized records that will be ready to go at tax time, thus maximizing your income and time, all in alignment with Internal Revenue Service (IRS) regulations.

DO YOUR HOMEWORK

Make some time in your schedule for becoming really familiar with the expenses that you can deduct on your tax return. Employ the same sound research skills that you use for writing an article to finding out about the expenses and what records you are required to keep to document them. In addition to the IRS website, the internet abounds with information for small business owners, and there are also entire books and websites dedicated to just this topic. Familiarize yourself with the eligible expenses; you might even find that there are some you have overlooked.

For the official word and to double-check your research, a good reference is IRS Publication 583, Starting A Business and Keeping Records. It provides an overview and refers the reader to other publications with more detail, said Smith. In addition, it includes some sample record-keeping systems.

Set up your structure

The first critical step in easy record keeping is setting up a system for filing the records of your business expenses. Don't be put off; it's easier and less time consuming than you might think.

Any organizer will tell you it's important to set up a style that fits your personality, which is key to following through with the actual filing of receipts and other supporting documentation of business expenses. This may be hanging file folders, an accordion style file, a day planner, a 3-ring binder, or for the techie-type, a software program on the computer or even an app on a smart phone. (Smith points out that the IRS website has a list of vendors who sell tax preparation software.) If you choose either of the electronic options, be sure to back up files regularly, and know that you also must retain receipts and other documentation that prove those expenses you recorded electronically. It's critical to be honest with yourself and choose the system that you are most likely to use.

USE THE SCHEDULE C FORM

Once you've chosen how to set up your files, decide on the categories for each file. If you're using an electronic system, the program will already have these set up for you. If you're using paper, the Schedule C form, available at www.irs.gov can help with this. Part II of the form lists the different categories of business expenses as they have to be recorded on the tax return. Since each person's expenses are different, make a study of the form to determine which files will be useful to you. For example, if you make business use of your home and take a deduction for that (Line 18), you'll want a file for records related to this expense. If your home office doubles as a guest room making you ineligible to take that deduction, you don't need a tab for that category. If you paid an independent contractor for business-related services, you will want a file for "Contract labor" (Line 11). If you didn't, you don't need this file. (Note that there is a separate line for "Legal and professional services," i.e., attorneys and accountants.)

If it sounds complicated to know what expense goes where, consult the "Instructions for Schedule C" booklet available online that provides details about these expenses as well as other publications to consult for further clarification.

Here are some of the categories that most all writers will have.

- **Vehicle expenses (Line 9).** There is a standard deduction for mileage (the amount changes every year and sometimes even in the middle of the year, so check the IRS website for the most up-to-date figure). This means that you need to document the business-related miles that you drive, and not just the date and mileage, but where you traveled and for what purpose. The simplest way to do this is to keep a mileage log right in your car to write down the date, place you traveled, the business purpose, and number of miles, the four requirements to satisfy an allowable business expense. Mueller, who has a free downloadable Vehicle Use Log on his website, said that mileage is an expense that people often forget to record. He suggests putting the mileage log right on the driver's seat so that you have to move it when you sit down, or to put it on the dashboard where you'll see it. If you do not want to use the standard deduction for mileage, there are additional records that you need to keep about your gas purchases and vehicle maintenance expenses.
- **Depreciation (Line 13).** This can look confusing, but it simply refers to equipment that you put into service in a given year whose life will extend beyond that year. (For writers, this most likely includes their computers and printers.) Reading the Schedule C Instruction booklet can give you a better idea of what is included in this

category and the receipts and records that you need to keep on file for this expense. Since the IRS requires paper (or scanned) receipts for expenses in excess of $75, it is important to keep these. If the receipt is printed on electrostatic paper, make a copy or scan it, Mueller said, because the print will fade over time.

- **Supplies (Line 22).** This is what it sounds like–paper clips, toner cartridges, paper, USB drives, file folders, etc.

- **Travel, meals and entertainment (Line 24).** The IRS asks that the travel costs (like airfare to a writer's conference and hotel expenses) be separated from meals and entertainment (for example, the bill for when you took a source to lunch for an interview, or the meals you incurred while attending the writers' conference). The IRS has very specific rules about which expenses are deductible and which are not, which it spells out in the Schedule C Instruction booklet. Mueller said that in order to claim entertainment expenses, there are five pieces of information that must be recorded: where, when, how much, the name of the person you entertained and the business objective.

- **Utilities (Line 25).** This can include your telephone if you have a separate line.

- **Other.** This is for expenses that don't fit into other categories, such as postage, photocopying fees, books and your *Writer's Digest* subscription.

- **Income.** This is where you can keep check stubs, invoices, and other records of payments you receive. When you're paid $600 or more in a year, you should receive a 1099-MISC, but for amounts under that, you might not receive this documentation at the end of the year.

THE SECRET: DO IT NOW, NEVER LATER

Once you've taken the time to set up your filing system, whether it be folders, a notebook, or whatever works best for you, you need to get into the habit of filing receipts there. "Records are your friends," said Smith. "The best records are those that you keep at the time that you're doing whatever it is. A lot of people know to keep a log book to write things down when they pay the expense. It helps them to really keep track of the expenses that they're legitimately entitled to," he said.

Your filing system won't serve you if you don't utilize it. The trick is to do it right away, whether it be recording that trip downtown to do an interview or printing a receipt for

ANOTHER RESOURCE

Ron Mueller's website is www.home-businesstaxsavings.com. There you'll find free and low-cost downloads, including a vehicle use log and year-end tax deduction memory jogger, as well as a newsletter with tax savings tips and the latest updates about changes to the tax law, among other information relating to home-based businesses

something ordered online and tucking it into the right file. If you wait to record a trip, for example, with our lives as busy as they are, you're likely to forget by the end of the week. If you receive an e-mail receipt, if you don't print it out and file it right away, you might forget about it come tax time and lose that deduction. I keep my notebook right on the bookshelf in the kitchen so that it's easily accessible for me to use.

Setting up a time daily to record business expenses and file any receipts you gather while you're out is a good idea. Go through your pocketbook or wallet and pull out any receipts you've acquired and file them. The longer you wait, the bigger the chance that those receipts will be lost or misplaced. Train yourself to get in the habit of recording and filing frequently. When tax time comes, all the receipts you need will be neatly filed away.

A trick that Mueller uses is to write in his day planner in pencil. At the end of each day, he goes through and erases what he didn't get done and writes in what he did do. Then he takes a moment to ask himself if he spent money on anything that might be deductible, and he writes those items in. If items are over $75, he files the receipts for those. "It's a discipline," Mueller said, noting that it only takes three to four minutes a day—the time you would take to brush your teeth—to keep good records.

Good records will serve you well whether you prepare your own return or have someone else do it. An accountant can only take into consideration the documentation you've presented when you go to have your taxes prepared. Maintaining thorough records of your writing expenses can help you to keep more of the income you earn.

PLE SCHEDULE C EXPENSE DOCUMENTATION:

Why (business purpose):

What (description, including itemized accounting of cost):

When (date):

Where (location):

Who (names of those for whom the expense was incurred; e.g., meals and entertainment):

Joanne E. McFadden has been a freelance writer for 21 years, although she admits it took her almost two decades to get so serious and organized about her bookkeeping. She's worked for three daily newspapers and has published articles in many more publications.

MAKING THE MOST OF THE MONEY YOU EARN

....

by Sage Cohen

Writers who manage money well can establish a prosperous writing life that meets their short-term needs and long-term goals. This article will introduce the key financial systems, strategies, attitudes and practices that will help you cultivate a writing life that makes the most of your resources and sustains you over time.

DIVIDING BUSINESS AND PERSONAL EXPENSES

If you are reporting your writing business to the IRS, it is important that you keep the money that flows from this source entirely separate from your personal finances. Here's what you'll need to accomplish this:

- **BUSINESS CHECKING ACCOUNT:** Only two types of money go into this account: money you have been paid for your writing and/or "capital investments" you make by depositing your own money to invest in the business. And only two types of payments are made from this account: business-related expenses (such as: subscriptions, marketing and advertisement, professional development, fax or phone service, postage, computer software and supplies), and "capital draws" which you make to pay yourself.
- **BUSINESS SAVINGS ACCOUNT OR MONEY MARKET ACCOUNT:** This account is the holding pen where your quarterly tax payments will accumulate and earn interest. Money put aside for your retirement account(s) can also be held here.
- **BUSINESS CREDIT CARD:** It's a good idea to have a credit card for your business as a means of emergency preparedness. Pay off the card responsibly every month and this will help you establish a good business credit record, which can be useful down the line should you need a loan for any reason.

When establishing your business banking and credit, shop around for the best deals, such as highest interest rates, lowest (or no) monthly service fees, and free checking. Mint.com is a good source for researching your options.

EXPENSE TRACKING AND RECONCILING

Once your bank accounts are set up, it's time to start tracking and categorizing what you earn and spend. This will ensure that you can accurately report your income and itemize your deductions when tax time rolls around every quarter. Whether you intend to prepare your taxes yourself or have an accountant help you, immaculate financial records will be the key to speed and success in filing your taxes.

For the most effective and consistent expense tracking, I highly recommend that you use a computer program such as QuickBooks. While it may seem simpler to do accounting by hand, I assure you that it isn't. Even a luddite such as I, who can't comprehend the most basic principles of accounting, can use QuickBooks with great aplomb to plug in the proper categories for income and expenses, easily reconcile bank statements, and with a few clicks prepare all of the requisite reports that make it easy to prepare taxes.

PAYING BILLS ONLINE

While it's certainly not imperative, you might want to check out your bank's online bill pay option if you're not using this already. Once you've set up the payee list, you can make payments in a few seconds every month or set up auto payments for expenses that are recurring. Having a digital history of bills paid can also come in handy with your accounting.

MANAGING TAXES

Self-employed people need to pay quarterly taxes. A quick, online search will reveal a variety of tax calculators and other online tools that can help you estimate what your payments should be. Programs such as TurboTax are popular and useful tools for automating and guiding you step-by-step through tax preparation. An accountant can also be helpful in understanding your unique tax picture, identifying and saving the right amount for taxes each quarter, and even determining SEP IRA contribution amounts (described later in this article). The more complex your finances (or antediluvian your accounting skills), the more likely that you'll benefit from this kind of personalized expertise.

Once you have forecasted your taxes either with the help of a specialized, tax-planning program or an accountant, you can establish a plan toward saving the right amount for quarterly payments. For example, once I figured out what my tax bracket was and the approximate percentage of income that needed to be set aside as taxes, I would immediately transfer a percentage of every deposit to my savings account, where it would sit and grow a little interest until quarterly tax time came around. When I could afford to do so, I would also set aside the appropriate percentage of SEP IRA contribution from each deposit so that I'd be ready at end-of-year to deposit as much as I possibly could for retirement.

THE PRINCIPLE TO COMMIT TO IS THIS: Get that tax-earmarked cash out of your hot little hands (i.e., checking account) as soon as you can, and create whatever deterrents you need to leave the money in savings so you'll have it when you need it.

INTELLIGENT INVESTING FOR YOUR CAREER

Your writing business will require not only the investment of your time but also the investment of money. When deciding what to spend and how, consider your values and your budget in these three, key areas:

EDUCATION	MARKETING AND PROMOTION	KEEPING THE WHEELS TURNING
Subscriptions to publications in your field	URL registration and hosting for blogs and websites	Technology and application purchase, servicing and back-up
Memberships to organizations in your field	Contact database subscription (such as Constant Contact) for communicating with your audiences	Office supplies and furniture
Books: on topics you want to learn, or in genres you are cultivating	Business cards and stationery	Insurances for you and/or your business
Conferences and seminars	Print promotions (such as direct mail), giveaways and schwag	Travel, gas, parking
Classes and workshops	Online or print ad placement costs	Phone, fax and e-mail

This is not an absolute formula for spending, by any means—just a snapshot of the types of expenses you may be considering and negotiating over time. My general rule would be: start small and modest with the one or two most urgent and/or inexpensive items in each list, and grow slowly over time as your income grows.

The good news is that these legitimate business expenses may all be deducted from your income—making your net income and tax burden less. Please keep in mind that the IRS allows losses as long as you make a profit for at least three of the first five years you are in business. Otherwise, the IRS will consider your writing a non-deductible hobby.

PREPARATION AND PROTECTION FOR THE FUTURE

As a self-employed writer, in many ways your future is in your hands. Following are some of the health and financial investments that I'd recommend you consider as you build and nurture The Enterprise of You. Please understand that these are a layperson's suggestions. I am by no means an accountant, tax advisor or financial planning guru. I am simply a person who has educated herself on these topics for the sake of her own writing business, made the choices I am recommending and benefited from them. I'd like you to benefit from them, too.

SEP IRAS

Individual Retirement Accounts (IRAs) are investment accounts designed to help individuals save for retirement. But I do recommend that you educate yourself about the Simplified Employee Pension Individual Retirement Account (SEP IRA) and consider opening one if you don't have one already.

A SEP IRA is a special type of IRA that is particularly beneficial to self-employed people. Whereas a Roth IRA has a contribution cap of $5,000 or $6,000, depending on your age, the contribution limit for self-employed people in 2011 is approximately 20% of adjusted earned income, with a maximum contribution of $49,000. Contributions for a SEP IRA are generally 100% tax deductible and investments grow tax deferred. Let's say your adjusted earned income this year is $50,000. This means you'd be able to contribute $10,000 to your retirement account. I encourage you to do some research online or ask your accountant if a SEP IRA makes sense for you.

CREATING A 9-MONTH SAVINGS BUFFER

When you're living month-to-month, you are extremely vulnerable to fluctuation in the economy, client budget changes, life emergencies and every other wrench that could turn a good working groove into a frightening financial rut. The best way to prepare for the unexpected is to start (or continue) developing a savings buffer. The experts these days are suggesting that we accumulate nine months of living expenses to help us navigate transition in a way that we feel empowered rather than scared and desperate to take the next thing that comes along.

When I paid off one of my credit cards in full, I added that monthly payment to the monthly savings transfer.

I started creating my savings buffer by opening the highest-interest money market account I could find and setting up a modest, monthly automatic transfer from my checking account. Then, when I paid off my car after five years of monthly payments, I added my car payment amount to the monthly transfer. (I'd been paying that amount for five years, so I was pretty sure I could continue to pay it to myself.) When I paid off one of my credit cards in full, I added that monthly payment to the monthly savings transfer. Within a year, I had a hefty sum going to savings every month before I had time to think about it, all based on expenses I was accustomed to paying, with money that had never been anticipated in the monthly cash flow.

What can you do today—and tomorrow—to put your money to work for your life, and start being as creative with your savings as you are with language?

DISABILITY INSURANCE

If writing is your livelihood, what happens if you become unable to write? I have writing friends who have become incapacitated and unable to work due to injuries to their brains, backs, hands and eyes. Disability insurance is one way to protect against such emergencies and ensure that you have an income in the unlikely event that you're not physically able to earn one yourself.

Depending on your health, age and budget, monthly disability insurance payments may or may not be within your means or priorities. But you won't know until you learn more about your coverage options. I encourage you to investigate this possibility with several highly rated insurance companies to get the lay of the land for your unique, personal profile and then make an informed decision.

HEALTH INSURANCE

Self-employed writers face tough decisions about health insurance. If you are lucky, there is someone in your family with great health coverage that is also available to you. Without the benefit of group health insurance, chances are that self-insuring costs are high and coverage is low. Just as in disability insurance, age and health status are significant variables in costs and availability of coverage. (Once again, I am no expert on this topic; only a novice who has had to figure things out for myself along the way, sharing the little I know with you.)

Ideally, of course, you'll have reasonably-priced health insurance that helps make preventive care and health maintenance more accessible and protects you in case of a major medical emergency. The following are a few possibilities to check out that could reduce costs and improve access to health coverage:

- Join a group that aggregates its members for group coverage, such as a Chamber of Commerce or AARP. Ask an insurance agent in your area if there are any other group coverage options available to you.

- Consider a high-deductible health plan paired with a Health Savings Account (HSA). Because the deductible is so high, these plans are generally thought to be most useful for a major medical emergency. But an HSA paired with such a plan allows you to put aside a chunk of pre-tax change every year that can be spent on medical expenses or remain in the account where it can be invested and grow. 2011 HSA investment limits, for example, are: $3,050 for individual coverage and $6,150 for family coverage.

Establishing effective financial systems for your writing business will take some time and energy at the front end. I suggest that you pace yourself by taking an achievable step or two each week until you have a baseline of financial management that works for you. Then, you can start moving toward some of your bigger, longer-term goals. Once it's established, your solid financial foundation will pay you in dividends of greater efficiency, insight and peace of mind for the rest of your writing career.

SAGE COHEN is the author of *The Productive Writer* and *Writing the Life Poetic*, both from Writer's Digest Books. She's been nominated for a Pushcart Prize, won first prize in the Ghost Road Press Poetry contest and published dozens of poems, essays and articles on the writing life. Sage holds an MFA in creative writing from New York University and a BA from Brown University. Since 1997, she has been a freelance writer serving clients including Intuit, Blue Shield, Adobe, and Kaiser Permanente..

PHOTO © Nyla Alisia

REPURPOSING WRITING FOR PLATFORM AND PROFIT

by Sage Cohen

Anything worth writing about is worth writing about repeatedly. The greater your command on a topic, the more leverage you have in the realm of publishing, income generation and platform building. Plus, when you consolidate knowledge by adapting writing in ways that improve your performance and results, you gain confidence in what you know and your ability to communicate it. Eventually, you may even come to consider yourself—and be considered by others—an expert in your chosen field. This article suggests strategies and systems that can help you maximize the value of your work by repurposing writing for fresh markets and media.

A STRATEGIC APPROACH TO CREATING CONTINUED VALUE FROM YOUR THINKING AND WRITING

Instead of starting from scratch each time you pitch an article, workshop, or class, I propose that you leverage the knowledge base you've already cultivated, while finding a new dimension to explore or a new audience to educate. I call this process repurposing.

Repurposing works best when you start cultivating a consciousness about what you're writing now, what you want to be writing more of over time, and charting out the path between the two. These simple steps can take you there.

Take stock of what you have already written.

Investigate your files, archives, clips, and notebooks to see what topics or themes are taking up the most real estate. Check out not only the themes you've been assigned by editors or clients, but also the writing you choose to do. Make a diagram or chart that helps you measure how much of each type of source information you already have on hand. Let's say you come up with this list of themes about which you could write and have written author-itatively: mortgage banking, health and wellness, positive discipline for preschoolers, and providing inspiration and instruction for writers.

Decide which theme(s) you'd enjoy exploring more deeply

I invite you to prioritize your list of themes in order of what you most want to pursue moving forward. Make sure you choose a topic that truly interests you, or else you're likely to limit your productivity through your own resistance.

Let's say you believe you should be writing about mortgage banking because that's been profitable for you, but what you really love writing about is skills and strategies for improving writing. I'd argue this: When you're writing about something that is of great interest to you, you'll have far more energy for exploring its nuances and finding surprising ways to publish and profit from it.

If you're just getting started, or you would like to start from scratch with a topic you've never covered before, no problem. Write that down at the top of your list. Everyone has to start repurposing somewhere.

Define the types of people you might want to reach.

Let's assume that your number one interest from the list you just made is "providing inspiration and instruction for writers." Now ask yourself what types of people would benefit from knowing about this? The obvious answer is, of course: Writers. But there could be dozens or even hundreds of sub-categories, and then sub-sub categories that could help you identify publications, speaking and teaching opportunities, and other media through which you might customize content that connects with each of these groups. Here's a sample brainstorm:

POETS	CREATIVE NONFICTION WRITERS	FICTION WRITERS	FREELANCE WRITERS (FOR MAGAZINES)	COPY WRITERS (FOR BUSINESS / MARKETING / ADVERTISING)
Members of writing organizations				
Blog readers / online media consumers				
Students: college / high school / elementary / adult education				
Magazine / literary publication subscribers				
Book club members				
Writing groups				
People who attend writing conferences				
Audiences at community literary events / lectures / readings				

Each of these groups could be broken down further into the following sub-categories:

- Writers wanting to publish / author
- Writers wanting to improve their craft
- Writers wanting to improve their process
- Writers with bad habits who want to learn better habits
- Writers wanting to make more money
- Writers wanting to know how to run their own writing business
- Writers wanting to understand and navigate brand or platform
- Writers wanting to get inspired
- Writers wanting to use social media more effectively

Spend some time getting as detailed as you can about the types of people who might be interested in your topic—including where they might go to learn about this topic, and the types of knowledge they might be seeking. (Don't worry yet about if you actually want to speak to all of these audiences. The point here is to dream big and capture a wide range of possibilities.)

Identify fresh ways to reach subsets of your identified audience

Staying with the "providing inspiration and instruction for writers" theme, let's say you just published an article about transforming fear into courage in a writing trade magazine. Now you want to find fresh ways to spin and sell this content. If you focused on the same general audience but targeted different sub-sets and/or media, you might consider the following:

- Present at writing conferences, high schools, or writing groups on this topic.
- Use the article's knowledge base as a jumping off point for developing a 25-page e-book on the topic.
- Offer a tele-class (or a series of tele-classes) where you teach writers about how to get a handle on their relationship with fear.
- Condense or expand your 10 best tips on fear in the writing life and offer them as a series for targeted subscribers, such as rewarding subscribers to your blog or website with a 10-week, free e-mail series, or pitching this content to literary blogs or other organizations as content for their readers.
- Create and sell a daily e-mail series where you offer writers one bite-sized thought, quote or tip about fear for (you define the time range).

You see what I mean? You could keep going and going and going with new ways to explore and package and market your interest in writers' relationship with fear. I call this process of finding and using new formats, media or experiences through which you reach similar audiences *lateral* repurposing.

Tap unprecedented markets

Another approach to repurposing, which I call *vertical* repurposing, involves re-slanting content for completely new markets or audiences. Because fear is something that every human negotiates at one time or another, there are likely to be principles in our example piece that translate to people of every stripe.

First, I recommend naming for yourself the universal, translatable nugget of truth that you believe you are offering. In this case, let's say: *Behaviors and attitudes that help you work with your fear to eliminate procrastination and perfectionism.*

Then, have fun brainstorming the various audiences you might target and channels through which you might reach them. The sky is literally the limit. A few examples of the result of this work might be:

- Offer a workshop (and accompanying training materials) to corporate teams or departments who want employees to become more productive.
- Pitch a piece to a psychology trade magazine on how fear influences human development and performance —and what can be done about it.
- Pitch an article to a performance arts publication that addresses their unique creative concerns in the context of fear.
- Write an article in publications for educators teaching them how to identify and address the signs of fear in low-performing students.
- Train entrepreneurs in "feeling the fear and doing it anyway."

Make a game plan

You've done the important work of brainstorming possibilities. Now it's time to get as specific as possible about how you intend to proceed with repurposing. I'm a big fan of making extremely detailed work plans—because they help prove to me that what I want to do is actually within my reach. Even if I don't follow the plan at all, which often I don't, I move forward anchored in a sense of certainty that it's only a matter of time before I accomplish what I've set out to do.

- Choose a piece of writing from your preferred arsenal of work. Again, make sure the topic still holds some interest for you.
- Make yourself a blueprint of possibilities that identifies who you want to pitch or sell or present it to next, why it might matter to them, and the ways that you might reach this audience. For example, I have culled some of the possibilities suggested above:

Lateral Repurposing Possibilities for Fear Article

MARKET OR CHANNEL	AUDIENCE	WHY THIS IS RELEVANT TO THEM	PIECE/S TO PITCH OR SELL
[Name of] Writing Conference	Conference attendees	Website says 50% of attendees want to learn about writing process and productivity.	Workshop on fear in the writing life
My Blog about the Writing Life	My blog subscribers, Facebook friends, Twitter followers	They've subscribed to or visited my blog to get tips on writing more effectively.	25-page e-book and/or daily e-mail series focused on transforming your relationship with fear in 30 days
Tele-class through [Name of Writer who features guest writing teachers]	[Name of Writer's] audience, my blog subscribers, Facebook friends, Twitter followers	They signed up to learn about tackling fear in the writing life.	FREE: Present class material distilled from workshop above and/or OFFERS of a 25-page e-book and/or daily e-mail series focused on transforming your relationship with fear in 30 days

Vertical Repurposing Possibilities for Fear Article

MARKET OR CHANNEL	AUDIENCE	WHY THIS IS RELEVANT TO THEM	PIECE/S TO PITCH OR SELL
Corporations	Employee teams or departments	It can help teams collaborate more effectively and become more productive.	Workshop, educational collateral, and/or training materials
Psychology Trade Magazine	People interested in human psychology	Provide education about the impact of fear on human development.	Magazine article
Education Trade Magazine	Educators	Help them identify and address fear's role in low academic performance.	Magazine article

You can refer to these lists again and again —and add to them over time to track the evolution of your expertise for preferred audiences and markets.

Repurpose

With all of the strategic heavy lifting complete, you can now choose one of the possibilities you've articulated above and do whatever next step makes sense to take your work forward, such as: create the product to sell, write the query, submit a proposal to the conference, etc. I suggest the following guidelines to steer your thinking and writing:

- Read your original piece a few times, ideally out loud at least once. This helps you re-establish your connection with what you already know about this topic. Then put it out of sight.
- Start a working draft; at the top, write down everything you know you are striving to accomplish, such as: word count, market or channel / audience, target publication / media / delivery channel.
- Draft a detailed outline or do a 10-minute free write (whatever your style may be) to capture in writing the essence of what you want to accomplish with this piece.
- Research and write as you would any article or query or [whatever you have determined your deliverable to be].
- This piece should reflect the next step in your investigation of this topic. Compare it to the original to ensure there are no exact overlaps or repeats of language. This new piece should read in some way fresh and new and authentically distinguished from all of your other writing about [fear in the writing life]. (Echoing similar strategies or tips is not necessarily a problem, as long as the audience and/or market are significantly different from those of the original.)
- If you are sending this out for publication, briefly explain in your query of the success you've already had on this topic (what you've published, where you've presented) and how it's relevant to the current application that you are proposing. The delicate dance here is demonstrating that you have established expertise, while also making it clear that you have something fresh and engaging to say to this publication's readers. (The same principle is true if you are marketing a writing product yourself.)

REPEAT AND PROSPER!

You can stay engaged in repurposing consciousness by asking yourself one simple question every time you write something: "Who else could benefit from knowing about this?" (Simply apply this process to flesh out the answer to that question.) Once you've repurposed a piece of writing a few times, you'll get a feel for how vast the opportunities might be for everything you write. And you'll be on your way to establishing a practice that can boost your confidence and expertise while fortifying your platform and your profits.

SUBMISSION TRACKER

Recordkeeping is an important tool for the successful freelance writer. It's important to keep accurate records for tax season, but it's equally important to keep accurate submission records. Failure to do so could lead to some embarrassing double submissions or result in missed opportunities to follow up. Plus, an organized writer always impresses editors and agents.

On the next page is a sample submission tracker spreadsheet. You can make copies of the one in this book to help you keep records, or you can create a similar spreadsheet on your computer using a spreadsheet program. WritersMarket.com also provides submission tracking tools as part of the My Markets feature of the site.

This submission tracker has nine columns:

- **MANUSCRIPT TITLE.** This is the title of your manuscript.
- **MARKET.** This is the name of the magazine, book publisher, contest, or other entity to which you've submitted your manuscript.
- **CONTACT NAME.** This is the name of the editor, agent, or other contact who's received your work.
- **DATE SENT.** The date you submitted your manuscript.
- **DATE RETURNED.** The date your manuscript was rejected.
- **DATE ACCEPTED.** The date your manuscript was accepted.
- **DATE PUBLISHED.** The date your manuscript was published.
- **PAYMENT RECEIVED.** Detail any payment received.
- **COMMENTS.** This column is for any other notes about your experience with the market.

SUBMISSION TRACKER

MANUSCRIPT TITLE	MARKET	CONTACT NAME	DATE SENT	DATE RETURNED	DATE ACCEPTED	DATE PUBLISHED	PAYMENT RECEIVED	COMMENTS

SHOULD YOUR WRITING BUSINESS BE AN LLC?

Business Structures Explained

by Carol Topp, CPA

A new member to my writers group told us her writing business was structured as a corporation. As a certified public accountant, I found that a little odd. I didn't know Connie well, but she had told us she had just written her first book, a self-published memoir. *Why would a brand new author want corporate status for her business?* I wondered. It seemed overly complex to me, so I asked her why she had formed a corporation. "I don't know," she said, "it's what my lawyer and CPA set up." Now I was really concerned. She'd had two professionals set her up in a complex business structure when she hadn't yet sold one copy of her book!

What was going on?

SOLE PROPRIETORSHIP

Most authors prefer the simplest business structure possible—what the IRS calls a sole proprietorship, meaning a business with one owner.

Sole proprietors may go by many names including:

- freelancer
- independent contractor
- self-employed writer
- independent publisher
- self-published or traditionally published author

During a consultation with a new author, I explained the advantages of sole proprietorship. She asked me, "Why would I want to be a sole proprietor? Why not just be a freelancer?" I explained that "sole proprietor" is a tax-related term to describe her profession as a freelance writer.

Sole proprietorships are easy and quick to start. You are in business as soon as you say that you are! Or at least when you are paid for your writing. I became a professional writer when I received $50 for writing a magazine article. A business had been born. Sole proprietorships have minimal government filings and licenses, if any. Usually a writer can use his or her own name as the business name, so business name filing is needed. Best of all, sole proprietorships have the simplest tax structure. Sole proprietors use a two-page form (Schedule C Business Income or Loss) and attach it to their Form 1040 tax return.

I would have thought that Connie's writing business would be structured as a sole proprietorship. Why then was she saying that her writing business was a corporation? I asked her a few more questions.

LIMITED LIABILITY STATUS

"Oh, they set up an LLC," she explained. Now I understood. Connie was talking about limited liability company (LLC) status. She had mistakenly thought that the "C" in LLC meant "corporation," but it means "company." They are quite different. LLC status is a legal standing granted by your state (not the IRS), and it offers limited liability to protect your personal assets from any business liabilities.

It's easy to get confused as Connie did; some advertising adds to the confusion. I've seen one ad that says "Get incorporated today" while showing a smiling woman holding a business card with "Your Business, LLC" circled in red. The ad confused incorporation with LLC status. Incorporating involves forming your business as a corporation for tax purposes; LLC status is a legal standing that limits liability.

LLCs are not one of the three business structures that the IRS recognizes for tax purposes. As a matter of fact, the IRS calls LLCs "disregarded entities." (We all wish the IRS would disregard us a little more!) Certainly, the IRS knows that LLCs exist, but for tax purposes, the LLC status is disregarded, and the business owner must choose one of three structures: sole proprietorship, partnership or corporation.

What LLC status will do for you

So why had Connie's lawyer and CPA set up her sole proprietorship with LLC status? Probably because they wanted to protect her personal assets from any business debts.

LLC status offers limited liability protection. When you read "liability," think "lawsuit" or, more specifically, the money you might owe if sued. LLC status cannot stop a lawsuit, but your liabilities may be limited to your business assets. As a writer, your business assets might include your laptop computer and the cash in your business checking account. The advantage of protecting your personal assets is the main reason why authors and other small business owners obtain LLC status for their businesses.

An example of how LLC status can help involved a ghostwriter who was sued for breach of contract. He was a sole proprietor with LLC status for his business. If he had lost, the lawsuit damages would have been limited to his business assets and could not have touched his personal assets, such as his house or savings. Fortunately, he won his case.

What LLC status won't do for you

Limited Liability Company status will not reduce your taxes. Your business files the same tax forms it did before having LLC status. "If an expense is business related, it's tax deductible, no matter what business structure you use," says tax attorney Julian Block, author of *Easy Tax Guide for Writers, Photographers and Other Freelancers*.

My tax client Russ showed me a handout from a seminar that claimed one of the benefits of LLC status was a health insurance tax deduction, leading Russ to believe he needed LLC status to receive this tax break. This health insurance deduction is available to all sole proprietorships, whether they have LLC status or not. The seminar handout had inadvertently confused him.

LLC STATUS IS NOT BULLETPROOF

For years the bulletproof vest of limited liability was only available to corporations. In the 1980s, LLC status became popular and sole proprietors signed up in droves. Finally, they could receive limited liability protection without the complexities of corporate status. It all seemed too good to be true, and perhaps it was.

Lately, limited liability status has been challenged in court, and several business owners found that their personal assets were at risk. The bulletproof vest has some cracks. "If an author were driving a car while on business and injured someone, he or she could still be sued," explains attorney Julian Block. "It's not a magic bullet."

To avoid piercing your limited liability, you must keep your business separate from your personal life. Mixing assets may lead a court to determine that your LLC status is weak and therefore hold you personally liable. "It isn't enough for business people merely to carry a liability shield; they must also take reasonable measures to this shield," cautions New Hampshire attorney John Cunningham.

There are several ways to protect your shield of limited liability:

- Don't commit fraud. Even LLC status can't protect you if you're a crook!
- Set up a separate checking account for your business.
- Avoid treating business assets as your own.
- Avoid personal guarantees on business loans.
- Purchase professional liability insurance.
- Sign contracts in the name of your LLC.
- Consider placing your home or investments into a trust to further protect your assets.

Disadvantages to LLC status

To obtain LLC status from your state, you file paperwork with an accompanying fee. Often, the paperwork is fairly straightforward, especially for single-member LLCs. Some individuals file for LLC status without assistance, but I recommend you seek professional advice to understand the pros and cons of LLC status for your business. If your LLC has multiple members or is a complex arrangement, you should hire a business attorney to assist you in establishing your LLC.

When should you consider LLC status for your writing business?

Consider LLC status when you wish to protect your personal assets. In Connie's case, her lawyer and CPA were possibly being overly cautious because she had no business income or assets yet.

I operated my accounting business as a sole proprietorship for its first six years. After that, I was attracting more clients and generating more income. I already had professional liability insurance, but I decided it was time to add limited liability status to my sole proprietorship. I applied to be a single member LLC in my state by filing the paperwork and paying a $125 fee. My business name is now Carol Topp, CPA, LLC (are you impressed?) but I still file the same tax forms I did before obtaining LLC status. I hope my limited liability status is never challenged in court, but I have it (and insurance) just in case I am ever sued.

PARTNERSHIPS ARE LIKE MARRIAGE

A second business structure is a partnership with two or more other people. Occasionally, a writer may coauthor a book, but these are usually collaborations, not formal business partnerships

I usually discourage coauthors from forming a business partnership, warning them that a partnership is like being married but not being in love. You may be responsible for debts the other person can take on. Partnerships have complex tax situations necessitating professional expertise, and they may require a lawyer to draft the partnership agreement.

"Forming a business partnership really isn't necessary, and that is especially true when it is a one-shot deal," explains Dr. Dennis Hensley, coauthor of more than six titles. Quite frequently a publisher will hire the coauthors and make all the business arrangements. "When I was teamed with Stanley Field to write *The Freelancer: A Writer's Guide to Success*, we signed an agreement defining our writing responsibilities, how we would share earnings, who would serve as lead writer for the project, and how we would communicate during the writing of the manuscript. The publisher was putting us together because we had separate areas of expertise that were needed for the book the publisher wanted to release."

Alternatively, you may come up with a book idea of your own. Dauna and Marcie, long-time friends, decided to write a book together, but they did not form a business partnership. Both women maintained separate sole proprietorships, agreeing on how to split expenses and share the royalties. This kept each of their businesses separate and made the book project easier to operate.

"Before jumping into a business partnership with your life partner, friend, family member or an entrepreneur you know, sit down and talk over expectations with each other,'" advises James Chartrand of Men With Pens. "Create an agreement for sharing work and profits. Decide who does what and when, and how to split up the money—or else you'll be splitting up, period."

WRITER, INC.

The third and most complex business structure is a corporation. There are two types of corporations, S corporations and C corporations. An S corporation has a limited number of shareholders and may have only one shareholder, the owner, while C corporations can have an unlimited number of shareholders and are typically run by a board of directors. If a writer forms a corporation, it is typically an S corporation.

S corporation status may be a desirable business structure for authors who form a publishing company. Felice Gerwitz self-published her books as a sole proprietor for many years. She started publishing other authors and found that forming an S corporation could save on taxes, particularly self-employment tax. "Self-employment taxes as a sole proprietor were killing me," says Gerwitz. "Fortunately, my CPA advised me to form an S corporation, and I saw my self-employment tax drop."

As an S corporation, Gerwitz takes some of her profit as wages and some as ordinary income, which is not subject to self-employment tax. An S corporation has more complex tax preparation than a sole proprietorship, so you should seek professional accounting advice for your record keeping and tax preparation.

CONCLUSION

A writer has three business structures from which to choose: sole proprietorship, partnership or corporate status (S or C). In addition, a writer may obtain limited liability company status to limit his or her liability. Each business structure has advantages and increasing complexity. For most writers, the sole proprietorship with LLC status will serve their needs well.

BUSINESS STRUCTURES

Word pictures can explain the different business structures an author might choose.

Picture a sole proprietorship as a single-family house. Single-family homes are very common, as is the sole proprietorship form of business (78 percent of all small businesses are sole proprietorships).

A partnership is like a duplex with two families living in one house. Living that close together can bring benefits but can also create friction, just like a business partnership.

A corporation is like an apartment building with many tenants in one building. In the same way, a corporation can have many owners called shareholders. Apartment buildings are expensive to start and can be difficult to maintain, just like a corporation.

A limited liability company (LLC) is not any of these. It is a legal status granted by your state, not a business structure in the eyes of the IRS. It is similar to a fence surrounding a building, providing protection. Picture the single family home with a fence protecting it. That would be a sole proprietorship with LLC status. A partnership or corporation can also have LLC protection, just as duplexes and apartment buildings may also have fences.

Carol Topp, CPA is a Certified Public Accountant and author of *Business Tips and Taxes for Writers* (Media Angels). She has authored 10 books, both as an indie publisher and author for a small press. Learn more at CarolToppCPA.com and TaxesForWriters.com.

HOW MUCH SHOULD I CHARGE?

····································

by Lynn Wasnak

If you're a beginning freelance writer, or don't know many other freelancers, you may wonder how anyone manages to earn enough to eat and pay the rent by writing or performing a mix of writing-related tasks. Yet, smart full-time freelance writers and editors annually gross $35,000 and up—sometimes into the $150,000-200,000 range. These top-earning freelancers rarely have names known to the general public. (Celebrity writers earn fees far beyond the rates cited in this survey.) But, year after year, they sustain themselves and their families on a freelance income, while maintaining control of their hours and their lives.

Such freelancers take writing and editing seriously—it's their business.

Periodically, they sit down and think about the earning potential of their work, and how they can make freelancing more profitable and fun. They know their numbers: what it costs to run their business; what hourly rate they require; how long a job will take. Unless there's a real bonus (a special clip, or a chance to try something new) these writers turn down work that doesn't meet the mark and replace it with a better-paying project.

If you don't know your numbers, take a few minutes to figure them out. Begin by choosing your target annual income—whether it's $25,000 or $100,000. Add in fixed expenses: social security, taxes, and office supplies. Don't forget health insurance and something for your retirement. Once you've determined your annual gross target, divide it by 1,000 billable hours—about 21 hours per week—to determine your target hourly rate.

Remember—this rate is flexible. You can continue doing low-paying work you love as long as you make up for the loss with more lucrative jobs. But you must monitor your rate of earning if you want to reach your goal. If you slip, remind yourself you're in charge. As a freelancer, you can raise prices, chase better-paying jobs, work extra hours, or adjust your spending."

"Sounds great," you may say. "But how do I come up with 1,000 billable hours each year? I'm lucky to find a writing-related job every month or two, and these pay a pittance."

That's where business attitude comes in: network, track your time, join professional organizations, and study the markets. Learn how to query, then query like mad. Take chances by reaching for the next level. Learn to negotiate for a fee you can live on—your plumber does! Then get it in writing.

You'll be surprised how far you can go, and how much you can earn, if you believe in your skills and act on your belief. The rates that follow are a guide to steer you in the right direction.

This report is based on input from sales finalized in 2009 and 2010 only. The data is generated from voluntary surveys completed by members of numerous professional writers' and editors' organizations and specialty groups. We thank these responding groups, listed below, and their members for generously sharing information. If you would like to contribute your input, e-mail lwasnak@fuse.net for a survey.

PARTICIPATING ORGANIZATIONS

Here are the organizations surveyed to compile the "How Much Should I Charge?" pay rate chart. You can also find Professional Organizations in the Resources.

- American Independent Writers (AIW), (202)775-5150. Website: www.amerindy writers.org.
- American Literary Translators Association (ALTA), (972)883-2093. Website: www. utdallas.edu/alta/.
- American Medical Writers Association (AMWA), (301)294-5303. Website: www. amwa.org.
- American Society of Journalists & Authors (ASJA), (212)997-0947. Website: www. asja.org.
- American Society of Media Photographers (ASMP), (215)451-2767. Website: www. asmp.org.
- American Society of Picture Professionals (ASPP), (703)299-0219. Website: www. aspp.com.
- American Translators Association (ATA), (703)683-6100. Website: www.atanet.org.
- Angela Hoy's Writers Weekly. Website: www.writersweekly.com.
- Association of Independents in Radio (AIR), (617)825-4400. Website: www.air media.org.
- Association of Personal Historians (APH). Website: www.personalhistorians.org.
- Educational Freelancers Association (EFA), (212)929-5400. Website: www.the-efa.org.

- Freelance Success (FLX), (877) 731-5411. Website: www.freelancesucess.com.
- International Association of Business Communicators (IABC), (415)544-4700. Website: www.iabc.com.
- Investigative Reporters & Editors (IRE), (573)882-2042. Website: www.ire.org.
- Media Communicators Association International (MCA-I), (888)899-6224. Website: www.mca-i.org.
- National Cartoonists Society (NCS), (407)647-8839. Website: www.reuben.org/main.asp.
- National Writers Union (NWU), (212)254-0279. Website: www.nwu.org.
- National Association of Science Writers (NASW), (510)647-9500. Website: www.nasw.org.
- Society of Professional Journalists (SPJ), (317)927-8000. Website: www.spj.org.
- Society for Technical Communication (STC), (703)522-4114. Website: www.stc.org.
- Women in Film (WIF). Website: www.wif.org.
- Writer's Guild of America East (WGAE), (212)767-7800. Website: www.wgaeast.org.
- Writer's Guild of America West (WGA), (323)951-4000. Website: www.wga.org.

LYNN WASNAK (www.lynnwasnak.com) was directed to the market for her first paid piece of deathless prose ("Fossils in Your Driveway" published by *Journeys* in 1968 for $4) by *Writer's Market*. In the 40 years since, she's made her living as a freelancer and has never looked back.

	PER HOUR			PER PROJECT			OTHER		
	HIGH	LOW	AVG	HIGH	LOW	AVG	HIGH	LOW	AVG
ADVERTISING & PUBLIC RELATIONS									
Advertising copywriting	$150	$35	$83	$9,000	$150	$2752	$3/word	25¢/word	$1.56/word
Advertising editing	$125	$20	$64	n/a	n/a	n/a	$1/word	25¢/word	65¢/word
Advertorials	$180	$50	$92	$1,875	$200	$479	$3/word	75¢/word	$1.57/word
Business public relations	$180	$30	$84	n/a	n/a	n/a	$500/day	$200/day	$356/day
Campaign development or product launch	$150	$35	$95	$8,750	$1,500	$4,540	n/a	n/a	n/a
Catalog copywriting	$150	$25	$71	n/a	n/a	n/a	$350/item	$25/item	$116/item
Corporate spokesperson role	$180	$70	$107	n/a	n/a	n/a	$1,200/day	$500/day	$740/day
Direct-mail copywriting	$150	$35	$84	$8,248	$500	$2,839	$4/word $400/page	$1/word $200/page	$2.17/word $314/page
Event promotions/publicity	$125	$30	$75	n/a	n/a	n/a	n/a	n/a	$500/day
Press kits	$180	$30	$82	n/a	n/a	n/a	$850/60sec	$120/60sec	$456/60sec
Press/news release	$180	$30	$78	$1,500	$125	$700	$2/word $750/page	40¢/word $150/page	$1.17/word $348/page
Radio commercials	$99	$30	$72	n/a	n/a	n/a	$850/60sec	$120/60sec	$456/60sec

	PER HOUR			PER PROJECT			OTHER		
	HIGH	LOW	AVG	HIGH	LOW	AVG	HIGH	LOW	AVG
Speech writing/editing for individuals or corporations	$167	$35	$90	$10,000	$2,700	$5,036	$350/minute	$100/minute	$204/minute
BOOK PUBLISHING									
Abstracting and abridging	$125	$30	$74	n/a	n/a	n/a	$2/word	$1/word	$1.48/word
Anthology editing	$80	$23	$51	$7,900	$1,200	$4,588	n/a	n/a	n/a
Book chapter	$100	$35	$60	$2,500	$1,200	$1,758	20¢/word	8¢/word	14¢/word
Book production for clients	$100	$40	$67	n/a	n/a	n/a	$17.50/page	$5/page	$10/page
Book proposal consultation	$125	$25	$66	$1,500	$250	$788	n/a	n/a	n/a
Book publicity for clients	n/a	n/a	n/a	$10,000	$500	$2,000	n/a	n/a	n/a
Book query critique	$100	$50	$72	$500	$75	$202	n/a	n/a	n/a
Children's book writing	$75	$35	$50	n/a	n/a	n/a	$5/word $5,000/adv	$1/word $450/adv	$2.75/word $2,286/adv
Content editing (scholarly/textbook)	$125	$20	$51	$15,000	$500	$4,477	$20/page	$3/page	$6.89/page
Content editing (trade)	$125	$19	$54	$20,000	$1,000	$6,538	$20/page	$3.75/page	$8/page
Copyediting (trade)	$100	$16	$46	$5,500	$2,000	$3,667	$6/page	$1/page	$4.22/page

	PER HOUR			PER PROJECT			OTHER		
	HIGH	LOW	AVG	HIGH	LOW	AVG	HIGH	LOW	AVG
Encyclopedia articles	n/a	n/a	n/a	n/a	n/a	n/a	50¢/word $3,000/item	15¢/word $50/item	35¢/word $933/item
Fiction book writing (own)	n/a	n/a	n/a	n/a	n/a	n/a	$40,000/adv	$525/adv	$14,193/adv
Ghostwriting, as told to	$125	$35	$67	$47,000	$5,500	$22,892	$100/page	$50/page	$87/page
Ghostwriting, no credit	$125	$30	$73	n/a	n/a	n/a	$3/word $500/page	50¢/word $50/page	$1.79/word $206/page
Guidebook writing/editing	n/a	n/a	n/a	n/a	n/a	n/a	$14,000/adv	$10,000/adv	$12,000/adv
Indexing	$60	$22	$35	n/a	n/a	n/a	$12/page	$2/page	$4.72/page
Manuscript evaluation and critique	$100	$23	$66	$2,000	$150	$663	n/a	n/a	n/a
Manuscript typing	n/a	n/a	$20	n/a	n/a	n/a	$3/page	95¢/page	$1.67/page
Movie novelizations	n/a	n/a	n/a	$15,000	$5,000	$9,159	n/a	n/a	n/a
Nonfiction book writing (collaborative)	$125	$40	$80	n/a	n/a	n/a	$110/page $75,000/adv	$50/page $1,300/adv	$80/page $22,684/adv
Nonfiction book writing (own)	$125	$40	$72	n/a	n/a	n/a	$110/page $50,000/adv	$50/page $1,300/adv	$80/page $14,057/adv
Novel synopsis (general)	$60	$30	$45	$450	$150	$292	$100/page	$10/page	$37/page

	PER HOUR			PER PROJECT			OTHER		
	HIGH	LOW	AVG	HIGH	LOW	AVG	HIGH	LOW	AVG
Personal history writing/editing (for clients)	$125	$30	$60	$40,000	$750	$15,038	n/a	n/a	n/a
Proofreading	$75	$15	$31	n/a	n/a	n/a	$5/page	$2/page	$3.26/page
Research for writers or book publishers	$150	$15	$52	n/a	n/a	n/a	$600/day	$450/day	$525/day
Rewriting/structural editing	$120	$25	$67	$50,000	$2,500	$13,929	15¢/word	6¢/word	11¢/word
Translation—literary	n/a	n/a	n/a	$10,000	$7,000	$8,500	20¢/target word	6¢/target word	11¢/target word
Translation—nonfiction/technical	n/a	n/a	n/a	n/a	n/a	n/a	35¢/target word	8¢/target word	16¢/target word
BUSINESS									
Annual reports	$180	$45	$92	$15,000	$500	$5,708	$600	$100	$349
Brochures, booklets, flyers	$150	$30	$81	$15,000	$300	$4,215	$2.50/word $800/page	35¢/word $50/page	$1.21/word $341/page
Business editing (general)	$150	$25	$70	n/a	n/a	n/a	n/a	n/a	n/a
Business letters	$150	$30	$74	n/a	n/a	n/a	$2/word	$1/word	$1.47/word
Business plan	$150	$30	$82	$15,000	$200	$4,100	n/a	n/a	n/a

	PER HOUR			PER PROJECT			OTHER		
	HIGH	LOW	AVG	HIGH	LOW	AVG	HIGH	LOW	AVG
Business writing seminars	$200	$60	$107	$8,600	$550	$2,919	n/a	n/a	n/a
Consultation on communications	$180	$40	$95	n/a	n/a	n/a	$1,200/day	$500/day	$823/day
Copyediting for business	$125	$25	$60	n/a	n/a	n/a	$4/page	$2/page	$3/page
Corporate histories	$180	$35	$86	160,000	$5,000	$54,500	$2/word	$1/word	$1.50/word
Corporate periodicals, editing	$125	$35	$69	n/a	n/a	n/a	$2.50/word	75¢/word	$1.42/word
Corporate periodicals, writing	$135	$35	$78	n/a	n/a	$1,875	$3/word	$1/word	$1.71/word
Corporate profiles	$180	$35	$88	n/a	n/a	$3,000	$2/word	$1/word	$1.50/word
Ghostwriting for business execs	$150	$25	$84	$3,000	$500	$1,393	$2.50/word	50¢/word	$2/word
Ghostwriting for businesses	$250	$35	$109	$3,000	$500	$1,756	n/a	n/a	n/a
Newsletters, desktop publishing/production	$135	$35	$71	$6,600	$1,000	$3,480	$750/page	$150/page	$429/page
Newsletters, editing	$125	$25	$67	n/a	n/a	$3,600	$230/page	$150/page	$185/page
Newsletters, writing	$125	$25	$77	$6,600	$800	$3,567	$5/word $1,250/page	$1/word $150/page	$2.30/word $514/page

	PER HOUR			PER PROJECT			OTHER		
	HIGH	LOW	AVG	HIGH	LOW	AVG	HIGH	LOW	AVG
Translation services for business use	$75	$35	$52	n/a	n/a	n/a	$35/ target word $1.40/ target line	6¢/ target word $1/ target line	$2.30/ target word $1.20/ target line
Resume writing	$100	$60	$72	$500	$150	$287	n/a	n/a	n/a
COMPUTER, INTERNET & TECHNICAL									
Blogging—paid	n/a	n/a	$100	$2,000	$500	$1,240	$500/post	$6/post	$49/post
E-mail copywriting	$125	$35	$85	n/a	n/a	$300	$2/word	30¢/word	91¢/word
Educational webinars	$500	$0	$195	n/a	n/a	n/a	n/a	n/a	n/a
Hardware/Software help screen writing	$95	$60	$81	$6,000	$1,000	$4,000	n/a	n/a	n/a
Hardware/Software manual writing	$165	$30	$80	$23,500	$5,000	$11,500	n/a	n/a	n/a
Internet research	$95	$25	$55	n/a	n/a	n/a	n/a	n/a	n/a
Keyword descriptions	n/a	n/a	n/a	n/a	n/a	n/a	$200/page	$135/page	$165/page
Online videos for clients	$95	$60	$76	n/a	n/a	n/a	n/a	n/a	n/a

	PER HOUR			PER PROJECT			OTHER		
	HIGH	LOW	AVG	HIGH	LOW	AVG	HIGH	LOW	AVG
Social media postings for clients	$95	$30	$62	n/a	n/a	$500	n/a	n/a	$10/word
Technical editing	$150	$25	$65	n/a	n/a	n/a	n/a	n/a	n/a
Technical writing	$160	$30	$80	n/a	n/a	n/a	n/a	n/a	n/a
Web editing	$100	$25	$57	n/a	n/a	n/a	$10/page	$3/page	$5.67/page
Webpage design	$150	$35	$80	$4,000	$200	$1,278	n/a	n/a	n/a
Website or blog promotion	n/a	n/a	n/a	$650	$195	$335	n/a	n/a	n/a
Website reviews	n/a	n/a	n/a	$900	$50	$300	n/a	n/a	n/a
Website search engine optimization	$89	$60	$76	$50,000	$8,000	$12,000		n/a	n/a
White papers	$135	$25	$82	$10,000	$2,500	$4,927	n/a	n/a	n/a
EDITORIAL/DESIGN PACKAGES									
Desktop publishing	$150	$25	$67	n/a	n/a	n/a	$750/page	$30/page	$202/page
Photo brochures	$125	$65	$87	$15,000	$400	$3,869	$65/picture	$35/picture	$48/picture
Photography	$100	$50	$71	$10,500	$50	$2,100	$2,500/day	$500/day	$1,340/day

	PER HOUR			PER PROJECT			OTHER		
	HIGH	LOW	AVG	HIGH	LOW	AVG	HIGH	LOW	AVG
Photo research	$75	$25	$49	n/a	n/a	n/a	n/a	n/a	n/a
Picture editing	$100	$40	$64	n/a	n/a	n/a	$65/picture	$35/picture	$53/picture
EDUCATIONAL & LITERARY SERVICES									
Author appearances at national events	n/a	n/a	n/a	n/a	n/a	n/a	$500/hour $30,000/event	$100/hour $500/event	$285/hour $5,000/event
Author appearances at regional events	n/a	n/a	n/a	n/a	n/a	n/a	$1,500/event	$50/event	$615/event
Author appearances at local groups	$63	$40	$47	n/a	n/a	n/a	$400/event	$75/event	$219/event
Authors presenting in schools	$125	$25	$78	n/a	n/a	n/a	$350/class	$50/class	$183/class
Educational grant and proposal writing	$100	$35	$67	n/a	n/a	n/a	n/a	n/a	n/a
Manuscript evaluation for theses/dissertations	$100	$15	$53	$1,550	$200	$733	n/a	n/a	n/a
Poetry manuscript critique	$100	$25	$62	n/a	n/a	n/a	n/a	n/a	n/a
Private writing instruction	$60	$50	$57	n/a	n/a	n/a	n/a	n/a	n/a

	PER HOUR			PER PROJECT			OTHER		
	HIGH	LOW	AVG	HIGH	LOW	AVG	HIGH	LOW	AVG
Readings by poets, fiction writers	n/a	n/a	n/a	n/a	n/a	n/a	$3,000/event	$50/event	$225/event
Short story manuscript critique	$150	$30	$75	$175	$50	$112	n/a	n/a	n/a
Teaching adult writing classes	$125	$35	$82	n/a	n/a	n/a	$800/class $5,000/course	$150/class $500/course	$450/class $2,667/course
Writer's workshop panel or class	$220	$30	$92	n/a	n/a	n/a	$5,000/day	$60/day	$1,186/day
Writing for scholarly journals	$100	$40	$63	$450	$100	$285	n/a	n/a	n/a
FILM, VIDEO, TV, RADIO, STAGE									
Book/novel summaries for film producers	n/a	n/a	n/a	n/a	n/a	n/a	$34/page	$15/page	$23/page $120/book
Business film/video scriptwriting	$150	$50	$97	n/a	n/a	$600	$1,000/run min	$50/run min	$334/run min $500/day
Comedy writing for entertainers	n/a	n/a	n/a	n/a	n/a	n/a	$150/joke $500/group	$5/joke $100/group	$50/joke $283/group
Copyediting audiovisuals	$90	$22	$53	n/a	n/a	n/a	n/a	n/a	n/a
Educational or training film/video scriptwriting	$125	$35	$81	n/a	n/a	n/a	$500/run min	$100/run min	$245/run min

	PER HOUR			PER PROJECT			OTHER		
	HIGH	LOW	AVG	HIGH	LOW	AVG	HIGH	LOW	AVG
Feature film options	First 18 months, 10% WGA minimum; 10% minimum each 18-month period thereafter.								
TV options	First 180 days, 5% WGA minimum; 10% minimum each 180-day period thereafter.								
Industrial product film/video scriptwriting	$150	$30	$99	n/a	n/a	n/a	$500/run min	$100/run min	$300/run min
Playwriting for the stage	5-10% box office/Broadway, 6-7% box office/off-Broadway; 10% box office/off-Broadway, 10% box office/regional theatre.								
Radio editorials	$70	$50	$60	n/a	n/a	n/a	$200/run min $400/day	$45/run min $250/day	$124/run min $325/day
Radio interviews	n/a	n/a	n/a	$1,500	$150	$633	n/a	n/a	n/a
Screenwriting (original screenplay-including treatment)	n/a	n/a	n/a	n/a	n/a	n/a	$117,602	$62,642	$90,122
Script synopsis for agent or film	$2,344/30 min, $4,441/60 min, $6,564/90 min								
Script synopsis for business	$75	$45	$62	n/a	n/a	n/a	n/a	n/a	n/a
TV commercials	$99	$60	$81	n/a	n/a	n/a	$2,500/30 sec	$150/30 sec	$1,204/30 sec
TV news story/feature	$1,455/5 min, $2,903/10 min, $4,105/15 min								
TV scripts (non-theatrical)	Prime Time: $33,681/60 min, $47,388/90 min Not Prime Time: $12,857/30 min, $23,370/60 min, $35,122/90 min								

	PER HOUR			PER PROJECT			OTHER		
	HIGH	LOW	AVG	HIGH	LOW	AVG	HIGH	LOW	AVG
TV scripts (teleplay/MOW)	$68,150/120 min								
MAGAZINES & TRADE JOURNALS									
Article manuscript critique	$125	$25	$64	n/a	n/a	n/a	n/a	n/a	n/a
Arts query critique	$100	$50	$75	n/a	n/a	n/a	n/a	n/a	n/a
Arts reviewing	$95	$60	$79	$325	$100	$194	$1.20/word	8¢/word	58¢/word
Book reviews	n/a	n/a	n/a	$900	$25	$338	$1.50/word	15¢/word	68¢/word
City magazine calendar	n/a	n/a	n/a	$250	$50	$140	$1/word	30¢/word	70¢/word
Comic book/strip writing				$200 original story, $500 existing story, $35 short script.					
Consultation on magazine editorial	$150	$30	$81	n/a	n/a	n/a	n/a	n/a	$100/page
Consumer magazine column	n/a	n/a	n/a	$2,500	$75	$898	$2.50/word	37¢/word	$1.13/word
Consumer front-of-book	n/a	n/a	n/a	$850	$350	$600	n/a	n/a	n/a
Content editing	$125	$25	$57	$6,500	$2,000	$3,819	15¢/word	6¢/word	11¢/word
Contributing editor	n/a	n/a	n/a	n/a	n/a	n/a	$156,000/contract	$20,000/contract	$51,000/contract

	PER HOUR			PER PROJECT			OTHER		
	HIGH	LOW	AVG	HIGH	LOW	AVG	HIGH	LOW	AVG
Copyediting magazines	$100	$18	$50	n/a	n/a	n/a	$10/page	$2.90/page	$5.68/page
Fact checking	$125	$15	$46	n/a	n/a	n/a	n/a	n/a	n/a
Gag writing for cartoonists	$35/gag; 25% sale on spec.								
Ghostwriting articles (general)	$200	$30	$102	$3,500	$1,100	$2,229	$10/word	60¢/word	$2.25/word
Magazine research	$100	$15	$47	n/a	n/a	n/a	$500/item	$100/item	$200/item
Proofreading	$75	$15	$35	n/a	n/a	n/a	n/a	n/a	n/a
Reprint fees	n/a	n/a	n/a	$1,500	$20	$461	$1.50/word	10¢/word	73¢/word
Rewriting	$125	$20	$68	n/a	n/a	n/a	n/a	n/a	$50/page
Trade journal feature article	$122	$40	$80	$4,950	$150	$1,412	$3/word	20¢/word	$1.16/word
Transcribing interviews	$180	$90	$50	n/a	n/a	n/a	$3/min	$1/min	$2/min
MEDICAL/SCIENCE									
Medical/scientific conference coverage	$125	$50	$85	n/a	n/a	n/a	$800/day	$300/day	$600/day
Medical/scientific editing	$125	$21	$73	n/a	n/a	n/a	$12.50/page $600/day	$3/page $500/day	$4.40/page $550/day

	PER HOUR			PER PROJECT			OTHER		
	HIGH	LOW	AVG	HIGH	LOW	AVG	HIGH	LOW	AVG
Medical/scientific writing	$250	$30	$95	$5,000	$1,000	$3,354	$2/word	25¢/word	$1.12/word
Medical/scientific multimedia presentations	$100	$50	$75	n/a	n/a	n/a	$100/slide	$50/slide	$77/slide
Medical/scientific proofreading	$125	$18	$64	n/a	n/a	$500	$3/page	$2.50/page	$2.75/page
Pharmaceutical writing	$125	$90	$105	n/a	n/a	n/a	n/a	n/a	n/a
NEWSPAPERS									
Arts reviewing	$69	$30	$53	$200	$15	$101	60¢/word	6¢/word	36¢/word
Book reviews	$69	$45	$58	$350	$15	$140	60¢/word	25¢/word	44¢/word
Column, local	n/a	n/a	n/a	$600	$25	$206	$1/word	38¢/word	65¢/word
Column, self-syndicated	n/a	n/a	n/a	n/a	n/a	n/a	$35/insertion	$4/insertion	$16/insertion
Copyediting	$35	$15	$27	n/a	n/a	n/a	n/a	n/a	n/a
Editing/manuscript evaluation	$75	$25	$35	n/a	n/a	n/a	n/a	n/a	n/a
Feature writing	$79	$40	$63	$1,040	$85	$478	$1.60/word	10¢/word	59¢/word
Investigative reporting	n/a	n/a	n/a	n/a	n/a	n/a	$10,000/grant	$250/grant	$2,250/grant

	PER HOUR			PER PROJECT			OTHER		
	HIGH	LOW	AVG	HIGH	LOW	AVG	HIGH	LOW	AVG
Obituary copy	n/a	n/a	n/a	$225	$35	$124	n/a	n/a	n/a
Proofreading	$45	$15	$23	n/a	n/a	n/a	n/a	n/a	n/a
Stringing	n/a	n/a	n/a	$2,400	$40	$525	n/a	n/a	n/a
NONPROFIT									
Grant writing for nonprofits	$150	$19	$70	$3,000	$500	$1,852	n/a	n/a	n/a
Nonprofit annual reports	$100	$30	$64	n/a	n/a	n/a	n/a	n/a	n/a
Nonprofit writing	$150	$20	$77	$17,600	$200	$4,706	n/a	n/a	n/a
Nonprofit editing	$125	$25	$54	n/a	n/a	n/a	n/a	n/a	n/a
Nonprofit fundraising literature	$110	$35	$74	$3,500	$300	$1,597	$1,000/day	$500/day	$767/day
Nonprofit presentations	$100	$50	$73	n/a	n/a	n/a	n/a	n/a	n/a
Nonprofit public relations	$100	$20	$60	n/a	n/a	n/a	n/a	n/a	n/a
POLITICS/GOVERNMENT									
Government agency writing/editing	$100	$20	$57	n/a	n/a	n/a	$1.25/word	25¢/word	75¢/word

	PER HOUR			PER PROJECT				OTHER		
	HIGH	LOW	AVG	HIGH	LOW	AVG	HIGH	LOW	AVG
Government grant writing/ editing	$150	$19	$68	n/a	n/a	n/a	n/a	n/a	n/a
Government-sponsored research	$100	$35	$66	n/a	n/a	n/a	n/a	n/a	$600/day
Public relations for political campaigns	$150	$40	$86	n/a	n/a	n/a	n/a	n/a	n/a
Speechwriting for government officials	$200	$30	$96	$4,500	$1,000	$2,750	$200/run min	$110/run min	$155/run min
Speechwriting for political campaigns	$150	$60	$101	n/a	n/a	n/a	$200/run min	$100/run min	$162/run min

BALANCE YOUR WRITING AND YOUR PLATFORM

In 8 Simple Steps

by Krissy Brady

Writers today have many hats to wear—writer, blogger, social media manager, publisher, marketer—so it's no wonder the balancing act becomes a challenge. This is especially the case when you're consumed by the *writing vs. platform* tug-of-war: either your writing is going well or your platform is going strong, but rarely do the two coexist peacefully.

If the quest for balance between your writing and platform hasn't been working out very well, strive for harmony instead. Both your writing and platform are important aspects of your career, but let's face it: nothing is *ever* more important than the writing itself. Your platform is supposed to complement your writing career, not distract you from it.

To prevent this from happening, follow these 8 simple steps:

STEP 1: PLAN PLATFORM AROUND YOUR WRITING SCHEDULE

Your writing must *always* come first; otherwise, there's no point to building a platform. The further ahead you plan your writing schedule, the easier it will be to plan your blogging schedule. Doing so will give you a bird's eye view of how much time you'll have to devote to any blog- and social media-related tasks you want to take on.

The key to building a successful platform your followers will depend on is *consistency*. Always post blog posts when you say you're going to, and do the same with your social media profiles. To be (and stay) consistent, create your writing schedule, then take a look at the busiest portions of it: how much of your platform can you build during these times? Use this as your guide when creating your overall social media strategy.

You'll never have to feel like you're choosing between the two because you'll have planned a realistic amount of time for both. You'll also never have to worry about over-scheduling yourself. (Bonus: during assignment lulls, you can bank additional blog posts and social media content for upcoming busy periods.)

STEP 2: ALIGN YOUR WRITING TASKS WITH BLOGGING TASKS

The process of completing a blog post is identical to that of a freelance article, just on a smaller scale. Organize your workday based on each phase of the creative process, and batch similar tasks together:

- During brainstorming sessions, choose the next phase of article pitches you'd like to work on. While you're at it, create complementary blog post ideas. This will not only give you the opportunity to repurpose your research for multiple projects, it will spread your wings further within your chosen area of expertise.
- Speaking of research, after you've batched together the article and post ideas that are of similar scope, make a list of the holes that need to be filled for each angle you're focusing on. You'll be able to accomplish research for multiple pieces in one sitting instead of several.
- When outlining your query letters, create outlines for your guest post pitches.
- Create a production line of sorts for revising your pitches and researching markets, then go on a pitching frenzy!

By bunching tasks together that are similar in scope, you'll be able to seamlessly shift over to your blogging tasks without having to shift your entire mindset.

STEP 3: CREATE AN INDEX OF BLOG POST IDEAS

Some blog posts fly from our keyboards and onto the screen, while others just won't… come… out. This is a writer's worst nightmare. There's nothing more frustrating than taking four hours to write a blog post that should've only taken an hour, especially when we have paid writing deadlines waiting in the wings.

Alleviate the pressure by creating an index of blog post ideas. That way, when it's time to sit down and write a post, you can choose your next topic based on your current inspiration level. You'll look through your list of ideas and will be automatically drawn toward certain ideas over others, making the writing process more fluent and less forced.

You can keep track of your blog post ideas quickly and easily through your Wordpress dashboard, thanks to a plugin called *Ideas* (http://bit.ly/Mz1sVG). Before, you had to create blog post drafts to keep track of your ideas, making your dashboard look cluttered and messy. Now, with the *Ideas* plugin, you can keep track of your ideas in a separate area, create outlines for each in the summary section, and list the links you'd like to include in the resources section.

The more information you can prepare for each post in advance, the faster you'll write them, and the less conflicted you'll feel about your writing and blogging tasks.

STEP 4: WORK ON BLOG POSTS IN BATCHES

The word "balance" makes you feel like you have to split your days evenly between all aspects of your writing career, which leads to feelings of being torn and distracted. It's much easier to complete creative tasks when you're focusing on them individually rather than stringing yourself too thin.

Choose one day a week (or every two weeks depending on how often you plan to post) and *only* work on your blog posts. (A great plugin to help you with the planning process is the *Editorial Calendar* plugin from WordPress: http://bit.ly/4eP5W6.) By dividing your efforts instead of trying to maintain your writing and blogging simultaneously, your mind will always be clear to focus on the task at hand. No longer will you be writing while thinking about your blog, or blogging while thinking about your writing.

STEP 5: CREATE STRATEGY FOR SOCIAL MEDIA ACCOUNTS

An editorial calendar is just as important for your social media accounts as it is for your blog. In the social media world, sporadic, inconsistent social media posts are called "random acts of marketing." They confuse your audience and cause your platform to stagnate. Until you make vivid, concise goals for each of your social media profiles, there's no way to gauge the progress you're making because it's not clear what you're working toward.

Know your goals. Know your audience. Know their needs. If you recycle the same content over all of your profiles, you won't give them a reason to follow you across all platforms. Each social media platform has its own strengths you can use to create unique content:

- **Facebook** has become more and more visual with each upgrade. Focus on stunning visuals your target audience will immediately share with their friends and followers.
- **Twitter** is all about the headlines: focus on making your headlines irresistible and watch your content spread like wildfire.
- **LinkedIn** focuses on business networking and building your client base. Here you can concentrate on sharing intriguing articles and news that will help you establish credibility in your niche (and help you make quality connections).
- **YouTube** is perfect for the how-to guru. Create videos to help your audience improve their lives in big and small ways, and you'll stay top of mind when they need help in the future.
- **Pinterest** took the social media world by storm, combining stunning imagery with ultimate ideas in creativity (and causing every social media platform to up the ante

with their own visual capabilities). Use Pinterest to help your followers make their dreams a reality.

Choose a specific focus for each of your social media accounts. For example, have each of your profiles represent a pressure point your target audience struggles with; this will encourage them to subscribe to all of your profiles. Clear profile definitions will ensure you won't become lost as you maintain them, and your followers won't as they visit them.

STEP 6: CURATE CONTENT FOR SOCIAL MEDIA ACCOUNTS

You know how important it is to share quality content through your social media profiles, but how do you go about doing so without it taking over your life? Browsing the Internet is a tricky business. Even if you subscribe to targeted blogs, you still have to sift through dozens of e-mails, dozens of shares and dozens of tweets. If you're not careful, hours could go by before you realize you're lost in the information sea.

Don't fret: there are now very handy, very convenient, and very free content curation tools at your disposal, including:

- **Google Alerts: google.com/alerts.** Choose search queries you want to be kept in the loop about, and have the results sent directly to your inbox as they happen, once a day, or once a week.
- **Social Mention: socialmention.com.** Similar to Google Alerts but for social media results—blogs, networks, comments, etc.—and you can have the results sent to your inbox on a daily basis.
- **News.me: news.me.** In an information overload society, we too easily miss out on fantastic content because it's buried underneath a pile of rubbish. When you sign up for News.me, it will keep track of your feeds and send you a daily newsletter of the five best links.
- **Prismatic: getprismatic.com.** Once you set up a Prismatic account, you'll wonder what you ever did without it. As you begin keeping track of the information that interests you and your followers, Prismatic keeps track of what you've read and what you're going to read, and uses this information to streamline a newsfeed that couldn't be more perfect for your needs.

Instead of spending hours scouring every blog for information to share, these tools will help you curate the best possible content for your readership (and in a fraction of the time).

STEP 7: CREATE A SEPARATE E-MAIL FOR SUBSCRIPTIONS

Admit it: there's nothing that clutters your mind more than a cluttered inbox. To alleviate said cluttered feeling, you spend hours reading and responding to all of your e-mails. Your inbox is eventually empty, and you feel a sense of accomplishment… for about five minutes, until the next flood of e-mails come in and you realize you haven't accomplished one word of writing.

If you want to boost your daily productivity level, the best decision you'll ever make is creating a separate e-mail account specifically for mailing list and blog subscriptions. Your primary inbox will then be dedicated to your writing assignments, which you'll be able to focus on distraction-free.

The same goes for when it's time to catch up on your reading: you'll be able to focus on the learning process without feeling guilty for not replying to work-related e-mails immediately.

STEP 8: SCHEDULE YOUR SOCIAL MEDIA POSTS IN ADVANCE

Once you have the editorial calendars for your blog and social media profiles in place, everything you post should be intentional toward your career goals. This is where scheduling your posts in advance comes in handy. Use a scheduling program like Buffer (bufferapp.com) or Hootsuite (hootsuite.com), and define a posting routine for each social media account.

Decide how many times you'll post to your Facebook page, Twitter account, and other social media profiles, and also decide on when. You can setup your scheduling program to automatically launch your posts at specific times so you can focus entirely on the quality of your content. To find out the best times to post—common times your following is online— sign up for a free Crowdbooster account (crowdbooster.com). Crowdbooster will continually analyze your Facebook and Twitter accounts and will regularly notify you of the best times to post content.

Scheduling your social media posts in advance means you'll have one less excuse to procrastinate during the week. Instead, unwind at the end of your productive day by engaging with your followers. (Just imagine!)

As you use the above steps to create harmony between your writing and platform, you'll naturally start refining each part of the process and making it your own. In no time, you'll be wearing all of your writing career hats in style.

KRISSY BRADY is a freelance writer from Gravenhurst, Ontario, Canada. Her articles have appeared in *Women's Health* and *The Writer*, and she's currently working on her first screenplay. You can learn more about Krissy at her website: www.writtenbykrissy.com.

HOW TO LAUNCH AN AUTHOR WEBSITE

....

by Karen M. Rider

A writer's website serves as a digital calling card to the world, one that should dynamically present your writing wares. Unlike a blog that aims to engage people in discussion, the purpose of a website is **to inform** people about who you are and **to promote** your offerings to your target audience: potential readers or clients, editors, publishers or agents. Whether you choose to design-it-yourself (DIY) or hire a Web design professional, you'll need a strategy that successfully leads you to the launch of your new website.

"If you strategize with clear goals and capture visitors' attention with compelling content that meets their needs right from the homepage," says Shaila Abdullah, owner, MyHouseofDesign.com, "then visitors are more likely to be excited about buying your book or hiring you." A website strategy consists of the following steps:

1. Know Cost Components
2. Understand Visitor Expectations
3. Know Your Audience
4. Set Relevant Goals and Objectives
5. Envision the Design
6. Create Error-free Content
7. Optimize & Market

COST COMPONENTS

"There are four components associated with the cost for a website: Domain, hosting, site development and site maintenance," explains Maddee James, owner of xuni.com Web Design.

Domain (URL) is the "street address" for your site, such as "yourname.com." Domains can be purchased from online registrars such as Register.com. The domain registration fee is paid in advance and for a specified period (e.g., 1-5 years). Hosting services such as HostGator.com charge to provide the Internet "house" for your website. Hosting is billed monthly or annually.

Site Development is the process through which a designer (or you, if DIY) builds a website before it "goes live" on the Web. For professionally designed sites, the bulk of cost is in development. Most DIY services charge a monthly or annual fee. Watch for add-on charges for things like additional pages or shopping carts for your site.

Writing consultant and novelist Patricia Sheehy has used a variety of website hosting and design services over the years. Based on her extensive research of DIY services, she advises writers to "look for a website service that offers a range of templates, shows 'live' websites using these templates, offers 24/7 technical support from real people, and the control panel is easy to learn to use."

Site Maintenance is the routine updating of a website after it is launched. Cost for maintenance depends on two factors: frequency and who makes the updates. Update schedules vary based on a writer's goals and the type of information they have to present to visitors. An author may update only when a new book is launched. Freelancers might update as often as they have new clips to post. If you handle updates on your own, as often as you like, there is no additional cost. However, if you have a designer do it for you, a fee will be assessed based on time involved.

The time, effort and technical aspects that go into the four components of site development renders the cost: For a professionally designed, entry-level website the price can range from $1,000-2,000. A DIY site may cost just a few hundred dollars, but a poorly designed site means a lackluster representation of your work on the Web. If you go the DIY route, be sure you have the time, patience and aptitude to create a website that meets both your writing goals and your visitor's expectations.

VISITOR EXPECTATIONS

You're not ready to design a website until you understand the types of pages visitors expect to see within a writer's website. Use the short list below to identify the pages you'll need for your website:

- Homepage with a welcome message
- Books or Portfolio Page
- Reviews/Testimonials Page
- Bio Page
- Contact Page

- Events Page
- Services Page (if applicable)
- Press Page or FAQ Page

Visitors also expect a website to have an inherent hierarchy that makes it easy for them to find their way around your home on the Web. Site Navigation (menu bar across the top or down the side) must use familiar titles (e.g., Connect, Store, About, Events). Visitors will not scroll to bottom of page to see what's hiding down there, so arrange essential information "above the fold" (i.e., the bottom of your screen). Essential information includes calls-to-action, which guide the visitor to do something that is meaningful to your goals: buy your book, e-mail you about an assignment, subscribe to a newsletter.

Visitors also do not want to swim in a sea of text; break it up with high quality graphics (photos, book or magazine cover, a call-out box). Use the same typeface throughout the site and be sure it is clear to read against the color palette. Bold and italic should be used sparingly; underline should be used only for hyperlinks. Also, make sure links work properly. Finally, visitors don't like to wait for a site to load—avoid using a Flash intro.

"If you don't provide this guidance throughout the pages of your site, your visitor won't be motivated to respond; you need to give them clear direction," says Penny Sansevieri, President, Author Marketing Experts. "Otherwise, you'll wind-up with lots of visitors and no tangible result" (e.g., sales, subscribers). This is why another important part of strategy is to…

KNOW YOUR AUDIENCE

If you want to turn visitors into fans or clients, provide content that immediately "speaks" to their needs. Visitors subconsciously ask themselves a set of questions when they visit a website. Take the time to answer the following questions to help you (or a designer) create a site that speaks to your target audience:

- What does this writer offer? How can s/he help me?
- Why should I read this book/hire this person, right now?
- What am I being asked to do here?
- How do I connect/learn more?
- What do other people have to say?
- Where do I buy this book?

SET GOALS & OBJECTIVES

Tangible results come from setting relevant goals that meet your needs as a writer as well as visitor expectations. To help you clarify primary goals for your website, Shaila Abdullah suggests answering these questions:

- What do you want your website to do for you?
- Who are you trying to attract to your work?
- What are you offering visitors?
- What action do you want visitors to take?
- Will you engage with visitors using social media?

For example, a freelancer's primary goal is to show why they're the person to hire for an assignment. She needs to provide concise, compelling information about why she's the writer an editor needs to hire. She'll back that up with a great testimonial. The unpublished author pitching a book wants to demonstrate why an agent should take a chance on him. He'll want to show a dynamite book cover, provide a short synopsis and a terrific blurb from someone with clout. If compelling enough, this information will lead the agent to contact the author.

For any of these writers, secondary objectives might be to book speaking engagements, build their subscription list or grow their following on social media. They can encourage site visitors to connect with them by using call-to-action statements or buttons (e.g., subscribe, a Twitter icon). Make sure your content crystalizes benefits visitors will receive if they take the action you've requested. This could be the offer of a thrilling read; expertise they won't find elsewhere; a chance to win something or exclusive content not published in the book.

One caveat: Even if you're a writer of many different talents, be careful not to confuse visitors. For example, a freelance writer with a big portfolio, coaching services and a novel to sell may acquire more clients and sell more books by having *two different* websites because the audience—and the goal (get hired versus sell books) for each—is different.

ENVISION THE DESIGN

What should your website look like? The answer depends on the kind of image you want to project to visitors. Mysterious? Edgy? Serious? Humorous? Color, font choices tone of voice and images all convey something about you. While you can borrow ideas from your favorite writer's website, "your website should be an authentic reflection of you and your writing," says James. You also have to be realistic about what you can afford in terms of design. A more intricate graphic design or the use of motion graphics will cost more. Most DIY services provide templates but do not give you the design range you receive from a web designer. There's a trade-off to be made and only you can decide where that line is drawn for your website.

CREATE ERROR-FREE, CURRENT CONTENT

The content you create follows naturally from goals and objectives, site structure and the needs of your audience. Writers often make two types of mistakes with their websites, and both interfere with the ability to generate interest in your work. The first mistake is filling each page with too much copy.

"Websites are not read like a magazine," explains Penny Sansevieri. "Writers need to convey who they are and what they have to offer with about 250 words per Page within a website."

The second mistake is a failure to correct errors. Sure, every work of literature has typos that weren't caught by the copyeditor. However, if you have more than just a misplaced comma on a page, or typos throughout the site, it reflects poorly on you and your work.

"Even if you work with a professional, have a third pair of eyes proofread every page of your website," suggests Abdullah.

No one likes to visit an outdated website. "To keep traffic moving to your site and to hold visitor interest," says Sansevieri, "provide current and relevant information that compels them to buy your book or to purchase services from you. A blog, incorporated into your website, is one way to keep content current." Additionally, most web designers (and DIY templates) incorporate social media bookmarking into website structure. This makes it easy for visitors to like, share or tweet from any page within a site.

OPTIMIZE & MARKET

Once your site is ready for launch, you will want to optimize the content so search engines (e.g., Firefox) can find your site and rank it for search results. "The purpose of Search Engine Optimization is to drive traffic to your website through strategic placement of keywords relevant to your site," explains Abdullah. DIY services usually offer an SEO package for a fee. A web designer should provide SEO for the major pages of your website.

Search Engine Marketing (SEM) consists of any type of paid or free promotion you do in order to increase the visibility and ranking of your website in a search result. SEM is akin to buying advertising for your website. Examples of SEM are Google AdWords, Facebook ads, listing your URL in a print ad. A type of SEM, Social Media Marketing, involves directing traffic to your website from your Twitter page, a book review site, a blog and other high ranking sites relevant to your writing.

Whether you choose to design-it-yourself (DIY) or hire a Web designer, your website should evolve with your career *and* pay you back the time, effort and money you invested in it. Here's to your successful launch!

KAREN M. RIDER enjoys writing success steps for writers and the creative process. She's been writing professionally since 2006, when the birth of her daughter prompted Karen to pursue a dream that had for too long lay dormant in her heart. www.karenmrider.com

HOW TO GET SOCIAL

20 Mistakes Writers Make When Using Social Media (& How to Avoid Them)

by Debbie Ridpath Ohi

Social media can be a great tool for writers but can also be damaging if misused. Here are the most common mistakes that authors tend to make, and how to avoid them.

1. Not deciding why they're using social media first.

Before you sign up for any social media network, think about why you're doing it. You need to be more specific than "I want to get published." Are you hoping to network with people in the industry who might be able to help you? For promotion purposes? To keep up with publishing industry trends and news? For mutual encouragement and fun chat with other writers? Knowing your goals will help you make the right choices.

2. Trying to be everywhere.

With so many social media networks to choose from, with new networks springing up every month, it's impossible and inadvisable for authors to join them all. Figuring out what you want (see Tip #1) will help you decide what networks to focus on and how to use them. At the time this article was written, Facebook and Twitter were the most popular social media venues, with Tumblr close behind and Google+ slowly gaining in popularity. My personal favorite is Twitter.

3. Not having a profile photo.

Some writers leave their profile photo blank, perhaps in a misguided effort to maintain privacy. My advice: If you're planning to use social media to network and promote yourself, you have to be willing to put yourself out there. I use a headshot photo, so people know what I look like. Some writers use the covers of their books while others use illustrations. Whatever you do, DON'T leave your profile photo blank—that tends to give the impression that you're a newbie who doesn't know what they're doing (even if that's true, you don't need to advertise the fact) or worse, that you're a spammer.

4. Having a blank or uninformative profile.

I'm amazed at how many writers don't bother filling in their profile bio info. This is one of the most important and useful opportunities for getting people interested in you and your work. As in a blank profile photo, a blank profile bio can give the impression that the user is a spammer, or may not be invested enough to put in the effort of writing a bio.

Some writers opt for one-sentence pithy profile bios which aim to be funny, mysterious or snarky. While this may intrigue some visitors enough to want to connect, writers need to think carefully about what kind of connections they're hoping to make. If you're hoping to be taken seriously by editors, publishers, agents and other writers, make sure your profile bio reflects your intention. This doesn't mean you can't inject some personality...just be wary of injecting too much. Always proofread your bio, and keep it updated. Include a URL where people can find out more info about you and your work.

I'm amazed at how many writers don't bother filling in their profile bio info. This is one of the most important and useful opportunities for getting people interested in you and your work.

5. Trying to be clever/funny when you're not.

Be wary of trying to be edgy, clever or funny in your social media unless you're very sure you ARE edgy, clever or funny. Because if you aren't, your post is more likely to fall flat and give readers the impression that you're trying too hard.

6. Missing opportunities to include links and tags, or over-tagging.

Social media platforms like Facebook and Twitter enable users to tag other users in posts, and can be a great way of connecting. Example: Suppose you're tweeting about a great blog post by author Gomer Glotz. Instead of "15 Tips for Dealing With Rejection by Gomer Glotz <link here>", it could be "15 Tips For Dealing With Rejection by @GomerGlotz <link here>". Gomer will get a notification in his Mentions feed of your tweet.

Tagging people in your posts can be an effective part of your networking efforts but it can also backfire if you overdo it. Tagging someone just because you want them to look at your post is like shouting their name across a crowded room. It may be fine once in a while if you're sure they would be interested and have the time to respond, but if you do it too often or inappropriately, people will start to ignore you. Or worse, get irritated.

7. Posting bare links or "check this out" on Twitter.

Never just post a bare link, expecting people to be curious enough to click through. Unless they're avid fans, most of them won't. Ditto for "check this out" posts with a link. What if a reader does click through and then feels let down or tricked when the page is something that doesn't interest him or her? Respect your reader's time and give them a reason to click the link.

Take the time to compose a succinct, informative and intriguing description when posting the link.

8. Spamming people's Facebook Walls.

Don't use other people's personal Facebook Walls as a billboard for your promo posts. That's like walking into someone's living room and slapping an advertising poster on their wall before leaving. And yes, this includes "I thought your readers would be interested in my FREE ebook giveaway and prize draw" type of posts.

9. Not taking the time to learn how a community works before they post.

Whether or not they're explicitly stated, every online community has its own rules of etiquette. Before you start participating, take the time to watch how other people behave and how they post. I've been in scheduled Twitter chats where someone kept posting "Buy my book!" promo throughout our discussion, oblivious. No one at the chat will buy his books.

My advice: Pick one or two social media channels in the beginning and focus on those. Learn how to use them properly. Find writers who write for a similar audience as you do, who are active and successful in social media. Watch what they do and how they do it.

....

Don't use other people's personal Facebook Walls as a billboard for your promo posts. That's like walking into someone's living room and slapping an advertising poster on their wall before leaving.

....

10. Only joining social media when they have a book to promote.

This is one of the most common errors I've seen writers make. "There's no point in me joining Twitter or Facebook yet," they'll say. "I don't have anything to promote yet." BIG MISTAKE. In my opinion, the best time to join social media is before you have anything to promote. Why? Because then people won't think you're one of the many authors who join social media just because they have a book or books to sell.

For authors who have an upcoming book to promote, I strongly advise joining social media NOW (after you've finished reading this article, that is) instead of waiting until closer to launch date.

11. Over-promoting.

Posting "Buy my book" over and over again on your social media feed will not help sell your book. No matter what your posting schedule, anyone visiting your page is going to be turned off. I've also seen authors who also go through their entire follower list, tagging a different person with each repetitive post.

A a general rule, try to reign in your pure promotional posts to 20% or less. The rest of the time, you should be sharing useful or interesting content, interacting with other people.

There are exceptions, such as when your book actually launches. But even then, try to make your promo posts more personal and interesting. Instead of saying, "My book just launched! Buy it!", say "I had so much fun at my book launch! Here are a few photos...".

12. Not proofreading before posting.

Proper spelling and grammar are especially important for writers. Even if you're posting from your mobile device, take the time to read over what you're about to post publicly before hitting Send. If you're posting a link, verify that the link works. When copying and pasting a link, it's easy to accidentally miss a character at the end of the URL. If you're tagging someone, make sure you're tagging the right person.

13. Forgetting that an online chat is still public

When everyone in an online chat room or Twitter chat is exchanging casual chat or rapid-fire repartee, it can be easy to forget that what you post is still public. Unlike a private conversation in a friend's living room, parts of your conversation may be copied and pasted elsewhere, or saved on someone's hard drive. No matter how casual the atmosphere, always be aware of what you are saying in a public online venue.

14. Posting in anger.

Think twice before posting in anger. Instead of blowing off steam in a public venue, call up a trusted friend instead. Sure, you get a momentary satisfaction for having vented, but chances are good that you'll regret making that post. Nearly everyone has heard the horror stories of well-known authors who have regretted a Twitter post and deleted it...only to find that it was too late since their tweet had already been shared with others.

If someone posts something upsetting about you, do NOT give in to the impulse to respond right away. Take a deep breath. Think hard about whether you need to reply at all. Is this something that would be better discussed in a private e-mail or a phone call? If a public reply is needed, always take the high road. Be brief and don't try to provoke, then switch to a more neutral topic.

15. Being overly negative.

Be aware that making a habit of whiny or complaining posts will give the impression that you are a whiny and complaining person. People who have not met you in person may assume that you're like this in real life as well, and may not want to work with you.

Never, ever bash a work or potential work colleague in public. It's unprofessional. I've heard agents and editors say they were about to sign on an author until they checked the author's blog or social media feed and were turned off by these kinds of posts.

Be aware of the image you are projecting. It's worth taking the time every so often and reviewing your posts to remind yourself how you are portraying yourself.

16. Obsessing about follower count.

Whatever the platform, don't let yourself get too hung up on follower count. I've seen Twitter profiles where the authors promise to follow back anyone who follows them...a sure sign that they're focus is on numbers instead of who their followers are. I would far rather have 100 people follow me who are actually interested in me and my work than 1,000 random strangers who are just after more followers.

Besides, be aware that what's popular in social media now may be old news next year when something shinier catches people's attention. A question to ask yourself: "If this social media site shut down right now, would I still consider the time I've spent here worth it?"

I would far rather have 100 people follow me who are actually interested in me and my work than 1,000 random strangers who are just after more followers.

17. Forgetting the "social" in "social media."

Some authors use social media just to post links to their new blog posts. They may even have software set up so that these links are automatically posted to their social media feed instead of logging in manually. While there's nothing wrong with this in itself, people are less likely to want to follow this type of feed unless they're already fans. To attract new followers and connections, you need to show you're interested and that you're genuinely engaged.

18. Believing that social media can replace engaging face-to-face.

As engaging and useful as social media can be, it can never replace face-to-face conversation. Engage in real-life: join your local writers' organization, attend writers' conferences and workshops.

19. Forcing themselves to use social media even if they hate it.

Given the potential benefits, I believe it's worth learning to use social media. However, if you've given it your best shot and still feel uncomfortable using it....then don't. Find other ways to achieve your goals that feel more natural.

If you force yourself to continue using social media just because everyone tells you that you should, your followers will be able to tell.

20. Spending too much time on social media.

It can be easy to convince yourself that the time you spend on social media is part of work. You're networking, after all, or doing promotion. Minutes can turn into hours before you know it, so keep track of your time. Be honest about what you're doing.

As fun and useful as social media can be, don't forget your first priority: writing.

Debbie Ridpath Ohi offers additional social media tips at http://inkygirl.com/a-writers-guide-to-twitter. Her illustrations appear in I'M BORED, a picture book written by Michael Ian Black (Simon & Schuster BFYR) that was chosen by The New York Times for its Notable Children's Books Of 2012 list. She is author of Writer's Online Marketplace (Writer's Digest Books). Twitter: @inkyelbows. Website: DebbieOhi.com.

HOW TO IMPROVE YOUR PRESENTATION SKILLS

by Brenda Collins

Given the emerging power and popularity of social media, do you still need to put your physical face on your author brand? Do you have to give presentations or workshops? According to many successful editors, agents and writers, the answer is "yes". In this competitive publishing environment, authors have to be skilled marketers. The experts report that live events can be very beneficial to an author's career. The good news is you can learn how to present effectively even if the thought scares you now.

"For certain audiences," notes Holly Root, of the Waxman Literary Agency, "it's absolutely expected that an author would be willing to appear—for instance, a very newsy nonfiction title, or a book with a huge publicity push, or a novel for kids, where school visits would be key. For the majority of novelists, it is optional, the kind of thing that if done well can be a terrific boost. The more people who know about you, the better your chances some of them will be your kind of readers." Root believes that appearances by one of her authors, Lisa Patton, absolutely contributed to her books becoming bestsellers.

If the thought of speaking in front of a crowd makes your stomach churn, you are not alone. Several studies have shown that public speaking is the number one fear for most people, followed by fear of death.

In my experience, though, even an introvert can become a great public speaker. When I was 10 years old, I stood in front of my Grade 5 class to give my first speech—and burst into tears. With practice, and maturity, I now deliver talks to audiences of all sizes. You just need the right skills, techniques and experience.

PREPARATION

Preparation is the secret to successful presentations. Preparation will ease the jitters when first you look out at your audience. Preparation will help you hide the fact you've lost your place in your notes. Preparation will ensure your presentation doesn't run too long or too short. And, more than anything else, preparation will make sure you say something that is worth the time your audience spends listening to you.

DEFINE OBJECTIVE

Jot down, in plain language, one sentence stating what you want to achieve through the presentation. That is not the same as what you want to say. Ask yourself why you are giving this particular presentation to this particular audience. What should they take away from it? This becomes your *key message*, which will shape the rest of your presentation. For example, "My presentation objective is to give writers the tools they need to deliver effective presentations with confidence."

REFINE CONTENT & STRUCTURE

List the important points you want to make in the presentation. For some this may be a neat list of bullet points, but for less linear thinkers, also known as *pantsers*, it could be a mind map, bubble drawing, or just scribbles all over a page.

Guided by your key message, arrange your notes so that each point flows naturally into the next, like a story plot. Think—beginning, middle, and end. This is your opportunity to make sure your message is clear.

Presentation structure is quite standardized. Your opening is like a novel or magazine article. You need to hook your audience right from the beginning with a relevant quotation, personal anecdote, a rhetorical question or other device.

There's a saying, "Tell them what you're going to say—, tell them—, then tell them what you told them!" That forms the body of your presentation: your objective, main points and summary.

Finally, you wrap up your presentation by linking back to your opening. Think of your opening and closing as the bookends of your presentation holding it all together for your audience.

EDIT

Eliminate unnecessary information and conflicting messages. Presentations are rarely too short; often they are too long. As operatic soprano and self-help guru Dorothy Sarnoff once noted, "Make sure you have finished speaking before your audience has finished listening."

Some of your revisions can help you prepare for audience questions. Don't worry about anticipating all possible questions. If you do not have the answer, either throw the question out to the audience to generate discussion or ask for the questioner's card so you can get back with an answer later.

AVOID DEATH BY POWERPOINT

Decide if and where you are going to use slides, handouts or other aids. Slides are *not* mandatory. In fact, they can be a distraction, and there's always a risk that the technology won't work on the big day.

Only use a slide or handout if it illustrates something that is otherwise hard to visualize or if it will support audience participation.

If you do want to use slides, there are a few rules.

- Assume two minutes talk time per slide to calculate how many you should have. Remember to number them.
- A picture or graph is worth a thousand words. Use them where possible.
- No more than three or four short bullets per slide. Overwhelming detail or animation is confusing.
- Use a clear (sans serif), large (minimum 24 point) font size.
- Use a consistent color scheme, of three or four high contrast colors at most. Remember some people have difficulty distinguishing between certain color combinations e.g. red-green, blue-yellow.

If you will be using slides, tell the organizers beforehand to ensure you'll have the equipment you need and that technical help will be available.

With or without technology, always have a contingency plan. Overhead lamps burn out. The projector provided might not work with your laptop, the thumb drive you had your presentation on could get lost. Bring a hard copy of your slides and notes so you can go ahead without a computer if need be.

The organizer may determine when handouts are distributed but, if you have a choice, consider these options.

BEFORE: Makes it easy for your audience to follow along with you and take notes. However, they also may be reading instead of listening to you and the paper rattling can be distracting.

DURING: This is my least favorite. It is difficult to distribute the handout quickly enough to be relevant to the point you're making without breaking the flow of your presentation.

AFTER: My preference is to let the audience know they will receive the slides at the end of the presentation so they can focus on what I'm saying but avoid taking unnecessary notes.

REHEARSE, REHEARSE, AND REHEARSE SOME MORE

One of the ways I learned to overcome the mind-numbing fear was to practice the presentation until I could give it in my sleep.

For notes, only write down key words, in large print so they are easy to read. Use these sparingly as memory joggers, not as a script. The fastest way to bore an audience is to read your presentation word for word.

Practice where you will pause throughout your presentation. You need time to take a breath and your audience needs time to digest your point before you move onto the next one.

Rehearse not only what you're going to say, but how. Use your voice and body language to make it interesting. Bob Mayer, best-selling author of over 40 books, publisher, and skilled professional speaker, notes, "as much as it is presenting information, it is also a form of entertainment. While content is important, presenting in an energetic and exciting manner is also important."

A run-through in front of the mirror is good. Even better is a trusted friend who will tell you if you unconsciously use any "ah, um, you know, like" empty fillers.

No friends available? Try recording your practice run, on video if possible. Early in my career, I was taped as part of a media training course. Watching that video was a shocker. As I spoke, my hands were flailing around as if I was swatting at wasps. You don't have to tie your hands behind your back but make sure you don't hold a pointer, pen or any other object you might play with if you're nervous. If you like putting your hands in your pockets, make sure there are no coins in there. You want your entire posture to project confidence and calm.

Your dress rehearsal should include the outfit you plan to wear for the presentation. What you wear should be appropriate and comfortable. You also want to be sure your shoes won't squeak and your jewelry won't rattle as you move.

THE BIG DAY

You are ready. Standing at the side of the stage, you hear your name called. Wait! If you want to deliver your presentation with energy and composure—I'm remembering my embarrassing episode of stage fright in Grade 5—the delivery of your presentation starts at least an hour before you get to the podium. You arrive before anyone else so that you can scope out the room in advance, place some water within easy reach, make sure your notes are in order, set up and test out any equipment you've requested.

With your environment arranged, you focus on making sure you are ready. My eldest brother had a long and successful career as an on-air morning show host on national public radio. He had to wake up his mouth and voice before flipping on the microphone. He might tighten and stretch his face muscles, rotate his lower jaw to loosen the jaw muscles, and recite a tongue twister, like "Rita wrote a ridiculous rhythm about racoons" or other sound combinations. Try it and your opening will slide out more smoothly.

Right before you begin is also the time to release any pent-up tension from your body by rolling your shoulders, stretching your neck, pulling your arms over your head and behind your back to open up your chest. Then take three deep abdominal breaths, straighten your shoulders and walk out to the podium with confidence.

While presenting, stay aware of your audience. If they are yawning or drooping, do not take it personally, especially if it's after lunch. Have you slipped into a monotone, or started reading your slides? Add an anecdote or stretch break to wake them up.

Presentations are both an art and a science. Consult your library or bookstore to learn more about giving presentations. I can add a few final lessons that the books often miss, and that I learned the hard way:

- Keep a bottle of water at hand for when your tongue threatens to stick to the roof of your mouth.
- Never drink coffee before you give a talk. Let's just say it makes men perspire and ladies glisten.
- When it comes to mistakes of any kind, laugh and the audience with laugh with you.
- If your talk is after lunch when everyone feels sluggish, turn down the thermostat a degree or two. You don't want to see their breath, but just enough to keep the audience feeling refreshed.
- Memorize your first three slides. I find that if nerves hit when I first look out at the audience, I can rely on rote to get started and usually by the fourth slide I've found my groove.

Writers are skilled wordsmiths. Presentations are one more way we can use our talent in crafting, polishing and delivering words to an audience. Any writer can learn to give presentations but Alicia Rasley, an award-winning author and nationally known teacher of writing workshops, advises, "Give presentations because it excites you, because it's fun, because you get to meet new people and see new places."

As Emily Ohanjanians, Associate Editor, HQN Books (Harlequin) says, "It is certainly not easy for everyone, but just be confident in who you are and what you have to say. After all, if people read your writing, you must have something good to say!"

....

BRENDA COLLINS has long believed that, for writers to succeed, writing talent must be supplemented with strong business skills. To support that view, she has published articles and delivered workshops to hundreds of writers on career planning, professional networking and presentation skills. Collins also serves annually as a judge for an international mystery / suspense fiction-writing contest. Her paranormal novella, *Witch in the Wind*, is available on Amazon. Prior to becoming a freelance writer, Collins spent 25 years in the corporate world where her work included award winning technical and corporate writing.

....

THE ART OF PROMOTING:

Advice From the Trenches

by Kerrie Flanagan

Author book promotion is not what it used to be. Both traditional and newer online strategies are needed to create an effective marketing plan because publishers now expect authors to carry the majority of the PR responsibilities. Marketing can feel overwhelming for an author but the good news is there are those who have found success in navigating this vast territory.

PLAN AN EVENT

To ensure a good turnout at a book signing or book launch, put in a little extra time to make it an event people will remember. Acclaimed YA author Laura Resau has perfected this idea over the years with the release of each of her books.

"Be creative and think outside the box," says Resau. "Include all ages if possible. Create a fun, lively, warm atmosphere. Make it a party that YOU would attend."

For the launch party of her fourth book, *The Indigo Notebook*, set in Ecuador, her Ecuadorian friend danced and explained the folklore behind the dance. With her latest book, *The Ruby Notebook*, set in France, she hired an accordionist who played while the young kids danced and the crowd enjoyed French pastries. She sets aside time to read excerpts and autograph books.

To promote the event, she uses listservs, her blog, Facebook, an e-newsletter, plus she enlists the help of her friends and writing group members to spread the word. She also sends postcard invitations with the book cover image on front.

"I think people are more likely to come to the release if they have the postcard hanging on their fridge staring at them every day for weeks before the event," she says.

An event can also happen online. For three years in a row, Christina Katz, author of *Get Known Before the Book Deal* and *Writer Mama*, hosted The Writer Mama Back-to-School Giveaway where she gave away a book on her blog every day for 30 days.

"I connected fellow authors with readers and in the process got to know my readers a lot better," said Katz. "One thing authors need to understand about marketing books today is that if you are not having an ongoing conversation with your fans, you are really missing out on the wealth of opportunities."

SPEAK UP

LeAnn Thieman, co-author of 11 Chicken Soup for the Soul books including the *New York Times* best-seller, *Chicken Soup for the Nurses Soul*, finds radio is an effective promotional outlet.

"There are over 10,000 radio stations in the United States, many with hosts looking for people to interview every day," said Thieman. "When I am going to be in an area for a speaking event or even just visiting, I call the local stations to see if they are interested in interviewing me on my topic, one I creatively relate to what's happening in the world today."

She advises authors to send a copy of their book and a synopsis to the station before the interview. Provide them with questions they can ask and have three to four talking points of your own ready. Weave your own sound bites and messages into the interview, but never overtly promote your book.

Greg Campbell, the best-selling nonfiction author of *Blood Diamonds: Tracing The Deadly Path Of The World's Most Precious Stones*, found promoting himself as an expert speaker to universities, nonprofits and trade shows to be an effective way to promote his books.

"When Scott Selby and I published *Flawless: Inside the Largest Diamond Heist in History*," Campbell said, "we searched for major trade shows on security and offered to speak to attendees about the real-life security failures described in the book. We ended up as keynote speakers at the International Security Conference in Las Vegas, with about 500 people in the audience."

With the help of their publisher, Selby and Campbell arranged to have the local Barnes & Noble set up a table to sell books at the event.

GET SOCIAL

Most authors would agree that staying connected with readers via social media is crucial in any successful publicity plan.

Campbell recently had social media thrust upon him by a pair of fans disappointed in his anemic online presence. They set up a Facebook author fan page as well as an author page on Goodreads.com for him. It pushed him to embrace social media.

"The fact that it took my readers to force me into this realm proved that there were readers out there hungry for information and new content," he said. "Even if it's just 140-character tweets. My education into this realm is continuing, but I plan to begin tweeting and blogging about the content of my newest book several months before it hits the shelves. In this way, I hope to have primed the pump and created online buzz for it long before it's available."

Jane Porter, author of six novels, including her latest, *She's Gone Country*, makes a point to stay connected with her readers.

"Sites like Facebook and Twitter have proved invaluable in providing a different platform to meet with my readers and spread the word," said Porter. "The more accessible you are the more readers get a chance to listen to what you have to share."

Romance author Ashley March finds blog tours highly successful. "I researched blogs and online romance community sites which had good followings and scheduled around 20 days where I visited each website with either an interview or guest blog. I always included a giveaway as a way to create more enthusiasm."

She attributes the buzz and success of her debut novel, *Seducing the Duchess*, with this blog tour.

PARTNER WITH YOUR PUBLISHER

Although publishers do expect authors to take on the role of publicist, it doesn't mean they are not willing to help at all. With her debut novel March took the lead and found her publisher eager to support her efforts.

They sent her book to every major romance reviewer online, provided her with her books to use as giveaways and when she couldn't reach someone at a blog she really wanted to visit, the publisher coordinated that specific blog visit for her. Because of the publisher's support, her March Madness blog party was a success.

"Throughout my debut experience," says March, "I truly felt like we were partners, and that's a great feeling to have."

Katz sums it up best. "Consistent and constant self-promotion are key to publishing success, regardless of whether you self-publish or traditionally publish...It's not any one self-promotion technique an author uses, it's using all of them."

KERRIE FLANAGAN is a freelance writer and the director of Northern Colorado Writers, an organization that supports and encourages writers of all levels and genres. Over the past decade she has published more than 125 articles in national and regional publications, enjoyed two years as contributing editor for Journey magazine, worked in PR for the Fort Collins CVB and for various authors and started The Writing Bug blog. www.KerrieFlanagan.com

PHOTO: Desiree Suchy

JEFF GOINS

Outlast the Lucky, Outwork the Lazy

....

by Robert Lee Brewer

For two years now, Jeff Goins has been atop the WriteToDone.com best writing blogs list. He has a legion of adoring fans and avid supporters. So he must be great at promoting himself online, right?

"You know," says Goins, "I really don't think that way. I use social media to help people, and I believe that makes people want to help my writing spread and succeed."

In fact, Goins, the author of *Wrecked: When a Broken World Slams Into Your Comfortable Life* (Moody Publishers), cites his best writing experience as a moment of helping his family.

"Telling my wife she didn't have to go back to work after having our son," explains Goins. "We were fortunate enough to make some side income through my book, e-book, and online course, that she could now be a full-time mom—something she'd wanted to do for a while. I'm more proud of that than any other writing accomplishment to date."

But maybe it was just payback to a person who helped him realize what he wanted to do with his life.

Let's start at the beginning. Was there a moment you realized you wanted to become a writer?

I always wanted to be a writer but would never admit it to myself. A few years ago, I attended a conference that was all about launching a dream. It was full of people who were ready to take the next step with their passion, but I was there to find mine.

But then the speaker said this, "Some of you have said you don't know what your dream is." I nodded along, resting in the fact that I wasn't the only one. "But I don't believe that's true; I believe you know what your dream is. You're just afraid to admit."

My heart sank.

I went home that night and told my wife I didn't know what my dream was, and she said, "Sure you do. It's to be a writer." And she was right. So I began to want to figure out how to be a writer.

Of course, it's one thing to want something and another to do it. It would be awhile before I'd actually start calling myself a writer—and that's when everything began to change.

I found you through your blog (goinswriter.com), which has built a following over the past few years. Could you explain the main thing you think your blog is doing that works?

Great question. It feels slightly weird to talk about my "success" because I still very much feel like I'm in process, on my way to where I want to be. That said, I know I've learned some things that could help others. So here are the three things I think I've done fairly well with my blog:

- **I only publish my very best content.** This is less common with bloggers than it should be; most are throwing a brain dump onto the screen and calling it "art." I really try to write articles for my blog that I would be proud of. As a result, I've built a resource of evergreen content.
- **I try to help people and be generous.** This means although I wrote for myself (passion must be primary), what I write—and how I write it—is intended to help others. I also try to give more than I take and ask permission every step of the way. As a result, my audience seems to really trust me, which I don't take lightly.
- **I guest post widely.** My blog is only two years old. The first year I wrote something like 100 posts for other blogs (in addition to the 300+ articles I wrote for my own blog), and many of those blogs were outside of my niche. Guest posting, I believe, is the single best way to expand your reach as a blogger. I still credit it as the main cause for my blog's growth.

Your writing presence seems to meld together two main goals—writing and making a difference. How do you personally manage to write while making a difference in the world?

I believe writers are difference-makers. It took me a long time to understand this, because I believed that words were cheap. They're not. They're invaluable. Words hold the power to give life or bring death; they can raise a person's spirit or destroy it.

Understanding that what we say has impact—and realizing we actually have a message to share—is the first step to making an impact in your family, your community, and your world.

Your recent book, *Wrecked,* **tackles misfortune and spins it into a positive. Could you share how inconvenience has opened opportunities in your life?**

I don't grow when I'm on the couch with a blanket on my lap (which happens to be the posture I'm currently in). I become a better me when I'm out there in the mess of the world, trying to make sense of things.

For example, getting my evening interrupted by a homeless man in Spain was the incident that gave me clarity about how I should be spending the rest of my life. And because it felt like a disruption to the "plan," I almost missed it.

Every major growth opportunity in my life has come disguised as an inconvenience. The more I talk with people about this idea, the more it seems to be a universal truth.

Earlier books you released were specifically for writers, including *The Writer's Manifesto* **and** *You Are a Writer: Start Acting Like One.* **Your manifesto, in particular, encourages writers to write for the sake of writing, which is how many of us get started. Could you elaborate on this a little?**

We all think we want the stage, the audience, the fanfare. But the reality is life is pretty lonely in the hotel room after the big show in the auditorium. We only have to read a few biographies of famous people to understand this.

Writers mistakenly believe fame is the answer to their problems—why they can't get published, why they're not a pro yet, etc.—but it's not. What holds us back is a lack of passion, a lack of effort due to indifference.

What sustains a writer to help her get through the ups and downs of the creative life isn't the handful of mountaintop experiences she might get. It's the love of the craft. That's the only way you can stick with writing long enough to succeed.

So write what you would enjoy even if nobody ever reads it (because sometimes, nobody ever does). The irony is this is how we create our best work.

Now I just wrote over 150 words, which is more than one-sixth the size of that manifesto (which is available for free on my website).

I believe both e-books were self-published. Could you share a little about your process with self-publishing?

The days of submitting to gatekeepers are over. I had those messages in me and wanted to get them out into the world. I didn't want to get anyone's permission and felt the urgency; they needed to be shared now.

The beauty of self-publishing is that's actually possible, easy, and cheap now. We truly live in the age of No Excuse. If you have a message or story the world needs to hear but hasn't, it's nobody's fault but your own.

You speak frequently on writing, marketing, and making a difference. What do you consider the top two or three things to deliver a good presentation?

One, make personal connections. If people wanted a monologue, they could listen to your podcast on iTunes. Be rough, spontaneous, and human.

Two, tell stories. People relate to what you've done more than to what you know. Show your scars, tell your truth.

Three, practice. Yes, be spontaneous and occasionally off-the-cuff, but don't be sloppy. People are giving you their trust; don't abuse it.

You're the Communications Director for Adventures in Missions, an international nonprofit organization. Could you first describe Adventures in Missions?

Adventures (adventures.org) is a mission organization that sends churches, individuals, and groups on mission trips around the world. We have an emphasis on prayer and personal development, while ministering first to the poorest areas in the world.

Then, could you share a little about what's involved in your role as Communications Director?

I oversee all the content that our organization puts out. This means I lead a team of writers, helping them grow in their craft and making sure all our content is consistent with our organization's voice. I also help our executive director with various writing and communication projects.

If you could pass on only one piece of advice for other writers just getting started on their journey, what would it be?

Don't quit. Outlast those who are lucky and outwork those who are lazy.

WILEY CASH

Homesick Success

....

by Robert Lee Brewer

Some authors appear to hit the ground running. For instance, Wiley Cash's first novel, *A Land More Kind Than Home* (William Morrow/HarperCollins), debuted on *The New York Times* bestsellers list. Since then, it's gone to paperback and been received well there too.

However, don't mistake Cash's success for luck. He's been writing and working on his craft for years, receiving grants and fellowships from the Asheville Area Arts Council, the Thomas Wolfe Society, the MacDowell Colony, and Yaddo. His stories have appeared in *Crab Orchard Review*, *Roanoake Review*, and *The Carolina Quarterly*. Plus, his essays on Southern literature have appeared in *American Literary Realism*, *The South Carolina Review*, and other publications.

To top it off, Cash has a Ph.D. in English from the University of Louisiana-Lafayette. In fact, it was when Cash moved to Louisiana that all his hard work started to pay dividends.

"I moved to Louisiana to attend graduate school in the fall of 2003," remembers Cash, "and I was immediately homesick for North Carolina. I started reading and re-reading my favorite North Carolina authors and listening to North Carolina music. When the central idea of *A Land More Kind Than Home* fell into my lap—I read a news story about a young boy being smothered during a healing service—I decided to set that story in the mountains of North Carolina. I realized that in doing that I could do two things: I could tell the story with authority because I know that place so well, and I could go home again."

That decision might seem like a lucky break to some writers, but it was the culmination of a lifetime devoted to writing and storytelling.

Let's start at the beginning. Was there a moment you realized you wanted to become a writer?

I was raised in a family of readers. In our family, on the day you turned six years old, you received your own library card. Even then I understood that that little paper card was a ticket to any place or time I wanted to visit. I worshipped books, and it wasn't long before I was trying to write stories of my own.

I chose to attend the University of North Carolina-Asheville because it offered an undergraduate major in Creative Writing through the Literature and Language department. I went there hoping to be a poet, but I arrived, read my peers' work and discovered that I was a pretty awful poet. But I wanted to write, and I'd always loved telling stories. So I gave fiction a try, and I've never looked back.

I found you through Twitter—after you responded to one of my tweets. Could you explain how you've used social media for your writing career?

Social media has served me well primarily *after* the publication of *A Land More Kind Than Home*. I've used it to stay in contact with booksellers and book bloggers I've either met in person or via the Internet. These folks really drive the success of a book like mine, and their support has been incredibly important. I also use social media to keep up with authors I like and admire.

I'm actually the member of a private Facebook group called Book Pregnant. We're a collection of 30 or so debut authors whose first books were all published around the same time. We use our private page to celebrate, lament, and support each other through the roller coaster ride of publishing. They've all been incredible friends to me over the past couple years.

Your debut novel, *A Land More Kind Than Home* (William Morrow), was released in hard cover and has already moved on to paperback. What has been the most surprising part of the entire process?

My publisher pushed for a huge release for the hardcover: it was well reviewed, there were a lot of stories/interviews in the media, and I was sent on a multi-city tour throughout the southeast. I was surprised that a debut novel set in Appalachia would get that kind of support these days, but I was even more surprised when the paperback released garnered the same level of support and excitement from my publisher.

The paperback release has been a great success, and I'm actually in the middle of a national tour in support of it now. I've been incredibly lucky to have the support of a big publishing house, and I know that support is driven by the love my editor has for this novel. He's a North Carolina guy too.

Your novel is considered a Southern novel. Could you explain the characteristics of Southern literature for people unfamiliar with this genre?

It's hard for me to say what makes a book distinctly Southern. Perhaps it's my dedication to getting the landscape right. There is no place in the world like the Blue Ridge Mountains in Southern Appalachia, and I wanted that place to live on the page for my reader, especially if they've never visited the area. When you have a strong sense of place in your work your characters spring from that place.

Even though my novel is set primarily in the 1980s, my characters' lives revolve around this place; they work the land, they're affected by the seasons, their families have owned these farms for generations. I know that kind of tie between people and land exists in the other parts of the country, but something about the South seems to make the representation of it more intrinsic to the portrayal of the people.

Your book weaves together multiple narrators. Did this present challenges in writing the novel?

It was a challenge. Each of these characters has his or her own story to tell, but I couldn't simply allow their stories to meander across the page and make the mistake of thinking I had a novel. That would be a collection of oral stories, and a novel is very different. I worked hard to corral their narratives and edit their narratives so that they fit into the classical structure of the novel.

Once I figured out what my plot would be I was able to structure these narratives around it while staying true to the individual stories. These characters and their stories definitely came first, and once I had them on the page I attached them to the frame of the plot. I ended up making outlines, calendars, and all kinds of things to help me track these voices and the knowledge they possessed on particular days. It was a tedious but very interesting process.

You've been busy touring for the paperback edition of your novel after touring for the hardcover. What have you learned from your book touring experiences?

I've learned the importance of the independent bookstores. When we think about our books coming out, we think about seeing them in big box stores and on Internet sites, and that is important too. But nothing is as important as getting a group of well-read, intelligent booksellers behind your book.

These folks read a lot, and they know their clientele. And if they get behind you they are behind you 100%. I like to tell readers that you may buy a book online or from a big box store, but chances are you know about the book because an intelligent independent bookseller knew about it first.

Excerpts of the novel were published in literary publications. Were these published as excerpts or as self-contained stories?

> They were published as self-contained stories. It's tough to publish novel excerpts that are clearly excerpts because people want complete stories. I've never submitted excerpts to magazines or journals.

You earned a Ph.D. from the University of Louisiana at Lafayette. How has your graduate program influenced your writing?

> I had the honor of studying fiction writing under Ernest J. Gaines, and that really changed my life. He always stressed the act of writing as work; it's not a hobby. You don't make a career out of a hobby. He also taught me how to write about the place you call home. There was an incredible writing community at the University of Louisiana-Lafayette. The students were very supportive of one another and very open to discussing one another's work. I still count some of my classmates as my best friends in the world.

What's been your best experience as a writer to this point?

> Calling my wife and telling her that my agent had sold *A Land More Kind Than Home* and the synopsis for a second novel.

On your site, you include your query letter to Nat Sobel of Sobel Weber Associates. Do you have a top tip on submitting queries to agents?

> Always, always, always read the submission guidelines and never submit form query letters. Make sure you know this particular agent's clientele, and make sure you share something with this agent's authors. Are they writing in the same genre as you? Are they writing about the same region? The last thing you want to do is to submit your sci-fi novel to someone who only represents romance. You've wasted your time, their time, and a stamp.

If you could pass on only one piece of advice for other novelists just getting started on their journey, what would it be?

> Don't see rejection as a reason to stop trying.

JEN MICHALSKI

Fiction Writing Trifecta

....

by Robert Lee Brewer

It is rare to run across a fiction writer who's released a collection of short stories, a collection of novellas, and a novel. Rarer still, a writer who has all three books published in the same year. Yet, that is exactly what Jen Michalski will accomplish in 2013.

Her novellas, *Could You Be With Her Now* (Dzanc Books), released in January; her novel, *The Tide King* (Black Lawrence Press), releases in May; and her short story collection, *From Here* (Aqueous Books), finishes off the year in November. Talk about a good year!

Michalski is also the author of the short story collection *Close Encounters* and founding editor of the literary quarterly *jmww*. She's the co-host of The 510 Readers and the biannual Lit Show and interviews writers at The Nervous Breakdown. She also is the editor of the well-received anthology *City Sages: Baltimore*, which *Baltimore Magazine* called a "Best of Baltimore" in 2010.

What are you currently up to?

I'm finishing up a second novel, tentatively called *Rabbits Singing*. I joke that it's my abridged love letter to Donna Tartt's *The Little Friend*, since it's about a third of its size. (Seriously, can anyone write a 30-page scene and make it as interesting as Tartt?) But it's not really the same. In *Rabbits*, a young girl, Kate, drives an ice cream truck in Newport, Rhode Island, during the summer. One of her favorite customers, a young boy who is a bit autistic or somewhere on the spectrum is accused of drowning a little girl, and Kate tries to solve the mystery.

Not only that, but she sort of befriends an old, reclusive movie star who lives in a dilapidated mansion and tries to help.

In 2013, you seem set to pull off a fiction trifecta I'm not sure has ever been accomplished before: releasing a new collection of short stories, a new novel, and a collection of novellas. How did you manage to get all three of these books published in the same year?

I think I sort of cheated because the couplet of novellas, *Could You Be With Her Now*, were taken a few years before the novel and short story collection were. Of course, I have no control over publishers' catalogs and schedules, and it just so happened that they all would release in the same year.

Thankfully, they're spaced out very well (January, May, November), so I'm not double and triple promoting books at once—I was a little worried about that, about having my publishers have to compete against each other or me not being able to give any one book the attention it deserves. I think it's just a lucky problem to have all around; it just means I'm going to have to work triple hard.

The collection of novellas is what really drew me to you at first, because novellas are often such a tough sell. What do you like about the novella form?

I don't set out to write novellas because, like you said, they are tough to sell. But for some reason, these two stories kept going past the 15, then the 20-page mark, and then I was like "oh crap."

What I love about the form is that you're not restricted to 5,000-7,000 words, but you're also not locked into several years of plotting and writing and revising a traditional novel. What happens in both of the novellas in *Could You Be With Her Now* happens over the course of days and weeks and represents such a small microcosm of the lives they show.

And I think that's what I like about that format—about really concentrating on this one episode in a life, very specifically, without having to have this wide thematic scope. Like when Virginia Woolf combined the short stories "Mrs Dalloway in Bond Street" and "The Prime Minister" into *Mrs. Dalloway*.

You've been nominated for the Pushcart for your short fiction. What do you think makes for a great short story?

The stories I love the most are the ones when, afterward, you're still thinking about the characters. They're so authentic and true to themselves that you're almost able to take them out of the story and imagine how their lives will continue to play out. I love thinking that those characters are still living somewhere in the world and I can go visit them and see what's new.

But I love words, too, how they sound, how dissonant or consonant, the repetition, the alliteration. Words that are alive but don't distract from the story.

Your novel, *The Tide King*, was the winner of the 2012 Big Moose Prize. What has the experience of entering a contest to publish your first novel been like?

It's been a dream. You never expect to win these sorts of things, which makes me wonder why I've entered so many over the years! But I've always had so much respect for Black Lawrence, and a chapter of *The Tide King* was a semifinalist in one of their chapbook contests, so I took a chance.

I didn't allow myself to think about winning at all, even as the long list became the short list and then suddenly getting a phone call on a Monday morning from a number I didn't recognize. Obviously I've received more attention, and I really feel like a novelist now and not just someone who's been publishing short stories for years.

You're a founding editor of the literary journal *jmww*. What was your role as a founder, and has it changed any over time?

Catherine Harrison and I founded *jmww* eight years ago. We'd just finished grad school and missed the interaction with other writing students. We also really wanted to start a journal as a way to navigate the scene in Baltimore, and we found it was a great way to go about it. In the beginning, it was the two of us, and we received three submissions for the first issue, one of which was mine and one of which was hers.

But over the years, we've gotten many more submissions, my html coding has gotten better, and now we also publish an annual print anthology of our best online work. An essay we published last year was short-listed for the *2012 Best American Essays*, and in 2013 we're holding our first poetry chapbook contest, which will be judged by a nationally known talent.

These days, Catherine is no longer actively working at the journal, and my role is more administrative, but I still oversee the day-to-day stuff and the website maintenance/design and answer e-mails. I love when someone writes in just to tell us they loved a story or a poem or a book review.

That's the best part of running a journal—knowing that you're exposing people to good work, and conversely, that you're helping good writers reach a good audience. That and all of the other writers and editors I've met—there are hundreds and hundreds of us out there doing this labor of love, and I think of us all as literary siblings.

Do you have any pet peeves in short fiction? Or things you try to avoid in your own stories?

I like strong characterization and carefully chosen prose. Words are more than just placeholders for the plot; words have texture and color and cadence. Too many stories feel black and white to me instead of in color because the words used just feel so overused or thoughtless. It's so important to find your voice, your own personal vocabulary, when writing.

Although I'm not necessarily turned off by bad people in fiction, I read a lot of stories in which people do terrible things for no reason. This seems too much like real life to me, and I read to escape (a little).

One other thing—the protagonist should do things, make choices—this provides tension and climax of the story. A lot of fiction (long and short) baffles me in that the protagonist just seems to be more a vessel to convey other things happening in a story other than actively being a part of it.

You're the co-host of the 510 Readings and the Lit Show. Could you explain what these events are?

The 510 Readings is a monthly fiction series I cohost with the novelist Michael Kimball, here in Baltimore. We have four readers—local, regional, national—who read for 10-12 minutes each, usually from their latest work. Then we all go out for drinks and dinner after at a local bar.

It's very relaxed and informal and we've hosted standing room-only crowds for years because local writers and readers come to think of it as more monthly literary social, where you meet new friends and keep the old, too. Writers from all other the United States, Canada, and Great Britain have read, and of course Baltimore, too.

The Lit Show is a little different, in terms of format, and wider in scope—think Conan with writers and playwrights and poets and also musicians instead of movie and television stars. Writer Betsy Boyd and I cohost, and in addition to chatting with us, our guests read or show movie clips or perform silly tricks and we just go with it in our quest to find the stories behind the stories.

At most readings, the focus is on the work. At the Lit Show, the focus is on the artist. Because of all the moving parts, we have the Lit Show only semiannually.

Do you feel it's important to be an active part of the writing community?

Absolutely. I don't think I would have three books out in 2013 if I didn't. The community plays so many parts in a writer's development—networking, writing groups, readings. In addition to other writers, you get to know the local booksellers and librarians and media so that when you do finally publish a novel or a chapbook or collection, you've got this built-in network, which is so important, because many publishers nowadays expect authors to act as their own publicists.

If your book is published and you haven't begun to reach out yet, it's not too late, but it's close to being too late. You need to be building your community—online or in person—while you're still writing.

And, in the end, the community is really a unique group of people who understand what you're going through as a writer—the writer's block, the rejections, the acceptances, the minutiae of revising and plotting. Also, there's usually a pretty good writers' softball team, too—at least there is in Baltimore.

I should also add that the best communities are symbiotic. Offer to review others' books or interview them for local publications. Become a reader at a literary journal. Start a blog and write about other writers. Start a reading series. You'd be surprised how little money is needed (close to none) and what a need you'd be filling.

If you could pass on only one piece of advice to your fellow fiction writers, what would it be?

In addition to the networking, invest in learning to write. You've probably heard this a million times, but I can't stress it enough. Most writers have some natural talent, but just because someone can throw 90 miles an hour doesn't mean he or she is a pitcher. There are techniques and skills only applicable to the trade that you must learn.

If you can't afford an MFA program, there are plenty of local and online classes, craft books and reading series and, well, good novels, to expose one to good writing. And remember that learning to write is ongoing; just as you always are growing in age and experiences, you are also growing as a writer.

BLOGGING BASICS:

Get the Most Out of Your Blog

by Robert Lee Brewer

In these days of publishing and media change, writers have to build platforms and learn how to connect to audiences if they want to improve their chances of publication and over-all success. There are many methods of audience connection available to writers, but one of the most important is through blogging.

Since I've spent several years successfully blogging—both personally and profession-ally—I figure I've got a few nuggets of wisdom to pass on to writers who are curious about blogging or who already are.

Here's my quick list of tips:

1. **START BLOGGING TODAY.** If you don't have a blog, use Blogger, WordPress, or some other blogging software to start your blog today. It's free, and you can start off with your very personal "Here I am, world" post.

2. **START SMALL.** Blogs are essentially very simple, but they can get very complicated (for people who like complications). However, I advise bloggers start small and evolve over time.

3. **USE YOUR NAME IN YOUR URL.** This will make it easier for search engines to find you when your audience eventually starts seeking you out by name. For instance, my url is http://robertleebrewer.blogspot.com. If you try Googling "Robert Lee Brewer," you'll notice that My Name Is Not Bob is one of the top 5 search results (behind my other blog: Poetic Asides).

4. **UNLESS YOU HAVE A REASON, USE YOUR NAME AS THE TITLE OF YOUR BLOG.** Again, this helps with search engine results. My Poetic Asides blog includes my name in the title, and it ranks higher than My Name Is Not Bob. However, I felt the play on my name was worth the trade off.

5. **FIGURE OUT YOUR BLOGGING GOALS.** You should return to this step every couple months, because it's natural for your blogging goals to evolve over time. Initially, your blogging goals may be to make a post a week about what you have written, submitted, etc. Over time, you may incorporate guests posts, contests, tips, etc.

6. **BE YOURSELF.** I'm a big supporter of the idea that your image should match your identity. It gets too confusing trying to maintain a million personas. Know who you are and be that on your blog, whether that means you're sincere, funny, sarcastic, etc.

7. **POST AT LEAST ONCE A WEEK.** This is for starters. Eventually, you may find it better to post once a day or multiple times per day. But remember: Start small and evolve over time.

8. **POST RELEVANT CONTENT.** This means that you post things that your readers might actually care to know.

9. **USEFUL AND HELPFUL POSTS WILL ATTRACT MORE VISITORS.** Talking about yourself is all fine and great. I do it myself. But if you share truly helpful advice, your readers will share it with others, and visitors will find you on search engines.

10. **TITLE YOUR POSTS IN A WAY THAT GETS YOU FOUND IN SEARCH ENGINES.** The more specific you can get the better. For instance, the title "Blogging Tips" will most likely get lost in search results. However, the title "Blogging Tips for Writers" specifies which audience I'm targeting and increases the chances of being found on the first page of search results.

11. **LINK TO POSTS IN OTHER MEDIA.** If you have an e-mail newsletter, link to your blog posts in your newsletter. If you have social media accounts, link to your blog posts there. If you have a helpful post, link to it in relevant forums and on message boards.

12. **WRITE WELL, BUT BE CONCISE.** At the end of the day, you're writing blog posts, not literary manifestos. Don't spend a week writing each post. Try to keep it to an hour or two tops and then post. Make sure your spelling and grammar are good, but don't stress yourself out too much.

13. **FIND LIKE-MINDED BLOGGERS.** Comment on their blogs regularly and link to them from yours. Eventually, they may do the same. Keep in mind that blogging is a form of social media, so the more you communicate with your peers the more you'll get out of the process.

14. **RESPOND TO COMMENTS ON YOUR BLOG.** Even if it's just a simple "Thanks," respond to your readers if they comment on your blog. After all, you want your readers to be engaged with your blog, and you want them to know that you care they took time to comment.

15. **EXPERIMENT.** Start small, but don't get complacent. Every so often, try something new. For instance, the biggest draw to my Poetic Asides blog are the poetry prompts

and challenges I issue to poets. Initially, that was an experiment—one that worked very well. I've tried other experiments that haven't panned out, and that's fine. It's all part of a process.

SEO TIPS FOR WRITERS

Most writers may already know what SEO is. If not, SEO stands for *search engine optimization*. Basically, a site or blog that practices good SEO habits should improve its rankings in search engines, such as Google and Bing. Most huge corporations have realized the importance of SEO and spend enormous sums of time, energy and money on perfecting their SEO practices. However, writers can improve their SEO without going to those same extremes.

In this section, I will use the terms of *site pages* and *blog posts* interchangeably. In both cases, you should be practicing the same SEO strategies (when it makes sense).

Here are my top tips on ways to improve your SEO starting today:

1. **USE APPROPRIATE KEYWORDS.** Make sure that your page displays your main keyword(s) in the page title, content, URL, title tags, page header, image names and tags (if you're including images). All of this is easy to do, but if you feel overwhelmed, just remember to use your keyword(s) in your page title and content (especially in the first and last 50 words of your page).

2. **USE KEYWORDS NATURALLY.** Don't kill your content and make yourself look like a spammer to search engines by overloading your page with your keyword(s). You don't get SEO points for quantity but for quality. Plus, one of the main ways to improve your page rankings is when you...

3. **DELIVER QUALITY CONTENT.** The best way to improve your SEO is by providing content that readers want to share with others by linking to your pages. Some of the top results in search engines can be years old, because the content is so good that people keep coming back. So, incorporate your keywords in a smart way, but make sure it works organically with your content.

4. **UPDATE CONTENT REGULARLY.** If your site looks dead to visitors, then it'll appear that way to search engines too. So update your content regularly. This should be very easy for writers who have blogs. For writers who have sites, incorporate your blog into your site. This will make it easier for visitors to your blog to discover more about you on your site (through your site navigation tools).

5. **LINK BACK TO YOUR OWN CONTENT.** If I have a post on Blogging Tips for Writers, for instance, I'll link back to it if I have a Platform Building post, because the two complement each other. This also helps clicks on my blog, which helps SEO. The one caveat is that you don't go crazy with your linking and that you make sure your links are relevant. Otherwise, you'll kill your traffic, which is not good for your page rankings.

6. **LINK TO OTHERS YOU CONSIDER HELPFUL.** Back in 2000, I remember being ordered by my boss at the time (who didn't last too much longer afterward) to ignore any competitive or complementary websites—no matter how helpful their content—because they were our competitors. You can try basing your online strategy on these principles, but I'm nearly 100 percent confident you'll fail. It's helpful for other sites and your own to link to other great resources. I shine a light on others to help them out (if I find their content truly helpful) in the hopes that they'll do the same if ever they find my content truly helpful for their audience.

7. **GET SPECIFIC WITH YOUR HEADLINES.** If you interview someone on your blog, don't title your post with an interesting quotation. While that strategy may help get readers in the print world, it doesn't help with SEO at all. Instead, title your post as "Interview With (insert name here)." If you have a way to identify the person further, include that in the title too. For instance, when I interview poets on my Poetic Asides blog, I'll title those posts like this: Interview With Poet Erika Meitner. Erika's name is a keyword, but so are the terms *poet* and *interview*.

8. **USE IMAGES.** Many expert sources state that the use of images can improve SEO, because it shows search engines that the person creating the page is spending a little extra time and effort on the page than a common spammer. However, I'd caution anyone using images to make sure those images are somehow complementary to the content. Don't just throw up a lot of images that have no relevance to anything. At the same time...

9. **OPTIMIZE IMAGES THROUGH STRATEGIC LABELING.** Writers can do this by making sure the image file is labeled using your keyword(s) for the post. Using the Erika Meitner example above (which does include images), I would label the file "Erika Meitner headshot.jpg"—or whatever the image file type happens to be. Writers can also improve image SEO through the use of captions and ALT tagging. Of course, at the same time, writers should always ask themselves if it's worth going through all that trouble for each image or not. Each writer has to answer that question for him (or her) self.

10. **USE YOUR SOCIAL MEDIA PLATFORM TO SPREAD THE WORD.** Whenever you do something new on your site or blog, you should share that information on your other social media sites, such as Twitter, Facebook, LinkedIn, online forums, etc. This lets your social media connections know that something new is on your site/blog. If it's relevant and/or valuable, they'll let others know. And that's a great way to build your SEO.

Programmers and marketers could get even more involved in the dynamics of SEO optimization, but I think these tips will help most writers out immediately and effectively while still allowing plenty of time and energy for the actual work of writing.

BLOG DESIGN TIPS FOR WRITERS

Design is an important element to any blog's success. But how can you improve your blog's design if you're not a designer? I'm just an editor with an English Lit degree and no formal training in design. However, I've worked in media for more than a decade now and can share some very fundamental and easy tricks to improve the design of your blog.

Here are my seven blog design tips for writers:

1. **USE LISTS.** Whether they're numbered or bullet points, use lists when possible. Lists break up the text and make it easy for readers to follow what you're blogging.

2. **BOLD MAIN POINTS IN LISTS.** Again, this helps break up the text while also highlighting the important points of your post.

3. **USE HEADINGS.** If your posts are longer than 300 words and you don't use lists, then please break up the text by using basic headings.

4. **USE A READABLE FONT.** Avoid using fonts that are too large or too small. Avoid using cursive or weird fonts. Times New Roman or Arial works, but if you want to get "creative," use something similar to those.

5. **LEFT ALIGN.** English-speaking readers are trained to read left to right. If you want to make your blog easier to read, avoid centering or right aligning your text (unless you're purposefully calling out the text).

6. **USE SMALL PARAGRAPHS.** A good rule of thumb is to try and avoid paragraphs that drone on longer than five sentences. I usually try to keep paragraphs to around three sentences myself.

7. **ADD RELEVANT IMAGES.** Personally, I shy away from using too many images. My reason is that I only like to use them if they're relevant. However, images are very powerful on blogs, so please use them—just make sure they're relevant to your blog post.

If you're already doing everything on my list, keep it up! If you're not, then you might want to re-think your design strategy on your blog. Simply adding a header here and a list there can easily improve the design of a blog post.

GUEST POSTING TIPS FOR WRITERS

Recently, I've broken into guest posting as both a guest poster and as a host of guest posts (over at my Poetic Asides blog). So far, I'm pretty pleased with both sides of the guest posting process. As a writer, it gives me access to an engaged audience I may not usually reach. As a blogger, it provides me with fresh and valuable content I don't have to create. Guest blogging is a rare win-win scenario.

That said, writers could benefit from a few tips on the process of guest posting:

1. **PITCH GUEST POSTS LIKE ONE WOULD PITCH ARTICLES TO A MAGAZINE.** Include what your hook is for the post, what you plan to cover, and a little about who you are.

Remember: Your post should somehow benefit the audience of the blog you'd like to guest post.

2. **OFFER PROMOTIONAL COPY OF BOOK (OR OTHER GIVEAWAYS) AS PART OF YOUR GUEST POST.** Having a random giveaway for people who comment on a blog post can help spur conversation and interest in your guest post, which is a great way to get the most mileage out of your guest appearance.

3. **CATER POSTS TO AUDIENCE.** As the editor of *Writer's Market* and *Poet's Market*, I have great range in the topics I can cover. However, if I'm writing a guest post for a fiction blog, I'll write about things of interest to a novelist—not a poet.

4. **MAKE PERSONAL, BUT PROVIDE NUGGET.** Guest posts are a great opportunity for you to really show your stuff to a new audience. You could write a very helpful and impersonal post, but that won't connect with readers the same way as if you write a very helpful and personal post that makes them want to learn more about you (and your blog, your book, your Twitter account, etc.). Speaking of which...

5. **SHARE LINKS TO YOUR WEBSITE, BLOG, SOCIAL NETWORKS, ETC.** After all, you need to make it easy for readers who enjoyed your guest post to learn more about you and your projects. Start the conversation in your guest post and keep it going on your own sites, profiles, etc. And related to that...

6. **PROMOTE YOUR GUEST POST THROUGH YOUR NORMAL CHANNELS ONCE THE POST GOES LIVE.** Your normal audience will want to know where you've been and what you've been doing. Plus, guest posts lend a little extra "street cred" to your projects. But don't stop there...

7. **CHECK FOR COMMENTS ON YOUR GUEST POST AND RESPOND IN A TIMELY MANNER.** Sometimes the comments are the most interesting part of a guest post (no offense). This is where readers can ask more in-depth or related questions, and it's also where you can show your expertise on the subject by being as helpful as possible. And guiding all seven of these tips is this one:

8. **PUT SOME EFFORT INTO YOUR GUEST POST.** Part of the benefit to guest posting is the opportunity to connect with a new audience. Make sure you bring your A-game, because you need to make a good impression if you want this exposure to actually help grow your audience. Don't stress yourself out, but put a little thought into what you submit.

ONE ADDITIONAL TIP: Have fun with it. Passion is what really drives the popularity of blogs. Share your passion and enthusiasm, and readers are sure to be impressed.

AUTHOR PLATFORM 2.0

....

by Jane Friedman

You've been through the drill already. You know about establishing your own website, being active on social media, plus networking up and down the food chain. You've heard all the advice about building your online and offline presence—and perhaps you've landed a book deal because of your strong platform.

But platform building is a career-long activity. It doesn't stop once your website goes live, or after you land a book deal. In fact, your continued career growth depends on extending your reach and uncovering new opportunities. So what's next?

I'll break it down into three categories:

- Optimize your online presence.
- Make your relationships matter.
- Diversify your content.

OPTIMIZE YOUR ONLINE PRESENCE

First things first. You need your own domain (e.g., JaneFriedman.com is the domain I own), and you should be self-hosted. If you're still working off Blogger or Wordpress.com, then you won't be able to implement all of my advice due to the limitations of having your site owned or hosted by someone else.

Once you truly own your site, hire a professional website designer to customize the look and feel to best convey your personality or brand. If you don't yet have a grasp on what your "personality" is, then hold off on a site revamp until you do. Or you might start simple, by getting a professionally designed header that's unique to your site.

Website and blog must-haves

Here's a checklist of things you should implement aside from a customized design.

- Readers should be able to subscribe to your blog posts via e-mail or RSS. You should be able to track the number of people who are signing up, and see when they are signing up.
- Customize the e-mails sent to anyone who subscribes to your blog posts. This can be done if you use Feedburner (free service) or MailChimp (free up to 2,000 names). Each e-mail that your readers receive should have the same look and feel as your website or whatever branding you typically use. You should also be able to see how many people open these e-mails and what they click on.
- If you do not actively blog, start an e-mail newsletter and post the sign-up form on your site. This way you can stay in touch with people who express interest in your news and updates. Again, MailChimp is a free e-mail newsletter delivery service for up to 2,000 names. You should also have e-newsletter sign-up forms with you at speaking engagements.
- Install Google Analytics, which offers valuable data on who visits your site, when they visit, what content they look at, how long they stay, etc.
- Add social sharing buttons to your site and each post, so people can easily share your content on Facebook, Google, etc. This functionality might have to be manually added if you have a self-hosted site.

Review your metrics

As I hope you noticed, many of the above items relate to metrics and measurement. Advance platform building requires that you study your numbers. Especially think about the following:

- How do people find your site? For example, if you're dumping a lot of energy into Twitter to drive traffic to your blog posts, but very few people visit your site from Twitter, that means your strategy is not working, and you might need to course correct.
- What content is the most popular on your site? This is like a neon sign, telling you what your readers want. Whatever it is, consider how you can build on it, repurpose it, or expand it.
- What causes a spike in traffic, followers, or subscribers? When you achieve spikes, you've done something right. How can you repeat the success?
- What's extending your reach? Most days, you're probably talking to the same crowd you were yesterday. But every so often, you'll be opened up to a new audience—and from that you can find new and loyal readers. Identify activities that have a broad ripple effect, and make you heard beyond your existing circles. (In Google Analytics, this would mean tracking how new visitors find you.)

Advanced social media monitoring and involvement

Just about everyone by now has a Facebook profile or page, a LinkedIn profile, a Twitter account, etc. But static profiles can only do so much for you. Social media becomes more valuable when you decide how to interact and how to facilitate valuable discussion among your followers. Here are a few areas to consider.

- Implement an advanced commenting system. Sometimes the most valuable part of a blog is having a comments section where people can contribute and interact with each other. But this usually means actively filtering the good comments from the bad. Using a robust system like Disqus or Livefyre (and paying for access to their filtering tools) can help you develop a quality discussion area that rewards the most thoughtful contributors.

- Add a forum or discussion board. Very popular bloggers, who may have hundreds of comments on a post, will often add a forum or discussion board so their community can interact in an extended way. If your site is Wordpress-based, plug-ins can help you add a forum to your site in one step. Or you can consider using a private Facebook group or Ning (ning.com) as the base for your community.

- Use HootSuite to be strategic with your social media updates. HootSuite is a free, Web-based software that helps you schedule updates primarily for Twitter, but also for other sites. It also helps you analyze the effectiveness of your tweets (e.g, how many people clicked on a link you tweeted?).

- Use Paper.li (free service) to automatically curate the best daily tweets, updates, and posts on whatever subject you're an expert on—based on the people or organizations you follow and trust. Sometimes curating is one of the best services you can provide for your community—not only do you provide valuable content, you help people understand *who else* provides valuable content!

A final word about social media: Everyone knows about the usual suspects (Facebook, Twitter, Google Plus). Make sure you're not missing a more niche, devoted community on your topic. For example, All About Romance (www.likesbooks.com) is a very popular site for readers and authors of romance.

MAKE YOUR RELATIONSHIPS MATTER

A key component to platform is the relationships you have and grow. Often when you see a successful author, it's only the *visible* aspects of their online presence or content that are apparent. What you can't see is all of the relationship-building and behind-the-scenes conversations that contribute to a more impactful and amplified reach.

Am I saying you have to know big-name people to have a successful platform? No! Do you need to build relationships with successful or authoritative people (or organizations/businesses) in your community? Yes. Here's how to amplify your efforts.

Make a list of who's interacting with you the most

Regardless of where it's happening (on your site or on social media), take note of who is reading, commenting on, or sharing your content. These are people who are already paying attention, like what you're doing, and are receptive to further interaction.

If you're ignoring these people, then you're missing an opportunity to develop a more valuable relationship (which will likely lead to new ones), as well as reward and empower those you're already engaged with.

What does "rewarding" and "empowering" look like? You might drop a personal note, offer an e-book or product for free, or involve them somehow in your online content. You might have a special newsletter for them. Do what makes sense—there are many ways to employ this principle. Christina Katz, who teaches classes to writers, creates "Dream Teams" of writers who are selected from previous students. It's a great idea that rewards both Christina and the students she coaches.

Make a list of your mentors and how you can help them

You should have a list (or wish list!) of mentors. If not, develop one. We all have people who are doing something we dream of, or operate a few steps beyond where we're currently at.

....

Do not approach this as something you're going to "get something" out of, or it will backfire.

....

If you're not already closely following your mentors on their most active channels of communication (blog, Twitter, Facebook, etc), then start. Begin commenting, sharing, and being a visible fan of what they do. Consider other ways you can develop the relationship, e.g., interview them on your blog or review their book. But most of all, brainstorm how you can serve them.

If you engage mentors in an intelligent way (not in a needy "look at me" sort of way), then you may develop a more meaningful relationship when they reach out to acknowledge your efforts. But be careful: Do not approach this as something you're going to "get something" out of, or it will backfire.

Do watch for opportunities that mentors will inevitably offer (e.g., "I'm looking for someone to help moderate my community. Who wants to help?") I once helped an author arrange a book event when he stopped in Cincinnati, and that helped solidify a relationship that had only been virtual up until that point.

Finally, don't forget a time-honored way to cozy up to mentors: offer a guest post for their blog. Just make sure that what you contribute is of the highest quality possible—more high quality than what you'd demand for your own site. If you bring a mentor considerable traffic, you'll earn their attention and esteem.

Look for partnerships with peers

Who is attempting to reach the same audience as you? Don't see them as competitors. Instead, align with them to do bigger and better things. You can see examples of partnership everywhere in the writing community, such as:

- Writer Unboxed website (where I participate)
- Jungle Red Writers blog
- The Kill Zone blog

We all have different strengths. Banding together is an excellent way to extend your platform in ways you can't manage on your own. When presented with opportunities to collaborate, say yes whenever you'll be exposed to a new audience or diversify your online presence.

Stay alert to your influencers and who you influence

There are many ways to identify important people in your community, but if you're not sure where to start, try the following.

- Blog rolls. Find just one blog that you know is influential. See who they're linking to and recommending. Identify sites that seem to be on everyone's "best of" list— or try searching for "best blogs" + your niche.
- Klout. This social media tool attempts to measure people's authority online by assigning a score. It will summarize who you influence, and who you are influenced by.
- If you use the Disqus commenting system, it will identify the most active commenters on your site.

DIVERSIFY YOUR CONTENT

Writers can easily fall into the trap of thinking only about new *written* content. It's a shame, because by repurposing existing content into new mediums, you can open yourself up to entirely new audiences.

For example, I have a friend who has a long solo commute by car, plus he walks his dogs while listening to his iPod. Nearly all of his media consumption is podcast driven. He rarely reads because his lifestyle doesn't support it. That means that if he can't get his content in audio form, he won't buy it.

Envision a day in the life of your readers. Are they likely to be using mobile devices? Tablets? (Guess what: Google Analytics tells you the percentage of mobile and tablet visits to your site!) Do your readers like to watch videos on YouTube? Do they buy e-books? Are they on Twitter?

If you adapt your content to different mediums, you will uncover a new audience who didn't know you existed. While not all content is fit for adaptation, brainstorm a list of all the content you currently own rights to, and think of ways it could be repurposed or redistributed.

> If you adapt your content to different mediums, you will uncover a new audience who didn't know you existed.

A popular repurposing project for longtime bloggers is to compile and edit a compilation of best blog posts, and make it available as an e-book (free or paid). Some bloggers will even do that with a handful of blog posts that can serve as a beginner or introductory guide to a specific topic. Fiction writers: How about a sampler of your work in e-book or PDF form? Poets: How about a podcast of you reading some of your favorite poems?

Some forms or mediums you might want to explore:

- Creating podcasts and distributing through your own site (or via iTunes)
- Creating videocasts and distributing through YouTube or Vimeo (did you know that YouTube is now the No. 2 search engine?)
- Creating tips or lessons in e-mail newsletter form
- Creating PDFs (free or paid), and using Scribd to help distribute
- Creating online tutorials or offering critiques through tools such as Google Hangouts, Google Docs, and/or Screencast.com
- Creating slide presentations and distributing through SlideShare

The only limit is your imagination!

HOUSEKEEPING

On a final note, I'd like to share a few housekeeping tips that can help boost your image and authority online. While they may seem trivial, they go a long way in making a good impression and spreading the word about what you do.

- Get professional headshots that accurately convey your brand or personality—what people know you and love you for.
- For your social media profiles, completely fill out *all* fields and maximize the functionality. This is important for search and discoverability. For instance, on LinkedIn, add keywords that cover all of your skill sets, pipe in your Twitter account and blog posts, and give complete descriptions of all positions you've held. On Google Plus, list all the sites that you're a contributor for. On Facebook, allow people to subscribe to your public updates even if they aren't your friends.

- Gather updated testimonials and blurbs, and use them on your site and/or your social media profiles if appropriate.

However you decide to tackle the next stage of your platform development, ensure consistency. Whether it's your website, e-newsletter, Facebook profile, business cards, or letterhead, be consistent in the look and feel of your materials and in the message you send. Unless you are appealing to different audiences with different needs, broadcast a unified message no matter where and how people find you. Believe me—it doesn't get boring. Instead, it helps people remember who you are and what you stand for.

JANE FRIEDMAN is a former publishing and media exec who now teaches full-time at the University of Cincinnati. She has spoken on writing, publishing, and the future of media at more than 200 events since 2001, including South by Southwest, BookExpo America, and the Association of Writers and Writing Programs. Find out more at http://janefriedman.com.

LITERARY AGENTS

The literary agencies listed in this section are open to new clients and are members of the Association of Authors' Representatives (AAR), which means they do not charge for reading, critiquing, or editing. Some agents in this section may charge clients for office expenses such as photocopying, foreign postage, long-distance phone calls, or express mail services. Make sure you have a clear understanding of what these expenses are before signing any agency agreement.

FOR MORE...

The *2014 Guide to Literary Agents* (Writer's Digest Books) offers more than 800 literary agents, as well as information on writers' conferences. It also offers a wealth of information on the author/agent relationship and other related topics. Also, WritersMarket.com offers hundreds of up-to-date listings for literary agents.

DOMINICK ABEL LITERARY AGENCY, INC.

146 W. 82nd St., #1A, New York NY 10024. (212)877-0710. **Fax:** (212)595-3133. **E-mail:** dominick@dalainc.com. Member AAR. Represents 100 clients. Currently handles: adult fiction and nonfiction.

HOW TO CONTACT Query via e-mail.

TERMS Agent receives 15% commission on domestic sales. Agent receives 20% commission on foreign sales.

ALIVE COMMUNICATIONS, INC.

7680 Goddard St., Suite 200, Colorado Springs CO 80920. (719)260-7080. **Fax:** (719)260-8223. **E-mail:** submissions@alivecom.com. **Website:** www.alivecom.com. **Contact:** Rick Christian. Other memberships include Authors Guild. Represents 100+ clients. 5% of clients are new/unpublished writers. Currently handles: nonfiction books 50%, novels 40%, juvenile books 10%.

MEMBER AGENTS Rick Christian, president (blockbusters, bestsellers); Lee Hough (popular/commercial nonfiction and fiction, thoughtful spirituality, children's); Andrea Heinecke (thoughtful/inspirational nonfiction, women's fiction/nonfiction, popular/commercial nonfiction & fiction); Joel Kneedler popular/commercial nonfiction and fiction, thoughtful spirituality, children's).

REPRESENTS Nonfiction books, novels, short story collections, novellas. **Considers these nonfiction areas:** autobiography, biography, business, child guidance, economics, how-to, inspirational, parenting, personal improvement, religious, self-help, women's issues, women's studies. **Considers these fiction areas:** adventure, contemporary issues, crime, family saga, historical, humor, inspirational, literary, mainstream, mystery, police, religious, satire, suspense, thriller.

HOW TO CONTACT Query via e-mail. "Be advised that this agency works primarily with well-established, best-selling, and career authors. Always looking for a breakout, blockbuster author with genuine talent." New clients come through recommendations from others.

TERMS Agent receives 15% commission on domestic sales. Offers written contract; 2-month notice must be given to terminate contract.

TIPS Rewrite and polish until the words on the page shine. Endorsements and great connections may help, provided you can write with power and passion. Network with publishing professionals by making contacts, joining critique groups, and attending writers' conferences in order to make personal connections and to get feedback. Alive Communications, Inc., has established itself as a premiere literary agency. We serve an elite group of authors who are critically acclaimed and commercially successful in both Christian and general markets.

BETSY AMSTER LITERARY ENTERPRISES

6312 SW Capitol Hwy #503, Portland OR 97239. **Website:** www.amsterlit.com. **Contact:** Betsy Amster (adult); Mary Cummings (children's and YA). Estab. 1992. Represents more than 65 clients. 35% of clients are new/unpublished writers. Currently handles: nonfiction books 65%, novels 35%.

REPRESENTS Nonfiction books, novels. **Considers these nonfiction areas:** art & design, biography, business, child guidance, cooking/nutrition, current affairs, ethnic, gardening, health/medicine, history, memoirs, money, parenting, popular culture, psychology, science/technology, self-help, sociology, travelogues, social issues, women's issues. **Considers these fiction areas:** ethnic, literary, women's, high quality.

HOW TO CONTACT For adult titles: b.amster.assistant@gmail.com. "For fiction or memoirs, please embed the first three pages in the body of your e-mail. For nonfiction, please embed your proposal." For children's and YA: b.amster.kidsbooks@gmail.com. See submission requirements online at website. "For picture books, please embed the entire text in the body of your e-mail. For novels, please embed the first three pages." Accepts simultaneous submissions. Responds in 1 month to queries. Responds in 2 months to mss. Obtains most new clients through recommendations from others, solicitations, conferences.

TERMS Agent receives 15% commission on domestic sales. Agent receives 20% commission on foreign sales. Offers written contract, binding for 1 year; 3-month notice must be given to terminate contract. Charges for photocopying, postage, messengers, galleys/books used in submissions to foreign and film agents and to magazines for first serial rights.

ANDERSON LITERARY MANAGEMENT, LLC

12 W. 19th St., New York NY 10011. (212)645-6045. **Fax:** (212)741-1936. **E-mail:** info@andersonliterary.com; kathleen@andersonliterary.com; claire@andersonliterary.com. **Website:** www.andersonliterary.com. **Contact:** Kathleen Anderson. Estab. 2006. Represents 100+ clients. 20% of clients are new/unpub-

lished writers. Currently handles: nonfiction books 50%, novels 50%.

MEMBER AGENTS Kathleen Anderson, Claire Wheeler.

REPRESENTS Nonfiction books, novels, short story collections, juvenile. **Considers these nonfiction areas:** anthropology, archeology, architecture, art, autobiography, biography, cultural interests, current affairs, dance, design, education, environment, ethnic, gay, government, history, law, lesbian, memoirs, music, nature, politics, psychology, women's issues, women's studies. **Considers these fiction areas:** action, adventure, ethnic, family saga, feminist, frontier, gay, historical, lesbian, literary, mystery, suspense, thriller, westerns, women's, young adult.

HOW TO CONTACT Query with SASE. Submit synopsis, first 3 sample chapters, proposal (for nonfiction). Snail mail queries only. Accepts simultaneous submissions. Responds in 6 weeks to queries. Obtains most new clients through recommendations from others, solicitations, conferences.

TERMS Agent receives 15% commission on domestic sales. Offers written contract.

TIPS "We do not represent plays or screenplays."

ARCADIA

31 Lake Place N., Danbury CT 06810. **E-mail:** arcadialit@sbcglobal.net. **Contact:** Victoria Gould Pryor.

REPRESENTS Nonfiction books, literary and commercial fiction. **Considers these nonfiction areas:** biography, business, current affairs, health, history, psychology, science, true crime, women's, investigative journalism; culture; classical music; life transforming self-help.

HOW TO CONTACT No unsolicited submissions. Query with SASE. This agency accepts e-queries (no attachments).

THE AXELROD AGENCY

55 Main St., P.O. Box 357, Chatham NY 12037. (518)392-2100. **E-mail:** steve@axelrodagency.com. **Website:** www.axelrodagency.com. **Contact:** Steven Axelrod. Represents 15-20 clients. 1% of clients are new/unpublished writers. Currently handles: novels 95%.

REPRESENTS Novels. **Considers these fiction areas:** mystery, romance, women's.

HOW TO CONTACT Query with SASE. Accepts simultaneous submissions. Responds in 3 weeks to queries. Responds in 6 weeks to mss. Obtains most new clients through recommendations from others.

TERMS Agent receives 15% commission on domestic sales. Agent receives 20% commission on foreign sales. No written contract.

LORETTA BARRETT BOOKS, INC.

220 E. 23rd St., 11th Floor, New York NY 10010. (212)242-3420. **E-mail:** query@lorettabarrettbooks. com. **Website:** www.lorettabarrettbooks.com. **Contact:** Loretta A. Barrett; Nick Mullendore; Gabriel Davis. Estab. 1990. Currently handles: nonfiction books 50%, novels 50%.

MEMBER AGENTS Loretta A. Barrett; Nick Mullendore.

REPRESENTS Nonfiction books, novels. **Considers these nonfiction areas:** biography, child guidance, current affairs, ethnic, government, health/nutrition, history, memoirs, money, multicultural, nature, popular culture, psychology, religion, science, self help, sociology, spirituality, sports, women's, young adult, creative nonfiction. **Considers these fiction areas:** contemporary, psychic, adventure, detective, ethnic, family, historical, literary, mainstream, mystery, thriller, young adult.

HOW TO CONTACT See guidelines online. Use e-mail (no attachments) or if by post, query with SASE. For hardcopy queries, please send a 1-2 page query letter and a synopsis or chapter outline for your project. In your letter, please include your contact information, any relevant background information on yourself or your project, and a paragraph of description of your project. If you are submitting electronically, then all of this material may be included in the body of your e-mail. Accepts simultaneous submissions. Responds in 3-6 weeks to queries.

TERMS Agent receives 15% commission on domestic sales. Agent receives 20% commission on foreign sales. Offers written contract. Charges clients for shipping and photocopying.

BARBARA BRAUN ASSOCIATES, INC.

7 E. 14th St., Suite 19F, New York NY 10003. **Fax:** (212)604-9023. **E-mail:** bbasubmissions@gmail.com. **Website:** www.barbarabraunagency.com. **Contact:** Barbara Braun.

MEMBER AGENTS Barbara Braun; John F. Baker.

REPRESENTS Nonfiction books, novels. **Considers these nonfiction areas:** "We represent both literary and commercial and serious nonfiction, including psychology, biography, history, women's issues, social and political issues, cultural criticism, as well as art, architecture, film, photography, fashion and design.". **Considers these fiction areas:** literary and commercial.

HOW TO CONTACT "E-mail submissions only, marked 'query' in subject line. We no longer accept submissions by regular mail. Your query should include: a brief summary of your book, word count, genre, any relevant publishing experience, and the first 5 pages of your ms pasted into the body of the e-mail. (No attachments--we will not open these.)"

TERMS Agent receives 15% commission on domestic sales. Agent receives 20% commission on foreign sales.

TIPS "Our clients' books are represented throughout Europe, Asia, and Latin America by various sub-agents. We are also active in selling motion picture rights to the books we represent, and work with various Hollywood agencies."

KIMBERLEY CAMERON & ASSOCIATES

1550 Tiburon Blvd., #704, Tiburon CA 94920. **Fax:** (415)789-9191. **E-mail:** info@kimberleycameron. com. **Website:** www.kimberleycameron.com. **Contact:** Kimberley Cameron. 30% of clients are new/unpublished writers.

MEMBER AGENTS Kimberley Cameron, Elizabeth Kracht, Pooja Menon, Amy Cloughley, and Ethan Vaughan.

REPRESENTS Nonfiction, fiction. **Considers these nonfiction areas:** biography, current affairs, foods, humor, language, memoirs, popular culture, science, true crime, women's issues, women's studies, lifestyle. **Considers these fiction areas:** adventure, contemporary issues, ethnic, family saga, historical, horror, mainstream, mystery, interlinked short story collections, thriller, women's, and sophisticated/crossover young adult.

HOW TO CONTACT Query via e-mail. "See our website for submission guidelines." Obtains new clients through recommendations from others, solicitations.

TERMS Agent receives 15% on domestic sales; 10% on film sales. Offers written contract, binding for 1 year.

TIPS "Please consult our submission guidelines and send a polite, well-written query to our e-mail address."

SANDRA DIJKSTRA LITERARY AGENCY

1155 Camino del Mar, PMB 515, Del Mar CA 92014. (858)755-3115. **Fax:** (858)794-2822. **E-mail:** elise@

dijkstraagency.com. **Website:** www.dijkstraagency. com. Other memberships include Authors Guild, PEN West, Poets and Editors, MWA. Represents 100+ clients. 30% of clients are new/unpublished writers. Currently handles: nonfiction books 50%, novels 45%, juvenile books 5%.

MEMBER AGENTS Sandra Dijkstra, president (adult only). Acquiring Sub-agents: Elise Capron (adult only), Jill Marr (adult only), Thao Le (adult and YA), Jennifer Azantian (YA only). Sub-rights agent: Andrea Cavallaro.

REPRESENTS Nonfiction books, novels. **Considers these nonfiction areas:** biography, business, history, memoirs, psychology, science, self-help, narrative. **Considers these fiction areas:** contemporary issues, fantasy, literary, science fiction, suspense, thriller, women's, young adult.

HOW TO CONTACT "Please see guidelines on our website, and please note that we now only accept e-mail submissions. Due to the large number of unsolicited submissions we receive, we are only able to respond those submissions in which we are interested." Accepts simultaneous submissions. Responds to queries of interest within 6 weeks.

TERMS Works in conjunction with foreign and film agents. Agent receives 15% commission on domestic sales and 20% commission on foreign sales. Offers written contract. No reading fee.

TIPS "Be professional and learn the standard procedures for submitting your work. Be a regular patron of bookstores, and study what kind of books are being published and will appear on the shelves next to yours. You'll also find lots of books on writing and the publishing industry that will help you. At conferences, ask published writers about their agents. Don't believe the myth that an agent has to be in New York to be successful. We've already disproved it!"

JANIS A. DONNAUD & ASSOCIATES, INC.

525 Broadway, Second Floor, New York NY 10012. (212)431-2664. **Fax:** (212)431-2667. **E-mail:** jdonnaud@aol.com; donnaudassociate@aol.com. **Contact:** Janis A. Donnaud. Signatory of WGA. Represents 40 clients. 5% of clients are new/unpublished writers. Currently handles: nonfiction books 100%.

REPRESENTS Nonfiction books. **Considers these nonfiction areas:** autobiography, African-American, biography, business, celebrity, child guidance, cooking, current affairs, diet/nutrition, foods, health, humor, medicine, parenting, psychology, satire, women's issues, women's studies, lifestyle.

HOW TO CONTACT Query with SASE. Submit description of book, 2-3 pages of sample material. Prefers to read materials exclusively. No phone calls. Responds in 1 month to queries and mss. Obtains most new clients through recommendations from others.

TERMS Agent receives 15% commission on domestic and film sales; 20% commission on foreign sales. Offers written contract; 1-month notice must be given to terminate contract.

FINEPRINT LITERARY MANAGEMENT

115 W. 29th, 3rd Floor, New York NY 10001. (212)279-1282. **E-mail:** stephany@fineprintlit.com. **Website:** www.fineprintlit.com.

MEMBER AGENTS **Peter Rubie**, CEO (nonfiction interests include narrative nonfiction, popular science, spirituality, history, biography, pop culture, business, technology, parenting, health, self help, music, and food; fiction interests include literate thrillers, crime fiction, science fiction and fantasy, military fiction and literary fiction, middle grade and YA fiction and nonfiction for boys); **Stephany Evans**, Nonfiction: health and wellness, especially women's health; spirituality, environment/sustainability, food and wine, memoir, and narrative nonfiction; Fiction: stories with a strong and interesting female protagonist, both literary and upmarket commercial/book club fiction, romance - all sub genres; mysteries; **Janet Reid**, Nonfiction: narrative nonfiction, history and biography; Fiction: thrillers, **Brooks Sherman**, Nonfiction: narrative nonfiction, history, pop culture, and food; Fiction: literary, upmarket, crime, science fiction grounded in realistic settings, high/contemporary/dark fantasy, magical realism, middle grade, young adult, and picture books; **Becky Vinter**, Nonfiction: travel, food, health, wellness, business/management, environment, current events, memoir; Fiction: women's fiction, romance, mysteries, literary, book club, young adult; **Laura Wood**, Nonfiction: nonfiction books, business, dance, economics, history, humor, law, science, narrative nonfiction, popular science; Fiction: fantasy, science fiction, suspense.

HOW TO CONTACT Query with SASE. Submit synopsis and first 3-5 pages of ms embedded in an e-mail proposal for nonfiction. Do not send attachments or manuscripts without a request. See contact page online at website for e-mails. Obtains most new clients through recommendations from others, solicitations.

TERMS Agent receives 15% commission on domestic sales. Agent receives 20% commission on foreign sales.

THE FRIEDRICH AGENCY

19 W. 21st St., Suite 201, New York NY 10010. **E-mail:** mfriedrich@friedrichagency.com; lcarson@friedrichagency.com; mschulman@friedrichagency.com; nichole@friedrichagency.com. **Website:** www.friedrichagency.com. **Contact:** Molly Friedrich; Lucy Carson. Signatory of WGA. Represents 50+ clients.

MEMBER AGENTS Molly Friedrich, founder and agent (open to queries); Lucy Carson, foreign rights director and agent (open to queries); Molly Schulman, assistant; Nichole LeFebvre, foreign rights assistant.

REPRESENTS Full-length fiction and nonfiction.

HOW TO CONTACT Query by e-mail (strongly preferred), or by mail with SASE. See guidelines on website.

GREYHAUS LITERARY

3021 20th St., PL SW, Puyallup WA 98373. **E-mail:** scott@greyhausagency.com. **Website:** www.greyhausagency.com. **Contact:** Scott Eagan, member RWA. Estab. 2003.

HOW TO CONTACT Send a query, the first 3 pages and a synopsis of no more than 3 pages. There is also a submission form on this agency's website.

JOHN HAWKINS & ASSOCIATES, INC.

71 W. 23rd St., Suite 1600, New York NY 10010. (212)807-7040. **Fax:** (212)807-9555. **E-mail:** jha@jhalit.com; moses@jhalit.com; Frazier@jhalit.com; Ahawkins@jhalit.com. **Website:** www.jhalit.com. **Contact:** Moses Cardona (rights and translations); Liz Free (permissions); Warren Frazier, literary agent; Anne Hawkins, literary agent. Represents over 100 clients. 5-10% of clients are new/unpublished writers. Currently handles: nonfiction books 40%, novels 40%, juvenile books 20%.

MEMBER AGENTS Moses Cardona; Liz Free; Warren Frazier; Anne Hawkins.

REPRESENTS Nonfiction books, novels. **Considers these nonfiction areas:** Americana, biography, business, cultural interests, current affairs, design, economics, education, ethnic, film, gardening, gay/lesbian, government, health, history, horticulture, memoirs, money, multicultural, popular culture, politics, psychology, recreation, science, self-help, sex, sociology, software, theater, travel, young adult, music, creative nonfiction. **Considers these fiction areas:** action, adventure, crime, detective, ethnic, experimental, family saga, gay, glitz, hi-lo, historical, inspirational, literary, mainstream, multicultural, multimedia, mystery, police, short story collections, sports, supernatural, suspense, thriller, translation, war, westerns, women's, young adult.

HOW TO CONTACT Submit query, proposal package, outline, SASE. Accepts simultaneous submissions. Responds in 1 month to queries. Obtains most new clients through recommendations from others.

TERMS Agent receives 15% commission on domestic sales. Agent receives 20% commission on foreign sales. Charges clients for photocopying.

LINDA KONNER LITERARY AGENCY

10 W. 15th St., Suite 1918, New York NY 10011. (212)691-3419. **E-mail:** ldkonner@cs.com. **Website:** www.lindakonnerliteraryagency.com. **Contact:** Linda Konner. Signatory of WGA. Other memberships include ASJA. Represents 85 clients. 30-35% of clients are new/unpublished writers. Currently handles: nonfiction books 100%.

REPRESENTS Nonfiction books. **Considers these nonfiction areas:** diet/nutrition, gay/lesbian, health, medicine, money, parenting, popular culture, psychology, self-help, women's issues, biography (celebrity), African American and Latino issues, relationships.

HOW TO CONTACT Query by e-mail or by mail with SASE, synopsis, author bio, sufficient return postage. Prefers to read materials exclusively for 2 weeks. Accepts simultaneous submissions. Obtains most new clients through recommendations from others, occasional solicitation among established authors/journalists.

TERMS Agent receives 15% commission on domestic sales. Agent receives 25% commission on foreign sales. Offers written contract. Charges one-time fee for domestic expenses; additional expenses may be incurred for foreign sales.

THE NED LEAVITT AGENCY

70 Wooster St., Suite 4F, New York NY 10012. (212)334-0999. **Website:** www.nedleavittagency.com. **Contact:** Ned Leavitt; Jillian Sweeney. Represents 40+ clients.

MEMBER AGENTS Ned Leavitt, founder and agent; Britta Alexander, agent.

REPRESENTS Nonfiction books, novels.

HOW TO CONTACT This agency now only takes queries/submissions through referred clients. Do *not* cold query.

TIPS "Look online for this agency's recently changed submission guidelines." or guidance in the writing process we strongly recommend the following books: *Writing Down The Bones* by Nathalie Goldberg; *Bird By Bird* by Anne Lamott.

LIVING WORD LITERARY AGENCY

P.O. Box 40974, Eugene OR 97414. **E-mail:** livingwordliterary@gmail.com. **Website:** livingwordliterary.wordpress.com. **Contact:** Kimberly Shumate, agent. Estab. 2009. Member Evangelical Christian Publishers Association

REPRESENTS **Considers these nonfiction areas:** health, parenting, self-help, relationships. **Considers these fiction areas:** inspirational, adult fiction, Christian living.

HOW TO CONTACT Submit a query with short synopsis and first chapter via Word document. Agency only responds if interested.

MARTIN LITERARY MANAGEMENT

7683 SE 27th St., #307, Mercer Island WA 98040. (206)486-1773. **E-mail:** sharlene@martinliterarymanagement.com. **Website:** www.MartinLiteraryManagement.com. **Contact:** Sharlene Martin.

MEMBER AGENTS Sharlene Martin (nonfiction).

REPRESENTS **Considers these nonfiction areas:** autobiography, biography, business, child guidance, current affairs, economics, health, history, how-to, humor, inspirational, investigative, medicine, memoirs, parenting, popular culture, psychology, satire, self-help, true crime, women's issues, women's studies.

HOW TO CONTACT Query via e-mail with MS Word only. No attachments on queries; place letter in body of e-mail. Accepts simultaneous submissions. Responds in 2 weeks to queries. Responds in 3-4 weeks to mss. Obtains most new clients through recommendations from others.

TERMS Agent receives 15% commission on domestic sales. Agent receives 25% commission on foreign sales. Offers written contract, binding for 1 year; 1-month notice must be given to terminate contract. Charges author for postage and copying if material is not sent electronically. 99% of materials are sent electronically to minimize charges to author for postage and copying.

TIPS "Have a strong platform for nonfiction. Please don't call. I welcome e-mail. I'm very responsive when I'm interested in a query and work hard to get my clients' materials in the best possible shape before submissions. Do your homework prior to submission and only submit your best efforts. Please review our website carefully to make sure we're a good match for your work. If you read my book, *Publish Your Nonfiction Book: Strategies For Learning the Industry, Selling Your Book and Building a Successful Career* (Writer's Digest Books) you'll know exactly how to charm me."

MENDEL MEDIA GROUP, LLC

115 W. 30th St., Suite 800, New York NY 10001. (646)239-9896. **Fax:** (212)685-4717. **E-mail:** scott@mendelmedia.com. **Website:** www.mendelmedia.com. Represents 40-60 clients.

REPRESENTS Nonfiction books, novels, scholarly, with potential for broad/popular appeal. **Considers these nonfiction areas:** Americana, animals, anthropology, architecture, art, biography, business, child guidance, cooking, current affairs, dance, diet//nutrition, education, environment, ethnic, foods, gardening, gay/lesbian, government, health, history, how-to, humor, investigative, language, medicine, memoirs, military, money, multicultural, music, parenting, philosophy, popular culture, psychology, recreation, regional, religious, science, self-help, sex, sociology, software, spirituality, sports, true crime, war, women's issues, women's studies, Jewish topics; creative nonfiction. **Considers these fiction areas:** action, adventure, contemporary issues, crime, detective, erotica, ethnic, feminist, gay, glitz, historical, humor, inspirational, juvenile, lesbian, literary, mainstream, mystery, picture books, police, religious, romance, satire, sports, thriller, young adult, Jewish fiction.

HOW TO CONTACT Query with SASE. Do not e-mail or fax queries. For nonfiction, include a complete, fully edited book proposal with sample chapters. For fiction, include a complete synopsis and no more than 20 pages of sample text. Responds in 2 weeks to queries. Responds in 4-6 weeks to mss. Obtains most new clients through recommendations from others.

TERMS Agent receives 15% commission on domestic sales. Agent receives 20% commission on foreign sales.

TIPS "While I am not interested in being flattered by a prospective client, it does matter to me that she knows why she is writing to me in the first place. Is one of my clients a colleague of hers? Has she read a book by one of my clients that led her to believe I might be interested in her work? Authors of descriptive nonfiction should have real credentials and expertise in their subject areas, either as academics, journalists, or policy experts, and authors of prescriptive nonfiction should have legitimate expertise and considerable experience communicating their ideas in seminars and workshops, in a successful business, through the media, etc."

NELSON LITERARY AGENCY

1732 Wazee St., Suite 207, Denver CO 80202. (303)292-2805. **E-mail:** query@nelsonagency.com. **Website:** www.nelsonagency.com. **Contact:** Kristin Nelson, president and senior literary agent; Sara Megibow, associate literary agent. RWA, SCBWI, SFWA.

REPRESENTS Novels, select nonfiction. **Considers these nonfiction areas:** memoirs. **Considers these fiction areas:** commercial, literary, mainstream, romance (includes fantasy with romantic elements, science fiction, fantasy, young adult).

HOW TO CONTACT Query by e-mail only.

THE VRICHARD PARKS AGENCY

P.O. Box 693, Salem NY 12865. (518)854-9466. **Fax:** (518)854-9466. **E-mail:** rp@richardparksagency.com. **Website:** www.richardparksagency.com. **Contact:** Richard Parks. Currently handles: nonfiction books 55%, novels 40%, story collections 5%.

REPRESENTS Nonfiction books, novels. **Considers these nonfiction areas:** animals, anthropology, archeology, art, autobiography, biography, business, child guidance, cooking, crafts, cultural interests, current affairs, dance, diet/nutrition, economics, environment, ethnic, film, foods, gardening, gay/lesbian, government, health, history, hobbies, how-to, humor, language, law, memoirs, military, money, music, parenting, popular culture, politics, psychology, science, self-help, sociology, technology, theater, travel, women's issues, women's studies.

HOW TO CONTACT Query with SASE. Does not accept queries by e-mail or fax. Responds in 2 weeks to queries. Obtains most new clients through recommendations/referrals.

TERMS Agent receives 15% commission on domestic sales. Agent receives 20% commission on foreign sales. Charges clients for photocopying or any unusual expense incurred at the writer's request.

RLR ASSOCIATES, LTD.

Literary Department, 7 W. 51st St., New York NY 10019. (212)541-8641. **Fax:** (212)262-7084. **E-mail:** sgould@rlrassociates.net. **Website:** www.rlrassociates.net. **Contact:** Scott Gould. Represents 50 clients. 25% of clients are new/unpublished writers. Currently handles: nonfiction books 70%, novels 25%, story collections 5%.

REPRESENTS Nonfiction books, novels, short-story collections, scholarly. **Considers these nonfiction areas:** animals, anthropology, archeology, art, autobiography, biography, business, child guidance, cooking, cultural interests, current affairs, decorating, diet/nutrition, economics, education, environment, ethnic, foods, gay/lesbian, government, health, history, humor, inspirational, interior design, language, law, memoirs, money, multicultural, music, parenting, photography, popular culture, politics, psychology, religious, science, self-help, sociology, sports, technology, translation, travel, true crime, women's issues, women's studies. **Considers these fiction areas:** action, adventure, cartoon, comic books, crime, detective, ethnic, experimental, family saga, feminist, gay, historical, horror, humor, lesbian, literary, mainstream, multicultural, mystery, police, satire, sports, suspense.

HOW TO CONTACT Query by either e-mail or mail. Accepts simultaneous submissions. Responds in 4-8 weeks to queries. Obtains most new clients through recommendations from others.

TERMS Agent receives 15% commission on domestic sales. Agent receives 20% commission on foreign sales. Offers written contract.

TIPS "Please check out our website for more details on our agency."

RITA ROSENKRANZ LITERARY AGENCY

440 West End Ave., #15D, New York NY 10024. (212)873-6333. **Website:** www.ritarosenkranzliteraryagency.com. **Contact:** Rita Rosenkranz. Represents 35 clients. 30% of clients are new/unpublished writers. Currently handles: nonfiction books 99%, novels 1%.

REPRESENTS Nonfiction books. **Considers these nonfiction areas:** animals, anthropology, art, autobiography, biography, business, child guidance, computers, cooking, crafts, cultural interests, current affairs, dance, decorating, economics, ethnic, film, gay, government, health, history, hobbies, how-to, humor, inspirational, interior design, language, law, lesbian, literature, medicine, military, money, music, nature, parenting, personal improvement, photography, popular

culture, politics, psychology, religious, satire, science, self-help, sports, technology, theater, war, women's issues, women's studies.

HOW TO CONTACT Send query letter only (no proposal) via regular mail or e-mail. Submit proposal package with SASE only on request. No fax queries. Accepts simultaneous submissions. Responds in 2 weeks to queries. Obtains most new clients through directory listings, solicitations, conferences, word of mouth.

TERMS Agent receives 15% commission on domestic sales. Agent receives 20% commission on foreign sales. Offers written contract, binding for 3 years; 3-month written notice must be given to terminate contract. Charges clients for photocopying. Makes referrals to editing services.

TIPS "Identify the current competition for your project to make sure the project is valid. A strong cover letter is very important."

THE SAGALYN AGENCY

1250 Connecticut Ave., 7th Floor, Washington DC 20036. **E-mail:** query@sagalyn.com. **Website:** www.sagalyn.com. Estab. 1980. Currently handles: nonfiction books 85%, novels 5%, scholarly books 10%.

MEMBER AGENTS Raphael Sagalyn; Shannon O'Neill.

REPRESENTS Nonfiction books. **Considers these nonfiction areas:** autobiography, biography, business, economics, history, memoirs, popular culture, science, technology, journalism.

HOW TO CONTACT Please send e-mail queries only (no attachments). Include 1 of these words in the subject line: query, submission, inquiry.

TIPS "We receive 1,000-1,200 queries a year, which in turn lead to 2 or 3 new clients. See our website for sales information and recent projects."

SUSAN SCHULMAN LITERARY AGENCY

454 W. 44th St., New York NY 10036. (212)713-1633. **Fax:** (212)581-8830. **E-mail:** schulmanqueries@yahoo.com. **Contact:** Susan Schulman. Estab. 1980. Signatory of WGA. Other memberships include Dramatists Guild. 10% of clients are new/unpublished writers. Currently handles: nonfiction books 50%, novels 25%, juvenile books 15%, stage plays 10%.

MEMBER AGENTS Linda Kiss, director of foreign rights; Katherine Stones, theater; Emily Uhry, submissions editor.

REPRESENTS **Considers these nonfiction areas:** anthropology, archeology, autobiography, biography, business, child guidance, cooking, cultural interests, current affairs, dance, diet/nutrition, economics, education, environment, ethnic, foods, gay/lesbian, government, health, history, how-to, inspirational, investigative, language, law, literature, medicine, memoirs, money, music, parenting, popular culture, politics, psychology, religious, self-help, sociology, sports, true crime, women's issues, women's studies. **Considers these fiction areas:** action, adventure, crime, detective, feminist, historical, humor, inspirational, juvenile, literary, mainstream, mystery, picture books, police, religious, suspense, women's, young adult.

HOW TO CONTACT Query with SASE. Submit outline, synopsis, author bio, 3 sample chapters. Accepts simultaneous submissions. Responds in 6 weeks to queries/mss. Obtains most new clients through recommendations from others, solicitations, conferences.

TERMS Agent receives 15% commission on domestic sales. Agent receives 20% commission on foreign sales. Offers written contract; 30-day notice must be given to terminate contract.

TIPS "Keep writing!" Schulman describes her agency as "professional boutique, long-standing, eclectic."

THE SEYMOUR AGENCY

475 Miner St., Canton NY 13617. (315)386-1831. E-mail: marysue@twcny.rr.com; nicole@theseymouragency.com. **Website:** www.theseymouragency.com. **Contact:** Mary Sue Seymour, Nicole Resciniti. Signatory of WGA. Other memberships include RWA, Authors Guild. Represents 50 clients. 5% of clients are new/unpublished writers. Currently handles: nonfiction books 50%, other 50% fiction.

MEMBER AGENTS Mary Sue Seymour (accepts queries in Christian, inspirational, romance, and nonfiction; Nicole Resciniti (accepts queries in same categories as Ms. Seymour in addition to action/suspense/thriller, mystery, sci-fi, fantasy, and YA/children's).

REPRESENTS Nonfiction books, novels. **Considers these nonfiction areas:** business, health, how-to, self help, Christian books; cookbooks; any well-written nonfiction that includes a proposal in standard format and 1 sample chapter. **Considers these fiction areas:** action, fantasy, mystery, religious, romance, science fiction, suspense, thriller, young adult.

HOW TO CONTACT Query with SASE, synopsis, first 50 pages for romance. Accepts e-mail queries. Accepts simultaneous submissions. Responds in 1 month to queries. Responds in 3 months to mss.

TERMS Agent receives 12-15% commission on domestic sales.

WENDY SHERMAN ASSOCIATES, INC.

27 W. 24th St., New York NY 10010. (212)279-9027. E-mail: wendy@wsherman.com. **E-mail:** submissions@wsherman.com. **Website:** www.wsherman.com. **Contact:** Wendy Sherman; Kim Perel. Represents 50 clients. 30% of clients are new/unpublished writers.

MEMBER AGENTS Wendy Sherman (board member of AAR), Kim Perel.

REPRESENTS Considers these nonfiction areas: memoirs, psychology, narrative nonfiction. **Considers these fiction areas:** mainstream, Mainstream fiction that hits the sweet spot between literary and commercial.

HOW TO CONTACT Query via e-mail only. Accepts simultaneous submissions. Responds in 1 month to queries. Obtains most new clients through recommendations from other writers.

TERMS Agent receives standard 15% commission. Offers written contract.

TIPS "The bottom line is: Do your homework. Be as well prepared as possible. Read the books that will help you present yourself and your work with polish. You want your submission to stand out."

STERLING LORD LITERISTIC, INC.

65 Bleecker St., 12th Floor, New York NY 10012. (212)780-6050. **Fax:** (212)780-6095. **E-mail:** info@sll.com. **Website:** www.sll.com. Signatory of WGA. Represents 600 clients. Currently handles: nonfiction books 50%, novels 50%.

MEMBER AGENTS Philippa Brophy; Laurie Liss; Sterling Lord; Peter Matson; Douglas Stewart; Neeti Madan; Robert Guinsler; George Nicholson; Jim Rutman; Celeste Fine; Judy Heiblum; Erica Rand Silverman.

HOW TO CONTACT Query with SASE via mail. Include synopsis of the work, a brief proposal or the first three chapters of the manuscript, and brief bio or resume. Does not respond to unsolicited e-mail queries. Does not represent screenplays. Responds in approximately 1 month.

TERMS Agent receives 15% commission on domestic sales; 20% commission on foreign sales. Offers written contract.

PAM STRICKLER AUTHOR MANAGEMENT

P.O. Box 505, New Paltz NY 12561. (845)255-0061. E-mail: pamstrickleragency@gmail.com. **Website:** www.

pamstrickler.com. **Contact:** Pamela Dean Strickler. An associate member of the Historical Novel Society and member of RWA.

REPRESENTS Novels. **Considers these fiction areas:** historical, romance, women's.

HOW TO CONTACT E-mail queries only, including a one-page letter with a brief description of your plot, plus the first 10 pages of your novel all pasted into the body of the e-mail. Sorry, unknown attachments will not be opened.

EMMA SWEENEY AGENCY, LLC

245 E 80th St., Suite 7E, New York NY 10075. **E-mail:** queries@emmasweeneyagency.com. **Website:** www. emmasweeneyagency.com. Represents 80 clients. 5% of clients are new/unpublished writers. Currently handles: nonfiction books 50%, novels 50%.

MEMBER AGENTS Emma Sweeney, president; Noah Ballard, agent (represents literary fiction, young adult novel, and narrative nonfiction. Considers nonfiction areas: popular science, pop culture, music history, biography, memoirs, cooking, and anything relating to animals. Considers these fiction areas: literary (of the highest writing quality possible), young adult; eva@ emmasweeneyagency.com); Justine Wenger, junior agent/assistant (justine@emmasweeneyagency.com).

REPRESENTS Nonfiction books, novels.

HOW TO CONTACT Send query letter and first 10 pages in body of e-mail (no attachments) to queries@ emmasweeneyagency.com. No snail mail queries.

TERMS Agent receives 15% commission on domestic sales. Agent receives 10% commission on foreign sales.

TESSLER LITERARY AGENCY, LLC

27 W. 20th St., Suite 1003, New York NY 10011. (212)242-0466. **Fax:** (212)242-2366. **Website:** www.tessleragency.com. **Contact:** Michelle Tessler. Currently handles: 90% nonfiction books, 10% novels.

HOW TO CONTACT Submit query through online query form only. Accepts simultaneous submissions. New clients by queries/submissions through the website and recommendations from others.

TERMS Receives 15% commission on domestic sales; 20% on foreign sales. Offers written contract.

WALES LITERARY AGENCY, INC.

P.O. Box 9426, Seattle WA 98109. (206)284-7114. **E-mail:** waleslit@waleslit.com. **Website:** www.waleslit.

com. **Contact:** Elizabeth Wales; Neal Swain. Other memberships include Book Publishers' Northwest, Pacific Northwest Booksellers Association, PEN. Represents 60 clients. 10% of clients are new/unpublished writers. Currently handles: nonfiction books 60%, novels 40%.

HOW TO CONTACT Accepts queries sent with cover letter and SASE, and e-mail queries with no attachments. No phone or fax queries. Guidelines and client list available online. Accepts simultaneous submissions. Responds 2 weeks to queries, 2 months to mss.

TERMS Agent receives 15% commission on domestic sales. Agent receives 20% commission on foreign sales.

TIPS "We are especially interested in work that espouses a progressive cultural or political view, projects a new voice, or simply shares an important, compelling story. We also encourage writers living in the Pacific Northwest, West Coast, Alaska, and Pacific Rim countries, and writers from historically underrepresented groups, such as gay and lesbian writers and writers of color, to submit work (but does not discourage writers outside these areas). Most importantly, whether in fiction or nonfiction, the agency is looking for talented storytellers."

WM CLARK ASSOCIATES

186 Fifth Ave., Second Floor, New York NY 10010. (212)675-2784. **Fax:** (347)-649-9262. **E-mail:** general@wmclark.com. **Website:** www.wmclark.com. Estab. 1997. 50% of clients are new/unpublished writers. Currently handles: nonfiction books 50%, novels 50%.

REPRESENTS Nonfiction books, novels. **Considers these nonfiction areas:** architecture, art, autobiography, biography, cultural interests, current affairs, dance, design, ethnic, film, history, inspirational, memoirs, music, politics, popular culture, religious, science, sociology, technology, theater, translation, travel memoir, Eastern philosophy. **Considers these fiction areas:** contemporary issues, ethnic, historical, literary, mainstream, Southern fiction.

HOW TO CONTACT Accepts queries via online form only at www.wmclark.com/queryguidelines.html. We respond to all queries submitted via this form. Responds in 1-2 months to queries.

TERMS Agent receives 15% commission on domestic sales. Agent receives 20% commission on foreign sales. Offers written contract.

BOOK PUBLISHERS

The markets in this year's Book Publishers section offer opportunities in nearly every area of publishing. Large, commercial houses are here as are their smaller counterparts.

When you have a good list, send for those publishers' catalogs and manuscript guidelines, or check publishers' websites, which often contain catalog listings, manuscript preparation guidelines, current contact names, and other information helpful to prospective authors. You want to use this information to make sure your book idea is in line with a publisher's list but is not a duplicate of something already published.

You should also visit bookstores and libraries to see if the publisher's books are well represented. When you find a couple of books the house has published that are similar to yours, write or call the company to find out who edited those books. This extra bit of research could be the key to getting your proposal to precisely the right editor.

Publishers prefer different methods of submission on first contact. Most like to see a one-page query with SASE, especially for nonfiction. Others will accept a brief proposal package that might include an outline and/or a sample chapter. Some publishers will accept submissions from agents only. Each listing in the Book Publishers section includes specific submission methods, if provided by the publisher. Make sure you read each listing carefully to find out exactly what the publisher wants to receive.

When you write your one-page query, give an overview of your book, mention the intended audience, the competition for your book (check local bookstore shelves), and what sets your book apart from the competition. You should also include any previous publishing experience or special training relevant to the subject of your book. For more on queries, read "Query Letter Clinic."

Personalize your query by addressing the editor individually and mentioning what you know about the company from its catalog or books. Never send a form letter as a query. Try your best to send your query to the appropriate editor. Editors move around all the time, so it's in your best interest to look online or call the publishing house to make sure the editor you are addressing your query to is still employed by that publisher.

AUTHOR-SUBSIDY PUBLISHERS' NOT INCLUDED

Writer's Market is a reference tool to help you sell your writing, and we encourage you to work with publishers that pay a royalty. Subsidy publishing involves paying money to a publishing house to publish a book. The source of the money could be a government, foundation or university grant, or it could be the author of the book. If one of the publishers listed in this book offers you an author-subsidy arrangement (sometimes called "cooperative publishing, co-publishing," or "joint venture"); or asks you to pay for part or all of the cost of any aspect of publishing (editing services, manuscript critiques, printing, advertising, etc.); or asks you to guarantee the purchase of any number of the books yourself, we would like you to inform us of that company's practices immediately.

AARDVARK PRESS

P.O. Box 203, Onrus River Cape Town 7201, South Africa. **Fax:** (27)(86)514-0793. **E-mail:** publish@aardvarkpress.co.za. **Website:** www.aardvarkpress.co.za. Aardvark Press works with authors who are entrepreneurs and leaders and who are willing to take their belief in their message further than the pages of a book. **NONFICTION** Subjects include animals, health, sports, travel, leisure, recreation, young families. "We look at most nonfiction projects. If we can't offer to publish (for a myriad reasons including full lists, subject/genre outside our core focus, etc.), we try to provide advice on where an author might improve a proposal, or submit his or her work." Query via e-mail.

ABBEVILLE FAMILY

Abbeville Press, 137 Varick St., New York NY 10013. (212)366-5585. **Fax:** (212)366-6966. **E-mail:** abbeville@abbeville.com. **Website:** www.abbeville.com. Estab. 1977. "Our list is full for the next several seasons." **Publishes 8 titles/year. 10% of books from first-time authors**

○ *Not accepting unsolicited book proposals at this time.*

FICTION Picture books: animal, anthology, concept, contemporary, fantasy, folktales, health, hi-lo, history, humor, multicultural, nature/environment, poetry, science fiction, special needs, sports, suspense. Average word length 300-1,000 words. Please refer to website for submission policy.

ABC-CLIO

Acquisitions Department, P.O. Box 1911, Santa Barbara CA 93116. (805)968-1911. **Website:** www.abc-clio.com; www.greenwood.com. Estab. 1955. ABC-CLIO is an award-winning publisher of reference titles, academic and general interest books, electronic resources, and books for librarians and other professionals. **Publishes 600 titles/year. 20% of books from first-time authors. 90% from unagented writers. Pays variable royalty on net price.** Accepts simultaneous submissions. Catalog and guidelines available online. Online request form.

IMPRINTS ABC-CLIO; Greenwood Press; Praeger; Linworth and Libraries Unlimited.

NONFICTION Subjects include business, child guidance, education, government, history, humanities, language, music, psychology, religion, social sciences, sociology, sports, women's issues. No memoirs, drama. Query with proposal package, including scope, organization, length of project, whether a complete ms is available or when it will be, CV or rèsumè and SASE.

TIPS "Looking for reference materials and materials for educated general readers. Many of our authors are college professors who have distinguished credentials and who have published research widely in their fields."

HARRY N. ABRAMS, INC.

115 W. 18th St., 6th Floor, New York NY 10011. (212)206-7715. **Fax:** (212)519-1210. **E-mail:** abrams@abramsbooks.com. **Website:** www.abramsbooks.com. **Contact:** Managing editor. Estab. 1951. Publishes hardcover and a few paperback originals. **Publishes 250 titles/year.**

IMPRINTS Stewart, Tabori & Chang and Abrams Appleseed; Abrams Books for Young Readers & Amulet Books.

○ Does not accept unsolicited materials.

NONFICTION Subjects include art, architecture, nature, environment, recreation, outdoor.

FICTION Subjects include young adult. Publishes hardcover and "a few" paperback originals. Averages 150 total titles/year.

TIPS "We are one of the few publishers who publish almost exclusively illustrated books. We consider ourselves the leading publishers of art books and high-quality artwork in the U.S. Once the author has signed a contract to write a book for our firm the author must finish the manuscript to agreed-upon high standards within the schedule agreed upon in the contract."

ABRAMS BOOKS FOR YOUNG READERS

115 W. 18th St., New York NY 10011. **Website:** www.abramsyoungreaders.com.

○ Abrams no longer accepts unsolicited manuscripts or queries. Abrams title *365 Penguins*, by Jean-Luc Fromental, illustrated by Joelle Jolivel, won a Boston Globe-Horn Book Picture Book Honor Award in 2007. *Abrams also publishes Laurent De Brunhoff, Graeme Base, and Laura Numeroff, among others.*

ACADEMY CHICAGO PUBLISHERS

363 W. Erie St., Suite 4W, Chicago IL 60654. (312)751-7300. **Fax:** (312)751-7306. **E-mail:** zhanna@academychicago.com. **Website:** www.academychicago.com. **Contact:** Zhanna Vaynberg, managing editor. Estab. 1975. Publishes hardcover and some paperback originals and trade paperback reprints. "We publish qual-

ity fiction and nonfiction. Our audience is literate and discriminating. No novelized biography, history, or science fiction." No electronic submissions. **Publishes 10 titles/year. Pays 7-10% royalty on wholesale price.** Publishes book 18 months after acceptance of ms. Responds in 3 months. Book catalog available online. Guidelines available online.

NONFICTION Subjects include history, travel. No religion, cookbooks, or self-help. Submit proposal package, outline, bio, 3 sample chapters.

FICTION Subjects include historical, mainstream, contemporary, military, war, mystery. "We look for quality work, but we do not publish experimental, avant garde, horror, science fiction, thrillers novels." Submit proposal package, synopsis, 3 sample chapters.

TIPS "At the moment, we are looking for good nonfiction; we certainly want excellent original fiction, but we are swamped. No fax queries, no disks. No electronic submissions. We are always interested in reprinting good out-of-print books."

⊕⊘ ACE SCIENCE FICTION AND FANTASY

Imprint of the Berkley Publishing Group, Penguin Group (USA), Inc., 375 Hudson St., New York NY 10014. (212)366-2000. **Website:** www.penguin.com. **Contact:** Ginjer Buchanan, editor-in-chief. Editorial Director: Susan Allison. Estab. 1953. Publishes hardcover, paperback, and trade paperback originals and reprints. Ace publishes science fiction and fantasy exclusively. **Publishes 75 titles/year. Pays royalty. Pays advance.**

◑ As imprint of Penguin, Ace is not open to unsolicited submissions.

FICTION Subjects include fantasy, science fiction. No other genre accepted. No short stories. Due to the high volume of manuscripts received, most Penguin Group (USA) Inc. imprints do not normally accept unsolicited manuscripts. Query first with SASE. Editors will not respond unless interested.

RECENT TITLE(S) *Od Magic*, by Patricia A. McKillip; *Accelerando*, by Charles Stross.

ADAMS-BLAKE PUBLISHING

8041 Sierra St. #321, Fair Oaks CA 95628. (916)962-9296. **Website:** www.adams-blake.com. **Contact:** Monica Blane, acquisitions editor. Estab. 1992. Publishes only e-books. "We are getting away from doing trade titles and are doing more short-run/high-priced specialized publications targeted to corporations, law,

medicine, engineering, computers, etc." **Publishes 5 titles/year. 50 queries received/year. 15 mss received/year. 80% of books from first-time authors. 99% from unagented writers. Pays 15% royalty on wholesale price.** Publishes book 2 months after acceptance. Accepts simultaneous submissions. Responds in 2 months.

NONFICTION Subjects include business, economics, computers, electronics, counseling, career guidance, labor, money, finance. "We like titles in sales and marketing, but which are targeted to a specific industry. We don't look for retail trade titles but more to special markets where we sell 10,000 copies to a company to give to their employees." Query. Does not review artwork/photos.

TIPS "If you have a book that a large company might buy and give away at sales meetings, send us a query. We like books on sales, especially in specific industries—Like 'How to Sell Annuities' or 'How to Sell High-Tech.' We look for the title that a company will buy several thousand copies of at a time. We often "personalize" for the company. We especially like short books, 50,000 words (more or less)."

ADAMS MEDIA

Division of F+W Media, Inc., 57 Littlefield St., Avon MA 02322. (508)427-7100. **Fax:** (800)872-5628. **E-mail:** AdamsMediaSubmissions@fwmedia.com. **Website:** www.adamsmedia.com. **Contact:** Lisa Laing; Brendan O'Neill; Victoria Sandbrook; Ross Weisman; Halli Melnitsky. Estab. 1980. Publishes hardcover originals, trade paperback, eBook originals and reprints. Adams Media publishes commercial nonfiction, including self-help, women's issues, pop psychology, relationships, business, careers, pets, parenting, New Age, gift books, cookbooks, how-to, reference, and humor. Does not return unsolicited materials. **Publishes more than 250 books and eBooks/year titles/year. 5,000 queries received/year. 1,500 mss received/year. 40% of books from first-time authors. Pays standard royalty or makes outright purchase. Pays variable advance.** Publishes book 12-18 months after acceptance. Accepts simultaneous submissions. Responds in 3 months to queries. Guidelines available online.

RECENT TITLE(S) *Dude, You're Gonna Be a Dad!, The Everything Juicing Book, The Unofficial Harry*

Potter Cookbook, Fake Science 101, 201 Organic Baby Purees.

ADDICUS BOOKS, INC.

P.O. Box 45327, Omaha NE 68145. (402)330-7493. **Fax:** (402)330-1707. **E-mail:** info@addicusbooks. com. **Website:** www.addicusbooks.com. Estab. 1994. Addicus Books, Inc. seeks mss with strong national or regional appeal. "We are dedicated to producing high-quality nonfiction books. Our focus is on consumer health titles, but we will consider other topics. In addition to working with a master book distributor, IPG Books of Chicago, which delivers books to stores and libraries, we continually seek special sales channels, outside traditional bookstores." **Publishes 10 titles/year. 90% of books from first-time authors. 95% from unagented writers.** Publishes ms 9 months after acceptance. Responds in 1 month to proposals. Catalog and guidelines available on website.

○ "Due to the amount of queries we receive our editors are not available for phone inquiries. If we're interested in taking a closer look at your book, we'll contact you after we receive your inquiry."

NONFICTION Subjects include business, economics, consumer health, investing. "We are expanding our line of consumer health titles. Query with a brief e-mail. Tell us what your book is about, who the audience is, and how that audience would be reached. If we are interested, we may ask for a proposal, outlining the nature of your work. See proposal guidelines on our website. Do not send entire ms unless requested. When querying electronically, send only 1-page e-mail, giving an overview of your book and its market Please do not send hard copies by certified mail or return receipt requested. Additional submission guidelines online."

RECENT TITLE(S) *Macular Degeneration—from Diagnosis to Treatment,* by David Boyer, M.D., and Homayoun Tabandeh, M.D.; *Lung Cancer—A Guide to Diagnosis and Treatment,* by Walter Scott, M.D.

TIPS "We are looking for compact, concise books on consumer health topics."

AERONAUTICAL PUBLISHERS

1 Oakglade Circle, Hummelstown PA 17036-9525. (717)566-0468. **Fax:** (717)566-6423. **E-mail:** info@ possibilitypress.com. **Website:** www.aeronautical-publishers.com. **Contact:** Mike Markowski, publisher. Estab. 1981. Publishes trade paperback originals.

"Our mission is to help people learn more about aviation and model aviation through the written word." **Pays variable royalty.** Responds in 2 months to queries. Guidelines available online.

IMPRINTS American Aeronautical Archives, Aviation Publishers, Aeronautical Publishers.

NONFICTION Subjects include history, aviation, hobbies, recreation, radio control, free flight, indoor models, micro radio control, home-built aircraft, ultralights, and hang gliders. Prefers submission by mail. Include SASE. See guidelines online. Reviews artwork/photos. Do not send originals.

RECENT TITLE(S) *Flying Models,* by Don Ross; *Those Magnificent Fast Flying Machines,* by C.B. Hayward.

TIPS "Our focus is on books of short to medium length that will serve the emerging needs of the hobby. We also want to help youth get started, while enhancing everyone's enjoyment of the hobby. We are looking for authors who are passionate about the hobby, and will champion their book and the messages of their books, supported by efforts at promoting and selling their books."

AHSAHTA PRESS

MFA Program in Creative Writing, Boise State University, 1910 University Dr., MS 1525, Boise ID 83725. (208)426-4210. **E-mail:** ahsahta@boisestate.edu. **E-mail:** jholmes@boisestate.edu. **Website:** ahsahtapress. boisestate.edu. **Contact:** Janet Holmes, director. Estab. 1974. Publishes trade paperback originals. **Publishes 7 titles/year. 800 mss received/year. 15% of books from first-time authors. 100% from unagented writers. Pays 8% royalty on retail price.** Publishes ms 2 years after acceptance. Accepts simultaneous submissions. Responds in 3 months to mss. Book catalog available online.

POETRY "We are booked years in advance and are not currently reading manuscripts, with the exception of the Sawtooth Poetry Prize competition, from which we publish 2-3 mss per year." Open readings during May beginning in 2013. Submit complete ms. Considers multiple and simultaneous submissions. Reading period is temporarily suspended due to backlog, but the press publishes runners-up as well as winners of the Sawtooth Poetry Prize. Forthcoming, new, and backlist titles available on website. Most backlist titles: $9.95; most current titles: $18.

RECENT TITLE(S) *Counterpart*, by Elizabeth Robinson; *Chinoiserie*, by Karen Rigby; *Pleasure*, by Brian Teare; *Obedience*, by Chris Vitiello.

TIPS "Ahsahta's motto is that poetry is art, so our readers tend to come to us for the unexpected—poetry that makes them think, reflect, and even do something they haven't done before."

⊘ ALADDIN

Simon & Schuster, 1230 Ave. of the Americas, 4th Floor, New York NY 10020. (212)698-7000. **Website:** www.simonsays.com. **Contact:** Acquisitions Editor. Publishes hardcover/paperback imprints of Simon & Schuster Children's Publishing Children's Division. Aladdin publishes picture books, beginning readers, chapter books, middle grade and tween fiction and nonfiction, and graphic novels and nonfiction in hardcover and paperback, with an emphasis on commercial, kid-friendly titles.

FICTION Simon & Schuster does not review, retain or return unsolicited materials or artwork. "We suggest prospective authors and illustrators submit their mss through a professional literary agent."

ALLWORTH PRESS

An imprint of Skyhorse Publishing, 307 West 36th St., 11th Floor, New York NY 10018. (212)643-6816. **Fax:** (212)643-6819. **Website:** www.allworth.com. **Contact:** Bob Porter, associate publisher; Tad Crawford, publisher. Estab. 1989. Publishes hardcover and trade paperback originals. "Allworth Press publishes business and self-help information for artists, designers, photographers, authors and film and performing artists, as well as books about business, money and the law for the general public. The press also publishes the best of classic and contemporary writing in art and graphic design. Currently emphasizing photography, graphic & industrial design, performing arts, fine arts and crafts, et al." **Publishes 12-18 titles/year. Pays advance.** Responds in 4-6 weeks. Book catalog and ms guidelines free.

NONFICTION Subjects include art, architecture, business, economics, film, cinema, stage, music, dance, photography, film, television, graphic design, performing arts, as well as business and legal guides for the public. "We are currently accepting query letters for practical, legal, and technique books targeted to professionals in the arts, including designers, graphic and fine artists, craftspeople, photographers, and those involved in film and the performing arts." Query with 1-2 page synopsis, chapter outline, market analysis, sample chapter, bio, SASE.

TIPS "We are helping creative people in the arts by giving them practical advice about business and success."

ALONDRA PRESS, LLC

4119 Wildacres Dr., Houston TX 77072. **E-mail:** lark@alondrapress.com. **Website:** www.alondrapress.com. **Contact:** Pennelope Leight, fiction editor; Solomon Tager, nonfiction editor. Estab. 2007. Publishes trade paperback originals and reprints. **Publishes 4 titles/year. 75% of books from first-time authors. 75% from unagented writers.** Publishes book 8 months after acceptance. Accepts simultaneous submissions. Responds in 1 month to queries/proposals; 3 months to mss. Guidelines available online.

NONFICTION Subjects include anthropology, archaeology, history, philosophy, psychology, translation. Submit complete ms.

FICTION Subjects include literary, all fiction genres. "Just send us a few pages in an email attachment, or the entire manuscript. We will look at it quickly and tell you if it interests us."

RECENT TITLE(S) *Nessus the Centaur*, by Henry Hollenbaugh (literary/adventure); *Canyon Chronicles*, by K. Gray Jones (historical fiction); *Spinoza's God*, by Franklin L. Dixon – philosophy.

TIPS "Be sure to read our guidelines before sending a submission. We will not respond to authors who do not observe our simple guidelines. Send your submissions in an e-mail attachment only."

ALPINE PUBLICATIONS

38262 Linman Road, Crawford CO 81415. (970)921-5005. **Fax:** (970)921-5081. **E-mail:** editorial@alpinepub.com. **Website:** alpinepub.com. **Contact:** Ms. B.J. McKinney, publisher. Estab. 1975. Publishes hardcover and trade paperback originals and reprints. **Publishes 6-10 titles/year. 40% of books from first-time authors. 95% from unagented writers. Pays 8-15% royalty on wholesale price. Pays advance.** Publishes ms 18 months after acceptance. Accepts simultaneous submissions. Responds in 1 month. Book catalog available free. Guidelines available online.

IMPRINTS Blue Ribbon Books.

NONFICTION Subjects include animals. Alpine specializes in books that promote the enjoyment of and responsibility for companion animals with emphasis on dogs and horses. No biographies. Query with a brief synopsis, chapter outline, bio, 1-3 sample chapters, and market analysis.

TIPS "Our audience is pet owners, breeders, exhibitors, veterinarians, animal trainers, animal care specialists, and judges. Our books are in-depth and most are heavily illustrated. Look up some of our titles before you submit. See what is unique about our books. Write your proposal to suit our guidelines."

⟳ THE ALTHOUSE PRESS

University of Western Ontario, Faculty of Education, 1137 Western Rd., London ON N6G 1G7, Canada. (519)661-2096. **Fax:** (519)661-3714. **E-mail:** press@uwo.ca. **Website:** www.edu.uwo.ca/althousepress. **Contact:** Katherine Butson, editorial assistant. Publishes trade paperback originals and reprints. "The Althouse Press publishes both scholarly research monographs in education and professional books and materials for educators in elementary schools, secondary schools, and faculties of education. De-emphasizing curricular or instructional materials intended for use by elementary or secondary school students." **Publishes 1-5 titles/year. 50-100 queries received/year. 14 mss received/year. 50% of books from first-time authors. 100% from unagented writers. Pays $300 advance.** Publishes ms 18 months after acceptance. Accepts simultaneous submissions. Responds in 1-2 months to queries; 4 months to mss. Book catalog available free. Guidelines available online.

NONFICTION Subjects include education, scholarly. "Do not send incomplete manuscripts that are only marginally appropriate to our market and limited mandate." Reviews artwork/photos. Send photocopies.

RECENT TITLE(S) *Pedagogy in Motion: A Community of Inquiry for Human Movement Students*, edited by Ellen Singleton and Aniko Varpalotai.

TIPS "Audience is practicing teachers and graduate education students."

AMACOM BOOKS

American Management Association, 1601 Broadway, New York NY 10019. (212)586-8100. **Fax:** (212)903-8168. **E-mail:** cparisi@amanet.org; ekadin@amanet.org; rnirkind@amanet.org. **Website:** www.amacombooks.org. **Contact:** Ellen Kadin, executive editor (marketing, career, personal development); Robert Nirkind, senior editor (sales, customer service, project management, finance); Christina Parisi, executive editor (human resources, leadership, training, management). Estab. 1923. Publishes hardcover and trade paperback originals, professional books. AMACOM is the publishing arm of the American Management Association, the world's largest training organization for managers and their organizations—advancing the skills of individuals to drive business success. AMACOM's books are intended to enhance readers' personal and professional growth, and to help readers meet the challenges of the future by conveying emerging trends and cutting-edge thinking.

NONFICTION Subjects include all business topics. Publishes books for consumer and professional markets, including general business, management, strategic planning, human resources, manufacturing, project management, training, finance, sales, marketing, customer service, career, technology applications, history, real estate, parenting, communications and biography. Submit proposals including brief book description and rationale, TOC, author bio and platform, intended audience, competing books and sample chapters. Proposals returned with SASE only.

TIPS "A proposal is usually between 10 and 20 pages in length."

AMADEUS PRESS

Hal Leonard Publishing Group, 33 Plymouth St., Suite 302, Montclair NJ 07402. (973)337-5034. **Fax:** (973)337-5227. **E-mail:** jcerullo@halleonard.com. **Website:** www.amadeuspress.com. **Contact:** John Cerullo, publisher.

NONFICTION "Amadeus Press welcomes submissions pertaining to classical and traditional music and opera. Send proposal including: a letter describing the purpose and audience for your book, along with your background and qualifications; please indicate which word-processing software you use as we ask that final ms be submitted on disk; an outline or table of contents and an estimate of the length of the completed ms in numbers of words or double-spaced pages; a sample chapter or two, printed out (no electronic file transfers, please); sample illustrations as well as an estimate of the total numbers and types (for example, pen-and-ink artwork for line drawings, black-and-white glossy photographic prints, camera-ready music examples) of illustrations planned for your book; your schedule to complete the book. Generally, we ask authors to submit book proposals early in the writing process as this allows us to give editorial advice during the development phase and cuts down the amount of revisions needed later. Due to the large volume of submissions, you may not receive a response from us. If you wish to have the materials you submit returned to you, please so indicate and include return postage."

AMERICAN BAR ASSOCIATION PUBLISHING

321 N. Clark St., Chicago IL 60654. (312)988-5000. **Fax:** (312)988-6030. **Website:** www.ababooks.org. **Contact:** Tim Brandhorst, director of new product development. Estab. 1878. Publishes hardcover and trade paperback originals. "We are interested in books that help lawyers practice law more effectively, whether it's how to handle clients, structure a real estate deal, or take an antitrust case to court." **Publishes 100 titles/year. 50 queries received/year. 20% of books from first-time authors. 95% from unagented writers.** Publishes ms 6 months after acceptance. Accepts simultaneous submissions. Responds in 1 month to queries and proposals; 3 months to mss. Book catalog and ms guidelines online.

NONFICTION Subjects include business, economics, computers, electronics, money, finance, software, legal practice. "Our market is not, generally, the public. Books need to be targeted to lawyers who are seeking solutions to their practice problems. We rarely publish scholarly treatises." All areas of legal practice. Query with SASE.

RECENT TITLE(S) *Model Rules of Professional Conduct, 2009 Ed.; How Brain Science Can Make You a Better Lawyer* by David A. Sousa; *McElhaney's Trial Notebook; The Creative Lawyer: A Practical Guide to Authentic Satisfaction*, by Michael F. Melcher

TIPS "ABA books are written for practicing lawyers. The most successful books have a practical, reader-friendly voice. Features like checklists, exhibits, sample contracts, and flow charts are preferred. The Association also publishes over 80 major national periodicals in a variety of legal areas. Contact Tim Brandhorst, Director of New Product Development, at the above address with queries."

AMERICAN CARRIAGE HOUSE PUBLISHING

P.O. Box 1130, Nevada City CA 95959. (530)432-8860. **Fax:** (530)432-7379. **Website:** www.americancarriagehousepublishing.com. **Contact:** Lynn Taylor, editor (parenting, reference, child, women). Estab. 2004. Publishes trade paperback and electronic originals.

Publishes 10 titles/year. 10% of books from first-time authors. 100% from unagented writers. Pays outright purchase of $300-3,000. Publishes ms 1 year after acceptance. Accepts simultaneous submissions. Responds in 3 months. Catalog free on request.

NONFICTION Subjects include child guidance, education, parenting, womens issues, womens studies, young adult. Query with SASE. Reviews artwork/photos. Send photocopies.

FICTION Subjects include religious, spiritual, young adult. Query with SASE.

POETRY Wholesome poetry.

TIPS "We are looking for proposals, both fiction and nonfiction, preferably wholesome topics."

AMERICAN CATHOLIC PRESS

16565 S. State St., South Holland IL 60473. (312)331-5845. **Fax:** (708)331-5484. **E-mail:** acp@acpress.org. **Website:** www.acpress.org. **Contact:** Rev. Michael Gilligan, PhD, editorial director. Estab. 1967. Publishes hardcover originals and hardcover and paperback reprints. **Publishes 4 titles/year. Makes outright purchase of $25-100.** Guidelines available online.

NONFICTION Subjects include education, music, dance, religion, spirituality. "We publish books on the Roman Catholic liturgy—for the most part, books on religious music and educational books and pamphlets. We also publish religious songs for church use, including Psalms, as well as choral and instrumental arrangements. We are interested in new music, meant for use in church services. Books, or even pamphlets, on the Roman Catholic Mass are especially welcome. We have no interest in secular topics and are not interested in religious poetry of any kind."

TIPS "Most of our sales are by direct mail, although we do work through retail outlets."

AMERICAN CHEMICAL SOCIETY

Publications/Books Division, 1155 16th St. NW, Washington DC 20036. (202)452-2120. **Fax:** (202)452-8913. **Website:** pubs.acs.org/books/. **Contact:** Bob Hauserman, acquisitions editor. Estab. 1876. Publishes hardcover originals. American Chemical Society publishes symposium-based books for chemistry. **Publishes 35 titles/year. Pays royalty.** Accepts simultaneous submissions. Responds in 2 months to proposals. Book catalog available free. Guidelines available online.

NONFICTION Subjects include science. Emphasis is on meeting-based books. Log in to submission site online.

AMERICAN CORRECTIONAL ASSOCIATION

206 N. Washington St., Suite 200, Alexandria VA 22314. (703)224-0194. **Fax:** (703)224-0179. **E-mail:** aliceh@aca.org; susanc@aca.org; rgibson@aca.org. **Website:** www.aca.org. **Contact:** Alice Heiserman, manager of publications and research. Estab. 1870. Publishes trade paperback originals. "American Correctional Association provides practical information on jails, prisons, boot camps, probation, parole, community corrections, juvenile facilities and rehabilitation programs, substance abuse programs, and other areas of corrections." **Publishes 18 titles/year. 90% of books from first-time authors. 100% from unagented writers.** Publishes ms 1 year after acceptance. Responds in 4 months to queries. Book catalog available free. Guidelines available online.

NONFICTION "We are looking for practical, how-to texts or training materials written for the corrections profession. We are especially interested in books on management, development of first-line supervisors, and security-threat group/management in prisons." No autobiographies or true-life accounts by current or former inmates or correctional officers, theses, or dissertations. No fiction or poetry. Query with SASE. Reviews artwork/photos.

RECENT TITLE(S) *TRY: Treatment Readiness for Youth at Risk; Changing Criminal Thinking; Decoming a Model Warden.*

TIPS "Authors are professionals in the field of corrections. Our audience is made up of corrections professionals and criminal justice students. No books by inmates or former inmates. This publisher advises out-of-town freelance editors, indexers, and proofreaders to refrain from requesting work from them."

AMERICAN COUNSELING ASSOCIATION

5999 Stevenson Ave., Alexandria VA 22304. (703)823-9800. **Fax:** (703)823-4786. **E-mail:** cbaker@counseling.org. **Website:** www.counseling.org. **Contact:** Carolyn C. Baker, director of publications. Estab. 1952. Publishes paperback originals. "The American Counseling Association is dedicated to promoting public confidence and trust in the counseling profession. We publish scholarly texts for graduate level students and mental health professionals. We do not publish books for the general public." **Publishes 8-10 titles/year. 1% of books from first-time authors. 90% from unagented writers.** Accepts simultaneous submissions. Responds in 1 month to queries. Guidelines available free.

NONFICTION Subjects include education, gay, lesbian, health, multicultural, psychology, religion, sociology, spirituality, women's issues. ACA does not publish self-help books or autobiographies. Query with SASE. Submit proposal package, outline, 2 sample chapters, vitae.

RECENT TITLE(S) *Counseling Around the World; Assessment in Counseling, Fifth Edition; Multicultural Issues in Counseling, Fourth Edition; Casebook for Counseling Lesbian, Gay, Bisexual, and Transgender Persons and Their Families; The Counselor and the Law, Sixth Edition.*

TIPS "Target your market. Your books will not be appropriate for everyone across all disciplines."

AMERICAN FEDERATION OF ASTROLOGERS

6535 S. Rural Rd., Tempe AZ 85283. (480)838-1751. **Fax:** (480)838-8293. **E-mail:** info@astrologers.com. **Website:** www.astrologers.com. Estab. 1938. Publishes trade paperback originals and reprints. American Federation of Astrologers publishes astrology books, calendars, charts, and related aids. **Publishes 10-15 titles/year. 10 queries received/year. 20 mss received/year. 50% of books from first-time authors. 100% from unagented writers. Pays 10% royalty.** Publishes book 10 months after acceptance of ms. Accepts simultaneous submissions. Responds in 6 months to mss. Book catalog available free. Guidelines available on website.

NONFICTION "Our market for beginner books, Sun-sign guides, and similar material is limited and we thus publish very few of these. The ideal word count for a book-length manuscript published by AFA is about 40,000 words, although we will consider manuscripts from 20,000 to 60,000 words." Submit complete ms.

TIPS "AFA welcomes articles for *Today's Astrologer*, our monthly journal for members, on any astrological subject. Most articles are 1,500-3,000 words, but we do accept shorter and longer articles. Follow the guidelines online for book manuscripts. You also can e-mail your article to info@astrologers.com, but any charts or illustrations must be submitted as attachments and not embedded in the body of the e-mail or in an attached document."

⊘ AMERICAN PRESS

60 State St., Suite 700, Boston MA 02109. (617)247-0022. **E-mail:** americanpress@flash.net. **Website:** www.americanpresspublishers.com. **Contact:** Jana Kirk, editor. Estab. 1911. Publishes college textbooks. **Publishes 25 titles/year. 350 queries received/year. 100 mss received/year. 50% of books from first-time authors. 90% from unagented writers. Pays 5-15% royalty on wholesale price.** Publishes book 9 months after acceotance. after acceptance of ms. Responds in 3 months to queries.

◯ "Mss proposals are welcome in all subjects & disciplines."

NONFICTION Subjects include agriculture, anthropology, archeology, art, architecture, business, economics, education, government, politics, health, medicine, history, horticulture, music, dance, psychology, science, sociology, sports. "We prefer that our authors actually teach courses for which the manuscripts are designed." Query, or submit outline with tentative TOC. *No complete mss.*

RECENT TITLE(S) *Athletic Administration 2nd Edition*, by William F. Stier, Jr.; *Fundraising and Promotion for Sport and Recreation Programs 3rd Edition*, by William F. Stier, Jr.; *Sport Biomechanics 7th Edition*, by Joe Bell & Tony Grice; *Integrating Technology into Physical Education and Health 5th Edition*, by Ken Felker; *Web 2.0 Tools for Teachers*, by Ken Felker and Andrew Swift; *Basic Communication Course Annual #24*, edited by Stephen K. Hunt; *Applied Research in Coaching and Athletics Annual #27*, edited by Warren K. Simpson.

AMERICAN QUILTER'S SOCIETY

Schroeder Publishing, P.O. Box 3290, Paducah KY 42002. (270)898-7903. **Fax:** (270)898-1173. **E-mail:** editor@aqsquilt.com. **Website:** www.americanquilter.com. **Contact:** Andi Reynolds, executive book editor (primarily how-to and patterns, but other quilting books sometimes published, including quilt-related fiction). Estab. 1984. Publishes trade paperbacks. "American Quilter's Society publishes how-to and pattern books for quilters (beginners through intermediate skill level). We are not the publisher for non-quilters writing about quilts. We now publish quilt-related craft cozy romance and mystery titles, series only. Humor is good. Graphic depictions and curse words are bad." **Publishes 20-24 titles/year. 100 queries received/year. 60% of books from first-time authors.**

Pays 5% royalty on retail price fir both nonfiction and fiction. Publishes nonfiction ms 9-18 months after acceptance. Fiction published on a different schedule TBD. after acceptance of ms. Responds in 2 months to proposals. Nonfiction proposal guidelines online.

◯ Accepts simultaneous nonfiction submissions. Does not accept simultaneous fiction submissions.

NONFICTION No queries; proposals only. Note: 1 or 2 completed quilt projects must accompany proposal. **FICTION** Submit a synopsis and 2 sample chapters, plus an outline of the next 2 books in the series. **RECENT TITLE(S)** *Liberated Quiltmaking II*, by Gwen Marston; *T-Shirt Quilts Made Easy*, by Martha Deleonardis; *Decorate Your Shoes*, by Annemart Berendse.

AMERICAN WATER WORKS ASSOCIATION

6666 W. Quincy Ave., Denver CO 80235. (303)347-6260. **Fax:** (303)794-7310. **E-mail:** submissions@awwa.org. **Website:** www.awwa.org. **Contact:** David Plank, manager, business and product development. Estab. 1881. Publishes hardcover and trade paperback originals. "AWWA strives to advance and promote the safety and knowledge of drinking water and related issues to all audiences—from kindergarten through post-doctorate." **Publishes 25 titles/year.** Responds in 4 months to queries. Book catalog and ms guidelines free.

NONFICTION Subjects include nature, environment, science, software, drinking water- and wastewater-related topics, operations, treatment, sustainability. Query with SASE. Submit outline, bio, 3 sample chapters. Reviews artwork/photos. Send photocopies.

TIPS "See website to download submission instructions."

AMHERST MEDIA INC.

175 Rano St., Suite 200, Buffalo NY 14207. (716)874-4450. **Fax:** (716)874-4508. **E-mail:** submissions@amherstmedia.com. **Website:** www.amherstmedia.com. **Contact:** Craig Alesse, publisher. Estab. 1974. Publishes trade paperback originals and reprints. Amherst Media publishes how-to photography books. **Publishes 30 titles/year. 60% of books from first-time authors. 90% from unagented writers. Pays 6-8% royalty. Pays advance.** Publishes book 1 year after acceptance. Accepts simultaneous submissions. Responds in 2 months to queries. Book catalog free

and online (catalog@amherstmedia.com). Guidelines free and available online.

NONFICTION Subjects include photography. Looking for well-written and illustrated photo books. Query with outline, 2 sample chapters, and SASE. Reviews artwork/photos.

RECENT TITLE(S) *Minimalist Lighting*, by Kirk Tuck; *Portrait Photographer's Handbook*, by Bill Hurter.

TIPS "Our audience is made up of beginning to advanced photographers. If I were a writer trying to market a book today, I would fill the need of a specific audience and self-edit in a tight manner."

AMIRA PRESS

2721 N. Rosedale St., Baltimore MD 21216, Wales. (704)858-7533. **E-mail:** submissions@amirapress.com. **Website:** www.amirapress.com. **Contact:** Yvette A. Lynn, CEO (any sub genre). Estab. 2007. Format publishes in paperback originals, e-books, POD printing. "We are a small press which publishes sensual and erotic romance. Our slogan is 'Erotic and Sensual Romance. Immerse Yourself.' Our authors and stories are diverse." **Published 30 new writers last year.** Averages 50 fiction titles/year. Member EPIC. Distributes/promotes titles through Amazon, Mobipocket, Fictionwise, BarnesandNoble.com, Target.com, Amirapress.com, AllRomance Ebooks, and Ingrams. **Pays royalties, 8.5% of cover price (print)—30-40% of cover price (e-books).** Publishes ms 1-4 months after acceptance. Accepts simultaneous submissions. Responds in 3 months. Guidelines available online.

FICTION Subjects include erotica. Submit complete ms with cover letter by e mail. "No snail mail." Include estimated word count, heat level, brief bio, list of publishing credits. Accepts unsolicited mss. Sometimes critiques/comments on rejected mss.

TIPS "Please read our submission guidelines thoroughly and follow them when submitting. We do not consider a work until we have all the requested information and the work is presented in the format we outline."

AMULET BOOKS

Abrams Books for Young Readers, 115 W. 18th St., New York NY 10001. **Website:** www.amuletbooks.com. **Contact:** Susan Van Metre, vice president/publisher; Tamar Brazis, editorial director; Cecily Kaiser, publishing director. Estab. 2004. **10% of books from first-time authors.**

○ *Does not accept unsolicited mss or queries.*

FICTION Middle readers: adventure, contemporary, fantasy, history, science fiction, sports. Young adults/teens: adventure, contemporary, fantasy, history, science fiction, sports, suspense. Recently published *Diary of a Wimpy Kid*, by Jeff Kinney; *The Sisters Grimm*, by Michael Buckley (mid-grade series); *ttyl*, by Lauren Miracle (YA novel); *Heart of a Samurai*, by Margi Preus (Newberry Honor Award winner).

ANACUS PRESS

Imprint of Finney Co., 8075 215th St. W, Lakeville MN 55044. (952)469-6699. **Fax:** (952)469-1968. **Website:** www.ecopress.com. **Contact:** Alan Krysan, president (bicycling guides, travel). Publishes trade paperback originals. Anacus Press specializes in bicycling and outdoor recreation publications for book and retail markets. **Publishes variable number of titles/year. Pays 10% royalty on wholesale price.** Responds in 3 months. Book catalog available online.

NONFICTION Subjects include environment, recreation, regional, travel. Query with SASE.

TIPS "Audience is cyclists and armchair adventurers."

ANAPHORA LITERARY PRESS

104 Banff Dr., Apt. 101, Edinboro PA 16412. (814)273-0004. **E-mail:** pennsylvaniajournal@gmail.com. **Website:** www.anaphoraliterary.com. **Contact:** Anna Faktorovich, editor-in-chief (general interest). Estab. 2007. Format publishes in trade paperback originals and reprints; mass market paperback originals and reprints. "In the Winter of 2010, Anaphora began accepting book-length single-author submissions. We are actively seeking single and multiple-author books in fiction (poetry, novels, and short story collections) and nonfiction (academic, legal, business, journals, edited and un-edited dissertations, biographies, and memoirs). E-mail submissions. Profits are split 50/50 with single-author writers. There are no costs to have a book produced by Anaphora. We do not offer any free contributor copies." **Publishes 3 titles/year. 200 queries/year; 100 mss/year 50% of books from first-time authors. 100% from unagented writers. Pays 10-30% royalty on retail price.** "We currently publish journals, which are authored by several people. If we publish a novel or a critical book by a single author, we will share our profits with the author." Publishes 2 months after acceptance. Accepts simultaneous submissions. Responds in 1 month on queries, proposals, and mss. Catalog and guidelines available online at website.

NONFICTION Subjects include communications, contemporary culture, creative nonfiction, education, entertainment, games, government, hobbies, humanities, language, literary criticism, literature, memoirs, multicultural, New Age, philosophy, politics, recreation, regional, travel, women's issues, academic, legal, business, journals, edited and un-edited dissertations. "We are actively seeking quality writing that is original, innovative, enlightening, intellectual and otherwise a pleasure to read. Our primary focus in nonfiction is literary criticism; but, there are many other areas of interest. Send a query letter if you are considering submitting anything in the other fields listed above." Query. Does not review artwork.

FICTION Subjects include adventure, comic books, confession, contemporary, experimental, fantasy, feminist, gothic, historical, humor, literary, mainstream, military, mystery, occult, picture books, plays, poetry, poetry in translation, regional, short story collections, suspense, war. "We are actively seeking submissions at this time. The genre is not as important as the quality of work. You should have a completed full-length ms ready to be emailed or mailed upon request." Looking for single and multiple-author books in fiction (poetry, novels, and short story collections). Query.

POETRY Looking for single and multiple-author books in poetry. Query with 10 sample poems.

TIPS "Our audience is academics, college students and graduates, as well as anybody who loves literature. Regardless of profits, we love publishing great books and we enjoy reading submissions. So, if you are reading this book because you love writing and hope to publish as soon as possible, send a query letter or a submission to us. But, remember—proofread your work (most of our editors are English instructors)."

ANDREWS MCMEEL UNIVERSAL

1130 Walnut St., Kansas City MO 64106. (816)581-7500. **Website:** www.amuniversal.com. **Contact:** Christine Schillig, vice president/editorial director. Estab. 1973. Publishes hardcover and paperback originals. Andrews McMeel publishes general trade books, humor books, miniature gift books, calendars, and stationery products. **Publishes 300 titles/year. Pays royalty on retail price or net receipts. Pays advance.**

NONFICTION Subjects include contemporary culture, general trade, relationships. Also produces gift books. Agented submissions only.

ANHINGA PRESS

P.O. Box 3665, Tallahassee FL 32315. (850)422-1408. **Fax:** (850)442-6323. **E-mail:** info@anhinga.org. **Website:** www.anhinga.org. **Contact:** Rick Campbell, editor. Publishes hardcover and trade paperback originals. Publishes only full-length collections of poetry (60-80 pages). No individual poems or chapbooks. **Publishes 5 titles/year. Pays 10% royalty on retail price. Offers Anhinga Prize of $2,000.** Accepts simultaneous submissions. Responds in 3 months to queries, proposals, and mss. Book catalog and contest for #10 SASE or online. Guidelines available online.

POETRY Query with SASE and 10-page sample (not full ms) by mail. No e-mail queries.

ANNICK PRESS, LTD.

15 Patricia Ave., Toronto ON M2M 1H9, Canada. (416)221-4802. **Fax:** (416)221-8400. **E-mail:** annickpress@annickpress.com. **Website:** www.annickpress.com. **Contact:** Rick Wilks, director; Colleen MacMillan, associate publisher; Sheryl Shapiro, creative director. Publishes picture books, juvenile and YA fiction and nonfiction; specializes in trade books. "Annick Press maintains a commitment to high quality books that entertain and challenge. Our publications share fantasy and stimulate imagination, while encouraging children to trust their judgment and abilities." Publishes 5 picture books/year; 6 young readers/year; 8 middle readers/year; 9 young adult titles/year. **Publishes 25 titles/year. 5,000 queries received/year. 3,000 mss received/year. 20% of books from first-time authors. 80-85% from unagented writers. Pays authors royalty of 5-12% based on retail price. Offers advances (average amount: $3,000). Pays illustrators royalty of 5% minimum.** Publishes a book 2 years after acceptance. Book catalog and guidelines available online.

Does not accept unsolicited mss.

NONFICTION Recently published *Pharaohs and Foot Soldiers: One Hundred Ancient Egyptian Jobs you Might Have Desired or Dreaded*, by Kristin Butcher, illustrations by Martha Newbigging, ages 9-12; *The Bite of the Mango*, by Mariatu Kamara with Susan McClelland, ages 14 and up; *Adventures on the Ancient Silk Road*, by Priscilla Galloway with Dawn Hunter, ages 10 and up; *The Chinese Thought of it: Amazing Inventions and Innovations,* by Ting-xing Ye, ages 9-11. Works with 20 illustrators/year. Illustrations only: Query with samples.

FICTION Publisher of children's books. Publishes hardcover and trade paperback originals. Average print order: 9,000. First novel print order: 7,000. Plans 18 first novels this year. Averages 25 total titles/year. Distributes titles through Firefly Books Ltd. Juvenile, young adult. Recently published *The Apprentice's Masterpiece: A Story of Medieval Spain*, by Melanie Little, ages 12 and up; Chicken, Pig, Cow series, written and illustrated by Ruth Ohi, ages 2-5; Single Voices series, Melanie Little, Editor, ages 14 and up; *Crusades*, by Laura Scandiffio, illustrated by John Mantha, ages 9-11. Not accepting picture books at this time.

RECENT TITLE(S) *Adventures on the Ancient Silk Road* by Priscilla Galloway with Dawn Hunter; a*nd Pharaohs and Foot Soldiers: One Hundred Ancient Egyptian Jobs You Might Have Desired or Dreaded*, by Kristin Butcher, illustrated by Martha Newbigging.

ANVIL PRESS

P.O. Box 3008 MPO, Vancouver BC V6B 3X5, Canada. (604)876-8710. **Fax:** (604)879-2667. **E-mail:** info@anvilpress.com. **Website:** www.anvilpress.com. **Contact:** Brian Kaufman. Estab. 1988. Publishes trade paperback originals. "Anvil Press publishes contemporary adult fiction, poetry, and drama, giving voice to up-and-coming Canadian writers, exploring all literary genres, discovering, nurturing, and promoting new Canadian literary talent. Currently emphasizing urban/suburban themed fiction and poetry, deemphasizing historical novels." **Publishes 8-10 titles/year. 300 queries received/year. 80% of books from first-time authors. 70% from unagented writers. Pays advance.** Publishes book 8 months after acceptance of ms. Accepts simultaneous submissions. Responds in 6 months. Book catalog for 9×12 SAE with 2 first-class stamps. Guidelines available online.

Canadian authors only. No e-mail submissions.

FICTION Subjects include experimental, literary, short story collections. Contemporary, modern literature; no formulaic or genre. Query with SASE.

POETRY "Get our catalog, look at our poetry. We do very little poetry-maybe 1-2 titles per year."

TIPS "Audience is young, informed, educated, aware, with an opinion, culturally active (films, books, the performing arts). No U.S. authors. Research the appropriate publisher for your work."

APA BOOKS

American Psychological Association, 750 First St., NE, Washington DC 20002. (800)374-2721 or (202)336-5500. **Website:** www.apa.org/books. Publishes hardcover and trade paperback originals. Book catalog available online. Guidelines available online.

IMPRINTS Magination Press (children's books).

NONFICTION Subjects include education, gay, lesbian, multicultural, psychology, science, social sciences, sociology, women's issues, women's studies. Submit cv and prospectus with TOC, intended audience, selling points, and outside competition.

TIPS "Our press features scholarly books on empirically supported topics for professionals and students in all areas of psychology."

APPALACHIAN MOUNTAIN CLUB BOOKS

5 Joy St., Boston MA 02108. (617)523-0636. **Fax:** (617)523-0722. **E-mail:** amcbooks@outdoors.org. **Website:** www.outdoors.org. Estab. 1876. Publishes hardcover and trade paperback originals. "AMC Books are written and published by the experts in the Northeast outdoors. Our mission is to publish authoritative, accurate, and easy-to-use books and maps based on AMC's expertise in outdoor recreation, education, and conservation. We are committed to producing books and maps that appeal to novices and day visitors as well as outdoor enthusiasts in our core activity areas of hiking and paddling. By advancing the interest of the public in outdoor recreation and helping our readers to access backcountry trails and waterways, and by using our books to educate the public about safety, conservation, and stewardship, we support AMC's mission of promoting the protection, enjoyment, and wise use of the Northeast outdoors. We work with the best professional writers possible and draw upon the experience of our programs staff and chapter leaders from Maine to Washington, D.C." Accepts simultaneous submissions. Guidelines available online.

NONFICTION Subjects include nature, environment, recreation, regional, Northeast outdoor recreation, literary nonfiction, guidebooks, Maps that are based on our direct work with land managers and our on-the-ground collection of data on trails, natural features, and points of interest. AMC Books also publishes narrative titles related to outdoor recreation, mountaineering, and adventure, often with a historical perspective. "Appalachian Mountain Club publishes hiking guides, paddling guides, nature, conservation, and mountain-subject guides for America's Northeast. We connect recreation to conservation and education." Query with proposal and the first 3 chapters of your ms.

TIPS "Our audience is outdoor recreationists, conservation-minded hikers and canoeists, family outdoor lovers, armchair enthusiasts. Visit our website for proposal submission guidelines and more information."

ARCADE PUBLISHING

Skyhorse Publishing, 307 W. 36th St., 11th Floor, New York NY 10018. (212)643-6816. **Fax:** (212)643-6819. **E-mail:** arcadesubmissions@skyhorsepublishing.com. **Website:** www.arcadepub.com. **Contact:** Acquisitions Editor. Estab. 1988. Publishes hardcover originals, trade paperback reprints. "Arcade prides itself on publishing top-notch literary nonfiction and fiction, with a significant proportion of foreign writers." **Publishes 35 titles/year. 5% of books from first-time authors. Pays royalty on retail price and 10 author's copies. Pays advance.** Publishes book 18 months after acceptance. Responds in 2 months if interested. Book catalog and ms guidelines for #10 SASE.

NONFICTION Subjects include history, memoirs, nature, environment, travel, popular science, current events. Submit proposal with brief query, 1-2 page synopsis, chapter outline, market analysis, sample chapter, bio.

FICTION Subjects include literary, mainstream, contemporary, short story collections, translation. No romance, historical, science fiction. Submit proposal with brief query, 1-2 page synopsis, chapter outline, market analysis, sample chapter, bio.

ARCADIA PUBLISHING

420 Wando Park Blvd., Mt. Pleasant SC 29464. (843)853-2070. **Fax:** (843)853-0044. **E-mail:** publishingnortheast@arcadiapublishing.com; publishingsouth@arcadiapublishing.com; publishingwest@arcadiapublishing.com; publishingmidwest@arcadiapublishing.com; publishingmidatlantic@arcadiapublishing.com; publishingsouthwest@arcadiapublishing.com. **Website:** www.arcadiapublishing.com. Estab. 1993. Publishes trade paperback originals. "Arcadia publishes photographic vintage regional histories. We have more than 3,000 Images of America series in print. We have expanded our California program." **Publishes 600 titles/year. Pays 8% royalty on retail price.** Publishes book 9 months after acceptance. Accepts simultaneous submissions. Book catalog available online. Guidelines available free.

NONFICTION Subjects include history, local, regional. "Arcadia accepts submissions year-round. Our editors seek proposals on local history topics and are able to provide authors with detailed information about our publishing program as well as book proposal submission guidelines. Due to the great demand for titles on local and regional history, we are currently searching for authors to work with us on new photographic history projects. Please contact one of our regional publishing teams if you are interested in submitting a proposal." Specific proposal form to be completed.

TIPS "Writers should know that we only publish history titles. The majority of our books are on a city or region, and contain vintage images with limited text."

ARCHAIA

1680 Vine St., Suite 912, Los Angeles CA 90028. **Website:** www.archaia.com. **Contact:** Mark Smylie, chief creative officer. Use online submission form.

FICTION Looking for graphic novel submissions that include finished art. "Archaia Entertainment, LLC is a multi-award-winning graphic novel publisher with more than 50 renowned publishing brands, including such domestic and international hits as *Artesia, Mouse Guard, The Killer, Gunnerkrigg Court, Awakening, Titanium Rain, Days Missing, Tumor, Syndrome, Okko, The Secret History*, and a line of Jim Henson graphic novels including *Fraggle Rock* and *The Dark Crystal*. Archaia has built an unparalleled reputation for producing meaningful content that perpetually transforms minds, building one of the industry's most visually stunning and eclectic slates of graphic novels. Archaia is the reigning 2010 Graphic Novel Publisher of the Year according to *Ain't It Cool News, Graphic Policy*, and *Comic Related*. Archaia has also successfully emerged as a prolific storyteller in all facets of the entertainment industry, extending its popular brands into film, television, gaming, and branded digital media."

⊕ ARCH ST. PRESS

1485 Valley Forge Rd., Valley Forge PA 19481. (484)823-0120. **E-mail:** contact@archSt.press.org. **E-mail:** development@archSt.press.org. **Website:** www.archSt.press.org. **Contact:** Robert Rimm, managing editor. Estab. 2011. Publishes hardcover, trade paperback, mass market paperback, and electronic originals. **Publishes 4 titles/year. 100 queries received/year. 5 mss received/year. 30% of books from first-**

time authors. **50% from unagented writers. Pays 6-20% royalty on retail price.** Publishes ms 1 year after acceptance. Accepts simultaneous submissions. Responds in 1 month to queries and proposals; 2 months to mss. Book catalog and guidelines available online at website.

◯ *Does not accept fiction or poetry.*

NONFICTION Subjects include architecture, art, business, communications, community, contemporary culture, creative nonfiction, dance, economics, education, environment, finance, government, health, history, humanities, labor, language, law, literary criticism, literature, memoirs, money, multicultural, music, nature, philosophy, social sciences, sociology, spirituality, translation, womens issues, womens studies, world affairs, leadership. Query with SASE. Submit proposal package including outline and 3 sample chapters. Review artwork. Writers should send photocopies.

RECENT TITLE(S) *Genership 1.0*, by David Castro (leadership); *Empathy*, by various authors (social entrepreneurship).

🌑 ARC PUBLICATIONS

Nanholme Mill, Shaw Wood Rd., Todmorden, Lancashire OL14 6DA, England. **E-mail:** editorarcuk@ btinternet.com. **Website:** www.arcpublications.co.uk. **Contact:** John W. Clarke. Estab. 1969. Responds in 6 weeks.

POETRY Publishes "contemporary poetry from new and established writers from the UK and abroad, specializing in the work of world poets writing in English, and the work of overseas poets in translation." Send 16-24 pages of poetry and short cover letter.

A-R EDITIONS, INC.

8551 Research Way, Suite 180, Middleton WI 53562. (608)203-2565. **E-mail:** pamela.whitcomb@areditions. com. **Website:** www.areditions.com. **Contact:** Pamela Whitcomb, managing editor (Recent Researches Series). Estab. 1962. **Publishes 30 titles/year. 40 queries received/year. 30 mss received/year. 75% of books from first-time authors. 100% from unagented writers. Pays royalty or honoraria.** Responds in 1 month to queries; 3 months to proposals; 6 months to mss. Book catalog available online. Guidelines available online.

◯ "A-R Editions publishes modern critical editions of music based on current musicological research. Each edition is devoted to works by a single composer or to a single genre of composition. The contents are chosen for their potential interest to scholars and performers, then prepared for publication according to the standards that govern the making of all reliable, historical editions."

NONFICTION Subjects include computers, electronics, music, dance, software, historical music editions. Computer Music and Digital Audio Series titles deal with issues tied to digital and electronic media, and include both textbooks and handbooks in this area. Query with SASE. Submit outline. "All material submitted in support of a proposal becomes the property of A-R Editions. Please send photocopies of all important documents (retain your originals). We suggest that you send your proposal either with delivery confirmation or by a service that offers package tracking to avoid misdirected packages."

☼ ARSENAL PULP PRESS

#101-211 East Georgia St., Vancouver BC V6A 1Z6, Canada. (604)687-4233. **Fax:** (604)687-4283. **E-mail:** info@arsenalpulp.com. **Website:** www.arsenalpulp. com. **Contact:** Editorial Board. Estab. 1980. Publishes trade paperback originals, and trade paperback reprints. "We are interested in literature that traverses uncharted territories, publishing books that challenge and stimulate and ask probing questions about the world around us. With a staff of five, located in a second-floor office in the historic Vancouver district of Gastown, we publish between 14 and 20 new titles per year, as well as an average of 12 to 15 reprints." **Publishes 14-20 titles/year. 500 queries received/ year. 300 mss received/year. 30% of books from first-time authors. 100% from unagented writers.** Publishes book 1 year after acceptance of ms. Accepts simultaneous submissions. Responds in 2 months to queries. Responds in 4 months to proposals and mss. Book catalog for 9×12 SAE with IRCs or online. Guidelines available online.

IMPRINTS Tillacum Library, Advance Editions.

NONFICTION Subjects include art, architecture, cooking, foods, nutrition, creative nonfiction, ethnic, Canadian, cultural studies, aboriginal issues, gay, health, lesbian, history, cultural, language, literature, multicultural, political/sociological studies, regional studies and guides, in particular for British Columbia, sex, sociology, travel, women's issues, women's studies, youth culture, film, visual art.

Rarely publishes non-Canadian authors. No poetry at this time. "We do not publish children's books." Each submission must include: a synopsis of the work, a chapter by chapter outline for nonfiction, writing credentials, a 50-page excerpt from the ms (*do not send more, it will be a waste of postage; if we like what we see, we'll ask for the rest of the manuscript*), and a marketing analysis. If our editorial board is interested, you will be asked to send the entire manuscript. We do not accept discs or submissions by fax or email, and we do not discuss concepts over the phone. Send submissions to: Editorial Board. Reviews artwork/photos.

FICTION Subjects include ethnic, general, feminist, gay, lesbian, literary, multicultural, short story collections. No children's books or genre fiction, i.e., westerns, romance, horror, mystery, etc. Submit proposal package, outline, clips, 2-3 sample chapters.

ARTE PUBLICO PRESS

University of Houston, 4902 Gulf Fwy, Bldg 19, Rm 100, Houston TX 77204-2004. **Fax:** (713)743-3080. **E-mail:** submapp@mail.uh.edu. **Website:** www.latinoteca.com/arte-publico-press. **Contact:** Nicolas Kanellos, editor. Estab. 1979. Publishes hardcover originals, trade paperback originals and reprints. **Publishes 25-30 titles/year. 1,000 queries received/year. 2,000 mss received/year. 50% of books from first-time authors. 80% from unagented writers. Pays 10% royalty on wholesale price. Provides 20 author's copies; 40% discount on subsequent copies. Pays $1,000-3,000 advance.** Publishes book 2 years. after acceptance of ms. Accepts simultaneous submissions. Responds in 1 month to queries and proposals. Responds in 4 months to mss. Book catalog available free. Guidelines available online.

IMPRINTS Piñata Books.

○ Arte Publico Press is the oldest and largest publisher of Hispanic literature for children and adults in the United States. "We are a showcase for **Hispanic** literary creativity, arts and culture. Our endeavor is to provide a national forum for U.S.-Hispanic literature."

NONFICTION Subjects include ethnic, language, literature, regional, translation, women's issues, women's studies. Hispanic civil rights issues for new series: The Hispanic Civil Rights Series. Submissions made through online submission form.

FICTION Subjects include contemporary, ethnic, literary, mainstream. "Written by U.S.-Hispanics. Submissions made through online submission form.

POETRY Submissions made through online submission form.

RECENT TITLE(S) *Butterflies on Carmen St./Mariposas en la calle Carmen*, by Monica Brown; *El corrido de Dante*, by Eduardo Gonzalez-Viana; *The Lady from Buenos Aires*, by Diane Gonzales Bertrane.

TIPS "Include cover letter in which you 'sell' your book—why should we publish the book, who will want to read it, why does it matter, etc. Use our ms submission online form. Format files accepted are: Word, plain/text, rich/text files. Other formats will not be accepted. Manuscript files cannot be larger than 5MB. Once editors review your ms, you will receive an e-mail with the decision. Revision process could take up to four months."

ASA, AVIATION SUPPLIES & ACADEMICS

7005 132 Place SE, Newcastle WA 98059. (425)235-1500. **E-mail:** feedback@asa2fly.com. **Website:** www.asa2fly.com. "ASA is an industry leader in the development and sales of aviation supplies, publications, and software for pilots, flight instructors, flight engineers and aviation technicians. All ASA products are developed by a team of researchers, authors and editors." Book catalog available free.

NONFICTION Subjects include education. "We are primarily an aviation publisher. Educational books in this area are our specialty; other aviation books will be considered." All subjects must be related to aviation education and training. Query with outline. Send photocopies.

RECENT TITLE(S) *Together We Fly: Voices from the DC-3*, by Julie Boatman Filucci; *Practical Aviation Law, 5th Edition*, by J. Scott Hamilton.

TIPS "Two of our specialty series include ASA's *Focus Series*, and ASA *Aviator's Library*. Books in our *Focus Series* concentrate on single-subject areas of aviation knowledge, curriculum and practice. The *Aviator's Library* is comprised of titles of known and/or classic aviation authors or established instructor/authors in the industry, and other aviation specialty titles."

ASCE PRESS

American Society of Civil Engineers, 1801 Alexander Bell Dr., Reston VA 20191. (703)295-6275. **Fax:** (703)295-6278. **Website:** www.asce.org/pubs. Estab. 1989. "ASCE Press publishes technical volumes that are useful to practicing civil engineers and civil engineering students, as well as allied professionals. We publish books by individual authors and editors to advance the civil engineering profession. Currently emphasizing geotechnical, structural engineering, sustainable engineering and engineering history. De-emphasizing highly specialized areas with narrow scope." **Publishes 10-15 titles/year. 20% of books from first-time authors. 100% from unagented writers.** Guidelines available online.

NONFICTION "We are looking for topics that are useful and instructive to the engineering practitioner." Query with proposal, sample chapters, CV, TOC, and target audience.

TIPS "As a traditional publisher of scientific and technical materials, ASCE Press applies rigorous standards to the expertise, scholarship, readability and attractiveness of its books."

ASHLAND POETRY PRESS

401 College Ave., Ashland OH 44805. (419)289-5957. **Fax:** (419)289-5255. **E-mail:** app@ashland.edu. **Web site:** www.ashland.edu/aupoetry. **Contact:** Sarah M. Wells, managing editor. Estab. 1969. Publishes trade paperback originals. **Publishes 2-3 titles/year. 400 mss received/year in Snyder Prize. 50% of books from first-time authors. 100% from unagented writers. Makes outright purchase of $500-1,000.** Publishes book 10 months after acceptance. Accepts simultaneous submissions. Responds in 1 month to queries; 6 months to mss. Book catalog available online. Guidelines available online.

POETRY "We accept unsolicited manuscripts through the Snyder Prize competition each spring-the deadline is April 30. Judges are mindful of dedication to craftsmanship and thematic integrity."

TIPS "We rarely publish a title submitted off the transom outside of our Snyder Prize competition."

ASM PRESS

Book division for the American Society for Microbiology, 1752 N. St., NW, Washington DC 20036. (202)737-3600. **Fax:** (202)942-9342. **E-mail:** lwilliams@asmusa.org. **Website:** www.asmpress.org. **Contact:** Lindsay Williams, editorial and rights coordinator. Estab. 1899. Publishes hardcover, trade paperback and electronic originals. **Publishes 30 titles/year. 40% of books from first-time authors. 95% from unagented writers. Pays 5-15% royalty on wholesale price. Pays $1,000-10,000 advance.** Publishes book 6-9 months after acceptance. Accepts simultaneous submissions. Responds in 2 months. Book catalog available online. Guidelines available online.

NONFICTION Subjects include agriculture, animals, education, health, medicine, history, horticulture, nature, environment, science, microbiology and related sciences. "Must have bona fide academic credentials in which they are writing." Query with SASE or by email. Submit proposal package, outline, prospectus. Proposals for journal articles must be submitted to the journals department at: journals@asmusa.com. Reviews artwork/photos. Send photocopies.

TIPS "Credentials are most important."

ASTRAGAL PRESS

Finney Company, 8075 215th St. West, Lakeville MN 55044. (866)543-3045. **Fax:** (952)669-1968. **Website:** www.astragalpress.com. Estab. 1983. Publishes trade paperback originals and reprints. "Our primary audience includes those interested in antique tool collecting, metalworking, carriage building, early sciences and early trades, and railroading." Accepts simultaneous submissions. Book catalog and ms guidelines free.

NONFICTION Wants books on early tools, trades & technology, and railroads. Query with SASE. Submit sample chapters, TOC, book overview, illustration descriptions. Submit complete ms.

TIPS "We sell to niche markets. We are happy to work with knowledgeable amateur authors in developing titles."

⚠ ⊘ ATHENEUM BOOKS FOR YOUNG READERS

Simon & Schuster, 1230 Ave. of the Americas, New York NY 10020. **Website:** imprints.simonandschuster.biz/atheneum; www.simonsayskids.com. **Contact:** Caitlyn Dlouhy, editorial director; Justin Chanda, vice president/publisher; Namrata Tripathi, executive editor; Anne Zafian, vice president. Estab. 1960. Publishes hardcover originals. "Atheneum Books for Young Readers publishes books aimed at children, pre-school through high school." Publishes hardcover originals, picture books for young kids, nonfiction for ages 8-12 and novels for middle-grade and young adults. Types of books include biography, historical fiction, history, nonfiction. Publishes 60 titles/year. 100% require freelance illustration.

NONFICTION Subjects include Americana, animals, art, architecture, business, economics, government, politics, health, medicine, history, music, dance, nature, environment, photography, psychology, recreation, religion, science, sociology, sports, travel. Publishes hardcover originals, picture books for young kids, nonfiction for ages 8-12 and novels for middle-grade and young adults. Types of books include biography, historical fiction, history, nonfiction. Publishes 60 titles/year. 100% require freelance illustration.

FICTION Subjects include adventure, ethnic, experimental, fantasy, gothic, historical, horror, humor, mainstream, contemporary, mystery, science fiction, sports, suspense, western, Animal. All in juvenile versions. "We have few specific needs except for books that are fresh, interesting and well written. Fad topics are dangerous, as are works you haven't polished to the best of your ability. We also don't need safety pamphlets, ABC books, coloring books and board books. In writing picture book texts, avoid the coy and 'cutesy,' such as stories about characters with alliterative names."

TIPS "Study our titles."

A.T. PUBLISHING

23 Lily Lake Rd., Highland NY 12528. (845)691-2021. **E-mail:** tjp2@optonline.net. **Contact:** Anthony Prizzia, publisher (education); John Prizzia, publisher. Estab. 2001. Publishes trade paperback originals. **Publishes 1-3 titles/year. 5-10 queries received/year. 100% of books from first-time authors. 100% from unagented writers. Pays 15-25% royalty on retail price. Makes outright purchase of $500-2,500. Pays $500-1,000 advance.** Accepts simultaneous submissions. Responds in 1 month to queries; 2 months to proposals; 4 months to mss.

NONFICTION Subjects include cooking, foods, nutrition, education, recreation, science, sports. Query with SASE. Submit complete ms. Reviews artwork/photos. Send photocopies.

RECENT TITLE(S) *It's Not Just Sauce*, by Tony Prizzia; *Welcome to My Nightmare, Classroom*, by Debra Craig; *Had To Take A Break*, written by Clayton Dorn Coburn, illustrated by Sharon Dorn Gill.

TIPS "Audience is people interested in a variety of topics, general. Submit typed manuscript for consideration, including a SASE for return of ms."

AUTUMN HOUSE PRESS

87½ Westwood St., Pittsburgh PA 15211. (412)381-4261. **E-mail:** info@autumnhouse.org. **Website:** www.autumnhouse.org. **Contact:** Michael Simms, editor-in-chief (fiction). Sharon Dilworth, fiction

editor. Estab. 1998. Hardcover, trade paperback, and electronic originals. Format: acid-free paper; offset printing; perfect and casebound (cloth) bound; sometimes contains illustrations. Average print order: 1,500. Debut novel print order: 1,500. "We are a non-profit literary press specializing in high-quality poetry and fiction. Our editions are beautifully designed and printed, and they are distributed nationally. Approximately one-third of our sales are to college literature and creative writing classes." Member CLMP, AWP, Academy of American Poets. "We distribute our own titles. We do extensive national promotion through ads, web-marketing, reading tours, bookfairs and conferences. We are open to all genres. The quality of writing concerns us, not the genre." You can also learn about our annual Fiction Prize, Poetry Prize and Chapbook Award competitions, as well as our online journal, *Coal Hill Review*. (Please note that Autumn House accepts unsolicited manuscripts *only* through these competitions.) **Publishes 8 titles/year. Receives 1,000 mss/year. 10% of books from first-time authors. 100% from unagented writers. Pays 7% royalty on wholesale price. Pays $0-2,500 advance.** Publishes 9 months after acceptance. Accepts simultaneous submissions. Responds in 1-3 days on queries and proposals; 3 months on mss. Catalog free on request. Guidelines online at website; free on request; or for #10 SASE.

FICTION Subjects include literary. Holds competition/award for short stories, novels, story collections, translations, memoirs, nonfiction. *We ask that all submissions from authors new to Autumn House come through one of our annual contests.* "To identify and publish the best fiction, nonfiction, and poetry manuscripts we can find." Annual. Prize: $2,500 and book publication. Entries should be unpublished. Open to all writers over the age of 18. Length: approx 200-300 pages. Results announced September. Winners notified by mail, by phone, by e-mail. Results made available to entrants with SASE, by fax, by e-mail, on website. Published *New World Order*, by Derek Green (collection of stories) and *Drift and Swerve*, by Samuel Ligon (collection of stories). All submissions come through our annual contests; deadline June 30 each year. See website for official guidelines. Responds to queries in 2 days. Accepts mss only through contest. Never critiques/comments on rejected mss. Responds to mss by August. Questions answered through email at: info@autumnhouse.org. "Submit only through our annual contest. See guidelines online. Submit completed ms. Cover letter should include name, address, phone, e-mail, novel/story title. The mss are judged blind, so please include two cover pages, one with contact information and one without. The competition is tough, so submit only your best work!"

POETRY Since 2003, the annual Autumn House Poetry Contest has awarded publication of a full-length manuscript and $2,500 to the winner. *We ask that all submissions from authors new to Autumn House come through one of our annual contests.* All finalists will be considered for publication. Submit only through our annual contest. See guidelines online.

RECENT TITLE(S) *Drift and Swerve*, by Samuel Ligon; *New World Order*, by Derek Green; *She Heads into the Wilderness*, by Anne Marie Macari; *The Song of the Horse*, by Samuel Hazo; *House Where a Woman*, by Lori Wilson.

TIPS "The competition to publish with Autumn House is very tough. Submit only your best work."

AVALON BOOKS

Thomas Bouregy & Sons, Inc., 1202 Lexington Ave., Suite 283, New York NY 10028. **E-mail:** editorial@avalonbooks.com; avalon@avalonbooks.com; lbrown@avalonbooks.com. **E-mail:** editorial@avalonbooks.com. **Website:** www.avalonbooks.com. **Contact:** Lia Brown, editor. Estab. 1950. Publishes hardcover originals. **Publishes 60 titles/year. Pays 10% royalty. Pays $1,000 advance.** Publishes a book 12-18 months after acceptance. Responds in 2-3 months to queries. Guidelines available online.

FICTION "We publish contemporary romances, historical romances, mysteries and westerns. Time period and setting are the author's preference. The historical romances will maintain the high level of reading expected by our readers. The books shall be wholesome fiction, without graphic sex, violence or strong language. We do accept unagented material. We no longer accept e-mail queries. When submitting, include a query letter, a 2-3 page (and no longer) synopsis of the entire ms, and the first three chapters. All submissions must be typed and double spaced. If we think that your novel might be suitable for our list, we will contact you and request that you submit the entire manuscript. There is no need to send your partial to any specific editor at Avalon. The editors read all the genres that are listed above. Address your letter to: **The Editors**."

TIPS "Avalon Books are geared and marketed for librarians to purchase and distribute."

AVON ROMANCE

Harper Collins Publishers, 10 E. 53 St., New York NY 10022. **E-mail:** info@avonromance.com. **Website:** www.avonromance.com. Estab. 1941. Publishes paperback and digital originals and reprints. "Avon has been publishing award-winning books since 1941. It is recognized for having pioneered the historical romance category and continues to bring the best of commercial literature to the broadest possible audience." **Publishes 400 titles/year.**

FICTION Subjects include historical, literary, mystery, romance, science fiction, young adult. Submit a query and ms via the online submission form at www.avonromance.com/impulse.

AZRO PRESS

PMB 342, 1704 Llano St. B, Santa Fe NM 87505. (505)989-3272. **Fax:** (505)989-3832. **E-mail:** books@azropress.com; azropress@gmail.com. **Website:** www.azropress.com. **Contact:** Gae Elsenhardt. Estab. 1997. **Pays authors royalty of 5-10% based on wholesale price. Pays illustrators by the project ($2,000) or royalty of 5%.** Publishes book 1-2 years after acceptance. Accepts simultaneous submissions. Responds to queries/mss in 3-4 months. Catalog available for #10 SASE and 3 first-class stamps or online.

"We like to publish illustrated children's books by Southwestern authors and illustrators. We are always looking for books with a Southwestern look or theme."

NONFICTION Picture books: animal, geography, history. Young readers: geography, history. Query or submit complete ms.

FICTION Picture books: animal, history, humor, nature/environment. Young readers: adventure, animal, hi-lo, history, humor. Average word length: picture books—1,200; young readers—2,000-2,500. Query or submit complete ms.

RECENT TITLE(S) *Triassic Hall: Building an Exhibit from the Ground Up*, by Jaenet Guggenheim and Dr. Spencer Lucas.

TIPS "We are not currently accepting new manuscripts. Please see our website for acceptance date."

B & H PUBLISHING GROUP

One Lifeway Plaza, Nashville TN 37234. (615)251-2000. **Website:** www.broadmanholman.com.

BACKBEAT BOOKS

Hal Leonard Publishing Group, 33 Plymouth St., Suite 302, Montclair NJ 07042. (800)637-2852. **E-mail:** jcerullo@halleonard.com. **Website:** www.backbeat-books.com. **Contact:** John Cerullo, group publisher. Publishes hardcover and trade paperback originals; trade paperback reprints. **Publishes 24 titles/year.**
NONFICTION Subjects include music (rock & roll), pop culture. Query with TOC, sample chapter, sample illustrations.

THE BACKWATERS PRESS

3502 N. 52nd St., Omaha NE 68104. (402)451-4052. **Website:** www.thebackwaterspress.org. **Contact:** Greg Kosmicki, editor.
POETRY "Only considers submissions to Backwaters Prize. More details on site."

BAEN BOOKS

P.O. Box 1188, Wake Forest NC 27588. (919)570-1640. **Website:** www.baen.com. Estab. 1983. "We publish only science fiction and fantasy. Writers familiar with what we have published in the past will know what sort of material we are most likely to publish in the future: powerful plots with solid scientific and philosophical underpinnings are the sine qua non for consideration for science fiction submissions. As for fantasy, any magical system must be both rigorously coherent and integral to the plot, and overall the work must at least strive for originality." Responds to mss within 12-18 months.
FICTION "Style: Simple is generally better; in our opinion good style, like good breeding, never calls attention to itself. Length: 100,000 - 130,000 words Generally we are uncomfortable with manuscripts under 100,000 words, but if your novel is really wonderful send it along regardless of length. Query letters are not necessary. We prefer to see complete manuscripts accompanied by a synopsis. We prefer not to see simultaneous submissions. Electronic submissions are strongly preferred. *We no longer accept submissions by e-mail.* Send ms by using the submission form at: ftp.baen.com/Slush/submit.aspx. No disks unless requested. Attach ms as a Rich Text Format (.rtf) file. Any other format will not be considered."

BAILIWICK PRESS

309 East Mulberry St., Fort Collins CO 80524. (970) 672-4878. **Fax:** (970) 672-4731. **E-mail:** info@baili-wickpress.com. **Website:** www.bailiwickpress.com. "We're a micro-press that produces books and other products that inspire and tell great stories. Our motto is 'books with something to say.' We are now considering submissions, agented and unagented, for children's and young adult fiction. We're looking for smart, funny, and layered writing that kids will clamor for. Authors who already have a following have a leg up. We are only looking for humorous children's fiction. Please do not submit work for adults. Illustrated fiction is desired but not required. (Illustrators are also invited to send samples.) Make us laugh out loud, ooh and aah, and cry, 'Eureka!' Please read the Aldo Zelnick series to determine if we might be on the same page, then fill out our submission form. Please do not send submissions via snail mail or phone calls. **You must complete the online submission form to be considered.** If, after completing and submitting the form, you also need to send us an e-mail attachment (such as sample illustrations or excerpts of graphics), you may e-mail them to info@bailiwick-press.com." Accepts simultaneous submissions. Responds in 6 months.

⊘ BAKER ACADEMIC

Division of Baker Publishing Group, 6030 E. Fulton Rd., Ada MI 49301. (616)676-9185. **Website:** www.ba-keracademic.com. Estab. 1939. Publishes hardcover and trade paperback originals. **Publishes 50 titles/year. 10% of books from first-time authors. 85% from unagented writers. Pays advance.** Publishes book 1 year after acceptance. Guidelines for #10 SASE.
"Baker Academic publishes religious academic and professional books for students and church leaders. Does not accept unsolicited queries. We will consider unsolicited work only through one of the following Ave.s. Materials sent to our editorial staff through a professional literary agent will be considered. In addition, our staff attends various writers' conferences at which prospective authors can develop relationships with those in the publishing industry."
NONFICTION Subjects include anthropology, archeology, education, psychology, religion, women's issues, women's studies, Biblical studies, Christian doctrine, books for pastors and church leaders, contemporary issues. Agented submissions only.

⊗⊘ BAKER BOOKS

6030 East Fulton Rd., Ada MI 49301. (616)676-9185. **Website:** www.bakerbooks.com. Estab. 1939. Publishes in hardcover and trade paperback originals, and trade paperback reprints. "We will consider unsolicited work only through one of the following Ave.s. Materials sent through a literary agent will be considered. In addition, our staff attends various writers' conferences at which prospective authors can develop relationships with those in the publishing industry." Book catalog for 9½×12½ envelope and 3 first-class stamps. Guidelines online.

○ "Baker Books publishes popular religious nonfiction reference books and professional books for church leaders. Most of our authors and readers are evangelical Christians, and our books are purchased from Christian bookstores, mail-order retailers, and school bookstores. Does not accept unsolicited queries."

NONFICTION Subjects include childe guidance, psychology, religion, women's issues, women's studies, Christian doctrines.

TIPS "We are not interested in historical fiction, romances, science fiction, biblical narratives or spiritual warfare novels. Do not call to 'pass by' your idea."

BALCONY MEDIA, INC.

512 E. Wilson, Suite 213, Glendale CA 91206. (818)956-5313. **E-mail:** ann@balconypress.com. **Contact:** Ann Gray, publisher. Publishes hardcover and trade paperback originals. **Publishes 6-8 titles/year. 75% of books from first-time authors. 90% from unagented writers. Pays 10% royalty on wholesale price.** Accepts simultaneous submissions. Responds in 1 month to queries/proposals; 3 months to mss. Book catalog available online.

○ "We also publish *Form: pioneering design magazine, bi-monthly to the architecture and design professions.* Editor: Alexi Drosu, www.form-mag.net."

NONFICTION Subjects include art, architecture, ethnic, gardening, history, relative to design, art, architecture, and regional. "We are interested in the human side of design as opposed to technical or how-to. We like to think our books will be interesting to the general public who might not otherwise select an architecture or design book." Query by e-mail or letter. Submit outline and 2 sample chapters with introduction, if applicable.

TIPS "Audience consists of architects, designers, and the general public who enjoy those fields. Our books typically cover California subjects, but that is not a restriction. It's always nice when an author has strong ideas about how the book can be effectively marketed. We are not afraid of small niches if a good sales plan can be devised."

BALZER & BRAY

HarperCollins Children's Books, 10 E. 53rd St., New York NY 10022. **Website:** www.harpercollinschildrens.com. Estab. 2008. **Publishes 10 titles/year. Offers advances. Pays illustrators by the project.** Publishes book 18 months after acceptance.

NONFICTION All levels: animal, biography, concept, cooking, history, multicultural, music/dance, nature/environment, science, self-help, social issues, special needs, sports. "We will publish very few nonfiction titles, maybe 1-2 per year." Agented submissions only.

FICTION Picture Books, Young Readers: adventure, animal, anthology, concept, contemporary, fantasy, history, humor, multicultural, nature/environment, poetry, science fiction, special needs, sports, suspense. Middle Readers, Young Adults/Teens: adventure, animal, anthology, contemporary, fantasy, history, humor, multicultural, nature/environment, poetry, science fiction, special needs, sports, suspense. Agented submissions only.

◑ BANCROFT PRESS

P.O. Box 65360, Baltimore MD 21209-9945. (410)358-0658. **Fax:** (410)764-1967. **E-mail:** bruceb@bancroftpress.com;. **Website:** www.bancroftpress.com. **Contact:** Bruce Bortz, editor/publisher (health, investments, politics, history, humor, literary novels, mystery/thrillers, chick lit, young adult). Publishes hardcover and trade paperback originals. "Bancroft Press is a general trade publisher. We publish young adult fiction and adult fiction, as well as occasional nonfiction. Our only mandate is 'books that enlighten.'" **Publishes 4-6 titles/year. Pays 6-8% royalty. Pays various royalties on retail price. Pays $750 advance.** Publishes book up to 3 years after acceptance of ms. Accepts simultaneous submissions. Responds in 6-12 months to queries, proposals and manuscripts. Guidelines available online.

NONFICTION Subjects include business, economics, government, politics, health, medicine, money, finance, regional, sports, women's issues, women's studies, popular culture. "We advise writers to visit the website." All quality books on any subject of interest to the publisher. Submit proposal package, outline, 2 sample chapters, competition/market survey.

FICTION Subjects include ethnic, general, feminist, gay, lesbian, historical, humor, literary, mainstream, contemporary, military, war, mystery, amateur sleuth, cozy, police procedural, private eye/hardboiled, regional, science fiction, hard science fiction/technological, soft/sociological, translation, frontier sage, traditional, young adult, historical, problem novels, series, thrillers. Submit complete ms.

TIPS "We advise writers to visit our website and to be familiar with our previous work. Patience is the number one attribute contributors must have. It takes us a very long time to get through submitted material, because we are such a small company. Also, we only publish 4-6 books per year, so it may take a long time for your optioned book to be published. We like to be able to market our books to be used in schools and in libraries. We prefer fiction that bucks trends and moves in a new direction. We are especially interested in mysteries and humor (especially humorous mysteries)."

⚠⊘ BANTAM BOOKS

Imprint of Random House, Inc., 1745 Broadway, New York NY 10019. (212)782-9000. **Website:** www.randomhouse.com.

◯ *Not seeking mss at this time.*

BARRICADE BOOKS, INC.

185 Bridge Plaza N., Suite 309, Fort Lee NJ 07024. (201)944-7600. **Fax:** (201)917-4951. **Website:** www.barricadebooks.com. **Contact:** Carole Stuart, publisher. Estab. 1991. Publishes hardcover and trade paperback originals, trade paperback reprints. "Barricade Books publishes nonfiction, mostly of the controversial type, and books we can promote with authors who can talk about their topics on radio and television and to the press." **Publishes 12 titles/year. 200 queries received/year. 100 mss received/year. 80% of books from first-time authors. 50% from unagented writers. Pays 10-12% royalty on retail price for hardcover. Pays advance.** Publishes book 18 months after acceptance. Responds in 1 month to queries.

NONFICTION Subjects include business, economics, ethnic, gay, lesbian, government, politics, health, medicine, history, nature, environment, psychology, sociology, true crime. We look for quality nonfiction manuscripts—preferably with a controversial lean. Query with SASE. Submit outline, 1-2 sample chapters. Material will not be returned or responded to without SASE. We do not accept proposals on disk or via e-mail. Reviews artwork/photos. Send photocopies.

TIPS "Do your homework. Visit bookshops to find publishers who are doing the kinds of books you want to write. Always submit to a person—not just 'Editor.'"

BAYLOR UNIVERSITY PRESS

One Bear Place 97363, Waco TX 76798. (254)710-3164; 3522. **Fax:** (254)710-3440. **E-mail:** carey_newman@baylor.edu. **Website:** www.baylorpress.com. **Contact:** Dr. Carey C. Newman, director. Publishes hardcover and trade paperback originals. "We publish contemporary and historical scholarly works about culture, religion, politics, science, and the arts." **Publishes 30 titles/year. Pays 10% royalty on wholesale price.** Publishes ms 1 year after acceptance. Accepts simultaneous submissions. Responds in 2 months to proposals. Guidelines available online.

NONFICTION Submit outline, 1-3 sample chapters.

BAYWOOD PUBLISHING CO., INC.

26 Austin Ave., P.O. Box 337, Amityville NY 11701. (631)691-1270. **Fax:** (631)691-1770. **Website:** www.baywood.com. **Contact:** Stuart Cohen, managing editor. Estab. 1964. "Baywood Publishing publishes original and innovative books in the humanities and social sciences, including areas such as health sciences, gerontology, death and bereavement, psychology, technical communications, and archaeology." **Pays 7-15% royalty on retail price.** Publishes book within 12 months of acceptance. after acceptance of ms. Book catalog and ms guidelines free or online.

NONFICTION Subjects include anthropology, archaeology, computers, electronics, education, health, environment, psychology, sociology, women's issues, gerontology, technical writing, death and bereavement, environmental issues, recreational mathematics, health policy, labor relations, workplace rights. Submit proposal package.

BEARMANOR MEDIA

P.O. Box 1129, Duncan OK 73534. (580)252-3547. **Fax:** (814)690-1559. **E-mail:** books@benohmart.com. **Website:** www.bearmanormedia.com. **Contact:** Ben Ohmart, publisher. Estab. 2000. Publishes trade paperback originals and reprints. **Publishes 70 titles/year. 90% of books from first-time authors. 90% from unagented writers. Negotiable per project. Pays upon acceptance.** Accepts simultaneous submissions. Responds only if interested. Book catalog vailable online, or free with a 9 x 12 SASE submission.

NONFICTION Subjects include old-time radio, voice actors, old movies, classic television. Query with SASE. E-mail queries preferred. Submit proposal package, outline, list of credits on the subject.

TIPS "My readers love the past. Radio, old movies, old television. My own tastes include voice actors and scripts, especially of radio and television no longer available. I prefer books on subjects that haven't previously been covered as full books. It doesn't matter to me if you're a first-time author or have a track record. Just know your subject!"

BEAR STAR PRESS

185 Hollow Oak Dr., Cohasset CA 95973. (530)891-0360. **Website:** www.bearstarpress.com. **Contact:** Beth Spencer, publisher/editor. Estab. 1996. Publishes trade paperback originals. "Bear Star is committed to publishing the best poetry it can attract. Each year it sponsors the Dorothy Brunsman contest, open to poets from Western and Pacific states. From time to time we add to our list other poets from our target area whose work we admire." **Publishes 1-3 titles/year. Pays $1,000, and 25 copies to winner of annual Dorothy Brunsman contest.** Publishes book 9 months after acceptance. Accepts simultaneous submissions. Responds in 2 weeks to queries. Guidelines available online.

FICTION Use our Online form. Mss should be between 50 and 65 pages in length. All work must be original and accompanied by a $20 reading fee. Previously published poems can be included in your ms if you retain the copyright (this is standard).

POETRY Wants well-crafted poems. No restrictions as to form, subject matter, style, or purpose. "Poets should enter our annual book competition. Other books are occasionally solicited by publisher, sometimes from among contestants who didn't win." Query and submit complete ms. Online form.

RECENT TITLE(S) *Keel Bone*, by Maya Khosla; *The Soup of Something Missing*, by Rick Bursky; *Death of a Mexican and Other Poems*, by Manuel Paul Lopez.

TIPS "Send your best work, consider its arrangement. A 'wow' poem early keeps me reading."

BEHRMAN HOUSE INC.

11 Edison Place, Springfield NJ 07081. (973)379-7200. **Fax:** (973)379-7280. Estab. 1921. Publishes books on all aspects of Judaism: history, cultural, textbooks, holidays. "Behrman House publishes quality books of Jewish content—history, Bible, philosophy, holidays, ethics—for children and adults." **12% of books from first-time authors. Pays authors royalty of 3-10% based on retail price or buys ms outright for $1,000-5,000. Offers advance. Pays illustrators by the project (range: $500-5,000).** Publishes book 18 months after acceptance. Accepts simultaneous submissions. Responds in 1 month to queries; 2 months to mss. Book catalog free on request.

NONFICTION All levels: Judaism, Jewish educational textbooks. Average word length: young reader—1,200; middle reader—2,000; young adult—4,000. Recently published *I Kid's Mensch Handbook*, by Scott E. Blumenthal; *Shalom Ivrit 3*, by Nili Ziv. Submit outline/synopsis and sample chapters.

FICTION Submit outline/synopsis and sample chapters.

TIPS Looking for "religious school texts" with Judaic themes or general trade Judaica.

FREDERIC C. BEIL, PUBLISHER, INC.

609 Whitaker St., Savannah GA 31401. (912)233-2446. **Fax:** (912)233-6456. **E-mail:** books@beil.com. **Website:** www.beil.com. **Contact:** Mary Ann Bowman, editor. Estab. 1982. Publishes hardcover originals and reprints. Frederic C. Beil publishes in the fields of history, literature, and biography. **Publishes 13 titles/year. 3,500 queries received/year. 13 mss received/year. 80% of books from first-time authors. 100% from unagented writers. Pays 7.5% royalty on retail price.** Responds in 1 week to queries. Book catalog available free.

IMPRINTS The Sandstone Press; Hypermedia, Inc.

NONFICTION Subjects include art, architecture, history, language, literature, book arts. Query with SASE. Reviews artwork/photos. Send photocopies.

FICTION Subjects include historical, literary, regional, short story collections, translation, biography. Query with SASE.

TIPS "Our objectives are (1) to offer to the reading public carefully selected texts of lasting value; (2) to adhere to high standards in the choice of materials and in bookmaking craftsmanship; (3) to produce books that exemplify good taste in format and design; and (4) to maintain the lowest cost consistent with quality."

BELLEVUE LITERARY PRESS

New York University School of Medicine, Dept. of Medicine, NYU School of Medicine, 550 First Ave., OBV A612, New York NY 10016. (212) 263-7802. E-mail: BLPsubmissions@gmail.com. Website: blpress. org. Estab. 2005. "Publishes literary and authoritative fiction and nonfiction at the nexus of the arts and the sciences, with a special focus on medicine. As our authors explore cultural and historical representations of the human body, illness, and health, they address the impact of scientific and medical practice on the individual and society."

NONFICTION "If you have a completed manuscript, a sample of a manuscript or a proposal that fits our mission as a press feel free to submit it to us by postal mail. Please keep in mind that at this time we are unable to return manuscripts. We will also accept short proposals by email. You may submit them to either Erika Goldman or her assistant Leslie Hodgkins at: leslie.hodgkins@med.nyu.edu."

TIPS "We are a project of New York University's School of Medicine and while our standards reflect NYU's excellence in scholarship, humanistic medicine, and science, our authors need not be affiliated with NYU. We are not a university press and do not receive any funding from NYU. Our publishing operations are financed exclusively by foundation grants, private donors, and book sales revenue."

BENBELLA BOOKS

10300 N. Central Expy., Suite 530, Dallas TX 75231. **Website:** www.benbellabooks.com. **Contact:** Glenn Yeffeth, publisher. Estab. 2001. Publishes hardcover and trade paperback originals. **Publishes 20-25 titles/year. Pays 6-15% royalty on retail price.** Publishes ms 10 months after acceptance. Accepts simultaneous submissions. Guidelines available online.

NONFICTION Subjects include pop contemporary culture, cooking, foods, nutrition, health, medicine, literary criticism, money, finance, science. Submit proposal package, including: outline, 2 sample chapters (via e-mail).

BENDALL BOOKS

P.O. BOX 115, Mill Bay BC V0R2P0, Canada. (250)743-2946. **Fax:** (250)743-2910. **E-mail:** admin@bendallbooks.com. **Website:** www.bendallbooks.com. **Contact:** Mary Moore, publisher. Publishes trade paperback originals. **Publishes 1 titles/year. 30 queries** received/year. 5 mss received/year. 50% of books from first-time authors. 100% from unagented writers. Pays 5-15% royalty on wholesale price. Publishes book 1 year after acceptance. Book catalog available free. Guidelines available online.

NONFICTION Subjects include education.

BENTLEY PUBLISHERS

1734 Massachusetts Ave., Cambridge MA 02138. (617)547-4170. **Fax:** (617)876-9235. **E-mail:** michael. bentley@bentleypublishers.com. **Website:** www.bentleypublishers.com. **Contact:** Michael Bentley, president. Estab. 1950. Publishes hardcover and trade paperback originals and reprints. "Bentley Publishers publishes books for automotive enthusiasts. We are interested in books that showcase good research, strong illustrations, and valuable technical information." Automotive subjects only. Query with SASE. Submit sample chapters, bio, synopsis, target market. Reviews artwork/photos. Book catalog and ms guidelines online.

NONFICTION Subjects include Automotive subjects only. Query with SASE. Submit sample chapters, bio, synopsis, target market. Rreviews artwork/photos.

TIPS "Our audience is composed of serious, intelligent automobile, sports car, and racing enthusiasts, automotive technicians and high-performance tuners."

⬤⊘ BERKLEY BOOKS

Penguin Group (USA) Inc., 375 Hudson St., New York NY 10014. **Website:** us.penguingroup.com/. **Contact:** Leslie Gelbman, president and publisher. Estab. 1955. Publishes paperback and mass market originals and reprints. The Berkley Publishing Group publishes a variety of general nonfiction and fiction including the traditional categories of romance, mystery and science fiction. **Publishes 500 titles/year.**

IMPRINTS Ace; Berkley; Jove.

○ "Due to high volume of manuscripts received, most Penguin imprints do not normally accept unsolicited manuscripts. The preferred method for having manuscripts considered for publication by a major publisher is to submit them through an established literary agent."

NONFICTION Subjects include business, economics, child guidance, creative nonfiction, gay, lesbian, health, medicine, history, New Age, psychology, true crime, job-seeking communication. *Prefers agented submissions.*

FICTION Subjects include adventure, historical, literary, mystery, romance, spiritual, suspense, western, young adult. No occult fiction. *Prefers agented submissions.*

BERRETT-KOEHLER PUBLISHERS, INC.

235 Montgomery St., Suite 650, San Francisco CA 94104. (415)288-0260. **Fax:** (415)362-2512. **E-mail:** bkpub@bkpub.com. **Website:** www.bkconnection.com. **Contact:** Jeevan Sivasubramaniam, senior managing editor. Publishes hardcover & trade paperback originals, mass market paperback originals, hardcover & trade paperback reprints. "Berrett-Koehler Publishers' mission is to publish books that support the movement toward a world that works for all. Our titles promote positive change at personal, organizational and societal levels." Please see proposal guidelines online. **Publishes 40 titles/year. 1,300 queries received/year. 800 mss received/year. 20-30% of books from first-time authors. 70% from unagented writers. Pays 10-20% royalty.** Publishes book 10 months after acceptance. Accepts simultaneous submissions. Responds in 1 month to queries, proposals and mss. Book catalog available online. Guidelines available online.

NONFICTION Subjects include business, economics, community, government, politics, New Age, spirituality. Submit proposal package, outline, bio, 1-2 sample chapters. Hard-copy proposals only. Do not e-mail, fax, or phone please. Reviews artwork/photos. Send photocopies or originals with SASE.

RECENT TITLE(S) *Citizen Wealth*, by Wade Rathke; *The Death of Why*, by Andrea Batista Schlesinger; *Unite and Conquer*, by Kyrsten Sinema; *Alternatives to Globalization*, by Jerry Mander & IFG (current affairs); *Leadership and the New Science*, by Margaret Wheatley (business); *Confessions of an Economic Hit Man*, by John Perkins (*New York Times* bestseller).

TIPS "Our audience is business leaders. Use common sense, do your research."

⊘ BETHANY HOUSE PUBLISHERS

Baker Publishing Group, 6030 E. Fulton Rd., Ada MI 49301. (616)676-9185. **Fax:** (616)676-9573. **Website:** www.bethanyhouse.com. Estab. 1956. Publishes hardcover and trade paperback originals, mass market paperback reprints. Bethany House Publishers specializes in books that communicate Biblical truth and assist people in both spiritual and practical areas of life. While we do not accept unsolicited queries or proposals via telephone or e-mail, we will consider 1-page queries sent by fax and directed to adult nonfiction, adult fiction, or young adult/children. **Publishes 90-100 titles/year. 2% of books from first-time authors. 50% from unagented writers. Pays royalty on net price. Pays advance.** Publishes a book 1 year after acceptance. Accepts simultaneous submissions. Responds in 3 months to queries. Book catalog for 9 x 12 envelope and 5 first-class stamps. Guidelines available online.

◖ *All unsolicited mss returned unopened.*

NONFICTION Subjects include child guidance, Biblical disciplines, personal and corporate renewal, emerging generations, devotional, marriage and family, applied theology, inspirational.

FICTION Subjects include historical, young adult, contemporary.

RECENT TITLE(S) *Under God*, by Toby Mae and Michael Tait (nonfiction); *Candle in the Darkness*, by Lynn Austin (fiction); *God Called a Girl*, by Shannon Kubiak Primicerio (YA nonfiction).

TIPS Bethany House Publishers' publishing program relates Biblical truth to all areas of life—whether in the framework of a well-told story, of a challenging book for spiritual growth, or of a Bible reference work. We are seeking high-quality fiction and nonfiction that will inspire and challenge our audience.

BETTERWAY HOME BOOKS

Imprint of F+W Media, Inc., 10151 Carver Rd., Suite 200, Cincinnati OH 45242. **E-mail:** jacqueline.musser@fwmedia.com. **Website:** www.betterwaybooks.com. **Contact:** Jacqueline Musser, acquisitions editor. Publishes trade paperback and hardcover originals. **Publishes 6-8 titles/year. 6 queries received/year. 60% of books from first-time authors. 95% from unagented writers. Pays 8-10% royalty on wholesale price. Pays $2,500-3,000 advance.** Publishes ms 18 months after acceptance. Accepts simultaneous submissions. Responds in 3 month to queries and proposals.

NONFICTION Subjects include gardening, house and home, home organization, homemaking, simple living, homesteading skills, personal finance. Query with SASE. Submit proposal package, outline, 1 sample chapter. Reviews artwork/photos. Send photocopies and PDFs (if submitting electronically).

RECENT TITLE(S) *Organize Now! Your Money, Business & Career*, by Jennifer Ford Berry; *Little House* *in the Suburbs,* by Deanna Caswell and Daisy Siskin; *Build the Perfect Bug Out Bag,* by Creek Stewart; *Home-Ec 101,* by Heather Solos; *The Easy Organizer,* by Marilyn Bohn.

TIPS "Looking for authors with a strong web following in their book topic."

BICK PUBLISHING HOUSE

16 Marion Rd., Branford CT 06405. Phone/**Fax:** (203)208-5253. **E-mail:** bickpubhse@aol.com. **Website:** www.bickpubhouse.com. **Contact:** Dale Carlson, president. Estab. 1994. Publishes trade paperback originals. Bick Publishing House publishes step-by-step, easy-to-read professional information for the general adult public about physical, psychological, and emotional disabilities or special needs. "The mission of Bick Publishing House for Teens/Young Adults is to relate modern science and its ethics, communications arts, philosophy, psychology to the teenager's world, so they can make their own responsible decisions about their own lives and future. The Life Sciences books in the series are presented with accessible texts, with glossary of terms, illustrations, index, resources, bibliography,websites. The mission of Bick Publishing House for Adults is to bring professional information to the general audience in mental illness and recovery, addictions and recovery, in the art of living with disabilities, and in wildlife rehabilitation." Currently emphasizing science, psychology for teens. **Publishes 4 titles/year. 100 queries received/year; 100 mss received/year. 55% of books from first-time authors. 55% from unagented writers. Pays $500-1,000 advance.** Publishes ms 1 year after acceptance. Responds in 1 month to queries; 2 months to proposals; 3 months to mss. Book catalog available free. Guidelines for #10 SASE.

NONFICTION Subjects include health, medicine, disability/special needs, psychology, young adult or teen science, psychology, wildlife rehabilitation. Query with SASE. Submit proposal package, outline, resumè, 3 sample chapters.

TIPS "Read our books!"

BIOGRAPHICAL PUBLISHING COMPANY

95 Sycamore Dr., Prospect CT 06712-1493. (203)758-3661. **Fax:** (253)793-2618. **E-mail:** biopub@aol.com. **Website:** www.biopub.us. **Contact:** John R. Guevin, editor. Estab. 1991. Hardcover originals & reprints; trade paperback originals & reprints. This is a Paid Services publisher. See website. **Publishes 6 titles/**

year. **Receives 300 queries/year; 25 mss/year. 50% of books from first-time authors. 90% from unagented writers. Pays 90-95% royalty on wholesale price.** Publishes book 4 months. after acceptance of ms. Responds in 1 month on queries, proposals, and mss. Catalog and guidelines free on request.

NONFICTION Subjects include animals, career guidance, child guidance, community, cooking, counseling, education, environment, ethnic, finance, foods, games, gardening, government, health, history, hobbies, house and home, humanities, language, literature, medicine, memoirs, military, money, multicultural, nature, nutrition, politics, psychology, public affairs, recreation, regional, science, social sciences, spirituality. True Query with SASE; submit completed ms. Reviews artwork/photos. Send photocopies.

FICTION Subjects include adventure, contemporary, ethnic, historical, humor, juvenile, literary, mainstream, military, multicultural, mystery, picture books, poetry, regional, religious, romance, science fiction, short story collections, spiritual, sports, suspense, war, western, young adult. Query with SASE; submit completed ms.

POETRY Query; submit complete ms.

BIRCH BOOK PRESS

P.O. Box 81, Delhi NY 13753. **Fax:** (607)746-7453. **E-mail:** birchbrook@copper.net. **Website:** www.birchbrookpress.info. **Contact:** Tom Tolnay, editor/publisher; Barbara dela Cuesta, associate editor. Estab. 1982. Occasionally publishes trade paperback originals. Birch Brook Press "is a letterpress book printer/typesetter/designer that uses monies from these activities to publish several titles of its own each year with cultural and literary interest." Specializes in literary work, flyfishing, baseball, outdoors, theme anthologies, occasional translations of classics, and books about books. Specializes "mostly in anthologies with specific themes." Books are "handset letterpress editions printed in our own shop." Member, Small Press Center, Publishers Marketing Association, Academy of American Poets. Distributes titles through Barnes&Noble.com, Amazon.com, Gazelle Book Services in Europe, Multicultural Books in Canada. Abe Books, and Alibris Books online. Promotes titles through website, catalogs, direct mail and group ads, book fairs. **Publishes 4 titles/year. 200+ queries received/year; 200+ mss received/year. 95% from unagented writers. Pays modest royalty on accep-**

tance. Publishes ms 10-18 months after acceptance. Accepts simultaneous submissions. Responds in 3 to 6 months to mss. Book catalog available online.

NONFICTION Subjects include film, music (rare), nonfiction of cultural interest, including stage, opera, including outdoors.

FICTION , Literary, regional (Adirondacks), popular culture, special interest (flyfishing, baseball, books about books, outdoors). "Mostly we do anthologies around a particular theme generated inhouse. We make specific calls for fiction when we are doing an anthology." Query with SASE or submit sample chapter(s), synopsis.

POETRY Query first with a few sample poems or chapters, or send entire ms. No e-mail submissions; submissions by postal mail only. Must include SASE with submissions. Occasionally comments on rejected poems. Royalty on co-op contracts.

TIPS "Write well on subjects of interest to BBP, such as outdoors, flyfishing, baseball, music, literary stories, fine poetry, and occasional novellas, books about books."

BIRDSONG BOOKS

1322 Bayview Rd., Middletown DE 19709. (302)378-7274. **E-mail:** birdsong@birdsongbooks.com. **Website:** www.BirdsongBooks.com. **Contact:** Nancy Carol Willis, president. Estab. 1998. "Birdsong Books seeks to spark the delight of discovering our wild neighbors and natural habitats. We believe knowledge and understanding of nature fosters caring and a desire to protect the Earth and all living things. Our emphasis is on North American animals and habitats, rather than people." Publishes book 2-3 years after acceptance. Accepts simultaneous submissions. Responds to mss in 3 months.

NONFICTION Picture books, young readers: activity books, animal, nature/environment. Average word length: picture books—800-1,000 plus content for 2-4 pages of back matter. Recently published *The Animals' Winter Sleep*, by Lynda-Graham Barber (age 3-6, nonfiction picture book); *Red Knot: A Shorebird's Incredible Journey*, by Nancy Carol Willis (age 6-9, nonfiction picture book); *Raccoon Moon*, by Nancy Carol Willis (ages 5-8, natural science picture book); *The Robins In Your Backyard*, by Nancy Carol Willis (ages 4-7, nonfiction picture book). Submit complete ms package with SASE.

TIPS "We are a small independent press actively seeking manuscripts that fit our narrowly defined niche. We are only interested in nonfiction, natural science picture books or educational activity books about North American animals and habitats. We are not interested in fiction stories based on actual events. Our books include several pages of back matter suitable for early elementary classrooms. Mailed submissions with SASE only. No e-mail submissions or phone calls, please. Cover letters should sell author/illustrator and book idea."

BKMK PRESS

University of Missouri - Kansas City, 5101 Rockhill Rd., Kansas City MO 64110-2499. (816)235-2558. **Fax:** (816)235-2611. **E-mail:** bkmk@umkc.edu. **Website:** www.umkc.edu/bkmk. **Contact:** Ben Furnish, managing editor. Estab. 1971. Publishes trade paperback originals. "BkMk Press publishes fine literature. Reading period January-June." **Publishes 4/year titles/year.** Accepts simultaneous submissions. Responds in 4-6 months to queries. Guidelines available online.

NONFICTION Creative nonfiction essays. Submit 25-50 pp. sample and SASE.

FICTION Subjects include literary, short story collections. Query with SASE.

POETRY Submit 10 sample poems and SASE.

TIPS "We skew toward readers of literature, particularly contemporary writing. Because of our limited number of titles published per year, we discourage apprentice writers or 'scattershot' submissions."

BLACK DOME PRESS CORP.

649 Delaware Ave., Delmar NY 12054. (518)439-6512. **Fax:** (518)439-1309. **E-mail:** blackdomep@aol.com. **Website:** www.blackdomepress.com. Estab. 1990. Publishes cloth and trade paperback originals and reprints. Accepts simultaneous submissions. Book catalog and guidelines available online.

Do not send the entire work. Mail a cover letter, table of contents, introduction, sample chapter (or two), and your C.V. or brief biography to the Editor. Please do not send computer disks or submit your proposal via e-mail. If your book will include illustrations, please send us copies of sample illustrations. Do not send originals.

NONFICTION Subjects include history, nature, environment, photography, regional, New York state, Native Americans, grand hotels, genealogy, colonial life, French & Indian War (NYS), American Revolution (NYS), quilting, architecture, railroads, hiking and kayaking guidebooks. New York state regional material only. Submit proposal package, outline, bio. **TIPS** "Our audience is comprised of New York state residents, tourists, and visitors."

BLACK HERON PRESS

P.O. Box 13396, Mill Creek WA 98082. **Website:** www.blackheronpress.com. **Contact:** Jerry Gold, publisher. Estab. 1984. Publishes hardcover and trade paperback originals, trade paperback reprints. "Black Heron Press publishes primarily literary fiction." **Publishes 4 titles/year. 1,500 queries received/year. 50% of books from first-time authors. 90% from unagented writers. Pays 8% royalty on retail price.** Publishes ms 2 years after acceptance. Accepts simultaneous submissions. Responds in 6 months to queries and mss. Catalog available online and for 6" x 9" SAE with 3 first-class stamps. Guidelines available for #10 SASE.

NONFICTION Subjects include military, war. Submit proposal package, include cover letter & first 30-50 pages of your completed novel. "We do not review artwork."

FICTION Subjects include confession, erotica, literary (regardless of genre), military, war, sci-fi, young adult, Some science fiction—not fantasy, not Dungeons & Dragons—that makes or implies a social statement. "All of our fiction is character driven. We don't want to see fiction written for the mass market. If it sells to the mass market, fine, but we don't see ourselves as a commercial press." Submit proposal package, including cover letter & first 40-50 pages pages of your completed novel.

TIPS "Our Readers love good fiction—they are scattered among all social classes, ethnic groups, and zip code areas. If you can't read our books, at least check out our titles on our website."

BLACK LAWRENCE PRESS

326 Bingham St., Pittsburgh PA 15211. **E-mail:** editors@blacklawrencepress.com. **Website:** www.blacklawrencepress.com. **Contact:** Diane Goettel, executive editor. Estab. 2003. Black Lawrence press seeks to publish intriguing books of literature—novels, short story collections, poetry collections, chapbooks, anthologies, and creative nonfiction. Will also publish the occasional translation from German. Has published books by Mary Biddinger, Marc McKee, Patrick Michael Finn, David Rigsbee, Laura McCullough,

Adam Prince, Charlotte Pence, and T.J. Beitelman. Publishes 15-20 books/year, mostly poetry and fiction. Manuscripts are selected through open submission and competition. Books are 20-400 pages, offset-printed or high-quality POD, perfect-bound, with 4-color cover. **Accepts submissions during the months of June and November. Pays royalties.** Responds in 6 months to mss.

⊕ BLACK MOUNTAIN PRESS

P.O. Box 9907, Asheville NC 28815. (828)273-3332. **E-mail:** jackmoe@theBlackMountainPress.com. **Website:** www.theBlackMountainPress.com. **Contact:** Jack Moe, editor (how-to, poetry); James Robiningski (short story collections, novels). Estab. 1994. Publishes hardcover, trade paperback, and electronic originals. **Publishes 4 titles/year. 150 mss received/year. 90% of books from first-time authors. 100% from unagented writers. Pays 5-10% royalty on retail price. Pays $100-500 advance.** Publishes ms 5 months after acceptance. Accepts simultaneous submissions. Responds in 4-6 months to mss. Book catalog and ms guidelines available online at website.

NONFICTION Subjects include architecture, art, language, literature, sports. "We are concentrating more on literary projects for the next 2 years." Submit complete ms. Reviews artwork. Send digital photos only on CD or DVD.

FICTION Subjects include comic books, experimental, literary, poetry, poetry in translation, short story collections, graphic novels. "Creative literary fiction and poetry or collection of short stories are wanted for the next few years." Submit complete ms.

POETRY Submit complete ms.

TIPS "Don't be afraid of sending your anti-government, anti-religion, anti-art, anti-literature, experimental, avant-garde efforts here. But don't send your work before it's fully cooked, we do, however, enjoy fresh, natural, and sometimes even raw material, just don't send in anything that is "glowing" unless it was savaged from a FoxNews book-burning event."

⊕ BLACK OCEAN

P.O. Box 52030, Boston MA 02205. **Fax:** (617)849-5678. **E-mail:** carrie@blackocean.org. **Website:** www.blackocean.org. **Contact:** Carrie Olivia Adams, poetry editor. Estab. 2006. **Publishes 3 titles/year.** Responds in 6 months to mss.

POETRY Wants poetry that is well-considered, risks itself, and by its beauty and/or bravery disturbs a tiny corner of the universe. Manuscripts are selected through open submission. Books are 60+ pages. Book/chapbook mss may include previously published poems. We have an open submission period in May of each year; specific guidelines are updated and posted on our website in the months preceding.

BLACK ROSE WRITING

P.O. Box 1540, Castroville TX 78009. **E-mail:** creator@blackrosewriting.com. **Website:** www.blackrosewriting.com. **Contact:** Reagan Rothe. Estab. 2006. Publishes majority trade paperback, occasional hard cover or children's book. "We publish only one genre—our genre." Black Rose Writing is an independent publishing house that believes in developing a personal relationship with our authors. We don't see them as clients or just another number on a page, but rather as people.. who we are willing to do whatever it takes to make them satisfied with their publishing choice. We are seeking growth in an array of different genres and searching for new publicity venues for our authors everyday. Black Rose Writing doesn't promise our authors the world, leading them to become overwhelmed by the competitive and difficult venture. We are honest with our authors, and we give them the insight to generate solid leads without wasting their time. Black Rose Writing works with our authors along many lines of promotion, (examples: showcasing your titles at festivals, scheduling book events, and sending out press releases and review copies) and provides a broad distribution that covers many book buyers and allows interested parties access to our titles easily. We want to make our authors' journeys into the publishing world a success and eliminate the fear of a toilsome and lengthy experience. **Publishes 75+ titles/year.** Accepts simultaneous submissions. Responds in 2-3 months to mss. Please check submission guidelines before contacting by e-mail.

○ Online store: www.blackrosewritingbooks.com

NONFICTION Subjects include science, sports, young adult, general. Query via e-mail. Submit synopsis and author bio. Please allow 3-4 weeks for response.
FICTION Subjects include adventure, fantasy, historical, horror, humor, juvenile, mainstream, mystery, picture books, plays, romance, short story collections, sports, western, young adult, detective. Query via e-mail. Submit synopsis and author bio. Please allow 3-4 weeks for response.

TIPS "Please query via email first with synopsis and author bio. Allow 4-6 weeks for response. Always spell-check and try and sent an edited manuscript. Do not forward your initial contact e-mails."

BLACK VELVET SEDUCTIONS PUBLISHING

1350-C W. Southport Rd., Box 249, Indianapolis IN 46217. (319)241-6556. **E-mail:** lauriesanders@blackvelvetseductions.com. **Website:** www.blackvelvetseductions.com. **Contact:** Laurie Sanders, acquisitions editor. Estab. 2005. Publishes trade paperback and electronic originals and reprints. "We publish two types of material: 1) romance novels and short stories and 2) romantic stories involving spanking between consenting adults. We look for well-crafted stories with a high degree of emotional impact. **No first person point of view.** All material must be in third person point of view." Publishes trade paperback and electronic originals. "We have a high interest in republishing backlist titles in electronic and trade paperback formats once rights have reverted to the author." Accepts only complete manuscripts. Query with SASE. Submit complete ms. **Publishes about 20 titles/year. 500 queries received/year. 1,000 mss received/year. 90% of books from first-time authors. 100% from unagented writers. Pays 10% royalty for paperbacks; 50% royalty for electronic books.** Publishes ms 6-12 months after acceptance. Accepts simultaneous submissions. Responds in 6 months to queries; 8 months to proposals; 8-12 months to mss. Catalog free or online. Guidelines online (guidelines@blackvelvetseductions.com).

IMPRINTS Forbidden Experiences (erotic romance of all types); Tender Destinations (sweet romance of all types); Sensuous Journeys (sensuous romance of all types); Amorous Adventures (romantic suspense); Erotic relationship stories (erotic short stories, usually including spanking, with a romantic relationship at their core).

FICTION Subjects include romance, erotic romance, historical romance, multicultural romance, romance, short story collections romantic stories, romantic suspense, western romance. All stories must have a strong romance element. "There are very few sexual taboos in our erotic line. We tend to give our authors the widest latitude. If it is safe, sane, and consensual we will allow our authors latitude to show us the eroticism. However, we will not consider manuscripts with any of the following: bestiality (sex with animals), necrophilia (sex with dead people), pedophillia (sex with children)." Only accepts electronic submissions. **TIPS** "We publish romance and erotic romance. We look for books written in very deep point of view. Shallow point of view remains the number one reason we reject manuscripts in which the storyline generally works."

JOHN F. BLAIR, PUBLISHER

1406 Plaza Dr., Winston-Salem NC 27103. (336)768-1374. **Fax:** (336)768-9194. **Website:** www.blairpub.com. **Contact:** Carolyn Sakowski, president. Estab. 1954. **Pays royalties. Pays negotiable advance.** Publishes ms 18 months after acceptance. Responds in 3-6 months.

FICTION "We specialize in regional books, with an emphasis on nonfiction categories such as history, travel, folklore, and biography. We publish only one or two works of fiction each year. Fiction submitted to us should have some connection with the Southeast. We do not publish children's books, poetry, or category fiction such as romances, science fiction, or spy thrillers. We do not publish collections of short stories, essays, or newspaper columns. Accepts unsolicited mss. Any fiction submitted should have some connection with the Southeast, either through setting or author's background. Send a cover letter, giving a synopsis of the book. Include the first two chapters (at least 50 pages) of the manuscript. You may send the entire manuscript if you wish. If you choose to send only samples, please include the projected word length of your book and estimated completion date in your cover letter. Send a biography of the author, including publishing credits and credentials."

TIPS "We are primarily interested in nonfiction titles. Most of our titles have a tie-in with North Carolina or the southeastern United States, we do not accept short-story collections. Please enclose a cover letter and outline with the manuscript. We prefer to review queries before we are sent complete manuscripts. Queries should include an approximate word count."

⊕ BLAZEVOX [BOOKS]

76 Inwood Place, Buffalo NY 14209. **E-mail:** editor@blazevox.org. **Website:** www.blazevox.org. **Contact:** Geoffrey Gatza, editor/publisher. Estab. 2005. "We are a major publishing presence specializing in innovative fictions and wide-ranging fields of innovative forms of poetry and prose. Our goal is to publish works that are challenging, creative, attractive, and yet affordable to individual readers. Articles of submission depend on many criteria, but overall items submitted must conform to one ethereal trait, your work must not suck. This put plainly, bad art should be punished; we will not promote it. However, all submissions will be reviewed and the author will receive feedback. We are human too." **Pays 10% royalties on fiction and poetry books, based on net receipts. This amount may be split across multiple contributors. "We do not pay advances."** Guidelines online.

FICTION Subjects include experimental, short story collections. Submit complete ms via e-mail.

POETRY Submit complete ms via e-mail.

TIPS "We actively contract and support authors who tour, read and perform their work, play an active part of the contemporary literary scene, and seek a readership."

BLOOMBERG PRESS

Imprint of John Wiley & Sons, Professional Development, 111 River St., Hoboken NJ 07030. **Website:** www.wiley.com. Estab. 1995. Publishes hardcover and trade paperback originals. Bloomberg Press publishes professional books for practitioners in the financial markets. We publish commercially successful, very high-quality books that stand out clearly from the competition by their brevity, ease of use, sophistication, and abundance of practical tips and strategies; books readers need, will use, and appreciate. **Publishes 18-22 titles/year. 200 queries received/year. 20 mss received/year. 45% from unagented writers. Pays negotiable, competitive royalty. Pays negotiable advance for trade books.** Publishes book 9 months after acceptance. Accepts simultaneous submissions. With SASE, responds in 1 month to queries. Book catalog for 10x13 envelope and 5 First-Class stamps.

NONFICTION Subjects include business, economics, money, finance, professional books on finance, investment and financial services, and books for financial advisors. We are looking for authorities and for experienced service journalists. Do not send us unfocused books containing general information already covered by books in the marketplace. We do not publish business, management, leadership, or career books. Submit outline, sample chapters, SAE with sufficient postage. Submit complete ms.

TIPS *Bloomberg Professional Library*: Audience is upscale, financial professionals—traders, dealers, brokers, planners and advisors, financial managers, money managers, company executives, sophisticated investors. Authors are experienced financial journalists and/or financial professionals nationally prominent in their specialty for some time who have proven an ability to write a successful book. Research Bloomberg and look at our books in a library or bookstore, and peruse our website.

Ⓐ BLOOMSBURY CHILDREN'S BOOKS

Imprint of Bloomsbury USA, 175 Fifth Ave., New York NY 10010. **E-mail:** bloomsbury.kids@bloomsburyusa.com. **Website:** www.bloomsburykids.com. **Publishes 60 titles/year. 25% of books from first-time authors. Pays royalty. Pays advance.** Accepts simultaneous submissions. Responds in 6 months to queries; 6 months to ms. Book catalog available online. *Agented submissions only.* Guidelines available online.
○ No phone calls or e-mails.

FICTION Subjects include adventure, fantasy, historical, humor, juvenile, multicultural, mystery, picture books, poetry, science fiction, sports, suspense, young adult, animal, anthology, concept, contemporary, folktales, problem novels. Picture books: adventure, animal, contemporary, fantasy, folktales, history, humor, multicultural, poetry, suspense/mystery. Young readers: adventure, animal, anthology, concept, contemporary, fantasy, folktales, history, humor, multicultural, suspense/mystery. Middle readers: adventure, animal, contemporary, fantasy,folktales, history, humor, multicultural, poetry, problem novels. Young adults: adventure, animal, anthology, contemporary, fantasy, folktales, history, humor, multicultural, problem novels, science fiction, sports, suspense/mystery. Query with SASE. Submit clips, first 3 chapters with SASE.

TIPS "All Bloomsbury Children's Books submissions are considered on an individual basis. Bloomsbury Children's Books will no longer respond to unsolicited manuscripts or art submissions. Please include a telephone AND e-mail address where we may contact you if we are interested in your work. Do NOT send a self-addressed stamped envelope. We regret the inconvenience, but unfortunately, we are too understaffed to maintain a correspondence with authors. There is no need to send art with a picture book manuscript. Artists should submit art with a picture book manuscript. We do not return art samples. Please do not send us original art! Please note that we do ac-

cept simultaneous submissions but please be courteous and inform us if another house has made an offer on your work. Do not send originals or your only copy of anything. We are not liable for artwork or manuscript submissions. Please address all submissions to the attention of 'Manuscript Submissions'. Please make sure that everything is stapled, paper-clipped, or rubber-banded together. We do not accept e-mail or CD/DVD submissions. Be sure your work is appropriate for us. Familiarize yourself with our list by going to bookstores or libraries."

BLUEBRIDGE

Imprint of United Tribes Media, Inc., P.O. Box 601, Katonah NY 10536. (914)301-5901. **E-mail:** janguerth@bluebridgebooks.com. **Website:** www.bluebridgebooks.com. **Contact:** Jan-Erik Guerth, publisher (general nonfiction). Estab. 2004. Publishes hardcover and trade paperback originals. BlueBridge is an independent publisher of international nonfiction based near New York City. The BlueBridge mission. Thoughtful Books for Mind and Spirit. **Publishes 6 titles/year. 1,000 queries received/year. Pays variable advance.** Accepts simultaneous submissions. Responds in 1 month to queries and proposals.

NONFICTION Subjects include Americana, anthropology, archaeology, art, architecture, business, economics, child guidance, contemporary culture, creative nonfiction, ethnic, gardening, gay, lesbian, government, politics, health, medicine, history, humanities, language, literature, literary criticism, multicultural, music, dance, nature, environment, philosophy, psychology, religion, science, social sciences, sociology, spirituality, travel, women's issues, world affairs. Query with SASE or preferably by e-mail.

TIPS "We target a broad general nonfiction audience."

BLUE LIGHT PRESS

1563 45th Ave., San Francisco CA 94122. **E-mail:** bluelightpress@aol.com. **Website:** www.bluelightpress.com. **Contact:** Diane Frank, chief editor. Estab. 1988. "We like poems that are imagistic, emotionally honest, and push the edge—where the writer pushes through the imagery to a deeper level of insight and understanding. No rhymed poetry." Has published poetry by Alice Rogoff, Tom Centolella, Rustin Larson, Tony Krunk, Lisha Adela Garcia, Becky Sakellariou, and Christopher Buckley. "Books are elegantly designed and artistic." Chapbooks are 30 pages, digest-sized, professionally printed, with original cover art.

POETRY "We have an online poetry workshop with a wonderful group of American and international poets—open to new members 3 times per year. Send an e-mail for info. We work in person with local poets, and will edit/critique poems by mail; $40 for four poems." Does not accept e-mail submissions. **Deadlines:** January 30 full-sized ms. and June 15 for chapbooks. "Read our guidelines before sending your ms."

⊕ BLUE MOUNTAIN PRESS

Blue Mountain Arts, Inc., P.O. Box 4219, Boulder CO 80306. (800)525-0642. **E-mail:** BMPbooks@sps. com. **Website:** www.sps.com. **Contact:** Patti Wayant, editorial director. Estab. 1971. Publishes hardcover originals, trade paperback originals, electronic originals. **Pays royalty on wholesale price.** Publishes ms 6-8 months after acceptance. Accepts simultaneous submissions. Responds in 2-4 months to queries, mss, and proposals. Guidelines available by e-mail.

> *"Please note: We are not accepting works of fiction, rhyming poetry, children's books, chapbooks, or memoirs."*

NONFICTION , Personal growth, teens/tweens, family, relationships, motivational, and inspirational but not religious. Query with SASE. Submit proposal package including outline and 3-5 sample chapters.

POETRY "We publish poetry appropriate for gift books, self-help books, and personal growth books. We do not publish chapbooks or literary poetry." Query. Submit 10+ sample poems.

BLUE POPPY PRESS

Imprint of Blue Poppy Enterprises, Inc., 1990 57th Court Unit A, Boulder CO 80301. (303)447-8372. **Fax:** (303)245-8362. **E-mail:** info@bluepoppy.com. **Website:** www.bluepoppy.com. **Contact:** Bob Flaws, editor-in-chief. Estab. 1981. Publishes hardcover and trade paperback originals. **Publishes 3-4 titles/year. 50 queries received/year. 5-10 mss received/year. 30-40% of books from first-time authors. 100% from unagented writers. Pays 8-12% royalty.** Publishes ms 1 year after acceptance. Responds in 1 month to queries. Book catalog available free. Guidelines available online.

> "Blue Poppy Press is dedicated to expanding and improving the English language literature on acupuncture and Asian medicine for both professional practitioners and lay readers."

NONFICTION Subjects include ethnic, health, medicine. We only publish books on acupuncture and Oriental medicine by authors who can read Chinese and have a minimum of 5 years clinical experience. We also require all our authors to use Wiseman's *Glossary of Chinese Medical Terminology* as their standard for technical terms. Query with SASE. Submit outline, 1 sample chapter.

TIPS "Audience is practicing acupuncturists interested in alternatives in healthcare, preventive medicine, Chinese philosophy, and medicine."

⊕ BLUE RIVER PRESS

Cardinal Publishers Group, 2402 N. Shadeland Ave., Suite A, Indianapolis IN 46219. (317)352-8200. **Fax:** (317)352-8202. **E-mail:** tdoherty@cardinalpub.com. **E-mail:** editorial@cardinalpub.com. **Website:** www. cardinalpub.com. **Contact:** Tom Doherty, president (adult nonfiction). Estab. 2000. Publishes hardcover, trade paperback and electronic originals and reprints. **Publishes 8-12 titles/year. 60 queries received/year. 25% of books from first-time authors. 80% from unagented writers. Pays 10-15% on wholesale price. Outright purchase of $500-5,000. Offers advance up to $5,000.** Publishes ms 6 months after acceptance. Accepts simultaneous submissions. Responds to queries in 2 months. Book catalog for #10 SASE or online at website. Guidelines available by e-mail at info@ cardinalpub.com.

NONFICTION "Most non-religious adult nonfiction subjects are of interest. We like concepts that can develop into series products. Most of our books are paperback or hardcover in the categories of sport, business, health, fitness, lifestyle, yoga, and educational books for teachers and students."

BNA BOOKS

Imprint of The Bureau of National Affairs, Inc., 1801 S. Bell St., Arlington VA 22202. (703)341-5777. **Fax:** (703)341-1610. **E-mail:** books@bna.com. **Website:** www.bnabooks.com. **Contact:** Jim Fattibene, acquisitions manager. Estab. 1929. Publishes hardcover and softcover originals. Accepts simultaneous submissions. Book catalog available online. Guidelines available online.

> BNA Books publishes professional reference books written by lawyers, for lawyers.

NONFICTION No fiction, biographies, bibliographies, cookbooks, religion books, humor, or trade books. Submit detailed TOC or outline, cv, intended market, estimated word length.

TIPS "Our audience is made up of practicing lawyers and law librarians. We look for authoritative and comprehensive treatises that can be supplemented or revised every year or 2 on legal subjects of interest to those audiences."

BOA EDITIONS, LTD.

250 N. Goodman St., Suite 306, Rochester NY 14607. (585)546-3410. **Fax:** (585)546-3913. **E-mail:** conners@boaeditions.org; hall@boaeditions.org. **Website:** www.boaeditions.org. **Contact:** Peter Conners, editor. Melissa Hall, development director/office manager. Estab. 1976. Publishes hardcover and trade paperback originals. "BOA Editions publishes distinguished collections of poetry, fiction and poetry in translation. Our goal is to publish the finest American contemporary poetry, fiction and poetry in translation." **Publishes 11-13 titles/year. 1,000 queries received/year. 700 mss received/year. 15% of books from first-time authors. 90% from unagented writers. Negotiates royalties. Pays variable advance.** Publishes ms 18 months after acceptance. Accepts simultaneous submissions. Responds in 1 week to queries; 5 months to mss. Book catalog available online. Guidelines available online.

FICTION Subjects include literary, poetry, poetry in translation, short story collections. "We now publish literary fiction through our American Reader Series. While aesthetic quality is subjective, our fiction will be by authors more concerned with the artfulness of their writing than the twists and turns of plot. Our strongest current interest is in short story collections (and short-short story collections), although we will consider novels. We strongly advise you to read our first published fiction collections. *We are temporarily closed to novel/collection submissions.*"

POETRY "Readers who, like Whitman, expect of the poet to `indicate more than the beauty and dignity which always attach to dumb real objects . They expect him to indicate the path between reality and their souls,' are the audience of BOA's books." BOA Editions, a Pulitzer Prize-winning, not-for-profit publishing house acclaimed for its work, reads poetry mss for the American Poets Continuum Series (new poetry by distinguished poets in mid- and late career), the Lannan Translations Selection Series (publication of 2 new collections of contemporary international poetry annually, supported by The Lannan Foundation of Santa Fe, NM), The A. Poulin, Jr. Poetry Prize (to honor a poet's first book; mss considered through competition), and The America Reader Series (short fiction and prose on poetics). Has published poetry by Naomi Shihab Nye, W.D. Snodgrass, Lucille Clifton, Brigit Pegeen Kelly, and Li-Young Lee. Check website for reading periods for the American Poets Continuum Series and The Lannan Translation Selection Series. "Please adhere to the general submission guidelines for each series." Guidelines available for SASE or on website.

BOLD STROKES BOOKS, INC.

P.O. Box 249, Valley Falls NY 12185. (518)677-5127. **Fax:** (518)677-5291. **E-mail:** publisher@boldstrokesbooks.com. **E-mail:** submissions@boldstrokesbooks.com. **Website:** www.boldstrokesbooks.com. **Contact:** Len Barot, president; Lee Ligon, operations manager; Cindy Cresap, senior consulting editor and production manager. Publishes trade paperback originals and reprints; electronic originals and reprints. **Publishes 85+ titles/year. 300 queries/year; 300 mss/year. 10-20% of books from first-time authors. Sliding scale based on sales volume and format.** Publishes ms 6-16 months after acceptance. Responds in 1 month to queries; 2 months to proposals; 4 months to mss. Catalog free on request - PDF. Guidelines online at website.

NONFICTION Subjects include gay, lesbian, memoirs, young adult. Submit completed ms with bio, cover letter, and synopsis electronically only. Does not review artwork.

FICTION Subjects include adventure, erotica, fantasy, gay, gothic, historical, horror, lesbian, literary, mainstream, mystery, romance, science fiction, suspense, western, young adult. "Submissions should have a gay, lesbian, transgendered, or bisexual focus and should be positive and life-affirming." Submit completed ms with bio, cover letter, and synopsis—electronically only.

TIPS "We are particularly interested in authors who are interested in craft enhancement, technical development, and exploring and expanding traditional genre definitions and boundaries and are looking for a long-term publishing relationship ."

✪➋ BOOKOUTURE

StoryFire Ltd., 23 Sussex Rd., Ickenham UB10 8P, United Kingdom. **E-mail:** questions@bookouture.com. **E-mail:** pitch@bookouture.com. **Website:** www.bookouture.com. **Contact:** Oliver Rhodes, founder and publisher. Estab. 2012. Publishes mass market paperback and electronic originals and reprints. **Publishes 20 titles/year. Receives 200 queries/year; 300 mss/year. Pays 45% royalty on wholesale price.** Publishes ms 4 months after acceptance. Accepts simultaneous submissions. Responds in 1 month. Book catalog available online at website.

IMPRINTS Imprint of StoryFire Ltd.

FICTION Subjects include contemporary, erotica, ethnic, fantasy, gay, historical, lesbian, mainstream, mystery, romance, science fiction, suspense, western. "We're looking for entertaining fiction targeted at modern women. That can be anything from Steampunk to Erotica, Historicals to thrillers. A distinctive author voice is more important than a particular genre or manuscript length." Submit complete ms.

TIPS "The most important question that we ask of submissions is why would a reader buy the NEXT book? What's distinctive or different about your storytelling that will mean readers will want to come back for more. We look to acquire global English language rights for eBook and Print on Demand."

BOREALIS PRESS, LTD.

8 Mohawk Crescent, Napean ON K2H 7G6, Canada. (613)829-0150. **Fax:** (613)829-7783. **E-mail:** drt@borealispress.com. **Website:** www.borealispress.com. Estab. 1972. Publishes hardcover and paperback originals and reprints. Our mission is to publish work that will be of lasting interest in the Canadian book market. Currently emphasizing Canadian fiction, nonfiction, drama, poetry. De-emphasizing children's books. **Publishes 20 titles/year. 80% of books from first-time authors. 95% from unagented writers. Pays 10% royalty on net receipts; plus 3 free author's copies.** Publishes book 18 months after acceptance. Responds in 2 months to queries; 4 months to mss. Book catalog available online. Guidelines available online.

IMPRINTS Imprint: Tecumseh Press.

NONFICTION Subjects include government, politics, history, language, literature, regional. Only material Canadian in content. Looks for style in tone and language, reader interest, and maturity of outlook. Query with SASE. Submit outline, 2 sample chapters. *No unsolicited mss.* Reviews artwork/photos.

FICTION Subjects include adventure, ethnic, historical, juvenile, literary, mainstream, contemporary, romance, short story collections, young adult. Only material Canadian in content and dealing with signifi-

cant aspects of the human situation. Query with SASE. Submit clips, 1-2 sample chapters. *No unsolicited mss.*

BOTTOM DOG PRESS, INC.

P.O. Box 425, Huron OH 44839. **E-mail:** LsmithDog@smithdocs.net. **Website:** smithdocs.net. **Contact:** Larry Smith, director; Allen Frost, Laura Smith, Susanna Sharp-Schwacke, associate editors. Bottom Dog Press, Inc., "is a nonprofit literary and educational organization dedicated to publishing the best writing and art from the Midwest and Appalachia."

"Query via e-mail first."

BRANDEN PUBLISHING CO., INC.

P.O. Box 812094, Wellesley MA 02482. (781)235-3634. **Fax:** (781)235-3634. **E-mail:** branden@brandenbooks.com. **Website:** www.brandenbooks.com. **Contact:** Adolph Caso, editor. Estab. 1909. Publishes hardcover and trade paperback originals, reprints, and software. "Branden publishes books by or about women, children, military, Italian-American, or African-American themes." **Publishes 15 titles/year. 80% of books from first-time authors. 90% from unagented writers.** Publishes ms 10 months after acceptance. Responds in 1 month to queries.

IMPRINTS International Pocket Library and Popular Technology; Four Seas and Brashear; Branden Books.

NONFICTION Subjects include Americana, art, architecture, computers, electronics, contemporary culture, education, ethnic, government, politics, health, medicine, history, military, war, music, dance, photography, sociology, software, classics. "Especially looking for about 10 manuscripts on national and international subjects, including biographies of well-known individuals. Currently specializing in Americana, Italian-American, African-American." No religion or philosophy. *No unsolicited mss.* Paragraph query only with SASE. No telephone, e-mail, or fax inquiries. Reviews artwork/photos.

FICTION Subjects include ethnic, histories, integration, historical, literary, military, war, religious, historical-reconstructive, short story collections, translation. Looking for contemporary, fast pace, modern society. No science, mystery, experimental, horor, or pornography. *No unsolicited mss.* Query with SASE. Paragraph query only with author bio.

NICHOLAS BREALEY PUBLISHING

20 Park Plaza, Suite 610, Boston MA 02116. (617)523-3801. **Fax:** (617)523-3708. **E-mail:** info@nicholasbrealey.com. **E-mail:** submissions@nicholasbrealey.com.

Website: www.nicholasbrealey.com. **Contact:** Vanessa Descalzi, assistant editor and digital director. Estab. 1992. "Nicholas Brealey Publishing has a reputation for publishing high-quality and thought-provoking business books with international appeal. Over time our list has grown to focus also on adjacent fields like careers, professional and personal development and crossing cultures—and we are now expanding further into narrative nonfiction, notably adventure and travel writing. We welcome fresh ideas and new insights in all of these subject areas." Submit via e-mail and follow the guidelines on the website.

BREWERS PUBLICATIONS

Imprint of Brewers Association, 736 Pearl St., Boulder CO 80302. (303)447-0816. **Fax:** (303)447-2825. **E-mail:** kristi@brewersassociation.org; webmaster@brewersassociation.org. **Website:** www.brewerspublications.com. **Contact:** Kristi Switzer, publisher. Estab. 1986. Publishes hardcover and trade paperback originals. "BP is the largest publisher of contemporary and relevant brewing literature for today's craft brewers and homebrewers." **Publishes 2 titles/year. 50% of books from first-time authors. 100% from unagented writers. Pays small advance.** Publishes book 9 months after acceptance. Accepts simultaneous submissions. Responds in 3 months to relevant queries. "Only those submissions relevant to our needs will receive a response to queries". Guidelines available online.

NONFICTION "BP is the largest publisher of contemporary and relevant brewing literature for today's craft brewers and homebrewers. We seek to do this in a positive atmosphere, create lasting relationships and shared pride in our contributions to the brewing and beer community. The books we select to carry out this mission include titles relevant to homebrewing, professional brewing, starting a brewery, books on particular styles of beer, industry trends, ingredients, processes and the occasional broader interest title on cooking or the history/impact of beer in our society." Query first with proposal and sample chapter.

♻ BRICK BOOKS

Box 20081, 431 Boler Rd., London ON N6K 4G6, Canada. (519)657-8579. **E-mail:** brick.books@sympatico.ca. **Website:** www.brickbooks.ca. **Contact:** Don McKay, Stan Dragland, Barry Dempster, editors. Estab. 1975. Publishes trade paperback originals. Brick Books has a reading period of January 1-April 30. Mss received outside that period will be returned. No multiple submissions. Pays 10% royalty in book copies only. **Publishes 7 titles/year. 30 queries received/year. 100 mss received/year. 30% of books from first-time authors. 100% from unagented writers.** Publishes ms 2 years after acceptance. Responds in 3-4 months to queries. Book catalog free or online. Guidelines available online.

POETRY Submit only poetry.

TIPS "Writers without previous publications in literary journals or magazines are rarely considered by Brick Books for publication."

BRICK ROAD POETRY PRESS, INC.

P.O. Box 751, Columbus GA 31902. (706)649-3080. **Fax:** (706)649-3094. **E-mail:** editor@brickroadpoetrypress.com. **Website:** www.brickroadpoetrypress.com. **Contact:** Ron Self and Keith Badowski, co-editors/founders. Estab. 2009.

POETRY Publishes poetry only: books (single author collections), e-zine, and annual anthology. "We prefer poetry that offers a coherent human voice, a sense of humor, attentiveness to words and language, narratives with surprise twists, persona poems, and/or philosophical or spiritual themes explored through the concrete scenes and images." Does not want overemphasis on rhyme, intentional obscurity or riddling, highfalutin vocabulary, greeting card verse, overt religious statements of faith and/or praise, and/or abstractions. Publishes 10-12 poetry books/year and 1 anthology/year. Accepted poems meeting our theme requirements are published on our website. Mss accepted through open submission and competition. Books are 110 pages, print-on-demand, perfect-bound, paperback with full color art or photograph covers. "We accept .doc, .rtf, or .pdf file formats. We prefer electronic submissions but will reluctantly consider hard copy submissions by mail if USPS Flat Rate Mailing Envelope is used and with the stipulation that, should the author's work be chosen for publication, an electronic version (.doc or .rtf) must be prepared in a timely manner and at the poet's expense." Please include cover letter with poetry publication/recognition highlights and something intriguing about your life story or ongoing pursuits. "We would like to develop a connection with the poet as well as the poetry." Please include the collection title in the cover letter. "We want to publish poets who are engaged in the literary community, including regular submission of work to various publications and participation in poetry readings, workshops, and writers' groups. That said, we would never rule out an emerging poet who demonstrates ability and motivation to move in that direction." Pays royalties and 15 author copies. Initial print run of 150, print-on-demand thereafter.

TIPS "The best way to discover all that poetry can be and to expand the limits of your own poetry is to read expansively. We recommend the following poets: Kim Addonizio, Ken Babstock, Coleman Barks, Billy Collins, Morri Creech, Alice Friman, Beth A. Gylys, Jane Hirshfield, Jane Kenyon, Ted Kooser, Stanley Kunitz, Thomas Lux, Barry Marks, Michael Meyerhofer, Linda Pastan, Mark Strand, and Natasha D. Trethewey."

BRIGHTER BOOKS PUBLISHING HOUSE

Brighter Brains, Inc., 4825 Fairbrook Crescent, Nanaimo B.C. V9T 6M6, Canada. (250)585-7372. **E-mail:** info@brighterbooks.com. **E-mail:** submissions@brighterbooks.com. **Website:** www.brighterbooks.com. **Contact:** Angela Souza, senior/chief editor. Dean Jurgensen, senior editor (sciences, technology, information). Estab. 2009. Publishes hardcover and electronic originals; hardcover and trade paperback reprints; trade paperback originals and reprints. **Publishes 10-15 titles/year. 50% of books from first-time authors. 50% from unagented writers. Pays royalty on wholesale price. Advances are negotiable.** Publishes book 1 year after acceptance. Accepts simultaneous submissions. Responds in 2 months to queries and proposals; 3-4 months to mss. Catalog available online at website. Guidelines online at website and by e-mail at info@brighterbooks.com.

IMPRINTS Juvenile: Picture books; young readers; middle reader; young adults.

NONFICTION , animals, art/architecture, child guidance/parenting, computers/electronics, crafts, education, entertainment/games, hobbies, money/finance for kids, nature/environment, science. "We focus on high-quality reading for children and also unique methods of teaching things to both adults and children." Query with SASE. Submit proposal package, including: outline, 3 sample chapters, and introduction. Submit completed ms for picture books and younger readers. Reviews artwork/photos. "We prefer digital samples, but photocopies are fine as well."

FICTION Subjects include adventure, fantasy, humor, juvenile, multicultural, multimedia, mystery, picture books, science fiction, young adult. "We are looking for a return to the quality of writing found in classical works of literature. We want to publish truly great fiction, no matter the target audience or age level. We believe that by exposing children and young adults to excellent literature on a day-to-day basis, we can change their lives, making them better thinkers, more creative and well-adjusted. Books change people, and we want to do our part to make it a positive change." Query with SASE. Submit proposal package, including synopsis, 3 sampe chapters. Submit completed ms for picture books and young readers.

TIPS "Our fiction readers are smart boys and girls of all ages who are looking for characters they can relate to, and love to read. Our El-Hi readers are looking for a different way of learning school subjects. They may have learning difficulties with traditional methods. Our adult readers are well educated, and looking for well-written books about their subject of interest. 55% of work must be Canadian or Resident. However, we are still looking for talent worldwide."

BRIGHT MOUNTAIN BOOKS, INC.

206 Riva Ridge Dr., Fairview NC 28730. (828)628-1768. **Fax:** (828)628-1755. **E-mail:** booksbmb@charter.net. **Website:** www.brightmountainbooks.com. **Contact:** Cynthia F. Bright, senior editor. Martha Fullington, editor Estab. 1983. Publishes trade paperback originals and reprints. Currently, Bright Mountain Books has nearly forty titles in print, all written by local authors or having subject matter relevant to the region of the Southern Appalachian Mountains. **Publishes 3 titles/year. 50% of books from first-time authors. 100% from unagented writers. Pays royalty.** Responds in 1 month to queries; 5 months to mss.

IMPRINTS Historical Images, Ridgetop Books.

NONFICTION Subjects include history, regional. "Our current emphasis is on regional titles set in the Southern Appalachians and Carolinas, which can include nonfiction by local writers." Query with SASE.

BRIGHT RING PUBLISHING, INC.

P.O. Box 31338, Bellingham WA 98228. (360)592-9201. **Fax:** (360)592-4503. **E-mail:** maryann@brightring.com. **Website:** www.brightring.com. **Contact:** MaryAnn Kohl, editor. Estab. 1985.

Bright Ring is no longer accepting manuscript submissions.

BROADWAY BOOKS

The Crown Publishing Group/Random House, 1745 Broadway, New York NY 10019. (212)782-9000. **Fax:**

(212)782-9411. **Website:** www.broadwaybooks.com. **Contact:** William Thomas, editor-in-chief. Estab. 1995. Publishes hardcover and trade paperback books. **Receives thousands of mss/year. Pays royalty on retail price. Pays advance.**

IMPRINTS Broadway Books; Broadway Business; Doubleday; Doubleday Image; Doubleday Religious Publishing; Main St. Books; Nan A. Talese.

○ "Broadway publishes high quality general interest nonfiction and fiction for adults."

NONFICTION Subjects include business, economics, child guidance, contemporary culture, cooking, foods, nutrition, gay, lesbian, government, politics, health, medicine, history, memoirs, money, finance, multicultural, New Age, psychology, sex, spirituality, sports, travel, narrative, womens' issues, women's studies, current affairs, motivational/inspirational, popular culture, consumer reference. *Agented submissions only.*

☺ BROKEN JAW PRESS

Box 596, STN A, Fredericton NB E3B 5A6, Canada. (506)454-5127. **E-mail:** editors@brokenjaw.com. **Website:** www.brokenjaw.com. "Publishes almost exclusively Canadian-authored literary trade paperback originals and reprints.". "We publish poetry, fiction, drama and literary nonfiction, including translations and multilingual books." **Publishes 3-6 titles/year. 20% of books from first-time authors. 100% from unagented writers. Pays 10% royalty on retail price. Pays $0-500 advance.** Publishes ms 18 months after acceptance. Responds in 1 year to mss. Book catalog for 6×9 SAE with 2 first-class Canadian stamps in Canada or download PDF from website. Guidelines available online.

IMPRINTS Book Rat; Broken Jaw Press; SpareTime Editions; Dead Sea Physh Products; Maritimes Arts Projects Productions.

○ *Currently not accepting unsolicited mss and queries.*

NONFICTION Subjects include history, literature, literary criticism, regional, women's issues, women's studies, contemporary culture.

FICTION Subjects include Literary novel and short story collections, poetry.

TIPS "Unsolicited queries and manuscripts are not welcome at this time."

BROOKS BOOKS

3720 N. Woodridge Dr., Decatur IL 62526. **E-mail:** brooksbooks@sbcglobal.net. **Website:** www.brooksbookshaiku.com. **Contact:** Randy Brooks, editor (haiku poetry, tanka poetry). Publishes hardcover, trade paperback, and electronic originals. "Brooks Books, formerly High/Coo Press, publishes English-language haiku books, chapbooks, magazines, and bibliographies." **Publishes 2-3 titles/year. 100 queries received/year. 25 mss received/year. 10% of books from first-time authors. 100% from unagented writers. Outright purchase based on wholesale value of 10% of a press run.** Publishes ms 1 year after acceptance. Responds in 2 months to queries; 3 months to proposals and mss. Book catalog free on request or online at website. Guidelines free on request.

POETRY "We celebrate English language haiku by promoting & publishing in a variety of media. Our goal is to share our joy of the art of reading & writing haiku through our little chapbook-size magazine, *Mayfly.* Also, we celebrate the art of haiga, lifetime contributions of haiku writers, the integration of visual arts (photography or painting) and contemporary English language haiku by leading poets. Query.

TIPS "The best haiku capture human perception—moments of being alive conveyed through sensory images. They do not explain nor describe nor provide philosophical or political commentary. Haiku are gifts of the here and now, deliberately incomplete so that the reader can enter into the haiku moment to open the gift and experience the feelings and insights of that moment for his or her self. Our readership includes the haiku community, readers of contemporary poetry, teachers and students of Japanese literature and contemporary Japanese poetics."

☺ THE BRUCEDALE PRESS

P.O. Box 2259, Port Elgin ON N0H 2C0, Canada. (519)832-6025. **E-mail:** brucedale@bmts.com. **Website:** brucedalepress.ca. Publishes hardcover and trade paperback originals. The Brucedale Press publishes books and other materials of regional interest and merit, as well as literary, historical, and/or pictorial works. **Publishes 3 titles/year. 50 queries received/year. 30 mss received/year. 75% of books from first-time authors. 100% from unagented writers. Pays royalty.** Publishes book 1 year after acceptance. Accepts simultaneous submissions. Book catalog for #10

SASE (Canadian postage or IRC) or online. Guide-lines available online.

 Accepts works by Canadian authors only. Sub-missions accepted in September and March ONLY.

NONFICTION Subjects include history, language, lit-erature, memoirs, military, war, nature, environment, photography. Reviews artwork/photos.

FICTION Subjects include fantasy, feminist, histori-cal, humor, juvenile, literary, mainstream, contem-porary, mystery, plays, poetry, romance, short story collections, young adult.

TIPS Our focus is very regional. In reading submis-sions, I look for quality writing with a strong connec-tion to the Queen's Bush area of Ontario. All authors should visit our website, get a catalog, and read our books before submitting.

BUSTER BOOKS

9 Lion Yard, Tremadoc Rd., London WA SW4 7NQ, United Kingdom. 020 7720 8643. **Fax:** 022 7720 8953. **E-mail:** enquiries@michaelomarabooks.com. **Web-site:** busterbooks.co.uk. "We are dedicated to pro-viding irresistible and fun books for children of all ages. We typically publish black-and-white nonfic-tion for children aged 8-12 novelty titles-including doodle books."

NONFICTION Prefers synopsis and sample text over complete ms.

TIPS "We do not accept fiction submissions. Please do not send original artwork as we cannot guarantee its safety." Visit website before submitting.

BY LIGHT UNSEEN MEDIA

P.O. Box 1233, Pepperell MA 01463. (978) 433-8866. **Fax:** (978) 433-8866. **E-mail:** vyrdolak@bylightun-seenmedia.com. **E-mail:** vyrdolak@bylightunseen-media.com. **Website:** www.bylightunseenmedia.com. **Contact:** Inanna Arthen, owner/editor-in-chief. Es-tab. 2006. Publishes hardcover, paperback and elec-tronic originals; trade paperback reprints. **Publishes 5 titles/year. 20 mss received/year; 5 queries received/year. 80% of books from first-time authors. 100% from unagented writers. Pays royalty of 20-50% on net as explicitly defined in contract. Payment quar-terly. Pays $200 advance.** Publishes book 4 months after acceptance. Accepts simultaneous submissions. Responds in 3 months to queries/proposals/mss. Cat-alog available online at website. Ms guidelines avail-able online at website.

NONFICTION Subjects include alternative lifestyles, contemporary culture, creative nonfiction, history, language, literary criticism, literature, New Age, sci-ence, social sciences, folklore, popular media. "We are a niche small press that will *only* consider nonfiction on the theme of vampires (vampire folklore, movies, television, literature, vampires in culture, etc.). We're especially interested in academic or other well-re-searched material, but will consider self-help/New Age types of books (e.g. the kind of material published by Llewellyn). We use digital printing so all interiors would need to be black and white, including illustra-tions." Submit proposal package including outline, 3 sample chapters, brief author bio. *All unsolicited mss will be returned unopened.* Reviews artwork. Send photocopies/scanned PDF/jpeg.

FICTION Subjects include fantasy, gay, gothic, horror, lesbian, mystery, occult, science fiction, short story collections, suspense, western, young adult, magical realism, thriller. "We are a niche small press that *only* publishes fiction relating in some way to vampires. Within that guideline, we're interested in almost any genre that includes a vampire trope, the more cre-ative and innovative, the better. Restrictions are not-ed in the submission guidelines (no derivative fiction based on other works, such as Dracula, no gore-for-gore's-sake "splatter" horror, etc.) We do not publish anthologies." Submit proposal package including syn-opsis, 3 sample chapters, brief author bio. *We encour-age electronic submissions. All unsolicited mss will be returned unopened.*

TIPS "We strongly urge authors to familiarize them-selves with the vampire genre and not imagine that they're doing something new and amazingly differ-ent just because they're not imitating the current fad. Our submission guidelines list two online articles we recommend prospective authors read: "7 Wrong Things You Should Know About Vampire Folklore," and "Think Outside the Coffin: Writing the Vampire Novel." We're looking for strong characters and good story-telling, not gimmicks. Our most successful pro-motional tag line is "vampire stories for grown-ups." That gives a good idea of what we're selling (and buy-ing from authors)."

C&R PRESS

812 Westwood Ave., Chattanooga TN 37405. (423)645-5375. **E-mail:** editor@crpress.org. **Website:** www.crpress.org. **Contact:** Chad Prevost, editorial di-

rector and publisher; Ryan G. Van Cleave, executive director and publisher. Estab. 2006. Publishes hardcover, trade paperback, mass market paperback, and electronic originals. **Publishes 8 titles/year. 20% of books from first-time authors. 75% from unagented writers.** Publishes ms 1 year after acceptance. Accepts simultaneous submissions. Responds in up to 1 month on queries and proposals, 1-2 months on mss. Catalog and guidelines available online at website.

IMPRINTS Illumis Books.

NONFICTION Subjects include contemporary culture, creative nonfiction, memoirs. Submit complete ms and query via e-mail. "C&R is a green company and we prefer all submissions to be done electronically."

FICTION Subjects include experimental, literary, poetry, regional. "We want dynamic, exciting literary fiction and we want to work with authors (not merely books) who are engaged socially and driven to promote their work because of their belief in the product, and because it's energizing and exciting to do so and a vital part of the process." Submit complete ms via e-mail.

POETRY "We remain committed to our annual first book of poetry contest, the De Novo Award. However, we also feature 1-2 montly paid reading periods when we consider any and all poetry projects. Please check the website for updated guidelines." Submit complete ms.

⊘ CALAMARI PRESS

Via Titta Scarpetta #28, Rome 00153, Italy. **E-mail:** derek@calamaripress.net. **Website:** www.calamaripress.com. Publishes paperback originals. Calamari Press publishes books of literary text and art. Publishes 1-2 books/year. Manuscripts are selected by invitation. Occasionally has open submission period—check website. Helps to be published in *SleepingFish* first." See separate listing in magazines/journals. Order books through the website, Powell's, or SPD. **Publishes 1-2/year titles/year. Pays in author's copies.** Publishes book Manuscript published 2-6 months after acceptance. Responds to mss in 2 weeks. Writer's guidelines on website.

FICTION Query with outline/synopsis and 3 sample chapters. Accepts queries by e-mail only. Include brief bio. Send SASE or IRC for return of ms.

CALKINS CREEK

Boyds Mills Press, 815 Church St., Honesdale PA 18431. **Website:** www.calkinscreekbooks.com. Estab. 2004. We aim to publish books that are a well-written blend of creative writing and extensive research, which emphasize important events, people, and places in U.S. history." **Pays authors royalty or work purchased outright.** Guidelines available on website.

NONFICTION All levels: history. Recently published *Farmer George Plants a Nation*, by Peggy Thomas (ages 8 and up, nonfiction picture book); *Robert H. Jackson*, by Gail Jarrow (ages 10 and up, historical fiction). Submit outline/synopsis and 3 sample chapters.

FICTION All levels: history. Recently published *Healing Water*, by Joyce Moyer Hostetter (ages 10 and up, historical fiction); *The Shakeress*, by Kimberly Heuston (ages 12 and up, historical fiction). Submit outline/synopsis and 3 sample chapters.

TIPS "Read through our recently published titles and review our catalog. When selecting titles to publish, our emphasis will be on important events, people, and places in U.S. history. Writers are encouraged to submit a detailed bibliography, including secondary and primary sources, and expert reviews with their submissions."

CAMINO BOOKS, INC.

P.O. Box 59026, Philadelphia PA 19102. (215)413-1917. **Fax:** (215)413-3255. **Website:** www.caminobooks.com. **Contact:** E. Jutkowitz, publisher. Estab. 1987. Publishes hardcover and trade paperback originals. "Camino Books was founded in 1987 for the purpose of publishing quality nonfiction books of regional interest to people in the Middle Atlantic states. Our list is especially strong in titles about cooking, travel, gardening, and history, but we also publish biographies, local reference books, and books concerning parenting and important health issues. We occasionally publish books of national interest as well. We currently publish about 6 to 10 books per year, and we are always looking for new material and projects." **Publishes 6-10 titles/year. 20% of books from first-time authors. Pays $2,000 average advance.** Publishes ms 1 year after acceptance. Responds in 2 weeks to queries. Guidelines available online.

NONFICTION Subjects include agriculture, Americana, art, architecture, child guidance, cooking, foods, nutrition, ethnic, gardening, government, politics,

237

history, regional, travel. Query with SASE. Submit outline, sample chapters.

TIPS "The books must be of interest to readers in the Middle Atlantic states, or they should have a clearly defined niche, such as cookbooks."

⊘ CANDLEWICK PRESS

99 Dover St., Somerville MA 02144. (617)661-3330. **Fax:** (617)661-0565. **E-mail:** bigbear@candlewick. com. **Website:** www.candlewick.com. **Contact:** Deb Wayshak, executive editor (fiction); Joan Powers, editor-at-large (picture books); Liz Bicknell, editorial director/associate publisher (poetry, picture books, fiction); Mary Lee Donovan, executive editor (picture books, nonfiction/fiction); Hilary Van Dusen, senior editor (nonfiction/fiction); Sarah Ketchersid, senior editor (board, toddler); Joan Powers, editor-at-large. Estab. 1991. Publishes hardcover and trade paperback originals, and reprints. "Candlewick Press publishes high-quality, illustrated children's books for ages infant through young adult. We are a truly child-centered publisher." Candlewick title *Good Masters! Sweet Ladies! Voices from a Medieval Village,* by Amy Schlitz, won the John Newbery Medal in 2008. Their title *Twelve Rounds to Glory: The Story of Muhammad Ali,* by Charles R. Smith Jr., illustrated by Bryan Collier, won a Coretta Scott King Author Honor Award in 2008. Their title *The Astonishing Life of Octavian Nothing,* by M.T. Anderson, won the Boston Globe-Hornbook Award for Fiction and Poetry in 2007. **Publishes 200 titles/year. 5% of books from first-time authors. Pays authors royalty of 2½-10% based on retail price. Offers advance.**

○   *Candlewick Press is not accepting queries or unsolicited mss at this time.*

NONFICTION Picture books: concept, biography, geography, nature/environment. Young readers: biography, geography, nature/environment.

FICTION Subjects include juvenile, picture books, young adult. Picture books: animal, concept, contemporary, fantasy, history, humor, multicultural, nature/environment, poetry. Middle readers, young adults: contemporary, fantasy, history, humor, multicultural, poetry, science fiction, sports, suspense/mystery. "We do not accept editorial queries or submissions online. If you are an author or illustrator and would like us to consider your work, please read our submissions policy (online) to learn more."

TIPS *"We no longer accept unsolicited mss.* See our website for further information about us."

⊕ CANTERBURY HOUSE PUBLISHING, LTD.

225 Ira Harmon Rd., Vilas NC 28692. (828)297-7127. **E-mail:** publisher@canterburyhousepublishing.com. **E-mail:** editor@canterburyhousepublishing.com. **Website:** www.canterburyhousepublishing.com. **Contact:** Wendy Dingwall, publisher; Sandra Horton, editor. Estab. 2009. Publishes hardcover, trade paperback, and electronic originals. "Our audience is made up of readers looking for wholesome fiction with good southern stories, with elements of mystery, romance, and inspiration and/or are looking for true stories of achievement and triumph over challenging circumstances." **Publishes 3-6 titles/year. 35% of books from first-time authors. 100% from unagented writers. Pays 10-15% royalty on wholesale price.** Publishes ms 9-12 months after acceptance. Accepts simultaneous submissions. Responds in 1 month to queries; 3 months to mss. Book catalog available online at website. Guidelines availably online, free on request by e-mail.

○   *"We are very strict on our submission guidelines due to our small staff, and our target market of Southern regional settings. The setting needs to be a strong component in the stories. Authors need to be willing to actively promote their books in the beginning 9 months of publication via signing events and social media."*

NONFICTION Subjects include business, creative nonfiction, economics, memoirs, regional. Query with SASE and through website e-mail upon request. Reviews artwork. Send photocopies.

FICTION Subjects include contemporary, fantasy, historical, literary, mainstream, mystery, regional, romance, suspense. Query with SASE and through website.

TIPS "Because of our limited staff, we prefer authors who have good writing credentials and submit edited manuscripts. We also look at authors who are business and marketing savvy and willing to help promote their books."

◐ CAPALL BANN PUBLISHING

Auton Farm, Milverton, Somerset TA4 1NE, United Kingdom. (44)(182)340-1528. **E-mail:** enquiries@capallbann.co.uk. **Website:** www.capallbann.co.uk. **Contact:** Julia Day (MBS, healing, animals); Jon Day

(MBS, religion). Publishes trade and mass market paperback originals and trade paperback and mass market paperback reprints. "Our mission is to publish books of real value to enhance and improve readers' lives." **Publishes 46 titles/year. 800 queries received/year. 450 mss received/year. 50% of books from first-time authors. 100% from unagented writers. Pays 10% royalty on net sales.** Publishes ms 4-8 months after acceptance. Accepts simultaneous submissions. Responds in 2-6 weeks to queries; 2 months to proposals and mss. Book catalogue free. Guidelines available online.

NONFICTION Subjects include animals, anthropology, archeology, gardening, health, medicine, music, dance, nature, environment, philosophy, religion, spirituality, women's issues, new age. Submit outline. Reviews artwork/photos. Send photocopies.

CAROLINA WREN PRESS

120 Morris St., Durham NC 27701. (919)560-2738. E-mail: carolinawrenpress@earthlink.net. **Website:** www.carolinawrenpress.org. **Contact:** Andrea Selch, president. Estab. 1976. "We publish poetry, fiction, and memoirs by, and/or about people of color, women, gay/lesbian issues, health and mental health topics in children's literature." Publishes ms 2 year after acceptance. Accepts simultaneous submissions. Responds in 3 months to queries; 6 months to mss. Guidelines are available on our website in December, with information about electronic submissions.

◯   Accepts simultaneous submissions, but "let us know if work has been accepted elsewhere."

NONFICTION Subjects include biography, autobiography, literary nonfiction work by, and/or about people of color, women, gay/lesbian issues, health and mental health topics in children's literature.

FICTION Subjects include ethnic, experimental, poetry, feminist, gay, lesbian, literary, short story collections. "We are no longer publishing children's literature of any topic." Books: 6×9 paper; typeset; various bindings; illustrations. **Published 2 debut authors within the last year.** Distributes titles through Amazon.com, Barnes & Noble, Baker & Taylor, and on their website. "We very rarely accept any unsolicited manuscripts, but we accept submissions for the Doris Bakwin Award for Writing by a Woman in Jan-March of even-numbered years." Published *Downriver,* by Jeanne Leiby in 2007, *All Eyes,* by Phoebe Hoss in 2009, *Relative Strangers,* by Margaret Hermes in 2012. Query by mail. "We will accept e-mailed queries—a letter in the body of the e-mail describing your project—but please do not send large attachments."

POETRY Publishes 2 poetry books/year, "usually through the Carolina Wren Press Poetry Series Contest. Otherwise we primarily publish women, minorities, and North Carolina authors." Has published "a half-red sea" by Evie Shockley, as well as poetry by Lee Ann Brown, Minnie Bruce Pratt, William Pitt Root and Erica Hunt. Guidelines on website. We are not accepting unsolicited submissions except through our Poetry Series Contest. Accepts e-mail queries, but send only letter and description of work, no large files. Carolina Wren Press Poetry Contest for a First of Second Book takes submissions, electronically, from January to March of odd-numbered years.

TIPS "Best way to get read is to submit to a contest."

CAROLRHODA BOOKS, INC.

1251 Washington Ave. N., Minneapolis MN 55401. **Website:** www.lernerbooks.com. Estab. 1959. "We will continue to seek targeted solicitations at specific reading levels and in specific subject areas. The company will list these targeted solicitations on our website and in national newsletters, such as the SCBWI Bulletin."

◯   *Starting in 2007, Lerner Publishing Group no longer accepts submissions to any of their imprints except for Kar-Ben Publishing.*

CARSTENS PUBLICATIONS, INC.

Hobby Book Division, 108 Phil Hardin Rd., Newton NJ 07860. (973)383-3355. **Fax:** (973)383-4064. **E-mail:** carstens@carstens-publications.com. **Website:** www.carstens-publications.com. **Contact:** Henry R. Carstens, publisher. Estab. 1933. Publishes paperback originals. Carstens specializes in books about railroads, model railroads, and airplanes for hobbyists. **Publishes 8 titles/year. 100% from unagented writers. Pays 10% royalty on retail price. Pays advance.** Publishes ms 1 year after acceptance. Responds in 2 months to queries. Book catalog for #10 SASE.

NONFICTION Authors must know their field intimately because our readers are active modelers. Writers cannot write about somebody else's hobby with authority. If they do, we can't use them. Our railroad books presently are primarily photographic essays on specific railroads. Query with SASE. Reviews artwork/photos.

TIPS We need lots of good photos. Material must be in model, hobby, railroad, and transportation field only.

⚠️⊘ CARTWHEEL BOOKS

Imprint of Scholastic Trade Division, 557 Broadway, New York NY 10012. (212)343-6100. **Website:** www. scholastic.com. Estab. 1991. Publishes novelty books, easy readers, board books, hardcover and trade paperback originals. Cartwheel Books publishes innovative books for children, up to age 8. We are looking for 'novelties' that are books first, play objects second. Even without its gimmick, a Cartwheel Book should stand alone as a valid piece of children's literature. Accepts simultaneous submissions. Book catalog for 9 x 12 SASE. Guidelines available free.

NONFICTION Subjects include animals, history, music, dance, nature, environment, recreation, science, sports. Cartwheel Books publishes for the very young, therefore nonfiction should be written in a manner that is accessible to preschoolers through 2nd grade. Often writers choose topics that are too narrow or 'special' and do not appeal to the mass market. Also, the text and vocabulary are frequently too difficult for our young audience. *Accepts mss from agents, previously published authors only.* Reviews artwork/photos. Please do not send original artwork.

FICTION Subjects include humor, juvenile, mystery, picture books. Again, the subject should have mass market appeal for very young children. Humor can be helpful, but not necessary. Mistakes writers make are a reading level that is too difficult, a topic of no interest or too narrow, or manuscripts that are too long. *Accepts mss from agents, previously publishes authors only.*

TIPS Audience is young children, ages 0-8. Know what types of books the publisher does. Some manuscripts that don't work for one house may be perfect for another. Check out bookstores or catalogs to see where your writing would 'fit' best.

CATHOLIC UNIVERSITY OF AMERICA PRESS

620 Michigan Ave. NE, 240 Leahy Hall, Washington DC 20064. (202)319-5052. **Fax:** (202)319-4985. **E-mail:** cua-press@cua.edu. **Website:** cuapress.cua. edu. **Contact:** James C. Kruggel, acquisitions editor (philosophy, theology); Dr. David J. McGonagle, director (all other fields). Estab. 1939. The Catholic University of America Press publishes in the fields of history (ecclesiastical and secular), literature and languages, philosophy, political theory, social studies, and theology. "We have interdisciplinary emphasis on patristics, and medieval studies. We publish works of original scholarship intended for academic libraries, scholars and other professionals and works that offer a synthesis of knowledge of the subject of interest to a general audience or suitable for use in college and university classrooms." **Publishes 30-35 titles/ year. 50% of books from first-time authors. 100% from unagented writers. Pays variable royalty on net receipts.** Publishes book 18 months after acceptance. Responds in 5 days to queries. Book catalog on request. Guidelines available online.

NONFICTION Subjects include government, politics, history, language, literature, philosophy, religion, Church-state relations. No unrevised doctoral dissertations. Length: 40,000-120,000 words. Query with outline, sample chapter, cv, and list of previous publications.

TIPS Scholarly monographs and works suitable for adoption as supplementary reading material in courses have the best chance.

CAVE HOLLOW PRESS

P.O. Drawer J, Warrensburg MO 64093. **E-mail:** gb-crump@cavehollowpress.com. **Website:** www.cave-hollowpress.com. **Contact:** G.B. Crump, editor. Estab. 2001. Publishes trade paperback originals. **Publishes 1 title/year. 70 queries received/year. 6 mss received/year. 80% of books from first-time authors. 100% from unagented writers. Pays 7-12% royalty on wholesale price. Pays negotiable amount in advance.** Publishes book 1 year after acceptance of ms. Accepts simultaneous submissions. Responds in 1-2 months to queries and proposals. Responds in 3-6 months to manuscripts. Book catalog for #10 SASE. Guidelines available free.

FICTION Subjects include : mainstream, contemporary. "Our website is updated frequently to reflect the current type of fiction Cave Hollow Press is seeking." Query with SASE.

TIPS "Our audience varies based on the type of book we are publishing. We specialize in Missouri and Midwest regional fiction. We are interested in talented writers from Missouri and the surrounding Midwest. Check our submission guidelines on the website for what type of fiction we are interested in currently."

MARSHALL CAVENDISH

99 White Plains Rd., Tarrytown NY 10591. (914)332-8888. **Fax:** (914)332-1082. **E-mail:** mcc@marshall-cavendish.com. **Website:** www.marshallcavendish.us. **Contact:** Margery Cuyler, publisher. "Marshall Cavendish is an international publisher that publishes books, directories, magazines and digital platforms. Our philosophy of enriching life through knowledge transcends boundaries of geography and culture. In line with this vision, our products reach across the globe in 13 languages, and our publishing network spans Asia and the USA. Our brands have garnered international awards for educational excellence, and they include Marshall Cavendish Reference, Marshall Cavendish Benchmark, Marshall Cavendish Children, Marshall Cavendish Education and Marshall Cavendish Editions. Several have also achieved household name status in the international market. We ceaselessly explore new Ave.s to convey our products to the world, with our extensive variety of genres, languages and formats. In addition, our strategy of business expansion has ensured that the reach and benefits of Marshall Cavendish's products extend across the globe, especially into previously uncharted markets in China and Eastern Europe. Our aspiration to further the desire for lifelong learning and self-development continues to guide our efforts." **Publishes 60-70 titles/year. Pays authors/illustrators advance and royalties.**

IMPRINTS Marshall Cavendish Children, Marshall Cavendish Education and Marshall Cavendish Editions, Marshall Cavendish Reference, Marshall Cavendish Benchmark.

○ *Marshall Cavendish is no longer accepting unsolicited mss. However, the company will continue to consider agented mss.*

CEDAR FORT, INC.

2373 W. 700 S, Springville UT 84663. (801)489-4084. **Fax:** (801)489-1097. **Website:** www.cedarfort.com. **Contact:** Shersta Gatica, acquisitions editor. Estab. 1986. Publishes hardcover, trade paperback originals and reprints, mass market paperback and electronic reprints. "Each year we publish well over 100 books, and many of those are by first-time authors. At the same time, we love to see books from established authors. As one of the largest book publishers in Utah, we have the capability and enthusiasm to make your book a success, whether you are a newauthor or a returning one. We want to publish uplifting and edifying books that help people think about what is important in life, books people enjoyreading to relax and feel better about themselves, and books to help improve lives. We like to publish a wide variety of books. We are always on thelookout for new and exciting material that will capture the public's interest. However, there are a few genres with which we are very selective. Wearely take biographies, autobiographies, or memoirs unless they have a very strong selling point (such as Mafia to Mormon). We do not publishpoetry. Although we do put out several children's books each year, we are extremely selective. Our children's books must have strong religious ormoral values, and must contain outstanding writing and an excellent storyline." **Publishes 120 titles/year. Receives 200 queries/year; 600 mss/year. 60% of books from first-time authors. 95% from unagented writers. Pays 10-12% royalty on wholesale price. Pays $2,000-50,000 advance.** Publishes book 10-14 months after acceptance. Responds in 1 month on queries; 2 months on proposals; 4 months on mss. Catalog and guidelines available online at website.

IMPRINTS Council Press, Sweetwater Books, Bonneville Books, Front Table Books, Hobble Creek Press, CFI.

NONFICTION Subjects include agriculture, Americana, animals, anthropology, archeology, business, child guidance, communications, cooking, crafts, creative nonfiction, economics, education, foods, gardening, health, history, hobbies, horticulture, house and home, military, nature, recreation, regional, religion, social sciences, spirituality, war, womens issues, young adult. Query with SASE; submit proposal package, including outline, 2 sample chapters; or submit completed ms. Reviews artwork as part of the ms package. Send photocopies.

FICTION Subjects include adventure, contemporary, fantasy, historical, humor, juvenile, literary, mainstream, military, multicultural, mystery, regional, religious, romance, science fiction, spiritual, sports, suspense, war, western, young adult. Submit completed ms.

TIPS "Our audience is rural, conservative, mainstream. The first page of your ms is very important because we start reading every submission, but good writing and plot keep us reading."

⊕ CENTER FOR THANATOLOGY RESEARCH & EDUCATION, INC.

391 Atlantic Ave., Brooklyn NY 11217. (718)858-3026. **E-mail:** thanatology@pipeline.com. **Website:** www.thanatology.org. Estab. 1980. **Publishes 7 titles/year. 10 queries received/year. 3 mss received/year. 15% of books from first-time authors. 100% from unagented writers. Pays 10% royalty on wholesale price.** Publishes ms 9 months after acceptance. Responds in 1 month to queries and proposals. Book catalog and ms guidelines free.

NONFICTION Subjects include education, health, medicine, humanities, psychology, religion, social sciences, sociology, women's issues, women's studies, anthropology. All proposals we feel are applicable are sent to a board of professional readers for comment. Query with SASE. Reviews artwork/photos. Send photocopies.

POETRY We are open to appropriate submissions. Query.

TIPS "We serve 2 different audiences: One is physicians/social workers/nurses dealing with dying patients and bereaved families. The second relates to all aspects of cemetery lore: recording, preservation, description, art of."

CENTERSTREAM PUBLISHING

P.O. Box 17878, Anaheim Hills CA 92817. (714)779-9390. **Fax:** (714)779-9390. **E-mail:** Centerstrm@aol.com. **Website:** www.centerstream-usa.com. **Contact:** Ron Middlebrook, Cindy Middlebrook, owners. Estab. 1980. Publishes music hardcover and mass market paperback originals, trade paperback and mass market paperback reprints. Centerstream publishes music history and instructional books, all instruments plus DVDs. **Publishes 12 titles/year. 15 queries received/year. 15 mss received/year. 80% of books from first-time authors. 100% from unagented writers. Pays 10-15% royalty on wholesale price. Pays $300-3,000 advance.** Publishes ms 8 months after acceptance. Accepts simultaneous submissions. Responds in 3 months to queries. Book catalog and ms guidelines for #10 SASE.

NONFICTION Query with SASE.

RECENT Title(s) *Guitar Chord Shapes of Charlie Christian.*

CHALICE PRESS

483 E. Lockwood Ave., Suite 100, St. Louis MO 63119. (314)231-8500. **Fax:** (314)231-8524. **E-mail:** submissions@chalicepress.com. **Website:** www.chalicepress.com. **Contact:** Bradley Lyons, president and publisher. Publishes hardcover and trade paperback originals. **Publishes 35 titles/year. 300 queries received/year. 250 mss received/year. 10% of books from first-time authors. 100% from unagented writers.** Publishes ms 1 year after acceptance. Accepts simultaneous submissions. Responds in 2 months to queries; 3 months to proposals and mss. Book catalog available online. Guidelines available online.

NONFICTION Subjects include religion, Christian spirituality. Submit query.

RECENT Title(s) *Unbinding the Gospel*, by Martha Grace Reese; *Sabbath in the Suburbs*, by MaryAnn McKibben Dana; *Banned Questions about Jesus*, by Christian Piatt; *Passage into Discipleship: Guide to Baptism*, by Christopher Wilson; *A New Evangelical Manifesto: A Kingdom Vision for the Common Good*, edited by David P. Gushee; *Only God Knows Why*, by Amy Lyon.

TIPS "We publish for professors, church ministers, and lay Christian readers."

CHARLESBRIDGE PUBLISHING

85 Main St., Watertown MA 02472. (617)926-0329. **Fax:** (617)926-5720. **E-mail:** tradeeditorial@charlesbridge.com. **Website:** www.charlesbridge.com. Estab. 1980. Publishes hardcover and trade paperback nonfiction and fiction, children's books for the trade and library markets. "Charlesbridge publishes high-quality books for children, with a goal of creating lifelong readers and lifelong learners. Our books encourage reading and discovery in the classroom, library, and home. We believe that books for children should offer accurate information, promote a positive worldview, and embrace a child's innate sense of wonder and fun. To this end, we continually strive to seek new voices, new visions, and new directions in children's literature." **Publishes 30 titles/year. 10-20% of books from first-time authors. 80% from unagented writers. Pays royalty. Pays advance.** Publishes ms 2-4 years after acceptance. Responds in 3 months. If you have not heard back from us after 3 months, you may assume we do not have a place for your project and submit it elsewhere. Guidelines available online.

IMPRINTS Charlesbridge, Imagine Publishing.

○ "We're always interested in innovative approaches to a difficult genre, the nonfiction picture book."

NONFICTION Subjects include animals, creative nonfiction, history, multicultural, nature, environment, science, social science. Strong interest in nature, environment, social studies, and other topics for trade and library markets. *Exclusive submissions only.* "Charlesbridge accepts unsolicited manuscripts submitted exclusively to us for a period of three months. 'Exclusive Submission' should be written on all envelopes and cover letters." Please submit only one or two chapters at a time. For nonfiction books longer than 30 manuscript pages, send a detailed proposal, a chapter outline, and one to three chapters of text. Manuscripts should be typed and double-spaced. Please do not submit material by email, by fax, or on a computer disk. Illustrations are not necessary. Please make a copy of your manuscript, as we cannot be responsible for submissions lost in the mail. Include your name and address on the first page of your manuscript and in your cover letter. Be sure to list any previously published work or relevant writing experience.

FICTION Strong stories with enduring themes. Charlesbridge publishes both picture books and transitional bridge books (books ranging from early readers to middle-grade chapter books). Our fiction titles include lively, plot-driven stories with strong, engaging characters. No alphabet books, board books, coloring books, activity books, or books with audiotapes or CD-ROMs. *Exclusive submissions only.* "Charlesbridge accepts unsolicited manuscripts submitted exclusively to us for a period of three months. 'Exclusive Submission' should be written on all envelopes and cover letters. Please submit only one or two manuscript(s) at a time. For picture books and shorter bridge books, please send a complete manuscript. For fiction books longer than 30 manuscript pages, please send a detailed plot synopsis, a chapter outline, and three chapters of text. Manuscripts should be typed and double-spaced. Please do not submit material by email, by fax, or on a computer disk. Illustrations are not necessary. Please make a copy of your manuscript, as we cannot be responsible for submissions lost in the mail. Include your name and address on the first page of your manuscript and in your cover letter. Be sure to list any previously published work or relevant writing experience."

TIPS "To become acquainted with our publishing program, we encourage you to review our books and visit our website (www.charlesbridge.com), where you will find our catalog. To request a printed catalog, please send a 9" x 12" SASE with $2.50 in postage."

THE CHARLES PRESS, PUBLISHERS

230 North 21st St., Philadelphia PA 19103. (215)561-2786. **Fax:** (215)561-0191. **E-mail:** mailbox@charlespresspub.com. **Website:** www.charlespresspub.com. **Contact:** Lauren Meltzer, publisher. Estab. 1982. Publishes hardcover and trade paperback originals. Currently emphasizing mental and physical health (especially holistic, complementary and alternative healthcare), psychology, animals/pets/veterinary medicine, how-to (especially relating to healthcare and wellness), comparative religion, aging/eldercare/geriatrics, medical reference books. Accepts simultaneous submissions. Responds in approximately 1 to 2 months to proposals; 2 months to manuscripts. Book catalog available online. Guidelines available online.

NONFICTION Subjects include child guidance, health, mental health, physical health, medicine, psychology, religion, nursing, health care, how-to, aging/eldercare, criminology, true crime. No fiction, autobiographies, children's books, or poetry Query first, then submit proposal package that includes a description of the book, a few representative sample chapters, intended audience, competing titles, author's qualifications/background and SASE. No e-mailed or faxed submissions. Reviews artwork/photos. Send photocopies or transparencies.

CHELSEA GREEN PUBLISHING CO.

85 N. Main St., Suite 120, White River Junction VT 05001. (802)295-6300. **Fax:** (802)295-6444. **E-mail:** editorial@chelseagreen.com. **E-mail:** submissions@chelseagreen.com. **Website:** www.chelseagreen.com. Estab. 1984. Publishes hardcover and trade paperback originals and reprints. "Since 1984, Chelsea Green has been the publishing leader for books on the politics and practice of sustainable living." **Publishes 18-25 titles/year. 600-800 queries received/year. 200-300 mss received/year. 30% of books from first-time authors. 80% from unagented writers. Pays royalty on publisher's net. Pays $2,500-10,000 advance.** Publishes book 18 months after aceeptance. after acceptance of ms. Responds in 2 weeks to queries; 1 month to proposals/mss. Book catalog free or online. Guidelines available online.

NONFICTION Subjects include agriculture, alternative lifestyles, ethical & sustainable business, environment, foods, organic gardening, health, green building, progressive politics, science, social justice, simple living, renewable energy; and other sustainability topics. "We seldom publish cookbooks." We prefer electronic queries and proposals via email (as a single attachment). If sending via snail mail, submissions will only be returned with SASE. Please review our guidelines carefully before submitting. Reviews artwork/photos.

FICTION We do not publish fiction or children's books.

TIPS "Our readers and our authors are passionate about finding sustainable and viable solutions to contemporary challenges in the fields of energy, food production, economics, and building. It would be helpful for prospective authors to have a look at several of our current books, as well as our website."

CHELSEA HOUSE PUBLISHERS

Infobase Publishing, 132 W. 31st St., 17th Floor, New York NY 10001. (800) 322-8755 or (212) 967-8800. **Fax:** (800)780-7300. **E-mail:** editorial@factsonfile. com. **Website:** www.chelseahouse.com. **Contact:** Editorial assistant. Publishes hardcover originals and reprints. We publish curriculum-based nonfiction books for middle school and high school students. Accepts simultaneous submissions. Book catalog available online. Guidelines for #10 SASE.

NONFICTION Subjects include Americana, animals, anthropology, archeology, ethnic, gay, lesbian, government, politics, health, medicine, history, hobbies, language, literature, military, war, multicultural, music, dance, nature, environment, recreation, regional, religion, science, sociology, sports, travel, women's issues, women's studies. We are interested in expanding our topics to include more on the physical, life and environmental sciences. Query with SASE. Submit proposal package, outline, 2-3 sample chapters, résumé. Reviews artwork/photos. Send photocopies.

TIPS "Please review our products online or in our bi-annual catalog. Please be sure submissions fit our market of the middle and high school student. Be professional. Send clean, clear submissions that show you read the preferred submission format. Always include SASE."

CHEMICAL PUBLISHING CO., INC.

P.O. Box 676, Revere MA 02151. (888)439-3976. **Fax:** (888)439-3976. **E-mail:** info@chemical-publishing. com. **Website:** www.chemical-publishing.com. **Contact:** B. Carr, publisher. Estab. 1934. Publishes hard-

cover originals. Chemical Publishing Co., Inc., publishes professional chemistry-technical titles aimed at people employed in the chemical industry, libraries and graduate courses. **Publishes 10-15 titles/year. 20 queries received/year. 50% of books from first-time authors. 100% from unagented writers. Pays 10% royalty on retail price or makes negotiable outright purchase. Pays negotiable advance.** Publishes ms 8 months after acceptance. Responds in 3 weeks to queries; 5 weeks to proposals; 1 months to mss. Book catalog available free. Guidelines available online.

○ "We invite the submission of manuscripts whether they are technical, scientific or serious popular expositions. All submitted manuscripts and planned works will receive prompt attention. The staff will consider finished and proposed manuscripts by authors whose works have not been previously published as sympathetically as those by experienced authors. Please do not hesitate to consult us about such manuscripts or about your ideas for writing them."

NONFICTION Subjects include agriculture, cooking, foods, nutrition, health, medicine, nature, environment, science, analytical methods, chemical technology, cosmetics, dictionaries, engineering, environmental science, food technology, formularies, industrial technology, medical, metallurgy, textiles. Submit outline, a few pages of 3 sample chapters, SASE. Download CPC submission form online and include with submission. Reviews, artwork and photos should also be part of the manuscript package.

TIPS Audience is professionals in various fields of chemistry, corporate and public libraries, college libraries. We request a fax letter with an introduction of the author and the kind of book written. Afterwards, we will reply. If the title is of interest, then we will request samples of the manuscript.

CHICAGO REVIEW PRESS

814 N. Franklin St., Chicago IL 60610. (312)337-0747. **Fax:** (312)337-5110. **E-mail:** frontdesk@chicagoreviewpress.com. **Website:** www.chicagoreviewpress. com. **Contact:** Cynthia Sherry, publisher; Allison Felus, managing editor. Estab. 1973. "Chicago Review Press publishes high-quality, nonfiction, educational activity books that extend the learning process through hands-on projects and accurate and interesting text. We look for activity books that are as much

fun as they are constructive and informative." **Pays authors royalty of 712-1212% based on retail price. Offers advances of $3,000-6,000. Pays illustrators by the project (range varies considerably). Pays photographers by the project (range varies considerably).** Publishes a book 1-2 years after acceptance. Accepts simultaneous submissions. Responds to queries/mss in 2 months. Book catalog available for $3. Ms guidelines available for $3.

◯ *Chicago Review Press does not publish fiction.*

NONFICTION Young readers, middle readers and young adults: activity books, arts/crafts, multicultural, history, nature/environment, science. "We're interested in hands-on, educational books; anything else probably will be rejected." Average length: young readers and young adults—144-160 pgs. Enclose cover letter and no more than a table of contents and 1-2 sample chapters; prefers not to receive e-mail queries.

TIPS "We're looking for original activity books for small children and the adults caring for them—new themes and enticing projects to occupy kids' imaginations and promote their sense of personal creativity. We like activity books that are as much fun as they are constructive. Please write for guidelines so you'll know what we're looking for."

CHILDREN'S BRAINS ARE YUMMY (CBAY) BOOKS

P.O. Box 92411, Austin TX 78709. (312)789-1004. **Fax:** (512)473-7710. **E-mail:** submissions@cbaybooks.com. **Website:** www.cbaybooks.com. **Contact:** Madeline Smoot, publisher. Estab. 2008. "CBAY Books currently focuses on quality fantasy and science fiction books for the middle grade and teen markets. Although we are exploring the possibility of publishing fantasy and science fiction books in the future, we are not seeking submissions for them at this time. We do welcome books that mix genres—a fantasy mystery for example—but since our press currently has a narrow focus, all submissions need to have fantasy or science fiction elements to fit in with our list." **Publishes 8 titles/year. 30% of books from first-time authors. 0% from unagented writers. Pays authors royalty 10%-15% based on wholesale price. Offers advances against royalties. Average amount $500.** Responds in 3 months to mss. Brochure and guidelines available online at website.

FICTION Subjects include adventure, mystery, science fiction, suspense, folktales. Accepts international material. Submit outline/synopsis and 3 sample chapters.

TIPS "CBAY Books only accepts unsolicited submissions from authors at specific times for specific genres. Please check the website to see if we are accepting books at this time. Manuscripts received when submissions are closed are not read."

CHILDREN'S PRESS/FRANKLIN WATTS

Imprint of Scholastic, Inc., 90 Old Sherman Turnpike, Danbury CT 06816. **Website:** scholastic.com/librarypublishing; www.scholastic.com/internationalschools/childrenspress.htm. Estab. 1946. Publishes nonfiction hardcover originals. Book catalog for #10 SASE.

◯ "Children's Press publishes 90% nonfiction for the school and library market, and 10% early reader fiction and nonfiction. Our books support textbooks and closely relate to the elementary and middle-school curriculum. Franklin Watts publishes nonfiction for middle and high school curriculum."

NONFICTION Subjects include animals, anthropology, archeology, art, architecture, ethnic, health, medicine, history, hobbies, multicultural, music, dance, nature, environment, science, sports, general children's nonfiction. We publish nonfiction books that supplement the school curriculum. No fiction, poetry, folktales, cookbooks or novelty books. Query with SASE.

TIPS Most of this publisher's books are developed in-house; less than 5% come from unsolicited submissions. However, they publish several series for which they always need new books. Study catalogs to discover possible needs.

CHILD'S PLAY (INTERNATIONAL) LTD.

Children's Play International, Ashworth Rd. Bridgemead, Swindon, Wiltshire SN5 7YD, United Kingdom. **E-mail:** allday@childs-play.com; neil@childs-play.com; office@childs-play.com. **Website:** www.childs-play.com. **Contact:** Sue Baker, Neil Burden, manuscript acquisitions. Annie Kubler, art director Estab. 1972. Specializes in nonfiction, fiction, educational material, multicultural material. Produces 30 picture books/year; 10 young readers/year; 2 middle readers/year. "A child's early years are more important than any other. This is when children learn most about the world around them and the language they need to survive and grow. Child's Play aims to create exactly the right material for this all-important time." **Publishes 45 titles/year. 20% of books from first-time authors.** Publishes book 2 years after acceptance. Accepts simultaneous submissions. Responds to queries in 10 weeks; mss in 15 weeks.

NONFICTION Picture books: activity books, animal, concept, multicultural, music/dance, nature/environment, science. Young readers: activity books, animal, concept, multicultural, music/dance, nature/environment, science. Average word length: picture books—2,000; young readers—3,000.

FICTION Picture books: adventure, animal, concept, contemporary, folktales, multicultural, nature/environment. Young readers: adventure, animal, anthology, concept, contemporary, folktales, humor, multicultural, nature/environment, poetry. Average word length: picture books—1,500; young readers—2,000.

TIPS "Look at our website to see the kind of work we do before sending. Do not send cartoons. We do not publish novels. We do publish lots of books with pictures of babies/toddlers."

CHILD WELFARE LEAGUE OF AMERICA

1726 M St. NW, Suite 500, Washington DC 20036. **E-mail:** books@cwla.org. **Website:** www.cwla.org/pubs. Publishes hardcover and trade paperback originals. CWLA is a privately supported, nonprofit, membership-based organization committed to preserving, protecting, and promoting the well-being of all children and their families. Accepts simultaneous submissions. Book catalog and ms guidelines online.

IMPRINTS CWLA Press (child welfare professional publications); Child & Family Press (children's books and parenting books for the general public).

NONFICTION Subjects include child guidance, sociology. Submit complete ms and proposal with outline, TOC, sample chapter, intended audience, and SASE.

TIPS We are looking for positive, kid-friendly books for ages 3-9. We are looking for books that have a positive message—a feel-good book.

CHOSEN BOOKS

a division of Baker Publishing Group, 3985 Bradwater St., Fairfax VA 22031. (703)764-8250. **Fax:** (703)764-3995. **E-mail:** jcampbell@chosenbooks.com. **Website:** www.chosenbooks.com. **Contact:** Jane Campbell, editorial director. Estab. 1971. Publishes hardcover and trade paperback originals. "We publish well-crafted books that recognize the gifts and ministry of the Holy Spirit, and help the reader live a more empow-

ered and effective life for Jesus Christ." **Publishes 20 titles/year. 10% of books from first-time authors. 99% from unagented writers. Pays small advance.** Publishes book 12-18 months after acceptance. Accepts simultaneous submissions. Responds in 2-3 months to queries. Guidelines sent electronically on request.

NONFICTION "We publish books reflecting the current acts of the Holy Spirit in the world, books with a charismatic Christian orientation, or thematic first-person narrative. Query briefly by e-mail first." No New Age, poetry, fiction, autobiographies, biographies, compilations, Bible studies, booklets, academic, or children's books. Submit synopsis, chapter outline, 2 chapters, resume and SASE or email address. No computer disks. E-mail attachments OK.

TIPS "We look for solid, practical advice for the growing and maturing Christian. Platform essential. No chronicling of life events, please. Narratives have to be theme-driven. State the topic or theme of your book clearly in your query."

CHRISTIAN BOOKS TODAY LTD

136 Main St., Buckshaw Village Chorley, Lancashire PR7 7BZ, United Kingdom. **E-mail:** md@christian-bookstoday.com. **E-mail:** submissions@christian-bookstoday.com. **Website:** www.christianbookstoday.com. **Contact:** Jason Richardson, MD (nonfiction); Lynda McIntosh, editor (fiction). Estab. 2009. Publishes trade paperback originals/reprints and electronic originals/reprints. **Publishes 39 titles/year. 75% of books from first-time authors. 100% from unagented writers. Pays 10% royalty on retail price or 50% of title profit.** Publishes ms 6 months after acceptance. Accepts simultaneous submissions. Responds in 1 month to queries; 2 months to proposals and mss. Catalog and guidelines available online.

NONFICTION Subjects include spirituality, Christian/Catholic. "We are not looking for nonfiction at this time. Please send us your fiction."

FICTION Subjects include adventure, mainstream, poetry, religious, spiritual, Catholic/Christian. "We're looking for writers who write about life, failures and all! Tackle the big issues but in a tasteful way. Deal with divorce, blended families, ecumenism, atheists, creationism, crazy preachers, celebrity culture, sexuality. Life doesn't conform to expectations – neither did Christ. Tackle the difficult and brutal. How do we as Christians deal with the messiness? Moralizing doesn't appeal to a broader audience. In your cover letter tell us how you intend to market the book, what sets it apart. No fantasy or sci-fi please." Submit "cover Letter, chapter by chapter outline, first 3 chapters & SASE. Or via the member section of our website."

TIPS "We appeal to a general Christian readership. We are not interested in Hallmark stories, nor fantasy, or mysticism. We want work by Christians rather than Christian writing. If you want to take a risk in subject, you are particularly encouraged to submit. We actively seek out writers who want to build a career with us and who understand we do what we do because we love it."

CHRISTIAN FOCUS PUBLICATIONS

Geanies House, Tain Ross-shire IV20 1TW, United Kingdom. 44 (0) 1862 871 011. **Fax:** 44 (0) 1862 871 699. **E-mail:** info@christianfocus.com. **Website:** www. christianfocus.com. **Contact:** Catherine Mackenzie, publisher. Estab. 1975. Specializes in Christian material, nonfiction, fiction, educational material. **Publishes 22-32 titles/year. 2% of books from first-time authors.** Publishes book 1 year after acceptance. Responds to queries in 2 weeks; mss in 3 months.

NONFICTION All levels: activity books, biography, history, religion, science. Average word length: picture books—5,000; young readers—5,000; middle readers—5,000-10,000; young adult/teens—10,000-20,000. Recently published *Moses the Child-Kept by God*, by Carine Mackenzie, illustrated by Graham Kennedy (young reader, Bible story); *Hearts and Hands-History Lives vol. 4*, by Mindy Withrow, cover illustration by Jonathan Williams (teen, church history); *Little Hands Life of Jesus*, by Carine Mackenzie, illustrated by Rafaella Cosco (picture book, Bible stories about Jesus). Query or submit outline/synopsis and 3 sample chapters. Will consider electronic submissions and previously published work.

FICTION Picture books, young readers, adventure, history, religion. Middle readers: adventure, problem novels, religion. Young adult/teens: adventure, history, problem novels, religion. Average word length: young readers—5,000; middle readers—max 10,000; YA/teen—max 20,000. Query or submit outline/synopsis and 3 sample chapters. Will consider electronic submissions and previously published work.

TIPS "Be aware of the international market as regards writing style/topics as well as illustration styles. Our company sells rights to European as well as Asian countries. Fiction sales are not as good as they were. Christian fiction for youngsters is not a product that is performing well in comparison to nonfiction such as Christian biography/Bible stories/church history, etc."

CHRONICLE BOOKS

680 Second St., San Francisco CA 94107. **E-mail:** submissions@chroniclebooks.com. **Website:** www. chroniclebooks.com. "We publish an exciting range of books, stationery, kits, calendars, and novelty formats. Our list includes children's books and interactive formats; young adult books; cookbooks; fine art, design, and photography; pop culture; craft, fashion, beauty, and home decor; relationships, mind body-spirit; innovative formats such as interactive journals, kits, decks, and stationery; and much, much more." **Publishes 90 titles/year. Generally pays authors in royalties based on retail price, "though we do occasionally work on a flat fee basis." Advance varies. Illustrators paid royalty based on retail price or flat fee.** Publishes a book 1-3 years after acceptance. Responds to queries in 1 month. Book catalog for 9x12 SAE and 8 first-class stamps. Ms guidelines for #10 SASE.

NONFICTION Subjects include art, beauty, cooking, crafts, house and home, New Age, pop culture. "We're always looking for the new and unusual. We do accept unsolicited manuscripts and we review all proposals. However, given the volume of proposals we receive, we are not able to personally respond to unsolicited proposals unless we are interested in pursuing the project." Submit via mail or e-mail (prefers e-mail for adult submissions; only by mail for children's submissions). Submit proposal (guidelines online) and allow 3 months for editors to review. If submitting by mail, do not include SASE since our staff will not return materials.

FICTION Only interested in fiction for children and young adults. No adult fiction. Submit complete ms (picture books); submit outline/synopsis and 3 sample chapters (for older readers). Will not respond to submissions unless interested. Will not consider submissions by fax, e-mail or disk. Do not include SASE; do not send original materials. No submissions will be returned.

CHRONICLE BOOKS FOR CHILDREN

680 Second St., San Francisco CA 94107. (415)537-4200. **Fax:** (415)537-4460. **E-mail:** frontdesk@ chroniclebooks.com. **Website:** www.chroniclekids.

com. Publishes hardcover and trade paperback originals. "Chronicle Books for Children publishes an eclectic mixture of traditional and innovative children's books. Our aim is to publish books that inspire young readers to learn and grow creatively while helping them discover the joy of reading. We're looking for quirky, bold artwork and subject matter. Currently emphasizing picture books. De-emphasizing young adult." **Publishes 50-60 titles/year. 30,000 queries received/year. 6% of books from first-time authors. 25% from unagented writers. Pays 8% royalty. Pays variable advance.** Publishes a book 18-24 months after acceptance. Accepts simultaneous submissions. Responds in 2-4 weeks to queries; 6 months to mss. Book catalog for 9x12 envelope and 3 first-class stamps. Guidelines available online.

NONFICTION Subjects include animals, art, architecture, multicultural, nature, environment, science. Query with synopsis. Reviews artwork/photos.

FICTION Subjects include mainstream, contemporary, multicultural, young adult, picture books. Does not accept proposals by fax, via e-mail, or on disk. When submitting artwork, either as a part of a project or as samples for review, do not send original art.

TIPS "We are interested in projects that have a unique bent to them—be it in subject matter, writing style, or illustrative technique. As a small list, we are looking for books that will lend our list a distinctive flavor. Primarily we are interested in fiction and nonfiction picture books for children ages up to eight years, and nonfiction books for children ages up to twelve years. We publish board, pop-up, and other novelty formats as well as picture books. We are also interested in early chapter books, middle grade fiction, and young adult projects."

CHURCH PUBLISHING INC.

445 Fifth Ave., New York NY 10016. (800)223-6602. **Fax:** (212)779-3392. **E-mail:** nabryan@cpg.org. **Website:** www.churchpublishing.org. **Contact:** Nancy Bryan, editorial director. Estab. 1884. "With a religious publishing heritage dating back to 1918 and headquartered today in New York City, CPI is an official publisher of worship materials and resources for The Episcopal Church, plus a multi-faceted publisher and supplier to the broader ecumenical marketplace. In the nearly 100 years since its first publication, Church Publishing has emerged as a principal provider of liturgical and musical resources for The Episcopal Church, along with works on church leadership, pastoral care and Christian formation. With its growing portfolio of professional books and resources, Church Publishing was recognized in 1997 as the official publisher for the General Convention of the Episcopal Church in the United States. Simultaneously through the years, Church Publishing has consciously broadened its program, reach, and service to the church by publishing books for and about the worldwide Anglican Communion."

IMPRINTS Our book publishing imprints include Church Publishing, Morehouse Publishing, and Seabury Books.

TIPS "Prefer using freelancers who are located in central Pennsylvania and are available for meetings when necessary."

CLARION BOOKS

Houghton Mifflin Co., 215 Park Ave. S., New York NY 10003. **Website:** www.houghtonmifflinbooks.com; www.hmco.com. **Contact:** Dinah Stevenson, vice president and publisher; Jennifer B. Greene, senior editor (contemporary fiction, picture books for all ages, nonfiction); Jennifer Wingertzahn, editor (fiction, picture books); Lynne Polvino, editor (fiction, nonfiction, picture books); Christine Kettner, art director. Estab. 1965. Publishes hardcover originals for children. "Clarion Books publishes picture books, nonfiction, and fiction for infants through grade 12. Avoid telling your stories in verse unless you are a professional poet." **Publishes 50 titles/year. Pays 5-10% royalty on retail price. Pays minimum of $4,000 advance.** Publishes a book 2 years after acceptance. Responds in 2 months to queries. Guidelines for #10 SASE or online.

"We are no longer responding to your unsolicited submission unless we are interested in publishing it. Please do not include a SASE. Submissions will be recycled, and you will not hear from us regarding the status of your submission unless we are interested. We regret that we cannot respond personally to each submission, but we do consider each and every submission we receive."

NONFICTION Subjects include Americana, history, language, literature, nature, environment, photography, holiday. No unsolicited mss. Query with SASE. Submit proposal package, sample chapters, SASE. Reviews artwork/photos. Send photocopies.

FICTION Subjects include adventure, historical, humor, suspense, strong character studies, contemporary. "Clarion is highly selective in the areas of historical fiction, fantasy, and science fiction. A novel must be superlatively written in order to find a place on the list. Mss that arrive without an SASE of adequate size will *not* be responded to or returned. Accepts fiction translations." Submit complete ms. No queries, please. Send to only *one* Clarion editor.

TIPS "Looks for freshness, enthusiasm—in short, life."

CLARITY PRESS, INC.

3277 Roswell Rd. NE, Suite 469, Atlanta GA 30305. (404)647-6501. **Fax:** (877)613-7868. **E-mail:** clari typress@usa.net. **Website:** www.claritypress.com. **Contact:** Diana G. Collier, editorial director (contemporary social justice issues). Estab. 1984. Publishes hardcover and trade paperback originals. **Publishes 8 titles/year.** Accepts simultaneous submissions. Responds to queries only if interested.

NONFICTION Subjects include ethnic, world affairs, human rights/socioeconomic and minority issues, globalization, social justice. Publishes books on contemporary global issues in U.S., Middle East and Africa. No fiction. Query by e-mail only with synopsis, TOC, résumé, publishing history.

TIPS "Check our titles on the website at www.claritypress.com."

CLEAR LIGHT PUBLISHERS

823 Don Diego, Santa Fe NM 87505. (505)989-9590. **Fax:** (505)989-9519. **E-mail:** market@clearlightbooks.com. **Website:** clearlightbooks.com. **Contact:** Harmon Houghton, publisher. Estab. 1981. Publishes hardcover and trade paperback originals. "Clear Light publishes books that accurately depict the positive side of human experience and inspire the spirit." **Publishes 20-24 titles/year. 100 queries received/year. 10% of books from first-time authors. 50% from unagented writers. Pays 10% royalty on wholesale price. Offers advance, a percent of gross potential.** Publishes a book 1 year after acceptance. Accepts simultaneous submissions. Responds in 3 months to queries. Book catalog free. Guidelines available online.

NONFICTION Subjects include Americana, anthropology, archeology, art, architecture, cooking, foods, nutrition, ethnic, history, nature, environment, philosophy, photography, regional, Southwest. Middle readers and young adults: multicultural, American Indian and Hispanic only. Submit complete ms with SASE. "No e-mail submissions. Authors supply art. Manuscripts not considered without art or artist's renderings." Reviews artwork/photos. Send photocopies.

CLEIS PVRESS

Cleis Press & Viva Editions, 2246 Sixth St., Berkeley CA 94710. (510)845-8000 or (800)780-2279. **Fax:** (510)845-8001. **E-mail:** cleis@cleispress.com. **E-mail:** bknight@cleispress.com. **Website:** www.cleispress.com and www.vivaeditions.com. **Contact:** Brenda Knight, associate publisher. Kara Wuest, publishing coordinator; Frédérique Delacoste, art director Estab. 1980. Publishes books that inform, enlighten, and entertain. Areas of interest include gift, inspiration, health, family and childcare, self-help, women's issues, reference, cooking. "We do our best to bring readers quality books that celebrate life, inspire the mind, revive the spirit, and enhance lives all around. Our authors are practical visionaries; people who offer deep wisdom in a hopeful and helpful manner.". Cleis Press publishes provocative, intelligent books in the areas of sexuality, gay and lesbian studies, erotica, fiction, gender studies, and human rights. **Publishes 45 titles/year. 10% of books from first-time authors. 90% from unagented writers. Pays royalty on retail price.** Publishes ms 2 years after acceptance. Responds in 2 month to queries.

IMPRINTS Viva Edition

NONFICTION Subjects include gay, lesbian, women's issues, women's studies, sexual politics. "Cleis Press is interested in books on topics of sexuality, human rights and women's and gay and lesbian literature. Please consult our website first to be certain that your book fits our list." Query or submit outline and sample chapters.

FICTION Subjects include feminist, gay, lesbian, literary. "We are looking for high quality fiction and nonfiction." Submit complete ms. Include brief bio, list of publishing credits. Send SASE for return of ms or send a disposable ms and SASE for reply only.

TIPS "Be familiar with publishers' catalogs; be absolutely aware of your audience; research potential markets; present fresh new ways of looking at your topic; avoid 'PR' language and include publishing history in query letter."

CLEVELAND STATE UNIVERSITY POETRY CENTER

2121 Euclid Ave., RT 1841, Cleveland OH 44115. (216)687-3986. **Fax:** (216)687-6943. **E-mail:** poetry-center@csuohio.edu. **Website:** www.csuohio.edu/poetrycenter. **Contact:** Frank Giampietro, manager. Estab. 1962.

POETRY The Cleveland State University Poetry Center publishes "full-length collections by established and emerging poets, through competition and solicitation, as well as occasional poetry anthologies, texts on poetics, and novellas. Eclectic in its taste and inclusive in its aesthetic, with particular interest in lyric poetry and innovative approaches to craft. Not interested in light verse, devotional verse, doggerel, or poems by poets who have not read much contemporary poetry." Recent CSU Poetry Center publications include *The Hartford Book*, by Samuel Amadon; *Mother Was a Tragic Girl*, by Sandra Simonds; *I Live in a Hut*, by S.E. Smith; *Uncanny Valley*, by Jon Woodward. "Most manuscripts we publish are accepted through the competitions. All manuscripts sent for competitions are considered for publication. Outside of competitions, manuscripts are accepted by solicitation only."

○ COACH HOUSE BOOKS

80 bpNichol Lane, Toronto ON M5S 3J4, Canada. (416)979-2217. **Fax:** (416)977-1158. **E-mail:** editor@chbooks.com. **Website:** www.chbooks.com. **Contact:** Alana Wilcox, editor. Publishes trade paperback originals by Canadian authors. **Publishes 16 titles/year. 80% of books from first-time authors. 100% from unagented writers. Pays 10% royalty on retail price.** Publishes ms 1 year after acceptance. Responds in 6 months to queries. Guidelines available online.

NONFICTION Query with SASE.

FICTION Subjects include experimental, literary, poetry. "Electronic submissions are welcome. Please send your complete manuscript, along with an introductory letter that describes your work and compares it to at least two current Coach House titles, explaining how your book would fit our list, and a literary CV listing your previous publications and relevant experience. If you would like your manuscript back, please enclose a large enough self-addressed envelope with adequate postage. If you don't want your ms back, a small stamped envelope or e-mail address is fine. We prefer electronic submissions. Please email PDF files

to editor@chbooks.com and include the cover letter and CV as a part of the ms. Please send your manuscript only once. Revised and updated versions will not be read, so make sure you're happy with your text before sending. You can also send your manuscript to 80 bpNichol Lane, Toronto, Ontario, M5S 3J4. Please do not send it by ExpressPost or Canada Post courier – regular Canada Post mail is much more likely to arrive here. Be patient. We try to respond promptly, but we do receive hundreds of submissions, so it may take us several months to get back to you. Please do not call or email to check on the status of your submission. We will answer you as promptly as possible."

TIPS "We are not a general publisher, and publish only Canadian poetry, fiction, artist books and drama. We are interested primarily in innovative or experimental writing."

COFFEE HOUSE PRESS

79 13th NE, Suite 110, Minneapolis MN 55413. (612)338-0125. **Fax:** (612)338-4004. **E-mail:** info@coffeehousepress.org. **Website:** www.coffeehousepress.org. **Contact:** Chris Fischbach, associate publisher. Estab. 1984. Publishes hardcover and trade paperback originals. This successful nonprofit small press has received numerous grants from various organizations including the NEA, the McKnight Foundation and Target. Books published by Coffee House Press have won numerous honors and awards. Example: The Book of Medicines by Linda Hogan won the Colorado Book Award for Poetry and the Lannan Foundation Literary Fellowship. **Publishes 16-18 titles/year.** Responds in 4-6 weeks to queries; up to 6 months to mss. Book catalog and ms guidelines online.

FICTION Fiction Seeks literary novels, short story collections and poetry. Query first with outline and samples (20-30 pages).

POETRY As of September 1, 2010, Coffee House Press will only accept submissions during two annual reading periods: September 1-October 31 and March 1-April 30. Submissions postmarked outside of these two reading periods will not be considered or returned. In addition, until further notice, Coffee House Press will not accept unsolicited poetry submissions. Please check our web page periodically for future updates to this policy.

TIPS Look for our books at stores and libraries to get a feel for what we like to publish. No phone calls, e-mails, or faxes."

COLLEGE PRESS PUBLISHING CO.

P.O.Box 1132, 2111 N. Main St., Suite C, Joplin MO 64801. (800)289-3300. **Fax:** (417)623-1929. **Website:** www.collegepress.com. Estab. 1959. Publishes hardcover and trade paperback originals and reprints. College Press is a traditional Christian publishing house. Seeks proposals for Bible studies, topical studies (biblically based), apologetic studies, historical biographies of Christians, Sunday/Bible School curriculum (adult electives). Accepts simultaneous submissions. Responds in 3 months to proposals; 2 months to mss. Book catalog for 9x12 envelope and 5 first-class stamps. Guidelines available online.

IMPRINTS HeartSpring Publishing (nonacademic Christian, inspirational, devotional and Christian fiction).

NONFICTION Seeks Bible studies, topical studies, apologetic studies, historical biographies of Christians, and Sunday/Bible school curriculum. No poetry, games/puzzles, books on prophecy from a premillennial or dispensational viewpoint, or any book without a Christian message. Query with SASE. Always send a proposal or query letter first and requested mss to: Acquisitions Editor.

TIPS "Our core market is Christian Churches/ Churches of Christ and conservative evangelical Christians. Have your material critically reviewed prior to sending it. Make sure that it is non-Calvinistic and that it leans more amillennial (if it is apocalyptic writing)."

CONARI PRESS

Red Wheel/Weiser, LLC., 665 Third St., Suite 400, San Francisco CA 94107. **E-mail:** info@redwheelweiser. com. **E-mail:** submissions@rwwbooks.com. **Website:** www.redwheelweiser.com. **Contact:** Pat Bryce, acquisitions editor. Estab. 1987. "Conari Press, an imprint of Red Wheel/Weiser, publishes books on topics ranging from spirituality, personal growth, and relationships to women's issues, parenting, and social issues. Our mission is to publish quality books that will make a difference in people's lives—how we feel about ourselves and how we relate to one another. We value integrity, compassion, and receptivity, both in the books we publish and in the way we do business."

NONFICTION Inspire, literally to breathe life into. That's what Conari Press books aim to do — inspire all walks of life, mind, body, and spirit; inspire creativity, laughter, gratitude, good food, good health, and all good things in life. We publish wellness and recovery books, particularly 12-step books, books on health and eating, books especially for women, and books on spirituality, personal growth, parenting, and social issues. Submit proposal, including: an overview of the book; a complete table of contents; a market/audience analysis, including similar titles; an up-to-date listing of your own marketing and publicity experience and/ or plans; your vita and/or qualifications to write the book; and two or three sample chapters. Send cover letter including author information and brief description of proposed work.

TIPS "Review our website to make sure your work is appropriate."

CONCORDIA PUBLISHING HOUSE

3558 S. Jefferson Ave., St. Louis MO 63118. (314)268-1187. **Fax:** (314)268-1329. **E-mail:** publicity@cph.org; rosemary.parkinson@cph.org. **Website:** www.cph. org. **Contact:** Peggy Kuethe, senior editor (children's product, adult devotional, women's resources), Dawn Weinstock, managing production editor (adult nonfiction on Christian spirituality and culture, academic works of interest in Lutheran markets). Estab. 1869. Publishes hardcover and trade paperback originals. "Concordia Publishing House produces quality resources that communicate and nurture the Christian faith and ministry of people of all ages, lay and professional. These resources include curriculum, worship aids, books, and religious supplies. We publish approximately 30 quality children's books each year. We boldly provide Gospel resources that are Christ-centered, Bible-based and faithful to our Lutheran heritage." **Pays authors royalties based on retail price or work purchased outright ($750-2,000).** Responds in 1 month to queries; 3 months to mss. Ms guidelines for 1 first-class stamp and a #10 envelope.

NONFICTION Subjects include child guidance, religion, science, child guidance in Christian context, inspirational. Picture books, young readers, young adults: Bible stories, activity books, arts/crafts, concept, contemporary, religion. "All books must contain explicit Christian content." Recently published *Three Wise Women of Christmas*, by Dandi Daley Mackall (picture book for ages 6-10); *The Town That Forgot About Christmas*, by Susan K. Leigh (ages 5-9, picture book); *Little Ones Talk With God* (prayer book compilation, aged 5 and up). Submit complete ms (picture books); submit outline/synopsis and samples for longer mss. May also query.

TIPS "Do not send finished artwork with the manuscript. If sketches will help in the presentation of the manuscript, they may be sent. If stories are taken from the Bible, they should follow the Biblical account closely. Liberties should not be taken in fantasizing Biblical stories."

⊛⊛ CONSTABLE & ROBINSON, LTD.

55-56 Russell Square, London WC1B 4HP, United Kingdom. 0208-741-3663. **Fax:** 0208-748-7562. **E-mail:** reader@constablerobinson.com. **Website:** constablerobinson.co.uk/. **Contact:** Krystyna Green, editorial director (crime fiction). lpoliticsautobiographyQuery with SASE. Submit synopsis, SAE.Reviews artwork/photos. Send photocopies. Publishes hardcover and trade paperback originals. **Publishes 60 titles/year. 3,000 queries/year; 1,000 mss/year Pays royalty Pays advance** Publishes book 1 year after acceptance of ms. Accepts simultaneous submissions. Responds in 1 month to queries and proposals; 3 months to mss. Book catalog available free.

IMPRINTS Corsair, Constable Hardback; Robinson Paperback.

NONFICTION Subjects include health, history, medicine, military, photography, politics, psychology, science, travel, war. Query with SASE. Submit synopsis. Reviews artwork/photos. Send photocopies.

TIPS Constable & Robinson Ltd. is looking for "crime novels with good, strong identities. Think about what it is that makes your book(s) stand out from the others. We do not publish thrillers."

CONSUMER PRESS

13326 SW 28 St., Suite 102, Ft. Lauderdale FL 33330. (954)370-9153. **E-mail:** info@consumerpress.com. **Contact:** Joseph Pappas, editorial director. Estab. 1989. Publishes trade paperback originals. **Publishes 2-5 titles/year. Pays royalty on wholesale price or on retail price, as per agreement.** Book catalog available free.

IMPRINTS Women's Publications.

    "Consumer Press is a full-spectrum publishing company specializing in literary works by noted personalities. Known for innovation and excellence in copy development, book design, publicity, and distribution, we provide an array of related services for the seasoned or first-time author. Our staff collaborates closely with clients from planning to promotion, with a focus on perennial exposure and global recognition of each title."

NONFICTION Subjects include child guidance, health, medicine, money, finance, women's issues, women's studies, homeowner guides, building/remodeling, food/nutrition. Query with SASE, call, email, or use online submission form.

CORWIN PRESS, INC.

2455 Teller Rd., Thousand Oaks CA 91320. (800)818-7243. **Fax:** (805)499-2692. **E-mail:** lisa.shaw@corwinpress.com. **Website:** www.corwinpress.com. **Contact:** Lisa Shaw, executive director, editorial. Hudson Perigo, executive editor (classroom management, new teacher induction, general teaching methods); Jessica Allan, senior acquisitions editor (science, special education, gifted education, early childhood education, and counseling). Estab. 1990. Publishes paperback originals. **Publishes 150 titles/year.** Publishes ms 7 months after acceptance. Responds in 1-2 months to queries. Guidelines available online.

    "Corwin Press, Inc., publishes leading-edge, user-friendly publications for education professionals."

NONFICTION Subjects include education. Seeking fresh insights, conclusions, and recommendations for action. Prefers theory or research-based books that provide real-world examples and practical, hands-on strategies to help busy educators be successful. Professional-level publications for administrators, teachers, school specialists, policymakers, researchers and others involved with Pre K-12 education. No textbooks that simply summarize existing knowledge or mass-market books. Query with SASE.

⊙ COTEAU BOOKS

Thunder Creek Publishing Co-operative Ltd., 2517 Victoria Ave., Regina SK S4P 0T2, Canada. (306)777-0170. **Fax:** (306)522-5152. **E-mail:** coteau@coteaubooks.com. **Website:** www.coteaubooks.com. **Contact:** Geoffrey Ursell, publisher. Estab. 1975. Publishes trade paperback originals and reprints. "Our mission is to publish the finest in Canadian fiction, nonfiction, poetry, drama, and children's literature, with an emphasis on Saskatchewan and prairie writers. De-emphasizing science fiction, picture books." **Publishes 16 titles/year. 200 queries received/year. 200 mss received/year. 25% of books from first-time authors. 90% from unagented writers. Pays 10% royalty on** retail price. **12 months.** Responds in 3 months to queries and manuscripts. Book catalog available free. Guidelines available online.

NONFICTION Subjects include creative nonfiction, ethnic, history, language, literature, memoirs, regional, sports, travel. *Canadian authors only.* Submit bio, 3-4 sample chapters, SASE.

FICTION Subjects include ethnic, fantasy, feminist, gay, lesbian, historical, humor, juvenile, literary, mainstream, contemporary, multicultural, multimedia, mystery, plays, poetry, regional, short story collections, spiritual, sports, teen/young adult, novels/short fiction, adult/middle years. *Canadian authors only.* No science fiction. No children's picture books. Submit bio, complete ms, SASE.

POETRY Submit 20-25 sample poems and complete ms.

TIPS "Look at past publications to get an idea of our editorial program. We do not publish romance, horror, or picture books but are interested in juvenile and teen fiction from Canadian authors. Submissions, even queries, must be made in hard copy only. We do not accept simultaneous/multiple submissions. Check our website for new submission timing guidelines."

COUNCIL ON SOCIAL WORK EDUCATION

1701 Duke St., Suite 200, Alexandria VA 22314. (703)683-8080. **Fax:** (703)683-8099. **E-mail:** info@cswe.org. **Website:** www.cswe.org. **Contact:** Elizabeth Simon, publications manager. Estab. 1952. Publishes trade paperback originals. "Council on Social Work Education produces books and resources for social work educators, students and practitioners." **Publishes 4 titles/year. 12 queries received/year. 8 mss received/year. 25% of books from first-time authors. 100% from unagented writers. Pays sliding royalty scale, starting at 10%.** Publishes ms 1 year after acceptance. Responds in 2 months to queries; 3 months to proposals and mss. Book catalog and ms guidelines free via website or with SASE.

NONFICTION Subjects include education, sociology, social work. Books for social work and other educators. Query via email only with proposal package, including CV, outline, expected audience, and 2 sample chapters.

TIPS "Audience is Social work educators and students and others in the helping professions. Check areas of publication interest on website."

COVENANT COMMUNICATIONS, INC.

920 E. State Rd., American Fork UT 84003. (801)756-9966. **Fax:** (801)756-1049. **E-mail:** submissionsdesk@covenant-lds; submissions@covenant-lds.com. **Website:** www.covenant-lds.com. **Contact:** Kathryn Jenkins, managing editor. Estab. 1958. "Currently emphasizing inspirational, doctrinal, historical, biography. Our fiction is also expanding, and we are looking for new approaches to LDS literature and storytelling." **Publishes 80-100 titles/year. 350 queries, 1,200 mss 60% of books from first-time authors. 99% from unagented writers. Pays 6 1/2-15% royalty on retail price.** Publishes book 6 months to a year after acceptance of ms. Accepts simultaneous submissions. Responds in 1 month on queries & proposals; 4 months on manuscripts. Guidelines available online.

NONFICTION Subjects include history, religion, spirituality. "We target an exclusive audience of members of The Church of Jesus Christ of Latter-day Saints. All mss must be written for that audience." Submit complete ms. Reviews artwork. Send photocopies.

FICTION Subjects include adventure, historical, mystery, regional, religious, romance, spiritual, suspense. "We publish exclusively to the 'Mormon' (The Church of Jesus Christ of Latter-Day Saints) market. Fiction must feature characters who are members of that church, grappling with issues relevant to that religion." Submit complete ms.

TIPS "Our audience is exclusively LDS (Latter Day Saints, 'Mormon')." We do not accept manuscripts that do not have a strong LDS theme or feature strong LDS characters.

CQ PRESS

2300 N St., NW, Suite 800, Washington DC 20037. (202)729-1800. **E-mail:** ckiino@cqpress.com. **Website:** www.cqpress.com. **Contact:** Charisse Kiino, chief acquisitions editor. Estab. 1945. Publishes hardcover and online paperback titles. Accepts simultaneous submissions. Book catalog available free.

IMPRINTS College, Library/Reference, Staff Directories; CQ Electronic Library/CQ Researcher.

○ CQ Press seeks to educate the public by publishing authoritative works on American and international politics, policy, and people.

NONFICTION Subjects include government, politics, history. "We are interested in American government, public administration, comparative government, and international relations." Submit proposal package, outline, bio.

TIPS "Our books present important information on American government and politics, and related issues, with careful attention to accuracy, thoroughness, and readability."

CRABTREE PUBLISHING COMPANY

PMB 59051, 350 Fifth Ave., 59th Floor, New York NY 10118. (212)496-5040; (800)387-7650. **Fax:** (800)355-7166. **Website:** www.crabtreebooks.com. Estab. 1978. Crabtree Publishing Company is dedicated to producing high-quality books and educational products for K-8+. Each resource blends accuracy, immediacy, and eye-catching illustration with the goal of inspiring nothing less than a life-long interest in reading and learning in children. The company began building its reputation in 1978 as a quality children's nonfiction book publisher with acclaimed author Bobbie Kalman's first series about the early pioneers. The Early Settler Life Series became a mainstay in schools as well as historic sites and museums across North America.

○   "Crabtree does not accept unsolicited manuscripts. Crabtree Publishing has an editorial team in-house that creates curriculum-specific book series."

TIPS "Since our books are for younger readers, lively photos of children and animals are always excellent." Portfolio should be diverse and encompass several subjects rather than just 1 or 2; depth of coverage of subject should be intense so that any publishing company could, conceivably, use all or many of a photographer's photos in a book on a particular subject."

CRAFTSMAN BOOK CO.

6058 Corte Del Cedro, Carlsbad CA 92011. (760)438-7828 or (800)829-8123. **Fax:** (760)438-0398. **Website:** www.craftsman-book.com. **Contact:** Laurence D. Jacobs, editorial manager. Estab. 1957. Publishes paperback originals. Publishes how-to manuals for professional builders. Currently emphasizing construction software. **Publishes 12 titles/year. 85% of books from first-time authors. 98% from unagented writers. Pays 7 1/2-12 1/2% royalty on wholesale price or retail price.** Publishes ms 2 years after acceptance. Accepts simultaneous submissions. Responds in 2 months to queries. Book catalog and ms guidelines free.

NONFICTION All titles are related to construction for professional builders. Reviews artwork/photos.

TIPS "The book submission should be loaded with step-by-step instructions, illustrations, charts, reference data, forms, samples, cost estimates, rules of thumb, and examples that solve actual problems in the builder's office and in the field. It must cover the subject completely, become the owner's primary reference on the subject, have a high utility-to-cost ratio, and help the owner make a better living in his chosen field."

⊕ CRAIGMORE CREATIONS

2900 SE Stark St., Suite 1A, Portland OR 97124. (503)477-9562. **E-mail:** info@craigmorecreations.com. **E-mail:** Submit by mail only. **Website:** www.craigmorecreations.com. Estab. 2009. Accepts simultaneous submissions.

NONFICTION Subjects include animals, anthropology, archeology, creative nonfiction, environment, multicultural, nature, regional, science, young adult, Earth sciences, natural history. "We publish books that make time travel seem possible: nonfiction that explores pre-history and Earth sciences for children. Submit proposal package. See website for detailed submission guidelines. Send photocopies.

CREATIVE COMPANY

P.O. Box 227, Mankato MN 56002. (800)445-6209. **Fax:** (507)388-2746. **E-mail:** info@thecreativecompany.us. **Website:** www.thecreativecompany.us. **Contact:** Aaron Frisch. Estab. 1932. The Creative Company has two imprints: Creative Editions (picture books), and Creative Education (nonfiction series). **Publishes 140 titles/year.** Publishes a book 2 years after acceptance. Responds in 3 months to queries/mss. Guidelines available for SAE.

○   "We are currently not accepting fiction submissions."

NONFICTION Picture books, young readers, young adults: animal, arts/crafts, biography, careers, geography, health, history, hobbies, multicultural, music/dance, nature/environment, religion, science, social issues, special needs, sports. Average word length: young readers—500; young adults—6,000. Recently published *Empire State Building*, by Kate Riggs (age 7, young reader); *The Assassination of Archduke Ferdinand*, by Valerie Bodden (age 14, young adult/teen). Submit outline/synopsis and 2 sample chapters, along with division of titles within the series.

TIPS "We are accepting nonfiction, series submissions only. Fiction submissions will not be reviewed or returned. Nonfiction submissions should be presented in series (4, 6, or 8) rather than single."

CREATIVE HOMEOWNER

One International Blvd., Suite 400, Mahwah NJ 07495. **E-mail:** info@creativehomeowner.com. **Website:** www.creativehomeowner.com. **Contact:** Rich Weisman, president; Mary Dolan, photo researcher. Estab. 1978. Publishes trade paperback originals. Creative Homeowner is a leading and trusted source for the best information, inspiration, and instruction related to the house and home. Over the past 25 years, Creative Homeowner has grown significantly to include titles covering all aspects of decorating and design; home repair and improvement; house plans; and gardening and landscaping. Creative Homeowner's books and online information are known by consumers for their complete and easy-to-follow instructions, up-to-date information, and extensive use of color photography. Among its best selling titles are *Decorating with Architectural Trimwork, Wiring, and Landscaping With Stone*. Book catalog available free. **NONFICTION** Subjects include gardening, Home remodeling/building. Query, or submit proposal package, including competitive books (short analysis), outline, and SASE. Reviews artwork/photos.

CRESCENT MOON PUBLISHING

P.O. Box 393, Maidstone Kent ME14 5XU, United Kingdom. (44)(162)272-9593. **E-mail:** cresmopub@yahoo.co.uk. **Website:** www.crescentmoon.org.uk. **Contact:** Jeremy Robinson, director (arts, media, cinema, literature); Cassidy Hushes (visual arts). Estab. 1988. Publishes hardcover and trade paperback originals. "Our mission is to publish the best in contemporary work, in poetry, fiction, and critical studies, and selections from the great writers. Currently emphasizing nonfiction (media, film, music, painting). De-emphasizing children's books." **Publishes 25 titles/year. 300 queries received/year. 400 mss received/year. 1% of books from first-time authors. 1% from unagented writers. Pays royalty. Pays negotiable advance.** Publishes ms 18 months after acceptance. Accepts simultaneous submissions. Responds in 2 months to queries; 4 months to proposals and mss. Book catalog and ms guidelines free.

IMPRINTS *Joe's Press, Pagan America Magazine, Passion Magazine.*

NONFICTION Subjects include Americana, art, architecture, gardening, government, politics, language, literature, music, dance, philosophy, religion, travel, women's issues, women's studies, cinema, the media, cultural studies. Query with SASE. Submit outline, 2 sample chapters, bio. Reviews artwork/photos. Send photocopies.

FICTION Subjects include erotica, experimental, feminist, gay, lesbian, literary, short story collections, translation. "We do not publish much fiction at present but will consider high quality new work." Query with SASE. Submit outline, clips, 2 sample chapters, bio.

POETRY "We prefer a small selection of the poet's very best work at first. We prefer free verse or non-rhyming poetry. Do not send too much material." Query and submit 6 sample poems.

TIPS "Our audience is interested in new contemporary writing."

CRICKET BOOKS

Imprint of Carus Publishing, 70 E. Lake St., Suite 300, Chicago IL 60601. (603)924-7209. **Fax:** (603)924-7380. **Website:** www.cricketmag.com. **Contact:** Submissions Editor. Estab. 1999. Publishes hardcover originals. Cricket Books publishes picture books, chapter books, and middle-grade novels. **Publishes 5 titles/year. Pays up to 10% royalty on retail price. Average advance: $1,500 and up.** Publishes ms 18 months after acceptance.

Currently not accepting queries or mss. Check website for submissions details and updates

FICTION Subjects include juvenile, adventure, easy-to-read, fantasy/science fiction, historical, horror, mystery/suspense, problem novels, sports, westerns.

TIPS "Take a look at the recent titles to see what sort of materials we're interested in, especially for nonfiction. Please note that we aren't doing the sort of strictly educational nonfiction that other publishers specialize in."

CRIMSON ROMANCE

Adams Media, a division of F+W Media, Inc., 57 Littlefield St., Avon MA 02322. (508)427-7100. **E-mail:** editorcrimson@gmail.com. **Contact:** Jennifer Lawler, editor. Publishes electronic originals. "Direct to e-book imprint of Adams Media."

FICTION "We're open to romance submissions in five popular subgenres: romantic suspense, contemporary, paranormal, historical, and erotic romance. Within those subgenres, we areflexible about what happens. It's romance, so there must be ahappily-ever-after, but we're open to how your characters get there. You won'tcome up against preconceived ideas about what can or can't happen in romance orwhat kind of characters you can or can't have. Our only rule is everyone has tobe a consenting adult. Other than that, we're looking for smart, savvy heroines, fresh voices, and new takes on old favorite themes. We're looking for full-length novels, and while we prefer to work on the shorter end of the spectrum (50,000words, give or take), we're not going to rule you out because you go shorter or longer. If you have a finished novel you'd like for us to consider, please just drop editor Jennifer Lawler a line at editorcrimson@gmail.com with a brief description of your work–please,no attachments until I know you're not a spambot. That's it! I'll get back to you as quickly as I can–within a few days for queries and within a few weeks if I request a full."

CROSS-CULTURAL COMMUNICATIONS

Cross-Cultural Literary Editions, Ltd.; Express Editions; Ostrich Editions, 239 Wynsum Ave., Merrick NY 11566. (516)869-5635. **Fax:** (516)379-1901. **E-mail:** cccpoetry@aol.com. **Website:** www.cross-cultural-communications.com. **Contact:** Stanley H. Barkan, publisher/editor-in-chief (bilingual poetry); Bebe Barkan, Mia Barkan Clarke, art editors (complementary art to poetry editions). Estab. 1971. Publishes hardcover and trade paperback originals. **Publishes 10 titles/year. 200 queries received/year. 50 mss received/year. 25% of books from first-time authors. 100% from unagented writers.** Publishes book 1 year after acceptance. Responds in 1 month to proposals; 2 months to mss. Book catalog (sample flyers) for #10 SASE.

IMPRINTS Expressive Editions (contact Mia Barkan Clarke).

NONFICTION Subjects include language, literature, memoirs, multicultural. "Query first; we basically do not want the focus on nonfiction." Query with SASE. Reviews artwork/photos. Send photocopies.

FICTION Subjects include historical, multicultural, poetry, poetry in translation, translation, Bilingual poetry. Query with SASE.

POETRY For bilingual poetry submit 3-6 short poems in original language with English translation, a brief (3-5 lines) bio of the author and translator(s).

CROWN BOOKS FOR YOUNG READERS

1745 Broadway, 10th Floor, New York NY 10019. (212)572-2600 or (800)200-3552. **Website:** www.randomhouse.com/kids.

Random House Children's Publishing only accepts submissions through agents.

CROWN BUSINESS

Random House, Inc., 1745 Broadway, New York NY 10019. (212)572-2275. **Fax:** (212)572-6192. **E-mail:** crownbiz@randomhouse.com. **Website:** crownpublishing.com. Estab. 1995. Publishes hardcover and trade paperback originals. Accepts simultaneous submissions. Book catalog available online.

Agented submissions only.

NONFICTION Subjects include business, economics, money, finance, management. Query with proposal package including outline, 1-2 sample chapters, market analysis and information on author platform.

CRYSTAL SPIRIT PUBLISHING, INC.

P.O. Box 12506, Durham NC 27709. **E-mail:** crystalspiritinc@gmail.com. **Website:** www.crystalspiritinc.com. **Contact:** Vanessa S. O'Neal, senior editor; Elise L. Lattier, editor. Estab. 2004. Publishes hardcover, trade paperback, mass market paperback, and electronic originals. "Our readers are lovers of high-quality books that are sold in book and gift stores and placed in libraries and schools. They support independent authors and they expect works that will provide them with entertainment, inspiration, romance, and education. Our audience loves to read and will embrace niche authors that love to write." **Publishes 3-4 titles/year. Receives 30 mss/year. 80% of books from first-time authors. 100% from unagented writers. Pays 20-45% royalty on retail price.** Publishes ms 3-6 months after acceptance. Accepts simultaneous submissions. Responds in 3-6 months to mss. Book catalog and ms guidelines available online at website.

NONFICTION Subjects include business, creative nonfiction, economics, ethnic, memoirs, multicultural, New Age, religion, sex, spirituality, young adult, inspirational, Christian romance. Submit cover letter, synopsis, and 30 pages (or 30 chapters) by USPS mail ONLY.

FICTION Subjects include confession, contemporary, erotica, ethnic, feminist, gay, humor, juvenile, lesbian, literary, mainstream, multicultural, poetry, religious, romance, short story collections, spiritual, young adult, inspirational, Christian romance. Submit cover letter, synopsis, and 30 pages (or 30 chapters) by USPS mail ONLY.

POETRY "All poetry must have titles. Include a description of the collective works and type of poetry." Submit 10 sample poems.

TIPS "Submissions are accepted for publication throughout the year, but the decisions for publishing considerations are made in March, June, September, and December. Works should be positive and nonthreatening. Typed pages only. Non-typed entries will not be reviewed or returned. Ensure that all contact information is correct, abide by the submission guidelines and do not send follow-up e-mails or calls."

⊕ CUP OF TEA BOOKS

PageSpring Publishing, P.O. Box 21133, Columbus OH 43221. **E-mail:** weditor@pagespringpublishing.com. **Website:** www.cupofteabooks.com. Estab. 2012. Publishes trade paperback and electronic originals. "Cup of Tea Books publishes novel-length women's fiction. We are interested in finely-drawn characters, a compelling story, and deft writing. We accept e-mail queries only; see our website for details." **Pays royalty.** Publishes ms 6 months after acceptance. Accepts simultaneous submissions. Responds in 1 month to queries and mss. Guidelines online at website.

IMPRINTS Imprint of PageSpring Publishing.

NONFICTION Does not accept nonfiction.

FICTION Subjects include adventure, contemporary, fantasy, feminist, historical, humor, literary, mainstream, mystery, regional, romance. Submit proposal package via e-mail. Include synopsis and the first 30 pages.

CYCLE PUBLICATIONS INC.

Van der Plas Publications, 1282 Seventh Ave., San Francisco CA 94112. (415)665-8214. **Fax:** (415)753-8572. **E-mail:** rvdp@cyclepublishing.com. **Website:** www.cyclepublishing.com. Estab. 1985. "Van der Plas Publications / Cycle Publishing was started in 1997 with four books. Since then, we have introduced about 4 new books each year, and in addition to our "mainstay" of cycling books, we now also have books on manufactured housing, golf, baseball, and strength training.Our offices are located in San Francisco, where we do editorial work, as well as administration, publicity, and design. Our books are warehoused in Kimball, Michigan, which is close to the companies that print most of our books and is conveniently located to supply our book trade distributors and the major book wholesalers."

CYCLOTOUR GUIDE BOOKS

160 Harvard St., Rochester NY 14607. (585)244-6157. **E-mail:** cyclotour@cyclotour.com. **Website:** www.cyclotour.com. Estab. 1994. Publishes trade paperback originals. **Publishes 2 titles/year. Receives 25 queries/year and 2 mss/year. 50% of books from first-time authors. 100% from unagented writers.** Publishes ms 2 years after acceptance. Accepts simultaneous submissions. Responds in 1 month to queries, proposals, and mss. Book catalog and ms guidelines online.

NONFICTION Subjects include sports (bicycle only), travel (bicycle tourism). No narrative accounts of their bicycle tour without distance indicators. Query with SASE. Reviews artwork/photos as part of ms package. Send photocopies.

TIPS Bicyclists. Folks with a dream of bicycle touring. "Check your grammar and spelling. Write logically."

⊘ DA CAPO PRESS

Perseus Books Group, 44 Farnsworth St., 3rd Floor, Boston MA 02210. (617)252-5200. **Website:** www.dacapopress.com. Estab. 1975. Publishes hardcover originals and trade paperback originals and reprints. **Publishes 115 titles/year. 500 queries received/year. 300 mss received/year. 35% of books from first-time authors. 1% from unagented writers. Pays 7-15% royalty. Pays $1,000-225,000 advance.** Publishes book 1 year after acceptance. Book catalog available online. Guidelines available online.

NONFICTION Subjects include art, architecture, contemporary culture, creative nonfiction, government, politics, history, language, literature, memoirs, military, war, social sciences, sports, translation, travel, world affairs.

⊗⊘ DAVID R. GODINE, PUBLISHER

15 Court Square, Suite 320, Boston MA 02108. (617)451-9600. **Fax:** (617)350-0250. **E-mail:** info@godine.com. **Website:** www.godine.com. Estab. 1970. "We publish books that matter for people who care."

⊖   This publisher is no longer considering unsolicited mss of any type. Only interested in agented material.

DAW BOOKS, INC.

Penguin Group (USA), 375 Hudson St., New York NY 10014-3658. (212)366-2096. **Fax:** (212)366-2090. **Web-**

site: www.dawbooks.com. **Contact:** Peter Stampfel, submissions editor. Estab. 1971. Publishes hardcover and paperback originals and reprints. DAW Books publishes science fiction and fantasy. **Publishes 50-60 titles/year. Pays in royalties with an advance negotiable on a book-by-book basis.** Responds in 3 months to manuscripts. Guidelines available online.

○ Simultaneous submissions not accepted, unless prior arrangements are made by agent.

NONFICTION We do not want any nonfiction.

FICTION Subjects include fantasy, science fiction, "Currently seeking modern urban fantasy and paranormals. We like character-driven books with appealing protagonists, engaging plots, and well-constructed worlds. We accept both agented and unagented manuscripts.". Submit entire ms, cover letter, SASE. Do not submit your only copy of anything. Responds within 3 months to mss. The average length of the novels we publish varies but is almost never less than 80,000 words. Send us the entire manuscript with a cover letter. We do not accept electronic submissions of any kind.

DAWN PUBLICATIONS

12402 Bitney Springs Rd., Nevada City CA 95959. (530)274-7775. **Fax:** (530)274-7778. **Website:** www.dawnpub.com. **Contact:** Glenn Hovemann, editor. Estab. 1979. Publishes hardcover and trade paperback originals. "Dawn Publications is dedicated to inspiring in children a sense of appreciation for all life on earth. Dawn looks for nature awareness and appreciation titles that promote a relationship with the natural world and specific habitats, usually through inspiring treatment and nonfiction." **Publishes 6 titles/year. 2,500 queries or mss received/year. 15% of books from first-time authors. 90% from unagented writers. Pays advance.** Publishes book 1-2 years after acceptance. Accepts simultaneous submissions. Responds in 2 months to queries. Book catalog available online. Guidelines available online.

○ Dawn accepts mss submissions by e-mail; follow instructions posted on website. Submissions by mail still OK.

NONFICTION Subjects include animals, nature, environment.

TIPS "Publishes mostly creative nonfiction with lightness and inspiration." Looking for "picture books expressing nature awareness with inspirational quality

leading to enhanced self-awareness." Does not publish anthropomorphic works; no animal dialogue.

DBS PRODUCTIONS

P.O. Box 94, Charlottesville VA 22902. (800)745-1581. **Fax:** (434)293-5502. **E-mail:** info@dbs-sar.com. **Website:** www.dbs-sar.com. **Contact:** Bob Adams, publisher. Estab. 1989. Publishes hardcover and trade paperback originals. **Publishes 4 titles/year. 10 queries received/year. 10% of books from first-time authors. 100% from unagented writers. Pays 5-20% royalty on retail price.** Publishes ms 1 year after acceptance. Responds in 2 weeks to queries. Book catalog available on request or on website. Guidelines for #10 SASE.

○ "dBS Productions produces search and rescue and outdoor first-aid related materials and courses. It offers a selection of publications, videotapes, management kits and tools, and instructional modules."

NONFICTION Subjects include health, medicine. Submit proposal package, outline, 2 sample chapters. Reviews artwork/photos. Send photocopies.

DELACORTE PRESS

1745 Broadway, New York NY 10019. (212)782-9000. **Website:** www.randomhouse.com/kids. Publishes middlegrade and young adult fiction in hard cover, trade paperback, mass market and digest formats. Publishes middle-grade and young adult fiction in hardcover, trade paperback, mass market and digest formats.

○ All other query letters or ms submissions must be submitted through an agent or at the request of an editor. No e-mail queries.

Ⓐ Ⓞ DELACORTE PRESS BOOKS FOR YOUNG READERS

Imprint of Random House Children's Books/Random House, Inc., 1745 Broadway, New York NY 10019. (212)782-9000. **Website:** www.randomhouse.com/kids; www.randomhouse.com/teens. Distinguished literary fiction and commercial fiction for the middle grade and young adult categories.

○ Not currently accepting unsolicited mss.

Ⓐ DEL REY BOOKS

Imprint of Random House Publishing Group, 1745 Broadway, 18th Floor, New York NY 10019. (212)782-9000. **E-mail:** delrey@randomhouse.com. **Website:** www.randomhouse.com. Estab. 1977. Publishes hardcover, trade paperback, and mass market originals and mass market paperback reprints. Del Rey publishes top level fantasy, alternate history, and science fiction. **Pays royalty on retail price. Pays competitive advance.**

FICTION Subjects include fantasy, should have the practice of magic as an essential element of the plot, science fiction, well-plotted novels with good characterizations, exotic locales and detailed alien creatures, alternate history. Agented submissions only.

TIPS "Del Rey is a reader's house. Pay particular attention to plotting, strong characters, and dramatic, satisfactory conclusions. It must be/feel believable. That's what the readers like. In terms of mass market, we basically created the field of fantasy bestsellers. Not that it didn't exist before, but we put the mass into mass market."

DEMONTREVILLE PRESS, INC.

P.O. Box 835, Lake Elmo MN 55042. **E-mail:** publisher@demontrevillepress.com. **Website:** www.demontrevillepress.com. **Contact:** Kevin Clemens, publisher (automotive fiction and nonfiction). Estab. 2006. Publishes trade paperback originals and reprints. **Publishes 4 titles/year. 150 queries received/year. 100 mss received/year. 90% of books from first-time authors. 90% from unagented writers. Pays 20% royalty on sale price.** Publishes book 18 months after acceptance. Accepts simultaneous submissions. Responds in 3 months to queries; 4 months to proposals; 6 months to mss. Book catalog available online. Guidelines available online.

NONFICTION Subjects include current events, automotive, environment, motorcycle. "We want novel length automotive or motorcycle historicals and/or adventures. Environmental energy and infrastructure books wanted." Submit proposal package online, outline, 3 sample chapters, bio. Reviews artwork/photos. Do not send photos until requested.

FICTION Subjects include current events, environment, adventure, mystery, sports, young adult, automotive, motorcycle. "We want novel length automotive or motorcycle historicals and/or adventures." Submit proposal package, 3 sample chapters, clips, bio.

TIPS "Environmental, energy and transportation nonfiction works are now being accepted. Automotive and motorcycle enthusiasts, adventurers, environmentalists and history buffs make up our audience."

Ⓐ DIAL BOOKS FOR YOUNG READERS

Imprint of Penguin Group USA, 375 Hudson St., New York NY 10014. (212)366-2000. **Website:** www.penguin.com/youngreaders. **Contact:** Lauri Hornik, president/publisher; Kathy Dawson, associate publisher; Kate Harrison, senior editor; Liz Waniewski, editor; Alisha Niehaus, editor; Jessica Garrison, editor; Lily Malcom, art director. Estab. 1961. Publishes hardcover originals. "Dial Books for Young Readers publishes quality picture books for ages 18 months-6 years; lively, believable novels for middle readers and young adults; and occasional nonfiction for middle readers and young adults." **Publishes 50 titles/year. 5,000 queries received/year. 20% of books from first-time authors. Pays royalty. Pays varies advance.** Responds in 4-6 months to queries. Book catalog for 9 X12 envelope and 4 first-class stamps.

NONFICTION "Due to the overwhelming number of unsolicited manuscripts we receive, we at Dial Books for Young Readers have had to change our submissions policy: As of August 1, 2005, Dial will no longer respond to your unsolicited submission unless interested in publishing it. Please do not include SASE with your submission. You will not hear from Dial regarding the status of your submission unless we are interested, in which case you can expect a reply from us within four months. We accept entire picture book manuscripts and a maximum of 10 pages for longer works (novels, easy-to-reads). When submitting a portion of a longer work, please provide an accompanying cover letter that briefly describes your manuscript's plot, genre (i.e. easy-to-read, middle grade or YA novel), the intended age group, and your publishing credits, if any."

FICTION Subjects include adventure, fantasy, juvenile, picture books, young adult. Especially looking for lively and well-written novels for middle grade and young adult children involving a convincing plot and believable characters. The subject matter or theme should not already be overworked in previously published books. The approach must not be demeaning to any minority group, nor should the roles of female characters (or others) be stereotyped, though we don't think books should be didactic, or in any way message-y. No topics inappropriate for the juvenile, young adult, and middle grade audiences. No plays. Accepts unsolicited queries and up to 10 pages for longer works and unsolicited mss for picture books.

TIPS "Our readers are anywhere from preschool age to teenage. Picture books must have strong plots, lots of action, unusual premises, or universal themes treated with freshness and originality. Humor works well in these books. A very well-thought-out and intelligently presented book has the best chance of being taken on. Genre isn't as much of a factor as presentation."

⊘ DISKUS PUBLISHING

P.O. Box 475, Eaton IN 47338. **E-mail:** editor@diskuspublishing.com. **Website:** www.diskuspublishing.com. **Contact:** Carol Davis, senior editor; Holly Janey, submissions editor. Estab. 1996. Publishes e-books and printed books. **Publishes 50 titles/year. Pays 40% royalty.** Publishes ms 9-12 months after acceotance. after acceptance of ms. Accepts simultaneous submissions. Book catalog is available online only. Guidelines for #10 SASE or online. "We prefer you get your guidelines online.".

○ *"At this time DiskUs Publishing is closed for submissions. Keep checking our website for updates on the status of our submissions reopen date"*

NONFICTION Subjects include crafts, foods, games, sports, jokes, scrap booking, sewing, general nonfiction. Submit publishing history, bio, estimated word count and genre. Submit complete ms. Send your e-mailed submission to diskuspublishing@aol.com with the words Diskus Submission in the subject line.

FICTION Subjects include adventure, contemporary, ethnic, fantasy, historical, horror, humor, juvenile, literary, mainstream, military, multicultural, mystery, religious, romance, science fiction, short story collections, suspense, war, western, young adult, family saga, psychic/supernatural, thriller/espionage. "We are actively seeking confessions for our Diskus Confessions line. As well as short stories for our Quick Pick line. We only accept e-mailed submissions for these lines." Send your submission to diskuspublishing@aol.com with the word Diskus Submission in the subject line.

DIVERSION PRESS

P.O. Box 3930, Clarksville TN 37043. **E-mail:** diversionpress@yahoo.com. **Website:** www.diversionpress.com. Estab. 2008. Publishes hardcover, trade and mass market paperback originals. **Publishes 5-10 titles/year. 75% of books from first-time authors. 100% from unagented writers. Pays 10% royalty on wholesale price.** Publishes ms 1-2 years after accep-

tance. Responds in 2 weeks to queries. Responds in 1 month to proposals. Guidelines available online.

NONFICTION Subjects include Americana, animals, community, contemporary culture, education, ethnic, government, politics, health, medicine, history, hobbies, humanities, language, literature, literary criticism, memoirs, military, war, multicultural, philosophy, psychology, recreation, regional, science, social sciences, sociology, travel, women's issues, women's studies, world affairs. "The editors have doctoral degrees and are interested in a broad range of academic works. We are also interested in how-to, slice of life, and other nonfiction areas." Does not review works that are sexually explicit, religious, or put children in a bad light. Send query/proposal first. Mss accepted by request only. Reviews artwork/photos. Send photocopies.

FICTION Subjects include adventure, fantasy, gothic, historical, horror, humor, literary, mainstream, contemporary, mystery, poetry, science fiction, short story collections, suspense, young adult. "We will happily consider any children's or young adult books if they are illustrated. If your story has potential to become a series, please address that in your proposal. Fiction short stories and poetry will be considered for our anthology series. See website for details on how to submit your ms."

POETRY "Poetry will be considered for anthology series and for our poetry award." Submit 5 sample poems.

TIPS "Read our website and blog prior to submitting. We like short, concise queries. Tell us why your book is different, not like other books. Give us a realistic idea of what you will do to market your book—that you will actually do. We will ask for more information if we are interested."

DIVERTIR

P.O. Box 232, North Salem NH 03073. **E-mail:** info@divertirpublishing.com; query@divertirpublishing.com. **Website:** www.divertirpublishing.com. **Contact:** Kenneth Tupper, publisher. Estab. 2009. Publishes trade paperback and electronic originals. **Publishes 6-12 titles/year. 80% of books from first-time authors. 100% from unagented writers. Pays 10-15% royalty on wholesale price (for novels and nonfiction); outright purchase: $10-50 (for short stories) with additional bonus payments to authors when certain sales milestones are met.** Publishes ms 6-9 months after acceptance. Accepts simultaneous submissions. Responds in 1-2 months on queries; 3-4 months on proposals and mss. Catalog available online at www.divertirpublishing.com/bookstore.html. Guidelines online at website: www.divertirpublishing.com/authorinfo.html.

NONFICTION Subjects include contemporary culture, crafts, government, history, hobbies, New Age, politics, psychic, world affairs. "We are particularly interested in the following: political/social commentary, current events, history, humor and satire, crafts and hobbies, inspirational, self-help, religious and spiritual, and metaphysics." Reviews artwork/photos as part of the ms package. Submit electronically.

FICTION Subjects include adventure, contemporary, fantasy, gothic, historical, horror, humor, literary, mainstream, mystery, occult, poetry, religious, romance, science fiction, short story collections, spiritual, translation, young adult. "We are particularly interested in the following: science fiction, fantasy, historical, alternate history, contemporary mythology, mystery and suspense, paranormal, and urban fantasy." Electronically submit proposal package, including synopsis and query letter with author's bio.

POETRY Query.

TIPS "Please see our Author Info page (online) for more information."

DK PUBLISHING

375 Hudson St., New York NY 10014. **Website:** www.dk.com. "DK publishes photographically illustrated nonfiction for children of all ages."

DK Publishing does not accept unagented mss or proposals.

DNA PRESS & NARTEA PUBLISHING

DNA Press, P.O. Box 9311, Glendale CA 91226. **E-mail:** editors@dnapress.com. **Website:** www.dnapress.com. Estab. 1998. Publishes hardcover and trade paperback originals. Book publisher for young adults, children, and adults. **Publishes 10 titles/year. 500 queries received/year. 400 mss received/year. 90% of books from first-time authors. 100% from unagented writers. Pays 10-15% royalty.** Publishes book 8 months after acceptance. Accepts simultaneous submissions. Responds in 6 weeks to mss. Book catalog and ms guidelines free.

NONFICTION "We publish business, real estate and investment books." Reviews artwork/photos.

FICTION Subjects include juvenile, science fiction, young adult. All books should be oriented to explaining science even if they do not fall 100% under the category of science fiction. Submit complete ms.

TIPS Quick response, great relationships, high commission/royalty.

DOG-EARED PUBLICATIONS

P.O. Box 620863, Middletown WI 53562. (608)831-1410. **Fax:** (608)831-1410. **E-mail:** field@dog-eared.com. **Website:** www.dog-eared.com. **Contact:** Nancy Field, publisher. Estab. 1977. The home of Dog-eared Publications is a perfect place to create children's nature books! Perched on a hilltop in Middleton, Wisconsin, we are surrounded by wild meadows and oak forests where deer, wild turkeys, and even bobcats leave their marks. **Pays author royalty based on wholesale price. Offers advance.** Brochure available for SASE and 1 first-class stamp or on website.

NONFICTION Middle readers: activity books, animal, nature/environment, science. Average word length: varies. *Currently not accepting unsolicited mss.*

DORAL PUBLISHING, INC.

3 Burroughs, Irvine CA 92618. (800)633-5385. **E-mail:** doralpub@mindspring.com. **Website:** www.doralpub.com. **Contact:** Alvin Grossman, publisher; Joe Liddy, marketing manager (purebred dogs). Estab. 1986. Publishes hardcover and trade paperback originals. **Publishes 10 titles/year. 30 queries received/year. 15 mss received/year. 85% from unagented writers. Pays 10% royalty on wholesale price.** Publishes ms 6 months after acceptance. Responds in 2 months to queries. Book catalog available free. Guidelines for #10 SASE.

"Doral Publishing publishes only books about dogs and dog-related topics, mostly geared for pure-bred dog owners and showing. Currently emphasizing breed books."

NONFICTION Subjects include animals, health, medicine. "We are looking for new ideas. No flowery prose. Manuscripts should be literate, intelligent, but easy to read. Subjects must be dog-related." Query with SASE. Submit outline, 2 sample chapters. Reviews artwork/photos. Send photocopies.

FICTION Subjects include juvenile. Subjects must center around dogs. Either the main character should be a dog or a dog should play an integral role. Query with SASE.

TIPS "We are currently expanding and are looking for new topics and fresh ideas while staying true to our niche. While we will steadfastly maintain that market—we are always looking for excellent breed books—we also want to explore more 'mainstream' topics."

DOUBLEDAY BOOKS FOR YOUNG READERS

1540 Broadway, New York NY 10036. (212)782-9000. **Website:** www.randomhouse.com/kids.

○ Only accepts mss submitted by an agent. Trade picture book list, from preschool to age 8.

⊘ DOUBLEDAY RELIGION

The Crown Publishing Group, a Division of Random House, Inc., 1745 Broadway, New York NY 10019. (212)782-9000. **Website:** www.randomhouse.com; crownpublishing.com. Estab. 1897. Publishes hardcover and trade paperback originals and reprints. Accepts simultaneous submissions.

IMPRINTS Image Books; Galilee; New Jerusalem Bible; Three Leaves Press.

○ "Random House, Inc. does not accept unsolicited submissions, proposals, manuscripts, or submission queries via e-mail at this time. If you would like to have your work or manuscript considered for publication by a major book publisher, we recommend that you work with an established literary agent. Each agency has manuscript submission guidelines."

NONFICTION Agented submissions only.

DOVER PUBLICATIONS, INC.

31 E. Second St., Mineola NY 11501. (516)294-7000. **Fax:** (516)873-1401. **E-mail:** hr@doverpublications. com. **Website:** www.doverpublications.com. **Contact:** John Grafton (math/science reprints). Estab. 1941. Publishes trade paperback originals and reprints. **Publishes 660 titles/year. Makes outright purchase.** Accepts simultaneous submissions. Book catalog available online.

○ Covers subjects from A - W, including Poetry - Fine Art - Recipes - Games - Puzzles - Famous Quotations - Clip Art - Great Literature - Craft Projects - Photography - Coloring Pages.

NONFICTION Subjects include agriculture, Americana, animals, anthropology, archeology, art, architecture, cooking, foods, nutrition, health, medicine, history, hobbies, language, literature, music, dance, nature, environment, philosophy, photography, religion, science, sports, translation, travel. Publishes mostly reprints. Accepts original paper doll collections, game books, coloring books (juvenile). Query with SASE. Reviews artwork/photos.

DOWN EAST BOOKS

Imprint of Down East Enterprise, Inc., P.O. Box 679, Camden ME 04843. (207)594-9544, 800-766-1670. **Fax:** (207)594-7215. **E-mail:** editorial@downeast.com. **E-mail:** submissions@downeast.com. **Website:** www. downeast.com. **Contact:** Paul Doiron, editor-in-chief. Estab. 1967. Publishes hardcover and trade paperback originals, trade paperback reprints. Down East Books publishes books that capture and illuminate the unique beauty and character of New England's history, culture, and wild places. **Publishes 24-30 titles/year. 50% of books from first-time authors. 90% from unagented writers. Pays $500 average advance.** Publishes ms 1 year after acceptance. Accepts simultaneous submissions. Responds in 3 months to queries. Send SASE for ms guidelines. Send 9 x 12 SASE for guidelines, plus recent catalog.

NONFICTION Subjects include Americana, history, nature, environment, recreation, regional, sports. Books about the New England region, Maine in particular. All of our regional books must have a Maine or New England emphasis. Query with SASE. Do not send CD, DVD, or disk. Reviews artwork/photos.

FICTION Subjects include juvenile, mainstream, contemporary, regional. We publish 2-4 juvenile titles/year (fiction and nonfiction), and 0-1 adult fiction titles/year. Query with SASE.

DOWN THE SHORE PUBLISHING

Box 100, West Creek NJ 08092. **Fax:** (609)597-0422. **E-mail:** info@down-the-shore.com. **Website:** www. down-the-shore.com. Publishes hardcover and trade paperback originals and reprints. "Bear in mind that our market is regional-New Jersey, the Jersey Shore, the mid-Atlantic, and seashore and coastal subjects." **Publishes 4-10 titles/year. Pays royalty on wholesale or retail price, or makes outright purchase.** Accepts simultaneous submissions. Responds in 3 months to queries. Book catalog for 8×10 SAE with 2 first-class stamps or on website. Guidelines available online.

NONFICTION Subjects include Americana, art, architecture, history, nature, environment, regional. Query with SASE. Submit proposal package, 1-2 sample chapters, synopsis. Reviews artwork/photos. Send photocopies.

FICTION Subjects include regional. Query with SASE. Submit proposal package, clips, 1-2 sample chapters.
POETRY "We do not publish poetry, unless it is to be included as part of an anthology."
TIPS "Carefully consider whether your proposal is a good fit for our established market."

DREAMLAND BOOKS INC.

P.O.Box 1714, Minnetonka MN 55345. (612)281-4704. **E-mail:** dreamlandbooks@inbox.com. **Website:** www.dreamlandbooks.inc.com. Estab. 2008.
FICTION "We are not accepting children's story submissions at this time. However, if you have a master or doctoral degree in creative writing, literature, or like field AND already have at least one non-vanity book published, we welcome query letters."
POETRY "We ARE accpeting poetry and flash story submissions for our poetry journal Cellar Door Poetry. We accept all forms of poetry, but will not publish any work that promotes violence or pornography."

DUFOUR EDITIONS

P.O. Box 7, 124 Byers Road, Chester Springs PA 19425. (610)458-5005 or (800)869-5677. **Fax:** (610)458-7103. **Website:** www.dufoureditions.com. Estab. 1948. Publishes hardcover originals, trade paperback originals and reprints. We publish literary fiction by good writers which is well received and achieves modest sales. De-emphasizing poetry and nonfiction. **Publishes 3-4 titles/year. 200 queries received/year. 15 mss received/year. 20-30% of books from first-time authors. 80% from unagented writers. Pays $100-500 advance.** Publishes book 18 months after acceptance of ms. Accepts simultaneous submissions. Responds in 3 months to queries. Responds in 3 months to proposals. Responds in 6 months to manuscripts. Book catalog available free.
NONFICTION Subjects include history, translation. Query with SASE. Reviews artwork/photos. Send photocopies.
FICTION Subjects include literary, short story collections, translation. We like books that are slightly off-beat, different and well-written. Query with SASE.
POETRY Query.
TIPS Audience is sophisticated, literate readers especially interested in foreign literature and translations, and a strong Irish-Celtic focus, as well as work from U.S. writers. Check to see if the publisher is really a good match for your subject matter.

DUNDURN PRESS, LTD.

3 Church St., Suite 500, Toronto ON M5E 1M2, Canada. (416)214-5544. **E-mail:** info@dundurn.com. **Website:** www.dundurn.com. **Contact:** Allison Hirst; Kirk Howard, president and publisher. Estab. 1972. Publishes hardcover, trade paperback, and ebook originals and reprints. Dundurn publishes books by Canadian authors. **600 queries received/year. 25% of books from first-time authors. 50% from unagented writers.** Publishes ms 1-2 year after acceptance. Accepts simultaneous submissions. Responds in 3 months to queries. Guidelines available on website.

"We *do not* publish poetry, short stories, children's books for readers under seven years of age, or picture books."

NONFICTION Subjects include art, architecture, history, Canadian and military, war, music, dance, drama, regional, art history, theater, serious and popular nonfiction. Submit cover letter, synopsis, CV, table of contents, writing sample, e-mail contact. Accepts submissions via postal mail only. Do not submit original materials. Submissions will not be returned.
FICTION Subjects include literary, mystery, young adult. No romance, science fiction, or experimental. Submit cover letter, 3 sample chapters, synopsis, CV, e-mail contact. Accepts submissions via postal mail only. Submissions will not be returned.

DUNEDIN ACADEMIC PRESS LTD

Hudson House, 8 Albany St., Edinburgh EH1 3QB, United Kingdom. (44)(131)473-2397. **E-mail:** mail@dunedinacademicpress.co.uk. **Website:** www.dunedinacademicpress.co.uk. **Contact:** Anthony Kinahan, director. Estab. 2001. **Publishes 15-20 titles/year. 10% of books from first-time authors. 90% from unagented writers. Pays royalty.** Book catalog and proposal guidelines available online.

"Read and respond to the proposal guidelines on our website before submitting. Do not send mss unless requested to do so. Do not send hard copy proposals. Approach first by e-mail, outlining proposal and identifying the market."

NONFICTION , earth science, education policy, health and social care, child protection. Reviews artwork/photos.
TIPS "Dunedin's list contains authors and subjects from across the international the academic world DAP?s horizons are far broader than our immediate Scottish environment. One of the strengths of Dune-

din is that we are able to offer our authors that individual support that comes from dealing with a small independent publisher committed to growth through careful treatment of its authors."

ⓐ THOMAS DUNNE BOOKS

Imprint of St. Martin's Press, 175 Fifth Ave., New York NY 10010. (212)674-5151. **Website:** www.thomasdunnebooks.com. Estab. 1986. Publishes hardcover and trade paperback originals, and reprints. "Thomas Dunne Books publishes popular trade fiction and nonfiction. With an output of approximately 175 titles each year, his group covers a range of genres including commercial and literary fiction, thrillers, biography, politics, sports, popular science, and more. The list is intentionally eclectic and includes a wide range of fiction and nonfiction, from first books to international bestsellers." Accepts simultaneous submissions. Book catalog and ms guidelines free.

O *Accepts agented submissions only.*

NONFICTION Subjects include government, politics, history, sports, political commentary. Author's attention to detail is important. We get a lot of manuscripts that are poorly proofread and just can't be considered. Agents submit query, or an outline and 1 sample pages. Reviews artwork/photos. Send photocopies.

FICTION Subjects include mainstream, contemporary, mystery, suspense, thrillers, women's. Agents submit query.

DUQUESNE UNIVERSITY PRESS

600 Forbes Ave., Pittsburgh PA 15282. (412)396-6610. Fax: (412)396-5984. **E-mail:** dupress@duq.edu. **Website:** www.dupress.duq.edu. **Contact:** Susan Wadsworth-Booth, director. Estab. 1927. Publishes hardcover and trade paperback originals. "Duquesne publishes scholarly monographs in the fields of literary studies (medieval & Renaissance), continental philosophy, ethics, religious studies and existential psychology. Interdisciplinary works are also of interest. Duquesne University Press does NOT publish fiction, poetry, children's books, technical or "hard" science works, or unrevised theses or dissertations." **Publishes 8-12 titles/year. 400 queries received/year. 65 mss received/year. 30% of books from first-time authors. 95% from unagented writers. Pays royalty on net price. Pays (some) advance.** Publishes ms 1 year after acceptance. Responds in 1 month to proposals; 3 months to mss. Book catalog and ms guidelines for #10 SASE. Guidelines available online.

NONFICTION Subjects include language, literature, philosophy, continental, psychology, existential, religion. "We look for quality of scholarship." For scholarly books, query or submit outline, 1 sample chapter, and SASE.

ⓐⓏ DUTTON ADULT TRADE

Imprint of Penguin Group (USA), Inc., 375 Hudson St., New York NY 10014. (212)366-2000. **Website:** us.penguingroup.com. Estab. 1852. Publishes hardcover originals. "*Dutton* publishes hardcover, original, mainstream, and contemporary fiction and nonfiction in the areas of memoir, self-help, politics, psychology, and science for a general readership. Dutton currently publishes 45 hardcovers a year, roughly half fiction and half nonfiction. It is currently home to many #1 *New York Times* best-selling authors, most notably **Harlan Coben**, author of *Hold Tight*, **Ken Follett**, author of *Pillars of the Earth* and *World Without End*, **Eckhart Tolle**, author of *A New Earth*, and **Al Franken**, author of *The Truth*. Dutton also publishes the *New York Times* best-selling authors **Eric Jerome Dickey**, author of *Pleasure* and *Waking with Enemies*, **Raymond Khoury**, author of *The Last Templar* and *The Sanctuary*, **John Lescroart**, author of *Betrayal* and *The Suspect*, **John Hodgman**, author of *The Areas of My Expertise* and *More Information Than You Require*, **John Jakes**, author of *Charleston* and *The Gods of Newport*, **Jenny McCarthy**, author of *Baby Laughs* and *Louder than Words*, and **Daniel Levitin**, author of *This is Your Brain on Music* and *The World in Six Songs*." **Pays royalty. Pays negotiable advance.** Accepts simultaneous submissions. Book catalog for #10 SASE.

O *Does not accept unsolicited ms. Agented submissions only.* "Query letters **only** (must include SASE) A query letter should be typed and, ideally, fit on one page. Please include a brief synopsis of your ms and your publishing credits, if any."

NONFICTION Agented submissions only. *No unsolicited mss.*

FICTION Subjects include adventure, historical, literary, mainstream, contemporary, mystery, short story collections, suspense. Agented submissions only. *No unsolicited mss.*

TIPS Write the complete ms and submit it to an agent or agents. They will know exactly which editor will be interested in a project.

DUTTON CHILDREN'S BOOKS

Penguin Group (USA), Inc., 375 Hudson St., New York NY 10014. **E-mail:** duttonpublicity@ us.penguingroup.com. **Website:** www.penguin.com. **Contact:** Sara Reynolds, art director. Estab. 1852. Publishes hardcover originals as well as novelty formats. Dutton Children's Books publishes high-quality fiction and nonfiction for readers ranging from preschoolers to young adults on a variety of subjects. Currently emphasizing middlegrade and young adult novels that offer a fresh perspective. De-emphasizing photographic nonfiction and picture books that teach a lesson. Approximately 80 new hardcover titles are published every year, fiction and nonfiction for babies through young adults. **Publishes 100 titles/year. 15% of books from first-time authors. Pays royalty on retail price. Pays advance.**

○ "Cultivating the creative talents of authors and illustrators and publishing books with purpose and heart continue to be the mission and joy at Dutton."

NONFICTION Subjects include animals, history, US, nature, environment, science. Query with SASE.

FICTION Dutton Children's Books has a diverse, general interest list that includes picture books; easy-to-read books; and fiction for all ages, from first chapter books to young adult readers. Query with SASE.

EAGLE'S VIEW PUBLISHING

168 W. 12th St., Ogden UT 84310. (801)393-3991. **Fax:** (801)393-4647. **E-mail:** sales@eaglefeathertrading. com. **Website:** www.eaglesviewpub.com. **Contact:** Denise Knight, editor-in-chief. Estab. 1982. Publishes trade paperback originals. "Eagle's View primarily publishes how-to craft books with a subject related to historical or contemporary Native American/Mountain Man/frontier crafts/bead crafts. Currently emphasizing bead-related craft books. De-emphasizing history except for historical Indian crafts." **Publishes 2-4 titles/year. 40 queries received/year. 20 mss received/year. 90% of books from first-time authors. 100% from unagented writers. Pays 8-10% royalty on net selling price.** Publishes ms 1 year after acceptance. Accepts simultaneous submissions. Responds in 1 year to proposals. Book catalog and ms guidelines for $4.00.

NONFICTION Subjects include anthropology, archaeology, Native American crafts, ethnic, Native American, history, American frontier historical patterns and books, hobbies, crafts, especially beadwork. Submit outline, 1-2 sample chapters. Reviews artwork/photos. Send photocopies and sample illustrations.

TIPS "We will not be publishing any new beaded earrings books for the foreseeable future. We are interested in other craft projects using seed beads, especially books that feature a variety of items, not just different designs for 1 item."

EAKIN PRESS

P.O. Box 21235, Waco TX 76702. (254)235-6161. **Fax:** (254)235-6230. **Website:** www.eakinpress.com. **Contact:** Kris Gholson, associate publisher. Estab. 1978. Publishes hardcover and paperback originals and reprints. "Our top priority is to cover the history and culture of the Southwest, especially Texas and Oklahoma. We also have successfully published titles related to ethnic studies. We publish very little fiction, other than for children." Accepts simultaneous submissions. Responds in up to 1 year to queries. Book catalog for $1.25. Guidelines available online.

○ No electronic submissions.

NONFICTION Subjects include Americana, Western, business, economics, cooking, foods, nutrition, ethnic, history, military, war, regional, sports, African American studies. Juvenile nonfiction: includes biographies of historic personalities, prefer with Texas or regional interest, or nature studies; and easy-read illustrated books for grades 1-3. Submit sample chapters, bio, synopsis, publishing credits, SASE.

FICTION Subjects include historical, juvenile. Juvenile fiction for grades K-12, preferably relating to Texas and the Southwest or contemporary. No adult fiction. Query or submit outline/synopsis

EASTLAND PRESS

P.O. Box 99749, Seattle WA 98139. (206)217-0204. **Fax:** (206)217-0205. **E-mail:** info@eastlandpress.com. **Website:** www.eastlandpress.com. **Contact:** John O'Connor, Managing Editor. Estab. 1981. Publishes hardcover and trade paperback originals. "Eastland Press is interested in textbooks for practitioners of alternative medical therapies, primarily Chinese and physical therapies, and related bodywork." **Publishes 4-6 titles/year. 25 queries received/year. 30% of books from first-time authors. 90% from unagented writers. Pays 12-15% royalty on receipts.** Publishes book 12 to 24 months after acceptance of ms. Accepts simultaneous submissions. Responds in 1 month to queries.

NONFICTION Subjects include health, medicine. "We prefer that a manuscript be completed or close to completion before we will consider publication. Proposals are rarely considered, unless submitted by a published author or teaching institution." Submit outline and 2-3 sample chapters. Reviews artwork/photos. Send photocopies.

RECENT Title(s) *Anatomy of Breathing*, by Blandine Calais-Germain; *The Fasciae: Anatomy, Dysfunction & Treatment*, by Serge Paoletti; *Chinese Herbal Medicine*, by Dan Bensky.

◎⊘ THE ECCO PRESS

10 E. 53rd St., New York NY 10022. (212)207-7000. **Fax:** (212)702-2460. **Website:** www.harpercollins.com. **Contact:** Daniel Halpern, editor-in-chief. Estab. 1970. Publishes hardcover and trade paperback originals and reprints. **Publishes 60 titles/year. Pays royalty. Pays negotiable advance.** Publishes ms 1 year after acceptance.

FICTION Literary, short story collections. "We can publish possibly one or two original novels a year." Published *Blonde*, by Joyce Carrol Oates; *Pitching Around Fidel*, by S.L. Price. *Does not accept unsolicited mss.*

TIPS "We are always interested in first novels and feel it's important that they be brought to the attention of the reading public."

♡ ÉCRITS DES FORGES

992-A, rue Royale, Trois-Rivières QC G9A 4H9, Canada. (819)840-8492. **Website:** www.ecritsdesforges.com. **Contact:** Stéphane Despatie, director. Estab. 1971. **Pays royalties of 10-20%.** Responds to queries in 6 months.

POETRY Écrits des Forges publishes poetry only that is "authentic and original as a signature. We have published poetry from more than 1,000 poets coming from most of the francophone countries: Andreé Romus (Belgium), Amadou Lamine Sall (Seéneégal), Nicole Brossard, Claude Beausoleil, Jean-Marc Desgent, and Jean-Paul Daoust (Québec)." Publishes 45-50 paperback books of poetry/year. Books are usually 80-88 pages, digest-sized, perfect-bound, with 2-color covers with art. Query first with a few sample poems and a cover letter with brief bio and publication credits. Order sample books by writing or faxing.

EDCON PUBLISHING GROUP

30 Montauk Blvd., Oakdale NY 11769. (631)567-7227. **Fax:** (631)567-8745. **E-mail:** dale@edconpublishing.com. **Website:** www.edconpublishing.com. **Work purchased outright from authors for up to $1,000.** Publishes book 6 months after acceptance. Accepts simultaneous submissions. Catalog available online.

◑　Looking for educational games and nonfiction work in the areas of math, science, reading and social studies.

NONFICTION Grades 1-12, though primarily 6-12 remedial.

FICTION Submit outline/synopsis and 1 sample chapter. Submission kept on file unless return is requested. Include SASE for return.

♡ EDGE SCIENCE FICTION AND FANTASY PUBLISHING/TESSERACT BOOKS

Hades Publications, Box 1714, Calgary AB T2P 2L7, Canada. (403)254-0160. **Fax:** (403)254-0456. **E-mail:** publisher@hadespublications.com. **Website:** www.edgewebsite.com. **Contact:** Editorial Manager. Estab. 1996.

TIPS "Send us your best, polished, completed manuscript. Use proper manuscript format. Take the time before you submit to get a critique from people who can offer you useful advice. When in doubt, visit our website for helpful resources, FAQs and other tips."

EDUPRESS, INC.

P.O. Box 8610, Madison WI 53708. (920)563-9571 ext. 332. **Fax:** (920)563-7395. **E-mail:** edupress@highsmith.com; LBowie@highsmith.com. **Website:** www.edupressinc.com. **Contact:** Liz Bowie. Estab. 1979. Edupress, Inc., publishes supplemental curriculum resources for PK-6th grade. Currently emphasizing reading and math materials, as well as science and social studies. **Work purchased outright from authors.** Publishes ms 1-2 years after acceptance. Responds in 2-4 months to queries and mss. Catalog available on website.

◑　"Our mission is to create products that make kids want to go to school!"

NONFICTION Submit complete ms via mail or e-mail with "Manuscript Submission" as the subject line.

TIPS "We are looking for unique, research-based, quality supplemental materials for Pre-K through eighth grade. We publish all subject areas in many different formats, including games. Our materials are intended for classroom and home schooling use."

EERDMANS BOOKS FOR YOUNG READERS

2140 Oak Industrial Dr. NE, Grand Rapids MI 49505. **E-mail:** youngreaders@eerdmans.com; gbrown@ eerdmans.com. **Website:** www.eerdmans.com/ youngreaders. **Contact:** Kathleen Merz, acquisitions editor. "We are seeking books that encourage independent thinking, problem-solving, creativity, acceptance, kindness. Books that encourage moral values without being didactic or preachy. Board books, picture books, middle reader fiction, young adult fiction, nonfiction, illustrated storybooks. A submission stands out when it's obvious that someone put time into it—the publisher's name and address are spelled correctly, the package is neat, and all of our submission requirements have been followed precisely. We look for short, concise cover letters that explain why the ms fits with our list, and/or how the ms fills an important need in the world of children's literature. Send exclusive ms submissions to acquisitions editor. We regret that due to the volume of material we receive, we cannot comment on ms we are unable to accept." **6,000 mss received/year. Pays 5-7% royalty on retail.** Publishes middle reader and YA books 1 year after acceptance; publishes picture books in 2-3 years. after acceptance of ms. Responds to mss in 3-4 months.

○ "We seek to engage young minds with words and pictures that inform and delight, inspire and entertain. From board books for babies to picture books, nonfiction, and novels for children and young adults, our goal is to produce quality literature for a new generation of readers. We believe in books!"

NONFICTION Middle readers: biography, history, multicultural, nature/environment, religion, social issues. Young adults/teens: biography, history, multicultural, nature/environment, religion, social issues. Average word length: middle readers—35,000; young adult books—35,000. Reviews artwork/photos. Send color photocopies rather than original art.

FICTION Picture books: animal, contemporary, folktales, history, humor, multicultural, nature/environment, poetry, religion, special needs, social issues, sports, suspense. Young readers: animal, contemporary, fantasy, folktales, history, humor, multicultural, poetry, religion, special needs, social issues, sports, suspense. Middle readers: adventure, contemporary, fantasy, history, humor, multicultural, nature/environment, problem novels, religion, social issues, sports, suspense. Young adults/teens: adventure, contemporary, fantasy, folktales, history, humor, multicultural, nature/environment, problem novels, religion, sports, suspense. Average word length: picture books—1,000; middle readers—15,000; young adult—45,000. "Right now we are not acquiring books that revolve around a holiday. (No Christmas, Thanksgiving, Easter, Halloween, Fourth of July, Hanukkah books.) We do not publish retold or original fairy tales, nor do we publish books about witches or ghosts or vampires." Send exclusive ms submissions (marked so on outside of envelope) to acquisitions editor.

TIPS "Find out who Eerdmans is before submitting a manuscript. Look at our website, request a catalog, and check out our books."

WILLIAM B. EERDMANS PUBLISHING CO.

2140 Oak Industrial Dr. NE, Grand Rapids MI 49505. (616)459-4591. **Fax:** (616)459-6540. **E-mail:** info@ eerdmans.com. **Website:** www.eerdmans.com. **Contact:** Jon Pott, editor-in-chief. Estab. 1911. Publishes hardcover and paperback originals and reprints. "The majority of our adult publications are religious and most of these are academic or semi-academic in character (as opposed to inspirational or celebrity books), though we also publish general trade books on the Christian life. Our nonreligious titles, most of them in regional history or on social issues, aim, similarly, at an educated audience." Accepts simultaneous submissions. Responds in 4 weeks to queries, possibly longer for mss. Please include e-mail and/or SASE. Book catalog and ms guidelines free.

IMPRINTS Eerdmans Books for Young Readers.

○ Will not respond to or accept mss, proposals, or queries sent by e-mail or fax.

NONFICTION Subjects include history, religious, language, literature, philosophy, of religion, psychology, regional, history, religion, sociology, translation, Biblical studies. "We prefer that writers take the time to notice if we have published anything at all in the same category as their manuscript before sending it to us." Query with TOC, 2-3 sample chapters, and SASE for return of ms. Reviews artwork/photos.

FICTION Subjects include religious, children's, general, fantasy. Query with SASE.

EGMONT USA

443 Park Ave. S, New York NY 10016. (212)685-0102. **E-mail:** Suite 806. **Website:** www.egmontusa.com. **Contact:** Elizabeth Law, vice president/publisher;

Regina Griffin, executive editor; Greg Ferguson, senior editor; Alison Weiss, assistant editor. Estab. 2008. Specializes in trade books. Publishes 1 picture book/year; 2 young readers/year; 20 middle readers/year; 20 young adult/year. "Egmont USA publishes quality commercial fiction. We are committed to editorial excellence and to providing first-rate care for our authors. Our motto is that we turn writers into authors and children into passionate readers." **25% of books from first-time authors. Pays authors royalties based on retail price.** Publishes book 18 months after acceptance. Accepts simultaneous submissions. Responds to queries in 4 weeks; mss in 6 weeks.

- *"Unfortunately, Egmont USA is not currently able to accept unsolicited submissions; we only accept submissions from literary agents."*

FICTION Young readers: adventure, animal, contemporary, humor, multicultural. Middle readers: adventure, animal, contemporary, fantasy, humor, multicultural, problem novels, science fiction, special needs. Young adults/teens: adventure, animal, contemporary, fantasy, humor, multicultural, paranormal, problem novels, religion, science fiction, special needs. Query or submit completed ms.

EDWARD ELGAR PUBLISHING, INC.

Edward Elgar Publishing Inc., The William Pratt House, 9 Dewey Court, Northampton MA 01060. (413)584-5551. **Fax:** (413)584-9933. **E-mail:** elgarsubmissions@e-elgar.com; submissions@e-elgar.co.uk. **Website:** www.e-elgar.com. **Contact:** Alan Sturmer; Tara Gorvine. Estab. 1986. "Specializing in research monographs, reference books and upper-level textbooks in highly focused areas, we are able to offer a unique service in terms of editorial, production and worldwide marketing.We have three offices, Cheltenham and Camberley in the UK and Northampton, MA, US."

- "We are actively commissioning new titles and are happy to consider and advise on ideas for monograph books, textbooks, professional law books and academic journals at any stage. Please complete a proposal form in as much detail as possible. We review all prososals with our academic advisors."

ELLORA'S CAVE PUBLISHING, INC.

1056 Home Ave., Akron OH 44310. **E-mail:** submissions@ellorascave.com. **Website:** www.ellorascave.com. Estab. 2000. Publishes electronic originals and reprints; print books. **Pays 45% royalty on amount received.** Accepts simultaneous submissions. Responds in 2-4 months to mss. No queries. Guidelines available online. "Read and follow detailed submission instructions.".

FICTION , Erotic romance and erotica fiction of every subgenre, including gay/lesbian, menage and more, and BDSM. All must have abundant, explicit, and graphic erotic content. Submit electronically only; cover e-mail as defined in our submission guidelines plus one attached .docx file containing full synopsis, first three chapters, and last chapter.

TIPS "Our audience is romance readers who want explicit sexual detail. They come to us because we offer sex with romance, plot, emotion. In addition to erotic romance with happy-ever-after endings, we also publish pure erotica, detailing sexual adventure, and experimentation."

EMIS, INC.

P.O. Box 270666, Fort Collins CO 80527. (214)349 0077; (800)225-0694. **Fax:** (970)672-8606. **Website:** www.emispub.com. **Contact:** Lynda Blake, president. Publishes trade paperback originals. **Publishes 2 titles/year. Pays 12% royalty on retail price.** Responds in 3 months to queries. Book catalog available free. Guidelines available free.

- "Medical text designed for physicians; fit in the lab coat pocket as a quick reference. Currently emphasizing women's health."

NONFICTION Subjects include health, medicine, psychology, women's health/medicine. Submit 3 sample chapters with SASE.

TIPS Audience is medical professionals and medical product manufacturers and distributors.

ENCOUNTER BOOKS

900 Broadway, Suite 601, New York NY 10003. (212)871-6310. **Fax:** (212)871-6311. **Website:** www.encounterbooks.com. **Contact:** Roger Kimball, editor and president. Hardcover originals and trade paperback reprints. Encounter Books publishes serious nonfiction—books that can alter our society, challenge our morality, stimulate our imaginations—in the areas of history, politics, religion, biography, education, public policy, current affairs, and social sciences. Encounter Books is an activity of Encounter for Culture and Education, a tax-exempt, non profit corporation dedicated to strengthening the marketplace of ideas and engaging in educational activities

to help preserve democratic culture. Accepts simultaneous submissions. Book catalog online. Guidelines available online.

○ *Accepts agented material only. No unsolicited mss/queries.*

NONFICTION Subjects include child guidance, education, ethnic, government, politics, health, medicine, history, language, literature, memoirs, military, war, multicultural, philosophy, psychology, religion, science, sociology, women's issues, women's studies, gender studies. Only considers agented submissions.

✚ ENETE ENTERPRISES

3600 Mission #10, San Diego CA 92109. **E-mail:** EneteEnterprises@gmail.com. **Website:** www.EneteEnterprises.com. **Contact:** Shannon Enete, editor. Estab. 2011. Publishes trade paperback originals, mass market paperback originals, electronic originals. **Publishes 6 titles/year. 60 queries received/year. 30 mss received/year. 95% of books from first-time authors. 100% from unagented writers. Pays royalties of 1-15%.** Publishes book 3-6 months after acceptance. Accepts simultaneous submissions. Responds to queries/proposals in 1 month; mss in 1-3 months. Guidelines available on website.

NONFICTION Subjects include cooking, creative nonfiction, education, foods, gay, government, health, lesbian, medicine, memoirs, multicultural, nutrition, photography, politics, science, spirituality, travel, world affairs. "Actively seeking books about healthcare / medicine. More specifically: back care, emergency medicine, international medicine, healthcare, insurance, EMT or Paramedic, or alternative medicine." Submit query, proposal, or ms by e-mail. Reviews artwork.

FICTION Subjects include adventure, gay, lesbian, romance, science fiction. Submit query, proposal, or ms by e-mail according to guidelines (do not forget a marketing plan).

TIPS "Send me your best work. Do not rush a draft."

ENGLISH TEA ROSE PRESS

The Wild Rose Press, P.O. Box 708, Adams Basin NY 14410. (585)752-8770. **E-mail:** queryus@thewildrosepress.com. **Website:** www.thewildrosepress.com. **Contact:** Nicole D'Arienzo, editor. Estab. 2006. Publishes paperback originals, reprints, and e-books in a POD format. Member: EPIC, Romance Writers of America. Distributes/promotes titles through major distribution chains, including iTunes, Kobo, Sony, Amazon.com, Kindle, as well as smaller and online distributors. **Pays royalty of 7% minimum; 35% maximum.** Publishes ms 1 year after acceptance. Responds in 4 weeks to queries; 3 months to mss. Guidelines available on website.

○ *Does not accept unsolicited mss.* Agented fiction less than 1%. Always comments on rejected mss. Sends prepublication galleys to author.

FICTION Wants contemporary, futuristic/time travel, gothic, historical, regency, romantic suspense, erotic, and paranormal romances. "In the English Tea Rose line we have conquering heroes, high seas adventure, and scandalous gossip. The love stories that will take you back in time. From the windswept moors of Scotland, to the Emerald Isle, to the elegant ballrooms of Regency England, the men and women of this time are larger than life and willing to risk it all for the love of a lifetime. English Tea Rose stories encompass historical romances set before 1900 which are not set on American soil. Send us your medieval knights, Vikings, Scottish highlanders, marauding pirates, and ladies and gentlemen of the Ton. English Tea Rose romances should have strong conflict and be emotionally driven; and, whether the story is medieval, Regency, set during the renaissance, or any other pre-1900 time, they must stay true to their period in historical accuracy and flavor. English Tea Roses can range from sweet to spicy, but should not contain overly explicit language." Send query letter with outline and a list of publishing credits. Include estimated word count, brief bio, and list of publishing credits.

TIPS "Polish your manuscript, make it as error free as possible, and follow our submission guidelines."

ENSLOW PUBLISHERS, INC.

40 Industrial Rd., Box 398, Berkeley Heights NJ 07922. (973)771-9400. **E-mail:** customerservice@enslow.com. **Website:** www.enslow.com. **Contact:** Brian D. Enslow, editor. Estab. 1977. Publishes hardcover originals. 10% require freelance illustration. **Publishes 250 titles/year. Pays royalty on net price with advance or flat fee. Pays advance.** Publishes ms 1 year after acceptance. Responds in 1 month to queries. Guidelines for #10 SASE.

IMPRINTS MyReportLinks.com Books, Enslow Elementary

○ "Enslow publishes hardcover nonfiction series books for young adults and school-age children."

NONFICTION Subjects include health, medicine, history, recreation, sports, science, sociology. "Interested in new ideas for series of books for young people." No fiction, fictionalized history, or dialogue.

RECENT Title(s) *TV News: Can It Be Trusted?*, by Ray Spangenburg and Kit Moser; *Resisters and Rescuers—Standing Up Against the Holocaust*, by Linda Jacobs Attman.

TIPS "We love to receive resumes from experienced writers with good research skills who can think like young people."

EOS

Imprint of HarperCollins General Books Group, 10 E. 53rd St., New York NY 10022. (212)207-7000. **Website:** www.eosbooks.com. Estab. 1998. Publishes hardcover originals, trade and mass market paperback originals, and reprints. Eos publishes quality science fiction/fantasy with broad appeal. **Pays royalty on retail price. Pays variable advance.** Guidelines for #10 SASE.

FICTION Subjects include fantasy, science fiction. No horror or juvenile. Agented submissions only. *All unsolicited mss returned.*

TIPS "Query via e-mail. Your query should be brief—no more than a 2-page description of your book. Do not send chapters or full synopsis at this time. You will receive a response—either a decline or a request for more material—in approximately 1-2 months."

EPICENTER PRESS, INC.

P.O. Box 82368, Kenmore WA 98028. **Fax:** (425)481-8253. **E-mail:** info@epicenterpress.com; laelmorgan@cs.com. **Website:** www.epicenterpress.com. **Contact:** Lael Morgan, acquisitions editor. Estab. 1987. Publishes hardcover and trade paperback originals. "We are a regional press founded in Alaska whose interests include but are not limited to the arts, history, environment, and diverse cultures and lifestyles of the North Pacific and high latitudes." **Publishes 4-8 titles/year. 200 queries received/year. 100 mss received/year. 75% of books from first-time authors. 90% from unagented writers.** Publishes book 1-2 years after acceptance. Responds in 3 months to queries. Book catalog and ms guidelines on website.

"Our affiliated company, Aftershocks Media, provides a range of services to self-publisher industry distributors."

NONFICTION Subjects include animals, ethnic, history, nature, environment, recreation, regional, women's issues. "Our focus is Alaska and the Pacific Northwest. We do not encourage nonfiction titles from outside this region." Submit outline and 3 sample chapters. Reviews artwork/photos. Send photocopies.

ERIE CANAL PRODUCTIONS

4 Farmdale St., Clinton NY 13323. **E-mail:** eriecanal@juno.com. **Website:** www.eriecanalproductions.com. **Contact:** Scott Fiesthumel, president. Estab. 2001. Publishes trade paperback originals. **Publishes 1-2 titles/year. 50% of books from first-time authors. 100% from unagented writers. Pays negotiable royalty on net profits.** Responds in 1 month to queries. Book catalog available free.

NONFICTION Subjects include Americana, history, sports. Query with SASE. *All unsolicited mss returned unopened.*

RECENT Title(s) *The Legend of Wild Bill Setley*, by Tony Kissel; *S. Fiesthumel*, (biography); *Diamond Dynasty*, by Billy Mills; *The Bank With the Gold Dome*, by Scott Fiesthumel.

TIPS "We publish nonfiction books that look at historical places, events, and people along the traditional route of the Erie Canal through New York State."

F+W MEDIA, INC. (BOOK DIVISION)

10151 Carver Rd., Suite 200, Blue Ash OH 45242. (513)531-2690. **Website:** www.fwmedia.com. **Contact:** President Sara Domville; President David Blansfield. Estab. 1913. "In October 2008, F+W Media moved from a divisionally structured company to a community structure, wherein the publisher and editorial director for each community has full responsibility for the books, magazines, online, events, and educational products associated with their community. F+W Media produces more than 400 new books per year, maintains a backlist of more than 2,500 titles, publishes 39 magazines, owns and operates dozens of informational and subscription-based websites, and operates a growing number of successful consumer shows annually." **Publishes 400+ titles/year.** Guidelines available online.

IMPRINTS Adams Media (general interest series); David & Charles (crafts, equestrian, railroads, soft crafts); HOW Books (graphic design, illustrated, humor, pop culture); IMPACT Books (fantasy art, manga, creative comics and popular culture); Krause Books (antiques and collectibles, automotive, coins and paper money, comics, crafts, games, firearms, militaria, outdoors and hunting, records and

CDs, sports, toys); Memory Makers (scrapbooking); North Light Books (crafts, decorative painting, fine art); Popular Woodworking Books (shop skills, woodworking); Warman's (antiques and collectibles, field guides); Writer's Digest Books (writing and reference).

⬤ Please see individual listings for specific submission information about the company's imprints.

FABER & FABER INC.

Farrar, Straus & Giroux, 18 W. 18th St., New York NY 10011. (212)741-6900. **E-mail:** fsg.editorial@fsgbooks. com. **Website:** us.macmillan.com/faberandfaber.aspx. Estab. 1976. Responds in 6-8 weeks.

NONFICTION "All submissions must be submitted through the mail—we do not accept electronic submissions, or submissions delivered in person. Please include a cover letter describing your submission, along with the first 50 pages of the manuscript."

POETRY "All submissions must be submitted through the mail—we do not accept electronic submissions, or submissions delivered in person. Please include a cover letter describing your submission, along with the first 50 pages of the manuscript. If you are submitting poems, please include 3-4 poems."

⬤ FABER & FABER LTD

Bloomsbury House, 74-77 Great Russell St., London WC1B 3DA, United Kingdom. **Website:** www.faber. co.uk. **Contact:** Lee Brackstone, Hannah Griffiths, Angus Cargill, (fiction); Walter Donohue (film); Dinah Wood, (plays); Julian Loose, Neil Belton, (nonfiction); Paul Keegan, (poetry); Belinda Matthews, (music); Suzy Jenvy, Julia Wells, (children's). Estab. 1925. Publishes hardcover and paperback originals and reprints. Faber & Faber have rejuvenated their nonfiction, music and children's titles in recent years and the film and drama lists remain market leaders. **Publishes 200 titles/year. Pays royalty. Pays varying advances with each project.** Accepts simultaneous submissions. Responds in 3 months to mss. Book catalog available online.

⬤ Faber & Faber will consider unsolicited proposals for poetry only.

NONFICTION Subjects include art, architecture, contemporary culture, cooking, foods, nutrition, creative nonfiction, government, politics, history, humanities, literary criticism, memoirs, military, war, multicultural, music, dance, psychology, recreation, science, sports, travel, world affairs, Children's. *No unsolicited nonfiction submissions.*

FICTION Subjects include adventure, ethnic, experimental, fantasy, historical, humor, literary, mystery, plays, poetry, short story collections, spiritual, sports, suspense, young adult, Drama, Plays, Screenplays, Children's Fiction, Arts & Literature. *No unsolicited fiction submissions.*

POETRY Address poetry to 'Poetry Submissions Department' and include an SAE for return. For more information, ring 020 7465 0045. Submit 6 sample poems.

TIPS Explore the website and downloadable book catalogues thoroughly to get a feel for the lists in all categories and genres.

FACTS ON FILE, INC.

Infobase Learning, 132 W. 31st St., 17th Floor, New York NY 10001. (800)322-8755. **Fax:** (800)678-3633. **E-mail:** llikoff@factsonfile.com; custserv@factsonfile. com. **Website:** www.factsonfile.com. **Contact:** Laurie Likoff, editorial director (science, fashion, natural history); Justine Ciovacco (science, nature, juvenile); Owen Lancer, senior editor (American history, women's studies); James Chambers, trade editor (health, pop culture, true crime, sports); Jeff Soloway, acquisitions editor (language/literature). Estab. 1941. Publishes hardcover originals and reprints. Facts on File produces high-quality reference materials on a broad range of subjects for the school library market and the general nonfiction trade. **Publishes 135-150 titles/ year. 25% from unagented writers. Pays 10% royalty on retail price. Pays $5,000-10,000 advance.** Accepts simultaneous submissions. Responds in 2 months to queries. Book catalog available free. Guidelines available online.

IMPRINTS Checkmark Books.

NONFICTION Subjects include contemporary culture, education, health, medicine, history, language, literature, multicultural, recreation, religion, sports, careers, entertainment, natural history, popular culture. "We publish serious, informational books for a targeted audience. All our books must have strong library interest, but we also distribute books effectively to the trade. Our library books fit the junior and senior high school curriculum." No computer books, technical books, cookbooks, biographies (except YA), pop psychology, humor, fiction or poetry. Query or submit outline and sample chapter with SASE. No submissions returned without SASE.

TIPS "Our audience is school and public libraries for our more reference-oriented books and libraries, schools and bookstores for our less reference-oriented informational titles."

FAIRLEIGH DICKINSON UNIVERSITY PRESS

285 Madison Ave., M-GH2-01, Madison NJ 07940. (973)443-8564. **Fax:** (973)443-8364. **E-mail:** fdupress@fdu.edu. **Website:** www.fdupress.org. **Contact:** Harry Keyishian, director. Estab. 1967. Publishes hardcover originals and occasional paperbacks, and all existing electronic formats. Fairleigh Dickinson publishes scholarly books for the academic market, in the humanities and social sciences through a co-publishing partnership that was established in 2010 with The Rowman & Littlefield Publishing Group, Lanham, MD. **Publishes 35-45 titles/year. 33% of books from first-time authors. 95% from unagented writers.** Publishes ms 6-7 months after acceptance. Responds in 2 weeks to queries.

○ " Contracts are arranged through The Rowman & Littlefield Publishing Group, which also handles editing and production. We are a selection committee."

NONFICTION Subjects include architecture, art, cinema, communications, contemporary culture, dance, economics, ethnic, film, gay, government, history, law, lesbian, literary criticism, multicultural, music, philosophy, psychology, regional, religion, sociology, womens issues, womens studies, world affairs, local, world literature, Italian Studies (series), Communication Studies (series), Willa Cather (series), American history and culture, Civil War, Jewish studies. "The Press discourages submissions of unrevised dissertations. We will consider scholarly editions of literary works in all fields, in English, or translation. We welcome inquiries about essay collections if the the material is previously unpublished, he essays have a unifying and consistent theme, and the editors provide a substantial scholarly introduction." No nonscholarly books. We do not publish textbooks, or original fiction, poetry or plays. Query with outline, detailed abstract, and sample chapters (if possible), and CV. Does not review artwork.

FANTAGRAPHICS BOOKS INC.

7563 Lake City Way NE, Seattle WA 98115. (206)524-1967. **Fax:** (206)524-2104. **E-mail:** fbicomix@fantagraphics.com. **Website:** www.fantagraphics.com. **Contact:** Submissions editor. Estab. 1976. Publishes original trade paperbacks. Publishes comics for thinking readers. Does not want mainstream genres of superhero, vigilante, horror, fantasy, or science fiction. Responds in 2-3 months to queries. Book catalog available online. Guidelines available online.

FICTION Subjects include comic books. "Fantagraphics is an independent company with a modus operandi different from larger, factory-like corporate comics publishers. If your talents are limited to a specific area of expertise (i.e. inking, writing, etc.), then you will need to develop your own team before submitting a project to us. We want to see an idea that is fully fleshed-out in your mind, at least, if not on paper. Submit a minimum of 5 fully-inked pages of art, a synopsis, SASE, and a brief note stating approximately how many issues you have in mind."

TIPS "Take note of the originality and diversity of the themes and approaches to drawing in such Fantagraphics titles as *Love & Rockets* (stories of life in Latin America and Chicano L.A.), *Palestine* (journalistic autobiography in the Middle East), *Eightball* (surrealism mixed with kitsch culture in stories alternately humorous and painfully personal), and *Naughty Bits* (feminist humor and short stories which both attack and commiserate). Try to develop your own, equally individual voice; originality, aesthetic maturity, and graphic storytelling skill are the signs by which Fantagraphics judges whether or not your submission is ripe for publication."

⊕◉ FANTASTIC BOOKS PUBLISHING

Lilac Tree Farm, Honeypots Ln., Elstronwick East Yorkshire HU12 9BP, United Kingdom. +44 (07415)388882. **E-mail:** fantasticbookspublishing@gmail.com. **Website:** www.fantasticbookspublishing.com. **Contact:** Daniel Grubb, CEO/COO. Estab. 2012. Publishes trade paperback and electronic originals. **Publishes 10-15 titles/year. 100+ queries received/year. 100+ mss received/year. 70% of books from first-time authors. 100% from unagented writers. Pays 40-100% on wholesale price. No advance.** Publishes ms 3-4 months after acceptance. Accepts simultaneous submissions. Responds in 1 week to queries; 1 month to proposals; 3 months to mss. Catalog and guidelines available online at website.

○ 50% author-subsidy published.

NONFICTION , Open to any subject. Submit proposal package, including outline, 3 sample chapters, and 5GBP submission fee to cover admin and reader report production. "All we ask is that you review our submission guidelines and follow them closely for your submission. Every submission to Fantastic Books Publishing will be returned with a readers report from our editorial team. This may be an offer of publication, suggestions for tightening the manuscript or simply to reject it. Even in the case of rejections, we usually suggest alternative routes to publication."

FICTION Subjects include adventure, confession, contemporary, erotica, ethnic, experimental, fantasy, feminist, gay, gothic, hi-lo, historical, horror, humor, juvenile, lesbian, literary, mainstream, military, multicultural, multimedia, mystery, occult, poetry, poetry in translation, regional, romance, science fiction, short story collections, sports, suspense, war, western, young adult. Submit proposal package, including synopsis, 3 sample chapters, and 5GBP submission fee to cover admin and reader report production. "All we ask is that you review our submission guidelines and follow them closely for your submission. Every submission to Fantastic Books Publishing will be returned with a readers report from our editorial team. This may be an offer of publication, suggestions for tightening the manuscript or simply to reject it. Even in the case of rejections, we usually suggest alternative routes to publication."

POETRY Submit 3 sample poems.

TIPS "Be yourself. Don't try to come across as anything different. We work very closely with our clients and it is our intention to get to know you and to welcome you into our publishing family. This helps us market and promote your book to your target audience. It also helps the reputation of the publishing industry which, in these times of constant change, is what we intend to do by being honest, transparent and, above all, sincere with our clients."

FARCOUNTRY PRESS

P.O. Box 5630, Helena MT 59604. (800)821-3874. **Fax:** (406)443-5480. **E-mail:** will@farcountrypress.com. **Website:** www.farcountrypress.com. **Contact:** Will Harmon. Award-winning publisher Farcountry Press specializes in softcover and hardcover color photography books showcasing the nation's cities, states, national parks, and wildlife. Farcountry also publishes several children's series, as well as guidebooks, cookbooks, and regional history titles nationwide. **Publishes The staff produces about 30 books annually; the backlist has grown to more than 300 titles titles/year.** Submission guidelines available on website.

FARRAR, STRAUS & GIROUX

18 W. 18th St., New York NY 10011. **E-mail:** childrenseditorial@fsgbooks.com. **Website:** www.fsgkidsbooks.com. **Contact:** Margaret Ferguson, editorial director; Wesley Adams, executive editor; Janine O'Malley, senior editor; Frances Foster, Frances Foster Books; Robbin Gourley, art director. Estab. 1946. Book catalog available for 9×12 SASE with $1.95 postage. Ms guidelines for SASE, with 1 first-class stamp, or can be viewed at www.fsgkidsbooks.com.

○ *As of January 2010, Farrar Straus & Giroux does not accept unsolicited manuscripts. "We recommend finding a literary agent to represent you and your work."*

NONFICTION All levels: all categories. "We publish only literary nonfiction."

FICTION All levels: all categories. "Original and well-written material for all ages."

TIPS "Study our catalog before submitting. We will see illustrators' portfolios by appointment. Don't ask for criticism and/or advice—due to the volume of submissions we receive, it's just not possible. Never send originals. Always enclose SASE."

○○ FARRAR, STRAUS & GIROUX/ BOOKS FOR YOUNG READERS

18 W. 18th St., New York NY 10011. **E-mail:** fsg.editorial@fsgbooks.com. **Website:** us.macmillan.com. Estab. 1946. Publishes hardcover originals and trade paperback reprints. "We publish original and well-written material for all ages." **Publishes 75 titles/year. 6,000 queries and mss received/year. 5% of books from first-time authors. 50% from unagented writers. Pays 2-6% royalty on retail price for paperbacks, 3-10% for hardcovers. Pays $3,000-25,000 advance.** Publishes book 18 months after acceptance of ms. Accepts simultaneous submissions. Responds in 2 months to queries. Responds in 3 months to manuscripts. For catalog fax request or email to: childrens.publicity@fsgbooks.com. Guidelines available online.

IMPRINTS Frances Foster Books.

FICTION Subjects include juvenile, picture books, young adult, nonfiction. True Do not query picture books; just send ms. Do not fax or e-mail queries or mss. Query with SASE. Hard copy submissions only. **TIPS** Audience is full age range, preschool to young adult. Specializes in literary fiction.

FATHER'S PRESS

2424 SE 6th St., Lee's Summit MO 64063. (816)600-6288. **E-mail:** mike@fatherspress.com. **Website:** www.fatherspress.com. **Contact:** Mike Smitley, owner (fiction, nonfiction). Estab. 2006. Publishes hardcover, trade paperback, and mass market paperback originals and reprints. **Publishes 6-10 titles/year. Pays 10-15% royalty on wholesale price.** Publishes book 6 months after acceptance of ms. Responds in 1 month to queries and proposals. Responds in 3 months to mss. Guidelines available online.

NONFICTION Subjects include animals, cooking, foods, nutrition, creative nonfiction, history, military, war, nature, regional, religion, travel, women's issues, world affairs. Query with SASE. Unsolicited mss returned unopened. Call or e-mail first. Reviews artwork/photos. Send photocopies.

FICTION Subjects include adventure, historical, juvenile, literary, mainstream, contemporary, military, war, mystery, regional, religious, suspense, western, young adult. Query with SASE. Unsolicited mss returned unopened. Call or e-mail first.

FREDERICK FELL PUBLISHERS, INC.

2131 Hollywood Blvd., Suite 305, Hollywood FL 33020. (954)925-5242. **Fax:** (954)455-4243. **E-mail:** fellpub@aol.com. **Website:** www.fellpub.com. **Contact:** Barbara Newman, senior editor. Publishes hardcover and trade paperback originals. **Publishes 25 titles/year. 4,000 queries received/year. 1,000 mss received/year. 95% of books from first-time authors. 95% from unagented writers. Pays negotiable royalty on retail price. Pays up to $10,000 advance.** Publishes book 1 year after acceptance of ms. Accepts simultaneous submissions. Responds in 1 month to queries. Responds in 3 months to proposals. Guidelines available online.

○ "Fell is now publishing 50 e-books per year."

NONFICTION Subjects include business, economics, child guidance, education, ethnic, film, cinema, stage, health, medicine, hobbies, money, finance, spirituality. "We are reviewing in all categories. Advise us of the top 3 competitive titles for your work and the reasons why the public would benefit by having your book published." Submit proposal package, including outline, 3 sample chapters, author bio, publicity ideas, market analysis. Reviews artwork/photos. Send photocopies.

TIPS "We are most interested in well-written, timely nonfiction with strong sales potential. We will not consider topics that appeal to a small, select audience. Learn markets and be prepared to help with sales and promotion. Show us how your book is unique or better than the competition."

FENCE BOOKS

Science Library 320, Univ. of Albany, 1400 Washington Ave., Albany NY 12222. (518)591-8162. **E-mail:** fence.fencebooks@gmail.com; robfence@gmail.com. **Website:** www.fenceportal.org. **Contact:** Rob Arnold, Submissions Manager. Hardcover originals. "*Fence is closed to submissions right now.* We'll have another reading period in the Spring. Fence Books offers 2 book contests (in addition to the National Poetry Series) with 2 sets of guidelines and entry forms on our website." Guidelines available online.

FICTION Subjects include poetry.

POETRY Enter National Poetry Series Contest. See Open Competition Guidelines online. Also the annual Fence Books Motherwell Prize 2011 ($5,000) for a first or second book of poetry by a woman. Submit 48-60 pages during the month of November; and Fence Modern Poets Series 2011, for a poet writing in English at any stage in his or her career. $25 entry fee. Submissions may be sent through regular USPS mail, UPS, Fedex-type couriers, or certified mail.

TIPS "At present Fence Books is a self-selecting publisher; mss come to our attention through our contests and through editors' investigations. We hope to become open to submissions of poetry and fiction mss in the near future."

FERGUSON PUBLISHING CO.

Infobase Publishing, 132 W. 31st St., 17th Floor, New York NY 10001. (800)322-8755. **E-mail:** editorial@factsonfile.com. **Website:** www.infobasepublishing.com. Estab. 1940. Publishes hardcover and trade paperback originals. "We are primarily a career education publisher that publishes for schools and libraries. We need writers who have expertise in a particular career or career field (for possible full-length books on a specific career or field)." **Publishes 50 titles/year. Pays by project.** Responds in 6 months to queries. Guidelines available online.

○ "Please provide an overview of the subject you wish to write on, the intended audience, a brief description of the contents, and a sample chapter or headword list. It is not advisable to send a complete manuscript at this point. Include a list of the relevant competition and an indication of how your book will improve upon the competition or fill a specific niche in the market. Include a brief curriculum vitae or your writing accomplishments and relevant experience. Send or email your proposal to: Editorial Director."

NONFICTION "We publish work specifically for the elementary/junior high/high school/college library reference market. Works are generally encyclopedic in nature. Our current focus is career encyclopedias and young adult career sets and series. We consider manuscripts that cross over into the trade market." No mass market, poetry, scholarly, or juvenile books, please. Query or submit an outline and 1 sample chapter.

TIPS "We like writers who know the market—former or current librarians or teachers or guidance counselors."

◉ DAVID FICKLING BOOKS

31 Beamont St., Oxford En OX1 2NP, United Kingdom. (018)65-339000. **Fax:** (018)65-339009. **E-mail:** DFickling@randomhouse.co.uk; tburgess@randomhouse.co.uk. **Website:** www.davidficklingbooks.co.uk. **Publishes 12 titles/year.** Responds to mss in 3 months.

FICTION Considers all categories. Submit 3 sample chapters.

◉ FIFTH HOUSE PUBLISHERS

Fitzhenry & Whiteside, 195 Allstate Parkway, Markham ON L3R 4&8, Canada. (403)571-5230; (800)387-9776. **E-mail:** tdettman@fifthhousepublishers.ca. **Website:** www.fifthhousepublishers.ca. **Contact:** Tracey Dettman. Estab. 1982. "Fifth House Publishers, a Fitzhenry & Whiteside company, is committed to "bringing the West to the rest" by publishing approximately fifteen books a year about the land and people who make this region unique. We publish the acclaimed Going Wild series, Pierre Berton's History for Young Canadians, Keepers of Life, the Western Canadian Classics series, the Prairie Gardening series, and more. Our books are selected for their quality and contribution to the understanding of western-Canadian (and Canadian) history, culture, and environment."

FILTER PRESS, LLC

P.O. Box 95, Palmer Lake CO 80133. (719)481-2420; (888)570-2663. **Fax:** (719)481-2420. **E-mail:** info@filterpressbooks.com. **Website:** www.filterpressbooks.com. **Contact:** Doris Baker, president. Estab. 1957. Publishes trade paperback originals and reprints. **Publishes 4-6 titles/year. Pays 10-12% royalty on wholesale price.** Publishes ms 18 months after acceptance.

○ "Filter Press specializes in nonfiction of the West.","Please submit in hardcopy (not a computer disk) to our address."

NONFICTION Subjects include Americana, anthropology, archeology, ethnic, history, regional, crafts and crafts people of the Southwest. Query with outline and SASE. Reviews artwork/photos.

◉ FINDHORN PRESS

Delft Cottage, Dyke, Forres Scotland IV36 2TF, United Kingdom. (44)(1309) 690-582. **Fax:** (44)(131) 777-2711. **E-mail:** submissions@findhornpress.com. **Website:** www.findhornpress.com. **Contact:** Thierry Bogliolo, publisher. Estab. 1971. Publishes trade paperback originals. **Publishes 20 titles/year. 1,000 queries received/year. 50% of books from first-time authors. 80% from unagented writers. Pays 10-15% royalty on wholesale price.** Publishes ms 12-18 months after acceptance. Responds in 3-4 months to proposals. Book catalog and ms guidelines online. **NONFICTION** Subjects include nature, spirituality, alternative health. No autobiographies.

FINNEY COMPANY, INC.

8075 215th St. W., Lakeville MN 55044. (952)469-6699. **Fax:** (952)469-1968. **E-mail:** feedback@finneyco.com. **Website:** www.finneyco.com. **Contact:** Alan E. Krysan, president. Publishes trade paperback originals. **Publishes 2 titles/year. Pays 10% royalty on wholesale price. Pays advance.** Publishes ms 1 year after acceptance. Responds in 2-3 months to queries. **NONFICTION** Subjects include business, economics, education, career exploration/development. Finney publishes career development educational materials. Query with SASE. Reviews artwork/photos.

FIRE ENGINEERING BOOKS & VIDEOS

Imprint of PennWell Corp., 1421 S. Sheridan Rd., Tulsa OK 74112. (918)831-9410. **Fax:** (918)831-9555.

E-mail: FireBookEditor@pennwell.com; sales@
pennwell.com. **Website:** www.pennwellbooks.com.
Contact: Maria Patterson. Publishes hardcover and
softcover originals. "Fire Engineering publishes textbooks relevant to firefighting and training. Currently emphasizing strategy and tactics, reserve training,
preparedness for terrorist threats, natural disasters,
first response to fires and emergencies." Responds
in 1 month to proposals. Book catalog available free.
NONFICTION Submit proposal via e-mail.
TIPS No human-interest stories; technical training
only.

⊕ FIRST EDITION DESIGN PUBLISHING

5202 Old Ashwood Dr., Sarasota FL 34233. (941)921-
2607. **Fax:** (617)249-1694. **E-mail:** support@firstedi-
tiondesign.com. **E-mail:** submission@firstedition-
design.com. **Website:** www.firsteditiondesignpub-
lishing.com. **Contact:** Deborah E. Gordon, executive
editor; Tom Gahan, marketing director. Estab. 1985.
**Publishes 750+ titles/year. 45% of books from first-
time authors. 95% from unagented writers. Pays
royalty 30-70% on retail price.** Publishes book Accept to publish time is 1 week to 2 months. after acceptance of ms. Accepts simultaneous submissions.
Send SAE for catalog. Guidelines available free on
request or online at website.
NONFICTION Subjects include agriculture, alternative lifestyles, Americana, animals, architecture, art, business, career guidance, contemporary
culture, counseling, creative nonfiction, education,
ethnic, gay, government, health, history, humanities,
language, law, memoirs, military, money, multicultural, nature, New Age, philosophy, psychology, recreation, regional, religion, science, sex, social sciences, sociology, spirituality, womens issues, womens
studies, world affairs, young adult. Send complete
ms electronically.
FICTION Subjects include adventure, confession,
ethnic, experimental, fantasy, feminist, gay, gothic, historical, horror, humor, literary, mainstream,
multicultural, mystery, occult, poetry, regional, religious, romance, science fiction, short story collections, spiritual, suspense, western, young adult. Submit complete ms electronically.
POETRY Submit complete ms electronically.
TIPS "Follow our FAQs listed on our website."

○ FITZHENRY & WHITESIDE LTD.

195 Allstate Pkwy., Markham ON L3R 4T8, Canada.
(905)477-9700. **Fax:** (905)477-9179. **E-mail:** fitzkids@
fitzhenry.ca; godwit@fitzhenry.ca; charkin@fitzhen-
ry.ca. **Website:** www.fitzhenry.ca/. **Contact:** Sharon
Fitzhenry, president; Cathy Sandusky, children's publisher; Christie Harkin, submissions editor. Emphasis on Canadian authors and illustrators, subject or
perspective. **Publishes 15 titles/year. 10% of books
from first-time authors. Pays authors 8-10% royalty
with escalations. Offers "respectable" advances for
picture books, split 50/50 between author and illustrator. Pays illustrators by project and royalty.
Pays photographers per photo.** Publishes book 1-2
years after acceptance.
TIPS "We respond to quality."

FIVE STAR PUBLICATIONS, INC.

P.O. Box 6698, Chandler AZ 85246. (480)940-8182.
Fax: (480)940-8787. **E-mail:** info@fivestarpublica-
tions.com. **Website:** www.fivestarpublications.com.
Contact: Linda F. Radke, president. Estab. 1985.
"Helps produce and market award-winning books."

○   "Five Star Publications publishes and promotes
award-winning fiction, nonfiction, cookbooks,
children's literature and professional guides.
More information about Five Star Publications,
Inc., a 25-year leader in the book publishing/
book marketing industry, is available online at
our website." Other websites: www.LittleFive-
star.com, www.FiveStarLegends.com; www.
FiveStarSleuths.com; www.SixPointsPress.
com.

TIPS Features the Purple Dragonfly Book Awards and
Royal Dragonfly Book Awards, which were conceived
and designed with children in mind. "Not only do we
want to recognize and honor accomplished authors
in the field of children's literature, but we also want
to highlight and reward up-and-coming newly published authors, as well as younger published writers.
In our efforts to include everyone, the awards are divided into distinct subject categories, ranging from
books on the environment and cooking to books on
sports and family issues. (Please see the complete categories list on the entry form on our website.)

○ FLARESTACK POETS

P.O. Box 14779, Birmingham, West Midlands B13
3GU, United Kingdom. **E-mail:** meria@btinternet.
com; jacquierowe@hotmail.co.uk. **Website:** www.

flarestackpoets.co.uk. **Contact:** Meredith Andrea and Jacqui Rowe. Estab. 2008. **Pays 25% royalty and 6 contributor's copies.** Responds in 6 weeks.

POETRY Flarestack Poets wants "poems that dare outside current trends, even against the grain." Does not want "poems that fail to engage with either language or feeling." First chapbooks appearing in Autumn 2009. Publishes 8 chapbooks/year and 1 anthology. Manuscripts are selected through open submission and competition. "Our first chapbooks are winners of the 2009 Flarestack Poets Pamphlet competition. Thereafter we will consider open submissions." Chapbooks are 20-30 pages, professional photocopy, saddle-stitched, card cover. Query first with a few sample poems and a cover letter with brief bio and publication credits. Ms may include previously published poems.

FLASHLIGHT PRESS

527 Empire Blvd., Brooklyn NY 11225. (718)288-8300. **Fax:** (718)972-6307. **E-mail:** editor@flashlightpress.com. **Website:** www.flashlightpress.com. **Contact:** Shari Dash Greenspan, editor. Estab. 2004. Publishes hardcover and trade paperback originals. **Publishes 2-3 titles/year. 1,200 queries received/year; 120 mss received/year. 50% of books from first-time authors. Pays 8-10% royalty on wholesale price.** Publishes ms 3 years after acceptance. Accepts simultaneous submissions. "Due to the large number of queries we receive, we are no longer able to send individual replies for queries we do not wish to pursue. You will receive an automated reply that we received your query." Responds in 3 months to mss. Book catalog available online. Guidelines available online.

FICTION Average word length: 1,000 words. Picture books: contemporary, humor, multicultural. "Query by e-mail only, after carefully reading our submission guidelines: www.flashlightpress.com/submissionguidelines.html. No e-mail attachments. Do not send anything by snail mail."

FLOATING BRIDGE PRESS

909 NE 43rd St., #205, Seattle WA 98105. **E-mail:** floatingbridgepress@yahoo.com. **Website:** www.floatingbridgepress.org. Estab. 1994.

POETRY Floating Bridge Press publishes chapbooks and anthologies by Washington State poets, selected through an annual competition (see below). The press also publishes *Floating Bridge Review*, an annual anthology featuring the work of Washington State poets.

Floating Bridge Review is 86-144 pages, digest-sized, offset-printed, perfect-bound, with glossy cardstock cover. For a sample chapbook or anthology, send $13 postpaid.

FLORIDA ACADEMIC PRESS

P.O. Box 357425, Gainesville FL 32635. (352)332-5104. **E-mail:** fapress@gmail.com. **Website:** www.floridaacademicpress.com. **Contact:** Max Vargas, CEO (nonfiction/scholarly); Linda Travis, assistant editor (fiction). Estab. 1997. Publishes trade paperback originals. **Publishes 10 titles/year. 1,200 queries received/year; 800 mss received/year. 80% of books from first-time authors. 100% from unagented writers. Pays 6-10% royalty on retail price and higher on sales of 2,500+ copies a year.** Publishes ms 3 months after acceptance. Responds in 3-4 months to mss. Catalog available online.

NONFICTION Subjects include government/politics, philosophy, psychology, social sciences, world affairs,. We only assess complete mss that do not require extensive copy-editing. SASE returns. Submit completed ms only and CV. Works in progress of no interest—submit only final ms. Reviews artwork/photos. Send photocopies.

FICTION Subjects include historical, literary. Serious fiction and scholarly social science manuscripts. Does not want "children's books, poetry, science fiction, religious tracts, anthologies, or booklets." Submit completed ms by hard copy only.

TIPS Considers complete mss only. "Manuscripts we decide to publish must be re-submitted by the author in ready-to-print PDF files. Match our needs—do not send blindly. Books we accept for publication must be submitted in camera-ready format. The Press covers all publication/promotional expenditures."

FLUX

Llewellyn Worldwide, Ltd., Llewellyn Worldwide, Ltd., 2143 Wooddale Dr., Woodbury, MN 55125. (651)312-8613. **Fax:** (651)291-1908. **Website:** www.fluxnow.com; fluxnow.blogspot.com. **Contact:** Brian Farrey, acquisitions editor. Estab. 2005. "Flux seeks to publish authors who see YA as a point of view, not a reading level. We look for books that try to capture a slice of teenage experience, whether in real or imagined worlds." **Publishes 21 titles/year. 50% of books from first-time authors. Pays royalties of 10-15% based on wholesale price.** Book catalog and guidelines available on website.

○ *Does not accept unsolicited mss.*

FICTION Young Adults: adventure, contemporary, fantasy, history, humor, problem novels, religion, science fiction, sports, suspense.

TIPS "Read contemporary teen books. Be aware of what else is out there. If you don't read teen books, you probably shouldn't write them. Know your audience. Write incredibly well. Do not condescend."

FLYING PEN PRESS LLC

1660 Niagara St., Denver CO 80228. (303)375-0499. **Fax:** (303)375-0499. **E-mail:** GeneralInquiries@FlyingPenPress.com; Publisher@FlyingPenPress.com. **E-mail:** Submissions@FlyingPenPress.com. **Website:** www.flyingpenpress.com. **Contact:** David A. Rozansky, publisher. Estab. 2007. Publishes trade paperback and electronic originals. **Publishes 5 titles/year. Receives 120 queries/year; 360 mss/year. 55% of books from first-time authors. 88% from unagented writers. Pays 35-46% royalty; share of gross profits (net receipts less printing costs). No advances.** Publishes book 6 months after acceptance. Accepts simultaneous submissions. Responds in less than 1 month to queries/proposals; 6 months to mss. Catalog free on request; available online at website. Guidelines free on request and available online.

○ *No unsolicited mss.*

NONFICTION Subjects include alternative lifestyles, Americana, animals, anthropology, archaeology, business, career guidance, child guidance, communications, community, computers, contemporary culture, counseling, creative nonfiction, economics, electronics, entertainment, environment, ethnic, finance, games, government, health, history, hobbies, humanities, labor, language, literature, medicine, memoirs, military, money, muticultural, nature, parenting, philosophy, politics, public affairs, recreation, regional (CO, S.W. U.S., Nat'l Parks, Rocky Mountains), science, social sciences, sociology, software, translation, transportation, travel, war, world affairs, aviation, aerospace, game books, travel guides, puzzle books. Submit book proposals and completed ms by e-mail only.

FICTION Subjects include adventure, comic books, contemporary, ethnic, experimental, fantasy, gothic, historical, horror, humor, literary, mainstream, military, multicultural, mystery, regional, romance, science fiction, short story collections, sports, suspense, translation, western. "We have changed our focus to be platform centric. We seek ideas for series, and we invite trademark holders and blogging personalities to submit ideas for a line of books." Submit completed ms by e-mail only.

TIPS "Create a series concept that will attract readers, which we can then assign to writers for several books in the line. Trademarked characters, movie and TV tie-ins, and popular blogs are suitable platforms."

FOCAL PRESS

711 3rd Ave., 8th Floor, New York NY 10017. **Website:** www.focalpress.com. **Contact:** Amorette Petersen, publishing director; for further editorial contacts, visit the contacts page on the company's Website. Estab. US, 1981; UK, 1938. Publishes hardcover and paperback originals and reprints. "Focal Press provides excellent books for students, advanced amateurs, and working professionals involved in all areas of media technology. Topics of interest include photography (digital and traditional techniques), film/video, audio, broadcasting, and cinematography, through to journalism, radio, television, video, and writing. Currently emphasizing graphics, gaming, animation, and multimedia." **Publishes 80-120 UK-US titles/year; entire firm publishes over 1,000 titles/year. 25% of books from first-time authors. 90% from unagented writers.** Publishes ms 6 months after acceptance. Accepts simultaneous submissions. Responds in 2 months to queries. Book catalog for #10 SASE. Guidelines available online.

NONFICTION Subjects include film, cinema, stage, photography, film, cinematography, broadcasting, theater and performing arts, audio, sound and media technology. We do not publish collections of photographs or books composed primarily of photographs. To submit a proposal for consideration by Elsevier, please fill in the **proposal form** online. Once we have had a chance to review your proposal in line with our publishing plan and budget, we will contact you to discuss the next steps. Reviews artwork/photos.

○ FODOR'S TRAVEL PUBLICATIONS, INC.

Imprint of Random House, Inc., 1745 Broadway, New York NY 10019. **E-mail:** editors@fodors.com. **Website:** www.fodors.com. Estab. 1936. Publishes trade paperback originals. Fodor's publishes travel books on many regions and countries. **Most titles are collective works, with contributions as works for hire. Most contributions are updates of previously published volumes.** Accepts simultaneous submissions.

Responds in 2 months to queries. Book catalog available free.

○ "If you're interested in working for Fodor's as a travel writer, send your resume and writing clips, together with a cover letter explaining your qualifications and areas of expertise, to editors@fodors.com. You may also mail materials to: Fodor's Travel Publications, Researcher Writer Positions, 1745 Broadway, 15th floor, New York, NY 10019. Remember that most Fodor's writers live in the areas they cover. Note that we do not accept unsolicited manuscripts."

NONFICTION Subjects include travel. We are interested in unique approaches to favorite destinations. Writers seldom review our catalog or our list and often query about books on topics that we're already covering. Beyond that, it's important to review competition and to say what the proposed book will add. Do not send originals without first querying as to our interest in the project. We're not interested in travel literature or in proposals for general travel guidebooks. Agented submissions only. Submit proposal and résumé via mail.

TIPS In preparing your query or proposal, remember that it's the only argument Fodor's will hear about why your book will be a good one, and why you think it will sell; and it's also best evidence of your ability to create the book you propose. Craft your proposal well and carefully so that it puts your best foot forward.

⊕ FOLDED WORD

5209 Del Vista Way, Rocklin CA 95765. Phone/**Fax:** (916)624-5088. **E-mail:** editors@foldedword.com. **Website:** www.foldedword.com. Editor-in-Chief: J.S. Graustein. Poetry Editor: Rose Auslander. Fiction Editor: Casey Murphy. Estab. 2008. "Folded Word is an independent literary press. Our focus? Connecting new voices to readers. Our goal? To make poetry and fiction accessible for the widest audience possible both on and off the page."

TIPS "E-mail is the best way to reach us."

FOREIGN POLICY ASSOCIATION

470 Park Ave. S., New York NY 10016. (212)481-8100. **Fax:** (212)481-9275. **E-mail:** info@fpa.org; rnolan@fpa.org. **Website:** www.fpa.org. Publishes 2 periodicals, an annual eight episode PBS Television series with DVD and an occasional hardcover and trade paperback original. The Foreign Policy Association, a nonpartisan, not-for-profit educational organization founded in 1918, is a catalyst for developing awareness, understanding of and informed opinion on US foreign policy and global issues. Through its balanced, nonpartisan publications, FPA seeks to encourage individuals in schools, communities and the workplace to participate in the foreign policy process. Accepts simultaneous submissions. Book catalog available free.

NONFICTION Subjects include government, politics, history, foreign policy.

TIPS "Audience is students and people with an interest, but not necessarily any expertise, in foreign policy and international relations."

FORTRESS PRESS

P.O. Box 1209, Minneapolis MN 55440. (612)330-3300. **Website:** www.fortresspress.com. Publishes hardcover and trade paperback originals. "Fortress Press publishes academic books in Biblical studies, theology, Christian ethics, church history, and professional books in pastoral care and counseling." **Pays royalty on retail price.** Accepts simultaneous submissions. Book catalog free (call 1-800-328-4648). Guidelines available online.

NONFICTION Subjects include religion, women's issues, women's studies, church history, African-American studies. Query with annotated TOC, brief cv, sample pages, SASE. Please study guidelines before submitting.

FORWARD MOVEMENT

412 Sycamore St., Cincinnati OH 45202. (513)721-6659; (800)543 1813. Fax: (513)721-0729. E-mail: rschmidt@forwarddaybyday.com. **Website:** www.forwardmovement.org. **Contact:** Rev. Dr. Richard H. Schmidt, editor and director. Estab. 1934. "Forward Movement was established to help reinvigorate the life of the church. Many titles focus on the life of prayer, where our relationship with God is centered, death, marriage, baptism, recovery, joy, the Episcopal Church and more. Currently emphasizing prayer/spirituality." **Publishes 30 titles/year.** Responds in 1 month. Book catalog and ms guidelines free. Guidelines available online.

○ "Forward Movement is an official agency of the Episcopal Church. In addition to Forward Day by Day, our daily devotional guide, we publish other books and tracts related to the life and concerns of the Christian church, especially within the Anglican Communion. These typically include material introducing the Episcopal Church, meditations and spiritual readings, prayers, liturgical resources, biblical reflections, and material on stewardship, church history, issues before the church, and Christian healing."

NONFICTION Subjects include religion. "We are an agency of the Episcopal Church.", "There is a special need for tracts of under 8 pages. (A page usually runs about 200 words.) On rare occasions, we publish a full-length book." Query with SASE or by email with complete ms attached.

FICTION Subjects include juvenile.

TIPS "Audience is primarily Episcopalians and other Christians."

WALTER FOSTER PUBLISHING, INC.

3 Wrigley, Suite A, Irvine CA 92618. (800)426-0099. **Fax:** (949)380-7575. **E-mail:** info@walterfoster.com. **Website:** www.walterfoster.com. Estab. 1922. Publishes trade paperback originals. "Walter Foster publishes instructional how-to/craft instruction as well as licensed products."

FOUR WAY BOOKS

Box 535, Village Station, New York NY 10014. **E-mail:** editors@fourwaybooks.com. **Website:** www.fourwaybooks.com. **Contact:** Martha Rhodes, director. Estab. 1993. "Four Way Books is a not-for-profit literary press dedicated to publishing poetry and short fiction by emerging and established writers. Each year, Four Way Books publishes the winners of its national poetry competitions, as well as collections accepted through general submission, panel selection, and solicitation by the editors."

FICTION Open reading period: June 1-30. Book-length story collections and novellas. Submission guidelines will be posted online at end of May. Does not want novels or translations.

POETRY Four Way Books publishes poetry and short fiction. Considers full-length poetry mss only. Publishes 8-11 books a year. Books are about 70 pages, offset-printed digitally, perfect-bound, with paperback binding, art/graphics on covers. Does not want individual poems or poetry intended for children/young readers. See website for complete submission guidelines and open reading period in June. Book mss may include previously published poems. Responds to submissions in 4 months. Payment varies. Order sample books from Four Way Books online or through bookstores.

FOX CHAPEL PUBLISHING

1970 Broad St., East Petersburg PA 17520. (800)457-9112. **Fax:** (717)560-4702. **E-mail:** CustomerService@FoxChapelPublishing.com. **Website:** www. foxchapelpublishing.com. **Contact:** Peg Couch, acquisitions editor. Publishes hardcover and trade paperback originals and trade paperback reprints. Fox Chapel publishes woodworking, woodcarving, and design titles for professionals and hobbyists. **Publishes 25-40 titles/year. 50% of books from first-time authors. 100% from unagented writers. Pays royalty or makes outright purchase. Pays variable advance.** Publishes ms 18 months after acceptance. Accepts simultaneous submissions. Responds in 2 months to queries.

NONFICTION Submission guidelines on website. Reviews artwork/photos. Send photocopies.

TIPS "We're looking for knowledgeable artists, craftspeople and woodworkers, all experts in their fields, to write books of lasting value."

⊕ FRANCES LINCOLN CHILDREN'S BOOKS

Frances Lincoln, 74-77 White Lion St., Islington, London N1 9PF, United Kingdom. 00442072844009. **E-mail:** flcb@franceslincoln.com. **Website:** www. franceslincoln.com. Estab. 1977. "Our company was founded by Frances Lincoln in 1977. We published our first books two years later, and we have been creating illustrated books of the highest quality ever since, with special emphasis on gardening, walking and the outdoors, art, architecture, design and landscape. In 1983, we started to publish illustrated books for children. Since then we have won many awards and prizes with both fiction and nonfiction children's books." **Publishes 100 titles/year. 6% of books from first-time authors.** Publishes book 18 months after acceptance. Accepts simultaneous submissions. Responds to mss in minimum of 6 weeks.

NONFICTION Picture books, young readers, middle readers, young adult: activity books, animal, biography, careers, cooking, graphic novels, history, multicultural, nature/environment, religion, social issues, special needs. Average word length: picture books—1,000; middle readers—29,768. Query by e-mail.

FICTION Picture books, young readers, middle readers, young adults: adventure, animal, anthology, fantasy, folktales, health, history, humor, multicultural, nature/environment, special needs, sports. Average word length: picture books—1,000; young readers—9,788; middle readers— 20,653; young adults— 35,407. Query by e-mail.

FRANKLIN WATTS

338 Euston Rd., London NW1 3BH, United Kingdom. +44 (0)20 7873 6000. **Fax:** +44 (0)20 7873 6024. **E-mail:** ad@hachettechildrens.co.uk. **Website:** www.franklinwatts.co.uk. Estab. 1942. Franklin Watts is well known for its high quality and attractive information books, which support the National Curriculum and stimulate children's enquiring minds. Reader Development is one of Franklin Watts' specialisations; the list offers titles on a wide array of subjects for beginner readers. It is also the proud publisher of many award-winning authors/illustrators, including Mick Manning and Brita Granstrom.

O   Generally does not accept unsolicited mss.

FREE SPIRIT PUBLISHING, INC.

217 Fifth Ave. N., Suite 200, Minneapolis MN 55401-1299. (612)338-2068. **Fax:** (612)337-5050. **E-mail:** acquisitions@freespirit.com. **Website:** www.freespirit.com. Estab. 1983. Publishes trade paperback originals and reprints. "We believe passionately in empowering kids to learn to think for themselves and make their own good choices." **Publishes 12-18 titles/year. 5% of books from first-time authors. 75% from unagented writers. Pays advance.** Book catalog and ms guidelines online.

O   Free Spirit does not accept fiction, poetry or storybook submissions.

NONFICTION Subjects include child guidance, education, pre-K-12, study and social sciences skills, special needs, differentiation but not textbooks or basic skills books like reading, counting, etc., health, medicine, mental/emotional health for/about children, psychology for/about children, sociology for/about children. "Many of our authors are educators, mental health professionals, and youth workers involved in helping kids and teens." No fiction or picture storybooks, poetry, single biographies or autobiographies, books with mythical or animal characters, or books with religious or New Age content. "We are not looking for academic or religious materials, or books that analyze problems with the nation's school systems."

Query with cover letter stating qualifications, intent, and intended audience and market analysis (how your book stands out from the field), along with outline, 2 sample chapters, rèsumè, SASE. Do not send original copies of work.

FICTION "Please review catalog and author guidelines (both available online) before submitting proposal." Reponds to queries in 4-6 months. "If you'd like material returned, enclose a SASE with sufficient postage." Accepts queries only—not submissions—by e-mail.

TIPS "Our books are issue-oriented, jargon-free, and solution-focused. Our audience is children, teens, teachers, parents and youth counselors. We are especially concerned with kids' social and emotional well-being and look for books with ready-to-use strategies for coping with today's issues at home or in school—written in everyday language. We are not looking for academic or religious materials, or books that analyze problems with the nation's school systems. Instead, we want books that offer practical, positive advice so kids can help themselves, and parents and teachers can help kids succeed."

FREESTONE/PEACHTREE, JR.

1700 Chattahoochee Ave., Atlanta GA 30318. (404)876-8761. **Fax:** (404)875-2578. **E-mail:** hello@peachtree-online.com. **Website:** www.peachtree-online.com. **Contact:** Helen Harriss, acquisitions; Loraine Joyner, art director; Melanie McMahon Ives, production manager. Estab. 1977. **Publishes 4-8 titles/year.** Publishes book 1-2 years after acceptance. Accepts simultaneous submissions. Responds in 6 months-1 year.

O   Freestone and Peachtree, Jr. are imprints of Peachtree Publishers. See the listing for Peachtree for submission information. No e-mail or fax queries or submissions, please.

NONFICTION Picture books, young readers, middle readers, young adults: history, sports. Picture books: animal, health, multicultural, nature/environment, science, social issues, special needs.

FICTION Middle Readers: adventure, animal, history, nature/environment, sports. Young Adults: fiction, history, biography, mystery, adventure. Does not want to see science fiction, religion, or romance. Submit 3 sample chapters by postal mail only. No query necessary.

FRONT ROW EXPERIENCE LLC

540 Discovery Bay Blvd., Discovery Bay CA 94505. (925)634-5710. **E-mail:** service@frontrowexperience. com. **Website:** www.frontrowexperience.com. **Contact:** Frank Alexander, editor. Estab. 1974. Publishes trade paperback originals and reprints. "Front Row publishes books on movement education and coordination activities for pre-K to 6th grade." **Publishes 1-2 titles/year.** Accepts simultaneous submissions. Responds in 1 month to queries.

IMPRINTS Kokono.

NONFICTION Subjects include movement education, perceptual-motor development, sensory motor development, hand-eye coordination activities. Query.

TIPS "Be on target—find out what we want, and only submit queries. If you want to send documents, send as a PDF file to our e-mail."

FRONT ST.

Boyds Mills Press, 815 Church St., Honesdale PA 18431. **Website:** www.frontSt.books.com. **Contact:** Acquisitions Editor. Estab. 1994. Publishes hardcover originals and trade paperback reprints. "We are an independent publisher of books for children and young adults." **Publishes 10-15 titles/year. 2,000 queries received/year. 5,000 mss received/year. 30% of books from first-time authors. 60% from unagented writers. Pays royalty on retail price. Pays advance.** Publishes book 1 year after acceptance of ms. Accepts simultaneous submissions. Responds in 3 months. Book catalog available online. Guidelines available online.

NONFICTION "Keep in mind that good children's nonfiction has a narrative quality—a story line—that encyclopedias do not; please consider whether both the subject and the language will appeal to children."

FICTION Subjects include adventure, historical, humor, juvenile, literary, picture books, young adult, adventure, fantasy/science fiction fiction, historical, mystery/suspense, problem novels, sports. Query with first 3 chapters and a plot summary and label the package "Manuscript Submission."

POETRY Submit book-length collection of poems. "Keep in mind that the strongest collections demonstrate a facility with multiple poetic forms."

TIPS "Read through our recently published titles and review our website. Check to see what's on the market and in our catalog before submitting your story. Feel free to query us if you're not sure."

FULCRUM PUBLISHING

4690 Table Mountain Dr., Suite 100, Golden CO 80403. **E-mail:** info@fulcrum-books.com. **Website:** www.fulcrum-books.com. **Contact:** T. Baker, acquisitions editor. Estab. 1984. **Pays authors royalty based on wholesale price. Offers advances.** Catalog available for SASE. Ms guidelines available online at website.

NONFICTION Middle and early readers: Western history, nature/ environment, Native American. Submit complete ms or submit outline/synopsis and 2 sample chapters. "Publisher does not send response letters unless we are interested in publishing." Do not send SASE.

TIPS "Research our line first. We look for books that appeal to the school market and trade. "

FUTURECYCLE PRESS

Website: www.futurecycle.org. **Contact:** Diane Kistner, director/editor-in-chief. Estab. 2007. **Pays 10% royalty and 25 author's copies.** Responds to mss in 3 months. Guidelines available online at website.

POETRY Wants "poetry from highly skilled poets, whether well known or emerging. With a few exceptions, we are eclectic in our editorial tastes." Does not want concrete or visual poetry. Publishes 4 poetry books/year and 2 chapbooks/year. Ms. selected through open submission and competition. "We read unsolicited mss. but also conduct a yearly poetry book competition." Books are 60-90 pages; offset print, perfect-bound, with glossy, full color cover stock, b&w inside. Chapbooks are 20-40 pages, offset print, saddle-stitched. Submit complete ms, no need to query.

GASLIGHT PUBLICATIONS

P.O. Box 1344, Studio City CA 91614. **Website:** playerspress.home.att.net/gaslight_catalogue.htm. **Contact:** Simon Waters, fiction editor (Sherlock Holmes only). Estab. 1950. Publishes hardcover and paperback originals and reprints. **Pays 8-10% royalty.** Publishes ms 1-6 months after acceptance. Responds in 2 weeks to queries; 1 year to mss.

FICTION Sherlock Holmes only. Query with SASE. Include estimated word count, brief bio, list of publishing credits.

TIPS "Please send only Sherlock Holmes material. Other stuff just wastes time and money."

✪ GENEALOGICAL PUBLISHING CO., INC.

3600 Clipper Mill Rd., Baltimore MD 21211. (410)837-8271. **Fax:** (410)752-8492. **E-mail:** info@genealogical.

com. **E-mail:** jgaronzi@genealogical.com. **Website:** www.genealogical.com. **Contact:** Joe Garonzik, mktg. dir. (history & genealogy). Estab. 1959. Hardcover and trade paperback originals and reprints. **Publishes 100 titles/year. 100 queries/year; 20 mss/year. 10% of books from first-time authors. 99% from unagented writers. 10-15% royalty on wholesale price.** Publishes book 6 months after acceptance of ms. Accepts simultaneous submissions. Responds in 1 month on queries, proposals, and mss. Catalog free on request. Guidelines not available.

NONFICTION Subjects include Americana, ethnic, history, hobbies. Submit outline, 1 sample chapter. Reviews artwork/photos as part of the mss package.

TIPS "Our audience is genealogy hobbyists."

GENESIS PRESS, INC.

P.O. Box 101, Columbus MS 39701. (888)463-4461. **Fax:** (662)329-9399. **E-mail:** customerservice@genesis-press.com. **Website:** www.genesis-press.com. Estab. 1993. Publishes hardcover and trade paperback originals and reprints. Genesis Press is the largest privately owned African-American book publisher in the country. Genesis has steadily increased its reach, and now brings its readers everything from suspense and science fiction to Christian-oriented romance and nonfiction. Responds in 2 months to queries. Responds in 4 months to manuscripts. Guidelines available online.

IMPRINTS Indigo (romance); Black Coral (fiction); Indigo Love Spectrum (interracial romance); Indigo after Dark (erotica); Obsidian (thriller/myster); Indigo Glitz (love stories for young adults); Indigo Vibe (for stylish audience under 35 years old); Mount Blue (Christian); Inca Books (teens); Sage (self-help/inspirational).

NONFICTION Submit outline, 3 sample chapters, SASE. If you would like your ms returned, you must follow all the rules on our website. Please use Priority or First Class mail-no Media Mail, Fed Ex, and no metered mail. We cannot return partials or manuscripts outside the US . No International Reply Coupons, please.

FICTION Subjects include adventure, erotica, ethnic, multicultural, mystery, romance, science fiction, women's. Submit clips, 3 sample chapters, SASE.

TIPS Be professional. Always include a cover letter and SASE. Follow the submission guidelines posted on our website or send SASE for a copy.

⊘ GHOST PONY PRESS

P.O. Box 260113, Madison WI 53726. **E-mail:** ghostponypress@hotmail.com. **Contact:** Ingrid Swanberg, editor/publisher. Estab. 1980. Ghost Pony Press has published 3 books of poetry by proóspero saiíz, including *the bird of nothing & other poems* (168 pages, 7x10, with sewn and wrapped binding; paperback available for $20, signed and numbered edition for $35). Also published *zen concrete & etc.* by d.a. levy (268 pages, magazine-sized, perfect-bound, illustrated; paperback available for $27.50).

POETRY Query first, with a few sample poems (5-10) and cover letter with brief bio and publication credits. Include SASE. Considers previously published material for book publication. Accepts submissions by postal mail only; no e-mail submissions. Editor sometimes comments briefly on rejected poems. No promised response time. "We currently have a considerable backlog."

GIBBS SMITH

P.O. Box 667, Layton UT 84041. (801)544-9800. **Fax:** (801)544-8853. **E-mail:** info@gibbs-smith.com. **Website:** www.gibbs-smith.com. **Contact:** Suzanne Taylor, associate publisher and creative director (children's activity books); Jennifer Grillone, art acquisitions. Estab. 1969. **Publishes 3 titles/year. 50% of books from first-time authors. 50% from unagented writers. Pays authors royalty of 2% based on retail price or work purchased outright ($500 minimum). Offers advances (average amount: $2,000).** Publishes ms 1-2 years after acceptance. Accepts simultaneous submissions. Responds to queries and mss in 2 months. Book catalog available for 9×12 SAE and $2.30 postage. Ms guidelines available by e-mail.

○   Gibbs Smith is not accepting fiction at this time.

NONFICTION Middle readers: activity, arts/crafts, cooking, how-to, nature/environment, science. Average word length: picture books—under 1,000 words; activity books—under 15,000 words. Recently published *Hiding in a Fort*, by G. Lawson Drinkard, illustrated by Fran Lee (ages 7-12); *Sleeping in a Sack: Camping Activities for Kids*, by Linda White, illustrated by Fran Lee (ages 7-12). Nonfiction: Submit an outline and writing samples for activity books; query for other types of books.

FICTION *Gibbs Smith is not accepting fiction at this time.*

TIPS "We target ages 5-11. We do not publish young adult novels or chapter books."

⊘ GIFTED EDUCATION PRESS

10201 Yuma Ct., Manassas VA 20109. (703)369-5017. **E-mail:** mfisher345@comcast.net. **Website:** www.giftedpress.com. **Contact:** Maurice Fisher, publisher. Estab. 1981. Publishes trade paperback originals. "Searching for rigorous texts on teaching science, math and humanities to gifted students." **Publishes 5 titles/year. 20 queries received/year. 10 mss received/year. 90% of books from first-time authors. 100% from unagented writers. Pays 10% royalty on retail price.** Publishes ms 4 months after acceptance. Accepts simultaneous submissions. Responds in 1 month to queries, proposals and mss. Book catalog available online. Guidelines available online.

NONFICTION Subjects include child guidance, computers, electronics, education, history, humanities, philosophy, science, teaching, math, biology, Shakespeare, chemistry, physics, creativity. Query with SASE. *All unsolicited mss returned unopened.* Reviews artwork/photos.

TIPS "Audience includes teachers, parents, gift program supervisors, professors. Be knowledgeable about your subject. Write clearly and don't use educational jargon."

● ⊘ GINNINDERRA PRESS

P.O. Box 3461, Port Adelaide 5015, Australia. (61)(2)6258-9060. **Fax:** (61)(2)6258-9069. **E-mail:** stephen@ginninderrapress.com.au. **Website:** www.ginninderrapress.com.au. **Contact:** Stephen Matthews, publisher. Estab. 1996. Ginninderra Press works "to give publishing opportunities to new writers." Has published poetry by Alan Gould and Geoff Page. Books are usually up to 72 pages, A5, laser-printed, saddle-stapled or thermal-bound, with board covers. Responds to queries within 1 week; mss in 2 months.

○ *Publishes books by Australian authors only.*

POETRY Query first, with a few sample poems and a cover letter with brief bio and publication credits. Considers previously published poems.

GIVAL PRESS

Gival Press, LLC, P.O. Box 3812, Arlington VA 22203. (703)351-0079. **E-mail:** givalpress@yahoo.com. **Website:** www.givalpress.com. **Contact:** Robert L. Giron, editor-in-chief (area of interest: literary). Estab. 1998. Publishes trade paperback, electronic originals, and reprints. **Publishes 5-6 titles/year. over 200 queries**

received/year. **60 mss received/year. 50% of books from first-time authors. 70% from unagented writers. Royalties (% varies).** Publishes book 12 months after acceptance of ms. Accepts simultaneous submissions. Responds in 1 month to queries, 3 months to proposals & mss. Book catalog available online, free on request/for #10 SASE. Guidelines available online, by email, free on request/for #10 SASE.

NONFICTION Subjects include gay, lesbian, memoirs, multicultural, translation, womens issues, womens studies, scholarly. Submit between October-December only. Always query first via email; provide plan/ms content, bio, and supportive material. Reviews artwork/photos; query first.

FICTION Subjects include gay, lesbian, literary, multicultural, poetry, translation. Always query first via email; provide description, author's bio, and supportive material.

POETRY Query via email; provide description, bio, etc.; submit 5-6 sample poems via email.

TIPS "Our audience is those who read literary works with depth to the work. Visit our website—there is much to be read/learned from the numerous pages."

GLENBRIDGE PUBLISHING, LTD.

19923 E. Long Ave., Centennial CO 80016. (800)986-4135; (720)870-8381. **Fax:** (720)230-1209. **Website:** www.glenbridgepublishing.com. Estab. 1986. Publishes hardcover originals and reprints, trade paperback originals. "Glenbridge has an eclectic approach to publishing. We look for titles that have long-term capabilities." **Publishes 6-8 titles/year. Pays 10% royalty.** Publishes ms 1 year after acceptance. Accepts simultaneous submissions. Responds in 2 months to queries. Book catalog available online. Guidelines for #10 SASE.

NONFICTION Subjects include Americana, animals, business, economics, education, environment, family, finance, parenting, writing, film, theatre, communication, cooking, foods, nutrition, health, medicine, history, philosophy, politics & government, psychology, sociology. Publishers for over 23 years, offering books from every genre, with the aim of uplifting, educating, and entertaining. Send e-mail on website. Query with outline/synopsis, sample chapters.

THE GLENCANNON PRESS

P.O. Box 1428, El Cerrito CA 94530. (510)528-4216. **Fax:** (510)528-3194. **E-mail:** merships@yahoo.com. **Website:** www.glencannon.com. **Contact:** Bill Harris (maritime, maritime children's). Estab. 1993. Publishes hardcover and paperback originals and hardcover reprints. "We publish quality books about ships and the sea." Average print order: 1,000. Member PMA, BAIPA. Distributes titles through Baker & Taylor. Promotes titles through direct mail, magazine advertising and word of mouth. Accepts unsolicited mss. Often comments on rejected mss. **Publishes 4-5 titles/year. Pays 10-20% royalty.** Publishes ms 6-24 months after acceptance. Accepts simultaneous submissions. Responds in 1 month to queries; 2 months to mss.

IMPRINTS Smyth: perfect binding; illustrations.

FICTION Submit complete ms. Include brief bio, list of publishing credits. Send SASE for return of ms or send a disposable ms and SASE for reply only.

TIPS "Write a good story in a compelling style."

DAVID R. GODINE, PUBLISHER, INC.
15 Court Square, Suite 320, Boston MA 02108. (617)451-9600. **Fax:** (617)350-0250. **E-mail:** info@ godine.com. **Website:** www.godine.com. Estab. 1970. Publishes hardcover and trade paperback originals and reprints. "Our particular strengths are books about the history and design of the written word, literary essays, and the best of world fiction in translation. We also have an unusually strong list of children's books, all of them printed in their entirety with no cuts, deletions, or side-stepping to keep the political watchdogs happy." **Publishes 35 titles/year. Pays royalty on retail price.** Publishes book 3 years after acceptance of ms. Book catalog for 5X8 envelope and 3 First-Class stamps.

NONFICTION Subjects include Americana, art, architecture, gardening, literary criticism, nature, environment, photography, book arts, typography. *No unsolicited mss*

FICTION Subjects include historical, literary, translation, literature, novels. *No unsolicited mss*

TIPS "Please visit our website for more information about our books and detailed submission policy. No phone calls, please. Have your agent contact us."

GOLDEN WEST BOOKS
P.O. Box 80250, San Marino CA 91118. (626)458-8148. **Fax:** (626)458-8148. **E-mail:** trainbook@earthlink. net. **Website:** www.goldenwestbooks.com. **Contact:** Donald Duke, publisher. Publishes hardcover originals. "Golden West Books specializes in railroad history." **Publishes 3-4 titles/year. 8-10 queries re-**ceived/year. 5 mss received/year. 75% of books from first-time authors. 100% from unagented writers. **Pays 8-10% royalty on wholesale price.** Publishes ms 3 months after acceptance. Responds in 3 months to queries. Book catalog and ms guidelines free.

"We are always interested in new material. Please use the form online to contact us; we will follow up with you as soon as possible."

NONFICTION Subjects include Americana, history. Query with SASE. Reviews artwork/photos.

GOLLEHON PRESS, INC.
6157 28th St. SE, Grand Rapids MI 49546. (616)949-3515. **Fax:** (616)949-8674. **E-mail:** editorial@gollehonbooks.com. **Website:** www.gollehonbooks.com. **Contact:** Lori Adams, editor. Publishes hardcover, trade paperback, and mass market paperback originals. "Currently emphasizing theology (life of Christ), political, current events, pets (dogs only, rescue/heroic), self-help, and gardening. *No unsolicited mss*; brief proposals only with first 5 pages of Chapter 1. Writer must have strong credentials to author work." **Publishes 6-8 titles/year. 100 queries received/year. 30 mss received/year. 85% of books from first-time authors. 90% from unagented writers. Pays 7% royalty on retail price. Pays $500-1,000 advance.** Publishes book 6 months after acceptance. Accepts simultaneous submissions. Responds in 1 month (if interested) to proposals; 3 months to mss. Book catalog and ms guidelines online.

NONFICTION Submit brief proposal package only with bio and first 5 pages of Chapter 1. "We do not return materials unless we specifically request the full manuscript." Reviews artwork/photos. Send Writer must be sure he/she owns all rights to photos, artwork, illustrations, etc., submitted for consideration (all submissions must be free of any third-party claims). Never send original photos or art.

TIPS "Mail brief book proposal, bio, and a few sample pages only. We will request a full manuscript if interested. We cannot respond to all queries. Full manuscript will be returned if we requested it, and if writer provides SASE. We do not return proposals. Simultaneous submissions are encouraged."

GOODMAN BECK PUBLISHING
E-mail: info@goodmanbeck.com. **Website:** www. goodmanbeck.com. Estab. 2007. Publishes trade paperback originals. "Our primary interest at this time is mental health, personal growth, aging well, positive

psychology, accessible spirituality, and self-help." **Publishes 5-6 titles/year. 65% of books from first-time authors. 90% from unagented writers. Pays 10% royalty on retail price.** Publishes book 6-9 months after acceptance. Accepts simultaneous submissions. "Due to high query volume, response not guaranteed.".

○ "Our audience is adults trying to cope with this 'upside down world.' With our self-help books, we are trying to improve the world one book at a time."

NONFICTION Subjects include creative nonfiction, health, medicine, philosophy, psychology, spirituality,. No religious or political works, textbooks, or how-to books at this time. Query with SASE. E-mail submissions only. Reviews artwork/photos. Send photocopies.

FICTION Subjects include contemporary, mainstream, mystery, poetry, short story collections, suspense. "Fiction books should be able to generate a passionate response from our adult readers." No science fiction, fantasy, or romance novels. Query with SASE. E-mail submissions only.

POETRY "We are interested in zen-inspired haiku and non-embellished, non-rhyming, egoless poems. Read Mary Oliver." Query, submit 3 sample poems. E-mail submissions only.

TIPS "Your book should be enlightening and marketable. Be prepared to have a comprehensive marketing plan. You will be very involved."

○ GOOSE LANE EDITIONS

500 Beaverbrook Ct., Suite 330, Fredericton, New Brunswick E3B 5X4, Canada. (506)450-4251. **Fax:** (506)459-4991. **Website:** www.gooselane.com/submissions.php. **Contact:** Angela Williams, publishing assistant. Estab. 1954. Publishes hardcover and paperback originals and occasional reprints. "Goose Lane publishes literary fiction and nonfiction from well-read and highly skilled Canadian authors." **Publishes 16-20 titles/year. 20% of books from first-time authors. 60% from unagented writers. Pays 8-10% royalty on retail price. Pays $500-3,000, negotiable advance.** Responds in 6 months to queries.

NONFICTION Subjects include art, architecture, history, language, literature, nature, environment, regional, women's issues, women's studies. Query with SASE.

GRANITE PUBLISHING, LLC

P.O. Box 1429, Columbus NC 28722. (828)894-8444. **Fax:** (828)894-8454. **E-mail:** brian@granitepublish-

ing.us; eileen@souledout.org. **Website:** www.granitepublishing.us/index.html. **Contact:** Brian Crissey. Publishes trade paperback originals and reprints. "Granite Publishing strives to preserve the Earth by publishing books that develop new wisdom about our emerging planetary citizenship, bringing information from the outerworlds to our world. Currently emphasizing indigenous ideas, planetary healing." **Publishes 4 titles/year. 50 queries received/year. 150 mss received/year. 70% of books from first-time authors. 90% from unagented writers. Pays 7 1/2-10% royalty.** Publishes ms 16 months after acceptance. Accepts simultaneous submissions. Responds in 6 months to mss.

IMPRINTS Wild Flower Press; Swan-Raven & Co.; Agents of Change.

○ Granite Publishing accepts only a few very fine mss in our niches each year, and those that are accepted must follow our rigid guidelines online at: www.granitepublishing.us/root/SubmissionGuidelines.html. Our Little Granite Books imprint publishes only our own writings for children.

NONFICTION Subjects include New Age, planetary paradigm shift. Submit proposal. Reviews artwork/photos. Send photocopies.

GRAPHIA

222 Berkeley St., Boston MA 02116. (617)351-5000. **E-mail:** anna.meier@hmhpub.com. **Website:** www.graphiabooks.com. **Contact:** Anna Meier. "Graphia publishes quality paperbacks for today's teen readers, ages 14 and up. From fiction to nonfiction, poetry to graphic novels, Graphia runs the gamut, all unified by the quality of writing that is the hallmark of this imprint." Accepts simultaneous submissions. Responds to queries in up to 3 months.

NONFICTION Young adults: biography, history, multicultural, nature/environment, science, social issues. Query.

FICTION Young adults: adventure, contemporary, fantasy, history, humor, multicultural, poetry. Query.

GRAYWOLF PRESS

250 Third Ave. N., Suite 600, Minneapolis MN 55401. **E-mail:** wolves@graywolfpress.org. **Website:** www.graywolfpress.org. **Contact:** Katie Dublinski, editorial manager (nonfiction, fiction). Estab. 1974. Publishes trade cloth and paperback originals. "Graywolf Press is an independent, nonprofit publisher dedicat-

ed to the creation and promotion of thoughtful and imaginative contemporary literature essential to a vital and diverse culture." **Publishes 23 titles/year. 3,000 queries received/year. 20% of books from first-time authors. 50% from unagented writers. Pays royalty on retail price. Pays $1,000-25,000 advance.** Publishes 18 months after acceptance. Responds in 3 months to queries. Book catalog available free. Guidelines available online.

NONFICTION Subjects include contemporary culture, language, literature, culture. Query with SASE.

FICTION Subjects include short story collections, literary novels. "Familiarize yourself with our list first." No genre books (romance, western, science fiction, suspense) Query with SASE. Please do not fax or e-mail.

POETRY "We are interested in linguistically challenging work." Query with SASE.

GREAT POTENTIAL PRESS

1325 N. Wilmot Ave., #300, Tucson AZ 85712. **Website:** www.giftedbooks.com. **Contact:** Janet Gore, editor; James T. Webb, Ph.D., president. Estab. 1986. Publishes trade paperback originals. Specializes in nonfiction books that address academic, social and emotional issues of gifted and talented children and adults. **Publishes 6-10 titles/year. 75 queries received/year. 20-30 mss received/year. 50% of books from first-time authors. 100% from unagented writers. Pays 10% royalty on retail price.** Publishes book 1 year after acceptance. Accepts simultaneous submissions. Responds in 2 months to queries, 3 months to proposals; 4 months to mss. Book catalog free or on website. Guidelines available online.

NONFICTION Subjects include child guidance, education, multicultural, psychology, translation, travel, women's issues, gifted/talented children and adults, misdiagnosis of gifted, parenting gifted, teaching gifted, meeting the social and emotional needs of gifted and talented, and strategies for working with gifted children and adults. Submit proposal package, including preface or introduction, TOC, chapter outline, 2-3 sample chapters and an explanation of how work differs from similar published books.

TIPS "Mss should be clear, cogent, and well-written and should pertain to gifted, talented, and creative persons and/or issues."

GREAT SOURCE EDUCATION GROUP

Houghton Mifflin Harcourt, Editorial Department, 181 Ballardvale St., Wilmington MA 01887. **Website:** www.greatsource.com. Great Source's main publishing efforts are instructional and focus on the school market. For all materials, the reading level must be appropriate to the skill level of the students and the nature of the materials. Guidelines available online.

NONFICTION Reading, writing, language arts, math, and science. Material must be appealing to students, proven classroom effective, be consistent with current research.

GREENHAVEN PRESS

27500 Drake Rd., Farmington Hills MI 48331. **E-mail:** betz.deschenes@cengage.com. **Website:** www.gale.com/greenhaven. **Contact:** Betz Des Chenes. Estab. 1970. Publishes 220 young adult academic reference titles/year. 50% of books by first-time authors. Greenhaven continues to print quality nonfiction anthologies for libraries and classrooms. Our well known Opposing Viewpoints series is highly respected by students and librarians in need of material on controversial social issues. Greenhaven accepts no unsolicited manuscripts. Send query, resume, and list of published works by e-mail. Work purchased outright from authors; write-for-hire, flat fee.

NONFICTION Young adults (high school): controversial issues, social issues, history, literature, science, environment, health.

⊘ GREENWILLOW BOOKS

HarperCollins Publishers, 10 E. 53rd St., New York NY 10022. (212)207-7000. **Website:** www.greenwillowblog.com. **Contact:** Virginia Duncan, vice president/publisher; Paul Zakris, art director. Estab. 1974. Publishes hardcover originals, paperbacks, ebooks, and reprints. **Publishes 40-50 titles/year. Pays 10% royalty on wholesale price for first-time authors. Average advance: variable.** Publishes ms 2 years after acceptance.

◗ Does not accept unsolicited mss. "Unsolicited mail will not be opened and will not be returned."

FICTION Subjects include fantasy, humor, literary, mystery, picture books.

⊘ GREENWOOD PRESS

ABC-CLIO, P.O. Box 1911, Santa Barbara CA 93116. (805)968-1911. **E-mail:** CustomerService@abc-clio.

com. **Website:** www.abc-clio.com. **Contact:** Vince Burns, vice president of editorial. Publishes hardcover originals. Greenwood Press publishes reference materials for high school, public and academic libraries in the humanities and the social and hard sciences. **Publishes 200 titles/year. 1,000 queries received/year. 25% of books from first-time authors. Pays variable royalty on net price. Pays rare advance.** Publishes book 1 year after acceptance. Accepts simultaneous submissions. Responds in 6 months to queries. Book catalog and ms guidelines online.

NONFICTION Subjects include humanities, literary criticism, social sciences, humanities and the social and hard sciences. Query with proposal package, including scope, organization, length of project, whether complete ms is available or when it will be, cv or resume and SASE. *No unsolicited mss.*

⊕ GREY GECKO PRESS

565 S. Mason Rd., Suite 154, Katy TX 77450. (866)535 6078. **Fax:** (866)535-6078. **E-mail:** info@greygeckopress.com. **E-mail:** submissions@greygeckopress.com. **Website:** www.greygeckopress.com. **Contact:** Hilary Comfort, editor-in-chief; Jason Aydelotte, executive director. Estab. 2011. Publishes hardcover, trade paperback, and electronic originals. **Publishes 10-20 titles/year. 200+ queries received/year; 10-20 mss received/year. 100% of books from first-time authors. 100% from unagented writers. Pays 50-80% royalties on wholesale price.** Publishes ms 3-6 months after acceptance. Accepts simultaneous submissions. Responds in 1-3 months to queries, proposals, and mss. Book catalog and ms guidelines for #10 SASE, by e-mail or online.

NONFICTION Subjects include architecture, art, contemporary culture, cooking, creative nonfiction, environment, foods, history, marine subjects, military, nature, photography, travel, war. "All nonfiction submissions are evaluated on a case by case basis. We focus mainly on fiction, but we'll take a look at nonfiction works. We prefer electronic submissions." Query with SASE. Submit proposal package including outline, detailed synopsis, and 3 sample chapters. Reviews artwork. Send photocopies or link to photo website.

FICTION Subjects include adventure, contemporary, ethnic, fantasy, feminist, gay, historical, horror, humor, juvenile, lesbian, literary, mainstream, military, multicultural, mystery, occult, regional, romance,

science fiction, short story collections, sports, suspense, war, western, young adult. "We do not publish extreme horror, erotica, or religious fiction. New and interesting stories by unpublished authors will always get our attention. Innovation is a core value of our company. We prefer electronic submissions but will accept: Query with SASE. Submit proposal package including outline, detailed, synopsis, and 3 sample chapters."

POETRY Not currently accepting poetry submissions.
TIPS "Be willing to be a part of the Grey Gecko family. Publishing with us is a partnership, not indentured servitude."

⊕ GRIT CITY PUBLICATIONS

309 Hill St., Pittsburgh PA 15140. (412)607-4592. **E-mail:** GritCityPublications@gmail.com. **Website:** www.GritCityPublications.com. **Contact:** Ron Gavalik, publisher. Estab. 2011. Publishes electronic originals. **90% of books from first-time authors. 100% from unagented writers. Pays 11.7-18.4% royalty on retail price. Does not offer advance.** Publishes ms 3-6 months after acceptance. Responds to queries in 1 month; mss in 3. Book catalog and guidelines available online at website.

FICTION Subjects include adventure, confession, erotica, fantasy, gothic, historical, horror, military, mystery, occult, romance, science fiction, short story collections, suspense, war, western, young adult, humor (dark only). "Please keep in mind we seek genre fiction for transformation into our unique fiction medium that's not published anywhere else. That's what makes EmotoBooks a hit with our fans. GCP publishes EmotoBooks. We seek shorter works of 6,000-10,000 words for EmotoSingles. We also seek works over 15,000 words for EmotoSerials. EmotoSerials are either short-term (novella length) or long-term (novel length). Writers are also required to read our "How To Create EmotoBooks handbook." This is a free download from the Write Emotobooks page on the website. Query EmotoSerials through e-mail; submit completed EmotoSingles only by e-mail.

TIPS "We ask writers to experience already published EmotoBooks to discover the new medium and learn our style."

⊕ ⊘ GROSSET & DUNLAP PUBLISHERS

Penguin Putnam Inc., 375 Hudson St., New York NY 10014. **Website:** www.penguingroup.com. **Contact:** Francesco Sedita, vice president/publisher. Estab.

1898. Publishes hardcover (few) and mass market paperback originals. Grosset & Dunlap publishes children's books that show children that reading is fun, with books that speak to their interests, and that are affordable so that children can build a home library of their own. Focus on licensed properties, series and readers. "Grosset & Dunlap publishes high-interest, affordable books for children ages 0-10 years. We focus on original series, licensed properties, readers and novelty books." **Publishes 140 titles/year. Pays royalty. Pays advance.**

Ⓞ *Not currently accepting submissions.*

NONFICTION Subjects include nature, environment, science. "We do not accept e-mail submissions. Unsolicited mss usually receive a response in 6-8 weeks."

FICTION Subjects include juvenile. All book formats except for picture books. Agented submissions only.

TIPS Nonfiction that is particularly topical or of wide interest in the mass market; new concepts for novelty format for preschoolers; and very well-written easy readers on topics that appeal to primary graders have the best chance of selling to our firm.

◎ GROUNDWOOD BOOKS

110 Spadina Ave. Suite 801, Toronto ON M5V 2K4, Canada. (416)363-4343. **Fax:** (416)363-1017. **E-mail:** ssutherland@groundwoodbooks.com. **Website:** www. houseofanansi.com. Publishes 12 picture books/year; 3 young readers/year; 5 middle readers/year; 5 young adult titles/year, approximately 2 nonfiction titles/year. **Offers advances.** Accepts simultaneous submissions. Responds to mss in 6-8 months. Visit web site for guidelines: www.houseofanansi.com/Groundwoodsubmissions.aspx.

FICTION Submit synopsis and sample chapters.

GROUP PUBLISHING, INC.

1515 Cascade Ave., Loveland CO 80539. **Website:** www.group.com. Estab. 1974. Publishes trade paperback originals. "Our mission is to equip churches to help children, youth, and adults grow in their relationship with Jesus." **Publishes 65 titles/year. 500 queries received/year. 500 mss received/year. 40% of books from first-time authors. 95% from unagented writers. Pays up to 10% royalty on wholesale price or makes outright purchase or work for hire. Pays up to $1,000 advance.** Publishes ms 18 months after acceptance. Accepts simultaneous submissions. Responds in 1 month to queries; 6 months to proposals

and mss. Book catalog for 9x12 envelope and 2 first-class stamps.

NONFICTION Subjects include education, religion. "We're an interdenominational publisher of resource materials for people who work with adults, youth or children in a Christian church setting. We also publish materials for use directly by youth or children (such as devotional books, workbooks or Bibles stories). Everything we do is based on concepts of active and interactive learning as described in *Why Nobody Learns Much of Anything at Church: And How to Fix It*, by Thom and Joani Schultz. We need new, practical, hands-on, innovative, out-of-the-box ideas—things that no one's doing.. yet." Query with SASE. Submit proposal package, outline, 3 sample chapters, cover letter, introduction to book, and sample activities if appropriate.

TIPS "Our audience consists of pastors, Christian education directors, youth leaders, and Sunday school teachers."

◎◎ GROVE/ATLANTIC, INC.

841 Broadway, 4th Floor, New York NY 10003. (212)614-7850. **Fax:** (212)614-7886. **E-mail:** info@groveatlantic.com. **Website:** www.groveatlantic.com. Estab. 1917. Publishes hardcover and trade paperback originals, and reprints. "Due to limited resources of time and staffing, Grove/Atlantic cannot accept manuscripts that do not come through a literary agent. In today's publishing world, agents are more important than ever, helping writers shape their work and navigate the main publishing houses to find the most appropriate outlet for a project." **Publishes 100 titles/year. 1,000+ queries received/year. 1,000+ mss received/year. 10% of books from first-time authors. Pays 7 ½-12 ½% royalty. Makes outright purchase of $5-500,000.** Publishes book Book published 9 months after acceptance of ms. after acceptance of ms. Accepts simultaneous submissions. Responds in 1 month to queries; 2 months to proposals; 4 months to mss. Book catalog available online.

IMPRINTS Black Cat, Atlantic Monthly Press, Grove Press.

NONFICTION Subjects include art, architecture, business, economics, creative nonfiction, education, government, politics, language, literature, memoirs, military, war, philosophy, psychology, science, social sciences, sports, translation. Agented submissions only.

FICTION Subjects include erotica, horror, literary, science fiction, short story collections, suspense, western. Agented submissions only.

POETRY Agented submissions only.

GRYPHON HOUSE, INC.

P.O. Box 10, 6848 Leon's Way, Lewisville NC 27203. **Website:** www.gryphonhouse.com. **Contact:** Kathy Charner, editor-in-chief. Estab. 1981. Publishes trade paperback originals. "Gryphon House publishes books that teachers and parents of young children (birth-age 8) consider essential to their daily lives." Publishes parent and teacher resource books, textbooks. "At Gryphon House, our goal is to publish books that help teachers and parents enrich the lives of children from birth through age 8. We strive to make our books useful for teachers at all levels of experience, as well as for parents, caregivers, and anyone interested in working with children." Query. Submit outline/synopsis and 2 sample chapters. Responds to queries/mss in 6 months. Publishes a book 18 months after acceptance. Will consider simultaneous submissions, e-mail submissions. Book catalog and ms guidelines available via website or with SASE. "We are looking for books of creative, participatory learning experiences that have a common conceptual theme to tie them together. The books should be on subjects that parents or teachers want to do on a daily basis." **Publishes 12-15 titles/year. Pays royalty on wholesale price.** Responds in 3-6 months to queries. Guidelines available online.

NONFICTION Subjects include child guidance, education, early childhood. Currently emphasizing social-emotional intelligence and classroom management; de-emphasizing literacy after-school activities. "We prefer to receive a letter of inquiry and/or a proposal, rather than the entire manuscript. Please include: the proposed title, the purpose of the book, table of contents, introductory material, 20-40 sample pages of the actual book. In addition, please describe the book, including the intended audience, why teachers will want to buy it, how it is different from other similar books already published, and what qualifications you possess that make you the appropriate person to write the book. If you have a writing sample that demonstrates that you write clear, compelling prose, please include it with your letter."

GRYPHON PUBLICATIONS

P.O. Box 209, Brooklyn NY 11228. **Website:** www.gryphonbooks.com. **Contact:** Gary Lovisi, owner/publisher. Publishes trade paperback originals and reprints. "I publish very genre-oriented work (science fiction, crime, pulps) and nonfiction on these topics, authors and artists. It's best to query with an idea first." **Publishes 10 titles/year. 500 queries received/year. 1,000 mss received/year. 20% of books from first-time authors. 90% from unagented writers. Makes outright purchase by contract, price varies. Pays no advance.** Publishes ms 1-2 years after acceptance. Responds in 1 month to queries. Book catalog and ms guidelines for #10 SASE.

IMPRINTS Paperback Parade Magazine; Hardboiled Magazine; Gryphon Books; Gryphon Doubles.

NONFICTION Subjects include hobbies, language, literature, book collecting. "We need well-written, well-researched articles, but query first on topic and length. Writers should not submit material that is not fully developed/researched." Query with SASE. Reviews artwork/photos. Send photocopies; slides, transparencies may be necessary later.

FICTION "We want cutting-edge fiction, under 3,000 words with impact."

TIPS "We are very particular about novels and book-length work. A first-timer has a better chance with a short story or article. On anything over 4,000 words do not send manuscript, send only query letter with SASE. Always query **first** with an SASE."

⊘ ⟳ GUERNICA EDITIONS

Box 117, Station P, Toronto ON M5S 2S6, Canada. (416)576-9403. **Fax:** (416)981-7606. **E-mail:** michaelmirolla@guernicaeditions.com. **Website:** www.guernicaeditions.com. **Contact:** Antonio D'Alfonso, editor/publisher (poetry, nonfiction, novels). Estab. 1978. Publishes trade paperback originals and reprints. Guernica Editions is a literary press that produces works of poetry, fiction and nonfiction often by writers who are ignored by the mainstream. **Publishes 15 titles/year. 750 mss received/year. 20% of books from first-time authors. 99% from unagented writers. Pays 8-10% royalty on retail price, or makes outright purchase of $200-5,000. Pays $200-2,000 advance.** Publishes 15 months after acceptance. Responds in 1 month to queries. Responds in 6 months to proposals. Responds in 1 year to manuscripts. Book catalog available online.

NONFICTION Subjects include art, architecture, creative nonfiction, ethnic, film, cinema, stage, gay, lesbian, government, politics, history, language, literature, lit-crit, memoirs, multicultural, music, dance, philosophy, psychology, regional, religion, sex, translation, women's issues. Query with SASE. *All unsolicited mss returned unopened.* Reviews artwork/photos. Send photocopies.

FICTION Subjects include erotica, feminist, gay, lesbian, literary, multicultural, plays, poetry, poetry in translation, translation. "We wish to open up into the fiction world and focus less on poetry. We specialize in European, especially Italian, translations." Query with SASE. *All unsolicited mss returned unopened.*

POETRY Feminist, gay/lesbian, literary, multicultural, poetry in translation. We wish to have writers in translation. Any writer who has translated Italian poetry is welcomed. Full books only. No single poems by different authors, unless modern, and used as an anthology. First books will have no place in the next couple of years. Query.

GULF PUBLISHING COMPANY

2 Greenway Plaza, Suite 1020, Houston TX 77046. (713)529-4301. **Fax:** (713)520-4433. **E-mail:** svb@gulfpub.com. **Website:** www.gulfpub.com. **Contact:** Katie Hammon. Estab. 1916. Publishes hardcover originals and reprints; electronic originals and reprints. "Gulf Publishing Company is the leading publisher to the oil and gas industry. Our specialized publications reach over 100,000 people involved in energy industries worldwide. Our magazines and catalogs help readers keep current with information important to their field and allow advertisers to reach their customers in all segments of petroleum operations. More than half of Gulf Publishing Company's editorial staff have engineering degrees. The others are thoroughly trained and experienced business journalists and editors." **Publishes 12-15 titles/year. 3-5 queries and mss received in a year. 30% of books from first-time authors. 80% from unagented writers. Royalties on retail price. Pays $1,000-$1,500 advance.** Publishes ms 8-9 months after acceptance. Accepts simultaneous submissions. Responds in 2 months to queries; 1 month to proposals and mss. Catalog free on request. Guidelines available by e-mail.

NONFICTION , Engineering. "We don't publish a lot in the year, therefore we are able to focus more on marketing and sales—we are hoping to grow in the future." Submit outline, 1-2 sample chapters, completed ms. Reviews artwork. Send high res. file formats with high dpi in b&w.

TIPS "Our audience would be engineers, engineering students, academia, professors, well managers, construction engineers. We recommend getting contributors to help with the writing process—this provides a more comprehensive overview for technical and scientific books. Work harder on artwork. It's expensive and time-consuming for a publisher to redraw a lot of the figures."

HACHAI PUBLISHING

527 Empire Blvd., Brooklyn NY 11225. (718)633-0100. **Fax:** (718)633-0103. **Website:** www.hachai.com. **Contact:** Devorah Leah Rosenfeld, editor. Estab. 1988. Publishes hardcover originals. Hachai is dedicated to producing high quality Jewish children's literature, ages 2-10. Story should promote universal values such as sharing, kindness, etc. **Publishes 4 titles/year. 75% of books from first-time authors. Work purchased outright from authors for $800-1,000. Accepts simultaneous submissions. Responds in 2 months to mss. Book catalog available free. Guidelines available online.

○ "All books have spiritual/religious themes, specifically traditional Jewish content. We're seeking books about morals and values; the Jewish experience in current and Biblical times, and Jewish observance, Sabbath and holidays."

NONFICTION Subjects include ethnic, religion. Submit complete ms. Reviews artwork/photos. Send photocopies.

FICTION Picture books and young readers: contemporary, historical fiction, religion. Middle readers: adventure, contemporary, problem novels, religion. Does not want to see fantasy, animal stories, romance, problem novels depicting drug use or violence. Submit complete ms.

TIPS "We are looking for books that convey the traditional Jewish experience in modern times or long ago; traditional Jewish observance such as Sabbath and holidays and mitzvos such as mezuzah, blessings etc.; positive character traits (middos) such as honesty, charity, respect, sharing, etc. We are also interested in historical fiction for young readers (7-10) written with a traditional Jewish perspective and highlighting the relevance of Torah in making important choices. Please, no animal stories, romance, violence, preachy sermonizing. Write a story that incorporates a moral, not a preachy morality tale. Originality is the key. We feel Hachai publications will appeal to a wider readership as parents become more interested in positive values for their children."

⊕ HADLEY RILLE BOOKS

P.O. Box 25466, Overland Park KS 66225. **E-mail:** subs@hadleyrillebooks.com. **Website:** www.hadleyrillebooks.com. **Contact:** Eric T. Reynolds, editor/publisher. Estab. 2005.

Currently closed to submissions. Check website for future reading periods.

FICTION Subjects include fantasy, science fiction, short story collections.

TIPS "We aim to produce books that are aligned with current interest in the genres. Anthology markets are somewhat rare in SF these days, we feel there aren't enough good anthologies being published each year and part of our goal is to present the best that we can. We like stories that fit well within the guidelines of the particular anthology for which we are soliciting manuscripts. Aside from that, we want stories with strong characters (not necessarily characters with strong personalities, flawed characters are welcome). We want a sense of wonder and awe. We want to feel the world around the character and so scene description is important (however, this doesn't always require a lot of text, just set the scene well so we don't wonder where the character is). We strongly recommend workshopping the story or having it critiqued in some way by readers familiar with the genre. We prefer clichés be kept to a bare minimum in the prose and avoid re-working old story lines."

HAMPTON ROADS PUBLISHING CO., INC.

665 Third St., Suite 400, San Francisco CA 94107. **E-mail:** submissions@hrpub.com; submissions@redwheelweiser.com. **Website:** www.hrpub.com. **Contact:** Ms. Pat Bryce, Acquisitions Editor. Estab. 1989. Publishes and distributes hardcover and trade paperback originals on subjects including metaphysics, health, complementary medicine, visionary fiction, and other related topics. "Our reason for being is to impact, uplift, and contribute to positive change in the world. We publish books that will enrich and empower the evolving consciousness of mankind. Though we are not necessarily limited in scope, we are most interested in manuscripts on the following subjects: Body/Mind/Spirit, Health and Healing, Self-Help. Please be advised that at the moment we are not accepting: Fiction or Novelized material that does not pertain to body/mind/spirit, Channeled writing. **Publishes 35-40 titles/year. 1,000 queries received/year. 1,500 mss received/year. 50% of books from first-time authors. 70% from unagented writers. Pays royalty. Pays $1,000-50,000 advance.** Publishes book 1 year after acceptance of ms. Accepts simultaneous submissions. Responds in 2-4 months to queries. Responds in 1 month to proposals. Responds in 6-12 months to manuscripts. Guidelines available online.

"Please know that we only publish a handful of books every year, and that we pass on many well written, important works, simply because we cannot publish them all. We review each and every proposal very carefully. However, due to the volume of inquiries, we cannot respond to them all individually. Please give us 30 days to review your proposal. If you do not hear back from us within that time, this means we have decided to pursue other book ideas that we feel fit better within our plan."

NONFICTION Subjects include New Age, spirituality. Query with SASE. Submit synopsis, SASE. No longer accepting electronic submissions. Reviews artwork/photos. Send photocopies.

FICTION Subjects include literary, spiritual, Visionary fiction, past-life fiction based on actual memories. Fiction should have 1 or more of the following themes: spiritual, inspirational, metaphysical, i.e., past-life recall, out-of-body experiences, near-death experience, paranormal. Query with SASE. Submit outline, 2 sample chapters, clips. Submit complete ms.

HANCOCK HOUSE PUBLISHERS

U.S. Office, 1431 Harrison Ave., Blaine WA 98230. (604)538-1114. **Fax:** (604)538-2262. **E-mail:** submissions@hancockhouse.com. **Website:** www.hancockhouse.com. Estab. 1971. Publishes hardcover, trade paperback, and eBook originals and reprints. "Hancock House Publishers is the largest North American publisher of wildlife and Native Indian titles. We also cover Pacific Northwest, fishing, history, Canadiana, biographies. We are seeking agriculture, natural history, animal husbandry, conservation, and popular science titles with a regional (Pacific Northwest), national, or international focus. Currently emphasizing nonfiction wildlife, cryptozoology, guide books, native history, biography, fishing." **Publishes 12-20 titles/year. 50% of books from first-time authors. 90% from unagented writers. Pays 10% royalty.** Publishes book 1 year after acceptance. Accepts simultaneous submissions. Responds to proposals in 3-6 months. Book catalog available free. Guidelines available online.

NONFICTION Subjects include agriculture, animals, ethnic, history, horticulture, nature, environment, regional. Centered around Pacific Northwest, local history, nature guide books, international ornithology, and Native Americans. Query via e-mail, including outline with word count, a short author bio, table of contents, 3 sample chapters. Accepts double-spaced word .docs or PDFs. Reviews artwork/photos. Send photocopies.

HANSER PUBLICATIONS

6915 Valley Ave., Cincinnati OH 45244. (513)527-8800; (800)950-8977. **Fax:** (513)527-8801. **E-mail:** info@hanserpublications.com. **Website:** www.hanserpublications.com. Estab. 1993. Publishes hardcover and paperback originals, and digital educational and training programs. "Hanser Publications publishes books and electronic media for the manufacturing (both metalworking and plastics) industries. Publications range from basic training materials to advanced reference books." **Publishes 10-15 titles/year. 100 queries received/year. 10-20 mss received/year. 50% of books from first-time authors. 100% from unagented writers.** Publishes ms 10 months after acceptance. Accepts simultaneous submissions. Responds in 2 weeks to queries; 1 month to proposals/mss. Book catalog available free. Guidelines available online.

○ "Hanser Publications is currently seeking technical experts with strong writing skills to author training and reference books and related products focused on various aspects of the manufacturing industry. Our goal is to provide manufacturing professionals with insightful, easy-to-reference information, and to educate and prepare students for technical careers through accessible, concise training manuals. Do your publishing ideas match this goal? If so, we'd like to hear from you. Submit your detailed product proposals, resume of credentials, and a brief writing sample to: Development Editor, Prospective Authors."

NONFICTION "We publish how-to texts, references, technical books, and computer-based learning materials for the manufacturing industries. Titles include award-winning management books, encyclopedic references, and leading references." Submit outline, sample chapters, resume, preface, and comparison to competing or similar titles.

TIPS "E-mail submissions speed up response time."

⚠⊘ HARCOURT, INC., TRADE DIVISION

Imprint of Houghton Mifflin Harcourt Book Group, 215 Park Ave. S., New York NY 10003. **Website:** www.harcourtbooks.com. Publishes hardcover and trade paperback originals and trade paperback reprints. **Publishes 120 titles/year. 5% of books from first-time authors. 5% from unagented writers. Pays 6-15% royalty on retail price. Pays $2,000 minimum advance.** Accepts simultaneous submissions. Book catalog for 9×12 envelope and first-class stamps. Guidelines available online.

NONFICTION *No unsolicited mss.* Agented submissions only.

FICTION Agented submissions only.

⊕ HARK! NEW ERA PUBLISHING, LLC

E-mail: staff@harknewerapublishing.com. **Website:** www.harknewerapublishing.com. **Contact:** Jonathan Katora, editor/co-managing member; Amana Katora, editor/co-managing member. Estab. 2012. Publishes electronic originals. We are targeting the growing eBook market. Our audience will be people who appreciate quality fiction." **Pays competitive royalties on retail sales.** Publishes ms 4 months after acceptance. Accepts simultaneous submissions. Responds to queries and mss in 1 month. Catalog and guidelines available online at website.

○ *Accepts electronic submissions only.*

NONFICTION Subjects include creative nonfiction. "We are looking for writers who are willing to work closely with our editors and staff. They must also be comfortable working with our virtual company and writers will be expected to navigate this medium." Submit query, 20 sample pages, 1 page author biography. Do not send SASE.

FICTION Subjects include contemporary, literary, mainstream, short story collections. "We are neither for, nor adverse to genre submissions of fiction. We look for quality fiction. Writers must be willing to work closely with our editors and staff. They must also be comfortable working with our virtual company and will be expected to navigate this medium." Submit query, 20 sample pages, 1 page author biography. Do not send SASE.

TIPS "Follow our submission guidelines on our website. Unsolicited submissions that do not follow our guidelines will not be considered. We are interested in writers who enjoy working with others."

HARLAN DAVIDSON, INC./FORUM PRESS, INC.

773 Glenn Ave., Wheeling IL 60090. (847)541-9720. **Fax:** (847)541-9830. **E-mail:** harlandavidson@harlandavidson.com. **Website:** www.harlandavidson. com. "Serving the needs of instructors and students of history in colleges, universities, and high schools throughout North America, Harlan Davidson, Inc., remains an independent publisher of textbooks and supplements. We invite you to browse our site. All of our publications are available for purchase or as complimentary examination copies to qualified instructors."

HARPERBUSINESS

Imprint of HarperCollins General Books Group, 10 E. 53rd St., New York NY 10022. (212)207-7000. **Website:** www.harpercollins.com. Estab. 1991. Publishes hardcover, trade paperback originals and reprints. HarperBusiness publishes the inside story on ideas that will shape business practices with cutting-edge information and visionary concepts. **Pays royalty on retail price. Pays advance.** Accepts simultaneous submissions.

○ "The gold standard of business book publishing for 50 years, Harper Business brings you innovative, authoritative, and creative works from world-class thinkers. Building upon this rich legacy of paradigm-shifting books, Harper Business authors continue to help readers see the future and to lead and live successfully."

NONFICTION Subjects include business, economics, Marketing subjects. We don't publish how-to, textbooks or things for academic market; no reference (tax or mortgage guides), our reference department does that. Proposals need to be top notch. We tend not to publish people who have no business standing. Must have business credentials. Agented submissions only.

HARPERCOLLINS PUBLISHERS

10 E. 53rd, New York NY 10022. (212)207-6901. **E-mail:** Dana.fritts@Harpercollins.com; Kate.eng-bring@Harpercollins.com. **Website:** www.harpercollins.com. **Contact:** Kate Engbring, assistant designer; Dana Fritts, designer. Publishes hardcover and paperback originals and paperback reprints. HarperCollins, one of the largest English language publishers in the world, is a broad-based publisher with strengths in academic, business and professional, children's, educational, general interest, and religious and spiritual books, as well as multimedia titles. **Publishes 500 titles/year. Negotiates a flat fee upon acceptance.** Accepts simultaneous submissions. Responds in 1 month, will contact if interested. Catalog available online.

IMPRINTS HarperCollins Australia/New Zealand: Angus & Robertson, Fourth Estate, HarperBusiness, HarperCollins, HarperPerenniel, HarperReligious, HarperSports, Voyager; **HarperCollins Canada**: HarperFlamingoCanada, PerennialCanada; **HarperCollins Children's Books Group:** Amistad, Julie Andrews Collection, Avon, Joanna Cotler Books, Eos, Laura Geringer Books, Greenwillow Books, HarperAudio, HarperCollins Children's Books, HarperFestival, HarperTempest, HarperTrophy, Rayo, Katherine Tegen Books; **HarperCollins General Books Group:** Access, Amistad, Avon, Caedmon, Ecco, Eos, Fourth Estate, HarperAudio, HarperBusiness, HarperCollins, HarperEntertainment, HarperLargePrint, HarperResource, HarperSanFrancisco, HarperTorch, Harper Design International, Perennial, PerfectBound, Quill, Rayo, ReganBooks, William Morrow, William Morrow Cookbooks; **HarperCollins UK:** Collins Bartholomew, Collins, HarperCollins Crime & Thrillers, Collins Freedom to Teach, HarperCollins Children's Books, Thorsons/Element, Voyager Books; **Zondervan:** Inspirio, Vida, Zonderkidz, Zondervan.

NONFICTION *No unsolicited mss or queries.* Agented submissions only. Unsolicited mss returned unopened.

FICTION "We look for a strong story line and exceptional literary talent." Agented submissions only. *All unsolicited mss returned.*

TIPS "We do not accept any unsolicited material."

HARVARD BUSINESS REVIEW PRESS

Imprint of Harvard Business School Publishing Corp., 60 Harvard Way, Boston MA 02163. (617)783-7400. **Fax:** (617)783-7489. **E-mail:** cschinke@harvardbusiness.org. **Website:** www.hbr.org. **Contact:** Courtney Schinke, editorial coordinator. Estab. 1984. Publishes hardcover originals and several paperback series. The Harvard Business Review Press publishes books for senior and general managers and business scholars. Harvard Business Review Press is the source of the most influential ideas and conversations that shape business worldwide. **Publishes 40-50 titles/year. Pays escalating royalty on retail price. Advances vary depending on author and market for the book.** Accepts simultaneous submissions. Responds in 1 month to proposals and mss. Book catalog available online. Guidelines available online.

NONFICTION Submit proposal package, outline, sample chapters.

TIPS "We do not publish books on real estate, personal finance or business parables."

THE HARVARD COMMON PRESS

535 Albany St., 5th Floor, Boston MA 02118. (617)423-5803. **Fax:** (617)695-9794. **E-mail:** info@harvardpress.com. **E-mail:** editorial@harvardcommonpress.com. **Website:** www.harvardcommonpress.com. **Contact:** Valerie Cimino, executive editor. Estab. 1976. Publishes hardcover and trade paperback originals and reprints. "We want strong, practical books that help people gain control over a particular area of their lives. Currently emphasizing cooking, child care/parenting, health. De-emphasizing general instructional books, travel." **Publishes 16 titles/year. 20% of books from first-time authors. 40% from unagented writers. Pays royalty. Pays average $2,500-10,000 advance.** Publishes ms 1 year after acceptance. Accepts simultaneous submissions. Responds in 2 months to queries. Book catalog for 9x12 envelope and 3 first-class stamps. Guidelines for #10 SASE or online.

IMPRINTS Gambit Books.

NONFICTION Subjects include child guidance, cooking, foods, nutrition, health, medicine. A large percentage of our list is made up of books about cooking, child care, and parenting; in these areas we are looking for authors who are knowledgeable, if not experts, and who can offer a different approach to the subject. We are open to good nonfiction proposals that show evidence of strong organization and writing, and clearly demonstrate a need in the marketplace. First-time authors are welcome. Submit outline. Potential authors may also submit a query letter or e-mail of no more than 300 words, rather than a full proposal; if interested, we will ask to see a proposal. Queries and questions may be sent via e-mail. We will not consider e-mail attachments containing proposals. No phone calls, please.

TIPS "We are demanding about the quality of proposals; in addition to strong writing skills and thorough knowledge of the subject matter, we require a detailed analysis of the competition."

HARVEST HOUSE PUBLISHERS

990 Owen Loop N, Eugene OR 97402. (541)343-0123. **Fax:** (541)302-0731. **Website:** www.harvesthousepublishers.com. Estab. 1974. Publishes hardcover, trade paperback, and mass market paperback originals and reprints. **Publishes 160 titles/year. 1,500 queries received/year. 1,000 mss received/year. 1% of books from first-time authors. Pays royalty.**

NONFICTION Subjects include anthropology, archeology, business, economics, child guidance, health, medicine, money, finance, religion, women's issues, women's studies, Bible studies. *No unsolicited mss.*

FICTION *No unsolicited mss, proposals, or artwork.* Agented submissions only.

TIPS "For first time/nonpublished authors we suggest building their literary résumé by submitting to magazines, or perhaps accruing book contributions."

HAYES SCHOOL PUBLISHING CO. INC.

321 Pennwood Ave., Wilkinsburg PA 15221. (412)371-2373. **Fax:** (800)543-8771. **E-mail:** chayes@hayespub.com. **Website:** www.hayespub.com. **Contact:** Clair N. Hayes. Estab. 1940. Produces folders, workbooks, stickers, certificates. Wants to see supplementary teaching aids for grades K-12. Interested in all subject areas. Will consider simultaneous and electronic submissions. Query with description or complete ms. Responds in 6 weeks. SASE for return of submissions. **Work purchased outright. Purchases all rights.**

HAY HOUSE INC.

P.O. Box 5100, Carlsbad CA 92018. (760)431-7695. **Fax:** (760)431-6948. **E-mail:** editorial@hayhouse.com. **Website:** www.hayhouse.com. **Contact:** Patty Gift, East Coast acquisitions (pgift@hayhouse.com); Alex Freemon, West Coast acquisitions (afreemon@hayhouse.com). Estab. 1985. Publishes hardcover, trade paperback and eBook/POD originals. "We publish books, audios, and videos that help heal the planet." **Publishes 50 titles/year. Pays standard royalty.** Accepts simultaneous submissions. Guidelines available online.

IMPRINTS Hay House Lifestyles; Hay House Insights; Hay House Visions; New Beginnings Press; SmileyBooks.

NONFICTION Subjects include cooking, foods, nutrition, education, health, medicine, money, finance, nature, environment, New Age, philosophy, psychology, sociology, women's issues, women's studies, mind/body/spirit. "Hay House is interested in a variety of subjects as long as they have a positive self-help slant to them. No poetry, children's books, or negative concepts that are not conducive to helping/healing ourselves or our planet." Accepts e-mail submissions from agents.

TIPS "Our audience is concerned with our planet, the healing properties of love, and general self-help principles. If I were a writer trying to market a book today, I would research the market thoroughly to make sure there weren't already too many books on the subject I was interested in writing about. Then I would make sure I had a unique slant on my idea. Simultaneous submissions from agents must include SASE's."

HEALTH COMMUNICATIONS, INC.

3201 SW 15th St., Deerfield Beach FL 33442. (954)360-0909, ext. 232. **Fax:** (954)360-0034. **E-mail:** Editorial@hcibooks.com. **Website:** www.hcibooks.com. Estab. 1976. Publishes hardcover and trade paperback nonfiction only. "While HCI is a best known for recovery publishing, today recovery is only one part of a publishing program that includes titles in self-help and psychology, health and wellness, spirituality, inspiration, women's and men's issues, relationships, family, teens and children, memoirs, mind/body/spirit integration, and gift books." **Publishes 60 titles/year.** Responds in 3-6 months to queries and proposals. See submission guidelines on website at www.hcibooks.com/t-submission_guidelines.aspx.

○ "Due to the volume of submissions, Health Communications cannot guarantee response times or personalize responses to individual proposals. Under no circumstances do we accept phone calls or e-mails pitching submissions."

NONFICTION Subjects include child guidance, health, parenting, psychology, women's issues, women's studies, young adult, Self-help.

HEALTH PROFESSIONS PRESS

P.O. Box 10624, Baltimore MD 21285-0624. (410)337-9585. **Fax:** (410)337-8539. **E-mail:** mmagnus@health-propress.com. **Website:** www.healthpropress.com. **Contact:** Mary Magnus, director of publications (aging, long-term care, health administration). Publishes hardcover and trade paperback originals. "We are a specialty publisher. Our primary audiences are professionals, students, and educated consumers interested in topics related to aging and eldercare." **Publishes 6-8 titles/year. 70 queries received/year. 12 mss received/year. 50% of books from first-time authors. 100% from unagented writers. Pays 8-18% royalty on wholesale price.** Publishes ms 10 months after acceptance. Accepts simultaneous submissions. Responds in 1 month to queries; 3 months to proposals; 4 months to mss. Book catalog free or online. Guidelines available online.

NONFICTION Subjects include health, medicine, psychology. Query with SASE. Submit proposal package, outline, resume, 1-2 sample chapters, cover letter.

WILLIAM S. HEIN & CO., INC.

2350 N. Forest Rd., Getzville NY 14068. **E-mail:** mail@wshein.com. **Website:** www.wshein.com. **Contact:** Sheila Jarrett, publications manager. Estab. 1961. "William S. Hein & Co. publishes reference books for law librarians, legal researchers, and those interested in legal writing. Currently emphasizing legal research, legal writing, and legal education." **Publishes 30 titles/year. 80 queries received/year. 40 mss received/year. 30% of books from first-time authors. 100% from unagented writers. Pays 10-20% royalty on net price.** Publishes book 9 months after acceptance. Accepts simultaneous submissions. Responds in 3 months to queries. Book catalog available online. Guidelines: send e-mail for info and mss proposal form.

NONFICTION Subjects include education, government, politics, women's issues, world affairs, legislative histories.

HEINEMANN EDUCATIONAL PUBLISHERS

P.O. Box 781940, Sandton 2146, South Africa. (27)(11)322-8600. **Fax:** 086 687 7822. **E-mail:** customerliaison@heinemann.co.za. **Website:** www.heinemann.co.za. Interested in textbooks for primary schools, literature and textbooks for secondary schools, and technical publishing for colleges/universities.

NONFICTION Subjects include animals, art, architecture, business, economics, education, ethnic, health, medicine, history, humanities, language, literature, music, dance, psychology, regional, religion, science, social sciences, sports, math, engineering, management, nursing, marketing.

HELLGATE PRESS

P.O. Box 3531, Ashland OR 97520. (541)973-5154. **E-mail:** harley@hellgatepress.com. **Website:** www. hellgatepress.com. **Contact:** Harley B. Patrick, editor. Estab. 1996. "Hellgate Press specializes in military history, other military topics, travel adventure, and historical/adventure fiction." **Publishes 15-20 titles/year. 85% of books from first-time authors. 95% from unagented writers. Pays royalty.** Publishes ms 6-9 months after acceptance. Responds in 2 months to queries.

NONFICTION Subjects include history, memoirs, military, war, travel adventure. Query/proposal by e-mail only. *Do not send mss.*

HENDRICK-LONG PUBLISHING CO., INC.

10635 Tower Oaks, Suite D, Houston TX 77070. (832)912-READ. **Fax:** (832)912-7353. **E-mail:** hendrick-long@att.net. **Website:** hendricklongpublishing.com. **Contact:** Vilma Long. Estab. 1969. Publishes hardcover and trade paperback originals and hardcover reprints. "Hendrick-Long publishes historical fiction and nonfiction about Texas and the Southwest for children and young adults." **Publishes 4 titles/year. 90% from unagented writers. Pays royalty on selling price. Pays advance.** Publishes book 18 months after acceptance of ms. Responds in 3 months to queries. Book catalog for 8½x11 or 9x12 SASE with 4 first-class stamps. Guidelines available online.

NONFICTION Subjects include history, regional. Subject must be Texas related; other subjects cannot be considered. We are particularly interested in material from educators that can be used in the classroom as workbooks, math, science, history with a Texas theme or twist. Query, or submit outline and 2 sample chapters. Reviews artwork/photos. Send photocopies.

FICTION Subjects include juvenile, young adult. Query with SASE. Submit outline, clips, 2 sample chapters.

HENDRICKSON PUBLISHERS, INC.

P.O. Box 3473, Peabody MA 01961. **Fax:** (978)573-8276. **E-mail:** editorial@hendrickson.com; orders@hendrickson.com. **Website:** www.hendrickson.com. **Contact:** Shirley Decker-Lucke, editorial director. Estab. 1983. Publishes trade reprints, bibles, and scholarly material in the areas of New Testament; Hebrew

Bible; religion and culture; patristics; Judaism; and practical, historical, and Biblical theology. "Hendrickson is an academic publisher of books that give insight into Bible understanding (academically) and encourage spiritual growth (popular trade). Currently emphasizing Biblical helps and reference, ministerial helps, and Biblical studies." **Publishes 35 titles/year. 800 queries received/year. 10% of books from first-time authors. 90% from unagented writers.** Publishes ms 1 year after acceptance. Responds in 3-4 months to queries. Book catalog and ms guidelines for #10 SASE.

NONFICTION Subjects include religion. "No longer accepting unsolicited manuscripts or book proposals. Cannot return material sent or respond to all queries." Submit outline, sample chapters, and CV.

HERITAGE BOOKS, INC.

518 Ruatan St., Berwyn Heights MD 20740. (301)345-2077. **E-mail:** Info@HeritageBooks.com. **E-mail:** Submissions@HeritageBooks.com. **Website:** www.heritagebooks.com. Estab. 1978. Publishes hardcover and paperback originals and reprints. "Our goal is to celebrate life by exploring all aspects of American life: settlement, development, wars, and other significant events, including family histories, memoirs, etc. Currently emphasizing early American life, early wars and conflicts, ethnic studies." **Publishes 200 titles/year. 25% of books from first-time authors. 100% from unagented writers. Pays 10% royalty on list price. Accepts simultaneous submissions. Responds** in 3 months to queries. Book catalog and ms guidelines free.

NONFICTION Subjects include Americana, ethnic, origins and research guides, history, memoirs, military, war, regional, history. Query with SASE. Submit outline via e-mail. Reviews artwork/photos.

TIPS "The quality of the book is of prime importance; next is its relevance to our fields of interest."

✪ HERITAGE HOUSE PUBLISHING CO., LTD.

#340-1105 Pandora Ave., Victoria BC V8V 3P9, Canada. 250-360-0829. **E-mail:** editorial@heritagehouse.ca. **Website:** www.heritagehouse.ca. **Contact:** Rodger Touchie, publisher. Publishes mostly trade paperback and some hardcovers. "Heritage House publishes books that celebrate the historical and cultural heritage of Canada, particularly Western Canada and, to an extent, the Pacific Northwest. We also publish some titles of national interest and a series of books aimed at young and casual readers, called *Amazing Stories*. We accept simultaneous submissions, but indicate on your query that it is a simultaneous submission." **Publishes 25-30 titles/year. 200 queries received/year. 100 mss received/year. 50% of books from first-time authors. 90% from unagented writers. Pays 12-15% royalty on net proceeds. Advances are rarely paid.** Publishes book within 1-2 years of acceptance. after acceptance of ms. Accepts simultaneous submissions. Responds in 6 months to queries. Catalogue and guidelines available online.

NONFICTION Subjects include history, regional, adventure, contemporary Canadian culture. Query with SASE. Include synopsis, outline, 2-3 sample chapters with indication of illustrative material available, and marketing strategy.

TIPS "Our books appeal to residents of and visitors to the northwest quadrant of the continent. We're looking for good stories and good storytellers. We focus on work by Canadian authors."

HEYDAY BOOKS

c/o Acquisitions Editor, Box 9145, Berkeley CA 94709. **Fax:** (510)549-1889. **E-mail:** heyday@heydaybooks.com. **Website:** www.heydaybooks.com. **Contact:** Gayle Wattawa, acquisitions and editorial director. Estab. 1974. Publishes hardcover originals, trade paperback originals and reprints. "Heyday Books publishes nonfiction books and literary anthologies with a strong California focus. We publish books about Native Americans, natural history, history, literature, and recreation, with a strong California focus." **Publishes 12-15 titles/year. 50% of books from first-time authors. 90% from unagented writers. Pays 8% royalty on net price.** Publishes book 18 months after acceptance. Responds in 3 months to queries/mss. Book catalog for 9 ×12 SAE with 4 first-class stamps.

NONFICTION Subjects include Americana, ethnic, history, nature, environment, recreation, regional, travel, California. Books about California only. Query with outline and synopsis. "Query or proposal by traditional post. Include a cover letter introducing yourself and your qualifications, a brief description of your project, a table of contents and list of illustrations, notes on the market you are trying to reach and why your book will appeal to them, a sample chapter, and a SASE if you would like us to return these materials to you." Reviews artwork/photos.

HIBBARD PUBLISHERS

P.O. Box 73182, Lynnwood Ridge 0040, South Africa. (27)(12)804-3990. **Fax:** (27)(12)804-1240. **E-mail:** publisher@hibbard.co.za;tersia@hibbard.co.za. **Website:** www.hibbard.co.za. "Our mission is to take the products of our authors' dreams and efforts, and to transform and shape these into the best possible product for end users, i.e. readers, teachers, learners and their parents."

IMPRINTS Bard (literature/academic); Thandi Art Press (African language literature); Galactic (math workbooks/poster series); Manx (fiction); Manx Juvenile (children's); GSAT (arts & culture); Five Star Study Guides.

TIPS "When the pressure is on, we make use of the services of some of the best free-lancers in various fields."

HIGHLAND PRESS PUBLISHING

P.O. Box 2292, High Springs FL 32655. (386) 454-3927. **Fax:** (386) 454-3927. **E-mail:** The.Highland.Press@gmail.com; Submissions.hp@gmail.com. **Website:** www.highlandpress.org. **Contact:** Leanne Burroughs, CEO (fiction); she will forward all mss to appropriate editor. Estab. 2005. Paperback originals. "With our focus on historical romances, Highland Press Publishing is known as your 'Passport to Romance.' We focus on historical romances and our award-winning anthologies. Our short stories/novellas are heart warming. As for our historicals, we publish historical novels like many of us grew up with and loved. History is a big part of the story and is tactfully woven throughout the romance." We have recently opened oursubmissions up to all genres, with the exception of erotica. Our newest lines are inspirational, regency, and young adult. **Publishes 30 titles/year. 90% from unagented writers. Pays royalties 7.5-8%** Publishes book within 18 months after acceptance of ms. Accepts simultaneous submissions. Responds in 8 weeks to queries; responds in 3-12 months to mss. Catalog and guidelines available online at website.

FICTION Send query letter. Query with outline/synopsis and sample chapters. Accepts queries by snail mail, e-mail. Include estimated word count, target market.

TIPS Special interests: Children's ms must come with illustrator. "We will always be looking for good historical manuscripts. In addition, we are actively seeking inspirational romances and Regency period romances." Numerous romance anthologies are planned. Topics and word count are posted on the Website. Writers should query with their proposal. After the submission deadline has passed, editors select the stories. "I don't publish based on industry trends. We buy what we like and what we believe readers are looking for. However, often this proves to be the genres and time-periods larger publishers are not currently interested in. Be professional at all times. Present your manuscript in the best possible light. Be sure you have run spell check and that the manuscript has been vetted by at least one critique partner, preferably more. Many times we receive manuscripts that have wonderful stories involved, but would take far too much time to edit to make it marketable."

HIGH PLAINS PRESS

P.O. Box 123, 403 Cassa Rd., Glendo WY 82213. (307)735-4370. **Fax:** (307)735-4590. **E-mail:** editor@highplainspress.com. **Website:** www.highplainspress.com. **Contact:** Nancy Curtis, publisher. Estab. 1984. Publishes hardcover and trade paperback originals. High Plains Press is a regional book publishing company specializing in books about the American West, with special interest in things relating to Wyoming. **Publishes 4 titles/year. 50 queries; 75 mss received/year. 75% of books from first-time authors. 100% from unagented writers. Pays 10% royalty on wholesale price. Pays $200-1,200 advance.** Publishes book 2 years after acceptance of ms. after acceptance of ms. Accepts simultaneous submissions. Responds in 3 months to queries and proposals; 12 months on mss. Book catalog available online. Guidelines available online.

NONFICTION Subjects include agriculture, Americana, environment, history, horticulture, memoirs, nature, regional. "We consider only books with strong connection to the West." Query with SASE. Reviews artwork/photos. Send photocopies.

POETRY "We publish 1 poetry volume a year. Require connection to West. Consider poetry in August." Submit 5 sample poems.

TIPS "Our audience comprises general readers interested in history and culture of the Rockies."

HIGH TIDE PRESS

2081 Calistoga Dr., Suite 2N, New Lenox IL 60451. (815)717-3780. **Website:** www.hightidepress.com. **Contact:** Monica Regan, senior editor. Estab. 1995. Publishes hardcover and trade paperback originals.

"High Tide Press is a leading provider of resources for disability and nonprofit professionals - publications and training materials on intellectual/developmental disabilities, behavioral health, and nonprofit management." **Publishes 2-3 titles/year. 20 queries received/year. 3 mss received/year. 50% of books from first-time authors. 100% from unagented writers. Pays royalty. Percentages vary.** Publishes book up to 1 year after acceptance. Accepts simultaneous submissions. Responds in 6 months to queries and proposals. Book catalog available online. Guidelines available online at website www.hightidepress.com/main/submissions.php.

NONFICTION Subjects include business, economics, education, health, medicine, how-to, human services, nonprofit management, psychology, reference, All of these topics as they relate to developmental, learning and intellectual disabilities, behavioral health, and human services management. "We do not publish personal stories. We produce materials for direct support staff, managers and professionals in the fields of disabilities and human services, as well as educators." Query via e-mail.

TIPS "Our readers are leaders and managers, mostly in the field of human services, and especially those who serve persons with intellectual disabilities or behavioral health needs."

HILL & WANG

Farrar, Straus and Giroux, 18 West 18th St., New York NY 10011. **E-mail:** fsg.editorial@fsgbooks.com. **Website:** us.macmillan.com. **Accepts unsolicited submissions by mail only.**

HINKLER

45-55 Fairchild St., Heatherton VI 3202, Australia. (61)(3)9552 1333. **Fax:** (61)(3)9558-2566. **E-mail:** enquiries@hinkler.com.au; Stevie.Brockley@hinkler.com.au. **Website:** www.hinklerbooks.com. **Contact:** Stephen Ungar, CEO/publisher. Estab. 1993. "Packaged entertainment affordable to every family."

HIPPOCRENE BOOKS INC.

171 Madison Ave., New York NY 10016. (718)454-2366. **E-mail:** info@hippocrenebooks.com. **Website:** www.hippocrenebooks.com. Estab. 1971. "Over the last forty years, Hippocrene Books has become one of America's foremost publishers of foreign language reference books and ethnic cookbooks. As a small publishing house in a marketplace dominated by conglomerates, Hippocrene has succeeded by con-

tinually reinventing its list while maintaining a strong international and ethnic orientation."

HIPPOPOTAMUS PRESS

22 Whitewell Rd., Frome Somerset BA11 4EL, United Kingdom. (44)(173)466-6653. **E-mail:** rjhippopress@aol.com. **Contact:** R. John, editor; M. Pargitter (poetry); Anna Martin (translation). Estab. 1974. Publishes hardcover and trade paperback originals. "Hippopotamus Press publishes first, full collections of verse by those well represented in the mainstream poetry magazines of the English-speaking world." **Publishes 6-12 titles/year. 90% of books from first-time authors. 90% from unagented writers. Pays 7½-10% royalty on retail price. Pays advance.** Publishes book 10 months after acceptance. Accepts simultaneous submissions. Responds in 1 month to queries. Book catalog available free.

NONFICTION Subjects include language, literature, translation. Query with SASE. Submit complete ms.

POETRY "Read one of our authors—poets often make the mistake of submitting poetry without knowing the type of verse we publish." Query and submit complete ms.

TIPS "We publish books for a literate audience. We have a strong link to the Modernist tradition. Read what we publish."

HISTORY PUBLISHING COMPANY, INC.

P.O. Box 700, Palisades NY 10964. **Fax:** (845)231-6167. **Website:** www.historypublishingco.com. **Contact:** Don Bracken, editorial director. Estab. 2001. Publishes hardcover and trade paperback originals and electronic books. "History Publishing is looking for interesting stories that make up history. If you have a story about an aspect of history that would have an appeal to a large niche or broad readership, History Publishing is interested." **Publishes 20 titles/year. 50% of books from first-time authors. 75% from unagented writers. Pays 7-10% royalty on wholesale list price. Does not pay advances to unpublished authors.** Publishes ms 1 year after acceptance. Responds in 2 months to full mss. Guidelines on website.

NONFICTION Subjects include Americana, business, contemporary culture, creative nonfiction, economics, government, history, military, politics, social sciences, sociology, war, world affairs. Query with SASE. Submit proposal package, outline, 3 sample chapters or submit complete ms. Reviews artwork/photos. Send photocopies.

TIPS "We focus on an audience interested in the events that shaped the world we live in and the events of today that continue to shape that world. Focus on interesting and serious events that will appeal to the contemporary reader who likes easy-to-read history that flows from one page to the next."

HIS WORK CHRISTIAN PUBLISHING

P.O. Box 563, Ward Cove AK 99928. (206)274-8474. **Fax:** (614)388-0664. **E-mail:** hiswork@hisworkpub.com. **Website:** www.hisworkpub.com. **Contact:** Angela J. Perez, acquisitions editor. Estab. 2005. Publishes trade paperback and electronic originals and reprints; also, hardcover originals. **Publishes 3-5 titles/year. 100% from unagented writers. Pays 10-20% royalty on wholesale price.** Publishes book 1-2 years after acceptance. Accepts simultaneous submissions. Responds in 1-3 months to queries; 1-2 months to *requested* manuscripts. Book catalog available online. "Guidelines available online and updated regularly. Please check these before submitting to see what we are looking for.".

NONFICTION Subjects include child guidance, cooking, foods, nutrition, creative nonfiction, gardening, health, medicine, history, hobbies, language, literature, memoirs, money, finance, music, dance, photography, recreation, religion, sports. "We only accept Christian material or material that does not go against Christian standards. This is a very strict policy that we enforce. Please keep this in mind before deciding to submit your work to us." Submit query/proposal package, 3 sample chapters, clips. Reviews artwork/photos. Send photocopies.

FICTION Subjects include humor, juvenile, mystery, picture books, poetry, religious, short story collections, sports, suspense, young adult. Submit query/proposal package, 3 sample chapters, clips.

POETRY "We only plan to publish 1-2 titles per year in poetry. Send us only your best work." Submit 15 sample poems.

TIPS "Audience is children and adults who are looking for the entertainment and relaxation you can only get from jumping into a good book. Submit only your best work to us. Submit only in the genres we are interested in publishing. Do not submit work that is not suitable for a Christian audience."

HOLIDAY HOUSE, INC.

425 Madison Ave., New York NY 10017. (212)688-0085. **Fax:** (212)421-6134. **E-mail:** info@holidayhouse.

com. **Website:** holidayhouse.com. **Contact:** Mary Cash, editor-in-chief. Estab. 1935. Publishes hardcover originals and paperback reprints. "Holiday House publishes children's and young adult books for the school and library markets. We have a commitment to publishing first-time authors and illustrators. We specialize in quality hardcovers from picture books to young adult, both fiction and nonfiction, primarily for the school and library market." **Publishes 50 titles/year. 5% of books from first-time authors. 50% from unagented writers. Pays royalty on list price, range varies. Agent's royalty.** Publishes 1-2 years after acceptance. Responds in 4 months. Guidelines for #10 SASE.

NONFICTION Subjects include Americana, history, science, Judaica. Please send the entire manuscript, whether submitting a picture book or novel. All submissions should be directed to the Editorial Department, Holiday House, 425 Madison Ave., New York, NY 10017. Send your manuscript via U.S. Mail. We do not accept certified or registered mail. There is no need to include a SASE. We do not consider submissions by e-mail or fax. Please note that you do not have to supply illustrations. However, if you have illustrations you would like to include with your submission, you may send detailed sketches or photocopies of the original art. Do not send original art. Reviews artwork/photos. Send photocopies-no originals.

FICTION Subjects include adventure, historical, humor, literary, mainstream, contemporary, Judaica and holiday, animal stories for young readers. Children's books only. Query with SASE. No phone calls, please.

TIPS "We need manuscripts with strong stories and writing."

HENRY HOLT

Macmillan, 175 Fifth Ave., New York NY 10010. **Website:** us.macmillan.com/henryholt.aspx. **Agented submissions only.**

HOLY CROSS ORTHODOX PRESS

Hellenic College, 50 Goddard Ave., Brookline MA 02445. (617)850-1321. **Fax:** (617)850-1457. **E-mail:** press@hchc.edu. **Contact:** Dr. Anton C. Vrame. Estab. 1974. Publishes trade paperback originals. "Holy Cross publishes titles that are rooted in the tradition of the Eastern Orthodox Church." **Publishes 8 titles/year. 10-15 queries received/year. 10-15 mss received/year. 85% of books from first-time authors. 100% from unagented writers. Pays 8-12% royalty**

on retail price. Publishes ms 2 years after acceptance. Accepts simultaneous submissions. Responds in 6 months to mss. Book catalog available online through Holy Cross Bookstore.

IMPRINTS Holy Cross Orthodox Press.

NONFICTION Subjects include ethnic, religion, Greek Orthodox. Holy Cross Orthodox Press publishes scholarly and popular literature in the areas of Orthodox Christian theology and Greek letters. Submissions are often far too technical usually with a very limited audiences. Submit outline. Submit complete ms. Reviews artwork/photos. Send photocopies.

HOPEWELL PUBLICATIONS

P.O. Box 11, Titusville NJ 08560. **Website:** www.hopepubs.com. **Contact:** E. Martin, publisher. Estab. 2002. Format publishes in hardcover, trade paperback, and electronic originals; trade paperback and electronic reprints. "Hopewell Publications specializes in classic reprints—books with proven sales records that have gone out of print—and the occasional new title of interest. Our catalog spans from one to sixty years of publication history. We print fiction and nonfiction, and we accept agented and unagented materials. Books are only accepted after a formal e-mail query." **Publishes 20-30 titles/year. Receives 2,000 queries/year; 500 mss/year. 25% of books from first-time authors. 75% from unagented writers. Pays royalty on retail price. Publishes ms 6-12 months after acceptance.** Accepts simultaneous submissions. Responds in 3 months to queries; 6 months to proposals; 9 months to mss. Catalog online at website. Guidelines online at website (e-mail query guidelines).

IMPRINTS Egress Books, Legacy Classics.

NONFICTION All nonfiction subjects acceptable. Query online using our online guidelines.

FICTION Subjects include adventure, contemporary, experimental, fantasy, gay, historical, humor, juvenile, literary, mainstream, mystery, plays, short story collections, spiritual, suspense, young adult, All fiction subjects acceptable. Query online using our online guidelines.

HOUGHTON MIFFLIN HARCOURT BOOKS FOR CHILDREN

Imprint of Houghton Mifflin Trade & Reference Division, 222 Berkeley St., Boston MA 02116. (617)351-5000. **Fax:** (617)351-1111. **E-mail:** children's_books@hmco.com. **Website:** www.houghtonmifflinbooks.com. **Contact:** Erica Zappy, associate editor; Kate

O'Sullivan, senior editor; Anne Rider, executive editor; Margaret Raymo, editorial director. Publishes hardcover originals and trade paperback originals and reprints. Houghton Mifflin Harcourt gives shape to ideas that educate, inform, and above all, delight. Query with SASE. Submit sample chapters, synopsis. Faxed or e-mailed manuscripts and proposals are not considered. Complete submission guidelines available on website. **Publishes 100 titles/year. 5,000 queries received/year. 14,000 mss received/year. 10% of books from first-time authors. 60% from unagented writers. Pays 5-10% royalty on retail price. Pays variable advance.** Publishes ms 2 years after acceptance. Accepts simultaneous submissions. Responds in 4-6 months to queries. Guidelines available online. **IMPRINTS** Sandpiper Paperback Books; Graphia.

◗ Does not respond to or return mss unless interested.

NONFICTION Subjects include animals, anthropology, archeology, art, architecture, ethnic, history, language, literature, music, dance, nature, environment, science, sports. Interested in innovative books and subjects about which the author is passionate. Query with SASE. Submit sample chapters, synopsis. Reviews artwork/photos. Send photocopies.

FICTION Subjects include adventure, ethnic, historical, humor, juvenile, early readers, literary, mystery, picture books, suspense, young adult, board books. Submit complete ms.

TIPS Faxed or e-mailed manuscripts and proposals are not considered. Complete submission guidelines available on website.

ⓐ HOUGHTON MIFFLIN HARCOURT CO.

222 Berkeley St., Boston MA 02116. (617)351-5000. **Website:** www.hmhco.com; www.hmhbooks.com. Estab. 1832. Publishes hardcover originals and trade paperback originals and reprints.

IMPRINTS American Heritage Dictionaries; Clarion Books; Great Source Education Group; Houghton Mifflin; Houghton Mifflin Books for Children; Houghton Mifflin Paperbacks; Mariner Books; McDougal Littell; Peterson Field Guides; Riverside Publishing; Sunburst Technology; Taylor's Gardening Guides; Edusoft; Promissor; Walter Lorraine Books; Kingfisher.

◗ "Houghton Mifflin Harcourt gives shape to ideas that educate, inform and delight. In a new era of publishing, our legacy of quality

thrives as we combine imagination with technology, bringing you new ways to know."

NONFICTION We are not a mass market publisher. Our main focus is serious nonfiction. We do practical self-help but not pop psychology self-help. Agented submissions only. Unsolicited mss returned unopened.

◷ ⊘ HOUSE OF ANANSI PRESS

110 Spadina Ave., Suite 801, Toronto ON M5V 2K4, Canada. (416)363-4343. **Fax:** (416)363-1017. **Website:** www.anansi.ca. Estab. 1967. **Pays 8-10% royalties. Pays $750 advance and 10 author's copies.** Publishes book Responds to queries within 1 year, to mss (if invited) within 4 months. after acceptance of ms.

POETRY House of Anansi publishes literary fiction and poetry by Canadian and international writers. "We seek to balance the list between well-known and emerging writers, with an interest in writing by Canadians of all backgrounds. We publish Canadian poetry only, and poets must have a substantial publication record—if not in books, then definitely in journals and magazines of repute." Does not want "children's poetry or poetry by previously unpublished poets." Has published *Power Politics* by Margaret Atwood and *Ruin & Beauty* by Patricia Young. Books are generally 96-144 pages, trade paperbacks with French sleeves, with matte covers. Canadian poets should query first with 10 sample poems (typed double-spaced) and a cover letter with brief bio and publication credits. Considers simultaneous submissions. Poems are circulated to an editorial board. Often comments on rejected poems.

HOW BOOKS

F+W Media, Inc., 10151 Carver Rd., Suite 200, Blue Ash OH 45242. (513)531-2690. **E-mail:** megan.patrick@fwmedia.com. **Website:** www.howdesign.com. **Contact:** Megan Patrick, content director. Estab. 1985. Publishes hardcover and trade paperback originals. **Publishes 15 titles/year. 50 queries received/year. 5 mss received/year. 50% of books from first-time authors. 50% from unagented writers. Pays 10% royalty on wholesale price. Pays $2,000-6,000 advance.** Publishes ms 18-24 months after acceptance. Accepts simultaneous submissions. Responds in 1 month to queries and proposals; 3 months to mss. Book catalog available online. Guidelines available online.

NONFICTION Graphic design, creativity, pop culture. "We look for material that reflects the cutting edge of trends, graphic design, and culture. Nearly all HOW Books are intensely visual, and authors must be able to create or supply art/illustration for their books." Query with SASE. Submit proposal package, outline, 1 sample chapter, sample art or sample design. Reviews artwork/photos. Send photocopies and PDF's (if submitting electronically).

TIPS "Audience comprised of graphic designers. Your art, design, or concept."

HQN BOOKS

Imprint of Harlequin, 233 Broadway, Suite 1001, New York NY 10279. **Website:** e.harlequin.com; www.hqn. com. **Contact:** Tara Parsons, senior editor. Publishes hardcover, trade paperback, and mass market paperback originals. **Pays royalty. Pays advance.**

"HQN publishes romance in all subgenres - historical, contemporary, romantic suspense, paranormal as long as the story's central focus is romance. Prospective authors can familiarize themselves with the wide range of books we publish by reading work by some of our current authors. These include Susan Andersen, Beth Ciotta, Nicola Cornick, Victoria Dahl, Susan Grant, Kristan Higgins, Susan Mallery, Kasey Michaels, Linda Lael Miller, Diana Palmer, Carly Phillips, Rosemary Rogers, Meryl Sawyer, Gena Showalter, Christina Skye, and Bertrice Small. The imprint is looking for a wide range of authors from known romance stars to first-time authors. At the moment, we are accepting only agented submissions - unagented authors may send a query letter to determine if their project suits our needs. Please send your projects to our New York Editorial Office."

FICTION Subjects include romance, contemporary and historical. Accepts unagented material. Length: 90,000 words.

HUDSON HILLS PRESS, INC.

P.O. Box 250, 116 Pleasant St., Suite 049, Easthampton MA 01027. **E-mail:** editorial@hudsonhills.com. **Website:** www.hudsonhills.com. Estab. 1978. Publishes hardcover and paperback originals. Hudson Hills Press publishes books about art and photography, including monographs. **Publishes 15+ titles/year. 15% of books from first-time authors. 90% from unagented writers. Pays 4-6% royalty on retail price. Pays $3,500 average advance.** Publishes ms 1 year after acceptance. Accepts simultaneous submissions. Responds in 2 months to queries. Book catalog for 6 x 9 SAE with 2 first-class stamps.

NONFICTION Subjects include art, architecture, photography. Query first, then submit outline and sample chapters. Reviews artwork/photos.

HUNTER HOUSE PUBLISHERS

P.O.Box 2914, Alameda CA 94501. **Website:** www. hunterhouse.com. Visit website for submission guidelines. Submit overview and chapter-by-chapter synopsis, sample chapters, and statistics on subject area, support organizations or networks, personal bio, and marketing ideas. "Testimonials from professionals or well-known authors are helpful, especially for health books." **Payment varies. Sends galleys to authors. Book catalog available. But most updated information is on website; ms guidelines for standard SAE and 1 first-class stamp.** Publishes ms 18 months after acceptance. Accepts simultaneous submissions. Responds to queries in 1-3 months; mss in 3-6 months.

NONFICTION Books are fitness/diet/exercise and activity games/social skills/classroom management-oriented. Does *not* want to see books for young children, fiction, illustrated picture books, memoir or autobiography. Published SmartFun activity book series (currently about 20 books): each has 101 games that encourage imagination, social interaction, and self-expression in children (generally between ages 3-15). Widely used in homes, schools, day-care centers, clubs, and camps. Each activity includes set-up, age range, difficulty level, materials list and a time suggestion.

TIPS "Looking for children's activity books focused on education, teamwork, skill-building, ETC. The children's books we publish are for a select, therapeutic audience. No fiction! Please, no fiction."

HUNTER HOUSE PUBLISHERS

P.O. Box 2914, 1515 1/2 Park St., Alameda CA 94501. (510)865-5282. **E-mail:** ordering@hunterhouse.com. **E-mail:** acquisitions@hunterhouse.com. **Website:** www.hunterhouse.com. **Contact:** Jeanne Brondino, acquisitions editor; Kiran S. Rana, publisher. Estab. 1978. Publishes trade paperback originals and reprints. Hunter House publishes health books (especially women's health), self-help health, sexuality and couple relationships, violence prevention and intervention. De-emphasizing reference, self-help psychology. **Publishes 10-12 titles/year. 300 queries re-**

ceived/year. 100 mss received/year. **50% of books from first-time authors. 90% from unagented writers. Pays 10-20% royalty on net receipts. Pays $500-3,000 advance.** Publishes book 18 months after acceptance. Accepts simultaneous submissions. Responds in 2 months to queries; 3 months to proposals. Book catalog available online at website. Guidelines available online and by e-mail request.

NONFICTION Subjects include child guidance, community, health, medicine, nutrition, parenting, psychology, sex, women's issues, self-help, women's health, fitness, relationships, sexuality, personal growth, and violence prevention. Health books (especially women's health) should focus on self-help, health. Family books: Our current focus is sexuality and couple relationships, and alternative lifestyles to high stress. Community topics include violence prevention/violence intervention. We also publish specialized curriculam for counselors and educators in the areas of violence prevention and trauma in children. Query with proposal package, including synopsis, TOC, and chapter outline, two sample chapters, target audience information, competition, and what distinguishes the book. We look for computer printouts of good quality or e-mail. Please inform us if a ms is available on computer disk (IBM format is preferable). Reviews artwork/photos. Send photocopies. Proposals generally not returned, requested mss returned with SASE. Reviews artwork/photos as part of ms package.

FICTION We do not publish fiction, autobiography, or general children's books, so those types of works get returned right away.

TIPS "Audience is concerned people who are looking to educate themselves and their community about real-life issues that affect them. Please send as much information as possible about who your audience is, how your book addresses their needs, and how you reach that audience in your ongoing work. Include a marketing plan. Explain how you will help us market your book. Have a Facebook account, Twitter, or a blog. List any professional organization of which you are a member."

IBEX PUBLISHERS

P.O. Box 30087, Bethesda MD 20824. (301)718-8188. **Fax:** (301)907-8707. **E-mail:** info@ibexpub.com. **Website:** www.ibexpublishers.com. Estab. 1979. Publishes hardcover and trade paperback originals and reprints.

"IBEX publishes books about Iran and the Middle East and about Persian culture and literature." **Publishes 10-12 titles/year. Payment varies.** Accepts simultaneous submissions. Book catalog available free.

IMPRINTS Iranbooks Press.

NONFICTION Subjects include cooking, foods, nutrition, language, literature. Query with SASE, or submit proposal package, including outline and 2 sample chapters.

POETRY "Translations of Persian poets will be considered."

ICONOGRAFIX, INC.

1830A Hanley Rd., P.O. Box 446, Hudson WI 54016. (715)381-9755. **Fax:** (715)381-9756. **E-mail:** dcfrautschi@iconografixinc.com. **Website:** www.enthusiastbooks.com. **Contact:** Dylan Frautschi, editorial director. Estab. 1992. Publishes trade paperback originals. "Iconografix publishes special, historical-interest photographic books for transportation equipment enthusiasts. Currently emphasizing emergency vehicles, buses, trucks, railroads, automobiles, auto racing, construction equipment, snowmobiles." **Publishes 24 titles/year. 100 queries received/year. 20 mss received/year. 50% of books from first-time authors. 100% from unagented writers. Pays 8-12% royalty on wholesale price. Pays $1,000-3,000 advance.** Publishes book 1 year after acceptance. Accepts simultaneous submissions. Responds in 1 month to queries; 3 months to proposals and mss. Book catalog and ms guidelines free.

NONFICTION Subjects include Americana, photos from archives of historic places, objects, people, history, hobbies, military, war, transportation (older photos of specific vehicles). Interested in photo archives. Query with SASE, or submit proposal package, including outline. Reviews artwork/photos. Send photocopies.

IDEALS PUBLICATIONS INC.

2630 Elm Hill Pike, Suite 100, Nashville TN 37214. (615)781-1451. **E-mail:** idealsinfo@guideposts.org. **Website:** www.idealsbooks.com. Estab. 1944. "Ideals Publications publishes 20-25 new children's titles a year, primarily for 2-8 year-olds. Our backlist includes more than 400 titles, and we publish picture books, activity books, board books, and novelty and sound books covering a wide array of topics, such as Bible stories, holidays, early learning, history, family relationships, and values. Our bestselling titles include *The Story of Christmas, The Story of Easter, Seaman's Journal, How Do I Love You?, God Made You Special* and *A View at the Zoo*. Through our dedication to publishing high-quality and engaging books, we never forget our obligation to our littlest readers to help create those special moments with books."

IMPRINTS Ideals, Ideals Children's Books, Candy-Cane Press, Williamson Books.

FICTION Ideals Children's Books publishes fiction and nonfiction picture books for children ages 4 to 8. Subjects include holiday, inspirational, and patriotic themes; relationships and values; and general fiction. Mss should be no longer than 800 words. CandyCane Press publishes board books and novelty books for children ages 2 to 5. Subject matter is similar to Ideals Children's Books, with a focus on younger children. Mss should be no longer than 250 words.

IDW PUBLISHING

5080 Santa Fe, San Diego CA 92109. **E-mail:** letters@idwpublishing.com. **Website:** www.idwpublishing.com. Estab. 1999. Publishes hardcover, mass market and trade paperback originals. IDW Publishing currently publishes a wide range of comic books and graphic novels including titles based on Angel, Doctor Who, GI Joe, Star Trek, Terminator: Salvation, and Transformers. Creator-driven titles include Fallen Angel by Peter David and JK Woodward, Locke & Key by Joe Hill and Gabriel Rodriguez, and a variety of titles by writer Steve Niles including Wake the Dead, Epilogue, and Dead, She Said.

IDYLL ARBOR, INC.

39129 264th Ave. SE, Enumclaw WA 98022. (360)825-7797. **Fax:** (360)825-5670. **E-mail:** editors@idyllarbor.com. **Website:** www.idyllarbor.com. **Contact:** Tom Blaschko. Estab. 1984. Publishes hardcover and trade paperback originals, and trade paperback reprints. "Idyll Arbor publishes practical information on the current state and art of healthcare practice. Currently emphasizing therapies (recreational, aquatic, occupational, music, horticultural), and activity directors in long-term care facilities. Issues Press looks at problems in society from video games to returning veterans and their problems reintegrating into the civilian world. Pine Winds Press publishes books about strange phenomena such as Bigfoot." **Publishes 6 titles/year. 50% of books from first-time authors. 100% from unagented writers. Pays 8-15% royalty on wholesale price or retail price.** Publishes book 1 year after acceptance. Accepts simultaneous submissions. Responds in 1 month; 2 months to proposals; 6 months to mss. Book catalog and ms guidelines free.

IMPRINTS Issues Press; Pine Winds Press.

NONFICTION Subjects include health, medicine, for therapists, activity directors, psychology, recreational therapy, horticulture (used in long-term care activities or health care therapy). "Idyll Arbor is currently developing a line of books under the imprint Issues Press, which treats emotional issues in a clear-headed manner. The latest books are *Science for Seniors, Lessons of the Inca Shamans, Mind on the Run*. Another series of *Personal Health* books explains a condition or a closely related set of medical or psychological conditions. The target audience is the person or the family of the person with the condition. We want to publish a book that explains a condition at the level of detail expected of the average primary care physician so that our readers can address the situation intelligently with specialists. We look for manuscripts from authors with recent clinical experience. Good grounding in theory is required, but practical experience is more important." Query preferred with outline and 1 sample chapter. Reviews artwork/photos. Send photocopies.

TIPS "The books must be useful for the health practitioner who meets face to face with patients or the books must be useful for teaching undergraduate and graduate level classes. We are especially looking for therapists with a solid clinical background to write on their area of expertise."

ILIUM PRESS

2407 S. Sonora Dr., Spokane WA 99037. (509)928-7950. **E-mail:** contact@iliumpress.com; submissions@iliumpress.com. **Website:** www.iliumpress.com. **Contact:** John Lemon, owner/editor (literature, epic poetry, how-to). Estab. 2010. Publishes trade paperback originals and reprints, electronic originals and reprints. **Publishes 1-3 titles/year. Pays 20%-50% royalties on receipts.** Publishes ms up to 1 year after acceptance. Accepts simultaneous submissions. Responds in 6 months to queries/proposals/mss. Guidelines available on website www.iliumpress.com.

NONFICTION Subjects include contemporary culture, memoirs, music, alt-pop music bios, writing, and "practical small business how-to that appeals to the DIY ethic and promoting creative work". Query with SASE or submit proposal package, with outline, 3 sample chapters, and SASE.

FICTION Subjects include adventure, erotica, literary, science fiction, gritty/noir mystery, dystopian science fiction. "See website for guidelines and preferred styles." Query with SASE or submit proposal package with outline, first 20 pages, and SASE.

POETRY "Submit only book-length narrative epic poems in metered blank or sprung verse. All others will be rejected. See submission guidelines on website." Query with first 20 pages and SASE.

TIPS "Read submission guidelines and literary preferences on the website: www.iliumpress.com."

ILLUMINATION ARTS

P.O. Box 1865, Bellevue WA 98009. **Website:** www. illumin.com. **Contact:** Ruth Thompson, editorial director. Estab. 1987. **Pays authors and illustrators royalty based on wholesale price. Book fliers available for SASE.**

○ "Note that our submission review process is on hold until notice on website so submissions are not currently being reviewed." Normal requirements include no electronic or CD submissions for text or art. Considers simultaneous submissions.

NONFICTION Uses color artwork only. Reviews both ms submissions from authors and illustration packages from artists. Artists may query with color samples, résumé and promotional material to be kept on file or returned with SASE only. Responds within 3 months with SASE only. Samples returned with SASE or filed.

FICTION Word length: Prefers under 1,000, but will consider up to 1,500 words.

TIPS "Read our books or visit website to see what our books are like. Follow submission guidelines found on website. Be patient. We are unable to track unsolicited submissions."

IMAGE COMICS

2134 Allston Way, 2nd Floor, Berkeley CA 94704. **E-mail:** submissions@imagecomics.com. **Website:** www.imagecomics.com. **Contact:** Eric Stephenson, publisher. Estab. 1992. Publishes comic books, graphic novels. See this company's website for detailed guidelines.

○ Does not accept writing samples without art.

IMAGES SI, INC

109 Woods of Arden Rd., Staten Island NY 10312. (718)966-3964. **Fax:** (718)966-3695. **Website:** www. imagesco.com. Estab. 1990. **Publishes 4 eBooks titles/year. Pays 10-20% royalty on wholesale price.** Publishes ms 6-24 months after acceptance.

NONFICTION Subjects include computers, electronics, science.

FICTION Subjects include science fiction.

IMMEDIUM

P.O. Box 31846, San Francisco CA 94131. (415)452-8546. **Fax:** (360)937-6272. **E-mail:** submissions@ immedium.com. **Website:** www.immedium.com. **Contact:** Amy Ma, acquisitions editor. Estab. 2005. Publishes hardcover and trade paperback originals. "*Immedium* focuses on publishing eye-catching children's picture books, Asian American topics, and contemporary arts, popular culture, and multicultural issues." **Publishes 4 titles/year. 50 queries received/year. 25 mss received/year. 50% of books from first-time authors. 90% from unagented writers. Pays 5% royalty on wholesale price. Pays on publication.** Publishes book 2 years after acceptance. Accepts simultaneous submissions. Responds in 1 month to queries; 2 months to proposals; 3 months to mss. Catalog available online. Guidelines available online.

NONFICTION Subjects include art, architecture, multicultural. Query with SASE. Submit proposal package, outline, 2 sample chapters. Submit complete ms. Reviews artwork/photos. Send photocopies.

FICTION Subjects include comic books, picture books. Submit complete ms.

TIPS "Our audience is children and parents. Please visit our site."

IMPACT BOOKS

F+W Media, Inc., 10151 Carver Road, Suite 200, Blue Ash OH 45242. (513)531-2690. **Fax:** (513)531-2686. **E-mail:** pam.wissman@fwmedia.com. **Website:** www. northlightshop.com; www.impact-books.com. **Contact:** Pamela Wissman, editorial director (art instruction for fantasy, comics, manga, anime, popular culture, graffiti, science fiction, cartooning, body art). Estab. 2004. Publishes trade paperback originals and reprints. **Publishes 8-9 titles/year. 50 queries received/year. 10-12 mss received/year. 80% of books from first-time authors. 100% from unagented writers.** Publishes book 11 months after acceptance of ms. Accepts simultaneous submissions. Responds in 4 months to queries. Responds in 4 months to proposals. Responds in 2 months to manuscripts. Book catalog available free. Guidelines available online.

○ IMPACT Books publishes titles that emphasize illustrated how-to-draw-manga, graffiti, fantasy and comics art instruction. Currently emphasizing fantasy art, traditional American comics styles, including humor; and Japanese-style (manga and anime) and graffiti. This market is for experienced artists who are willing to work with an IMPACT editor to produce a step-by-step how-to book about the artist's creative process. See also separate listing for F+W Media in this section.

NONFICTION Subjects include art, art instruction, contemporary culture, creative nonfiction, hobbies. Submit proposal package, outline, 1 sample chapter, at least 1 example of sample art. Reviews artwork/photos. Send digital art, hard copies, or anything that represents the art well, preferably in the form the author plans to submit art if contracted.

TIPS "Audience comprised primarily of 12- to 18-year-old beginners along the lines of comic buyers, in general—mostly teenagers—but also appealing to a broader audience of young adults 19-30 who need basic techniques. Art must appeal to teenagers and be submitted in a form that will reproduce well. Authors need to know how to teach beginners step-by-step. A sample step-by-step demonstration is important."

IMPACT PUBLISHERS, INC.

P.O. Box 6016, Atascadero CA 93423. **E-mail:** submissions@impactpublishers.com. **Website:** www.impact-publishers.com. **Contact:** Freeman Porter, submissions editor. Estab. 1970. Imprints: Little Imp Books, Rebuilding Books, The Practical Therapist Series. "Our purpose is to make the best human services expertise available to the widest possible audience. We publish only popular psychology and self-help materials written in everyday language by professionals with advanced degrees and significant experience in the human services." **Publishes 3-5 titles/year. 20% of books from first-time authors. Pays authors royalty of 10-12%. Offers advances.** Accepts simultaneous submissions. Responds to queries/mss in 3 months. Book catalog for #10 SASE with 2 first-class stamps. Guidelines for SASE.

NONFICTION Young readers, middle readers, young adults: self-help. Recently published *Jigsaw Puzzle*

Family: The Stepkids' Guide to Fitting It Together, by Cynthia MacGregor (ages 8-12, children's/divorce/emotions). Query or submit complete ms, cover letter, résumé.

TIPS "Please do not submit fiction, poetry or narratives."

INCENTIVE PUBLICATIONS, INC.

233 N. Michigan Ave., Suite 2000, Chicago IL 60601.. **Website:** www.incentivepublications.com. **Contact:** Patience Camplair, editor. Estab. 1970. Publishes paperback originals. "Incentive publishes developmentally appropriate teacher/parent resource materials and educational workbooks for children in grades K-12. Currently emphasizing primary material. Also interested in character education, English as a second language programs, early learning, current technology, related materials." **Publishes 25-30 titles/year. 25% of books from first-time authors. 100% from unagented writers. Pays royalty, or makes outright purchase.** Publishes book an average of 1 year after acceptance of ms. Responds in 1 month to queries. Guidelines available online.

NONFICTION Subjects include education. Teacher resource books in pre-K through 12th grade. Query with synopsis and detailed outline.

INFORMATION TODAY, INC.

143 Old Marlton Pike, Medford NJ 08055. (609)654-6266. **Fax:** (609)654-4309. **E-mail:** jbryans@infotoday.com. **Website:** www.infotoday.com. **Contact:** John B. Bryans, editor-in-chief/publisher. Publishes hardcover and trade paperback originals. "We look for highly-focused coverage of cutting-edge technology topics. Written by established experts and targeted to a tech-savvy readership. Virtually all our titles focus on how information is accessed, used, shared, and transformed into knowledge that can benefit people, business, and society. Currently emphasizing Internet/online technologies, including their social significance: biography, how-to, technical, reference, scholarly. De-emphasizing fiction." **Publishes 15-20 titles/year. 200 queries received/year. 30 mss received/year. 30% of books from first-time authors. 90% from unagented writers. Pays 10-15% royalty on wholesale price. Pays $500-2,500 advance.** Publishes book 9 months after acceptance. Accepts simultaneous submissions. Responds in 1 month to queries; 2 months to proposals; 3 months to mss. Book catalog free or on website. Proposal guidelines free or via e-mail as attachment.

IMPRINTS ITI (academic, scholarly, library science); CyberAge Books (high-end consumer and business technology books-emphasis on Internet/WWW topics including online research).

NONFICTION Subjects include business, economics, computers, electronics, education, science, Internet and cyberculture. Query with SASE. Reviews artwork/photos. Send photocopies.

TIPS "Our readers include scholars, academics, indexers, librarians, information professionals (ITI imprint), as well as high-end consumer and business users of Internet/WWW/online technologies, and people interested in the marriage of technology with issues of social significance (i.e., cyberculture)."

INGALLS PUBLISHING GROUP, INC

P.O. Box 2500, Banner Elk NC 28604. (828)297-6884. **Fax:** (828)297-6880. **E-mail:** editor@ingallspublishinggroup.com; sales@ingallspublishinggroup.com. **Website:** www.ingallspublishinggroup.com. **Contact:** Rebecca Owen. Estab. 2001. Publishes hardcover originals, paperback originals and paperback reprints. "We are a small regional house focusing on popular fiction and memoir. At present, we are most interested in regional fiction, historical fiction and mystery fiction." Exploring digital technologies for printing and e-books. Member IBPA, MWA, SIBA. Accepts unsolicited mss. Query first. Will specifically request if interested in reading synopsis and 3 sample chapters. Accepts queries by e-mail. Include estimated word count, brief bio, list of publishing credits. Agented fiction 10%. Accepts electronic submissions. No submissions on disk. Often comments on rejected mss. **Pays 10% royalty.** Publishes ms 6 months-2 years after acceptance. Accepts simultaneous submissions. Responds in 6 weeks to queries or mss. Guidelines available online.

FICTION Subjects include historical, mystery, regional. Query first. Will specifically request if interested in reading synopsis and 3 sample chapters. Accepts queries by e-mail. Include estimated word count, brief bio, list of publishing credits. No submissions on disk.

⊕ INNOVATIVE PUBLISHERS INC.

44 Highland St., Boston MA 02119. (617)963-0886. **Fax:** (617)861-8533. **E-mail:** pub@innovative-publishers.com. **Website:** www.innovative-publishers.com. Estab. 2000. Publishes hardcover, trade paperback, mass market, and electronic originals; trade paperback and mass market reprints. **Publishes**

350-600 titles/year. Receives 4,500 queries/year. Receives 800-1,000 mss/year. 45% of books from first-time authors. 50% from unagented writers. Pays 5-17% royalty on retail price. Offers $1,500-$125,000 advance. Publishes ms 2 years after acceptance. Accepts simultaneous submissions. Responds in 3 months to queries; 4-6 months to mss and proposals. Book catalog for 9x12 SASE with 7 first-class stamps. Guidelines for #10 SASE.

NONFICTION Subjects include Americana, anthropology, archeology, architecture, art, business, career guidance, child guidance, communications, community, contemporary culture, cooking, counseling, crafts, creative nonfiction, economics, education, entertainment, finance, foods, games, gardening, government, health, history, hobbies, house and home, humanities, language, law, literary criticism, literature, memoirs, money, multicultural, music, New Age, philosophy, photography, psychology, real estate, religion, science, social sciences, sociology, spirituality, translation, transportation, travel, womens issues, womens studies, world affairs, young adult. "We want books from dedicated writers and not those who are writing on the latest trend. Our audience is broad, educated, and insightful." Query with SASE. Reviews artwork.

FICTION Subjects include adventure, comic books, confession, contemporary, erotica, ethnic, experimental, fantasy, feminist, gothic, historical, horror, humor, juvenile, literary, mainstream, multicultural, mystery, picture books, plays, poetry, religious, romance, science fiction, short story collections, spiritual, suspense, translation, young adult. "Primarily seeking artists that are immersed in their topic. If you live, eat, and sleep your topic, it will show. Our focus is a wide demographic." Query with SASE.

POETRY "Some works may be slated for anthologies. Readers are from diverse demographic. Seeking innovative styles. Especially seeking emerging ethnic poets from Asia, Europe, and Spanish-speaking countries." Query. Submit 4 sample poems.

☾ INSOMNIAC PRESS

520 Princess Ave., London ON N6B 2B8, Canada. (416)504-6270. **E-mail:** mike@insomniacpress.com. **Website:** www.insomniacpress.com. **Contact:** Mike O'Connor, publisher. Estab. 1992. Publishes trade paperback originals and reprints, mass market paperback originals, and electronic originals and reprints.

Publishes 20 titles/year. 250 queries received/year. **1,000 mss received/year. 50% of books from first-time authors. 80% from unagented writers. Pays 10-15% royalty on retail price. Pays $500-1,000 advance.** Publishes book 6 months after acceptance of ms. Accepts simultaneous submissions. Guidelines available online.

NONFICTION Subjects include business, creative nonfiction, gay, lesbian, government, politics, health, medicine, language, literature, money, finance, multicultural, religion, true crime. Very interested in areas such as true crime and well-written and well-researched nonfiction on topics of wide interest. Query via e-mail, submit proposal package including outline, 2 sample chapters, or submit complete ms. Reviews artwork/photos. Send photocopies.

FICTION Subjects include comic books, ethnic, experimental, gay, lesbian, humor, literary, mainstream, multicultural, mystery, poetry, suspense. "We publish a mix of commercial (mysteries) and literary fiction." Query via e-mail, submit proposal.

POETRY "Our poetry publishing is limited to 2-4 books per year and we are often booked up a year or two in advance." Submit complete ms.

TIPS "We envision a mixed readership that appreciates up-and-coming literary fiction and poetry as well as solidly researched and provocative nonfiction. Peruse our website and familiarize yourself with what we've published in the past."

INTERLINK PUBLISHING GROUP, INC.

46 Crosby St., Northampton MA 01060. (413)582-7054. **Fax:** (413)582-7057. **E-mail:** info@interlinkbooks.com; editor@interlinkbooks.com. **Website:** www.interlinkbooks.com. **Contact:** Michel Moushabeck, publisher; Pam Thompson, editor. Estab. 1987. Publishes hardcover and trade paperback originals. Interlink is a independent publisher of a general trade list of adult fiction and nonfiction with an emphasis on books that have a wide appeal while also meeting high intellectual and literary standards. **Publishes 90 titles/year. 30% of books from first-time authors. 50% from unagented writers. Pays 6-8% royalty on retail price. Pays small advance.** Publishes book 18 months after acceptance of ms. Accepts simultaneous submissions. Responds in 3-6 months to queries. Book catalog and guidelines available free online.

IMPRINTS Crocodile Books, USA; Codagan Guides, USA; Interlink Books; Olive Branch Press; Clockroot Books.

NONFICTION Subjects include world travel, world literature, world history and politics, art, world music & dance, international cooking, children's books from around the world. Submit outline and sample chapters.

FICTION Subjects include ethnic, international adult. "We are looking for translated works relating to the Middle East, Africa or Latin America." No science fiction, romance, plays, erotica, fantasy, horror. Query with SASE. Submit outline, sample chapters.

TIPS "Any submissions that fit well in our publishing program will receive careful attention. A visit to our website, your local bookstore, or library to look at some of our books before you send in your submission is recommended."

INTERNATIONAL FOUNDATION OF EMPLOYEE BENEFIT PLANS

18700 W. Bluemound Rd., Brookfield WI 53045. (262)786-6700. **Fax:** (262)786-8780. **E-mail:** bookstore@ifebp.org. **Website:** www.ifebp.org. **Contact:** Kelli Kolsrud, director, information services and publications. Estab. 1954. Publishes trade paperback originals. IFEBP publishes general and technical monographs on all aspects of employee benefits—pension plans, health insurance, etc. **Publishes 10 titles/year. 15% of books from first-time authors. 80% from unagented writers. Pays 5-15% royalty on wholesale and retail price.** Publishes ms 1 year after acceptance. Responds in 3 months to queries. Book catalog available free. Guidelines available online.

NONFICTION Subjects limited to health care, pensions, retirement planning and employee benefits and compensation. Query with outline.

TIPS "Be aware of interests of employers and the marketplace in benefits topics, for example, pension plan changes, healthcare cost containment."

INTERNATIONAL PRESS

P.O. Box 43502, Somerville MA 02143. (617)623-3855. **Fax:** (617)623-3101. **E-mail:** ipb-mgmt@intlpress.com. **Website:** www.intlpress.com. **Contact:** Brian Bianchini, general manager (research math and physics). Estab. 1992. Publishes hardcover originals and reprints. International Press of Boston, Inc. is an academic publishing company that welcomes book publication inquiries from prospective authors on all topics in Mathematics and Physics. International Press also publishes high-level mathematics and mathematical physics book titles and textbooks. **Publishes 12 titles/year. 200 queries received/year. 500 mss received/year. 10% of books from first-time authors. 100% from unagented writers. Pays 3-10% royalty.** Publishes ms 6 months after acceptance. Responds in 5 months to queries and proposals; 1 year to mss. Book catalog available free. Guidelines available online.

O   With close ties to the Chinese math community and the community of Chinese American mathematicians, International Press is developing a strong partnership with publishers and distributors of academic books throughout China.

NONFICTION Subjects include science. All our books will be in research mathematics. Authors need to provide ready to print latex files. Submit complete ms. Reviews artwork/photos. Send EPS files.

TIPS "Audience is PhD mathematicians, researchers and students."

INTERNATIONAL PUBLISHERS CO., INC.

235 W. 23 St., New York NY 10011. (212)366-9816. **Fax:** (212)366-9820. **E-mail:** service@intpubnyc.com. **Website:** www.intpubnyc.com. **Contact:** Betty Smith, president. Estab. 1924. Publishes hardcover originals, trade paperback originals and reprints. "International Publishers Co., Inc. emphasizes books based on Marxist science." **Publishes 5-6 titles/year. 50-100 mss received/year. 10% of books from first-time authors. Pays 5-7½% royalty on paperbacks; 10% royalty on cloth.** Publishes book 6 months after acceptance of ms. Accepts simultaneous submissions. Responds in 1 month to queries; 6 months to mss. Book catalog online at website. Guidelines online at website.

NONFICTION Subjects include art, architecture, economics, government, politics, history, philosophy. Books on labor, black studies, and women's studies based on Marxist science have high priority. Query, or submit outline, sample chapters, and SASE. Reviews artwork/photos.

TIPS "No fiction or poetry."

INTERNATIONAL WEALTH SUCCESS

P.O. Box 186, Merrick NY 11570. (516)766-5850. **Fax:** (516)766-5919. **Website:** www.iwsmoney.com. **Contact:** Tyler G. Hicks, editor. Estab. 1967. **Publishes 10 titles/year. 100% of books from first-time authors. 100% from unagented writers. Pays 10% royalty on wholesale or retail price. Offers usual advance of $1,000, but this varies depending on author's reputation and nature of book. Buys all rights.** Publishes ms 4 months after acceptance. Responds in 1 month to queries. Book catalog and ms guidelines for 9x12 SAE with 3 first-class stamps.

O   "Our mission is to publish books, newsletters, and self-study courses aimed at helping beginners and experienced business people start, and succeed in, their own small business in the fields of real estate, import-export, mail order, licensing, venture capital, financial brokerage, etc. The large number of layoffs and downsizings have made our publications of greater importance to people seeking financial independence in their own business, free of layoff threats and snarling bosses."

NONFICTION Subjects include business, economics, financing, business success, venture capital, etc. Techniques, methods, sources for building wealth. Highly personal, how-to-do-it with plenty of case histories. Books are aimed at wealth builders and are highly sympathetic to their problems. These publications present a wide range of business opportunities while providing practical, hands-on, step-by-step instructions aimed at helping readers achieve their personal goals in as short a time as possible while adhering to ethical and professional business standards. Length: 60,000-70,000 words. Query. Reviews artwork/photos.

TIPS "With the mass layoffs in large and medium-size companies there is an increasing interest in owning your own business. So we focus on more how-to, hands-on material on owning—and becoming successful in—one's own business of any kind. Our market is the BWB—Beginning Wealth Builder. This person has so little money that financial planning is something they never think of. Instead, they want to know what kind of a business they can get into to make some money without a large investment. Write for this market and you have millions of potential readers. Remember—there are a lot more people without money than with money."

INTERVARSITY PRESS

P.O. Box 1400, Downers Grove IL 60515. **E-mail:** email@ivpress.com. **Website:** www.ivpress.com/submissions. **Contact:** David Zimmerman, associate editor (Likewise); Cindy Bunch, senior editor (IVP Connect, Formatio); Brannon Ellis, associate editor (academic, reference); David Congdon, senior editor (IVP Academic) or Dan Reid, senior editor (reference, academic); Al Hsu, associate editor (IVP Books). Estab. 1947. Publishes hardcover originals, trade paperback and mass market paperback originals. "InterVarsity Press publishes a full line of books from an evangelical Christian perspective targeted to an open-minded audience. We serve those in the university, the church, and the world, by publishing books from an evangelical Christian perspective." **Publishes 110-130 titles/ year. 450 queries received/year. 900 mss received/ year. 13% of books from first-time authors. 86% from unagented writers. Pays 14-16% royalty on retail price. Outright purchase is $75-1,500. Pays negotiable advance.** Publishes book 18 months after acceptance. Accepts simultaneous submissions. Responds in 3 months to proposals "from pastors, professors, or previously published authors. We are unable to respond to other proposals or queries.". Book catalog for 9 ×12 SAE and 5 first-class stamps, or on line at website. Guidelines available online.

IMPRINTS IVP Academic; IVP Connect; IVP Books.

◯ "We think of ourselves as the leading publisher of thoughtful Christian books, and we envision our audience to be similarly thoughtful about their Christian lives—people who really want to think through what it means to be a Christ-follower and to live biblically, and then take some concrete steps toward living more in that direction."

NONFICTION Subjects include business, child guidance, contemporary culture, economics, ethnic, history, memoirs, multicultural, philosophy, psychology, religion, science, social sciences, sociology, spirituality. "InterVarsity Press publishes a full line of books from an evangelical Christian perspective targeted to an open-minded audience. We serve those in the university, the church, and the world, by publishing books from an evangelical Christian perspective." Very few business/economics, child guidance/parenting, memoirs. Submit proposal that includes chapter-by-chapter summary, 2 complete sample chapters, and bio. Does not review artwork.

TIPS "The best way to submit to us is to go to a conference where one of our editors are. Networking is key. We're seeking writers who have good ideas and a presence/platform where they've been testing their ideas out (a church, university, on a prominent blog).

We need authors who will bring resources to the table for helping to publicize and sell their books (speaking at seminars and conferences, writing for national magazines or newspapers, etc.)."

INTERWEAVE

F+W Media, Inc., 201 E. Fourth St., Loveland CO 80537. **E-mail:** akorleski@interweave.com. **Website:** www.interweave.com. **Contact:** Allison Korleski, editorial director. Looking for instructional books on knitting, crochet, sewing & quilting, beading, jewelry making, metalwork, mixed-media, spinning, weaving, and fiber arts. Submit book proposal with 7-10 images via e-mail only.

💿 IRISH ACADEMIC PRESS

2 Brookside, Dundrum Road, Dundrum Dublin 14, Ireland. (353)(1)2989937. **Fax:** (353)(1)2982783. **E-mail:** info@iap.ie. **E-mail:** lisa.hyde@iap.ie. **Website:** www.iap.ie. **Contact:** Lisa Hyde, editor. Estab. 1974. **Publishes 15 titles/year. Pays royalty.** Accepts simultaneous submissions. Guidelines available free.

IMPRINTS Vallentine-Mitchell Publishers.

◯ Request submission guidelines before submitting.

NONFICTION Subjects include art, architecture, government, politics, history, literary criticism, military, war, womens issues, womens studies, genealogy, Irish history. Does not want fiction or poetry. Query with SASE. Submit proposal package, outline, resume, publishing history, bio, target audience, competing books, SASE.

IRON GATE PUBLISHING

P.O. Box 999, Niwot CO 80544. (303)530-2551. **Fax:** (303)530-5273. **E-mail:** editor@irongate.com. **Website:** www.irongate.com. **Contact:** Dina C. Carson, publisher (how-to, genealogy, local history). Publishes hardcover and trade paperback originals. "Our readers are people who are looking for solid, how-to advice on planning reunions or self-publishing a genealogy." **Publishes 6-10 titles/year. 100 queries received/year. 20 mss received/year. 30% of books from first-time authors. 10% from unagented writers. Pays royalty on a case-by-case basis.** Publishes book 1 year after acceptance. Accepts simultaneous submissions. Responds in 2 months to proposals. Book catalog and writer's guidelines free or online.

IMPRINTS Reunion Solutions Press; KinderMed Press.

NONFICTION , hobbies, genealogy, local history, reunions, party planning. Query with SASE, or submit proposal package, including outline, 2 sample chapters, and marketing summary. Reviews artwork/photos. Send photocopies.

TIPS "Please look at the other books we publish and tell us in your query letter why your book would fit into our line of books."

ITALICA PRESS

595 Main St., Suite 605, New York NY 10044-0047. (917)371-0563. **E-mail:** inquiries@italicapress.com. **Website:** www.italicapress.com. **Contact:** Ronald G. Musto and Eileen Gardiner, publishers. Estab. 1985. Publishes trade paperback originals. "Italica Press publishes English translations of modern Italian fiction and medieval and Renaissance nonfiction." **Publishes 6 titles/year. 600 queries received/year. 60 mss received/year. 5% of books from first-time authors. 100% from unagented writers. Pays 7-15% royalty on wholesale price; author's copies.** Publishes book 1 year after acceptance of ms. Accepts simultaneous submissions. Responds in 1 month to queries. Responds in 4 months to manuscripts. Book catalog and guidelines available online.

NONFICTION Subjects include translation. "We publish English translations of medieval and Renaissance source materials and English translations of modern Italian fiction." Query with SASE. Reviews artwork/photos. Send photocopies.

FICTION Query with SASE.

POETRY Poetry titles are always translations and generally dual language.

TIPS "We are interested in considering a wide variety of medieval and Renaissance topics (not historical fiction), and for modern works we are only interested in translations from Italian fiction by well-known Italian authors." *Only* fiction that has been previously published in Italian. A *brief* call saves a lot of postage. 90% of proposals we receive are completely off base—but we are very interested in things that are right on target. Please send return postage if you want your ms returned.

JAIN PUBLISHING CO.

P.O. Box 3523, Fremont CA 94539. (510)659-8272. **Fax:** (510)659-0501. **E-mail:** mail@jainpub.com. **Website:** www.jainpub.com. **Contact:** M. Jain, editor-in-chief. Estab. 1989. Publishes hardcover and paperback originals and reprints. Jain Publishing Co. is a humanities and social sciences publisher that publishes college textbooks and supplements, as well as professional and scholarly references, e-books and e-courses. It also publishes in the areas of humanities and societies pertaining specifically to ask, commonly categorized as "Asian Studies". **Publishes 12-15 titles/year. 300 queries received/year. 100% from unagented writers. Pays 5-15% royalty on net sales.** Publishes ms 1-2 years after acceptance. Responds in 3 months to mss. Book catalog and ms guidelines online.

NONFICTION Subjects include humanities, social sciences, Asian studies, medical, business, scientific/technical. Submit proposal package, publishing history. Reviews artwork/photos. Send photocopies.

ALICE JAMES BOOKS

238 Main St., Farmington ME 04938. (207)778-7071. **Fax:** (207)778-7766. **E-mail:** interns@alicejamesbooks.org; frank@alicejamesbooks.org. **Website:** www.alicejamesbooks.org. **Contact:** Meg Willing, managing editor; Carey Salerno, executive director; Ellen Marlow, editorial assistant. Estab. 1973. Publishes trade paperback originals. "Alice James Books is a nonprofit cooperative poetry press. The founders' objectives were to give women access to publishing and to involve authors in the publishing process. The cooperative selects mss for publication through both regional and national competitions." **Publishes 6 titles/year. Approximately 1,000 mss received/year. 50% of books from first-time authors. 100% from unagented writers. Pays through competition awards.** Publishes ms 1 year after acceptance. Accepts simultaneous submissions. Responds promptly to queries; 4 months to mss. Book catalog for free or on website. Guidelines for #10 SASE or on website.

POETRY "Alice James Books is a nonprofit cooperative poetry press. The founders' objectives were to give women access to publishing and to involve authors in the publishing process. The cooperative selects mss for publication through both regional and national competitions." Seeks to publish the best contemporary poetry by both established and beginning poets, with particular emphasis on involving poets in the publishing process. Has published poetry by Jane Kenyon, Jean Valentine, B.H. Fairchild, and Matthea Harvey. Publishes flat-spined paperbacks of high quality, both in production and contents. Does not want children's poetry or light verse. Publishes 6 paperback books/year, 80 pages each, in editions of approximately 1,500. Query.

TIPS "Send SASE for contest guidelines or check website. Do not send work without consulting current guidelines."

JEWISH LIGHTS PUBLISHING

LongHill Partners, Inc., Sunset Farm Offices, Rt. 4, P.O. Box 237, Woodstock VT 05091. (802)457-4000. **Fax:** (802)457-4004. **E-mail:** editorial@jewishlights.com; sales@jewishlights.com. **Website:** www.jewishlights.com. **Contact:** Tim Holtz, art acquisitions. Estab. 1990. Publishes hardcover and trade paperback originals, trade paperback reprints. "Jewish Lights publishes books for people of all faiths and all backgrounds who yearn for books that attract, engage, educate and spiritually inspire. Our authors are at the forefront of spiritual thought and deal with the quest for the self and for meaning in life by drawing on the Jewish wisdom tradition. Our books cover topics including history, spirituality, life cycle, children, self-help, recovery, theology and philosophy. We do not publish autobiography, biography, fiction, haggadot, poetry or cookbooks. At this point we plan to do only two books for children annually, and one will be for younger children (ages 4-10)." Fiction/nonfiction: Query with outline/synopsis and 2 sample chapters; submit complete ms for picture books. Include SASE. Responds to queries/mss in 4 months. **Publishes 30 titles/year. 50% of books from first-time authors. 75% from unagented writers. Pays authors royalty of 10% of revenue received; 15% royalty for subsequent printings.** Publishes ms 1 year after acceptance. Accepts simultaneous submissions. Responds in 3 months to queries. Book catalog and ms guidelines online.

NONFICTION Subjects include business, economics, with spiritual slant, finding spiritual meaning in one's work, health, medicine, healing/recovery, wellness, aging, life cycle, history, nature, environment, philosophy, religion, theology, spirituality, and inspiration, women's issues, women's studies. Picture book, young readers, middle readers: activity books, spirituality. "We do *not* publish haggadot, biography, poetry, or cookbooks." Reviews artwork/photos. Send photocopies. Works with 2 illustrators/year. Reviews ms/illustration packages from artists. Query. Illustrations only: Query with samples; provide résumé. Samples returned with SASE; samples filed.

FICTION Picture books, young readers, middle readers: spirituality. "We are not interested in anything other than spirituality."

TIPS "We publish books for all faiths and backgrounds that also reflect the Jewish wisdom tradition. Explain in your cover letter why you're submitting your project to us in particular. Make sure you know what we publish."

JIST PUBLISHING

875 Montreal Way, St. Paul MN 55102. **Website:** www.jist.com. **Contact:** Susan Pines, associate publisher (career and education reference and library titles, assessments, videos, e-products); Lori Cates Hand, product line manager, trade and workbooks (career, job search, and education trade and workbook titles). Estab. 1981. Publishes hardcover and trade paperback originals. "Our purpose is to provide quality job search, career development, occupational, and life skills information, products, and services that help people manage and improve their lives and careers-and the lives of others. Publishes practical, self-directed tools and training materials that are used in employment and training, education, and business settings. Whether reference books, trade books, assessment tools, workbooks, or videos, JIST products foster self-directed job-search attitudes and behaviors." **Publishes 60 titles/year. Receives 40 submissions/year. 25% of books from first-time authors. 75% from unagented writers. Pays 8-10% royalty on net receipts. Pays advance: 12 months.** Accepts simultaneous submissions. Responds in 6 months to queries, proposals, and mss. Book catalog available online. Guidelines available online.

NONFICTION Subjects include : business, economics, education. Specializes in job search, career development, occupational information, character education, and domestic abuse topics. "We want text/workbook formats that would be useful in a school or other institutional setting. We also publish trade titles for all reading levels. Will consider books for professional staff and educators, appropriate software and videos." Submit proposal package, including outline, 1 sample chapter, and author resume, competitive analysis, marketing ideas. Does not review artwork/photos.

TIPS "Our audiences are students, job seekers, and career changers of all ages and occupations who want to find good jobs quickly and improve their futures. We sell materials through the trade as well as to institutional markets like schools, colleges, and one-stop career centers."

THE JOHNS HOPKINS UNIVERSITY PRESS

2715 N. Charles St., Baltimore MD 21218. (410)516-6900. **Fax:** (410)516-6968. **E-mail:** jmm@press.jhu.edu. **Website:** www.press.jhu.edu. **Contact:** Jacqueline C. Wehmueller, executive editor (consumer health, psychology and psychiatry, and history of medicine; jcw@press.jhu.edu); Matthew McAdam, editor (mxm@jhu.press.edu); Robert J. Brugger, senior acquisitions editor (American history; rjb@press.jhu.edu); Vincent J. Burke, exec. editor (biology; vjb@press.jhu.edu); Juliana McCarthy, acquisitions editor (humanities, classics, and ancient studies; jmm@press.jhu.edu); Ashleigh McKown, assistant editor (higher education, history of technology, history of science; aem@press.jhu.edu); Suzanne Flinchbaugh, Associate Editor (Political Science, Health Policy, and Co-Publishing Liaison; skf@press.jhu.edu; Greg Nicholl, Assistant Editor (Regional Books, Poetry and Fiction, and Anabaptist and Pietist Studies; gan@press.jhu.edu). Estab. 1878. Publishes hardcover originals and reprints, and trade paperback reprints. **Publishes 140 titles/year. Pays royalty.** Publishes ms 1 year after acceptance.

NONFICTION Subjects include government, politics, health, medicine, history, humanities, literary criticism, regional, religion, science. Submit proposal package, outline, 1 sample chapter, curriculum vita. Reviews artwork/photos. Send photocopies.

POETRY "One of the largest American university presses, Johns Hopkins publishes primarily scholarly books and journals. We do, however, publish short fiction and poetry in the series Johns Hopkins: Poetry and Fiction, edited by John Irwin."

JONATHAN DAVID PUBLISHERS, INC.

68-22 Eliot Ave., Middle Village NY 11379. (718)456-8611. **Fax:** (718)894-2818. **E-mail:** submission@jdbooks.com. **Website:** www.jdbooks.com. **Contact:** David Kolatch, editorial director. Estab. 1948. Publishes hardcover and trade paperback originals and reprints. Jonathan David publishes popular Judaica. **Publishes 20-25 titles/year. 50% of books from first-time authors. 90% from unagented writers. Pays royalty, or makes outright purchase.** Publishes ms 18 months after acceptance. Responds in 1 month to queries and proposals; 2 months to mss. Book catalog available online. Guidelines available online.

NONFICTION Subjects include cooking, foods, nutrition, creative nonfiction, ethnic, multicultural, religion, sports. Query with SASE. Submit proposal package, outline, résumé, 3 sample chapters. Reviews artwork/photos. Send photocopies.

JOURNEYFORTH

Imprint of BJU Press, 1700 Wade Hampton Blvd., Greenville SC 29614. (864)242-5100, ext. 4350. **Fax:** (864)298-0268. **E-mail:** jb@bju.edu. **Website:** www.journeyforth.com. **Contact:** Nancy Lohr. Estab. 1974. Publishes paperback originals. "Small independent publisher of trustworthy novels and biographies for readers pre-school through high school from a conservative Christian perspective, Christian living books, and Bible studies for adults." **Publishes 25 titles/year. 10% of books from first-time authors. 8% from unagented writers. Pays royalty.** Publishes book 12-18 months after acceptance of ms. Does accept simultaneous submissions. Responds in 1 month to queries. Responds in 3 months to manuscripts. Book catalog available free. Guidelines available online at www.bjupress.com/books/freelance.php.

NONFICTION Subjects include animals, contemporary culture, creative nonfiction, environment, history, music, nature, religion, spirituality, sports, young adult. Nonfiction Christian living, Bible studies, church and ministry, church history. We produce books for the adult Christian market that are from a conservative Christian worldview.

FICTION Subjects include adventure, historical, animal, easy-to-read, series, mystery, sports, children's/juvenile, suspense, young adult, western. Our fiction is all based on a moral and Christian worldview. Does not want short stories. Submit 5 sample chapters, synopsis, SASE.

TIPS "Study the publisher's guidelines. No picture books and no submissions by e-mail."

JUPITER GARDENS PRESS

Jupiter Gardens, LLC, P.O. Box 191, Grimes IA 50111. **E-mail:** submissions@jupitergardens.com. **Website:** www.jupitergardens.com. **Contact:** Mary Wilson, publisher (romance, sf/f, new age). Estab. 2007. Format publishes in trade paperback originals and reprints; electronic originals and reprints. **Publishes 30+ titles/year. Pays 40% royalty on retail price.** Publishes ms 4 months after acceptance. Accepts simultaneous submissions. Responds in 1 months on proposals, 2 months on mss. Catalog available online at website. Guidelines available online at website.

IMPRINTS Pink Petal Books, Mary Wilson, publisher; Jupiter Storm, Sasha Vivelo, senior editor.

NONFICTION Subjects include alternative lifestyles, animals, astrology, environment, gay, health, lesbian, medicine, nature, psychic, religion, sex, spirituality, womens issues, world affairs, young adult, romance, science fiction, fantasy, and metaphysical fiction & nonfiction. "We only publish metaphysical/New Age nonfiction, or nonfiction related to science fiction & fantasy." Submit proposal package, including: outline, 3 sample chapters, and promotional plan/market analysis. Does not review artwork. Writers should send electronic submissions only.

FICTION Subjects include fantasy, gay, lesbian, occult, religious, romance, science fiction, spiritual, young adult, New Age/metaphysical. "We only publish romance (all sub-genres), science fiction & fantasy & metaphysical fiction. Our science fiction and fantasy covers a wide variety of topics, such as feminist fantasy, or more hard science fiction and fantasy which looks at the human condition. Our young adult imprint, Jupiter Storm, with thought provoking reads that explore the full range of speculative fiction, includes science fiction or fantasy and metaphysical fiction. These readers would enjoy edgy contemporary works. Our romance readers love seeing a couple, no matter the gender, overcome obstacles and grow in order to find true love. Like our readers, we believe that love can come in many forms. To submit your work for consideration, please email submissions@jupitergardens.com with a cover letter detailing your writing experience (if any, we do welcome new authors), and attach in DOC or RTF format, a 2-4 page synopsis, and the first 3 chapters."

TIPS "No matter which line you're submitting to, know your genre and your readership. We publish a diverse catalog, and we're passionate about our main focus. We want romance that takes your breath away and leaves you with that warm feeling that love does conquer all. Our science fiction takes place in wild and alien worlds, and our fantasy transports readers to mythical realms and finds strange worlds within our own. And our metaphysical nonfiction will help readers gain new skills and awareness for the coming age. We want authors who engage with their readers and who aren't afraid to use social media to connect. Read and follow our submission guidelines."

KAEDEN BOOKS

P.O. Box 16190, Rocky River OH 44116. **Website:** www.kaeden.com. **Contact:** Lisa Stenger, editor. Estab. 1986. Publishes paperback originals. "Children's book publisher for education K-3 market: reading stories, fiction/nonfiction, chapter books, science, and social studies materials." **Publishes 12-20 titles/year. 1,000 mss received/year. 30% of books from first-time authors. 95% from unagented writers. Work purchased outright from authors. Pays royalties to previous authors.** Publishes ms 6-9 months after acceptance. Accepts simultaneous submissions. Responds only if interested. Book catalog and guidelines available online.

NONFICTION Subjects include animals, creative nonfiction, science, social sciences. Manuscripts should have interesting topics and information presented in language comprehensible to young students. Content should be supported with details and accurate facts. Submit complete ms. "Can be as minimal as 25 words for the earliest reader or as much as 2,000 words for the fluent reader. Beginning chapter books are welcome. Our readers are in kindergarten to third grade, so vocabulary and sentence structure must be appropriate for young readers. Make sure that all language used in the story is of an appropriate level for the students to read independently. Sentences should be complete and grammatically correct." Reviews artwork/photos. Send photocopies.

FICTION Subjects include adventure, fantasy, historical, humor, mystery, short story collections, sports, suspense. "We are looking for stories with humor, surprise endings, and interesting characters that will appeal to children in kindergarten through third grade. No sentence fragments. Please do not submit: queries, manuscript summaries, or résumés, manuscripts that stereotype or demean individuals or groups, manuscripts that present violence as acceptable behavior." Submit complete ms. "Can be as minimal as 25 words for the earliest reader or as much as 2,000 words for the fluent reader. Beginning chapter books are welcome. Our readers are in kindergarten to third grade, so vocabulary and sentence structure must be appropriate for young readers. Make sure that all language used in the story is of an appropriate level for the students to read independently. Sentences should be complete and grammatically correct."

TIPS "Our audience ranges from kindergarten-third grade school children. We are an educational publisher. We are particularly interested in humorous stories with surprise endings and beginning chapter books."

KALMBACH PUBLISHING CO.

21027 Crossroads Circle, P.O. Box 1612, Waukesha WI 53187. (262)796-8776. **Fax:** (262)798-6468. **E-mail:** books@kalmbach.com. **Website:** www.kalmbach. com. **Contact:** Ronald Kovach, senior editor. Estab. 1934. Publishes paperback originals and reprints. **Publishes 40-50 titles/year. 50% of books from first-time authors. 99% from unagented writers. Pays 7% royalty on net receipts. Pays $1,500 advance.** Publishes ms 18 months after acceptance. Responds in 2 months to queries.

NONFICTION "Focus on beading, wirework, and one-of-a-kind artisan creations for jewelry-making and crafts and in the railfan, model railroading, plastic modeling and toy train collecting/operating hobbies. Kalmbach publishes reference materials and how-to publications for hobbyists, jewelry-makers, and crafters." Query with 2-3 page detailed outline, sample chapter with photos, drawings, and how-to text. Reviews artwork/photos.

TIPS "Our how-to books are highly visual in their presentation. Any author who wants to publish with us must be able to furnish good photographs and rough drawings before we'll consider his or her book."

KAMEHAMEHA PUBLISHING

567 S. King St., Honolulu HI 96813. **Website:** www. KamehamehaPublishing.org. Estab. 1933. "Kamehameha Schools Press publishes in the areas of Hawaiian history, Hawaiian culture, Hawaiian language and Hawaiian studies." **Work purchased outright from authors or by royalty agreement.** Publishes ms 2 years after acceptance. Responds in 3 months to queries and mss. Call or write for book catalog.

NONFICTION Young reader, middle readers, young adults: biography, history, multicultural, Hawaiian folklore.

FICTION Young reader, middle readers, young adults: biography, history, multicultural, Hawaiian folklore.

TIPS "Writers and illustrators must be knowledgeable in Hawaiian history/culture and be able to show credentials to validate their proficiency. Greatly prefer to work with writers/illustrators available in the Honolulu area."

KANE/MILLER BOOK PUBLISHERS

Kane/Miller: A Division of EDC Publishing, 4901 Morena Blvd., Suite 213, San Diego CA 92117. (858)456-0540. **Fax:** (858)456-9641. **E-mail:** info@ kanemiller.com. **E-mail:** submissions@kanemiller. com. **Website:** www.kanemiller.com. **Contact:** Kira Lynn, editorial department. Estab. 1985. "Kane/Miller Book Publishers is a division of EDC Publishing, specializing in award-winning children's books from around the world. Our books bring the children of the world closer to each other, sharing stories and ideas, while exploring cultural differences and similarities. Although we continue to look for books from other countries, we are now actively seeking works that convey cultures and communities within the US. We are looking for picture book fiction and nonfiction on those subjects that may be defined as particularly American: sports such as baseball, historical events, American biographies, American folk tales, etc. We are committed to expanding our early and middlegrade fiction list. We're interested in great stories with engaging characters in all genres (mystery, fantasy, adventure, historical, etc.) and, as with picture books, especially those with particularly American subjects. All submissions sent via USPS should be sent to: Editorial Department. Please do not send anything requiring a signature. Work submitted for consideration may also be sent via e-mail. Please send either the complete picture book ms, the published book (with a summary and outline in English, if that is not the language of origin) or a synopsis of the work and two sample chapters. Do not send originals. Illustrators may send color copies, tear sheets, or other non-returnable illustration samples. If you have a website with additional samples of your work, please include the web address. Please do not send original artwork, or samples on CD. A SASE must be included if you send your submission via USPS; otherwise you will not receive a reply. If we wish to follow up, we will notify you." Responds in 90 days.

○ "We like to think that a child reading a Kane/ Miller book will see parallels between his own life and what might be the unfamiliar setting and characters of the story. And that by seeing how a character who is somehow or in some way dissimilar—an outsider—finds a way to fit comfortably into a culture or community or situation while maintaining a healthy sense of self and self-dignity, she might be empowered to do the same."

NONFICTION Subjects include Americana, history, sports, young adult.

FICTION Subjects include adventure, fantasy, historical, juvenile, mystery, picture books. Picture Books: concept, contemporary, health, humor, multicultural. Young Readers: contemporary, multicultural, suspense. Middle Readers: contemporary, humor, multicultural, suspense.

KAR-BEN PUBLISHING

Lerner Publishing Group, 1251 Washington Ave. N., Minneapolis MN 55401. (612)332-3344, ext. 229. **Fax:** 612-332-7615. **E-mail:** Editorial@Karben.com. **Website:** www.karben.com. Estab. 1974. Publishes hardcover, trade paperback and electronic originals. **Publishes 10-15 titles/year. 800 mss received/year. 20% of books from first-time authors. 70% from unagented writers. Pays 3-5% royalty on NET price. Pays $500-2,500 advance.** Publishes book Most manuscripts published within 2 years. after acceptance of ms. Accepts simultaneous submissions. Responds in 6 weeks. Book catalog available online; free upon request. Guidelines available online.

NONFICTION Subjects include Jewish content children's books only. "In addition to traditional Jewish-themed stories about Jewish holidays, history, folktales and other subjects, we especially seek stories that reflect the rich diversity of the contemporary Jewish community." Picture books, young readers: activity books, arts/crafts, biography, careers, concept, cooking, history, how-to, multicultural, religion, social issues, special needs; must be of Jewish interest. No textbooks, games, or educational materials. Submit completed ms. Reviews artwork separately. Works with 10-12 illustrators/year. Prefers four-color art in any medium that is scannable. Reviews illustration packages from artists. Submit sample of art or online portfolio (no originals).

FICTION Subjects include juvenile; Jewish content only. "We seek picture book mss of about 1,000 words on Jewish-themed topics for children." Picture books: Adventure, concept, folktales, history, humor, multicultural, religion, special needs; must be on a Jewish theme. Average word length: picture books—1,000. Recently published *Engineer Ari and the Rosh Hashanah Ride*, by Deborah Bodin Cohen, illustrated by Shahar Kober; and *The Wedding That Saved a Town*, by Yale Strom, illustrated by Jenya Prosmitsky. Submit full ms. Picture books only.

TIPS "Authors: Do a literature search to make sure similar title doesn't already exist. Illustrators: Look at our online catalog for a sense of what we like—bright colors and lively composition."

⊕ KELLY POINT PUBLISHING LLC

Martin Sisters Publishing LLC, P.O. Box 1154, Barbourville KY 40906. **E-mail:** publisher@kellypointpublishing.com. **E-mail:** submissions@kellypointpublishing.com. **Website:** www.kellypointpublishing.com. **Contact:** Melissa Newman, publisher. Estab. 2012. Publishes trade paperback, mass market, and electronic originals. Subsidiary of Martin Sisters Publishing LLC. **Publishes 12 titles/year. Receives 100 queries/year; 30 mss/year. 75% of books from first-time authors. 100% from unagented writers. Pays 7.5% royalty on retail price.** Publishes ms 3-6 months after acceptance. Accepts simultaneous submissions. Responds in 1 month to queries; 2 months to proposals; 4 months to mss. Book catalog available online at website. Guidelines available online at website or by e-mail at submissions e-mail address.

IMPRINTS Kelly Point Books, KP Mystery, KP Romance.

○ *All unsolicited mss returned unopened.*

NONFICTION Subjects include memoirs, young adult. "While Kelly Point Publishing focuses mainly on publishing fiction, we do look at a few memoirs and self-help mss if they are well written and researched." Query with SASE.

FICTION Subjects include adventure, contemporary, historical, humor, juvenile, literary, mainstream, mystery, romance, science fiction, short story collections, spiritual, sports, western, young adult, women's fiction and chick lit. "Please visit our website and read the submissions guidelines for aspiring authors before submitting your query." Query with SASE.

TIPS "Write a good query letter with a hook and follow the submissions guidelines on our website."

KEY CURRICULUM PRESS

1150 65th St., Emeryville CA 94608. (800)995-6284. **Fax:** (800)541-2442. **Website:** www.keypress.com. Estab. 1971. "It's our mission to: Engage students with effective, relevant, high-quality mathematics and science instructional materials and software that open their eyes to math and science in the world around them, develop both conceptual understanding and skills, and ignite their interest in learning. Support mathematics and science educators by partnering with them to promote an inclusive and compelling learning environment that facilitates their success in meeting the educational needs of all students. Advocate for research, ideas, strategies, and policies that lead to excellence and equity in education, as well as a better educational experience for all students. Provide a respectful, collaborative, and forward-thinking workplace that promotes open communication, values people, nurtures their ideas, and helps Key Curriculum Press achieve sustainable growth."

TIPS "Provide website gallery. Call prior to dropping off portfolio."

KIDS CAN PRESS

25 Dockside Dr., Toronto ON M5A 0B5, Canada. (416)479-7000. **Fax:** (416)960-5437. **E-mail:** info@ kidscan.com; kkalmar@kidscan.com. **Website:** www. kidscanpress.com. Estab. 1973. Publishes book 18-24 months after acceptance. Responds in 6 months only if interested.

Kids Can Press is currently accepting unsolicited mss from Canadian adult authors only.

NONFICTION Picture books: activity books, animal, arts/crafts, biography, careers, concept, health, history, hobbies, how-to, multicultural, nature/environment, science, social issues, special needs, sports. Young readers: activity books, animal, arts/crafts, biography, careers, concept, history, hobbies, how-to, multicultural. Middle readers: cooking, music/dance. Average word length: picture books 500-1,250; young readers 750-2,000; middle readers 5,000-15,000. Submit outline/synopsis and 2-3 sample chapters. For picture books submit complete ms.

FICTION Picture books, young readers: concepts. We do not accept young adult fiction or fantasy novels for any age. Adventure, animal, contemporary, folktales, history, humor, multicultural, nature/environment, special needs, sports, suspense/mystery. Average word length: picture books 1,000-2,000; young readers 750-1,500; middle readers 10,000-15,000; young adults over 15,000. Submit outline/synopsis and 2-3 sample chapters. For picture books submit complete ms.

KINDRED PRODUCTIONS

1310 Taylor Ave., Winnipeg MB R3M 3Z6, Canada. (204)669-6575. **Fax:** (204)654-1865. **E-mail:** kindred@mbconf.ca. **Website:** www.kindredproductions.com. **Contact:** Renita Kornelsen, acquisitions. Publishes trade paperback originals and reprints. "Kindred Productions publishes, promotes, and markets print and nonprint resources that will shape our

Christian faith and discipleship from a Mennonite Brethren perspective. Currently emphasizing Mennonite Brethren Resources. De-emphasizing personal experience, biographical. No children's books or fiction." **Publishes 3 titles/year. 1% of books from first-time authors. 100% from unagented writers.** Publishes book 18 months after acceptance. Accepts simultaneous submissions. Responds in 3 months to queries; 5 months to mss. Guidelines available by e-mail request.

NONFICTION Subjects include religion, historical, i. "Our books cater primarily to our Mennonite Brethren denomination readers." Query with SASE. Submit outline, 2-3 sample chapters.

TIPS "Most of our books are sold to churches, religious bookstores, and schools. We are concentrating on books with a Mennonite Brethren perspective. We do not accept children's manuscripts."

KIRKBRIDE BIBLE CO. INC.

Office/HQ, 1102 Deloss St., Indianapolis IN 46203. (800)428-4385. **Fax:** (317)633-1444. **E-mail:** info@ kirkbride.com. **Website:** www.kirkbride.com. Estab. 1915. Publishes Thompson Chain-Reference Bible hardcover originals and quality leather bindings styles and translations of the Bible. Types of books include reference and religious. Specializes in reference and study material.

ALFRED A. KNOPF

1745 Broadway, 21st Floor, New York NY 10019. **Website:** knopf.knopfdoubleday.com. Estab. 1915. Publishes hardcover and paperback originals. **Publishes 200 titles/year. Royalties vary. Offers advance.** Publishes ms 1 year after acceptance. Responds in 2-6 months to queries.

FICTION Publishes book-length fiction of literary merit by known or unknown writers. Length: 40,000-150,000 words. *Agented submissions only.*

KNOPF PUBLISHING GROUP

Imprint of Random House, 1745 Broadway, New York NY 10019. (212)751-2600. **Website:** www.randomhouse.com/knopf. **Contact:** Senior Editor. Estab. 1915. Publishes hardcover and paperback originals.

IMPRINTS Alfred A. Knopf; Everyman's Library; Pantheon Books; Schocken Books; Vintage Anchor Publishing (Vintage Books, Anchor Books).

Knopf is a general publisher of quality nonfiction and fiction. "We usually only accept work through an agent, but you may still send a query to our slush pile.

KNOX ROBINSON PUBLISHING

244 Fifth Ave., Suite 1861, New York NY 10001. E-mail: subs@knoxrobinsonpublishing.com. **Website:** www.knoxrobinsonpublishing.com. **Contact:** Dana Celeste Robinson, managing director (historical fiction, historical romance, fantasy). Estab. 2010. Knox Robinson Publishing is an international, independent, specialist publisher of historical fiction, historical romance and fantasy. **Publishes 5 titles/year. Pays royalty.** Accepts simultaneous submissions. Responds in 2 months to submissions of first 3 chapters. "We do not accept proposals.". Knox Publishing has 10 books in print and 14 scheduled for release in 2012. Guidelines free on request.

○ "KRP publishes historical fiction and historical romance; any story set in an era prior to 1960 is acceptable. We also publish medieval fantasy. We do not publish science fiction. We do not publish fantasy with children and/or animal protagonists. We do not publish novels that involve any aspects of time travel. We welcome the submission of a well-written, detailed synopsis and the first 3 chapters of completed mss directly from authors."

NONFICTION Subjects include history, humanities, religion, general nonfiction, scholarly, history monographs. "Our goal is to publish history books, monographs and historical fiction that satisfies history buffs and encourages general readers to learn more." Submit first 3 chapters and author questionnaire found on website. Reviews artwork/photos. Send photocopies. Does not accept printed submissions; electronic only.

FICTION Wants historical, historical romance. "We are seeking historical fiction featuring obscure historical figures." Submit first 3 chapters and author questionnaire found on website.

KRAUSE PUBLICATIONS

A Division of F+W Media, Inc., 700 E. State St., Iola WI 54990. (715)445-2214. **Fax:** (715)445-4087. **Website:** www.krausebooks.com. **Contact:** Paul Kennedy (antiques and collectibles, music, sports, militaria, humor, numismatics); Corrina Peterson (firearms); Brian Lovett (outdoors); Brian Earnest (automotive). Publishes hardcover and trade paperback originals. "We are the world's largest hobby and collectibles publisher." **Publishes 80 titles/year. 200 queries received/year. 40 mss received/year. 50% of books from first-time authors. 95% from unagented writers. Pays advance. Photo budget.** Publishes ms 18 months after acceptance. Responds in 3 months to proposals. Responds in 2 months to manuscripts. Book catalog for free or on website. Guidelines available free upon request.

NONFICTION Submit proposal package, including outline, table of contents, a sample chapter, and letter explaining your project's unique contributions. Reviews artwork/photos. Accepts only digital photography. Send sample photos.

TIPS Audience consists of serious hobbyists. "Your work should provide a unique contribution to the special interest."

KREGEL PUBLICATIONS

Kregel, Inc., P.O. Box 2607, Grand Rapids MI 49501. (616)451-4775. **Fax:** (616)451-9330. **E-mail:** kregelbooks@kregel.com. **Website:** www.kregelpublications.com. **Contact:** Dennis R. Hillman, publisher. Estab. 1949. Publishes hardcover and trade paperback originals and reprints. "Our mission as an evangelical Christian publisher is to provide—with integrity and excellence—trusted, Biblically based resources that challenge and encourage individuals in their Christian lives. Works in theology and Biblical studies should reflect the historic, orthodox Protestant tradition." **Publishes 90 titles/year. 20% of books from first-time authors. 35% from unagented writers. Pays royalty on wholesale price. Pays negotiable advance.** Publishes ms 16 months after acceptance. Guidelines available online.

IMPRINTS Editorial Portavoz (Spanish-language works); Kregel Academic & Professional; Kregel Kidzone.

NONFICTION "We serve evangelical Christian readers and those in career Christian service."

FICTION Subjects include religious, children's, general, inspirational, mystery/suspense, relationships, young adult. Fiction should be geared toward the evangelical Christian market. Wants books with fast-paced, contemporary storylines presenting a strong Christian message in an engaging, entertaining style.

TIPS "Our audience consists of conservative, evangelical Christians, including pastors and ministry students."

LAKE CLAREMONT PRESS

P.O. Box 711, Chicago IL 60690. (312)226-8400. **Fax:** (312)226-8420. **E-mail:** sharon@lakeclaremont.com. **Website:** www.lakeclaremont.com. **Contact:** Sharon Woodhouse, publisher. Estab. 1994. Publishes trade paperback originals. "We specialize in nonfiction books on the Chicago area and its history, particularly by authors with a passion or organizations with a mission." **Publishes 2-3 titles/year. 250 queries received/ year. 100 mss received/year. 50% of books from first-time authors. 100% from unagented writers. Pays 10-15% royalty on net sales. Pays $500-1,000 advance.** Publishes book 12-18 months after acceptance of ms. Accepts simultaneous submissions. Responds in 1 month to queries. Responds in 2 months to proposals. Responds in 2-6 months to mss. Book catalog available online.

NONFICTION Subjects include Americana, ethnic, history, nature, environment, regional, travel, women's issues, film/cinema/stage (regional)—as long as it is primarily a Chicago book. Query with SASE, or submit proposal package, including outline and 2 sample chapters, or submit complete ms (e-mail queries and proposals preferred).

TIPS "Please include a market analysis in proposals (who would buy this book and where) and an analysis of similar books available for different regions. Please know what else is out there."

WENDY LAMB BOOKS

Imprint of Random House Children's Books/Random House, Inc., 1745 Broadway, New York NY 10019. (212)782-9000. **Fax:** (212)782-9452. **E-mail:** wlamb@randomhouse.com; cmeckler@randomhouse.com. **Website:** www.randomhouse.com. Estab. 2001. Publishes hardcover originals. "Query letter with SASE for reply. A query letter should briefly describe the book you have written, the intended age group, and your brief biography and publishing credits, if any. Please send the first 10 pages (or to the end of the chapter) of your manuscript. Our turn around time is approximately 4-8 weeks." **Pays royalty.** Accepts simultaneous submissions. Guidelines for #10 SASE.

◗ Literary fiction and nonfiction for readers 8-15.

FICTION Subjects include middle grade and young adult. Recently published *When You Reach Me*, by Rebecca Stead; *Love, Aubrey*, by Suzanne LaFleur; *Eyes of the Emporer*, by Graham Salisbury; *A Brief Chapter in My Impossible Life*, by Dana Reinhardt; *What*

They Found: Love on 145th St., by Walter Dean Myers; *Eleven*, by Patricia Reilly Giff. Other WLB authors include Christopher Paul Curtis, Gary Paulsen, Donna Jo Napoli, Peter Dickinson, Marthe Jocelyn, Graham McNamee.

POETRY Submit 4 sample poems.

TIPS "Please note that we do not publish picture books. Please send the first 10 pages of your ms (or until the end of the first chapter) along with a cover letter, synopsis, and SASE. Before you submit, please take a look at some of our recent titles to get an idea of what we publish."

⟲ ⊘ LAPWING PUBLICATIONS

1 Ballysillan Dr., Belfast BT14 8HQ, Northern Ireland. +44 2890 500 796. **Fax:** +44 2890 295 800. **E-mail:** lapwing.poetry@ntlworld.com. **Website:** www.lapwingpoetry.com. **Contact:** Dennis Greig, editor. Estab. 1989. **Pays 20 author's copies, no royalties.** Responds to queries in 1 month; mss in 2 months.

◗ Lapwing will produce work only if and when resources to do so are available.

POETRY Lapwing publishes "emerging Irish poets and poets domiciled in Ireland, plus the new work of a suitable size by established Irish writers. Non-Irish poets are also published. Poets based in continental Europe have become a major feature. Emphasis on first collections preferrably not larger than 80 pages. Logistically, publishing beyond the British Isles is always difficult for 'hard copy' editions. PDF copies via e-mail are £3 or 3€ per copy. No fixed upperl limit to number of titles per year. Hard copy prices are £8 to £10 per copy. No e-reader required." Wants poetry of all kinds, but, "no crass political, racist, sexist propaganda, even of a positive or 'pc' tenor." Has published Alastair Thomson, Clifford Ireson, Colette Wittorski, Gilberte de Leger, Aubrey Malone, and Jane Shaw Holiday. Pamphlets up to 32 pages, chapbooks up to 44 pages, books 48-112 pages; New Belfast binding, simulated perfect binding for books, otherwise saddle stitching. "Submit 6 poems in the first instance; depending on these, an invitation to submit more may follow." Considers simultaneous submissions. Accepts e-mail submissions in body of message or in DOC format. Cover letter is required. "All submissions receive a first reading. If these poems have minor errors or faults, the writer is advised. If poor quality, the poems are returned. Those 'passing' first reading are retained, and a letter of conditional offer is sent." Often comments on rejected poems. "After initial publication, irrespective of the quantity, the work will be permanently available using 'print-on-demand' production; such publications will not always be printed exactly as the original, although the content will remain the same."

TIPS "At present we are unable to accept new work from beyond mainland Europe and the British Isles due to increased delivery costs."

⊘⊘ LAUREL-LEAF

Imprint of Random House Children's Books/Random House, Inc., 1745 Broadway, New York NY 10019. (212)782-9000. **Website:** www.randomhouse.com/teens.

◐ Quality reprint paperback imprint for young adult paperback books. *Does not accept unsolicited mss.*

⊕ LEDGE HILL PUBLISHING

P.O. Box 337, Alton NH 03809. **E-mail:** info@ledge-hillpublishing.com. **Website:** www.ledgehillpublishing.com. **Contact:** Amanda Eason. Estab. 2011. Publishes hardcover, trade paperback, and mass market paperback originals. **Publishes 10-15 titles/year. 20-40 queries received/year. 15-30 mss received/year. 100% of books from first-time authors. 100% from unagented writers. Pays 2-15% royalty.** Publishes ms 3 months after acceptance. Responds in 1 month to queries and proposals; 2 months to mss. Book catalog available online at website. Guidelines free on request by e-mail or online at website.

NONFICTION Subjects include agriculture, animals, anthropology, archeology, astrology, automotive, career guidance, child guidance, contemporary culture, crafts, creative nonfiction, education, entertainment, environment, ethnic, games, gardening, health, history, hobbies, horticulture, humanities, marine subjects, medicine, memoirs, nature, New Age, sex, social sciences, womens issues, womens studies, young adult. Submit proposal package including an outline, 3 sample chapters or submit complete ms. Reviews artwork. Send photocopies or compressed .jpegs.

FICTION Subjects include adventure, confession, contemporary, experimental, hi-lo, humor, juvenile, literary, mainstream, mystery, occult, picture books, poetry, regional, religious, science fiction, short story collections, spiritual, suspense, young adult. Submit proposal package, including syopsis and 4 sample chapters or submit complete ms.

POETRY Submit complete ms.

LEE & LOW BOOKS

95 Madison Ave., #1205, New York NY 10016. (212)779-4400. **E-mail:** general@leeandlow.com. **Website:** www.leeandlow.com. **Contact:** Louise May, editor-in-chief (multicultural children's fiction/nonfiction). Jennifer Fox, senior editor; Emily Hazel, assistant editor Estab. 1991. Publishes hardcover originals and trade paperback reprints. "Our goals are to meet a growing need for books that address children of color, and to present literature that all children can identify with. We only consider multicultural children's books. Currently emphasizing material for 5-12 year olds. Sponsors a yearly New Voices Award for first-time picture book authors of color. Contest rules online at website or for SASE." **Publishes 12-14 titles/year. Receives 100 queries/year; 1,200 mss/year. 20% of books from first-time authors. 50% from unagented writers. Pays net royalty. Pays authors advances against royalty. Pays illustrators advance against royalty. Photographers paid advance against royalty.** Publishes book 2 years after acceptance. Responds in 6 months to mss if interested. Book catalog available online. Guidelines available online or by written request with SASE.

NONFICTION Picture books: concept. Picture books, middle readers: biography, history, multicultural, science and sports. Average word length: picture books 1,500-3,000. Recently published *Seeds of Change*, by Jen Cullerton Johnson; *Sharing Our Homeland*, by Trish Marx. Submit complete ms. Reviews artwork/photos only if writer is also a professional illustrator or photographer. Send photocopies and nonreturnable art samples only.

FICTION Subjects include contemporary and historical fiction featuring people of color. Also accepts thematic or narrative poetry collections with a multicultural focus. Picture books, young readers: anthology, contemporary, history, multicultural, poetry. Picture book, middle reader: contemporary, history, multicultural, nature/environment, poetry, sports. Average word length: picture books—1,000-1,500 words. Recently published *Gracias~Thanks*, by Pat Mora; *Balarama*, by Ted and Betsy Lewin; *Yasmin's Hammer*, by Ann Malaspina; *Only One Year*, by Andrea Cheng (chapter book). "We do not publish folklore or animal stories." Submit complete ms.

POETRY Submit complete ms.

TIPS "Check our website to see the kinds of books we publish. Do not send mss that don't fit our mission."

LEGACY PRESS

P.O. Box 261129, San Diego CA 92196. (858)277-1167. **E-mail:** john.gregory@rainbowpublishers.com. **Website:** www.rainbowpublishers.com; www.legacy-presskids.com. Estab. 1979. Publishes 4 young readers/year; 4 middle readers/year; 4 young adult titles/year. 50% of books by first-time authors. "Our mission is to publish Bible-based, teacher resource materials that contribute to and inspire spiritual growth and development in kids ages 2-12." **For authors work purchased outright (range: $500 and up). Pays illustrators by the project (range: $300 and up). Sends galleys to authors.** Accepts simultaneous submissions. Responds to queries in 6 weeks, mss in 3 months.

NONFICTION Young readers, middle readers, young adult/teens: activity books, arts/crafts, how-to, reference, religion. Works with 25 illustrators/year. Reviews ms/illustration packages from artists. Submit ms with 2-5 pieces of final art. Illustrations only: Query with samples. Responds in 6 weeks. Samples returned with SASE; samples filed.

TIPS "Our Rainbow imprint publishes reproducible books for teachers of children in Christian ministries, including crafts, activities, games and puzzles. Our Legacy imprint publishes titles for children such as devotionals, fiction and Christian living. Please write for guidelines and study the market before submitting material."

⊕ HAL LEONARD BOOKS

Hal Leonard Publishing Group, 33 Plymouth St., Suite 302, Montclair NJ 07042. (973)337-5034. **Fax:** (973)337-5227. **Contact:** John Cerullo, publisher. Kristina Radka **Publishes 30 titles/year.**

NONFICTION Subjects include music. Query with SASE.

⊕ LES FIGUES PRESS

P.O. Box 7736, Los Angeles CA 90007. **E-mail:** info@lesfigues.com. **Website:** www.lesfigues.com. **Contact:** Teresa Carmody and Vanessa Place, co-directors. Les Figues Press is an independent, nonprofit publisher of poetry, prose, visual art, conceptual writing, and translation. With amission is to create aesthetic conversations between readers, writers, and artists, Les-Figues Press favors projects which push the boundaries of genre, form, and general acceptability. Sub-

missions are only reviewed through its annual NOS Book Contest.

⊘ LETHE PRESS

118 Heritage Ave., Maple Shade NJ 08052. (609)410-7391. **E-mail:** editor@lethepressbooks.com. **Website:** www.lethepressbooks.com. **Contact:** Steve Berman, publisher. Estab. 2001.

ARTHUR A. LEVINE BOOKS

Scholastic, Inc., 557 Broadway, New York NY 10012. (212)343-4436. **Fax:** (212)343-6143. **E-mail:** arthuralevinebooks@scholastic.com. **Website:** www.arthuralevinebooks.com. **Contact:** Arthur A. Levine, VP/publisher; Cheryl Klein, executive editor; Emily Clement, assistant editor. Estab. 1996. Publishes hardcover, paperback, and ebook editions. Imprint of Scholastic, Inc. Publishes a book 18 months after acceptance. Responds in 1 month to queries; 5 months to mss.

NONFICTION Please follow submission guidelines at www.arthuralevinebooks.com/submission.asp. Works with 8 illustrators/year. Will review ms/illustration packages from artists. Query first. Illustrations only: Send postcard sample with tearsheets. Samples not returned.

FICTION Subjects include juvenile, picture books, young adult. "Arthur A. Levine is looking for distinctive literature, for children and young adults, for whatever's extraordinary." Averages 18-20 total titles/year.

LIFE CYCLE BOOKS

P.O. Box 799, Fort Collins CO 80522. **Website:** www.lifecyclebooks.com. **Contact:** Paul Broughton, general manager. Estab. 1973. Publishes trade paperback originals and reprints, and mass market reprints. **Publishes 6 titles/year. 100+ queries received/year. 50% of books from first-time authors. 100% from unagented writers. Pays 8-10% royalty on wholesale price. Pays $250-1,000 advance.** Publishes book 1 year after acceptance. Responds in 1 month to queries, proposals, and mss. Book catalog available online.

NONFICTION Subjects include health, medicine, religion, social sciences, womens issues, womens studies. We specialize in human life issues. Query with SASE. Submit complete ms. Reviews artwork/photos.

LIGHTHOUSE POINT PRESS

100 First Ave., Suite 525, Pittsburgh PA 15222-1517. (412)323-9320. **Fax:** (412)323-9334. **E-mail:** ryearick@yearick-millea.com. **Contact:** Ralph W. Yearick,

publisher (business/career/general nonfiction). Estab. 1993. Publishes hardcover and trade paperback originals. "Lighthouse Point Press specializes in business/career nonfiction titles, and books that help readers improve their quality of life. We do not re-publish self-published books." **Pays 5-10% royalty on retail price.** Responds in 6 months to queries.

NONFICTION Subjects include business, economics. "We are open to all types of submissions related to general nonfiction, but most interested in business/career manuscripts." Submit proposal package, outline, 1-2 sample chapters and bio. Complete ms preferred.

TIPS "When submitting a manuscript or proposal, please tell us what you see as the target market/audience for the book. Also, be very specific about what you are willing to do to promote the book."

LILLENAS PUBLISHING CO.

Imprint of Lillenas Drama Resources, P.O. Box 419527, Kansas City MO 64109. (816)931-1900. **Fax:** (816)412-8390. **E-mail:** drama@lillenas.com. **Website:** www.lillenasdrama.com. Publishes mass market paperback and electronic originals. "We purchase only original, previously unpublished materials. Also, we require that all scripts be performed at least once before it is submitted for consideration. We do not accept scripts that are sent via fax or e-mail. Direct all manuscripts to the Drama Resources Editor." **Publishes 50+ titles/year. Pays royalty on net price. Makes outright purchase.** Responds in 4-6 months to material. See guidelines online at website.

NONFICTION Subjects include religion, life issues. No musicals. Query with SASE. Submit complete ms.

FICTION "Looking for sketch and monologue collections for all ages – adults, children and youth. For these collections, we request 12 - 15 scripts to be submitted at one time. Unique treatments of spiritual themes, relevant issues and biblical messages are of interest. Contemporary full-length and one-act plays that have conflict, characterization, and a spiritual context that is neither a sermon nor an apologetic for youth and adults. We also need wholesome so-called secular full-length scripts for dinner theatres and schools." No musicals.

TIPS "We never receive too many manuscripts."

LINDEN PUBLISHING, INC.

2006 S. Mary, Fresno CA 93721. (559)233-6633. **Fax:** (559)233-6933. **E-mail:** richard@lindenpub.com. **Website:** www.lindenpub.com. **Contact:** Richard Sor-

sky, president; Kent Sorsky, vice president. Estab. 1976. Publishes trade paperback originals; hardcover and trade paperback reprints. **Publishes 10-12 titles/year. 30+ queries received/year. 5-15 mss received/year. 40% of books from first-time authors. 50% from unagented writers. Pays 7½ -12% royalty on wholesale price. Pays $500-6,000 advance.** Publishes ms 18 months after acceptance. Responds in 1 month to queries and proposals. Book catalog available online. Guidelines available via e-mail.

NONFICTION Subjects include history, regional, hobbies, woodworking, Regional California history. Submit proposal package, outline, 3 sample chapters, bio. Reviews artwork/photos. Send electronic files, if available.

✪ R.C. LINNELL PUBLISHING

2100 Tyler Ln., Louisville KY 40205. **E-mail:** info@LinnellPublishing.com. **Website:** www.linnellpublishing.com. **Contact:** Cheri Powell, owner. Estab. 2010. Publishes print on demand paperbacks. "We are currently very small and have published a limited number of books. We would review books on other subjects on a case-by-case basis. If a book is well-written and has an audience we would consider it." **Publishes 3 titles/year. 5 queries received/year. 5 mss received/year. 83% of books from first-time authors. 100% from unagented writers. Pays 10-40% royalty on retail price.** Publishes ms 3 months after acceptance. Accepts simultaneous submissions. Responds in 1 month to mss. Book catalog and guidelines available online at website.

NONFICTION Subjects include alternative lifestyles, Americana, astrology, career guidance, contemporary culture, cooking, counseling, creative nonfiction, ethnic, foods, language, literature, memoirs, multicultural, New Age, philosophy, psychic, psychology, regional, religion, sociology, spirituality, translation, travel, womens issues, womens studies, young adult. Submit complete ms.

FICTION Subjects include adventure, confession, contemporary, experimental, fantasy, feminist, gay, gothic, hi-lo, historical, humor, lesbian, literary, mainstream, multicultural, mystery, occult, regional, religious, romance, science fiction, short story collections, spiritual, suspense, translation, western, young adult. Submit complete ms.

TIPS "Visit our web site to understand the business model and the relationship with authors. All sales are through the internet. Author should have a marketing plan in mind. We can help expand the plan but we do not market books. Author should be comfortable with using the internet and should know their intended readers. We offer translation services for English to Spanish and Spanish to English. We are especially interested in books that inspire, motivate, amuse and challenge readers."

LIQUID SILVER BOOKS

10509 Sedgegrass Dr., Indianapolis IN 46235. **E-mail:** tracey@liquidsilverbooks.com. **Website:** www.liquidsilverbooks.com. **Contact:** Tracey West, acquisitions editor; Terri Schaefer, editorial director. Estab. 1999. Liquid Silver Books is an imprint of Atlantic Bridge Publishing, a royalty paying, full-service ePublisher. Atlantic Bridge has been in business since June 1999. Liquid Silver Books is dedicated to bringing high quality erotic romance to our readers. Liquid Silver Books, Romance's Silver Lining. Publishes ms 4-5 months after acceptance. Accepts simultaneous submissions. Responds to mss in 4-6 weeks.

> "We are foremost an ePublisher. We believe the market will continue to grow for eBooks. It is our prime focus. At this time our print publishing is on hiatus. We will update the submission guidelines if we reinstate this aspect of our publishing."

FICTION Needs contemporary, gay and lesbian, paranormal, supernatural, sci-fi, fantasy, historical, suspense, and western romances. We do not accept literary Erotica submissions. E-mail entire ms as an attachment in .RTF format in Arial 12pt. "Include in the body of the email: author bio, your thoughts on ePublishing, a blurb of your book, including title and series title if applicable. Ms must include Pen name, real name, snail mail and email contact information on the first page, top left corner." More writer's guidelines available online at website.

Ⓐ LITTLE, BROWN AND CO. ADULT TRADE BOOKS

237 Park Ave., New York NY 10017. **E-mail:** publicity@littlebrown.com. **Website:** www.hachettebookgroup.com. **Contact:** Michael Pietsch, publisher. Estab. 1837. Publishes hardcover originals and paperback originals and reprints. "The general editorial philosophy for all divisions continues to be broad and flexible, with high quality and the promise of commercial success as always the first considerations."

Publishes 100 titles/year. Pays royalty. Offer advance. Guidelines available online.

FICTION Literary, mainstream/contemporary. *Agented submissions only.*

Ⓐ LITTLE, BROWN AND CO. BOOKS FOR YOUNG READERS

Hachette Book Group USA, 237 Park Ave., New York NY 10017. (212)364-1100. **Fax:** (212)364-0925. **E-mail:** pamela.gruber@hbgusa.com. **Website:** www.lb-kids.com; www.lb-teens.com. Estab. 1837. "Little, Brown and Co. Children's Publishing publishes all formats including board books, picture books, middle grade fiction, and nonfiction YA titles. We are looking for strong writing and presentation, but no predetermined topics." *Only interested in solicited agented material.* Fiction: Submit complete ms. Nonfiction: Submit cover letter, previous publications, a proposal, outline and 3 sample chapters. Do not send originals. **Publishes 100-150 titles/year. Pays authors royalties based on retail price. Pays illustrators and photographers by the project or royalty based on retail price. Sends galleys to authors; dummies to illustrators. Pays negotiable advance.** Publishes ms 2 years after acceptance. Accepts simultaneous submissions. Responds in 1 month to queries; 2 months to proposals and mss.

NONFICTION Subjects include animals, art, architecture, ethnic, gay, lesbian, history, hobbies, nature, environment, recreation, science, sports. Writers should avoid looking for the 'issue' they think publishers want to see, choosing instead topics they know best and are most enthusiastic about/inspired by. Middle readers, young adults: arts/crafts, history, multicultural, nature, self help, social issues, sports, science. Average word length: middle readers—15,000-25,000; young adults—20,000-40,000. Recently published *American Dreaming*, by Laban Carrick Hill; *Exploratopia*, by the Exploratorium; *Yeah! Yeah! Yeah!: The Beatles, Beatlemania, and the Music that Changed the World*, by Bob Spitz. *Agented submissions only.*

FICTION Subjects include adventure, fantasy, feminist, gay, lesbian, historical, humor, mystery, science fiction, suspense, chick lit, multicultural. Picture books: humor, adventure, animal, contemporary, history, multicultural, folktales. Young adults: contemporary, humor, multicultural, suspense/mystery, chick lit. Multicultural needs include "any material by, for and about minorities." Average word length: picture books—1,000; young readers—6,000; middle readers—15,000- 50,000; young adults—50,000 and up. *Agented submissions only.*

TIPS "In order to break into the field, authors and illustrators should research their competition and try to come up with something outstandingly different."

LITTLE TIGER PRESS

1 The Coda Centre, 189 Munster Rd., London En SW6 6AW, United Kingdom. 44)20-7385 6333. **E-mail:** info@littletiger.co.uk; malperin@littletiger.co.uk. **Website:** www.littletigerpress.com.

FICTION Picture books: animal, concept, contemporary, humor. Average word length: picture books—750 words or less. Recently published *Gruff the Grump*, by Steve Smallman and Cee Biscoe (ages 3-7, picture book); *One Special Day*, by M. Christina Butler and Tina Macnaughton (ages 3-7, touch-and-feel, picture book).

TIPS "Every reasonable care is taken of the manuscripts and samples we receive, but we cannot accept responsibility for any loss or damage. Try to read or look at as many books on the Little Tiger Press list before sending in your material. Refer to our website www.littletigerpress.com for further details."

LLEWELLYN PUBLICATIONS

Imprint of Llewellyn Worldwide, Ltd., 2143 Wooddale Dr., Woodbury MN 55125. (651)291-1970. **Fax:** (651)291-1908. **E-mail:** Publicity@llewellyn.com. **Website:** www.llewellyn.com. Estab. 1901. Publishes trade and mass market paperback originals. "Llewellyn publishes New Age fiction and nonfiction exploring new worlds of mind and spirit. Currently emphasizing astrology, alternative health and healing, tarot. De-emphasizing fiction, channeling." **Publishes 100+ titles/year. 30% of books from first-time authors. 50% from unagented writers. Pays 10% royalty on wholesale or retail price.** Accepts simultaneous submissions. Responds in 3 months to queries. Book catalog for 9 x 12 SAE with 4 first-class stamps.

NONFICTION Subjects include cooking, foods, nutrition, health, medicine, nature, environment, New Age, psychology, women's issues, women's studies. Submit outline, sample chapters. Reviews artwork/photos.

LOOSE ID

P.O. Box 425690, San Francisco CA 94142-5960. **E-mail:** submissions@loose-id.com. **Website:** www.

loose-id.com. **Contact:** Treva Harte, editor-in-chief. Estab. 2004. "*Loose Id* is love unleashed. We're taking romance to the edge." Publishes e-books and some print books. Distributes/promotes titles. "The company promotes itself through web and print advertising wherever readers of erotic romance may be found, creating a recognizable brand identity as the place to let your id run free and the people who unleash your fantasies. It is currently pursuing licensing agreements for foreign translations, and has a print program of 2 to 5 titles per month." **Pays e-book royalties of 35%.** Publishes ms 1 year after acceptance. Responds to queries in 1 month. Guidelines available online at website.

◯   "Loose Id is actively acquiring stories from both aspiring and established authors."

FICTION Wants nontraditional erotic romance stories, including gay, lesbian, heroes and heroines, multi-culturalism, cross-genre, fantasy, and science fiction, straight contemporary or historical romances. Query with outline/synopsis and three sample chapters. Accepts queries by e-mail. Include estimated word count, list of publishing credits, and why your submission is "Love Unleashed. Before submitting a query or proposal, please read the guidelines on our website. Please don't hesitate to contact us at submissions@loose-id.com for any information you don't see there."

LOST HORSE PRESS

105 Lost Horse Lane, Sandpoint ID 83864. (208)255-4410. **E-mail:** losthorsepress@mindspring.com. **Website:** www.losthorsepress.org. **Contact:** Christine Holbert, publisher; Carolyne Wright, editor; Christi Kramer, editor. Estab. 1998. Publishes hardcover and paperback originals. Distributed by University of Washington Press. **Publishes 8-10 titles/year.** Publishes ms 6-12 months after acceptance.

◯   "*Does not accept unsolicited mss.* However, we welcome submissions for the *Idaho Prize for Poetry*, a national competition offering $1,000 prize money plus publication for a book-length manuscript. Please check the submission guidelines for the *Idaho Prize for Poetry* online."

FICTION Subjects include literary, poetry, regional, Pacific Northwest, short story collections.

LOUISIANA STATE UNIVERSITY PRESS

3990 W. Lakeshore Dr., Baton Rouge LA 70808. (225)578-6294. **Fax:** (225)578-6461. **E-mail:** mkc@lsu.edu. **Website:** www.lsupress.org. **Contact:** MK Callaway, director. John Easterly, excecutive editor (poetry, fiction, literary studies); Rand Dotson, senior editor (U.S. History & Southern Studies). Estab. 1935. Publishes hardcover and paperback originals, and reprints. Publishes 8 poetry titles per year and 2 works of original fiction as part of the Yellow Shoe Fiction series. Publishes in the fall and spring. **Publishes 80-90 titles/year. 33% of books from first-time authors. 95% from unagented writers. Pays royalty.** Publishes ms 1 year after acceptance. Responds in 1 month to queries. Book catalog and ms guidelines free and online.

NONFICTION Subjects include Americana, animals, anthropology, archeology, art, architecture, ethnic, government, politics, history, language, literature, literary criticism, memoirs, military, war, Civil & WWII, music, dance, Southern, Jazz, nature, environment, philosophy, Political, photography, regional, sociology, women's issues, women's studies, world affairs, geography and environmental studies. "We publish general interest books about Louisiana and the South, Atlantic and European and World History. Prizes are regularly awarded to LSU Press authors for the excellence of their general body of work. All books must undergo a rigorous approval process." Query with SASE. Submit proposal package, outline, sample chapters, cover letter, resume. *No unsolicited submissions by email attachment.*

FICTION Query with SASE. Submit proposal package, sample chapters, resume, clips, and cover letter.

POETRY A highly respected publisher of collections by poets such as Claudia Emerson, David Kirby, Brendan Galvin, Fred Chappell, Marilyn Nelson, and Henry Taylor. Publisher of the Southern Messenger Poets series edited by Dave Smith. No unsolicited poetry mss. for the foreseeable future. We have filled our slots until 2014."

⊘ LOVING HEALING PRESS INC.

5145 Pontiac Trail, Ann Arbor MI 48105. (888)761-6268. **Fax:** (734)663-6861. **E-mail:** info@lovinghealing.com. **Website:** www.lovinghealing.com. **Contact:** Victor R. Volkman, senior editor (psychology, self-help, personal growth, trauma recovery). Estab. 2003. Publishes hardcover and trade paperback originals and reprints. **Publishes 20 titles/year. Receives 200 queries/year; 100 mss/year. 50% of books from first-time authors. 80% from unagented writers. Pays 6-12% royalty on retail price.** Publishes book 10 months after acceptance. Accepts simultaneous submissions. Responds in 1 month on queries and proposals, 2 months on mss. Catalog available online at website. Guidelines online at website.

◯ *Currently not accepting mss.*

NONFICTION Subjects include child guidance, health, memoirs, psychology, social work. We are primarily interested in self-help books which are person-centered and non-judgmental. Submit proposal package, including: outline, 3 sample chapters; submit complete ms. Reviews artwork/photos as part of the ms package; send JPEG files.

FICTION Subjects include multicultural, social change. Submit complete ms.

LRP PUBLICATIONS, INC.

360 Hiatt Dr., Palm Beach Gardens FL 33418. **E-mail:** dshadovitz@lrp.com. **Website:** www.lrp.com. Estab. 1977. Publishes hardcover and trade paperback originals. **Pays royalty.** Book catalog available free. Guidelines available free.

◯ "LRP publishes two industry-leading magazines, *Human Resource Executive®* and *Risk & Insurance®*, as well as hundreds of newsletters, books, videos and case reporters in the fields of: human resources, federal employment, workers' compensation, public employment law, disability, bankruptcy, education administration and law."

NONFICTION Subjects include business, economics, education. Submit proposal package, outline.

⊘ LUCENT BOOKS

Attn: Publisher - Lucent Books, 27500 Drake Rd., Farmington Hills MI 48331. **E-mail:** betz.deschenes@cengage.com. **Website:** www.gale.com/lucent. **Contact:** Betz Des Chenes. Estab. 1988. Lucent Books is a nontrade publisher of nonfiction for the middle school audience providing students with resource material for academic studies and for independent learning.

NONFICTION Potential writers should familiarize themselves with the material. All are works for hire, by assignment only. *No unsolicited mss.* E-mail query with cover letter, résumé and list of publications.

⊕ LUCKY MARBLE BOOKS

PageSpring Publishing, P.O. Box 21133, Columbus OH 43221 **E-mail:** yaeditor@pagespringpublishing.com. **Website:** www.luckymarblebooks.com. Estab. 2012. Publishes trade paperback and electronic originals. "Lucky Marble Books publishes novel-length young adult and middle grade fiction. We are looking for engaging characters and well-crafted plots that keep our readers turning the page. We accept e-mail queries only; see our website for details." **Pays royalty.** Publishes ms 6-9 months after acceptance. Accepts simultaneous submissions. Responds in 1 month to queries and mss. Guidelines available on website.

IMPRINTS Imprint of PageSpring Publishing

NONFICTION Does not accept nonfiction.

FICTION Subjects include adventure, contemporary, fantasy, feminist, historical, humor, juvenile, literary, mainstream, multicultural, mystery, regional, romance, science fiction, sports, suspense, young adult. Submit proposal package via e-mail. Include synopsis and 3 sample chapters.

TIPS "We love books that jump right into the story and sweep us along!"

⊘ LUNA BISONTE PRODS

137 Leland Ave., Columbus OH 43214-7505. **E-mail:** bennett.23@osu.edu. **Website:** www.johnmbennett.net. **Contact:** John M. Bennett, editor/publisher. Estab. 1967.

POETRY "Interested in avant-garde and highly experimental work only." Has published poetry by Jim Leftwich, Sheila E. Murphy, Al Ackerman, Richard Kostelanetz, Carla Bertola, Olchar Lindsann, and many others. Query first, with a few sample poems and cover letter with brief bio and publication credits. "Keep it brief. Chapbook publishing usually depends on grants or other subsidies, and is usually by solicitation. **Will also consider subsidy arrangements on negotiable terms.**" A sampling of various Luna Bisonte Prods products is available for $20.

THE LYONS PRESS

The Globe Pequot Press, Inc., Box 480, 246 Goose Ln., Guilford CT 06437. (203)458-4500. **Fax:** (203)458-4668. **E-mail:** info@globepequot.com. **Website:** www.lyonspress.com. Estab. 1984 (Lyons & Burford), 1997 (The Lyons Press). Publishes hardcover and trade paperback originals and reprints. The Lyons Press publishes practical and literary books, chiefly centered on outdoor subjects—natural history, all sports, gardening, horses, fishing, hunting, survival, self-reliant living, plus cooking, memoir, bio, nonfiction. **Pays $3,000-25,000 advance.** Accepts simultaneous submissions. Responds in 4 months to queries, proposals and tmss. Book catalog available online. Guidelines available online.

◗ The Lyons Press has teamed up to develop books with The Explorers Club, Orvis, L.L. Bean, *Field & Stream*, Outward Bound, Buckmasters, and *Golf Magazine*.

NONFICTION Subjects include agriculture, Americana, animals, art & reference, cooking, foods & wine, nutrition, history, military, war, nature, environment, recreation, sports, adventure, fitness, the sea, woodworking. Visit our website and note the featured categories. Query with SASE. Submit proposal package, outline, 3 sample chapters. marketing description. Reviews artwork/photos. Send photocopies and non-original prints.

MACMILLAN

Macmillan, 175 Fifth Ave., New York NY 10010. **Website:** us.macmillan.com/. **Agented submissions only.**

♡ MAGENTA PUBLISHING FOR THE ARTS

151 Winchester St., Toronto ON M4X 1B5, Canada. **E-mail:** info@magentafoundation.org. **Website:** www.magentafoundation.org. **Contact:** Submissions. Estab. 2004. "The Magenta Foundation is Canada's pioneering non-profit arts publishing house. Magenta was created to organize promotional opportunities for Canadian artists in the international arts community through circulated exhibitions and publications. Projects mounted by Magenta are supported by credible international media coverage and critical reviews in all mainstream media formats (radio, television and print).

MAGINATION PRESS

750 First St., NE, Washington DC 20002. (202)336-5618. **Fax:** (202)336-5624. **E-mail:** rteeter@apa.org. **Website:** www.apa.org. **Contact:** Kristine Enderle, managing editor. Estab. 1988. Magination Press is an imprint of the American Psychological Association. "We publish books dealing with the psycho/therapeutic resolution of children's problems and psychological issues with a strong self-help component." Submit complete ms. Materials returned only with SASE. **Publishes 12 titles/year. 75% of books from first-time authors.** Publishes a book 18-24 months

after acceptance. Accepts simultaneous submissions. Responds to queries in 1-2 months; mss in 2-6 months.

NONFICTION All levels: psychological and social issues, self-help, health, multicultural, special needs.

FICTION All levels: psychological and social issues, self-help, health, parenting concerns and, special needs. Picture books, middle school readers.

MAGNUS PRESS

1647 Shire Ave., Oceanside CA 92057. **E-mail:** magnuspres@aol.com. **Website:** www.magnuspress. com. **Contact:** Warren Angel, editorial director. Estab. 1997. Publishes trade paperback originals and reprints. **Publishes 1-3 titles/year. 120 queries received/year. 75 mss received/year. 44% of books from first-time authors. 89% from unagented writers. Pays 6-15% royalty on retail price.** Publishes ms 1 year after acceptance. Accepts simultaneous submissions. Responds in 1 month to queries, proposals and mss. Book catalog and ms guidelines for #10 SASE.

IMPRINTS Canticle Books.

NONFICTION Subjects include religion, from a Christian perspective. "Writers must be well-grounded in Biblical knowledge and must be able to communicate effectively with the lay person." Submit proposal package, outline, sample chapters, bio.

TIPS "Magnus Press's audience is mainly Christian lay persons, but also includes anyone interested in spirituality and/or Biblical studies and the church. Study our listings and catalog; learn to write effectively for an average reader; read any one of our published books."

MAIN ST. RAG PUBLISHING COMPANY

P.O. Box 690100, Charlotte NC 28227. (704)573-2516. **E-mail:** editor@mainSt.rag.com. **Website:** www. mainSt.rag.com. **Contact:** M. Scott Douglass, publisher, editor. Estab. 1996. "There are 4 ways to get a book of poetry published: 1) self-publish using our imprint; 2) Enter one of our contests; 3) Be invited; 4) Be recommended." Responds in 3-6 weeks to queries.

Main St. Rag (our poetry label); Mint Hill Books (fiction label); Pure Heart Press (self-publishing label).

NONFICTION Subjects include art (mostly photographs, prefer images of people in action), creative nonfiction, photography, interview, reviews, essays. "Pissing off politicians, corporations, zealots, and/or lawyers is acceptable and encouraged." Nothing derogatory on the basis of race, gender, sexual orientation, or religious persuasion. Query with SASE. Reviews artwork/photos.

FICTION Subjects include literary, poetry, cartoons, short fiction. "See Current themes online. Address to Short Fiction Anthology for consideration for our anthology. We are not open to unsolicited submissions of full-length mss. of short fiction." Query with SASE. Submit 2 short stories.

POETRY "We are interested in any style, subject, with emphasis on edgier materials, and we enjoy humor. We prefer work alive with the poet's own experiences. We don't want much formal poetry, but will consider it if formal poems maintain the integrity of the form without becoming stiff, uninteresting, or losing their vitality. Poems of 40 lines or less are more acceptable. Submit 6 pages per submission, 1 typed page per 8.5 X 11 page. We are not interested in the graphic details of your love life. We are least likely to accept garden poetry, poetry about poems or Greek & Roman mythology." Query.

TIPS "You can request a free electronic newsletter which is a reference for writers, readers and publishers by providing limited information and directing them to links and emails. Current features include: Call for Submissions; Contests; and New Releases. (No email submissions unless overseas, reviews, images, subscribers to *The MainSt. Rag*.) In all cases, query prior to submitting for instructions."

MANAGEMENT ADVISORY PUBLICATIONS

P.O. Box 81151, Wellesley Hills MA 02481. (781)235-2895. **Fax:** (781)235-5446. **E-mail:** info@masp.com. **Website:** www.masp.com. **Contact:** Jay Kuong, editor (corporate governance, compliance, security, audit, IT, business continuity). Estab. 1972. Publishes mass market paperback originals. Trade books on corporate and IT governance, risk management, compliance, security, auditing and contingency planning and business continuity publications. **Publishes 2-10 titles/year. Receives 25 queries/year; 10 mss/year. 5% of books from first-time authors. Pays 5-10% royalty on wholesale price.** Publishes book 6 months after acceptance. Responds in 4 months on queries. Catalog not available. Guidelines not available.

NONFICTION Subjects include business, computers, economics, electronics. Submit proposal package.

TIPS "Our audience is primarily business and IT professionals and University and Company libraries."

MANDALA PUBLISHING

Mandala Publishing and Earth Aware Editions, 10 Paul Dr., San Rafael CA 94903. **E-mail:** info@mandalapublishing.com. **Website:** www.mandalapublishing.com. Estab. 1989. Publishes hardcover, trade paperback, and electronic originals. "In the traditions of the East, wisdom, truth, and beauty go hand in- hand. This is reflected in the great arts, music, yoga, and philosophy of India. Mandala Publishing strives to bring to its readers authentic and accessible renderings of thousands of years of wisdom and philosophy from this unique culture-timeless treasures that are our inspirations and guides. At Mandala, we believe that the arts, health, ecology, and spirituality of the great Vedic traditions are as relevant today as they were in sacred India thousands of years ago. As a distinguished publisher in the world of Vedic literature, lifestyle, and interests today, Mandala strives to provide accessible and meaningful works for the modern reader." **Publishes 12 titles/year. 200 queries received/year. 100 mss received/year, 40% of books from first-time authors. 100% from unagented writers. Pays 3-15% royalty on retail price.** Publishes ms 8 months after acceptance. Accepts simultaneous submissions. Responds in 6 months to queries, proposals, and mss. Book catalog available online.

NONFICTION Subjects include alternative, cooking, foods, nutrition, education, health, medicine, philosophy, photography, religion, spirituality. Query with SASE. Reviews artwork/photos. Send photocopies and thumbnails.

FICTION Subjects include juvenile, religious, spiritual. Query with SASE.

○ MANOR HOUSE PUBLISHING, INC.

452 Cottingham Crescent, Ancaster ON L9G 3V6, Canada. **E-mail:** mbdavie@manor-house.biz. **Website:** www.manor-house.biz. **Contact:** Mike Davie, president (novels, poetry, and nonfiction). Estab. 1998. Publishes hardcover, trade paperback, and mass market paperback originals reprints. **Publishes 5-6 titles/year. 30 queries received/year; 20 mss received/year. 90% of books from first-time authors. 90% from unagented writers. Pays 10% royalty on retail price.** Publishes book 1 year after acceptance. Accepts simultaneous submissions. Queries and mss to be sent by e-mail only. "We will respond in 30 days if interested-if not, there is no response. Do not follow up

unless asked to do so.". Book catalog available online. Guidelines available via e-mail.

NONFICTION Subjects include alternative, anthropology, business, community, history, sex, social sciences, sociology, spirituality. "We are a Canadian publisher, so mss should be Canadian in content and aimed as much as possible at a wide, general audience. At this point in time, we are only publishing books by Canadian citizens residing in Canada." Query via e-mail. Submit proposal package, outline, bio, 3 sample chapters. Submit complete ms. Reviews artwork/photos. Send photocopies.

FICTION Subjects include adventure, experimental, gothic, historical, horror, humor, juvenile, literary, mystery, occult, poetry, regional, romance, short story collections, young adult. Stories should have Canadian settings and characters should be Canadian, but content should have universal appeal to wide audience. Query via e-mail. Submit proposal package, clips, bio, 3 sample chapters. Submit complete ms.

POETRY Poetry should engage, provoke, involve the reader.

TIPS "Our audience includes everyone-the general public/mass audience. Self-edit your work first, make sure it is well written with strong Canadian content."

◉ MANTRA LINGUA

Global House, 303 Ballards Ln., London N12 8NP, United Kingdom. (44)(208)445 5123. **E-mail:** jean@mantralingua.com. **Website:** www.mantralingua.com.

Mantra Lingua publishes dual-language books in English and more that 42 languages. They also publish talking books and resources with their Talking Pen technology, which brings sound and interactivity to their products. They will consider good contemporary stories, myths and folklore for picture books only.

FICTION Picture books, young readers, middle readers: folktales, multicultural stories, myths. Average word length: picture books—1,000-1,500; young readers—1,000-1,500. Submit outline/synopsis (250 words) via postal mail. Incluse SASE for returns.

MARINE TECHNIQUES PUBLISHING

126 Western Ave., Suite 266, Augusta ME 04330. (207)622-7984. **E-mail:** info@marinetechpublishing.com. **Website:** www.marinetechpublishing.com. **Contact:** James L. Pelletier, president/owner(commercial maritime); Maritime Associates

Globally (commercial maritime). Estab. 1983. Trade paperback originals and reprints. "Publishes only books related to the commercial marine/maritime industry." **Publishes 2-5 titles/year. 20+ queries received/year. 40+ mss received/year. 50% of books from first-time authors. 75% from unagented writers. Pays 25-55% royalty on wholesale or retail price. Makes outright purchase.** Publishes ms 1 year after acceptance. Accepts simultaneous submissions. Responds in 2 months to queries, proposals, and mss. Book catalog available online, by e-mail, and for #10 SASE for $5. Guidelines available by e-mail, and for #10 SASE for $5.

NONFICTION Subjects include maritime education, marine subjects, counseling, career guidance, maritime labor, marine engineering, global water transportation, marine subjects, water transportation. "We are concerned with 'maritime related works' and not recreational boating, but rather commercial maritime industries, such as deep-sea water transportation, offshore oil & gas, inland towing, coastal tug boat, 'water transportation industries.'" Submit proposal package, including all sample chapters; submit completed ms. Reviews artwork/photos as part of the ms package; send photocopies.

FICTION Subjects include adventure, military, war, maritime. Must be commercial maritime/marine related. Submit proposal package, including all sample chapters. Submit complete ms.

TIPS "Audience consists of commercial marine/maritime firms, persons employed in all aspects of the marine/maritime commercial water-transportation-related industries and recreational fresh and salt water fields, persons interested in seeking employment in the commercial marine industry; firms seeking to sell their products and services to vessel owners, operators, and managers; shipyards, vessel repair yards, recreational and yacht boat building and national and international ports and terminals involved with the commercial marine industry globally worldwide, etc."

⊘ MARLOR PRESS, INC.

4304 Brigadoon Dr., St. Paul MN 55126. (651)484-4600. **E-mail:** marlin.marlor@minn.net. **Contact:** Marlin Bree, publisher. Estab. 1981. Publishes trade paperback originals. "Currently emphasizing general interest nonfiction children's books and nonfiction boating books." **Publishes 2 titles/year. 200 queries received/year. 25 mss received/year. 100% of books from first-time authors. Pays 8-10% royalty on wholesale price.** Publishes ms 1 year after acceptance. Responds in 3-6 weeks to queries.

NONFICTION Subjects include travel, boating. Primarily how-to stuff. *No unsolicited mss.* No anecdotal reminiscences or biographical materials. No fiction or poetry. Query first; submit outline with sample chapters only when requested. Do not send full ms. Reviews artwork/photos.

MARTIN SISTERS PUBLISHING, LLC

P.O. Box 1749, Barbourville KY 40906-1499. **E-mail:** publisher@martinsisterspublishing.com. **Website:** www.martinsisterspublishing.com. **Contact:** Denise Melton, Publisher/Editor (Fiction/nonfiction); Melissa Newman, Publisher/Editor (Fiction/nonfiction). Estab. 2011. Firm/imprint publishes trade and mass market paperback originals; electronic originals. **Publishes 12 titles/year. 75% of books from first-time authors. 100% from unagented writers. Pays 7.5% royalty/max on retail price. No advance offered.** Publishes book Time between acceptance of ms and publication is 6 months. after acceptance of ms. Accepts simultaneous submissions. Responds in 1 month on queries, 2 months on proposals, 3-6 months on mss. Catalog and guidelines available online.

IMPRINTS Ivy House Books — literary/mainstream fiction; rainshower books — christian fiction and nonfiction; Skyvine Books — science fiction/fantasy/paranormal; romance; Martin Sisters Books — nonfiction/short story collections/coffee table books/cookbooks; Barefoot Books — young adult. Query Ms. Newman or Ms. Melton for all imprints listed at submissions@martinsisterspublishing.com.

NONFICTION Subjects include Americana, child guidance, contemporary culture, cooking, creative nonfiction, education, gardening, history, house and home, humanities, labor, language, law, literature, memoirs, money, nutrition, parenting, psychology, regional, sociology, spirituality, womens issues, womens studies, western. Send query letter only to submissions@martinsisterspublishing.com Does not review artwork.

FICTION Subjects include adventure, confession, fantasy, historical, humor, juvenile, literary, mainstream, military, mystery, poetry in translation, regional, religious, romance, science fiction, short story collections, spiritual, sports, suspense, war, western, young adult.

🌑 MASKEW MILLER LONGMAN

Subsidiary of Pearson Education and Caxton Publishers, P.O. Box 396, Cape Town 8000, South Africa. (27) (21)531-8103. **E-mail:** mmlwCape@mml.co.za. **Website:** www.mml.co.za. "The Maskew Miller Longman Group has over 100 years of publishing experience in southern Africa, with staff and offices in countries throughout southern, central and east Africa. As partners to government in the educational arena, we develop local materials for local needs. We are one of the leading educational publishers in Africa. We tap into global expertise: whether it be in education, technology or customer services, we benefit from being part of Pearson Education, which is the largest educational publisher in the world and which produces the best and most up-to-date learning material available. We publish in more than 50 languages, including all of South Africa's official languages as well as French, Portuguese, and numerous African languages in each of the countries in which we operate. Publishes teacher references and dictionaries for educational markets. Interested in all genres (poetry/novels/short stories/plays) of African language literature, as well as material for the Young Africa and They Fought for Freedom series in English."

NONFICTION Subjects include education, literature, young adult.

MASTER BOOKS

P.O. Box 726, Green Forest AR 72638. (870)438-5288. **Fax:** (870)438-5120. **E-mail:** nlp@newleafpress.net; amanda@newleafpress.net, **Website:** www.masterbooks.net. **Contact:** Craig Forman, acquisitions editor. Estab. 1975. Publishes 3 middle readers/year; 2 young adult nonfiction titles/year; 15 adult trade books/year. **10% of books from first-time authors. Pays authors royalty of 3-15% based on wholesale price.** Publishes book 1 year after acceptance. Responds to queries and mss in 4 months. Book catalog available upon request. Guidelines available on website.

NONFICTION Picture books: activity books, animal, nature/environment, creation. Young readers, middle readers, young adults: activity books, animal, biography Christian, nature/environment, science, creation. Recently published *Passport to the World* (middle readers); *The Earth* (science book); *Demolishing Supposed Bible Contradictions*, compiled by Ken Ham (adult series). Submission guidelines on website.

TIPS "All of our children's books are creation-based, including topics from the Book of Genesis. We look also for home school educational material that would be supplementary to a home school curriculum."

MAUPIN HOUSE PUBLISHING, INC.

1710 Roe Crest Dr., N. Mankato MN 56003. **E-mail:** info@maupinhouse.com. **Website:** www.maupinhouse.com. **Contact:** Julie Graddy, publisher (areas of interest: education, professional development). Publishes trade paperback originals and reprints. "Maupin House publishes professional resource books for language arts teachers K-12." **Publishes 6-8 titles/year. 60% of books from first-time authors. 100% from unagented writers. Pays 10% royalty on retail price.** Publishes ms 18 months after acceptance. Accepts simultaneous submissions. Responds in less than 1 month to queries, proposals, and mss. Catalog and guidelines free on request and available online at website and by email at: publisher@maupinhouse.com.

NONFICTION Subjects include education, language arts, literacy and the arts, reading comprehension, writing workshop. "Study the website to understand our publishing preferences. Successful authors are all teachers or former teachers." Query with SASE or via e-mail. Submit proposal package, including outline, 1-2 sample chapters, and TOC/marketing ideas. Reviews artwork/photos as part of the mss package. Writers should send photocopies, digital.

TIPS "Our audience is K-12 educators, teachers. Be familiar with our publishing areas and tell us why your book idea is better/different than what is out there. How do you plan to promote it? Successful authors help promote books via speaking engagements, conferences, etc."

⊕ MAVEN HOUSE PRESS

316 W. Bernard St., West Chester PA 19382. (610)883-7988. **Fax:** (888)894-3403. **E-mail:** info@mavenhousepress.com. **Website:** www.mavenhousepress.com. **Contact:** Jim Pennypacker, publisher. Estab. 2012. Publishes hardcover, trade paperback, and electronic originals. Maven House Press publishes business books for executives and managers to help them lead their organizations to greatness. **Publishes 6 titles/year. Pays 10-50% royalty based on wholesale price.** Publishes ms 9 months after acceptance. Accepts simultaneous submissions. Responds in 1 month.

NONFICTION Subjects include business, economics, Business/management. Submit proposal package including: outline, 1-2 sample chapters. See submission form online at website.

⊘ MAVERICK DUCK PRESS

NJ **E-mail:** maverickduckpress@yahoo.com. **Website:** www.maverickduckpress.com. **Contact:** Kendall A. Bell, editor. Estab. 2005. Maverick Duck Press is a "publisher of chapbooks from undiscovered talent. We are looking for fresh and powerful work that shows a sense of innovation or a new take on passion or emotion. Previous publication in print or online journals could increase your chances of us accepting your manuscript." Does not want "unedited work." **Pays 20 author's copies (out of a press run of 50).**
POETRY Send ms in Microsoft Word format with a cover letter with brief bio and publication credits. Chapbook mss may include previously published poems. "Previous publication is always a plus, as we may be more familiar with your work. Chapbook mss should have 16-24 poems, but no more than 24 poems."

◐ MAVERICK MUSICALS AND PLAYS

89 Bergann Rd., Maleny QLD 4552, Australia. Phone/**Fax:** (61)(7)5494-4007. **E-mail:** helen@mavmuse.com. **Website:** www.mavmuse.com. Estab. 1978. Guidelines available online.
FICTION Subjects include plays and musicals. "Looking for two-act musicals and one- and two-act plays. See website for more details."

⊘ MCBOOKS PRESS

ID Booth Building, 520 N. Meadow St., Ithaca NY 14850. (607)272-2114. **Fax:** (607)273-6068. **E-mail:** mcbooks@mcbooks.com. **Website:** www.mcbooks.com. **Contact:** Alexander G. Skutt, publisher. Estab. 1979. Publishes trade paperback and hardcover originals and reprints. **Publishes 5 titles/year.** Accepts simultaneous submissions. Guidelines available online.
◐ "Currently not accepting submissions or queries for fiction or nonfiction."
FICTION Publishes Julian Stockwin, John Biggins, Colin Sargent, and Douglas W. Jacobson. Distributes titles through Independent Publishers Group.
TIPS "We are currently only publishing authors with whom we have a pre-existing relationship. If this policy changes, we will announce the change on our website."

THE MCDONALD & WOODWARD PUBLISHING CO.

431 E. College St., Granville OH 43023. (740)321-1140. **Fax:** (740)321-1141. **E-mail:** mwpubco@mwpubco.com. **Website:** www.mwpubco.com. **Contact:** Jerry N. McDonald, publisher. Estab. 1986. Publishes hardcover and trade paperback originals. McDonald & Woodward publishes books in natural history, cultural history, and natural resources. Currently emphasizing travel, natural and cultural history, and natural resource conservation. **Publishes 5 titles/year. 25 queries received/year. 20 mss received/year. Pays 10% royalty.** Accepts simultaneous submissions. Responds in less than 1 month to queries, proposals & mss. Book catalog available online. Guidelines free on request; by e-mail.
NONFICTION Subjects include animals, architecture, environment, history, nature, science, travel, natural history. Query with SASE. Reviews artwork/photos. Photos are not required.
FICTION Subjects include historical. Query with SASE.
TIPS Our books are meant for the curious and educated elements of the general population.

⊘ MARGARET K. MCELDERRY BOOKS

Imprint of Simon & Schuster Children's Publishing Division, Simon & Schuster, 1230 Sixth Ave., New York NY 10020. (212)698-7200. **Website:** www.simonsayskids.com. **Contact:** Justin Chanda, vice president; Karen Wojtyla, editorial director; Gretchen Hirsch, associate editor; Emily Fabre, assistant editor. Ann Bobco, executive art director. Estab. 1971. "Margaret K. McElderry Books publishes hardcover and paperback trade books for children from pre-school age through young adult. This list includes picture books, middle grade and teen fiction, poetry, and fantasy. The style and subject matter of the books we publish is almost unlimited. We do not publish textbooks, coloring and activity books, greeting cards, magazines, pamphlets, or religious publications." **Publishes 30 titles/year. 15% of books from first-time authors. 50% from unagented writers. Pays authors royalty based on retail price. Pays illustrator royalty of by the project. Pays photographers by the project. Original artwork returned at job's completion. Offers $5,000-8,000 advance for new authors.** Guidelines for #10 SASE.

NONFICTION Subjects include history, adventure. Looks for originality of ideas, clarity and felicity of expression, well-organized plot and strong characterization (fiction) or clear exposition (nonfiction); quality. Accept query letters with SASE only for picture books; query letter with first 3 chapters, SASE for middle grades and young adult novels. *No unsolicited mss.*

FICTION Subjects include adventure, fantasy, historical, mainstream, contemporary, mystery, picture books, young adult, or middle grade, All categories (fiction and nonfiction) for juvenile and young adult. We will consider any category. Results depend on the quality of the imagination, the artwork, and the writing. Average word length: picture books—500; young readers—2,000; middle readers—10,000-20,000; young adults—45,000 50,000. Recently Published: *Monster Mess*, by Margery Cuyler, illustrated by S. D. Schindler (picture book); *The Joy of Spooking: Fiendish Deeds*, by P. J. Bracegirdle (MGF); *Identical*, by Ellen Hopkins (teen); *Where is Home, Little Pip?*, by Karma Wilson, illustrated by Jane Chapman (picture book); *Dr. Ted*, by Andrea Beaty, illustrated by Pascal LeMaitre (picture book); *To Be Mona*, by Kelly Easton (teen). *No unsolicited mss.* Send query letter with SASE.

POETRY *No unsolicited mss.* Query and submit 3 sample poems.

TIPS "Read! The children's book field is competitive. See what's been done and what's out there before submitting. We look for high quality: an originality of ideas, clarity and felicity of expression, a well organized plot, and strong character-driven stories. We're looking for strong, original fiction, especially mysteries and middle grade humor. We are always interested in picture books for the youngest age reader. Study our titles."

MCFARLAND & CO., INC., PUBLISHERS

Box 611, Jefferson NC 28640. (336)246-4460. **Fax:** (336)246-5018. **E-mail:** info@mcfarlandpub.com. **Website:** www.mcfarlandpub.com. **Contact:** Steve Wilson, editorial director (automotive, general); David Alff, editor (general); Gary Mitchem, acquisitions editor (general, baseball). Estab. 1979. Publishes hardcover and quality paperback originals; a nontrade publisher. "McFarland publishes serious nonfiction in a variety of fields, including general reference, performing arts, popular culture, sports (particularly baseball); women's studies, librarianship, literature, Civil War, history and international studies. Currently emphasizing medieval history, automotive history. De-emphasizing memoirs." **Publishes 350 titles/year. 50% of books from first-time authors. 95% from unagented writers.** Publishes book 10 months after acceptance. Responds in 1 month to queries. Guidelines available online.

NONFICTION Subjects include art, architecture, automotive, health, medicine, history, military, war/war, popular contemporary culture, music, dance, recreation, sociology, world affairs, sports (very strong), African-American studies (very strong). Reference books are particularly wanted—fresh material (i.e., not in head-to-head competition with an established title). We prefer manuscripts of 250 or more double-spaced pages or at least 75,000 words. No fiction, New Age, exposes, poetry, children's books, devotional/inspirational works, Bible studies, or personal essays. Query with SASE. Submit outline, sample chapters. Reviews artwork/photos.

TIPS "We want well-organized knowledge of an area in which there is not information coverage at present, plus reliability so we don't feel we have to check absolutely everything. Our market is worldwide and libraries are an important part. McFarland also publishes six journals: the *Journal of Information Ethics, North Korean Review, Base Ball: A Journal of the Early GameBlack Ball: A Negro Leagues Journal, Clues: A Journal of Detection*, and *Minerva Journal of Women and War*."

MC PRESS

3695 W. Quail Heights Ct., Boise ID 83703. **Fax:** (208)639-1231. **E-mail:** duptmor@mcpressonline.com. **Website:** www.mcpressonline.com. **Contact:** David Uptmor, publisher. Estab. 2001. Publishes trade paperback originals. **Publishes 40 titles/year. 100 queries received/year. 50 mss received/year. 5% of books from first-time authors. 5% from unagented writers. Pays 10-16% royalty on wholesale price.** Publishes book 5 months after acceptance. Accepts simultaneous submissions. Responds in 1 month to queries/proposals/mss. Book catalog and ms guidelines free.

IMPRINTS MC Press, IBM Press.

NONFICTION Subjects include computers, electronics. "We specialize in computer titles targeted at IBM technologies." Submit proposal package, outline, 2 sample chapters, abstract. Reviews artwork/photos. Send photocopies.

ME & MI PUBLISHING

English-Spanish Foundation, 2600 Beverly Dr., Unit 113, Aurora IL 60502. **Fax:** (630)588-9804. **Website:** www.memima.com. **Contact:** Mark Wesley, acquisition editor (pre-K-1). Estab. 2001. Publishes hardcover originals. **Publishes 10 titles/year. 30 queries received/year. 30 mss received/year. 30% of books from first-time authors. 70% from unagented writers. Pays 5% royalty on wholesale price. Makes outright purchase of $1,000-3,000.** Publishes ms 1 year after acceptance. Accepts simultaneous submissions. Responds in 1 month to queries; 3 months to proposals; 4 months to mss. Book catalog available online. Guidelines available via e-mail.

NONFICTION Subjects include ethnic, language, literature, multicultural. Submit complete ms. Reviews artwork/photos. Send photocopies.

TIPS "Our audience is pre-K to 2nd grade. Our books are bilingual (Spanish and English)."

MEDALLION MEDIA GROUP

100 S. River St., Aurora IL 60506. (630)513-8316. **E-mail:** emily@medallionpress.com. **E-mail:** submissions@medallionpress.com. **Website:** medallionmediagroup.com. **Contact:** Emily Steele, editorial director. Estab. 2003. Publishes trade paperback, hardcover, e-book originals, book apps, and TREEbook™. "We are an independent, innovative publisher looking for compelling, memorable stories told in distinctive voices." Online submission form: medallionmediagroup.com/submissions. **Offers advance.** Publishes ms 1-2 years after acceptance. Responds in 2-3 months to mss. Guidelines available online at website.

NONFICTION Subjects include art, health, design, fitness. *Agented only.* Please query.

FICTION Subjects include fantasy, historical, horror, literary, mainstream, mystery, romance, science fiction, suspense, young adult, thriller, Christian, YA-YA (YA written by young adults). Minimum word count: 60,000. (40,000 for YA-YA). No short stories, anthologies, erotica. Submit first 3 consecutive chapters and a synopsis through our online submission form, medallionmediagroup.com/submissions.

TIPS "We are not affected by trends. We are simply looking for well-crafted, original, compelling works of fiction and nonfiction. Please visit our website at medallionmediagroup.com/submissions/ for the most current guidelines prior to submitting anything to us."

MEDICAL GROUP MANAGEMENT ASSOCIATION

104 Inverness Terrace E., Englewood CO 80112. (303)799-1111. **E-mail:** support@mgma.com; connexion@mgma.com. **Website:** www.mgma.com. Estab. 1926. Publishes professional and scholarly hardcover, paperback, and electronic originals, and trade paperback reprints. **Publishes 6 titles/year. 18 queries received/year. 6 mss received/year. 30% of books from first-time authors. 100% from unagented writers. Pays 8-17% royalty on net sales (twice a year). Pays $2,000-5,000 advance.** Publishes ms 6 months after acceptance. Accepts simultaneous submissions. Responds in less than 3 weeks to queries; months to proposals and mss. Book catalog available online. Writer's guidelines online or via e-mail.

NONFICTION Subjects include audio, business, economics, education, health. Submit proposal package, outline, 3 sample chapters. Submit complete ms. Reviews artwork/photos. Send photocopies.

TIPS Audience includes medical practice managers and executives. Our books are geared at the business side of medicine.

MERIWETHER PUBLISHING LTD.

885 Elkton Dr., Colorado Springs CO 80907. (719)594-9916. **Fax:** (719)594-4422. **E-mail:** editor@meriwether.com. **Website:** www.meriwether.com. **Contact:** Ted Zapel; Rhonda Wray. Estab. 1969. "Our niche is drama. Our books cover a wide variety of theatre subjects from play anthologies to theatrecraft. We publish books of monologs, duologs, short one-act plays, scenes for students, acting textbooks, how-to speech and theatre textbooks, improvisation and theatre games. We also publish anthologies of Christian sketches. We do not publish works of fiction or devotionals." **75% of books from first-time authors. Pays authors royalty of 10% based on retail or wholesale price.** Publishes book 6-12 months after acceptance. Accepts simultaneous submissions. Responds to queries in 3 weeks, mss in 2 months or less.

NONFICTION Middle readers: activity books, how-to, religion, textbooks. Young adults: activity books, drama/theater arts, how-to church activities, religion. Average length: 250 pages.

FICTION Middle readers, young adults: anthology, contemporary, humor, religion. "We publish plays, not prose-fiction. Our emphasis is comedy plays instead of educational themes."

TIPS "We are currently interested in finding unique treatments for theater arts subjects: scene books, how-to books, musical comedy scripts, monologs and short comedy plays for teens."

MERRIAM PRESS

133 Elm St., Suite 3R, Bennington VT 05201. (802)447-0313. **E-mail:** ray@merriam-press.com. **Website:** www.merriam-press.com. Estab. 1988. Publishes hardcover and softcover trade paperback originals and reprints. "Merriam Press specializes in military history - particularly World War II history. We are also branching out into other genres." **Publishes 20+ titles/year. 70-90% of books from first-time authors. 100% from unagented writers. Pays 10% royalty on actual selling price.** Publishes ms 6 months or less after acceptance. Responds quickly (e-mail preferred) to queries. Book catalog available for $5 or visit website to view all available titles and access writer's guidelines and info.

NONFICTION Especially but not limited to: military, war, World War II. Query with SASE or by e-mail first. Send copies of sample chapters or entire ms by mail or on disk/flash drive or as an e-mail attachment (preferred in Word .doc/.docx file format). Reviews artwork/photos.

FICTION Especially but not limited to military, war, World War II. Query with SASE or by e-mail first.

TIPS "Our military history books are geared for military historians, collectors, model kit builders, wargamers, veterans, general enthusiasts. We now publish some historical fiction and poetry and will consider well-written books on a variety of non-military topics."

MESSIANIC JEWISH PUBLISHERS

6120 Day Long Lane, Clarksville MD 21029. (410)531-6644. **E-mail:** website@messianicjewish.net. **Website:** www.messianicjewish.net. **Contact:** Janet Chaier, managing editor. Publishes hardcover and trade paperback originals and reprints. **Publishes 6-12 titles/year. Pays 7-15% royalty on wholesale price.** Guidelines available via e-mail.

IMPRINTS Lederer Books.

NONFICTION Subjects include religion, Messianic Judaism, Jewish roots of the Christian faith. Text must demonstrate keen awareness of Jewish culture

and thought, and Biblical literacy. Jewish themes only. Query with SASE. Unsolicited mss are not returned.

FICTION Subjects include religious. "We publish very little fiction. Jewish or Biblical themes are a must. Text must demonstrate keen awareness of Jewish culture and thought." Query with SASE. Unsolicited mss are not return

METROPOLITAN BOOKS

Henry Holt & Co., 175 Fifth Ave., New York NY 10010. **Website:** us.macmillan.com/metropolitan.aspx. **Agented submissions only.**

⊘ MIAMI UNIVERSITY PRESS

356 Bachelor Hall, Miami University, Oxford OH 45056. **E-mail:** tumakw@muohio.edu. **Website:** www.muohio.edu/mupress. **Contact:** Keith Tuma, editor; Dana Leonard, managing editor. Estab. 1992. Publishes 1-2 books of poetry/year and one novella, in paperback editions.

POETRY Miami University Press is unable to respond to unsolicited mss and queries.

MICHIGAN STATE UNIVERSITY PRESS

1405 S. Harrison Rd., Suite 25, East Lansing MI 48823-5202. (517)355-9543. **Fax:** (517)432-2611. **E-mail:** msupress@msu.edu. **Website:** msupress.msu.edu/. **Contact:** Martha Bates and Julie Loehr, acquisitions. Estab. 1947. Publishes hardcover and softcover originals. **Pays variable royalty.** Book catalog and ms guidelines for 9×12 SASE or online.

Michigan State University Press has notably represented both scholarly publishing and the mission of Michigan State University with the publication of numerous award-winning books and scholarly journals. In addition, they publish nonfiction that addresses, in a more contemporary way, social concerns, such as diversity and civil rights. They also publish literary fiction and poetry.

NONFICTION Subjects include Nonfiction Americana, American Studies, business, economics, creative nonfiction, ethnic, Afro-American studies, government, politics, history, contemporary civil rights, language, literature, literary criticism, regional, Great Lakes regional, Canadian studies, women's studies, environmental studies, and American Indian Studies. Distributes books for: University of Calgary Press, University of Alberta Press, and University of Manitoba Press. Submit proposal/outline and sample chapter. Hard copy is preferred but email proposals are also accepted. Initial submissions to MSU Press should be in the form of a short letter of inquiry and a sample chapter(s), as well as our preliminary Marketing Questionnaire, which can be downloaded from their website. We do not accept: Festschrifts, conference papers, or unrevised dissertations. (Festschrift: A complimentary or memorial publication usually in the form of a collection of essays, addresses, or biographical, bibliographic, scientific, of other contributions). Reviews artwork/photos.

MICROSOFT PRESS

E-mail: 4bkideas@microsoft.com. **Website:** www.microsoft.com/learning/en/us/microsoft-press-books.aspx. **Publishes 80 titles/year. 25% of books from first-time authors. 90% from unagented writers.** Book proposal guidelines available online.

NONFICTION Subjects include software. A book proposal should consist of the following information: a table of contents, a resumè with author biography, a writing sample, and a questionnaire. "We place a great deal of emphasis on your proposal. A proposal provides us with a basis for evaluating the idea of the book and how fully your book fulfills its purpose."

MILKWEED EDITIONS

1011 Washington Ave. S., Suite 300, Minneapolis MN 55415. (612)332-3192. **Fax:** (612)215-2550. **E-mail:** submissions@milkweed.org. **Website:** www.milkweed.org. Estab. 1979. Publishes hardcover, trade paperback, and electronic originals; trade paperback and electronic reprints. "Milkweed Editions publishes with the intention of making a humane impact on society, in the belief that literature is a transformative art uniquely able to convey the essential experiences of the human heart and spirit. To that end, Milkweed Editions publishes distinctive voices of literary merit in handsomely designed, visually dynamic books, exploring the ethical, cultural, and esthetic issues that free societies need continually to address." **Publishes 15-20 titles/year. 25% of books from first-time authors. 75% from unagented writers. Pays authors variable royalty based on retail price. Offers advance against royalties. Pays varied advance from $500-10,000.** Publishes book in 18 months. after acceptance of ms. Accepts simultaneous submissions. Responds in 6 months to queries, proposals, and mss. Book catalog available online. Guidelines available online.

NONFICTION Subjects include agriculture, animals, archaeology, art, contemporary culture, creative nonfiction, environment, gardening, gay, government, history, humanities, language, literature, multicultural, nature, politics, literary, regional, translation, women's issues, world affairs. Does not review artwork.

FICTION Subjects include experimental, short story collections, translation, young adult. Novels for adults and for readers 8-13. High literary quality. For adult readers: literary fiction, nonfiction, poetry, essays. Middle readers: adventure, contemporary, fantasy, multicultural, nature/environment, suspense/mystery. Does not want to see folktales, health, hi-lo, picture books, poetry, religion, romance, sports. Average length: middle readers—90-200 pages. No romance, mysteries, science fiction. Query with SASE, submit completed ms.

POETRY Query with SASE; submit completed ms

TIPS "We are looking for excellent writing with the intent of making a humane impact on society. Please read submission guidelines before submitting and acquaint yourself with our books in terms of style and quality before submitting. Many factors influence our selection process, so don't get discouraged. Nonfiction is focused on literary writing about the natural world, including living well in urban environments."

MILKWEEDS FOR YOUNG READERS

Milkweed Editions, Open Book Building, 1011 Washington Ave. S., Suite 300, Minneapolis MN 55415. (612)332-3192. **Fax:** (612)215-2550. **E-mail:** submissions@milkweed.org. **Website:** www.milkweed.org. Estab. 1984. Publishes hardcover and trade paperback originals. "We are looking first of all for high quality literary writing. We publish books with the intention of making a humane impact on society." **Publishes 3-4 titles/year. 25% of books from first-time authors. 50% from unagented writers. Pays 7% royalty on retail price. Pays variable advance.** Publishes ms 1 year after acceptance. Accepts simultaneous submissions. Responds in 6 months to queries. Book catalog for $1.50. Guidelines for #10 SASE or on the website.

FICTION Subjects include adventure, fantasy, historical, humor, mainstream, contemporary, animal, environmental. Query with SASE. "Milkweed Editions now accepts manuscripts online through ourSubmission Manager. If you're a first-time submitter, you'll need to fill in a simple form and then follow the instructions for selecting and uploading your manuscript. Please make sure that your manuscript follows the submission guidelines."

THE MILLBROOK PRESS

Lerner Publishing Group, 1251 Washington Ave N, Minneapolis MN 55401. **Website:** www.lernerbooks.com. **Contact:** Carol Hinz, editorial director. "Millbrook Press publishes informative picture books, illustrated nonfiction titles, and inspiring photo-driven titles for grades K–5. Our authors approach curricular topics with a fresh point of view. Our fact-filled books engage readers with fun yet accessible writing, high-quality photographs, and a wide variety of illustration styles. We cover subjects ranging from the parts of speech and other language arts skills; to history, science, and math; to art, sports, crafts, and other interests. Millbrook Press is the home of the best-selling Words Are CATegorical® series and Bob Raczka's Art Adventures."

"We do not accept unsolicited manuscripts from authors. Occasionally, we may put out a call for submissions, which will be announced on our website."

MINNESOTA HISTORICAL SOCIETY PRESS

Minnesota Historical Society, 345 Kellogg Blvd. W., St. Paul MN 55102-1906. (651)259-3200. **Fax:** (651)297-1345. **Website:** shop.mnhs.org. **Contact:** Ann Regan, editor-in-chief. Estab. 1852. Publishes hardcover, trade paperback and electronic originals; trade paperback and electronic reprints. "Minnesota Historical Society Press publishes both scholarly and general interest books that contribute to the understanding of the Midwest." **Publishes 30 titles/year. 300 queries received/year. 150 mss received/year. 60% of books from first-time authors. 95% from unagented writers. Royalties are negotiated; 5-10% on wholesale price. Pays $1,000 and up.** Publishes book 16 months after acceptance of ms. Accepts simultaneous submissions. Responds in 1 month to queries, 2 months on proposals, 2-4 months on mss. Book catalog online and available free. Guidelines available online and are free.

IMPRINTS Borealis Books, Minnesota Historical Society Press; Ann Regan, editor-in-chief.

NONFICTION Subjects include scholarly, Americana, anthropology, archaeology, art, architecture, community, cooking, foods, nutrition, creative nonfiction, ethnic, government, politics, history, memoirs, multicultural, nature, environment, photography, regional, women's issues, women's studies, Native American studies. Books must have a connection to the Midwest. Regional works only. Submit proposal package, outline, 1 sample chapter and other materials listed in our online website in author guidelines: CV, brief description, intended audience, readership, length of ms, schedule. Reviews artwork/photos. Send photocopies.

MITCHELL LANE PUBLISHERS INC.

P.O. Box 196, Hockessin DE 19707. (302)234-9426. **Fax:** (866)834-4164. **E-mail:** barbaramitchell@mitchelllane.com. **Website:** www.mitchelllane.com. **Contact:** Barbara Mitchell, publisher. Estab. 1993. Publishes hardcover and library bound originals. **Publishes 80 titles/year. 100 queries received/year. 5 mss received/year. 0% of books from first-time authors. 90% from unagented writers. Work purchased outright from authors (range: $350-2,000). Pays illustrators by the project (range: $40-400).** Publishes ms 1 year after acceptance. Responds only if interested to queries. Book catalog available free.

NONFICTION Subjects include ethnic, multicultural. Young readers, middle readers, young adults: biography, nonfiction, and curriculum-related subjects. Average word length: 4,000-50,000 words. Recently published Katy Perry and Prince William (both Blue Banner Biographies); Justin Bieber (A Robbie Reader); Earth Science Projects for Kids series; Your Land and My Land: Middle East series; and World Crafts and Recipes series. Query with SASE. *All unsolicited mss discarded.*

TIPS "We hire writers on a 'work-for-hire' basis to complete book projects we assign. Send résumé and writing samples that do not need to be returned."

MODERN PUBLISHING

155 E. 55th St., New York NY 10022. (212)826-0850. **Fax:** (212)759-9069. **Website:** www.modernpublishing.com. "Modern Publishing is a privately owned mass-market children's book publisher specializing in coloring and activity books, hardcover and paperback picture storybooks, puzzle and crossword collections, educational workbooks, board books, beginning readers, novelty and holiday books and other genres in various trim sizes and formats. Our titles feature both time-tested favorites and the hottest new licensed characters; generic characters; and characters from our Honey Bear imprint. Our titles

are geared for children from infancy through ten years of age. Modern Publishing's history spans 40 years offering the highest quality book products at unbeatable prices. Our distribution includes chain drug stores, mass market, trade outlets, educational and specialty stores in the U.S. and Canada, including book clubs and fairs, for all of the 250+ titles we publish yearly. We also offer full creative services to develop and print proprietary book products and premium promotional items."

○ "Modern Publishing is currently focusing on licensed properties and coloring and activity books. We are no longer considering submissions that don't fall within those categories."

MOMENTUM BOOKS, LLC

117 W. Third St., Royal Oak MI 48067. (248)691-1800. **Fax:** (248)691-4531. **E-mail:** info@momentumbooks. com. **Website:** www.momentumbooks.com. **Contact:** Franklin Foxx, editor. Estab. 1987. Momentum Books publishes Midwest regional nonfiction. **Publishes 6 titles/year. 100 queries received/year; 30 mss received/year. 95% of books from first-time authors. 100% from unagented writers. Pays 10-15% royalty.** Guidelines available online.

NONFICTION Needs history, sports, travel, automotive, current events, biography, entertainment. Submit proposal package, outline, 3 sample chapters, marketing outline.

TIPS Also, custom publishing services are available for authors who are considering self-publishing.

MONDIAL

203 W. 107th St., Suite 6C, New York NY 10025. (212)851-3252. **Fax:** (208)361-2863. **E-mail:** contact@ mondialbooks.com. **Website:** www.mondialbooks. com; www.librejo.com. **Contact:** Andrew Moore, editor. Estab. 1996. Publishes trade paperback originals and reprints. **Publishes 20 titles/year. 2,000 queries received/year. 500 mss received/year. 20% of books from first-time authors. Pays 10% royalty on wholesale price.** Publishes ms 4 months after acceptance. Accepts simultaneous submissions. Responds to queries in 3 months. Guidelines available online.

NONFICTION Subjects include alternative, ethnic, gay, lesbian, history, language, literature, literary criticism, memoirs, multicultural, philosophy, psychology, sex, sociology, translation. Submit proposal package, outline, 1 sample chapters. Send only electronically by e-mail.

FICTION Subjects include adventure, erotica, ethnic, gay, lesbian, historical, literary, mainstream, contemporary, multicultural, mystery, poetry, romance, short story collections, translation. Query through online submission form.

MOODY PUBLISHERS

Moody Bible Institute, 820 N. LaSalle Blvd., Chicago IL 60610. (800)678-8812. **Fax:** (312)329-4157. **E-mail:** authors@moody.edu. **Website:** www.moodypublishers.org. Estab. 1894. Publishes hardcover, trade, and mass market paperback originals. "The mission of Moody Publishers is to educate and edify the Christian and to evangelize the non-Christian by ethically publishing conservative, evangelical Christian literature and other media for all ages around the world, and to help provide resources for Moody Bible Institute in its training of future Christian leaders." **Publishes 60 titles/year. 1,500 queries received/year. 2,000 mss received/year. 1% of books from first-time authors. 80% from unagented writers. Royalty varies.** Publishes book 1 year after acceptance. Responds in 2-3 months to queries. Book catalog for 9×12 envelope and 4 first-class stamps. Guidelines for SASE and on website.

IMPRINTS Northfield Publishing; Lift Every Voice (African American-interest).

NONFICTION Subjects include child guidance, money, finance, religion, spirituality, women's issues, women's studies. We are no longer reviewing queries or unsolicited manuscripts unless they come to us through an agent. Unsolicited proposals will be returned only if proper postage is included. We are not able to acknowledge the receipt of your unsolicited proposal. Does not accept unsolicited nonfiction submissions.

FICTION Subjects include fantasy, historical, mystery, religious, children's religious, inspirational, religious mystery/suspense, science fiction, young adult, adventure, fantasy/science fiction, historical, mystery/suspense, series. Submit query letter, bio, one-page description of book, word count, table of contents, two chapters fully written, marketing information and SASE. "Mss should be neatly typed, double-spaced, on white letter-size typing paper. Grammar, style and punctuation should follow normal English usage. We use The Chicago Manual of Style (University of Chicago Press) for fine points."

TIPS "In our fiction list, we're looking for Christian storytellers rather than teachers trying to present a message. Your motivation should be to delight the reader. Using your skills to create beautiful works is glorifying to God."

MOON TIDE PRESS

P.O. Box 50184, Irvine CA 92619. **E-mail:** publisher@moontidepress.com. **Website:** www.moontidepress.com. **Contact:** Michael Miller, publisher. Estab. 2006. **POETRY** Query first.

TIPS "Keep in mind that when we open and read your ms, it will probably be in the middle of a large stack of other submissions, and many of those will be well-meaning but undistinguished collections about the same few themes. So don't be afraid to take risks. Surprise and entertain us. Give us something that the next ten poets in the stack won't."

☮ MOOSE ENTERPRISE BOOK & THEATRE PLAY PUBLISHING

684 Walls Rd., Sault Ste. Marie ON P6A 5K6, Canada. (705) 779-3331. **Fax:** (705) 779-3331. **E-mail:** mooseenterprises@on.aibn.com. **Website:** www.moosehidebooks.com. **Contact:** Edmond Alcid. Estab. 1996. Editorial philosophy: "To assist the new writers of moral standards." **Pays royalties.** Publishes book 1 year after acceptance. Responds to queries in 1 month; mss in 3 months. Ms guidelines available for SASE.

🎧 This publisher does not offer payment for stories published in its anthologies and/or book collections. Be sure to send a SASE for guidelines.

NONFICTION Middle readers, young adults: biography, history, multicultural. Query.

FICTION Middle readers, young adults: adventure, fantasy, humor, suspense/mystery, story poetry. Query.

TIPS "Do not copy trends; be yourself—give me something new, something different."

MOREHOUSE PUBLISHING CO.

Church Publishing Incorporated, 4475 Linglestown Rd., Harrisburg PA 17112. **Fax:** (717)541-8136. **E-mail:** dperkins@cpg.org. **Website:** www.morehousepublishing.org. **Contact:** Davis Perkins. Estab. 1884. Publishes hardcover and paperback originals. Morehouse Publishing publishes mainline Christian books, primarily Episcopal/Anglican works. Currently emphasizing Christian spiritual direction. **Publishes 35 titles/year. 50% of books from first-time authors.**

Pays small advance. Publishes book 18 months after acceptance. Accepts simultaneous submissions. Responds in 2-3 months to queries. Guidelines available online.

NONFICTION Subjects include religion, Christian, women's issues, women's studies, Christian spirituality, liturgies, congregational resources, issues around Christian life. Submit outline, résumé, 1-2 sample chapters, market analysis.

MOTORBOOKS

Quayside Publishing Group, Motorbooks, MBI Publishing Company, 400 First Ave. North, Suite 300, Minneapolis MN 55401. (612)344-8100. **Fax:** (612)344-8691. **E-mail:** dholmstrom@quaysidepub.com. **Website:** www.motorbooks.com. **Contact:** Lee Klancher, senior editor; Darwin Holmstrom (motorcycles); Peter Bodensteiner (racing, how-to); Dennis Pernu (Americana, trains & boats); Steve Gansen (military, aviation, tractors). Estab. 1973. Publishes hardcover and paperback originals. "Motorbooks is one of the world's leading transportation publishers, covering subjects from classic motorcycles to heavy equipment to today's latest automotive technology. We satisfy our customers' high expectations by hiring top writers and photographers and presenting their work in handsomely designed books that work hard in the shop and look good on the coffee table." **Publishes 200 titles/year. 300 queries received/year. 50 mss received/year. 95% from unagented writers. Pays $5,000 average advance.** Publishes ms 1 year after acceptance. Accepts simultaneous submissions. Responds in 6-8 months to proposals. Book catalog available free. Guidelines for #10 SASE or online.

IMPRINTS Motorbooks International, Crestline.

NONFICTION Subjects include Americana, history, hobbies, military, war, photography, translation, nonfiction. State qualifications for doing book. Transportation-related subjects. Query with SASE. Reviews artwork/photos. Send photocopies.

MOTORCYCLING

Imprint of Far Horizons Media Company, P.O. Box 560989, Rockledge FL 32956. (321)690-2224. **Fax:** (321)690-0853. **E-mail:** postmaster@farhorizonsmedia.com. **Website:** www.farhorizonsmedia.com. Publishes trade paperback originals and limited hardback. **Publishes 15-25 titles/year. 100 queries received/year. 50 mss received/year. 50% of books from first-time authors. 99% from unagented writers.** Publishes ms 3 months after acceptance. Responds in 1 month to queries. Guidelines available by e-mail.

O   Motorcycling publishes books on motorcycling and motorcycling history.

NONFICTION "General interest relating to touring, guide books, how-to subjects, and motorcycling history. We are interested in any title related to these fields. Query with a list of ideas. Include phone number. Our title plans rarely extend past 6 months, although we know the type and quantity of books we will publish over the next 2 years. We prefer good knowledge with simple-to-understand writing style containing a well-rounded vocabulary." Query with SASE. Reviews artwork/photos. Send photocopies and JPEG files on CD.

TIPS "All of our staff and editors are riders. As such, we publish what we would want to read relating to the subject. Our audience in general are active riders at the beginner and intermediate level of repair knowledge and riding skills, and history buffs wanting to learn more about the history of motorcycles in this country. Many are people new to motorcycles, attempting to learn all they can before starting out on that first long ride or even buying their first bike. Keep it easy and simple to follow. Use motorcycle jargon sparingly. Do not use complicated technical jargon, terms, or formulas without a detailed explanation of the same. Use experienced riders and mechanics as a resource for knowledge."

MOUNTAIN PRESS PUBLISHING CO.

P.O. Box 2399, Missoula MT 59806. (406)728-1900 or (800)234-5308. **Fax:** (406)728-1635. **E-mail:** info@mtnpress.com. **Website:** www.mountain-press.com. **Contact:** Jennifer Carey, editor. Estab. 1948. Publishes hardcover and trade paperback originals. "We are expanding our Roadside Geology, Geology Underfoot, and Roadside History series (done on a state-by-state basis). We are interested in well-written regional field guides—plants and flowers—and readable history and natural history." **Publishes 15 titles/year. 50% of books from first-time authors. 90% from unagented writers. Pays 7-12% royalty on wholesale price.** Publishes ms 2 years after acceptance. Responds in 3 months to queries. Book catalog available online.

O   Expanding children's/juvenile nonfiction titles.

NONFICTION Subjects include animals, history, Western, nature, environment, regional, science, Earth science. No personal histories or journals, poetry or fiction. Query with SASE. Submit outline, sample chapters. Reviews artwork/photos.

TIPS "Find out what kind of books a publisher is interested in and tailor your writing to them; research markets and target your audience. Research other books on the same subjects. Make yours different. Don't present your manuscript to a publisher—sell it. Give the information needed to make a decision on a title. Please learn what we publish before sending your proposal. We are a 'niche' publisher."

Ø MOVING PARTS PRESS

10699 Empire Grade, Santa Cruz CA 95060. (831)427-2271. **E-mail:** frice@movingpartspress.com. **Website:** www.movingpartspress.com. **Contact:** Felicia Rice, poetry editor. Estab. 1977. Moving Part Press publishes handsome, innovative books, broadsides, and prints that "explore the relationship of word and image, typography and the visual arts, the fine arts and popular culture."

POETRY Does not accept unsolicited mss.

MSI PRESS

1760-F Airline Hwy, #203, Hollister CA 95023. **E-mail:** editor@msipress.com. **Website:** www.msipress.com. **Contact:** Betty Leaver, managing editor (foreign language, humanities, humor, spirituality). Estab. 2003. Publishes trade paperback originals. **Publishes 8-12 titles/year. 10% of books from first-time authors. 100% from unagented writers. Pays 10% royalty on wholesale price.** Publishes ms 6 months after acceptance. Accepts simultaneous submissions. Responds in 1 month to queries and proposals; 2 months to mss. Catalog available online at website. Guidelines available by e-mail: info@msipress.com.

NONFICTION Subjects include education, health, humanities, language, medicine, psychology, spirituality. "We are hoping to expand our spirituality, psychology, and self-help line." Submit proposal package, including: outline, 1 sample chapter, and professional résumè. Prefers electronic submissions. Reviews artwork/photos; send computer disk, or, preferably, e-file.

FICTION "We have no current plans to publish any more fiction."

TIPS "We are interested in helping to develop new writers who have good literacy skills. We also have the capacity to work with authors with limited English skills whose first language is Arabic, Russian, Spanish, French, German, or Czech."

Ⓐ MVP BOOKS

MBI Publishing and Quayside Publishing Group, 400 First Ave. N, Suite 300, Minneapolis MN 55401. (612)344-8160. **E-mail:** jleventhal@mbipublishing.com. **Website:** www.mvpbooks.com. **Contact:** Josh Leventhal, publisher. Estab. 2009. Publishes hardcover and trade paperback originals. "We publish books for enthusiasts in a wide variety of sports, recreation, and fitness subjects, including heavily illustrated celebrations, narrative works, and how-to instructional guides." **Publishes 15-20 titles/year. Pays royalty or fees. Pays advance.** Publishes ms 1 year after acceptance. Responds in 3 months to queries.

○ "We seek authors who are strongly committed to helping us promote and sell their books. Please present as focused an idea as possible in a brief submission. Note your credentials for writing the book. Tell all you know about the market niche, existing competition, and marketing possibilities for proposed book."

NONFICTION Subjects include sports (baseball, football, basketball, hockey, surfing, golf, bicycling, martial arts, etc.); outdoor activities (hunting and fishing); health and fitness. No children's books. Query with SASE. "We consider queries from both first-time and experienced authors as well as agented or unagented projects. Submit outline." Reviews artwork/photos. Send sample digital images or transparencies (duplicates and tearsheets only).

Ⓒ MY GREEN PUBLISHER LLC

P.O. Box 702, Richland MT 49083. **E-mail:** mygreenpublisher@gmail.com. **Website:** www.mygreenpublisher.com. **Contact:** Fiona Thomas, editor-in-chief. Estab. 2011. Publishes trade paperback and electronic originals. **Publishes 36-48 titles/year. 100 queries received/year; 100 mss received/year. 85% of books from first-time authors. 100% from unagented writers. Pays 15% royalty on wholesale price (paperback); 20% royalty on wholesale price (ebook).** Publishes ms 6-12 months after acceptance. Accepts simultaneous submissions. Responds in 3 days to queries; 1 month to proposals and mss. Book catalog available online. Guidelines availble online or by e-mail.

NONFICTION , Interested in all subjects. Submit complete ms. Reviews artwork. Send high-res jpegs.

FICTION , Interested in all subjects. Submit complete ms.

POETRY Submit complete ms.

Ⓒ NAPOLEON & COMPANY

500-3 Church St., Toronto ON M5E 1M2, Canada. **E-mail:** submissions@dundurn.com. **Website:** www.napoleonandcompany.com. **Contact:** A. Thompson, editor. Estab. 1990. Publishes hardcover and trade paperback originals and reprints. Rendezvous publishes adult fiction. Napoleon publishes children's books. **Publishes 15 titles/year. 200 queries received/year. 100 mss received/year. 50% of books from first-time authors. 75% from unagented writers.** Publishes ms 18 months after acceptance. Accepts simultaneous submissions. Responds in 1 month to queries; 3 months to proposals; 6 months to mss. Book catalog and guidelines available online.

○ "Napoleon is not accepting children's picture books at this time. Rendezvous Crime is not accepting mysteries. Check website for updates. We are accepting general adult fiction only for RendezVous Press and Darkstar Fiction."

NONFICTION Query with SASE. Submit outline, 1 sample chapter.

TIPS Canadian resident authors only.

NAR ASSOCIATES

P.O. Box 233, Barryville NY 12719. (845)557-8713. **Website:** www.aodceus.com. **Contact:** Nick Roes, acquisitions editor. Estab. 1977. Publishes trade paperback originals. **Publishes 6 titles/year. 10 queries received/year. 10 mss received/year. 80% of books from first-time authors. 100% from unagented writers. Makes outright purchase of $500.** Publishes ms 1 month after acceptance. Accepts simultaneous submissions. Responds in 1 month to queries, proposals and mss. Book catalog available online. Guidelines available via e-mail.

NONFICTION Subjects include education, psychology, counseling techniques, professional ethics. "We publish home study courses for addiction and social work professionals." Query with SASE. Reviews artwork/photos. Send photocopies.

TIPS "Our audience consists of addiction counselors, social workers, and other counseling professionals. Use same format as existing coursework currently in publication."

NATIONAL ASSOCIATION FOR MUSIC EDUCATION

1806 Robert Fulton Dr., Reston VA 20191-4348. **Fax:** (703)860-1531. **E-mail:** ellaw@nafme.org. **Website:** www.nafme.org. **Contact:** Ella Wilcox, editor; Linda

Brown, editor. Sue Rarus, Dir. of Informaton Resources and Publications Estab. 1907. "JOURNALS: See www.menc.org for our guidelines for contributors. Our mission is to advance music education by encouraging the study and making of music by all. *Music Educators Journal* and *Teaching Music* are two of our journal publications. *Music Educators Journal (MEJ)* encourages music education professionals who are MENC members to submit mss about all phases of music education in schools and communities, practical instructional techniques, teaching philosophy, and current issues in music teaching and learning. (See separate listing for Teaching Music.) BOOKS: Publishes hardcover and trade paperback originals. Publishes 10 titles/year. 75 queries received/year. 50 mss received/year. 40% of books from first-time authors. 100% from unagented writers. Pays royalty on retail price. Publishes book 1-2 years after acceptance of ms. Responds in 2 months to queries. Responds in 4 months to proposals. Book catalog available online. Guidelines available online. **Pays royalty on retail price.**

NONFICTION Subjects include child guidance, education, multicultural, music, dance, music education. Mss evaluated by professional music educators. Submit proposal package, outline, 1-3 sample chapters, bio, CV, marketing strategy. For journal articles, submit electronically to mc.manuscriptcentral.com/mej. Authors will be required to set up an online account on the SAGETRACK system powered by ScholarOne (this can take about 30 minutes). From their account, a new submission can be initiated.

TIPS "Look online for book proposal guidelines. No telephone calls. We are committed to music education books that will serve as the very best resources for music educators, students and their parents."

NATUREGRAPH PUBLISHERS, INC.

P.O. Box 1047, Happy Camp CA 96039. **Fax:** (530)493-5240. **E-mail:** nature@sisqtel.net. **Website:** www.naturegraph.com. **Contact:** Barbara Brown, owner. Estab. 1946. Publishes trade paperback originals. **Publishes 2 titles/year. 300 queries received/year. 12 mss received/year. 80% of books from first-time authors. 0% from unagented writers.** Publishes ms 2 years after acceptance. Accepts simultaneous submissions. Responds in 1 month to queries; 2 months to mss. Book catalog for #10 SASE.

NONFICTION Subjects include anthropology, archaeology, multicultural, nature, environment, science, natural history: biology, geology, ecology, astronomy, crafts.

TIPS "Please-always send a stamped reply envelope. Publishers get hundreds of manuscripts yearly."

NAVAL INSTITUTE PRESS

US Naval Institute, 291 Wood Rd., Annapolis MD 21402. (410)268-6110. **Fax:** (410)295-1084. **E-mail:** cparkinson@usni.org; books@usni.org. **Website:** www.usni.org. Estab. 1873. "The Naval Institute Press publishes trade and scholarly nonfiction. We are interested in national and international security, naval, military, military jointness, intelligence, and special warfare, both current and historical." **Publishes 80-90 titles/year. 50% of books from first-time authors. 90% from unagented writers.** Guidelines available online.

NONFICTION Submit proposal package with outline, author bio, TOC, description/synopsis, sample chapter(s), page/word count, number of illustrations, ms completion date, intended market; or submit complete ms. Send SASE with sufficient postage for return of ms. Send by postal mail only. No e-mail submissions, please.

⊘ NAVPRESS, (THE PUBLISHING MINISTRY OF THE NAVIGATORS)

P.O. Box 35002, Colorado Springs CO 80935. **Fax:** (719)260-7223. **E-mail:** customerservice@navpress.com. **Website:** www.navpress.com. Estab. 1975. Publishes hardcover, trade paperback, direct and mass market paperback originals and reprints; electronic books and Bible studies. **Pays royalty. Pays low or no advances.** Book catalog available free.

NONFICTION Subjects include child guidance, parenting, sociology, spirituality and contemporary culture, Christian living, marriage.

NBM PUBLISHING

160 Broadway, Suite 700, East Bldg., New York NY 10038. **E-mail:** nbmgn@nbmpub.com. **Website:** nbmpub.com. **Contact:** Terry Nantier, editor/art director. Estab. 1976. Publishes graphic novels for an audience of adults. Types of books include fiction, mystery and social parodies.

NEAL-SCHUMAN PUBLISHERS, INC.

50 E. Huron St., Chicago IL 60611. (312)280-5846. **Fax:** (312)280-5275. **E-mail:** info@neal-schuman.com. **Website:** www.neal-schuman.com. **Contact:** J. Michael Jeffers, vice president/ director of publishing.

Estab. 1976. Publishes trade paperback originals. "Neal-Schuman publishes books about library management, archival science, records management, digital curation, information literary, the Internet and information technology. Especially submitting proposals for undergraduate information studies, archival science, records management, and knowledge management textbooks." **Publishes 36 titles/year. 150 queries received/year. 80% of books from first-time authors. 100% from unagented writers. Pays 10-15% royalty on wholesale price. Pays infrequent advance.** Publishes ms 1 year after acceptance. Accepts simultaneous submissions. Responds in 1 month to queries, proposals, and mss. Book catalog free. Mss guidelines not available.

NONFICTION Subjects include computers, electronics, education, software, Internet guides, library and information science, archival studies, records management. Submit proposal package, outline, 1 sample chapter. Reviews artwork. Send photocopies.

TIPS "Our audience are professional librarians, archivists, and records managers."

NEW AFRICA BOOKS

New Africa Books (Pty) Ltd, P.O. Box 46962, Glosderry 7702, South Africa. (27)(21)467-5860. **Fax:** (27)(21)467-5895. **E-mail:** info@newafricabooks.co.za. **Website:** www.newafricabooks.co.za. **Contact:** David Philip, publisher. "New Africa Books strives to be the leading African publisher – the world's definitive gateway to African content and information." **Publishes 8-10 titles/year. 40% of books from first-time authors. 80% from unagented writers. Pays royalty.**

NONFICTION Subjects include art, architecture, education, history, memoirs, politics, science, lifestyle.

FICTION Subjects include juvenile, literary.

NEW FORUMS PRESS

New Forums, 1018 S. Lewis St., Stillwater OK 74074. (405)372-6158. **Fax:** (405)377-2237. **E-mail:** contact@newforums.com. **E-mail:** submissions@newforums.com. **Website:** www.newforums.com. **Contact:** Doug Dollar, president (interests: higher education, Oklahoma-Regional). Estab. 1981. Hardcover and trade paperback originals. "New Forums Press is an independent publisher offering works devoted to various aspects of professional development in higher education, home and office aides, and various titles of a regional interest. We welcome suggestions for thematic series of books and thematic issues of our academic journals—addressing a single issue, problem, or theory." **60% of books from first-time authors. 100% from unagented writers.** Use Author Guidelines online or call (800)606-3766 with any questions.

NONFICTION Subjects include business, finance, history, literature, money, music, politics, regional, sociology, young adult. "We are actively seeking new authors—send for review copies and author guidelines, and visit our website." Mss should be submitted as a Microsoft Word document, or a similar standard word processor document (saved in RTF rich text), as an attachment to an email sent to submissions@newforums.com. Otherwise, submit your manuscript on 8 ½ x 11 inch white bond paper (one original). The name and complete address, telephone, fax number, and email address of each author should appear on a separate cover page, so it can be removed for the blind review process.

✚ NEW ISSUES POETRY & PROSE

Western Michigan University, 1903 W. Michigan Ave., Kalamazoo MI 49008-5463. (269)387-8185. **Fax:** (269)387-2562. **E-mail:** new-issues@wmich.edu. **Website:** wmich.edu/newissues. **Contact:** Managing Editor. Estab. 1996. **50% first time authors% of books from first-time authors. 95% unagented writers% from unagented writers.** Publishes 18 months after acceptance. Accepts simultaneous submissions. Guidelines available online, by e-mail, or by SASE.

FICTION Subjects include literary, poetry.

POETRY New Issues Poetry & Prose offers two contests annually. The Green Rose Prize is awarded to an author who has previously published at least one full-length book of poems. The New Issues Poetry Prize, an award for a first book of poems, is chosen by a guest judge. Past judges have included Philip Levine, C.K. Williams, C.D. Wright, and Campbell McGrath. New Issues does not read manuscripts outside our contests. Graduate students in the Ph.D. and M.F.A. programs of Western Michigan Univ. often volunteer their time reading manuscripts. Finalists are chosen by the editors. New Issues often publishes up to two additional manuscripts selected from the finalists.

NEW LIBRI PRESS

4230 95th Ave. SE, Mercer Island WA 98040. **E-mail:** query@newlibri.com. **Website:** www.newlibri.com. **Contact:** Michael Muller, editor (nonfiction and foreign writers); Stanislav Fritz (literary). Estab. 2011. Publishes hardcover, trade paperback, mass market paperback, electronic original, electronic reprints. **Publishes 10 titles/year. 80% of books from first-time authors. 90% from unagented writers. Pays 20-35% royalty on wholesale price. No advance.** Publishes ms 9-12 months after acceptance. Responds in 1 month to ms. No proposals; only complete mss. Catalog not available yet.

NONFICTION Subjects include agriculture, automotive, business, child guidance, computers, cooking, creative nonfiction, economics, electronics, environment, gardening, hobbies, house and home, nature, parenting, recreation, science, sex, software, translation, travel. "Writers should know we embrace ebooks. This means that some formats and types of books work well and others don't." Prefers e-mail. Submit proposal package, including outline, 2 sample chapters, and summary of market from author's perspective. Prefers complete ms.

FICTION Subjects include adventure, experimental, fantasy, historical, horror, literary, mainstream, military, mystery, science fiction, translation, war, western, young adult. "Open to most ideas right now; this will change as we mature as a press." As a new press, we are more open than most and time will probably shape the direction. That said, trite as it is, we want good writing that is fun to read. While we currently are not looking for some sub-genres, if it is well written and a bit off the beaten path, submit to us. We are ebook friendly, which means some fiction may be less likely to currently sell (e.g. picture books would work only on an iPad or Color Nook as of this writing)." Submit proposal package, including synopsis. Prefers complete ms.

POETRY "Poetry is not our focus. We will probably only examine poetry in the author-subsidized model."

TIPS "Our audience is someone who is comfortable reading an ebook,or someone who is tired of the recycled authors of mainstream publishing, but still wants a good, relatively fast, reading experience. The industry is changing, while we accept for the traditional model, we are searching for writers who are interested in sharing the risk and controlling their own destiny. We embrace writers with no agent."

NEW RIVERS PRESS

MSU Moorhead, 1104 Seventh Ave. S., Moorhead MN 56563. **E-mail:** kelleysu@mnstate.edu. **Website:** www.newriverspress.com. **Contact:** Alan Davis. Suzzanne Kelley, managing editor. Estab. 1968. New Riv-

ers Press publishes collections of poetry, novels, nonfiction, translations of contemporary literature, and collections of short fiction and nonfiction. "We continue to publish books regularly by new and emerging writers, but we also welcome the opportunity to read work of every character and to publish the best literature available nationwide. Each fall through the Many Voices Project competition, we choose 2 books: 1 poetry and 1 prose."

POETRY The Many Voices Project awards $1,000, a standard book contract, publication of a book-length ms by New Rivers Press, and national distribution. All previously published poems must be acknowledged. "We will consider simultaneous submissions if noted as such. If your manuscript is accepted elsewhere during the judging, you must notify New Rivers Press immediately. If you do not give such notification and your manuscript is selected, your entry gives New Rivers Press permission to go ahead with publication." Submit 50-80 pages of poetry. Entry form (required) and guidelines available on website. **Entry fee:** $25. **Deadline:** submit September 15-November 1 (postmark). Guidelines available on website.

RECENT Title(s) *The Hunger Bone*, by Deb Marquart; *Real Karaoke People*, by Ed Bok-Lee; *Haints*, by Clint McCown; *Girl Held in Home*, by Elizabeth Searle; *And Then*, by Tim Nolan; *It Takes You Over*, by Nick Healy; *Good Things*, by Nick Knittel.

NEWSAGE PRESS

P.O. Box 607, Troutdale OR 97060-0607. (503)695-2211. **E-mail:** info@newsagepress.com. **Website:** www.newsagepress.com. **Contact:** Maureen R. Michelson, publisher; Sherry Wachter, design. Estab. 1985. Publishes trade paperback originals. "We focus on nonfiction books. No `how to' books or cynical, despairing books. Photo-essay books in large format are no longer published by Newsage Press. No novels or other forms of fiction." Guidelines available online.

NONFICTION Subjects include animals, multicultural, nature, environment, womens issues, womens studies, death/dying. Submit 2 sample chapters, proposal (no more than 1 page), SASE.

NEW VICTORIA PUBLISHERS

2455 W. Warner Ave., Chicago IL 60613. (773)793-2244. **E-mail:** newvictoriapub@att.net. **Website:** www.newvictoria.com. **Contact:** Patricia Feuerhaken, president. Estab. 1976. Publishes trade paperback originals. "Publishes mostly lesbian fiction—strong female protagonists. Most well known for Stoner McTavish mystery series." Distributes titles through Amazon Books, Bella books, Bulldog Books (Sydney, Australia), and Women and Children First Books (Chicago). Promotes titles "mostly through lesbian feminist media." **Publishes 3 titles/year. Pays 10% royalty.** Publishes ms 1 year after acceptance. Accepts simultaneous submissions. Catalog free on request; for #10 SASE; or online at website. Guidelines free on request; for #10 SASE; or online.

○ *Mommy Deadest*, by Jean Marcy, won the Lambda Literary Award for Mystery. *Mommy Deadest*, by Jean Marcy, won the Lambda Literary Award for Mystery.

NONFICTION Subjects include alternative, biography, lesbian, history, language, poetry, fiction, literature, memoirs, multicultural, music/dance, mystery, nature, environment, New Age, erotica, translation, women's issues/studies, world affairs, contemporary culture, autobiography, biography, general nonfiction, humor, reference, science fiction. "We will consider well-researched nonfiction of interest to women, as well as lesbian feminist herstory, or biography of interest to a general as well as academic audience." Query with SASE. Reviews artwork/photos; send photocopies.

FICTION Lesbian, feminist fiction including adventure, erotica, fantasy, historical, humor, mystery (amateur sleuth), or science fiction. Accepts unsolicited mss, but prefers query first. Submit outline, synopsis, and sample chapters (50 pages). No queries by e-mail or fax; please send SASE or IRC. No simultaneous submissions.

TIPS "We are especially interested in lesbian or feminist novels, ideally with a character or characters who can evolve through a series of books. Stories should involve a complex plot, accurate details, and protagonists with full emotional lives. Pay attention to plot and character development. Read guidelines carefully. We advise you to look through our catalog or visit our website to see our past editorial decisions as well as what we are currently marketing. Our books average 80-100,000 words, or 200-220 single-spaced pages."

NEW WORLD LIBRARY

14 Pamaron Way, Novato CA 94949. (415)884-2100. **Fax:** (415)884-2199. **E-mail:** submit@newworldlibrary.com. **Website:** www.newworldlibrary.com. **Contact:** Jonathan Wichmann, submissions editor.

Estab. 1979. Publishes hardcover and trade paperback originals and reprints. "NWL is dedicated to publishing books that inspire and challenge us to improve the quality of our lives and our world." **Publishes 35-40 titles/year. 10% of books from first-time authors. 40% from unagented writers.** Accepts simultaneous submissions. Responds in 3 months to queries. Book catalog available free. Guidelines available online.

IMPRINTS H.J. Kramer.

○ Prefers e-mail submissions. No longer accepting children's mss.

NONFICTION Submit outline, bio, 2-3 sample chapters, SASE.

⊘ NINETY-SIX PRESS

Furman University, 3300 Poinsett Hwy., Greenville SC 29613. (864)294-3152. **Fax:** (864)294-2224. **E-mail:** gil.allen@furman.edu. **Website:** library.furman.edu/specialcollections/96Press/index.htm. **Contact:** Gilbert Allen, editor. Estab. 1991. For a sample, send $10.

TIPS "South Carolina poets only. Check our website for guidelines."

NOMAD PRESS

2456 Christain St., White River Junction VT 05001. (802)649-1995. **Fax:** (802)649-2667. **E-mail:** rachel@nomadpress.net; info@nomadpress.net. **Website:** www.nomadpress.net. **Contact:** Alex Kahan, publisher. Estab. 2001. "We produce nonfiction children's activity books that bring a particular science or cultural topic into sharp focus. Nomad Press does not accept unsolicited manuscripts. If authors are interested in contributing to our children's series, please send a writing resume that includes relevant experience/expertise and publishing credits." **Pays authors royalty based on retail price or work purchased outright. Offers advance against royalties.** Publishes book 1 year after acceptance. Responds to queries in 3-4 weeks. Catalog available on website.

○ Nomad Press does not accept picture books or fiction.

NONFICTION Middle readers: activity books, history, science. Average word length: middle readers—30,000.

TIPS "We publish a very specific kind of nonfiction children's activity book. Please keep this in mind when querying or submitting."

⊕ NORTH ATLANTIC BOOKS

2526 MLK Jr. Way, Berkeley CA 94704. **Website:** www.northatlanticbooks.com. **Contact:** Douglas Reil, associate publisher; Erin Wiegand, senior acquisitions editor. Estab. 1974. Publishes hardcover, trade paperback, and electronic originals; trade paperback and electronic reprints. **Publishes 60 titles/year. Receives 200 mss/year. 50% of books from first-time authors. 75% from unagented writers. Pays royalty percentage on wholesale price.** Publishes ms 14 months after acceptance. Accepts simultaneous submissions. Responds in 3-6 months to queries, proposals, mss. Book catalog free on request (if available). Guidelines online.

IMPRINTS Evolver Editions, Blue Snake Books.

NONFICTION Subjects include agriculture, anthropology, archeology, architecture, art, astrology, business, child guidance, community, contemporary culture, cooking, economics, electronics, environment, finance, foods, gardening, gay, health, horticultural, lesbian, medicine, memoirs, money, multicultural, nature, New Age, nutrition, philosophy, politics, psychic, psychology, public affairs, religion, science, social sciences, sociology, spirituality, sports, travel, womens issues, womens studies, world affairs. "See our submission guidelines on our website." Submit proposal package including an outline, 3-4 sample chapters, and "a 75-word statement about the book, your qualifications as an author, marketing plan/audience, for the book, and comparable titles." Reviews artwork with ms package.

FICTION Subjects include adventure, literary, multicultural, mystery, regional, science fiction, spiritual. "We only publish fiction on rare occasions." Submit proposal package including an outline, 3-4 sample chapters, and "a 75-word statement about the book, your qualifications as an author, marketing plan/audience, for the book, and comparable titles."

POETRY Submit 15-20 sample poems.

NORTH CAROLINA OFFICE OF ARCHIVES AND HISTORY

Historical Publications Section, 4622 Mail Service Center, Raleigh NC 27699. (919)733-7442. **Fax:** (919)733-1439. **E-mail:** historical.publications@ncdcr.gov. **Website:** www.ncpublications.com. **Contact:** Donna E. Kelly, administrator (North Carolina and southern history). Publishes hardcover and trade paperback originals. "We publish *only* titles that relate to North Carolina. The North Carolina Office of Archives and History also publishes the *North Carolina Historical Review*, a quarterly scholarly journal of history." **Publishes 4 titles/year. 20 queries received/year. 25 mss received/year. 5% of books**

from first-time authors. 100% from unagented writers. Makes one-time payment upon delivery of completed ms. Publishes ms 2 years after acceptance. Accepts simultaneous submissions. Responds in 1 week to queries and to proposals; 2 months to mss. Guidelines for $3.

NONFICTION Subjects include history, related to North Carolina, military, war, related to North Carolina, regional, North Carolina and Southern history. Query with SASE. Reviews artwork/photos. Send photocopies.

NORTH LIGHT BOOKS

F+W Media, Inc., 10151 Carver Rd., Suite 200, Blue Ash OH 45242. **Fax:** (513)891-7153. **E-mail:** jamie.markle@fwmedia.com; pam.wissman@fwmedia.com; vanessa.lyman@fwmedia.com;. **Website:** www.fwmedia.com. **Contact:** Jamie Markle, fine art publisher; Pam Wissman, senior content director fine arts; Vanessa Lyman, editorial director craft. Publishes hardcover and trade paperback how-to books. "North Light Books publishes art and craft books, including watercolor, drawing, mixed media, acrylic, knitting, jewelry making, sewing, and needle arts that emphasize illustrated how-to art instruction. Currently emphasizing drawing including traditional, fantasy art, and Japanese-style comics as well as creativity and inspiration. The KP Craft imprint publishes quilting, sewing, knitting, crochet, jewelry making, sewing and needle arts." **Publishes 70-75 titles/year. Pays 8% royalty on net receipts and $3,500 advance.** Accepts simultaneous submissions. Responds in 2 months to queries. available as PDF on www.fwmedia.com.

This market is for experienced fine artists and crafters who are willing to work with an North Light editor to produce a step-by-step how-to book about the artist's creative process. See also separate listing for F+W Media, Inc., in this section.

NONFICTION Subjects include hobbies, watercolor, realistic drawing, creativity, decorative painting, comics drawing, paper arts, sewing, quilting, knitting, collage and other craft instruction books. Interested in books on acrylic painting, basic drawing and sketching, journaling, pen and ink, colored pencil, decorative painting, and beading, art, how-to. Do not submit coffee table art books without how-to art instruction. Query with SASE. Submit outline.

NORTH POINT PRESS

Farrar, Straus and Giroux, 18 West 18th St., New York NY 10010. **E-mail:** fsg.editorial@fsgbooks.com. **Website:** us.macmillan.com. **Considers unsolicited submissions by mail only.**

NORTIA PRESS

Mission Viejo CA **E-mail:** acquisitions@nortiapress. com. **Website:** www.NortiaPress.com. Estab. 2009. Publishes trade paperback and electronic originals. **Publishes 6 titles/year. 0% of books from first-time authors. 80% from unagented writers. Pays negotiable royalties on wholesale price.** Publishes ms 7 months after acceptance. Accepts simultaneous submissions. Responds in 1 month to queries and proposals.

NONFICTION Subjects include ethnic, government, humanities, military, public affairs, religion, social sciences, sociology, war, womens issues.

FICTION Subjects include ethnic, historical, literary, military, war. "We focus mainly on nonfiction as well as literary and historical fiction, but are open to other genres. No vampire stories, science fiction, or erotica, please. Submit a brief e-mail query. Please include a short bio, approximate word count of book, and expected date of completion (fiction titles should be completed before sending a query, and should contain a sample chapter in the body of the e-mail). All unsolicited snail mail or attachments will be discarded without review.

TIPS "We specialize in working with experienced authors who seek a more collaborative and fulfilling relationship with their publisher. As such, we are less likely to accept pitches form first-time authors, no matter how good the idea. As with any pitch, please make your e-mail very brief and to the point, so the reader is not forced to skim it. Always include some biographic information. Your life is interesting."

W.W. NORTON & COMPANY, INC.

500 Fifth Ave., New York NY 10110. (212)354-5500. **Fax:** (212)869-0856. **Website:** www.wwnorton.com. **Contact:** Trish Marks. Estab. 1923. "W. W. Norton & Company, the oldest and largest publishing house owned wholly by its employees, strives to carry out the imperative of its founder to "publish books not for a single season, but for the years" in fiction, nonfiction, poetry, college textbooks, cookbooks, art books and professional books."

"Due to the workload of our editorial staff and the large volume of materials we receive, *Norton is no longer able to accept unsolicited submissions*. If you are seeking publication, we suggest working with a literary agent who will represent you to the house."

NO STARCH PRESS, INC.

38 Ringold St., Suite 250, San Francisco CA 94103. (415)863-9900. **Fax:** (415)863-9950. **E-mail:** info@ nostarch.com. **Website:** www.nostarch.com. **Contact:** William Pollock, publisher. Estab. 1994. Publishes trade paperback originals. "No Starch Press publishes the finest in geek entertainment—unique books on technology, with a focus on open source, security, hacking, programming, alternative operating systems, LEGO, science, and math. Our titles have personality, our authors are passionate, and our books tackle topics that people care about. No Starch Press titles have received numerous awards, including gold medals from the Independent Publisher Book Awards (the "IPPYs") and ForeWord's Book of the Year Awards, and have been showcased in the prestigious STEP Inside Design 100 and Communication Arts Design Annual. Visit www.nostarch.com for a complete catalog." **Publishes 20-25 titles/year. 100 queries received/year. 5 mss received/year. 80% of books from first-time authors. 90% from unagented writers. Pays 10-15% royalty on wholesale price. Pays advance.** Publishes book 4 months after acceptance of ms. Accepts simultaneous submissions. Book catalog available online.

NONFICTION Subjects include science, technology, computing, lego. Submit outline, bio, 1 sample chapter, market rationale. Reviews artwork/photos. Send photocopies.

TIPS "Books must be relevant to tech-savvy, geeky readers."

NOVA PRESS

9058 Lloyd P;ace, West Hollywood CA 90069. (310)275-3513. **Fax:** (310)281-5629. **E-mail:** novapress@aol.com. **Website:** www.novapress.net. **Contact:** Jeff Kolby, president. Estab. 1993. Publishes trade paperback originals. "Nova Press publishes only test prep books for college entrance exams (SAT, GRE, GMAT, LSAT, etc.), and closely related reference books, such as college guides and vocabulary books." **Publishes 4 titles/year.** Publishes book 6 months after acceptance. Book catalog available free.

NONFICTION Subjects include education, software.

NURSESBOOKS.ORG

American Nurses Association, 8515 Georgia Ave., Suite 400, Silver Spring MD 20901. 1-800-274-4ANA. **Fax:** (301)628-5003. **E-mail:** anp@ana.org. **Website:** www.nursesbooks.org. **Contact:** Rosanne Roe, publisher; Eric Wurzbacher, editor/project manager; Camille Walker, business operations coordinator/project manager. Publishes professional paperback originals and reprints. "Nursebooks.org publishes books designed to help professional nurses in their work and careers. Through the publishing program, Nursebooks.org provides nurses in all practice settings with publications that address cutting edge issues and form a basis for debate and exploration of this century's most critical health care trends." **Publishes 10 titles/year. 50 queries received/year. 8-10 mss received/year. 75% of books from first-time authors. 100% from unagented writers.** Publishes ms 4 months after acceptance. Responds in 3 months to proposals and mss. Book catalog available online. Guidelines available free.

NONFICTION Subjects include advanced practice, computers, continuing education, ethics, health care policy, nursing administration, psychiatric and mental health, quality, nursing history, workplace issues, key clinical topics, such as geriatrics, pain management, public health, spirituality and home health. Submit outline, 1 sample chapter, CV, list of 3 reviewers and paragraph on audience and how to reach them. Reviews artwork/photos. Send photocopies.

OAK KNOLL PRESS

310 Delaware St., New Castle DE 19720. (302)328-7232. **Fax:** (302)328-7274. **E-mail:** Laura@oakknoll.com. **Website:** www.oakknoll.com. **Contact:** Laura R. Williams, publishing director. Estab. 1976. Publishes hardcover and trade paperback originals and reprints. "Oak Knoll specializes in books about books and manuals on the book arts: preserving the art and lore of the printed word." **Publishes 40 titles/year. 250 queries received/year. 100 mss received/year. 50% of books from first-time authors. 100% from unagented writers.** Publishes ms 1 year after acceptance. Accepts simultaneous submissions. Guidelines available online.

NONFICTION Reviews artwork/photos. Send photocopies.

OAK TREE PRESS

140 E. Palmer, Taylorville IL 62568. (217)824-6500. **E-mail:** oaktreepub@aol.com. **E-mail:** queryotp@aol.com. **Website:** www.oaktreebooks.com. **Contact:** Billie Johnson, publisher (mysteries, romance, nonfiction); Sarah Wasson, acquisitions editor (all); Barbara Hoffman, senior editor (children's, young adult, educational). Estab. 1998. Publishes trade paperback and hardcover books. "Oak Tree Press is an independent publisher that celebrates writers, and is dedicated to the many great unknowns who are just waiting for the opportunity to break into print. We're looking for mainstream, genre fiction, narrative nonfiction, how-to. Sponsors 3 contests annually: Dark Oak Mystery, Timeless Love Romance and CopTales for true crime and other stories of law enforcement professionals." **Royalties based on sales. No advance.** Publishes ms 9-18 months after acceptance. Responds in 4-6 weeks. Catalog and guidelines available online.

FICTION Adventure, confession, ethnic, fantasy (romance), feminist, humor, mainstream/contemporary, mystery (amateur sleuth, cozy, police procedural, private eye/hard-boiled), new age/mystic, picture books, romance (contemporary, futuristic/time travel, romantic suspense), suspense, thriller/espionage, young adult (adventure, mystery/suspense, romance). Emphasis on mystery and romance novels. "No science fiction or fantasy novels, or stories set far into the future. Next, novels substantially longer than our stated word count are not considered, regardless of genre. We look for manuscripts of 70-90,000 words. If the story really charms us, we will bend some on either end of the range. No right-wing political or racist agenda, gratuitous sex or violence, especially against women, or depict harm of animals." Does not accept or return unsolicited mss. Query with SASE. Accepts queries by e-mail. Include estimated word count, brief bio, list of publishing credits, brief description of ms. Send SASE for return of ms or send a disposable ms and SASE for reply only.

TIPS "Perhaps my most extreme pet peeve is receiving queries on projects which we've clearly advertised we don't want: science fiction, fantasy, epic tomes, bigoted diatribes and so on. Second to that is a practice I call 'over-taping,' or the use of yards and yards of tape, or worse yet, the filament tape so that it takes forever to open the package. Finding story pitches on my voice mail is also annoying."

OBERLIN COLLEGE PRESS

50 N. Professor St., Oberlin College, Oberlin OH 44074. (440)775-8408. **Fax:** (440)775-8124. **E-mail:** oc.press@oberlin.edu. **Website:** www.oberlin.edu/ocpress. **Contact:** Linda Slocum, managing editor. Estab. 1969. Publishes hardcover and trade paperback originals. **Publishes 2-3 titles/year. Pays 7½-10% royalty.** Accepts simultaneous submissions. Responds promptly to queries; 2 months to mss.

POETRY "*FIELD Magazine*—submit 2-6 poems through website "submissions" tab; FIELD Translation Series—query with SASE and sample poems; FIELD Poetry Series—*no unsolicited mss.* Enter mss in FIELD Poetry Prize ($1,000 and a standard royalty contract) held annually in May. Submit electronically through field poetry prize link on website at www.oberlin.edu/ocpress." Submit 2-6 sample poems.

TIPS "Queries for the FIELD Translation Series: send sample poems and letter describing project. Winner of the annual FIELD poetry prize determines publication. Do not send unsolicited manuscripts."

OCEANVIEW PUBLISHING

595 Bay Isles Rd., Suite 120-G, Longboat Key FL 34228. **E-mail:** submissions@oceanviewpub.com. **Website:** www.oceanviewpub.com. **Contact:** Robert Gussin, CEO. Estab. 2006. Publishes hardcover and electronic originals. Independent publisher of nonfiction and fiction, with primary interest in original mystery, thriller and suspense titles. Accepts new and established writers." Responds in 3 months on mss. Catalog and guidelines available online.

NONFICTION Accepts nonfiction but specializes in original mystery, thriller and suspense titles. Query.

FICTION Subjects include mystery, suspense, thriller. Accepting adult mss with a primary interest in the mystery, thriller and suspense genres—from new & established writers. No children's or YA literature, poetry, cookbooks, technical manuals or short stories. Within body of e-mail only, include author's name and brief bio (Indicate if this is an agent submission), ms title and word count, author's mailing address, phone number and e-mail address. Attached to the e-mail should be the following: A synopsis of 750 words or fewer. The first 30 pages of the ms. Please note that we accept only Word documents as attachments to the submission e-mail. Do not send query letters or proposals.

ONEWORLD PUBLICATIONS

10 Bloomsbury St., London WC1B 3SR, United Kingdom. (44)(20)7307-8900. **E-mail:** submissions@oneworld-publications.com. **Website:** www.oneworld-publications.com. Estab. 1986. Publishes hardcover and trade paperback originals and mass market paperback reprints. "We publish general trade nonfiction, which must be accessible but authoritative, mainly by academics or experts for a general readership and where appropriate a cross-over student market. Currently emphasizing current affairs, popular science, history, psychology and business; de-emphasizing self help.We also publish literary fiction by international authors, both debut and established, throughout the English language world as well as selling translation rights. Our focus is on well-written literary and high-end commercial fiction from a variety of cultures and periods, many exploring interesting issues and global problems. In addition we publish fiction in translation." **Publishes 50 titles/year. 300 queries received/year; 200 mss received/year. 20% of books from first-time authors. 50% from unagented writers. Pays 10% royalty on wholesale price for academic books; standard royalties for trade titles. Pays $1,000-50,000 advance.** Publishes ms 12-15 months after acceptance. Book catalog available online. Guidelines available online.

NONFICTION Subjects include business, economics. Submit through online proposal form.

FICTION Subjects include politics, history, multicultural, philosophy, psychology, religion, science, sociology, women's issues, women's studies. Submit through online proposal forms.

TIPS "We don't require agents—just good proposals with enough hard information."

ONSTAGE PUBLISHING

190 Lime Quarry Rd., Suite 106-J, Madison AL 35758-8962. (256)461-0661. **E-mail:** onstage123@knology.net. **Website:** www.onstagepublishing.com. **Contact:** Dianne Hamilton, senior editor. Estab. 1999. At this time, we only produce fiction books for ages 8-18. We are adding an eBook only side of the house for mysteries for grades 6-12. See our website for more information. We will not do anthologies of any kind. Query first for nonfiction projects as nonfiction projects must spark our interest. Now accepting e-mail queries and submissions. For submissions: Put the first 3 chapters in the body of the e-mail. Do not use

attachments! We will no longer return any mss. Only an SASE envelope is needed. Send complete ms if under 20,000 words, otherwise send synopsis and first 3 chapters. **80% of books from first-time authors. Pays authors/illustrators/photographers advance plus royalties.**

FICTION Middle readers: adventure, contemporary, fantasy, history, nature/environment, science fiction, suspense/mystery. Young adults: adventure, contemporary, fantasy, history, humor, science fiction, suspense/mystery. Average word length: chapter books—4,000-6,000 words; middle readers—5,000 words and up; young adults—25,000 and up. "We do not produce picture books."

TIPS "Study our titles and get a sense of the kind of books we publish, so that you know whether your project is likely to be right for us."

ON THE MARK PRESS

15 Dairy Ave., Napanee ON K7R 1M4. 800-463-6367. **Fax:** 800-290-3631. **E-mail:** productdevelopment@onthemarkpress.com. **Website:** www.onthemarkpress.com. Estab. 1986. **15% of books from first-time authors.**

OOLIGAN PRESS

369 Neuberger Hall, 724 SW Harrison St., Portland OR 97201. **E-mail:** ooligan@ooliganpress.pdx.edu. **Website:** www.ooliganpress.pdx.edu. Estab. 2001. Publishes trade paperback, and electronic originals and reprints. **Publishes 4-6 titles/year. 250-500 queries received/year. 100 mss received/year. 90% of books from first-time authors. 90% from unagented writers. Pays negotiable royalty on retail price.** Book catalog available online. Guidelines available online.

NONFICTION Subjects include agriculture, alternative, anthropology, archeology, art, architecture, community, contemporary culture, cooking, foods, nutrition, creative nonfiction, education, ethnic, film, cinema, stage, gay, lesbian, government, politics, history, humanities, language, literature, literary criticism, memoirs, multicultural, music, dance, nature, environment, philosophy, regional, religion, social sciences, sociology, spirituality, translation, travel, women's issues, women's studies, world affairs, young adult. Young adult: open to all categories. Query with SASE. Submit proposal package, outline, 4 sample chapters, projected page count, audience, marketing ideas and a list of similar titles. Reviews artwork/photos.

FICTION Subjects include adventure, ethnic, experimental, fantasy, feminist, gay, lesbian, historical, horror, humor, literary, mainstream, contemporary, multicultural, mystery, plays, poetry, poetry in translation, regional, science fiction, short story collections, spiritual, suspense, translation, young adult, and middle grade. "Ooligan Press is a general trade press at Portland State University. As a teaching press, Ooligan makes as little distinction as possible between the press and the classroom. Under the direction of professional faculty and staff, the work of the press is done by students enrolled in the Book Publishing graduate program at PSU. We are especially interested in works with social, literary, or educational value. Though we place special value on local authors, we are open to all submissions, including translated works and writings by children and young adults. We do not currently publish picture books, board books, easy readers, or pop-up books or middle grade readers." Query with SASE. *"At this time we cannot accept science fiction or fantasy submissions."*

POETRY Ooligan is a general trade press that "specializes in publishing authors from the Pacific Northwest and/or works that have specific value to that community. We are limited in the number of poetry titles that we publish as poetry represents only a small percentage of our overall acquisitions. We are open to all forms of style and verse; however, we give special preference to translated poetry, prose poetry, and traditional verse. Although spoken word, slam, and rap poetry are of interest to the press, we will not consider such work if it does not translate well to the written page. Ooligan does not publish chapbooks." Query, submit 20 sample poems, submit complete ms.

TIPS "For children's books, our audience will be middle grades and young adult, with marketing to general trade, libraries, and schools. Good marketing ideas increase the chances of a manuscript succeeding."

OPEN COURT PUBLISHING CO.

70 E. Lake St., Suite 300, Chicago IL 60601. **Website:** www.opencourtbooks.com. Estab. 1887. Publishes hardcover and trade paperback originals. **Publishes 20 titles/year. Pays 5-15% royalty on wholesale price.** Publishes ms 2 years after acceptance. Book catalog available online. Guidelines available online.

NONFICTION Subjects include philosophy, Asian thought, religious studies and popular culture. Query with SASE. Submit proposal package, outline, 1 sample chapter, TOC, author's cover letter, intended audience.

TIPS "Audience consists of philosophers and intelligent general readers."

OPEN ROAD TRAVEL GUIDES

P.O. Box 284, Cold Spring Harbor NY 11724. (631)692-7172. **E-mail:** jopenroad@aol.com. **Website:** www.openroadguides.com. Estab. 1993. Publishes trade paperback originals. "Open Road publishes travel guides and, in its Cold Spring Press imprint, now publishes genealogy books (8 in print to date) and welcomes submissions in this area." **Publishes 20-22 titles/year. 200 queries received/year. 75 mss received/year. 30% of books from first-time authors. 98% from unagented writers. Pays 5-6% royalty on retail price. Pays $1,000-3,500 advance.** Publishes book 3 months after acceptance of ms. Accepts simultaneous submissions. Responds in 1 month to queries. Responds in 2 months to proposals. Book catalog online. Ms guidelines sent if proposal is accepted.

NONFICTION Subjects include travel guides and travelogues. Query with SASE.

ORANGE FRAZER PRESS, INC.

P.O. Box 214, 37½ W. Main St., Wilmington OH 45177. (937)382-3196. **Fax:** (937)383-3159. **E-mail:** publisher@orangefrazer.com. **Website:** www.orangefrazer.com; www.orangefrazercustombooks.com. **Contact:** Marcy Hawley (custom book publishing); John Baskin (trade publishing). Publishes hardcover and trade paperback originals. "Orange Frazer Press accepts nonfiction only: corporate histories, town celebrations, and anniversary books. We now focus mostly on custom books/self-publishing, but do still take on some trade books." **Publishes 25 titles/year. 50 queries received/year. 35 mss received/year. 80% of books from first-time authors. 100% from unagented writers. Pays 10% royalty on wholesale price. "50% of our books are author-subsidy published/year if the author can afford it." Pays advance.** Publishes book 10 months after acceptance of ms. Accepts simultaneous submissions. Responds in 6 months to proposals. Book catalog and guidelines available free.

NONFICTION Subjects include audio, anthropology, archaeology, art, architecture, business, economics, cooking, foods, nutrition, education, history, nature, environment, photography, regional, sports, travel. "Sports and personalities are our main focus. Accepts Ohio nonfiction only." Submit proposal package, out-

line, 3 sample chapters, and marketing plan. Reviews artwork/photos. Send photocopies.

TIPS "For our commercial titles, we focus mainly on sports and biographies. Our readers are interested in sports or curious about famous persons/personalities. Also, we mainly publish custom books now—90% custom titles, 10% trade titles."

ORCA BOOK PUBLISHERS

P.O. Box 5626, Stn. B, Victoria BC V8R 6S4, Canada. **Fax:** (877)408-1551. **E-mail:** orca@orcabook.com. **Website:** www.orcabook.com. **Contact:** Christi Howes, editor (picture books); Sarah Harvey, editor (young readers); Andrew Wooldridge, editor (juvenile and teen fiction); Bob Tyrrell, publisher (YA, teen). Estab. 1984. Publishes hardcover and trade paperback originals, and mass market paperback originals and reprints. **Publishes 30 titles/year. 2,500 queries received/year. 1,000 mss received/year. 20% of books from first-time authors. 75% from unagented writers. Pays 10% royalty.** Publishes book 12-18 months after acceptance. Responds in 1 month to queries; 2 months to proposals and mss. Book catalog for 8½x11 SASE. Guidelines available online.

Only publishes Canadian authors.

NONFICTION Subjects include multicultural, picture books. Only publishes Canadian authors. Query with SASE.

FICTION Subjects include hi-lo, juvenile (5-9), literary, mainstream, contemporary, young adult (10-18). Picture books: animals, contemporary, history, nature/environment. Middle readers: contemporary, history, fantasy, nature/environment, problem novels, graphic novels. Young adults: adventure, contemporary, hi-lo (Orca Soundings), history, multicultural, nature/environment, problem novels, suspense/mystery, graphic novels. Average word length: picture books—500-1,500; middle readers—20,000-35,000; young adult—25,000-45,000; Orca Soundings—13,000-15,000; Orca Currents—13,000-15,000. Query with SASE. Submit proposal package, outline, clips, 2-5 sample chapters, SASE.

RECENT Title(s) *Sister Wife*, by Shelley Hrdlitschka (teen fiction); *Buttercup's Lovely Day*, by Carolyn Beck (picture book)

TIPS "Our audience is students in grades K-12. Know our books, and know the market."

ORCHARD BOOKS

557 Broadway, New York NY 10012. **E-mail:** mcroland@scholastic.com. **Website:** www.scholastic.com. **Contact:** Ken Geist, vice president/editorial director; David Saylor, vice president/creative director. **Publishes 20 titles/year. 10% of books from first-time authors. Most commonly offers an advance against list royalties.**

○   *Orchard is not accepting unsolicited manuscripts.*

FICTION Picture books, early readers, and novelty: animal, contemporary, history, humor, multicultural, poetry.

TIPS "Read some of our books to determine first whether your manuscript is suited to our list."

⊘ ORCHISES PRESS

P.O. Box 320533, Alexandria VA 22320. (703)683-1243. **E-mail:** lathbury@gmu.edu. **Website:** mason.gmu.edu/~lathbury. **Contact:** Roger Lathbury, editor-in-chief. Estab. 1983. Publishes hardcover and trade paperback originals and reprints. Orchises Press is a general literary publisher specializing in poetry with selected reprints and textbooks. No new fiction or children's books. **Publishes 2-3 titles/year. 1% of books from first-time authors. 95% from unagented writers. Pays 36% of receipts after Orchises has recouped its costs.** Publishes book 1 year after acceptance. Accepts simultaneous submissions. Responds in 3 months to queries. Guidelines available online.

NONFICTION No real restrictions on subject matter. Query with SASE. Reviews artwork/photos. Send photocopies.

POETRY Poetry must have been published in respected literary journals. *Orchises Press no longer reads unsolicited mss.* Publishes free verse, but has strong formalist preferences. Query and submit 5 sample poems.

OTTN PUBLISHING

16 Risler St., Stockton NJ 08559. (609)397-4005. **Fax:** (609)397-4007. **E-mail:** inquiries@ottnpublishing.com. **Website:** www.ottnpublishing.com. Estab. 1998. Publishes hardcover and trade paperback originals. **Publishes 5-10 titles/year. Receives 50 queries/year. 50% of books from first-time authors. 100% from unagented writers. Pays outright purchase of $1,200 to $5,000.** Publishes book 9 months after acceptance. Accepts simultaneous submissions. Responds in 6 months to queries. Catalog available online at website. Guidelines available online at website.

NONFICTION Subjects include government, history, military, politics, war. Query with SASE.

TIPS Most of our books are published for the school library market, although we do publish some books for an adult audience.

OUR CHILD PRESS

P.O. Box 4379, Philadelphia PA 19118. Phone/fax: (610)308-8088. **E-mail:** info@ourchildpress.com. **Website:** www.ourchildpress.com. **Contact:** Carol Perrott, president. **90% of books from first-time authors. Pays authors royalty of 5-10% based on wholesale price. Pays illustrators royalty of 5-10% based on wholesale price.** Publishes a book 6-12 months after acceptance. Responds to queries/mss in 6 months. Book catalog for business-size SAE and 67 cents.

FICTION All levels: adoption, multicultural, special needs.

OUR SUNDAY VISITOR, INC.

200 Noll Plaza, Huntington IN 46750. **E-mail:** jlindsey@osv.com. **Website:** www.osv.com. **Contact:** Jacquelyn Lindsey; David Dziena; Bert Ghezzi; Cindy Cavnar; Tyler Ottinger, art director. Publishes paperback and hardbound originals. "We are a Catholic publishing company seeking to educate and deepen our readers in their faith. Currently emphasizing devotional, inspirational, Catholic identity, apologetics, and catechetics." **Publishes 40-50 titles/year. Pays authors royalty of 10-12% net. Pays illustrators by the project (range: $25-1,500).** Publishes ms 1-2 years after acceptance. Accepts simultaneous submissions. Responds in 2 months to queries/mss. Book catalog for 9×12 envelope and first-class stamps; ms guidelines available online.

○   Our Sunday Visitor, Inc. is publishing only those children's books that are specifically Catholic. See website for submission guidelines."

NONFICTION Prefers to see well-developed proposals as first submission with annotated outline and definition of intended market; Catholic viewpoints on family, prayer, and devotional books, and Catholic heritage books. Picture books, middle readers, young readers, young adults. Query, submit complete ms, or submit outline/synopsis and 2-3 sample chapters. Reviews artwork/photos.

TIPS "Stay in accordance with our guidelines."

OUTRIDER PRESS, INC.

2036 North Winds Dr., Dyer IN 46311. (219)322-7270. **Fax:** (219)322-7085. **E-mail:** outriderpress@sbcglobal.net. **Website:** www.outriderpress.com. **Contact:** Whitney Scott, editor. Estab. 1988. Publishes trade paperback originals. **Receives 2,400 queries/year; 200 mss/year. 90% from unagented writers. Pays honorarium.** Publishes ms 6 months after acceptance. Responds in 6 weeks to queries; 4 months to proposals and mss. Guidelines available online.

Ⓞ Accepts unsolicited mss. Query with SASE. Accepts queries by mail. Include estimated word count, brief bio, list of publishing credits. Accepts simultaneous submissions, electronic submissions, submissions on disk. Sometimes comments on rejected mss. In affiliation with Tallgrass Writers Guild, publishes an annual anthology with $1,000 in cash prizes for short fiction, nonfiction, and poetry. Anthology theme for 2013 was: "'Music to my ear.' As Always, boradly interpreted; we welcome nature's music as subjects as well as human-made compositions and whatever constitutes music to your ears." Guidelines via e-mail at outriderpress@sbcglobal.net. Was a *Small Press Review* "Pick" for 2000. Sponsors an anthology competition for short stories, poetry, and creative nonfiction.

NONFICTION Subjects include creative nonfiction, language, literature, general nonfiction.

FICTION Subjects include contemporary, ethnic, experimental, feminist, gay, historical, humor, lesbian, literary, mainstream, short story collections, fantasy (space fantasy, sword and sorcery), family saga, horror (psychological/supernatural), mystery (amateur sleuth, cozy, police procedural, private eye/hardboiled), psychic/supernatural, romance (contemporary, futuristic/time travel), western (frontier saga, traditional). Ethnic, experimental, family saga, fantasy (space fantasy, sword and sorcery), feminist, gay/lesbian, historical, horror (psychological, supernatural), humor, lesbian, literary, mainstream/contemporary, mystery (amateur sleuth, cozy, police procedural, private eye/hard-boiled), new age/mystic, psychic/supernatural, romance (contemporary, futuristic/time travel, gothic, historical, regency period, romantic suspense), science fiction (soft/sociological), short story collections, thriller/espionage, western (frontier saga, traditional). Published *Telling Time*, by Cherie

Caswell Dost; *If Ever I Cease to Love*, by Robert Klein Engler; *62000 Reasons*, by Paul Miller; *Aquarium Octopus*, by Claudia Van Gerven; and *Heat*, by Deborah Thompson. Query with SASE.

TIPS "It's always best to familiarize yourself with our publications. We're especially fond of humor/irony."

Ⓞ THE OVERLOOK PRESS

141 Wooster St., New York NY 10012. (212)673-2210. **Fax:** (212)673-2296. **E-mail:** sales@overlookny.com. **Website:** www.overlookpress.com. Estab. 1971. Publishes hardcover and trade paperback originals and hardcover reprints. "Overlook Press publishes fiction, children's books, and nonfiction." **Publishes 100 titles/year.** Book catalog available free.

NONFICTION Subjects include art, architecture, film, cinema, stage, history, regional, New York State, current events, design, health/fitness, how-to, lifestyle, martial arts. The Overlook Press is an independent general-interest publisher. The publishing program consists of nearly 100 new books per year, evenly divided between hardcovers and trade paperbacks. The list is eclectic, but areas of strength include interesting fiction, history, biography, drama, and design. No pornography. Agented submissions only.

FICTION Subjects include literary, some commercial, foreign literature in translation. Agented submissions only.

RICHARD C. OWEN PUBLISHERS, INC.

P.O. Box 585, Katonah NY 10536. (914)232-3903; (800)262-0787. **E-mail:** richardowen@rcowen.com. **Website:** www.rcowen.com. **Contact:** Richard Owen, publisher. Estab. 1982. "We publish child-focused books, with inherent instructional value, about characters and situations with which five-, six-, and seven-year-old children can identify—books that can be read for meaning, entertainment, enjoyment and information. We include multicultural stories that present minorities in a positive and natural way. Our stories show the diversity in America." Not interested in lesson plans, or books of activities for literature studies or other content areas. Submit complete ms and cover letter. **Pays authors royalty of 5% based on net price or outright purchase (range: $25-500). Offers no advances. Pays illustrators by the project (range: $100-2,000) or per photo (range: $100-150).** Publishes a book 2-3 years after acceptance. Accepts simultaneous submissions. Responds to mss in 1 year.

Book catalog available with SASE. Ms guidelines with SASE or online.

○ "Due to high volume and long production time, we are currently limiting to nonfiction submissions only."

NONFICTION Subjects include art, architecture, history, nature, environment, recreation, science, sports, women's issues, women's studies, music, diverse culture, nature. Our books are for kindergarten, first- and second-grade children to read on their own. The stories are very brief—under 1,000 words—yet well structured and crafted with memorable characters, language, and plots. Picture books, young readers: animals, careers, history, how-to, music/dance, geography, multicultural, nature/environment, science, sports. Multicultural needs include: "Good stories respectful of all heritages, races, cultural—African-American, Hispanic, American Indian." Wants lively stories. No "encyclopedic" type of information stories. Average word length: under 500 words. Recently published *The Coral Reef*.

TIPS "We don't respond to queries or e-mails. Please do not fax or e-mail us. Because our books are so brief, it is better to send an entire manuscript. We publish story books with inherent educational value for young readers—books they can read with enjoyment and success. We believe students become enthusiastic, independent, life-long learners when supported and guided by skillful teachers using good books. The professional development work we do and the books we publish support these beliefs."

⊜ PETER OWEN PUBLISHERS

81 Ridge Rd., London N8 9NP, United Kingdom. (44)(208)350-1775. **Fax:** (44)(208)340-9488. **E-mail:** aowen@peterowen.com. **Website:** www.peterowen.com. **Contact:** Antonia Owen, editorial director. Publishes hardcover originals and trade paperback originals and reprints. "We are far more interested in proposals for nonfiction than fiction at the moment. No poetry or short stories." **Publishes 20-30 titles/year. 3,000 queries received/year. 800 mss received/year. 70% from unagented writers. Pays 7½-10% royalty. Pays negotiable advance.** Publishes ms 1 year after acceptance. Responds in 2 months to queries; 3 months to proposals and mss. Book catalog for SASE, SAE with IRC or on website.

NONFICTION Subjects include history, literature, memoirs, translation, travel, art, drama, literary, bi-

ography. Query with SASE. Submit outline, 1-3 sample chapters. Submit complete ms with return postage or email with attachments including synopsis.

FICTION Subjects include literary and translation. "No first novels-Authors should be aware that we publish very little new fiction these days. Will consider excerpts from novels of normal length from established authors if they submit sample chapters and synopses." Query with SASE or by e-mail.

OXFORD UNIVERSITY PRESS

198 Madison Ave., New York NY 10016. (212)726-6000. **E-mail:** custserv.us@oup.com. **Website:** www.oup.com/us.

OZARK MOUNTAIN PUBLISHING, INC.

P.O. Box 754, Huntsville AR 72740, U.S. (479)738-2348. **Fax:** (479)738-2448. **E-mail:** info@ozarkmt.com. **Website:** www.ozarkmt.com. **Contact:** Julia Degan, director (New Age/metaphysics/spiritual). Estab. 1991. Publishes trade paperback originals. **Publishes 8-10 titles/year. 50-75 queries; 150-200 mss. 50% of books from first-time authors. 95% from unagented writers. Pays 10-15% royalty on retail or wholesale price. Pays $250-500 advance.** Publishes ms 6-9 months after acceptance. Accepts simultaneous submissions. Responds in 6 months to queries, 7 months to mss. Book catalog free on request. Guidelines available online at website www.ozarkmt.com/submissions.htm.

NONFICTION Subjects include new age/metaphysical/body-mind-spirit, philosophy, spirituality. No phone calls please. Query with SASE. Submit 4-5 sample chapters.

TIPS "We envision our audience to be open minded, spiritually expanding. Please do not call to check on submissions. Do not submit electronically. Send hard copy only."

P & R PUBLISHING CO.

P.O. Box 817, Phillipsburg NJ 08865. **Fax:** (908)859-2390. **E-mail:** editorial@prpbooks.com. **Website:** www.prpbooks.com. Estab. 1930. Publishes hardcover originals and trade paperback originals and reprints. **Publishes 40 titles/year. Up to 300 queries received/year. 100 mss received/year. 5% of books from first-time authors. 95% from unagented writers. Pays 10-16% royalty on wholesale price.** Accepts simultaneous submissions. Responds in 3 months to proposals. Guidelines available online.

NONFICTION Subjects include history, religion, spirituality, translation. Only accepts electronic submission with completion of online Author Guidelines. Hard copy mss will not be returned.

TIPS "Our audience is evangelical Christians and seekers. All of our publications are consistent with Biblical teaching, as summarized in the Westminster Standards."

PACIFIC PRESS PUBLISHING ASSOCIATION

Trade Book Division, 1350 N. Kings Rd., Nampa ID 83687. (208)465-2500. **Fax:** (208)465-2531. **E-mail:** booksubmissions@pacificpress.com. **Website:** www.pacificpress.com. **Contact:** Scott Cady, acquisitions editor (children's stories, biography, Christian living, spiritual growth); David Jarnes, book editor (theology, doctrine, inspiration). Estab. 1874. Publishes hardcover and trade paperback originals and reprints. "We publish books that fit Seventh-day Adventist beliefs only. All titles are Christian and religious. For guidance, see www.adventist.org/beliefs/index.html. Our books fit into the categories of this retail site: www.adventistbookcenter.com." **Publishes 35 titles/year. 35% of books from first-time authors. 100% from unagented writers. Pays 8-16% royalty on wholesale price.** Publishes book 2 years after acceptance. Responds in 3 months to queries. Guidelines available online.

NONFICTION Subjects include child guidance, cooking, foods, nutrition, vegetarian only, health, history, nature, environment, philosophy, religion, spirituality, women's issues, family living, Christian lifestyle, Bible study, Christian doctrine, prophecy. Query with SASE or e-mail, or submit 3 sample chapters, cover letter with overview of book. Electronic submissions accepted. Reviews artwork/photos.

FICTION Subjects include religious. "Pacific Press rarely publishes fiction, but we're interested in developing a line of Seventh-day Adventist fiction in the future. Only proposals accepted; no full manuscripts."

TIPS "Our primary audience is members of the Seventh-day Adventist denomination. Almost all are written by Seventh-day Adventists. Books that do well for us relate the Biblical message to practical human concerns and focus more on the experiential rather than theoretical aspects of Christianity. We are assigning more titles, using less unsolicited material—although we still publish manuscripts from freelance submissions and proposals."

⊕ PAGESPRING PUBLISHING

P.O. Box 2113, Columbus OH 43221. **E-mail:** ps@pagespringpublishing.com. **E-mail:** yaeditor@pagespringpublishing.com; weditor@pagespringpublishing.com. **Website:** www.pagespringpublishing.com. Estab. 2012. Publishes trade paperback and electronic originals. "PageSpring Publishing publishes young adult and middle grade titles under the Lucky Marble Books imprint and women's fiction under the Cup of Tea imprint. See imprint websites for submission details." **Publishes 10-20 titles/year. Pays royalty on wholesale price.** Publishes ms 6 months after acceptance. Accepts simultaneous submissions. Responds to queries in 1 month. Guidelines available online at website.

IMPRINTS Lucky Marble Books, Cup of Tea Books.

FICTION Subjects include adventure, contemporary, fantasy, feminist, historical, humor, literary, mainstream, mystery, regional, romance, young adult. Submit proposal package including synopsis and 3 sample chapters.

PALARI PUBLISHING

P.O. Box 4, Montpelier VA 23192. (866)570-6724. **Fax:** (866)570-6724. **E-mail:** dave@palaribooks.com. **Website:** www.palaribooks.com. **Contact:** David Smitherman, publisher/editor. Estab. 1998. Publishes hardcover and trade paperback originals. "Palari provides authoritative, well-written nonfiction that addresses topical consumer needs and fiction with an emphasis on intelligence and quality. We accept solicited and unsolicited manuscripts, however we prefer a query letter and SASE, describing the project briefly and concisely. This letter should include a complete address and telephone number. Palari Publishing accepts queries or any other submissions by e-mail, but prefers queries submitted by US mail. All queries must be submitted by mail according to our guidelines. Promotes titles through book signings, direct mail and the Internet." **Pays royalty.** Publishes ms 1 year after acceptance. Responds in 1 month to queries; 2-3 months to mss. Guidelines available online.

◑ Member of Publishers Marketing Association.

NONFICTION Subjects include business, economics, memoirs.

FICTION Subjects include adventure, ethnic, gay, lesbian, historical, literary, mainstream, contemporary, multicultural. Tell why your idea is unique or interesting. Make sure we are interested in your genre before submitting. Query with SASE. Submit bio, estimated word count, list of publishing credits. Accepts queries via e-mail (prefer US Mail), fax.

TIPS "Send a good bio. I'm interested in a writer's experience and unique outlook on life."

PALETTES & QUILLS

330 Knickerbocker Ave., Rochester NY 14615. (585)456-0217. **E-mail:** palettesnquills@gmail.com. **Website:** www.palettesnquills.com. **Contact:** Donna M. Marbach, publisher/owner. Estab. 2002.

NONFICTION Does not want political and religious diatribes.

POETRY Palettes & Quills "is at this point, a poetry press only, and produces only a handful of publications each year, specializing in anthologies, individual chapbooks, and broadsides." Wants "work that should appeal to a wide audience." Does not want "poems that are sold blocks of text, long-lined and without stanza breaks. Wildly elaborate free-verse would be difficult and in all likelihood fight with art background, amateurish rhyming poem, overly sentimental poems, poems that use excessive profanity, or which denigrate other people, or political and religious diatribes." Query first with 3-5 poems and a cover letter with brief bio and publication credits for individual unsolicited chapbooks. May include previously published poems. Chapbook poets would get 20 copies of a run; broadside poets and artists get 5-10 copies and occasionally paid $10 for reproduction rights. Anthology poets get 1 copy of the anthology. All poets and artists get a discount on purchases that include their work.

PANTHEON BOOKS

Random House, Inc., 1745 Broadway, 3rd Floor, New York NY 10019. **E-mail:** pantheonpublicity@randomhouse.com. **Website:** www.pantheonbooks.com. Estab. 1942. Publishes hardcover and trade paperback originals and trade paperback reprints.

○ Pantheon Books publishes both Western and non-Western authors of literary fiction and important nonfiction. "We only accept mss submitted by an agent. You may still send a 20-50 page sample and a SASE to our slushpile. Allow 2-6 months for a response."

FICTION *Agented submissions only.*

PARADISE CAY PUBLICATIONS

P.O. Box 29, Arcata CA 95518-0029. (800)736-4509. **Fax:** (707)822-9163. **E-mail:** info@paracay.com; jim@paracay.com. **Website:** www.paracay.com. **Contact:** Matt Morehouse, publisher. Publishes hardcover and trade paperback originals and reprints. "Paradise Cay Publications, Inc. is a small independent publisher specializing in nautical books, videos, and art prints. Our primary interest is in manuscripts that deal with the instructional and technical aspects of ocean sailing. We also publish and will consider fiction if it has a strong nautical theme." **Publishes 5 titles/year. 360-480 queries received/year. 240-360 mss received/year. 10% of books from first-time authors. 100% from unagented writers. Pays 10-15% royalty on wholesale price. Makes outright purchase of $1,000-10,000. Does not normally pay advances to first-time or little-known authors.** Publishes book 4 months after acceptance. Responds in 1 month to queries/proposals; 2 months to mss. Book catalog and ms guidelines free on request or online.

IMPRINTS Pardey Books.

NONFICTION Subjects include cooking, foods, nutrition, recreation, sports, travel. Must have strong nautical theme. Include a cover letter containing a story synopsis and a short bio, including any plans to promote their work. The cover letter should describe the book's subject matter, approach, distinguishing characteristics, intended audience, author's qualifications, and why the author thinks this book is appropriate for Paradise Cay. Call first. Reviews artwork/photos. Send photocopies.

FICTION Subjects include adventure, nautical, sailing. All fiction must have a nautical theme. Query with SASE. Submit proposal package, clips, 2-3 sample chapters.

TIPS Audience is recreational sailors. Call Matt Morehouse (publisher).

PARADISE RESEARCH PUBLICATIONS, INC.

P.O. Box 837, Kihei HI 96753. (808)874-4876. **Fax:** (808)874-4876. **E-mail:** dickb@dickb.com. **Website:** www.dickb.com/index.shtml. Publishes trade paperback originals. Paradise Research Publications wants only books on Alcoholics Anonymous and its spiritual roots. **Publishes 3 titles/year. 5 queries received/year. 1 mss received/year. 20% of books from first-time authors. 100% from unagented writers. Pays 10% royalty.** Publishes ms 3 months after acceptance. Accepts simultaneous submissions. Responds in 1 month to queries. Book catalog available online.

NONFICTION Subjects include health, medicine, psychology, religion, spirituality, recovery, alcoholism, addictions, Christian recovery, history of Alcoholics Annonymous. Query with SASE.

PARAGON HOUSE PUBLISHERS

1925 Oakcrest Ave., Suite 7, St. Paul MN 55113. (651)644-3087. **Fax:** (651)644-0997. **E-mail:** paragon@paragonhouse.com. **Website:** www.paragonhouse.com. **Contact:** Gordon Anderson, acquisitions editor. Estab. 1962. Publishes hardcover and trade paperback originals and trade paperback reprints and eBooks. "We publish general-interest titles and textbooks that provide the readers greater understanding of society and the world. Currently emphasizing religion, philosophy, economics, and society." **Publishes 5-10 titles/year. 1,500 queries received/year. 150 mss received/year. 7% of books from first-time authors. 90% from unagented writers. Pays $500-1,000 advance.** Publishes ms 1 year after acceptance. Accepts simultaneous submissions. Guidelines available online.

IMPRINTS *Series*: Paragon Issues in Philosophy; Genocide and Holocaust Studies; Omega Books.

NONFICTION Subjects include government, politics, multicultural, nature, environment, philosophy, psychology, religion, sociology, women's issues, world affairs. Submit proposal package, outline, 2 sample chapters, market breakdown. SASE.

PASSKEY PUBLICATIONS

P.O. Box 580465, Elk Grove CA 95758. (916)712-7446. **Fax:** (916)427-5765. **Website:** www.passkeypublications.com. **Contact:** Christine P. Silva, president. Estab. 2007. Publishes trade paperback originals. **Publishes 15 titles/year. Receives 375 queries/year; 120 mss/year. 15% of books from first-time authors. 90% from unagented writers. Pay varies on retail price.** Publishes ms 1 year after acceptance. Accepts simultaneous submissions. Responds in 1 month on queries, proposals, and mss (for tax & accounting only). All others 1-3 months. Catalog and guidelines online at website www.passkeypublications.com.

IMPRINTS Passkey Publications, PassKey EA Review.

NONFICTION Subjects include business, economics, finance, money, real estate, accounting, taxation, study guides for professional examinations. "Books on taxation and accounting are generally updated every year to reflect tax law changes, and the turnaround on a ms must be less than 3 months for ac-

counting and tax subject matter. Books generally remain in publication only 11 months and are generally published every year for updates." Submit complete ms. Nonfiction mss only. Reviews artwork/photos as part of ms package. Send electronic files on disk, via e-mail, or jump drive.

TIPS "Accepting business, accounting, tax, finance and other related subjects only."

PASSPORT PRESS

E-mail: travelbook@yahoo.com. **Website:** www.paulglassman.com. **Contact:** Paul Glassman. Estab. 1975. Publishes trade paperback originals. "Passport Press publishes practical travel guides on specific countries. Currently emphasizing offbeat countries." **Publishes 4 titles/year. 25% of books from first-time authors. 100% from unagented writers. Pays 6% royalty on retail price. Pays advance.** Publishes ms 9 months after acceptance.

IMPRINTS Travel Line Press.

NONFICTION Subjects include travel. "Especially looking for mss on practical travel subjects and travel guides on specific countries." No travelogues. Send 1-page query only. Reviews artwork/photos.

PAUL DRY BOOKS

1700 Sanson St., Suite 700, Philadelphia PA 19103. (215)231-9939. **Fax:** (215)231-9942. **E-mail:** pdry@pauldrybooks.com; editor@pauldrybooks.com. **Website:** pauldrybooks.com. Hardcover and trade paperback originals, trade paperback reprints. "We publish fiction, both novels and short stories, and nonfiction, biography, memoirs, history, and essays, covering subjects from Homer to Chekhov, bird watching to jazz music, New York City to shogunate Japan." Book catalog available online. Guidelines available online.

"Take a few minutes to familiarize yourself with the books we publish. Then if you think your book would be a good fit in our line, we invite you to submit the following: A one- or two-page summary of the work. Be sure to tell us how many pages or words the full book will be; a sample of 20 to 30 pages; your bio. A brief description of how you think the book (and you, the author) could be marketed."

NONFICTION Subjects include agriculture, contemporary culture, history, literary criticism, memoirs, multicultural, philosophy, religion, translation, popular mathematics. Submit proposal package.

FICTION Subjects include literary, short story collections, translation, young adult, novels. Submit sample chapters, clips, bio.

TIPS "Our aim is to publish lively books 'to awaken, delight, & educate'—to spark conversation. We publish fiction and nonfiction, and essays covering subjects from Homer to Chekhov, bird watching to jazz music, New York City to shogunate Japan."

PAULINE BOOKS & MEDIA

50 St. Paul's Ave., Boston MA 02130. (617)522-8911. **Fax:** (617)541-9805. **E-mail:** design@paulinemedia. com; editorial@paulinemedia.com. **Website:** www. pauline.org. Estab. 1932. Publishes trade paperback originals and reprints. "Submissions are evaluated on adherence to Gospel values, harmony with the Catholic tradition, relevance of topic, and quality of writing." For board books and picture books, the entire manuscript should be submitted. For easy-to-read, young readers, and middle reader books and teen books, please send a cover letter accompanied by a synopsis and two sample chapters. "Electronic submissions are encouraged. We make every effort to respond to unsolicited submissions within 2 months." **Publishes 40 titles/year. 15% of books from first-time authors. 5% from unagented writers. Varies by project, but generally are royalties with advance. Flat fees sometimes considered for smaller works.** Publishes a book approximately 11-18 months after acceptance. Accepts simultaneous submissions. Responds in 2 months to queries, proposals, & mss. Book catalog available online. Guidelines available online & by e-mail.

NONFICTION Subjects include child guidance, religion, spirituality. Picture books, young readers, middle readers, teen: religion and fiction. Average word length: picture books—500-1,000; young readers—8,000-10,000; middle readers—15,000-25,000; teen—30,000-50,000. No biography/autobiography, poetry, or strictly nonreligious works considered. Submit proposal package, including outline, 1- 2 sample chapters, cover letter, synopsis, intended audience and proposed length. Reviews artwork; send photocopies.

FICTION Subjects include juvenile. Children's and teen fiction only. We are now accepting submissions for easy-to-read and middle reader chapter, and teen fiction. Please see our Writer's Guidelines. "Submit proposal package, including synopsis, 2 sample chapters, and cover letter; complete ms."

TIPS "Manuscripts may or may not be explicitly catechetical, but we seek those that reflect a positive worldview, good moral values, awareness and appreciation of diversity, and respect for all people. All material must be relevant to the lives of readers and must conform to Catholic teaching and practice."

PAULIST PRESS

997 MacArthur Blvd., Mahwah NJ 07430. (201)825-7300. **Fax:** (201)825-8345. **Website:** www.paulistpress. com. **Contact:** Donna Crilly, managing editor. Estab. 1865. "Paulist Press publishes ecumenical theology, Roman Catholic studies, and books on scripture, liturgy, spirituality, church history, and philosophy, as well as works on faith and culture. Our publishing is oriented toward adult-level nonfiction. We do not publish poetry or works of fiction, and we have scaled back our involvement in children's publishing." **Receives 250 submissions/year. Royalties and advances are negotible. Illustrators sometimes receive a flat fee when all we need are spot illustrations.** Publishes a book 12-18 months after acceptance. Accepts simultaneous submissions. Responds in 3 months to queries and proposals; 3-4 months on mss. Book catalog available online. Guidelines available online and by e-mail.

PAYCOCK PRESS

3819 N. 13th St., Arlington VA 22201. (703)525-9296. **E-mail:** gargoyle@gargoylemagazine.com. **Website:** www.gargoylemagazine.com. **Contact:** Lucinda Ebersole and Richard Peabody. Estab. 1976. "Too academic for underground, too outlaw for the academic world. We tend to be edgy and look for ultra-literary work." Publishes paperback originals. Books: POD printing. Average print order: 500. Averages 1 total title/year. Member CLMP. Distributes through Amazon and website. Publishes ms 1 year after acceptance. Accepts simultaneous submissions. Responds to queries in 1 month; mss in 4 months.

FICTION Wants: experimental, literary, short story collections. Accepts unsolicited mss. Accepts queries by e-mail. Include brief bio. Send SASE for return of ms or send a disposable ms and SASE for reply only.

TIPS "Check out our website. Two of our favorite writers are Paul Bowles and Jeanette Winterson."

PEACE HILL PRESS

Affiliate of W.W. Norton, 18021 The Glebe Ln., Charles City VA 23030. (804)829-5043. **Fax:** (804)829-5704. **E-mail:** info@peacehillpress.com. **Website:** www.peace-hillpress.com. **Contact:** Peter Buffington, acquisitions editor. Estab. 2001. Publishes hardcover and trade paperback originals. **Publishes 4-8 titles/year. Pays 6-10% royalty on retail price. Pays $500-1,000 advance.** Publishes a book 18 months after acceptance. Accepts simultaneous submissions.

NONFICTION Subjects include education, history, language, literature. Submit proposal package, outline, 1 sample chapter. Reviews artwork/photos. Send photocopies.

FICTION Subjects include historical, juvenile, picture books, young adult. Submit proposal package, outline, 1 sample chapter.

PEACHTREE CHILDREN'S BOOKS

Peachtree Publishers, Ltd., 1700 Chattahoochee Ave., Atlanta GA 30318-2112. (404)876-8761. **Fax:** (404)875-2578. **E-mail:** hello@peachtree-online.com. **Website:** www.peachtree-online.com. **Contact:** Helen Harriss, submissions editor. Publishes hardcover and trade paperback originals. "We publish a broad range of subjects and perspectives, with emphasis on innovative plots and strong writing." **Publishes 30 titles/year. 25% of books from first-time authors. 25% from un-agented writers. Pays royalty on retail price.** Publishes ms 1 year after acceptance. Accepts simultaneous submissions. Responds in 6 months and mss. Book catalog for 6 first-class stamps. Guidelines available online.

NONFICTION Subjects include animals, child guidance, creative nonfiction, education, ethnic, gardening, health, medicine, history, language, literature, literary criticism, multicultural, music, dance, nature, environment, recreation, regional, science, social sciences, sports, travel. No e-mail or fax queries of mss. Submit complete ms with SASE, or summary and 3 sample chapters with SASE.

FICTION Subjects include juvenile, picture books, young adult. Looking for very well-written middle grade and young adult novels. Juvenile, picture books, young adult. Looking for very well written middle grade and young adult novels. No adult fiction. No short stories. No collections of poetry or short stories; no romance or science fiction. Submit complete ms with SASE.

⚪ ⊘ PEDLAR PRESS

113 Bond St., St. John's NL A16 1T6, Canada. (709)738-6702. **E-mail:** feralgrl@interlog.com. **Website:** www.pedlarpress.com. **Contact:** Beth Follett, owner/editor. Distributes in Canada through LitDistCo.; in the US distributes directly through publisher. **Publishes 7 titles/year. Pays 10% royalty on retail price. Average advance: $200-400.** Publishes ms 1 year after acceptance.

FICTION Experimental, feminist, gay/lesbian, literary, short story collections. Canadian writers only. Query with SASE, sample chapter(s), synopsis.

TIPS "I select manuscripts according to my taste, which fluctuates. Be familiar with some if not most of Pedlar's recent titles."

PELICAN PUBLISHING COMPANY

1000 Burmaster St., Gretna LA 70053. (504)368-1175. **Fax:** (504)368-1195. **E-mail:** editorial@pelicanpub.com. **Website:** www.pelicanpub.com. **Contact:** Nina Kooij, editor-in-chief. Estab. 1926. Publishes hardcover, trade paperback and mass market paperback originals and reprints. "We believe ideas have consequences. One of the consequences is that they lead to a best-selling book. We publish books to improve and uplift the reader. Currently emphasizing business and history titles." Publishes 20 young readers/year; 1 middle reader/year. "Our children's books (illustrated and otherwise) include history, biography, holiday, and regional. Pelican's mission is to publish books of quality and permanence that enrich the lives of those who read them." **Pays authors in royalties; buys ms outright "rarely." Illustrators paid by "various arrangements." Advance considered.** Publishes a book 9-18 months after acceptance. Responds in 1 month to queries; 3 months to mss. Book catalog and ms guidelines online.

NONFICTION Subjects include Americana, especially Southern regional, Ozarks, Texas, Florida, and Southwest, art, architecture, ethnic, government, politics, special interest in conservative viewpoint, history, popular, multicultural, American artforms, but will consider others: jazz, blues, Cajun, R&B, regional, religion, for popular audience mostly, but will consider others, sports, motivational (with business slant). "We look for authors who can promote successfully. We require that a query be made first. This greatly expedites the review process and can save the writer additional postage expenses." Young readers: biography, history, holiday, multicultural. Middle readers: Louisiana history, holiday, regional. No multiple queries or submissions. Query with SASE. Reviews artwork/photos.

FICTION Subjects include historical, juvenile, regional or historical focus. We publish no adult fiction. Young readers: history, holiday, science, multicultural and regional. Middle readers: Louisiana History. Multicultural needs include stories about African-Americans, Irish-Americans, Jews, Asian-Americans, and Hispanics. Does not want animal stories, general Christmas stories, "day at school" or "accept yourself" stories. Maximum word length: young readers—1,100; middle readers—40,000. No young adult, romance, science fiction, fantasy, gothic, mystery, erotica, confession, horror, sex, or violence. Also no psychological novels. Query with SASE. Submit outline, clips, 2 sample chapters, SASE.

POETRY Pelican Publishing Company is a medium-sized publisher of popular histories, cookbooks, regional books, children's books, and inspirational/motivational books. Considers poetry for "hardcover children's books only (1,100 words maximum), preferably with a regional focus. However, our needs for this are very limited; we publish 20 juvenile titles per year, and most of these are prose, not poetry." Two of Pelican's popular series are prose books about Gaston the Green-Nosed Alligator by James Rice, and Clovis Crawfish by Mary Alice Fontenot. Books are 32 pages, magazine-sized, include illustrations.

TIPS "We do extremely well with cookbooks, popular histories, and business. We will continue to build in these areas. The writer must have a clear sense of the market and knowledge of the competition. A query letter should describe the project briefly, give the author's writing and professional credentials, and promotional ideas."

PEMMICAN PUBLICATIONS, INC.

90 Sutherland Ave., Winnipeg MB R2W 3C7, Canada. (204)589-6346. **Fax:** (204)589-2063. **E-mail:** pemmican@pemmican.mb.ca. **Website:** www.pemmican.publications.ca. **Contact:** Randal McIlroy, managing editor (Metis culture & heritage). Estab. 1980. Publishes trade paperback originals and reprints. "Pemmican Publications is a Metis publishing house, with a mandate to publish books by Metis authors and illustrators and with an emphasis on culturally relevant stories. We encourage writers to learn a little about Pemmican before sending samples. Pemmican publishes titles in the following genres: Adult Fiction, which includes novels, story collections and anthologies; Nonfiction, with an emphasis on social history and biography reflecting Metis experience; Children's and Young Adult titles; Aboriginal languages, including Michif and Cree." **Publishes 5-6 titles/year. 120 queries received/year. 120 mss received/year. 50% of books from first-time authors. 100% from unagented writers. Pays 10% royalty on retail price.** Publishes book 1-2 years after acceptance. Accepts simultaneous submissions. Responds to queries, proposals, and mss in 3 months. Book catalog available free with SASE. Guidelines available online.

NONFICTION Subjects include alternative, creative nonfiction, education, ethnic, history, language, literature, military, war, nature, environment. All mss must be Metis culture and heritage related. Submit proposal package including outline and 3 sample chapters. Reviews artwork/photos. Send photocopies.

FICTION Subjects include adventure, ethnic, historical, juvenile, literary, mystery, picture books, short story collections, sports, suspense, young adult. All manuscripts must be Metis culture and heritage related. Submit proposal package including outline and 3 sample chapters.

POETRY Submit 10 sample poems and complete ms.

TIPS "Our mandate is to promote Metis authors, illustrators and stories. No agent is necessary."

PENGUIN GROUP USA

375 Hudson St., New York NY 10014. (212)366-2000. **Website:** www.penguin.com. **Contact:** Peter Stampfel, submission editor (DAW Books). General interest publisher of both fiction and nonfiction. Responds in 3 months generally. Guidelines available online at website.

IMPRINTS Exceptions are DAW Books and G.P. Putnam's Sons Books for Young Readers, which are accepting submissions. See individual listings for more information. **Penguin Adult Division:** Ace Books, Alpha Books, Avery, Berkley Books, Dutton, Gotham Books, HPBooks, Hudson St. Press, Jove, New American Library, Penguin, The Penguin Press, Perigee, Plume, Portfolio, G.P. Putnam's Sons, Riverhead, Sentinel, Jeremy P. Tarcher, Viking; **Penguin Children's Division:** Dial Books for Young Readers, Dutton Children's Books, Firebird, Grosset & Dunlap, Philomel, Price Stern Sloan, Puffin Books, G.P. Putnam's Sons, Speak, Viking Children's Books, Frederick Warne.

○ *No unsolicited mss.* Submit work through a literary agent.

FICTION "We publish first novels if they are of professional quality. A literary agent is not required for submission. We will not consider mss that are currently on submission to another publisher unless prior arrangements have been made with a literary agent. Please enclose a SASE with your submission for our correspondence. We ask that you only send us disposable copies of your ms, which will be recycled in the event they are not found suitable for publication. We regret that we are no longer able to return submitted ms copies, as the process resulted in too many difficulties with the postal service and unnecessary expense for the prospective authors. It may require up to three months or more for our editors to review a submission and come to a decision. If you want to be sure we have received your manuscript, please enclose a stamped, self-addressed postcard that we will return when your ms. It is not necessary for you to register or copyright your work before publicationit is protected by law as long as it has not been published. When published, we will copyright the book in the author's name and register that copyright with the Library of Congress. DAW Books is currently accepting manuscripts in the science fiction/fantasy genre. We publish science fiction and fantasy novels. The average length of the novels we publish varies but is almost never less than 80,000 words. Do not submit handwritten material." We do not want short stories, short story collections, novellas, or poetry. "Due to the high volume of mss we receive, Penguin Group (USA) Inc. imprints do not normally accept unsolicited mss. On rare occasion, however, a particular imprint may be open to reading such. The Penguin Group (USA) web site features a listing of which imprints (if any) are currently accepting unsolicited manuscripts." Continue to check website for updates to the list.

PENNY-FARTHING PRESS INC.

2000 W. Sam Houston Pkwy. S, Houston TX 77042. (713)780-0300 or (800)926-2669. **Fax:** (713)780-4004. **E-mail:** submissions@pfpress.com; corp@pfpress.com. **Website:** www.pfpress.com. **Contact:** Ken White, publisher; Marlaine Maddox, editor-in-chief. Estab. 1998. "Penny-Farthing Press officially opened its doors in 1998 with a small staff and a plan to create comic books and children's books that exemplified quality storytelling, artwork, and printing.Starting with only one book, The Victorian, Penny-Farthing Press has expanded its line to six titles, but keeps its yearly output small enough to maintain the highest quality. This "boutique approach" to publishing has won the recognition of the comics and fine arts industries, and PFP has won numerous awards including the Gutenberg D'Argent Medal and several Spectrum Awards." Guidelines available online at website.

FICTION "Please make sure all submissions include a synopsis that is brief and to the point. Remember, the synopsis is the "first impression" of your submission and you know what they say about first impressions. If you are submitting just one single-issue story (standard 32 pp.), you may send the full script with your submission. If you are submitting a story for any kind of series or graphic novel, please send only the first chapter of the series. If we like what we see, we will contact you to see more. If you are submitting a completed work (script, art work and lettering) copies of this may be sent instead."

◐⊘ PERENNIAL

HarperCollins Publishers, 10 E. 53rd St., New York NY 10022. (212)207-7000. **Website:** www.harpercollins.com. **Contact:** Acquisitions Editor. Estab. 1963. Publishes trade paperback originals and reprints. Perennial publishes a broad range of adult literary fiction and nonfiction paperbacks that create a record of our culture. Book catalog available free.

○ "With the exception of Avon romance, HarperCollins does not accept unsolicited submissions or query letters. Please refer to your local bookstore, the library, or a book entitled *Literary Marketplace* on how to find the appropriate agent for you."

NONFICTION Subjects include Americana, animals, business, economics, child guidance, cooking, foods, nutrition, education, ethnic, gay, lesbian, history, language, literature, military, war, money, finance, music, dance, nature, environment, and environment, philosophy, psychology, self-help psychotherapy, recreation, regional, religion, spirituality, science, sociology, sports, translation, travel, womens issues, womens studies, mental health, health, classic literature. Our focus is ever-changing, adjusting to the marketplace. Mistakes writers often make are not giving their background and credentials-why they are qualified to write the book. A proposal should explain why the author wants to write this book; why it will sell; and why it is better or different from others of its kind. Agented submissions only.

FICTION Subjects include ethnic, feminist, literary. Agented submissions only.

POETRY Don't send poetry unless you have been published in several established literary magazines already. *Agented submissions only.*

TIPS See our website for a list of titles or write to us for a free catalog.

THE PERMANENT PRESS

Attn: Judith Shepard, 4170 Noyac Rd., Sag Harbor NY 11963. (631)725-1101. **Fax:** (631)725-8215. **E-mail:** judith@thepermanentpress.com; shepard@thepermanentpress.com. **Website:** www.thepermanentpress.com. **Contact:** Judith and Martin Shepard, acquisitions/co-publishers. Blog: www.thecockeyedpessimist.com Estab. 1978. Publishes hardcover originals. Mid-size, independent publisher of literary fiction. "We keep titles in print and are active in selling subsidiary rights." Average print order: 1,500. Averages 14 total titles. Accepts unsolicited mss. Pays 10-15% royalty on wholesale price. Offers $1,000 advance. **Pays 10-15% royalty on wholesale price. Offers $1,000 advance.** Publishes ms within 18 months after acceptance. Responds in weeks or months to queries and submissions.

◑ *Will NOT accept simultaneous submissions.*

FICTION Promotes titles through reviews. Literary, mainstream/contemporary, mystery. Especially looking for high-line literary fiction, "artful, original and arresting." Accepts any fiction category as long as it is a "well-written, original full-length novel."

TIPS "We are looking for good books—be they 10th novels or first ones, it makes little difference. The fiction is more important than the track record. Send us the first 25 pages; it's impossible to judge something that begins on page 302. Also, no outlines—let the writing present itself."

⊕ PERSEA BOOKS

277 Broadway, Suite 708, New York NY 10007. (212)260-9256. **Fax:** (212)267-3165. **E-mail:** info@perseabooks.com. **Website:** www.perseabooks.com. Estab. 1975. "We are pleased to receive query letters from authors and literary agents for fiction and nonfiction manuscripts." Responds in 8 weeks to proposals; 10 weeks to mss. Guidelines online.

NONFICTION Subjects include contemporary culture, literary criticism, literature, memoirs, translation, travel, young adult. Queries should include a cover letter, author background and publication history, a detailed synopsis of the proposed work, and a sample chapter. Please indicate if the work is simultaneously submitted.

FICTION Subjects include contemporary, literary, short story collections, translation, young adult. Queries should include a cover letter, author background and publication history, a detailed synopsis of the proposed work, and a sample chapter. Please indicate if the work is simultaneously submitted.

POETRY "We have a longstanding commitment to publishing extraordinary contemporary poetry and maintain an active poetry program. At this time, due to our commitment to the poets we already publish, we are limited in our ability to add new collections." Send an e-mail to poetry@perseabooks.com describing current project and publication history, attaching a pdf or Word document with up to 12 sample pages of poetry. "If the timing is right and we are interested in seeing more work, we will contact you."

PERSEUS BOOK GROUP

250 W. 57th St., 15th Floor, New York NY 10107. **Website:** www.perseusbooksgroup.com. **Agented submissions only.**

⊘ PERUGIA PRESS

P.O. Box 60364, Florence MA 01062. **E-mail:** info@perugiapress.com. **Website:** www.perugiapress.com. **Contact:** Susan Kan, director. Estab. 1997.

PETER PAUPER PRESS, INC.

202 Mamaroneck Ave., White Plains NY 10601. **E-mail:** customerservice@peterpauper.com. **Website:** www.peterpauper.com. **Contact:** Barbara Paulding, editorial director. Estab. 1928. Publishes hardcover originals. "PPP publishes small and medium format, illustrated gift books for occasions and in celebration of specific relationships such as mom, sister, friend, teacher, grandmother, granddaughter. PPP has expanded into the following areas: books for teens and tweens, activity books for children, organizers, books on popular topics of nonfiction for adults and licensed books by best-selling authors." **Publishes 40-50 titles/year. 100 queries received/year. 150 mss received/year. 5% from unagented writers. Makes outright purchase only. Pays advance.** Publishes ms 1 year after acceptance. Responds in 2 months to

queries. Ms guidelines for #10 SASE or may request via e-mail.

NONFICTION "We do not publish fiction or poetry. We publish brief, original quotes, aphorisms, and wise sayings. Please do not send us other people's quotes." Query with SASE.

TIPS "Our readers are primarily female, age 10 and over, who are likely to buy a 'gift' book or gift book set in a stationery, gift, book, or boutique store or national book chain. Writers should become familiar with our previously published work. We publish only small- and medium-format, illustrated, hardcover gift books and sets of between 1,000-4,000 words. We have much less interest in work aimed at men."

PFLAUM PUBLISHING GROUP

2621 Dryden Rd., Suite 300, Dayton OH, 45439. **Contact:** Cullen W. Schippe, president and publisher Pflaum Publishing Division. "Pflaum Publishing Group, a division of Peter Li, Inc., serves the specialized market of religious education, primarily Roman Catholic. We provide high quality, theologically sound, practical, and affordable resources that assist religious educators of and ministers to children from preschool through senior high school." **Publishes 20 titles/year. Payment by outright purchase.** Book catalog and ms guidelines free.

NONFICTION Query with SASE.

RECENT Title(s) *Absolutely Advent; Totally Lent; Days of Faith Student Planners.*

⊘ PHILOMEL BOOKS

Imprint of Penguin Group (USA), Inc., 375 Hudson St., New York NY 10014. (212)414-3610. **Website:** www.us.penguingroup.com. **Contact:** Michael Green, president/publisher; Annie Ericsson, junior designer. Estab. 1980. Publishes hardcover originals. "We look for beautifully written, engaging manuscripts for children and young adults." **Publishes 8-10 titles/ year. 5% of books from first-time authors. 20% from unagented writers. Pays authors in royalties. Average advance payment "varies." Illustrators paid by advance and in royalties. Pays negotiable advance.** Accepts simultaneous submissions. Book catalog for 9×12 envelope and 4 first-class stamps. Guidelines for #10 SASE.

NONFICTION Picture books.

FICTION Subjects include adventure, ethnic, fantasy, historical, juvenile, literary, picture books, regional, short story collections, translation, western, young adult. All levels: adventure, animal, boys, contemporary, fantasy, folktales, historical fiction, humor, sports, multicultural. Middle readers, young adults: problem novels, science fiction, suspense/mystery. No concept picture books, mass-market "character" books, or series. Average word length: picture books—1,000; young readers—1,500; middle readers—14,000; young adult—20,000. No series or activity books. No generic, mass-market oriented fiction. *No unsolicited mss.*

TIPS Wants "unique fiction or nonfiction with a strong voice and lasting quality. Discover your own voice and own story and persevere." Looks for "something unusual, original, well written. Fine art or illustrative art that feels unique. The genre (fantasy, contemporary, or historical fiction) is not so important as the story itself and the spirited life the story allows its main character."

PIANO PRESS

P.O. Box 85, Del Mar CA 92014. (619)884-1401. **Fax:** (858)755-1104. **E-mail:** pianopress@pianopress.com. **Website:** www.pianopress.com. **Contact:** Elizabeth C. Axford, editor. Estab. 1998. "We publish music-related books, either fiction or nonfiction, coloring books, songbooks, and poetry." **Pays authors, illustrators, and photographers royalty of 5-10% based on retail price.** Publishes book 1 year after acceptance. Accepts simultaneous submissions. Responds to queries in 3 months; mss in 6 months. Book catalog available for #10 SASE and 2 first-class stamps.

NONFICTION Picture books, young readers, middle readers, young adults: multicultural, music/dance. Average word length: picture books—1,500-2,000.

FICTION Picture books, young readers, middle readers, young adults: folktales, multicultural, poetry, music. Average word length: picture books—1,500-2,000.

TIPS "We are looking for music-related material only for any juvenile market. Please do not send non-music-related materials. Query first before submitting anything."

⬤ PIATKUS BOOKS

Little, Brown Book Group, 100 Victoria Embankment, London WA EC4Y 0DY, United Kingdom. 0207 911 8000. **Fax:** 0207 911 8100. **E-mail:** info@ littlebrown.co.uk. **Website:** piatkus.co.uk. **Contact:** Emma Beswetherick, senior editor. Donna Condon, editor; Kim Mackay, editorial assistant Estab. 1979. Publishes hardcover originals, paperback originals, and paperback reprints. "Until 2007, Piatkus operated as an independent publishing house. Now it exists as a commercial imprint of Hachette-owned Little, Brown Book Group." **10% from unagented writers.** Publishes ms 1 year after acceptance. Responds in 3 months to mss. Guidelines available online.

○ Piatkus no longer accepts fiction proposals.

NONFICTION To submit a nonfiction proposal to Piatkus, please send a letter of enquiry outlining the work and 3 sample chapters. We do not accept e-mailed book proposals. Accepts unsolicited mss. Query with SASE or submit first 3 sample chapter(s), synopsis. Accepts queries by mail. Include estimated word count, brief bio, list of publishing credits. Send SASE for return of ms or send a disposable ms and SASE for reply only. Accepts simultaneous submissions. No submissions on disk or via e-mail. Rarely comments on rejected mss.

FICTION Quality family saga, historical, literary. Best-selling authors include: Nora Roberts, JD Robb, Christina Jones, Julia Quinn, Nick Brownlee.

TIPS "Study our list before submitting your work."

ⒶPICADOR USA

MacMillan, 175 Fifth Ave., New York NY 10010. (212)674-5151. **E-mail:** david.saint@picadorusa.com; pressinquiries@macmillanusa.com. **Website:** www.picadorusa.com. **Contact:** Frances Coady, publisher (literary fiction). Joshua Kendall, associate editor (literary fiction); Sam Douglas, associate editor; David Rogers, assistant editor Estab. 1994. Picador publishes high-quality literary fiction and nonfiction. "We are open to a broad range of subjects, well written by authoritative authors." Publishes hardcover and trade paperback originals and reprints. Averages 70-80 total titles/year. Titles distributed through Von Holtzbrinck Publishers. Titles promoted through national print advertising and bookstore co-op. **Pays 7-15% on royalty. Advance varies.** Publishes ms 18 months after acceptance. Accepts simultaneous submissions. Responds to queries in 2 months. Book catalog for 9×12 SASE and $2.60 postage. Ms guidelines for #10 SASE or online.

○ Does not accept unsolicited mss. *Agented submissions only.*

PICCADILLY BOOKS, LTD.

P.O. Box 25203, Colorado Springs CO 80936. (719)550-9887. **Fax:** (719) 550-8810. **Website:** www.piccadillybooks.com. Estab. 1985. Publishes hard-cover originals and trade paperback originals and reprints. "Picadilly publishes nonfiction, diet, nutrition, and health-related books with a focus on alternative and natural medicine." **Publishes 5-8 titles/year. 70% of books from first-time authors. 95% from unagented writers. Pays 6-10% royalty on retail price.** Publishes ms 1 year after acceptance. Accepts simultaneous submissions. Responds only if interested, unless accompanied by a SASE to queries.

NONFICTION Subjects include cooking, foods, nutrition, health, medicine, performing arts. "Do your research. Let us know why there is a need for your book, how it differs from other books on the market, and how you will promote the book. No phone calls. We prefer to see the entire ms, but will accept a minimum of 3 sample chapters on your first inquiry. A cover letter is also required; please provide a brief overview of the book, information about similar books already in print and explain why yours is different or better. Tell us the prime market for your book and what you can do to help market it. Also, provide us with background information on yourself and explain what qualifies you to write this book."

TIPS "We publish nonfiction, general interest, self-help books currently emphasizing alternative health."

PICCADILLY PRESS

5 Castle Rd., London NW1 8PR, United Kingdom. (44)(207)267-4492. **Fax:** (44)(207)267-4493. **E-mail:** books@piccadillypress.co.uk. **Website:** www.piccadillypress.co.uk. "Piccadilly Press is the perfect choice for variety of reading for everyone aged 2-16! We're an independent publisher, celebrating 26 years of specialising in teen fiction and nonfiction, childrens fiction, picture books and parenting books by highly acclaimed authors and illustrators and fresh new talents too. We hope you enjoy reading the books as much as we enjoy publishing them." Responds to mss in 6 weeks.

NONFICTION Young adults: self help (humorous). Average word length: young adults—25,000-35,000. Submit outline/synopsis and 2 sample chapters.

FICTION Picture books: animal, contemporary, fantasy, nature/environment. Young adults: contemporary, humor, problem novels. Average word length: picture books—500-1,000; young adults—25,000-35,000. Submit complete ms for picture books or submit outline/synopsis and 2 sample chapters for YA. Enclose a brief cover letter and SASE for reply.

TIPS "Take a look in bookshops to see if there are many other books of a similar nature to yours—this is what your book will be competing against, so make sure there is something truly unique about your story. Looking at what else is available will give you ideas as to what topics are popular, but reading a little of them will also give you a sense of the right styles, language and length appropriate for the age-group."

PINEAPPLE PRESS, INC.

P.O. Box 3889, Sarasota FL 34230. (941)739-2219. **Fax:** (941)739-2296. **E-mail:** info@pineapplepress.com. **Website:** www.pineapplepress.com. **Contact:** June Cussen, executive editor. Estab. 1982. Publishes hardcover and trade paperback originals. "We are seeking quality nonfiction on diverse topics for the library and book trade markets. Our mission is to publish good books about Florida." **Publishes 25 titles/year. 1,000 queries received/year. 500 mss received/year. 50% of books from first-time authors. 95% from unagented writers. Pays authors royalty of 10-15%.** Publishes a book 1 year after acceptance. Accepts simultaneous submissions. Responds to queries/samples/mss in 2 months. Book catalog for 9×12 SAE with $1.25 postage. Guidelines available online.

NONFICTION Subjects include regional, Florida. Picture books: animal, history, nature/environmental, science. Young readers, middle readers, young adults: animal, biography, geography, history, nature/environment, science. We will consider most nonfiction topics when related to Florida. Query or submit outline/synopsis and intro and 3 sample chapters. Reviews artwork/photos. Send photocopies.

FICTION Subjects include regional, Florida. Picture books, young readers, middle readers, young adults: animal, folktales, history, nature/environment. Query or submit outline/synopsis and 3 sample chapters.

TIPS "Quality first novels will be published, though we usually only do one or two novels per year and they must be set in Florida. We regard the author/editor relationship as a trusting relationship with communication open both ways. Learn all you can about the publishing process and about how to promote your book once it is published. A query on a novel without a brief sample seems useless."

PIÑATA BOOKS

Imprint of Arte Publico Press, University of Houston, 4902 Gulf Fwy, Bldg 19, Rm 100, Houston TX 77204-2004. (713)743-2845. **Fax:** (713)743-3080. **E-mail:** submapp@mail.uh.edu. **Website:** www.latinoteca.com/arte-publico-press. **Contact:** Nicolas Kanellos, director. Estab. 1994. Publishes hardcover and trade paperback originals. "Piñata Books is dedicated to the publication of children's and young adult literature focusing on U.S. Hispanic culture by U.S. Hispanic authors. Arte Publico's mission is the publication, promotion and dissemination of Latino literature for a variety of national and regional audiences, from early childhood to adult, through the complete gamut of delivery systems, including personal performance as well as print and electronic media." **Publishes 10-15 titles/year. 80% of books from first-time authors. Pays 10% royalty on wholesale price. Pays $1,000-3,000 advance.** Publishes book 2 years after acceptance. Accepts simultaneous submissions. Responds in 2-3 months to queries; 4-6 months to mss. Book catalog and ms guidelines available via website or with #10 SASE.

○ Accepts material from U.S./Hispanic authors only (living abroad OK). Mss, queries, synopses, etc., are accepted in either English or Spanish.

NONFICTION Subjects include ethnic. Piñata Books specializes in publication of children's and young adult literature that authentically portrays themes, characters and customs unique to U.S. Hispanic culture. Submissions made through online submission form.

FICTION Subjects include adventure, juvenile, picture books, young adult. Submissions made through online submission form.

POETRY Appropriate to Hispanic theme. Submissions made through online submission form.

TIPS "Include cover letter with submission explaining why your manuscript is unique and important, why we should publish it, who will buy it, etc."

PITSPOPANY PRESS

Simcha Media, P.O. Box 5329, Englewood NJ 07631. (212)444-1657. **Fax:** (866)205-3966. **E-mail:** pitspop@netvision.net.il. **Website:** www.pitspopany.com. Estab. 1992. "Pitspopany Press is dedicated to bringing quality children's books of Jewish interest into the marketplace. Our goal is to create titles that will appeal to the esthetic senses of our readers and, at the same time, offer quality Jewish content to the discerning parent, teacher, and librarian. While the people working for Pitspopany Press embody a wide spectrum of Jewish belief and opinion, we insist that our titles be respectful of the mainstream Jewish viewpoints and beliefs. We are especially interested in chapter books for kids. Most of all, we are committed to creating books that all Jewish children can read, learn from, and enjoy." **Pays authors royalty or work purchased outright.** Publishes book 9 months after acceptance. Accepts simultaneous submissions. Responds to queries/mss in 6 weeks. Catalog on website. Writer's guidelines available for SASE.

NONFICTION All levels: activity books, animal, arts/crafts, biography, careers, concept, cooking, geography, health, history, hobbies, how-to, multicultural, music/dance, nature/environment, reference, religion, science, self help, social issues, special needs, sports. Submit outline/synopsis.

FICTION Picture books: animal, anthology, fantasy, folktales, history, humor, multicultural, nature/environment, poetry. Young readers: adventure, animal, anthology, concept, contemporary, fantasy, folktales, health, history, humor, multicultural, nature/environment, poetry, religion, science fiction, special needs, sports, suspense. Middle readers: animal, anthology, fantasy, folktales, health, hi-lo, history, humor, multicultural, nature/environment, poetry, religion, science fiction, special needs, sports, suspense. Young adults/teens: animal, anthology, contemporary, fantasy, folktales, health, hi-lo, history, humor, multicultural, nature/environment, poetry, religion, science fiction, special needs, sports, suspense. Submit outline/synopsis.

⊘ PLAN B PRESS

P.O. Box 4067, Alexandria VA 22303. (215)732-2663. **E-mail:** planbpress@gmail.com. **Website:** www.planbpress.com. **Contact:** Steven Allen May, president. Estab. 1999. Plan B Press is a "small publishing company with an international feel. Our intention is to have Plan B Press be part of the conversation about the direction and depth of literary movements and genres. Plan B Press's new direction is to seek out authors rarely-to-never published, sharing new voices that might not otherwise be heard. Plan B Press is determined to merge text with image, writing with art." Publishes poetry and short fiction. Wants "ex-

perimental poetry, concrete/visual work." Publishes 1 poetry book/year and 5-10 chapbooks/year. Mss are selected through open submission and through competition (see below). Books/chapbooks are 24-48 pages, with covers with art/graphics. **Pays author's copies.** Responds to queries in 1 month; mss in 3 months.

POETRY Wants to see: experimental, concrete, visual poetry. Does not want "sonnets, political or religious poems, work in the style of Ogden Nash." Query first, with a few sample poems and a cover letter with brief bio and publication credits. Book/chapbook mss may include previously published poems.

PLANNERS PRESS

Imprint of the American Planning Association, 205 N. Michigan Ave., Suite 1200, Chicago IL 60601. (312)431-9100. **Fax:** (312)786-6700. **E-mail:** plannerspress@planning.org. **Website:** www.planning.org/plannerspress/index.htm. **Contact:** Timothy Mennel, Ph.D. (planning practice, urban issues, land use, transportation). Estab. 1970. Publishes hardcover, electronic, and trade paperback originals; and trade paperback and electronic reprints. "Our books often have a narrow audience of city planners and frequently focus on the tools of city planning." **Publishes 12 titles/year. 50 queries received/year. 35 mss received/year. 25% of books from first-time authors. 100% from unagented writers. Pays 10-15% royalty on net receipts. Pays advance.** Publishes ms 15 months after acceptance. Accepts simultaneous submissions. Responds in 1 month to queries; 2 months to proposals and mss. Book catalog online at website www.planning.org/apastore. Guidelines available by e-mail at plannerspress@planning.org.

NONFICTION Subjects include agriculture, business, economics, community, contemporary culture, economics, environment, finance, government, politics, history, horticulture, law, money, finance, nature, environment, politics, real estate, science, social sciences, sociology, transportation, world affairs. Submit proposal package, including: outline, 1 sample chapter and c.v. Submit completed ms. Reviews artwork/photos. Send photocopies.

TIPS "Our audience is professional planners but also anyone interested in community development, urban affairs, sustainability, and related fields."

PLEXUS PUBLISHING, INC.

143 Old Marlton Pike, Medford NJ 08055. (609)654-6500. **Fax:** (609)654-4309. **E-mail:** jbryans@plexus-

publishing.com. **Website:** www.plexuspublishing.com. **Contact:** John B. Bryans, editor-in-chief/publisher. Estab. 1977. Publishes hardcover and paperback originals. Plexus publishes regional-interest (southern New Jersey and the greater Philadelphia area) fiction and nonfiction including mysteries, field guides, nature, travel and history. Also a limited number of titles in health/medicine, biology, ecology, botany, astronomy. **Pays $500-1,000 advance.** Accepts simultaneous submissions. Responds in 3 months to proposals. Book catalog and book proposal guidelines for 10x13 SASE.

NONFICTION Query with SASE.

FICTION Mysteries and literary novels with a strong regional (southern New Jersey) angle. Query with SASE.

ⒶⓄ POCKET BOOKS

Simon & Schuster, 1230 Ave. of the Americas, New York NY 10020. (212)698-7000. **Website:** www.simonsays.com. **Contact:** Jennifer Bergstrom, editor-in-chief. Estab. 1939. Publishes paperback originals and reprints, mass market and trade paperbacks. Pocket Books publishes commercial fiction and genre fiction (WWE, Downtown Press, Star Trek). Book catalog available free. Guidelines available online.

○ Pocket Books remains the mass market imprint of Simon & Schuster] in the Gallery family publishing titles from authors like Stephen King, Mary Higgins Clark, Vince Flynn, Sandra Brown, Greg Iles, Kresley Cole, and Julia London.

NONFICTION Subjects include cooking, foods, nutrition. *Agented submissions only.*

FICTION Subjects include mystery, romance, suspense, psychological suspense, thriller, western, *Star Trek. Agented submissions only.*

POCOL PRESS

Box 411, Clifton VA 20124. (703)830 5862. **Website:** www.pocolpress.com. **Contact:** J. Thomas Hetrick, editor. Estab. 1999. Publishes trade paperback originals. "Pocol Press is dedicated to producing high-quality print books ans eBooks from first-time, non-agented authors. However, all submissions are welcome. We're dedicated to good storytellers and to the written word, specializing in short fiction and baseball. Several of our books have been used as literary texts at universities and in book group discussions around the nation. Pocol Press does not publish children's books, romance novels, or graphic novels." **Publishes 6 titles/year. 90 queries received/year. 20 mss received/year. 90% of books from first-time authors. 100% from unagented writers. Pays 10-12% royalty on wholesale price.** Publishes book less than 1 year after acceptance. Responds in 1 month to queries; 2 months too mss. Book catalog and guidelines available online.

○ "Our authors are comprised of veteran writers and emerging talents."

FICTION Subjects include historical, horror, literary, mainstream, contemporary, military, war, mystery, short story collections, thematic, spiritual, sports, western, baseball fiction. "We specialize in thematic short fiction collections by a single author and baseball fiction. Expert storytellers welcome." Horror (psychological, supernatural), literary, mainstream/contemporary, short story collections, baseball. Published *Gulf,* by Brock Adams (short fiction); *The Last of One* by Stephan Solberg (novel); *A Good Death* by David F. Lawrence. Does not accept or return unsolicited mss. Query with SASE or submit 1 sample chapter(s).

TIPS "Our audience is aged 18 and over. Pocol Press is unique; we publish good writing and great storytelling. Write the best stories you can. Read them to you friends/peers. Note their reaction. Publishes some of the finest fiction by a small press."

⊙ THE POISONED PENCIL

Poisoned Pen Press, 6962 E. 1st Ave., Suite 103, Scottsdale AZ 85251. (480)945-3375. **Fax:** (480)949-1707. **E-mail:** info@thepoisonedpencil.com. **E-mail:** www.thepoisonedpencil.submittable.com/submit. **Website:** www.thepoisonedpencil.com. **Contact:** Ellen Larson, editor. Estab. 2012. Publishes trade paperback and electronic originals. **250 submissions received/year. Pays 9-15% for trade paperback; 25-35% for eBooks. Pays advance of $1,000.** Publishes ms 15 months after acceptance. Responds in 6 weeks to mss. Guidelines available online at website.

IMPRINTS Imprint of Poisoned Pen Press.

○ *Accepts young adult mysteries only.*

FICTION Subjects include mystery, young adult. "We publish only young adult mystery novels, 45,000 to 90,000 words in length. For our purposes, a young adult book is a book with a protagonist between the ages of 12 and 18. We are looking for both traditional and cross-genre young adult mysteries. We encourage off-beat approaches and narrative choices that reflect the complexity and ambiguity of today's world. Submissions from teens are very welcome. Avoid serial killers, excessive gore, and vampires (and other heavy supernatural themes). We only consider authors who live in the US or Canada, due to practicalities of marketing promotion. Avoid coincidence in plotting. Avoid having your sleuth leap to conclusions rather than discover and deduce. Pay attention to the resonance between character and plot; between plot and theme; between theme and character. We are looking for clean style, fluid storytelling, and solid structure. Unrealistic dialog is a real turn-off." Submit proposal package including synopsis, complete ms, and cover letter.

TIPS "Our audience is young adults and adults who love YA mysteries."

POISONED PEN PRESS

6962 E. 1st Ave., Suite 103, Scottsdale AZ 85251. (480)945-3375. **Fax:** (480)949-1707. **E-mail:** submissions@poisonedpenpress.com. **Website:** www.poisonedpenpress.com. **Contact:** Jessica Tribble, publisher; Barbara Peters, editor-in-chief. Estab. 1996. Publishes hardcover originals, and hardcover and trade paperback reprints. "Our publishing goal is to offer well-written mystery novels of crime and/or detection where the puzzle and its resolution are the main forces that move the story forward." **Publishes 36 titles/year. 1,000 queries received/year. 300 mss received/year. 35% of books from first-time authors. 65% from unagented writers. Pays 9-15% royalty on retail price.** Publishes book 10-12 months after acceptance. Responds in 2-3 months to queries and proposals; 6 months to mss. Book catalog and guidelines available online at website.

IMPRINTS The Poisoned Pencil.

○ *Not currently accepting submissions. Check website.*

FICTION Subjects include mystery. Mss should generally be longer than 65,000 words and shorter than 100,000 words. Member Publishers Marketing Associations, Arizona Book Publishers Associations, Publishers Association of West. Distributes through Ingram, Baker & Taylor, Brodart. Does not want novels centered on serial killers, spousal or child abuse, drugs, or extremist groups, although we do not entirely rule such works out. Accepts unsolicited mss. Electronic queries only. "Query with SASE. Submit clips, first 3 pages. We must receive both the synopsis

and ms pages electronically as separate attachments to an e-mail message or as a disk or CD which we will not return."

TIPS "Audience is adult readers of mystery fiction."

POPULAR WOODWORKING BOOKS

Imprint of F+W Media, Inc., 10151 Carver Rd., Suite 200, Blue Ash OH 45242. (513)531-2690. **Website:** www.popularwoodworking.com. **Contact:** David Thiel, executive editor. Publishes trade paperback and hardcover originals and reprints. "Popular Woodworking Books is one of the largest publishers of woodworking books in the world. From perfecting a furniture design to putting on the final coat of finish, our books provide step-by-step instructions and trusted advice from the pros that make them valuable tools for both beginning and advanced woodworkers. Currently emphasizing woodworking jigs and fixtures, furniture and cabinet projects, smaller finely crafted boxes, all styles of furniture. De-emphasizing woodturning, woodcarving, scroll saw projects." **Publishes 6-8 titles/year. 20 queries received/year. 10 mss received/year. 20% of books from first-time authors. 95% from unagented writers.** Accepts simultaneous submissions. Responds in 1 month to queries.

NONFICTION Subjects include hobbies, woodworking/wood crafts. "We publish heavily illustrated how-to woodworking books that show, rather than tell, our readers how to accomplish their woodworking goals." Query with SASE, or electronic query. Proposal package should include an outline and digital photos.

TIPS "Our books are for beginning to advanced woodworking enthusiasts."

POSSIBILITY PRESS

1 Oakglade Circle, Hummelstown PA 17036. **E-mail:** info@possibilitypress.com. **Website:** www.possibilitypress.com. **Contact:** Mike Markowski, publisher. Estab. 1981. Publishes trade paperback originals. "Our mission is to help the people of the world grow and become the best they can be, through the written and spoken word." **Publishes 2-3 titles/year. 90% of books from first-time authors. 100% from unagented writers. Royalties vary.** Responds in 1 month to queries. Catalog available online. Guidelines available online.

IMPRINTS Aeronautical Publishers; Possibility Press; Markowski International Publishers.

NONFICTION Subjects include psychology, pop psychology, self-help, leadership, relationships, attitude, business, success/motivation, inspiration, entrepreneurship, sales marketing, MLM and home-based business topics, and human interest success stories. Prefers submissions to be mailed. Include SASE. Submit ms in Microsoft Word. Your submission needs to be made both in hard copy and on a CD. Label it clearly with the book title and your name. Be sure to keep a backup CD for yourself. Save your ms as a .doc file name. Save your file a second time with an rtf (Rich Text Format) extension. See guidelines online. Reviews artwork/photos. Do not send originals.

FICTION Needs: parable that teach lessons about life and success.

TIPS "Our focus is on co-authoring and publishing short (15,000-30,000 words) bestsellers. We're looking for kind and compassionate authors who are passionate about making a difference in the world, and will champion their mission to do so, especially by public speaking. Our dream author writes well, knows how to promote, will champion their mission, speaks for a living, has a following and a platform, is cooperative and understanding, humbly handles critique and direction, is grateful, intelligent, and has a good sense of humor."

PPI (PROFESSIONAL PUBLICATIONS, INC.)

1250 Fifth Ave., Belmont CA 94002. (650)593-9119. **Fax:** (650)592-4519. **E-mail:** info@ppi2pass.com. **Website:** www.ppi2pass.com. Estab. 1975. Publishes hardcover, paperback, and electronic products, CD-ROMs and DVDs. "PPI publishes professional, reference, and licensing preparation materials. PPI wants submissions from both professionals practicing in the field and from experienced instructors. Currently emphasizing engineering, interior design, architecture, landscape architecture and LEED exam review." **Publishes 10 titles/year. 5% of books from first-time authors. 100% from unagented writers.** Publishes ms 4-18 months after acceptance. Accepts simultaneous submissions. Responds in 1 month to queries. Book catalog and ms guidelines free.

NONFICTION Subjects include architecture, science, landscape architecture, engineering mathematics, engineering, surveying, interior design, greenbuilding, sustainable development, and other professional licensure subjects. Especially needs review and reference books for all professional licensing examinations. Please submit ms and proposal outlining market po-

tential, etc. Proposal template available upon request. Reviews artwork/photos.

TIPS "We specialize in books for those people who want to become licensed and/or accredited professionals: engineers, architects, surveyors, interior designers, LEED APs, etc. Exam Prep Lines generally include online and print products such as review manuals, practice problems, sample exams, E-Learning Modules, IPhone Apps, and more. Demonstrating your understanding of the market, competition, appropriate delivery methods, and marketing ideas will help sell us on your proposal."

☼ PRAIRIE JOURNAL PRESS

P.O. Box 68073, Calgary AB T3G 3N8, Canada. **E-mail:** prairiejournal@yahoo.com. **Website:** www.geocities.com/prairiejournal/. **Contact:** Anne Burke, literary editor. Estab. 1983. **Pays 1 author's copy; honorarium depends on grant/award provided by the government or private/corporate donations.**

Prairie Journal Press authors have been nominees for The Journey Prize in fiction and finalists and honorable mention for the National Magazine awards. Prairie Journal Press authors have been nominees for The Journey Prize in fiction and finalists and honorable mention for the National Magazine awards.

FICTION Literary, short story collections. Published *Prairie Journal Fiction, Prairie Journal Fiction II* (anthologies of short stories); *Solstice* (short fiction on the theme of aging); and *Prairie Journal Prose*. Submit with SAE with IRC for individuals. No U.S. stamps please. Accepts unsolicited mss. Sometimes comments on rejected mss.

TIPS "We wish we had the means to promote more new writers. We look for something different each time and try not to repeat types of stories if possible. We receive fiction of very high quality. Short fiction is preferable although excerpts from novels are considered if they stand alone on their own merit."

PRAKKEN PUBLICATIONS, INC.

P.O. Box 8623, Ann Arbor MI 48107. (734)975-2800. **Fax:** (734)975-2787. **E-mail:** pam@eddigest.com. **E-mail:** susanne@eddigest.com. **Contact:** Susanne Peckham, book editor; Sharon K. Miller, art/design/production manager. Estab. 1934. Publishes educational hardcover and paperback originals, as well as educational magazines. "We publish books for educators in career/vocational and technology education, as well as books for the machine trades and machinists' education. Currently emphasizing machine trades." **Publishes 3 titles/year.** Accepts simultaneous submissions. Responds in 2 months to queries. Book catalog for #10 SASE.

NONFICTION Subjects include education. "We are currently interested in manuscripts with broad appeal in any of the specific subject areas of machine trades, technology education, career-technical education, and reference for the general education field." Submit outline, sample chapters.

TIPS "We have a continuing interest in magazine and book manuscripts which reflect emerging issues and trends in education, especially career-technical, industrial, and technology education."

PRESA :S: PRESS

P.O. Box 792, 8590 Belding Rd. NE, Rockford MI 49341. **E-mail:** presapress@aol.com. **Website:** www.presapress.com. **Contact:** Roseanne Ritzema, editor. Estab. 2003. Presa :S: Press publishes "perfect-bound paperbacks and saddle-stitched chapbooks of poetry. Wants "imagistic poetry where form is an extension of content, surreal, experimental, and personal poetry." Does not want "overtly political or didactic material." **Pays 10-25 author\quotes copies.** Publishes book Time between acceptance and publication is 8-12 weeks. after acceptance of ms. Responds to queries in 2-4 weeks; to mss in 8-12 weeks. Guidelines available in magazine, for SASE, and by e-mail. **POETRY** Needs poems, reviews, essays, photos, criticism, and prose. Dedicates 6-8 pages of each issue to a featured poet. Considers previously published poems. (Considers poetry posted on a public website/blog/forum and poetry posted on a private, password-protected forum as published.) Acquires first North American serial rights and the right to reprint in anthologies. Rights revert to poets upon publication. Accepts postal submissions only. Cover letter is preferred. Reads submissions year round. Poems are circulated to an editorial board. Never comments on rejected poems. Never publishes theme issues. Reviews books and chapbooks of poetry. Send materials for review consideration to Roseanne Ritzema. Query first, with a few sample poems and a cover letter with brief bio and publication credits. Book/chapbook mss may include previously published poems.

 PRESS 53

P.O. Box 30314, Winston-Salem NC 27101. **E-mail:** kevin@press53.com. **Website:** www.press53.com. **Contact:** Kevin Morgan Watson, publisher. "Press 53 was founded in October 2005 and quickly began earning a reputation as a quality publishing house of short story and poetry collections." Open submission period in November each year. **Publishes 16-18 titles/year.** Responds in 6 months to mss. Guidelines online. **FICTION** Subjects include literary, short story collections. "We publish roughly 8 short story collections each year by writers who are active and earning recognition through publication and awards." Collections should include 10-15 short stories with 70% or more of those stories previously published. Does not want novels. November submission period. Submit via Submittable on site a letter of introduction (information about yourself and your collection), where the stories have been published, a few ideas for marketing your book, and the complete ms.

POETRY "We love working with poets who have been widely published and are active in the poetry community. We publish only full-length poetry collections of roughly 70 pages or more." Prefers that at least 30-40% of the poems in the collection be previously published. In November, submit via Submittable on site: letter of introduction with info about yourself and poetry collection, the number of poems in collection, where the poems have been published, and a few ideas for marketing book, along with complete ms.

TIPS "We are looking for writers who are actively involved in the writing community, writers who are submitting their work to journals, magazines and contests, and who are getting published and earning a reputation for their work."

PRICE STERN SLOAN, INC.

Penguin Group, 375 Hudson St., New York NY 10014. (212)366-2000. **Website:** us.penguingroup.com/static/pages/publishers/index.html. **Contact:** Francesco Sedita, vice-president/publisher. Estab. 1963. "Price Stern Sloan publishes quirky mass market novelty series for childrens as well as licensed movie tie-in books." Price Stern Sloan only responds to submissions it's interested in publishing. Book catalog online.

Price Stern Sloan does not accept e-mail submissions.

FICTION Publishes picture books and novelty/board books including Mad Libs Movie and Television Tie-ins, and unauthorized biographies. All book formats except for picture books. "We publish unique novelty formats and fun, colorful paperbacks and activity books. We also publish the Book with Audio Series *Wee Sing* and *Baby Loves Jazz*." Submit a summary and first chapter or two for longer works.

TIPS "Price Stern Sloan publishes unique, fun titles."

PRICE WORLD PUBLISHING, LLC

1300 W. Belmont Ave., 20G, Chicago IL 60657. (866) S-WORKOUT; (888)234-6896. **Fax:** (216)803-0350. **E-mail:** publishing@priceworldpublishing.com. **Website:** www.priceworldpublishing.com. **Contact:** Robert Price, president/executive editor. Estab. 2002. Trade and mass market paperback and hardcover originals. **Publishes 200+ titles/year. Several hundred queries and mss received/year. 33% of books from first-time authors. 50% from unagented writers. Pays 8-15% royalty on wholesale price.**

NONFICTION Subjects include sports. Submit proposal package, including outline, completed ms; visit www.priceworldpublishing.com for proposal submission information. Reviews artwork/photos; send PDF or MS Word docs.

FICTION All fiction.

TIPS "We accept books of all genres and we work with authors of all backgrounds. Our focus is on emerging trends and unique topics that target specific niche markets. Visit www.PriceWorldPublishing.com for more information."

PRINCETON ARCHITECTURAL PRESS

37 E. 7th St., New York NY 10003. (212)995-9620. **Fax:** (212)995-9454. **E-mail:** submissions@papress.com. **Website:** www.papress.com. Publishes hardcover and trade paperback originals. **Publishes 50 titles/year. 300 queries received/year. 150 mss received/year. 65% of books from first-time authors. 95% from unagented writers. Pays royalty on wholesale price.** Publishes ms 1 year after acceptance. Accepts simultaneous submissions. Responds in 2 months to queries, proposals and mss. Book catalog available online. Guidelines available online.

NONFICTION Subjects include art, architecture. Submit proposal package, outline, 1 sample chapters, table of contents, sample of art, and survey of competitive titles. Reviews artwork/photos. Do not send originals.

TIPS "Princeton Architecture Press publishes fine books on architecture, design, photography, land-scape, and visual culture. Our books are acclaimed for their strong and unique editorial vision, unrivaled design sensibility, and high production values at affordable prices."

PRINCETON UNIVERSITY PRESS

41 William St., Princeton NJ 08540. (609)258-4900. **Fax:** (609)258-6305. **Website:** www.pupress.princeton.edu. **Contact:** Hanne Winarsky, editor. "The Lockert Library of Poetry in Translation embraces a wide geographic and temporal range, from Scandinavia to Latin America to the subcontinent of India, from the Tang Dynasty to Europe of the modern day. It especially emphasizes poets who are established in their native lands and who are being introduced to an English-speaking audience. The series, many of whose titles are bilingual editions, calls attention to some of the most widely-praised poetry available today. In the Lockert Library series, each book is given individual design treatment rather than stamped into a series mold. We have published a wide range of poets from other cultures, including well-known writers such as Hoolderlin and Cavafy, and those who have not yet had their due in English translation, such as Goöran Sonnevi. Manuscripts are judged with several criteria in mind: the ability of the translation to stand on its own as poetry in English; fidelity to the tone and spirit of the original, rather than literal accuracy; and the importance of the translated poet to the literature of his or her time and country."

POETRY Submit hard copy of proposal with sample poems or full ms. Cover letter is required. Reads submissions year round. Mss will not be returned. Comments on finalists only. Responds in 3-4 months.

PRINTING INDUSTRIES OF AMERICA

200 Deer Run Rd., Sewickley PA 15143. (412)741-6860. **Fax:** (412)741-2311. **E-mail:** awoodall@printing.org. **Website:** www.printing.org. **Contact:** Amy Woodall, director (printing, graphic arts, communication). Estab. 1921. Publishes trade paperback originals and hardcover reference texts. "Printing Industries of America, along with its affiliates, delivers products and services that enhance the growth and profitability of its members and the industry through advocacy, education, research, and technical information." Printing Industries of America's mission is to serve the graphic communications community as the major resource for technical information and services through research and education. **Publishes 20 titles/**

year. **20 mss received/year; 30 queries received/year. 50% of books from first-time authors. 100% from unagented writers. Pays 15-20% royalty on wholesale price.** Publishes ms 18 months after acceptance. Accepts simultaneous submissions. Responds in 1 month to queries.

NONFICTION Subjects include business, communications, economics, education, printing and graphic arts reference, technical, textbook. Currently emphasizing technical textbooks as well as career guides for graphic communications and turnkey training curricula. Query with SASE, or submit outline, sample chapters, and SASE. Reviews artwork. Send photocopies.

PROSTAR PUBLICATIONS INC.

East Coast, 3 Church Circle, Suite 109, Annapolis MD 21401. (800)481-6277. **Fax:** (800)487-6277. **E-mail:** editor@prostarpublications.com. **Website:** www.prostarpublications.com. Estab. 1991. "ProStar Publications, Inc. is the largest publisher and distributor of U.S. Nautical publications world wide. Our titles include all U.S. Sailing Directions, U.S.C.G. Light Lists, Navigation Rules (International & Inland), NOAA Tide & Tidal Current Tables, Code of Federal Regulations (CFR™s), Boating Almanacs and the U.S. Notice to Mariners on a weekly basis."

PRUFROCK PRESS, INC.

P.O. Box 8813, Waco TX 76714. (800)988-2208. **Fax:** (800)240-0333. **E-mail:** info@prufrock.com. **Website:** www.prufrock.com. **Contact:** Joel McIntosh, publisher and marketing director. "Prufrock Press offers award-winning products focused on gifted education, gifted children, advanced learning, and special needs learners. For more than 20 years, Prufrock has supported gifted children and their education and development. The company publishes more than 300 products that enhance the lives of gifted children and the teachers and parents who support them." **50 queries received/year. 40 mss received/year. 20% of books from first-time authors. 100% from unagented writers.** Publishes ms 1-2 year after acceptance. Accepts simultaneous submissions. Book catalog for 10×12 envelope and 2 first-class stamps. Guidelines available online.

◘   Accepts simultaneous submissions, but must be notified about it.

NONFICTION Subjects include education, language, literature. "We are always looking for truly original,

creative materials for teachers." Query with SASE. Submit outline, 1-3 sample chapters.

FICTION Prufrock Press "offers award-winning products focused on gifted education, gifted children, advanced learning, and special needs learners. For more than 20 years, Prufrock has supported gifted children and their education and development. The company publishes more than 300 products that enhance the lives of gifted children and the teachers and parents who support them." No picture books. "Prufrock Press does not consider unsolicited manuscripts."

PUFFIN BOOKS

Imprint of Penguin Group (USA), Inc., 375 Hudson St., New York NY 10014. (212)366-2000. **Website:** www.penguinputnam.com. **Contact:** Kristin Gilson, editorial director. Sharyn November, senior editor Publishes trade paperback originals and reprints. "Puffin Books publishes high-end trade paperbacks and paperback reprints for preschool children, beginning and middle readers, and young adults." **Publishes 175-200 titles/year. Receives 600 queries and mss/year. 1% of books from first-time authors. 5% from unagented writers. Royalty varies. Pays varies advance.** Publishes book 1 year after acceptance. Responds in 5 months. Book catalog for 9×12 SAE with 7 first-class stamps.

IMPRINTS Speak, Firebird, Sleuth.

NONFICTION Subjects include education, for teaching concepts and colors, not academic, history, women's issues, women's studies. Biography, illustrated books, young children's concept books (counting, shapes, colors). Subjects include education (for teaching concepts and colors, not academic), women in history. "Women in history books interest us." *No unsolicited mss.* Submit 5 pages of ms with SASE.

FICTION Subjects include picture books, young adult, middle grade, easy-to-read grades 1-3. Picture books, young adult novels, middle grade and easy-to-read grades 1-3: fantasy and science fiction, graphic novels, classics. *No unsolicited mss.* Submit 3 sample chapters with SASE.

TIPS "Our audience ranges from little children 'first books' to young adult (ages 14-16). An original idea has the best luck."

PURDUE UNIVERSITY PRESS

Stewart Center 370, 504 West State St., West Lafayette IN 47907-2058. (765)494-2038. **E-mail:** pupress@purdue.edu. **Website:** www.thepress.purdue.edu. **Contact:** Charles Watkinson, director; Katherine Purple, lead production editor. Estab. 1960. Publishes hardcover and trade paperback originals and trade paperback reprints. "We look for books that look at the world as a whole and offer new thoughts and insights into the standard debate. Currently emphasizing technology, human-animal issues, business. De-emphasizing literary studies." **Publishes 20-25 titles/year.** Book catalog and ms guidelines for 9×12 SASE.

NONFICTION Subjects include agriculture, Americana, business,government, politics, health, history, language, literary criticism, philosophy, regional, science, social sciences, sociology. Dedicated to the dissemination of scholarly and professional information, Purdue University Press provides quality resources in several key subject areas including business, technology, health, veterinary medicine, and other selected disciplines in the humanities and sciences. As the scholarly publishing arm of Purdue University and a unit of Purdue Libraries, the Press is also a partner for university faculty and staff, centers and departments, wishing to disseminate the results of their research. Query before submitting.

PURICH PUBLISHING

Box 23032, Market Mall Post Office, Saskatoon SK S7J 5H3, Canada. (306)373-5311. **Fax:** (306)373-5315. **E-mail:** purich@sasktel.net. **Website:** www.purich-publishing.com. **Contact:** Donald Purich, publisher; Karen Bolstad, publisher. Estab. 1992. Publishes trade paperback originals. "Purich publishes books on law, Aboriginal/Native American issues, and Western Canadian history for the academic and professional trade reference market." **Publishes 3-5 titles/year. 20% of books from first-time authors. 100% from unagented writers. Pays 8-12% royalty on retail price.** Publishes ms 4 months after acceptance. Responds in 1 month to queries; months to mss. Book catalog available free.

NONFICTION , Aboriginal and social justice issues, Western Canadian history. "We are a specialized publisher and only consider work in our subject areas." Query with SASE.

PUSH

Scholastic, 557 Broadway, New York NY 10012. **E-mail:** DLevithan@Scholastic.com. **Website:** www.thisispush.com. Estab. 2002. PUSH publishes new voices in teen literature. **Publishes 6-9 titles/year. 50% of books from first-time authors.**

PUSH does not accept unsolicited mss or queries, only agented or referred fiction/memoir.

NONFICTION Young adults: memoir. *Does not accept unsolicited mss.*

FICTION Young adults: contemporary, multicultural, poetry. *Does not accept unsolicited mss.*

TIPS "We only publish first-time writers (and then their subsequent books), so authors who have published previously should not consider PUSH. Also, for young writers in grades 7-12, we run the PUSH Novel Contest with the Scholastic Art & Writing Awards. Every year it begins in October and ends in March. Rules can be found on our website."

G.P. PUTNAM'S SONS HARDCOVER

Imprint of Penguin Group (USA), Inc., 375 Hudson, New York NY 10014. (212)366-2000. **Fax:** (212)366-2664. **Website:** www.penguinputnam.com. Publishes hardcover originals. **Pays variable royalties on retail price. Pays varies advance.** Accepts simultaneous submissions. Request book catalog through mail order department.

NONFICTION Subjects include animals, business, economics, child guidance, contemporary culture, cooking, foods, nutrition, health, medicine, military, war, nature, environment, religion, science, sports, travel, women's issues, women's studies, celebrity-related topics. Agented submissions only. *No unsolicited mss.*

FICTION Subjects include adventure, literary, mainstream, mystery, suspense, women's. Agented submissions only. *No unsolicited mss.*

QUEST BOOKS

Imprint of Theosophical Publishing House, 306 W. Geneva Rd., P.O. Box 270, Wheaton IL 60187. **E-mail:** submissions@questbooks.net. **Website:** www.quest-books.net. **Contact:** Richard Smoley, editor. Idarmis Rodriguez, associate editor. Estab. 1965. Publishes hardcover and trade paperback originals and reprints. "Quest Books is the imprint of the Theosophical Publishing House, the publishing arm of the Theosophical Society in America. Since 1965, Quest books has sold millions of books by leading cultural thinkers on such increasingly popular subjects as transpersonal psychology, comparative religion, deep ecology, spiritual growth, the development of creativity, and alternative health practices." **Publishes 10 titles/year. 150** mss received/year; 350 queries received/year. 20% of books from first-time authors. 80% from unagented writers. **Pays royalty on retail price. Pays varying advance.** Publishes ms 1 year after acceptance. Accepts simultaneous submissions. Responds in 2 months to queries, proposals, and mss. Book catalog available free. Guidelines available online at: www. questbooks.net/aboutquest.cfm#submission.

NONFICTION Subjects include philosophy, psychology, religion, spirituality, New Age, astrology/psychic. Our speciality is high-quality spiritual nonfiction with a self-help aspect. Great writing is a must. We seldom publish 'personal spiritual awakening' stories. No submissions accepted that do not fit the needs outlined above. No fiction, poetry, children's books, or any literature based on channeling or personal psychic impressions. Submit proposal package, including outline, 1 sample chapter. Prefer online submissions; attachments must be sent as a single file in Microsoft Word, Rich Text, or PDF formats. Reviews artwork/photos. Hard copies of mss. and artwork will not be returned. Reviews artwork/photos. Writers should send photocopies or transparencies, but note that none will be returned.

TIPS "Our audience includes readers interested in spirituality, particularly the world's mystical traditions. Read a few recent Quest titles and submission guidelines before submitting. Know our books and our company goals. Explain how your book or proposal relates to other Quest titles. Quest gives preference to writers with established reputations/successful publications. Please be advised that proposals or manuscripts WILL NOT BE ACCEPTED if they fall into any of the following categories: Works intended for or about children, teenagers, or adolescents; Fiction or literary works (novels, short stories, essays, or poetry); Autobiographical material (memoirs, personal experiences, or family stories); Works received through mediumship, trance, or channeling; Works related to UFOs or extraterrestrials; Works related to self-aggrandizement (e.g., "how to make a fortune") or "how to" books."

⊘ QUITE SPECIFIC MEDIA GROUP, LTD.

7373 Pyramid Place, Hollywood CA 90046. (323)851-5797. **Fax:** (323)851-5798. **E-mail:** info@quitespecificmedia.com. **Website:** www.quitespecificmedia.com. **Contact:** Ralph Pine, editor-in-chief. Estab. 1967. Publishes hardcover originals, trade paperback origi-

inals and reprints. "Quite Specific Media Group is an umbrella company of 5 imprints specializing in costume and fashion, theater and design." **Publishes 12 titles/year. 75 queries received/year. 30 mss received/year. 75% of books from first-time authors. 85% from unagented writers. Pays royalty on wholesale price. Pays varies advance.** Publishes ms 18 months after acceptance. Accepts simultaneous submissions. Responds to queries. Book catalog available online. Guidelines available free.

IMPRINTS Imprints: Costume & Fashion Press; Drama Publishers; By Design Press; Entertainment Pro; Jade Rabbit.

NONFICTION Subjects include fashion, film, cinema, stage, history, literary criticism, translation. Accepts nonfiction and technical works in translations also. For and about performing arts theory and practice: acting, directing; voice, speech, movement; makeup, masks, wits; costumes, sets, lighting, sound; design and execution; technical theater, stagecraft, equipment; stage management; producing; arts management, all varieties; business and legal aspects; film, radio, television, cable, video; theory, criticism, reference; theater and performance history; costume and fashion. Query by e-mail please. Reviews artwork/photos.

QUIXOTE PRESS

3544 Blakslee St., Wever IA 52658. (800)571-2665. **Fax:** (319)372-7485. **Website:** www.heartsntummies.com. **Contact:** Bruce Carlson.

○   Quixote Press specializes in humorous and/or regional folklore and special-interest cookbooks. Publishes trade paperback originals and reprints. Website: www.heartsntummies.com. Published many debut authors within the last year. Needs humor, short story collections. Query with SASE. Accepts simultaneous submissions. Pays 10% royalty on wholesale price. Publishes ms 1 year after acceptance.

TIPS "Carefully consider marketing considerations. Audience is women in gift shops, on farm sites, direct retail outlets, wineries, outdoor sport shops, etc. Contact us at *you idea* stage, not complete ms stage. Be receptive to design input by us."

⊕ RAGGED SKY PRESS

P.O. Box 312, Annandale NJ 08801. **E-mail:** info@raggedsky.com. **Website:** www.raggedsky.com. **Contact:** Ellen Foos, publisher; Vasiliki Katsarou, managing editor; Arlene Weiner, editor. Produces books of poetry and inspired prose. Ragged Sky is a small, highly selective cooperative press. "We work with our authors closely." Learn more online.

RAINBOW PUBLISHERS

P.O. Box 261129, San Diego CA 92196. (858)277-1167. **E-mail:** editor@rainbowpublishers.com. **Website:** www.rainbowpublishers.com; www.legacypresskids. com. Estab. 1979. "Our mission is to publish Bible-based, teacher resource materials that contribute to and inspire spiritual growth and development in kids ages 2-12." **For authors work purchased outright (range: $500 and up).** Accepts simultaneous submissions. Responds to queries in 6 weeks; mss in 3 months.

NONFICTION Young readers, middle readers, young adult/teens: activity books, arts/crafts, how-to, reference, religion.

TIPS "Our Rainbow imprint publishes reproducible books for teachers of children in Christian ministries, including crafts, activities, games and puzzles. Our Legacy imprint publishes titles for children such as devotionals, fiction and Christian living. Please write for guidelines and study the market before submitting material."

RAIN TOWN PRESS

1111 E. Burnside St. #309, Portland OR 97214. (503)962-9618. E-mail: submissions@raintownpress.com. **Website:** www.raintownpress.com. **Contact:** Misty V'Marie, acquisitions editor; Ellery Harvey, art director. Estab. 2009. **Publishes 1-4 middle readers; 1-4 young adult titles/year. 100% of books from first-time authors. Pays 8-15% royalty on net sales. Does not pay advance.** Publishes ms 1 year after acceptance. Accepts simultaneous submissions. Responds to queries and mss in 1-6 months. Catalog available on website. Imprints included in a single catalog. Guidelines available on website for writers, artists, and photographers.

IMPRINTS In The Future: Raintown Kids, Mary Darcy, Misty V'Marie, William Softich, Leah Brown.

"We are Portland, Oregon's first independent press dedicated to publishing literature for middle grade and young adult readers. We hope to give rise to their voice, speaking directly to the spirit they embody through our books and other endeavors. The gray days we endure in the Pacific Northwest are custom-made for reading a good book—or in our case, making one. The rain inspires, challenges, and motivates us. To that end, we say: Let it drizzle. We will soon publish picture books."

NONFICTION Subjects include animals, contemporary culture, environment, health, history, multicultural, nature, sports. Middle Readers/YA/Teens: biography, concept, graphic novels, hi-lo, how-to. Query. Submit outline/synopsis and 2 sample chapters. See online submission guide for detailed instructions.

FICTION Subjects include fantasy, folktales, graphic novels, hi-lo, problem novels, science fiction, special needs, concept. Middle Readers/YA/Teens: Wants adventure, animal, contemporary, fantasy, folktales, graphic novels, health, hi-lo, history, humor, multicultural, nature/environment, problem novels, sci-fi, special needs, sports. Catalog available on website. Query. Submit complete ms. See online submission guide for detailed instructions.

TIPS "The middle grade and YA markets have sometimes very stringent conventions for subject matter, theme, etc. It's most helpful if an author knows his/her genre inside and out. Read, read, read books that have successfully been published for your genre. This will ultimately make your writing more marketable. Also, follow a publisher's submission guidelines to a tee. We try to set writers up for success. Send us what we're looking for."

RANDOM HOUSE

1745 Broadway, New York NY 10019. **Website:** www.randomhouse.com. **Agented submissions only.**

⊗⊘ RANDOM HOUSE CHILDREN'S BOOKS

1745 Broadway, New York NY 10019. (212)782-9000. **Website:** www.randomhouse.com. Estab. 1925. "Producing books for preschool children through young adult readers, in all formats from board to activity books to picture books and novels, Random House Children's Books brings together world-famous franchise characters, multimillion-copy series and top-flight, award-winning authors, and illustrators."

IMPRINTS BooksReportsNow.com, GoldenBooks. com, Junie B. Jones, Kids@Random, Seusville, Teachers@Random, Teens@Random; **Knopf/Delacorte/ Dell Young Readers Group:** Bantam, Crown, David Fickling Books, Delacorte Press, Dell Dragonfly, Dell Laurel-Leaf, Dell Yearling, Doubleday, Alfred A. Knopf, Wendy Lamb Books; **Random House Young**

Readers Group: Akiko, Arthur, Barbie, Beginner Books, The Berenstain Bears, Bob the Builder, Disney, Dragon Tales, First Time Books, Golden Books, Landmark Books, Little Golden Books, Lucas Books, Mercer Mayer, Nickelodeon, Nick, Jr., pat the bunny, Picturebacks, Precious Moments, Richard Scarry, Sesame St. Books, Step Into Reading, Stepping Stones, Star Wars, Thomas the Tank Engine and Friends.

○ Submit mss through a literary agent.

FICTION "Random House publishes a select list of first chapter books and novels, with an emphasis on fantasy and historical fiction." Chapter books, middle-grade readers, young adult. *Does not accept unsolicited mss.*

TIPS "We look for original, unique stories. Do something that hasn't been done before."

○⊘ RANDOM HOUSE-GOLDEN BOOKS FOR YOUNG READERS GROUP

1745 Broadway, New York NY 10019. **Website:** www.randomhouse.com. Estab. 1935. "Random House Books aims to create books that nurture the hearts and minds of children, providing and promoting quality books and a rich variety of media that entertain and educate readers from 6 months to 12 years." **2% of books from first-time authors. Pays authors in royalties; sometimes buys mss outright.** Book catalog free on request.

○ Random House-Golden Books does not accept unsolicited manuscripts, only agented material. They reserve the right not to return unsolicited material.

⊘ RAVEN TREE PRESS

A Division of Delta Publishing Company, 1400 Miller Pkwy., McHenry IL 60050. (800)323-8270. **Fax:** (800)909-9901. **E-mail:** raven@raventreepress.com. **Website:** www.raventreepress.com. Estab. 2000. Publishes hardcover and trade paperback originals. "We publish entertaining and educational picture books in a variety of formats. Bilingual (English/Spanish), English-only, Spanish-only, and wordless editions." **Publishes 8-10 titles/year. 1,500 mss received/year. 50% of books from first-time authors. 90% from unagented writers. Pays royalty. Pays variable advance.** Accepts simultaneous submissions. Book catalog online. Guidelines online.

○ Currently closed to submissions. Check website for updates.

NONFICTION "Submission guidelines available online. Do not query or send mss without first checking submission guidelines on our website for most current information."

TIPS "Submit only based on guidelines. No e-mail or snail mail queries please. Word count is a definite issue, since we are bilingual."

RAZORBILL

Penguin Group, 375 Hudson St., New York NY 10014. (212)414-3448. **Fax:** (212)414-3343. **E-mail:** laura.schechter@us.penguingroup.com; Ben.Schrank@us.penguingroup.com. **Website:** www.razorbillbooks.com. **Contact:** Gillian Levinson, assistant edtor; Jessica Rothenberg, editor; Brianne Mulligan, editor. Estab. 2003. "This division of Penguin Young Readers is looking for the best and the most original of commercial contemporary fiction titles for middle grade and YA readers. A select quantity of nonfiction titles will also be considered." **Publishes 30 titles/year. Offers advance against royalties.** Publishes book 1-2 after acceptance. Responds to queries/mss in 1-3 months.

NONFICTION Middle readers and young adults/teens: concept. Submit outline/synopsis and 3 sample chapters along with query and SASE.

FICTION Middle Readers: adventure, contemporary, graphic novels, fantasy, humor, problem novels. Young adults/teens: adventure, contemporary, fantasy, graphic novels, humor, multicultural, suspense, paranormal, science fiction, dystopian, literary, romance. Average word length: middle readers—40,000; young adult—60,000. Submit outline/synopsis and 3 sample chapters along with query and SASE.

TIPS "New writers will have the best chance of acceptance and publication with original, contemporary material that boasts a distinctive voice and well-articulated world. Check out www.razorbillbooks.com to get a better idea of what we're looking for."

⊖ REALITY ST.

63 All Saints St., Hastings, E. Sussex TN34 3BN, United Kingdom. +44(0)1424 431271. **E-mail:** info@realitySt..co.uk. **Website:** www.realitySt..co.uk. **Contact:** Ken Edwards, editor and publisher. Estab. 1993. Publishes trade paperback originals. Reality St. is based in Hastings, UK, publishing new and innovative writing in English and in translation from other languages. Some established writers whose books they have published are Nicole Brossard, Allen Fisher, Barbara Guest, Fanny Howe, Denise Riley, Peter Riley, and

Maurice Scully. **Publishes 3-4 titles/year.** Book catalog available online.

⬤ *Does not accept unsolicited submissions.*

FICTION Subjects include poetry, poetry in translation, translation, experimental fiction, anthologies.

✪ RECLINER BOOKS

P.O. Box 64128, Calgary AB T2K 1A9, Canada. (403)668-9746. **E-mail:** info@reclinerbooks.com. **E-mail:** submission@reclinerbooks.com. **Website:** www.reclinerbooks.com. **Contact:** Dustin Smith, editor (fiction, literary nonfiction). Estab. 2009. Publishes trade paperback originals. **Publishes 4-8 titles/year. 50% of books from first-time authors. 100% from unagented writers. Pays 10-15% royalty on retail price. Pays $250-500 advance.** Publishes ms 1 year after acceptance. Accepts simultaneous submissions. Responds in 3 months on queries and proposals; 6 months on mss. Soon available online at www.writtenindust.com/catalogue.html. Guidelines available online at www.writtenindust.com/submission.

NONFICTION Subjects include animals, anthropology, business, creative nonfiction, economics, environment, gay, health, history, language, law, lesbian, literature, medicine, memoirs, money, nature, politics, religion, science, sex, social sciences, sociology, womens issues, womens studies, world affairs, literary nonfiction. "We are currently seeking literary nonfiction titles only, the more literary the better." Submit proposal package, including: outline, 3 sample chapters; submit completed mss. Reviews artwork/photos as part of ms package; send photocopies.

FICTION Subjects include adventure, contemporary, experimental, feminist, gay, historical, humor, lesbian, literary, mainstream, military, multicultural, religious. True "We are not currently accepting anything targeted at children, young adults, or science fiction readers." Submit proposal package, including: synopsis, 3 sample chapters, completed mss.

TIPS "Our audience is 24 years and older, 70% female, 30% male, 90% Canadian."

✪ RED DEER PRESS

195 Allstate Pkwy., Markham ON L3R 4TB, Canada. (905)477-9700. **Fax:** (905)477-9179. **E-mail:** rdp@reddeerpress.com; dionne@reddeerpress.com; val@reddeerpress.com. **Website:** www.reddeerpress.com. **Contact:** Richard Dionne, publisher. Estab. 1975. **Pays 8-10% royalty.** Publishes ms 18 months after acceptance. Accepts simultaneous submissions. Re-

sponds to queries in 6 months. Book catalog for 9 x 12 SASE.

⬤ Red Deer Press has received numerous honors and awards from the Book Publishers Association of Alberta, Canadian Children's Book Centre, the Governor General of Canada and the Writers Guild of Alberta.

FICTION Publishes young adult, adult nonfiction, science fiction, fantasy, and paperback originals "focusing on books by, about, or of interest to Canadians." Books: offset paper; offset printing; hardcover/perfect-bound. Average print order: 5,000. First novel print order: 2,500. Distributes titles in Canada and the US, the UK, Australia and New Zealand. Young adult (juvenile and early reader), contemporary. No romance or horror. Accepts unsolicited mss. Query with SASE. No submissions on disk.

TIPS "We're very interested in young adult and children's fiction from Canadian writers with a proven track record (either published books or widely published in established magazines or journals) and for manuscripts with regional themes and/or a distinctive voice. We publish Canadian authors exclusively."

⊘ RED HEN PRESS

P.O. Box 3537, Granada Hills CA 91394. (818)831-0649. **Fax:** (818)831-6659. **E-mail:** redhenpressbooks.com. **Website:** www.redhen.org. **Contact:** Mark E. Cull, publisher/editor (fiction). Estab. 1993. Publishes trade paperback originals. "*Red Hen Press is not currently accepting unsolicited material.* At this time, the best opportunity to be published by Red Hen is by entering one of our contests. Please find more information in our award submission guidelines." **Publishes 22 titles/year. 2,000 queries received/year. 500 mss received/year. 10% of books from first-time authors. 90% from unagented writers.** Publishes ms 1 year after acceptance. Accepts simultaneous submissions. Responds in 1 month to queries; 2 months to proposals; months to mss. Book catalog available free. Guidelines available online.

NONFICTION Subjects include ethnic, gay, lesbian, language, literature, memoirs, women's issues, women's studies, political/social interest. Currently not accepting submissions.

FICTION Subjects include ethnic, experimental, feminist, gay, lesbian, historical, literary, mainstream, contemporary, poetry, poetry in translation, short story collections. Ethnic, experimental, feminist, gay/

lesbian, historical, literary, mainstream/contemporary, short story collections. "We prefer high-quality literary fiction." Currently not accepting submissions.

TIPS "Audience reads poetry, literary fiction, intelligent nonfiction. If you have an agent, we may be too small since we don't pay advances. Write well. Send queries first. Be willing to help promote your own book."

RED MOON PRESS

P.O. Box 2461, Winchester VA 22604. (540)722-2156. **E-mail:** jim.kacian@redmoonpress.com. **Website:** www.redmoonpress.com. **Contact:** Jim Kacian, editor/publisher. Estab. 1993. Red Moon Press "is the largest and most prestigious publisher of English-language haiku and related work in the world." Publishes 6-8 volumes/year, usually 3-5 anthologies and individual collections of English-language haiku, as well as 1-3 books of essays, translations, or criticism of haiku. Under other imprints, the press also publishes chapbooks of various sizes and formats.

POETRY Query with book theme and information, and 30-40 poems or draft of first chapter. Responds to queries in 2 weeks, to mss (if invited) in 3 months. "Each contract separately negotiated."

RED ROCK PRESS

331 W. 57th St., Suite 175, New York NY 10019. **Fax:** (212)362-6216. **E-mail:** info@redrockpress.com. **Website:** www.redrockpress.com. **Contact:** Ilene Barth. Estab. 1998. Publishes hardcover and trade paperback originals. **Publishes 6-8 titles/year. Pays royalty on wholesale price. The amount of the advance offered depends on the project.** Responds in 3-4 months to queries. Book catalog for #10 SASE.

NONFICTION Subjects include creative nonfiction. All of our books are pegged to gift-giving holidays.

RED SAGE PUBLISHING, INC.

P.O. Box 4844, Seminole FL 33775. (727)391-3847. **E-mail:** submissions@eredsage.com. **Website:** www.eredsage.com. **Contact:** Alexandria Kendall, publisher; Theresa Stevens, managing editor. Estab. 1995. Publishes books of romance fiction, written for the adventurous woman. **Publishes 4 titles/year. 50% of books from first-time authors. Pays advance.** Guidelines available online.

FICTION Submission guidelines online at www.eredsage.com/store/RedSageSubmissionGuidelines_HowToSendSubmission.html

RED TUQUE BOOKS, INC.

477 Martin St., Unit #6, Penticton BC V2A 5L2, Canada. (778)476-5750. **Fax:** (778)476-5651. **Website:** www.redtuquebooks.ca. **Contact:** David Korinetz, executive editor. **Pays 5-7% royalties on net sales. Pays $250 advance.** Publishes ms 1 year after acceptance. Responds in 3 weeks.

FICTION Subjects include adventure, fantasy, science fiction, short story collections, young adult. Submit a query letter and first five pages. Include total word count. A one-page synopsis is optional. Accepts queries by e-mail and mail. SASE for reply only.

TIPS "Well-plotted, character-driven stories, preferably with happy endings, will have the best chance of being accepted. Keep in mind that authors who like to begin sentences with 'and, or, and but' are less likely to be considered. Don't send anything gruesome or overly explicit; tell us a good story, but think PG."

RED WHEEL/WEISER, CONARI PRESS, HAMPTON ROADS

665 Third St., Suite 400, San Francisco CA 94107. (415)978-2665. **Fax:** (415)359-0142. **Website:** www.redwheelweiser.com. **Contact:** Pat Bryce, acquisitions editor. Estab. 1956. Publishes hardcover and trade paperback originals and reprints. **Publishes 60-75 titles/year. 2,000 queries received/year; 2,000 mss received/year. 20% of books from first-time authors. 50% from unagented writers. Pays royalty.** Publishes book 1 year after acceptance of ms. Accepts simultaneous submissions. Responds in 3 months to queries. Responds in 3-6 months to proposals. Responds in 3-6 months to mss. Book catalog available free. Guidelines available online.

IMPRINTS Conari Press; Weiser.

NONFICTION Subjects include New Age, spirituality, womens issues, womens studies, parenting. Query with SASE. Submit proposal package, outline, 2 sample chapters, table of contents. Reviews artwork/photos. Send photocopies.

REFERENCE SERVICE PRESS

5000 Windplay Dr., Suite 4, El Dorado Hills CA 95762. (916)939-9620. **Fax:** (916)939-9626. **E-mail:** info@rspfunding.com. **Website:** www.rspfunding.com. **Contact:** Stuart Hauser, acquisitions editor. Estab. 1977. Publishes hardcover originals. "Reference Service Press focuses on the development and publication of financial aid resources in any format (print, electronic, e-book, etc.). We are interested in financial aid publications aimed at specific groups (e.g., minorities, women, veterans, the disabled, undergraduates majoring in specific subject areas, specific types of financial aid, etc.)." **Publishes 10-20 titles/year. 100% from unagented writers. Pays 10% royalty. Pays advance.** Publishes book 6 months after acceptance. Accepts simultaneous submissions. Responds in 2 months to queries. Book catalog for #10 SASE.

NONFICTION Subjects include agriculture, art, architecture, business, economics, education, ethnic, health, medicine, history, religion, science, sociology, women's issues, women's studies, disabled. Submit outline, sample chapters.

TIPS "Our audience consists of librarians, counselors, researchers, students, re-entry women, scholars, and other fundseekers."

RENAISSANCE HOUSE

465 Westview Ave., Englewood NJ 07631. (201)408-4048. **E-mail:** info@renaissancehouse.net. **Website:** www.renaissancehouse.net. Publishes biographies, folktales, coffee table books, instructional, textbooks, adventure, picture books, juvenile and young adult. Specializes in multicultural and bilingual titles, Spanish-English. Submit outline/synopsis. Will consider e-mail submissions. Children's, educational, multicultural, and textbooks. Represents 80 illustrators. 95% of artwork handled is children's book illustration. Currently open to illustrators seeking representation. Open to both new and established illustrators. Publishes ms 1 year after acceptance. Accepts simultaneous submissions. Responds to queries/mss in 2 months.

FICTION Subjects include fantasy, juvenile, picture books, legends, fables. Picture books: animal, folktales, multicultural. Young readers: animal, anthology, folktales, multicultural. Middle readers, young adult/teens: anthology, folktales, multicultural, nature/environment.

REPUBLIC OF TEXAS PRESS

Imprint of Taylor Trade Publishing, and part of Rowman and Littlefield Publishing Group, 5360 Manhattan Circle, #101, Boulder CO 80303. (303)543-7835, ext. 318. **E-mail:** tradeeditorial@rowman.com. **Website:** www.rlpgtrade.com. **Contact:** Rick Rinehart, editorial director. Publishes trade and paperback originals. **Publishes 10-15 titles/year. 95% from unagented writers. Pays industry-standard royalty on net receipts. Pays small advance.** Publishes ms 1 year after acceptance. Accepts simultaneous submissions. Responds in 2 months to queries.

NONFICTION "Republic of Texas Press specializes in Texas history and general Texana nonfiction, including ethnic, history, nature/environment, regional, sports, travel, women's issues/studies, Old West, Texas military, and ghost accounts." Proposals should be limited to a query letter; an email will generate the quickest response. If querying by email, please note in the memo box "book proposal." Send no attachments unless requested. What we look for at this stage is suitability of the proposed book to our publishing program (see categories) as well as the author's unique qualifications for writing his or her book.

TIPS "Do not submit any original materials, as they will not be returned. Our market is adult."

RING OF FIRE PUBLISHING LLC

6523 California Ave. SW #409, Seattle WA 98136. **E-mail:** contact@ringoffirebooks.com. **E-mail:** submissions@ringoffirebooks.com. **Website:** www.ringoffirebooks.com. Estab. 2011. "Our audience is comprised of well read fiction enthusiasts. Let us tell your story." **Publishes 6-12 titles/year. 75% of books from first-time authors. 100% from unagented writers. Pays royalties.** Publishes ms 6 months after acceptance. Accepts simultaneous submissions. Responds in 1 month to queries; 2 months to mss. Book catalog and ms guidelines available online at website.

IMPRINTS Publishes trade paperback and electronic originals.

FICTION Subjects include adventure, contemporary, experimental, fantasy, gothic, horror, juvenile, literary, mainstream, mystery, occult, romance, science fiction, short story collections, suspense, western, young adult. Query online. Submit synopsis and 3 sample chapters.

RIO NUEVO PUBLISHERS

Imprint of Treasure Chest Books, P.O. Box 5250, Tucson AZ 85703. **Fax:** (520)624-5888. **E-mail:** info@rionuevo.com. **Website:** www.rionuevo.com. Estab. 1975. Publishes hardcover and trade paperback originals and reprints. **Publishes 12-20 titles/year. 20 queries received/year. 10 mss received/year. 30% of books from first-time authors. 100% from unagented writers. Pays $1,000-4,000 advance.** Publishes book 1 year after acceptance. Accepts simultaneous submissions. Responds in 6 months to queries/

proposals/mss. Book catalog available online. Guidelines available via e-mail.

NONFICTION Subjects include animals, cooking, foods, nutrition, gardening, history, nature, environment, regional, religion, spirituality, travel. "We cover the Southwest but prefer titles that are not too narrow in their focus. We want our books to be of broad enough interest that people from other places will also want to read them." Query with SASE. Submit proposal package, outline, 2 sample chapters. Reviews artwork/photos. Send photocopies.

TIPS "We have a general audience of intelligent people interested in the Southwest-nature, history, culture. Many of our books are sold in gift shops throughout the region; we are also distributed nationally by W.W. Norton."

RIVERHEAD BOOKS

Penguin Putnam, 375 Hudson St., Office #4079, New York NY 10014. **E-mail:** ecommerce@us.penguingroup.com. **E-mail:** riverhead.web@us.penguingroup.com. **Website:** www.riverhead-books.com. **Contact:** Megan Lynch, senior editor.
FICTION Literary, mainstream, contemporary. *Submit through agent only. No unsolicited mss.*

ROARING BROOK PRESS

175 Fifth Ave., New York NY 10010. (646)307-5151. **E-mail:** david.langva@roaringbrookpress.com. **E-mail:** press.inquiries@macmillanusa.com. **Website:** us.macmillan.com/RoaringBrook.aspx. **Contact:** David Langva. Estab. 2000. Roaring Brook Press is an imprint of MacMillan, a group of companies that includes Henry Holt and Farrar, Straus & Giroux. Roaring Brook is not accepting unsolicited manuscripts. **Pays authors royalty based on retail price.**
NONFICTION Picture books, young readers, middle readers, young adults: adventure, animal, contemporary, fantasy, history, humor, multicultural, nature/environment, poetry, religion, science fiction, sports, suspense/mystery. *Not accepting unsolicited mss or queries.*
FICTION Picture books, young readers, middle readers, young adults: adventure, animal, contemporary, fantasy, history, humor, multicultural, nature/environment, poetry, religion, science fiction, sports, suspense/mystery. *Not accepting unsolicited mss or queries.*
TIPS "You should find a reputable agent and have him/her submit your work."

RONSDALE PRESS

3350 W. 21st Ave., Vancouver BC V6S 1G7, Canada. (604)738-4688. **Fax:** (604)731-4548. **E-mail:** ronsdale@shaw.ca. **Website:** ronsdalepress.com. **Contact:** Ronald B. Hatch (fiction, poetry, nonfiction, social commentary); Veronica Hatch (YA novels and short stories). Estab. 1988. Publishes trade paperback originals. "Ronsdale Press is a Canadian literary publishing house that publishes 12 books each year, four of which are young adult titles. Of particular interest are books involving children exploring and discovering new aspects of Canadian history." **Publishes 12 titles/year. 40 queries received/year. 800 mss received/year. 40% of books from first-time authors. 95% from unagented writers. Pays 10% royalty on retail price.** Publishes book 1 year after acceptance. Accepts simultaneous submissions. Responds to queries in 2 weeks; mss in 2 months. Book catalog for #10 SASE. Guidelines available online.

NONFICTION Subjects include history, Canadian, language, literature, nature, environment, regional. Middle readers, young adults: animal, biography, history, multicultural, social issues. Average word length: young readers—90; middle readers—90. "We publish a number of books for children and young adults in the age 10 to 15 range. We are especially interested in YA historical novels. **We regret that we can no longer publish picture books.**" Submit complete ms.
FICTION Subjects include literary, short story collections, novels. Young adults: Canadian novels. Average word length: middle readers and young adults—50,000. Submit complete ms.
POETRY Poets should have published some poems in magazines/journals and should be well-read in contemporary masters. Submit complete ms.
TIPS "Ronsdale Press is a literary publishing house, based in Vancouver, and dedicated to publishing books from across Canada, books that give Canadians new insights into themselves and their country. We aim to publish the best Canadian writers."

ROSE ALLEY PRESS

4203 Brooklyn Ave. NE, #103A, Seattle WA 98105. (206)633-2725. **E-mail:** rosealleypress@juno.com. **Website:** www.rosealleypress.com. **Contact:** David D. Horowitz. Estab. 1995. "Rose Alley Press primarily publishes books featuring rhymed metrical poetry and an annually updated booklet about writing and publication. We do not read or consider unsolicited manuscripts."

⚈ ROTOVISION

Sheridan House, 114 Western Rd., Hove East Sussex BN3 IDD, England. (44)(127)371-6010. **Fax:** (44)(127)372-7269. **E-mail:** isheetam@rotovision.com. **Website:** www.rotovision.com. **Contact:** Isheeta Mustafi. Publishes hardcover and trade paperback originals, and trade paperback reprints. Accepts simultaneous submissions. Book catalog available free. Guidelines available free.

○ "RotoVision books showcase the works of top writers and designers reflecting excellence and innovation in the visual arts. If you wish to submit a book proposal, in the first instance please familiarise yourself with our publishing portfolio to ensure your proposal fits into our focus area."

NONFICTION Subjects include art, creative nonfiction, design, fashion, graphic design, photography. "Our books are aimed at keen amateurs and professionals who want to improve their skills." Submit an e-mail with "Book Proposal" in the subject line. Reviews artwork/photos. Send transparencies and PDFs.

TIPS "Our audience includes professionals, keen amateurs, and students of visual arts including graphic design, general design, advertising, and photography. Make your approach international in scope. Content not to be less than 35% US."

ROWMAN & LITTLEFIELD PUBLISHING GROUP

4501 Forbes Blvd., Suite 200, Lanham MD 20706. (301)459-3366. **Fax:** (301)429-5748. **E-mail:** jsisk@rowmanlittlefield.com. **Website:** www.rowmanlittlefield.com. **Contact:** Jonathan Sisk, vice president/executive editor (American government, public policy, political theory); Susan McEachern, vice president/editorial director (international studies); Sarah Stanton and Patti Davis, acquisitions editors. Estab. 1949. Publishes hardcover and trade paperback originals and reprints. "We are an independent press devoted to publishing scholarly books in the best tradition of university presses; innovative, thought-provoking texts for college courses; and crossover trade books intended to convey scholarly trends to an educated readership. Our approach emphasizes substance and quality of thought over ephemeral trends. We offer a forum for responsible voices representing the diversity of opinion on college campuses, and take special pride in several series designed to provide students with the pros and cons of hotly contested issues." **Pays advance.** Book catalog online. Guidelines available online.

IMPRINTS Lexington Books; Rowman & Littlefield Publishers; Madison Books; Scarecrow Press; Cooper Square.

NONFICTION "Rowman & Littlefield is seeking proposals in the serious nonfiction areas of history, politics, current events, religion, sociology, philosophy, communication and education. All proposal inquiries can be emailed or mailed to the respective acquisitions editor listed on the contacts page on our website."

RUKA PRESS

P.O. Box 1409, Washington DC 20013. **E-mail:** contact@rukapress.com. **E-mail:** submissions@rukapress.com. **Website:** www.rukapress.com. **Contact:** Daniel Kohan, owner. Estab. 2010. Publishes in trade paperback originals, electronic. "We publish nonfiction books with a strong environmental component for a general audience. We are looking for books that explain things, that make an argument, that demystify. We are interested in economics, science, nature, climate change, and sustainability. We like building charts and graphs, tables and timelines. Our politics are progressive, but our books need not be political." Publishes 3-4/year titles/year. **Pays advance. Royalties are 10-25% on wholesale price.** Publishes book 9-12 months (between acceptance and publication). after acceptance of ms. Accepts simultaneous submissions. Responds in 1 month to queries and proposals. Book catalogue available online. Guidelines available online.

NONFICTION Subjects include environment, nature, science. Submit proposal package, including outline, resume, bio, or CV, and 1 sample chapter.

TIPS "We appeal to an audience of intelligent, educated readers with broad interests. Be sure to tell us why your proposal is unique, and why you are especially qualified to write this book. We are looking for originality and expertise."

SAE INTERNATIONAL

400 Commonwealth Dr., Warrendale PA 15096-0001. (724)776-4841. **E-mail:** writeabook@sae.org. **Website:** www.sae.org/writeabook. **Contact:** Martha Swiss, intellectual property manager; Kevin Jost, editorial director. Estab. 1905. Publishes hardcover

and trade paperback originals, eBooks. Automotive means anything self-propelled. We are a professional society serving engineers, scientists, and researchers in the automobile, aerospace, and off-highway industries. **Publishes approximately 10 titles/year. 50 queries received/year. 20 mss received/year. 70% of books from first-time authors. 100% from unagented writers. Pays royalty. Pays possible advance.** Publishes book 9-10 months after acceptance of ms. Accepts simultaneous submissions. Responds in 4 months to queries. Book catalog free. Guidelines available online.

NONFICTION Query with proposal—see www.sae.org/writeabook for details on submitting a proposal.

TIPS "Audience is automotive and aerospace engineers and managers, automotive safety and biomechanics professionals, students, educators, enthusiasts, and historians."

SAFARI PRESS, INC.

15621 Chemical Lane, Building B, Huntington Beach CA 92649. (714)894-9080. **Fax:** (714)894-4949. **E-mail:** info@safaripress.com. **Website:** www.safaripress.com. **Contact:** Jacqueline Neufeld, editor. Estab. 1985. Publishes hardcover originals and reprints, and trade paperback reprints. Safari Press publishes books only on big-game hunting, sporting, firearms, and wingshooting; this includes African, North American, European, Asian, and South American hunting and wingshooting. Does not want books on 'outdoors' topics (hiking, camping, canoeing, etc.). **Publishes 25-30 titles/year. 70% of books from first-time authors. 80% from unagented writers. Pays 8-15% royalty on wholesale price.** Book catalog for $1. Guidelines available online.

The editor notes that she receives many mss outside the areas of big-game hunting, wingshooting, and sporting firearms, and these are always rejected.

NONFICTION "We discourage autobiographies, unless the life of the hunter or firearms maker has been exceptional. We routinely reject manuscripts along the lines of 'Me and my buddies went hunting for.. and a good time was had by all!" No outdoors topics (hiking, camping, canoeing, fishing, etc.) Query with SASE. Submit outline.

SAINT MARTIN'S PRESS

175 Fifth Ave., New York NY 10010.

No unsolicited mss. Accepts agented submissions only.

SAINT MARY'S PRESS

702 Terrace Heights, Winona MN 55987. (800)533-8095. **Fax:** (800)344-9225. **E-mail:** submissions@smp.org. **Website:** www.smp.org. Ms guidelines online or by e-mail.

NONFICTION Subjects include religion, prayers, spirituality. Titles for Catholic youth and their parents, teachers, and youth ministers. High school Catholic religious education textbooks and primary source readings. Query with SASE. Submit proposal package, outline, 1 sample chapter, SASE. Brief author biography.

TIPS "Request product catalog and/or do research online of Saint Mary Press book lists before submitting proposal."

SAKURA PUBLISHING & TECHNOLOGIES

P.O. Box 1681, Hermitage PA 16148. (330)360-5131. **E-mail:** skpublishing124@gmail.com. **Website:** www.sakura-publishing.com. **Contact:** Derek Vasconi, talent finder and CEO. Estab. 2010. Publishes hardcover, trade paperback, mass market paperback and electronic originals and reprints. **Publishes 10-12 titles/year. 90% of books from first-time authors. 99% from unagented writers. Pays royalty of 20-60% on wholesale price or retail price.** Publishes ms 6 months after acceptance. Accepts simultaneous submissions. Responds in 1 month to queries, mss, proposals. Book catalog available for #10 SASE. Guidelines available online at website or by e-mail.

NONFICTION Subjects include alternative lifestyles, Americana, animals, architecture, art, contemporary culture, creative nonfiction, entertainment, games, gay, history, hobbies, humanities, memoirs, military.

SAME OLD STORY PRODUCTIONS

P.O. Box 606, Halfway OR 97834. (541)742-4121. **E-mail:** submissions@sameoldstory.net. **Website:** www.sameoldstory.net. **Contact:** Doug McKim, editor and founder; Cindy Womack-Steele, editor. Estab. 2012. Publishes hardcover, trade paperback, mass market paperback, and electronic originals and reprints. "We are a **self-publishing, subsidy publisher**. We offer competitive rates that are both fair and affordable. For price details or further information please visit our website. Or e-mail: questions@sameoldstory.net."

Publishes 12-24 titles/year. 50-100% of books from first-time authors. 100% from unagented writers. Publishes ms 6 months after acceptance. Accepts simultaneous submissions. Responds to queries, proposals, and mss in 1 month. Catalog available online. Guidelines by e-mail.

NONFICTION Subjects include alternative lifestyles, Americana, animals, ethnic, gay, history, lesbian, memoirs, military, multicultural, regional, religion, social sciences, spirituality, war, young adult. Query with SASE. Submit proposal package including an outline and 3 sample chapters. Reviews art with ms package. Send photocopies; CD-Rom.

FICTION Subjects include adventure, contemporary, erotica, ethnic, experimental, fantasy, feminist, gay, gothic, historical, horror, humor, juvenile, lesbian, literary, mainstream, military, multicultural, mystery, regional, religious, romance, science fiction, short story collections, spiritual, sports, suspense, war, western, young adult. "Please send us a great story you truly believe in!" Query with SASE. Submit proposal package with synopsis and 3 sample chapters.

TIPS "Our audience is young, open-minded, daring, imaginitive, and fun-loving. Be honest with yourself and your abilities as a writer. Work very hard and have fun with your writing."

SAMHAIN PUBLISHING, LTD

11821 Mason Montgomery Rd., Cincinnati OH 45249. (478)314-5144. **Fax:** (478)314-5148. **E-mail:** editor@samhainpublishing.com. **Website:** www.samhainpublishing.com. **Contact:** Heather Osborn, editorial director. Estab. 2005. Publishes e-books and paperback originals. POD/offset printing; line illustrations. "A small, independent publisher, Samhain's motto is 'It's all about the story.' We look for fresh, unique voices who have a story to share with the world. We encourage our authors to let their muse have its way and to create tales that don't always adhere to current trends. One never knows what the next hot genre will be or when it will start, so write what's in your soul. These are the books that, whether the story is based on formula or is an original, when written from the heart will earn you a life-time readership." **Pays royalties 30-40% for e-books, average of 8% for trade paper, and author's copies (quantity varies).** Publishes ms 18 months after acceptance. Responds in 4 months to queries and mss. Guidelines available online.
Preditor and Editors Best Publisher 2006.

FICTION Needs erotica and all genres and all heat levels of romance (contemporary, futuristic/time travel, gothic, historical, paranormal, regency period, romantic suspense, fantasy, action/adventure, etc.), as well as fantasy, urban fantasy or science fiction with strong romantic elements, with word counts between 12,000 and 120,000 words. "Samhain is now accepting submissions for our line of horror novels. We are actively seeking talented writers who can tell an exciting, dramatic and frightening story, and who are eager to promote their work and build their community of readers. We are looking for novels 'either supernatural or non-supernatural, contemporary or historical' that are original and compelling. Authors can be previously unpublished or established, agented or un-agented. Content can range from subtle and unsettling to gory and shocking. The writing is what counts." Accepts unsolicited mss. Query with outline/synopsis and either 3 sample chapters or the full ms. Accepts queries by e-mail only. Include estimated word count, brief bio, list of publishing credits, and "how the author is working to improve craft: association, critique groups, etc."

TIPS "Because we are an e-publisher first, we do not have to be as concerned with industry trends and can publish less popular genres of fiction if we believe the story and voice are good and will appeal to our customers. Please follow submission guidelines located on our website, include all requested information and proof your query/manuscript for errors prior to submission."

SANTA MONICA PRESS LLC

P.O. Box 850, Solana Beach CA 92075. (858)793-1890; (800)784-9553. **E-mail:** books@santamonicapress.com. **Website:** www.santamonicapress.com. Estab. 1994. Publishes hardcover and trade paperback originals. "At Santa Monica Press, we're not afraid to cast a wide editorial net. Our eclectic list of lively and modern nonfiction titles includes books in such categories as popular culture, film history, photography, humor, biography, travel, and reference." **Publishes 15 titles/year. 25% of books from first-time authors. 75% from unagented writers. Pays 6-10% royalty on net price. Pays $500-10,000+ advance.** Publishes book 1 year after acceptance. Accepts simultaneous submissions. Responds in 1-2 months to proposals. Guidelines available online.

NONFICTION Subjects include Americana, architecture, art, contemporary culture, creative nonfiction, education, entertainment, film, games, humanities, language, literature, memoirs, regional, social sciences, sports, travel, Biography, coffee table book, general nonfiction, gift book, humor, illustrated book, reference. Submit proposal package, including outline, 2-3 sample chapters, biography, marketing and publicity plans, analysis of competitive titles, SASE with appropriate postage. Reviews artwork/photos. Send photocopies.

TIPS "Visit our website before submitting to view our author guidelines and to get a clear idea of the types of books we publish. Carefully analyze your book's competition and tell us what makes your book different— and what makes it better. Also let us know what promotional and marketing opportunities you, as the author, bring to the project."

⊕ SATURNALIA BOOKS

105 Woodside Rd., Ardmore PA 19003. (267) 278-9541. **E-mail:** info@saturnaliabooks.com. **Website:** www.saturnaliabooks.org. **Contact:** Henry Israeli, publisher. Estab. 2002. Publishes trade paperback originals and digital versions for e-readers. "We do not accept unsolicited submissions. We hold a contest, the Saturnalia Books Poetry Prize, annually in which 1 anonymously submitted title is chosen by a poet with a national reputation for publication. Submissions are accepted during the month of March. The submission fee is $30, and the prize is $2,000 and 20 copies of the book. See website for details." **Publishes 4 titles/year. Receives 500 mss a year. 33% of books from first-time authors. 100% from unagented writers. Pays authors 4-6% royalty on retail price. Pays $400-2,000 advance.** Accepts simultaneous submissions. Responds in 4 months on mss. Catalog on website. Guidelines available on website.

POETRY "Saturnalia Books has no bias against any school of poetry, but we do tend to publish writers who take chances and push against convention in some way, whether it's in form, language, content, or musicality." Submit complete ms to contest only.

TIPS "Our audience tend to be young avid readers of contemporary poetry. Read a few sample books first."

⊕ SCHIFFER PUBLISHING, LTD.

4880 Lower Valley Rd., Atglen PA 19310. (610)593-1777. **Fax:** (610)593-2002. **E-mail:** info@schifferbooks. com; Schifferbk@aol.com. **Website:** www.schiffer-books.com. **Contact:** Tina Skinner. Estab. 1975. **Publishes 10-20 titles/year. Pays royalty on wholesale price.** Responds in 2 weeks to queries. Book catalog available free. Guidelines available online.

NONFICTION Art-quality illustrated regional histories. Looking for informed, entertaining writing and lots of subject areas to provide points of entry into the text for non-history buffs who buy a beautiful book because they are from, or love, an area. Full color possible in the case of historic postcards. Fax or e-mail outline, photos, and book proposal.

TIPS "We want to publish books for towns or cities with relevant population or active tourism to support book sales. A list of potential town vendors is a helpful start toward selling us on your book idea."

✚⊘ SCHOCKEN BOOKS

Imprint of Knopf Publishing Group, Division of Random House, Inc., 1745 Broadway 21-1, New York NY 10019. (212)572-9000. **Fax:** (212)572-6030. **Website:** www.schocken.com. Estab. 1945. Publishes hardcover and trade paperback originals and reprints. "Schocken publishes quality Judaica in all areas-fiction, history, biography, current affairs, spirituality and religious practices, popular culture, and cultural studies." **Publishes 9-12 titles/year. Pays varied advance.** Accepts simultaneous submissions.

🗨 Does not accept unsolicited mss.

Ⓐ SCHOLASTIC PRESS

Imprint of Scholastic, Inc., 557 Broadway, New York NY 10012. (212)343-6100. **Fax:** (212)343-4713. **Website:** www.scholastic.com. **Contact:** David Saylor, editorial director, Scholastic Press, creative director and associate publisher for all Scholastic hardcover imprints. David Levithan, executive editorial director; Lisa Sandell, acquiring editor; Dianne Hess, executive editor; Tracy Mack, executive editor; Rachel Griffiths, editor; Jennifer Rees, associate editor. Publishes hardcover originals. Scholastic Press publishes fresh, literary picture book fiction and nonfiction; fresh, literary nonseries or nongenre-oriented middle grade and young adult fiction. Currently emphasizing subtly handled treatments of key relationships in children's lives; unusual approaches to commonly dry subjects, such as biography, math, history, or science. De-emphasizing fairy tales (or retellings), board books, genre, or series fiction (mystery, fantasy, etc.). **Publishes 60 titles/year. 2,500 queries received/year. 1% of books from first-time authors. Pays royalty on** retail price. **Pays variable advance.** Publishes book 2 years after acceptance. Responds in 3 months to queries; 6-8 months to mss.

NONFICTION *Agented submissions and previously published authors only.*

FICTION Subjects include juvenile, picture books, novels. Looking for strong picture books, young chapter books, appealing middle grade novels (ages 8-11) and interesting and well-written young adult novels. Wants fresh, exciting picture books and novels—inspiring, new talent. *Agented submissions and previously published authors only.*

TIPS Read *currently* published children's books. Revise, rewrite, rework and find your own voice, style and subject. We are looking for authors with a strong and unique voice who can tell a great story and have the ability to evoke genuine emotion. Children's publishers are becoming more selective, looking for irresistible talent and fairly broad appeal, yet still very willing to take risks, just to keep the game interesting."

SCRIBE PUBLICATIONS

18-20 Edward St., Brunswick VIC 3056, Australia. (61)(3)9388-8780. **Fax:** (61)(3)9388-8787. **E-mail:** info@scribepub.com.au. **Website:** www.scribepublications.com.au. Estab. 1976. **Publishes 70 titles/year. 10-25% of books from first-time authors. 10-20% from unagented writers.** Submission guidelines available on website under About Us.

NONFICTION Subjects include environment, government, politics, history, memoirs, nature, environment, psychology, current affairs, social history. "Please refer first to our website before contacting us or submitting anything, because we explain there who we will accept proposals from."

SEAL PRESS

1700 4th St., Berkeley CA 94710. (510)595-3664. **E-mail:** Seal.Press@perseusbooks.com. **E-mail:** sealacquisitions@avalonpub.com. **Website:** www.sealpress.com. Estab. 1976. Publishes trade paperback originals. "Seal Press is an imprint of Avalon Publishing Group, feminist book publisher interested in original, lively, radical, empowering and culturally diverse nonfiction by women addressing contemporary issues from a feminist perspective or speaking positively to the experience of being female. Currently emphasizing women outdoor adventurists, young feminists, political issues for women, health issues, and surviving abuse. *Not accepting fiction at this time.*" **Publishes**

30 titles/year. 1,000 queries received/year. 750 mss received/year. 25% of books from first-time authors. 50% from unagented writers. Pays 7-10% royalty on retail price. Pays variable royalty on retail price. Pays $3,000-10,000 advance. Pays variable advance.** Publishes ms 1 year after acceptance. Accepts simultaneous submissions. Responds in 2 months to queries. Book catalog and ms guidelines for SASE or online.

NONFICTION Subjects include Americana, child guidance, contemporary culture, creative nonfiction, ethnic, gay, lesbian, memoirs, multicultural, nature, environment, sex, travel, women's issues, women's studies, popular culture, politics, domestic violence, sexual abuse. Query with SASE. Reviews artwork/photos. Send photocopies. No original art or photos accepted.

FICTION Ethnic, feminist, gay/lesbian, literary, multicultural. "We are interested in alternative voices." *Does not accept fiction at present.* Query with SASE or submit outline, 2 sample chapters, synopsis.

TIPS "Our audience is generally composed of women interested in reading about women's issues addressed from a feminist perspective."

SEARCH INSTITUTE PRESS

Search Institute, 615 First Ave. NE, Suite 125, Minneapolis MN 55413. (612)399-0200. **Fax:** (612)692-5553. **E-mail:** acquisitions@search-institute.org. **Website:** www.search-institute.org. Estab. 1958. Publishes trade paperback originals. **Publishes 12-15 titles/year. Pays royalty.** Publishes book 1 year after acceptance. Accepts simultaneous submissions. Responds in 6 months to queries, proposals, mss. Catalog free on request, online at website. Guidelines online at website.

NONFICTION Subjects include career guidance, child guidance, community, counseling, education, entertainment, games, parenting, public affairs, social sciences, youth leadership, prevention, activities. Does not want children's picture books, poetry, New Age and religious-themes, memoirs, biographies, and autobiographies. Query with SASE. Does not review artwork/photos.

TIPS "Our audience is educators, youth program leaders, mentors, parents."

SEAWORTHY PUBLICATIONS, INC.

2020 N. Atlantic Ave., #226, Cocoa Beach FL 32931. (321)610-3634. **Fax:** (321)400-1006. **E-mail:** orders@seaworthy.com. **Website:** www.seaworthy.com. **Con-**

tact: Joseph F. Janson, publisher. Publishes trade paperback originals, hardcover originals, and reprints. "Seaworthy Publications is a nautical book publisher that primarily publishes books of interest to recreational boaters and bluewater cruisers, including cruising guides, how-to books about boating. Currently emphasizing cruising guides." **Publishes 8 titles/year. 150 queries received/year. 40 mss received/year. 60% of books from first-time authors. 100% from unagented writers. Pays 15% royalty on wholesale price. Pays $1,000 advance.** Publishes ms 6 months after acceptance. Responds in 1 month to queries. Book catalog and guidelines available online.

NONFICTION Subjects include regional, sailing, boating, regional, boating guide books. Regional guide books, first-person adventure, reference, technical—all dealing with boating. Query with SASE. Submit 3 sample chapters, TOC. Prefers electronic query via e-mail. Reviews artwork/photos. Send photocopies or color prints.

TIPS "Our audience consists of sailors, boaters, and those interested in the sea, sailing, or long-distance cruising."

⬤⊘ SECOND AEON PUBLICATIONS

19 Southminster Rd., Roath, Cardiff CF23 5AT, Wales. +44(29)2049-3093. **Fax:** +44(29)2049-3093. **E-mail:** peter@peterfinch.co.uk. **Website:** www.peterfinch.co.uk. **Contact:** Peter Finch, poetry editor. Estab. 1966.

◯ Does not accept unsolicited mss.

POETRY *Does not accept unsolicited mss.*

◯ SECOND STORY PRESS

20 Maud St., Suite 401, Toronto ON M5V 2M5, Canada. (416)537-7850. **Fax:** (416)537-0588. **E-mail:** info@secondstorypress.ca; marketing@secondstorypress.com. **Website:** www.secondstorypress.ca.

NONFICTION Picture books: biography. *Accepts appropriate material from residents of Canada only.* Submit complete ms or submit outline and sample chapters by postal mail only. No electronic submissions or queries.

FICTION Considers non-sexist, non-racist, and non-violent stories, as well as historical fiction, chapter books, picture books. *Accepts appropriate material from residents of Canada only.* Submit outline and sample chapters by postal mail only. No electronic submissions or queries.

SEEDLING CONTINENTAL PRESS

520 E. Bainbridge St., Elizabethtown PA 17022. **E-mail:** bspencer@continentalpress.com. **Website:** www.continentalpress.com. **Contact:** Megan Bergonzi. Publishes books for classroom use only for the beginning reader in English. "Natural language and predictable text are requisite. Patterned text is acceptable, but must have a unique story line. Poetry, books in rhyme and full-length picture books are not being accepted. Illustrations are not necessary." **Work purchased outright from authors.** Publishes book 1-2 years after acceptance. Accepts simultaneous submissions. Responds to mss in 6 months.

NONFICTION Young readers: animal, arts/crafts, biography, careers, concept, multicultural, nature/environment, science. Does not accept texts longer than 12 pages or over 300 words. Average word length: young readers—100. Submit complete ms.

FICTION Young readers: adventure, animal, folktales, humor, multicultural, nature/environment. Does not accept texts longer than 12 pages or over 300 words. Average word length: young readers—100. Submit complete ms.

TIPS "See our website. Follow writers' guidelines carefully and test your story with children and educators."

SENTIENT PUBLICATIONS

1113 Spruce St., Boulder CO 80302. **E-mail:** contact@sentientpublications.com. **Website:** www.sentientpublications.com. **Contact:** Connie Shaw, acquisitions editor. Estab. 2001. Publishes hardcover and trade paperback originals; trade paperback reprints. **Publishes 12 titles/year. 200 queries received/year. 100 mss received/year. 70% of books from first-time authors. 50% from unagented writers. Pays royalty on wholesale price. Pays advance.** Publishes ms 6 months after acceptance. Accepts simultaneous submissions. Responds in 1 month to queries; 2 months to proposals and mss. Book catalog available online.

NONFICTION Subjects include child guidance, contemporary culture, creative nonfiction, education, gardening, history, memoirs, New Age, philosophy, photography, psychology, science, social sciences, sociology, spirituality, travel. "We're especially looking for holistic health books that have something new to say." Submit proposal package, See our website. Submit complete ms. Does not review artwork/photos.

SERIOUSLY GOOD BOOKS

999 Vanderbilt Beach Rd., Naples FL 34119. **E-mail:** seriouslygoodbks@aol.com. **Website:** www.seriously-goodbks.net. Estab. 2010. Publishes trade paperback and electronic originals. Publishes historial fiction only. **Publishes 2-5 titles/year. Pays 15% minimum royalties.** Respons in 1 month to queries. Book catalog and writers guidelines online at website.

FICTION Subjects include historical. Query by e-mail.

TIPS "Looking for historial fiction with substance. We seek well-researched historical fiction in the vein of Rutherfurd, Mary Renault, Maggie Anton, Robert Harris, etc. Please don't query with historical fiction mixed with other genres (romance, time travel, vampires, etc.)."

SEVEN STORIES PRESS

140 Watts St., New York NY 10013. (212)226-8760. **Fax:** (212)226-1411. **E-mail:** anna@sevenstories.com. **Website:** www.sevenstories.com. **Contact:** Daniel Simon; Anna Lui. Estab. 1995. Publishes hardcover and trade paperback originals. Founded in 1995 in New York City, and named for the seven authors who committed to a home with a fiercely independent spirit, Seven Stories Press publishes works of the imagination and political titles by voices of conscience. While most widely known for its books on politics, human rights, and social and economic justice, Seven Stories continues to champion literature, with a list encompassing both innovative debut novels and National Book Award–winning poetry collections, as well as prose and poetry translations from the French, Spanish, German, Swedish, Italian, Greek, Polish, Korean, Vietnamese, Russian, and Arabic. **Publishes 40-50 titles/year. 15% of books from first-time authors. 50% from unagented writers. Pays 7-15% royalty on retail price. Pays advance.** Publishes ms 1-3 years after acceptance. Accepts simultaneous submissions. Responds in 1 month to queries and mss. Book catalog and ms guidelines free.

NONFICTION Responds only if interested.

FICTION Subjects include literary. "We are currently unable to accept any unsolicited full manuscripts. We do accept query letters and sample chapters. Please send no more than a cover letter and two sample chapters, along with a 44-cent SASE or postcard for reply. (If you would like your submission materials returned to you, please include sufficient postage.)"

TIPS "Each year we also publish an annual compilation of censored news stories by Project Censored. Features of this series include the Top 25 Censored News Stories of the year—which has a history of identifying important neglected news stories and which is widely disseminated in the alternative press—as well as the "Junk Food News" chapter and chapters on hot-button topics for the year. Seven Stories also maintains a publishing partnership with Human Rights Watch through the yearly publication of the World Report, a preeminent account of human rights abuse around the world—a report card on the progress of the world's nations towards the protection of human rights for people everywhere."

SHAMBHALA PUBLICATIONS, INC.

300 Massachusetts Ave., Boston MA 02115. (617)424-0030. **Fax:** (617)236-1563. **E-mail:** editors@shambhala.com. **Website:** www.shambhala.com. Estab. 1969. Publishes hardcover and trade paperback originals and reprints. **Publishes 90-100 titles/year. 500 queries received/year. 1,200 mss/proposals received/year. 30% of books from first-time authors. 80% from unagented writers. Pays 8% royalty on retail price.** Publishes ms 1 year after acceptance. Accepts simultaneous submissions. Responds in 4 months to queries, proposals, and mss. Book catalog and ms guidelines free.

NONFICTION Subjects include cooking, crafts, parenting, Buddhism, martial arts, yoga, natural health, Eastern philosophy, creativity, green living, nature writing. To send a book proposal, include a synopsis of the book, a table of contents or outline, a copy of the author's resume or some other brief biographical statement, along with two or three sample chapters (they do not need to be in consecutive order). The chapters should be double-spaced. Include SASE. Publishes very little fiction or poetry.

FICTION Submit proposal package, outline, résumé, clips, 2 sample chapters, table of contents.

SHEARSMAN BOOKS, LTD

50 Westons Hills Dr., Emersons Green Bristol BS16 7DF, United Kingdom. **E-mail:** editor@shearsman.com. **Website:** www.shearsman.com. **Contact:** Tony Frazer, editor. Estab. 1981. Publishes trade paperback originals. **Publishes 45-60 titles/year. Pays 10% royalty on retail price after 150 copies have sold; authors also receive 10 free copies of their books.** Re-

sponds in 2-3 months to mss. Book catalog available online. Guidelines available online.

NONFICTION Subjects include memoirs, translation, essays.

POETRY "Shearsman only publishes poetry, poetry collections, and poetry in translation (from any language but with an emphasis on work in Spanish & in German). Some critical work on poetry and also memoirs and essays by poets. Mainly poetry by British, Irish, North American, & Australian poets." No children's books.

TIPS "Book ms submission: most of the ms must have already appeared in the UK or USA magazines of some repute, & it has to fill 70-72 pages of half letter or A5 pages. You must have sufficient return postage. Submissions can also be made by email. It is unlikely that a poet with no track record will be accepted for publication as there is no obvious audience for the work. Try to develop some exposure to UK & US magazines & try to assemble a ms only later."

SHEN'S BOOKS

1547 Palos Verdes Mall #291, Walnut Creek CA 94597. (925)262-8108. **Fax:** (888)269-9092. **E-mail:** info@ shens.com. **Website:** www.shens.com. **Contact:** Renee Ting, president. Estab. 1986. **Authors pay negotiated by project.** Publishes book 1-2 years after acceptance. Accepts simultaneous submissions. Responds to queries in 1-2 weeks; mss in 6-12 months. Catalog available on website.

NONFICTION Picture books, young readers: multicultural.

FICTION Picture books, young readers: folktales, multicultural with Asian Focus.

TIPS "Be familiar with our catalog before submitting."

SILVERFISH REVIEW PRESS

P.O. Box 3541, Eugene OR 97403. (541)344-5060. **E-mail:** sfrpress@earthlink.net. **Website:** www.silverfishreviewpress.com. **Contact:** Rodger Moody, series editor. Estab. 1978. Trade paperback originals. "Sponsors the Gerald Cable Book Award. This prize is awarded annually to a book length manuscript of original poetry by an author who has not yet published a full-length collection. There are no restrictions on the kind of poetry or subject matter; translations are not acceptable. Winners will receive one thousand dollars, publication, and twenty-five copies of the book. The winner will be announced in late March, 2012. Entries must be postmarked by October

15. Entries may be submitted by e-mail. See website for instructions." **Publishes 2-3 titles/year. 50% of books from first-time authors. 100% from unagented writers.** Guidelines available online.

TIPS "Read recent Silverfish titles."

SILVER LEAF BOOKS, LLC

P.O. Box 6460, Holliston MA 01746. **E-mail:** editor@ silverleafbooks.com. **Website:** www.silverleafbooks. com. **Contact:** Brett Fried, editor. "Silver Leaf Books is a small press featuring primarily new and upcoming talent in the fantasy, science fiction, mystery, thrillers, suspense, and horror genres. Our editors work closely with our authors to establish a lasting and mutually beneficial relationship, helping both the authors and company continue to grow and thrive." Publishes hardcover originals, trade paperback originals, paperback originals, electronic/digital books. Average print order: 3,000. Debut novel print order: 3,000. **Published 1 new writer last year.** Plans 4 debut novels this year. Averages 6 total titles/year; 6 fiction titles/year. Distributes/promotes titles through Baker & Taylor Books and Ingram. **75% from unagented writers. Pays royalties, and provides author's copies.** Publishes ms 1-2 years after acceptance. Responds to queries in 6 months; mss in 4 months. Guidelines available online at website.

FICTION Fantasy (space fantasy, sword and sorcery), horror (dark fantasy, futuristic, psychological, supernatural), mystery/suspense (amateur sleuth, cozy, police procedural, private eye/hard-boiled), science fiction (hard science/technological, soft/sociological), young adult (adventure, fantasy/science fiction, horror, mystery/suspense). Query with outline/synopsis and 3 sample chapters. Accepts queries by snail mail. Include estimated word count, brief bio and marketing plan. Send SASE or IRC for return of ms or disposable copy of ms and SASE/IRC for reply only.

TIPS "Follow the online guidelines, be thorough and professional."

SILVER MOON PRESS

400 E. 85th St., New York NY 10028. (800)874-3320. **Fax:** (212)988-8112. **E-mail:** mail@silvermoonpress. com. **Website:** silvermoonpress.com. Publishes hardcover originals. Publishes educational material for grades 3-8. **Publishes 1-2 prep workbooks and 1-2 historical fiction. titles/year. 600 queries received/ year. 400 mss received/year. 60% of books from first-time authors. 70% from unagented writers.**

Pays 7-10% royalty. Pays 500-1,000 advance. Publishes ms 18 months after acceptance. Accepts simultaneous submissions. Responds in 6-12 months to queries, proposals and mss. Book catalog with 9 x 12 SASE. Guidelines with #10 SASE.

○ *Does not accept unsolicited mss.*

NONFICTION Subjects include education, history, language, literature, multicultural.

FICTION Subjects include historical, multicultural, biographical. Middle readers: historical, multicultural and mystery. Average word length: 14,000.

TIPS "We do not accept biographies, poetry, or romance. We do not accept fantasy, science fiction, or historical fiction with elements of either. No picture books. Submissions that fit into New York State curriculum topics such as the Revolutionary War, Colonial times, and New York state history in general stand a greater chance of acceptance than those that do not."

ⓐ SIMON & SCHUSTER

1230 Ave. of the Americas, New York NY 10020. (212)698-7000. **Website:** www.simonsays.com.

○ *Accepts agented submissions only.*

ⓞ SIMON & SCHUSTER BOOKS FOR YOUNG READERS

Imprint of Simon & Schuster Children's Publishing, 1230 Ave. of the Americas, New York NY 10020. (212)698-7000. **Fax:** (212)698-2796. **Website:** www. simonsayskids.com. Publishes hardcover originals. "Simon and Schuster Books For Young Readers is the Flagship imprint of the S&S Children's Division. We are committed to publishing a wide range of contemporary, commercial, award-winning fiction and nonfiction that spans every age of children's publishing. BFYR is constantly looking to the future, supporting our foundation authors and franchises, but always with an eye for breaking new ground with every publication. We publish high-quality fiction and nonfiction for a variety of age groups and a variety of markets. Above all, we strive to publish books that we are passionate about." **Publishes 75 titles/year. Pays variable royalty on retail price.** Publishes ms 2-4 years after acceptance. Accepts simultaneous submissions. Responds in 2 months to queries and mss. Guidelines for #10 SASE.

IMPRINTS Paula Wiseman Books.

○ *No unsolicited mss.* All unsolicited mss returned unopened. Queries are accepted via mail.

NONFICTION Subjects include history, nature, environment, biography. Picture books: concept. All levels: narrative, current events, biography, history. "We're looking for picture books or middle grade nonfiction that have a retail potential. No photo essays." Recently published Insiders Series (picture book nonfiction, all ages). Query with SASE only.

FICTION Subjects include fantasy, historical, humor, juvenile, mystery, picture books, science fiction, young adult, adventure, historical, mystery, contemporary fiction. Query with SASE only.

TIPS "We're looking for picture books centered on a strong, fully-developed protagonist who grows or changes during the course of the story; YA novels that are challenging and psychologically complex; also imaginative and humorous middle-grade fiction. And we want nonfiction that is as engaging as fiction. Our imprint's slogan is 'Reading You'll Remember.' We aim to publish books that are fresh, accessible and family-oriented; we want them to have an impact on the reader."

SKINNER HOUSE BOOKS

The Unitarian Universalist Association, 25 Beacon St., Boston MA 02108. (617)742-2100 ext. 603. **Fax:** (617)742-7025. **E-mail:** info@uua.org. **Website:** www. uua.org/skinner. **Contact:** Mary Benard, senior editor. Estab. 1975. Publishes trade paperback originals and reprints. "We publish titles in Unitarian Universalist faith, liberal religion, history, biography, worship, and issues of social justice. Most of our children's titles are intended for religious education or worship use. They reflect Unitarian Universalist values. We also publish inspirational titles of poetic prose and meditations. Writers should know that Unitarian Universalism is a liberal religious denomination committed to progressive ideals. Currently emphasizing social justice concerns." **Publishes 10-20 titles/year. 50% of books from first-time authors. 100% from unagented writers.** Publishes book 1 year after acceptance. Accepts simultaneous submissions. Responds to queries in 3 weeks. Book catalog for 6×9 SAE with 3 first-class stamps. Guidelines available online.

NONFICTION Subjects include gay, lesbian, memoirs, religion, women's issues, women's studies, inspirational, church leadership. All levels: activity books, multicultural, music/dance, nature/environment, religion. Query or submit outline/synopsis and 2 sample chapters. Reviews artwork/photos. Send photocopies.

FICTION All levels: anthology, multicultural, nature/environment, religion. Query or submit outline/synopsis and 2 sample chapters.

TIPS "From outside our denomination, we are interested in manuscripts that will be of help or interest to liberal churches, Sunday School classes, parents, ministers, and volunteers. Inspirational/spiritual and children's titles must reflect liberal Unitarian Universalist values."

SLACK, INC.

6900 Grove Rd., Thorofare NJ 08086. (856)848-1000. **Fax:** (856)853-5991. **E-mail:** bookspublishing@slack-inc.com. **Website:** www.slackbooks.com. **Contact:** John Bond, publisher. Estab. 1960. Publishes hardcover and paperback originals. SLACK INC. publishes academic textbooks and professional reference books on various medical topics in an expedient manner. **Publishes 35 titles/year. 80 queries received/year. 23 mss received/year. 75% of books from first-time authors. 100% from unagented writers. Pays 10% royalty. Pays advance.** Publishes book 8 months after acceptance. Accepts simultaneous submissions. Responds in 1 month to queries/proposals; 3 months to mss. Book catalog and ms guidelines free. Guidelines available online.

NONFICTION Subjects include health, medicine, ophthalmology. Submit proposal package, outline, 2 sample chapters, market profile and cv. Reviews artwork/photos. Send photocopies.

⊘ SLEEPING BEAR PRESS

315 East Eisenhower Pkwy, Suite 200, Ann Arbor MI 48108. (800)487-2323. **Fax:** (734)794-0004. **E-mail:** customerservice@sleepingbearpress.com. **Website:** www.sleepingbearpress.com. **Contact:** Heather Hughes. Estab. 1998. Book catalog available via e-mail.

○ *Currently not accepting ms submissions or queries at this time.* "Please check back for further updates."

FICTION Picture books: adventure, animal, concept, folktales, history, multicultural, nature/environment, religion, sports. Young readers: adventure, animal, concept, folktales, history, humor, multicul-

tural, nature/environment, religion, sports. Average word length: picture books—1,800.

SMALL BEER PRESS

150 Pleasant St., #306, Easthampton MA 01027. (413) 203-1636. **Fax:** (413) 203-1636. **E-mail:** info@smallbeerpress.com. **Website:** www.smallbeerpress.com. **Contact:** Gavin J. Grant, acquisitions. Estab. 2000.

○ Small Beer Press also publishes the zine *Lady Churchill's Rosebud Wristlet*. "SBP's books have recently received the Tiptree and Crawford Awards."

FICTION Literary, experimental, speculative, story collections. Recently published *The Monkey's Wedding and Other Stories*, by Joan Aiken; *Meeks*, by Julia Holmes; *What I Didn't See and Other Stories*, by Karen Joy Fowler. "We do not accept unsolicited novel or short story collection manuscripts. Queries are welcome. Please send queries with an SASE by mail."

TIPS "Please be familiar with our books first to avoid wasting your time and ours, thank you."

SOFT SKULL PRESS INC.

Counterpoint, 1919 Fifth St., Berkeley CA 94710. (510)704-0230. **Fax:** (510)704-0268. **E-mail:** info@softskull.com. **Website:** www.softskull.com. Publishes hardcover and trade paperback originals. "Here at Soft Skull we love books that are new, fun, smart, revelatory, quirky, groundbreaking, cage-rattling and/or otherwise unusual." **Publishes 40 titles/year. Pays 7-10% royalty. Average advance: $100-15,000.** Publishes ms 6 months after acceptance. Responds in 2 months to proposals; 3 months to mss. Book catalog and guidelines on website.

NONFICTION Subjects include contemporary culture, creative nonfiction, entertainment, literature, pop culture. Send a cover letter describing your project and a full proposal along with two sample chapters.

FICTION Subjects include comic books, confession, contemporary, erotica, experimental, gay, lesbian, literary, mainstream, multicultural, short story collections. Does not consider poetry. Soft Skull Press no longer accepts digital submissions. Send a cover letter describing your project in detail and a completed ms. For graphic novels, send a minimum of five fully inked pages of art, along with a synopsis of your storyline. "Please do not send original material, as it will not be returned."

TIPS "See our website for updated submission guidelines."

SOHO PRESS, INC.

853 Broadway, New York NY 10003. **E-mail:** soho@sohopress.com. **Website:** www.sohopress.com. **Contact:** Bronwen Hruska, publisher; Katie Herman, editor. Mark Doten, editor Estab. 1986. Publishes hardcover and trade paperback originals; trade paperback reprints. Soho Press publishes primarily fiction, as well as some narrative literary nonfiction and mysteries set abroad. No electronic submissions, only queries by e-mail. **Publishes 60-70 titles/year. 15-25% of books from first-time authors. 10% from unagented writers. Pays 10-15% royalty on retail price (varies under certain circumstances).** Publishes ms 18 months after acceptance. Accepts simultaneous submissions. Responds in 3 months to queries and mss. Guidelines available online.

NONFICTION Subjects include creative nonfiction, ethnic, memoirs. "Independent publisher known for sophisticated fiction, mysteries set abroad, women's interest (no genre) novels and multicultural novels." Publishes hardcover and trade paperback originals and reprint editions. Books: perfect binding; halftone illustrations. First novel print order varies. We do not buy books on proposal. We always need to see a complete ms before we buy a book, though we prefer an initial submission of 3 sample chapters. We do not publish books with color art or photographs or a lot of graphical material." No self-help, how-to, or cookbooks. Submit 3 sample chapters and a cover letter with a synopsis and author bio; SASE. Send photocopies.

FICTION Subjects include ethnic, historical, humor, literary, mystery, In mysteries, we only publish series with foreign or exotic settings, usually procedurals. Adventure, ethnic, feminist, historical, literary, mainstream/contemporary, mystery (police procedural), suspense, multicultural. Submit 3 sample chapters and cover letter with synopsis, author bio, SASE. *No e-mailed submissions.*

TIPS "Soho Press publishes discerning authors for discriminating readers, finding the strongest possible writers and publishing them. Before submitting, look at our website for an idea of the types of books we publish, and read our submission guidelines."

SOLAS HOUSE/TRAVELERS' TALES

2320 Bowdoin St., Palo Alto CA 94306. (650)462-2110. **Fax:** (650)462-2114. **E-mail:** submit@travelerstales.com. **Website:** www.travelerstales.com; www.besttravelwriting.com. **Contact:** James O'Reilly; Larry Habegger; Sean O'Reilly, series editors. Publishes inspirational travel books, mostly anthologies and travel advice books. **Publishes 8-10 titles/year. Pays $100 honorarium for anthology pieces.** Accepts simultaneous submissions. Guidelines available online. Sponsors and operates annual Solas Awards for Best Travel Writing.

○ "Due to the volume of submissions, we do not respond unless the material submitted meets our immediate editorial needs. All stories are read and filed for future use contingent upon meeting editorial guidelines."

NONFICTION Subjects include all aspects of travel.

TIPS "We publish personal nonfiction stories and anecdotes—funny, illuminating, adventurous, frightening, or grim. Stories should reflect that unique alchemy that occurs when you enter unfamiliar territory and begin to see the world differently as a result. Stories that have already been published, including book excerpts, are welcome as long as the authors retain the copyright or can obtain permission from the copyright holder to reprint the material. We publish nonfiction for the most part, but in 2012 we published our first novel."

SOL BOOKS

An imprint of Skywater Publishing Company, P.O. Box 24668, Minneapolis MN 55424. **E-mail:** info@solbooks.com. **E-mail:** submissions@solbooks.com. **Website:** www.solbooks.com. **Contact:** S. R. Welvaert, prose editor. Connie Colwell Miller, poetry editor (poetry and mainstream prose) Estab. 2005. Publishes mass market paperback and electronic originals and reprints. **Publishes 2-4 titles/year. 500 queries received/year. 25% of books from first-time authors. 100% from unagented writers. Pays 15% royalty. Pays $250-1,000 advance.** Publishes ms 1-2 years after acceptance. Accepts simultaneous submissions. Responds in 3 months to queries/proposals; 3-6 months to ms. Guidelines available online.

FICTION Subjects include adventure, ethnic, experimental, fantasy, gothic, historical, horror, humor, literary, mainstream, contemporary, military, war, multicultural, mystery, poetry, poetry in translation, regional, science fiction, short story collections, sports, suspense, translation, western. "We're open to all styles of writing, but what we find more important than scintillating prose is a good story well told, with intriguing characters and a captivating plot." Submit complete ms.

POETRY "We seek accessible poetry. That does not mean we're willing to sacrifice literary quality. Rather, we feel that poetry should not be overtly convoluted, but reach toward a wider audience than other writers of poetry." Submit complete ms.

◎ SOURCEBOOKS

Sourcebooks, Inc., 232 Madison Ave., Suite 1100, New York NY 10016. **E-mail:** editorialsubmissions@sourcebooks.com. **Website:** www.sourcebooks.com. Does not accept hard copy submissions. Submit via e-mail.

◎ SOURCEBOOKS LANDMARK

Sourcebooks, Inc., 232 Madison Ave., Suite 1100, New York NY 10016. **E-mail:** romance@sourcebooks.com. **Website:** www.sourcebooks.com. **Contact:** Leah Haltenschmidt. "Our fiction imprint, Sourcebooks Landmark, publishes a variety of commercial fiction, including specialties in historical fiction and Austenalia. We are interested first and foremost in books that have a story to tell."

◐ "We publish a variety of titles. We are currently only reviewing agented fiction manuscripts with the exception of Romance fiction. Find out more information about our Romance fiction submission guidelines online at our website."

FICTION "We are actively acquiring single-title and single-title series Romance fiction (90,000 to 120,000 actual digital words) for our Casablanca imprint. We are looking for strong writers who are excited about marketing their books and building their community of readers, and whose books have something fresh to offer in the genre of Romance." Receipt of email submissions will be acknowledged within 21 days via email. Responds to queries in 6-8 weeks. Email: romance@sourcebooks.com.

SOUTH END PRESS

P.O. Box 382132, Cambridge MA 02238. (718)874-0089. **Fax:** (800)960-0778. **E-mail:** southend@southendpress.org. **Website:** www.southendpress.org. Estab. 1977. Publishes library and trade paperback and eBook originals and reprints, in English and some Spanish. "South End Press publishes nonfiction political books with a left/feminist/antiracist perspective." **Publishes 10 titles/year. 400 queries received/year. 100 mss received/year. 30% of books**

from first-time authors. 95% from unagented writers. Pays 11% royalty on wholesale price. Pays occasionally $500-2,500 advance. Publishes ms 9 months after acceptance. Accepts simultaneous submissions. Responds in up to 3 months to queries and proposals only if interested. Book catalog available free. Guidelines available online.

NONFICTION Subjects include economics, environment, government, health, history, medicine, nature, philosophy, science, sociology, womens issues, womens studies, world affairs, critical ethnic studies, queer studies, disability studies, culture & media studies. Query with SASE. Submit 2 sample chapters, intro or conclusion, and annotated TOC. Reviews artwork/photos. Send photocopies.

SPEAK UP PRESS

P.O. Box 100506, Denver CO 80250. (303)715-0837. **Fax:** (303)715-0793. **E-mail:** info@speakuppress.org. **E-mail:** submit@speakuppress.org. **Website:** www.speakuppress.org. Estab. 1999. As a 501(c)3 nonprofit organization, Speak Up Press is supported by individuals, corporations, and foundations from across the country. Speak Up Press publishes *Speak Up Online* quarterly, featuring the original fiction, nonfiction, and poetry of teens (13-19 years old).

◐ *Only accepts submissions via e-mail.*

NONFICTION Nonfiction: Young adult nonfiction, with an emphasis on stories about overcoming adversity and finding a voice. No more than 2,500 words. Submit via e-mail only. Include work in body of e-mail. No attachments.

TIPS "Follow submission guidelines."

THE SPEECH BIN INC.

P.O. Box 1579, Appleton WI 54912-1579. (888)388-3224. **Fax:** (888)388-6344. **E-mail:** customercare@schoolspecialty.com. **Website:** www.speechbin.com. Estab. 1984. "The Speech Bin® products provide you with tools for children with speech, language, and communication needs. We equip you to help with articulation, phonology, oral-motor, apraxia, fluency, voice, early education, language and communication, auditory processing/listening, reading/literacy, autism/pervasive developmental delay, pragmatics and social skills, cognition, word finding, augmentative alternative communication, and more! Our products are hand-selected by experienced special needs professionals. Not only do they meet our high quality standards, they are also kid-tested and therapist, teacher and parent approved."

SPINNER BOOKS

University Games, 2030 Harrison St., San Francisco CA 94107. (415)503-1600. **Fax:** (415)503-0085. **E-mail:** info@ugames.com. **Website:** www.ugames.com. Estab. 1985. "Spinners Books publishes books of puzzles, games and trivia." Publishes book 6 months after acceptance. Responds to queries in 3 months; mss in 2 months only if interested.

NONFICTION Picture books: games & puzzles. Query.

STACKPOLE BOOKS

5067 Ritter Rd., Mechanicsburg PA 17055. **Fax:** (717)796-0412. **E-mail:** jschnell@stackpolebooks. com. **E-mail:** cevans@stackpolebooks.com; kweaver@stackpolebooks.com; mallison@stackpolebooks. com; jnichols@stackpolebooks.com. **Website:** www. stackpolebooks.com. **Contact:** Judith Schnell, editorial director (outdoor sports); Chris Evans, editor (history); Mark Allison, editor (nature); Kyle Weaver, editor (regional/Pennsylvania). Estab. 1935. Publishes hardcover and trade paperback originals, reprints, and ebooks 100/yr. "Stackpole maintains a growing and vital publishing program by featuring authors who are experts in their fields." **Pays industry standard advance.** Publishes book 1 year after acceptance. Responds in 1 month to queries. See catalog and guidelines online.

NONFICTION Subjects include history, military, outdoor sports. "First of all, send your query to an individual editor. The more information you can supply, the better." Reviews artwork/photos.

TIPS "Stackpole seeks well-written, authoritative mss for specialized and general trade markets. Proposals should include chapter outline, sample chapter, illustrations, and author's credentials."

STANDARD PUBLISHING

Standex International Corp., 8805 Governor's Hill Dr., Suite 400, Cincinnati OH 45249. (800)543-1353. **E-mail:** customerservice@standardpub.com. **E-mail:** adultministry@standardpub.com; ministrytochildren@standardpub.com; ministrytoyouth@ standardpub.com. **Website:** www.standardpub.com. Mark Taylor, adult ministry resources; Ruth Frederick, children and youth ministry resources; Diane Stortz, family resources. Estab. 1866. Publishes resources that meet church and family needs in the area of children's ministry. Guidelines and current publishing objectives available online.

STANFORD UNIVERSITY PRESS

1450 Page Mill Rd., Palo Alto CA 94304. (650)723-9434. **Fax:** (650)725-3457. **E-mail:** info@www.sup. org. **Website:** www.sup.org. **Contact:** Stacy Wagner (Asian studies, US foreign policy, Asian-American studies); Kate Wahl (law, political science, public policy); Margo Beth Crouppen (economics, finance, business). Estab. 1925. "Stanford University Press publishes scholarly books in the humanities and social sciences, along with professional books in business, economics and management science; also high-level textbooks and some books for a more general audience." **Pays variable royalty (sometimes none). Pays occasional advance.** Guidelines available online.

NONFICTION Subjects include anthropology, archeology, business, economics, ethnic, studies, gay, lesbian, government, politics, history, humanities, language, literature, literary criticism, and literary theory, nature, environment, philosophy, psychology, religion, science, social sciences, sociology, political science, law, education, history and culture of China, Japan and Latin America, European history, linguistics, geology, medieval and classical studies. Query with prospectus and an outline. Reviews artwork/photos.

TIPS "The writer's best chance is a work of original scholarship with an argument of some importance."

STARCHERONE BOOKS

Dzanc Books, P.O. Box 303, Buffalo NY 14201, (716)885-2726. **E-mail:** starcherone@gmail.com; publisher@starcherone.com. **Website:** www.starcherone.com. **Contact:** Ted Pelton, publisher; Carra Stratton, acquisitions editor. Estab. 2000. Non-profit publisher of literary and experimental fiction. Publishes paperback originals and reprints. Books: acid-free paper; perfect bound; occasional illustrations. Average print order: 1,000. Average first novel print order: 1,000. **Published 2 debut authors within the last year.** Member CLMP. Titles distributed through website, Small Press Distribution, Amazon, independent bookstores. **Pays 10-12.5% royalty.** Publishes ms 18 months after acceptance. Responds in 2 months to queries; 6-10 months to mss. Catalog and guidelines available online at website.

FICTION Accepts queries by mail or e-mail during August and September of each year. Submissions of unsolicited mss will risk being returned or discarded, unread. Include brief bio, list of publishing credits. Always query before sending ms.

STEEL TOE BOOKS

Department of English, Western Kentucky University, 1906 College Heights Blvd. #11086, Bowling Green KY 42101. (270)745-5769. **E-mail:** tom.hunley@wku. edu. **Website:** www.steeltoebooks.com. **Contact:** Dr. Tom C. Hunley, director. Estab. 2003. Steel Toe Books publishes "full-length, single-author poetry collections. Our books are professionally designed and printed. We look for workmanship (economical use of language, high-energy verbs, precise literal descriptions, original figurative language, poems carefully arranged as a book); a unique style and/or a distinctive voice; clarity; emotional impact; humor (word plays, hyperbole, comic timing); performability (a Steel Toe poet is at home on the stage as well as on the page)." Does not want "dry verse, purposely obscure language, poetry by people who are so wary of being called 'sentimental' they steer away from any recognizable human emotions, poetry that takes itself so seriously that it's unintentionally funny." Has published poetry by Allison Joseph, Susan Browne, James Doyle, Martha Silano, Mary Biddinger, John Guzlowski, Jeannine Hall Gailey, and others. Publishes 1-3 poetry books/year. Manuscripts are normally selected through open submission.

POETRY "Check the website for news about our next open reading period." Book mss may include previously published poems. Responds to mss in 3 months. Pays $500 advance on 10% royalties and 10 author's copies. Order sample books by sending $12 to Steel Toe Books. *Must purchase a manuscript in order to submit.* See website for submission guidelines.

STEEPLE HILL BOOKS

Imprint of Harlequin Enterprises, 233 Broadway, Suite 1001, New York NY 10279. (212)553-4200. **Fax:** (212)227-8969. **Website:** www.eharlequin.com. **Contact:** Joan Marlow Golan, executive editor; Melissa Endlich, senior editor (inspirational contemporary romance, historical romance, romantic suspense); Tina James, senior editor (inspirational romantic suspense and historical romance); Emily Rodmell, associate editor. Estab. 1997. Publishes mass market paperback originals and reprints. "This series of contemporary, inspirational love stories portrays Christian characters facing the many challenges of life, faith, and love in today's world." **Publishes 144 titles/year. Pays royalty on retail price. Pays advance.** Responds in 3 months to proposals and mss. Guidelines available online, free on request, for #10 SASE.

IMPRINTS Love Inspired; Love Inspired Suspense; Love Inspired Historical.

FICTION , Romance (Christian, 70,000-75,000 words). Wants all genres of inspirational woman's fiction including contemporary and historical romance, chick/mom-lit, relationship novels, romantic suspense, mysteries, family sagas, and thrillers. "We are looking for authors writing from a Christian worldview and conveying their personal faith and ministry values in entertaining fiction that will touch the hearts of believers and seekers everywhere." Query with SASE and synopsis, submit completed ms.

TIPS "Drama, humor, and even a touch of mystery all have a place in Steeple Hill. Subplots are welcome and should further the story's main focus or intertwine in a meaningful way. Secondary characters (children, family, friends, neighbors, fellow church members, etc.) may all contribute to a substantial and satisfying story. These wholesome tales include strong family values and high moral standards. While there is no premarital sex between characters, in the case of romance, a vivid, exciting tone presented with a mature perspective is essential. Although the element of faith must clearly be present, it should be well integrated into the characterizations and plot. The conflict between the main characters should be an emotional one, arising naturally from the well-developed personalities you've created. Suitable stories should also impart an important lesson about the powers of trust and faith."

STEMMER HOUSE PUBLISHERS

4 White Brook Rd., P.O. Box 89, Gilsum NH 03448. (800)345-6665. **Fax:** (603)357-2073. **E-mail:** info@ stemmer.com; editor@stemmer.com. **Website:** www. stemmer.com. Estab. 1975. **Pays advance.** Publishes ms 1-2 years after acceptance. Accepts simultaneous submissions.

IMPRINTS The International Design Library®; The NatureEncyclopedia Series.

NONFICTION Subjects include animals, arts, multicultural, nature, environment. Query with SASE.

STENHOUSE PUBLISHERS

480 Congress St., Portland ME 04101. **E-mail:** editors@stenhouse.com. **Website:** www.stenhouse.com.

Contact: Jill Cooley, editorial assistant. Estab. 1993. Publishes paperback originals. Stenhouse publishes exclusively professional books for teachers, K-12. **Publishes 15 titles/year. 300 queries received/year. 30% of books from first-time authors. 99% from unagented writers. Pays royalty on wholesale price.** Accepts simultaneous submissions. Responds in 2 weeks to queries; 1 month to mss. Book catalog free or online. Guidelines available online.

NONFICTION Subjects include education, specializing in literary with offerings in elementary and middle level math and science. All of our books are a combination of theory and practice. No children's books or student texts. Query by e-mail (preferred) or SASE. Reviews artwork/photos. Send photocopies.

STERLING PUBLISHING CO., INC.

387 Park Ave. S 10th Floor, New York NY 10016. (212)532-7160. **Fax:** (212)981-0508. **E-mail:** ragis@sterlingpublishing.com. **E-mail:** info@sterlingpublishing.com. **Website:** www.sterlingpublishing.com. Publishes hardcover and paperback originals and reprints. "Sterling publishes highly illustrated, accessible, hands-on, practical books for adults and children." **15% of books from first-time authors. Pays royalty or work purchased outright. Offers advances (average amount: $2,000).** Accepts simultaneous submissions. Catalog available on website. Guidelines available online.

IMPRINTS Sterling/Books; Sterling/Ethos; Lark; Sterling/Children's; Sterling/Epicure; Ecosystem; Puzzlewright Press; Union Square Press; Ecosystem; Sandy Creek; Sterling/Innovation; Fall River Press; Metro Books; Flashkids; Quamut; Silver Lining Calendars; Hearst Books.

○ "Our mission is to publish high-quality books that educate, entertain, and enrich the lives of our readers."

NONFICTION Subjects include alternative, animals, art, architecture, ethnic, gardening, health, medicine, hobbies, New Age, recreation, science, sports, fiber arts, games and puzzles, children's humor, children's science, nature and activities, pets, wine, home decorating, dolls and puppets, ghosts, UFOs, woodworking, crafts, medieval, Celtic subjects, alternative health and healing, new consciousness. Proposals on subjects such as crafting, decorating, outdoor living, and photography should be sent directly to Lark Books at their Asheville, North Carolina offices.

Complete guidelines can be found on the Lark site: www.larkbooks.com/submissions. Publishes nonfiction only. Submit outline, publishing history, 1 sample chapter (typed and double-spaced), SASE. Explain your idea. Send sample illustrations where applicable. For children's books, please submit full mss. We do not accept electronic (e-mail) submissions. Be sure to include information about yourself with particular regard to your skills and qualifications in the subject area of your submission. It is helpful for us to know your publishing history—whether or not you've written other books and, if so, the name of the publisher and whether those books are currently in print. Reviews artwork/photocopies.

FICTION "At present we do not accept fiction."

TIPS "We are primarily a nonfiction activities-based publisher. We have a picture book list, but we do not publish chapter books or novels. Our list is not trend-driven. We focus on titles that will backlist well. "

STIPES PUBLISHING LLC

P.O. Box 526, Champaign IL 61824. (217)356-8391. **Fax:** (217)356-5753. **E-mail:** stipes01@sbcglobal.net. **Website:** www.stipes.com. **Contact:** Benjamin H. Watts, (engineering, science, business); Robert Watts (agriculture, music, and physical education). Estab. 1925. Publishes hardcover and paperback originals. "Stipes Publishing is oriented towards the education market and educational books with some emphasis in the trade market." **Publishes 15-30 titles/year. 50% of books from first-time authors. 95% from unagented writers. Pays 15% maximum royalty on retail price.** Publishes ms 4 months after acceptance. Responds in 2 months to queries. Guidelines available online.

NONFICTION Subjects include agriculture, business, economics, music, dance, nature, environment, recreation, science. "All of our books in the trade area are books that also have a college text market. No books unrelated to educational fields taught at the college level." Submit outline, 1 sample chapter.

ST. JOHANN PRESS

P.O. Box 241, Haworth NJ 07641. (201)387-1529. **E-mail:** d.biesel@verizon.net. **Website:** www.stjohannpress.com. Estab. 1991. Publishes hardcover originals, trade paperback originals and reprints. **Publishes 6-8 titles/year. Receives 15 submissions/year. 50% of books from first-time authors. 95% from unagented writers. Pays 10-15% royalty on whole-**

sale price. Publishes book 15 months after acceptance. Accepts simultaneous submissions. Responds in 1 month on queries. Catalog online at website. Guidelines free on request.

NONFICTION Subjects include cooking, crafts, foods, history, hobbies, memoirs, military, nutrition, religion, sports (history), war (USMC), Black history in sports. "We are a niche publisher with interests in titles that will sell over a long period of time. For example, the World Football League Encyclopedia, Chicago Showcase of Basketball, will not need to be redone. We do baseball but prefer soccer, hockey, etc." Query with SASE. Reviews artwork/photos as part of the ms package. Send photocopies.

TIPS "Our readership is libraries, individuals with special interests, (e.g. sports historians); we also do specialized reference."

STONE BRIDGE PRESS

P.O. Box 8208, Berkeley CA 94707. **Website:** www.stonebridge.com. **Contact:** Peter Goodman, publisher. Estab. 1989. "Independent press focusing on books about Japan and Asia in English (business, language, culture, literature, animation)." Publishes hardcover and trade paperback originals. Books: 60-70 lb. offset paper; web and sheet paper; perfect bound; some illustrations. Averages 12 total titles/year. Distributes titles through Consortium. Promotes titles through Internet announcements, special-interest magazines and niche tie-ins to associations. **75% from unagented writers. Pays royalty on wholesale price.** Publishes ms 2 years after acceptance. Responds to queries in 4 months, mss in 8 months. Book catalog for 2 first-class stamps and SASE. Ms guidelines online.

FICTION Experimental, gay/lesbian, literary, Japan-themed. "Primarily looking at material relating to Japan. Translations only." Does not accept unsolicited mss. Query with SASE. Accepts queries by e-mail, fax.

TIPS "Fiction translations only for the time being. No poetry."

✪ STONESLIDE BOOKS

Stoneslide Media LLC, P.O. Box 8331, New Haven CT 06530. **E-mail:** editors@stoneslidecorrective.com. **E-mail:** submissions@stoneslidecorrective.com. **Website:** www.stoneslidecorrective.com. **Contact:** Jonathan Weisberg, editor; Christopher Wachlin, editor. Estab. 2012. Publishes trade paperback and electronic originals. **Publishes 3-5 titles/year. Receives 300 queries/year; 150 mss/year. Pays royalty of 20% minimum to 80% maximum.** Publishes book 8 months after acceptance. Responds in 1 month to queries/proposals; 2 months to mss. Book catalog and guidelines available online.

FICTION Subjects include adventure, contemporary, experimental, fantasy, gothic, historical, humor, literary, mainstream, mystery, science fiction, short story collections, suspense. "We will look at any genre. The importatn factor for us is that the story use plot, characters, emotions, and other elements of storytelling to think and move the mind forward." Submit proposal package via e-mail including: synopsis and 3 sample chapters.

TIPS "Read the Stoneslide Corrective to see if your work fits with our approach."

STOREY PUBLISHING

210 MASS MoCA Way, North Adams MA 01247. (800)793-9396. **Fax:** (413)346-2196. **E-mail:** webmaster@storey.com. **Website:** www.storcy.com. **Contact:** Deborah Balmuth, editorial director (building, sewing, gift). Estab. 1983. Publishes hardcover and trade paperback originals and reprints. "The mission of Storey Publishing is to serve our customers by publishing practical information that encourages personal independence in harmony with the environment. We seek to do this in a positive atmosphere that promotes editorial quality, team spirit, and profitability. The books we select to carry out this mission include titles on gardening, small-scale farming, building, cooking, homebrewing, crafts, part-time business, home improvement, woodworking, animals, nature, natural living, personal care, and country living. We are always pleased to review new proposals, which we try to process expeditiously. We offer both work-for-hire and standard royalty contracts." **Publishes 40 titles/year. 600 queries received/year. 150 mss received/year. 25% of books from first-time authors. 60% from unagented writers. We offer both work-for-hire and standard royalty contracts. Pays advance.** Publishes book 2 years after acceptance. Accepts simultaneous submissions. Responds in 1 month to queries; 3 months to proposals/mss. Book catalog available free. Guidelines available online at website.

NONFICTION Subjects include animals, gardening, nature, environment, home, mind/body/spirit, birds, beer and wine, crafts, building, cooking. Reviews artwork/photos.

ST PAULS/ALBA HOUSE

Society of St. Paul, 2187 Victory Blvd., Staten Island NY 10314. (718)761-0047. **Fax:** (718)761-0057. **E-mail:** edmund_lane@juno.com; albabooks@aol.com. **Website:** www.stpauls.us; www.albahouse.org. **Contact:** Edmund C. Lane, SSP, acquisitions editor. Estab. 1957. Publishes trade paperback and mass market paperback originals and reprints. **Publishes 22 titles/year. 250 queries received/year. 150 mss received/year. 10% of books from first-time authors. 100% from unagented writers. Pays 5-10% royalty.** Publishes ms 10 months after acceptance. Responds in 1 month to queries and proposals; 2 months to mss. Book catalog and ms guidelines free.

NONFICTION Subjects include philosophy, religion, spirituality. Alba House is the North American publishing division of the Society of St. Paul, an International Roman Catholic Missionary Religious Congregation dedicated to spreading the Gospel message via the media of communications. Does not want fiction, children's books, poetry, personal testimonies, or autobiographies. Submit complete ms. Reviews artwork/photos. Send photocopies.

TIPS "Our audience is educated Roman Catholic readers interested in matters related to the Church, spirituality, Biblical and theological topics, moral concerns, lives of the saints, etc."

STRIDER NOLAN PUBLISHING, INC.

702 Cricket Ave., Glenside PA 19038. **E-mail:** infostridernolan@yahoo.com. **Website:** www.stridernolanmedia.com. Publishes hardcover, trade paperback. "At this time, Strider Nolan is only seeking stories or art for our Visions anthology. Feel free to contact us via e-mail. If you would like to submit a novel to us, we have plenty of material in the pipeline but are always willing to listen. We cannot guarantee anything, so your project would really have to be something special to get us to look at it. We do accept unagented material, although a prior history of published work (even self-published) is preferable. Favored genres include science fiction, horror, and historical fiction (especially westerns or Civil War)." **Publishes 5-10 titles/year. 1,000-2,000 queries received/year. 500-1,000 mss received/year. 50% of books from first-time authors. 50% from unagented writers. Pays royalty on retail price.** Accepts simultaneous submissions. Book catalog available online. Guidelines available online.

SUBITO PRESS

University of Colorado at Boulder, Dept. of English, 226 UCB, Boulder CO 80309-0226. **E-mail:** subitopressucb@gmail.com. **Website:** www.subitopress.org. Trade paperback originals. Subito Press is a nonprofit publisher of literary works. Each year Subito publishes one work of fiction and one work of poetry through its contest. Submissions are open annually during the month of July. Accepts simultaneous submissions. Guidelines online.

FICTION Subjects include experimental, literary, translation. Submit complete ms to contest.

POETRY Submit complete ms to contest.

TIPS "We publish two books of innovative writing a year through our poetry and fiction contests. All entries are also considered for publication with the press."

SUN BOOKS / SUN PUBLISHING

P.O. Box 5588, Santa Fe NM 87502. (505)471-5177. **E-mail:** info@sunbooks.com. **Website:** www.sunbooks.com. **Contact:** Skip Whitson, director. Estab. 1973. Publishes trade paperback originals and reprints. **Publishes 10-15 titles/year. 5% of books from first-time authors. 90% from unagented writers. Pays 5% royalty on retail price. Occasionally makes outright purchase.** Publishes ms 16-18 months after acceptance. "Will respond within 2 months, via e-mail, to queries if interested.". Book catalog available online at www.sunbooks.com or www.abooksource.com. Queries via e-mail only, please.

NONFICTION , self-help, leadership, motivational, recovery, inspirational.

SUNBURY PRESS, INC.

50 W. Main St., Mechanicsburg PA 17055. **E-mail:** info@sunburypress.com. **E-mail:** proposals@sunburypress.com. **Website:** www.sunburypress.com. Estab. 2004. Publishes trade paperback originals and reprints; electronic originals and reprints. **Publishes 75 titles/year. 750 queries/year; 500 mss/year. 40% of books from first-time authors. 90% from unagented writers. Pays 10% royalty on wholesale price.** Publishes ms 3 months after acceptance. Accepts simultaneous submissions. Responds in 2 months. Catalog and guidelines available online at website.

○ "Please use our online submission form."

NONFICTION Subjects include Americana, animals, anthropology, archeology, architecture, art, astrology, business, career guidance, child guidance, communications, computers, contemporary culture, counseling, crafts, creative nonfiction, dance, economics, education, electronics, entertainment, ethnic, government, health, history, hobbies, house and home, humanities, language, literature, memoirs, military, money, multicultural, music, nature, New Age, photography, regional, religion, science, sex, spirituality, sports, transportation, travel, war, world affairs, young adult. "We are currently seeking Civil War era memoirs and unpublished or new material regarding the Civil War. We are also seeking biographies / histories of local/regional figures who were noteworthy but unpublished or sparsely published." Reviews artwork.

FICTION Subjects include adventure, confession, contemporary, ethnic, experimental, fantasy, gothic, historical, horror, humor, juvenile, mainstream, military, multicultural, mystery, occult, picture books, poetry, regional, religious, romance, science fiction, short story collections, spiritual, sports, suspense, western, young adult. "We are especially seeking historical fiction regarding the Civil War and books of regional interest."

POETRY Submit complete ms.

TIPS "Our books appeal to very diverse audiences. We are building our list in many categories, focusing on many demographics. We are not like traditional publishers—we are digitally adept and very creative. Don't be surprised if we move quicker than you are accustomed to!"

SUNRISE RIVER PRESS

39966 Grand Ave., North Branch MN 55056. (800)895-4585. **Fax:** (651)277-1203. **E-mail:** editorial@sunriseriverpress.com. **Website:** www.sunriserverpress.com. Estab. 1992. "E-mail is preferred method of contact." **Publishes 30 titles/year. Pays advance.** Accepts simultaneous submissions. Guidelines available online.

○ Sunrise River Press is part of a 3-company publishing house that also includes CarTech Books and Specialty Press. "Sunrise River Press is currently seeking book proposals from health/medical writers or experts who are interested in authoring consumer-geared trade paperbacks on healthcare, fitness, and nutrition topics."

NONFICTION Subjects include cooking, foods, nutrition, health, medicine, genetics, immune system maintenance, fitness; also some professional healthcare titles. Check website for submission guidelines. No phone calls, please; no originals.

FICTION "Although we don't solicit article-length manuscripts, short humour contributions or jokes are welcome." Submit online at: www2.readersdigest.ca/laugh_submit.html.

SUPERCOLLEGE

2713 Newlands Ave., Belmont CA 94002. Phone/**Fax:** (650)618-2221. **E-mail:** supercollege@supercollege.com. **Website:** www.supercollege.com. Estab. 1998. Publishes trade paperback originals. "We only publish books on admission, financial aid, scholarships, test preparation, student life, and career preparation for college and graduate students." **Publishes 8-10 titles/year. 50% of books from first-time authors. 70% from unagented writers. Pays royalty on wholesale price or makes outright purchase.** Publishes ms 7-9 months after acceptance. Book catalog and writers guidelines online.

NONFICTION Subjects include education, admissions, financial aid, scholarships, test prep, student life, career prep. Submit complete ms. Reviews artwork/photos. Send photocopies.

TIPS "We want titles that are student and parent friendly, and that are different from other titles in this category. We also seek authors who want to work with a small but dynamic and ambitious publishing company."

⊕ SWAN ISLE PRESS

P.O. Box 408790, Chicago IL 60640. (773)728-3780. **E-mail:** info@swanislepress.com. **Website:** www.swanislepress.com. Estab. 1999. Publishes hardcover and trade paperback originals. **Publishes 3 titles/year. 1,500 queries received/year. 0% of books from first-time authors. Pays 7 1/2-10% royalty on wholesale price.** Publishes book 18 months after acceptance. Responds in 6 months to queries. Responds in 12 months to manuscripts. Book catalog available online. Guidelines available online.

○ *"We do not accept unsolicited mss."*

NONFICTION Subjects include art, architecture, creative nonfiction, ethnic, history, humanities, language, literature, literary criticism, memoirs, multicultural, translation. Query with SASE. Submit complete mss only if author receives affirmative response to query. Reviews artwork/photos. Send photocopies.

FICTION Subjects include ethnic, historical, literary, multicultural, poetry, poetry in translation, short story collections, translation. Query with SASE. Submit complete mss.

POETRY Query and submit complete ms.

⊕ SWEETGRASS BOOKS

Farcounty Press, P.O. Box 5630, Helena MT 59604. (800)821-3874. **Fax:** (406)443-5480. **E-mail:** kathy@farcountypress.com; kathy@sweetgrassbooks.com. **Website:** www.sweetgrassbooks.com. Estab. 2012. The custom publishing division of Farcounty Press, offering the same professional editorial, design, production, print management, and distribution services as Farcounty Press to self publishers.

SYLVAN DELL PUBLISHING

612 Johnnie Dodds, Suite A2, Mt. Pleasant SC 29464. (843)971-6722. **Fax:** (843)216-3804. **E-mail:** donnagerman@sylvandellpublishing.com. **Website:** www.sylvandellpublishing.com. **Contact:** Donna German, editor. Estab. 2004. Publishes hardcover, trade paperback, and electronic originals. "The picture books we publish are usually, but not always, fictional stories that relate to animals, nature, the environment, and science. All books should subtly convey an educational theme through a warm story that is fun to read and that will grab a child's attention. Each book has a 3-5 page '*For Creative Minds*' section to reinforce the educational component. This section will have a craft and/or game as well as 'fun facts' to be shared by the parent, teacher, or other adult. Authors do not need to supply this information. Mss. should be less than 1,500 words and meet all of the following 4 criteria: Fun to read—mostly fiction with nonfiction facts woven into the story; National or regional in scope; Must tie into early elementary school curriculum; must be marketable through a niche market such as a zoo, aquarium, or museum gift shop." **Publishes 10 titles/year. 2,000 mss received/year. 50% of books from first-time authors. 100% from unagented writers. Pays 6-8% royalty on wholesale price. Pays small advance.** Publishes book 18 months after acceptance. May hold onto mss of interest for 1 year until acceptance. after acceptance of ms. Accepts simultaneous submissions. Acknowledges receipt of ms submission within one week. Book catalog and guidelines available online.

NONFICTION Subjects include science, math. "We are not looking for mss. about: pets (dogs or cats in particular); new babies; local or state-specific; mag-

ic; biographies; history-related; ABC books; poetry; series; young adult books or novels; holiday-related books. We do not consider mss. that have been previously published in any way, including e-books or self-published." Accepts electronic submissions only. Snail mail submissions are discarded without being opened. Reviews artwork/photos. Send 1-2 JPEGS.

FICTION Subjects include picture books. Picture books: animal, folktales, nature/environment, math-related. Word length—picture books: no more than 1500. Accepts electronic submissions only. Snail mail submissions are discarded without being opened.

TIPS "Please make sure that you have looked at our website to read our complete submission guidelines and to see if we are looking for a particular subject. Manuscripts must meet all four of our stated criteria. We look for fairly realistic, bright and colorful art—no cartoons. We want the children excited about the books. We envision the books being used at home and in the classroom."

SYRACUSE UNIVERSITY PRESS

621 Skytop Rd., Suite 110, Syracuse NY 13244. (315)443-5534. **Fax:** (315)443-5545. **E-mail:** seguiod@syr.edu; dhmccay@syr.edu; jsbaines@syr.edu; klbalens@syr.edu. **Website:** syracuseuniversitypress.syr.edu. **Contact:** Suzanne Guiod, editor-in-chief; Deanna McCay, acquisitions editor; Jennika Baines, acquisitions editor; Kelly Balenske, editorial assistant; Alice Randel Pfeiffer, director. Estab. 1943. "Currently emphasizing Middle East studies, Jewish studies, Irish studies, peace studies, disability studies, television and popular culture, sports and entertainment, Native American studies, gender and ethnic studies, New York State." **Publishes 50 titles/year. 25% of books from first-time authors. 95% from unagented writers.** Publishes book 15 months after acceptance. Book catalog available online at website. Guidelines available online at website.

NONFICTION "Special opportunity in our nonfiction program for books on New York state, sports history, Jewish studies, Irish studies, the Middle East, religion and politics, television, and popular culture, disability studies, peace studies, Native American studies. Provide precise descriptions of subjects, along with background description of project. The author must make a case for the importance of his or her subject." Submit query via e-mail with the book vproposal form found on our website and a copy of your CV. Reviews artwork/photos.

TIPS "We're seeking well-written and thoroughly researched books that will make a significant contribution to the subject areas listed above and will be favorably received in the marketplace."

TAFELBERG PUBLISHERS

Imprint of NB Publishers, P.O. Box 879, Cape Town 8000, South Africa. (27)(21)406-3033. **Fax:** (27)(21)406-3812. **E-mail:** nb@nb.co.za. **Website:** www.tafelberg.com. **Contact:** Danita van Romburgh, editorial secretary; Louise Steyn, publisher. General publisher best known for Afrikaans fiction, authoritative political works, children's/youth literature, and a variety of illustrated and nonillustrated nonfiction. **Publishes 10 titles/year. Pays authors royalty of 15-18% based on wholesale price.** Publishes book 1 year after acceptance. Responds to queries in 2 weeks; mss in 6 months.

NONFICTION Subjects include health, medicine, memoirs, politics. Submit complete ms.

FICTION Subjects include juvenile, romance. Picture books, young readers: animal, anthology, contemporary, fantasy, folktales, hi-lo, humor, multicultural, nature/environment, scient fiction, special needs. Middle readers, young adults: animal (middle reader only), contemporary, fantasy, hi-lo, humor, multicultural, nature/environment, problem novels, science fiction, special needs, sports, suspense/mystery. Average word length: picture books—1,500-7,500; young readers—25,000; middle readers—15,000; young adults—40,000. Query or submit complete ms.

TIPS "Writers: Story needs to have a South African or African style. Illustrators: I'd like to look, but the chances of getting commissioned are slim. The market is small and difficult. Do not expect huge advances. Editorial staff attended or plans to attend the following conferences: IBBY, Frankfurt, SCBWI Bologna."

NAN A. TALESE

Imprint of Doubleday, Random House, Inco, 1745 Broadway, New York NY 10019. (212)782-8918. **Fax:** (212)782-8448. **Website:** www.nanatalese.com. **Contact:** Nan A. Talese, publisher and editorial director; Ronit Feldman, assistant editor. Publishes hardcover originals. Nan A. Talese publishes nonfiction with a powerful guiding narrative and relevance to larger cultural interests, and literary fiction of the highest quality. **Publishes 15 titles/year. 400 queries received/year. 400 mss received/year. Pays variable royalty on retail price. Pays varying advance.** *Agented submissions only.*

NONFICTION Subjects include contemporary culture, history, philosophy, sociology.

FICTION Subjects include literary. Well-written narratives with a compelling story line, good characterization and use of language. We like stories with an edge.

TIPS "Audience is highly literate people interested in story, information and insight. We want well-written material submitted by agents only. See our website."

TANGLEWOOD BOOKS

P.O. Box 3009, Terre Haute IN 47803. **E-mail:** ptierney@tanglewoodbooks.com. **Website:** www.tanglewoodbooks.com. **Contact:** Kairi Hamlin, acquisitions editor; Peggy Tierney, publisher. Estab. 2003. "Tanglewood Press strives to publish entertaining, kid-centric books." **Publishes 10 titles/year. 20% of books from first-time authors.** Publishes book 2 years after acceptance. Accepts simultaneous submissions. Responds to mss in up to 18 months.

NONFICTION Does not generally publish nonfiction.

FICTION Picture books: adventure, animal, concept, contemporary, fantasy, humor. Average word length: picture books—800. Query with 3-5 sample chapters.

TIPS "Please see lengthy 'Submissions' page on our website."

TAYLOR TRADE PUBLISHING

The Rowman & Littlefield Publishing Group, 5360 Manhattan Circle, #101, Boulder CO 80303. (303)543-7835. **Fax:** (303)543-0043. **E-mail:** tradeeditorial@rowman.com. **Website:** www.rowman.com/TaylorTrade. **Contact:** Acquisitions Editor. Publishes hardcover originals, trade paperback originals and reprints. Taylor Trade Publishing does not publish fiction or poetry. "Proposals from institutions such as museums or galleries pertaining to their collections are strongly encouraged." **Publishes 70 titles/year. 15% of books from first-time authors. 65% from unagented writers.** Publishes book 1 year after acceptance of ms. after acceptance of ms. Responds in 2 months to queries. See catalog online at website. Submission guidelines available on website under "Author Resources.".

NONFICTION Subjects include art, child guidance, cooking, entertainment, gardening, history, nature, regional, sports. "Proposals should be limited to a query letter; an e-mail will generate the quickest response. If querying by e-mail, please note in the memo box 'book proposal.' Send no attachments unless requested. If using postal mail, query with SASE. What we look for at this stage is suitability of the proposed book to our publishing program (see categories) as well as the author's unique qualifications for writing his or her book."

⊘ TEBOT BACH

P.O. Box 7887, Huntington Beach CA 92615. (714)968-0905. **E-mail:** info@tebotbach.org. **Website:** www.tebotbach.org. **Contact:** Mifanwy Kaiser, editor/publisher. Publishes book 2 years after acceptance of ms. Responds to queries and mss, if invited, in 3 months.
POETRY Offers two contests per year. The Patricia Bibby First Book Contest and The Clockwise Chapbook contest. Go to www.tebotbach.org and www.spillway.org for further information on programs and guidelines for submission. Query first via e-mail, with a few sample poems and cover letter with brief bio.

TEMPLE UNIVERSITY PRESS

1852 N. 10th St., Philadelphia PA 19122. (215)926-2140. **Fax:** (215)926-2141. **E-mail:** tempress@temple.edu. **Website:** www.temple.edu/tempress/. **Contact:** Alex Holzman, director; Janet Francendese, editor-in-chief; Micah Kleit, executive editor. Estab. 1969. "Temple University Press has been publishing path-breaking books on Asian-Americans, law, gender issues, film, women's studies and other interesting areas for nearly 40 years." **Publishes 60 titles/year. Pays advance.** Publishes ms 10 months after acceptance. Responds in 2 months to queries. Book catalog available free. Guidelines available online.
NONFICTION Subjects include ethnic, government, politics, health, medicine, history, photography, regional, Philadelphia, sociology, labor studies, urban studies, Latin American/Latino, Asian American, African American studies, public policy, women's studies. No memoirs, fiction or poetry. Query with SASE. Reviews artwork/photos.

TEN SPEED PRESS

The Crown Publishing Group, Attn: Acquisitions, 2625 Alcatraz Ave. #505, Berkeley CA 94705. (510)559-1600. **Fax:** (510)524-1052. **E-mail:** CrownBiz@randomhouse.com. **Website:** www.crownpublishing.com/imprint/ten-speed-press. Estab. 1971. Publishes trade paperback originals and reprints. "Ten Speed Press publishes authoritative books for an audience interested in innovative ideas. Currently emphasizing cookbooks, career, business, alternative education, and offbeat general nonfiction gift books." **Publishes 120 titles/year. 40% of books from first-time authors. 40% from unagented writers. Pays $2,500 average advance.** Publishes book 1 year after acceptance of ms. Accepts simultaneous submissions. Responds in 3 months to queries; 6-8 weeks to proposals. Book catalog for 9×12 envelope and 6 first-class stamps. Guidelines available online.
NONFICTION Subjects include business, career guidance, cooking, crafts, relationships, how-to, humor, and pop culture. No fiction. "Please read our submission guidelines online. Before submitting your manuscript, you should first familiarize yourself with our publishing areas and imprints. Note that we do not consider certain genres, including fiction, poetry, memoir, and most photography." Agented submissions only.
TIPS "We like books from people who really know their subject, rather than people who think they've spotted a trend to capitalize on. We like books that will sell for a long time, rather than 9-day wonders. Our audience consists of a well-educated, slightly weird group of people who like food, the outdoors, and take a light, but serious, approach to business and careers. Study the backlist of each publisher you're submitting to and tailor your proposal to what you perceive as their needs. Nothing gets a publisher's attention like someone who knows what he or she is talking about, and nothing falls flat like someone who obviously has no idea who he or she is submitting to."

TEXAS A&M UNIVERSITY PRESS

John H. Lindsey Building, Lewis St., 4354 TAMU, College Station TX 77843. (979)845-1436. **Fax:** (979)847-8752. **E-mail:** katie.cowart@tamu.edu. **Website:** www.tamupress.com. **Contact:** Katie Cowart, acquisitions assistant. Estab. 1974. "Texas A&M University Press publishes a wide range of nonfiction, scholarly, trade, and crossover books of regional and national interest, reflecting the interests of the university, the broader scholarly community, and the people of our state and region." **Publishes 60 titles/year. Pays royalty.** Publishes ms 1 year after acceptance. Responds in 1 month to queries. Book catalog available free. Guidelines available online.
NONFICTION Subjects include agriculture, anthropology, archeology, architecture, art, environment,

history, language, literature, military, nature, regional, war, Mexican-US borderlands studies, nautical archaeology, ethnic studies, presidential studies. Nonreturnable queries; e-mail preferred.

TIPS "Proposal requirements are posted on the website."

TEXAS TECH UNIVERSITY PRESS

P.O. Box 41037, 3003 15th St., Suite 201, Lubbock TX 79409. (806)742-2982. **Fax:** (806)742-2979. **E-mail:** judith.keeling@ttu.edu. **Website:** www.ttupress.org. **Contact:** Judith Keeling, editor-in-chief; Robert Mandel, director. Estab. 1971. Texas Tech University Press, the book publishing office of the university since 1971 and an AAUP member since 1986, publishes nonfiction titles in the areas of natural history and the natural sciences; eighteenth-century and Joseph Conrad studies; studies of modern Southeast Asia, particularly the Vietnam War; costume and textile history; Latin American literature and culture; and all aspects of the Great Plains and the American West, especially history, biography, memoir, sports history, and travel. In addition, the Press publishes several scholarly journals, acclaimed series for young readers, an annual invited poetry collection, and literary fiction of Texas and the West. Guidelines online.

NONFICTION Subjects include environment, ethnic, history, law, literary criticism, literature, regional, sports. Submit proposal that includes introduction, 2 sample chapters, cover letter, working title, anticipated ms length, description of audience, comparison of book to others published on the subject, brief bio or CV.

FICTION Subjects include ethnic, multicultural, religious, western. Fiction rooted in the American West and Southwest, Jewish literature, Latin American and Latino fiction (in translation or English).

POETRY "TTUP publishes an annual invited first-book poetry manuscript (please note that we cannot entertain unsolicited poetry submissions)."

TEXAS WESTERN PRESS

The University of Texas at El Paso, 500 W. University Ave., El Paso TX 79968. (915)747-5688. **Fax:** (915)747-5345. **E-mail:** twpress@utep.edu; ctavarez@utep.edu. **Website:** twp.utep.edu. **Contact:** Robert L. Stakes, director. Estab. 1952. Publishes hardcover and paperback originals. "Texas Western Press publishes books on the history and cultures of the American Southwest, particularly historical and biographical works

about West Texas, New Mexico, northern Mexico, and the U.S. borderlands. The Press also publishes selected books in the areas of regional art, photography, Native American studies, geography, demographics, border issues, politics, and natural history." **Publishes 1 title/year. Pays standard 10% royalty. Pays advance.** Responds in 2 months to queries. Book catalog available free. Guidelines available online.

IMPRINTS Southwestern Studies.

NONFICTION Subjects include education, health, medicine, history, language, literature, nature, environment, regional, science, social sciences. "Historic and cultural accounts of the Southwest (West Texas, New Mexico, northern Mexico). Also art, photographic books, Native American and limited regional fiction reprints. Occasional technical titles. Our *Southwestern Studies* use manuscripts of up to 30,000 words. Our hardback books range from 30,000 words and up. The writer should use good exposition in his work. Most of our work requires documentation. We favor a scholarly, but not overly pedantic, style. We specialize in superior book design." Query with SASE, or submit résumé, 2-3 sample chapters, cover letter, description of ms and special features, TOC, list of competing titles.

TIPS "Texas Western Press is interested in books relating to the history of Hispanics in the US. Will experiment with photo-documentary books, and is interested in seeing more contemporary books on border issues. We try to treat our authors professionally, produce handsome, long-lived books and aim for quality, rather than quantity of titles carrying our imprint."

☼ THISTLEDOWN PRESS LTD.

118 20th St. West, Saskatoon SK S7M 0W6, Canada. (306)244-1722. **Fax:** (306)244-1762. **Website:** www.thistledownpress.com. **Contact:** Allan Forrie, publisher. **Pays authors royalty of 10-12% based on net dollar sales. Pays illustrators and photographers by the project (range: $250-750).** Publishes book 1 year after acceptance. Responds to queries in 4 months. Book catalog free on request. Guidelines available for #10 envelope and IRC.

○ "Thistledown originates books by Canadian authors only, although we have co-published titles by authors outside Canada. We do not publish children's picture books."

FICTION Middle readers, young adults: adventure, anthology, contemporary, fantasy, humor, poetry, romance, science fiction, suspense/mystery, short stories. Average word length: young adults—40,000. Submit outline/synopsis and sample chapters. *Does not accept mss.* Do not query by e-mail.

TIPS "Send cover letter including publishing history and SASE."

TIA CHUCHA PRESS

c/o Tia Chucha's Centro Cultural, 13197-A Gladstone Blvd., Sylmar CA 91342. **E-mail:** info@tiachucha.com. **Website:** www.tiachucha.com. **Contact:** Luis Rodriguez, director. Estab. 1989. Publishes hardcover and trade paperback originals. Tia Chucha's Centro Cultural is a nonprofit learning and cultural arts center. We support and promote the continued growth, development and holistic learning of our community through the many powerful means of the arts. Tia Centra provides a positive space for people to activate what we all share as humans: the capacity to create, to imagine and to express ourselves in an effort to improve the quality of life for our community. **Publishes 2-4 titles/year. 25-30 queries received/year. 150 mss received/year. Pays 10% royalty on wholesale price.** Publishes ms 1 year after acceptance. Responds in 9 months to mss. Guidelines available free.

NONFICTION Subjects include agriculture, Americana, art, architecture, community, computers, electronics, contemporary culture, creative nonfiction, ethnic, government, politics, history, humanities, language, literature, memoirs, multicultural, music, dance, New Age, philosophy, photography, regional, sociology, software, translation, travel, womens issues, womens studies, world affairs. Celebrating Words, literature and art; festivals, book readings, signings.

FICTION Subjects include ethnic, feminist, historical, humor, juvenile, literary, mainstream, contemporary, multicultural, multimedia, plays, poetry, regional, short story collections, translation, young adult.

POETRY No restrictions as to style or content. We do cross-cultural and performance-oriented poetry. It has to work on the page, however. Query and submit complete ms.

TIPS We will cultivate the practice. Audience is those interested.

TILBURY HOUSE

Harpswell Press, Inc., 103 Brunswick Ave., Gardiner ME 04345. (800)582-1899. **Fax:** (207)582-8227. **E-mail:** tilbury@tilburyhouse.com. **Website:** www.tilburyhouse.com. **Contact:** Karen Fisk, associate children's book editor; Jennifer Bunting, publisher. Estab. 1990. **Publishes 10 titles/year. Pays royalty based on wholesale price.** Publishes ms 1 year after acceptance. Responds to mss in 2 months. Book catalog available free. Guidelines available online.

NONFICTION Regional adult biography/history/maritime/nature, and children's picture books that deal with issues, such as bullying, multiculturalism, etc. Submit complete ms or outline/synopsis. Reviews artwork/photos. Send photocopies.

FICTION Picture books: multicultural, nature/environment. Special needs include books that teach children about tolerance and honoring diversity. Recently published *One of Us*, by Peggy Moss; *Moonwatchers: Shirin's ramadan Miracle*, by Reza Jalali; and *The Lunch Thief*, by Anne Bromely, illustrated by Rober Casilla. Submit complete ms or outline/synopsis.

TIPS "We are always interested in stories that will encourage children to understand the natural world and the environment, as well as stories with social justice themes. We really like stories that engage children to become problem solvers as well as those that promote respect, tolerance and compassion." We do not publish books with personified animal characters; historical fiction; chapter books; fantasy."

TIMBERLINE PRESS

5710 S. Kimbark #3, Chicago IL 60637. **E-mail:** timberlinc@vacpoetry.org. **Website:** vacpoetry.org/timberline. Estab. 1975. "Since January 2011, Timberline Press (founded by Clarence Wolfshohl in 1975) has been the fine press imprint of Virtual Artists Collective. We print chapbooks—usually poetry—usually 20-30 pages, hand bound, limited editions of 50-100. We generally print no more than 2 or 3 books a year."

"Please note that we are not currently accepting new submissions."

TIN HOUSE BOOKS

2617 NW Thurman St., Portland OR 97210. (503)473-8663. **Fax:** (503)473-8957. **E-mail:** meg@tinhouse.com. **Website:** www.tinhouse.com. **Contact:** Meg Storey, editor; Tony Perez, editor; Masie Cochran, associate editor. Publishes hardcover originals, paperback originals, paperback reprints. "We are a small independent publisher dedicated to nurturing new, promising talent as well as showcasing the work of established writers. Our Tin House New Voice series features work by authors who have not previously published a book." Distributes/promotes titles through Publishers Group West. **Publishes 8-10 titles/year. 20% from unagented writers.** Publishes ms 1 year after acceptance. Accepts simultaneous submissions. Responds to queries in 2-3 weeks; mss in 2-3 months. Guidelines available on website.

NONFICTION *Agented mss only.* We no longer read unsolicited submissions by authors with no representation. We will continue to accept submissions from agents.

FICTION *Agented mss only.* We no longer read unsolicited submissions by authors with no representation. We will continue to accept submissions from agents.

TITAN PRESS

PMB 17897, Encino CA 91416. **E-mail:** titan91416@ yahoo.com. **Website:** www.calwriterssfv.com. **Contact:** Stefanya Wilson, editor. Estab. 1981. Publishes hardcover and paperback originals. **Publishes 12 titles/year. 50% from unagented writers. Pays 20-40% royalty.** Publishes ms 1 year after acceptance. Responds to queries in 3 months. Ms guidelines for #10 SASE.

FICTION Literary, mainstream/contemporary, short story collections. Published *Orange Messiahs*, by Scott Sonders (fiction). Does not accept unsolicited mss. Query with SASE. Include brief bio, social security number, list of publishing credits.

TIPS "Look, act, sound, and *be* professional."

TOKYO ROSE RECORDS/CHAPULTEPEC PRESS

4222 Chambers, Cincinnati OH 45223. **E-mail:** ChapultepecPress@hotmail.com. **Website:** www.tokyoroserecords.com. **Contact:** David Garza. Estab. 2001. Publishes trade paperback originals. **Publishes 1-2 titles/year. 50 queries received/year. 10 mss received/year. 50% of books from first-time authors. 100% from unagented writers. Pays 50% of profits and author's copies.** Publishes book 6 months after acceptance. Accepts simultaneous submissions. Book catalog available online.

NONFICTION Subjects include alternative, art, architecture, contemporary culture, creative nonfiction, ethnic, government, politics, history, humanities, language, literature, literary criticism, memoirs, multicultural, music, dance, nature, environment, philosophy, photography, recreation, regional, translation, world affairs. Submit proposal package, outline, 2-3 sample chapters, artwork samples. Reviews artwork/photos. Send photocopies.

FICTION Subjects include comic books, erotica, ethnic, experimental, humor, literary, multicultural, multimedia, occult, picture books, plays, poetry, poetry in translation, regional, short story collections stories, translation. Submit proposal package, clips, 2-3 sample chapters, artwork samples.

POETRY Chapultepec Press publishes books of poetry/literature, essays, social/political issues, art, music, film, history, popular science; library/archive issues, and bilingual works. Wants "poetry that works as a unit, that is caustic, fun, open-ended, worldly, mature, relevant, stirring, evocative. Bilingual. Looking for authors who have a publishing history. No poetry collections without a purpose, that are mere collections. Also looking for broadsides/posters/illuminations." Publishes 1-2 books/year. Books are usually 1-100 pages. Query first. Submit 5-15 sample poems.

TIPS Tokyo Rose Records/Chapultepec Press specializes in shorter-length publications (100 pages or less). Order sample books by sending $5 payable to David Garza.

⊘ TOP COW PRODUCTIONS, INC.

3812 Dunn Dr., Culver City CA 90232. **Website:** www.topcow.com.

FICTION *No unsolicited submissions.* Prefers submissions from artists. See website for details and advice on how to break into the market.

TOP PUBLICATIONS, LTD.

12221 Merit Dr., Suite 950, Dallas TX 75251. (972)628-6414. **Fax:** (972)233-0713. **E-mail:** info@toppub.com. **E-mail:** submissions@toppub.com. **Website:** www.toppub.com. Estab. 1999. Publishes hardcover and paperback originals. Primarily a mainstream fiction publisher. **Publishes 2-3 titles/year. 200 queries received/year. 20 mss received/year. 90% of books from first-time authors. 95% from unagented writers. Pays 15% royalty on wholesale price. Pays $250-$1,000 advance.** Publishes book 6 months after acceptance. Accepts simultaneous submissions. Acknowledges receipt of queries but only responds if interested in seeing ms. Responds in 6 months to mss. Tear sheets available on new titles. Guidelines available online.

○   "It is imperative that our authors realize they will be required to promote their book extensively for it to be a success. Unless they are willing to make this commitment, they shouldn't submit to TOP."

NONFICTION "We are primarily a fiction publisher and do not solicit submissions of nonfiction works."

FICTION Subjects include adventure, contemporary, historical, horror, juvenile, military, mystery, regional, romance, science fiction, short story collections, suspense, young adult.

TIPS "We recommend that our authors write books that appeal to a large mainstream audience to make marketing easier and increase the chances of success. We only publish a few titles a year so the odds at getting published at TOP are slim. If we don't offer you a contract it doesn't mean we didn't like your submission. We have to pass on a lot of good material each year simply by the limitations of our time and budget."

TOR BOOKS

175 Fifth Ave., New York NY 10010. **Website:** www.tor-forge.com. **Contact:** Juliet Pederson, publishing coordinator, Susan Change, senior editor **Publishes Publishes 5-10 middle readers/year; 5-10 young adult titles/year. titles/year. Pays author royalty. Pays illustrators by the project.** Book catalog available for 9x12 SAE and 3 first-class stamps. See website for latest submission guidelines.

IMPRINTS Forge, Orb, Starscape, Tor Teen.

Tor Books is the "world's largest publisher of science fiction and fantasy, with strong category publishing in historical fiction, mystery, western/Americana, thriller, YA."

NONFICTION Middle readers and young adult: geography, history, how-to, multicultural, nature/environment, science, social issues. Does not want to see religion, cooking. Average word length: middle readers—25,000-35,000; young adults—70,000.

FICTION Subjects include Middle readers, young adult titles: adventure, animal, anthology, concept, contemporary, fantasy, history, humor, multicultural, nature/environment, problem novel, science fiction, suspense/mystery. Average word length: middle readers—30,000; young adults—60,000-100,000. We do not accept queries.

TIPS "Know the house you are submitting to, familiarize yourself with the types of books they are publishing. Get an agent. Allow him/her to direct you to publishers who are most appropriate. It saves time and effort."

TORQUERE PRESS

P.O. Box 2545, Round Rock TX 78680. (512)586-3553. **Fax:** (866)287-2968. **E-mail:** editor@torquerepress. com. **E-mail:** submissions@torquerepress.com. **Website:** www.torquerepress.com. **Contact:** Shawn Clements, submissions editor (homoerotica, suspense, gay/lesbian); Lorna Hinson, senior editor (gay/lesbian romance, historicals). Estab. 2003. Publishes trade paperback originals and electronic originals and reprints. "We are a gay and lesbian press focusing on romance and genres of romance. We particularly like paranormal and western romance." **Publishes 140 titles/year. 500 queries received/year. 200 mss received/year. 25% of books from first-time authors. 100% from unagented writers. Pays 8-40% royalty. Pays $35-75 for anthology stories.** Publishes ms 6 months after acceptance. Responds in 1 month to queries and proposals; 2-4 months to mss. Book catalog available online. Guidelines available online.

IMPRINTS Top Shelf (Shawn Clements, editor); Single Shots (Kil Kenny, editor); Screwdrivers (M. Rode, editor); High Balls (Vincent Diamond, editor).

FICTION Subjects include adventure, erotica, gay, lesbian, historical, horror, mainstream, contemporary, multicultural, mystery, occult, romance, science fiction, short story collections, suspense, western. All categories gay and lesbian themed. Adventure, erotica, historical, horror, mainstream, multicultural, mystery, occult, romance, science fiction, short story collections, suspense, western. Imprints accepting submissions. Submit proposal package, 3 sample chapters, clips.

TIPS "Our audience is primarily people looking for a familiar romance setting featuring gay or lesbian protagonists. Please read guidelines carefully and familiarize yourself with our lines."

TORREY HOUSE PRESS, LLC

2806 Melony Dr., SLC UT 84124. (801)810-9THP. **E-mail:** mark@torreyhouse.com. **Website:** torreyhouse. com. **Contact:** Mark Bailey, publisher. Estab. 2010. Publishes hardcover, trade paperback, and electronic originals. "Torrey House Press (THP) publishes literary fiction and creative nonfiction about the world environment with a tilt toward the American West. See the website at www.torreyhouse.com for guidelines about submitting your work; peruse the columns and book reviews and read some of THP's favorite fiction and nonfiction excerpts to get a sense of the writing that the company seeks. Follow us at Torrey House Press on Facebook and on our website for contest updates, and please contact us any time with questions." **Publishes 10 titles/year. 500 queries/year; 200 mss/year. 80% of books from first-time authors. 80% from unagented writers. Pays 5-15% royalty on retail price.** Publishes ms 6-12 months after acceptance. Accepts simultaneous submissions. Responds in 3 months to queries, proposals, and mss. Catalog online at website. Guidelines online at website.

NONFICTION Subjects include anthropology, creative nonfiction, environment, nature. Query; submit proposal package, including: outline, ms, bio. Does not review artwork.

FICTION Subjects include historical, literary. "Torrey House Press publishes literary fiction and creative nonfiction about the world environment and the American West." Submit proposal package including: synopsis, complete ms, bio.

POETRY Query; submit complete ms.

TIPS "Include writing experience (none okay)."

☼ TOUCHWOOD EDITIONS

The Heritage Group, 340-1105 Pandora Ave., Victoria BC V8V 3P9, Canada. (250)360-0829. **Fax:** (250)386-0829. **E-mail:** info@touchwoodeditions.com. **Website:** www.touchwoodeditions.com. Ruth Linka Publishes trade paperback originals and reprints. **Publishes 20-25 titles/year. 40% of books from first-time authors. 70% from unagented writers. Pays 15% royalty on net price.** Publishes book 12-24 months after acceptance of ms. Accepts simultaneous submissions. Responds in 3 months to queries. Book catalog and submission guidelines available online for free.

NONFICTION Subjects include anthropology, archeology, art, architecture, creative nonfiction, government, politics, history, nature, environment, recreation, regional, nautical. Submit TOC, outline, word count, 2-3 sample chapters, synopsis. Reviews artwork/photos. Send photocopies.

FICTION Subjects include historical, mystery. Submit TOC, outline, word count.

TIPS "Our area of interest is Western Canada. We would like more creative nonfiction and books about people of note in Canada's history."

TOWER PUBLISHING

588 Saco Rd., Standish ME 04084. (207)642-5400. **Fax:** (207)642-5463. **E-mail:** info@towerpub.com. **Website:** www.towerpub.com. **Contact:** Michael Ly-ons, president. Estab. 1772. Publishes hardcover originals and reprints, trade paperback originals. Tower Publishing specializes in business and professional directories and legal books. **Publishes 22 titles/year. 60 queries received/year. 30 mss received/year. 10% of books from first-time authors. 90% from unagented writers.** Publishes ms 6 months after acceptance. Accepts simultaneous submissions. Responds in 1 month to queries; 2 months to proposals and mss. Book catalog and ms guidelines online.

NONFICTION Subjects include business, economics. Looking for legal books of a national stature. Query with SASE. Submit outline.

⊘ TOY BOX PRODUCTIONS

7532 Hickory Hills Ct., Whites Creek TN 37189. (615)299-0822. **Fax:** (615)876-3931. **E-mail:** toybox@crttoybox.com. **Website:** www.crttoybox.com. Estab. 1995. Publishes mass market paperback originals. **Publishes 4 titles/year. 100% of books from first-time authors. 100% from unagented writers. Pays 10-15% royalty on wholesale price.** Book catalog available online.

◒ We are not accepting new submissions at this time.

NONFICTION Subjects include audio, Americana, education, religion. *All unsolicited mail returned unopened.*

☼ TRADEWIND BOOKS

202-1807 Maritime Mews, Granville Island, Vancouver BC V6H 3W7, Canada. (604)662-4405. **E-mail:** tradewindbooks@mail.lycos.com. **Website:** www.tradewindbooks.com. **Contact:** Michael Katz, publisher; Carol Frank, art director; R. David Stephens, senior editor. Publishes hardcover and trade paperback originals. "Tradewind Books publishes juvenile picture books and young adult novels. Requires that submissions include evidence that author has read at least 3 titles published by Tradewind Books." **Publishes 5 titles/year. 15% of books from first-time authors. 50% from unagented writers. Pays 7% royalty on retail price. Pays variable advance.** Publishes book 3 years after acceptance. Accepts simultaneous submissions. Responds to mss in 2 months. Book catalog and ms guidelines online.

FICTION Subjects include juvenile, picture books. Picture books: adventure, multicultural, folktales. Average word length: 900 words. Send complete ms for picture books. *YA novels by Canadian authors only. Chapter books by US authors considered.*

TRAFALGAR SQUARE BOOKS

P.O. Box 257, 388 Howe Hill Road, North Pomfret VT 05053. (802)457-1911. **Website:** www.horseandrider-books.com. **Contact:** Martha Cook, managing director; Rebecca Didier, senior editor. Estab. 1985. Publishes hardcover and trade paperback originals. "We publish high quality instructional books for horsemen and horsewomen, always with the horse's welfare in mind." **Publishes 12 titles/year. 50% of books from first-time authors. 80% from unagented writers. Pays royalty. Pays advance.** Publishes ms 18 months after acceptance. Responds in 1 month to queries, 2 months to proposals, 2-3 months to mss. Catalog free on request and by e-mail.

NONFICTION Subjects include animals, horses/dogs. We rarely consider books for complete novices. Query with SASE. Submit proposal package including outline, 1-3 sample chapters, letter of introduction including qualifications for writing on the subject and why the proposed book is an essential addition to existing publications. Reviews artwork/photos as part of the ms package. We prefer color laser thumbnail sheets or duplicate prints (do not send original photos or art!).

TIPS "Our audience is horse lovers and riders interested in doing what is best in the interest of horses."

TRISTAN PUBLISHING

2355 Louisiana Ave. N, Golden Valley MO 55427. (763)545-1383. **Fax:** (763)545-1387. **E-mail:** info@tristanpublishing.com or manuscripts@tristanpublishing.com. **Website:** www.tristanpublishing.com. **Contact:** Brett Waldman, publisher. Estab. 2002. Publishes hardcover originals. **Publishes 6-10 titles/year. 1,000 queries and manuscripts/year. 15% of books from first-time authors. 100% from unagented writers. Pays royalty on wholesale or retail price; outright purchase.** Publishes book 2 years after acceptance. Accepts simultaneous submissions. Responds in 3 months on queries/proposals/mss. Catalog and guidelines free on request. Guidelines available online at website.

IMPRINTS Tristan Publishing; Waldman House Press; Tristan Outdoors.

NONFICTION Inspirational. "Our mission is to create books with a message that inspire and uplift in typically 1,000 words or less." Query with SASE;

submit completed mss. Reviews artwork/photos; send photocopies.

FICTION Inspirational, gift books. Query with SASE; submit completed mss.

TIPS "Our audience is adults and children."

TRUMAN STATE UNIVERSITY PRESS

100 E. Normal Ave., Kirksville MO 63501. (660)785-7336. **Fax:** (660)785-4480. **E-mail:** tsup@truman.edu. **Website:** tsup.truman.edu. **Contact:** Barbara Smith-Mandell, copy editor/acquisitions editor; Judith Sharp, production editor. Estab. 1986. Truman State University Press (TSUP) publishes peer-reviewed research in the humanities for the scholarly community and the broader public, and publishes creative literary works. Guidelines available online.

NONFICTION , contemporary nonfiction, early modern, American studies, poetry. Submit book ms proposals in American Studies to Barbara Smith-Mandell, at bsm@truman.edu; nonfiction to Monica Barron at tsupnonfiction@truman.edu; early modern studies to wolfem1@stjohns.edu

TUPELO PRESS

P.O. Box 1767, North Adams MA 01247. (413)664-9611. **E-mail:** publisher@tupelopress.org. **E-mail:** www.tupelopress.org/submissions. **Website:** www.tupelopress.org. **Contact:** Jeffrey Levine, publish/editor-in-chief; Elyse Newhouse, associate publisher; Jim Schley, managing editor. Estab. 2001. "We're an independent nonprofit literary press. Also sponsor these upcoming competitions: Dorset Prize: $10,000. Entries must be postmarked between September 1 and December 31, 2011. Guidelines are online; Snowbound Series chapbook Award: $1,000 and 50 copies of chapbook. See website for submission period and guidelines. Every July we have Open Submissions. We accept book-length poetry, poetry collections (48 + pages), short story collections, novellas, literary nonfiction/memoirs and up to 80 pages of a novel." Guidelines available online.

NONFICTION Subjects include memoirs. No cookbooks, children's books, inspirational books, graphic novels, or religious books.

FICTION Subjects include poetry, short story collections, Novels. "For Novels—submit no more than 100 pages along with a summary of the entire book. If we're interested we'll ask you to send the rest. We accept very few works of prose (1 or 2 per year)." Submit complete ms. **Charges a $45 reading fee.**

POETRY "Our mission is to publish thrilling, visually and emotionally and intellectually stimulating books of the highest quality, inside and out. We want contemporary poetry, etc. by the most diverse list of emerging and established writers in the U.S." Submit complete ms.

☺ TURNSTONE PRESS

206-100 Arthur St., Winnipeg MB R3B 1H3, Canada. (204)947-1555. **Fax:** (204)942-1555. **E-mail:** info@turnstonepress.com. **E-mail:** editor@turnstonepress.com. **Website:** www.turnstonepress.com. Estab. 1976. "Turnstone Press is a literary publisher, not a general publisher, and therefore we are only interested in literary fiction, literary nonfiction—including literary criticism—and poetry. We do publish literary mysteries, thrillers, and noir under our Ravenstone imprint. We publish only Canadian authors or landed immigrants, we strive to publish a significant number of new writers, to publish in a variety of genres, and to have 50% of each year's list be Manitoba writers and/or books with Manitoba content." Publishes ms 2 years after acceptance. Responds in 4-7 months. Guidelines available online at website.

NONFICTION "Samples must be 40 to 60 pages, typed/printed in a minimum 12 point serif typeface such as Times, Book Antiqua, or Garamond."

FICTION "Samples must be 40 to 60 pages, typed/printed in a minimum 12 point serif typeface such as Times, Book Antiqua, or Garamond."

POETRY Poetry manuscripts should be a minimum 70 pages. Submit complete ms. Include cover letter.

TIPS "As a Canadian literary press, we have a mandate to publish Canadian writers only. Do some homework before submitting works to make sure your subject matter/genre/writing style falls within the publishers area of interest."

⊕ TURN THE PAGE PUBLISHING LLC

P.O. Box 3179, Upper Montclair NJ 07043. **E-mail:** rlentin@turnthepagepublishing.com. **E-mail:** inquiry@turnthepagepublishing.com. **Website:** www.turnthepagepublishing.com. **Contact:** Roseann Lentin, editor-in-chief; Ann Kolakowski, editor. Estab. 2009. Publishes hardcover, trade paperback, electronic originals and trade paperback, electronic reprints. **Publishes 12-15 titles/year. Receives 100 queries/year; 50 mss/year. 95% of books from first-time authors. 100% from unagented writers. Pays 8-15% royalty on retail price.** Publishes ms 8 months after acceptance. Accepts simultaneous submissions. Responds in 3 months to queries; 2 months to proposals/mss. Book catalog available online at website. Guidelines by e-mail.

NONFICTION Subjects include alternative lifestyles, Americana, animals, astrology, child guidance, cooking, creative nonfiction, finance, foods, memoirs, military, money, New Age, parenting, spirituality, war, womens studies, young adult. Submit proposal package including outline, 3 sample chapters, author bio. Reviews artwork. Send photocopies.

FICTION Subjects include contemporary, humor, juvenile, literary, mainstream, military, picture books, spiritual, suspense, war, young adult. "We like new, fresh voices who are not afraid to 'step outside the box,' with unique ideas and storylines. We prefer 'edgy' rather than 'typical.'" Submit proposal package including synopsis and 3 sample chapters.

TIPS "Our audience is made up of intelligent, sophisticated, forward-thinking, progressive readers, who are not afraid to consider reading something different to Turn the Page of their lives. We're an independent publisher, we're avant-garde, so if you're looking for run of the mill, don't submit here."

TUTTLE PUBLISHING

364 Innovation Dr., North Clarendon VT 05759. (802)773-8930. **Fax:** (802)773-6993. **E-mail:** info@tuttlepublishing.com. **Website:** www.tuttlepublishing.com. Estab. 1832. Publishes hardcover and trade paperback originals and reprints. Tuttle is America's leading publisher of books on Japan and Asia. **Publishes 125 titles/year. 1,000 queries received/year. 20% of books from first-time authors. 40% from unagented writers. Pays 5-10% royalty on net or retail price, depending on format and kind of book. Pays advance.** Publishes book 18 months after acceptance. Accepts simultaneous submissions. Responds in 2-3 months to proposals.

☺ "Familiarize yourself with our catalog and/or similar books we publish. Send complete book proposal with cover letter, table of contents, 1-2 sample chapters, target audience description, SASE. No e-mail submissions."

NONFICTION Query with SASE.

TWILIGHT TIMES BOOKS

P.O. Box 3340, Kingsport TN 37664. **Website:** www.twilighttimesbooks.com. **Contact:** Andy M. Scott, managing editor. Estab. 1999. "We publish compelling literary fiction by authors with a distinctive voice." Published 5 debut authors within the last year. Averages 120 total titles; 15 fiction titles/year. Member: AAP, PAS, SPAN, SLF. **90% from unagented writers. Pays 8-15% royalty.** Responds in 4 weeks to queries; 2 months to mss. Guidelines available online.

FICTION Accepts unsolicited mss. Do not send complete mss. Queries via e-mail only. Include estimated word count, brief bio, list of publishing credits, marketing plan.

TIPS "The only requirement for consideration at Twilight Times Books is that your novel must be entertaining and professionally written."

⚠ ⊘ TYNDALE HOUSE PUBLISHERS, INC.

351 Executive Dr., Carol Stream IL 60188. (800)323-9400. **Fax:** (800)684-0247. **Website:** www.tyndale.com. **Contact:** Katara Washington Patton, acquisitions; Talinda Iverson, art acquisitions. Estab. 1962. Publishes hardcover and trade paperback originals and mass paperback reprints. "Tyndale House publishes practical, user-friendly Christian books for the home and family." **Publishes 15 titles/year. Pays negotiable royalty. Pays negotiable advance.** Accepts simultaneous submissions. Guidelines for 9×12 SAE and $2.40 for postage or visit website.

NONFICTION Subjects include child guidance, religion, devotional/inspirational. Prefers agented submissions.

FICTION Subjects include juvenile, romance, Christian (children's, general, inspirational, mystery/suspense, thriller, romance). "Christian truths must be woven into the story organically. No short story collections. Youth books: character building stories with Christian perspective. Especially interested in ages 10-14. We primarily publish Christian historical romances, with occasional contemporary, suspense, or standalones." Agented submissions only. *No unsolicited mss.*

TIPS "All accepted manuscripts will appeal to Evangelical Christian children and parents."

UNBRIDLED BOOKS

200 N. Ninth St., Suite A, Columbia MO 65201. **Website:** unbridledbooks.com. Estab. 2004. "Unbridled Books is a premier publisher of works of rich literary quality that appeal to a broad audience."

FICTION Please query first by e-mail. Due to the heavy volume of submissions, we regret that at this time we are not able to consider uninvited mss. Please query either Fred Ramey or Greg Michalson, but not both.

TIPS "We try to read each ms that arrives, so please be patient."

UNION SQUARE PUBLISHING

Sterling, 387 Park Ave. South, 11th Floor, New York NY 10016-8810. **E-mail:** submissions@cardozapub.com. **Website:** www.sterlingpublishing.com. **Contact:** Acquisition Editor (biographies, word books, cultural studies, sports, general nonfiction and fiction). Estab. 2002. Publishes hardcover originals, trade paperback originals and reprints, mass market paperback originals. **Publishes 5-10 titles/year. 10 queries received/year. 5 mss received/year. 80% of books from first-time authors. 95% from unagented writers. Pays 5-6% royalty on retail price. Pays $1,000-10,000 advance.** Publishes book 7 months after acceptance of ms. Accepts simultaneous submissions. Responds in 1-2 months to queries. Responds in 1-2 months to proposals. Responds in 2-3 months to manuscripts. Guidelines available via e-mail.

NONFICTION Subjects include anthropology, archeology, community, contemporary culture, cooking, foods, nutrition, education, ethnic, government, politics, history, hobbies, humanities, language, literature, memoirs, multicultural, music, dance, nature, environment, philosophy, recreation, religion, social sciences, sociology, spirituality, sports, translation. "Union Square Publishing is a new imprint of a long-established company, and we have yet to determine the exact role it will fill in the publishing world. We began by publishing books on writing, words, and language." Query with SASE. Submit complete ms. Reviews artwork/photos. Send photocopies.

TIPS "We will never reject a book based solely on genre. Our audience is the general market interested in original concepts."

THE UNIVERSITY OF AKRON PRESS

120 E. Mill St., Suite 415, Akron OH 44325. (330)972-5342. **Fax:** (330)972-8364. **E-mail:** uapress@uakron.edu. **Website:** www.uakron.edu/uapress. **Contact:** Thomas Bacher, director and acquisitions. Estab. 1988. Publishes hardcover and paperback originals and reissues. "The University of Akron Press is the publishing arm of The University of Akron and is dedicated to the dissemination of scholarly, professional, and regional books and other content." **Publishes 10-12 titles/year. 200-300 queries received/year. 50-75 mss**

received/year. **40% of books from first-time authors. 80% from unagented writers. Pays 7-15% royalty.** Publishes book 9-12 months after acceptance. Accepts simultaneous submissions. Responds in 2 weeks to queries/proposals; 3-4 months to solicited mss. Query prior to submitting. Guidelines available online.

NONFICTION Subjects include Applied politics, early American literature, emerging technologies, history of psychology, history of technology, interdisciplinary studies, Northeast Ohio history and culture, Ohio politics, poetics. Query by email. Mss cannot be returned unless SASE is included.

POETRY Follow the guidelines and submit mss only for the contest: www.uakron.edu/uapress/poetry.html. "We publish two books of poetry annually, one of which is the winner of The Akron Poetry prize. We also are interested in literary collections based around one theme, especially collections of translated works." If you are interested in publishing with The University of Akron Press, please fill out form online.

THE UNIVERSITY OF ALABAMA PRESS

P.O. Box 870380, Tuscaloosa AL 35487. (205)348-5180 or (205)348-1571. **Fax:** (205)348-9201. **E-mail:** rcook@uapress.ua.edu. **Website:** www.uapress.ua.edu. **Contact:** Rick Cook, production manager; Michele Myatt Quinn, designer; Kaci Lane Hindman, production editor. Publishes nonfiction hardcover and paperbound originals, and fiction paperback reprints. **Publishes 70-75 titles/year. 70% of books from first-time authors. 95% from unagented writers. Pays advance.** Responds in 2 weeks to queries. Book catalog available free.

NONFICTION Subjects include anthropology, archeology, community, government, politics, history, language, literature, literary criticism, religion, translation. Considers upon merit almost any subject of scholarly interest, but specializes in communications, military history, public administration, literary criticism and biography, history, Jewish studies, and American archaeology. Accepts nonfiction translations. Query with SASE. Reviews artwork/photos.

FICTION Reprints of works by contemporary, Southern writers. Distributor of Fiction Collective 2 (FC@), avant garde fiction. Query with SASE.

TIPS "Please direct inquiry to appropriate acquisitions editor. University of Alabama Press responds to an author within 2 weeks upon receiving the ms. If they think it is unsuitable for Alabama's program,

they tell the author at once. If the ms warrants it, they begin the peer-review process, which may take 2-4 months to complete. During that process, they keep the author fully informed."

THE UNIVERSITY OF ARKANSAS PRESS

McIlroy House, 105 N. McIlroy Ave., Fayetteville AR 72701. (479)575-3246. **Fax:** (479)575-6044. **E-mail:** lmalley@uark.edu; jewatki@uark.edu. **Website:** uapress.com. **Contact:** Lawrence J. Malley, director and editor-in-chief and Julie Watkins, editor. Estab. 1980. Publishes hardcover and trade paperback originals and reprints. "The University of Arkansas Press publishes series on Ozark studies, the Civil War in the West, poetry and poetics, and sport and society." **Publishes 30 titles/year. 30% of books from first-time authors. 95% from unagented writers.** Publishes book 1 year after acceptance. Responds in 3 months to proposals. Book catalog and ms guidelines on website or on request.

NONFICTION Subjects include government, politics, history, Southern, humanities, literary criticism, nature, environment, regional, Arkansas. Accepted mss must be submitted on disk. Query with SASE. Submit outline, sample chapters, resume.

POETRY University of Arkansas Press publishes four poetry books per year through the Miller Williams Poetry Prize. See Contests section of this book for more information.

UNIVERSITY OF CALGARY PRESS

2500 University Dr. NW, Calgary AB T2N 1N4, Canada. (403)220-7578. **Fax:** (403)282-0085. **Website:** www.uofcpress.com. **Contact:** John King, senior editor. Publishes scholarly and trade paperback originals and reprints. **Publishes 10 titles/year.** Publishes ms 20 months after acceptance. Book catalog available for free. Guidelines available online through ms submission website.

NONFICTION Subjects include art, architecture, philosophy women's studies, world affairs, Canadian studies, post-modern studies, native studies, history, international relations, arctic studies, Africa, Latin American and Caribbean studies, and heritage of the Canadian and American heartland.

THE UNIVERSITY OF CHICAGO PRESS

1427 E. 60th St., Chicago IL 60637. Voicemail: (773)702-7700. **Fax:** (773)702-2705 or (773)702-9756. **Website:** www.press.uchicago.edu. **Contact:** Randolph Petilos, poetry and medieval studies editor. Estab. 1891. "The University of Chicago Press has been publishing scholarly books and journals since 1891. Annually, we publish an average of four books in our Phoenix Poets series and two books of poetry in translation. Occasionally, we may publish a book of poetry outside Phoenix Poets, or as a paperback reprint from another publisher."

UNIVERSITY OF GEORGIA PRESS

Main Library, Third Floor, 320 S. Jackson St., Athens GA 30602. (706)369-6130. **Fax:** (706)369-6131. **E-mail:** books@ugapress.uga.edu. **Website:** www.ugapress.org. Estab. 1938. Publishes hardcover originals, trade paperback originals, and reprints. University of Georgia Press is a midsized press that publishes fiction only through the Flannery O'Connor Award for Short Fiction competition. **Publishes 85 titles/year. Pays 7-10% royalty on net receipts. Pays rare, varying advance.** Publishes book 1 year after acceptance. Responds in 2 months to queries. Book catalog and ms guidelines for #10 SASE or online.

NONFICTION Subjects include government, politics, history, American, nature, environment, regional, environmental studies, literary nonfiction. Query with SASE. Submit bio, 1 sample chapter. Reviews artwork/photos. Send if essential to book.

FICTION Short story collections published in Flannery O'Connor Award Competition. Mss for Flannery O'Connor Award for Short Fiction accepted in April and May.

TIPS "Please visit our website to view our book catalogs and for all manuscript submission guidelines."

UNIVERSITY OF ILLINOIS PRESS

1325 S. Oak St., Champaign IL 61820-6903. (217)333-0950. **Fax:** (217)244-8082. **E-mail:** uipress@uillinois.edu. **Website:** www.press.uillinois.edu. **Contact:** Willis Regier, director (literature, classics, ancient religion, sports history); Larin McLaughlin, senior acquisitions editor (women's studies, American studies, religion); Laurie Matheson, senior acquisitions editor (history, appalachian studies, labor studies, music, folklore); Daniel Nasset, acquisitions editor (film studies, anthropology, communication studies. Estab. 1918. Publishes hardcover and trade paperback originals and reprints. University of Illinois Press publishes scholarly books and serious nonfiction with a wide range of study interests. Currently emphasizing American history, especially immigration, labor, African-American, and military; American religion, music, women's studies, and film. **Publishes 150 titles/year. 35% of books from first-time authors. 95% from unagented writers. Pays $1,000-1,500 (rarely) advance.** Publishes book 1 year after acceptance of ms. Responds in 1 month to queries. Book catalog for 9x12 envelope and 2 first-class stamps. Guidelines available online.

NONFICTION Subjects include Americana, animals, cooking, foods, nutrition, government, politics, history, especially American history, language, literature, military, war, music, especially American music, dance, philosophy, regional, sociology, sports, translation, film/cinema/stage. "Always looking for solid, scholarly books in American history, especially social history; books on American popular music, and books in the broad area of American studies." Query with SASE. Submit outline.

TIPS "As a university press, we are required to submit all mss to rigorous scholarly review. Mss need to be clearly original, well written, and based on solid and thorough research. We cannot encourage memoirs or autobiographies."

UNIVERSITY OF IOWA PRESS

100 Kuhl House, 119 W. Park Rd., Iowa City IA 52242. (319)335-2000. **Fax:** (319)335-2055. **E-mail:** uipress@uiowa.edu. **Website:** www.uiowapress.org. **Contact:** Holly Carver, director; Joseph Parsons, acquisitions editor. Estab. 1969. Publishes hardcover and paperback originals. "We publish authoritative, original nonfiction that we market mostly by direct mail to groups with special interests in our titles, and by advertising in trade and scholarly publications." **Publishes 35 titles/year. 30% of books from first-time authors. 95% from unagented writers. Pays 7-10% royalty on net receipts.** Publishes book 1 year after acceptance. Book catalog available free. Guidelines available online.

NONFICTION Subjects include anthropology, archeology, creative nonfiction, history, regional, language, literature, nature, environment, American literary studies, medicine and literature. "Looks for evidence of original research, reliable sources, clarity of organization, complete development of theme with documentation, supportive footnotes and/or bibliography, and a substantive contribution to knowledge in the field treated. Use *Chicago Manual of Style*." Query with SASE. Submit outline. Reviews artwork/photos.

FICTION Currently publishes the Iowa Short Fiction Award selections.

POETRY Currently publishes winners of the Iowa Poetry Prize Competition, Kuhl House Poets, poetry anthologies. Competition guidelines available on website.

UNIVERSITY OF NEBRASKA PRESS

1111 Lincoln Mall, Lincoln NE 68588. (800)755-1105. **Fax:** (402)472-6214. **E-mail:** pressmail@unl.edu. **E-mail:** arold1@unl.edu. **Website:** nebraskapress.unl. edu. **Contact:** Heather Lundine, editor-in-chief; Alison Rold, production manager. Publishes hardcover and trade paperback originals and trade paperback reprints. "We primarily publish nonfiction books and scholarly journals, along with a few titles per season in contemporary and regional prose and poetry. On occasion, we reprint previously published fiction of established reputation, and we have several programs to publish literary works in translation." Book catalog available free. Guidelines available online.

IMPRINTS Bison Books (paperback reprints of classic books).

NONFICTION Subjects include agriculture, animals, anthropology, archeology, creative nonfiction, history, memoirs, military, war, multicultural, nature, environment, religion, sports, translation, women's issues, women's studies, Native American studies, American Lives series, experimental fiction by American-Indian writers. Submit book proposal with overview, audience, format, detailed chapter outline, sample chapters, sample bibliography, timetable, CV.

FICTION Series and translation only. Occasionally reprints fiction of established reputation.

POETRY Contemporary, regional.

UNIVERSITY OF NEVADA PRESS

Morrill Hall, Mail Stop 0166, Reno NV 89557. (775)784-6573. **Fax:** (775)784-6200. **Website:** www. unpress.nevada.edu. **Contact:** Joanne O'Hare, director. Estab. 1961. Publishes hardcover and paperback originals and reprints. "Small university press. Publishes fiction that primarily focuses on the American West." Member: AAUP **Publishes 25 titles/year.** Publishes ms 18 months after acceptance. Responds in 2 months. Guidelines available online.

NONFICTION Subjects include anthropology, archeology, ethnic, studies, history, regional and natural, nature, environment, regional, history and geography, western literature, current affairs, gambling and

gaming, Basque studies. No juvenile books. Submit proposal. No online submissions. Reviews artwork/photos. Send photocopies.

FICTION "We publish in Basque Studies, Gambling Studies, Western literature, Western history, Natural science, Environmental Studies, Travel and Outdoor books, Archeology, Anthropology, and Political Studies, all focusing on the West". The Press also publishes creative nonfiction and books on regional topics for a general audience. Submit proposal package, outline, clips, 2-4 sample chapters. Include estimated word count, brief bio, list of publishing credits. Send SASE or IRC. No e-mail submissions.

UNIVERSITY OF NORTH TEXAS PRESS

1155 Union Circle, #311336, Denton TX 76203. (940)565-2142. **Fax:** (940)565-4590. **E-mail:** ronald. chrisman@unt.edu; Karen.DeVinney@unt.edu. **Website:** untpress.unt.edu. **Contact:** Ronald Chrisman, director; Paula Oates, assistant editor; Lori Belew, administrative assistant. Estab. 1987. Publishes hardcover and trade paperback originals and reprints. "We are dedicated to producing the highest quality scholarly, academic, and general interest books. We are committed to serving all peoples by publishing stories of their cultures and experiences that have been overlooked. Currently emphasizing military history, Texas history and literature, music, Mexican-American studies." **Publishes 14-16 titles/year. 500 queries received/year. 50% of books from first-time authors. 95% from unagented writers.** Publishes ms 1-2 years after acceptance. Responds in 1 month to queries. Book catalog for 8 ½×11 SASE. Guidelines available online.

NONFICTION Subjects include Americana, ethnic, government, politics, history, music, dance, biography, military, war, nature, regional, women's issues/studies. Query with SASE. Reviews artwork/photos. Send photocopies.

FICTION "The only fiction we publish is the winner of the Katherine Anne Porter Prize in Short Fiction, an annual, national competition with a $1,000 prize, and publication of the winning ms each Fall."

POETRY "The only poetry we publish is the winner of the Vassar Miller Prize in Poetry, an annual, national competition with a $1,000 prize and publication of the winning ms each Spring." Query.

TIPS "We publish series called War and the Southwest; Texas Folklore Society Publications; the Western Life Series; Practical Guide Series; Al-Filo: Mexican-American studies; North Texas Crime and Criminal Justice; Katherine Anne Porter Prize in Short Fiction; and the North Texas Lives of Musicians Series."

UNIVERSITY OF OKLAHOMA PRESS

2800 Venture Dr., Norman OK 73069. **E-mail:** cerankin@ou.edu. **Website:** www.oupress.com. **Contact:** Charles E. Rankin, editor-in-chief. Estab. 1928. Publishes hardcover and paperback originals and reprints. University of Oklahoma Press publishes books for both scholarly and nonspecialist readers. **Publishes 90 titles/year. Pays standard royalty.** Responds promptly to queries. Book catalog for 9×12 SAE with 6 first-class stamps.

IMPRINTS Plains Reprints.

NONFICTION Subjects include political science (Congressional, area and security studies), history (regional, military, natural), language/literature (American Indian, US West), American Indian studies, classical studies. Query with SASE or by email. Submit outline, resume, 1-2 sample chapters. Use *Chicago Manual of Style* for ms guidelines. Reviews artwork/photos.

UNIVERSITY OF OTTAWA PRESS

542 King Edward, Ottawa ON K1N 6N5, Canada. (613)562-5246. **Fax:** (613)562-5247. **E-mail:** puo-uop@uottawa.ca. **Website:** www.press.uottawa.ca. Estab. 1936. "UOP publishes books and journals, in French and English, and in any and all editions and formats, that touch upon the human condition: anthropology, sociology, political science, psychology, criminology, media studies, economics, education, language and culture, law, history, literature, translation studies, philosophy, public administration, health sciences, and religious studies." Accepts simultaneous submissions. Book catalog and ms guidelines free online at website.

NONFICTION "Submit outline www.press.uottawa.ca/info/submissions, proposal form (please see website), CV, 1-2 sample chapters (for monographs only), manuscript (for collected works only), table of contents, 2-5 page proposal/summary, contributor names, short bios, and citizenships (for collected works only)."

TIPS "Please note that the University of Ottawa Press does not accept: bilingual works (texts must be either entirely in English or entirely in French), undergraduate or masters theses, or doctoral theses that have not been substantially revised."

UNIVERSITY OF PENNSYLVANIA PRESS

3905 Spruce St., Philadelphia PA 19104. (215)898-6261. **Fax:** (215)898-0404. **Website:** www.pennpress.org. **Contact:** Jerome Singerman, humanities editor; Peter Agree, editor-in-chief and social sciences editor; Jo Joslyn, art and architecture editor; Robert Lockhart, history editor; Bill Finan, politics, international relations; John Hubbard, art director. Estab. 1890. Publishes hardcover and paperback originals, and reprints. "Manuscript submissions are welcome in fields appropriate for Penn Press's editorial program. The Press's acquiring editors, and their fields of responsibility, are listed in the Contact Us section of our Web site. Although we have no formal policies regarding manuscript proposals and submissions, what we need minimally, in order to gauge our degree of interest, is a brief statement describing the manuscript, a copy of the contents page, and a reasonably current vita. Initial inquiries are best sent by letter, in paper form, to the appropriate acquiring editor." **Publishes 100+ titles/year. 20-30% of books from first-time authors. 95% from unagented writers. Royalty determined on book-by-book basis. Pays advance.** Publishes ms 10 months after acceptance. Responds in 3 months to queries. Book catalog available online. Guidelines available online.

NONFICTION Subjects include Americana, art, architecture, history, American, art, architecture, literary criticism, sociology, anthropology, literary criticism, cultural studies, ancient studies, medieval studies, urban studies, human rights. Follow the *Chicago Manual of Style*. "Serious books that serve the scholar and the professional, student and general reader." *No unsolicited mss.* Query with SASE. Submit outline, resume. Reviews artwork/photos. Send photocopies.

UNIVERSITY OF TAMPA PRESS

University of Tampa, 401 W. Kennedy Blvd., Box 19F, Tampa FL 33606-1490. (813)253-6266. **Fax:** (813)258-7593. **E-mail:** utpress@ut.edu. **Website:** www.utpress.ut.edu. **Contact:** Richard Mathews, editor. Publishes hardcover originals and reprints; trade paperback originals and reprints. Responds in 3-4 months to queries. Book catalog available online.

NONFICTION Florida history. Reviews artwork/photos.

FICTION Subjects include literary, poetry.

POETRY Submit 3-6 sample poems.

TIPS We only consider book-length poetry submitted through the annual Tampa Review Prize for Poetry, and rarely publish excerpts. No e-mail or handwritten submissions. Submit between Sept. 1 and Dec. 31.

UNIVERSITY OF WISCONSIN PRESS

1930 Monroe St., 3rd Floor, Madison WI 53711. (608)263-1110. **Fax:** (608)263-1132. **E-mail:** uwiscpress@uwpress.wisc.edu. **E-mail:** kadushin@wisc.edu. **Website:** www.wisc.edu/wisconsinpress. **Contact:** Raphael Kadushin, senior acquisitions editor; Gwen Walker, acquisitions editor. Gwen Walker, acquisitions editor Estab. 1937. Publishes hardcoveroriginals, paperback originals, and paperback reprints. **Publishes 98 total titles (average); 15 fiction titles/year. titles/year. Pays royalty.** Publishes ms 9-18 months after acceptance. Responds in 2 weeks toqueries; 8 weeks to mss. Rarely comments on rejected mss. Guidelines online.

○ Check online guidelines for latest submission guidelines.

NONFICTION Subjects include anthropology, dance, environment, film, foods, gay, history, lesbian, memoirs, travel, African Studies, classical studies, human rights, Irish studies, Jewish studies, Latin American studies, Latino/a memoirs, modern Western European history, performance studies, Slavic studies, Southeast Asian studies. Does not accept unsolicited mss. Query with SASE or submit outline, 1-2 sample chapter(s), synopsis. Accepts queries by e-mail, mail, fax. Include estimated word count, brief bio. Send copy of ms and SASE. Direct your inquiries in the areas of autobiography/memoir, biography, classical studies, dance and performance studies, film, food, gender studies, GLBT studies, Jewish studies, Latino/amemoirs, and travel to Raphael Kadushin, kadushin@wisc.edu. Agented fiction: 40%. Direct nonfiction inquiries in the areas of African studies, anthropology, environmental studies, human rights, Irish studies, Latin American studies, Slavic studies, Southeast Asian studies, and U.S. History to Gwen Walker, gcwalker@uwpress.wisc.edu. See website for more contact info.

FICTION Gay/lesbian, historical,lesbian, mystery, regional (Wisconsin), short story collections.

POETRY The University of Wisconsin Press Awards the Brittingham Prize in Poetry and Felix Pollack Prize in Poetry. Each winning poet receives $2,500 ($1,000 cash prize and $1,500 honorarium to cover expenses of reading in Madison). Prizes awarded annually for the two best book-length manuscripts of original poetry submitted in the open competition. Submission period September 1-30. More details online.

TIPS "Make sure the query letter and sample text are well-written, and read guidelines carefully to make sure we accept the genre you are submitting."

UNIVERSITY PRESS OF KANSAS

2502 Westbrooke Circle, Lawrence KS 66045. (785)864-4154. **Fax:** (785)864-4586. **E-mail:** upress@ku.edu. **Website:** www.kansaspress.ku.edu; www.facebook.com/kansaspress. **Contact:** Michael J. Briggs, editor-in-chief (military history, political science, law); Fred M. Woodward, director, (political science, presidency, regional). Estab. 1946. Publishes hardcover originals, trade paperback originals and reprints. "The University Press of Kansas publishes scholarly books that advance knowledge and regional books that contribute to the understanding of Kansas, the Great Plains, and the Midwest." **Publishes 55 titles/year. 600 queries received/year. 20% of books from first-time authors. 98% from unagented writers. Pays selective advance.** Publishes book 10 months after acceptance. Responds in 1 month to proposals. Book catalog and ms guidelines free.

NONFICTION Subjects include Americana, archeology, environment, government, military, nature, politics, regional, war, American History, Native Studies, American Cultural Studies. "We are looking for books on topics of wide interest based on solid scholarship and written for both specialists and informed general readers. Do not send unsolicited, complete manuscripts." Submit outline, sample chapters, cover letter, cv, prospectus. Reviews artwork/photos. Send photocopies.

UNIVERSITY PRESS OF MISSISSIPPI

3825 Ridgewood Rd., Jackson MS 39211. (601)432-6205. **Fax:** (601)432-6217. **E-mail:** press@mississippi.edu. **Website:** www.upress.state.ms.us. **Contact:** Craig Gill, editor-in-chief (regional studies, history, folklore, music). Estab. 1970. Publishes hardcover and paperback originals and reprints and eBooks. "University Press of Mississippi publishes scholarly and trade titles, as well as special series, including: American Made Music; Conversations with Comic Artists; Conversations with Filmmakers; Faulkner and Yoknapatawpha; Literary Conversations; Hollywood Legends; Caribbean Studies." **Publishes 60** titles/year. **80% of books from first-time authors. 90% from unagented writers. Competitive royalties and terms. Pays advance.** Publishes ms 1 year after acceptance. Responds in 3 months to queries.

NONFICTION Subjects include Americana, art, architecture, ethnic, minority studies, politics, history, literature, literary criticism, music, photography, regional, Southern, folklife, literary criticism, popular culture with scholarly emphasis, literary studies. "We prefer a proposal that describes the significance of the work and a chapter outline." Submit outline, sample chapters, cv.

UPPER ACCESS, INC.

87 Upper Access Rd., Hinesburg VT 05461. (802)482-2988. **Fax:** (802)304-1005. **E-mail:** info@upperaccess.com. **Website:** www.upperaccess.com. **Contact:** Steve Carlson, publisher. Estab. 1986. Publishes hardcover and trade paperback originals; hardcover and trade paperback reprints. Publishes nonfiction to improve the quality of life. **Publishes 2-3 titles/year. 200 queries received/year. 40 mss received/year. 50% of books from first-time authors. 80% from unagented writers. Pays 10-20% royalty on wholesale price. $200-500. Advances are tokens of our good faith; author earnings are from royalties a book sells.** Publishes ms 8 months after acceptance. Accepts simultaneous submissions. Responds in 1 month to queries/mss. Catalog online at website. Guidelines available online.

NONFICTION Subjects include alternative lifestyles, child guidance, community/public affairs, contemporary culture, cooking, foods, nutrition, creative nonfiction, education, ethnic, gardening, government, politics/politics, health, medicine, history, humor, humanities, language, literature, multicultural, nature, environment, philosophy, psychology, science, sex, social sciences, sociology, womens issues, womens studies, world affairs affairs, (gay, lesbian possible). "We are open to considering almost any nonfiction topic that has some potential for national general trade sales." Query with SASE. "We strongly prefer an initial e-mail describing your proposed title. No attachments please. We will look at paper mail if there is no other way, but email will be reviewed much more quickly and thoroughly." Will request artwork, etc. if and when appropriate. "Discuss this with us in your initial e-mail query."

FICTION "Note: Please do not submit fiction, even if it relates to nonfiction subjects. We cannot take novels or poetry of any kind at this time."

TIPS "We target intelligent adults willing to challenge the status quo, who are interested in more self-sufficiency with respect for the environment. Most of our books are either unique subjects or unique or different ways of looking at major issues or basic education on subjects that are not well understood by most of the general public. We make a long-term commitment to each book that we publish, trying to find its market as long as possible. Please note that as a tiny company, we go through periods when we cannot even look at new manuscripts while we catch up with the projects we are committed to. During such periods, we will respond to e-mail queries, but with standardized responses."

⊕ URJ PRESS

633 Third Ave., 7th Floor, New York NY 10017. (212)650-4120. **Fax:** (212)650-4119. **E-mail:** press@urj.org. **Website:** www.urjpress.com. **Contact:** Rabbi Hara Person, editor. Publishes hardcover and trade paperback originals. "URJ publishes textbooks for the religious classroom, children's tradebooks and scholarly work of Jewish education import—no adult fiction and no YA fiction." **Publishes 22 titles/year. 500 queries received/year. 400 mss received/year. 70% of books from first-time authors. 90% from unagented writers. Pays 3-5% royalty on retail price. Makes outright purchase of 500-2,000. Pays $500-2,000 advance.** Publishes book 18-24 months after acceptance. Responds to queries/mss in 4 months. Book catalog and ms guidelines free or on website.

◑ *URJ Press publishes books related to Judaism.*

NONFICTION Subjects include art, architecture, synagogue, child guidance, cooking, foods, nutrition, Jewish, education, ethnic, Judaism, government, politics, Israeli/Jewish, history, language, literature, Hebrew, military, war, as relates to Judaism, music, dance, nature, environment, philosophy, Jewish, religion, Judaism only, sex, as it relates to Judaism, spirituality, Jewish. Picture books, young readers, middle readers: religion. Average word length: picture books—1,500. Recently published *The Seven Spices: Stories and Recipes Inspired by the Foods of the Bible*, by Matt Biers-Ariel, illustrated by Tama Goodman (story and recipe book). Submit proposal package, outline, bio, 1-2 sample chapters.

FICTION Subjects include juvenile, children's picture books. Picture books: religion. Average word length: picture books—1,500. Recently published *The Purim Costume*, by Peninnah Schran, illustrated by Tammy L. Keiser (ages 4-8, picture book); *A Year of Jewish Stories: 52 Tales for Children and Their Families*, by Grace Ragues Maisel and Samantha Shubert, illustrated by Tammy L. Keiser (ages 4-12, picture book). Submit complete ms with author bio.

TIPS "Look at some of our books. Have an understanding of the Reform Judaism community. In addition to bookstores, we sell to Jewish congregations and Hebrew day schools."

USBORNE PUBLISHING

83-85 Saffron Hill, London En EC1N 8RT, United Kingdom. (44)(020)7430-2800. **Fax:** (44)(020)7430-1562. **E-mail:** mail@usborne.co.uk; pippas@usborne.co.uk; alicep@usborne.co.uk; Graeme@usborne.co.uk. **Website:** www.usborne.com. "Usborne Publishing is a multiple-award winning, world-wide children's publishing company specializing in superbly researched and produced information books with a unique appeal to young readers." **Pays authors royalty.**

FICTION Young readers, middle readers: adventure, contemporary, fantasy, history, humor, multicultural, nature/environment, science fiction, suspense/mystery, strong concept-based or character-led series. Average word length: young readers—5,000-10,000; middle readers—25,000-50,000.

TIPS "Do not send any original work and, sorry, but we cannot guarantee a reply."

VANDERBILT UNIVERSITY PRESS

VU Station B 351813, Nashville TN 37235. (615)322-3585. **Fax:** (615)343-8823. **E-mail:** vupress@vanderbilt.edu. **Website:** www.vanderbiltuniversitypress.com. **Contact:** Michael Ames, director. Publishes hardcover originals and trade paperback originals and reprints. "Vanderbilt University Press publishes books on healthcare, social sciences, education, and regional studies, for both academic and general audiences that are intellectually significant, socially relevant, and of practical importance." **Publishes 20-25 titles/year. 500 queries received/year. 25% of books from first-time authors. 90% from unagented writers. Pays rare advance.** Publishes ms 10 months after acceptance. Accepts simultaneous submissions. Responds in 2 weeks to proposals. Book catalog available free online. Guidelines available online.

Also distributes for and co-publishes with Country Music Foundation.

NONFICTION Subjects include Americana, anthropology, archeology, education, ethnic, government, politics, health, medicine, history, language, literature, multicultural, music, dance, nature, environment, philosophy, women's issues, women's studies. Submit prospectus, sample chapter, cv. Does not accept electronic submissions. Reviews artwork/photos. Send photocopies.

TIPS "Our audience consists of scholars and educated, general readers."

VANHOOK HOUSE

925 Orchard St., Charleston WV 25302. **E-mail:** editor@vanhookhouse.com. **E-mail:** acquisitions@vanhookhouse.com. **Website:** www.vanhookhouse.com. **Contact:** Jim Whyte, acquisitions, all fiction/true crime/military/war. Estab. 2009. Publishes hardcover and trade paperback originals; trade paperback reprints. "VanHook House is a small press focused on the talents of new, unpublished authors. We are looking for works of fiction and nonfiction to add to our catalog. No erotica or sci-fi, please. Query via email. Queries accepted ONLY during submissions periods." **Publishes 6 titles/year. Receives 20 mss/year. 100% of books from first-time authors. 100% from unagented writers. Pays authors 8-10% royalty on wholesale price. Advance negotiable.** Publishes ms 6 months after acceptance. Responds in 1 month on queries; 2 months on proposals; 3 months on mss. Book catalog and guidelines free on request and available online at website.

NONFICTION Subjects include agriculture, Americana, animals, anthropology, architecture, art, automotive, business, career guidance, child guidance, communications, community, computers, contemporary culture, cooking, counseling, crafts, creative nonfiction, dance, education, electronics, entertainment, environment, ethnic, foods, games, gardening, government, health, history, house and home, humanities, labor, language, law, literature, marine subjects, medicine, memoirs, military, muticultural, music, nature, New Age, nutrition, philosophy, photography, politics, psychology, public affairs, real estate, recreation, regional, religion, science, sex, social sciences, sociology, software, spirituality, sports, transportation, travel, women's issues/studies, war, world affairs. Reviews artwork.

POETRY "A collection must contain 200 individual poems to be considered." Query; submit 3 sample poems.

TIPS "Visit our website."

VÉHICULE PRESS

3861 Boulevard st-Laurent, P.O.B. 42094 BP Roy, Montreal QC H2W 2T3, Canada. (514)844-6073. **Fax:** (514)844-7543. **E-mail:** vp@vehiculepress.com. **Website:** www.vehiculepress.com. **Contact:** Simon Dardick, president/publisher. Estab. 1973. Publishes trade paperback originals by Canadian authors mostly. "Montreal's Véhicule Press has published the best of Canadian and Quebec literature-fiction, poetry, essays, translations, and social history." **Publishes 15 titles/year. 20% of books from first-time authors. 95% from unagented writers. Pays 10-15% royalty on retail price. Pays $200-500 advance.** Publishes ms 1 year after acceptance. Responds in 4 months to queries. Book catalog for 9 x 12 SAE with IRCs.

IMPRINTS Signal Editions (poetry); Dossier Quebec (history, memoirs); Esplanade Editions (fiction).

NONFICTION Subjects include government, politics, history, language, literature, memoirs, regional, sociology. Especially looking for Canadian social history. Query with SASE. Reviews artwork/photos.

FICTION Subjects include feminist, literary, translation, literary novels. Contact Andrew Steinmetz. Literary, regional, short story collections. No romance or formula writing. Query with SASE.

POETRY Contact Carmine Starnino with SASE. Véhicule Press is a "literary press with a poetry series, Signal Editions, publishing the work of Canadian poets only." Publishes flat-spined paperbacks. Publishes Canadian poetry that is "first-rate, original, content-conscious."

TIPS "Quality in almost any style is acceptable. We believe in the editing process."

VERTIGO

DC Universe, Vertigo-DC Comics, 1700 Broadway, New York NY 10019. **Website:** www.dccomics.com.

FICTION "The DC TALENT SEARCH program is designed to offer aspiring artists the chance to present artwork samples directly to the DC Editors and Art Directors. The process is simple: during your convention visit, drop off photocopied samples of your work and enjoy the show! No lines, no waiting. If the DC folks like what they see, a time is scheduled for you the following day to meet a DC representative personally and discuss your artistic interests and portfolio.

At this time, DC Comics does not accept unsolicited writing submissions by mail. See submission guidelines online. "We're seeking artists for all our imprints, including the DC Universe, Vertigo, WildStorm, Mad magazine, Minx, kids comics and more!"

VIEWPOINT PRESS

PMB 400 785 Tucker Rd. #G, Tehachapi CA 93561. (661)821-5110. **Fax:** (661)821-7515. **E-mail:** joie99@aol.com. **Website:** www.viewpointpress.com/products.html. We have been in business for 25 years and have three children's books: *Seeds of Violence: the Autobiography of a Subversive; Fiddler of the Opry: The Howdy Forrester Story; and Footprints of the Soul: a Novel.*

Not currently accepting mss.

VIKING

Imprint of Penguin Group (USA), Inc., 375 Hudson St., New York NY 10014. (212)366-2000. **Website:** us.penguingroup.com/static/pages/publishers/adult/viking.html. Estab. 1925. Publishes hardcover and originals. Viking publishes a mix of academic and popular fiction and nonfiction. **Publishes 100 titles/year. Pays 10-15% royalty on retail price.** Publishes ms 18 months after acceptance. Accepts simultaneous submissions.

NONFICTION Subjects include business, economics, child guidance, cooking, foods, nutrition, health, medicine, history, language, literature, music, dance, philosophy, womens issues, womens studies. Agented submissions only.

FICTION Subjects include literary, mainstream, contemporary, mystery, suspense. Literary, mainstream/contemporary, mystery, suspense. Agented submissions only.

VIKING CHILDREN'S BOOKS

375 Hudson St., New York NY 10014. **E-mail:** averystudiopublicity@us.penguingroup.com. **Website:** www.penguingroup.com. **Contact:** Catherine Frank, executive editor. Joy Peskin, Anne Gunton, Tracy Gates, associate editorial editors; Joy Peskin, executive editor; Janet Pascal, editor; Kendra Levin, associate editor; Leila Sales, editorial assistant. Publishes hardcover originals. "Viking Children's Books is known for humorous, quirky picture books, in addition to more traditional fiction. We publish the highest quality fiction, nonfiction, and picture books for pre-schoolers through young adults." **Publishes 70 titles/year. Pays 2-10% royalty on retail price or flat fee. Pays negotia-**

ble **advance.** Publishes book 1-2 years after acceptance. Responds to queries/mss in 6 months.

○ *Does not accept unsolicited submissions.*

NONFICTION All levels: biography, concept, history, multicultural, music/dance, nature/environment, science, and sports.

FICTION All levels: adventure, animal, contemporary, fantasy, history, humor, multicultural, nature/environment, poetry, problem novels, romance, science fiction, sports, suspense/mystery. *Accepts agented mss only.*

TIPS No "cartoony" or mass-market submissions for picture books.

◐ VILLARD BOOKS

Imprint of Random House Publishing Group, 1745 Broadway, New York NY 10019. (212)572-2600. **Website:** www.atrandom.com. Estab. 1983. Publishes hardcover and trade paperback originals. "Villard Books is the publisher of savvy and sometimes quirky, best-selling hardcovers and trade paperbacks." **Pays negotiable royalty Pays negotiable advance.** Accepts simultaneous submissions.

NONFICTION , Commercial nonfiction. Agented submissions only.

FICTION Commercial fiction. Agented submissions only.

◐ VINTAGE ANCHOR PUBLISHING

1745 Broadway, New York NY 10019. **E-mail:** vintageanchorpublicity@randomhouse.com. **Website:** www.randomhouse.com. **Contact:** Furaha Norton, editor. **Pays 4-8% royalty on retail price. Average advance: $2,500 and up.** Publishes ms 1 year after acceptance.

FICTION Literary, mainstream/contemporary, short story collections. *Agented submissions only.* Accepts simultaneous submissions. No electronic submissions.

VIVISPHERE PUBLISHING

675 Dutchess Turnpike, Poughkeepsie NY 12603. (845)463-1100, ext. 314. **Fax:** (845)463-0018. **E-mail:** cs@vivisphere.com. **Website:** www.vivisphere.com. **Contact:** Lisa Mays. Estab. 1995. Publishes trade paperback originals and reprints and e-books. Vivisphere Publishing is now considering new submissions from any genre as follows: game of bridge (cards), nonfiction, history, military, new age, fiction, feminist/gay/lesbian, horror, contemporary, self-help, science fiction and cookbooks. **Pays royalty.** Publishes ms 6 months-2 years after acceptance. Accepts simultaneous submissions. Responds in 6-12 months to queries, proposals, mss. Book catalog and ms guidelines online.

○ "Cookbooks should have a particular slant or appeal to a certain niche. Also publish out-of-print books."

NONFICTION Subjects include history, military, New Age, Game of Bridge. "Query with SASE. Please submit a proposal package (printed paper copy) including: outline and 1st chapter along with your contact information to: Attn: New Submissions, at our address. Or, opt to submit via e-mail at cs@vivisphere.com."

FICTION Subjects include feminist, gay, lesbian, historical, horror, literary, contemporary, military, self help, science fiction. Query with SASE.

VIZ MEDIA LLC

P.O. Box 77010, 295 Bay St., San Francisco CA 94133. (415)546-7073. **E-mail:** evelyn.dubocq@viz.com. **Website:** www.viz.com. "VIZ Media, LLC is one of the most comprehensive and innovative companies in the field of manga (graphic novel) publishing, animation and entertainment licensing of Japanese content. Owned by three of Japan's largest creators and licensors of manga and animation, Shueisha Inc., Shogakukan Inc., and Shogakukan-Shueisha Productions, Co., Ltd., VIZ Media is a leader in the publishing and distribution of Japanese manga for English speaking audiences in North America, the United Kingdom, Ireland, and South Africa and is a global ex-Asia licensor of Japanese manga and animation. The company offers an integrated product line including magazines such as SHONEN JUMP and SHOJO BEAT, graphic novels, and DVDs, and develops, markets, licenses, and distributes animated entertainment for audiences and consumers of all ages."

FICTION VIZ Media is currently accepting submissions and pitches for original comics. Keep in mind that all submissions must be accompanied by a signed release form.

VOYAGEUR PRESS

Quayside Publishing Group, 400 First Ave. N., Suite 300, Minneapolis MN 55401. (800)458-0454. **Fax:** (612)344-8691. **E-mail:** mdregni@voyageurpress.com. **Website:** voyageurpress.com. **Contact:** Michael Dregni, publisher. Estab. 1972. Publishes hardcover and trade paperback originals. "Voyageur Press (and its sports imprint MVP Books) is internationally known as a leading publisher of quality music, sports, country living, crafts, natural history, and regional books. No children's or poetry books." **Publishes 80 titles/year. 1,200 queries received/year. 500 mss received/year. 10% of books from first-time authors. 90% from un-**

agented writers. **Pays royalty. Pays advance.** Publishes ms 1 year after acceptance. Accepts simultaneous submissions. Responds in 3 months to queries.

IMPRINTS MVP Books.

NONFICTION Subjects include Americana, cooking, environment, history, hobbies, music, nature, regional, sports, collectibles, country living, knitting and quilting, outdoor recreation. Query with SASE. Submit outline. Send sample digital images or transparencies (duplicates and tearsheets only).

TIPS "We publish books for an audience interested in regional, natural, and cultural history on a wide variety of subjects. We seek authors strongly committed to helping us promote and sell their books. Please present as focused an idea as possible in a brief submission (1-page cover letter; 2-page outline or proposal). Note your credentials for writing the book. Tell all you know about the market niche and marketing possibilities for proposed book. We use more book designers than artists or illustrators, since most of our books are illustrated with photographs."

W&A PUBLISHING

One Peregrine Way, P.O. Box 849, Cedar Falls IA 50613. (319)266-0441; (800)927-8222. **Fax:** (319)266-1695. **E-mail:** kgolden@w-apublishing.com. **E-mail:** editorial@w-apublishing.com. **Website:** www.w-apublishing.com. **Contact:** Karris Golden, executive editor. Estab. 2006. Publishes hardcover and electronic originals and hardcover reprints. **Publishes 10-12/year titles/year. 90% of books from first-time authors. 100% from unagented writers. Pays 15% royalty.** Publishes ms 3-6 months after acceptance. Accepts simultaneous submissions. Responds in 1-2 months on queries and proposals. Catalog available online at website. Guidelines available online at website and by e-mail at editorial@w-apublishing.com.

NONFICTION Subjects include business, economics, finance, money, Investing/trading; investment/trading strategies, systems, and techniques; hot trends; trading/investment psychology; trading guidelines and how-to; new, tested trading/investment methods; anthologies of articles related to the above. "We are always interested in great ideas, fresh voices, and new methods, strategies, and approaches that will educate readers interested in improving their skills as traders and investors." No proposals based on get-rich-quick schemes or 'foolproof, can't lose' strategies. Submit proposal packages, including: outline/synopsis, 1-3 sample

chapters(s), table of contents and author's biographical information; prefer e-mailed submissions. Writers should send photocopies; scans; computer-generated graphics.

TIPS "Our readers have increased knowledge and awareness of discrete investment products and tools. They are interested in an education and want to learn from practicing financial professionals. Our goal is to offer readers materials highlighting new techniques, in-depth analysis, and solid information that helps them hone their skills and make informed decisions. We are interested in providing accompanying workbook materials in print and electronic form to augment the published book. (We prefer workbook/training materials that are supplemental rather than incorporated into the book.)"

WAKE FOREST UNIVERSITY PRESS

P.O. Box 7333, Winston-Salem NC 27109. (336)758-5448. **Fax:** (336)758-5636. **E-mail:** wfupress@wfu.edu. **Website:** www.wfu.edu/wfupress. **Contact:** Jefferson Holdridge, director/poetry editor; Dillon Johnston, advisory editor. Estab. 1976. "We publish only poetry from Ireland. I am able to consider only poetry written by native Irish poets. I must return, unread, poetry from American poets." Query with 4-5 samples and cover letter. Sometimes sends prepublication galleys. Buys North American or U.S. rights. **Pays on 10% royalty contract, plus 6-8 author's copies. Negotiable advance.** Responds to queries in 1-2 weeks; to submissions (*if invited*) in 2-3 months.

WALKER AND CO.

Walker Publishing Co., 175 Fifth Ave., 7th Floor, New York NY 10010. (212)727-8300. **Fax:** (212)727-0984. **E-mail:** rebecca.mancini@bloomsburyusa.com. **Website:** bloomsbury.com/us/children. **Contact:** Emily Easton, publisher (picture books, middle grade & young adult novels); Stacy Cantor, associate editor (picture books, middle grade, and young adult novels); Mary Kate Castellani, assistant editor (picture books, middle grade, and young adult novels). Estab. 1959. Publishes hardcover trade originals. "Walker publishes general nonfiction on a variety of subjects, as well as children's books." **Pays 5-10% royalty.** Publishes ms 1 year after acceptance. Book catalog for 9×12 envelope and 3 first-class stamps.

NONFICTION Subjects include business, economics, health, medicine, history, (science and technology), nature, environment, science, sports, mathematics, self-help. *Adult: agented submissions only*; Juvenile: send synopsis.

FICTION Subjects include juvenile, mystery, adult, picture books. Accepts unsolicited mss. Query with SASE. Include "a concise description of the story line, including its outcome, word length of story, writing experience, publishing credits, particular expertise on this subject and in this genre. Common mistake: not researching our publishing program and forgetting SASE." Query with SASE. Send complete ms for picture books.

⊕ WALTSAN PUBLISHING

P.O. Box 821803, Vancouver WA 98682. **E-mail:** williamkercher@gmail.com. **E-mail:** acqs@WaltsanPublishing.com. **Website:** www.WaltsanPublishing.com. **Contact:** William Kercher, acquisitions editor. Estab. 2010. Trade paperback originals, mass market paperback originals, electronic originals. Waltsan publishing publishes biographies, general nonfiction, how-tos, and illustrated, reference, scholary, self-help, technical books, and textbooks. **Publishes 12 titles/year. Accepts electronic submissions only. "See website for details." Pays royalty minimum of 20%, maximum of 50% Does not pay advance.** Accepts simultaneous submissions. Responds in 1 month on queries, proposals, and mss. Cataog available for SAE with 1 first class stamp. Guidelines available online.

○   "Waltsan looks at author credentials, manuscript length, suitability of topic, believability, marketability, and writing skills. Looking for appropriate number and quality of graphics when appropriate."

NONFICTION Interested in all topics. Reviews artwork as part of the ms package.

FICTION Interested in all topics. "Make sure your writing is polished, believable, and the manuscript is not too short. Pay attention to details and don't try to fool the readers. Check for continuity of details by making sure what is written in one chapter coincides with what is written in other chapters. Don't guess. Check your facts." Accepts electronic submissions ONLY. "See website for details."

POETRY Accepts electronic submissions ONLY. "See website for details."

TIPS "Waltsan Publishing's audience is the 'on-the-go' person, electronic reader or android in hand, that wants to read whenever and wherever they get a chance. Generally younger, technologically savvy, and intelligent. Truly a 21st century individual."

WASHINGTON STATE UNIVERSITY PRESS

P.O. Box 645910, Pullman WA 99164-5910. (800)354-7360. **Fax:** (509)335-8568. **E-mail:** wsupress@wsu.edu. **Website:** wsupress.wsu.edu. **Contact:** Acquisitions editor. Estab. 1928. Publishes hardcover originals, trade paperback originals, and reprints. WSU Press publishes scholarly nonfiction books on the history, pre-history, culture, and politics of the West, particularly the Pacific Northwest. **Publishes 4-6 titles/year. 40% of books from first-time authors. 95% from unagented writers. Pays 5% royalty graduated according to sales.** Publishes book 18 months after acceptance of ms. Responds in 2 months to queries. Submission guidelines available online.

NONFICTION Subjects include , but are not limited to, archaeology, biography, cultural studies, cooking and food history, environment, government, history, politics, nature, railroads, science, essays. "We welcome engaging and thought-provoking mss that focus on the greater Pacific Northwest (primarily Washington, Oregon, Idaho, British Columbia, western Montana, and southeastern Alaska). Currently we are not accepting how-to books, literary criticism, memoirs, novels, or poetry." Submit outline, sample chapters. Reviews artwork/photos.

TIPS "We have developed our marketing in the direction of regional and local history, and use this as the base upon which to expand our publishing program. For history, the secret is to write strong narratives on significant topics or events. Stories should be told in imaginative, clever ways and be substantiated factually. Have visuals (photos, maps, etc.) available to help the reader envision what has happened. Explain stories in ways that tie them to wider-ranging regional, national—or even international—events. Weave them into the large pattern of history."

WASHINGTON WRITERS' PUBLISHING HOUSE

P.O. Box 15271, Washington DC 20003. **E-mail:** wwphpress@gmail.com. **Website:** www.washingtonwriters.org. **Contact:** Patrick Pepper, president. Estab. 1975. Guidelines for SASE or on website.

FICTION Washington Writers' Publishing House considers book-length mss for publication by fiction writers living within 75 driving miles of the U.S. Capitol, Baltimore area included, through competition only.

Has published fiction books by Andrew Wingfield, David Taylor, Elizabeth Bruce, Phil Kurata, Gretchen Roberts, Denis Collins, Elisavietta Ritchie, Laura Brylawski-Miller, Hilary Tham, Catherine Kimrey. Offers $1,000 and 50 copies of published book plus additional copies for publicity use. Manuscripts may include previously published stories and excerpts. "Author should indicate where they heard about WWPH." **Entry fee:** $25. **Deadline:** July 1-November 1 (postmark). Order sample fiction books on website or by sending $16 plus $3 s&h to Washington Writers' Publishing House, P.O. Box 15271, Washington DC 20003. Submit an electronic copy by e-mail to wwphpress@gmail.com (use PDF, .doc, or rich text format) or 2 hard copies by snail mail of a short story collection or novel (no more than 350 pages, double or 1-1/2 spaced; author's name should not appear on any ms pages). Include separate page of publication acknowledgments plus 2 cover sheets: one with ms title, poet's name, address, telephone number, and e-mail address, the other with ms title only. Include SASE for results only; mss will not be returned (will be recycled).

POETRY Washington Writers' Publishing House considers book-length mss for publication by poets living within 75 driving miles of the U.S. Capitol (Baltimore area included) through competition only. Publishes 1-2 poetry books/year. "No specific criteria, except literary excellence."

ⓐ WATERBROOK MULTNOMAH PUBLISHING GROUP

Random House, 12265 Oracle Blvd., Suite 200, Colorado Springs CO 80921. (719)590-4999. **Fax:** (719)590-8977. **Website:** www.waterbrookmultnomah.com. Estab. 1996. Publishes hardcover and trade paperback originals. **Publishes 70 titles/year. 2,000 queries received/year. 15% of books from first-time authors. Pays royalty.** Publishes book 1 year after acceptance. Accepts simultaneous submissions. Responds in 2-3 months to queries/proposals/mss. Book catalog available online.

NONFICTION Subjects include child guidance, money, finance, religion, spirituality, marriage, Christian living. We publish books on unique topics with a Christian perspective. Agented submissions only.

FICTION Subjects include adventure, historical, literary, mainstream, contemporary, mystery, religious, inspirational, religious mystery/suspense, religious thriller, religious romance, romance, contemporary, historical, science fiction, spiritual, suspense. Adventure, historical, literary, mainstream/contemporary, mystery, religious (inspirational, religious mystery/suspense, religious thriller, religious romance), romance (contemporary, historical), science fiction, spiritual, suspense. Agented submissions only.

WAVE BOOKS

1938 Fairview Ave. E., Suite 201, Seattle WA 98102. (206)676-5337. **E-mail:** info@wavepoetry.com. **Website:** www.wavepoetry.com. **Contact:** Charlie Wright, publisher; Joshua Beckman and Matthew Zapruder, editors; Heidi Broadhead, managing editor. Estab. 2005. Publishes hardcover and trade paperback originals. "Wave Books is an independent poetry press based in Seattle, Washington, dedicated to publishing the best in contemporary American poetry, poetry in translation, and writing by poets. The Press was founded in 2005, merging with established publisher Verse Press. By publishing strong innovative work in finely crafted trade editions and handmade ephemera, we hope to continue to challenge the values and practices of readers and add to the collective sense of what's possible in contemporary poetry." Catalog online.

○ "No children's fiction or nonfiction for Wave library. Please no unsolicited mss or queries. We will post calls for submissions on our website."

WAVELAND PRESS, INC.

4180 Illinois Route 83, Suite 101, Long Grove IL 60047-9580. (847)634-0081. **Fax:** (847)634-9501. **E-mail:** info@waveland.com. **Website:** www.waveland.com. Estab. 1975. Waveland Press, Inc. is a publisher of college textbooks and supplements. We are committed to providing reasonably priced teaching materials for the classroom and actively seek to add new titles to our growing lists in a variety of academic disciplines. If you are currently working on a project you feel serves a need and would have promise as an adopted text in the college market, we would like to hear from you.

WEIGL PUBLISHERS INC.

350 Fifth Ave. 59th Floor, New York NY 10118. (866)649-3445. **Fax:** (866)449-3445. **E-mail:** linda@weigl.com. **Website:** www.weigl.com. **Contact:** Heather Kissock, acquisitions. Estab. 2000. Publishes 25 young readers/year; 40 middle readers/year; 20 young adult titles/year. "Our mission is to provide innovative high-quality learning resources for schools and libraries worldwide at a competitive price." **Publishes 85 titles/year. 15% of books from first-time authors.**

Publishes book 6-9 months after acceptance. Accepts simultaneous submissions.

NONFICTION Young readers: animal, biography, geography, history, multicultural, nature/environment, science. Middle readers: animal, biography, geography, history, multicultural, nature/environment, science, social issues, sports. Young adults: biography, careers, geography, history, multicultural, nature/environment, social issues. Average word length: young readers—100 words/page; middle readers—200 words/page; young adults—300 words/page. Recently published *Amazing Animals* (ages 9 and up, science series); *U.S. Sites and Symbols* (ages 8 and up, social studies series); *Science Q&A* (ages 9 and up, social studies series). Query by e-mail only.

WESLEYAN PUBLISHING HOUSE

P.O. Box 50434, Indianapolis IN 46250. **E-mail:** submissions@wesleyan.org. **Website:** www.wesleyan.org/wg. **Contact:** Rachael Stevenson, associate production editor. Estab. 1843. Publishes hardcover and trade paperback originals. **150-175 submissions received/year. Pays royalty on wholesale price.** Publishes book 11 months after acceptance. Accepts simultaneous submissions. Responds within 2 months to proposals. Catalog available online at website. Guidelines available online at website.

NONFICTION Subjects include Christianity/religion. No hard-copy submissions. Submit proposal package, including outline, 3-5 sample chapters, bio. See writer's guidelines. Does not review artwork.

TIPS "Our books help evangelical Christians learn about the faith or grow in their relationship with God."

⊘ WESLEYAN UNIVERSITY PRESS

215 Long Lane, Middletown CT 06459. (860)685-7711. **Fax:** (860)685-7712. **E-mail:** stamminen@wesleyan.edu. **Website:** www.wesleyan.edu/wespress. **Contact:** Suzanna Tamminen, director and editor-in-chief. Estab. 1959. Publishes hardcover originals and paperbacks. "Wesleyan University Press is a scholarly press with a focus on poetry, music, dance and cultural studies." Wesleyan University Press is one of the major publishers of poetry in the nation. Publishes 4-6 titles/year. Responds to queries in 2 months; to mss in 4 months. Pays royalties plus 10 author's copies. Poetry publications from Wesleyan tend to get widely (and respectfully) reviewed. **"We are accepting manuscripts by invitation only until further notice."** Accepts simul-

taneous submissions. Book catalog available free. Ms guidelines online or with #10 SASE.

NONFICTION Subjects include music, dance, film/TV & media studies, science fiction studies, dance and poetry. Submit proposal package, outline, sample chapters, cover letter, CV, TOC, anticipated length of ms and date of completion. Reviews artwork/photos. Send photocopies.

POETRY We do not accept unsolicited manuscripts. Query first with SASE. Considers simultaneous submissions.

WESTMINSTER JOHN KNOX PRESS

Division of Presbyterian Publishing Corp., 100 Witherspoon St., Louisville KY 40202. **Fax:** (502)569-5113. **E-mail:** submissions@wjkbooks.com. **Website:** www.wjkbooks.com. **Contact:** Jana Riess, acquisitions editor. Publishes hardcover and paperback originals and reprints. "All WJK books have a religious/spiritual angle, but are written for various markets-scholarly, professional, and the general reader. Westminster John Knox is affiliated with the Presbyterian Church USA. No phone queries. We do not publish fiction, poetry, memoir, children's books, or dissertations. We will not return or respond to submissions without an accompanying SASE with sufficient postage." **Publishes 70 titles/year. 2,500 queries received/year. 750 mss received/year. 10% of books from first-time authors. Pays royalty on net price.** Responds in 3 months. Proposal guidelines online.

NONFICTION Subjects include religion, spirituality. Submit proposal package according to the WJK book proposal guidelines found online.

⊘ WHITAKER HOUSE

1030 Hunt Valley Circle, New Kensington PA 15068. **E-mail:** publisher@whitakerhouse.com. **Website:** www.whitakerhouse.com. **Contact:** Tom Cox, managing editor. Estab. 1970. Publishes hardcover, trade paperback, and mass market originals. **Publishes 50 titles/year. 600 queries received/year. 200 mss received/year. 15% of books from first-time authors. 60% from unagented writers. Pays 5-15% royalty on wholesale price.** Publishes ms 7 months after acceptance. Accepts simultaneous submissions. Responds in 3 months to queries, proposals and mss. Book catalog available online. Guidelines available online and by e-mail.

NONFICTION Subjects include religion, Christian. Accepts submissions on topics with a Christian perspective. Subjects include Christian living, prayer, spiritual warfare, healing, gifts of the spirit, etc. Accepts submissions on any topic as long as they have a Christian perspective. Query with SASE. Does not review artwork/photos.

FICTION Subjects include religious, Christian, historial romance, African American romance and Amish fiction. All fiction must have a Christian perspective. Query with SASE.

TIPS "Audience includes those seeking uplifting and inspirational fiction and nonfiction."

☺ WHITECAP BOOKS, LTD.

351 Lynn Ave., North Vancouver BC V7J 2C4, Canada. (905)477-9700 ext. 244. **Fax:** (905)477-9179. **E-mail:** whitecap@whitecap.ca. **Website:** www.whitecap.ca. Publishes hardcover and trade paperback originals. "Whitecap Books is a general trade publisher with a focus on food and wine titles. Although we are interested in reviewing unsolicited ms submissions, please note that we only accept submissions that meet the needs of our current publishing program. Please see some of most recent releases to get an idea of the kinds of titles we are interested in." **Publishes 40 titles/year. 500 queries received/year; 1,000 mss received/year. 20% of books from first-time authors. 90% from unagented writers. Pays royalty. Pays negotiated advance.** Publishes book 1 year after acceptance. Accepts simultaneous submissions. Responds in 2-3 months to proposals. Catalog and guidelines available online at website.

NONFICTION Subjects include animals, cooking, foods, nutrition, gardening, history, nature, environment, recreation, regional, travel. Young children's and middle reader's nonfiction focusing mainly on nature, wildlife and animals. "Writers should take the time to research our list and read the submission guidelines on our website. This is especially important for children's writers and cookbook authors. We will only consider submissions that fall into these categories: cookbooks, wine and spirits, regional travel, home and garden, Canadian history, North American natural history, juvenile series-based fiction. At this time, we are not accepting the following categories: self-help or inspirational books, political, social commentary, or issue books, general how-to books, biographies or memoirs, business and finance, art and architecture, religion and spirituality." Submit cover letter, synopsis, SASE via ground mail. See guidelines online at website. Reviews artwork/photos. Send photocopies.

TIPS "We want well-written, well-researched material that presents a fresh approach to a particular topic."

WHITE PINE PRESS

P.O. Box 236, Buffalo NY 14201. (716)627-4665. **Fax:** (716)627-4665. **E-mail:** wpine@whitepine.org. **Website:** www.whitepine.org. **Contact:** Dennis Maloney, editor. Estab. 1973. Publishes trade paperback originals. **Publishes 10-12 titles/year. 500 queries/yearly 1% of books from first-time authors. 100% from unagented writers. Pays contributor's copies.** Publishes ms 18 months after acceptance. Accepts simultaneous submissions. Responds in 1 month to queries and proposals; 4 months to mss. Catalog available online at website; for #10 SASE. Guidelines available online at website.

NONFICTION Subjects include language, literature, multicultural, translation, poetry. "*We are currently not considering nonfiction mss. We do not review artwork/photos.*"

FICTION Subjects include poetry, poetry in translation, translation. "We are currently not reading U.S. fiction. We are currently reading unsolicited poetry only as part of our Annual Poetry Contest. The reading period is July 1 - November 30 for fiction and poetry in translation only." For fiction and poetry in translation ONLY-query with SASE; submit proposal package, including synopsis and 2 sample chapters."

ALBERT WHITMAN & COMPANY

250 S. Northwest Hwy., Suite 320, Park Ridge IL 60068. (800)255-7675. **Fax:** (847)581-0039. **E-mail:** mail@awhitmanco.com. **Website:** www.albertwhitman.com. Estab. 1919. Publishes in original hardcover, paperback, boardbooks. Albert Whitman's special interest and issue titles address subjects such as disease, social issues, and disabilities. Many books deal in a caring and respectful manner with the challenging situations and learning experiences encountered by children, helping them to grow intellectually and emotionally. **Publishes 40 titles/year. 10% of books from first-time authors. 50% from unagented writers. On retail price: Pays 10% royalty for novels; 5% for picture books. Pays advance.** Publishes a book 18 months after acceptance. Accepts simultaneous submissions. Responds within 3 months to queries; 4 months to proposals and mss. "Send a self-addressed, stamped 9x12 envelope with your request, and address your letter to "Catalog Request" at our main address. Please include three first-class stamps (U.S. postage) with your SASE. Unless you

specify otherwise, we will send our most recent catalog.". Guidelines available on website.

NONFICTION Subjects include Americana, animals, character education, disabilities, family issues, holidays, multicultural, sports. Picture books, young readers, middle readers: animal, arts/crafts, health, history, hobbies, multicultural, music/dance, nature/environment, science, sports, special needs. Does not want to see, "religion, any books that have to be written in, or fictionalized biographies. Submit query, outline, and sample chapter. For picture books send entire ms. Include cover letter. Reviews artwork/photos. Send photocopies.

FICTION Subjects include juvenile, picture books, sports. Picture books, young readers, middle readers: adventure, concept (to help children deal with problems), fantasy, history, humor, multicultural, suspense. Middle readers: problem novels, suspense/mystery. "We are interested in contemporary multicultural stories—stories with holiday themes, and exciting distinctive novels. We publish a wide variety of topics and are interested in stories that help children deal with their problems and concerns. Does not want to see, "religion-oriented, ABCs, pop-up, romance, counting." Submit query, outline, and sample chapter. For picture books send entire ms. Include cover letter.

TIPS "In both picture books and nonfiction, we are seeking stories showing life in other cultures and the variety of multicultural life in the U.S. We also want fiction and nonfiction about mentally or physically challenged children; some recent topics have been autism, stuttering, and diabetes. Look up some of our books first to be sure your submission is appropriate for Albert Whitman & Co. We publish trade books that are especially interesting to schools and libraries. We recommend you study our website before submitting your work."

WILDSTORM

DC Universe, 1700 Broadway, New York NY 10019. **Website:** www.dccomics.com/wildstorm/.
Does not accept unsolicited mss.

JOHN WILEY & SONS, INC.

Wiley-Blackwell, 111 River St., Hoboken NJ 07030. (201)748-6000. **Fax:** (201)748-6088. **E-mail:** vicky.kinsman@wiley.com. **Website:** www.wiley.com. **Contact:** Editorial Department. Estab. 1807. Publishes hardcover originals, trade paperback originals and reprints. "The General Interest group publishes nonfiction books for the consumer market. There is also a Higher Education Division. See proposal guideines online." **Pays competitive rates. Pays advance.** Accepts simultaneous submissions. Book catalog available online. Guidelines available online.

IMPRINTS Jossey-Bass, Pfeiffer, Capstone.

NONFICTION Subjects include history, memoirs, psychology, science, popular, African-American interest, health/self-improvement, technical, medical. If you have an idea for a new book, journal, or electronic product that falls into the chemistry, the life sciences, medicine, mathematical and physical sciences, humanities, and social sciences arena, please send your proposal or manuscript to Wiley-Blackwell. See website for more details.

TIPS "Include a brief description of the publication and overall objective. Describe exactly what the publication will be about. What will there be about your selection, organization, or treatment of the subject that will make the readers buy the publication? Address why there is a need for the proposed publication."

WILLIAM MORROW

HarperCollins, 10 E. 53rd St., New York NY 10022. (212)207-7000. **Fax:** (212)207-7145. **Website:** www.harpercollins.com. Estab. 1926. "William Morrow publishes a wide range of titles that receive much recognition and prestige—a most selective house." **Pays standard royalty on retail price. Pays varying advance.** Book catalog available free.

NONFICTION Subjects include art, architecture, cooking, foods, nutrition, history. Length 50,000-100,000 words. *No unsolicited mss or proposals.* Agented submissions only.

FICTION Publishes adult fiction. Morrow accepts only the highest quality submissions in adult fiction. *No unsolicited mss or proposals.* Agented submissions only.

WILLIAMSON BOOKS

2630 Elm Hill Pike, Suite 100, Nashville TN 37214. **E-mail:** pjay@guideposts.org. **Website:** www.idealspublications.com. Estab. 1983. Publishes "very successful nonfiction series (Kids Can! Series) on subjects such as history, science, arts/crafts, geography, diversity, multiculturalism. Little Hands series for ages 2-6, Kaleidoscope Kids series (age 7 and up) and Quick Starts for Kids! series (ages 8 and up). Our goal is to help every child fulfill his/her potential and experience personal growth." **Pays authors advance against future royalties based on wholesale price or purchases outright.**

Pays illustrators by the project. Pays photographers per photo. Publishes book 1 year after acceptance. Responds to queries and mss in 4 months. Guidelines available for SASE.

NONFICTION Hands-on active learning books, animals, African-American, arts/crafts, Asian, biography, diversity, careers, geography, health, history, hobbies, how-to, math, multicultural, music/dance, nature/environment, Native American, science, writing and journaling. Does not want to see textbooks, picture books, fiction. "Looking for all things African American, Asian American, Hispanic, Latino, and Native American including crafts and traditions, as well as their history, biographies, and personal retrospectives of growing up in U.S. for grades pre K-8th. We are looking for books in which learning and doing are inseparable." Recently published *Keeping Our Earth Green; Leap Into Space; China!; Big Fun Craft Book.* Query with annotated TOC/synopsis and 1 sample chapter.

TIPS "Please do not send any fiction or picture books of any kind—those should go to Ideals Children's Books. Look at our books to see what we do. We're interested in interactive learning books with a creative approach packed with interesting information, written for young readers ages 3-7 and 8-14. In nonfiction children's publishing, we are looking for authors with a depth of knowledge shared with children through a warm, embracing style. Our publishing philosophy is based on the idea that all children can succeed and have positive learning experiences. Children's lasting learning experiences involve their participation."

WILLOW CREEK PRESS

P.O. Box 147, 9931 Highway 70 W., Minocqua WI 54548. (715)358-7010. **Fax:** (715)358-2807. **E-mail:** jpetrie@willowcreekpress.com. **Website:** www.willowcreekpress.com. **Contact:** Jeremy Petrie, vice president of sales. Estab. 1986. Publishes hardcover and trade paperback originals and reprints. "We specialize in nature, outdoor, and sporting topics, including gardening, wildlife, and animal books. Pets, cookbooks, and a few humor books and essays round out our titles. Currently emphasizing pets (mainly dogs and cats), wildlife, outdoor sports (hunting, fishing). De-emphasizing essays, fiction." **Publishes 25 titles/year. 400 queries received/year. 150 mss received/year. 15% of books from first-time authors. 50% from unagented writers. Pays 6-15% royalty on wholesale price. Pays $2,000-5,000 advance.** Publishes ms 18 months after accep-

tance. Accepts simultaneous submissions. Responds in 2 months to queries. Guidelines available online.

NONFICTION Subjects include animals, cooking, foods, nutrition, gardening, nature, environment, recreation, sports, travel, wildlife, pets. Submit outline, 1 sample chapter, SASE. Reviews artwork/photos.

WILSHIRE BOOK COMPANY

9731 Variel Ave., Chatsworth CA 91311. (818)700-1522. **Fax:** (818)700-1527. **E-mail:** mpowers@mpowers.com. **Website:** www.mpowers.com. **Contact:** Rights Department. Estab. 1947. Publishes trade paperback originals and reprints. **Publishes 25 titles/year. 1,200 queries received/year. 70% of books from first-time authors. 90% from unagented writers. Pays standard royalty. Pays advance.** Publishes ms 6-9 months after acceptance. Accepts simultaneous submissions. Responds in 2 months. Ms guidelines online.

NONFICTION Subjects include psychology, personal success. Minimum 30,000 words Submit 3 sample chapters. Submit complete ms. Include outline, author bio, analysis of book's competition and SASE. No e-mail or fax submissions. Reviews artwork/photos. Send photocopies.

FICTION "You are not only what you are today, but also what you choose to become tomorrow." Looking for adult fables that teach principles of psychological growth. Distributes titles through wholesalers, bookstores and mail order. Promotes titles through author interviews on radio and television. Wants adult allegories that teach principles of psychological growth or offer guidance in living. Minimum 30,000 words. No standard fiction. Submit 3 sample chapters. Submit complete ms. Include outline, author bio, analysis of book's, competition and SASE.

TIPS "We are vitally interested in all new material we receive. Just as you are hopeful when submitting your manuscript for publication, we are hopeful as we read each one submitted, searching for those we believe could be successful in the marketplace. Writing and publishing must be a team effort. We need you to write what we can sell. We suggest you read the successful books similar to the one you want to write. Analyze them to discover what elements make them winners. Duplicate those elements in your own style, using a creative new approach and fresh material, and you will have written a book we can catapult onto the bestseller list. You are welcome to telephone or e-mail us for immediate feedback on any book concept you may have.

To learn more about us and what we publish, and for complete manuscript guidelines, visit our website."

WINDWARD PUBLISHING

Finney Company, 8075 215th St. W., Lakeville MN 55044. (952)469-6699. **Fax:** (952)469-1968. **E-mail:** feedback@finney-hobar.com. **Website:** www.finney-hobar.com. **Contact:** Alan E. Krysan, president. Estab. 1973. Publishes trade paperback originals. Windward publishes illustrated natural history, recreation books, and children's books. "Covers topics of natural history and science, outdoor recreation, and children's literature. Its principal markets are book, retail, and specialty stores. While primarily a nonfiction publisher, we will occasionally accept fiction books with educational value." **Publishes 6-10 titles/year. 120 queries received/year. 50 mss received/year. 50% of books from first-time authors. 100% from unagented writers. Pays 10% royalty on wholesale price. Pays advance.** Publishes book 1 year after acceptance. Accepts simultaneous submissions. Responds in 8-10 weeks to queries.

NONFICTION Subjects include agriculture, animals, gardening, nature, environment, recreation, science, sports, natural history. Young readers, middle readers, young adults: activity books, animal, careers, nature/environment, science. Young adults: textbooks. Query with SASE. Does not accept e-mail or fax submissions. Reviews artwork/photos.

WISCONSIN HISTORICAL SOCIETY PRESS

816 State St., Madison WI 53706. (608)264-6465. **Fax:** (608)264-6486. **E-mail:** whspress@wisconsinhistory.org. **Website:** www.wisconsinhistory.org/whspress/. **Contact:** Kate Thompson, editor. Estab. 1855. Publishes hardcover and trade paperback originals; trade paperback reprints. **Publishes 12-14 titles/year. 60-75 queries received/year. 20% of books from first-time authors. 90% from unagented writers. Pays royalty on wholesale price.** Publishes ms 2 years after acceptance. Book catalog available free. Guidelines available online.

IMPRINTS Wisconsin Magazine of History.

NONFICTION Subjects include Wisconsin history and culture: archaeology, architecture, cooking, foods, ethnic, history (Wisconsin), memoirs, regional, sports. Submit proposal package, form from website. Reviews artwork/photos. Send photocopies.

TIPS "Our audience reads about Wisconsin. Carefully review the book."

WISDOM PUBLICATIONS

199 Elm St., Somerville MA 02144. (617)776-7416, ext. 28. **Fax:** (617)776-7841. **E-mail:** editors@wisdompubs.org. **Website:** www.wisdompubs.org. **Contact:** David Kittlestrom, senior editor. Estab. 1976. Publishes hardcover originals and trade paperback originals and reprints. "Wisdom Publications is dedicated to making available authentic Buddhist works for the benefit of all. We publish translations, commentaries, and teachings of past and contemporary Buddhist masters and original works by leading Buddhist scholars. Currently emphasizing popular applied Buddhism, scholarly titles." **Publishes 20-25 titles/year. 300 queries received/year. 50% of books from first-time authors. 95% from unagented writers. Pays 4-8% royalty on wholesale price. Pays advance.** Publishes ms within 2 years of acceptance. after acceptance of ms. Book catalog and ms guidelines online.

NONFICTION Subjects include philosophy, Buddhist or comparative Buddhist/Western, psychology, religion, Buddhism, Tibet. Submissions should be made electronically.

TIPS "We are basically a publisher of Buddhist books-all schools and traditions of Buddhism. Please see our catalog or our website before you send anything to us to get a sense of what we publish."

PAULA WISEMAN BOOKS

1230 Sixth Ave., New York NY 10020. (212)698-7272. **Fax:** (212)698-2796. **E-mail:** paula.wiseman@simonandschuster.com; Alexandra.Penfold@simonandschuster.com. **Website:** kids.simonandschuster.com. **Publishes 20 titles/year. 10% of books from first-time authors.**

NONFICTION Picture books: animal, biography, concept, history, nature/environment. Young readers: animal, biography, history, multicultural, nature/environment, sports. Average word length: picture books—500; others standard length. *Does not accept unsolicited or unagented mss.*

FICTION Considers all categories. Average word length: picture books—500; others standard length. Recently published *Outfoxed*, by Mike Twohy. *Does not accept unsolicited or unagented mss.*

WOODBINE HOUSE

6510 Bells Mill Rd., Bethesda MD 20817. (301)897-3570. **Fax:** (301)897-5838. **E-mail:** ngpaul@woodbinehouse.com. **Website:** www.woodbinehouse.com. **Contact:** Nancy Gray Paul, acquisitions editor. Estab. 1985. Publishes trade paperback originals. Woodbine House publishes books for or about individuals with disabilities to help those individuals and their families live fulfilling and satisfying lives in their homes, schools, and communities. **Publishes 10 titles/year. 15% of books from first-time authors. 90% from unagented writers. Pays 10-12% royalty.** Publishes ms 18 months after acceptance. Accepts simultaneous submissions. Responds in 3 months to queries. Book catalog for 6x9 SAE with 3 first-class stamps. No metered mail or international reply coupons (IRC's) please. Guidelines available online.

NONFICTION Subjects include specific issues related to a given disability (e.g., communication skills, social sciences skills, feeding issues) and practical guides to issues of concern to parents of children with disabilities (e.g., special education, sibling issues). Publishes books for and about children with disabilities. No personal accounts or general parenting guides. Submit outline, and at least 3 sample chapters. Reviews artwork/photos.

FICTION Subjects include picture books, children's. Receptive to stories re: developmental and intellectual disabilities, e.g., autism and cerebral palsy. Submit complete ms with SASE.

TIPS "Do not send us a proposal on the basis of this description. Examine our catalog or website and a couple of our books to make sure you are on the right track. Put some thought into how your book could be marketed (aside from in bookstores). Keep cover letters concise and to the point; if it's a subject that interests us, we'll ask to see more."

WRITER'S DIGEST BOOKS

Imprint of F+W Media, Inc., 10151 Carver Rd., Suite #200, Cincinnati OH 45242. **E-mail:** writersdigest@fwmedia.com. **Website:** www.writersdigest.com. **Contact:** Rachel Scheller; James Duncan. Estab. 1920. Publishes hardcover originals and trade paperbacks. "Writer's Digest Books is the premiere source for instructional books on writing and publishing for an audience of aspirational writers. Typical mss are 80,000 words. E-mail queries strongly preferred; no phone calls please." **Publishes 18-20 titles/year. 300 queries received/year. 50 mss received/year. 30% from unagented writers. Pays average $3,000 advance.** Publishes book 1 year after acceptance. Accepts simultaneous submissions. Responds in 3 months to queries. "Our catalog of titles is available to view online at www.WritersDigestShop.com.".

Writer's Digest Books accepts query letters and complete proposals via e-mail at writersdigest@fwmedia.com.

NONFICTION "Our instruction books stress results and how specifically to achieve them. Should be well-researched, yet lively and readable. We do not want to see books telling readers how to crack specific nonfiction markets: *Writing for the Computer Market* or *Writing for Trade Publications,* for instance. We are most in need of fiction-technique books written by published authors. Be prepared to explain how the proposed book differs from existing books on the subject." No fiction or poetry. Query with SASE. Submit outline, sample chapters, SASE.

YALE UNIVERSITY PRESS

P.O. Box 209040, New Haven CT 06520. (203)432-0960. **Fax:** (203)432-0948. **E-mail:** niamh.cunningham@yale.edu. **Website:** www.yale.edu/yup. **Contact:** Niamh Cunningham, (203)432-0975. Christopher Rogers, editorial director (history and current events); Jean E. Thomson Black, executive editor (science, medicine); Vadim Staklo, Associate Editor (reference books, Annals of Communism, Slavic Studies); William Frucht, Executive Editor (politics, law, and economics); Michelle Komie, Senior Editor (art, architecture); Patricia Fidler, Publisher (art, architecture); Tim Shea, Editor (languages, ESL); Alison Mackeen, Editor (literature, literary studies, media studies); Sarah Miller, Associate Editor, General Interest; Ileene Smith, Exec. Editor at large, General Interest; Laura Davulis, Editor (digital development); Jennifer Banks, Senior Editor (Religion, Religious History, Classics). Estab. 1908. Estab. 1908. Publishes hardcover and trade paperback originals. "Yale University Press publishes scholarly and general interest books." Accepts simultaneous submissions. Book catalog and ms guidelines online.

NONFICTION Subjects include Americana, anthropology, archeology, art, architecture, business, economics, education, health, medicine, history, language, literature, military, war, music, dance, philosophy, psychology, religion, science, sociology, women's issues, women's studies. Our nonfiction has to be at a very high level. Most of our books are written by professors or journalists, with a high level of expertise. *Submit proposals only.* We'll ask if we want to see more. *No unsolicited mss.* We won't return them. Submit sample chapters, cover letter, prospectus, cv, table of contents, SASE. Reviews artwork/photos. Send photocopies.

POETRY Publishes 1 book each year. Submit to Yale Series of Younger Poets Competition. Open to poets under 40 who have not had a book previously published. Submit ms of 48-64 pages by November 15. Rules and guidelines available online or with SASE. Submit complete ms.

TIPS "Audience is scholars, students and general readers."

ⒶⓄ YEARLING BOOKS

Imprint of Random House Children's Books/Random House, Inc., 1745 Broadway, New York NY 10019. (212)782-9000. **Website:** www.randomhouse.com/kids.

IMPRINTS *Does not accept unsolicited mss.*

◯ "Quality reprint paperback imprint for middle grade paperback books."

YELLOW SHOE FICTION SERIES

P.O. Box 25053, Baton Rouge LA 70894. **Website:** www.lsu.edu/lsupress. **Contact:** Michael Griffith, editor. Estab. 2004. **Publishes 2 titles/year. Pays royalty. Offers advance.**

◯ "Looking first and foremost for literary excellence, especially good manuscripts that have fallen through the cracks at the big commercial presses. I'll cast a wide net."

FICTION Does not accept unsolicited mss. Accepts queries by mail, Attn: Rand Dotson. No electronic submissions.

YMAA PUBLICATION CENTER

P.O. Box 480, Wolfeboro NH 03894. (603)569-7988. **Fax:** (603)569-1889. **E-mail:** info@ymaa.com. **Contact:** David Ripianzi, director. Estab. 1982. Publishes trade paperback originals and reprints. YMAA publishes books on Chinese Chi Kung (Qigong), Taijiquan, (Tai Chi) and Asian martial arts. We are expanding our focus to include books on healing, wellness, meditation and subjects related to Asian culture and Asian medicine. De-emphasizing fitness books. **Publishes 6 titles/year. 50 queries received/year. 20 mss received/year. 25% of books from first-time authors. 100% from unagented writers.** Publishes ms 18 months after acceptance. Accepts simultaneous submissions. Responds in 3 months to proposals. Book catalog available online. Guidelines available free.

NONFICTION Subjects include ethnic, health, medicine, Chinese, history, philosophy, spirituality, sports, Asian martial arts, Chinese Qigong. We no longer publish or solicit books for children. We also produce instructional DVDs and videos to accompany our books on traditional Chinese martial arts, meditation, massage, and Chi Kung. We are most interested in Asian martial arts, Chinese medicine, and Chinese Qigong. We publish Eastern thought, health, meditation, massage, and East/West synthesis. Submit proposal package, outline, bio, 1 sample chapter, SASE. Reviews artwork/photos. Send Send photocopies and 1-2 originals to determine quality of photo/line art.

FICTION We are excited to announce a new category: **martial arts fiction**. We are seeking mss that bring the venerated tradition of true Asian martial arts to readers. Your novel length ms should be a thrilling story that conveys insights into true martial techniques and philosophies.

Ⓐ ZEBRA BOOKS

Kensington, 119 W. 40th St., New York NY 10018. **E-mail:** mrecords@kensingtonbooks.com. **Website:** www.kensingtonbooks.com. **Contact:** Megan Records, associate editor. Publishes hardcover originals, trade paperback and mass market paperback originals and reprints. Zebra Books is dedicated to women's fiction, which includes, but is not limited to romance. Publishes ms 12-18 months after acceptance. Accepts simultaneous submissions. Book catalog available online.

NONFICTION For nonfiction, send cover letter/query, including the author's qualifications and connections relevant to the book's content and marketing, and summary or outline of book's content. All submissions should be double-spaced, paginated, cleanly printed and readable. Do not bind pages together.

FICTION Mostly historical romance. Some contemporary romance, westerns, horror, and humor. Agented submissions only. You may query only by e-mail. Do not attach manuscripts or proposals to e-mail queries. An editor will respond if he or she is interested in seeing your material based on your query. submit to one editor only. For fiction, send cover letter, first three chapters, and synopsis (no more than five pages). Note that we do not publish science fiction or fantasy. We do not publish poetry.

ZENITH PRESS

Quayside Publishing Group, 400 First Ave. N., Suite 300, Minneapolis MN 55401. (612)344-8100; (800)328-0590. **Fax:** (612)344-8691. **E-mail:** egilg@quaysidepub.com. **E-mail:** egilg@quaysidepub.com; spearson@quaysidepub.com. **Website:** www.qbookshop.com; zenithpress.com. **Contact:** Eric Gilg, editorial director; Scott Pearson, acquisitions editor. Richard Kane, senior acquisitions editor (American military history, politics/current events) Estab. 2004. Publishes hardcover and trade paperback originals, electronic originals and reprints, hardcover and trade paperback reprints. "Zenith Press publishes an eclectic collection of historical nonfiction and current affairs in both narrative and illustrated formats. Building on a core of military history, particularly from World War II forward, Zenith reaches out to other historical, aviation, and science topics with compelling narrative hooks or eye-catching photography. From a history of WWII aviation wrecks to an illustrated celebration of the space shuttle program, Zenith books are engaging true stories with historical, military, or science foundations—sometimes all three at once." **Publishes 210 titles/year. Receives 250 queries/year; 100 mss/year. 25% of books from first-time authors. 50% from unagented writers. Pays authors 8-15% royalty on wholesale price.** Publishes ms 1 year after acceptance. Accepts simultaneous submissions. Responds in 1 month on queries, proposals, and mss. Catalog available online. Guidelines available online at www.quaysidepub.com/submissions.php.

NONFICTION Subjects include history, military, politics, science, world affairs, aviation. Submit proposal package, including outline, 1-3 sample chapters, and author biography. Reviews artwork. Send digital files.

ZONDERVAN, A HARPERCOLLINS COMPANY

Division of HarperCollins Publishers, 5300 Patterson Ave. SE, Grand Rapids MI 49530. (616)698-6900. **Fax:** (616)698-3454. **E-mail:** submissions@zondervan.com. **E-mail:** christianmanuscriptsubmissions.com. **Website:** www.zondervan.com. Estab. 1931. Publishes hardcover and trade paperback originals and reprints. "Our mission is to be the leading Christian communications company meeting the needs of people with resources that glorify Jesus Christ and promote biblical principles." **Publishes 200 titles/year. 10% of books from first-time authors. 60% from unagented writers. Pays 14% royalty on net amount received on sales of cloth and softcover trade editions; 12% royalty on net amount received on sales of mass market paperbacks. Pays variable advance.** Responds in 2 months to queries; 3 months to proposals; 4 months to mss. Guidelines available online.

IMPRINTS Zondervan, Zonderkidz, Youth Specialties, Editorial Vida.

NONFICTION Subjects include history, humanities, memoirs, religion, Christian living, devotional, bible study resources, preaching, counseling, college and seminary textbooks, discipleship, worship, church renewal for pastors, professionals and lay leaders in ministry, theological, and biblical reference books. All religious perspective (evangelical). "We're currently accepting unsolicited book proposals only for the following categories: Academic (only college and seminary textbooks in the areas of theology, biblical studies, church history, etc.) Reference (commentaries, handbooks, encyclopedias, etc.) Ministry Resources (books and resources for pastors and ministry professionals). Proposals should be saved as a Microsoft Word document (unless it contains Hebrew, Greek, or language other than English, in which case it should be saved as an Adobe PDF document) and sent electronically as an attachment to submissions@zondervan.com, putting the appropriate category in the subject line. Your proposal should include the book title a table of contents, including a 2 or 3-sentence description of each chapter, a brief description of the proposed book, including the unique contribution of the book and why you feel it must be published, your intended reader and your vita, including your qualifications to write the book. The proposal should be no more than 5 pages. If we're interested in reviewing more material from you, we'll respond within 6 weeks." *No longer accepts unsolicited mailed submissions.* Instead, submissions may be submitted electronically to (ChristianManuscriptSubmissions.com).

FICTION Refer to nonfiction. Inklings-style fiction of high literary quality. Christian relevance in all cases. Will not consider collections of short stories or poetry. Submit TOC, curriculum vitae, chapter outline, intended audience.

ZUMAYA PUBLICATIONS, LLC

3209 S. Interstate 35, Austin TX 78741. **E-mail:** business@zumayapublications.com. **E-mail:** acquisitions@zumayapublications.com. **Website:** www.zumayapublications.com. **Contact:** Adrienne Rose, acquisitions editor. Estab. 1999. Publishes trade paperback and electronic originals and reprints. **Publishes 20-25 titles/year. 1,000 queries received/year. 100 mss received/year. 75% of books from first-time authors. 98% from unagented writers.** Publishes book 2 years after acceptance. Accepts simultaneous submissions. Responds in

6 months to queries and proposals; 9 months to mss. Guidelines available online.

IMPRINTS Zumaya Arcane (New Age, inspirational fiction & nonfiction), Zumaya Boundless (GLBT); Zumaya Embraces (romance/women's fiction); Zumaya Enigma (mystery/suspense/thriller); Zumaya Thresholds (YA/middle grade); Zumaya Otherworlds (SF/F/H), Zumaya Yesterdays (memoirs, historical fiction, fiction, western fiction); Zumaya Fabled Ink (graphic novels).

"We accept only electronic queries; all others will be discarded unread. A working knowledge of computers and relevant software is a necessity, as our production process is completely digital."

NONFICTION Subjects include creative nonfiction, memoirs, New Age, spirituality, true ghost stories. "The easiest way to figure out what we're looking for is to look at what we've already done. Our main nonfiction interests are in collections of true ghost stories, ones that have been investigated or thoroughly documented, memoirs that address specific regions and eras and books on the craft of writing. That doesn't mean we won't consider something else." Electronic query only. Reviews artwork/photos. Send digital format.

FICTION Subjects include adventure, fantasy, bisexual, gay, lesbian, historical, horror, humor, juvenile, literary, mainstream, contemporary, multicultural, mystery, occult, romance, science fiction, short story collections, spiritual, suspense, transgender, western, young adult. "We are currently oversupplied with speculative fiction and are reviewing submissions in SF, fantasy and paranormal suspense by invitation only. We are much in need of GLBT and YA/middle grade, historical and western, New Age/inspirational (no overtly Christian materials, please), non-category romance, thrillers. As with nonfiction, we encourage people to review what we've already published so as to avoid sending us more of the same, at least, insofar as the plot is concerned. While we're always looking for good specific mysteries, we want original concepts rather than slightly altered versions of what we've already published." Electronic query only.

TIPS "We're catering to readers who may have loved last year's best seller but not enough to want to read 10 more just like it. Have something different. If it does not fit standard pigeonholes, that's a plus. On the other hand, it has to have an audience. And if you're not prepared to work with us on promotion and marketing, it would be better to look elsewhere."

CONSUMER MAGAZINES

Selling your writing to consumer magazines is as much an exercise of your marketing skills as it is of your writing abilities. Editors are looking not only for good writing, but for good writing which communicates pertinent information to a specific audience—their readers.

APPROACHING THE CONSUMER MAGAZINE MARKET

Marketing skills will help you successfully discern a magazine's editorial slant, and write queries and articles that prove your knowledge of the magazine's readership. You can gather clues about a magazine's readership—and establish your credibility with the magazine's editor—in a number of ways:

- **READ** the magazine's listing in *Writer's Market*.
- **STUDY** a magazine's writer's guidelines.
- **CHECK** a magazine's website.
- **READ** several current issues of the target magazine.

Writers who can correctly and consistently discern a publication's audience and deliver stories that speak to that target readership will win out every time over writers who submit haphazardly.

ANIMAL

⊕⊗ AKC GAZETTE

American Kennel Club, (212)696-8295. **Fax:** (212)696-8239. **Website:** www.akc.org/pubs/gazette. **Contact:** Tilly Grassa, creative director. **85% freelance written.** Monthly magazine. "Geared to interests of fanciers of purebred dogs as opposed to commercial interests or pet owners. We require solid expertise from our contributors—we are *not* a pet magazine." Estab. 1889. Circ. 60,000. Byline given. Pays on publication. Offers 10% kill fee. Publishes ms an average of 6 months after acceptance. Submit seasonal material 6 months in advance. Accepts queries by mail. Responds in 2 months to queries. Guidelines for #10 SASE.

NONFICTION Needs general interest, how-to, humor, interview, photo feature, travel, dog art, training and canine performance sports. No poetry, tributes to individual dogs, or fiction. **Buys 30-40 mss/year.** Length: 1,000-3,000 words. **Pays $300-500.** Pays expenses of writers on assignment.

FICTION Annual short fiction contest only. Guidelines for #10 SASE. Send entries to AKC Publications Fiction Contest.

⊕⊗ APPALOOSA JOURNAL

2720 West Pullman Rd., Moscow ID 83843. (208)882-5578. **Fax:** (208)882-8150. **E-mail:** editor@appaloosajournal.com; designer2@appaloosajournal.com. **Website:** www.appaloosajournal.com. **Contact:** Dana Russell, editor; John Langston, art director. **40% freelance written.** Monthly magazine covering Appaloosa horses. "*Appaloosa Journal* is the authoritative, association-based source for information about the Appaloosa Horse Club, the Appaloosa breed and the Appaloosa industry. Our mission is to cultivate a broader membership base and instill enthusiasm for the breed by recognizing the needs and achievements of the Appaloosa, ApHC members, enthusiasts and our readers. The Appaloosa Horse Club is a not-for-profit organization. Serious inquiries within specified budget only." Estab. 1946. Circ. 25,000. Byline given. Pays on publication. Publishes ms an average of 3 months after acceptance. Responds in 1 month to queries. Responds in 2 months to mss. Sample copy free. Guidelines available online.

NONFICTION Needs historical, interview, photo feature, breeders, trainers, specific training methods, influential horses, youth and non-pro competi-tors, breed history, trail riding, and artists using Appaloosa subjects. **Buys 15-20 mss/year.** Send complete ms. *Appaloosa Journal* is not responsible for unsolicited materials. All freelance correspondence should be directed to editor Dana Russell via e-mail, with the subject line "'Freelance.' Article-length reports of timely and newsworthy events, such as shows, races, and overseas competition, are welcome but must be pre-approved by the editor. Mss exceeding the preferred word length will be evaluated according to relevance and content matter. Lengthy stories, opinion pieces, or poorly written pieces will be rejected. Mss may be sent on a CD or via e-mail in Microsoft Word or text-only format. If sent via CD, an accompanying hard copy should be printed, double spaced, following the guidelines." Length: 1,500-1,800 words (features); 600-800 words (article-length). **Pays $200-400.**

⊗⊕ BIRDING WORLD

Sea Lawn, Coast Rd., Cley next the Sea, Holt Norfolk NR25 7RZ United Kingdom. (44)(126)374-0913. **E-mail:** steve@birdingworld.co.uk. **Website:** www.birdingworld.co.uk. **Contact:** Steve Gantlett. "Monthly magazine publishing notes about birds and birdwatching. The emphasis is on rarer British and Western Palearctic birds with topical interest." Estab. 1987. No kill fee. Accepts queries by mail, e-mail. Sample copy for free. Guidelines by email.

⊕⊗ CAT FANCY

I-5 Publishing, P.O. Box 6050, Mission Viejo CA 92690. (949)855-8822. **Fax:** (949)855-3045. **E-mail:** slogan@bowtieinc.com. **E-mail:** query@catfancy.com. **Website:** www.catchannel.com. **Contact:** Susan Logan, editor. **90% freelance written.** Monthly magazine covering all aspects of responsible cat ownership. "*Cat Fancy* is the undisputed premier feline magazine that is dedicated to better lives for pet cats. Always a presence within the cat world, *Cat Fancy* and its sister website, CatChannel.com, are where cat owners, lovers, and rescue organizations go for education and entertainment. With a readership that is highly receptive to its credible advice, news, lifestyle information, *Cat Fancy* and CatChannel.com are the ultimate places to read about cat news, breeds, care and products and services." Estab. 1965. Circ. 290,000. Pays on publication. Editorial lead time 6 months. Accepts queries by mail, e-mail. Responds in 3 months to queries. Guidelines available online.

NONFICTION Needs how-to, humor, photo feature, travel, behavior, health, lifestyle, cat culture, entertainment. "We no longer publish any fiction or poetry." **Buys 70 mss/year.** Feature Articles: "We are open to working with new contributors and fresh voices in addition to drawing from a talented crop of established contributors. Each month, we provide our readers with a mix of informative articles on various topics, including breed profiles, feline health, nutrition, grooming, behavior, training, as well as lifestyle and special interest articles on cat culture, the human-animal bond and personalities. Query first." Length: 100-1,000 words. **Pays $50-450.**

☉☉ THE CHRONICLE OF THE HORSE

P.O. Box 46, Middleburg VA 20118. (540)687-6341. **Fax:** (540)687-3937. **E-mail:** slieser@chronofhorse. com. **E-mail:** bethr@chronofhorse.com (feature stories); results@chronofhorse.com (news stories). **Website:** www.chronofhorse.com. **Contact:** Sara Lieser, managing editor; Beth Rasin, executive editor. **80% freelance written.** Weekly magazine covering horses. "We cover English riding sports, including horse showing, grand prix jumping competitions, steeplechase racing, foxhunting, dressage, endurance riding, handicapped riding, and combined training. We are the official publication for the national governing bodies of many of the above sports. We feature news, how-to articles on equitation and horse care and interviews with leaders in the various fields." Estab. 1937. Circ. 18,000. Byline given. Pays for features on acceptance; news and other items on publication. Publishes ms an average of 4 months after acceptance. Submit seasonal material 3 months in advance. Accepts queries by mail, e-mail. Responds in 5-6 weeks to queries. Sample copy for $2 and 9x12 SASE. Guidelines available online.

NONFICTION Needs general interest, historical, history of breeds, use of horses in other countries and times, art, etc., how-to, trailer, train, design a course, save money, etc., humor, centered on living with horses or horse people, interview, of nationally known horsemen or the very unusual, technical, horse care, articles on feeding, injuries, care of foals, shoeing, etc. Special issues: Steeplechase Racing (January); American Horse in Sport and Grand Prix Jumping (February); Horse Show (March); Intercollegiate (April); Kentucky 4-Star Preview (April); Junior and Pony (April); Dressage (June); Horse Care (July);

Combined Training (August); Hunt Roster (September); Amateur (November); Stallion (December). No poetry, Q&A interviews, clinic reports, Western riding articles, personal experience or wild horses. **Buys 300 mss/year.** Send complete ms. Length: 1,500-2,500 words. **Pays $150-250.**

COLUMNS/DEPARTMENTS Dressage, Combined Training, Horse Show, Horse Care, Racing over Fences, Young Entry (about young riders, geared for youth), Horses and Humanities, Hunting, Vaulting, Handicapped Riding, Trail Riding, 1,000-1,225 words; News of major competitions (clear assignment with us first), 1,500 words. Query with or without published clips or send complete ms. **Pays $25-200.**

☉ COONHOUND BLOODLINES

United Kennel Club, Inc., 100 E. Kilgore Rd., Kalamazoo MI 49002-5584. (269)343-9020. **Fax:** (269)343-7037. **E-mail:** vrand@ukcdogs.com. **Website:** www.ukcdogs.com. **Contact:** Vicki Rand, editor. **40% freelance written.** Monthly magazine covering all aspects of the 6 Coonhound dog breeds. Estab. 1925. Circ. 16,000. Byline given. Pays on publication. No kill fee. Publishes ms an average of 6 months after acceptance. Editorial lead time 6 months. Submit seasonal material 6 months in advance. Accepts queries by mail, e-mail, fax, phone. Accepts simultaneous submissions. Responds in 6 weeks to queries. Sample copy for $4.50.

NONFICTION Needs general interest, historical, humor, interview, new product, personal experience, photo feature; breed-specific. Special issues: Six of the magazine's 12 issues are each devoted to a specific breed of Coonhound. Treeing Walker (February); English (July); Black & Tan (April); Bluetick (May); Redbone (June); Plott Hound (August), 1,000-3,000 words and photos. **Buys 12-36 mss/year.** Query. Length: 1,000-5,000 words. **Pays variable amount.** Sometimes pays expenses of writers on assignment.

FICTION Must be about the Coonhound breeds or hunting with hounds. Needs adventure, historical, humorous, mystery. **Buys 3-6 mss/year.** Query. Length: 1,000-3,000 words. **Pay varies.**

☉☉ DOG FANCY

BowTie Inc., P.O. Box 6050, Mission Viejo CA 92690. (949)855-8822. **Fax:** (949)855-3045. **E-mail:** barkback@dogfancy.com. **Website:** www.dogfancy.com; www.dogchannel.com. **95% freelance written.** Monthly magazine for men and women of all ages interested in all phases of dog ownership. Estab. 1970.

Circ. 268,000. Byline given. Pays on publication. Offers kill fee. Publishes ms an average of 6 months after acceptance. Accepts queries by e-mail. Responds in 2 months to queries. Guidelines available online.

NONFICTION Needs general interest, how-to, humor, inspirational, interview, photo feature, travel. "No stories written from a dog's point of view." **Buys 10 or fewer from new writers; 80 mss/year.** Query. Length: 850-1,200 words. **Pays 40¢/word.**

COLUMNS/DEPARTMENTS News hound, fun dog. **Buys 6 mss/year.** Query by e-mail. **Pays 40¢/word.**

EQUESTRIAN MAGAZINE

United States Equestrian Federation (USEF), 4047 Iron Works Pkwy., Lexington KY 40511. (859)225-6934. **Fax:** (859)231-6662. **E-mail:** bsosby@usef.org. **Website:** www.usef.org. **Contact:** Brian Sosby, editor. **10-30% freelance written.** Magazine published 6 times/year covering the equestrian sport. Estab. 1937. Circ. 77,000. Byline given. Pays on publication. Offers 50% kill fee. Editorial lead time 1-5 months. Accepts queries by mail, e-mail, fax, phone. Sample copy and writer's guidelines free.

NONFICTION Needs interview, technical, all equestrian-related. **Buys 20-30 mss/year.** Query with published clips. Length: 500-3,500 words. **Pays $200-400.**

EQUINE JOURNAL

83 Leicester St., North Oxford MA 01537. (508)987-5886. **Fax:** (508)987-5887. **E-mail:** editorial@equine-journal.com. **Website:** www.equinejournal.com. **Contact:** Kelly Ballou, editor. **90% freelance written.** Monthly tabloid covering horses—all breeds, all disciplines. "*Equine Journal* is a monthly, all-breed/discipline regional publication for horse enthusiasts. The purpose of our editorial is to educate, entertain, and enable amateurs and professionals alike to stay on top of new developments in the field. Every month, the *Equine Journal* presents feature articles and columns spanning the length and breadth of horse-related activities and interests from all corners of the country." Estab. 1988. Circ. 26,000. Byline given. Pays on publication. Editorial lead time 4 months. Accepts queries by mail, e-mail, fax, phone. Responds in 2 months to queries. Guidelines available online.

NONFICTION Needs general interest, how-to, interview. **Buys 100 mss/year.** Send complete ms. Length: 1,500-2,200 words.

COLUMNS/DEPARTMENTS Horse Health (health-related topics), 1,200-1,500 words. **Buys 12 mss/year.** Query.

FIDO FRIENDLY MAGAZINE

Fido Friendly, Inc., P.O. Box 160, Marsing ID 83639. **E-mail:** fieldeditor@fidofriendly.com. **Website:** www.fidofriendly.com. **95% freelance written.** Bimonthly magazine covering travel with your dog. "We want articles about all things travel related with your dog." Estab. 2,000. Circ. 44,000. Byline given. Pays on publication. No kill fee. Publishes ms an average of 2 months after acceptance. Editorial lead time 1-3 months. Submit seasonal material 3 months in advance. Accepts queries by e-mail. Accepts simultaneous submissions. Responds in 2 weeks to queries. Responds in 1 month to mss. Sample copy for $7. Guidelines free.

NONFICTION Contact: Susan Sims, publisher. Needs essays, general interest, how-to, travel with your dog, humor, inspirational, interview, personal experience, travel. No articles about dog's point of view - dog's voice. **Buys 24 mss/year.** Query with published clips. Length: 600-1,200 words. **Pays 10-20¢ for assigned articles. Pays 10-20¢ for unsolicited articles.**

COLUMNS/DEPARTMENTS Fido Friendly City (City where dogs have lots of options to enjoy restaurants, dog retail stores, dog parks, sports activity.) **Buys 6 mss/year.** Query with published clips. **Pays 10-20¢/word**

FICTION Contact: Susan Sims. Needs adventure, (dog). Nothing from dog's point of view. **Buys 0 mss/year.** Query. Length: 600-1,200 words. **Pays 10¢-20¢.**

FRESHWATER AND MARINE AQUARIUM

Bowtie, Inc., 3 Burroughs, Irvine CA 92618. (949)855-8822. **E-mail:** emizer@bowtieinc.com. **Website:** www.fishchannel.com. Clay Jackson. **Contact:** Ethan Mizer, senior associate editor. **95% freelance written.** The freshwater and marine aquarium hobby. "Our audience tends to be more advanced fish-and coral-keepers as well as planted tank fans. Writers should have aquarium keeping experience themselves. FAMA covers all aspects of fish and coral husbandry." Estab. 1978. Circ. 14,000. Byline given. Pays on publication. Pays $50 kill fee. Publishes ms 6-8 months after acceptance. 3.5 months editorial lead time. Accepts queries by mail, e-mail. Accepts simultaneous submissions. 3 weeks on queries, 2 months on mss. "If we are interested in a query or ms, we'll e-mail an assignment with guidelines included."

NONFICTION **Contact:** Ethan Mizer, senior associate editor. Needs general interest, how-to, interview, new product, personal experience, technical, aquarium-related articles. Special issues: Three special issues every year. Past issues have included aquarium lighting, invertebrates, planted tanks, food, etc. "No beginner articles, such as keeping guppies and goldfish. If mid-level to advanced aquarists wouldn't get anything new by reading it, don't send it." Writer should query. 1,500-2,000/words. **Pay $300-400; 20¢/word.**

COLUMNS/DEPARTMENTS "All of our columns are assigned and written by established columnists." **Pays $250.**

$ THE GREYHOUND REVIEW

P.O. Box 543, Abilene KS 67410. (785)263-4660. **E-mail:** nga@ngagreyhounds.com. **Website:** www.ngagreyhounds.com. **20% freelance written.** Monthly magazine covering greyhound breeding, training, and racing. Estab. 1911. Circ. 3,500. Byline given. Pays on acceptance. No kill fee. Submit seasonal material 2 months in advance. Responds in 2 weeks to queries. Responds in 1 month to mss. Sample copy for $3. Guidelines free.

NONFICTION Needs how-to, interview, personal experience. Do not submit gambling systems. **Buys 21 mss/year.** Query. Length: 1,000-10,000 words. **Pays $85-150.**

REPRINTS Send photocopy. Pays 100% of amount paid for original article.

$$$ HORSE&RIDER

2520 55th St., #210, Boulder CO 80301. **E-mail:** horseandrider@aimmedia.com. **Website:** www.horseandrider.com. **Contact:** Julie Preble, assistant editor. **10% freelance written. "Very little unsolicited freelance accepted."** Monthly magazine covering Western horse industry, competition, recreation. "*Horse&Rider*'s mission is to enhance the enjoyment and satisfaction readers derive from horse involvement. We strive to do this by providing the insights, knowledge, and horsemanship skills they need to safely and effectively handle, ride, and appreciate their horses, in and out of the competition arena. We also help them find the time, resources, and energy they need to enjoy their horse to the fullest." Estab. 1961. Circ. 150,000. Byline given. Pays after publication. Publishes ms an average of 1 year after acceptance. Editorial lead time 2 months. Submit seasonal material 6 months in advance. Accepts queries by mail (must be on a CD in a digital format), e-mail (preferred). Responds in 3 months to queries and to mss. Sample copy and writer's guidelines online.

NONFICTION Needs book excerpts, general interest, how-to, horse training, horsemanship, humor, interview, new product, personal experience, photo feature, travel. **Buys 5-10 mss/year.** Send complete ms. Length: 1,000-3,000 words. **Pay depends on length, use, and quality.**

$$$ THE HORSE

P.O. Box 919003, Lexington KY 40591. (859)278-2361. **Fax:** (859)276-4450. **E-mail:** editorial@thehorse.com. **Website:** www.thehorse.com. **85% freelance written.** Monthly magazine covering equine health, care, management and welfare. *The Horse* is an educational/news magazine geared toward the hands-on horse owner. Estab. 1983. Circ. 55,000. Byline given. Pays on acceptance. Publishes ms an average of 6 months after acceptance. Accepts queries by mail, e-mail. Responds in 3 months to queries. Sample copy for $3.95 or online. Guidelines available online.

NONFICTION Needs how-to, technical, topical interviews. No first-person experiences not from professionals; this is a technical magazine to inform horse owners. **Buys 90 mss/year.** Query with published clips. Length: 250-4,000 words. **Pays $60-850.**

COLUMNS/DEPARTMENTS News Front (news on horse health), 100-500 words; Equinomics (economics of horse ownership); Step by Step (feet and leg care); Nutrition; Reproduction; Back to Basics, all 1,500-2,200 words. **Buys Accepts 50 column articles/year. mss/year.** Query with published clips. **Pays $50-450.**

$$ HORSE ILLUSTRATED

I-5 Publishing, P.O. Box 8237, Lexington KY 40533. (859)260-9800. **Fax:** (859)260-1154. **E-mail:** horseillustrated@bowtieinc.com. **Website:** www.horseillustrated.com. **Contact:** Elizabeth Moyer, editor. **90% freelance written. Prefers to work with published/established writers, but will work with new/unpublished writers.** Monthly magazine covering all aspects of horse ownership. "Our readers are adults, mostly women, between the ages of 18 and 40; stories should be geared to that age group and reflect responsible horse care." Estab. 1976. Circ. 160,660. Byline given. Pays on publication. Publishes ms an average of 8 months after acceptance. Submit seasonal material 6 months in advance. Accepts queries by mail. Responds in 3 months to queries. Guidelines available at www.horsechannel.com/horse-magazines/horse-illustrated/submission-guidelines.aspx.

NONFICTION Needs general interest, how-to, horse care, training, veterinary care, inspirational, photo feature. "No little girl horse stories, cowboy and Indian stories, or anything not *directly* relating to horses." **Buys 20 mss/year.** Query or send complete ms. Length: 1,000-2,000 words. **Pays $200-400.**

○ HORSEPOWER

Box 670, Aurora ON L4G 4J9 Canada. (800)505-7428. **Fax:** (905)841-1530. **E-mail:** ftdesk@horse-canada.com. **Website:** www.horsepowermagazine.ca. **Contact:** Susan Stafford, managing editor. Bimonthly 16-page magazine, bound into *Horse Canada*, a bimonthly family horse magazine. "*Horsepower* offers how-to articles and stories relating to horse care for kids ages 6-16, with a focus on safety." Estab. 1988. Circ. 17,000. Pays on publication. Responds to mss in 3 months. Guidelines available for SASE.

NONFICTION Needs Middle readers, young adults: arts/crafts, biography, careers, fashion, games/puzzles, health, history, hobbies, how-to, humorous, interview/profile, problem-solving, travel. **Buys 6-10 mss/year.** Submit complete ms. Length: 500-1,200 words.

○○ JUST LABS

Village Press, 2779 Aero Park Dr., Traverse City MI 49686. (231)946-3712; (800)447-7367. **E-mail:** jake@villagepress.com. **E-mail:** jillianlacross@villagepress.com. **Website:** www.justlabsmagazine.com. **Contact:** Jason Smith, editor; Jill LaCross, managing editor. **50% freelance written.** Bimonthly magazine covering all aspects of teh Labrador Retriever. "*Just Labs* is targeted toward the family Labrador Retriever, and all of our articles help people learn about, live with, train, take care of, and enjoy their dogs. We do not look for articles that pull at the heart strings (those are usually staff-written), but rather we look for articles that teach, inform, and entertain." Estab. 2001. Circ. 20,000. Byline given. Pays on publication. Offers 40% kill fee. Publishes ms an average of 6 months after acceptance. Editorial lead time 6 months. Submit seasonal material 6-8 months in advance. Accepts queries by mail. Responds in 4-6 weeks to queries. Responds in 2 months to mss. Guidelines for #10 SASE.

NONFICTION Needs essays, how-to, (train, health, lifestyle), humor, inspirational, interview, photo feature, technical, travel. "We don't want tributes to dogs that have passed on. This is a privilege we reserve for our subscribers." **Buys 30 mss/year.** Query. Length: 1,000-1,800 words. **Pays $250-400 for assigned articles. Pays $250-400 for unsolicited articles.**

○ MINIATURE DONKEY TALK

Miniature Donkey Talk, Inc., P.O. Box 982, Cripple Creek CO 80813. (719)689-2904. **E-mail:** mike@donkeytalk.info. **Website:** www.web-donkeys.com. **Contact:** Mike Gross. **65% freelance written.** Quarterly magazine covering donkeys, with articles on healthcare, promotion, and management of donkeys for owners, breeders, and donkey lovers. Estab. 1987. Circ. 4,925. Byline given. Pays on acceptance. Publishes ms an average of 4 months after acceptance. Editorial lead time 2 months. Submit seasonal material 3 months in advance. Accepts queries by mail, e-mail. Responds in 2 weeks to queries. Responds in 1 month to mss. Sample copy for $5. Guidelines free.

NONFICTION Needs book excerpts, humor, interview, personal experience. **Buys 6 mss/year.** Query with published clips. Length: 700-5,000 words. **Pays $25-150.**

COLUMNS/DEPARTMENTS Humor, 2,000 words; Healthcare, 2,000-5,000 words; Management, 2,000 words. **Buys 50 mss/year.** Query. **Pays $25-100.**

○○ PAINT HORSE JOURNAL

American Paint Horse Association, P.O. Box 961023, Fort Worth TX 76161-0023. (817)834-2742. **E-mail:** jhein@apha.com. **Website:** www.painthorsejournal.com. **Contact:** Jessica Hein, editor. **10% freelance written. Works with a small number of new/unpublished writers each year.** Monthly magazine for people who raise, breed, and show Paint Horses. Estab. 1966. Circ. 12,000. Byline given. Pays on acceptance. Offers negotiable kill fee. Submit seasonal material 3 months in advance. Accepts queries by mail, e-mail, fax. Sample copy for $7 (includes shipping). Guidelines available online.

NONFICTION Needs general interest, personality pieces on well-known owners of Paints, historical, Paint Horses in the past—particular horses and the breed in general, how-to, train and show horses, photo feature of Paint Horses. **Buys 4-5 mss/year.** Query. Length: 1,000-2,000 words. **Pays $100-500.**

⊕⊕ REPTILES

BowTie, Inc., P.O. Box 6050, Mission Viejo CA 92690. (949)855-8822. **E-mail:** reptiles@bowtieinc.com. **Website:** www.reptilesmagazine.com. **20% freelance written.** Monthly magazine covering reptiles and amphibians. *Reptiles* covers "a wide range of topics relating to reptiles and amphibians, including breeding, captive care, field herping, etc." Estab. 1992. Byline given. Pays on publication. Offers 20% kill fee. Publishes ms an average of 6-8 months after acceptance. Accepts queries by mail, e-mail. Responds in 1 month to queries. Responds in 1-2 months to mss. Sample copy available online. Guidelines available online.

NONFICTION Needs general interest, historical, how-to, interview, personal experience, photo feature, travel. **Buys 10 mss/year.** Query. Length: 1,000-2,000 words. **Pays $250-500.**

⊕ ROCKY MOUNTAIN RIDER MAGAZINE

P.O. Box 995, Hamilton MT 59840. (406)363-4085. **E-mail:** info@rockymountainrider.com. **Website:** www.rockymountainrider.com. **Contact:** Natalie Riehl, publisher. **90% freelance written.** Monthly regional (Idaho, Montana, Nevada, Oregon, Utah, Washington, Wyoming) all-breed magazine for horse owners and enthusiasts. Estab. 1993. Circ. 14,000. Byline given. Pays on publication. No kill fee. Publishes ms an average of 6 months after acceptance. Submit seasonal material 6 months in advance. Accepts queries by mail, e-mail. Accepts simultaneous submissions. Responds in 2 months to queries. Responds in 3 months to mss. Sample copy for $3. Guidelines on website.

NONFICTION Needs horse care, horse health issues, anecdotes, historical, humor, personal experience. **Buys 50 mss/year.** Send complete ms. Length: 500-2,000 words. **Pays $35 per 1,000 words (approximately).**

POETRY Needs light verse, traditional. Wants "cowboy poetry; western or horse-themed poetry." Submit 1-10 poems at a time. Considers previously published poems and simultaneous submissions. No e-mail submissions; postal submissions only. Cover letter is preferred. Include SASE. Seldom comments on rejected poems. Occasionally publishes theme issues. Reviews books of poetry. Send materials for review consideration. Include SASE for returns. Buys 25 poems/year. **Pays $10/poem.**

FILLERS Needs anecdotes, facts, gags, short humor. Length: 200-750 words. **Pays $15-30.**

⊕⊕ TROPICAL FISH HOBBYIST MAGAZINE

TFH Publications, Inc., One TFH Plaza, Neptune City NJ 07753. **E-mail:** associateeditor@tfh.com. **Website:** www.tfhmagazine.com. **90% freelance written.** Monthly magazine covering tropical fish. Estab. 1952. Circ. 35,000. Byline given. Pays on acceptance. No kill fee. Editorial lead time 3 months. Submit seasonal material 6 months in advance. Accepts queries by e-mail. Responds immediately on electronic queries. Guidelines available online.

NONFICTION Buys 100-150 mss/year. Manuscripts should be submitted as e-mail attachments to associateeditor@tfh.com. Most articles are between 10,000 and 20,000 characters-with-spaces long. Please break up the text using subheads to categorize topics. We prefer articles that are submitted with photos. Do not insert photos into the text. Photos must be submitted separately." Length: 10,000 - 20,000 characters-with-spaces. **Pays $100-250.**

ART AND ARCHITECTURE

⊕⊕ AMERICAN INDIAN ART MAGAZINE

American Indian Art, Inc., 7314 E. Osborn Dr., Scottsdale AZ 85251. (480)994-5445. **Fax:** (480)945-9533. **E-mail:** info@aiamagazine.com. **E-mail:** editorial@aiamagazine.com. **Website:** www.aiamagazine.com. **97% freelance written. Works with many new/unpublished writers/year.** Quarterly magazine covering Native American art, historic and contemporary, including new research on any aspect of Native American art north of the US-Mexico border. American Indian Art Magazine is a quarterly art journal that presents art by all North American Indians through articles and illustrations designed to be of interest to both casual readers and professionals. All articles, whether solicited or volunteered, are subject to review by members of the Magazine's Editorial Advisory Board and/or other authorities in the field. Articles reflecting original research are preferred over summaries and reviews of previously discussed material. The Magazine pays an author's fee of $400, upon publication, for research articles, $200 for museum collection articles and $400 for exhibition features. Estab. 1975. Circ. 22,000. Byline given. Pays on publication. No kill fee. Publishes ms an average of 6 months after acceptance. Accepts queries by e-mail, online submission form. Responds in 6 weeks to queries; 3 months to mss. Guidelines for #10 SASE or online.

NONFICTION No previously published work or personal interviews with artists. **Buys 12-18 mss/year.** Query. Prefers e-mail submissions as an attachment or on CD (prefers Microsoft Word) Length: 6,000-7,000 words. **Pays $150-300.**

💲💲💲 AMERICANSTYLE MAGAZINE

The Rosen Group, 3000 Chestnut Ave., Suite 300, Baltimore MD 21211. (410)889-3093. **Fax:** (410)243-7089. **E-mail:** info@americanstyle.com. **Website:** www.americanstyle.com. **70% freelance written.** Bimonthly magazine covering arts, crafts, travel, and interior design. "*AmericanStyle* is a full-color lifestyle publication for people who love art. Our mandate is to nurture collectors with information that will increase their passion for contemporary art and craft and the artists who create it. *AmericanStyle*'s primary audience is contemporary craft collectors and enthusiasts. Readers are college-educated, age 35+, high-income earners with the financial means to collect art and craft, and to travel to national art and craft events in pursuit of their passions." Estab. 1994. Circ. 60,000. Pays on publication. Publishes ms an average of 9-12 months after acceptance. Editorial lead time 9-12 months. Submit seasonal material at least 1 year in advance. Accepts queries by mail, e-mail. Sample copy for $3. Guidelines available online.

NONFICTION Emailed submissions are to be followed by hard copy submissions. Length: 600-800 words. **Pays $400-800.** Sometimes pays expenses of writers on assignment.

COLUMNS/DEPARTMENTS Portfolio (profiles of emerging and established artists); Arts Tour; Arts Walk; Origins; One on One, all appx. 600 words. Query with published clips. **Pays $400-600.**

💲💲 THE ARTIST'S MAGAZINE

F+W Media, Inc., 10151 Carver Rd., Blue Ash OH 45242. (513)531-2690, ext. 11731. **Fax:** (513)891-7153. **Website:** www.artistsmagazine.com. **Contact:** Maureen Bloomfield, editor-in-chief; Brian Roeth, senior art director. **80% freelance written.** Magazine published 10 times/year covering primarily two-dimensional art for working artists. Maureen Bloomfield says, "Ours is a highly visual approach to teaching serious amateur and professional artists techniques that will help them improve their skills and market their work. The style should be crisp and immediately engaging, written in a voice that speaks directly to artists. We do not accept unsolicited manuscripts. Artists should send digital images of their work; writers should send clips of previously published work, along with a query letter." Circ. 100,000. Bionote given for feature material. Pays on publication. Offers 8% kill fee. Publishes ms an average of 6 months-1 year after acceptance. Responds in 6 months to queries. Sample copy for $5.99. Guidelines available online.

NONFICTION No unillustrated articles. **Buys 60 mss/year.** Length: 500-1,200 words. **Pays $300-500.**

💲💲 ART PAPERS

Atlanta Art Papers, Inc., P.O. Box 5748, Atlanta GA 31107. (404)588-1837. **Fax:** (404)588-1836. **E-mail:** editor@artpapers.org. **Website:** www.artpapers.org. **Contact:** Editor-in-chief. **95% freelance written.** Bimonthly magazine covering contemporary art and artists. "*Art Papers*, about regional and national contemporary art and artists, features a variety of perspectives on current art concerns. Each issue presents topical articles, interviews, reviews from across the U.S., and an extensive and informative artists' classified listings section. Our writers and the artists they cover represent the scope and diversity of the country's art scene." Estab. 1977. Circ. 12,000. Byline given. Pays on publication. No kill fee. Publishes ms an average of 3 months after acceptance. Editorial lead time 2 months. Submit seasonal material 2 months in advance.

NONFICTION **Buys 240 mss/year. Pays $60-325.**
COLUMNS/DEPARTMENTS Current art concerns and news. **Buys 8-10 mss/year.** Query. **Pays $100-175.**

💲 AUSTRALIAN ART COLLECTOR

Gadfly Media, Level 1, 579 Harris St., Ultimo, Sydney NSW 2007 Australia. (61)02 8204 1000. **Fax:** (61)(2)9281-7529. **E-mail:** hmckissockdavis@artcollector.net.au. **Website:** www.artcollector.net.au. **Contact:** Hannah McKissock-Davis, editor. Quarterly magazine covering Australian art collecting. "*Australian Art Collector* is the only Australian publication targeted specifically at people who buy art."

NONFICTION Needs exposé, general interest, interview. Query.

⊘ 💲💲💲💲 AZURE DESIGN, ARCHITECTURE AND ART

460 Richmond St. W, Suite 601, Toronto ON M5V 1Y1 Canada. (416)203-9674. **Fax:** (416)203-9842. **E-mail:** editorial@azuremag.com; azure@azureonline.com.

Website: www.azuremagazine.com. **Contact:** Nina Boccia, assistant editor. **75% freelance written.** Magazine covering design and architecture. Estab. 1985. Circ. 20,000. Pays on publication. Offers variable kill fee. Publishes ms an average of 1 month after acceptance. Editorial lead time up to 45 days. Responds in 6 weeks to queries.

NONFICTION Buys 25-30 mss/year. Length: 350-2,000 words. **Pays $1/word (Canadian).**

COLUMNS/DEPARTMENTS Trailer (essay/photo on something from the built environment); and Forms & Functions (coming exhibitions, happenings in world of design), both 300-350 words. **Buys 30 mss/year.** Query. **Pays $1/word (Canadian).**

◐ⓈⒺ C

C The Visual Arts Foundation, P.O. Box 5, Station B, Toronto ON M5T 2T2 Canada. (416)539-9495. **Fax:** (416)539-9903. **Website:** www.cmagazine.com. **80% freelance written.** Quarterly magazine covering international contemporary art. C provides a vital and vibrant forum for the presentation of contemporary art and the discussion of issues surrounding art in our culture, including feature articles, reviews and reports, as well as original artists' projects. Estab. 1983. Circ. 7,000. Byline given. Pays on publication. Offers kill fee. Publishes ms an average of 4 months after acceptance. Editorial lead time 3 months. Accepts queries by mail, e-mail, fax. Accepts simultaneous submissions. Responds in 6 weeks to queries. Responds in 4 months to mss. Sample copy for $10 (US). Guidelines online.

NONFICTION Needs essays, general interest, opinion, personal experience. **Buys 50 mss/year.** Length: 1,000-3,000 words. **Pays $150-500 (Canadian), $105-350 (US).**

COLUMNS/DEPARTMENTS Reviews (review of art exhibitions), 500 words. **Buys 30 mss/year.** Query. **Pays $125 (Canadian)**

⒮Ⓢ DIRECT ART MAGAZINE

Slow Art Productions, 123 Warren St., Hudson NY 12534. **E-mail:** slowart@aol.com; directartmag@aol.com. **Website:** www.slowart.com. **75% freelance written.** Semiannual fine art magazine covering alternative, anti-establishment, left-leaning fine art. Estab. 1996. Circ. 10,000. Byline sometimes given. Pays on acceptance. No kill fee. Editorial lead time 2 months. Submit seasonal material 3 months in advance. Accepts queries by mail, e-mail. Accepts simultaneous

submissions. Responds in 2 weeks to queries. Responds in 1 month to mss. Sample copy for sae with 9x12 envelope and 10 first-class stamps. Guidelines for #10 SASE.

NONFICTION Needs essays, exposé, historical, how-to, humor, inspirational, interview, opinion, personal experience, photo feature, technical. **Buys 4-6 mss/year.** Query with published clips. Length: 1,000-3,000 words. **Pays $100-500.**

COLUMNS/DEPARTMENTS Query with published clips. **Pays $100-500.**

◐ⓈⒺ ESPACE

Le Centre de Diffusion 3D, 4888 rue Saint-Denis, Montreal QC H2J 2L6 Canada. (514)844-9858. **Fax:** (514)844-3661. **E-mail:** espace@espace-sculpture.com. **Website:** www.espace-sculpture.com. **Contact:** Serge Fisette, editor. **95% freelance written.** Quarterly magazine covering sculpture events. Estab. 1987. Circ. 1,400. Byline given. Pays on publication. No kill fee. Publishes ms an average of 3 months after acceptance. Editorial lead time 5 months. Submit seasonal material 3 months in advance. Accepts queries by mail. Accepts simultaneous submissions. Sample copy free.

NONFICTION Needs essays, exposé. **Buys 60 mss/year.** Query. Length: 1,000 words. **Pays $65/page and a copy of the magazine.**

⒮⒮Ⓔ METROPOLIS

Bellerophon Publications, 61 W. 23rd St., 4th Floor, New York NY 10010. (212)627-9977. **Fax:** (212)627-9988. **E-mail:** edit@metropolismag.com. **Website:** www.metropolismag.com. **Contact:** Shannon Sharpe, managing editor. **80% freelance written.** Monthly magazine (combined issue July/August) for consumers interested in architecture and design. "*Metropolis* examines contemporary life through design—architecture, interior design, product design, graphic design, crafts, planning, and preservation. Subjects range from the sprawling urban environment to intimate living spaces to small objects of everyday use. In looking for why design happens in a certain way, *Metropolis* explores the economic, environmental, social, cultural, political, and technological context. With its innovative graphic presentation and its provocative voice, *Metropolis* shows how richly designed our world can be." Estab. 1981. Circ. 45,000. Byline given. Pays 60-90 days after acceptance. No kill fee. Publishes ms an average of 3 months after acceptance. Submit seasonal material 3 months in advance. Accepts queries by mail, e-mail, fax. Responds in 8 months to queries. Sample copy for $7. Guidelines available online.

NONFICTION Contact: Martin C. Pedersen, executive editor. Needs essays, design, architecture, urban planning issues and ideas, interview, of multi-disciplinary designers/architects. No profiles on individual architectural practices, information from public relations firms, or fine arts. **Buys 30 mss/year.** "Send query letters, not complete mss, describing your idea and why it would be good for our magazine. Be concise, specific, and clear. Also, please include clips and a résumé. The ideal *Metropolis* story is based on strong reporting skills and includes an examination of current critical issues. A design firm's newest work isn't a story, but the issues that their work brings to light might be. We do not cover conferences or seminars. Please send these announcements to the general magazine address or e-mail. Send query letters for potential articles for *MetropolisMag.com*, the online home of *Metropolis* Magazine, to Susan Szenasy at susans@metropolismag.com. The same guidelines as above applies." Length: 1,500-4,000 words. **Pays $1,500-4,000.**

COLUMNS/DEPARTMENTS The Metropolis Observed (architecture, design, and city planning news features), 100-1,200 words, pays $100-1,200; Perspective (opinion or personal observation of architecture and design), 1,200 words, pays $1,200; Enterprise (the business/development of architecture and design), 1,500 words, pays $1,500; In Review (architecture and book review essays), 1,500 words, pays $1,500. Direct queries to Belinda Lanks, managing editor. **Buys 40 mss/year.** Query with published clips.

$$ MODERNISM MAGAZINE

199 George St., Lambertville NJ 08530. (609)397-4104. **Fax:** (609)397-4409. **E-mail:** andrea@modernismmagazine.com. **Website:** www.modernismmagazine.com. **Contact:** Andrea Truppin, editor-in-chief. **70% freelance written.** Quarterly magazine covering 20th century design, architecture and decorative arts. "We are interested in design, architecture and decorative arts and the people who created them. Our coverage begins in the 1920s with Art Deco and related movements, and ends with 1980s Post-Modernism, leaving contemporary design to other magazines." Estab. 1998. Circ. 35,000. Byline given. Pays on publication. Offers 25% kill fee. Publishes ms an average of 4 months after acceptance. Editorial lead time 6 months.

Submit seasonal material 6 months in advance. Accepts queries by mail, e-mail. Accepts simultaneous submissions. Responds in 1 month to queries. Sample copy for $6.95. Guidelines free.

NONFICTION Needs book excerpts, essays, historical, interview, new product, photo feature. No first-person. **Buys 20 mss/year.** "To propose an article, send an email or letter to Andrea Truppin describing your subject matter, angle and illustration material. Please include a résumé and two samples of previously published writing, as well as a sample of unpublished writing. It helps to include images, but for the initial query, these can be low resolution digital files or photocopies. Proposals are submitted on a speculative basis." Length: 1,000-2,500 words. **Pays $300-600.**

REPRINTS Accepts previously published submissions.

ASSOCIATIONS

$$$$ AAA LIVING

Pace Communications, 1301 Carolina St., Greensboro NC 27401. **Fax:** (336)383-8272. **E-mail:** martha.leonard@paceco.com. **Website:** www.aaa.com/aaaliving. **Contact:** Martha Leonard. **20% freelance written.** Published 4 times a year/print; 6 times a year/digital. "AAA Living magazine, published for the Auto Club Group of Dearborn, Michigan, is for members of AAA clubs in 8 Midwest states (IL, N. IN, IA, MI, MN, NE, ND, & WI). Our magazine features lifestyle & travel articles about each state, written by knowledgeable resident writers. This is the best opportunity for freelancers." Estab. 1917. Circ. 2.5 million. Pays on acceptance. Offers 10% kill fee. Editorial lead time 6 months. Accepts queries by mail, e-mail. Responds in 6 months to mss. Samples available online at aaa.com/aaaliving. Guidelines are not available online.

NONFICTION Needs travel. Query with published clips. Length: 150-1,600 words. **Pays $1/word for assigned articles.** Sometimes pays expenses of writers on assignment.

$$$$ AMERICAN EDUCATOR

American Federation of Teachers, 555 New Jersey Ave. NW, Washington DC 20001. **E-mail:** amered@aft.org. **Website:** www.aft.org/ae. **Contact:** Lisa Hansel, editor. **5% freelance written.** Quarterly magazine covering education, condition of children, and labor issues. *American Educator*, the quaterly magazine of the American Federation of Teachers, reaches over

900,000 public school teachers, higher education faculty, and education researchers and policymakers. The magazine concentrates on significant ideas and practices in education, civics, and the condition of children in America and around the world. Estab. 1977. Circ. 900,000. Byline given. Pays on publication. Offers 50% kill fee. Publishes ms an average of 2-6 months after acceptance. Editorial lead time 1 year. Submit seasonal material 6 months in advance. Accepts queries by mail, e-mail. Accepts simultaneous submissions. Responds in 2 months to queries. Responds in 6 months to mss. Sample copy and guidelines available online.

NONFICTION Needs book excerpts, essays, historical, interview, discussions of educational research. No pieces that are not supportive of the public schools. **Buys 8 mss/year.** Query with published clips. Length: 1,000-7,000 words. **Pays $750-3,000 for assigned articles. Pays $300-1,000 for unsolicited articles.** Pays expenses of writers on assignment.

DAC NEWS

Detroit Athletic Club, 241 Madison Ave., Detroit MI 48226. (313)442-1034. **Fax:** (313)442-1047. **E-mail:** kenv@thedac.com. **Website:** www.thedac.com. **20% freelance written.** *DAC News* is the magazine for Detroit Athletic Club members. It covers club news and events, plus general interest features. Published 10 times/year. Estab. 1916. Circ. 5,000. Byline given. Pays on publication. No kill fee. Publishes ms an average of 3 months after acceptance. Editorial lead time 3 months. Submit seasonal material 3 months in advance. Accepts queries by mail, phone. Responds in 1 month to queries. Sample copy free.

NONFICTION Needs general interest, historical, photo feature. "No politics or social issues—this is an entertainment magazine. We do not acccept unsolicited mss or queries for travel articles." **Buys 2-3 mss/year.** Length: 1,000-2,000 words. **Pays $100-500.** Sometimes pays expenses of writers on assignment.

DCM

AFCOM, 742 E. Chapman Ave., Orange CA 92866. **Fax:** (714)997-9743. **E-mail:** afcom@afcom.com; jmoore@afcom.com. **Website:** www.afcom.com. **Contact:** Karen Riccio, managing editor. **50% freelance written.** Bimonthly magazine covering data center management. *DCM* is the slick, 4-color, bimonthly publication for members of AFCOM, the leading association for data center management. Es-

tab. 1988. Circ. 4,000 worldwide. Byline given. Pays on acceptance for assigned articles and on publication for unsolicited articles. Offers 0-10% kill fee. Publishes ms an average of 3 months after acceptance. Editorial lead time 6-12 months. Submit seasonal material 6 months in advance. Responds in 1-3 weeks to queries. Responds in 1-3 months to mss. Guidelines available online.

NONFICTION Needs how-to, technical, management as it relates to and includes examples of data centers and data center manager. Special issues: The January/February issue is the annual 'Emerging Technologies' issue. Articles for this issue are visionary and product neutral. No product reviews or general tech articles. **Buys 15+ mss/year.** Query with published clips. Length: 2,000 word maximum. **Pays 50¢/word and up, based on writer's expertise.**

THE ELKS MAGAZINE

2750 N. Lakeview Ave., Chicago IL 60614. (773)755-4740. **E-mail:** elksmag@elks.org. **Website:** www.elks.org/elksmag. **Contact:** Cheryl T. Stachura, editor/publisher. **25% freelance written.** Magazine covers nonfiction only; published 10 times/year with basic mission of being the voice of the elks. All material is written in-house. Estab. 1922. Circ. 1,037,000. Pays on acceptance. No kill fee. Accepts queries by mail, e-mail. Responds in 1 month with a yes/no on ms purchase. Guidelines available online.

NONFICTION No fiction, religion, controversial issues, first-person, fillers, or verse. **Buys 20-30 mss/year.** Send complete ms. Length: 1,200-2,000 words. **Pays 25¢/word.**

COLUMNS/DEPARTMENTS "The invited columnists are already selected."

HUMANITIES

National Endowment for the Humanities, 1100 Pennsylvania Ave. NW, Washington DC 20506. (202)606-8435. **Fax:** (202)606-8451. **E-mail:** dskinner@neh.gov; info@neh.gov. **Website:** www.neh.gov/humanities. **Contact:** David Skinner, editor. **50% freelance written.** Bimonthly magazine covering news in the humanities focused on projects that receive financial support from the agency. Estab. 1980. Circ. 6,000. Byline given. Pays on publication. Publishes ms an average of 2 months after acceptance. Editorial lead time 3 months. Submit seasonal material 4 months in advance. Accepts queries by mail, e-mail, fax, phone. YesSample copy available online.

NONFICTION Needs book excerpts, historical, interview, photo feature. **Buys 25 mss/year.** Query with published clips. Length: 400-2,500 words. **Pays $300-600.** Sometimes pays expenses of writers on assignment.

COLUMNS/DEPARTMENTS In Focus (directors of state humanities councils), 700 words; Breakout (special activities of state humanities councils), 750 words. **Buys 12 mss/year.** Query with published clips. **Pays $300.**

⊙⊙ LIFE IN ACTION

United Spinal Association, 75-20 Astoria Blvd., East Elmhurst NY 11370-1177. (718)803-3782, ext. 7224. **E-mail:** lifeinaction@unitedspinal.org. **Website:** www.spinalcord.org/life-in-action. **Contact:** Ian Ruder, editor. **50% freelance written.** Bimonthly magazine covering living with spinal cord injury/disorder (SCI/D). "The bimonthly membership magazine for the National Spinal Cord Injury Association, a program of United Spinal Association. Members include people with spinal cord injury or disorder, as well as caregivers, parents, and some spinal cord injury/disorder professionals. All articles should reflect this common interest of the audience. Assume that your audience is better educated in the subject of spinal cord injury than average, but be careful not to be too technical. Each issue has a theme (available from editor) that unites features in addition to a series of departments focused on building community and providing solutions for the SCI/D community. Articles that feature members, chapters or the organization are preferred, but any article that deals with issue pertinent to SCI/D community will be considered." Estab. 2011. Circ. 35,000. Byline given. Pays on publication. No kill fee. Publishes ms an average of 1-2 months after acceptance. Accepts queries by e-mail. Sample copy and guidelines available on website.

NONFICTION Needs essays, general interest, how-to, humor, interview, new product, personal experience, photo feature, travel, medical research. Does not want "articles that treat disabilities as an affliction or cause for pity, or that show the writer does not get that people with disabilities are people like anyone else." **Buys 36 mss/year.** Query. "All queries should be submitted electronically to lifeinaction@unitedspinal.org in MS Word or a compatible program." Length: 800-1,600 words. **Pays $200-400.**

COLUMNS/DEPARTMENTS Travel (report on access of a single travel destination based on conversations with disabled travelers), Access (hands-on look at how to improve access for a specific type of area), Ask Anything (tap members and experts to answer community question relating to life w/SCI/D), Advocacy (investigation of ongoing advocacy issue related to SCI/D). **Buys 40 mss/year.** Length: 800 words. Query with published clips. **Pays $200.**

⊙⊙ LION

Lions Clubs International, 300 W. 22nd St., Oak Brook IL 60523-8842. **Fax:** (630)571-1685. **E-mail:** magazine@lionsclubs.org. **Website:** www.lionsclubs.org. **Contact:** Jay Copp, senior editor. **35% freelance written. Works with a small number of new/unpublished writers each year.** Monthly magazine covering service club organization for Lions Club members and their families. Estab. 1918. Circ. 490,000. Byline given. Pays on acceptance. No kill fee. Publishes ms an average of 5 months after acceptance. Accepts queries by mail, e-mail, fax, phone. Responds in 1 month to queries. Sample copy and writer's guidelines free.

NONFICTION Needs photo feature, must be of a Lions Club service project, informational (issues of interest to civic-minded individuals). No travel, biography, or personal experiences. **Buys 40 mss/year.** "Article length should not exceed 2,000 words, and is subject to editing. No gags, fillers, quizzes or poems are accepted. Photos must be color prints or sent digitally. *LION* magazine pays upon acceptance of material. Advance queries save your time and ours. Address all submissions to Jay Copp, senior editor, by mail or e-mail text and .tif or .jpg (300 dpi) photos." Length: 500-2,000 words. **Pays $100-750.** Sometimes pays expenses of writers on assignment.

⊙⊙ PENN LINES

Pennsylvania Rural Electric Association, 212 Locust St., P.O. Box 1266, Harrisburg PA 17108. **E-mail:** editor@prea.com. **Website:** www.prea.com/content/penn_lines_2012.asp. Monthly magazine covering rural life in Pennsylvania. "News magazine of Pennsylvania electric cooperatives. Features should be balanced, and they should have a rural focus. Electric cooperative sources (such as consumers) should be used." Estab. 1966. Circ. 140,000. Byline given. Pays on publication. No kill fee. Publishes ms an average of 3 months after acceptance. Editorial lead time 4 months. Submit seasonal material 4 months in advance. Accepts queries by mail, e-mail. Sample copy available online.

NONFICTION Needs general interest, historical, how-to, interview, travel; rural PA only. **Buys 6 mss/year.** Query or send complete ms. Length: 500-2,000 words. **Pays $300-650.**

THE ROTARIAN

Rotary International, One Rotary Center, 1560 Sherman Ave., Evanston IL 60201. (847)866-3000. **Fax:** (847)328-8554. **E-mail:** rotarian@rotary.org. **Website:** www.rotary.org. **40% freelance written.** Monthly magazine for Rotarian business and professional men and women and their families, schools, libraries, hospitals, etc. "Articles should appeal to an international audience and in some way help Rotarians help other people. The organization's rationale is one of hope, encouragement, and belief in the power of individuals talking and working together." Estab. 1911. Circ. 510,000. Byline sometimes given. Pays on acceptance. Offers kill fee. Kill fee negotiable. Editorial lead time 4-8 months. Accepts queries by mail, e-mail. YesSample copy for $1 (edbrookc@rotaryintl.org). Guidelines available online.

NONFICTION Needs general interest, humor, inspirational, photo feature, technical, science, travel, lifestyle, sports, business/finance, environmental, health/medicine, social issues. No fiction, religious, or political articles. Query with published clips. Length: 1,500-2,500 words. **Pays negotiable rate.** Answer.

REPRINTS "Send tearsheet, photocopy or typed ms with rights for sale noted and information about when and where the material previously appeared." Negotiates payment.

COLUMNS/DEPARTMENTS Health; Management; Finance; Travel, all 550-900 words. Query.

⑤⑤⑤ SCOUTING

Boy Scouts of America, 1325 W. Walnut Hill Lane, P.O. Box 152079, Irving TX 75015-2079. **Website:** www.scoutingmagazine.org. **Contact:** John R. Clark, managing editor; Bryan Wendell, senior editor; Gretchen Sparling, associate editor; Linda Lawrence, assistant to the managing editor. **80% freelance written.** Magazine published 6 times/year covering Scouting activities for adult leaders of the Boy Scouts, Cub Scouts, and Venturing. Estab. 1913. Circ. 1 million. Byline given. Pays on acceptance for major features and some shorter features. Publishes ms an average of 18 months after acceptance. Editorial lead time 1

year. Submit seasonal material 1 year in advance. Accepts queries by mail. Accepts simultaneous submissions. Responds in 3 weeks to queries. Responds in 2 months to mss. Sample copy for $2.50 and 9x12 SAE with 4 first-class stamps, or online. Guidelines available online.

NONFICTION Needs inspirational, interview. **Buys 20-30 mss/year.** "Query with published clips and SASE. A query with a synopsis or outline of a proposed story is essential. Include a SASE. We do not buy fiction or poetry. We purchase first rights unless otherwise specified (purchase does not necessarily guarantee publication). Photos, if of acceptable quality, are usually included in payment for certain assignments. (We normally assign professional photographers to take photographs for major story assignments.) Writers or photographers should be familiar with the Scouting program and *Scouting* magazine." Length: short features, 500-700 words; some longer features, up to 1,200 words, usually the result of a definite assignment to a professional writer. **Pays $650-800 for major articles, $300-500 for shorter features. Rates depend on professional quality an article.** Pays expenses of writers on assignment.

REPRINTS Send photocopy of article and information about when and where the article previously appeared. First-person accounts of meaningful Scouting experiences (previously published in local newspapers, etc.) are a popular subject.

COLUMNS/DEPARTMENTS Way It Was (Scouting history), 600-750 words; Family Talk (family—raising kids, etc.), 600-750 words. **Buys 8-12 mss/year.** Query. **Pays $300-500.**

FILLERS Limited to personal accounts of humorous or inspirational Scouting experiences. Needs anecdotes, short humor. **Buys 15-25 mss/year.** Length: 50-150 words. **Pays $25 on publication.**

⑨ ⑤⑤ THE TOASTMASTER

Toastmasters International, P.O. Box 9052, Mission Viejo CA 92690. (949)858-8255. **E-mail:** submissions@toastmasters.org. **Website:** www.toastmasters.org. **Contact:** Suzanne Frey, editor; Susan Campbell, graphic design manager. **50% freelance written.** Monthly magazine on public speaking, leadership, and club concerns. "This magazine is sent to members of Toastmasters International, a nonprofit educational association of men and women throughout the world who are interested in developing their communication and leadership skills. Members range from novice to professional speakers and from a wide variety of ethnic and cultural backgrounds, as Toastmasters is an international organization." Estab. 1933. Circ. 235,000 in 11,700 clubs worldwide. Byline given. Pays on acceptance. No kill fee. Publishes ms an average of 1 year after acceptance. Submit seasonal material 3-4 months in advance. Accepts queries by mail, e-mail. Accepts simultaneous submissions. Responds in 6-8 weeks to queries. Sample copy for 9x12 SASE with 4 first-class stamps. Guidelines available online.

NONFICTION Needs how-to, humor, interview, well-known speakers and leaders, communications, leadership, language use. **Buys 50 mss/year.** "Please read our guidelines first, then when you are ready, submit through e-mail. Query with published clips." Length: 700-1,800 words. **"Compensation for accepted articles depends on whether our submission guidelines are followed, the amount of research involved, and the article's general value to us."** Sometimes pays expenses of writers on assignment.

REPRINTS Send typed ms with rights for sale noted and information about when and where the material previously appeared. Pays 50-70% of amount paid for an original article.

$ TRAIL & TIMBERLINE

The Colorado Mountain Club, 710 10th St., Suite 200, Golden CO 80401. (303)996-2745. **Fax:** (303)279-3080. **E-mail:** editor@cmc.org. **Website:** http://cmc.org/tnt/Home.aspx. **Contact:** Editor. **80% freelance written.** Official quarterly publication for the Colorado Mountain Club. "Articles in *Trail & Timberline* conform to the mission statement of the Colorado Mountain Club to unite the energy, interest, and knowledge of lovers of the Colorado mountains, to collect and disseminate information 'regarding the Colorado mountains in the areas of art, science, literature and recreaetion,' to stimulate public interest, and to encourage preservation of the mountains of Colorado and the Rocky Mountain region." Estab. 1918. Circ. 10,500. Byline given. Pays on acceptance. No kill fee. Publishes ms an average of 2 months after acceptance. Editorial lead time 6 months. Submit seasonal material 6 months in advance. Accepts queries by mail, e-mail. Responds in 1 week to queries. Responds in 1 month to mss. Sample copy for $5. Guidelines available online.

NONFICTION Needs essays, humor, opinion, Switchbacks, personal experience, photo feature, travel, trip reports. **Buys 10-15 mss/year.** Send complete ms. Length: 500-2,000 words. **Pays $50.**

POETRY Needs avant-garde, free verse, traditional. Buys 6-12 poems/year. **Pays $50.**

$$$ VFW MAGAZINE

Veterans of Foreign Wars of the United States, 406 W. 34th St., Suite 523, Kansas City MO 64111. (816)756-3390. **Fax:** (816)968-1169. **E-mail:** magazine@vfw.org. **Website:** www.vfwmagazine.org. Tim Dyhouse, senior editor. **Contact:** Rich Kolb, editor-in-chief. **40% freelance written.** Monthly magazine on veterans' affairs, military history, patriotism, defense, and current events. "*VFW Magazine* goes to its members worldwide, all having served honorably in the armed forces overseas from World War II through the Iraq and Afghanistan Wars." Estab. 1904. Circ. 1.5 million. Byline given. Pays on acceptance. Offers 50% kill fee. Publishes ms 3-6 months after acceptance. Editorial lead time is 6 months. Submit seasonal material 6 months in advance. Accepts queries by mail, e-mail, fax. Responds in 2 months to queries. Sample copy for 9x12 SAE with 5 first-class stamps. Guidelines available by e-mail.

NONFICTION Contact: Richard Kolb. Needs general interest, historical, inspirational. **Buys 25-30 mss/year.** Query with 1-page outline, résumé, and published clips. Length: 1,000-1,500 words. **Pays up to $500-$1,000 maximum for assigned articles; $500-$750 maximum for unsolicited articles.**

ASTROLOGY & NEW AGE

$$ FATE MAGAZINE

Fate Magazine, Inc., P.O. Box 460, Lakeville MN 55044 US. (952)431-2050. **Fax:** (952)891-6091. **E-mail:** submissions@fatemag.com. **Website:** www.fatemag.com. **Contact:** Phyllis Galde, editor-in-chief; David Godwin, managing editor. **75% freelance written.** Covering the paranormal, ghosts, ufos, strange science. "Reports a wide variety of strange and unknown phenomena. We are open to receiving any well-written, well-documented article. Our readers especially like reports of current investigations, experiments, theories, and experiences. See topics on website at http://www.fatemag.com/fatemagold/WritersGuidelines.pdf." Estab. 1948. Circ. 15,000. Byline given. Pays after publication.

Publishes ms 3-6 months after acceptance. Editorial lead time 3-6 months. Accepts queries by mail, e-mail, fax. Accepts simultaneous submissions. Responds in 1-3 months to queries. Sample copy available for free online, by e-mail. Guidelines available online.

NONFICTION Contact: Editor. Needs general interest, historical, how-to, personal experience, photo feature, technical. "We do not publish poetry, fiction, editorial/opinion pieces, or book-length mss." **Buys 100 mss/year mss/year.** Query. 500-4,000 words **Pays 5¢/word.** Pays with merchandise or ad space if requested.

COLUMNS/DEPARTMENTS Contact: Editor. True Mystic Experiences: Short reader-submitted stories of strange experiences; My Proof of Survival: Short, reader-submitted stories of proof of life after death, 300-1,000 words. Writer should query. **$25**

FILLERS Fillers are especially welcomed and must be be fully authenticated also, and on similar topics. Length: 100-1,000 words. **Pays 5¢/word**

$ WHOLE LIFE TIMES

Whole Life Media, LLC, 23705 Vanowen St., #306, West Hills CA 91307. (877)807-2599. **Fax:** (310)933-1693. **E-mail:** editor@wholelifemagazine.com. **Website:** www.wholelifemagazine.com. Bimonthly regional glossy on holistic living. "*Whole Life Times* relies almost entirely on freelance material. We depend on freelancers like you." Open to stories on natural health, alternative healing, green living, sustainable and local food, social responsibility, conscious business, the environment, spirituality and personal growth—anything that deals with a progressive, healthy lifestyle. Estab. 1978. Circ. 42,000 (print); 5,000 (digital). Byline given. Pays within 30-45 days of publication. 50% kill fee on assigned stories. No kill fee to first-time *WLT* writers, or for unsolicited submissions. Publishes ms 2-4 months after acceptance. Accepts queries by e-mail only. Sample copy for $3. Guidelines available online and via e-mail.

NONFICTION Special issues: Healing Arts, Food and Nutrition, Spirituality, New Beginnings, Relationships, Longevity, Arts/Cultures Travel, Vitamins and Supplements, Women's Issues, Sexuality, Science and Metaphysics, eco lifestyle. **Buys 60 mss/year.** Send complete ms. Submissions are accepted via e-mail. Artwork should also be sent via e-mail as hard copies will not be returned. "Queries should be professionally written and show an awareness of current topics of interest in our subject area. We welcome investigative reporting and are happy to see queries that address topics in a political context. We are especially looking for articles on health and nutrition. No regular columns sought. Submissions should be double-spaced in AP style as an attached unformatted MS Word file (.doc). If you do not have Microsoft Word and must e-mail in another program, please also copy and paste your story in the message section of your e-mail." **Payment varies. "*WLT* accepts up to 3 longer stories (800-1,100 words) per issue, and pay ranges from $100-175 depending on topic, research required and writer experience. In addition, we have a number of regular departments that pay $75-150 depending on topic, research required and writer experience. We pay by invoice, so please be sure to submit one, and name the file with your name."**

REPRINTS Rarely publishes reprints.

COLUMNS/DEPARTMENTS Local News, Taste of Health, Yoga & Spirit, Healthy Living, Art & Soul. Length: 750-900 words. Send complete ms. Submissions are accepted via e-mail. Artwork should also be sent via e-mail as hard copies will not be returned. "Queries should be professionally written and show an awareness of current topics of interest in our subject area. We welcome investigative reporting and are happy to see queries that address topics in a political context. We are especially looking for articles on health and nutrition. No regular columns sought. Submissions should be double-spaced in AP style as an attached unformatted MS Word file (.doc). If you do not have Microsoft Word and must e-mail in another program, please also copy and paste your story in the message section of your e-mail. **City of Angels is our FOB section featuring short, newsy blurbs on our coverage topics, generally in the context of Los Angeles. These are generally 350-450 words and pay $25-35 depending on length and topic. This is a great section for writers who are new to us. Back-Words is a 750-word personal essay that often highlights a seminal moment or event in the life of the writer and pays $100. We pay by invoice, so be sure to submit one, and name the file with your name."**

$ WITCHES AND PAGANS

BBI Media, Inc., P.O. Box 687, Forest Grove OR 97116. (888)724-3966. **E-mail:** editor2@bbimedia.

com. **Website:** www.witchesandpagans.com. Quarterly magazine covering paganism, wicca and earth religions. *Witches and Pagans* is dedicated to witches, wiccans, neo-pagans, and various other earth-based, pre-Christian, shamanic, and magical practitioners. We hope to reach not only those already involved in what we cover, but the curious and completely new as well. Estab. 2002. Circ. 10,000. Byline given. Pays on publication. Editorial lead time 3-4 months. Submit seasonal material 6 months in advance. Accepts queries by mail, e-mail, fax, phone. Responds in 1-2 weeks to queries. Responds in 1 month to mss.

NONFICTION Needs book excerpts, essays, historical, how-to, humor, inspirational, interview, new product, opinion, personal experience, photo feature, religious, travel. Special issues: Features (articles, essays, fiction, interviews, and rituals) should range between 1,000 - 5,000 words. We most often publish items between 1500 - 3000 words; we prefer in-depth coverage to tidbits in most cases, and the upper ranges are usually reserved for lead pieces assigned to specific writers. Send complete ms. "Submit all written material in electronic format. Our first choice is Open Office writer file attachments emailed directly to editor2@bbimedia.com. This e-mail address is being protected from spambots. You need JavaScript enabled to view it; other acceptable file attachment formats include text files and commonly used word processing programs; you may also paste the text of your ms directly into an email message. Use a plain, legible font or typeface large enough to read easily. Sidebars can be 500-1,300 words or so. Reviews have specific lengths and formats, email editor2@bbimedia.com. This e-mail address is being protected from spambots. You need JavaScript enabled to view it ." Length: 1,000-4,000 words.

FICTION Needs adventure, erotica, ethnic, fantasy, historical, horror, humorous, mainstream, mystery, novel concepts, religious, romance, suspense. Avoid gratuitous sex, violence, sentimentality and pagan moralizing. Don't beat our readers with the Rede or the Threefold Law. **Buys 3-4 mss/year.** Send complete ms. Length: 1,000-5,000 words. **Pays 2¢/word minimum.**

POETRY Needs avant-garde, free verse, haiku, light verse, traditional. Submit maximum 3-5 poems.

AUTOMOTIVE AND MOTORCYCLE

$ AMERICAN MOTORCYCLIST

American Motorcyclist Association, 13515 Yarmouth Dr., Pickerington OH 43147. (614)856-1900. **E-mail:** grassroots@ama-cycle.org. **Website:** www.americanmotorcyclist.com. **Contact:** Bill Wood, director of communications; Grant Parsons, managing editor. **10% freelance written.** Monthly magazine for enthusiastic motorcyclists investing considerable time and money in the sport, emphasizing the motorcyclist, not the vehicle. Monthly magazine of the American Motorcyclist Association. Emphasizes people involved in, and events dealing with, all aspects of motorcycling. Readers are "enthusiastic motorcyclists, investing considerable time in road riding or all aspects of the sport." Estab. 1947. Circ. 260,000. Byline given. Pays on publication. No kill fee. Editorial lead time 3 months. Submit seasonal material 4 months in advance. Accepts queries by mail, e-mail. Responds in 5 weeks to queries. Responds in 6 weeks to mss. Sample copy for $1.50. Guidelines free.

NONFICTION Needs interview, with interesting personalities in the world of motorcycling, personal experience, travel. **Buys 8 mss/year.** Send complete ms. Length: 1,000-2,500 words. **Pays minimum $8/published column inch.**

$$ AUTOMOBILE QUARTERLY

Automobile Heritage Publishing & Communications LLC, 800 E. 8th St., New Albany IN 47150. **Fax:** (812)948-2816. **E-mail:** info@autoquarterly.com; tpowell@autoquarterly.com. **Website:** www.autoquarterly.com. **Contact:** Tracy Powell, managing editor. **85% freelance written.** Quarterly magazine covering "automotive history, with excellent photography." Estab. 1962. Circ. 8,000. Byline given. Pays on acceptance. Publishes ms an average of 1 year after acceptance. Editorial lead time 9 months. Responds in 1 month to queries. Responds in 2 months to mss. Sample copy for $19.95.

NONFICTION Needs historical, photo feature, technical, biographies. **Buys 25 mss/year.** Query. Length: 2,500-5,000 words. **Pays approximately 35¢/word or more.** Sometimes pays expenses of writers on assignment.

⊛⊛⊛⊛ AUTOWEEK

Crain Communications, Inc., 1155 Gratiot Ave., Detroit MI 48207. (313)446-6000. **Fax:** (313)446-1027. **Website:** www.autoweek.com. **5% freelance written, most by regular contributors.** *AutoWeek* is a biweekly magazine for auto enthusiasts. Estab. 1958. Circ. 300,000. Byline given. Pays on publication. Publishes ms an average of 1 month after acceptance. Accepts queries by e-mail.

NONFICTION Needs historical, interview. **Buys 5 mss/year.** Query. Length: 100-400 words. **Pays $1/word.**

✆⊛⊛⊛ CANADIAN BIKER MAGAZINE

735 Market St., Victoria BC V8T 2E2 Canada. (250)384-0333. **Fax:** (250)384-1832. **E-mail:** edit@canadianbiker.com. **Website:** www.canadianbiker.com. **65% freelance written.** Magazine covering motorcycling. Estab. 1980. Circ. 20,000. Byline given. Publishes ms an average of 1 year after acceptance. Editorial lead time 3 months. Accepts queries by mail, e-mail, fax, phone. Responds in 6 weeks to queries. Responds in 6 months to mss. Sample copy for $5 or online. Guidelines free.

NONFICTION Needs general interest, historical, how-to, interview, Canadian personalities preferred, new product, technical, travel. **Buys 12 mss/year.** Send complete ms. Length: 500-1,500 words. **Pays $100-200 for assigned articles. Pays $80-150 for unsolicited articles.**

⊘ ⊛⊛⊛⊛ CAR AND DRIVER

Hearst Communications, Inc., 1585 Eisenhower Place, Ann Arbor MI 48108. (734)971-3600. **Fax:** (734)971-9188. **E-mail:** editors@caranddriver.com. **Website:** www.caranddriver.com. **Contact:** Eddie Alterman, editor-in-chief. Monthly magazine for auto enthusiasts; college-educated, professional, median 24-35 years of age. Estab. 1956. Circ. 1,212,555. Byline given. Pays on acceptance. Offers 25% kill fee. Accepts queries by mail, e-mail. Responds in 2 months to queries.

NONFICTION Buys 1 mss/year. Pays maximum $3,000/feature; $750-1,500/short piece. Pays expenses of writers on assignment.

⊛⊛ CLASSIC TRUCKS

Primedia/McMullen Argus Publishing, 1733 Alton Parkway, Irvine CA 92606. **E-mail:** inquiries@automotive.com. **Website:** www.classictrucks.com. Monthly magazine covering classic trucks from the 1930s to 1973. Estab. 1994. Circ. 60,000. Byline given. Pays on publication. Editorial lead time 4 months. Submit seasonal material 4 months in advance. Guidelines free.

NONFICTION Needs how-to, interview, new product, technical, travel. Query. Length: 1,500-5,000 words. **Pays $75-200/page. Pays $100/page maximum for unsolicited articles.**

COLUMNS/DEPARTMENTS Buys 24 mss/year. Query.

⊛⊛⊛ FOUR WHEELER MAGAZINE

831 S. Douglas Street, El Segundo CA 90245. **Website:** www.fourwheeler.com. **20% freelance written. Works with a small number of new/unpublished writers each year.** Monthly magazine covering four-wheel-drive vehicles, back-country driving, competition, and travel adventure. Estab. 1963. Circ. 355,466. Pays on publication. No kill fee. Publishes ms an average of 4 months after acceptance. Submit seasonal material 4 months in advance. Accepts queries by mail.

NONFICTION Query with photos. 1,200-2,000 words; average 4-5 pages when published. **Pays $200-300/feature vehicles; $350-600/travel and adventure; $100-800/technical articles.**

⊘⊛⊛ FRICTION ZONE

44489 Town Center Way, Suite D497, Palm Desert CA 92260. (951)751-0442. **E-mail:** amy@friction-zone.com. **Website:** www.friction-zone.com. **60% freelance written.** Monthly magazine covering motorcycles. Estab. 1999. Circ. 26,000. Byline given. Pays on publication. No kill fee. Publishes ms an average of 1 month after acceptance. Editorial lead time 6 weeks. Submit seasonal material 2 months in advance. Responds in to queries. Sample copy for $4.50 or on website.

NONFICTION Needs general interest, historical, how-to, humor, inspirational, interview, new product, opinion, photo feature, technical, travel, medical (relating to motorcyclists), book reviews (relating to motorcyclists). Does not accept first-person writing. **Buys 1 mss/year.** Query. Length: 1,000-3,000 words. **Pays 20¢/word.** Sometimes pays expenses of writers on assignment.

COLUMNS/DEPARTMENTS Health Zone (health issues relating to motorcyclists); Motorcycle Engines 101 (basic motorcycle mechanics); Road Trip (California destination review including hotel, road, restaurant), all 2,000 words. **Buys 60 mss/year.** Query. **Pays 20¢/word**

FICTION We want stories concerning motorcycling or motorcyclists. No 'first-person' fiction. Query. Length: 1,000-2,000 words. **Pays 20¢/word.**

FILLERS Needs anecdotes, facts, gags, newsbreaks, short humor. Length: 2,000-3,000 words. **Pays 20¢/word**.

⊛⊛ RIDER MAGAZINE

2575 Vista Del Mar Dr., Ventura CA 93001. (805)667-4314. **Fax:** (805)667-4378. **Website:** www.ridermagazine.com. **60% freelance written.** Monthly magazine covering motorcycling. *Rider* serves the all-brand motorcycle lifestyle/enthusiast with a slant toward travel and touring. Estab. 1974. Circ. 127,000. Byline given. Pays on publication. Offers 25% kill fee. Publishes ms an average of 6-12 months after acceptance. Editorial lead time 3 months. Submit seasonal material 6 months in advance. Accepts queries by mail only. Responds in 2 months to queries. Sample copy for $2.95. Guidelines on website.

NONFICTION Needs general interest, historical, how-to, humor, interview, personal experience, travel. Does not want to see fiction or "How I Began Motorcycling" articles. **Buys 40-50 mss/year.** Query. Length: 750-1,800 words. **Pays $150-750.**

COLUMNS/DEPARTMENTS Favorite Rides (short trip), 850-1,100 words. **Buys 12 mss/year.** Query. **Pays $150-750.**

⊛⊛ ROADBIKE

TAM Communications, 1010 Summer St., Stamford CT 06905. (203)425-8777. **Fax:** (203)425-8775. **E-mail:** info@roadbikemag.com. **Website:** www.roadbikemag.com. **40% freelance written.** Monthly magazine covering motorcycling tours, project and custom bikes, products, news, and tech. Estab. 1993. Circ. 50,000. Byline given. Pays on publication. No kill fee. Publishes ms an average of 6 months after acceptance. Editorial lead time 4 months. Submit seasonal material 6 months in advance. Accepts queries by mail, e-mail, fax, online submission form. Guidelines free.

NONFICTION Needs how-to, motorcycle tech, travel, camping, interview, motorcycle related, new product, photo feature, motorcycle events or gathering places with maximum of 1,000 words text, travel. No fiction. **Buys 100 mss/year.** Send complete ms. Length: 1,000-2,500 words. **Pays $15-400.**

FILLERS Needs facts.

⊛⊛ ROAD KING

Parthenon Publishing, 102 Woodmount Blvd., Suite 450, Nashville TN 37205. **Website:** www.roadking.com. **25% freelance written.** Bimonthly magazine covering the trucking industry. Byline given. Pays 3 weeks from acceptance. Offers 30% kill fee. Publishes ms an average of 3 months after acceptance. Editorial lead time 3-4 months. Submit seasonal material 4 months in advance. Accepts queries by mail. Accepts simultaneous submissions. Responds in 3-4 weeks to queries. Sample copy for #10 SASE. Guidelines free.

NONFICTION No essays, no humor, no cartoons. **Buys 12 mss/year.** Query with published clips. Length: 100-1,000 words. **Pays $50-500.**

⊛ TRUCKIN' MAGAZINE

Source Interlink Media, Inc., 1733 Alton Parkway, Irvine CA 92606. **E-mail:** inquiries@automotive.com. **Website:** www.truckinweb.com. Monthly magazine. Written for pickup drivers and enthusiasts. Circ. 186,606. No kill fee. Editorial lead time 3 months.

NONFICTION Query first. Submit through mail.

AVIATION

⊛⊛⊛⊛ AIR & SPACE MAGAZINE

Smithsonian Institution, P.O. Box 37012, MRC 951, Washington DC 20013. (202)633-6070. **Fax:** (202)633-6085. **E-mail:** editors@si.edu. **Website:** www.airspacemag.com. **80% freelance written.** Bimonthly magazine covering aviation and aerospace for a nontechnical audience. 'Emphasizes the human rather than the technological, on the ideas behind the events. Features are slanted to a technically curious, but not necessarily technically knowledgeable, audience. We are looking for unique angles to aviation/aerospace stories, history, events, personalities, current and future technologies, that emphasize the human-interest aspect." Estab. 1985. Circ. 225,000. Byline given. Pays on acceptance. Offers kill fee. Accepts queries by mail, e-mail, fax. Responds in 3 months to queries. Sample copy for $7. Guidelines available online.

NONFICTION Needs book excerpts, essays, general interest, on aviation/aerospace, historical, humor, photo feature, technical. **Buys 50 mss/year.** Query with published clips. Length: 1,500-3,000 words. **Pays $1,500-3,000.** Pays expenses of writers on assignment.

COLUMNS/DEPARTMENTS Above and Beyond (first person), 1,500-2,000 words; Flights and Fancy (whimsy), approximately 800 words. Soundings (brief items, timely but not breaking news), 500-700 words. **Buys 25 mss/year.** Query with published clips. **Pays $150-300.**

AVIATION HISTORY

Weider History Group, 19300 Promenade Dr., Leesburg VA 20176. **E-mail:** aviationhistory@weiderhistorygroup.com. **Website:** www.thehistorynet.com. **95% freelance written.** Bimonthly magazine covering military and civilian aviation from first flight to the jet age. "It aims to make aeronautical history not only factually accurate and complete, but also enjoyable to a varied subscriber and newsstand audience." Estab. 1990. Circ. 45,000. Byline given. Pays on publication. No kill fee. Publishes ms an average of 2 years after acceptance. Editorial lead time 6 months. Submit seasonal material 1 year in advance. Accepts queries by mail, e-mail, fax. Accepts simultaneous submissions. Responds in 2 months to queries. Responds in 3 months to mss. Sample copy for $5. Guidelines with #10 SASE or online.

NONFICTION Needs historical, interview, personal experience. **Buys 24 mss/year.** Query. Feature articles should be 3,000-3,500 words, each with a 500-word sidebar where appropriate, author's biography, and book suggestions for further reading **Pays $300.**

COLUMNS/DEPARTMENTS Aviators, Restored, Extremes all 1,500 words or less. Pays $150 and up. Book reviews, 250-500 words, pays minimum $50.

CESSNA OWNER MAGAZINE

Jones Publishing, Inc., N7528 Aanstad Rd., Iola WI 54945. (715)445-5000. **Fax:** (715)445-4053. **E-mail:** editor@cessnaowner.org. **Website:** www.cessnaowner.org. **50% freelance written.** Monthly magazine covering Cessna single and twin-engine aircraft. "*Cessna Owner Magazine* is the official publication of the Cessna Owner Organization (C.O.O.). Therefore, our readers are Cessna aircraft owners, renters, pilots, and enthusiasts. Articles should deal with buying/selling, flying, maintaining, or modifying Cessnas. The purpose of our magazine is to promote safe, fun, and affordable flying." Estab. 1975. Circ. 6,000. Byline given. Pays on publication. No kill fee. Publishes ms an average of 3 months after acceptance. Accepts queries by mail, e-mail. Responds in 2 weeks to queries. Responds in 1 month to mss.

NONFICTION Needs historical of specific Cessna models, how-to, aircraft repairs and maintenance, new product, personal experience, photo feature, technical, aircraft engines and airframes. Special issues: Engines (maintenance, upgrades); Avionics (purchasing, new products). **Buys 48 mss/year.** Query. Length: 1,500-2,000 words. **Pays 12¢/word.**

REPRINTS Send mss via e-mail with rights for sale noted and information about when and where the material previously appeared.

FLIGHT JOURNAL

Air Age Media, 88 Danbury Rd., Rte. 7, Wilton CT 06897. (203)529-4630. **Fax:** (203)529-3010. **E-mail:** flightjournal@airage.com. **Website:** www.flightjournal.com. Bimonthly magazine covering aviation-oriented material, for the most part with a historical overtone, but also with some modern history in the making reporting. "*Flight Journal* is like no other aviation magazine in the world, covering the world of flight from its simple beginnings to its high-tech, no-holds-barred future. We put readers in the cockpit and let them live the thrill and adventure of the aviation experience, narrated by those who know the technology and made the history. Each issue brings the stories of flight--past, present and future--to life." No kill fee. Accepts queries by mail, e-mail. Guidelines available.

NONFICTION Needs exposé, historical, humor, interview, new product, personal experience, photo feature, technical. "We do not want any general aviation articles as in 'My Flight to Baja in my 172,' nor detailed recitations of the technical capabilities of an aircraft. Avoid historically accurate but bland chronologies of events." Length: 2,500-3,000 words. Lengthier pieces should be discussed in advance with the editors. **Pays $600.**

FLYING ADVENTURES

Aviation Publishing Corporation, El Monte Airport (EMT), P.O. Box 93613, Pasadena CA 91109-3613. (626)618-4000. **E-mail:** editor@flyingadventures.com; info@flyingadventures.com. **Website:** www.flyingadventures.com. **20% freelance written.** Bimonthly magazine covering lifestyle travel for owners and passengers of private aircraft. "Our articles cover upscale travelers." Estab. 1994. Circ. 135,858. Byline given for features. Pays on acceptance. No kill fee. Editorial lead time 2 weeks to 2 months. Accepts queries by e-mail. Accepts simultaneous submissions. Responds immediately. Sample copy and guidelines free.

NONFICTION Needs travel, lifestyle. "Nothing non-relevant or not our style. See magazine." Query with published clips. Length: 500-1,500 words. **Pays $150-300 for assigned and unsolicited articles.** Sometimes pays expenses of writers on assignment.

COLUMNS/DEPARTMENTS Contact: Editor. "Numerous departments; see magazine." **Buys 100+ mss/year.** Query with published clips. **Pays $-$150.**

🖙🖙 PIPERS MAGAZINE

Jones Publishing, Inc., N7450 Aanstad Rd., Iola WI 54945. (866)697-4737. **Website:** www.piperowner.org. **50% freelance written.** Monthly magazine covering Piper single and twin engine aircraft. *Pipers Magazine* is the official publication of the Piper Owner Society (P.O.S). Therefore, our readers are Piper aircraft owners, renters, pilots, mechanics, and enthusiasts. Articles should deal with buying/selling, flying, maintaining, or modifying Pipers. The purpose of our magazine is to promote safe, fun and affordable flying. Estab. 1988. Circ. 5,000. Pays on publication. Publishes ms an average of 3 months after acceptance. Editorial lead time 1 month. Submit seasonal material 3 months in advance. Accepts queries by mail, e-mail, fax, phone. Responds in 2 weeks to queries. Responds in 1 month to mss. Sample copy free. Guidelines free.

NONFICTION Needs historical, of specific models of Pipers, how-to, aircraft repairs and maintenance, new product, personal experience, photo feature, technical, aircraft engines and airframes. **Buys 48 mss/year.** Query. Length: 1,500-2,000 words. **Pays 12¢/word.**

REPRINTS Send mss by e-mail with rights for sale noted and information about when and where the material previously appeared.

BUSINESS AND FINANCE

BUSINESS NATIONAL

🖙🖙🖙🖙 CORPORATE BOARD MEMBER

Board Member Inc., 5110 Maryland Way, Suite 250, Brentwood TN 37027. **Fax:** (615)371-0899. **E-mail:** boardmember@boardmember.com. **Website:** www. boardmember.com. **100% freelance written.** Bimonthly magazine covering corporate governance. "Our readers are the directors and top executives of publicly-held US corporations. We look for detailed and preferably narrative stories about how individual boards have dealt with the challenges that face them

on a daily basis: reforms, shareholder suits, CEO pay, firing and hiring CEOs, setting up new boards, firing useless directors. We're happy to light fires under the feet of boards that are asleep at the switch. We also do service-type pieces, written in the second person, advising directors about new wrinkles in disclosure laws, for example." Estab. 1999. Circ. 60,000. Byline given. Pays on acceptance. Offers 25% kill fee. Publishes ms an average of 3 months after acceptance. Editorial lead time 4-5 months. Submit seasonal material 4-5 months in advance. Accepts queries by e-mail. Responds in 1 week to queries. Responds in 1 week to mss. Sample copy available online. Guidelines by e-mail.

NONFICTION Special issues: Best Law Firms in America (July/August); What Directors Think (November/December). Does not want views from 35,000 feet, pontification, opinion, humor, anything devoid of reporting. **Buys 100 mss/year.** Query. Length: 650-2,500 words. **Pays $1,200-5,000.** Pays expenses of writers on assignment.

🖙🖙 DOLLARS & SENSE: THE MAGAZINE OF ECONOMIC JUSTICE

Economic Affairs Bureau, Inc., One Milk St., 5th Floor, Boston MA 02109. (617)447-2177. **Fax:** (617)477-2179. **E-mail:** dollars@dollarsandsense.org. **Website:** www.dollarsandsense.org. **10% freelance written.** Bimonthly magazine covering economic, environmental, and social justice. "We explain the workings of the US and international economics, and provide left perspectives on current economic affairs. Our audience is a mix of activists, organizers, academics, unionists, and other socially concerned people." Estab. 1974. Circ. 8,000. Byline given. Pays on publication. No kill fee. Publishes ms an average of 4 months after acceptance. Editorial lead time 3 months. Submit seasonal material 2 months in advance. Accepts queries by mail, e-mail (preferred). Sample copy for $5 or on website. Guidelines available on website.

NONFICTION Needs exposé, political economics. **Buys 6 mss/year.** Query with published clips. Length: 250-3,000 words. **Pays $0-200.** Sometimes pays expenses of writers on assignment.

🖙🖙 ENTREPRENEUR MAGAZINE

Entrepreneur Media Inc., 2445 McCabe Way, Suite 400, Irvine CA 92614. (949)261-2325. **E-mail:** queries@entrepreneur.com. **Website:** www.entrepreneur. com. **60% freelance written.** *"Entrepreneur* readers already run their own businesses. They have been in business for several years and are seeking innovative methods and strategies to improve their business operations. They are also interested in new business ideas and opportunities, as well as current issues that affect their companies." Circ. 600,000. Byline given. Pays on acceptance. No kill fee. Publishes ms an average of 5 months after acceptance. Submit seasonal material 6 months in advance. Accepts queries by e-mail. Responds in 3 months to queries. Sample copy for $7.20. Guidelines available at /www.entrepreneur.com/entmagwg.html.

NONFICTION Needs how-to, information on running a business, dealing with the psychological aspects of running a business, profiles of unique entrepreneurs, current news/trends (and their effect on small business). **Buys 10-20 mss/year.** Query with published clips. Length: 1,800 words. **Payment varies.**

COLUMNS/DEPARTMENTS Snapshots (profiles of interesting entrepreneurs who exemplify innovation in their marketing/sales technique, financing method or management style, or who have developed an innovative product/service or technology); Money Smarts (financial management); Marketing Smarts; Web Smarts (Internet news); Tech Smarts; Management Smarts; Viewpoint (first-person essay on entrepreneurship), all 300 words. **Pays $1/word.**

⊘ FORTUNE

Time, Inc., 1271 Avenue of the Americas, New York NY 10020. (212)522-1212. **Fax:** (212)522-0810. **E-mail:** letters@fortune.com. **Website:** www.fortune.com. Andrew Serwer, managing editor. Biweekly magazine covering business and finance. Edited primarily for high-demographic business people. Specializes in big stories about companies, business personalities, technology, managing, Wall Street, media, marketing, personal finance, politics, and policy. Circ. 1,066,000. No kill fee. Editorial lead time 6 weeks.

⊛⊛⊛⊛ HISPANIC BUSINESS

Hispanic Business, Inc., 5385 Hollister Ave., Suite 204, Santa Barbara CA 93111. (800)806-4268. **Fax:** (805)964-5539. **Website:** www.hispanicbusiness.com. **40-50% freelance written.** Monthly magazine covering Hispanic business. For more than 2 decades, *Hispanic Business* magazine has documented the growing affluence and power of the Hispanic community. Our magazine reaches the most educated, affluent Hispanic business and community leaders. Stories should

have relevance for the Hispanic business community. Estab. 1979. Circ. 220,000 (rate base); 990,000 (readership base). Byline given. Pays on publication. Offers 50% kill fee. Publishes ms an average of 1 month after acceptance. Editorial lead time 1-3 months. Submit seasonal material 2 months in advance. Accepts queries by mail. Accepts simultaneous submissions. Responds in 3 weeks to queries. Responds in 1 month to mss. Sample copy free.

NONFICTION Needs interview, travel. **Buys 120 mss/year.** Query résumé and published clips. Length: 650-2,000 words. **Pays $50-1,500.** Sometimes pays expenses of writers on assignment.

COLUMNS/DEPARTMENTS Tech Pulse (technology); Money Matters (financial), both 800 words. **Buys 40 mss/year.** Query with résumé and published clips. **Pays $50-450.**

⊛⊛⊛ MYBUSINESS MAGAZINE

Imagination Publishing, 600 W. Fulton St., 6th Floor, Chicago IL 60661. (615)872-5800; (800)634-2669). **E-mail:** nfib@imaginepub.com. **Website:** www.mybusinessmag.com. **75% freelance written.** Bimonthly magazine for small businesses. "We are a guide to small business success, however that is defined in the new small business economy. We explore the methods and minds behind the trends and celebrate the men and women leading the creation of the new small business economy." Estab. 1999. Circ. 100,000. Byline given. Pays on publication. Offers 30% kill fee. Publishes ms an average of 4 months after acceptance. Editorial lead time 4-6 months. Submit seasonal material 5 months in advance. Accepts queries by e-mail. Accepts simultaneous submissions. Responds in 3 weeks to queries. Sample copy free. Guidelines available online.

NONFICTION Needs how-to, new product. **Buys 8 mss/year.** "Query with résumé and 2 published clips. We accept pitches for feature stories, which fall under 1 of 3 categories: Own, Operate, and Grow. Story ideas should be small-business focused, with an emphasis on timely problems that small business owners face and real, workable solutions. Trend pieces are also of interest. Copy should be submitted as a Microsoft Word enclosure. Deadlines are 90 days before publication." Length: 200-1,800 words. **Pays $75-1,000.**

⊛⊛ THE NETWORK JOURNAL

The Network Journal Communication, 39 Broadway, Suite 2430, New York NY 10006. (212)962-3791. **Fax:**

(212)962-3537. **E-mail:** tnjeditors@tnj.com. **Website:** www.tnj.com. **25% freelance written.** Monthly magazine covering business and career articles. *The Network Journal* caters to black professionals and small-business owners, providing quality coverage on business, financial, technology and career news germane to the black community. Estab. 1993. Circ. 25,000. Byline given. Pays on publication. Editorial lead time 2 months. Submit seasonal material 3 months in advance. Accepts queries by mail, e-mail, fax, phone. Accepts simultaneous submissions. Sample copy for $1 or online. Writer's guidelines for SASE or online.

NONFICTION Needs how-to, interview. Send complete ms. Length: 1,200-1,500 words. **Pays $150-200.** Sometimes pays expenses of writers on assignment.

COLUMNS/DEPARTMENTS Book reviews, 700-800 words; career management and small business development, 800 words. **Pays $100.**

🍁 ◐ $$$$ PROFIT

Rogers Media, 1 Mt. Pleasant Rd., 11th Floor, Toronto ON M4Y 2Y5 Canada. (416)764-1402. **Fax:** (416)764-1404. **Website:** www.profitguide.com. **80% freelance written.** Magazine published 6 times/year covering small and medium businesses. "We specialize in specific, useful information that helps our readers manage their businesses better. We want Canadian stories only." Estab. 1982. Circ. 110,000. Byline given. Pays on acceptance. Offers variable kill fee. Publishes ms an average of 2 months after acceptance. Submit seasonal material 6 months in advance. Accepts queries by mail, fax, phone. Responds in 1 month to queries. Responds in 6 weeks to mss. Sample copy for 9x12 SAE with 84¢ postage. Guidelines free.

NONFICTION Needs how-to, business management tips, strategies and Canadian business profiles. **Buys 50 mss/year.** Query with published clips. Length: 800-2,000 words. **Pays $500-2,000.** Pays expenses of writers on assignment.

COLUMNS/DEPARTMENTS Finance (info on raising capital in Canada), 700 words; Marketing (marketing strategies for independent business), 700 words. **Buys 80 mss/year.** Query with published clips. **Pays $150-600.**

$$ TECHNICAL ANALYSIS OF STOCKS & COMMODITIES

4757 California Ave. SW, Seattle WA 98116. (206)938-0570. **E-mail:** editor@traders.com. **Website:** www.traders.com. **Contact:** Jayanthi Gopalakrishnan, editor; Christine Morrison, art director; Elizabeth M.S. Flynn, managing editor. **90% freelance written.** "Magazine covers methods of investing and trading stocks, bonds and commodities (futures), options, mutual funds, and precious metals using technical analysis." Estab. 1982. Circ. 60,000. Byline given. Pays on publication. No kill fee. Publishes ms an average of 4 months after acceptance. Responds in 2 months to queries. Sample copy for $5. Guidelines available online.

NONFICTION Needs how-to, trade, technical, cartoons, trading and software aids to trading, Product reviews, utilities, real-world trading (actual case studies of trades and their results). No newsletter-type, buy-sell recommendations. The article subject must relate to technical analysis, charting or a numerical technique used to trade securities or futures. Almost universally requires graphics with every article. **Buys 150 mss/year.** Send complete ms. Length: 1,000-4,000 words. **Pays $100-500.**

REPRINTS Send tearsheet with rights for sale noted and information about when and where the material previously appeared.

COLUMNS/DEPARTMENTS Length: 800-1,600 words. **Buys 100 columns. mss/year.** Query. **Pays $50-300**

FILLERS Contact: Karen Wasserman, fillers editor. "Must relate to trading stocks, bonds, options, mutual funds, commodities, or precious metals." **Buys 20 fillers. mss/year.** Length: 500 words. **Pays $20-50.**

BUSINESS REGIONAL

$$ ALASKA BUSINESS MONTHLY

Alaska Business Publishing, 501 W. Northern Lights Blvd., Suite 100, Anchorage AK 99503-2577. (907)276-4373. **Fax:** (907)279-2900. **E-mail:** editor@akbizmag.com. **Website:** www.akbizmag.com. **Contact:** Susan Harrington, managing editor. **75% freelance written.** "Our audience is Alaska businessmen and businesswomen who rely on us for timely features and up-to-date information about doing business in Alaska." Estab. 1985. Circ. 12,000-15,000. Byline given. Pays on publication. Offers $50 kill fee. Publishes ms an average of 2 months after acceptance. Assignments are due 2 months before date published. Editorial lead time 3-6 months. Submit seasonal material 6 months in advance. Accepts queries by e-mail, online submission form. Responds in 1 month to queries. Order sample copy through website store or download off website under "archives." Guidelines online.

NONFICTION Needs Alaska-centric, profiles of leaders, thought-provoking articles about the economy, companies and projects in all economic sectors of Alaska. Special issues: "A different industry is featured each month in a special section. Read our magazine and editorial calendar for an idea of the material we assign." No fiction, poetry, or anything not pertinent to Alaska business. Rarely uses any unsolicited or unassigned articles. **Buys approximately 200 mss/year.** Send query and half a dozen clips of previously published articles. Do not send complete mss. Length: 500-1,800 words. **Pays $100-350 for assigned articles.**

☼ ❸❸❸❸ ALBERTA VENTURE

Venture Publishing Inc., 10259–105 St., Edmonton AB T5J 1E3 Canada. (780)990-0839. **E-mail:** admin@albertaventure.com. **Website:** www.albertaventure.com. **70% freelance written.** Monthly magazine covering business in Alberta. "Our readers are mostly business owners and managers in Alberta who read the magazine to keep up with trends and run their businesses better." Estab. 1997. Circ. 35,000. Byline given. Pays on publication. Offers 30% kill fee. Publishes ms an average of 2 months after acceptance. Editorial lead time 3 months. Submit seasonal material 3 months in advance. Accepts queries by e-mail. Responds in 2 weeks to queries. Sample copy available online. Guidelines by e-mail.

NONFICTION Needs how-to, business narrative related to Alberta. Does not want company or product profiles. **Buys 75 mss/year.** Query. Length: 1,000-3,000 words. **Pays $300-2,000 (Canadian).** Pays expenses of writers on assignment.

☼ ❸❸ ATLANTIC BUSINESS MAGAZINE

Communications Ten, Ltd., P.O. Box 2356, Station C, St. John's NL A1C 6E7 Canada. (709)726-9300. **Fax:** (709)726-3013. **E-mail:** dchafe@atlanticbusinessmagazine.com. **Website:** www.atlanticbusinessmagazine.com. **Contact:** Dawn Chafe, editor. **80% freelance written.** Bimonthly magazine covering business in Atlantic Canada. "We discuss positive business developments, emphasizing that the 4 Atlantic provinces are a great place to do business." Estab. 1989. Circ. 30,000. Byline given. Pays within 30 days of publication. No kill fee. Publishes ms an average of 2 months after acceptance. Editorial lead time 6 months. Ac-

cepts queries by mail, e-mail, fax. Sample copy free. Guidelines available on website.

NONFICTION Needs exposé, general interest, interview, new product. "We don't want religious, technical, or scholarly material. We are not an academic magazine. We are interested only in stories concerning business topics specific to the 4 Canadian provinces of Nova Scotia, New Brunswick, Prince Edward Island, and Newfoundland and Labrador." **Buys 36 mss/year.** Query with published clips. Length: 1,000-1,200 words for features; 3,500-4,000 for cover stories. **Pays 40¢/word.** Sometimes pays expenses of writers on assignment.

COLUMNS/DEPARTMENTS Query with published gested story ideas."

❸❸ CINCY MAGAZINE

Great Lakes Publishing Co., Cincinnati Club Building, 30 Garfield Place, Suite 440, Cincinnati OH 45202. (513)421-2533. **Fax:** (513)421-2542. **E-mail:** dgebhardt-french@cincymagazine.com. **Website:** www.cincymagazine.com. **Contact:** Dianne Gebhardt-French, editor; Tim Curtis, managing editor. **80% freelance written.** Glossy bimonthly color magazine written for business professionals in Greater Cincinnati, published 10 times annually. *Cincy* is written and designed for the interests of business professionals and executives both at work and away from work, with features, trend stories, news and opinions related to business, along with lifestyle articles on home, dining, shopping, travel, health and more. Estab. 2003. Circ. 15,300. Byline given. Pays on publication. Offers 100% kill fee. Publishes ms an average of 3 months after acceptance. Editorial lead time 1-3 months. Submit seasonal material 4 months in advance. Accepts queries by mail, e-mail.

NONFICTION Needs general interest, interview. Does not want stock advice. Length: 200-2,000 words. **Pays $75-600.**

❸❸❸ COLORADOBIZ

6160 S. Syracuse Way, #300, Greenwood Village CO 80111. (303)662-5200. **E-mail:** mtaylor@cobizmag.com. **Website:** www.cobizmag.com. **Contact:** Mike Taylor, managing editor. **70% freelance written.** "*ColoradoBiz* is a monthly magazine that covers people, issues and trends statewide for a sophisticated audience of business owners and executives." Estab. 1973. Circ. 20,000+. Byline given. Pays on publication. Publishes ms 2 months after acceptance. Editorial lead time is

2-3 months. Submit seasonal material 3 months in advance. Accepts queries by e-mail. Responds in 2 weeks to queries. Sample copy available for $2.95 with SASE. Writer's guidelines free online.

NONFICTION Needs book excerpts, exposé, technical, Colorado business. Special issues: Minority business. Does not want humor, first-person, self-promotional. **Buys up to 100 mss/year mss/year.** Query with published clips. Length: 300-3,000 words. Sometimes pays expenses of writers on assignment.

COLUMNS/DEPARTMENTS State of the State, 150 to 300 word briefs on Colorado business issues. Query.

⊜ ⊜ CORPORATE CONNECTICUT MAGAZINE

Corporate World LLC, P.O. Box 290726, Wethersfield CT 06129. **Fax:** (860)257-1924. **E-mail:** editor@corpct.com. **Website:** www.corpct.com. **50% freelance written.** Quarterly magazine covering regional reporting, global coverage of corporate/business leaders, entrepreneurs. *Corporate Connecticut* is devoted to people who make business happen in the private sector and who create innovative change across public arenas. Centered in the Northeast between New York and Boston, Connecticut is positioned in a coastal corridor with a dense affluent population who are highly mobile, accomplished and educated. Estab. 2001. Byline given. Pays on publication. Offers 25% kill fee. Publishes ms an average of 2-3 months after acceptance. Editorial lead time 3-6 months. Submit seasonal material 10-12 months in advance. Accepts queries by mail, e-mail. Responds in 2 weeks to queries. Sample copy for #10 SASE.

NONFICTION Query with published clips. **Pays 35¢/ word minimum with varying fees for excellence.**

⊜ CRAIN'S DETROIT BUSINESS

Crain Communications, Inc., 1155 Gratiot, Detroit MI 48207. (313)446-0419. **Fax:** (313)446-1687. **E-mail:** kcrain@crain.com. **Website:** www.crainsdetroit.com. **10% freelance written.** Weekly tabloid covering business in the Detroit metropolitan area—specifically Wayne, Oakland, Macomb, Washtenaw, and Livingston counties. Estab. 1985. Circ. 150,000. Byline given. Pays on publication. No kill fee. Publishes ms an average of 1 month after acceptance. Accepts queries by mail, e-mail. Sample copy for $1.50. Guidelines available online.

NONFICTION Needs new product, technical, business. **Buys 20 mss/year.** Query with published clips.

30-40 words/column inch **Pays $10-15/column inch.** Pays expenses of writers on assignment.

⊜ ⊜ INGRAM'S

Show-Me Publishing, Inc., P.O. Box 411356, Kansas City MO 64141. (816)842-9994. **Fax:** (816)474-1111. **E-mail:** editorial@ingramsonline.com. **Website:** www. ingramsonline.com. **Contact:** Joe Sweeney, editor-in-chief and publisher. **10% freelance written.** Monthly magazine covering Kansas City business and economic development. *"Ingram's* readers are top-level corporate executives and community leaders, officials and decision makers. Our editorial content must provide such readers with timely, relevant information and insights."* Estab. 1975. Circ. 105,000. Byline given. Pays on publication. No kill fee. Publishes ms an average of 1 month after acceptance. Editorial lead time 1 month. Submit seasonal material 5 months in advance. Accepts queries by e-mail. Sample copy free.

NONFICTION Needs interview, technical. Does not want humor, inspirational, or anything not related to Kansas City business. **Buys 4-6 mss/year.** Query. Length: 500-1,500 words. **Pays $75-200 depending on research/feature length.** Sometimes pays expenses of writers on assignment.

COLUMNS/DEPARTMENTS Say So (opinion), 1,500 words. **Buys 12 mss/year. Pays $75-100 maximum.**

⊜ MERCER BUSINESS MAGAZINE

2550 Kuser Rd., Trenton NJ 08691. (609)586-2056. **Fax:** (609)586-8052. **E-mail:** maggih@mercerbusiness.com. **Website:** www.mercerbusiness.com. **Contact:** Maggi Hill, managing editor. **100% freelance written.** Monthly magazine covering national and local business-related, theme-based topics. *Mercer Business* is a Chamber of Commerce publication, so the slant is pro-business primarily. Also covers nonprofits, education and other related issues. Estab. 1924. Circ. 8,500. Byline given. Pays on publication. Publishes ms an average of 1 month after acceptance. Editorial lead time 6 weeks. Submit seasonal material 6 weeks in advance. Accepts queries by e-mail. Accepts simultaneous submissions. Responds in 1 week to queries. Sample copy for #10 SASE. Guidelines by e-mail.

NONFICTION Needs humor. Query with published clips. Length: 1,000-1,800 words. **Pays $150 for assigned articles.** Sometimes pays expenses of writers on assignment.

FILLERS Needs gags. **Buys 24 mss/year.** Length: 300-500 words.

⊘ $$$$ OREGON BUSINESS

MEDIAmerica, Inc., 715 SW Morrison St, Suite 800, Portalnd OR 97205. (503)223-0304. **Fax:** (503)221-6544. **E-mail:** lindab@oregonbusiness.com. **E-mail:** editor@oregonbusiness.com. **Website:** www.oregonbusiness.com. **Contact:** Linda Baker, editor. **15-25% freelance written.** Monthly magazine covering business in Oregon. Our subscribers inlcude owners of small and medium-sized businesses, government agencies, professional staffs of banks, insurance companies, ad agencies, attorneys and other service providers. We accept *only* stories about Oregon businesses, issues and trends. Estab. 1981. Circ. 50,000. Byline given. Pays on publication. No kill fee. Editorial lead time 2 months. Accepts queries by mail, e-mail. Sample copy for $4. Guidelines available online.

NONFICTION Query with résumé and 2-3 published clips. Length: 1,200-3,000 words.

COLUMNS/DEPARTMENTS First Person (opinion piece on an issue related to business), 750 words; Around the State (recent news and trends, and how they might shape the future), 100-600 words; Business Tools (practical, how-to suggestions for business managers and owners), 400-600 words; In Character (profile of interesting or quirky member of the business community), 850 words. Query with résumé and 2-3 published clips.

$$ PACIFIC COAST BUSINESS TIMES

14 E. Carrillo St., Suite A, Santa Barbara CA 93101. (805)560-6950. **E-mail:** hdubroff@pacbiztimes.com. **Website:** www.pacbiztimes.com. **Contact:** Henry Dubroff, founder and editor. **10% freelance written.** Weekly tabloid covering financial news specific to Santa Barbara, Ventura, San Luis Obispo counties in California. Estab. 2000. Circ. 5,000. Byline given. No kill fee. Editorial lead time 1 month. Accepts queries by e-mail, phone. Sample copy free. Guidelines free.

NONFICTION Needs interview, opinion, personal finance. Does not want first person, promo or fluff pieces. **Buys 20 mss/year.** Query. Length: 500-800 words. **Pays $75-175.** Pays expenses of writers on assignment.

COLUMNS/DEPARTMENTS Harvey Mackay (management), 600 words. Query. **Pays $10-50.**

$$ PRAIRIE BUSINESS

Grand Forks (ND), Forum Communications Company, 808 Third Ave., #400, Fargo ND 58103. **Fax:** (701)280-9092. **E-mail:** info@prairiebizmag.com; kbevill@prairiebizmag.com. **Website:** www.prairiebizmag.com. **Contact:** Kris Bevill, editor. **30% freelance written.** Monthly magazine covering business on the Northern Plains (North Dakota, South Dakota, Minnesota). "We attempt to be a resource for business owners/managers, policymakers, educators, and nonprofit administrators, acting as a catalyst for growth in the region by reaching out to an audience of decision makers within the region and also venture capitalists, site selectors, and angel visitors from outside the region." Estab. 2000. Circ. 20,000. Byline given. Pays within 2 weeks of mailing date. No kill fee. Publishes ms an average of 1-2 months after acceptance. Editorial lead time 2 months. Submit seasonal material 2 months in advance. Accepts queries by e-mail. Accepts simultaneous submissions. Responds in 2 weeks to queries. Sample copy free. Guidelines free.

NONFICTION Needs interview, technical, basic online research. "Does not want articles that are blatant self-promotion for any interest without providing value for readers." **Buys 36 mss/year.** Query. Length: 800-1,500 words. **Pays 15¢/word.**

PROVIDENCE BUSINESS NEWS

400 Westminster St., Suite 600, Providence RI 02903. (401)273-2201, ext. 215. **Fax:** (401)274-0670. **E-mail:** murphy@pbn.com. **Website:** www.pbn.com. Business magazine covering news of importance to the Providence area.

💬 Query before submitting.

$ ROCHESTER BUSINESS JOURNAL

Rochester Business Journal, Inc., 45 E. Ave., Suite 500, Rochester NY 14604. (585)546-8303. **Fax:** (585)546-3398. **E-mail:** rbj@rbj.net. **Website:** www.rbj.net. **10% freelance written.** Weekly tabloid covering local business. The *Rochester Business Journal* is geared toward corporate executives and owners of small businesses, bringing them leading-edge business coverage and analysis first in the market. Estab. 1984. Circ. 10,000. Byline given. Pays on publication. No kill fee. Publishes ms an average of 1 month after acceptance. Editorial lead time 6 weeks. Accepts queries by mail, fax. Responds in 1 week to queries. Sample copy for free or by e-mail. Guidelines available online.

NONFICTION Needs how-to, business topics, news features, trend stories with local examples. Do not query about any topics that do not include several local examples—local companies, organizations, universities, etc. **Buys 110 mss/year.** Query with published clips. Length: 1,000-2,000 words. **Pays $150.**

⊚⊚ SMARTCEO MAGAZINE

SmartCEO, 2700 Lighthouse Point E., Suite 220A, Baltimore MD 21224. (410)342-9510. **Fax:** (410)675-5280. **E-mail:** editorial@smartceo.com. **Website:** www.smartceo.com. **25% freelance written.** Monthly magazine covering regional business in the Baltimore, MD and Washington, DC areas. "*SmartCEO* is a regional 'growing company' publication. We are not news; we are a resource full of smart ideas to help educate and inspire decision-makers in the Baltimore and DC areas. Each issue contains features, interviews, case studies, columns and other departments designed to help this region's CEOs face the daily challenges of running a business." Estab. 2001. Circ. 34,000. Byline given. Pays on publication. No kill fee. Publishes ms an average of 2 months after acceptance. Editorial lead time 5 months. Submit seasonal material 5 months in advance. Accepts queries by e-mail, phone. Responds in 4 weeks to queries. Responds in 2 months to mss. Sample copy available online. Guidelines by e-mail.

NONFICTION Needs essays, interview, Business features or tips. "We do not want pitches on CEOs or companies outside the Baltimore, MD or Washington, DC areas; no product reviews, lifestyle content or book reviews, please." **Buys 20 mss/year.** Query. Length: 2,000-5,000 words. **Pays $300-600.** Sometimes pays expenses of writers on assignment.

COLUMNS/DEPARTMENTS Project to Watch (overview of a local development project in progress and why it is of interest to the business community), 600 words; Q&A and tip-focused coverage of business issues and challenges (each article includes the opinions of 10-20 CEOs), 500-1,000 words. **Buys 0-5 mss/year mss/year.** Query.

⊚⊚ THE LANE REPORT

Lane Communications Group, 201 E. Main St., 14th Floor, Lexington KY 40507. (859)244-3500. **Fax:** (859)244-3555. **E-mail:** markgreen@lanereport.com; editorial@lanereport.com. **Website:** www.lanereport.com. **70% freelance written.** Monthly magazine covering statewide business. Estab. 1986. Circ. 15,000. Byline given. Pays on publication. No kill fee. Editorial lead time 6 weeks. Submit seasonal material 3 months in advance. Accepts queries by mail, e-mail, fax. Accepts simultaneous submissions. Responds in 1 month to queries. Sample copy and writer's guidelines free.

NONFICTION Needs essays, interview, new product, photo feature. **Buys 30-40 mss/year.** Query with published clips. Length: 500-2,000 words. **Pays $150-375.** Sometimes pays expenses of writers on assignment.

COLUMNS/DEPARTMENTS Technology and Business in Kentucky; Advertising; Exploring Kentucky; Perspective; Spotlight on the Arts, all less than 1,000 words.

⊚⊚ VERMONT BUSINESS MAGAZINE

365 Dorset St., South Burlington VT 05403. (802)863-8038. **Fax:** (802)863-8069. **Website:** www.vermontbiz.com. **Contact:** Tim McQuiston, editor. **80% freelance written.** Monthly tabloid covering business in Vermont. Circ. 8,000. Byline given. Pays on publication. No kill fee. Publishes ms an average of 1 month after acceptance. Responds in 2 months to queries. Sample copy for SAE with 11x14 envelope and 7 first-class stamps.

NONFICTION **Buys 200 mss/year.** Query with published clips. Length: 800-1,800 words. **Pays $100-200.**

REPRINTS Send tearsheet and information about when and where the material previously appeared.

CAREER, COLLEGE AND ALUMNI

⊚⊚ AFRICAN-AMERICAN CAREER WORLD

Equal Opportunity Publications, Inc., 445 Broad Hollow Rd., Suite 425, Melville NY 11747. (631)421-9421. **Fax:** (631)421-1352. **E-mail:** info@eop.com. **Website:** www.eop.com. **60% freelance written.** Semiannual magazine focused on African-American students and professionals in all disciplines. Estab. 1969. Byline given. Pays on publication. No kill fee. Publishes ms an average of 3 months after acceptance. Editorial lead time 3 months. Accepts queries by mail, e-mail, fax, phone. Accepts simultaneous submissions. Sample copy free. Guidelines free.

NONFICTION Needs how-to, get jobs, interview, personal experience. We do not want articles that are too general. Query. Length: 1,500-2,500 words. **Pays $350 for assigned articles.**

⊚⊚ AMERICAN CAREERS

Career Communications, Inc., 6701 W. 64th St., Suite 210, Overland Park KS 66202. (800)669-7795. **E-mail:** ccinfo@carcom.com. **Website:** www.carcom.com; www.americancareersonline.com. **Contact:** Mary

Pitchford, editor-in-chief; Jerry Kanabel, art director. **10% freelance written.** "*American Careers* provides career, salary, and education information to middle school and high school students. Self-tests help them relate their interests and abilities to future careers." Estab. 1989. Circ. 500,000. Byline given. Pays 1 month after acceptance. No kill fee. Accepts queries by mail. Accepts simultaneous submissions. Sample copy for $4. Guidelines for #10 SASE.

NONFICTION No "preachy" advice to teens or articles that talk down to students. **Buys 5 mss/year.** Query by mail only with published clips. Length: 300-1,000 words. **Pays $100-450.**

⊛⊛⊛⊛ HARVARD MAGAZINE

7 Ware St., Cambridge MA 02138. (617)495-5746. **Fax:** (617)495-0324. **E-mail:** jon_shaw@harvard. edu; harvard_magazine@harvard.edu. **Website:** www.harvardmagazine.com. **Contact:** Jonathan S. Shaw, managing editor. **35-50% freelance written.** Bimonthly magazine for Harvard University faculty, alumni, and students. Estab. 1898. Circ. 245,000. Byline given. Pays on publication. No kill fee. Publishes ms an average of 4 months after acceptance. Editorial lead time 1 year. Accepts queries by mail, fax. Responds in 1 month to queries and mss. Sample copy available online.

NONFICTION Needs book excerpts, essays, interview, journalism on Harvard-related intellectual subjects. **Buys 20-30 mss/year.** Query with published clips. Length: 800-10,000 words. **Pays $400-3,000.** Pays expenses of writers on assignment.

⊛⊛ HISPANIC CAREER WORLD

Equal Opportunity Publications, Inc., 445 Broad Hollow Rd., Suite 425, Melville NY 11747. (631)421-9421. **Fax:** (631)421-1352. **E-mail:** info@eop.com. **Website:** www.eop.com. **Contact:** James Schneider, editorial and production director. **60% freelance written.** Semiannual magazine aimed at Hispanic students and professionals in all disciplines. Estab. 1969. Byline given. Pays on publication. No kill fee. Publishes ms an average of 3 months after acceptance. Editorial lead time 3 months. Accepts queries by mail, e-mail, fax, phone. Accepts simultaneous submissions. Responds in 2 weeks to queries; 2 months to mss. Sample copy free. Guidelines free.

NONFICTION Needs how-to, find jobs, interview, personal experience. Query. Length: 1,500-2,500 words. **Pays $350 for assigned articles.**

⊛ NEXTSTEPU MAGAZINE

Next Step Publishing, Inc., 2 W. Main St., Suite 200, Victor NY 14564. **E-mail:** info@NextStepU.com. **Website:** www.nextstepmag.com. **Contact:** Katie Barry, editor. **75% freelance written.** Bimonthly magazine covering LINK Newsletter, Transfer Guide. "Our magazine is a 5-times-a-school-year objective publication that prepares students for life after high school." Articles cover college, careers, life, and financial aid. Estab. 1995. Circ. distributed in 20,500+ high schools. No kill fee. Editorial lead time 6 months. Submit seasonal material 6 months in advance. Accepts queries by e-mail. NoSample copy available online. Guidelines online a www.nextstepu.com/pdf-handouts/WriterGuidelines.pdf.

NONFICTION Needs book excerpts, general interest, how-to, interview, personal experience, travel. Special issues: *Link* is a newsletter published 5 times a year for high school counselors. Articles run 800-1,500 words and "should be focused on helping counselors do their jobs better." Past articles have included counseling students with AD/HD, sports scholarships, and motivation tactics.

COLUMNS/DEPARTMENTS Contact: Laura Jeanne Hammond. College Planning (college types, making a decision, admissions); Financial Air (scholarships, financial aid options);SAT/ACT (preparing for the SAT/ACT, study tips), 400-1,000 words; Career Profiles (profile at least 3 professionals in different aspects of a specific industry), 800-1,000 words; Military (careers in the military, different branches, how to join), 400-600 words.

⊛⊛⊛⊛ NOTRE DAME MAGAZINE

University of Notre Dame, 500 Grace Hall, Notre Dame IN 46556-5612. (574)631-5335. **E-mail:** ndmag@nd.edu. **Website:** magazine.nd.edu. Kerry Prugh, art director. **50% freelance written.** "We are a university magazine with a scope as broad as that found at a university, but we place our discussion in a moral, ethical, and spiritual context reflecting our Catholic heritage." Estab. 1972. Circ. 150,000. Byline given. Pays on acceptance. No kill fee. Publishes ms an average of 1 year after acceptance. Accepts queries by mail, e-mail, fax. Responds in 2 months to queries. Sample copy available online and by request. Guidelines available online.

NONFICTION Needs opinion, personal experience, religious. **Buys 35 mss/year.** Query with published clips. Length: 600-3,000 words. **Pays $250-3,000.** Sometimes pays expenses of writers on assignment.

COLUMNS/DEPARTMENTS CrossCurrents (essays, deal with a wide array of issues—some topical, some personal, some serious, some light). Query with or without published clips or send complete ms.

⊛⊛ OREGON QUARTERLY

5228 University of Oregon, Eugene OR 97403. (541)346-5048. **E-mail:** quarterly@uoregon.edu. **Website:** www.oregonquarterly.com. **85% freelance written.** Quarterly magazine covering people and ideas at the University of Oregon and the Northwest. Estab. 1919. Circ. 100,000. Byline given. Pays on acceptance. Offers 20% kill fee. Publishes ms an average of 3 months after acceptance. Accepts queries by mail (preferred), e-mail ("grumpily"). Guidelines available online.

NONFICTION Buys 30 mss/year. Query with published clips. Length: 300-3,000 words. **Payment varies—30¢-50C/per word for departments; features more.** Sometimes pays expenses of writers on assignment.

REPRINTS See Upfront/Excerpts section for examples. Send photocopy and information about when and where the material previously appeared.

♡ ⊛⊛ QUEEN'S ALUMNI REVIEW

Department of Marketing and Communications, Office of Advancement, Queen's University, Kingston ON K7L 3N6 Canada. **Fax:** (613)533-2060. **E-mail:** ken.cuthbertson@queensu.ca. **E-mail:** review@queensu.ca. **Website:** http://alumnireview.queensu.ca. **Contact:** Ken Cuthbertson, editor. **25% freelance written.** Quarterly magazine covering Queen's University alumni. Estab. 1927. Circ. 121,000. Byline given. Pays on publication. Publishes ms an average of 3 months after acceptance. Editorial lead time 3 months. Submit seasonal material 9 months in advance. Accepts queries by mail, e-mail. Responds in 2 weeks. Sample copy and writer's guidelines online.

NONFICTION "Does not want religious or political rants, travel articles, how-to, or general interest pieces that do not refer to or make some reference to our core audience." **Buys 10 mss/year.** Send complete ms. Length: 200-2,500 words. **Pays 50¢/word (Canadian), plus 10% e-rights fee for assigned articles.** Sometimes pays expenses of writers on assignment.

COLUMNS/DEPARTMENTS "Potential freelancers should study our magazine before submitting a query for a column." **Buys 10 mss/year.** Query with published clips or send complete ms. **Pays 50¢/word (Canadian), plus a 10% e-right fee.**

⊛⊛⊛ UAB MAGAZINE

UAB Publications and Periodicals (University of Alabama at Birmingham), AB 340, 1530 3rd Ave. S., Birmingham AL 35294-0103. (205)934-9420. **Fax:** (205)975-4416. **E-mail:** mwindsor@uab.edu; charlesb@uab.edu; periodicals@uab.edu. **Website:** www.uab.edu/uabmagazine. **Contact:** Matt Windsor, editor. **70% freelance written.** University magazine published 3 times/year covering University of Alabama at Birmingham. *UAB Magazine* informs readers about the innovation and creative energy that drives UAB's renowned research, educational, and health care programs. The magazine reaches active alumni, faculty, friends and donors, patients, corporate and community leaders, media and the public. Estab. 1980. Circ. 33,000. Byline given. Pays on acceptance. Offers 50% kill fee. Publishes ms an average of 3-4 months after acceptance. Editorial lead time 3 months. Accepts queries by mail, e-mail. Sample copy available online. Guidelines free.

NONFICTION Needs general interest, interview. **Buys 40-50 mss/year.** Query with published clips. Length: 500-5,000 words. **Pays $100-1,200.** Sometimes pays expenses of writers on assignment.

⊛⊛ WORKFORCE DIVERSITY FOR ENGINEERING & IT PROFESSIONALS

Equal Opportunity Publications, Inc., 445 Broad Hollow Rd., Suite 425, Melville NY 11747. (631)421-9421. **Fax:** (631)421-1352. **E-mail:** info@eop.com. **Website:** www.eop.com. **60% freelance written.** Quarterly magazine addressing workplace issues affecting technical professional women, members of minority groups, and people with disabilities. Estab. 1969. Byline given. Pays on publication. No kill fee. Publishes ms an average of 3 months after acceptance. Editorial lead time 3 months. Accepts queries by mail, e-mail, fax, phone. Accepts simultaneous submissions. Responds in 2 weeks to queries. Responds in 2 months to mss. Sample copy free. Guidelines free.

NONFICTION Needs how-to, find jobs, interview, personal experience. We do not want articles that are too general. Query. Length: 1,500-2,500 words. **Pays $350 for assigned articles.**

CHILD CARE AND PARENTAL GUIDANCE

💲💲💲 AMERICAN BABY MAGAZINE

Meredith Corp., 375 Lexington Ave., 9th Floor, New York NY 10017. **E-mail:** abletters@americanbaby.com. **Website:** www.americanbaby.com. **70% freelance written.** Monthly magazine covering health, medical, and child care concerns for expectant and new parents, particularly those having their first child or those whose child is between the ages of birth and 2 years old. Mothers are the primary readers, but fathers' issues are equally important. Estab. 1938. Circ. 2,000,000. Byline given. Pays on acceptance. Offers 25% kill fee. Publishes ms an average of 6 months after acceptance. Editorial lead time 5 months. Submit seasonal material 6 months in advance. Accepts queries by mail. Responds in 3 months to queries. Responds in 3 months to mss. Sample copy for 9x12 SAE with 6 first-class stamps. Guidelines for #10 SASE.

NONFICTION Needs book excerpts, essays, general interest, how-to, some aspect of pregnancy or child care, humor, new product, personal experience, fitness, beauty, health, h=. No 'hearts and flowers' or fantasy pieces. **Buys 60 mss/year.** Send complete ms. Length: 1,000-2,000 words. **Pays $750-1,200 for assigned articles. Pays $600-800 for unsolicited articles.** Pays expenses of writers on assignment.

REPRINTS Send photocopy and information about when and where the material previously appeared. Pays 50% of original price.

COLUMNS/DEPARTMENTS Personal essays (700-1,000 words) and shorter items for Crib Notes (news and features) and Health Briefs (50-150 words) are also accepted. **Pays $200-1,000.**

💲 ATLANTA PARENT

2346 Perimeter Park Dr., Atlanta GA 30341. (770)454-7599. **E-mail:** editor@atlantaparent.com. **Website:** www.atlantaparent.com. **Contact:** Editor. **50% freelance written.** Monthly magazine for parents in the Atlanta metro area with children from birth to 18 years old. "*Atlanta Parent* magazine has been a valuable resource for Atlanta families since 1983. It is the only magazine in the Atlanta area providing pertinent, local, and award-winning family-oriented articles and information. Atlanta parents rely on us for features that are timely, informative, and reader-friendly on important issues such as childcare, fam

ily life, education, adolescence, motherhood, health, and teens. Fun, easy, and inexpensive family activities and crafts as well as the humorous side of parenting are also important to our readers." Estab. 1983. Byline given. Pays on publication. Publishes ms an average of 3 months after acceptance. Submit seasonal material 6 months in advance. Accepts queries by mail, e-mail. Responds in 4 months to queries. Sample copy for $3.

NONFICTION Needs general interest, how-to, humor, interview, travel. Special issues: Private School (January); Camp (February); Birthday Parties (March and September); Maternity and Mothering (May and October); Childcare (July); Back-to-School (August); Teens (September); Holidays (November/December). No religious or philosophical discussions. **Buys 60 mss/year.** Send complete ms. Length: 800-1,200 words. **Pays $5-50.** Sometimes pays expenses of writers on assignment.

REPRINTS Send tearsheet or photocopy with rights for sale noted and information about when and where the material previously appeared. Pays $30-50.

💲💲💲💲 BABY TALK

2 Park Ave., 10th Floor, New York NY 10016. (212)522-4327. **Fax:** (212)522-8699. **E-mail:** letters@babytalk.com. **Website:** www.babytalk.com. Estab. 1935. Circ. 2,000,000. Byline given. Accepts queries by mail, online form. Responds in 2 months to queries.

NONFICTION No phone calls. Query with SASE. Length: 1,000-2,000 words. **Pays $500-2,000 depending on length, degree of difficulty, and the writer's experience.**

COLUMNS/DEPARTMENTS Several departments are written by regular contributors. 100 1,250 words. Query with SASE **Pays $100-1,000.**

💲💲 BIRMINGHAM PARENT

Evans Publishing LLC, 700-C Southgate Dr., Pelham AL 35124. (205)987-7700. **Fax:** (205)987-7600. **E-mail:** editor@birminghamparent.com; carol@biringhamparent.com. **Website:** www.birminghamparent.com. **Contact:** Carol Muse Evans, publisher/editor; Lori Chandler Pruitt, associate editor. **75% freelance written.** Monthly magazine covering family issues, parenting, education, babies to teens, health care, anything involving parents raising children. "We are a free, local parenting publication in central Alabama. All of our stories carry some type of local slant. Parenting magazines abound: we are the source for the local market." Estab. 2004. Circ. 30,000. Byline given.

Pays within 30 days of publication. Offers 20% kill fee. Publishes ms an average of 3-4 months after acceptance. Editorial lead time 3-4 months. Submit seasonal material 4 months in advance. Accepts queries by e-mail. Accepts simultaneous submissions. Responds in 2-3 weeks to queries. Responds in 2-3 months to mss. Sample copy for $3. Guidelines available online. **NONFICTION** Needs book excerpts, general interest, how-to, interview, parenting. Does not want first person pieces. "Our pieces educate and inform; we don't take stories without sources." **Buys 24 mss/year.** Send complete ms. Length: 350-2,500 words. **Pays $50-350 for assigned articles. Pays $35-200 for unsolicited articles.**

COLUMNS/DEPARTMENTS Parenting Solo (single parenting), 650 words; Baby & Me (dealing with newborns or pregnancy), 650 words; Teens (raising teenagers), 650-1,500 words. **Buys 36 mss/year.** Query with published clips or send complete ms. **Pays $35-200.**

CHESAPEAKE FAMILY

Jefferson Communications, 929 West St., Suite 307, Annapolis MD 21401. (410)263-1641. **Fax:** (410)280-0255. **E-mail:** editor@chesapeakefamily.com; calendar@chesapeakefamily.com. **Website:** www.chesapeakefamily.com. **Contact:** Betsy Stein, editor; Karen Gaspers, managing editor. **80% freelance written.** Monthly magazine covering parenting. *Chesapeake Family* is a free, regional parenting publication serving readers in the Anne Arundel, Calvert, Prince George's, and Queen Anne's counties of Maryland. Our goal is to identify tips, resources, and products that will make our readers' lives easier. We answer the questions they don't have time to ask, doing the research for them so they have the information they need to make better decisions for their families' health, education, and well-being. Articles must have local angle and resources. Estab. 1990. Circ. 40,000. Byline given. Publishes ms an average of 2 months after acceptance. Editorial lead time 3-6 months. Submit seasonal material 4 months in advance. Accepts queries by mail, e-mail, fax. Accepts simultaneous submissions. Guidelines available online. **NONFICTION** Needs how-to, parenting topics: sign your kids up for sports, find out if your child needs braces, etc., interview, local personalities, travel, family-fun destinations. No general, personal essays (however, personal anecdotes leading into a story with

general applicability is fine). **Buys 25 mss/year.** Send complete ms. Length: 800-1,200 words. **Pays $75-125. Pays $35-50 for unsolicited articles.**

COLUMNS/DEPARTMENTS Buys 25 mss/year. **Pays $35-50.**

CHICAGO PARENT

141 S. Oak Park Ave., Oak Park IL 60302. (708)386-5555. **Website:** www.chicagoparent.com. **Contact:** Tamara O'Shaughnessy, editor. **60% freelance written.** Monthly tabloid. "*Chicago Parent* has a distinctly local approach. We offer information, inspiration, perspective and empathy to Chicago-area parents. Our lively editorial mix has a 'we're all in this together' spirit, and articles are thoroughly researched and well written." Estab. 1988. Circ. 125,000 in 3 zones covering the 6-county Chicago metropolitan area. Byline given. Pays on publication. Offers 10-50% kill fee. Publishes ms an average of 2 months after acceptance. Editorial lead time 4 months. Submit seasonal material 4 months in advance. Accepts queries by mail. Responds in 6 weeks to queries. Sample copy for $3.95 and 11×17 SAE with $1.65 postage. Guidelines for #10 SASE.

NONFICTION Needs essays, exposé, how-to, parent-related, humor, interview, travel, local interest. Special issues: include Chicago Baby and Healthy Child. No pot-boiler parenting pieces, simultaneous submissions, previously published pieces or non-local writers (from outside the 6-county Chicago metropolitan area). **Buys 40-50 mss/year.** Query with published clips. Length: 200-2,500 words. **Pays $25-300 for assigned articles. Pays $25-100 for unsolicited articles.** Pays expenses of writers on assignment.

COLUMNS/DEPARTMENTS Healthy Child (kids' health issues), 850 words; Getaway (travel pieces), up to 1,200 words; other columns not open to freelancers. **Buys 30 mss/year.** Query with published clips or send complete ms. **Pays $100.**

COLUMBUS PARENT MAGAZINE

Consumer News Service, 34 S. Third St., Columbus OH 43215. (614)461-8878. **E-mail:** jhawes@columbusparent.com; contact@columbusparent.com. **Website:** www.columbusparent.com. **Contact:** Jane Hawes, editor. **50% freelance written.** Monthly magazine covering parenting. A hip, reliable resource for Central Ohio parents who are raising children from birth to 18. Estab. 1988. Circ. 60,000. Byline given. Pays on publication. Offers 10% kill fee. Publishes ms an average of 2 months after acceptance. Editorial lead time 3 months. Submit seasonal material 5 months in advance. Accepts queries by mail, e-mail, fax. Sample copy available online. Guidelines available online.

NONFICTION Needs general interest, how-to, interview, new product. Does not want personal essays. **Buys 80 mss/year.** Send complete ms. Length: 500-900 words. **Pays 10¢/word.**

$ GRAND RAPIDS FAMILY MAGAZINE

Gemini Publications, 549 Ottawa Ave. NW, Suite 201, Grand Rapids MI 49503-1444. (616)459-4545. **Fax:** (616)459-4800. **E-mail:** cvalade@geminipub.com. **Website:** www.grfamily.com. **Contact:** Carole Valade, editor. Monthly magazine covering local parenting issues. *Grand Rapids Family* seeks to inform, instruct, amuse, and entertain its readers and their families. Circ. 30,000. Byline given. Pays on publication. Offers $25 kill fee. Editorial lead time 3 months. Submit seasonal material 4 months in advance. Accepts simultaneous submissions. Responds in 2 months to queries. Responds in 6 months to mss. Guidelines with #10 SASE.

NONFICTION Query. **Pays $25-50.**

COLUMNS/DEPARTMENTS All local: law, finance, humor, opinion, mental health. **Pays $25.**

$ HOME EDUCATION MAGAZINE

P.O. Box 1083, Tonasket WA 98855. (800)236-3278; (509)486-1351. **Fax:** (509)486-2753. **E-mail:** articles@homeedmag.com. **Website:** www.homeedmag.com. **Contact:** Jeanne Faulconer, articles editor. **80% freelance written.** Bimonthly magazine covering home-based education. "We feature articles which address the concerns of parents who want to take a direct involvement in the education of their children—concerns such as socialization, how to find curriculums and materials, testing and evaluation, how to tell when your child is ready to begin reading, what to do when homeschooling is difficult, teaching advanced subjects, etc." Estab. 1983. Circ. 120,000. Byline given. Pays on publication. Publishes ms an average of 6 months after acceptance. Submit seasonal material 6 months in advance. Accepts queries by mail. Responds in 2 months to queries. Sample copy for $6.50. Writer's guidelines via e-mail, or on website.

NONFICTION Needs essays, how-to, related to homeschooling, humor, interview, personal experience, photo feature, technical. **Buys 40-50 mss/year.** Send complete ms. Length: 750-2,500 words. **Pays $50-150.**

$ HOMESCHOOLING TODAY

P.O. Box 244, Abingdon VA 24212. (866)804-4478; 276-466-4478. **Fax:** (888)333-4478. **E-mail:** management@homeschooltoday.com. **Website:** www.homeschooltoday.com. **Contact:** Alex Wiggers, publisher; Ashley Wiggers and Debbie Strayer, executive editors. **75% freelance written.** Bimonthly magazine covering homeschooling. "We are a practical magazine for homeschoolers with a broadly Christian perspective." Estab. 1992. Circ. 13,000. Byline given. Pays on publication. Offers 25% kill fee. Publishes ms an average of 1 year after acceptance. Editorial lead time 6 months. Submit seasonal material 1 year in advance. Accepts simultaneous submissions. Responds in 4 months to mss. Sample copy free. Guidelines available on website.

NONFICTION Needs book excerpts, how-to, interview, new product. **Buys 30 mss/year.** Send complete ms. Length: 500-2,000 words. **Pays 10¢/word.**

$$ INDY'S CHILD MAGAZINE

Midwest Parenting Publications, 921 E. 86th St., Suite 130, Indianapolis IN 46240. (317)722-8500. **Fax:** (317)722-8510. **E-mail:** indyschild@indyschild.com. **Website:** www.indyschild.com. **Contact:** Susan Bryant, editor. **100% freelance written.** Monthly magazine covering a myriad of parenting topics and pieces of information relative to families and children in greater Cincinnati and Indianapolis. Sister publication is *Cincinnati Parent*. Estab. 1985. Byline given. Pays on publication. No kill fee. Publishes ms an average of 6 months after acceptance. Editorial lead time 3 months. Submit seasonal material 6 months in advance. Accepts queries by mail, e-mail. Guidelines available online. "We ask that you read this entire page then complete the writer's agreement by clicking on the link at the bottom (or top) of the page. Please note that you must follow these guidelines for every piece of editorial that is submitted to our office. Failure to do so may prevent us from using your editorial."

NONFICTION Needs exposé, general interest, historical, how-to, family projects, crafts, humor, inspirational, interview, opinion, photo feature, travel. **Buys 50 mss/year.** Send complete ms. **Pays .10 cents per word for first publication rights to an article and no more. Feature articles must be no less than**

1500-2000 words. Fees include the rights to use your article once published.

REPRINTS *Actively seeking reprints from freelancers.* Reprint articles are paid $35 for articles under 500 words and $50 for articles up to 1000 words.

COLUMNS/DEPARTMENTS Most Indy's Child Parenting Magazine articles are purchased from freelance writers. In a typical issue, readers will find a variety of regular columns. We also run two to three feature articles at 1500 words per article and six - 10 shorter articles at about 500-800 words per article which are reprints only. The topics must pertain to Indiana parents and families in general. Features consistently require in-depth research and interviews with sources in Indiana (or Cincinnati, Ohio for our sister publication). Rave Reviews, Publisher's Note, Women's Health, Museum Note, Local Profiles, News You Can Use, Mayor's column, and more.

Ⓢ METROFAMILY MAGAZINE

Inprint Publishing, 725 NW 11th St., Suite 204, Oklahoma City OK 73103. (405)601-2081. **E-mail:** editor@metrofamilymagazine.com. **Website:** www.metrofamilymagazine.com. **Contact:** Mari Farthing, editor. **20% freelance written.** Monthly tabloid covering parenting. Circ. 35,000. Byline given. Pays on publication. No kill fee; assignments given to local writers only. Requests ms an average of 2-3 months after acceptance. Editorial lead time 3-6 months. Accepts queries by e-mail. Accepts simultaneous submissions. Responds in 3 weeks to queries (only if interested). Responds in 1 month to mss. Sample copy for sae with 10x13 envelope and 3 first-class stamps. Guidelines via e-mail or return with #10 SASE.

NONFICTION Needs Family or mom-specific articles; see website for themes. No poetry, fiction (except for humor column), or anything that doesn't support good, solid family values. Send complete ms. Submit via e-mail only. Length: 800-1,200 words. **Pays $40-60, plus 1 contributor's copy.**

Ⓢ METROKIDS

Kidstuff Publications, Inc., 1412-1414 Pine St., Philadelphia PA 19102. (215)291-5560, ext. 102. **Fax:** (215)291-5563. **E-mail:** editor@metrokids.com. **Website:** www.metrokids.com. **Contact:** Tom Livingston, executive editor. **25% freelance written.** Monthly tabloid providing information for parents and kids in Philadelphia and surrounding counties, South Jersey, and Delaware. "*MetroKids*, a free monthly magazine, is a resource for parents living in the greater Delaware Valley. The Pennsylvania, South Jersey, and Delaware editions of *MetroKids* are available in supermarkets, libraries, daycares, and hundreds of other locations. The magazine features the Never a Dull Moment calendar of day-by-day family events; child-focused camp, day care and party directories, and articles that offer parenting advice and insights. Other *MetroKids* publications include the Family Find-It Book, a guide to area attractions, service providers and community resources; SpecialKids, a resource guide for families of children with special needs; and Educator's Edition, a directory of field trips, assemblies, and school enrichment programs." Estab. 1990. Circ. 115,000. Byline given. Pays on publication. Submit seasonal material 4 months in advance. Accepts queries by e-mail. Guidelines available by e-mail.

NONFICTION Needs general interest, how-to, new product, travel, parenting, health. Special issues: Educator's Edition—field trips, school enrichment, teacher, professional development (March and September); SpecialKids—children with special needs (August). **Buys 40 mss/year.** Query with published clips. Length: 800-1,500 words. **Pays $50.**

REPRINTS E-mail summary or complete article and information about when and where the material previously appeared. Pays $35, or $50 if localized after discussion.

COLUMNS/DEPARTMENTS Techno Family (CD-ROM and website reviews); Body Wise (health); Style File (fashion and trends); Woman First (motherhood); Practical Parenting (financial parenting advice); Kids 'N Care (toddlers and daycare); Special Kids (disabilities), all 650-850 words. **Buys 25 mss/year.** Query. **Pays $25-50.**

Ⓢ Ⓢ METRO PARENT MAGAZINE

Metro Parent Publishing Group, 22041 Woodward Ave., Ferndale MI 48220. (248)398-3400. **Fax:** (248)339-4215. **E-mail:** editor@metroparent.com; jelliott@metroparent.com; kkovelle@metroparent.com. **Website:** www.metroparent.com. **Contact:** Julia Elliott, executive editor; Kim Kovelle, senior editor. **75% freelance written.** Monthly magazine covering parenting, women's health, education. "MetroParent.com is an online parenting community offering expert advice, stories on parenting trends and issues, and numerous ways for parents to enrich their experience raising the next generation. It is part of Metro

Parent Publishing Group, which began in suburban Detroit in 1986. Publications include Metro Parent magazine, Metro Baby, Going Places, Special Edition, Party Book and Big Book of Schools. Metro Parent Publishing Group also brings family-friendly events to southeast Michigan as part of its events department." Circ. 80,000. Byline given. Pays on publication. Publishes ms an average of 3 months after acceptance. Editorial lead time 3 months. Submit seasonal material 3 months in advance. Accepts queries by mail, e-mail. Accepts simultaneous submissions. Responds in 2 weeks to queries. Responds in 3 months to mss. Sample copy for $2.50.

NONFICTION Needs essays, humor, inspirational, personal experience. **Buys 100 mss/year.** Send complete ms. Length: 1,500-2,500 words. **Pays $50-300 for assigned articles.**

COLUMNS/DEPARTMENTS Women's Health (latest issues of 20-40 year olds), 750-900 words; Solo Parenting (advice for single parents); Family Finance (making sense of money and legal issues); Tweens 'N Teens (handling teen issues), 750-800 words. **Buys 50 mss/year.** Send complete ms. **Pays $75-150.**

⊛⊛ PARENT:WISE AUSTIN

Pleticha Publishing Inc., 7301 Ranch Rd. 620 N, Suite 155, 388, Austin TX 78726. (877)MAMA-304. **Fax:** (866)MAMA-591. **E-mail:** editor@parentwiseaustin.com. **Website:** www.parentwiseaustin.com. 25% freelance written. Monthly magazine covering parenting news, features and issues; mothering issues; maternal feminism; feminism as it pertains to motherhood and work/life balance; serious/thoughtful essays about the parenting experience; humor articles pertaining to the parenting experience. *"Parent:Wise Austin* targets educated, thoughtful readers who want solid information about the parenting experience. We seek to create a warm, nurturing community by providing excellent, well researched articles, thoughtful essays, humor articles, and other articles appealing to parents. Our readers demand in-depth, well written articles; we do not accept, nor will we print, 're-worked' articles on boiler plate topics." Estab. 2004. Circ. 32,000. Byline given. Pays on publication. No kill fee. Publishes ms an average of 2 months after acceptance. Editorial lead time 6 months. Submit seasonal material 6 months in advance. Accepts queries by e-mail. Responds in 1 week to queries. Responds in 1 month to mss. Sample copy for $1.50 postage. "How-ever, sample copies can be viewed online." Guidelines available online.

NONFICTION Needs essays, humor, opinion, personal experience, travel, hard news, features on parenting issues. Special issues: Mother's Day issue (May); Father's Day issue (June). "Does not want boiler plate articles or generic articles that have been customized for our market." **Buys 12-20 mss/year.** All articles should be submitted in their entirety—no queries—via email. You should receive a response within 60-days (if not, please email us again to ensure that we received your submission). Please do NOT send us your article via snail mail (snail-mailed submissions will not be read or returned). Length: 500-2,500 words. **Pays $50-200.** Sometimes pays expenses of writers on assignment.

COLUMNS/DEPARTMENTS My Life as a Parent (humor), 500-700 words; Essay (first-person narrative), 500-1,000 words. **Buys 24-50 mss/year.** Send complete ms. **Pays $50.**

POETRY Needs avant-garde, free verse, haiku, light verse, traditional. "Does not want poetry that does not pertain to parenting or the parenting experience." Buys 3-5 poems/year. Submit maximum 3 poems. Length: 25 lines.

⊛⊛⊛⊛ PARENTING MAGAZINE (EARLY YEARS AND SCHOOL YEARS EDITIONS)

Bonnier Corporation, 2 Park Ave., 10th Floor, New York NY 10016. (212)779-5000. **Website:** www.parenting.com. **"Largely freelance written."** Magazine published 10 times/year for mothers of children from birth to 12, and covering both the emotional and practical aspects of parenting. Estab. 1987. Circ. 2,100,000. Byline given. Pays on acceptance. Offers 25% kill fee. Accepts queries by mail. Responds in 2 months. Samples not available. Guidelines for #10 SASE.

NONFICTION Contact: Articles Editor. Needs book excerpts, personal experience, child development/behavior/health. **Buys 20-30 mss/year.** Query. Length: 1,000-2,500 words. **Pays $1,000-3,000.** Pays expenses of writers on assignment.

COLUMNS/DEPARTMENTS Contact: Query to the specific departmental editor. **Buys 50-60 mss/year.** Query. **Pays $50-400.**

PEDIATRICS FOR PARENTS

Pediatrics for Parents, Inc., 120 Western Ave., Gloucester MA 01930. (215)253-4543. **Fax:** (973)302-4543. **E-mail:** richsagall@pedsforparents.com. **Website:** www.pedsforparents.com. **Contact:** Richard J. Sagall, M.D., editor. **50% freelance written.** Monthly newsletter covering children's health. "*Pediatrics For Parents* emphasizes an informed, common-sense approach to childhood health care. We stress preventative action, accident prevention, when to call the doctor and when and how to handle a situation at home. We are also looking for articles that describe general, medical and pediatric problems, advances, new treatments, etc. All articles must be medically accurate and useful to parents with children—prenatal to adolescence." Estab. 1981. Circ. 120,000. Byline given. Pays on publication. Publishes ms an average of 4 months after acceptance. Accepts queries by mail, e-mail, fax. Accepts simultaneous submissions. Responds in 1 month to queries. Sample copy available online. Guidelines available online.

NONFICTION No first person or experience. **Buys 25 mss/year.** Send complete ms. Length: 1,000-1,500 words. **Pays $10-25.**

PIKES PEAK PARENT

The Gazette/Freedom Communications, 30 S. Prospect St., Colorado Springs CO 80903. **Fax:** (719)476-1625. **Website:** www.pikespeakparent.com. **10% freelance written.** Monthly tabloid covering parenting, family, and grandparenting. We prefer stories with local angle and local stories. We do not accept unsolicited manuscripts. Estab. 1994. Circ. 35,000. Byline given. Pays on publication. No kill fee. Editorial lead time 3 months. Submit seasonal material 4 months in advance. Accepts queries by e-mail. Accepts simultaneous submissions. Responds in 1 month to queries. Sample copy available online.

NONFICTION Needs essays, general interest, how-to, medical related to parenting. **Buys 10 mss/year.** Query with published clips. Length: 800-1,000 words. **Pays $20-120.**

SACRAMENTO PARENT

Family Publishing Inc., 457 Grass Valley Hwy., Suite 5, Auburn CA 95603. (530)888-0573. **Fax:** (530)888-1536. **E-mail:** shelly@sacramentoparent.com. **Website:** www.sacramentoparent.com. **Contact:** Shelly Bokman, editor-in-chief. **50% freelance written.** Monthly magazine covering parenting in the Sacra-

mento region. "We look for articles that promote a developmentally appropriate, healthy, and peaceful environment for children." Estab. 1992. Circ. 50,000. Byline given. Pays on publication. Offers 10% kill fee. Publishes ms an average of 2 months after acceptance. Editorial lead time 3 months. Submit seasonal material 4 months in advance. Accepts queries by e-mail. Sample copy free. Guidelines by e-mail.

NONFICTION Needs book excerpts, general interest, how-to, humor, interview, opinion, personal experience. **Buys 36 mss/year.** Query. Length: 300-1,000 words. **Pays $50-200 for original articles.**

COLUMNS/DEPARTMENTS Let's Go! (Sacramento regional family-friendly day trips/excursions/activities), 600 words. **Pays $25-45.**

SAN DIEGO FAMILY MAGAZINE

1475 Sixth Ave., 5th Floor, San Diego CA 92101-3200. (619)685-6970. **Fax:** (619)685-6978. **E-mail:** family@sandiegofamily.com. **Website:** www.sandiegofamily.com. **100% freelance written.** "*SDFM* is a regional family monthly publication. We focus on providing current, informative and interesting editorial about parenting and family life that educates and entertains." Estab. 1982. Circ. 100,000. Byline given. Pays on publication. No kill fee. Publishes ms an average of 1-6 months after acceptance. Editorial lead time 4 months. Submit seasonal material 6 months in advance. Accepts queries by mail, e-mail. Accepts simultaneous submissions. Responds in 1 month to queries. Responds in 2 months to mss. Sample copy for $4.50 to P.O. Box 23960, San Diego CA 92193. Guidelines available online.

NONFICTION Needs essays, general interest, how-to, interview, technical, travel, informational articles. Does not want humorous personal essays, opinion pieces, religious or spiritual. **Buys 350-500 mss/year.** Query. Length: 600-1,250 words. **Pays $22-90.**

REPRINTS Send typed ms with rights for sale, ted and information about when and where the material previously appeared. Will respond only if SASE is included.

FILLERS Buys 0-12 mss/year. Send complete ms. Length: 200-600 words.

SCHOLASTIC PARENT & CHILD

Scholastic, Inc., 557 Broadway, New York NY 10012. (212)343-6100. **Fax:** (212)343-4801. **E-mail:** parentandchild@scholastic.com. **Website:** parentandchildonline.com. **Contact:** Nick Friedman, editor-in-chief; Elizabeth Anne Shaw, executive editor. Bimonthly magazine published to keep active parents up-to-date on children's learning and development while in pre-school or child-care environment. Circ. 1,224,098. No kill fee. Editorial lead time 10 weeks.

SOUTH FLORIDA PARENTING
1701 Green Rd., Suite B, Deerfield Beach FL 33064. (954)698-6397. **Fax:** (954)421-9002. **E-mail:** klcamarena@tribune.com. **Website:** www.sfparenting.com. **Contact:** Kyara Lome-Camarenar, editor. **90% freelance written.** Monthly magazine covering parenting, family. *"South Florida Parenting* provides news, information, and a calendar of events for readers in Southeast Florida (Palm Beach, Broward and Miami-Dade counties). The focus is on parenting issues, things to do, information about raising children in South Florida."* Estab. 1990. Circ. 110,000. Byline given. Pays on publication. No kill fee. Editorial lead time 4 months. Submit seasonal material 4 months in advance. Accepts queries by e-mail, fax. Responds in 3 months to queries.

NONFICTION Needs how-to (parenting issues), interview/profile, family, parenting and children's issues. Special issues: family fitness, education, spring party guide, fall party guide, kids and the environment, toddler/preschool, preteen. Length: 500-1,000 words. **Pays $40-165.**

REPRINTS Pays $25-50.

COLUMNS/DEPARTMENTS Dad's Perspective, Family Deals, Products for Families, Health/Safety, Nutrition, Baby Basics, Travel, Toddler/Preschool, Preteen, South Florida News.

SOUTHWEST FLORIDA PARENT & CHILD
The News-Press, A Gannett Company, 2442 Dr. Martin Luther King, Jr. Blvd., Fort Myers FL 33901. (239)335-0200. **Fax:** (239)344-0708. **E-mail:** editor@swflparentchild.com; phayford@fortmyer.gannett.com. **Website:** http://news-press.com/moms. **Contact:** Pamela Smith Hayford, editor. **75% freelance written.** Monthly magazine covering parenting. *"Southwest Florida Parent & Child* is a regional parenting magazine with an audience of mostly moms but some dads, too. With every article, we strive to give readers information they can use. We aim to be an indispensable resource for our local parents."* Estab. 2000. Circ. 25,000. Byline given. Pays on publica-

tion. Publishes ms an average of 2-3 months after acceptance. Editorial lead time 2-3 months. Submit seasonal material 3+ months in advance. Accepts queries by mail, e-mail. Accepts simultaneous submissions.

NONFICTION Needs book excerpts, general interest, how-to, humor, interview, new product, personal experience, photo feature, religious, travel. Does not want personal experience or opinion pieces. **Buys 96-120 mss/year.** Send complete ms. Length: 500-700 words. **Pays $25-200.** Sometimes pays expenses of writers on assignment.

TODAY'S PARENT
Rogers Media, Inc., One Mt. Pleasant Rd., 8th Floor, Toronto ON M4Y 2Y5 Canada. (416)764-2883. **Fax:** (416)764-2894. **E-mail:** editors@todaysparent.com. **Website:** www.todaysparent.com. **Contact:** Jackie Shipley, art director. Monthly magazine for parents with children up to the age of 12. Circ. 2,000,000. No kill fee. Editorial lead time 5 months.

NONFICTION Length: 1,800-2,500 words. **Pays $1,500-2,200.**

COLUMNS/DEPARTMENTS What's New (games/apps/movies/toys); Health (parents and children); Behaviour; Relationships; Steps and Stages; How Does He/She Do It; Bright Idea; Food/In the Kitchen.

TODAY'S PARENT PREGNANCY & BIRTH
Rogers Media, Inc., One Mt. Pleasant Rd., 8th Floor, Toronto ON M4Y 2Y5 Canada. (416)764-2883. **Fax:** (416)764-2894. **E-mail:** editors@todaysparent.com. **Website:** www.todaysparent.com. **100% freelance written.** Magazine published 3 times/year. *"P&B* helps, supports and encourages expectant and new parents with news and features related to pregnancy, birth, human sexuality and parenting."* Estab. 1973. Circ. 190,000. Pays on acceptance. Publishes ms an average of 8 months after acceptance. Editorial lead time 6 months. Accepts queries by mail. Responds in 6 weeks to queries. Guidelines for SASE.

NONFICTION Buys 12 mss/year. Query with published clips; send detailed proposal. Length: 1,000-2,500 words. **Pays up to $1/word.** Sometimes pays expenses of writers on assignment.

TOLEDO AREA PARENT NEWS
Adams Street Publishing, Co., 1120 Adams St., Toledo OH 43604. (419)244-9859. **E-mail:** cjacobs@toledocitypaper.com; editor@toledocitypaper.com. **Website:** www.toledoparent.com. **Contact:** Collette Jacobs,

editor-in-chief and publisher; Alia Orra, assignment editor. Monthly tabloid for Northwest Ohio/Southeast Michigan parents. Estab. 1992. Circ. 40,000. Byline given. Pays on publication. No kill fee. Publishes ms an average of 1 month after acceptance. Editorial lead time 3 months. Accepts queries by mail, e-mail, fax. Responds in 1 month to queries. Sample copy for $1.50.

NONFICTION Needs general interest, interview, opinion. **Buys 10 mss/year.** Length: 1,000-2,500 words. **Pays $75-125.**

$$ TWINS™ MAGAZINE

30799 Pinetree Road, #256, Cleveland OH 44124. (855)758-9567. **Fax:** (855)758-9567. **E-mail:** twinseditor@twinsmagazine.com. **Website:** www.twinsmagazine.com. **Contact:** Christa Reed, editor. **50% freelance written.** "We now publish eight (8) issues per year—4 print/4 digital covering all aspects of parenting twins/multiples. *Twins* is a national/international publication that provides informational and educational articles regarding the parenting of twins, triplets, and more. All articles must be multiple specific and have an upbeat, hopeful, and/or positive ending." Estab. 1984. Circ. 35,000. Byline given. Pays on publication. Editorial lead time 4 months. Submit seasonal material 6 months in advance. Accepts queries by U.S. mail, e-mail only. Response time varies. Sample copy for $5 or on website. Guidelines available online.

NONFICTION Needs personal experience, first-person parenting experience, professional experience as it relates to multiples. Nothing on cloning, pregnancy reduction, or fertility issues. **Buys 12 mss/year.** Send complete ms. Length: 650-1,200 words. **Pays $25-250 for assigned articles. Pays $25-125 for unsolicited articles.**

COLUMNS/DEPARTMENTS A Word From Dad; Mom-2-Mom; LOL: Laugh Out Loud; Family Health; Resource Round Up; Tales From Twins; & Research. Pays $25-75. **Buys 8-10 mss/year.** Query with or without published clips or send complete ms. **Pays $40-75.**

COMIC BOOKS

$ THE COMICS JOURNAL

Fantagraphics Books, 7563 Lake City Way NE, Seattle WA 98115. (206)524-1967. **Fax:** (206)524-2104. **E-mail:** editorial@tcj.com. **Website:** www.tcj.com. Magazine covering the comics medium from an arts-first perspective on a six-week schedule. "*The Comics Journal* is one of the nation's most respected single-arts magazines, providing its readers with an eclectic mix of industry news, professional interviews, and reviews of current work. Due to its reputation as the American magazine with an interest in comics as an art form, the *Journal* has subscribers worldwide, and in this country serves as an important window into the world of comics for several general arts and news magazines." Byline given. Accepts queries by mail, e-mail. Guidelines available online.

NONFICTION Needs essays, interview, opinion, reviews. Send complete ms. Length: 2,000-3,000 words. **Pays 4¢/word, and 1 contributor's copy.**

COLUMNS/DEPARTMENTS On Theory, Art and Craft (2,000-3,000 words); Firing Line (reviews 1,000-5,000 words); Bullets (reviews 400 words or less). Send inquiries, samples **Pays 4¢/word, and 1 contributor's copy.**

CONSUMER SERVICE AND BUSINESS OPPORTUNITY

$$ HOME BUSINESS MAGAZINE

20711 Holt Ave, #807, Lakeville MN 55044. **E-mail:** editor@homebusinessmag.com; publisher@homebusinessmag.com. **Website:** www.homebusinessmag.com. **75% freelance written.** "Covers every angle of the home-based business market including: cutting edge editorial by well-known authorities on sales and marketing, business operations, the home office, franchising, business opportunities, network marketing, mail order, and other subjects to help readers choose, manage, and prosper in a home-based business; display advertising, classified ads and a directory of home-based businesses; technology, the Internet, computers, and the future of home-based business; home-office editorial including management advice, office set-up, and product descriptions; business opportunities, franchising and work-from-home success stories." Estab. 1993. Circ. 105,000. No kill fee. Publishes ms an average of 6 months after acceptance. Editorial lead time 6 months. Submit seasonal material 6 months in advance. Accepts queries by e-mail. Accepts simultaneous submissions. Sample copy for sae with 9x12 envelope and 8 first-class stamps. Guidelines for #10 SASE.

NONFICTION Needs book excerpts, general interest, how-to, home business, inspirational, interview, new product, personal experience, photo feature, technical, mail order, franchise, business management, Internet, finance network marketing. No non-home business related topics. **Buys 40 mss/year.** Send complete ms. Length: 200-1,000 words. **Pays 20¢/published word for work-for-hire assignments; 50-word byline for unsolicited articles.**

COLUMNS/DEPARTMENTS Marketing & Sales; Money Corner; Home Office; Management; Technology; Working Smarter; Franchising; Network Marketing, all 650 words. Send complete ms.

KIPLINGER'S PERSONAL FINANCE

1100 13th St. NW, Washington DC 20005. (202)887-6400. **Fax:** (202)331-1206. **E-mail:** jbodnar@kiplinger.com. **Website:** www.kiplinger.com. **Contact:** Janet Bodnar, editor; Stacie Harrison, art director. **10% freelance written. Prefers to work with published/established writers.** Monthly magazine for general, adult audience interested in personal finance and consumer information. *"Kiplinger's* is a highly trustworthy source of information on saving and investing, taxes, credit, home ownership, paying for college, retirement planning, automobile buying, and many other personal finance topics." Estab. 1947. Circ. 800,000. Pays on acceptance. No kill fee. Publishes ms an average of 2 months after acceptance. Responds in 1 month to queries.

NONFICTION Query with published clips. Pays expenses of writers on assignment.

CONTEMPORARY CULTURE

⟳ ⑤⑤⑤ ADBUSTERS

Adbusters Media Foundation, 1243 W. 7th Ave., Vancouver BC V6H 1B7 Canada. (604)736-9401. **Fax:** (604)737-6021. **E-mail:** editor@adbusters.org. **Website:** www.adbusters.org. **50% freelance written.** Bimonthly magazine on consumerism. "We are an activist journal of the mental environment." Estab. 1989. Circ. 90,000. Byline given. Pays 1 month after publication. Accepts queries by mail, e-mail, fax. Accepts simultaneous submissions. Guidelines available online.

NONFICTION Needs essays, exposé, interview, opinion. **Buys variable mss/year.** Query. Length: 250-3,000 words. **Pays $100/page for unsolicited articles; 50¢/word for solicited articles.**

FICTION Inquire about themes.

POETRY Inquire about themes.

⑤⑤ BUST MAGAZINE

Bust, Inc., 18 W. 27th St., 9th Floor, New York NY 10001. **E-mail:** debbie@bust.com. **E-mail:** submissions@bust.com. **Website:** www.bust.com. **Contact:** Debbie Stoller, editor-in-chief/publisher. **60% freelance written.** Bimonthly magazine covering pop culture for young women. *"Bust* is the groundbreaking, original women's lifestyle magazine & website that is unique in its ability to connect with bright, cutting-edge, influential young women." Estab. 1993. Circ. 100,000. Byline given. Pays on publication. No kill fee. Publishes ms an average of 4 months after acceptance. Editorial lead time 3-4 months. Submit seasonal material 6 months in advance. Accepts queries by mail, e-mail. Accepts simultaneous submissions. Response time varies. Guidelines online at www.bust.com/info/submit.html.

NONFICTION Needs book excerpts, exposé, general interest, historical, how-to, humor, inspirational, interview, new product, personal experience, photo feature, travel. Special issues: No dates are currently set, but we usually have a fashion issue, a music issue and a *Men We Love* issue periodically. We do not want poetry; no stories not relating to women. **Buys 60+ mss/year.** Query with published clips. Length: 350-3,000 words. **Pays 0-$250/max for assigned articles. Pays 0-$250/max for unsolicited articles.** Sometimes pays expenses of writers on assignment.

COLUMNS/DEPARTMENTS Contact: Emily Rems, Managing Editor. Books (Reviews of books by women) assigned by us, Music (Reviews of music by/about women), Movies (Reviews of movies by/about women), 300 words; One-Handed-Read (Erotic Fiction for Women), 1,200 words. **Buys 6 mss/year.** Query with published clips. **Pays $-$100.**

FICTION Contact: Lisa Butterworth, Assoc. Editor. Needs erotica. "We only publish erotic fiction. All other content is nonfiction." **Buys 6 mss/year.** Query with published clips. Length: 1,000-1,500 words. **Pays $0-$100.**

⑤⑤⑤ COMMENTARY

561 7th Ave., 16th Floor, New York NY 10018. (212)891-1400. **E-mail:** submissions@commentarymagazine.com. **Website:** www.commentarymagazine.com. **Contact:** John Podhoretz, editor. Monthly magazine covering Judaism, politics, and culture. *"Commentary* is America's premier monthly magazine of opinion and a pivotal voice in American intellectual

life. Since its inception in 1945, and increasingly after it emerged as the flagship of neoconservatism in the 1970s, the magazine has been consistently engaged with several large, interrelated questions: the fate of democracy and of democratic ideas in a world threatened by totalitarian ideologies; the state of American and Western security; the future of the Jews, Judaism, and Jewish culture in Israel, the United States, and around the world; and the preservation of high culture in an age of political correctness and the collapse of critical standards." Estab. 1945. Byline given. Pays on publication. No kill fee. Publishes ms an average of 2 months after acceptance. Accepts queries by mail. **NONFICTION** Needs essays, opinion. **Buys 4 mss/ year.** Query. Length: 2,000-8,000 words. **Pays $400-1,200.**

⟳ 💲💲 COMMON GROUND

Common Ground Publishing, 204-4381 Fraser St., Vancouver BC V5V 4G4 Canada. (604)733-2215. **Fax:** (604)733-4415. **E-mail:** admin@commonground.ca. **E-mail:** editor@commonground.ca. **Website:** www. commonground.ca. **90% freelance written.** Monthly tabloid covering health, environment, spirit, creativity, and wellness. "We serve the cultural creative community." Estab. 1982. Circ. 70,000. Byline given. Pays on publication. No kill fee. Publishes ms an average of 1 month after acceptance. Editorial lead time 2 months. Submit seasonal material 3 months in advance. Accepts queries by e-mail. Accepts simultaneous submissions. Responds in 6 weeks to queries. Responds in 3 months to mss. Sample copy for $5. Guidelines available online.
NONFICTION Needs book excerpts, how-to, inspirational, interview, opinion, personal experience, travel, call to action. Send complete ms. Length: 500-2,500 words. **Pays 10¢/word (Canadian).**

💲💲💲 FIRST THINGS

Institute on Religion & Public Life, 35 East 21st St., 6th floor, New York NY 10010. (212)627-1985. **E-mail:** ft@firstthings.com. **Website:** www.firstthings.com. **70% freelance written.** Covers social and intellectual commentary. "Intellectual journal published 10 times/year containing social and ethical commentary in a broad sense, religious and ethical perspectives on society, culture, law, medicine, church and state, morality, and more." Estab. 1990. Circ. 32,000. Byline given. Pays on publication. Publishes ms an average of 4 months after acceptance. Editorial lead time 2

months. Submit seasonal material 5 months in advance. Responds in 6 weeks to mss. Sample copy and writer's guidelines for #10 SASE.
NONFICTION Needs essays, opinion. **Buys 60 mss/ year.** Send complete ms. Length: 1,000-5,000 words. **Pays $400-1,000.** Sometimes pays expenses of writers on assignment.
POETRY Contact: Paul Lake, poetry editor. Needs traditional. Buys 25-30 poems/year. Length: 4-40 lines. **Pays $50.**

💲💲💲 FLAUNT

1422 N. Highland Ave., Los Angeles CA 90028. (323)836-1000. **E-mail:** info@flauntmagazine.com. **Website:** www.flaunt.com. **Contact:** Luis Barajas, editor-in-chief. **40% freelance written.** Monthly magazine covering culture, arts, entertainment, music, fashion, and film. "*Flaunt* features the bold work of emerging photographers, writers, artists and musicians. The quality of the content is mirrored in the sophisticated, interactive format of the magazine, using advanced printing techniques, fold-out articles, beautiful papers and inserts to create a visually stimulating, surprisingly readable, and intelligent book that pushes the magazine into the realm of art-object. *Flaunt* has, since 1998, made it a point to break new ground, earning itself a reputation as an engine of the avant-garde and an outlet for the culture of the cutting edge. *Flaunt* takes pride in reinventing itself each month, while consistently representing a hybrid of all that is interesting in entertainment, fashion, music, design, film, art, and literature." Estab. 1998. Circ. 100,000. Byline given. No kill fee. Publishes ms an average of 3 months after acceptance. Editorial lead time 3 months. Submit seasonal material 3 months in advance. Accepts queries by mail, e-mail. Accepts simultaneous submissions. Responds in 2 weeks to queries. Responds in 1 month to mss. Guidelines by e-mail.
NONFICTION Needs book excerpts, essays, exposé, general interest, historical, humor, interview, new product, opinion, personal experience, photo feature, travel. Special issues: September and March (fashion issues); February (men's issue); May (music issue). **Buys 20 mss/year.** Query with published clips. Length: 500-5,000 words. **Pays up to $500.** Sometimes pays expenses of writers on assignment.
FICTION Contact: Contact Andrew Pogany, senior editor. **Buys 4 mss/year.**

$$ NATURALLY

Internaturally, Inc., P.O. Box 317, Newfoundland NJ 07435. (973)697-3552. **Fax:** (973)697-8313. **E-mail:** naturally@internaturally.com. **Website:** www.internaturally.com. **80% freelance written.** Quarterly magazine covering nudism and naturism. "A full color, glossy magazine with online editions, and the foremost naturist/nudist magazine in the US with international distribution. *Naturally* focuses on the clothes-free lifestyle, publishing articles about worldwide destinations, first-time nudist experiences, with news information pertaining to the clothes-free lifestyle. Our mission is to demystify the human form, and allow each human to feel comfortable in their own skin, in a non-sexual environment. We offer a range of books, DVDs, magazines, and other products useful to naturists/nudists in their daily lives, and for the education of non-naturists. Travel DVDs featuring resorts to visit; books on Christianity and nudity, nudist plays, memoirs, cartoons, and novellas; and also towels, sandals, calendars, and more." Estab. 1980. Circ. 30,000. Byline given. Pays on publication. No kill fee. Publishes ms an average of 3 months after acceptance. Editorial lead time 3-6 months. Submit seasonal material 6 months in advance. Accepts queries by mail, phone. Accepts simultaneous submissions. Responds in 2 weeks to queries. Responds in 3 months to mss. Sample copy available online.

NONFICTION Needs book excerpts, essays, exposé, general interest, historical, how-to, for first-time visitors to nudist park., humor, inspirational, interview, new product, personal experience, photo feature, travel. Special issues: Free-beach activities, public nude events. "We don't want opinion pieces and religious slants." **Buys 50 mss/year.** Send complete ms. Length: 500-2,000 words. **Pays $80 per page, text or photos minimum; $300 maximum for assigned articles.**

COLUMNS/DEPARTMENTS Health (nudism/naturism), Travel (nudism/naturism), Celebrities (nudism/naturism). **Buys 8 mss/year.** Send complete ms.

FICTION Needs humorous. No science fiction. **Buys 6-8 mss/year.** Send complete ms. Length: 800-2,000 words. **Pays $0-$80 per page.**

POETRY Needs avant-garde, free verse, haiku, light verse, traditional. Buys 3-6 poems/year. Submit maximum 3 poems.

FILLERS Needs anecdotes, facts, gags, newsbreaks, short humor. **Buys 4 mss/year.**

$ NEW HAVEN ADVOCATE

New Mass Media, Inc., 900 Chapel St., New Haven CT 06510. (203)789-0010. **Fax:** (203)787-1418. **E-mail:** jadamian@hartfordadvocate.com. **Website:** www.ct.com/news/advocates. **Contact:** John Adamian, editor. **10% freelance written.** Weekly tabloid covering alternative, investigative, cultural reporting. "Alternative, investigative, cultural reporting with a strong voice. We like to shake things up." Estab. 1975. Circ. 55,000. Byline given. Pays on publication. No kill fee. Editorial lead time 1 month. Submit seasonal material 2 months in advance. Accepts simultaneous submissions. Responds in 1 month to queries.

NONFICTION Needs book excerpts, essays, exposé, general interest, humor, interview. **Buys 15-20 mss/year.** Query with published clips. Length: 750-2,000 words. **Pays $50-150.** Sometimes pays expenses of writers on assignment.

$$ SHEPHERD EXPRESS

The Brooklyn Company, Inc., 207 E. Buffalo St., Suite 410, Milwaukee WI 53202. (414)276-2222. **Fax:** (414)276-3312. **E-mail:** info@expressmilwaukee.com. **Website:** http://expressmilwaukee.com. **Contact:** Louis Fortis, editor-in-chief and publisher. **50% freelance written.** Weekly tabloid covering news and arts with a progressive news edge and a hip entertainment perspective. Home of Sheprd Flickr interactive photo feature—Milwaukee-related photography. Estab. 1982. Circ. 58,000. Pays 1 month after publication. No kill fee. Publishes ms an average of 1 month after acceptance. Submit seasonal material 2 months in advance. Accepts simultaneous submissions. Sample copy for $3.

NONFICTION Needs book excerpts, essays, exposé, opinion. **Buys 200 mss/year.** Send complete ms. Length: 900-2,500 words. **Pays $35-300 for assigned articles. Pays $10-200 for unsolicited articles.** Sometimes pays expenses of writers on assignment.

COLUMNS/DEPARTMENTS Opinions (social trends, politics, from progressive slant), 800-1,200 words; Books Reviewed (new books only: Social trends, environment, politics), 600-1,200 words. **Buys 10 mss/year.** Send complete ms.

$$$ THE SUN

107 N. Roberson St., Chapel Hill NC 27516. (919)942-5282. **Fax:** (919)932-3101. **Website:** www.thesunmagazine.org. Sy Safransky, editor. **Contact:** Luc Sanders, assistant editor. **90% freelance written.** Monthly

magazine publishing essays, inverviews, fiction, and poetry. "We are open to all kinds of writing, though we favor work of a personal nature." Estab. 1974. Circ. 69,500. Byline given. Pays on publication. Publishes ms an average of 6-12 months after acceptance. Accepts queries by mail. Responds in 3-6 months to queries. Responds in 3-6 months to mss. Sample copy for $5. Guidelines available online.

NONFICTION Contact: Sy Safransky, editor. Needs essays, personal experience, spiritual, interview. **Buys 50. mss/year.** Send complete ms. 7,000 words maximum **Pays $300-2,000.** .

REPRINTS Send photocopy and information about when and where the material previously appeared.

FICTION Contact: Sy Safransky, editor. Open to all fiction. Receives 800 unsolicited mss/month. Accepts 20 short stories/year. Recently published work by Tony Hoagland, David James Duncan, Poe Ballantine, Linda McCullough Moore, Brenda Miller. No science fiction, horror, fantasy, or other genre fiction. "Read an issue before submitting." **Buys 20/year mss/year.** Send complete ms. Accepts reprint submissions. Length: 7,000 words maximum. **Pays $300-1,500.**

POETRY Contact: Sy Safransky, editor. Needs free verse. Submit up to 6 poems at a time. Considers previously published poems but strongly prefers unpublished work; no simultaneous submissions. "Poems should be typed and accompanied by a cover letter and SASE." Guidelines available with SASE or on website. Responds within 3-6 months. Acquires first serial or one-time rights. Rarely publishes poems that rhyme. **Pays $100-500 on publication plus contributor's copies and subscription.**

UTNE READER

1503 SW 42nd St, Topeka KS 66609. (785)274-4300. **E-mail:** editor@utne.com. **Website:** www.utne.com. **Contact:** Carolyn Lang, art director. Estab. 1984. Circ. 250,000. Accepts queries by mail, e-mail. Guidelines available online.

REPRINTS Send tearsheet or photocopy with rights for sale noted and information about when and where the material previously appeared.

🍁 $ CANADIAN DIMENSION

2E-91 Albert St., Winnipeg MB R3B 1G5 Canada. (204)957-1519. **Fax:** (204)943-4617. **E-mail:** editor@canadiandimension.com; letters@canadiandimension.com. **Website:** www.canadiandimension.com. **Contact:** Cy Gonick, publisher and coordinating editor. **80% freelance written.** Bimonthly magazine covering politics and wold issues from a socialist perspective. "We bring a socialist perspective to bear on events across Canada and around the world. Our contributors provide in-depth coverage on popular movements, peace, labour, women, aboriginal justice, environment, third world, and eastern Europe." Estab. 1963. Circ. 3,000. Pays on publication. Publishes ms an average of 6 months after acceptance. Accepts simultaneous submissions. Responds in 6 weeks to queries. Sample copy for $2. Guidelines available online.

NONFICTION Needs interview, opinion, reviews. **Buys 8 mss/year.** Length: 500-2,000 words. **Pays $25-100.**

REPRINTS Send typed ms with rights for sale noted and information about when and where the material previously appeared.

DISABILITIES

🍁 $$ ABILITIES

Canadian Abilities Foundation, 340 College St., Suite 270, Toronto ON M5T 3A9 Canada. (416)923-1885. **Fax:** (416)923-9829. **Website:** www.abilities.ca. **50% freelance written.** Quarterly magazine covering disability issues. *Abilities* provides information, inspiration, and opportunity to its readers with articles and resources covering health, travel, sports, products, technology, profiles, employment, recreation, and more. Estab. 1987. Circ. 20,000. Byline given. Pays on publication. Offers 50% kill fee. Publishes ms an average of 3 months after acceptance. Editorial lead time 3 months. Submit seasonal material 4 months in advance. Accepts queries by mail, e-mail, fax. Responds in 3 months to queries. Sample copy free. Writer's guidelines for #10 SASE, online, or by e-mail.

NONFICTION Needs general interest, how-to, humor, inspirational, interview, new product, personal experience, photo feature, travel. Does not want articles that 'preach to the converted'—this means info that people with disabilities likely already know, such as what it's like to have a disability. **Buys 30-40 mss/year.** Query or send complete ms. Length: 500-2,500 words. **Pays $50-400 (Canadian) for assigned articles. Pays $50-350 (Canadian) for unsolicited articles.**

REPRINTS Sometimes accepts previously published submissions (if stated as such).

COLUMNS/DEPARTMENTS The Lighter Side (humor), 700 words; Profile, 1,200 words.

💲💲💲💲 ARTHRITIS TODAY

Arthritis Foundation, 1330 W. Peachtree St., Suite 100, Atlanta GA 30309. (404)872-7100. **Fax:** (404)872-9559. **Website:** www.arthritistoday.org. **50% freelance written.** Bimonthly magazine covering living with arthritis and the latest in research/treatment. *Arthritis Today* is a consumer health magazine and is written for the more than 70 million Americans who have arthritis and for the millions of others whose lives are touched by an arthritis-related disease. The editorial content is designed to help the person with arthritis live a more productive, independent, and pain-free life. The articles are upbeat and provide practical advice, information, and inspiration. Estab. 1987. Circ. 650,000. Byline given. Pays on acceptance. Offers kill fee. Offers kill fee. Editorial lead time 6 months. Submit seasonal material 6 months in advance. Accepts queries by mail, online submission form. Accepts simultaneous submissions. Responds in 2 months to queries. Sample copy for 9x11 SAE with 4 first-class stamps.

NONFICTION Needs general interest, how-to, tips on any aspect of living with arthritis, inspirational, new product, arthritis related, opinion, personal experience, photo feature, technical, travel, tips, news, service, nutrition, general health, lifestyle. **Buys 12 unsolicited mss/year.** Query with published clips. Length: 150-2,500 words. **Pays $100-2,500.** Pays expenses of writers on assignment.

COLUMNS/DEPARTMENTS Nutrition, 100-600 words; Fitness, 100-600 words; Balance (emotional coping), 100-600 words; MedWatch, 100-800 words; Solutions, 100-600 words; Life Makeover, 400-600 words.

FILLERS Needs facts, gags, short humor. **Buys 2 mss/year.** Length: 40-100 words. **Pays $80-150.**

💲💲 DIABETES HEALTH

King's Publishing, Inc., 365 Bel Marin Keys Blvd., Suite 100, Novato CA 94949. (415)883-1990. **Fax:** (415)883-1932. **E-mail:** editor@diabeteshealth.com. **Website:** www.diabeteshealth.com. **Contact:** Nadia Al-Samarrie, publisher and editor-in-chief. **40% freelance written.** Monthly tabloid covering diabetes care. "*Diabetes Health* covers the latest in diabetes care, medications, and patient advocacy. Personal accounts are welcome as well as medical-oriented articles by MDs, RNs, and CDEs (certified diabetes educators)." Estab. 1991. Circ. 40,000. Byline given. Pays on publication. No kill fee. Publishes ms an average of 2 months after acceptance. Editorial lead time 2 months. Submit seasonal material 2 months in advance. Accepts queries by e-mail, online submission form. Sample copy available online. Guidelines free.

NONFICTION Needs essays, how-to, humor, inspirational, interview, new product, opinion, personal experience. **Buys 25 mss/year.** Send complete ms. "Our feature stories run at a maximum of 1,500 words. Features should have at least 3-5 outside sources. We also accept shorter opinion pieces, columns (500 words each) and letters to the editor. We are not responsible for returning unsolicited content or photos. All content should be balanced, informative, lively, timely, concise and easy to read for a lay audience. *Diabetes Health* does not accept mss that promote a product, philosophy, or personal view. When discussing products or treatment techniques, you should include experiences of a person with diabetes. Never make sweeping generalizations that cannot be supported by published research or highly credible sources. All mss should be sent as a Word file. Do not fax or mail mss. Do not copy and paste ms into the body of an e-mail. All mss will be edited for style, length, and substance. Upon receiving a ms, we will either query you for additional information or, if the material is unacceptable, return the ms with rewrite instructions. We encourage writers to submit photographs or other art that will help illustrate the story." Length: 500-1,500 words. **Pays about 20¢/word. "Payment varies with experience and is based on the final length as it appears in the magazine."**

💲💲 DIABETES SELF-MANAGEMENT

R.A. Rapaport Publishing, Inc., 150 W. 22nd St., Suite 800, New York NY 10011. (212)989-0200. **Fax:** (212)989-4786. **E-mail:** editor@rapaportpublishing.com. **Website:** www.diabetesselfmanagement.com. **20% freelance written.** Bimonthly magazine. "We publish how-to health care articles for motivated, intelligent readers who have diabetes and who are actively involved in their own health care management. All articles must have immediate application to their daily living." Estab. 1983. Circ. 410,000. Byline given. Pays on publication. Offers 20% kill fee. Submit seasonal material 6 months in advance. Accepts queries by mail, e-mail, fax. Responds in 6 weeks to queries.

Sample copy for $4 and 9x12 SAE with 6 first-class stamps, or online. Guidelines for #10 SASE.

NONFICTION Needs how-to, exercise, nutrition, diabetes self-care, product surveys, technical, reviews of products available, foods sold by brand name, pharmacology, travel, considerations and prep for people with diabetes. No personal experiences, personality profiles, exposés, or research breakthroughs. **Buys 10-12 mss/year.** Query with published clips. Length: 2,000-2,500 words. **Pays $400-700 for assigned articles. Pays $200-700 for unsolicited articles.**

$ DIALOGUE

Blindskills, Inc., P.O. Box 5181, Salem OR 97304. **E-mail:** magazine@blindskills.com. **Website:** www.blindskills.com. **60% freelance written.** Quarterly journal covering visually impaired people. Estab. 1962. Circ. 1,100. Byline given. Pays on publication. Publishes ms an average of 6 months after acceptance. Editorial lead time 3 months. Accepts queries by e-mail. One free sample on request. Available in large print, Braille, digital audio cassette, and e-mail. Guidelines available online.

NONFICTION Needs essays, general interest, historical, how-to, life skills methods used by visually impaired people, humor, interview, personal experience, sports, recreation, hobbies. No controversial, explicit sex, religious, or political topics. **Buys 50-60 mss/year.** Send complete ms. Length: 200-1,200/ words. **Pays $15-35 for assigned articles. Pays $15-25 for unsolicited articles.**

COLUMNS/DEPARTMENTS All material should be relative to blind and visually impaired readers. Living with Low Vision, 1,000 words; Hear's How (dealing with sight loss), 1,000 words. Technology Answer Book, 1,000 words. **Buys 80 mss/year.** Send complete ms. **Pays $10-25.**

HEARING HEALTH

Hearing Health, 363 Seventh Ave., 10th Floor, New York NY 10001. **E-mail:** info@hearinghealthfoundation.org. **Website:** www.hearinghealthfoundation.org. Magazine covering issues and concerns pertaining to hearing health and hearing loss. Byline given. Pays with contributor copies. Accepts queries by mail, e-mail. Accepts simultaneous submissions. Guidelines available online.

NONFICTION Send complete ms.

REPRINTS "Please do not submit a previously published article unless permission has been obtained in writing that allows the article's use in *Hearing Health*."

COLUMNS/DEPARTMENTS Features (800-1,500 words); First-person stories (500-1,500 words); Humor (500-750 words); Viewpoints/Op-Ed (350-500 words). Send complete ms.

$$ PN

PVA Publications, 2111 E. Highland Ave., Suite 180, Phoenix AZ 85016-4702. (602)224-0500. **E-mail:** andy@pvamag.com. **Website:** www.pn-magazine.com. **Contact:** Andy Nemann, editorial coordinator. Monthly magazine covering news and information for wheelchair users. Estab. 1946. Circ. 40,000. Byline given. Pays on publication. Publishes ms an average of 2-4 months after acceptance. Editorial lead time 3 months. Submit seasonal material 3 months in advance. Accepts queries by mail, e-mail, fax. Sample copy and guidelines free.

NONFICTION Needs how-to, interview, new product, opinion. **Buys 10-12 mss/year.** Send complete ms. Length: 1,200-2,500 words. **Pays $25-250.**

$$ SPECIALIVING

P.O. Box 1000, Bloomington IL 61702. (309)962-2003. **E-mail:** gareeb@aol.com. **Website:** www.specialiving.com. **90% freelance written.** Quarterly online magazine covering the physically disabled/mobility impaired. "We are now an online-only magazine. There is no subscription fee. Subject matter is the same. Payment is still the same, (max 800 words). Need photos with ms." Estab. 2001. Circ. 12,000. Byline given. Pays on publication. Editorial lead time 3 months. Submit seasonal material 6 months in advance. Accepts queries by mail, e-mail, fax, phone. Accepts simultaneous submissions. Responds in 3 weeks to queries.

NONFICTION Needs how-to, humor, inspirational, interview, new product, personal experience, technical, travel. **Buys 40 mss/year.** Query. Length: 800 words. **Pays 10¢/word.**

COLUMNS/DEPARTMENTS Shopping Guide; Items. **Buys 30 mss/year.** Query.

$$ SPORTS 'N SPOKES

The Magazine for Wheelchair Sports and Recreation, PVA Publications, 2111 E. Highland Ave., Suite 180, Phoenix AZ 85016-4702. (602)224-0500. **Fax:** (602)224-0507. **E-mail:** brenda@pvamag.com; richard@pvamag.com. **Website:** www.sportsnspokes.

com. Richard Hoover, editor. **Contact:** Brenda Martin, editorial coordinator. Bimonthly magazine covering wheelchair sports and recreation. Writing must pertain to wheelchair sports and recreation. Estab. 1974. Circ. 25,000. Byline given. Pays on publication. Publishes ms an average of 2-3 months after acceptance. Editorial lead time 2-3 months. Submit seasonal material 2-3 months in advance. Accepts queries by mail, e-mail. Sample copy and guidelines free.

NONFICTION Needs general interest, interview, new product. **Buys 5-6 mss/year.** Send complete ms. Length: 1,200-2,500 words. **Pays $20-250.**

ENTERTAINMENT

💲 CINEASTE

Cineaste Publishers, Inc., 243 Fifth Ave., #706, New York NY 10016. (212)366-5720. **E-mail:** cineaste@cineaste.com. **Website:** www.cineaste.com. **30% freelance written.** Quarterly magazine covering motion pictures with an emphasis on social and political perspective on cinema. Estab. 1967. Circ. 11,000. Byline given. Pays on publication. Offers 50% kill fee. Publishes ms an average of 4 months after acceptance. Editorial lead time 3 months. Submit seasonal material 4 months in advance. Accepts queries by mail, e-mail, fax. Responds in 1 month to queries. Sample copy for $5. Writer's guidelines on website.

NONFICTION Needs book excerpts, essays, exposé, historical, humor, interview, opinion. **Buys 20-30 mss/year.** Query with published clips. Length: 2,000-5,000 words. **Pays $30-100.**

COLUMNS/DEPARTMENTS Homevideo (topics of general interest or a related group of films); A Second Look (new interpretation of a film classic or a reevaluation of an unjustly neglected release of more recent vintage); Lost and Found (film that may or may not be released or otherwise seen in the US but which is important enough to be brought to the attention of our readers); all 1,000-1,500 words. Query with published clips. **Pays $50 minimum.**

☺ 💲 DANCE INTERNATIONAL

Scotiabant Dance Centre, Level 6 677 Davie St., Vancouver BC V6B 2G6 Canada. (604)681-1525. **Fax:** (604)681-7732. **E-mail:** Editor@DanceInternational.org. **Website:** www.danceinternational.org. **100% freelance written.** Quarterly magazine covering dance arts. Articles and reviews on current activities in world dance, with occasional historical essays; re-

views of dance films, video, and books. Estab. 1973. Circ. 4,500. Byline given. Pays on publication. Offers 50% kill fee. Publishes ms an average of 3 months after acceptance. Editorial lead time 3 months. Submit seasonal material 6 weeks in advance. Accepts queries by mail, e-mail, fax, phone. Responds in 2 weeks to queries. Responds in 1 month to mss. Sample copy for $7. Guidelines for #10 SASE.

NONFICTION Needs book excerpts, essays, historical, interview, personal experience, photo feature. **Buys 100 mss/year.** Query. Length: 1,200-2,200 words. **Pays $40-150.**

COLUMNS/DEPARTMENTS Dance Bookshelf (recent books reviewed), 700-800 words; Regional Reports (events in each region), 1,200 words. **Buys 100 mss/year.** Query. **Pays $80.**

💲💲 FLICK MAGAZINE

Decipher, Inc., 259 Granby St., 3rd Floor, Norfolk VA 23510. (757)623-3600. **Fax:** (757)623-8368. **E-mail:** julie.matthews@decipher.com. **Website:** www.flick-magazine.com. **30-40% freelance written.** Mini-magazine distributed in movie theaters that comes out in conjunction with selected movies covering one specific movie per issue. *Flick's* mission is to match the passion and personality of fans, taking readers inside Hollywood and increasing their connection to the film they are about to view. Estab. 2005. Circ. 2.5 million. Pays on acceptance. No kill fee. Publishes ms an average of 4 months after acceptance. Editorial lead time 4-5 months. Accepts queries by mail, e-mail.

NONFICTION Needs essays, humor, interview, opinion, personal experience. Query. Length: 500-1,000 words. **Pays $200-500.** Sometimes pays expenses of writers on assignment.

COLUMNS/DEPARTMENTS **Pays $200-500.**

FILLERS Needs gags, short humor. **Buys 5-10 mss/year. Pays $200-500.**

💲 IN TOUCH WEEKLY

270 Sylvan Ave., Englewood Cliffs NJ 07632. (201)569-6699. **E-mail:** breakingnews@intouchweekly.com; contactintouch@intouchweekly.com. **Website:** www.intouchweekly.com. **10% freelance written.** Weekly magazine covering celebrity news and entertainment. Estab. 2002. Circ. 1,300,000. No byline given. Pays on publication. Editorial lead time 1 week. Accepts queries by e-mail.

NONFICTION Needs interview, gossip. **Buys 1,300 mss/year.** Query. Send a tip about a celebrity by e-mail. Length: 100-1,000 words. **Pays $50.**

💲💲💲 OK! MAGAZINE

American Media, Inc., 1155 Avenue of the Americas, New York NY 10036. **Website:** www.okmagazine.com. **10% freelance written.** Weekly magazine covering entertainment news. "We are a celebrity friendly magazine. We strive not to show celebrities in a negative light. We consider ourselves a cross between *People* and *In Style*." Estab. 2005. Circ. 1,000,000. Byline sometimes given. Pays after publication. Publishes ms an average of 1 month after acceptance. Editorial lead time 2 weeks. Accepts queries by mail, e-mail. **NONFICTION** Needs interview, photo feature. **Buys 50 mss/year.** Query with published clips. Length: 500-2,000 words. **Pays $100-1,000.**

♻ 💲💲 RUE MORGUE

Marrs Media, Inc., 1411 Dufferin St., Toronto ON M6H 4C7 Canada. **E-mail:** dave@rue-morgue.com. **Website:** www.rue-morgue.com. **Contact:** Dave Alexander, editor-in-chief. **50% freelance written.** Monthly magazine covering horror entertainment. "A knowledge of horror entertainment (films, books, games, toys, etc.)." Estab. 1997. Byline given. Pays on publication. No kill fee. Publishes ms an average of 2-4 months after acceptance. Editorial lead time 2 months. Submit seasonal material 4 months in advance. Accepts queries by e-mail. Responds in 6 weeks to queries. Responds in 2 months to mss. Guidelines available by e-mail.

NONFICTION Needs essays, exposé, historical, interview, travel, new product. No reviews. Query with published clips or send complete ms. Length: 500-3,500 words.

COLUMNS/DEPARTMENTS Classic Cut (historical essays on classic horror films, books, games, comic books, music), 500-700 words. Query with published clips.

💲💲💲💲 SOUND & VISION

Bonnier Corp., 2 Park Ave., 10th Floor, New York NY 10016. (212)767-5000. **Fax:** (212)767-5200. **E-mail:** feedback@soundandvisionmag.com. **Website:** www.soundandvisionmag.com. **Contact:** Mike Mettler, editor-in-chief. **40% freelance written.** Magazine published 8 times/year covering home theater consumer products. "Provides readers with authoritative information on the home entertainment technologies and products that will impact their lives." Estab. 1958. Circ. 400,000. Byline given. Pays on acceptance. Publishes ms an average of 4 months after acceptance. Accepts queries by mail, e-mail. Sample copy for SAE with 9x12 envelope and 11 first-class stamps.

NONFICTION **Buys 25 mss/year.** Query with published clips. Length: 1,500-3,000 words. **Pays $1,000-1,500.**

💲 TELEREVISTA

304 Indian Trace #238, Weston FL 33326. (954)689-2428. **Fax:** (954)689-2428. **E-mail:** info@telerevista.com. **Website:** www.telerevista.com. **Contact:** Salvatore Trimarchi, editor. **100% freelance written.** Monthly magazine written in Spanish covering Hispanic entertainment (U.S. and Puerto Rico). "We feature interviews, gossip, breaking stories, behind-the-scenes happenings, etc." Estab. 1986. Byline sometimes given. Pays on publication. Publishes ms an average of 3 months after acceptance. Editorial lead time 2 months. Submit seasonal material 3 months in advance. Accepts queries by mail, e-mail, fax. Sample copy free.

NONFICTION Needs exposé, interview, opinion, photo feature. **Buys 200 mss/year.** Query. **Pays $25-75.**

COLUMNS/DEPARTMENTS Buys 60 mss/year. Query. **Pays $25-75.**

FILLERS Needs anecdotes, facts, gags, newsbreaks, short humor.

ETHNIC AND MINORITY

💲💲💲💲 AARP SEGUNDA JUVENTUD

AARP, 601 E St. NW, Washington DC 20049. **E-mail:** segundajuventud@aarp.org. **Website:** www.aarpsegundajuventud.org. **75% freelance written.** Bimonthly Spanish language magazine geared toward 50+ Hispanics. With fresh and relevant editorial content and a mission of inclusiveness and empowerment, *AARP Segunda Juventud* serves more than 800,000 Hispanic AARP members and their families in all 50 states, the District of Columbia, Puerto Rico, and the US Virgin Islands. Estab. 2002. Circ. 800,000. Byline given. Pays on acceptance. Offers 33.33% kill fee. Publishes ms an average of 4 months after acceptance. Editorial lead time 2-12 months. Submit seasonal material 4-12 months in advance. Accepts queries by mail, e-mail. Accepts simultaneous submissions. Responds in 4 months to queries and mss. Sample copy available online.

NONFICTION Needs general interest, interview, new product, travel, reviews (book, film, music). **Buys 36 mss/year.** Query with published clips. Length: 200-1,500 words. **Pays $1-2/word.** Sometimes pays expenses of writers on assignment.

COLUMNS/DEPARTMENTS Health; Finance; Travel; Celebrity profile; Encore (Hispanic 50+ individuals re-inventing themselves). **Buys 24 mss/year.** Query with published clips. **Pays $1-2/word.**

FILLERS Needs facts. **Buys 6 mss/year.** Length: 200-250 words. **Pays $1-2/word.**

$ AIM MAGAZINE

Aim Publication Association, P.O. Box 856, Forest Grove OR 97116. (253)815-9030. **E-mail:** editor@aimmagazine.com; apiladoone@aol.com. **Website:** aimmagazine.org. **75% freelance written. Works with a small number of new/unpublished writers each year.** Quarterly magazine on social betterment that promotes racial harmony and peace for high school, college, and general audience. Publishes material to purge racism from the human bloodstream through the written word. Estab. 1975. Circ. 10,000. Byline given. Pays on publication. Offers 60% kill fee. Publishes ms an average of 3 months after acceptance. Submit seasonal material 6 months in advance. Accepts queries by mail, e-mail. Does not accept previously published submissions.Responds in 2 months to queries. Responds in 1 month to mss. Sample copy and writer's guidelines for $5 and 9x12 SAE with correct postage or online. Guidelines available online: http://www.aimmagazine.org/submit.htm.

NONFICTION Needs exposé, education, general interest, social significance, historical, Black or Indian, how-to, create a more equitable society, interview, one who is making social contributions to community, book reviews, reviews of plays. No religious material. **Buys 16 mss/year.** Send complete ms. Length: 500-800 words. **Pays $25-35.**

FICTION Contact: Ruth Apilado, associate editor. Fiction that teaches the brotherhood of man. Needs ethnic, historical, mainstream, suspense. Open. No religious mss. **Buys 20 mss/year.** Send complete ms. Length: 1,000-1,500 words. **Pays $25-35.**

POETRY Needs avant-garde, free verse, light verse. No preachy poetry. Buys 20 poems/year. Submit maximum 5 poems. Length: 15-30 lines. **Pays $3-5.**

FILLERS Needs anecdotes, newsbreaks, short humor. **Buys 30 mss/year.** Length: 50-100 words. **Pays $5.**

$$$ B'NAI B'RITH MAGAZINE

2020 K St. NW, 7th Floor, Washington DC 20006. (202)857-6527. **E-mail:** bbmag@bnaibrith.org. **Website:** www.bnaibrith.org. **90% freelance written.** Quarterly magazine specializing in social, political, historical, religious, cultural, 'lifestyle,' and service articles relating chiefly to the Jewish communities of North America and Israel. Write for the American Jewish audience, i.e., write about topics from a Jewish perspective, highlighting creativity and innovation in Jewish life. Estab. 1886. Circ. 110,000. Byline given. Pays on publication. Publishes ms an average of 6 months after acceptance. Editorial lead time 3 months. Submit seasonal material 5 months in advance. Accepts queries by mail, e-mail, fax. Accepts simultaneous submissions. Responds in 1 month to queries. Responds in 6 weeks to mss. Sample copy for $2. Writer's guidelines for #10 SASE or by e-mail.

NONFICTION Needs interview, photo feature, religious, travel. No Holocaust memoirs, first-person essays/memoirs, fiction, or poetry. **Buys 14-20 mss/year.** Query with published clips. Length: 1,000-2,500 words. **Pays $300-800 for assigned articles. Pays $300-700 for unsolicited articles.** Sometimes pays expenses of writers on assignment.

🍁 $ CELTICLIFE INTERNATIONAL

Clansman Publishing, Ltd., P.O. Box 8805, Station A, Halifax NS B3K 5M4 Canada. (902)835-2358. **Fax:** (902)835-0080. **E-mail:** editor@celticlife.ca. **Website:** www.celticlifeintl.com. **Contact:** Stephen Patrick Clarke, managing editor. **95% freelance written.** Quarterly magazine covering culture of those with an interest in Celtic culture around the world. "The magazine chronicles the stories of Celtic people from around the world, with a focus on the stories of those who are not mentioned in history books. We also feature Gaelic language articles, history of Celtic people, traditions, music, and folklore. We profile Celtic musicians and include reviews of Celtic books, music, and videos." Estab. 1987. Circ. distribution: 173,740; readership 880,000. Byline given. Pays after publication. No kill fee. Editorial lead time 2 months. Submit seasonal material 3 months in advance. Accepts queries by e-mail only. Responds in 1 week to queries. Responds in 1 month to mss.

NONFICTION Needs essays, general interest, historical, interview, opinion, personal experience, travel, Gaelic language, Celtic music reviews, profiles of Celtic musicians, Celtic history, traditions, and folklore. Also buys short fiction. No fiction, poetry, historical stories already well publicized. **Buys 100 mss/year.** Query or send complete ms. Length: 800-2,500 words. **All writers receive a complimentary subscription. COLUMNS/DEPARTMENTS** Query.

⊗⊗ HADASSAH MAGAZINE

50 W. 58th St., New York NY 10019. (212)688-0227. **Fax:** (212)446-9521. **E-mail:** magazine@hadassah. org. **Website:** www.hadassah.org/magazine. **Contact:** Elizabeth Goldberg. **90% freelance written.** Monthly magazine. "*Hadassah* is a general interest Jewish feature and literary magazine. We speak to our readers on a vast array of subjects ranging from politics to parenting, to midlife crisis to Mideast crisis. Our readers want coverage on social and economic issues, Jewish women's (feminist) issues, the arts, travel and health." Circ. 243,000. Pays on acceptance. Responds in 4 months to mss. Sample copy and writer's guidelines with 9x12 SASE.

NONFICTION Buys 10 unsolicited mss/year. Query. Length: 1,500-2,000 words. Sometimes pays expenses of writers on assignment.

COLUMNS/DEPARTMENTS "We have a family column and a travel column, but a query for topic or destination should be submitted first to make sure the area is of interest and the story follows our format."

FICTION Contact: Zelda Shluker, managing editor. Short stories with strong plots and positive Jewish values. Needs ethnic, Jewish. No personal memoirs, schmaltzy or shelter magazine fiction. Length: 1,500-2,000 words. **Pays $500 minimum.**

⊗ INTERNATIONAL EXAMINER

622 S. Washington St., Seattle WA 98104. (206)624-3925. **Fax:** (206)624-3046. **E-mail:** editor@iexaminer. org. **Website:** www.iexaminer.org. **Contact:** Christina Twu, editor-in-chief. **75% freelance written.** Biweekly journal of Asian-American news, politics, and arts. "*International Examiner* is about Asian-American issues and things of interest to Asian-Americans. We do not want stuff about Asian things (stories on your trip to China, Japanese Tea Ceremony, etc. will be rejected). Yes, we are in English." Estab. 1974. Circ. 12,000. Pays on publication. No kill fee. Publishes ms an average of 1 month after acceptance. Editorial lead

time 1 month. Submit seasonal material 2 months in advance. Accepts queries by mail, e-mail, fax. Accepts simultaneous submissions. Guidelines for #10 SASE.

NONFICTION Needs essays, exposé, general interest, historical, humor, interview, opinion, personal experience, photo feature. **Buys 100 mss/year.** Query by mail, fax, or e-mail with published clips. 750-5,000 words, depending on subject. **Pays $25-100.** Sometimes pays expenses of writers on assignment.

REPRINTS Accepts previously published submissions (as long as published in same area). Send typed ms with rights for sale noted and information about when and where the material previously appeared. Payment negotiable.

FICTION Asian-American authored fiction by or about Asian-Americans only. Needs novel concepts. **Buys 1-2 mss/year.** Query.

⊗⊗ ITALIAN AMERICA

219 E St. NE, Washington DC 20002. (202)547-2900. **Fax:** (202)546-8168. **E-mail:** ddesanctis@osia.org. **Website:** www.osia.org. **Contact:** Dona De Sanctis, editor. **20% freelance written.** Quarterly magazine. *Italian America* provides timely information about OSIA, while reporting on individuals, institutions, issues, and events of current or historical significance in the Italian-American community. Estab. 1996. Circ. 65,000. Byline given. Pays on publication. Offers 50% kill fee. Publishes ms an average of 3 months after acceptance. Editorial lead time 3 months. Accepts queries by mail, e-mail, fax. Accepts simultaneous submissions. Sample copy free. Guidelines available online.

NONFICTION Needs historical, little known historical facts that must relate to Italian Americans, interview, opinion, current events. **Buys 8 mss/year.** Query with published clips. Length: 750-1,000 words. **Pays $50-250.**

⊗⊗ JEWISH ACTION

Orthodox Union, 11 Broadway, New York NY 10004. (212)613-8146. **Fax:** (212)613-0646. **E-mail:** ja@ ou.org. **Website:** www.ou.org/jewish_action. **Contact:** Nechama Carmel, editor; Rashel Zywica, assistant editor. **80% freelance written.** Quarterly magazine covering a vibrant approach to Jewish issues, Orthodox lifestyle, and values. Estab. 1986. Circ. 40,000. Byline given. Pays 2 months after publication. Submit seasonal material 4 months in advance. Accepts queries by mail, e-mail, fax. Responds in 3 months to queries. Sample copy available online. Guidelines with #10 SASE or by e-mail.

NONFICTION "We are not looking for Holocaust accounts. We welcome essays about responses to personal or societal challenges." **Buys 30-40 mss/year.** Query with published clips. Length: 1,000-3,000 words. **Pays $100-400 for assigned articles. Pays $75-150 for unsolicited articles.**

COLUMNS/DEPARTMENTS Just Between Us (personal opinion on current Jewish life and issues), 1,000 words. **Buys 4 mss/year.**

FICTION Must have relevance to Orthodox reader. Length: 1,000-2,000 words.

POETRY Buys limited number of poems/year. **Pays $25-75.**

KHABAR

Khabar, Inc., 3790 Holcomb Bridge Rd., Suite 101, Norcross GA 30092. (770)451-7666, ext. 115. **Fax:** (770)234-6115. **E-mail:** parthiv@khabar.com; info@khabar.com. **Website:** www.khabar.com. **50% freelance written.** "Monthly magazine covering the Asian Indian community in and around Georgia." Content relating to Indian-American and/or immigrant experience. Estab. 1992. Circ. 27,000. Pays on publication. Offers 25% kill fee. Publishes ms an average of 2 months after acceptance. Editorial lead time 2 months. Submit seasonal material 2 months in advance. Accepts queries by e-mail. Accepts simultaneous submissions. Sample copy free. Guidelines by e-mail.

NONFICTION Needs essays, interview, opinion, personal experience, travel. **Buys 5 mss/year.** Send complete ms. Length: 750-4,000 words. **Pays $100-300 for assigned articles. Pays $75 for unsolicited articles.**

COLUMNS/DEPARTMENTS Book Review, 1,200 words; Music Review, 800 words; Spotlight (profiles), 1,200-3,000 words. **Buys 5 mss/year.** Query with or without published clips or send complete ms. **Pays $75+.**

FICTION Needs ethnic, Indian American/Asian immigrant. **Buys 5 mss/year.** Query or send complete ms. **Pays $50-100.**

LATINA MAGAZINE

Latina Media Ventures, LLC, 625 Madison Ave., 3rd Floor, New York NY 10022. (212)642-0200. **E-mail:** editor@latina.com. **Website:** www.latina.com. **Contact:** Damarys Ocaña, executive editor. **40-50% freelance written.** Monthly magazine covering Latina lifestyle. *Latina Magazine* is the leading bilingual lifestyle publication for Hispanic women in the US today. Covering the best of Latino fashion, beauty, culture, and food, the magazine also features celebrity profiles and interviews. Estab. 1996. Circ. 250,000. Byline given. Pays on publication. Offers 25% kill fee. Publishes ms an average of 2-3 months after acceptance. Editorial lead time 3 months. Submit seasonal material 4-5 months in advance. Accepts queries by e-mail. Responds in 1 month to queries. Responds in 1-2 months to mss. Sample copy available online.

NONFICTION Needs essays, how-to, humor, inspirational, interview, new product, personal experience. Special issues: The 10 Latinas Who Changed the World (December). We do not feature an extensive amount of celebrity content or entertainment content, and freelancers should be sensitive to this. The magazine does not contain book or album reviews, and we do not write stories covering an artist's new project. We do not attend press junkets and do not cover press conferences. Please note that we are a lifestyle magazine, not an entertainment magazine. **Buys 15-20 mss/year.** Query with published clips. Length: 300-2,200 words. **Pays $1/word.** Pays expenses of writers on assignment.

MOMENT

4115 Wisconsin Ave. NW, Suite 102, Washington DC 20016. (202)363-6422. **Fax:** (202)362-2514. **E-mail:** editor@momentmag.com. **Website:** www.momentmag.com. **90% freelance written.** Bimonthly magazine on Judaism. *Moment* is committed to portraying intellectual, political, cultural, and religious debates within the community, and to educating readers about Judaism's rich history and contemporary movements, ranging from left to right, fundamentalist to secular. Estab. 1975. Circ. 65,000. Byline given. Pays on publication. Publishes ms an average of 6 months after acceptance. Editorial lead time 3 months. Submit seasonal material 6 months in advance. Accepts queries by mail, e-mail. Accepts simultaneous submissions. Responds in 1 month to queries. Responds in 3 months to mss. Sample copy for $4.50 and SAE. Guidelines available online.

NONFICTION **Buys 25-30 mss/year.** Query with published clips. Length: 2,500-7,000 words. **Pays $200-1,200 for assigned articles. Pays $40-500 for unsolicited articles.**

COLUMNS/DEPARTMENTS 5765 (snappy pieces about quirky events in Jewish communities, news and ideas to improve Jewish living), 250 words maximum; Olam (first-person pieces, humor, and colorful reportage), 600-1,500 words; Book reviews (fiction and nonfiction) are accepted but generally assigned, 400-800 words. **Buys 30 mss/year.** Query with published clips. **Pays $50-250.**

⊙⊙ NATIVE PEOPLES MAGAZINE

5333 N. Seventh St., Suite C-224, Phoenix AZ 85014. (602)265-4855. **Fax:** (602)265-3113. **E-mail:** dgibson@nativepeoples.com; kcoochwytewa@nativepeoples.com. **Website:** www.nativepeoples.com. **Contact:** Daniel Gibson, editor; Kevin Coochwytewa, art director. Bimonthly magazine covering Native Americans. High-quality reproduction with full color throughout. The primary purpose of this magazine is to offer a sensitive portrayal of the arts and lifeways of native peoples of the Americas. Estab. 1987. Circ. 40,000. Byline given. Pays on publication. Accepts queries by mail, e-mail, fax. Responds in 2 months to queries. Guidelines by request.

NONFICTION Needs interviews of interesting and leading Natives from all walks of life, with an emphasis on arts, personal experience. **Buys 35 mss/year.** Length: 1,000-2,500 words. **Pays 25¢/word.**

⊙⊙ RUSSIAN LIFE

RIS Publications, P.O. Box 567, Montpelier VT 05601. **Website:** www.russianlife.com. **75% freelance written.** Bimonthly magazine covering Russian culture, history, travel, and business. "Our readers are informed Russophiles with an avid interest in all things Russian. But we do not publish personal travel journals or the like." Estab. 1956. Circ. 15,000. Byline given. Pays on publication. Publishes ms an average of 3-6 months after acceptance. Editorial lead time 2 months. Submit seasonal material 3 months in advance. Accepts queries by mail. TrueResponds in 1 month to queries. Sample copy with 9x12 SASE and 6 first-class stamps. Guidelines available online.

NONFICTION Needs general interest, photo feature, travel. No personal stories, i.e., How I came to love Russia. **Buys 15-20 mss/year.** Query. Length: 1,000-6,000 words. **Pays $100-300.**

REPRINTS Accepts previously published submissions rarely.

⊙⊙ SCANDINAVIAN REVIEW

The American-Scandinavian Foundation, 58 Park Ave., New York NY 10016. (212)779-3587. **E-mail:** info@amscan.org. **Website:** www.amscan.org. **75% freelance written.** Triannual magazine for contemporary Scandinavia. Audience: Members, embassies, consulates, libraries. Slant: Popular coverage of contemporary affairs in Scandinavia. Estab. 1913. Circ. 4,000. Byline given. Pays on publication. No kill fee. Publishes ms an average of 2 months after acceptance. Editorial lead time 3 months. Submit seasonal material 3 months in advance. Responds in 6 weeks to queries. Sample copy available online. Guidelines free.

NONFICTION Needs general interest, interview, photo feature, travel, must have Scandinavia as topic focus. Special issues: Scandinavian travel. No pornography. **Buys 30 mss/year.** Query with published clips. Length: 1,500-2,000 words. **Pays $300 maximum.**

⊙ ⊙ WINDSPEAKER

Aboriginal Multi-Media Society of Alberta, 13245-146 St., Edmonton AB T5L 4S8 Canada. (780)455-2700. **Fax:** (780)455-7639. **E-mail:** market@ammsa.com; dsteel@ammsa.com. **Website:** www.ammsa.com/windspeaker. **Contact:** Paul Macedo, director of publishing operations; Debora Steel, contributing news editor. **25% freelance written.** Monthly tabloid covering native issues. Focus on events and issues that affect and interest native peoples, national or local. Estab. 1983. Circ. 27,000. Byline given. Pays on publication. Offers kill fee. Publishes ms an average of 1 month after acceptance. Editorial lead time 1 month. Submit seasonal material 2 months in advance. Accepts queries by mail, e-mail, phone. Accepts simultaneous submissions. Sample copy free. Guidelines available online.

NONFICTION Needs opinion, photo feature, travel, news interview/profile, reviews: books, music, movies. Special issues: Powwow (June); Travel supplement (May). **Buys 200 mss/year.** Query with published clips and SASE or by phone. Length: 500-800 words. **Pays $3-3.60/published inch.** Sometimes pays expenses of writers on assignment.

FOOD AND DRINK

AMERICAN WINE SOCIETY JOURNAL

American Wine Society, 2881 S. Lake Leelanau Dr., Lake Leelanau MI 49653. (586)946-0049. **E-mail:** rink@americanwinesociety.org. **Website:** www.americanwinesociety.org. **Contact:** Jim Rink, editor. **100% freelance written.** "The non-profit American Wine Society is the largest consumer based wine education organization in the U.S. The *Journal* reflects the varied interests of AWS members, which may include wine novices, experts, grape growers, amateur and professional winemakers, chefs, wine appreciators, wine educators, restauranteurs, and anyone wanting to learn more about wine and gastronomy." Estab. 1967. Circ. 5,000. Byline given. Pays on publication. No kill fee. Publishes 3 months after acceptance. Editorial lead time is 3 months. Accepts queries by mail, e-mail. TrueAccepts simultaneous submissions. Responds in 2 weeks on queries, 3 months on mss. Sample copy available on website. Writer's guidelines available by e-mail at rink@americanwinesociety.org.

NONFICTION Needs general interest, historical, how-to, nostalgic, technical, travel. Submit query with published clips.

COLUMNS/DEPARTMENTS Columns include wine reviews, book reviews, food and wine articles. Writer should send query with published clips.

⊖⊖⊖ DRAFT

Draft Publishing, 4742 N. 24th St., Suite 210, Phoenix AZ 85016. (888)806-4677. **E-mail:** jessica.daynor@draftmag.com. **Website:** www.draftmag.com. **60% freelance written.** Bimonthly magazine covering beer and men's lifestyle (including food, travel, sports and leisure). "*DRAFT* is a national men's magazine devoted to beer, breweries and the lifestyle and culture that surrounds it. Read by nearly 300,000 men aged 21-45, *DRAFT* offers formal beer reviews, plus coverage of food, travel, sports and leisure. Writers need not have formal beer knowledge (though that's a plus!), but they should be experienced journalists who can appreciate beer and beer culture." Estab. 2006. Circ. 275,000. Byline given. Pays on publication. Offers 20% kill fee. Publishes ms an average of 2 months after acceptance. Editorial lead time 4 months. Submit seasonal material 6 months in advance. Accepts queries by e-mail. Accepts simultaneous submissions. Responds in 3 weeks to queries. Sample copy for $3 (magazine can also be found on most newsstands for $4.99). Guidelines available at www.draftmag.com/submissions.

NONFICTION Needs features, short front-of-book pieces, how-to's, interviews, travel, food, restaurant and bar pieces, sports and adventure; anything guy-related. Special issues: The editorial calendar is as follows: November/December: Holiday issue; Jan/Feb: Best of issue; May/June: Food issue; Mar/Apr: Travel

issue; July/Aug: All-American issue; Sept/Oct Anniversary issue. Do not want unsolicited mss., beer reviews, brewery profiles. **Buys 80/year. mss/year.** Query with published clips. Length: 250-2,500 words. **50-90¢ for assigned articles.** sometimes (limit agreed upon in advance).

COLUMNS/DEPARTMENTS Contact: Chris Staten, associate editor, (chris.staten@draftmag.com) for On-Tap and OnTap llife, Jessica Daynor, managing editor, for all other departments. 'On Tap' (short FOB pieces on beer-related subjects, 350 words; 'On Tap Life' (short FOB pieces on NON -beer-related subjects (travel, food, sports, home, leisure), 350 words; 'Trek' (travel pieces [need not relate to beer, but it's a plus]), 950 words; 'Taste' (beer-and-food-related incident or unique perspective on beer), 750 words. **Buys 50 mss/year.** Query with published clips. **Pays 50¢-80¢.**

⊘ FOOD & WINE

American Express Publishing Corp., 1120 Avenue of the Americas, 9th Floor, New York NY 10036. (212)382-5600. **Fax:** (212)764-2177. **Website:** www.foodandwine.com. Monthly magazine for the reader who enjoys the finer things in life. Editorial focuses on upscale dining, covering resturants, entertaining at home, and travel destinations. Circ. 964,000. No kill fee. Editorial lead time 6 months.

◯ Does not buy freelance material or use freelance writers.

⊖⊖ KASHRUS MAGAZINE

The Kashrus Institute, P.O. Box 204, Brooklyn NY 11204. (718)336-8544. **E-mail:** editorial@kashrus-magazine.com. **Website:** www.kashrusmagazine.com. **Contact:** Rabbi Wikler, editor. Estab. 1981. Circ. 10,000. Byline given. Pays on publication. Offers 50% kill fee. Publishes ms an average of 2 months after acceptance. Submit seasonal material 2 months in advance. Accepts queries by mail, phone. Accepts simultaneous submissions. Responds in 2 weeks. Sample copy - e-mail kashrus@aol.com and ask for "writer's sample copy."

NONFICTION Needs health, travel, new product, personal experience, photo feature, religious, technical. Special issues: International Kosher Travel (October); Passover Shopping Guide (March); Domestic Kosher Travel Guide (June). **Buys 8-12 mss/year.** Query with published clips. Length: 1,000-1,500 words. **Pays $100-250 for assigned articles. Pays up**

to **$100 for unsolicited articles.** Sometimes pays expenses of writers on assignment.

REPRINTS Send tearsheet or photocopy and information about when and where the material previously appeared. Pays 25-50% of amount paid for an original article.

TEA MAGAZINE

1000 Germantown Pike., F-2, Plymouth Meeting PA 19462. (484)688-0300. **Fax:** (484)688-0303. **E-mail:** teamag@teamag.com; Dan@teamag.com. **Website:** www.teamag.com. **Contact:** Dan Bolton, editor and publisher. **75% freelance written.** Quarterly magazine covering anything tea related. "TEA is a lifestyle publication celebrating tea and tea culture. It exists to encourage people to drink fine tea. Online and in print it articulates a forward-looking vision of nourishing, healthy, modern tea. TEA's content educates and excites enthusiasts. It offers new energy, new direction – with opportunities for tea enthusiasts young and old to share their discoveries via mobile, web and at retail locations where the publication is sold." Estab. 1994. Circ. 9,500. Byline given. Pays on publication. Publishes ms an average of 1 year after acceptance. Editorial lead time 9 months. Submit seasonal material 6 months in advance. Responds in 6 months to mss. Guidelines by e-mail.

NONFICTION Needs book excerpts, essays, general interest, historical, how-to, humor, interview, personal experience, photo feature, travel. Send complete ms. **Pays negotiable amount.** Sometimes pays expenses of writers on assignment.

COLUMNS/DEPARTMENTS Readers' Stories (personal experience involving tea); Book Reviews (review on tea books). Send complete ms. **Pays negotiable amount**

FICTION Does not want anything that is not tea related. Send complete ms. **Pays negotiable amount.**

POETRY Needs avant-garde, free verse, haiku, light verse, traditional. Does not want anything that is not tea related.

⑨⑨ WINE PRESS NORTHWEST

333 W. Canal Dr., Kennewick WA 99336. (509)582-1564. **Fax:** (509)585-7221. **E-mail:** editor@winepressnw.com; info@winepressnw.com. **Website:** www.winepressnw.com. **50% freelance written.** Quarterly magazine covering Pacific Northwest wine (Washington, Oregon, British Columbia, Idaho). "Wine Press Northwest is a quarterly magazine for those with an interest in wine, from the novice to the veteran. We publish in March, June, September and December. We focus on Washington, Oregon, Idaho and British Columbia's talented winemakers and the wineries, vintners and restaurants that showcase Northwest wines. We are dedicated to all who savor the fruits of their labor." Estab. 1998. Circ. 12,000. Byline given. Pays on publication. Offers 20% kill fee. Publishes ms an average of 3 months after acceptance. Editorial lead time 3 months. Submit seasonal material 3 months in advance. Accepts queries by mail, e-mail, fax. Accepts simultaneous submissions. Responds in 1 month to queries. Sample copy free or online. Guidelines free.

NONFICTION Needs general interest, historical, interview, new product, photo feature, travel. No beer, spirits, non-NW (California wine, etc.). **Buys 30 mss/year.** Query with published clips. Length: 1,500-2,500 words. **Pays $300.** Sometimes pays expenses of writers on assignment.

⑨⑨⑨ WINE SPECTATOR

M. Shanken Communications, Inc., 387 Park Ave. S., New York NY 10016. **E-mail:** wsonline@mshanken.com. **Website:** www.winespectator.com. **20% freelance written. Prefers to work with published/established writers.** Monthly news magazine. Estab. 1976. Circ. 350,000. Byline given. Pays within 30 days of publication. No kill fee. Publishes ms an average of 2 months after acceptance. Submit seasonal material 4 months in advance. Accepts queries by mail, fax. Responds in 3 months to queries. Guidelines for #10 SASE.

NONFICTION Needs general interest, news about wine or wine events, interview, of wine, vintners, wineries, opinion, photo feature, travel, dining and other lifestyle pieces. No winery promotional pieces or articles by writers who lack sufficient knowledge to write below just surface data. Query. Length: 100-2,000 words. **Pays $100-1,000.**

⑨⑨⑨⑨ WINE ENTHUSIAST MAGAZINE

Wine Enthusiast Media, 333 North Bedford Rd., Mt. Kisco NY 10549. **E-mail:** editor@wineenthusiast.net. **Website:** www.winemag.com. **Contact:** Mike Dawson, senior editor of digital and print (mdawson@wineenthusiast.net), for short, front-of-the-book items; Joe Czerwinski, managing editor (jczerwin@wineenthusiast.net), for feature stories aimed at the Pairings department and short back-of-the-book items. **40% freelance written.** Monthly magazine covering the lifestyle of wine. "Our readers are upscale and educated, but not necessarily super-sophisticated about wine itself. Our informal, irreverent approach appeals to savvy enophiles and newbies alike." Estab. 1988. Circ. 80,000. Byline given. Pays on acceptance. Offers 25% kill fee. Editorial lead time 4 months. Submit seasonal material 5 months in advance. Accepts queries by e-mail. Responds in 2 weeks to queries. Responds in 2 months to mss.

NONFICTION Needs essays, humor, interview, new product, personal experience. **Buys 5 mss/year. Pays $750-2,500 for assigned articles. Pays $750-2,000 for unsolicited articles. Pays 50¢/word for website articles.**

GAMES AND PUZZLES

💲 THE BRIDGE BULLETIN

American Contract Bridge League, 6575 Windchase Dr., Horn Lake MS 38637-1523. (662)253-3156. **Fax:** (662)253-3187. **E-mail:** editor@acbl.org. **E-mail:** brent. manley@acbl.org. **Website:** www.acbl.org. Paul Linxwiler, managing editor. **Contact:** Brent Manley, editor. **20% freelance written.** Monthly magazine covering duplicate (tournament) bridge. Estab. 1938. Circ. 155,000. Byline given. Pays on publication. Publishes ms an average of 3 months after acceptance. Editorial lead time 2 months. Accepts queries by mail, e-mail. Accepts simultaneous submissions.

NONFICTION Needs book excerpts, essays, how-to, play better bridge, humor, interview, new product, personal experience, photo feature, technical, travel. **Buys 6 mss/year.** Query. Length: 500-2,000 words. **Pays $100/page.**

💲💲 CHESS LIFE

P.O. Box 3967, Crossville TN 38557. (931)787-1234. **Fax:** (931)787-1200. **E-mail:** dlucas@uschess.org; fbutler@uschess.org. **Website:** www.uschess.org. **Contact:** Daniel Lucas, editor; Francesca "Frankie" Butler, art director. **15% freelance written. Works with a small number of new/unpublished writers/year.** Monthly magazine. "*Chess Life* is the official publication of the United States Chess Federation, covering news of most major chess events, both here and abroad, with special emphasis on the triumphs and exploits of American players." Estab. 1939. Circ. 85,000. Byline given. No kill fee. Publishes ms an average of 6 months after acceptance. Submit seasonal material 6 months in advance. Accepts queries by mail, e-mail, fax, phone. TrueAccepts simultaneous submissions. Responds in 3 months to mss. Sample copy and writer's guidelines with 9×11 SASE with 5 first-class stamps.

NONFICTION Needs general interest, historical, humor, interview, of a famous chess player or organizer, photo feature, chess centered, technical. No stories about personal experiences with chess. **Buys 30-40 mss/year.** Query with samples if new to publication. 3,000 words maximum. **Pays $100/page (800-1,000 words).** Sometimes pays expenses of writers on assignment.

REPRINTS "Send tearsheet, photocopy or typed ms with rights for sale noted and information about when and where the material previously appeared."

FILLERS Submit with samples and clips. Buys first or negotiable rights to cartoons and puzzles. **Pays $25 upon acceptance.**

💲💲💲 GAMES MAGAZINE

Kappa Publishing Group, Inc., 6198 Butler Pike, Suite 200, Blue Bell PA 19422. (215)643-6385. **Fax:** (215)628-3571. **E-mail:** games@kappapublishing.com. **Website:** www.gamesmagazine-online.com. **Contact:** R. Wayne Schmittberger, editor-in-chief. **50% freelance written.** Online magazine covering puzzles and games. *Games* is a magazine of puzzles, contests, and features pertaining to games and ingenuity. It is aimed primarily at adults and has an emphasis on pop culture. Estab. 1977. Circ. 75,000. Byline given. Pays on publication. Offers 25% kill fee. Publishes ms an average of 4 months after acceptance. Editorial lead time 3 months. Submit seasonal material 6 months in advance. Accepts queries by mail, e-mail. Accepts simultaneous submissions. Responds in 6 weeks to queries. Responds in 3 months to mss. Sample copy for $5. Guidelines for #10 SASE.

NONFICTION Needs photo feature, puzzles. **Buys 100 puzzles/year and 3 mss/year.** Query. Length: 1,500-2,500 words. **Pays $300-1,000.** Sometimes pays expenses of writers on assignment.

COLUMNS/DEPARTMENTS Gamebits (game/puzzle news), 250 words; Games & Books (product reviews), 350 words; Wild Cards (short text puzzles), 100 words. **Buys 50 mss/year.** Query. **Pays $25-250.**

FICTION Needs adventure, interactive, mystery. **Buys 1-2 mss/year.** Query. Length: 1,500-2,500 words. **Pays $500-1,200.**

$$ POKER PRO MAGAZINE

Poker Pro Media, 2101 NE Corporate Blvd., Boca Raton FL 33432. **E-mail:** jwenzel@pokerpromedia.com. **Website:** www.pokerpromagazine.com. **Contact:** John Wenzel, editor. **75% freelance written.** Monthly magazine covering poker, gambling, and nightlife. "We want articles about poker and gambling-related articles only; also nightlife in gaming cities and articles on gaming destinations." Estab. 2005. Circ. 150,000. Byline given. Pays on publication. No kill fee. Publishes ms an average of 1 month after acceptance. Editorial lead time 1 1/2 months. Submit seasonal material 2 months in advance. Accepts queries by e-mail. Responds in 1 week to queries. Responds in 1 month to mss. Sample copy and guidelines by e-mail.

NONFICTION Needs book excerpts, essays, exposé, general interest, historical, how-to, humor, interview, new product, opinion, personal experience, photo feature, travel. **Buys 125 mss/year.** Query. Length: 800-2,500 words. **Pays $100-$200 for assigned articles. Pays $100-$200 for unsolicited articles.** Sometimes pays expenses of writers on assignment.

GAY & LESBIAN INTEREST

$ THE GAY & LESBIAN REVIEW

Gay & Lesbian Review, Inc., P.O. Box 180300, Boston MA 02118. (617)421-0082. **E-mail:** editor@glreview.com. **Website:** www.glreview.com. **100% freelance written**. Bimonthly magazine covers gay and lesbian history, culture, and politics. In-depth essays on GLBT history, biography, the arts, political issues, written in clear, lively prose targeted to the 'literate nonspecialist.' Estab. 1994. Circ. 12,000. Byline given. Pays on publication. No kill fee. Editorial lead time 2 months. Accepts queries by mail, e-mail, phone. Accepts simultaneous submissions. Sample copy free. Guidelines free.

NONFICTION Needs essays, historical, humor, interview, opinion, book reviews. Does not want fiction, memoirs, personal reflections. Query. Length: 1,500-5,000 words. **Pays $100.**

POETRY Needs avant-garde, free verse, traditional. **No payment for poems.**

$$$$ THE GUIDE

2 Carlton St., Suite 1600, Toronto ON M5B 1J3. (416)925-6665. **Fax:** (416)925-6674. **E-mail:** brandon.matheson@xtra.ca. **Website:** www.guidemag.com. **Contact:** Brandon Matheson, publisher and editor-in-chief. **75% freelance written.** Monthly magazine on the gay and lesbian news, features, and travel. Estab. 1981. Pays on publication. Offers 50% kill fee. Publishes ms an average of 2 months after acceptance. Submit seasonal material 4 months in advance. Accepts queries by mail, e-mail. Accepts simultaneous submissions. Responds in 3 months to queries.

NONFICTION Needs general interest, historical, humor, personal experience, photo feature, travel, gay, lesbian, video. Send complete ms. Length: 500-800 words. **Pays $100-1,000.**

REPRINTS Occasionally buys previously published submissions. Pays 100% of amount paid for an original article.

$$ INSTINCT MAGAZINE

303 N. Glenoaks Blvd., Suite L-120, Burbank CA 91502. (818)286-0071; (818)843-1536 x102. **E-mail:** editor@instinctmag.com. **Website:** instinctmagazine.com. **Contact:** Mike Wood, editor-in-chief. **40% freelance written.** Gay men's monthly lifestyle and entertainment magazine. "*Instinct* is a blend of *Cosmo* and *Maxim* for gay men. We're smart, sexy, irreverent, and we always have a sense of humor—a unique style that has made us the #1 gay men's magazine in the US." Estab. 1997. Circ. 115,000. Byline given. Pays on publication. Offers 20% kill fee. Editorial lead time 2-3 months. Accepts queries by mail, e-mail. Accepts simultaneous submissions. Sample copy available online. Guidelines available online. Register online first.

NONFICTION Needs exposé, general interest, humor, interview, celebrity and non-celebrity, travel, basically anything of interest to gay men will be considered. Does not want first-person accounts or articles. Send complete ms via online submissions manager. Length: 850-2,000 words. **Pays $50-300.** Sometimes pays expenses of writers on assignment.

COLUMNS/DEPARTMENTS Health (gay, off-kilter), 800 words; Fitness (irreverent), 500 words; Movies, Books (edgy, sardonic), 800 words; Music, Video Games (indie, underground), 800 words. **Pays $150-250.**

$$ MENSBOOK JOURNAL

CQS Media, Inc., P.O. Box 418, Sturbridge MA 01566. **Fax:** (508)347-8150. **E-mail:** features@mensbook.com. **Website:** www.mensbook.com. **Contact:** P.C. Carr, editor/publisher. **75% freelance written.** Quarterly online download for gay men. "We target bright, inquisitive, discerning gay men who want more non-commercial substance from gay media. We seek primarily first-person autobiographical pieces—then: biographies, political and social analysis, cartoons, short fiction, commentary, travel, and humor." Estab. 2008. Circ. 5,000. Byline given. Pays on publication. Editorial lead time 4 months. Submit seasonal material 6 months in advance. Accepts queries by e-mail. Responds in 8 weeks to queries. Sample copy sent free by PDF. Guidelines online at www.mensbook.com/writersguidelines.htm.

NONFICTION Needs first-person pieces; essays; think-pieces; exposé; humor; inspirational profiles of courage and triumph over adversity; interview/profile; religion/philosophy vis-a-vis the gay experience; opinion; travel. "We do not want celebrity profiles/commentary, chatty, campy gossip; sexual conjecture about famous people; or film reviews." **Buys 25 mss/year.** Query by e-mail. Length: 1,000-2,500 words. **Pays stipend for assigned articles and for unsolicited articles.**

FICTION Needs adventure, erotica, fantasy, mystery/suspense, slice-of-life vignettes. **Buys 10-12 fiction mss/year.** Send complete ms. Length: 750-3,000 words.

POETRY Needs Needs avant-garde, free verse, haiku, light verse, traditional. Buys 8 poems/year.

TIPS "Be a tight writer with a cogent, potent message. Structure your work with well-organized progressive sequencing. Edit everything down before you send it over so we know it is the best you can do, and we'll work together from there."

⊛⊛ METROSOURCE MAGAZINE

137 W. 19th St., 2nd Floor, New York NY 10011. (212)691-5127. **E-mail:** letters@metrosource.com. **Website:** www.metrosource.com. **75% freelance written.** Magazine published 6 times/year. "*MetroSource* is an upscale, glossy, 4-color lifestyle magazine targeted to an urban, professional gay and lesbian readership." Estab. 1990. Circ. 145,000. Byline given. Pays on publication. Publishes ms an average of 2 months after acceptance. Editorial lead time 4 months. Submit seasonal material 4 months in advance. Accepts queries by mail, e-mail, fax, phone. Accepts simultaneous submissions. Sample copy for $5.

NONFICTION Needs exposé, interview, opinion, photo feature, travel. **Buys 20 mss/year.** Query with published clips. Length: 1,000-1,800 words. **Pays $100-400.**

PHOTOS State availability. Captions, model releases required. Negotiates payment individually.

COLUMNS/DEPARTMENTS Book, film, television, and stage reviews; health columns; and personal diary and opinion pieces. Word lengths vary. Query with published clips. **Pays $200.**

⊛⊛ THE ADVOCATE

Here Media, Inc., 10990 Wilshire Blvd., Penthouse, Los Angeles CA 90024. (310)943-5858. **Fax:** (310)806-6350. **E-mail:** newsroom@advocate.com. **Website:** www.advocate.com. **Contact:** Neal Broverman, managing editor. Biweekly magazine covering national news events with a gay and lesbian perspective on the issues. Estab. 1967. Circ. 120,000. Byline given. Pays on publication. Responds in 1 month to queries. Sample copy for $3.95. Guidelines on website.

NONFICTION Needs exposé, interview, news reporting, investigating. Query. Length: 1,200 words. **Pays $550.**

COLUMNS/DEPARTMENTS Arts & Media (news and profiles of well-known gay or lesbians in entertainment) is most open to freelancers; 750 words. Query. **Pays $100-500.**

TIPS "*The Advocate* is a unique newsmagazine. While we report on gay and lesbian issues and are published by 1 of the country's oldest and most established gay-owned companies, we also play by the rules of mainstream-not-gay-community journalism."

⊛ THE WASHINGTON BLADE

P.O. Box 53352, Washington DC 20009. (202)747-2077. **Fax:** (202)747-2070. **E-mail:** knaff@washblade.com. **Website:** www.washblade.com. **Contact:** Kevin Naff, editor. **20% freelance written.** Nation's oldest and largest weekly newspaper covering the lesbian, gay, bisexual and transgender issues. Articles (subjects) should be written from or directed to a gay perspective. Estab. 1969. Circ. 30,000. Byline given. No kill fee. Submit seasonal material one month in advance. Accepts queries by mail, e-mail, fax. Responds in within one month to queries.

REPRINTS Send typed manuscript with rights for sale noted and information about when and where the material previously appeared.

PHOTOS A photo or graphic with feature articles is particularly important. Photos with news stories are appreciated. Send photos by mail or e-mail to mkey@

washblade.com. No Answer. Captions required. Pay varies. Photographers on assignment are paid mutually agreed upon fee.

COLUMNS/DEPARTMENTS Send feature submissions to Joey DiGuglielmo, arts editor (joeyd@washblade.com). Sent opinion submissions to Kevin Naff, editor (knaff@washblade.com). Pay varies. No sexually explicit material.

TIPS "We maintain a highly competent and professional staff of news reporters, and it is difficult to break in here as a freelancer covering news. Include a résumé, good examples of your writing, and know the paper before you send a manuscript for publication. We look for writers who are credible and professional, and for copy that is accurate, fair, timely, and objective in tone. We do not work with writers who play fast and loose with the facts, or who are unprofessional in presentation. Before you send anything, become familiar with our publication. Do not send sexually explicit material."

○ ⑤⑤ XTRA

Pink Triangle Press, 2 Carlton St., Suite 1600, Toronto ON M5B 1J3 Canada. (416)925-6665; (800)268-9872. **Fax:** (416)925-6674. **E-mail:** info.toronto@xtra.ca. **E-mail:** matt.mills@xtra.ca. **Website:** www.xtra.ca. **Contact:** Matt Mills, associate publisher and editor-in-chief. **80% freelance written.** Biweekly tabloid covering gay, lesbian, bisexual, and transgender issues, news, arts, and events of interest in Toronto. "*Xtra* is dedicated to lesbian and gay sexual liberation. We publish material that advocates this end, according to the mission statement of the not-for-profit organization Pink Triangle Press, which operates the paper." Estab. 1984. Circ. 45,000. Byline given. Pays on publication. No kill fee. Editorial lead time 1 month. Accepts queries by e-mail. Accepts simultaneous submissions. Responds in 2 weeks to queries. Sample copy available online. Guidelines by e-mail.

NONFICTION Needs book excerpts, essays, interview, opinion, personal experience, travel. Does not want US-based stories or profiles of straight people who do not have a direct connection to the LGBT community. Query with published clips. Length: 200-1,600 words. Sometimes pays expenses of writers on assignment. Payment: Limit agreed upon in advance. **PHOTOS** Send photos. Captions, identification of subjects, model releases required. Offers $60 minimum.

COLUMNS/DEPARTMENTS *Xtra* rarely publishes unsolicited columns. **Buys 6 columns/year. mss/year.** Query with published clips.

⑤ ECHO MAGAZINE

ACE Publishing, Inc., P.O. Box 16630, Phoenix AZ 85011. (602)266-0550. **Fax:** (602)266-0773. **E-mail:** editor@echomag.com. **Website:** www.echomag.com. **Contact:** Glenn Gullickson, managing editor. **30-40% freelance written.** Biweekly magazine covering gay and lesbian issues. *Echo Magazine* is a newsmagazine for gay, lesbian, bisexual, and transgendered persons in the Phoenix metro area and throughout the state of Arizona. Editorial content needs to be pro-gay, that is, supportive of GLBT equality in all areas of American life. Estab. 1989. Circ. 15,000-18,000. Byline given. Pays on publication. No kill fee. Publishes ms an average of less than 1 month after acceptance. Editorial lead time 1-2 months. Submit seasonal material 1-2 months in advance. Accepts queries by e-mail. Responds in 2 weeks to queries. Responds in 1 month to mss. Sample copy available online. Guidelines by e-mail.

NONFICTION Needs book excerpts, essays, historical, humor, interview, opinion, personal experience, photo feature, travel. Special issues: Pride Festival (April); Arts issue (August); Holiday Gift/Decor (December). No articles on topics unrelated to our GLBT readers, or anything that is not pro-gay. **Buys 10-20 mss/year.** Query. Length: 500-2,000 words. **Pays $30-40.**

PHOTOS State availability. Captions, identification of subjects, model releases required. Reviews contact sheets, GIF/JPEG files. Negotiates payment individually.

COLUMNS/DEPARTMENTS Guest Commentary (opinion on GLBT issues), 500-1,000 words; Arts/Entertainment (profiles of GLBT or relevant celebrities, or arts issues), 800-1,500 words. **Buys 5-10 mss/year.** Query. **Pays $30-40.**

TIPS "Know Phoenix (or other areas of Arizona) and its GLBT community. Please don't send non-gay-related or non-pro-gay material. Research your topics thoroughly and write professionally. Our print content and online content are very similar."

GENERAL INTEREST

⑤⑤ THE AMERICAN LEGION MAGAZINE

P.O. Box 1055, Indianapolis IN 46206-1055. (317)630-1200. **Fax:** (317)630-1280. **E-mail:** magazine@legion.org. **E-mail:** mgrills@legion.org;hsoria@legion.org.

Website: www.legion.org. **Contact:** Matt Grills, cartoon editor; Holly Soria, art director. **70% freelance written. Prefers to work with published/established writers, but works with a small number of new/unpublished writers each year.** Monthly magazine. "Working through 15,000 community-level posts, the honorably discharged wartime veterans of The American Legion dedicate themselves to God, country, and traditional American values. They believe in a strong defense; adequate and compassionate care for veterans and their families; community service; and the wholesome development of our nation's youth. We publish articles that reflect these values. We inform our readers and their families of significant trends and issues affecting our nation, the world and the way we live. Our major features focus on the American flag, national security, foreign affairs, business trends, social issues, health, education, ethics and the arts. We also publish selected general feature articles, articles of special interest to veterans, and question-and-answer interviews with prominent national and world figures." Estab. 1919. Circ. 2,550,000. Byline given. Pays on acceptance. No kill fee. Publishes ms an average of 6 months after acceptance. Accepts queries by mail, e-mail, fax. Responds in 2 months to queries. Sample copy for $3.50 and 9x12 SAE with 6 first-class stamps. Guidelines for #10 SASE.

NONFICTION Needs general interest, interview. No regional topics or promotion of partisan political agendas. No personal experiences or war stories. **Buys 50-60 mss/year.** Query with SASE should explain the subject or issue, article's angle and organization, writer's qualifications, and experts to be interviewed. Length: 300-2,000 words. **Pays 40¢/word and up.**

⊗⊗ THE AMERICAN SCHOLAR

Phi Beta Kappa, 1606 New Hampshire Ave. NW, Washington DC 20009. (202)265-3808. **Fax:** (202)265-0083. **E-mail:** scholar@pbk.org. **Website:** www.theamericanscholar.org. **Contact:** Sandra Costich, editor at large. **100% freelance written.** Quarterly magazine dedicated to current events, politics, history, science, culture and the arts. "Our intent is to have articles written by scholars and experts but written in nontechnical language for an intelligent audience. Material covers a wide range in the arts, sciences, current affairs, history, and literature." Estab. 1932. Circ. 30,000. Byline given. Pays on publication. Offers 50% kill fee. Publishes ms an average of 1 year after

acceptance. Editorial lead time 6 months. Submit seasonal material 6 months in advance. Accepts queries by mail, e-mail, fax. Responds in 2 weeks to queries; 2 months to mss. Sample copy for $9. Guidelines for #10 SASE or via e-mail.

NONFICTION Needs essays, historical, humor. **Buys 40 mss/year.** Query. Length: 3,000-5,000 words. **Pays $500 maximum.**

POETRY Contact: Sandra Costich. "We're not considering any unsolicited poetry."

THE ATLANTIC MONTHLY

The Watergate, 600 New Hampshire Ave., NW, Washington DC 20037. (202)266-6000. **Website:** www.theatlantic.com. **Contact:** James Bennet, editor; C. Michael Curtis, fiction editor; David Barber, poetry editor. Covers poetry, fiction, and articles of the highest quality. General magazine for an educated readership with broad cultural and public-affairs interests. "The Atlantic considers unsolicited manuscripts, either fiction or nonfiction. A general familiarity with what we have published in the past is the best guide to our needs and preferences. Manuscripts must be typewritten and double-spaced. Receipt of manuscripts will be acknowledged if accompanied by a self-addressed stamped envelope. Manuscripts will not be returned. **At this time, the print magazine does not read submissions sent via fax or e-mail.** TheAtlantic.com no longer accepts unsolicited submissions." Estab. 1857. Circ. 500,000. Byline given. No kill fee. Accepts queries by mail. Guidelines available onine.

NONFICTION Needs book excerpts, essays, general interest, humor, travel. Query with or without published clips or send complete ms to "Editorial Department" at address above. All unsolicited mss must be accompanied by SASE. A general familiarity with what we have published in the past is the best guide to our needs and preferences. Simply send your manuscript—typewritten, double-spaced—to the Editorial Director, The Atlantic. Receipt of manuscripts will be acknowledged if accompanied by a self-addressed stamped envelope. Manuscripts will not be returned. Length: 1,000-6,000 words **Payment varies** Sometimes pays expenses.

FICTION Contact: C. Michael Curtis, fiction editor. Literary and contemporary fiction. "Seeks fiction that is clear, tightly written with strong sense of 'story' and well-defined characters." No longer publishes fiction in the regular magazine. Instead, it will appear in a special newsstand-only fiction issue. Send complete ms. Preferred length: 2,00-6,000 words.

POETRY Contact: David Barber, poetry editor. *The Atlantic Monthly* publishes some of the most distinguished poetry in American literature. "We read with interest and attention every poem submitted to the magazine and, quite simply, we publish those that seem to us to be the best." Has published poetry by Maxine Kumin, Stanley Plumly, Linda Gregerson, Philip Levine, Ellen Bryant Voigt, and W.S. Merwin. Receives about 60,000 poems/year. Subscription: $24.50 for 10 issues. Sample: $7.50 (back issue). Buys Accepts 30-35 poems/year poems/year. Submit maximum 6 poems/max poems.

THE CHRISTIAN SCIENCE MONITOR

The Home Forum Page, 210 Massachussetts Ave., P02-30, Boston MA 02115. **E-mail:** homeforum@csmonitor.com. **Website:** www.csmonitor.com; http://www.csmonitor.com/About/Contributor-guidelines#homeforum. **Contact:** Susan Leach, Marjorie Kehe, editors. *The Christian Science Monitor*, an international daily newspaper, regularly features poetry in The Home Forum section. Wants "finely crafted poems that explore and celebrate daily life; that provide a respite from daily news and from the bleakness that appears in so much contemporary verse." Considers free verse and fixed forms. Has published poetry by Diana Der-Hovanessian, Marilyn Krysl, and Michael Glaser. Publishes 1-2 poems/week. Estab. 1908.

POETRY Submit up to 5 poems at a time. Lines/poem: Prefers short poems under 20 lines. No previously published poems or simultaneous submissions. Accepts e-mail submissions only (by attachment in MS Word, 1 poem/e-mail). Pays $20/haiku; $40/poem. Does not want "work that presents people in helpless or hopeless states; poetry about death, aging, or illness; or dark, violent, sensual poems. No poems that are overtly religious or falsely sweet."

$$ FORUM

Business Journals, Inc., 1384 Broadway, 11th Floor, New York NY 10018. (212)710-7442. **E-mail:** jillianl@busjour.com. **Website:** www.busjour.com. Lisa Montemorra, project manager. **Contact:** Jillian LaRochelle, managing editor. **80% freelance written.** Semiannual magazine covering luxury fashion (men's 70%, women's 30%), luxury lifestyle. "*Forum* directly targets a very upscale reader interested in profiles and service pieces on upscale designers, new fashion trends, and traditional suiting. Lifestyle articles—including wine and spirits, travel, cars, boating, sports, collecting, etc.—are upscale top of the line (i.e., don't write how expensive taxis are)." Circ. 150,000. Byline given. Pays on publication. Publishes ms an average of 3-4 months after acceptance. Editorial lead time 6 months. Submit seasonal material 6 months in advance. Accepts queries by mail, e-mail. Responds in 2-3 weeks to queries. Guidelines by e-mail.

NONFICTION Needs general interest, interview, travel, luxury lifestyle trends, fashion service pieces. Does not want personal essays ("we run a few but commission them"). No fiction or single product articles; "in other words, an article should be on what's new in Italian wines, not about 1 superspecial brand." **Buys 20-25 mss/year.** Query. Length: 300-1,500 words. **Pays $300-500.**

COLUMNS/DEPARTMENTS Travel, 1,000-1,500 words; Wine + Spirits, 600-1,200 words; Gourmet, 600-1,200 words; Wheels, 600 words. **Buys 10-15 mss/year.** Query. **Pays $300-500.**

$$$$ HARPER'S MAGAZINE

666 Broadway, 11th Floor, New York NY 10012. (212)420-5720. **Fax:** (212)228-5889. **E-mail:** readings@harpers.org. **Website:** www.harpers.org. **90% freelance written**. Monthly magazine for well-educated, socially concerned, widely read men and women who value ideas and good writing. *Harper's Magazine* encourages national discussion on current and significant issues in a format that offers arresting facts and intelligent opinions. By means of its several shorter journalistic forms—Harper's Index, Readings, Forum, and Annotation—as well as with its acclaimed essays, fiction, and reporting, *Harper's* continues the tradition begun with its first issue in 1850: to inform readers across the whole spectrum of political, literary, cultural, and scientific affairs. Estab. 1850. Circ. 230,000. Pays on acceptance. Offers negotiable kill fee. Publishes ms an average of 3 months after acceptance. Responds in 6 weeks to queries. Sample copy for $5.95.

NONFICTION Needs humor. No interviews; no profiles. **Buys 2 mss/year.** Query. Length: 4,000-6,000 words.

REPRINTS Accepted for Readings section. Send typed ms with rights for sale ted and information about when and where the article previously appeared.

FICTION Will consider unsolicited fiction. Needs humorous. **Buys 12 mss/year.** Query. Length: 3,000-5,000 words. **Generally pays 50¢-$1/word.**

❸❸❸❸ NATIONAL GEOGRAPHIC MAGAZINE

1145 17th St. NW, Washington DC 20036. (202)857-7000. **Fax:** (202)492-5767. **Website:** www.national-geographic.com. Chris Johns, editor-in-chief. **60% freelance written. Prefers to work with published/established writers.** Monthly magazine for members of the National Geographic Society. "Timely articles written in a compelling, 'eyewitness' style. Arresting photographs that speak to us of the beauty, mystery, and harsh realities of life on earth. Maps of unprecedented detail and accuracy. These are the hallmarks of *National Geographic* magazine. Since 1888, the *Geographic* has been educating readers about the world." Estab. 1888. Circ. 6,800,000.

NONFICTION Query (500 words with clips of published articles) by mail to editor. Do not send mss. Length: 2,000-8,000 words. Pays expenses of writers on assignment.

❸❸❸ NEWSWEEK

The Daily Beast, 251 W. 57th St., New York NY 10019. (212)445-4000. **Website:** www.newsweek.com. *Newsweek* is edited to report the week's developments on the newsfront of the world and the nation through news, commentary, and analysis. Circ. 3,180,000.

COLUMNS/DEPARTMENTS Contact: myturn@newsweek.com. "We are no longer accepting submissions for the print edition. To submit an essay to our website, please e-mail it to: myturn@newsweek.com. The My Turn essay should be: A) an original piece, B) 850-900 words, C) generally personal in tone, and D) about any topic, but not framed as a response to a Newsweek story or another My Turn essay. Submissions must not have been published elsewhere. Please include your full name, phone number, and address with your entry. The competition is very stiff-we get 600 entries per month-and we can only print 1 a week. *Due to the number of submissions we receive, we cannot respond unless we plan to publish your essay;* if your story is tied to current events, it may not be appropriate. We are fully aware of the time and effort involved in preparing an essay, and each ms is given careful consideration. For an automated message with further details about My Turn, you may call: (212) 445-4547." **Pays $1,000 on publication.**

❸❸❸ THE NEW YORK TIMES MAGAZINE

620 8th Ave., New York NY 10018. (212)556-1234. **Fax:** (212)556-3830. **E-mail:** magazine@nytimes.com; nytnews@nytimes.com; executive-editor@nytimes.com. **Website:** www.nytimes.com/pages/magazine. **Contact:** Margaret Editor, public editor. *The New York Times Magazine* appears in *The New York Times* on Sunday. The *Arts and Leisure* section appears during the week. The *Op Ed* page appears daily.

❸❸❸ THE OLD FARMER'S ALMANAC

Yankee Publishing, Inc., P.O. Box 520, Dublin NH 03444. (603)563-8111. **Website:** www.almanac.com. **Contact:** Janice Stillman, editor. **95% freelance written.** Annual magazine covering weather, gardening, history, oddities, and lore. "*The Old Farmer's Almanac* is the oldest continuously published periodical in North America. Since 1792, it has provided useful information for people in all walks of life: tide tables for those who live near the ocean; sunrise tables and planting charts for those who live on the farm or simply enjoy gardening; recipes for those who like to cook; and forecasts for those who don't like the question of weather left up in the air. The words of the *Almanac*'s founder, Robert B. Thomas, guide us still: 'Our main endeavor is to be useful, but with a pleasant degree of humour.'" Estab. 1792. Circ. 3,100,000. Byline given. Pays on acceptance. Offers 25% kill fee. Publishes ms an average of 9 months after acceptance. Editorial lead time 6 months. Submit seasonal material 1 year in advance. Accepts queries by mail. Responds in 3 weeks to queries. Responds in 2 months to mss. Sample copy for $6 at bookstores or online. Guidelines available at www.almanac.com/content/writers-guidelines.

NONFICTION Needs general interest, historical, how-to, garden, cook, save money, humor, weather, natural remedies, obscure facts, history, popular culture. No personal recollections/accounts, personal/family histories. Query with published clips. Length: 800-2,500 words. **Pays 65¢/word.** Sometimes pays expenses of writers on assignment.

FILLERS Needs anecdotes, short humor. **Buys 1-2 mss/year.** Length: 100-200 words. **Pays $25.**

❸❸❸❸ OUTSIDE

Mariah Media, Inc., 400 Market St., Santa Fe NM 87501. (505)989-7100. **Fax:** (505)989-4700. **Website:** www.outsidemag.com. **60% freelance written.**

Monthly magazine covering active lifestyle. Estab. 1977. Circ. 665,000. Byline given. Pays on acceptance. Offers 25% kill fee. Publishes ms an average of 3-6 months after acceptance. Accepts queries by mail. Responds is 6-8 weeks. Guidelines on website.

NONFICTION Needs book excerpts, new product, travel. **Buys 300 mss/year.** Query with 2 or 3 relevant clips along with a SASE to: Editorial Department at address above. "Queries should present a clear, original, and provocative thesis, not merely a topic or idea, and should reflect familiarity with the magazine's content and tone. Features are generally 1,500-5,000 words in length. Dispatches articles (100-800 words) cover timely news, events, issues, and short profiles. Destinations pieces (300-1,000 words) include places, news, and advice for adventurous travelers. Review articles (200-1,500 words) examine and evaluate outdoor gear and equipment." Length: 100-5,000 words. **Pays $1.50-2/word for assigned articles. Pays $1-1.50/word for unsolicited articles.** Pays expenses of writers on assignment.

COLUMNS/DEPARTMENTS Pays $1.50-$2/word.

PARADE

ParadeNet, Inc., 711 Third Ave., New York NY 10017-4014. (212)450-7000. **Website:** www.parade.com. **Contact:** Megan Brown, articles editor. **95% freelance written.** Weekly magazine for a general interest audience. Estab. 1941. Circ. 32,000,000. Pays on acceptance. Offers kill fee. Kill fee varies in amount. Publishes ms an average of 5 months after acceptance. Editorial lead time 1 month. Accepts queries by mail, online submission form. Accepts simultaneous submissions. Sample copy and guidelines available online.

NONFICTION Spot news events are not accepted, as *Parade* has a 2-month lead time. No fiction, fashion, travel, poetry, cartoons, nostalgia, regular columns, personal essays, quizzes, or fillers. Unsolicited queries concerning celebrities, politicians or sports figures are rarely assigned. **Buys 150 mss/year.** Query with published clips. Length: 1,200-1,500 words. **Pays very competitive amount.** Pays expenses of writers on assignment.

PEOPLE

Time, Inc., 1271 Avenue of the Americas, New York NY 10020. (212)522-1212. **Fax:** (212)522-1359. **E-mail:** editor@people.com. **Website:** www.people.com. Weekly magazine. Designed as a forum for personality journalism through the use of short articles on contemporary news events and people. Circ. about 3.7 million. No kill fee. Editorial lead time 3 months.

PORTLAND MONTHLY

165 State St., Portland ME 04101. (207)775-4339. **E-mail:** staff@portlandmonthly.com. **Website:** www.portlandmagazine.com. **Contact:** Colin Sargent, editor. Monthly city lifestyle magazine—fiction, style, business, real estate, controversy, fashion, cuisine, interviews and art relating to the Maine area. Estab. 1985. Circ. 100,000. Pays on publication. No kill fee. Accepts queries by mail, e-mail.

NONFICTION Query first. "Clips and a bio note are appreciated, but we take no responsibility for returning unsolicited materials."

FICTION Send complete ms. 700 words or less

READER'S DIGEST

The Reader's Digest Association, Inc., Box 100, Pleasantville NY 10572. **E-mail:** letters@rd.com. **E-mail:** articleproposals@rd.com. **Website:** www.rd.com. Monthly magazine. No kill fee.

COLUMNS/DEPARTMENTS Life; @Work; Off Base, **pays $300.** Laugh; Quotes, **pays $100.** Address your submission to the appropriate humor category.

READER'S DIGEST (CANADA)

1100 Rene Le vesque Blvd. W, Montreal QC H3B 5H5 Canada. **E-mail:** originals@rd.com. **Website:** www.readersdigest.ca. **30-50% freelance written.** Monthly magazine of general interest articles and subjects. Estab. 1948. Circ. 1,000,000. Byline given. **Pays on acceptance for original works.** Pays on publication for pickups. Offers $500 (Canadian) kill fee. Submit seasonal material 5 months in advance. Accepts queries by mail, online submission form. Guidelines available online.

NONFICTION Needs general interest, how-to, general interest, humor, jokes, inspirational, personal experience, travel, adventure, crime, health. Query with published clips. Proposals can be mailed to the above address. We are looking for dramatic narratives, inspirational stories, articles about crime, adventure, travel and health issues. Download our writer's guidelines. If we are interested in pursuing your idea, an editor will contact you. Length: 2,000-2,500 words. **Pays $1.50-2.50/word (CDN) depending on story type.** Pays expenses of writers on assignment.

REPRINTS Query. Payment is negotiable.

◎◎◎◎ ROBB REPORT

CurtCo Media Labs, 29160 Heathercliff Rd., Suite #200, Malibu CA 90265. (310)589-7700. **Fax:** (310)589-7701. **E-mail:** editorial@robbreport.com. **Website:** www.robbreport.com. **Contact:** Brett Anderson, editor-in-chief. **60% freelance written.** Monthly lifestyle magazine geared toward active, affluent readers. Addresses upscale autos, luxury travel, boating, technology, lifestyles, watches, fashion, sports, investments, collectibles. "For over 30 years, *Robb Report* magazine has served as the definitive authority on connoisseurship for ultra-affluent consumers. *Robb Report* not only showcases the products and services available from the most prestigious luxury brands around the globe, but it also provides its sophisticated readership with detailed insight into a range of these subjects, which include sports and luxury automobiles, yachts, real estate, travel, private aircraft, fashion, fine jewelry and watches, art, wine, state-of-the-art home electronics, and much more. For connoisseurs seeking the very best that life has to offer, *Robb Report* remains the essential luxury resource." Estab. 1976. Circ. 104,000. Byline given. Pays on publication. Offers 25% kill fee. Submit seasonal material 5 months in advance. Accepts queries by mail, fax. Responds in 2 months to queries. Responds in 1 month to mss. Sample copy for $10.95, plus shipping and handling. Guidelines for #10 SASE.

NONFICTION Needs new product, autos, boats, aircraft, watches, consumer electronics, travel, international and domestic, dining. Special issues: Home (October); Recreation (March). **Buys 60 mss/year.** Query with published clips. Length: 500-2,000 words. **Pays $1/word.** Sometimes pays expenses of writers on assignment.

◎ SENIOR LIVING

Stratis Publishing Ltd, 153, 1581-H Hillside Ave., Victoria BC V8T 2CI Canada. (250)479-4705. **Fax:** (250)479-4808. **E-mail:** editor@seniorlivingmag.com. **Website:** www.seniorlivingmag.com. **Contact:** Bobbie Jo Reid, managing editor. **100% freelance written.** 12 times per yr. magazine covering active 50+ living. "Inspiring editorial profiling 'seniors' (50+) who are active & lead interesting lives. Include articles on health, housing, accessibility, sports, travel, recipes, etc." Estab. 2004. Circ. 41,000. Byline given. Pays quarterly. No kill fee. Publishes an average of 2-3 months after acceptance. Editorial lead time 3 months. Submit seasonal material 6 months in advance. Accepts queries by e-mail. Accepts simultaneous submissions.

NONFICTION Needs historical, how-to, humor, inspirational, interview, personal experience, travel, active living for 50+. All editorial must be about or reflect the lifestyles of people living in British Columbia. Do not want politics, religion, promotion of business, service or products, humor that demeans 50+ demographic or aging process. **Buys 150 mss/year.** Query. Does not accept previously published material. Length: 500-1,200 words. **Pays $35-150 for assigned articles. Pays $35-150 for unsolicited articles.** Sometimes pays expenses (limit agreed upon in advance).

COLUMNS/DEPARTMENTS Buys 5-6 mss/yr mss/year. Query with published clips. **Pays $25-$50.**

◎◎◎◎ SMITHSONIAN MAGAZINE

Capital Gallery, Suite 6001, MRC 513, P.O. Box 37012, Washington DC 20013. (202)275-2000. **E-mail:** smithsonianmagazine@si.edu. **Website:** www.smithsonianmag.com. **Contact:** Molly Roberts, photo editor; Jeff Campagna, art services coordinator. **90% freelance written.** Monthly magazine for associate members of the Smithsonian Institution; 85% with college education. "*Smithsonian Magazine's* mission is to inspire fascination with all the world has to offer by featuring unexpected and entertaining editorial that explores different lifestyles, cultures and peoples, the arts, the wonders of nature and technology, and much more. The highly educated, innovative readers of *Smithsonian* share a unique desire to celebrate life, seeking out the timely as well as timeless, the artistic as well as the academic, and the thought-provoking as well as the humorous." Circ. 2,300,000. Pays on acceptance. Offers 33% kill fee. Publishes ms an average of 6 months after acceptance. Editorial lead time 2 months. Submit seasonal material 3 months in advance. Accepts queries by online submission form only. Responds in 3 weeks to queries from the web form. Sample copy for $5. Guidelines available online.

NONFICTION Buys 120-130 feature (up to 5,000 words) and 12 short (500-650 words) mss/year. Use online submission form. "*Smithsonian* magazine accepts unsolicited proposals from established freelance writers for features and some departments. Please use the Web submission form to submit a written proposal of 250 to 300 words as a preliminary query. The proposal should convince us that we should cover the subject, offer descriptive information on how you, the writer, would treat the subject, and offer us an opportunity to judge your writing ability. Background information and writing credentials are helpful. The proposal text box on the Web submission form holds 10,000 characters (approximately 2,000 words), ample room for a cover letter and proposal. All unsolicited proposals are sent to us on speculation, and you should receive a reply within three weeks to queries sent using the Web form. If you have supporting material or clips of your previously published work available on-line, please include the URLs (links) in the area provided on the web form. If we decide to commission an article, the writer receives full payment on acceptance of the manuscript. If the article is found unsuitable, one-third of the payment serves as a kill fee. Our article length ranges from a 700-word humor column to a 4,000-word full-length feature. We consider focused subjects that fall within the general range of Smithsonian Institution interests, such as: cultural history, physical science, art and natural history. We are always looking for offbeat subjects and profiles. We do not consider fiction, poetry, political and news events, or previously published articles. Read more: www.smithsonianmag.com/contact-us/submission-guidelines.html#ixzz1JcrD2vnl." **Pays various rates per feature, $1,500 per short piece.** Pays expenses of writers on assignment.

COLUMNS/DEPARTMENTS Buys 12-15 department articles/year. Length: 1,000-2,000 words. Last Page humor, 550-700 words. Use online submission form. **Pays $1,000-1,500.**

THE NEW YORKER

4 Times Square, New York NY 10036. (212) 286-5900. **E-mail:** beth_lusko@newyorker.com; toon@cartoonbank.com. **Website:** www.newyorker.com; www.cartoonbank.com. **Contact:** Bob Mankoff, cartoon; David Remnick, editor-in-chief. A quality weekly magazine of distinct news stories, articles, essays, and poems for a literate audience. Estab. 1925. Circ. 938,600. Pays on acceptance. No kill fee. Accepts queries by mail, e-mail. Responds in 3 months to mss.

NONFICTION "Submissions: Fiction, poetry, Shouts & Murmurs, and newsbreaks should be sent as pdf attachments. Do not paste them into the message field. Due to volume, we cannot consider unsolicited 'Talk of the Town' stories or other nonfiction." Submit at www.newyorker.com/contact/contactus.

FICTION Publishes 1 ms/issue. Send complete ms. Fiction, poetry, Shouts & Murmurs, and newsbreaks should be sent as pdf attachments. Do not paste them into the message field. Submit at www.newyorker.com/contact/contactus. **Payment varies.**

POETRY Send poetry to Poetry Department. Submit no more than 6 poems at a time. No previously published poems or simultaneous submissions. Use online e-mail source and upload as pdf attachment. Include poet's name in the subject line and as the title of attached document. "We prefer to receive no more than 2 submissions per writer per year." **Pays top rates.**

[$] [$] THE SATURDAY EVENING POST

1100 Waterway Blvd., Indianapolis IN 46202. (317)634-1100. **E-mail:** editor@saturdayeveningpost.com. **Website:** www.saturdayeveningpost.com. Steve Slon, editorial director/associate publisher. **30% freelance written.** Bimonthly general interest, family-oriented magazine focusing on lifestyle, physical fitness, and preventive medicine. "Ask almost any American if he or she has heard of *The Saturday Evening Post*, and you will find that many have fond recollections of the magazine from their childhood days. Many readers recall sitting with their families on Saturdays awaiting delivery of their *Post* subscription in the mail. *The Saturday Evening Post* has forged a tradition of 'forefront journalism.' *The Saturday Evening Post* continues to stand at the journalistic forefront with its coverage of health, nutrition, and preventive medicine." Estab. 1728. Circ. 355,537. Byline given. Pays on publication. Publishes ms an average of 3 months after acceptance. Submit seasonal material 4 months in advance. Accepts queries by mail, fax. Accepts simultaneous submissions. Responds in 3 weeks to queries. Responds in 6 weeks to mss.

NONFICTION Needs how-to, gardening, home improvement, humor, interview, medical, health, fitness. No political articles or articles containing sexual innuendo or hypersophistication. **Buys 25 mss/year.** Send complete ms. Length: 1,000-2,500 words. **Pays $25-400.**

COLUMNS/DEPARTMENTS Travel (destinations); Post Scripts (well-known humorists); Post People (activities of celebrities). Length 750-1,500. **Buys 16 mss/year.** Query with published clips or send complete ms. **Pays $150 minimum, negotiable maximum.**

FICTION Query.

POETRY Needs light verse.

FILLERS Needs anecdotes, short humor. **Buys 200 mss/year.** Length: 300 words. **Pays $15.**

⑨⑨⑨ YES! MAGAZINE

284 Madrona Way NE, Suite 116, Bainbridge Island WA 98110. **E-mail:** editors@yesmagazine.org. **E-mail:** submissions@yesmagazine.org. **Website:** www.yesmagazine.org. **70% freelance written.** Quarterly magazine covering sustainability, social justice, grassroots activism, contemporary culture; nature, conservation, ecology, politics, and world affairs. "*YES! Magazine* documents how people are creating a more just, sustainable and compassionate world. Each issue includes articles focused on a theme—about solutions to a significant challenge facing our world—and a number of timely, non-theme articles. Our non-theme section provides ongoing coverage of issues like health, climate change, globalization, media reform, faith, democracy, economy and labor, social and racial justice and peace building. To inquire about upcoming themes, send an email to submissions@yesmagazine.org; please be sure to type 'themes' as the subject line." Estab. 1997. Circ. 55,000. Byline given. Pays on publication. Rarely offers kill fee. Publishes ms an average of 1-6 months after acceptance. Editorial lead time 3-6 months. Submit seasonal material 2-6 months in advance. Accepts queries by e-mail. Sample copy and writer's guidelines online.

NONFICTION Needs book excerpts, opinion. "We don't want stories that are negative or too politically partisan." **Buys 30 mss/year mss/year.** Query with published clips. Length: 100-2,500 words. **Pays $50-1,250 for assigned articles. Pays $50-600 for unsolicited articles.**

REPRINTS Send photocopy or typed ms with rights for sale noted and information about when and where the material previously appeared.

COLUMNS/DEPARTMENTS Signs of Life (positive news briefs), 100-250 words; Commentary (opinion from thinkers and experts), 500 words; Book and film reviews, 500-800 words. **Pays $20-$300.**

HEALTH AND FITNESS

⑨⑨ AMERICAN FITNESS

15250 Ventura Blvd., Suite 200, Sherman Oaks CA 91403. (800)446-2322, ext. 200. **E-mail:** americanfitness@afaa.com. **Website:** www.afaa.com. **Contact:** Meg Jordan, editor. **75% freelance written.** Bimonthly magazine covering exercise and fitness, health, and nutrition. "We need timely, in-depth, informative articles on health, fitness, aerobic exercise, sports nutrition, age-specific fitness, and outdoor activity. Absolutely no first-person accounts. Need well-researched articles for professional readers." Estab. 1983. Circ. 42,900. Byline given. Pays 30 days after publication. No kill fee. Publishes ms an average of 6 months after acceptance. Submit seasonal material 4 months in advance. Accepts queries by mail, fax. Accepts simultaneous submissions. Responds in 2 months to queries. Sample copy for $4.50 and SASE with 6 first-class stamps.

NONFICTION Needs historical, history of various athletic events, inspirational, sport's leaders motivational pieces, interview, fitness figures, new product, plus equipment review, personal experience, successful fitness story, photo feature, on exercise, fitness, new sport, travel, activity adventures. No articles on unsound nutritional practices, popular trends, or unsafe exercise gimmicks. **Buys 18-25 mss/year.** Send complete ms. Length: 800-1,200 words. **Pays $200 for features, $80 for news.** Sometimes pays expenses of writers on assignment.

COLUMNS/DEPARTMENTS Research (latest exercise and fitness findings); Alternative paths (non-mainstream approaches to health, wellness, and fitness); Strength (latest breakthroughs in weight training); Clubscene (profiles and highlights of fitness club industry); Adventure (treks, trails, and global challenges); Food (low-fat/nonfat, high-flavor dishes); Homescene (home-workout alternatives); Clip 'n' Post (concise exercise research to post in health clubs, offices or on refrigerators). Length: 800-1,000 words. Query with published clips or send complete ms. **Pays $100-200.**

⑨⑨ CLIMBING

Cruz Bay Publishing, Inc., 2520 55th St., Suite 210, Boulder CO 80302. (303)625-1600. **Fax:** (303)440-3618. **E-mail:** sdavis@climbing.com. **E-mail:** contribute@climbing.com. **Website:** www.climbing.com. Magazine published 9 times/year covering climbing and mountaineering. Provides features on rock climbing and mountaneering worldwide. Estab. 1970. Circ. 51,000. Pays on publication. No kill fee. Editorial lead time 6 weeks. Accepts queries by e-mail. Sample copy for $4.99. Guidelines available online.

NONFICTION Needs interview, interesting climbers, personal experience, climbing adventures, surveys of different areas. Query. Length: 1,500-3,500 words. **Pays 35¢/word.**

COLUMNS/DEPARTMENTS Query. **Payment varies.**

⊖⊖⊖⊖ FITNESS MAGAZINE

Meredith Corp., 805 Third Ave., 25th Floor, New York NY 10022. **E-mail:** fitnessmail@fitnessmagazine.com. **Website:** www.fitnessmagazine.com. Monthly magazine for women in their 20s and 30s who are interested in fitness and living a healthy life. Circ. 1.5 million. Byline given. Pays on acceptance. Offers 20% kill fee. Responds in 2 months to queries.

NONFICTION **Buys 60-80 mss/year.** Query. Length: 1,500-2,500 words. **Pays $1,500-2,500.** Pays expenses of writers on assignment.

REPRINTS Send photocopy. Negotiates fee.

COLUMNS/DEPARTMENTS Length: 600-1,200 words. **Buys 30 mss/year.** Query. **Pays $800-1,500.**

⊖⊖ HEALING LIFESTYLES & SPAS

P.O. Box 271207, Louisville CO 80027. (202)441-9557. **Fax:** (303)926-4099. **E-mail:** melissa@healinglifestyles.com; editorial@healinglifestyles.com. **Website:** www.healinglifestyles.com. **Contact:** Melissa B. Williams, editor-in-chief. **90% freelance written.** Estab. 1996. Circ. 45,000. Pays on publication. No kill fee. Publishes ms an average of 2-10 months after acceptance. Editorial lead time 6 months. Submit seasonal material 6-9 months in advance. Accepts queries by mail, e-mail. Responds in 6 weeks to queries.

NONFICTION Needs travel, domestic and international. No fiction or poetry. Query. Length: 1,000-2,000 words. **Pays $150-500, depending on length, research, experience, and availability and quality of images.**

COLUMNS/DEPARTMENTS All Things New & Natural (short pieces outlining new health trends, alternative medicine updates, and other interesting tidbits of information), 50-200 words; Urban Retreats (focuses on a single city and explores its spas and organic living features), 1,200-1,600 words; Health (features on relevant topics ranging from nutrition to health news and updates), 900-1,200 words; Food (nutrition or spa-focused food articles and recipes), 1,000-1,200 words; Ritual (highlights a specific at-home ritual), 500 words; Seasonal Spa (focuses on a seasonal ingredient on the spa menu), 500-700 words; Spa Origins

(focuses on particular modalities and healing beliefs from around the world, 1,000-1,200 words; Yoga, 400-800 words; Retreat (highlights a spa or yoga retreat), 500 words; Spa a la carte (explores a new treatment or modality on the spa menu), 600-1,000 words; Insight (focuses on profiles, theme-related articles, and new therapies, healing practices, and newsworthy items), 1,000-2,000 words. Query.

○ ⊖⊖ IMPACT MAGAZINE

IMPACT Productions, 2007 2nd St. SW, Calgary AB T2S 1S4 Canada. (403)228-0605. **E-mail:** editor@impactmagazine.ca; info@impactmagazine.ca. **Website:** www.impactmagazine.ca. **Contact:** Chris Welner, editor. **10% freelance written.** Bimonthly magazine covering fitness and sport performance. "A leader in the industry, *IMPACT Magazine* is committed to publishing content provided by the best experts in their fields for those who aspire to higher levels of health, fitness, and sport performance." Estab. 1992. Circ. 90,000. Byline given. Pays 30 days after publication. Offers 25% kill fee. Publishes ms an average of 4-6 months after acceptance. Editorial lead time 6 months. Submit seasonal material 6 months in advance. Accepts queries by e-mail. Accepts simultaneous submissions. Responds in 4 weeks to queries. Sample copy and guidelines available online.

NONFICTION Needs general interest, how-to, interview, new product, opinion, technical. **Buys 4 mss/year.** Query. Length: 600-1,800 words. **Pays $0.25/max. for assigned articles. Pays $0.25/max. for unsolicited articles.**

⊖⊖⊖⊖ MEN'S HEALTH

Rodale, 33 E. Minor St., Emmaus PA 18098. (610)967-5171. **Fax:** (610)967-7725. **E-mail:** mhletters@rodale.com. **Website:** www.menshealth.com. **50% freelance written.** Magazine published 10 times/year covering men's health and fitness. *Men's Health* is a lifestyle magazine showing men the practical and positive actions that make their lives better, with articles covering fitness, nutrition, relationships, travel, careers, grooming, and health issues. Estab. 1986. Circ. 1,600,000. Pays on acceptance. Offers 25% kill fee. Accepts queries by mail, e-mail. Responds in 3 weeks to queries. Guidelines for #10 SASE.

NONFICTION **Buys 30 features/year; 360 short mss/year.** Query with published clips. Length: 1,200-4,000 words for features; 100-300 words for short pieces. **Pays $1,000-5,000 for features; $100-500 for short pieces.**

COLUMNS/DEPARTMENTS Length: 750-1,500 words. **Buys 80 mss/year. Pays $750- 2,000.**

☻☻☻ MUSCLE & FITNESS

Weider Publications, part of American Media, Inc., 21100 Erwin St., Woodland Hills CA 91367. (818)884-6800. **Fax:** (818)595-0463. **Website:** www.muscleand-fitness.com. **50% freelance written.** Monthly magazine covering bodybuilding and fitness for healthy, active men and women. "*Muscle & Fitness* contains a wide range of features and monthly departments devoted to all areas of bodybuilding, health, fitness, sport, injury prevention and treatment, and nutrition. Editorial fulfills 2 functions: information and entertainment. "Special attention is devoted to how-to advice and accuracy. Estab. 1950. Circ. 500,000. Pays on publication. No kill fee. Publishes ms an average of 2 months after acceptance. Editorial lead time 5 months. Submit seasonal material 6 months in advance. Accepts queries by mail. Responds in 1 month to queries.

NONFICTION Needs book excerpts, how-to, training, humor, interview, photo feature. **Buys 120 mss/year.** Query with published clips. Length: 800-1,800 words. **Pays $400-1,000.** Pays expenses of writers on assignment.

REPRINTS Send photocopy with rights for sale noted and information about when and where the material previously appeared. Payment varies.

☺ ☻ MUSCLEMAG

Robert Kennedy Publishing, Inc., 400 Matheson Blvd. W., Mississauga ON L5R 3M1, Canada. (905)507-3545. **Fax:** (905)507-2372. **E-mail:** editorial@musclemag.com. **Website:** www.musclemag.com. **80% freelance written.** Covers hardcore bodybuilding. Monthly magazine on building health, fitness, and physique. Byline given. Pays on acceptance. Publishes ms an average of 6 months after acceptance. Accepts queries by mail, e-mail. Responds in 4 months to queries. Responds in 4 months to mss. Guidelines available.

NONFICTION Needs how-to, interview, new product, personal experience, photo feature, bodybuilding, strenth training, health, nutrition, fitness. **Pays $80-400 for assigned accepted articles submitted on spec.**

FILLERS Needs anecdotes, facts, gags, newsbreaks, fitness, nutrition, health, short humor. **Buys 50-100 mss/year.** Length: 100-200 words.

☺ ☻☻☻ OXYGEN

Robert Kennedy Publishing, 400 Matheson Blvd. W., Mississauga ON L5R 3M1 Canada. (905)507-3545; (888)254-0767. **Fax:** (905)507-2372. **Website:** www.oxygenmag.com. **70% freelance written.** Monthly magazine covering women's health and fitness. *Oxygen* encourages various exercise, good nutrition to shape, and condition the body. Estab. 1997. Circ. 340,000. Byline given. Pays on acceptance. Offers 25% kill fee. Publishes ms an average of 4 months after acceptance. Editorial lead time 3 months. Submit seasonal material 6 months in advance. Accepts queries by mail, fax. Responds in 5 weeks to queries. Responds in 2 months to mss. Sample copy for $5.

NONFICTION Needs exposé, how-to, training and nutrition, humor, inspirational, interview, new product, personal experience, photo feature. No poorly researched articles that do not genuinely help the readers toward physical fitness, health, and physique. **Buys 100 mss/year.** Send complete ms with SASE and $5 for return postage. Length: 1,400-1,800 words. **Pays $250-1,000.** Sometimes pays expenses of writers on assignment.

COLUMNS/DEPARTMENTS Nutrition (low-fat recipes), 1,700 words; Weight Training (routines and techniques), 1,800 words; Aerobics (how-tos), 1,700 words. **Buys 50 mss/year.** Send complete ms. **Pays $150-500.**

☻☻☻☻ SHAPE MAGAZINE

American Media, 21100 Erwin St., Woodland Hills CA 91367. (818)884-6800. **Website:** www.shape.com. **70% freelance written. Prefers to work with published/established writers.** Monthly magazine covering health, fitness, nutrition, and beauty for women ages 18-34. "*Shape* reaches women who are committed to healthful, active lifestyles. Our readers are participating in a variety of fitness-related activities, in the gym, at home and outdoors, and they are also proactive about their health and are nutrition conscious." Estab. 1981. Circ. 1,600,000. Pays on acceptance. Offers 33% kill fee. Submit seasonal material 8 months in advance. Accepts queries by mail. Responds in 2 months to queries. Sample copy for SAE with 9x12 envelope and 4 First-Class stamps.

NONFICTION Needs book excerpts, exposé, health, fitness, nutrition related, how-to, get fit, health/fitness, recipe. "We rarely publish celebrity question and answer stories, celebrity profiles, or menopausal/hormone replacement therapy stories." Query with published clips. Length: 2,500 words/features; 1,000 words/shorter pieces. **Pays $1.50/word (on average).**

⊖⊖⊖ SPIRITUALITY & HEALTH MAGAZINE

Spirituality & Health Media, LLC, 107 Cass St., Suite C, Traverse City MI 49684. (231)933-5660. **E-mail:** editors@spiritualityhealth.com. **Website:** www.spiritualityhealth.com. **Contact:** Karen Bouris, editor-in-chief; Ilima Loomis, managing editor. Bimonthly magazine covering research-based spirituality and health. "We look for formally credentialed writers in their fields. We are nondenominational and non-proselytizing. We are not New Age. We appreciate well-written work that offers spiritual seekers from all different traditions help in their unique journeys." Estab. 1998. Circ. 95,000. Byline given. Pays on acceptance. Offers 25% kill fee. Editorial lead time 4 months. Submit seasonal material 6 months in advance. Accepts queries by e-mail. Accepts simultaneous submissions. Responds in 3-4 months to queries. Responds in 2-4 months to mss. Sample copy and writer's guidelines online.

NONFICTION Does not want proselytizing, New Age cures with no scientific basis, "how I recovered from a disease personal essays," psychics, advice columns, profiles of individual healers or practitioners, pieces promoting one way or guru, reviews, poetry or columns.

⊘ ⊖⊖ VIBRANT LIFE

Review and Herald Publishing Association, 55 W. Oak Ridge Dr., Hagerstown MD 21740-7390. (301)393-4019. **Fax:** (301)393-4055. **E-mail:** vibrantlife@rhpa.org; hquintana@rhpa.org. **Website:** www.vibrantlife.com. **Contact:** Heather Quintana, editor. **80% freelance written. Enjoys working with published/established writers; works with a small number of new/unpublished writers each year.** Bimonthly magazine covering health articles (especially from a prevention angle and with a Christian slant). "Whether you are fit and vigorous or have just received a frightening diagnosis, *Vibrant Life* has health information that will help you move closer to the life you were designed to live. It is perfect for sharing with people who may have never heard of this Christian approach to whole-person health. It's a wonderful way to introduce people to God's plan for us to have harmony of mind, body, and spirit. You can give a subscription to neighbors, friends, or coworkers; order a stack to place in a local grocery store, business, or doctor's office; or use it as a part of local church health initiatives, such as blood drives or cooking classes." Estab. 1885. Circ. 30,000. Byline given. Pays on acceptance. Offers 50% kill fee. Submit seasonal material 9 months in advance. Accepts queries by mail, e-mail, fax. Responds in 1 month to queries. Sample copy for $1. Guidelines available online.

NONFICTION Needs interview, with personalities on health. **Buys 50-60 feature articles/year and 6-12 short mss/year.** Send complete ms. Length: 500-1,500 words for features; 25-250 words for short pieces. **Pays $75-300 for features, $50-75 for short pieces.**

REPRINTS Send tearsheet and information about when and where the material previously appeared. Pays 50% of amount paid for an original article.

COLUMNS/DEPARTMENTS Buys 12-18 department articles/year. Length: 500-650 words. **Pays $75-175.**

⊖⊖⊖⊖ VIM & VIGOR

1010 E. Missouri Ave., Phoenix AZ 85014. (602)395-5850. **Fax:** (602)395-5853. **Website:** www.comhs.org/vim_vigor/. **90% freelance written.** Quarterly magazine covering health and healthcare. Estab. 1985. Circ. 800,000. Byline given. Pays on acceptance. Publishes ms an average of 6 months after acceptance. Sample copy for 9x12 SAE with 8 first-class stamps. Guidelines for #10 SASE.

NONFICTION Send published clips and résumé by mail or e-mail. Length: 500-1,200 words. **Pays 90¢-$1/word.** Pays expenses of writers on assignment.

⊖⊖⊖⊖ YOGA JOURNAL

Active Interest Media, Healthy Living Group, 475 Sansome St., Suite 850, San Francisco CA 94111. (415)591-0555. **Fax:** (415)591-0733. **E-mail:** queries@yjmag.com. **Website:** www.yogajournal.com. **Contact:** Kaitlin Quistgaard, editor-in-chief. **75% freelance written.** Magazine published 9 times a year covering the practice and philosophy of yoga. "With comprehensive features on the practice, fitness, well-being, and everyday balance, we deliver the yoga tradition suited to today's lifestyle. We welcome professional queries for these departments: **Om**: Covers myriad aspects of the yoga lifestyle (150-400 words). This department includes Yoga Diary, a 250-word story about a pivotal moment in your yoga practice. **Eating Wisely**: A popular, 1,400-word department about relationship to food. Most stories focus on vegetarian and whole-foods cooking, nutritional healing, and contemplative pieces about the relationship between yoga and food. **Well Being**: This 1,500-word department presents reported pieces about holistic health practices." Estab. 1975. Circ. 300,000. Byline given. Pays within 90 days of acceptance. Offers kill fee. Offers kill fee on assigned articles. Publishes ms an average of 10 months after acceptance. Submit seasonal material 7 months in advance. Accepts queries by e-mail. Responds in 6 weeks to queries if interested. Sample copy for $4.99. Guidelines on website.

NONFICTION Needs book excerpts, how-to, yoga, exercise, inspirational, yoga or related, interview, opinion, photo feature, travel, yoga-related. Does not want unsolicited poetry or cartoons. "Please avoid New Age jargon and in-house buzz words as much as possible." **Buys 50-60 mss/year.** Query with SASE. Length: 3,000-5,000 words. **Pays $800-2,000.**

REPRINTS Send tearsheet or photocopy with rights for sale noted and information about when and where the material previously appeared.

COLUMNS/DEPARTMENTS Health (self-care; well-being); Body-Mind (hatha Yoga, other body-mind modalities, meditation, yoga philosophy, Western mysticism); Community (service, profiles, organizations, events), all 1,500-2,000 words. **Pays $400-800.** Living (books, video, arts, music), 800 words. **Pays $200-250.** World of Yoga, Spectrum (brief yoga and healthy living news/events/fillers), 150-600 words. **Pays $50-150.**

HISTORY

AMERICAN HISTORY

Weider History Group, 19300 Promenade Dr., Leesburg VA 20176. (703)771-9400. **Fax:** (703)779-8345. **Website:** www.historynet.com. **60% freelance written.** Bimonthly magazine of cultural, social, military, and political history published for a general audience. "Presents the history of America to a broad spectrum of general-interest readers in an authoritative, informative, thought-provoking and entertaining style. Lively narratives take readers on an adventure with history, complemented by rare photographs, paintings, illustrations and maps." Estab. 1966. Circ. 95,000. Byline given. Pays on acceptance. No kill fee. Responds in 10 weeks to queries. Sample copy and guidelines for $5 (includes 3rd class postage) or $4

and 9x12 SAE with 4 first-class stamps. Guidelines for #10 SASE.

NONFICTION Needs Key prerequisites for publication are thorough research and accurate presentation, precise English usage, and sound organization, a lively style, and a high level of human interest. *Unsolicited manuscripts not considered.* Inappropriate materials include: book reviews, travelogues, personal/family narratives not of national significance, articles about collectibles/antiques, living artists, local/individual historic buildings/landmarks, and articles of a current editorial nature. **Buys 20 mss/year.** Query by mail only with published clips and SASE. 2,000-4,000 words depending on type of article.

💲💲 AMERICA'S CIVIL WAR

Weider History Group, 19300 Promenade Dr., Leesburg VA 20176-6500. (703)771-9400. **Fax:** (703)779-8345. **E-mail:** acw@weiderhistorygroup.com. **Website:** www.historynet.com. **95% freelance written.** Bimonthly magazine covering popular history and straight historical narrative for both the general reader and the American Civil War buff covering strategy, tactics, personalities, arms, and equipment. Estab. 1988. Circ. 78,000. Byline given. Pays on publication. No kill fee. Accepts queries by mail, e-mail. Sample copy for $5. Guidelines for #10 SASE.

NONFICTION Needs historical, book notices, preservation news. **Buys 24 mss/year.** "Query. Submit a page outlining the subject and your approach to it, and why you believe this would be an important article for the magazine. Briefly summarize your prior writing experience in a cover note." Length: 3,500-4,000 words; 500-word sidebar. **Pays $300 and up.**

COLUMNS/DEPARTMENTS Personality (profiles of Civil War personalities); Men & Material (about weapons used); Commands (about units); Eyewitness to War (historical letters and diary excerpts). Length: 2,000 words. **Buys 24 mss/year.** Query. **Pays $150 and up.**

💲 BRITISH HERITAGE

Weider History Group, 19300 Promenade Dr., Leesburg VA 20176. (703)771-9400. **Fax:** (703)779-8345. **E-mail:** dana.huntley@weiderhistorygroup.com. **Website:** www.thehistorynet.com. Bimonthly magazine covering British travel and culture. "The magazine of travel, culture and adventure, especially written for those who love England, Scotland, and Wales. A must-read for Anglophiles, *British Heritage* shows them what they can see and do, how to get there and where to stay, with information that even veteran travelers may overlook." Circ. 77,485. Pays on acceptance. Pays kill fee, "though never had to." Editorial lead time 6 months. Accepts queries by e-mail.

NONFICTION Buys 50 mss/year. Query by e-mail. Length: 1,000-2,500 words.

💲💲💲 CIVIL WAR TIMES

Weider History Group, 19300 Promenade Dr., Leesburg VA 20176-6500. (703)779-8371. **Fax:** (703)779-8345. **E-mail:** civilwartimes@weiderhistorygroup.com; cwt@weiderhistorygroup.com. **Website:** www.historynet.com. **90% freelance written. Works with a small number of new/unpublished writers each year.** Magazine published 6 times/year covering the history of the American Civil War. *"Civil War Times* is the full-spectrum magazine of the Civil War. Specifically, we look for nonpartisan coverage of battles, prominent military, and civilian figures, the home front, politics, military technology, common soldier life, prisoners and escapes, period art and photography, the naval war, blockade-running, specific regiments, and much more." Estab. 1962. Circ. 108,000. Pays on acceptance and on publication. Publishes ms an average of 18 months after acceptance. Submit seasonal material 1 year in advance. Responds in 3-6 months to queries. Sample copy for $6. Guidelines for #10 SASE.

NONFICTION Needs interview, photo feature, Civil War historical material. "Don't send us a comprehensive article on a well-known major battle. Instead, focus on some part or aspect of such a battle, or some group of soldiers in the battle. Similar advice applies to major historical figures like Lincoln and Lee. Positively no fiction or poetry." Buys 20 freelance mss/year. Query with clips and SASE. **Pays $75-800.**

⟳ 💲💲 HISTORY MAGAZINE

Moorshead Magazines, 505 Consumers Rd., Suite 312, Toronto ON M2J 4V8 Canada. **E-mail:** edward@moorshead.com. **E-mail:** hm_queries@moorshead.com. **Website:** www.history-magazine.com. **Contact:** Edward Zapletal, publisher/editor. **90% freelance written.** Bimonthly magazine covering social history. A general interest history magazine, focusing on social history up to the outbreak of World War II. Estab. 1999. Byline given. Pays on publication. Publishes ms an average of 6 months after acceptance. Editorial lead time 6 months. Submit seasonal ma-

terial 6 months in advance. Accepts queries by mail, e-mail. Responds in 1 month to queries. Responds in 1 month to mss. Sample copy available online. Guidelines available online.

NONFICTION Needs book excerpts, historical. Does not want first-person narratives or revisionist history. **Buys 50 mss/year.** Query. Do not submit complete ms. "PLEASE NOTE: Submissions must be accompanied by the author's name, telephone number, postal address and e-mail address. If not present in the manuscript, we will delay publication until we receive the necessary contact information." Length: 400-2,500 words. **Pays $50-250.**

💲 LEBEN

City Seminary Press, 2150 River Plaza Dr., Suite 150, Sacramento CA 95833. **E-mail:** editor@leben.us. **Website:** www.leben.us. **40% freelance written.** Estab. 2004. Circ. 5,000. Byline given. Pays on acceptance. Offers 25% kill fee. Publishes ms an average of 6 months after acceptance. Editorial lead time 6 months. Submit seasonal material 6 months in advance. Accepts queries by online submission form. Accepts simultaneous submissions. Responds in 3 weeks to queries. Responds in 2 months to mss. Sample copy for $1.50 (order online or request via e-mail). Guidelines by e-mail.

○ Quarterly magazine presenting the people and events of Christian history from a Reformation perspective. We are not a theological journal, per se, but rather a popular history magazine."

NONFICTION Needs historical, reformed biography. Does not want articles that argue theological issues. "There is a place for that, but not in a popular history/biography magazine aimed at general readership." Query. Length: 500-2,500 words. **Pays up to $100.**

TIPS "Visit our website and read our publication. We are a niche magazine, but a person knowledgeable about the Reformation should be able to write for."

LIGHTHOUSE DIGEST

Lighthouse Digest, P.O. Box 250, East Machias ME 04630. (207)259-2121. **E-mail:** Editor@LighthouseDigest.com. **Website:** www.lighthousedigest.com. **Contact:** Tim Harrison, editor. **15% freelance written.** Monthly magazine covering historical, fiction and news events about lighthouses and similar maritime stories. Estab. 1989. Circ. 24,000. Byline given. No kill fee. Publishes ms an average of 4 months after acceptance. Editorial lead time 3 months. Submit seasonal material 3 months in advance. Accepts queries by e-mail. Accepts simultaneous submissions. Responds in 6 weeks to queries. Sample copy free.

NONFICTION Needs exposé, general interest, historical, humor, inspirational, personal experience, photo feature, religious, technical, travel. No historical data taken from books. **Buys 30 mss/year.** Send complete ms. Length: 2,500 words maximum.

FICTION Needs adventure, historical, humorous, mystery, religious, romance, suspense. **Buys 2 mss/ year.** Send complete ms. 2,500 words maximum.

💲💲 PERSIMMON HILL

1700 NE 63rd St., Oklahoma City OK 73111. (405)478-2250, ext. 213. **Fax:** (405)478-4714. **E-mail:** editor@ nationalcowboymuseum.org. **Website:** www.nationalcowboymuseum.org. **Contact:** Judy Hilovsky. **70% freelance written. Prefers to work with published/ established writers; works with a small number of new/unpublished writers each year.** Biannual magazine for an audience interested in Western art, Western history, ranching, and rodeo, including historians, artists, ranchers, art galleries, schools, and librarios. Publication of the National Cowboy and Western Heritage Museum. Estab. 1970. Circ. 7,500. Byline given. Pays on publication. No kill fee. Publishes ms an average of 18 months after acceptance. Responds in 3 months to queries. Sample copy for $11. Writer's guidelines available on website.

NONFICTION Buys 50-75 mss/year. Query with clips. Length: 1,500 words. **Pays $150-300.**

💲💲💲 TIMELINE

Ohio Historical Society, 800 E. 17th Ave., Columbus OH 43211-2474. (614)297-2360. **Fax:** (614)297-2367. **E-mail:** timeline@ohiohistory.org. **Website:** www.ohiohistory.org/resource/publicat/timeline. **90% freelance written. Works with a small number of new/ unpublished writers each year.** Quarterly magazine covering history, prehistory, and the natural sciences, directed toward readers in the Midwest. Estab. 1984. Circ. 6,000. Byline given. Pays on final edit. Offers $75 minimum kill fee. Publishes ms an average of 1 year after acceptance. Submit seasonal material 6 months in advance. Accepts queries by mail, e-mail, fax. Responds in 3 weeks to queries. Responds in 6 weeks to mss. Sample copy for $12 and 9x12 SAE. Guidelines for #10 SASE.

NONFICTION Needs book excerpts, essays, historical, photo feature. **Buys 22 mss/year.** Query. 1,500-4,000 words. Also vignettes of 500-1,000 words. **Pays $100-800.**

🚫 💲💲💲 TRUE WEST

True West Publishing, Inc., P.O. Box 8008, Cave Creek AZ 85327. (888)687-1881. **Fax:** (480)575-1903. **E-mail:** editor@twmag.com. **Website:** www.truewestmagazine.com. **Contact:** Meghan Saar, editor-in-chief; Bob Boze Bell, executive editor. **45% freelance written. Works with a small number of new/unpublished writers each year.** Magazine published 10 times/year covering Western American history from prehistory 1800 to 1930. "We want reliable research on significant historical topics written in lively prose for an informed general audience. More recent topics may be used if they have a historical angle or retain the Old West flavor of trail dust and saddle leather. True West magazine's features and departments tie the history of the American West (between 1800-1930) to the modern western lifestyle through enticing narrative and intelligent analyses." Estab. 1953. Byline given. Pays on publication. Kill fee applicable only to material assigned by the editor, not for stories submitted on spec based on query written to the editor. 50% of original fee should the story have run in the publication. Editorial lead time 6 months. Accepts queries by mail, e-mail. Sample copy for $3. Guidelines available online.

NONFICTION No fiction, poetry, or unsupported, undocumented tales. **Buys 30 mss/year.** No unsolicited mss. True West seeks to establish long-term relationships with writers who conduct excellent research, provide a fresh look at an old subject, write well, hit deadlines and provide manuscripts at the assigned word length. Such writers tend to get repeat assignments. Send your query and accompanying MSS and photos to: **Meghan Saar,** editor-in-chief, via mail (SASE). Length: no more than 1,500 words. **Pays $50-800.** "Features pay $150-500 with a $20 payment for each photo the author provides that is published with the article and not already part of True West archives."

FILLERS Needs anecdotes, facts, gags, newsbreaks, short humor. **Buys 30 mss/year.** Length: 50-300 words.

💲💲 WILD WEST

Weider History Group, 19300 Promenade Dr., Leesburg VA 20176-6500. (703)771-9400. **Fax:** (703)779-8345. **E-mail:** wildwest@weiderhistorygroup.com. **Website:** www.historynet.com. **Contact:** Eric Weider, publisher. **95% freelance written.** Bimonthly magazine covering the history of the American frontier, from its eastern beginnings to its western terminus. "*Wild West* covers the popular (narrative) history of the American West—events, trends, personalities, anything of general interest." Estab. 1988. Circ. 83,500. Byline given. Pays on publication. No kill fee. Publishes ms an average of 2 years after acceptance. Editorial lead time 10 months. Submit seasonal material 1 year in advance. Accepts queries by mail, e-mail. Accepts simultaneous submissions. Responds in 3 months to queries. Responds in 6 months to mss. Sample copy for $6. Writer's guidelines for #10 SASE or online.

NONFICTION Needs historical, Old West. No excerpts, travel, etc. Articles can be adapted from book. No fiction or poetry. Nothing current. **Buys 36 mss/year.** Query. Length: 3,500 words with a 500-word sidebar. **Pays $300.**

COLUMNS/DEPARTMENTS Gunfighters & Lawmen, 2,000 words; Westerners, 2,000 words; Warriors & Chiefs, 2,000 words; Western Lore, 2,000 words; Guns of the West, 1,500 words; Artists West, 1,500 words; Books Reviews, 250 words. **Buys 36 mss/year.** Query. **Pays $150 for departments; book reviews paid by the word, minimum $40.**

HOBBY AND CRAFT

⊕⊕⊕⊕ AMERICAN CRAFT

American Craft Council, 1224 Marshall St. NE, Suite 200, Minneapolis MN 55413. (612)206-3100. **E-mail:** mmoses@craftcouncil.org. **E-mail:** query@craftcouncil.org. **Website:** www.americancraftmag.org. **Contact:** Monica Moses, editor. **75% freelance written.** Bimonthly magazine covering art/craft/design. Estab. 1943. Circ. 40,000. Byline given. Pays 30 days after acceptance. Offers 25% kill fee. Publishes ms an average of 2 months after acceptance. Editorial lead time 3 months. Submit seasonal material 3 months in advance. Accepts queries by mail, e-mail. Accepts simultaneous submissions. Responds in 1 month to queries. Responds in 2 months to mss. Sample copy free. Guidelines available on website.

NONFICTION Needs essays, general interest, interview, new product, opinion, photo feature, travel. Query with published clips. Length: 1,200-3,000 words. Pays expenses of writers on assignment.

COLUMNS/DEPARTMENTS Critics's Corner (critical essays), 200-2,500 words; Wide World of Craft (travel), 800-1,000 words; Material Culture (material studies), 600-800 words; outskirts (a look at peripheral disciplines), 600-800 words. **Buys 10-12 mss/year.** Query with published clips. **Pays $1-1.50/word.**

⊕⊕ ANTIQUE TRADER

F+W Media, Inc., 700 E. State St., Iola WI 54990. (715)445-2214. **Fax:** (715)445-4087. **E-mail:** toni.rahn@fwmedia.com; karen.knapstein@fwmedia.com. **Website:** www.antiquetrader.com. **Contact:** Antoinette (Toni) Rahn, editor and online content manager; Karen Knapstein, print editor. **60% freelance written.** Published 26 times per year. "We publish quote-heavy stories of timely interest in the antiques field. We cover antiques shows, auctions, and news events." Estab. 1957. Circ. 50,000. Byline given. Pays on publication. No kill fee. Publishes ms an average of 1-3 months after acceptance. Editorial lead time 2 months. Accepts queries by mail, e-mail, fax. Responds in 1 week to queries. Responds in 2 months to mss Sample copy for cover price, plus postage. Guidelines available online.

NONFICTION Needs book excerpts, general interest, interview, personal experience, show and auction coverage. Does not want the same, dry textbook, historical stories on antiques that appear elsewhere. Our readers want personality and timeliness. **Buys 1,000+ mss/year.** Send complete ms. Length: 750-1,200 words. **Pays $50-150, plus contributor copy.**

COLUMNS/DEPARTMENTS Dealer Profile (interviews with interesting antiques dealers), 750-1,200 words; Collector Profile (interviews with interesting collectors), 750-1,000 words. **Buys 30-60 mss/year.** Query with or without published clips or send complete ms.

⊕⊕ BEAD & BUTTON

Kalmbach Publishing, P.O. Box 1612, 21027 Crossroads Circle, Waukesha WI 53187-1612. **E-mail:** editor@beadandbutton.com. **Website:** www.beadandbutton.com. **Contact:** Julia Gerlach, editor; Jane Danley Cruz, Stacy Werkheiser, and Connie Whittaker, associate editors; Lora Groszkiewicz, editorial assistant. **50% freelance written.** "*Bead & Button* is a bimonthly magazine devoted to techniques, projects, designs, and materials relating to making beaded jewelry. Our readership includes both professional and amateur bead and button makers, hobbyists, and enthusiasts who find satisfaction in making beautiful things." Estab. 1994. Circ. 100,000. Byline given. Pays on acceptance. Offers $75 kill fee. Publishes ms an average of 4-12 months after acceptance. Accepts queries by mail, e-mail, fax. Guidelines available online.

NONFICTION Needs historical, on beaded jewelry history, how-to, make beaded jewelry and accessories, humor, inspirational, interview. **Buys 20-25 mss/year.** E-mail complete ms as a Word attachment. Length: 1,000-1,200 words. **Pays $75-400.**

⊛⊛ BLADE MAGAZINE

F+W Media, Inc., 700 E. State St., Iola WI 54990-0001. (715)445-2214. **Fax:** (715)445 4087. **E-mail:** joe.kertzman@fwmedia.com. **Website:** www.blademag.com. **Contact:** Joe Kertzman, managing editor. **5% freelance written.** Monthly magazine covering working and using collectible, popular knives. *Blade* prefers in-depth articles focusing on groups of knives, whether military, collectible, high-tech, pocket knives or hunting knives, and how they perform. Estab. 1973. Circ. 39,000. Byline given. Pays on publication. No kill fee. Publishes ms an average of 9 months after acceptance. Editorial lead time 9 months. Submit seasonal material 9 months in advance. Accepts queries by mail, e-mail, fax. Responds in 3 months to queries. Responds in 6 months to mss. Sample copy for $4.99. Guidelines for SAE with 8x11 envelope and 3 first-class stamps.

NONFICTION Needs general interest, historical, how-to, interview, new product, photo feature, technical. "We assign profiles, show stories, hammer-in stories, etc. We don't need those. If you've seen the story on the Internet or in another knife or knife/gun magazine, we don't need it. We don't do stories on knives used for self-defense." Send complete ms. Length: 700-1,400 words. **Pays $150-300.**

FILLERS Needs anecdotes, facts, newsbreaks. **Buys 1-2 fillers. mss/year.** Length: 50-200 words. **Pays $25-50.**

⊛ BREW YOUR OWN

Battenkill Communications, 5515 Main St., Manchester Center VT 05255. (802)362-3981. **Fax:** (802)362-2377. **E-mail:** edit@byo.com. **Website:** www.byo.com. **Contact:** Chris Colby, editor. **85% freelance written.** Monthly magazine covering home brewing. "Our mission is to provide practical information in an entertaining format. We try to capture the spirit and challenge of brewing while helping our readers

brew the best beer they can." Estab. 1995. Circ. 50,000. Byline given. Pays on acceptance. Offers 25% kill fee. Publishes ms an average of 4 months after acceptance. Editorial lead time 3 months. Submit seasonal material 3 months in advance. Accepts queries by mail, e-mail, fax. Responds in 2 months to queries. Guidelines available on website.

NONFICTION Needs historical, how-to, home brewing, humor, related to home brewing, interview, of professional brewers who can offer useful tips to home hobbyists, personal experience, trends. **Buys 75 mss/year.** Query with published clips or description of brewing expertise Length: 800 3,000 words. **Pays $50-350, depending on length, complexity of article, and experience of writer.** Sometimes pays expenses of writers on assignment.

COLUMNS/DEPARTMENTS News (humorous, unusual news about homebrewing), 50-250 words; Last Call (humorous stories about homebrewing), 700 words. **Buys 12 mss/year.** Query with or without published clips. **Pays $75.**

⊙ ⊛⊛ CANADIAN WOODWORKING AND HOME IMPROVEMENT

Sawdust Media, Inc., 51 Maple Ave. N., RR #3, Burford ON N0E 1A0 Canada. (519)449-2444. **Fax:** (519)449-2445. **E-mail:** pfulcher@canadianwoodworking.com. **Website:** www.canadianwoodworking.com. **20% freelance written.** Bimonthly magazine covering woodworking; only accepts work from Canadian writers. Estab. 1999. Byline given. Pays on publication. Offers 50% kill fee. Accepts queries by e-mail. Sample copy available online. Guidelines by e-mail.

NONFICTION Needs how to, humor, inspirational, new product, personal experience, photo feature, technical. Does not want profile on a woodworker. Query. Length: 500-4,000 words. **Pays $100-600 for assigned articles. Pays $50-400 for unsolicited articles.**

⊛ CARVING MAGAZINE

All American Crafts, P.O. Box 611, Faribault MN 55021. **E-mail:** editors@carvingmagazine.com. **Website:** www.carvingmagazine.com. **Contact:** Chris Whillock, editor. **95% freelance written.** Quarterly magazine covering woodcarving. "*Carving Magazine* specializes in woodcarving articles including step-by-steps, techniques, profiles, and photo galleries." Estab. 2002. Circ. 20,000. Byline given. Pays on publication. Publishes ms an average of 6 months after acceptance.

Editorial lead time 6 months. Submit seasonal material 6 months in advance. Accepts queries by mail, e-mail. Guidelines available online.

NONFICTION Needs general interest, historical, how-to, interview, photo feature. Does not want anything other than woodcarving. **Buys 40 mss/year.** Length: 2,000 words. **Pays $50-100.**

FILLERS Needs gags.

⊘⊖ CERAMICS MONTHLY

600 N. Cleveland Ave., Suite 210, Westerville OH 43082. (614)794-5867. **Fax:** (614)891-8960. **E-mail:** editorial@ceramicsmonthly.org. **Website:** www.ceramicsmonthly.org. **70% freelance written.** Monthly magazine (except July and August) covering the ceramic art and craft field. "Each issue of *Ceramics Monthly* includes articles on potters and ceramics artists from throughout the world, exhibitions, and production processes, as well as critical commentary, book and video reviews, clay and glaze recipes, kiln designs and firing techniques, advice from experts in the field, and ads for available materials and equipment. While principally covering contemporary work, the magazine also looks back at influential artists and events from the past." Estab. 1953. Circ. 39,000. Byline given. Pays on publication. Editorial lead time 3 months. Submit seasonal material 6 months in advance. Accepts queries by mail, e-mail, fax, phone. Responds in 2 months to mss. Guidelines available online.

NONFICTION Needs essays, how-to, interview, opinion, personal experience, technical. **Buys 100 mss/year.** Send complete ms. Length: 500-1,500 words. **Pays 10¢/word.**

COLUMNS/DEPARTMENTS Upfront (workshop/exhibition review), 500-1,000 words. **Buys 20 mss/year.** Send complete ms.

⊘⊖ CLASSIC TOY TRAINS

Kalmbach Publishing Co., P.O. Box 1612, 21027 Crossroads Cir., Waukesha WI 53187. (262)796-8776, ext. 524. **Fax:** (262)796-1142. **E-mail:** manuscripts@classictoytrains.com. **Website:** www.classictoytrains.com. **Contact:** Carl Swanson, editor. **80% freelance written.** Magazine published 9 times/year covering collectible toy trains (O, S, Standard) like Lionel and American Flyer, etc. "For the collector and operator of toy trains, *CTT* offers full-color photos of layouts and collections of toy trains, restoration tips, operating information, new product reviews and informa-

tion, and insights into the history of toy trains." Estab. 1987. Circ. 50,000. Byline given. Pays on acceptance. Publishes ms an average of 1 year after acceptance. Editorial lead time 3 months. Submit seasonal material 6 months in advance. Accepts queries by mail, e-mail. Responds in 3 weeks to queries. Responds in 1 month to mss. Sample copy for $5.95, plus postage. Guidelines available online.

NONFICTION Needs general interest, historical, how-to, restore toy trains; design a layout; build accessories; fix broken toy trains, interview, personal experience, photo feature, technical. **Buys 90 mss/year.** Query. Length: 500-5,000 words. **Pays $75-500.** Sometimes pays expenses of writers on assignment.

⊖ CQ AMATEUR RADIO

CQ Communications, Inc., 25 Newbridge Rd., Hicksville NY 11801. (516)681-2922. **Fax:** (516)681-2926. **E-mail:** cq@cq-amateur-radio.com. **E-mail:** w2vu@cq-amateur-radio.com. **Website:** www.cq-amateur-radio.com. **Contact:** Richard Moseson, editor. **40% freelance written.** Monthly magazine covering amateur (ham) radio. "*CQ* is published for active ham radio operators and is read by radio amateurs in over 100 countries. All articles must deal with amateur radio. Our focus is on operating and on practical projects. A thorough knowledge of amateur radio is required." Estab. 1945. Circ. 60,000. Byline given. Pays on publication. No kill fee. Publishes ms an average of 6 months after acceptance. Editorial lead time 4 months. Submit seasonal material 4 months in advance. Accepts queries by mail, e-mail, fax. Responds in 3 weeks to queries. Responds in 3 months to mss. Sample copy free. Guidelines available online.

NONFICTION Needs historical, how-to, interview, personal experience, technical, all related to amateur radio. **Buys 50-60 mss/year.** Query. Length: 2,000-4,000 words. **Pays $40/published page.** Pays writer expenses rarely and only by prior arrangement.

⊘⊖ DOLLS

Jones Publishing, Inc., P.O. Box 5000, N7528 Aanstad Rd., Iola WI 54945. (715)445-5000. **Fax:** (715)445-4053. **E-mail:** joyceg@jonespublishing.com; jonespub@jonespublishing.com. **Website:** www.dollsmagazine.com. **Contact:** Joyce Greenholdt, editor. **75% freelance written.** Magazine published 10 times/year covering dolls, doll artists, and related topics of interest to doll collectors and enthusiasts. "*Dolls* enhances the joy of collecting by introducing readers to the best new dolls from around the world, along with the artists and designers who create them. It keeps readers up-to-date on shows, sales and special events in the doll world. With beautiful color photography, *Dolls* offers an array of easy-to-read, informative articles that help our collectors select the best buys." Estab. 1982. Circ. 100,000. Byline given. Pays on publication. No kill fee. Accepts queries by mail, e-mail. Responds in 1 month to queries.

NONFICTION Needs historical, how-to, interview, new product, photo feature. **Buys 55 mss/year.** Send complete ms. Length: 750-1,200 words. **Pays $75-300.**

F+W MEDIA, INC. (MAGAZINE DIVISION)

10151 Carver Rd., Suite 200, Cincinnati OH 45242. (513)531-2690. **E-mail:** dave.pulvermacher@fwmedia.com. **Website:** www.fwmedia.com. **Contact:** Dave Pulvermacher, marketing research supervisor. "Each month, millions of enthusiasts turn to the magazines from F+W for inspiration, instruction, and encouragement. Readers are as varied as our categories, but all are assured of getting the best possible coverage of their favorite hobby." Publishes magazines in the following categories: **antiques and collectibles** (*Antique Trader*); **automotive** (*Military Vehicles, Old Cars Report Price Guide, Old Cars Weekly*); **coins and paper money** (*Bank Note Reporter, Coins Magazine, Coin Prices, Numismatic News, World Coin News*); **comics** (*Comics Buyer's Guide*); **construction** (*Frame Building News, Metal Roofing, Rural Builder*); **fine art** (*Collector's Guide, Pastel Journal, Southwest Art, The Artist's Magazine, Watercolor Artist*), **firearms and knives** (*Blade, Gun Digest—The Magazine,*); **genealogy** (*Family Tree Magazine*); **graphic design** (*HOW Magazine, PRINT*); **horticulture** (*Horticulture*); **militaria** (*Military Trader*); **outdoors and hunting** (*Deer & Deer Hunting, Trapper & Predator Caller, Turkey & Turkey Hunting*); **records and CDs** (*Goldmine*); **sports** (*Sports Collectors Digest*); **woodworking** (*Popular Woodworking Magazine*); **writing** (*Writer's Digest*). Please see individual listings in the Consumer Magazines and Trade Journals sections for specific submission information about each magazine.

$$$ FAMILY TREE MAGAZINE

F+W Media, Inc., 10151 Carver Rd., Suite 200, Cincinnati OH 45242. (513)531-2690. **Fax:** (513)891-7153. **E-mail:** ftmedit@fwpubs.com. **Website:** www.familytreemagazine.com. **75% freelance written.** Magazine covering family history, heritage, and genealogy research. "*Family Tree Magazine* is a general-interest consumer magazine that helps readers discover, preserve, and celebrate their family's history. We cover genealogy, ethnic heritage, genealogy websites and software, photography and photo preservation, and other ways that families connect with their past." Estab. 1999. Circ. 75,000. Byline given. Pays on acceptance. Offers 25% kill fee. Publishes ms an average of 6 months after acceptance. Editorial lead time 8 months. Submit seasonal material 8 months in advance. Accepts queries by mail, e-mail. Responds in 1 month to queries. Sample copy for $8 from website. Guidelines available online.

NONFICTION Needs book excerpts, historical, how-to, genealogy, new product, photography, computer, technical, genealogy software, photography equipment. **Buys 60 mss/year.** Query with published clips. Length: 250-4,500 words. **Pays $25-800.** Does not pay expenses.

☉ $ FIBRE FOCUS

Magazine of the Ontario Handweavers & Spinners, 17 Robinson Rd., RR4, Waterford ON N0E 1Y0 Canada. (519)443-7104. **E-mail:** ffeditor@ohs.on.ca. **Website:** www.ohs.on.ca. **Contact:** Dawna Beatty, editor. **90% freelance written.** Quarterly magazine covering handweaving, spinning, basketry, beading, and other fibre arts. "Our readers are weavers and spinners who also do dyeing, knitting, basketry, feltmaking, papermaking, sheep raising, and craft supply. All articles deal with some aspect of these crafts." Estab. 1957. Circ. 1,000. Byline given. Pays within 30 days after publication. Editorial lead time 6 months. Submit seasonal material 6 months in advance. Responds in 1 month to queries. Sample copy for $8 (Canadian). Guidelines available online.

NONFICTION Needs how-to, interview, new product, opinion, personal experience, technical, travel, book reviews. **Buys 40-60 mss/year.** "Please contact the *Fibre Focus* editor before undertaking a project or an article. Mss may be submitted c/o Dawna Beatty by e-mail for anything you have to contribute for upcoming issues. **Feature article deadlines: December 31, March 31, June 30, and September 15.** Please read the guidelines for contributing an article to *Fibre Focus*." Word length varies. **Pays $30 (Canadian) per published page.**

FINE BOOKS & COLLECTIONS

OP Media, LLC, 101 Europa Dr., Suite 150, Chapel Hill NC 27517. (800)662-4834. **Fax:** (919)945-0700. **E-mail:** rebecca@finebooksmagazine.com. **Website:** www.finebooksmagazine.com. **90% freelance written.** Bimonthly magazine covering used and antiquarian bookselling and book collecting. We cover all aspects of selling and collecting out-of-print books. We emphasize good writing, interesting people, and unexpected view points. Estab. 2002. Circ. 5,000. Byline given. Pays on publication. Offers negotiable kill fee. Publishes ms an average of 4 months after acceptance. Editorial lead time 6+ months. Submit seasonal material 4 months in advance. Accepts queries by mail, e-mail. Accepts simultaneous submissions. Responds in 2 months to queries and mss. Sample copy for $6.50 + shipping. Guidelines available online.

NONFICTION Needs book excerpts, essays, exposé, general interest, historical, how-to, travel. Does not want tales of the 'gold in my attic' vein; how to collect; bibliographies/lists; stories emphasizing books/art as an investment **Buys 25 mss/year.** Query with published clips. Length: 500-2,000 words. **Pays $125-400.** Sometimes pays expenses of writers on assignment.

COLUMNS/DEPARTMENTS Digest (news about collectors, booksellers, and bookselling), 500 words.

FINESCALE MODELER

Kalmbach Publishing Co., 21027 Crossroads Circle, P.O. Box 1612, Waukesha WI 53187-1612. (414)796-8776. **Website:** www.finescale.com. **80% freelance written. Eager to work with new/unpublished writers.** Magazine published 10 times/year devoted to how-to-do-it modeling information for scale model builders who build non-operating aircraft, tanks, boats, automobiles, figures, dioramas, and science fiction and fantasy models. Circ. 60,000. Byline given. Pays on acceptance. No kill fee. Publishes ms an average of 14 months after acceptance. Responds in 6 weeks to queries. Responds in 3 months to mss. Sample copy with 9x12 SASE and 3 first-class stamps. Guidelines available on website.

NONFICTION Needs how-to, build scale models, technical, research information for building models. Query or send complete ms via www.contribute.kalmbach.com. Length: 750-3,000 words. **Pays $60/ published page minimum.**

COLUMNS/DEPARTMENTS *FSM* Showcase (photos plus description of model); *FSM* Tips and Techniques (model building hints and tips). Buys 25-50 mss/year. Send complete ms. **Pays $25-50.**

THE FINE TOOL JOURNAL LLC

P.O. Box 737, 9325 Dwight Boyer Rd., Watervliet MI 49098. (269)463-8255. **Fax:** (269)463-3767. **E-mail:** finetoolj@gmail.com; jim@finetooljournal.net. **Website:** www.finetooljournal.net. **Contact:** Jim Gehring. **90% freelance written.** "Quarterly magazine specializing in older or antique hand tools from all traditional trades. Readers are primarily interested in woodworking tools, but some subscribers have interests in such areas as leatherworking, wrenches, kitchen, and machinist tools. Readers range from beginners just getting into the hobby to advanced collectors and organizations." Estab. 1970. Circ. 2,500. Byline given. Pays on publication. Offers $50 kill fee. Publishes ms an average of 6 months after acceptance. Editorial lead time 9 months. Submit seasonal material 6 months in advance. Accepts queries by mail, online submission form. Responds in 2 months to queries; 3 months to mss. Sample copy for $5. Guidelines for #10 SASE.

NONFICTION Needs general interest, historical, how-to, make, use, fix and tune tools, interview, personal experience, photo feature, technical. **Buys 24 mss/year.** Send complete ms. Length: 1,000-3,000 words. **Pays $50-200.** Pays expenses of writers on assignment.

COLUMNS/DEPARTMENTS Stanley Tools (new finds and odd types), 300-400 words; Tips of the Trade (how to use tools), 100-200 words. **Buys 12 mss/ year.** Send complete ms. **Pays $30-60.**

FINE WOODWORKING

The Taunton Press, Inc., 63 South Main St., P.O. Box 5506, Newtown CT 06470-5506. (203)426-8171. **Fax:** (203)426-3434. **E-mail:** fw@taunton.com. **Website:** www.finewoodworking.com. **Contact:** Tom McKenna, senior editor. Bimonthly magazine on woodworking in the small shop. Estab. 1975. Circ. 270,000. Byline given. Pays on acceptance. Offers variable kill fee. Submit seasonal material 6 months in advance. Accepts simultaneous submissions. Responds in 1 month to queries. Guidelines online at www.finewoodworking.com/pages/fw_authorguideline.asp.

NONFICTION Needs how-to, woodworking. **Buys 120 mss/year.** Send article outline, helpful drawings or photos, and proposal letter. **Pays $150/magazine**

page. Sometimes pays expenses of writers on assignment.

COLUMNS/DEPARTMENTS Fundamentals (basic how-to and concepts for beginning woodworkers); Master Class (advanced techniques); Finish Line (finishing techniques); Question & Answer (woodworking Q&A); Methods of Work (shop tips); Tools & Materials (short reviews of new tools). **Buys 400 mss/year. Pays $50-150/published page.**

$$ THE HOME SHOP MACHINIST

P.O. Box 629, Traverse City MI 49685. (231)946-3712. **Fax:** (231)946-6180. **E-mail:** gbulliss@villagepress.com; daronklooster@villagepress.com. **Website:** www.homeshopmachinist.net. **Contact:** George Bulliss, editor; Daron Klooster, managing editor. **95% freelance written.** Bimonthly magazine covering machining and metalworking for the hobbyist. Circ. 34,000. Byline given. Pays on publication. Publishes ms an average of 2 years after acceptance. Responds in 2 months to queries. Sample copy free. Guidelines for 9x12 SASE.

NONFICTION Needs how-to, projects designed to upgrade present shop equipment or hobby model projects that require machining, technical, should pertain to metalworking, machining, drafting, layout, welding or foundry work for the hobbyist. No fiction or people features. **Buys 40 mss/year.** Send complete ms. Length: open—"whatever it takes to do a thorough job." **Pays $40/published page, plus $9/published photo.**

COLUMNS/DEPARTMENTS "Become familiar with our magazine before submitting." Book Reviews; New Product Reviews; Micro-Machining; Foundry. Length: 600-1,500 words. **Buys 25-30 mss/year.** Query. **Pays $40-70.**

FILLERS **Buys 12-15 mss/year.** Length: 100-300 words. **Pays $30-48.**

$$ KITPLANES

P.O. Box 856, Friendswood TX 77549. (832)851-6665. **E-mail:** editorial@kitplanes.com. **Website:** www.kitplanes.com. **Contact:** Paul Dye, editor-in-chief. **50% freelance written. Eager to work with new/unpublished writers.** Monthly magazine covering self-construction of private aircraft for pilots and builders. Estab. 1984. Circ. 72,000. Byline given. Pays on publication. Publishes ms an average of 3 months after acceptance. Submit seasonal material 6 months in advance. Accepts queries by mail, e-mail. Responds in 4 weeks to queries. Responds in 6 weeks to mss. Sample copy for $6. Guidelines available online.

NONFICTION Needs general interest, how-to, interview, new product, personal experience, photo feature, technical. No general-interest aviation articles, or "My First Solo" type of articles. **Buys 80 mss/year.** Query. Length: 500-3,000 words. **Pays $250-1,000, including story photos.**

$$ THE LEATHER CRAFTERS & SADDLERS JOURNAL

222 Blackburn St., Rhinelander WI 54501-2902. (715)362-5393. **Fax:** (715)362-5391. **E-mail:** journal@newnorth.net. **Website:** http://leathercraftersjournal.com. **Contact:** Dot Reis, publisher. **100% freelance written.** Bimonthly magazine covering leatherwork. "A leather-working publication with how-to, step-by-step instructional articles using patterns for leathercraft, leather art, custom saddle, boot, etc. A complete resource for leather, tools, machinery, and allied materials, plus leather industry news." Estab. 1990. Circ. 8,000. Byline given. Pays on publication. Publishes ms an average of 4 months after acceptance. Submit seasonal material 6 months in advance. Accepts queries by mail, e-mail, fax, phone. Accepts simultaneous submissions. Responds in 1 month to mss. Sample copy for $7. Guidelines available on website.

NONFICTION **Buys 75 mss/year.** Send complete ms. Length: 500-2,500 words. **Pays $20-250 for assigned articles. Pays $25-150 for unsolicited articles.**

REPRINTS Send tearsheet or photocopy. Pays 50% of amount paid for an original article.

COLUMNS/DEPARTMENTS Beginners; Intermediate; Artists; Western Design; Saddlemakers; International Design; and Letters (the open exchange of information between all peoples). Length: 500-2,500 words on all.

$ LINN'S STAMP NEWS

Amos Press, P.O. Box 29, Sidney OH 45365. (937)498-0801. **Fax:** (937)498-0886. **E-mail:** linns@linns.com. **Website:** www.linns.com. **Contact:** Michael Baadke, editor. **50% freelance written.** Weekly tabloid on the stamp collecting hobby. "All articles must be about philatelic collectibles. Our goal at *Linn's* is to create a weekly publication that is indispensable to stamp collectors." Estab. 1928. Circ. 32,000. Byline given. Pays within 1 month of publication. Publishes ms an average of 4 months after acceptance. Submit seasonal material 2 months in advance. Responds in 6 weeks

CONSUMER MAGAZINES

to queries. Sample copy online. Guidelines available online.

NONFICTION Needs general interest, historical, how-to, interview, technical, club and show news, current issues, auction realization, and recent discoveries. "No articles merely giving information on background of stamp subject. Must have philatelic information included." **Buys 25 mss/year.** Send complete ms. Length: 1,200 words maximum. **Pays $40-100.** Sometimes pays expenses of writers on assignment.

LOST TREASURE, INC.

P.O. Box 451589, Grove OK 74345. (866)469-6224. **Fax:** (918)786-2192. **E-mail:** managingeditor@lost-treasure.com. **Website:** www.losttreasure.com. **Contact:** Carla Banning, managing editor. **75% freelance written.** Monthly and annual magazines covering lost treasure. Estab. 1966. Circ. 55,000. Byline given. Pays on publication. Accepts queries by mail, e-mail, fax. Responds in 1 month to queries. Responds in 2 months to mss. Sample copy for #10 SASE. Guidelines for 10×13 SAE with $1.70 postage or online.

NONFICTION Buys 225 mss/year. Query on *Treasure Cache* only. "Will buy articles, photographs, and cartoons that meet our editorial approval." Enclose SASE with all editorial submissions. Length: 1,000-2,000 words. **Pays 4¢/word.**

MILITARY VEHICLES

F+W Media, Inc., 700 E. State St., Iola WI 54990-0001. (715)445-4612. **Fax:** (715)445-4087. **E-mail:** john.adams-graf@fwmedia.com. **Website:** www.militarytrader.com. **Contact:** John Adams-Graf, editor. **50% freelance written.** Bimonthly magazine covering historic military vehicles. Dedicated to serving people who collect, restore, and drive historic military vehicles. Circ. 18,500. Byline given. Pays on publication. No kill fee. Publishes ms an average of 1 month after acceptance. Accepts queries by mail, e-mail. Accepts simultaneous submissions. Responds in 1 week to queries. Responds in 1 month to mss. Sample copy for $5.

NONFICTION Needs historical, how-to, technical. **Buys 20 mss/year.** Send complete ms. Length: 1,300-2,600 words. **Pays $0-200.**

COLUMNS/DEPARTMENTS Pays $0-75.

MODEL CARS MAGAZINE

Golden Bell Press, 2403 Champa St., Denver CO 80205. (808)754-1378. **E-mail:** gregg@modelcars-

mag.com. **Website:** www.modelcarsmag.com. **25% freelance written.** Magazine published 9 times year covering model cars, trucks, and other automotive models. "*Model Cars Magazine* is the hobby's how-to authority for the automotive modeling hobbiest. We are on the forefront of the hobby, our editorial staff are model car builders, and every single one of our writers have a passion for the hobby that is evident in the articles and stories that we publish. We are the model car magazine written by and for model car builders." Estab. 1999. Circ. 7,000. Byline given. Pays on publication. Publishes ms an average of 2-3 months after acceptance. Editorial lead time 2-3 months. Accepts queries by mail, e-mail. Sample copy online.

NONFICTION Needs how-to. Length: 600-3,000 words. **Pays $50/page. Pays $25/page for unsolicited articles.**

MONITORING TIMES

Grove Enterprises, Inc., 7540 Hwy. 64 W., Brasstown NC 28904. (828)837-9200. **E-mail:** editor@monitoringtimes.com. **Website:** www.monitoringtimes.com. **Contact:** Ken Reitz. **15% freelance written.** Monthly magazine for radio hobbyists. Estab. 1982. Circ. 15,000. Byline given. Pays on publication. Publishes ms an average of 4 months after acceptance. Submit seasonal material 4 months in advance. Accepts queries by mail, e-mail. Responds in 1 month to queries. Sample copy for 9x12 SAE and 9 first-class stamps. Guidelines available online.

NONFICTION Needs general interest, how-to, humor, interview, personal experience, photo feature, technical. **Buys 50 mss/year.** Query. Length: 1,500-3,000 words. **Pays average of $90-100 per published page.**

REPRINTS Send photocopy and information about when and where the material previously appeared. Pays 50% of amount paid for an original article.

COLUMNS/DEPARTMENTS Query editor.

NATIONAL COMMUNICATIONS

Norm Schrein, Inc., P.O. Box 291918, Kettering OH 45429. (937)299-7226. **Fax:** (937)299-1323. **E-mail:** norm@bearcat1.com. **Website:** www.nat-com.org. **Contact:** Norm Schrein, editor. **100% freelance written.** Bimonthly magazine covering radio as a hobby. "*National Communications* is the magazine for every radio user." Estab. 1990. Circ. 5,000. Byline given. Pays on publication. No kill fee. Publishes ms an average of 2 months after acceptance. Editorial lead time

2 months. Submit seasonal material 2 months in advance. Accepts queries by phone. Accepts simultaneous submissions. Sample copy for $4.

NONFICTION Needs how-to, interview, new product, personal experience, photo feature, technical. Does not want articles off topic of the publication's audience (radio hobbyists). **Buys 2-3 mss/year.** Query. Length: 300 words. **Pays $75+.**

$$ PAPER CRAFTS MAGAZINE

Primedia Magazines, 14850 Pony Express Rd., Suite 200, Bluffdale UT 84065. (801)816-8300. **Fax:** (801)816-8302. **E-mail:** editor@papercraftsmag.com. **Website:** www.papercraftsmag.com. **Contact:** Jennifer Schaerer, editor-in-chief; Kerri Miller, managing editor. Magazine published 10 times/year designed to help readers make creative and rewarding handmade crafts. The main focus is fresh, craft-related projects our reader can make and display in her home or give as gifts. Estab. 1978. Circ. 300,000. Byline given. Pays on acceptance. Editorial lead time 6 months. Accepts queries by mail, e-mail. Responds in 1 month to queries. Guidelines for #10 SASE.

NONFICTION Needs how-to. **Buys 300 mss/year.** Query with photo or sketch of how-to project. Do not send the actual project until request. **Pays $100-500.**

$ PIECEWORK MAGAZINE

Interweave Press, Inc., 201 E. 4th St., Loveland CO 80537. (800) 272-2193. **Fax:** (970)669-6117. **E-mail:** piecework@interweave.com. **Website:** www.interweave.com. **90% freelance written.** Bimonthly magazine covering needlework history. *PieceWork* celebrates the rich tradition of needlework and the history of the people behind it. Stories and projects on embroidery, cross-stitch, knitting, crocheting, and quilting, along with other textile arts, are featured in each issue. Estab. 1993. Circ. 30,000. Byline given. Pays on publication. Offers 25% kill fee. Editorial lead time 6 months. Submit seasonal material 6 months in advance. Accepts queries by mail, e-mail, fax, phone. Responds in 6 months to queries. Sample copy and writer's guidelines free.

NONFICTION Needs book excerpts, historical, how-to, interview, new product. No contemporary needlework articles. **Buys 25-30 mss/year.** Send complete ms. Length: 1,000-5,000 words. **Pays $100/printed page.**

$ POPULAR COMMUNICATIONS

CQ Communications, Inc., 25 Newbridge Rd., Hicksville NY 11801. (516)681-2922. **Fax:** (516)681-2926. **E-mail:** cq@cq-amateur-radio.com. **Website:** www.popular-communications.com. **25% freelance written.** Monthly magazine covering the radio communications hobby. Estab. 1982. Circ. 40,000. Byline given. Pays on publication. Publishes ms an average of 6 months after acceptance. Editorial lead time 3 months. Submit seasonal material 6 months in advance. Accepts queries by mail, e-mail. Responds in 1 month to queries. Responds in 2 months to mss. Sample copy free. Guidelines for #10 SASE.

NONFICTION Needs general interest, how-to, antenna construction, humor, new product, photo feature, technical. **Buys 6-10 mss/year.** Query. Length: 1,800-3,000 words. **Pays $135/printed page.**

$$$$ POPULAR MECHANICS

Hearst Corp., 300 W. 57th St., New York NY 10019. (212)649-2000. **E-mail:** popularmechanics@hearst.com; pmwebmaster@hearst.com. **Website:** www.popularmechanics.com. **Up to 50% freelance written.** Monthly magazine on technology, science, automotive, home, outdoors. "We are a men's service magazine that addresses the diverse interests of today's male, providing him with information to improve the way he lives. We cover stories from do-it-yourself projects to technological advances in aerospace, military, automotive, and so on." Estab. 1902. Circ. 1,200,000. Pays on acceptance. Offers 25% kill fee. Publishes ms an average of 6 months after acceptance. Submit seasonal material 6 months in advance. Guidelines available on website.

NONFICTION Pays $1/word and up.

$$ POPULAR WOODWORKING MAGAZINE

F+W Media, Inc., 8469 Blue Ash Rd., Suite 100, Cincinnati OH 45236. (513)531-2690, ext. 11348. **E-mail:** megan.fitzpatrick@fwmedia.com. **Website:** www.popularwoodworking.com. **45% freelance written.** Magazine published 7 times/year. "*Popular Woodworking Magazine* invites woodworkers of all skill levels into a community of professionals who share their hard-won shop experience through in-depth projects and technique articles, which help the readers hone their existing skills and develop new ones for both hand and power tools. Related stories increase the readers' understanding and enjoyment of their craft.

Any project submitted must be aesthetically pleasing, of sound construction, and offer a challenge to readers. On the average, we use 2 freelance features per issue. Our primary needs are 'how-to' articles on woodworking. Our secondary need is for articles that will inspire discussion concerning woodworking. Tone of articles should be conversational and informal but knowledgeable, as if the writer is speaking directly to the reader. Our readers are the woodworking hobbyist and small woodshop owner. Writers should have an extensive knowledge of woodworking and excellent woodworking techniques and skills." Estab. 1981. Circ. 150,000. Byline given. Pays on acceptance. No kill fee. Publishes ms an average of 10 months after acceptance. Submit seasonal material 6 months in advance. Accepts queries by mail, e-mail, phone. Responds in 2 months to queries. Sample copy for $5.99 and 9x12 SAE with 6 first-class stamps or online. Guidelines available online.

NONFICTION Needs how-to (on woodworking projects, with plans), humor (woodworking anecdotes), technical (woodworking techniques). No tool reviews. **Buys 12 mss/year.** Send complete ms. **Pay starts at $250/published page.**

REPRINTS Send photocopy with rights for sale noted and information about when and where the material previously appeared. Pays 25% of amount paid for an original article.

COLUMNS/DEPARTMENTS Tricks of the Trade (helpful techniques), End Grain (thoughts on woodworking as a profession or hobby, can be humorous or serious), 500-550 words. **Buys 20 columns/yr mss/year.** Query.

THE QUILTER

All American Crafts, Inc., 7 Waterloo Rd., Stanhope NJ 07874. (973)347-6900, ext. 135. **E-mail:** editors@ thequiltermag.com. **Website:** www.thequiltermag. com. **Contact:** Laurette Koserowski, editor. **45% freelance written.** Bimonthly magazine on quilting. "*The Quilter* is an instructional magazine that features patterns in patchwork and appliquè techniques. The editors accept articles relating to quilting, detailed quilting projects, and profiles of outstanding quilting instructors and their techniques. Holiday items are always welcome." Estab. 1988. Byline given. Pays on publication. Publishes ms an average of 6 months after acceptance. Submit seasonal material 6 months in advance. Accepts queries by mail, phone. Responds

in 6 weeks to queries. Sample copy for SAE with 9x12 envelope and 4 first-class stamps. Guidelines available online.

NONFICTION Query with published clips. Length: 350-1,000 words. **Pays $150-250/article for original, unpublished mss. Project payments are a flat rate of $175-$375/project.**

COLUMNS/DEPARTMENTS Feature Teacher (qualified quilt teachers with teaching involved—with slides); Profile (award-winning and interesting quilters). Length: 1,000 words maximum. **Pays 10¢/word, $15/photo.**

RENAISSANCE MAGAZINE

80 Hathaway Dr., Stratford CT 06615. (800)232-2224. **Fax:** (800)775-2729. **E-mail:** editortom@renaissancemagazine.com. **Website:** www.renaissancemagazine.com. **Contact:** Tom Hauck, editor. **90% freelance written.** Bimonthly magazine covering the history of the Middle Ages and the Renaissance. "Our readers include historians, reenactors, roleplayers, medievalists, and Renaissance Faire enthusiasts." Estab. 1996. Circ. 33,000. Byline given. Pays on publication. Publishes ms an average of 1 year after acceptance. Editorial lead time 6 months. Submit seasonal material 4 months in advance. Accepts queries by mail, e-mail, fax, phone. Responds in 3 weeks to queries. Responds in 2 months to mss. Sample copy for $9. Guidelines available online.

NONFICTION Needs essays, exposé, historical, how-to, interview, new product, opinion, photo feature, religious, travel. **Buys 25 mss/year.** Query or send ms. Length: 1,000-5,000 words. **Pays 8¢/word.**

ROCK & GEM

Miller Magazines, Inc., 3585 Maple St., Suite 232, Ventura CA 93003. (805)644-3824. **Fax:** (805)644-3875. **E-mail:** editor@rockngem.com. **Website:** www.rockngem.com. **99% freelance written.** Monthly magazine covering rockhounding field trips, how-to lapidary projects, minerals, fossils, gold prospecting, mining, etc. See guidelines. "This is not a scientific journal. Its articles appeal to amateurs, beginners, and experts, but its tone is conversational and casual, not stuffy. It's for hobbyists." Estab. 1971. Circ. 55,000. Byline given. Pays on publication. No kill fee. Editorial lead time 4 months. Submit seasonal material 6 months in advance. Accepts queries by mail. Guidelines available online.

NONFICTION Needs general interest, how-to, personal experience, photo feature, travel. Does not want to see The 25th Anniversary of the Pet Rock, or anything so scientific that it could be a thesis. **Buys 156-200 mss/year.** Send complete ms. Length: 2,000-4,000 words. **Pays $100-250.**

💲💲 SEWNEWS

Creative Crafts Group, 741 Corporate Circle, Suite A, Golden CO 80401. (303)215-5600. **Fax:** (303)215-5601. **E-mail:** sewnews@sewnews.com. **Website:** www.sewnews.com. **Contact:** Ellen March, editor-in-chief. **70% freelance written. Works with a small number of new/unpublished writers each year.** Monthly magazine covering fashion, gift, and home-dec sewing. "Our magazine is for the beginning home sewer to the professional dressmaker. It expresses the fun, creativity, and excitement of sewing." Estab. 1980. Circ. 185,000. Byline given. Pays on publication. No kill fee. Publishes ms an average of 6 months after acceptance. Submit seasonal material 6 months in advance. Accepts queries by mail, e-mail. Responds in 2 months to mss. Sample copy for $5.99. Guidelines available on website.

NONFICTION Needs how-to, sewing techniques, interview, interesting personalities in home-sewing field. **Buys 200-240 mss/year.** Query with published clips if available. Length: 500-2,000 words. **Pays $50-500.**

💲 SHUTTLE SPINDLE & DYEPOT

Handweavers Guild of America, Inc., 1255 Buford Hwy., Suite 211, Suwanee GA 30024. (678)730-0010. **Fax:** (678)730-0836. **E-mail:** hga@weavespindye.org. **Website:** www.weavespindye.org. **60% freelance written.** Quarterly magazine. "Quarterly membership publication of the Handweavers Guild of America, Inc., *Shuttle Spindle & Dyepot* magazine seeks to encourage excellence in contemporary fiber arts and to support the preservation of techniques and traditions in fiber arts. It also provides inspiration for fiber artists of all levels and develops public awareness and appreciation of the fiber arts. *Shuttle Spindle & Dyepot* appeals to a highly educated, creative, and very knowledgeable audience of fiber artists and craftsmen, weavers, spinners, dyers, and basket makers." Estab. 1969. Circ. 30,000. Byline given. Pays on publication. Publishes ms an average of 6 months after acceptance. Editorial lead time 8 months. Submit seasonal material 8 months in advance. Accepts queries by mail, e-mail, fax, phone. Sample copy for $8.00 plus shipping. Guidelines available online.

NONFICTION Needs inspirational, interview, new product, personal experience, photo feature, technical, travel. No self-promotional and no articles from those without knowledge of area/art/artists. **Buys 40 mss/year.** Query with published clips. Length: 1,000-2,000 words. **Pays $75-150.**

COLUMNS/DEPARTMENTS Books and Videos, News and Information, Calendar and Conference, Travel and Workshop (all fiber/art related).

💲 SUNSHINE ARTIST

Palm House Publishing Inc., 4075 L.B. McLeod Rd., Suite E, Orlando FL 32811. (800)597-2573. **Fax:** (407)228-9862. **E-mail:** business@sunshineartist.com. **Website:** www.sunshineartist.com. Monthly magazine covering art shows in the US. We are the premiere marketing/reference magazine for artists and crafts professionals who earn their living through art shows nationwide. We list more than 2,000 shows monthly, critique many of them, and publish articles on marketing, selling and other issues of concern to professional show circuit artists. Estab. 1972. Circ. 12,000. Byline given. Pays on publication. Publishes ms an average of 3 months after acceptance. Responds in 2 months to queries. Sample copy for $5.

NONFICTION No how-to. **Buys 5-10 freelance mss/year.** Send complete ms. Length: 1,000-2,000 words. **Pays $50-150.**

REPRINTS Send photocopy and information about when and where the material previously appeared.

💲💲 TEDDY BEAR & FRIENDS

P.O. Box 5000, Iola WI 54945-5000. (800)331-0038. **Fax:** (715)445-4053. **Website:** www.teddybearandfriends.com. **65% freelance written. Works with a small number of new/unpublished writers each year.** Bimonthly magazine on teddy bears for collectors, enthusiasts and bearmakers. Estab. 1985. Byline given. Payment upon publication on the last day of the month the issue is mailed. Submit seasonal material 6 months in advance. Sample copy and writer's guidelines for $2 and 9x12 SAE.

NONFICTION Needs historical, how-to, interview. No articles from the bear's point of view. **Buys 30-40 mss/year.** Query with published clips. Length: 900-1,500 words. **Pays $100-350.**

⊖⊜ THREADS

Taunton Press, 63 S. Main St., P.O. Box 5506, Newtown CT 06470. (203)426-8171. **Fax:** (203)426-3434. **E-mail:** th@taunton.com. **Website:** www.threadsmagazine.com. Bimonthly magazine covering garment sewing, garment design, and embellishments (including quilting and embroidery). Written by sewing experts; magazine is geared primarily to intermediate/advanced sewers. "We're seeking proposals from hands-on authors who first and foremost have a skill. Being an experienced writer is of secondary consideration." Estab. 1985. Circ. 129,000. Byline given. Offers $150 kill fee. Editorial lead time minimum 4 months. Responds in 1-2 months to queries. Guidelines available online.

NONFICTION $150/page.

COLUMNS/DEPARTMENTS Product reviews; book reviews; Tips; Closures (stories of a humorous nature). Query. **Closures pays $150/page. Each sewing tip printed pays $25.**

⊜⊜ TOY FARMER

Toy Farmer Publications, 7496 106 Ave. SE, LaMoure ND 58458-9404. (701)883-5206. **Fax:** (701)883-5209. **E-mail:** info@toyfarmer.com. **Website:** www.toyfarmer.com. **70% freelance written.** Monthly magazine covering farm toys. Estab. 1978. Circ. 27,000. Byline given. Pays on publication. Editorial lead time 2 months. Submit seasonal material 3 months in advance. Accepts queries by mail, e-mail, fax. Responds in 1 month to queries. Responds in 2 months to mss. Guidelines available upon request.

NONFICTION Needs general interest, historical, interview, new product, personal experience, technical, book introductions. **Buys 100 mss/year.** Query with published clips. Length: 800-1,500 words. **Pays 10¢/word.** Sometimes pays expenses of writers on assignment.

⊜ TREASURES: ANTIQUE TO MODERN COLLECTIBLES

Pioneer Communications, Inc., The Plaza, 300 Walnut, Suite 6, Des Moines IA 50309. (319)415-5839. **Fax:** (319)824-3414. **E-mail:** lkruger@pioneermagazines.com; info@treasuresmagazine.com. **Website:** www.treasuresmagazine.com. **Contact:** Linda Kruger, editor. **20% freelance written. Works with a small number of new/unpublished writers each year.** Magazine-size publication on glossy stock, full cover, covering antiques, collectibles, and nostalgic memo-rabilia and modern collectibles. Ten issues/year. Estab. 1959. Circ. 11,000. Byline given. Pays on publication. Publishes ms an average of 1 year after acceptance. Submit seasonal material 3 months in advance. Accepts queries by e-mail. Responds in 2 weeks to queries. Responds in 6 weeks to mss. Sample copy for $4 and 9x12 SAE. Guidelines free.

NONFICTION Needs general interest, collectibles, antique to modern, historical, relating to collections or collectors, how-to, display your collection, care for, restore, appraise, locate, add to, etc., interview, covering individual collectors and their hobbies, unique or extensive; celebrity collectors, and limited edition artists, technical, in-depth analysis of a particular antique, collectible, or collecting field, travel, hot antiquing places in the U.S. Special issues: Twelve-month listing of antique and collectible shows, flea markets, and conventions (January includes events January-December; June includes events June-May); Care & Display of Collectibles (September); holidays (October-December). **Buys 36 mss/year.** Query with sample of writing. Length: 800-1,000 words. **Pays $1.10/column inch.**

⊜ WESTERN & EASTERN TREASURES

People's Publishing Co., Inc., P.O. Box 219, San Anselmo CA 94979. **E-mail:** westeast@wetreasures.com. **Website:** www.wetreasures.com. **100% freelance written.** Monthly magazine covering hobby/sport of metal detecting/treasure hunting. *"Western & Eastern Treasures* provides concise, yet comprehensive coverage of every aspect of the sport/hobby of metal detecting and treasure hunting with a strong emphasis on current, accurate information; innovative, field-proven advice and instruction; and entertaining, effective presentation."* Estab. 1966. Circ. 50,000. Byline given. Pays on publication. No kill fee. Publishes ms an average of 4+ months after acceptance. Editorial lead time 4 months. Submit seasonal material 3-4 months in advance. Responds in 3 months to mss. Sample copy for SAE with 9x12 envelope and 5 First-Class stamps. Guidelines for #10 SASE.

NONFICTION Needs how-to, tips and finds for metal detectorists, interview, only people in metal detecting, personal experience, positive metal detector experiences, technical, only metal detecting hobby-related, helping in local community with metal detecting skills (i.e., helping local police locate evidence at crime scenes—all volunteer basis). Special issues: *Sil-*

ver & Gold Annual (editorial deadline February each year)—looking for articles 1,500+ words, plus photos on the subject of locating silver and/or gold using a metal detector. No fiction, poetry, or puzzles. **Buys 150+ mss/year.** Send complete ms. Length: 1,000-1,500 words. **Pays 3¢/word.**

⊖⊖ WOODSHOP NEWS

Cruz Bay Publishing Inc., an Active Interest Media company, 10 Bokum Rd., Essex CT 06426. (860)767-8227. **Fax:** (860)767-1048. **E-mail:** editorial@woodshopnews.com. **Website:** www.woodshopnews.com. **Contact:** Tod Riggio, editor. **20% freelance written.** Monthly tabloid covering woodworking for professionals. Solid business news and features about woodworking companies. Feature stories about interesting professional woodworkers. Some how-to articles. Estab. 1986. Circ. 60,000. Byline given. Pays on publication. Publishes ms an average of 3 months after acceptance. Submit seasonal material 4 months in advance. Accepts queries by mail, e-mail, fax. Responds in 1 month to queries. Sample copy available online. Guidelines free.

O *Woodshop News* needs writers in major cities in all regions except the Northeast. Also looking for more editorial opinion pieces.

NONFICTION Needs how-to, query first, interview, new product, opinion, personal experience, photo feature. "Keyword is *newsworthy*. No general interest profiles of folksy woodworkers." **Buys 15-25 mss/ year.** Send complete ms. Length: 100-1,200 words. **Pays $50-500 for assigned articles. Pays $40-250 for unsolicited articles.** Pays expenses of writers on assignment.

PHOTOS Captions, identification of subjects required. Reviews contact sheets, prints.

COLUMNS/DEPARTMENTS Pro Shop (business advice, marketing, employee relations, taxes, etc., for the professional written by an established professional in the field); Finishing (how-to and techniques, materials, spraybooths, staining; written by experienced finishers), both 1,200-1,500 words. **Buys 18 mss/year.** Query. **Pays $200-300.**

TIPS "The best way to start is a profile of a professional woodworker in your area. Find a unique angle about the person or business and stress this as the theme of your article. Avoid a broad, general-interest theme that would be more appropriate to a daily newspaper. Our readers are professional woodworkers who want more depth and more specifics than would a general readership. If you are profiling a business, we need standard business information such as gross annual earnings/sales, customer base, product line and prices, marketing strategy, etc. Color 35mm or high-res digital photos are a must."

HOME AND GARDEN

⊖⊖ THE AMERICAN GARDENER

7931 E. Boulevard Dr., Alexandria VA 22308-1300. (703)768-5700. **Fax:** (703)768-7533. **E-mail:** editor@ahs.org; myee@ahs.org. **Website:** www.ahs.org. **Contact:** Mary Yee, art director. **60% freelance written.** Bimonthly, 64-page, four-color magazine covering gardening and horticulture. "This is the official publication of the American Horticultural Society (AHS), a national, nonprofit, membership organization for gardeners, founded in 1922. The AHS mission is 'to open the eyes of all Americans to the vital connection between people and plants, and to inspire all Americans to become responsible caretakers of the earth, to celebrate America's diversity through the art and science of horticulture, and to lead this effort by sharing the society's unique national resources with all Americans.' All articles are also published on members-only website." Estab. 1922. Circ. 20,000. Byline given. Pays on publication. Offers 25% kill fee. Publishes ms an average of 6 months after acceptance. Editorial lead time 6 months. Submit seasonal material at least 1 year in advance. Accepts queries by mail with SASE. Responds in 3 months to queries. Sample copy for $5. Writer's guidelines by e-mail and online.

NONFICTION Buys 20 mss/year. Query with published clips. No fax, phone, or e-mail submissions. Length: 1,500-2,500 words. **Pays $300-500, depending on complexity and author's experience.**

REPRINTS Rarely purchases second rights. Send photocopy of article with information about when and where the material previously appeared. Payment varies.

COLUMNS/DEPARTMENTS Natural Connections (explains a natural phenomenon—plant and pollinator relationships, plant and fungus relationships, parasites—that may be observed in nature or in the garden), 750-1,200 words. Homegrown Harvest (articles on edible plants delivered in a personal, reassuring voice. Each issue focuses on a single crop, such as carrots, blueberries, or parsley), 800-900 words; Plant in the Spotlight (profiles of a single plant species or cultivar, including a personal perspective on why it's a favored plant), 600 words. **Buys 5 mss/year.** Query with published clips. **Pays $100-250.**

⊛⊛ ATLANTA HOMES AND LIFESTYLES

Network Communications, Inc., 1100 Johnson Ferry Rd., Suite 685, Atlanta GA 30342. (404)252-6670. **Fax:** (404)252-6673. **E-mail:** gchristman@nci.com. **Website:** www.atlantahomesmag.com. **Contact:** Clinton Ross Smith, editor; Elizabeth Anderson, art director. **65% freelance written.** Magazine published 12 times/year. *Atlanta Homes and Lifestyles* is designed for the action-oriented, well-educated reader who enjoys his/her shelter, its design and construction, its environment, and living and entertaining in it. Estab. 1983. Circ. 30,000. Byline given. Pays on publication. Publishes ms an average of 6 months after acceptance. Accepts queries by mail, fax. Responds in 3 months to queries. Sample copy for $3.95.

NONFICTION Needs interview, new product, photo feature, well-designed homes, gardens, local art, remodeling, food, preservation, entertaining. "We do not want articles outside respective market area, not written for magazine format, or that are excessively controversial, investigative, or that cannot be appropriately illustrated with attractive photography." **Buys 35 mss/year.** Query with published clips. Length: 500-1,200 words. **Pays $100-500.** Sometimes pays expenses of writer on assignment.

COLUMNS/DEPARTMENTS Pays $50-200.

⊛ BACKHOME

Wordsworth Communications, Inc., P.O. Box 70, Hendersonville NC 28793. (828)696-3838. **Fax:** (828)696-0700. **E-mail:** backhome2622@att.net. **Website:** www.backhomemagazine.com. **80% freelance written.** Bimonthly magazine. "*BackHome* encourages readers to take more control over their lives by doing more for themselves: productive organic gardening; building and repairing their homes; utilizing renewable energy systems; raising crops and livestock; building furniture; toys and games and other projects; creative cooking. *BackHome* promotes respect for family activities, community programs, and the environment." Estab. 1990. Circ. 42,000. Byline given. Pays on publication. Offers $25 kill fee at publisher's discretion. Publishes ms an average of 1 year after acceptance. Editorial lead time 3 months. Submit seasonal material 6 months in advance. Accepts queries

by mail, e-mail, fax, phone. Responds in 6 weeks to queries. Responds in 2 months to mss. Sample copy $5 or online. Guidelines available online.

NONFICTION Needs how-to, gardening, construction, energy, homebusiness, interview, personal experience, technical, self-sufficiency. No essays or old-timey reminiscences. **Buys 80 mss/year.** Query. Length: 750-5,000 words. **Pays $35 (approximately)/printed page.**

REPRINTS Send photocopy and information about when and where the material previously appeared. Pays $35/printed page.

⊛⊛⊛⊛ BETTER HOMES AND GARDENS

1716 Locust St., Des Moines IA 50309-3023. (515)284-3044. **Fax:** (515)284-3763. **Website:** www.bhg.com. Brenda Lesch, creative director. **Contact:** Gayle Goodson Butler, editor-in-chief. **10-15% freelance written.** Magazine "providing home service information for people who have a serious interest in their homes." "We read all freelance articles, but much prefer to see a letter of query rather than a finished manuscript." Estab. 1922. Circ. 7,605,000. Pays on acceptance.

NONFICTION Needs travel, education, gardening, health, cars, home, entertainment. "We do not deal with political subjects or with areas not connected with the home, community, and family. No poetry or fiction." **Pay rates vary.**

⊛⊛ BIRDS & BLOOMS

Reiman Media Group, 5400 S. 60th St., Greendale WI 53129-1404. (414)423-0100. **E-mail:** editors@birdsandblooms.com. **Website:** www.birdsandblooms.com. **15% freelance written.** Bimonthly magazine focusing on "the beauty in your own backyard." "*Birds & Blooms* is a sharing magazine that lets backyard enthusiasts chat with each other by exchanging personal experiences. This makes *Birds & Blooms* more like a conversation than a magazine, as readers share tips and tricks on producing beautiful blooms and attracting feathered friends to their backyards." Estab. 1995. Circ. 1,900,000. Byline given. Pays on publication. No kill fee. Publishes ms an average of 7 months after acceptance. Editorial lead time 2 months. Submit seasonal material 4 months in advance. Accepts queries by mail, online submission form. Accepts simultaneous submissions. Responds in 2 months to queries and mss. Sample copy for $2, 9x12 SAE and $1.95 postage.

Guidelines available at www.birdsandblooms.com/contributor-s-guidelines.

NONFICTION Needs essays, how-to, humor, inspirational, personal experience, photo feature, natural crafting and plan items for building backyard accents. No bird rescue or captive bird pieces. **Buys 12-20 mss/year.** Send complete ms, along with full name, daytime phone number, e-mail address and mailing address. "If you're submitting for a particular column, note that as well. Each reader contributor whose story, photo, or short item is published receives a *Birds & Blooms* tote bag. See guidelines online." Length: 250-1,000 words. **Pays $100-400.**

COLUMNS/DEPARTMENTS Backyard Banter (odds, ends, and unique things); Bird Tales (backyard bird stories); Local Lookouts (community backyard happenings), all 200 words. **Buys 12-20 mss/year.** Send complete ms. **Pays $50-75.**

FILLERS Needs anecdotes, facts, gags. **Buys 25 mss/year.** Length: 10-250 words. **Pays $10-75.**

❤❤ CALIFORNIA HOMES

McFadden-Bray Publishing Corp., 417 31st St., Suite B, Newport Beach CA 92663. (949)640-1484. **Fax:** (949)640-1665. **E-mail:** edit@calhomesmagazine.com; susan@calhomesmagazine.com; larissa@calhomesmagazine.com. **Website:** www.calhomesmagazine.com. Larissa Linn, art director. **Contact:** Kathy Bryant, managing editor; Vanessa Brunner, assistant editor. **80% freelance written.** Bimonthly magazine covering California interiors, architecture, some food, travel, history, and current events in the field. Estab. 1997. Circ. 80,000. Byline given. Pays on publication. Offers 50% kill fee. Publishes ms an average of 3 months after acceptance. Editorial lead time 3 months. Submit seasonal material 6 months in advance. Accepts queries by mail, e-mail, fax. Responds in 1 month to queries. Responds in 2 months to mss. Sample copy for $7.50. Guidelines for #10 SASE.

NONFICTION Query. Length: 500-1,000 words. **Pays $250-750.** Sometimes pays expenses of writers on assignment.

❤ ⊘ CANADIAN HOMES & COTTAGES

The In-Home Show, Ltd., 2650 Meadowvale Blvd., Unit 4, Mississauga ON L5N 6M5 Canada. (905)567-1440. **Fax:** (905)567-1442. **E-mail:** jnaisby@homesandcottages.com; editorial@homesandcottages.com. **Website:** www.homesandcottages.com. **Contact:** Janice E. Naisby, editor-in-chief. **75% freelance written.** Magazine published 6 times/year covering home building and renovating in Canada. "*Homes & Cottages* is Canada's largest home improvement magazine. Publishes articles that have a technical slant, as well as those with a more general lifestyle feel." Estab. 1987. Circ. 92,340. Byline given. Pays on acceptance. Offers 10% kill fee. Publishes ms an average of 6 months after acceptance. Editorial lead time 3 months. Submit seasonal material 6 months in advance. Accepts queries by mail. Sample copy for SAE. Guidelines for #10 SASE.

NONFICTION Needs humor, building and renovation related, new product, technical. **Buys 32 mss/year.** Query. Length: 800-1,500 words. **Pays $3500-650.** Sometimes pays expenses of writers on assignment.

❤❤ THE CANADIAN ORGANIC GROWER

39 McArthur Ave., Ottawa ON K1L 8L7 Canada. **E-mail:** editor@cog.ca; office@cog.ca. **Website:** http://magazine.cog.ca. **Contact:** Managing editor. **100% freelance written.** Magazine published 3 times/year covering organic gardening and farming. "We publish articles that are of interest to organic gardeners, farmers and consumers in Canada. We're always looking for practical how-to articles, as well as farmer profiles. At times, we include news about the organic community, recipes and stories about successful marketing strategies." Estab. 1975. Circ. 4,000. Byline given. Pays on publication. Publishes ms an average of 2-3 months after acceptance. Editorial lead time 6 months. Submit seasonal material 6 months in advance. Accepts queries by mail, e-mail. Responds in 3 weeks to queries. Responds in 1 month to mss. Sample copy and guidelines available online.

NONFICTION Needs essays, general interest, how-to, garden, farm, market, process organic food, interview, new product, opinion, technical, "If you would like to write an article for *The Canadian Organic Grower*, please email the editor to discuss your idea before you start to write. If you would like to submit a book review, please contact the COG Librarian for detailed guidelines and, if necessary, suggestions about books to review: library@cog.ca." Does not want "rants." **Buys 25 mss/year.** Query. Length: 500-2,500 words. **Pays $150-350 for assigned articles. Pays $150-350 for unsolicited articles.**

⊕ $ CHARLESTON STYLE & DESIGN

P.O. Box 20098, Charleston SC 29413. **E-mail:** editor@charlestonstyleanddesign.com. **Website:** www.charlestonstyleanddesign.com. **Contact:** Mary K. Love, editor. **85% freelance written.** Quarterly magazine covering design (architecture and interior design) and lifestyle (wines, restaurants, fashion, local retailers, and travel). "Charleston Style & Design is a full-color magazine for discriminating readers eager to discover new horizons in Charleston and the world beyond. We offer vivid, well-researched articles on trends in home design, fashion, food and wine, health/fitness, antiques/collectibles, the arts, travel, and more. We also profile celebrities and opinion leaders who have a link with Charleston or the area." Estab. 2008. Circ. 45,000. Byline given. Pays on publication. Pays 50% kill fee. Publishes ms 4 months after acceptance. Editorial lead time 3-6 months. Submit seasonal material 3 months in advance. Accepts queries by e-mail. Accepts simultaneous submissions. Responds in 2 weeks on queries; 2 months on mss. Sample copy available online. Guidelines via e-mail.

NONFICTION Needs essays. Does not want submissions of anything other than essays. Query with published clips. Length: 300-1,200 words. **Pays $120-500 for assigned articles.** Sometimes pays expenses of writers on assignment.

COLUMNS/DEPARTMENTS Reflections (personal essays), 600 words. "Your essay should present an idea, concept or experience that you think would be of interest to our readers. We believe that the best personal essays have all the characteristics of a good story, offering compelling descriptions, a narrative line and, of course, a personal point of view. Beyond that, we look for essays that give readers a 'takeaway,' a thought or insight to which they can relate." Submit personal essay and short 2-sentence bio via e-mail with the words "personal essay" in the subject line. **Pays $180.**

$$$$ COASTAL LIVING

Southern Progress Corp., 2100 Lakeshore Dr., Birmingham AL 35209. (205)445-6007. **Fax:** (205)445-8655. **E-mail:** mamie_walling@timeinc.com. **Website:** www.coastalliving.com. **Contact:** Mamie Walling. "Bimonthly magazine for those who live or vacation along our nation's coasts. The magazine emphasizes home design and travel, but also covers a wide variety of other lifestyle topics and coastal concerns." Estab. 1997. Circ. 660,000. Pays on acceptance. Offers 25% kill fee. Responds in 2 months to queries. Sample copy available online. Guidelines available online.

NONFICTION Query with clips and SASE. **Pays $1/word.**

$$ COLORADO HOMES & LIFESTYLES

Network Communications, Inc., 1780 S. Bellaire St., Suite 505, Denver CO 80222. (303)248-2060. **Fax:** (303)248-2066. **E-mail:** mabel@coloradohomesmag.com. **Website:** www.coloradohomesmag.com. **Contact:** Mary Barthelme Abel, editor-in-chief. **75% freelance written.** Upscale shelter magazine published 9 times/year containing beautiful homes, landscapes, architecture, calendar, antiques, etc. All of Colorado is included. Geared toward home-related and lifestyle areas, personality profiles, etc. Estab. 1981. Circ. 36,000. Byline given. Pays on acceptance. Offers 15% kill fee. Publishes ms an average of 3 months after acceptance. Editorial lead time 3 months. Submit seasonal material 1 year in advance. Accepts queries by mail, e-mail. Accepts simultaneous submissions. Responds in 2 months to queries. Sample copy for #10 SASE.

NONFICTION No personal essays, religious, humor, or technical submissions. **Buys 50-75 mss/year.** Query with published clips. Provide sources with phone numbers with submissions. Length: 900-1,500 words. **Pays $200-400.** Sometimes pays expenses of writers on assignment.

COUNTRY LIVING

The Hearst Corp., 300 W. 57th St., New York NY 10019. (212)649-3501. **E-mail:** countryliving@hearst.com. **Website:** www.countryliving.com. **Contact:** Sarah Gray Miller, editor-in-chief. Monthly magazine covering home design and interior decorating with an emphasis on country style. Estab. 1978. Circ. 1,600,000. No kill fee.

NONFICTION Buys 20-30 mss/year. Send complete ms and SASE. **Payment varies.**

COLUMNS/DEPARTMENTS Query first.

$$ EARLY AMERICAN LIFE

Firelands Media Group LLC, P.O. Box 221228, Shaker Heights OH 44122. **E-mail:** queries@firelandsmedia.com. **Website:** www.ealonline.com. **Contact:** Tess Rosch, publisher; Jeanmarie Andrews, executive editor. **60% freelance written.** Bimonthly magazine for people who are interested in capturing the warmth and beauty of the 1600-1840 period and using it in their homes and lives today. They are interested in antiques, traditional crafts, architecture, restoration, and collecting. Estab. 1970. Circ. 90,000. Byline given. Pays on acceptance. 25% kill fee. Publishes ms an average of 1 year after acceptance. Accepts queries by mail, e-mail. Responds in 3 months to queries. Sample copy and writer's guidelines for 9x12 SAE with $2.50 postage. Guidelines available online at: www.ealonline.com/editorial/guidelines.php.

NONFICTION **Buys 40 mss/year.** Query us first before sending ms. Length: 750-3,000 words. **Pays $250-700, additionally for photos.**

$$$ FINE GARDENING

Taunton Press, 63 S. Main St., P.O. Box 5506, Newtown CT 06470-5506. (203)426-8171. **Fax:** (203)426-3434. **E-mail:** fg@taunton.com. **Website:** www.finegardening.com. Bimonthly magazine covering gardening. High-value magazine on landscape and ornamental gardening. Articles written by avid gardeners—first person, handson gardening experiences. Estab. 1988. Circ. 200,000. Byline given. Pays on acceptance. No kill fee. Publishes an average of 6 months after acceptance. Editorial lead time 1 year. Submit seasonal material 1 year in advance. Accepts queries by mail, e-mail. Guidelines free.

NONFICTION Needs how-to, personal experience, photo feature.

$$$$ HORTICULTURE

F+W Media, Inc., 10151 Carver Rd., Suite #200, Blue Ash OH 45242. (513)531-2690. **Fax:** (513)891-7153. **E-mail:** edit@hortmag.com. **Website:** www.hortmag.com. Bimonthly magazine. *Horticulture*, the country's oldest gardening magazine, is designed for active home gardeners. Our goal is to offer a blend of text, photographs and illustrations that will both instruct and inspire readers. Circ. 160,000. Byline given. Offers kill fee. Submit seasonal material 10 months in advance. Accepts queries by mail, e-mail, fax. Responds in 3 months to queries. Guidelines for SASE or by e-mail.

NONFICTION **Buys 70 mss/year.** Query with published clips, subject background material and SASE. Length: 800-1,000 words. **Pays $500.**

COLUMNS/DEPARTMENTS Length: 200-600 words. Query with published clips, subject background material and SASE. Include disk where possible. **Pays $250.**

$$$$ HOUSE BEAUTIFUL

The Hearst Corp., 300 W. 57th St., 27th Floor, New York NY 10019. (212)903-5000. **E-mail:** readerservices@housebeautiful.com. **Website:** www.housebeautiful.com. Monthly magazine covering home decoration and design. Targeted toward affluent, educated readers ages 30-40. Covers home design and decoration, gardening and entertaining, interior design, architecture, and travel. Circ. 865,352. No kill fee. Editorial lead time 3 months.

LOG HOME LIVING

Home Buyer Publications, Inc., 4125 Lafayette Center Dr., Suite 100, Chantilly VA 20151. (703)222-9411; (800)826-3893. **Fax:** (703)222-3209. **E-mail:** editor@timberhomeliving.com. **Website:** www.loghomeliving.com. **90% freelance written.** Monthly magazine for enthusiasts who are dreaming of, planning for, or actively building a log home. Estab. 1989. Circ. 132,000. Byline given. Pays on acceptance. Offers $100 kill fee. Publishes ms an average of 6 months after acceptance. Editorial lead time 6 months. Submit seasonal material 6 months in advance. Accepts queries by mail, e-mail. Responds in 6 weeks to queries. Sample copy for $4. Guidelines available online.

NONFICTION Needs how-to (build or maintain log home), interview of log home owners, personal experience, photo feature (log homes), technical, design/decor topics, travel. **Buys 60 mss/year.** Query with SASE. Length: 1,000-2,000 words. **Payment depends on length, nature of the work, and writer's expertise.** Pays expenses of writers on assignment.

REPRINTS Send tearsheet, photocopy or typed ms and information about when and where the material previously appeared.

$$ MOUNTAIN LIVING

Network Communications, Inc., 1780 S. Bellaire St., Suite 505, Denver CO 80222. (303)248-2060. **Fax:** (303)248-2066. **E-mail:** hscott@mountainliving.com; cdeorio@mountainliving.com. **Website:** www.mountainliving.com. **Contact:** Holly Scott, publisher; Christine DeOrio, editor-in-chief. **50% freelance written.** Magazine published 10 times/year covering architecture, interior design ,and lifestyle issues for people who live in, visit, or hope to live in the mountains. Estab. 1994. Circ. 48,000. Byline given. Pays on acceptance. Offers 15% kill fee. Publishes ms an average of 4 months after acceptance. Editorial lead time 6 months. Submit seasonal material 8-12 months in advance. Accepts queries by mail, e-mail. Responds in 6 weeks to queries. Responds in 2 months to mss. Sample copy for $7. Guidelines by e-mail.

NONFICTION Needs photo feature, travel, home features. **Buys 30 mss/year.** Query with published clips. Length: 500-1,000 words. **Pays $250-600.** Sometimes pays expenses of writers on assignment.

COLUMNS/DEPARTMENTS ML Recommends; Short Travel Tips; New Product Information; Art; Insider's Guide; Entertaining. Length: 300-800 words. **Buys 35 mss/year.** Query with published clips. **Pays $50-500.**

$$$$ ORGANIC GARDENING

Rodale, 400 S. 10th S., Emmaus PA 18098-0099. E-mail: og@rodale.com. **Website:** www.organicgardening.com. **75% freelance written.** Bimonthly magazine covering gardening. "*Organic Gardening* is for gardeners who enjoy gardening as an integral part of a healthy lifestyle. Editorial shows readers how to grow flowers, edibles, and herbs, as well as information on ecological landscaping. Also covers organic topics including soil building and pest control." Estab. 1942. Circ. 300,000. Byline given. Pays between acceptance and publication. No kill fee. Accepts queries by mail, fax. Responds in 3 months to queries.

NONFICTION Query with published clips and outline. **Pays up to $1/word for experienced writers.**

$$ ROMANTIC HOMES

Y-Visionary Publishing, 2400 East Katella Ave., Suite 300, Orange CA 92868. **E-mail:** jdemontravel@beckett.com. **Website:** www.romantichomesmag.com. **Contact:** Jacqueline DeMontravel, editor. **70% freelance written.** Monthly magazine covering home decor. *Romantic Homes* is the magazine for women who want to create a warm, intimate, and casually elegant home—a haven that is both a gathering place for family and friends and a private refuge from the pressures of the outside world. The *Romantic Homes* reader is personally involved in the decor of her home. Features offer unique ideas and how-to advice on decorating, home furnishings, and gardening. Departments focus on floor and wall coverings, paint, textiles, refinishing, architectural elements, artwork, travel, and entertaining. Every article responds to the reader's need to create a beautiful, attainable environment, providing her with the style ideas and resources to achieve her own romantic home. Estab. 1994. Circ. 200,000. Byline given. Pays 30-60 days upon receipt of invoice.

No kill fee. Publishes ms an average of 4 months after acceptance. Editorial lead time 5 months. Submit seasonal material 6 months in advance. Accepts queries by mail, fax. Accepts simultaneous submissions. Responds in 2 weeks to queries. Responds in 2 months to mss. Guidelines for #10 SASE.

NONFICTION Needs essays, how-to, new product, personal experience, travel. **Buys 150 mss/year.** Query with published clips. Length: 1,000-1,200 words. **Pays $500.**

COLUMNS/DEPARTMENTS Departments cover antiques, collectibles, artwork, shopping, travel, refinishing, architectural elements, flower arranging, entertaining, and decorating. Length: 400-600 words. **Pays $250.**

$$$ SU CASA

Bella Media, 215 W. San Francisco St., Santa Fe NM 87501. (505)344-1783. **Fax:** (505)983-1555. **E-mail:** amygross@sucasamagazine.com. **Website:** www. sucasamagazine.com. **Contact:** Amy Gross, editor. **80% freelance written.** Magazine published 4 times/ year covering southwestern homes, building, design, architecture for the reader comtemplating building, remodeling, or decorating a Santa Fe style home. "*Su Casa* is tightly focused on Southwestern home building, architecture and design. In particular, we feature New Mexico homes. We also cover alternative construction, far-out homes and contemporary design. We also cover alternative construction, contemporary design, and some Southwestern trend architecture." Estab. 1995. Circ. 40,000. Byline given. Pays on acceptance. Offers 50% kill fee. Publishes ms an average of 6 months after acceptance. Editorial lead time 6-9 months. Submit seasonal material 9 months in advance. Accepts queries by mail, e-mail, fax, phone. Responds in 1 week to queries. Responds in 1 month to mss. Sample copy free. Guidelines free.

NONFICTION Needs book excerpts, essays, interview, personal experience, photo feature. Special issues: The summer issue covers kitchen and bath topics. Does not want how-to articles, product reviews or features, no trends in southwest homes. **Buys 30 mss/ year.** Query with published clips. Length: 1,000-2,500 words. **Pays $250-1,000.** Sometimes pays expenses of writers on assignment. Limit agreed upon in advance.

$$ TEXAS GARDENER

Suntex Communications, Inc., P.O. Box 9005, Waco TX 76714. (254)848-9393. **Fax:** (254)848-9779. **E-**

mail: info@texasgardener.com. **Website:** www.texasgardener.com. **80% freelance written. Works with a small number of new/unpublished writers each year.** Bimonthly magazine covering vegetable and fruit production, ornamentals, and home landscape information for home gardeners in Texas. Estab. 1981. Circ. 20,000. Byline given. Pays on publication. No kill fee. Publishes ms an average of 4 months after acceptance. Submit seasonal material 6 months in advance. Accepts queries by mail, e-mail, fax. Responds in 2 months to queries. Sample copy for $4.25 and SAE with 5 first-class stamps. Writers' guidelines available online at website.

NONFICTION Needs how-to, humor, interview, photo feature. **Buys 50-60 mss/year.** Query with published clips. Length: 800-2,400 words. **Pays $50-200.**

COLUMNS/DEPARTMENTS Between Neighbors. **Pays $25.**

$$ TEXAS HOME & LIVING

Publications & Communications, Inc., 13581 Pond Springs Rd., Suite 450, Austin TX 78729. (512)381-0576. **Fax:** (512)331-3950. **E-mail:** bronas@pcinews.com. **Website:** www.texasHomeandLiving.com. **75% freelance written.** Bimonthly magazine. "*Texas Home & Living*..the magazine of design, architecture and Texas lifestyle." Estab. 1994. Circ. 50,000. Byline given. Pays on publication. Offers 100% kill fee. Publishes ms an average of 4 months after acceptance. Editorial lead time 4 months. Submit seasonal material 6 months in advance. Accepts queries by mail, e-mail, fax. Responds in 1 month to queries; 2 months to mss. Sample copy free. Guidelines available online.

NONFICTION Needs how-to, interview, new product, travel. **Buys 18 mss/year.** Query with published clips. Length: 500-2,000 words. **Pays $200 for assigned articles.** Pays expenses of writers on assignment.

$$$$ THIS OLD HOUSE MAGAZINE

Time Inc., 135 W. 50th St., 10th Floor, New York NY 10020. (212)522-9465. **Fax:** (212)522-9435. **E-mail:** toh_letters@thisoldhouse.com. **Website:** www.thisoldhouse.com. **40% freelance written.** Magazine published 10 times/year covering home design, renovation, and maintenance. "*This Old House* is the ultimate resource for readers whose homes are their passions. The magazine's mission is threefold: to inform with lively service journalism and reporting on innovative new products and materials, to inspire with beautiful examples of fine craftsmanship and elegant architectural design, and to instruct with clear step-by-step projects that will enhance a home or help a homeowner maintain one. The voice of the magazine is not that of a rarefied design maven or a linear Mr. Fix It, but rather that of an eyes-wide-open, in-the-trenches homeowner who's eager for advice, tools, and techniques that'll help him realize his dream of a home." Estab. 1995. Circ. 960,000. Byline given. Pays on acceptance. Publishes ms an average of 3-6 months after acceptance. Editorial lead time 3-12 months. Submit seasonal material 1 year in advance. Accepts queries by mail, e-mail.

NONFICTION Needs essays, how-to, new product, technical; must be house-related. **Buys 70 mss/year.** Query with published clips. Length: 250-2,500 words. **Pays $1/word.** Sometimes pays expenses of writers on assignment.

COLUMNS/DEPARTMENTS Around the House (news, new products). 250 words. **Pays $1/word.**

TIMBER HOME LIVING

4125 Lafayette Center Dr., Suite 100, Chantilly VA 20151. (703)222-9411. **E-mail:** editor@timberhomeliving.com. **Website:** www.timberhomeliving.com. **75% freelance written.** Bimonthly magazine for people who own or are planning to build contemporary timber frame homes. It is devoted exclusively to timber frame homes that have a freestanding frame and wooden joinery. Our interest in historical, reconstructed timber frames and one-of-a-kind owner-built homes is secondary and should be queried first. Estab. 1991. Circ. 92,500. Byline given. Pays on acceptance. Offers $100 kill fee. Publishes ms an average of 3 months after acceptance. Accepts queries by mail, e-mail. Sample copy for $4. Guidelines available online.

NONFICTION Needs general interest, how-to, construction advice, interview, timber home owners, new product, photo feature, technical, design/decor. No historical articles. **Buys 15 mss/year.** Query with SASE. Length: 1,200-1,400 words. **Payment depends on the story's length, the nature of the work, and the expertise of the writer.** Sometimes pays expenses of writers on assignment.

$$ VICTORIAN HOMES

Beckett Media, 22840 Savi Ranch Pkwy., Suite 200, Yorba Linda CA 92887. (714)939-9991. **Fax:** (714)939-9909. **E-mail:** ephillips@beckett.com. **Website:** www.victorianhomesmag.com. **Contact:** Elaine K. Phillips, editor; Jacqueline deMontravel, editorial director. **90% freelance written.** Quarterly magazine covering Victorian home restoration and decoration. *Victorian Homes* is read by Victorian home owners, restorers, house museum management, and others interested in the Victorian revival. Feature articles cover home architecture, interior design, furnishings, and the home's history. Photography is very important to the feature. Estab. 1981. Circ. 100,000. Byline given. Pays on acceptance. Offers $50 kill fee. Publishes ms an average of 1 year after acceptance. Editorial lead time 4 months. Submit seasonal material 1 year in advance. Accepts queries by e-mail only. Accepts simultaneous submissions. Responds in 6 weeks to queries. Responds in 2 months to mss. Sample copy and writer's guidelines for SAE.

NONFICTION Needs how-to create period decor, renovation tutorials, photo-based features. **Buys 30-35 mss/year.** Query. Length: 500-1,200 words. **Pays $50-150.** Sometimes pays expenses of writers on assignment.

HUMOR

🕑🕑 MAD MAGAZINE

1700 Broadway, New York NY 10019. (212)506-4850. **Fax:** (212)506-4848. **E-mail:** submissions@madmagazine.com. **Website:** www.madmag.com. **100% freelance written.** Monthly magazine always on the lookout for new ways to spoof and to poke fun at hot trends. Estab. 1952. Byline given. Pays on acceptance. Publishes ms an average of 6 months after acceptance. Submit seasonal material 6 months in advance. Responds in 10 weeks to queries. Sample copy available online. Guidelines available online.

NONFICTION "We're not interested in formats we're already doing or have done to death like 'what they say and what they really mean.' Don't send previously published submissions, riddles, advice columns, TV or movie satires, book manuscripts, top 10 lists, articles about Alfred E. Neuman, poetry, essays, short stories or other text pieces." **Buys 400 mss/year. Pays minimum of $500/page.**

INFLIGHT

🕑🕑🕑 GO

INK Publishing, 68 Jay St., Suite 315, Brooklyn NY 11201. (347)294-1220. **Fax:** (917)591-6247. **E-mail:** editorial@airtranmagazine.com. **Website:** www. airtranmagazine.com. **Contact:** Orion Ray-Jones, editor-in-chief; Jaime Lowe, executive editor; Sophie-Claire Hoeller, assistant editor. **80% freelance written.** Monthly magazine covering travel. "*Go Magazine* is an inflight magazine covering travel, general interest and light business." Estab. 2003. Circ. 100,000. Byline given. net 45 days upon receipt of invoice. Offers 50% kill fee. Publishes ms an average of 3 months after acceptance. Editorial lead time 4 months. Submit seasonal material 5 months in advance. Accepts queries by e-mail. Sample copy available online. Guidelines online at website.

NONFICTION Needs general interest, interview, photo feature, travel, light business. Does not want first-person travelogues. **Buys 200 mss/year.** Query with published clips. Length: 400-2,000 words. **Pay is negotiable.**

🕑🕑🕑 HEMISPHERES

Ink Publishing, 68 Jay St., Brooklyn NY 11201. (347)294-1220. **Fax:** (917)591-6247. **E-mail:** editorial@hemispheresmagazine.com. **Website:** www.hemispheresmagazine.com. **Contact:** Joe Keohane, editor-in-chief. **95% freelance written.** Monthly magazine for the educated, business, and recreational frequent traveler on an airline that spans the globe. "*Hemispheres* is an inflight magazine that interprets 'inflight' to be a mode of delivery rather than an editorial genre. *Hemispheres'* task is to engage, intrigue and entertain its primary readers—an international, culturally diverse group of affluent, educated professionals and executives who frequently travel for business and pleasure on United Airlines. The magazine offers a global perspective and a focus on topics that cross borders as often as the people reading the magazine. Emphasizes ideas, concepts, and culture rather than products, presented in a fresh, artful, and sophisticated graphic environment." Estab. 1992. Circ. 12.3 million. Byline given. Pays on acceptance. Offers 20% kill fee. Publishes ms an average of 4-6 months after acceptance. Editorial lead time 8 months. Submit seasonal material 8 months in advance. Accepts queries by mail. Responds in 2 months to queries. Responds in 4 months to mss. Sample copy for $7.50. Guidelines on website.

NONFICTION Needs general interest, humor, personal experience. No "in this country" phraseology. "Too American" is a frequent complaint for queries.

Query with published clips. Length: 500-3,000 words. **Pays 50¢/word and up.**

COLUMNS/DEPARTMENTS Making a Difference (Q&A format interview with world leaders, movers, and shakers; a 500-600 word introduction anchors the interview. "We want to profile an international mix of men and women representing a variety of topics or issues, but all must truly be making a difference. No puffy celebrity profiles.); 15 Fascinating Facts (a snappy selection of 1- or 2-sentence obscure, intriguing, or travel-service-oriented items that the reader never knew about a city, state, country, or destination.); Executive Secrets (things that top executives know); Case Study (business strategies of international companies or organizations. No lionizations of CEOs. Strategies should be the emphasis. "We want international candidates.); Weekend Breakway ("takes us just outside a major city after a week of business for several activities for an action-packed weekend"); Roving Gourmet (insider's guide to interesting eating in major city, resort area, or region. The slant can be anything from ethnic to expensive; not just best. The 4 featured eateries span a spectrum from hole in the wall, to expense account lunch, and on to big deal dining.); Collecting (occasional 800-word story on collections and collecting that can emphasize travel); Eye on Sports (global look at anything of interest in sports); Vintage Traveler (options for mature, experienced travelers); Savvy Shopper (insider's tour of best places in the world to shop. Savvy Shopper (steps beyond all those stories that just mention the great shopping at a particular destination. A shop-by-shop, gallery-by-gallery tour of the best places in the world.); Science and Technology (substantive, insightful stories on how technology is changing our lives and the business world. "Not just another column on audio components or software. No gift guides!"); Aviation Journal (for those fascinated with aviation; topics range widely.); Terminal Bliss ("a great airports guide series"); Grape And Grain (wine and spirits with emphasis on education, "not one-upmanship"); Show Business (films, music, and entertainment); Musings (humor or just curious musings); Quick Quiz (tests to amuse and educate); Travel Trends (brief, practical, invaluable, global, trend-oriented); Book Beat (tackles topics like the Wodehouse Society, the birth of a book, the competition between local bookshops, and national chains. "Please, no review proposals."); What the World's Reading (residents explore how current bestsellers tell us what their country is thinking). Length: 1,400 words. Query with published clips. **Pays 50¢/word and up.**

FICTION Needs adventure, ethnic, historical, humorous, mainstream, mystery, explorations of those issues common to all people but within the context of a particular culture. **Buys 14 mss/year.** Send complete ms. Length: 1,000-4,000 words. **Pays 50¢/word and up.**

$$$$ SPIRIT MAGAZINE

Pace Communications, Inc., Suite 360, 2811 McKinney Ave., Dallas TX 75204. (214)580-8070. **Fax:** (214)580-2491. **Website:** www.spiritmag.com. **Contact:** Jay Heinrichs, editorial director. Monthly magazine for passengers on Southwest Airlines. Estab. 1992. Circ. 380,000. Byline given. Pays on acceptance. Responds in 1 month to queries. Guidelines available online.

NONFICTION Buys about 40 mss/year. Query by mail only with published clips. 3,000-6,000 words (features). **Pays $1/word.** Pays expenses of writers on assignment.

COLUMNS/DEPARTMENTS Length: 800-900 words. **Buys about 21 mss/year.** Query by mail only with published clips.

FILLERS Buys 12 mss/year. 250 words. **variable amount.**

JUVENILE

$$$$ BOYS' LIFE

Boy Scouts of America, P.O. Box 152079, 1325 West Walnut Hill Lane, Irving TX 75015. (972)580-2366. **Fax:** (972)580-2079. **Website:** www.boyslife.org. **Contact:** J.D. Owen, editor-in-chief; Michael Goldman, managing editor; Paula Murphey, senior editorAaron Derr, senior writer. **75% freelance written. Prefers to work with published/established writers; works with small number of new/unpublished writers each year.** *Boys' Life* is a monthly 4-color general interest magazine for boys 7-18, most of whom are Cub Scouts, Boy Scouts or Venturers. Estab. 1911. Circ. 1.1 million. Byline given. Pays on acceptance. Publishes approximately one year after acceptance. Accepts queries by mail. Responds to queries/mss in 2 months. Sample copies for $3.95 plus 9x12 SASE. Guidelines available with SASE and online.

NONFICTION Contact: Send article queries to the attention of the senior editor; column queries to the attention of the associate editor. Needs Scouting activities and general interests (nature, Earth, health, cars, sports, science, computers, space and aviation, entertainment, history, music, animals, how-to's, etc.). **Buys 60 mss/year.** Query with SASE. No phone queries. Averge word length for articles: 500-1,500 words, including sidebars and boxes. Average word length for columns: 300-750. **Pay ranges from $300 and up.** Pays expenses of writers on assignment.

COLUMNS/DEPARTMENTS Contact: Columns query associate editor with SASE for response.

FICTION Needs All fiction is assigned.

BREAD FOR GOD'S CHILDREN

P.O. Box 1017, Arcadia FL 34265. (863)494-6214. **Fax:** (863)993-0154. **E-mail:** bread@breadministries.org. **Website:** www.breadministries.org. **Contact:** Judith M. Gibbs, editor. **10% freelance written.** An interdenominational Christian teaching publication published 6-8 times/year written to aid children and youth in leading a Christian life. Estab. 1972. Circ. 10,000 (U.S. & Canada). Byline given. No kill fee. Publishes ms an average of 6 months after acceptance. Accepts queries by mail. Accepts simultaneous submissions. Responds to mss in 6 months. Three sample copies for 9x12 SAE and 5 first-class stamps. Guidelines for #10 SASE.

NONFICTION Needs All levels: how-to. "We do not want anything detrimental to solid family values. Most topics will fit if they are slanted to our basic needs." Buys 3-4 mss/year. Length: 500-800 words.

REPRINTS Send tearsheet and information about when and where the material previously appeared.

COLUMNS/DEPARTMENTS Freelance columns: Let's Chat (children's Christian values), 500-700 words; Teen Page (youth Christian values), 600-800 words; Idea Page (games, crafts, Bible drills). **Buys 5-8 mss/year.** Send complete ms. **Pays $30.**

FICTION "We are looking for writers who have a solid knowledge of Biblical principles and are concerned for the youth of today living by those principles. Our stories must be well written, with the story itself getting the message across—no preaching, moralizing, or tag endings." Young readers, middle readers, young adult/teen: adventure, religious, problem-solving, sports. Looks for "teaching stories that portray Christian lifestyles without preaching." Buys approximately 10-15 mss/year. Send complete ms. Length: young

children—600-800 words; older children—900-1,500 words. **Pays $40-50.**

💲 CADET QUEST MAGAZINE

P.O. Box 7259, Grand Rapids MI 49510-7259. (616)241-5616. **Fax:** (616)241-5558. **E-mail:** submissions@calvinistcadets.org. **Website:** www.calvinistcadets.org. **Contact:** G. Richard Broene, editor. **40% freelance written. Works with a small number of new/unpublished writers each year.** Magazine published 7 times/year. "*Cadet Quest Magazine* shows boys 9-14 how God is at work in their lives and in the world around them." Estab. 1958. Circ. 6,000. Byline given. Pays on acceptance. No kill fee. Publishes ms an average of 4-11 months after acceptance. Accepts simultaneous submissions. Responds in 2 months to mss. Sample copy for 9x12 SASE. Guidelines for #10 SASE.

NONFICTION Needs how-to, humor, inspirational, interview, personal experience, informational. Special issues: Write for new themes list in January. **Buys 6-12 mss/year.** Send complete ms. Length: 500-1,500 words. **Pays 4-6¢/word.**

REPRINTS Send typed ms with rights for sale noted. Payment varies.

COLUMNS/DEPARTMENTS Freelance column: Project Page (uses simple projects boys 9-14 can do on their own made with easily accessible materials; must provide clear, accurate instructions).

FICTION Middle readers, boys/early teens: adventure, arts/craft, games/puzzles, hobbies, how-to, humorous, interview/profile, multicultural, problem-solving, religious, science, sports. Fast-moving stories that appeal to a boy's sense of adventure or sense of humor are welcome. Needs adventure, religious, spiritual, sports. Avoid preachiness. Avoid simplistic answers to complicated problems. Avoid long dialogue and little action. No fantasy, science fiction, fashion, horror or erotica. **Buys 14 mss/year.** Send complete ms. Length: 900-1,500 words. **Pays 4-6¢/word, and 1 contributor's copy.**

💲💲 CLUBHOUSE MAGAZINE

Focus on the Family, 8605 Explorer Dr., Colorado Springs CO 80920. **Website:** www.clubhousemagazine.com. **Contact:** Stephen O'Rear, editorial assistant. **25% freelance written.** Monthly magazine. *Clubhouse* readers are 8-12 year old boys and girls who desire to know more about God and the Bible. Their parents (who typically pay for the membership) want wholesome, educational material with Scriptural or moral insight. The kids want excitement, adventure, action, humor, or mystery. Your job as a writer is to please both the parent and child with each article. Estab. 1987. Circ. 85,000. Byline given. Pays on acceptance. No kill fee. Publishes ms an average of 12-18 months after acceptance. Editorial lead time 5 months. Submit seasonal material 9 months in advance. Responds in 2 months to mss. Sample copy for $1.50 with 9x12 SASE. Guidelines for #10 SASE.

NONFICTION Contact: Jesse Florea, editor. Needs essays, how-to, humor, inspirational, interview, personal experience, photo feature, religious. Avoid Bible stories. Avoid informational-only, science, or educational articles. Avoid biographies told encyclopedia or textbook style. **Buys 6 mss/year.** Send complete ms. Length: 800-1,200 words. **Pays $25-450 for assigned articles. Pays 15-25¢/word for unsolicited articles.**

FICTION Contact: Jesse Florea, editor. Needs adventure, humorous, mystery, religious, suspense, holiday. Avoid contemporary, middle-class family settings (existing authors meet this need), poems (rarely printed), stories dealing with boy-girl relationships. **Buys 10 mss/year.** Send complete ms. Length: 400-1,500 words. **Pays $200 and up for first time contributor and 5 contributor's copies; additional copies available.**

FILLERS Needs facts, newsbreaks. **Buys 2 mss/year.** Length: 40-100 words.

⊙⊙ CRICKET

Carus Publishing Co., 70 E. Lake St., Suite 300, Chicago IL 60601. (312)701-1720, ext. 10. **Website:** www.cricketmag.com. **Contact:** Marianne Carus, editor-in chief; Lonnie Plecha, editor; Alice Letvin, editorial director; Karen Kohn, senior art director. Monthly magazine for children ages 9-14. "*Cricket* is looking for more fiction and nonfiction for the older end of its 9-14 age range, as well as contemporary stories set in other countries. It also seeks humorous stories and mysteries (not detective spoofs), fantasy and original fairy tales, stand-alone excerpts from unpublished novels, and well-written/researched science articles." Estab. 1973. Circ. 73,000. Byline given. Pays on publication. Accepts queries by mail. Responds in 4-6 months to mss. Guidelines available online.

NONFICTION Middle readers, young adults/teens: adventure, architecture, archaeology, biography, foreign culture, games/puzzles, geography, natural history, science and technology, social science, sports, trav-

el. Multicultural needs include articles on customs and cultures. Requests bibliography with submissions. Buys 30 mss/year. Submit complete ms, SASE. Length: 200-1,500 words. **Pays 25¢/word maximum.**

FICTION Middle readers, young adults/teens: contemporary, fantasy, folk and fairy tales, history, humorous, legends/myths, realistic, science fiction, suspense/mystery. Buys 70 mss/year. Recently published work by Aaron Shepard, Arnold Adoff, and Nancy Springer. No didactic, sex, religious, or horror stories. **Buys 75-100 mss/year.** Submit complete ms. Length: 200-2,000 words. **Pays 25¢/word maximum, and 6 contributor's copies; $2.50 charge for extras.**

POETRY Reviews poems. Limit submission to 5 poems or less. Serious, humorous, nonsense rhymes. Buys 20-30 poems/year. Length: 50 lines maximum. **Pays $3/line maximum.**

FILLERS Crossword puzzles, logic puzzles, math puzzles, crafts, recipes, science experiments, games and activities from other countries, plays, music, art.

⊙⊙ DIG MAGAZINE

Carus Publishing Co., 30 Grove St., Suite C, Peterborough NH 03458. (603)924-7209. **Fax:** (603)924-7380. **Website:** www.digonsite.com. **Contact:** Rosalie Baker, editor. **75% freelance written.** Magazine published 9 times/year covering archaeology for kids ages 9-14. Estab. 1999. Circ. 20,000. Byline given. Pays on publication. No kill fee. Publishes ms an average of 1 year after acceptance. Editorial lead time 1 year. Accepts queries by mail. Responds in several months. Sample copy for $5.95 with 8x11 SASE or $10 without SASE. Guidelines available online.

NONFICTION Needs personal experience, photo feature, travel, archaeological excavation reports. No fiction. Occasional paleontology stories accepted. **Buys 30-40 mss/year.** Query with published clips. Length: 100-1,000 words. **Pays 20-25¢/word.**

POETRY Query. Length: up to 100 lines.

⊙⊙ FACES

Cobblestone Publishing, 30 Grove St., Suite C, Peterborough NH 03458. (603)924-7209; (800)821-0115. **Fax:** (603)924-7380. **E-mail:** customerservice@caruspub.com. **Website:** www.cobblestonepub.com. **90-100% freelance written.** "Published 9 times/year, *Faces* covers world culture for ages 9-14. It stands apart from other children's magazines by offering a solid look at one subject and stressing strong editorial content, color photographs throughout, and original illustrations. *Faces* offers an equal balance of feature articles and activities, as well as folktales and legends." Estab. 1984. Circ. 15,000. Byline given. Pays on publication. Offers 50% kill fee. Accepts queries by mail, e-mail. Accepts simultaneous submissions. Sample copy for $6.95, $2 shipping and handling, 10 x 13 SASE. Guidelines with SASE or online.

NONFICTION Needs historical, humor, interview, personal experience, photo feature, travel, recipes, activities, crafts. **Buys 45-50 mss/year.** Query with writing sample, 1-page outline, bibliography, SASE. Length: 800 words/feature articles; 300-600/supplemental nonfiction; 700 words maximum/activities. **Pays 20-25¢/word.**

FICTION Needs ethnic, historical, retold legends/ folktales, original plays. Length: 800 words maximum. **Pays 20-25¢/word.**

POETRY Serious and light verse considered. Must have clear, objective imagery. Length: 100 lines maximum. **Pays on an individual basis.**

FILLERS "Crossword and other word puzzles (no word finds), mazes, and picture puzzles that use the vocabulary of the issue's theme or otherwise relate to the theme." **Pays on an individual basis.**

$ $ GIRLS' LIFE

Monarch Publishing, 4529 Harford Rd., Baltimore MD 21214. (410)426-9600. **Fax:** (410)254-0991. **E-mail:** jessica@girlslife.com. **Website:** www.girlslife.com. **Contact:** Jessica D'Argenio Waller, associate fashion editor; Chun Kim, art director. Bimonthly magazine covering girls ages 9-15. Estab. 1994. Circ. 363,000. Byline given. Pays on publication. Publishes ms an average of 3 months after acceptance. Editorial lead time 4 months. Submit seasonal material 5 months in advance. Accepts queries by mail, e-mail. Responds in 1 month to queries. Sample copy for $5 or online. Guidelines available online.

NONFICTION Needs book excerpts, essays, general interest, how-to, humor, inspirational, interview, new product, travel. Special issues: Special issues: Back to School (August/September); Fall, Halloween (October/November); Holidays, Winter (December/January); Valentine's Day, Crushes (February/March); Spring, Mother's Day (April/May); and Summer, Father's Day (June/July). **Buys 40 mss/year.** Query by mail with published clips. Submit complete mss on spec only. "Features and articles should speak to young women ages 10-15 looking for new ideas about relationships, family, friends, school, etc. with fresh, savvy advice. Front-of-the-book columns and quizzes are a good place to start." Length: 700-2,000 words. **Pays $350/regular column; $500/feature.**

COLUMNS/DEPARTMENTS Buys 20 mss/year. Query with published clips. **Pays $150-450.**

FICTION "We accept short fiction. They should be stand-alone stories and are generally 2,500-3,500 words."

$ HIGHLIGHTS FOR CHILDREN

803 Church St., Honesdale PA 18431. (570)253-1080. **Fax:** (570)251-7847. **Website:** www.highlights.com. **Contact:** Christine French Cully, editor-in-chief; Drew Hires, art director. **80% freelance written.** Monthly magazine for children up to age 12. "This book of wholesome fun is dedicated to helping children grow in basic skills and knowledge, in creativeness, in ability to think and reason, in sensitivity to others, in high ideals, and worthy ways of living—for children are the world's most important people. We publish stories for beginning and advanced readers. Up to 500 words for beginners (ages 3-7), up to 800 words for advanced (ages 8-12)." Estab. 1946. Circ. approximately 2 million. Pays on acceptance. Accepts queries by mail. Responds in 2 months to queries. Sample copy free. Guidelines on website in "About Us" area.

NONFICTION "Generally we prefer to see a manuscript rather than a query. However, we will review queries regarding nonfiction." Length: 800 words maximum. **Pays $25 for craft ideas and puzzles; $25 for fingerplays; $150 and up for articles.**

FICTION Meaningful stories appealing to both girls and boys, up to age 12. Vivid, full of action. Engaging plot, strong characterization, lively language. Prefers stories in which a child protagonist solves a dilemma through his or her own resources. Seeks stories that the child ages 8-12 will eagerly read, and the child ages 2-7 will like to hear when read aloud (500-800 words). Stories require interesting plots and a number of illustration possiblities. Also need rebuses (picture stories 120 words or under), stories with urban settings, stories for beginning readers (100-500 words), sports and humorous stories, adventures, holiday stories, and mysteries. We also would like to see more material of 1-page length (300 words), both fiction and factual. Needs adventure, fantasy, historical, humorous, animal, contemporary, folktales, multi-cultural, problem-solving, sports. No war, crime or violence. Send complete ms. **Pays $100 minimum plus 2 contributor's copies.**

POETRY Lines/poem: 16 maximum ("most poems are shorter"). Considers simultaneous submissions ("please indicate"); no previously published poetry. No e-mail submissions. "Submit typed manuscript with very brief cover letter." Occasionally comments on submissions "if manuscript has merit or author seems to have potential for our market." Guidelines available for SASE. Responds "generally within one month." Always sends prepublication galleys. Pays 2 contributor's copies; "money varies." Acquires all rights.

◉◉ JACK AND JILL

U.S. Kids, 1100 Waterway Blvd., Indianapolis IN 46206-0567. (317)634-1100. **E-mail:** editor@saturdayeveningpost.com. **Website:** www.jackandjillmag. org. **50% freelance written.** Bimonthly magazine published for children ages 8-12. Estab. 1938. Circ. 200,000. Byline given. Pays on publication. Publishes ms an average of 8 months after acceptance. Submit seasonal material 8 months in advance. Responds to mss in 3 months. Guidelines available online.

NONFICTION Needs Young readers, middle readers: animal, arts, crafts, cooking, games, puzzles, history, hobbies, how-to, humorous, interviews, profile, nature, science, sports. **Buys 8-10 mss/year.** Submit complete ms. Queries not accepted. Length: 700 words. **Pays 30¢/word.**

FICTION Needs Young readers and middle readers: adventure, contemporary, folktales, health, history, humorous, nature, sports. **Buys 30-35 mss/year.** Submit complete ms. Queries not accepted. Length: 600-800 words. **Pays 30¢/word.**

POETRY Wants light-hearted poetry appropriate for the age group. Mss must be typewritten with poet's contact information in upper right-hand corner of each poem's page. SASE required. **Pays $25-50.**

◉◉◉ JUNIOR SCHOLASTIC

Scholastic, Inc., 557 Broadway, New York NY 10012. (212)343-6100. **Fax:** (212)343-6945. **E-mail:** junior@scholastic.com. **Website:** www.juniorscholastic.com. Magazine published 18 times/year. Edited for students ages 11-14. Circ. 535,000. No kill fee. Editorial lead time 6 weeks.

KEYS FOR KIDS

Box 1001, Grand Rapids MI 49501-1001. (616)647-4950. **Fax:** (616)647-4950. **E-mail:** hazel@cbhministries.org. **Website:** www.cbhministries.org. **Contact:** Hazel Marett, fiction editor. "CBH Ministries is an international Christian ministry based on the gospel of Jesus Christ, which produces and distributes excellent media resources to evangelize and disciple kids and their families." Estab. 1982. Pays on acceptance. Accepts simultaneous submissions. Sample copy for 6x9 SAE and 3 first-class stamps. Guidelines for SASE.

FICTION Buys 40 mss/year. Needs religious. "Tell a story (not a Bible story) with a spiritual application." Submit complete ms. Length: 400 words. **Pays $25 for stories.**

◉◉ LADYBUG

Carus Publishing Co., 700 E. Lake St., Suite 300, Chicago IL 60601. (312)701-1720. **Website:** www.cricketmag.com. **Contact:** Marianne Carus, editor-in-chief; Suzanne Beck, managing art director. Monthly magazine for children ages 2-6. *LADYBUG Magazine*, published monthly, is a reading and listening magazine for young children (ages 2-6). "We look for quality literature and nonfiction." Subscription: $35.97/year (12 issues). sample: $5; sample pages available on website. Estab. 1990. Circ. 125,000. Byline given. Pays on publication. Responds in 6 months to mss. Guidelines available online.

NONFICTION Needs Picture-oriented material: activities, animal, arts/crafts, concept, cooking, humorous, math, nature/environment, problem-solving, science. **Buys 35 mss/year.** Send complete ms, SASE. Length: 400-700 words. **Pays 25¢/word minimum.**

FICTION Picture-oriented material: adventure, animal, fantasy, folktales, humorous, multicultural, nature/environment, problem-solving, science fiction, sports, suspense/mystery. "Open to any easy fiction stories." Buys 50 mss/year. **Buys 30 mss/year.** Submit complete ms, include SASE. Length: 800 words maximum. **Pays 25¢/word minimum.**

POETRY Needs light verse, traditional. Wants poetry that is "rhythmic, rhyming; serious, humorous, active." Buys 40 poems/year. Submit maximum 5 poems. Length: 20 lines maximum. **Pays $3/line ($25 minimum).**

FILLERS Learning activities, games, crafts, songs, finger games. See back issues for types, formats, and length.

$ NATURE FRIEND MAGAZINE

4253 Woodcock Lane, Dayton VA 22821. (540)867-0764. **E-mail:** info@naturefriendmagazine.com; editor@naturefriendmagazine.com; photos@naturefriendmagazine.com. **Website:** www.naturefriendmagazine.com. **Contact:** Kevin Shank, editor. **80% freelance written.** Monthly children's magazine covering creation-based nature. "*Nature Friend* includes stories, puzzles, science experiments, nature experiments—all submissions need to honor God as creator." Estab. 1982. Circ. 13,000. Byline given. Pays on publication. No kill fee. Editorial lead time 4 months. Submit seasonal material 6 months in advance. Accepts simultaneous submissions. Responds in 6 months to mss. Sample copy for $5 postage paid. Guidelines available on website.

NONFICTION Needs how-to, nature, photo feature, science experiments (for ages 8-12), articles about interesting/unusual animals. No poetry, evolution, animals depicted in captivity, talking animal stories, or evolutionary material. **Buys 50 mss/year.** Send complete ms. Length: 250-900 words. **Pays 5¢/word.**

COLUMNS/DEPARTMENTS Learning By Doing, 500-900 words. **Buys 12 mss/year.** Send complete ms.

FILLERS Needs facts, puzzles, short essays on something current in nature. **Buys 35 mss/year.** Length: 150-250 words. **5¢/word.**

$$ NEW MOON GIRLS

New Moon Girl Media, P.O. Box 161287, Duluth MN 55816. (218)728-5507. **Fax:** (218)728-0314. **E-mail:** newmoon@newmoon.com. **Website:** www.newmoon.org. **25% freelance written.** Bimonthly magazine covering girls ages 8-14, edited by girls aged 8-14. "*New Moon Girls* is for every girl who wants her voice heard and her dreams taken seriously. *New Moon* celebrates girls, explores the passage from girl to woman, and builds healthy resistance to gender inequities. The *New Moon* girl is true to herself and *New Moon Girls* helps her as she pursues her unique path in life, moving confidently into the world." Estab. 1992. Circ. 30,000. Byline given. Pays on publication. Publishes ms an average of 6 months after acceptance. Editorial lead time 6 months. Submit seasonal material 8 months in advance. Accepts queries by mail, e-mail, fax. Accepts simultaneous submissions. Responds in 2 months to mss. Sample copy for $7 or online. Guidelines available at website.

NONFICTION Needs essays, general interest, humor, inspirational, interview, opinion, personal experience, written by girls, photo feature, religious, travel, multicultural/girls from other countries. No fashion, beauty, or dating. **Buys 20 mss/year.** Send complete ms. Publishes nonfiction by adults in Herstory and Women's Work departments only. Length: 600 words. **Pays 6-12¢/word.**

COLUMNS/DEPARTMENTS Women's Work (profile of a woman and her job relating the the theme), 600 words; Herstory (historical woman relating to theme), 600 words. **Buys 10 mss/year.** Query. **Pays 6-12¢/word.**

FICTION Prefers girl-written material. All girl-centered. Needs adventure, fantasy, historical, humorous, slice-of-life vignettes. **Buys 6 mss/year.** Send complete ms. Length: 900-1,600 words. **Pays 6-12¢/word.**

$ SHINE BRIGHTLY

GEMS Girls' Clubs, P.O. Box 7259, Grand Rapids MI 49510. (616)241-5616. **Fax:** (616)241-5558. **E-mail:** shinebrightly@gemsgc.org. **Website:** www.gemsgc.org. **Contact:** Jan Boone, executive director; Kelli Gilmore, managing editor. **80% freelance written. Works with new and published/established writers.** Monthly magazine (with combined June/July, August summer issue). "Our purpose is to lead girls into a living relationship with Jesus Christ and to help them see how God is at work in their lives and the world around them. Puzzles, crafts, stories, and articles for girls ages 9-14." Estab. 1970. Circ. 17,000. Byline given. Pays on publication. No kill fee. Publishes ms an average of 1 year after acceptance. Submit seasonal material 1 year in advance. Accepts simultaneous submissions. Responds in 2 months to mss. Sample copy with 9x12 SASE with 3 first class stamps and $1. Guidelines available online.

NONFICTION Needs humor, inspirational, seasonal and holiday, interview, personal experience, photo feature, religious, travel, adventure, mystery. Avoid the testimony approach. **Buys 35 unsolicited mss/year.** Submit complete ms in body of e-mail. No attachments. Length: 100-800 words. **Pays up to $35, plus 2 copies.**

REPRINTS Send typed manuscript with rights for sale noted and information about when and where the material previously appeared.

COLUMNS/DEPARTMENTS How-to (crafts); puzzles and jokes; quizzes. Length: 200-400 words. Send complete ms. **Pay varies.**

FICTION Does not want "unrealistic stories and those with trite, easy endings. We are interested in manuscripts that show how girls can change the world." Needs adventure experiences girls could have in their hometowns or places they might realistically visit, ethnic, historical, humorous, mystery, religious, omance, slice-of-life vignettes, suspense,. Believable only. Nothing too preachy. **Buys 30 mss/year.** Submit complete ms in body of e-mail. No attachments. Length: 700-900 words. **Pays up to $35, plus 2 copies.**

POETRY Needs free verse, haiku, light verse, traditional. **Limited need for poetry. Pays $5-15.**

⑤ SPARKLE

GEMS Girls' Clubs, P.O. Box 7259, Grand Rapids MI 49510. (616)241-5616. **Fax:** (616)241-5558. **E-mail:** kelli@gemsgc.org. **Website:** www.gemsgc.org. **Contact:** Kelli Gilmore, managing editor; Nicole Zaagman, art director/photo editor. **80% freelance written.** Bimonthly magazine for girls ages 6-9. "Our mission is to prepare young girls to live out their faith and become world-changers. We strive to help girls make a difference in the world. We look at the application of scripture to everyday life. We strive to delight the reader and cause the reader to evalute her own life in light of the truth presented. Finally, we strive to teach practical life skills." Estab. 2002. Circ. 5,000. Byline given. Pays on publication. Offers $20 kill fee. Editorial lead time 3 months. Submit seasonal material 1 year in advance. Accepts queries by mail, e-mail. Accepts simultaneous submissions. Responds in 3 weeks to queries; 3 months to mss. Sample copy for 9x13 SAE, 3 first-class stamps, and $1 for coverage/publication cost. Writer's guidelines for #10 SASE or online.

NONFICTION Young readers: animal, arts/crafts, biography, careers, cooking, concept, games/puzzles, geography, health, history, hobbies, how-to, humor, inspirational, interview/profile, math, multicultural, music/drama/art, nature/environment, personal experience, photo feature, problem-solving, quizzes, recipes, religious, science, social issues, sports, travel. Looking for inspirational biographies, stories from Zambia, and ideas on how to live a green lifestyle. Constant mention of God is not necessary if the moral tone of the story is positive. **Buys 15 mss/year.**

Send complete ms. Length: 100-400 words. **Pays $35 maximum.**

COLUMNS/DEPARTMENTS Crafts; puzzles and jokes; quizzes, all 200-400 words. Send complete ms. **Payment varies.**

FICTION Young readers: adventure, animal, contemporary, ethnic/multcultural, fantasy, folktale, health, history, humorous, music and musicians, mystery, nature/environment, problem-solving, religious, recipes, service projects, slice-of-life, sports, suspense/mystery, vignettes, interacting with family and friends. **Buys 10 mss/year.** Send complete ms. Length: 100-400 words. **Pays $35 maximum.**

POETRY Prefers rhyming. "We do not wish to see anything that is too difficult for a first grader to read. We wish it to remain light. The style can be fun, but also teach a truth." No violence or secular material. Buys 4 poems/year. Submit maximum 4 poems.

FILLERS Needs facts, short humor. **Buys 6 mss/year.** Length: 50-150 words. **Pays $10-15.**

⑤ STONE SOUP

Children's Art Foundation, P.O. Box 83, Santa Cruz CA 95063-0083. (831)426-5557. **E-mail:** editor@ stonesoup.com. **Website:** http://stonesoup.com. **Contact:** Ms. Gerry Mandel, editor. **100% freelance written.** Bimonthly magazine of writing and art by children age 13 under, including fiction, poetry, book reviews, and art. *Stone Soup* is 48 pages, 7x10, professionally printed in color on heavy stock, saddle-stapled, with coated cover with full-color illustration. Receives 5,000 poetry submissions/year, accepts about 12. Press run is 15,000. Subscription: $37/year (U.S.). "We have a preference for writing and art based on real-life experiences; no formula stories or poems. We only publish writing by children ages 8 to 13. We do not publish writing by adults." Estab. 1973. Pays on publication. Publishes ms an average of 4 months after acceptance. Submit seasonal material 6 months in advance. Sample copy by phone only. Guidelines available online.

NONFICTION Needs historical, personal experience, book reviews. **Buys 12 mss/year.** Submit complete ms; no SASE. **Pays $40, a certificate and 2 contributor's copies, plus discounts.**

FICTION Needs adventure, ethnic, experimental, fantasy, historical, humorous, mystery, science fiction, slice-of-life vignettes, suspense. "We do not like assignments or formula stories of any kind." **Buys 60**

mss/year. Send complete ms; no SASE. Length: 150-2,500 words. **Pays $40 for stories, a certificate and 2 contributor's copies, plus discounts.**

POETRY Needs avant-garde, free verse. Wants free verse poetry. Does not want rhyming poetry, haiku, or cinquain. Buys 12 poems/year. **Pays $40/poem, a certificate, and 2 contributor's copies, plus discounts.**

LITERARY & LITTLE

ACM (ANOTHER CHICAGO MAGAZINE)

P.O. Box 408439, Chicago IL 60640. **E-mail:** editors@anotherchicagomagazine.net. **Website:** www.anotherchicagomagazine.net. **Contact:** Jacob S. Knabb, editor-in-chief; Caroline Eick Kasner, managing editor. "*Another Chicago Magazine* is a biannual literary magazine that publishes work by both new and established writers. We look for work that goes beyond the artistic and academic to include and address the larger world. The editors read submissions in fiction, poetry, creative nonfiction, etc. year round. We often publish special theme issues and sections. We will post upcoming themes on our website. Fiction: Short stories and novel excerpts of 15-20 pages or less. Poetry: Usually no more than 4 pages. Creative Nonfiction: Usually no more than 20 pages. Et Al.: Work that doesn't quite fit into the other genres such as Word & Image Texts, Satire, and Interviews." Estab. 1977. Circ. 2,000. Byline given. Accepts queries by mail. Accepts simultaneous submissions. Responds in 3 months to queries; 6 months to mss. Sample copy available for $8.

NONFICTION Contact: Ling Ma, nonfiction editor. "Please include the following contact information in your cover letter and on your manuscript: Byline (name as you want it to appear if published), mailing address, phone number, and e-mail. Include a self-addressed stamped envelope (SASE). If a SASE is not enclosed, you will only hear from us if we are interested in your work. Include the genre (e.g., nonfiction, et al.) of your work in the address." Accepts simultaneous, multiple submissions.

FICTION Contact: Paul Genesius Durica, fiction editor. Needs ethnic, experimental, contemporary, feminist, gay, lesbian, literary. "Please include the following contact information in your cover letter and on your ms: Byline (name as you want it to appear if published), mailing address, phone number, and e-mail. Include a self-addressed stamped envelope (SASE). If a SASE is not enclosed, you will only hear from us if we are interested in your work. Include the genre (e.g., fiction) of your work in the address." Short stories and novel excerpts of 15-20 pages or less. **Pays small honorarium when possible, contributor's copies and 1 year subscription.**

POETRY Contact: David Welch, poetry editor. Submit 3-4 typed poems at a time, usually no more than 4 pages. Considers simultaneous submissions with notification; no previously published poems. Reads submissions year-round. Guidelines available on website; however, "The best way to know what we publish is to read what we publish. If you haven't read *ACM* before, order a sample copy to know if your work is appropriate." Responds in 3 months. Sends prepublication galleys. Pays monetary amount "if funds permit," and/or one contributor's copy and one-year subscription. Acquires first serial rights. Reviews books of poetry in 250-800 words. Send materials for review consideration. No more than 4 pages.

$ AGNI

Creative Writing Program, Boston University, 236 Bay State Rd., Boston MA 02215. (617)353-7135. **Fax:** (617)353-7134. **E-mail:** agni@bu.edu. **Website:** www.agnimagazine.org. **Contact:** Sven Birkerts, editor. Biannual literary magazine. "Eclectic literary magazine publishing first-rate poems, essays, translations, and stories." Estab. 1972. Circ. 3,000 in print, plus more than 60,000 distinct readers online per year. Byline given. Pays on publication. Publishes ms an average of 6 months after acceptance. Editorial lead time 1 year. Accepts queries by mail. Accepts simultaneous submissions. Responds in 2 weeks to queries. Responds in 4 months to mss. Sample copy for $10 or online. Guidelines available online.

FICTION Buys stories, prose poems. "No science fiction or romance." **Buys 20+ mss/year.** Query by mail. **Pays $10/page up to $150, a 1-year subscription, and for print publication: 2 contributor's copies and 4 gift copies.**

POETRY Submit no more than 5 poems at a time. Considers simultaneous submissions; no previously published poems. No e-mail submissions. Cover letter is required ("brief, sincere"). "No fancy fonts, gimmicks. Include SASE or e-mail address; no preformatted reply cards." Buys 120+ poems/year. **Pays $20/page up to $150.**

✪ ⑤ THE ANTIGONISH REVIEW

St. Francis Xavier University, P.O. Box 5000, Antigonish NS B2G 2W5 Canada. (902)867-3962. **Fax:** (902)867-5563. **E-mail:** tar@stfx.ca. **Website:** www.antigonishreview.com. **Contact:** Bonnie McIsaac, office manager. **100% freelance written.** Quarterly literary magazine for educated and creative readers. Estab. 1970. Circ. 850. Byline given. Pays on publication. Offers variable kill fee. Publishes ms an average of 8 months after acceptance. Editorial lead time 4 months. Submit seasonal material 4 months in advance. Accepts queries by mail, fax. Responds in 1 month to queries; 6 months to mss. Sample copy for $7 or online. Guidelines for #10 SASE or online.

NONFICTION Needs essays, interview, book reviews/articles. No academic pieces. **Buys 15-20 mss/year.** Query. Length: 1,500-5,000 words **Pays $50 and 2 contributor's copies.**

FICTION Send complete ms. Accepts submissions by fax. Accepts electronic (disk compatible with Word-Perfect/IBM and Windows) submissions. Prefers hard copy. Needs literary, translations, contemporary, prose poem. No erotica. **Buys 35-40 mss/year.** Send complete ms. Length: 500-5,000 words. **Pays $50 and 2 contributor's copies for stories.**

POETRY *The Antigonish Review*, published quarterly, tries "to produce the kind of literary and visual mosaic that the modern sensibility requires or would respond to." Open to poetry on any subject written from any point of view and in any form. However, writers should expect their work to be considered within the full context of old and new poetry in English and other languages. No more than 6-8 poems should be submitted at any one time. A preferable submission would be from 3-4 poems. No previously published poems or simultaneous submissions. Has published poetry by Andy Wainwright, W.J. Keith, Michael Hulse, Jean McNeil, M. Travis Lane, and Douglas Lochhead. Buys 100-125 poems/year. Submit maximum 5 poems. Submit 6-8 poems at a time. Lines/poem: not over 80, i.e., 2 pages. **Pays $10/page to a maximum of $50 and 2 contributor's copies. Acquires first North American serial rights.**

⑤ ANTIOCH REVIEW

P.O. Box 148, Yellow Springs OH 45387-0148. **E-mail:** mkeyes@antiochreview.org. **Website:** www.antiochreview.org. **Contact:** Robert S. Fogarty, editor; Judith Hall, poetry editor. Quarterly magazine for general, literary, and academic audience. Literary and cultural review of contemporary issues, and literature for general readership. *The Antioch Review* "is an independent quarterly of critical and creative thought. For well over 70 years, creative authors, poets, and thinkers have found a friendly reception—regardless of formal reputation. We get far more poetry than we can possibly accept, and the competition is keen. Here, where form and content are so inseparable and reaction is so personal, it is difficult to state requirements or limitations. Studying recent issues of *The Antioch Review* should be helpful." Has published poetry by Richard Howard, Jacqueline Osherow, Alice Fulton, Richard Kenney, and others. Receives about 3,000 submissions/year. Estab. 1941. Circ. 3,000. Byline given. Pays on publication. Publishes ms an average of 10 months after acceptance. Responds in 3-6 months to mss. Sample copy for $7. Guidelines available online.

NONFICTION Length: 2,000-8,000 words. **Pays $20/printed page, plus 2 contributor's copies.**

FICTION Contact: Fiction editor. Quality fiction only, distinctive in style with fresh insights into the human condition. Needs experimental, contemporary. No science fiction, fantasy, or confessions. Send complete ms with SASE, preferably mailed flat. Length: generally under 8,000 words. **Pays $20/printed page, plus 2 contributor's copies.**

POETRY Submit 3-6 poems at a time. No previously published poems or simultaneous submissions. Include SASE with all submissions. No light or inspirational verse. Poetry submissions are not accepted between between May 1 and September 1. **Pays $20/printed page, plus 2 contributor's copies.**

✪ ⑤ ARC

Arc Poetry Society, P.O. Box 81060, Ottawa ON K1P 1B1 Canada. **E-mail:** managingeditor@arcpoetry.ca; coordinatingeditor@arcpoetry.ca. **Website:** www.arcpoetry.ca. **Contact:** Monty Reid, managing editor; Robyn Jeffrey, coordinating editor. Semiannual magazine featuring poetry, poetry-related articles, and criticism. "Our focus is poetry, and Canadian poetry in general, although we do publish writers from elsewhere. We are looking for the best poetry from new and established writers. We often have special issues. Send a SASE for upcoming special issues and contests." Estab. 1978. Circ. 1,500. Byline given. Pays on publication. Publishes ms an average of 6 months af-

ter acceptance. Accepts queries by online submission form. Responds in 4 months. Guidelines for #10 SASE. **NONFICTION** Needs essays, interview, book reviews. Query first. Length: 500-4,000 words. **Pays $40/printed page (Canadian), and 2 copies.**
POETRY Needs avant-garde, free verse. E-mail submissions not accepted. Buys 60 poems/year. Submit maximum 5 poems. **Pays $40/printed page (Canadian).**

ARSENIC LOBSTER

E-mail: lobster@magere.com. **Website:** http://arsenic-lobster.magere.com. Annual anthology journal and book covering poetry. New online issues released in April, August, and December. No kill fee. Accepts simultaneous submissions. Guidelines available at http://arseniclobster.magere.com/1submission.html.
POETRY Contact: Susan Yount, poetry editor. Needs free verse. E-mail submissions to lobster@magere.com; submit 3-5 poems. "Poems should be timeless, rich in imagery, and edgy; seeking elegant emotion, articulate experiment. Be compelled to write." "We do not want political rants or Hallmark poetry."

⊙ ARTFUL DODGE

Dept. of English, College of Wooster, Wooster OH 44691. (330)263-2577. **E-mail:** artfuldodge@wooster.edu. **Website:** www.wooster.edu/artfuldodge. **Contact:** Daniel Bourne, editor-in-chief; Karin Lin-Greenberg, fiction editor; Marcy Campbell, associate fiction editor; Carolyne Wright, translation editor. Annual magazine that takes a strong interest in poets who are continually testing what they can get away with successfully in regard to subject, perspective, language, etc., but who also show mastery of the current American poetic techniques—its varied textures and its achievement in the illumination of the particular. There is no theme in this magazine, except literary power. We also have an ongoing interest in translations from Central/Eastern Europe and elsewhere. Estab. 1979. Circ. 1,000. Accepts queries by mail. Accepts simultaneous submissions. Responds in 1-6 months to mss. Sample copy for $7. Guidelines for #10 SASE.
FICTION Contact: Marcy Campbell, fiction editor. Needs experimental, prose poem. We judge by literary quality, not by genre. We are especially interested in fine English translations of significant prose writers. Translations should be submitted with original texts. **Pays 2 contributor's copies and honorarium**

of $5/page, thanks to funding from the Ohio Arts Council.
POETRY Contact: Philip Brady, poetry editor. We are interested in poems that utilize stylistic persuasions both old and new to good effect. We are not afraid of poems which try to deal with large social, political, historical, and even philosophical questions—especially if the poem emerges from one's own life experience and is not the result of armchair pontificating. We don't want cute, rococo surrealism, someone's warmed-up, left-over notion of an avant-garde that existed 10-100 years ago, or any last bastions of rhymed verse in the civilized world. Buys 20 poems/year. Submit maximum 6 poems. **Pays $5/page honorarium and 2 contributor's copies.**

ASHEVILLE POETRY REVIEW

P.O. Box 7086, Asheville NC 28802. (828)450-0357. **Website:** www.ashevillereview.com. **Contact:** Keith Flynn, founder/managing editor. *Asheville Poetry Review*, published annually, prints "the best regional, national, and international poems we can find. We publish translations, interviews, essays, historical perspectives, and book reviews as well." Wants "quality work with well-crafted ideas married to a dynamic style. Any subject matter is fit to be considered so long as the language is vivid with a clear sense of rhythm. We subscribe to the Borges dictum that great poetry is a combination of 'algebra and fire.' Estab. 1994. Up to 1 year from acceptance to publishing time. Responds in up to 4 months. Sample: $13. **"We prefer poets purchase a sample copy prior to submitting."** Guidelines available for SASE or on website.
POETRY Submit 3-5 poems at a time. No previously published poems or simultaneous submissions. No e-mail submissions. Cover letter is required. Include comprehensive bio, recent publishing credits, and SASE. Reads submissions January 15-July 15. Poems are circulated to an editorial board. Seldom comments on rejected poems. **Sponsors the William Matthews Poetry Prize: $1,000 awarded for a single poem, reads submissions September 15-January 15. See website for complete guidelines. Pays 1 contributor's copy.**

BIG PULP

Exter Press, P.O. Box 92, Cumberland MD 21501. **E-mail:** editors@bigpulp.com. **E-mail:** editors@bigpulp.com. **Website:** www.bigpulp.com. **Contact:** Bill Olver, editor. Quarterly literary magazine. Submissions accepted by e-mail only. "We define 'pulp fiction' very broadly—it's lively, challenging, thought-provoking, thrilling and fun, regardless of how many or how few genre elements are packed in. We don't subscribe to the theory that genre fiction is disposable; in our opinion, a great deal of literary fiction could easily fall under one of our general categories. We place a higher value on character and story than genre elements." Byline given. Pays on publication. 100% kill fee. Publishes ms 1 year after acceptance. TrueAccepts simultaneous submissions. Responds in 2 months to mss. Sample copy available for $10; excerpts available online at no cost. Guidelines available online at website.

FICTION Needs adventure, fantasy, horror, mystery, romance, science fiction, suspense, western, superhero. Does not want generic slice-of-life, memoirs, inspirational, political, pastoral odes. **Buys 70 mss/year.** Submit complete ms. Length: 10,000 words maximum. **Pays $5-25.**

POETRY Needs avant-garde, free verse, haiku, light verse, traditional. "All types of poetry are considered, but poems should have a genre connection." Buys 20 poems/year. Submit maximum 5 poems. Length: 100 lines maximum. **Pays $5/poem.**

$ BOMB MAGAZINE

New Arts Publications, 80 Hanson Place, Suite 703, Brooklyn NY 11217. (718)636-9100. **Fax:** (718)636-9200. **E-mail:** firstproof@bombsite.com; generalinquiries@bombsite.com. **Website:** www.bombsite.com. **Contact:** Monica de la Torre, senior editor. Quarterly magazine providing interviews between artists, writers, musicians, directors, and actors. "Written, edited and produced by industry professionals and funded by those interested in the arts. Publishes work which is unconventional and contains an edge, whether it be in style or subject matter." Estab. 1981. Circ. 36,000. Pays on publication. No kill fee. Publishes ms an average of 3-6 months after acceptance. Editorial lead time 3-4 months. Accepts queries by mail. Responds in 3-5 months to mss. Sample copy for $10. Guidelines by e-mail.

FICTION Written, edited and produced by industry professionals and funded by those interested in the arts. Publishes writing which is unconventional and contains an edge, whether it be in style or subject matter. Submit complete ms. Needs experimental, novel concepts, contemporary. No genre: romance, science fiction, horror, western. E-mailed submissions will not be considered. Length: less than 25 pages. **Pays $100, and contributor's copies.**

POETRY *BOMB Magazine* accepts unsolicited poetry and prose submissions for our literary pull-out *First Proof* by mail from January 1-August 31. Submissions sent outside these dates will be returned unread. Submit maximum 4-6 poems. **Pays $100, and contributor's copies. Sends galleys to author.**

FILLERS No more than 25 pages in length.

$$ BOULEVARD

Opojaz, Inc., 6614 Clayton Rd., Box 325, Richmond Heights MO 63117. (314)862-2643. **Fax:** (314)862-2982. **E-mail:** richardburgin@att.net; jessicarogen@boulevardmagazine.org; kellyleavitt@boulevardmagazine.com. **Website:** www.boulevardmagazine.org. **Contact:** Richard Burgin, editor; Jessica Rogen, managing editor; Kelly Leavitt, associate editor. **100% freelance written.** Triannual magazine covering fiction, poetry, and essays. "*Boulevard* is a diverse literary magazine presenting original creative work by well-known authors, as well as by writers of exciting promise." Estab. 1985. Circ. 11,000. Byline given. Pays on publication. Offers no kill fee. Publishes ms an average of 9 months after acceptance. Accepts queries by mail. Accepts simultaneous submissions. Responds in 2 weeks to queries. Responds in 3 months to mss. Sample copy for $10. Guidelines available online.

NONFICTION Needs book excerpts, essays, interview, opinion, photo feature. No pornography, science fiction, children's stories, or westerns. **Buys 10 mss/year.** Send complete ms. Now has online submissions link. 10,000 words maximum. **Pays $20/page, minimum $150.**

FICTION Contact: Richard Burgin, editor. Also sponsors the Short Fiction Contest for Emerging Writers. $1,500 and publication in Boulevard awarded to the winning story by a writer who has not yet published a book of fiction, poetry, or creative nonfiction with a nationally distributed press. All entries must be postmarked by December 31, 2010. Entry fee is $15 for each individual story, with no limit per author. Entry fee includes a one-year subscription to Boulevard (one per author). Make check payable to Boulevard. Needs confession, experimental, mainstream, novel excerpts. "We do not want erotica, science fiction, romance, western, horror, or children's stories." **Buys 20 mss/year.** Send complete ms. Now takes online submissions: pdf, doc, docx, txt, rtf, jpg, gif, mp3, mp4, m4a, zip, tiff, png Length: 8,000 words maximum. **Pays $50-500 (sometimes higher) for accepted work.**

POETRY Needs avant-garde, free verse, haiku, traditional. *Boulevard*, published 3 times/year, strives "to publish only the finest in fiction, poetry, and nonfiction (essays and interviews). While we frequently publish writers with previous credits, we are very interested in publishing less experienced or unpublished writers with exceptional promise. We've published everything from John Ashbery to Donald Hall to a wide variety of styles from new or lesser known poets. We're eclectic. We are interested in original, moving poetry written from the head as well as the heart. It can be about any topic." Buys 80 poems/year. Submit maximum 5 poems. Length: 200/max lines. **Pays $25-300 (sometimes higher) depending on length, plus one contributor's copy.**

🍁 $$ BRICK

Brick, P.O. Box 609, Station P, Toronto ON M5S 2Y4 Canada. **E-mail:** info@brickmag.com. **Website:** www.brickmag.com. **Contact:** Nadia Szilvassy, publisher and managing editor. **90% freelance written.** Semiannual magazine covering literature and the arts. "We publish literary nonfiction of a very high quality on a range of arts and culture subjects." Estab. 1977. Circ. 4,000. Byline given. Pays on publication. No kill fee. Publishes ms 3-5 months after acceptance. Editorial lead time 5 months. Responds in 6 months to mss. Sample copy for $15, plus shipping. Guidelines available online.

NONFICTION Needs essays, historical, interview, opinion, travel. No fiction, poetry, personal memoir, or art. **Buys 30-40 mss/year.** Send complete ms. Length: 250-3,000 words. **Pays $75-500 (Canadian).**

$ BUTTON

P.O. Box 77, Westminster MA 01473. **E-mail:** sally@moonsigns.net. **Website:** www.moonsigns.net. **30% freelance written.** Annual literary magazine. "*Button* is New England's tiniest magazine of poetry, fiction, and gracious living, published once a year. As 'gracious living' is on the cover, we like wit, brevity, cleverly-conceived essay/recipe, poetry that isn't sentimental, or song lyrics. I started *Button* so that a century from now, when people read it in landfills or, preferably, libraries, they'll say, 'Gee, what a great time to have lived. I wish I lived back then." Estab. 1993. Circ. 750. Byline given. Pays on publication. No kill fee. Publishes ms 3-9 months after acceptance. Editorial lead time 6 months. Responds in 1 month to queries. Responds in 2 months to mss. Sometimes comments on rejected mss. Sample copy for $2.50. Guidelines available online.

NONFICTION Needs personal experience, cooking stories. Does not want "the tired, the trite, the sexist, the multiply-folded, the single-spaced, the sentimental, the self-pitying, the swaggering, the infantile (i.e., coruscated whimsy and self-conscious quaint), poems about Why You Can't Be Together and stories about How Complicated Am I. Before you send us anything, sit down and read a poem by Stanley Kunitz or a story by Evelyn Waugh, Louisa May Alcott, or anyone who's visited the poles, and if you still think you've written a damn fine thing, have at it. A word-count on the top of the page is fine—a copyright or 'all rights reserved' reminder makes you look like a beginner." **Buys 3-6 mss/year.** Length: 300-2,000 words. **Pays small honorarium and copies.**

FICTION Contact: W.M. Davies, fiction editor. Seeks quality fiction. No genre fiction, science fiction, techno-thriller. "Wants more of anything Herman Melville, Henry James, or Betty MacDonald would like to read." **Buys 1-2 mss/year.** Send complete ms with bio, list of publications, and explain how you found the magazine. Include SASE. Length: 300-2,000 words. **Pays honorarium and subscriptions.**

POETRY Contact: Maude Piper, poetry editor. Needs free verse, traditional. Wants quality poetry; "poetry that incises a perfect figure 8 on the ice, but also cuts beneath that mirrored surface. Minimal use of vertical pronoun. Do not submit more than twice in 1 year." No previously published poems. Cover letter is required. Does not want "sentiment; no 'musing' on who or what done ya wrong." Buys 2-4 poems/year. Submit maximum 3 poems. **Pays honorarium and at least 2 contributor's copies.**

$$ CHICKEN SOUP FOR THE SOUL PUBLISHING, LLC

Chicken Soup for the Soul Publishing, LLC, **Fax:** (203)861-7194. **E-mail:** webmaster@chickensoupforthesoul.com (for all inquires). **Website:** www.chickensoup.com. **95% freelance written.** Paperback with 12 publications/year featuring inspirational, heartwarming, uplifting short stories. Estab. 1993. Circ. Over 200 titles; 100 million books in print. Byline given. Pays on publication. No kill fee. Accepts simultaneous submissions. Responds upon consideration. Guidelines available online.

NONFICTION No sermon, essay, eulogy, term paper, journal entry, political, or controversial issues. **Buys 1,000 mss/year.** Send complete ms. Length: 300-1,200 words. **Pays $200.**

POETRY Needs traditional. No controversial poetry.

COLORADO REVIEW

Center for Literary Publishing, Colorado State University, 9105 Campus Delivery, Fort Collins CO 80523. (970)491-5449. **E-mail:** creview@colostate.edu. **Website:** http://coloradoreview.colostate.edu. **Contact:** Stephanie G'Schwind, editor-in-chief and nonfiction editor. Literary magazine published 3 times/year. Circ. 1,000. Byline given. Pays on publication. No kill fee. Publishes ms an average of 6 months after acceptance. Editorial lead time 1 year. Accepts simultaneous submissions. Responds in 2 months to mss. Sample copy for $10. Guidelines available online.

NONFICTION **Buys 6-9 mss/year.** Mss for nonfiction stories are read year round. Send no more than 1 story at a time. **Pays $25 or $5/page, whichever is greater.**

FICTION **Contact:** Steven Schwartz. Needs contemporary, ethnic, experimental, mainstream, short fiction. No genre fiction. Send complete ms. Fiction mss are read August 1-April 30. Mss received May 1-July 31 will be returned unread. Send no more than 1 story at a time. Length: under 30 ms pages. **Pays $25 or $5/page, whichever is greater.**

POETRY **Contact:** Don Revell, Sasha Steensen, and Matthew Cooperman, poetry editors; Dan Beachy-Quick, book review editor. Considers poetry of any style. Poetry mss are read August 1-April 30. Mss received May 1-July 31 will be returned unread. Has published poetry by Sherman Alexie, Laynie Browne, John Gallaher, Kevin Prufer, Craig Morgan Teicher, Susan Tichy, Elizabeth Robinson, Elizabeth Willis, and Keith Waldrop. Buys 60-100 poems/year. Submit maximum 5 poems. **Pays minimum of $25 or $5/page.**

CONFRONTATION

English Department, LIU Post, Brookville NY 11548. (516)299-2720. **E-mail:** confrontationmag@gmail.com. **Website:** www.confrontationmagazine.org. **Contact:** Jonna Semeiks, editor-in-chief. **75% freelance written.** Semiannual magazine comprising all forms and genres of stories, poems, essays, memoirs, and plays. A special section contains book reviews. "We also publish the work of 1 visual artist per issue, selected by the editors." *Confrontation* has been in continuous publication since 1968. Our taste and our magazine is eclectic, but we always look for excellence in style, an important theme, a memorable voice. We enjoy discovering and fostering new talent. Each issue contains work by both well-established and new writers. In addition, *Confrontation* often features a thematic special section that "confronts" a topic. The ensuing confrontation is an attempt to see the many sides of an issue or theme, rather than to present a formed conclusion. "We prefer single submissions. Clear copy. No e-mail submissions unless writer resides outside the U.S. Mail submissions with a SASE. We read August 16-May 15. Do not send mss or e-mail submissions between May 16 and August 15. We publish theme issues. Upcoming themes are announced on our website and Facebook page and in our magazine." Estab. 1968. Circ. 2,000. Byline given. Pays on publication. Offers kill fee. Publishes work in the first or second issue after acceptance. Accepts queries by mail, e-mail, phone. Accepts simultaneous submissions. Responds in 3 weeks to queries; 8-10 weeks to mss.

NONFICTION Needs essays, personal experience. Special issues: "We publish personal as well as cultural, political and other kinds of essays as well as (self-contained) sections of memoirs." **Buys 12 mss/year.** Send complete ms. Length: 1,500-5,000 words. **Pays $50-125; more for commissioned work.**

FICTION "We judge on quality of writing and thought or imagination, so we will accept genre fiction. However, it must have literary merit or it must transcend or challenge genre." Needs experimental as well as more traditional fiction, self-contained novel excerpts, slice-of-life vignettes, lyrical or philosophical fiction. No "proselytizing" literature or conventional genre fiction. **Buys 30-40 mss/year.** Send complete ms. Length: Up to 7,200 words **Pays $50-125; more for commissioned work.**

POETRY **Contact:** Belinda Kremer, poetry editor. Needs avant-garde or experimental as well as traditional poems (and forms), lyric poems, dramatic monologues, satiric or philosophical poems. In short, a wide range of verse. *Confrontation* is interested in all poetic forms. Our only criterion is high literary merit. We think of our audience as an educated, lay group of intelligent readers. Has published poetry by

David Ray, T. Alan Broughton, David Ignatow, Philip Appleman, Jane Mayhall, and Joseph Brodsky. Submit no more than 10 pages at a time (up to 6 poems). Buys 60 poems per year. *Confrontation* also offers the biennial Confrontation Poetry Prize. No sentimental verse. No previously published poems. Lines/poem: Length should generally be kept to 2 pages. **Pays $25-75; more for commissioned work.**

CONTRARY

3133 S. Emerald Ave., Chicago IL 60616-3299. **E-mail:** chicago@contrarymagazine.com (no submissions). **Website:** www.contrarymagazine.com. **Contact:** Jeff McMahon, editor. "*Contrary* publishes fiction, poetry, literary commentary, and prefers work that combines the virtues of all those categories. Founded at the University of Chicago, it now operates independently and not-for-profit on the South Side of Chicago. We like work that is not only contrary in content, but contrary in its evasion of the expectations established by its genre. Our fiction defies traditional story form. For example, a story may bring us to closure without ever delivering an ending. We don't insist on the ending, but we do insist on the closure. And we value fiction as poetic as any poem." Quarterly. Member CLMP. Estab. 2003. Circ. 38,000. Pays on publication. Mss published no more than 21 days after acceptance. Responds to queries in 2 weeks; 3 months to mss. Rarely comments on/critiques rejected mss. Guidelines available on website.

FICTION Contact: Frances Badgett, fiction editor. Needs literary. Accepts submissions through website only: www.contrarymagazine.com/Contrary/Submissions.html. Include estimated word count, brief bio, list of publications. Considers simultaneous submissions. Length: 2,000 words (maximum); average length: 750 words. Publishes short shorts. Average length of short shorts: 750 words. **Pays $20-60.**

POETRY Contact: Shaindel Beers, poetry editor. No mail or e-mail submissions; submit work via the website. Considers simultaneous submissions; no previously published poems. Accepts submissions through online form only. Often comments on rejected poems. Submit maximum 3 poems. **$20 per byline, $60 for featured work.**"Upon acceptance, *Contrary* acquires the following rights: 1) exclusive rights for the three-month period that the accepted work appears in the current issue of *Contrary* magazine, 2) the right to permanent inclusion of the work in *Contrary's* electronic archive, and 3) the right to reproduce the work in print and electronic collections of our content. After the current issue expires, the author is free to seek republication elsewhere, but *Contrary* must be credited upon republication."**

CRAB ORCHARD REVIEW

Department of English, Southern Illinois University at Carbondale, Faner Hall 2380, Mail Code 4503, 1000 Faner Dr., Carbondale IL 62901. (618)453-6833. **Fax:** (618)453-8224. **Website:** www.craborchardreview.siuc.edu. "We are a general interest literary journal published twice/year. We strive to be a journal that writers admire and readers enjoy. We publish fiction, poetry, creative nonfiction, fiction translations, interviews and reviews." Estab. 1995. Circ. 2,500. No kill fee. Publishes ms an average of 9-12 months after acceptance. Accepts simultaneous submissions. Responds in 3 weeks to queries. Responds in 9 months to mss. Sample copy for $8. Guidelines for #10 SASE.

FICTION Contact: Jon Tribble, managing editor. Needs ethnic, excerpted novel. No science fiction, romance, western, horror, gothic or children's. Wants more novel excerpts that also stand alone as pieces. Send SASE for reply, return of ms. Length: 1,000-6,500 words. **Pays $100 minimum; $20/page maximum, 2 contributor's copies and a year subscription.**

POETRY Wants all styles and forms from traditional to experimental. Does not want greeting card verse; literary poetry only. Has published poetry by Luisa A. Igloria, Erinn Batykefer, Jim Daniels, Bryan Tso Jones. Submit up to 5 poems at a time. Considers simultaneous submissions with notification; no previously published poems. Postal submissions only. Cover letter is preferred. "Indicate stanza breaks on poems of more than 1 page." Reads submissions April-November for Summer/Fall special theme issue, February-April for regular, non-thematic Winter/Spring issue. Time between acceptance and publication is 6 months to a year. "Poems that are under serious consideration are discussed and decided on by the managing editor and poetry editor." Submit maximum 5 poems.

CRAZYHORSE

College of Charleston, Department of English, 66 George St., Charleston SC 29424. (843)953-4470. **E-mail:** crazyhorse@cofc.edu. **Website:** http://crazyhorse.cofc.edu. Semiannual magazine. "We like to print a mix of writing regardless of its form, genre, school, or politics. We're especially on the lookout for original writing that doesn't fit the categories and that engages in the work of honest communication." Estab. 2,000. Circ. 1,500. No kill fee. Publishes ms an average of 6-12 months after acceptance. Accepts simultaneous submissions. Responds in 1 week to queries. Responds in 3-5 months to mss. Sample copy for $5. Guidelines for SASE or by e-mail.

FICTION Accepts all fiction of fine quality, including short shorts and literary essays. **Buys 12-15 mss/ year. Pays 2 contributor's copies and $20 per page.**

POETRY Submit 3-5 poems at a time. Considers simultaneous submissions. No previously published poems. No fax, e-mail or disk submissions. Cover letter is preferred. Reads submissions year round, but slows down during the summer. Buys 80 poems/year. Submit maximum 5 poems. **Pays $20-35/page and 2 contributor's copies.**

⊖⊖⊖ DELAWARE BEACH LIFE

Endeavours LLC, Endeavours, LLC, P.O. Box 417, Rehoboth Beach DE 19927. (302)227-9499. **E-mail:** info@delawarebeachlife.com. **Website:** www.delawarebeachlife.com. **Contact:** Terry Plowman, publisher/editor. Covering coastal Delaware. "Delaware Beach Life focuses on coastal Delaware: Fenwick to Lewes. You can go slightly inland as long as there's water and a natural connection to the coast, e.g., Angola or Long Neck." Publishes 8 issues/year. Estab. 2002. Circ. 15,000. Byline given. Pays on acceptance. 50% kill fee. Publishes ms 4 months after acceptance. Editorial lead time is 6 months. Submit seasonal material 12 months in advance. Accepts queries by e-mail. Accepts previously published mss. Reports in 8 weeks to queries; 6 months to mss. Sample copy available online at website. Guidelines free and by e-mail.

NONFICTION Needs book excerpts, essays, general interest, humor, interview, opinion, photo feature. Does not want anything not focused on coastal Delaware. Query with published clips. Length: 1,200-3,000 words. **Pays $400-1,000 for assigned articles.** Does not pay expenses of writers on assignment.

COLUMNS/DEPARTMENTS Profiles, History, and Opinion (all coastal DE)—1,200/words each. **Buys 32 mss/year.** Query with published clips. **Pays $150-350.**

FICTION Needs adventure, condensed novels, historical, humorous, novel excerpts, Must have coastal theme. Does not want anything not coastal. **Buys 3 mss/year.** Query with published clips. Length: 1,000-2,000 words.

POETRY Needs We use avant-garde, free verse, haiku, light verse, and traditional. Does not want anything not coastal. No erotic poetry. Buys 6 poems/ year. Submit maximum 3 poems. Length: 6-15/lines. **Pays up to $50.**

DENVER QUARTERLY

University of Denver, 2000 E. Asbury, Denver CO 80208. (303)871-2892. **Website:** www.denverquarterly. com. **Contact:** Bill Ramke. "We publish fiction, articles and poetry for a generally well-educated audience, primarily interested in literature and the literary experience. They read *DQ* to find something a little different from a stictly academic quarterly or a creative writing outlet." Quarterly. Reads between September 15 and May 15. Estab. 1996. Circ. 2,000. Publishes ms 1 year after acceptance. Responds in 3 months.

FICTION "We are interested in experimental fiction (minimalism, magic realism, etc.) as well as in realistic fiction and in writing about fiction. No sentimental, science fiction, romance or spy thrillers. No stories longer than 15 pages!" Submit ms by mail, include SASE. **Pays $5/page for fiction and poetry and 2 contributor's copies.**

POETRY Poetry submissions should be comprised of 3-5 poems. Submit ms by mail, include SASE. Accepts simultaneous submissions. Sample copy for $10. **Pays $5/page for fiction and poetry and 2 contributor's copies.**

⟳ ⊖ DESCANT

P.O. Box 314, Station P, Toronto ON M5S 2S8 Canada. (416)593-2557. **Fax:** (416)593-9362. **E-mail:** info@descant.ca. **E-mail:** submit@descant.ca. **Website:** www. descant.ca. Quarterly Journal. Estab. 1970. Circ. 1,200. Pays on publication. No kill fee. Publishes ms an average of 16 months after acceptance. Editorial lead time 1 year. Accepts queries by mail, e-mail, phone. Sample copy for $8.50 plus postage. Guidelines available online.

NONFICTION Needs book excerpts, essays, interview, personal experience, historical.

FICTION Contact: Karen Mulhallen, editor. Short stories or book excerpts. Maximum length 6,000 words; 3,000 words or less preferred. Needs ethnic, experimental, historical, humorous. No erotica, fantasy, gothic, horror, religious, romance, beat. Send complete ms with cover letter. Include estimated word count and brief bio. **Pays $100 (Canadian).**

POETRY Needs free verse, light verse, traditional. "*Descant* seeks high quality poems and stories in both traditional and innovative form." Annual. Circ. 500-750. Member CLMP. Literary. Submit maximum 6 poems. **Pays $100.**

EPOCH

251 Goldwin Smith Hall, Cornell University, Ithaca NY 14853. (607)255-3385. **Fax:** (607)255-6661. **Website:** http://english.arts.cornell.edu/publications/epoch. **100% freelance written.** Literary magazine published 3 times/year. "Well-written literary fiction, poetry, personal essays. Newcomers always welcome. Open to mainstream and avant-garde writing." Estab. 1947. Circ. 1,000. Byline given. Pays on publication. Offers 100% kill fee. Publishes ms an average of 6 months after acceptance. Editorial lead time 6 months. Submit seasonal material 8 months in advance. Accepts queries by mail. Responds in 2 weeks to queries. Responds in 6 weeks to mss. Sometimes comments on rejected mss. Sample copy for $5. Guidelines online and for #10 SASE.

NONFICTION Needs essays, interview. No inspirational. **Buys 6-8 mss/year.** Send complete ms. **Pays $5 up/printed page.**

FICTION Needs ethnic, experimental, mainstream, novel concepts, literary short stories. No genre fiction. "Would like to see more Southern fiction (Southern U.S.)." **Buys 25-30 mss/year.** Send complete ms. **Pays $5 and up/printed page.**

POETRY Needs avant-garde, free verse, haiku, light verse, traditional. No simultaneous submissions. Mss not accompanied by SASE will be discarded unread. Occasionally provides criticism on poems. Buys 30-75 poems/year. Submit maximum 7 poems. **Pays $5 up/printed page.**

EVENT

Douglas College, P.O. Box 2503, New Westminster BC V3L 5B2 Canada. (604)527-5293. **Fax:** (604)527-5095. **E-mail:** event@douglascollege.ca. **Website:** www.event.douglas.bc.ca. **100% freelance written.** Magazine published 3 times/year containing fiction, poetry, creative nonfiction, notes on writing, and reviews. "We are eclectic and always open to content that invites involvement. Generally, we like strong narrative." Estab. 1971. Circ. 1,250. Byline given. Pays on publication. Publishes ms an average of 8 months after acceptance. Accepts queries by mail. Accepts simultaneous submissions. Responds in 1 month to queries. Responds in 6 months to mss. Guidelines available online.

FICTION "We look for readability, style, and writing that invites involvement." Submit maximum 2 stories. Needs humorous, contemporary. No technically poor or unoriginal pieces. **Buys 12-15 mss/year.** Send complete ms. Length: 5,000 words maximum. **Pays $25/page up to $500.**

POETRY Needs free verse. "We tend to appreciate the narrative and sometimes the confessional modes." No light verse. Buys 30-40 poems/year. Submit maximum 10 poems. **Pays $25-500.**

EYE ON LIFE ONLINE MAGAZINE

P.O. Box 534, Brookline MA 02445. **E-mail:** eyeonlife.ezine@gmail.com. **Website:** http://eyeonlifemag.com. **Contact:** Tom Rubenoff, senior poetry editor. Estab. 2009. Byline given. Responds in 4-6 weeks.

NONFICTION Publishes 6 articles or book reviews per year. Submit using online submission manager only. **Pays $20/article. Pays $25/article covering poetry event with photo.**

POETRY Publishes up to 5 poems/week. Submissions through online submission form only. Seeking poetry with vivid imagery that either works well within its form or transcends it in less than 400 words. **Does not pay for poetry at this time.**

FEMINIST STUDIES

0103 Taliaferro, University of Maryland, College Park MD 20742. (301)405-7415. **Fax:** (301)405-8395. **E-mail:** atambe@umd.edu. **E-mail:** kmantilla@feministstudies.org. **Website:** www.feministstudies.org. **Contact:** Ashwini Tambe, editorial director; Karla Mantilla, managing editor. "Over the years, Feminist Studies has been a reliable source of significant writings on issues that are important to all classes and races of women. Those familiar with the literature on women's studies are well aware of the importance and vitality of the journal and the frequency with which articles first published in Feminist Studies are cited and/or reprinted elsewhere. Indeed, no less than four anthologies have been created from articles originally published in Feminist Studies: Clio's Consciousness Raised: New Perspectives on the History of Women; Sex and Class in Women's History; U.S. Women in Struggle: A Feminist Studies Anthology; and Lesbian Subjects: A Feminist Studies Reader." Estab. 1974. Guidelines available online.

NONFICTION "We accept submissions in the following categories: research & criticism, creative writing, art & art essays, review essays. We will only review work that is not under consideration elsewhere, including in electronic format or on any kind of Web page or elsewhere on the internet. We use the 16th edition of the Chicago Manual of Style for manuscript and citation style." See website for detailed guidelines. Length: up to 10,500 words.

THE FIDDLEHEAD

University of New Brunswick, Campus House, 11 Garland Court, Box 4400, Fredericton NB E3B 5A3 Canada. (506)453-3501. **Fax:** (506) 453-5069. **E-mail:** fiddlehd@unb.ca. **Website:** www.thefiddlehead.ca. Mark Anthony Jarman and Gerard Beirne, fiction editors; Sarah Bernstein, Phillip Crymble, Claire Kelly, and Ian LeTourneau, poetry editors. **Contact:** Kathryn Taglia, managing editor. "Canada's longest living literary journal, *The Fiddlehead* is published 4 times a year at the University of New Brunswick, with the generous assistance of the University of New Brunswick, the Canada Council for the Arts, and the Province of New Brunswick. It is experienced; wise enough to recognize excellence; always looking for freshness and surprise. *The Fiddlehead* publishes short stories, poems, book reviews, and a small number of personal essays. Our full-colour covers have become collectors' items, and feature work by New Brunswick artists and from New Brunswick museums and art galleries. *The Fiddlehead* also sponsors an annual writing contest. The journal is open to good writing in English from all over the world, looking always for freshness and surprise. Our editors are always happy to see new unsolicited works in fiction and poetry. Work is read on an ongoing basis; the acceptance rate is around 1-2%. Apart from our annual contest, we have no deadlines for submissions." Estab. 1945. Circ. 1,500. Pays on publication for first or one-time serial rights. Responds in 3-9 months to mss. Occasionally comments on rejected mss. Sample copy for $15 (U.S.).

FICTION Receives 100-150 unsolicited mss/month. Accepts 4-5 mss/issue; 20-40 mss/year. Agented fiction: small percentage. Publishes high percentage of new writers/year. Needs literary. Send SASE and *Canadian* stamps or IRCs for return of mss. No e-mail submissions. Simultaneous submissions only if stated on cover letter; must contact immediately if accepted elsewhere. Average length: 3,000-6,000 words. Also publishes short shorts. **Pays up to $40 (Canadian)/ published page and 2 contributor's copies.**

POETRY Send SASE and *Canadian* stamps or IRCs for return of mss. No email submissions. Simultaneous submissions only if stated on cover letter; must contact immediately if accepted elsewhere. **Pays up to $40 (Canadian)/published page and 2 contributor's copies.**

FIELD: CONTEMPORARY POETRY & POETICS

Oberlin College Press, 50 N. Professor St., Oberlin OH 44074-1091. (440)775-8408. **Fax:** (440)775-8124. **E-mail:** oc.press@oberlin.edu. **Website:** www.oberlin.edu/ocpress. **Contact:** managing editor. **60% freelance written.** Biannual magazine of poetry, poetry in translation, and essays on contemporary poetry by poets. *FIELD: Contemporary Poetry and Poetics*, published semiannually in April and October, is a literary journal with "emphasis on poetry, translations, and essays by poets. See electronic submission guidelines." Estab. 1969. Circ. 1,500. Byline given. Pays on publication. Editorial lead time 4 months. Accepts queries by mail, e-mail, fax, phone, online submission form. Responds in 6-8 weeks to mss. Sample copy for $8. Guidelines available online and for #10 SASE.

POETRY Needs contemporary, prose poems, free verse, traditional. Submissions are read August 1 through May 31. Submit 3-5 of your best poems. No previously published poems or simultaneous submissions. No e-mail submissions. Include cover letter and SASE. Submit using submission manager: www.oberlin.edu/ocpress/submissions.html. Buys 120 poems/year. Submit maximum 5 poems. **Pays $15/page and 2 contributor's copies.**

FIVE POINTS

Georgia State University, P.O. Box 3999, Atlanta GA 30302-3999. **E-mail:** info@langate.gsu.edu. **Website:** www.fivepoints.gsu.edu. Triannual literary journal publishing short shorts, literary essays, poetry. *"Five Points* is committed to publishing work that compels the imagination through the use of fresh and convincing language." Estab. 1996. Circ. 2,000. No kill fee. Publishes ms an average of 6 months after acceptance. Sample copy for $7.

FICTION **Contact:** Megan Sexton, co-editor. List of upcoming themes available for SASE. Receives 250 unsolicited mss/month. Accepts 4 mss/issue; 15-20 mss/year. Does not read mss April 30-September 1.

Publishes 1 new writer/year. Sometimes comments on rejected mss. Recently published work by Frederick Busch, Ursula Hegi, Melanie Rae Thon. Sponsors awards/contests. Average length: 7,500 words. **Pays $15/page minimum; $250 maximum, free subscription to magazine and 2 contributor's copies; additional copies $4.**

THE GEORGIA REVIEW

The University of Georgia, Athens GA 30602. (706)542-3481. **Fax:** (706)542-0047. **E-mail:** garev@uga.edu. **Website:** www.uga.edu/garev. **Contact:** Stephen Corey, editor. **99% freelance written.** Quarterly journal. Our readers are educated, inquisitive people who read a lot of work in the areas we feature, so they expect only the best in our pages. All work submitted should show evidence that the writer is at least as well-educated and well-read as our readers. Essays should be authoritative but accessible to a range of readers. Estab. 1947. Circ. 3,500. Byline given. Pays on publication. No kill fee. Publishes ms an average of 6 months after acceptance. Accepts queries by mail. Responds in 2 weeks to queries. Responds in 2-3 months to mss. Sample copy for $10. Guidelines available online.

NONFICTION Needs essays. **Buys 12-20 mss/year.** For the most part we are not interested in scholarly articles that are narrow in focus and/or overly burdened with footnotes. The ideal essay for *The Georgia Review* is a provocative, thesis-oriented work that can engage both the intelligent general reader and the specialist. Send complete ms. "We do not consider unsolicited manuscripts between May 15 and August 15. Submissions received during that period will be returned unread. Work previously published in any form or submitted simultaneously to other journals will not be considered." **Pays $40/published page.**

FICTION "We seek original, excellent writing not bound by type." "Ordinarily we do not publish novel excerpts or works translated into English, and we strongly discourage authors from submitting these." **Buys 12-20 mss/year.** Send complete ms. "We do not consider unsolicited manuscripts between May 15 and August 15. Submissions received during that period will be returned unread. Work previously published in any form or submitted simultaneously to other journals will not be considered." **Pays $50/published page.**

POETRY "We seek original, excellent poetry. Submit 3-5 poems at a time." Buys 60-75 poems/year. Submit maximum 5 poems. **Pays $4/line.**

GLIMMER TRAIN STORIES

Glimmer Train Press, Inc., P.O. Box 80430, Portland OR 97280. **Fax:** (503)221-0837. **E-mail:** eds@glimmertrain.org. **Website:** www.glimmertrain.org. **90% freelance written.** Quarterly magazine of literary short fiction. "We are interested in literary short stories, particularly by new and lightly published writers." Estab. 1991. Circ. 12,000. Byline given. Pays on acceptance. Publishes ms an average of 15 months after acceptance. Accepts simultaneous submissions. Responds in 2 months to mss. Sometimes comments on rejected mss. Sample copy for $14 on website. Guidelines available online.

FICTION Buys 40 mss/year. Submit via the website. "In a pinch, send a hard copy and include SASE for response." Length: 1,200-12,000 words. **Pays $700 for standard submissions, up to $2,500 for contest-winning stories.**

GRAIN

P.O. Box 67, Saskatoon SK S7K 3K1 Canada. (306)244-2828. **Fax:** (306)244-0255. **E-mail:** grainmag@sasktel.net. **Website:** www.grainmagazine.ca. **Contact:** Rilla Friesen, editor. Quarterly magazine covering poetry, fiction, creative nonfiction. "*Grain, The Journal Of Eclectic Writing,* is a literary quarterly that publishes engaging, diverse, and challenging writing and art by some of the best Canadian and international writers and artists. Every issue features superb new writing from both developing and established writers. Each issue also highlights the unique artwork of a different visual artist. *Grain* has garnered national and international recognition for its distinctive, cutting-edge content and design." Estab. 1973. Circ. 1,600. Byline given. Pays on publication for first Canadian serial rights. Typically responds in 3-6 months. Guidelines available by SASE (or SAE and IRC), e-mail, or on website.

NONFICTION No academic papers or reportage. "No fax or e-mail submissions; postal submissions only. Send typed, unpublished material only (we consider work published online to be previously published). Please only submit work in 1 genre at 1 time." Length: 5,000 words maximum. **Pays $50-225 CAD (depending on number of pages) and 2 contributor's copies.**

FICTION Needs experimental, literary, mainstream, contemporary. No romance, confession, science fiction, vignettes, mystery. "Submissions must be typed in readable font (ideally 12 point, Times Roman or Courier), free of typos, printed on 1 side only. No staples. Your name and address must be on every page. Pieces of more than 1 page must be numbered. Cover letter with all contact information, title(s) and genre of work is required." Length: 5,000/words max; "stories at the longer end of the word count must be of exceptional quality."

POETRY Needs individual poems, sequences, suites. Wants "High quality, imaginative, well-crafted poetry." Submit up to 12 pages of poetry, typed in readable font on 1 side only. No previously published poems or simultaneous submissions. No fax or e-mail submissions; postal submissions only. Cover letter with all contact information, title(s), and genre of work is required. "No staples. Your name and address must be on every page. Pieces of more than 1 page must be numbered. Please only submit work in one genre at one time." **Pays $50-225 CAD (depending on number of pages) and 2 contributor's copies.**

$ GULF COAST: A JOURNAL OF LITERATURE AND FINE ARTS

University of Houston, Department of English, University of Houston, Houston TX 77204-3013. (713)743-3223. **E-mail:** editors@gulfcoastmag.org. **Website:** www.gulfcoastmag.org. **Contact:** Zachary Martin, editor; Karyna McGlynn, managing editor; Michelle Oakes, Justine Post, Kimberly Bruss, poetry editors; Aja Gabel, D'Lynn Barham, Ashley Wurzbacher, fiction editors; Jameelah Lang, Beth Lyons, nonfiction editors. Biannual magazine covering innovative fiction, nonfiction, and poetry for the literary-minded. Estab. 1986. No kill fee. Publishes ms 6 months-1 year after acceptance. Accepts queries by mail, phone. Accepts simultaneous submissions. Responds in 4-6 months to mss. Sometimes comments on rejected mss. Back issue for $8, 7x10 SASE with 4 first-class stamps. Writer's guidelines for #10 SASE or on website.

NONFICTION Contact: Nonfiction editor. Needs interview, reviews. *Gulf Coast* reads general submissions, submitted by post or through the online submissions manager September 1-March 1. Submissions e-mailed directly to the editors or postmarked March 1-September 1 will not be read or responded to. "Please visit our contest page for contest submission guidelines." **Pays $50 per review, and $100 per interview.** Sometimes pays expenses of writers on assignment.

FICTION Contact: Fiction editor. "Please do not send multiple submissions; we will read only one submission per author at a given time, except in the case of our annual contests." Needs ethnic, experimental, multicultural, literary, regional, translations, contemporary. No children's, genre, religious/inspirational. *Gulf Coast* reads general submissions, submitted by post or through the online submissions manager September 1-March 1. Submissions e-mailed directly to the editors or postmarked March 1-September 1 will not be read or responded to. "Please visit our contest page for contest submission guidelines." **Pays $150.**

POETRY Contact: Poetry editor. Submit up to 5 poems at a time. Considers simultaneous submissions with notification; no previously published poems. Cover letter is required. List previous publications and include a brief bio. Reads submissions September-April. Submit maximum 1-5 poems. **Pays $30/poem.**

HANGING LOOSE

Hanging Loose Press, 231 Wyckoff St., Brooklyn NY 11217. **E-mail:** editor@hangingloosepress.com. **Website:** www.hangingloosepress.com. **Contact:** Robert Hershon, Dick Lourie, and Mark Pawlak, poetry editors. *Hanging Loose*, published in April and October, "concentrates on the work of new writers." Wants "excellent, energetic" poems. Estab. 1966. Responds in 3 months. Sample: $12.

POETRY Submit up to 6 poems at a time. No fax or e-mail submissions; postal submissions only. No simultaneous submissions. "Would-be contributors should read the magazine first." **Pays small fee and 2 contributor's copies.**

$ HAYDEN'S FERRY REVIEW

c/o Virginia G. Piper Center for Creative Writing, Arizona State University, P.O. Box 875002, Tempe AZ 85287. (480)965-1337. **E-mail:** HFR@asu.edu. **Website:** www.haydensferryreview.org. **Contact:** Beth Staples, managing editor. **85% freelance written.** Semiannual magazine. "*Hayden's Ferry Review* publishes the best quality fiction, poetry, and creative nonfiction from new, emerging, and established writers." Estab. 1986. Circ. 1,300. Byline given. Pays on publication. No kill fee. Publishes ms an average of 6 months after acceptance. Editorial lead time 5 months.

Accepts queries by online submission form. Accepts simultaneous submissions. Responds in 1 week or less to e-mail queries. Responds in 3-4 months to mss. Sample copy for $7.50. Guidelines available online.

NONFICTION Needs essays, interview, personal experience. **Buys 2 mss/year.** Send complete ms. Word length open **Pays $50.**

FICTION Contact: Editors change every 1-2 years. Needs ethnic, experimental, humorous, slice-of-life vignettes, contemporary, prose poem. **Buys 10 mss/year.** Send complete ms. Word length open.

POETRY Needs avant-garde, free verse, haiku, light verse, traditional. Buys 60 poems/year. Submit maximum 6 poems. Word length open. **Pays $50.**

⊗ THE HOLLINS CRITIC

P.O. Box 9538, Hollins University, Roanoke VA 24020-1538. **E-mail:** acockrell@hollins.edu. **Website:** www.hollins.edu/academics/critic. **Contact:** Cathryn Hankla. **100% freelance written.** Magazine published 5 times/year. Estab. 1964. Circ. 400. Byline given. Pays on publication. No kill fee. Publishes ms an average of 1 year after acceptance. Accepts queries by online submission form. Submit at www.hollinscriticssubmissions.com. Accepts simultaneous submissions. Responds in 2 months to mss. Sample copy for $3. Guidelines for #10 SASE.

POETRY Needs avant-garde, free verse, traditional. Submit up to 5 poems at a time using the online submission form at www.hollinscriticssubmissions.com, available September 15-December 1. Submissions received at other times will be returned unread. Responds in 6 weeks. "We read poetry only from September 1-December 15." Publishes 16-20 poems/year. **Pays $25/poem plus 5 contributor's copies.**

HOOT

A postcard review of {mini} poetry and prose, 1413 Academy Lane, Elkins Park PA 19027. **E-mail:** info@hootreview.com. **E-mail:** onlinesubmissions@hootreview.com. **Website:** www.hootreview.com. **Contact:** Amanda Vacharat and Dorian Geisler, editors. **100% freelance written.** "*HOOT* publishes 1 piece of writing, designed with original art/photographs, on the front of a postcard every month. The postcards are intended for sharing, to be hung on the wall, etc. Therefore, we look for very brief, surprising-yet-gimmick-free writing that can stand on its own, that also follows 'The Refrigerator Rule'—something that you would hang on your refrigerator and would want to read and look at for a whole month. This 'rule' applies to our online content as well." Estab. 2011. Pays on publication. Publishes ms 2 months after acceptance. Accepts queries by e-mail. Accepts simultaneous submissions. Sample copy available for $2. Writer's guidelines available on website.

NONFICTION Needs personal experience, creative nonfiction. **Buys 6 mss/year.** Submit complete ms. Length: 150 words maximum. **Pays $10-100 for assigned and unsolicited pieces.**

FICTION Needs experimental, literary, flash/short-short. **Buys 14 mss/year.** Submit complete ms. Length: 150 words maximum. **Pays $10-100 for print publication.**

POETRY Needs avant-garde, free verse, haiku, light verse, traditional, prose. Buys 14 poems/year. Submit maximum 2 per submission poems. Length: 10 lines. **Pays $10-100 for print publication.**

HOSPITAL DRIVE

Hospital Drive, P.O. Box 800761, Charlottesville VA 22908-0761. **E-mail:** hospitaldrive@virginia.edu. **Website:** http://hospitaldrive.med.virginia.edu. **Contact:** Dr. Daniel Becker, editor. *Hospital Drive* "encourages original creative work that examines themes of health, illness, and healing. Submissions will be accepted from anyone, but preference is given to those involved in providing, teaching, studying, or researching patient care. All work will be judged anonymously by reviewers and the editorial board. Poems, short fiction, personal essays, reviews, photography, and visual art (painting, drawing, sculpture, mixed media) will be considered. Issues will be released at least twice a year, and may include invited work. Please review our web site thoroughly and direct any additional questions to query@hospitaldrive.med.virginia.edu." Estab. 2006. Time between acceptance and publication is 3-6 months. Guidelines available on website.

POETRY Submit up to 5 poems. Accepts e-mail submissions as attachment; no fax or disk submissions. Cover letter is unnecessary. All works must be submitted by e-mail (mailed, printed submissions cannot be accepted for review), accompanied by basic contact information and the titles of each piece. Attach each poem as a separate document to 1 e-mail. Put "poetry submission" in the e-mail subject line. "All submissions will be reviewed anonymously by the editorial board, and only the highest quality work will be published." Never comments on rejected poems.

HUBBUB

5344 SE 38th Ave., Portland OR 97202. **E-mail:** lisa. steinman@reed.edu. **Website:** www.reed.edu/hubbub/. J. Shugrue and Lisa M. Steinman, co-editors. *Hubbub*, published once/year in the spring, is designed "to feature a multitude of voices from interesting contemporary American poets." Wants "poems that are well-crafted, with something to say. We have no single style, subject, or length requirement and, in particular, will consider long poems." Estab. 1983. Responds in 4 months. Guidelines available for SASE.
POETRY Submit 3-6 typed poems at a time. No previously published poems or simultaneous submissions. Include SASE. "We review 2-4 poetry books/year in short (3-page) reviews; all reviews are solicited. We do, however, list books received/recommended." Send materials for review consideration. Does not want light verse. **Pays $20/poem.**

☉ THE HUDSON REVIEW

The Hudson Review, Inc., 684 Park Ave., New York NY 10065. **E-mail:** info@hudsonreview.com. **Website:** www.hudsonreview.com. **Contact:** Paula Deitz, editor. **100% freelance written.** Quarterly magazine publishing fiction, poetry, essays, book reviews; criticism of literature, art, theatre, dance, film and music, and articles on contemporary cultural developments. Estab. 1948. Circ. 2,000. Byline given. Pays on publication. No kill fee. Publishes ms an average of 6 months after acceptance. Editorial lead time 3 months. Accepts queries by mail. Responds in 6 months. Sample copy for $10. Guidelines for #10 SASE or online.
NONFICTION Contact: Paula Deitz. Needs essays, general interest, historical, opinion, personal experience, travel. **Buys 4-6 mss/year.** Send complete ms between January 1 and March 31 only. Length: up to 3,500 words.
FICTION Reads between September 1 and November 30 only. **Buys 4 mss/year.** Length: up to 10,000 words.
POETRY Reads poems only between April 1 and June 30. Buys 12-20 poems/year. Submit maximum 7 poems. **Pays 50¢/line.**

☉ ILLUMEN

Sam's Dot Publishing, Inc., P.O. Box 782, Cedar Rapids IA 52406-0782. **E-mail:** illumensdp@yahoo.com. **Website:** www.samsdotpublishing.com/aoife/cover. htm. **Contact:** Karen L. Newman, editor. **100% free-**

lance written. Semiannual magazine. "*Illumen* publishes speculative poetry and articles about speculative poetry, and reviews of poetry and collections." Estab. 2004. Circ. 40. Byline given. Offers 100% kill fee. Editorial lead time 2 months. Submit seasonal material 6 months in advance. Accepts queries by e-mail. Responds in 2 weeks to queries. Responds in 3-4 months to mss. Sample copy for $8. Guidelines available online.
NONFICTION Buys 5-8 mss/year. Send complete ms. Length: 2,000 words. **Pays $10 for unsolicited articles.**
POETRY Needs avant-garde, free verse, haiku, light verse, traditional. "Scifaiku is a difficult sell with us because we also publish a specialty magazine—*Scifaikuest*—for scifaiku and related forms." Buys 40-50 poems/year. Submit maximum 5 poems. Length: 200 lines. **Pays 1-2¢/word.**

IMAGE

3307 Third Ave. W., Seattle WA 98119. (206)281-2988. **Fax:** (206)281-2979. **E-mail:** image@imagejournal.org. **Website:** www.imagejournal.org. **Contact:** Gregory Wolfe, publisher/editor. **50% freelance written.** Quarterly magazine covering the intersection between art and faith. "*Image* is a unique forum for the best writing and artwork that is informed by—or grapples with—religious faith. We have never been interested in art that merely regurgitates dogma or falls back on easy answers or didacticism. Instead, our focus has been on writing and visual artwork that embody a spiritual struggle, that seek to strike a balance between tradition and a profound openness to the world. Each issue explores this relationship through outstanding fiction, poetry, painting, sculpture, architecture, film, music, interviews, and dance. *Image* also features 4-color reproductions of visual art." Estab. 1989. Circ. 4,500. Byline given. Pays on acceptance. No kill fee. Publishes ms an average of 8 months after acceptance. Accepts queries by mail, e-mail. Responds in 1 month to queries. Responds in 5 months to mss. Send SASE for reply, return of ms, or send disposable copy of ms. Sample copy available online or for $16. Guidelines online.
NONFICTION "No sentimental, preachy, moralistic, or obvious essays." **Buys 10 mss/year.** Send complete ms. Does not accept e-mail submissions. Length: 4,000-6,000 words. **Pays $10/page; $150 maximum for all prose articles.**

FICTION "No sentimental, preachy, moralistic, obvious stories, or genre stories (unless they manage to transcend their genre)." **Buys 8 mss/year.** Send complete ms. Does not accept e-mail submissions. Length: 4,000-6,000 words. **Pays $10/page ($150 maximum) and 4 contributor's copies.**

$ INDIANA REVIEW

Ballantine Hall 465, 1020 E. Kirkwood, Indiana University, Bloomington IN 47405. (812)855-3439. **E-mail:** inreview@indiana.edu. **Website:** www.indiana.edu/~inreview. **Contact:** Jennifer Luebbers, editor. **100% freelance written.** Biannual magazine. "*Indiana Review*, a nonprofit organization run by IU graduate students, is a journal of previously unpublished poetry and fiction. Literary interviews and essays are also considered. We publish innovative fiction, nonfiction, and poetry. We're interested in energy, originality, and careful attention to craft. While we publish many well-known writers, we also welcome new and emerging poets and fiction writers." Estab. 1976. Circ. 5,000. Byline given. Pays on publication. Publishes ms an average of 3-6 months after acceptance. Accepts queries by mail, e-mail. Accepts simultaneous submissions. Responds in 2 or more weeks to queries. Responds in 4 or more months to mss. Sample copy for $9. Guidelines available online.

NONFICTION Contact: Justin Wolfe, nonfiction editor. Needs essays, interview, creative nonfiction, reviews. No coming of age/slice of life pieces. **Buys 5-7 mss/year.** Send complete ms. 9,000 words maximum. **Pays $5/page ($10 minimum), plus 2 contributor's copies.**

FICTION Contact: Joe Hiland, fiction editor. "We look for daring stories which integrate theme, language, character, and form. We like polished writing, humor, and fiction which has consequence beyond the world of its narrator." Needs ethnic, experimental, mainstream, novel concepts, literary, short fictions, translations. No genre fiction. **Buys 14-18 mss/year.** Send complete ms. Cover letters should be *brief* and demonstrate specific familiarity with the content of a recent issue of *Indiana Review*. Include SASE. Length: 250-10,000 words. **Pays $5/page ($10 minimum), plus 2 contributor's copies.**

POETRY Contact: Michael Mlekoday, poetry editor. "We look for poems that are skillful and bold, exhibiting an inventiveness of language with attention to voice and sonics. Experimental, free verse, prose poem, traditional form, lyrical, narrative." Buys 80 poems/year. Submit maximum 6 poems. 5 lines minimum. **Pays $5/page ($10 minimum), plus 2 contributor's copies.**

$ THE IOWA REVIEW

308 EPB, The University of Iowa, Iowa City IA 52242. (319)335-0462. **Website:** www.iowareview.org. **Contact:** Russell Scott Valentino, editor. Triannual magazine. *The Iowa Review*, published 3 times/year, prints fiction, poetry, essays, reviews, and, occasionally, interviews. *The Iowa Review* is 5½ ×8½, approximately 200 pages, professionally printed, flat-spined, first-grade offset paper, Carolina CS1 10-point cover stock. Receives about 5,000 submissions/year, accepts up to 100. Press run is 2,900; 1,500 distributed to stores. Subscription: $25. Stories, essays, and poems for a general readership interested in contemporary literature. Estab. 1970. Circ. 3,500. Pays on publication. Publishes ms an average of 12-18 months after acceptance. Accepts queries by mail. Accepts simultaneous submissions. Responds in 4 months to mss. Sample copy for $9.95 and online. Guidelines available online.

FICTION "We are open to a range of styles and voices and always hope to be surprised by work we then feel we need." Receives 600 unsolicited mss/month. Accepts 4-6 mss/issue; 12-18 mss/year. Does not read mss January-August. Publishes ms an average of 12-18 months after acceptance. Agented fiction less than 2%. **Publishes some new writers/year.** Recently published work by Bradley Bazzle, Chris Offutt, Alison Ruch. Send complete ms with cover letter. "Don't bother with queries." SASE for return of ms. SASE required. Responds in 4 months to mss. Accepts mss by snail mail and online submission form at https://iowareview.submittable.com/submit; no e-mail submissions. Simultaneous submissions accepted. **Pays $.08 per word ($100 minimum), plus 2 contributor's copies.**

POETRY Submit up to 8 poems at a time. Online submissions accepted, but no e-mail submissions. Cover letter (with title of work and genre) is encouraged. SASE required. Reads submissions "only during the fall semester, September through November, and then contest entries in the spring." Time between acceptance and publication is "around a year." Occasionally comments on rejected poems or offers suggestions on accepted poems. Pays $1.50/line of poetry, $40 minimum. "We simply look for poems that, at the time we read and choose, we find we admire. No specifications as to form, length, style, subject matter, or purpose. Though we print work from established writers, we're always delighted when we discover new talent."

🌑 ⑤ ISLAND

P.O. Box 210, Sandy Bay Tasmania 7006 Australia. (61)(3)6226-2325. **E-mail:** island.magazine@utas.edu. au. **Website:** www.islandmag.com. Quarterly magazine. "*Island* seeks quality fiction, poetry, essays, and articles. A literary magazine with an environmental heart." Circ. 1,500. Accepts queries by e-mail and submissions only online via website. Subscriptions and sample copies available for purchase online. Guidelines available online.

NONFICTION Pays $150 (Australian)/1,000 words.

FICTION Length: up to 2,500 words. **Pays $150 (Australian).**

POETRY Pays $100.

⑤ THE KENYON REVIEW

Finn House, 102 W. Wiggin, Gambier OH 43022. (740)427-5208. **Fax:** (740)427-5417. **E-mail:** kenyon-review@kenyon.edu. **Website:** www.kenyonreview. org. **Contact:** Marlene Landefeld. **100% freelance written.** Quarterly magazine covering contemporary literature and criticism. "An international journal of literature, culture, and the arts, dedicated to an inclusive representation of the best in new writing (fiction, poetry, essays, interviews, criticism) from established and emerging writers." Estab. 1939. Circ. 6,000. Byline given. Pays on publication. No kill fee. Publishes ms an average of 1 year after acceptance. Editorial lead time 1 year. Submit seasonal material 1 year in advance. Responds in 4 months to mss. Sample copy $10, includes postage and handling. Call or e-mail to order. Guidelines available online.

NONFICTION Needs essays, interview, criticism. Only accepts mss via online submissions program; visit website for instructions. Do not submit via e-mail or snail mail. Receives 900 unsolicited mss/month. Unsolicited mss read September 15-January 15 only. Length: 3-15 typeset pages preferred. **Pays $15-40/page.**

FICTION Receives 900 unsolicited mss/month. Unsolicited mss read September 15-January 15 only. Recently published work by Alice Hoffman, Beth Ann Fennelly, Romulus Linney, John Koethe, Albert Goldbarth, Erin McGraw Needs condensed novels, ethnic, experimental, historical, humorous, mainstream, contemporary, excerpts from novels, gay/lesbian, lit-

erary, translations. Only accepts mss via online submissions program; visit website for instructions. Do not submit via e-mail or snail mail. Length: 3-15 typeset pages preferred. **Pays $15-40/page.**

POETRY Features all styles, forms, lengths, and subject matters. Considers translations. Has published poetry by Billy Collins, Diane Ackerman, John Kinsella, Carol Muske-Dukes, Diane di Prima, and Seamus Heaney. Submit up to 6 poems at a time. No previously published poems or simultaneous submissions. Accepts submissions through online registration only at www.kenyon-review.org/submissions (group poems in a single document; do not submit poems individually). Reads submissions September 15-January 15.

◑ ⑤ THE MALAHAT REVIEW

The University of Victoria, P.O. Box 1700, STN CSC, Victoria BC V8W 2Y2 Canada. (250)721-8524. **E-mail:** malahat@uvic.ca (for queries only). **Website:** www.malahatreview.ca. **Contact:** John Barton, editor. **100% freelance written. Eager to work with new/unpublished writers.** Quarterly magazine covering poetry, fiction, creative nonfiction, and reviews. "We try to achieve a balance of views and styles in each issue. We strive for a mix of the best writing by both established and new writers." Estab. 1967. Circ. 1,500. Byline given. Pays on acceptance. No kill fee. Publishes ms an average of 6 months after acceptance. Accepts queries by mail. Responds in 2 weeks to queries. Responds in 3-10 months to mss. Sample copy for $16.95 (US). Guidelines available online.

NONFICTION Include SASE with Canadian postage or IRCs. **Pays $35/magazine page.**

FICTION Needs general fiction and creative nonfiction. **Buys 12-14 mss/year.** Send complete ms. Length: 8,000 words maximum. **Pays $35/magazine page**.

POETRY Needs avant-garde, free verse, traditional. Buys 100 poems/year. Length: 5-10 pages **Pays $35/magazine page.**

⑤ THE MASSACHUSETTS REVIEW

South College, University of Massachusetts, Amherst MA 01003. (413)545-2689. **Fax:** (413)577-0740. **E-mail:** massrev@external.umass.edu. **Website:** www. massreview.org. **Contact:** Jim Hicks, editor. Quarterly magazine. Estab. 1959. Circ. 1,200. Pays on publication. Publishes ms an average of 18 months after acceptance. Accepts queries by mail. Accepts simultaneous submissions. Responds in 3 months to mss. Sample copy for $8. Guidelines available online.

NONFICTION No reviews of single books. "Articles and essays of breadth and depth are considered, as well as discussions of leading writers; of art, music, and drama; analyses of trends in literature, science, philosophy, and public affairs. Please include your name and contact information on the first page. We encourage page numbers." Send complete ms or query with SASE Length: 6,500 words maximum. **Pays $50.**

FICTION Wants short stories. Accepts one short story per submission. "Please include your name and contact information on the first page, and we encourage page numbers." Has published work by Ahdaf Soueif, Elizabeth Denton, Nicholas Montemarano. **Buys 10 mss/year.** Send complete ms. Length: "a maximum of 30 pages or 8000 words." **Pays $50.**

POETRY Has published poetry by Catherine Barnett, Billy Collins, and Dara Wier. "A poetry submission may consist of up to 6 poems. Please include your name and contact on every page." Submit maximum 6 poems. Length: "There are no restrictions for length, but generally our poems are less than 100 lines." **Pays 50¢/line to $25 maximum.**

⊕ MICHIGAN QUARTERLY REVIEW

0576 Rackham Bldg., 915 E. Washington, University of Michigan, Ann Arbor MI 48109-1070. (734)764-9265. **E-mail:** mqr@umich.edu. **Website:** www.michiganquarterlyreview.com. **Contact:** Jonathan Freedman, editor; Vicki Lawrence, managing editor. **75% freelance written.** Quarterly journal of literature and the humanities publishing literary essays, fiction, poetry, creative nonfiction, memoir, interviews, and book reviews. "*MQR* is an eclectic interdisciplinary journal of arts and culture that seeks to combine the best of poetry, fiction, and creative nonfiction with outstanding critical essays on literary, cultural, social, and political matters. The flagship journal of the University of Michigan, *MQR* draws on lively minds here and elsewhere, seeking to present accessible work of all varieties for sophisticated readers from within and without the academy." Estab. 1962. Circ. 1,000. Byline given. Pays on publication. No kill fee. Publishes ms an average of 1 year after acceptance. Accepts queries by mail. Responds in 2 months to queries. Responds in 2 months to mss. Sample copy for $4. Guidelines available online.

NONFICTION Special issues: Publishes theme issues. Upcoming themes available in magazine and on website. **Buys 35 mss/year.** Query. Length: 2,000-5,000 words. **Pays $10/published page.**

FICTION Contact: Fiction Editor. "No restrictions on subject matter or language. We are very selective. We like stories which are unusual in tone and structure, and innovative in language. No genre fiction written for a market. Would like to see more fiction about social, political, cultural matters, not just centered on a love relationship or dysfunctional family." Receives 300 unsolicited mss/month. Accepts 3-4 mss/issue; 12-16 mss/year. Publishes 1-2 new writers/year. Has published work by Rebecca Makkai, Peter Ho Davies, Laura Kasischke, Gerald Shapiro, Alan Cheuse. Needs literary. "No genre fictionwritten for a market. Would like to see more fiction about social, political, cultural matters, not just centered on a love relationship or dysfunctional family." **Buys 10 mss/year.** Send complete ms. Length: 1,500-7,000 words; average length: 5,000 words. **Pays $10/published page.**

POETRY No previously published poems or simultaneous submissions. No e-mail submissions. Cover letter is preferred. "It puts a human face on the ms. A few sentences of biography is all I want, nothing lengthy or defensive." Prefers typed mss. Reviews books of poetry. "All reviews are commissioned.> **Pays $8-12/published page.**

⊕ MID-AMERICAN REVIEW

Bowling Green State University, Department of English, Bowling Green OH 43403. (419)372-2725. **E-mail:** mar@bgsu.edu. **Website:** www.bgsu.edu/midamericanreview. **Contact:** Abigail Cloud, editor-in-chief. Semiannual magazine of the highest quality fiction, poetry, and translations of contemporary poetry and fiction. Also publishes critical articles and book reviews of contemporary literature. Reads mss all year. Publishes new and established writers. "We aim to put the best possible work in front of the biggest possible audience. We publish contemporary fiction, poetry, creative nonfiction, translations and book reviews." Estab. 1981. Circ. 1,400. Byline given. Pays on publication when funding is available. No kill fee. Publishes mss an average of 6 months after acceptance. Accepts queries by online submission form. Responds in 5 months to mss. Sample copy for $9 (current issue); $5 (back issue); $10 (rare back issues). Guidelines available online.

NONFICTION Needs creative nonfiction, leaning toward lyrical essays; short book reviews (400-500 words). Submit ms by post with SASE or with online submission manager. Selects 12 mss/year of 4,500 mss submitted. **Pays $10/page up to $50, pending funding.**

FICTION Contact: Abigail Cloud, editor. Publishes traditional, character-oriented, literary, experimental, prose poem, and short-short stories. Needs experimental, Memoir, prose poem, traditional. No genre fiction. **Buys 12 mss/year.** Submit ms by post with SASE or with online submission manager. Selects 12 mss/year of 4,500 mss submitted. Agented fiction 5%. Recently published work by Matthew Eck and J. David Stevens. Length: 6,000 words maximum. **Pays $10/page up to $50, pending funding.**

POETRY Contact: Jessica Zinz, editor. Submit by mail with SASE or through online submissions form at website. Publishes poems with "textured, evocative images, an awareness of how words sound and mean, and a definite sense of voice. Each line should help carry the poem, and an individual vision must be evident." Send 1-6 poems. Recently published work by Mary Ann Samyn, Sydney Lea, Bob Hicok, and Amy Newman. **Pays $10/page up to $50, pending funding.**

$$$ THE MISSOURI REVIEW

357 McReynolds Hall, University of Missouri, Columbia MO 65211. (573)882-4474. **Fax:** (573)884-4671. **E-mail:** question@moreview.com. **Website:** www.missourireview.com. **Contact:** Speer Morgan, editor. **90% freelance written.** Quarterly magazine. Estab. 1978. Circ. 6,500. Byline given. Offers signed contract. Editorial lead time 6 months. Accepts queries by mail. Responds in 2 weeks to queries. Responds in 10 weeks to mss. Sample copy for $8.95 or online. Guidelines available online.

NONFICTION Contact: Evelyn Somers, associate editor. Needs book excerpts, essays. No literary criticism. **Buys 10 mss/year.** Send complete ms. **Pays $1,000.**

FICTION Contact: Speer Morgan, editor. Needs ethnic, humorous, mainstream, novel concepts, literary. No genre or flash fiction. **Buys 25 mss/year.** Send complete ms. **Pays $30/printed page.**

POETRY Contact: Austin Segrest, poetry editor. Submit 6-12 poems at a time. Buys 50 poems/year. **Pays $30/printed page and 3 contributor's copies.**

$ MODERN HAIKU

P.O. Box 33077, Santa Fe NM 87594-3077. **E-mail:** modernhaiku@gmail.com. **Website:** http://modernhaiku.org. **85% freelance written.** Magazine published 3 times/year in February, June, and October covering haiku poetry. "*Modern Haiku* "the foremost international journal o fEnglish-language haiku and criticism, and publishes high quality material only. Haiku and related genres, articles on haiku, haiku book reviews, and translations comprise its contents. It has an international circulation; subscribers include many university, school, and public libraries." Estab. 1969. Circ. 650. Byline given. Pays on acceptance. No kill fee. Publishes ms an average of 6 months after acceptance. Editorial lead time 4 months. Accepts queries by mail, e-mail. "Now accepts submissions by e-mail; please review submission guidelines 7 policies on website." Responds in 1 week to queries. Responds in 6-8 weeks to mss. Sample copy for $15 in North America, $16 in Canada, $20 in Mexico, $22 overseas. Subscription: $35 ppd by regular mail in the U.S. Pay ment possible by PayPal on the *Modern Haiku* website. Guidelines available for SASE or on website.

NONFICTION Needs essays, anything related to haiku. Send complete ms. **Pays $5/page.**

COLUMNS/DEPARTMENTS Haiku & Senryu; Haibun; Essays (on haiku and related genres); Reviews (books of haiku or related genres). **Buys 40 essays and reviews (most are commissioned) mss/year.** Send complete ms. **Pays $5/page.**

POETRY Needs haiku, senryu, haibun, haiga. Postal submissions: "Send 5-15 haiku on 1 or 2 letter sized sheets. Put name and address at the top of each sheet. Include SASE." E-mail submissions: "May be attachments (recommended) or pasted in body of message. Subject line must read: MH Submission. Adhere to guidelines on the website. No payment for haiki sent/accepted by e-mail." Reviews of books of haiku by staff and freelancers by invitation in 350-1,000 words, usually single-book format. Send materials for review consideration with complete ordering information. Does not want "general poetry, tanka, renku, linked verse forms. No special consideration given to work by children and teens." Buys Publishes 750 poems/year. poems/year. Submit maximum Maximum number of poems: 24. poems. **Pays $1 per haiku by postal mail only (not for e-mail).**

$ NEW ENGLAND REVIEW

Middlebury College, Middlebury VT 05753. (802)443-5075. **E-mail:** nereview@middlebury.edu. **E-mail:** Carolyn Kuebler, editor. **Website:** www.nereview.com. Quarterly literary magazine. *New England Review* is a prestigious, nationally distributed literary journal. Reads September 1-May 31 (postmarked dates). Estab. 1978. Circ. 2,000. Byline given. Pays on publication. No kill fee. Publishes ms an average of 6 months after acceptance. Accepts simultaneous submissions. Responds in 2 weeks to queries. Responds in 3 months to mss. Sometimes comments on rejected mss. Sample copy for $10 (add $5 for overseas). Guidelines available online.

NONFICTION **Buys 20-25 mss/year.** Send complete ms via online submission manager or postal mail (with SASE). No e-mail submissions. Length: 7,500 words maximum, though exceptions may be made. **Pays $10/page ($20 minimum), and 2 contributor's copies.**

FICTION Send 1 story at a time, unless it is very short. Serious literary only, novel excerpts. Needs literary. **Buys 25 mss/year.** Send complete ms via online submission manager or postal mail (with SASE). No e-mail submissions. "Will consider simultaneous submissions, but must be stated as such and you must notify us immediately if the ms accepted for publication elsewhere." Prose length: not strict on word count. **Pays $10/page ($20 minimum), and 2 contributor's copies.**

POETRY Submit up to 6 poems at a time. No previously published poems or simultaneous submissions. Accepts submissions by postal mail or online submission manager only; accepts questions by e-mail. "Cover letters are useful." Address submissions to "Poetry Editor." Reads submissions postmarked September 1-May 31 only. Buys 75-90 poems/year. Submit maximum 6 poems. **Pays $10/page ($20 minimum), and 2 contributor's copies.**

$ NEW LETTERS

University of Missouri-Kansas City, 5101 Rockhill Rd., Kansas City MO 64110. (816)235-1168. **Fax:** (816)235-2611. **E-mail:** newletters@umkc.edu. **Website:** www.newletters.org. **Contact:** Robert Stewart, editor-in-chief. **100% freelance written.** Quarterly magazine. Estab. 1934. Circ. 5,000. Byline given. Pays on publication. No kill fee. Publishes ms an average of 6 months after acceptance. Editorial lead time 6 months. Submit seasonal material 6 months in advance. Accepts queries by mail. Responds in 1 month to queries; 5 months to mss. Sample copy for $10 or sample articles on website. Guidelines available online.

NONFICTION Needs essays. No self-help, how-to, or nonliterary work. **Buys 8-10 mss/year.** Send complete ms. 5,000 words maximum. **Pays $40-100.**

FICTION **Contact:** Robert Stewart, editor. Needs ethnic, experimental, humorous, mainstream, contemporary. No genre fiction. **Buys 15-20 mss/year.** Send complete ms. 5,000 words maximum. **Pays $30-75.**

POETRY Needs avant-garde, free verse, haiku, traditional. No light verse. Buys 40-50 poems/year. Submit maximum 6 poems. Open. **Pays $10-25.**

NEW OHIO REVIEW

English Department, 360 Ellis Hall, Ohio University, Athens OH 45701. (740)597-1360. **E-mail:** noreditors@ohio.edu. **Website:** www.ohiou.edu/nor. **Contact:** Jill Allyn Rosser, editor. *NOR*, published biannually in spring and fall, publishes fiction, nonfiction, and poetry. Single: $9; Subscription: $16. Member: CLMP. Reading period is September 15th to December 15th and January 15th to April 1st. Estab. 2007. Byline given. No kill fee. Accepts queries by mail, e-mail, online submission form. Accepts simultaneous submissions. Responds in 2-4 months. Guidelines available online.

NONFICTION Needs essays, humor. Submit complete ms. **Pays minimum of $30 in addition to 2 contributor's copies and 1-year subscription.**

FICTION Needs confessions, experimental, humorous, mainstream. Send complete ms. **Pays $30 minimum in addition to 2 contributor's copies and 1-year subscription.**

POETRY Needs Needs avant-garde, free verse, haiku, light verse, traditional. Submit up to 6 poems at a time. "Do not submit more than once every six months. Submit maximum 6 poems.

🍁 $$ THE NEW QUARTERLY

St. Jerome's University, 290 Westmount Rd. N., Waterloo ON N2L 3G3 Canada. (519)884-8111, ext. 28290. **E-mail:** editor@tnq.ca; pmulloy@tnq.ca. **Website:** www.tnq.ca. **95% freelance written.** Quarterly book covering Canadian fiction and poetry. "Emphasis on emerging writers and genres, but we publish more traditional work as well if the language and narrative structure are fresh." Estab. 1981. Circ. 1,000. Byline given. Pays on publication. No kill fee. Publishes ms an average of 4 months after acceptance. Editorial lead time 6 months. Accepts queries by mail. Accepts simultaneous submissions. Responds in 2 weeks to queries; 4 months to mss. Sample copy for $16.50 (cover price, plus mailing). Guidelines for #10 SASE or online.

FICTION *"Canadian work only.* We are not interested in genre fiction. We are looking for innovative, beautifully crafted, deeply felt literary fiction."* **Buys 20-25 mss/year.** Send complete ms. Does not accept submissions by e-mail. Accepts simultaneoues submissions if indicated in cover letter. 20 pages maximum **Pays $200/story.**

POETRY Needs avant-garde, free verse, traditional. *Canadian work only.* Buys 40 poems/year. Submit maximum 3 poems. **Pays $40/poem.**

THE NEW WRITER

P.O. Box 60, Cranbrook Kent TN17 2ZR United Kingdom. (44)(158)021-2626. **E-mail:** editor@thenewwriter.com. **Website:** www.thenewwriter.com. **Contact:** Abegail Morley, poetry editor. Publishes 6 issues per 18 months. Quarterly. "Contemporary writing magazine which publishes the best in fact, fiction and poetry." Estab. 1996. Circ. 1,500. Pays on publication. No kill fee. Publishes ms an average of 1 year after acceptance. Accepts queries by e-mail. Accepts simultaneous submissions. Responds in 2 months to queries. Responds in 4 months to mss. Sample copy for SASE and A4 SAE with IRCs only. Guidelines for SASE.

NONFICTION Query. Length: 1,000-2,000 words. **Pays £20-40.**

FICTION *No unsolicited mss.* Accepts fiction from subscribers only. "We will consider most categories apart from stories written for children. No horror, erotic, or cosy fiction." Query with published clips. Length: 2,000-5,000 words. **Pays £10 per story by credit voucher; additional copies for £1.50.**

POETRY Buys 50 poems/year. Submit maximum 3 poems. Length: 40 lines maximum. **Pays £5/poem.**

NINTH LETTER

Department of English, University of Illinois, 608 S. Wright St., Urbana IL 61801. (217)244-3145. **E-mail:** info@ninthletter.com; editor@ninthletter.com. **Website:** www.ninthletter.com. **Contact:** Jodee Stanley, editor. *"Ninth Letter* accepts submissions of fiction, poetry, and essays from September 1 to February 28 (postmark dates). *Ninth Letter* is published semi-annually at the University of Illinois, Urbana-Cham-

paign. We are interested in prose and poetry that experiment with form, narrative, and nontraditional subject matter, as well as more traditional literary work." Pays on publication. Accepts queries by mail, online submission form.

NONFICTION Contact: nonfiction@ninthletter.com. "Please send only one story or essay at a time. All mailed submissions must include an SASE for reply." Length: up to 8,000 words. **Pays $25 per printed page and 2 contributor's copies.**

FICTION Contact: fiction@ninthpoetry.com. "Please send only one story or essay at a time. All mailed submissions must include an SASE for reply." Length: up to 8,000 words. **Pays $25 per printed page and 2 contributor's copies.**

POETRY Contact: poetry@ninthletter.com. Submit 3-6 poems (no more than 10 pages) at a time. "All mailed submissions must include an SASE for reply." **Pays $25 per printed page and 2 contributor's copies.**

NORTH AMERICAN REVIEW

University of Northern Iowa, 1222 W. 27th St., Cedar Falls IA 50614. (319)273-6455. **Fax:** (319)273-4326. **E-mail:** nar@uni.edu. **Website:** northamericanreview.org. **Contact:** Kim Groninga, nonfiction editor. **90% freelance written.** Published 4 times/year. "The *NAR* is the oldest literary magazine in America and one of the most respected; though we have no prejudices about the subject matter of material sent to us, our first concern is quality." Estab. 1815. Circ. under 5,000. Byline given. Pays on publication. No kill fee. Publishes ms an average of 1 year after acceptance. Accepts queries by mail. Responds in 4 months to mss. Sample copy for $7. Guidelines available online.

NONFICTION Contact: Ron Sandvik, nonfiction editor. Length: Open. **Pays $5/350 words; $20 minimum, $100 maximum.**

FICTION Open (literary). "No flat narrative stories where the inferiority of the character is the paramount concern." Wants to see more "well-crafted literary stories that emphasize family concerns. We'd also like to see more stories engaged with environmental concerns." Reads fiction mss all year. Publishes ms an average of 1 year after acceptance. **Publishes 2 new writers/year.** Recently published work by Lee Ann Roripaugh, Dick Allen, Rita Welty Bourke. Needs Wants more well-crafted literary stories that emphasize family concerns. No flat narrative stories where the inferiority of the character is the paramount concern. Accepts submissions by USPS mail only. Send complete ms with SASE. Responds in 3 months to queries; 4 months to mss. No simultaneous submissions. Sample copy for $7. **Pays $5/350 words; $20 minimum, $100 maximum.**

POETRY No restrictions; highest quality only. **Pays $1/line; $20 minimum, $100 maximum.**

NOW & THEN; THE APPALACHIAN MAGAZINE

East Tennessee State University, Box 70556, Johnson City TN 37614-1707. (423)439-5348. **Fax:** (423)439-6340. **E-mail:** nowandthen@etsu.edu. **E-mail:** wardenc@etsu.edu. **Website:** www.etsu.edu/cass/nowandthen. **Contact:** Jane Woodside, editor. Literary magazine published twice/year. "*Now & Then* accepts a variety of writing genres: fiction, poetry, nonfiction, essays, interviews, memoirs, and book reviews. All submissions must relate to Appalachia and to the issue's specific theme. Our readership is educated and interested in the region." Estab. 1984. Circ. 1,000. Sample copy available for $8 plus $3 shipping. Guidelines and upcoming themes available on website.

FICTION Accepts 2-3 mss/issue. Publishes ms 4 months after acceptance. Publishes some new writers/year. Needs adventure, ethnic/multicultural, experimental, fantasy, historical, humor/satire, literary, mainstream, regional, slice-of-life vignettes, excerpted novel, prose poem, "Absolutely has to relate to Appalachian theme. Can be about adjustment to new environment, themes of leaving and returning, for instance. Nothing unrelated to region." Send complete ms. Accepts submissions by mail, e-mail. Include "information we can use for contributor's note." SASE (or IRC). Responds in 5 months to queries; 5 months to mss. Accepts simultaneous submissions "but let us know when it has been accepted elsewhere right away." Sample copy for $5. Writer's guidelines online. Reviews fiction. Length: 1,000-1,500 words. **Pays $30-100. Pays on publication.**

POETRY Submit up to 5 poems, with SASE and cover letter including "a few lines about yourself for a contributor's note and whether the work has been published or accepted elsewhere." Will consider simultaneous submissions; occasionally accepts previously published poems. Put name, address and phone number on every poem. Deadlines: March 31 (spring/summer issue) and August 31 (fall/winter issues). Publishes theme issues. Responds within 6 months.

Sends prepublication galleys. Pays $20/poem plus 2 contributor's copies.

🌑🌑🌑 THE PARIS REVIEW

62 White St., New York NY 10013. (212)343-1333. **E-mail:** queries@theparisreview.org. **Website:** www.theparisreview.org. Nathaniel Rich, fiction editor. **Contact:** Lorin Stein, editor. Quarterly magazine. "Fiction and poetry of superlative quality, whatever the genre, style or mode. Our contributors include prominent, as well as less well-known and previously unpublished writers. Writers at Work interview series includes important contemporary writers discussing their own work and the craft of writing." Pays on publication. No kill fee. Accepts queries by mail. Accepts simultaneous submissions. Responds in 4 months to mss. Sample copy for $12 (includes postage). Guidelines available online.

FICTION Study the publication. Annual Aga Khan Fiction Contest award of $1,000. Recently published work by Karl Taro Greenfeld, J. Robert Lennon, and Belle Boggs. Send complete ms. no limit **Pays $500-1,000.**

POETRY Contact: Richard Howard, poetry editor. Submit no more than six poems at a time. Poetry can be sent to the poetry editor (please include a self-addressed, stamped envelope), or submitted online at http://www.theparisreview.org/poetry/. **Pays $35 minimum varies according to length. Awards $1,000 in Bernard F. Conners Poetry Prize contest.**

🌑🌑 PARNASSUS: POETRY IN REVIEW

Poetry in Review Foundation, 205 W. 89th St., #8F, New York NY 10024. (212)362-3492. **E-mail:** parnew@aol.com. **Website:** www.parnassusreview.com. **Contact:** Herbert Leibowitz, editor and publisher. Annual magazine covering poetry and criticism. "We now publish 1 double issue a year." Estab. 1972. Circ. 1,800. Byline given. Pays on publication. No kill fee. Publishes ms an average of 12-14 months after acceptance. Accepts queries by mail. Responds in 2 months to mss. Sample copy for $15.

NONFICTION Needs essays. **Buys 30 mss/year.** Query with published clips. Length: 1,500-7,500 words. **Pays $200-750.**

POETRY Needs avant garde, free verse, traditional. Accepts most types of poetry. Buys 3-4 unsolicited poems/year.

PEARL

3030 E. Second St., Long Beach CA 90803. (562)434-4523. **E-mail:** pearlmag@aol.com. **Website:** www.pearlmag.com. **Contact:** Joan Jobe Smith and Marilyn Johnson, poetry editors. Biannual magazine featuring poetry, short fiction, and black and white artwork. We also sponsor the Pearl Poetry Prize, an annual contest for a full length book, as well as the Pearl Short Story Prize. *"Pearl* is an eclectic publication, a place for lively, readable poetry and prose that speaks to real people about real life in direct, living language, profane or sublime." Estab. 1974. Pays with contributor's copy. No kill fee. Publishes ms an average of 6-12 months after acceptance. Accepts queries by mail. Accepts simultaneous submissions. Sample copy for $10. Guidelines available online.

FICTION "Our annual fiction issue features the winner of our Pearl Short Story Prize contest as well as 'short-shorts,' and some of the longer stories in our contest. Length: 1,200 words. No obscure, experimental fiction. The winner of the Pearl Short Story Prize receives $250 and 10 copies of the issue the story appears in . A $15 entry fee includes a copy of the magazine; all entries are considered for publication." Nothing sentimental, obscure, predictable, abstract or cliché-ridden poetry or fiction. Length: 1,200 words. **Short Story Prize of $250, 100 copies of the issue the story appears in.**

POETRY "Our poetry issue contains a 12-15 page section featuring the work of a single poet. Entry fee for the Pearl Poetry Prize is $20, which includes a copy of the winning book." No sentimental, obscure, predictable, abstract or cliché-ridden poetry. Submit maximum 3-5 poems. 40 lines max. Send with cover letter and SASE.

THE PEDESTAL MAGAZINE

6815 Honors Court, Charlotte NC 28210. (704)643-0244. **E-mail:** pedmagazine@carolina.rr.com. **Website:** www.thepedestalmagazine.com. **Contact:** John Amen, editor-in-chief. Bimonthly website currently accepting submissions of poetry, fiction, and nonfiction. "We are committed to promoting diversity and celebrating the voice of the individual." Estab. 2000. No kill fee. Publishes ms 2-4 weeks after acceptance. Accepts queries by e-mail. Accepts simultaneous submissions. Responds in 4-6 weeks to mss. Guidelines available online.

NONFICTION Needs essays, Reviews, interview. **Pays 2¢/word. Pays for unsolicited articles.**

FICTION "We are receptive to all sorts of high-quality literary fiction. Genre fiction is encouraged as long as it crosses or comments upon its genre and is both character-driven and psychologically acute. We encourage submissions of short fiction, no more than 3 flash fiction pieces at a time. There is no need to query prior to submitting; please submit via the submission form—no email to the editor." Needs adventure, ethnic, experimental, historical, horror, humorous, mainstream, mystery, romance, science fiction, Works that don't fit into a specific category. **Buys 10-25 mss/year.** Query by e-mail. Length: 4,000 words. **Pays $40/poem ; 8¢/word.**

POETRY "We are open to a wide variety of poetry, ranging from the highly experimental to the traditionally formal. Submit all poems in 1 form. No need to query before submitting." Submit maximum 6 poems. No length restriction.

PLOUGHSHARES

Emerson College, Ploughshares, 120 Boylston St., Boston MA 02116. **Website:** www.pshares.org. **Contact:** Ladette Randolph, editor-in-chief/executive director; Andrea Martucci, managing editor. *Ploughshares*, published 3 times/year, is "a journal of new writing guest-edited by prominent poets and writers to reflect different and contrasting points of view. Translations are welcome if permission has been granted. Our mission is to present dynamic, contrasting views on what is valid and important in contemporary literature and to discover and advance significant literary talent. Each issue is guest-edited by a different writer. We no longer structure issues around preconceived themes." Editors have included Carolyn Forché, Gerald Stern, Rita Dove, Chase Twichell, and Marilyn Hacker. Has published poetry by Donald Hall, Li-Young Lee, Robert Pinsky, Brenda Hillman, and Thylias Moss. Ploughshares is 200 pages, digest-sized. Receives about 11,000 poetry, fiction, and essay submissions/year. Press run is 6,000. Subscription: $30 domestic, $30 plus shipping (see website) foreign. Sample: $14 current issue, $7 back issue, please inquire for shipping rates. Estab. 1971. Circ. 6,000. Pays on publication. Publishes ms an average of 6 months after acceptance. Accepts queries by mail, online submission form. Accepts simultaneous submissions. Responds in 5 months to mss. Guidelines available online.

NONFICTION Needs essays. Length: 3,00-10,000 words. **Pays $25/printed page; $50 minimum, $250 maximum.**

FICTION Recently published work by ZZ Packer, Antonya Nelson, Stuart Dybek. Needs mainstream, literary. "No genre (science fiction, detective, gothic, adventure, etc.), popular formula or commerical fiction whose purpose is to entertain rather than to illuminate."

POETRY Needs Needs avant-garde, free verse, traditional. Submit 1-3 poems at a time.

POEM

Huntsville Literary Association, P.O. Box 2006, Huntsville AL 35804. **E-mail:** poem@hla-hsv.org. **Website:** www.hlahsv.org. **Contact:** Rebecca Harbor, editor; Peggy Brosious, assistant editor; Harry V. Moore, assistant editor. *Poem*, published twice/year in the spring and fall, consists entirely of poetry. "We publish both traditional forms and free verse." Wants poems "characterized by compression, rich vocabulary, significant content, and evidence of 'a tuned ear and practiced pen.' We want coherent work that moves through the particulars of the poem to make a point. We equally welcome submissions from established poets as well as from less-known and beginning poets." Does not want translations. Has published poetry by Kathryn Kirkpatrick, Peter Serchuk, and Kim Bridgford. *Poem* is 90 pages, digest-sized, flat-spined, printed on good stock paper, with a clean design and a matte cover. Prints more than 60 poems/issue, generally featured 1 to a page. Press run is 500. Single copy: $10; subscription: $20. Sample: $7 (back issue). Estab. 1967. Circ. 500. Accepts queries by mail. Responds in 1-3 months.

POETRY "Submit 3-5 poems, preferably with a cover letter. Place name, address, telephone number, and email address on cover letter and on each poem. Include SASE with sufficient postage. Submissions are read throughout the year. We equally welcome submissions from established poets as well as from less known and beginning poets. We publish both traditional forms and free verse. We want poems characterized by compression, rich vocabulary, significant content, and evidence of 'a tuned ear and practiced pen.' We want coherent work that moves through the particulars of the poem to make a point." "We do not

want "greeting card verse" or proselytizing or didactic poems." **Pays 2 contributor's copies.**

ⓢ POETRY

The Poetry Foundation, 61 W. Superior St., Chicago IL 60654. (312)787-7070. **Fax:** (312)787-6650. **E-mail:** editors@poetrymagazine.org. **Website:** www.poetrymagazine.org. Christian Wiman, Editor. **Contact:** Helen Klaviter. **100% freelance written.** Monthly magazine. *Poetry*'s website offers featured poems, letters, reviews, interviews, essays, and web-exclusive features. *Poetry*, published monthly by The Poetry Foundation (see separate listing in Organizations), "has no special manuscript needs and no special requirements as to form or genre: We examine in turn all work received and accept that which seems best." Has published poetry by the major voices of our time as well as new talent. *Poetry* is elegantly printed, flat-spined. Receives 90,000 submissions/year, accepts about 300-350. Press run is 16,000. Single copy: $3.75; subscription: $35 ($38 for institutions). Sample: $5.50. Estab. 1912. Circ. 31,000. Byline given. Pays on publication. No kill fee. Publishes ms an average of 9 months after acceptance. Accepts queries by mail. Responds in 1-2 months to mss and queries. Sample copy for $3.75 or online at website. Guidelines available online.

NONFICTION Buys 14 mss/year. Query. Length: 1,000-2,000 words. **Pays $150/page.**

POETRY Accepts all styles and subject matter. Submit no more than 4 poems at a time. No previously published poems or simultaneous submissions. Electronic submission preferred. When submitting by post put return address on outside of envelope; include SASE. Submissions must be typed, single-spaced, with poet's name and address on every page. Pays $10/line (with a minimum payment of $300). Reviews books of poetry in multi-book formats of varying lengths. Does not accept unsolicited reviews. Buys 180-250 poems/year. Submit maximum 4 poems. **Pays $10/line ($150 minimum payment).**

◎ ⓢ THE PRAIRIE JOURNAL

P.O. Box 68073, 28 Crowfoot Terrace NW, Calgary AB Y3G 3N8 Canada. **E-mail:** editor@prairiejournal.org (queries only); prairiejournal@yahoo.com. **Website:** www.prairiejournal.org. **Contact:** A.E. Burke, literary editor. **100% freelance written.** Semiannual magazine publishing quality poetry, short fiction, drama, literary criticism, reviews, bibliography, interviews, profiles, and artwork. "The audience is literary, university, library, scholarly, and creative readers/writers." Estab. 1983. Circ. 650-750. Byline given. Pays on publication. No kill fee. Publishes ms an average of 4-6 months after acceptance. Editorial lead time 2-6 months. Accepts queries by mail, e-mail. Responds in 2 weeks to queries; 2-6 months to mss. Sample copy for $5. Guidelines available online.

NONFICTION Needs essays, humor, interview, literary. No inspirational, news, religious, or travel. **Buys 25-40 mss/year.** Query with published clips. Length: 100-3,000 words. **Pays $50-100, plus contributor's copy.**

COLUMNS/DEPARTMENTS Reviews (books from small presses publishing poetry, short fiction, essays, and criticism), 200-1,000 words. **Buys 5 mss/year.** Query with published clips. **Pays $10-50.**

FICTION No genre (romance, horror, western—sagebrush or cowboys), erotic, science fiction, or mystery. **Buys 6 mss/year.** Send complete ms. No e-mail submissions. Length: 100-3,000 words. **Pays $10-75.**

POETRY Needs avant-garde, free verse, haiku. *The Prairie Journal*, published twice/year, seeks poetry "of any length; free verse, contemporary themes (feminist, nature, urban, non-political), aesthetic value, a poet's poetry." Does not want to see "most rhymed verse, sentimentality, egotistical ravings. No cowboys or sage brush." Has published poetry by Liliane Welch, Cornelia Hoogland, Sheila Hyland, Zoe Lendale, and Chad Norman. *The Prairie Journal* is 40-60 pages, digest-sized, offset-printed, saddle-stapled, with card cover, includes ads. Receives about 1,000 poems/year, accepts 10%. Press run is 600; the rest are sold on newsstands. Subscription: $10 for individuals, $18 for libraries. Sample: $8 ("use postal money order"). No U.S. stamps. No heroic couplets or greeting card verse. Buys 25-35 poems/year. Submit maximum 6-8 poems. Length: 3-50 lines. **Pays $5-50.**

↻ Ⓢ PRISM INTERNATIONAL

Department of Creative Writing, Buch E462, 1866 Main Mall, University of British Columbia, Vancouver BC V6T 1Z1 Canada. (604)822-2514. **Fax:** (604)822-3616. **E-mail:** prismcirculation@gmail.com. **Website:** www.prismmagazine.ca. **100% freelance written. Works with new/unpublished writers.** A quarterly international journal of contemporary writing—fiction, poetry, drama, creative nonfiction and translation. *PRISM international* is 80 pages, digest-sized, elegantly printed, flat-spined, with original color artwork on a glossy card cover. Readership: public and university libraries, individual subscriptions, bookstores—a world-wide audience concerned with the contemporary in literature. "We have no thematic or stylistic allegiances: Excellence is our main criterion for acceptance of manuscripts." Receives 1,000 submissions/year, accepts about 80. Circulation is for 1,200 subscribers. Subscription: $35/year for Canadian subscriptions, $40/year for US subscriptions, $45/year for international. Sample: $12. Estab. 1959. Circ. 1,200. Pays on publication. No kill fee. Publishes ms an average of 4 months after acceptance. Accepts queries by mail and online. Responds in 4 months to queries. Responds in 3-6 months to mss. Sample copy for $12, more info online. Guidelines available online.

NONFICTION No reviews, tracts, or scholarly essays. **Pays $20/printed page, and 1-year subscription.**

FICTION For Drama: one-acts/excerpts of no more than 1500 words preferred. Also interested in seeing dramatic monologues. Needs experimental, novel concepts, traditional, "New writing that is contemporary and literary. Short stories and self-contained novel excerpts. Works of translation are eagerly sought and should be accompanied by a copy of the original. Would like to see more translations. No gothic, confession, religious, romance, pornography, or science fiction." **Buys 12-16 mss/year.** Send complete ms. 25 pages maximum **Pays $20/printed page, and 1-year subscription**.

POETRY Needs avant-garde, traditional. Wants "fresh, distinctive poetry that shows an awareness of traditions old and new. We read everything." Considers poetry by children and teens. "Excellence is the only criterion." Has published poetry by Margaret Avison, Elizabeth Bachinsky, John Pass, Warren Heiti, Don McKay, Bill Bissett, and Stephanie Bolster. Submit maximum 6 poems. **Pays $40/printed page, and 1-year subscription**.

QUARTERLY WEST

University of Utah, 255 S. Central Campus Dr., Room 3500, Salt Lake City UT 84112. **E-mail:** quarterlywest@gmail.com. **Website:** www.quarterlywest.utah.edu. **Contact:** C.A. Schaefer & Sadie Hoagland, editors. Semiannual magazine. "We publish fiction, poetry, and nonfiction in long and short formats, and will consider experimental as well as traditional works." Estab. 1976. Circ. 1,900. Pays on publication.

Publishes ms an average of 6 months after acceptance. Accepts queries by online submission form. Accepts simultaneous submissions. Responds in 6 months to mss. Sample copy for $7.50 or online. Guidelines available online.

NONFICTION Needs essays, interview, personal experience, travel, book reviews. **Buys 6-8 mss/year.** Send complete ms using online submissions manager. 10,000 words maximum. **Pays $20-100.**

FICTION No preferred lengths; interested in longer, fuller short stories and short shorts. Needs ethnic, experimental, humorous, mainstream, novel concepts, slice-of-life vignettes, short shorts, translations. No detective, science fiction or romance. **Buys 6-10 mss/year.** Send complete ms using online submissions manager. **Pays $15-100, and 2 contributor's copies.**

POETRY Needs avant-garde, free verse, traditional. Submit 3-5 poems at a time using online submissions manager. Buys 40-50 poems/year. Submit maximum 5 poems. **Pays $15-100.**

🌐 $$ QUEEN'S QUARTERLY

144 Barrie St., Queen's University, Kingston ON K7L 3N6 Canada. (613)533-2667. **Fax:** (613)533-6822. **E-mail:** queens.quarterly@queensu.ca. **Website:** www.queensu.ca/quarterly. **Contact:** Joan Harcourt, editor. **95% freelance written.** Quartlery literary magazine. *Queen's Quarterly* is "a general interest intellectual review featuring articles on science, politics, humanities, arts and letters, extensive book reviews, some poetry and fiction." Estab. 1893. Circ. 3,000. Byline given. Pays on publication. Publishes ms on average 6-12 months after acceptance. Accepts queries by e-mail. Responds in 2-3 months to queries. Free sample copy and guidelines online.

NONFICTION Contact: Boris Castel, editor (articles, essays and reviews).

FICTION Contact: Joan Harcourt, literary editor (fiction and poetry). Needs historical, literary, mainstream, novel excerpts, short stories, women's. "Special emphasis on work by Canadian writers." Send complete ms with SASE and/or IRC. No reply with insufficient postage. Accepts 2 mss/issue; 8 mss/year. Publishes 5 new writers/year. Length: 2,500-3,000 words. "Submissions over 3,000 words shall not be accepted." **Pays on publication for first North American serial rights. Sends galleys to author.**

POETRY Submit up to 6 poems at a time. No simultaneous submissions. Submissions can be sent on hard copy with a SASE (no replies/returns for foreign submissions unless accompanied by an IRC) or by e-mail and will be responded to by same. Responds in 1 month. "We are especially interested in poetry by Canadian writers. Shorter poems preferred." Has published poetry by Evelyn Lau, Sue Nevill, and Raymond Souster. Each issue contains about 12 pages of poetry. Buys 25 poems/year. **Pays usually $50 (Canadian)/poem, "but it varies," plus 2 copies.**

🌐 $ THE SAVAGE KICK LITERARY MAGAZINE

Murder Slim Press, 29 Alpha Rd., Gorleston Norfolk NR31 0EQ United Kingdom. **E-mail:** moonshine@murderslim.com. **Website:** www.murderslim.com. **100% freelance written.** Semiannual magazine. "*Savage Kick* primarily deals with viewpoints outside the mainstream: honest emotions told in a raw, simplistic way. It is recommended that you are very familiar with the *SK* style before submitting. We have only accepted 8 new writers in 4 years of the magazine. Ensure you have a distinctive voice and story to tell." Estab. 2005. Circ. 500+. Byline given. Pays on acceptance. Publishes ms an average of up to 2 months after acceptance. Accepts queries by mail, e-mail. Accepts simultaneous submissions. Responds in 7-10 days to queries. Guidelines free.

NONFICTION Needs interview, personal experience. **Buys 10-20 mss/year.** Send complete ms. Length: 500-3,000 words. **Pays $25-35.**

COLUMNS/DEPARTMENTS Buys up to 4 mss/year. Query. **Pays $25-35.**

FICTION Needs mystery, slice-of-life vignettes, crime. "Real-life stories are preferred, unless the work is distinctively extreme within the crime genre. No poetry of any kind, no mainstream fiction, Oprah-style fiction, Internet/chat language, teen issues, excessive Shakespearean language, surrealism, overworked irony, or genre fiction (horror, fantasy, science fiction, western, erotica, etc.)." **Buys 10-25 mss/year.** Send complete ms. Length: 500-6,000 words. **Pays $35.**

THE SEWANEE REVIEW

University of the South, 735 University Ave., Sewanee TN 37383-1000. (931)598-1000. **Website:** www.sewanee.edu/sewanee_review. The *Sewanee Review* is America's oldest continuously published literary quarterly. Publishes "original fiction, poetry, essays on literary and related subjects, and book reviews for well-educated readers who appreciate good American and English literature." Only erudite work representing depth of knowledge and skill of expression is published. Estab. 1892. Circ. 2,200. Pays on publication. Responds in 6-8 weeks to mss. Sample copy for $8.50 ($9.50 outside US). Guidelines available online.

FICTION Send query letter for reviews. Send complete ms for fiction. Needs literary, contemporary. No erotica, science fiction, fantasy or excessively violent or profane material. **Buys 10-15 mss/year.** Length: 3,500-7,500 words. **Pays $10-12/printed page, plus 2 contributor's copies.**

POETRY Submit up to 6 poems at a time. "Please keep in mind that for each poem published in *The Sewanee Review*, approximately 250 poems are considered." Submit maximum 6 poems. Length: 40 lines maximum/poem. **Pays $2.50/line, plus 2 contributor's copies (and reduced price for additional copies).**

SHENANDOAH

Washington and Lee University, 17 Courthouse Square, Lexington VA 24450. (540)458-8908. **Fax:** (540)458-8461. **E-mail:** shenandoah@wlu.edu. **Website:** http://shenandoahliterary.org. **Contact:** R.T. Smith, editor. Semiannual digital-only literary journal. "For over half a century, *Shenandoah* has been publishing splendid poems, stories, essays, and reviews which display passionate understanding, formal accomplishment and serious mischief." Estab. 1950. Circ. 2,000. Byline given. Pays on publication. No kill fee. Publishes ms an average of 10 months after acceptance. Responds in 3 months to mss. Sample copy for $12. Guidelines available online.

NONFICTION Needs essays, book reviews. **Buys 6 mss/year.** Send complete ms. **Pays $25/page ($250 maximum).**

FICTION Needs mainstream, novel excerpts. "No sloppy, hasty, slight fiction." **Buys 15 mss/year.** Send complete ms. **Pays $25/page ($250 maximum).**

POETRY Considers simultaneous submissions "only if we are immediately informed of acceptance elsewhere." No e-mail submissions. All submissions should be typed on 1 side of the paper only, with name and address clearly written on the upper right corner of the ms. Staff reviews books of poetry in 7-10 pages, multibook format. Send materials for review consideration. (Most reviews are solicited.) "No inspirational, confessional poetry." Buys 70 poems/year.

Submit maximum 5 poems. **Pays $2.50/line, 1-year subscription, and 1 contributor's copy.**

SHORT STUFF

Bowman Publications, 2001 I St., #5, Fairbury NE 68352. (402)587-5003. **E-mail:** shortstf89@aol.com. **98% freelance written.** Bimonthly magazine publishing short fiction that is holiday oriented. "We are perhaps an enigma in that we publish only clean stories in any genre. We'll tackle any subject, but don't allow obscene language or pornographic description. Our magazine is for grown-ups, not X-rated 'adult' fare." Estab. 1989. Circ. 5,000. Byline given. Payment and contract upon publication. Editorial lead time 3 months. Submit seasonal material 3 months in advance. Responds in 6 months to mss. Sample copy: send 9x12 SAE with 5 first-class (44¢) stamps. Guidelines for #10 SASE.

NONFICTION Needs humor. Special issues: "We are holiday oriented and each issue reflects the appropriate holidays." Issues are Valentine's (February/March); Easter (April/May), Mom's and Dad's (June/July); Americana (August/September); Halloween (October/November); and Holiday (December/January). **Buys 30 mss/year.** Send complete ms. Include cover letter about the author and synopsis of the story. Length: 500-1,500 words. **Payment varies.**

FICTION Receives 500 unsolicited mss/month. Accepts 9-12 mss/issue; 76 mss/year. Has published work by Bill Hallstead, Dede Hammond, Skye Gibbons. Needs adventure, historical, humorous, mainstream, mystery, romance, science fiction, (seldom), suspense, western. "We want to see more humor—not essay format—real stories with humor; 1,000-word mysteries, modern lifestyles. The 1,000-word pieces have the best chance of publication. No erotica; nothing morbid or pornographic. **Buys 144 mss/year.** Send complete ms. Length: 500-1,500 words. **Payment varies.**

FILLERS Needs anecdotes, short humor. **Buys 200 mss/year.** Length: 20-500 words. **Filler pays variable amount.**

SNOWY EGRET

The Fair Press, P.O. Box 9265, Terre Haute IN 47808. **Website:** www.snowyegret.net. *Snowy Egret*, published in spring and autumn, specializes in work that is "nature-oriented: poetry that celebrates the abundance and beauty of nature or explores the interconnections between nature and the human psyche." Has published poetry by Conrad Hilberry, Lyn Lifshin,

Gayle Eleanor, James Armstrong, and Patricia Hooper. *Snowy Egret* is 60 pages, magazine-sized, offset-printed, saddle-stapled. Receives about 500 poems/year, accepts about 30. Press run is 400. Sample: $8; subscription: $15/year, $25 for 2 years. Semiannual. Estab. 1922. Circ. 400. Pays on publication. Submission guidelines online at website.

FICTION "We publish works which celebrate the abundance and beauty of nature and examine the variety of ways in which human beings interact with landscapes and living things. Nature writing from literary, artistic, psychological, philosophical and historical perspectives." "No genre fiction, e.g., horror, western, romance, etc." Send complete ms with SASE. Cover letter optional: do not query. Responds in 2 months to mss. Accepts simultaneous submissions if noted. **Pays $2/page plus 2 contributor's copies.**

POETRY Guidelines available on website. Responds in 1 month. Always sends prepublication galleys. **Pays $4/poem or $4/page plus 2 contributor's copies. Acquires first North American and one-time reprint rights.**

SO TO SPEAK

George Mason University, 4400 University Dr., MSN 2C5, Fairfax VA 22030-4444. **E-mail:** sts@gmu.edu (inquiries only). **Website:** http://sotospeakjournal.org. **Contact:** Kate Partridge, editor-in-chief. *So to Speak*, published semiannually, prints "high-quality work relating to feminism, including poetry, fiction, nonfiction (including book reviews and interviews), photography, artwork, collaborations, lyrical essays, and other genre-questioning texts." Wants "work that addresses issues of significance to women's lives and movements for women's equality and are especially interested in pieces that explore issues of race, class, and sexuality in relation to gender." Estab. 1993. Publishes ms 6-8 months after acceptance. Accepts simultaneous submissions. Responds in 6 months to mss. Sample copy: $7.

NONFICTION Contact: Christine Widmayer, nonfiction editor. Needs ethnic/multicultural, experimental, feminist, lesbian, literary, mainstream, regional, translations. Receives 100 unsolicited mss/month. Accepts 3-5 mss/issue; 6-10 mss/year. Accepts submissions only via submissions manager on website. Does not accept paper or e-mail submissions. "Nonfiction submitted during the August 1–October 15 reading period will be considered for our Spring annual nonfiction contest and must be accompanied by a $15 reading fee. Nonfiction submitted during the January 1–March 15 reading period will be considered for our Fall Issue and requires no reading fee." Sponsors awards/contests. Length: 4,500 words maximum. **Pays contributor copies.**

FICTION Contact: Dan Hong, fiction editor. Receives 100 unsolicited mss/month. Accepts 3-5 mss/issue; 6-10 mss/year. Publishes 7 new writers/year. Sponsors awards/contests. Needs ethnic/multicultural, experimental, feminist, lesbian, literary, mainstream, regional, translations. No science fiction, mystery, genre romance. Accepts submissions only via submissions manager on website. Does not accept paper or e-mail submissions. "Fiction submitted during the August 1–October 15 reading period will be considered for our Spring Issue and requires no reading fee. Fiction submitted during the January 1–March 15 reading period will be considered for our Fall annual fiction contest and must be accompanied by a $15 reading fee. See contest guidelines. Contest entries will not be returned." Length: 4,500 words maximum. **Pays contributor copies.**

POETRY Contact: Sheila McMullin, poetry editor. Receives about 800 poems/year; accepts 10%. Accepts submissions only via submissions manager on website. Submit 3-5 poems at a time. Considers simultaneous submissions; no previously published poems. No e-mail or paper submissions. "Please submit poems as you wish to see them in print. Be sure to include a cover letter with full contact info, publication credits, and awards received." Reads submissions August 15-October 15 and December 31-March 15. Seldom comments on rejected poems. Responds in 3 months if submissions are received during reading period. **Pays 2 contributor's copies.** *So to Speak* **holds an annual poetry contest that awards $500. Guidelines available for SASE, by e-mail, or on website.**

THE SOUTHERN REVIEW

Louisiana State University, Old President's House, Baton Rouge LA 70803-5001. (225)578-5108. **Fax:** (225)578-5098. **E-mail:** southernreview@lsu.edu. **Website:** www.lsu.edu/tsr. **Contact:** Jeanne Leiby, Editor. **100% freelance written. Works with a moderate number of new/unpublished writers each year; reads unsolicited mss.** Quarterly magazine with emphasis on contemporary literature in the US and abroad. Reading period: September1-June 1. All mss. submitted during summer months will be recycled. Estab. 1935. Circ. 2,900. Byline given. Pays on publication. No kill fee. Publishes ms an average of 6 months after acceptance. Accepts queries by mail. Does not accept previously published work.Responds in 2 months. Sample copy for $8. Guidelines available online.

NONFICTION **Buys 25 mss/year.** Length: 4,000-10,000 words. **Pays $30/page.**

FICTION **Contact:** Jessica Faust-Spitzfaden, assistant editor. Short stories of lasting literary merit, with emphasis on style and technique; novel excerpts. "We emphasize style and substantial content. No mystery, fantasy or religious mss." Submit one ms. in any genre at a time. "We rarely publish work that is longer than 8,000 words. We consider novel excerpts if they stand alone." Length: 4,000-8,000 words. **Pays $30/page.**

POETRY Submit maximum 5/time poems. 1-4 pages **Pays $30/page.**

$$ THE STRAND MAGAZINE

P.O. Box 1418, Birmingham MI 48012-1418. (248)788-5948. **Fax:** (248)874-1046. **E-mail:** strandmag@strandmag.com. **Website:** www.strandmag.com. Quarterly magazine covering mysteries, short stories, essays, book reviews. After an absence of nearly half a century, the magazine known to millions for bringing Sir Arthur Conan Doyle's ingenious detective, Sherlock Holmes, to the world has once again appeared on the literary scene. First launched in 1891, *The Strand*,included in its pages the works of some of the greatest writers of the 20th century: Agatha Christie, Dorothy Sayers, Margery Allingham, W. Somerset Maugham, Graham Greene, P.G. Wodehouse, H.G. Wells, Aldous Huxley and many others. In 1950, economic difficulties in England caused a drop in circulation which forced the magazine to cease publication. Estab. 1998. Circ. 50,000. Byline given. Pays on acceptance. No kill fee. Publishes ms an average of 4 months after acceptance. Accepts queries by e-mail. Responds in 1 month to queries. Guidelines for #10 SASE.

FICTION **Contact:** A.F. Gulli, editor. Needs horror, humorous, mystery, detective stories, suspense, tales of the unexpected, tales of terror and the supernatural written in the classic tradition of this century's great authors. We are not interested in submissions with any sexual content. Query first. Include SASE. Length: 2,000-6,000 words. **Pays $50-175.**

$$$ SUBTROPICS

University of Florida, P.O. Box 112075, 4008 Turlington Hall, Gainesville FL 32611-2075. **E-mail:** subtropics@english.ufl.edu. **Website:** www.english.ufl.edu/subtropics. **Contact:** David Leavitt. **100% freelance written.** Publishes "the best new fiction, poetry, literary nonfiction, and translation by emerging and established writers. In addition to new work, *Subtropics* also, from time to time, republishes important and compelling stories, essays, and poems that have lapsed out of print." "Magazine published twice year through the University of Florida's English department. *Subtropics* seeks to publish the best literary fiction, essays, and poetry being written today, both by established and emerging authors. We will consider works of fiction of any length, from short shorts to novellas and self-contained novel excerpts. We give the same latitude to essays. We appreciate work in translation and, from time to time, republish important and compelling stories, essays, and poems that have lapsed out of print by writers no longer living." Member CLMP. Estab. 2005. Byline given. Pays on acceptance. Publishes ms an average of 6 months after acceptance. Responds in 1 month to queries and mss. Rarely comments on/critiques rejected mss Sample copy available for $12.95. Guidelines available on website.

NONFICTION Needs essays, literary nonfiction. No book reviews. **Buys 4-5 mss/year.** Send complete ms. **Pays $1,000.**

FICTION Receives 1,000 mss/month. Accepts 5-6 mss/issue; 10-12 mss/year. Does not read May 1-August 31. Agented fiction 33%. Publishes 1-2 new writers/year. Has published John Barth, Ariel Dorfman, Tony D'Souza, Allan Gurganus, Frances Hwang, Kuzhali Manickavel, Eileen Pollack, Padgett Powell, Nancy Reisman, Jarret Rosenblatt, Joanna Scott, and Olga Slavnikova. Needs literary fiction, short shorts. No genre fiction. **Buys 20 mss/year.** Send complete ms with cover letter. Send disposable copy of ms. Replies via e-mail only. Do not include SASE. Considers simultaneous submissions. Average length: 5,000 words. Average length of short shorts: 400 words. **Pays $500 for short shorts; $1,000 for full stories; 2 contributor's copies.**

POETRY Submit in hard copy by mail. Include cover letter with contact information on both letter and on submission. Responds by e-mail. Submission period September 1-May 1. Does not return ms. "We do not accept simultaneous submissions in poetry." Buys 50 poems/year. Submit maximum 5 poems. **Pays $100 per poem.**

◎ TAMPA REVIEW

University of Tampa Press, 401 W. Kennedy Blvd., Tampa FL 33606. (813)253-6266. **Fax:** (813)258-7593. **E-mail:** utpress@ut.edu. **Website:** www.ut.edu/tampareview. **Contact:** Richard Mathews, editor. Semiannual magazine published in hardback format. An international literary journal publishing art and literature from Florida and Tampa Bay as well as new work and translations from throughout the world. Estab. 1988. Circ. 500. Byline given. Pays on publication. No kill fee. Publishes ms an average of 10 months after acceptance. Editorial lead time 18 months. Accepts queries by mail. Responds in 5 months to mss. Sample copy for $7. Guidelines available online.

NONFICTION Contact: Elizabeth Winston. Needs general interest, interview, personal experience, creative nonfiction. No how-to articles, fads, journalistic reprise, etc. **Buys 6 mss/year.** Send complete ms. Length: 250-7,500 words. **Pays $10/printed page.**

FICTION Contact: Audrey Colombe; Julie Iromuanya. Needs ethnic, experimental, fantasy, historical, mainstream, literary. "We are far more interested in quality than in genre. Nothing sentimental as opposed to genuinely moving, nor self-conscious style at the expense of human truth." **Buys 6 mss/year.** Send complete ms. Include brief bio. Length: 200-5,000 words. **Pays $10/printed page.**

POETRY Contact: Elizabeth Winston. Needs avantgarde, free verse, haiku, light verse, traditional. No greeting card verse, hackneyed, sing-song, rhymefor-the-sake-of-rhyme. Buys 45 poems/year. Submit maximum 10 poems. Length: 2-225 lines.

THEMA

Thema Literary Society, P.O. Box 8747, Metairie LA 70011-8747. **E-mail:** thema@cox.net. **Website:** http://themaliterarysociety.com. **Contact:** Gail Howard, poetry editor. **100% freelance written.** "THEMA is designed to stimulate creative thinking by challenging writers with unusual themes, such as 'The Box Under the Bed' and 'Put It In Your Pocket, Lillian.' Appeals to writers, teachers of creative writing, and general reading audience." Estab. 1988. Byline given. Pays on acceptance. No kill fee. Publishes ms, on average, within 6 months after acceptance. Responds in 1 week to queries. Responds in 5 months to mss. Sample $10 U.S./$15 foreign. Upcoming themes and guidelines available in magazine, for SASE, by e-mail, or on website.

◯ *THEMA* is 100 pages, digest-sized professionally printed, with glossy card cover. Receives about 400 poems/year, accepts about 8%. Press run is 400 (230 subscribers, 30 libraries). Subscription: $20 U.S./$30 foreign. Has published poetry by Beverly Boyd, Elizabeth Creith, James Penha and Matthew J. Spireng.

FICTION Needs adventure, ethnic, experimental, fantasy, historical, humorous, mainstream, mystery, novel concepts, religious, science fiction, slice-of-life vignettes, suspense, western, contemporary, sports, prose poem. No erotica. Send complete ms with SASE, cover letter; include "name and address, brief introduction, specifying the intended target issue for the mss." SASE. Accepts simultaneous, multiple submissions, and reprints. Does not accept e-mailed submissions. **Pays $10-25.**

POETRY Submit up to 3 poems at a time. Include SASE. "All submissions should be typewritten on standard 812x11 paper. Submissions are accepted all year, but evaluated after specified deadlines." Specify target theme. Editor comments on submissions. "Each issue is based on an unusual premise. Please send SASE for guidelines before submitting poetry to find out the upcoming themes." Does not want "scatologic language, alternate lifestyle, explicit love poetry." **Pays $10/poem and 1 contributor's copy.**

THIRD WEDNESDAY: A LITERARY ARTS MAGAZINE

174 Greenside Up, Ypsilanti MI 48197. (734) 434-2409. **E-mail:** submissions@thirdwednesday.org; LaurenceWT@aol.com. **Website:** http://thirdwednesday.org. **Contact:** Laurence Thomas, editor. "*Third Wednesday* publishes quality (a subjective term at best) poetry, short fiction, and artwork by experienced writers and artists. We welcome work by established writers/artists, as well as those who are not yet well known, but headed for prominence." Estab. 2007. Pays on acceptance. Publishes ms 3 months after acceptance. Accepts queries by e-mail. Does not welcome submissions by snail mail. Accepts simultaneous submissions. Responds to mss in 6-8 weeks. Sometimes comments on/critiques rejected mss. Sample copy available for $8. Guidelines available for SASE, or via e-mail.

FICTION Needs experimental, fantasy, humorous, mainstream, romance, literary, satire. Does not want "purely anecdotal accounts of incidents, sentimentality, pointless conclusions, or stories without some characterization or plot development." Send complete ms with cover letter. Include estimated word count and brief bio. Length: 1,500 words (maximum); average length: 1,000 words. **Pays $3 and 1 contributor's copy.** **POETRY** Submit 1-5 poems at a time. Wants "all styles and forms of poetry, from formal to experimental. Emphasis is placed on the ideas conveyed, craft and language, beauty of expression, and the picture that extends beyond the frame of the poem." Does not want "hate-filled diatribes, pornography (though eroticism is acceptable), prose masquerading as poetry, first drafts of anything." Acquires first North American serial rights, electronic rights. "*TW* retains the right to reproduce accepted work as samples on our website." Rights revert to poet upon publication. **Pays $3 and 1 contributor's copy.**

☾ VALLUM: CONTEMPORARY POETRY

P.O. Box 598, Victoria Station, Montreal QC H3Z 2Y6 Canada. (514)937-8946. **Fax:** (514)937-8946. **E-mail:** info@vallummag.com. **Website:** www.vallummag.com. **Contact:** Joshua Auerbach and Eleni Zisimatos, editors. "Poetry/fine arts magazine published twice/year. Publishes exciting interplay of poets and artists. Content for magazine is selected according to themes listed on website. Material is not filed but is returned by SASE. E-mail response is preferred. Seeking exciting, unpublished, traditional or avant-garde poetry that reflects contemporary experience." Estab. 2000. Circ. 3,200. Pays on publication. Sample copies available for $10. Guidelines available on website.

NONFICTION Needs reviews, essays on poetry. **Pays $65 for accepted reviews or essays on poetry.**
POETRY Does not want "hate" poetry. **Pays $30 honorarium for accepted poems.**

☾☾ VESTAL REVIEW

2609 Dartmouth Dr., Vestal NY 13850. **E-mail:** submissions@vestalreview.net. **Website:** www.vestalreview.net. Semi-annual print magazine specializing in flash fiction. Circ. 1,500. Pays on publication. No kill fee. Publishes ms an average of 3-4 months after acceptance. Accepts queries by e-mail. Accepts simultaneous submissions. Responds in 1 week to queries. Responds in 4 months to mss. Guidelines available online.

FICTION Needs ethnic, horror, mainstream, speculative fiction. Does not read new submissions in January,

June, July, and December. All submissions received during these months will be returned unopened. "We accept submissions only through our submission manager." Length: 50-500 words. **Pays 3-10¢/word and 1 contributor's copy; additional copies for $10 (plus postage).**

☾ VIRGINIA QUARTERLY REVIEW

University of Virginia, 5 Boar's Head Lane, P.O. Box 400223, Charlottesville VA 22904. (434)243-4995. **Fax:** (434)924-1397. **E-mail:** editors@vqronline.org. **Website:** www.vqronline.org. **Contact:** Paul Reyes, deputy editor; Jane Friedman, web editor. Quarterly magazine. A national journal of literature and thought. A lay, intellectual audience; people who are not out-and-out scholars but who are interested in ideas and literature. Estab. 1925. Circ. 7,000. Byline given. Pays on publication. No kill fee. Publishes ms an average of 4 months after acceptance. Editorial lead time 6 months. Submit seasonal material 6 months in advance. Accepts queries by online submission form. Responds in 4 months to mss. Sample copy for $14. Guidelines available online.

NONFICTION Needs book excerpts, essays, general interest, historical, reportage, travel. Send complete ms. Length: 2,000-7,000 words. **Pays $.20/word.**
FICTION Needs ethnic, historical, humorous, mainstream, mystery, novel excerpts, serialized novels, suspense, multicultural, feminist. Send complete ms. Length: 2,000-8,000 words. **Pays $100/page maximum.**
POETRY Submit maximum 5 poems. **Pays $5/line, minimum of $200.**

WASHINGTON SQUARE

Creative Writing Program, New York University, 58 West 10th St., New York NY 10011. **E-mail:** washingtonsquarereview@gmail.com. **Website:** www.washingtonsquarereview.com. Semiannual magazine covering fiction and poetry by emerging and established writers. *Washington Square* is a nonprofit, innovative, nationally-distributed literary journal edited and produced by students of the NYU Graduate Creative Writing Program. It is published semiannually and features fiction and poetry by emerging and established writers. *Washington Square* also includes interviews and an artist portfolio. There is no submission fee. It accepts simultaneous submissions and queries by mail. It does not offer monetary compensation, other than its $500 prize for annual competitions in poetry, fiction, and flash fiction. No kill fee. Accepts queries by mail. Accepts simultaneous submissions. **NONFICTION** Needs interview, Translation. **FICTION** Length: 1 short story up to 20 pages. **POETRY** Length: 5-10 pages total.

WEBER: THE CONTEMPORARY WEST

Weber State University, 1405 University Circle, Ogden UT 84408-1405. **Website:** www.weber.edu/weber-journal. *Weber: The Contemporary West*, published 3 times/year, is "an interdisciplinary journal interested in relevant works covering a wide range of topics." Wants "three or four poems; we publish multiple poems from a poet." Does not want "poems that are flippant, prurient, sing-song, or preachy." Has published poetry by Naomi Shihab Nye, Carolyn Forche, Stephen Dunn, Billy Collins, William Kloefkorn, David Lee, Gary Gildner, and Robert Dana. *Weber* is 150 pages, offset-printed on acid-free paper, perfect-bound, with color cover. Receives about 250-300 poems/year, accepts 30-40. Press run is 1,000; 90% libraries. Subscription: $20 ($30 for institutions); $40 for outside the US. Sample: $10 (back issue). Estab. 1983. Publishes ms 15 months after acceptance. Responds in 6 months. Themes and guidelines available in magazine, for SASE, by e-mail, or on website.
POETRY Submit 3-4 poems at a time, 2 copies of each (one without name). Considers simultaneous submissions; no previously published poems. Cover letter is preferred. Poems are selected by an anonymous (blind) evaluation. Always sends prepublication galleys. **Pays 2 contributor's copies, a year's subscription, and a small honorarium ($100-300) depending on fluctuating grant monies.**

ⓢ WEST BRANCH

Stadler Center for Poetry, Bucknell University, Lewisburg PA 17837-2029. (570)577-1853. **Fax:** (570)577-1885. **E-mail:** westbranch@bucknell.edu. **Website:** www.bucknell.edu/westbranch. Semiannual literary magazine. *West Branch* publishes poetry, fiction, and nonfiction in both traditional and innovative styles. Byline given. Pays on publication. No kill fee. Accepts queries by online submission form. Sample copy for $3. Guidelines available online.
NONFICTION Needs essays, general interest, literary. **Buys 4-5 mss/year.** Send complete ms. **Pays $20-100 ($10/page).**

FICTION Needs novel excerpts, short stories. No genre fiction. **Buys 10-12 mss/year.** Send complete ms. **Pays $20-100 ($10/page).**
POETRY Needs free and formal verse. Buys 30-40 poems/year. Submit maximum 6 poems. **Pays $20-100 ($10/page).**

ⓢ WESTERN HUMANITIES REVIEW

University of Utah, English Department, 255 S. Central Campus Dr., Room 3500, Salt Lake City UT 84112-0494. (801)581-6070. **Fax:** (801)585-5167. **E-mail:** whr@mail.hum.utah.edu. **Website:** www.hum.utah.edu/whr. **Contact:** Barry Weller, editor; Nate Liederbach, managing editor. A tri-annual magazine for educated readers. Estab. 1947. Circ. 1,000. Pays in contributor copies. Publishes ms an average of 1 year after acceptance. Accepts simultaneous submissions. Responds in 6 months. Sample copy for $10. Guidelines available online.
NONFICTION **Contact:** Stuart Culver, nonfiction editor. **Buys 6-8unsolicited/year mss/year.** Send complete ms. **Pays $5/published page.**
FICTION **Contact:** Lance Olsen, Fiction Editor. Needs experimental, and innovative voices. Does not want genre (romance, sci-fi, etc.). **Buys 5-8 mss/year mss/year.** Send complete ms. Length: 5,000 words. **Pays $5/published page (when funds available).**
POETRY **Contact:** Poetry editors: Craig Dworkin, Paisley Rekdal, Tom Stillinger. Considers simultaneous submissions but no more than 5 poems or 25 pages per reading period. No fax or e-mail submissions. Reads submissions October 1-April 1 only. Wants "quality poetry of any form, including translations." Has published poetry by Charles Simic, Olena Kalytiak Davis, Ravi Shankar, Karen Volkman, Dan Beachy-Quick, Lucie Brock-Broido, Christine Hume, and Dan Chiasson. Innovative prose poems may be submitted as fiction or non-fiction to the appropriate editor. **Pays 2 contributor's copies.**

ⓒ ⓢ WINDSOR REVIEW

Department of English, University of Windsor, Windsor ON N9B 3P4 Canada. (519)253-3000; (519) 253-4232, ext. 2290. **Fax:** (519)971-3676. **E-mail:** uwrevu@uwindsor.ca. **Website:** www.uwindsor.ca. **Contact:** Marty Gervais, art editor. Semiannual magazine. "We try to offer a balance of fiction and poetry distinguished by excellence." Estab. 1965. Circ. 250. Pays on publication. Publishes ms an average of 6 months after acceptance. Accepts queries by e-mail. Responds in 1 month to queries; 6 weeks to mss. Sample copy for $7 (U.S.). Guidelines available online.

FICTION Contact: Alistair MacLeod, fiction editor. Needs experimental. No genre fiction (science fiction, romance), but would consider if writing is good enough. Send complete ms. Length: 1,000-5,000 words. **Pays $25, 1 contributor's copy and a free subscription.**

POETRY Submit maximum 6 poems.

😊😊 THE YALE REVIEW

Yale University, P.O. Box 208243, New Haven CT 06520. (203)432-0499. **Fax:** (203)432-0510. **Website:** www.yale.edu/yalereview. **Contact:** J.D. McClatchy, editor. **20% freelance written.** Quarterly magazine. Estab. 1911. Circ. 7,000. Pays prior to publication. No kill fee. Publishes ms an average of 6 months after acceptance. Responds in 2 months to queries. Responds in 2 months to mss. Sample copy for $9, plus postage. Guidelines available online.

NONFICTION No previously published submissions. Send complete ms with cover letter and SASE. Length: 3,000-5,000 words. **Pays $400-500.**

FICTION Buys quality fiction. Submit complete ms with SASE. All submissions should be sent to the editorial office. Length: 3,000-5,000 words. **Pays $400-500.**

POETRY Pays $100-250.

😊😊😊 ZOETROPE: ALL-STORY

Zoetrope: All Story, The Sentinel Bldg., 916 Kearny St., San Francisco CA 94133. (415)788-7500. **Website:** www.all-story.com. **Contact:** Michael Ray, editor. Quarterly magazine specializing in the best of contemporary short fiction. *Zoetrope: All Story* presents a new generation of classic stories. Estab. 1997. Circ. 20,000. Byline given. No kill fee. Publishes ms an average of 5 months after acceptance. Accepts queries by mail. Accepts simultaneous submissions. Responds in 8 months (if SASE included). Sample copy for $8.00. Guidelines available online.

FICTION Buys 25-35 mss/year. "Writers should submit only one story at a time and no more than two stories a year. Before submitting, non-subscribers should read several issues of the magazine to determine if their works fit with *All-Story*. Electronic versions of the magazine are available to read, in part, at the website; and print versions are available for purchase by single-issue order and subscription. We consider unsolicited submissions of short stories and one-act plays no longer than 7,000 words. Excerpts from larger works, screen-

plays, treatments, and poetry will be returned unread. We do not accept artwork or design submissions. We do not accept unsolicited revisions nor respond to writers who don't include an SASE." Send complete ms. **Pays up to $1,000.**

MEN'S

😊😊😊😊 CIGAR AFICIONADO

M. Shanken Communications, Inc., 387 Park Ave. S., 8th Floor, New York NY 10016. (212)684-4224. **Fax:** (212)684-5424. **E-mail:** gmott@mshanken.com. **Website:** www.cigaraficionado.com. **75% freelance written.** Bimonthly magazine for affluent men about the world of cigars. Estab. 1992. Circ. 275,000. Byline given. Pays on acceptance. Offers 25% kill fee. Publishes ms an average of 3-6 months after acceptance. Editorial lead time 6 months. Submit seasonal material 6 months in advance. Accepts queries by e-mail. Responds in 1 month to queries. Responds in 2 months to mss. Sample copy free.

NONFICTION Needs general interest. Query. Length: 1,500-4,000 words. **Pays variable amount.** Pays expenses of writers on assignment.

😊😊😊😊 KING

Harris Publications, Inc., 1115 Broadway, 8th Floor, New York NY 10010. **Fax:** (212)807-0216. **E-mail:** king@harris-pub.com. **Website:** www.king-mag.com **75% freelance written.** Men's lifestyle magazine published 80 times/year. *King* is a general interest men's magazine with a strong editorial voice. Topics include lifestyle, entertainment, news, women, cars, music, fashion, investigative reporting. Estab. 2001. Circ. 270,000. Byline given. Pays on publication. Offers 25% kill fee. Editorial lead time 2-3 months. Submit seasonal material 4 months in advance. Accepts queries by e-mail. Responds in 1 month to queries. Guidelines free.

NONFICTION Needs essays, exposé, general interest. Does not want completed articles. Pitches only. Query with published clips. Length: 2,000-5,000 words. **Pays $1-1.50/word.** Sometimes pays expenses of writers on assignment.

MILITARY

🔄 😊😊 AIRFORCE

Air Force Association of Canada, P.O Box 2460, Stn D, Ottawa ON K1P 5W6 Canada. (613)232-2303. **Fax:** (613)232-2156. **E-mail:** director@airforce.ca. **Web-**

site: www.airforce.ca. **5% freelance written.** Quarterly magazine covering Canada's air force heritage. Stories center on Canadian military aviation—past, present and future. Estab. 1977. Circ. 16,000. Byline given. Pays on publication. Publishes ms an average of 6 months after acceptance. Editorial lead time 3 months. Submit seasonal material 3 months in advance. Accepts queries by mail, e-mail, fax, phone. Accepts simultaneous submissions. Responds in 2 weeks to queries; 1 month to mss. Sample copy free. Guidelines by e-mail.

NONFICTION Needs historical, interview, personal experience, photo feature. **Buys 2 mss/year.** Query with published clips. Length: 1,500-3,500 words. Sometimes pays expenses of writers on assignment. Limit agreed upon in advance.

FILLERS Needs anecdotes, facts. About 800 words. **Negotiable.**

⊛⊛ AIR FORCE TIMES

Gannett Government Media, 6883 Commercial Dr., Springfield VA 22159. (703)750-8646. **Fax:** (703)750-8601. **E-mail:** airlet@airforcetimes.com. **Website:** www.airforcetimes.com. **Contact:** Becky Iannotta, managing editor. "Weeklies edited separately for Army, Navy, Marine Corps, and Air Force military personnel and their families. They contain career information such as pay raises, promotions, news of legislation affecting the military, housing, base activities, and features of interest to military people." Estab. 1940. Byline given. Pays on acceptance. Offers kill fee. Accepts queries by mail, e-mail, phone. Accepts simultaneous submissions. Responds in 1 month to queries. Sample copy for #10 SASE. Guidelines for #10 SASE.

NONFICTION No advice pieces. **Buys 150-175 mss/year.** Query. Length: 750-2,000 words. **Pays $100-500.**

COLUMNS/DEPARTMENTS Length: 500-900 words. **Buys 75 mss/year. Pays $75-125.**

⊛⊛ ARMY MAGAZINE

Association of the U.S. Army, 2425 Wilson Blvd., Arlington VA 22201. (800)336-4570. **E-mail:** armymag@ausa.org. **Website:** www.ausa.org. **Contact:** Editorial assistant. **70% freelance written. Prefers to work with published/established writers.** Monthly magazine emphasizing military interests. Estab. 1904. Circ. 70,000. Byline given. Pays on publication. Publishes ms an average of 5 months after acceptance. Submit seasonal material 3 months in advance. Accepts queries by mail. Sample copy and writer's guidelines for 9x12 SAE with $1 postage or online.

NONFICTION Needs historical, military and original, humor, military feature-length articles and anecdotes, interview, photo feature. Special issues: "We would like to see more pieces about little-known episodes involving interesting military personalities. We especially want material lending itself to heavy, contributor-supplied photographic treatment. The first thing a contributor should recognize is that our readership is very savvy militarily. 'Gee-whiz' personal reminiscences get short shrift, unless they hold their own in a company in which long military service, heroism and unusual experiences are commonplace. At the same time, *ARMY* readers like a well-written story with a fresh slant, whether it is about an experience in a foxhole or the fortunes of a corps in battle." No rehashed history. No unsolicited book reviews. **Buys 40 mss/year.** Submit complete ms (hard copy and disk). Length: 1,000-1,500 words. **Pays 12-18¢/word.**

⊛⊛⊛ MILITARY OFFICER

201 N. Washington St., Alexandria VA 22314-2539. (800)234-6622. **Fax:** (703)838-8179. **E-mail:** editor@moaa.org. **Website:** www.moaa.org. **60% freelance written. Prefers to work with published/established writers.** Monthly magazine for officers of the 7 uniformed services and their families. Estab. 1945. Circ. 325,000. Byline given. Pays on acceptance. Publishes ms an average of 1 year after acceptance. Accepts queries by e-mail. Responds in 3 months to queries. Sample copy and guidelines available online.

NONFICTION "We rarely accept unsolicited mss." **Buys 50 mss/year.** Query with résumé, sample clips. Length: 1,000-2,000 words (features). **Pays 80¢/word (features).**

⊛⊛ PROCEEDINGS

U.S. Naval Institute, 291 Wood Rd., Annapolis MD 21402-5034. (410)268-6110. **Fax:** (410)295-7940. **E-mail:** articlesubmissions@usni.org. **Website:** www.usni.org/magazines/proceedings. **Contact:** Richard G. Latture, editor-in-chief; Amy Voight, photo editor. **80% freelance written.** Monthly magazine covering Navy, Marine Corps, and Coast Guard issues. Estab. 1873. Circ. 60,000. Byline given. Pays on publication. Publishes ms an average of 9 months after acceptance. Editorial lead time 3 months. Responds in 2 months to queries. Sample copy for $3.95. Guidelines available on website.

NONFICTION Needs essays, historical, interview, photo feature, technical. **Buys 100-125 mss/year.** Send complete ms. 3,000 words. **Pays $60-150/printed page for unsolicited articles.**

COLUMNS/DEPARTMENTS Comment & Discussion (letters to editor), 500 words; Commentary (opinion), 700 words; Nobody Asked Me, But.. (opinion), less than 700 words. **Buys 150-200 mss/year.** Query or send complete ms. **Pays $34-150.**

FILLERS Needs anecdotes. **Buys 20 mss/year.** Length: 100 words. **Pays $25.**

❸❸❸❸ SOLDIER OF FORTUNE

2135 11th St., Boulder CO 80302. (303)449-3750. **E-mail:** editorsof@aol.com. **Website:** www.sofmag.com. **Contact:** Lt. Col. Robert A. Brown, editor/publisher. **50% freelance written.** Monthly magazine covering military, paramilitary, police, combat subjects, and action/adventure. "We are an action-oriented magazine; we cover combat hot spots around the world. We also provide timely features on state of the-art weapons and equipment; elite military and police units; and historical military operations. Readership is primarily active-duty military, veterans, and law enforcement." Estab. 1975. Circ. 60,000. Byline given. Offers 25% kill fee. Responds in 3 weeks to queries. Responds in 1 month to mss. Sample copy for $5. Guidelines with #10 SASE.

NONFICTION Needs exposé, general interest, historical, how-to, on weapons and their skilled use, humor, interview, new product, personal experience, photo feature, No. 1 on our list, technical, travel, combat reports, military unit reports, and solid Vietnam and Operation Iraqi Freedom articles. No `How I won the war' pieces; no op-ed pieces unless they are fully and factually backgrounded; no knife articles (staff assignments only). All submitted articles should have good art; art will sell us on an article. **Buys 75 mss/year.** Query with or without published clips or send complete ms. Send mss to articles editor; queries to managing editor Length: 2,000-3,000 words. **Pays $150-250/page.**

REPRINTS Send disk copy, photocopy of article and information about when and where the material previously appeared. Pays 25% of amount paid for an original article.

FILLERS Contact: Bulletin board editor. Needs newsbreaks, military/paramilitary related has to be documented. Length: 100-250 words. **Pays $50.**

MUSIC CONSUMER

ALARM

Alarm Press, 205 N. Michigan Ave., Suite 3200, Chicago IL 60601. (312)341-1290. **E-mail:** info@alarmpress.com. **Website:** www.alarmpress.com/alarm-magazine. *ALARM*, published 6 times/year, "does one thing, and it does it very well: it publishes the best new music and art in *ALARM* magazine and alarmpress.com. From our headquarters in a small Chicago office, along with a cast of contributing writers spread across the country, we listen to thousands of CDs, view hundreds of gallery openings, and attend lectures and live concerts in order to present inspirational artists who are fueled by an honest and contagious obsession with their art." Accepts queries by mail, e-mail. Only responds if interested. Submit by e-mail with the subject line "ALARM magazine submissions. Please send your work as part of the body of an e-mail; we cannot accept attachments." Alternatively, submissions may be sent by regular mail to Submissions Dept. "*ALARM* is not responsible for the return, loss of, or damage to unsolicited manuscripts, unsolicited art work, or any other unsolicited materials. Those submitting manuscripts, art work, or any other materials should not send originals."

❸❸ BLUEGRASS UNLIMITED

Bluegrass Unlimited, Inc., P.O. Box 771, Warrenton VA 20188. (540)349-8181 or (800)BLU-GRAS. **Fax:** (540)341-0011. **E-mail:** editor@bluegrassmusic.com; info@bluegrassmusic.com. **Website:** www.bluegrassmusic.com. **10% freelance written. Prefers to work with published/established writers.** Monthly magazine covering bluegrass, acoustic, and old-time country music. Estab. 1966. Circ. 20,000. Byline given. Pays on publication. Offers negotiated kill fee. Publishes ms an average of 4 months after acceptance. Submit seasonal material 4 months in advance. Accepts queries by mail, e-mail, fax. Responds in 2 weeks to queries. Responds in 2 months to mss. Sample copy free. Guidelines for #10 SASE.

NONFICTION Needs general interest, historical, how-to, interview, personal experience, photo feature, travel. No fan-style articles. **Buys 30-40 mss/year.** Query. Length: Open. **Pays 10-13¢/word.**

REPRINTS Send photocopy with rights for sale noted and information about when and where the material previously appeared. Payment is negotiable.

FICTION Needs ethnic, humorous. **Buys 3-5 mss/ year.** Query. Length: Negotiable. **Pays 10-13¢/word.**

⊗⊗ CHAMBER MUSIC

Chamber Music America, 99 Madison Ave., 5th Floor, New York NY 10016. (212)242-2022. **Fax:** (212)242-7955. **E-mail:** egoldensohn@chamber-music.org. **E-mail:** Ellen Goldensohn, publications director. **Website:** www.chamber-music.org. Bimonthly magazine covering chamber music. Estab. 1977. Circ. 13,000. Byline given. Pays on publication. Offers kill fee. Publishes ms an average of 5 months after acceptance. Editorial lead time 4 months. Accepts queries by mail, phone.

NONFICTION Needs book excerpts, essays, humor, opinion, personal experience, issue-oriented stories of relevance to the chamber music fields written by top music journalists and critics, or music practitioners. No artist profiles, no stories about opera or symphonic work. **Buys 35 mss/year.** Query with published clips. Length: 2,500-3,500 words. **Pays $500 minimum.** Sometimes pays expenses of writers on assignment.

⊗ CHURCH MUSIC QUARTERLY

The Royal School of Church Music, 19 The Close, Salisbury Wiltshire SP1 2EB United Kingdom. (44)(1722)424848. **Fax:** (44)(172)242-4849. **E-mail:** cmq@rscm.com. **Website:** www.rscm.com. Quarterly publication that offers advice, information, and inspiration to church music enthusiasts around the world. Each issue offers a variety of articles and interviews by distinguished musicians, theologians, and scholars. Circ. 13,500. Pays upon publication. No kill fee. Accepts queries by e-mail. Guidelines by e-mail.

NONFICTION Submit ms, bio. Length: 1,200-1,400 words. **Pays £60/page for commissioned articles.**

GUITAR WORLD

NewBay Media, LLC, E. 28th St., 12th Floor, New York NY 10016. (212)378-0400. **Fax:** (212)281-4704. **E-mail:** soundingboard@guitarworld.com. **Website:** www.guitarworld.com. Monthly magazine for guitarists. Written for guitar players categorized as either professionals, semi-professionals or amateur players. Every issue offers broad-ranging interviews that cover technique, instruments, and lifestyles. Circ. 150,000. No kill fee. Editorial lead time 2 months.

⊘ ROLLING STONE

Wenner Media, 1290 Avenue of the Americas, New York NY 10104. (212)484-1616. **Fax:** (212)484-1664. **E-mail:** rseditors@rollingstone.com; photo@rollingstone.com. **Website:** www.rollingstone.com. Biweekly magazine geared towards young adults interested in news of popular music, entertainment and the arts, current news events, politics and American culture. Circ. 1,464,943. No kill fee. Editorial lead time 1 month.

⊗⊗⊗ SYMPHONY

League of American Orchestras, 33 W. 60th St., Fifth Floor, New York NY 10023. (212)262-5161. **Fax:** (212)262-5198. **E-mail:** clane@americanorchestras.org; jmelick@americanorchestras.org; editor@americanorchestras.org. **Website:** www.symphony.org. **Contact:** Chester Lane, senior editor; Jennifer Melick, managing editor. **50% freelance written.** Bimonthly magazine for the orchestra industry and classical music enthusiasts covering classical music, orchestra industry, musicians. "*Symphony*, the quarterly magazine of the League of American Orchestras, reports on the critical issues, trends, personalities, and developments of the orchestra world. Every issue includes news, provocative essays, in-depth articles, and cutting-edge research relevant to the entire orchestra field. *Symphony* profiles take readers behind the scenes to meet the people who are making a difference in the orchestra world, while wide-ranging survey articles reveal the strategies and tactics that are helping orchestras meet the challenges of the 21st century. Symphony is a matchless source of meaningful information about orchestras, and serves as an advocate and connector for the orchestra field." Circ. 18,000. Byline given. Pays on acceptance. No kill fee. Publishes ms an average of 10 weeks after acceptance. Editorial lead time 6 months. Submit seasonal material 8 months in advance. Accepts queries by mail, e-mail. Accepts simultaneous submissions. Guidelines available online.

NONFICTION Needs book excerpts, essays, inspirational, interview, opinion, personal experience, rare, photo feature, rare, issue features, trend pieces (by assignment only; pitches welcome). Does not want to see reviews, interviews. **Buys 30 mss/year.** Query with published clips. Length: 1,500-3,500 words. **Pays $500-900.** Sometimes pays expenses of writers on assignment.

COLUMNS/DEPARTMENTS Repertoire (orchestral music—essays); Comment (personal views and opinions); Currents (electronic media developments); In Print (books); On Record (CD, DVD, video), all 1,000-2,500 words. **Buys 12 mss/year.** Query with published clips.

MYSTERY

ALFRED HITCHCOCK'S MYSTERY MAGAZINE

Dell Magazines, 267 Broadway, 4th Floor, New York NY 10007. (212)686-7188. **E-mail:** alfredhitchcockmm@dellmagazines.com. **Website:** www.themysteryplace.com/ahmm. **100% freelance written.** Monthly magazine featuring new mystery short stories. Estab. 1956. Circ. 90,000 readers. Byline given. Pays on publication. No kill fee. Submit seasonal material 7 months in advance. Responds in 3-5 months to mss. Sample copy for $5. Guidelines for SASE or on website.

FICTION Contact: Linda Landrigan, editor. "Original and well-written mystery and crime fiction. Because this is a mystery magazine, the stories we buy must fall into that genre in some sense or another. We are interested in nearly every kind of mystery: stories of detection of the classic kind, police procedurals, private eye tales, suspense, courtroom dramas, stories of espionage, and so on. We ask only that the story be about crime (or the threat or fear of one). We sometimes accept ghost stories or supernatural tales, but those also should involve a crime." Needs mystery, suspense. No sensationalism. Send complete ms. Length: up to 12,000 words. **Payment varies.**

$ ELLERY QUEEN'S MYSTERY MAGAZINE

Dell Magazines, 267 Broadway, 4th Floor, New York NY 10017. (212)686-7188. **Fax:** (212)686-7414. **E-mail:** elleryqueenmm@dellmagazines.com. **Website:** www.themysteryplace.com/eqmm. **Contact:** Jackie Sherbow, assistant editor. **100% freelance written.** Featuring mystery fiction. "*Ellery Queen's Mystery Magazine* welcomes submissions from both new and established writers. We publish every kind of mystery short story: the psychological suspense tale, the deductive puzzle, the private eye case—the gamut of crime and detection from the realistic (including the policeman's lot and stories of police procedure) to the more imaginative (including 'locked rooms' and 'impossible crimes'). We look for strong writing, an original and exciting plot, and professional craftsmanship. We encourage writers whose work meets these general criteria to read an issue of *EQMM* before making a submission." Estab. 1941. Circ. 100,000. Byline given. Pays on acceptance. No kill fee. Publishes ms an average of 6-12 months after acceptance. Accepts queries by online submission form. Accepts simultaneous submissions. Responds in 3 months to mss. Sample copy for $5.50. Guidelines for SASE or online.

FICTION Contact: Janet Hutchings, editor. "We always need detective stories. Special consideration given to anything timely and original." Needs mystery. No explicit sex or violence, no gore or horror. Seldom publishes parodies or pastiches. **Buys up to 120 mss/year.** *EQMM* uses an online submission system (http://eqmm.magazinesubmissions.com) that has been designed to streamline our process and improve communication with authors. We ask that all submissions be made electronically, using this system, rather than on paper. All stories should be in standard manuscript format and submitted in .DOC format. For detailed submission instructions, see http://eqmm.magazinesubmissions.com or our writers guidelines page (http://www.themysteryplace.com/eqmm/guidelines). Most stories 2,500-8,000 words. Accepts longer and shorter submissions—including minute mysteries of 250 words, and novellas of up to 20,000 words from established authors. **Pays 5-8¢/word; occasionally higher for established authors.**

POETRY Short mystery verses, limericks. Length: 1 page, double spaced maximum.

NATURE, CONSERVATION AND ECOLOGY

♻ $ ALTERNATIVES JOURNAL

200 University Ave. W., Waterloo ON N2L 3G1 Canada. (519)888-4505. **Fax:** (519)746-0292. **E-mail:** editor@alternativesjournal.ca; marcia@alternativesjournal.ca. **Website:** www.alternativesjournal.ca. **Contact:** Eric Rumble, editor; Marcia Ruby, creative director. **90% freelance written.** Magazine published 6 times/year covering international environmental issues. "*Alternatives Journal*, Canada's national environmental magazine, delivers thoughtful analysis and intelligent debate on Canadian and world environmental issues, the latest news and ideas, as well as profiles of environmental leaders who are making a difference. *A/J* is a bimonthly magazine featuring bright,

lively writing by the nation's foremost environmental thinkers and researchers. *A/J* offers a vision of a more sustainable future as well as the tools needed to take us there." Estab. 1971. Circ. 5,000. Byline given. Pays on publication. Offers 50% kill fee. Publishes ms an average of 5 months after acceptance. Editorial lead time 7 months. Submit seasonal material 5 months in advance. Accepts queries by mail, e-mail, fax. Accepts simultaneous submissions. Sample copy free for Canadian writers only. Guidelines available on website.

NONFICTION Needs book excerpts, essays, exposé, humor, interview, opinion. **Buys 50 mss/year.** Query with published clips. Length: 800-3,000 words. **Pays $.10/word (Canadian).** Sometimes pays expenses of writers on assignment.

PHOTOS State availability. Identification of subjects required. Offers $35-75/photo.

TIPS "Before responding to this call for submissions, please read several back issues of the magazine so that you understand the nature of our publication. We also suggest you go through our detailed submission procedures to understand the types and lengths of articles we accept. Queries should explain, in less than 300 words, the content and scope of your article, and should convey your intended approach, tone, and style. Please include a list of people you will interview, potential images or sources for images, and the number of words you propose to write. We would also like to receive a very short bio. And if you have not written for *Alternatives* before, please include other examples of your writing. Articles range from about 500 to 4,000 words in length. Keep in mind that our lead time is several months. Articles should not be so time-bound that they will seem dated once published. Alternatives has a limited budget of $.10 per word for several articles. This stipend is available to professional and amateur writers and students only. Please indicate your interest in this funding in your submission."

ARIZONA WILDLIFE VIEWS

5000 W. Carefee Hwy., Phoenix AZ 85086. (800)777-0015. **E-mail:** awv@azgfd.gov; hrayment@azgfd.gov. **Website:** www.azgfd.gov/magazine. **Contact:** Heidi Rayment. **50% freelance written.** Bimonthly magazine covering Arizona wildlife, wildlife management, and outdoor recreation (specifically hunting, fishing, wildlife watching, boating and off-highway vehicle recreation). "*Arizona Wildlife Views* is a general interest magazine about Arizona wildlife, wildlife management and outdoor recreation. We publish material that conforms to the mission and policies of the Arizona Game and Fish Department. In addition to Arizona wildlife and wildlife management, topics include habitat issues, outdoor recreation involving wildlife, boating, fishing, hunting, bird-watching, animal observation, off-highway vehicle use, etc., and historical articles about wildlife and wildlife management." Circ. 22,000. Byline given. Pays on publication. No kill fee. Publishes ms an average of 10 months after acceptance. Editorial lead time 1 year. Submit seasonal material 2 months in advance. Accepts queries by mail, e-mail (preferred). Accepts simultaneous submissions. Responds in 1 month to queries. Responds in 2 months to mss. Sample copy free. Guidelines available online.

NONFICTION Needs general interest, historical, how-to, interview, photo feature, technical, travel, scientific for a popular audience. Does not want "Me and Joe" articles, anthropomorphism of wildlife, or opinionated pieces not based on confirmable facts. **Buys 20 mss/year.** Query. Length: 1,000-2,500 words. **Pays $450-800.**

✪ $$$ THE ATLANTIC SALMON JOURNAL

The Atlantic Salmon Federation, P.O. Box 5200, St. Andrews NB E5B 3S8 Canada. (506)529-4581. **Fax:** (506)529-4438. **E-mail:** savesalmon@asf.ca. **Website:** www.asf.ca. **Contact:** Martin Silverstone, editor. **50-68% freelance written.** Quarterly magazine covering conservation efforts for the Atlantic salmon, catering to the dedicated angler and conservationist. Circ. 11,000. Byline given. Pays on publication. No kill fee. Publishes ms an average of 6 months after acceptance. Submit seasonal material 3 months in advance. Accepts simultaneous submissions. Responds in 2 months to queries. Sample copy for 9x12 SAE with $1 (Canadian), or IRC. Guidelines free.

NONFICTION Needs exposé, historical, how-to, humor, interview, new product, opinion, personal experience, photo feature, technical, travel, conservation. **Buys 15-20 mss/year.** Query with published clips. Length: 2,000 words. **Pays $400-800 for articles with photos.** Sometimes pays expenses of writers on assignment.

COLUMNS/DEPARTMENTS Fit To Be Tied (Conservation issues and salmon research; the design, construction and success of specific flies); interesting characters in the sport and opinion pieces by knowledgeable writers, 900 words; Casting Around (short, informative, entertaining reports, book reviews and quotes from the world of Atlantic salmon angling and conservation). Query. **Pays $50-300.**

THE BEAR DELUXE MAGAZINE

Orlo, 810 SE Belmont, Studio 5, Portland OR 97214. (503)242-1047. **E-mail:** bear@orlo.org. **Website:** www.orlo.org. **Contact:** Tom Webb, editor-in-chief; Kristin Rogers Brown, art director. **80% freelance written.** Covers fiction/essay/poetry/other. 750-4,500 words. Do not combine submissions, rather submit poetry, fiction and essay in separate packages. News essays, on occasion, are assigned out if they have a strong element of reporting. Artists contribute to *The Bear Deluxe* in various ways, including: editorial illustration, editorial photography, spot illustration, independent art, cover art, graphic design, and cartoons. "*The Bear Deluxe Magazine* is a national independent environmental arts magazine publishing significant works of reporting, creative nonfiction, literature, visual art and design. Based in the Pacific Northwest, it reaches across cultural and political divides to engage readers on vital issues effecting the environment. Published twice per year, *The Bear Deluxe* includes a wider array and a higher-percentage of visual art work and design than many other publications. Artwork is included both as editorial support and as stand alone or independent art. It has included nationally recognized artists as well as emerging artists. As with any publication, artists are encouraged to review a sample copy for a clearer understanding of the magazine's approach. Unsolicited submissions and samples are accepted and encouraged." Estab. 1993. Circ. 19,000. Byline given. Pays on publication. Offers 25% kill fee. Publishes ms an average of 6 months after acceptance. Editorial lead time 6 months. Submit seasonal material 9 months in advance. Accepts queries by mail, e-mail. Accepts simultaneous submissions. Responds in 3-6 months to mail queries. Only responds to e-mail queries if interested. Sample copy for $3. Guidelines for #10 SASE or on website.

NONFICTION Needs book excerpts, essays, exposé, general interest, interview, new product, opinion, personal experience, photo feature, travel, artist profiles. Special issues: Publishes 1 theme/2 years. **Buys 40 mss/year.** Query with published clips. Length: 250-4,500 words. Essays: 750-3,000 words. **Pays $25-400, depending on piece.** Sometimes pays expenses.

COLUMNS/DEPARTMENTS Reviews (almost anything), 300 words; Front of the Book (mix of short news bits, found writing, quirky tidbits), 300-500 words; Portrait of an Artist (artist profiles), 1,200 words; Back of the Book (creative opinion pieces), 650 words. **Buys 16 mss/year.** Query with published clips. **Pays $25-400, depending on piece.**

FICTION "Stories must have some environmental context, but we view that in a broad sense." Needs adventure, condensed novels, historical, horror, humorous, mystery, novel concepts, western. No detective, children's, or horror. **Buys 8 mss/year.** Query or send complete ms. Length: 750-4,500 words. **Pays free subscription to the magazine, contributor's copies and $25-400, depending on piece; additional copies for postage.**

POETRY Needs avant-garde, free verse, haiku, light verse, traditional. Submit 3-5 poems at a time. Considers previously published poems and simultaneous submissions "so long as noted." Poems are reviewed by a committee of 3-5 people. Publishes 1 theme issue/year. Acquires first or one-time rights. Buys 16-20 poems/year. Submit maximum 3-5 poems. Length: 50 lines maximum. **Pays $20, subscription, and copies.**

FILLERS Needs facts, newsbreaks, short humor. **Buys 10 mss/year.** Length: 100-750 words.

BIRD WATCHER'S DIGEST

P.O. Box 110, Marietta OH 45750. (740)373-5285; (800)879-2473. **Fax:** (740)373-8443. **E-mail:** editor@birdwatchersdigest.com. **E-mail:** submissions@birdwatchersdigest.com. **Website:** www.birdwatchersdigest.com. **Contact:** Bill Thompson III, editor. **60% freelance written.** Bimonthly magazine covering natural history—birds and bird watching. "*BWD* is a nontechnical magazine interpreting ornithological material for amateur observers, including the knowledgeable birder, the serious novice and the backyard bird watcher; we strive to provide good reading and good ornithology. Works with a small number of new/unpublished writers each year." Estab. 1978. Circ. 125,000. Byline given. Pays on publication. Publishes ms an average of 2 years after acceptance. Submit seasonal material 6 months in advance. TrueResponds in 10-12 weeks to queries. Sample copy for $3.99 or access online. Guidelines available online.

NONFICTION Needs book excerpts, how-to, relating to birds, feeding and attracting, etc., humor, personal experience, travel. No articles on pet or caged birds, or raising a baby bird. **Buys 45-60 mss/year.** "We gladly accept e-mail queries and ms submissions but aren't not able to respond immediately to most inquiries via e-mail. When submitting by e-mail, please make the subject line read 'Submission—[your topic].' Attach your submission to your e-mail in either MS Word (.doc) or RichText Format (.rtf). Please do not copy and paste your submission into the body of the e-mail. Whether submitting by regular mail or e-mail, please include your full contact information on every page. We ask that you allow 10 to 12 weeks for a response." Length: 600-3,500 words. **Pays from $100.**

⊕⊕ BIRDWATCHING

Kalmbach Publishing Co., 85 Quincy Ave., Suite 2, Quincy MA 02169. **Fax:** (262)798-6468. **E-mail:** mail@birdwatchingdaily.com. **Website:** www.birdwatchingdaily.com. Bimonthly magazine for bird-watchers who actively look for wild birds in the field. "*BirdWatching* concentrates on where to find, how to attract, and how to identify wild birds, and on how to understand what they do." Estab. 1987. Circ. 40,000. Byline given. Pays on publication. Accepts queries by mail. Guidelines available online.

NONFICTION Needs essays, how-to, attracting birds, interview, personal experience, photo feature, bird photography, travel, birding hotspots in North America and beyond, product reviews/comparisons, bird biology, endangered or threatened birds. No poetry, fiction, or puzzles. **Buys 60 mss/year.** Query with published clips. Length: 500-2,400 words. **Pays $200-450.**

⊕⊕ E THE ENVIRONMENTAL MAGAZINE

Earth Action Network, 28 Knight St., Westport CT 06851. (203)854-5559. **Fax:** (203)866-0602. **E-mail:** info@emagazine.com; brita@emagazine.com. **Website:** www.emagazine.com. **60% freelance written.** Bimonthly magazine. *E Magazine* was formed for the purpose of acting as a clearinghouse of information, news, and commentary on environmental issues. Estab. 1990. Circ. 50,000. Byline given. Pays on publication. No kill fee. Editorial lead time 3 months. Submit seasonal material 6 months in advance. Accepts queries by mail, e-mail, fax. Accepts simultaneous submissions. Sample copy for $5 or online. Guidelines available online.

NONFICTION Needs exposé, environmental, how-to, new product, book review, feature (in-depth articles on key natural environmental issues). **Buys 100 mss/year.** Query with published clips. Length: 100-4,000 words. **Pays 30¢/word.**

COLUMNS/DEPARTMENTS On spec or free contributions welcome. In Brief/Currents (environmental news stories/trends), 400-1,000 words; Conversations (Q&As with environmental movers and shakers), 2,000 words; Tools for Green Living; Your Health; Eco-Travel; Eco-Home; Eating Right; Green Business; Consumer News (each 700-1,200 words). Query with published clips.

⊙ GREEN TEACHER

Green Teacher, 95 Robert St., Toronto ON M2S 2K5 Canada. (416)960-1244. **Fax:** (416)925-3474. **E-mail:** tim@greenteacher.com; info@greenteacher.com. **Website:** www.greenteacher.com. **Contact:** Tim Grant, co-editor; Brandon Quigley, editorial assistant. "*Green Teacher* is a magazine that helps youth educators enhance environmental and global education inside and outside of schools." Estab. 1991. Circ. 15,000. Pays on acceptance. Publishes ms 8 months after acceptance. Accepts queries by mail, e-mail. Responds to queries in 1 week.

NONFICTION Needs multicultural, nature, environment. Query. Submit one-page summary or outline. Length: 750-2,500 words.

⊕⊕⊕ MINNESOTA CONSERVATION VOLUNTEER

Minnesota Department of Natural Resources, 500 Lafeyette Rd., St. Paul MN 55155-4046. **Website:** www.dnr.state.mn.us/magazine. **50% freelance written.** Bimonthly magazine covering Minnesota natural resources, wildlife, natural history, outdoor recreation, and land use. "*Minnesota Conservation Volunteer* is a donor-supported magazine advocating conservation and careful use of Minnesota's natural resources. Material must reflect an appreciation of nature and an ethic of care for the environment. We rely on a variety of sources in our reporting. More than 130,000 Minnesota households, businesses, schools, and other groups subscribe to this conservation magazine." Estab. 1940. Circ. 131,000. Byline given. Pays on acceptance. Offers 30% kill fee. Publishes ms an average of 2 months after acceptance. Editorial lead time 9 months. Submit seasonal material 9 months in advance. Accepts queries by mail, e-mail. Responds in 1 month to queries. Responds in 2 months to mss. Sample copy free or on website. Guidelines available online.

NONFICTION Needs essays, exposé, general interest, historical, humor, interview, opinion, personal experience, photo feature, travel, Young Naturalists for children. Rarely publishes poetry or uncritical advocacy. **Buys 12 mss/year.** Query with published clips. Length: up to 1,800 words. **Pays 50¢/word for full-length feature articles.** Pays expenses of writers on assignment.

COLUMNS/DEPARTMENTS Close Encounters (unusual, exciting, or humorous personal wildlife experience in Minnesota), up to 1,500 words; Sense of Place (first- or third-person essay developing character of a Minnesota place), up to 1,500 words; Viewpoint (well-researched and well-reasoned opinion piece), up to 1,500 words; Minnesota Profile (concise description of emblematic state species or geographic feature), 400 words. **Buys 12 mss/year.** Query with published clips. **Pays 50¢/word.**

⊖⊖⊖ ⊘ NATIONAL PARKS MAGAZINE

National Parks Conservation Association, 777 Sixth St. NW, Suite 700, Washington DC 20001. (202)223-6722; (800)628-7275. Fax: (202)454-3333. **E-mail:** npmag@npca.org. **Website:** www.npca.org/magazine/. **Contact:** Scott Kirkwood, editor-in-chief. **60% freelance written. Prefers to work with published/established writers.** Quarterly magazine for a largely unscientific but highly educated audience interested in preservation of National Park System units, natural areas, and protection of wildlife habitat. "*National Parks* magazine publishes articles about areas in the National Park System, proposed new areas, threats to parks or park wildlife, scientific discoveries, legislative issues, and endangered species of plants or animals relevant to national parks. We do not publish articles on general environmental topics, nor do we print articles about land managed by the Fish and Wildlife Service, Bureau of Land Management, or other federal agencies." Estab. 1919. Circ. 340,000. Pays on acceptance. Offers 33% kill fee. Publishes ms an average of 2 months after acceptance. Responds in 3-4 months to queries. Sample copy for $3 and 9x12 SASE or online. Guidelines available online.

NONFICTION Needs exposé, on threats, wildlife problems in national parks, descriptive articles about new or proposed national parks and wilderness parks. No poetry, philosophical essays, or first-person narratives. No unsolicited mss. Length: 1,500 words. **Pays $1,300 for 1,500-word features and travel articles.**

⊖⊖ NORTHERN WOODLANDS MAGAZINE

Center for Woodlands Education, Inc., 1776 Center Rd., P.O. Box 471, Corinth VT 05039-0471. (802)439-6292. **Fax:** (802)439-6296. **E-mail:** dave@northernwoodlands.org. **Website:** www.northernwoodlands.org. **40-60% freelance written.** Quarterly magazine covering natural history, conservation, and forest management in the Northeast. "*Northern Woodlands* strives to inspire landowners' sense of stewardship by increasing their awareness of the natural history and the principles of conservation and forestry that are directly related to their land. We also hope to increase the public's awareness of the social, economic, and environmental benefits of a working forest." Estab. 1994. Circ. 15,000. Byline given. Pays 1 month prior to publication. Publishes ms an average of 6 months after acceptance. Editorial lead time 6 months. Submit seasonal material 6 months in advance. Accepts queries by mail, e-mail. Accepts simultaneous submissions. Responds in 1 month to queries. Responds in 1-2 months to mss. Sample copy and guidelines available online.

NONFICTION No product reviews, first-person travelogues, "cute" animal stories, opinion, or advocacy pieces. **Buys 15-20 mss/year.** Query with published clips. Length: 500-3,000 words. **Pay varies per piece.** Sometimes pays expenses of writers on assignment.

⊖⊖ OCEAN MAGAZINE

P.O. Box 84, Rodanthe NC 27968-0084. (252)256-2296. **E-mail:** diane@oceanmagazine.org. **Website:** www.oceanmagazine.org. **100% freelance written.** "*OCEAN* magazine serves to celebrate and protect the greatest, most comprehensive resource for life on earth, our world's ocean. *OCEAN* publishes articles, stories, poems, essays, and photography about the ocean—observations, experiences, scientific and environmental discussions—written with fact and feeling, illustrated with images from nature." Estab. 2004. Circ. 40,000. Byline given. Pays on publication. Publishes ms an average of 2-4 months after acceptance. Editorial lead time 3-6 months. Submit seasonal material 3-6 months in advance. Accepts queries by e-mail. Yes. Accepts simultaneous submissions. Responds in 1 day to 2 months. Sample copy available for $3 digital, $8.45 print. Guidelines available online.

NONFICTION Needs book excerpts, essays, general interest, historical, inspirational, interview, opinion, personal experience, photo feature, technical, travel, spiritual. Does not want "poor writing." **Buys 24-36 mss/year.** Query. Length: 75-5,000 words. **Pays $75-250.**

FICTION Needs adventure, fantasy, historical, novel concepts, romance, slice-of-life vignettes. **Buys 1-2 mss/year.** Query. Length: 100-2,000 words. **Pays $75-150.**

POETRY Needs avant-garde, free verse, haiku, light verse, traditional. Buys 12 poems/year. Submit maximum 6 poems. **Pays $25-75.**

FILLERS Needs anecdotes, facts. **Buys Reflections facts 4-12 mss/year.** Length: 20-100 words. **Pays $25-75.**

⊖⊖⊖⊖ SIERRA

85 Second St., 2nd Floor, San Francisco CA 94105. (415)977-5656. **Fax:** (415)977-5799. **E-mail:** sierra. magazine@sierraclub.org. **Website:** www.sierraclub. org. **Contact:** Martha Geering, art director. **Works with a small number of new/unpublished writers each year.** Bimonthly magazine emphasizing conservation and environmental politics for people who are well educated, activist, outdoor-oriented, and politically well informed with a dedication to conservation. Estab. 1893. Circ. 695,000. Byline given. Pays on acceptance. Offers negotiable kill fee. Publishes ms an average of 4 months after acceptance. Accepts queries by mail, fax. Responds in 2 months to queries. Sample copy for $3 and SASE, or online. Guidelines available online.

NONFICTION Needs exposé, well-documented articles on environmental issues of national importance such as energy, wilderness, forests, etc., general interest, well-researched nontechnical pieces on areas of particular environmental concern, interview, photo feature, photo feature essays on threatened or scenic areas, journalistic treatments of semitechnical topic (energy sources, wildlife management, land use, waste management, etc.). "No 'My trip to ..' or 'Why we must save wildlife/nature' articles; no poetry or general superficial essays on environmentalism; no reporting on purely local environmental issues. **Buys 30-36 mss/**

year. Query with published clips. Length: 1,000-3,000 words. **Pays $800-3,000.**

REPRINTS Send photocopy with rights for sale noted and information about when and where the material previously appeared. Payment negotiable.

COLUMNS/DEPARTMENTS Food for Thought (food's connection to environment); Good Going (adventure journey); Hearth & Home (advice for environmentally sound living); Body Politics (health and the environment); Profiles (biographical look at environmentalists); Hidden Life (exposure of hidden environmental problems in everyday objects); Lay of the Land (national/international concerns), 500-700 words; Mixed Media (essays on environment in the media; book reviews), 200-300 words. **Pays $50-500.**

⊖⊖⊖⊖ WILDLIFE CONSERVATION

2300 Southern Blvd., Bronx NY 10460. (718)220-5100. **E-mail:** nsimmons@wcs.org; membership@ wcs.org. **Website:** www.wcs.org. Bimonthly magazine for environmentally aware readers. Offers 25% kill fee. Accepts simultaneous submissions. Responds in 1 month to queries. Sample copy for $4.95 (plus $1 postage). Writer's guidelines available for SASE or via e-mail.

NONFICTION Buys 30 mss/year. Query with published clips. Length: 300-2,000 words. **Pays $1/word for features and department articles, and $150 for short pieces**

PERSONAL COMPUTERS

⊖⊖⊖ SMART COMPUTING

Sandhills Publishing, 120 W. Harvest Dr., Lincoln NE 68521. (800)544-1264. **Fax:** (402)479-2104. **E-mail:** editor@smartcomputing.com. **Website:** www.smart-computing.com. **45% freelance written.** Monthly magazine. "We focus on plain-English computing articles with an emphasis on tutorials that improve productivity without the purchase of new hardware." Estab. 1990. Circ. 200,000. Byline given. Pays on acceptance. Offers 25% kill fee. Publishes ms an average of 2 months after acceptance. Editorial lead time 4 months. Submit seasonal material 4 months in advance. Accepts queries by mail, e-mail. Accepts simultaneous submissions. Responds in 1 month to queries. Sample copy for $7.99. Guidelines for #10 SASE.

NONFICTION Needs how-to, new product, technical. No humor, opinion, personal experience. **Buys 250 mss/year.** Query with published clips. Length:

800-3,200 words. **Pays $240-960.** Pays expenses of writers on assignment up to $75.

PHOTOGRAPHY

APOGEE PHOTO MAGAZINE

Jacksonville FL (904)619-2010. **E-mail:** meier@qa-das.com. **Website:** apogeephoto.com. **Contact:** Marla Meier, editorial director. "A free online monthly magazine designed to inform, educate and entertain photographers of all ages and levels. Take online photography courses, read photo articles covering a wide range of photo topics and see listings of photo workshops and tours, camera clubs, and books. Submit your articles for publication."

PHOTOS "*Apogee Photo* is interested in providing an electronic forum for high quality work from photographic writers and photographers. We will accept articles up to 2000 words on any photographic subject geared towards the beginning to advanced photographer. Articles must have a minimum of 4-6 photographs accompanying them. You must hold the copyright and/or have a copyright release from a 3rd party and you must have signed model releases where applicable for any identifiable person or persons which appear in your photographs." Accepts reviews of new products, 1,000/words max.

PHOTOGRAPHER'S FORUM MAGAZINE

813 Reddick St., Santa Barbara CA 93103. (805)965-6425. **Fax:** (805)965-0496. **E-mail:** julie@serbin.com. **Website:** www.pfmagazine.com. **Contact:** Julie Simpson, managing editor. Quarterly magazine for the serious student and emerging professional photographer. Includes feature articles on historic and contemporary photographers, interviews, book reviews, workshop listings, and new products.

NONFICTION Needs historical, interview, new product, photo feature, profile, reviews.

PIX

DGR Media, 8 Ngobit Rd., Sunninghill South Africa. (011)234-6997. **Fax:** (011)803-3278. **E-mail:** tracey@pixmag.co.za. **Website:** www.pixmag.co.za. **Contact:** Tracey Simpson. **75% freelance written.** Bimonthly magazine covering techniques and new products (cameras/accessories) for consumer and professional photographers. Estab. 2003. Circ. 8,000. Byline given. Pays on publication. No kill fee. Publishes ms an average of 3 months after acceptance. Editorial lead time 1 month. Submit seasonal material 1 weeks in advance. Accepts queries by e-mail. Accepts simultaneous submissions. Guidelines by e-mail.

NONFICTION Needs how-to, interview, photo feature, technical, travel. **Buys 10 mss/year.** Query. Length: 600-1,800 words. **Pays maximum R300 for assigned articles. Pays maximum R250 for unsolicited articles.** Sometimes pays expenses of writers on assignment.

POLITICS AND WORLD AFFAIRS

THE AMERICAN DISSIDENT: A JOURNAL OF LITERATURE, DEMOCRACY & DISSIDENCE

217 Commerce Rd., Barnstable MA 02630. **E-mail:** todslone@hotmail.com. **Website:** www.theamericandissident.org. **Contact:** G. Tod Slone, editor. Journal, published 2 times/year, provides "a forum for, amongst other things, criticism of the academic/literary established order, which clearly discourages vigorous debate, cornerstone of democracy, to the evident detriment of American Literature. The Journal seeks rare poets daring to risk going against that established-order grain." Wants "poetry, reviews, artwork, and short (1,000 words) essays in English, French, or Spanish, written on the edge with a dash of personal risk and stemming from personal experience, conflict with power, and/or involvement." Submissions should be "iconoclastic and parrhesiastic in nature." Estab. 1998. Circ. 200. Up to 2 months between acceptance and publication. Accepts queries by e-mail. Responds in 1 month. Guidelines available for SASE.

NONFICTION Needs exposé, opinion, reviews.

POETRY Submit 3 poems at a time. Considers simultaneous submissions; no previously published poems. E-mail submissions from subscribers only. "Far too many poets submit without even reading the guidelines. Include SASE and cover letter containing not credits, but rather personal dissident information, as well as incidents that provoked you to 'go upright and vital, and speak the rude truth in all ways' (Emerson)." Time between acceptance and publication is up to 2 months. Almost always comments on rejected poems. Guidelines available for SASE. Responds in 1 month. Pays 1 contributor's copy. Acquires first North American serial rights. Reviews books/chapbooks of poetry and other magazines in 250 words, single-book format. Send materials for review consideration.

HE AMERICAN SPECTATOR

1611 N. Kent St., Suite 901, Arlington VA 22209. (703)807-2011. **Fax:** (703)807-2013. **E-mail:** editor@spectator.org. **Website:** www.spectator.org. Monthly conservative magazine covering U.S. politics. "For many years, one ideological viewpoint dominated American print and broadcast journalism. Today, that viewpoint still controls the entertainment and news divisions of the television networks, the mass-circulation news magazines, and the daily newspapers. *The American Spectator* has attempted to balance the Left's domination of the media by debunking its perceived wisdom and advancing alternative ideas through spirited writing, insightful essays, humor and, most recently, through well-researched investigative articles that have themselves become news." Estab. 1967. Circ. 50,000. No kill fee. Accepts queries by mail, e-mail. Responds only if interested in 3-4 weeks.

NONFICTION No unsolicited poetry, fiction, satire, or crossword puzzles. Query with résumé, clips and SASE.

COLUMNS/DEPARTMENTS The Continuing Crisis and Current Wisdom (humor); On the Prowl (Washington insider news). Query with résumé, clips and SASE.

◉◉ CHURCH & STATE

1301 K Street NW, Suite 850E, Washington DC 20005. (202)466-3234. **Fax:** (202)466-2587. **E-mail:** americansunited@au.org. **Website:** www.au.org. **10% freelance written.** Monthly magazine emphasizing religious liberty and church/state relations matters. "Strongly advocates separation of church and state. Readership is well-educated." Estab. 1947. Circ. 40,000. Pays on acceptance. No kill fee. Publishes ms an average of 2 months after acceptance. Accepts queries by mail. Accepts simultaneous submissions. Responds in 2 months to queries. Sample copy and writer's guidelines for 9x12 SAE with 3 first-class stamps.

NONFICTION Needs exposé, general interest, historical, interview. **Buys 11 mss/year.** Query. Length: 800-1,600 words. **Pays $150-300.** Sometimes pays expenses of writers on assignment.

REPRINTS Send tearsheet, photocopy or typed ms with rights for sale noted and information about when and where the material previously appeared.

◉◉ THE FREEMAN: IDEAS ON LIBERTY

30 S. Broadway, Irvington-on-Hudson NY 10533. (914)591-7230. **Fax:** (914)591-8910. **E-mail:** freeman@fee.org. **E-mail:** mnolan@fee.org. **Website:** www.thefreemanonline.org. Max Borders, editor. **Contact:** Michael Nolan, managing editor. **85% freelance written.** Monthly publication for the layman and fairly advanced students of liberty. Estab. 1946. Byline given. Pays on publication. No kill fee. Publishes ms an average of 5 months after acceptance. Sample copy for 7 1/2x10 1/2 SASE with 4 first-class stamps. Guidelines available on website.

NONFICTION **Buys 100 mss/year.** Query with SASE. Length: 3,500 words. **Pays 10¢/word.** Sometimes pays expenses of writers on assignment.

LEFT CURVE

P.O. Box 472, Oakland CA 94604-0472. (510)763-7193. **E-mail:** editor@leftcurve.org. **Website:** www.leftcurve.org. **Contact:** Csaba Polony, editor. "*Left Curve* is an artist-produced journal addressing the problem(s) of cultural forms emerging from the crises of modernity that strive to be independent from the control of dominant institutions, based on the recognition of the destructiveness of commodity (capitalist) systems to all life." Published irregularly. Estab. 1974. Circ. 2,000. Publishes ms 6-12 months after acceptance. Responds in 6 months to mss and poems. Sometimes comments on rejected mss. Sample copy for $12; back copies $10. Guidelines available for SASE, by e-mail, or on website.

FICTION Needs ethnic/multicultural, experimental, historical, literary, regional, science fiction, translations, contemporary, prose poem, political. "No topical satire, religion-based pieces, melodrama. We publish critical, open, social/political-conscious writing." Send complete ms with cover letterl. Include "statement of writer's intent, brief bio, and reason for submitting to *Left Curve*. We accept electronic submissions and hard copy, though for accepted work we request e-mail copy, either in body of text or as attachments. For accepted longer work, we prefer submission of final draft in digital form via disk or e-mail." Length: 500-5,000 words; average length: 1,200 words. Also ublishes short shorts. **Pays in contributor's copies.**

POETRY Submit up to 5 poems at a time. Accepts e-mail or disk submissions. Cover letter is required. "Explain why you are submitting." Publishes theme issues. Lines/poem: "most of our published poetry is 1 page in length, though we have published longer poems of up to 8 pages." **Pays 2-3 contributor's copies.**

THE NATION

33 Irving Place, 8th Floor, New York NY 10003. **E-mail:** submissions@thenation.com. **Website:** www. thenation.com. Steven Brower, art director. **Contact:** Jordan Davis, poetry editor. *The Nation*, published weekly, is a journal of left/liberal opinion, with arts coverage that includes poetry. The only requirement for poetry is "excellence." Estab. 1865. Circ. 100,000. Guidelines available online.

NONFICTION Needs civil liberties, civil rights, labor, economics, environmental, feminist issues, politics, the arts. Queries accepted via e-mail only to submissions@thenation.com. Length: 750-2,500 words. **Pays $150-500, depending on length.**

POETRY Submit up to 3 poems at a time, no more than 8 poems within the calendar year. No simultaneous submissions. No fax, e-mail disk submissions. Doesn't reply to or return poems sent by fax or e-mail or submitted without an SASE.

THE NEW VERSE NEWS

Tangerang Indonesia. **E-mail:** nvneditor@yahoo. com; nvneditor@gmail.com. **Website:** www.new-versenews.com. **Contact:** James Penha, editor. *The New Verse News*, published online and updated "every day or two," has "a clear liberal bias, but will consider various visions and views." Wants "poems, both serious and satirical, on current events and topical issues; will also consider prose poems and short-short stories and plays." Does not want "work unrelated to the news." Receives about 1,200 poems/year; accepts about 300. "Normally, poems are published immediately upon acceptance." Submit seasonal poems 1 month in advance. Responds in 1-3 weeks. Sometimes comments on rejected poems. Guidelines available on website.

POETRY Submit 1-5 poems at a time. No previously published poems or simultaneous submissions. Accepts only e-mail submissions (pasted into body of message); use "Verse News Submission" as the subject line; no disk or postal submissions. Send brief bio. Reads submissions year-round. Poems are circulated to an editorial board. Lines/poem: no length restrictions. **No payment.**

THE PROGRESSIVE

409 E. Main St., Madison WI 53703. (608)257-4626. **Fax:** (608)257-3373. **E-mail:** editorial@progressive. org; mattr@progressive.org. **Website:** www.progressive.org. **Contact:** Matthew Rothschild, editor. **75% freelance written.** Monthly magazine of investigative reporting, political commentary, cultural coverage, activism, interviews, poetry, and humor. Estab. 1909. Byline given. Pays on publication. Publishes ms an average of 6 weeks after acceptance. Accepts queries by mail. Responds in 1 month to queries. Sample copy for 9x12 SASE with 4 first-class stamps or sample articles online. Guidelines available online.

NONFICTION Query. Length: 500-4,000 words. **Pays $500-1,300.**

POETRY Publishes 1 original poem a month. "We prefer poems that connect up—in 1 fashion or another, however obliquely—with political concerns." **Pays $150.**

THEORIA

Berghahn Books, Inc., c/o Turpin North America, 143 West St., New Milford CT 06776. (860)350-0041. **Fax:** (860)350-0039. **E-mail:** theoriasa@gmail.com; editorial@journals.berghahnbooks.com. **Website:** http:// journals.berghahnbooks.com/th. **Contact:** Chris Allsobrook, managing editor. **100% freelance written.** Academic journal published 1 times/year. "*Theoria* is an engaged, multidisciplinary peer-reviewed journal of social and political theory. Its purpose is to address—through scholarly debate—the many challenges posed to intellectual life by the major social, political, and economic forces that shape the contemporary world. Thus, it is principally concerned with questions such as how modern systems of power, processes of globalization, and capitalist economic organization bear on matters such as justice, democracy, and truth." Estab. 1947. Circ. 300. Byline sometimes given. No kill fee. Publishes ms an average of 6 months after acceptance. Editorial lead time 3 months. Submit seasonal material 3 months in advance. Accepts queries by mail, e-mail, fax, phone. Responds in 1 week to queries. Responds in 3-4 months to mss. Sample copy free online. Guidelines online or via e-mail.

NONFICTION Needs book excerpts, essays, exposé, general interest, historical, interview, review articles, book reviews, theoretical, philosophical, political. **Buys 1 mss/year.** Send complete ms. "Ms must comply with guidelines." Length: 6,000-9,000 words. "Ms must be ready for blind peer review." **No payment.**

PHOTOS State availability. Identification of subjects required. Reviews GIF/JPEG files. Negotiates payment individually.

COLUMNS/DEPARTMENTS Book Reviews, 1,000-1,500 words; Review Articles, 3,000-5,000 words. **Buys 1 mss/year.** Send complete ms.

PSYCHOLOGY & SELF-IMPROVEMENT

THE AWAKENINGS REVIEW

P.O. Box 177, Wheaton IL 60187. **E-mail:** info@awakeningsproject.org. **Website:** www.awakeningsproject.org. **Contact:** Robert Lundin, director. *The Awakenings Review* is published by the Awakenings Project. Begun in cooperation with the University of Chicago Center for Psychiatric Rehabilitation in 2000, *The Awakenings Review* has been acclaimed internationally and draws writers from all over the United States and from several other countries including Israel, South Africa, Australia, Finland, Switzerland, the United Kingdom, and Canada. Estab. 1999. Publishes ms 8 months after acceptance. Submit seasonal poems 6 months in advance. Responds in 1 month. Guidelines available in magazine, for SASE, by e-mail, or on website.

POETRY Submit 5 poems at a time. No previously published poems or simultaneous submissions. No e-mail submissions. Cover letter is preferred. Include SASE and short bio. Poems are read by a board of editors. Often comments on rejected poems. Occasionally publishes theme issue. **Pays 1 contributor's copy, plus discount on additional copies.**

REGIONAL

ALABAMA

$ ALABAMA LIVING

Alabama Rural Electric Association, 340 Techna-Center Dr., Montgomery AL 36117. (800)410-2737. **Website:** www.alabamaliving.com. **Contact:** Lenore Vickrey, editor; Michael Cornelison, art director. **80% freelance written.** Monthly magazine covering topics of interest to rural and suburban Alabamians. "Our magazine is an editorially balanced, informational and educational service to members of rural electric cooperatives. Our mix regularly includes Alabama history, Alabama features, gardening, outdoor, and consumer pieces." Estab. 1948. Circ. 400,000. Byline given. Pays on acceptance. No kill fee. Editorial lead time 4 months. Submit seasonal material 4 months in advance. Accepts queries by mail, e-mail. Accepts simultaneous submissions. Responds in 1 month to queries. Sample copy free.

NONFICTION Needs historical, rural-oriented, Alabama slant, Alabama. Special issues: Gardening (March); Travel (April); Home Improvement (May); Holiday Recipes (December). **Buys 20 mss/year.** Send complete ms. Length: 500-750 words. **Pays $250 minimum for assigned articles. Pays $150 minimum for unsolicited articles.**

REPRINTS Send typed manuscript with rights for sale noted. Pays $100.

ARIZONA

$$ ARIZONA FOOTHILLS MAGAZINE

8132 N. 87th Place, Scottsdale AZ 85258. (480)460-5203. **Fax:** (480)443-1517. **E-mail:** editorial@azfoothillsmag.com; publisher@azfoothillsmag.com. **Website:** www.azfoothillsmag.com. **Contact:** Michael Dee, publisher. **10% freelance written.** Monthly magazine covering Arizona lifestyle. Estab. 1996. Circ. 60,000. Byline given. Pays on publication. No kill fee. Publishes ms an average of 6 months after acceptance. Editorial lead time 6 months. Submit seasonal material at least 4 months in advance. Accepts queries by mail, e-mail. Responds in 1 month to queries. Sample copy for #10 SASE.

NONFICTION Needs general interest, photo feature, travel, fashion, decor, arts, interview. **Buys 10 mss/year.** Query with published clips. Length: 900-2,000 words. **Pays 35-40¢/word for assigned articles.**

COLUMNS/DEPARTMENTS Travel, dining, fashion, home decor, design, architecture, wine, shopping, golf, performance & visual arts.

$ PHOENIX MAGAZINE

Cities West Publishing, Inc., 15169 N. Scottsdale Rd., Suite C-310, Scottsdale AZ 85254. (866)481-6970. **Fax:** (602)604-0169. **E-mail:** phxmag@citieswestpub.com. **Website:** www.phoenixmag.com. **70% freelance written.** Monthly magazine covering regional issues, personalities, events, neighborhoods, customs, and history of metro Phoenix. Estab. 1966. Circ. 60,000. Byline given. Pays on publication. No kill fee. Publishes ms an average of 3 months after acceptance. Submit seasonal material 1 year in advance. Accepts queries by mail, e-mail. Responds in 2 months to queries. Responds in 2 months to mss. Sample copy for $3.95 and 9x12 SASE with 5 first-class stamps. Guidelines for #10 SASE.

NONFICTION Needs general interest, interview, investigative, historical, service pieces (where to go and what to do around town). "We do not publish fiction, poetry, personal essays, book reviews, music reviews, or product reviews, and our travel stories are staff written. With the exception of our travel stories, all of the content in *Phoenix* magazine is geographically specific to the Phoenix-metro region. We do not publish any non-travel news or feature stories that are outside the Phoenix area, and we prefer that our freelancers are located in the Phoenix metro area." **Buys 50 mss/year.** Query with published clips via e-mail. "Include a short summary, a list of sources, and an explanation of why you think your idea is right for the magazine and why you're qualified to write it." Length: 150-2,000 words.

CALIFORNIA

⊗⊗ CARLSBAD MAGAZINE

Wheelhouse Media, P.O. Box 2089, Carlsbad CA 92018. (760)729-9099. **Fax:** (760)729-9011. **E-mail:** tim@wheelhousemedia.com. **Website:** www.click-oncarlsbad.com. **Contact:** Tim Wrisley. **80% freelance written.** Bimonthly magazine covering people, places, events, arts in Carlsbad, California. "We are a regional magazine highlighting all things pertaining specifically to Carlsbad. We focus on history, events, people, and places that make Carlsbad interesting and unique. Our audience is both Carlsbad residents and visitors or anyone interested in learning more about Carlsbad. We favor a conversational tone that still adheres to standard rules of writing." Estab. 2004. Circ. 35,000. Byline given. Pays on publication. Publishes ms an average of 6 months after acceptance. Editorial lead time 4 months. Submit seasonal material 6-12 months in advance. Accepts queries by mail, e-mail. Accepts simultaneous submissions. Responds in 2 months to queries and to mss. Sample copy for $2.31. Guidelines by e-mail.

NONFICTION Needs historical, interview, photo feature, home, garden, arts, events. Does not want self-promoting articles for individuals or businesses, real estate how-to's, advertorials. **Buys 3 mss/year.** Query with published clips. Length: 300-2,700 words. **Pays 20-30¢/word for assigned articles. Pays 20¢/word for unsolicited articles.** Sometimes pays expenses of writers on assignment.

COLUMNS/DEPARTMENTS Carlsbad Arts (people, places or things related to cultural arts in Carlsbad); Happenings (events that take place in Carlsbad); Carlsbad Character (unique Carlsbad residents who have contributed to Carlsbad's character); Commerce (Carlsbad business profiles); Surf Scene (subjects pertaining to the beach/surf in Carlsbad), all 500-700 words. Garden (Carlsbad garden feature); Home (Carlsbad home feature), both 700-1,200 words. **Buys 60 mss/year.** Query with published clips. **Pays $50 flat fee or 20¢/word.**

⊗ JOURNAL PLUS MAGAZINE

654 Osos St., San Luis Obispo CA 93401. (805)546-0609; (805)544-8711. **Fax:** (805)546-8827. **E-mail:** slojournal@fix.net. **Website:** www.slojournal.com. **Contact:** Steve Owens, publisher. "*The Journal* is strictly local to the Central Coast of California, and the writers are local as well." Sample copy for SASE with $2 postage. Guidelines available online.

NONFICTION Needs general interest. Query. Length: 600-1,400 words. **Pays $50 for articles under 850 words, with artwork or photos; $75 for articles under 850 words, with artwork or photos.**

⊗ NOB HILL GAZETTE

Nob Hill Gazette, Inc., 5 Third St., Suite 222, San Francisco CA 94103. (415)227-0190. **Fax:** (415)974-5103. **E-mail:** email@nobhillgazette.com; claudia@nobhillgazette.com; lois@nobhillgazette.com; shara@nobhillgazette.com;. **Website:** www.nobhillgazette.com. **Contact:** Claudia Zaik, editor; Lois Lehrman, publisher; Shara Hall, photo editor. **95% freelance written.** Monthly magazine covering upscale lifestyles in the Bay Area. "The *Gazette* caters to an audience upscale in taste and lifestyle. Our main purpose is to publicize events that raise millions of dollars for local cultural programs and charities, and to recognize the dedicated volunteers who work behind the scenes. With publisher Lois Lehrman at the helm, each trendsetting issue of our monthly magazine includes about 200 photos and 15 or more local interest stories. Our features, often 'tongue-in-chic,' cover art, beauty, books, entertainment, fashion, health, history, interiors, profiles, travels, and much, much more." Estab. 1978. Circ. 82,000. Byline given. Pays on 15th of month following publication. Offers $50 kill fee. Publishes ms an average of 2-3 months after acceptance. Editorial lead time 1-2 months. Submit seasonal material 1-2 months in advance. Accepts queries by e-mail. Responds in 2 weeks to queries. Responds in 2 months to mss. Sample copy available online. Guidelines free. **NONFICTION** Contact: Claudia Zaik, editor. Needs general interest, historical, interview, opinion, photo feature, trends, lifestyles, fashion, health, fitness, entertaining, decor, real estate, charity and philanthropy, culture and the arts. Does not want first person articles, anything commercial (from a business or with a product to sell), profiles of people not active in the community, anything technical, anything on people or events not in the Bay Area. **Buys 75 mss/ year.** Query with published clips. Length: 1,200-2,000 words. **Pays $100.** Sometimes pays expenses of writers on assignment.

COLUMNS/DEPARTMENTS Contact: Lois Lehrman, publisher. "All our columnists are freelancers, but they write for us regularly, so we don't take other submissions."

⊕⊖ SACRAMENTO NEWS & REVIEW

Chico Community Publishing, 1124 Del Paso Blvd., Sacramento CA 95815. (916)498-1234. **Fax:** (916)498-7920. **Website:** www.newsreview.com. **Contact:** Rachel Leibrock, editor; Nick Miller, editor. **25% freelance written.** Alternative news and entertainment weekly magazine. We maintain a high literary standard for submissions; unique or alternative slant. Publication aimed at a young, intellectual audience; submissions should have an edge and strong voice. We have a decided preference for stories with a strong local slant. "Our mission: To publish great newspapers that are successful and enduring. To create a quality work environment that encourages employees to grow professionally while respecting personal welfare. To have a positive impact on our communities and make them better places to live. " Estab. 1989. Circ. 87,000. Byline given. Pays on publication. Offers 10% kill fee. Publishes ms an average of 2 months after acceptance. Editorial lead time 2 months. Submit seasonal material 2 months in advance. Accepts queries by mail, e-mail. Accepts simultaneous submissions. Responds in 1 month to queries. Responds in 2 months to mss. Sample copy for 50¢. Guidelines available online.

NONFICTION Needs essays, exposé, general interest, humor, interview, personal experience. Does not want to see travel, product stories, business profile. **Buys 20-30 mss/year.** Query with published clips. Length: 750-5,000 words. **Pays $40-500.** Sometimes pays expenses of writers on assignment.

SONG OF THE SAN JOAQUIN

P.O. Box 1161, Modesto CA 95353. **E-mail:** cleor36@ yahoo.com. **Website:** www.ChaparralPoets.org/SSJ. html. **Contact:** Cleo Griffith, editor. *Song of the San Joaquin*, published quarterly, features "subjects about or pertinent to the San Joaquin Valley of Central California. This is defined geographically as the region from Fresno to Stockton, and from the foothills on the west to those on the east." Wants all forms and styles of poetry. "Keep subject in mind." Does not want "pornographic, demeaning, vague, or trite approaches." Considers poetry by children and teens. Estab. 2003. Publishes ms 3-6 months after acceptance. Submit seasonal poems at least 3 months in advance. Occasionally publishes theme issues. Upcoming themes available for SASE, by e-mail, or on website. TrueResponds in up to 3 months.

POETRY This is a quarterly, please keep in mind the sesons of the year. Considers previously published poems. E-mail submissions are preferred; no disk submissions. Cover letter is preferred. "SASE required. All submissions must be typed on 1 side of the page only. Proofread submissions carefully. Name, address, phone number, and e-mail address should appear on all pages. Cover letter should include any awards, honors, and previous publications for each poem, and a biographical sketch of 75 words or less." Reads submissions "periodically throughout the year." Has published poetry by Robert Cooperman, Taylor Graham, Carol Louise Moon, Mimi Moriarty, Charles Rammelkamp. Submit maximum 3 poems. Open ("however, poems under 40 lines have the best chance"). **Pays 1 contributor's copy.**

CANADA/INTERNATIONAL

⊕⊖ ABACO LIFE

Caribe Communications, P.O. Box 37487, Raleigh NC 27627. (919)859-6782. **Fax:** (919)859-6769. **E-mail:** jimkerr@mindspring.com. **Website:** www.abacolife. com. **Contact:** Jim Kerr, publisher and editor. **50% freelance written.** Quarterly magazine covering Abaco, an island group in the Northeast Bahamas. "*Ab-*

aco Life editorial focuses entirely on activities, history, wildlife, resorts, people and other subjects pertaining to the Abacos. Readers include locals, vacationers, second-home owners, and other visitors whose interests range from real estate and resorts to scuba, sailing, fishing, and beaches. The tone is upbeat, adventurous, humorous. No fluff writing for an audience already familiar with the area." Estab. 1979. Circ. 10,000. Byline given. Pays on publication. Offers 40% kill fee. Publishes ms an average of 2 months after acceptance. Editorial lead time 2 months. Submit seasonal material 4 months in advance. Accepts queries by mail, e-mail. Accepts simultaneous submissions. Responds in 2 weeks to queries. Responds in 2 months to mss. Sample copy for $2. Guidelines free.

NONFICTION Needs general interest, historical, how-to, interview, personal experience, photo feature, travel. No general first-time impressions. Articles must be specific, show knowledge and research of the subject and area—'Abaco's Sponge Industry'; 'Diving Abaco's Wrecks'; 'The Hurricane of '36.' **Buys 8-10 mss/year.** Query or send complete ms Length: 700-2,000 words. **Pays $400-1,000.**

🍁 $$$$ ALBERTA VIEWS

Alberta Views, Ltd., Suite 208, 320 23rd Ave. SW, Calgary AB T2S 0J2 Canada. (403)243-5334l; (877)212-5334. **Fax:** (403)243-8599. **E-mail:** queries@albertaviews.ab.ca. **Website:** www.albertaviews.ab.ca. **Contact:** Evan Osenton, editor. **50% freelance written.** Bimonthly magazine covering Alberta culture: politics, economy, social issues, and art. "We are a regional magazine providing thoughtful commentary and background information on issues of concern to Albertans. Most of our writers are Albertans." Estab. 1997. Circ. 30,000. Byline given. Pays on publication. Offers 50% kill fee. Publishes ms an average of 3 months after acceptance. Editorial lead time 4 months. Submit seasonal material 3 months in advance. Accepts queries by e-mail. Responds in 6 weeks to queries. Responds in 2 months to mss. Sample copy free. "If you are a writer, illustrator, or photographer interested in contributing to *Alberta Views*, please see our contributor's guidelines online."

NONFICTION Needs essays. **Buys 18 mss/year.** "Query with written proposal of 300–500 words outlining your intended contribution to *Alberta Views*, why you are qualified to write about your subject, and what sources you intend to use; a résumé outlining your experience and education; recent examples of your published work (tear sheets)." Length: 3,000-5,000 words. **Pays $1,000-1,500 for assigned articles. Pays $350-750 for unsolicited articles.** Sometimes pays expenses of writers on assignment.

FICTION Only fiction by Alberta writers via the annual *Albera Views* fiction contest. **Buys 6 mss/year.** Send complete ms. Length: 2,500-4,000 words. **Pays $1,000 maximum.**

🍁 $$ COTTAGE

OP Publishing, Ltd., Suite 500-200, West Esplanade, North Vancouver BC V7M 1A4 Canada. (604)998-3327. **Fax:** (604)998-3320. **E-mail:** editor@cottagemagazine.com. **Website:** www.cottagemagazine.com. **80% freelance written.** "Bimonthly magazine covering do-it-yourself projects, profiles of people and their innovative solutions to building and maintaining their country homes, issues that affect rural individuals and communities, and the R&R aspect of country living." "Our readers want solid, practical information about living in the country—including alternative energy and sustainable living. They also like to have fun in a wide range of recreational pursuits, from canoeing, fishing, and sailing to water skiing, snowmobiling, and entertaining." Estab. 1992. Circ. 20,000. Byline given. Pays within 1 month of publication. Offers 25% kill fee. Publishes ms an average of 6 months after acceptance. Accepts queries by e-mail. Accepts simultaneous submissions. Responds in 1 month to queries.

NONFICTION Buys 18-24 mss/year. Query. Up to 1,500 words. **Pays $100-450 (including visuals).**

COLUMNS/DEPARTMENTS Utilities (solar and/or wind power), 800 words; Weekend Project (a how-to most homeowners can do themselves), 800 words; Government (new regulations, processes, problems), 800 words; Diversions (advisories, ideas, and how-to's about the fun things that people do), 800 words; InRoads (product reviews), 50-600 words; This Land (personal essays or news-based story with a broader context), 800 words; Last Word or Cabin Life (personal essays and experiences), 800 words; Elements (short articles focusing on a single feature of a cottage), 600 words; Alternatives (applied alternative energy), 600 words. Query. **Pays $75-250.**

FILLERS Needs anecdotes, facts, newsbreaks, seasonal tips. **Buys 12 mss/year.** Length: 50-200 words. **20¢/word.**

🍁 $$$$ HAMILTON MAGAZINE

Town Media, a division of Sun Media, 1074 Cooke Blvd., Burlington ON L7T 4A8 Canada. (905)522-6117 or (905)634-8003. **Fax:** (905)634-7661 or (905)634-8804. **E-mail:** marc.skulnick@sunmedia.ca; tm.info@sunmedia.ca. **Website:** www.hamiltonmagazine.com. **Contact:** Marc Skulnick, editor; Kate Sharrow, art director. **50% freelance written.** Quarterly magazine devoted to the Greater Hamilton and Golden Horseshoe area (Ontario, Canada). "Our mandate: to entertain and inform by spotlighting the best of what our city and region has to offer. We invite readers to take part in a vibrant community by supplying them with authoritative and dynamic coverage of local culture, food, fashion, and design. Each story strives to expand your view of the area, every issue an essential resource for exploring, understanding and unlocking the region. Packed with insight, intrigue and suspense, *Hamilton Magazine* delivers the city to your doorstep." Estab. 1978. Byline given. Pays on publication. Offers 50% kill fee. Editorial lead time 2-3 months. Submit seasonal material 2-3 months in advance. Accepts queries by e-mail. Responds in 1 week to queries and to mss. Sample copy with #10 SASE. Guidelines by e-mail.

NONFICTION Needs book excerpts, essays, exposé, historical, how-to, humor, inspirational, interview, personal experience, photo feature, religious, travel. Does not want generic articles that could appear in any mass-market publication. Send complete ms. Length: 800-2,000 words. **Pays $200-1,600 for assigned articles; $100-800 for unsolicited articles.** Sometimes pays expenses of writers on assignment.

COLUMNS/DEPARTMENTS A&E Art, 1,200-2,000 words; A&E Music, 1,200-2,000 words; A&E Books, 1,200-1,400 words. **Buys 12 columns/year.** Send complete ms. **Pays $200-400.**

🍁 $$ MONDAY MAGAZINE

Black Press Ltd., 818 Broughton St., Victoria BC V8W 1E4 Canada. **E-mail:** editor@mondaymag.com. **Website:** www.mondaymag.com. **Contact:** Grant McKenzie, editor-in-chief. **10% freelance written.** Weekly tabloid covering local news. "*Monday Magazine* is Victoria's only alternative newsweekly. For more than 35 years, we have published fresh, informative, and alternative perspectives on local events. We prefer lively, concise writing with a sense of humor and insight." Estab. 1975. Circ. 20,000. Byline given. **Currently not accepting freelance articles requiring payment.** Pays 1 month after publication. No kill fee. Publishes ms an average of 1 month after acceptance. Editorial lead time 1-2 months. Submit seasonal material 2 months in advance. Accepts queries by e-mail (preferred). Responds in 6-8 weeks to queries. Responds in up to 3 months to mss. Guidelines available on website.

NONFICTION Needs local exposé, general interest, humor, interview, personal experience. Special issues: Body, Mind, Spirit (October); Student Survival Guide (August). Does not want fiction, poetry, or conspiracy theories. Send complete ms. Length: 300-1,000 words. **Pays $25-50. Currently not accepting freelance articles requiring payment.**

🍁 $$ ⊘ OUTDOOR CANADA MAGAZINE

54 St. Patrick St., Toronto ON M5T 1V1 Canada. (416)599-2000. **E mail:** editorial@outdoorcanada.ca. **Website:** www.outdoorcanada.ca. **90% freelance written. Works with a small number of new/unpublished writers each year.** Estab. 1972. Circ. 90,000. Byline given. Pays on publication. No kill fee. Publishes ms an average of 8 months after acceptance. Submit seasonal material 1 year in advance. Accepts queries by mail, e-mail. Responds in 1 month to queries. Guidelines available online.

NONFICTION Needs how-to, fishing, hunting, outdoor issues, outdoor destinations in Canada. **Buys 35-40 mss/year.** Does not accept unsolicited mss. 2,500 words **Pays $500 and up.**

REPRINTS Send information about when and where the article previously appeared. Payment varies

FILLERS Buys 30-40 mss/year. Length: 100-500 words. **Pays $50 and up.**

🍁 $$$$ TORONTO LIFE

111 Queen St. E., Suite 320, Toronto ON M5C 1S2 Canada. (416)364-3333. **Fax:** (416)861-1169. **E-mail:** editorial@torontolife.com. **Website:** www.torontolife.com. **95% freelance written. Prefers to work with published/established writers.** Monthly magazine emphasizing local issues and social trends, short humor/satire, and service features for upper income, well-educated and, for the most part, young Torontonians. Circ. 92,039. Byline given. Pays on acceptance. Offers kill fee. Pays 50% kill fee for commissioned articles only. Publishes ms an average of 4 months after

acceptance. Responds in 3 weeks to queries. Sample copy for $4.95 with SAE and IRCs.

NONFICTION Query with published clips and SASE. Length: 1,000-6,000 words. **Pays $500-5,000.**

COLUMNS/DEPARTMENTS We run about 5 columns an issue. They are all freelanced, though most are from regular contributors. They are mostly local in concern and cover politics, business, performing arts, media, design, and food. Length: 2,000 words. Query with published clips and SASE. **Pays $2,000**

🍁 UP HERE

P.O. Box 1350, Yellowknife NT X1A 3T1 Canada. (867)766-6710. **Fax:** (867)873-9876. **E-mail:** aaron@uphere.ca; katharine@uphere.ca. **Website:** www.uphere.ca. **Contact:** Aaron Spitzer, editor; Eva Holland, associate editor; Samia Madwar, associate editor. **50% freelance written.** Magazine published 8 times/year covering general interest about Canada's Far North. We publish features, columns, and shorts about people, wildlife, native cultures, travel, and adventure in Yukon, Northwest Territories, and Nunavut. Be informative, but entertaining. Estab. 1984. Circ. 22,000. Byline given. Pays on publication. Offers 50% kill fee. Editorial lead time 6 months. Accepts queries by e-mail. Sample copy for $4.95 (Canadian) and 9x12 SASE.

NONFICTION Needs essays, general interest, how-to, humor, interview, personal experience, photo feature, technical, travel, lifestyle/culture, historical. **Buys 25-30 mss/year.** Query. Length: 1,500-3,000 words. **Fees are negotiable.**

COLUMNS/DEPARTMENTS Write for updated guidelines, visit website, or e-mail. **Buys 25-30 mss/year.** Query with published clips.

COLORADO

$$ STEAMBOAT MAGAZINE

Ski Town Publications, Inc., 1120 S. Lincoln Ave., Suite F, Steamboat Springs CO 80487. (970)871-9413. **Fax:** (970)871-1922. **E-mail:** info@steamboatmagazine.com. **Website:** www.steamboatmagazine.com. **Contact:** Deborah Olsen, president/publisher; Jennie Lay, editor. **80% freelance written.** "Quarterly magazine showcasing the history, people, lifestyles, and interests of Northwest Colorado. Our readers are generally well-educated, well-traveled, upscale, active people visiting our region to ski in winter and recreate in summer. They come from all 50 states and many foreign countries. Writing should be fresh, entertaining, and informative." Estab. 1978. Circ. 20,000. Byline given. Pays 50% on acceptance, 50% on publication. No kill fee. Submit seasonal material 1 year in advance. Accepts queries by mail, e-mail, fax, phone. Responds in 3 months to queries. Sample copy for $5.95 and SAE with 10 first-class stamps. Guidelines free.

NONFICTION Needs book excerpts, essays, general interest, historical, humor, interview, photo feature, travel. **Buys 10-15 mss/year.** Query with published clips. Length: 150-1,500 words. **Pays $50-300 for assigned articles.** Sometimes pays expenses of writers on assignment.

TELLURIDE MAGAZINE

Big Earth Publishing, Inc., P.O. Box 3488, Telluride CO 81435. (970)728-4245. **Fax:** (866)936-8406. **E-mail:** deb@telluridemagazine.com. **Website:** www.telluridemagazine.com. **Contact:** Deb Dion Kees, editor-in-chief. **75% freelance written.** Telluride: community, events, recreation, ski resort, surrounding region, San Juan Mountains, history, tourism, mountain living. "*Telluride Magazine* speaks specifically to Telluride and the surrounding mountain environment. Telluride is a resort town supported by the ski industry in winter, festivals in summer, outdoor recreation year round and the unique lifestyle all of that affords. As a National Historic Landmark District with a colorful mining history, it weaves a tale that readers seek out. The local/visitor interaction is key to Telluride's success in making profiles an important part of the content. Telluriders are an environmentally minded and progressive bunch who appreciate efforts toward sustainability and protecting the natural landscape and wilderness that are the region's number one draw." Estab. 1982. Circ. 70,000. Byline given. Pays 60 days from publication. Editorial lead time and advance on seasonal submissions is 6 months. Accepts queries by e-mail. Responds in 2 weeks on queries; 2 months on mss. Sample copy online at website. Guidelines by e-mail.

NONFICTION Needs historical, humor, nostalgic, personal experience, photo feature, travel, recreation, lifestyle. No articles about places or adventures other than Telluride. **Buys 10 mss/year.** Query with published clips. 1,000-2,000 words. **$200-700 for assigned articles; $100-700 for unsolicited articles.** Does not pay expenses.

COLUMNS/DEPARTMENTS Telluride Turns (news and current topics); Mountain Health (health issues related to mountain sports, and living at altitude); Nature Notes (explores the flora, fauna, geology and climate of San Juan Mountains); Green Bytes (sustainable & environmentally sound ideas and products for home building), all 500 words. **Buys 40/year mss/year.** Query. **Pays $50-200.**

FICTION "Please contact us; we are very specific about what we will accept." Needs adventure, historical, humorous, slice-of-life vignettes, western, recreation in the mountains. **Buys 2 mss/year.** Query with published clips. 800-1,200 words.

POETRY Needs Any poetry; must reflect mountains or mountain living. Buys 1/year poems/year. Length: 3 lines minimum. **Pays up to to $100.**

FILLERS anecdotes, facts, short humor. **Buys seldom buys fillers. mss/year.** 300-1,000 words. **Pays up to $500.**

CONNECTICUT

$$$ CONNECTICUT MAGAZINE

Journal Register Co., 40 Sargent Dr., New Haven CT 06511. (203)789-5226. **Fax:** (203)789-5255. **E-mail:** cmonagan@connecticutmag.com. **Website:** www.connecticutmag.com. **Contact:** Charles A. Monagam, editor; Dale B. Salm, managing editor. **75% freelance written. "Prefers to work with published/established writers who know the state and live/have lived here.** Monthly magazine for an affluent, sophisticated, suburban audience. We want only articles that pertain to living in Connecticut." Estab. 1971. Circ. 93,000. Byline given. Pays on publication. Offers 20% kill fee. Publishes ms an average of 4 months after acceptance. Submit seasonal material 4 months in advance. Accepts queries by mail, e-mail, fax. Responds in 6 weeks to queries. Guidelines for #10 SASE.

NONFICTION Needs book excerpts, exposé, general interest, interview, topics of service to Connecticut readers. Special issues: Dining/entertainment, northeast/travel, home/garden and Connecticut bride twice/year. Also, business (January) and healthcare 4-6x/year. No personal essays. **Buys 50 mss/year.** Query with published clips. 3,000 words maximum. **Pays $600-1,200.** Sometimes pays expenses of writers on assignment.

COLUMNS/DEPARTMENTS Business, Health, Politics, Connecticut Calendar, Arts, Dining Out, Gardening, Environment, Education, People, Sports, Media, From the Field (quirky, interesting regional stories with broad appeal). Length: 1,500-2,500 words. **Buys 50 mss/year.** Query with published clips. **Pays $400-700.**

FILLERS Short pieces about Connecticut trends, curiosities, interesting short subjects, etc. Length: 150-400 words. **Pays $75-150.**

DELAWARE

$$ DELAWARE TODAY

3301 Lancaster Pike, Suite 5C, Wilmington DE 19805. (302)656-1809. **Fax:** (302)656-5843. **E-mail:** editors@delawaretoday.com. **Website:** www.delawaretoday.com. **50% freelance written.** Monthly magazine geared toward Delaware people, places and issues. All stories must have Delaware slant. No pitches such as Delawareans will be interested in a national topic. Estab. 1962. Circ. 25,000. Byline given. Pays on publication. Offers 50% kill fee. Publishes ms an average of 4 months after acceptance. Editorial lead time 3 months. Submit seasonal material 6 months in advance. Responds in 2 months to queries. Sample copy for $2.95.

NONFICTION Needs historical, interview, photo feature, lifestyles, issues. Special issues: Newcomer's Guide to Delaware. **Buys 40 mss/year.** Query with published clips. Length: 100-3,000 words. **Pays $50-750.** Sometimes pays expenses of writers on assignment.

COLUMNS/DEPARTMENTS Business, Health, History, People, all 1,500 words. **Buys 24 mss/year.** Query with published clips. **Pays $150-250.**

FILLERS Needs anecdotes, newsbreaks, short humor. **Buys 10 mss/year.** Length: 100-200 words. **Pays $50-75.**

DISTRICT OF COLUMBIA

$$ WASHINGTON CITY PAPER

2390 Champlain St. NW, Washington DC 20009. (202)332-2100. **Fax:** (202)332-8500. **E-mail:** mail@washingtoncitypaper.com. **Website:** www.washingtoncitypaper.com. **Contact:** Jonathan L. Fischer, managing editor. **50% freelance written.** Relentlessly local alternative weekly in nation's capital covering city and regional politics, media and arts. No national stories. Estab. 1981. Circ. 95,000. Byline given. Pays on publication. Offers kill fee. Offers 10% kill fee for assigned stories. Publishes ms an average of 6 weeks after acceptance. Editorial lead time 7-10 days. Responds in 1 month to queries. Guidelines available online.

NONFICTION **Buys 100 mss/year.** District Line: 800-1,500 words; Covers: 2,500-10,000 words **Pays 10-40¢/word.** Sometimes pays expenses of writers on assignment.

COLUMNS/DEPARTMENTS Music Writing (eclectic). **Buys 100 mss/year.** Query with published clips or send complete ms. **Pays 10-40¢/word.**

FLORIDA

$$$$ BOCA RATON MAGAZINE

JES Publishing, 5455 N. Federal Hwy., Suite M, Boca Raton FL 33487. (561)997-8683. **Fax:** (561)997-8909. **E-mail:** editor@bocamag.com; kevin@bocamag.com. **Website:** www.bocamag.com. **Contact:** Marie Speed, editor-in-chief; Kevin Kaminski, editor. **70% freelance written.** Bimonthly lifestyle magazine devoted to the residents of South Florida, featuring fashion, interior design, food, people, places, and issues that shape the affluent South Florida market. Estab. 1981. Circ. 20,000. Byline given. Pays on acceptance. No kill fee. Publishes ms an average of 3 months after acceptance. Submit seasonal material 7 months in advance. Accepts simultaneous submissions. Responds in 1 month to queries. Sample copy for $4.95 and 10x13 SAE with 10 first-class stamps. Guidelines for #10 SASE.

NONFICTION Needs general interest, historical, humor, interview, photo feature, travel. Special issues: Interior Design (September-October); Real Estate (March-April), Best of Boca (July-August). Send complete ms. Length: 800-2,500 words. **Pays $350-1,500.**

REPRINTS Send tearsheet. Payment varies.

COLUMNS/DEPARTMENTS Body & Soul (health, fitness and beauty column, general interest); Hitting Home (family and social interactions); History or Arts (relevant to South Florida); all 1,000 words. Query with published clips or send complete ms. **Pays $350-400.**

$$ EMERALD COAST MAGAZINE

Rowland Publishing, Inc., 1932 Miccosukee Rd., Tallahassee FL 32308. (850)878-0554. **Fax:** (850)656-1871. **E-mail:** editorial@rowlandinc.com. **Website:** www.emeraldcoastmagazine.com. **25% freelance written.** Bimonthly magazine. Lifestyle publication celebrating life on Florida's Emerald Coast. All content has an Emerald Coast (Northwest Florida) connection. This includes Sandestin, Destin, Fort Walton Beach. Estab. 2000. Circ. 18,000. Byline given. Pays on acceptance. No kill fee. Publishes ms an average of 3 months after acceptance. Editorial lead time 4 months. Submit seasonal material 6 months in advance. Accepts queries by mail, e-mail. Accepts simultaneous submissions. Responds in 3 months to queries. Responds in 3 months to mss. Sample copy for $4. Guidelines by e-mail.

NONFICTION Needs essays, historical, inspirational, interview, new product, personal experience, photo feature. No fiction, poetry, or travel. No general interest—be Northwest Florida specific. **Buys 5 mss/year.** Query with published clips. Length: 1,800-2,000 words. **Pays $100-250.**

$ FT. MYERS MAGAZINE

15880 Summerlin Rd., Suite 189, Fort Myers FL 33908. (941)433-3884. **E-mail:** ftmyers@optonline.net. **Website:** www.ftmyersmagazine.com. **90% freelance written.** Bimonthly magazine covering regional arts and living for educated, active, successful and creative residents of Lee & Collier counties (FL) and guests at resorts and hotels in Lee County. "Content: Arts, entertainment, media, travel, sports, health, home, garden, environmental issues." Estab. 2001. Circ. 20,000. Byline given. 30 days after publication. No kill fee. Publishes ms an average of 2-6 months after acceptance. Editorial lead time 2-4 months. Submit seasonal material 2-4 months in advance. Accepts queries by e-mail. Accepts simultaneous submissions. Responds in 3 months to queries and to mss. Guidelines available online.

NONFICTION Needs essays, general interest, historical, how-to, humor, interview, personal experience, reviews, previews, news, informational. **Buys 10-25 mss/year.** Send complete ms. Length: 750-1,500 words. **Pays $50-150 or approximately 10¢/word.** Sometimes pays expenses of writers on assignment.

COLUMNS/DEPARTMENTS Media: books, music, video, film, theater, Internet, software (news, previews, reviews, interviews, profiles), 750-1,500 words. Lifestyles: art & design, science & technology, house & garden, health & wellness, sports & recreation, travel & leisure, food & drink (news, interviews, previews, reviews, profiles, advice), 750-1,500 words. **Buys 60 mss/year.** Query with or without published clips or send complete ms. **Pays $50-150.**

⊖⊖ TALLAHASSEE MAGAZINE

Rowland Publishing, Inc., 1932 Miccosukee Rd., Tallahassee FL 32308. **E-mail:** editorial@rowland-publishing.com. **Website:** www.rowlandpublishing.com/tallahassee-magazine. **20% freelance written.** Bimonthly magazine covering life in Florida's Capital Region. All content has a Tallahassee, Florida connection. Estab. 1978. Circ. 18,000. Byline given. Pays on acceptance. No kill fee. Publishes ms an average of 2 months after acceptance. Editorial lead time 4 months. Submit seasonal material 6 months in advance. Accepts queries by mail, e-mail. Accepts simultaneous submissions. Responds in 3 months to queries & mss. Sample copy for $4. Guidelines by e-mail.

NONFICTION Needs book excerpts, essays, historical, inspirational, interview, new product, personal experience, photo feature, travel, sports, business, Calendar items. No fiction, poetry, or travel. No general interest. **Buys 15 mss/year.** Query with published clips. Length: 500-2,500 words. **Pays $100-350.**

⊖⊖ WHERE MAGAZINE (WHERE GUESTBOOK, WHERE MAP, WHERE NEWSLETTER)

Morris Visitor Publications, 699 Broad St., Suite 500, Augusta GA 30901. **Fax:** (305)892-2991. **E-mail:** editorial@wheretraveler.com. **Website:** www.wheretraveler.com. **40% freelance written.** Monthly magazine covering tourism in U.S. cities, certain European cities, and Singapore. Estab. 1936. Circ. 30,000. Byline for features only, but all writers listed on masthead. Pays on publication. Editorial lead time 3 months. Submit seasonal material 3 months in advance. Accepts queries by mail, e-mail. Responds in 1 week to queries Sample copy available online. Guidelines by e-mail.

NONFICTION Needs new product, photo feature, travel. Query. Length: 500 words.

COLUMNS/DEPARTMENTS Dining; Entertainment; Museums & Attractions; Art Galleries; Shops & Services; all 50 words. Queries for writer clips only per page of 1 blurbs per page.

GENERAL REGIONAL

⊖⊖ BLUE RIDGE COUNTRY

Leisure Publishing, 3424 Brambleton Ave., Roanoke VA 24018. (540)989-6138. **Fax:** (540)989-7603. **E-mail:** krheinheimer@leisurepublishing.com. **Web-**site: www.blueridgecountry.com. **Contact:** Kurt Rheinheimer, editor. **90% freelance written.** Bimonthly, full-color magazine covering the Blue Ridge region. "The magazine is designed to celebrate the history, heritage and beauty of the Blue Ridge region. It is aimed at adult, upscale readers who enjoy living or traveling in the mountain regions of Virginia, North Carolina, West Virginia, Maryland, Kentucky, Tennessee, South Carolina, Alabama, and Georgia." Estab. 1988. Circ. 425,000. Byline given. Pays on publication. Offers kill fee. Offers $50 kill fee for commissioned pieces only. Publishes ms an average of 8 months after acceptance. Submit seasonal material 6 months in advance. Accepts queries by mail, e-mail, fax; prefer e-mail. Responds in 3-4 months to queries. Responds in 2 months to mss. Sample copy with 9x12 SASE with 6 first-class stamps. Guidelines available online.

NONFICTION Needs essays, general interest, historical, personal experience, photo feature, travel. Special issues: "The photo essay will continue to be part of each issue, but for the foreseeable future will be a combination of book and gallery/museum exhibit previews, and also essays of work by talented individual photographers—though we cannot pay, this is a good option for those who are interested in editorial coverage of their work. Those essays will include short profile, web link and contact information, with the idea of getting them, their work and their business directly in front of 425,000 readers' eyes." **Buys 25-30 mss/year.** Send complete ms. Length: 200-1,500 words. **Pays $50-250.**

COLUMNS/DEPARTMENTS Inns and Getaways (reviews of inns); Mountain Delicacies (cookbooks and recipes); Country Roads (shorts on regional news, people, destinations, events, history, antiques, books); Inns and Getaways (reviews of inns); On the Mountainside (first-person outdoor recreation pieces excluding hikes). **Buys 30-42 mss/year.** Query. **Pays $25-125.**

THE OXFORD AMERICAN

P.O. BOX 3235, Little Rock AR 72203. (501)374-0000. **Fax:** (501)374-0001. **E-mail:** info@oxfordamerican.org. **Website:** www.oxfordamerican.org. **Contact:** Roger D. Hodge, editor; Jullianne Ballou, managing editor; Warwick Sabin, publisher. Quarterly literary magazine from the South with a national audience. Circ. 55,000. Pays on publication. Accepts queries by mail. Responds in 2-3 months or sooner to mss.

Guidelines available at www.oxfordamerican.org/pages/submission-guidelines.

NONFICTION Needs short and long essays (500 to 3,000 words), general interest, how-to, humor, personal experience, travel, reporting, business. Query with SASE or send complete ms.

COLUMNS/DEPARTMENTS Odes, Travel, Politics, Business, Writing on Writing, Southerner Abroad, Reports, Literature.

FICTION Stories should be from or about the South. Send complete ms.

POETRY Poems should be from or about the South. Submit maximum 3-5 poems.

SOUTHERN LIVING

Time Inc. Lifestyle Group, 2100 Lakeshore Dr., Birmingham AL 35209. (205)445-6000. **Fax:** (205)445-6700. **E-mail:** slonline@timeinc.com. **Website:** www.southernliving.com. **Contact:** Claire Machamer, online editor. Monthly magazine covering southern lifestyle. Publication addressing the tastes and interest of contemporary southerners. Estab. 1966. Circ. 2,510,000. No kill fee. Editorial lead time 3 months. Accepts queries by mail. NoSample copy for $4.99 at newsstands. Guidelines by e-mail.

NONFICTION Needs essays. Send ms (typed, double-spaced) by postal mail. Southern Living column: "Above all, it must be southern. We need comments on life in this region—written from the standpoint of a person who is intimately familiar with this part of the world. It's personal, almost always involving something that happened to the writer or someone he or she knows very well. We take special note of stories that are contemporary in their point of view." Length: 500-600 words.

YANKEE

Yankee Publishing, Inc., P.O. Box 520, Dublin NH 03444-0520. (603)563-8111. **Fax:** (603)563-8298. **E-mail:** editors@yankeepub.com. **Website:** www.yankeemagazine.com. **Contact:** Debbie Despres, assistant editor; Heather Marcus, photo editor. **60% freelance written.** Monthly magazine covering the New England states of Connecticut, Massachusetts, Maine, New Hampshire, Rhode Island, and Vermont. "Our feature articles, as well as the departments of Home, Food, and Travel, reflect what is happening currently in these New England states. Our mission is to express and perhaps, indirectly, preserve the New England culture—and to do so in an entertaining way. Our audi-

ence is national and has 1 thing in common—it loves New England." Estab. 1935. Circ. 317,000. Byline given. Pays on acceptance. Offers kill fee. Editorial lead time 6 months. Submit seasonal material 1 year in advance. Accepts queries by mail. Accepts simultaneous submissions. Responds in 2 months to queries. Guidelines available on website.

NONFICTION Needs essays, general interest, interview. Does not want "good old days" pieces or dialect, humor, or anything outside New England. **Buys 30 mss/year.** Query with published clips and SASE. Length: 2,500 words maeximum. **Pays per assignment.** Pays expenses of writers on assignment when appropriate.

GEORGIA

GEORGIA MAGAZINE

Georgia Electric Membership Corp., P.O. Box 1707, Tucker GA 30085. (770)270-6951. **Fax:** (770)270-6995. **E-mail:** ann.orowski@georgiaemc.com. **Website:** www.georgiamagazine.org. **Contact:** Ann Orowski, editor. **50% freelance written.** We are a monthly magazine for and about Georgians, with a friendly, conversational tone and human interest topics. Estab. 1945. Circ. 509,000. Byline given. Pays on publication. No kill fee. Publishes ms an average of 6 months after acceptance. Editorial lead time 2 months. Submit seasonal material 6 months in advance. Accepts simultaneous submissions. Responds in 1 month to subjects of interest. Sample copy for $2. Guidelines for #10 SASE, or by e-mail.

NONFICTION Needs general interest, Georgia focused, historical, how-to, in the home and garden, humor, inspirational, interview, photo feature, travel. Query with published clips. Length: 1,000-1,200 words; 800 words for smaller features and departments. **Pays $350-500.**

POINTS NORTH MAGAZINE ATLANTA

All Points Interactive Media Corp., 568 Peachtree Pkwy., Cumming GA 30041-6820. (770)844-0969. **Fax:** (770)844-0968. **E-mail:** bre@ptsnorth.com; heather@ptsnorth.com; editorial@ptsnorth.com. **Website:** www.pointsnorthatlanta.com. **Contact:** Bre Humphries, editor; Heather Brown, senior editor. **15% freelance written.** Monthly magazine covering lifestyle in Atlanta, Georgia. "*Points North* specializes in providing pertinent information for our prestigious audience. In each issue we feature intriguing personalities that have a connection to the Atlanta area, fabulous travel destinations, upcoming local and regional events, topics relating to home improvement, recreation, cultural arts and entertainment, fashion, health, retail shopping and the latest news and information from those north Atlanta communities in our primary coverage area." Estab. 2000. Circ. 70,000. Byline given. Pays on publication. Offers negotiable (for assigned articles only) kill fee. Publishes ms an average of 3 months after acceptance. Editorial lead time 3 months. Submit seasonal material 6 months in advance. Accepts queries by e-mail only. Responds in 6-8 weeks to queries. Responds in 6-8 months to mss. Sample copy for $3.

NONFICTION **Contact:** Managing editor. Needs general interest, only topics pertaining to Atlanta area, historical, interview, travel. **Buys 50-60 mss/year.** Query with published clips. Length: 1,200-2,500 words. **Pays $100-250.**

$$ SAVANNAH MAGAZINE

Morris Publishing Group, P.O. Box 1088, Savannah GA 31402. **Fax:** (912)525-0611. **E-mail:** editor@savannahmagazine.com. **Website:** www.savannahmagazine.com. **Contact:** Annabelle Carr, editor; Andrea Goto, associate editor. **95% freelance written.** Bimonthly magazine focusing on homes and entertaining covering coastal lifestyle of Savannah and South Carolina area. "*Savannah Magazine* publishes articles about people, places and events of interest to the residents of the greater Savannah areas, as well as coastal Georgia and the South Carolina low country. We strive to provide our readers with information that is both useful and entertaining—written in a lively, readable style." Estab. 1990. Circ. 16,000. Byline given. Pays on publication. Offers 20% kill fee. Publishes ms an average of 2 months after acceptance. Accepts queries by mail, e-mail, fax. Accepts simultaneous submissions. Responds in 4 weeks to queries; 6 weeks to mss. Sample copy free. Guidelines by e-mail.

NONFICTION Needs general interest, historical, humor, interview, travel. Does not want fiction or poetry. Query with published clips. Length: 500-750 words. **Pays $250-450.**

HAWAII

$$$ HONOLULU MAGAZINE

PacificBasin Communications, 1000 Bishop St., Suite 405, Honolulu HI 96813. (808)537-9500. **Fax:** (808)537-6455. **E-mail:** akamn@honolulumagazine.com. **Website:** www.honolulumagazine.com. **Contact:** A. Kam Napier, editor. **Prefers to work with published/established writers.** Monthly magazine covering general interest topics relating to Hawaii residents. Estab. 1888. Circ. 30,000. Byline given. Pays about 30 days after publication. Where appropriate, kill fee of half of assignment fee. Accepts queries by mail, e-mail. Guidelines available online.

NONFICTION Needs historical, interview, sports, politics, lifestyle trends, all Hawaii-related. "We write for Hawaii residents, so travel articles about Hawaii are not appropriate." Send complete ms. determined when assignments discussed. **Pays $250-1,200.** Sometimes pays expenses of writers on assignment.

COLUMNS/DEPARTMENTS Length determined when assignments discussed. Query with published clips or send complete ms. **Pays $100-300.**

IDAHO

$$ SUN VALLEY MAGAZINE

Valley Publishing, LLC, 111 First Ave. N #1M, Meriwether Building, Hailey ID 83333. (208)788-0770. **Fax:** (208)788-3881. **E-mail:** michael@sunvalleymag.com; robinleahy@sunvalleymag.com. **Website:** www.sunvalleymag.com. **Contact:** Mike McKenna, editor; Robin Leahy, art director. **95% freelance written.** Quarterly magazine covering the lifestyle of the Sun Valley area. *Sun Valley Magazine* presents the lifestyle of the Sun Valley area and the Wood River Valley, including recreation, culture, profiles, history and the arts. Estab. 1973. Circ. 17,000. Byline given. Pays on publication. No kill fee. Publishes ms an average of 5 months after acceptance. Editorial lead time 1 year. Submit seasonal material 14 months in advance. Accepts queries by mail. Accepts simultaneous submissions. Responds in 5 weeks to queries. Responds in 2 months to mss. Sample copy for $4.95 and $3 postage. Guidelines for #10 SASE.

NONFICTION Needs historical, interview, photo feature, travel. Special issues: Sun Valley home design and architecture (spring); Sun Valley weddings/wedding planner (summer). Query with published clips. **Pays $40-500.** Sometimes pays expenses of writers on assignment.

REPRINTS Only occasionally purchases reprints.

COLUMNS/DEPARTMENTS Conservation issues, winter/summer sports, health and wellness, mountain-related activities and subjects, home (interior design), garden. All columns must have a local slant. Query with published clips. **Pays $40-300.**

ILLINOIS

🟡🟡🟡🟡 CHICAGO MAGAZINE

435 N. Michigan Ave., Suite 1100, Chicago IL 60611. (312)222-8999. **E-mail:** bfenner@chicagomag.com; cwalker@chicagomag.com. **Website:** www.chicago-mag.com. **Contact:** Elizabeth Fenner, editor-in-chief; Cassie Walker Burke, executive editor. **50% freelance written. Prefers to work with published/established writers.** Monthly magazine for an audience which is 95% from Chicago area; 90% college educated; upper income, overriding interests in the arts, politics, dining, good life in the city and suburbs. Most are in 25-50 age bracket, well-read and articulate. "Produced by the city's best magazine editors and writers, Chicago Magazine is the definitive voice on top dining, entertainment, shopping and real estate in the region. It also offers provocative narrative stories and topical features that have won numerous awards. Chicago Magazine reaches 1.5 million readers and is published by Tribune Company." Estab. 1968. Circ. 182,000. Pays on acceptance. No kill fee. Publishes ms an average of 3 months after acceptance. Submit seasonal material 4 months in advance. Accepts queries by mail, e-mail. Responds in 1 month to queries. For sample copy, send $3 to Circulation Department. Guidelines for #10 SASE.

NONFICTION Needs exposé, humor, personal experience, think pieces, profiles, spot news, historical articles. Does not want anything about events outside the city or profiles on people who no longer live in the city. **Buys 100 mss/year.** Query; indicate specifics, knowledge of city and market, and demonstrable access to sources. Length: 200-6,000 words. **Pays $100-3,000 and up.** Pays expenses of writers on assignment.

🟡🟡🟡🟡 CHICAGO READER

Sun-Times Media, LLC, 350 N. Orleans St., Chicago IL 60654. (312)321-9613. **E-mail:** letters@chicagoreader.com. **E-mail:** mail@chicagoreader.com. **Website:** www.chicagoreader.com. **Contact:** Mara Shalhoup, editor. **50% freelance written.** Weekly alternative tabloid for Chicago. Estab. 1971. Circ. 120,000. Byline given. Pays on publication. Occasional kill fee. Publishes ms an average of 2 weeks after acceptance. Editorial lead time up to 6 months. Accepts queries by mail, e-mail. Accepts simultaneous submissions.

Responds if interested. Sample copy free. Guidelines available online.

NONFICTION Buys 500 mss/year. Send complete ms. Length: 250-2,500 words. **Pays $100-3,000.** Sometimes pays expenses of writers on assignment.

REPRINTS Occasionally accepts previously published submissions.

COLUMNS/DEPARTMENTS Local color, 500-2,500 words; arts and entertainment reviews, up to 1,200 words.

🟡🟡 CHICAGO SCENE MAGAZINE

233 E. Erie St., Suite 603, Chicago IL 60611. **Fax:** (312)587-7397. **E-mail:** email@chicago-scene.com. **Website:** www.chicago-scene.com. **Contact:** Ted Widen, publisher; Robert Luce, editor. **95% freelance written.** Monthly magazine covering dining, nightlife, travel, beauty, entertainment, fitness, style, drinks. *Chicago Scene Magazine* is the premier news and entertainment publication for Chicago's young professional. Estab. 2001. Byline given. Pays on publication. No kill fee. Publishes ms an average of 2 months after acceptance. Submit seasonal material 3 months in advance. Accepts queries by e-mail. Sample copy available online. Guidelines free.

NONFICTION Needs how-to, interview, new product, travel. Does not want personal experiences, essays, technical. Query with published clips. Length: 600-2,400 words. **Pays $25-250.**

COLUMNS/DEPARTMENTS Beauty, 840 words; Dining, 1,260-1,680 words; Drinks, 1,260-1,680 words; Fitness, 420-630 words; Travel, 1,260-1,680 words; Nightlife, 1,050-1,680 words; Personal Style, 420 words. Query with published clips. **Pays $25-250.**

🟡 ILLINOIS ENTERTAINER

4223 W. Lake St., Suite 420, Chicago IL 60624. (773)533-9333. **Fax:** (312)922-9341. **E-mail:** service@illinoisentertainer.com. **Website:** www.illinoisentertainer.com. **80% freelance written.** Monthly free magazine covering popular and alternative music, as well as other entertainment (film, media) in Illinois. Estab. 1974. Circ. 55,000. Byline given. Pays on publication. Offers 50% kill fee. Publishes ms an average of 2 months after acceptance. Editorial lead time 2 months. Submit seasonal material 2 months in advance. Accepts queries by mail. Accepts simultaneous submissions. Responds in 2 months to queries. Sample copy for $5.

NONFICTION Needs exposé, how-to, humor, interview, new product, reviews. No personal, confessional, or inspirational articles. **Buys 75 mss/year.** Query with published clips. Length: 600-2,600 words. **Pays $15-160.** Sometimes pays expenses of writers on assignment.

REPRINTS Send typed ms with rights for sale noted and information about when and where the material previously appeared. Pays 100% of amount paid for an original article.

COLUMNS/DEPARTMENTS Spins (LP reviews), 100-400 words. **Buys 200-300 mss/year.** Query with published clips. **Pays $8-25.**

$ MIDWESTERN FAMILY MAGAZINE

P.O. Box 9302, Peoria IL 61612. (309)303-7309. **Fax:** (866)412-3835. **E-mail:** jrudd@midwesternfamily.com. **Website:** www.midwesternfamily.com. **90% freelance written.** Bimonthly magazine covering family living in Central Illinois. *Midwestern Family* is a comprehensive guide to fun, health and happiness for Central Illinois families. Estab. 2003. Circ. 23,000. Byline given. Pays on publication. No kill fee. Publishes ms an average of 2 months after acceptance. Editorial lead time 4-6 weeks. Submit seasonal material 4-6 weeks in advance. Accepts queries by e-mail, online submission form. Responds in 2 weeks to queries. Responds in 4 months to mss. Sample copy for $1.50. Guidelines by e-mail.

NONFICTION Query. Length: 1,000-1,500 words. **Pays $100.** Sometimes pays expenses of writers on assignment.

COLUMNS/DEPARTMENTS Home; Fun; Life; Food; Health; Discovery, all 1,000-1,250 words. **Buys 40 mss/year.** Query. **Pays $100.**

$$ OUTDOOR ILLINOIS

Illinois Department of Natural Resources, P.O. Box 19225, Dept. NL, Springfield IL 62794. (217)785-4193. **E-mail:** dnr.editor@illinois.gov. **Website:** www.dnr.state.il.us/oi. **25% freelance written.** Monthly magazine covering Illinois cultural and natural resources. *Outdoor Illinois* promotes outdoor activities, Illinois State parks, Illinois natural and cultural resources. Estab. 1973. Circ. 30,000. Byline given. Pays on acceptance. Editorial lead time 4 months. Submit seasonal material 1 year in advance. Accepts queries by mail, e-mail. Responds in 2 weeks to queries. Sample copy free. Guidelines by e-mail.

NONFICTION Needs historical, how-to, humor, interview, photo feature, travel. Does not want first person unless truly has something to say. Query with published clips. Length: 350-1,500 words. **Pays $100-250.**

$$ WEST SUBURBAN LIVING

C2 Publishing, Inc., P.O. Box 111, Elmhurst IL 60126. (630)834-4995. **Fax:** (630)834-4996. **Website:** www.westsuburbanliving.net. **Contact:** Chuck Cozette, editor. **80% freelance written.** Bimonthly magazine focusing on the western suburbs of Chicago. Estab. 1996. Circ. 25,000. Byline given. Pays on publication. Publishes ms an average of 2-4 months after acceptance. Accepts queries by mail, e-mail, fax. NoSample copy available online.

NONFICTION Needs general interest, how-to, travel. "Does not want anything that does not have an angle or tie-in to the area we cover—Chicago's western suburbs." **Buys 15 mss/year. Pays $100-500.** Sometimes pays expenses of writers on assignment.

INDIANA

$$ EVANSVILLE LIVING

Tucker Publishing Group, 223 NW Second St., Suite 200, Evansville IN 47708. (812)426-2115. **Fax:** (812)426-2134. **Website:** www.evansvilleliving.com. **Contact:** Kristen K. Tucker. **80-100% freelance written.** Bimonthly magazine covering Evansville, Indiana, and the greater area. *Evansville Living* is the only full-color, glossy, 100+ page city magazine for the Evansville, Indiana, area. Regular departments include: Home Style, Garden Style, Day Tripping, Sporting Life, and Local Flavor (menus). Estab. 2000. Circ. 50,000. Byline given. Pays on acceptance. No kill fee. Publishes ms an average of 3 months after acceptance. Editorial lead time 6 months. Submit seasonal material 6 months in advance. Accepts queries by mail, e-mail, fax. YesSample copy for $5 or online. Guidelines for free or by e-mail.

NONFICTION Needs essays, general interest, historical, photo feature, travel. **Buys 60-80 mss/year.** Query with published clips. Length: 200-2,000 words. **Pays $100-300.** Sometimes pays expenses of writers on assignment.

COLUMNS/DEPARTMENTS Home Style (home); Garden Style (garden); Sporting Life (sports); Local Flavor (menus), all 1,500 words. Query with published clips. **Pays $100-300.**

⊙⊙⊙ INDIANAPOLIS MONTHLY

Emmis Communications, 1 Emmis Plaza, 40 Monument Circle, Suite 100, Indianapolis IN 46204. (317)237-9288. **E-mail:** deborah@emmis.com. **Website:** www.indianapolismonthly.com. **Contact:** Deborah Paul, editorial director. **30% freelance written. Prefers to work with published/established writers.** "*Indianapolis Monthly* attracts and enlightens its upscale, well-educated readership with bright, lively editorial on subjects ranging from personalities to social issues, fashion to food. Its diverse content and attention to service make it the ultimate source by which the Indianapolis area lives." Estab. 1977. Circ. 50,000. Byline given. Pays on publication. Offers kill fee. Offers negotiable kill fee. Publishes ms an average of 2 months after acceptance. Editorial lead time 3 months. Submit seasonal material 3 months in advance. Accepts queries by mail, e-mail. Responds in 6 weeks to queries. Sample copy for $6.10.

NONFICTION Needs book excerpts by Indiana authors or with strong Indiana ties, essays, exposé, general interest, interview, photo feature. "No poetry, fiction, or domestic humor; no 'How Indy Has Changed Since I Left Town', 'An Outsider's View of the 500', or generic material with no or little tie to Indianapolis/Indiana." **Buys 35 mss/year.** Query by mail with published clips. Length: 200-3,000 words. **Pays $50-1,000.**

IOWA

⊙⊙ THE IOWAN

Pioneer Communications, Inc., 300 Walnut, Suite 6, Des Moines IA 50309. (515)246-0402. **Fax:** (515)282-0125. **E-mail:** editor@iowan.com. **Website:** www.iowan.com. **Contact:** Beth Wilson, editor. **75% freelance written.** Bimonthly magazine covering the state of Iowa. "*The Iowan* is a bimonthly magazine exploring everything Iowa has to offer. Each issue travels into diverse pockets of the state to discover the sights, meet the people, learn the history, taste the cuisine, and experience the culture." Estab. 1952. Circ. 20,000. Byline given. Pays on acceptance. Offers $100 kill fee. Publishes ms an average of 3 months after acceptance. Editorial lead time 9-10 months. Submit seasonal material 6-12 months in advance. Accepts queries by mail, e-mail. Responds to queries received twice/year. Sample copy for $4.95, plus s&h. Guidelines available at www.iowan.com/about/contributors.

NONFICTION Needs essays, general interest, historical, interview, photo feature, travel. **Buys 30 mss/year.** Query with published clips. Length: 700-1,500 words. **Pays $150-450.** Sometimes pays expenses of writers on assignment. ; pre-approved only

COLUMNS/DEPARTMENTS Last Word (essay), 800 words. **Buys 6 mss/year.** Query with published clips. **Pays $100.**

KANSAS

⊙⊙ KANSAS!

Travel & Tourism Development Division of the Kansas Department of Commerce, 1000 S.W. Jackson St., Suite 100, Topeka KS 66612-1354. (785)296-3479. **Fax:** (785)296-6988. **E-mail:** kansas.mag@travelks.com. **Website:** www.kansasmag.com. **90% freelance written.** Quarterly magazine emphasizing Kansas travel attractions and events. Estab. 1945. Circ. 45,000. Byline and courtesy bylines are given to all content. Pays on acceptance. No kill fee. Purchased content will publish an average of 1 year after acceptance. Submit seasonal material 8 months in advance. Accepts queries by mail. Responds in 2 months to queries. Guidelines available on website.

NONFICTION Needs general interest, photo feature, travel. Query by mail. Length: 750-1,250 words. **Pays $200-350.** Mileage reimbursement is available for writers on assignment in the state of Kansas; TBD by assignment editor.

KENTUCKY

FORT MITCHELL LIVING

Community Publications, Inc., 179 Fairfield Ave., Bellevue KY 41073. (859)291-1412. **Fax:** (859)291-1417. **E-mail:** fortmitchell@livingmagazines.com. **Website:** www.livingmagazines.com. Estab. 1983. Circ. 4,700. Byline given. Pays on publication. Editorial lead time 2 months. Submit seasonal material 3 months in advance. Guidelines by e-mail.

NONFICTION Query.

FORT THOMAS LIVING

Community Publications, Inc., 179 Fairfield Ave., Bellevue KY 41073. (859)291-1412. **Fax:** (859)291-1417. **E-mail:** fortthomas@livingmagazines.com. **Website:** www.livingmagazines.com. **Contact:** Linda Johnson, editor. Monthly magazine covering Fort Thomas community. "Magazine focuses upon people living and working in Fort Thomas and promoting acitvities of interest to this community." Estab. 1977. Circ. 4,400. Byline given. Pays on publication. Editorial lead time 2 months. Submit seasonal material 3 months in advance. Accepts queries by mail, e-mail. Guidelines by email.

NONFICTION Does not want any material unrelated to Fort Thomas, Kentucky. Query. Prefers email submissions.

$ $ KENTUCKY LIVING

Kentucky Association of Electric Co-Ops, P.O. Box 32170, Louisville KY 40232. (502)451-2430. **Fax:** (502)459-1611. **E-mail:** e-mail@kentuckyliving.com. **Website:** www.kentuckyliving.com. **Mostly freelance written. Prefers to work with published/established writers.** Monthly feature magazine primarily for Kentucky residents. Estab. 1948. Circ. 500,000. Byline given. Pays on acceptance. No kill fee. Publishes ms an average of 12 months after acceptance. Submit seasonal material at least 6 months in advance. Accepts simultaneous submissions. Responds in 1 month to queries. Sample copy with SASE (9x12 envelope and 4 first-class stamps).

NONFICTION Needs Emphasis on electric industry and ties to Kentucky's electric co-op areas of readership. **Buys 18-24 mss/year.** Send complete ms. **Pays $75-935** Sometimes pays expenses of writers on assignment.

$ $ KENTUCKY MONTHLY

P.O. Box 559, Frankfort KY 40602-0559. (502)227-0053; (888)329-0053. **Fax:** (502)227-5009. **E-mail:** kymonthly@kentuckymonthly.com; steve@kentuckymonthly.com. **Website:** www.kentuckymonthly.com. **Contact:** Stephen Vest, editor. **50% freelance written.** Monthly magazine. "We publish stories about Kentucky and by Kentuckians, including those who live elsewhere." Estab. 1998. Circ. 42,000. Byline given. Pays within 3 months of publication. No kill fee. Publishes ms an average of 3 months after acceptance. Editorial lead time 3 months. Submit seasonal material 4 months in advance. Accepts queries by mail, e-mail, fax. Accepts simultaneous submissions. Responds in 1 month to queries. Responds in 1 month to mss. Sample copy and writer's guidelines online.

NONFICTION Needs book excerpts, general interest, historical, how-to, humor, interview, photo feature, religious, travel, all with a Kentucky angle. **Buys 50 mss/year.** Query. Length: 300-2,000 words. **Pays**

$75-350 for assigned articles. Pays $50-200 for unsolicited articles.

FICTION Needs adventure, historical, mainstream, novel concepts, all Kentucky-related stories. **Buys 30 mss/year.** Query with published clips. Length: 1,000-5,000 words. **Pays $50-100.**

LOUISIANA

$ $ PRESERVATION IN PRINT

Preservation Resource Center of New Orleans, 923 Tchoupitoulos St., New Orleans LA 70130. (504)581-7032. **Fax:** (504)636-3073. **E-mail:** mfitzpatrick@prcno.org; prc@prcno.org. **Website:** www.prcno.org. **Contact:** Mary Fitzpatrick, editor. **30% freelance written.** Monthly magazine covering preservation. "We want articles about interest in the historic architecture of New Orleans." Estab. 1974. Circ. 10,000. Byline given. Pays on acceptance. No kill fee. Publishes ms an average of 1 month after acceptance. Editorial lead time 1 month. Submit seasonal material 1-2 months in advance. Accepts queries by mail, e-mail, fax, phone. Accepts simultaneous submissions. Sample copy available online. Guidelines free.

NONFICTION Needs essays, historical, interview, photo feature, technical. **Buys 30 mss/year.** Query. Length: 700-1,000 words. **Pays $100-200 for assigned articles.** Sometimes pays expenses of writers on assignment.

MAINE

$ DISCOVER MAINE MAGAZINE

10 Exchange St., Suite 208, Portland ME 04101. (207)874-7720. **Fax:** (207)874-7721. **E-mail:** info@discovermainemagazine.com. **Website:** www.discovermainemagazine.com. **Contact:** Jim Burch, editor and publisher. **100% freelance written.** Monthly magazine covering Maine history and nostalgia. Sports and hunting/fishing topics are also included. "Discover Maine Magazine is dedicated to bringing the amazing history of the great state of Maine to readers in every corner of the state and to those from away who love the rich heritage and traditions of Maine. From the history of Maine's mill towns, to the traditions of family farming and coastal fishing, nine times a year Discover Maine's stories tell of life in the cities and towns across Maine as it was years ago." Estab. 1992. Circ. 12,000. Byline given. Pays on publication. No

kill fee. Publishes ms an average of 2-3 months after acceptance. Accepts queries by mail, fax, phone. Accepts simultaneous submissions. Responds in 2 weeks to queries; 1 month to mss.

NONFICTION Needs historical. Does not want to receive poetry. **Buys 200 mss/year.** Send complete ms. Length: 500-2,000 words. **Pays $20-30**

MARYLAND

💲💲 BALTIMORE MAGAZINE

Inner Harbor, E. 1000 Lancaster St., Suite 400, Baltimore MD 21202. (410)752-4200. **Fax:** (410)625-0280. **E-mail:** Send correspondence to the appropriate editor. **Website:** www.baltimoremagazine.net. **Contact:** Max Weiss, managing editor; Ken Inglehart, managing editor, special editions. **50-60% freelance written.** Monthly city magazine featuring news, profiles and service articles. "Pieces must address an educated, active, affluent reader and must have a very strong Baltimore angle." Estab. 1907. Circ. 70,000. Byline given. Pays within 1 month of publication. Accepts queries by mail, e-mail (preferred).

NONFICTION Needs book excerpts, Baltimore subject or author, essays, exposé, general interest, historical, humor, interview, with a Baltimorean, new product, personal experience, photo feature, travel, local and regional to Maryland. "Nothing that lacks a strong Baltimore focus or angle. Unsolicited personal essays are almost never accepted. We've printed only two over the past few years; the last was by a 19-year veteran city judge reminiscing on his time on the bench and the odd stories and situations he encountered there. Unsolicited food and restaurant reviews, whether positive or negative, are likewise never accepted." Query by e-mail or mail with published clips or send complete ms. Length: 1,600-2,500 words. **Pays 30-40¢/word.** Sometimes pays expenses.

COLUMNS/DEPARTMENTS "The shorter pieces are the best places to break into the magazine." Hot Shot, Health, Education, Sports, Parenting, Politics. Length: 1,000-2,500 words. Query with published clips.

MASSACHUSETTS

💲💲 CAPE COD MAGAZINE

Rabideau Media Group, P.O. Box 208, Yarmouth Port MA 02765. (508)771-6549. **Fax:** (508)771-3769.

E-mail: editor@capecodmagazine.com. **Website:** www.capecodmagazine.com. **80% freelance written.** Magazine published 9 times/year covering Cape Cod lifestyle. Estab. 1996. Circ. 16,000. Byline given. Pays 30 days after publication. Offers 25% kill fee. Publishes ms an average of 3 months after acceptance. Editorial lead time 6 months. Submit seasonal material 1 year in advance. Accepts queries by mail, e-mail. Responds in 3 weeks to queries. Responds in 2 months to mss. Sample copy for $5. Guidelines by e-mail.

NONFICTION Needs book excerpts, essays, general interest, historical, humor, interview, personal experience. Does not want clichéd pieces, interviews, and puff features. **Buys 3 mss/year.** Send complete ms. Length: 800-2,500 words. **Pays $300-500 for assigned articles. Pays $100-300 for unsolicited articles.** Sometimes pays expenses of writers on assignment.

COLUMNS/DEPARTMENTS Last Word (personal observations in typical back page format), 700 words. **Buys 4 mss/year.** Query with or without published clips or send complete ms. **Pays $150-300.**

💲💲 CHATHAM MAGAZINE

Rabideau Publishing, P.O. Box 208, Yarmouth Port MA 02675. (508)771-6549. **Fax:** (508)771-3769. **E-mail:** editor@capecodmagazine.com. **Website:** www.chathammag.com. **Contact:** Michael Rabideau, publisher; Liz Rabideau, associate publisher. **80% freelance written.** Annual magazine covering Chatham, MA lifestyle. Estab. 2006. Byline given. Pays 30 days after publication. Offers 25% kill fee. Publishes ms an average of 3 months after acceptance. Editorial lead time 6 months. Submit seasonal material 1 year in advance. Accepts queries by mail, e-mail. Responds in 3 weeks to queries. Responds in 2 months to mss. Sample copy for $5. Guidelines by e-mail.

NONFICTION Needs book excerpts, essays, general interest, historical, humor, interview, personal experience. Send complete ms. Length: 800-2,500 words. **Pays $300-500 for assigned articles. Pays $100-300 for unsolicited articles.** Sometimes pays expenses of writers on assignment.

COLUMNS/DEPARTMENTS Hooked (fishing issues), 700 words. **Buys 4 mss/year.** Query with or without published clips or send complete ms. **Pays $150-300.**

$$ PROVINCETOWN ARTS

Provincetown Arts, Inc., 650 Commercial St., P.O. Box 35, Provincetown MA 02657. (508)487-3167. **E-mail:** cbusa@comcast.net. **Website:** www.provincetownarts.org. **90% freelance written.** Annual magazine covering contemporary art and writing. "*Provincetown Arts* focuses broadly on the artists and writers who inhabit or visit the Lower Cape, and seeks to stimulate creative activity and enhance public awareness of the cultural life of the nation's oldest continuous art colony. Drawing upon a 75-year tradition rich in visual art, literature, and theater, *Provincetown Arts* offers a unique blend of interviews, fiction, visual features, reviews, reporting, and poetry. Has published poetry by Bruce Smith, Franz Wright, Sandra McPherson, and Cyrus Cassells. 170 pages, magazine-sized, perfect-bound, with full-color glossy cover. Press run is 10,000. Estab. 1985. Circ. 8,000. Pays on publication. Offers 50% kill fee. Publishes ms an average of 4 months after acceptance. Editorial lead time 6 months. Submit seasonal material 6 months in advance. Accepts simultaneous submissions. Responds in 3 weeks to queries; 2 months to mss. Sample copy for $10. Guidelines for #10 SASE.

NONFICTION Needs book excerpts, essays, humor, interview. **Buys 40 mss/year.** Send complete ms. Length: 1,500-4,000 words. **Pays $150 minimum for assigned articles. Pays $125 minimum for unsolicited articles.**

FICTION Contact: Christopher Busa, editor. Needs mainstream, novel concepts. **Buys 7 mss/year.** Send complete ms. Length: 500-5,000 words. **Pays $75-300.**

POETRY Submit up to 3 poems at a time. No e-mail submissions; "all queries and submissions should be sent via postal mail." Submissions must be typed. Buys 25 poems/year poems/year. Submit maximum 3 poems. **Pays $25-100/poem plus 2 contributor's copies. Acquires first rights.**

$$ WORCESTER MAGAZINE

101 Water St., Worcester MA 01604. (508)749-3166. **Fax:** (508)749-3165. **E-mail:** bdurgin@worcestermag.com. **Website:** www.worcestermag.com. **Contact:** Brittany Durgin, editor; Kathleen Real, publisher. **10% freelance written.** Weekly tabloid emphasizing the central Massachusetts region, especially the city of Worcester. Estab. 1976. Circ. 40,000. Byline given. Pays on publication. No kill fee. Publishes ms an average of 3 weeks after acceptance. Submit seasonal material 2 months in advance. Accepts queries by mail, e-mail, fax.

NONFICTION Needs essays, exposé, area government, corporate, general interest, historical, humor, opinion, local, personal experience, photo feature, religious, interview (local). **Buys less than 75 mss/year.** Length: 500-1,500 words. **Pays 10¢/word.**

MICHIGAN

$$$ ANN ARBOR OBSERVER

Ann Arbor Observer Co., 2390 Winewood, Ann Arbor MI 48103. **Fax:** (734)769-3375. **E-mail:** hilton@aaobserver.com. **Website:** www.annarborobserver.com. **50% freelance written**. Monthly magazine. "We depend heavily on freelancers and we're always glad to talk to new ones. We look for the intelligence and judgment to fully explore complex people and situations, and the ability to convey what makes them interesting." Estab. 1976. Circ. 60,000. Byline given in some sections. Pays on publication. No kill fee. Publishes ms an average of 2 months after acceptance. Accepts queries by mail, e-mail, fax, phone. Responds in 3 weeks to queries. Responds in several months to mss. Sample copy for 12½ x 15 SAE with $3 postage. Guidelines for #10 SASE.

NONFICTION Buys 75 mss/year. Length: 100-2,500 words. **Pays up to $1,000.** Sometimes pays expenses of writers on assignment.

COLUMNS/DEPARTMENTS Up Front (short, interesting tidbits), 150 words. **Pays $100.** Inside Ann Arbor (concise stories), 300-500 words. **Pays $200.** Around Town (unusual, compelling ancedotes), 750-1,500 words. **Pays $150-200.**

$$ GRAND RAPIDS MAGAZINE

Gemini Publications, 549 Ottawa Ave. NW, Suite 201, Grand Rapids MI 49503. (616)459-4545. **Fax:** (616)459-4800. **E-mail:** cvalade@geminipub.com. **Website:** www.grmag.com. *Grand Rapids* is a general interest life and style magazine designed for those who live in the Grand Rapids metropolitan area or desire to maintain contact with the community. Estab. 1964. Circ. 20,000. Byline given. Pays on publication. No kill fee. Editorial lead time 2 months. Submit seasonal material 2 months in advance. Sample copy for $2 and SASE with $1.50 postage. Guidelines with #10 SASE.

NONFICTION Query. **Pays $25-500.**

😊💲 MICHIGAN HISTORY

The Historical Society of Michigan, 5815 Executive Dr., Lansing MI 48911. (517)332-1828. **Fax:** (517)324-4370. **E-mail:** mhmeditor@hsmichigan.org; hsm@hsmichigan.org. **E-mail:** majher@hsmichigan.org. **Website:** www.hsmichigan.org. **Contact:** Patricia Majher, editor. Covers exciting stories of Michigan people and their impact on their communities, the nation and the world. *Michigan History* overflows with intriguing feature articles, bold illustrations and departments highlighting history-related books, travel and events 6 time each year. Bimonthly magazine, 64 colorful pages. "A thoroughly entertaining read, Michigan History specializes in stories from Michigan's colorful past. Within its pages, you'll learn about logging, mining, manufacturing, and military history as well as art and architecture, music, sports, shipwrecks, and more. Requires idea queries first." In addition to payment, authors receive 5 free copies of issues in which their work appears. Estab. 1917. Circ. 22,000. Byline given. Pays on publication. Publishes ms 6 months after acceptance. Editorial lead time 1 year. Accepts queries by mail, e-mail. Guidelines for authors at www.hsmichigan.org/michiganhistory/contribute.

NONFICTION Needs feature articles, bold illustrations and departments highlighting history-related books, travel and events., Remember the Time features (first-person, factual, personal experiences that happened in Michigan—750 words) pay $100. Other features pay $200-$400, depending on word length and cooperation in gathering photos. "We are not a scholarly journal and do not accept academic papers." **Buys 50-55/mss/year mss/year.** "When you are ready to submit a manuscript, please provide a digital copy of the text, and also list your research sources for fact-checking purposes. Include with your ms a summary of your writing experience and "in the interest of full disclosure" any relationship you have to your subject. You are expected to gather your own graphics (provided digitally and with captions, if possible) or at least suggest possible graphics." Length: 750-2,500 words. **Pays $100-400.**

😊💲 TRAVERSE

Prism Publications, Inc., 148 E. Front St., Traverse City MI 49684. (231)941-8174. **Fax:** (231)941-8391. **Website:** www.mynorth.com. **20% freelance written.** Monthly magazine covering northern Michigan life. "Since 1981, our company, Prism Publications, Inc., has been dedicated to sharing stories and photos that embody life in Northern Michigan. For more than 25 years we have accomplished this through our award-winning flagship publication *Traverse, Northern Michigan's Magazine.*" Estab. 1981. Circ. 30,000. Byline given. Pays on acceptance. Offers 10% kill fee. Editorial lead time 1 year. Submit seasonal material 1 year in advance. Accepts queries by mail, fax, phone. Accepts simultaneous submissions. Responds in 2 months to queries. Sample copy for $3. Guidelines for #10 SASE.

NONFICTION Needs book excerpts, essays, general interest, historical, humor, interview, personal experience, photo feature, travel. No fiction or poetry. **Buys 24 mss/year.** Send complete ms. Length: 1,000-3,200 words. **Pays $150-500.** Sometimes pays expenses of writers on assignment.

PHOTOS State availability. Negotiates payment individually.

COLUMNS/DEPARTMENTS Up in Michigan Reflection (essays about northern Michigan); Reflection on Home (essays about northern homes), both 700 words. **Buys 18 mss/year.** Query with published clips or send complete ms. **Pays $100-200.**

TIPS "When shaping an article for us, consider first that it must be strongly rooted in our region. If you send us a piece about peaches, even if it does an admirable job of relaying the history of peaches, their medicinal qualities, their nutritional magnificence, and so on, we are likely to reject if it doesn't include local farms as a reference point. We want sidebars and extended captions designed to bring in a reader not enticed by the main subject. We cover the northern portion of the Lower Peninsula and to a lesser degree the Upper Peninsula. General categories of interest include nature and the environment, regional culture, personalities, the arts (visual, performing, literary), crafts, food & dining, homes, history, and outdoor activities (e.g., fishing, golf, skiing, boating, biking, hiking, birding, gardening). We are keenly interested in environmental and land-use issues but seldom use material dealing with such issues as health care, education, social services, criminal justice, and local politics. We use service pieces and a small number of how-to pieces, mostly focused on small projects for the home or yard. Also, we value research. We need articles built with information. Many of the pieces we reject use writing style to fill in for information voids."

Style and voice are strongest when used as vehicles for sound research."

MINNESOTA

💲💲 LAKE COUNTRY JOURNAL

1022 Madison St., P.O. Box 978, Brainerd MN 56401. (218)828-6424, ext. 14. **Fax:** (218)825-7816. **E-mail:** jodi@lakecountryjournal.com. **Website:** www.lakecountryjournal.com. **Contact:** Jodi Schwen, editor. **90% freelance written.** Bimonthly magazine covering central Minnesota's lake country. "Lake Country is one of the fastest-growing areas in the midwest. Each bimonthly issue of *Lake Country Journal* captures the essence of why we work, play, and live in this area. Through a diverse blend of articles from features and fiction, to recreation, recipes, gardening, and nature, this quality lifestyle magazine promotes positive family and business endeavors, showcases our natural and cultural resources, and highlights the best of our people, places, and events." Estab. 1996. Circ. 14,500. Byline given. Pays on publication. Offers 25% kill fee. Publishes ms an average of 6 months after acceptance. Submit seasonal material 1 year in advance. Accepts queries by mail, e-mail. Responds in 2 months to queries. Responds in 3 months to mss. Sample copy for $6. Guidelines available online.

NONFICTION Needs essays, general interest, how-to, humor, interview, personal experience, photo feature. "No articles that come from writers who are not familiar with our target geographical location." **Buys 30 mss/year.** Query with or without published clips. Length: 1,000-1,500 words. **Pays $100-200.** Sometimes pays expenses of writers on assignment.

COLUMNS/DEPARTMENTS Profile-People from Lake Country, 800 words; Essay, 800 words; Health (topics pertinent to central Minnesota living), 500 words. **Buys 40 mss/year.** Query with published clips. **Pays $50-75.**

FICTION Needs adventure, humorous, mainstream, slice-of-life vignettes, literary; also family fiction appropriate to Lake Country and seasonal fiction. **Buys 6 mss/year.** Length: 1,500 words. **Pays $100-200.**

POETRY Needs free verse. "Never use rhyming verse, avant-garde, experimental, etc." Buys 6 poems/year. Submit maximum 4 poems. Length: 8-32 lines. **Pays $25.**

FILLERS Needs anecdotes, short humor. **Buys 20 mss/year.** Length: 100-300 words. **Pays $25/filler.**

💲💲💲 MPLS. ST. PAUL MAGAZINE

MSP Communications, 220 S. 6th St., Suite 500, Minneapolis MN 55402. (612)339-7571. **Fax:** (612)339-5806. **E-mail:** edit@mspmag.com. **Website:** www.mspmag.com. **Contact:** Adam Platt, executive editor. Monthly magazine covering the Minneapolis-St. Paul area. *Mpls. St. Paul Magazine* is a city magazine serving upscale readers in the Minneapolis-St. Paul metro area. Circ. 80,000. Pays on publication. Editorial lead time 3 months. Accepts queries by mail, e-mail, fax. Sample copy for $10.

NONFICTION Needs book excerpts, essays, general interest, historical, interview, personal experience, photo feature, travel. **Buys 150 mss/year.** Query with published clips. Length: 500-4,000 words. **Pays 50-75¢/word for assigned articles.**

MISSISSIPPI

💲💲 MISSISSIPPI MAGAZINE

Downhome Publications, 5 Lakeland Circle, Jackson MS 39216. (601)982-8418. **Fax:** (601)982-8447. **E-mail:** editor@mismag.com. **Website:** www.mississippimagazine.com. **Contact:** Melanie M. Ward, editor. **90% freelance written.** Bimonthly magazine covering Mississippi—the state and its lifestyles. "We are interested in positive stories reflecting Mississippi's rich traditions and heritage and focusing on the contributions the state and its natives have made to the arts, literature, and culture. In each issue we showcase homes and gardens, in-state travel, food, design, art, and more." Estab. 1982. Circ. 40,000. Byline given. Pays on publication. Offers 25% kill fee. Publishes ms an average of 6 months after acceptance. Accepts queries by mail, fax. Responds in 2 months to queries. Guidelines for #10 SASE or online.

NONFICTION Needs general interest, historical, how-to, home decor, interview, personal experience, travel, in-state. No opinion, political, sports, exposé. **Buys 15 mss/year.** Query. Length: 100-1,200 words. **Pays $25-350.**

COLUMNS/DEPARTMENTS Southern Scrapbook (see recent issues for example), 100-600 words; Gardening (short informative article on a specific plant or gardening technique), 800-1,200 words; Culture Center (story about an event or person relating to Mississippi's art, music, theatre, or literature), 800-1,200 words; On Being Southern (personal essay about life in Mississippi; only ms submissions accepted), 750 words. **Buys 6 mss/year.** Query. **Pays $150-225.**

MISSOURI

⊛⊛ 417 MAGAZINE

Whitaker Publishing, 2111 S. Eastgate Ave., Springfield MO 65809. (417)883-7417. **Fax:** (417)889-7417. **E-mail:** editor@417mag.com. **Website:** www.417mag.com. **Contact:** Katie Pollock Estes, editor. **50% freelance written.** Monthly magazine. *"417 Magazine* is a regional title serving southwest Missouri. Our editorial mix includes service journalism and lifestyle content on home, fashion and the arts; as well as narrative and issues pieces. The audience is affluent, educated, mostly female." Estab. 1998. Circ. 20,000. Byline given. Pays on acceptance. Publishes ms an average of 2-3 months after acceptance. Editorial lead time 6 months. Accepts queries by e-mail. Responds in 1-2 months to queries. Sample copy by e-mail. Guidelines available online.

NONFICTION Needs essays, exposé, general interest, how-to, humor, inspirational, interview, new product, personal experience, photo feature, travel, local book reviews. "We are a local magazine, so anything not reflecting our local focus is something we have to pass on." **Buys 175 mss/year.** Query with published clips. Length: 300-3,500 words. **Pays $30-500, sometimes more. Sometimes pays expenses of writers on assignment.**

⊛⊛ KANSAS CITY HOMES & GARDENS

Network Communications, Inc., 9647 Lackman Rd., Lenexa KS 66219. (913)648-5757. **Fax:** (913)648-5783. **E-mail:** bpearl@nci.com. **Website:** www.kchandg.com. **Contact:** Brooke Pearl, editor. Magazine published 8 times annually cover homes and gardening in the Kansas City, Missouri area. *"KCH&G* creates inspirational, credible, and compelling content about trends and events in local home and design for affluent homeowners, with beautiful photography, engaging features, and expert insight. We help our readers get smarter about where to find and how to buy the best solutions for enhancing their homes." Estab. 1986. Circ. 18,000. Byline given. Pays on publication. No kill fee. Editorial lead time 4 months. Submit seasonal material 4 months in advance. Accepts queries by mail, e-mail, fax. Accepts simultaneous submissions. Responds in 1 month to queries. Responds in 1 month to mss. Sample copy for $5.

NONFICTION Buys 8 mss/year. Query with published clips. Length: 600-1,000 words. **Pays $100-350.** Sometimes pays expenses of writers on assignment.

KC MAGAZINE

7101 College Blvd., Suite 400, Overland Park KS 66210. (913)894-6923. **Website:** www.kcmag.com. **Contact:** Pete Dulin, editor-in-chief. **75% freelance written.** Monthly magazine covering life in Kansas City, Kansas. "Our mission is to celebrate living in Kansas City. We are a consumer lifestyle/general interest magazine focused on Kansas City, its people, and places." Estab. 1994. Circ. 31,000. Byline given. Pays on acceptance. Offers 10% kill fee. Publishes ms an average of 3 months after acceptance. Editorial lead time 4 months. Submit seasonal material 6 months in advance. Accepts queries by mail, e-mail, fax. Accepts simultaneous submissions. Sample copy for 8 1/2x11 SAE or online.

NONFICTION Needs exposé, general interest, interview, photo feature. **Buys 15-20 mss/year.** Query with published clips. Length: 250-3,000 words.

COLUMNS/DEPARTMENTS Entertainment (Kansas City only), 1,000 words; Food (Kansas City food and restaurants only), 1,000 words. **Buys 12 mss/year.** Query with published clips.

⊛⊛ MISSOURI LIFE

Missouri Life, Inc., 501 High St., Suite A, Boonville MO 65233. (660)882-9898. **Fax:** (660)882-9899. **E-mail:** lauren@missourilife.com. **Website:** www.missourilife.com. **Contact:** Lauren Licklider, associate editor. **85% freelance written.** Bimonthly magazine covering the state of Missouri. *"Missouri Life's* readers are mostly college-educated people with a wide range of travel and lifestyle interests. Our magazine discovers the people, places, and events—both past and present—that make Missouri a great place to live and/or visit." Estab. 1973. Circ. 96,800. Byline given. Pays on publication. Editorial lead time 6 months. Submit seasonal material 6 months in advance. Accepts queries by mail, e-mail, fax. Responds in approximately 2 months to queries. Sample copy available for $4.95 and SASE with $2.44 first-class postage (or a digital version can be purchased online). Guidelines available online.

NONFICTION Needs general interest, historical, travel, all Missouri related. Length: 300-2,000 words. **No set amount per word.**

COLUMNS/DEPARTMENTS "All Around Missouri (people and places, past and present, written in an almanac style); Missouri Artist (features a Missouri artist), 500 words; Made in Missouri (products and businesses native to Missouri), 500 words. Contact assistant manager for restaurant review queries.

⊛⊛ RELOCATING TO THE LAKE OF THE OZARKS

Showcase Publishing, 2820 Bagnell Dam Blvd., #1B, Lake Ozark MO 65049. (573)365-2323. **Fax:** (573)365-2351. **E-mail:** spublishingco@msn.com. **Website:** www.relocatingtothelakeoftheozarks.com. **Contact:** Dave Leathers, publisher. Semi-annual relocation guide; free for people moving to the area. Byline given. Pays on publication. No kill fee. Publishes ms an average of 6 months after acceptance. Accepts queries by e-mail. Sample copy for $8.95.

NONFICTION Needs historical, travel, local issues. Length: 600-1,000 words.

⊛ RIVER HILLS TRAVELER

Traveler Publishing Co., P.O. Box 245, St. Clair MO 63077-0245. (800)874-8423. **Fax:** (800)874-8423. **E-mail:** stories@rhtrav.com. **Website:** www.riverhillstraveler.com. **Contact:** Emery Styron, editor. **80% freelance written.** Monthly tabloid covering outdoor sports and nature in the southeast quarter of Missouri, the east and central Ozarks. Topics like those in *Field & Stream* and *National Geographic*. Estab. 1973. Circ. 5,000. Byline given. Pays on publication. No kill fee. Publishes ms an average of 2 months after acceptance. Editorial lead time 2 months. Submit seasonal material 1 year in advance. Accepts queries by e-mail. Accepts simultaneous submissions. Responds in 2 months to queries. Sample copy for SAE or online. Guidelines available online.

NONFICTION Needs historical, how-to, humor, opinion, personal experience, photo feature, technical, travel. No stories about other geographic areas. **Buys 80 mss/year.** Query with writing samples. Length: 1,500 word maximum. **Pays $15-50.**

REPRINTS E-mail ms with rights for sale noted and information about when and where the material previously appeared.

⊛ RURAL MISSOURI MAGAZINE

Association of Missouri Electric Cooperatives, P.O. Box 1645, Jefferson City MO 65102. **E-mail:** hberry@ruralmissouri.coop. **Website:** www.ruralmissouri.coop. **5% freelance written.** Monthly magazine covering rural interests in Missouri; people, places and sights in Missouri. "Our audience is comprised of rural electric cooperative members in Missouri. We describe our magazine as 'being devoted to the rural way of life.'" Estab. 1948. Circ. 555,000. Byline given. Pays on acceptance. Publishes ms an average of 6 months after acceptance. Editorial lead time 6 months. Submit seasonal material 6 months in advance. Accepts queries by mail, e-mail. Responds in 6-8 weeks to queries and to mss. Sample copy available online. Guidelines available online.

NONFICTION Needs general interest, historical. Does not want personal experiences or nostalgia pieces. Send complete ms. Length: 1,000-1,100 words. **Pays variable amount for each piece.**

MONTANA

⊛⊛ MONTANA MAGAZINE

Lee Enterprises, P.O. Box 5630, Helena MT 59604. **E-mail:** editor@montanamagazine.com; butch.larcombe@lee.net. **Website:** www.montanamagazine.com. **Contact:** Butch Larcombe, editor. **90% freelance written.** Bimonthly magazine. Strictly Montana-oriented magazine that features community profiles, contemporary issues, wildlife and natural history, travel pieces. Estab. 1970. Circ. 40,000. Byline given. No kill fee. Publishes ms an average of 1 year after acceptance. Submit seasonal material 1 year in advance. Accepts queries by e-mail. Accepts simultaneous submissions. Responds in 6 months to queries. Sample copy for $5 or online. Guidelines available online.

NONFICTION Needs essays, general interest, interview, photo feature, travel. Special issues: Special features on summer and winter destination points. No 'me and Joe' hiking and hunting tales; no blood-and-guts hunting stories; no poetry; no fiction; no sentimental essays. **Buys 30 mss/year.** Query with samples and SASE. Length: 800-1,000 words. **Pays 20¢/word.** Sometimes pays expenses of writers on assignment.

REPRINTS Send photocopy of article with rights for sale and information about when and where the material previously appeared. Pays 50% of amount paid for an original article.

PHOTOS Send photos. Captions, identification of subjects, model releases required. Reviews contact sheets, 35mm or larger format transparencies, 5x7

CONSUMER MAGAZINES

prints. Offers additional payment for photos accepted with ms.

COLUMNS/DEPARTMENTS Memories (reminisces of early-day Montana life), 800-1,000 words; Outdoor Recreation, 1,500-2,000 words; Community Festivals, 500 words, plus b&w or color photo; Montana-Specific Humor, 800-1,000 words. Query with samples and SASE.

TIPS "We avoid commonly known topics so Montanans won't ho-hum through more of what they already know. If it's time to revisit a topic, we look for a unique slant."

NEVADA

⊗⊗ NEVADA MAGAZINE

401 N. Carson St., Carson City NV 89701. (775)687-5416. **Fax:** (775)687-6159. **E-mail:** editor@nevadamagazine.com. **Website:** www.nevadamagazine.com. **25% freelance written. Works with a small number of new/unpublished writers each year.** Bimonthly magazine published by the state of Nevada to promote tourism. Estab. 1936. Circ. 20,000. Byline given. Pays on publication. No kill fee. Publishes ms an average of 6 months after acceptance. Submit seasonal material 6 months in advance. Accepts queries by e-mail (preferred). Responds in 1 month to queries.

NONFICTION Length: 700-1,000 words. **Pays $50-250.**

PHOTOS Contact: Query art director Tony deRonnebeck (tony@nevadamagazine.com). Reviews digital images. Pays $25-250; cover, $250.

TIPS "Keep in mind the magazine's purpose is to promote Nevada tourism. We look for a light, enthusiastic tone of voice without being too 'cute.'"

NEW HAMPSHIRE

⊗⊗ NEW HAMPSHIRE MAGAZINE

McLean Communications, Inc., 150 Dow St., Manchester NH 03101. (603)624-1442. **E-mail:** editor@nhmagazine.com; bcoles@nhmagazine.com. **Website:** www.nhmagazine.com. **Contact:** Rick Broussard, executive editor; Barbara Coles, editor. **50% freelance written.** Monthly magazine devoted to New Hampshire. "We want stories written for, by, and about the people of New Hampshire with emphasis on qualities that set us apart from other states.

We feature lifestyle, adventure, and home-related stories with a unique local angle." Estab. 1986. Circ. 32,000. Byline given. Pays on publication. Offers 25% kill fee. Editorial lead time 3 months. Submit seasonal material 3 months in advance. Accepts queries by mail, e-mail, fax. Accepts simultaneous submissions. Responds in 2 months to queries. Responds in 3 months to mss. Guidelines available online.

NONFICTION Needs essays, general interest, historical, photo feature, business. **Buys 30 mss/year.** Query with published clips. Length: 800-2,000 words. **Pays $50-500.** Sometimes pays expenses of writers on assignment.

PHOTOS State availability. Captions, identification of subjects, model releases required. Possible additional payment for photos accepted with ms.

FILLERS Length: 200-400 words.

NEW JERSEY

⊗⊗⊗ NEW JERSEY MONTHLY

55 Park Place, P.O. Box 920, Morristown NJ 07963-0920. (973)539-8230. **Fax:** (973)538-2953. **E-mail:** dingram@njmonthly.com; dcarter@njmonthly.com. **E-mail:** research@njmonthly.com. **Website:** www.njmonthly.com. **75-80% freelance written.** Monthly magazine covering just about anything to do with New Jersey, from news, politics, and sports to decorating trends and lifestyle issues. Our readership is well-educated, affluent, and on average our readers have lived in New Jersey 20 years or more. Estab. 1976. Circ. 92,000. Byline given. Pays on completion of fact-checking. Offers 20% kill fee. Publishes ms an average of 3 months after acceptance. Editorial lead time 3 months. Submit seasonal material 6 months in advance. Accepts queries by mail, e-mail, fax, phone. Accepts simultaneous submissions. Responds in 2-3 months to queries.

NONFICTION Needs book excerpts, essays, exposé, general interest, historical, humor, interview, personal experience, photo feature, travel, within New Jersey, arts, sports, politics. No experience pieces from people who used to live in New Jersey or general pieces that have no New Jersey angle. **Buys 90-100 mss/year.** Query with published magazine clips and SASE. Length: 250-3,000 words. **Pays $750-2,500.** Pays reasonable expenses of writers on assignment with prior approval.

PHOTOS Contact: Donna Panagakos, art director. State availability. Identification of subjects, model releases required. Reviews transparencies, prints. Payment negotiated.

COLUMNS/DEPARTMENTS Exit Ramp (back page essay usually originating from personal experience but written in a way that tells a broader story of statewide interest), 1,200 words. **Buys 12 mss/year.** Query with published clips. **Pays $400.**

FILLERS Needs anecdotes, for front-of-book. **Buys 12-15 mss/year.** Length: 200-250 words. **$100.**

TIPS "The best approach: Do your homework! Read the past year's issues to get an understanding of our well-written, well-researched articles that tell a tale from a well-established point of view."

⊛⊛ THE SANDPAPER

The SandPaper, Inc., 1816 Long Beach Blvd., Surf City NJ 08008. (609)494-5900. **Fax:** (609)494-1437. **E-mail:** jaymann@thesandpaper.net; letters@thesandpaper.net; photo@thesandpaper.net. **Website:** www.thesandpaper.net. **Contact:** Jay Mann, managing editor; Gail Travers, executive editor; Ryan Morrill, photography editor. Weekly tabloid covering subjects of interest to Long Island Beach area residents and visitors. Each issue includes a mix of news, human interest features, opinion columns, and entertainment/calendar listings. Estab. 1976. Circ. 30,000. Byline given. Pays on publication. Offers 100% kill fee. Publishes ms an average of 1 month after acceptance. Submit seasonal material 3 months in advance. Accepts queries by mail, e-mail, fax, phone. Accepts simultaneous submissions. Responds in 1 month to queries.

COLUMNS/DEPARTMENTS Speakeasy (opinion and slice-of-life, often humorous); Commentary (forum for social science perspectives); both 1,000-1,500 words, preferably with local or Jersey Shore angle. **Buys 50 mss/year.** Send complete ms. **Pays $40**

NEW MEXICO

⊛⊛ NEW MEXICO MAGAZINE

Lew Wallace Bldg., 495 Old Santa Fe Trail, Santa Fe NM 87501-2750. (505)827-7447. **E-mail:** letters@nmmagazine.com. **E-mail:** queries@nmmagazine.com. **Website:** www.nmmagazine.com. **70% freelance written.** Covers areas throughout the state. "We want to publish a lively editorial mix, covering both the down-home (like a diner in Tucumcari) and

the upscale (a new bistro in world-class Santa Fe)." Explore the gamut of the Old West and the New Age. "Our magazine is about the power of place—in particular more than 120,000 square miles of mountains, desert, grasslands, and forest inhabited by a culturally rich mix of individuals. It is an enterprise of the New Mexico Tourism Department, which strives to make potential visitors aware of our state's multicultural heritage, climate, environment, and uniqueness." Estab. 1923. Circ. 100,000. Pays on acceptance. 20% kill fee. Publishes ms an average of 3 months after acceptance. Submit seasonal material 1 year in advance. Accepts queries by mail, e-mail (preferred). Does not accept previously published submissions. Responds to queries if interested. Sample copy for $5. Guidelines available online.

NONFICTION "Submit your story idea along with a working head and subhead and a paragraph synopsis. Include published clips and a short sum-up about your strengths as a writer. We will consider your proposal as well as your potential to write stories we've conceptualized."

REPRINTS Rarely publishes reprints, but sometimes publishes excerpts from novels and nonfiction books.

PHOTOS "Purchased as portfolio or on assignment. Photographers interested in photo assignments should reference submission guidelines on the contributors' page of our website."

TRADICION REVISTA

LPD Press, 925 Salamanca N.W., Los Ranchos NM 87107-5647. (505)344-9382. **Fax:** (505)345-5129. **E-mail:** LPDPress@q.com. **Website:** www.LPDPress.com. **75% freelance written.** Quarterly magazine covering Southwest history and culture. "We publish Southwest art and history, especially the art of New Mexico." Estab. 1995. Circ. 5,000. Byline given. Does not pay for articles. No kill fee. Editorial lead time 6 months. Submit seasonal material 4 months in advance. Accepts queries by e-mail, phone. Accepts simultaneous submissions. Responds in 1 week to queries. Responds in 1 month to mss. Sample copy free.

NONFICTION Needs essays, general interest, historical, interview, photo feature, travel. **Buys 20 (no pay) mss/year.** Query. Length: 500-2,000 words.

PHOTOS Send photos. Captions required. Reviews GIF/JPEG/PDF files. Offers no additional payment for photos accepted with ms.

COLUMNS/DEPARTMENTS Query. **No pay.**

NEW YORK

💲 ARTSNEWS

ArtsWestchester, 31 Mamaroneck Ave., White Plains NY 10601. **Fax:** (914)428-4306. **E-mail:** jormond@artswestchester.org. **Website:** www.artswestchester.org. **Contact:** Jim Ormond, editor. **20% freelance written.** Monthly tabloid covering arts and entertainment in Westchester County, New York. "We profile artists, arts organizations and write teasers about upcoming exhibitions, concerts, events, theatrical performances, etc." Estab. 1975. Circ. 20,000. Byline given. Pays on publication. Editorial lead time 1 month. Submit seasonal material 2 months in advance. Accepts queries by mail, e-mail. Sample copy free.

NONFICTION Query with published clips. Length: 400-500 words. **Pays $75-100.** Pays expenses of writers on assignment.

TIPS "Please e-mail cover letter, résumé, 2 clips. No phone calls please."

💲💲 BUFFALO SPREE MAGAZINE

Buffalo Spree Publishing, Inc., 100 Corporate Pkwy., Suite 200, Buffalo NY 14226. (716)783-9119. **Fax:** (716)783-9983. **E-mail:** elicata@buffalospree.com. **Website:** www.buffalospree.com. **Contact:** Elizabeth Licata, editor. **90% freelance written.** City regional magazine published 12 times/year. Estab. 1967. Circ. 25,000. Byline given. Pays on publication. No kill fee. Publishes ms an average of 2 months after acceptance. Accepts queries by e-mail. Responds in 6 months to queries. Sample copy for $4.95 and 9x12 SAE with 12 first-class stamps.

NONFICTION Needs interview, travel, issue-oriented features, arts, living, food, regional. Query with résumé and published clips. Length: 1,000-2,000 words. **Pays $125-250.**

TIPS "Send a well-written, compelling query or an interesting topic, and *great* clips. We no longer regularly publish fiction or poetry. Prefers material that is Western New York related."

CITY LIMITS

Community Service Society of New York, 105 E. 22nd St., Suite 901, New York NY 10010. (212)614-5397. **E-mail:** magazine@citylimits.org; editor@citylimits.org. **Website:** www.citylimits.org. **Contact:** Mark Anthony Thomas, director; Jarrett Murphy, editor-in-chief. **50% freelance written.** Monthly magazine covering urban politics and policy in New York City. "*City Limits* is a nonprofit online magazine focusing on issues facing New York City and its neighborhoods, particularly low-income communities. The magazine is strongly committed to investigative journalism, in-depth policy analysis, hard-hitting profiles, and investigation of pressing civic issues in New York City. Driven by a mission to inform public discourse, the magazine provides the factual reporting, human faces, data, history, and breadth of knowledge necessary to understanding the nuances, complexities, and hard truths of the city, its politics, and its people." Estab. 1976. Byline given. Pays on publication. Offers 50% kill fee. Publishes ms an average of 3 months after acceptance. Editorial lead time 2 months. Accepts queries by mail, e-mail, fax. Accepts simultaneous submissions. Responds in 1 month. Sample copy for $2.95. Guidelines free.

NONFICTION Needs book excerpts, exposé, humor, interview, opinion, photo feature. No essays, polemics. **Buys 25 mss/year.** Query with published clips. Length: 400-3,500 words. **Pays $150-2,000 for assigned articles. Pays $100-800 for unsolicited articles.** Pays expenses of writers on assignment.

PHOTOS State availability. Model release required for children. Reviews contact sheets, negatives, transparencies. Buys 20 photos from freelancers/issue; 200 photos/year. Pays $100 for color cover; $50-100 for b&w inside. Pays on publication. Credit line given. Buys rights for use in *City Limits* in print and online; higher rate given for online use.

COLUMNS/DEPARTMENTS Making Change (nonprofit business), Big Idea (policy news), Book Review—all 800 words; Urban Legend (profile), First Hand (Q&A)—both 350 words. **Buys 15 mss/year.** Query with published clips.

TIPS "Our specialty is covering low-income communities. We want to report untold stories about news affecting neighborhoods at the grassroots. We're looking for stories about housing, health care, criminal justice, child welfare, education, economic development, welfare reform, politics, and government. We need good photojournalists who can capture the emotion of a scene. We offer huge pay for great photos."

💲 HUDSON VALLEY LIFE

The Professional Image, 174 South St., Newburgh NY 12550. (845)562-3606. **Fax:** (845)562-3681. **E-mail:** editor@excitingread.com. **Website:** www.hvlife.com. **Contact:** M.J. Goff, editor. **95% freelance written.**

Monthly magazine serving parents and active adults by providing reliable local information of interest. "We are a local resource of information and introduce ideas that lead to enjoyable experiences for the readers in our community. Our readers turn to us for great ideas on travel, health, home improvement and so much more. We continually work at meeting the diverse needs of our ever-changing market. *Hudson Valley Life* magazine offers trusted editorial, extensive resource guides, listings of places to go and things to do and advertisers that are interested in providing products and services for this unique market." Estab. 1999. Circ. 15,000. Pays on publication. No kill fee. Publishes ms an average of 3 months after acceptance. Guidelines available online.

NONFICTION Needs exposé, general interest, humor, interview, personal experience. **Buys 15 mss/year.** Query. Length: 700-1,200 words. **Pays $60-120 for assigned articles. Pays $25-35 for unsolicited articles.**

REPRINTS Pays $25-35.

⊗⊗⊗⊗ NEW YORK MAGAZINE

New York Media, 75 Varick St., New York NY 10013. **E-mail:** editorialsubmissions@nymag.com. **Website:** www.newyorkmag.com. **25% freelance written.** Weekly magazine focusing on current events in the New York metropolitan area. Circ. 405,149. Pays on acceptance. Offers 25% kill fee. Submit seasonal material 2 months in advance. Responds in 1 month to queries. Sample copy for $3.50 or on website.

NONFICTION Query by e-mail. No unsolicited ms. **Pays $1/word.** Pays expenses of writers on assignment.

NORTH CAROLINA

⊗⊗ AAA CAROLINAS GO MAGAZINE

6600 AAA Dr., Charlotte NC 28212. **Fax:** (704)569-7815. **Website:** www.aaacarolinas.com. **Contact:** Tom Crosby, VP of communications. **20% freelance written.** Member publication for the Carolina affiliate of American Automobile Association covering travel and auto-related issues. Estab. 1922. Circ. 1.1 million. Byline given. Pays on publication. No kill fee. Editorial lead time 2 months. Accepts queries by mail. Sample copy and writer's guidelines for #10 SASE.

NONFICTION Needs travel, auto safety. Length: 750 words. **Pays $150.**

PHOTOS Send photos. Identification of subjects required. Reviews slides. Offers no additional payment for photos accepted with ms.

TIPS "Submit regional stories that focus on travel and auto safety in North and South Carolina and surrounding states."

⊗⊗ CARY MAGAZINE

S&A Cherokee, Westview at Weston, 301 Cascade Pointe Lane, #101, Cary NC 27513. (919)674-6020. **Fax:** (919)674-6027. **E-mail:** editor@carymagazine. com. **Website:** www.carymagazine.com. **Contact:** Emily Uhland, editor; Nancy Pardue, editor; Tara Croft, web editor. **40% freelance written.** Publishes 8 times/year. "Lifestyle publication for the affluent communities of Cary, Apex, Morrisville, Holly Springs and Fuquay-Varina. Our editorial objective is to entertain, enlighten and inform our readers with unique and engaging editorial and vivid photography." Estab. 2004. Circ. 18,000. Byline given. Kill fee negotiated. Editorial lead time 3 months. Submit seasonal material 3 months in advance. Accepts queries by mail, e-mail. Responds in 2-4 weeks to queries. Responds in 1 month to mss. Sample copy for $4.95. Guidelines free.

NONFICTION Needs historical, specific to Western Wake County, North Carolina, inspirational, interview, human interest, personal experience. Don't submit articles with no local connection. **Buys 2 mss/year.** Query with published clips. Sometimes pays expenses of writers on assignment.

PHOTOS Freelancers should state the availability of photos with their submission or send the photos with their submission. Identification of subjects required. Reviews GIF/JPEG files. Negotiates payment individually.

TIPS "Prefer experienced feature writers with exceptional interviewing skills who can take a fresh perspective on a topic; writes with a unique flare, but clearly with a good hook to engage the reader and evoke emotion; adheres to AP Style and follows basic journalism conventions; and takes deadlines seriously. E-mail inquiries preferred."

⊗⊗ CHARLOTTE MAGAZINE

Morris Visitor Publications, 309 E. Morehead St., Suite 50, Charlotte NC 28202. (704)335-7181. **Fax:** (704)335-3757. **E-mail:** richard.thurmond@charlottemagazine.com. **Website:** www.charlottemagazine. com. Carrie Campbell, art director (carrie.campbell@charlottemagazine.com). **75% freelance writ-**

ten. Monthly magazine covering Charlotte life. This magazine tells its readers things they didn't know about Charlotte in an interesting, entertaining, and sometimes provocative style. Circ. 40,000. Byline given. Pays within 30 days of acceptance. Offers 25% kill fee. Publishes ms an average of 3 months after acceptance. Editorial lead time 3 months. Submit seasonal material 6 months in advance. Accepts queries by mail, e-mail. Accepts simultaneous submissions. Responds in 6 months to mss. Sample copy for $6.

NONFICTION Needs book excerpts, exposé, general interest, interview, photo feature, travel. **Buys 35-50 mss/year.** Query with published clips. Length: 200-3,000 words. **Pays 20-40¢/word.** Sometimes pays expenses of writers on assignment.

PHOTOS State availability. Identification of subjects required. Negotiates payment individually.

COLUMNS/DEPARTMENTS Buys 35-50 mss/year. **Pays 20-40¢/word**

TIPS "A story for *Charlotte* magazine could only appear in *Charlotte* magazine. That is, the story and its treatment are particularly germane to this area. Because of this, we rarely work with writers who live outside the Charlotte area."

$$ FIFTEEN 501

Weiss and Hughes Publishing, 189 Wind Chime Court, Suite 104, Raleigh NC 27615. (919)870-1722. **Fax:** (919)719-5260. **E-mail:** djackson@whmags. com. **Website:** www.fifteen501.com. **Contact:** Danielle Jackson, editor. **50% freelance written.** Quarterly magazine covering lifestyle issues relevant to residents in the U.S. 15/501 corridor of Durham, Orange, and Chatham counties in North Carolina. "We cover issues important to residents of Durham, Orange and Chatham counties. We're committed to improving our readers' overall quality of life and keeping them informed of the lifestyle amenities there." Estab. 2006. Circ. 30,000. Byline given. Pays within 30 days of publication. Offers 25% kill fee. Publishes ms an average of 2 months after acceptance. Editorial lead time 2-3 months. Submit seasonal material 6 months in advance. Accepts queries by mail, e-mail. Accepts simultaneous submissions. Responds in 2-4 weeks to queries. Sample copy available online. Guidelines by e-mail.

NONFICTION Needs general interest, historical, how-to, home interiors, landscaping, gardening, technology, inspirational, interview, personal experi-

rience, photo feature, technical, travel. Does not want opinion pieces or political or religious topics. Query. Length: 600-1,200 words. **Pays 35¢/word.** Sometimes pays expenses of writers on assignment.

PHOTOS State availability. Captions, identification of subjects required. Reviews transparencies, GIF/JPEG files. Offers no additional payment for photos accepted with ms.

COLUMNS/DEPARTMENTS Around Town (local lifestyle topics), 1,000 words; Hometown Stories, 600 words; Travel (around North Carolina), 1,000 words; Home Interiors/Landscaping (varies), 1,000 words; Restaurants (local, fine dining), 600-1,000 words. **Buys 20-25 mss/year.** Query. **Pays 35¢/word.**

TIPS "All queries must be focused on the issues that make Durham, Chapel Hill, Carrboro, Hillsborough, and Pittsboro unique and wonderful places to live."

$$ WAKE LIVING

Weiss and Hughes Publishing, 189 Wind Chime Ct., Suite 104, Raleigh NC 27615. (919)870-1722. **Fax:** (919)719-5260. **E-mail:** dhughes@wakeliving. com. **Website:** www.wakeliving.com. **Contact:** David Hughes, president and publisher. **50% freelance written.** Quarterly magazine covering lifestyle issues in Wake County, North Carolina. "We cover issues important to residents of Wake County. We are committed to improving our readers' overall quality of life and keeping them informed of the lifestyle amenities here." Estab. 2003. Circ. 40,000. Byline given. Pays within 30 days of publication. Offers 25% kill fee. Publishes ms an average of 2 months after acceptance. Editorial lead time 2-3 months. Submit seasonal material 6 months in advance. Accepts queries by mail, e-mail. Accepts simultaneous submissions. Responds in 2-4 weeks to queries. Sample copy available online. Guidelines available online.

NONFICTION Needs general interest, historical, how-to, home interiors, technology, landscaping, gardening, inspirational, interview, personal experience, photo feature, technical, travel. Does not want opinion pieces, political topics, religious articles. Query. Length: 600-1,200 words. **Pays 35¢/word. Pay is per article and varies by complexity of assignment** Sometimes pays expenses of writers on assignment.

PHOTOS State availability. Captions, identification of subjects required. Reviews transparencies, GIF/JPEG files. Offers no additional payment for photos accepted with ms.

COLUMNS/DEPARTMENTS Around Town (local lifestyle topics); Hometown Stories, 600 words; Travel (around North Carolina); Home Interiors/Landscaping, all 1,000 words. Restaurants (local restaurants, fine dining), 600-1,000 words. **Buys 20-25 mss/year.** Query. **Pays 35¢/word. Pay is per article and varies by complexity of assignment.**

TIPS "Articles must be specifically focused on Wake County/Raleigh metro issues. We like unusual angles about what makes living here unique from other areas."

NORTH DAKOTA

$$ NORTH DAKOTA LIVING MAGAZINE

North Dakota Association of Rural Electric Cooperatives, 3201 Nygren Dr. NW, P.O. Box 727, Mandan ND 58554-0727. (701)663-6501. **Fax:** (701)663-3745. **E-mail:** kbrick@ndarec.com; cdevney@ndarec.com. **Website:** www.ndarec.com/dakotaLiving. **20% freelance written.** Monthly magazine covering information of interest to memberships of electric cooperatives and telephone cooperatives. "We publish a general interest magazine for North Dakotans. We treat subjects pertaining to living and working in the northern Great Plains. We provide progress reporting on electric cooperatives and telephone cooperatives." Estab. 1954. Circ. 70,000. Byline given. Pays on acceptance. No kill fee. Publishes ms an average of 6 months after acceptance. Editorial lead time 6 months. Submit seasonal material 6 months in advance. Accepts queries by mail, e-mail. Accepts simultaneous submissions. Sample copy and writer's guidelines not available.

NONFICTION Needs general interest, historical, how-to, humor, interview, new product, travel. **Buys 20 mss/year.** Query with published clips. Length: 1,500-2,000 words. **Pays $100-500 minimum for assigned articles. Pays $300-600 for unsolicited articles.** Sometimes pays expenses of writers on assignment.

COLUMNS/DEPARTMENTS Energy Use and Financial Planning, both 750 words. **Buys 6 mss/year.** Query with published clips. **Pays $100-300.**

FICTION Needs historical, humorous, slice-of-life vignettes, western. **Buys 1 mss/year.** Query with published clips. Length: 1,000-2,500 words. **Pays $100-400.**

OHIO

$$ AKRON LIFE

Baker Media Group, 1653 Merriman Rd., Suite 116, Akron OH 44313. (330)253-0056. **Fax:** (330)253-5868. **E-mail:** info@bakermediagroup.com. **E-mail:** editor@bakermediagroup.com; acymerman@bakermediagroup.com. **Website:** www.akronlife.com. **Contact:** Abby Cymerman, managing editor. **10% freelance written.** Monthly regional magazine covering Summit, Stark, Portage and Medina counties. "*Akron Life & Leisure* is a monthly lifestyles publication committed to providing information that enhances and enriches the experience of living in or visiting Akron and the surrounding region of Summit, Portage, Medina and Stark counties. Each colorful, thoughtfully designed issue profiles interesting places, personalities and events in the arts, sports, entertainment, business, politics and social scene. We cover issues important to the Greater Akron area and significant trends affecting the lives of those who live here." Estab. 2002. Circ. 15,000. Byline given. Pays on publication. Offers 50% kill fee. Publishes ms an average of 4-6 months after acceptance. Editorial lead time 2+ months. Submit seasonal material 6 months in advance. Accepts queries by mail, e-mail, fax. Sample copy free. Guidelines free.

NONFICTION Needs essays, general interest, historical, how-to, humor, interview, photo feature, travel. Query with published clips. Length: 300-2,000 words. **Pays $0.10 max/word for assigned and unsolicited articles.**

PHOTOS State availability. Captions, identification of subjects, model releases required. Reviews GIF/JPEG files. Negotiates payment individually.

TIPS "It's best to submit a detailed query along with samples of previously published works. Include why you think the story is of interest to our readers, and be sure to have a fresh approach."

$ BEND OF THE RIVER MAGAZINE

P.O. Box 859, Maumee OH 43537. (419)893-0022. **Website:** http://bendoftherivermagazine.com. **98% freelance written. This magazine reports that it is eager to work with all writers. "We buy material that we like whether it is by an experienced writer or not."** Monthly magazine for readers interested in northwestern Ohio history and nostalgia. Estab. 1972. Circ. 6,500. Byline given. Pays on publication. No kill fee. Publishes ms an average of 1 month after acceptance. Submit seasonal material 2 months in advance. Responds in 1 week to queries. Sample copy for $1.25.

NONFICTION Needs historical. **Buys 75 unsolicited mss/year.** Send complete ms. 1,500 words. **Pays $50 on average.**

TIPS "Our stockpile is low. Send us something!"

$$$ CINCINNATI MAGAZINE

Emmis Publishing Corp., 441 Vine St., Suite 200, Cincinnati OH 45202-2039. (513)421-4300. **Fax:** (513)562-2746. **Website:** www.cincinnatimagazine.com. **Contact:** Jay Stowe, editor; Amanda Boyd Walters, deputy editor. Monthly magazine emphasizing Cincinnati living. Circ. 38,000. Byline given. Pays on publication. No kill fee. Accepts queries by mail, e-mail. Send SASE for writer's guidelines; view content on magazine website.

NONFICTION **Buys 12 mss/year.** Query. Length: 2,500-3,500 words. **Pays $500-1,000.**

COLUMNS/DEPARTMENTS Topics are Cincinnati media, arts and entertainment, people, politics, sports, business, regional. Length: 1,000-1,500 words. **Buys 10-15 mss/year.** Query. **Pays $200-400.**

TIPS "It's most helpful on us if you query in writing, with clips. All articles have a local focus. No generics, please. Also: No movie, book, theater reviews, poetry, or fiction. For special advertising sections, query special sections editor Marnie Hayutin; for *Cincinnati Wedding*, query custom publishing editor Kara Renee Hagerman."

$$$ CLEVELAND MAGAZINE

City Magazines, Inc., 1422 Euclid Ave., Suite 730, Cleveland OH 44115. (216)771-2833. **Fax:** (216)781-6318. **E-mail:** gleydura@clevelandmagazine.com; miller@clevelandmagazine.com. **Website:** www.clevelandmagazine.com. **Contact:** Kristen Miller, art director; Steve Gleydura, editor. **60% freelance written. Mostly by assignment.** Monthly magazine with a strong Cleveland/Northeast Ohio angle. Estab. 1972. Circ. 50,000. Byline given. Pays on publication. No kill fee. Publishes ms an average of 3 months after acceptance. Editorial lead time 6 months. Submit seasonal material 8 months in advance. Accepts queries by mail, e-mail, fax. Accepts simultaneous submissions. Responds in 2 months to queries.

NONFICTION Needs general interest, historical, humor, interview, travel, home and garden. Query with published clips. Length: 800-4,000 words. **Pays $250-1,200.**

PHOTOS Buys an average of 50 photos from freelancers/issue; 600 photos/year. Model release required for portraits; property release required for individual homes. Photo captions required; include names, date, location, event, phone. Pays on publication. Credit line given. Buys one-time publication, electronic and promotional rights.

COLUMNS/DEPARTMENTS Talking Points (opinion or observation-driven essay), approximately 1,000 words. Query with published clips. **Pays $300.**

$$$ COLUMBUS MONTHLY

Dispatch Magazines, 34 S. Third St., Columbus OH 43215. (614)888-4567. **Fax:** (614)848-3838. **E-mail:** kschmidt@columbusmonthly.com; jross@columbusalive.com. **Website:** www.columbusmonthly.com. **Contact:** Kristen Schmitt, editor; John Ross, assistant editor. **40-60% freelance written. Prefers to work with published/established writers.** Monthly magazine emphasizing subjects specifically related to Columbus and Central Ohio. Circ. 35,000. Byline given. Pays on publication. No kill fee. Publishes ms an average of 2 months after acceptance. Responds in 1 month to queries. Sample copy for $6.50.

NONFICTION **Buys 2-3 unsolicited mss/year.** Query. Length: 250-4,000 words. **Pays $85-900.** Sometimes pays expenses of writers on assignment.

TIPS "It makes sense to start small—something for our City Journal section, perhaps. Stories for that section run between 250-500 words."

INDIAN HILL LIVING

Community Publications, Inc., 179 Fairfield Ave., Bellevue KY 41074. (859)291-1412. **Fax:** (859)291-1417. **E-mail:** indianhill@livingmagazines.com. **Website:** www.livingmagazines.com. **Contact:** Moira Grainger, editor. Monthly magazine covering Indian Hill community. Estab. 1983. Circ. 3,000. Byline given. Pays on publication. Editorial lead time 2 months. Submit seasonal material 3 months in advance. Accepts queries by mail, e-mail, fax. Guidelines by e-mail.

NONFICTION Needs book excerpts, essays, exposé, general interest, historical, humor, inspirational, interview, new product, personal experience, photo feature, travel. Does not want anything unrelated to Indian Hill, Ohio. Query.

PHOTOS State availability. Captions, identification of subjects, model releases required. Reviews contact sheets, negatives, transparencies, prints, GIF/JPEG files. Negotiates payment individually.

COLUMNS/DEPARTMENTS Financial; Artistic (reviews, etc.); Historic; Food. Query.

FICTION Needs adventure, historical, humorous, mainstream, slice-of-life vignettes. Query.

POETRY Needs free verse, light verse, traditional. Please query.

FILLERS Please query. Needs anecdotes, short humor.

💲💲💲 OHIO MAGAZINE

Great Lakes Publishing Co., 1422 Euclid Ave., Suite 730, Cleveland OH 44115. (216)771-2833. **E-mail:** editorial@ohiomagazine.com. **E-mail:** vpospisil@ohiomagazine.com; lblake@ohiomagazine.com. **Website:** www.ohiomagazine.com. **Contact:** Vivian Pospisil, executive editor; Lesley Blake, art director. **50% freelance written.** Monthly magazine emphasizing Ohio-based travel, news, and feature material that highlights what's special and unique about the state. Estab. 1978. Circ. 80,000. Byline given. Pays on publication. 20% kill fee. Publishes ms an average of 6 months after acceptance. Submit seasonal material 6 months in advance. Accepts queries by mail, e-mail. Responds in 3 months to queries. Responds in 3 months to mss. Sample copy for $3.95 and 9x12 SAE or online. Guidelines available on website.

NONFICTION Query with résumé and at least 3 published clips. Length: 1,000-3,000 words. **Pays $300-1,200.** Sometimes pays expenses of writers on assignment.

REPRINTS Contact Emily Vanuch, advertising coordinator. Pays 50% of amount paid for an original article.

PHOTOS Rate negotiable.

COLUMNS/DEPARTMENTS **Buys minimum 5 unsolicited mss/year. Pays $100-600.**

TIPS "Freelancers should send all queries in writing (either by mail or e-mail), not by telephone. Successful queries demonstrate an intimate knowledge of the publication. We are looking to increase our circle of writers who can write about the state in an informative and upbeat style. Strong reporting skills are highly valued."

SYCAMORE LIVING

Community Publications, Inc., 179 Fairfield Ave., Bellevue KY 41073. (859)291-1412. **Fax:** (859)291-1417. **E-mail:** sycamore@livingmagazines.com. **Website:** www.livingmagazines.com. **Contact:** Vicki Black,

editor. Monthly magazine covering the Sycamore community, a Greater Cincinnati area. Estab. 1983. Circ. 6,600. Byline given. Pays on publication. Editorial lead time 2 months. Submit seasonal material 3 months in advance. Accepts queries by mail, e-mail, fax. Guidelines by e-mail.

NONFICTION Needs book excerpts, essays, exposé, general interest, historical, humor, inspirational, interview, new product, personal experience, photo feature, travel. Does not want anything unrelated to Sycamore, Ohio. Query.

PHOTOS State availability. Captions, identification of subjects, model releases required. Reviews contact sheets, negatives, transparencies, prints, GIF/JPEG files. Negotiates payment individually.

COLUMNS/DEPARTMENTS Financial; Artistic (reviews, etc.); Historic; Food. Query.

FICTION Needs adventure, historical, humorous, mainstream, slice-of-life vignettes. Query.

POETRY Needs free verse, light verse, traditional. Please query.

FILLERS Please query. Needs anecdotes, short humor.

OKLAHOMA

💲💲 INTERMISSION

Langdon Publishing, 110 E. 2nd St., Tulsa OK 74103-3212. (918)596-2368. **Fax:** (918)596-7144. **E-mail:** nbizjack@cityoftulsa.org. **Website:** www.tulsapac.com. **Contact:** Nancy Bizjack, editor. **30% freelance written.** Monthly magazine covering events held at the Tulsa Performing Arts Center. "We feature profiles of entertainers appearing at our center, Q&As, stories on the events, and entertainers slated for the Tulsa PAC." Byline given. Pays on publication. Offers 50% kill fee. Publishes ms an average of 1 month after acceptance. Editorial lead time 2 months. Submit seasonal material 2 months in advance. Accepts queries by mail, e-mail. Accepts simultaneous submissions. Responds in 2 weeks to queries. Sample copy available online. Guidelines by e-mail.

NONFICTION Needs general interest, interview. Does not want personal experience articles. **Buys 35 mss/year.** Query with published clips. Length: 600-1,400 words. **Pays $100-200.**

COLUMNS/DEPARTMENTS Q&A (personalities and artists tied into the events at the Tulsa PAC), 1,100 words. **Buys 12 mss/year.** Query with published clips. **Pays $100-150.**

TIPS "Look ahead at our upcoming events, find an interesting slant on an event. Interview someone who would be of general interest."

⚙️⚙️ OKLAHOMA TODAY

P.O. Box 1468, Oklahoma City OK 73101-1468. (405)230-8450. **Fax:** (405)230-8650. **E-mail:** steffie@ oklahomatoday.com. **Website:** www.oklahomatoday. com. **Contact:** Steffie Corcoran, editor. **80% freelance written. Works with approximately 25 new/unpublished writers each year.** Bimonthly magazine covering people, places, and things of Oklahoma. "We are interested in showing off the best Oklahoma has to offer; we're pretty serious about our travel slant but regularly run history, nature, and personality profiles." Estab. 1956. Circ. 45,000. Byline given. Pays on publication. No kill fee. Publishes ms an average of 6 months after acceptance. Submit seasonal material 1 year in advance. Accepts queries by mail, e-mail. Responds in 4 months to queries. Sample copy for $4.95 and 9x12 SASE or online. Guidelines available on website.

NONFICTION Needs book excerpts, on Oklahoma topics, historical, Oklahoma only, interview, Oklahomans only, photo feature, in Oklahoma, travel, in Oklahoma. No phone queries. **Buys 20-40 mss/year.** Query with published clips. Length: 250-3,000 words. **Pays $25-750.**

PHOTOS "We are especially interested in developing contacts with photographers who live in Oklahoma or have shot here. Send samples. Photo guidelines with SASE." No answer. Captions, identification of subjects required. Reviews 4x5, 2¼x2¼, and 35mm color transparencies, high-quality transparencies, slides, and b&w prints. Pays $50-750 for color.

TIPS "The best way to become a regular contributor to *Oklahoma Today* is to query us with 1 or more story ideas, each developed to give us an idea of your proposed slant. We're looking for lively, concise, well-researched and reported stories, stories that don't need to be heavily edited and are not newspaper style. We have a 3-person full-time editorial staff, and freelancers who can write and have done their homework get called again and again."

OREGON

⚙️⚙️ OREGON COAST

4969 Hwy. 101 N, Suite 2, Florence OR 97439. (800)348-8401. **E-mail:** Alicia@nwmags.com. **Web-**site: www.northwestmagazines.com. **Contact:** Alicia Spooner. **65% freelance written.** Bimonthly magazine covering the Oregon Coast. Estab. 1982. Circ. 50,000. Byline given. Pays after publication. Offers 33% (on assigned stories only, not on stories accepted on spec) kill fee. Publishes ms an average of up to 1 year after acceptance. Submit seasonal material 6 months in advance. Accepts queries by mail, e-mail. Responds in 3 months to queries. Sample copy for $4.50. Guidelines available on website.

NONFICTION Buys 55 mss/year. Query with published clips. Length: 500-1,500 words. **Pays $75-350, plus 2 contributor copies.**

REPRINTS Send tearsheet or photocopy and information about when and where the material previously appeared. Pays an average of 60% of the amount paid for an original article.

PHOTOS Photo submissions with no ms or stand alone or cover photos. Send photos. Captions, identification of subjects, Slides or high-resolution digital.

TIPS "Slant article for readers who do not live at the Oregon Coast. At least 1 historical article is used in each issue. Manuscript/photo packages are preferred over manuscripts with no photos. List photo credits and captions for each photo. Check all facts, proper names, and numbers carefully in photo/manuscript packages. Must pertain to Oregon Coast somehow."

PENNSYLVANIA

⚙️⚙️ BERKS COUNTY LIVING

201 Washington St., Suite 525, GoggleWorks Center for the Arts, Reading PA 19601. (610)898-1928. **Fax:** (610)898-1933. **E-mail:** nmurry@berkscountyliving. com. **Website:** www.berkscountyliving.com. **Contact:** Nikki M. Murry, editor-in-chief. **90% freelance written.** Bimonthly magazine covering topics of interest to people living in Berks County, Pennsylvania. Estab. 2000. Circ. 36,000. Byline given. Pays on publication. Offers 25% kill fee. Publishes ms an average of 4 months after acceptance. Editorial lead time 3 months. Submit seasonal material 4 months in advance. Accepts queries by mail, e-mail. Accepts simultaneous submissions. Responds in 1 week to queries. Responds in 1 month to mss. Sample copy for SAE with 9x12 envelope and 2 first-class stamps.

NONFICTION Needs exposé, general interest, historical, how-to, humor, inspirational, interview, new product, photo feature, travel, food, health. **Buys 25**

mss/year. Query. Length: 750-2,000 words. **Pays $150-400.** Sometimes pays expenses of writers on assignment.

PHOTOS State availability. Captions, identification of subjects, model releases required. Reviews 35mm or greater transparencies, any size prints. Negotiates payment individually.

$$ MAIN LINE TODAY

Today Media, Inc., 4699 West Chester Pike, Newtown Square PA 19073. (610)325-4630. **Fax:** (610)325-4636. **E-mail:** hrowland@mainlinetoday.com; tbehan@mainlinetoday.com. **Website:** www.mainlinetoday.com. **Contact:** Hobart Rowland, editor-in-chief; Tara Behan, senior editor. **60% freelance written.** Monthly magazine serving Philadelphia's main line and western suburbs. *Main Line Today*'s high-quality print and electronic media provide authoritative, current and entertaining information on local lifestyle trends, while examining the people, issues and institutions that shape life in Philadelphia's western suburbs. Estab. 1996. Circ. 20,000. Byline given. Pays on publication. Offers 25% kill fee. Publishes ms an average of 3 months after acceptance. Editorial lead time 5 months. Submit seasonal material 5 months in advance. Accepts queries by fax. Accepts simultaneous submissions. Responds in 2 weeks to queries. Responds in 1 month to mss. Sample copy free. Guidelines free.

NONFICTION Needs book excerpts, historical, how-to, humor, interview, opinion, photo feature, travel. Special issues: Health & Wellness Guide (September and March). Query with published clips. Length: 400-3,000 words. **Pays $125-650.** Sometimes pays expenses of writers on assignment.

PHOTOS State availability. Identification of subjects, model releases required. Reviews GIF/JPEG files. Negotiates payment individually.

COLUMNS/DEPARTMENTS Profile (local personality); Neighborhood (local people/issues); End of the Line (essay/humor); Living Well (health/wellness), all 1,600 words. **Buys 50 mss/year.** Query with published clips. **Pays $125-350.**

TIPS "*Main Line Today* values good living, social responsibility and community engagement. We treat all subjects with respect, and always strive to be truthful, fair, accurate and insightful. Main Line Today is opinionated, smart, stylish and witty, with an emphasis on superior writing, photography and design."

$$ PENNSYLVANIA

Pennsylvania Magazine Co., P.O. Box 755, Camp Hill PA 17001-0755. (717)697-4660. **E-mail:** editor@pa-mag.com. **Website:** www.pa-mag.com. **90% freelance written.** Bimonthly magazine covering people, places, events, and history in Pennsylvania. Estab. 1981. Circ. 33,000. Byline given. Pays on acceptance except for articles (by authors unknown to us) sent on speculation. Offers 25% kill fee for assigned articles. Publishes ms an average of 9 months after acceptance. Submit seasonal material 9 months in advance. Accepts queries by mail, e-mail. Responds in 4-6 weeks to queries. Sample copy free. Guidelines for #10 SASE or by e-mail.

NONFICTION Nothing on Amish topics, hunting, or skiing. **Buys 75-120 mss/year.** Query. Length: 750-2,500 words. **Pays 15¢/word.**

REPRINTS Send photocopy with rights for sale noted and information about when and where the material previously appeared. Pays 5¢/word.

PHOTOS "Contact editor via e-mail for photography instructions. We work primarily with digital images and prefer raw when possible." Photography Essay (highlights annual photo essay contest entries and showcases individual photographers). Captions required. Digital photos (send printouts and CD OR DVD or contact to upload to dropbox folder. Pays $25-35 for inside photos; $150 for covers.

COLUMNS/DEPARTMENTS Round Up (short items about people, unusual events, museums, historical topics/events, family and individually owned consumer-related businesses), 250-1,300 words; Town and Country (items about people or events illustrated with photos or commissioned art), 500 words. Include SASE. Query. **Pays 15¢/word.**

TIPS "Our publication depends upon freelance work—send queries. Remember that a subject isn't an idea. Send the topic and your approach to the topic when you query. Answer the question: Would this be interesting to someone across the state? Find things that interest you enough that you'd travel 30-50 miles in a car to see/do/explore it, and send a query on that."

$$ PENNSYLVANIA HERITAGE

Pennsylvania Historical and Museum Commission and the Pennsylvania Heritage Society, Commonwealth Keystone Bldg., Plaza Level, 400 North St., Harrisburg PA 17120. (717)787-2407. **Fax:** (717)346-9099. **E-mail:** miomalley@state.pa.us. **Website:** www.

paheritage.org. **Contact:** Michael J. O'Malley III, editor. **75% freelance written. Prefers to work with published/established writers.** Quarterly magazine covering history and culture in Pennsylvania. "*Pennsylvania Heritage* introduces readers to Pennsylvania's rich culture and historic legacy; educates and sensitizes them to the value of preserving that heritage; and entertains and involves them in such a way as to ensure that Pennsylvania's past has a future. The magazine is intended for intelligent lay readers." Estab. 1974. Circ. 10,000. Byline given. Pays on publication. Publishes ms an average of 1 year after acceptance. Accepts queries by mail, e-mail. Responds in 10 weeks to queries. Responds in 8 months to mss. Sample copy for $5 and 9x12 SAE or online. Guidelines for #10 SASE.

Pennsylvania Heritage is now considering freelance submissions that are shorter in length (2,000-3,000 words); pictorial/photographic essays; biographies of famous (and not-so-famous) Pennsylvanians; and interviews with individuals who have helped shape, make, and preserve the Keystone State's history and heritage.

NONFICTION No articles which do not relate to Pennsylvania history or culture. **Buys 20-24 mss/year.** Prefers to see mss with suggested illustrations. Length: 2,000-3,500 words. **Pays $100-500.**

PHOTOS State availability of or send photos. Captions, identification of subjects required. Pays $25-200 for transparencies; $5-75 for b&w photos.

TIPS "We are looking for well-written, interesting material that pertains to any aspect of Pennsylvania history or culture. Potential contributors should realize that, although our articles are popularly styled, they are not light, puffy, or breezy; in fact they demand strident documentation and substantiation (sans footnotes). The most frequent mistake made by writers in completing articles for us is making them either too scholarly or too sentimental or nostalgic. We want material which educates, but also entertains. Authors should make history readable and enjoyable. Our goal is to make the Keystone State's history come to life in a meaningful, memorable way."

PHILADELPHIA STYLE
Philadelphia Style Magazine, LLC, 141 League St., Philadelphia PA 19147. (215)468-6670. **Fax:** (215)223-3095. **E-mail:** info@phillystylemag.com. **Website:** www.phillystylemag.com. **Contact:** Kristin Detterline-Munro. **50% freelance written.** "Bimonthly magazine covering upscale living in the Philadelphia region. Topics include: celebrity interviews, fashion (men's and women's), food, home and design, real estate, dining, beauty, travel, arts and entertainment, and more. Our magazine is a positive look at the best ways to live in the Philadelphia region. Submitted articles should speak to an upscale, educated audience of professionals that live in the Delaware Valley." Estab. 1999. Circ. 60,000. Byline given. Pays on publication. Offers 25% kill fee. Publishes ms an average of 3 months after acceptance. Editorial lead time 2-4 months. Submit seasonal material 6 months in advance. Accepts queries by mail, e-mail, fax.

NONFICTION Needs general interest, interview, travel, region-specific articles. "We are not looking for articles that do not have a regional spin." **Buys 100+ mss/year.** Send complete ms. Length: 300-2,500 words. **Pays $50-500.**

COLUMNS/DEPARTMENTS Declarations (celebrity interviews and celebrity contributors); Currents (fashion news); Manor (home and design news); Liberties (beauty and travel news); Dish (dining news); Life in the City (fresh, quirky, regional reporting on books, real estate, art, retail, dining, events, and little-known stories/facts about the region), 100-500 words; Vanguard (people on the forefront of Philadelphia's arts, media, fashion, business, and social scene), 500-700 words; In the Neighborhood (reader-friendly reporting on up-and-coming areas of the region including dining, shopping, attractions, and recreation), 2,000-2,500 words. Query with published clips or send complete ms. **Pays $50-500.**

TIPS "Mail queries with clips or manuscripts. Articles should speak to a stylish, educated audience."

PITTSBURGH MAGAZINE
WiesnerMedia, Washington's Landing, 600 Waterfront Dr., Suite 100, Pittsburgh PA 15222-4795. (412)304-0900. **Fax:** (412)304-0938. **E-mail:** editors@pittsburghmagazine.com. **Website:** www.pittsburghmag.com. **Contact:** Julie Talerico, editor-in-chief; Betsy Benson, publisher and vice president. **70% freelance written.** Monthly magazine covering the Pittsburgh metropolitan area. "*Pittsburgh* presents issues, analyzes problems, and strives to encourage a better understanding of the community. Our region is Western Pennsylvania, Eastern Ohio, Northern

West Virginia, and Western Maryland." Estab. 1970. Circ. 75,000. Byline given. Pays on publication. Offers kill fee. Offers kill fee. Publishes ms an average of 2 months after acceptance. Submit seasonal material 6 months in advance. Accepts queries by mail. Responds in 2 months to queries. Sample copy for $2 (old back issues). Guidelines online at www.pittsburghmagazine.com/Pittsburgh-Magazine/Writers-Guidelines, or via SASE.

NONFICTION Needs exposé, lifestyle, sports, informational, service, business, medical, profile. "We have minimal interest in historical articles and we do not publish fiction, poetry, advocacy, or personal reminiscence pieces." Query in writing with outline and clips. Length: 1,200-4,000 words. **Pays $300-1,500+.**

PHOTOS Query. Model releases required. Pays prenegotiated expenses of writer on assignment.

TIPS "Best bet to break in is through hard news with a region-wide impact or service pieces or profiles with a regional interest. The point is that we want more stories that reflect our region, not just a tiny part. And we *never* consider any story without a strong regional focus."

💲 SUSQUEHANNA LIFE

637 Market St., Lewisburg PA 17837. (800)232-1670. **Fax:** (570)524-7796. **E-mail:** susquehannalife@gmail.com. **Website:** www.susquehannalife.com. **80% freelance written.** Quarterly magazine covering Central Pennsylvania lifestyle. Estab. 1993. Circ. 45,000. Byline given. Pays on publication. Offers 50% kill fee. Publishes ms an average of 6-9 months after acceptance. Editorial lead time 3-6 months. Submit seasonal material 4-6 months in advance. Accepts queries by e-mail. Responds in 4-6 weeks to queries. Responds in 1-3 months to mss. Sample copy for $4.95, plus 5 first-class stamps. Guidelines for #10 SASE.

NONFICTION Needs book excerpts, general interest, historical, how-to, inspirational, related to the region, interview, photo feature, travel. Does not want fiction. **Buys 30-40 mss/year.** Query or send complete ms. Length: 800-1,200 words. **Pays $75-125.** Sometimes pays expenses of writers on assignment.

PHOTOS Send photos. Captions, identification of subjects, model releases required. Reviews contact sheets, prints, GIF/JPEG files. Offers $20-25/photo; $100+ for cover photos.

POETRY Must have a Central Pennsylvania angle.

TIPS "When you query, do not address letter to 'Dear Sir'—address the letter to the name of the publisher/editor. Demonstrate your ability to write. You need to be familiar with the type of articles we use and the particular flavor of the region. Only accepts submissions with a Central Pennsylvania angle."

RHODE ISLAND

💲💲💲 RHODE ISLAND MONTHLY

717 Allens Ave., Suite 105, Providence RI 02905. (401)649-4800. **E-mail:** tstrasberg@rimonthly.com. **Website:** www.rimonthly.com. **Contact:** Tina Strasberg, art director. **50% freelance written.** Monthly magazine covering Rhode Island. *Rhode Island Monthly* is a general interest consumer magazine with a strict Rhode Island focus. Estab. 1988. Circ. 41,000. Byline given. Pays on acceptance. Offers 25% kill fee. Publishes ms an average of 3 months after acceptance. Editorial lead time 3 months. Submit seasonal material 6 months in advance. Accepts queries by mail, e-mail, fax. Responds in 6 weeks to queries. Guidelines free.

NONFICTION Needs exposé, general interest, interview, photo feature. **Buys 40 mss/year.** Query with published clips. Length: 1,800-3,000 words. **Pays $600-1,200.** Sometimes pays expenses of writers on assignment.

SOUTH CAROLINA

CHARLESTON MAGAZINE

P.O. Box 1794, Mt. Pleasant SC 29465. (843)971-9811 or (888)242-7624. **E-mail:** dshankland@charlestonmag.com; anna@charlestonmag.com; jed@charlestonmag.com. **Website:** www.charlestonmag.com. **Contact:** Darcy Shankland, editor-in-chief; Anna Evans, managing editor; Jed Drew, publisher. **80% freelance written.** Bimonthly magazine covering current issues, events, arts and culture, leisure pursuits, travel, and personalities, as they pertain to the city of Charleston and surrounding areas. A Lowcountry institution for more than 30 years, *Charleston Magazine* captures the essence of Charleston and her surrounding areas—her people, arts and architecture, culture and events, and natural beauty. Estab. 1972. Circ. 25,000. Byline given. Pays 1 month after publication. No kill fee. Submit seasonal material 4 months in advance. Accepts queries by mail, e-mail, fax. Sample copies may be ordered at cover price from office. Guidelines for #10 SASE.

NONFICTION Needs general interest, humor, interview, opinion, photo feature, travel, food, architecture, sports, current events/issues, art. Not interested in 'Southern nostalgia' articles or gratuitous history pieces. **Buys 40 mss/year.** Query with published clips and SASE. Length: 150-1,500 words. **Payment negotiated.** Sometimes pays expenses of writers on assignment.

REPRINTS Send photocopy and information about when and where the material previously appeared. Payment negotiable.

PHOTOS Send photos. Identification of subjects required. Reviews contact sheets, transparencies, slides.

COLUMNS/DEPARTMENTS Channel Markers (general local interest), 50-400 words; Local Seen (profile of local interest), 500 words; In Good Taste (restaurants and culinary trends in the city), 1,000-1,200 words, plus recipes; Chef at Home (profile of local chefs), 1,200 words, plus recipes; On the Road (travel opportunities near Charleston), 1,000-1,200 words; Southern View (personal experience about Charleston life), 750 words; Doing Business (profiles of exceptional local businesses and entrepreneurs), 1,000-1,200 words; Native Talent (local profiles), 1,000-1,200 words; Top of the Shelf (reviews of books with Southern content or by a Southern author), 750 words.

TIPS "Charleston, although a city with a 300-year history, is a vibrant, modern community with a tremendous dedication to the arts and no shortage of newsworthy subjects. We're looking for the freshest stories about Charleston—and those don't always come from insiders, but also outsiders who are keenly observant."

☻☻ HILTON HEAD MONTHLY

P.O. Box 5926, Hilton Head Island SC 29938. **Fax:** (843)842-5743. **E-mail:** editor@hiltonheadmonthly. com. **Website:** www.hiltonheadmonthly.com. **Contact:** Barry Kaufman, editor. **75% freelance written.** Monthly magazine covering the people, business, community, environment, and lifestyle of Hilton Head, SC, and the surrounding Lowcountry. "Our mission is to offer lively, fresh writing about Hilton Head Island, an upscale, environmentally conscious and intensely pro-active resort community on the coast of South Carolina." Circ. 35,000. Byline given. Pays on publication. Offers 50% kill fee. Publishes ms an average of 6 months after acceptance. Edito-

rial lead time 3 months. Submit seasonal material 4 months in advance. Accepts queries by mail, e-mail, . Accepts simultaneous submissions. Responds in 1 week to queries. Responds in 4 months to mss. Sample copy for $3.

NONFICTION Needs general interest, historical, history only, how-to, home related, humor, interview, Hilton Head residents only, opinion, general humor or Hilton Head Island community affairs, personal experience, travel. "Everything is local, local, local, so we're especially interested in profiles of notable residents (or those with Lowcountry ties) and original takes on home design/maintenance, environmental issues, entrepreneurship, health, sports, arts and entertainment, humor, travel and volunteerism. We like to see how national trends/issues play out on a local level." **Buys 225-250 mss/year.** Query with published clips.

PHOTOS State availability. Reviews contact sheets, prints, digital samples. Negotiates payment individually.

COLUMNS/DEPARTMENTS News; Business; Lifestyles (hobbies, health, sports, etc.); Home; Around Town (local events, charities and personalities); People (profiles, weddings, etc.). Query with synopsis. **Pays 20¢/word.**

TIPS "Sure, Hilton Head is known primarily as an affluent resort island, but there's plenty more going on than just golf and tennis; this is a lively community with a strong sense of identity and decades-long tradition of community, volunteerism, and environmental preservation. We don't need any more tales of why you chose to retire here or how you fell in love with the beaches, herons, or salt marshes. Seek out lively, surprising characters—there are plenty—and offer fresh (but not trendy) takes on local personalities, Southern living, and green issues."

TENNESSEE

☻☻ AT HOME TENNESSEE

671 N. Ericson Rd., Suite 200, Cordova TN 38018. (901)684-4155. **Fax:** (901)684-4156. **E-mail:** jherbison@athometn.com. **Website:** www.athometn.com. **Contact:** Janna Herbison, editor; Margaret Monger, publisher and editorial director. **50% freelance written.** Monthly magazine covering décor, design, and fashion of Tennessee homes. Estab. 2002. Circ. 37,000. Byline given. Pays on publication. Offers 50% kill fee.

Editorial lead time 2 months. Submit seasonal material 2-3 months in advance. Accepts queries by e-mail. Responds in 1-2 months to queries. Sample copy for $4.99. Guidelines free.

NONFICTION Needs general interest, how-to, interview, travel, landscaping, arts, design. Does not want opinion pieces. Query with published clips. Length: 400-900 words. **Pays $50-200.**

PHOTOS Send photos. Reviews GIF/JPEG files.

💲💲 MEMPHIS

Contemporary Media, P.O. Box 1738, Memphis TN 38101. (901)521-9000. **Fax:** (901)521-0129. **E-mail:** murtaugh@memphismagazine.com. **Website:** www. memphismagazine.com. **Contact:** Frank Murtaugh, managing editor. **30% freelance written. Works with a small number of new/unpublished writers.** Monthly magazine covering Memphis and the local region. Our mission is to provide Memphis with a colorful and informative look at the people, places, lifestyles and businesses that make the Bluff City unique. Estab. 1976. Circ. 24,000. No byline given. Pays on publication. Submit seasonal material 3 months in advance. Accepts queries by mail, e-mail, fax.

NONFICTION Needs essays, general interest, historical, interview, photo feature, travel, Interiors/exteriors, local issues and events. Special issues: Restaurant Guide and City Guide. **Buys 20 mss/year.** Query with published clips. Length: 500-3,000 words. **Pays 10-30¢/word.** Sometimes pays expenses of writers on assignment.

PHOTOS State availability. Reviews contact sheets, transparencies.

FICTION One story published annually as part of contest. Open only to those within 150 miles of Memphis. See website for details.

💲💲 MEMPHIS DOWNTOWNER MAGAZINE

Downtown Productions, Inc., 408 S. Front St., Suite 109, Memphis TN 38103. (901)525-7118. **Fax:** (901)525-7128. **E-mail:** editor@memphisdowntowner.com. **Website:** www.memphisdowntowner.com. **Contact:** Terre Gorham, editor. **50% freelance written.** Monthly magazine covering features on positive aspects with a Memphis tie-in, especially to downtown. "We feature people, companies, nonprofits, and other issues that the general Memphis public would find interesting, entertaining, and informative. All editorial focuses on the positives Memphis has. No

negative commentary or personal judgements. Controversial subjects should be treated fairly and balanced without bias." Estab. 1991. Circ. 30,000. Byline given. Pays on 15th of month in which assignment is published. Offers 25% kill fee. Publishes ms an average of 2-6 months after acceptance. Editorial lead time 3-6 months. Submit seasonal material 3-6 months in advance. Accepts queries by mail, e-mail. Responds in 2 weeks to queries. Sample copy free. Guidelines by e-mail.

NONFICTION Needs general interest, historical, how-to, humor, interview, personal experience, photo feature. **Buys 40-50 mss/year.** Query with published clips. Length: 600-2,000 words. **Pays scales vary depending on scope of assignment, but typically runs 15¢/word.** Sometimes pays expenses of writers on assignment.

PHOTOS State availability. Identification of subjects required. Reviews GIF/JPEG files (300 DPI). Negotiates payment individually.

COLUMNS/DEPARTMENTS So It Goes (G-rated humor), 600-800 words; Discovery 901 (Memphis one-of-a-kinds), 1,000-1,200 words. **Buys 6 mss/year.** Query with published clips. **Pays $100-150.**

FILLERS "Unusual, interesting, or how-to or what to look for appealing to a large, general audience." Needs facts.

TIPS "Always pitch an actual story idea. E-mails that simply let us know you're a freelance writer mysteriously disappear from our inboxes. Actually read the magazine before you pitch. Get to know the regular columns and departments. In your pitch, explain where in the magazine you think your story idea would best fit. See website for magazine samples and past issues."

TEXAS

💲💲💲 HOUSTON PRESS

1621 Milam, Suite 100, Houston TX 77002. (713)280-2400. **Fax:** (713)280-2444. **Website:** www.houstonpress.com. **Contact:** Margaret Downing, editor. **40% freelance written.** "Weekly tabloid covering news and arts stories of interest to a Houston audience. If the same story could run in Seattle, then it's not for us." Estab. 1989. Byline given. Pays on publication. No kill fee. Publishes ms an average of 2 weeks after acceptance. Editorial lead time 2 months. Submit seasonal material 3 months in advance. Sample copy for $3.

NONFICTION Needs exposé, general interest, interview, arts reviews. Query with published clips. Length: 300-4,500 words. **Pays $10-1,000.** Sometimes pays expenses of writers on assignment.

PHOTOS State availability. Identification of subjects required. Negotiates payment individually.

💲💲💲 TEXAS HIGHWAYS

P.O. Box 141009, Austin TX 78714-1009. (800)839-4997. **Website:** www.texashighways.com. **70% freelance written.** Monthly magazine encourages travel within the state and tells the Texas story to readers around the world. Estab. 1974. Circ. 250,000. Pays on acceptance. No kill fee. Publishes ms an average of 1 year after acceptance. Accepts queries by mail. Responds in 2 months to queries. Guidelines available online.

NONFICTION Query with description, published clips, additional background materials (charts, maps, etc.) and SASE. Length: 1,200-1,500 words. **Pays 40-50¢/word.**

TIPS "We like strong leads that draw in the reader immediately and clear, concise writing. Be specific and avoid superlatives. Avoid overused words. Don't forget the basics—who, what, where, when, why, and how."

💲💲💲💲 TEXAS MONTHLY

Emmis Publishing LP, P.O. Box 1569, Austin TX 78767. (512)320-6900. **Fax:** (512)476-9007. **E-mail:** lbaldwin@texasmonthly.com. **Website:** www.texasmonthly.com. **Contact:** Jake Silverstein, editor; Leslie Baldwin, photo editor; Andi Beierman, deputy art director. **10% freelance written.** Monthly magazine covering Texas. Estab. 1973. Circ. 300,000. Byline given. Pays on acceptance, $1/word and writer's expenses. Publishes ms an average of 1-3 months after acceptance. Editorial lead time 2 months. Submit seasonal material 3 months in advance. Accepts queries by mail, e-mail, fax. Responds in 6-8 weeks to queries. Responds in 6-8 weeks to mss. Sample copy for $7. Guidelines available online.

NONFICTION Contact: John Broders, associate editor (jbroders@texasmonthly.com). Needs book excerpts, essays, exposé, general interest, interview, personal experience, photo feature, travel. Does not want articles without a Texas connection. **Buys 15**

mss/year. Query. Length: 2,000-5,000 words. Pays expenses of writers on assignment.

TIPS "Stories must appeal to an educated Texas audience. *Texas Monthly* covers the state's politics, sports, business, culture and changing lifestyles. We like solidly researched reporting that uncovers issues of public concern, reveals offbeat and previously unreported topics, or uses a novel approach to familiar topics. It contains lengthy features, interviews, essays, book excerpts, and reviews of books and movies. Does not want articles without a Texas connection. Any issue of the magazine would be a helpful guide; sample copy for $7. Guidelines available online."

💲💲 TEXAS PARKS & WILDLIFE

4200 Smith School Rd., Bldg. D, Austin TX 78744. (800)937-9393. **Fax:** (512)389-8397. **E-mail:** magazine@tpwd.state.tx.us. **Website:** www.tpwmagazine.com. **80% freelance written.** Monthly magazine featuring articles about "Texas hunting, fishing, birding, outdoor recreation, game and nongame wildlife, state parks, environmental issues." All articles must be about Texas. Estab. 1942. Circ. 150,000. Byline given. Pays on acceptance. Offers kill fee. Kill fee determined by contract, usually $200-250. Publishes ms an average of 4 months after acceptance. Accepts queries by mail. Responds in 1 month to queries; 3 months to mss. Sample copy and guidelines available online.

NONFICTION Needs general interest (Texas only), how-to, outdoor activities, photo feature, travel, state parks, and small towns. **Buys 60 mss/year.** Query with published clips; follow up by e-mail 1 month after submitting query. Length: 500-2,500 words. **Pays 50¢/word.**

PHOTOS Send photos to photo editor. Captions, identification of subjects required. Reviews transparencies. Offers $65-500/photo.

TIPS "Queries with a strong seasonal peg are preferred. Our planning progress begins 7 months before the date of publication. That means you have to think ahead: *What will Texas outdoor enthusiasts want to read about 7 months from today?*"

VIRGINIA

💲💲 VIRGINIA LIVING

Cape Fear Publishing, 109 E. Cary St., Richmond VA 23219. (804)343-7539. **Fax:** (804)649-0306. **E-mail:** ErinParkhurst@CapeFear.com. **Website:** www.virginialiving.com. **Contact:** Erin Parkhurst, editor.

80% freelance written. Bimonthly magazine covering life and lifestyle in Virginia. "We are a large-format (10x13) glossy magazine covering life in Virginia, from food, architecture, and gardening, to issues, profiles, and travel." Estab. 2002. Circ. 70,000. Byline given. Pays on publication. Publishes ms an average of 4-6 months after acceptance. Editorial lead time 2-6 months. Submit seasonal material 1 year in advance. Accepts queries by mail. Accepts simultaneous submissions. Responds in 1 month to queries. Responds in 1 month to mss. Sample copy for $5.

NONFICTION Needs book excerpts, essays, exposé, general interest, historical, interview, new product, personal experience, photo feature, travel, architecture, design. No fiction, poetry, previously published articles, or stories with a firm grasp of the obvious. **Buys 180 mss/year.** Query with published clips or send complete ms. Length: 300-3,000 words. **Pays 50¢/word.**

PHOTOS Contact: Brandon Peck, art director. Captions, identification of subjects, model releases required. Reviews contact sheets, 6x7 transparencies, 8x10 prints, GIF/JPEG files. Negotiates payment individually.

COLUMNS/DEPARTMENTS Beauty; Travel; Books; Events; Sports (all with a unique Virginia slant), all 1,000-1,500 words. **Buys 50 mss/year.** Send complete ms. **Pays $120-200.**

TIPS "Queries should be about fresh subjects in Virginia. Avoid stories about Williamsburg, Chincoteague ponies, Monticello, the Civil War, and other press release-type topics. We prefer to introduce new subjects, faces, and ideas, and get beyond the many clichés of Virginia. Freelancers would also do well to think about what time of the year they are pitching stories for, as well as art possibilities. We are a large-format magazine close to the size of the old-look magazine, so photography is a key component to our stories."

WASHINGTON

⊕⊕ PUGET SOUND MAGAZINE

2115 Renee Place, Port Townsend WA 98368. (206)414-1589. **Fax:** (206)932-2574. **E-mail:** editorial@pugetsoundmagazine.com. **Website:** www.pugetsoundmagazine.com. **Contact:** David Petrich. **50% freelance written.** Online magazine covering regional focus on adventure, travel, recreation, art,

food, wine, culture, wildlife, plants, and healthy living on the shoreline communities of Puget Sound and the Salish Sea. Olympia WA to Campbell River, BC. Writing from a personal experience, human interest perspective. We do profiles, historic pieces, how to—mostly features on water-centric lifestyles. Estab. 2008. Circ. 30,000. Byline given. No kill fee. Publishes ms an average of 2 months after acceptance. Editorial lead time 2 months. Accepts queries by mail, e-mail. Accepts simultaneous submissions. Responds in 4 weeks to queries. Sample copy free. Guidelines available online.

NONFICTION Contact: Kathleen McKelvey. Needs book excerpts, essays, general interest, historical, how-to, humor, inspirational, interview, personal experience, photo feature, travel. Special issues: No special issues at this time. Nothing negative, political, pornographic, religious. Send complete ms. Length: 800-2,000 words. **Pays 10¢ for assigned articles and for unsolicited articles.**

PHOTOS Contact: Dave Petrich, graphics/creative. State availability of or send photos. Photos require captions, identification of subjects. Reviews contact sheets. Negotiates payment individually.

FICTION Contact: Katherine McKelvey. Needs adventure, historical, humorous, mainstream, mystery, western. **Buys 6 mss/year.** Query with published clips. Word length: 800-1,000 words. **Pays 10¢ word.**

POETRY Contact: Terry Persun, editor. Needs free verse, traditional. Buys 6/yr. poems/year. Submit maximum 3 poems. Length: 25 lines.

TIPS "Pay attention to what we ask for. Read the magazine to get the feel of what we do."

⊕⊕ SEATTLE MAGAZINE

Tiger Oak Publications Inc., 1518 First Ave. S, Suite 500, Seattle WA 98134. (206)284-1750. **Fax:** (206)284-2550. **E-mail:** rachel.hart@tigeroak.com. **Website:** www.seattlemag.com. **Contact:** Rachel Hart, editorial director; Lisa Wogan, managing editor. **75% freelance written.** "Monthly magazine serving the Seattle metropolitan area. Articles should be written with our readers in mind. They are interested in social issues, the arts, politics, homes and gardens, travel and maintaining the region's high quality of life." Estab. 1992. Circ. 45,000. Byline given. Pays on or about 30 days after publication. Offers 25% kill fee. Publishes ms an average of 3 months after acceptance. Editorial lead time 6 months. Submit seasonal material 6 months in advance. Accepts queries by mail, e-mail, fax. Responds in 2 months to queries. Sample copy for #10 SASE. Guidelines available online.

NONFICTION Needs book excerpts, local, essays, exposé, general interest, humor, interview, photo feature, travel, local/regional interest. No longer accepting queries by mail. Query with published clips. Length: 200-4,000 words. **Pays $50 minimum.**

PHOTOS State availability. Negotiates payment individually.

COLUMNS/DEPARTMENTS Scoop, Urban Safari, Voice, Trips, People, Environment, Hot Button, Fitness, Fashion, Eat and Drink Query with published clips. **Pays $225-400.**

TIPS "The best queries include some idea of a lead and sources of information, plus compelling reasons why the article belongs specifically in *Seattle Magazine*. In addition, queries should demonstrate the writer's familiarity with the magazine. New writers are often assigned front- or back-of-the-book contents, rather than features. However, the editors do not discourage writers from querying for longer articles and are especially interested in receiving trend pieces, in-depth stories with a news hook and cultural criticism with a local angle."

SEATTLE WEEKLY

307 Third Ave. S., Second Floor, Seattle WA 98104. (206)623-0500. **Fax:** (206)467-4338. **Website:** www.seattleweekly.com. **20% freelance written.** Weekly tabloid covering arts, politics, food, business and books with local and regional emphasis. The *Seattle Weekly* publishes stories on Northwest politics and art, usually written by regional and local writers, for a mostly upscale, urban audience; writing is high-quality magazine style. Estab. 1976. Circ. 105,000. Byline given. Pays on publication. Offers variable kill fee. Publishes ms an average of 1 month after acceptance. Submit seasonal material 2 months in advance. Responds in 1 month to queries. Sample copy for $3.

NONFICTION Needs book excerpts, exposé, general interest, historical, Northwest, humor, interview, opinion. **Buys 6-8 mss/year.** Query with cover letter, résumé, published clips, and SASE. Length: 300-4,000 words. **Pays $50-800.** Sometimes pays expenses of writers on assignment.

REPRINTS Send tearsheet. Payment varies.

WISCONSIN

MADISON MAGAZINE

Morgan Murphy Media, 7025 Raymond Rd., Madison WI 53719. (608)270-3600. **Fax:** (608)270-3636. **E-mail:** bnardi@madisonmagazine.com. **Website:** www.madisonmagazine.com. **Contact:** Brennan Nardi, editor. **75% freelance written.** Monthly magazine covering life in the greater Madison, Wisconsin, area. Estab. 1978. Byline given. Pays on publication. Offers 33% kill fee. Publishes ms an average of 2 months after acceptance. Editorial lead time 3 months. Submit seasonal material 3-4 months in advance. Accepts queries by mail, e-mail. Accepts simultaneous submissions. Responds in 3 weeks to queries. Responds in 3 weeks to mss. Sample copy free. Guidelines available.

NONFICTION Needs book excerpts, essays, exposé, general interest, historical, how-to, humor, inspirational, interview, new product, opinion, personal experience, photo feature, religious, technical, travel.

PHOTOS State availability. Reviews contact sheets. Negotiates payment individually.

COLUMNS/DEPARTMENTS Your Town (local events) and OverTones (local arts/entertainment), both 300 words; Habitat (local house/garden) and Business (local business), both 800 words. **Buys 120 mss/year.** Query with published clips. **Pays variable amount.**

FILLERS Needs anecdotes, facts, gags, newsbreaks, short humor. Length: 100 words. **Pays 20-30¢/word.**

TIPS "Our magazine is local, so only articles pertaining to Madison, Wisconsin, are considered. Specific queries are heavily appreciated. We like fresh, new content taken in a local perspective. Show us what you're like to write for us."

MILWAUKEE MAGAZINE

126 N. Jefferson St., Milwaukee WI 53202. (414)273-1101. **Fax:** (414)273-0016. **E-mail:** milmag@milwaukeemagazine.com; cristina.daglas@milwaukeemag.com. **Website:** www.milwaukeemagazine.com. **Contact:** Cristina Daglas, editor; Ann Christianson, senior editor/dining critic; Howie Magner, senior editor. **40% freelance written.** Monthly magazine covering the people, issues, and places of theMilwaukee, Wisconsin, area. "We publish stories about Milwaukee, of service to Milwaukee-area residents and exploring the area's changing lifestyle, business, arts, politics, and dining. Our goal has always been to create an

informative, literate and entertaining magazine that will challenge Milwaukeeans with in-depth reporting and analysis of issues of the day, provide useful service features, and enlighten readers with thoughtful stories, essays and columns. Underlying this mission is the desire to discover what is unique about Wisconsin and its people, to challenge conventional wisdom when necessary, criticize when warranted, heap praise when deserved, and season all with affection and concern for the place we call home." Circ. 40,000. Byline given. Pays on publication. Offers 20% kill fee. Publishes ms an average of 2 months after acceptance. Submit seasonal material 6 months in advance. Accepts queries by mail, e-mail. Responds in 6 weeks to queries. Sample copy for $6. Guidelines available on website.

NONFICTION Needs essays, exposé, general interest, historical, interview, photo feature, travel, food and dining, and other services. No articles without a strong Milwaukee or Wisconsin angle. **Buys 30-50 mss/year.** Query with published clips. Length: 2,500-5,000 words for full-length features; 800 words for 2-page breaker features (short on copy, long on visuals). **Pays $700-2,000 for full-length articles.** Sometimes pays expenses of writers on assignment.

COLUMNS/DEPARTMENTS Insider (inside information on Milwaukee, exposé, slice-of-life, unconventional angles on current scene), up to 500 words; Mini Reviews for Insider, 125 words. Query with published clips.

TIPS "Pitch something for the Insider, or suggest a compelling profile we haven't already done. Submit clips that prove you can do the job. The department most open is Insider. Think short, lively, offbeat, fresh, people-oriented. We are actively seeking freelance writers who can deliver lively, readable copy that helps our readers make the most out of the Milwaukee area. Because we're only human, we'd like writers who can deliver copy on deadline that fits the specifications of our assignment. If you fit this description, we'd love to work with you."

WISCONSIN NATURAL RESOURCES

Wisconsin Department of Natural Resources, P.O. Box 7921, Madison WI 53707-7921. (608)266-1510. **Fax:** (608)264-6293. **E-mail:** natasha.kassulke@wisconsin.gov. **E-mail:** Natasha Kassulke. **Website:** www.wnrmag.com. **30% freelance written.** Bimonthly magazine covering environment, natural resource

management, and outdoor skills. "We cover current issues in Wisconsin aimed to educate and advocate for resource conservation, outdoor recreation, and wise land use." Estab. 1931. Circ. 77,000. Byline given. Publishes ms an average of 8 months after acceptance. Editorial lead time 6 months. Submit seasonal material 1 year in advance. Accepts queries by mail, e-mail. Accepts simultaneous submissions. Responds in 3 weeks to queries. Responds in 6 months to mss. Sample copy free. Guidelines available online.

NONFICTION Needs essays, how-to, photo feature, features on current outdoor issues and environmental issues. Does not want animal rights pieces, poetry or fiction. Query. Length: 1,500-2,700 words.

PHOTOS Also seeks photos of pets at state properties like wildlife areas, campsites, and trails. Send photos. Identification of subjects required. Reviews transparencies, JPEG files. Offers no additional payment for photos accepted with ms.

TIPS "Provide images that match the copy."

💲💲 WISCONSIN TRAILS

333 W. State St., Milwaukee WI 53201. **Fax:** (414)647-4723. **E-mail:** clewis@wistrails.com. **Website:** www.wisconsintrails.com. **Contact:** Chelsey Lewis, assistant editor. **40% freelance written.** Bimonthly magazine for readers interested in Wisconsin and its contemporary issues, personalities, recreation, history, natural beauty, and arts. Estab. 1960. Circ. 55,000. Byline given. Pays 1 month from publication. Kill fee 20%, up to $75. Publishes ms an average of 6 months after acceptance. Submit seasonal material 1 year in advance. Accepts queries by mail, e-mail, fax. Responds in 2-3 months to queries. Sample copy for $4.95. Guidelines for #10 SASE or online.

NONFICTION Does not accept unsolicited mss. Query or send outline. Length: 250-1,500 words. **Pays 25¢/word.** Sometimes pays expenses of writers on assignment.

PHOTOS "Because *Wisconsin Trails* works primarily with professional photographers, we do not pay writers for accompanying images nor do we reimburse for any related expenses. Photos will be credited and the photographer retains all rights." Contact editor. Pays $75-250.

TIPS "When querying, submit well-thought-out ideas about stories specific to people, places, events, arts, outdoor adventures, etc., in Wisconsin. Include published clips with queries. Do some research—many queries we receive are pitching ideas for stories we recently have published. Know the tone, content, and audience of the magazine. Refer to our writer's guidelines, or request them, if necessary."

WYOMING

$ WYOMING RURAL ELECTRIC NEWS (WREN)

2312 Carey Ave., Cheyenne WY 82001. (307)772-1986. **Fax:** (307)634-0728. **E-mail:** wren@wyomingrea.org. **Website:** www.wyomingrea.org/publications.asp. **20% freelance written.** Monthly magazine (except in January) for audience of small town residents, vacation-home owners, farmers, and ranchers. Estab. 1954. Circ. 41,000. Byline given. Pays on acceptance. No kill fee. Publishes ms an average of 2 months after acceptance. Submit seasonal material 2 months in advance. Accepts queries by mail, e-mail, fax. Responds in 3 months to queries. Sample copy for $2.50 and 9x12 SASE. Guidelines for #10 SASE.

NONFICTION No nostalgia, sarcasm, or tongue-in-cheek. **Buys 4-10 mss/year.** Send complete ms. Length: 500-800 words. **Pays up to $140, plus 4 copies.**

REPRINTS Send tearsheet or photocopy and information about when and where the material previously appeared.

PHOTOS Color only.

TIPS "Always looking for fresh, new writers. Submit entire ms. Don't submit a regionally set story from some other part of the country. Photos and illustrations (if appropriate) are always welcomed. We want factual articles that are blunt, to the point, accurate."

RELIGIOUS

$ BIBLE ADVOCATE

Bible Advocate, Church of God (Seventh Day), P.O. Box 33677, Denver CO 80233. (303)452-7973. **E-mail:** bibleadvocate@cog7.org. **Website:** http://baonline.org/. **Contact:** Sherri Langton, associate editor. **25% freelance written.** Religious magazine published 6 times/year. "Our purpose is to advocate the Bible and represent the Church of God (Seventh Day) to a Christian audience." Estab. 1863. Circ. 13,500. Byline given. Pays on publication. No kill fee. Publishes ms an average of 9 months after acceptance. Editorial lead time 3 months. Submit seasonal material 6 months in advance. Accepts queries by mail, e-mail; prefers e-mail; attachments ok. Accepts simultaneous submissions. Responds in 2 months to queries. Sample copy for sae with 9x12 envelope and 3 first-class stamps. Guidelines available online.

NONFICTION Needs inspirational, personal experience, religious, Biblical studies. No articles on Christmas or Easter. **Buys 10-15 mss/year.** Send complete ms and SASE. Length: 1,000-1,200 words. **Pays $25-55.**

REPRINTS E-mail ms with rights for sale noted.

POETRY Needs free verse, traditional, Christian/Bible themes. Prefers e-mail submissions. Cover letter is preferred. "No handwritten submissions, please." Time between acceptance and publication is up to 1 year. "I read them first and reject those that won't work for us. I send good ones to editor for approval." Seldom comments on rejected poems. No avant-garde. Buys 10-12 poems/year. Submit maximum 5/poems. poems. Length: 5-20 lines. **Pays $20 and 2 contributor's copies.**

TIPS "Be fresh, not preachy! Articles must be in keeping with the doctrinal understanding of the Church of God (Seventh Day). Therefore, the writer should become familiar with what the Church generally accepts as truth as set forth in its doctrinal beliefs. We reserve the right to edit manuscripts to fit our space requirements, doctrinal stands and church terminology. Significant changes are referred to writers for approval. No fax or handwritten submissions, please."

THE BREAKTHROUGH INTERCESSOR

Breakthrough, Inc., P.O. Box 121, Lincoln VA 20160. **E-mail:** breakthrough@intercessors.org. **Website:** http://intercessors.org. *The Breakthrough Intercessor*, published quarterly, focuses on "encouraging people in prayer and faith; preparing and equipping those who pray." Accepts multiple articles per issue: 300-1,000 word true stories on prayer. Estab. 1980. Time between acceptance and publication varies. Guidelines available on website.

NONFICTION Needs essays, memoir. Send complete ms, along with article name, author's name, address, phone number, and e-mail. Considers previously published articles. Accepts fax, e-mail (pasted into body of message or attachment), and mailed hard copy. Articlesare circulated to an editorial board. Length: approximately 1,000 words.

⊙⊙ CATHOLIC ANSWERS

Catholic Answers, 2020 Gillespie Way, El Cajon CA 92020. (619)387-7200. **Fax:** (619)387-0042. **Website:** www.catholic.com. **60% freelance written.** Monthly magazine covering Catholic apologetics and evangelization. Our content explains, defends and promotes Catholic teaching. Estab. 1990. Circ. 24,000. Byline given. Pays on acceptance. Offers variable kill fee. Publishes ms an average of 4 months after acceptance. Accepts queries by e-mail. Responds in 2-4 weeks to queries. Responds in 1-2 months to mss. Sample copy available online. Guidelines by e-mail.

NONFICTION Needs book excerpts, essays, religious, conversion stories. **Buys 50 mss/year.** Send complete ms. Length: 1,500-3,000 words. **Pays $200-350.**

COLUMNS/DEPARTMENTS Damascus Road (stories of conversion to the Catholic Church), 2,000 words. **Buys 10 mss/year.** Send complete ms. **Pays $200.**

⊙⊙ CATHOLIC DIGEST

P.O. Box 6015, New London CT 06320. (800)321-0411. **Fax:** (860)457-3013. **E-mail:** queries@catholicdigest. com. **Website:** www.catholicdigest.com. **12% freelance written.** Monthly magazine. Publishes features and advice on topics ranging from health, psychology, humor, adventure, and family, to ethics, spirituality, and Catholics, from modern-day heroes to saints through the ages. Helpful and relevant reading culled from secular and religious periodicals. Estab. 1936. Circ. 275,000. Byline given. Pays on publication. No kill fee. Editorial lead time 3 months. Submit seasonal material 4-5 months in advance. Accepts queries by mail, e-mail. Responds in 2 months to mss. Sample copy free. Guidelines available on website.

NONFICTION Needs book excerpts, essays, general interest, historical, how-to, humor, inspirational, interview, personal experience, religious, travel. Does not accept unsolicited submissions. Send complete ms. Length: 350-1,500 words. **Pays $200-300.**

REPRINTS Send tearsheet or typed ms with rights for sale noted and information about when and where the material previously appeared. Pays $100.

PHOTOS State availability. "If your query is accepted and you have photos that may be used to accompany your submission, please attach them as JPEG files. Photos must be at least 300 dpi to be used in the magazine. Appropriate credit lines and captions should also accompany the photos." Reviews contact sheets, transparencies, prints. Negotiates payment individually.

FILLERS Contact: Filler Editor. Open Door (statements of true incidents through which people are brought into the Catholic faith, or recover the Catholic faith they had lost), 350-600 words. Send to opendoor@catholicdigest.com. Good Egg (stories about a Catholic who has demonstrated their faith through commitment to their family, community, and church), 350-600 words. Send to goodegg@catholicdigest.com. **Buys 200 mss/year.** 350-600 words.

TIPS "Spiritual, self-help, and all wellness is a good bet for us. We would also like to see material with an innovative approach to daily living, articles that show new ways of looking at old ideas, problems. You've got to dig beneath the surface."

⊙⊙ CATHOLIC FORESTER

Catholic Order of Foresters, 355 Shuman Blvd., P.O. Box 3012, Naperville IL 60566-7012. **Fax:** (630)983-3384. **E-mail:** magazine@catholicforester.org. **Website:** www.catholicforester.org. **Contact:** Editor; art director. **20% freelance written.** Quarterly magazine for members of the Catholic Order of Foresters, a fraternal insurance benefit society. "*Catholic Forester* is a quarterly magazine filled with product features, member stories, and articles affirming fraternalism, unity, friendship, and true Christian charity among members. Although a portion of each issue is devoted to the organization and its members, a few freelance pieces are published in most issues. These articles cover varied topics to create a balanced issue for the purpose of informing, educating, and entertaining our readers." Estab. 1883. Circ. 77,000. Pays on acceptance. Editorial lead time 6 months. Submit seasonal material 6 months in advance. TrueResponds in 3 months to mss. Sample copy for 9x12 SAE and 4 first-class stamps. Guidelines available on website.

NONFICTION Needs health and wellness, money management and budgeting, parenting and family life, insurance, nostalgia, humor, inspirational, religious, Will consider previously published work. **Buys 6-10 mss/year.** Send complete ms by mail, fax, or e-mail. Rejected material will not be returned without accompanying SASE. Length: 500-1,000 words. **Pays 50¢/word.**

PHOTOS State availability. Negotiates payment individually.

FICTION Needs humorous, religious, inspirational. **Buys 6-10 mss/year.** Length: 500-1,500 words. **Pays 50¢/word.**

POETRY Needs light verse, traditional. Buys 3 poems/year. Length: 15 lines maximum. **Pays 30¢/word.**

TIPS "Our audience includes a broad age spectrum, ranging from youth to seniors. A good children's story with a positive lesson or message would rate high on our list."

$$ CELEBRATE LIFE MAGAZINE

American Life League, P.O. Box 1350, Stafford VA 22555. (540)659-4171. **Fax:** (540)659-2586. **E-mail:** clmag@all.org. **Website:** www.clmagazine.org. **Contact:** Editor. **50% freelance written.** Quarterly magazine "publishing educational articles and human-interest stories on the right to life and dignity of all human beings." Estab. 1979. Circ. 30,000. Byline given. Pays on publication. Submit seasonal material 4 months in advance. Accepts queries by mail, e-mail. No.Responds in 6 months to mss. For sample copy, send 9x12 SAE and 4 first-class stamps. Guidelines available on website.

NONFICTION "Nonfiction only; no fiction, poetry, songs, music, allegory, or devotionals." Does not publish reprints. Query with published clips or send complete ms. Length: 600-1,800 words.

PHOTOS Identification of subjects in photos required.

TIPS "Articles must not contradict the teachings of the Catholic church. Our common themes include: abortion, post-abortion healing, sidewalk counseling, adoption, contraception, sterilization, chastity, euthanasia, eugenics, infertility, marriage based on pro-life principles, miscarriage/stillbirth, marriage, opposition to exceptions in pro-life legislation, false definition of death, organ donation, pro-life parenting, pro-life/anti-life activities and legislation, population control/decline, pro-life heroes, sex education, human cloning, stem cell research/therapy, special needs children/parenting/adoption, care and dignity of the elderly/disabled/chronically ill and young people in pro-life action."

$$$ CHARISMA & CHRISTIAN LIFE

Charisma Media, 600 Rinehart Rd., Lake Mary FL 32746. (407)333-0600. **Fax:** (407)333-7133. **E-mail:** charisma@charismamedia.com. **Website:** www.charismamag.com. **Contact:** Marcus Yoars. **80% freelance written.** Monthly magazine covering items of interest to the Pentecostal or independent charismatic reader. Now also online. "More than half of our readers are Christians who belong to Pentecostal or independent charismatic churches, and numerous others participate in the charismatic renewal in mainline denominations." Estab. 1975. Circ. 250,000. Byline given. Pays on publication. Offers $50 kill fee. Publishes ms an average of 3 months after acceptance. Editorial lead time 4 months. Submit seasonal material 5 months in advance. Accepts queries by mail, e-mail. Sample copy for $4. Guidelines by e-mail and online.

NONFICTION Needs book excerpts, exposé, general interest, interview, religious. No fiction, poetry, columns/departments, or sermons. **Buys 40 mss/year.** Query. Length: 1,800-2,500 words. Pays expenses of writers on assignment.

PHOTOS State availability. Model releases required. Reviews contact sheets, 2 1/4x2 1/4 transparencies, 3x5 or larger prints, TIF/JPEG files. Negotiates payment individually.

TIPS "Be especially on the lookout for news stories, trend articles, or interesting personality profiles that relate specifically to the Christian reader."

$$ CHRISTIAN HOME & SCHOOL

Christian Schools International, 3350 E. Paris Ave. SE, Grand Rapids MI 49512. (616)957-1070, ext. 239. **Fax:** (616)957-5022. **E-mail:** rheyboer@csionline.org. **Website:** www.csionline.org/chs. **30% freelance written. Works with a small number of new/unpublished writers each year.** Magazine published 2 times/year during the school year covering family life and Christian education. In addition, a special high school issue is published each spring. "*Christian Home & School* is designed for parents in the United States and Canada who send their children to Christian schools and are concerned about the challenges facing Christian families today. These readers expect a mature, Biblical perspective in the articles, not just a Bible verse tacked onto the end." Estab. 1922. Circ. 66,000. Byline given. Pays on publication. No kill fee. Publishes ms an average of 4 months after acceptance. Submit seasonal material 4 months in advance. Accepts queries by mail, e-mail. Responds in 1 month to queries. Sample copy for 9x12 SAE with 4 first-class stamps. Guidelines only for #10 SASE or online. For article topics, refer to the editorial calendar on website.

NONFICTION Needs book excerpts, interview, opinion, personal experience, articles on parenting and school life. **Buys 30 mss/year.** Send complete ms. Length: 1,000-2,000 words. **Pays $175-250.**

TIPS "Features are the area most open to freelancers. We are publishing articles that deal with contemporary issues that affect parents. Use an informal easy-to-read style rather than a philosophical, academic tone. Try to incorporate vivid imagery and concrete, practical examples from real life. We look for manuscripts with a mature Christian perspective."

COLUMBIA

1 Columbus Plaza, New Haven CT 06510. (203)752-4398. **Fax:** (203)752-4109. **E-mail:** columbia@kofc.org. **Website:** www.kofc.org/columbia. **Contact:** Alton Pelowski, managing editor. Monthly magazine for Catholic families. Caters primarily to members of the Knights of Columbus. Estab. 1921. Circ. 1,700,000. Pays on acceptance. No kill fee. Accepts queries by mail, e-mail. Sample copy and writer's guidelines on website.

NONFICTION No reprints, poetry, cartoons, puzzles, short stories/fiction. Query with SASE or by e-mail. Length: 750-1,500 words. **Payment varies.**

CONSCIENCE

Catholics for Choice, 1436 U St. NW, Suite 301, Washington D.C. 20009. (202)986-6093. **E-mail:** conscience@catholicsforchoice.org. **Website:** www.catholicsforchoice.org. **Contact:** Jon O'Brien, executive editor. **80% written by nonstaff writers. Publishes 40 freelance submissions yearly; 10% by unpublished writers, 50% by authors who are new to the magazine, 70% by experts.** "Conscience offers in-depth coverage of a range of topics, including contemporary politics, Catholicism, women's rights in society and in religions, U.S. politics, reproductive rights, sexuality and gender, ethics and bioethics, feminist theology, social justice, church and state issues, and the role of religion in formulating public policy." Estab. 1980. Circ. 12,000. Byline given. Pays on publication. No kill fee. Publishes ms an average of 2 months after acceptance. Accepts queries by mail, e-mail. Responds in 4 months to queries. Sample copy free with 9x12 envelope and $1.85 postage. Guidelines with #10 SASE.

NONFICTION Needs book excerpts, interview, opinion, personal experience, a small amount, issue analysis. **Buys 4-8 mss/year.** Send complete ms. Length: 1,500-3,500 words. **Pays $200 negotiable.**

REPRINTS Send typed manuscript with rights for sale noted and information about when and where the

material previously appeared. Pays 20-30% of amount paid for an original article.

PHOTOS Sample copies available. Buys up to 25 photos/year. Model/property release preferred. Photo captions preferred; include title, subject, photographer's name. Reviews photos with or without a manuscript. Pays $300 maximum for color cover; $50 maximum for b&w inside. Pays on publication. Credit line given.

COLUMNS/DEPARTMENTS Book Reviews, 600-1,200 words. **Buys 4-8 mss/year. Pays $75.**

TIPS "Our readership includes national and international opinion leaders and policymakers, librarians, members of the clergy and the press, and leaders in the fields of theology, ethics, and women's studies. Articles should be written for a diverse and educated audience."

DAVEY AND GOLIATH'S DEVOTIONS

Evangelical Lutheran Church in America, ELCA Churchwide Ministries, 8765 W. Higgins Rd., Chicago IL 60631. **E-mail:** daveyandgoliath@elca.org. **Website:** www.daveyandgoliath.org. "*Davey and Goliath's Devotions* is a magazine with concrete ideas that families can use to build Biblical literacy and share faith and serve others. It includes Bible stories, family activities, crafts, games, and a section of puzzles, and mazes." Pays on acceptance of final ms.

TIPS "Pay attention to details in the sample devotional. Follow the process laid out in the information for prospective writers. Ability to interpret Bible texts appropriately for children is required. Content must be doable and fun for families on the go."

$$ DECISION

Billy Graham Evangelistic Association, P.O. Box 668886, Charlotte NC 28266. (704)401-2432. **Fax:** (704)401-3009. **E-mail:** submissions@bgea.org. **Website:** www.decisionmag.org. **Contact:** Bob Paulson, editor. **5% freelance written. Works each year with small number of new/unpublished writers.** "Magazine published 11 times/year with a mission to extend the ministry of Billy Graham Evangelistic Association; to communicate the Good News of Jesus Christ in such a way that readers will be drawn to make a commitment to Christ; and to encourage, strengthen and equip Christians in evangelism and discipleship." Estab. 1960. Circ. 400,000. Byline given. Pays on publication. Publishes ms an average of up to 18 months after acceptance. Editorial lead time 6 months. Submit seasonal material 6 months in advance. Sample copy for sae with 9x12 envelope and 4 first-class stamps. Guidelines available online.

NONFICTION Needs personal experience, testimony. **Buys approximately 8 mss/year.** Send complete ms. Length: 400-1,500 words. **Pays $200-400.** Pays expenses of writers on assignment.

PHOTOS State availability. Captions, identification of subjects, model releases required. Reviews prints.

COLUMNS/DEPARTMENTS Finding Jesus (people who have become Christians through Billy Graham Ministries), 500-900 words. **Buys 11 mss/year.** Send complete ms. **Pays $200.**

TIPS "Articles should have some connection to the ministry of Billy Graham or Franklin Graham. For example, you may have volunteered in one of these ministries or been touched by them. The article does not need to be entirely about that connection, but it should at least mention the connection. Testimonies and personal experience articles should show how God intervened in your life and how you have been transformed by God. SASE required with submissions."

EFCA TODAY

Evangelical Free Church of America, 418 Fourth St., NE, Charlottesville VA 22902. **E-mail:** dianemc@ journeygroup.com. **Website:** www.efca.org. **30% freelance written.** Quarterly digital magazine. "*EFCA Today*'s purpose is to unify church leaders around the overall mission of the EFCA by bringing its stories and vision to life, and to sharpen those leaders by generating conversations over topics pertinent to faith and life in this 21st century." Estab. 1931. Byline given. Pays on acceptance. Offers 50% kill fee. Publishes ms an average of 3 months after acceptance. Editorial lead time 5 months. Submit seasonal material 6 months in advance. Accepts queries by mail, e-mail. Rarely accepts previously published material.Responds in 6 weeks. Sample copy for $1 with SAE and 5 first-class stamps. Guidelines by e-mail.

NONFICTION Needs interview, of EFCA-related subjects, feature articles of EFCA interest, highlighting EFCA subjects. No general interest inspirational articles. Send complete ms. Length: 200-1,100 words and related/approved expenses for assigned articles. **Pays 23¢/word for first rights, including limited subsidiary rights (free use within an EFCA context).**

REPRINTS varies.

COLUMNS/DEPARTMENTS Engage (out of the church and into the world); Leader to Leader (what leaders are saying, doing, learning); Catalyst (the passion of EFCA's young leaders; Face to Face (our global family), all between 200 and 600/words. Send complete ms. **Pays 23¢/word and related/approved expenses for assigned articles.**

TIPS "One portion of each *EFCA Today* is devoted to a topic designed to stimulate thoughtful dialog and leadership growth, and to highlight how EFCA leaders are already involved in living out that theme. Examples of themes are: new paradigms for 'doing church,' church planting and the 'emerging' church. These articles differ from those in the above sections, in that their primary focus in on the issue rather than the person; the person serves to illustrate the issue. These articles should run between 400 and 800 words. Include contacts for verification of article."

EVANGEL

Light and Life Communications, 770 N. High School Rd., Indianapolis IN 46214. (317)244-3660. **Contact:** Julie Innes, editor. *Evangel,* published quarterly, is an adult Sunday School paper. "Devotional in nature, it lifts up Christ as the source of salvation and hope. The mission of *Evangel* is to increase the reader's understanding of the nature and character of God and the nature of a life lived for Christ. Material that fits this mission and isn't longer than 1 page will be considered." Estab. 1897 by free Methodist denomination. Circ. less than 10,000. Pays on publication. Publishes ms 18-36 months after acceptance. Submit seasonal poems 1 year in advance. Responds in 4-6 weeks to queries. Responds in up to 2 months to poems. Seldom comments on rejected poems. Sample copy and writer's guidelines for #10 SASE. "Write 'guidelines request' on your envelope so we can sort it from the submissions."

FICTION Receives 300 unsolicited mss/month. Accepts 3-4 mss/issue; 156-200 mss/year. Publishes 7 new writers/year. Needs true religious/inspirational. "No fiction without any semblance of Christian message or where the message clobbers the reader. Looking for devotional style short pieces 500 words or less." Send complete ms. Accepts multiple submissions. **Pays 4¢/word and 2 contributor's copies.**

POETRY Submit no more than 5 poems at a time. Considers simultaneous submissions. Cover letter ispreferred. "Poetry must be typed on 8.5 x 11 white paper. In the upper left-hand corner of each page, include your name, address, phone number, and social security number. In the upper right-hand corner of cover page, specify what rights you are offering. One-eighth of the way down the page, give the title. All subsequent material must be double-spaced, with 1-inch margins." **Pays $10 plus 2 contributor's copies.**

TIPS "Desire, concise, tight writing that supports a solid thesis and fits the mission expressed in the guidelines."

$ EVANGELICAL MISSIONS QUARTERLY

Billy Graham Center/Wheaton College, P.O. Box 794, Wheaton IL 60187. (630)752-7158. **Fax:** (630)752-7155. **E-mail:** emq@wheaton.edu. **Website:** www.emisdirect.com. **Contact:** Laurie Fortunak Nichols, managing editor. **67% freelance written.** Quarterly magazine covering evangelical missions. *Evangelical Missions Quarterly* is a professional journal for evangelical missionaries, agency executives, and church members who support global missions ministries. Estab. 1964. Circ. 7,000. Byline given. Pays on publication. Offers negotiable kill fee. Publishes ms an average of 18 months after acceptance. Editorial lead time 1 year. Accepts queries by e-mail. Responds in 2 weeks to queries. Sample copy free. Guidelines available online.

NONFICTION Needs book reviews, essays, interview, opinion, personal experience, religious. No sermons, poetry, or straight news. **Buys 24 mss/year.** Query. Length: 800-3,000 words. **Pays $25-100.**

PHOTOS Send photos. Identification of subjects required. Offers no additional payment for photos accepted with ms.

COLUMNS/DEPARTMENTS In the Workshop (practical how to's), 800-2,000 words; Perspectives (opinion), 800 words. **Buys 8 mss/year.** Query. **Pays $50-100.**

TIPS "We prefer articles about deeds done, showing the why and the how, claiming not only success but also admitting failure. Principles drawn from one example must be applicable to missions more generally. *EMQ* does not include articles which have been previously published in journals, books, websites, etc."

🍁 $$ FAITH TODAY

Evangelical Fellowship of Canada, P.O. Box 5885, West Beaver Creek Post Office, Richmond Hill ON L4B 0B8 Canada. (905)479-5885. **Fax:** (905)479-4742. **Website:** www.faithtoday.ca. Bimonthly magazine. "*FT* is the magazine of an association of more than 40 evangelical denominations, but serves evangelicals in all denominations. It focuses on church issues, social issues and personal faith as they are tied to the Canadian context. Writing should explicitly acknowledge that Canadian evangelical context." Estab. 1983. Circ. 20,000. Byline given. Pays on publication. Offers 30-50% kill fee. Publishes ms an average of 4 months after acceptance. Editorial lead time 4 months. Accepts queries by mail, e-mail, fax. Responds in 6 weeks to queries. Sample copy for SASE in Canadian postage. Guidelines available online at www.faithtoday.ca/writers. "View complete back issues at www.faithtoday.ca/digital. Or download one of our free apps from www.faithtoday.ca."

NONFICTION Needs book excerpts, Canadian authors only, essays, Canadian authors only, interview, Canadian subjects only, opinion, religious, news feature. **Buys 75 mss/year.** Query. Length: 400-2,000 words. **Pays $100-500 Canadian.** Sometimes pays expenses of writers on assignment.

REPRINTS Send photocopy. Rarely used. Pays 50% of amount paid for an original article.

PHOTOS State availability. Reviews contact sheets.

TIPS "Query should include brief outline and names of the sources you plan to interview in your research. Use Canadian postage on SASE."

$$ FCA MAGAZINE

Fellowship of Christian Athletes, 8701 Leeds Rd., Kansas City MO 64129. (816)921-0909. **Fax:** (816)921-8755. **E-mail:** mag@fca.org. **Website:** www.fca.org/mag. **Contact:** Clay Meyer, editor; Matheau Casner, creative director. **50% freelance written. Prefers to work with published/established writers, but works with a growing number of new/unpublished writers each year.** Published 6 times/year. "We seek to serve as a ministry tool of the Fellowship of Christian Athletes by informing, inspiring, and involving coaches, athletes, and all whom they influence, that they may make an impact for Jesus Christ." Estab. 1959. Circ. 80,000. Byline given. Pays on publication. No kill fee. Publishes ms an average of 4 months after acceptance. Submit seasonal material 6 months in advance. Responds to queries/mss in 3 months. Sample copy for $2 and 9x12 SASE with 3 first-class stamps. Guidelines available at www.fca.org/mag/media-kit.

NONFICTION Needs inspirational, interview (with name athletes and coaches solid in their faith), personal experience, photo feature. **Buys 5-20 mss/year.**

"Articles should be accompanied by at least 3 quality photos." Query. Considers electronic sumbissions via e-mail. Length: 1,000-2,000 words. **Pays $150-400 for assigned and unsolicited articles.**

PHOTOS State availability. Reviews contact sheets. Payment based on size of photo.

TIPS "Profiles and interviews of particular interest to coed athlete, primarily high school and college age. Our graphics and editorial content appeal to youth. The area most open to freelancers is profiles on or interviews with well-known athletes or coaches (male, female, minorities) who have been or are involved in some capacity with FCA."

THE FRIEND

The Friend Publications Ltd, 173 Euston Rd., London England NW1 2BJ United Kingdom. (44)(207)663-1010. **Fax:** (44)(207)663-1182. **E-mail:** editorial@the-friend.org. **Website:** www.thefriend.org. **Contact:** Ian Kirk Smith. Weekly magazine. Completely independent, *The Friend* brings readers news and views from a Quaker perspective, as well as from a wide range of authors whose writings are of interest to Quakers and non-Quakers alike. There are articles on issues such as peace, spirituality, Quaker belief, and ecumenism, as well as news of Friends from Britain and abroad. Circ. 3,250. Byline given. No kill fee. Accepts queries by mail, e-mail, phone. Guidelines available online.

NONFICTION Query. Length: 550 words/full page; 1,100 words/double page spread.

PHOTOS Accepts illustrations (photos or drawings). Reviews color or b&w prints. Covers costs if photographs are commissioned.

COLUMNS/DEPARTMENTS Art reviews (new books, plays, videos, exhibitions), 550 words.

POETRY There are no rules regarding poetry, but doesn't want particularly long poems.

GUIDE

55 W. Oak Ridge Dr., Hagerstown MD 21740. (301)393-4037. **Fax:** (301)393-4055. **E-mail:** guide@rhpa.org. **Website:** www.guidemagazine.org. **Contact:** Randy Fishell, editor; Brandon Reese, designer. "*Guide* is a Christian story magazine for young people ages 10-14. The 32-page, 4-color publication is published weekly by the Review and Herald Publishing Association. Our mission is to show readers, through stories that illustrate Bible truth, how to walk with God now and forever." Estab. 1953. Byline given. Pays on acceptance. Accepts queries by mail, e-mail.

Responds in 6 weeks to mss. Sample copy free with 6x9 SAE and 2 first-class stamps. Guidelines available on website.

NONFICTION Send complete ms. "Each issue includes 3-4 true stories. *Guide* does not publish fiction, poetry, or articles (devotionals, how-to, profiles, etc.). However, we sometimes accept quizzes and other unique nonstory formats. Each piece should include a clear spiritual element." Length: 1,000-1,200 words. **Pays 6-12¢/word.**

TIPS "Children's magazines want mystery, action, discovery, suspense, and humor—no matter what the topic. For us, truth is stronger than fiction."

GUIDEPOSTS MAGAZINE

Suite 2AB, 39 Old Ridgebury Rd., Danbury IA 06810. **E-mail:** submissions@guidepostsmag.com. **Website:** www.guideposts.com. **40% freelance written. Works with a small number of new/unpublished writers each year.** Monthly magazine featuring personal inspirational stories. "*Guideposts* is an inspirational monthly magazine for people of all faiths, in which men and women from all walks of life tell in true, first person narrative how they overcame obstacles, rose above failures, handled sorrow, gained new spiritual insight, and became more effective people through faith in God." Estab. 1945. Pays on publication. Offers kill fee. Offers 20% kill fee on assigned stories, but not to first-time freelancers. Publishes ms an average of several months after acceptance. Guidelines available online.

NONFICTION Buys 40-60 unsolicited mss/year. Length: 250-1,500 words. **Pays $100-500.** Pays expenses of writers on assignment.

TIPS "Study the magazine before you try to write for it. Each story must make a single spiritual point that readers can apply to their own daily lives. And it may be easier to just sit down and write them than to have to go through the process of preparing a query. They should be warm, well written, intelligent, and upbeat. We require personal narratives that are true and have some spiritual aspect, but the religious element can be subtle and should *not* be sermonic. A writer succeeds with us if he or she can write a true article using short-story techniques with scenes, drama, tension, and a resolution of the problem presented."

HIGHWAY NEWS

Transport For Christ, P.O. Box 117, 1525 River Rd., Marietta PA 17547. (717)426-9977. **Fax:** (717)426-

9980. **E-mail:** editor@transportforchrist.org. **Website:** www.transportforchrist.org. **Contact:** Inge Koenig. **50% freelance written.** Monthly magazine covering trucking and Christianity. "We publish human interest stories, testimonials, and teachings that have a foundation in Biblical/Christian values. Since truck drivers and their families are our primary readers, we publish works that they will find edifying and helpful." Estab. 1957. Circ. 29,000. Byline given. No kill fee. Publishes ms an average of 1 year after acceptance. Submit seasonal material 1 year in advance. Accepts queries by mail, e-mail, fax. Accepts simultaneous submissions. Responds in 1 month to queries. Responds in 2 months to mss. Sample copy free. Writer's guidelines by e-mail.

NONFICTION Needs trucking-related essays, general interest, humor, inspirational, interview, personal experience, photo feature, religious, trucking. No sermons full of personal opinions. Nothing of political nature. **Buys 10-15 mss/year.** Send complete ms. Length: 600-800 words.

PHOTOS Send photos. Captions, identification of subjects, model releases required. Reviews prints, GIF/JPEG files. Does not pay for photos.

COLUMNS/DEPARTMENTS From the Road (stories by truckers on the road); Devotionals with Trucking theme; both 600 words. Send complete ms.

FICTION Needs humorous, religious, slice-of-life vignettes. No romance or fantasy. "We use very little fiction." **Buys 1 or fewer mss/year.** Send complete ms. Length: 600-800 words.

POETRY Needs traditional. Accepts very little poetry. "Don't send anything unrelated to the trucking industry." Buys Accepts 2 mss/year. poems/year. Length: 4-20 lines.

FILLERS Needs anecdotes, facts, short humor. Length: 20-200 words.

TIPS "We are especially interested in human interest stories about truck drivers. Find a trucker doing something unusual or good and write a story about him or her. Be sure to send pictures."

HOLINESS TODAY

Nazarene Global Ministry Center, 17001 Prairie Star Pkwy., Lenexa KS 66220. (913)577-0500. **E-mail:** holinesstoday@nazarene.org. **Website:** www.holinesstoday.org. **Contact:** Carmen J. Ringhiser, managing editor; Devid J. Felter, editor-in-chief. *Holiness Today*, published bimonthly online and in print, is "the primary print voice of the Church of the Nazarene, with articles geared to enhance holiness living by connecting Nazarenes with our heritage, vision, and mission through real life stories of God at work in the world." Holiness Today (print) is 40 pages. Subscription: $12/year U.S. Circ. 30,000.

⊗⊗ LIGHT & LIFE MAGAZINE [LLM]

Free Methodist Church-USA, 770 N. High School Rd., Indianapolis IN 46214. (317)616-4776. **Fax:** (317)244-1247. **E-mail:** jeff.finley@fmcusa.org. **Website:** http://llcomm.org; http://fmcusa.org. **Contact:** Jeff Finley, managing editor. **20% freelance written.** "Light & Life Magazine [LLM] is a monthly magazine by Light & Life Communications, the publishing arm of the Free Methodist Church–USA. Each issue focuses on a specific theme with a cohesive approach in which the articles complement each other." Estab. 1868. Circ. 53,000 (English); 6,000 (Spanish). Byline given. Pays on publication. No kill fee. Accepts queries by e-mail. Responds in 2 months. Guidelines available at http://llcom.org/writersguidelines.

NONFICTION Query. Length: 325 words (feature: 1,100 words). **Pays $75/article ($200/feature).**

⊗⊗ LIGUORIAN

One Liguori Dr., Liguori MO 63057. (636)464-2500. **Fax:** (636)464-8449; (636)464-2503. **E-mail:** liguorianeditor@liguori.org. **Website:** www.liguorian.org. **Contact:** Cheryl Plass, managing editor. **25% freelance written. Prefers to work with published/established writers.** Magazine published 10 times/year for Catholics. "Our purpose is to lead our readers to a fuller Christian life by helping them better understand the teachings of the gospel and the church and by illustrating how these teachings apply to life and the problems confronting them as members of families, the church, and society." Estab. 1913. Circ. 100,000. Pays on acceptance. Submit seasonal material 8 months in advance. Accepts queries by mail, e-mail, fax, phone. Responds in 3 months to mss. Sample copy for 9x12 SAE with 3 first-class stamps or online. Guidelines for #10 SASE and on website.

NONFICTION "No travelogue approach or un-researched ventures into controversial areas. Also, no material found in secular publications—fad subjects that already get enough press, pop psychology, negative or put-down articles. *Liguorian* does not consider retold Bible stories." **Buys 30-40 unsolicited mss/**

year. Length: 400-2,200 words. **Pays 12-15¢/word and 5 contributor's copies.**

PHOTOS Photographs on assignment only unless submitted with and specific to article.

FICTION Needs religious, inspirational, senior citizen/retirement. Send complete ms. Length: 1,500-2,200 words. **Pays 12-15¢/word and 5 contributor's copies.**

TIPS "First read several issues containing short stories. We look for originality and creative input in each story we read. Since most editors must wade through mounds of manuscripts each month, consideration for the editor requires that the market be studied, the manuscript be carefully presented and polished before submitting. Our publication uses only one story a month. Compare this with the 25 or more we receive over the transom each month. Also, many fiction mss are written without a specific goal or thrust, i.e., an interesting incident that goes nowhere is *not a story*. We believe fiction is a highly effective mode for transmitting the Christian message and also provides a good balance in an unusually heavy issue."

LIVE WIRE

8805 Governor's Hill Dr., Suite 400, Cincinnati OH 45249. (513)931-4050. **Fax:** (877)867-5751. **E-mail:** mredford@standardpub.com. **Website:** www.standardpub.com. Estab. 1949.

💲 THE LIVING CHURCH

Living Church Foundation, P.O. Box 514036, Milwaukee WI 53203-3436. (414)276-5420. **Fax:** (414)276-7483. **E-mail:** tlc@livingchurch.org. **Website:** www.livingchurch.org. **Contact:** John Schuessler, managing editor; Douglas LeBlanc, associate editor. **50% freelance written.** Magazine covering news or articles of interest to members of the Episcopal Church. Weekly magazine that presents news and views of the Episcopal Church and the wider Anglican Communion, along with articles on spirituality, Anglican heritage, and the application of Christianity in daily life. There are commentaries on scripture, book reviews, editorials, letters to the editor, and special thematic issues. Estab. 1878. Circ. 9,500. Byline given. Does not pay unless article is requested. No kill fee. Publishes ms an average of 3 months after acceptance. Editorial lead time 3 weeks. Submit seasonal material 2 months in advance. Accepts queries by mail, e-mail, fax. Responds in 2 weeks to queries. Responds in 1 month to mss. Sample copy free.

NONFICTION Needs opinion, personal experience, photo feature, religious. **Buys 10 mss/year.** Send complete ms. Length: 1,000 words. **Pays $25-100.** Sometimes pays expenses of writers on assignment.

PHOTOS Send photos. Reviews any size prints. Offers $15-50/photo.

COLUMNS/DEPARTMENTS Benediction (devotional), 250 words; Viewpoint (opinion), under 1,000 words. Send complete ms. **Pays $50 maximum.**

POETRY Needs light verse, traditional.

💲💲 THE LOOKOUT

Standard Publishing, 8805 Governor's Hill Dr., Suite 400, Cincinnati OH 45249. (513)931-4050. **Fax:** (513)931-0950. **E-mail:** lookout@standardpub.com. **Website:** www.lookoutmag.com. **Contact:** Shawn McMullen, editor. **50% freelance written.** Weekly magazine for Christian adults, with emphasis on spiritual growth, family life, and topical issues. "Our purpose is to provide Christian adults with practical, Biblical teaching and current information that will help them mature as believers." Estab. 1894. Circ. 45,000. Byline given. Pays on acceptance. Offers 33% kill fee. Publishes ms an average of 1 year after acceptance. Editorial lead time 9 months. Submit seasonal material 1 year in advance. Accepts queries by mail, e-mail. No previously published material. Accepts simultaneous submissions. Responds in 10 weeks to queries and mss. Sample copy for $1. Guidelines by e-mail or online.

NONFICTION Needs inspirational, interview, opinion, personal experience, religious. No fiction or poetry. **Buys 100 mss/year.** Send complete ms. Length: 1,200-1,400 words. **Pays 11-17¢/word.**

PHOTOS State availability. Identification of subjects required. Offers no additional payment for photos accepted with ms.

TIPS "*The Lookout* publishes from a theologically conservative, nondenominational, and noncharismatic perspective. We aim primarily for those aged 30-55. Most readers are married and have elementary to young adult children. Our emphasis is on the needs of ordinary Christians who want to grow in their faith. We value well-informed articles that offer lively and clear writing as well as strong application. We often address tough issues and seek to explore fresh ideas or recent developments affecting today's Christians."

$ $ THE LUTHERAN

8765 W. Higgins Rd., 5th Floor, Chicago IL 60631-4183. (770)380-2540. **Fax:** (773)380-2409. **E-mail:** lutheran@lutheran.org. **Website:** www.thelutheran. org. **Contact:** Daniel J. Lehmann, editor; Michael D. Watson, art director. **15% freelance written.** Monthly magazine for lay people in church covering news and activities of the Evangelical Lutheran Church in America, news of the world of religion, ethical reflections on issues in society, andpersonal Christian experience. Estab. 1988. Circ. 300,000. Byline given. Pays on acceptance. Offers 50% kill fee. Publishes ms an average of 6 months after acceptance. Submit seasonal material 4 months in advance. Accepts queries by mail, e-mail. Responds in 6 weeks to queries. Sample copy free. Guidelines available online.

NONFICTION Needs inspirational, interview, personal experience, photo feature, religious. No articles unrelated to the world of religion. **Buys 40 mss/year.** Query with published clips. Length: 250-1,200 words. **Pays $75-600.** Pays expenses of writers on assignment.

PHOTOS Send photos. Captions, identification of subjects required. Reviews contact sheets, transparencies, prints. Offers $50-175/photo.

COLUMNS/DEPARTMENTS Contact editor.

TIPS "Writers have the best chance selling us feature articles."

$ THE LUTHERAN DIGEST

The Lutheran Digest, Inc., 6160 Carmen Ave. E, Inver Grove Heights MN 55076. (952)933-2820. **Fax:** (952)933-5708. **E-mail:** editor@lutherandigest.com. **Website:** www.lutherandigest.com. **Contact:** Nicholas A. Skapyak, editor. **95% freelance written.** Quarterly magazine covering Christianity from a Lutheran perspective. Publishes articles and poetry. "Articles frequently reflect a Lutheran Christian perspective, but are not intended to be sermonettes. Popular stories show how God has intervened in a person's life to help solve a problem." Estab. 1953. Circ. 50,000. Byline given. Pays on publication. No kill fee. Publishes ms an average of 6 months after acceptance. Editorial lead time 9 months. Submit seasonal material 9 months in advance. "No queries, please." Accepts queries by e-mail mss only as Microsoft Word or PDF attachments. Accepts simultaneous submissions. Re-

sponds in 1 month to queries. Responds in 4 months to mss. No response to e-mailed mss unless selected for publication. Sample copy for $3.50. Guidelines available online.

NONFICTION Needs general interest, historical, how-to, personal or spiritual growth, humor, inspirational, personal experience, religious, nature, God's unique creatures. Does not want "to see personal tributes to deceased relatives or friends. They are seldom used unless the subject of the article is well known. We also avoid articles about the moment a person finds Christ as his or her personal savior." **Buys 50-60 mss/year.** Send complete ms. Length: No more than 1,500 words. **Pays $35-50.**

REPRINTS Accepts previously published submissions. "We prefer this as we are a digest and 70-80% of our articles are reprints."

PHOTOS "We seldom print photos from outside sources." State availability.

POETRY Submit 3 poems at a time. Lines/poem: 25 maximum. Considers previously published poems and simultaneous submissions. Accepts fax and e-mail (as attachment) submissions. Cover letter is preferred. "Include SASE if return is desired." Time between acceptance and publication is up to 9 months. "Poems are selected by editor and reviewed by publication panel." Guidelines available for SASE or on website. Responds in 3 months. Pays credit and 1 contributor's copy. Acquires one-time rights.

TIPS "Reading our writers' guidelines and sample articles online is encouraged and is the best way to get a 'feel' of the type of material we publish."

THE MENNONITE

718 N. Main St., Newton KS 67114-1703. (866)866-2872 ext. 34398. **Fax:** (316)283-0454. **E-mail:** gordonh@themennonite.org. **Website:** www.themennonite.org. **Contact:** Gordon Houser, associate editor. *The Mennonite*, published monthly, seeks "to help readers glorify God, grow in faith and become agents of healing and hope in the world. Our readers are primarily people in Mennonite churches." Single copy: $3; subscription: $46 U.S. Estab. 2001. Circ. 9,000. Publishes ms up to 1 year after acceptance. Responds in 2 weeks. Guidelines online.

NONFICTION Needs general interest, religious, Bible study, prayer, environment, aging, death/dying, Christmas, Easter, children, parenting, marriage, singleness, racism, peace and justice, worship, health issues, arts, "personal stories of Mennonites exercising their faith. Query via e-mail (preferred). Include name, address, phone number, one-sentence summary of the article and "three catchy, creative titles. Illustrations, charts, graphs, and photos (in color) to go with the article are welcome." If sending by regular mail, also include an SASE. Length: 1,200-1,500 words for feature articles. **Payment varies.**

TIPS "Writing should be concise, accessible to the general reader, and with strong lead paragraphs. This last point cannot be overemphasized. The lead paragraph is the foundation of a good article. It should provide a summary of the article. We are especially interested in personal stories of Mennonites exercising their faith."

⊛⊛ MESSAGE MAGAZINE

Review and Herald Publishing Association, 55 West Oak Ridge Dr., Hagerstown MD 21740. (301)393-4099. **Fax:** (301)393-4103. **E-mail:** ccrawford@rhpa.org. **E-mail:** Message@rhpa.org. **Website:** www.messagemagazine.org. **Contact:** Carmela Monk Crawford, editor. **10-20% freelance written.** Bimonthly magazine. "*Message* is the oldest religious journal addressing ethnic issues in the country. Our audience is predominantly Black and Seventh-day Adventist; however, *Message* is an outreach magazine for the churched and un-churched across cultural lines." Estab. 1898. Circ. 110,000. Byline given. Pays on acceptance. No kill fee. Publishes ms an average of 12 months after acceptance. Editorial lead time 6 months. Submit seasonal material 6 months in advance. Responds in 9 months to queries. Sample copy by e-mail. Guidelines by e-mail and online.

NONFICTION Needs general interest; how-to (overcome depression, overcome defeat, get closer to God, learn from failure, deal with the economic crises, etc.). **Buys variable number of mss/year.** Send complete ms. Length: 800-1,200 words. **Payment varies. Payment upon acceptance.**

PHOTOS State availability. Identification of subjects required.

TIPS "Please look at the magazine before submitting manuscripts. *Message* publishes a variety of writing styles as long as the writing style is easy to read and flows—please avoid highly technical writing styles."

MESSAGE OF THE OPEN BIBLE

Open Bible Churches, 2020 Bell Ave., Des Moines IA 50315-1096. (515)288-6761. **Fax:** (515)288-2510. E-mail: andrea@openbible.org. **Website:** www.openbible.org. **5% freelance written.** "*The Message of the Open Bible* is the official bimonthly publication of Open Bible Churches. Its readership consists mostly of people affiliated with Open Bible." Estab. 1932. Circ. 2,700. Byline given. No kill fee. Publishes ms an average of 4-6 months after acceptance. Editorial lead time 6 months. Submit seasonal material 6 months in advance. Accepts queries by mail. Responds in 1 month to queries. Responds in 2 months to mss. Sample copy for SAE with 9x12 envelope and 3 first-class stamps. Writer's guidelines for #10 SASE or by e-mail (message@openbible.org).

NONFICTION Needs inspirational, teachings or challenges, interview, personal experience, religious, testimonies, news. No sermons. Send complete ms. Length: 650 words maximum.

PHOTOS State availability. Reviews 5x7 prints, GIF/JPEG files. Does not pay for photos.

⊛⊛ MY DAILY VISITOR

Our Sunday Visitor, Inc., Publishing Division, 200 Noll Plaza, Huntington IN 46750. (260)356-8400. **Fax:** (260)356-8472. **E-mail:** mdvisitor@osv.com; mhogan@osv.com. **Website:** www.osv.com. **Contact:** Michelle Hogan, executive assistant. **99% freelance written.** Bimonthly magazine of scripture meditations based on the day's Catholic Mass readings. Circ. 33,000. Byline given. Pays on acceptance. No kill fee. Publishes ms an average of 6 months after acceptance. Accepts queries by mail, e-mail. Responds in 2 months to queries. Sample copy and writer's guidelines for #10 SAE with 3 first-class stamps.

NONFICTION Needs inspirational, personal experience, religious. **Buys 12 mss/year.** Query with published clips. Length: 130-140 words times the number of days in month. **Pays $500 for 1 month (28-31) of meditations and 5 free copies.**

TIPS "Previous experience in writing scripture-based Catholic meditations or essays is helpful."

A NEW HEART

Hospital Christian Fellowship, Inc., P.O. Box 4004, San Clemente CA 92674. (949)496-7655. **Fax:** (949)496-8465. **E-mail:** hcfusa@gmail.com. **Website:** www.hcfusa.com. **50% freelance written.** Quarterly magazine covering articles and true stories that are health-related, with a Christian message, to encourage healthcare workers, patients, and volunteers to meet specific needs. Estab. 1978. Circ. 5,000. Byline given. No kill fee. Publishes ms an average of 4-6 months after acceptance. Editorial lead time 6 months. Submit seasonal material 6 months in advance. Accepts queries by mail, e-mail, fax, phone. Accepts simultaneous submissions. Responds in 2 weeks to queries. Sample copy free. Guidelines free.

NONFICTION Needs humor, inspirational, personal experience, religious. No fiction. **Buys 10-20 mss/year.** Query. Length: 500-1,500 words.

PHOTOS State availability of or send photos. Captions, identification of subjects required. Offers no additional payment for photos accepted with ms.

COLUMNS/DEPARTMENTS Book Review (medical/Christian), 200 words; Events (medical/Christian), 100-200 words; Chaplains (medical/Christian/inspirational), 200-250 words; On the Lighter Side (medical/clean fun), 100-200 words. **Buys 4-6 mss/year.** Send complete ms. **Pays in copies.**

FILLERS Needs anecdotes, gags, short humor. **Buys 4-10 mss/year.** Length: 50-100 words. **Pays in copies.**

💲💲 ONE

Catholic Near East Welfare Association, 1011 First Ave., New York NY 10022-4195. (212)826-1480. **Fax:** (212)838-1344. **E-mail:** cnewa@cnewa.org. **Website:** www.cnewa.org. **Contact:** Deacon Greg Kandra, executive editor. **75% freelance written.** Bimonthly magazine for a Catholic audience with interest in the Near East, particularly its current religious, cultural and political aspects. Estab. 1974. Circ. 100,000. Byline given. Pays on publication. No kill fee. Publishes ms an average of 6 months after acceptance. Accepts queries by mail, fax. Responds in 1 month to queries. Sample copy and writer's guidelines for 7 1/2 x 10 1/2 SAE with 2 first-class stamps.

NONFICTION Length: 1,200-1,800 words. **Pays 20¢/edited word.**

PHOTOS "Photographs to accompany ms are welcome; they should illustrate the people, places, ceremonies, etc. which are described in the article. We prefer color transparencies but occasionally use b&w." Pay varies depending on use—scale from $50-300.

TIPS "We are interested in current events in the Near East as they affect the cultural, political, and religious lives of the people."

💲💲 OUR SUNDAY VISITOR

Our Sunday Visitor, Inc., 200 Noll Plaza, Huntington IN 46750. (260)356-8400. **Fax:** (260)356-8472. **E-mail:** oursunvis@osv.com; bmcnamara@osv.com;

gcrowe@osv.com. **Website:** www.osv.com. **Contact:** Beth McNamara, editorial director; Gretchen Crowe, editor. **70% freelance written. (Mostly assigned.).** Weekly publication covering world events and culture from a Catholic perspective. "We are a Catholic publishing company seeking to educate and deepen our readers in their faith. Currently emphasizing devotional, inspirational, catholic identity, apologetics, and catechetics." Estab. 1912. Circ. 60,000. Byline given. Pays on acceptance. No kill fee. Publishes ms an average of 2-3 weeks after acceptance. Accepts queries by mail, e-mail. Responds within 4 to 6 weeks. Sample copy for $2. Send a 10x13 SASE with 93 cents in postage affixed. Detailed guidelines online at: www.osv.com/AboutUsNav/WritersGuidelines/OSVNewsweeklyGuidelines/tabid/1389/Default.aspx.

NONFICTION Needs personal experience, profile, religious, reviews, family, essay, news analysis. "When submitting via e-mail, always include QUERY or MANUSCRIPT in the subject line."

💲💲 OUTREACH MAGAZINE

2231 Faraday Way, Suite 120, Carlsbad CA 92008-7728. (760)940-0600. **Fax:** (760)597-2314. **E-mail:** tellus@outreachmagazine.com. **Website:** www.outreachmagazine.com. **80% freelance written.** Bimonthly magazine covering outreach in Christianity. "*Outreach* is designed to inspire, challenge, and equip churches and church leaders to reach out to their communities with the love of Jesus Christ." Circ. 30,000. Byline given. Pays on publication. Offers 10% kill fee. Publishes ms an average of 2-4 months after acceptance. Editorial lead time 6 months. Submit seasonal material 6 months in advance. Accepts queries by mail, e-mail. Accepts simultaneous submissions. Responds in 2 months to queries. Responds in 8 months to mss. Sample copy free. Guidelines available online.

NONFICTION Needs book excerpts, how-to, humor, inspirational, interview, personal experience, photo feature, religious. Special issues: Vacation Bible School (January); Church Growth—America's Fastest-Growing Churches (Special Issue). Does not want fiction, poetry, non-outreach-related articles. **Buys 30 mss/year.** Query with published clips. Length: 1,500-2,500 words. **Pays $375-600 for assigned articles; $375-500 for unsolicited articles.** Sometimes pays expenses of writers on assignment.

PHOTOS Send photos. Identification of subjects required. Reviews GIF/JPEG files. Negotiates payment individually.

COLUMNS/DEPARTMENTS Pulse (short stories about outreach-oriented churches and ministries), 250-350 words; Soulfires (an as-told-to interview with a person about the stories and people that have fueled their passion for outreach), 900 words; Ideas (a profile of a church that is using a transferable idea or concept for outreach), 300 words, plus sidebar; Soulfires (short interviews with known voices about the stories and people that have informed their worldview and faith perspective), 600 words. **Buys 6 mss/year.** Query with published clips. **Pays $100-375.**

FILLERS Needs facts, gags. **Buys 6 mss/year.** Length: 25-100 words. **Pays negotiated fee.**

TIPS "Study our magazine and writer's guidelines. Send published clips that showcase tight, bright writing as well as your ability to interview; research; and organize numerous sources into an article; and write a 100-word piece as well as a 1,600-word piece."

PENTECOSTAL EVANGEL

The General Council of the Assemblies of God, 1445 N. Boonville Ave., Springfield MO 65802. (417)862-2781. **Fax:** (417)862-0416. **E-mail:** pe@ag.org. **Website:** pe.ag.org. **Contact:** Ken Horn, editor. **5-10% freelance written.** Weekly magazine emphasizing news of the Assemblies of God for members of the Assemblies and other Pentecostal and charismatic Christians. "Articles should be inspirational without being preachy. Any devotional writing should take a literal approach to the Bible. A variety of general topics and personal experience accepted with inspirational tie-in." Estab. 1913. Circ. 180,000. Byline given. Pays on acceptance. Offers 100% kill fee. Publishes ms an average of 6 months or more after acceptance. Editorial lead time 3 months. Submit seasonal material 6 months in advance. Accepts queries by e-mail. Responds in 2 weeks to queries. Responds in 2 months to mss. Sample copy free. Guidelines available online.

NONFICTION Needs book excerpts, general interest, inspirational, personal experience, religious. Does not want poetry, fiction, self-promotional. **Buys 10-15 mss/year.** Send complete ms. Length: 700-1,200 words. **Pays $25-200.**

TIPS "We publish first-person articles concerning spiritual experiences; that is, answers to prayer for help in a particular situation, of unusual conversions or healings through faith in Christ. All articles submitted to us should be related to religious life. We are Protestant, evangelical, Pentecostal, and any doctrines or practices portrayed should be in harmony with the official position of our denomination (Assemblies of God)."

THE PENTECOSTAL MESSENGER

Pentecostal Church of God, P.O. Box 211866, Bedford TX 76095. (817)554-5900; (417)624-7050. **Fax:** (817)391-4101. **E-mail:** info@pcg.org. **Website:** www.pcg.org. Monthly magazine covering Christian, inspirational, religious, leadership news. "Our organization is Pentecostal in nature. Our publication goes out to our ministers and laypeople to educate, inspire and inform them of topics around the world and in our organization that will help them in their daily walk." Estab. 1919. Circ. 5,000. Byline given. Pays on publication. Editorial lead time 6 months. Submit themed material 6 months in advance. Accepts queries by mail. Accepts simultaneous submissions. May contact the *Pentecostal Messenger* for a list of monthly themes.

NONFICTION Needs book excerpts, essays, exposé, general interest, inspirational, interview, new product, personal experience, religious. **Buys 12-24 mss/year.** Send complete ms. Length: 750-2,000 words. **Pays $15-40.**

PHOTOS Send photos. Identification of subjects required. Reviews prints. Offers no additional payment for photos accepted with ms.

THE PENWOOD REVIEW

P.O. Box 862, Los Alamitos CA 90720. **E-mail:** lcameron65@verizon.net. **E-mail:** submissions@penwoodreview.com. **Website:** www.penwoodreview.com. **Contact:** Lori Cameron, editor. **100%.** *The Penwood Review* has been established to embrace high quality poetry of all kinds, and to provide a forum for poets who want to write intriguing, energetic, and disciplined poetry as an expression of their faith in God. We encourage writing that elevates the sacred while exploring its mystery and meaning in our lives. Semiannual. Wants "disciplined, high-quality, well-crafted poetry on any subject. Rhyming poetry must be written in traditional forms (sonnets, tercets, villanelles, sestinas, etc.)." Estab. 1997. Circ. 50-100. No byline given. No kill fee. Publishes ms 1 year after acceptance. Accepts queries by e-mail. Responds in up to 4 months. Sample copy for $6.

POETRY Submit 3-5 poems at a time. Lines/poem: less than 2 pages preferred. No previously published poems or simultaneous submissions. Prefers e-mail submissions (pasted into body of message). Cover letter is optional. One poem to a page with the author's full name, address, and phone number in the upper right corner. "Submissions are circulated among an editorial staff for evaluations." Never comments on rejected poems. Does not want "light verse, doggerel, or greeting card-style poetry. Also, nothing racist, sexist, pornographic, or blasphemous. Submit maximum 5 poems.

THE PINK CHAMELEON

E-mail: dpfreda@juno.com. **Website:** www.thepink-chameleon.com. **Contact:** Dorothy Paula Freda, editor/publisher. *The Pink Chameleon*, published annually online, contains "family-oriented, upbeat poetry and stories, any genre in good taste that gives hope for the future." Estab. 2000. Time between acceptance and publication is up to 1 year, depending on date of acceptance. Publishes ms within 1 year after acceptance. Responds in 1 month to ms. Sometimes comments on rejected mss. Sample copy and writer's guidelines online.

NONFICTION Needs nonfiction short stories, articles. Send complete ms in the body of the e-mail. No attachments. Accepts reprints. No simultaneous submissions. Reading period is January 1-April 30 and September 1-October 31. Length: 500-2,500 words; average length: 2,000 words. **No payment.**

FICTION Reading period is January 1-April 30 and September 1-October 31. Needs short stories, adventure, family saga, fantasy, humor/satire, literary, mainstream, mystery/suspense, religious/inspirational, romance, science fiction, western, young adult/teen, psychic/supernatural. "No violence for the sake of violence." No novels or novel excerpts. Send complete ms in the body of the e-mail. No attachments. Accepts reprints. No simultaneous submissions. Length: 500-2,500 words; average length: 2,000 words. **No payment.**

POETRY Needs Wants "poems about nature, loved ones, rare moments in time." Reading period is January 1-April 30 and September 1-October 31. Considers poetry by children and teens. Submit 1-4 poems at a time. Considers previously published poems; no simultaneous submissions. Accepts e-mail submissions only (pasted into body of message; no attach-

ments. Use plain text and include a brief bio. Often comments on rejected poems. Does not want "pornography, cursing, swearing; nothing evoking despair." Submit maximum 4 poems. Line length: 6-24 lines. **No payment.**

TIPS "Simple, honest, evocative emotion, upbeat fiction and nonfiction submissions that give hope for the future; well-paced plots; stories, poetry, articles, essays that speak from the heart. Read guidelines carefully. Use a good, but not ostentatious, opening hook. Stories should have a beginning, middle and end that make the reader feel the story was worth his or her time. This also applies to articles and essays. In the latter 2, wrap your comments and conclusions in a neatly packaged final paragraph. Turnoffs include violence and bad language. Simple, genuine and sensitive work does not need to shock with vulgarity to be interesting and enjoyable."

⊘ ⊖⊖ THE PLAIN TRUTH

Plain Truth Ministries, 300 W. Green St., Pasadena CA 91129. (800)309-4466. **Fax:** (626)358-4846. **E-mail:** managing.editor@ptm.org. **Website:** www.ptm. org. **90% freelance written.** Bimonthly magazine. "We seek to reignite the flame of shattered lives by illustrating the joy of a new life in Christ." Estab. 1935. Circ. 70,000. Byline given. Pays on publication. Offers $50 kill fee. Publishes ms an average of 8 months after acceptance. Editorial lead time 6 months. Submit seasonal material 6 months in advance. Accepts queries by mail, e-mail. Accepts simultaneous submissions. Sample copy for sae with 9x12 envelope and 5 first-class stamps. Guidelines available online.

NONFICTION Needs inspirational, interview, personal experience, religious. **Buys 48-50 mss/year.** Query with published clips and SASE. *No unsolicited mss.* Length: 750-2,500 words. **Pays 25Â¢/word.**

REPRINTS Send tearsheet or photocopy of article or typed ms with rights for sale ted and information about when and where the article previously appeared with SASE for response. Pays 15Â¢/word.

PHOTOS State availability. Captions required. Reviews transparencies, prints. Negotiates payment individually.

TIPS "Material should offer Biblical solutions to real-life problems. Both first-person and third-person illustrations are encouraged. Articles should take a unique twist on a subject. Material must be insightful and practical for the Christain reader. All articles must be well researched and Biblically accurate without becoming overly scholastic. Use convincing arguments to support your Christian platform. Use vivid word pictures, simple and compelling language, and avoid stuffy academic jargon. Captivating anecdotes are vital."

⊖⊛ POINT

Converge Worldwide (Baptist General Conference), Mail Code 200, 11002 Lake Hart Dr., Orlando FL 32832. **Fax:** (866)990-8980. **E-mail:** bob.putman@ convergeww.org. **Website:** www.convergeworldwide.org. **5% freelance written.** Nonprofit, religious, evangelical Christian magazine published 4 times/ year covering Converge Worldwide. "*Point* is the official magazine of Converge Worldwide (BCG). Almost exclusively uses articles related to Converge, our churches, or by/about Converge people." Circ. 43,000. Byline given. Pays on publication. Offers 50% kill fee. Editorial lead time 6 months. Submit seasonal material 6 months in advance. Accepts queries by e-mail. Responds in 1 month to queries. Responds in 3 months to mss. Sample copy for #10 SASE. Guidelines and theme list free.

NONFICTION Buys 20-30 mss/year. Query with published clips. Wnats "articles about our people, churches, missions. View online at: www.convergeworldwide.org. before sending anything." Length: 300-1,500 words. **Pays $60-280.** Sometimes pays expenses of writers on assignment.

PHOTOS State availability. Captions, identification of subjects, model releases required. Reviews prints, some high-resolution digital. Offers $15-60/photo.

COLUMNS/DEPARTMENTS Converge Connection (blurbs of news happening in Converge Worldwide), 50-150 words. Send complete ms. **Pays $30.**

TIPS "Please study the magazine and the denomination. We will send sample copies to interested freelancers and give further information about our publication needs upon request. Freelancers from our churches who are interested in working on assignment are especially welcome."

○ ⊛ PRAIRIE MESSENGER

Benedictine Monks of St. Peter's Abbey, P.O. Box 190, Muenster SK S0K 2Y0 Canada. (306)682-1772. **Fax:** (306)682-5285. **E-mail:** pm.canadian@stpeterspress.ca. **Website:** www.prairiemessenger.ca. **Contact:** Maureen Weber, associate editor. **10% Freelance written.** Weekly Catholic publication published by

the Benedictine Monks of St. Peter's Abbey. Has a strong focus on ecumenism, social justice, interfaith relations, aboriginal issues, arts and culture. Estab. 1904. Circ. 5,000. Byline given. Pays on publication. No kill fee. Publishes ms an average of 4 months after acceptance. Submit seasonal material 3 months in advance. Accepts queries by mail, e-mail, fax, phone. TrueAccepts simultaneous submissions. Responds only if interested; send nonreturnable samples. Sample copy for 9x12 SASE with $1 Canadian postage or IRCs. Guidelines available online. "Because of government subsidy regulations, we are no longer able to accept non-Canadian freelance material."

NONFICTION Needs interview, opinion, religious. "No articles on abortion." **Buys 15 mss/year.** Send complete ms. Length: 500-800 words. **Pays $60/article.** Sometimes pays expenses of writers on assignment.

PHOTOS Send photos. Captions required. Reviews 3x5 prints. Offers $25/photo.

⊖⊛ PRESBYTERIANS TODAY

Presbyterian Church (U.S.A.), 100 Witherspoon St., Louisville KY 40202-1396. (502)569-5520. **Fax:** (502)569-8887. **E-mail:** today@pcusa.org. **Website:** www.pcusa.org/today. **Contact:** Patrick David Heery, editor. **25% freelance written. Prefers to work with published/established writers.** Denominational magazine published 10 times/year covering religion, denominational activities, and public issues for members of the Presbyterian Church (U.S.A.). "The magazine's purpose is to increase understanding and appreciation of what the church and its members are doing to live out their Christian faith." Estab. 1867. Circ. 40,000. Byline given. Pays on acceptance. Offers 50% kill fee. Publishes ms an average of 6 months after acceptance. Editorial lead time 3 months. Submit seasonal material 3 months in advance. Accepts queries by mail, e-mail, fax. Responds in 2 weeks to queries. Sample copy free. Guidelines available online.

NONFICTION Needs how-to, inspirational, Presbyterian programs, everyday Christian issues. **Buys 20 mss/year.** Send complete ms. Length: 1,000-1,800 words. **Pays $300 maximum for assigned articles; $75-300 for unsolicited articles.**

PHOTOS State availability. Identification of subjects required. Reviews contact sheets, transparencies, color prints, digital images. Negotiates payment individually.

⊕⊕ PRISM MAGAZINE

Evangelicals for Social Action, P.O. Box 367, Wayne PA 19087. (484)384-2990. **E-mail:** kkomarni@eastern.edu. **Website:** www.prismmagazine.org. **50% freelance written.** Bimonthly magazine covering Christianity and social justice. "For holistic, Biblical, socially-concerned, progressive Christians." Estab. 1993. Circ. 2,500. Byline given. Pays on publication. Publishes ms an average of 4-6 months after acceptance. Editorial lead time 4 months. Submit seasonal material 4 months in advance. Accepts queries by mail, e-mail. Responds in 1 month to queries; 3 months to mss. Hardcover sample copy for $3. PDF sample copy free. Request via website. Guidelines on website.

○ We're a nonprofit; some writers are pro bono. Rarely accepts previously published material."

NONFICTION Needs essays on culture/faith, interviews, ministry profiles, reviews, etc. **Buys 10-12 mss/year.** Send complete ms. Length: 500-3,000 words. **Pays $50-75 per printed page.**

PHOTOS Send photos. Reviews JPEG files. Pays $25/photo published; $200 if photo used on cover.

TIPS "We look closely at stories of holistic ministry. It's best to request a sample copy to get to know *PRISM*'s focus/style before submitting—we receive many submissions that are not appropriate."

⊕ PURPOSE

1251 Virginia Ave., Harrisonburg VA 22802. **E-mail:** CarolD@MennoMedia.org; purposeeditor@mpn.net. **Website:** www.mennomedia.org. **Contact:** Carol Duerksen, editor. **75% freelance written.** Magazine focuses on Christian discipleship—how to be a faithful Christian in the midst of everyday life situations. Uses personal story form to present models and examples to encourage Christians in living a life of faithful discipleship. *Purpose*, published monthly by Faith & Life Resources, an imprint of the Mennonite Publishing Network (the official publisher for the Mennonite Church in the US and Canada), is a "religious young adult/adult monthly." Focuses on "action-oriented, discipleship living." *Purpose* is digest-sized with 4-color printing throughout. Press run is 8,000. Receives about 2,000 poems/year, accepts 150. Sample (with guidelines): $2 and 9x12 SAE. Estab. 1968. Circ. 8,500. Pays on acceptance. No kill fee. Publishes ms an average of 18 months after acceptance. Submit seasonal material 1 year in advance. Accepts queries by e-mail. Accepts simultaneous submissions. Responds in

3 months to queries. Sample copy and writer's guidelines for 6x9 SAE and $2.

NONFICTION Buys 140 mss/year. E-mail submissions preferred. **Pays $20-50 for articles.**

REPRINTS Send tearsheet, photocopy or typed ms with rights for sale noted and information about when and where the material previously appeared.

PHOTOS Photos purchased with ms must be sharp enough for reproduction; requires prints in all cases. Captions required.

FICTION Contact: Carol Duerksen, editor. Produce the story with specificity so that it appears to take place somewhere and with real people. Needs historical, related to discipleship theme, humorous, religious. No militaristic/narrow patriotism or racism. Send complete ms. Length: 600 words. **Pays up to 7¢ for stories, and 2 contributor's copies.**

POETRY Needs free verse, light verse, traditional. Buys 140 poems/year. Length: 12 lines maximum. **Pays $7.50-20/poem depending on length and quality. Buys one-time rights only.**

FILLERS 6¢/word maximum.

TIPS "Many stories are situational, how to respond to dilemmas. Looking for first-person storylines. Write crisp, action moving, personal style, focused upon an individual, a group of people, or an organization. The story form is an excellent literary device to help readers explore discipleship issues. The first 2 paragraphs are crucial in establishing the mood/issue to be resolved in the story. Work hard on the development of these."

QUAKER LIFE

Friends United Meeting, 101 Quaker Hill Dr., Richmond IN 47374. (765)962-7573. **Fax:** (765)966-1293. **E-mail:** quakerlife@fum.org; annieg@fum.org. **Website:** www.fum.org. **Contact:** Annie Glen, communications editor. **50% freelance written.** A Christian Quaker magazine published 6 times/year that covers news, inspirational, devotional, peace, equality, and justice issues. Estab. 1960. Circ. 3,000. Byline given. No kill fee. Publishes ms an average of 3-6 months after acceptance. Editorial lead time 2-3 months. Submit seasonal material 4-6 months in advance. Accepts queries by mail, e-mail. Accepts simultaneous submissions. Responds in 1 week to queries. Responds in 1-3 months to mss. Sample copy and writer's guidelines free.

NONFICTION Needs book excerpts, general interest, humor, inspirational, interview, personal experience, photo feature, religious, travel, Bible study. No poetry or fiction. Query. Length: 400-1,500 words. **Pays 3 contributor's copies.**

PHOTOS Reviews b&w or color prints and JPEG files. Occasionally, line drawings and b&w cartoons are used. Send photos. Does not pay for photos.

COLUMNS/DEPARTMENTS News Brief (newsworthy events among Quakers), 75-200 words; Devotional/Inspirational (personal insights or spiritual turning points), 750 words; Ideas That Work (ideas from meetings that could be used by others), 750 words; Book/Media Reviews, 75-300 words.

RAILROAD EVANGELIST

Railroad Evangelist Association, Inc., P.O. Box 5026, Vancouver WA 98668. (360)699-7208. **E-mail:** rrjoe@comcast.net. **Website:** www.railroadevangelist.com. **80% freelance written.** Magazine published 3 times/year covering the railroad industry. "The *Railroad Evangelist*'s purpose and intent is to reach people everywhere with the life-changing gospel of Jesus Christ. The railroad industry is our primary target, along with model railroad and rail fans." Estab. 1938. Circ. 3,000/issue. Byline sometimes given. No kill fee. Editorial lead time 6 weeks. Submit seasonal material 6 weeks in advance. Accepts queries by mail, e-mail. YesSample copy for SAE with 10x12 envelope and 3 first-class stamps. Guidelines for #10 SASE.

NONFICTION Needs inspirational, interview, personal experience, religious. Query. Length: 300-800 words. **Pays in contributor copies.**

PHOTOS State availability. Captions required. Reviews 3x5, 8x10 prints, GIF/JPEG files. Offers no additional payment for photos accepted with ms.

COLUMNS/DEPARTMENTS Right Track (personal testimony), 300-800 words; Ladies Line (personal testimony), 300-500 words; Kids Corner (geared toward children), 50-100 words. Query. **Pays in contributor copies.**

FICTION Needs historical, religious. Query. Length: 300-800 words. **Pays in contributor copies.**

POETRY Needs traditional. Length: 10-100 lines. **Pays in contributor copies.**

💲💲 REFORM JUDAISM

633 Third Ave., 7th Floor, New York NY 10017-6778. (212)650-4240. **Fax:** (212)650-4249. **E-mail:** rjmagazine@urj.org. **Website:** www.reformjudaismmag.org.

Contact: Joy Weinberg, managing editor. **30% freelance written.** Quarterly magazine of Jewish issues for contemporary Jews. "*Reform Judaism* is the official voice of the Union for Reform Judaism, linking the institutions and affiliates of Reform Judaism with every Reform Jew. *RJ* covers developments within the movement while interpreting events and Jewish tradition from a Reform perspective." Estab. 1972. Circ. 310,000. Byline given. Pays on publication. Offers kill fee for commissioned articles. Publishes ms an average of 3 months after acceptance. Submit seasonal material 6 months in advance. Accepts simultaneous submissions. Responds in 2 months to queries and to mss. Sample copy for $3.50. Guidelines available online.

NONFICTION Buys 30 mss/year. Submit complete ms. SASE is preferrable and will elicit a faster response. Cover stories: 2,500-3,500 words; major feature: 1,800-2,500 words; secondary feature: 1,200-1,500 words; department (e.g., travel): 1,200 words. **Pays 30¢/published word.** Sometimes pays expenses of writers on assignment.

REPRINTS Send tearsheet, photocopy or typed ms with rights for sale and information about when and where the material previously appeared. Usually doesn't publish reprints.

PHOTOS Send photos. Identification of subjects required. Reviews 8x10/color or slides, b&w prints, and printouts of electronic images. Payment varies.

FICTION Needs humorous, religious, sophisticated, cutting-edge, superb writing. **Buys 4 mss/year.** Send complete ms. Length: 600-2,500 words. **Pays 30¢/published word.**

TIPS "We prefer a stamped postcard including the following information/checklist: __ Yes, we are interested in publishing; __No, unfortunately the submission doesn't meet our needs; __Maybe, we'd like to hold on to the article for now. Submissions sent this way will receive a faster response."

💲💲 RELEVANT

Relevant Media Group, 900 N. Orange Ave., Winter Park FL 32789. (407)660-1411. **Fax:** (407)660-8555. **E-mail:** ryan@relevantmediagroup.com; alyce@relevantmediagroup.com. **Website:** www.relevantmagazine.com. **Contact:** Ryan Hamm, managing editor; Alyca Giligan, associate editor. **80% freelance written.** Bimonthly magazine covering God, life, and progressive culture. *Relevant* is a lifestyle magazine for Christians in their 20s and 30s. Estab. 2002. Circ. 83,000. Byline given. Pays 45 days after publication. Offers 50% kill fee. Publishes ms an average of 6 months after acceptance. Editorial lead time 4 months. Submit seasonal material 5 months in advance. Accepts queries by e-mail. Accepts simultaneous submissions. Responds in 6 weeks to queries. Responds in 3 months to mss. Sample copy available online. Guidelines available online.

NONFICTION Needs general interest, how-to, inspirational, interview, new product, personal experience, religious. Don't submit anything that doesn't target ages 18-34. Query with published clips. Length: 600-1,000 words. **Pays 10-15¢/word for assigned articles. Pays 10¢/word for unsolicited articles.** Sometimes pays expenses of writers on assignment.

TIPS "The easiest way to get noticed by our editors is to first submit (donate) stories for online publication."

🜂 RIVER REGION'S JOURNEY

P.O. Box 230367, Montgomery AL 36123. (334)213-7940. **Fax:** (334)213-7990. **E-mail:** info@readjourney-magazine.com. **Website:** www.readjourneymagazine.com. **Contact:** DeAnne Watson, editor. **50% freelance written.** Monthly magazine covering Christian living. Includes Protestant Christian writing, topical articles on Christian living, and Christian living articles with helpful information for walking with Christ daily. Estab. 1999. Circ. 8,000. Byline given. Pays on publication. Offers 25% kill fee. Publishes ms an average of 6-12 months after acceptance. Editorial lead time 1 year. Submit seasonal material 1 year in advance. Accepts queries by e-mail. Accepts simultaneous submissions. Sample copy for $1.75 and self-addressed magazine-size envelope. Guidelines by e-mail.

NONFICTION Needs inspirational, religious. No fiction, poetry, or autobiography. Submit query or complete ms. Length: 1,300-2,200 words. **Pays $25-50 for assigned articles. Pays $25 for unsolicited articles.**

SACRED JOURNEY

Fellowship in Prayer, Inc., 291 Witherspoon St., Princeton NJ 08542. (609)924-6863. **Fax:** (609)924-6910. **E-mail:** submissions@sacredjourney.org; lbaumann@fellowshipinprayer.org. **Website:** www.fellowshipinprayer.org. **70% freelance written.** *Sacred Journey: The Journal of Fellowship in Prayer* is a quarterly multi-faith journal published winter, spring, summer, and autumn. Estab. 1950. Circ. 5,000. No kill fee. Editorial lead time 3 months. Submit seasonal material 4

months in advance. Accepts queries by e-mail (preferably). Accepts simultaneous submissions. Responds within 4 months of receipt. Submission is considered permission for publication. "We reserve the right to edit. We will make every effort to contact the author with content revisions. Please include or be prepared to provide a bio of 50-words or less and/or a headshot phot to accompany your work, should it be selected for the print journal." Free sample copy available online. Writer guidelines are available online or by request.

NONFICTION Buys 30 mss/year. Send complete ms. Length: Approx. 750-1,500 words, double-spaced. **"If your work is selected for publication in the journal or on our website, you will receive a complimentary 1-year subscription to** *Sacred Journey* **if you work is selected for publication in the journal or on our website. For publication in the print journal you will also receive 5 copies of the issue in which your work appears."**

PHOTOS "We accept hi-res digital photographs and illlustrations for possible publication. Cover photos are typically in color while interior photos are usually in b&w. We favor vertical images, but consider horizontal ones."

POETRY "No poetry highly specific to a certain faith tradition. Nothing laden with specific faith terminology, nor a lot of Bible quotes or other quotes." Submit maximum 5 per submission poems. Limited to 35 lines (occasionally longer).

TIPS "We are always seeking original prayers to share the richness of the world's religious traditions."

🜂 THE SECRET PLACE

American Baptist Home Mission Societies, ABC/USA, P.O. Box 851, Valley Forge PA 19482. (610)768-2434. **E-mail:** thesecretplace@abc-usa.org. **100% freelance written.** Quarterly devotional covering Christian daily devotions. Estab. 1937. Circ. 250,000. Byline given. Pays on acceptance. No kill fee. Editorial lead time 1 year. Submit seasonal material 9 months in advance. For free sample and guidelines, send 6x9 SASE.

NONFICTION Needs inspirational. **Buys about 400 mss/year.** Send complete ms. Length: 100-200 words. **Pays $20.**

POETRY Needs avant-garde, free verse, light verse, traditional. Buys Publishes 12-15 poems/year. poems/year. Submit maximum Maximum number of poems: 6. poems. Length: 4-30 lines. **Pays $20.**

TIPS "Prefers submissions via e-mail."

$ SEEK

8805 Governor's Hill Dr., Suite 400, Cincinnati OH 45239. (513)931-4050, ext. 351. **E-mail:** seek@standardpub.com. **Website:** www.standardpub.com. Contains art and photos in each issue. "Inspirational stories of faith-in-action for Christian adults; a Sunday School take-home paper." Quarterly. Religious/inspirational, religious fiction and religiously slanted historical and humorous fiction. No poetry. List of upcoming themes available online. Accepts 150 mss/year. Send complete ms. Prefers submissions by e-mail. "*SEEK* corresponds to the topics of Standard Publishing's adult curriculum line and is designed to further apply these topics to everyday life." "Unsolicited mss must be written to a theme list." Estab. 1970. Circ. 27,000. Byline given. Pays on acceptance. No kill fee. Acceptance to publishing time is 1 year. Accepts queries by e-mail. Writer's guidelines online.

NONFICTION Send complete ms. **Pays 7 cents/word for first rights; 5 cents/word for reprint rights.**

REPRINTS Reprints pay 5 cents/word.

FICTION Needs religious/inspirational, religious fiction and religiously slanted historical and humorous fiction. Send complete ms. Prefers submissions by e-mail. **Pays 7¢/word.**

TIPS "Write a credible story with a Christian slant—no preachments; avoid overworked themes such as joy in suffering, generation gaps, etc. Most manuscripts are rejected by us because of irrelevant topic or message, unrealistic story, or poor character and/or plot development. We use fiction stories that are believable."

$ SOCIAL JUSTICE REVIEW

3835 Westminster Place, St. Louis MO 63108. (314)371-1653. **Fax:** (314)371-0889. **Website:** www.socialjusticereview.org. **25% freelance written. Works with a small number of new/unpublished writers each year.** Bimonthly magazine "to promote a true Christian humanism with respect for the dignity and rights of all human beings." Estab. 1908. No kill fee. Publishes ms an average of 1 year after acceptance. Accepts queries by mail. Sample copy for SAE with 9x12 envelope and 3 first-class stamps.

NONFICTION Query by mail only with SASE. Length: 2,500-3,000 words. **Pays about 2¢/word.**

REPRINTS Send typed ms with rights for sale noted and information about when and where the material previously appeared. Pays about 2¢/word.

TIPS "Write moderate essays completely compatible with papal teaching and readable to the average person."

$ $ ST. ANTHONY MESSENGER

Franciscan Media, 28 W. Liberty St., Cincinnati OH 45202-6498. (513)241-5615. **Fax:** (513)241-0399. **E-mail:** mageditors@franciscanmedia.org. **Website:** www.stanthonymessenger.org. **Contact:** John Feister, editor. **55% freelance written.** Monthly general interest magazine for a national readership of Catholic families, most of which have children or grandchildren in grade school, high school, or college. "*St. Anthony Messenger* is a Catholic family magazine which aims to help its readers lead more fully human and Christian lives. We publish articles which report on a changing church and world, opinion pieces written from the perspective of Christian faith and values, personality profiles, and fiction which entertains and informs." Estab. 1893. Circ. 305,000. Byline given. Pays on acceptance. No kill fee. Publishes ms an average of 1 year after acceptance. Submit seasonal material 6 months in advance. Accepts queries by mail, e-mail, fax. Responds in 3 weeks to queries. Responds in 2 months to mss. Sample copy for 9x12 SAE with 4 first-class stamps. Guidelines available online.

NONFICTION Needs how-to, on psychological and spiritual growth, problems of parenting/better parenting, marriage problems/marriage enrichment, humor, inspirational, interview, opinion, limited use; writer must have special qualifications for topic, personal experience, if pertinent to our purpose, photo feature, informational, social issues. **Buys 35-50 mss/year.** Query with published clips. Length: 2,000-2,500 words. **Pays 20¢/word.** Sometimes pays expenses of writers on assignment.

FICTION Needs mainstream, religious, senior citizen/retirement. "We do not want mawkishly sentimental or preachy fiction. Stories are most often rejected for poor plotting and characterization, bad dialogue (listen to how people talk), and inadequate motivation. Many stories say nothing, are 'happenings' rather than stories. No fetal journals, no rewritten Bible stories." **Buys 12 mss/year.** Send complete ms. Length: 2,000-2,500 words. **Pays 20¢/word maximum and 2 contributor's copies; $1 charge for extras.**

POETRY Contact: Poetry Editor. Submit "a few" poems at a time. "Please include your phone number and

CONSUMER MAGAZINES

a SASE with your submission. Do not send us your entire collection of poetry. Poems must be original." Submit seasonal poems several months in advance. "Our poetry needs are very limited." Submit maximum 4-5 poems. Length: up to 20-25 lines; "the shorter, the better." **Pays $2/line; $20 minimum.**

TIPS "The freelancer should consider why his or her proposed article would be appropriate for us, rather than for *Redbook* or *Saturday Review*. We treat human problems of all kinds, but from a religious perspective. Articles should reflect Catholic theology, spirituality, and employ a Catholic terminology and vocabulary. We need more articles on prayer, scripture, Catholic worship. Get authoritative information (not merely library research); we want interviews with experts. Write in popular style; use lots of examples, stories, and personal quotes. Word length is an important consideration."

SUCCESS STORIES

Franklin Publishing Company, 2723 Steamboat Circle, Arlington TX 76006. (817)548-1124. **E-mail:** ludwigotto@sbcglobal.net. **Website:** www.franklin-publishing.net; www.londonpress.us. **Contact:** Dr. Ludwig Otto. **59% freelance written.** Monthly journal covering positive responses to the problems in life. Estab. 1983. Circ. 1,000. Byline given. Does not pay, but offers 15% discount on issues purchased and 1-year free membership in the International Association of Professionals. No kill fee. Publishes ms an average of 1 month after acceptance. Editorial lead time 1 month. Submit seasonal material 3 months in advance. Accepts queries by mail, e-mail. Accepts simultaneous submissions. Responds in 1 week to queries and to mss. Guidelines available online.

NONFICTION Needs book excerpts, essays, general interest, historical, how-to, humor, inspirational, interview, new product, opinion, personal experience, religious, technical, travel. Send complete ms. Length: 750-6,000 words.

FICTION Needs adventure, condensed novels, ethnic, horror, humorous, mainstream, mystery, novel concepts, religious, science fiction, slice-of-life vignettes of life, suspense, western. Send complete ms.

POETRY Needs avant-garde, free verse, haiku, light verse, traditional.

FILLERS Needs anecdotes, facts, gags.

⟳ ⑤ THRIVE - THE EB ONLINE

Fellowship of Evangelical Baptist Churches in Canada, P.O. Box 457, Guelph ON N1H 6K9 Canada. (519)821-4830, ext. 229. **Fax:** (519)821-9829. **E-mail:** eb@fellowship.ca. **Website:** www.thrive-magazine.ca; www.fellowship.ca. **10% freelance written.** Online magazine covering religious, spiritual, Christian living, denominational, and missionary news. "We exist to enhance the life and ministry of the church leaders and members in Fellowship Congregations." Estab. 1953. Byline given. Pays on publication. No kill fee. Publishes ms an average of 6 months after acceptance. Editorial lead time 4 months. Accepts queries by e-mail. Accepts simultaneous submissions. Sample copy available online. Guidelines available online.

NONFICTION Needs religious. No poetry, fiction, puzzles. **Buys 4-6 mss/year.** Send complete ms. Length: 600-2,400 words. **Pays $50.**

TRICYCLE

1115 Broadway Suite 1113, New York NY 10010. (646)461-9847. **E-mail:** editorial@tricycle.com. **Website:** www.tricycle.com. **80% freelance written.** Quarterly magazine providing a unique and independent public forum for exploring Buddhist teachings and practices, establishing a dialogue between Buddhism and the broader culture, and introducing Buddhist thinking to Western disciplines. "*Tricycle* readers tend to be well educated and open minded." Estab. 1991. Circ. 50,000. Byline given. Pays on publication. Offers 25% kill fee. Editorial lead time 3 months. Accepts queries by mail, e-mail (preferable). Accepts simultaneous submissions. Responds in 3 months to queries and mss. Sample copy for $7.95 or online at website. Guidelines available online.

NONFICTION Needs book excerpts, essays, general interest, historical, humor, inspirational, interview, personal experience, photo feature, religious, travel. **Buys 4-6 mss/year.** Length: 1,000-5,000 words.

PHOTOS State availability. Captions, identification of subjects required. Reviews contact sheets. Negotiates payment individually.

COLUMNS/DEPARTMENTS Reviews (film, books, tapes), 600 words; Science and Gen Next, both 700 words. **Buys 6-8 mss/year.** Query.

TIPS "For your submission to be considered, we ask that you first send us a 1-page query outlining your idea, relevant information about your writing background and any Buddhist background, your familiarity with the subject of your proposal, and so on. If you have clips or writing samples, please send these along with your proposal."

☯ ☺ THE UNITED CHURCH OBSERVER

478 Huron St., Toronto ON M5R 2R3 Canada. (416)960-8500. **Fax:** (416)960-8477. **E-mail:** dnwilson@ucobserver.org. **Website:** www.ucobserver.org. **50% freelance written. Prefers to work with published/established writers.** Monthly general interest magazine for people associated with The United Church of Canada and non-churchgoers interested in issues of faith, justice and ethical living. Deals primarily with events, trends, and policies having religious significance. Most coverage is Canadian, but reports on international or world concerns will be considered. Byline usually given. Pays on publication. No kill fee. Publishes ms an average of 4 months after acceptance. Accepts queries by mail, e-mail, fax.

NONFICTION No poetry. Queries preferred. **Rates depend on subject, author, and work involved.** Pays expenses of writers on assignment as negotiated.

REPRINTS Send tearsheet or photocopy and information about when and where the material previously appeared. Payment negotiated.

PHOTOS Buys color photographs with mss. Send via e-mail. Payment varies.

TIPS "The writer has a better chance of breaking in at our publication with short articles. Include samples of previous magazine writing with query."

☺ ☺ THE UPPER ROOM

1908 Grand Ave., P.O. Box 310004, Nashville TN 37203. (615)340-7252. **Fax:** (615)340-7267. **E-mail:** theupperroommagazine@upperroom.org. **Website:** www.upperroom.org. **95% freelance written. Eager to work with new/unpublished writers.** Bimonthly magazine offering a daily inspirational message which includes a Bible reading, text, prayer, "Thought for the Day," and suggestion for further prayer. Each day's meditation is written by a different person and is usually a personal witness about discovering meaning and power for Christian living through scripture study which illuminates daily life. Circ. 2.2 million (U.S.); 385,000 outside U.S. Byline given. Pays on publication. No kill fee. Publishes ms an average of 1 year after acceptance. Submit seasonal material 14 months in advance. Sample copy and writer's guidelines with a 4x6 SAE and 2 first-class stamps. Guidelines only for #10 SASE or online.

NONFICTION Needs inspirational, personal experience, Bible-study insights. Special issues: Lent and Easter; Advent. No poetry, lengthy spiritual journey stories. **Buys 365 unsolicited mss/year.** Send complete ms by mail or e-mail. Length: 300 words. **Pays $25/meditation.**

TIPS "The best way to break in to our magazine is to send a well-written ms that looks at the Christian faith in a fresh way. Standard stories and sermon illustrations are immediately rejected. We want to find new writers and welcome good material. We are interested in meditations based on Old Testament characters and stories. Good repeat meditations can lead to work on longer assignments for our other publications, which pay more. A writer who can deal concretely with everyday situations, relate them to the Bible and spiritual truths, and write clear, direct prose should be able to write for *The Upper Room*. We want material that provides for interaction on the part of the reader—meditation suggestions, journaling suggestions, space to reflect and link personal experience with the meditation for the day. Meditations that are personal, authentic, exploratory, and full of sensory detail make good devotional writing."

☺☺ THE WAR CRY

The Salvation Army, 615 Slaters Lane, Alexandria VA 22314. (703)684-4128. **Fax:** (703)684-5539. **E-mail:** war_cry@usn.salvationarmy.org. **Website:** http://publications.salvationarmyusa.org. **10% freelance written.** "General interest magazine with evangelical emphasis and portrayals that express the mission of the Salvation Army. Fifteen issues are published per year, including special Easter and Christmas issues." Estab. 1881. Circ. 288,000. Byline given. Pays on publication. No kill fee. Publishes ms an average of 2 months to 1 year after acceptance. Editorial lead time 3 months before issue date, Christmas and Easter. Submit seasonal material 6 months in advance. Responds in 3-4 weeks to mss. Sample copy, theme list, and writer's guidelines free for #10 SASE or online.

NONFICTION Needs inspirational, interview, personal experience, religious. No missionary stories, confessions. **Buys 30 mss/year.** Complete mss, queries, and reprints accepted via mail or e-mail. Submissions strengthened when photos included where appropriate. **Pays $0.25/word for articles.**

PHOTOS Purchases limited number of photos. Identification of subjects required.

POETRY Purchases limited number of poetry.

FILLERS Needs anecdotes, inspirational. **Buys 10-20 mss/year mss/year.** Length: 50-350 words. **Pays $0.25/word.**

$ WESLEYAN LIFE

The Wesleyan Publishing House, P.O. Box 50434, Indianapolis IN 46250. (317)774-7909. **Fax:** (317)774-3924. **E-mail:** communications@wesleyan.org; macbethw@wesleyan.org; kindk@wesleyan.org. **Website:** www.wesleyanlifeonline.com. **Contact:** Wayne MacBeth, general editor; Kerry Kind, managing editor. Quarterly magazine of The Wesleyan Church. Estab. 1842. Circ. 50,000. Byline given. Pays on publication. No kill fee. Submit seasonal material 6 months in advance. Accepts simultaneous submissions.

NONFICTION Needs inspirational, religious. No poetry accepted. Send complete ms. Length: 250-400 words. **Pays $25-150.**

$ WOMAN ALIVE

Christian Publishing and Outreach, Garcia Estate, Canterbury Rd., Worthing West Sussex BN13 1BW United Kingdom. (44)(1903) 60-4379. **E-mail:** womanalive@cpo.org.uk. **Website:** www.womanalive.co.uk. **Contact:** Jackie Harris, editor; Sharon Barnard, assistant editor. "*Woman Alive* is a Christian magazine geared specifically toward women. It covers all denominations and seeks to inspire, encourage, and provide resources to women in their faith, helping them to grow in their relationship with God and providing practical help and biblical perspective on the issues impacting their livves." Pays on publication. No kill fee. Accepts queries by mail, e-mail. Sample copy for £1.50, plus postage. Guidelines available on website.

NONFICTION Needs how-to, personal experience, travel; also, building life skills and discipleship, interviews with Christian women in prominent positions or who are making a difference in their communities/jobs, women facing difficult challenges or taking on new challenges, affordable holiday destinations written from a Christian perspective. Submit clips, bio, article summary, ms, SASE. Length: 750-850 words/1-page article; 1,200-1,500 words/2-page article; 1,600-1,800 words/3-page article. **Pays £70/1-page article; £95/2-page article; £125/3-page article.**

PHOTOS Send photos. Reviews 300 dpi digital images.

RETIREMENT

$$$$ AARP THE MAGAZINE

AARP, c/o Editorial Submissions, 601 E. St. NW, Washington DC 20049. **E-mail:** aarpmagazine@aarp.org. **Website:** www.aarp.org/magazine. **50% freelance written. Prefers to work with published/established writers.** Bimonthly magazine covering issues that affect people over the age of 50. "*AARP The Magazine* is devoted to the varied needs and active life interests of AARP members, age 50 and over, covering such topics as financial planning, travel, health, careers, retirement, relationships, and social and cultural change. Its editorial content serves the mission of AARP seeking through education, advocacy, and service to enhance the quality of life for all by promoting independence, dignity, and purpose." Circ. 22,721,661. Byline given. Pays on acceptance. Offers 25% kill fee. Publishes ms an average of 6 months after acceptance. Submit seasonal material 6 months in advance. Accepts queries by mail, e-mail only. Responds in 3 months to queries. Sample copy free. Guidelines available online.

NONFICTION No previously published articles. Query with published clips. *No unsolicited mss.* Length: Up to 2,000 words. **Pays $1/word.** Sometimes pays expenses of writers on assignment.

PHOTOS Photos purchased with or without accompanying mss. Pays $250 and up for color; $150 and up for b&w.

TIPS "The most frequent mistake made by writers in completing an article for us is poor follow-through with basic research. The outline is often more interesting than the finished piece. We do not accept unsolicited mss."

$ MATURE YEARS

The United Methodist Publishing House, 201 Eighth Ave. S., P.O. Box 801, Nashville TN 37202-0801. (615)749-6292. **Fax:** (615)749-6512. **E-mail:** matureyears@umpublishing.org. **80% freelance written. Prefers to work with published/established writers.** Quarterly magazine designed to help persons in and nearing the retirement years understand and appropriate the resources of the Christian faith in dealing with specific problems and opportunities related to aging. Estab. 1954. Circ. 55,000. Pays on acceptance. No kill fee. Publishes ms an average of 1 year after acceptance. Submit seasonal material 14 months in advance. Responds in 2 weeks to queries. Responds in 2 months to mss. Sample copy for $6 and 9x12 SAE. Writer's guidelines for #10 SASE or by e-mail.

NONFICTION Needs how-to, hobbies, inspirational, religious, travel, special guidelines, older adult health, finance issues. **Buys 75-80 mss/year.** Send complete ms; e-mail submissions preferred. Length: 900-2,000 words. **Pays $45-125.** Sometimes pays expenses of writers on assignment.

REPRINTS Send tearsheet, photocopy, or typed ms with rights for sale noted and information about when and where the material previously appeared. Pays at same rate as for previously unpublished material.

PHOTOS Send photos. Captions, model releases required. Negotiates pay individually.

COLUMNS/DEPARTMENTS Health Hints (retirement, health), 900-1,500 words; Going Places (travel, pilgrimage), 1,000-1,500 words; Fragments of Life (personal inspiration), 250-600 words; Modern Revelations (religious/inspirational), 900-1,500 words; Money Matters (personal finance), 1,200-1,800 words; Merry-Go-Round (cartoons, jokes, 4-6 line humorous verse); Puzzle Time (religious puzzles, crosswords). **Buys 4 mss/year.** Send complete ms. **Pays $25-45.**

FICTION Contact: Marvin Cropsey, editor. Needs humorous, religious, slice-of-life vignettes, retirement years nostalgia, intergenerational relationships. "We don't want anything poking fun at old age, saccharine stories, or anything not for older adults. Must show older adults (age 55 plus) in a positive manner." **Buys 4 mss/year.** Send complete ms. Length: 1,000-2,000 words. **Pays $60-125.**

POETRY Needs free verse, haiku, light verse, traditional. Submit seasonal and nature poems for spring from December through February; for summer, March through May; for fall, June through August; and for winter, September through November. Accepts fax and e-mail submissions (e-mail preferred). Buys 24 poems/year. Submit maximum 6 poems. Length: 3-16 lines of up to 50 characters maximum. **Pays $5-20.**

TIPS "Practice writing dialogue! Listen to people talk; take notes; master dialogue writing! Not easy, but well worth it! Most inquiry letters are far too long. If you can't sell me an idea in a brief paragraph, you're not going to sell the reader on reading your finished article or story."

RURAL

⊖⊖ BACKWOODS HOME MAGAZINE

P.O. Box 712, Gold Beach OR 97444. (541)247-8900. **Fax:** (541)247-8600. **E-mail:** editor@backwoodshome. com. **E-mail:** article-submission@backwoodshome. com. **Website:** www.backwoodshome.com. **Contact:** Dave Duffy, editor and publisher. **90% freelance written.** Bimonthly magazine covering self-reliance. "*Backwoods Home Magazine* is written for people who have a desire to pursue personal independence, self-sufficiency, and their dreams. We offer 'how-to' articles on self-reliance." Estab. 1989. Circ. 38,000. Byline given. Pays on acceptance. Editorial lead time 4-6 months. Submit seasonal material 4-6 months in advance. Accepts queries by mail, e-mail. Sample copy for 9x10 SAE and 6 first-class stamps. Guidelines available online.

NONFICTION Needs general interest, how-to, humor, personal experience, technical. **Buys 120 mss/year.** Send complete ms via e-mail; no attachments. Length: 500 words. **Pays $30-200.**

PHOTOS Send photos. Captions, identification of subjects, model releases required. Offers no additional payment for photos accepted with ms.

⊙ ⊖⊖ THE COUNTRY CONNECTION

Pinecone Publishing, 691 Pinecrest Rd., Boulter ON K0L 1G0 Canada. (866)332-3651; (613)332-3651. **Website:** www.pinecone.on.ca. **Contact:** Gus Zylstra, publisher. **100% freelance written.** Magazine published 4 times/year covering nature, environment, history, heritage, nostalgia, travel and the arts. *The Country Connection* is a magazine for true nature lovers and the rural adventurer. Building on our commitment to heritage, cultural, artistic, and environmental themes, we continually add new topics to illuminate the country experience of people living within nature. Our goal is to chronicle rural life in its many aspects, giving 'voice' to the countryside. Estab. 1989. Circ. 4,000. Byline given. Pays on publication. No kill fee. Publishes ms an average of 4 months after acceptance. Editorial lead time 4 months. Accepts queries by mail, e-mail, phone. Sample copy for $5.64. Guidelines available online.

NONFICTION Needs general interest, historical, humor, opinion, personal experience, travel, lifestyle, leisure, art and culture, vegan recipes. No hunting, fishing, animal husbandry, or pet articles. **Buys 60 mss/**

year. Send complete ms. Length: 500-2,000 words. **Pays 10Â¢/word.**

PHOTOS Send photos. Captions required. Reviews transparencies, prints, digital photos on CD. Offers $10-50/photo.

FICTION Needs adventure, fantasy, historical, humorous, slice-of-life vignettes, country living. **Buys 10 mss/year.** Send complete ms. Length: 500-1,500 words. **Pays 10Â¢/word.**

TIPS Canadian content only with a preference for Ontario subject matter. Send manuscript with appropriate support material such as photos, illustrations, maps, etc.

🟡🟡 FARM & RANCH LIVING

Reiman Media Group, Farm & Ranch Living, 5400 S. 60th St., Greendale WI 53129. (414)423-0100. **Fax:** (414)423-8463. **E-mail:** editors@farmandranchliving. com. **Website:** www.farmandranchliving.com. **30% freelance written. Eager to work with new/unpublished writers.** Bimonthly magazine aimed at families that farm or ranch full time. *F&RL* is *not* a 'how-to' magazine—it focuses on people rather than products and profits. Estab. 1978. Circ. 400,000. Byline given. Pays on publication. No kill fee. Publishes ms an average of 6 months after acceptance. Submit seasonal material 6 months in advance. Accepts queries by mail, e-mail, fax. Responds in 6 weeks to queries. Sample copy for $2. Guidelines for #10 SASE.

NONFICTION Needs humor, rural only, inspirational, interview, personal experience, farm/ranch related, photo feature, nostalgia, prettiest place in the country (photo/text tour of ranch or farm). No issue-oriented stories (pollution, animal rights, etc.). **Buys 30 mss/ year.** Send complete ms. Length: 600-1,200 words. **Pays up to $300 for text/photo package. Payment for Prettiest Place negotiable.**

REPRINTS Send photocopy with rights for sale noted. Payment negotiable.

PHOTOS Scenic. State availability. Pays $75-200 for 35mm color slides.

TIPS "Our readers enjoy stories and features that are upbeat and positive. A freelancer must see *F&RL* to fully appreciate how different it is from other farm publications—ordering a sample is strongly advised (not available on newsstands). Photo features (about interesting farm or ranch families) and personality profiles are most open to freelancers."

🟡🟡 HOBBY FARMS

Bowtie, Inc., P.O. Box 12106, Lexington KY 40580. **Fax:** (859)252-7480. **E-mail:** hobbyfarms@bowtieinc. com. **Website:** www.hobbyfarms.com. **75% freelance written.** Bimonthly magazine covering small farms and rural lifestyle. "*Hobby Farms* is the magazine for rural enthusiasts. Whether you have a small garden or 100 acres, there is something in *Hobby Farms* to educate, enlighten, or inspire you." Estab. 2001. Circ. 252,801. Byline given. Pays on publication. Publishes ms an average of 6 months after acceptance. Editorial lead time 4 months. Submit seasonal material 6 months in advance. Accepts queries by mail, e-mail. Responds in 2 months to queries. Responds in 2 months to mss. Guidelines free.

NONFICTION Needs historical, how-to, farm or livestock management, equipment, etc., interview, personal experience, technical, breed or crop profiles. **Buys 10 mss/year.** Send complete ms. Length: 1,500-2,500 words. Sometimes pays expenses of writers on assignment. Limit agreed upon in advance.

PHOTOS State availability of or send photos. Identification of subjects, model releases required. Reviews GIF/JPEG files. Negotiates payment individually.

TIPS "Please state your specific experience with any aspect of farming (livestock, gardening, equipment, marketing, etc)."

MONADNOCK TABLE: THE GUIDE TO OUR REGION'S FOOD, FARMS, & COMMUNITY

P.O. Box 1504, Keene NH 03431. (603)357-8761. **E-mail:** marcia@monadnocktable.com; jodi@monadnocktable.com; info@monadnocktable.com. **Website:** www.monadnocktable.com. **Contact:** Marcia Passos Duffy, co-publisher & editorial director; Jodi Genest, co-publisher & creative director. Quarterly Magazine for local food/farms in the Monadnock Region of New Hampshire. Estab. 2010. Circ. 10,000. Byline given. Pays on publication. 25% kill fee. Publishes ms 3 months after acceptance. Editorial lead time 3 months. Submit seasonal material 3 months in advance. Accepts queries by e-mail. Reports in 1 month to queries and mss. Sample copy available online. Guidelines are available on website.

NONFICTION Contact: Marcia Passos Duffy, editorial director. Needs book excerpts, essays, how-to, interview, opinion, personal experience. Length: 500-1,000 words. **Pays 10¢ per word.** Sometimes pays expenses of writers on assignment. (limit agreed upon in advance)

PHOTOS Contact: Jodi Genest, creative director. Freelancers should state of photos with submission. Captions required. Reviews GIF/JPEG files. Offers no additional payment for photos accepted with ms.

COLUMNS/DEPARTMENTS Our Local Farmer (profile of local farmer in Monadnock Region), up to 800 words; Local Eats (profile of local chef and/or restaurant using local food), up to 800 words; Feature (how-to or "think" piece about local foods), up 1,000; Books/Opinion/Commentary (review of books, book excerpt, commentary, opinion pieces about local food), up to 500 words. **Buys 10 mss/year.** Query.

TIPS "Please query first with your qualifications. Please read magazine first for style (magazines available online). Must have a local (Monadnock Region, New Hampshire) angle."

[$] MOTHER EARTH NEWS

Ogden Publications, 1503 SW 42nd St., Topeka KS 66609-1265. (785)274-4300. **E-mail:** letters@motherearthnews.com. **Website:** www.motherearthnews.com. **Contact:** Cheryl Long, editor-in-chief. **Mostly written by staff and team of established freelancers.** Bimonthly magazine emphasizing country living, country skills, natural health, and sustainable technologies for both long-time and would-be ruralists. "*Mother Earth News* promotes self-sufficient, financially independent, and environmentally aware lifestyles. Many of our feature articles are written by our Contributing Editors, but we also assign articles to freelance writers, particularly those who have experience with our subject matter (both firsthand and writing experience." Circ. 350,000. Byline given. Pays on publication. No kill fee. Submit seasonal material 5 months in advance. Responds in 6 months to mss. Sample copy for $5. Guidelines for #10 SASE.

NONFICTION Needs how-to, green building, do-it-yourself, organic gardening, whole foods & cooking, natural health, livestock & sustainable farming, renewable energy, 21st century homesteading, nature-environment-community, green transportation. No fiction, please. **Buys 35-50 mss/year.** "Query. Please send a short synopsis of the idea, a one-page outline and any relevant digital photos, and samples. If available, please send us copies of 1 or 2 published articles, or tell us where to find them online." Country Lore length: 100-300/words. Firsthand Reports length: 1,500-2,000/words. **Pays $25-150.**

PHOTOS "We welcome quality photographs for our 2 departments."

COLUMNS/DEPARTMENTS Country Lore (helpful how-to tips); 100-300/words; Firsthand Reports (first-person stories about sustainable lifestyles of all sorts), 1,500-2,000/words.

TIPS "Read our magazine and take a close look at previous issues to learn more abut the various topics we cover. We assign articles about 6-8 months ahead of publication date, so keep in mind timing and the seasonality of some topics. Our articles provide hands-on, useful information for people who want a more fun, conscientious, sustainable, secure and satisfying lifestyle. Practicality is critical; freelance articles must be informative, well-documented and tightly written in an engaging and energetic voice. For how-to articles, complete, easy-to-understand instructions are essential."

[$][$] RANGE MAGAZINE

Purple Coyote Corp., 106 E. Adams St., Suite 201, Carson City NV 89706. (775)884-2200. **Fax:** (775)884-2213. **E-mail:** edit@rangemagazine.com. **Website:** www.rangemagazine.com. **70% freelance written.** Quarterly magazine covering ranching, farming, and the issues that affect agriculture. "*RANGE* magazine is devoted to the issues that threaten the West, its people, lifestyles, lands and wildlife. No stranger to controversy, *RANGE* is the leading forum for opposing viewpoints in the search for solutions that will halt the deletion of a national resource—the American rancher." Estab. 1991. Pays on publication. Publishes ms an average of 3-6 months after acceptance. Accepts queries by e-mail. Responds in 4-8 weeks to queries. Responds in 1-6 months to mss. Sample copy for $2. Guidelines available online.

NONFICTION Needs major ranch features in American West, issues that affect ranchers, profiles, short book excerpts that suit range, humor, photo essays. No sports or events. No book reviews. Writer must be familiar with *RANGE*. Query. Length: 500-2,000 words. **Pays $50-500.**

PHOTOS Contact: C.J. Hadley, editor/publisher. State availability of photography. Captions and identification must be included with all photos. Reviews high-res digitals on disk or flash drive with contact sheets. FTP site available. Slides and prints also reviewed. Negotiates payment individually.

$ RURAL HERITAGE

P.O. Box 2067, Cedar Rapids IA 52406. (319)362-3027. **E-mail:** info@ruralheritage.com. **Website:** www.ruralheritage.com. **Contact:** Joe Mischka, editor. **98% freelance written. Willing to work with a small number of new/unpublished writers.** Bimonthly magazine devoted to the training and care of draft animals. Estab. 1976. Circ. 9,500. Byline given. Pays on publication. No kill fee. Publishes ms an average of 6 months after acceptance. Submit seasonal material 6 months in advance. Accepts queries by mail, e-mail. Responds in 3 months to queries. Sample copy for $8. Guidelines available online.

NONFICTION Needs how-to, farming with draft animals, interview, people using draft animals, photo feature. No articles on *mechanized* farming. **Buys 200 mss/year.** Query or send complete ms. Length: 1,200-1,500 words. **Pays 5¢/word.**

PHOTOS 6 covers/year, animals in harness $200. Photo guidelines with #10 SASE or online. Captions, identification of subjects required. Pays $10.

POETRY Needs traditional. **Pays $5-25.**

TIPS "Thoroughly understand our subject: working draft animals in harness. We'd like more pieces on plans and instructions for constructing various horse-drawn implements and vehicles. Always welcome are: 1.) Detailed descriptions and photos of horse-drawn implements, 2.) Prices and other details of draft animal and implement auctions and sales."

$$ RURALITE

P.O. Box 558, Forest Grove OR 97116-0558. (503)357-2105. **Fax:** (503)357-8615. **E-mail:** editor@ruralite.org. **E-mail:** curtisc@ruralite.org. **Website:** www.ruralite.org. **Contact:** Curtis Condon, editor. **80% freelance written. Works with new, unpublished writers.** Monthly magazine aimed at members of consumer-owned electric utilities throughout 7 western states. General-interest publication used by 47 rural electric cooperatives and PUDs. Readers are predominantly rural and small-town residents interested in stories about people and issues that affect Northwest lifestyles. Estab. 1954. Circ. 325,000. Byline given. Pays on acceptance. No kill fee. Accepts queries by mail. Responds in 1 month to queries. Sample copy for 9x12 SAE with $1.52 of postage affixed. Guidelines available online.

NONFICTION Buys 50-60 mss/year. Query. Length: 100-2,000 words. **Pays $50-500.**

REPRINTS Send typed ms with rights for sale noted and information about when and where the material previously appeared.

PHOTOS Illustrated stories are the key to a sale. Stories without art rarely make it. Color prints/negatives, color slides, all formats accepted. No black & white. Inside color is $25-100; cover photo is $250-350.

TIPS "Study recent issues. Follow directions when given an assignment. Be able to deliver a complete package (story and photos). We're looking for regular contributors to whom we can assign topics from our story list after they've proven their ability to deliver quality mss."

SCIENCE

$$ AD ASTRA

National Space Society, 1155 15th St. NW, Suite 500, Washington DC 20005. (202)429-1600. **Fax:** (202)463-0659. **E-mail:** adastra@nss.org. **Website:** www.nss.org/adastra. **Contact:** Gary Barnhard, editor-in-chief. **90% freelance written.** "We publish non-technical, lively articles about all aspects of international space programs, from shuttle missions to planetary probes to plans for the future and commercial space." Estab. 1989. Circ. 25,000. Byline given. Pays on publication. No kill fee. Responds only when interested. Sample copy for 9x12 SASE.

NONFICTION Needs book excerpts, essays, exposé, general interest, interview, opinion, photo feature, technical. No science fiction or UFO stories. Query with published clips. Length: 1,000-2,400 words. **Pays $200-500 for features.**

PHOTOS State availability. Identification of subjects required. Reviews color prints, digital, JPEG-IS, GISS. Negotiates pay.

TIPS "We require mss to be in Word or text file formats. Know the field of space technology, programs, and policy. Know the players. Look for fresh angles. And, please, know how to write!"

$$$$ AMERICAN ARCHAEOLOGY

The Archaeological Conservancy, 5301 Central Ave. NE, #902, Albuquerque NM 87108. (505)266-9668. **Fax:** (505)266-0311. **E-mail:** tacmag@nm.net. **Website:** www.americanarchaeology.org. **Contact:** Michael Bawaya, editor; Vicki Singer, art director. **60% freelance written.** Quarterly magazine. "We're a popular archaeology magazine. Our readers are very interested in this science. Our features cover important digs, prominent archaeologists, and most any aspect of the science. We only cover North America." Estab. 1997. Circ. 35,000. Byline given. Pays on acceptance. Offers 20% kill fee. Publishes ms an average of 3 months after acceptance. Editorial lead time 3 months. Accepts queries by mail, e-mail, fax. Responds in 3 weeks to queries. Responds in 1 month to mss

NONFICTION No fiction, poetry, humor. **Buys 15 mss/year.** Query with published clips. Length: 1,500-3,000 words. **Pays $1,000-2,000.** Pays expenses of writers on assignment.

PHOTOS State availability. Identification of subjects required. Reviews transparencies, prints. Pays $50 and up for occasional stock images; assigns work by project (pay varies); negotiable. **Pays on acceptance.** Credit line given. Buys one-time rights. Offers $400-600/photo shoot. Negotiates payment individually.

TIPS "Read the magazine. Features must have a considerable amount of archaeological detail."

⊛⊛⊛⊛ ARCHAEOLOGY

Archaeological Institute of America, 36-36 33rd St., Long Island NY 11106. (718)472-3050. **Fax:** (718)472-3051. **E-mail:** cvalentino@archaeology.org. **E-mail:** editorial@archaeology.org. **Website:** www.archaeology.org. **Contact:** Editor-in-chief. **50% freelance written.** *ARCHAEOLOGY* combines worldwide archaeological findings with photography, specially rendered maps, drawings, and charts. Covers current excavations and recent discoveries, and includes personality profiles, technology updates, adventure, travel and studies of ancient cultures. "*ARCHAEOLOGY* magazine is a publication of the Archaeological Institute of America, a 130-year-old nonprofit organization. The magazine has been published continuously for more than 60 years. We have a total audience of nearly 750,000, mostly in the United States and Canada. Our readership is a combination of the general public, enthusiastic amateurs, and scholars in the field. Publishing bimonthly, we bring our readers all the exciting aspects of archaeology: adventure, discovery, culture, history, technology, and travel. Authors include both professional journalists and professional archaeologists. If you are a scientist interested in writing about your research for *ARCHAEOLOGY*, see tips and suggestions on writing for a general audience online." Estab. 1948. Circ. 750,000. Byline given. Pays on

acceptance. Offers 25% kill fee. Submit seasonal material 6 months in advance. Accepts queries by mail, e-mail, fax. Accepts simultaneous submissions. Sample copy and writer's guidelines free. Guidelines online. Request photographer's sample copy for $6 through paypal to scribblesbyshannon@yahoo.com.

NONFICTION Needs essays, general interest. "Our reviews department looks for short (250- to 500-word) articles on museums, books, television shows, movies, websites, and games of interest to our readers. While the material reviewed may not be purely archaeological in nature, it should have a strong archaeological element to it. Reviews should not simply summarize the material, but provide a critical evaluation." **Buys 6 mss/year.** Query preferred. "Preliminary queries should be no more than 1 or 2 pages (500 words max.) in length and may be sent to the Editor-in-Chief by mail or via e-mail to editorial@archaeology.org. We do not accept telephone queries. Check our online index and search to make sure that we have not already published a similar article. Your query should tell us the following: who you are, why you are qualified to cover the subject, how you will cover the subject (with an emphasis on narrative structure, new knowledge, etc.), and why our readers would be interested in the subject." Length: 1,000-3,000 words. **Pays $2,000 maximum.** Sometimes pays expenses of writers on assignment.

PHOTOS Clips and credentials are helpful. While illustrations are not the sole responsibility of the author, it helps to give us a sense of how the article could be illustrated; if possible, e-mail an example of 2 or 3 images that might accompany the article (noting where and from whom such images may be obtained). Please do not e-mail unusually large images or too many images at a time; we will request additional ones if needed. Please do not mail us unsolicited CDs, transparencies, or slides as they will not be returned. If you do not have access to images, referrals to professional photographers with relevant material are appreciated. Send photos. Identification of subjects, Reviews 4x5 color transparencies, 35mm color slides.

COLUMNS/DEPARTMENTS Insider is a piece of about 2,500 words dealing with subject matter with which the author has an intimate, personal interest. **Conversation** is a one-page interview in a Q&A format with someone who has made a considerable impact on the field of archaeology or has done something unusual or intriguing. **Letter From..** is an account of a personal experience involving a particular topic or site. "Letters" have included a visit to an alien-archaeology theme park, the account of an archaeologist caught in a civil war, and an overnight stay with the guards at Angkor Wat. "Letters" are usually about 2,500 to 3,000 words in length. **Artifact** is the last editorial page of the magazine. Its purpose is to introduce the reader to a single artifact that reveals something surprising about a site or an historical event. Unusual artifacts recently excavated are preferred and visuals must be of the highest quality. The writer must explain the archaeological context, date, site found, etc., as well as summarize the artifact's importance in about 200 words or less. First person accounts by the actual excavators or specialists are preferred, although exceptions are be made.

TIPS "We reach nonspecialist readers interested in art, science, history, and culture. Our reports, regional commentaries, and feature-length articles introduce readers to recent developments in archaeology worldwide."

⊖⊖ ASTRONOMY

Kalmbach Publishing, 21027 Crossroads Circle, P.O. Box 1612, Waukesha WI 53187-1612. (800)533-6644. **Fax:** (262)798-6468. **Website:** www.astronomy.com. David J. Eicher, editor. **Contact:** LuAnn Williams Belter, art director (for art and photography). **50% of articles submitted and written by science writers; includes commissioned and unsolicited.** Monthly magazine covering the science and hobby of astronomy. "Half of our magazine is for hobbyists (who are active observers of the sky); the other half is directed toward armchair astronomers who are intrigued by the science." Estab. 1973. Circ. 108,000. Byline given. Pays on acceptance. Does pay a kill fee, although rarely used. Responds in 1 month to queries. Responds in 3 months to mss. on website.

NONFICTION Needs book excerpts, new product, announcements, photo feature, technical, space, astronomy. **Buys 75 mss/year.** Please query on all article ideas Length: 500-3,000 words. **Pays $100-1,000.**

TIPS "Submitting to *Astronomy* could be tough—take a look at how technical astronomy is. But if someone is a physics teacher or an amateur astronomer, he or she might want to study the magazine for a year to see the sorts of subjects and approaches we use, and then submit a proposal. Submission guidelines available online."

⊖⊖⊖⊖ BIOSCIENCE

American Institute of Biological Sciences, 1900 Campus Commons Dr., Suite 200, Reston VA 20191. (202)628-1500. **Fax:** (202)628-1509. **E-mail:** tbeardsley@aibs.org. **Website:** www.aibs.org. **Contact:** Dr. Timothy M. Beardsley, editor-in-chief. **5% freelance written.** Monthly peer-reviewed scientific journal covering organisms from molecules to the environment. "We contract professional science writers to write features on assigned topics, including organismal biology and ecology, but excluding biomedical topics." Estab. 1951. Byline given. Publishes ms an average of 3 months after acceptance. Editorial lead time 2 months. Accepts queries by e-mail. Responds in 2-3 weeks to queries. Sample copy on website. Guidelines free.

NONFICTION Does not want biomedical topics. **Buys 10 mss/year.** Query. Length: 1,500-3,000 words. **Pays $1,500-3,000.** Sometimes pays expenses of writers on assignment.

TIPS "Queries can cover any area of biology. The story should appeal to a wide scientific audience, yet be accessible to the interested (and somewhat science-literate) layperson. *BioScience* tends to favor research and policy trend stories and avoids personality profiles."

⊖⊖⊖ CHEMICAL HERITAGE

Chemical Heritage Foundation (CHF), 315 Chestnut St., Philadelphia PA 19106. (215)925-2222. **E-mail:** editor@chemheritage.org. **Website:** www.chemheritage.org. **40% freelance written.** The magazine is published three times per year. *Chemical Heritage* reports on the history of the chemical and molecular sciences and industries, on CHF activities, and on other activities of interest to our readers. Estab. 1982. Circ. 20,000. Byline given. Pays on acceptance. Publishes ms an average of 6-12 months after acceptance. Editorial lead time 4 months. Accepts queries by mail, e-mail, phone. Responds in 1 month to queries and to mss. Sample copy free.

NONFICTION Needs book excerpts, essays, historical, interview. No exposés or excessively technical material. Many of our readers are highly educated professionals, but they may not be familiar with, for example, specific chemical processes. **Buys 3-5 mss/year.** Query. Length: 1,000-3,500 words. **Pays 50¢ to $1/word.**

PHOTOS State availability. Captions required. Offers no additional payment for photos accepted with ms.

COLUMNS/DEPARTMENTS Book reviews: 200 or 750 words; CHF collections: 300-500 words; policy: 1,000 words; personal remembrances: 750 words; profiles of CHF awardees and oral history subjects: 600-900 words: buys 3-5 mms/year. **Buys 10 mss/ year.** Query.

TIPS "CHF attends exhibits at many scientific trade shows and scholarly conferences. Our representatives are always happy to speak to potential authors genuinely interested in the past, present and future of chemistry. We are a good venue for scholars who want to reach a broader audience or for science writers who want to bolster their scholarly credentials."

CHEMMATTERS

1155 16th St., NW, Washington DC 20036. (202)872-6164. **Fax:** (202)833-7732. **E-mail:** chemmatters@acs.org. **Website:** www.acs.org/chemmatters. **Contact:** Pat Pages, editor; Cornithia Harris, art director. Covers content covered in a standard high school chemistry textbook. Estab. 1983. Pays on acceptance. Publishes ms 6 months after acceptance. Accepts queries by mail, e-mail. Accepts simultaneous submissions. Responds to queries/mss in 2 weeks. Sample copies free for 10x13 SASE and 3 first-class stamps. Writer's guidelines free for SASE (available as e-mail attachment upon request).

NONFICTION Query with published clips. **Pays $500-1,000 for article. Additional payment for mss/ illustration packages and for photos accompanying articles.**

TIPS "Be aware of the content covered in a standard high school chemistry textbook. Choose themes and topics that are timely, interesting, fun, *and* that relate to the content and concepts of the first-year chemistry course. Articles should describe real people involved with real science. Best articles feature young people making a difference or solving a problem."

⊗⊗⊗⊗ INVENTORS DIGEST

Inventors Digest, LLC, 520 Elliot St., Suite 200, Charlotte NC 28202. (704)369-7312. **Fax:** (704)333-5115. **E-mail:** info@inventorsdigest.com. **Website:** www.inventorsdigest.com/about-us. **50% freelance written.** Monthly magazine covering inventions, technology, engineering, intellectual property issues. Inventors Digest is committed to educating and inspiring entry- and enterprise-level inventors and professional innovators. As the leading print and online publication for the innovation culture, *Inventors Digest* delivers useful, entertaining and cutting-edge information to help its readers succeed. Estab. 1983. Circ. 40,000. Byline given. Pays on publication. Offers 40% kill fee. Publishes ms an average of 2 months after acceptance. Editorial lead time 2 months. Submit seasonal material 4 months in advance. Accepts queries by mail, e-mail. Responds in 3 weeks to queries; 1 month to mss. Sample copy available online. Guidelines free.

NONFICTION Needs book excerpts, historical, how-to, secure a patent, find a licensing manufacturer, avoid scams, inspirational, interview, new product, opinion, (does not mean letters to the editor), personal experience, technical. Special issues: Our editorial calendar is available at our website, http://inventorsdigest.com/images/Inventors%20Digest%20Media%20Kit_R08.pdf. "We don't want poetry. No stories that talk about readers—stay away from 'one should do X' construction. Nothing that duplicates what you can read elsewhere." **Buys 4 mss/year.** Query. Length: 2,500 words. **Pays $50-TBD for assigned articles. Pays $50-TBD for unsolicited articles.**

PHOTOS Contact: Mike Drummond. State availability. Identification of subjects required. Reviews GIF/JPEG files. Negotiates payment individually.

COLUMNS/DEPARTMENTS Contact: Brandon Phillips. Cover (the most important package-puts a key topic in compelling context), 2,000-3,000 words; Radar (news/product snippets), 1,200; Bookshelf (book reviews), 700; Pro Bono (legal issues), 850; Profile (human interest stories on inventors and innovators), BrainChild (celebration of young inventors and innovators), FirstPerson (inventors show how they've overcome hurdles), 1,000; MeetingRoom (learn secrets to success of best inventor groups in the country), 900; TalkBack (Q&A with manufacturers, retailers, etc. in the innovation industry), Five Questions With.. (a conversation with some of the brightest and most controversial minds in Technology, manufacturing, academia and other fields), 800. **Buys 4 mss/year mss/ year.** Query. **Pays $20.**

TIPS "We prefer e-mail. If it's a long piece (more than 2,000 words), send a synopsis, captivating us in 300 words. Put 'Article Query' in the subject line. A great story should have conflict or obstacles to overcome. Show us something surprising and why we should care, and put it in context. Sweep, color, scene and strong character anecdotes are important. If there's no conflict-moral, institutional, cultural, obstacles to overcome-there's no story. If you send it in analog form, write to: *Inventors Digest*, Article Query, P.O. Box 36761, Charlotte, NC 28236."

SCIENCE EDITOR

Council of Science Editors, 10200 W. 44th Ave., Suite 304, Wheat Ridge CO 80033. (720)881-6046. **Fax:** (303)422-8894. **E-mail:** pkbaskin@gmail.com. **Website:** www.councilscienceeditors.org. **Contact:** Patty Baskin, editor. *Science Editor*, published quarterly, is "a forum for the exchange of information and ideas among professionals concerned with publishing in the sciences." Wants "up to 90 typeset lines of poetry on the intersection of science (including but not limited to biomedicine) and communication. Geared toward adult scholars, writers, and editors in communication and the sciences." Estab. 2000. Publishes ms 3-6 months after acceptance. Submit seasonal material 9 months in advance. Responds in 3-6 weeks. Guidelines by e-mail.

POETRY Submit up to 3 poems at a time, maximum 90 lines. Does not consider previously published poems or simultaneous submissions. Accepts e-mail submissions (pasted into the body of message), no fax or disk. "Submit both cover letter and poetry by e-mail only in the body of the same e-mail message, with no attachments." Sometimes comments on rejected poems. "*Science Editor* is posted online. Issues at least 1 year old are openly displayed accessible. Issues less than 1 year old can be accessed only by Council of Science Editors members." Rights revert to poet upon publication. **Pays 3 contributor's copies.**

🟦🟦🟦🟦 SCIENTIFIC AMERICAN

75 Varick St., 9th Floor, New York NY 10013-1917. (212)451-8200. **E-mail:** editors@sciam.com. **Website:** www.sciam.com. **Contact:** Mariette DiChristina, editor-in-chief. Monthly magazine covering developments and topics of interest in the world of science. "*Scientific American* brings its readers directly to the wellspring of exploration and technological innovation. The magazine specializes in first-hand accounts by the people who actually do the work. Their personal experience provides an authoritative perspective on future growth. Over 100 of our authors have won Nobel Prizes. Complementing those articles are regular departments written by *Scientific American*'s staff of professional journalists, all specialists in their fields. *Scientific American* is the authoritative source of advance information. Authors are the first to report on important breakthroughs, because they're the

people who make them. It all goes back to *Scientific American*'s corporate mission: to link those who use knowledge with those who create it." Estab. 1845. Circ. 710,000. Byline given. Pays on publication. No kill fee. Guidelines available on website.

NONFICTION Query before submitting. **Pays $1/word average.** Pays expenses of writers on assignment.

⊘ 🟦🟦🟦🟦 STARDATE

University of Texas, 1 University Station, A2100, Austin TX 78712. (512)471-5285. **Fax:** (512)471-5060. **Website:** http://stardate.org. **80% freelance written.** Bimonthly magazine covering astronomy. "*StarDate* is written for people with an interest in astronomy and what they see in the night sky, but no special astronomy training or background." Estab. 1975. Circ. 10,000. Byline given. Pays on acceptance. Offers 25% kill fee. Publishes ms an average of 4 months after acceptance. Editorial lead time 6 months. Submit seasonal material 6 months in advance. Accepts queries by mail, e-mail, fax. Responds in 6 weeks to queries. Sample copy and writer's guidelines free.

NONFICTION Needs general interest, historical, interview, photo feature, technical, travel, research in astronomy. No first-person; first stargazing experiences; paranormal. **Buys 8 mss/year.** Query with published clips. Length: 1,500-3,000 words. **Pays $500-1,500.** Sometimes pays expenses of writers on assignment.

PHOTOS Send photos. Identification of subjects required. Reviews transparencies, prints. Negotiates payment individually.

COLUMNS/DEPARTMENTS Astro News (short astronomy news item), 250 words. **Buys 6 mss/year.** Query with published clips. **Pays $100-200.**

TIPS "Keep up to date with current astronomy news and space missions. No technical jargon."

🟦🟦 WEATHERWISE

Taylor & Francis Group, 325 Chestnut St., Suite 800, Philadelphia PA 19106. (215)625-8900. **E-mail:** margaret.benner@taylorandfrancis.com. **Website:** www.weatherwise.org. **Contact:** Margaret Benner Smidt, editor-in-chief. **75% freelance written.** Bimonthly magazine covering weather and meteorology. "*Weatherwise* is America's only magazine about the weather. Our readers range from professional weathercasters and scientists to basement-bound hobbyists, but all share a common interest in craving information about weather as it relates to the atmospheric sciences, technology, history, culture, society, art, etc." Estab. 1948. Circ. 11,000. Byline given. Pays on publication. No kill fee. Publishes ms an average of 6 months after acceptance. Editorial lead time 6-9 months. Submit seasonal material 9 months in advance. Accepts queries by mail, e-mail, fax, phone. Responds in 2 months to queries. Guidelines available online.

NONFICTION Needs book excerpts, essays, general interest, historical, how-to, interview, new product, opinion, personal experience, photo feature, technical, travel. Special issues: Photo Contest (September/October deadline June 2). No blow-by-blow accounts of the biggest storm to ever hit your backyard. **Buys 15-18 mss/year.** Query with published clips. Length: 2,000-3,000 words. **Pays $200-500 for assigned articles. Pays $0-300 for unsolicited articles.**

PHOTOS Captions, identification of subjects required. Reviews contact sheets, negatives, prints, electronic files. Negotiates payment individually.

COLUMNS/DEPARTMENTS Weather Front (news, trends), 300-400 words; Weather Talk (folklore and humor), 650-1,000 words. **Buys 12-15 mss/year.** Query with published clips. **Pays $0-200.**

TIPS "Don't query us wanting to write about broad types like the Greenhouse Effect, the Ozone Hole, El Niño, etc. Although these are valid topics, you can bet you won't be able to cover it all in 2,000 words. With these topics and all others, find the story within the story. And whether you're writing about a historical storm or new technology, be sure to focus on the human element—the struggles, triumphs, and other anecdotes of individuals."

SCIENCE FICTION, FANTASY AND HORROR

ANALOG SCIENCE FICTION & FACT

Dell Magazines, 267 Broadway, 4th Floor, New York NY 10007-2352. (212)686-7188. **Fax:** (212)686-7414. **E-mail:** analog@dellmagazines.com. **Website:** www. analogsf.com. **Contact:** Dr. Stanley Schmidt, editor. **100% freelance written. Eager to work with new/unpublished writers.** Monthly magazine for general future-minded audience. Estab. 1930. Circ. 50,000. Byline given. Pays on acceptance. No kill fee. Publishes ms an average of 10 months after acceptance. Accepts queries by mail. Sample copy for $5. Guidelines available online.

Fiction published in *Analog* has won numerous Nebula and Hugo Awards. Fiction published in *Analog* has won numerous Nebula and Hugo Awards.

NONFICTION Buys 11 mss/year. Send complete ms. 5,000 words **Pays 6¢/word.**

FICTION "Basically, we publish science fiction stories. That is, stories in which some aspect of future science or technology is so integral to the plot that, if that aspect were removed, the story would collapse. The science can be physical, sociological, or psychological. The technology can be anything from electronic engineering to biogenetic engineering. But the stories must be strong and realistic, with believable people doing believable things—no matter how fantastic the background might be." Needs science fiction, hard science/technological, soft/sociological. No fantasy or stories in which the scientific background is implausible or plays no essential role. **Buys 60-100 unsolicited mss/year.** Submit via online submissions manager. Prefers lengths between 2,000 and 7,000 words for shorts, 10,000-20,000 words for novelettes, and 40,000-80,000 for serials **Analog pays 6-8 cents per word for short stories up to 7,500 words, $450-600 for stories between 7,500 and 10,000 words, and 5-6 cents per word for longer material.**

TIPS "I'm looking for irresistibly entertaining stories that make me think about things in ways I've never done before. Read several issues to get a broad feel for our tastes, but don't try to imitate what you read." "In your query give clear indication of central ideas and themes and general nature of story line—and what is distinctive or unusual about it. We have no hard-and-fast editorial guidelines, because science fiction is such a broad field that I don't want to inhibit a new writer's thinking by imposing 'Thou Shalt Not's.' Besides, a really good story can make an editor swallow his preconceived taboos. I want the best work I can get, regardless of who wrote it—and I need new writers. So I work closely with new writers who show definite promise, but of course it's impossible to do this with every new writer. No occult or fantasy."

APEX MAGAZINE

Apex Publications, LLC, P.O. Box 24323, Lexington KY 40524. (859)312-3974. **E-mail:** jason@apexbookcompany.com. **Website:** www.apexbookcompany. com. **100% freelance written.** Monthly e-zine publishing dark speculative fiction. "An elite repository for new and seasoned authors with an other-worldly interest in the unquestioned and slightly bizarre parts of the universe." Estab. 2004. Circ. 10,000 unique visits per month. Byline given. Pays on publication. Offers 30% kill fee. Publishes ms an average of 2 months after acceptance. Editorial lead time 2 months. Submit seasonal material 2 months in advance. Accepts queries by e-mail. Responds in 20-30 days to queries and to mss. Sample copy available online. Guidelines available online.

FICTION "We publish dark speculative fiction with horror elements. Our readers are those that enjoy speculative fiction with dark themes." Needs science fiction, dark speculative fiction. Does not want monster fiction. **Buys 24 mss/year.** Send complete ms with cover letter. Include estimated word count, brief bio. Length: 100-7,500 words. **Pays $20-200.**

TIPS "See submissions guidelines at submissions@ apexdigest.com."

ASCENT ASPIRATIONS

1560 Arbutus Dr., Nanoose Bay BC C9P 9C8 Canada. **E-mail:** ascentaspirations@shaw.ca. **Website:** www. ascentaspirations.ca. **Contact:** David Fraser, editor. E-zine specializing in short fiction (all genres) and poetry, spoken work videos, essays, visual art. "*Ascent Aspirations* magazine publishes monthly online and once in print. The print issues are operated as contests. Please refer to current guidelines before submitting. *Ascent Aspirations* is a quality electronic publication dedicated to the promotion and encouragement of aspiring writers of any genre. The focus however is toward interesting experimental writing in dark mainstream, literary, science fiction, fantasy and horror. Poetry can be on any theme. Essays need to be unique, current and have social, philosophical commentary." Estab. 1997. Accepts simultaneous, multiple submissions, and reprints. Responds in 1 week to queries; 3 months to mss. Sometimes comments on rejected mss. Guidelines by e-mail or on website.

NONFICTION Needs literary essays, literary criticism. Query by e-mail with Word attachment. Include estimated word count, brief bio, and list of publications. "If you have to submit by mail because it is your only avenue, provide a SASE with either International Coupons or Canadian stamps only." Length: 1,000 words or less. **"No payment at this time."**

FICTION Needs erotica, experimental, fantasy (space fantasy), feminist, horror (dark fantasy, futuristic,

psychological, supernatural), literary, mainstream, mystery/suspense, New Age, psychic/supernatural/ occult, science fiction (hard science/technological, soft/sociological). Query by e-mail with Word attachment. Include estimated word count, brief bio, and list of publications. "If you have to submit by mail because it is your only avenue, provide a SASE with either International Coupons or Canadian stamps only." Length: 1,000 words or less. Publishes short shorts. **"No payment at this time."**

POETRY Submit 1-5 poems at a time. Considers previously published poems and simultaneous submissions. Prefers e-mail submissions (pasted into body of message or as attachment in Word); no disk submissions. "If you must submit by postal mail because it is your only avenue, provide a SASE with IRCs or Canadian stamps." Reads submissions on a regular basis year round. "We accept all forms of poetry on any theme. Poetry needs to be unique and touch the reader emotionally with relevant human, social, and philosophical imagery." Considers poetry by children and teens. Does not want poetry "that focuses on mainstream overtly religious verse." **"No payment at this time."**

TIPS "Short fiction should, first of all tell, a good story, take the reader to new and interesting imaginary or real places. Short fiction should use language lyrically and effectively, be experimental in either form or content and take the reader into realms where they can analyze and think about the human condition. Write with passion for your material, be concise and economical and let the reader work to unravel your story. In terms of editing, always proofread to the point where what you submit is the best it possibly can be. Never be discouraged if your work is not accepted; it may just not be the right fit for a current publication."

ASIMOV'S SCIENCE FICTION

Dell Magazine Fiction Group, 267 Broadway, 4th Floor, New York NY 10007. (212)686-7188. **Fax:** (212)686-7414. **E-mail:** asimovssf@dellmagazines. com. **Website:** www.asimovs.com. **Contact:** Sheila Williams, editor; Victoria Green, senior art director; June Levine, associate art director. **98% freelance written. Works with a small number of new/unpublished writers each year.** Magazine published 10 times/year, including 2 double issues. "Magazine consists of science fiction and fantasy stories for adults and young adults. Publishes the best short science fiction available." Estab. 1977. Circ. 50,000. Pays on acceptance. No kill fee. Publishes ms an average of 6-12 months after acceptance. Accepts queries by mail. Responds in 2 months to queries. Responds in 3 months to mss. Sample copy for $5. Guidelines for #10 SASE or online.

FICTION "Science fiction primarily. Some fantasy and humor but no sword and sorcery. No explicit sex or violence that isn't integral to the story. It is best to read a great deal of material in the genre to avoid the use of some very old ideas. Send complete ms and SASE with *all* submissions." Needs fantasy, science fiction, hard science, soft sociological. No horror or psychic/supernatural. Would like to see more hard science fiction. **Buys 10 mss/issue mss/year.** Length: 750-15,000 words. **Pays 5-8¢/word.**

POETRY 40 lines maximum. **Pays $1/line.**

TIPS "In general, we're looking for 'character-oriented' stories, those in which the characters, rather than the science, provide the main focus for the reader's interest. Serious, thoughtful, yet accessible fiction will constitute the majority of our purchases, but there's always room for the humorous as well. Borderline fantasy is fine, but no Sword & Sorcery, please. A good overview would be to consider that all fiction is written to examine or illuminate some aspect of human existence, but that in science fiction the backdrop you work against is the size of the universe. Please do not send us submissions on disk or via e-mail. We've bought some of our best stories from people who have never sold a story before."

CHIZINE: TREATMENT OF LIGHT AND SHADE IN WORDS

Canada. "Subtle, sophisticated dark fiction with a literary bent." Quarterly. Estab. 1997. Accepts queries by e-mail. Responds in 3 months to mss. Guidelines on website.

FICTION Needs experimental, fantasy, horror, mystery, science fiction. Does not want "tropes of vampires, werewolves, mummies, monsters, or anything that's been done to death." Send complete ms with cover letter.

POETRY **Contact:** Brett Alexander Savory. "Subtle, sophisticated dark fiction with a literary bent." Quarterly. Experimental, fantasy, horror (dark fantasy, futuristic, psychological, supernatural), literary, mystery, science fiction (soft/sociological). Does not want "tropes of vampires, werewolves, mummies, monsters, or anything that's been done to death."

HORROR HOUND

P.O. Box 710, Milford OH 45150. **E-mail:** support@horrorhound.com. **Website:** www.horrorhound.com. **Contact:** Nathan Hanneman, editor. *Horror Hound* offers retrospectives, film facts, exclusive photos, interviews, fan contributions, a look at horror fan lifestyles, original art, theme based issues, and more. "Our goals is to offer the most fan-friendly publication available at the best price to the readers with enough incentives in each issue to keep you coming back for more."

NONFICTION Query first.

HUNGUR MAGAZINE

P.O. Box 782, Cedar Rapids IA 52406-0782. **E-mail:** hungurmagazine@yahoo.com. **Website:** www.samsdotpublishing.com. **Contact:** Terrie Leigh Relf, editor. *Hungur Magazine*, published biannually, features "stories and poems about vampires, and especially about vampires on other worlds." Prefers a "decadent literary style." Estab. 2004. Pays on publication. Publishes ms 4-6 months after acceptance. Responds in 2-3 weeks. Guidelines online at www.samsdotpublishing.com/HungurGL.htm.

NONFICTION Needs essays, reviews. No simultaneous submissions. Accepts e-mail submissions (pasted into body of message); no disk submissions. Reads submissions year round. Length: 2,000 words maximum. **Pays $10 per article; $7 per review.**

REPRINTS Pays $5 per story reprints; $3 per article reprint; $2 per poem reprints.

FICTION Needs vampire stories. No simultaneous submissions. Accepts e-mail submissions (pasted into body of message); no disk submissions. Reads submissions year round. Length: 2,500-6,000 words. Flash fiction: 1,000 words maximum. **Pays $12 for stories; $4 for flash fiction.**

POETRY Submit up to 5 poems at a time. No simultaneous submissions. Accepts e-mail submissions (pasted into body of message); no disk submissions. Reads submissions year round. Reviews books and chapbooks of poetry. Send materials for review consideration to Tyree Campbell. Lines/poem: prefers less than 100. **Pays $4/poem and 1 contributor's copy.**

$ LEADING EDGE

4087 JKB, Provo UT 84602. **E-mail:** editor@leadingedgemagazine.com; fiction@leadingedgemagazine.

com; art@leadingedgemagazine.com. **Website:** www. leadingedgemagazine.com. **Contact:** Nyssa Silvester, senior editor. **90% freelance written.** Semiannual magazine covering science fiction and fantasy. "We strive to encourage developing and established talent and provide high quality speculative fiction to our readers." Does not accept mss with sex, excessive violence, or profanity. "*Leading Edge* is a magazine dedicated to new and upcoming talent in the field of science fiction and fantasy." Estab. 1980. Circ. 200. Byline given. Pays on publication. No kill fee. Publishes ms an average of 2-4 months after acceptance. Responds in 2-4 months to mss. Single copy: $5.95; subscription: $10 (2 issues), $20 (4 issues), $27.50 (6 issues). Guidelines available online at website.

FICTION Needs fantasy, science fiction. **Buys 14-16 mss/year mss/year.** Send complete ms with cover letter and SASE. Include estimated word count. Length: 15,000 words maximum. **Pays 1¢/word; $10 minimum.**

POETRY Needs avant-garde, haiku, light verse, traditional. "Publishes 2-4 poems per issue. Poetry should reflect both literary value and popular appeal and should deal with science fiction- or fantasy-related themes." Submit 1 or more poems at a time. No e-mail submissions. Cover letter is preferred. Include name, address, phone number, length of poem, title, and type of poem at the top of each page. Please include SASE with every submission." Submit maximum 10 poems. Pays $10 for first 4 pages; $1.50/each subsequent page.

TIPS "Buy a sample issue to know what is currently selling in our magazine. Also, make sure to follow the writer's guidelines when submitting."

THE MAGAZINE OF FANTASY & SCIENCE FICTION

P.O. Box 3447, Hoboken NJ 07030. (201) 876-2551. **E-mail:** fandsf@aol.com. **Website:** www.fandsf.com. **Contact:** Gordon Van Gelder, editor. **100% freelance written.** "*The Magazine of Fantasy and Science Fiction* publishes various types of science fiction and fantasy short stories and novellas, making up about 80% of each issue. The balance of each issue is devoted to articles about science fiction, a science column, book and film reviews, cartoons, and competitions." Bimonthly. Estab. 1949. Circ. 40,000. Byline given. Pays on acceptance. No kill fee. Publishes ms an average of 9-12 months after acceptance. Submit seasonal material 8 months in advance. Responds in 2 months to queries.

Sample copy for $6. Guidelines for SASE, by e-mail or website.

COLUMNS/DEPARTMENTS Curiosities (Reviews of odd & obscure books), 270 words max. Accepts 6 mss/year. Query. **Pays $-$50.**

FICTION Contact: Gordon Van Gelder, Editor. "Prefers character-oriented stories. We receive a lot of fantasy fiction, but never enough science fiction." Needs adventure, fantasy, horror, space fantasy, sword & sorcery, dark fantasy, futuristic, psychological, supernatural, science fiction, hard science/technological, soft/sociological. **Buys Accepts 60-90/mss. mss/year.** No electronic submissions. Send complete Ms. Length: up to 25,000 words **Pays 7-10¢/word.**

POETRY *The Magazine of Fantasy & Science Fiction*, published bimonthy, is "one of the longest-running magazines devoted to the literature of the fantastic." Wants only poetry that deals with the fantastic or the science-fictional. Has published poetry by Rebecca Kavaler, Elizabeth Bear, Sophie M. White, and Robert Frazier. "I buy poems very infrequently—just when one hits me right." **Pays $50/poem and 2 contributor's copies. Acquires first North American serial rights.**

TIPS "Good storytelling makes a submission stand out. Regarding manuscripts, a well-prepared manuscript (i.e., one that follows the traditional format, like that describted here: www.sfwa.org/writing/vonda/vonda.htm) stands out more than any gimmicks. Read an issue of the magazine before submitting. New writers should keep their submissions under 15,000 words—we rarely publish novellas by new writers."

MORPHEUS TALES

116 Muriel St., London N1 9QU United Kingdom. **E-mail:** morpheustales@blueyonder.co.uk. **Website:** www.morpheustales.com. **Contact:** Adam Bradley, publisher. **100% freelance written.** Quarterly magazine covering horror, science fiction, fantasy. "We publish the best in horror, science fiction and fantasy—both fiction and nonfiction." Estab. 2008. Circ. 1,000. No kill fee. Publishes ms an average of 18 months after acceptance. Editorial lead time 3 months. Submit seasonal material 6 months in advance. Accepts queries by e-mail. Responds in 1 week to queries. Responds in 1 month to mss. Sample copy for $7. Guidelines available online.

NONFICTION Needs book excerpts, essays, general interest, how-to, inspirational, interview, new product, opinion, photo feature, Letters to the Editor. "All material must be based on horror, science fiction, or fantasy genre." **Buys 6 mss/year.** Query. Length: 1,000-3,000 words. Sometimes pays expenses of writers on assignment.

PHOTOS Model and property release are required.

FICTION Needs experimental, fantasy, horror, mystery, novel concepts, science fiction, serialized, suspense. **Buys 20 mss/year.** Send complete ms. Length: 800-3,000 words.

ON SPEC

P.O. Box 4727, Station South, Edmonton AB T6E 5G6 Canada. (780)628-7121. **E-mail:** onspec@onspec.ca. **E-mail:** onspecmag@gmail.com. **Website:** www.on-spec.ca. **95% freelance written.** Quarterly magazine covering Canadian science fiction, fantasy and horror. "We publish speculative fiction and poetry by new and established writers, with a strong preference for Canadian authored works." Estab. 1989. Circ. 2,000. Byline given. Pays on acceptance. No kill fee. Publishes ms an average of 6-18 months after acceptance. Editorial lead time 6 months. Accepts queries by mail. Accepts simultaneous submissions. Responds in 2 weeks to queries; 6 months after deadline to mss. Sample copy for $8. Guidelines for #10 SASE or on website.

FICTION Needs fantasy, horror, science fiction, magic realism, ghost stories, fairy stories. No media tie-in or shaggy-alien stories. No condensed or excerpted novels, religious/inspirational stories, fairy tales. **Buys 50 mss/year.** Send complete ms. Electronic submissions preferred. Length: 1,000-6,000 words.

POETRY Needs avant-garde, free verse. No rhyming or religious material. Buys 6 poems/year. Submit maximum 10 poems. Length: 4-100 lines. **Pays $50 and 1 contributor's copy.**

TIPS "We want to see stories with plausible characters, a well-constructed, consistent, and vividly described setting, a strong plot and believable emotions; characters must show us (not tell us) their emotional responses to each other and to the situation and/or challenge they face. Also: don't send us stories written for television. We don't like media tie-ins, so don't watch TV for inspiration! Read, instead! Strong preference given to submissions by Canadians."

SCARY MONSTERS MAGAZINE

Dennis Druktenis Publishing and Mail Order, Inc., 348 Jocelyn Place, Highwood IL 60040. **E-mail:** scaremail@aol.com. **Website:** www.scarymonsters-magazine.com. Horror magazine specializing in scary monsters.

NONFICTION Query first.

SCREEM MAGAZINE

41 Mayer St., Wilkes Barre PA 18702. **E-mail:** screemagazine@msn.com. **Website:** www.screemag.com. Magazine covering everything related to horror. Sample copy online at website. Back copies between $7.95 and $20.

NONFICTION Query first.

TALES OF THE TALISMAN

Hadrosaur Productions, P.O. Box 2194, Mesilla Park NM 88047-2194. **E-mail:** hadrosaur@zianet.com. **Website:** www.talesofthetalisman.com. **Contact:** David Lee Summers, editor. **95% freelance written.** Quarterly magazine covering science fiction and fantasy. "*Tales of the Talisman* is a literary science fiction and fantasy magazine. We publish short stories, poetry, and articles with themes related to science fiction and fantasy. Above all, we are looking for thought-provoking ideas and good writing. Speculative fiction set in the past, present, and future is welcome. Likewise, contemporary or historical fiction is welcome as long as it has a mythic or science fictional element. Our target audience includes adult fans of the science fiction and fantasy genres along with anyone else who enjoys thought-provoking and entertaining writing." Estab. 1995. Circ. 200. Byline given. Pays on acceptance. Offers 100% kill fee. Publishes ms an average of 9 months after acceptance. Editorial lead time 9-12 months. Submit seasonal material 1 year in advance. Accepts queries by mail, e-mail. Responds in 1 week to queries. Responds in 1 month to mss. Sample copy for $8. Guidelines available online.

NONFICTION Needs interview, technical, articles on the craft of writing. "We do not want to see unsolicited articles—please query first if you have an idea that you think would be suitable for *Tales of the Talisman*'s audience. We do not want to see negative or derogatory articles." **Buys 1-3 mss/year.** Query. Length: 1,000-3,000 words. **Pays $10 for assigned articles.**

FICTION Contact: David L. Summers, editor. Needs fantasy, space fantasy, sword and sorcery, horror, science fiction, hard science/technological, soft/sociological. "We do not want to see stories with graphic violence. Do not send 'mainstream' fiction with no science fictional or fantastic elements. Do not send stories with copyrighted characters, unless you're the copyright holder." **Buys 25-30 mss/year.** Send complete ms. Length: 1,000-6,000 words. **Pays $6-10.**

POETRY Needs avant-garde, free verse, haiku, light verse, traditional. "Do not send 'mainstream' poetry with no science fictional or fantastic elements. Do not send poems featuring copyrighted characters, unless you're the copyright holder." Buys 24-30 poems/year. Submit maximum 5 poems. Length: 3-50 lines.

SEX

$$ EXOTIC MAGAZINE

X Publishing Inc., 818 SW 3rd Ave., Suite 1324, Portland OR 97204. (503)816-4174. **Fax:** (503)241-7239. **E-mail:** editorial@xmag.com. **Website:** www.xmag.com. Monthly magazine covering adult entertainment and sexuality. "*Exotic* is pro-sex, informative, amusing, mature, and intelligent. Our readers rent and/or buy adult videos, visit strip clubs, and are interested in topics related to the adult entertainment industry and sexuality/culture. Don't talk down to them or fire too far over their heads. Many readers are computer literate and well-traveled. We're also interested in insightful fetish material. We are not a 'hard core' publication." Estab. 1993. Circ. 75,000+. Byline given. Pays 30 days after publication. No kill fee. Accepts queries by fax. Accepts simultaneous submissions. Responds in 2 weeks to queries. Responds in 2 months to mss. Sample copy for SAE with 9x12 envelope and 5 first-class stamps. Guidelines for #10 SASE.

NONFICTION Needs exposé, general interest, historical, how-to, humor, interview, travel, news. No men writing as women, articles about being a "horny guy," or opinion pieces pretending to be fact pieces. **Buys 36 mss/year.** Send complete ms. Length: 1,000-1,800 words. **Pays 10¢/word, up to $150.**

REPRINTS Send typed ms with rights for sale noted and information about when and where the material previously appeared. Pays 100% of amount paid for an original article.

PHOTOS Rarely buys photos. Most provided by staff. Model releases required. Reviews prints. Negotiates payment individually.

FICTION "We are currently overwhelmed with fiction submissions. Please only send fiction if it's really amazing." Needs erotica, slice-of-life vignettes, must present either erotic element or some vice of modern culture, such as gambling, music, dancing. Send complete ms. Length: 1,000-1,800 words. **Pays 10¢/word, up to $150.**

TIPS "Read adult publications, spend time in the clubs doing more than just tipping and drinking. Look for new insights in adult topics. For the industry to continue to improve, those who cover it must also be educated consumers and affiliates. Please type, spell-check and be realistic about how much time the editor can take 'fixing' your ms."

$$$$ HUSTLER

HG Inc., 8484 Wilshire Blvd., Suite 900, Beverly Hills CA 90211. **Fax:** (323)651-2741. **Website:** www.hustler.com. **60% freelance written.** Magazine published 13 times/year. *Hustler* is the no-nonsense men's magazine, one that is willing to speak frankly about society's sacred cows and exposé its hypocrites. The *Hustler* reader expects honest, unflinching looks at hard topicsÃ³sexual, social, political, personality profile, true crime. Estab. 1974. Circ. 750,000. Byline given. Pays as boards ship to printer. Offers 20% kill fee. Publishes ms an average of 3 months after acceptance. Editorial lead time 4 months. Submit seasonal material 6 months in advance. Accepts queries by mail, e-mail, fax. Responds in 2 weeks to queries. Responds in 1 month to mss. Guidelines for #10 SASE.

NONFICTION Needs book excerpts, exposé, general interest, how-to, interview, personal experience, trends. **Buys 30 mss/year.** Query. Length: 3,500-4,000 words. **Pays $1,500.** Sometimes pays expenses of writers on assignment.

COLUMNS/DEPARTMENTS Sex play (some aspect of sex that can be encapsulated in a limited space), 2,500 words. **Buys 13 mss/year.** Send complete ms. **Pays $750.**

FILLERS Jokes and Graffilthy, bathroom wall humor. **Pays $50-100.**

TIPS "Don't try and mimic the *Hustler* style. If a writer needs to be molded into our voice, we'll do a better job of it than he or she will. Avoid first- and second-person voice. The ideal manuscript is quote-rich, visual and is narratively driven by events and viewpoints that push one another forward."

$$$$ ⊘ PENTHOUSE

General Media Communications, 2 Penn Plaza, 11th Floor, New York NY 10121. (212)702-6000. **Fax:** (212)702-6279. **E-mail:** pbloch@pmgi.com. **Website:** www.penthouse.com. Monthly magazine. *Penthouse* is for the sophisticated male. Its editorial scope ranges from outspoken contemporary comment to photography essays of beautiful women. *Penthouse* features interviews with personalities, sociological studies, humor, travel, food and wine, and fashion and grooming for men. Estab. 1969. Circ. 640,000. Byline given. Pays 2 months after acceptance. Offers 25% kill fee. Editorial lead time 3 months. Accepts simultaneous submissions. Guidelines for #10 SASE.

NONFICTION Needs exposé, general interest, to men, interview. **Buys 50 mss/year.** Send complete ms. Length: 4,000-6,000 words. **Pays $3,000.**

COLUMNS/DEPARTMENTS Length: 1,000 words. **Buys 25 mss/year.** Query with published clips or send complete ms. **Pays $500.**

TIPS "Because of our long lead time, writers should think at least 6 months ahead. We take chances. Go against the grain; we like writers who look under rocks and see what hides there."

M.I.P. COMPANY

P.O. Box 27484, Minneapolis MN 55427. (763)544-5915. **Website:** www.mipco.com. **Contact:** Michael Peltsman, editor. Specializes in Russian erotica poetry. "The publisher of controversial Russian literature (erotic poetry)." Estab. 1984. Accepts simultaneous submissions. Responds to queries in 1 month. Seldom comments on rejected poems.

POETRY Considers simultaneous submissions; no previously published poems.

✚ TALENT DRIPS EROTIC LITERARY EZINE

Cleveland OH 44102. (216)799-9775. **E-mail:** talentdripseroticpublishing@yahoo.com. **Website:** http://eroticatalentdrips.wordpress.com. **Contact:** Kimberly Steele, founder. *Talent Drips*, published monthly online, focuses solely on showcasing new erotic fiction. Estab. 2007. Time between acceptance and publication is 2 months. Accepts queries by e-mail. Accepts previously published material and poetry. Accepts simultaneous submissions. Responds in 3 weeks. Guidelines on website.

FICTION Needs erotic short stories. Submit short stories between 5,000 and 10,000 words by e-mail to talentdripseroticpublishing@yahoo.com. Stories should be pasted into body of message. Reads submissions during publication months only. **Pays $15 for each accepted short story.**

POETRY Needs erotic. Submit 2-3 poems at a time, maximum 30 lines each by e-mail to talentdripse-

roticpublishing@yahoo.com. Considers previously published and simultaneous submissions. Accepts e-mail pasted into body of message. Reads submissions during publication months only. **Pays $10 for each accepted poem.**

TIPS "Please read our take on the difference between *erotica* and *pornography*; it's on the website. *Talent Drips* does not accept pornography. And please keep poetry 30 lines or less."

SPORTS

ARCHERY AND BOWHUNTING

⊛⊛ BOW & ARROW HUNTING

Beckett Media LLC, 22840 Savi Ranch Pkwy., Suite 200, Yorba Linda CA 92887. (714)200-1900. **Fax:** (800)249-7761. **E-mail:** JBell@Beckett.com; editorial@bowandarrowhunting.com. **Website:** www.bowandarrowhunting.com. **70% freelance written.** Magazine published 9 times/year covering bowhunting. "Dedicated to serve the serious bowhunting enthusiast. Writers must be willing to share their secrets so our readers can become better bowhunters." Estab. 1962. Circ. 90,000. Byline given. Pays on publication. No kill fee. Publishes ms an average of 2 months after acceptance. Submit seasonal material 6 months in advance. Accepts queries by mail, e-mail. Accepts simultaneous submissions. Responds in 1 month to queries; 6 weeks to mss. Sample copy and writer's guidelines free.

NONFICTION Needs how-to, humor, interview, opinion, personal experience, technical. **Buys 60 mss/year.** Send complete ms. Length: 1,700-3,000 words. **Pays $200-450.**

PHOTOS Send photos. Captions required. Reviews contact sheets, digital images only; no slides or prints accepted. Offers no additional payment for photos accepted with ms.

FILLERS Needs facts, newsbreaks. **Buys 12 mss/year.** Length: 500 words. **Pays $20-100.**

TIPS "Inform readers how they can become better at the sport, but don't forget to keep it fun! Sidebars are recommended with every submission."

⊛⊛ BOWHUNTER

InterMedia Outdoors, 6385 Flank Dr., Suite 800, Harrisburg PA 17112. (717)695-8085. **Fax:** (717)545-

2527. **E-mail:** curt.wells@imoutdoors.com. **Website:** www.bowhunter.com. Mark Olszewski, art director; Jeff Waring, publisher. **Contact:** Curt Wells, editor. **50% freelance written.** Bimonthly magazine covering hunting big and small game with bow and arrow. "We are a special-interest publication, produced by bowhunters for bowhunters, covering all aspects of the sport. Material included in each issue is designed to entertain and inform readers, making them better bowhunters." Estab. 1971. Circ. 126,480. Byline given. Pays on acceptance. No kill fee. Submit seasonal material 8 months in advance. Accepts queries by mail, e-mail, fax. Responds in 1 month to queries. Responds in 2 months to mss. Sample copy for $2 and 8 1/2x11 SASE with appropriate postage. Guidelines for #10 SASE or on website.

NONFICTION Needs general interest, how-to, interview, opinion, personal experience, photo feature. **Buys 60-plus mss/year.** Query. Length: 250-2,000 words. **Pays $500 maximum for assigned articles. Pays $100-400 for unsolicited articles.** Sometimes pays expenses of writers on assignment.

PHOTOS Send photos. Captions required. Reviews high-res digital images. Reviews photos with or without a manuscript. Offers $50-300/photo. Pays $50-125 for b&w inside; $75-300 for color inside; $600 for cover, "occasionally more if photo warrants it." **Pays on acceptance**. Credit line given. Buys one-time publication rights.

TIPS "A writer must know bowhunting and be willing to share that knowledge. Writers should anticipate *all* questions a reader might ask, then answer them in the article itself or in an appropriate sidebar. Articles should be written with the reader foremost in mind; we won't be impressed by writers seeking to prove how good they are—either as writers or bowhunters. We care about the reader and don't need writers with 'I' trouble. Features are a good bet because most of our material comes from freelancers. The best advice is: Be yourself. Tell your story the same as if sharing the experience around a campfire. Don't try to write like you think a writer writes."

$$ BOWHUNTING WORLD

Grand View Media Group, 5959 Baker Rd., Suite 300, Minnetonka MN 55345. (888)431-2877. **E-mail:** molis@grandviewmedia.com. **Website:** www.bowhuntingworld.com. **Contact:** Mark Olis. **50% freelance written.** Bimonthly magazine with 3 additional issues for bowhunting and archery enthusiasts who participate in the sport year-round. Estab. 1952. Circ. 95,000. Byline given. Pays on acceptance. No kill fee. Publishes ms an average of 5 months after acceptance. Responds in 1 week (e-mail queries). Responds in 6 weeks to mss. Sample copy for $3 and 9x12 SASE with 10 first-class stamps. Guidelines with #10 SASE.

NONFICTION Buys 60 mss/year. Send complete ms. Length: 1,500-2,500 words. **Pays $350-600.**

PHOTOS "We are seeking cover photos that depict specific behavioral traits of the more common big game animals (scraping whitetails, bugling elk, etc.) and well-equipped bowhunters in action. Must include return postage."

TIPS "Writers are strongly advised to adhere to guidelines and become familiar with our format, as our needs are very specific. Writers are urged to query by e-mail. We prefer detailed outlines of 6 or so article ideas/query. Assignments are made for the next 18 months."

BASEBALL

$ JUNIOR BASEBALL

JSAN Publishing LLC, Wilton CT 06897. (203)210-5726. **E-mail:** publisher@juniorbaseball.com. **Website:** www.juniorbaseball.com. **Contact:** Jim Beecher, publisher. **25% freelance written.** Bimonthly magazine focused on youth baseball players ages 7-17 (including high school) and their parents/coaches. Edited to various reading levels, depending upon age/skill level of feature. Estab. 1996. Circ. 20,000. Byline given. Pays on publication. No kill fee. Publishes ms an average of 4 months after acceptance. Editorial lead time 3 months. Submit seasonal material 4 months in advance. Accepts simultaneous submissions. Responds in 2 weeks to queries; 1 month to mss. Sample copy for $5 and online.

NONFICTION Needs how-to, skills, tips, features, how-to play better baseball, etc., interview, with major league players; only on assignment, personal experience, from coaches' or parents' perspective. No trite first-person articles about your kid. No fiction or poetry. **Buys 8-12 mss/year.** Query. Length: 500-1,000 words. **Pays $50-100.**

PHOTOS Photos can be e-mailed in 300 dpi JPEGs. State availability. Captions, identification of subjects required. Reviews 35mm transparencies, 3x5 prints.

Offers $10-100/photo; negotiates payment individually.

COLUMNS/DEPARTMENTS Freelance columns: When I Was a Kid (a current Major League Baseball player profile); Parents Feature (topics of interest to parents of youth ball players); all 1,000-1,500 words. In the Spotlight (news, events, new products), 50-100 words; Hot Prospect (written for the 14 and older competitive player. High school baseball is included, and the focus is on improving the finer points of the game to make the high school team, earn a college scholarship, or attract scouts, written to an adult level), 500-1,000 words. **Buys 8-12 mss/year. Pays $50-100.**

TIPS "Must be well-versed in baseball! Have a child who is very involved in the sport, or have extensive hands-on experience in coaching baseball, at the youth, high school or higher level. We can always use accurate, authoritative skills information, and good photos to accompany is a big advantage! This magazine is read by experts. No fiction, poems, games, puzzles, etc." Does not want first-person articles about your child.

BICYCLING

⊙⊙⊛ ADVENTURE CYCLIST

Adventure Cycling Assn., Box 8308, Missoula MT 59807. (406)721-1776, ext. 222. **Fax:** (406)721-8754. **E-mail:** magazine@adventurecycling.org. **Website:** www.adventurecycling.org. **Contact:** Greg Siple, art director; Michael Deme, editor. **75% freelance written.** Published 9 times/year for Adventure Cycling Association members, emphasizing bicycle tourism and travel. Estab. 1975. Circ. 45,500. Byline given. Pays on publication. Kill fee 25%. Submit seasonal material 12 months in advance. Sample copy and guidelines for 9x12 SAE with 4 first-class stamps. Info available at www.adventurecycling.org/mag.

NONFICTION Needs first-person bike-travel accounts (U.S. and worldwide), essays, how-to, profiles, photo feature, technical, U.S. or foreign tour accounts. **Buys 20-25 mss/year.** Send complete ms. Length: 1,400-3,500 words. **Inquiries requested prior to complete manuscripts. Pays sliding scale per word. PHOTOS** State availability.

⊙⊛ BIKE MAGAZINE

Source Interlink Media, P.O. Box 1028, Dana Point CA 926229. (949)325-6200. **Fax:** (949)325-6196. **E-mail:** bikemag@sorc.com. **Website:** www.bikemag.com. **Contact:** Joe Parkin, editor; Brice Minnigh, managing editor. **35% freelance written.** Magazine publishes 8 times/year covering mountain biking. Estab. 1993. Circ. 170,000. Byline given. Pays on publication. Offers 25% kill fee. Publishes ms an average of 2 months after acceptance. Editorial lead time 4 months. Submit seasonal material 6 months in advance. Responds in 2 months to queries. Sample copy for $8. Guidelines for #10 SASE.

NONFICTION Needs humor, interview, personal experience, photo feature, travel. **Buys 20 mss/year.** Length: 1,000-2,500 words. **Pays 50¢/word.** Sometimes pays expenses of writers on assignment. $500 maximum.

PHOTOS Contact: David Reddick, photo editor. Send photos. Captions, identification of subjects required. Reviews color transparencies, b&w prints. Negotiates payment individually.

COLUMNS/DEPARTMENTS Splatter (news), 300 words; Urb (details a great ride within 1 hour of a major metropolitan area), 600-700 words. **Buys 20 mss/year. Pays 50¢/word.**

TIPS "Remember that we focus on hard core mountain biking, not beginners. We're looking for ideas that deliver the excitement and passion of the sport in ways that aren't common or predictable. Ideas should be vivid, unbiased, irreverent, probing, fun, humorous, funky, quirky, smart, good. Great feature ideas are always welcome, especially features on cultural matters or issues in the sport. However, you're much more likely to get published in *Bike* if you send us great ideas for short articles. In particular we need stories for our Splatter, a front-of-the-book section devoted to news, funny anecdotes, quotes, and odds and ends. These stories range from 50 to 300 words. We also need personality profiles of 600 words or so for our People Who Ride section. Racers are OK but we're more interested in grassroots people with interesting personalities—it doesn't matter if they're Mother Theresas or scumbags, so long as they make mountain biking a little more interesting. Short descriptions of great rides are very welcome for our Urb column; the length should be from 600-700 words."

⊙⊛ CYCLE CALIFORNIA! MAGAZINE

1702-L Meridian Ave. #289, San Jose CA 95125. (408)924-0270. **Fax:** (408)292-3005. **E-mail:** tcorral@cyclecalifornia.com; BMack@cyclecalifornia.com.

Website: www.cyclecalifornia.com. **Contact:** Tracy L. Corral; Bob Mack, publisher. **75% freelance written.** Magazine published 11 times/year covering Northern California bicycling events, races, people. Issues (topics) covered include bicycle commuting, bicycle politics, touring, racing, nostalgia, history—anything at all to do with riding a bike. Estab. 1995. Circ. 26,000 print; 4,700 digital. Byline given. Pays on publication. No kill fee. Publishes ms an average of 3 months after acceptance. Editorial lead time 6 weeks. Submit seasonal material 6 weeks in advance. Accepts queries by e-mail. Accepts simultaneous submissions. Responds in 1 month to queries. Sample copy with 10x13 SASE and 3 first-class stamps. Guidelines with #10 SASE.

NONFICTION Needs historical, how-to, interview, opinion, personal experience, technical, travel. Special issues: Bicycle Tour & Travel (January/February). No articles about any sport that doesn't relate to bicycling. No product reviews. **Buys 36 mss/year.** Query. Length: 500-1,500 words. **Pays 10-15¢/word.**

PHOTOS Send photos. Identification of subjects preferred. Negotiates payment individually.

COLUMNS/DEPARTMENTS Buys 2-3 mss/year. Query with published clips. **Pays 10-15¢/word.**

TIPS "E-mail us with good ideas. While we don't exclude writers from other parts of the country, articles really should reflect a Northern California slant, or be of general interest to bicyclists. We prefer stories written by people who like and use their bikes."

💲💲 VELONEWS

Inside Communications, Inc., 3002 Sterling Circle, Suite 100, Boulder CO 80301. (303)440-0601. **Fax:** (303)444-6788. **E-mail:** webletters@competitorgroup. com. **E-mail:** nrogers@competitorgroup.com. **Website:** www.velonews.com. **Contact:** Neal Rogers, editor-in-chief. **40% freelance written.** Monthly tabloid covering bicycle racing. Estab. 1972. Circ. 48,000. Byline given. Pays on publication. No kill fee. Publishes ms an average of 1 month after acceptance. Responds in 3 weeks to queries.

NONFICTION Buys 80 mss/year. Query. Length: 300-1,200 words. **Pays $100-400.**

REPRINTS Send typed manuscript with rights for sale noted and information about when and where the material previously appeared.

PHOTOS State availability. Captions, identification of subjects required.

BOATING

⊘ 💲💲💲 BOATING

Bonnier Corporation, 460 N. Orlando Ave., Winter Park FL 32789. (407)628-4802. **Fax:** (407)628-7061. **E-mail:** editor@boatingmag.com. **Website:** www.boatingmag.com. **Contact:** Kevin Falvey, editor-in-chief. **25% freelance written.** Magazine published 11 times/year covering performance boating. Estab. 1973. Circ. 50,000. Byline given. Pays on publication. Offers negotiable kill fee. Publishes ms an average of 3 months after acceptance. Editorial lead time 3 months. Submit seasonal material 4 months in advance. Accepts queries by mail, e-mail, fax. Sample copy available online.

NONFICTION Needs how-to, interview, new product, photo feature. No general interest boating stories. **Buys numerous mss/year.** Query. Length: 300-2,000 words. **Pays $125-1,200.** Sometimes pays expenses of writers on assignment.

PHOTOS State availability. Captions required. Reviews negatives.

💲💲💲 CANOE & KAYAK

GrindMedia, LLC, 236 Avenida Fabricante, Suite 201, San Clemente CA 92672. (425)827-6363. **E-mail:** jeff@canoekayak.com; joe@canoekayak.com; dave@canoekayak.com. **Website:** www.canoekayak. com. **Contact:** Jeff Moag, editor-in-chief; Joe Carberry, senior editor; Dave Shively, managing editor. **75% freelance written.** Bimonthly magazine covering paddlesports. "*Canoe & Kayak* is North America's No. 1 paddlesports resource. Our readers include flatwater and whitewater canoeists and kayakers of all skill levels. We provide comprehensive information on destinations, technique and equipment. Beyond that, we cover canoe and kayak camping, safety, the environment, and the history of boats and sport." Estab. 1972. Circ. 70,000. Byline given. Pays on publication. No kill fee. Publishes ms an average of 6 months after acceptance. Editorial lead time 6 months. Submit seasonal material 8 months in advance. Accepts queries by mail, e-mail. Responds in 2 months to queries. Sample copy and writer's guidelines for 9x12 SAE with 7 first-class stamps.

NONFICTION Needs historical, how-to, canoe, kayak camp, load boats, paddle whitewater, etc., personal experience, photo feature, technical, travel. Special issues: Whitewater Paddling; Beginner's Guide; Kayak Touring; Canoe Journal. No cartoons, poems, stories in which bad judgement is portrayed or 'Me and Molly' articles. **Buys 25 mss/year.** Send complete ms. Length: 400-2,500 words. **Pays $100-800 for assigned articles. Pays $100-500 for unsolicited articles.**

PHOTOS "Some activities we cover are canoeing, kayaking, canoe fishing, camping, canoe sailing or poling, backpacking (when compatible with the main activity) and occasionally inflatable boats. We are not interested in groups of people in rafts, photos showing disregard for the environment or personal safety, gasoline-powered engines unless appropriate to the discussion, or unskilled persons taking extraordinary risks." State availability. Captions, identification of subjects, model releases required. Reviews 35mm transparencies, 4x6 prints. Offers $75-500/photo.

COLUMNS/DEPARTMENTS Put In (environment, conservation, events), 500 words; Destinations (canoe and kayak destinations in US, Canada), 1,500 words; Essays, 750 words. **Buys 40 mss/year.** Send complete ms. **Pays $100-350.**

FILLERS Needs anecdotes, facts, newsbreaks. **Buys 20 mss/year.** Length: 200-500 words. **Pays $25-50.**

TIPS "Start with Put-In articles (short featurettes) or short, unique equipment reviews. Or give us the best, most exciting article we've ever seen—with great photos. Read the magazine before submitting."

$$$ CHESAPEAKE BAY MAGAZINE

1819 Bay Ridge Ave., Annapolis MD 21403. (410)263-2662, ext. 32. **Fax:** (410)267-6924. **E-mail:** editor@chesapeakeboating.net. **Website:** www.chesapeakeboating.net. **Contact:** Ann Levelle, managing editor; T.F. Sayles, editor. **60% freelance written.** Monthly magazine covering boating and the Chesapeake Bay. "Our readers are boaters. Our writers should know boats and boating. Read the magazine before submitting." Estab. 1972. Circ. 46,000. Byline given. Pays within 2 months after acceptance. No kill fee. Publishes ms an average of 1 year after acceptance. Editorial lead time 1 year. Submit seasonal material 1 year in advance. Accepts queries by mail, e-mail, fax, phone. Accepts simultaneous submissions. Responds in 2 months to queries. Responds in 3 months to mss. Sample copy for $5.19 prepaid.

NONFICTION Buys 30 mss/year. Query with published clips. Length: 300-3,000 words. **Pays $100-1,000.** Pays expenses of writers on assignment.

PHOTOS Captions, identification of subjects required. Offers $75-250/photo, $400/day rate for assignment photography. Pays $400 for color cover; $75-250 for color *stock* inside, depending on size; $200-1,200 for *assigned* photo package. Pays on publication. Credit line given. Buys one-time rights.

TIPS "Send us unedited writing samples (not clips) that show the writer can write, not just string words together. We look for well-organized, lucid, lively, intelligent writing."

○ $ COAST&KAYAK MAGAZINE

Wild Coast Publishing, P.O. Box 24 Stn. A, Nanaimo BC V9R 5K4 Canada. (250)244-6437; (866)984-6437. **Fax:** (866)654-1937. **E-mail:** editor@coastandkayak.com. **Website:** www.coastandkayak.com. **Contact:** John Kimantas, editor. **75% freelance written.** Quarterly magazine with a major focus on paddling the Pacific coast. "We promote safe paddling, guide paddlers to useful products and services, and explore coastal environmental issues." Estab. 1991. Circ. 65,000 print and electronic readers. Byline given. Pays on publication. Publishes ms an average of 4 months after acceptance. Editorial lead time 4 months. Submit seasonal material 4 months in advance. Accepts queries by mail, e-mail. Sample copy and guidelines available online.

NONFICTION Needs how-to, paddle, travel, humor, new product, personal experience, technical, travel, trips. **Buys 25 mss/year.** Query. Length: 1,000-1,500 words. **Pays $50-75.**

PHOTOS State availability. Captions, identification of subjects required. Reviews low-res JPEGs. Offers $25-50/photo.

TIPS "You must know paddling—though novice paddlers are welcome. A strong environmental or wilderness appreciation component is advisable. We are willing to help refine work with flexible people. E-mail queries preferred. Check out our editorial calendar for our upcoming features."

$$$$ CRUISING WORLD

The Sailing Co., 55 Hammarlund Way, Middletown RI 02842. (401)845-5100. **Fax:** (401)845-5180. **E-mail:** cw.manuscripts@gmail.com; elaine.lembo@cruisingworld.com; bill.roche@bonniercorp.com. **Website:** www.cruisingworld.com. **Contact:** Elaine Lembo, deputy editor; Bill Roche, art director. **60% freelance written.** Monthly magazine covering sailing, cruising/adventuring, do-it-yourself boat improvements. "*Cruising World* is a publication by and for sailboat owners who spend time in home waters as well as voyaging the world. Its readership is extremely loyal, savvy, and driven by independent thinking." Estab. 1974. Circ. 155,000. Byline given. **Pays on acceptance for articles;** on publication for photography. No kill fee. Publishes ms an average of 18 months after acceptance. Editorial lead time 3 months. Submit seasonal material 1 year in advance. Accepts queries by mail. Responds in 2 months to queries. Responds in 4 months to mss. Sample copy free. Guidelines available online.

NONFICTION Needs book excerpts, essays, exposé, general interest, historical, how-to, humor, interview, new product, opinion, personal experience, photo feature, technical, travel. No travel articles that have nothing to do with cruising aboard sailboats from 20-50 feet in length. **Buys dozens mss/year.** Send complete ms. **Pays $50-1,500 for assigned articles. Pays $50-1,000 for unsolicited articles.** Sometimes pays expenses of writers on assignment.

PHOTOS Send high-res (minimum 300 DPI) images on CD. Send photos. Captions required. Reviews negatives, transparencies, color slides preferred. Payment upon publication. Also buys stand-alone photos.

COLUMNS/DEPARTMENTS Shoreline (sailing news, people, and short features; contact Elaine Lembo), 300 words maximum; Hands-on Sailor (refit, voyaging, seamanship, how-to), 1,000-1,500 words. **Buys dozens mss/year.** Query with or without published clips or send complete ms.

TIPS *"Cruising World's* readers know exactly what they want to read, so our best advice to freelancers is to carefully read the magazine and envision which exact section or department would be the appropriate place for proposed submissions."

GOOD OLD BOAT

Partnership for Excellence, Inc., 7340 Niagara Lane N., Maple Grove MN 55311. (763)494-0314. **E-mail:** karen@goodoldboat.com. **Website:** www.goodoldboat.com. **Contact:** Karen Larson, editor. **90% freelance written.** Bimonthly magazine covering sailing. *"Good Old Boat* magazine focuses on maintaining, upgrading, and loving fiberglass cruising sailboats from the 1960s through the early 2000s. Readers see themselves as part of a community of sailors who share similar maintenance and replacement concerns not generally addressed in the other sailing publications. Our readers do much of the writing about projects they have done on their boats and the joy they receive

from sailing them." Estab. 1998. Circ. 30,000. Pays 2 months in advance of publication. No kill fee. Publishes ms an average of 12-18 months after acceptance. Editorial lead time 4 months. Submit seasonal material 12-15 months in advance. Accepts queries by mail, e-mail. Accepts simultaneous submissions. Responds in 1-2 weeks to queries. Responds in 2-6 months to mss. Downloadable sample copy free. Guidelines available online.

NONFICTION Needs general interest, historical, how-to, interview, personal experience, photo feature, technical. "Articles written by non-sailors serve no purpose for us." **Buys 150 mss/year.** Query or send complete ms. **Payment varies; refer to published rates on website.**

PHOTOS State availability of or send photos. "We do not pay additional fees for photos except when they run as covers, or are specifically requested to support an article."

TIPS "Our shorter pieces are the best way to break into our magazine. We publish many Simple Solutions and Quick & Easy pieces. These are how-to tips that have worked for sailors on their boats. In addition, our readers send lists of projects which they've done on their boats and which they could write for publication. We respond to these queries with a thumbs up or down by project. Articles are submitted on speculation, but they have a better chance of being accepted once we have approved of the suggested topic."

💲💲 HEARTLAND BOATING

The Waterways Journal, Inc., 319 N. Fourth St., Suite 650, St. Louis MO 63102. (314)241-4310. **Fax:** (314)241-4207. **E-mail:** lbraff@heartlandboating.com. **Website:** www.heartlandboating.com. **Contact:** Brad Kovach, editor. **90% freelance written.** Magazine published 8 times/year covering recreational boating on the inland waterways of mid-America, from the Great Lakes south to the Gulf of Mexico and over to the east. "Our writers must have experience with, and a great interest in, boating, particularly in the area described above. *Heartland Boating's* content is both informative and humorous—describing boating life as the heartland boater knows it. The content reflects the challenge, joy, and excitement of our way of life afloat. We are devoted to both power and sailboating enthusiasts throughout middle America; houseboats are included. The focus is on the freshwater inland rivers and lakes of the heartland, primarily the waters of the Arkansas, Tennessee, Cumberland, Ohio, Missouri, Illinois, and Mississippi rivers, the Tennessee-Tombigbee Waterway, The Gulf Intracoastal Waterway, and the lakes along these waterways." Estab. 1989. Circ. 10,000. Byline given. Pays on publication. No kill fee. Editorial lead time 3 months. Accepts queries by mail. Responds only if interested. Sample copy upon request. Guidelines for #10 SASE.

NONFICTION Needs how-to, articles about navigation maintenance, upkeep, or making time spent aboard easier and more comfortable, humor, personal experience, technical, Great Loop leg trips, along waterways and on-land stops. Special issues: Annual houseboat issue in March looks at what is coming out on the houseboat market for the coming year. **Buys 100 mss/year.** Send complete ms. Length: 850-1,500 words. **Pays $40-285.**

REPRINTS Send tearsheet, photocopy or typed ms and information about when and where the material previously appeared.

PHOTOS Magazine published 8 times/year covering recreational boating on the inland waterways of mid America, from the Great Lakes south to the Gulf of Mexico and over to the east. Send photos. Model release is required, property release is preferred, photo captions are required. Include names and locations. Reviews prints, digital images. Offers no additional payment for photos accepted with ms.

COLUMNS/DEPARTMENTS Books Aboard (assigned book reviews), 400 words. Buys 8-10 mss/year. Pays $40. Handy Hints (boat improvement or safety projects), 1,000 words. Buys 8 mss/year. Pays $180. Heartland Haunts (waterside restaurants, bars or B&Bs), 1,000 words. Buys 16 mss/year. Pays $160. Query with published clips or send complete ms.

TIPS "We plan the next year's schedule starting in May. So submitting material between May 1 and July 15 is the best way to proceed."

⊘ $ $ HOUSEBOAT MAGAZINE

Harris Publishing, Inc., 360 B St., Idaho Falls ID 83402. **Fax:** (208)522-5241. **E-mail:** blk@houseboatmagazine.com. **Website:** www.houseboatmagazine.com. **Contact:** Brady L. Kay, executive editor. **35% freelance written.** "Quarterly magazine for houseboaters who enjoy reading everything that reflects the unique houseboating lifestyle. If it is not a houseboat-specific article, please do not query." Estab. 1990. Circ. 25,000. Byline given. Pays on acceptance. Offers 25% kill fee. Publishes ms an average of 3 months after acceptance. Editorial lead time 6 months. Submit seasonal material 6 months in advance. Accepts simultaneous submissions. Responds in 1 month to queries. Sample copy for $5. Guidelines by e-mail.

NONFICTION Needs how-to, interview, new product, personal experience, travel. **Buys 36 mss/year.** Query. Length: 1,500-2,200 words. **Pays $200-500.**

PHOTOS Often required as part of submission package. Color prints discouraged. Digital prints are unacceptable. Seldom purchases photos without ms, but occasionally buys cover photos. Captions, model releases required. Reviews transparencies, high-resolution electronic images. Offers no additional payment for photos accepted with ms.

COLUMNS/DEPARTMENTS Pays $150-300.

TIPS "As a general rule, how-to articles are always in demand. So are stories on unique houseboats or houseboaters. You are less likely to break in with a travel piece that does not revolve around specific people or groups. Personality profile pieces with excellent supporting photography are your best bet."

$ $ LAKELAND BOATING

O'Meara-Brown Publications, Inc., 727 S. Dearborn St., Suite 812, Chicago IL 60605. (312)276-0610. **Fax:** (312)276-0619. **E-mail:** info@lakelandboating.com; ljohnson@lakelandboating.com. **Website:** www.lakelandboating.com. **Contact:** Lindsey Johnson, editor. **50% freelance written.** Magazine covering Great Lakes boating. Estab. 1946. Circ. 60,000. Byline given. Pays on publication. No kill fee. Accepts queries by e-mail. Responds in 4 months to queries. Sample copy for $5.50 and 9x12 SAE with 6 first-class stamps. Guidelines free.

NONFICTION Needs book excerpts, historical, how-to, interview, personal experience, photo feature, technical, travel, must relate to boating in Great Lakes. No inspirational, religious, exposé, or poetry. **Buys 20-30 mss/year.** Length: 300-1,500 words. **Pays $100-600.**

PHOTOS State availability. Captions required. Reviews prefers 35mm transparencies, high-res digital shots.

COLUMNS/DEPARTMENTS Bosun's Locker (technical or how-to pieces on boating), 100-1,000 words. **Buys 40 mss/year.** Query. **Pays $25-200.**

$ NORTHERN BREEZES, SAILING MAGAZINE

Northern Breezes, Inc., 3949 Winnetka Ave. N, Minneapolis MN 55427. (763)542-9707. **Fax:** (763)542-8998. **E-mail:** info@sailingbreezes.com. **Website:** www.sailingbreezes.com. **70% freelance written.** Magazine published 8 times/year for the Great Lakes and Midwest sailing community. Focusing on regional cruising, racing, and day sailing. Estab. 1989. Circ. 22,300. Byline given. Pays on publication. No kill fee. Editorial lead time 1 months. Submit seasonal material 3 months in advance. Accepts queries by mail, e-mail, fax. Responds in 1 month to queries. Responds in 2 months to mss. Sample copy free.

NONFICTION Needs book excerpts, how-to, sailing topics, humor, inspirational, interview, new product, personal experience, photo feature, technical, travel. No boating reviews. **Buys 24 mss/year.** Query with published clips. Length: 300-3,500 words.

PHOTOS Send photos. Captions required. Reviews negatives, 35mm slides, 3x5 or 4x6 prints. "Digital submission preferred." Offers no additional payment for photos accepted with ms.

COLUMNS/DEPARTMENTS This Old Boat (sailboat), 500-1,000 words; Surveyor's Notebook, 500-800 words. **Buys 8 mss/year.** Query with published clips. **Pays $50-150.**

TIPS "Query with a regional connection already in mind."

🍁 $$ PACIFIC YACHTING

OP Publishing, Ltd., 200 West Esplanade, Suite 500, North Vancouver BC V7M 1A4 Canada. (604)998-3310. **Fax:** (604)998-3320. **E-mail:** editor@pacificyachting.com. **Website:** www.pacificyachting.com. **Contact:** Dale Miller, editor; Arran Yates, art director. **90% freelance written.** Monthly magazine covering all aspects of recreational boating in the Pacific Northwest. "The bulk of our writers and photographers not only come from the local boating community, many of them were long-time *PY* readers before coming aboard as a contributor. The *PY* reader buys the magazine to read about new destinations or changes to old haunts on the British Columbia coast and the Pacific Northwest and to learn the latest about boats and gear." Estab. 1968. Circ. 19,000. Byline given. Pays on publication. No kill fee. Publishes ms an average of 6 months after acceptance. Editorial lead time 4 months. Submit seasonal material 6 months in advance. Accepts queries by mail, e-mail, fax. Sample copy for $6.95, plus postage charged to credit card. Guidelines available online.

NONFICTION Needs historical, British Columbia coast only, how-to, humor, interview, personal experience, technical, boating related, travel, cruising, and destination on the British Columbia coast. "No articles from writers who are obviously not boaters!" Query. Length: 800-2,000 words. **Pays $150-500. Pays some expenses of writers on assignment for unsolicited articles.** Pays expenses of writers on assignment.

PHOTOS Send photos. Identification of subjects required. Reviews digital photos transparencies, 4 x 6 prints, and slides. Offers no additional payment for photos accepted with ms. Offers $25-400 for photos accepted alone.

COLUMNS/DEPARTMENTS Currents (current events, trade and people news, boat gatherings, and festivities), 50-250 words. Reflections; Cruising, both 800-1,000 words. Query. **Pay varies.**

TIPS "Our reader wants you to balance important navigation details with first-person observations, blending the practical with the romantic. Write tight, write short, write with the reader in mind, write to inform, write to entertain. Be specific, accurate, and historic."

$$ PONTOON & DECK BOAT

Harris Publishing, Inc., 360 B. St., Idaho Falls ID 83402. (208)524-7000. **Fax:** (208)522-5241. **E-mail:** blk@pdbmagazine.com. **Website:** www.pdbmagazine.com. **Contact:** Brady L. Kay, editor. **15% freelance written.** Magazine published 11 times/year covering boating. "We are a boating niche publication geared toward the pontoon and deck boating lifestyle and consumer market. Our audience is comprised of people who utilize these boats for varied family activities and fishing. Our magazine is promotional of the PDB industry and its major players. We seek to give the reader a twofold reason to read our publication: to celebrate the lifestyle, and to do it aboard a first-class craft." Estab. 1995. Circ. 84,000. Byline given. Pays on publication. No kill fee. Editorial lead time 2 months. Submit seasonal material 3 months in advance. Accepts simultaneous submissions. Responds in 6 weeks to queries. Responds in 3 months to mss. Sample copy and writer's guidelines free.

NONFICTION Needs how-to, personal experience, technical, remodeling, rebuilding. "We are saturated with travel pieces; no general boating, humor, fiction, or poetry." **Buys 15 mss/year.** Send complete ms. Length: 600-2,000 words. **Pays $50-300.** Sometimes pays expenses of writers on assignment.

PHOTOS State availability. Captions, model releases required. Reviews transparencies.

COLUMNS/DEPARTMENTS No Wake Zone (short, fun quips); Better Boater (how-to). **Buys 6-12 mss/year.** Query with published clips. **Pays $50-150.**

TIPS "Be specific to pontoon and deck boats. Any general boating material goes to the slush pile. The more you can tie together the lifestyle, attitudes, and the PDB industry, the more interest we'll take in what you send us."

⊛⊛⊛ POWER & MOTORYACHT

10 Bokum Rd., Essex CT 06426. (860)767-3200. **E-mail:** gsass@aimmedia.com; cwhite@aimmedia.com. **Website:** www.powerandmotoryacht.com. Aimee Colon, art director. **Contact:** George Sass, editor-in-chief; Chris White, managing editor. **25% freelance written.** Monthly magazine covering powerboats 24 feet and larger with special emphasis on the 35-foot-plus market. "Readers have an average of 33 years experience boating, and we give them accurate advice on how to choose, operate, and maintain their boats as well as what electronics and gear will help them pursue their favorite pastime. In addition, since powerboating is truly a lifestyle and not just a hobby for them, *Power & Motoryacht* reports on a host of other topics that affect their enjoyment of the water: chartering, sportfishing, and the environment, among others. Articles must therefore be clear, concise, and authoritative; knowledge of the marine industry is mandatory. Include personal experience and information for marine industry experts where appropriate." Estab. 1985. Circ. 157,000. Byline given. Pays on acceptance. Offers 33% kill fee. Publishes ms an average of 4-6 months after acceptance. Editorial lead time 4-6 months. Submit seasonal material 4-6 months in advance. Accepts queries by mail, e-mail. Responds in 1 month to queries. Sample copy with 10x12 SASE. Guidelines with #10 SASE or via e-mail.

NONFICTION Needs how-to, interview, personal experience, photo feature, travel. No unsolicited mss or articles about sailboats and/or sailing yachts (including motorsailers or cruise ships). **Buys 20-25 mss/year.** Query with published clips. Length: 800-1,500 words. **Pays $500-1,000 for assigned articles.** Sometimes pays expenses of writers on assignment.

PHOTOS State availability. Captions, identification of subjects required. Reviews 8x10 transparencies, GIF/JPEG files (minimum 300 dpi). Offers no additional payment for photos accepted with ms.

TIPS "Take a clever or even unique approach to a subject, particularly if the topic is dry/technical. Pitch us on yacht cruises you've taken, particularly if they're in off-the-beaten-path locations."

⊙ ⊛⊛ POWER BOATING CANADA

1121 Invicta Drive Unit 2, Oakville ON L6H 2R2 Canada. (800)354-9145. **Fax:** (905)844-5032. **E-mail:** editor@powerboating.com. **Website:** www.powerboating.com. **70% freelance written.** Bimonthly magazine covering recreational power boating. *Power Boating Canada* offers boating destinations, how-to features, boat tests (usually staff written), lifestyle pieces—with a Canadian slant—and appeal to recreational power boaters across the country. Estab. 1984. Circ. 42,000. Byline given. Pays on publication. No kill fee. Publishes ms an average of 3 months after acceptance. Editorial lead time 2 months. Submit seasonal material 3 months in advance. Responds in 1 month to queries. Responds in 2 months to mss. Sample copy free.

NONFICTION Needs historical, how-to, interview, personal experience, travel, boating destinations. No general boating articles or personal anecdotes. **Buys 40-50 mss/year.** Query. Length: 1,200-2,500 words. **Pays $150-300 (Canadian).** Sometimes pays expenses of writers on assignment.

REPRINTS Send photocopy with rights for sale noted and information about when and where the material previously appeared.

PHOTOS Send photos. Captions, identification of subjects required. Reviews contact sheets, negatives, transparencies, prints. Pay varies; no additional payment for photos accepted with ms.

⊛⊛⊛ SAIL

98 N. Washington St., Suite 107, Boston MA 02114. (617)720-8600. **Fax:** (617)723-0912. **E-mail:** sailmail@sailmagazine.com. **Website:** www.sailmagazine.com. **Contact:** Peter Nielsen, editor-in-chief. **30% freelance written.** Monthly magazine written and edited for everyone who sails—aboard a coastal or bluewater cruiser, trailerable, one-design or offshore racer, or daysailer. How-to and technical articles concen-

trate on techniques of sailing and aspects of design and construction, boat systems, and gear; the feature section emphasizes the fun and rewards of sailing in a practical and instructive way. Estab. 1970. Circ. 180,000. Byline given. Pays on acceptance. No kill fee. Publishes ms an average of 1 year after acceptance. Accepts queries by mail, e-mail, fax. Responds in 3 months to queries. Guidelines with SASE or online (download).

NONFICTION Needs how-to, personal experience, technical, distance cruising, destinations. Special issues: Cruising, chartering, commissioning, fitting-out, special race (e.g., America's Cup), Top 10 Boats. **Buys 50 mss/year.** Query. Length: 1,500-3,000 words. **Pays $200-800.** Sometimes pays expenses of writers on assignment.

PHOTOS Prefers transparencies. High-res digital photos (300 dpi) are also accepted, as are high-quality color prints (preferably with negatives attached). Captions, identification of subjects, Payment varies, up to $1,000 if photo used on cover.

COLUMNS/DEPARTMENTS Sailing Memories (short essay); Sailing News (cruising, racing, legal, political, environmental); Under Sail (human interest). Query. **Pays $50-400.**

TIPS "Request an articles' specification sheet. We look for unique ways of viewing sailing. Skim old issues of *Sail* for ideas about the types of articles we publish. Always remember that *Sail* is a sailing magazine. Stay away from gloomy articles detailing all the things that went wrong on your boat. Think constructively and write about how to avoid certain problems. You should focus on a theme or choose some aspect of sailing and discuss a personal attitude or new philosophical approach to the subject. Notice that we have certain issues devoted to special themes—for example, chartering, electronics, commissioning, and the like. Stay away from pieces that chronicle your journey in the day-by-day style of a logbook. These are generally dull and uninteresting. Select specific actions or events (preferably sailing events, not shorebound activities), and build your articles around them. Emphasize the sailing."

$$$ SAILING MAGAZINE

125 E. Main St., Port Washington WI 53074. (262)284-3494. **Fax:** (262)284-7764. **E-mail:** editorial@sailingmagazine.net. **Website:** www.sailingmagazine.net. Monthly magazine for the experienced sailor. Estab. 1966. Circ. 45,000. Pays after publication. No kill fee. Accepts queries by mail, e-mail. Responds in 2 months to queries.

NONFICTION Needs book excerpts, how-to, tech pieces on boats and gear, interview, personal experience, travel by sail. **Buys 15-20 mss/year.** Send complete ms. Prefers text in Word on disk for Mac or to e-mail address. Length: 750-2,500 words. **Pays $100-800.**

PHOTOS Captions required. Reviews color transparencies. Pays $50-400.

$$ SAILING WORLD

Bonnier Corporation, 55 Hammarlund Way, Middletown RI 02842. (401)845-5100. **Fax:** (401)848-5180. **E-mail:** editor@sailingworld.com. **Website:** www.sailingworld.com. **Contact:** Dave Reed, editor. **40% freelance written.** Magazine published 10 times/year covering performance sailing. Estab. 1962. Circ. 65,000. Byline given. Pays on publication. No kill fee. Publishes ms an average of 4 months after acceptance. Responds in 1 month to queries. Sample copy for $5. Guidelines available on website.

NONFICTION Needs how-to, for racing and performance-oriented sailors, interview, photo feature, Regatta sports and charter. No travelogs. **Buys 5-10 unsolicited mss/year.** "Prospective contributors to Sailing World should study recent issues of the magazine to determine appropriate subject matter. The emphasis here is on performance sailing: keep in mind that the Sailing World readership is relatively educated about the sport. Unless you are dealing with a totally new aspect of sailing, you can and should discuss ideas on an advanced technical level; however, extensive formulae and graphs don't play well to our audience. When in doubt as to the suitability of an article or idea, submit a written query before time and energy are misdirected. (Because of the volume of queries received, editors cannot accept phone calls.)" Length: 400-1,500 words. **Pays $400 for up to 2,000 words.** Does not pay expenses of writers on assignment unless pre-approved.

TIPS "Send query with outline and include your experience. Prospective contributors should study recent issues of the magazine to determine appropriate subject matter. The emphasis here is on performance sailing: keep in mind that the *Sailing World* readership is relatively educated about the sport. Unless you are dealing with a totally new aspect of sailing, you can and should discuss ideas on an advanced technical level. 'Gee-whiz' impressions from beginning sailors are generally not accepted."

⊛⊛ SEA KAYAKER

Sea Kayaker, Inc., P.O. Box 17029, Seattle WA 98127. (206)789-1326. **Fax:** (206)781-1141. **E-mail:** editorial@seakayakermag.com. **Website:** www.seakayakermag.com. **95% freelance written.** *Sea Kayaker* is a bimonthly publication with a worldwide readership that covers all aspects of kayak touring. It is well known as an important source of continuing education by the most experienced paddlers. Estab. 1984. Circ. 30,000. Byline given. Pays on publication. Offers 10% kill fee. Publishes ms an average of 6 months after acceptance. Editorial lead time 4 months. Submit seasonal material 4 months in advance. Accepts queries by mail, e-mail, fax, phone. Responds in 2 months to queries. Sample copy for $7.30 (US), samples to other countries extra. Guidelines available online.

NONFICTION Needs essays, historical, how-to, on making equipment, humor, new product, personal experience, technical, travel. Unsolicited gear reviews are not accepted. **Buys 50 mss/year.** Send complete ms. Length: 1,500-5,000 words. **Pays 18-20¢/word for assigned articles. Pays 15-17¢/word for unsolicited articles.**

PHOTOS Send photos. Captions, identification of subjects required. Reviews transparencies, prints. Offers $15-400.

COLUMNS/DEPARTMENTS Technique; Equipment; Do-It-Yourself; Food; Safety; Health; Environment; Book Reviews; all 1,000-2,500 words. **Buys 40-45 mss/year.** Query. **Pays 15-20¢/word.**

TIPS "We consider unsolicited manuscripts that include a SASE, but we give greater priority to brief descriptions (several paragraphs) of proposed articles accompanied by at least 2 samples—published or unpublished—of your writing. Enclose a statement as to why you're qualified to write the piece and indicate whether photographs or illustrations are available to accompany the piece."

SEA MAGAZINE

Duncan McIntosh Co., 17782 Cowan, Suite C, Irvine CA 92614. (949)660-6150. **Fax:** (949)660-6172. **E-mail:** mike@seamag.com. **Website:** www.goboatingamerica.com. Monthly magazine covering West Coast power boating. Estab. 1908. Circ. 55,000. Byline given. Pays on publication. Publishes ms an average of 6 months after acceptance. Editorial lead time 3 months. Submit seasonal material 6 months in advance. Accepts simultaneous submissions. Responds in 3 months to queries.

NONFICTION Needs how-to, new product, personal experience, technical, travel. **Buys 36 mss/year.** Send complete ms. Length: 1,000-1,500 words. **Payment varies.** Pays expenses of writers on assignment.

PHOTOS State availability of photos. Captions, identification of subjects, model releases required. Reviews transparencies, high-res digital. Offers $50-250/photo.

⊛ ⊛⊛⊛⊛ SHOWBOATS INTERNATIONAL

Published by Boat International Media, 41-47 Hartfield Rd., London SW19 3RQ United Kingdom. (954)522-2628 (U.S. number). **Fax:** (954)522-2240. **E-mail:** marilyn.mower@boatinternationalmedia.com. **Website:** www.boatinternational.com. **Contact:** Marilyn Mower, editorial director - U.S.; Richard Taranto, art director. **70% freelance written.** Magazine published 10 times/year covering luxury superyacht industry. Estab. 1995. Circ. 55,000. Byline given. Pays on publication. Offers 30% kill fee. Editorial lead time 2 months. Submit seasonal material 4 months in advance. Accepts queries by e-mail. Responds in 2 months to mss. Sample copy for $6.00. Guidelines free.

NONFICTION Travel/destination pieces that are superyacht related. **Buys 3/year mss/year.** Query. Length: 700-2,500 words. **Pays $300 minimum, $2,000 maximum for assigned articles.** Sometimes pays expenses of writers on assignment.

PHOTOS State availability. Captions required. Reviews contact sheets, GIF/JPEG files. negotiates payment individually.

⊛⊛ SOUTHERN BOATING

Southern Boating & Yachting, Inc., 330 N. Andrews Ave., Ft. Lauderdale FL 33301. (954)522-5515. **Fax:** (954)522-2260. **E-mail:** liz@southernboating.com; jon@southernboating.com. **Website:** www.southernboating.com. **Contact:** Liz Pasch, executive editor; Jon Hernandez, art director. **50% freelance written.** Monthly boating magazine. Upscale monthly yachting magazine focusing on the Southeast U.S., Bahamas, Caribbean, and Gulf of Mexico. Estab. 1972. Circ. 40,000. Byline given. Pays within 30 days of publication. No kill fee. Publishes ms an average of 2 months after acceptance. Editorial lead time 3 months. Submit seasonal material 3 months in advance. Accepts queries by e-mail. Sample copy for $8.

NONFICTION Needs how-to, boat maintenance, travel, boating related, destination pieces. **Buys 50 mss/year.** Query. Length: 900-1,200 words. **Pays $500-750 with art.**

PHOTOS State availability of or send photos. Captions, identification of subjects, model releases required. Reviews transparencies, prints, digital files. Offers $75/photo minimum.

COLUMNS/DEPARTMENTS Weekend Workshop (how-to/maintenance), 900 words; What's New in Electronics (electronics), 900 words; Engine Room (new developments), 1,000 words. **Buys 24 mss/year.** Query first; see media kit for special issue focus. **Pays $600.**

WATERFRONT TIMES

Storyboard Media Inc., 2787 E. Oakland Park Blvd., Suite 205, Ft. Lauderdale FL 33306. (954)524-9450. **Fax:** (954)524-9464. **E-mail:** editor@waterfronttimes. com. **Website:** www.waterfronttimes.com. **Contact:** Jennifer Heit, editor. **20% freelance written.** Monthly tabloid covering marine and boating topics for the Greater Ft. Lauderdale waterfront community. Estab. 1984. Circ. 20,000. Byline given. Pays on publication. No kill fee. Publishes ms an average of 2 months after acceptance. Submit seasonal material 3 months in advance. Responds in 1 month to queries. Sample copy for SAE with 9x12 envelope and 4 first-class stamps.

NONFICTION Needs interview of people important in boating, i.e., racers, boat builders, designers, etc. from south Florida; regional articles on south Florida's waterfront issues; marine communities; travel pieces of interest to boaters, including docking information. Length: 500-1,000 words. **Pays $100-125 for assigned articles.**

PHOTOS Send photos. Reviews JPEG/TIFF files.

TIPS "No fiction. Keep it under 1,000 words. Photos or illustrations help. Send for a sample copy of *Waterfront Times* so you can acquaint yourself with our publication and our unique audience. Although we're not necessarily looking for technical articles, it helps if the writer has sailing or powerboating experience. Writers should be familiar with the region and be specific when dealing with local topics."

WATERWAY GUIDE

P.O. Box 1125, 16273 General Puller Hwy., Deltaville VA 23043. (804)776-8999. **Fax:** (804)776-6111.

E-mail: joan@waterwayguide.com. **Website:** www. waterwayguide.com. **Contact:** Tom Hale, editor. **90% freelance written.** Annual magazine covering intracoastal waterway travel for recreational boats. Six editions cover coastal waters from Maine to Florida, the Bahamas, the Gulf of Mexico, the Great Lakes, and the Great Loop Cruise of America's inland waterways. "Writer must be knowledgeable about navigation and the areas covered by the guide." Estab. 1947. Circ. 30,000. Byline given. Pays on publication. No kill fee. Publishes ms an average of 3 months after acceptance. Editorial lead time 4 months. Submit seasonal material 3 months in advance. Accepts queries by mail, phone. Responds in 6 weeks to queries. Responds in 2 months to mss. Sample copy for $39.95 with $3 postage.

NONFICTION Needs essays, historical, how-to, photo feature, technical, travel. **Buys 6 mss/year.** Send complete ms. Length: 250-5,000 words. **Pays $50-500.**

PHOTOS Send photos. Captions, identification of subjects required. Reviews transparencies, 3 x 5 prints. Offers $25-50/photo.

TIPS "Must have on-the-water experience and be able to provide new and accurate information on geographic areas covered by *Waterway Guide*."

WATERWAYS WORLD

Waterways World Ltd, 151 Station St., Burton-on-Trent Staffordshire DE14 1BG United Kingdom. 01283 742950. **E-mail:** editorial@waterwaysworld.com. **Website:** www.waterwaysworld.com. **Contact:** Bobby Cowling, editor. Monthly magazine publishing news, photographs, and illustrated articles on all aspects of inland waterways in Britain, and on limited aspects of waterways abroad. Estab. 1972. Pays on publication. No kill fee. Editorial lead time 2 months. Accepts queries by mail, e-mail. NoGuidelines by e-mail.

NONFICTION Does not want poetry or fiction. Submit query letter or complete ms, SAE.

PHOTOS Captions required. Reviews transparencies, gloss prints, 300 dpi digital images, maps/diagrams.

WOODENBOAT MAGAZINE

WoodenBoat Publications, Inc., P.O. Box 78, Brookline ME 04616. (207)359-4651. **Website:** www.woodenboat.com. **Contact:** Matt Murphy, editor. **50% freelance written.** Bimonthly magazine for wooden boat owners, builders, and designers. "We are devoted exclusively to the design, building, care, preservation, and use of wooden boats, both commercial and pleasure, old and new, sail and power. We work to convey quality, integrity, and involvement in the creation and care of these craft, to entertain, inform, inspire, and to provide our varied readers with access to individuals who are deeply experienced in the world of wooden boats." Estab. 1974. Circ. 90,000. Byline given. Pays on publication. Offers variable kill fee. Publishes ms an average of 1 year after acceptance. Accepts queries by online submission form. Accepts simultaneous submissions. Responds in 2 months to queries and mss. Sample copy for $5.99. Guidelines available online.

NONFICTION Needs technical, repair, restoration, maintenance, use, design, and building wooden boats. No poetry, fiction. **Buys 50 mss/year.** Query with published clips. Length: 1,500-5,000 words. **Pays $300/1,000 words.** Sometimes pays expenses of writers on assignment.

REPRINTS Send tearsheet or typed ms with rights for sale noted and information about when and where the material previously appeared.

PHOTOS Send photos. Identification of subjects required. Reviews negatives. Pays $15-75 b&w, $25-350 color.

COLUMNS/DEPARTMENTS Currents pays for information on wooden boat-related events, projects, boatshop activities, etc. Uses same columnists for each issue. Length: 250-1,000 words. Send complete information. **Pays $5-50.**

TIPS "We appreciate a detailed, articulate query letter, accompanied by photos, that will give us a clear idea of what the author is proposing. We appreciate samples of previously published work. It is important for a prospective author to become familiar with our magazine. Most work is submitted on speculation. The most common failure is not exploring the subject material in enough depth."

$$$ YACHTING

Bonnier Corporation, 55 Hammarlund Way, Middletown RI 02842. **Fax:** (401)845-5180. **E-mail:** letters@yachtingmagazine.com. **Website:** www.yachtingmagazine.com. **30% freelance written.** Monthly magazine covering yachts, boats. Monthly magazine written and edited for experienced, knowledgeable yachtsmen. Estab. 1907. Circ. 132,000. Byline given. Pays on acceptance. No kill fee. Editorial lead time 2 months. Submit seasonal material 6 months in advance. Accepts queries by mail, e-mail, fax. Responds in 1 month to queries. Responds in 3 months to mss. Sample copy free. Guidelines available online.

NONFICTION Needs personal experience, technical. **Buys 50 mss/year.** Query with published clips. Length: 750-800 words. **Pays $150-1,500.** Pays expenses of writers on assignment.

PHOTOS Send photos. Captions, identification of subjects, model releases required. Reviews transparencies. Negotiates payment individually.

TIPS "We require considerable expertise in our writing because our audience is experienced and knowledgeable. Vivid descriptions of quaint anchorages and quainter natives are fine, but our readers want to know how the yachtsmen got there, too. They also want to know how their boats work. *Yachting* is edited for experienced, affluent boatowners—power and sail—who don't have the time or the inclination to read sub-standard stories. They love carefully crafted stories about places they've never been or a different spin on places they have, meticulously reported pieces on issues that affect their yachting lives, personal accounts of yachting experiences from which they can learn, engaging profiles of people who share their passion for boats, insightful essays that evoke the history and traditions of the sport and compelling photographs of others enjoying the game as much as they do. They love to know what to buy and how things work. They love to be surprised. They don't mind getting their hands dirty or saving a buck here and there, but they're not interested in learning how to make a masthead light out of a mayonnaise jar. If you love what they love and can communicate like a pro (that means meeting deadlines, writing tight, being obsessively accurate and never misspelling a proper name), we'd love to hear from you."

GENERAL INTEREST

$ OUTDOORS NW

PMB Box 331, 10002 Aurora Ave. N. #36, Seattle WA 98133. (206)418-0747; (800) 935-1083. **Fax:** (206)418-0746. **E-mail:** info@outdoorsnw.com. **Website:** www.outdoorsnw.com. **80% freelance written.** Monthly magazine covering outdoor recreation in the Pacific Northwest. "Writers must have a solid knowledge of the sport they are writing about. They must be doers." Estab. 1988. Circ. 40,000. Byline given. Pays on publication. No kill fee. Publishes ms an average of 3 months after acceptance. Editorial lead time 2 months. Submit seasonal material 4 months in advance. Accepts queries by mail, e-mail, fax. Accepts simultaneous submissions. Sample copy and writer's guidelines for $3.

NONFICTION Needs interview, new product, travel. Query with published clips. Length: 750-1,500 words. **Pays $25-125.** Sometimes pays expenses of writers on assignment.

PHOTOS Send photos. Captions, identification of subjects, model releases required. Reviews electronic images only.

COLUMNS/DEPARTMENTS Faces, Places, Puruits (750 words). **Buys 4-6 mss/year.** Query with published clips. **Pays $40-75.**

TIPS "*Outdoors NW* is written for the serious Pacific Northwest outdoor recreationalist. The magazine's look, style and editorial content actively engage the reader, delivering insightful perspectives on the sports it has come to be known for—alpine skiing, bicycling, adventure racing, triathlon and multi-sport, hiking, kayaking, marathons, mountain climbing, Nordic skiing, running, and snowboarding. *Outdoors NW* magazine wants vivid writing, telling images, and original perspectives to produce its smart, entertaining monthly."

$ SILENT SPORTS

Journal Community Publishing Group, P.O. Box 620583, Middleton WI 53562. (715)258-4354; (715)369-4859. **E-mail:** info@silentsports.net. **E-mail:** editor@silentsports.net. **Website:** www.silentsports.net. **Contact:** Joel Patenaude, editor. **75% freelance written.** Monthly magazine covering running, cycling, cross-country skiing, canoeing, kayaking, snowshoeing, in-line skating, camping, backpacking, and hiking aimed at people in Wisconsin, Minnesota, northern Illinois, and portions of Michigan and Iowa. "Not a coffee table magazine. Our readers are participants from rank amateur weekend athletes to highly competitive racers." Estab. 1984. Circ. 10,000. Byline given. Pays on publication. Offers 20% kill fee. Publishes ms an average of 3 months after acceptance. Submit seasonal material 4 months in advance. Accepts queries by mail, e-mail, fax. Responds in 3 months to queries. Sample copy and writer's guidelines for 10x13 SAE with 7 first-class stamps.

NONFICTION Needs general interest, how-to, interview, opinion, technical, travel. **Buys 25 mss/year.** Query. Length: 2,500 words maximum. **Pays $15-100.** Sometimes pays expenses of writers on assignment.

REPRINTS Send typed manuscript with rights for sale noted and information about when and where the material previously appeared. Pays 50% of amount paid for an original article.

PHOTOS State availability. Reviews transparencies. Pays $5-15 for b&w story photos; $50-100 for color covers.

TIPS "Where-to-go and personality profiles are areas most open to freelancers. Writers should keep in mind that this is a regional, Midwest-based publication. We want only stories/articles with a focus on our region."

SPORTS ILLUSTRATED

Time, Inc., 1271 Avenue of the Americas, New York NY 10020. (212)522-1212. **E-mail:** story_queries@simail.com. **Website:** www.si.com. Terry McDonell, editor. Weekly magazine covering sports. *Sports Illustrated* reports and interprets the world of sport, recreation, and active leisure. It previews, analyzes, and comments upon major games and events, as well as those noteworthy for character and spirit alone. It features individuals connected to sport and evaluates trends concerning the part sport plays in contemporary life. In addition, the magazine has articles on such subjects as sports gear and swim suits. Special departments deal with sports equipment, books, and statistics. Estab. 1954. Circ. 3,339,000. No kill fee. Accepts queries by mail. Responds in 4-6 weeks to queries.

NONFICTION Query.

GOLF

$$ AFRICAN AMERICAN GOLFER'S DIGEST

80 Wall St., Suite 720, New York NY 10005. (212)571-6559. **E-mail:** debertcook@aol.com. **Website:** www.africanamericangolfersdigest.com. **Contact:** Debert Cook, managing editor. **100% freelance written.** Quarterly. Covering golf lifestyle, health, travel destinations and reviews, golf equipment, golfer profiles. "Editorial should focus on interests of our market demographic of African Americans with historical, artistic, musical, educational (higher learning), automotive, sports, fashion, entertainment, and other categories of high interest to them." Estab. 2003. Circ. 20,000. Byline given. No kill fee. Publishes ms an aver-

age of 3 months after acceptance. Editorial lead time 3-6 months. Submit seasonal material 3-6 months in advance. Accepts queries by e-mail. Accepts simultaneous submissions. Responds in 3 weeks to queries. Responds in 3 months to mss. Sample copy for $6. Guidelines by e-mail.

NONFICTION Needs how-to, interview, new product, personal experience, photo feature, technical, travel., golf-related. **Buys 3 mss/year.** Query. Length: 250-1,500 words. **Pays 10-50¢/word.**

PHOTOS State availability. Captions, identification of subjects, model releases required. Reviews GIF/JPEG files (300 dpi or higher at 4x6). Negotiates payment individually. Credit line given.

COLUMNS/DEPARTMENTS Profiles (celebrities, national leaders, entertainers, corporate leaders, etc., who golf); Travel (destination/golf course reviews); Golf Fashion (jewelry, clothing, accessories). **Buys 3 mss/year.** Query. **Pays 10-50¢/word.**

FILLERS Needs anecdotes, facts, gags, newsbreaks, short humor. **Buys 3 mss/year.** Length: 20-125 words. **Pays 10-50¢/word.**

TIPS "Emphasize golf and African American appeal."

⊖⊖ AZ GOLF INSIDER

Arizona Golf Association, 7226 N. 16th St., Suite 200, Phoenix AZ 85020. (602)944-3035. **Fax:** (602)944-3228. **Website:** www.azgolf.org. **Contact:** Brian Foster, director of marketing and communications. **50% freelance written.** Quarterly magazine covering golf in Arizona, the official publication of the Arizona Golf Association. Estab. 1999. Circ. 45,000. Byline given. Pays on acceptance. No kill fee. Editorial lead time 6 months. Submit seasonal material 3 months in advance. Accepts queries by mail. Accepts simultaneous submissions. Sample copy and writer's guidelines free.

NONFICTION Needs book excerpts, essays, historical, how-to, golf, humor, inspirational, interview, new product, opinion, personal experience, photo feature, travel, destinations. **Buys 5-10 mss/year.** Query. Length: 500-2,000 words. **Pays $50-500.** Sometimes pays expenses of writers on assignment.

PHOTOS State availability. Captions, identification of subjects required. Reviews contact sheets. Negotiates payment individually.

COLUMNS/DEPARTMENTS Short Strokes (golf news and notes), Improving Your Game (golf tips), Out of Bounds (guest editorial, 800 words). Query.

⊙ ⊚ ⊖⊖⊖ GOLF CANADA

Chill Media Inc., 482 S. Service Rd. E., Suite 103, Oakville ON L6J 2X6 Canada. (905)337-1886. **Fax:** (905)337-1887. **E-mail:** scotty@ichill.ca; alison@ichill.ca. **Website:** www.golfcanada.ca. Alison King, managing editor. **Contact:** Scott Stevenson, publisher. **80% freelance written.** Magazine published 4 times/year covering Canadian golf. *Golf Canada* is the official magazine of the Royal Canadian Golf Association, published to entertain and enlighten members about RCGA-related activities and to generally support and promote amateur golf in Canada. Estab. 1994. Circ. 159,000. Byline given. Pays 30 days after publication. Offers 25% kill fee. Editorial lead time 3 months. Submit seasonal material 6 months in advance. Accepts queries by mail, e-mail, fax, phone. Sample copy free.

NONFICTION Needs historical, interview, new product, opinion, photo feature, travel. Query with published clips. Length: word counts vary. **Rates are negotiated upon agreement.** Sometimes pays expenses of writers on assignment.

PHOTOS State availability. Captions required. Reviews contact sheets, negatives, transparencies, prints. Rates negotiated upon agreement.

COLUMNS/DEPARTMENTS Guest Column (focus on issues surrounding the Canadian golf community), 700 words. Query. **Rates are negotiated upon agreement.**

TIPS "Keep story ideas focused on Canadian competitive golf."

⊖⊖ THE GOLFER

59 E. 72nd St., New York NY 10021. (212)867-7070. **Fax:** (212)867-8550. **E-mail:** info@thegolferinc.com. **Website:** www.thegolfermag.com; www.thegolferinc.com. **40% freelance written.** Bimonthly magazine covering golf. A sophisticated tone for a lifestyle-oriented magazine. "The Golfer Inc. is an international luxury brand, a new media company that is a driving force in the game. Its website is the source for those who want the best the game has to offer—the classic courses, great destinations, finest accoutrements, most intriguing personalities and latest trends on and off the course.The magazine has distinguished itself as the highest quality, most innovative in its field. It is written for the top of the market—those who live a lifestyle shaped by their passion for the game. With its stunning photography, elegant design and evocative writing, The Golfer speaks to its affluent readers with

a sense of style and sophistication—it is a world class publication with an international flair, celebrating the lifestyle of the game." Estab. 1994. Circ. 253,000. Byline given. Pays on publication. Offers negotiable kill fee. Publishes ms an average of 2 months after acceptance. Editorial lead time 2 months. Submit seasonal material 4 months in advance. Accepts queries by mail, e-mail, fax. Accepts simultaneous submissions. Sample copy free.

NONFICTION Needs book excerpts, essays, general interest, historical, how-to, humor, inspirational, interview, new product, opinion, personal experience, photo feature, technical, travel. Send complete ms. Length: 300-2,000 words. **Pays $150-600.**

PHOTOS Send photos. Reviews any size digital files.

❸❸❸ GOLFING MAGAZINE

Golfer Magazine, Inc., 274 Silas Dean Hwy., Wethersfield CT 06109. (860)563-1633. **Fax:** (646)607-3001. **E-mail:** tlanders@golfingmagazine.net; JTorsiello@golfingMagazine.net. **Website:** www.golfingmagazineonline.com. **Contact:** Tom Landers, president and publisher; John Torsiello, editor. **30% freelance written.** Bimonthly magazine covering golf, including travel, products, player profiles and company profiles. Estab. 1999. Circ. 175,000. Byline given. Pays on publication. Offers negotiable kill fee. Editorial lead time 2 months. Submit seasonal material 2 months in advance. Accepts queries by mail, e-mail. YesSample copy free.

NONFICTION Needs book excerpts, new product, photo feature, travel. **Buys 4-5 mss/year.** Query. Length: 700-2,500 words. **Pays $250-1,000 for assigned articles. Pays $100-500 for unsolicited articles.**

PHOTOS State availability. Captions required. Reviews GIF/JPEG files. Negotiates payment and rights individually.

FILLERS Needs facts, gags. **Buys 2-3 mss/year. Payment individually determined.**

❸❸ GOLF NEWS

P.O. Box 1040, Rancho Mirage CA 92270. (760)321-8800. **Fax:** (760)328-3013. **E-mail:** golfnews@aol.com. **Website:** www.golfnewsmag.com. **Contact:** Dan Poppers, editor-in-chief. **40% freelance written.** Monthly magazine covering golf. "Our publication specializes in the creative treatment of the sport of golf, offering a variety of themes and slants as related to golf. If it's good writing and relates to golf, we're interested." Estab. 1984. Circ. 15,000. Byline given. Pays on ac-

ceptance. Publishes ms an average of 3 months after acceptance. Editorial lead time 2 months. Submit seasonal material 2 months in advance. Accepts queries by mail, e-mail. Accepts simultaneous submissions. Responds in 3 weeks to queries. Responds in 3 weeks to mss. Sample copy for $2 and 9x12 SAE with 4 first class stamps.

NONFICTION Needs book excerpts, essays, exposé, general interest, historical, humor, inspirational, interview, opinion, personal experience, real estate. **Buys 20 mss/year.** Query with published clips. **Pays $75-350.**

PHOTOS State availability. Identification of subjects required. Negotiates payment individually.

COLUMNS/DEPARTMENTS Submit ideas. **Buys 10 mss/year.** Query with published clips.

TIPS "Solid, creative, excellent, professional writing. Only good writers need apply. We are a national award-winning magazine looking for the most creative writers we can find."

❸❸❸ GOLF TIPS

Werner Publishing Corp., 12121 Wilshire Blvd., 12th Floor, Los Angeles CA 90025-1176. (310)820-1500. **Fax:** (310)826-5008. **E-mail:** editors@golftipsmag.com. **Website:** www.golftipsmag.com. **95% freelance written.** Magazine published 9 times/year covering golf instruction and equipment. "We provide mostly concise, very clear golf instruction pieces for the serious golfer." Estab. 1986. Circ. 300,000. Byline given. Pays on publication. Offers 33% kill fee. Publishes ms an average of 2 months after acceptance. Editorial lead time 3 months. Submit seasonal material 4 months in advance. Responds in 1 month to queries. Sample copy free. Guidelines on website.

NONFICTION Needs book excerpts, how-to, interview, new product, photo feature, technical, travel: all golf related. "Generally, golf essays rarely make it." **Buys 125 mss/year.** Send complete ms. Length: 250-2,000 words. **Pays $300-1,000 for assigned articles. Pays $300-800 for unsolicited articles.** Sometimes pays expenses of writers on assignment.

PHOTOS State availability. Captions, identification of subjects required. Reviews 2x2 transparencies. Negotiates payment individually.

COLUMNS/DEPARTMENTS Stroke Saver (very clear, concise instruction), 350 words; Lesson Library (book excerpts—usually in a series), 1,000 words; Travel Tips (formatted golf travel), 2,500 words. **Buys**

40 mss/year. Query with or without published clips or send complete ms. **Pays $300-850.**

TIPS "Contact a respected PGA professional and find out if they're interested in being published. A good writer can turn an interview into a decent instruction piece."

💲💲💲 MINNESOTA GOLFER

Minnesota Golf Association, 6550 York Ave. S., Suite 211, Edina MN 55435. (952)927-4643. **Fax:** (952)927-9642. **E-mail:** wp@mngolf.org; editor@mngolf.org. **Website:** www.www.mngolf.org/magazine. **Contact:** W.P. Ryan, editor. **75% freelance written.** Bimonthly magazine covering golf in Minnesota; the official publication of the Minnesota Golf Association. Estab. 1975. Circ. 66,000. Byline given. Pays on acceptance or publication. No kill fee. Editorial lead time 3 months. Accepts queries by mail, e-mail, fax.

NONFICTION Needs historical, interview, new product, travel, book reviews, instruction, golf course previews. Query with published clips. Length: 400-2,000 words. **Pays $50-750.** Sometimes pays expenses of writers on assignment.

PHOTOS State availability. Captions, identification of subjects required. Reviews contact sheets, transparencies, digital images. Negotiates payment individually.

COLUMNS/DEPARTMENTS Punch shots (golf news and notes); Q School (news and information targeted to beginners, junior golfers and women); Great Drives (featuring noteworthy golf holes in Minnesota); Instruction.

💲💲 TEXAS GOLFER MAGAZINE

Texas Golder Media, 15721 Park Row, Suite 100, Houston TX 77084. (888)863-9899. **E-mail:** george@texasgolfermagazine.com. **Website:** www.texasgolfermagazine.com. **Contact:** George Fuller, editor-in-chief/associate publisher. **10% freelance written.** Bimonthly magazine covering golf in Texas. Estab. 1984. Circ. 50,000. Byline given. Pays 10 days after publication. No kill fee. Publishes ms an average of 2 months after acceptance. Editorial lead time 2 months. Submit seasonal material 3 months in advance. Responds in 2 weeks to queries; 1 month to mss. Sample copy free. Prefers direct phone discussion for writer's guidelines.

NONFICTION Needs book excerpts, humor, personal experience, all golf-related. Travel pieces accepted about golf outside of Texas. **Buys 20 mss/year.** Query. **Pays 25-40¢/word.**

PHOTOS State availability. Captions, identification of subjects required. Reviews contact sheets, prints. No additional payment for photos accepted with ms, but pays $125 for cover photo.

TIPS "Most of our purchases are in the how-to area, so writers must know golf quite well and play the game."

💲💲 VIRGINIA GOLFER

Touchpoint Publishing, Inc., 600 Founders Bridge Blvd., Midlothian VA 23113. (804)378-2300, ext. 12. **Fax:** (804)378-2369. **E-mail:** ablair@vsga.org. **Website:** www.vsga.org. **Contact:** Andrew Blair, editor. **65% freelance written.** Bimonthly magazine covering golf in Virginia, the official publication of the Virginia State Golf Association. Estab. 1983. Circ. 45,000. Byline given. Pays on publication. No kill fee. Editorial lead time 6 months. Submit seasonal material 3 months in advance. Accepts queries by mail, e-mail. Accepts simultaneous submissions. Sample copy and writer's guidelines free.

NONFICTION Needs book excerpts, essays, historical, how-to, golf, humor, inspirational, interview, personal experience, photo feature, technical, golf equipment, where to play, golf business. **Buys 30-40 mss/year.** Send complete ms. Length: 500-2,500 words. **Pays $50-200.** Sometimes pays expenses of writers on assignment.

PHOTOS State availability. Captions, identification of subjects required. Reviews contact sheets. Negotiates payment individually.

COLUMNS/DEPARTMENTS Chip ins & Three Putts (news notes), Rules Corner (golf rules explanations and discussion), Your Game, Golf Travel (where to play), Great Holes, Q&A, Golf Business (what's happening?), Fashion. Query.

GUNS

💲💲 GUN DIGEST THE MAGAZINE

F+W Media, 700 E. State St., Iola WI 54990. (715)445-2214. **Fax:** (715)445-4087. **E-mail:** kevin.michalowski@fwmedia.com. **Website:** www.gundigest.com. **Contact:** Kevin Michalowski, senior editor. **Uses 90% freelancers.** Bimonthly magazine covering firearms. "*Gun Digest* the magazine covers all aspects of the firearms community; from collectible guns to tactical gear to reloading and accessories. We also publish gun reviews and tests of new and collectible firearms and news features about firearms legislation. We are 100 percent pro-gun, fully support the NRA and make no bones about our support of Constitutional freedoms." Byline given. Pays on publication. Publishes ms 2 months after acceptance. Editorial lead time 3 months. Accepts queries by e-mail. Responds in 3 weeks on queries; 1 month on mss. Free sample copy. Guidelines available via e-mail.

NONFICTION Needs general interest (firearms related), historical, how-to, interview, new product, nostalgic, profile, technical, All submissions must focus on firearms, accessories or the firearms industry and legislation. Stories that include hunting reference must have as their focus the firearms or ammunition used. The hunting should be secondary. Special issues: *Gun Digest* magazine also publishes an annual gear guide and 4 issues each year of *Tactical Gear Magazine*. *Tactical Gear* is designed for readers interested in self-defense, police and military gear including guns, knives, accessories and fitness. "We do not publish 'Me and Joe' hunting stories." **Buys 50-75 mss/year.** Query. 500-3,500 max. **$175-500 for assigned and for unsolicited articles. Does not pay in contributor copies.** Does not pay expenses.

PHOTOS Send photos with submission. Requires captions, identification of subjects. Reviews GIF/JPEG files (and TIF files); 300 DPI submitted on a CD (size). Offers no additional payment for photos accepted with ms.

TIPS "Be an expert in your field. Submit clear copy using the AP stylebook as your guide. Submissions are most easily handled if submitted on a CD. Ms should be saved as an MS Word Doc with photo captions at the bottom of the text. Photo captions and files should have the same names. Do not send mss with photos embedded. Well-researched stories about odd or interesting firearms are always welcomed, should have solid photo support. The Senior Editor will assign gun reviews and tests."

🜲🜲 MUZZLE BLASTS

P.O. Box 67, Friendship IN 47021. (812)667-5131. **Fax:** (812)667-5136. **E-mail:** mblastdop@seidata.com. **Website:** www.nmlra.org. **65% freelance written.** Monthly magazine. "Articles must relate to muzzleloading or the muzzleloaing era of American history." Estab. 1939. Circ. 18,500. Byline given. Pays on publication. Offers $50 kill fee. Publishes ms an average of 6 months after acceptance. Editorial lead time 4 months. Submit seasonal material 6 months in advance. Responds in 1 month to mss. Sample copy and writer's guidelines free.

NONFICTION Needs book excerpts, general interest, historical, how-to, humor, interview, new product, personal experience, photo feature, technical, travel. No subjects that do not pertain to muzzleloading. **Buys 80 mss/year.** Query. Length: 2,500 words. **Pays $150 minimum for assigned articles. Pays $50 minimum for unsolicited articles.**

PHOTOS Send photos. Captions, model releases required. Reviews prints and digital images. Negotiates payment individually.

COLUMNS/DEPARTMENTS Buys 96 mss/year. Query. **Pays $50-200.**

FICTION Must pertain to muzzleloading. Needs adventure, historical, humorous. **Buys 6 mss/year.** Query. Length: 2,500 words. **Pays $50-300.**

FILLERS Needs facts. **Pays $50.**

HIKING AND BACKPACKING

🜲🜲🜲🜲 BACKPACKER MAGAZINE

Cruz Bay Publishing, Inc., an Active Interest Media Co., 2520 55th St., Suite 210, Boulder CO 80301. **E-mail:** gfullerton@backpacker.com. **Website:** www.backpacker.com. Dennis Lewon, editor-in-chief (Features & People), dlewon@backpacker.com; Rachel Zurer, associate editor, (Destinations & Heroes), rzurer@backpacker.com; Kristy Holland, associate editor (Skills & Survival), kholland@aimmedia.com; Kristin Hostetter, gear editor (Gear), khostetter1@gmail.com. **50% freelance written.** Magazine published 9 times/year covering wilderness travel for backpackers. Estab. 1973. Circ. 340,000. Byline given. Pays on acceptance. 25% kill fee. 6 months. Accepts queries by mail (include SASE for returns), e-mail (preferred, with attachments and web links). Responds in 2-4 weeks to queries. Free sample copy. Guidelines available online.

NONFICTION Needs Primarily service based, *Backpacker* needs how-to, inspirational, interview, new product, personal experience, technical, travel., Occasionally accepts feature essays, exposé and historical stories from proven freelancers. *Backpacker* primarily covers hiking. When warranted, we cover canoeing, kayaking, snowshoeing, cross-country skiing, and other human-powered modes of travel. Wilderness or backcountry: The true backpacking experience means getting away from the trailhead and into the wilds. Whether a dayhike or a weeklong trip, out-of-the-way, unusual destinations are what we're looking for. No step-by-step accounts of what you did on your summer vacation—stories that chronicle every rest stop and gulp of water. Query with published clips before sending complete ms. Length: 150-3,000 words. **Pays 10¢-$1/word.**

PHOTOS Buys 80 photos from freelancers/issue; 720 photos/year. Needs transparencies or hi-res digital of people backpacking, camping, landscapes/scenics. Reviews photos with or without a manuscript. Model/property release required (if necessary). Accepts images in digital format. Send via ZIP, e-mail as JPEG files at 72 dpi for review (300 dpi needed to print). State availability. Payment varies.

COLUMNS/DEPARTMENTS Life List (personal essay telling a story about a premier wildnerness destination or experience) 400 words; Top 3 (great hiking destinations around a theme), 350 words; Rip & Go (weekend backpacking destinations) 400 words; Trail Mix (themed local hikes e.g. 'See This Now,' 'Braggin' Rights,' and 'Secrets of a Ranger') 50-200 words; Master Class (expert-based skills blowout, organized by beginner, intermediate and expert, on a hiking-specific theme) 900 words; Test Kitchen (food-related field test and recipes) 500 words; Out Alive (first-person, skills-based survival account) 900 words; Troubleshoot This (skills to face a specific hazard) 200 words; Chart of Death (infographic presentation of skills related to a particular survival hazard), research-based, 300-500 words; Field Notes (first-person reviews of new gear) 150 words. **Buys 50-75 mss/year.**

TIPS Our best advice is to read the publication—most freelancers don't know the magazine at all. The best way to break in is with an article for the Top 3, Rip & Go, Heroes, Trail Mix, Troubleshoot This or Out Alive departments. The ability/willingness to provide web content (GPS tracks, how-to video, audio, slideshows) may also help land an assignment.

HOCKEY

$$ MINNESOTA HOCKEY JOURNAL

Touchpoint Sports, 505 N. Hwy 169, Ste. 465, Minneapolis MN 55441. (763)595-0808. **Fax:** (763)595-0016. **E-mail:** mhj@touchpointsports.com; greg@touchpointsports.com. **Website:** www.minnesotahockeyjournal.com. **50% freelance written.** Journal published 4 times/year covering Minnesota hockey. Estab. 2000. Circ. 40,000. Byline given. Pays on publication. No kill fee. Editorial lead time 6 months. Submit seasonal material 4 months in advance. Accepts simultaneous submissions. Sample copy and writer's guidelines free.

NONFICTION Needs essays, general interest, historical, how-to, play hockey, humor, inspirational, interview, new product, opinion, personal experience, photo feature, travel, hockey camps, pro hockey, juniors, college, Olympics, youth. **Buys 3-5 mss/year.** Query. Length: 500-1,500 words. **Pays $100-300.**

PHOTOS State availability. Captions, identification of subjects required. Reviews contact sheets. Negotiates payment individually.

$$$ USA HOCKEY MAGAZINE

Touchpoint Sports, 1775 Bob Johnson Dr., Colorado Springs CO 80906. (719)576-8724. **Fax:** (763)538-1160. **E-mail:** usah@usahockey.org; info@touchpointsports.com. **Website:** www.usahockeymagazine.com; www.usahockey.com. **Contact:** Harry Thompson, editor-in-chief. **60% freelance written.** Magazine published 10 times/year covering amateur hockey in the U.S. The world's largest hockey magazine, *USA Hockey Magazine* is the official magazine of USA Hockey, Inc., the national governing body of hockey. Estab. 1980. Circ. 444,000. Byline given. Pays on acceptance or publication. No kill fee. Editorial lead time 6 months. Submit seasonal material 4 months in advance. Accepts simultaneous submissions. Sample copy and writer's guidelines free.

NONFICTION Needs essays, general interest, historical, how-to, play hockey, humor, inspirational, interview, new product, opinion, personal experience, photo feature, travel, hockey camps, pro hockey, juniors, college, NCAA hockey championships, Olympics, youth, etc. **Buys 20-30 mss/year.** Query. Length: 500-5,000 words. **Pays $50-750.** Pays expenses of writers on assignment.

PHOTOS State availability. Captions, identification of subjects required. Reviews contact sheets. Negotiates payment individually.

COLUMNS/DEPARTMENTS Short Cuts (news and notes); Coaches' Corner (teaching tips); USA Hockey; Inline Notebook (news and notes). **Pays $150-250.**

FICTION Needs adventure, humorous, slice-of-life vignettes. **Buys 10-20 mss/year. Pays $150-1,000.**

FILLERS Needs anecdotes, facts, gags, newsbreaks, short humor. **Buys 20-30 mss/year.** Length: 10-100 words. **Pays $25-250.**

TIPS "Writers must have a general knowledge and enthusiasm for hockey, including ice, inline, street, and other. The primary audience is youth players in the U.S."

HORSE RACING

⊜⊜ HOOF BEATS

750 Michigan Ave., Columbus OH 43215. **E-mail:** hoofbeats@ustrotting.com. **Website:** www.hoofbeats-magazine.com. **60% freelance written.** Monthly magazine covering harness racing and standardbred horses. "Articles and photos must relate to harness racing or standardbreds. We do not accept any topics that do not touch on these subjects." Estab. 1933. Circ. 10,000. Byline given. Pays on publication. Offers 25% kill fee. Publishes ms an average of 2-4 months after acceptance. Editorial lead time 6 months. Submit seasonal material 6 months in advance. Accepts queries by mail, e-mail, fax. Accepts simultaneous submissions. Responds in 2 weeks to queries. Responds in 1 month to mss. Sample copy available online. Guidelines free.

NONFICTION Needs general interest, how-to, interview, personal experience, photo feature, technical. "We do not want any fiction or poetry." **Buys 48-72 mss/year.** Query. Length: 750-3,000 words. **Pays $100-500. Pays $100-500 for unsolicited articles.**

PHOTOS State availability. Identification of subjects required. Reviews contact sheets. We offer $25-100 per photo.

COLUMNS/DEPARTMENTS Equine Clinic (standardbreds who overcame major health issues), 900-1,200 words; Profiles (short profiles on people or horses in harness racing), 600-1,000 words; Industry Trends (issues impacting standardbreds & harness racing), 1,000-2,000 words. **Buys 60 mss/year mss/year.** Query. **Pays $100-500.**

TIPS "We welcome new writers who know about harness racing or are willing to learn about it. Make sure to read *Hoof Beats* before querying to see our slant & style. We look for informative/promotional stories on harness racing—not exposés on the sport."

HUNTING AND FISHING

⊜⊜ ALABAMA GAME & FISH

Game & Fish, 2250 Newmarket Pkwy., Suite 110, Marietta GA 30067. (770)953-9222. **Fax:** (678)279-7512. **E-mail:** ken.dunwoody@imoutdoors.com. **Website:** www.alabamagameandfish.com. Jimmy Jacobs, editor. **Contact:** Ken Dunwoody, editorial director. See *Game & Fish.* Pays a kill fee.

⊜⊜ AMERICAN ANGLER

735 Broad St., Augusta GA 30904. (706)828-3971. **E-mail:** steve.walburn@morris.com; wayne.knight@morris.com. **Website:** www.americanangler.com. **Contact:** Steve Walburn, editor; Wayne Knight, art director. **95% freelance written.** Bimonthly magazine covering fly fishing. "*American Angler* is devoted exclusively to fly fishing. We focus mainly on coldwater fly fishing for trout, steelhead, and salmon, but we also run articles about warmwater and saltwater fly fishing. Our mission is to supply our readers with well-written, accurate articles on every aspect of the sport—angling techniques and methods, reading water, finding fish, selecting flies, tying flies, fish behavior, places to fish, casting, managing line, rigging, tackle, accessories, entomology, and any other relevant topics. Each submission should present specific, useful information that will increase our readers' enjoyment of the sport and help them catch more fish." Estab. 1976. Circ. 35,000. Byline given. Pays on publication. No kill fee. Publishes ms an average of 6 months after acceptance. Editorial lead time 3 months. Submit seasonal material 5 months in advance. Accepts queries by e-mail only to steve.walburn@morris.com. Accepts simultaneous submissions. Responds in 6 weeks to queries. Responds in 2 months to mss.

NONFICTION Needs how-to, most important, personal experience, photo feature, seldom, technical. No superficial, broad-brush coverage of subjects. **Buys 45-60 mss/year.** Query with published clips. Length: 800-2,200 words. **Pays $200-600.**

REPRINTS Send information about when and where the material previously appeared. Pay negotiable.

PHOTOS "How-to pieces—those that deal with tactics, rigging, fly tying, and the like—must be accompanied by appropriate photography or rough sketches for our illustrator. Naturally, where-to stories must be illustrated with shots of scenery, people fishing, anglers holding fish, and other pictures that help flesh out the story and paint the local color. Do not bother sending sub-par photographs. We only accept photos that are well lit, tack sharp, and correctly framed. A fly-tying submission should always include samples of flies to send to our staff photographer, even if photos of the flies are included." Send photos. Captions, identification of subjects required. Digital photos only. Offers no additional payment for photos accepted with ms. Pays $600-700 for color cover; $30-350 for color inside. Pays on publication. Credit line given. Buys one-time rights, first rights for covers. "Payment is made just prior to publication. "We don't pay by the word, and length is only one of the variables considered. The quality and completeness of a submission may be more important than its length in determining rates, and articles that include good photography are usually worth more. As a guideline, the following rates generally apply: Feature articles pay $450 (and perhaps a bit more if we're impressed), while short features pay $200 to $400. Generally, these rates assume that useful photos, drawings, or sketches accompany the words.

COLUMNS/DEPARTMENTS One-page shorts (problem solvers), 350-750 words. Query with published clips. **Pays $100-300.**

TIPS "If you are submitting for the first time, please submit complete queries."

⊛⊛⊛ AMERICAN HUNTER

National Rifle Association, 11250 Waples Mill Rd., Fairfax VA 22030-9400. (703)267-1336. **Fax:** (703)267-3971. **E-mail:** publications@nrahq.org; americanhunter@nrahq.org; lcromwell@nrahq.org. **Website:** www.americanhunter.org. **Contact:** J. Scott Olmsted, editor-in-chief. Monthly magazine for hunters who are members of the National Rifle Association (NRA). "*American Hunter* contains articles dealing with various sport hunting and related activities both at home and abroad. With the encouragement of the sport as a prime game management tool, emphasis is on technique, sportsmanship and safety. In each issue hunting equipment and firearms are evaluated, legislative happenings affecting the sport are reported, lore and legend are retold and the business of the Association is recorded in the Official Journal section." Circ. 1,000,000. Byline given. Pays on publication. No kill fee. Accepts queries by mail, e-mail. Responds in 6 months to queries. Guidelines with #10 SASE.

NONFICTION Special issues: Pheasants, whitetail tactics, black bear feed areas, mule deer, duck hunters' transport by land and sea, tech topics to be decided; rut strategies, muzzleloader moose and elk, fall turkeys, staying warm, goose talk, long-range muzzleloading. Not interested in material on fishing, camp-

ing, or firearms knowledge. Query. Length: 1,800-2,000 words. **Pays up to $1,000.**

REPRINTS Copies for author will be provided upon publication. No reprints possible.

PHOTOS Captions preferred. Accepts images in digital format only, no slides. Model release required "for every recognizable human face in a photo." Pays $125-600/image; $1,000 for color cover; $400-1,400 for text/photo package. Pays on publication. Credit line given. No additional payment made for photos used with ms. Photos purchased with or without accompanying mss.

COLUMNS/DEPARTMENTS Hunting Guns, Hunting Loads, destination and adventure, and Public Hunting Grounds. Study back issues for appropriate subject matter and style. Length: 800-1,500 words. **Pays $300-800.**

TIPS "Although unsolicited mss are accepted, detailed query letters outlining the proposed topic and approach are appreciated and will save both writers and editors a considerable amount of time. If we like your story idea, you will be contacted by mail or phone and given direction on how we'd like the topic covered. NRA Publications accept all mss and photographs for consideration on a speculation basis only. Story angles should be narrow, but coverage must have depth. How-to articles are popular with readers and might range from methods for hunting to techniques on making gear used on successful hunts. Where-to articles should contain contacts and information needed to arrange a similar hunt. All submissions are judged on three criteria: Story angle (it should be fresh, interesting, and informative); quality of writing (clear and lively—capable of holding the readers' attention throughout); and quality and quantity of accompanying photos (sharpness, reproducability, and connection to text are most important.)"

⊛⊛ ARKANSAS SPORTSMAN

Game & Fish, 2250 Newmarket Pkwy., Suite 110, Marietta GA 30067. (770)953-9222. **Fax:** (678)279-7512. **E-mail:** ken.dunwoody@imoutdoors.com. **Website:** www.arkansassportsmanmag.com. Nick Gilmore, editor. **Contact:** Ken Dunwoody, editorial director. See *Game & Fish*. Pays a kill fee.

⊛ BACON BUSTERS

Yaffa Publishing, 17-21 Bellevue St., Surry Hills NSW 2010 Australia. (61)(2)9281-2333. **Fax:** (61)(2)9281-2750. **E-mail:** editor@baconbusters.com.au. **Website:** www.yaffa.com.au. **Contact:** Clint Magro, editor. Bimonthly magazine covering the hog hunting scene in Australia. "*Bacon Busters* content includes readers' short stories, how-to articles, pig hunting features, technical advice, pig dog profiles, and Australia's biggest collection of pig hunting photos. Not to mention the famous Babes & Boars section!" Estab. 1995.

NONFICTION Needs exposé, general interest, how-to, interview. Query.

BASSMASTER MAGAZINE

B.A.S.S. Publications, 1170 Celebration Blvd., Suite 200, Celebration FL 32830. (407)566-2277. **Fax:** (407)566-2072. **E-mail:** editorial@bassmaster.com. **Website:** www.bassmaster.com. **80% freelance written.** Magazine published 11 times/year about largemouth, smallmouth, and spotted bass, offering how-to articles for dedicated beginning and advanced bass fishermen, including destinations and new product reviews. Estab. 1968. Circ. 600,000. Byline given. Pays on acceptance. No kill fee. Publishes ms an average of less than 1 year after acceptance. Editorial lead time 2 months. Submit seasonal material 6 months in advance. Accepts queries by mail, e-mail. Responds in 2 months to queries. Sample copy upon request. Guidelines for #10 SASE.

Needs destination stories (how to fish a certain area) for the Northwest and Northeast.

NONFICTION Needs historical, how-to, patterns, lures, etc., interview, of knowledgeable people in the sport, new product, reels, rods, and bass boats, travel, where to go fish for bass, conservation related to bass fishing. No first-person, personal experience-type articles. **Buys 100 mss/year.** Query. Length: 500-1,500 words. **Pays $100-300.**

PHOTOS Send photos. Captions, model releases required. Reviews transparencies. Offers no additional payment for photos accepted with ms, but pays $800 for color cover transparencies.

COLUMNS/DEPARTMENTS Short Cast/News/Views/Notes/Briefs (upfront regular feature covering news-related events such as new state bass records, unusual bass fishing happenings, conservation, new products, and editorial viewpoints). Length: 250-400 words. **Pays $100-300.**

TIPS "Editorial direction continues in the short, more direct how-to article. Compact, easy-to-read information is our objective. Shorter articles with good graphics, such as how-to diagrams, step-by-step instruction, etc., will enhance a writer's articles submitted to *Bass-*

master Magazine. The most frequent mistakes made by writers in completing an article for us are poor grammar, poor writing, poor organization, and superficial research. Send in detailed queries outlining specific objectives of article, obtain writer's guidelines. Be as concise as possible."

BC OUTDOORS HUNTING AND SHOOTING

Outdoor Group Media, #201a-7261 River Place, Mission BC T4S 0A2 Canada. (604)820-3400. **Fax:** (604)820-3477. **E-mail:** info@outdoorgroupmedia. com; mmitchell@outdoorgroupmedia.com; production@outdoorgroupmedia.com. **Website:** www. bcoutdoorsmagazine.com. **Contact:** Mike Mitchell, editor. **80% freelance written.** Biannual magazine covering hunting, shooting, camping, and backroads in British Columbia, Canada. "*BC Outdoors Magazine* publishes 7 sport fishing issues a year with 2 hunting and shooting supplement issues each summer and fall. Our magazine is about the best outdoor experiences in BC. Whether you're camping on an ocean shore, hiking into your favorite lake, or learning how to fly-fish on your favourite river, we want to showcase what our province has to offer to sport fishing and outdoor enthusiasts. *BC Outdoors Hunting and Shooting* provides trusted editorial for trapping, deer hunting, big buck, bowhunting, bag limits, baitling, decoys, calling, camouflage, tracking, trophy hunting, pheasant hunting, goose hunting, hunting regulations, duck hunting, whitetail hunting, hunting regulations, hunting trips, and mule deer hunting." Estab. 1945. Circ. 30,000. Byline given. Pays on publication. Offers kill fee. Publishes ms an average of 3 months after acceptance. Accepts queries by e-mail. Guidelines for 8x10 SASE with 7 Canadian first-class stamps.

NONFICTION Needs how-to, new or innovative articles on hunting subjects, personal experience, outdoor adventure, outdoor topics specific to British Columbia. **Buys 50 mss/year.** "Please query the publication before submitting. Please do not send unsolicited mss or photos. Your pitch should be no more than 100-words outlining exactly what your story will be. You should be able to encapsulate the essence of your story and show us why our readers would be interested in reading or knowing what you are writing about. Queries need to be clear, succinct and straight to the point. Show us why we should publish your article in

150 words or less." Length: 1,700-2,000 words. **Pays $300-500.**

PHOTOS Biannual magazine emphasizing hunting, RV camping, canoeing, wildlife and management issues in British Columbia only. Sample copy available for $4.95 Canadian. Family oriented. "By far, most photos accompany manuscripts. We are always on the lookout for good covers—wildlife, recreational activities, people in the outdoors—of British Columbia, vertical and square format. Photos with manuscripts must, of course, illustrate the story. There should, as far as possible, be something happening. Photos generally dominate lead spread of each story. They are used in everything from double-page bleeds to thumbnails." State availability. Model/property release preferred. Photo captions or at least full identification required.

COLUMNS/DEPARTMENTS Column needs basically supplied in-house.

TIPS "Send us material on fishing and hunting. We generally just send back nonrelated work. We want in-depth information and professional writing only. Emphasis on environmental issues. Those pieces with a conservation component have a better chance of being published. Subject must be specific to British Columbia. We receive many mss written by people who obviously do not know the magazine or market. The writer has a better chance of breaking in with short, lesser-paying articles and fillers, because we have a stable of regular writers who produce most main features."

🌐💲 CALIFORNIA GAME & FISH

Game & Fish, 2250 Newmarket Pkwy., Suite 110, Marietta GA 30067. (770)953-9222. **Fax:** (678)279-7512. **E-mail:** ken.dunwoody@imoutdoors.com. **Website:** www.californiagameandfish.com. Daniel McElrath, editor. See *Game & Fish*. Pays a kill fee.

🌐💲 DEER & DEER HUNTING

F+W Media, Inc., 700 E. State St., Iola WI 54990. (715)445-2214. **E-mail:** dan.schmidt@fwmedia.com. **Website:** www.deeranddeerhunting.com. **Contact:** Dan Schmidt, editor-in-chief. **95% freelance written.** Magazine published 10 times/year covering white-tailed deer. "Readers include a cross section of the deer hunting population—individuals who hunt with bow, gun, or camera. The editorial content of the magazine focuses on white-tailed deer biology and behavior, management principle and practices, habitat requirements, natural history of deer, hunt-

ing techniques, and hunting ethics. We also publish a wide range of how-to articles designed to help hunters locate and get close to deer at all times of the year. The majority of our readership consists of 2-season hunters (bow & gun) and approximately one-third camera hunt." Estab. 1977. Circ. 200,000. Byline given. Pays on acceptance. No kill fee. Publishes ms an average of 18 months after acceptance. Editorial lead time 6 months. Submit seasonal material 12 months in advance. Accepts queries by mail, e-mail. Responds in 1 month to queries. Responds in 2 months to mss. Sample copy for 9x12 SASE. Guidelines available on website.

NONFICTION Needs general interest, historical, how-to, photo feature, technical. No "Joe and me" articles. **Buys 100 mss/year.** Send complete ms. Length: 1,000-2,000 words. **Pays $150-600 for assigned articles. Pays $150-400 for unsolicited articles.** Sometimes pays expenses of writers on assignment.

PHOTOS Send photos. Captions required. Reviews transparencies. Offers $75-250/photo; $600 for cover photos.

COLUMNS/DEPARTMENTS Deer Browse (odd occurrences), 500 words. **Buys 10 mss/year.** Query. **Pays $25-250.**

FICTION Mood deer hunting pieces. **Buys 9 mss/year.** Send complete ms.

FILLERS Needs facts, newsbreaks. **Buys 40-50 mss/year.** Length: 100-500 words. **Pays $15-150.**

TIPS "Feature articles dealing with deer biology or behavior should be documented by scientific research (the author's or that of others) as opposed to a limited number of personal observations."

🌐💲 THE DRAKE MAGAZINE

P.O. Box 11546, Denver CO 80211. (949)218-8642. **E-mail:** info@drakemag.com. **Website:** www.drakemag. com. **70% freelance written.** Quarterly magazine for people who love flyfishing. Estab. 1998. Byline given. Pays 1 month after publication. No kill fee. Publishes ms an average of 1 year after acceptance. Editorial lead time 1 year. Submit seasonal material 1 year in advance. Accepts queries by e-mail. Responds in 6 months to mss. Guidelines available online.

NONFICTION Needs flyfishing news items from your local area, historical, humor, opinion, personal experience, photo feature, short essays, travel, flyfishing related. **Buys 20-30 mss/year.** Query. Length:

650-2,000 words. **Pays 25¢/word, "depending on the amount of work we have to put into the piece."**

PHOTOS State availability. Offers $50-200/photo.

💲💲💲 FIELD & STREAM

2 Park Ave., New York NY 10016. (212)779-5296. **Fax:** (212)779-5114. **E-mail:** fsletters@bonniercorp.com. **Website:** www.fieldandstream.com. **50% freelance written.** Broad-based monthly service magazine for the hunter and fisherman. Editorial content consists of articles of penetrating depth about national hunting, fishing, and related activities. Also humor, personal essays, profiles on outdoor people, conservation, sportsmen's insider secrets, tactics and techniques, and adventures. Estab. 1895. Circ. 1,500,000. Byline given. Pays on acceptance for most articles. No kill fee. Accepts queries by mail. Responds in 1 month to queries. Guidelines available online.

PHOTOS Contact: Photo editor. Send photos. Reviews slides (prefers color). When purchased separately, pays $450 minimum for color.

TIPS "Above all, study the magazine before submitting anything."

💲💲 FLORIDA GAME & FISH

Game & Fish, 2250 Newmarket Pkwy., Suite 110, Marietta GA 30067. (770)953-9222. **Fax:** (678)279-7512. **E-mail:** ken.dunwoody@imoutdoors.com. **Website:** www.floridagameandfish.com. Jimmy Jacobs, editor. **Contact:** Ken Dunwoody, editorial director. See *Game & Fish*. Pays a kill fee.

💲💲 FLORIDA SPORTSMAN

Wickstrom Communications, Intermedia Outdoors, 2700 S. Kanner Hwy., Stuart FL 34994. (772)219-7400. **Fax:** (772)219-6900. **E-mail:** editor@floridasportsman.com. **Website:** www.floridasportsman.com. **30% freelance written.** Monthly magazine covering fishing, boating, hunting, and related sports—Florida and Caribbean only. Edited for the boatowner and offshore, coastal, and fresh water fisherman. It provides a how, when, and where approach in its articles, which also includes occasional camping, diving, and hunting stories—plus ecology; in-depth articles and editorials attempting to protect Florida's wilderness, wetlands, and natural beauty. Circ. 115,000. Byline given. Pays on acceptance. No kill fee. Publishes ms an average of 6 months after acceptance. Submit seasonal material 6 months in advance. Accepts queries by mail, e-mail. Responds in 2 months to queries. Re-

sponds in 1 month to mss. Sample copy free. Guidelines available at www.floridasportsman.com/submission_guidelines.

NONFICTION Needs essays, environment or nature, how-to, fishing, hunting, boating, humor, outdoors angle, personal experience, in fishing, etc., technical, boats, tackle, etc., as particularly suitable for Florida specialties. **Buys 40-60 mss/year.** Query. Length: 1,500-2,500 words. **Pays $475.**

PHOTOS Send photos. High-res digital images on CD preferred. Reviews 35mm transparencies, 4×5 and larger prints. Offers no additional payment for photos accepted with ms. Pays up to $750 for cover photos.

TIPS "Feature articles are sometimes open to freelancers; however there is little chance of acceptance unless contributor is an accomplished and avid outdoorsman *and* a competent writer-photographer with considerable experience in Florida."

💲💲 FLW BASS FISHING MAGAZINE

FLW Outdoors, 30 Gamble Lane, Benton KY 42025. **E-mail:** cmoore@flwoutdoors.com. **Website:** www.flwoutdoors.com. **Contact:** Colin Moore, editor. **40% freelance written.** Magazines published 8 times/year covering bass. "*FLW Bass Fishing Magazine* and *FLW Walleye Fishing Magazine* caters to all anglers from beginning weekend anglers to hardcore professional anglers. Our magazine seeks to educate as well as entertain anglers with cutting-edge techniques and new product innovations being used by America's top fishermen." Estab. 1979. Circ. 100,000+. Byline given. Pays on acceptance. Publishes ms an average of 4 months after acceptance. Editorial lead time 5 months. Submit seasonal material 1 year in advance. Accepts queries by mail, e-mail. NoSample copy free. Guidelines free.

NONFICTION Needs how-to, new product, photo feature, technical. Does not want "me-and-Bubba-went-fishing type stories"; stories about author's first trip to catch a certain type of fish; orstories in the first person about catching a fish. **Buys 50-75 mss/year.** Query. Length: 800-1,250 words. **Pays $400-500.** Sometimes pays expenses of writers on assignment.

PHOTOS State availability. Captions required. Reviews contact sheets, GIF/JPEG files. Offers $50-200/photo.

COLUMNS/DEPARTMENTS Destinations; Environment; Boat Tech; Tackle Maintenance. **Buys 20-30 mss/year.** Query. **Pays $100-300.**

TIPS "This how-to fishing magazine provide readers with information on the tactics and techniques that the pros who win FLW Bass Fishing Tournaments use. Emphasis is placed on seasonal fishing techniques that work."

🅢 FLY FISHERMAN MAGAZINE

P.O. Box 420235, Palm Coast FL 32142. **E-mail:** fly-fish@emailcustomerservice.com. **Website:** www.fly-fisherman.com. **Contact:** Jeff Simpson. Published 6 times/year covering fly fishing. Written for anglers who fish primarily with a fly rod and for other anglers who would like to learn more about fly fishing. Circ. 120,358. No kill fee.

🅢🅢 FUR-FISH-GAME

2878 E. Main St., Columbus OH 43209-9947. **E-mail:** ffgcox@ameritech.net. **Website:** www.furfishgame.com. **Contact:** Mitch Cox, editor. **65% freelance written.** Monthly magazine for outdoorsmen of all ages who are interested in hunting, fishing, trapping, dogs, camping, conservation, and related topics. Estab. 1900. Circ. 118,000. Byline given. Pays on acceptance. No kill fee. Publishes ms an average of 4 months after acceptance. Responds in 2 months to queries. Sample copy for $1 and 9x12 SASE. Guidelines with #10 SASE.
NONFICTION Query. Length: 500-3,000 words. **Pays $50-250 or more for features depending upon quality, photo support, and importance to magazine.**
PHOTOS Send photos. Captions. Reviews transparencies, color 5×7 or 8×10 prints, digital photos on CD only with thumbnail sheet of small images and a numbered caption sheet. Pays $35 for separate freelance photos.
TIPS "We are always looking for quality how-to articles about fish, game animals, or birds that are popular with everyday outdoorsmen but often overlooked in other publications, such as catfish, bluegill, crappie, squirrel, rabbit, crows, etc. We also use articles on standard seasonal subjects such as deer and pheasant, but like to see a fresh approach or new technique. Instructional trapping articles are useful all year. Articles on gun dogs, ginseng, and do-it-yourself projects are also popular with our readers. An assortment of photos and/or sketches greatly enhances any manuscript, and sidebars, where applicable, can also help. No phone queries, please."

🅢🅢 GAME & FISH

2250 Newmarket Pkwy., Suite 110, Marietta GA 30067. (770)953-9222. **Fax:** (678)279-7512. **E-mail:** ken.dunwoody@imoutdoors.com. **Website:** www.gameandfishmag.com. **Contact:** Ken Dunwoody, editorial director; Ron Sinfelt, photo editor; Allen Hansen, graphic artist. **90% freelance written.** Publishes 28 different monthly outdoor magazines, each one covering the fishing and hunting opportunities in a particular state or region (see individual titles to contact editors). Estab. 1975. Circ. 570,000 for 28 state-specific magazines. Byline given. Pays 3 months prior to cover date of issue. Offers negotiable kill fee. Publishes ms an average of 7 months after acceptance. Submit seasonal material 8 months in advance. Accepts queries by mail, e-mail, fax. Responds in 3 months to queries. Sample copy for $3.50 and 9x12 SASE. Guidelines for #10 SASE.
NONFICTION Length: 1,500-2,400 words. **Pays $150-300; additional payment made for electronic rights.**
PHOTOS Captions, identification of subjects required. Reviews transparencies, prints, digital images. Cover photos $250, inside color $75, and b&w $25.
TIPS "Our readers are experienced anglers and hunters, and we try to provide them with useful, specific articles about where, when, and how to enjoy the best hunting and fishing in their state or region. We also cover topics concerning game and fish management. Most articles should be tightly focused and aimed at outdoorsmen in 1 particular state. After familiarizing themselves with our magazine(s), writers should query the appropriate state editor (see individual listings) or send to Ken Dunwoody."

🅢🅢 GEORGIA SPORTSMAN

Game & Fish, 2250 Newmarket Pkwy., Suite 110, Marietta GA 30067. (770)953-9222. **Fax:** (678)279-7512. **E-mail:** ken.dunwoody@imoutdoors.com. **Website:** www.georgiasportsmanmag.com. Jimmy Jacobs, editor. **Contact:** Ken Dunwoody, editorial director. See *Game & Fish.* Pays a kill fee.

🅢🅢🅢 GRAY'S SPORTING JOURNAL

Morris Communications Corp., 735 Broad St., Augusta GA 30901. (706)724-0851. **E-mail:** editorgsj@gmail.com; russ.lumpkin@morris.com. **Website:** www.grayssportingjournal.com. **Contact:** James R. Babb, editor; Russ Lumpkin, managing editor. **75% freelance written.** 7 issues per year magazine High-end hunting and fishing—think *Field & Stream* meets *The New Yorker.* "We expect competent, vividly written prose—fact or fiction—that has high entertainment value for a very sophisticated audience of experienced hunters and anglers. We do not consider previously published material. We do, however, occasionally run prepublication book excerpts. To get a feel for what Gray's publishes, review several back issues. Note that we do not, as a rule, publish 'how-to' articles; this is the province of our regular columnists." Estab. 1975. Circ. 32,000. Byline given. Pays on publication. No kill fee. Publishes ms an average of 1 year after acceptance. Editorial lead time 14 months. Submit seasonal material 16 months in advance. Accepts simultaneous submissions. Responds in 3 months to mss. Guidelines available online.

NONFICTION Needs essays, historical, humor, personal experience, photo feature, travel. Special issues: Gray's publishes three themed issues each year: August is always entirely devoted to upland bird-hunting; April to fly fishing; December to sporting travel. All other issues—February, May, September, November—focus on seasonally appropriate themes. Each issue always features a travel piece, from exotic destinations to right around the corner. We publish no how-to of any kind. **Buys 20-30 mss/year.** Send complete ms. Length: 1,500-12,000 words. **Pays $600-1,000 for unsolicited articles.**

PHOTOS State availability. Reviews contact sheets, GIF/JPEG files. We negotiate payment individually.

FICTION Accepts quality fiction with some aspect of hunting or fishing at the core. Needs adventure, experimental, historical, humorous, slice-of-life vignettes. If some aspect of hunting or fishing isn't at the core of the story, it has zero chance of interesting *Gray's.* **Buys 20 mss/year mss/year.** Send complete ms. Length: 1,500-12,000 words. **Pays $600-1,000.**

POETRY Needs avant-garde, haiku, light verse, traditional. Buys 7/year poems/year. Submit maximum 3 poems. Length: 10-40 lines.

TIPS "Write something different, write something well—fiction or nonfiction—write something that goes to the heart of hunting or fishing more elegantly, more inspirationally, than the 1,500 or so other unsolicited manuscripts we review each year. For best results, submit by e-mail. Mail submissions can take weeks longer to hear back."

🐟🐟 ILLINOIS GAME & FISH

Game & Fish, 2250 Newmarket Pkwy., Suite 110, Marietta GA 30067. (770)953-9222. **Fax:** (678)279-7512. **E-mail:** ken.dunwoody@imoutdoors.com. **Website:** www.illinoisgameandfish.com. Daniel McElrath, editor. **Contact:** Ken Dunwoody, editorial director. See *Game & Fish.* Pays a kill fee.

🐟🐟 IOWA GAME & FISH

Game & Fish, 2250 Newmarket Pkwy., Suite 110, Marietta GA 30067. (770)953-9222. **Fax:** (678)279-7512. **E-mail:** ken.dunwoody@imoutdoors.com. **Website:** www.iowagameandfish.com. Daniel McElrath, editor. **Contact:** Ken Dunwoody, editorial director. See *Game & Fish.* Pays a kill fee.

🐟🐟 KENTUCKY GAME & FISH

Game & Fish, 2250 Newmarket Pkwy., Suite 110, Marietta GA 30067. (770)953-9222. **Fax:** (678)279-7512. **E-mail:** ken.dunwoody@imoutdoors.com. **Website:** www.kentuckygameandfish.com. Jimmy Jacobs, editor. **Contact:** Ken Dunwoody, editorial director. See *Game & Fish.* Pays a kill fee.

🐟🐟 THE MAINE SPORTSMAN

183 State St., Augusta ME 04330. (207)622-4242. **Fax:** (207)622-4255. **E-mail:** harry@mainesportsman.com. **Website:** www.mainesportsman.com. **80% freelance written.** Monthly tabloid covering Maine's outdoor. "Eager to work with new/unpublished writers, but because we run over 30 regular columns, it's hard to get into *The Maine Sportsman* as a beginner." Estab. 1972. Circ. 30,000. Byline given. Pays during month of publication. No kill fee. Publishes ms an average of 3 months after acceptance. Accepts queries by mail, e-mail. Responds in 2 weeks to queries.

NONFICTION Buys 25-40 mss/year. Send complete ms via e-mail Length: 200-2,000 words. **Pays $20-300.** Sometimes pays expenses of writers on assignment.

REPRINTS Send typed ms via e-mail or query with rights for sale noted. Pays 100% of amount paid for an original article.

PHOTOS Send color slides, color prints, or JPGs/TIFFs via e-mail. Pays $5-50 for b&w print.

TIPS "We publish numerous special sections each year and are eager to buy Maine-oriented articles on snowmobiling, ice fishing, boating, salt water and deer hunting. Send articles or queries."

❸❸ MARLIN

P.O. Box 8500, Winter Park FL 32790. (407)628-4802. **Fax:** (407)628-7061. **E-mail:** editor@marlinmag.com. **Website:** www.marlinmag.com. **90% freelance written.** Magazine published 8 times/year covering the sport of big game fishing (billfish, tuna, dorado, and wahoo). "Our readers are sophisticated, affluent, and serious about their sport—they expect a high-class, well-written magazine that provides information and practical advice." Estab. 1982. Circ. 50,000. Byline given. Pays on acceptance. No kill fee. Publishes ms an average of 3 months after acceptance. Submit seasonal material 3 months in advance. YesSample copy free with SASE. Guidelines available online.

NONFICTION Needs general interest, how-to, bait-rigging, tackle maintenance, etc., new product, personal experience, photo feature, technical, travel. No freshwater fishing stories. No 'Me & Joe went fishing' stories. **Buys 30-50 mss/year.** Query with published clips. Length: 800-3,000 words. **Pays $250-500.**

REPRINTS Send photocopy and information about when and where the material previously appeared. Pays 50-75% of amount paid for original article.

PHOTOS State availability. Reviews original slides. Offers $50-300 for inside use, $1,000 for a cover.

COLUMNS/DEPARTMENTS Tournament Reports (reports on winners of major big game fishing tournaments), 200-400 words; Blue Water Currents (news features), 100-400 words. **Buys 25 mss/year.** Query. **Pays $75-250.**

TIPS "Tournament reports are a good way to break in to *Marlin*. Make them short but accurate, and provide photos of fishing action or winners' award shots (*not* dead fish hanging up at the docks). We always need how-tos and news items. Our destination pieces (travel stories) emphasize where and when to fish, but also include information on where to stay. For features: Crisp, high-action stories with emphasis on exotic nature, adventure, personality, etc.—nothing flowery or academic. Technical/how-to: concise and informational—specific details. News: Again, concise with good details—watch for legislation affecting big game fishing, outstanding catches, new clubs and organizations, new trends, and conservation issues."

❸ MICHIGAN OUT-OF-DOORS

P.O. Box 30235, Lansing MI 48909. (517)371-1041. **Fax:** (517)371-1505. **E-mail:** thansen@mucc.org; magazine@mucc.org. **Website:** www.michiganoutofdoors.

com. **Contact:** Tony Hansen, editor. **75% freelance written.** Monthly magazine emphasizing Michigan hunting and fishing with associated conservation issues. Estab. 1947. Circ. 40,000. Byline given. Pays on acceptance. No kill fee. Publishes ms an average of 6 months after acceptance. Submit seasonal material 6 months in advance. Accepts queries by e-mail only. Responds in 1 month to queries. Sample copy for $3.50. Guidelines for free.

NONFICTION Needs exposé, historical, how-to, interview, opinion, personal experience, photo feature. All topics must pertain to hunting and fishing topics in Michigan. Special issues: Archery Deer and Small Game Hunting (October); Firearm Deer Hunting (November); Cross-country Skiing and Early-ice Lake Fishing (December or January); Camping/Hiking (May); Family Fishing (June). No humor or poetry. **Buys 96 mss/year.** Send complete ms. Length: 1,000-2,000 words. **Pays $150 minimum for feature stories. Photos must be included with story.**

PHOTOS Captions required. Offers no additional payment for photos accepted with ms; others $20-175.

TIPS "Top priority is placed on queries that offer new ideas on hard-core hunting and fishing topics. Submit seasonal material 6 months in advance. Wants to see new approaches to subject matter."

❸❸ MICHIGAN SPORTSMAN

Game & Fish, 2250 Newmarket Pkwy., Suite 110, Marietta GA 30067. (770)953-9222. **Fax:** (678)279-7512. **E-mail:** ken.dunwoody@imoutdoors.com. **Website:** www.michigansportsmanmag.com. Nick Gilmore, editor. **Contact:** Ken Dunwoody, editorial director. See *Game & Fish*. Pays a kill fee.

❸ MIDWEST OUTDOORS

MidWest Outdoors, Ltd., 111 Shore Dr., Burr Ridge IL 60527. (630)887-7722. **Fax:** (630)887-1958. **Website:** www.midwestoutdoors.com. **100% freelance written.** Monthly tabloid emphasizing fishing, hunting, camping, and boating. Estab. 1967. Byline given. Pays on publication. No kill fee. Publishes ms an average of 3 months after acceptance. Submit seasonal material 2 months in advance. Accepts simultaneous submissions. Responds in 3 weeks to queries. Sample copy for $1 or online. Guidelines for #10 SASE.

NONFICTION Needs how-to, fishing, hunting, camping in the Midwest, where-to-go (fishing, hunting, camping within 500 miles of Chicago). "We do not want to see any articles on 'my first fishing, hunting, or camping experiences,' 'cleaning my tackle box,' 'tackle tune-up,' 'making fishing fun for kids,' or 'catch and release.'" **Buys 1,800 unsolicited mss/year.** Send complete ms. "Submissions must be e-mailed to info@ midwestoutdoors.com (Microsoft Word format preferred)." Length: 1,000-1,500 words. **Pays $15-30.**

PHOTOS Captions required. Reviews slides and b&w prints. Offers no additional payment for photos accompanying ms.

COLUMNS/DEPARTMENTS Fishing; Hunting. Send complete ms. **Pays $30.**

TIPS "Break in with a great unknown fishing hole or new technique within 500 miles of Chicago. Where, how, when, and why. Know the type of publication you are sending material to."

💲💲 MINNESOTA SPORTSMAN

Game & Fish, 2250 Newmarket Pkwy., Suite 110, Marietta GA 30067. (770)953-9222. **Fax:** (678)279-7512. **E-mail:** ken.dunwoody@imoutdoors.com. **Website:** www.minnesotasportsmanmag.com. Nick Gilmore, editor. **Contact:** Ken Dunwoody, editorial director. See *Game & Fish*. Pays a kill fee.

💲💲 MISSISSIPPI/LOUISIANA GAME & FISH

Game & Fish, 2250 Newmarket Pkwy., Suite 110, Marietta GA 30067. (770)953-9222. **Fax:** (678)279-7512. **E-mail:** ken.dunwoody@imoutdoors.com. **Website:** www.mississippigameandfish.com. Jimmy Jacobs, editor. **Contact:** Ken Dunwoody, editorial director. See *Game & Fish*. Pays a kill fee.

💲💲 MUSKY HUNTER MAGAZINE

P.O. Box 340, 7978 Hwy. 70 E., St. Germain WI 54558. (715)477-2178. **Fax:** (715)477-8858. **E-mail:** editor@ muskyhunter.com. **Website:** www.muskyhunter.com. **Contact:** Jim Saric, editor. **90% freelance written.** Bimonthly magazine on musky fishing. Serves the vertical market of musky fishing enthusiasts. "We're interested in how-to, where-to articles." Estab. 1988. Circ. 37,000. Byline given. Pays on publication. No kill fee. Publishes ms an average of 4 months after acceptance. Submit seasonal material 4 months in advance. Responds in 2 months to queries. Sample copy with 9x12 SASE and $2.79 postage. Guidelines with #10 SASE.

NONFICTION Needs historical, related only to musky fishing, how-to, catch muskies, modify lures, boats, and tackle for musky fishing, personal experience (must be musky fishing experience), technical, fishing equipment, travel, to lakes and areas for musky

fishing. **Buys 50 mss/year.** Send complete ms. Length: 1,000-2,500 words. **Pays $100-300 for assigned articles. Pays $50-300 for unsolicited articles.**

PHOTOS Send photos. Identification of subjects required. Reviews 35mm transparencies, 3x5 prints, high-res digital images preferred. Offers no additional payment for photos accepted with ms.

💲💲 NEW ENGLAND GAME & FISH

Game & Fish, 2250 Newmarket Pkwy., Suite 110, Marietta GA 30067. (770)953-9222. **Fax:** (678)279-7512. **E-mail:** ken.dunwoody@imoutdoors.com. **Website:** www.newenglandgameandfish.com. David Johnson, editor. **Contact:** Ken Dunwoody, editorial director. See *Game & Fish*. Pays a kill fee.

💲💲 NEW YORK GAME & FISH

Game & Fish, 2250 Newmarket Pkwy., Suite 110, Marietta GA 30067. (770)953-9222. **Fax:** (678)279-7512. **E-mail:** ken.dunwoody@imoutdoors.com. **Website:** www.newyorkgameandfish.com. David Johnson, editor. **Contact:** Ken Dunwoody, editorial director. See *Game & Fish*. Pays a kill fee.

💲💲 NORTH AMERICAN WHITETAIL

Game & Fish, 2250 Newmarket Pkwy., Suite 110, Marietta GA 30067. (770)953-9222. **Fax:** (678)279-7512. **E-mail:** ken.dunwoody@imoutdoors.com. **Website:** www.northamericanwhitetail.com. **Contact:** Ken Dunwoody, editorial director. **70% freelance written.** Magazine published 8 times/year about hunting trophy-class white-tailed deer in North America, primarily the U.S. "We provide the serious hunter with highly sophisticated information about trophy-class whitetails and how, when, and where to hunt them. We are not a general hunting magazine or a magazine for the very occasional deer hunter." Estab. 1982. Circ. 150,000. Byline given. Pays 65 days prior to cover date of issue. Offers negotiable kill fee. Publishes ms an average of 6 months after acceptance. Submit seasonal material 10 months in advance. Accepts queries by mail, e-mail, phone. Responds in 3 months to mss. Sample copy for $3.50 and 9x12 SAE with 7 first-class stamps. Guidelines for #10 SASE.

NONFICTION Needs how-to, interview. **Buys 50 mss/year.** Query. Length: 1,000-3,000 words. **Pays $150-400.**

PHOTOS Send photos. Captions, identification of subjects required. Reviews 35mm transparencies, color prints, high quality digital images. Offers no additional payment for photos accepted with ms.

COLUMNS/DEPARTMENTS Trails and Tails (nostalgic, humorous, or other entertaining styles of deer-hunting material, fictional or nonfictional), 1,200 words. **Buys 8 mss/year.** Send complete ms. **Pays $150.**

TIPS "Our articles are written by persons who are deer hunters first, writers second. Our hard-core hunting audience can see through material produced by non-hunters or those with only marginal deer-hunting expertise. We have a continual need for expert profiles/interviews. Study the magazine to see what type of hunting expert it takes to qualify for our use, and look at how those articles have been directed by the writers. Good photography of the interviewee and his hunting results must accompany such pieces."

⊛⊛ NORTH CAROLINA GAME & FISH

Game & Fish, 2250 Newmarket Pkwy., Suite 110, Marietta GA 30067. (770)953-9222. **Fax:** (678)279-7512. **E-mail:** ken.dunwoody@imoutdoors.com. **Website:** www.ncgameandfish.com. David Johnson, editor. **Contact:** Ken Dunwoody, editorial director. See *Game & Fish*. Pays a kill fee.

⊛⊛ OHIO GAME & FISH

Game & Fish, 2250 Newmarket Pkwy., Suite 110, Marietta GA 30067. (770)953-9222. **Fax:** (678)279-7512. **E-mail:** ken.dunwoody@imoutdoors.com. **Website:** www.ohiogameandfish.com. David Johnson, editor. **Contact:** Ken Dunwoody, editorial director. See *Game & Fish*. Pays a kill fee.

⊛⊛ OKLAHOMA GAME & FISH

Game & Fish, 2250 Newmarket Pkwy., Suite 110, Marietta GA 30067. (770)953-9222. **Fax:** (678)279-7512. **E-mail:** ken.dunwoody@imoutdoors.com. **Website:** www.oklahomagameandfish.com. Nick Gilmore, editor. **Contact:** Ken Dunwoody, editorial director. See *Game & Fish*. Pays a kill fee.

⊛⊛ PENNSYLVANIA GAME & FISH

Game & Fish, 2250 Newmarket Pkwy., Suite 110, Marietta GA 30067. (770)953-9222. **Fax:** (678)279-7512. **E-mail:** ken.dunwoody@imoutdoors.com. **Website:** www.pagameandfish.com. David Johnson, editor. **Contact:** Ken Dunwoody, editorial director. See *Game & Fish*. Pays a kill fee.

⊛⊛ RACK MAGAZINE

Buckmasters, Ltd., 10350 U.S. Hwy. 80 E., Montgomery AL 36117. (800)240-3337. **Fax:** (334)215-3535. E-mail: mhandley@buckmasters.com. **Website:** www.buckmasters.com. **50% freelance written.** Monthly (July-December) magazine covering big game hunting. "All features are either first- or third-person narratives detailing the successful hunts for world-class, big game animals—mostly white-tailed deer and other North American species." Estab. 1998. Circ. 75,000. Byline given. Pays on publication. No kill fee. Publishes ms an average of 9 months after acceptance. Editorial lead time 9-12 months. Submit seasonal material 9 months in advance. Accepts queries by e-mail. Accepts simultaneous submissions. Responds in 1 month to queries. Responds in 2 months to mss. Sample copy free. Guidelines free.

NONFICTION Needs personal experience. "We're interested only in articles chronicling successful hunts." **Buys 40-50 mss/year.** Query. Length: 1,000 words. **Pays $100-325 for assigned and unsolicited articles.**

PHOTOS Send photos. Captions, identification of subjects required. Reviews transparencies, prints, GIF/JPEG files.

TIPS "Ask for and read the writer's guidelines."

⊛⊛ ROCKY MOUNTAIN GAME & FISH

Game & Fish, 2250 Newmarket Pkwy., Suite 110, Marietta GA 30067. (770)935-9222. **Fax:** (678)279-7512. **E-mail:** ken.dunwoody@imoutdoors.com. **Website:** www.rmgameandfish.com. Daniel McElrath, editor. **Contact:** Ken Dunwoody, editorial director. See *Game & Fish*. Pays a kill fee.

⊛⊛ SALT WATER SPORTSMAN

Bonnier Corporation, 460 N. Orlando Ave., Suite 200, Winter Park FL 32789. (407)628-4802. **E-mail:** editor@saltwatersportsman.com. **Website:** www.saltwatersportsman.com. **Contact:** John Brownlee, editor-in-chief. **85% freelance written.** Monthly magazine covering saltwater sport fishing. *Salt Water Sportsman* is edited for serious marine sport fishermen whose lifestyle includes the pursuit of game fish in U.S. waters and around the world. It provides information on fishing trends, techniques, and destinations, both local and international. Each issue reviews offshore and inshore fishing boats, high-tech electronics, innovative tackle, engines, and other new products. Coverage also focuses on sound fisheries management and conservation. Circ. 170,000. Byline given. Pays on acceptance. Offers kill fee. Publishes ms an average of 5 months after acceptance. Submit seasonal material 8 months in advance. Accepts queries by mail, e-mail, fax. Responds in 1 month to queries. Sample copy for #10 SASE. Guidelines available by request.

NONFICTION Needs how-to, personal experience, technical, travel, to fishing areas. **Buys 100 mss/year.** Query. Length: 1,200-2,000 words. **Pays $300-750.**

REPRINTS Send tearsheet. Pays up to 50% of amount paid for original article.

PHOTOS Captions required. Reviews color slides. Pays $1,500 minimum for 35mm, 2¼×2¼ or 8×10 transparencies for cover.

COLUMNS/DEPARTMENTS Sportsman's Tips (short, how-to tips and techniques on salt water fishing, emphasis is on building, repairing, or reconditioning specific items or gear). Send complete ms.

TIPS "There are a lot of knowledgeable fishermen/budding writers out there who could be valuable to us with a little coaching. Many don't think they can write a story for us, but they'd be surprised. We work with writers. Shorter articles that get to the point which are accompanied by good, sharp photos are hard for us to turn down. Having to delete unnecessary wordage—conversation, clichés, etc.—that writers feel is mandatory is annoying. Often they don't devote enough attention to specific fishing information."

🐟🐟 SHOTGUN SPORTS MAGAZINE

P.O. Box 6810, Auburn CA 95604. (530)889-2220. **Fax:** (530)889-9106. **E-mail:** shotgun@shotgunsportsmagazine.com. **Website:** www.shotgunsportsmagazine.com. **Contact:** Johnny Cantu, editor-in-chief. **50% freelance written. Welcomes new writers.** Monthly magazine covering all the shotgun sports and shotgun hunting—sporting clays, trap, skeet, hunting, gunsmithing, shotshell patterning, shotsell reloading, mental training for the shotgun sports, shotgun tests, anything shotgun. Pays on publication. No kill fee. Publishes ms an average of 1-6 months after acceptance. Sample copy and writer's guidelines available on the website.

NONFICTION Needs Currently needs anything with a 'shotgun' subject. Think pieces, roundups, historical, interviews, etc. No articles promoting a specific club or sponsored hunting trip, etc. Submit complete ms with photos by mail with SASE. Can submit by e-mail. Make Length: 1,500-3,000 words. **Pays $50-150.**

REPRINTS Photo

PHOTOS 5x7 or 8x10 b&w or 4-color with appropriate captions. On disk or e-mailed at least 5-inches and 300 dpi (contact Graphics Artist for details). Reviews

transparencies (35 mm or larger), b&w, or 4-color. Send photos.

TIPS "Do not fax manuscript. Send good photos. Take a fresh approach. Create a professional, yet friendly article. Send diagrams, maps, and photos of unique details, if needed. For interviews, more interested in 'words of wisdom' than a list of accomplishments. Reloading articles must include source information and backup data. Check your facts and data! If you can't think of a fresh approach, don't bother. If it's not about shotguns or shotgunners, don't send it. Never say, 'You don't need to check my data; I never make mistakes.'"

🐟🐟 SOUTH CAROLINA GAME & FISH

Game & Fish, 2250 Newmarket Pkwy., Suite 110, Marietta GA 30067. (770)953-9222. **Fax:** (678)279-7512. **E-mail:** ken.dunwoody@imoutdoors.com. **Website:** www.scgameandfish.com. David Johnson, editor. **Contact:** Ken Dunwoody, editorial director. See *Game & Fish.* Pays a kill fee.

🐟🐟🐟🐟 SPORT FISHING

Bonnier Corporation, 460 N. Orlando Ave., Suite 200, Winter Park FL 32789. (407)628-4802. **Fax:** (407)628-7061. **E-mail:** Editor@sportfishingmag.com. **Website:** www.sportfishingmag.com. **50% freelance written.** Magazine published 10 times/year covering saltwater angling, saltwater fish and fisheries. "*Sport Fishing's* readers are middle-aged, affluent, mostly male, who are generally proficient in and very educated to their sport. We are about fishing from boats, not from surf or jetties." Estab. 1985. Circ. 250,000. Byline given. Pays on acceptance. Offers 25% kill fee. Publishes ms an average of 6-12 months after acceptance. Editorial lead time 2-12 months. Submit seasonal material 1 year in advance. Accepts queries by e-mail. Responds in 1 week to queries. Responds in 1 month to mss. Sample copy with #10 SASE. Guidelines available online.

NONFICTION Needs general interest, how-to. Query. Length: 2,500-3,000 words. **Pays $500-750 for text only; $1,500+ possible for complete package with photos.** Answer.

PHOTOS State availability. Reviews GIF/JPEG files. Offers $75-400/photo.

TIPS "Queries please; no over-the-transom submissions. Meet or beat deadlines. Include quality photos when you can. Quote the experts. Balance information with readability. Include sidebars."

❸❸❸ SPORTS AFIELD

Field Sports Publishing, 15621 Chemical Ln., Suite B, Huntington Beach CA 92649. (714)373-4910. **E-mail:** letters@sportsafield.com. **Website:** www.sportsafield. com. **Contact:** Jerry Gutierrez, art director. **60% freelance written.** Magazine published 6 times/year covering big game hunting. "We cater to the upscale hunting market, especially hunters who travel to exotic destinations like Alaska and Africa. We are not a deer hunting magazine, and we do not cover fishing." Estab. 1887. Circ. 50,000. Byline given. Pays 1 month prior to publication. Publishes ms an average of 6 months after acceptance. Editorial lead time 4 months. Submit seasonal material 5 months in advance. Accepts queries by mail, e-mail. Responds in 2 months to queries and to mss Sample copy for $7.99. Guidelines available online.

NONFICTION Needs personal experience, travel. **Buys 6-8 mss/year.** Query. Length: 1,500-2,500 words. **Pays $500-800.**

PHOTOS State availability. Captions, model releases required. Reviews 35mm slides transparencies, TIFF/JPEG files. Offers no additional payment for photos accepted with ms.

FILLERS Needs newsbreaks. **Buys 30 mss/year.** Length: 200-500 words. **Pays $75-150.**

❸❸ TENNESSEE SPORTSMAN

Game & Fish, 2250 Newmarket Pkwy., Suite 110, Marietta GA 30067. (770)953-9222. **Fax:** (678)279 7512. **E-mail:** ken.dunwoody@imoutdoors.com. **Website:** www.tennesseesportsmanmag.com. Jimmy Jacobs, editor. **Contact:** Ken Dunwoody, editorial director See *Game & Fish.* Pays a kill fee.

❸❸ TEXAS SPORTSMAN

Game & Fish, 2250 Newmarket Pkwy., Suite 110, Marietta GA 30067. (770)953-9222. **Fax:** (678)279-7512. **E-mail:** ken.dunwoody@imoutdoors.com. **Website:** www.texassportsmanmag.com. Nick Gilmore, editor. **Contact:** Ken Dunwoody, editorial director. See *Game & Fish.* Pays a kill fee.

❸❸ TURKEY & TURKEY HUNTING

F+W Media, Inc., 700 E. State St., Iola WI 54990. (715)445-4612. **E-mail:** brian.lovett@fwmedia.com. **Website:** www.turkeyandturkeyhunting.com. **Contact:** Brian Lovett, editor. **50% freelance written.** Bimonthly magazine filled with practical and comprehensive information for wild turkey hunters. Estab. 1982. Circ. 40,000. Byline given. Pays on acceptance. Offers 50% kill fee. Publishes ms an average of 8 months after acceptance. Editorial lead time 1 year. Submit seasonal material 1 year in advance. Acccpts queries by mail, e-mail. Responds in 1 month to queries. Responds in 6 months to mss. Sample copy for $4.

NONFICTION Does not want "Me and Joe went hunting and here's what happened" articles. **Buys 20 mss/year.** Send complete ms. Length: 1,500-2,500 words. **Pays $275-400.**

PHOTOS Send photos. Identification of subjects required. Reviews 2x2 transparencies, any size prints, digital images with contact sheets. Offers $75-200/photo. Negotiates payment individually.

TIPS "Turkey hunting is a continually growing and changing sport. Search for topics that reflect this trend. Our audience is sophisticated and experienced. We have several contributing editors who write most of our how-to articles, so we buy few articles of this type from freelancers. Well-written mood/essay articles are always welcome for review. If you have not written for *Turkey & Turkey Hunting*, it is best to send a finished ms. We do not assign articles based on query letters."

❸❸ TURKEY COUNTRY

National Wild Turkey Federation, P.O. Box 530, Edgefield SC 29824-0530. (803)637-3106. **Fax:** (803)637-0034. **E-mail:** info@nwtf.net; turkeycountry@nwtf.net. **E-mail:** klee@nwtf.net. **Website:** www.turkeycountrymagazine.com. **Contact:** Karen Lee, editor; Gregg Powers, managing editor; P.J. Perea, senior editor; Matt Lindler, photo editor. **50-60% freelance written.** Bimonthly educational magazine for members of the National Wild Turkey Federation. Topics covered include hunting, history, restoration, management, biology, and distribution of wild turkey. Estab. 1973. Circ. 180,000. Byline given. Pays on acceptance. No kill fee. Publishes ms an average of 6 months after acceptance. Editorial lead time 1 year. Accepts queries by mail, e-mail. Responds in 2 months to queries Sample copy for $3 and 9x12 SAE. Guidelines available online.

NONFICTION Query (preferred) or send complete ms. Length: 500-1,200 words. **Pays $250-550.**

PHOTOS "We want quality photos submitted with features. Illustrations also acceptable. We are using more and more inside color illustrations. No typical hunter-holding-dead-turkey photos or setups using mounted birds or domestic turkeys. Photos with how-to stories must make the techniques clear (i.e., how to make a turkey call; how to sculpt or carve a bird in wood)." Identification of subjects, model releases required. Reviews transparencies, high resolution digital images.

FICTION Must contribute to the education, enlightenment, or entertainment of readers in some special way.

TIPS "The writer should simply keep in mind that the audience is 'expert' on wild turkey management, hunting, life history, and restoration/conservation history. He/she must know the subject. We are buying more third person, more fiction, more humor—in an attempt to avoid the 'predictability trap' of a single subject magazine."

💲💲 WASHINGTON-OREGON GAME & FISH

Game & Fish, 2250 Newmarket Pkwy., Suite 110, Marietta GA 30067. (770)953-9222. **Fax:** (678)279-7512. **E-mail:** ken.dunwoody@imoutdoors.com. **Website:** www.wogameandfish.com. Daniel McElrath, editor. **Contact:** Ken Dunwoody, editorial director. See *Game & Fish*. Pays a kill fee.

💲💲 WEST VIRGINIA GAME & FISH

Game & Fish, 2250 Newmarket Pkwy., Suite 110, Marietta GA 30067. (770)953-9222. **Fax:** (678)279-7512. **Website:** www.wvgameandfish.com. "This is the ultimate resource for West Virginia outdoor enthusiasts that are passionate about hunting, shooting and fishing." Pays a kill fee.

💲💲 WISCONSIN SPORTSMAN

Game & Fish, 2250 Newmarket Pkwy., Suite 110, Marietta GA 30067. (770)953-9222. **Fax:** (678)279-7512. **E-mail:** ken.dunwoody@imoutdoors.com. **Website:** www.wisconsinsportsmanmag.com. Nick Gilmore, editor. **Contact:** Ken Dunwoody, editorial director. See *Game & Fish*. Pays a kill fee.

MARTIAL ARTS

💲 BLITZ AUSTRALASIAN MARTIAL ARTS MAGAZINE

Blitz Publications, P.O. Box 4075, Mulgrave VIC 3170 Australia. (61)(3)9574-8999. **Fax:** (61)(3)9574-8899. **E-mail:** ben@blitzmag.com.au. **Website:** www.blitzmag. net. "*Blitz Australasian Martial Arts* monthly magazine features interviews and articles on the world's best martial arts and combat sports personalities, unique styles, technique and fitness tips, health and self-defense strategies, combat psychology, as well as unrivaled coverage of local fight news and events." **NONFICTION** Needs general interest, how-to. Query.

FIGHT! MAGAZINE

The Premier Mixed Martial Arts Magazine, 1200 Laker Hearn Dr., Suite 450, Atlanta GA 30319. **Website:** www.fightmagazine.com. **Contact:** Ladd Dunwoody, editor. Monthly magazine covering mixed martial arts. Fight! Magazine offers mixed martial arts news, UFC results, and more. Read magazine for more details.

NONFICTION Query first.

💲💲 JOURNAL OF ASIAN MARTIAL ARTS

Via Media Publishing Co., 941 Calle Mejia, #822, Santa Fe NM 87501. (505)983-1919. **E-mail:** info@goviamedia.com. **Website:** www.goviamedia.com. **90% freelance written.** "Quarterly magazine covering all historical and cultural aspects related to Asian martial arts, offering a mature, well-rounded view of this uniquely fascinating subject. Although the journal treats the subject with academic accuracy (references at end), writing need not lose the reader!". Estab. 1991. Circ. 10,000. Byline given. Pays on publication. No kill fee. Publishes ms an average of 1 year after acceptance. Submit seasonal material 6 months in advance. Responds in 1 month to queries. Responds in 2 months to mss. Sample copy for $10. Guidelines with #10 SASE or online.

NONFICTION Needs essays, exposé, historical, how-to, martial art techniques and materials, e.g., weapons, interview, personal experience, photo feature, place or person, religious, technical, travel. No articles overburdened with technical/foreign/scholarly vocabulary, or material slanted as indirect advertising or for personal aggrandizement. **Buys 30 mss/year.** Query with short background and martial arts experience. Length: 1,000-10,000 words. **Pays $150-500.**

PHOTOS State availability. Identification of subjects, model releases required. Reviews contact sheets, negatives, transparencies, prints. Offers no additional payment for photos accepted with ms.

COLUMNS/DEPARTMENTS Location (city, area, specific site, Asian or non-Asian, showing value for martial arts, researchers, history); Media Review (film, book, video, museum for aspects of academic and artistic interest). Length: 1,000-2,500 words. **Buys 16 mss/year.** Query. **Pays $50-200.**

FICTION Needs adventure, historical, humorous, slice-of-life vignettes, translation. No material that does not focus on martial arts culture. **Buys 1 mss/year.** Query. Length: 1,000-10,000 words. **Pays $50-500, or copies.**

POETRY Needs avant-garde, free verse, haiku, light verse, traditional. No poetry that does not focus on martial arts culture. Buys 2 poems/year. Submit maximum 10 poems. **Pays $10-100, or copies.**

FILLERS Needs anecdotes, facts, gags, newsbreaks, short humor. **Buys 2 mss/year.** Length: 25-500 words. **Pays $1-50, or copies.**

TIPS "Always query before sending a manuscript. We are open to varied types of articles; most however require a strong academic grasp of Asian culture. For those not having this background, we suggest trying a museum review, or interview, where authorities can be questioned, quoted, and provide supportive illustrations. We especially desire articles/reports from Asia, with photo illustrations, particularly of a martial art style, so readers can visually understand the unique attributes of that style, its applications, evolution, etc. Location and media reports are special areas that writers may consider, especially if they live in a location of martial art significance."

⊙ KUNG FU TAI CHI

Pacific Rim Publishing, 40748 Encyclopedia Circle, Fremont CA 94538. (510)656-5100. **Fax:** (510)656-8844. **E-mail:** gene@kungfumagazine.com. **Website:** www.kungfumagazine.com. **70% freelance written.** Bimonthly magazine covering Chinese martial arts and culture. "*Kung Fu Tai Chi* covers the full range of Kung Fu culture, including healing, philosophy, meditation, Fengshui, Buddhism, Taoism, history, and the latest events in art and culture, plus insightful features on the martial arts." Circ. 15,000. Byline given. Pays on publication. No kill fee. Editorial lead time 4 months. Submit seasonal material 4 months in advance. Accepts queries by mail, e-mail, fax, phone. Responds in 2 months to queries. Responds in 3 months to mss. Sample copy for $4.99 or online. Guidelines available online.

NONFICTION Needs general interest, historical, interview, personal experience, religious, technical, travel, cultural perspectives. No poetry or fiction.

Buys 70 mss/year. Query. Length: 500-2,500 words. **Pays $35-125.**

PHOTOS Send photos. Captions, identification of subjects required. Reviews 5x7 prints, GIF/JPEG files. Offers no additional payment for photos accepted with ms.

TIPS "Check out our website and get an idea of past articles."

⊙⊙ T'AI CHI

Wayfarer Publications, P.O. Box 39938, Los Angeles CA 90039. (323)665-7773. **Fax:** (323)665-1627. **E-mail:** taichi@tai-chi.com. **Website:** www.tai-chi.com. **Contact:** Marvin Smalheiser, editor. **90% freelance written.** Quarterly magazine covering T'ai Chi Ch'uan as a martial art and for health and fitness. "Covers T'ai Chi Ch'uan and other internal martial arts, plus qigong and Chinese health, nutrition, and philosophical disciplines. Readers are practitioners or laymen interested in developing skills and insight for self-defense, health, and self-improvement." Estab. 1977. Circ. 50,000. Byline given. Pays on publication. No kill fee. Published ms an average of 3 months after acceptance. Editorial lead time 3 months. Submit seasonal material 6 months in advance. Accepts queries by mail, e-mail, fax. Responds in 3 weeks to queries. Responds in 3 months to mss. Sample copy for $5.99. Guidelines available online.

NONFICTION Needs essays, how-to, on T'ai Chi Ch'uan, qigong, and related Chinese disciplines, interview, personal experience. "Do not want articles promoting an individual, system, or school." Send complete ms. Length: 1,200-4,500 words. **Pays $75-500.**

PHOTOS Send photos. Captions, identification of subjects, model releases required. Reviews color or b&w 4x6 or 5x7 prints, digital files suitable for print production. "Offers no additional payment for photos accepted with ms, but overall payment takes into consideration the number and quality of photos."

TIPS "Think and write for practitioners and laymen who want information and insight, and who are trying to work through problems to improve skills and their health. No promotional material."

⊙⊙ ULTIMATE MMA

Beckett Media, 22840 Savi Ranch Pkwy., Suite 200, Yorba Linda CA 92887. (714)200-1930. **E-mail:** djeffrey@beckett.com. **Website:** www.ultimatemmamag.com. **Contact:** Doug Jeffrey, editor. Monthly magazine covering mixed martial arts, grappling. "We are interested in anything and everything about mixed martial arts—lifestyle to events to training to strategy." Estab. 2000. Byline given. Pays on publication. Offers 20% kill fee. Publishes ms an average of 1-3 months after acceptance. Editorial lead time 3 months. Submit seasonal material 3 months in advance. Accepts queries by mail, e-mail. Responds in 2 months to mss. Sample copy free. Guidelines free.

NONFICTION Needs book excerpts, exposé, general interest, historical, how-to, inspirational, interview, new product, personal experience, photo feature, technical. **Buys 30 mss/year.** Query. Length: 500-1,500 words. **Pays $150-500 for assigned articles. Pays $150-500 for unsolicited articles.** Sometimes pays expenses of writers on assignment.

PHOTOS State availability.

COLUMNS/DEPARTMENTS Beyond Fighting (lifestyle of fighters); Exercises to bolster MMA game and general fitness. **Buys 30 mss/year.** Query with or without published clips. **Pays $0-125.**

MISCELLANEOUS SPORTS

⊛⊛ AMERICAN CHEERLEADER

Macfadden Performing Arts Media LLC, 110 William St., 23rd Floor, New York NY 10038. (646)459-4800. **Fax:** (646)459-4900. **E-mail:** mwalker@americancheerleader.com; acmail@americancheerleader.com. **Website:** www.americancheerleader.com. **Contact:** Marisa Walker, editor-in-chief. **30% freelance written.** Bimonthly magazine covering high school, college, and competitive cheerleading. "We try to keep a young, informative voice for all articles—'for cheerleaders, by cheerleaders.'" Estab. 1995. Circ. 200,000. Byline given. Pays on publication. Offers 25% kill fee. Publishes ms an average of 4 months after acceptance. Editorial lead time 3 months. Submit seasonal material 4 months in advance. Accepts queries by mail, e-mail, online submission form. Responds in 4 weeks to queries. Responds in 2 months to mss. Sample copy for $2.95. Guidelines free.

NONFICTION Needs young adults: biography, interview/profile (sports personalities), careers, fashion, beauty, health, how-to (cheering techniques, routines, pep songs, etc.), problem-solving, sports, cheerleading-specific material. Special issues: Special issues: Tryouts (April); Camp Basics (June); College (October); Competition (December). No professional cheerleading stories, i.e., no Dallas Cowboy cheerleaders. **Buys 20 mss/year.** Query with published clips; provide résumé, business card, and tearsheets to be kept on file. "We're looking for authors who know cheerleading." Length: 750-2,000 words. **Pays $100-250 for assigned articles; $100 maximum for unsolicited articles.** Sometimes pays expenses of writers on assignment.

PHOTOS State availability. Model releases required. Reviews transparencies, 5x7 prints. Offers $50/photo.

COLUMNS/DEPARTMENTS Freelance columns: Gameday Beauty (skin care, celeb how-tos), 600 words; Health & Fitness (teen athletes), 1,000 words; Profiles (winning squads), 1,000 words. **Buys 12 mss/year.** Query with published clips. **Pays $100-250.**

TIPS "We invite proposals from freelance writers who are involved in or have been involved in cheerleading—i.e., coaches, sponsors, or cheerleaders. Our writing style is upbeat and 'sporty' to catch and hold the attention of our teenaged readers. Articles should be broken down into lots of sidebars, bulleted lists, Q&As, etc."

⊛⊛⊛ ATV RIDER MAGAZINE

GrindMedia, LLC, 1733 Alton Pkwy., Irvine CA 92606. **Fax:** (763)383-4499. **Website:** www.atvrideronline.com. **Contact:** John Prusak, editor. **20% freelance written.** Bimonthly magazine covering all-terrain vehicles. Devoted to covering all the things ATV owners enjoy, from hunting to racing, farming to trail riding. Byline given. Pays on magazine shipment to printer. Editorial lead time 6 months. Accepts queries by mail, e-mail, fax. Responds in 3 weeks to queries. Sample copy and writer's guidelines for #10 SASE.

NONFICTION Needs how-to, interview, new product, personal experience, photo feature, technical, travel. **Buys 15-20 mss/year.** Query with published clips. Length: 200-2,000 words. **Pays $100-1,000.** Sometimes pays expenses of writers on assignment.

PHOTOS State availability. Captions, identification of subjects required. Negotiates payment individually.

TIPS "Writers must have experience with ATVs, and should own 1 or have regular access to at least 1 ATV."

☺ ⊛ CANADIAN RODEO NEWS

Canadian Rodeo News, Ltd., 272245 RR 2, Airdrie AB T4A 2L5 Canada. (403)945-7393. **Fax:** (403)945-0936. **E-mail:** editor@rodeocanada.com. **Website:** www.rodeocanada.com. **80% freelance written.** Monthly tabloid covering Canada's professional rodeo (CPRA) personalities and livestock. Read by rodeo participants and fans. Estab. 1964. Circ. 4,000. Byline given. Pays on publication. No kill fee. Publishes ms an average of 1 month after acceptance. Editorial lead time 1 month. Submit seasonal material 1 month in advance. Accepts queries by mail, e-mail, fax. Accepts simultaneous submissions. Responds in 1 month to queries. Responds in 2 months to mss.

NONFICTION Needs general interest, historical, interview. **Buys 70-80 mss/year.** Query. Length: 400-1,200 words. **Pays $30-60.**

REPRINTS Send photocopy of article or typed ms with rights for sale noted and information about when and where the material previously appeared. Pays 100% of amount paid for an original article.

PHOTOS Send photos. Reviews digital only. Offers $15-25/cover photo.

TIPS "Best to call first with the story idea to inquire if it is suitable for publication. Readers are very knowledgeable of the sport, so writers need to be as well."

LACROSSE MAGAZINE

113 W. University Pkwy., Baltimore MD 21210. (410)235-6882. **Fax:** (410)366-6735. **E-mail:** feedback@laxmagazine.com. **Website:** www.laxmagazine.com; www.uslacrosse.org. **Contact:** Matt DaSilva, editor; Gabriella O'Brien, art director;. **60% freelance written.** Monthly magazine covering the sport of lacrosse. "*Lacrosse* is the only national feature publication devoted to the sport of lacrosse. It is a benefit of membership in U.S. Lacrosse, a nonprofit organization devoted to promoting the growth of lacrosse and preserving its history. U.S. Lacrosse maintains *Lacrosse Magazine Online* (LMO) at www.laxmagazine.com. *LMO* features daily lacrosse news and scores directly from lacrosse-playing colleges. *LMO* also includes originally-produced features and news briefs covering all levels of play. Occasional feature articles printed in *Lacrosse* are re-published at *LMO*, and vice versa. The online component of *Lacrosse* will do things that a printed publication can't—provide news, scores and information in a timely manner." Estab. 1978. Circ. 235,000. Byline given. Pays on publication. No kill fee. Publishes ms an average of 2 months after acceptance. Editorial lead time 2 months. Submit seasonal material 2 months in advance. Sample copy free. Guidelines at www.uslacrosse.org.

NONFICTION Needs book excerpts, general interest, historical, how-to, drills, conditioning, x's and o's, etc., interview, new product, opinion, personal experience, photo feature, technical. **Buys 30-40 mss/year.** Length: 500-1,750 words. **Payment negotiable.** Sometimes pays expenses of writers on assignment.

PHOTOS State availability. Captions, identification of subjects required. Reviews contact sheets, 4x6 prints. Negotiates payment individually.

COLUMNS/DEPARTMENTS First Person (personal experience), 1,000 words; Fitness (conditioning/strength/exercise), 500-1,000 words; How-to, 500-1,000 words. **Buys 10-15 mss/year. Payment negotiable.**

TIPS "As the national development center of lacrosse, we are particularly interested in stories about the growth of the sport in non-traditional areas of the U.S. and abroad, written for an audience already knowledgeable about the game."

POINTE MAGAZINE

MacFadden Performing Arts Media, LLC, 333 Seveneth Ave., 11th Floor, New York NY 10001. (212)979-4862. **Fax:** (646)459-4848. **E-mail:** pointe@dancemedia.com. **Website:** www.pointemagazine.com. **Contact:** Amy Cogan, publisher. Bimonthly magazine covering ballet. *Pointe Magazine* is the only magazine dedicated to ballet. It offers practicalities on ballet careers as well as news and features. Estab. 2000. Circ. 38,000. Byline given. Pays on publication. Responds in 1 month to queries. Responds in 1 month to mss. Sample copy for SAE with 9x12 envelope and 6 first-class stamps.

NONFICTION Needs historical, how-to, interview, biography, careers, health, news. **Buys 60 mss/year.** Query with published clips. Length: 400-1,500 words. **Pays $125-400.**

PHOTOS Contact: Colin Fowler, photo editor. State availability. Captions required. Reviews 2 1/4 x 2 1/4 or 35 mm transparencies, 8 x 11 prints. Negotiates payment individually.

POLO PLAYERS' EDITION

9011 Lake Worth Rd., Suite B, Lake Worth FL 33467. (561)968-5208. **Fax:** (561)968-5209. **E-mail:** gwen@poloplayersedition.com. **Website:** www.poloplayersedition.com. **Contact:** Gwen Rizzo, editor/publisher. Monthly magazine on the sport and lifestyle polo. "Our readers are affluent, well educated, well read, and highly sophisticated." Circ. 6,150. Pays on acceptance. Offers kill fee; varies. Publishes ms an average of 2 months after acceptance. Submit seasonal material 3 months in advance. Accepts queries by mail, e-mail. Accepts simultaneous submissions. Responds in 3 months to queries. Guidelines for #10 SAE with 2 stamps.

NONFICTION Needs historical, interview, personal experience, photo feature, technical, travel. Special issues: Annual Art Issue/Gift Buying Guide; Winter Preview/Florida Supplement. **Buys 20 mss/year.** Send complete ms. Length: 800-3,000 words. **Pays $150-400 for assigned articles. Pays $100-300 for unsolicited articles.** Sometimes pays expenses of writers on assignment.

REPRINTS Send tearsheet or typed ms with rights for sale noted and information about when and where the material previously appeared. Pays 50% of amount paid for an original article.

PHOTOS State availability of or send photos. Captions required. Reviews contact sheets, transparencies, prints. Offers $20-150/photo.

COLUMNS/DEPARTMENTS Yesteryears (historical pieces), 500 words; Profiles (clubs and players), 800-1,000 words. **Buys 15 mss/year.** Query with published clips. **Pays $100-300.**

TIPS "Query us on a personality or club profile or historic piece or, if you know the game, state availability to cover a tournament. Keep in mind that ours is a sophisticated, well-educated audience."

$ PRORODEO SPORTS NEWS

Professional Rodeo Cowboys Association, 101 ProRodeo Dr., Colorado Springs CO 80919. (719)593-8840. **Fax:** (719)548-4889. **Website:** www.prorodeo.com. **Contact:** Neal Reid, managing editor. **10% freelance written.** Biweekly magazine covering professional rodeo. "Our readers are extremely knowledgeable about the sport of rodeo, and anyone who writes for us should have that same in-depth knowledge. Estab. 1952. Circ. 27,000. Byline given. Pays on publication. No kill fee. Publishes ms an average of 1 month after acceptance. Editorial lead time 2 months. Submit seasonal material 2 months in advance. Responds in 2 weeks to queries Sample copy for #10 SASE. Guidelines free.

NONFICTION Needs historical, how-to, interview, photo feature, technical. **Pays $50-100.**

PHOTOS State availability. Identification of subjects required. Reviews digital images and hard copy portfolios. Offers $15-85/photo.

$ RUGBY MAGAZINE

Rugby Press, Ltd., 459 Columbus Ave., #1200, New York NY 10024. (212)787-1160. **Fax:** (212)787-1161. **E-mail:** alex@rugbymag.com. **Website:** www.rugbymag.com. **Contact:** Alex Goff, editor-in-chief. **75% freelance written.** Monthly magazine. Estab. 1975. Circ. 10,000. Byline given. Pays on publication. No kill fee. Publishes ms an average of 2 months after acceptance. Editorial lead time 1 month. Submit seasonal material 2 months in advance. Accepts queries by mail, e-mail, fax, phone. Accepts simultaneous submissions. Responds in 2 weeks to queries. Responds in 1 month to mss. Sample copy for $4. Guidelines free.

NONFICTION Needs book excerpts, essays, general interest, historical, how-to, humor, interview, new product, opinion, personal experience, photo feature, technical, travel. **Buys 15 mss/year.** Send complete ms. Length: 600-2,000 words. **Pays $50 minimum.** Pays expenses of writers on assignment.

REPRINTS Send tearsheet or typed ms with rights for sale noted and information about when and where the material previously appeared. Payment varies.

PHOTOS Send photos. Reviews negatives, transparencies, prints. Offers no additional payment for photos accepted with ms.

COLUMNS/DEPARTMENTS Nutrition (athletic nutrition), 900 words; Referees' Corner, 1,200 words. **Buys 2-3 mss/year.** Query with published clips. **Pays $50 maximum.**

FICTION Needs cond novels, humorous, novel concepts, slice-of-life vignettes. **Buys 1-3 mss/year.** Query with published clips. Length: 1,000-2,500 words. **Pays $100.**

TIPS "Give us a call. Send along your stories or photos; we're happy to take a look. Tournament stories are a good way to get yourself published in *Rugby Magazine*."

$ SKYDIVING

1665 Lexington Ave., Suite 102, DeLand FL 32724. (386)736-9779. **Fax:** (386)736-9786. **E-mail:** sue@skydivingmagazine.com; mike@skydivingmagazine.com. **Website:** www.skydivingmagazine.com. **Contact:** Sue Clifton, editor; Mike Truffer, publisher. **25% freelance written.** Monthly tabloid featuring skydiving for sport parachutists, worldwide dealers and equipment manufacturers. "*Skydiving* is a news magazine. Its purpose is to deliver timely, useful and interesting information about the equipment, techniques, events, people and places of parachuting. Our scope is national. *Skydiving*'s audience spans the entire spectrum of jumpers, from first-jump students to veterans with thousands of skydives. Some readers are riggers with a keen interest in the technical aspects of parachutes, while others are weekend 'fun' jumpers who want information to help them make travel plans and equipment purchases." Estab. 1979. Circ. 14,200. Byline given. Pays on publication. No kill fee. Publishes ms an average of 3 months after acceptance. Accepts simultaneous submissions. Responds in 1 month to queries. Sample copy for $2. Guidelines available online.

NONFICTION No personal experience or human interest articles. Query. Length: 500-1,000 words. **Pays $25-100.** Sometimes pays expenses of writers on assignment.

PHOTOS State availability. Captions required. Reviews 5x7 and larger b&w glossy prints. Offers no additional payment for photos accepted with ms.

FILLERS Needs newsbreaks. Length: 100-200 words. **Pays $25 minimum.**

TIPS "The most frequent mistake made by writers in completing articles for us is that the writer isn't knowledgeable about the sport of parachuting. Articles about events are especially time-sensitive so yours must be submitted quickly. We welcome contributions about equipment. Even short, 'quick look' articles about new products are appropriate for *Skydiving*. If you know of a drop zone or other place that jumpers would like to visit, write an article describing its features and tell them why you liked it and what they can expect to find if they visit it. Avoid first-person articles."

⊘ TRANSWORLD SKATEBOARDING

2052 Corte del Nogal, Suite 100, Carlsbad CA 92011. (760)722-7777. **E-mail:** lauren.machen@transworld. net. **Website:** www.skateboarding.transworld.net. **Contact:** Kevin Duffel, editor; Joey Shigeo-Mueliner, managing editor; Monica Campana, publisher; Oliver Barton, director of video and photo; Sam Muller, senior photographer. Monthly magazine for skateboarding enthusiasts. *"TransWorld SKATEboarding* has been the largest, most progressive and most respected skateboarding magazine in the world for nearly 25 years. Delivering the most innovative photography and cutting-edge editorial content, it offers readers an inside look at skate culture through news, product reviews and in-depth profiles of the world's top skateboarders. It covers the American and global skateboard scenes from street and vert-ramp skating to international competition, and it features in-depth interviews with the top pros and up-and-coming riders. Designed to spread the culture of skateboarding in its purest form, the magazine provides bold, inside coverage of events, personalities, equipment and techniques. A market leader in skateboarding video production and events, *TransWorld SKATEboarding* founded the TransWorld SKATEboarding Awards, the first and largest professional skateboarding awards ceremony in the world, and has produced more than 25 feature films, by far the most within the skateboarding industry." Circ. 243,000. No kill fee. Editorial lead time 3 months.

MOTOR SPORTS

⊛ DIRT RIDER

GrindMedia, LLC, 1733 Alton Pkwy., Suite 100, Irvine CA 92606. **Website:** www.dirtrider.com. Monthly magazine devoted to the sport of off-road motorcycle riding that showcases the many ways enthusiasts can enjoy dirt bikes. Circ. 201,342. No kill fee.

⊛ THE HOOK MAGAZINE

P.O. Box 51324, Bowling Green KY 42104. (270)202-6742. **E-mail:** editor@hookmagazine.com; rblively@ hotmail.com. **Website:** www.hookmagazine.com. **Contact:** Bryan Lively, editor-in-chief. **80% freelance written.** Bimonthly magazine covering tractor pulling. Estab. 1992. Circ. 6,000. Byline given. Pays on publication. No kill fee. Editorial lead time 6 months. Submit seasonal material 6 months in advance. Accepts queries by mail, e-mail, fax. Accepts simultaneous submissions. Responds in 3 weeks to queries. Responds in 2 months to mss. Sample copy for 8 1/2x11 SAE with 4 first-class stamps or online. Guidelines for #10 SASE.

NONFICTION Needs how-to, interview, new product, personal experience, photo feature, technical, event coverage. **Buys 25 mss/year.** Send complete ms. Length: 500-1,500 words. **Pays $70 for technical articles; $35 for others.**

PHOTOS Send photos. Captions, identification of subjects, model releases required. Reviews 3x5 prints. Negotiates payment individually.

FILLERS Needs anecdotes, short humor. **Buys 6 mss/ year.** Length: 100 words.

TIPS "Write 'real'; our readers don't respond well to scholarly tomes. Use your everyday voice in all submissions and your chances will go up radically."

💲💲 ROAD RACER X

Filter Publications, 122 Vista Del Rio Dr., Morgantown WV 26508. (304)284-0080. **Fax:** (304)284-0081. **E-mail:** online@racerxonline.com. **Website:** www.roadracerx.com. **25% freelance written.** Magazine published 8 times/year covering motorcycle road racing. "We cover the sport of motorcycle road racing from a lifestyle/personality perspective. We don't do many technical stories or road tests." Estab. 2003. Circ. 35,000. Byline given. Pays on publication. No kill fee. Publishes ms an average of 2 months after acceptance. Editorial lead time 2 months. Submit seasonal material 1 month in advance. Accepts queries by e-mail. Responds in 1 month to queries. Sample copy for #10 SASE. Guidelines available.

NONFICTION Needs historical, (road racing), interview, (racers). Special issues: "We publish official event programs for several important events, including the Red Bull U.S. Grand Prix and the Miller Motorsports Park World Superbike race. We do not want road tests." **Buys 8 mss/year.** Query. Length: 2,000-3,000 words. **Pays $400-600 for assigned and unsolicited articles.** Sometimes pays expenses of writers on assignment.

PHOTOS State availability. Reviews GIF/JPEG files. Negotiates payment individually.

COLUMNS/DEPARTMENTS Buys 8 mss/year. Query. **Pays $25-$100.**

TIPS "In order for your work to appeal to our readers, you must know the world of motorcycle road racing."

💲💲 SAND SPORTS MAGAZINE

Wright Publishing Co., Inc., P.O. Box 2260, Costa Mesa CA 92628. (714)979-2560, ext. 107. **Fax:** (714)979-3998. **E-mail:** msommer@hotvws.com. **Website:** www.sandsports.net. **Contact:** Michael Sommer, editor. **20% freelance written.** Bimonthly magazine covering vehicles for off-road and sand dunes. Estab. 1995. Circ. 35,000. Byline given. Pays on publication. Editorial lead time 3 months. Submit seasonal material 6 months in advance. Accepts queries by mail. Sample copy and writer's guidelines free.

NONFICTION Needs how-to, technical-mechanical, photo feature, technical. **Buys 20 mss/year.** Query. 1,500 words minimum **Pays $175/page.** Sometimes pays expenses of writers on assignment.

PHOTOS Send photos. Captions, identification of subjects, model releases required. Reviews color slides or high res digital images. Negotiates payment individually.

RUNNING

💲 INSIDE TEXAS RUNNING

P.O. Box 19909, Houston TX 77224. (713)935-0555. **Fax:** (713)935-0559. **Website:** www.insidetexasrunning.com. **Contact:** Lance Phegley, editor. **70% freelance written.** Monthly (except June and August) tabloid covering running and running-related events. Our audience is made up of Texas runners who may also be interested in cross training. Estab. 1977. Circ. 10,000. Byline given. Pays on publication. No kill fee. Publishes ms an average of 2 months after acceptance. Submit seasonal material 2 months in advance. Responds in 1 month to mss. Sample copy for $4.95. Guidelines for #10 SASE.

NONFICTION Special issues: Shoe Review (March); Fall Race Review (September); Marathon Focus (October); Resource Guide (December). **Buys 20 mss/year.** Send complete ms. Length: 500-1,500 words. **Pays $100 maximum for assigned articles. Pays $50 maximum for unsolicited articles.**

REPRINTS Send tearsheet, photocopy or typed ms with rights for sale noted and information about when and where the material previously appeared.

PHOTOS Send photos. Captions required. Offers $25 maximum/photo.

TIPS Writers should be familiar with the sport and the publication.

💲💲💲💲 RUNNER'S WORLD

Rodale, 400 S. 10th St., Emmaus PA 18098. (610)967-8441. **Fax:** (610)967-8883. **E-mail:** rwedit@rodale.com. **Website:** www.runnersworld.com. **Contact:** David Willey, editor-in-chief; Benjamen Purvis, design director. **5% freelance written.** Monthly magazine on running—mainly long-distance running. Estab. 1966. Circ. 500,000. Byline given. Pays on publication. No kill fee. Publishes ms an average of 6 months after acceptance. Submit seasonal material 6 months in advance. Accepts queries by mail. Responds in 2 months to queries. Guidelines available online.

NONFICTION Needs how-to, train, prevent injuries, interview, personal experience. No "my first marathon" stories. No poetry. **Buys 5-7 mss/year.** Query. **Pays $1,500-2,000.** Pays expenses of writers on assignment.

PHOTOS State availability. Identification of subjects required.

COLUMNS/DEPARTMENTS Finish Line (back-of-the-magazine essay, personal experience, humor). **Buys 24 mss/year.** Send complete ms. **Pays $300.**

TIPS "We are always looking for 'Adventure Runs' from readers—runs in wild, remote, beautiful, and interesting places. These are rarely race stories but more like backtracking/running adventures. Great color slides are crucial; 2,000 words maximum."

$$ RUNNING TIMES

Rodale, Inc., 400 S. 10th St., Emmaus PA 18098-0099. (610)967-5171. **Fax:** (610)967-8964. **E-mail:** editor@runningtimes.com. **Website:** www.runningtimes.com. **Contact:** Jonathan Beverly, editor-in-chief. **40% freelance written.** Magazine published 10 times/year covering distance running and racing. "*Running Times* is the national magazine for the experienced running participant and fan. Our audience is knowledgeable about the sport and active in running and racing. All editorial relates specifically to running: improving performance, enhancing enjoyment, or exploring events, places, and people in the sport." Estab. 1977. Circ. 102,000. Byline given. Pays on publication. No kill fee. Publishes ms an average of 3 months after acceptance. Editorial lead time 4-6 months. Submit seasonal material 6 months in advance. Accepts queries by mail, e-mail. Responds in 1 month to queries. Responds in 2 months to mss. Sample copy for $8. Guidelines available online.

NONFICTION Needs book excerpts, essays, historical, how-to, training, humor, inspirational, interview, new product, opinion, personal experience, with theme, purpose, evidence of additional research and/or special expertise, photo feature, news, reports. No basic, beginner how-to, generic fitness/nutrition, or generic first-person accounts. **Buys 35 mss/year.** Query. Length: 1,500-3,000 words. **Pays $300-2,000 for assigned articles. Pays $150-1,000 for unsolicited articles.** Sometimes pays expenses of writers on assignment.

PHOTOS State availability. Identification of subjects required. Negotiates payment individually.

COLUMNS/DEPARTMENTS Training (short topics related to enhancing performance), 1,000 words; Sports-Med (application of medical knowledge to running), 1,000 words; Nutrition (application of nutritional principles to running performance), 1,000 words. **Buys 10 mss/year.** Query. **Pays $200-400.**

FICTION Any genre, with running-related theme or characters. Buys 1 ms/year. Send complete ms. Length: 1,500-3,000 words. **Pays $100-500.**

TIPS "Thoroughly get to know runners and the running culture, both at the participant level and the professional, elite level."

$$ TRAIL RUNNER

Big Stone Publishing, 2567 Dolores Way, Carbondale CO 81623. (970)704-1442. **Fax:** (970)963-4965. **E-mail:** aarnold@bigstonepub.com. **Website:** www.trailrunnermag.com. **Contact:** Michael Benge, editor; Ashley Arnold, associate editor. **50% freelance written.** Bimonthly magazine covering trail running, adventure racing, snowshoeing. Covers all aspects of off-road running. "North America's only magazine dedicated to trail running. In-depth editorial and compelling photography informs, entertains and inspires readers of all ages and abilities to enjoy the outdoors and to improve their health and fitness through the sport of trail running." Estab. 1999. Circ. 29,000. Byline given. Pays on publication. Offers $50 kill fee. Publishes ms an average of 2 months after acceptance. Editorial lead time is 3 months. Submit seasonal material 5 months in advance. Accepts queries by e-mail. Accepts simultaneous submissions. Responds in 4 weeks to queries. Sample copy for $5. Guidelines available online at http://trailrunnermag.com/contri_guidelines.php.

NONFICTION Needs exposé, historical, how-to, humor, inspirational, interview, personal experience, technical, travel, racing. Does not want "My first trail race." **Buys 30-40 mss/year.** Query with one or two writing samples (preferably previously published articles), including your name, phone number and email address. Identify which department your story would be best suited for. **Pays 30¢/word for assigned and unsolicited articles.**

PHOTOS "*Trail Runner* regularly features stunning photography of trail running destinations, races, adventures and faces of the sport." State availability of photos with submission. Captions, Identification of subjects. Reviews GIF/JPEG files. Offers $50-250/photo.

COLUMNS/DEPARTMENTS **Contact:** Michael Benge, editor, or Ashley Arnold, associate editor. Making Tracks (news, race reports, athlete Q&A, nutrition tips), 300-800 words; Adventure (adventure stories, athlete profiles); Nutrition (sports nutrition, health news), 800-1,000 words; Great Escapes (running destinations/trails), 1,200 words **Buys 30 mss/year.** Query with published clips. **Pays 30 cents/word.**

FICTION Pays 25-35 cents/word.

FILLERS Needs anecdotes, facts, newsbreaks, short humor. **Buys 10 mss/year.** Length: 75-400 words. **Pays 30 cents/word.**

TIPS "Demonstrate familiarity with the sport. Best way to break in is with interesting and unique news, facts, insights. Check website for more information."

SKIING AND SNOW SPORTS

💲 AMERICAN SNOWMOBILER

Kalmbach Publishing Co., 21027 Crossroads Circle, P.O. Box 1612, Waukesha WI 53187-1612. **E-mail:** editor@amsnow.com. **Website:** www.amsnow.com. **Contact:** Mark Savage, editor. **30% freelance written.** Magazine published 6 times seasonally covering snowmobiling. Estab. 1985. Circ. 54,000. Byline given. Pays on acceptance. No kill fee. Publishes an average of 4 months after acceptance. Editorial lead time 4 months. Submit seasonal material 6 months in advance. Accepts queries by mail, e-mail, fax. Responds in 1 month to queries. Responds in 2 months to mss. Guidelines available online.

NONFICTION Needs general interest, historical, how-to, interview, personal experience, photo feature, travel. **Buys 10 mss/year.** Query with published clips. Length: 500-1,200 words. **Pay varies for assigned articles. Pays $100 minimum for unsolicited articles.**

PHOTOS State availability. Captions, identification of subjects, model releases required. Offers no additional payment for photos accepted with ms.

💲 SKATING

United States Figure Skating Association, 20 First St., Colorado Springs CO 80906. (719)635-5200. **Fax:** (719)635-9548. **E-mail:** info@usfigureskating.org. **Website:** www.usfsa.org. "*Skating* magazine is the official publication of U.S. Figure Skating, and thus we cover skating at both the championship and grass roots level." Published 10 times/year. Estab. 1923. Circ. 42,000. Byline given. Pays on publication. No kill fee. Publishes ms an average of 3 months after acceptance. Accepts queries by mail, e-mail, fax.

NONFICTION Needs general interest, historical, how-to, interview, background and interests of skaters, volunteers, or other U.S. Figure Skating members, photo feature, technical and competition reports, figure skat-

ing issues and trends, sports medicine. **Buys 10 mss/year.** Query. Length: 500-2,500 words. **Payment varies.**

PHOTOS Photos purchased with or without accompanying ms. Query. Pays $10 for 8x10 or 5x7 b&w glossy prints, and $25 for color prints or transparencies.

COLUMNS/DEPARTMENTS Ice Breaker (news briefs); Foreign Competition Reports; Health and Fitness; In Synch (synchronized skating news); Takeoff (up-and-coming athletes), all 500-2,000 words.

TIPS "We want writing by experienced persons knowledgeable in the technical and artistic aspects of figure skating with a new outlook on the development of the sport. Knowledge and background in technical aspects of figure skating is helpful, but not necessary to the quality of writing expected. We would like to see articles and short features on U.S. Figure Skating volunteers, skaters, and other U.S. Figure Skating members who normally wouldn't get recognized, as opposed to features on championship-level athletes, which are usually assigned to regular contributors. Good quality color photos are a must with submissions. Also would be interested in seeing figure skating 'issues and trends' articles, instead of just profiles. No professional skater material. Synchronized skating and adult skating are the 2 fastest growing aspects of the U.S. Figure Skating. We would like to see more stories dealing with these unique athletes."

💲💲💲💲 SKIING

Bonnier Corporation, 5720 Flatiron Pkwy., Boulder CO 80301. (303)253-6300. **E-mail:** editor@skiingmag.com. **Website:** www.skinet.com. **Contact:** Sam Bass, editor-in-chief. Magazine published 7 times/year for skiers who "deeply love winter, and who live for travel, adventure, instruction, gear, and news." "*Skiing* is the user's guide to winter adventure. It is equal parts jaw-dropping inspiration and practical information, action and utility, attitude, and advice. It relates the lifestyles of dedicated skiers and captures their spirit of daring and exploration. Dramatic photography transports readers to spine-tingling mountains with breathtaking immediacy. Reading *Skiing* is almost as much fun as being there." Estab. 1948. Circ. 400,000. Byline given. Offers 40% kill fee. No

NONFICTION Buys 10-15 (feature) and 12-24 (short) mss/year. Query. Length: 1,500-2,000 words (feature); 100-500 words (short). **Pays $1,000-2,500/feature; $100-500/short piece.**

COLUMNS/DEPARTMENTS Length: 200-1,000 words. **Buys 2-3 mss/year.** Query. **Pays $150-1,000.**

TIPS "Consider less obvious subjects: smaller ski areas, specific local ski cultures, unknown aspects of popular resorts. Be expressive, not merely descriptive. We want readers to feel the adventure in your writing—to tingle with the excitement of skiing steep powder, of meeting intriguing people, of reaching new goals or achieving dramatic new insights. We want readers to have fun, to see the humor in and the lighter side of skiing and their fellow skiers."

⊘❸❸❸ SKIING MAGAZINE

Bonnier Corp., 5720 Flatiron Pkwy., Boulder CO 80301. (303)253-6300. **Fax:** (303)448-7638. **E-mail:** editor@skiingmag.com. **Website:** www.skinet.com/skiing. **60% freelance written.** Magazine published 8 times/year. *Skiing Magazine* is an online ski-lifestyle publication written and edited for recreational skiers. Its content is intended to help them ski better (technique), buy better (equipment and skiwear), and introduce them to new experiences, people, and adventures. Estab. 1936. Circ. 430,000. Byline given. Pays on acceptance. Offers 15% kill fee. Publishes ms an average of 3 months after acceptance. Submit seasonal material 8 months in advance. Accepts queries by mail, e-mail. Sample copy with 9 x 12 SASE and 5 first-class stamps.

NONFICTION Needs essays, historical, how-to, humor, interview, personal experience. **Buys 5-10 mss/year.** Send complete ms. Length: 1,000-3,500 words. **Pays $500-1,000 for assigned articles. Pays $300-700 for unsolicited articles.** Pays expenses of writers on assignment.

PHOTOS Sponsors 12-week-long internship based at editorial headquarters in Boulder, CO. Intern workload includes: assisting in our photo studio and on assignment, photo retouching, coordinating photography, working with our art department to build cohesive features, invoicing, production workflow, and participating in staff meetings. "We try to keep the grunt work to a minimum. *Skiing Magazine* is a small staff (4 editors and 2 art directors), so interns work closely with staffers. Interns should be dedicated, hard-working, conscientious, and fun-loving, with a career interest in photography. A very strong foundation in the CS3 Creative Suite, as well as previous journalism or photography experience is required. A passion for the sport of skiing helps." All internships are unpaid. E-mail résumé, cover letter, and portfolio to: Niall@skiingmag.

com. Send photos. Captions, identification of subjects, model releases required. Offers $75-300/photo.

FILLERS Needs facts, short humor. **Buys 10 mss/year.** Length: 60-75 words. **Pays $50-75.**

TIPS "Writers must have an extensive familiarity with the sport and know what concerns, interests, and amuses skiers. Start with short pieces ('hometown hills,' 'dining out,' 'sleeping in'). Columns are most open to freelancers."

❸❸ SNOWEST MAGAZINE

Harris Publishing, 360 B St., Idaho Falls ID 83402. (208)524-7000. **Fax:** (208)522-5241. **E-mail:** lindstrm@snowest.com. **Website:** http://snowest.com. **10-25% freelance written.** Monthly magazine covering snowmobiling. "*SnoWest* covers the sport of snowmobiling, products, and personalities in the western states. This includes mountain riding, deep powder, and trail riding, as well as destination pieces, tech tips, and new model reviews." Estab. 1972. Circ. 140,000. Byline given. Pays on publication. No kill fee. Publishes ms an average of 2 months after acceptance. Editorial lead time 6 months. Submit seasonal material 3 months in advance. Sample copy and writer's guidelines free.

NONFICTION Needs how-to, fix a snowmobile, make it high performance, new product, technical, travel. **Buys 3-5 mss/year.** Query with published clips. Length: 500-1,500 words. **Pays $150-300.**

PHOTOS Send photos. Captions, identification of subjects required. Negotiates payment individually.

❸❸ SNOW GOER

3300 Fernbrook Lane N., Suite #200, Plymouth MN 55447. **Fax:** (763) 383-4499. **Website:** www.snowgoer.com. **5% freelance written.** Magazine published 7 times/year covering snowmobiling. "*Snow Goer* is a hard-hitting, tell-it-like-it-is magazine designed for the ultra-active snowmobile enthusiast. It is fun, exciting, innovative, and on the cutting edge of technology and trends." Estab. 1967. Circ. 66,000. Byline given. Pays on publication. No kill fee. Publishes ms an average of 5 months after acceptance. Editorial lead time 5 months. Submit seasonal material 6 months in advance. Accepts queries by mail. Accepts simultaneous submissions. Responds in 3 months to queries. Sample copy for SAE with 8x10 envelope and 4 First-Class stamps.

NONFICTION Needs general interest, how-to, interview, new product, personal experience, photo feature, technical, travel. **Buys 6 mss/year.** Query. Length: 500-

4,000 words. **Pays $50-500.** Sometimes pays expenses of writers on assignment.

PHOTOS State availability. Captions, identification of subjects required. Reviews contact sheets, prints. Negotiates payment individually.

TIPS "*Snow Goer* magazine is written for, and by, mature and discerning snowmobile riders. If you wish to contribute articles and photos to *Snow Goer* please carefully read our editorial guidelines (available by request) before submitting your query. Please query us *by regular mail*; do not e-mail article queries."

WATER SPORTS

🍁 $ DIVER

216 East Esplanade, North Vancouver BC V7L 1A3 Canada. (604)988-0711. **Fax:** (604)988-0747. **E-mail:** editor@divermag.com. **Website:** www.divermag.com. Magazine published 8 times/year emphasizing sport scuba diving, ocean science, and technology for a well-educated, active readership across North America and around the world. Circ. 30,000. No kill fee. Accepts queries by e-mail.

NONFICTION Query first. Length: 500-3,000 words. **Pays 12.5 cents/word, $25/photo inside, $350 for cover photo.**

PHOTOS Captions, identification of subjects required. Reviews JPEG/TIFF files (300 dpi), slides, maps, drawings.

$ $ ROWING NEWS

The Independent Rowing News, Inc., Rivermill Suite 440, 85 Mechanic St., Lebanon NH 03766. (603)448-5090. **E-mail:** editor@rowingnews.com. **Website:** www.rowingnews.com. **Contact:** Ed Winchester, editor. **75% freelance written.** Monthly magazine covering rowing (the Olympic sport). "We write for a North American readership, serving the rowing community with features, how-to, and dispatches from the rowing world at large." Estab. 1994. Circ. 20,000. Byline given. Pays on publication. No kill fee. Publishes ms an average of 1-2 months after acceptance. Editorial lead time 1-12 months. Submit seasonal material 1-2 months in advance. Responds in 6 weeks to queries. Sample copy available online. Guidelines free.

NONFICTION Needs essays, how-to, rowing only, interview, new product, personal experience, rowing, travel. **Buys 12 mss/year.** Query with published clips. "Everything must be directedly related to rowing." Length: 1,500-5,000 words. Sometimes pays expenses of writers on assignment.

PHOTOS Reviews JPEG/TIFF. Negotiates payment.

TIPS "Make sure you are familiar with the magazine."

⊘ $ SURFER MAGAZINE

Source Interlink, P.O. Box 1028, Dana Point CA 92629-5028. (949)325-6212. **E-mail:** brendon@surfermag.com; janna@surfermag.com. **Website:** www.surfermag.com. **Contact:** Brendon Thomas, editor; Janna Irons, managing editor. Monthly magazine edited for the avid surfers and those who follow the beach, wave riding scene. Circ. 118,570. No kill fee. Editorial lead time 10 weeks.

$ $ SWIMMING WORLD MAGAZINE

Sports Publications International, P.O. Box 20337, Sedona AZ 86341. (928)284-4005. **Fax:** (928)284-2477. **E-mail:** editorial@swimmingworldmagazine.com. **Website:** www.swimmingworldmagazine.com. **Contact:** Jason Marsteller, managing editor. **30% freelance written.** Bimonthly magazine about competitive swimming. Readers are fitness-oriented adults from varied social and professional backgrounds who share swimming as part of their lifestyle. Estab. 1960. Circ. 50,000. Byline given. Pays on publication. Editorial lead time 2 months. Submit seasonal material 3 months in advance. Accepts queries by mail, e-mail, fax. Accepts simultaneous submissions. Responds in 1 month to queries. Guidelines available online.

NONFICTION Needs book excerpts, essays, exposé, general interest, historical, how-to, training plans and techniques, humor, inspirational, interview, people associated with fitness and competitive swimming, new product, articles describing new products for fitness and competitive training, personal experience, photo feature, technical, travel, general health. **Buys 30 mss/year.** Query with a 250-word synopsis of article. Length: 250-2,500 words. **Pays $75-400.**

PHOTOS Send photos. Captions, identification of subjects, model releases required. Reviews high-resolution digital images. Negotiates payment.

$ THE WATER SKIER

1251 Holy Cow Rd., Polk City FL 33868. (863)324-4341. **Fax:** (863)325-8259. **E-mail:** satkinson@usawaterski.org. **Website:** www.usawaterski.org. **Contact:** Scott Atkinson, editor. **10-20% freelance written.** Magazine published 7 times/year. *The Water Skier* is the membership magazine of USA Water Ski, the national governing body for organized water skiing in the United States. The magazine has a controlled circulation and is available only to USA Water Ski's membership, which is made up of 20,000 active competitive water skiers and 10,000 members who are supporting the sport. These supporting members may participate in the sport but they don't compete. The editorial content of the magazine features distinctive and informative writing about the sport of water skiing only. Estab. 1951. Circ. 30,000. Byline given. Offers 30% kill fee. Editorial lead time 4 months. Submit seasonal material 6 months in advance. Responds in 2 weeks to queries. Sample copy for $3.50. Guidelines with #10 SASE.

NONFICTION Needs historical, has to pertain to water skiing, interview, call for assignment, new product, boating and water ski equipment, travel, water ski vacation destinations. **Buys 10-15 mss/year.** Query. Length: 1,500-3,000 words. **Pays $100-150.**

REPRINTS Send photocopy. Payment negotiable.

PHOTOS State availability. Captions, identification of subjects required. Reviews contact sheets. Negotiates payment individually.

COLUMNS/DEPARTMENTS The Water Skier News (small news items about people and events in the sport), 400-500 words. Other topics include safety, training (3-event, barefoot, disabled, show ski, ski race, kneeboard, and wakeboard); champions on their way; new products. Query. **Pays $50-100.**

TIPS "Contact the editor through a query letter (please, no phone calls) with an idea. Avoid instruction, these articles are written by professionals. Concentrate on articles about the people of the sport. We are always looking for interesting stories about people in the sport. Also, short news features which will make a reader say to himself, 'Hey, I didn't know that.' Keep in mind that the publication is highly specialized about the sport of water skiing."

TEEN AND YOUNG ADULT

$ $ CICADA MAGAZINE

Cricket Magazine Group, 70 E. Lake St., Suite 300, Chicago IL 60601. (312)701-1720. **Fax:** (312)701-1728. **E-mail:** cicada@cicadamag.com. **Website:** www.cicadamag.com. **Contact:** Marianne Carus, editor-in-chief; Deborah Vetter, executive editor; John Sandford, art director. **80% freelance written.** Bimonthly literary magazine for ages 14 and up. Publishes original short stories, poems, and first-person essays written for teens and young adults. *Cicada* publishes fiction and poetry with a genuine teen sensibility, aimed at the high school and college-age market. The editors are looking for stories and poems that are thought-provoking but entertaining. Estab. 1998. Circ. 10,000. Byline given. Pays on publication. Accepts simultaneous submissions. Responds in 4-6 months to mss. Guidelines available online at www.cricketmag.com (adults) and www.cicadamag.com (young adults 14-23).

NONFICTION Needs essays, personal experience, First-person, coming-of-age experiences that are relevant to teens and young adults (example: life in the Peace Corps). Buys up to 6 mss/year. Submit complete ms, SASE. Length: 5,000 words maximum; **Pays up to 25¢/word.**

REPRINTS Payment varies.

PHOTOS Send photocopies/tearsheets of artwork.

FICTION Young adults: adventure, contemporary, fantasy, historical, humor/satire, mainstream, multicultural, nature/environment, novel excerpts, novellas (1/issue), realistic, romance, science fiction, sports, suspense/mystery. Buys up to 42 mss/year. The main protagonist should be at least 14 and preferably older. Stories should have a genuine teen sensibility and be aimed at readers in high school or college. Length: 5,000 words maximum (up to 9,000 words/novellas). **Pays up to 25¢/word.**

POETRY Needs free verse, light verse, traditional. Reviews serious, humorous, free verse, rhyming (if done well) poetry. Limit submissions to 5 poems. Length: 25 lines maximum. **Pays up to $3/line on publication.**

TIPS "Quality writing, good literary style, genuine teen sensibility, depth, humor, good character development, avoidance of stereotypes. Read several issues to familiarize yourself with our style."

$ INSIGHT

The Review and Herald Publishing Association, 55 W. Oak Ridge Dr., Hagerstown MD 21740. (301)393-4038. **E-mail:** insight@rhpa.org. **Website:** www.insightmagazine.org. **80% freelance written.** Weekly magazine covering spiritual life of teenagers. *Insight* publishes true dramatic stories, interviews, and community and mission service features that relate directly to the lives of Christian teenagers, particularly those with a Seventh-day Adventist background. Estab. 1970. Circ. 8,000. Byline given. Pays on publication. No kill fee. Publishes ms an average of 4 months after acceptance. Editorial lead time 6 months. Submit seasonal material

6 months in advance. Accepts queries by mail, e-mail, fax. Responds in 1 month to mss. Sample copy for $2 and #10 SASE. Guidelines available online.

NONFICTION Needs how-to, teen relationships and experiences, humor, interview, personal experience, photo feature, religious. **Buys 120 mss/year.** Send complete ms. Length: 500-1,000 words. **Pays $25-150 for assigned articles. Pays $25-125 for unsolicited articles.**

REPRINTS Send typed ms with rights for sale noted and information about when and where the material previously appeared. Pays $50.

PHOTOS State availability. Model releases required. Reviews contact sheets, negatives, transparencies, prints. Negotiates payment individually.

COLUMNS/DEPARTMENTS Columns: Big Deal (topic of importance to teens) 800-1,000 words; Interviews (Christian culture figures, especially musicians), 1,000 words; It Happened to Me (first-person teen experiences containing spiritual insights), 1,000 words; On the Edge (dramatic true stories about Christians), 800-1,000 words; So I Said..(true short stories in the first person of common, everyday events and experiences that taught the writer something), 300-500 words. Send complete ms. **Pays $25-125.**

TIPS "Skim 2 months of *Insight*. Write about your teen experiences. Use informed, contemporary style and vocabulary. Follow Jesus' life and example."

$$$$ SEVENTEEN

300 W. 57th St., 17th Floor, New York NY 10019. (917)934-6500. **Fax:** (917)934-6574. **Website:** www.seventeen.com. **20% freelance written.** Monthly magazine. *Seventeen* is a young woman's first fashion and beauty magazine. Tailored for young women in their teens and early twenties, *Seventeen* covers fashion, beauty, health, fitness, food, college, entertainment, fiction, plus crucial personal and global issues. Estab. 1944. Circ. 2,400,000. Byline given. Pays on acceptance. Offers 25% kill fee. Publishes ms an average of 6 months after acceptance. Accepts queries by mail. Responds in 3 months to queries.

NONFICTION Length: 1,200-2,500 words. **Pays $1/word, occasionally more.** Pays expenses of writers on assignment.

PHOTOS Photos usually by assignment only.

TIPS "Writers have to ask themselves whether or not they feel they can find the right tone for a *Seventeen* article—a tone which is empathetic, yet never patronizing; lively, yet not superficial. Not all writers feel comfortable with, understand, or like teenagers. If you don't like them, *Seventeen* is the wrong market for you. An excellent way to break in to the magazine is by contributing ideas for quizzes or the 'My Story' (personal essay) column."

TRAVEL, CAMPING AND TRAILER

$ AAA GOING PLACES

AAA Auto Club South, 1515 N. Westshore Blvd., Tampa FL 33607. (813)289-5923. **Fax:** (813)288-7935. **Website:** www.aaagoingplaces.com. **50% freelance written.** Bimonthly magazine on auto tips, cruise travel, tours. Estab. 1982. Circ. 2,500,000. Byline given. Pays on publication. No kill fee. Publishes ms an average of 6 months after acceptance. Submit seasonal material 9 months in advance. Accepts simultaneous submissions. Responds in 2 months to mss. Writer's guidelines for SAE.

NONFICTION Needs historical, how-to, humor, interview, personal experience, photo feature, travel. **Buys 15 mss/year.** Send complete ms. Length: 500-1,200 words. **Pays $50/printed page.**

PHOTOS State availability. Captions required. Reviews 2â—Š2 transparencies, 300 dpi digital images. Offers no additional payment for photos accepted with ms.

COLUMNS/DEPARTMENTS What's Happening (local attractions in Florida, Georgia, or Tennessee).

TIPS We prefer lively, upbeat stories that appeal to a well-traveled, sophisticated audience, bearing in mind that AAA is a conservative company.

$ CAMPING TODAY

126 Hermitage Rd., Butler PA 16001-8509. (724)283-7401. **E-mail:** d_johnston01@msn.com. **Website:** www.fcrv.org. **Contact:** DeWayne Johnston, editor. **30% freelance written.** Bimonthly official membership publication of the FCRV. "*Camping Today* is the largest nonprofit family camping and RV organization in the U.S. and Canada. Members are heavily oriented toward RV travel. Concentration is on member activities in chapters. Group is also interested in conservation and wildlife. The majority of members are retired." Estab. 1983. Circ. 10,000. Byline given. Pays on publication. No kill fee. Publishes ms an average of 6 months after acceptance. Submit seasonal material 3 months in ad-

vance. Accepts simultaneous submissions. Responds in 2 months to queries and mss. Sample copy and guidelines for 4 first-class stamps. Guidelines for #10 SASE.

NONFICTION Needs humor, camping or travel related, interview, interesting campers, new product, technical, RVs related, travel, interesting places to visit by RV, camping. **Buys 10-15 mss/year.** Query by mail or e-mail or send complete ms with photos. Length: 750-2,000 words. **Pays $50-150.**

REPRINTS Send typed ms with rights for sale noted and information about when and where the material previously appeared. Pays 35-50% of amount paid for original article.

PHOTOS Need b&w or sharp color prints. Send photos. Captions required.

TIPS "Freelance material on RV travel, RV maintenance/safety, and items of general camping interest throughout the U.S. and Canada will receive special attention. Good photos increase your chances. See website."

FAMILY MOTOR COACHIING

8291 Clough Pike, Cincinnati OH 45244. (513)474-3622. **Fax:** (513)388-5286. **E-mail:** rgould@fmca.com; magazine@fmca.com. **Website:** www.fmca.com. **Contact:** Robbin Gould, editor. **80% freelance written. We prefer that writers be experienced RVers.** Monthly magazine emphasizing travel by motorhome, motorhome mechanics, maintenance, and other technical information. *"Family Motor Coaching* magazine is edited for the members and prospective members of the Family Motor Coach Association who own or are about to purchase self-contained, motorized recreational vehicles known as motorhomes. Featured are articles on travel and recreation, association news and activities, plus articles on new products and motorhome maintenance and repair. Approximately 1/3 of editorial content is devoted to travel and entertainment, 1/3 to association news, and 1/3 to new products, industry news, and motorhome maintenance." Estab. 1963. Circ. 140,000. Byline given. Pays on acceptance. Publishes ms an average of 8 months after acceptance. Submit seasonal material 4 months in advance. Accepts queries by mail, e-mail, fax. Responds in 3 months to queries. Sample copy for $3.99; $5 if paying by credit card. Guidelines with #10 SASE or request PDF by e-mail.

NONFICTION Needs how-to, do-it-yourself motorhome projects and modifications, humor, interview, new product, technical, motorhome travel (various ar-

eas of North America accessible by motorhome), bus conversions, nostalgia. **Buys 50-75 mss/year.** Query with published clips. Length: 1,000-2,000 words. **Pays $100-500, depending on article category.**

PHOTOS State availability. Captions, model releases, Offers no additional payment for b&w contact sheets, 35mm 21/4x21/4 color transparencies, or high-res electronic images (300 dpi and at least 4x6 in size).

TIPS "The greatest number of contributions we receive are travel; therefore, that area is the most competitive. However, it also represents the easiest way to break into our publication. Articles should be written for those traveling by self-contained motorhome. The destinations must be accessible to motorhome travelers and any peculiar road conditions should be mentioned."

HIGHROADS

AAA Arizona, 3144 N. 7th Ave., Phoenix AZ 85013. (602)650-2732. **Fax:** (602)241-2917. **E-mail:** highroads@arizona.aaa.com. **Website:** www.aaa.com. **50% freelance written.** Bimonthly magazine covering travel/automotive for A A A Arizona members. "Our magazine goes out to our 470,000+ AAA Arizona members on a bimonthly basis. The mean age of our audience is around 60 years old. We look for intelligent, engaging writing covering auto and travel-related topics." Byline given. Pays on publication. Offers 30% kill fee. Editorial lead time 6 months. Submit seasonal material 6 months in advance. Accepts queries by mail, e-mail, fax. Accepts simultaneous submissions. Sample copy for #10 SASE. Guidelines by e-mail.

NONFICTION Needs travel, auto-related. Does not want articles unrelated to travel, automotive, or Arizona living. **Buys 21 mss/year.** Query with published clips. Length: 500-2,000 words. **Pays $0.35/word for assigned articles; $0.35/word for unsolicited articles.**

PHOTOS Identification of subjects required. Offers $75-500 per photo.

COLUMNS/DEPARTMENTS **Contact:** Jill Schildhouse. Weekender (weekend destinations near Arizona), Road Trip (day activities in Arizona), Charming Stays (a charming inn or B&B in Arizona); 500-700 words. **Buys 10 mss/year. Pays $0-35.**

INNS MAGAZINE

Harworth Publishing Inc., P.O. Box 998, Guelph ON N1H 6N1 Canada. (519)767-6059. **Fax:** (519)821-0479. **E-mail:** info@harworthpublishing.com. **Website:** www.innsmagazine.com. **Contact:** Mary Hughes, editor. *Inns* is a national publication for travel, dining, and pastimes. It focuses on inns, beds and breakfasts, resorts, and travel in North America. The magazine is targeted to travelers looking for exquisite getaways. Accepts queries by e-mail. Guidelines by e-mail.

NONFICTION Needs general interest, interview, new product, opinion, personal experience, travel. Query. Length: 300-600 words. **Pays $175-250 (Canadian).**

FILLERS Short quips or nominations at 75 words are **$25 each**. All stories submitted have to accompany photos. E-mail photos to designer@harworthpublishing.com.

⚫ ⊕⊕ INTERNATIONAL LIVING

International Living Publishing, Ltd., Elysium House, Ballytruckle, Waterford Ireland (800)643-2479. **Fax:** 353-51-304-561. **E-mail:** editor@internationalliving.com. **Website:** www.internationalliving.com. **Contact:** Eoin Bassett, managing editor. **50% freelance written.** Monthly magazine covering retirement, travel, investment, and real estate overseas. "We do not want descriptions of how beautiful places are. We want specifics, recommendations, contacts, prices, names, addresses, phone numbers, etc. We want offbeat locations and off-the-beaten-track spots." Estab. 1981. Circ. 500,000. Byline given. Pays on publication. Offers 25-50% kill fee. Publishes ms an average of 3 months after acceptance. Editorial lead time 2 months. Submit seasonal material 3 months in advance. Accepts queries by mail, e-mail, fax. Accepts simultaneous submissions. Responds in 2 months to mss. Sample copy for #10 SASE. Guidelines available online.

NONFICTION Needs how-to, get a job, buy real estate, get cheap airfares overseas, start a business, etc., interview, entrepreneur or retiree abroad, new product, travel, personal experience, travel, shopping, cruises. No descriptive, run-of-the-mill travel articles. **Buys 100 mss/year.** Send complete ms. Length: 500-2,000 words. **Pays $200-500 for assigned articles. Pays $100-400 for unsolicited articles.**

PHOTOS State availability. Identification of subjects required. Reviews contact sheets, negatives, transparencies, prints. Offers $50/photo.

FILLERS Needs facts. **Buys 20 mss/year.** Length: 50-250 words. **Pays $25-50.**

TIPS "Make recommendations in your articles. We want first-hand accounts. Tell us how to do things: how to catch a cab, order a meal, buy a souvenir, buy property, start a business, etc. *International Living's* philosophy is that the world is full of opportunities to do whatever you want, whenever you want. We will show you how."

⊕⊕⊕⊕ ISLANDS

Bonnier Corp., 460 N. Orlando Ave., Suite 200, Winter Park FL 32789. (407)628-4802. **E-mail:** editor@islands.com. **Website:** www.islands.com. **80% freelance written.** Magazine published 8 times/year. "We cover accessible and once-in-a-lifetime islands from many different perspectives: travel, culture, lifestyle. We ask our authors to give us the essence of the island and do it with literary flair." Estab. 1981. Circ. 250,000. Byline given. Pays on publication. Offers 25% kill fee. Publishes ms an average of 8 months after acceptance. Accepts queries by e-mail. Responds in 2 months to queries. Responds in 6 weeks to mss. Sample copy for $6. "E-mail us for writer's guidelines."

NONFICTION Needs book excerpts, essays, general interest, interview, photo feature, travel, service shorts, island-related material. **Buys 25 feature mss/year.** Send complete ms. Length: 2,000-4,000 words. **Pays $750-2,500.** Sometimes pays expenses of writers on assignment.

PHOTOS "Fine color photography is a special attraction of *Islands*, and we look for superb composition, technical quality, and editorial applicability. Will not accept or be responsible for unsolicited images or artwork."

COLUMNS/DEPARTMENTS Discovers section (island related news), 100-250 words; Taste (island cuisine), 900-1,000 words; Travel Tales (personal essay), 900-1,100 words; Live the Life (island expat Q&A). Query with published clips. **Pays $25-1,000.**

⊕⊕ MOTORHOME

2575 Vista Del Mar Dr., Ventura CA 93001. (805)667-4100. **Fax:** (805)667-4484. **E-mail:** info@motorhomemagazine.com. **Website:** www.motorhomemagazine.com. **Contact:** Eileen Hubbard, editor. **60% freelance written.** Monthly magazine covering topics for RV enthusiasts. "*MotorHome* is a magazine for owners and prospective buyers of motorized recreational vehicles who are active outdoorsmen and wide-ranging travelers. We cover all aspects of the RV lifestyle; editorial material is both technical and nontechnical in nature. Regular features include tests and descriptions of various models of motorhomes, travel adventures, and hobbies pursued in such vehicles, objective analysis of equipment and supplies for such vehicles, and do-it-yourself articles. Guides within the magazine provide listings of manufacturers, rentals, and other sources of equipment and accessories of interest to enthusiasts. Articles must have an RV slant and excellent photography accompanying text." Estab. 1968. Circ. 150,000. Byline given. Pays on acceptance. Offers 30% kill fee. Publishes ms an average of within 1 year after acceptance. Editorial lead time 4 months. Submit seasonal material 6 months in advance. Accepts queries by mail, fax. Responds in 1 month to queries. Responds in 2 months to mss. Sample copy free. Guidelines available online.

NONFICTION Needs general interest, historical, how-to, humor, interview, new product, personal experience, photo feature, technical, travel, celebrity profiles, recreation, lifestyle, legislation; all RV related. No diaries of RV trips or negative RV experiences. **Buys 120 mss/year.** Query with published clips. Length: 250-2,500 words. **Pays $300-600.**

PHOTOS Digital photography accepted. Send photos. Captions, identification of subjects, model releases required. Reviews 35mm slides. Offers no additional payment for art accepted with ms. Pays $500 for covers.

COLUMNS/DEPARTMENTS Crossroads (offbeat briefs of people, places, and events of interest to travelers), 100-200 words; Keepers (tips, resources). Query with published clips or send complete ms. **Pays $100.**

TIPS "If a freelancer has an idea for a good article, it's best to send a query and include possible photo locations to illustrate the article. We prefer to assign articles and work with the author in developing a piece suitable to our audience. We are in a specialized field with very enthusiastic readers who appreciate articles by authors who actually enjoy motorhomes. The following areas are most open: Crossroads—brief descriptions of places to see or special events, with 1 photo/slide, 100-200 words; travel—places to go with a motorhome, where to stay, what to see and do, etc.; and how-to—personal projects on author's motorhomes to make travel easier, unique projects, accessories. Also articles on motorhome-owning celebrities, humorous experiences. Be sure to submit appropriate photography with at least 1 good motorhome shot to illustrate travel articles. No phone queries, please."

$ PATHFINDERS

6325 Germantown Ave., Philadelphia PA 19144. (215)438-2140. **Fax:** (215)438-2144. **E-mail:** editors@pathfinderstravel.com; info@pathfinderstravel.com. **Website:** www.pathfinderstravel.com. **75% freelance written.** Bimonthly magazine covering travel for people of color, primarily African-Americans. We look for lively, original, well-written stories that provide a good sense of place, with useful information and fresh ideas about travel and the travel industry. Our main audience is African-Americans, though we do look for articles relating to other persons of color: Native Americans, Hispanics and Asians. Pathfinders Travel Magazine for People of Color is is published quarterly. The magazine, which enjoys a circulation of 100,000 copies, reaches an affluent audience of African American travelers interested in enjoying the good life. Pathfinders tells readers where to go, what to do, where to dine and how to `get there from a cultural perspective. Pathfinders covers domestic and international destinations. The slick, glossy, color magazine is available nationally in Barnes & Nobel, Crown, Borders, Hastings and other independent book stores. Estab. 1997. Circ. 100,000. Byline given. Pays on publication. Accepts queries by mail, e-mail. Responds in 1 month to queries. Responds in 2 months to mss. Sample copy at bookstores (Barnes & Noble). Guidelines available online.

NONFICTION Needs essays, historical, how-to, personal experience, photo feature, travel, all vacation travel oriented. "No more pitches on Jamaica. We get these all the time." **Buys 16-20 mss/year.** Send complete ms. Length: 1,200-1,400 words for cover stories; 1,000-1,200 words for features. **Pays $200.**

PHOTOS State availability.

COLUMNS/DEPARTMENTS Chef's Table, Post Cards from Home; Looking Back; City of the Month, 500-600 words. Send complete ms. **Pays $150.**

TIPS We prefer seeing finished articles rather than queries. All articles are submitted on spec. Articles should be saved in either WordPerfect or Microsoft Word, double-spaced and saved as a text-only file. Include a hard copy. E-mail articles are accepted only by request of the editor. No historical articles.

$$ PILOT GETAWAYS MAGAZINE

Airventure Publishing LLC, P.O. Box 550, Glendale CA 91209. (818)241-1890. **Fax:** (818)241-1895. **E-mail:** info@pilotgetaways.com; editor@pilotgetaways.com. **Website:** www.pilotgetaways.com. **Contact:** John T. Kounis, editor. **90% freelance written.** Bimonthly magazine covering aviation travel for private pilots. *Pilot Getaways* is a travel magazine for private pilots. Our articles cover destinations that are easily accessible by private aircraft, including details such as airport transportation, convenient hotels, and attractions. Other regular features include fly-in dining, flying tips, and bush flying. Estab. 1999. Circ. 25,000. Byline given. Pays on publication. No kill fee. Editorial lead time 4 months. Submit seasonal material 9 months in advance. Accepts queries by mail, e-mail, fax, phone. Accepts simultaneous submissions. Responds in 2 weeks to queries; 2 months to mss. Sample copy and writer's guidelines free.

NONFICTION Needs travel, specifically travel guide articles. "We rarely publish articles about events that have already occurred, such as travel logs about trips the authors have taken or air show reports." **Buys 30 mss/year.** Query. Length: 1,000-3,500 words. **Pays $100-500.**

PHOTOS State availability. Captions, identification of subjects required. Reviews contact sheets, negatives, 35mm transparencies, prints, GIF/JPEG/TIFF files. Negotiates payment individually.

COLUMNS/DEPARTMENTS Weekend Getaways (short fly-in getaways), 2,000 words; Fly-in Dining (reviews of airport restaurants), 1,200 words; Flying Tips (tips and pointers on flying technique), 1,000 words; Bush Flying (getaways to unpaved destinations), 1,500 words. **Buys 20 mss/year.** Query. **Pays $100-500.**

TIPS *Pilot Getaways* follows a specific format, which is factual and informative. We rarely publish travel logs that chronicle a particular journey. Rather, we prefer travel guides with phone numbers, addresses, prices, etc., so that our readers can plan their own trips. The exact format is described in our writer's guidelines.

$$$ PORTHOLE CRUISE MAGAZINE

Panoff Publishing, 4517 NW 31st Ave., Ft. Lauderdale FL 33309-3403. (954)377-7777. **Fax:** (954)377-7000. **E-mail:** editorial@ppigroup.com. **Website:** www.porthole.com. **Contact:** Bill Panoff, publisher/editor-in-chief. **70% freelance written.** Bimonthly magazine covering the cruise industry. *Porthole Cruise Magazine* entices its readers to take a cruise vacation by delivering information that is timely, accurate, colorful, and entertaining. Estab. 1992. Circ. 80,000. Byline given. Pays on publication. Offers 20% kill fee. Publishes ms an average of 6 months after acceptance. Editorial lead time 8 months. Submit seasonal material 5 months in advance. Accepts queries by e-mail. Accepts simultaneous submissions. Guidelines available online.

NONFICTION Needs general interest, cruise related, historical, how-to, pick a cruise, not get seasick, travel tips, humor, interview, crew on board or industry executives, new product, personal experience, photo feature, travel, off-the-beaten-path, adventure, ports, destinations, cruises, onboard fashion, spa articles, duty-free shopping, port shopping, ship reviews. No articles on destinations that can't be reached by ship. **Buys 60 mss/year.** Length: 1,000-1,200 words. **Pays $500-600 for assigned feature articles.**

PHOTOS Contact: Linda Douthat, creative director. State availability. Captions, identification of subjects, model releases required. Reviews digital images and original transparencies. Rates available upon request to ldouthat@ppigroup.com.

$$ RECREATION NEWS

Official Publication of the RecGov.org, 204 Greenwood Rd., Linthicum MD 21090. (410)944-4852. **Website:** www.recreationnews.com. **Contact:** Marvin Bond, editor. **75% freelance written.** Monthly guide to leisure-time activities for federal and private industry workers covering Mid-Atlantic travel destinations, outdoor recreation, and cultural activities. Estab. 1982. Circ. 115,000. Byline given. Pays on publication. No kill fee. Publishes ms an average of 6 months after acceptance. Submit seasonal material 10 months in advance. Accepts queries by mail, e-mail, phone. Accepts simultaneous submissions. Responds in 2 months to queries. See sample copy and writer's guidelines online.

NONFICTION Needs Mid-Atlantic travel destinations, outdoor recreation. Special issues: Skiing (December), Golf (April), Theme Parks (July). Query with published clips or links. Length: 600-900 words. **Pays $50-300.**

REPRINTS Send tearsheet or typed ms with rights for sale noted and information about when and where the material previously appeared. Pays $50.

TIPS "Our articles are lively and conversational and deal with specific travel destinations in the Mid-Atlantic. We do not buy international or Caribbean stories. Outdoor recreation of all kinds is good, but avoid first-person narrative. Stories need to include info on nearby places of interest, places to eat, and places to stay. Keep contact information in separate box at end of story."

🍁 $$ SPA LIFE

Harworth Publishing, Inc., P.O. Box 998, Guelph ON N1H 6N1 Canada. (519)767-6059. **Fax:** (519)821-0479. **E-mail:** editor@harworthpublishing.com. **Website:**

www.spalifemagazine.com. "*Spa Life* is about more than just spas. With favorite recipes from featured spa destinations, mouth-watering treats are at your fingertips. *Spa Life* is also dedicated to personal and health issues." Estab. 2000. No kill fee. Accepts queries by e-mail. Guidelines by e-mail.

NONFICTION Needs general interest, interview, new product, personal experience, travel. Length: 300-600 words. **Pays $25-50 (Canadian).**

PHOTOS Contact Bruce Anderson, art director, at designer@harworthpublishing.com.

TIPS "Describe the treatments/food and surroundings. Include all information to make it easy for readers to get more info and make reservations. Make it personal and fun; the reader has to feel they know you and can relate."

🌣🌣 TRAILER LIFE

GS Media & Events, 3300 Fernbrook Lane N., Suite 200, Plymouth MN 55447. **Fax:** (805)667 4484. **E-mail:** info@trailerlife.com. **Website:** www.trailerlife.com. **Contact:** Tom Kaiser, managing editor. **40% freelance written.** Monthly magazine covering RV traveling. "*Trailer Life* magazine is written specifically for active people whose overall lifestyle is based on travel and recreation in their RV. Every issue includes product tests, travel articles, and other features—ranging from lifestyle to vehicle maintenance." Estab. 1941. Circ. 270,000. Byline given. Pays on acceptance. Offers kill fee. Offers 30% kill fee for assigned articles that are not acceptable. Publishes ms an average of 6 months after acceptance. Editorial lead time 4 months. Submit seasonal material 6 months in advance. Accepts queries by mail. Responds in 2 months to queries. Responds in 2 months to mss. Sample copy free. Guidelines available online.

NONFICTION Needs historical, how-to, technical, humor, new product, opinion, personal experience, travel. "No vehicle tests, product evaluations or road tests; tech material is strictly assigned. No diaries or trip logs, no non-RV trips; nothing without an RV-hook." Buys 75 mss/year. Query. Length: 250-2,500 words. **Pays $125-700.** Sometimes pays expenses of writers on assignment.

PHOTOS Send photos. Identification of subjects, model releases required. Reviews transparencies, b&w contact sheets . Offers no additional payment for photos accepted with ms, does pay for supplemental photos.

COLUMNS/DEPARTMENTS Around the Bend (news, trends of interest to RVers), 100 words. **Buys 70 mss/year.** Query or send complete ms **Pays $75-250.**

TIPS "Prerequisite: Must have RV focus, and photos must be magazine quality. These are the 2 biggest reasons why mss are rejected. Our readers are travel enthusiasts who own all types of RVs (travel trailers, truck campers, van conversions, motorhomes, tent trailers, fifth-wheels) in which they explore North America and beyond, embrace the great outdoors in national, state and private parks. They're very active and very adventurous."

🌣🌣🌣🌣 TRAVEL + LEISURE

American Express Publishing Corp., 1120 Avenue of the Americas, New York NY 10036. (212)382-5600. **Website:** www.travelandleisure.com. **95% freelance written.** *Travel + Leisure* is a monthly magazine edited for affluent travelers. It explores the latest resorts, hotels, fashions, foods, and drinks, as well as political, cultural, and economic issues affecting travelers. Circ. 950,000. Byline given. Pays on acceptance. Offers 25% kill fee. Accepts queries by mail, online submission form. Responds in 6 weeks to queries and mss. Sample copy for $5.50 from (800)888-8728. Guidelines available online.

NONFICTION Needs travel. **Buys 40-50 feature (3,000-5,000 words) and 200 short (125-500 words) mss/year.** Query (e-mail preferred) **Pays $4,000-6,000/feature; $100-500/short piece.** Pays expenses of writers on assignment.

PHOTOS **Contact:** Photo Dept. Discourages submission of unsolicited transparencies. Captions required. Payment varies.

COLUMNS/DEPARTMENTS Length: 2,500-3,500 words. **Buys 125-150 mss/year. Pays $2,000-3,500.**

TIPS Queries should not be generic, but should specify what is new or previously uncovered in a destination or travel-related subject area.

🌣 TRAVEL NATURALLY

Internaturally, Inc., P.O. Box 317, Newfoundland NJ 07435-0317. (973)697-3552. **Fax:** (973)697-8313. **E-mail:** naturally@internaturally.com. **Website:** www. internaturally.com. **90% freelance written.** Quarterly magazine covering wholesome family nude recreation and travel locations. "*Travel Naturally* looks at why millions of people believe that removing clothes in public is a good idea, and at places specifically created for that purpose—with good humor, but also in earnest. *Travel*

Naturally takes you to places where your personal freedom is the only agenda, and to places where textile-free living is a serious commitment." Estab. 1981. Circ. 35,000. Byline given. Pays on publication. No kill fee. Editorial lead time 4 months. Submit seasonal material 4 months in advance. Accepts queries by mail, e-mail, fax. Accepts simultaneous submissions. Sample copy for $9. Guidelines available.

NONFICTION Needs general interest, interview, personal experience, photo feature, travel. **Buys 12 mss/year.** Send complete ms. Length: 2 pages. **Pays $80/published page, including photos.**

REPRINTS Pays 50% of original rate.

PHOTOS Send photos. Reviews contact sheets, negatives, transparencies, prints, high resolution digital images.

POETRY Wants poetry about the naturalness of the human body and nature; any length. Consideers previously published poems and simultaneous submissions. Accepts e-mail and fax submissions. "Name and address must be submitted with e-mail."

FILLERS Needs anecdotes, facts, gags, newsbreaks, short humor, poems, artwork. **Payment is pro-rated based on length.**

TIPS "*Travel Naturally* invokes the philosophies of naturism and nudism, but also activities and beliefs in the mainstream that express themselves, barely: spiritual awareness, New Age customs, pagan and religious rites, alternative and fringe lifestyle beliefs, artistic expressions, and many individual nude interests. Our higher purpose is simply to help restore our sense of self. Although the term 'nude recreation' may, for some, conjure up visions of sexual frivolities inappropriate for youngsters—because that can also be technically true—these topics are outside the scope of *Travel Naturally*. Here the emphasis is on the many varieties of human beings, of all ages and backgrounds, recreating in their most natural state, at extraordinary places, their reasons for doing so, and the benefits they derive. We incorporate a travel department to advise and book vacations in locations reviewed in travel articles."

🟢 TRAVEL SMART

Communications House, Inc., P.O. Box 397, Dobbs Ferry NY 10522. (800)327-3633. **E-mail:** travelsmartnow@aol.com. **Website:** www.travelsmartnewsletter.com. Monthly newsletter covering information on good-value travel. Estab. 1976. Circ. 20,000. Pays on publication. No kill fee. Accepts queries by mail, e-mail.

Responds in 6 weeks to queries. Responds in 6 weeks to mss. Sample copy and guidelines for SAE with 9x12 envelope and 3 first-class stamps.

NONFICTION Query. Length: 100-1,500 words. **Pays $150 maximum.**

TIPS When you travel, check out small hotels offering good prices, good restaurants, and send us brief rundown (with prices, phone numbers, addresses). Information must be current. Include your phone number with submission, because we sometimes make immediate assignments.

🟢🟢 WOODALL'S REGIONALS

2575 Vista Del Mar Dr., Ventura CA 93001. **Website:** www.woodalls.com. Monthly magazine for RV and camping enthusiasts. Woodall's Regionals include *CamperWays*, *Midwest RV Traveler*, *Northeast Outdoors*, *Florida RV Traveler*. Byline given. Accepts queries by mail, e-mail. Responds in 1-2 months to queries. Sample copy free. Guidelines free.

NONFICTION **Buys 300 mss/year.** Query with published clips. Length: 1,000-1,400 words. **Pays $180-220/feature; $75-100/department article and short piece.**

WOMEN'S

🟢🟢🟢 BRIDAL GUIDE

RFP, LLC, 228 E. 45th St., 11th Floor, New York NY 10017. (212)838-7733; (800)472-7744. **Fax:** (212)308-7165. **E-mail:** editorial@bridalguide.com. **Website:** www.bridalguide.com. **20% freelance written.** Bimonthly magazine covering relationships, sexuality, fitness, wedding planning, psychology, finance, and travel. Only works with experienced/published writers. Pays on acceptance. No kill fee. Accepts queries by mail. Responds in 3 months to queries and mss. Sample copy for $5 and SAE with 4 first-class stamps. Guidelines available.

NONFICTION "Please do not send queries concerning beauty, fashion, or home design stories since we produce them in-house. We do not accept personal wedding essays, fiction, or poetry. Address travel queries to travel editor. All correspondence accompanied by an SASE will be answered." **Buys 100 mss/year.** Query with published clips from national consumer magazines. Length: 1,000-2,000 words. **Pays 50¢/word.**

PHOTOS Photography and illustration submissions should be sent to the art department.

TIPS "We are looking for service-oriented, well-researched pieces that are journalistically written. Writers we work with use at least 3 top expert sources, such as physicians, book authors, and business people in the appropriate field. Our tone is conversational, yet authoritative. Features are also generally filled with real-life anecdotes. We also do features that are completely real-person based—such as roundtables of bridesmaids discussing their experiences, or grooms-to-be talking about their feelings about getting married. In queries, we are looking for a well-thought-out idea, the specific angle of focus the writer intends to take, and the sources he or she intends to use. Queries should be brief and snappy—and titles should be supplied to give the editor an even better idea of the direction the writer is going in."

THE BROADSHEET

Broad Universe, 1812 E. Madison St., #208, Seattles WA 98122. **E-mail:** broadsheet@broaduniverse.org. **Website:** http://broaduniverse.org. **Contact:** Lillian Cohen-Moore, editor-in-chief. Covers articles about women writers of science fiction, fantasy, and horror genre fiction. "*The Broadsheet* is a small web-based zine published 3 times a year. *The Broadsheet* accepts art, articles, interviews, book reviews, and commentaries about any topic involving women writers and artists in science fiction, fantasy, and horror. It also accepts general articles on the writing or marketing of science fiction/fiction/horror. We only print nonfiction. Anyone may submit, whether female or male, new writer or experienced pro." Estab. 2000. Pays on acceptance. Accepts queries by e-mail. Accepts simultaneous submissions.

NONFICTION Query first via e-mail, according to topic: For Art: Constance Burris at art@broaduniverse.org. For Create: Carol Ullmann at editor3@ broaduniverse.org. All other topics: *Broadsheet* editor Lillian Cohen-Moore at broadsheet@broaduniverse. org. "Interviews should be 3,000-5,000 words. Brief articles (2,000 words or less) are preferred for Create, Sell, Read, and Think. However, excellent interviews and articles of shorter or longer lengths will also receive consideration." **Art and Interviews: $50; Create, Sell, Think: $40; Read: $25 for the usual brief review, up to $40 for pieces that deliver something more. "A brief biography of the contributor, including any link to the artist or author's website, will also run with the piece if so desired. Art and articles appearing in past issues of** *The Broadsheet* **are made available in** our public archives unless the artist or author states otherwise in writing."

PHOTOS Contact: Constance Burris.

CHATELAINE

One Mount Pleasant Rd., 8th Floor, Toronto ON M4Y 2Y5 Canada. (416)764-1888. **Fax:** (416)764-2891. **E-mail:** storyideas@chatelaine.rogers.com. **Website:** www.chatelaine.com. **Contact:** Samantha Grice, managing editor. Monthly magazine covering Canadian women's lifestyles. "*Chatelaine* is edited for Canadian women ages 25-49, their changing attitudes and lifestyles. Key editorial ingredients include health, finance, social issues, and trends, as well as fashion, beauty, food and home decor. Regular departments include Health pages, Entertainment, Money, Home, Humour, How-to." Byline given. Pays on acceptance. Offers 25-50% kill fee. Accepts queries by mail, e-mail (preferred). Responds in 4-6 weeks to 1 month to queries; up to 2 months to proposals. Guidelines available on website.

NONFICTION Query. **Pays $1/word.**

COMPLETE WOMAN

Associated Publications, Inc., 875 N. Michigan Ave., Suite 3434, Chicago IL 60611. (312)266-8680. **Fax:** (312)573-3020. **Website:** www.thecompletewoman-magazine.com. Kourtney McKay, art director. **90% freelance written.** Estab. 1980. Circ. 300,000. Byline given. Pays 45 days after acceptance. No kill fee. Publishes ms an average of 6 months after acceptance. Editorial lead time 6 months. Submit seasonal material 5 months in advance. Accepts queries by mail. Accepts simultaneous submissions. Responds in 2 months to queries. Responds in 2 months to mss. Guidelines with #10 SASE.

NONFICTION Needs book excerpts, exposé, of interest to women, general interest, how-to, beauty/diet-related, humor, inspirational, interview, celebrities, new product, personal experience, photo feature, sex, love, relationship advice. **Buys 60-100 mss/year.** Send complete ms. Length: 800-2,000 words. **Pays $160-500.** Sometimes pays expenses of writers on assignment.

REPRINTS Send tearsheet, photocopy or typed ms with rights for sale noted and information about when and where the material previously appeared.

PHOTOS Photo features with little or no copy should be sent to Kourtney McKay. Send photos. Captions, identification of subjects, model releases required. Reviews 2.25 or 35mm transparencies, 5x7 prints. Pays $35-100/photo.

TIPS "Freelance writers should review publication, review writer's guidelines, then submit their articles for review. We're looking for new ways to explore the usual topics, written in a format that will be easy for our readers (ages 24-40+) to understand. We also like sidebar information that readers can review quickly before or after reading the article. Our focus is relationship-driven, with an editorial blend of beauty, health, and career."

COUNTRY WOMAN

Reiman Publications, 5400 S. 60th St., Greendale WI 53129. (414)423-0100. **E-mail:** editors@countrywomanmagazine.com. **Website:** www.countrywomanmagazine.com. **Contact:** Lori Lau Grzybowski, editor. **75-85% freelance written.** Bimonthly magazine. *Country Woman* is for contemporary rural women of all ages and backgrounds and from all over the U.S. and Canada. It includes a sampling of the diversity that makes up rural women's lives—love of home, family, farm, ranch, community, hobbies, enduring values, humor, attaining new skills and appreciating present, past and future all within the context of the lifestyle that surrounds country living. Estab. 1970. Byline given. Pays on acceptance. No kill fee. Submit seasonal material 5 months in advance. Accepts queries by mail. Accepts simultaneous submissions. Responds in 2 months to queries. Responds in 3 months to mss. Sample copy for $2 and SASE. Guidelines with #10 SASE.

NONFICTION Needs general interest, historical, how-to, crafts, community projects, decorative, antiquing, etc., humor, inspirational, interview, personal experience, photo feature, packages profiling interesting country women-all pertaining to rural women's interests. Query. 1,000 words maximum.

REPRINTS Send typed manuscript with rights for sale noted and information about when and where the material previously appeared. Payment varies

PHOTOS Uses only excellent quality color photos. No b&w. We pay for photo/feature packages. State availability of or send photos. Captions, identification of subjects, model releases required. Reviews 35mm or 2.25 transparencies, excellent-quality color prints.

COLUMNS/DEPARTMENTS Why Farm Wives Age Fast (humor), I Remember When (nostalgia), and Country Decorating. Length: 500-1,000 words. **Buys 10-12 mss/year.** Query or send ms.

FICTION Contact: Kathleen Anderson, managing editor. Main character *must* be a country woman. All fiction must have a country setting. Fiction must have a positive, upbeat message. Includes fiction in every issue. Would buy more fiction if stories suitable for our audience were sent our way. No contemporary, urban pieces that deal with divorce, drugs, etc. Send complete ms. Length: 750-1,000 words.

POETRY Needs light verse, traditional. Poetry must have rhythm and rhyme. It must be country-related, positive, and upbeat. Always looking for seasonal poetry. Buys 6-12 poems/year. Submit maximum 6 poems. Length: 4-24 lines. **Pays $10-25/poem plus one contribtor's copy.**

TIPS "We have broadened our focus to include country women, not just women on farms and ranches but also women who live in a small town or country home and/or simply have an interest in country-oriented topics. This allows freelancers a wider scope in material. Write as clearly and with as much zest and enthusiasm as possible. We love good quotes, supporting materials (names, places, etc.) and strong leads and closings. Readers relate strongly to where they live and the lifestyle they've chosen. They want to be informed and entertained, and that's just exactly why they subscribe. Readers are busy—not too busy to read—but when they do sit down, they want good writing, reliable information and something that feels like a reward. How-to, humor, personal experience and nostalgia are areas most open to freelancers. Profiles, to a certain degree, are also open. Be accurate and fresh in approach."

$$$$ ELLE

Hachette Filipacchi Media U.S., Inc., 1271 Avenue of the Americas, 41st Floor, New York NY 10020. (212)767-5800. **Fax:** (212)489-4210. **Website:** www.elle.com. Monthly magazine. Edited for the modern, sophisticated, affluent, well-traveled woman in her twenties to early thirties. Circ. 1,100,000. No kill fee. Editorial lead time 3 months.

$$$$ FAMILY CIRCLE

Meredith Corporation, 375 Lexington Ave., 9th Floor, New York NY 10017. **Website:** www.familycircle.com. Lisa Kelsey, art director. **Contact:** Linda Fears, editor-in-chief. **80% freelance written.** Magazine published every 3 weeks. We are a national women's service magazine which covers many stages of a woman's life, along with her everyday concerns about social, family, and health issues. Submissions should focus on families with children ages 8-16. Estab. 1932. Circ. 4,200,000. Byline given. Offers 20% kill fee. Editorial lead time 4 months. Submit seasonal material 4 months in advance. Responds in 2 months to queries. Responds in 2 months to mss. For back issues, send $6.95 to P.O. Box 3156, Harlan IA 51537. Guidelines available online.

NONFICTION Needs essays, opinion, personal experience, women's interest subjects such as family and personal relationships, children, physical and mental health, nutrition and self-improvement. No fiction or poetry. **Buys 200 mss/year.** Submit detailed outline, 2 clips, cover letter describing your publishing history, SASE or IRCs. Length: 1,000-2,500 words. **Pays $1/word.**

TIPS Query letters should be concise and to the point. Also, writers should keep close tabs on *Family Circle* and other women's magazines to avoid submitting recently run subject matter. *Note*: Family Circle Fiction Contest: Contest begins March 1, 2010 and ends September 8, 2010. Entries must be postmarked on or before September 8, 2010 and received by September 15, 2010. Entries will not be acknowledged or returned. Sponsor: Meredith Corporation. ENTRY: Submit an original (written by entrant), fiction short story of no more than 2,500 words, typed on 8-1/2x11 paper. Entries must be unpublished and may not have won any prize or award. See website.

✪ $$$$ FLARE MAGAZINE

Rogers Communications, One Mt. Pleasant Rd., 8th Floor, Toronto ON M4Y 2Y5 Canada. (416)764-1829. **Fax:** (416)764-2866. **E-mail:** editors@flare.com. **Website:** www.flare.com. **Contact:** Miranda Purves, editor. Monthly magazine for women ages 17-35. Byline given. Offers 50% kill fee. Accepts queries by e-mail. Response time varies. Sample copy for #10 SASE. Guidelines available online at www.flare.com/about/writers-guidelines.

NONFICTION Buys 24 mss/year. Query. Length: 200-1,200 words. **Pays $1/word.** Pays expenses of writers on assignment.

TIPS Study our masthead to determine if your topic is handled by regular contributing staff or a staff member.

GIRLFRIENDZ MAGAZINE

6 Brookville Dr., Cherry Hill NJ 08003. **E-mail:** tobi@girlfriendzmag.com. **Website:** www.girlfriendzmag.com; www.facebook.com/girlfriendz. **80% freelance written.** Bimonthly magazine covering Baby Boomer women. "As a publication by and for Baby Boomer women, we are most interested in entertaining, educating, and empowering our readers. Our target is smart women born between 1946 and 1964. We like a little humor in our articles, but only if it's appropriate and subtle. And most importantly, all facts must be checked for accuracy. We insist on well-researched and well-documented information." Estab. 2007. Circ. 22,000. Byline given. Headshot and 50-word bio included. "As a startup, we are unable to pay our writers." No kill fee. Editorial lead time 3 months. Submit seasonal material 4 months in advance. Accepts queries by e-mail only. Accepts simultaneous submissions. Responds in 2 weeks to queries. Sample copy for $5. Guidelines available online.

NONFICTION Needs book excerpts, how-to, humor, interview (celebrities only), new product, articles of interest to women born 1946-1964; "especially interested in local and national celebrities. Examples of those we've already profiled: Marlo Thomas, Tina Louise, Mayim Bialik, Cokie Roberts, Dr. Ruth, Joan Lunden, Fran Drescher." "We do not want fiction, essays, or poetry." **Buys 20 mss/year.** Query. Length: 735-1,200 words. Sometimes pays expenses of writers on assignment.

PHOTOS State availability. Captions, identification of subjects required. Reviews JPEGs and/or PDFs, 300 dpi. Offers no additional payment for photos accepted with mss.

TIPS "Please do not call us or fax a query or ms; e-mail only. Please query only—no mss. And please, no fiction, essays, or poetry. We are interested in nonfiction articles that will make Boomer women think. We also like articles with subjects that our audience can identify with, though we're not looking for Sandwich Generation articles. Also, no articles on pre-schoolers or pregnancy. Our readers have children who are either just starting to exit elementary school, are in middle school, high school, or college; are just getting married; are just having children, or already have children. We are also looking for an ethnic mix of writers."

$$$$ GLAMOUR

Conde Nast Publications, Inc., 4 Times Square, 16th Floor, New York NY 10036. (212)286-2860. **Fax:** (212)286-8336. **Website:** www.glamour.com. **Contact:** Cynthia Leive, editor-in-chief. Monthly magazine covering subjects ranging from fashion, beauty and health, personal relationships, career, travel, food and entertainment. "*Glamour* is edited for the contemporary woman, and informs her of the trends and recommends how she can adapt them to her needs, and motivates her to take action." Estab. 1939. Circ. 2,320,325. No kill fee. Accepts queries by mail.

NONFICTION Needs personal experience, relationships, travel. **Pays 75¢-$1/word.**

PHOTOS Only uses professional photographers.

❸❸❸❸ GOOD HOUSEKEEPING

Hearst Corp., 300 W. 57th St., 28th Floor, New York NY 10019. (212)649-2200. **Website:** www.goodhousekeeping.com. **Contact:** Rosemary Ellis, editor. Monthly magazine covering women's interests. "*Good Housekeeping* is edited for the 'new traditionalist.' Articles which focus on food, fitness, beauty, and childcare draw upon the resources of the Good Housekeeping Institute. Editorial includes human interest stories, articles that focus on social issues, money management, health news, and travel." Circ. 4,000,000. Byline given. Pays on acceptance. Offers 25% kill fee. Submit seasonal material 6 months in advance. Responds in 2-3 months to queries. Responds in 2-3 months to mss. For sample copy, call (212)649-2359. Guidelines at www.goodhousekeeping.com/about/good-housekeeping-contributors-guidelines.

NONFICTION Buys 4-6 mss/year. Query. Length: 1,500-2,500 words. Pays expenses of writers on assignment.

PHOTOS Photos purchased mostly on assignment. State availability. Model releases required. Pays $100-350 for b&w; $200-400 for color photos.

COLUMNS/DEPARTMENTS Profiles (inspirational, activist or heroic women), 400-600 words. Query with published clips. **Pays $1/word for items 300-600 words.**

TIPS "Always send an SASE and clips. We prefer to see a query first. Do not send material on subjects already covered in-house by the Good Housekeeping Institute—these include food, beauty, needlework and crafts."

❸❸ GRACE ORMONDE WEDDING STYLE

Elegant Publishing, Inc., P.O. Box 89, Barrington RI 02806. (401)245-9726. **Fax:** (401)245-5371. **E-mail:** contact@weddingstylemagazine.com. **Website:** www.weddingstylemagazine.com. **Contact:** Human Resources. **90% freelance written.** Quarterly magazine covering weddings catering to the affluent bride. Estab. 1997. Circ. 400,000. Pays on publication. No kill fee. Publishes ms an average of 4 months after acceptance. Editorial lead time 3 months. Sample copy available online. Guidelines by e-mail.

PHOTOS State availability. Reviews transparencies. Negotiates payment individually.

TIPS E-mail résumé and 5 clips/samples in any area of writing.

❸❸❸❸ HARPER'S BAZAAR

The Hearst Corp., 300 W. 57th St., New York NY 10019. (212)903-5000. **E-mail:** editors@harpersbazaar.com. **Website:** www.harpersbazaar.com. "*Harper's Bazaar* is a specialist magazine published 10 times/year for women who enjoy fashion and beauty. It is edited for sophisticated women with exceptional taste. *Harper's Bazaar* offers ideas in fashion and beauty, and reports on issues and interests relevant to the lives of modern women." Estab. 1867. Circ. 734,504. Byline given. Pays on publication. Offers 25% kill fee. Responds in 2 months to queries.

NONFICTION Buys 36 mss/year. Query with published clips. Length: 2,000-3,000 words. **Payment negotiable.**

COLUMNS/DEPARTMENTS Length: 500-700 words. **Payment negotiable.**

⊘ ❸❸❸❸ LADIES' HOME JOURNAL

Meredith Corp., 375 Lexington Ave., 9th Floor, New York NY 10017. (212)557-6600. **E-mail:** lhj@mdp.com. **Website:** www.lhj.com. **50% freelance written.** Monthly magazine focusing on issues of concern to women 30-45. "*Ladies' Home Journal* is for active, empowered women who are evolving in new directions. It addresses informational needs with highly focused features and articles on a variety of topics: self, style, family, home, world, health, and food." Estab. 1882. Circ. 4.1 million. Pays on acceptance. Offers 25% kill fee. Publishes ms an average of 4-12 months after acceptance. Editorial lead time 4 months. Accepts queries by mail, e-mail. Accepts simultaneous submissions. Responds in 3 months to queries. Guidelines available online at www.lhj.com/lhj/file.jsp?item=/help/writers-Guidelines.

NONFICTION Send 1-2 page query, SASE, résumé, and clips via mail or e-mail (preferred). Length: 2,000-3,000 words. **Pays $2,000-4,000.** Pays expenses of writers on assignment.

PHOTOS *LHJ* arranges for its own photography almost all the time. State availability. Captions, identification of subjects, model releases required. Offers variable payment for photos accepted with ms.

FICTION Only short stories and novels submitted by an agent or publisher will be considered. No poetry of any kind. **Buys 12 mss/year.** Send complete ms. Length: 2,000-2,500 words.

⭘ $$ THE LINK & VISITOR

Canadian Baptist Women of Ontario and Quebec, 100-304 The East Mall, Etobicoke ON M9B 6E2 Canada. (416)651-8967. **E-mail:** rsejames@gmail.com. **Website:** www.baptistwomen.com. **Contact:** Renee James, editor/director of communications. **50% freelance written.** Magazine published 6 times/year designed to help Baptist women grow their world, faith, relationships, creativity, and mission vision—evangelical, egalitarian, Canadian. Estab. 1878. Circ. 3,500. Byline given. Pays on publication. No kill fee. Publishes ms an average of 6 months after acceptance. Editorial lead time 2 months. Submit seasonal material 4 months in advance. Accepts simultaneous submissions. Sample copy for 9x12 SAE with 2 first-class Canadian stamps.

NONFICTION Needs inspirational, interview, religious. **Buys 30-35 mss/year.** Query first. Unsolicited mss not accepted. Length: 650-800 words. **Pays 5-12¢/word (Canadian).** Sometimes pays expenses of writers on assignment.

PHOTOS State availability. Captions required. Offers no additional payment for photos accepted with ms.

TIPS "We cannot use unsolicited mss from non-Canadian writers. When submitting by e-mail, please send stories as messages, not as attachments."

$ LONG ISLAND WOMAN

P.O. Box 176, Malverne NY 11565. (516)505-0555. **Fax:** (516)505-1753. **E-mail:** editor@liwomanonline.com. **Website:** www.liwomanonline.com. **40% freelance written.** Monthly magazine covering issues of importance to women in Nassau and Suffolk counties in New York—health, family, finance, arts, entertainment, fitness, travel, home. Estab. 2001. Circ. 40,000. Byline given. Pays within 1 month of publication. Offers 20% kill fee. Publishes ms an average of 3 months after acceptance. Editorial lead time 3 months. Submit seasonal material 3 months in advance. Accepts queries by mail, e-mail. Accepts simultaneous submissions. Responds in 8 weeks to queries. Responds in 3 months to mss. Sample copy for $5. Guidelines available on website.

NONFICTION Needs book excerpts, general interest, how-to, humor, interview, new product, reviews, travel. **Buys 25-30 mss/year.** Send complete ms. Length: 500-2,250 words. **Pays $70-200.**

REPRINTS Length: 500-2,250 words. Pays $40-100.

PHOTOS State availability of or send photos. Captions, identification of subjects, model releases required. Reviews 5x7 prints.

COLUMNS/DEPARTMENTS Humor; Health Issues; Family Issues; Financial and Business Issues; Book Reviews and Books; Arts and Entertainment; Travel and Leisure; Home and Garden; Fitness.

$ MADISON

Bauer Media Group, 54-58 Park St., Sydney NSW 2000 Australia. (61)(2)9282-8000. **Fax:** (61)(2)9267-4361. **E-mail:** madison@acpmagazines.com.au. **Website:** www.madisonmag.com.au. **Contact:** Elizabeth Renkert, editor. Monthly magazine offering intelligent news and features, real women and their stories, beautiful fashion, sexy beauty, inspiring homes, and impress-your-friends food. "She is 25-39. Ambitious, sexy and socially aware. The *madison* woman actively enjoys her life. She loves fashion but will dress to suit a style she's developed. She's seriously interested in beauty but her health is just as important as finding the perfect lipgloss." Circ. 65,310.

$$$$ MARIE CLAIRE

The Hearst Publishing Corp., Feature Submissions, Marie Claire Magazine, 300 W. 57th St., 34th Floor, New York NY 10019. (212)649-5000. **Fax:** (212)649-5050. **Website:** www.marieclaire.com. **Contact:** Joanna Coles, editor-in-chief. Monthly magazine written for today's younger working woman with a smart service-oriented view. Estab. 1937. Circ. 952,223. No kill fee. Editorial lead time 6 months. Responds in 4-6 weeks.

NONFICTION Prefers to receive story proposals. Query. Include previously published clips.

$$$$ MS. MAGAZINE

433 S. Beverly Dr., Beverly Hills CA 90212. (310)556-2515. **Fax:** (310)556-2514. **E-mail:** mkort@msmagazine.com. **Website:** www.msmagazine.com. **Contact:** Michele Kort, senior editor. **70% freelance written.** Quarterly magazine on women's issues and news. Estab. 1972. Circ. 150,000. Byline given. Offers 25% kill fee. Responds in 3 months to queries. Responds in 3 months to mss. Sample copy for $9. Guidelines available online.

NONFICTION Needs international and national women's news, investigative reporting, personal narratives of prize-winning journalists and feminist thinkers. **Buys 4-5 feature (2,000-3,000 words) and**

4-5 short (500 words) mss/year. Query with published clips. Length: 300-3,500 words. **Pays $1/word; 50¢/word for news stories and book reviews.**
COLUMNS/DEPARTMENTS Buys 6-10 mss/year. **Pays $1/word.**
FICTION "*Ms.* welcomes the highest-quality original fiction and poetry, but is publishing these infrequently as of late."

NA'AMAT WOMAN

505 8th Ave., Suite 2302, New York NY 10018. (212)563-5222. **Fax:** (212)563-5710. **E-mail:** naamat@naamat.org; judith@naamat.org. **Website:** www.naamat.org. **Contact:** Judith Sokoloff, editor. **80% freelance written.** Quarterly magazine covering Jewish issues/subjects. "We cover issues and topics of interest to the Jewish community in the U.S., Israel, and the rest of the world with emphasis on Jewish women's issues." Estab. 1926. Circ. 12,000. Byline given. Pays on publication. No kill fee. Publishes ms an average of 6 months after acceptance. Submit seasonal material 6 months in advance. Accepts queries by mail, e-mail. Accepts simultaneous submissions. Responds in 4 weeks to queries. Responds in 3 months to mss. Sample copy for $2. Guidelines by e-mail.
NONFICTION Needs book excerpts, essays, historical, interview, personal experience, photo feature, travel, Jewish topics & issues, political & social issues & women's issues. **Buys 16-20 mss/year.** Send complete ms. **Pays 10-20¢/word for assigned and unsolicited articles.** Some
PHOTOS State availability. Reviews GIF/JPEG files. Negotiates payment individually.
FICTION "We want serious fiction, with insight, reflection and consciousness." Needs novel excerpts, literary with Jewish content. "We do not want fiction that is mostly dialogue. No corny Jewish humor. No Holocaust fiction." **Buys 1-2 mss/year.** Query with published clips or send complete ms. Length: 2,000-3,000 words. **Pays 10-20¢/word for assigned articles and for unsolicited articles.**
TIPS "No maudlin nostalgia or romance; no hackneyed Jewish humor."

PREGNANCY

Pregnancy Magazine Group, 4000 Shoreline Ct., Suite 400, S. San Francisco CA 94080-1960. **E-mail:** editors@pregnancymagazine.com. **Website:** www.pregnancymagazine.com. **Contact:** Abigail Tuller, editor-in-chief. **40% freelance written.** Magazine covering products, wellness, technology fashion, and beauty for pregnant women; and products, health, and child care for babies up to 12 months old. "A large part of our audience is first-time moms who seek advice and information about health, relationships, diet, celebrities, fashion, and green living for pregnant women and babies up to 12 months old. Our readers are first-time and experienced moms (and dads) who want articles that are relevant to their modern lives. Our goal is to help our readers feel confident and prepared for pregnancy and parenthood by providing the best information for today's parents." Estab. 2000. Circ. 250,000. Offers kill fee. Editorial lead time 5 months. Submit seasonal material 5-6 months in advance. Guidelines available at www.pregnancymagazine.com/writers.
NONFICTION Buys 60 mss/year. Length: 350-2,000 words.
TIPS "Interested freelancers should first read *Pregnancy's* Writer's Guidelines, which are available at www.pregnancymagazine.com/writers. When sending pitch ideas, be sure to follow those guidelines carefully."

P31 WOMAN

Proverbs 31 Ministries, 616-G Matthews-Mint Hill Rd., Charlotte NC 28105. (704)849-2270. **E-mail:** janet@proverbs31.org. **Website:** www.proverbs31.org. Janet Burke. **Contact:** Glynnis Whitwer, editor. **50% freelance written.** Monthly magazine covering Christian issues for women. "The *P31 Woman* provides Christian wives and mothers with articles that encourage them in their faith and support them in the many roles they have as women. We look for articles that have a Biblical foundation and offer inspiration, yet have a practical application to everyday life." Estab. 1992. Circ. 10,000. Byline given. No kill fee. Publishes ms an average of 6 months after acceptance. Editorial lead time 5 months. Submit seasonal material 5-6 months in advance. Accepts queries by mail, e-mail. Accepts simultaneous submissions. Responds in 2-4 weeks to queries; 1-2 months to mss. Sample copy online or $2 for hard copy. Guidelines available online.
NONFICTION Needs humor, inspirational, personal experience, religious. No biographical stories or articles about men's issues. Send complete ms. Length: 200-1,000 words. **Pays in contributor copies.**

REDBOOK MAGAZINE

Hearst Corp., Articles Department, Redbook, 300 W. 57th St., 22nd Floor, New York NY 10019. **Website:** www.redbookmag.com/writersguidelines. Monthly magazine covering women's issues. "*Redbook* is targeted to women between the ages of 25 and 45 who define themselves as smart, capable, and happy with their lives. Many, but not all, of our readers are going through 1 of 2 key life transitions: single to married and married to mom. Each issue is a provocative mix of features geared to entertain and inform them, including: News stories on contemporary issues that are relevant to the reader's life and experience, and explore the emotional ramifications of cultural and social changes; girst-person essays about dramatic pivotal moments in a woman's life; marriage articles with an emphasis on strengthening the relationship; short parenting features on how to deal with universal health and behavioral issues; reporting on exciting trends in women's lives." Estab. 1903. Circ. 2,200,000. Pays on acceptance. No kill fee. Publishes ms an average of 6 months after acceptance. Responds in 3 months to queries. Responds in 3 months to mss. Guidelines available online.

NONFICTION Query with published clips and SASE. Length: 2,500-3,000 words/features; 1,000-1,500 words/short articles.

TIPS "Most *Redbook* articles require solid research, well-developed anecdotes from on-the-record sources, and fresh, insightful quotes from established experts in a field that pass our 'reality check' test. Articles must apply to women in our demographics. Writers are advised to read at least the last 6 issues of the magazine (available in most libraries) to get a better understanding of appropriate subject matter and treatment. We prefer to see detailed queries rather than completed mss, and suggest that you provide us with some ideas for sources/experts. Please enclose 2 or more samples of your writing, as well as a SASE."

⊘ RESOURCES FOR FEMINIST RESEARCH

RFR/DRF (Resources for Feminist Research), OISE, University of Toronto, 252 Bloor St. W., Toronto ON M5S 1V6 Canada. **E-mail:** rfr@utoronto.ca. **Website:** www.oise.utoronto.ca/rfr. Semiannual academic journal covering feminist research in an interdisciplinary, international perspective. Estab. 1972. Circ. 2,500. Byline given. Publishes ms an average of 1 year after acceptance. Editorial lead time 1 year. Accepts queries by e-mail. Responds in 2 weeks to queries. Responds in 6-8 months to mss. Guidelines free.

NONFICTION Needs essays, academic articles and book reviews. Does not want nonacademic articles. Send complete ms. Length: 3,000-5,000 words.

PHOTOS Send photos. Identification of subjects required. Reviews prints, GIF/JPEG files. Offers no additional payment for photos accepted with ms.

❸❸❸❸ SELF

Conde Nast, 4 Times Square, New York NY 10036. (212)286-2860. **Fax:** (212)286-8110. **E-mail:** comments@self.com. **Website:** www.self.com. Monthly magazine for women ages 20-45. Self-confidence, self-assurance, and a healthy, happy lifestyle are pivotal to *Self* readers. This healthy lifestyle magazine delivers by addressing real-life issues from the inside out, with unparalleled energy and authority. From beauty, fitness, health and nutrition to personal style, finance, and happiness, the path to total well-being begins with *Self*. Circ. 1,300,000. Byline given on features and most short items. Pays on acceptance. No kill fee. Accepts queries by online submission form. Accepts simultaneous submissions. Responds in 1 month to queries. Guidelines for #10 SASE.

NONFICTION Buys 40 mss/year. Query with published clips. Length: 1,500-5,000 words. **Pays $1-2/word**

COLUMNS/DEPARTMENTS Uses short, news-driven items on health, fitness, nutrition, money, jobs, love/sex, psychology and happiness, travel. Length: 300-1,000 words. **Buys 50 mss/year.** Query with published clips. **Pays $1-2/word.**

❸❸ SKIRT!

Morris Communications, 1 Henrietta St., First Floor, Charleston SC 29403. (843)958-0027. **Fax:** (843)958-0029. **E-mail:** submissions@skirt.com; digitalmedia@skirt.com. **Website:** www.skirt.com. **Contact:** Nikki Hardin, publisher. **50% freelance written.** Monthly magazine covering women's interest. "*Skirt!* is all about women—their work, play, families, creativity, style, health, wealth, bodies, and souls. The magazine's attitude is spirited, independent, outspoken, serious, playful, irreverent, sometimes controversial, and always passionate." Estab. 1994. Circ. 285,000. Byline given. Pays on publication. No kill fee. Publishes ms an average of 2 months after acceptance. Editorial lead time 2-3 months. Submit seasonal material 2-3 months in advance. Accepts queries by e-mail (preferred). Accepts simultaneous submissions. Responds in 6-8 weeks to queries. Responds in 1-2 months to mss. Guidelines on website.

NONFICTION Needs essays, humor, personal experience. "Do not send feature articles. We only accept submissions of completed personal essays that will work with our monthly themes available online." **Buys 100+ mss/year.** Send complete ms. "We prefer e-mail submissions." Length: 900-1,200 words. **Pays $150-200.**

PHOTOS "We feature a different color photo, painting, or illustration on the cover each month. Each issue also features a b&w photo by a female photographer. Submit artwork via e-mail." Reviews slides, high-resolution digital files. Does not pay for photos or artwork, but the artist's bio is published.

TIPS "Surprise and charm us. We look for fearless essays that take chances with content and subject. *Skirt!* is not your average women's magazine. We push the envelope and select content that makes our readers think. Please review guidelines and themes online before submitting."

🌑 💲💲 THAT'S LIFE!

H Bauer Publishing, Academic House, 24-28 Oval Rd., London England NW1 7DT United Kingdom. (44)(207)241-8000. **E-mail:** stories@thatslife.co.uk. **Website:** www.thatslife.co.uk. **Contact:** Sophie Hearsey, editor. "*that's life!* is packed with the most amazing true-life stories and fab puzzles offering big money prizes including family sunshine holidays, and even a car! We also have bright, up-to-date fashion, health, and beauty pages with top tips and readers' letters. And just to make sure we get you smiling too, there's our rib-tickling rude jokes and 'aren't men' daft tales." Estab. 1995. Circ. 550,000. No kill fee. Submit seasonal material 3 months in advance. Accepts queries by mail. Responds in 6 weeks to mss. Guidelines by e-mail.

FICTION "Stories should have a strong plot and a good twist. A sexy relationships/scene can feature strongly, but isn't essential—the plot twist is much more important. The writing should be chronological and fast moving. A maximum of 4 characters is advisable. Avoid straightforward romance, historical backgrounds, science fiction, and stories told by animals or small children. Graphic murders and sex crimes—especially those involving children—are not acceptable." Send complete ms. Length: 700 words. **Pays £400.**

TIPS "Study the magazine for a few weeks to get an idea of our style and flavor."

♻ 💲💲 TODAY'S BRIDE

Family Communications, 65 The East Mall, Toronto ON M8Z SW3 Canada. (416)537-2604. **Fax:** (416)538-1794. **E-mail:** info@canadianbride.com. **Website:** www.todaysbride.ca; www.canadianbride.com. **20%**

freelance written. Semiannual magazine on wedding planning. Magazine provides information to engaged couples on all aspects of wedding planning, including tips, fashion advice, etc. Also contains beauty, home, groom, and honeymoon travel sections. Estab. 1979. Circ. 102,000. Byline given. Pays on acceptance. No kill fee. Editorial lead time 6 months. Accepts queries by mail, e-mail. Accepts simultaneous submissions. Responds in 2 weeks-1 month.

NONFICTION Needs humor, opinion, personal experience. No travel pieces. Send complete ms. Length: 800-1,400 words. **Pays $250-300.**

PHOTOS Send photos. Identification of subjects required. Reviews transparencies, prints. Negotiates payment individually.

TIPS "Send us tight writing about topics relevant to all brides and grooms. Stories for grooms, especially those written by/about grooms, are also encouraged."

💲💲 WOMAN'S LIFE

A Publication of Woman's Life Insurance Society, 1338 Military St., P.O. Box 5020, Port Huron MI 48061-5020. (800)521-9292, ext. 281. **Fax:** (810)985-6970. **E-mail:** wkrabach@womanslife.org. **Website:** www.womanslife.org. **Contact:** Wendy Krabach, managing editor. **30% freelance written.** Quarterly magazine published for a primarily female membership to help them care for themselves and their families. Estab. 1892. Circ. 32,000. Byline given. Pays on publication. No kill fee. Publishes ms an average of 1 year after acceptance. Submit seasonal material 6 months in advance. Accepts queries by mail, e-mail, fax. Accepts simultaneous submissions. Responds in 1 year to queries and to mss. Sample copy for sae with 9 X 12 envelope and 4 first-class stamps. Guidelines for #10 SASE.

NONFICTION **Buys 4-10 mss/year.** Send complete ms. Length: 1,000-2,000 words. **Pays $150-500.**

REPRINTS Send tearsheet, photocopy or typed ms with rights for sale noted and information about when and where the material previously appeared. Pays 15% of amount paid for an original article

PHOTOS Only interested in photos included with ms. Identification of subjects, model releases required.

💲💲💲 WOMAN'S WORLD

Bauer Publishing Co., 270 Sylvan Ave., Englewood Cliffs NJ 07632. (201)569-6699. **Fax:** (201)569-3584. **E-mail:** dearww@bauerpublishing.com; dearww@aol.com. **Website:** http://winit.womansworldmag.com. **Contact:** Stephanie Saible, editor-in-chief. Weekly magazine covering human interest and service pieces of interest to family-oriented women across the nation. *Woman's World* is a women's service magazine. It offers a blend of fashion, food, parenting, beauty, and relationship features coupled with the true-life human interest stories. "We publish short romances and mini-mysteries for all women, ages 18-68." Estab. 1980. Circ. 1,625,779. Pays on acceptance. No kill fee. Publishes ms an average of 4 months after acceptance. Submit seasonal material 4 months in advance. Accepts queries by mail. Responds in 2 months to mss. Guidelines for #10 SASE.

NONFICTION Pays $500/1,000 words.

FICTION Contact: Johnene Granger, fiction editor. "Short story, romance, and mainstream of 800 words and mini-mysteries of 1,000 words. Each of our stories has a light romantic theme and can be written from either a masculine or feminine point of view. Women characters may be single, married, or divorced. Plots must be fast moving with vivid dialogue and action. The problems and dilemmas inherent in them should be contemporary and realistic, handled with warmth and feeling. The stories must have a positive resolution. Specify Fiction on envelope. Always enclose SASE. Responds in 4 months. No phone or fax queries. Pays $1,000 for romances on acceptance for North American serial rights for 6 months. The 1,000 word mini-mysteries may feature either a 'whodunnit' or 'howdunnit' theme. The mystery may revolve around anything from a theft to murder. However, we are not interested in sordid or grotesque crimes. Emphasis should be on intricacies of plot rather than gratuitous violence. The story must include a resolution that clearly states the villain is getting his or her come-uppance. Submit complete mss. Specify Mini-Mystery on envelope. Enclose SASE. No phone queries." Needs mystery, romance, contemporary. Not interested in science fiction, fantasy, historical romance, or foreign locales. No explicit sex, graphic language, or seamy settings. Send complete ms. Romances—800 words; mysteries—1,000 words. **Pays $1,000/romances; $500/mysteries**.

TIPS The whole story should be sent when submitting fiction. Stories slanted for a particular holiday should be sent at least 6 months in advance. "Familiarize yourself totally with our format and style. Read at least a year's worth of *Woman's World* fiction. Analyze and dissect it. Regarding romances, scrutinize them not only for content but tone, mood and sensibility."

⊕ WOMEN IN BUSINESS

American Business Women's Association (The ABWA Co., Inc.), 11050 Roe Ave., Suite 200, Overland Park KS 66211. (816)361-6621. **Fax:** (816)361-4991. **E-mail:** abwa@abwa.org. **Website:** www.abwa.org. **Contact:** Rene Street, executive director. **30% freelance written.** Bimonthly magazine covering issues affecting working women. "How-to features for career women on business trends, small-business ownership, self-improvement, and retirement issues. Profiles business women." Estab. 1949. Circ. 45,000. Byline given. Pays on acceptance. No kill fee. Publishes ms an average of 3 months after acceptance. Editorial lead time 3 months. Accepts queries by mail, e-mail, fax. Accepts simultaneous submissions. Responds in 3 weeks to queries. Responds in 2 months to mss. Sample copy for SAE with 9x12 envelope and 4 first-class stamps. Guidelines for #10 SASE.

NONFICTION Needs how-to, interview, computer/Internet. No fiction or poetry. **Buys 3% of submitted mss/year.** Query. Length: 500-1,000 words. **Pays $100/500 words.**

PHOTOS State availability. Identification of subjects required. Reviews prints. Offers no additional payment for photos accepted with ms.

COLUMNS/DEPARTMENTS Life After Business (concerns of retired business women); It's Your Business (entrepreneurial advice for business owners); Health Spot (health issues that affect women in the work place). Length: 500-750 words. Query. **Pays $100/500 words.**

ZINK

304 Park Ave. S., 11th Floor, New York NY 10010. (212)260-9725. **E-mail:** jennifer.swanson@zinkmediagroup.com. **Website:** www.zinkmagazine.com. **Contact:** Jennifer Swanson, managing editor. *Zink* is a monthly fashion magazine catering to a savvy, well-cultured, and upscale audience.

NONFICTION Query first.

TRADE JOURNALS

///

Many writers who pick up *Writer's Market* for the first time do so with the hope of selling an article to one of the popular, high-profile consumer magazines found on newsstands and in bookstores. Many of those writers are surprised to find an entire world of magazine publishing exists outside the realm of commercial magazines—trade journals. Writers who have discovered trade journals have found a market that offers the chance to publish regularly for pay rates that rival those of the big-name magazines.

Trade journal is the general term for any publication focusing on a particular occupation or industry. Other terms used to describe the different types of trade publications are business, technical, and professional journals. They are read by truck drivers, farmers, fishermen, and just about everyone else working in a trade or profession. Trade periodicals are sharply angled to the specifics of the professions on which they report. They offer business-related news, features, and service articles that will foster their readers' professional development.

Editors at trade journals tell us their audience is made up of knowledgeable and highly interested readers. Writers for trade journals have to either possess knowledge about the field in question or be able to report it accurately from interviews with those who do. Writers who have or can develop a good grasp of a specialized body of knowledge will find trade magazine editors who are eager to hear from them.

An ideal way to begin your foray into trade journals is to write for those that report on your present profession. Begin by familiarizing yourself with the magazines that serve your occupation. After you've read enough issues to have a feel for the kinds of pieces the magazines run, approach the editors with your own article ideas. If you don't have experience in a profession but can demonstrate an ability to understand (and write about) the intricacies and issues of a particular trade that interests you, editors will still be willing to hear from you.

ADVERTISING, MARKETING AND PR

$$$ BRAND PACKAGING

BNP Media, 155 Pfingsten Rd., Suite 205, Deerfield IL 60015. (248)786-1680. **Fax:** (847)405-4100. **E-mail:** zielinskil@bnpmedia.com. **Website:** www.brandpackaging.com. **Contact:** Laura Zielinski, editor-in-chief. **15% freelance written.** Magazine published 10 times/year covering how packaging can be a marketing tool. "We publish strategies and tactics to make products stand out on the shelf. Our market is brand managers who are marketers but need to know something about packaging." Estab. 1997. Circ. 33,000. Byline given. Pays on acceptance. Publishes ms an average of 2 months after acceptance. Editorial lead time 3 months. Submit seasonal material 3 months in advance. Accepts queries by mail, fax. Sample copy free. Guidelines available on website.

NONFICTION Needs how-to, interview, new product. **Buys 10 mss/year.** Send complete ms. Length: 600-2,400 words. **Pays 40-50¢/word.**

PHOTOS State availability. Identification of subjects required. Reviews contact sheets, 35mm transparencies, 4x5 prints. Negotiates payment individually.

COLUMNS/DEPARTMENTS Emerging Technology (new packaging technology), 600 words. **Buys 10 mss/year.** Query. **Pays $150-300.**

TIPS "Be knowledgeable on marketing techniques and be able to grasp packaging techniques. Be sure you focus on packaging as a marketing tool. Use concrete examples. We are not seeking case histories at this time."

$ DECA DIMENSIONS

1908 Association Dr., Reston VA 20191. (703)860-5000. **Fax:** (703)860-4013. **E-mail:** publications@deca.org. **Website:** www.deca.org. **30% freelance written.** Quarterly magazine covering marketing, professional development, business, career training during school year (no issues published May-August). *DECA Dimensions* is the membership magazine for DECA—The Association of Marketing Students, primarily ages 15-19 in all 50 states, the U.S. territories, Germany, and Canada. The magazine is delivered through the classroom. Students are interested in developing professional, leadership, and career skills. Estab. 1947. Circ. 160,000. Byline given. Pays on publication. No kill fee. Editorial lead time 3 months. Submit seasonal material 4 months in advance. Accepts queries by mail, e-mail, fax, phone. Accepts simultaneous submissions. Sample copy free.

NONFICTION Needs essays, general interest, how-to, get jobs, start business, plan for college, etc., interview, business leads, personal experience, working, leadership development. **Buys 10 mss/year.** Send complete ms. Length: 800-1,000 words. **Pays $125 for assigned articles. Pays $100 for unsolicited articles.**

REPRINTS Send typed ms and information about when and where the material previously appeared. Pays 85% of amount paid for an original article.

COLUMNS/DEPARTMENTS Professional Development; Leadership, 350-500 words. **Buys 6 mss/year.** Send complete ms. **Pays $ 75-100.**

$$ O'DWYER'S PR REPORT

271 Madison Ave., #600, New York NY 10016. (212)679-2471; (866)395-7710. **Fax:** (212)683-2750. **E-mail:** john@odwyerpr.com. **Website:** www.odwyerpr.com. **Contact:** John O'Dwyer, editor. Monthly magazine providing PR articles. *O'Dwyer's* has been covering public relations, marketing communications, and related fields for over 40 years. The company provides the latest news and information about PR firms and professionals, the media, corporations, legal issues, jobs, technology, and much more through its website, weekly newsletter, monthly magazine, directories, and guides. Many of the contributors are PR people publicizing themselves while analyzing something. Byline given. No kill fee. Accepts queries by mail.

NONFICTION Needs opinion. Query. **Pays $250.**

$$$ PROMO MAGAZINE

Access Intelligence, (203)899-8442. **E-mail:** podell@accessintel.com. **Website:** www.chiefmarketer.com/promotional-marketing. **Contact:** Patricia Odell, executive editor. **5% freelance written.** Monthly magazine covering promotion marketing. Estab. 1987. Circ. 25,000. Byline given. Pays on publication. Offers 25% kill fee. Publishes ms an average of 2 months after acceptance. Editorial lead time 3 months. Submit seasonal material 3 months in advance. Responds in 1 month to queries. Sample copy for $5.

NONFICTION Needs exposé, general interest, how-to, marketing programs, interview, new product, promotion. No general marketing stories not heavily involved in promotions. Generally does not accept unsolicited mss; query first. **Buys 6-10 mss/year.** Query with published clips. **Pays $1,000 maximum**

for assigned articles. Pays $500 maximum for unsolicited articles. Sometimes pays expenses of writers on assignment.

PHOTOS State availability. Captions, identification of subjects, model releases required. Reviews contact sheets, negatives. Negotiates payment individually.

TIPS "Understand that our stories aim to teach marketing professionals about successful promotion strategies. Case studies or new promos have the best chance."

⊛⊛ SIGN BUILDER ILLUSTRATED

Simmons-Boardman Publishing Corp., 55 Broad St., 26th Floor, New York NY 10004. (252)355-5806. **E-mail:** jwooten@sbpub.com; abray@sbpub.com. **Website:** www.signshop.com. **Contact:** Jeff Wooten, editor; Ashley Bray, associate editor. **40% freelance written.** Monthly magazine covering sign and graphic industry. Estab. 1987. Circ. 14,500. Byline given. Pays on acceptance. Offers 10% kill fee. Publishes ms an average of 3 months after acceptance. Editorial lead time 3 months. Submit seasonal material 4 months in advance. Accepts queries by mail, e-mail, fax, phone. Accepts simultaneous submissions. Responds in 1 month to queries. Sample copy and writer's guidelines free.

NONFICTION Needs historical, how-to, humor, interview, photo feature, technical. **Buys 50-60 mss/year.** Query. Length: 1,000-1,500 words. **Pays $250-550 for assigned articles.**

PHOTOS Send photos. Captions, identification of subjects required. Reviews 3x5 prints. Negotiates payment individually,.

TIPS "Be very knowledgeable about a portion of the sign industry you are covering. We want our readers to come away from each article with at least 1 good idea, 1 new technique, or 1 more 'trick of the trade.' At the same time, we don't want a purely textbook listing of 'do this, do that.' Our readers enjoy *Sign Builder Illustrated* because the publication speaks to them in a clear and lively fashion, from 1 sign professional to another. We want to engage the reader who has been in the business for some time. While there might be a place for basic instruction in new techniques, our average paid subscriber has been in business over 20 years, employs over 7 people, and averages $800,000 in annual sales. These people aren't neophytes content with retread articles they can find anywhere. It's im-

portant for our writers to use anecdotes and examples drawn from the daily sign business."

SHOPPER MARKETING

Path to Purchase Institute, 8550 W. Bryn Mawr Ave., Suite 200, Chicago IL 60631. (773)992-4450. **Fax:** (773)992-4455. **E-mail:** shoppermarketing@p2pi.org. **Website:** www.shoppermarketingmag.com. **80% freelance written.** Monthly publication covering advertising and primarily the shopper marketing industry. "We cover how brands market to the shopper at retail, what insights/research did they gather to reach that shopper and how did they activate the program at retail. We write case studies on shopper marketing campaigns, displays, packaging, retail media, and events. We write major category reports, company profiles, trends features, and more. Our readers are marketers and retailers, and a small selection of P-O-P producers (the guys that build the displays)." Estab. 1988. Circ. 18,000. Byline given. Pays on acceptance. Offers no kill fee. Editorial lead time 2 months. Submit seasonal material 3 months in advance. Accepts queries by e-mail. Accepts simultaneous submissions. Responds in 1 month to queries. Sample copy and guidelines free.

⊛⊛⊛ SOCAL MEETINGS + EVENTS MAGAZINE

Tiger Oak Publications, One Tiger Oak Plaza, 900 S. Third St., Minneapolis MN 55415. **Fax:** (612)338-0532. **E-mail:** bobby.hart@tigeroak.com. **Website:** http://meetingsmags.com. **Contact:** Bobby Hart, managing editor. **80% freelance written.** "*SoCal Meetings & Events* magazine is the premier trade publication for meetings planners and hospitality service providers in Southern California. This magazine aims to report on and promote businesses involved in the meetings and events industry. The magazine covers current and emerging trends, people and venues in the meetings and events industry in Southern California." Quarterly magazine. Estab. 1993. Circ. 20,000. Byline given. Pays on acceptance. Offers 20% kill fee. Publishes ms an average of 4 months after acceptance. Editorial lead time 4-6 months. Submit seasonal material 6 months in advance. Accepts queries by mail. Accepts simultaneous submissions. Responds in 1-2 weeks to queries.

NONFICTION Needs general interest, historical, interview, new product, opinion, personal experience, photo feature, technical, travel. **Buys 30 mss/**

year. "Each query should tell us: What the story will be about; how you will tell the story (what sources you will use, how you will conduct research, etc.); why is the story pertinent to the market audience. Please also attach PDFs of 3 published magazine articles." Length: 600-1,500 words. **The average department length story (4-700 words) pays about $2-300 and the average feature length story (1,000-1,200 words) pays from $5-600, depending on the story. These rates are not guaranteed and vary.**

PHOTOS State availability. Identification of subjects, model releases required. Negotiates payment individually.

COLUMNS/DEPARTMENTS Meet + Eat (restaurant reviews); Facility Focus (venue reviews); Regional Spotlight (city review), 1,000 words. **Buys 30 mss/year.** Query with published clips. **Pays $400-600.**

TIPS "Familiarization with the meetings and events industry is critical, as well as knowing how to write for a trade magazine. Writers experienced in writing for the trade magazine business industry are preferred."

ART, DESIGN AND COLLECTIBLES

$$ AIRBRUSH ACTION MAGAZINE

Action, Inc., P.O. Box 438, Allenwood NJ 08720. (732)223-7878; (800)876-2473. **Fax:** (732)223-2855. **E-mail:** ceo@airbrushaction.com. **Website:** www.airbrushaction.com. **Contact:** Cliff Stieglitz, publisher. **80% freelance written.** Bimonthly magazine covering the spectrum of airbrush applications: automotive and custom paint applications, illustration, T-shirt airbrushing, fine art, automotive and sign painting, hobby/craft applications, wall murals, fingernails, temporary tattoos, artist profiles, reviews, and more. Estab. 1985. Circ. 35,000. Byline given. Pays 1 month after publication. Publishes ms an average of 6 months after acceptance. Editorial lead time 6 months. Submit seasonal material 6 months in advance. Accepts queries by mail, e-mail, fax. Accepts simultaneous submissions.

NONFICTION Needs how-to, humor, inspirational, interview, new product, personal experience, technical. Doesn't want anything unrelated to airbrush. Query with published clips. **Pays 15¢/word.** Sometimes pays expenses of writers on assignment.

PHOTOS Digital images preferred. Send photos. Captions, identification of subjects, model releases required. Negotiates payment individually.

COLUMNS/DEPARTMENTS Query with published clips.

TIPS "Send bio and writing samples. Send well-written technical information pertaining to airbrush art. We publish a lot of artist profiles—they all sound the same. Looking for new pizzazz!"

$$ ANTIQUEWEEK

MidCountry Media, 27 N. Jefferson St., P.O. Box 90, Knightstown IN 46148. (800)876-5133, ext. 189. **Fax:** (800)345-3398. **E-mail:** connie@antiqueweek.com; tony@antiqueweek.com. **Website:** www.antiqueweek.com. **Contact:** Connie Swaim, managing editor; Tony Gregory, publisher. **80% freelance written.** Weekly tabloid covering antiques and collectibles with 3 editions: Eastern, Central, and National, plus the monthly *AntiqueWest*. "*AntiqueWeek* has a wide range of readership from dealers and auctioneers to collectors, both advanced and novice. Our readers demand accurate information presented in an entertaining style." Estab. 1968. Circ. 50,000. Byline given. Pays on publication. Offers 10% kill fee or $25. Submit seasonal material 1 month in advance. Accepts queries by mail, e-mail. Sample copy free. Guidelines by e-mail.

NONFICTION Needs historical, how-to, interview, opinion, personal experience, antique show and auction reports, feature articles on particular types of antiques and collectibles. **Buys 400-500 mss/year.** Query. Length: 1,000-2,000 words. **Pays $50-250.**

REPRINTS Send electronic copy with rights for sale noted and information about when and where the material previously appeared.

PHOTOS All material must be submitted electronically via e-mail or on CD. Send photos. Identification of subjects required.

TIPS "Writers should know their topics thoroughly. Feature articles must be well researched and clearly written. An interview and profile article with a knowledgeable collector might be the break for a first-time contributor. We seek a balanced mix of information on traditional antiques and 20th century collectibles."

$$ ART MATERIALS RETAILER

Fahy-Williams Publishing, Inc., 171 Reed St., P.O. Box 1080, Geneva NY 14456. (315)789-0458. **Fax:** (315)789-4263. **E-mail:** tmanzer@fwpi.com. **Website:** www.artmaterialsretailer.com. J. Kevin Fahy,

TRADE JOURNALS

publisher (kfahy@fwpi.com). **Contact:** Tina Manzer, editorial director. **10% freelance written.** Quarterly magazine covering retail stores that sell art materials. Estab. 1998. Byline given. Pays on publication. No kill fee. Editorial lead time 2 months. Submit seasonal material 3 months in advance. Accepts simultaneous submissions. Responds in 3 weeks to queries. Responds in 3 months to mss. Sample copy and writer's guidelines free.

NONFICTION Needs book excerpts, how-to, interview, personal experience. **Buys 2 mss/year.** Send complete ms. Length: 1,500-3,000 words. **Pays $50-250.** Sometimes pays expenses of writers on assignment.

PHOTOS State availability. Identification of subjects required. Reviews transparencies. Offers no additional payment for photos accepted with ms.

FILLERS Needs anecdotes, facts, newsbreaks. **Buys 5 mss/year.** Length: 500-1,500 words. **Pays $50-125.**

TIPS "We like to review mss rather than queries. Artwork (photos, drawings, etc.) is a real plus. We (and our readers) enjoy practical, nuts-and-bolts, news-you-can-use articles."

FAITH + FORM

47 Grandview Terrace, Essex CT 06426. (860)575-4702. **E-mail:** mcrosbie@faithandform.com. **Website:** www.faithandform.com. **Contact:** Michael J. Crosbie, editor-in-chief. **50% freelance written.** Quarterly magazine covering relgious buildings and art. *Faith + Form*, devoted to religious art and architecture, is read by artists, designers, architects, clergy, congregations, and all who care about environments for worship. Writers must be knowledgeable about environments for worship, or able to explain them. Estab. 1967. Circ. 4,500. Byline given. Publishes ms an average of 6 months after acceptance. Editorial lead time 6 months. Submit seasonal material 6 months in advance. Accepts queries by online submission form. Accepts simultaneous submissions. Responds in 2 weeks to queries. Responds in 1 month to mss. Sample copy available online. Guidelines available.

NONFICTION Needs book excerpts, essays, how-to, inspirational, interview, opinion, personal experience, photo feature, religious, technical. **Buys 6 mss/year.** Query. Length: 500-2,500 words.

PHOTOS State availability. Captions required. Reviews GIF/JPEG files. Offers no additional payment for photos accepted with ms.

COLUMNS/DEPARTMENTS News, 250-750 words; Book Reviews, 250-500 words. **Buys 3 mss/year.** Query.

HOW

F+W Media, Inc., 10151 Carver Rd., Suite 200, Blue Ash OH 45242. (513)531-2690. **Fax:** (513)531-2902. **E-mail:** editorial@howdesign.com. **Website:** www.howdesign.com. **75% freelance written.** Bi-monthly magazine covering graphic design profession. Estab. 1985. Circ. 40,000. Byline given. Pays on acceptance. No kill fee. Responds in 6 weeks to queries.

NONFICTION Special issues: Self-Promotion Annual (September/October); Business Annual (November/December); International Annual of Design (March/April); Creativity/Paper/Stock Photography (May/June); Digital Design Annual (July/August). No how-to articles for beginning artists or fine-art-oriented articles. **Buys 40 mss/year.** Query with published clips and samples of subject's work, artwork, or design. Length: 1,500-2,000 words. **Pays $700-900.** Sometimes pays expenses of writers on assignment.

PHOTOS State availability. Captions required. Reviews information updated and verified.

COLUMNS/DEPARTMENTS Creativity (focuses on creative exercises and inspiration) 1,200-1,500 words. In-House Issues (focuses on business and creativity issues for corporate design groups), 1,200-1,500 words. Business (focuses on business issue for design firm owners), 1,200-1, 500 words. **Buys Number of columns: 35. mss/year.** Query with published clips. **Pays $250-400.**

TIPS "We look for writers who can recognize graphic designers on the cutting-edge of their industry, both creatively and business-wise. Writers must have an eye for detail, and be able to relay *HOW*'s editorial style in an interesting, concise manner—without omitting any details. Showing you've done your homework on a subject—and that you can go beyond asking those same old questions—will give you a big advantage."

THE PASTEL JOURNAL

F+W Media, Inc., 10151 Carver Rd., Suite #200, Cincinnati OH 45242. (513)531-2690. **Fax:** (513)891-7153. **E-mail:** pjedit@fwmedia.com. **Website:** www.pasteljournal.com. **Contact:** Anne Hevener. Bimonthly magazine covering pastel art. "*The Pastel Journal* is the only national magazine devoted to the medium of pastel. Addressing the working professional as well as passionate amateurs, *The Pastel Journal* offers inspiration, information, and instruction to our readers." Estab. 1999. Circ. 22,000. Byline given. Pays on acceptance. Offers 25% kill fee. Publishes ms an average of 3-6 months after acceptance. Editorial lead time 6 months. Submit seasonal material 6 months in advance. Accepts queries by mail. Accepts simultaneous submissions. Responds in 4-6 weeks to queries. Guidelines on website.

NONFICTION Needs how-to, interview, new product, profile. Does not want articles that aren't art-related. Review magazine before submitting. Query with or without published clips. Length: 500-2,500 words. **Pays $150-750.**

PHOTOS State availability of or send photos. Captions required. Reviews transparencies, prints, GIF/JPEG files. Offers no additional payment for photos accepted with ms.

💲💲💲 PRINT

F+W Media, Inc., 38 E. 29th St., 4th Floor, New York NY 10016. (212)447-1400. **Fax:** (212)447-5231. **E-mail:** Aaron.Kenedi@fwmedia.com. **E-mail:** info@printmag.com. **Website:** www.printmag.com. **Contact:** Aaron Kenedi. **75% freelance written.** Bimonthly magazine covering graphic design and visual culture. "*PRINT*'s articles, written by design specialists and cultural critics, focus on the social, political, and historical context of graphic design, and on the places where consumer culture and popular culture meet. We aim to produce a general interest magazine for professionals with engagingly written text and lavish illustrations. By covering a broad spectrum of topics, both international and local, we try to demonstrate the significance of design in the world at large." Estab. 1940. Circ. 45,000. Byline given. Pays on acceptance. Offers 25% kill fee. Publishes ms an average of 3 months after acceptance. Editorial lead time 3 months. Submit seasonal material 3 months in advance. Accepts queries by e-mail. Responds in 2 weeks to queries. Responds in 1 month to mss.

NONFICTION Needs essays, interview, opinion. **Buys 35-40 mss/year.** Query with published clips. Length: 1,000-2,500 words. **Pays $1,250.** Sometimes pays expenses of writers on assignment.

COLUMNS/DEPARTMENTS Query with published clips. **Pays $800.**

TIPS "Be well versed in issues related to the field of graphic design; don't submit ideas that are too general or geared to nonprofessionals."

💲💲 PROFESSIONAL ARTIST

Turnstile Publishing, 1500 Park Center Dr., Orlando FL 32835. (407)563-7000. **Fax:** (407)563-7099. **E-mail:** khall@artcalendar.com. **Website:** www.professionalartistmag.com. Louise Buyo at lbuyo@professionalartistmag.com. **Contact:** Kim Hall. **75% freelance written.** Monthly magazine. Estab. 1986. Circ. 20,000. Pays on publication. No kill fee. Sample print copy for $5. Guidelines available online.

NONFICTION Needs essays, the psychology of creativity, how-to, interview, successful artists with a focus on what made them successful, networking articles, marketing topics, technical articles (new equipment, new media, computer software, Internet marketing.), cartoons, art law, including pending legislation that affects artists (copyright law, Internet regulations, etc.). "We like nuts-and-bolts information about making a living as an artist. We do not run reviews or art historical pieces, nor do we like writing characterized by 'critic-speak,' philosophical hyperbole, psychological arrogance, politics, or New Age religion. Also, we do not condone a get-rich-quick attitude." Send complete ms. **Pays $250.**

REPRINTS Send photocopy or typed ms and information about when and where the material previously appeared. Pays $50.

PHOTOS Reviews b&w glossy or color prints. Pays $25.

COLUMNS/DEPARTMENTS "If an artist or freelancer sends us good articles regularly, and based on results we feel that he is able to produce a column at least 3 times per year, we will invite him to be a contributing writer. If a gifted artist-writer can commit to producing an article on a monthly basis, we will offer him a regular column and the title contributing editor." Send complete ms.

TIPS "We strongly suggest that you read a copy of the publication before submitting a proposal. Most queries are rejected because they are too general for our audience."

💲 TEXAS ARCHITECT

Texas Society of Architects, 500 Chicon St., Austin TX 78702. (512)478-7386. **Fax:** (512)478-0528. **Website:** www.texasarchitect.org. **Contact:** Catherine Gavin, editor. **30% freelance written. Mostly written by un-**

paid members of the professional society. Bimonthly journal covering architecture and architects of Texas. "*Texas Architect* is a highly visually-oriented look at Texas architecture, design, and urban planning. Articles cover varied subtopics within architecture. Readers are mostly architects and related building professionals." Estab. 1951. Circ. 12,500. Byline given. Pays on publication. No kill fee. Publishes ms an average of 3 months after acceptance. Submit seasonal material 4 months in advance. Accepts queries by mail, e-mail. Responds in 6 weeks to queries. Guidelines available online.

NONFICTION Needs interview, photo feature, technical, book reviews. Query with published clips. Length: 100-2,000 words. **Pays $50-100 for assigned articles.**

PHOTOS Send photos. Identification of subjects required. Reviews contact sheets, 35mm or 4x5 transparencies, 4x5 prints. Offers no additional payment for photos accepted with ms.

COLUMNS/DEPARTMENTS News (timely reports on architectural issues, projects, and people), 100-500 words. **Buys 10 articles/year mss/year.** Query with published clips. **Pays $50-100.**

⊕⊕ WATERCOLOR ARTIST

F+W Media, Inc., 10151 Carver Rd., Suite #200, Blue Ash OH 45242. (513)531-2690. **Fax:** (513)891-7153. **Website:** www.watercolorartistmagazine.com. **Contact:** Jennifer Hoffman, art director; Kelly Kane, editor. Bimonthly magazine covering water media arts. Estab. 1984. Circ. 42,000. Byline given. Pays on acceptance. Publishes ms an average of 3-6 months after acceptance. Editorial lead time 6 months. Submit seasonal material 6 months in advance. Accepts queries by mail. Accepts simultaneous submissions. Writer's guidelines available at http://www.artistsnetwork.com/contactus.

NONFICTION Needs book excerpts, essays, how-to, inspirational, interview, new product, personal experience. Does not want articles that aren't art-related. Review magazine before submitting. **Buys 36 mss/year.** Send query letter with images. Length: 350-2,500 words. **Pays $150-600.**

PHOTOS State availability of or send photos. Captions required. Reviews transparencies, prints, slides, GIF/JPEG files.

AUTO AND TRUCK

AFTERMARKET BUSINESS WORLD

Advanstar Communications, 24950 Country Club Blvd., Suite 200, North Olmsted OH 44070. (440)891-2746. **Fax:** (440)891-2675. **E-mail:** kmcnamara@advanstar.com. **Website:** www.aftermarketbusiness.com. **Contact:** Krista McNamara, managing editor. "The mission of *Aftermarket Business World* (formerly *Aftermarket Business*) involves satisfying the needs of U.S. readers who want to do business here and elsewhere and helping readers in other countries who want to do business with U.S. companies. Being an electronic publication assures us that we can reach just about anybody, anywhere. Editorial material for *Aftermarket Business World* focuses on news, trends, and analysis about the international automotive aftermarket. Written for corporate executives and key decision makers responsible for buying automotive products (parts, accessories, chemicals) and other services sold at retail to consumers and professional installers, it's the oldest continuously published business magazine covering the retail automotive aftermarket, and is the only publication dedicated to the specialized needs of this industry." Estab. 1936. Circ. 120,000. Byline given. "Corporate policy requires all freelancers to sign a print and online usage contract for stories." Pays on publication. Payment is negotiable. Sample copies available; call (888)527-7008 for rates.

TIPS "We can't stress enough the importance of knowing our audience. We are not a magazine aimed at car dealers or consumers. Our readers are auto parts distributors. Looking through sample issues will show you a lot about what we need."

⊕⊕ AUTOINC.

Automotive Service Association, P.O. Box 929, Bedford TX 76095-0929. (800)272-7467. **Fax:** (817)685-0225. **E-mail:** editor@asashop.org. **Website:** www.autoinc.org. **10% freelance written.** Monthly magazine covering independent automotive repair. The mission of *AutoInc.*, ASA's official publication, is to be the informational authority for ASA and industry members nationwide. Its purpose is to enhance the professionalism of these members through management, technical and legislative articles, researched and written with the highest regard for accuracy, quality, and integrity. Estab. 1952. Circ. 14,000. Byline given. Pays on publication. No kill fee. Publishes ms an average of 3 months after acceptance. Editorial lead time 2 months. Accepts queries by mail, e-mail, fax. Accepts simultaneous submissions. Responds in 6 weeks to queries.

Responds in 2 months to mss. Sample copy for $5 or online. Guidelines available online.

NONFICTION Needs how-to, automotive repair, technical. No coverage of staff moves or financial reports. **Buys 6 mss/year.** Query with published clips. Length: 1,200 words. **Pays $300.** Sometimes pays phone expenses of writers on assignment.

PHOTOS State availability of or send photos. Captions, identification of subjects, model releases required. Reviews 2×3 transparencies, 3×5 prints, high resolution digital images. Negotiates payment individually.

TIPS "Learn about the automotive repair industry, specifically the independent shop segment. Understand the high-tech requirements needed to succeed today. We target professional repair shop owners rather than consumers."

$$ BUSINESS FLEET

Bobit Publishing, 3520 Challenger St., Torrance CA 90501. (310)533-2400. **E-mail:** chris.brown@bobit.com. **Website:** www.businessfleet.com. **Contact:** Chris Brown, executive editor. **10% freelance written.** Bimonthly magazine covering businesses which operate 10-50 company vehicles. Estab. 2000. Circ. 100,000. Byline given. Pays on publication. Offers 25% kill fee. Publishes ms an average of 3 months after acceptance. Editorial lead time 2 months. Submit seasonal material 2 months in advance. Accepts queries by mail, e-mail, fax. Responds in 3 weeks to queries. Responds in 2 months to mss. Sample copy and writer's guidelines free.

NONFICTION Needs how-to, interview, new product, personal experience, photo feature, technical. **Buys 16 mss/year.** Query with published clips. Length: 500-2,000 words. **Pays $100-400.** Sometimes pays expenses of writers on assignment.

PHOTOS State availability. Captions required. Reviews 3x5 prints. Negotiates payment individually.

TIPS "Our mission is to educate our target audience on more economical and efficient ways of operating company vehicles, and to inform the audience of the latest vehicles, products, and services available to small commercial companies. Be knowledgeable about automotive and fleet-oriented subjects."

$$ FENDERBENDER

DeWitt Publishing, 1043 Grand Ave. #372, St. Paul MN 55105. (651)224-6207. **Fax:** (651)224-6212. **E-mail:** news@fenderbender.com; jweyer@fenderbender.com. **Website:** www.fenderbender.com. **Contact:** Jake Weyer, editor. **50% freelance written.** Monthly magazine covering automotive collision repair. Estab. 1999. Circ. 58,000. Byline given. Pays on publication. Offers 20% kill fee. Publishes ms an average of 2 months after acceptance. Editorial lead time 3 months. Submit seasonal material 6 months in advance. Accepts queries by e-mail. Accepts simultaneous submissions. Responds in 1-2 months to queries. Responds in 2-3 months to mss. Sample copy for SAE with 10x13 envelope and 6 first-class stamps. Guidelines available online.

NONFICTION Needs exposé, how-to, inspirational, interview, technical. Does not want personal narratives or any other first-person stories. No poems or creative writing mss. Query with published clips. Length: 1,800-2,500 words. **Pays 25-60¢/word.** Sometimes pays expenses of writers on assignment.

PHOTOS Send photos. Captions, identification of subjects, model releases required. Reviews PDF, GIF/JPEG files. Offers no additional payment for photos accepted with ms.

COLUMNS/DEPARTMENTS Q&A, 600 words; Shakes, Rattles & Rollovers; Rearview Mirror. Query with published clips. **Pays 25-35¢/word.**

TIPS "Potential writers need to be knowledgeable about the auto collision repair industry. They should also know standard business practices and be able to explain to shop owners how they can run their businesses better."

$$ FLEETSOLUTIONS

NAFA Fleet Management Association, 125 Village Blvd., Suite 200, Princeton NJ 08540. (609)986-1053; (609)720-0882. **Fax:** (609)720-0881; (609)452-8004. **E-mail:** publications@nafa.org; info@nafa.org. **Website:** www.nafa.org. **10% freelance written.** Magazine published 6 times/year covering automotive fleet management. Estab. 1957. Circ. 4,000. Bylines provided. Pays on publication. No kill fee. Publishes ms an average of 4 months after acceptance. Editorial lead time 2 months. Accepts queries by mail. Accepts simultaneous submissions. Responds in 1 month to queries. Sample copy available online. Guidelines free.

NONFICTION Needs interview, technical. **Buys 24 mss/year.** Query with published clips. Length: 500-3,000 words. **Pays $500 maximum.**

PHOTOS State availability. Reviews electronic images.

OLD CARS WEEKLY

F+W Media, Inc., 700 E. State St., Iola WI 54990-0001. (715)445-4612. **Fax:** (715)445-2214. **E-mail:** angelo. vanbogart@fwmedia.com. **Website:** www.oldcarsweekly.com. **Contact:** Angelo Van Bogart, editor. **30% freelance written.** Weekly tabloid for anyone restoring, selling, or driving an old car. Estab. 1971. Circ. 55,000. Byline given. Pays within 3 months after publication date. No kill fee. Publishes ms an average of 6 months after acceptance. Call circulation department for sample copy. Guidelines for #10 SASE.

NONFICTION Needs how-to, technical, auction prices realized lists. No "Grandpa's Car," "My First Car," or "My Car" themes from freelance contributors. **Buys 1,000 mss/year.** Send complete ms. Length: 400-1,600 words. **Payment varies.**

PHOTOS Send photos. Captions, identification of subjects required. Pays $5/photo. Offers no additional payment for photos accepted with ms.

TIPS "Seventy-five percent of our freelance material is done by a small group of regular contributors. Many new writers break in here, but we are usually overstocked with material and rarely seek nostalgic or historical pieces from new authors. We are searching for news stories and in-depth historical features that fit the needs of a nostalgic, car-oriented audience. Authors with good skills can work up to longer stories. The best queries are *checklists* where we can quickly mark a *yes* or *no* to article ideas."

⑨⑨⑨ OVERDRIVE

Randall-Reilly Publishing, 3200 Rice Mine Rd. NE, Tuscaloosa AL 35406. (205)349-2990. **Fax:** (205)750-8070. **E-mail:** mheine@rrpub.com. **Website:** www. etrucker.com. **Contact:** Max Heine, editorial director. **5% freelance written.** Monthly magazine for independent truckers. Estab. 1961. Circ. 100,000. Byline given. Pays on publication. Offers 10% kill fee. Publishes ms an average of 2 months after acceptance. Responds in 2 months to queries. Sample copy for 9x12 SASE.

NONFICTION Needs essays, exposé, how-to, truck maintenance and operation, interview, successful independent truckers, personal experience, photo feature, technical. Send complete ms. Length: 500-2,500 words. **Pays $300-1,500 for assigned articles.**

PHOTOS Photo fees negotiable.

TIPS "Talk to independent truckers. Develop a good knowledge of their concerns as small-business owners, truck drivers, and individuals. We prefer articles that quote experts, people in the industry, and truckers, to first-person expositions on a subject. Get straight facts. Look for good material on truck safety, on effects of government regulations, and on rates and business relationships between independent truckers, brokers, carriers, and shippers."

☺ ⑨⑨ TIRE NEWS

Rousseau Automotive Communication, 455, Notre-Dame East, Suite 311, Montreal QC H2Y 1C9 Canada. (514)289-0888; 1-877-989-0888. **Fax:** (514)289-5151. **E-mail:** info@autosphere.ca; daniel.lafrance@autosphere.ca. **Website:** www.autosphere.ca. **Contact:** Daniel Lafrance, editor-in-chief. Bimonthly magazine covering the Canadian tire industry. *Tire News* focuses on education/training, industry image, management, new tires, new techniques, marketing, HR, etc. Estab. 2004. Circ. 16,000. Byline given. Pays on publication. Publishes ms an average of 2 months after acceptance. Editorial lead time 2 months. Submit seasonal material 2 months in advance. Accepts simultaneous submissions. Responds in 2 weeks to queries. Responds in 2 months to mss. Sample copy free. Guidelines by e-mail.

NONFICTION Needs general interest, how-to, inspirational, interview, new product, technical. Does not want opinion pieces. **Buys 5 mss/year.** Query with published clips. Length: 550-610 words. **Pays up to $200 (Canadian).**

PHOTOS Send photos. Captions required. Reviews GIF/JPEG files. Offers no additional payment for photos accepted with ms.

FILLERS Needs facts. **Buys 2 mss/year.** Length: 550-610 words. **Pays $0-200.**

☺ ⑨⑨ WESTERN CANADA HIGHWAY NEWS

Craig Kelman & Associates, 2020 Portage Ave., 3rd Floor, Winnipeg MB R3J 0K4 Canada. (204)985-9785. **Fax:** (204)985-9795. **E-mail:** terry@kelman.ca. **Website:** http://highwaynews.ca. **Contact:** Terry Ross, editor. **30% freelance written.** Quarterly magazine covering trucking. "The official magazine of the Alberta, Saskatchewan, and Manitoba trucking associations." Estab. 1995. Circ. 4,500. Byline given. Pays on publication. No kill fee. Publishes ms an average of 2 months after acceptance. Editorial lead time 3 months. Submit seasonal material 3 months in advance. Accepts simultaneous submissions. Responds in 1 month to queries and mss. Sample copy for 10x13 SAE with 1 IRC. Guidelines for #10 SASE.

NONFICTION Needs essays, general interest, how-to, run a trucking business, interview, new product, opinion, personal experience, photo feature, technical, profiles in excellence (bios of trucking or associate firms enjoying success). **Buys 8-10 mss/year.** Query. Length: 500-3,000 words. **Pays 18-25¢/word.** Sometimes pays expenses of writers on assignment.

PHOTOS State availability. Identification of subjects required. Reviews 4x6 prints.

COLUMNS/DEPARTMENTS Safety (new safety innovation/products), 500 words; Trade Talk (new products), 300 words. Query. **Pays 18-25¢/word.**

TIPS "Our publication is fairly time sensitive regarding issues affecting the trucking industry in Western Canada. Current 'hot' topics are international trucking, security, driver fatigue, health and safety, emissions control, and national/international highway systems."

AVIATION AND SPACE

$$ AEROSAFETY WORLD MAGAZINE

Flight Safety Foundation, 801 Madison St., Suite 400, Alexandria VA 22314. (703)739-6700. **Fax:** (703)739-6708. **E-mail:** jackman@flightsafety.org. **Website:** www.flightsafety.org. **Contact:** Frank Jackman, director of publications. Monthly newsletter covering safety aspects of airport operations. Full-color monthly magazine offers in-depth analysis of important safety issues facing the industry, with emphasis on timely news coverage in a convenient format and eye-catching contemporary design. Estab. 1974. Pays on publication. Accepts queries by mail, e-mail. "Generally, the ms must be unpublished and must not be under consideration for publication elsewhere. In some circumstances, the Foundation may consider a previously published ms if it has been rewritten and adapted for Foundation readers. If your ms has been copyrighted, a copyright transfer may be required before your ms will be published by the Foundation."Catalog available on website. Guidelines available on website.

NONFICTION Needs technical. Query. **Pays $300-1,500.**

PHOTOS Pays $75 for each piece of original art.

TIPS "Few aviation topics are outside its scope."

$$ AVIATION INTERNATIONAL NEWS

The Convention News Co., 214 Franklin Ave., Midland Park NJ 07432. (201)444-5075. **Fax:** (201)444-4647. **E-mail:** nmoll@ainonline.com; editor@ainonline.com; ayannaco@ainonline.com. **Website:** www.ainonline.com. **Contact:** Nigel Moll, editor; Annmarie Yannaco, managing editor. **30-40% freelance written.** Monthly magazine, with daily onsite issues published at 3 conventions and 2 international air shows each year, and twice-weekly AINalerts via e-mail covering business and commercial aviation with news features, special reports, aircraft evaluations, and surveys on business aviation worldwide, written for business pilots and industry professionals. "While the heartbeat of *AIN* is driven by the news it carries, the human touch is not neglected. We pride ourselves on our people stories about the industry's 'movers and shakers' and others in aviation who make a difference." Estab. 1972. Circ. 40,000. Byline given. Pays on acceptance and upon receipt of writer's invoice. Offers variable kill fee. Publishes ms an average of 2 months after acceptance. Editorial lead time 2 months. Submit seasonal material 3 months in advance. Accepts queries by mail, e-mail, fax. Responds in 6 weeks to queries. Responds in 2 months to mss. Sample copy for $10. Writer's guidelines for 9x12 SAE with 3 first-class stamps.

NONFICTION Needs how-to, aviation, interview, new product, opinion, personal experience, photo feature, technical. No puff pieces. "Our readers expect serious, real news. We don't pull any punches. *AIN* is not a 'good news' publication; it tells the story, both good and bad." **Buys 150-200 mss/year.** Query with published clips. Do not send mss by e-mail unless requested. Length: 200-3,000 words. **Pays 40¢/word to first timers, higher rates to proven *AIN* freelancers.** Pays expenses of writers on assignment.

PHOTOS Send photos. Captions required. Reviews contact sheets, transparencies, prints, TIFF files (300 dpi). Negotiates payment individually.

TIPS "Our core freelancers are professional pilots with good writing skills, or good journalists and reporters with an interest in aviation (some with pilot licenses) or technical experts in the aviation industry. The ideal *AIN* writer has an intense interest in and strong knowledge of aviation, a talent for writing news stories, and journalistic cussedness. Hit me with a strong news story relating to business aviation that takes me by surprise—something from your local area or area of expertise. Make it readable, fact-filled, and in the inverted-pyramid style. Double-check facts and names. Interview the right people. Send me good, clear photos and illustrations. Send me well-written, logically ordered copy. Do this for me consistently and we may take you along on our staff to 1 of the conventions in the US or an airshow in Paris, Singapore, London, or Dubai."

$$ GROUND SUPPORT WORLDWIDE MAGAZINE

Cygnus Business Media, 1233 Janesville Ave., Fort Atkinson WI 53538. (800)547-7377, ext. 1370. **Fax:** (920)563-1699. **E-mail:** steve.smith@AviationPros.com. **Website:** www.groundsupportworldwide.com. **Contact:** Steve Smith, editor; Phil Saran, publisher. **20% freelance written.** Magazine published 10 times/year. "Our readers are those aviation professionals who are involved in ground support—the equipment manufacturers, the suppliers, the ramp operators, ground handlers, and airport and airline managers. We cover issues of interest to this community—deicing, ramp safety, equipment technology, pollution, etc." Estab. 1993. Circ. 15,000+. Pays on publication. No kill fee. Publishes ms an average of 2 months after acceptance. Editorial lead time 2 months. Accepts queries by mail, e-mail, fax. Responds in 3 weeks to queries; 3 months to mss. Sample copy for SAE with 9x11 envelope and 5 first-class stamps.

NONFICTION Needs how-to, use or maintain certain equipment, interview, new product, opinion, photo feature, technical aspects of ground support and issues, industry events, meetings, new rules and regulations. **Buys 12-20 mss/year.** Send complete ms. Length: 500-2,000 words. **Pays $100-300.**

PHOTOS Send photos. Identification of subjects required. Reviews 35mm prints, electronic preferred, slides. Offers additional payment for photos accepted with ms.

TIPS "Write about subjects that relate to ground services. Write in clear and simple terms—personal experience is always welcome. If you have an aviation background or ground support experience, let us know."

$$$ PROFESSIONAL PILOT

Queensmith Communications Corp., 30 S. Quaker Lane, Suite 300, Alexandria VA 22314. (703)370-0606. **Fax:** (703)370-7082. **E-mail:** editor@propilotmag.com; prose@propilotmag.com; editorial@propilotmag.com. **Website:** www.propilotmag.com. Murray Smith, editor and publisher. **Contact:** Phil Rose, managing editor. **75% freelance written.** Monthly magazine covering corporate, noncombat government, law enforcement, and various other types of professional aviation. "The typical reader of *Professional Pilot* has a sophisticated grasp of piloting/aviation knowledge and is interested in articles that help him/her do the job better or more efficiently." Estab. 1967. Circ. 40,000. Byline given. Pays on publication. Offers kill fee. Kill fee negotiable. Publishes ms an average of 2-3 months after acceptance. Accepts queries by mail, e-mail.

NONFICTION Buys 40 mss/year. Query. Length: 750-2,500 words. **Pays $200-1,000, depending on length. A fee for the article will be established at the time of assignment.** Sometimes pays expenses of writers on assignment.

PHOTOS Prefers transparencies or high resolution 300 JPEG digital images. Send photos. Captions, identification of subjects required. Additional payment for photos negotiable.

TIPS "Query first. Freelancer should be a professional pilot or have background in aviation. Authors should indicate relevant aviation experience and pilot credentials (certificates, ratings and hours). We place a greater emphasis on corporate operations and pilot concerns."

BEAUTY AND SALON

$$ BEAUTY STORE BUSINESS

Creative Age Communications, 7628 Densmore Ave., Van Nuys CA 91406. (818)782-7328, ext. 353; (800)442-5667. **Fax:** (818)782-7450. **E-mail:** mbatist@creativeage.com; mbirenbaum@creativeage.com; skelly@creativeage.com. **Website:** www.beautystorebusiness.com. Shelley Moench-Kelly, managing editor. **Contact:** Manyesha Batist, editor/online editor. **50% freelance written.** Monthly magazine covering beauty store business management, news, and beauty products. Estab. 1994. Circ. 15,000. Byline given. Pays on acceptance. Offers kill fee. Offers negotiable kill fee. Publishes ms an average of 3 months after acceptance. Editorial lead time 3 months. Submit seasonal material 4 months in advance. Accepts queries by mail, e-mail, fax. Responds in 1 week to queries. Responds in 2 weeks, if interested. Sample copy free.

NONFICTION Needs how-to, business management, merchandising, e-commerce, retailing, interview, industry leaders/beauty store owners. **Buys 20-30 mss/ year.** Query. Length: 1,800-2,200 words. **Pays $250-525 for assigned articles.** Sometimes pays expenses of writers on assignment.

PHOTOS Do not send computer art electronically. State availability. Captions, identification of subjects required. Reviews transparencies, computer art (artists work on Macs, request 300 dpi, on CD or Zip disk, saved as JPEG, TIFF, or EPS). Negotiates payment individually.

☼ $$ COSMETICS

Rogers Publishing Limited, One Mount Pleasant Rd., 7th Floor, Toronto ON M4Y 2Y5 Canada. (416)764-1680. **Fax:** (416)764-1704. **E-mail:** kristen.vinakmens@cosmetics.rogers.com. **Website:** www.cosmeticsmag.com. **Contact:** Kristen Vinakmens, editor. **10% freelance written.** Bimonthly magazine covering cosmetics for industry professionals. Estab. 1972. Circ. 13,000. Byline given. Pays on acceptance. Offers 50% kill fee. Publishes ms an average of 3 months after acceptance. Editorial lead time 4 months. Submit seasonal material 4 months in advance. Accepts queries by mail. Responds in 1 month to queries. Sample copy for $6 (Canadian) and 8% GST.

NONFICTION Needs general interest, interview, photo feature. **Buys 1 mss/year.** Query. Length: 250-1,200 words. **Pays 25¢/word.** Sometimes pays expenses of writers on assignment.

PHOTOS Send photos. Captions, identification of subjects, model releases required. Reviews 2 1/2 up to 8x10 transparencies, 4x6 up to 8x10 prints, 35mm slides; e-mail pictures in 300 dpi JPEG format. Offers no additional payment for photos accepted with ms.

COLUMNS/DEPARTMENTS "All articles assigned on a regular basis from correspondents and columnists that we know personally from the industry."

TIPS "Must have broad knowledge of the Canadian cosmetics, fragrance, and toiletries industry and retail business. 99.9% of freelance articles are assigned by the editor to writers involved with the Canadian cosmetics business."

$$ DAYSPA

Creative Age Publications, 7628 Densmore Ave., Van Nuys CA 91406. (818)782-7328, ext. 301. **Fax:** (818)782-7450. **Website:** www.dayspamagazine.com. **Contact:** Linda Kossoff, executive editor. **50% free-lance written.** Monthly magazine covering the business of day spas, multi-service/skincare salons, and resort/hotel spas. "*Dayspa* includes only well-targeted business and trend articles directed at the owners and managers. It serves to enrich, enlighten, and empower spa/salon professionals." Estab. 1996. Circ. 31,000. Byline given. Pays on acceptance. No kill fee. Publishes ms an average of 4 months after acceptance. Editorial lead time 4 months. Submit seasonal material 4 months in advance. Accepts queries by mail, e-mail, fax, phone, online submission form. Responds in 2 months to queries. Sample copy for $5.

NONFICTION Buys 40 mss/year. Query. Length: 1,500-1,800 words. **Pays $150-500.**

PHOTOS Send photos. Identification of subjects, model releases required. Negotiates payment individually.

COLUMNS/DEPARTMENTS Legal Pad (legal issues affecting salons/spas); Money Matters (financial issues); Management Workshop (spa management issues); Health Wise (wellness trends), all 1,200-1,500 words. **Buys 20 mss/year.** Query. **Pays $150-400.**

$$ MASSAGE MAGAZINE

5150 Palm Valley Rd., Suite 103, Ponte Vedra Beach FL 32082. (904)285-6020. **Fax:** (904)285-9944. **E-mail:** kmenahan@massagemag.com. **Website:** www.massagemag.com. **Contact:** Karen Menahan. **60% free-lance written.** Bimonthly magazine covering massage and other touch therapies. "Most of our readers are professional therapists who have been in practice for several years. About 80 percent are self-employed; 95 percent live in the United States. The vast majority of our readers have completed formal training in massage therapy. The techniques they practice include Swedish, sports and geriatric massage, energy work and myotherapy, among many others. Our readers work in settings ranging from home-based studios to spas to integrated clinics." Estab. 1985. Circ. 50,000. Byline given. Pays on publication. Publishes ms an average of 2 months-24 months after acceptance. Accepts queries by e-mail. Responds in 2 months to queries. Responds in 3 months to mss. Sample copy for $6.95. Guidelines available online.

NONFICTION Needs book excerpts, essays, general interest, how-to, interview, personal experience, photo feature, technical, experiential. No multiple submissions. Length: 600-2,000 words. **Pays $50-400.**

REPRINTS Send tearsheet of article and electronic ms with rights for sale noted and information about when and where the material previously appeared. Pays 50-75% of amount paid for an original article

PHOTOS Send photos with submission via e-mail. Identification of subjects required. Offers $15-40/photo; $40-100/illustration.

COLUMNS/DEPARTMENTS Profiles; News and Current Events; Practice Building (business); Technique; Body/Mind. Length: 800-1,200 words. **Pays $75-300 for assigned articles.**

FILLERS Needs facts, newsbreaks. Length: 100-800 words. **Pays $125 maximum.**

TIPS "Our readers seek practical information on how to help their clients, improve their techniques, and/or make their businesses more successful, as well as feature articles that place massage therapy in a positive or inspiring light. Since most of our readers are professional therapists, we do not publish articles on topics like 'How Massage Can Help You Relax.' Please study a few back issues so you know what types of topics and tone we're looking for."

$$ PULSE MAGAZINE

HOST Communications Inc., 2365 Harrodsburg Rd., Suite A325, Lexington KY 40504. (859)226-4326. **Fax:** (859)226-4445. **E-mail:** mae.manacap-johnson@ispastaff.com. **Website:** www.experienceispa.com/media/pulse-magazine. **Contact:** Mae Manacap-Johnson, editor. **20% freelance written.** Magazine published 10 times/year covering spa industry. Estab. 1991. Circ. 5,300. Byline given. Pays on publication. Publishes ms an average of 1 month after acceptance. Editorial lead time 3 months. Submit seasonal material 4 months in advance. Accepts queries by e-mail. Sample copy for #10 SASE. Guidelines by e-mail.

NONFICTION Needs general interest, how-to, interview, new product. Does not want articles focused on spas that are not members of ISPA, consumer-focused articles (market is the spa industry professional), or features on hot tubs ("not *that* spa industry"). **Buys 8-10 mss/year.** Query with published clips. Length: 800-2,000 words. **Pays $250-500.** Sometimes pays expenses of writers on assignment.

PHOTOS Send photos. Captions required. Reviews GIF/JPEG files. Negotiates payment individually.

TIPS "Understand the nuances of association publishing (different than consumer and B2B). Send published clips, not Word documents. Experience in writing for health and wellness market is helpful. Only feature ISPA member companies in the magazine; visit our website to learn more about our industry and to see if your pitch includes member companies before making contact."

$$ SKIN DEEP

Associated Skin Care Professionals, 25188 Genesee Trail Rd., Suite 200, Golden CO 80401. (800)789-0411. **E-mail:** editor@ascpskincare.com. **Website:** www.ascpskincare.com. **Contact:** Carrie Patrick, editor. **80% freelance written.** Bimonthly magazine covering technical, educational, and business information for estheticians with an emphasis on solo practitioners and spa/salon employees or independent contractors. "Our audience is the U.S. individual skin care practitioner who may work on her own and/or in a spa or salon setting. We keep her up to date on skin care trends and techniques and ways to earn more income doing waxing, facials, peels, microdermabrasion, body wraps and other skin treatments. Our product-neutral stories may include novel spa treatments within the esthetician scope of practice. We do not cover mass-market retail products, hair care, nail care, makeup, physician only treatments/products, cosmetic surgery, or invasive treatments like colonics or ear candling. Successful stories have included how-tos on paraffin facials, aromatherapy body wraps, waxing tips, how to read ingredient labels, how to improve word-of-mouth advertising, and how to choose an online scheduling software package." Estab. 2003. Circ. 12,000+. Byline given. Pays on acceptance. No kill fee. Publishes ms an average of 4-6 months after acceptance. Editorial lead time 4-5 months. Submit seasonal material 7 months in advance. Accepts queries by e-mail. Responds in 2 weeks to queries.

NONFICTION "We don't run general consumer beauty material or products that are very rarely run a new product that is available through retail outlets. 'New' products means introduced in the last 12 months. We do not run industry personnel announcements or stories on individual spas/salons or getaways. We don't cover hair or nails." **Buys 12 mss/year.** Query. Length: 1,200-1,600 words. **Pays $75-300 for assigned articles.**

TIPS "Visit www.ascpskincare.com to read previous issues and learn about what we do. Submit a brief query with an idea to determine if you are on the right track. State specifically what value this has to estheticians and their work/income. Please note that we do not publish fashion, cosmetics, hair, or consumer-focused articles."

💲💲 SKIN INC. MAGAZINE

Allured Business Media, 336 Gundersen Dr., Suite A, Carol Stream IL 60188. (630)653-2155. **Fax:** (630)653-2192. **E-mail:** cchristensen@allured.com. **Website:** www.skininc.com. **Contact:** Cathy Christensen, senior editor. **30% freelance written.** Magazine published 12 times/year. "Mss considered for publication that contain original and new information in the general fields of skin care and makeup, dermatological and esthetician-assisted surgical techniques. The subject may cover the science of skin, the business of skin care and makeup, and plastic surgeons on healthy (i.e., nondiseased) skin." Estab. 1988. Circ. 30,000. Byline given. Pays on publication. No kill fee. Publishes ms an average of 6 months after acceptance. Editorial lead time 6 months. Submit seasonal material 1 year in advance. Accepts queries by mail, e-mail, fax, phone. Responds in 3 weeks to queries. Responds in 1 month to mss. Sample copy and writer's guidelines free.

NONFICTION Needs general interest, how-to, interview, personal experience, technical. **Buys 6 mss/year.** Query with published clips. Length: 2,000 words. **Pays $100-300 for assigned articles. Pays $50-200 for unsolicited articles.**

PHOTOS State availability. Captions, identification of subjects, model releases required. Reviews 3x5 prints. Offers no additional payment for photos accepted with ms.

COLUMNS/DEPARTMENTS Finance (tips and solutions for managing money), 2,000-2,500 words; Personnel (managing personnel), 2,000-2,500 words; Marketing (marketing tips for salon owners), 2,000-2,500 words; Retail (retailing products and services in the salon environment), 2,000-2,500 words. Query with published clips. **Pays $50-200.**

FILLERS Needs facts, newsbreaks. **Buys Buys 6 mss/year.** Length: 250-500 words. **Pays $50-100.**

TIPS "Have an understanding of the professional spa industry."

BEAUTY/SALON

DERMASCOPE MAGAZINE

Aesthetics International Association, 310 E. I-30, Suite B107, Garland TX 75043. (469)429-9300. **Fax:** (469)429-9301. **E-mail:** amckay@dermascope.com; press@dermascope.com. **Website:** www.dermascope.com. **Contact:** Amy McKay. Monthly magazine covering aesthetics (skin care) and body and spa therapy. "Our magazine is a source of practical advice and continuing education for skin care, body, and spa therapy professionals. Our main readers are salon, day spa, and destination spa owners, managers, or technicians and aesthetics students." Estab. 1978. Circ. 16,000. No byline given. No kill fee. Publishes ms an average of 6 months after acceptance. Editorial lead time 3 months. Submit seasonal material 6 months in advance. Accepts queries by mail, e-mail, fax. Responds in 4-6 months. Sample copy available by phone. Guidelines available online at website.

NONFICTION Needs book excerpts, general interest, historical, how-to, inspirational, personal experience, photo feature, technical. Query with published clips. "How-tos, skin therapy, body therapy, diet, nutrition, spa, equipment, medical procedures, makeup, and business articles should be approximately 1,500-2,000 words. Feature stories should be 1,800-2,500 words. Sidebars are a plus. Stories exceeding 2,500 may be printed in part and run in concurrent issues."

REPRINTS Does not accept reprints.

BEVERAGES AND BOTTLING

AMERICAN BAR ASSOCIATION JOURNAL

321 N. Clark St., 20th Floor, Chicago IL 60654. (312)988-5822. **E-mail:** debora.clark@americanbar.org. **Website:** www.abajournal.com. **Contact:** Debora Clark, deputy design director. Monthly membership magazine of the American Bar Association. Emphasizes law and the legal profession. Readers are lawyers. Estab. 1915. Circ. 330,000.

TIPS "No phone calls! The *ABA Journal* does not hire beginners."

💲💲 MICHIGAN HOSPITALITY REVIEW

Michigan Licensed Beverage Association, 920 N. Fairview, Lansing MI 48912. (517)374-9611; (800)292-2896. **Fax:** (517)374-1165. **E-mail:** editor@mlba.org. **Website:** www.mlba.org. **Contact:** Nicole Hanselman, editor. **40-50% freelance written.** Monthly magazine covering the spirit industry in Michigan. Estab. 1983. Circ. 4,200. Pays on publication. No kill fee. Editorial lead time 3 months. Submit seasonal material 3 months in advance. Accepts queries by mail, e-mail.

Responds in 2 weeks to queries. Responds in 1 month to mss. Sample copy for $5 or online.

NONFICTION Needs essays, general interest, historical, how-to, make a drink, human resources, tips, etc., humor, interview, new product, opinion, personal experience, photo feature, technical. **Buys 24 mss/year.** Send complete ms. Length: 1,000 words. **Pays $20-200.**

COLUMNS/DEPARTMENTS Open to essay content ideas. Interviews (legislators, others), 750-1,000 words; personal experience (waitstaff, customer, bartenders), 500 words. **Buys 12 mss/year.** Send complete ms. **Pays $25-100.**

TIPS "We are particularly interested in nonfiction concerning responsible consumption/serving of alcohol. We are looking for product reviews, company profiles, personal experiences, and news articles that would benefit our audience. Our audience is a busy group of business owners and hospitality professionals striving to obtain pertinent information that is not too wordy."

$$ PRACTICAL WINERY & VINEYARD

PWV, Inc., 58-D Paul Dr., San Rafael CA 94903-2054. (415)479-5819. **Fax:** (415)492-9325. **E-mail:** office@practicalwinery.com; tina@practicalwinery.com. **Website:** www.practicalwinery.com. **Contact:** Don Neel, publisher/editor; Tina Vierra, associate publisher. **50% freelance written.** Bimonthly magazine covering winemaking, grapegrowing, and wine marketing. "*Practical Winery & Vineyard* is a technical trade journal for winemakers and grapegrowers. All articles are fact-checked and peer-reviewed prior to publication to ensure 100% accuracy, readability, and practical useful application for readers. No consumer-focused wine articles, please." Estab. 1979. Circ. 4,000. Byline given. Pays on publication. No kill fee. Publishes ms an average of 6-9 months after acceptance. Editorial lead time 6-9 months. Submit seasonal material 9 months in advance. Accepts queries by mail, e-mail, fax. Responds in 1-2 weeks to queries. Responds in 1 month to mss. Guidelines by e-mail.

NONFICTION Contact: Tina L. Vierra, associate publisher. Needs how-to, technical. Special issues: "Each issue has a specific topic/focus. Please see Editorial Calendar. We do not want any wine consumer trends, retail info, or wine tasting notes; no food, travel, wine lifestyles." **Buys 25 mss/year.** Query with published clips. Length: 1,000-3,000 words. **Pays 25-50¢/word for assigned articles. Pays 25-35¢/word for unsolicited articles.**

PHOTOS Contact: Tina L. Vierra, associate publisher. State availability. Captions required. Reviews GIF/JPEG files. Offers no additional payment for photos accepted with ms.

TIPS "Query with cover. Tech articles only; must have knowledge of technical aspects of winemaking/grapegrowing."

$$$ VINEYARD & WINERY MANAGEMENT

P.O. Box 14459, Santa Rosa CA 95402. (707)577-7700. **Fax:** (707)577-7705. **E-mail:** tcaputo@vwm-online.com. **Website:** www.vwm-online.com. **Contact:** Tina Caputo, editor-in-chief. **80% freelance written.** Bimonthly magazine of professional importance to grape growers, winemakers, and winery sales and business people. "Headquartered in Sonoma County, California, we proudly remain as a leading independent wine trade magazine serving all of North America." Estab. 1975. Circ. 6,500. Byline given. Pays on publication. 20% kill fee. Accepts queries by e-mail. Responds in 3 weeks to queries. Responds in 1 month to mss. Sample copy free. Guidelines for by e-mail.

NONFICTION Needs how-to, interview, new product, technical. **Buys 30 mss/year.** Query. Length: 1,500-2,000 words. **Pays approximately $500/feature.** Sometimes pays expenses of writers on assignment.

PHOTOS State availability. Captions, identification of subjects required. Digital photos preferred, JPEG or TIFF files 300 pixels/inch resolution at print size. Pays $20/each photo published.

TIPS "We're looking for long-term relationships with authors who know the business and write well. Electronic submissions required; query for formats."

$$ WINES & VINES

Wine Communications Group, 65 Mitchell Blvd., Suite A, San Rafael CA 94903. (415)453-9700. **Fax:** (415)453-2517. **E-mail:** edit@winesandvines.com; info@winesandvines.com. **Website:** www.winesandvines.com. **Contact:** Jim Gordon, editor; Kate Lavin, managing editor. **50% freelance written.** Monthly magazine covering the North American winegrape and winemaking industry. "Since 1919, *Wines & Vines Magazine* has been the authoritative voice of the wine and grape industry—from prohibition to phylloxera, we have covered it all. Our paid circulation reaches all 50 states and many foreign countries. Because we are intended for the trade—including growers, winemakers, winery owners, wholesalers, restauranteurs, and serious amateurs—we accept more technical, informative articles. We do not accept wine reviews, wine country tours, or anything of a wine consumer nature." Estab. 1919. Circ. 5,000. Byline given. Pays 30 days after acceptance. No kill fee. Publishes ms an average of 3 months after acceptance. Editorial lead time 2 months. Submit seasonal material 4 months in advance. Accepts queries by e-mail. Responds in 2-3 weeks to queries. Sample copy for $5. Guidelines free.

NONFICTION Needs interview, new product, technical. "No wine reviews, wine country travelogues, 'lifestyle' pieces, or anything aimed at wine consumers. Our readers are professionals in the field." **Buys 60 mss/year.** Query with published clips. Length: 1,000-2,000 words. **Pays flat fee of $500 for assigned articles.**

PHOTOS Prefers JPEG files (JPEG, 300 dpi minimum). Can use high-quality prints. State availability of or send photos. Captions, identification of subjects required. Does not pay for photos submitted by author, but will give photo credit.

BOOK AND BOOKSTORE

$ THE BLOOMSBURY REVIEW

1553 Platte St., Suite 206, Denver CO 80202. (303)455-3123. **Fax:** (303)455-7039. **E-mail:** info@bloomsburyreview.com. **E-mail:** editors@bloomsburyreview.com. **Website:** www.bloomsburyreview.com. **Contact:** Marilyn Auer, editor-in-chief/publisher. **75% freelance written.** Quarterly tabloid covering books and book-related matters. "We publish book reviews, interviews with writers and poets, literary essays, and original poetry. Our audience consists of educated, literate, nonspecialized readers." Estab. 1980. Circ. 35,000. Byline given. Pays on publication. No kill fee. Publishes ms an average of 4-6 months after acceptance. Accepts queries by mail. Responds in 4 months to queries. Sample copy for $5 and 9x12 SASE. Guidelines for #10 SASE.

NONFICTION Needs essays, interview, book reviews. **Buys 60 mss/year.** Send complete ms. Length: 800-1,500 words. **Pays $10-20. Sometimes pays writers with contributor copies or other premiums if writer agrees.**

PHOTOS State availability of photos. Reviews prints. Offers no additional payment for photos accepted with ms.

COLUMNS/DEPARTMENTS Book reviews and essays, 500-1,500 words. **Buys 6 mss/year.** Query with published clips or send complete ms. **Pays $10-20.**

POETRY Contact: Ray Gonzalez, poetry editor. Needs avant-garde, free verse, haiku, traditional. Buys 20 poems/year. Submit maximum 5 poems. **Pays $5-10.**

TIPS "We appreciate receiving published clips and/or completed mss. Please—no rough drafts. Book reviews should be of new books (within 6 months of publication)."

$$ FOREWORD REVIEWS

425 Boardman Ave., Suite B, Traverse City MI 49684. (231)933-3699. **Fax:** (231)933-3899. **E-mail:** julie@forewordreviews.com; victoria@forewordreviews.com. **Website:** www.forewordreviews.com. **Contact:** Julie Eakin, book review editor; Victoria Sutherland, publisher. **95% freelance written.** Bimonthly magazine covering reviews of good books independently published. "In each issue of the magazine, there are 3 to 4 feature *ForeSight* articles focusing on trends in popular categories. These are in addition to the 75 or more critical reviews of forthcoming titles from independent presses in our *Review* section. While we try very hard to communicate with publicity departments concerning calls for submissions to the *ForeSight* features, we also hope that publishers will keep these forms handy to track what's happening at *ForeWord*. Look online for our review submission guidelines or view our editorial calendar." Estab. 1998. Circ. 20,000 (about 85% librarians, 12% bookstores, 3% publishing professionals). Byline given. Pays 2 months after publication. No kill fee. Publishes ms an average of 2-3 months after acceptance. Editorial lead time 3-4 months. Submit seasonal material 5 months in advance. Accepts queries by mail, e-mail. Responds in 1 month to queries. Responds in 1 month to mss. Sample copy for $10 and 8 ½ x11 SASE with $1.50 postage.

NONFICTION Query with published clips. All review submissions should be sent to the book review editor. Submissions should include a fact sheet or press release. Length: 400-1,500 words. **Pays $25-200 for assigned articles.**

TIPS "Be knowledgeable about the needs of book-sellers and librarians—remember we are an industry trade journal, not a how-to or consumer publication. We review books prior to publication, so book reviews are always assigned—but send us a note telling subjects you wish to review, as well as a résumé."

THE HORN BOOK MAGAZINE

The Horn Book, Inc., 56 Roland St., Suite 200, Boston MA 02129. (617)628-0225. **Fax:** (617)628-0882. **Website:** www.hbook.com. Cynthia Ritter, editorial assistant. **75% freelance written. Prefers to work with published/established writers.** Bimonthly magazine covering children's literature for librarians, booksellers, professors, teachers and students of children's literature. Estab. 1924. Circ. 8,000. Byline given. Pays on publication. No kill fee. Publishes ms an average of 4 months after acceptance. Submit seasonal material 6 months in advance. Accepts queries by mail, e-mail, fax. Accepts simultaneous submissions. Responds in 3 months to queries. Sample copy and writer's guidelines online.

NONFICTION Needs interviews with children's book authors and illustrators, topics of interest to the children's book world. **Buys 20 mss/year.** Query or send complete ms. Preferred length: 1,000-2,500 words. **Pays honorarium upon publication.**

TIPS "Writers have a better chance of breaking into our publication with a query letter on a specific article they want to write."

Ⓢ VIDEO LIBRARIAN

3435 NE Nine Boulder Dr., Poulsbo WA 98370. (360)626-1259. **Fax:** (360)626-1260. **E-mail:** vidlib@videolibrarian.com. **Website:** www.videolibrarian.com. **75% freelance written.** Bimonthly magazine covering DVD reviews for librarians. "*Video Librarian* reviews approximately 225 titles in each issue: children's, documentaries, how-to's, movies, TV, music and anime." Estab. 1986. Circ. 2,000. Byline given. Pays on publication. Publishes ms an average of 2 months after acceptance. Editorial lead time 2 months. Accepts queries by e-mail. Accepts simultaneous submissions. Responds in 1 week to queries. Sample copy for $11.

NONFICTION Buys 500+ mss/year. Query with published clips. Length: 200-300 words. **Pays $10-20/review.**

TIPS "We are looking for DVD reviewers with a wide range of interests, good critical eye, and strong writing skills."

BRICK, GLASS AND CERAMICS

Ⓢ STAINED GLASS

Stained Glass Association of America, 9313 East 63rd St., Raytown MO 64133. (800)438-9581. **Fax:** (816)737-2801. **E-mail:** quarterly@sgaaonline.com; webmaster@sgaaonline.com. **Website:** www.stainedglass.org. **Contact:** Richard Gross, editor and media director. **70% freelance written.** Quarterly magazine. "Since 1906, *Stained Glass* has been the official voice of the Stained Glass Association of America. As the oldest, most respected stained glass publication in North America, *Stained Glass* preserves the techniques of the past as well as illustrates the trends of the future. This vital information, of significant value to the professional stained glass studio, is also of interest to those for whom stained glass is an avocation or hobby." Estab. 1906. Circ. 8,000. Byline given. Pays on publication. No kill fee. Publishes ms an average of 1 year after acceptance. Editorial lead time 6 months. Submit seasonal material 8 months in advance. Accepts queries by mail, e-mail, fax. Responds in 3 months to queries. Sample copy free. Guidelines on website.

NONFICTION Needs how-to, humor, interview, new product, opinion, photo feature, technical. **Buys 9 mss/year.** Query or send complete ms, but must include photos or slides—very heavy on photos. Length: 2,500-3,500 words. **Pays $125/illustrated article; $75/nonillustrated.**

REPRINTS Accepts previously published submissions from stained glass publications only. Send tearsheet of article. Payment negotiable.

PHOTOS Send photos. Identification of subjects required. Reviews 4x5 transparencies, send slides with submission. Pays $75 for non-illustrated. Pays $125, plus 3 copies for line art or photography.

COLUMNS/DEPARTMENTS Columns must be illustrated. Teknixs (technical, how-to, stained and glass art), word length varies by subject. **Buys 4 mss/year.** Query or send complete ms, but must be illustrated.

TIPS "We need more technical articles. Writers should be extremely well versed in the glass arts. Photographs are extremely important and must be of very high quality. Submissions without photographs or illustrations are seldom considered unless something special and writer states that photos are available. However, prefer to see with submission."

⊖⊖ US GLASS, METAL & GLAZING

Key Communications, Inc., P.O. Box 569, Garrisonville VA 22463. (540)720-5584, ext.114. **Fax:** (540)720-5687. **E-mail:** info@glass.com; erogers@glass.com. **Website:** www.usglassmag.com. **Contact:** Ellen Rogers, editor. **25% freelance written.** Monthly magazine for companies involved in the flat glass trades. Estab. 1966. Circ. 27,000. Byline given. Pays on publication. No kill fee. Publishes ms an average of 3 months after acceptance. Editorial lead time 3 months. Submit seasonal material 2 months in advance. Accepts queries by mail, e-mail. Accepts simultaneous submissions. Responds in 1 month to queries. Responds in 2 months to mss. Sample copy online.

NONFICTION Buys 12 mss/year. Query with published clips. **Pays $300-600 for assigned articles.** Sometimes pays expenses of writers on assignment.

PHOTOS State availability. Captions, identification of subjects required. Reviews contact sheets. Offers no additional payment for photos accepted with ms.

BUILDING INTERIORS

⊖⊖ FABRICS + FURNISHINGS INTERNATIONAL

SIPCO Publications + Events, 3 Island Ave., Suite 6i, Miami Beach FL 33139. **E-mail:** eric@sipco.net. **Website:** www.fandii.com. **Contact:** Eric Schneider, editor/publisher. **10% freelance written.** Bimonthly magazine covering commercial, hospitality interior design, and manufacturing. *F+FI* covers news from vendors who supply the hospitality interiors industry. Estab. 1990. Circ. 11,000+. Byline given. Pays on publication. Offers $100 kill fee. Editorial lead time 3 months. Submit seasonal material 3 months in advance. Accepts queries by e-mail. Accepts simultaneous submissions. Sample copy available online.

NONFICTION Needs interview, technical. "Does no opinion or consumer pieces. Our readers must learn something from our stories." Query with published clips. Length: 500-1,000 words. **Pays $250-350.**

PHOTOS Send photos. Captions, identification of subjects required. Reviews GIF/JPEG files. Offers no additional payment for photos accepted with ms.

TIPS "Give us a lead on a new project that we haven't heard about. Have pictures of space and ability to interview designer on how they made it work."

⊖⊖ KITCHEN & BATH DESIGN NEWS

Cygnus Business Media, 3 Huntington Quadrangle, Suite 301N, Melville NY 11747. **Fax:** (631)845-7218. **E-mail:** janice.costa@cygnuspub.com. **Website:** www.kitchenbathdesign.com. **15% freelance written.** "Monthly tabloid for kitchen and bath dealers and design professionals, offering design, business and marketing advice to help our readers be more successful. It is not a consumer publication about design, a book for do-it-yourselfers, or a magazine created to showcase pretty pictures of kitchens and baths. Rather, we cover the professional kitchen and bath design industry in depth, looking at the specific challenges facing these professionals, and how they address these challenges." Estab. 1983. Circ. 51,000. Byline given. Pays on publication. Publishes ms an average of 2-3 months after acceptance. Editorial lead time 2 months. Accepts queries by mail, e-mail, fax. Responds in 2-4 weeks to queries. Sample copy available online. Guidelines by e-mail.

NONFICTION Needs how-to, interview. Does not want consumer stories, generic business stories, or "I remodeled my kitchen and it's so beautiful" stories. "This is a magazine for trade professionals, so stories need to be both slanted for these professionals, as well as sophisticated enough so that people who have been working in the field 30 years can still learn something from them." Buys 16 mss/year. Query with published clips. Length: 1,100-3,000 words. **Pays $200-650.** Sometimes pays expenses of writers on assignment.

PHOTOS Send photos. Identification of subjects required. Offers no additional payment for photos accepted with ms.

TIPS "This is a trade magazine for kitchen and bath dealers and designers, so trade experience and knowledge of the industry are essential. We look for writers who already know the unique challenges facing this industry, as well as the major players, acronyms, etc. This is not a market for beginners, and the vast majority of our freelancers are either design professionals, or experienced in the industry."

⊖⊖ QUALIFIED REMODELER

Cygnus Business Media, 1233 Janesville Ave., Fort Atkinson WI 53538. **E-mail:** Rob.Heselbarth@cygnus.com. **Website:** www.forresidentialpros.com. **Contact:**

Rob Heselbarth, editorial director. **5% freelance written.** Monthly magazine covering residential remodeling. Estab. 1975. Circ. 83,500. Byline given. Pays on acceptance. No kill fee. Publishes ms an average of 1 month after acceptance. Editorial lead time 3 months. Submit seasonal material 2 months in advance. Accepts queries by mail, e-mail, fax, phone. Sample copy available online.

NONFICTION Needs how-to, business management, new product, photo feature, best practices articles, innovative design. **Buys 12 mss/year.** Query with published clips. Length: 1,200-2,500 words. **Pays $300-600 for assigned articles. Pays $200-400 for unsolicited articles.** Sometimes pays expenses of writers on assignment.

PHOTOS Send photos. Reviews negatives, transparencies. Negotiates payment individually.

COLUMNS/DEPARTMENTS Query with published clips. **Pays $400**

TIPS "We focus on business management issues faced by remodeling contractors. For example, sales, marketing, liability, taxes, and just about any matter addressing small business operation."

⊜⊜ WALLS & CEILINGS

2401 W. Big Beaver Rd., Suite 700, Troy MI 48084. (313)894-7380. **Fax:** (248)362-5103. **E-mail:** wyattj@ bnpmedia.com; mark@wwcca.org. **Website:** www. wconline.com. Mark Fowler, editorial director. **Contact:** John Wyatt, editor. **20% freelance written.** Monthly magazine for contractors involved in lathing and plastering, drywall, acoustics, fireproofing, curtain walls, and movable partitions, together with manufacturers, dealers, and architects. Estab. 1938. Circ. 30,000. Byline given. Pays on publication. No kill fee. Publishes ms an average of 6 months after acceptance. Submit seasonal material 4 months in advance. Accepts queries by mail, e-mail. Accepts simultaneous submissions. Responds in 6 months to queries. Sample copy for 9x12 SAE with $2 postage. Guidelines for #10 SASE.

NONFICTION Needs how-to, drywall and plaster construction and business management, technical. **Buys 20 mss/year.** Query or send complete ms. Length: 1,000-1,500 words. **Pays $50-500.** Sometimes pays expenses of writers on assignment.

REPRINTS Send tearsheet or photocopy with rights for sale noted and information about when and where the material previously appeared. Pays 50% of the amount paid for an original article.

PHOTOS Send photos. Captions, identification of subjects required. Reviews contact sheets, negatives, transparencies, prints.

BUSINESS MANAGEMENT

⊜ ⊜⊜⊜⊜ BEDTIMES

International Sleep Products Association, 501 Wythe St., Alexandria VA 22314. (571)482-5442. **E-mail:** jpalm@sleepproducts.org. **Website:** www.bedtimes-magazine.com; www.sleepproducts.org. **Contact:** Julie Palm, editor. **20-40% freelance written.** Monthly magazine covering the mattress manufacturing industry. "Our news and features are straightforward—we are not a lobbying vehicle for our association. No special slant." Estab. 1917. Circ. 3,800. Byline given. Pays on acceptance. No kill fee. Publishes ms an average of 3 months after acceptance. Editorial lead time 2 months. Accepts queries by e-mail. Accepts simultaneous submissions. Responds in 1 month to queries. Sample copy for $4. Guidelines by e-mail.

NONFICTION No pieces that do not relate to business in general or mattress industry in particular. **Buys 15-25/year mss/year.** Query with published clips. Length: 500-2,500 words. **Pays 50-$1/word for short features; $2,000 for cover story.**

PHOTOS State availability. Identification of subjects required. Negotiates payment individually.

TIPS "Cover topics have included: annual industry forecast; e-commerce; flammability and home furnishings; the risks and rewards of marketing overseas; the evolving family business; the shifting workplace environment; and what do consumers really want?"

⊜⊜⊜⊜ BLACK MBA MAGAZINE

9730 S. Western Ave., Suite 320, Evergreen Park IL 60805. (800)856-8092 (toll free); (850)668-7400 (direct). **Fax:** (708)422-1507. **E-mail:** elaine@naylor.com. **Website:** www.blackmbaonline.com. **Contact:** Elaine Richardson, Naylor LLC, managing editor. **80% freelance written.** Online magazine covering business career strategy, economic development, and financial management. Estab. 1997. Circ. 45,000. Byline given. Pays after publication. Offers 10-20% or $500 kill fee. Publishes ms an average of 1 month after acceptance. Editorial lead time 2-3 months. Submit seasonal material 3-4 months in advance. Accepts queries by mail, e-mail, fax. No

PHOTOS State availability of or send photos. Identification of subjects required. Reviews ZIP disk. Offers no additional payment for photos accepted with ms.

COLUMNS/DEPARTMENTS Management Strategies (leadership development), 1,200-1,700 words; Features (business management, entreprenuerial finance); Finance; Technology. Send complete ms. **Pays $500-1,000.**

💲💲💲 BUSINESS TRAVEL EXECUTIVE

5768 Remington Dr., Winston-Salem NC 27104. (336)766-1961. **E-mail:** DBooth@askbte.com. **Website:** www.askbte.com. **Contact:** Gerald Allison, publisher. **90% freelance written.** Monthly magazine covering corporate procurement of travel services. "We are not a travel magazine. We publish articles designed to help corporate purchasers of travel negotiate contracts, enforce policy, select automated services, track business travelers, and account for their safety and expenditures, understand changes in the various industries associated with travel. Do not submit mss without an assignment. Look at the website for an idea of what we publish." Byline given. Pays on publication. No kill fee. Publishes ms an average of 2 months after acceptance. Editorial lead time 0-3 months. Accepts queries by e-mail.

NONFICTION Needs how-to, technical. **Buys 48 mss/year.** "Please send unsolicited submissions, at your own risk. Please enclose aSASE for return of material. Submission of letters implies the right to edit and publish all or in part." Length: 800-2,000 words. **Pays $200-800.**

COLUMNS/DEPARTMENTS Meeting Place (meeting planning and management); Hotel Pulse (hotel negotiations, contracting and compliance); Security Watch (travel safety); all 1,000 words. **Buys 24 mss/year.** Query. **Pays $200-400.**

💲💲 CBA RETAILERS + RESOURCES

CBA, the Association for Christian Retail, 9240 Explorer Dr., Suite 200, Colorado Springs CO 80920. **Fax:** (719)272-3510. **E-mail:** ksamuelson@cbaonline.org. **Website:** www.cbaonline.org. **30% freelance written.** Monthly magazine covering the Christian retail industry. "Writers must have knowledge of and direct experience in the Christian retail industry. Subject matter must specifically pertain to the Christian retail audience." Estab. 1968. Byline given. Pays on publication. No kill fee. Publishes ms an average of 3 months after acceptance. Editorial lead time 3 months.

Submit seasonal material 6 months in advance. Accepts queries by e-mail. Responds in 2 months to queries. Sample copy for $9.50 or online.

NONFICTION Buys 24 mss/year. Query. Length: 750-1,500 words. **Pays 30¢/word upon publication.**

TIPS "Only experts on Christian retail industry, completely familiar with retail audience and their needs and considerations, should submit a query. Do not submit articles unless requested."

💲💲 CONTRACTING PROFITS

Trade Press Publishing, 2100 W. Florist Ave., Milwaukee WI 53209. (414)228-7701; (800)727-7995. **Fax:** (414)228-1134. **E-mail:** dan.weltin@tradepress.com. **Website:** www.cleanlink.com/cp. **Contact:** Dan Weltin, editor-in-chief. **40% freelance written.** Magazine published 10 times/year covering building service contracting and business management advice. "We are the pocket MBA for this industry—focusing not only on cleaning-specific topics, but also discussing how to run businesses better and increase profits through a variety of management articles." Estab. 1995. Circ. 32,000. Byline given. Pays within 30 days of acceptance. No kill fee. Editorial lead time 2 months. Submit seasonal material 3 months in advance. Accepts queries by mail, e-mail. Responds in weeks to queries. Sample copy available online. Guidelines free.

NONFICTION Needs exposé, how-to, interview, technical. No product-related reviews or testimonials. **Buys 30 mss/year.** Query with published clips. Length: 1,000-1,500 words. **Pays $100-500.** Sometimes pays expenses of writers on assignment.

COLUMNS/DEPARTMENTS Query with published clips.

TIPS "Read back issues on our website and be able to understand some of those topics prior to calling."

💲💲 CONTRACT MANAGEMENT

National Contract Management Association, 21740 Beaumeade Circle, Suite 125, Ashburn VA 20147. (571)382-0082. **Fax:** (703)448-0939. **E-mail:** khansen@ncmahq.org. **Website:** www.ncmahq.org. **Contact:** Kerry McKinnon Hansen, editor-in-chief. **10% freelance written.** Monthly magazine covering contract and business management. Most of the articles published in *Contract Management (CM)* are written by NCMA members, although one does not have to be an NCMA member to be published in the magazine. Articles should concern some aspect of the contract management profession, whether at the level of a beginner or that of the advanced practitioner. Estab. 1960. Circ. 23,000. Byline given. Pays on publication. No kill fee. Publishes ms an average of 3 months after acceptance. Editorial lead time 10 weeks. Submit seasonal material 3 months in advance. Accepts queries by mail, e-mail, fax, phone. Accepts simultaneous submissions. Responds in 2 weeks to queries. Responds in 1 month to mss. Sample copy and writer's guidelines available online.

NONFICTION Needs essays, general interest, how-to, humor, inspirational, new product, opinion, technical. No company or CEO profiles—"please read a copy of publication before submitting." **Buys 6-10 mss/year.** Query with published clips. "Send an inquiry including a brief summary (150 words) of the proposed article to the managing editor before you write the article." Length: 1,800-4,000 words. **Pays $300.**

PHOTOS State availability. Captions, identification of subjects required. Offers no additional payment for photos accepted with ms.

COLUMNS/DEPARTMENTS Professional Development (self-improvement in business), 1,000-1,500 words; Back to Basics (basic how-tos and discussions), 1,500-2,000 words. **Buys 2 mss/year.** Query with published clips. **Pays $300.**

TIPS "Query and read at least 1 issue. Visit website to better understand our audience."

⬤⬤ EXPANSION MANAGEMENT

Penton Media, Inc., 1300 E. 9th St., Cleveland OH 44114. (877)530-8801. **E-mail:** aselko@industryweek.com. **Website:** www.industryweek.com/expansion-management. **Contact:** Adrienne Selko, senior editor. **50% freelance written.** Monthly magazine covering economic development. Estab. 1986. Circ. 45,000. Byline given. Pays on acceptance. No kill fee. Publishes ms an average of 1 month after acceptance. Editorial lead time 2 months. Sample copy for $7. Guidelines free.

NONFICTION **Buys 120 mss/year.** Query with published clips. Length: 800-1,200 words. **Pays $200-400 for assigned articles.** Sometimes pays expenses of writers on assignment.

PHOTOS Send photos. Captions required. Offers no additional payment for photos accepted with ms.

TIPS "Send clips first, then call."

⬤⬤⬤ EXPO

Red 7 Media, 10 Norden Place, Norwalk CT 06855. (203)899-8438. **E-mail:** traphael@red7media.com; mhart@red7media.com. **E-mail:** tsilber@red7media.com. **Website:** www.expoweb.com. **Contact:** Tony Silber, general manager; T.J. Raphael, associate editor; Michael Hart, editor. **80% freelance written.** Magazine covering expositions. Byline given. Pays on publication. Offers 50% kill fee. Editorial lead time 3 months. Accepts queries by mail, e-mail, fax. Responds in 3 weeks to queries. Sample copy and guidelines free.

NONFICTION Needs how-to, interview. Query with published clips. Length: 600-2,400 words. **Pays 50¢/word.** Pays expenses of writers on assignment.

PHOTOS State availability.

COLUMNS/DEPARTMENTS Profile (personality profile), 650 words; Exhibitor Matters (exhibitor issues) and EXPOTech (technology), both 600-1,300 words. **Buys 10 mss/year.** Query with published clips.

TIPS "*EXPO* offers shorter features and departments, while continuing to offer in-depth reporting. Editorial is more concise, using synopsis, bullets, and tidbits whenever possible. Every article needs sidebars, call-outs, graphs, charts, etc., to create entry points for readers. Headlines and leads are more provocative. And writers should elevate the level of shop talk, demonstrating that *EXPO* is the leader in the industry. We plan our editorial calendar about 1 year in advance, but we are always open to new ideas. Please query before submitting a story to *EXPO*—tell us about your idea and what our readers would learn. Include your qualifications to write about the subject and the sources you plan to contact."

⬤⬤ INTENTS

Industrial Fabrics Association International, 1801 County Rd. B W, Roseville MN 55113. (651)225-2508; (800)-225-4324. **Fax:** (651)631-9334. **E-mail:** srniemi@ifai.com; jclafferty@ifai.com; generalinfo@ifai.com. **Website:** www.ifai.com/publications/intents. **Contact:** Susan R. Niemi, publisher; Jill C. Lafferty, editor. **50% freelance written.** Bimonthly magazine covering tent-rental and special-event industries. "In-Tents is the official publication of IFAI's Tent Rental Division, delivering 'the total tent experience.' In-Tents offers focused, credible information needed to stage and host safe, successful tented events. Issues of the magazine include news, trends and behind-the-scenes coverage of the latest events in tents." Estab. 1995. Circ. 12,000. Byline given. Pays on acceptance. No kill fee. Publishes ms an average of 2 months after acceptance. Editorial lead time 3 months. Accepts queries by mail, e-mail, fax. Sample copy and writer's guidelines free.

NONFICTION Needs how-to, interview, new product, photo feature, technical. **Buys 12-18 mss/year.** Query. Length: 800-2,000 words. **Pays $300-500.** Sometimes pays expenses of writers on assignment.

PHOTOS State availability. Captions, identification of subjects, model releases required. Reviews contact sheets, negatives, prints, digital images. Negotiates payment individually.

TIPS "We look for lively, intelligent writing that makes technical subjects come alive."

RETAIL INFO SYSTEMS NEWS

Edgell Communications, 4 Middlebury Blvd., Randolph NJ 07869. (973)607-1300. **Fax:** (973)607-1395. **E-mail:** ablair@edgellmail.com; jskorupa@edgellmail. com. **Website:** www.risnews.com. **Contact:** Adam Blair, editor; Joe Skorupa, group editor-in-chief, **65% freelance written.** Monthly magazine covering retail technology. Estab. 1988. Circ. 22,000. Byline sometimes given. Pays on publication. No kill fee. Publishes ms an average of 2 months after acceptance. Editorial lead time 3 months. Submit seasonal material 3 months in advance. Accepts queries by mail. Sample copy available online.

NONFICTION Needs essays, exposé, how-to, humor, interview, technical. **Buys 80 mss/year.** Query with published clips. Length: 700-1,900 words. **Pays $600-1,200 for assigned articles.** Sometimes pays expenses of writers on assignment.

PHOTOS State availability of or send photos. Identification of subjects required. Negotiates payment individually.

COLUMNS/DEPARTMENTS News/trends (analysis of current events), 150-300 words. **Buys 4 articles/year mss/year.** Query with published clips. **Pays $100-300.**

TIPS "Case histories about companies achieving substantial results using advanced management practices and/or advanced technology are best."

SECURITY DEALER & INTEGRATOR

Cygnus Business Media, 12735 Morris Rd., Bldg. 200, Suite 180, Alpharetta GA 30004. (800)547-7377, ext 2730. **E-mail:** deborah.omara@cygnus.com. **Web-**site: www.securityinfowatch.com/magazine. **Contact:** Deborah O'Mara, editor-in-chief. **25% freelance written.** Circ. 25,000. Byline sometimes given. Pays 3 weeks after publication. No kill fee. Publishes ms an average of 3 months after acceptance. Accepts queries by e-mail. Accepts simultaneous submissions.

NONFICTION Needs how-to, interview, technical. No consumer pieces. Query by e-mail. Length: 1,000-3,000 words. **Pays $300 for assigned articles; $100-200 for unsolicited articles.** Sometimes pays expenses of writers on assignment.

PHOTOS State availability. Captions, identification of subjects required. Reviews contact sheets, transparencies. Offers $25 additional payment for photos accepted with ms.

COLUMNS/DEPARTMENTS Closed Circuit TV, Access Control (both on application, installation, new products), 500-1,000 words. **Buys 25 mss/year.** Query by mail only. **Pays $100-150.**

TIPS "The areas of our publication most open to freelancers are technical innovations, trends in the alarm industry, and crime patterns as related to the business as well as business finance and management pieces."

SMART BUSINESS

Smart Business Network, Inc., 835 Sharon Dr., Suite 200, Cleveland OH 44145. (440)250-7000. **Fax:** (440)250-7001. **E-mail:** tshryock@sbnonline.com. **Website:** www.sbnonline.com. **Contact:** Todd Shryock, managing editor. **5% freelance written.** Monthly business magazine with an audience made up of business owners and top decision makers. "*Smart Business* is one of the fastest growing national chains of regional management journals for corporate executives. Every issue delves into the minds of the most innovative executives in each of our regions to report on how market leaders got to the top and what strategies they use to stay there." Estab. 1989. Byline given. Pays on publication. Offers 50% kill fee. Publishes ms an average of 2 months after acceptance. Editorial lead time 3 months. Submit seasonal material 3 months in advance. Accepts queries by mail, e-mail. Responds in 2 weeks to queries. Responds in 1 month to mss. Guidelines by e-mail.

NONFICTION Needs how-to, interview. No breaking news or news features. **Buys 10-12 mss/year.** Query with published clips. Length: 1,150-2,000 words. **Pays $200-500.** Sometimes pays expenses of writers on assignment.

PHOTOS State availability. Identification of subjects required. Reviews negatives, prints. Offers no additional payment for photos accepted with ms.

TIPS "The best way to submit to *Smart Business* is to read us—either online or in print. Remember, our audience is made up of top level business executives and owners."

⬤⬤ STAMATS MEETINGS MEDIA

655 Montgomery St., Suite 900, San Francisco CA 94111. **Fax:** (415)788-1358. **E-mail:** tyler.davidson@ meetingsfocus.com. **Website:** www.meetingsmedia. com. **Contact:** Tyler Davidson, chief content director. **75% freelance written.** Monthly tabloid covering meeting, event, and conference planning. Estab. 1986. Circ. *Meetings East* and *Meetings South* 22,000; *Meetings West* 26,000. Byline given. Pays 1 month after publication. No kill fee. Publishes ms an average of 1 month after acceptance. Editorial lead time 3 months. Submit seasonal material 3 months in advance. Accepts queries by mail, e-mail, fax. Responds in 3 weeks to queries. Sample copy for DSR with 9x13 envelope and 5 first-class stamps.

NONFICTION Needs how-to, travel, as it pertains to meetings and conventions. "No first-person fluff—this is a business magazine." **Buys 150 mss/year.** Query with published clips. Length: 1,200-2,000 words. **Pays $500 flat rate/package.**

PHOTOS State availability. Identification of subjects required. Offers no additional payment for photos accepted with ms.

TIPS "We're always looking for freelance writers who are local to our destination stories. For Site Inspections, get in touch in late September or early October, when we usually have the following year's editorial calendar available."

⬤ THE STATE JOURNAL

WorldNow, P.O. Box 11848, Charleston WV 25339. (304)344-1630; (304)395-3649. **E-mail:** jross@state-journal.com. **Website:** www.statejournal.com. **Contact:** Jim Ross, managing editor. **30% freelance written.** "We are a weekly journal dedicated to providing stories of interest to the business community in West Virginia." Estab. 1984. Circ. 10,000. Byline given. Pays on publication. No kill fee. Publishes ms an average of 3 weeks after acceptance. Submit seasonal material 4 months in advance. Accepts queries by mail, e-mail, fax. Sample copy and writer's guidelines for #10 SASE.

NONFICTION Needs general interest, interview, new product, (all business related). **Buys 400 mss/year.** Query. Length: 250-1,500 words. **Pays $50.** Sometimes pays expenses of writers on assignment.

PHOTOS State availability. Captions required. Reviews contact sheets. Offers $15/photo.

TIPS "Localize your work—mention West Virginia specifically in the article; or talk to business people in West Virginia."

⬤⬤ SUSTAINABLE INDUSTRIES

Sustainable Industries Media, LLC, P.O. Box 460324, San Francisco CA 94146. (415)762-3945. **E-mail:** sarah@sustainableindustries.com. **Website:** www.sustainableindustries.com. **Contact:** Sara Stroud, associate editor. **20% freelance written.** Bimonthly magazine covering environmental innovation in business. "We seek high quality, balanced reporting aimed at business readers. More compelling writing than is typical in standard trade journals." Estab. 2003. Circ. 2,500. Byline sometimes given. Pays on publication. No kill fee. Publishes ms an average of 1-3 months after acceptance. Editorial lead time 1-2 months. Accepts queries by mail, e-mail. Accepts simultaneous submissions.

NONFICTION Needs general interest, how-to, interview, new product, opinion, news briefs. Special issues: Themes rotate on the following topics: Agriculture & Natural Resources; Green Building; Energy; Government; Manufacturing & Technology; Retail & Service; Transportation & Tourism—though all topics are covered in each issue. No prosaic essays or extra-long pieces. Query with published clips. Length: 500-1,500 words. **Pays $0-500.**

PHOTOS State availability. Reviews prints, GIF/JPEG files. Offers no additional payment for photos accepted with ms.

COLUMNS/DEPARTMENTS Guest columns accepted, but not compensated. Business trade columns on specific industries: 500-1,000 words. Query.

CHURCH ADMINISTRATION AND MINISTRY

⬤ CHRISTIAN COMMUNICATOR

9118 W. Elmwood Dr., Suite 1G, Niles IL 60714-5820. (847)296-3964. **Fax:** (847)296-0754. **E-mail:** ljohnson@wordprocommunications.com. **Website:** acwriters.com. **Contact:** Lin Johnson, managing editor. **50%**

freelance written. Monthly magazine covering Christian writing and speaking. Circ. 4,000. Byline given. Pays on publication. No kill fee. Publishes ms an average of 6-12 months after acceptance. Editorial lead time 3 months. Submit seasonal material 9 months in advance. Accepts queries by e-mail. Responds in 6-8 weeks to queries. Responds in 8-12 weeks to mss. Sample copy for SAE and 5 first-class stamps. Writer's guidelines by e-mail or on website.

NONFICTION Needs how-to, interview, book reviews. **Buys 90 mss/year.** Query or send complete ms only by e-mail. Length: 650-1,000 words. **Pays $10. $5 for reviews. ACW CD for anecdotes.** True

COLUMNS/DEPARTMENTS Speaking, 650-1,000 words. **Buys 11 mss/year.** Query. **Pays $10.**

POETRY Needs free verse, light verse, traditional. Buys Publishes 22 poems/year. poems/year. Submit maximum Maximum number of poems: 3. poems. Length: 4-20 lines. **Pays $5.**

FILLERS Needs anecdotes, short humor. **Buys 10 30 mss/year.** Length: 75-300 words. **Pays CD.**

TIPS "We primarily use how-to articles and profiles of editors. However, we're willing to look at any other pieces geared to the writing life."

💲 CREATOR MAGAZINE

P.O. Box 3538, Pismo Beach CA 93448. (800)777-6713. **E-mail:** customerservice@creatormagazine.com. **Website:** www.creatormagazine.com. **Contact:** Bob Burroughs, editor. **35% freelance written.** Bimonthly magazine. Most readers are church music directors and worship leaders. Content focuses on the spectrum of worship styles from praise and worship to traditional to liturgical. All denominations subscribe. Articles on worship, choir rehearsal, handbells, children's/youth choirs, technique, relationships, etc. Estab. 1978. Circ. 6,000. Byline given. Pays on publication. No kill fee. Publishes ms an average of 3 months after acceptance. Editorial lead time 3 months. Submit seasonal material 4 months in advance. Accepts queries by mail. Accepts simultaneous submissions. Sample copy for SAE with 9x12 envelope and 5 first-class stamps. Guidelines free.

NONFICTION Needs essays, how-to, be a better church musician, choir director, rehearsal technician, etc., humor, short personal perspectives, inspirational, interview, call first, new product, call first, opinion, personal experience, photo feature, religious, technical, choral technique. Special issues: July/August

is directed toward adult choir members, rather than directors. **Buys 20 mss/year.** Query or send complete ms. Length: 1,000-10,000 words. **Pays $30-75 for assigned articles. Pays $30-60 for unsolicited articles.** Pays expenses of writers on assignment.

PHOTOS State availability of or send photos. Captions required. Reviews negatives, 8x10 prints. Offers no additional payment for photos accepted with ms.

COLUMNS/DEPARTMENTS Hints & Humor (music ministry short ideas, cute anecdotes, ministry experience), 75-250 words; Inspiration (motivational ministry stories), 200-500 words; Children/Youth (articles about specific choirs), 1,000-5,000 words. **Buys 15 mss/year.** Query or send complete ms. **Pays $20-60.**

TIPS "Request guidelines and stick to them. If theme is relevant and guidelines are followed, we'll probably publish your article."

💲💲 GROUP MAGAZINE

Simply Youth Ministry, 1515 Cascade Ave., Loveland CO 80538. (970)669-3836. **E-mail:** sfirestone@group.com. **Website:** www.groupmagazine.com. **Contact:** Scott Firestone IV, associate editor. **50% freelance written.** Bimonthly magazine for Christian youth workers. "*Group* is the interdenominational magazine for leaders of Christian youth groups. *Group*'s purpose is to supply ideas, practical help, inspiration, and training for youth leaders." Estab. 1974. Circ. 55,000. Byline sometimes given. Pays on acceptance. No kill fee. Editorial lead time 4 months. Submit seasonal material 5 months in advance. Accepts queries by mail, e-mail, fax. Responds in 8-10 weeks to queries. Responds in 2 months to mss. Sample copy for $2, plus 10x12 SAE and 3 first-class stamps.

NONFICTION Needs inspirational, personal experience, religious. No fiction, prose, or poetry. **Buys 30 mss/year.** Query. Length: 200-2,000 words. **Pays $50-250.** Sometimes pays expenses of writers on assignment.

COLUMNS/DEPARTMENTS "Try This One" section needs short ideas (100-250 words) for youth group use. These include games, fundraisers, crowdbreakers, Bible studies, helpful hints, outreach ideas, and discussion starters. "Hands-on Help" section needs mini-articles (100-350 words) that feature practical tips for youth leaders on working with students, adult leaders, and parents. **Pays $50.**

TIPS "We are always looking for submissions for short, novel, practical ideas that have worked in actual youth ministry settings. It's best to familiarize yourself with *Group Magazine* before sending in ideas for our departments."

🌑🌑 THE JOURNAL OF ADVENTIST EDUCATION

General Conference of SDA, 12501 Old Columbia Pike, Silver Spring MD 20904. (301)680-5069. **Fax:** (301)622-9627. **E-mail:** rumbleb@gc.adventist.org; goffc@gc.adventist.org. **Website:** http://jae.adventist.org. Chandra Goff. **Contact:** Beverly J. Robinson-Rumble, editor. Bimonthly (except skips issue in summer) professional journal covering teachers and administrators in Seventh Day Adventist school systems. Published 5 times/year in English, 2 times/year in French, Spanish, and Portuguese. Emphasizes procedures, philosophy and subject matter of Christian education. Estab. 1939. Circ. 14,000 in English; 13,000 in other languages. Byline given. Pays on publication. No kill fee. Publishes ms an average of 1 year after acceptance. Editorial lead time 1 year. Accepts queries by mail, e-mail, fax, phone. Responds in 6 weeks to queries. Responds in 4 months to mss. Sample copy for sae with 10x12 envelope and 5 first-class stamps. Guidelines available online.

NONFICTION Needs book excerpts, essays, howto, education-related, personal experience, photo feature, religious, education. "No brief first-person stories about Sunday Schools." "Query. Articles submitted on disk or by e-mail as attached files are welcome. Store in MS Word or WordPerfect format. If you submit a CD, be sure to include a printed copy of the article with the CD. Articles should be 6-8 pages long, with a max of 10 pages, including references. Two-part articles will be considered." Length: 1,000-1,500 words. **Pays $25-300.**

REPRINTS "Send tearsheet or photocopy and information about when and where the material previously appeared."

PHOTOS Buys 5-15 photos from freelancers/issue; up to 75 photos/year. Photos of children/teens, multicultural, parents, education, religious, health/fitness, technology/computers with people, committees, offices, school photos of teachers, students, parents, activities at all levels, elementary though graduate school. Reviews photos with or without a ms. Model release preferred. Photo captions preferred. Uses mostly digital color images but also accepts color prints; 35mm, 21/4x21/4, 4x5 transparencies. Send digital photos via ZIP, CD, or DVD (preferred); e-mail as TIFF, GIF, JPEG files at 300 DPI. Contact the editor to obtain instructions for posting photos on the magazine's FTP site. Do not send large numbers of photos as e-mail attachments. Send query letter with prints, photocopies, transparencies. Provide self-promotion piece to be kept on file for possible future assignments. Responds in 1 month to queries. Simultaneous submissions and previously published work OK. State availability of or send photos. Pays $100-350 for color cover; $50-100 for color inside. Willing to negotiate on electronic usage of photos. Pays on publication. Credit line given.

TIPS "Articles may deal with educational theory or practice, although the *Journal* seeks to emphasize the practical. Articles dealing with the creative and effective use of methods to enhance teaching skills or learning in the classroom are especially welcome. Whether theoretical or practical, such essays should demonstrate the skillful integration of Seventh-day Adventist faith/values and learning."

🌑 KIDS' MINISTRY IDEAS

Review and Herald Publishing Association, 55 W. Oak Ridge Dr., Hagerstown MD 21740. (301)393-3178. **Fax:** (301)393-3209. **E-mail:** kidsmin@rhpa.org. **Website:** www.kidsministryideas.com. **Contact:** Editor. **95% freelance written.** "A quarterly resource for children's leaders, those involved in Vacation Bible School and Story Hours, home school teachers, etc., *Kids' Ministry Ideas* provides affirmation, pertinent and informative articles, program ideas, resource suggestions, and answers to questions from a Seventh-day Adventist Christian perspective." Estab. 1991. Circ. 3,000. Byline given. Pays on acceptance. Publishes ms an average of 3 months after acceptance. Editorial lead time 3 months. Submit seasonal material 6 months to 1 year in advance. Accepts queries by mail, e-mail, fax. Responds in 3 weeks to queries. Responds in 3 months to mss. Sample copy free. Writer's guidelines online.

NONFICTION Needs inspirational, new products related to children's ministry, articles fitting the mission of *Kids' Ministry Ideas.* **Buys 40-60 mss/year.** Send complete ms. **Features:** Articles generally cover a 2-page spread and should be no more than 800 words. One-page articles should be 300 words. Queries are welcome. Length: 300-800 words. **Pays $20-100 for assigned articles. Pays $20-70 for unsolicited articles. Writers can expect payment within 5-6 weeks**

of acceptance. **Upon publication, authors are sent 1 complimentary copy of the issue in which their material appears.**

PHOTOS State availability. Captions required.

COLUMNS/DEPARTMENTS Buys 20-30 mss/year. Query. **Pays $20-100.**

TIPS "*Kids' Ministry Ideas* is a resource that is practical. Material needs to provide specific, helpful how-to's for children's leaders. Articles on a wide range of subjects appear in *KMI*, but they generally have 1 thing in common—practical ideas and easy-to-understand instructions that people can implement in their area of ministry. Use of sidebars, boxes, and lists of information is encouraged, as this dilutes copy intensity and makes articles more readable."

LEADERSHIP JOURNAL

Christianity Today International, 465 Gundersen Dr., Carol Stream IL 60188. (630)260-6200. **Fax:** (630)260-0114. **E-mail:** ljeditor@leadershipjournal.net. **Website:** www.leadershipjournal.net. Skye Jethani, managing editor. **Contact:** Marshall Shelley, editor-in-chief. **75% freelance written. Works with a small number of new/unpublished writers each year.** Quarterly magazine. "Writers must have a knowledge of and sympathy for the unique expectations placed on pastors and local church leaders. Each article must support points by illustrating from real life experiences in local churches." Estab. 1980. Circ. 48,000. Byline given. Pays on acceptance. Offers 33% kill fee. Publishes ms an average of 6 months after acceptance. Editorial lead time 6 months. Submit seasonal material 6 months in advance. Accepts queries by mail, e-mail, fax. Responds in 2 weeks to queries. Responds in 2 months to mss. Sample copy for free or online.

NONFICTION Needs how-to, humor, interview, personal experience, sermon illustrations. No articles from writers who have never read our journal. No unsolicited ms. **Buys 60 mss/year.** Query with proposal. Send a brief query letter describing your idea and how you plan to develop it. Length: 300-3,000 words. **Pays $35-400.** Sometimes pays expenses of writers on assignment.

COLUMNS/DEPARTMENTS Contact: Skye Jethanis, managing editor. Toolkit (book/software reviews), 500 words. **Buys 8 mss/year.** Query.

TIPS "Every article in *Leadership* must provide practical help for problems that church leaders face. *Leadership* articles are not essays expounding a topic or editorials arguing a position or homilies explaining Biblical principles. They are how-to articles, based on first-person accounts of real-life experiences in ministry. They allow our readers to see `over the shoulder' of a colleague in ministry who then reflects on those experiences and identifies the lessons learned. As you know, a magazine's slant is a specific personality that readers expect (and it's what they've sent us their subscription money to provide). Our style is that of friendly conversation rather than directive discourse—what I learned about local church ministry rather than what you need to do."

MOMENTUM

National Catholic Educational Association, 1005 N. Glebe Rd., Suite 525, Arlington VA 22201. (571)257-0010. **Fax:** (703)243-0025. **E-mail:** momentum@ncea.org. **Website:** www.ncea.org. **Contact:** Brian E. Gray, editor. **65% freelance written.** Quarterly educational journal covering educational issues in Catholic schools and parishes. *Momentum* is a membership journal of the National Catholic Educational Association. The audience is educators and administrators in Catholic schools K-12, and parish programs. Estab. 1970. Circ. 19,000. Byline given. Pays on publication. No kill fee. Publishes ms an average of 3 months after acceptance. Accepts queries by e-mail. Sample copy for $5 SASE and 8 first-class stamps. Guidelines available online.

NONFICTION No articles unrelated to educational and catechesis issues. **Buys 40-60 mss/year.** Query and send complete ms. Length: 1,500 words for feature articles; 3,500-5,000 for research articles; 500-750 words for book reviews. **Pays $75 maximum.**

PHOTOS State availability of photos. Captions, identification of subjects required. Reviews prints. Offers no additional payment for photos accepted with ms.

COLUMNS/DEPARTMENTS : From the Field (practical application in classroom); DRE Directions (parish catechesis), both 700 words. **Buys 10 mss/year.** Query and send complete ms. **Pays $50.**

THE PRIEST

Our Sunday Visitor, Inc., 200 Noll Plaza, Huntington IN 46750. (800)348-2440. **Fax:** (260)359-9117. **E-mail:** tpriest@osv.com. **Website:** www.osv.com. **Contact:** Editorial Department. **40% freelance written.** Monthly magazine. Byline given. Pays on acceptance. No kill fee. Editorial lead time 3 months. Submit seasonal material 4 months in advance. Accepts queries by mail, e-mail, fax, phone. Responds in 5 weeks to queries. Responds in 3 months to mss. Sample copy free. Guidelines on website.

NONFICTION Needs essays, historical/nostalgic, humor, inspirational, interview/profile, opinion, personal experience, photo feature, religious. **Buys 96 mss/year.** Send complete ms. Length: 1,500 words maximum. **Pays $200 minimum for assigned articles. Pays $50 minimum for unsolicited articles.**

PHOTOS Send photos. Captions, identification of subjects required. Reviews prints. Negotiates payment individually.

COLUMNS/DEPARTMENTS Viewpoints (whatever applies to priests and the Church): 1,000 words or less; send complete ms.

TIPS "Please do not stray from the magisterium of the Catholic Church."

$ RTJ'S CREATIVE CATECHIST

Twenty-Third Publications, P.O. Box 6015, New London CT 06320. (800)321-0411, ext. 188. **Fax:** (860)437-6246. **E-mail:** creativesubs@rtjscreativecatechist.com; rosanne.coffey@bayard-inc.com. **Website:** www.rtjscreativecatechist.com. **Contact:** Rosanne Coffey, editor. Monthly magazine for Catholic catechists and religion teachers. Estab. 1966. Circ. 30,000. Byline given. Pays on acceptance. Publishes ms an average of 3-20 months after acceptance. Editorial lead time 4 months. Submit seasonal material 6 months in advance. Accepts queries by mail, e-mail. Accepts simultaneous submissions. Responds in 1-2 weeks to queries. Responds in 1-2 months to mss. Sample copy for SAE with 9x12 envelope and 3 first-class stamps. Guidelines free.

NONFICTION Needs how-to, inspirational, personal experience, religious, articles on celebrating church seasons, sacraments, on morality, on prayer, on saints. Special issues: Sacraments; Prayer; Advent/Christmas; Lent/Easter. All should be written by people who have experience in religious education, or a good background in Catholic faith. Does not want fiction, poems, plays, articles written for Catholic school teachers (i.e., math, English, etc.), or articles that are academic rather than catechetical in nature. **Buys 35-40 mss/year.** Send complete ms. Length: 600-1,300 words. **Pays $100-125 for assigned articles. Pays $75-125 for unsolicited articles.**

COLUMNS/DEPARTMENTS Catechist to Catechist (brief articles on crafts, games, etc., for religion lessons); Faith and Fun (full-page religious word games, puzzles, mazes, etc., for children). **Buys 30 mss/year.** Send complete ms. **Pays $20-125.**

TIPS "We look for clear, concise articles written from experience. Articles should help readers move from theory/doctrine to concrete application. Unsolicited mss not returned without SASE. No fancy formatting; no handwritten mss. Author should be able to furnish article on disk or via e-mail if possible."

$$$ WORSHIP LEADER MAGAZINE

32234 Paseo Adelanto, Suite A, San Juan Capistrano CA 92675. (888)881-5861. **Fax:** (949)240-0038. **Website:** www.worshipleader.com. **Contact:** Jeremy Armstrong, managing editor. **80% freelance written.** Bimonthly magazine covering all aspects of Christian worship. "*Worship Leader Magazine* exists to challenge, serve, equip, and train those involved in leading the 21st century church in worship. The intended readership is the worship team (all those who plan and lead) of the local church." Estab. 1990. Circ. 40,000. Byline given. Pays on publication. Offers 50% kill fee. Editorial lead time 3 months. Submit seasonal material 6 months in advance. Accepts queries by online submission form. Responds in 6 weeks to queries. Responds in 3 months to mss. Sample copy for $5.

NONFICTION Needs general interest, how-to, related to purpose/audience, inspirational, interview, opinion. **Buys 15-30 mss/year.** "Unsolicited articles are only accepted for the web and should be between 700 and 900 words. Web articles are published on a gratis basis and are often the first step in creating a relationship with us and our readers, which could lead to more involvement as a writer." Length: 1,200-2,000 words for print version articles. **Pays $200-800 for assigned articles. Pays $200-500 for unsolicited articles.** Sometimes pays expenses of writers on assignment.

PHOTOS State availability. Identification of subjects required. Negotiate payment individually.

FICTION "You can also submit a song; see www.songdiscovery.com/submit-a-song."

TIPS "Our goal has been and is to provide the tools and information pastors, worship leaders, and ministers of music, youth, and the arts need to facilitate and enhance worship in their churches. In achieving this goal, we strive to maintain high journalistic standards, Biblical soundness, and theological neutrality. Our intent is to present the philosophical, scholarly insight on worship, as well as the day-to-day, 'putting it all together' side of worship, while celebrating our unity and diversity."

$$ YOUTHWORKER JOURNAL

Salem Publishing/CCM Communications, 402 BNA Dr., Suite 400, Nashville TN 37217-2509. **E-mail:** articles@youthworker.com. **E-mail:** ALee@SalemPublishing.com. **Website:** www.youthworker.com. **Contact:** Steve Rabey, editor; Amy L. Lee, managing editor. **100% freelance written.** Website and bimonthly magazine covering professional youth ministry in the church and parachurch. "We exist to help meet the personal and professional needs of career, Christian youth workers in the church and parachurch. Proposals accepted on the posted theme, according to the writer's guidelines on our website. It's not enough to write well—you must know youth ministry." Estab. 1984. Circ. 20,000. Byline given. Pays on publication. No kill fee. Publishes ms an average of 3 months after acceptance for print; immediately online. Editorial lead time 6 months for print; immediately online. Submit seasonal material 6 months in advance for print. Accepts queries by e-mail, online submission form. Responds within 6 weeks to queries. Sample copy for $5. Guidelines available online.

NONFICTION Needs essays, new product, youth ministry books only, personal experience, photo feature, religious. Query. Length: 250-3,000 words. **Pays $15-200.**

PHOTOS Send photos. Reviews GIF/JPEG files. Negotiates payment individually.

CLOTHING

$$$ FOOTWEAR PLUS

9 Threads, 36 Cooper Square, 4th Floor, New York NY 10003. (646)278-1550. **Fax:** (646)278-1553. **Website:** www.footwearplusmagazine.com. **20% freelance written.** Monthly magazine covering footwear fashion and business. "A business-to-business publication targeted at footwear retailers. Covering all categories of footwear and age ranges with a focus on new trends, brands and consumer buying habits, as well as retailer advice on operating the store more effectively." Estab. 1990. Circ. 18,000. Byline given. Pays on publication. No kill fee. Publishes ms an average of 1-2 months after acceptance. Editorial lead time 1-2 months. Sample copy for $5.

NONFICTION Needs interview, new product, technical. Does not want pieces unrelated to footwear/fashion industry. **Buys 10-20 mss/year.** Query. Length: 500-2,500 words. **Pays $1,000 maximum.** Sometimes pays expenses of writers on assignment.

$$ TEXTILE WORLD

Billian Publishing Co., 2100 RiverEdge Pkwy., Suite 1200, Atlanta GA 30328. (770)955-5656. **Fax:** (770)952-0669. **E-mail:** editor@textileworld.com. **Website:** www.textileworld.com. **Contact:** James Borneman, editor-in-chief. **5% freelance written.** Bimonthly magazine covering the business of textile, apparel, and fiber industries with considerable technical focus on products and processes. Estab. 1868. Byline given. Pays on publication. No kill fee.

NONFICTION Needs business, technical. No puff pieces pushing a particular product. **Buys 10 mss/year.** Query. Length: 500 words minimum. **Pays $200/published page.**

PHOTOS Send photos. Captions required. Reviews prints. Offers no additional payment for photos accepted with ms.

CONSTRUCTION AND CONTRACTING

$$ AUTOMATED BUILDER

CMN Associates, Inc., 2401 Grapevine Dr., Oxnard CA 93036. (805)351-5931. **Fax:** (805)351-5755. **E-mail:** cms03@pacbell.net. **Website:** www.automatedbuilder.com. **Contact:** Don O. Carlson, editor/publisher. **5% freelance written.** "*Automated Builder* provides management, production and marketing information on all 7 segments of home, apartment and commercial construction. These include: (1) production (site) builders, (2) panelized home manufacturers, (3) HUD-code (mobile) home manufacturers, (4) modular home manufacturers, (5) component manufacturers, (6) special unit (commercial) manufacturers, and (7) all types of builders and builders/dealers. The in-plant material is technical in content and covers new machine technologies and improved methods for in-plant building. Home and commercial buys will see the latest in homes and commercial structures." Estab. 1964. Circ. 75,000 when printed. Byline given if desired. Pays on acceptance. Publishes ms an average of 2 months after acceptance. Editorial lead time 2 months. Submit seasonal material 2 months in advance. Accepts queries by mail, e-mail, fax. Responds in 2 weeks to queries.

NONFICTION "No planned 'dreams.' Housing projects must be built or under construction. Same for commercial structures" **Buys 6-8 mss/year.** Phone queries OK. Length: 500-750 words. **Pays $250 for stories including photos.**

PHOTOS Captions are required for each photo. Offers no additional payment for photos accepted with ms. Payment is on acceptance.

TIPS "Stories often are too long, too loose; we prefer 500-750 words plus captions. We prefer a phone query on feature articles. If accepted on query, articles will not usually be rejected later. It is required that every story and photos are cleared with the source before sending to *Automated Builder*."

🌑🌑 BUILDERNEWS MAGAZINE

PNW Publishing, BUILDERnews Magazine, 2105 C St., Vancouver WA 98663, (360)906-0793; (800)401-0696. **Fax:** (360)906-0794. **E-mail:** editing@bnmag.com. **Website:** www.bnmag.com. Estab. 1996. Circ. 35,000. Byline given. Pays on acceptance of revised ms. No kill fee. Publishes ms an average of 1 month after acceptance. Editorial lead time 2 months. Submit seasonal material 3 months in advance. Accepts queries by mail, e-mail, fax. Responds in 1 week to queries. Responds in 1 month to mss. Sample copy for free or online. Guidelines free.

NONFICTION Needs how-to, interview, new product, technical. "No personal bios, unless they teach a valuable lesson to those in the building industry." **Buys 400 mss/year.** Query. Length: 500-2,500 words. **Pays $200-500.** Sometimes pays expenses of writers on assignment.

PHOTOS State availability. Captions, identification of subjects, model releases required. Offers no additional payment for photos accepted with ms.

COLUMNS/DEPARTMENTS Engineering; Construction; Architecture & Design; Tools & Materials; Heavy Equipment; Business & Economics; Legal Matters; E-build; Building Green; all 750-2,500 words. Query.

TIPS "Writers should have an understanding of the residential building industry and its terminology and be prepared to provide a résumé, writing samples, and story synopsis."

🌑🌑🌑 THE CONCRETE PRODUCER

Hanley-Wood, LLC, 8725 W. Higgins Rd., Suite 600, Chicago IL 60631. (773)824-2400; (773)824-2496. **E-mail:** smitchell@hanleywood.com; ryelton@hanleywood.com. **Website:** www.theconcreteproducer.com. **Contact:** Shelby O. Mitchell, editor; Richard Yelton, editor-at-large. **25% freelance written.** Monthly magazine covering concrete production. "Our audience consists of producers who have succeeded in making concrete the preferred building material through management, operating, quality control, use of the latest technology, or use of superior materials." Estab. 1982. Circ. 18,000. Byline given. Pays on acceptance. No kill fee. Publishes ms an average of 2 months after acceptance. Editorial lead time 4 months. Accepts queries by mail, e-mail, fax, phone. Responds in 1 week to queries. Responds in 2 months to mss. Sample copy for $4. Guidelines free.

NONFICTION Needs how-to, promote concrete, new product, technical. **Buys 10 mss/year.** Send complete ms. Length: 500-2,000 words. **Pays $200-1,000.** Sometimes pays expenses of writers on assignment.

PHOTOS Scan photos at 300 dpi. State availability. Captions, identification of subjects required. Reviews transparencies, prints. Offers no additional payment for photos accepted with ms.

🌑 HARD HAT NEWS

Lee Publications, Inc., 6113 State Hwy. 5, P.O. Box 121, Palatine Bridge NY 13428. (518)673-3237. **Fax:** (518)673-2381. **E-mail:** jcasey@leepub.com. **Website:** www.hardhat.com. **Contact:** Jon Casey, editor. **50% freelance written.** Biweekly tabloid covering heavy construction, equipment, road, and bridge work. "Our readers are contractors and heavy construction workers involved in excavation, highways, bridges, utility construction, and underground construction." Estab. 1980. Circ. 15,000. Byline given. No kill fee. Editorial lead time 2 weeks. Submit seasonal material 2 weeks in advance. Accepts queries by mail, e-mail, fax, phone. Sample copy and writer's guidelines free.

NONFICTION Needs interview, new product, opinion, photo feature, technical. Send complete ms. Length: 800-2,000 words. **Pays $2.50/inch.** Sometimes pays expenses of writers on assignment.

PHOTOS Send photos. Captions, identification of subjects required. Reviews prints, digital preferred. Offers $15/photo.

COLUMNS/DEPARTMENTS Association News; Parts and Repairs; Attachments; Trucks and Trailers; People on the Move.

TIPS "Every issue has a focus—see our editorial calendar. Special consideration is given to a story that coincides with the focus. A color photo is necessary for the front page. Vertical shots work best. We need more writers in metro New York area. Also, we are expanding our distribution into the Mid-Atlantic states and need writers in New York, Massachusetts, Vermont, Connecticut, and New Hampshire."

HOME ENERGY MAGAZINE

Home Energy Magazine, 1250 Addison St., Suite 211B, Berkeley CA 94702. (510)524-5405. **Fax:** (510)981-1406. **E-mail:** contact@homeenergy.org. **Website:** www.homeenergy.org. Alan Meier, senior executive editor. **Contact:** Jim Gunshinan, managing editor. **10% freelance written.** Bimonthly magazine covering green home building and renovation. Estab. 1984. Circ. 5,000. Byline given. Pays on publication. Offers 10% kill fee. Publishes ms an average of 4 months after acceptance. Editorial lead time 4 months. Accepts queries by e-mail. Responds in 2 weeks to queries. Responds in 2 months to mss. Guidelines by e-mail.

NONFICTION Needs interview, technical. "We do not want articles for consumers/general public." **Buys 6 mss/year.** Query with published clips. Length: 900-3,500 words. **Pays 20¢/word; $400 maximum for assigned articles. Pays 20¢/word; $400 maximum for unsolicited articles.**

INTERIOR CONSTRUCTION

Ceilings & Interior Systems Construction Association, 1010 Jorie Blvd., Suite 30, Oak Brook IL 60523. (630)584-1919. **Fax:** (630)584-2003. **E-mail:** rmgi@comcast.net; cisca@cisca.org. **Website:** www.cisca.org. **Contact:** Rick Reuland, managing editor. Quarterly magazine on acoustics and commercial specialty ceiling construction. Estab. 1950. Circ. 3,000. Byline given. Pays on publication. No kill fee. Publishes ms an average of 1 1/2 months after acceptance. Editorial lead time 2-3 months. Accepts queries by e-mail. Sample copy by e-mail. Guidelines available.

NONFICTION Needs new product, technical. Query with published clips. Publishes 1-2 features per issue. Length: 700-1,700 words. **Pays $400 minimum, $800 maximum for assigned articles.**

KEYSTONE BUILDER MAGAZINE

Pennsylvania Builders Association, 600 N. 12th St., Lemoyne PA 17043. (717)730-4380; 800-692-7339. **Fax:** (717)730-4396. **E-mail:** admin@pabuilders.org; metshied@pabuilders.org. **Website:** www.pabuilders.org. **10% freelance written.** Bimonthly trade publication for builders, remodelers, subcontractors, and other affiliates of the home building industry in Pennsylvania. Estab. 1988. Circ. 9,300. Byline given. Pays on publication. No kill fee. Publishes ms an average of 1 year after acceptance. Editorial lead time 3 months. Submit seasonal material 9 months in advance. Accepts queries by mail, e-mail. Accepts simultaneous submissions. Responds in 2 weeks to queries. Responds in 3 months to mss. Sample copy free. Guidelines by e-mail.

NONFICTION Needs general interest, how-to, new product, technical. No personnel or company profiles. **Buys 1-2 mss/year.** Send complete ms. Length: 200-500 words. **Pays $200.**

PHOTOS Send photos. Captions, identification of subjects required. Reviews digital images. Negotiates payment individually.

METAL ROOFING MAGAZINE

a Division of F+W Media, Inc., 700 E. Iola St., Iola WI 54990-0001. (715)445-4612, ext. 13281. **Fax:** (715)445-4087. **E-mail:** jim.austin@fwmedia.com. **Website:** www.metalroofingmag.com. **Contact:** Jim Austin, editor. **10% freelance written.** Bimonthly magazine covering roofing. *Metal Roofing Magazine* offers contractors, designers, suppliers, architects, and others in the construction industry a wealth of information on metal roofing—a growing segment of the roofing trade. Estab. 2000. Circ. 26,000. Byline given. Pays on publication. Publishes ms an average of 3 months after acceptance. Editorial lead time 3 months. Submit seasonal material 3 months in advance. Accepts queries by mail. Accepts simultaneous submissions. Sample copy free.

NONFICTION Needs book excerpts, historical, how-to, interview, new product, opinion, photo feature, technical. No advertorials. **Buys 15 mss/year.** Query with published clips. Length: 750 words minimum. **Pays $100-500 for assigned articles.**

PHOTOS Send photos. Captions, identification of subjects required. Reviews GIF/JPEG files. Negotiates payment individually.

COLUMNS/DEPARTMENTS Gutter Opportunities; Stay Cool; Metal Roofing Details; Spec It. **Buys 15 mss/year.** Send complete ms. **Pays $0-500.**

TIPS "Read our magazine online for a sense of our typical subject matter and audience. Contact by regular mail is best."

🌐 $ $ NETCOMPOSITES

4a Broom Business Park, Bridge Way Chesterfield S41 9QG UK. **E-mail:** info@netcomposites.com. **Website:** www.netcomposites.com. **1% freelance written.** Bimonthly newsletter covering advanced materials and fiber-reinforced polymer composites, plus a weekly electronic version called *Composite eNews*, reaching over 15,000 subscribers and many more pass-along readers. *Advanced Materials & Composites News* covers markets, applications, materials, processes, and organizations for all sectors of the global hi-tech materials world. Audience is management, academics, researchers, government, suppliers, and fabricators. Focus on news about growth opportunities. Estab. 1978. Circ. 15,000+. Byline sometimes given. Pays on publication. No kill fee. Publishes ms an average of 1 month after acceptance. Editorial lead time 2 weeks. Submit seasonal material 1 month in advance. Accepts queries by e-mail. Responds in 1 week to queries. Responds in 1 month to mss. Sample copy for #10 SASE.

NONFICTION Needs new product, technical, industry information. **Buys 4-6 mss/year.** Query. 300 words. **Pays $200/final printed page.**

PHOTOS State availability. Captions, identification of subjects, model releases required. Reviews 4x5 transparencies, prints, 35mm slides, JPEGs (much preferred). Offers no additional payment for photos accepted with ms.

$ $ POB MAGAZINE

BNP Media, 2401 W. Big Beaver Rd., Suite 700, Troy MI 48084. (248)362-3700. **E-mail:** pobeditor@bnpmedia.com. **Website:** www.pobonline.com. **Contact:** Christine Grahl. **5% freelance written,.** Monthly magazine covering surveying, mapping, and geomatics. Estab. 1975. Circ. 39,000. Byline given. Pays on publication. Publishes ms an average of 3 months after acceptance. Editorial lead time 3 months. Accepts queries by e-mail, phone. Sample copy and guidelines available online.

NONFICTION "Query. Please ensure the document is saved in MS-Word or text-only format. Please also include an author byline and biography." Length: 1,700-2,200 words, with 2 graphics included. **Pays $400.**

PHOTOS State availability. Captions, identification of subjects required. Reviews GIF/JPEG files. Offers no additional payment for photos accepted with ms.

TIPS "Authors must know our profession and industry."

$ $ UNDERGROUND CONSTRUCTION

Oildom Publishing Company of Texas, Inc., P.O. Box 941669, Houston TX 77094-8669. (281)558-6930, ext. 220. **Fax:** (281)558-7029. **E-mail:** rcarpenter@oildom.com; oklinger@oildom.com. **Website:** www.undergroundconstructionmagazine.com. **Contact:** Robert Carpenter, editor; Oliver Klinger, publisher. **35% freelance written.** Monthly magazine covering underground oil and gas pipeline, water and sewer pipeline, cable construction for contractors, and owning companies. Circ. 38,000. No kill fee. Publishes ms an average of 6 months after acceptance. Accepts queries by mail, e-mail, fax, phone. Responds in 1 month to mss. Sample copy for SAE.

NONFICTION Needs how-to, , job stories and industry issues. Query with published clips. Length: 1,000-2,000 words. **Pays $3-500.** Sometimes pays expenses of writers on assignment.

PHOTOS Send photos. Captions required. Reviews color prints and slides.

DRUGS, HEALTH CARE AND MEDICAL PRODUCTS

AMERICAN MEDICAL NEWS

American Medical Association, 515 N. State St., Chicago IL 60654. (312)464-4432. **Fax:** (312)464-4445. **E-mail:** bmindell@amednews.com; jcapaldi@amednews.com; jwenger@amednews.com. **Website:** www.amednews.com. **Contact:** Ben Mindell, editor; Jef Capaldi, art director; Jennifer Wenger, assistant art director. Primarily covers the business and political side of medical current events. "*American Medical News* is the nation's most widely circulated newspaper focusing on socioeconomic issues in medicine." Estab.

1958. Circ. 375,000. Pays on publication. Responds in 1 month to queries. Guidelines for #10 SASE.

NONFICTION Needs physician-oriented features reporting developments that affect the practice of medicine, 20-25. Query with SASE. Length: 1,500-2,000 words.

⚓ AUSTRALIAN HEALTH REVIEW

CSIRO Publishing, 150 Oxford St., Collingwood VIC 3066 Australia. (61)(2)9562-6640. **Fax:** (61)(2)9562-6699. **E-mail:** publishing.ahr@csiro.au. **Website:** www.publish.csiro.au/journals/ahr. Quarterly magazine for the Australian Healthcare and Hospitals Association. "*AHR* provides information for decision makers in the health care industry and is read by health care professionals, managers, planners, and policy makers throughout Australia and the region." Byline given. Guidelines available online.

NONFICTION Needs opinion, feature articles, research notes, case studies, book reviews, editorials. Send complete ms. Length: 500-5,000 words.

PHOTOS Send photos. Offers no additional payment for photos accepted with ms.

💲💲 LABTALK

LabTalk, P.O. Box 1945, Big Bear Lake CA 92315. (909)547-2234. **E-mail:** cwalker@jobson.com. **Website:** www.LabTalkOnline.com. **Contact:** Christie Walker, editor. **20% freelance written.** Magazine published 6 times/year for the eye wear industry. Estab. 1970. Accepts simultaneous submissions.

TIPS "Write for the optical laboratory owner and manager."

💲💲💲 VALIDATION TIMES

Washington Information Source Co., 19-B Wirt St. SW, Leesburg VA 20175. (703)779-8777. **Fax:** (703)779-2508. **E-mail:** kreid@fdainfo.com. **Website:** www.fdainfo.com. **Contact:** Ken Reid. Monthly newsletters covering regulation of pharmaceutical and medical devices. "We write to executives who have to keep up on changing FDA policies and regulations, and on what their competitors are doing at the agency." Estab. 1999. Byline given. Pays on publication. No kill fee. Publishes ms an average of 1 month after acceptance. Editorial lead time 1 month. Submit seasonal material 1 month in advance. Accepts queries by mail. Responds in 1 month to queries. Sample copy and writer's guidelines free.

NONFICTION Needs how-to, technical, regulatory. No lay interest pieces. **Buys 50-100 mss/year.** Query. Length: 600-1,500 words. **Pays $100/half day; $200 full day to cover meetings and same rate for writing.** Sometimes pays expenses of writers on assignment.

TIPS "If you're covering a conference for non-competing publications, call me with a drug or device regulatory angle."

EDUCATION AND COUNSELING

💲 ARTS & ACTIVITIES

Publishers' Development Corp., 12345 World Trade Dr., San Diego CA 92128. (858)605-0242. **Fax:** (858)605-0247. **E-mail:** ed@artsandactivities.com. **Website:** www.artsandactivities.com. **Contact:** Maryellen Bridge, editor-in-chief. **95% freelance written. Eager to work with new/unpublished writers.** Monthly (except July and August) magazine covering art education at levels from preschool through college for educators and therapists engaged in arts and crafts education and training. Estab. 1932. Circ. 20,000. Byline given. Pays on publication. No kill fee. Publishes ms 6 months to 3 years after acceptance. Submit seasonal material 6 months in advance. Accepts queries by mail, e-mail. Responds in 3 months to queries. Sample copy for SAE with 9x12 envelope and 8 first-class stamps. Guidelines available on website.

NONFICTION Needs historical, arts, activities, history, how-to, classroom art experiences, artists' techniques, interviews of artists, opinion on arts activities curriculum, ideas of how-to do things better, philosophy of art education, personal experience (ties in with the how-to) articles of exceptional art programs. **Buys 80-100 mss/year.** Length: 500-1,500 words. **Pays $35-150.**

TIPS "Frequently in unsolicited mss, writers obviously have not studied the magazine to see what style of articles we publish. Send for a sample copy to familiarize yourself with our style and needs. The best way to find out if his/her writing style suits our needs is for the author to submit a ms on speculation. We prefer an anecdotal style of writing so that readers will feel as though they are there in the art room as the lesson/project is taking place. Also, good quality photographs of student artwork are important. We are a visual art magazine!"

☼ ⑤ THE ATA MAGAZINE

11010 142nd St. NW, Edmonton AB T5N 2R1 Canada. (780)447-9400. **Fax:** (780)455-6481. **E-mail:** government@teachers.ab.ca. **Website:** www.teachers.ab.ca. Quarterly magazine covering education. Estab. 1920. Circ. 42,100. Byline given. Pays on publication. No kill fee. Publishes ms an average of 4 months after acceptance. Editorial lead time 2 months. Submit seasonal material 2 months in advance. Accepts queries by mail, e-mail, fax, phone. Accepts simultaneous submissions. Responds in 2 months to queries. Sample copy free. Guidelines available online.

NONFICTION Query with published clips. Length: 500-1,500 words. **Pays $75 (Canadian).**

PHOTOS Send photos. Captions required. Reviews 4x6 prints. Negotiates payment individually.

● AUSTRALASIAN JOURNAL OF EARLY CHILDHOOD

Early Childhood Australia, P.O. Box 86, Deakin West ACT 2600 Australia. (61)(2)6242-1800. **Fax:** (61)(2)6242-1818. **E-mail:** publishing@earlychildhood.org.au. **Website:** www.earlychildhoodaustralia.org.au. **Contact:** Chris Jones, publishing manager. Nonprofit early childhood advocacy organization, acting in the interests of young children aged from birth to 8 years of age, their families and those in the early childhood field. Specialist publisher of early childhood magazines, journals, and booklets. Guidelines available online.

NONFICTION Needs essays. Send complete ms. Length: Magazine articles, 600-1,000 words; research-based papers, 3,000-6,500 words; submissions for booklets, approximately 5,000 words.

COLLEGEXPRESS MAGAZINE

Carnegie Communications, LLC, 2 LAN Dr., Suite 100, Westford MA 01886. **E-mail:** info@carnegiecomm.com. **Website:** www.collegexpress.com. "*CollegeXpress Magazine,* formerly *Careers and Colleges,* provides juniors and seniors in high school with editorial, tips, trends, and websites to assist them in the transition to college, career, young adulthood, and independence." Byline given. Pays on acceptance plus 45 days. Accepts queries by mail, e-mail. Responds to queries in 6 weeks. Contributor's guidelines available electronically.

NONFICTION Needs Young adults/teens: careers, college, health, how-to, humorous, interview/profile, personal development, problem-solving, social issues, sports, travel. **Buys 10-20 mss/year.** Query. Length: 1,000-1,500 words.

TIPS "Articles with great quotes, good reporting, good writing. Rich with examples and anecdotes. Must tie in with the objective to help teenaged readers plan for their futures. Current trends, policy changes and information regarding college admissions, financial aid, and career opportunities."

⑤ THE FORENSIC TEACHER

Wide Open Minds Educational Services, P.O. Box 5263, Wilmington DE 19808. **E-mail:** admin@theforensicteacher.com. **Website:** www.theforensicteacher.com. **Contact:** Mark R. Feil, editor. **70% freelance written.** Quarterly magazine covering forensic education. "Our readers are middle, high and postsecondary teachers who are looking for better, easier and more engaging ways to teach forensics as well as law enforcement and scientific forensic experts. Our writers understand this and are writing from a forensic or educational background, or both. Prefer a first person writing style." Estab. 2006. Circ. 30,000. Byline given. Pays 60 days after publication. No kill fee. Publishes ms an average of 6 months after acceptance. Editorial lead time 6 months. Submit seasonal material 6 months in advance. Accepts queries by mail, e-mail. Accepts simultaneous submissions. Responds in 2 weeks to queries; 2 months to mss. Sample copy for $5. Guidelines available online.

NONFICTION Needs how-to, personal experience, photo feature, technical, lesson plans. Does not want poetry, fiction or anything unrelated to medicine, law, forensics or teaching. **Buys 18 mss/year.** Send complete ms. Length: 400-2,000 words. **Pays 2¢/word.**

PHOTOS State availability. Captions required. Reviews GIF/JPEG files/pdf. Send photos separately in e-mail, not in the article. Negotiates payment individually.

COLUMNS/DEPARTMENTS Needs lesson experiences or ideas, personal or professional experiences with a branch of forensics. "If you've done it in your classroom please share it with us. Also, if you're a professional, please tell our readers how they can duplicate the lesson/demo/experiment in their classrooms. Please share what you know."

FILLERS Needs : facts, newsbreaks. **Buys 15 fillers/year. mss/year.** Length: 50-200 words. **Pays 2¢/word.**

TIPS "Your article will benefit forensics teachers and their students. It should inform, entertain and enlighten the teacher and the students. Would you read it if you were a busy forensics teacher?"

$$ THE HISPANIC OUTLOOK IN HIGHER EDUCATION

80 Route 4 E., Suite 203, Paramus NJ 07652. (201)587-8800, ext. 100. **Fax:** (201)587-9105. **Website:** www.hispanicoutlook.com. **50% freelance written.** Biweekly magazine (except in summer) covering higher education of Hispanics. "We're looking for higher education story articles, with a focus on Hispanics and the advancements made by and for Hispanics in higher education." Circ. 28,000. Byline given. Pays on publication. No kill fee. Publishes ms an average of 2 months after acceptance. Editorial lead time 2 months. Submit seasonal material 3 months in advance. Accepts queries by mail, e-mail, fax. Accepts simultaneous submissions. Sample copy free.

NONFICTION Needs historical, interview of academic or scholar, opinion on higher education, personal experience egarding higher education only. **Buys 20-25 mss/year.** Query with published clips. Length: 1,800-2,200 words. **Pays $100 minimum for print articles, and $300 for online articles when accepted.** Pays expenses of writers on assignment.

PHOTOS Send photos. Reviews color or b&w prints, digital images must be 300 dpi (call for e-mail photo address). Offers no additional payment for photos accepted with ms.

TIPS "Articles explore the Hispanic experience in higher education. Special theme issues address sports, law, health, corporations, heritage, women, and a wide range of similar issues; however, articles need not fall under those umbrellas."

$$ PTO TODAY

PTO Today, Inc., 100 Stonewall Blvd., Suite 3, Wrentham MA 02093. (800)644-3561. **Fax:** (508)384-6108. **E-mail:** editor@ptotoday.com. **Website:** www.ptotoday.com. **Contact:** Craig Bystrynski, editor-in-chief. **50% freelance written.** Magazine published 6 times during the school year covering the work of school parent-teacher groups. "We celebrate the work of school parent volunteers and provide resources to help them do that work more effectively." Estab. 1999. Circ. 80,000. Byline given. Pays on acceptance. Offers 30% kill fee. Publishes ms an average of 4-6 months after acceptance. Editorial lead time 4 months. Submit seasonal material 4 months in advance. Accepts queries by e-mail. Guidelines by e-mail.

NONFICTION Needs general interest, how-to, interview, personal experience. **Buys 20 mss/year.** Query. "We review but do not encourage unsolicited submissions." Features are roughly 1,200-2,200 words. Average assignment is 1,200 words. Department pieces are 600-1,200 words. **Payment depends on the difficulty of the topic and the experience of the writer. "We pay by the assignment, not by the word; our pay scale ranges from $200 to $700 for features and $150 to $400 for departments. We occasionally pay more for high-impact stories and highly experienced writers. We buy all rights, and we pay on acceptance (within 30 days of invoice)."** Sometimes pays expenses of writers on assignment.

PHOTOS State availability. Identification of subjects required. Negotiates payment individually.

TIPS "It's difficult for us to find talented writers with strong experience with parent groups. This experience is a big plus. Also, it helps to review our writer's guidelines before querying. All queries must have a strong parent group angle."

READING TODAY

800 Barksdale Rd., P.O. Box 8139, Newark DE 19714-8139. (800)336-7323. **Fax:** (302)731-1057. **E-mail:** readingtoday@reading.org. **Website:** www.reading.org. Bimonthly magazine covering teaching literacy, children's and young adult's literature, and reading education. *Reading Today* is the membership magazine of the International Reading Association (IRA). Emphasizes reading education. Readers are educators who belong to the IRA. Estab. 1983. Circ. 70,000. Byline given. Pays on acceptance. Responds in 1 month. Simultaneous submissions and previously published work OK. Sample copy and guidelines online.

NONFICTION Send complete mss. "Use the IRA Style Guide at www.reading.org/styleguide.aspx. Consider inserting short section headers every 3 or 4 paragraphs. Include captions for photos. You can include references, but keep them to a minimum (this is a magazine, not a journal). Include a short bio: 'Name is position at organization, email@email.com.'" Length: 300-1,500 words.

$ SCHOOLARTS MAGAZINE

Davis Art, Production Department, Attn: Article Submissions, 50 Portland St., Worcester MA 01608. **E-mail:** nwalkup@davisart.com. **Website:** www.davisart.com. **Contact:** Nancy Walkup, editor. **85% freelance written.** Monthly magazine (August/September-May/June), serving arts and craft education profession, K-12, higher education, and museum education programs written by and for art teachers. Estab. 1901. Pays on publication (honorarium and 4 copies). No kill fee. Publishes ms an average of 24 months after acceptance. Accepts queries by mail. Responds in 1-2 months to queries. Guidelines available online. **NONFICTION** Query or send complete ms and SASE. Mail a CD containing article's text and photographs, along with signed permission forms (online under Guidelines). No e-mail submissions. Length: 600-1,400 words. **Pays $30-150.**

TIPS "We prefer articles on actual art projects or techniques done by students in actual classroom situations. Philosophical and theoretical aspects of art and art education are usually handled by our contributing editors. Our articles are reviewed and accepted on merit and each is tailored to meet our needs. Keep in mind that art teachers want practical tips above all—more hands-on information than academic theory. Write your article with the accompanying photographs in hand. The most frequent mistakes made by writers are bad visual material (photographs, drawings) submitted with articles, a lack of complete descriptions of art processes, and no rationale behind programs or activities. Familiarity with the field of art education is essential. Review recent issues of *SchoolArts*."

TEACHERS & WRITERS MAGAZINE

Teachers & Writers Collaborative, 520 Eighth Ave., Suite 2020, New York NY 10018. (212)691-6590. **Fax:** (212)675-0171. **E-mail:** editors@twc.org. **Website:** www.twc.org/magazine. **75% freelance written.** Quarterly magazine covering how to teach creative writing (kindergarten through university). *"Teachers & Writers Magazine* covers a cross-section of contemporary issues and innovations in education and writing, and engages writers, educators, critics, and students in a conversation on the nature of creativity and the imagination." Estab. 1967. Circ. 5,000. Byline given. Pays on publication. No kill fee. Publishes ms an average of 4-6 months after acceptance. Editorial lead time 4 months. Submit seasonal material 4-6 months in advance. Accepts queries by e-mail, as an attachment (preferred). Accepts simultaneous submissions. Responds in 4-8 weeks to queries. Responds in 3-6 months to mss. Sample copy for $5. Guidelines by e-mail.

NONFICTION Needs book excerpts, on creative writing education, essays, interview, opinion, personal experience, creative writing exercises. Length: 500-2,500 words.

TEACHERS OF VISION

A Publication of Christian Educators Association, 227 N. Magnolia Ave., Suite 2, Anaheim CA 92801. (714)761-1476. **E-mail:** TOV@ceai.org. **Website:** www.ceai.org. **70% freelance written.** Magazine published 4 times/year for Christians in public education. *"Teachers of Vision*'s articles inspire, inform, and equip teachers and administrators in the educational arena. Readers look for teacher tips, integrating faith and work, and general interest education articles. Topics include subject matter, religious expression and activity in public schools, and legal rights of Christian educators. Our audience is primarily public school educators. Other readers include teachers in private schools, university professors, school administrators, parents, and school board members." Estab. 1953. Circ. 10,000. Byline given. Pays on publication. No kill fee. Publishes ms an average of 6 months after acceptance. Editorial lead time 4 months. Submit seasonal material 4 months in advance. Accepts queries by mail, e-mail. Accepts simultaneous submissions. Responds in 1 month to queries; 3-4 months to mss. Sample copy for SAE with 9x12 envelope and 4 first-class stamps. Guidelines available online.

NONFICTION Needs how-to, humor, inspirational, interview, opinion, personal experience, religious. No preaching. **Buys 50-60 mss/year.** Query or send complete ms if 2,000 words or less. Length: 1,500 words. **Pays $40-50.**

REPRINTS Buys reprints.

PHOTOS State availability of photos. Offers no additional payment for photos accepted with ms.

COLUMNS/DEPARTMENTS Query. **Pays $10-40.**

POETRY Will accept poetry if pertains to public schools.

FILLERS Send with SASE—must relate to public education.

TIPS "We are looking for material on living out one's faith in appropriate, legal ways in the public school setting."

TEACHING MUSIC

MENC: The National Association for Music Education, 1806 Robert Fulton Dr., Reston VA 20191. **E-mail:** lindab@nafme.org. **Website:** www.menc.org.

Contact: Linda C. Brown, editor. Journal covering music education issued 6 times a year. "*Teaching Music* offers music educators a forum for the exchange of practical ideas that will help them become more effective teachers. Written in an easy-to-read, conversational style, the magazine includes timely information to interest, inform, and inspire music teachers and those who support their work." Byline given. *Does not pay writers at this time.* No kill fee. Publishes ms an average of 24 months after acceptance. Editorial lead time 12-18 months. Accepts queries by e-mail (preferably in Word). Responds in 2 weeks to queries. Responds in 3 months to mss. Guidelines available online.

NONFICTION Needs how-to, inspirational, personal experience, mss for the Lectern section that describe effective and innovative instructional strategies or thoughtful solutions to problems faced by music educators at all levels, from PreK through college. Major article categories are General Music, Band, Orchestra, Chorus, Early Childhood, Advocacy, and Teacher Education/Professional Development. Send complete ms. Length: 1,000-1,400 words.

PHOTOS Send in color photographs or other graphics that illustrate the main points of their articles. Photographers should obtain permission from the parents/guardians of minors whose photographs are submitted. Release form is online. Send photos after ms accepted.

TEACHING THEATRE

Educational Theatre Association, 2343 Auburn Ave., Cincinnati OH 45219-2815. (513)421-3900. **E-mail:** jpalmarini@edta.org. **Website:** www.edta.org. **Contact:** James Palmarini, editor. **65% freelance written.** Quarterly magazine covering education theater K-12; primary emphasis on middle and secondary level education. Estab. 1989. Circ. 5,000. Byline given. Pays on acceptance. No kill fee. Publishes ms an average of 3 months after acceptance. Editorial lead time 2 months. Accepts queries by mail, e-mail. Accepts simultaneous submissions. Responds in 4-6 weeks to queries. Responds in 3 months to mss. Sample copy for $2. Guidelines available online.

NONFICTION Needs book excerpts, essays, how-to, interview, opinion, technical theater. **Buys 12-15 mss/year.** Query. "A typical issue might include: an article on theatre curriculum development; a profile of an exemplary theatre education program; a how-to

teach piece on acting, directing, or playwriting; and a news story or 2 about pertinent educational theatre issues and events. Once articles are accepted, authors are asked to supply their work electronically via e-mail (jpalmarini@edta.org) or on IBM compatible diskettes." Length: 750-4,000 words **Pays $50-350.**

PHOTOS State availability. Reviews contact sheets, 5x7 and 8x10 transparencies, prints, digital images (150 dpi minimum). Unless other arrangements are made, payment for articles includes payment for the photos and illustrations.

TIPS Wants "articles that address the needs of the busy but experienced high school theater educators. Fundamental pieces on the value of theater education are not of value to us—our readers already know that."

TEACHING TOLERANCE

A Project of The Southern Poverty Law Center, 400 Washington Ave., Montgomery AL 36104. (334)956-8200. **Fax:** (334)956-8488. **Website:** www.teaching-tolerance.org. **30% freelance written.** Semiannual magazine. Estab. 1991. Circ. 400,000. Byline given. Pays on acceptance. No kill fee. Editorial lead time 6 months. Submit seasonal material 6 months in advance. Accepts queries by mail, fax, online submission form. Sample copy and writer's guidelines free or online.

NONFICTION Needs essays, how-to, classroom techniques, personal experience, classroom, photo feature. No jargon, rhetoric or academic analysis. No theoretical discussions on the pros/cons of multicultural education. **Buys 2-4 mss/year.** Submit outlines or complete mss. Length: 1,000-3,000 words. **Pays $500-3,000.** Pays expenses of writers on assignment.

PHOTOS State availability. Captions, identification of subjects required. Reviews contact sheets, transparencies.

COLUMNS/DEPARTMENTS Essays (personal reflection, how-to, school program), 400-800 words; Idea Exchange (special projects, successful anti-bias activities), 250-500 words; Student Writings (short essays dealing with diversity, tolerance, justice), 300-500 words. **Buys 8-12 mss/year.** Query with published clips. **Pays $50-1,000.**

TIPS "We want lively, simple, concise writing. Be descriptive and reflective, showing the strength of programs dealing successfully with diversity by employing clear descriptions of real scenes and interactions, and by using quotes from teachers and students. Study previous issues of the magazine before submitting. Most open to articles that have a strong classroom focus. We are interested in approaches to teaching tolerance and promoting understanding that really work that we might not have heard of. We want to inform, inspire and encourage our readers. We know what's happening nationally; we want to know what's happening in your neighborhood classroom."

ELECTRONICS AND COMMUNICATION

THE ACUTA JOURNAL

Information Communications Technology in Higher Education, ACUTA, 152 W. Zandale Dr., Suite 200, Lexington KY 40503. (859)278-3338. **Fax:** (859)278-3268. **E-mail:** aburton@acuta.org; pscott@acuta.org. **Website:** www.acuta.org. **Contact:** Amy Burton; Patricia Scott, director of communications. **20% freelance written.** Quarterly professional association journal covering information communications technology (ICT) in higher education. "Our audience includes, primarily, middle to upper management in the IT/telecommunications department on college/university campuses. They are highly skilled, technology-oriented professionals who provide data, voice, and video communications services for residential and academic purposes." Estab. 1997. Circ. 2,200. Byline given. Pays on publication. No kill fee. Publishes ms an average of 6 months after acceptance. Editorial lead time 6 months. Accepts queries by mail, e-mail, fax, phone. Responds in 1 month to queries. Responds in 2 months to mss. Sample copy for SAE with 9x12 envelope and 6 first-class stamps. Guidelines free.

NONFICTION Needs how-to, ICT, technical, technology, case study, college/university application of technology. **Buys 6-8 mss/year.** Query. Length: 1,200-4,000 words. **Pays 8-10¢/word.** Sometimes pays expenses of writers on assignment.

PHOTOS State availability. Captions, model releases required. Reviews prints. Offers no additional payment for photos accepted with ms.

TIPS "Our audience expects every article to be relevant to information communications technology on the college/university campus, whether it is related to technology, facilities, or management. Writers must read back issues to understand this focus and the level of technicality we expect."

TECH TRADER MAGAZINE

The Intermedia Group, Ltd., Tech Trader Magazine, 41 Bridge Rd., Glebe NSW 2037 Australia. (61)(2)9660-2113. **Fax:** (61)(2)9660-4419. **E-mail:** info@intermedia.com.au. **Website:** www.intermedia.com.au. **Contact:** Simon Grover, managing director/publisher; Mark Kuban, group publisher. "Tech Trader Magazine delivers the latest news, opinion, features, product reviews, overseas reports, and new products together in one lively publication."

NONFICTION Needs general interest, new product. Query.

ENERGY AND UTILITIES

ELECTRICAL APPARATUS

Barks Publications, Inc., Suite 901, 500 N. Michigan Ave., Chicago IL 60611. (312)321-9440. **Fax:** (312)321-1288. **E-mail:** eamagazine@barks.com. **Website:** www.barks.com/eacurr.html. **Contact:** Elsie Dickson, acting publisher; Kevin N. Jones, senior editor. Monthly magazine for persons working in electrical and electronic maintenance, in industrial plants and service and sales centers, who install and service electric motors, transformers, generators, controls, and related equipment. Contact staff members by telephone for their preferred e-mail addresses. Estab. 1967. Circ. 16,000. Byline given. Pays on publication. No kill fee. Publishes ms an average of 1 month after acceptance. Accepts queries by mail, fax. Responds in 1 week to queries. Responds in 2 weeks to mss.

NONFICTION Needs technical. Length: 1,500-2,500 words. **Pays $250-500 for assigned articles.**

TIPS "All feature articles are assigned to staff and contributing editors and correspondents. Professionals interested in appointments as contributing editors and correspondents should submit résumé and article outlines, including illustration suggestions. Writers should be competent with a camera, which should be described in résumé. Technical expertise is absolutely necessary, preferably an E.E. degree, or practical experience. We are also book publishers and some of the material in *EA* is now in book form, bringing the authors royalties. Also publishes an annual directory, subtitled *ElectroMechanical Bench Reference*."

PIPELINE & GAS JOURNAL

Oildom Publishing, 1160 Dairy Ashford, Suite 610, Houston TX 77079. (281)558-6930. **Fax:** (281)558-

7029. **E-mail:** rtubb@oildom.com. **Website:** www.pg-jonline.com; www.oildompublishing.com. Rita Tubb, man. ed. **Contact:** Jeff Share, editor. **15% freelance written.** Covers pipeline operations worldwide. "Edited for personnel engaged in energy pipeline design construction operations, as well as marketing, storage, supply, risk management and regulatory affairs, natural gas transmission and distribution companies." Estab. 1859. Circ. 29,000. Byline givien. Pays on publication. Publishes ms 2 months after acceptance. Editorial lead time 1 month. Accepts queries by e-mail to jshare@oildom.com. Responds in 2-3 weeks to queries; 1-2 months to mss. Sample copy free. Guidelines available online at http://pgjonline.com.

NONFICTION Contact: Editor. Needs interview, new product, travel, case studies. Query. Length: 2,000-3,000 words.

COLUMNS/DEPARTMENTS Contact: Senior editor: lbullion@oildom.com. What's New: Product type items, 100 words; New Products: Product items, 50-100 words; Business New: Personnel Change, 25-35 words, Company New: 35-50 words.

😊😊 PUBLIC POWER

1875 Connecticut Ave. NW, Suite 1200, Washington DC 20009-5715. (202)467-2900. **Fax:** (202)467-2910. **E-mail:** magazine@publicpower.org; dblaylock@publicpower.org **Website:** www.publicpower-media.org. **Contact:** David L. Blaylock, editor. **60% freelance written. Prefers to work with published/established writers.** Publication of the American Public Power Association, published 8 times a year. Emphasizes electric power provided by cities, towns, and utility districts. Estab. 1942. Byline given. Pays on acceptance. No kill fee. Publishes ms an average of 3 months after acceptance. Accepts queries by mail, e-mail, fax. Responds in 6 months to queries. Sample copy and writer's guidelines free.

NONFICTION Pays $500 and up.

PHOTOS Reviews electronic photos (minimum 300 dpi at reproduction size).

TIPS "We look for writers who are familiar with energy policy issues."

😊😊😊 TEXAS CO-OP POWER

Texas Electric Cooperatives, Inc., 1122 Colorado St., 24th Floor, Austin TX 78701. (512)486-6242. **E-mail:** editor@texas-ec.org. **Website:** www.texascooppower. com. **50% freelance written.** Monthly magazine covering rural and suburban Texas life, people, and plac-

es. "*Texas Co-op Power* provides 1 million households and businesses educational and technical information about electric cooperatives in a high-quality and entertaining format to promote the general welfare of cooperatives, their member-owners, and the areas in which they serve. *Texas Co-op Power* is published by your electric cooperative to enhance the quality of life of its member-customers in an educational and entertaining format." Estab. 1948. Circ. 1.2 million. Byline given. Pays after any necessary rewrites. No kill fee. Publishes ms an average of 6 months after acceptance. Editorial lead time 4-5 months. Submit seasonal material 6 months in advance. Accepts queries by mail, e-mail, fax, online submission form. Accepts simultaneous submissions. Responds in 1 month to queries. Responds in 3 months to mss. Sample copy available online. Guidelines for #10 SASE.

NONFICTION Needs general interest, historical, interview, photo feature, travel. **Buys 30 mss/year.** Query with published clips. Length: 800-1,200 words. **Pays $400-1,000.** Sometimes pays expenses of writers on assignment.

PHOTOS State availability. Identification of subjects, model releases required. Reviews transparencies, prints. Negotiates payment individually.

TIPS "We're looking for Texas-related, rural-based articles, often first-person, always lively and interesting."

ENGINEERING AND TECHNOLOGY

⊙ 😊😊😊 CABLING NETWORKING SYSTEMS

Business Information Group, 80 Valleybrook Dr., Toronto ON M3B 2S9 Canada. (416)510-6752. **Fax:** (416)510-5134. **E-mail:** pbarker@cnsmagazine.com. **Website:** www.cnsmagazine.com. **Contact:** Paul Barker, editor. **50% freelance written.** Magazine published 6 times/year covering the structured cabling/telecommunications industry. Estab. 1998. Circ. 11,000. Byline given. Pays on publication. No kill fee. Publishes ms an average of 1 month after acceptance. Editorial lead time 3 months. Submit seasonal material 1 month in advance. Accepts queries by mail, e-mail, phone. Accepts simultaneous submissions. Sample copy available online. Guidelines free.

NONFICTION Needs technical, case studies, features. No reprints or previously written articles. All articles are assigned by editor based on query or need of publication. **Buys 12 mss/year.** Query with published clips. Length: 1,500-2,500 words. **Pays 40-50¢/word.** Sometimes pays expenses of writers on assignment.

PHOTOS State availability. Captions, identification of subjects required. Reviews contact sheets, prints. Negotiates payment individually.

COLUMNS/DEPARTMENTS Focus on Engineering/Design; Focus on Installation; Focus on Maintenance/Testing; all 1,500 words. **Buys 7 mss/year.** Query with published clips. **Pays 40-50¢/word.**

TIPS "Visit our website to see back issues, and visit links on our website for background."

[C] $$$ CANADIAN CONSULTING ENGINEER

Business Information Group, 80 Valleybrook Dr., Toronto ON M3B 2S9 Canada. (416)510-5119. **Fax:** (416)510-5134. **E-mail:** bparsons@ccemag.com. **Website:** www.canadianconsultingengineer.com. **Contact:** Bronwen Parsons, editor. **20%% freelance written.** Bimonthly magazine covering consulting engineering in private practice. Estab. 1958. Circ. 8,900. Byline given depending on length of story. Pays on publication. Offers 50% kill fee. Publishes ms an average of 4 months after acceptance. Editorial lead time 6 months. Responds in 3 months to mss. Sample copy free.

NONFICTION Needs historical, new product, technical, engineering/construction projects, environmental/construction issues. **Buys 8-10 mss/year.** Length: 300-1,500 words. **Pays $200-1,000 (Canadian).** Sometimes pays expenses of writers on assignment.

PHOTOS State availability. Negotiates payment individually.

COLUMNS/DEPARTMENTS Export (selling consulting engineering services abroad); Management (managing consulting engineering businesses); On-Line (trends in CAD systems); Employment; Business; Construction and Environmental Law (Canada); all 800 words. **Buys 4 mss/year.** Query with published clips. **Pays $250-400.**

$$ COMPOSITES MANUFACTURING MAGAZINE

(formerly *Composites Fabrication Magazine*), American Composites Manufacturers Association, 3033 Wilson Blvd., Suite 420, Arlington VA 22201. (703)525-0511. **E-mail:** communications@acmanet.org. **Website:** www.acmanet.org. Monthly magazine covering any industry that uses reinforced composites: marine, aerospace, infrastructure, automotive, transportation, corrosion, architecture, tub and shower, sports, and recreation. "Primarily, we publish educational pieces, the how-to of the shop environment. We also publish marketing, business trends, and economic forecasts relevant to the composites industry." Estab. 1979. Circ. 12,000. Byline given. Pays on acceptance. No kill fee. Publishes ms an average of 2-3 months after acceptance. Editorial lead time 2 months. Accepts queries by e-mail. Accepts simultaneous submissions. Responds in 1 week to queries. Responds in 1 month to mss. Sample copy free. Guidelines by e-mail and online.

NONFICTION Needs how-to, composites manufacturing, new product, technical, marketing, related business trends and forecasts. Special issues: "Each January we publish a World Market Report where we cover all niche markets and all geographic areas relevant to the composites industry. Freelance material will be considered strongly for this issue." No need to query company or personal profiles unless there is an extremely unique or novel angle. **Buys 5-10 mss/year.** Query. *Composites Manufacturing* invites freelance feature submissions, all of which should be sent via e-mail as a Microsoft Word attachment. A query letter is required. Length: 1,500-4,000 words. **Pays 20-40¢/word (negotiable).** Sometimes pays expenses of writers on assignment.

COLUMNS/DEPARTMENTS "We publish columns on HR, relevant government legislation, industry lessons learned, regulatory affairs, and technology. Average word length for columns is 500 words. We would entertain any new column idea that hits hard on industry matters." Query. **Pays $300-350.**

TIPS "The best way to break into the magazine is to empathize with the entrepreneurial and technical background of readership, and come up with an exclusive, original, creative story idea. We pride ourselves on not looking or acting like any other trade publication (composites industry or otherwise). Our editor is very open to suggestions, but they must be unique. Don't waste his time with canned articles dressed up to look exclusive. This is the best way to get on the 'immediate rejection list.'"

EMBEDDED TECHNOLOGY

Tech Briefs Media Group, 261 Fifth Ave., New York NY 10016. (212)490-3999. **E-mail:** bruce@abpi.net. **Website:** www.techbriefsmediagroup.com. **100% freelance written.** Bimonthly magazine covering embedded, industrial, and COTS computers. *"Embedded Technology's* audience consists of computer and electronics engineers, designers, scientists, technicians, and systems integrators, and since ET is published in conjunction with NASA Tech Briefs, we probably have a few rocket scientists in the mix as well. Articles tend to be highly technical in nature and cover everything from the latest ASICs and FPGAs to single board computers and data transfer protocols." Estab. 2005. Circ. 71,000. Byline given. No monetary payment. No kill fee. Publishes ms an average of 3-6 months after acceptance. Editorial lead time 3-6 months. Accepts queries by e-mail. Sample copy and guidelines available online.

NONFICTION Contact: Bruce A. Bennett. Needs technical. "We don't want anything non-technical," Query. Length: 1,200-1,500 words.

TIPS "Our authors tend to work in the embedded computing industry and have solid academic and professional credentials. They're writing for professional and peer recognition, not monetary reward."

🟢🟢🟢 ENTERPRISE MINNESOTA MAGAZINE

Enterprise Minnesota, Inc., 310 4th Ave. S., Suite 7050, Minneapolis MN 55415. (612)373-2900; (800)325-3073. **Fax:** (612)373-2901. **E-mail:** editor@enterpriseminnesota.org. **Website:** www.enterpriseminnesota.org. **Contact:** Tom Mason, editor. **90% freelance written.** Magazine published 5 times/year. Estab. 1991. Circ. 16,000. Byline given. Pays on publication. Offers 10% kill fee. Publishes ms an average of 3 months after acceptance. Editorial lead time 1 month. Submit seasonal material 1 year in advance. Accepts queries by mail, e-mail. Guidelines free.

NONFICTION Needs general interest, how-to, interview. **Buys 60 mss/year.** Query with published clips. **Pays $150-1,000.**

COLUMNS/DEPARTMENTS Feature Well (Q&A format, provocative ideas from Minnesota business and industry leaders), 2,000 words; Up Front (mini profiles, anecdotal news items), 250-500 words. Query with published clips.

🟢🟢 LD+A

Illuminating Engineering Society of North America, 120 Wall St., 17th Floor, New York NY 10005-4001. (212)248-5000, ext. 108. **Fax:** (212)248-5017. **E-mail:** ptarricone@ies.org. **Website:** www.ies.org. **Contact:** Paul Tarricone, editor/associate publisher. **10% freelance written.** Estab. 1971. Circ. 10,000. Byline given. Pays on acceptance. No kill fee. Publishes ms an average of 4 months after acceptance. Editorial lead time 2 months. Submit seasonal material 4 months in advance. Accepts queries by mail, e-mail, fax, phone. Accepts simultaneous submissions. Responds in 2 weeks to queries. Sample copy free. Guidelines available on website.

NONFICTION Needs historical, how-to, opinion, personal experience, photo feature, technical. No articles blatantly promoting a product, company, or individual. **Buys 6-10 mss/year.** Query. Length: 1,500-2,000 words.

PHOTOS Send photos. Captions required. Reviews JPEG/TIFF files. Offers no additional payment for photos accepted with ms.

COLUMNS/DEPARTMENTS Essay by Invitation (industry trends), 1,200 words. Query. **Does not pay for columns.**

TIPS "Most of our features detail the ins and outs of a specific lighting project. From museums to stadiums and highways, *LD+A* gives its readers an in-depth look at how the designer(s) reached their goals."

🟢🟢 MFRTECH EJOURNAL

Manufacturers Group Inc., P.O. Box 4310, Lexington KY 40544. **E-mail:** editor@mfrtech.com. **Website:** www.mfrtech.com. **40% freelance written.** Magazine published daily online covering manufacturing and technology from news throughout the U.S. Editorial includes manufacturing news, expansions, acquisition white papers, case histories, new product announcements, feature submissions, book synopsis. Estab. 1976 (print). Circ. 60,000+ weekly subscribers (e-mail); 750,000 monthly online visitors. Byline given. 30 days following publication. Offers 25% kill fee. Publishes ms 3-4 days after acceptance. Editorial lead time 2 weeks. Submit seasonal material 2 weeks in advance. Sample copy available online. Guidelines by e-mail.

NONFICTION Needs new product, opinion, technical. General interest, inspirational, personal, travel, book excerpts. Length: 750-1,200 words; byline: 75 words. **Pays $0.20/word published.**

PHOTOS Up to 3 photo or graphic images permitted; must come as an attachment to ms submissions via e-mail as JPEGs and no larger than 300x300 pixels each.

COLUMNS/DEPARTMENTS New Plant Announcement, Acquisitions, Expansions, New Technology, Federal, Case Histories, Human Resources, Marketing. Query. **Pays $0.20/word.**

PHOTONICS TECH BRIEFS

Tech Briefs Media Group, 261 Fifth Ave., Suite 1901, New York NY 10016. (212)490-3999. **E-mail:** bruce@abpi.net. **Website:** www.techbriefsmediagroup.com. **100% freelance written.** Magazine published 6 times/year covering lasers, optics, and photonic systems. "*Photonics Tech Briefs*' audience consists of engineers, designers, scientists, and technicians working in all aspects of the laser, optics, and photonics industries. Since we're published in conjunction with NASA Tech Briefs, we probably have a few honest-to-goodness rocket scientists in the mix as well. Articles tend to be highly technical in nature and cover everything from lasers, fiber optics and infrared technology to biophotonics, photovoltaics, and digital imaging systems." Circ. 102,698. Byline given. No monetary payment. No kill fee. Publishes ms an average of 3-6 months after acceptance. Editorial lead time 3-6 months. Accepts queries by e-mail. Sample copy and guidelines available online.

NONFICTION Contact: Bruce A. Bennett. Needs technical. "We don't want anything non-technical." Query without published clips or send complete ms. Length: 1,200-1,500 words.

TIPS "Our authors tend to work in the photonics/optics industry and have solid academic and professional credentials. They're writing for professional and peer recognition, not monetary reward."

$$$$ RAILWAY TRACK AND STRUCTURES

Simmons-Boardman Publishing, 20 S. Clark St., Suite 2450, Chicago IL 60603. (312)683-0130. **Fax:** (312)683-0131. **E-mail:** Mischa@sbpub-chicago.com; Jnunez@sbpub-chicago.com. **Website:** www.rtands.com. **Contact:** Mischa Wanek-Libman, editor; Jennifer Nunez, assistant editor. **1% freelance written.** Monthly magazine covering railroad civil engineering. "*RT&S* is a nuts-and-bolts journal to help railroad civil engineers do their jobs better." Estab. 1904. Circ. 9,500. Byline given. Pays on publication. Offers 90% kill fee. Publishes ms an average of 1 month after acceptance. Editorial lead time 2 months. Submit seasonal material 3 months in advance. Accepts queries by mail, fax, phone. Accepts simultaneous submissions. Responds in 1 month to queries and to mss. Sample copy available online.

NONFICTION Needs how-to, new product, technical. Does not want nostalgia or "railroadiana." **Buys 1 mss/year.** Query. Length: 900-2,000 words. **Pays $500-1,000.** Sometimes pays expenses of writers on assignment.

PHOTOS State availability. Captions, identification of subjects, model releases required. Reviews GIF/JPEG files. Negotiates payment individually.

TIPS "We prefer writers with a civil engineering background and railroad experience."

$$ WOMAN ENGINEER

Equal Opportunity Publications, Inc., 445 Broad Hollow Rd., Suite 425, Melville NY 11747. (631)421-9421. **Fax:** (631)421-1352. **E-mail:** info@eop.com; jschneider@eop.com. **Website:** www.eop.com. **Contact:** James Schneider, editor. **60% freelance written. Works with a small number of new/unpublished writers each year.** Triannual magazine aimed at advancing the careers of women engineering students and professional women engineers. Estab. 1968. Circ. 16,000. Byline given. Pays on publication. No kill fee. Publishes ms an average of 3 months after acceptance. Editorial lead time 3 months. Accepts queries by mail, e-mail, fax, phone. Responds in 2 weeks to queries. Responds in 2 months to mss. Sample copy and writer's guidelines free.

NONFICTION Needs how-to, find jobs, interview, personal experience. Query. Length: 1,500-2,500 words. **Pays $350 for assigned articles.**

PHOTOS Captions, identification of subjects required. Reviews color slides but will accept b&w.

TIPS "We are looking for first-person 'As I See It' personal perspectives. Gear it to our audience."

ENTERTAINMENT AND THE ARTS

$$$ AMERICAN CINEMATOGRAPHER

American Society of Cinematographers, 1782 N. Orange Dr., Hollywood CA 90028. (800)448-0145; outside US: (323)969-4333. **Fax:** (323)876-4973. **E-mail:** stephen@ascmag.com. **Website:** www.theasc.com. **Contact:** Stephen Pizzello, executive editor. **90% freelance written.** Monthly magazine covering cinematography (motion picture, TV, music video, commercial). *"American Cinematographer* is a trade publication devoted to the art and craft of cinematography. Our readers are predominantly film-industry professionals." Estab. 1919. Circ. 45,000. Byline given. Pays on publication. Offers 50% kill fee. Publishes ms an average of 2-3 months after acceptance. Editorial lead time 2 months. Submit seasonal material 3 months in advance. Accepts queries by mail, e-mail, phone. NoResponds in 2 weeks to queries; 2 months to mss. Sample copy and writer's guidelines free.

NONFICTION Contact: Stephen Pizzello, editor. Needs interview, new product, technical. No reviews or opinion pieces. **Buys 20-25 mss/year.** Query with published clips. Length: 1,500-4,000 words. **Pays $600-1,200.** Sometimes pays expenses of writers on assignment.

TIPS "Familiarity with the technical side of film production and the ability to present that information in an articulate fashion to our audience are crucial."

⊗⊗ AMERICAN THEATRE

Theatre Communications Group, 520 8th Ave., 24th Floor, New York NY 10018. (212)609-5900. **E-mail:** jim@tcg.org. **Website:** www.tcg.org. **Contact:** Jim O'Quinn, editor-in-chief. **60% freelance written.** Monthly magazine covering theatre. "Our focus is American regional nonprofit theatre. American Theatre typically publishes 2 or 3 features and 4-6 back-of-the-book articles covering trends and events in all types of theatre, as well as economic and legislative developments affecting the arts." Estab. 1982. Circ. 100,000. Byline given. Pays on publication. Editorial lead time 2 months. Submit seasonal material 3 months in advance. Accepts queries by mail, e-mail, online submission form. Accepts simultaneous submissions. Responds in 2 months to queries. Sample copy and guidelines available online.

NONFICTION Needs book excerpts, essays, exposé, general interest, historical, how-to, humor, inspirational, interview, opinion, personal experience, photo feature, travel. Special issues: Training (January); International (May/June); Season Preview (October). No unsolicited submissions (rarely accepted). No reviews. Query with outlined proposal and published clips. Include brief rèsumè and SASE. Length: 200-2,000 words.

"While fees are negotiated per ms, we pay an average of $350 for full-length (2,500-3,500 words) features, and less for shorter pieces."

PHOTOS Contact: Kitty Suen, creative director: atphoto@tcg.com. Send photos. Captions required. Reviews JPEG files. Negotiates payment individually.

TIPS "The main focus is on professional American nonprofit theatre. Don't pitch music or film festivals. Must be about theatre."

⊗⊗ DANCE TEACHER

McFadden Performing Arts Media, 333 Seventh Ave., 11th Floor, New York NY 10001. **Fax:** (646)459-4000. **E-mail:** khildebrand@dancemedia.com. **Website:** www.dance-teacher.com. **Contact:** Karen Hildebrand, editor-in-chief; Joe Sullivan, managing editor. **60% freelance written.** Monthly magazine. Estab. 1979. Circ. 25,000. Byline given. Pays on publication. No kill fee. Publishes ms an average of 3 months after acceptance. Submit seasonal material 6 months in advance. Accepts queries by mail, e-mail, fax, phone, online submission form. Responds in 3 months to mss. Sample copy for SAE with 9x12 envelope and 6 first-class stamps. Guidelines available for free.

NONFICTION Needs how-to, teach, health, business, legal. Special issues: Summer Programs (January); Music & More (May); Costumes and Production Preview (November); College/Training Schools (December). No PR or puff pieces. All articles must be well researched. **Buys 30 mss/year.** Query. Length: 700-2,000 words. **Pays $100-300.**

PHOTOS Send photos. Reviews contact sheets, negatives, transparencies, prints. Limited photo budget.

TIPS "Read several issues—particularly seasonal. Stay within writer's guidelines."

DRAMATICS MAGAZINE

Educational Theatre Association, 2343 Auburn Ave., Cincinnati OH 45219. (513)421-3900. **E-mail:** dcorathers@edta.org. **Website:** www.edta.org. **Contact:** Don Corathers, editor. *"Dramatics* is for students (mainly high school age) and teachers of theater. Mix includes how-to (tech theater, acting, directing, etc.), informational, interview, photo feature, humorous, profile, technical. We want our student readers to grow as theater artists and become a more discerning and appreciative audience. Material is directed to both theater students and their teachers, with strong student slant." Estab. 1929. Circ. 35,000. Byline given. Pays on acceptance. Publishes ms 3 months after acceptance.

TrueAccepts simultaneous submissions. Sample copy available for 9x12 SAE with 4-ounce first-class postage. Guidelines available for SASE.

NONFICTION Needs Young adults: arts/crafts, careers, how-to, interview/profile, multicultural (all theater-related). "We try to portray the theater community in all its diversity." Does not want to see academic treatises. **Buys 50 mss/year.** Submit complete ms. Length: 750-3,000 words. **Pays $50-500 for articles.**

FICTION Young adults: drama (one-act and full-length plays). "We prefer unpublished scripts that have been produced at least once." Does not want to see plays that show no understanding of the conventions of the theater. No plays for children, no Christmas or didactic "message" plays. Submit complete ms. Buys 5-9 plays/year. Emerging playwrights have better chances with résumé of credits. Length: 750-3,000 words. **Pays $100-500 for plays.**

TIPS "Obtain our writer's guidelines and look at recent back issues. The best way to break in is to know our audience—drama students, teachers, and others interested in theater—and write for them. Writers who have some practical experience in theater, especially in technical areas, have an advantage, but we'll work with anybody who has a good idea. Some freelancers have become regular contributors."

⊖⊖⊖ EMMY MAGAZINE

Academy of Television Arts & Sciences, 5220 Lankershim Blvd., North Hollywood CA 91601. **E-mail:** emmymag@emmys.org. **Website:** www.emmymagazine.com; www.emmys.tv/emmy-magazine. **Contact:** Juan Morales, editor-in-chief; Gail Polevoi, editor. **90% freelance written. Prefers to work with published/established writers.** Bimonthly magazine on television for TV professionals. Circ. 14,000. Byline given. Pays on publication or within 6 months. Offers 25% kill fee. Publishes ms an average of 4 months after acceptance. Accepts queries by mail. Responds in 1 month to queries. Sample copy for sae with 9x12 envelope and 6 first-class stamps. Guidelines available online.

NONFICTION Query with published clips. Length: 1,500-2,000 words. **Pays $1,000-1,200.**

COLUMNS/DEPARTMENTS Mostly written by regular contributors, but newcomers can break in with filler items with In the Mix or short profiles in Labors of Love. Length: 250-500 words, depending on department. Query with published clips. **Pays $250-500.**

TIPS "Please review recent issues before querying us. Query with published, television-related clips. No fanzine, academic, or nostalgic approaches, please. Demonstrate experience in covering the business of television and your ability to write in a lively and compelling manner about programming trends and new technology. Identify fascinating people behind the scenes, not just in the executive suites, but in all ranks of the industry."

⊖⊖ MAKE-UP ARTIST MAGAZINE

12808 NE 95th St., Vancouver WA 98682. (360)882-3488. **E-mail:** news@makeupmag.com. **Website:** www.makeupmag.com; www.makeup411.com; www.imats.net. **Contact:** Heather Wisner, managing editor; Michael Key, publisher/editor-in-chief. **90% freelance written.** Bimonthly magazine covering all types of professional make-up artistry. "Our audience is a mixture of high-level make-up artists, make-up students, and movie buffs. Writers should be comfortable with technical writing, and should have substantial knowledge of at least 1 area of makeup, such as effects or fashion. This is an entertainment-industry magazine, so writing should have an element of fun and storytelling. Good interview skills required." Estab. 1996. Circ. 16,000. Byline given. Pays within 30 days of publication. No kill fee. Editorial lead time 6 weeks. Submit seasonal material 2 months in advance. Accepts queries by e-mail. Accepts simultaneous submissions. Sample copy for $7. Guidelines available via e-mail.

NONFICTION Needs features, how-to, new products, photo features, profile. "Does not want fluff pieces about consumer beauty products." **Buys 20+ mss/year.** Query with published clips. Length: 500-3,000 words. **Pays 20-50¢/word.** Sometimes pays expenses of writers on assignment.

PHOTOS Send photos. Captions, identification of subjects required. Reviews prints, GIF/JPEG files. Negotiates payment individually.

COLUMNS/DEPARTMENTS Cameo (short yet thorough look at a make-up artist not covered in a feature story), 800 words (15 photos); Lab Tech (how-to advice for effects artists, usually written by a current make-up artist working in a lab), 800 words (3 photos); Backstage (analysis, interview, tips, and behind the scenes info on a theatrical production's make-up), 800 words (3 photos). **Buys Buys 30 columns/year. mss/year.** Query with published clips. **Pays $100.**

TIPS "Read books about professional make-up artistry (see http://makeupmag.com/shop). Read online interviews with make-up artists. Read make-up oriented mainstream magazines, such as *Allure*. Read *Cinefex* and other film-industry publications. Meet and talk to make-up artists and make-up students."

⊛ SCREEN MAGAZINE

Screen Enterprises, Inc., 676 N. LaSalle Blvd., #501, Chicago IL 60654. (312)640-0800. **Fax:** (312)640-1928. **E-mail:** editor@screenmag.com. **Website:** www.screenmag.com. **Contact:** Andrew Schneider, editor. **5% freelance written.** Biweekly Chicago-based trade magazine covering advertising and film production in the Midwest and national markets. *Screen* is written for Midwest producers (and other creatives involved) of commercials, AV, features, independent corporate, and multimedia. Estab. 1979. Circ. 15,000. Byline given. Pays on publication. No kill fee. Accepts queries by e-mail. Responds in 3 weeks to queries. Sample copy available online.

NONFICTION Needs interview, new product, technical. No general AV; nothing specific to other markets; no no-brainers or opinion. **Buys 26 mss/year.** Query with published clips. Length: 750-1,500 words. **Pays $50.**

PHOTOS Send photos. Captions required. Reviews prints. Offers no additional payment for photos accepted with ms.

TIPS "Our readers want to know facts and figures. They want to know the news about a company or an individual. We provide exclusive news of this market, in as much depth as space allows without being boring, with lots of specific information and details. We write knowledgably about the market we serve. We recognize the film/video-making process is a difficult one because it 1) is often technical, 2) has implications not immediately discerned."

⊛ SOUTHERN THEATRE

Southeastern Theatre Conference, P.O. Box 9868, 3309 Northampton Dr., Greensboro NC 27429-0868. (336)292-6041. **E-mail:** deanna@setc.org. **Website:** www.setc.org/southern-theatre. **Contact:** Deanna Thompson, editor. **100% freelance written.** Quarterly magazine covering all aspects of theater in the Southeast, from innovative theater companies, to important trends, to people making a difference in the region. All stories must be written in a popular magazine style but with subject matter appropriate for theater professionals (not the general public). The audience includes members of the Southeastern Theatre Conference, founded in 1949 and the nation's largest regional theater organization. These members include individu-

als involved in professional, community, college/university, children's, and secondary school theater. The magazine also is purchased by more than 100 libraries. Estab. 1962. Circ. 4,200. Byline given. Pays on publication. No kill fee. Publishes ms an average of 3 months after acceptance. Editorial lead time 3 months. Submit seasonal material 6 months in advance. Accepts queries by mail, e-mail. Responds in 3 months to queries. Responds in 6 months to mss. Sample copy for $10. Guidelines available online.

NONFICTION Needs general interest, innovative theaters and theater programs, trend stories, interview, people making a difference in Southeastern theater. Special issues: Playwriting (Fall issue, all stories submitted by January 1). No scholarly articles. **Buys 15-20 mss/year.** Send complete ms. Length: 1,000-3,000 words. **Pays $50 for feature stories.**

PHOTOS State availability of or send photos. Captions, identification of subjects, model releases required. Reviews transparencies, prints. Offers no additional payment for photos accepted with ms.

COLUMNS/DEPARTMENTS *Outside the Box* (innovative solutions to problems faced by designers and technicians), 800-1,000 words; *400 Words* (column where the theater professionals can sound off on issues), 400 words; 800-1,000 words; *Words, Words, Words* (reviews of books on theater), 400 words. Query or send complete ms **No payment for columns.**

TIPS "Look for a theater or theater person in your area that is doing something different or innovative that would be of interest to others in the profession, then write about that theater or person in a compelling way. We also are looking for well-written trend stories (talk to theaters in your area about trends that are affecting them), and we especially like stories that help our readers do their jobs more effectively. Send an e-mail detailing a well-developed story idea, and ask if we're interested."

FARM

AGRICULTURAL EQUIPMENT

⊛ AG WEEKLY

Lee Agri-Media, P.O. Box 918, Bismarck ND 58501. (701)255-4905. **Fax:** (701)255-2312. **E-mail:** mark.conlon@lee.net. **Website:** www.agweekly.com. **Contact:** Mark Conlon, editor. **40% freelance written.** Monthly tabloid covering regional farming and ranching, with emphasis on Idaho. *Ag Weekly* is an agricultural publication covering production, markets, regulation, politics. Writers need to be familiar with Idaho agricultural commodities. Circ. 12,402. Byline given. Pays on publication. Publishes ms an average of 1 month after acceptance. Editorial lead time 1 month. Submit seasonal material 1 month in advance. Accepts queries by e-mail. Accepts simultaneous submissions. Responds in 2 weeks to queries. Responds in 1 month to mss. Sample copy available online. Guidelines with #10 SASE.

NONFICTION Needs interview, new product, opinion, travel, ag-related. Does not want anything other than local/regional ag-related articles. No cowboy poetry. **Buys 100 mss/year.** Query. Length: 250-700 words. **Pays $40-70.**

PHOTOS State availability. Captions required. Reviews GIF/JPEG files. Offers $10/photo.

IMPLEMENT & TRACTOR

Farm Journal, 222 S. Jefferson St., Mexico MO 65265. (573)581-6387. **E-mail:** jrussell@farmjournal.com. **Website:** www.implementandtractor.com. **Contact:** Jenn Russell, managing editor. **10% freelance written.** Bimonthly magazine covering the agricultural equipment industry. *"Implement & Tractor* offers equipment reviews and business news for agricultural equipment dealers, ag equipment manufacturers, distributors, and aftermarket suppliers." Estab. 1895. Circ. 5,000. Byline given. Pays on publication. No kill fee. Publishes ms an average of 3-4 months after acceptance. Editorial lead time 2 months. Accepts queries by mail, e-mail. Responds in 2 months to queries. Sample copy for $6.

CROPS AND SOIL MANAGEMENT

AMERICAN/WESTERN GROWER

Meister Media Worldwide, 37733 Euclid Ave., Willoughby OH 44094. (440)942-2000. **E-mail:** avazzano@meistermedia.com; deddy@meistermedia.com. **Website:** www.fruitgrower.com. **Contact:** Ann-Marie Vazzano, managing editor; David Eddy, editor. **3% freelance written.** Annual magazine covering commercial fruit growing. Estab. 1880. Circ. 44,000. Byline given. Pays on publication. No kill fee. Publishes ms an average of 4 months after acceptance. Editorial lead time 2 months. Submit seasonal material 4

months in advance. Accepts queries by mail, e-mail, fax, phone. Responds in 2 weeks to queries. Responds in 2 months to mss. Sample copy and writer's guidelines free.

NONFICTION Needs how-to, better grow fruit crops. **Buys 6-10 mss/year.** Send complete ms. Length: 800-1,200 words. **Pays $200-250.** Sometimes pays expenses of writers on assignment.

PHOTOS Send photos. Reviews prints, slides. Negotiates payment individually.

TIPS "How-to articles are best."

COTTON GROWER MAGAZINE

Meister Media Worldwide, Cotton Media Group, 8000 Centerview Pkwy., Suite #114, Cordova TN 38018-4246. (901)756-8822. **E-mail:** hgantz@meistermedia.com. **Website:** www.cotton247.com. **Contact:** Harry Gantz, editor. **5% freelance written.** Monthly magazine covering cotton production, cotton markets, and related subjects. Circ. 43,000. Byline given. Pays on acceptance. No kill fee. Publishes ms an average of 2 months after acceptance. Editorial lead time 2 months. Submit seasonal material 2 months in advance. Accepts queries by mail, e-mail, fax, phone. Accepts simultaneous submissions. Sample copy free.

NONFICTION Needs interview, new product, photo feature, technical. No fiction or humorous pieces. **Buys 5-10 mss/year.** Query with published clips. Length: 500-800 words. **Pays $200-400.** Sometimes pays expenses of writers on assignment.

PHOTOS State availability. Captions, identification of subjects required. Reviews transparencies. Offers no additional payment for photos accepted with ms.

FRUIT GROWERS NEWS

Great American Publishing, P.O. Box 128, Sparta MI 49345. (616)887-9008. **Fax:** (616)887-2666. **E-mail:** fgnedit@fruitgrowersnews.com. **Website:** www.fruitgrowersnews.com. **Contact:** Matt Milkovich, managing editor; Lee Dean, editorial director. **10% freelance written.** Monthly tabloid covering agriculture. "Our objective is to provide commercial fruit growers of all sizes with information to help them succeed." Estab. 1961. Circ. 16,429. Pays on publication. No kill fee. Publishes ms an average of 2 months after acceptance. Editorial lead time 1-2 months. Submit seasonal material 3 months in advance. Accepts queries by mail, e-mail, fax. Accepts simultaneous submissions. Responds in 2 weeks to queries. Responds in 1 month to mss. Sample copy free.

NONFICTION Needs general interest, interview, new product. No advertorials or other puff pieces. **Buys 25 mss/year.** Query with published clips and résumé. Length: 600-1,000 words. **Pays $150-250.** Sometimes pays expenses of writers on assignment.

PHOTOS Send photos. Captions required. Reviews prints. Offers $15/photo.

⊕⊕ GOOD FRUIT GROWER

Washington State Fruit Commission, 105 S. 18th St., #217, Yakima WA 98901. (509)575-2315. **E-mail:** jim.black@goodfruit.com. **Website:** www.goodfruit.com. **Contact:** Jim Black, managing editor. **10% freelance written.** Semi-monthly magazine covering tree fruit/grape growing. Estab. 1946. Circ. 11,000. Byline given. Pays on acceptance. Publishes ms an average of 2 months after acceptance. Accepts queries by mail, e-mail. Accepts simultaneous submissions. Responds in 1 week to queries. Responds in 1 month to mss. Sample copy free. Guidelines free.

NONFICTION Buys 20 mss/year. Query. Length: 500-1,500 words. **Pays 40-50¢/word.** Sometimes pays expenses of writers on assignment.

PHOTOS Contact: Jim Black. Reviews GIF/JPEG files. Negotiates payment individually.

TIPS "We want well-written, accurate information. We deal with our writers honestly and expect the same in return."

⊕ GRAIN JOURNAL

Country Journal Publishing Co., 3065 Pershing Court, Decatur IL 62526. (800)728-7511. **E-mail:** ed@grain-net.com. **Website:** www.grainnet.com. **Contact:** Ed Zdrojewski, editor. **5% freelance written.** Bimonthly magazine covering grain handling and merchandising. *Grain Journal* serves the North American grain industry, from the smallest country grain elevators and feed mills to major export terminals. Estab. 1972. Circ. 12,000. Byline sometimes given. Pays on publication. No kill fee. Publishes ms an average of 2 months after acceptance. Editorial lead time 2 months. Submit seasonal material 2 months in advance. Accepts simultaneous submissions. Sample copy free.

NONFICTION Needs how-to, interview, new product, technical. Query. 750 words maximum. **Pays $100.**

PHOTOS Send photos. Captions, identification of subjects required. Reviews contact sheets, negatives, transparencies, 3x5 prints, electronic files. Offers $50-100/photo.

TIPS "Call with your idea. We'll let you know if it is suitable for our publication."

⊕ ONION WORLD

Columbia Publishing, 8405 Ahtanum Rd., Yakima WA 98903. (509)248-2452, ext. 105. **Fax:** (509)248-4056. **E-mail:** dbrent@columbiapublications.com. **Website:** www.onionworld.net. **Contact:** Brent Clement, editor. **25% freelance written.** Monthly magazine covering the world of onion production and marketing for onion growers and shippers. Estab. 1985. Circ. 5,500. Byline given. Pays on publication. No kill fee. Publishes ms an average of 1 month after acceptance. Submit seasonal material 1 month in advance. Accepts queries by e-mail or phone. Accepts simultaneous submissions. Responds in 1 month to queries. Sample copy for SAE with 9x12 envelope and 5 first-class stamps.

NONFICTION Needs general interest, historical, interview. **Buys 30 mss/year.** Query. Length: 1,200-1,250 words. **Pays $100-250 per article, depending upon length. Mileage paid, but query first.**

REPRINTS Send photocopy and information about when and where the material previously appeared. Pays 50% of amount paid for an original article.

PHOTOS Send photos. Captions, identification of subjects required. Offers no additional payment for photos accepted with ms, unless it's a cover shot.

TIPS "Writers should be familiar with growing and marketing onions. We use a lot of feature stories on growers, shippers, and others in the onion trade—what they are doing, varieties grown, their problems, solutions, marketing plans, etc."

⊕ SPUDMAN

Great American Publishing, P.O. Box 128, Sparta MI 49345. (616)887-9008. **Fax:** (616)887-2666. **E-mail:** bills@spudman.com. **Website:** www.spudman.com. **Contact:** Bill Schaefer, managing editor. **10% freelance written.** Monthly magazine covering potato industry's growing, packing, processing, and chipping. Estab. 1964. Circ. 10,000. Byline given. Pays on publication. Offers $75 kill fee. Publishes ms an average of 2 months after acceptance. Editorial lead time 2 months. Submit seasonal material 4 months in advance. Accepts queries by mail, e-mail. YesResponds in 2-3 weeks to queries. Sample copy for SAE with 8½ x 11 envelope and 3 first-class stamps. Guidelines for #10 SASE.

$ THE VEGETABLE GROWERS NEWS

Great American Publishing, P.O. Box 128, Sparta MI 49345. (616)887-9008, ext. 102. **Fax:** (616)887-2666. **E-mail:** vgnedit@vegetablegrowersnews.com. **Website:** www.vegetablegrowersnews.com. **Contact:** Matt Milkovich, managing editor. **10% freelance written.** Monthly tabloid covering agriculture. Estab. 1970. Circ. 16,000. Pays on publication. No kill fee. Publishes ms an average of 2 months after acceptance. Editorial lead time 1-2 months. Submit seasonal material 3 months in advance. Accepts queries by mail, e-mail, fax. Accepts simultaneous submissions. Responds in 2 weeks to queries. Responds in 1 month to mss. Sample copy free.

NONFICTION Needs general interest, interview, new product. No advertorials, other puff pieces. **Buys 25 mss/year.** Query with published clips and résumé. Length: 800-1,200 words. **Pays $100-125.** Sometimes pays expenses of writers on assignment.

PHOTOS Send photos. Captions required. Reviews prints. Offers $15/photo.

DAIRY FARMING

$$ HOARD'S DAIRYMAN

W.D. Hoard and Sons, Co., 28 Milwaukee Ave., W., P.O. Box 801, Fort Atkinson WI 53538. (920)563-5551. **Fax:** (920)563-7298. **E-mail:** hoards@hoards.com. **Website:** www.hoards.com. Tabloid published 20 times/year covering dairy industry. "We publish semi-technical information published for dairy-farm families and their advisors. If you have a handy way to handle something on your farm, submit it as 1 of our famed Handy Hints." Estab. 1885. Circ. 100,000. Byline given. Pays on acceptance. No kill fee. Publishes ms an average of 4 months after acceptance. Editorial lead time 2 months. Submit seasonal material 3 months in advance. Accepts queries by mail, e-mail, fax. Responds in 2 weeks to queries. Responds in 1 month to mss. Guidelines for #10 SASE.

NONFICTION Needs how-to, technical. **Buys 60 mss/year.** Query. Length: 800-1,500 words. **Pays $150-350.**

PHOTOS Send photos. Reviews 2x2 transparencies. Offers no additional payment for photos.

COLUMNS/DEPARTMENTS "Handy Hints that are published receive $30, and if you include a clear, reproducible photo, that earns you an additional $20. The photo should be at least 240 dpi and approximately 4x 6 in size to print well in our magazine. And, when you provide your full mailing address with your hint, payment will be sent promptly. (Hints and photos can also be mailed to the Hoard's Dairyman office)."

LIVESTOCK

$$ ANGUS BEEF BULLETIN

Angus Productions, Inc., 3201 Frederick Ave., St. Joseph MO 64506-2997. (816)383-5270. **Fax:** (816)233-6575. **E-mail:** shermel@angusjournal.com. **Website:** www.angusbeefbulletin.com. **Contact:** Shauna Rose Hermel, editor. **45% freelance written.** Tabloid published 5 times/year covering commercial cattle industry. The *Bulletin* is mailed free to commercial cattlemen who have purchased an Angus bull and had the registration transferred to them and to others who sign a request card. Estab. 1985. Circ. 65,000-70,000. Byline given. Pays on publication. No kill fee. Publishes ms an average of 3 months after acceptance. Editorial lead time 3 months. Submit seasonal material 3 months in advance. Accepts queries by mail, e-mail. Accepts simultaneous submissions. Responds in 3 weeks to queries. Responds in 3 months to mss. Sample copy for $5. Guidelines for #10 SASE.

NONFICTION Needs how-to, cattle production, interview, technical, cattle production. **Buys 10 mss/year.** Query with published clips. Length: 800-2,500 words. **Pays $50-600.** Pays expenses of writers on assignment.

PHOTOS Send photos. Identification of subjects required. Reviews 5×7 transparencies, 5×7 glossy prints. Offers $25/photo.

TIPS Read the publication and have a firm grasp of the commercial cattle industry and how the Angus breed fits in that industry.

$$$ ANGUS JOURNAL

Angus Productions Inc., 3201 Frederick Ave., St. Joseph MO 64506-2997. (816)383-5270. **Fax:** (816)233-6575. **E-mail:** shermel@angusjournal.com. **Website:** www.angusjournal.com. **40% freelance written.** Monthly magazine covering Angus cattle. The *Angus Journal* is the official magazine of the American Angus Association. Its primary function as such is to report to the membership association activities and information pertinent to raising Angus cattle. Estab. 1919. Circ. 13,500. Byline given. Pays on publication. No kill fee. Publishes ms an average of 3 months after acceptance. Editorial lead time 2 months. Submit seasonal material 3 months in advance. Accepts queries by mail, e-mail, fax. Accepts simultaneous submissions. Responds in 3 weeks to queries. Responds in 2 months to mss. Sample copy for $5. Guidelines with #10 SASE.

NONFICTION Needs how-to, cattle production, interview, technical, related to cattle. **Buys 20-30 mss/ year.** Query with published clips. Length: 800-3,500 words. **Pays $50-1,000.** Pays expenses of writers on assignment.

PHOTOS Send photos. Identification of subjects required. Reviews 5×7 glossy prints. Offers $25-400/ photo.

TIPS "Have a firm grasp of the cattle industry."

BACKYARD POULTRY

Countryside Publications, Ltd., 145 Industrial Dr., Medford WI 54451. (715)785-7979. **Fax:** (715)785-7414. **E-mail:** byp@tds.net. **Website:** www.backyard-poultrymag.com. **Contact:** Elaine Belanger, editor. Bimonthly magazine covering breed selection, housing, management, health and nutrition, and other topics of interest to promote more and better raising of small-scale poultry. Query first.

THE BRAHMAN JOURNAL

Carl and Victoria Lambert, 915 12th St., Hempstead TX 77445. (979)826-4347. **Fax:** (979)826-2007. **E-mail:** info@brahmanjournal.com; vlambert@brahmanjournal.com. **Website:** www.brahmanjournal. com. **Contact:** Victoria Lambert, editor. **10% freelance written.** Monthly magazine covering Brahman cattle. *The Brahman Journal* provides timely and useful information about one of the largest and most dynamic breeds of beef cattle in the world. In each issue, *The Brahman Journal* reports on Brahman shows, events, and sales as well as technical articles and the latest research as it pertains to the Brahman Breed. Estab. 1971. Circ. 4,000. Byline given. Pays on publication. No kill fee. Publishes ms an average of 2 months after acceptance. Submit seasonal material 3 months in advance. Sample copy for SAE with 9x12 envelope and 5 first-class stamps.

NONFICTION Needs general interest, historical, interview. Special issues: See the Calendar online for special issues. **Buys 3-4 mss/year.** Query with published clips. Length: 1,200-3,000 words. **Pays $100-250.**

REPRINTS Send typed ms with rights for sale noted. Pays 50% of amount paid for an original article.

PHOTOS Photos needed for article purchase. Send photos. Captions required. Reviews 4x5 prints. Offers no additional payment for photos accepted with ms.

TIPS "Since *The Brahman Journal* is read around the world, being sent to 48 different countries, it is important that the magazine contain a wide variety of information. *The Brahman Journal* is read by seed stock producers, show ring competitors, F-1 breeders and Brahman lovers from around the world."

THE CATTLEMAN

Texas and Southwestern Cattle Raisers Association, 1301 W. Seventh St., Suite 201, Fort Worth TX 76102. **E-mail:** ehbrisendine@tscra.org. **Website:** www.the-cattlemanmagazine.com. **Contact:** Ellen H. Brisendine, editor. **25% freelance written.** Monthly magazine covering the Texas/Oklahoma beef cattle industry. "We specialize in in-depth, management-type articles related to range and pasture, beef cattle production, animal health, nutrition, and marketing. We want 'how-to' articles." Estab. 1914. Circ. 15,400. Byline given. Pays on acceptance. No kill fee. Publishes ms an average of 2 months after acceptance. Editorial lead time 2 months. Submit seasonal material 6 months in advance. Accepts queries by mail, e-mail. Sample copy free. Guidelines available online.

NONFICTION Needs how-to, interview, new product, personal experience, technical, ag research. Special issues: Editorial calendar themes include: Horses (January); Range and Pasture (February); Livestock Marketing (July); Hereford and Wildlife (August); Feedlots (September); Bull Buyers (October); Ranch Safety (December). Does not want to see anything not specifically related to beef production in the Southwest. **Buys 20 mss/year.** Query with published clips. Length: 1,500-2,000 words. **Pays $200-350 for assigned articles. Pays $100-350 for unsolicited articles.** Sometimes pays expenses of writers on assignment.

PHOTOS Identification of subjects required. Reviews transparencies, prints, digital files. Offers no additional payment for photos accepted with ms.

TIPS "Subscribers said they were most interested in the following topics in this order: range/pasture, property rights, animal health, water, new innovations, and marketing. *The Cattleman* prefers to work on an assignment basis. However, prospective contributors are urged to write the managing editor of the magazine to inquire of interest on a proposed subject. Occasionally, the editor will return a manuscript to a potential contributor for cutting, polishing, checking, rewriting, or condensing. Be able to demonstrate background/knowledge in this field. Include tearsheets from similar magazines."

💲💲 FEED LOT MAGAZINE

Feed Lot Magazine, Inc., P.O. Box 850, Dighton KS 67839. (620)397-2838. **Fax:** (620)397-2839. **E-mail:** feedlot@st-tel.net. **Website:** www.feedlotmagazine. com. **60% freelance written.** Bimonthly magazine that provides readers with the most up-to-date information on the beef industry in concise, easy-to-read articles designed to increase overall awareness among the feedlot community. "The editorial information content fits a dual role: large feedlots and their related cow/calf operations, and large 500pl cow/calf, 100pl stocker operations. The information covers all phases of production from breeding, genetics, animal health, nutrition, equipment design, research through finishing fat cattle. *Feed Lot* publishes a mix of new information and timely articles which directly affect the cattle industry." Estab. 1992. Circ. 12,000. Byline given. Pays on publication. Offers 50% kill fee. Publishes ms an average of 2 months after acceptance. Editorial lead time 2 months. Submit seasonal material 6 months in advance. Accepts queries by mail, e-mail, fax. Responds in 1 month to queries. Sample copy and writer's guidelines e-mailed.

NONFICTION Needs interview, new product, cattle-related, photo feature. Send complete ms; original material only. Length: 100-400 words. **Pays 30¢/word.**

PHOTOS State availability of or send photos. Captions, model releases required. Reviews contact sheets. Negotiates payment individually.

TIPS "Know what you are writing about—have a good knowledge of the subject."

💲 SHEEP! MAGAZINE

Countryside Publications, Ltd., 145 Industrial Dr., Medford WI 54451. (715)785-7979; (800)551-5691. **Fax:** (715)785-7414. **E-mail:** sheepmag@tds.net. **Website:** www.sheepmagazine.com. **35% freelance written. Prefers to work with published/established writers.** Bimonthly magazine published in north-central Wisconsin. Estab. 1980. Circ. 11,000. Byline given. Pays on publication. Offers $30 kill fee. Submit seasonal material 3 months in advance.

NONFICTION Needs book excerpts, how-to, on innovative lamb and wool marketing and promotion techniques, efficient record-keeping systems, or specific aspects of health and husbandry, interview, on experienced sheep producers who detail the economics and management of their operation, new product, of value to sheep producers; should be written by someone who has used them, technical, on genetics health and nutrition. **Buys 80 mss/year.** Send complete ms. Length: 750-2,500 words. **Pays $45-150.**

PHOTOS Color—vertical compositions of sheep and/or people—for cover. 35mm photos or other visuals improve chances of a sale. Identification of subjects required.

TIPS "Send us your best ideas and photos! We love good writing!"

MANAGEMENT

💲 AG JOURNAL

Arkansas Valley Publishing, 422 Colorado Ave., (P.O. Box 500), La Junta CO 81050. (719)384-1453. **E-mail:** publisher@ljtdmail.com; bcd@ljtdmail.com. **Website:** www.agjournalonline.com. **Contact:** Candi Hill, publisher/editor; Jennifer Justice, assistant editor. **20% freelance written.** Weekly journal covering agriculture. Estab. 1949. Circ. 11,000. Byline given. Pays on publication. No kill fee. Publishes ms an average of 2 weeks after acceptance. Editorial lead time 1 month. Submit seasonal material 1 month in advance. Accepts queries by e-mail. YesResponds in 2 weeks to queries. Sample copy and writer's guidelines free.

NONFICTION Needs how-to, interview, new product, opinion, photo feature, technical. Query by e-mail only. **Pays 4¢/word.** Sometimes pays expenses of writers on assignment.

PHOTOS State availability. Captions, identification of subjects required. Offers $8/photo.

💲💲 SMALLHOLDER MAGAZINE

Newsquest Media Group, 3 Falmouth Business Park, Bickland Water Rd., Falmouth Cornwall TR11 4SZ United Kingdom. (01)326-213338. **Fax:** (01)326-212084. **E-mail:** editorial@smallholder.co.uk. **Website:** www.smallholder.co.uk. **Contact:** Graham Smith. No kill fee. Accepts queries by e-mail. Sample copy available online. Guidelines by e-mail.

NONFICTION Length: 700-1,400 words. **Pays 4£/ word.**

PHOTOS Send photos. Reviews 300 dpi digital images. Pays £5-50.

MISCELLANEOUS FARM

🌐💲 ACRES U.S.A.

P.O. Box 301209, Austin TX 78703. (512)892-4400. **Fax:** (512)892-4448. **E-mail:** editor@acresusa.com. **Website:** www.acresusa.com. "Monthly trade journal written by people who have a sincere interest in the principles of organic and sustainable agriculture." Estab. 1970. Circ. 18,000. Byline given. Pays on publication. No kill fee. Editorial lead time 4 months. Submit seasonal material 6 months in advance. Accepts queries by mail, e-mail, fax. Accepts simultaneous submissions. Sample copy and writer's guidelines free. **NONFICTION** Needs exposé, how-to, personal experience. Special issues: Seeds (January), Poultry (February), Certified Organic (May), Livestock (June), Homesteading (August), Soil Fertility & Testing (October). Does not want poetry, fillers, product profiles, or anything with a promotional tone. **Buys about 50 mss/year.** Send complete ms. Length: 1,000-2,500 words. **Pays 10¢/word**

PHOTOS State availability of or send photos. Captions, identification of subjects required. Reviews GIF/JPEG/TIF files. Negotiates payment individually.

🌐💲 BEE CULTURE

P.O. Box 706, Medina OH 44256-0706. **Fax:** (330)725-5624. **E-mail:** kim@beeculture.com. **Website:** www.beeculture.com. **Contact:** Mr. Kim Flottum, editor. **50% freelance written.** Covers the natural science of honey bees. "Monthly magazine for beekeepers and those interested in the natural science of honey bees, with environmentally-oriented articles relating to honey bees or pollination." Estab. 1873. Pays on publication. No kill fee. Publishes ms an average of 4 months after acceptance. Accepts queries by mail, e-mail, fax, phone. Responds in 1 month to mss. Sample copy with 9x12 SASE and 5 first-class stamps. Guidelines and sample copy available online.

NONFICTION Needs interview, personal experience, photo feature. No "How I Began Beekeeping" articles. Highly advanced, technical, and scientific abstracts accepted for review for quarterly Refered section. Length: 2,000 words average. **Pays $200-250.**

REPRINTS Send photocopy and information about when and where the material previously appeared.

Pays about the same as for an original article, on negotiation.

PHOTOS Color prints, 5x7 standard, but 3x5 are OK. Electronic images encouraged. Digital JPEG, color only, at 300 dpi best, prints acceptable. Model release required. Photo captions preferred. Pays $50 for cover photos. Photos payment included with article payment.

TIPS "Do an interview story on commercial beekeepers who are cooperative enough to furnish accurate, factual information on their operations. Frequent mistakes made by writers in completing articles are that they are too general in nature and lack management knowledge."

🌐💲💲 PRODUCE BUSINESS

Phoenix Media Network Inc., P.O. Box 810425, Boca Raton FL 33481-0425. (561)994-1118. **E-mail:** kwhitacre@phoenixmedianet.com; info@producebusiness.com. **Website:** www.producebusiness.com. **Contact:** Ken Whitacre, publisher/editorial director. **90% freelance written.** Monthly magazine covering produce and floral marketing. Estab. 1985. Circ. 16,000. Byline given. Pays 30 days after publication. Offers $50 kill fee. Editorial lead time 2 months. Accepts queries by e-mail. NoSample copy and guidelines free.

NONFICTION Does not want unsolicited articles. **Buys 150 mss/year.** Query with published clips. Length: 1,200-10,000 words. **Pays $240-1,200.** Pays expenses of writers on assignment.

REGIONAL FARM

🌐💲 AMERICAN AGRICULTURIST

5227 Baltimore Pike, Littlestown PA 17340. (717)359-0150. **Fax:** (717)359-0250. **E-mail:** jvogel@farmprogress.com. **Website:** www.farmprogress.com. **20% freelance written.** Monthly magazine covering "cutting-edge technology and news to help farmers improve their operations." "We publish cutting-edge technology with ready on-farm application." Estab. 1842. Circ. 32,000. Pays on publication. No kill fee. Publishes ms an average of 3 months after acceptance. Editorial lead time 3 months. Submit seasonal material 3 months in advance. Accepts queries by e-mail, fax. Responds in 2 weeks to queries. Responds in 1 month to mss. Guidelines for #10 SASE.

NONFICTION Needs how-to, humor, inspirational, interview, new product, technical, "No stories without a strong tie to Mid-Atlantic farming." **Buys 20**

mss/year. Query. Length: 500-1,000 words. **Pays $250-500.** Sometimes pays expenses of writers on assignment.

PHOTOS Send photos. Captions, identification of subjects, model releases required. Reviews transparencies, JPEG files. Offers $75-200/photo.

COLUMNS/DEPARTMENTS Country Air (humor, nostalgia, inspirational), 300-400 words. **Buys Buys 12 mss/year mss/year.** Send complete ms. **Pays $100.**

⊗⊗ FLORIDA GROWER

Meister Media Worldwide, 37733 Euclid Ave., Willoughby OH 44094. (440)942-2000. **E-mail:** fgiles@ meistermedia.com; pprusnak@meistermedia.com. **Website:** www.growingproduce.com/floridagrower. **Contact:** Frank Giles, editor; Paul Rusnak, managing editor. **10% freelance written.** "Monthly magazine edited for the Florida farmer with commercial production interest primarily in citrus, vegetables, and other ag endeavors. Our goal is to provide articles which update and inform on such areas as production, ag financing, farm labor relations, technology, safety, education, and regulation". Estab. 1907. Circ. 12,200. Byline given. Pays on publication. No kill fee. Editorial lead time 2 months. Submit seasonal material 3 months in advance. Accepts queries by mail, e-mail, fax, phone. Responds in 1 month to queries. Sample copy for SAE with 9x12 envelope and 5 First-Class stamps. Guidelines free.

NONFICTION Needs interview, photo feature, technical. Query with published clips. Length: 700-1,000 words. **Pays $150-250.**

PHOTOS Send photos.

⊗ THE LAND

Free Press Co., P.O. Box 3169, Mankato MN 56002-3169. (507)345-4523. **E-mail:** editor@thelandonline. com. **Website:** www.thelandonline.com. **40% freelance written.** Weekly tabloid covering farming in Minnesota and Northern Iowa. "Although we're not tightly focused on any one type of farming, our articles must be of interest to farmers. In other words, will your article topic have an impact on people who live and work in rural areas? Prefers to work with Minnesota or Iowa writers." Estab. 1976. Circ. 33,000. Byline given. Pays on acceptance. No kill fee. Publishes ms an average of 2 months after acceptance. Editorial lead time 2 months. Submit seasonal material 2 months in advance. Accepts queries by mail, e-mail.

Responds in 3 weeks to queries. Responds in 2 months to mss. Sample copy free. Guidelines with #10 SASE.

NONFICTION Needs general interest, ag, how-to, crop, livestock production, marketing. **Buys 80 mss/ year.** Query. Length: 500-750 words. **Pays $50-70 for assigned articles.**

PHOTOS Send photos. Reviews contact sheets. Negotiates payment individually.

COLUMNS/DEPARTMENTS Query. **Pays $10-50.**

TIPS "Be enthused about rural Minnesota and Iowa life and agriculture, and be willing to work with our editors. We try to stress relevance. When sending me a query, convince me the story belongs in a Minnesota farm publication."

FINANCE

○ ⊗⊗⊗ ADVISOR'S EDGE

Rogers Media, Inc., 333 Bloor St. E., 6th Floor, Toronto ON M4W 1G6 Canada. **E-mail:** philip.porado@rci. rogers.com. **Website:** www.advisor.ca. **Contact:** Philip Porado, executive editor. Monthly magazine covering the financial industry (financial advisors and investment advisors). "*Advisor's Edge* focuses on sales and marketing opportunities for the financial advisor (how they can build their business and improve relationships with clients)." Estab. 1998. Circ. 36,000. Byline given. Pays on publication. Offers 25% kill fee. Publishes ms an average of 3 months after acceptance. Editorial lead time 3 months. Accepts queries by e-mail. Sample copy available online.

NONFICTION Needs how-to, interview. No articles that aren't relevant to how a financial advisor does his/ her job. **Buys 12 mss/year.** Query with published clips. Length: 1,500-2,000 words. **Pays $900 (Canadian).**

○ ◐ ⊗⊗⊗ AFP EXCHANGE

Association for Financial Professionals, 4520 East-West Hwy., Suite 750, Bethesda MD 20814. (301)907-2862. **E-mail:** exchange@afponline.org. **Website:** www.afponline.org/exchange. **20% freelance written.** Monthly magazine covering corporate treasury, corporate finance, B2B payments issues, corporate risk management, accounting and regulatory issues from the perspective of corporations. Welcomes interviews with CFOs and senior level practitioners. "Best practices and practical information for corporate CFOs and treasurers. Tone is professional, intended to appeal to financial professionals on the job. Most accepted articles are written by professional journalists and editors, many featuring high-level AFP members in profile and case studies." Estab. 1979. Circ. 25,000. Byline given. Pays on publication. Offers kill fee. Pays negotiable kill fee in advance. Editorial lead time 2 months. Submit seasonal material 3 months in advance. Accepts queries by e-mail. Responds in 1 week to queries. Responds in 1 month to mss.

NONFICTION Needs book excerpts, how-to, interview, personal experience, technical. No PR-type articles pointing to any type of product or solution. **Buys 3-4 mss/year.** Query. Length: 1,100-1,800 words. **Pays 75¢-$1 for assigned articles.**

COLUMNS/DEPARTMENTS Cash Flow Forecasting (practical tips for treasurers, CFOs); Financial Reporting (insight, practical tips); Risk Management (practical tips for treasurers, CFOs); Corporate Payments (practical tips for treasurers), all 1,000-1,300 words; Professional Development (success stories, career related, about high level financial professionals), 1,100 words. **Buys 10 mss/year.** Query. **Pays $75¢-$1/word.**

FILLERS Needs anecdotes. Length: 400-700 words. **Pays 75¢/word.**

TIPS "Accepted submissions deal with high-level issues relevant to today's corporate CFO or treasurer, including issues of global trade, global finance, accounting, M&A, risk management, corporate cash management, international regulatory issues, communications issues with corporate boards and shareholders, and especially new issues on the horizon. Preference given to articles by or about corporate practitioners in the finance function of mid-to large-size corporations in the U.S. or abroad. Also purchase articles by accomplished financial writers. Cannot accept content that points to any product, 'solution' or that promotes any vendor. Should not be considered a PR outlet. Authors may be required to sign agreement."

$$$ COLLECTIONS & CREDIT RISK

SourceMedia, One State St. Plaza, 27th Floor, New York NY 10004. **E-mail:** darren.waggoner@sourcemedia.com. **Website:** www.creditcollectionsworld.com. **Contact:** Darren Waggoner, chief editor. **33% freelance written.** Monthly journal covering debt collections and credit risk management. "*Collections & Credit Risk* is the only magazine that brings news and trends of strategic and competitive importance to collections and credit-policy executives who are driving the collections industry's growth and diversification in both commercial and consumer credit. These executives work for financial institutions, insurance companies, collections agencies, law firms and attorney networks, health-care providers, retailers, telecoms and utility companies, manufacturers, wholesalers, and government agencies." Estab. 1996. Circ. 30,000. Byline given. Pays on acceptance. Offers kill fee. Kill fee determined case by case. Publishes ms an average of 3 months after acceptance. Editorial lead time 3 months. Accepts queries by mail. Sample copy free or online.

NONFICTION Needs interview, technical, business news and analysis. No unsolicited submissions accepted—freelancers work on assignment only. **Buys 30-40 mss/year.** Query with published clips. Length: 1,000-2,500 words. **Pays $800-1,000.** Sometimes pays expenses of writers on assignment.

TIPS "This is a business news and analysis magazine focused on events and trends affecting the credit-risk management and collections professions. Our editorial approach is modeled after *Business Week, Forbes, Fortune, Wall Street Journal.* No fluff accepted."

$$$ CREDIT TODAY

P.O. Box 720, Roanoke VA 24004. (540)343-7500. **E-mail:** robl@credittoday.net; editor@credittoday.net. **Website:** www.credittoday.net. **Contact:** Rob Lawson, publisher. **50% freelance written.** Monthly newsletter covering business or trade credit. Estab. 1997. No byline given. Pays on acceptance. Publishes ms an average of 2 months after acceptance. Editorial lead time 1-2 months. Accepts queries by e-mail. NoSample copy free. Guidelines free.

NONFICTION Needs how-to, interview, technical. Does not want "puff" pieces promoting a particular product or vendor. **Buys 20 mss/year.** Send complete ms. Length: 700-1,800 words. **Pays $200-1,400.**

TIPS "Make pieces actionable, personable, and a quick read."

$$ CREDIT UNION MANAGEMENT

Credit Union Executives Society, 5510 Research Park Dr., Madison WI 53711. (608)271-2664. **E-mail:** lisa@cues.org; cues@cues.org. **Website:** www.cumanagement.org. **Contact:** Lisa Hochgraf, editor. **44% freelance written.** Monthly magazine covering credit union, banking trends, management, HR, and marketing issues. "Our philosophy mirrors the credit union industry of cooperative financial services." Estab. 1978. Circ. 7,413. Pays on acceptance. No kill fee. Publishes ms an average of 2 months after acceptance. Editorial lead time 3 months. Submit seasonal material 4 months in advance. Accepts queries by mail. Accepts simultaneous submissions. Responds in 2 weeks to queries; 1 month to mss. Sample copy and writer's guidelines free.

NONFICTION Needs book excerpts, how-to, be a good mentor/leader, recruit, etc., interview, technical. **Buys 74 mss/year.** Query with published clips. Length: 700-2,400 words. **$250-350 for assigned features.** Phone expenses only

COLUMNS/DEPARTMENTS Management Network (book/Web reviews, briefs), 300 words; e-marketing, 700 words; Point of Law, 700 words; Best Practices (new technology/operations trends), 700 words. Query with published clips.

TIPS "The best way is to e-mail an editor; include rèsumè, cover letter and clips. Knowledge of financial services is very helpful."

$$ SERVICING MANAGEMENT

Zackin Publications, P.O. Box 2180, Waterbury CT 06722. (800)325-6745. **Fax:** (203)262-4680. **E-mail:** hallp@sm-online.com. **Website:** www.sm-online.com. **Contact:** Phil Hall, editor. **15% freelance written.** Monthly magazine covering residential mortgage servicing. Estab. 1989. Circ. 20,000. Byline given. Pays on acceptance. No kill fee. Publishes ms an average of 2 months after acceptance. Accepts queries by mail, e-mail, fax, phone. Responds in 2 weeks to queries. Sample copy free. Guidelines available online.

NONFICTION Needs how-to, interview, new product, technical. **Buys 10 mss/year.** Query. Length: 1,500-2,500 words.

PHOTOS State availability. Identification of subjects required. Reviews contact sheets. Offers no additional payment for photos accepted with ms.

COLUMNS/DEPARTMENTS **Buys 5 mss/year.** Query. **Pays $200.**

$$$ THE FEDERAL CREDIT UNION

National Association of Federal Credit Unions, 3138 10th St. N., Arlington VA 22201. (703)522-4770; (800)336-4644. **Fax:** (703)524-1082. **E-mail:** rtaylor@nafcu.org. **Website:** www.nafcu.org/tfcuonline. **Contact:** Rick Taylor, associate editor. **30% freelance written.** Estab. 1967. Circ. 8,000. Byline given. Pays on publication. No kill fee. Publishes ms an average of 3 months after acceptance. Submit seasonal material 5 months in advance. Accepts queries by mail, e-mail, fax. Accepts simultaneous submissions. Responds in 2 months to queries. Sample copy for SAE with 10x13 envelope and 5 first-class stamps. Guidelines for #10 SASE.

NONFICTION Needs humor, inspirational, interview. Query with published clips and SASE. Length: 1,200-2,000 words. **Pays $400-1,000.**

PHOTOS Send photos. Identification of subjects, model releases required. Reviews 35mm transparencies, 5x7 prints, high-resolution photos. Offers no additional payment for photos accepted with ms. Pays $50-500.

TIPS "We would like more articles on how credit unions are using technology to serve their members and more articles on leading-edge technologies they can use in their operations. If you can write on current trends in technology, human resources, or strategic planning, you stand a better chance of being published than if you wrote on other topics."

$$$$ USAA MAGAZINE

USAA, 9800 Fredericksburg Rd., San Antonio TX 78288. **E-mail:** usaamagazine@usaa.com. **Website:** www.usaa.com/maglinks. **80% freelance written.** Quarterly magazine covering financial security for USAA members. "Conservative, common-sense approach to personal finance issues. Especially interested in how-to articles and pieces with actionable tips." Estab. 1970. Circ. 4.2 million. Byline given. Pays on acceptance. Offers 25% kill fee. Publishes ms an average of 4 months after acceptance. Editorial lead time 6 months. Submit seasonal material 6 months in advance. Accepts queries by e-mail. Responds in 6-8 weeks to queries. No mss accepted. Sample copy available online. Guidelines by e-mail.

NONFICTION Needs general interest, (finance), historical, (military), how-to, (personal finance), interview, (military/financial), personal experience, (finance). No poetry, photos, lifestyle unrelated to military or personal finance. **Buys 20 mss/year.** Query with published clips. Length: 750-1,500 words. **Pays $750-1,500 for assigned articles.** Sometimes pays expenses of writers on assignment.

TIPS "Story must take a unique or innovative approach to the personal finance topic. Piece must be actionable and useful. (Not philosophical or academic.)"

FISHING

🌐 AUSMARINE

Baird Publications, Suite 3, 20 Cato St., Hawthorne East 3123 Australia. (61)(3)9824-6055. **Fax:** (61)(3)9824-6588. **E-mail:** marinfo@baird.com.au. **Website:** www.bairdmaritime.com. Monthly magazine covering the Australian commercial fishing and government marine industry. "*Ausmarine* offers its readers information and ideas as to how to improve the efficiency and profitability of their business operations through the adoption of new technology and equipment, improved operational techniques and systems, and by simply providing them with the information required to make the right business decisions." Estab. 1978.

NONFICTION Query.

FLORIST, NURSERIES AND LANDSCAPERS

$$ DIGGER

Oregon Association of Nurseries, 29751 S.W. Town Center Loop W., Wilsonville OR 97070. (503)682-5089; (800) 342-6401. **Fax:** (503)682-5099. **E-mail:** ckipp@oan.org; info@oan.org. **Website:** www.oan.org. **Contact:** Curt Kipp, publications manager. **50% freelance written.** Monthly magazine covering nursery and greenhouse industry. "*Digger* is a monthly magazine that focuses on industry trends, regulations, research, marketing, and membership activities. In August the magazine becomes *Digger Farwest Edition*, with all the features of *Digger* plus a complete guide to the annual Farwest Show, 1 of North America's top-attended nursery industry trade shows." Circ. 8,000. Byline given. Pays on receipt of copy. Offers 100% kill fee. Publishes ms an average of 2 months after acceptance. Editorial lead time 6 weeks. Submit seasonal material 2 months in advance. Accepts queries by mail, e-mail, fax, phone. Sample copy and writer's guidelines free.

NONFICTION Needs general interest, how-to, propagation techniques, other crop-growing tips, interview, personal experience, technical. Special issues: "Farwest Edition (August)—this is a triple-size issue that runs in tandem with our annual trade show (14,500 circulation for this issue)." No articles not related or pertinent to nursery and greenhouse industry. **Buys 20-30 mss/year.** Query. Length: 800-2,000 words. **Pays $125-400 for assigned articles. Pays $100-300 for unsolicited articles.** Sometimes pays expenses of writers on assignment.

PHOTOS State availability. Captions, identification of subjects required. Reviews high-res digital images sent by e-mail or on CD preferred. Offers $25-150/photo.

TIPS "Our best freelancers are familiar with or have experience in the horticultural industry. Some 'green' knowledge is a definite advantage. Our readers are mainly nursery and greenhouse operators and owners who propagate nursery stock/crops, so we write with them in mind."

$ GROWERTALKS

Ball Publishing, 622 Town Rd., P.O. Box 1660, West Chicago IL 60186. (630)588-3385; (630)588-3401. **Fax:** (630)208-9350. **E-mail:** jzurko@ballpublishing.com; cbeytes@growertalks.com. **Website:** www.growertalks.com. **Contact:** Jen Zurko. **50% freelance written.** Monthly magazine covering horticulture. Estab. 1937. Circ. 9,500. Byline given. Pays on publication. No kill fee. Publishes ms an average of 3 months after acceptance. Editorial lead time 4 months. Submit seasonal material 3 months in advance. Accepts queries by mail, e-mail, fax. Responds in 1 month to queries. Sample copy and writer's guidelines free.

NONFICTION Needs how-to, time- or money-saving projects for professional flower/plant growers, interview, ornamental horticulture growers, personal experience, of a grower, technical, about growing process in greenhouse setting. No articles that promote only 1 product. **Buys 36 mss/year.** Query. Length: 1,200-1,600 words. **Pays $125 minimum for assigned articles. Pays $75 minimum for unsolicited articles.**

PHOTOS State availability. Captions, identification of subjects, model releases required. Reviews 2 1/2x2 1/2 slides and 3x5 prints. Negotiates payment individually.

TIPS "Discuss magazine with ornamental horticulture growers to find out what topics that have or haven't appeared in the magazine interest them."

$$ TREE CARE INDUSTRY MAGAZINE

Tree Care Industry Association, 136 Harvey Rd., Suite 101, Londonderry NH 03053. (800)733-2622 or (603)314-5380. **Fax:** (603)314-5386. **E-mail:** editor@tcia.org. **Website:** www.tcia.org. **Contact:** Don Staruk, editor. **50% freelance written.** Monthly magazine covering tree care and landscape maintenance. Estab. 1990. Circ. 27,500. Byline given. Pays within 1 month of publication. No kill fee. Publishes manuscripts an average of 3 months after acceptance. Editorial lead time 10 weeks. Submit seasonal material 3 months in advance. Accepts queries by e-mail. Responds within 2 days to queries. Responds in 2 months to mss. Sample copies: View PDFs online. Guidelines free.

NONFICTION Needs book excerpts, historical, interview, new product, technical. **Buys 60 mss/year.** Query with published clips. Length: 900-3,500 words. **Pays negotiable rate.**

PHOTOS Send photos with submission by e-mail or FTP site. Captions, identification of subjects required. Reviews prints. Negotiate payment individually.

COLUMNS/DEPARTMENTS Buys 40 mss/year. Send complete ms. **Pays $100 and up.**

TIPS "Preference is given to writers with background and knowledge of the tree care industry; our focus is relatively narrow."

GOVERNMENT AND PUBLIC SERVICE

💲💲 AMERICAN CITY & COUNTY

Penton Media, 6151 Powers Ferry Rd. NW, Suite 200, Atlanta GA 30339. (770)618-0199. **Fax:** (770)618-0349. **E-mail:** bill.wolpin@penton.com; lindsay.isaacs@penton.com. **Website:** www.americancityandcounty.com. **Contact:** Bill Wolpin, editorial director. **40% freelance written.** Monthly magazine covering local and state government in the U.S. Estab. 1909. Circ. 65,000. Byline given. Pays on publication. Offers 25% kill fee. Publishes ms an average of 2 months after acceptance. Editorial lead time 3 months. Accepts queries by e-mail. Accepts simultaneous submissions. Sample copy available online. Guidelines by e-mail.

NONFICTION Needs new product, local and state government news analysis. **Buys 36 mss/year.** Query. Length: 600-2,000 words. **Pays 30¢/published word.** Sometimes pays expenses of writers on assignment.

PHOTOS State availability. Captions required. Reviews GIF/JPEG files. Negotiates payment individually.

COLUMNS/DEPARTMENTS Issues & Trends (local and state government news analysis), 500-700 words. **Buys Buys 24 ms/year. mss/year.** Query. **Pays $150-250.**

TIPS "We use only third-person articles. We do not tell the reader what to do; we offer the facts and assume the reader will make his or her own informed decision. We cover city and county government and state highway departments. We do not cover state legislatures or the federal government, except as they affect local government."

🌐 BLUE LINE MAGAZINE

12A-4981 Highway 7 East, Suite 254, Markham ON L3R 1N1 Canada. (905)640-3048. **Fax:** (905)640-7547. **E-mail:** blueline@blueline.ca. **Website:** www.blueline.ca. Monthly magazine keeping readers on the leading edge of law enforcement information, whether it be case law, training issues or technology trends. Estab. 1989. Circ. 12,000.

NONFICTION Needs general interest, how-to, interview, new product. Query.

💲💲 COUNTY

Texas Association of Counties, P.O. Box 2131, Austin TX 78768-2131. (512)478-8753. **Fax:** (512)481-1240. **E-mail:** marias@county.org. **Website:** www.county.org. **Contact:** Maria Sprow, managing editor. **15% freelance written.** Bimonthly magazine covering county and state government in Texas. "We provide elected and appointed county officials with insights and information that help them do their jobs and enhances communications among the independent office-holders in the courthouse." Estab. 1988. Circ. 5,500. Byline given. Pays on acceptance. No kill fee. Publishes ms an average of 2 months after acceptance. Editorial lead time 2 months. Submit seasonal material 4 months in advance. Accepts queries by mail, e-mail, phone. Responds in 2 weeks to queries. Responds in 1 month to mss. Sample copy and writer's guidelines for 8x10 SAE with 3 first-class stamps.

NONFICTION Needs historical, photo feature, government innovations. **Buys 5 mss/year.** Query with published clips. Length: 1,000-3,000 words. **Pays $500-700.** Sometimes pays expenses of writers on assignment.

PHOTOS State availability. Captions, identification of subjects, model releases required. Negotiates payment individually.

COLUMNS/DEPARTMENTS Safety; Human Resources; Risk Management (all directed toward education of Texas county officials), maximum length 1,000 words. **Buys Buys 2 mss/year.** Query with published clips. **Pays $500.**

TIPS "Identify innovative practices or developing trends that affect Texas county officials, and have the basic journalism skills to write a multi-sourced, informative feature."

EVIDENCE TECHNOLOGY MAGAZINE

P.O. Box 555, Kearney MO 64060. **E-mail:** kmayo@evidencemagazine.com. **Website:** www.evidencemagazine.com. **Contact:** Kristi Mayo, editor. Bimonthly magazine providing news and information relating to the collection, processing, and preservation of evidence. "This is a business-to-business publication, not a peer reviewed journal. We look for mainstream pieces. Our readers want general crime scenes and forensic science articles." Accepts queries by e-mail. Guidelines available online.

NONFICTION Needs general interest, how-to, interview, new product, technical. Query. **Pays 2 contributor copies.**

PHOTOS Provide photos and/or illustrations. Reviews JPEG files (300 dpi or larger).

TIPS "Opening a dialogue with the editor will give you the opportunity to get guidelines on length, style, and deadlines."

⊕⊕ FIRE CHIEF

Primedia Business, 330 N. Wabash Ave., Suite 2300, Chicago IL 60611. (312)595-1080. **Fax:** (312)595-0295. **E-mail:** lisa@firechief.com. **Website:** www.firechief.com. **Contact:** Lisa Allegretti, editor. **60% freelance written.** Monthly magazine covering the fire chief occupation. "*Fire Chief* is the management magazine of the fire service, addressing the administrative, personnel, training, prevention/education, professional development, and operational issues faced by chiefs and other fire officers, whether in paid, volunteer, or combination departments. We're potentially interested in any article that can help them do their jobs better, whether that's as incident commanders, financial managers, supervisors, leaders, trainers, planners, or ambassadors to municipal officials or the public." Estab. 1956. Circ. 53,000. Byline given. Pays on publication. Offers kill fee. Kill fee negotiable. Publishes ms an average of 6 months after acceptance. Editorial lead time 2 months. Submit seasonal material 4 months in advance. Accepts queries by mail, e-mail, fax. Responds in 1 month to queries. Responds in 2 months to mss. Sample copy and submission guidelines free.

NONFICTION Needs how-to, technical. "We do not publish fiction, poetry, or historical articles. We also aren't interested in straightforward accounts of fires or other incidents, unless there are one or more specific lessons to be drawn from a particular incident, especially lessons that are applicable to a large number of departments." **Buys 50-60 mss/year.** Query first with published clips. Length: 1,000-10,000 words. **Pays $50-400.** Sometimes pays expenses of writers on assignment.

PHOTOS State availability. Captions, identification of subjects required. Reviews transparencies, prints.

COLUMNS/DEPARTMENTS Training Perspectives; EMS Viewpoints; Sound Off; Volunteer Voice; all 1,000-1,800 words.

TIPS "Writers who are unfamiliar with the fire service are very unlikely to place anything with us. Many pieces that we reject are either too unfocused or too abstract. We want articles that help keep fire chiefs well informed and effective at their jobs."

FIRE ENGINEERING

PennWell Corporation, 21-00 Rt. 208 S., Fair Lawn NJ 07410-2602. (800)962-6484, ext. 5047. **E-mail:** dianef@pennwell.com. **Website:** www.fireengineering.com. **Contact:** Diane Feldman, executive editor. Monthly magazine covering issues of importance to firefighters. Estab. 1877. Accepts queries by mail, e-mail. Responds in 2-3 months to mss. Guidelines available online.

NONFICTION Needs how-to, new product, incident reports, training. Send complete ms.

PHOTOS Reviews electronic format only: JPEG/TIFF/EPS files (300 dpi).

COLUMNS/DEPARTMENTS Volunteers Corner; Training Notebook; Rescue Company; The Engine Company; The Truck Company; Fire Prevention Bureau; Apparatus; The Shops; Fire Service EMS; Fire Service Court; Speaking of Safety; Fire Commentary; Technology Today; and Innovations: Homegrown. Send complete ms.

FIRE PROTECTION CONTRACTOR

550 High St., Suite 220, Auburn CA 95603. (530)823-0706. **Fax:** (530)823-6937. **E-mail:** info@fpcmag.com. **Website:** www.fpcmag.com. **Contact:** Brant Brumbeloe, editor. Monthly magazine for the benefit of fire protection contractors, engineers, designers, sprinkler fitters, apprentices, fabricators, manufacturers, and distributors of fire protection products used in

automatic fire sprinkler systems. Estab. 1978. Guidelines available on website.

NONFICTION Needs general interest, how-to, interview, new product, technical. Query.

FIRERESCUE

525 B St., Suite 1800, San Diego CA 92101. (619)699-6807. **Fax:** (619)699-6396. **E-mail:** janellef@pennwell.com. **Website:** www.firefighternation.com. **Contact:** Janelle Foskett, managing editor. "FireRescue covers the fire and rescue markets. Our 'Read It Today, Use It Tomorrow' mission weaves through every article and image we publish. Our readers consist of fire chiefs, company officers, training officers, firefighters, and technical rescue personnel." Estab. 1997. Circ. 50,000. Pays on publication. Accepts queries by mail, e-mail. Responds in 1 month to mss. Guidelines available online.

NONFICTION Needs general interest, how-to, interview, new product, technical. "All story ideas must be submitted with a cover letter that outlines your qualifications and includes your name, full address, phone, fax, social security or tax ID number, and e-mail address. We accept story submissions in 1 of the following 2 formats: query letters and mss." Length: 800-2,200 words. **Pays $100—$200 for features.**

PHOTOS Looks for "photographs that show firefighters in action, using proper techniques and wearing the proper equipment. Submit timely photographs that show the technical aspects of firefighting and rescue. Tight shots/close-ups preferred." Digital images in JPEG, TIFF, or EPS format at 72 dpi for initial review. We require 300 dpi resolution for publication. If you send images as attachments via e-mail, compress your files with Stuffit, Disk Doubler, etc.

TIPS "Read back issues of the magazine to learn our style. Research back issues to ensure we haven't covered your topic within the past three years. Read and follow the instructions on our guidelines page."

⊗⊗ LAW ENFORCEMENT TECHNOLOGY MAGAZINE

Cygnus Business Media, 1233 Janesville Ave., Fort Atkinson WI 53538. (800)547-7377. **E-mail:** officer@corp.officer.com; jonathan.kozlowski@cygnusb2b.com. **Website:** www.officer.com. **Contact:** Jonathan Kozlowski, editor. **40% freelance written.** Monthly magazine covering police management and technology. Estab. 1974. Circ. 30,000. Byline given. Pays on publication. No kill fee. Publishes ms an average of 4

months after acceptance. Editorial lead time 6 months. Responds in 1 month to queries. Responds in 2 months to mss. Guidelines free.

NONFICTION Needs how-to, interview, photo feature, police management and training. **Buys 30 mss/year.** Query. Length: 1,200-2,000 words. **Pays $75-400 for assigned articles.**

REPRINTS Send typed ms with rights for sale noted and information about when and where the material previously appeared. Payment negotiable.

PHOTOS Send photos. Captions required. Reviews contact sheets, negatives, 5x7 or 8x10 prints. Offers no additional payment for photos accepted with ms.

TIPS "Writer should have background in police work or currently work for a police agency. Most of our articles are technical or supervisory in nature. Please query first after looking at a sample copy. Prefers mss, queries, and images be submitted electronically."

⊗⊗ PLANNING

American Planning Association, 205 N. Michigan Ave., Suite 1200, Chicago IL 60601. (312)431-9100. **Fax:** (312)786-6700. **E-mail:** slewis@planning.org. **Website:** www.planning.org. **Contact:** Sylvia Lewis, editor; Joan Cairney, art director. **30% freelance written.** Monthly magazine emphasizing urban planning for adult, college-educated readers who are regional and urban planners in city, state, or federal agencies or in private business, or university faculty or students. Estab. 1972. Circ. 44,000. Byline given. Pays on publication. No kill fee. Publishes ms an average of 2 months after acceptance. Accepts queries by mail, e-mail, fax. Responds in 5 weeks to queries. Guidelines available online.

NONFICTION Special issues: Transportation Issue. Also needs news stories up to 500 words. **Buys 44 features and 33 news story mss/year.** Length: 500-3,000 words. **Pays $150-1,500.**

PHOTOS "We prefer authors supply their own photos, but we sometimes take our own or arrange for them in other ways." State availability. Captions required. Pays $100 minimum for photos used on inside pages and $300 for cover photos.

⊗⊗⊗⊗ YOUTH TODAY

Kennesaw State University, 1000 Chastain Rd., MD 2212, Bldg. 22, Kennesaw GA 30144. (202)785-0764. **E-mail:** jfleming@youthtoday.org. **Website:** www.youthtoday.org. **Contact:** John Fleming, editor. **50% freelance written.** Newspaper published 10 times a year covering businesses that provide services to youth.

Audience is people who run youth programs—mostly nonprofits and government agencies—who want help in providing services and getting funding. Estab. 1994. Circ. 9,000. Byline given. Pays on publication. Offers $200 kill fee for features. Editorial lead time 2 months. Accepts queries by mail, e-mail, or disk. Accepts simultaneous submissions. Responds in 2 weeks to queries. Responds in 1 month to mss. Sample copy for $5. Guidelines available on website.

NONFICTION Needs exposé, general interest, technical. "No feel-good stories about do-gooders. We examine the business of youth work." **Buys 5 mss/year.** Query. Send rèsumè, short cover letter, clips. Length: 600-2,500 words. **Pays $150-2,000 for assigned articles.** Pays expenses of writers on assignment.

PHOTOS Identification of subjects required. Offers no additional payment for photos accepted with ms.

COLUMNS/DEPARTMENTS *"Youth Today* also publishes 750-word guest columns, called Viewpoints. These pieces can be based on the writer's own experiences or based on research, but they must deal with an issue of interest to our readership and must soundly argue an opinion, or advocate for a change in thinking or action within the youth field."

TIPS "Business writers have the best shot. Focus on evaluations of programs, or why a program succeeds or fails. Please visit online."

GROCERIES AND FOOD PRODUCTS

⊛⊛⊛ CONVENIENCE DISTRIBUTION

American Wholesale Marketers Association, 2750 Prosperity Ave., Suite 530, Fairfax VA 22031. (703)208-3358. **Fax:** (703)573-5738. **E-mail:** info@awmanet.org. **Website:** www.awmanet.org. **70% freelance written.** Magazine published 10 times/year. "We cover trends in candy, tobacco, groceries, beverages, snacks, and other product categories found in convenience stores, grocery stores, and drugstores, plus distribution topics. Contributors should have prior experience writing about the food, retail, and/or distribution industries. Editorial includes a mix of columns, departments, and features (2-6 pages). We also cover AWMA programs." Estab. 1948. Circ. 11,000. Byline given. Pays on acceptance. No kill fee. Publishes ms an average of 2 months after acceptance. Editorial lead time 3-4 months. Accepts queries by e-mail only. Guidelines available online.

NONFICTION Needs how-to, technical, industry trends, also profiles of distribution firms. No comics, jokes, poems, or other fillers. **Buys 40 mss/year.** Query with published clips. Length: 1,200-3,600 words. **Pays 50¢/word.** Pays expenses of writers on assignment.

PHOTOS Authors must provide artwork (with captions) with articles.

TIPS "We're looking for reliable, accurate freelancers with whom we can establish a long-term working relationship. We need writers who understand this industry. We accept very few articles on speculation. Most are assigned. To consider a new writer for an assignment, we must first receive his or her résumé , at least 2 writing samples, and references."

⊛⊛⊛⊛ FOOD PRODUCT DESIGN MAGAZINE

P.O. Box 3439, Northbrook IL 60065-3439. (480)990-1101 ext. 1241; (800)581-1811. **E-mail:** lkuntz@vpico.com. **Website:** www.foodproductdesign.com. **Contact:** Lynn A. Kuntz, editor-in-chief. **50% freelance written.** Monthly magazine covering food processing industry. Written for food technologists by food technologists. No foodservice/restaurant, consumer, or recipe development. "Official media for SupplySide, *Food Product Design* delivers practical, use-it-now, take-it-to-the-bench editorial for product development professionals, as well as market intelligence and analysis of industry news for the executive-level reader. *Food Product Design* is the industry's leading product development content and information source." Estab. 1991. Circ. 30,000. Byline given. Pays on acceptance. Publishes ms an average of 2 months after acceptance. Editorial lead time 4 months. Sample copy for SAE with 9x12 envelope and 5 first-class stamps.

NONFICTION Needs technical. **Buys 30 mss/year.** Length: 1,500-7,000 words. **Pays $100-1,500.** Sometimes pays expenses of writers on assignment.

REPRINTS Accepts previously published submissions, depending on where it was published.

PHOTOS State availability. Captions required. Reviews transparencies, prints. Offers no additional payment for photos accepted with ms.

COLUMNS/DEPARTMENTS Pays $100-500.

TIPS "If you haven't worked in the food industry in research and development, or QA/QC, don't bother to call us. If you can't communicate technical information in a way that is clear, easy-to-understand, and well organized, don't bother to call us. While perfect grammar is not expected, good grammar and organization is."

🟢 FRESH CUT MAGAZINE

Great American Publishing, P.O. Box 128, 75 Applewood Dr., Suite A, Sparta MI 49345. (616)887-9008. **Fax:** (616)887-2666. **E-mail:** fcedit@freshcut.com. **Website:** www.freshcut.com. **Contact:** Lee Dean, editorial director. **20% freelance written.** Monthly magazine covering the value-added and pre-cut fruit and vegetable industry. The editor is interested in articles that focus on what different fresh-cut processors are doing. Estab. 1993. Circ. 16,000. Byline given. Pays on publication. No kill fee. Publishes ms an average of 2 months after acceptance. Editorial lead time 2 months. Accepts queries by mail, e-mail, fax, phone, online submission form. Responds in 1 month to queries. Responds in 2 months to mss. Sample copy for SAE with 9x12 envelope. Guidelines for #10 SASE.

NONFICTION Needs historical, new product, opinion, technical. **Buys 2-4 mss/year.** Query with published clips.

REPRINTS Send tearsheet with rights for sale noted and information about when and where the material previously appeared. Pays 50% of amount paid for an original article.

PHOTOS Send photos. Identification of subjects required. Reviews transparencies. Offers no additional payment for photos accepted with ms.

COLUMNS/DEPARTMENTS Packaging; Food Safety; Processing/Engineering. **Buys 20 mss/year.** Query. **Pays $125-200.**

🟢🟢🟢 NATURAL FOOD NETWORK MAGAZINE

1030 W. Higgins Rd., Suite 230, Park Ridge IL 60068. (847)720-5600. **E-mail:** news@naturalfoodnet.com; pan@m2media360.com. **Website:** www.natural-foodnet.com. **Contact:** Pan Demetrakakes, editor. **70% freelance written.** Bimonthly magazine covering natural and certified organic food industry (domestic and international). Estab. 2003. Circ. 15,000. Byline given. Pays on publication. Offers 10% (up to $50 maximum) kill fee. Publishes ms an average of 2 months after acceptance. Editorial lead time 2 months. Submit seasonal material 2 months in advance. Accepts queries by e-mail. Accepts simulta-

neous submissions. Responds in 1 week to queries. Responds in 1 month to mss. Sample copy and guidelines free.

NONFICTION Does not want work with a consumer angle. **Buys 50 mss/year.** Query. Length: 250-1,500 words. **Pays $250-750.** Sometimes pays expenses of writers on assignment.

PHOTOS State availability. Captions, identification of subjects required. Reviews JPEG files. Offers no additional payment for photos accepted with ms.

COLUMNS/DEPARTMENTS Q&A with industry leaders (natural and organic specialists in academia, trade associations and business); Worldview (interviews with internationally recognized leaders in organic food supply), both 750 words. **Buys 6 mss/year mss/year.** Query. **Pays $500.**

TIPS "Our magazine encourages writers to work closely with editors using online story pitch and assignment software. This collaborative software permits writers to see what is being pitched (anonymously) and to track their own assignments, download materials like story guidelines and monitor deadlines."

🟢🟢 THE PRODUCE NEWS

800 Kinderkamack Rd., Suite 100, Oradell NJ 07649. (201)986-7990. **Fax:** (201)986-7996. **E-mail:** groh@theproducenews.com. **Website:** www.theproduce-news.com. **Contact:** John Groh, editor and publisher. **10% freelance written. Works with a small number of new/unpublished writers each year.** Weekly magazine for commercial growers and shippers, receivers, and distributors of fresh fruits and vegetables, including chain store produce buyers and merchandisers. Estab. 1897. Pays on publication. No kill fee. Publishes ms an average of 2 weeks after acceptance. Accepts queries by mail, e-mail. Responds in 1 month to queries. Sample copy and writer's guidelines for 10x13 SAE and 4 first-class stamps.

NONFICTION Query. **Pays $1/column inch minimum.** Sometimes pays expenses of writers on assignment.

PHOTOS B&W glossies or color prints. Pays $8-10/photo.

TIPS "Stories should be trade oriented, not consumer oriented. As our circulation grows, we are interested in stories and news articles from all fresh-fruit-growing areas of the country."

HOME FURNISHINGS AND HOUSEHOLD GOODS

ENLIGHTENMENT

Bravo Integrated Media, 620 W. Germantown Pike, Suite 440, Plymouth Meeting PA 19462. (800)774-9861. **E-mail:** news@enlightenmentmag.com. **Website:** www.enlightenmentmag.com. **25% freelance written. Prefers to work with published/established writers.** Monthly magazine for lighting showrooms/department stores. Estab. 1923. Circ. 10,000. Pays on publication. No kill fee. Publishes ms an average of 6 months after acceptance. Submit seasonal material 6 months in advance. Accepts queries by mail. Responds in 2 months to queries. Sample copy for SAE with 9x12 envelope and 4 first-class stamps.

NONFICTION Needs interview, with lighting retailers, personal experience, as a businessperson involved with lighting, technical, concerning lighting or lighting design, profile (of a successful lighting retailer/lamp buyer). **Buys less than 10 mss/year.** Query.

REPRINTS Send tearsheet and information about when and where the material previously appeared.

PHOTOS State availability. Captions required.

TIPS "Have a unique perspective on retailing lamps and lighting fixtures. We often use freelancers located in a part of the country where we'd like to profile a specific business or person. Anyone who has published an article dealing with any aspect of home furnishings will have high priority."

$$ HOME FURNISHINGS RETAILER

National Home Furnishings Association (NHFA), 3910 Tinsley Dr., Suite 101, High Point NC 27265-3610. (336)801-6156. **Fax:** (336)801-6102. **E-mail:** wynnryan@rcn.com. **Website:** www.nhfa.org. **Contact:** Mary Wynn Ryan, editor-in-chief. **75% freelance written.** Monthly magazine published by NHFA covering the home furnishings industry. "We hope home furnishings retailers view our magazine as a profitability tool. We want each issue to help them make or save money." Estab. 1927. Circ. 15,000. Byline given. Pays on acceptance. No kill fee. Publishes ms an average of 6 weeks after acceptance. Editorial lead time 3 months. Accepts queries by mail, e-mail. Responds in 1 month to queries. Sample copy available with proper postage. Guidelines available.

NONFICTION Query. "When submitting a query or requesting a writing assignment, include a résumé, writing samples, and credentials. When articles are assigned, *Home Furnishings Retailer* will provide general direction along with suggestions for appropriate artwork. The author is responsible for obtaining photographs or other illustrative material. Assigned articles should be submitted via e-mail or on disc along with a list of sources with telephone numbers, fax numbers, and e-mail addresses." Length: 3,000-5,000 words (features). **Pays $350-500.**

PHOTOS Author is responsible for obtaining photos or other illustrative material. State availability. Identification of subjects required. Reviews transparencies. Negotiates payment individually.

COLUMNS/DEPARTMENTS Columns cover business and product trends that shape the home furnishings industry. Advertising and Marketing; Finance; Technology; Training; Creative Leadership; Law; Style and Operations. Length: 1,200-1,500 words. Query with published clips.

TIPS "Our readership includes owners of small 'ma and pa' furniture stores, executives of medium-sized chains (2-10 stores), and executives of big chains. Articles should be relevant to retailers and provide them with tangible information, ideas, and products to better their business."

HOSPITALS, NURSING AND NURSING HOMES

$$$ HOSPITALS & HEALTH NETWORKS

Health Forum Inc., 155 N. Wacker Dr., Suite 400, Chicago IL 60606. (312)893-6800. **Fax:** (312)422-4500. **E-mail:** rhill@healthforum.com; bsantamour@healthforum.com. **Website:** www.hhnmag.com. **Contact:** Richard Hill, editor; Bill Santamour, managing editor. **25% freelance written.** Monthly magazine covering hospitals. "We are a business publication for hospital and health system executives. We use only writers who are thoroughly familiar with the hospital field." Estab. 1926. Circ. 85,000. Byline given. Pays on acceptance. Offers variable kill fee. Publishes ms an average of 3 months after acceptance. Editorial lead time 2-3 months. Accepts queries by e-mail. Responds in 2-4 months to queries. Guidelines available online.

NONFICTION Needs interview, technical. Query with published clips. "Submit résumé and up to 5 samples of health care-related articles. We assign all articles and do not consider mss." Length: 350-2,000 words. **Pays $300-1,500 for assigned articles.**

TIPS "If you demonstrate via published clips that you are thoroughly familiar with the business issues facing health-care executives, and that you are a polished reporter and writer, we will consider assigning you an article for our InBox section to start out. These are generally 350 words on a specific development of interest to hospitals and health system executives. Persistence does not pay with us. Once you've sent your résumé and clips, we will review them. If we have no assignment at that time, we will keep promising freelance candidates on file for future assignments."

◎ ⑤⑤ LONG TERM CARE

Ontario Long Term Care Association, 345 Renfrew Dr., Third Floor, Markham ON L3R 9S9 Canada. (905)470-8995. **Fax:** (905)470-9595. **E-mail:** info@oltca.com. **Website:** www.oltca.com. **Contact:** Karen Milligan; Tracey Ann Coveart. Quarterly magazine covering professional issues and practical articles of interest to staff working in a long-term care setting (nursing home, retirement home). Information must be applicable to a Canadian setting; focus should be on staff and on resident well-being. Estab. 1990. Circ. 6,000. Byline given. Pays on publication. No kill fee. Publishes ms an average of 4 months after acceptance. Editorial lead time 3 months. Submit seasonal material 5 months in advance. Responds in 3 months to queries. Sample copy and guidelines free.

NONFICTION Needs general interest, how-to, practical, of use to long term care practitioners, inspirational, interview. No product-oriented articles. Query with published clips. Individuals should submit their ideas and/or completed articles to: justwrite@powergate.ca. Electronic versions in either Wordperfect or MS Word are preferred. Length:400-2,500 words. **Pays up to $500 (Canadian).**

PHOTOS Send photos. Captions, model releases required. Reviews contact sheets, 5x5 prints. Offers no additional payment for photos accepted with ms.

COLUMNS/DEPARTMENTS Query with published clips. **Pays up to $500 (Canadian).**

TIPS "Articles must be positive, upbeat, and contain helpful information that staff and managers working in the long-term care field can use. Focus should be on staff and resident well being. Articles that highlight new ways of doing things are particularly useful.

Please call the editor to discuss ideas. Must be applicable to Canadian settings."

⑤⑤⑤ NURSEWEEK

Gannett Healthcare Group, 1721 Moon Lake Blvd., Suite 540, Hoffman Estates IL 60169. **E-mail:** editor@nurse.com. **Website:** www.nurse.com. **Contact:** Jennifer Thew, RN. **98% freelance written.** Biweekly magazine covering nursing news. "Registered nurses read our magazine, which they receive for free by mail. We cover nursing news about people, practice, and the profession. Before you begin to write, we recommend that you review several of our magazines for content and style. We also suggest e-mailing your idea to the editorial director in your region (See list online). The editorial director can help you with the story's focus or angle, along with the organization and development of ideas." Estab. 1999. Circ. 155,000. Byline given. Pays on publication. Offers $200 kill fee. Publishes ms an average of 2 months after acceptance. Editorial lead time 2-3 months. Submit seasonal material 4 months in advance. Accepts queries by e-mail. Accepts simultaneous submissions. Sample copy free. Guidelines on website.

NONFICTION Needs interview, personal experience, , articles on innovative approaches to clinical care and evidence-based nursing practice, health-related legislation and regulation, community health programs, healthcare delivery systems, and professional development and management, advances in nursing specialties such as critical care, geriatrics, perioperative care, women's health, home care, long-term care, emergency care, med/surg, pediatrics, advanced practice, education, and staff development. "We don't want poetry, fiction, or technical pieces." **Buys 20 mss/year.** Query. Length: 900 words. **Pays $200-800 for assigned or unsolicited articles.**

PHOTOS Send photos. Captions, model releases required. Reviews contact sheets, GIF/JPEG files. Offers no additional payment for photos accepted with ms.

TIPS "Pitch us nursing news, AP style, minimum 3 sources, incorporate references. The stories we publish are short and written in a conversational, magazine-style rather than a scholarly tone. In keeping with any article appearing in a nursing publication, clinical accuracy is essential."

⑤⑤ NURSING2013

(formerly *Nursing2012*), Lippincott Williams & Wilkins, 323 Norristown Rd., Suite 200, Ambler PA

19002-2758. (215)646-8700. **Fax:** (215)654-1328. **E-mail:** nursingeditor@wolterskluwer.com. **Website:** www.nursing2013.com; http://journals.lww.com/nursing/pages/default.aspx. **Contact:** Linda Laskowski-Jones, RN, ACNS-BC, CCRN, CEN, MS, FAWM. **100% freelance written.** Monthly magazine written by nurses for nurses. "We look for practical advice for the direct caregiver that reflects the author's experience. Any form acceptable, but focus must be nursing." Estab. 1971. Circ. over 300,000. Byline given. Pays on publication. Offers 50% kill fee. Publishes ms an average of 18 months after acceptance. Submit seasonal material 8 months in advance. Responds in 2 weeks to queries. Responds in 3 months to mss. Sample copy for $5. "Specific instructions and guidelines for submitting articles are readily available on the submission service site. Please read and review them carefully."

NONFICTION Needs book excerpts, exposé, how-to, specifically as applies to nursing field, inspirational, opinion, personal experience, photo feature No articles from patients' point of view, poetry, etc. **Buys 100 mss/year.** "Query. All mss can be submitted online through the journal's submission website at www.LWWeSubmissions.com. Using this process will expedite review and feedback, and you can see where your ms is in the editorial process at any time after it's accepted. So we strongly encourage you to register there as an author and follow the directions." Length: 3,500 words (continuing ed feature); 2,100 words (features); short features/departments, 700 words. **Pays $50-400 for assigned articles.**

REPRINTS Send photocopy and information about when and where the material previously appeared. Pays 50% of amount paid for an original articles.

PHOTOS State availability. Model releases required. Offers no additional payment for photos accepted with ms.

TIPS "Basically, *Nursing2013* is a how-to journal, full of hands-on, practical articles. We look for the voice of experience from authors and for articles that help our readers deal with problems they face. We're always interested in taking a look at mss that fall into the following categories: clinical articles, drug articles, charting/documentation, emotional problems, legal problems, ethical dilemnas, and difficult or challenging cases."

$ SCHOOL NURSE NEWS

Franklin Communications, Inc., 71 Redner Rd., Morristown NJ 07960. (973)644-4003. **Fax:** (973)644-4062. **E-mail:** michael@schoolnursenews.org. **Website:** www.schoolnursenews.org. **Contact:** Michael Franklin, publisher. **10% freelance written.** Magazine published 5 times/year covering school nursing. "*School Nurse News* focuses on topics related to the health issues of school-aged children and adolescents (grades K-12), as well as the health and professional issues that concern school nurses. We believe this is an excellent opportunity for both new and experienced writers. *School Nurse News* publishes feature articles as well as news articles and regular departments, such as Asthma & Allergy Watch, Career & Salary Survey, Oral Health, Nursing Currents, and Sights & Sounds." Estab. 1982. Circ. 7,500. Byline given. Pays on publication. Publishes ms an average of 3-6 months after acceptance. Editorial lead time 3-6 months. Submit seasonal material 6 months in advance. Accepts queries by e-mail, fax, phone. Sample copy free. Guidelines available on website.

NONFICTION Needs how-to, interview, new product, personal experience. **Buys 1-2 mss/year.** Query. Send via e-mail or forward ms with disk. "Mss can include case histories, scenarios of health office situations, updates on diseases, reporting of research, and discussion of procedures and techniques, among others. The author is responsible for the accuracy of content. References should be complete, accurate, and in APA format. Tables, charts and photographs are welcome. Authors are responsible for obtaining permission to reproduce any material that has a pre-existing copyright. The feature article, references, tables, and charts should total 8-10 typewritten pages, double-spaced. The author's name should be included only on the top sheet. The top sheet should also include the title of the article, the author's credentials, current position, address, and phone." **Pays $100.**

HOTELS, MOTELS, CLUBS AND RESTAURANTS

$$ BARTENDER MAGAZINE

Foley Publishing, P.O. Box 158, Liberty Corner NJ 07938. (908)766-6006. **Fax:** (908)766-6607. **E-mail:** barmag@aol.com. **Website:** www.bartender.com. **Contact:** Jackie Foley, editor. **100% freelance written.**

Prefers to work with published/established writers; eager to work with new/unpublished writers. Quarterly magazine emphasizing liquor and bartending for bartenders, tavern owners, and owners of restaurants with full-service liquor licenses. Estab. 1979. Circ. 150,000. Byline given. Pays on publication. No kill fee. Publishes ms an average of 3 months after acceptance. Submit seasonal material 3 months in advance. Accepts simultaneous submissions. Responds in 2 months to mss. Sample copy with 9x12 SAE and 4 first-class stamps.

NONFICTION Needs general interest, historical, how-to, humor, interview with famous bartenders or ex-bartenders, new product, opinion, personal experience, photo feature, travel, nostalgia, unique bars, new techniques, new drinking trends, bar sports, bar magic tricks. Special issues: Special issues: Annual Calendar and Daily Cocktail Recipe Guide. Send complete ms and SASE. Length: 100-1,000 words.

REPRINTS Send tearsheet and information about when and where the material previously appeared. Pays 25% of amount paid for an original article.

PHOTOS Send photos. Captions, model releases required. Pays $7.50-50 for 8x10 b&w glossy prints; $10-75 for 8x10 color glossy prints.

COLUMNS/DEPARTMENTS Bar of the Month; Bartender of the Month; Creative Cocktails; Bar Sports; Quiz; Bar Art; Wine Cellar; Tips from the Top (from prominent figures in the liquor industry); One For the Road (travel); Collectors (bar or liquor-related items); Photo Essays. Length: 200-1,000 words. Query by mail only with SASE. **Pays $50-200.**

FILLERS Needs anecdotes, newsbreaks, short humor, clippings, jokes, gags. Length: 25-100 words. **Pays $5-25.**

TIPS "To break in, absolutely make sure your work will be of interest to all bartenders across the country. Your style of writing should reflect the audience you are addressing. The most frequent mistake made by writers in completing an article for us is using the wrong subject."

◎◎ EL RESTAURANTE MEXICANO

P.O. Box 2249, Oak Park IL 60303-2249. (708)267-0023. **E-mail:** kfurore@comcast.net. **Website:** www.restmex.com. **Contact:** Kathleen Furore, editor. Bimonthly magazine covering Mexican and other Latin cuisines. "*El Restaurante Mexicano* offers features and business-related articles that are geared specifi-

cally to owners and operators of Mexican, Tex-Mex, Southwestern, and Latin cuisine restaurants and other foodservice establishments that want to add that type of cuisine." Estab. 1997. Circ. 27,000. Byline given. Pays on publication. No kill fee. Publishes ms an average of 3 months after acceptance. Responds in 2 months to queries. Sample copy free.

NONFICTION "No specific knowledge of food or restaurants is needed; the key qualification is to be a good reporter who knows how to slant a story toward the Mexican restaurant operator." **Buys 4-6 mss/year.** Query with published clips. Length: 800-1,200 words. **Pays $250-300.** Pays expenses of writers on assignment.

TIPS "Query with a story idea, and tell how it pertains to Mexican restaurants."

⊘ ◎◎◎◎ HOSPITALITY TECHNOLOGY

Edgell Communications, 4 Middlebury Blvd., Randolph NJ 07869. (973)607-1300. **E-mail:** alorden@edgellmail.com. **Website:** www.htmagazine.com. **Contact:** Abigail Lorden, editor-in-chief. **70% freelance written.** Magazine published 9 times/year covering restaurant and lodging executives who manage hotels, casinos, cruise lines, quick service restaurants, etc. "We cover the technology used in foodservice and lodging. Our readers are the operators, who have significant IT responsibilities." Estab. 1996. Circ. 16,000. Byline given. Pays on acceptance. No kill fee. Publishes ms an average of 1 month after acceptance. Editorial lead time 2 months. Accepts queries by mail, e-mail. Responds in 2 weeks to queries.

NONFICTION Needs how-to, interview, new product, technical. Special issues: "We publish 2 studies each year: the Restaurant Industry Technology Study and the Lodging Industry Technology Study." No unsolicited mss. **Buys 40 mss/year.** Query with published clips. Length: 800-1,200 words. **Pays $1/word.** Sometimes pays expenses of writers on assignment.

TIPS "Given the vast amount of inquiries we receive, it's impossible for us to respond to all. We can only respond to those that are of particular interest."

◎ ◎◎ HOTELIER

Kostuch Media Ltd., 101-23 Lesmill Rd., Toronto ON M3B 3P6 Canada. (416)447-0888. **Fax:** (416)447-5333. **E-mail:** rcaira@foodservice.ca. **Website:** www.hoteliermagazine.com. **Contact:** Rosanna Caira, editor & publisher. **40% freelance written.** Magazine pubwww queries by mail, fax. Accepts simultaneous submissions. Responds in 2 weeks to queries. Sample copy and writer's guidelines free.

NONFICTION Needs how-to, train staff, interview. Industry reports and profiles on companies. Query with published clips. Length: 500-9,000 words. **Pays 25-35¢/word.** Sometimes pays expenses of writers on assignment.

PHOTOS State availability. Captions required. Reviews negatives, transparencies, 3x5 prints, JPEG, EPS, or TIF files. Negotiates payment individually.

TIPS "E-mail, fax, or mail a query outlining your experience, interests, and pay expectations. Include clippings."

☺ ☻☻ WESTERN RESTAURANT NEWS

Mercury Publications, Ltd., 1740 Wellington Ave., Winnipeg MB R3H 0E8 Canada. (204)954-2085. **Fax:** (204)954-2057. **E-mail:** editorial@mercury.mb.ca. **Website:** www.westernrestaurantnews.com; www.mercury.mb.ca. **Contact:** Nicole Sherwood, editorial coordinator. **20% freelance written.** Bimonthly magazine covering the restaurant trade in Western Canada. Reports profiles and industry reports on associations, regional business developments, etc. "*Western Restaurant News* is the authoritative voice of the foodservice industry in Western Canada. Offering a total package to readers, *WRN* delivers concise news articles, new product news, and coverage of the leading trade events in the West, across the country, and around the world." Estab. 1994. Circ. 14,532. Byline given. Pays 30-45 days from receipt of invoice. Offers 33% kill fee. Submit seasonal material 3 months in advance. Accepts queries by mail, fax. Accepts simultaneous submissions. Sample copy and writer's guidelines free.

NONFICTION Needs how-to, interview. Industry reports and profiles on companies. Query with published clips. Length: 500-9,000 words. **Pays 25-35¢/word.** Sometimes pays expenses of writers on assignment.

PHOTOS State availability. Captions required. Reviews negatives, transparencies, 3x5 prints, JPEG, EPS, or TIFF files. Negotiates payment individually.

TIWW2

INDUSTRIAL OPERATIONS

☺ ☻☻ COMMERCE & INDUSTRY

Mercury Publications, Ltd., 1740 Wellington Ave., Winnipeg MB R3H 0E8 Canada. (204)954-2085. **Fax:** (204)954-2057. **E-mail:** editorial@mercury.mb.ca. **Website:** www.commerceindustry.ca. **Contact:** Nicole Sherwood, editorial coordinator. **75% freelance written.** Bimonthly magazine covering the business and industrial sectors. "Offers new product news, industry event coverage, and breaking trade specific business stories. Industry reports and company profiles provide readers with an in-depth insight into key areas of interest in their profession." Estab. 1947. Circ. 18,876. Byline given. Pays 30-45 days from receipt of invoice. Offers 33% kill fee. Submit seasonal material 3 months in advance. Accepts queries by mail, e-mail, fax. Accepts simultaneous submissions. Responds in 2 weeks to queries. Sample copy and writer's guidelines free or by e-mail.

NONFICTION Needs how-to, interview. Industry reports and profiles on companies. Query with published clips. Length: 500-9,000 words. **Pays 25-35¢/word.** Sometimes pays expenses of writers on assignment.

PHOTOS State availability. Captions required. Reviews negatives, transparencies, 3x5 prints, JPEG, EPS or TIF files. Negotiates payment individually.

TIPS "E-mail, fax, or mail a query outlining your experience, interests and pay expectations. Include clippings."

☻☻ INDUSTRIAL WEIGH & MEASURE

WAM Publishing Co., P.O. Box 2247, Hendersonville TN 37077. (615)239-8087. **E-mail:** dave.mathieu@comcast.net. **Website:** www.iwammag.com. **Contact:** David M. Mathieu, publisher. Bimonthly magazine for users of industrial scales; covers material handling and logistics industries. Estab. 1914. Circ. 13,900. Byline given. Pays on acceptance. Offers 20% kill fee. Accepts queries by mail, e-mail, phone. Responds in 2 weeks to queries. Sample copy available online.

NONFICTION Needs interview with presidents of companies, personal experience, guest editorials on government involvement in business, technical, profilse (about users of weighing and measurement equipment). **Buys 15 mss/year.** Query on technical articles; submit complete ms for general interest material. Length: 1,000-2,500 words. **Pays $175-300.**

○ 🍁 $$$ PEM PLANT ENGINEERING & MAINTENANCE

CLB Media, Inc., 222 Edward St., Aurora ON L4G 1W6 Canada. (905)727-0077. **Fax:** (905)727-0017. **E-mail:** avoshart@clbmedia.ca. **Website:** www.pem-mag.com. **Contact:** André Voshart, editor. **30% freelance written.** Bimonthly magazine looking for informative articles on issues that affect plant floor operations and maintenance. Estab. 1977. Circ. 18,500. Byline given. Pays on publication. No kill fee. Publishes ms an average of 3 months after acceptance. Editorial lead time 4 months. Submit seasonal material 4 months in advance. Accepts simultaneous submissions. Responds in 3 weeks to queries. Responds in 1 month to mss. Sample copy free. Guidelines available.

NONFICTION Needs how-to, keep production downtime to a minimum, better operate an industrial operation, new product, technical. **Buys 6 mss/year.** Query with published clips. Length: 750-4,000 words. **Pays $500-1,400 (Canadian).** Sometimes pays expenses of writers on assignment.

PHOTOS State availability. Captions required. Reviews transparencies, prints. Negotiates payment individually.

COLUMNS/DEPARTMENTS , .

TIPS "Information can be found at our website. Call us for sample issues, ideas, etc."

INFORMATION SYSTEMS

$$$ DESKTOP ENGINEERING

Level 5 Communications, Inc., 1283 Main St., P.O. Box 1039, Dublin NH 03444. (603)563-1631. **Fax:** (603)563-8192. **E-mail:** jgooch@deskeng.com. **E-mail:** de-editors@deskeng.com. **Website:** www.deskeng.com. **Contact:** Jamie Gooch, managing editor. **90% freelance written.** Monthly magazine covering computer hardware/software for hands-on design and mechanical engineers, analysis engineers, and engineering management. Ten special supplements/year. Estab. 1995. Circ. 63,000. Byline given. Pays in month of publication. Kill fee for assigned story. Publishes ms an average of 2 months after acceptance. Editorial lead time 3 months. Accepts queries by mail, e-mail, phone. Responds in 2 weeks to queries; 1 month to mss. Sample copy for free with 8x10 SASE. Guidelines available on website.

NONFICTION Needs how-to, new product, reviews, technical, design. No fluff. **Buys 50-70 mss/year.** Query. Submit outline before you write an article. Length: 1,000-1,200 words. **Pays per project. Pay negotiable for unsolicited articles.** Sometimes pays expenses of writers on assignment.

PHOTOS "No matter what type of article you write, it must be supported and enhanced visually. Visual information can include screen shots, photos, schematics, tables, charts, checklists, time lines, reading lists, and program code. The exact mix will depend on your particular article, but each of these items must be accompanied by specific, detailed captions." Send photos. Captions required. Negotiates payment individually.

COLUMNS/DEPARTMENTS Product Briefs (new products), 50-100 words; Reviews (software, hardware), 500-1,500 words.

TIPS Call or e-mail the editors for submission tips.

$$$ GAME DEVELOPER

United Business Media LLC, 303 Second St., South Tower, 9th Floor, San Francisco CA 94107. (415)947-6000. **Fax:** (415)947-6090. **E-mail:** editors@gdmag.com. **Website:** www.gdmag.com. **Contact:** Patrick Miller, editor. **90% freelance written.** Monthly magazine covering computer game development. Estab. 1994. Circ. 35,000. Byline given. Pays on publication. No kill fee. Publishes ms an average of 3-6 months after acceptance. Editorial lead time 3 months. Submit seasonal material 4 months in advance. Accepts queries by e-mail. Sample copy free. Guidelines available online.

NONFICTION Needs how-to, personal experience, technical. **Buys 50 mss/year.** Query. Length: 3,500 words for Feature articles and the Postmortem column; 600-1,200 words for product reviews (game development tools). **Pays $150/page.**

PHOTOS State availability.

TIPS "We're looking for writers who are professional game developers with published game titles. We do not target the hobbyist or amateur market."

$ JOURNAL OF INFORMATION ETHICS

McFarland & Co., Inc., Publishers, P.O. Box 611, Jefferson NC 28640. (336)246-4460. **E-mail:** hauptman@stcloudstate.edu. **90% freelance written.** Semiannual scholarly journal covering all of the information sciences. "Addresses ethical issues in all of the information sciences with a deliberately interdisciplinary approach. Topics range from electronic mail monitoring to library acquisition of controversial material to archival ethics. The *Journal*'s aim is to present thoughtful considerations of ethical dilemmas that arise in a rapidly evolving system of information exchange and dissemination." Estab. 1992. Byline given. Pays on publication. No kill fee. Publishes ms an average of 2 years after acceptance. Submit seasonal material 8 months in advance. Accepts queries by mail, e-mail, phone. Sample copy for $30. Guidelines free.

NONFICTION Needs essays, opinion, book reviews. **Buys 10-12 mss/year.** Send complete ms. Length: 500-3,500 words. **Pays $25-50, depending on length.**

TIPS "Familiarize yourself with the many areas subsumed under the rubric of information ethics, e.g., privacy, scholarly communication, errors, peer review, confidentiality, e-mail, etc. Present a well-rounded discussion of any fresh, current, or evolving ethical topic within the information sciences or involving real-world information collection/exchange."

⊛⊛⊛ SYSTEM INEWS

Penton Technology Media, 748 Whalers Way, Fort Collins CO 80525. (970)663-4700; (800)621-1544. **E-mail:** editors@iprodeveloper.com. **Website:** www.iseriesnetwork.com. **40% freelance written.** Magazine, published 12 times/year, focused on programming, networking, IS management, and technology for users of IBM AS/400, iSERIES, SYSTEM i, AND IBM i platform. Estab. 1982. Circ. 30,000 (international). Byline given. Pays on publication. Offers 50% kill fee. Publishes ms an average of 3 months after acceptance. Editorial lead time 4 months. Submit seasonal material 4 months in advance. Accepts queries by e-mail. Responds in 3 weeks to queries. Responds in 5 weeks to mss. Guidelines available online.

NONFICTION Needs technical. Query. Length: 1,500-2,500 words. **Pays $300/$500 flat fee for assigned articles, depending on article quality and technical depth.**

REPRINTS Send photocopy. Payment negotiable.

PHOTOS State availability. Offers no additional payment for photos accepted with ms.

COLUMNS/DEPARTMENTS Load'n'go (complete utility).

TIPS "Must have in-depth knowledge of IBM AS/400/iSERIES/SYSTEM i/IBM i computer platform."

INSURANCE

⊛⊛⊛⊛ ADVISOR TODAY

NAIFA, 2901 Telestar Court, Falls Church VA 22042. (703)770-8204. **E-mail:** amseka@naifa.org. **Website:** www.advisortoday.com. **Contact:** Ayo Mseka. **25% freelance written.** Monthly magazine covering life insurance and financial planning. "Writers must demonstrate an understanding at what insurance agents and financial advisors do to earn business and serve their clients." Estab. 1906. Circ. 110,000. Pays on acceptance or publication (by mutual agreement with editor). No kill fee. Publishes ms an average of 3 months after acceptance. Editorial lead time 3 months. Submit seasonal material 6 months in advance. Accepts queries by mail, e-mail, fax, phone. Accepts simultaneous submissions. Sample copy free. Guidelines available online at www.advisortoday.com/about/contribute.cfm.

NONFICTION Buys 8 mss/year. "We prefer e-mail submissions in Microsoft Word format. For other formats and submission methods, please query first. For all articles and queries, contact Ayo Mseka. Web articles should cover the same subject matter covered in the magazine. The articles can be between 300-800 words and should be submitted to Ayo Mseka. Please indicate where a story has been previously published articles have been accepted." Length: 1,500-6,000 words. **Pays $800-2,000.**

JEWELRY

⊛⊛ THE ENGRAVERS JOURNAL

P.O. Box 318, Brighton MI 48116. (810)229-5725. **Fax:** (810)229-8320. **E-mail:** editor@engraversjournal.com. **Website:** www.engraversjournal.com. **Contact:** Managing editor. **70% freelance written.** Monthly magazine covering the recognition and identification industry (engraving, marking devices, awards, jewelry, and signage). "We provide practical information for the education and advancement of our readers, mainly retail business owners." Estab. 1975. Byline given. Pays on acceptance. No kill fee. Publishes ms an average of 3-9 months after acceptance. Accepts queries by mail, e-mail, fax. Responds in 2 weeks to mss. Sample copy free. Guidelines free.

NONFICTION Needs general interest, industry related, how-to, small business subjects, increase sales, develop new markets, use new sales techniques, etc., technical. No general overviews of the industry. Length: 1,000-5,000 words. **Pays $200 and up.**

REPRINTS Send tearsheet, photocopy or typed ms with rights for sale noted, and information about when and where the material previously appeared. Pays 50-100% of amount paid for original article.

PHOTOS Send photos. Captions, identification of subjects, model releases required. Pays variable rate.

JOURNALISM AND WRITING

⊗⊗⊗⊗ AMERICAN JOURNALISM REVIEW

University of Maryland Foundation, 1117 Journalism Bldg., University of Maryland, College Park MD 20742. (301)405-8803. **Fax:** (301)405-8323. **E-mail:** rrieder@ajr.umd.edu; editor@ajr.umd.edu. **Website:** www.ajr.org. **Contact:** Rem Rieder, editor. **80% freelance written.** Bimonthly magazine covering print, broadcast, and online journalism. "American Journalism Review covers ethical issues, trends in the industry, and coverage that falls short." Circ. 25,000. Byline given. Pays within 1 month after publication. Offers 25% kill fee. Publishes ms an average of 2 months after acceptance. Editorial lead time 1 month. Accepts queries by mail, e-mail. Responds in 1 month to queries and unsolicited mss. Sample copy for $4.95 pre-paid or online. Guidelines available online.

NONFICTION Needs exposé, personal experience, ethical issues. **Buys many mss/year.** Send complete ms. Length: 2,000-4,000 words. **Pays $1,500-2,000.** Pays expenses of writers on assignment.

FILLERS Needs anecdotes, facts, short humor, short pieces. Length: 150-1,000 words. **Pays $100-250.**

TIPS "Write a short story for the front-of-the-book section. We prefer queries to completed articles. Include in a page what you'd like to write about, who you'll interview, why it's important, and why you should write it."

⊗ AUTHORSHIP

National Writers Association, 10940 S. Parker Rd., #508, Parker CO 80134. (303)841-0246. **E-mail:** natlwritersassn@hotmail.com. **Website:** www.nationalwriters.com. Quarterly magazine covering writing articles only. "Association magazine targeted to beginning and professional writers. Covers how-to, humor, marketing issues. Disk and e-mail submissions preferred." Estab. 1950s. Circ. 4,000. Byline given. Pays on acceptance. No kill fee. Editorial lead time 3 months. Submit seasonal material 6 months in advance. Accepts simultaneous submissions. Responds in 2 months to queries. Sample copy for stamped, self-addressed, 8½x11 envelope.

NONFICTION **Buys 25 mss/year.** Query or send complete ms. Length: 1,200 words. **Pays $10, or discount on memberships and copies.**

PHOTOS State availability. Identification of subjects, model releases required. Reviews 5x7 prints. Offers no additional payment for photos accepted with ms.

TIPS "Members of National Writers Association are given preference."

⊗ BOOK DEALERS WORLD

North American Bookdealers Exchange, P.O. Box 606, Cottage Grove OR 97424. (541)942-7455. **Fax:** (541)942-7455. **E-mail:** nabe@bookmarketingprofits.com. **Website:** www.bookmarketingprofits.com. **50% freelance written.** Quarterly magazine covering writing, self-publishing, and marketing books by mail. Circ. 20,000. Byline given. Pays on publication. No kill fee. Publishes ms an average of 3 months after acceptance. Accepts simultaneous submissions. Responds in 1 month to queries. Sample copy for $3.

NONFICTION Needs book excerpts, writing, mail order, direct mail, publishing, how-to, home business by mail, advertising, interview, of successful self-publishers, positive articles on self-publishing, new writing angles, marketing. **Buys 10 mss/year.** Send complete ms. Length: 1,000-1,500 words. **Pays $25-50.**

REPRINTS Send typed ms with rights for sale noted and information about when and where the material previously appeared. Pays 80% of amount paid for an original article.

COLUMNS/DEPARTMENTS Publisher Profile (on successful self-publishers and their marketing strategy). Length: 250-1,000 words. **Buys 20 mss/year.** Send complete ms. **Pays $5-20.**

FILLERS Fillers concerning writing, publishing, or books. **Buys 6 mss/year.** Length: 100-250 words. **Pays $3-10.**

TIPS "Query first. Get a sample copy of the magazine."

◯ ⊗⊗ CANADIAN SCREENWRITER

Writers Guild of Canada, 366 Adelaide St. W., Suite 401, Toronto ON M5V 1R9 Canada. (416)979-7907. **Fax:** (416)979-9273. **E-mail:** info@wgc.ca; m.parker@wgc.ca. **Website:** www.wgc.ca. **Contact:** Maureen Parker, executive director. **80% freelance written.** Magazine published 3 times/year covering Canadian screenwriting for television, film, radio, and digital media. *Canadian Screenwriter* profiles

Canadian screenwriters, provides industry news, and offers practical writing tips for screenwriters. Estab. 1998. Circ. 4,000. Byline given. Pays on acceptance. Offers 50% kill fee. Publishes ms an average of 1 month after acceptance. Editorial lead time 2 months. Submit seasonal material 2 months in advance. Accepts queries by e-mail. YesResponds in 1 week to queries. Responds in 1 month to mss. Sample copy free. Guidelines by e-mail.

NONFICTION Needs how-to, humor, interview. Does not want writing on foreign screenwriters; the focus is on Canadian-resident screenwriters. **Buys 12 mss/year.** Query with published clips. Length: 750-2,200 words. **Pays 50¢/word.** Sometimes pays expenses of writers on assignment.

PHOTOS State availability. Identification of subjects required. Reviews GIF/JPEG files. Negotiates payment individually.

TIPS "Read other Canadian film and television publications."

☺ $ CANADIAN WRITER'S JOURNAL

Box 1178, New Liskeard ON P0J 1P0 Canada. (705)647-5424. **Fax:** (705)647-8366. **E-mail:** editor@cwj.ca. **Website:** www.cwj.ca. **Contact:** Deborah Ranchuk, editor. **75% freelance written.** Bimonthly magazine for writers. "Digest-size magazine for writers emphasizing short 'how-to' articles, which convey easily understood information useful to both apprentice and professional writers. General policy and postal subsidies require that the magazine must carry a substantial Canadian content. We try for about 90% Canadian content, but prefer good material over country of origin, or how well you're known. Writers may query, but unsolicited mss are welcome." Estab. 1984. Circ. 350. Byline given. Pays on publication. No kill fee. Publishes ms an average of 2-9 months after acceptance. Accepts queries by mail, e-mail, fax, phone; preference will be given to the article that can be submitted electronically. Responds in 2 months to queries. Sample copy for $8, including postage. Guidelines available online.

NONFICTION Needs how-to, articles for writers, , humorous and seasonal items. **Buys 200 mss/year.** Query optional. 400-2,500/words for articles; 250-500/words for book reviews **Pays $7.50/published magazine page (approx. 450 words), plus 1 complimentary copy. A $2 premium is paid for electronic submissions.**

REPRINTS Send typed ms with rights for sale noted and information about when and where the material previously appeared.

FICTION Fiction is published only through semiannual short fiction contest with April 30 deadline. Send SASE for rules, or see guidelines on website. Does not want gratuitous violence or sex subject matters. Accepts submissions by e-mail. Responds in 2 months to queries. Pays on publication for one-time rights.

POETRY Poetry must be unpublished elsewhere; short poems or extracts used as part of articles on the writing of poetry. Submit up to 5 poems at a time. No previously published poems. Accepts e-mail submissions (pasted into body of message, with 'Submission' in the subject line). Include SASE with postal submissions. "U.S. postage accepted; do not affix to envelope. Poems should be titled." Responds in 3-6 months. **Pays $2-5 per poem published (depending on length) and 1 contributor's copy. SASE required for response and payment.**

TIPS "We prefer short, tightly written, informative how-to articles. US writers: note that US postage cannot be used to mail from Canada. Obtain Canadian stamps, use IRCs, or send small amounts in cash."

$$$ ECONTENT MAGAZINE

Information Today, Inc., 143 Old Marlton Pike, Medford NJ 08055. (203)761-1466; (800)248-8466. **Fax:** (203)761-1444; (203)304-9300. **E-mail:** theresa.cramer@infotoday.com. **Website:** www.econtentmag.com. **Contact:** Theresa Cramer, editor. **90% freelance written.** Monthly magazine covering digital content trends, strategies, etc. "*EContent* is a business publication. Readers need to stay on top of industry trends and developments." Estab. 1979. Circ. 12,000. Byline given. Pays within 1 month of publication. Editorial lead time 3-4 months. Accepts queries by email. Responds in 3 weeks to queries. Responds in 1 month to mss. Sample copy and writer's guidelines online.

NONFICTION Needs exposé, how-to, interview, new product, opinion, technical, news features, strategic and solution-oriented features. No academic or straight Q&A. **Buys 48 mss/year.** Query with published clips. Submit electronically as e-mail attachment. Length: 500-700 words. **Pays 40-50¢/word.** Sometimes pays expenses of writers on assignment.

PHOTOS State availability. Captions required. Negotiates payment individually.

COLUMNS/DEPARTMENTS Profiles (short profile of unique company, person or product), 1,200 words; New Features (breaking news of content-related topics), 500 words maximum. **Buys 40 mss/year.** Query with published clips. **Pays 30-40¢/word.**

TIPS "Take a look at the website. Most of the time, an e-mail query with specific article ideas works well. A general outline of talking points is good, too. State prior experience."

FELLOWSCRIPT

InScribe Christian Writers' Fellowship, *FellowScript*, c/o P.O. Box 6201, Wetaskiwin AB T9A 2E9 Canada. **E-mail:** Pamela Mytroen, acquisitions editor, fellowscript@gmail.com. **Website:** www.inscribe.org. **Contact:** Bonnie Way, editor. **100% freelance written.** Quarterly writers' newsletter featuring Christian writing. "Our readers are Christians with a commitment to writing. Among our readership are best-selling authors and unpublished beginning writers. Submissions to us should include practical information, something the reader can immediately put into practice." Estab. 1983. Circ. 200. Byline given. Pays on publication. No kill fee. Publishes ms an average of 6-12 months after acceptance. Editorial lead time 3 months. Submit seasonal material 4 months in advance. Accepts queries by e-mail, prefers full ms by email; postal submissions only accepted from InScribe members. Accepts simultaneous submissions. Responds in 1 month to queries and mss. Sample copy for $5, 9x12 SAE, and 3 first-class stamps (Canadian) or IRCs. Guidelines available online.

NONFICTION Needs essays, exposé, how-to, for writers, interview, new product. Does not want poetry, fiction, personal experience, testimony or think piece, commentary articles. **Buys 30-45 mss/year.** Send complete ms attached in rtf or doc format. Length: 400-1,200 words. **Pays 2 1/2¢/word (first rights); 1 1/2¢/word reprints (Canadian funds).**

COLUMNS/DEPARTMENTS Book reviews, 150-300 words; Market Updates, 50-300 words. **Buys 1-3. mss/year.** Send complete ms. **Pays 1 contributor's copy.**

FILLERS Needs facts, newsbreaks. **Buys 5-10 mss/year.** Length: 25-300 words. **Pays 1 contributor's copy.**

TIPS "Send your complete ms by e-mail (pasted into the message, no attachments). E-mail is preferred. Tell us a bit about yourself. Write in a casual, first-person, anecdotal style. Be sure your article is full of practical material, something that can be applied. Most of our accepted freelance submissions fall into the 'how-to' category, and involve tasks, crafts, or procedures common to writers. Please do not send inspirational articles (i.e., 'How I sold My First Story')."

FREELANCE MARKET NEWS

The Writers Bureau Ltd., 8-10 Dutton St., Manchester M3 1LE England. (44)(161)819-9922. **Fax:** (44)(161)819-2842. **E-mail:** fmn@writersbureau.com. **Website:** www.freelancemarketnews.com. **15% freelance written.** Monthly newsletter covering freelance writing. Estab. 1968. Byline given. Pays on acceptance. No kill fee. Publishes ms an average of 3 months after acceptance. Editorial lead time 3 months. Submit seasonal material 3 months in advance. Accepts queries by mail, e-mail, fax. Sample copy and guidelines available online.

NONFICTION Needs how-to sell your writing/improve your writing. **Buys 12 mss/year.** Length: 1,00 words. **Pays £50/1,000 words.**

COLUMNS/DEPARTMENTS New Markets (magazines which have recently been published); Fillers & Letters; Overseas Markets (obviously only English-language publications); Market Notes (established publications accepting articles, fiction, reviews, or poetry). All should be between 40 and 200 words. **Pays £40/1,000 words.**

FREELANCE WRITER'S REPORT

CNW Publishing, Inc., 45 Main St., P.O. Box A, North Stratford NH 03590-0167. (603)922-8338. **E-mail:** fwrwm@writers-editors.com. **Website:** www.writers-editors.com. **25% freelance written.** Monthly newsletter covering the business of freelance writing. "*FWR* covers the marketing and business/office management aspects of running a freelance writing business. Articles must be of value to the established freelancer; nothing basic." Estab. 1982. Byline given. Pays on publication. No kill fee. Publishes ms an average of 6 months after acceptance. Editorial lead time 2 months. Submit seasonal material 2 months in advance. Accepts simultaneous submissions. Responds in 1 week to queries. Responds in 2 weeks to mss. Sample copy for 6x9 SAE with 2 first-class stamps (for back copy); $4 for current copy. Guidelines and sample copy available online.

NONFICTION Needs book excerpts, how-to (market, increase income or profits). "No articles about the basics of freelancing." **Buys 50 mss/year.** Send complete ms by e-mail. Length: up to 900 words. **Pays 10¢/word.**

TIPS "Write in a terse, newsletter style."

● ⊛⊛ MSLEXIA

Mslexia Publications Ltd., P.O. Box 656, Newcastle upon Tyne NE99 1PZ United Kingdom. (44)(191)204-8860. **E-mail:** submissions@mslexia.co.uk; postbag@mslexia.co.uk. **Website:** www.mslexia.co.uk. **Contact:** Debbie Taylor, editorial director. **60% freelance written.** Quarterly magazine offering advice and publishing opportunities for women writers, plus poetry and prose submissions on a different theme each issue. "*Mslexia* tells you all you need to know about exploring your creativity and getting into print. No other magazine provides *Mslexia*'s unique mix of advice and inspiration; news, reviews, interviews; competitions, events, grants; all served up with a challenging selection of new poetry and prose. *Mslexia* is read by authors and absolute beginners. A quarterly master class in the business and psychology of writing, it's the essential magazine for women who write." Estab. 1998. Circ. 9,000. Byline given. Pays on publication. Offers 50% kill fee. Publishes ms an average of 1 month after acceptance. Editorial lead time 3 months. Submit seasonal material 3 months in advance. Accepts queries by mail, e-mail, phone. Accepts simultaneous submissions. Responds in 3 months to mss. Sample copy available online. Writer's guidelines online or by e-mail.

NONFICTION Needs how-to, interview, opinion, personal experience. No general items about women or academic features. "We are only interested in features (for tertiary-educated readership) about women's writing and literature." **Buys 40 mss/year.** Query with published clips. Length: 500-2,200 words. **Pays $70-400 for assigned articles. Pays $70-300 for unsolicited articles.** Sometimes pays expenses of writers on assignment.

COLUMNS/DEPARTMENTS "We are open to suggestions, but would only commission 1 new column/year, probably from a UK-based writer." **Buys 12 mss/year.** Query with published clips.

FICTION See guidelines on website. "Submissions not on one of our current themes will be returned (if sub-mitted with a SASE) or destroyed." **Buys 30 mss/year.** Send complete ms. Length: 50-2,200 words.

POETRY Needs avant-garde, free verse, haiku, traditional. Buys 40 poems/year. Submit maximum 4 poems. **Pays £25 per poem; £15 per 1,000 words prose; features by negotiation. Plus contributors' copies.**

TIPS "Read the magazine; subscribe if you can afford it. *Mslexia* has a particular style and relationship with its readers which is hard to assess at a quick glance. The majority of our readers live in the UK, so feature pitches should be aware of this. We never commission work without seeing a written sample first. We rarely accept unsolicited manuscripts, but prefer a short letter suggesting a feature, plus a brief bio and writing sample."

⊛⊛ NOVEL & SHORT STORY WRITER'S MARKET

F+W Media, Inc., 10151 Carver Rd., Suite 200, Blue Ash OH 45242. (513)531-2690. **Fax:** (513)531-2686. **E-mail:** marketbookupdates@fwmedia.com. **Website:** www.writersmarket.com. **Contact:** Rachel Randall, content editor. **85% freelance written.** Annual resource book covering the fiction market. "In addition to thousands of listings for places to get fiction published, we feature articles on the craft and business of fiction writing, as well as interviews with successful fiction writers, editors, and agents. Our articles are unique in that they always offer an actionable take-away. In other words, readers must learn something immediately useful about the creation or marketing of fiction." Estab. 1981. Byline given. Pays on acceptance plus 45 days. Offers 25% kill fee. Accepts queries by e-mail only. Include "NSSWM Query" in the subject line. Responds in 4 weeks to queries.

NONFICTION Needs how-to, write, sell and promote fiction; find an agent; etc., interview, personal experience. **Buys 12-15 mss/year.** Length: 1,500-2,500 words. **Pays $400-700.**

PHOTOS Send photos. Identification of subjects required. Reviews prints, GIF/JPEG files (hi-res). Offers no additional payment for photos accepted with ms.

TIPS "The best way to break into this book is to review the last few years' editions and look for aspects of the fiction industry that we haven't covered recently. Send a specific, detailed pitch stating the topic, angle, and 'take-away' of the piece, what sources you intend to use, and what qualifies you to write this article. Freelancers who have published fiction and/or have contacts in the industry have an advantage."

💲💲 POETS & WRITERS MAGAZINE

90 Broad St., Suite 2100, New York NY 10004. (212)226-3586. **E-mail:** editor@pw.org. **Website:** www.pw.org/magazine. **Contact:** Kevin Larimer, editor. **95% freelance written.** Bimonthly professional trade journal for poets and fiction writers and creative nonfiction writers. Estab. 1987. Circ. 60,000. Byline given. Pays on publication. Offers 25% kill fee. Publishes ms an average of 4 months after acceptance. Submit seasonal material 4 months in advance. Accepts queries by mail, e-mail. Responds in 2 months to mss. Sample copy for $5.95. Guidelines available online.

NONFICTION Needs how-to, craft of poetry, fiction or creative nonfiction writing, interviews, with poets or writers of fiction and creative nonfiction, personal essays about literature, regional reports of literary activity, reports on small presses, service pieces about publishing trends. **Buys 35 mss/year.** Send complete ms. Length: 700-3,000 (depending on topic) words.

PHOTOS State availability. Reviews color prints. Offers no additional payment for photos accepted with ms.

COLUMNS/DEPARTMENTS Literary and Publishing News, 700-1,000 words; Profiles of Emerging and Established Poets, Fiction Writers and Creative Nonfiction Writers, 2,000-3,000 words; Craft Essays and Publishing Advice, 2,000-2,500 words. Query with published clips or send complete ms. **Pays $225-500.**

TIPS "We typically assign profiles to coincide with an author's forthcoming book publication. We are not looking for the Get Rich Quick or 10 Easy Steps variety of writing and publishing advice."

💲💲 QUILL & SCROLL MAGAZINE

Quill and Scroll International Honorary Society for High School Journalists, University of Iowa, School of Journalism and Mass Communication, 100 Adler Journalism Bldg., Iowa City IA 52242. (319)335-3457. **Fax:** (319)335-3989. **E-mail:** quill-scroll@uiowa.edu. **Website:** www.quillandscroll.org. **Contact:** Vanessa Shelton, executive director. **20% freelance written.** Bimonthly magazine covering scholastic journalism-related topics during school year. "Our primary audience is high school journalism students working on and studying topics related to newspapers, yearbooks, radio, television, and online media; secondary audi-

ence is their teachers and others interested in this topic. We invite journalism students and advisers to submit mss about important lessons learned or obstacles overcome." Estab. 1926. Circ. 10,000. Byline given. Pays on acceptance and publication. No kill fee. Publishes ms an average of 4 months after acceptance. Editorial lead time 2 months. Accepts queries by mail, e-mail. Accepts simultaneous submissions. Responds in 2 weeks to queries. Guidelines available.

NONFICTION Needs essays, how-to, humor, interview, new product, opinion, personal experience, photo feature, technical, travel, types on topic. Does not want articles not pertinent to high school student journalists. Query. Length: 600-1,000 words. **Pays $100-500 for assigned articles. Pays complementary copy and $200 maximum for unsolicited articles.** Sometimes pays expenses of writers on assignment.

PHOTOS State availability. Reviews GIF/JPEG files. Offers no additional payment for photos accepted with ms.

💲💲💲 WRITER'S DIGEST

F+W Media, Inc., 10151 Carver Rd., Suite #200, Blue Ash OH 45242. (513)531-2690. **E-mail:** wdsubmissions@fwmedia.com. **Website:** www.writersdigest.com. **75% freelance written.** Magazine for those who want to write better, get published and participate in the vibrant culture of writers. "Our readers look to us for specific ideas and tips that will help them succeed, whether success means getting into print, finding personal fulfillment through writing or building and maintaining a thriving writing career and network." Estab. 1920. Byline given. Pays on acceptance. Offers 25% kill fee. Publishes ms an average of 6-9 months after acceptance. Accepts queries by e-mail only. Responds in 2-4 months to queries and mss. Guidelines and editorial calendar available online (writersdigest.com/submissionguidelines).

NONFICTION Needs essays, how-to, humor, inspirational, interviews, profiles. Does not accept phone, snail mail, or fax queries. "We don't buy newspaper clippings or reprints of articles previously published in other writing magazines. Book and software reviews are handled in-house, as are most *WD* interviews." **Buys 40 mss/year.** Send complete ms. Length: 800-1,500 words. **Pays 30-50¢/word.**

TIPS "*InkWell* is the best place for new writers to break in. We recommend you consult our editorial calendar before pitching feature-length articles. Check our writer's guidelines for more details."

☺ WRITER'S WEB WATCH

Communications Concepts, Inc., 7481 Huntsman Blvd., #720, Springfield VA 22153-1648. (703)643-2200. **Website:** www.writerswebwatch.com. Monthly newsletter on business writing and communications. "Our readers are company writers, editors, communicators, and executives. They need specific, practical advice on how to write well as part of their job." Estab. 1983. Byline sometimes given. Pays within 45 days of acceptance. No kill fee. Publishes ms an average of 3 months after acceptance. Editorial lead time 3 months. Accepts queries by mail, e-mail, online submission form. Responds in 1 month to queries. Sample copy online.

NONFICTION Needs how-to. **Buys 90 mss/year.** Accepts electronic final mss. E-mail attached word processing files. Length: 100-600 words. **Pays $35-150.**

COLUMNS/DEPARTMENTS Writing Techniques (how-to business writing advice); Style Matters (grammar, usage, and editing); Online Publishing (writing, editing, and publishing for the Web); Managing Publications; PR & Marketing (writing).

FILLERS Short tips on writing or editing. Mini-reviews of communications websites for business writers, editors, and communicators. Length: 100-250 words. **Pays $35.**

TIPS "We do not use material on how to get published or how to conduct a freelancing business. Format your copy to follow *Writer's Web Watch* style. Include postal and e-mail addresses, phone numbers, website URLs, and prices for products/services mentioned in articles."

☺☺☺☺ WRITTEN BY

7000 W. Third St., Los Angeles CA 90048. (323)782-4522. **Fax:** (323)782-4800. **Website:** www.wga.org/writtenby/writtenby.aspx. **40% freelance written.** Magazine published 9 times/year. "*Written By* is the premier magazine written by and for America's screen and TV writers. We focus on the craft of screenwriting and cover all aspects of the entertainment industry from the perspective of the writer. We are read by all screenwriters and most entertainment executives." Estab. 1987. Circ. 12,000. Byline given. Pays on acceptance. Offers 10% kill fee. Publishes ms an average of 2 months after acceptance. Editorial lead time 4 months. Submit seasonal material 4 months in advance. Ac-

cepts queries by mail, e-mail, fax, phone, online submission form. Guidelines for #10 SASE.

NONFICTION Needs book excerpts, essays, historical, humor, interview, opinion, personal experience, photo feature, technical, software. No beginner pieces on how to break into Hollywood, or how to write scripts. **Buys 20 mss/year.** Query with published clips. Length: 500-3,500 words. **Pays $500-3,500 for assigned articles.** Sometimes pays expenses of writers on assignment.

PHOTOS State availability. Captions, identification of subjects, model releases required. Reviews transparencies. Offers no additional payment for photos accepted with ms.

COLUMNS/DEPARTMENTS Pays $1,000 maximum.

TIPS "We are looking for more theoretical essays on screenwriting past and/or present. Also, the writer must always keep in mind that our audience is made up primarily of working writers who are inside the business; therefore all articles need to have an 'insider' feel and not be written for those who are still trying to break in to Hollywood. We prefer a hard copy of submission or e-mail."

LAW

☺☺☺☺ ABA JOURNAL

American Bar Association, 321 N. Clark St., 20th Floor, Chicago IL 60654. (312)988-6018. **Fax:** (312)988-6014. **E-mail:** releases@americanbar.org. **Website:** www.abajournal.com. **Contact:** Allen Pusey, editor and publisher. **10% freelance written.** Monthly magazine covering the trends, people and finances of the legal profession from Wall Street to Main Street to Pennsylvania Avenue. The *ABA Journal* is an independent, thoughtful, and inquiring observer of the law and the legal profession. The magazine is edited for members of the American Bar Association. Circ. 380,000. Byline given. Pays on acceptance. No kill fee. Accepts queries by e-mail, fax. Sample copy free. Guidelines available online.

NONFICTION "We don't want anything that does not have a legal theme. No poetry or fiction." **Buys 5 mss/year.** "We use freelancers with experience reporting for legal or consumer publications; most have law degrees. If you are interested in freelancing for the *Journal*, we urge you to include your résumé and published clips when you contact us with story ideas." Length: 500-3,500 words. **Pays $300-2,000 for assigned articles.**

COLUMNS/DEPARTMENTS The National Pulse/Ideas from the Front (reports on legal news and trends), 650 words; eReport (reports on legal news and trends), 500-1,500 words. "The *ABA Journal eReport* is our weekly online newsletter sent out to members." **Buys 25 mss/year.** Query with published clips. **Pays $300, regardless of story length.**

💲💲💲 BENCH & BAR OF MINNESOTA

Minnesota State Bar Association, 600 Nicollet Mall #380, Minneapolis MN 55402. (612)333-1183; 800-882-6722. **Fax:** (612)333-4927. **E-mail:** jhaverkamp@mnbar.org. **Website:** www.mnbar.org. **Contact:** Judson Haverkamp, editor. **5% freelance written.** Magazine published 11 times/year. *Bench & Bar* seeks reportage, analysis, and commentary on changes in the law, trends and issues in the law and the legal profession, especially in Minnesota. Preference to items of practical/professional human interest to lawyers and judges. Audience is mostly Minnesota lawyers. Estab. 1931. Circ. 17,000. Byline given. Pays on acceptance. No kill fee. Publishes ms an average of 3 months after acceptance. Responds in 1 month to queries. Guidelines for free online or by mail.

NONFICTION Needs analysis and exposition of current trends, developments and issues in law, legal profession, especially in Minnesota. Balanced commentary and "how-to" considered. "We do not want one-sided opinion pieces or advertorial." **Buys 2-3 mss/year.** Send query or complete ms. Length: 1,000-3,500 words. **Pays $500-1,500.** Some expenses of writers on assignment.

PHOTOS State availability. Identification of subjects, model releases required. Reviews 5x7 prints. Pays $25-100 upon publication.

💲💲💲💲 CALIFORNIA LAWYER

Daily Journal Corp., 44 Montgomery St., Suite 250, San Francisco CA 94104. (415)296-2400. **Fax:** (415)296-2440. **E-mail:** bo_links@dailyjournal.com. **Website:** www.callawyer.com. **Contact:** Bo Links, legal editor. **30% freelance written.** Monthly magazine of law-related articles and general-interest subjects of appeal to lawyers and judges. "Our primary mission is to cover the news of the world as it affects the law and lawyers, helping our readers better comprehend the issues of the day and to cover changes and trends in the legal profession. Our readers are all California lawyers, plus judges, legislators, and corporate executives. Although we focus on California and the West, we have subscribers in every state. *California Lawyer* is a general interest magazine for people interested in law. Our writers are journalists." Estab. 1981. Circ. 140,000. Byline given. Pays on acceptance. Offers 25% kill fee. Publishes ms an average of 3 months after acceptance. Editorial lead time 3 months. Accepts queries by e-mail. No previously published articles. Sample copy and writer's guidelines for #10 SASE.

NONFICTION Needs essays, general interest, interview, news and feature articles on law-related topics. **Buys 12 mss/year.** Send complete ms. "We are interested in concise, well-written and well-researched articles on issues of current concern, as well as well-told feature narratives with a legal focus. We would like to see a description or outline of your proposed idea, including a list of possible sources." Length: 500-5,000 words. **Pays $50-2,000.** Pays expenses of writers on assignment.

PHOTOS Contact: Marsha Sessa, art director. State availability. Identification of subjects, model releases required. Reviews prints.

COLUMNS/DEPARTMENTS California Esq. (current legal trends), 300 words. **Buys 6 mss/year.** Query with or without published clips. **Pays $50-250.**

💲💲💲💲 INSIDECOUNSEL

222 S. Riverside Plaza, Suite 620, Chicago IL 60606. (312)654-3500. **E-mail:** apost@insidecounsel.com. **Website:** www.insidecounsel.com. **Contact:** Ashley Post, managing editor. **50% freelance written.** Monthly tabloid covering legal information for attorneys. "*InsideCounsel* is a monthly national magazine that gives general counsel and inhouse attorneys information on legal and business issues to help them better manage corporate law departments. It routinely addresses changes and trends in law departments, litigation management, legal technology, corporate governance and inhouse careers. Law areas covered monthly include: intellectual property, international, technology, project finance, e-commerce, and litigation. All articles need to be geared toward the inhouse attorney's perspective." Estab. 1991. Circ. 45,000. Byline given. Pays on publication. No kill fee. Publishes ms an average of 3 months after acceptance. Editorial lead time 3 months. Submit seasonal material 3 months in advance. Accepts queries by mail, e-mail.

Responds in 3 weeks to queries. Sample copy for $17. Guidelines available online.

NONFICTION Needs interview, news about legal aspects of business issues and events. **Buys 12-25 mss/year.** Query with published clips. Length: 500-3,000 words. **Pays $500-2,000.**

PHOTOS Freelancers should state availability of photos with submission. Identification of subjects required. Reviews color transparencies, b&w prints. Offers $25-150/photo.

TIPS "Our publication targets general counsel and in-house lawyers. All articles need to speak to them—not to the general attorney population. Query with clips and a list of potential in-house sources."

$$$ JCR

National Court Reporters Association, 8224 Old Courthouse Rd., Vienna VA 22180. (800)272-6272, ext. 164. **E-mail:** jschmidt@ncrahq.org. **Website:** www.ncraonline.org. **Contact:** Jacqueline Schmidt, editor. **10% freelance written.** Monthly, except bimonthly July/August and November/December, magazine covering court reporting, captioning, and CART provision. "The *JCR* has 2 complementary purposes: to communicate the activities, goals and mission of its publisher, the National Court Reporters Association; and, simultaneously, to seek out and publish diverse information and views on matters significantly related to the court reporting and captioning professions." Estab. 1899. Circ. 20,000. Byline sometimes given. Pays on acceptance. No kill fee. Publishes ms an average of 4-5 months after acceptance. Editorial lead time 4 months. Submit seasonal material 4 months in advance. Accepts queries by mail, e-mail. Sample copy free. Ms guidelines are available on NCRAonline.org under *JCR*.

NONFICTION Needs book excerpts, how-to, interview, technical, legal issues. **Buys 6-10 mss/year.** Query. Length: 1,000-2,500 words. **Pays $1,000 maximum for assigned articles. Pays $100 maximum for unsolicited articles.** Sometimes pays expenses of writers on assignment.

COLUMNS/DEPARTMENTS Language (proper punctuation, grammar, dealing with verbatim materials); Technical (new technologies, using mobile technology, using technology for work); Book excerpts (language, crime, legal issues)—all 1,000 words. **Pays up to $100.**

$ PARALEGAL TODAY

Conexion International Media, Inc., Editorial Department, 118 Steiner Dr., Pittsburgh PA 15236. (412)653-2262. **E-mail:** skane@conexionmedia.com. **Website:** www.paralegaltoday.com; www.conexioninternationalltd.com. **Contact:** Sally A. Kane, Esq., editor-in-chief. "Quarterly magazine geared toward all legal assistants/paralegals throughout the U.S. and Canada, regardless of specialty (litigation, corporate, bankruptcy, environmental law, etc.). How-to articles to help paralegals perform their jobs more effectively are most in demand, as are career and salary information, technolgoy tips, and trends pieces." Estab. 1983. Circ. 8,000. Byline given. Pays on publication. Offers kill fee ($25-50 standard rate). Editorial lead time is 10 weeks. Submit seasonal material 3 months in advance. Accepts queries by mail, e-mail, fax, online submission form. Accepts simultaneous submissions. Responds in 2 months to mss. Sample copy and writer's guidelines available online.

NONFICTION Needs interview, unique and interesting paralegals in unique and particular work related situations, news (brief, hard news topics regarding paralegals), features (present information to help paralegals advance their careers). Send query letter first; if electronic, send as attachment. **Pays $75-300.**

TIPS "Query editor first. Features run 1,500-2,500 words with sidebars. Writers must understand our audience. There is some opportunity for investigative journalism as well as the usual features, profiles, and columns. How-to articles are especially desired. If you are a great writer who can interview effectively and really dig into the topic to grab readers' attention, we need you."

STUDENT LAWYER

ABA Publishing, Law Student Division, American Bar Association, 321 N. Clark St., Chicago IL 60654. (312)988-6049. **Fax:** (312)988-6081. **E-mail:** studentlawyer@americanbar.org. **Website:** www.abanet.org/lsd/studentlawyer. **Contact:** Angela Gwizdala, editor. **Works with a small number of new writers each year.** Monthly magazine (September-May) for law student members of the American Bar Association. "*Student Lawyer* is a legal-affairs features magazine that competes for a share of law students' limited spare time, so the articles we publish must be informative, well-researched, good reads. We are especially interested in articles that provide students with practical advice for navigating the challenges of law school and developing their careers." Estab. 1972. Circ. 32,000. Byline given. No kill fee. Editorial lead time 6 months. Accepts queries by e-mail. Guidelines available online.

NONFICTION No fiction; no footnoted academic articles or briefs. Query with published clips. Submit by MS Word attachment. Length: 2,000-2,500 words.

TIPS "We are not a law review; we are a features magazine with law school (in the broadest sense) as the common denominator. Write clearly and well. Expect to work with editor to polish manuscripts to perfection. We do not make assignments to writers with whose work we are not familiar. If you're interested in writing for us, send a detailed, thought-out query with 3 previously published clips. We are always willing to look at material on spec. Sorry, we don't return mss."

🌐🌐🌐🌐 SUPER LAWYERS

Thomson Reuters, 610 Opperman Dr., Eagan MN 55123. (877)787-5290. **Website:** www.superlawyers. com. **Contact:** Erik Lundegaard, editor. **100% freelance written.** Monthly magazine covering law and politics. "We publish glossy magazines in every region of the country; all serve a legal audience and have a storytelling sensibility. We write profiles of interesting attorneys exclusively." Estab. 1990. Byline given. Pays on acceptance. Offers 25% kill fee. Publishes ms an average of 1 month after acceptance. Editorial lead time 6 months. Submit seasonal material 6 months in advance. Accepts queries by phone, online submission form. Accepts simultaneous submissions. Sample copy free. Guidelines free.

NONFICTION Needs general interest, historical. Query. Length: 500-2,000 words. **Pays 50¢-$1.50/ word.**

LUMBER

🌐🌐 PALLET ENTERPRISE

Industrial Reporting, Inc., 10244 Timber Ridge Dr., Ashland VA 23005. (804)550-0323. **Fax:** (804)550-2181. **E-mail:** edb@ireporting.com; chaille@ire-porting.com. **Website:** www.palletenterprise.com. **Contact:** Edward C. Brindley, Jr., Ph.D., publisher. **40% freelance written.** Monthly magazine covering lumber and pallet operations. "The *Pallet Enterprise* is a monthly trade magazine for the sawmill, pallet, remanufacturing, and wood processing industries. Articles should offer technical, solution-oriented information. Anti-forest articles are not accepted. Ar-

ticles should focus on machinery and unique ways to improve profitability/make money." Estab. 1981. Circ. 14,500. Pays on publication. Editorial lead time 2 months. Submit seasonal material 2 months in advance. Accepts queries by mail, e-mail, fax, phone. Accepts simultaneous submissions. Sample copy available online. Guidelines free.

NONFICTION Needs interview, new product, opinion, technical, industry news, environmental, forests operation/plant features. No lifestyle, humor, general news, etc. **Buys 20 mss/year.** Query with published clips. Length: 1,000-3,000 words. **Pays $200-400 for assigned articles. Pays $100-400 for unsolicited articles.** Sometimes pays expenses of writers on assignment.

PHOTOS State availability. Captions, identification of subjects required. Reviews 3x5 prints. Negotiates payment individually.

COLUMNS/DEPARTMENTS Green Watch (environmental news/opinion affecting US forests), 1,500 words. **Buys 12 mss/year.** Query with published clips. **Pays $200-400.**

TIPS "Provide unique environmental or industry-oriented articles. Many of our freelance articles are company features of sawmills, pallet manufacturers, pallet recyclers, and wood waste processors."

🌐🌐 TIMBERLINE

Industrial Reporting, Inc., 10244 Timber Ridge Dr., Ashland VA 23005. (804)550-0323. **Fax:** (804)550-2181. **E-mail:** chaille@ireporting.com. **Website:** www. timberlinemag.com. **Contact:** Chaille Brindley, assistant publisher. **50% freelance written.** Monthly tabloid covering the forest products industry. Estab. 1994. Circ. 30,000. Byline given. Pays on publication. Editorial lead time 2 months. Submit seasonal material 2 months in advance. Accepts queries by mail, e-mail, fax. Accepts simultaneous submissions.

NONFICTION **Contact:** Tim Cox, editor. Needs historical, interview, new product, opinion, technical, industry news, environmental operation/plant features. No lifestyles, humor, general news, etc. **Buys 25 mss/ year.** Query with published clips. Length: 1,000-3,000 words. **Pays $200-400 for assigned articles. Pays $100-400 for unsolicited articles.** Sometimes pays expenses of writers on assignment.

PHOTOS State availability. Captions, identification of subjects required. Reviews 3x5 prints. Negotiates payment individually.

COLUMNS/DEPARTMENTS Contact: Tim Cox, editor. From the Hill (legislative news impacting the forest products industry), 1,800 words; Green Watch (environmental news/opinion affecting U.S. forests), 1,500 words. **Buys 12 mss/year.** Query with published clips. **Pays $200-400.**

TIPS "Provide unique environmental or industry-oriented articles. Many of our freelance articles are company features of logging operations or sawmills."

$$ TIMBERWEST

TimberWest Publications, LLC, P.O. Box 610, Edmonds WA 98020. (425)778-3388. **Fax:** (425)771-3623. **E-mail:** timberwest@forestnet.com. **Website:** www.forestnet.com. **Contact:** Diane Mettler, managing editor. **75% freelance written.** Monthly magazine covering logging and lumber segment of the forestry industry in the Northwest. "We publish primarily profiles on loggers and their operations—with an emphasis on the machinery—in Washington, Oregon, Idaho, Montana, Northern California, and Alaska. Some timber issues are highly controversial, and although we will report on the issues, this is a pro-logging publication. We don't publish articles with a negative slant on the timber industry." Estab. 1975. Circ. 10,000. Byline given. Pays on acceptance. No kill fee. Editorial lead time 3 months. Accepts queries by mail, fax. Responds in 3 weeks to queries. Sample copy for $2. Guidelines for #10 sase.

NONFICTION Needs historical, interview, new product. "No articles that put the timber industry in a bad light—such as environmental articles against logging." **Buys 50 mss/year.** Query with published clips. Length: 1,100-1,500 words. **Pays $350.** Pays expenses of writers on assignment.

PHOTOS Send photos. Captions, identification of subjects required. Reviews contact sheets, transparencies, prints, GIF/JPEG files. Offers no additional payment for photos accepted with ms.

FILLERS Needs facts, newsbreaks. **Buys 10 mss/year.** Length: 400-800 words. **Pays $100-250.**

TIPS "We are always interested in profiles of loggers and their operations in Alaska, Oregon, Washington, Montana, and Northern California. We also want articles pertaining to current industry topics, such as fire abatement, sustainable forests, or new technology. Read an issue to get a clear idea of the type of material *TimberWest* publishes. The audience is primarily loggers and topics that focus on an 'evolving' timber industry versus a 'dying' industry will find a place in the magazine. When querying, a clear overview of the article will enhance acceptance."

MACHINERY AND METAL

$$$ CUTTING TOOL ENGINEERING

CTE Publications, Inc., 1 Northfield Plaza, Suite 240, Northfield IL 60093. (847)714-0175. **Fax:** (847)559-4444. **E-mail:** alanr@jwr.com. **Website:** www.ctemag.com. **Contact:** Alan Richter, editor. **40% freelance written.** Monthly magazine covering industrial metal cutting tools and metal cutting operations. "*Cutting Tool Engineering* serves owners, managers, and engineers who work in manufacturing, specifically manufacturing that involves cutting or grinding metal or other materials. Writing should be geared toward improving manufacturing processes." Circ. 48,000. Byline given. Pays on publication. Offers 50% kill fee. Publishes ms an average of 2 months after acceptance. Editorial lead time 2 months. Accepts queries by mail, fax. Responds in 2 months to mss. Sample copy and writers guidelines free.

NONFICTION Needs how-to, opinion, personal experience, technical. "No fiction or articles that don't relate to manufacturing." **Buys 10 mss/year.** Length: 1,500-3,000 words. **Pays $750-1,500.** Pays expenses of writers on assignment.

PHOTOS State availability. Captions required. Reviews transparencies, prints. Negotiates payment.

TIPS "For queries, write 2 clear paragraphs about how the proposed article will play out. Include sources that would be in the article."

✪ $$ EQUIPMENT JOURNAL

Pace Publishing, 5160 Explorer Dr., Unit 6, Mississauga ON L4W 4T7 Canada. (416)459-5163. **E-mail:** editor@equipmentjournal.com. **Website:** www.equipmentjournal.com. "We are Canada's national heavy equipment newspaper. We focus on the construction, material handling, mining, forestry and on-highway transportation industries." Estab. 1964. Circ. 23,000 subscriber. Byline given. Pays on publication. No kill fee. Publishes ms an average of 1-2 months after acceptance. Editorial lead time 2-3 months. Accepts queries by mail. Accepts simultaneous submissions. Sample copy and guidelines free.

NONFICTION Needs how-to, interview, new product, photo feature, technical. No material that falls outside of *EJ*'s mandate—the Canadian equipment industry. **Buys 15 mss/year.** Send complete ms. "We prefer electronic submissions. We do not accept unsolicited freelance submissions." Length: 500-1,500 words. **$250-400 for assigned and unsolicited articles.** Sometimes pays expenses of writers on assignment.

PHOTOS Contact: Nathan Medcalf, editor. State availability. Identification of subjects required. 4 x 6 prints. Negotiates payment individually.

TIPS "Please pitch a story, instead of asking for an assignment. We are looking for stories of construction sites."

MACHINE DESIGN

Penton Media, Penton Media Bldg., 1300 E. 9th St., Cleveland OH 44114. (216)931-9412. **Fax:** (216)621-8469. **E-mail:** mdeditor@penton.com. **Website:** www.machinedesign.com. Semimonthly magazine covering machine design. Covers the design engineering of manufactured products across the entire spectrum of the idustry for people who perform design engineering functions. Circ. 185,163. No kill fee. Editorial lead time 10 weeks. Accepts queries by mail, e-mail. No

NONFICTION Needs how-to, new product, technical. Send complete ms.

COLUMNS/DEPARTMENTS Query with or without published clips, or send complete ms.

⊛⊛ SPRINGS

Spring Manufacturers Institute, 2001 Midwest Rd., Suite 106, Oak Brook IL 60523-1335. (630)495-8588. **Fax:** (630)495-8595. **E-mail:** lynne@smihq.org. **Website:** www.smihq.org. **Contact:** Lynne Carr, general manager. **10% freelance written.** Quarterly magazine covering precision mechanical spring manufacture. Articles should be aimed at spring manufacturers. Estab. 1962. Circ. 10,800. Byline given. Pays on publication. No kill fee. Publishes ms an average of 3-6 months after acceptance. Editorial lead time 4 months. Accepts simultaneous submissions. Sample copy free. Guidelines available online.

NONFICTION Needs general interest, how-to, interview, opinion, personal experience, technical. **Buys 4-6 mss/year.** Length: 2,000-10,000 words. **Pays $100-600 for assigned articles.**

PHOTOS State availability. Captions required. Reviews prints, digital photos. Offers no additional payment for photos accepted with ms.

TIPS Call the editor. Contact springmakers and spring industry suppliers and ask about what inter-

ests them. Include interviews/quotes from people in the spring industry in the article. The editor can supply contacts. See guidelines on website.

⊛⊛⊛ STAMPING JOURNAL

Fabricators & Manufacturers Association (FMA), 833 Featherstone Rd., Rockford IL 61107. (815)399-8700. **Fax:** (815)381-1370. **E-mail:** dand@thefabricator.com; timh@thefabricator.com. **Website:** www.thefabricator.com. **Contact:** Dan Davis, editor-in-chief; Tim Heston, senior editor. **15% freelance written.** Bimonthly magazine covering metal stamping. "We look for how-to and educational articles—non-promotional." Estab. 1989. Circ. 35,000. Byline given. Pays on publication. No kill fee. Editorial lead time 6 months. Accepts queries by mail, e-mail, fax, phone. Responds in 2 weeks to queries. Responds in 2 months to mss. Sample copy and writer's guidelines free.

NONFICTION Needs how-to, technical, company profile. Special issues: Forecast issue (January). No unsolicited case studies. **Buys 5 mss/year.** Query with published clips. 1,000 words **Pays 40-80¢/word.** Sometimes pays expenses of writers on assignment.

PHOTOS State availability. Captions, identification of subjects required. Reviews contact sheets. Negotiates payment individually.

TIPS "Articles should be impartial and should not describe the benefits of certain products available from certain companies. They should not be biased toward the author's or against a competitor's products or technologies. The publisher may refuse any article that does not conform to this guideline."

⊛⊛⊛⊛ TODAY'S MACHINING WORLD

Screw Machine World, Inc., 4235 W. 166th St., Oak Forest IL 60452. (708)535-2237. **Fax:** (708)535-0103. **E-mail:** emily@todaysmachiningworld.com; lloydgrafftmw@yahoo.com; noah@todaysmachiningworld.com. **Website:** www.todaysmachiningworld.com. **Contact:** Emily Halgrimson, managing editor; Lloyd Graff, writer; Noah Graff, writer/website editor. **40% freelance written.** Monthly magazine covering metal turned parts manufacturing in the US and global. "We hire writers to tell a success story or challenge regarding our industry. There are **no** advertorials coming from advertisers." Estab. 2001. Circ. 18,500. Byline given. Pays on publication. Offers $500 kill fee. Publishes ms an average of 2 months after acceptance. Editorial lead time 2-4 months. Submit seasonal material 2 months in advance. Responds in 1 month to mss. Guidelines free.

NONFICTION Needs general interest, how-to. "We do not want unsolicited articles." **Buys 12-15 mss/year.** Query. Length: 1,500-2,500 words. **Pays $1,500-2,000 for assigned articles.**

PHOTOS State availability. Captions required. Reviews GIF/JPEG files. Negotiates payment individually.

COLUMNS/DEPARTMENTS Shop Doc (manufacturing problem/solution), 500 words. Query. **Pays $-$250.**

TIPS "You may submit an idea related to manufacturing that would be of interest to our readers. If you pitch it, we'll respond!"

THE WORLD OF WELDING

Hobart Institute of Welding Technology, 400 Trade Square E, Troy OH 45373. (937)332-5603. **Fax:** (937)332-5220. **E-mail:** hiwt@welding.org. **Website:** www.welding.org. **10% freelance written.** Quarterly magazine covering welding training and education. Estab. 1930. Circ. 6,500. Byline given. Publishes ms an average of 3 months after acceptance. Editorial lead time 3 months. Submit seasonal material 3 months in advance. Accepts queries by mail, e-mail, fax. Accepts simultaneous submissions. Responds in 1 week to queries. Responds in 3 months to mss. Sample copy and guidelines free.

NONFICTION Needs general interest, historical, how-to, interview, personal experience, photo feature, technical, welding topics. Query with published clips.

PHOTOS Send photos. Captions, identification of subjects, model releases required. Reviews GIF/JPEG files. Offers no additional payment for photos accepted with ms.

FILLERS Needs facts, newsbreaks. Query.

TIPS "Writers must be willing to donate material on welding and metallurgy related topics, welded art/sculpture, personal welding experiences. An editorial committee reviews submissions and determines acceptance."

MAINTENANCE AND SAFETY

☻☻ AMERICAN WINDOW CLEANER MAGAZINE

12 Publishing Corp., 750-B NW Broad St., Southern Pines NC 28387. (910)693-2644. **Fax:** (910)246-1681. **E-mail:** info@awcmag.com. **Website:** www.awcmag.

com. Bob Lawrence editor; Karen Grinter, creative director. **20% freelance written.** Bimonthly magazine on window cleaning. Articles to help window cleaners become more profitable, safe, professional, and feel good about what they do. Estab. 1986. Circ. 8,000. Byline given. Pays on acceptance. Offers 33% kill fee. Publishes ms an average of 4-8 months after acceptance. Editorial lead time 2 months. Submit seasonal material 3 months in advance. Responds in 2 weeks to queries. Responds in 1 month to mss. Sample copy free.

NONFICTION Needs how-to, humor, inspirational, interview, personal experience, photo feature, technical, add-on business. "We do not want PR-driven pieces. We want to educate—not push a particular product." **Buys 20 mss/year.** Query. Length: 500-5,000 words. **Pays $50-250.**

PHOTOS State availability. Captions required. Reviews contact sheets, transparencies, 4x6 prints. Offers $10 per photo.

COLUMNS/DEPARTMENTS Window Cleaning Tips (tricks of the trade), 1,000-2,000 words; Humor-anecdotes-feel good-abouts (window cleaning industry); Computer High-Tech (tips on new technology), all 1,000 words **Buys 12 mss/year.** Query. **Pays $50-100.**

☻☻ EXECUTIVE HOUSEKEEPING TODAY

The International Executive Housekeepers Association, 1001 Eastwind Dr., Suite 301, Westerville OH 43081-3361. (614)895-7166. **Fax:** (614)895-1248. **E-mail:** ldriscoll@ieha.org. **Website:** www.ieha.org. **Contact:** Leah Driscoll, editor. **50% freelance written.** "Monthly magazine for nearly 5,000 decision makers responsible for housekeeping management (cleaning, grounds maintenance, laundry, linen, pest control, waste management, regulatory compliance, training) for a variety of institutions: hospitality, healthcare, education, retail, government." Estab. 1930. Circ. 5,500. Byline given. No kill fee. Publishes ms an average of 6 months after acceptance. Editorial lead time 2 months. Submit seasonal material 3 months in advance. Accepts queries by mail, e-mail, fax, phone.

NONFICTION Needs general interest, interview, new product, related to magazine's scope, personal experience, in housekeeping profession, technical. **Buys 30 mss/year.** Query with published clips. Length: 1,500-2,000 words.

PHOTOS State availability. Identification of subjects required. Offers no additional payment for photos accepted with ms.

COLUMNS/DEPARTMENTS Federal Report (OSHA/EPA requirements), 1,000 words; Industry News; Management Perspectives (industry specific), 1,500-2,000 words. Query with published clips.

TIPS "Have a background in the industry or personal experience with any aspect of it."

MANAGEMENT AND SUPERVISION

$ $ $ HUMAN RESOURCE EXECUTIVE

LRP Publications Magazine Group, P.O. Box 980, Horsham PA 19044-0980. (215)784-0910. **Fax:** (215)784-0275. **E-mail:** kfrasch@lrp.com. **E-mail:** mobrien@lrp.com. **Website:** www.hronline.com. **Contact:** Kristen B. Frasch, managing editor. **30% freelance written.** Magazine published 16 times/year serving the information needs of chief human resource professionals/executives in companies, government agencies, and nonprofit institutions with 500 or more employees. Estab. 1987. Circ. 75,000. Byline given. Pays on acceptance. Offers kill fee. Pays 50% kill fee on assigned stories. Publishes ms an average of 2 months after acceptance. Accepts queries by mail, e-mail, fax. Responds in 1 month to mss. Guidelines available online.

NONFICTION Needs book excerpts, interview. **Buys 16 mss/year.** Query with published clips. News, editorial and byline submissions: Michael O'Brien, web editor, mobrien@lrp.com. Length: 1,800 words. **Pays $200-1,000.** Sometimes pays expenses of writers on assignment.

PHOTOS State availability. Identification of subjects required. Reviews contact sheets. Offers no additional payment for photos accepted with ms.

$ $ INCENTIVE

Northstar Travel Media LLC, 100 Lighting Way, Secaucus NJ 07094. (201)902-2000; (201)902-1975. **E-mail:** lcioffi@ntmllc.com. **Website:** www.incentivemag.com. **Contact:** Lori Cioffi, editorial director. Monthly magazine covering sales promotion and employee motivation: managing and marketing through motivation. Estab. 1905. Circ. 41,000. Byline given. Pays on acceptance. No kill fee. Publishes ms an average of 3 months after acceptance. Accepts queries by mail, e-mail, fax. Responds in 1 month to queries. Responds in 2 months to mss. Sample copy for SAE with 9x12 envelope.

NONFICTION Needs general interest, motivation, demographics, how-to, types of sales promotion, buying product categories, using destinations, interview, sales promotion executives, travel, incentive-oriented, corporate case studies. **Buys 48 mss/year.** Query with published clips. Length: 1,000-2,000 words. **Pays $250-700 for assigned articles. Does not pay for unsolicited articles.** Pays expenses of writers on assignment.

REPRINTS Send tearsheet and information about when and where the material previously appeared. Pays 50% of the amount paid for an original article.

PHOTOS Send photos. Identification of subjects required. Reviews contact sheets, transparencies. Offers some additional payment for photos accepted with ms.

TIPS "Read the publication, then query."

$ $ PLAYGROUND MAGAZINE

Harris Publishing, 360 B St., Idaho Falls ID 83402. (208)542-2271. **Fax:** (208)522-5241. **E-mail:** lindstrm@playgroundmag.com. **Website:** www.playgroundmag.com. **Contact:** Lane Lindstrom, editor. **25% freelance written.** Magazine published quarterly covering playgrounds, play-related issues, equipment, and industry trends. "*Playground Magazine* targets park and recreation management, elementary school teachers and administrators, child care facilities, and parent-group leader readership. Articles should focus on play and the playground market as a whole, including aquatic play and surfacing." Estab. 2000. Circ. 35,000. Byline given. Pays on publication. No kill fee. Publishes ms an average of 6 months after acceptance. Editorial lead time 2 months. Submit seasonal material 1 year in advance. Accepts queries by mail, e-mail. Accepts simultaneous submissions. Responds in 1 month to queries. Responds in 2 months to mss. Sample copy for $5. Guidelines for #10 SASE.

NONFICTION Needs how-to, interview, new product, opinion, personal experience, photo feature, technical, travel. *Playground Magazine* does not publish any articles that do not directly relate to play and the playground industry. **Buys 4-6 mss/year.** Query. Length: 800-1,500 words. **Pays $50-300 for assigned articles.** Sometimes pays expenses of writers on assignment.

PHOTOS State availability of or send photos. Captions, identification of subjects, model releases required. Reviews 35mm transparencies, GIF/JPEG files (350 dpi or better). Offers no additional payment for photos accepted with ms.

COLUMNS/DEPARTMENTS Dream Spaces (an article that profiles a unique play area and focuses on community involvement, unique design, or human interest), 800-1,200 words. **Buys 2 mss/year.** Query. **Pays $100-300.**

TIPS "We are looking for articles that managers can use as a resource when considering playground construction, management, safety, installation, maintenance, etc. Writers should find unique angles to playground-related features such as current trends in the industry, the value of play, natural play, the need for recess, etc. We are a trade journal that offers up-to-date industry news and features that promote play and the playground industry."

MARINE AND MARITIME INDUSTRIES

🌀💲 CURRENTS

Marine Technology Society, 1100 H St. NW, Suite LL-100, Washington DC 20005. (202)717-8705. **Fax:** (202)347-4302. **E-mail:** publications@mtsociety.org. **Website:** www.mtsociety.org. **Contact:** Mary Beth Loutinsky, communications manager. Bimonthly newsletter covering commercial, academic, scientific marine technology. Estab. 1963. Circ. 3,200. Byline given. Pays on acceptance. No kill fee. Editorial lead time 1-2 months. Accepts queries by e-mail. Accepts simultaneous submissions. Responds in 4 weeks to queries Sample copy free.

NONFICTION Needs interview, technical. **Buys 1-6 mss/year.** Query. Length: 250-500 words. **Pays $100-500 for assigned articles.** Sometimes pays expenses of writers on assignment.

🌀💲 PROFESSIONAL MARINER

Navigator Publishing, P.O. Box 569, Portland ME 04112. (207)772-2466, ext. 204. **Fax:** (207)772-2879. **E-mail:** jgormley@professionalmariner.com. **Website:** www.professionalmariner.com. **Contact:** John Gormley, editor. **75% freelance written.** Bimonthly magazine covering professional seamanship and maritime industry news. Estab. 1993. Circ. 29,000. Byline given. Pays on publication. No kill fee. Editorial lead

time 3 months. Accepts queries by mail, e-mail. Accepts simultaneous submissions.

NONFICTION Buys 15 mss/year. Query. Length: varies; short clips to long profiles/features. **Pays 25¢/word.** Sometimes pays expenses of writers on assignment.

PHOTOS Send photos. Captions, identification of subjects required. Reviews prints, slides. Negotiates payment individually.

TIPS "Remember that our audience comprises maritime industry professionals. Stories must be written at a level that will benefit this group."

🌀 WORK BOAT WORLD

Baird Maritime, Suite 3, 20 Cato St., Hawthorn East Victoria 3123 Australia. (61)(3)9824-6055. **Fax:** (61)(3)9824-6588. **E-mail:** marinfo@baird.com.au; editor@baird.com.au. **Website:** www.bairdmaritime.com. Monthly magazine covering all types of commercial, military, and government vessels to around 130 meters in length. Maintaining close contact with ship builders, designers, owners and operators, suppliers of vessel equipment and suppliers of services on a worldwide basis, the editors and journalists of *Work Boat World* seek always to be informative. They constantly put themselves in the shoes of readers so as to produce editorial matter that interests, educates, informs, and entertains. Estab. 1982.

NONFICTION Needs general interest, how-to, interview, new product. Query.

MEDICAL

CALIFORNIA

🌀💲 SOUTHERN CALIFORNIA PHYSICIAN

Physicians News Network, 707 Wilshire Blvd., Suite 3800, Los Angeles CA 90017. (213)226-0335. **Fax:** (213)226-0350. **E-mail:** cheryle@lacmanet.org. **Website:** www.socalphysician.net. **Contact:** Cheryl England, publisher/editor. **25% freelance written.** Monthly magazine covering non-technical articles of relevance to physicians. Estab. 1908. Circ. 18,000. Byline given. Pays on acceptance. Offers 10% kill fee. Publishes ms an average of 2-3 months after acceptance. Editorial lead time 2-3 months. Accepts queries by e-mail. Accepts simultaneous submissions. Responds in 4 weeks to queries. Responds in 2 months to mss. Sample copy available online.

NONFICTION Needs general interest. **Buys 12-24 mss/year.** Query with published clips. Length: 600-3,000 words. **Pays $200-600 for assigned articles.**

PHOTOS State availability.

COLUMNS/DEPARTMENTS Medical World (tips/how-to's), 800-900 words. Query with published clips. **Pays $$200-$600.**

TIPS "We want professional, well-researched articles covering policy, issues, and other concerns of physicians. No personal anecdotes or patient viewpoints."

$ ADVANCE FOR RESPIRATORY CARE & SLEEP MEDICINE

Merion Publications, Inc., 2900 Horizon Dr., Box 61556, King of Prussia PA 19406. (800)355-5627, ext. 1324. **Fax:** (610)278-1425. **E-mail:** sgeorge@advanceweb.com; advance@merion.com. **Website:** http://respiratory-care-sleep-medicine.advanceweb.com; www.advanceweb.com. **Contact:** Sharlene George, editor. **50% freelance written.** Biweekly magazine covering clinical, technical and business management trends for professionals in pulmonary, respiratory care, and sleep. "*ADVANCE for Respiratory Care & Sleep Medicine* welcomes original articles, on speculation, from members of the respiratory care and sleep professions. Once accepted, mss become the property of *ADVANCE for Respiratory Care & Sleep Medicine* and cannot be reproduced elsewhere without permission from the editor. An honorarium is paid for published articles. **For information on preparing your manuscript, please** download our Writer's Guidelines (PDF format)." Estab. 1988. Circ. 45,500. Byline given. Pays on publication. Offers 75% kill fee. Publishes ms an average of 6 months after acceptance. Editorial lead time 1 month. Submit seasonal material 3 months in advance. Accepts queries by mail, e-mail. Accepts simultaneous submissions. Responds in 2 weeks to queries. Responds in up to 6 months to mss. Sample copy available online. Guidelines available at http://respiratory-care-sleep-medicine.advanceweb.com/Editorial/Content/editorial.aspx?CTIID=3587.

NONFICTION Needs technical. "We do not want to get general information articles about specific respiratory care related diseases. For example, our audience is all too familiar with cystic fibrosis, asthma, COPD, bronchitis, Alpha 1 Antitrypsin Defiency, pulmonary hypertension and the like." **Buys 2-3 mss/year.** Query. E-mail article and send printout by mail. Length: 1,500-2,000/words; double-spaced, 4-7 pages. **Pays honorarium.** Sometimes pays expenses of writers on assignment.

PHOTOS State availability. Captions, identification of subjects, model releases required. Reviews GIF/JPEG files. Negotiates payment individually.

TIPS "The only way to truly break into the market for this publication on a freelance basis is to have a background in health care. All of our columnists are caregivers; most of our freelancers are caregivers. Any materials that come in of a general nature like 'contact me for freelance writing assignments or photography' are discarded."

$ ADVANCE NEWSMAGAZINES

Merion Publications Inc., 2900 Horizon Dr., King of Prussia PA 19406. (610)278-1400. **Fax:** (610)278-1425. **E-mail:** advance@merion.com. **Website:** www.advanceweb.com. More than 30 magazines covering allied health fields, nursing, age management, long-term care, and more. Byline given. Pays on publication. Editorial lead time 3 months. Accepts queries by e-mail only.

NONFICTION Needs interview, new product, personal experience, technical. Query with published clips. Include name, and phone and fax number for verification. Length: 2,000 words.

COLUMNS/DEPARTMENTS Phlebotomy Focus, Safety Solutions, Technology Trends, POL Perspectives, Performance in POCT, Eye on Education.

$ $ $ AHIP COVERAGE

America's Health Insurance Plans, 601 Pennsylvania Ave. NW, South Bldg., Suite 500, Washington DC 20004. (202)778-8493. **Fax:** (202)331-7487. **E-mail:** ahip@ahip.org. **Website:** www.ahip.org. **75% freelance written.** Bimonthly magazine geared toward administrators in America's health insurance companies. Articles should inform and generate interest and discussion about topics on anything from patient care to regulatory issues. Estab. 1990. Circ. 12,000. Byline given. Pays within 30 days of acceptance of article in final form. Offers 30% kill fee. Publishes ms an average of 2 months after acceptance. Editorial lead time 2 months. Submit seasonal material 4 months in advance. Accepts queries by mail, e-mail, fax. Accepts simultaneous submissions. Sample copy free.

NONFICTION Needs book excerpts, how-to, how industry professionals can better operate their health plans, opinion. "We do not accept stories that promote products." Send complete ms. Length: 1,800-

2,500 words. **Pays 65¢/word minimum.** Pays phone expenses of writers on assignment.

TIPS "Look for health plan success stories in your community; we like to include case studies on a variety of topics—including patient care, provider relations, regulatory issues—so that our readers can learn from their colleagues. Our readers are members of our trade association and look for advice and news. Topics relating to the quality of health plans are the ones more frequently assigned to writers, whether a feature or department. We also welcome story ideas. Just send us a letter with the details."

AMERICA'S PHARMACIST

National Community Pharmacists Association, 100 Daingerfield Rd., Suite 205, Alexandria VA 22314-2885. (703)683-8200. **Fax:** (703)683-3619. **E-mail:** mike.conlan@ncpanet.org. **Website:** www.ncpanet. org. Chris Linville, man. ed. **10% freelance written.** Monthly magazine. *America's Pharmacist* publishes business and management information and personal profiles of independent community pharmacists, the magazine's principal readers. Articles feature the very latest in successful business strategies, specialty pharmacy services, medication safety, consumer advice, continuing education, legislation, and regulation. Estab. 1904. Circ. 25,000. Byline given. Pays on publication. No kill fee. Publishes ms an average of 3 months after acceptance. Editorial lead time 3 months. Submit seasonal material 3 months in advance. Accepts queries by mail, e-mail, fax. Accepts simultaneous submissions. Responds in 1 week to queries. Responds in 2 weeks to mss. Sample copy free.

NONFICTION Needs interview, business information. **Buys 3 mss/year.** Query. Length: 1,500-2,500 words.

PHOTOS State availability. Captions, identification of subjects, model releases required. Reviews contact sheets. Negotiates payment individually.

AT THE CENTER

Right Ideas, Inc., P.O. Box 309, Fleetwood PA 19522. (800)588-7744. **Fax:** (800)588-7744. **E-mail:** info@atcmag.com. **Website:** www.atcmag.com. **20% freelance written.** Webzine published 4 times/year that provides encouragement and education to the staff, volunteers, and board members working in crisis pregnancy centers. Estab. 2000. Circ. 30,000. Byline given. Pays on publication. No kill fee. Publishes ms an average of 1 year after acceptance. Editorial lead time 6 months. Submit seasonal material 1 year in advance. Accepts queries by mail, e-mail, fax. Accepts simultaneous submissions. Responds in 1 month to queries. Responds in 3-4 months to mss. Sample copy available online. Guidelines for #10 SASE or by e-mail.

NONFICTION Buys about 12 mss/year. Query. Length: 800-1,200 words. **Pays $150 for assigned articles. Pays $50-150 for unsolicited articles.**

TIPS "Generally, we don't have enough space to print personal stories. If your story is relevant to the things you want to share with staff and volunteers of the centers, your best chance to get it published is to keep it brief (a couple paragraphs). Any scripture references should be quoted from KJV or ESV."

JEMS

PennWell Corporation, 525 B St., Suite 1800, San Diego CA 92101. (800)266-5367. **E-mail:** editor.jems@elsevier.com; aheightman@pennwell.com. **E-mail:** jenniferb@pennwell.com. **Website:** www.jems. com. **Contact:** Jennifer Berry, managing editor; A.J. Heightman, MPA, EMT-P, editor-in-chief. **95% freelance written.** Monthly magazine directed to personnel who serve the pre-hospital emergency medicine industry: paramedics, EMTs, emergency physicians and nurses, administrators, EMS consultants, etc. Estab. 1980. Circ. 45,000. Byline given. Pays on publication. No kill fee. Publishes ms an average of 6 months after acceptance. Submit seasonal material 6 months in advance. Accepts queries by e-mail. Responds in 2-3 months to queries. Sample copy free. Guidelines available at www.jems.com/about/author-guidelines.

NONFICTION Needs essays, exposé, general interest, how-to, humor, interview, new product, opinion, personal experience, photo feature, technical; continuing education. **Buys 50 mss/year.** Submit cover letter and outline/ms to managing editor Jennifer Berry. **Pays $100-350.**

PHOTOS State availability. Identification of subjects, model releases required. Reviews 4x6 prints, digital images. Offers $25 minimum per photo.

COLUMNS/DEPARTMENTS Length: 850 words maximum. Query with or without published clips. **Pays $50-250.**

TIPS "Please submit a 1-page cover letter with your ms. Your letter should answer these questions: 1) What specifically are you going to tell *JEMS* readers about pre-hospital medical care? 2) Why do *JEMS* readers need to know this? 3) How will you make your case (i.e., literature review, original research, interviews, personal experience, observation)? Your query should explain your qualifications, as well as include previous writing samples."

💲💲💲 MANAGED CARE

780 Township Line Rd., Yardley PA 19067. (267)685-2788. **Fax:** (267)685-2966. **E-mail:** jmarcille@managedcaremag.com. **Website:** www.managedcaremag.com. **Contact:** John Marcille, editor. **75% freelance written.** Monthly magazine. "We emphasize practical, usable information that helps HMO medical directors and pharmacy directors cope with the options, challenges, and hazards in the rapidly changing health care industry." Estab. 1992. Circ. 44,000. Byline given. Pays on acceptance. Offers 20% kill fee. Publishes ms an average of 6 weeks after acceptance. Editorial lead time 3 months. Submit seasonal material 4 months in advance. Accepts queries by mail, e-mail, fax. Responds in 3 weeks to queries. Responds in 2 months to mss. Sample copy free. Writer's guidelines on request.

NONFICTION Needs book excerpts, general interest, trends in health-care delivery and financing, quality of care, and employee concerns, how-to, deal with requisites of managed care, such as contracts with health plans, affiliation arrangements, accreditation, computer needs, etc., original research and review articles that examine the relationship between health care delivery and financing. Also considered occasionally are personal experience, opinion, interview/profile, and humor pieces, but these must have a strong managed care angle and draw upon the insights of (if they are not written by) a knowledgeable managed care professional. **Buys 40 mss/year.** Query with published clips. Length: 1,000-3,000 words. **Pays 75¢/word.** Pays expenses of writers on assignment.

PHOTOS State availability. Reviews contact sheets, negatives, transparencies, prints. Negotiates payment individually.

TIPS "Know our audience (health plan executives) and their needs. Study our website to see what we cover."

MEDESTHETICS

Creative Age Communications, 7628 Densmore Ave., Van Nuys CA 91406. **E-mail:** ihansen@creativeage.com. **Website:** www.medestheticsmagazine.com. **Contact:** Inga Hansen, associate publisher/executive editor. **50% freelance written.** Bimonthly magazine covering noninvasive medical aesthetic services such as laser hair removal, skin rejuvenation, injectable fillers, and neurotoxins. "*MedEsthetics* is a business-to-business magazine written for and distributed to dermatologists, plastic surgeons, and other physicians offering noninvasive medical aesthetic services. We cover the latest equipment and products as well as legal and management issues specific to medspas, laser centers, and other medical aesthetic practices." Estab. 2005. Circ. 20,000. Byline given. Pays on acceptance. Publishes ms an average of 3 months after acceptance. Editorial lead time 3 months. Submit seasonal material 3 months in advance. Accepts queries by e-mail. Responds in 1 month to queries.

NONFICTION Needs new product, technical. Does not want articles directed at consumers. **Buys 25 mss/year.** Query.

PHOTOS State availability. Identification of subjects, model releases required. Reviews transparencies, prints. Negotiates payment individually.

TIPS "We work strictly on assignment. Query with article ideas; do not send mss. We respond to queries with article assignments that specify article requirements."

MIDWIFERY TODAY

P.O Box 2672, Eugene OR 97402. (541)344-7438. **Fax:** (541)344-1422. **E-mail:** editorial@midwiferytoday.com and jan@midwiferytoday.com (editorial only); layout@midwiferytoday.com (photography). **Website:** www.midwiferytoday.com. **Contact:** Jan Tritten, editor-in-chief and publisher. **95% freelance written.** Quarterly magazine. Estab. 1986. Circ. 3,000. Byline given. No kill fee. Publishes ms an average of 5 months after acceptance. Editorial lead time 3-9 months. Submit seasonal material 6 months in advance. Accepts queries by e-mail. Accepts simultaneous submissions. Responds in 2 weeks to queries. Responds in 1 month to mss. Sample copy and guidelines available online.

NONFICTION Needs book excerpts, essays, how-to, humor, inspirational, interview, opinion, personal experience, photo feature, clinical research, herbal articles, birth stories, business advice. **Buys 60 mss/year.** Send complete ms. Length: 300-3,000 words.

PHOTOS Contact: Contact layout designer. State availability. Model releases required. Reviews prints, GIF/JPEG files. $15-$50 per photo.

COLUMNS/DEPARTMENTS News: "In My Opinion" (150-750 words). **Buys Buys 8 columns/year. mss/year.** Send complete ms.

POETRY Needs avant-garde, haiku, light verse, traditional. Accepts e-mail submissions (pasted into body of message or as attachment). Cover letter is required. Does not want poetry unrelated to pregnancy or birth. Does not want poetry that is "off subject or puts down the subject." Buys 4/year poems/year. Maximum line length: 25. **Pays 2 contributor's copies. Acquires first rights.**

FILLERS Needs anecdotes, facts, newsbreaks. Length: 100-600 words.

TIPS "Use Chicago Manual of Style formatting."

$$$$ MODERN PHYSICIAN

Crain Communications, 360 N. Michigan Ave., Chicago IL 60601-3806. (312)649-5439. **Fax:** (312)280-3183. **E-mail:** mgoozner@modernhealthcare.com. **Website:** www.modernphysician.com. **Contact:** Merrill Goozner, editor. **10% freelance written.** Monthly magazine covering business and management news for doctors. "*Modern Physician* offers timely topical news features with lots of business information—revenues, earnings, financial data." Estab. 1997. Circ. 24,000. Byline given. Pays on acceptance. No kill fee. Publishes ms an average of 2 months after acceptance. Editorial lead time 2 months. Accepts queries by mail, e-mail. Responds in 6 weeks to queries. Sample copy free. Writer's guidelines sent after query.

NONFICTION Length: 750-1,000 words. **Pays 75¢-$1/word. (Does not pay for Guest Commentaries.)**

TIPS "Read the publication, know our audience, and come up with a good story idea that we haven't thought of yet."

$$ OPTICAL PRISM

250 The East Mall, Suite 1113, Toronto ON M9B 6L3 Canada. (416)233-2487. **Fax:** (416)233-1746. **E-mail:** info@opticalprism.ca. **Website:** www.opticalprism.ca. **30% freelance written.** Magazine published 10 times/year. "We cover the health, fashion, and business aspects of the optical industry in Canada. Estab. 1982. Circ. 10,000. Byline given. Pays on publication. Publishes ms an average of 2 months after acceptance. Editorial lead time 3 months. Submit seasonal material 3 months in advance. Accepts queries by mail, e-mail. Accepts simultaneous submissions.

NONFICTION Needs interview, related to optical industry. Query. Length: 1,000-1,600 words. **Pays 40¢/word (Canadian).** Sometimes pays expenses of writers on assignment.

COLUMNS/DEPARTMENTS Insight (profiles on people in the eyewear industry—also sometimes schools and businesses), 700-1,000 words. **Buys 5 mss/year.** Query. **Pays 40¢/word.**

TIPS "Please look at our editorial themes, which are on our website, and pitch articles that are related to the themes for each issue."

$$ PODIATRY MANAGEMENT

Kane Communications, Inc., P.O. Box 750129, Forest Hills NY 11375. (718)897-9700. **Fax:** (718)896-5747. **E-mail:** bblock@podiatrym.com. **Website:** www.podiatrym.com. Magazine published 9 times/year for practicing podiatrists. "Aims to help the doctor of podiatric medicine to build a bigger, more successful practice, to conserve and invest his money, to keep him posted on the economic, legal, and sociological changes that affect him." Estab. 1982. Circ. 16,500. Byline given. Pays on publication. $75 kill fee. Submit seasonal material 4 months in advance. Accepts queries by e-mail. Accepts simultaneous submissions. Responds in 2 weeks to queries. Sample copy for $5 and 9x12 SAE. Guidelines for #10 SASE.

NONFICTION Buys 35 mss/year. Length: 1,500-3,000 words. **Pays $350-600.**

REPRINTS Send photocopy. Pays 33% of amount paid for an original article.

PHOTOS State availability. Pays $15 for b&w contact sheet.

TIPS "Articles should be tailored to podiatrists, and preferably should contain quotes from podiatrists."

$$ PRIMARY CARE OPTOMETRY NEWS

SLACK Inc., 6900 Grove Rd., Thorofare NJ 08086-9447. (856)848-1000. **Fax:** (856)848-5991. **E-mail:** optometry@healio.com. **Website:** www.healio.com/optometry. **Contact:** Nancy Hemphill, editor-in-chief. **5% freelance written.** Monthly tabloid covering optometry. "*Primary Care Optometry News* strives to be the optometric professional's definitive information source by delivering timely, accurate, authoritative and balanced reports on clinical issues, socioeconomic and legislative affairs, ophthalmic industry, and research developments, as well as updates on diagnostic and thereapeutic regimens and techniques to enhance the quality of patient care." Estab. 1996. Circ. 39,000. Byline given. Pays on publication. Offers 50% kill fee. Publishes ms an average of 2 months after acceptance. Editorial lead time 2 months. Accepts queries by mail, e-mail, fax, phone. Responds in 2 weeks to queries. Sample copy available online. Guidelines by e-mail.

NONFICTION Needs how-to, interview, new product, opinion, technical. **Buys 20 mss/year.** Query. Length: 800-1,000 words. **Pays $350-500.** Sometimes pays expenses of writers on assignment.

PHOTOS State availability. Captions, model releases required. Reviews GIF/JPEG files. Offers no additional payment for photos accepted with ms.

COLUMNS/DEPARTMENTS What's Your Diagnosis (case presentation), 800 words. **Buys 40 mss/year.** Query. **Pays $100-500.**

TIPS "Either e-mail or call the editor-in-chief with questions or story ideas."

⊘ $$ STRATEGIC HEALTH CARE MARKETING

Health Care Communications, 11 Heritage Lane, P.O. Box 594, Rye NY 10580. (914)967-6741. **Fax:** (914)967-3054. **E-mail:** healthcomm@aol.com. **Website:** www. strategichealthcare.com. **Contact:** Michele von Dambrowski, editor and publisher. **90% freelance written.** Monthly newsletter covering health care marketing and management in a wide range of settings, including hospitals, medical group practices, home health services, and managed care organizations. Emphasis is on strategies and techniques employed within the health care field and relevant applications from other service industries. Works with published/established writers only. *Strategic Health Care Marketing* is specifically seeking writers with expertise/contacts in managed care, patient satisfaction, and e-health. Estab. 1984. Byline given. Pays on publication. Offers 25% kill fee. Publishes ms an average of 2 months after acceptance. Accepts queries by mail, e-mail. Responds in 1 month to queries. Sample copy for SAE with 9x12 envelope and 3 first-class stamps. Guidelines sent with sample copy only.

NONFICTION Needs how-to, interview, new product, technical. **Buys 50 mss/year.** Query. Length: 1,000-1,800 words. **Pays $100-500.** Sometimes pays expenses of writers on assignment with prior authorization.

PHOTOS Photos, unless necessary for subject explanation, are rarely used. State availability. Captions, model releases required. Reviews contact sheets. Offers $10-30/photo.

TIPS "Writers with prior experience on the business beat for newspapers or newsletters will do well. We require a sophisticated, in-depth knowledge of health care and business. This is not a consumer publication—the writer with knowledge of both health care and marketing will excel. Absolutely no unsolicited mss; any received will be returned or discarded unread."

MUSIC TRADE

$$ CLASSICAL SINGER MAGAZINE

Classical Publications, Inc., P.O. Box 1710, Draper UT 84020. (801)254-1025, ext. 14. **Fax:** (801)254-3139. **E-mail:** editorial@classicalsinger.com. **Website:** www. classicalsinger.com. **Contact:** Sara Thomas. Monthly magazine covering classical singers. Estab. 1988. Circ. 7,000. Byline given, plus bio and contact info. Pays on publication. No kill fee. Publishes ms an average of 3 months after acceptance. Editorial lead time 3 months. Submit seasonal material 3 months in advance. Accepts queries by e-mail. YesResponds in 1 month to queries. Potential writers will be given password to website version of magazine and writer's guidelines online.

NONFICTION Needs book excerpts, exposé, carefully done, how-to, humor, interview, new product, personal experience, photo feature, religious, technical, travel, , crossword puzzles on opera theme. Does not want reviews unless they are assigned. Query with published clips. Length: 500-3,000 words. **Pays 5¢/word ($50 minimum). Writers also receive 10 contributor's copies.** Pays telephone expenses of writers with assignments when Xerox copy of bill submitted.

PHOTOS Send photos. Captions required.

TIPS "*Classical Singer Magazine* has a full-color glossy cover and glossy b&w and color pages inside. It ranges in size from 56 pages during the summer to 120 pages in September. Articles need to meet this mission statement: 'Information for a classical singer's career, support for a classical singer's life, and enlightenment for a classical singer's art.'"

⊘ $ INTERNATIONAL BLUEGRASS

International Bluegrass Music Association, 608 W. Iris Dr., Nashville TN 37204. (615)256-3222. **Fax:** (615)256-0450. **E-mail:** info@ibma.org. **Website:** www.ibma.org. **10% freelance written.** Bimonthly newsletter of the International Bluegrass Music Association. "We are the business publication for the bluegrass music industry. IBMA believes that our music has growth potential. We are interested in hard news and features concerning how to reach that potential and how to conduct business more effectively." Estab. 1985. Circ. 4,500. Byline given. Pays on publication. No kill fee. Publishes ms an average of 2 months after acceptance. Submit seasonal material 4 months in advance. Accepts queries by mail, e-mail, phone. Accepts simultaneous submissions. Responds in 1 month to queries. Sample copy for SAE with 6x9 envelope and 2 first-class stamps.

NONFICTION Needs book excerpts, essays, how-to, conduct business effectively within bluegrass music, new product, opinion. No interview/profiles/feature stories of performers (rare exceptions) or fans. **Buys 6 mss/year.** Query. Length: 1,000-1,200 words. **Pays up to $150/article for assigned articles.**

REPRINTS Send photocopy of article and information about when and where the article previously appeared. Does not pay for reprints.

PHOTOS Send photos. Captions, identification of subjects, Required. Offers no additional payment for photos accepted with ms.

COLUMNS/DEPARTMENTS Staff written.

TIPS "We're interested in a slant strongly toward the business end of bluegrass music. We're especially looking for material dealing with audience development and how to book bluegrass bands outside of the existing market."

⊖⊖ THE MUSIC & SOUND RETAILER

Testa Communications, 25 Willowdale Ave., Port Washington NY 11050. (516)767-2500. **E-mail:** dferrisi@testa.com. **Website:** www.msretailer.com. **Contact:** Dan Ferrisi, editor. **10% freelance written.** Monthly magazine covering business to business publication for music instrument products. *The Music & Sound Retailer* covers the music instrument industry and is sent to all dealers of these products, including Guitar Center, Sam Ash, and all small independent stores. Estab. 1983. Circ. 11,700. Byline given. Pays on publication. Offers $100 kill fee. Editorial lead time 1 month. Submit seasonal material 2 months in advance. Accepts queries by e-mail. Accepts simultaneous submissions. Responds in 2 weeks to queries. Responds in 1 month to mss. Sample copy for #10 SASE. Guidelines free.

NONFICTION Needs how-to, new product, opinion, (does not mean letters to the editor), personal experience. Concert and CD reviews are never published; neiter are interviews with musicians. **Buys 25 mss/**year. Query with published clips. Length: 1,000-2,000 words. **Pays $300-400 for assigned articles; $300-400 for unsolicited articles.** Sometimes pays expenses of writers on assignment.

PHOTOS Send photos. Captions required. Reviews GIF/JPEG files. Offers no additional payment for photos accepted with ms.

⊖⊖⊖ OPERA NEWS

Metropolitan Opera Guild, Inc., 70 Lincoln Center Plaza, 6th Floor, New York NY 10023. (212)769-7080. **Fax:** (212)769-8500. **E-mail:** info@operanews.com. **Website:** www.operanews.com. **Contact:** Kitty March. **75% freelance written.** Monthly magazine for people interested in opera—the opera professional as well as the opera audience. Estab. 1936. Circ. 105,000. Byline given. Pays on publication. No kill fee. Publishes ms an average of 4 months after acceptance. Editorial lead time 4 months. Accepts queries by e-mail. Sample copy for $5.

NONFICTION Needs historical, interview, informational, think pieces, opera, and CD, DVD and book reviews. "We do not accept works of fiction or personal remembrances. No phone calls, please." Query. Length: 1,500-2,800 words. **Pays $450-1,200.** Sometimes pays expenses of writers on assignment.

PHOTOS State availability.

COLUMNS/DEPARTMENTS Buys 24 mss/year.

⊖ OVERTONES

Handbell Musicians of America, P.O. Box 1765, Findlay OH 45839-1765. **E-mail:** jrsmith@handbellmusicians.org. **Website:** http://handbellmusicians.org/music-resources/overtones. **Contact:** J.R. Smith, publications director. **80% freelance written.** Bimonthly magazine covering English handbell ringing and conducting. "*Overtones* is a 48-page magazine with extensive educational articles, photos, advertisements, and graphic work. Handbell Musicians of America is dedicated to advancing the musical art of handbell/handchime ringing through education, community, and communication. The purpose of *Overtones* is to provide a printed resource to support that mission. We offer how-to articles, inspirational stories, and interviews with well-known people and unique ensembles." Estab. 1954. Circ. 8,000. Byline given. Pays on publication. No kill fee. Publishes ms an average of 4 months after acceptance. Editorial lead time 4 months. Submit seasonal material 4 months in advance. Accepts queries by mail, e-mail. YesResponds in 1 month to queries and to mss. Sample copy and guidelines by e-mail.

NONFICTION Needs essays, general interest, historical, how-to, inspirational, interview, religious, technical. Does not want product news or promotional material. **Buys 8-12 mss/year.** Send complete ms. Length: 1,200-2,400 words. **Pays $120.** Sometimes pays expenses of writers on assignment.

PHOTOS State availability of or send photos. Captions required. Reviews 8x10 prints, JPEG/TIFF files. Offers no additional payment for photos accepted with ms.

COLUMNS/DEPARTMENTS Handbells in Education (topics covering the use of handbells in school setting, teaching techniques, etc.); Handbells in Worship (topics and ideas for using handbells in a church setting); Tips & Tools (variety of topics from ringing and conducting techniques to score study to maintenance); Community Connections (topics covering issues relating to the operation/administration/techniques for community groups); Music Reviews (recommendations and descriptions of music following particular themes, i.e., youth music, difficult music, seasonal, etc.); all 800-1,200 words. Query. **Pays $80.**

TIPS "When writing profiles/interviews, try to determine what is especially unique or inspiring about the individual or ensemble and write from that viewpoint. Please have some expertise in handbells, education, or church music to write department articles."

⊛⊛ VENUES TODAY

18350 Mt. Langley, Suite 201, Fountain Valley CA 92708. (714)378-5400. **Fax:** (714)378-0040. **E-mail:** linda@venuestoday.com. **Website:** www.venuestoday.com. **Contact:** Linda Deckard, publisher/editor-in-chief. **70% freelance written.** Weekly magazine covering the live entertainment industry and the buildings that host shows and sports. "We need writers who can cover an exciting industry from the business side, not the consumer side. The readers are venue managers, concert promoters, those in the concert and sports business, not the audience for concerts and sports. So we need business journalists who can cover the latest news and trends in the market." Estab. 2002. Byline given. Pays on publication. Publishes ms an average of 1 month after acceptance. Editorial lead time 1-2 months. Submit seasonal material 1-2 months in advance. Accepts queries by mail, e-mail, fax. Accepts simultaneous submissions. Responds

in 1 week to queries. Sample copy available online. Guidelines free.

NONFICTION Needs interview, photo feature, technical, travel. Does not want customer slant, marketing pieces. Query with published clips. Length: 500-1,500 words. **Pays $100-250.** Pays expenses of writers on assignment.

PHOTOS State availability. Captions, identification of subjects required. Reviews GIF/JPEG files. Negotiates payment individually.

COLUMNS/DEPARTMENTS Venue News (new buildings, trend features, etc.); Bookings (show tours, business side); Marketing (of shows, sports, convention centers); Concessions (food, drink, merchandise). Length: 500-1,200 words. **Buys 250 mss/year.** Query with published clips. **Pays $100-250.**

FILLERS Needs gags. **Buys 6 mss/year. Pays $100-300.**

PAPER

⊛⊛ THE PAPER STOCK REPORT

McEntee Media Corp., 9815 Hazelwood Ave., Strongsville OH 44149. (440)238-6603. **Fax:** (440)238-6712. **E-mail:** ken@recycle.cc. **Website:** www.recycle.cc. **Contact:** Ken McEntee, editor/publisher. Biweekly newsletter covering market trends and news in the paper recycling industry. "Audience is interested in new innovative markets, applications for recovered scrap paper, as well as new laws and regulations impacting recycling." Estab. 1990. Circ. 2,000. Byline given. Pays on publication. No kill fee. Publishes ms an average of 1 month after acceptance. Editorial lead time 2 months. Submit seasonal material 2 months in advance. Accepts queries by mail, e-mail, fax, phone. Accepts simultaneous submissions. Responds in 1 month to queries. Sample copy for #10 SAE with 55¢ postage.

NONFICTION Needs book excerpts, essays, exposé, general interest, historical, interview, new product, opinion, photo feature, technical, all related to paper recycling. **Buys 0-13 mss/year.** Send complete ms. Length: 250-1,000 words. **Pays $50-250 for assigned articles. Pays $25-250 for unsolicited articles.** Pays expenses of writers on assignment.

PHOTOS State availability. Identification of subjects required. Reviews contact sheets. Negotiates payment individually.

TIPS "Articles must be valuable to readers in terms of presenting new market opportunities or cost-saving measures."

⊕⊕ RECYCLED PAPER NEWS

McEntee Media Corp., 9815 Hazelwood Ave., Strongsville OH 44149. (440)238-6603. **Fax:** (440)238-6712. **E-mail:** ken@recycle.cc. **Website:** www.recycle.cc. **Contact:** Ken McEntee, owner. **10% freelance written.** Monthly newsletter covering the recycling and composting industries. "We are interested in any news impacting the paper recycling industry, as well as other environmental issues in the paper industry, i.e., water/air pollution, chlorine-free paper, forest conservation, etc., with special emphasis on new laws and regulations." Estab. 1990. Pays on publication. No kill fee. Publishes ms an average of 2 months after acceptance. Editorial lead time 1 month. Submit seasonal material 1 month in advance. Accepts queries by mail, e-mail, fax, phone. Accepts simultaneous submissions. Responds in 2 months to queries. Sample copy for 9x12 SAE and 55¢ postage. Guidelines for #10 SASE.

NONFICTION Needs book excerpts, essays, how-to, interview, new product, opinion, personal experience, photo feature, technical, new business, legislation, regulation, business expansion. **Buys 0-5 mss/year.** Query with published clips. **Pays $10-500.**

COLUMNS/DEPARTMENTS Query with published clips. **Pays $10-500.**

TIPS "We appreciate leads on local news regarding recycling or composting, i.e., new facilities or businesses, new laws and regulations, unique programs, situations that impact supply and demand for recyclables, etc. International developments are also of interest."

PETS

⊕⊕ PET AGE

Journal Multimedia, 220 Davidson Ave., Suite 302, Somerset NJ 08873. (732)246-5722. **Website:** www.petage.com. **Contact:** Michelle Maskaly, editor-in-chief. **90% freelance written.** Monthly magazine for pet/pet supplies retailers, covering the complete pet industry. Estab. 1971. Circ. 23,022. Byline given. Pays on acceptance. No kill fee. Publishes ms an average of 3 months after acceptance. Sample copy and writer's guidelines available.

NONFICTION No profiles of industry members and/or retail establishments or consumer-oriented pet ar-

ticles. **Buys 80 mss/year.** Query with published clips. Length: 1,500-2,200 words. **Pays 15¢/word for assigned articles.** Pays documented telephone expenses.

PHOTOS Captions, identification of subjects required. Reviews transparencies, slides, and 5x7 glossy prints.

TIPS "This is a business publication for busy people, and must be very informative in easy-to-read, concise style. Articles about animal care or business practices should have the pet-retail angle or cover issues specific to this industry."

PLUMBING, HEATING, AIR CONDITIONING AND

⊕⊕ SNIPS MAGAZINE

BNP Media, 2401 W. Big Beaver Rd., Suite 700, Troy MI 48084. (248)244-6416. **Fax:** (248)362-0317. **E-mail:** mcconnellm@bnpmedia.com. **Website:** www.snipsmag.com. **Contact:** Michael McConnell. **2% freelance written.** Monthly magazine for sheet metal, heating, ventilation, air conditioning, and metal roofing contractors. Estab. 1932. No kill fee. Publishes ms an average of 3 months after acceptance. Accepts queries by mail, e-mail, fax, phone. Call for writer's guidelines.

NONFICTION Length: under 1,000 words unless on special assignment. **Pays $200-300.**

PHOTOS Negotiable.

PRINTING

⊕⊕ THE BIG PICTURE

ST Media Group International, 11262 Cornell Park Dr., Cincinnati OH 45242. (513)421-2050. **E-mail:** gregory.sharpless@stmediagroup.com. **Website:** http://bigpicture.net. **Contact:** Gregory Sharpless. **20% freelance written.** Magazine published 9 times/year covering wide-format digital printing. "*The Big Picture* covers wide-format printing as well as digital workflow, finishing, display, capture, and other related topics. Our 21,500 readers include digital print providers, sign shops, commercial printers, in-house print operations, and other print providers across the country. We are primarily interested in the technology and work processes behind wide-format printing, but also run trend features on segments of the industry (innovations in point-of-purchase displays, floor graphics, fine-art printing, vehicle wrapping, textile printing, etc.)." Estab. 1996. Circ. 21,500 controlled. Byline given. Pays on publication. Offers 20% kill fee. Publishes ms an average of 2 months after acceptance. Editorial lead time 2 months. Accepts queries by e-mail. Accepts simultaneous submissions. Responds in 2 weeks to queries. Responds in 1 month to mss. Sample copy available online. Guidelines available.

NONFICTION Needs how-to, interview, new product, technical. Does not want broad consumer-oriented pieces that do not speak to the business and technical aspects of producing print for pay. **Buys 15-20 mss/year.** Query with published clips. Length: 1,500-2,500 words. **Pays $500-700 for assigned articles.**

PHOTOS Send photos. Reviews GIF/JPEG files hi-res. Offers no additonal payment for photos accepted with ms.

TIPS "Interest in and knowledge of the digital printing industry will position you well to break into this market. You have to be willing to drill down into the production aspects of digital printing to write for us."

IN-PLANT GRAPHICS

North American Publishing Co., 1500 Spring Garden St., 12th Floor, Philadelphia PA 19130. (215)238-5321. **Fax:** (215)238-5457. **E-mail:** bobneubauer@napco.com. **Website:** www.ipgonline.com. **Contact:** Bob Neubauer, editor. **40% freelance written.** Estab. 1951. Circ. 23,100. Byline given. Pays on publication. No kill fee. Publishes ms an average of 3 months after acceptance. Editorial lead time 2 months. Submit seasonal material 3 months in advance. Accepts queries by mail, e-mail, fax. Guidelines available online.

NONFICTION Needs new product, graphic arts, technical, graphic arts/printing/prepress. No articles on desktop publishing software or design software. No Internet publishing articles. **Buys 5 mss/ year.** Query with published clips. Length: 800-1,500 words. **Pays $350-500.**

PHOTOS State availability. Captions, identification of subjects required. Reviews transparencies, prints. Negotiates payment individually.

TIPS "To get published in *IPG*, writers must contact the editor with an idea in the form of a query letter that includes published writing samples. Writers who have covered the graphic arts in the past may be assigned stories for an agreed-upon fee. We don't want stories that tout only 1 vendor's products and serve as glorified commercials. All profiles must be well bal-anced, covering a variety of issues. If you can tell us about an in-house printing operation is doing innovative things, we will be interested."

SCREEN PRINTING

ST Media Group International, 11262 Cornell Park Dr., Cincinnati OH 45242. (513)421-2050, ext. 331. **Fax:** (513)421-5144. **E-mail:** gail.flower@stmedia-group.com. **Website:** www.screenweb.com. **Contact:** Gail Flower. **30% freelance written.** Monthly magazine for the screen printing industry, including screen printers (commercial, industrial, and captive shops), suppliers and manufacturers, ad agencies, and allied profession. Estab. 1953. Circ. 17,500. Byline given. Pays on publication. No kill fee. Publishes ms an average of 3 months after acceptance. Accepts queries by mail, e-mail, fax. Sample copy available. Guidelines for #10 SASE.

NONFICTION Unsolicited mss not returned. **Buys 10-15 mss/year.** Query. **Pays $400 minimum for major features.**

PHOTOS Cover photos negotiable; b&w or color. Published material becomes the property of the magazine.

TIPS "Be an expert in the screen-printing industry with supreme or special knowledge of a particular screen-printing process, or have special knowledge of a field or issue of particular interest to screen-printers. If the author has a working knowledge of screen printing, assignments are more readily available. General management articles are rarely used."

PROFESSIONAL PHOTOGRAPHY

NEWS PHOTOGRAPHER

National Press Photographers Association, Inc., 6677 Whitemarsh Valley Walk, Austin TX 78746-6367. **E-mail:** magazine@nppa.org. **Website:** www.nppa.org. **Contact:** Donald R. Winslow, editor. Magazine on photojournalism published 10 times/year. *"News Photographer* magazine is dedicated to the advancement of still and television news photography. The magazine presents articles, interviews, profiles, history, new products, electronic imaging, and news related to the practice of photojournalism." Estab. 1946. Circ. 11,000. Byline given. Pays on acceptance. Offers 100% kill fee. Publishes ms an average of 4 months after acceptance. Editorial lead time 2 months. Submit seasonal material 2 months in advance. Accepts queries by mail, e-mail, fax, phone. Accepts simultaneous submissions. Responds in 1 month to queries. Sample copy for SAE with 9x12 envelope and 3 first-class stamps. Guidelines free.

NONFICTION Needs historical, how-to, interview, new product, opinion, personal experience, photo feature, technical. **Buys 10 mss/year.** Query. Length: 1,500 words. **Pays $300.** Pays expenses of writers on assignment.

PHOTOS State availability. Captions, identification of subjects required. Reviews high resolution, digital images only. Negotiates payment individually.

COLUMNS/DEPARTMENTS Query.

⑤⑤ THE PHOTO REVIEW

140 E. Richardson Ave., Suite 301, Langhorne PA 19047. (215)891-0214. **Fax:** (215)891-9358. **E-mail:** info@photoreview.org. **Website:** www.photoreview.org. **50% freelance written.** Quarterly magazine covering art photography and criticism. "*The Photo Review* publishes critical reviews of photography exhibitions and books, critical essays, and interviews. We do not publish how-to or technical articles." Estab. 1976. Circ. 2,000. Byline given. Pays on publication. No kill fee. Publishes ms an average of 9-12 months after acceptance. Editorial lead time 3 months. Submit seasonal material 6 months in advance. Accepts queries by mail. Accepts simultaneous submissions. Responds in 2 months to queries. Responds in 3 months to mss. Sample copy for $7. Guidelines for #10 SASE.

NONFICTION Needs interview, photography essay, critical review. No how-to articles. **Buys 20 mss/year.** Send complete ms. 2-20 typed pages **Pays $10-250.**

REPRINTS "Send tearsheet, photocopy, or typed ms with rights for sale noted and information about when and where the material previously appeared." Payment varies.

PHOTOS Send photos. Captions required. Reviews contact sheets, transparencies, prints. Offers no additional payment for photos accepted with ms.

SHUTTERBUG

Source Interlink Media, 1415 Chaffee Dr., Suite 1, Titusville FL 32780. **Fax:** (321)225-3149. **E-mail:** editorial@shutterbug.com. **Website:** www.shutterbug.com. **90% freelance written.** Monthly covering photography and digial imaging. Written for the avid amateur, part-time, and full-time professional photographers. Covers equipment techniques, profiles, tech-

nology, and news in photography. Estab. 1972. Circ. 90,000. Byline given. Pays on publication. Editorial lead time minimum 3 months. Submit seasonal material 6 months in advance. Accepts queries by mail, e-mail. Responds in 1 month to queries. Responds in 1 month to mss.

NONFICTION Query. Length: Depends on subject matter and content. **Payment rate is on published page including photographs.**

PHOTOS Send photos. Captions, model releases required. Reviews contact sheets, transparencies, CD-ROMs. Offers no additional payment for photos, except for cover shot.

TIPS "Write first for submission requirements and please be familiar with a few months of the magazine's content before submitting. No over the transom material—photos or mss—accepted."

REAL ESTATE

◯ ⑨ ⑤⑤ CANADIAN PROPERTY MANAGEMENT

Mediaedge Communications Inc., 5255 Yonge St., Toronto ON M2N 6P4 Canada. (416)512-8186. **Fax:** (416)512-8344. **E-mail:** barbc@mediaedge.ca. **Website:** www.canadianpropertymanagement.ca; www.mediaedge.ca. **Contact:** Barbara Carss, editor-in-chief. **10% freelance written.** Magazine published 8 times/year covering Canadian commercial, industrial, institutional (medical and educational), and residential properties. *Canadian Property Management* magazine is a trade journal supplying building owners and property managers with Canadian industry news, case law reviews, technical updates for building operations and events listings. Building and professional profile articles are regular features. Estab. 1985. Circ. 12,500. Byline given. Pays on publication. No kill fee. Publishes ms an average of 3 months after acceptance. Editorial lead time 2 months. Submit seasonal material 2 months in advance. Accepts queries by mail, e-mail, fax, phone. Accepts simultaneous submissions. Responds in 3 weeks to queries. Responds in 2 months to mss. Sample copy for $5, subject to availability. Guidelines free.

NONFICTION Needs interview, technical. No promotional articles (i.e., marketing a product or service geared to this industry) Query with published clips. Length: 700-1,200 words. **Pays 35¢/word.**

PHOTOS State availability. Captions, identification of subjects, model releases required. Reviews transparencies, 3x5 prints, digital (at least 300 dpi). Offers no additional payment for photos accepted with ms.

TIPS "We do not accept promotional articles serving companies or their products. Freelance articles that are strong, information-based pieces that serve the interests and needs of property managers and building owners stand a better chance of being published. Proposals and inquiries with article ideas are appreciated the most. A good understanding of the real estate industry (management structure) is also helpful for the writer."

$$ THE COOPERATOR

Yale Robbins, Inc., 102 Madison Ave., 5th Floor, New York NY 10016. (212)683-5700. **Fax:** (212)545-0764. **E-mail:** editorial@cooperator.com. **Website:** www.cooperator.com. **70% freelance written.** Monthly tabloid covering real estate in the New York City metro area. *The Cooperator* covers condominium and cooperative issues in New York and beyond. It is read by condo unit owners and co-op shareholders, real estate professionals, board members and managing agents, and other service professionals. Estab. 1980. Circ. 40,000. Byline given. Pays on publication. No kill fee. Publishes ms an average of 3 months after acceptance. Submit seasonal material 3 months in advance. Accepts queries by mail, e-mail, fax. Responds in 1 month to queries. Sample copy and writer's guidelines free.

NONFICTION Needs interview, new product, personal experience. No submissions without queries. Query with published clips. Length: 1,500-2,000 words. **Pays $325-425.** Sometimes pays expenses of writers on assignment.

PHOTOS State availability.

COLUMNS/DEPARTMENTS Profiles of co-op/condo-related businesses with something unique; Building Finance (investment and financing issues); Buying and Selling (market issues, etc.); Design (architectural and interior/exterior design, lobby renovation, etc.); Building Maintenance (issues related to maintaining interior/exterior, facades, lobbies, elevators, etc.); Legal Issues Related to Co-Ops/Condos; Real Estate Trends, all 1,500 words. **Buys 100 mss/year.** Query with published clips.

TIPS "You must have experience in business, legal, or financial. Must have published clips to send in with rèsumè and query."

$$ FLORIDA REALTOR MAGAZINE

Florida Association of Realtors, 7025 Augusta National Dr., Orlando FL 32822. (407)438-1400. **Fax:** (407)438-1411. **E-mail:** flrealtor@floridarealtors.org. **Website:** www.floridarealtormagazine.com. **Contact:** Doug Damerst, editor-in-chief. **70% freelance written.** Journal published 10 times/year covering the Florida real estate profession. "As the official publication of the Florida Association of Realtors, we provide helpful articles for our 115,000 members. We report new practices that lead to successful real estate careers and stay up on the trends and issues that affect business in Florida's real estate market." Estab. 1925. Circ. 112,205. Byline given. Pays on publication. No kill fee. Publishes ms an average of 2 months after acceptance. Editorial lead time 3 months. Accepts queries by mail, e-mail, fax. Sample copy available online.

NONFICTION No fiction or poetry. **Buys varying number of mss/year.** Query with published clips. Length: 800-1,500 words. **Pays $500-700.** Sometimes pays expenses of writers on assignment.

PHOTOS State availability of photos. Captions, identification of subjects, model releases required. Negotiates payment individually.

COLUMNS/DEPARTMENTS Some written in-house: Law & Ethics, 900 words; Market It, 600 words; Technology & You, 800 words; ManageIt, 600 words. **Buys varying number of mss/year. Payment varies.**

TIPS "Build a solid reputation for specializing in real estate business writing in state/national publications. Query with specific article ideas."

$$ OFFICE BUILDINGS MAGAZINE

Yale Robbins, Inc., 102 Madison Ave., New York NY 10016. (212)683-5700. **Fax:** (646)405-9751. **E-mail:** mrosupport@mrofficespace.com. **Website:** http://marketing.yrpubs.com/officebuildings. **15% freelance written.** Covers market statistics and trends. Annual magazine published in 12 separate editions covering market statistics, trends, and thinking of area professionals on the current and future state of the real estate market. Estab. 1987. Circ. 10,500. Byline sometimes given. Pays 1 month after publication.

Offers kill fee. Editorial lead time 2 months. Accepts queries by mail, e-mail.

NONFICTION **Buys 15-20 mss/year.** Query with published clips. Length: 1,500-2,000 words. **Pays $600-700.** Sometimes pays expenses of writers on assignment.

$$ PROPERTIES MAGAZINE

Properties Magazine, Inc., 3826 W. 158th St., Cleveland OH 44111. (216)251-0035. **Fax:** (216)251-0064. **E-mail:** kkrych@propertiesmag.com. **Website:** www.propertiesmag.com. **Contact:** Kenneth C. Krych, editor/publisher. **25% freelance written.** Monthly magazine covering real estate, residential, commerical construction. "*Properties Magazine* is published for executives in the real estate, building, banking, design, architectural, property management, tax, and law community—busy people who need the facts presented in an interesting and informative format." Estab. 1946. Circ. over 10,000. Byline given. Pays on publication. No kill fee. Publishes ms an average of 2 months after acceptance. Editorial lead time 2 months. Submit seasonal material 2 months in advance. Accepts queries by mail, fax. Responds in 3 weeks to queries. Sample copy for $3.95.

NONFICTION Needs general interest, how-to, humor, new product. Special issues: Environmental issues (September); Security/Fire Protection (October); Tax Issues (November); Computers In Real Estate (December). **Buys 30 mss/year.** Send complete ms. Length: 500-2,000 words. **Pays 50¢/column line.** Sometimes pays expenses of writers on assignment.

PHOTOS Send photos. Captions required. Reviews prints. Offers no additional payment for photos accepted with ms. Negotiates payment individually.

COLUMNS/DEPARTMENTS **Buys 25 mss/year.** Query or send complete ms. **Pays 50¢/column line.**

🍁 $$ REM

2255B Queen St. E., Suite #1178, Toronto ON M4E 1G3 Canada. (416)425-3504. **E-mail:** jim@remonline.com. **Website:** www.remonline.com. **Contact:** Jim Adair, managing editor. **35% freelance written.** Monthly Canadian trade journal covering real estate. "*REM* provides Canadian real estate agents and brokers with news and opinions they can't get anywhere else. It is an independent publication and not affiliated with any real estate board, association, or company." Estab. 1989. Circ. 38,000. Pays on acceptance. Offers 25% kill fee. Publishes ms an average of 2 months after acceptance. Editorial lead time 3 months. Submit seasonal material 3 months in advance. Accepts queries by mail, e-mail, fax. Accepts simultaneous submissions. Sample copy free.

NONFICTION Needs book excerpts, exposé, inspirational, interview, new product, personal experience. "No articles geared to consumers about market conditions or how to choose a realtor. Must have Canadian content." **Buys 60 mss/year.** Query. Length: 500-1,500 words. **Pays $200-400.**

PHOTOS Send photos. Captions, identification of subjects required. Reviews transparencies, prints, GIF/JPEG files. Offers $25/photo.

TIPS "Stories must be of interest or practical use for Canadian realtors. Check out our website to see the types of stories we require."

$$ ZONING PRACTICE

American Planning Association, 205 N. Michigan Ave., Suite 1200, Chicago IL 60601. (312)431-9100. **Fax:** (312)786-6700. **E-mail:** zoningpractice@planning.org. **Website:** www.planning.org/zoningpractice/index.htm. **90% freelance written.** Monthly newsletter covering land-use regulations including zoning. "Our publication is aimed at practicing urban planners and those involved in land-use decisions, such as zoning administrators and officials, planning commissioners, zoning boards of adjustment, land-use attorneys, developers, and others interested in this field. The material we publish must come from writers knowledgeable about zoning and subdivision regulations, preferably with practical experience in the field. Anything we publish needs to be of practical value to our audience in their everyday work." Estab. 1984. Circ. 2,000. Byline given. Pays on publication. Offers 50% kill fee. Publishes ms an average of 3 months after acceptance. Editorial lead time 6 months. Accepts queries by mail, e-mail, fax, phone. Responds in 2 weeks to queries. Responds in 1 month to mss. Sample copy free. Guidelines available atwww.planning.org/zoningpractice/contribguidelines.htm.

NONFICTION Needs technical. "See our description. We do not need general or consumer-interest articles about zoning because this publication is aimed at practitioners." **Buys 12 mss/year.** Query. Length: 3,000-5,000 words. **Pays $300 minimum for assigned articles.** Sometimes pays expenses of writers on assignment.

PHOTOS State availability. Captions required. Reviews GIF/JPEG files. Negotiates payment individually.

TIPS "Breaking in is easy if you know the subject matter and can write in plain English for practicing planners. We are always interested in finding new authors. We generally expect authors will earn another $200 premium for participating in an online forum called Ask the Author, in which they respond to questions from readers about their article. This requires a deep practical sense of how to make things work with regard to your topic."

RESOURCES AND WASTE REDUCTION

ⓈⓈ COMPOSTING NEWS

McEntee Media Corp., 9815 Hazelwood Ave., Cleveland OH 44149. (440)238-6603. **Fax:** (440)238-6712. **E-mail:** ken@recycle.cc. **Website:** www.compostingnews.com. **Contact:** Ken McEntee, editor. **5% freelance written.** Monthly newsletter about the composting industry. *Composting News* features the latest news and vital issues of concern to the producers, marketers, and end-users of compost, mulch and other organic waste-based products. Estab. 1992. Circ. 1,000. Pays on publication. No kill fee. Publishes ms an average of 1 month after acceptance. Editorial lead time 1 month. Submit seasonal material 1 month in advance. Accepts queries by mail, e-mail, fax, phone. Accepts simultaneous submissions. Responds in 2 months to queries. Sample copy for 9x12 SAE and 55¢ postage. Guidelines for #10 SASE.

NONFICTION Needs book excerpts, essays, general interest, how-to, interview, new product, opinion, personal experience, photo feature, technical, new business, legislation, regulation, business expansion. **Buys 0-5 mss/year.** Query with published clips. Length: 100-5,000 words. **Pays $10-500.**

COLUMNS/DEPARTMENTS Query with published clips. **Pays $10-500.**

TIPS "We appreciate leads on local news regarding composting, i.e., new facilities or business, new laws and regulations, unique programs, situations that impact supply and demand for composting. International developments are also of interest."

ⓈⓈⓈ EROSION CONTROL

Forester Media Inc., 2946 De La Vina St., Santa Barbara CA 93105. (805)682-1300. **Fax:** (805)682-0200. **E-mail:** eceditor@forester.net. **Website:** www.erosion-control.com. **Contact:** Janice Kaspersen, editor. **60% freelance written.** Magazine published 7 times/year covering all aspects of erosion prevention and sediment control. "*Erosion Control* is a practical, hands-on, 'how-to' professional journal. Our readers are civil engineers, landscape architects, builders, developers, public works officials, road and highway construction officials and engineers, soils specialists, farmers, landscape contractors, and others involved with any activity that disturbs significant areas of surface vegetation." Estab. 1994. Circ. 23,000. Byline given. Pays 1 month after acceptance. No kill fee. Publishes ms an average of 3 months after acceptance. Editorial lead time 4 months. Submit seasonal material 4 months in advance. Accepts queries by mail, e-mail, fax, phone. Responds in 3 weeks to queries. Sample copy and writer's guidelines free.

NONFICTION Needs photo feature, technical. **Buys 15 mss/year.** Query with published clips. Length: 3,000-4,000 words. **Pays $700-850.** Sometimes pays expenses of writers on assignment.

PHOTOS Send photos. Captions, identification of subjects, model releases required. Reviews transparencies, prints. Offers no additional payment for photos accepted with ms.

TIPS "Writers should have a good grasp of technology involved and good writing and communication skills. Most of our freelance articles include extensive interviews with engineers, contractors, developers, or project owners, and we often provide contact names for articles we assign."

ⓈⓈⓈ STORMWATER

Forester Media Inc., 2946 De La Vina St., Santa Barbara CA 93105. (805)682-1300. **Fax:** (805)682-0200. **E-mail:** sweditor@forester.net. **Website:** www.storm-h2o.com. **Contact:** Janice Kaspersen, editor. **10% freelance written.** Magazine published 8 times/year covering stormwater issues. "*Stormwater* is a practical business journal for professionals involved with surface water quality issues, protection, projects, and programs. Our readers are municipal employees, regulators, engineers, and consultants concerned with stormwater management." Estab. 2000. Circ. 20,000. Byline given. Pays 1 month after acceptance. No kill fee. Publishes ms an average of 3 months after acceptance. Editorial lead time 4 months. Submit seasonal material 4 months in advance. Accepts queries by mail, e-mail. Responds in 3 weeks to queries. Guidelines free.

NONFICTION Needs technical. **Buys 8-10 mss/year.** Query with published clips. Length: 3,000-4,000 words. **Pays $500-900.** Sometimes pays expenses of writers on assignment.

TIPS "Writers should have a good grasp of the technology and regulations involved in stormwater management and good interviewing skills. Our freelance articles include extensive interviews with engineers, stormwater managers, and project owners, and we often provide contact names for articles we assign. See past editorial content online."

⊖⊖ WATER WELL JOURNAL

National Ground Water Association, 601 Dempsey Rd., Westerville OH 43081. **Fax:** (614)898-7786. **E-mail:** tplumley@ngwa.org. **Website:** www.ngwa.org. **Contact:** Thad Plumley, director of publications; Mike Price, associate editor. Each month the *Water Well Journal* covers the topics of drilling, rigs and heavy equipment, pumping systems, water quality, business management, water supply, on-site waste water treatment, and diversification opportunities, including geothermal installations, environmental remediation, irrigation, dewatering, and foundation installation. It also offers updates on regulatory issues that impact the ground water industry. Circ. 24,000. Byline given. Pays on publication. Publishes ms an average of 3 months after acceptance. Editorial lead time 6 weeks. Submit seasonal material 3 months in advance. Accepts queries by mail. Responds in 2 weeks to queries. Responds in 1 month to mss. Guidelines free.

NONFICTION Needs essays, sometimes, historical, sometimes, how-to, recent examples include how-to chlorinate a well; how-to buy a used rig; how-to do bill collections, interview, new product, personal experience, photo feature, technical, business management. No company profiles or extended product releases. **Buys up to 30 mss/year.** Query with published clips. Length: 1,000-3,000 words. **Pays $150-400.**

PHOTOS State availability. Captions, identification of subjects required. Offers $50-250/photo.

TIPS "Some previous experience or knowledge in groundwater/drilling/construction industry helpful. Published clips are a must."

SELLING AND MERCHANDISING

⊖⊖ BALLOONS & PARTIES MAGAZINE

PartiLife Publications, 65 Sussex St., Hackensack NJ 07601. (201)441-4224. **Fax:** (201)342-8118. **E-mail:** mark@balloonsandparties.com. **Website:** www.balloonsandparties.com. **Contact:** Mark Zettler, publisher. **10% freelance written.** International trade journal published bi-monthly for professional party decorators and gift delivery businesses. "*BALLOONS & Parties Magazine* is published 6 times a year by PartiLife Publications, L.L.C., for the balloon, party and event fields. New product data, letters, mss, and photographs should be sent as 'Attention: Editor' and should include sender's full name, address, and telephone number. SASE required on all editorial submissions. All submissions considered for publication unless otherwise noted. Unsolicited materials are submitted at sender's risk and *BALLOONS & Parties*/PartiLife Publications, L.L.C., assumes no responsibility for unsolicited materials." Estab. 1986. Circ. 7,000. Byline given. Pays on publication. No kill fee. Publishes ms an average of 3 months after acceptance. Submit seasonal material 6 months in advance. Accepts queries by mail, e-mail, fax, phone. Responds in 6 weeks to queries. Sample copy for SAE with 9x12 envelope.

NONFICTION Needs essays, how-to, interview, new product, personal experience, photo feature, technical, craft. **Buys 12 mss/year.** Send complete ms. Length: 500-1,500 words. **Pays $100-300 for assigned articles. Pays $50-200 for unsolicited articles.** Sometimes pays expenses of writers on assignment.

REPRINTS Send typed ms with rights for sale noted and information about when and where the material previously appeared. Length: up to 2,500 words. Pays 10¢/word.

PHOTOS Send photos. Captions, identification of subjects, model releases required. Reviews 2x2 transparencies, 3x5 prints.

COLUMNS/DEPARTMENTS Problem Solver (small business issues); Recipes That Cook (centerpiece ideas with detailed how-to); 400-1,000 words. Send complete ms with photos.

TIPS "Show unusual, lavish, and outstanding examples of balloon sculpture, design and decorating, and other craft projects. Offer specific how-to information. Be positive and motivational in style."

🌑🌑 CASUAL LIVING MAGAZINE

Sandow Media Furniture/Today Group, 7025 Albert Pick Rd., Suite 200, Greensboro NC 27409. (336)605-1122. **Fax:** (336)605-1143. **E-mail:** cingram@casualliving.com. **Website:** www.casualliving.com. **Contact:** Cinde Ingram, editor-in-chief. **10% freelance written.** Monthly magazine covering outdoor furniture and accessories, barbecue grills, spas, and more. "Casual Living is a trade only publication for the casual furnishings and related industries, published monthly. We write about new products, trends, and casual furniture retailers, plus industry news." Estab. 1958. Circ. 10,000. Pays on publication. Publishes ms an average of 1-2 months after acceptance. Editorial lead time 1-2 months. Submit seasonal material 2 months in advance. Accepts queries by mail, e-mail. Responds in 2 weeks to queries. Sample copy available online.

NONFICTION Needs how-to, interview. **Buys 20 mss/year.** Query with published clips. Length: 300-1,000 words. **Pays $300-700.** Sometimes pays expenses of writers on assignment.

PHOTOS Contact: Jesse Burkhart, editorial assistant. Identification of subjects required. Reviews GIF/JPEG files. Negotiates payment individually.

🌑🌑🌑🌑 CONSUMER GOODS TECHNOLOGY

Edgell Communications, 4 Middlebury Blvd., Randolph NJ 07869. (973)607-1300. **Fax:** (973)607-1395. **E-mail:** aackerman@edgellmail.com. **Website:** www.consumergoods.com. **Contact:** Alliston Ackerman, editor. **40% freelance written.** Monthly tabloid benchmarking business technology performance. Estab. 1987. Circ. 25,000. Byline given. Pays on publication. No kill fee. Publishes ms an average of 2 months after acceptance. Editorial lead time 3 months. Accepts queries by e-mail. Sample copy available online. Guidelines by e-mail.

NONFICTION Needs essays, exposé, interview. **Buys 60 mss/year.** Query with published clips. Length: 700-1,900 words. **Pays $600-1,200.** Sometimes pays expenses of writers on assignment.

PHOTOS Identification of subjects, model releases required. Negotiates payment individually.

COLUMNS/DEPARTMENTS Columns 400-750 words—featured columnists. **Buys 4 mss/year.** Query with published clips. **Pays 75¢-$1/word.**

TIPS "All stories in *Consumer Goods Technology* are told through the voice of the consumer goods executive. We only quote VP-level or C-level CG executives. No vendor quotes. We're always on the lookout for freelance talent. We look in particular for writers with an in-depth understanding of the business issues faced by consumer goods firms and the technologies that are used by the industry to address those issues successfully. 'Bits and bytes' tech writing is not sought; our focus is on benchmarketing the business technology performance of CG firms, CG executives, CG vendors, and CG vendor products. Our target reader is tech-savvy, CG C-level decision maker. We write to, and about, our target reader."

🌑🌑 NICHE

The Rosen Group, 3000 Chestnut Ave., Suite 304, Baltimore MD 21211. (410)889-3093, ext. 231. **Fax:** (410)243-7089. **E-mail:** hoped@rosengrp.com. **Website:** www.nichemagazine.com. **Contact:** Hope Daniels, editor-in-chief. **80% freelance written.** Quarterly trade magazine for the progressive craft gallery retailer. Each issue includes retail gallery profiles, store design trends, management techniques, financial information, and merchandising strategies for small business owners, as well as articles about craft artists and craft mediums. Estab. 1988. Circ. 25,000. Byline given. Pays on publication. No kill fee. Publishes ms an average of 6-9 months after acceptance. Editorial lead time 9 months. Submit queries for seasonal material 1 year in advance. Accepts queries by e-mail. Responds in 4-6 weeks to queries. Responds in 3 months to mss. Sample copy for $3.

NONFICTION Needs interview, photo feature, articles targeted to independent retailers and small business owners. **Buys 15-20 mss/year.** Query with published clips. **Pays $300-700.** Sometimes pays expenses of writers on assignment.

PHOTOS Send photos. Captions required. Reviews e-images only. Negotiates payment individually.

COLUMNS/DEPARTMENTS Retail Details (short items at the front of the book, general retail information); Artist Profiles (short biographies of American Craft Artists); Retail Resources (including book/video/seminar reviews and educational opportunities pertaining to retailers). Query with published clips. **Pays $25-100 per item.**

🟢 O&A MARKETING NEWS

KAL Publications, Inc., 559 S. Harbor Blvd., Suite A, Anaheim CA 92805-4525. (714)563-9300. **Fax:** (714)563-9310. **E-mail:** kathy@kalpub.com. **Website:** www.kalpub.com. **3% freelance written.** Bimonthly tabloid. *O&A Marketing News* is editorially directed to people engaged in the distribution, merchandising, installation, and servicing of gasoline, oil, TBA, quick lube, carwash, convenience store, alternative fuel, and automotive aftermarket products in the 13 Western states. Estab. 1966. Circ. 7,500. Byline sometimes given. Pays on publication. No kill fee. Publishes ms an average of 2 months after acceptance. Editorial lead time 1 month. Submit seasonal material 1 month in advance. Accepts queries by mail, e-mail, fax. Accepts simultaneous submissions. Responds in 2 months to queries. Responds in 2 months to mss. Sample copy for SASE with 9x13 envelope and 10 first-class stamps. **NONFICTION** Needs interview, photo feature, industry news. Does not want anything that doesn't pertain to the petroleum marketing industry in the 13 Western states. **Buys 35 mss/year.** Send complete ms. Length: 100-500 words. **Pays $1.25/column inch.** **PHOTOS** State availability of or send photos. Captions, identification of subjects required. Reviews contact sheets, 4x6 prints, digital images. Offers $5/photo. **COLUMNS/DEPARTMENTS** Oregon News (petroleum marketing news in state of Oregon). **Buys 7 mss/ year.** Send complete ms. **Pays $1.25/column inch.** **FILLERS** Needs gags, short humor. **Buys Buys 7 fillers/year mss/year.** Length: 1-200 words. **Pays per column inch.**
TIPS "Seeking Western industry news pertaining to the petroleum marketing industry. It can be something simple—like a new gas station or quick lube opening. News from 'outlying' states such as Montana, Idaho, Wyoming, New Mexico, and Hawaii is always needed—but any timely, topical news-oriented stories will also be considered."

🟢🟢 SMART RETAILER

Emmis Communications, 707 Kautz Rd., St. Charles IL 60174. (630)377-8000; (888)228-7624. **Fax:** (630)377-8194. **E-mail:** edit@smart-retailer.com. **E-mail:** swagner@smart-retailer.com. **Website:** www. smart-retailer.com. **Contact:** Susan Wagner, editor. **50% freelance written.** Magazine published 7 times/ year covering independent retail, gift, and home decor. *Smart Retailer* is a trade publication for independent retailers of gifts and home accents. Estab. 1993. Circ. 32,000. Byline given. Pays 1 month after acceptance of final ms. Offers $50 kill fee. Publishes ms an average of 4-6 months after acceptance. Editorial lead time 4-6 months. Submit seasonal material 8-10 months in advance. Accepts queries by mail, e-mail, fax. Accepts simultaneous submissions. Usually responds in 4-6 weeks (only if accepted). Sample articles are available on website. Guidelines by e-mail.
NONFICTION Needs how-to, pertaining to retail, interview, new product, finance, legal, marketing, small business. No fiction, poetry, fillers, photos, artwork, or profiles of businesses, unless queried and first assigned. **Buys 20 mss/year.** Send complete ms, with résumé and published clips to: Writers Query, *Smart Retailer.* Length: 1,000-2,500 words. **Pays $275-500 for assigned articles. Pays $200-350 for unsolicited articles.** Sometimes pays expenses of writers on assignment. Limit agreed upon in advance.
COLUMNS/DEPARTMENTS Display & Design (store design and product display), 1,500 words; Retailer Profile (profile of retailer—assigned only), 1,800 words; Vendor Profile (profile of manufacturer—assigned only), 1,200 words; Technology (Internet, computer-related articles as applies to small retailers), 1,500 words; Marketing (marketing ideas and advice as applies to small retailers), 1,500 words; Finance (financial tips and advice as applies to small retailers), 1,500 words; Legal (legal tips and advice as applies to small retailers), 1,500 words; Employees (tips and advice on hiring, firing, and working with employees as applies to small retailers), 1,500 words. **Buys 15 mss/ year.** Query with published clips or send complete ms. **Pays $250-350.**

🟢🟢 TRAVEL GOODS SHOWCASE

Travel Goods Association, 301 North Harrison St., #412, Princeton NJ 08540. (877)842-1938. **Fax:** (877)842-1938. **E-mail:** info@travel-goods.org; cathy@travel-goods.org. **Website:** www.travel-goods. org. **Contact:** Cathy Hays. **5-10% freelance written.** Magazine published quarterly. "*Travel Goods Showcase* contains articles for retailers, dealers, manufacturers, and suppliers about luggage, business cases, personal leather goods, handbags, and accessories. Special articles report on trends in fashion, promotions, selling and marketing techniques, industry statistics, and other educational and promotional improvements and advancements." Estab. 1975. Circ. 21,000. Byline given. Pays on acceptance. Offers $50 kill fee. Publishes ms an average of 2 months after acceptance. Editorial lead time 3 months. Submit seasonal material 2 months in advance. Accepts queries by mail, e-mail. Responds in 2 weeks to queries. Responds in 1 month to mss. Sample copy and writer's guidelines free.

NONFICTION Needs interview, new product, technical, travel, retailer profiles with photos. No manufacturer profiles. **Buys 3 mss/year.** Query with published clips. Length: 1,200-1,600 words. **Pays $200-400.**

$$$ VERTICAL SYSTEMS RESELLER

Edgell Communications, Inc., 4 Middlebury Blvd., Randolph NJ 07869. (973)607-1300. **Fax:** (973)607-1395. **E-mail:** alorden@edgellmail.com. **Website:** www.verticalsystemsreseller.com. **Contact:** Abigail Lorden, editor-in-chief. **60% freelance written.** Monthly journal covering channel strategies that build business. Estab. 1992. Circ. 30,000. Byline given. Pays on acceptance. No kill fee. Publishes ms an average of 2 months after acceptance. Editorial lead time 3 months. Accepts queries by mail, e-mail, fax. Accepts simultaneous submissions. Responds in 2 weeks to queries. Responds in 2 months to mss. Sample copy available online.

NONFICTION Needs interview, opinion, technical, technology/channel issues. **Buys 36 mss/year.** Query with published clips. Length: 1,000-1,700 words. **Pays $200-800 for assigned articles.** Sometimes pays expenses of writers on assignment.

SPORT TRADE

$$ AQUATICS INTERNATIONAL

Hanley Wood, LLC, 6222 Wilshire Blvd., Suite 600, Los Angeles CA 90048. **Fax:** (323)801-4972. **E-mail:** etaylor@hanleywood.com. **Website:** www.aquaticsintl.com. **Contact:** Erika Taylor, editor. Magazine published 10 times/year covering public swimming pools and waterparks. Devoted to the commercial and public swimming pool industries. The magazine provides detailed information on designing, building, maintaining, promoting, managing, programming, and outfitting aquatics facilities. Estab. 1989. Circ. 30,000. Byline given. Pays on publication. No kill fee. Publishes ms an average of 3 months after acceptance. Editorial lead time 3 months. Responds in 1 month to queries. Sample copy for $10.50.

NONFICTION Needs how-to, interview, technical. **Buys 6 mss/year.** Send query letter with published clips/samples. Length: 1,500-2,500 words. **Pays $525 for assigned articles.**

COLUMNS/DEPARTMENTS Pays $250.

$$ ARROWTRADE MAGAZINE

Arrow Trade Publishing Corp., 3479 409th Ave. NW, Braham MN 55006. (320)396-3473. **Fax:** (320)396-3206. **E-mail:** timdehn@arrowtrademag.com. **Website:** www.arrowtrademag.com. **60% freelance written.** Bimonthly magazine covering the archery industry. "Our readers are interested in articles that help them operate their businesses better. They are primarily owners or managers of sporting goods stores and archery pro shops." Estab. 1996. Circ. 10,500. Byline given. Pays on publication. No kill fee. Publishes ms an average of 2 months after acceptance. Editorial lead time 2 months. Accepts queries by mail, e-mail, fax. Responds in 2 weeks to queries. Responds in 2 weeks to mss. Sample copy for SAE with 9x12 envelope and 10 First-Class stamps.

NONFICTION Needs interview, new product. "Generic business articles won't work for our highly specialized audience." **Buys 24 mss/year.** Query with published clips. Length: 2,400-4,800 words. **Pays $350-550.** Sometimes pays expenses of writers on assignment.

PHOTOS Send photos. Captions required. Must provide digital photos on CD or DVD. Offers no additional payment for photos accepted with ms.

TIPS "Our readers are hungry for articles that help them decide what to stock and how to do a better job selling or servicing it. Articles needed typically fall into 1 of these categories: business profiles on outstanding retailers, manufacturers, or distributors; equipment articles that cover categories of gear, citing trends in the market, and detailing why products have been designed a certain way and what type of use they're best suited for; basic business articles that help dealers do a better job of promoting their business, managing their inventory, training their staff, etc. Good interviewing skills are a must, as especially in the equipment articles we like to see a minimum of 6 sources."

⊗⊗ BOATING INDUSTRY

GS Media & Events, 3300 Fernbrook Lane N., Suite 200, Plymouth MN 55447. (763)383-4400. **E-mail:** jonathan.sweet@boatingindustry.com. **Website:** www.boatingindustry.com. **Contact:** Jonathan Sweet, editor-in-chief. **10-20% freelance written.** Bimonthly magazine covering recreational marine industry management. "We write for those in the industry—not the consumer. Our subject is the business of boating. All of our articles must be analytical and predictive, telling our readers where the industry is going, rather than where it's been." Estab. 1929. Circ. 23,000. Byline given. Pays on acceptance. Offers 50% kill fee. Publishes ms an average of 2 months after acceptance. Editorial lead time 2 months. Submit seasonal material 2 months in advance. Accepts queries by mail, e-mail. Responds in 1 month to queries. Sample copy available online. Guidelines free.

NONFICTION Needs technical, business. **Buys 30 mss/year.** Query with published clips. Length: 250-2,500 words. **Pays $25-250.** Sometimes pays expenses of writers on assignment.

PHOTOS State availability. Captions, identification of subjects required. Reviews 2X2 transparencies, 4x6 prints. Negotiates payment individually.

⊗⊗ BOWLING CENTER MANAGEMENT

Luby Publishing, 122 S. Michigan Ave., Suite 1806, Chicago IL 60605. (312)541-1110. **Fax:** (312)541-1180. **E-mail:** mikem@lubypublishing.com. **Website:** www.bcmmag.com. **Contact:** Michael Mazek, editor. **50% freelance written.** Monthly magazine covering bowling centers, family entertainment. "Bowling Center Management is the industry's leading business publication and offical trade magazien of the Bowling Proprietor's Association of America. Our readers are looking for novel ways to draw more customers. Accordingly, we look for articles that effectively present such ideas." Estab. 1995. Circ. 12,000. Byline given. Pays on acceptance. Publishes ms an average of 3 months after acceptance. Editorial lead time 3 months. Submit seasonal material 6 months in advance. Accepts queries by e-mail. Accepts simultaneous submissions. Responds in 2-3 weeks to queries. Sample copy for $10.

NONFICTION Needs how-to, interview. **Buys 10-20 mss/year.** Query. Length: 750-1,500 words. **Pays $150-350.**

TIPS "Send a solid, clever query by e-mail with knowledge and interest in an industry trend."

⊗⊗ GOLF COURSE MANAGEMENT

Golf Course Superintendents Association of America, 1421 Research Park Dr., Lawrence KS 66049. (800)472-7878. **Fax:** (785)832-3643. **E-mail:** shollister@gcsaa.org; bsmith@gcsaa.org; tcarson@gcsaa.org. **Website:** www.gcsaa.org. **Contact:** Scott Hollister, editor-in-chief; Bunny Smith, senior managing editor; Teresa Carson, senior science editor. **50% freelance written.** Monthly magazine covering the golf course superintendent. *GCM* helps the golf course superintendent become more efficient in all aspects of their job. Estab. 1924. Circ. 40,000. Byline given. Pays on acceptance. No kill fee. Publishes ms an average of 6 months after acceptance. Editorial lead time 6 months. Submit seasonal material 6 months in advance. Accepts simultaneous submissions. Responds in 3 weeks to queries. Responds in 1 month to mss. Sample copy free. Guidelines available at www2.gcsaa.org/gcm/ed_features.asp and www2.gcsaa.org/gcm/ed_research.asp.

NONFICTION Needs how-to, interview. No articles about playing golf. **Buys 40 mss/year.** Query for either feature, research, or superintendent article. Submit electronically, preferably as e-mail attachment. Send 1-page synopsis or query for feature article to Scott Hollister (shollister@gcsaa.org). For research articles, submit to Teresa Carson (tcarson@gcsaa.org). If you are a superintendent, contact Bunny Smith (bsmith@gcsaa.org). Length: 1,500-2,000 words. **Pays $400-600.** Sometimes pays expenses of writers on assignment.

PHOTOS Send photos. Identification of subjects required. Offers no additional payment for photos accepted with ms.

TIPS "Writers should have prior knowledge of golf course maintenance, agronomy and turfgrass science, and the overall profession of the golf course superintendent."

⊗⊗ INTERNATIONAL BOWLING INDUSTRY

B2B Media, Inc., 13245 Riverside Dr., Suite 501, Sherman Oaks CA 91423. (818)789-2695. **Fax:** (818)789-2812. **E-mail:** info@bowlingindustry.com. **Website:** www.bowlingindustry.com. **40% freelance written.** Monthly magazine covering ownership and management of bowling centers (alleys) and pro shops.

"*IBI* publishes articles in all phases of bowling center and bowling pro shop ownership and management, among them finance, promotion, customer service, relevant technology, architecture, and capital improvement. The magazine also covers the operational areas of bowling centers and pro shops such as human resources, food and beverage, corporate and birthday parties, ancillary attractions (go-karts, gaming and the like), and retailing. Articles must have strong how-to emphasis. They must be written specifically in terms of the bowling industry, although content may be applicable more widely." Estab. 1993. Circ. 10,200. Byline given. Pays on acceptance. Offers $50 kill fee. Publishes ms an average of 3 months after acceptance. Submit seasonal material 3 months in advance. Accepts queries by mail, e-mail, fax. Accepts simultaneous submissions. Responds in 2 weeks to queries. Responds in 1 month to mss. Sample copy for #10 SASE. Guidelines free.

NONFICTION Needs how-to, interview, new product, technical. **Buys 40 mss/year.** Send complete ms. Length: 1,100-1,400 words. **Pays $250.** Sometimes pays expenses of writers on assignment.

PHOTOS State availability. Identification of subjects required. Reviews JPEG photos. Offers no additional payment for photos accepted with ms.

TIPS "Please supply writing samples, applicable list of credits. and bio."

$$ POOL & SPA NEWS

Hanley Wood, LLC, 6222 Wilshire Blvd., Suite 600, Los Angeles CA 90048. (323)801-4972. **Fax:** (323)801-4986. **E-mail:** etaylor@hanleywood.com. **Website:** http://poolspanews.com. **Contact:** Erika Taylor, editor. **15% freelance written.** Semimonthly magazine covering the swimming pool and spa industry for builders, retail stores, and service firms. Estab. 1960. Circ. 16,300. Pays on publication. No kill fee. Publishes ms an average of 2 months after acceptance. Accepts queries by mail, e-mail. Responds in 1 month to queries. Sample copy for $5 and 9x12 SAE and 11 first-class stamps.

NONFICTION Needs interview, technical. Send résumé with published clips. Length: 500-2,000 words. **Pays $150-550.** Pays expenses of writers on assignment.

REPRINTS Send typed ms with rights for sale noted and information about when and where the material previously appeared. Payment varies.

PHOTOS Payment varies.

COLUMNS/DEPARTMENTS Payment varies.

$$ REFEREE

Referee Enterprises, Inc., 2017 Lathrop Ave., Racine WI 53405. (800)733-6100. **Fax:** (262)632-5460. **E-mail:** submissions@referee.com. **Website:** www.referee.com. **Contact:** Julie Sternberg, managing editor. **75% freelance written.** Monthly magazine covering sports officiating. *Referee* is a magazine for and read by sports officials of all kinds with a focus on baseball, basketball, football, softball, and soccer officiating. Estab. 1976. Circ. 40,000. Byline given. Pays on acceptance. Offers kill fee. Kill fee negotiable. Publishes ms an average of 6 months after acceptance. Editorial lead time 6 months. Accepts queries by mail, e-mail. Responds in 2 weeks to queries. Responds in 1 month to mss. Sample copy with #10 SASE. Guidelines available at www.referee.com/index.php/referee-magazine/writers-guidlines.

NONFICTION Needs book excerpts, essays, historical, how-to, sports officiating related, humor, interview, opinion, photo feature, technical, as it relates to sports officiating. "We don't want to see articles with themes not relating to sport officiating. General sports articles, although of interest to us, will not be published." **Buys 40 mss/year.** Query with published clips. Length: 500-3,500 words. **Pays $50-400.** Sometimes pays expenses of writers on assignment.

PHOTOS State availability. Identification of subjects required. Reviews contact sheets, negatives, transparencies, prints. Offers $35-40 per photo.

TIPS "Query first and be persistent. We may not like your idea, but that doesn't mean we won't like your next one. Professionalism pays off."

STONE, QUARRY AND MINING

⊙ $$ CANADIAN MINING JOURNAL

Business Information Group, 80 Valleybrook Dr., Toronto ON M3B 2S9 Canada. (416)510-6742. **Fax:** (416)510-5138. **E-mail:** rnoble@canadianminingjournal.com. **Website:** www.canadianminingjournal.com. **Contact:** Russell Noble, editor. **5% freelance written.** Magazine covering mining and mineral exploration by Canadian companies. *Canadian Mining Journal* provides articles and information of practical use to those who work in the technical, administrative, and supervisory aspects of exploration, mining, and processing in the Canadian mineral exploration and mining industry. Estab. 1882. Circ. 11,000. Byline given. Pays on publication. No kill fee. Publishes ms an average of 3 months after acceptance. Submit seasonal material 3 months in advance. Accepts queries by mail, e-mail, fax, phone. Responds in 1 week to queries. Responds in 1 month to mss.

NONFICTION Needs opinion, technical, operation descriptions. **Buys 6 mss/year.** Query with published clips. Length: 500-1,400 words. **Pays $100-600.** Pays expenses of writers on assignment.

PHOTOS State availability. Captions, identification of subjects, Required. Reviews 4x6 prints or high-resolution files. Negotiates payment individually.

COLUMNS/DEPARTMENTS Guest editorial (opinion on controversial subject related to mining industry), 600 words. **Buys 3 mss/year.** Query with published clips. **Pays $150.**

TIPS "I need articles about mine sites that would be expensive/difficult for me to reach. I also need to know the writer is competent to understand and describe the technology in an interesting way."

❸ CONTEMPORARY STONE & TILE DESIGN

Business News Publishing Media, 210 Route 4 East, Suite 203, Paramus NJ 07652. (201)291-9001, ext. 8611. **Fax:** (201)291-9002. **E-mail:** jennifer@stoneworld.com. **Website:** www.stoneworld.com. **Contact:** Jennifer Adams, editor. Quarterly magazine covering the full range of stone and tile design and architecture—from classic and historic spaces to current projects. Estab. 1995. Circ. 21,000. Byline given. Pays on publication. No kill fee. Publishes ms an average of 3 months after acceptance. Submit seasonal material 6 months in advance. Responds in 3 weeks to queries. Sample copy for $10.

NONFICTION Needs interview, prominent architect/designer or firm, photo feature, technical, architectural design. **Buys 8 mss/year.** Query with published clips. Length: 1,500-3,000 words. **Pays $6/column inch.** Pays expenses of writers on assignment.

PHOTOS State availability. Captions, identification of subjects required. Reviews transparencies, prints. Pays $10/photo accepted with ms.

COLUMNS/DEPARTMENTS Upcoming Events (for the architecture and design community); Stone Classics (featuring historic architecture); question and an-swer session with a prominent architect or designer. Length: 1,500-2,000 words. **Pays $6/inch.**

TIPS "The visual aspect of the magazine is key, so architectural photography is a must for any story. Cover the entire project, but focus on the stonework or tile work and how it relates to the rest of the space. Architects are very helpful in describing their work and often provide excellent quotes. As a relatively new magazine, we are looking for freelance submissions and are open to new feature topics. This is a narrow subject, however, so it's a good idea to speak with an editor before submitting anything."

❸ STONE WORLD

BNP Media, 210 Rt. 4 E., Suite 203, Paramus NJ 07652. (201)291-9001. **Fax:** (201)291-9002. **E-mail:** michael@stoneworld.com. **Website:** www.stoneworld.com. **Contact:** Michael Reis, editor/associate publisher. Monthly magazine on natural building stone for producers and users of granite, marble, limestone, slate, sandstone, onyx, and other natural stone products. Estab. 1984. Circ. 21,000. Byline given. Pays on publication. No kill fee. Publishes ms an average of 4 months after acceptance. Submit seasonal material 6 months in advance. Responds in 2 months to queries. Sample copy for $10.

NONFICTION Needs how-to, fabricate and/or install natural building stone, interview, photo feature, technical, architectural design, artistic stone uses, statistics, factory profile, equipment profile, trade show review. **Buys 10 mss/year.** Send complete ms. Length: 600-3,000 words. **Pays $6/column inch.** Pays expenses of writers on assignment.

REPRINTS Send photocopy with rights for sale noted and information about when and where the material previously appeared. Pays 50% of amount paid for an original article.

PHOTOS State availability. Captions, identification of subjects required. Reviews transparencies, prints, slides, digital images. Pays $10/photo accepted with ms.

COLUMNS/DEPARTMENTS News (pertaining to stone or design community); New Literature (brochures, catalogs, books, videos, etc., about stone); New Products (stone products); New Equipment (equipment and machinery for working with stone); Calendar (dates and locations of events in stone and design communities). Query or send complete ms. Length 300-600 words. **Pays $6/inch.**

TIPS "Articles about architectural stone design accompanied by professional color photographs and quotes from designing firms are often published, especially when 1 unique aspect of the stone selection or installation is highlighted. We are also interested in articles about new techniques of quarrying and/or fabricating natural building stone."

TOY, NOVELTY AND HOBBY

💲💲 MODEL RETAILER

Kalmach Publishing, 21027 Crossroads Circle, P.O. Box 1612, Waukesha WI 53187. (262)796-8776. **Fax:** (262)796-1142. **E-mail:** jreich@modelretailer.com. **E-mail:** editor@modelretailer.com. **Website:** www.modelretailer.com. **Contact:** Jeff Reich, editor. **5% freelance written.** Monthly magazine covering the business of hobbies. "*Model Retailer* covers the business of hobbies, from financial and shop management issues to industry trends and the latest product releases. Our goal is to provide hobby shop entrepreneurs with the tools and information they need to be successful retailers." Estab. 1987. Circ. 6,000. Byline given. Pays on acceptance. No kill fee. Publishes ms an average of 3 months after acceptance. Editorial lead time 3 months. Submit seasonal material 6 months in advance. Accepts queries by mail, e-mail. Sample copy free. Guidelines available online.

NONFICTION Needs how-to, business, new product. No articles that do not have a strong hobby or small retail component. **Buys 2-3 mss/year.** Query with published clips. "Freelance stories generally are assigned in advance, but we welcome proposals for feature articles and columns, or the submission of articles sent on speculation. You may send the ms as an e-mail attachment or via postal mail." Length: 750-1,500 words. **Pays $250-500 for assigned articles; $100-250 for unsolicited articles.** Sometimes pays expenses of writers on assignment.

PHOTOS State availability. Captions, identification of subjects required. Reviews 4x6 prints. Negotiates payment individually.

COLUMNS/DEPARTMENTS Shop Management; Sales Marketing; Technology Advice; Industry Trends; all 500-750 words. **Buys 2-3 mss/year.** Query with published clips. **Pays $100-200.**

PEN WORLD

Masterpiece Litho, Inc., P.O. Box 550246, Houston TX 77255-0246. (713)869-9997. **Fax:** (713)869-9993. **E-mail:** editor@penworld.com. **Website:** www.penworld.com. **Contact:** Laura Chandler, editor. Magazine published 6 times/year covering fine writing instruments. Published for writing instrument enthusiasts. Circ. 30,000. No kill fee.

TRANSPORTATION

LIMOUSINE DIGEST

Digest Publications, 3 Reeves Station Rd., Medford NJ 08055. (609)953-4900. **Fax:** (609)953-4905. **E-mail:** info@limodigest.com. **Website:** www.limodigest.com. **Contact:** Dawn Sheldon, assistant publisher. **10% freelance written.** Monthly magazine covering ground transportation. "*Limousine Digest* is 'the voice of the luxury ground transportation industry.' We cover all aspects of ground transportation, from vehicles to operators, safety issues, and political involvement." Estab. 1990. Circ. 10,000. Byline given. Pays on publication. No kill fee. Publishes ms an average of 3 months after acceptance. Editorial lead time 1 year. Submit seasonal material 3 months in advance. Accepts queries by mail, e-mail, fax. Accepts simultaneous submissions. Sample copy free.

NONFICTION Needs historical, how-to, start a company, market your product, humor, inspirational, interview, new product, personal experience, photo feature, technical, travel, industry news, business. **Buys 7-9 mss/year.** Send complete ms. Length: 700-1,900 words. **Negotiates flat-fee and per-word rates individually. Will pay authors in advertising trade-outs.**

PHOTOS Must include photos to be considered. Send photos. Captions, identification of subjects, model releases required. Reviews negatives. Negotiates payment individually.

COLUMNS/DEPARTMENTS New Model Showcase (new limousines, sedans, buses), 1,000 words; Player Profile (industry members profiled), 700 words; Hall of Fame (unique vehicles featured), 500-700 words. **Buys 5 mss/year.** Query. **Negotiates flat-fee and per-word rates individually. Will pay authors in advertising trade-outs.**

💲💲 METRO MAGAZINE

Bobit Business Media, 3520 Challenger St., Torrance CA 90503. (310)533-2400. **Fax:** (310)533-2502. **E-mail:** info@metro-magazine.com. **E-mail:** alex.roman@bobit.com. **Website:** www.metro-magazine.com. **Contact:** Alex Roman, managing editor. **10% freelance written.** Magazine published 10 times/year covering transit bus, passenger rail, and motorcoach operations. METRO's coverage includes both public transit systems and private bus operators, addressing topics such as funding mechanisms, procurement, rolling stock maintenance, privatization, risk management, and sustainability. *Metro Magazine* delivers business, government policy, and technology developments that are *industry specific* to public transportation. Estab. 1904. Circ. 20,500. Byline given. Pays on acceptance. Offers 10% kill fee. Publishes ms an average of 2 months after acceptance. Editorial lead time 3 months. Submit seasonal material 3 months in advance. Accepts queries by e-mail. Responds in 2 weeks to queries. Responds in 1 month to mss. Sample copy for $8. Guidelines by e-mail.

NONFICTION Needs how-to, interview, of industry figures, new product, related to transit—bus and rail—private bus, technical. **Buys 6-10 mss/year.** Query. Length: 400-1,500 words. **Pays $80-400.**

PHOTOS State availability. Captions, identification of subjects, model releases required. Negotiates payment individually.

COLUMNS/DEPARTMENTS Query. **Pays 20¢/word.**

TRAVEL TRADE

CRUISE INDUSTRY NEWS

441 Lexington Ave., Suite 809, New York NY 10017. (212)986-1025. **Fax:** (212)986-1033. **E-mail:** oivind@ cruiseindustrynews.com. **Website:** www.cruiseindustrynews.com. **Contact:** Oivind Mathisen, editor. **20% freelance written.** Quarterly magazine covering cruise shipping. "We write about the business of cruise shipping for the industry. That is, cruise lines, shipyards, financial analysts, etc." Estab. 1991. Circ. 10,000. Byline given. Pays on acceptance or on publication. Offers 25% kill fee. Publishes ms an average of 4 months after acceptance. Editorial lead time 3 months. Accepts queries by mail. Reponse time varies. Sample copy for $15. Guidelines for #10 SASE.

NONFICTION Needs interview, new product, photo feature, business. No travel stories. **Buys more than 20 mss/year.** Query with published clips. Length: 500-1,500 words. **Pays $.50/word published.** Sometimes pays expenses of writers on assignment.

PHOTOS State availability. Pays $25-50/photo.

LEISURE GROUP TRAVEL

Premier Tourism Marketing, 621 Plainfield Rd., Suite 406, Willowbrook IL 60527. (630)794-0696. **Fax:**

(630)794-0652. **E-mail:** randy@ptmgroups.com. **E-mail:** editor@ptmgroups.com. **Website:** www.premiertourismmarketing.com. **Contact:** Randy Mink, managing editor. **35% freelance written.** Bimonthly magazine covering group travel. "We cover destinations and editorial relevant to the group travel market." Estab. 1994. Circ. 15,012. Byline given. Pays on publication. No kill fee. Editorial lead time 6 months. Submit seasonal material 6 months in advance. Accepts queries by mail, e-mail.

NONFICTION Needs travel. **Buys 75 mss/year.** Query with published clips. Length: 1,200-3,000 words. **Pays $0-1,000.**

LL&A MAGAZINE

Media Diversified, Inc., 96 Karma Rd., Markham ON L3R 4Y3 Canada. (905)944-0265. **Fax:** (416)296-0994. **E-mail:** info@mediadiversified.com. **Website:** www. llanda.com. **5% freelance written.** Quarterly magazine for the travel, business, and fashion accessory market Estab. 1966. Circ. 7,000. Byline given. Pays on publication. No kill fee. Editorial lead time 6 weeks. Accepts queries by e-mail. Sample copy and guidelines free.

NONFICTION Needs general interest, how-to, new product, technical.

MIDWEST MEETINGS®

Hennen Publishing, 302 Sixth St. W, Brookings SD 57006. (605)692-9559. **Fax:** (605)692-9031. **E-mail:** info@midwestmeetings.com; editor@midwestmeetings.com. **Website:** www.midwestmeetings.com. **Contact:** Randy Hennen. **20% freelance written.** Quarterly magazine covering meetings/conventions industry. We provide information and resources to meeting/convention planners with a Midwest focus. Estab. 1996. Circ. 28,500. Byline given. Pays on acceptance. Publishes ms an average of 5 months after acceptance. Editorial lead time 3 months. Submit seasonal material 3 months in advance. Accepts queries by e-mail. Sample copy free. Guidelines by e-mail.

NONFICTION Needs essays, general interest, historical, how-to, humor, interview, personal experience, travel. Does not want marketing pieces related to specific hotels/meeting facilities. **Buys 15-20 mss/year.** Send complete ms. Length: 500-1,000 words. **Pays 5-50¢/word.**

PHOTOS Send photos. Captions, identification of subjects and permission statements/photo releases re-

quired. Reviews JPEG/EPS/TIF files (300 dpi). Offers no additional payment for photos accepted with ms.
TIPS If you were a meeting/event planner, what information would help you to perform your job better? We like lots of quotes from industry experts, insider tips, personal experience stories, etc. If you're not sure, e-mail the editor.

$$$ RV BUSINESS

G&G Media Group, 2901 E. Bristol St., Suite B, Elkhart IN 46514. (574)266-7980, ext. 13. **Fax:** (574)266-7984. **E-mail:** bhampson@rvbusiness.com; bhampson@g-gmediagroup.com. **Website:** www.rvbusiness.com. **Contact:** Bruce Hampson, editor. **50% freelance written.** *RV Business* caters to a specific audience of people who manufacture, sell, market, insure, finance, service and supply, components for recreational vehicles. Bimonthly. Estab. 1972. Circ. 21,000. Byline given. Pays on acceptance. Offers kill fee. Publishes ms an average of 2 months after acceptance. Editorial lead time 2 months. Accepts queries by e-mail only. Sample copy free.
NONFICTION Needs new product, photo feature, industry news and features. "No general articles without specific application to our market." **Buys 50 mss/year.** Query with published clips. Length: 125-2,200 words. **Pays $50-1,000.** Sometimes pays expenses of writers on assignment.
COLUMNS/DEPARTMENTS Top of the News (RV industry news), 75-400 words; Business Profiles, 400-500 words; Features (indepth industry features), 800-2,000 words. **Buys 300 mss/year.** Query. **Pays $50-1,000.**
TIPS "Query. Send 1 or several ideas and a few lines letting us know how you plan to treat it/them. We are always looking for good authors knowledgeable in the RV industry or related industries. We need more articles that are brief, factual, hard hitting, and business oriented. Review other publications in the field, including enthusiast magazines."

$$ SCHOOL TRANSPORTATION NEWS

STN Media Co., 5334 Torrance Blvd., 3rd Fl., Torrance CA 90503. (310)792-2226. **Fax:** (310)792-2231. **E-mail:** ryan@stnonline.com. **Website:** www.stnonline.com. **Contact:** Ryan Gray, editor-in-chief. **20% freelance written.** Monthly magazine covering school bus and pupil transportation industries in North America. "Contributors to *School Transportation News* must have a basic understanding of K-12 education and automotive fleets and specifically of school buses. Articles cover such topics as manufacturing, operations, maintenance and routing software, GPS, security and legislative affairs. A familiarity with these principles is preferred. Additional industry information is available on our website. New writers must perform some research of the industry or exhibit core competencies in the subject matter." Estab. 1991. Circ. 23,633. Byline given. Pays on publication. No kill fee. Editorial lead time 1-2 months. Submit seasonal material 3 months in advance. Accepts queries by e-mail. Accepts simultaneous submissions. Sample copy free. Guidelines free.
NONFICTION Needs book excerpts, general interest, historical, humor, inspirational, interview, new product, personal experience, photo feature, technical. "Does not want strictly localized editorial. We want articles that put into perspective the issues of the day." Query with published clips. Length: 600-1,200 words. **Pays $150-300.** Sometimes pays expenses of writers on assignment.
PHOTOS Contact: Sylvia Arroyo, managing editor. No Answer. Captions, model releases required. Reviews GIF/JPEG files. Offers $150-200/photo.
COLUMNS/DEPARTMENTS Creative Special Report, Cover Story, Top Story; Book/Video Reviews (new programs/publications/training for pupil transporters), both 600 words. **Buys 40 mss/year.** Query with published clips. **Pays $150.**
TIPS "Potential freelancers should exhibit a basic proficiency in understanding school bus issues and demonstrate the ability to report on education, legislative and business affairs, as well as a talent with feature writing. It would be helpful if the writer has previous contacts within the industry. Article pitches should be e-mailed only."

$$ SPECIALTY TRAVEL INDEX

Alpine Hansen, P.O. Box 458, San Anselmo CA 94979. (415)455-1643. **E-mail:** info@specialtytravel.com. **Website:** www.specialtytravel.com. **90% freelance written.** Semiannual magazine covering adventure and special interest travel. Estab. 1980. Circ. 35,000. Byline given. Pays on receipt and acceptance of all materials. No kill fee. Editorial lead time 3 month. Submit seasonal material 3 months in advance. Accepts queries by mail, e-mail. Writer's guidelines on request.

NONFICTION Needs how-to, personal experience, photo feature, travel. **Buys 15 mss/year.** Query. Length: 1,250 words. **Pays $300 minimum.**
REPRINTS Send tearsheet. Pays 100% of amount paid for an original article.
PHOTOS State availability. Captions, identification of subjects required. Reviews EPS/TIFF files. Negotiates payment individually.
TIPS "Write about group travel and be both creative and factual. The articles should relate to both the travel agent booking the tour and the client who is traveling."

$ TRAVEL42

NORTHSTAR Travel Media, 200 Brookstown Ave., Suite 301, Winston-Salem NC 27101. (336)714-3328. **Fax:** (336)714-3168. **E-mail:** csheaffer@ntmllc.com. **Website:** www.travel-42.com. **Contact:** Cindy Sheaffer, editorial director. Estab. 2011. No byline given. Pays 1 month after acceptance. No kill fee. Accepts queries by e-mail preferred.
TIPS "We may require sample hotel or cruise reports on facilities near freelancer's hometown before giving the first assignment. No byline because of sensitive nature of reviews."

VETERINARY

ANIMAL SHELTERING

2100 L St. NW, Washington DC 20037. (202)452-1100. **Fax:** (301)721-6468. **E-mail:** asm@humanesociety.org. **Website:** www.animalsheltering.org. **Contact:** Shevaun Brannigan, production/marketing manager; Carrie Allan, editor. **20% freelance written.** Magazine for animal care professionals and volunteers, dealing with animal welfare issues faced by animal shelters, animal control agencies, and rescue groups. Emphasis on news for the field and professional, hands-on work. Readers are shelter and animal control directors, kennel staff, field officers, humane investigators, animal control officers, animal rescuers, foster care volunteers, general volunteers, shelter veterinarians, and anyone concerned with local animal welfare issues. Estab. 1978. Circ. 6,000. Sample copies are free; contact Shevaun Brannigan at sbrannigan@hsus.org. Guidelines available by e-mail.
NONFICTION Approximately 6-10 submissions published each year from non-staff writers; of those submissions, 50% are from writers new to the publication. **"Payment varies depending on length and complexity of piece. Longer features generally $400–600; short news pieces generally $200. We rarely take unsolicited work, so it's best to contact the editor with story ideas."**
REPRINTS "Aquires first publication rights. We also grant permission, with a credit to the magazine and writer, to readers who want to use the materials to educate their supporters, staff and volunteers. Contact asm@humanesociety.org for writers' guidelines."
PHOTOS Pays $150 for cover; $75 for inside.
TIPS "We almost always need good photos of people working with animals in an animal shelter or in the field. We do not use photos of individual dogs, cats, and other companion animals as often as we use photos of people working to protect, rescue or care for dogs, cats, and other companion animals."

$ $ VETERINARY ECONOMICS

8033 Flint St., Lenexa KS 66214. (800)255-6864. **Fax:** (913)871-3808. **E-mail:** ve@advanstar.com. **Website:** http://veterinarybusiness.dvm360.com. **20% freelance written.** Monthly magazine covering veterinary practice management. "We address the business concerns and management needs of practicing veterinarians." Estab. 1960. Circ. 54,000. Byline given. Pays on publication. No kill fee. Publishes ms an average of 6 months after acceptance. Editorial lead time 3 months. Submit seasonal material 3 months in advance. Accepts queries by mail, e-mail. Accepts simultaneous submissions. Responds in 3 months to queries. Sample copy free. Guidelines available online.
NONFICTION Needs how-to, interview, personal experience. **Buys 24 mss/year.** Send complete ms. Length: 1,000-2,000 words. **Pays $40-350.**
PHOTOS Send photos. Captions, identification of subjects required. Reviews transparencies, prints. Offers no additional payment.
COLUMNS/DEPARTMENTS Practice Tips (easy, unique business tips), 250 words or fewer. Send complete ms. **Pays $40.**
TIPS "Among the topics we cover: veterinary hospital design, client relations, contractual and legal matters, investments, day-to-day management, marketing, personal finances, practice finances, personnel, collections, and taxes. We also cover news and issues within the veterinary profession; for example, articles might cover the effectiveness of Yellow Pages advertising, the growing number of women veterinarians, restrictive-covenant cases, and so on. Freelance writ-

ers are encouraged to submit proposals or outlines for articles on these topics. Most articles involve interviews with a nationwide sampling of veterinarians; we will provide the names and phone numbers if necessary. We accept only a small number of unsolicited mss each year; however, we do assign many articles to freelance writers. All material submitted by first-time contributors is read on speculation, and the review process usually takes 12-16 weeks. Our style is concise yet conversational, and all mss go through a fairly rigorous editing process. We encourage writers to provide specific examples to illustrate points made throughout their articles."

CONTESTS & AWARDS

The contests and awards listed in this section are arranged by subject. Nonfiction writers can turn immediately to nonfiction awards listed alphabetically by the name of the contest or award. The same is true for fiction writers, poets, playwrights and screenwriters, journalists, children's writers, and translators.

New contests and awards are announced in various writer's publications nearly every day. However, many lose their funding or fold—and sponsoring magazines go out of business just as often. We have contacted the organizations whose contests and awards are listed here with the understanding that they are valid through 2013-2014.

To make sure you have all the information you need about a particular contest, always send a SASE (self-addressed, stamped envelope) to the contact person in the listing and/or check their website before entering a contest. The listings in this section are brief, and many contests have lengthy, specific rules and requirements that we could not include in our limited space. Often a specific entry form must accompany your submission. Some require writers to submit through an online submission form.

When you receive a set of guidelines, you will see that some contests are not applicable to all writers. The writer's age, previous publication, geographic location, and length of the work are common matters of eligibility. Read the requirements carefully to ensure you don't enter a contest for which you are not qualified.

Winning a contest or award can launch a successful writing career. Take a professional approach by doing a little extra research. Find out who the previous winner of the award was by investing in a sample copy of the magazine in which the prize-winning article, poem, or short story appeared. Attend the staged reading of an award-winning play. Your extra effort will be to your advantage in competing with writers who simply submit blindly.

PLAYWRITING & SCRIPTWRITING

✚ 10 MINUTE PLAY CONTEST & FESTIVAL

Weathervane Playhouse, 1301 Weathervane Lane, Akron OH 44313. (330)836-2626. **E-mail:** info@weathervaneplayhouse.com. **Website:** www.weathervaneplayhouse.com. Annual 8x10 TheatreFest. Must be US citizen 18 years or older. All rights remain with writers. "The mission of the Weathervane Playhouse 8x10 TheatreFest is to promote the art of play writing, present new works, and introduce area audiences to the short play form. The competition will provide Weathervane with recognition for quality and innovative theatre." Deadline: mid-May. Prize: Prizes: 1st Place: $350; 2nd Place: $250; Audience Favorite: $150; 5 runners-up: $50. Eight finalists receive full productions of their plays during TheatreFest, held in mid-July. First round judges include individuals with experience in every area of stagecraft, including tech designers, actors, directors, stage managers, and playwrights.

TIPS "Please see visit www.weathervaneplayhouse. com/special-events for this year's specific dates, guidelines, etc."

ACADEMY NICHOLL FELLOWSHIPS IN SCREENWRITING

Academy of Motion Picture Arts & Sciences, 1313 N. Vine St., Hollywood CA 90028-8107. (310)247-3010. **E-mail:** nicholl@oscars.org. **Website:** www.oscars.org/nicholl. "Offered annually for unproduced feature film screenplays to identify talented new screenwriters. Open to writers who have not earned more than $5,000 writing for films or TV." Deadline: May 1. Prize: Up to 5 $35,000 fellowships awarded each year.

ALLIANCE OF WOMEN FILMMAKERS SCRIPT COMPETITION

Alliance of Women Filmmakers, 1317 N. San Fernando Blvd. #340, Burbank CA 91504. (818)749-6162. **E-mail:** info@womenfilmmakersalliance.org. **E-mail:** dmeans25@yahoo.com. **Website:** www.lawomensfest.com. Deadline: October 1. Prize: Prizes are sponsored and vary from year to year.

THE ANNUAL CONTEST OF CONTEST WINNERS™ COMPETITION

ScriptDoctor.com, 3661 N. Campbell Ave., Suite 222, Tucson AZ 85719. **E-mail:** thedoc@scriptdoctor.com. **Website:** www.scriptdoctor.com. **Contact:** Howard

Allen. Must be at least 18 years of age. No entry may have earned money or other consideration for more than $5,000.

ANNUAL NATIONAL PLAYWRITING COMPETITION

Wichita State University, School of Performing Arts, 1845 Fairmount, Box 153, Wichita KS 67260. (316)978-3646. **Fax:** (316)978-3202. **E-mail:** bret.jones@wichita.edu. **Contact:** Bret Jones, director of theatre. The contest will be open to all undergraduate and graduate students enrolled at any college or university in the United States. Please indicate school affiliation. All submissions must be original, unpublished and unproduced. Both full-length and one-act plays may be submitted. Full-length plays in 1 or more acts should be a minimum of 90 minutes playing time. Two or 3 short plays on related themes by the same author will be judged as 1 entry. The total playing time should be a minimum of 90 minutes. One-act plays should be a minimum of 30 minutes playing time to a maximum of 60 minutes playing time. Musicals should be a minimum of 90 minutes playing time and must include a CD of the accompanying music. Scripts should contain no more than 4-6 characters and setting must be suitable for an 85-seat Black box theatre. Eligible playwrights may submit up to 2 entries per contest year. One typewritten, bound copy should be submitted. Scripts must be typed and arranged in professional play script format. See information provided in *The Dramatist's Sourcebook* or the following website (www.pubinfo.vcu.edu/artweb/playwriting/format.html) for instruction on use of professional format. Two title pages must be included: 1 bound and the other unbound. The unbound title page should display the author's name, address, telephone number, and e-mail address if applicable. The bound title page should only display the name of the script; do not include any personal identifying information on the bound title page. Scripts may be submitted electronically to bret.jones@wichita.edu. Submit in PDF format. "Please include all information requested for mail in scripts with your electronic submission." Deadline: January 16. Prize: Production by the Wichita State University Theatre. Winner will be announced after March 15. No entry may be withdrawn after March 1. Judging will be conducted by a panel of 3 or more selected from the school faculty and may also include up to 3 experienced, faculty approved WSU School of Performing Arts students.

BIG BREAK INTERNATIONAL SCREENWRITING COMPETITION

Final Draft, Inc., 26707 W. Agoura Rd., Suite 205, Calabasas CA 91302. (818)995-8995. **E-mail:** bigbreak@finaldraft.com. **Website:** www.finaldraft.com/bigbreak. **Contact:** Shelly Mellott, VP events and services. "Big Break, a Final Draft, Inc. contest, is an annual, global screenwriting competition designed to promote emerging creative talent. Big Break rewards screenwriters with cash, prizes and A-list executive meetings. Since its inception in 2000, Big Break has awarded screenwriters with over $280,000 in cash and prizes and invaluable industry exposure. No rights to submitted materials are acquired or purchased. Contest is open to any writer. Guidelines and rules available online." No paper submissions. Submissions must be unpublished. Enter online. The contest objective is to bring recognition to promising screenwriters. June 1/ June 15 (extended). Prize: Prizes: 1st Place prizes: $15,000 total cash, plus finalist prizes, airfare to L.A., 3-night hotel stay (unless winner resides in or around L.A.), lunch with executives. 2nd Place prizes: $4,000 total cash, plus finalist prizes, airfare to L.A., 3-night hotel stay (unless winner resides in or around L.A.), lunch with executives. 3rd Place prizes: $2,000 total cash, plus finalist prizes, airfare to L.A., 3-night hotel stay (unless winner resides in or around L.A.), lunch with executives. 4th and 5th Place prizes: $250 total cash, plus finalist prizes. See 6th through 20th Place Finalist Prizes on website. Industry readers complete the first 2 rounds of judging. A panel of notable industry professionals conducts the final judging. Information on previous judges can be found on website.

BUNTVILLE CREW'S AWARD BLUE

Buntville Crew, 118 N. Railroad Ave., Buckley IL 60918-0445. **E-mail:** buntville@yahoo.fr. **Contact:** Steven Packard, artistic director. "Presented annually for the best unpublished/unproduced play script under 15 pages, written by a student enrolled in any Illinois high school. Submit 1 copy of the script in standard play format, a brief biography, and a SASE (scripts will not be returned). Include name, address, telephone number, age, and name of school." Deadline: May 31. Prize: Cash prize and possible productions in Buckley and/or New York City. Judged by panel selected by the theater.

CALIFORNIA YOUNG PLAYWRIGHTS CONTEST

Playwrights Project, 2590 Truxton Rd., Suite 202, San Diego CA 92106-6145. (619)239-8222. **Fax:** (619)239-8225. **E-mail:** write@playwrightsproject.org. **Website:** www.playwrightsproject.org. **Contact:** Cecelia Kouma, executive director. **Open to Californians under age 19.** Annual contest. Estab. 1985. "Our organization and the contest is designed to nurture promising young writers. We hope to develop playwrights and audiences for live theater. We also teach playwriting." Submissions required to be unpublished and not produced professionally. Submissions made by the author. Deadline for entries: June 1. SASE for contest rules and entry form. No entry fee. Judging by professionals in the theater community, a committee of 5-7; changes somewhat each year. Works performed in San Diego at a professional theatre. Writers submitting scripts of 10 or more pages receive a detailed script evaluation letter upon request. "Offered annually for previously unpublished plays by young writers to stimulate young people to create dramatic works, and to nurture promising writers. Scripts must be a minimum of 10 standard typewritten pages; send 2 copies. Scripts will *not* be returned. If requested, entrants receive detailed evaluation letter. Guidelines available online." See website for current year's deadline. Prize: Scripts will be produced in spring at a professional theatre in San Diego.

COE COLLEGE PLAYWRITING FESTIVAL

Coe College, 1220 First Ave. NE, Cedar Rapids IA 52402-5092. (319)399-8624. **Fax:** (319)399-8557. **E-mail:** swolvert@coe.edu. **Website:** www.theatre.coe.edu. **Contact:** Susan Wolverton. "Offered biennially for unpublished work to provide a venue for new works for the stage. We are interested in full-length productions, not one-acts or musicals. Open to any writer." One clean, bound script; a resume; the play's development history; and a statement of development goals for your play (one page). Deadline: November 1 (even years). Residency: April (odd years). Prize: $500, plus 1-week residency as guest artist with airfare, room and board provided.

CONTEST OF CONTEST WINNERS, THE

ScriptDoctor, 3661 N. Campbell Ave., Suite 222, Tucson AZ 85719. **E-mail:** thedoc@scriptdoctor.com. **Website:** www.scriptdoctor.com. **Contact:** Howard Allen. The Contest of Contest Winners™ is a special screenplay challenge reserved for the screenwriting elite - those who have won or placed as a finalist or quarter-finalist in a screenplay competition within the last six years. See website for the list of qualifying contests. Must be at least 18 years of age to enter. Deadline: December 30 (early) or January 10 (late). Prize: Cash $1,000 and story notes from a ScriptDoctor partner.

DRURY UNIVERSITY ONE-ACT PLAY CONTEST

Drury University, 900 N. Benton Ave., Springfield MO 65802-3344. **E-mail:** msokol@drury.edu. **Contact:** Mick Sokol. Offered in even-numbered years for unpublished and professionally unproduced plays. One play per playwright. Guidelines for SASE or by e-mail. Deadline: December 1. Prize: 1st Place: $300; Honorable Mention: $150.

ESSENTIAL THEATRE PLAYWRITING AWARD

The Essential Theatre, 1414 Foxhall Ln., #10, Atlanta GA 30316. (404) 212-0815. **E-mail:** pmhardy@aol.com. **Website:** www.essentialtheatre.com. **Contact:** Peter Hardy. "Offered annually for unproduced, full-length plays by Georgia resident writers. No limitations as to style or subject matter." Deadline: April 23. Prize: $600 and full production.

FLICKERS: RHODE ISLAND INTERNATIONAL FILM FESTIVAL SHORT SCREENPLAY COMPETITION

P.O. Box 162, Street Address: 36 RI Ave., Newport, RI 02840, Newport RI 02840. (401)861-4445. **Fax:** (401)490-6735. **E-mail:** info@film-festival.org. **Website:** www.film-festival.org/enterascreenplay.php. "Designed to showcase of the art of the short film in the written medim." Full-length scripts, no more than 130 pages. Half-hour shorts or teleplays, no more than 40 pages. Submissions must be in English. Submissions must use 12-point Courier font. Pages should be numbered. 3-hole punch and brads with front and back cover for non-digital files. No promotional material. No shooting scripts. See website for more details. "The purpose of the contest is to promote, embolden and cultivate screenwriters in their quest for opportunities within the industry." Deadline: July 15. Prize: software from Final Draft, magazine subscriptions from MovieMaker Magazine and Creative Screenwriting, web placement from Inktip.com, listings from Sell-a-Script and free passes to the 2014

Rhode Island International Film Festival and Script-Biz Screenwriter's Workshop. Prizes are worth over $10,000 in value.

⟳ GOVERNOR GENERAL'S LITERARY AWARD FOR DRAMA

Canada Council for the Arts, 350 Albert St., P.O. Box 1047, Ottawa ON K1P 5V8 Canada. (613)566-4414, ext. 5573. **Fax:** (613)566-4410. **Website:** www.canadacouncil.ca/prizes/ggla. Offered for the best English-language and the best French-language work of drama by a Canadian. Publishers submit titles for consideration. Deadline depends on the book's publication date. Books in English: March 15, June 1 or August 7. Books in French: March 15 or July 15. Prize: Each laureate receives $25,000; non-winning finalists receive $1,000.

⊕ THE MARILYN HALL AWARDS FOR YOUTH THEATRE

P.O. Box 148, Beverly Hills CA 90213. **Website:** www.beverlyhillstheatreguild.com. **Contact:** Candace Coster, competition coordinator. Unpublished submissions only. Authors must be U.S. citizens or legal residents and must sign entry form personally. "To encourage the creation and development of new plays for youth theatre." Deadline: Postmarked between January 15 and the last day of February. Prize: 1st Prize: $700; 2nd Prize: $300.

HENRICO THEATRE COMPANY ONE-ACT PLAYWRITING COMPETITION

P.O. Box 90775, Henrico VA 23273. (804)501-5138. **Fax:** (804)501-5284. **E-mail:** per22@co.henrico.va.us. **Contact:** Amy A. Perdue, cultural arts senior coordinator. "Offered annually for previously unpublished or unproduced plays or musicals to produce new dramatic works in one-act form. Scripts with small casts and simpler sets given preference. Controversial themes and excessive language should be avoided. Only one-act plays or musicals will be considered. The manuscript should be a one-act original (not an adaptation), unpublished, and unproduced, free of royalty and copyright restrictions. Scripts with smaller casts and simpler sets may be given preference. Controversial themes and excessive language should be avoided. Standard play script form should be used. All plays will be judged anonymously; therefore, there should be two title pages; the first must contain the play's title and the author's complete address and telephone number. The second title page must contain only the play's title. The playwright must submit two excellent quality copies. Receipt of all scripts will be acknowledged by mail. Scripts will be returned if SASE is included. No scripts will be returned until after the winner is announced. The HTC does not assume responsibility for loss, damage or return of scripts. All reasonable care will be taken." Deadline: July 1. Prize: Prizes: $300 prize. $200 to runner-up. Winning entries may be produced; videotape sent to author.

HORROR SCREENPLAY CONTEST

Cherub Productions, P.O. Box 540, Boulder Co 80306. (303)629-3072. **E-mail:** Cherubfilm@aol.com. **Website:** www.horrorscreenplaycontest.com. "This contest is looking for horror scripts." Contest is limited to the first 600 entries. Screenplays must be between 90-125 pages. Deadline: July 20. Prize: More than $5,000 in cash and prizes.

MCKNIGHT ADVANCEMENT GRANT

The Playwrights' Center, 2301 Franklin Ave. E., Minneapolis MN 55406-1099. (612)332-7481. **Fax:** (612)332-6037. **Website:** www.pwcenter.org. **Contact:** Amanda Robbins-Butcher, artistic administrator. The Playwrights' Center today serves more playwrights in more ways than any other organization in the country. Applications are screened for eligibility by the Playwrights' Center and evaluated by an initial select panel of professional theater artists; finalists are then evaluated by a second panel of national theater artists. Selection is based on artistic excellence and professional achievement, and is guided by the Playwrights' Center's mission statement. The McKnight Advancement Grants recognize playwrights whose work demonstrates exceptional artistic merit and excellence in the field, and whose primary residence is in the state of Minnesota. Deadline: January 10. Prize: two grants of $25,000 each will be awarded. Additional funds of $2,000 can be used to support a play development workshop and other professional expenses.

MOONDANCE INTERNATIONAL FILM FESTIVAL

970 Ninth St., Boulder CO 80302. (303)545-0202. **E-mail:** director@moondancefilmfestival.com; moondancefestival@gmail.com. **Website:** www.moondancefilmfestival.com; www.moondancefestival.com/blog. WRITTEN WORKS SUBMISSIONS: feature screenplays, short screenplays, feature & short musical screenplays, feature & short screenplays for children, 1, 2 or 3-act stageplays, mini-series for TV, television movies of the week, television pilots, libretti, musical film scripts, short stories, radio plays & short stories for children. Submission service: www.withoutabox.com/login/1240. Postmark Deadline: June 31.

NATIONAL CHILDREN'S THEATRE FESTIVAL

Actors' Playhouse at the Miracle Theatre, 280 Miracle Mile, Coral Gables FL 33134. (305)444-9293, ext. 615. **Fax:** (305)444-4181. **E-mail:** maulding@actorsplayhouse.org. **Website:** www.actorsplayhouse.org. **Contact:** Earl Maulding. Purpose is to bring together the excitement of the theater arts and the magic of young audiences through the creation of new musical works and to create a venue for playwrights/composers to showcase their artistic products. While scripts should target the appropriate audience, those musicals appealing to adults as well as children will be at an advantage. Contemporary relevance is to be preferred over mere topicality—we seek plays whose appeal will last beyond this season's headlines. Deadline: April 1. Prize: $500.
TIPS "Travel and lodging during the festival based on availability."

ONE-ACT PLAY CONTEST

Tennessee Williams/New Orleans Literary Festival, 938 Lafayette St., Suite 514, New Orleans LA 70113. (504)581-1144. **E-mail:** info@tennesseewilliams.net. **Website:** www.tennesseewilliams.net/contests. **Contact:** Paul J. Willis. "Annual contest for an unpublished play." Plays should run no more than one hour in length. Unlimited entries per person. Production criteria include scripts requiring minimal technical support for a 100-seat theater. Cast of characters must be small. See website for additional guidelines. "The One-Act Play Competition is an opportunity for playwrights to see their work fully produced before a large audience during one of the largest literary festivals in the nation, and for the festival to showcase undiscovered talent." Deadline: November 1. Prize: $1,500, staged read at the next festival, full production at the festival the following year, VIP All-Access Festival pass for two years ($1,000 value), and publication in Bayou. Judged by an anonymous expert panel.
TIPS Guidelines and entry forms can be found at www.tennesseewilliams.net/contests.

THE PAGE INTERNATIONAL SCREENWRITING AWARDS

The PAGE Awards Committee, 7510 Sunset Blvd., #610, Hollywood CA 90046-3408. **E-mail:** info@ PAGEawards.com. **Website:** www.PAGEawards.com. **Contact:** Zoe Simmons, Contest Coordinator. Annual competition to discover the most talented new screenwriters from across the country and around the world. "Each year, awards are presented to 31 screenwriters in 10 different genre categories: action/adventure, comedy, drama, family film, historical film, science fiction, thriller/horror, short film script, TV drama pilot, and TV sitcom pilot. Guidelines and entry forms are online. The contest is open to all writers 18 years of age and older who have not previously earned more than $25,000 writing for film and/or television. Please visit contest website for a complete list of rules and regulations." See the website for contest rules. Deadline: January 15 (early); March 1 (regular); April 1 (late). Prize: Prizes: Over $50,000 in cash and prizes, including a $25,000 grand prize, plus gold, silver, and bronze prizes in all 10 categories. Most importantly, the award-winning writers receive extensive publicity and industry exposure. Judging is done entirely by Hollywood professionals, including industry script readers, consultants, agents, managers, producers, and development executives.

SCRIPTAPALOOZA SCREENPLAY COMPETITION

Supported by Write Brothers, 7775 Sunset Blvd., #200, Hollywood CA 90046. (323)654-5809. **E-mail:** info@ scriptapalooza.com. **Website:** www.scriptapalooza. com. **Contact:** Mark Andrushko, president. "Annual competition for unpublished scripts from any genre. Open to any writer, 18 or older. Submit 1 copy of a 90- to 130-page screenplay. Body pages must be numbered, and scripts must be in industry-standard format. All entered scripts will be read and judged by more than 90 production companies." Early Deadline: January 7; Deadline: March 5; Late Deadline: April 16. Prize: 1st Place: $10,000 and software package from Write Brothers, Inc.; 2nd Place, 3rd Place, and 10 Runners-Up: Software package from Write Brothers, Inc. The top 100 scripts will be considered by over 90 production companies.

SCRIPTAPALOOZA TELEVISION WRITING COMPETITION

7775 Sunset Blvd., Suite #200, Hollywood CA 90046. (323)654-5809. **E-mail:** info@scriptapalooza.com.

Website: www.scriptapaloozatv.com. "Biannual competition accepting entries in 4 categories: Reality shows, sitcoms, original pilots, and 1-hour dramas. There are more than 25 producers, agents, and managers reading the winning scripts. Two past winners won Emmys because of Scriptapalooza and 1 past entrant now writes for Comedy Central." Winners announced February 15 and August 30. For contest results, visit website. Length: Standard television format whether 1 hour, 1-half hour, or pilot. Open to any writer 18 or older. Guidelines available now for SASE or on website. Accepts inquiries by e-mail, phone. "Pilots should be fresh and new and easy to visualize. Spec scripts should stay current with the shows, up-to-date story lines, characters, etc." Deadline: October 1 and April 15. Prize: 1st Place: $500; 2nd Place: $200; 3rd Place: $100 (in each category); production company consideration.

SHRIEKFEST HORROR/SCI-FI FILM FESTIVAL & SCREENPLAY COMPETITION

P.O. Box 950921, Lake Mary FL 32795. **E-mail:** shriekfest@aol.com. **Website:** www.shriekfest.com. **Contact:** Denise Gossett and Todd Beeson. "Our awards are to help screenwriters move their script up the ladder and hopefully have it made into a film. Our winners take that win and parlay it into agents, film deals, and options. No, we don't use loglines anywhere; we keep your script private." "We accept award-winning screenplays. No restrictions as long as it's in the horror/thriller or scifi/fantasy genres. We accept shorts and features. No specific lengths." Deadline: May 22 and July 10. Prize: Trophies, product awards, usually cash. "Our awards are updated all year long as sponsors step onboard. The winners go home with lots of stuff. We have at least 20-30 judges and they are all in different aspects of the entertainment industry, such as producers, directors, writers, actors, agents."

DOROTHY SILVER PLAYWRITING COMPETITION

The Mandel Jewish Community Center of Cleveland, 26001 S. Woodland Rd., Beachwood OH 44122. (216)831-0700. **Fax:** (216)831-7796. **E-mail:** dbobrow@mandeljcc.org. **E-mail:** info@mandeljcc.org. **Website:** www.mandeljcc.org. **Contact:** Deborah Bobrow, competition coordinator. "All entries must be original works, not previously produced, suitable for a full-length presentation, and directly concerned with the Jewish experience." Designed to encourage new plays that provide significant, fresh perspectives on the range of Jewish experience. Deadline: December 31. Prize: $1,000 and a staged reading.

SOUTHEASTERN THEATRE CONFERENCE HIGH SCHOOL NEW PLAY CONTEST

SETC, 1175 Revolution Mill Dr., Suite 14, Greensboro NC 27405. **E-mail:** setc_hs_new_plays@Yahoo.com. **Website:** www.setc.org. **Contact:** Meredith Levy. Annual contest for one-act plays (no musicals, adaptations, or collaborations) on any subject. The script should be a one-act play that has not been published or professionally produced. Each applicant may submit one play only. E-mail play as a PDF and application form to setc_hs_new_plays@Yahoo.com. Visit website for additional details and required application form. High school student playwrights who currently reside in 1 of the 10 states in the SETC region are eligible. These states include Alabama, Florida, Georgia, Kentucky, Mississippi, North Carolina, South Carolina, Tennessee, Virginia, and West Virginia. Deadline: Submit October 1-December 1. Prize: $250, subsidy to attend the annual SETC convention in March with an adult chaperone, and a staged reading followed by a talkback.

SOUTHERN PLAYWRIGHTS COMPETITION

Jacksonville State University, Department of English, 700 Pelham Rd. N., Jacksonville AL 36265-1602. (256)782-5498. **Fax:** (256)782-5441. **E-mail:** smoersch@jsu.edu. **E-mail:** swhitton@jsu.edu. **Website:** www.jsu.edu/depart/english/southpla.htm. **Contact:** Sarah Moersch. Playwrights must be native to or a resident of Alabama, Arkansas, Florida, Georgia, Kentucky, Louisiana, Mississippi, North Carolina, South Carolina, Tennessee, Texas, Virginia, or West Virginia. Plays must deal with the Southern experience. Entries must be original, full-length plays. No musicals or adaptations will be accepted. The playwright may submit only one play. All entries must be typed, securely bound, and clearly identified. Synopsis of script must be included. Legal clearance of all materials not in the public domain will be the responsibility of the playwright. The Southern Playwrights Competition seeks to identify and encourage the best of Southern playwriting. Deadline: January 15. Prize: $1,000 and production of the play.

THEATRE CONSPIRACY ANNUAL NEW PLAY CONTEST

Theatre Conspiracy, 10091 McGregor Blvd., Ft. Myers FL 33919. (239)936-3239. **Fax:** (239)936-0510. **E-mail:** info@theatreconspiracy.org. **Website:** theatreconspiracy.org. **Contact:** Bill Taylor, producing artistic director. Offered annually for full-length plays that are unproduced. Work submitted to the contest must be a full length play with eight characters or less and have simple to moderate technical demands. Plays having up to three previous productions are welcome. No musicals. Deadline: March 30. Prize: $700 and full production. Judged by a panel of qualified theatre teachers, directors and performers.

☺ THEATRE IN THE RAW BIENNIAL ONE-ACT PLAY WRITING CONTEST

Theatre In the Raw, 3521 Marshall St., Vancouver BC V5N 4S2 Canada. (604)708-5448. **E-mail:** theatreintheraw@telus.net. **Website:** www.theatreintheraw.ca. Biennial contest for an original one-act play, presented in proper stage-play format, that is unpublished and unproduced. The play (with no more than 6 characters) cannot be longer than 25 double-spaced, typed pages equal to 30 minutes. Scripts must have page numbers. Scripts are to be mailed only & will not be accepted by e-mail. Deadline: December 31, 2011. Prize: 1st Place: $200, at least 1 dramatic reading or staging of the play at a Theatre In the Raw Cafe/Venue, or as part of a mini-tour program for the One-Act Play Series Nights; 2nd Place: $100; 3rd Place: $75. Winners announced June 30.

TRUSTUS PLAYWRIGHTS' FESTIVAL

Trustus Theatre, 520 Lady St., Columbia SC 29201. (803)254-9732. **Fax:** (803)771-9153. **E-mail:** shammond@trustus.org. **E-mail:** shammond@trustus.org. **Website:** www.trustus.org. **Contact:** Sarah Hammond, literary manager. "Trustus Theatre announces its Annual Playwrights' Festival, a National Contest culminating in the Professional World Premier of an original play." In its 24th year, Trustus is one of America's longest-running play festivals. Since 1988, many of Trustus's winners have been published and produced off-Broadway, in Hollywood or at the Actors Theatre of Louisville. Full-length plays only, with no previous professional productions. Academic productions and workshops are okay. No musicals or no children's shows. One set, minimal production needs preferred. Cast of eight or fewer preferred, ages 15-60. One script per author. No re-submissions. Deadline: March 1. Prize: The winning play will receive a staged-reading at the 2013 Festival and $250. During the following year, the playwright will develop the script for production as he/she wishes and in consultation with members of the Trustus staff and company. In August, the play receive a full production—and the playwright an additional $500.

☺ THE HERMAN VOADEN NATIONAL PLAYWRITING COMPETITION

Drama Department, Queen's University, Kingston ON K7L 3N6 Canada. (613)533-6000, ext. 74336. E-mail: carolanne.hanna@queensu.ca. E-mail: drama@queensu.car. Website: www.queensu.ca/drama. Contact: Carol Anne Hanna. Offered every 2 years for unpublished plays to discover and develop new Canadian plays. See website for deadlines and guidelines. Open to Canadian citizens or landed immigrants. Deadline: January 15. Prize: 1st Prize: $3,000; 2nd Prize: $2,000; and 8 honorable mentions. 1st- and 2nd-prize winners are offered a 1-week workshop and public reading by professional director and cast. The 2 authors will be playwrights-in-residence for the rehearsal and reading period.

WATERFRONT FILM FESTIVAL AND INDIE SCREENPLAY COMPETITION

Waterfront Film Festival, P.O. Box 904, South Haven MI 49090. (269)857-8351. Fax: (269)857-1072. E-mail: info@waterfrontfilm.org. Website: www.waterfrontfilm.org. The festival is non-competitive and open to films of any genre: features, shorts, documentaries, animation, etc. The contest is now accepting entries from writers in any state. Previously, the contest was only for local writers. Scripts must be 80-130 pages in length. Entries are accepted through Withoutabox. Deadline: February 29. Prize: Prize includes cash, an industry reception in the winner's honor, lodging, and VIP pass to the festival.

WRITE NOW

Indiana Repertory Theatre, 140 W. Washington St., Indianapolis IN 46204. 480-921-5770. E-mail: info@writenow.co. Website: www.writenow.co. A national effort to advocate for playwrights and promote the development of new work for young audiences by: supporting the work of emerging and established playwrights through a biennial national competition and process-focused workshop; engaging a broad representation of the TYA field in an ongoing conversation about new play development; creating a stronger environment for new work by fostering connections and collaborations; cultivating a common language of shared values about new work from the perspectives of playwrights, producers, community stakeholders, and academia. The purpose of this biennial workshop is to encourage writers to create strikingly original scripts for young audiences. Playwrights from across the country are invited to submit scripts for review by a panel of peers. All submitted scripts will receive constructive feedback at the request of the playwright. At least four scripts will be selected as finalists to participate in the full workshop process, which includes a week on site at Childsplay with a development team, followed by a reading of the script at the Write Now gathering (transportation, housing, and a cash prize will be provided to the finalists). Semi-finalists will also be invited to read excerpts from their scripts at the Write Now gathering. Deadline: July 31.

YOUNG PLAYWRIGHTS INC. WRITE A PLAY! NYC COMPETITION

Young Playwrights, Inc., Young Playwrights Inc. NYC, P.O. Box 5134, New York NY 10185. (212)594-5440. Fax: (212)684-4902. E-mail: literary@youngplaywrights.org. Website: www.youngplaywrights.org. Contact: Literary Manager. "Offered annually for stage plays of any length (no musicals, screenplays, or adaptations) by NYC elementary, middle, and high school students only." "Play must be submitted by students, not teachers. There are no restrictions on length, style, or subject, but collaborations of more than 3 writers will not be accepted. Screenplays and musicals are not eligible, nor are adaptations. Scripts should be typed and stapled, and pages must be numbered. Scripts must have a cover page with title of play, playwright's name, home address (with apartment number and zip code), phone number, school, grade, and date of birth. Submit a copy of your play and keep the original; scripts will not be returned." Deadline: postmarked on or before March 1. Prize: Prize varies.

ANNA ZORNIO MEMORIAL CHILDREN'S THEATRE PLAYWRITING COMPETITION

University of New Hampshire, Department of Theatre and Dance, PCAC, 30 Academic Way, Durham NH 03824. (603)862-3044. Fax: (603)862-0298. E-mail: mike.wood@unh.edu. Website: www.unh.edu/theatre-dance/zornio. Contact: Michael Wood. Offered every 4 years for unpublished well-written plays or musicals appropriate for young audiences with a maximum length of 60 minutes. May submit more than 1 play, but not more than 3. Purpose of the award: "to honor the late Anna Zornio, an alumna of The University of New Hampshire, for dedication to and inspiration of playwriting for young people, K-12th grade." Deadline: March of 2016. Prize: $500.

ARTS COUNCILS & FELLOWSHIPS

☼ ADVANCED ARTIST AWARD

Government of Yukon, P.O. Box 2703, (L-3), Whitehorse YT Y1A 2C6 Canada. (867)667-8789. **Fax:** (867)393-6456. **E-mail:** artsfund@gov.yk.ca. **Website:** www.tc.gov.yk.ca/arts.html. The Advanced Artist Award (AAA) assists individual Yukon visual, literary and performing artists practicing at a senior level with innovative projects, travel, or educational pursuits that contribute to their personal artistic development and to their community. The intended results and outcomes of the Advanced Artist Award are toencourage artistic creativity, to enable artists to develop their skills, and toimprove the ability of artists to promote their works or talents. Deadlines: April 1 and October 1. Prize: Prizes: Level A artists: up to $5,000; Level B artists: up to $2,500. peer assessment (made up of senior Yukon artists representing the various disciplines seen in applicants for that round).

ALABAMA STATE COUNCIL ON THE ARTS INDIVIDUAL ARTIST FELLOWSHIP

201 Monroe St., Montgomery AL 36130. (334)242-4076, ext. 236. **Fax:** (334)240-3269. **E-mail:** anne.kimzey@arts.alabama.gov. **Website:** www.arts.state.al.us. **Contact:** Anne Kimzey, literature program manager. Purpose: To recognize the achievements and potential of Alabama writers. Must be a legal resident of Alabama who has lived in the state for 2 years prior to application. Competition receives 25 submissions annually. Accepts inquiries by e-mail and phone. "The following should be submitted: a résumé and a list of published works with reviews, if available; and a minimum of 10 pages of poetry or prose, but no more than 20 pages. Please label each page with title, artist's name, and date. If published, indicate where and the date of publication. Please do not submit bound material." Guidelines available in January on website. Deadline: March 1. Applications must be submitted online by eGRANT. Judged by independent peer panel. Winners notified by mail and announced on website in June.

GEORGE BENNETT FELLOWSHIP

Phillips Exeter Academy, Phillips Exeter Academy, 20 Main St., Exeter NH 03833. **E-mail:** teaching_opportunities@exeter.edu. **Website:** www.exeter.edu. Annual award for fellow and family "to provide time and freedom from material considerations to a person seriously contemplating or pursuing a career as a writer. Applicants should have a manuscript in progress which they intend to complete during the fellowship period." Duties: To be in residency at the Academy for the academic year; to make oneself available informally to students interested in writing. The committee favors writers who have not yet published a book with a major publisher. Deadline for application: December 1. A choice will be made, and all entrants notified in mid-April. Prize: Cash stipend, room and board. Judged by committee of the English department.

CHLA RESEARCH GRANTS

Children's Literature Association, 1301 W. 22nd Street, Suite 202, Oak Brook IL 60523. (630)571-4520. **Fax:** (708)876-5598. **E-mail:** info@childlitassn.org. **Website:** www.childlitassn.org. **Contact:** ChLA Grants Chair. Offered annually. Two types of grants area available: Faculty Research Grants and Beiter Graduate Student Research Grants. The grants are awarded for proposals dealing with criticism or original scholarship with the expectation that the undertaking will lead to publication (or a conference presentation for student awards) and make a significant contribution to the field of children's literature in the area of scholarship or criticism. Funds are not intended for work leading to the completion of a professional degree. Guidelines available online. Deadline: February 1. Prize: $500-1,500. Judged by the ChLA Grants Committee.

DOBIE PAISANO PROJECT

The Graduate School, The University of Texas at Austin, Attn: Dobie Paisano Program, 110 Inner Campus Drive Stop G0400, Austin TX 78712-0531. (512)232-3609. **Fax:** (512)471-7620. **E-mail:** gbarton@austin.utexas.edu. **Website:** www.utexas.edu/ogs/Paisano. **Contact:** Gwen Barton. "Sponsored by the Graduate School at The University of Texas at Austin and the Texas Institute of Letters, the Dobie Paisano Fellowship Program provides solitude, time, and a comfortable place for Texas writers or writers who have written significantly about Texas." "At the time of the application, the applicant must meet one of the following requirements: (1) be a native Texan, (2) have resided in Texas at least three years at some time, or (3) have published significant work with a Texas subject. Those who meet requirement 1 or 2 do not have to meet the Texas subject matter restriction." Deadline: January 15. Prize: "The Ralph A. Johnston memorial Fellowship is for a period of 4 months with a stipend of $5,000 per month. It is aimed at writers who have already demonstrated some publishing and critical success. The Jesse H. Jones Writing Fellowship is for a period of approximately 6 months with a stipend of $3,000 per month. It is aimed at, but not limited to, writers who are early in their careers."

TIPS "Guidelines and application forms are on the website or may be requested by sending a SASE (2-ounce postage) to the above address and attention of 'Dobie Paisano Fellowship Project.'"

DOCTORAL DISSERTATION FELLOWSHIPS IN JEWISH STUDIES

Foundation for Jewish Culture, P.O. Box 489, New York NY 10113-0489. (212)629-0500, ext. 215. **Fax:** (212)629-0508. **E-mail:** grants@jewishculture.org. **E-mail:** pzak@jewishculture.org. **Website:** www.jewishculture.org. **Contact:** Paul Zakrzewski. Open annually to students who have completed their course work and need funding for research in order to finish their dissertation thesis or a PhD in a Jewish field of study. The Foundation of Jewish Culture awards four to five Doctoral Dissertation fellowships per year to emerging scholars who are working in their last year of thesis writing within recognized fields associated with Jewish studies. Deadline: September 15. Prize: $16,000-20,000 grant.

JOSEPH R. DUNLAP FELLOWSHIP

William Morris Society in the US, Department of English, University of Iowa, Iowa City IA 52242. **E-mail:** us@morrissociety.org. **Website:** www.morrissociety.org. **Contact:** Prof. Florence Boos. Offered annually "to promote study of the life and work of William Morris (1834-96), British poet, designer, and socialist. Award may be for research or a creative project." Curriculum vitae, 1-page proposal, and 2 letters of recommendation required for application. Applicants must be US citizens or permanent residents. Deadline: December 15 of the year before the award is to be applied. Prize: Up to $1,000; multiple and partial awards possible.

GAP (GRANTS FOR ARTIST PROJECTS) PROGRAM

Artist Trust, 1835 12th Ave., Seattle WA 98122. (206)467-8734 ext. 11. **Fax:** (866)218-7878. **E-mail:** miguel@artisttrust.org. **Website:** www.artisttrust.org. **Contact:** Miguel Guillén, program manager. The GAP grant is awarded annually to 60 Washington state artists of all disciplines. Artist projects may include (but are not limited to): The development, completion or presentation of new work; publication; travel for artistic research or to present or complete work; documentation of work; and advanced workshops for professional development. Full-time students are not eligible. Guidelines will be posted on website in March. Deadline: April. Prize: Award: Up to $1,500 for artist-generated projects.

☻ THE HODDER FELLOWSHIP

Lewis Center for the Arts, 185 Nassau Street, Princeton NJ 08544. (609)258-1500. **E-mail:** anikolop@princeton.edu. **Website:** www.princeton.edu/arts/lewis_center/society_of_fellows. **Contact:** Angelo Nikolopoulos, program assistant, Creative Writing. Preference is given to applicants outside academia. Candidates for the Ph.D. are not eligible. Submit a resumè, sample of previous work (10 pages maximum, not returnable), and a project proposal of 2-3 pages. Guidelines available on website. Princeton University is an equal opportunity employer and complies with applicable EEO and affirmative action regulations. Apply online. The Hodder Fellowship will be given to writers of exceptional promise to pursue independent projects at Princeton University during the current academic year. Typically the fellows are poets, playwrights, novelists, creative nonfiction writers and translators who have published one highly acclaimed work and are undertaking a significant new project that might not be possible without the "studious leisure" afforded by the fellowship. Deadline: November 1, 2010 (postmarked). Prize: $68,000 stipend.

MASSACHUSETTS CULTURAL COUNCIL ARTIST FELLOWSHIP PROGRAM

Massachusetts Cultural Council, 10 St. James Ave., 3rd Floor, Boston MA 02116-3803. (617)727-3668. **Fax:** (617)727-0044. **E-mail:** mcc@art.state.ma.us. **Website:** www.massculturalcouncil.org; http://artsake.massculturalcouncil.org. **Contact:** Dan Blask, prog. coordinator. Awards in poetry, fiction/creative nonfiction, and dramatic writing (among other discipline categories) are given in recognition of exceptional original work (check website for award amount). Artistic excellence and creative ability, based on work submitted for review. Must be 18 years or older and a legal residents of Massachusetts for the last 2 years and at time of award. This excludes students in directly-related degree programs and grant recipients within the last 3 years. Judged by independent peer panels composed of artists and arts professionals.

TIPS Accepts inquiries by fax, e-mail and phone. "Send in your best work and follow guidelines (available on website)."

JENNY MCKEAN MOORE VISITING WRITER

English Deptartment, George Washington University, Rome Hall, 801 22nd St. NW, Suite 760, Washington DC 20052. (202)994-6180. **Fax:** (202)994-7915. **E-mail:** tvmallon@gwu.edu. **Website:** http://columbian.gwu.edu/departmentsprograms/english/creativewriting/activitiesevents. **Contact:** Thomas Mallon, director of Creative Writing. "The position is filled annually, bringing a visiting writer to The George Washington University. During each semester the Writer teaches 1 creative-writing course at the university as well as a community workshop. Each year we seek someone specializing in a different genre—fiction, poetry, creative nonfiction. For the 2012-13 academic year we will be looking for a poet. Guidelines for application will be announced in *The Writer's Chronicle*. Annual stipend between $50,000 and $60,000, plus reduced-rent townhouse on campus (not guaranteed)." Application Deadline: November 1. Prize: Annual stipend varies, depending on endowment performance; most recently, stipend was $58,000, plus reduced-rent townhouse (not guaranteed).

NEBRASKA ARTS COUNCIL INDIVIDUAL ARTISTS FELLOWSHIPS

Nebraska Arts Council, 1004 Farnam St., Plaza Level, Omaha NE 68102. (402)595-2122. **Fax:** (402)595-2334. **E-mail:** nac.info@nebraska.gov. **Website:** www.nebraskaartscouncil.org. Offered every 3 years (literature alternates with other disciplines) to recognize exemplary achievements by originating artists in their fields of endeavor and support the contributions made by Nebraska artists to the quality of life in this state. Generally, distinguished achievement awards are $5,000 and merit awards are $1,000-2,000. Funds available are announced in September prior to the deadline. Must be a resident of Nebraska for at least 2 years prior to submission date; 18 years of age; and not enrolled in an undergraduate, graduate, or certificate-granting program in English, creative writing, literature, or related field. Deadline: November 15.

NORTH CAROLINA WRITERS' FELLOWSHIPS

North Carolina Arts Council, North Carolina Arts Council, Writers' Fellowships, Department of Cultural Resources, Raleigh NC 27699-4632. (919)807-6512. **Fax:** (919)807-6532. **E-mail:** debbie.mcgill@ncmail.net. **Website:** www.ncarts.org. **Contact:** Debbie McGill, literature director. The North Carolina Arts Council offers grants in two categories to writers, spoken-word artists, playwrights, and screenwriters: fellowships (every other year) and residency grants (every year). Writers must be current residents of North Carolina for at least 1 year, must remain in residence in North Carolina during the grant year, and may not pursue academic or professional degrees while receiving grant. Fellowships offered to support writers in the development and creation of their work. See website for details. Offered every even year to support writers of fiction, poetry, literary nonfiction, literary translation, and spoken word. See website for guidelines and other eligibility requirements. Deadline: November 1. Prize: $10,000 grant. Reviewed by a panel of literature professionals (writers and editors).

SCREENPLAY FESTIVAL

11693 San Vicente Blvd., Ste. 806, Los Angeles CA 90049. (424)248-9221. **Fax:** (866)770-2994. **E-mail:** info@screenplayfestival.com. **Website:** www.screenplayfestival.com. This festival is an opportunity to give all scriptwriters a chance to be noticed and have their work read by the power players. Entries in the feature-length competition must be more than 60 pages; entries in the short screenplay contest must be fewer than 60 pages. "The Screenplay Festival was established to solve two major problems: Problem Number One: It is simply too difficult for talented writers who have no 'connections' to gain recognition and get their material read by legitimate agents, producers, directors and investors. Problem Number Two: Agents, producers, directors, and investors complain that they cannot find any great material, but they will generally not accept 'unsolicited material.' This means that unless the script comes from a source that is known to them, they will not read it. Screenplay Festival was established to help eliminate this 'chicken and egg' problem. By accepting all submitted screenplays and judging them based upon their quality — not their source or their standardized formatting or the quality of the brads holding them together — Screenplay Festival looks to give undiscovered screenwriters an opportunity to rise above the crowd." Deadline: September 1. Prize: In all categories, there is a $1,000 prize.

FICTION

24-HOUR SHORT STORY CONTEST

WritersWeekly.com, 5726 Cortez Rd. W., #349, Bradenton FL 34210. **E-mail:** writersweekly@writersweekly.com. **Website:** www.writersweekly.com/misc/contest.php. **Contact:** Angela Hoy. "Quarterly contest in which registered entrants receive a topic at start time (usually noon Central Time) and have 24 hours to write a story on that topic. All submissions must be returned via e-mail. Each contest is limited to 500 people. Guidelines via e-mail or online." Deadline: Quarterly—see website for dates. Prize: 1st Place: $300; 2nd Place: $250; 3rd Place: $200. There are also 20 honorable mentions and 60 door prizes. The top 3 winners' entries are posted on WritersWeekly.com (non-exclusive electronic rights only). Writers retain all rights to their work. Angela Hoy (publisher of WritersWeekly.com and Booklocker.com).

THE SHERWOOD ANDERSON FOUNDATION FICTION AWARD

12330 Ashton Mill Terrace, Glen Allen VA 23059. **E-mail:** sherwoodandersonfoundation@gmail.com. **Website:** sherwoodandersonfoundation.org. **Contact:** Anna McKean, foundation president. Contest is to honor, preserve and celebrate the memory and literary work of Sherwood Anderson, American realist for the first half of the 20th century. Annual award supports developing writers of short stories and novels. Entrants must have published at least one book of fiction or have had several short stories published in major literary and/or commercial publication. Self-published stories do not qualify. Send a detailed resumé that includes a bibliography of your publications. Include a cover letter that provides a history of your writing experience and your plans for writing projects. Also, submit 2 or 3 examples of what you consider to be your best work. Do not send manuscripts by e-mail. Only mss in English will be accepted. Open to

any writer who meets the qualifications listed above. Accepts inquiries by e-mail. Mail your application to the above address. No mss or publications will be returned. Deadline: April 1. Prize: $20,000 grant award.

THE BALTIMORE REVIEW FICTION CONTEST

The Baltimore Review, P.O. Box 529, Fork MD 21051. **Website:** www.baltimorereview.org. **Contact:** Barbara Westwood Diehl, senior editor. Biannual, critically acclaimed literary journal that accepts fiction, creative nonfiction, and poetry. Submit via postal mail and not through online submissions email, which is for regular submissions only. "The Annual Fiction Award aims to recognize the best new fiction today, from Baltimore and beyond. Submit one short story per entry fee. All styles and forms are accepted. Maximum word count is 6,000. Simultaneous submissions are fine, but alert us if your story has been accepted elsewhere. Judges vary each year." Submission Periods: August 1 through November 30 and February 1 through May 31. Prize: 1st Place: $500 and publication; 2nd Place: $250; 3rd Place: $100. Editors of *The Baltimore Review*

BELLEVUE LITERARY REVIEW GOLDENBERG PRIZE FOR FICTION

Bellevue Literary Review, NYU Dept of Medicine, 550 First Ave., OBV-A612, New York NY 10016. (212)263-3973. **E-mail:** info@blreview.org; stacy@blreview.org. **Website:** www.blreview.org. **Contact:** Stacy Bodziak, managing editor. The BLR prizes award outstanding writing related to themes of health, healing, illness, the mind and the body. Annual. Competition/award for short stories. Receives about 200-300 entries per category. Send credit card information or make checks payable to Bellevue Literary Review. Guidelines available in February. Accepts inquiries by e-mail, phone, mail. Submissions open in February. Results announced in December and made available to entrants with SASE, by e-mail, on website. Winners notified by mail, by e-mail. Entries should be unpublished. Anyone may enter contest. Length: No minimum; maximum of 5,000 words. Writers may submit own work. Deadline: July 1. Prize: $1,000 and publication in *The Bellevue Literary Review*. BLR editors select semi-finalists to be read by an independent judge who chooses the winner. Previous judges include Amy Hempel, Rick Moody, Rosellen Brown, and Andre Dubus III.

BINGHAMTON UNIVERSITY JOHN GARDNER FICTION BOOK AWARD

Creative Writing Program, Binghamton University, Binghamton University, Department of English, General Literature, and Rhetoric, Library North Room 1149, P.O. Box 6000, Binghamton NY 13902-6000. (607)777-2713. **E-mail:** cwpro@binghamton.edu. **Website:** http://binghamton.edu/english/creative-writing/. **Contact:** Maria Mazziotti Gillan, director. Contest offered annually for a novel or collection of fiction published in previous year. Offered annually for a novel or collection of short stories published that year in a press run of 500 copies or more. Each book submitted must be accompanied by an application form. Publisher may submit more than 1 book for prize consideration. Send 3 copies of each book. Guidelines available on website. Award's purpose is "to serve the literary community by calling attention to outstanding books of fiction." Deadline: March 1. Prize: $1,000. Judged by a professional writer not on Binghamton University faculty.

◐ THE CAINE PRIZE FOR AFRICAN WRITING

The Menier Gallery, Menier Chocolate Factory, 51 Southwark St., London SE1 1RU United Kingdom. (44)(207)378-6234. **Fax:** (44)(207)378-6235. **E-mail:** info@caineprize.com. **Website:** www.caineprize.com. **Contact:** Nick Elam. "Annual award for a short story (3,000-10,000 words) in English by an African writer. An 'African writer' is normally taken to mean someone who was born in Africa; who is a national of an African country; or whose parents are African, and whose work has reflected African sensibilities. Entries must have appeared for the first time in the 5 years prior to the closing date for submissions, which is January 31 each year. Publishers should submit 6 copies of the published original with a brief cover note (no pro forma application). Guidelines for SASE or online." Deadline: January 31. Prize: $15,000 (£10,000). a panel of judges appointed each year.

THE ALEXANDER PATTERSON CAPPON FICTION AWARD

New Letters, University of Missouri-Kansas City, 5101 Rockhill Rd., Kansas City MO 64110. (816)235-1168. **Fax:** (816)235-2611. **E-mail:** newletters@umkc.edu. **Website:** www.newletters.org. **Contact:** Ashley Kaine. Offered annually for unpublished work to discover and reward new and upcoming writers. Buys first North American serial rights. Open to any writer. Deadline: May 18. Prize: 1st Place: $1,500 and publication in a volume of *New Letters*; runner-up will receive a complimentary copy of a recent book of poetry or fiction courtesy of BkMk Press. All entries will be given consideration for publication in future issues of *New Letters*.

KAY CATTARULLA AWARD FOR BEST SHORT STORY

Texas Institute of Letters, P.O. Box 609, Round Rock TX 78680. **E-mail:** tilsecretary@yahoo.com. **Website:** http://texasinstituteofletters.org. Offered annually for work published January 1-December 31 of previous year to recognize the best short story. The story submitted must have appeared in print for the first time to be eligible. Writers must have been born in Texas, must have lived in Texas for at least 2 consecutive years, or the subject matter of the work must be associated with Texas. See website for guidelines. Deadline: See website for exact date. Prize: $1,000.

◐ TOM COLLINS POETRY PRIZE COMPETITION FELLOWSHIP OF AUSTRALIAN WRITERS (WA)

Fellowship of Australian Writers (WA), P.O. Box 6180, Swanbourne WA 6910. (61)(8)9384-4771. **Fax:** (61)(8)9384-4854. **E-mail:** admin@fawwa.org.au. **Website:** www.fawwa.org.au. Annual contest for unpublished poems maximum 60 lines. "We reserve the right to publish entries in a FAWWA publication or on its website." Guidelines online or for SASE. Deadline: December 15. Prize: 1st Place: $1,000; 2nd Place; $400; Highly Commended: $150.

CRAZYHORSE FICTION PRIZE

College of Charleston, Department of English, 66 George St., Charleston SC 29424. (843)953-4470. **Fax:** (843)953-7740. **E-mail:** crazyhorse@cofc.edu. **Website:** http://crazyhorse.cofc.edu. The journal's mission is to publish the entire spectrum of today's fiction, essays, and poetry—from the mainstream to the avant-garde, from the established to the undiscovered writer. The editors are especially interested in original writing that engages in the work of honest communication. *Crazyhorse* publishes writing of fine quality regardless of style, predilection, subject. Contest open to any writer. To enter, please send up to 25 pages of prose. Send SASE or see website. Deadline: January 31 of each year; see website. Prize: $2,000 and publication in *Crazyhorse*. Judged by anonymous writer whose identity is disclosed when the winners are announced in April. Past judges: Diana Abu-Jaber (2004), T.M. McNally (2005), Dan Chaon (2006), Antonya Nelson (2007), Ha Jin (2008); Ann Pratchett (2009).

DEAD OF WINTER

E-mail: editors@toasted-cheese.com. **Website:** www.toasted-cheese.com. **Contact:** Stephanie Lenz, editor. The contest is a winter-themed horror fiction contest with a new topic each year. Topic and word limit announced October 1. The topic is usually geared toward a supernatural theme. Categories: Short stories. No entry fee. Results announced January 31. Winners notified by e-mail. List of winners on website. Entries must be unpublished. Accepts inquiries by e-mail. Cover letter should include name, address, e-mail, word count, and title. Word limit varies each year. Open to any writer. Guidelines available in October on website. Deadline: December 21. Prize: Amazon gift certificates and publication in *Toasted Cheese*. Also offers honorable mention. Judged by 2 *Toasted Cheese* editors who blind judge each contest. Each judge uses her own criteria to rate entries.

TIPS "Follow online submission guidelines."

JACK DYER FICTION PRIZE

Crab Orchard Review, Department of English, Mail Code 4503, Faner Hall 2380, Southern Illinois University at Carbondale, 1000 Faner Drive, Carbondale IL 62901. **E-mail:** jtribble@siu.edu. **Website:** www.craborchardreview.siu.edu. **Contact:** Jon C. Tribble, man. editor. Offered annually for unpublished short fiction. *Crab Orchard Review* acquires first North American serial rights to all submitted work. Entries must be unpublished. Length: 6,000 words maximum. Please note that no stories will be returned. Results announced by end of August. Guidelines available on website. Deadline: May 4. Prize: $2,000, publication and 1-year subscription to *Crab Orchard Review*. Judged by editorial staff (pre-screening); winner chosen by genre editor.

TIPS "Carefully read directions for entering and follow them exactly. Send us your best work. Note that simultaneous submissions are accepted for this prize, but the winning entry must NOT be accepted elsewhere. No electronic submissions."

MARY KENNEDY EASTHAM FLASH FICTION PRIZE

Category in the Soul Making Keats Literary Competition, The Webhallow House, 1544 Sweetwood Dr., Broadmoor Village CA 94015-2029. **E-mail:** Eileen-Malone@comcast.net. **Website:** www.soulmaking-contest.us. **Contact:** Eileen Malone. "Keep each story under 500 words. Three stories per entry. One story per page, typed, double-spaced, and unidentified. Send me your best stuff but more than that make my heart beat faster. Surprise me. Read great writing daily and WRITE. WRITE. WRITE. To be successful you need to do your best every day for a very long time." Deadline: November 30. Prize: Prizes: 1st Place: $100; 2nd Place: $50; 3rd Place: $25.

THE FAR HORIZONS AWARD FOR SHORT FICTION

The Malahat Review, University of Victoria, P.O. Box 1700, Stn CSC, Victoria BC V8W 2Y2 Canada. (250)721-8524. **Fax:** (250)472-5051. **E-mail:** malahat@uvic.ca. **Website:** www.malahatreview.ca. **Contact:** John Barton, editor. Open to "emerging short fiction writers from Canada, the US, and elsewhere" who have not yet published their fiction in a full-length book (48 pages or more). 2011 winner: Zoey Peterson. Winner and finalists contacted by e-mail. Submissions must be unpublished. No simultaneous submissions. Submit 1 piece of short fiction, 3,500 words maximum; no restrictions on subject matter or aesthetic approach. Include separate page with author's name, address, e-mail, and title; no identifying information on mss pages. No e-mail submissions. Do not include SASE for results; mss will not be returned. Guidelines available on website. Deadline: May 1 of odd-numbered years. Prize: Offers $1,000 CAD, publication in fall issue of *The Malahat Review* (see separate listing in Magazines/Journals). Announced in fall on website, Facebook page, and in quarterly e-newsletter, *Malahat Lite*.

FIRSTWRITER.COM INTERNATIONAL SHORT STORY CONTEST

firstwriter.com, United Kingdom. **Website:** www.firstwriter.com. **Contact:** J. Paul Dyson, managing editor. "Accepts short stories up to 3,000 words on any subject and in any style." Deadline: April 1. Prize: Prize total about $300. Ten special commendations will also be awarded and all the winners will be published in *firstwriter* magazine and receive a $36 subscription voucher, allowing an annual subscription to be taken out for free. All submissions are automatically considered for publication in *firstwriter* magazine and may be published there online. Judged by *firstwriter* magazine editors.

● FISH PUBLISHING FLASH FICTION COMPETITION

Durrus, Bantry, County Cork Ireland. **E-mail:** info@fishpublishing.com. **Website:** www.fishpublishing.com. The Fish Flash Fiction Prize has been an annual event since 2004. Max length: 300 words. You may enter as many times as you wish. See website for details and rules. "This is an opportunity to attempt what is one of the most difficult and rewarding tasks - to create, in a tiny fragment, a completely resolved and compelling story in 300 words or less." Deadline: February 28. Prize: First Prize: €1,000. The ten published authors will receive five copies of the Anthology and will be invited to read at the launch during the West Cork Literary Festival in July. 2013 competition judged by Peter Benson.

H.E. FRANCIS SHORT STORY COMPETITION

Ruth Hindman Foundation, University of Alabama in Huntsville, Department of English, Morton Hall Room 222, Huntsville AL 35899. **Website:** www.hefranciscompetition.com. "Offered annually for unpublished work, not to exceed 5,000 words. Acquires first-time publication rights." Using the electronic submission system or by mail, submit a story of up to 5,000 words. If submitting by mail, include three copies of the story. Send an SASE or visit the website for complete guidelines. Deadline: December 31. Prize: $2,000. Judged by a panel of nationally recognized, award-winning authors, directors of creative writing programs, and editors of literary journals.

GIVAL PRESS NOVEL AWARD

Gival Press, LLC, P.O. Box 3812, Arlington VA 22203. (703)351-0079. **E-mail:** givalpress@yahoo.com. **Website:** www.givalpress.com. **Contact:** Robert L. Giron. Offered annually for a previously unpublished original novel (not a translation). Guidelines by phone, on website, via e-mail, or by mail with SASE. Results announced late fall of same year. Winners notified by phone. Results made available to entrants with SASE, by e-mail, on website. Open to any author who writes original work in English. Length: 30,000-100,000 words. Cover letter should include name, address, phone, e-mail, word count, novel title; include a short bio and short synopsis. Only the title and word count should appear on the actual ms. Writers may submit own work. "Review the types of mss Gival Press has published. We stress literary works." "To award the best literary novel." Deadline: May 30. Prize: $3,000, plus publication of book with a standard contract and author's copies. Final judge is announced after winner is chosen. Entries read anonymously.

GLIMMER TRAIN'S FAMILY MATTERS

Glimmer Train, 4763 SW Maplewood Rd., P.O. Box 80430, Portland OR 97280. (503)221-0836. **Fax:** (503)221-0837. **E-mail:** eds@glimmertrain.org. **Website:** www.glimmertrain.org. **Contact:** Susan Burmeister-Brown. "This contest is now held twice a year, during the months of April and October. Winners are contacted two months after the close of each contest, and results officially announced one week later. Submit online at www.glimmertrain.org. Prize: 1st Place: $1,500, publication in *Glimmer Train Stories*, and 20 copies of that issue; 2nd Place: $500; 3rd Place: $300. **TIPS** "The word count for this contest generally ranges from 1,500 to 5,000, though up to 12,000 words is fine."

GLIMMER TRAIN'S FAMILY MATTERS CONTEST

Glimmer Train Press, Inc., 4763 SW Maplewood, P.O. Box 80403, Portland OR 97280-1430. **Fax:** (503)221-0837. **E-mail:** editors@glimmertrain.org. **Website:** www.glimmertrain.org. **Contact:** Linda Swanson-Davies. Open in the months of April and October. Winners will be called two months after the close of each competition, and results announced in their respective bulletins, on their website, and in a number of additional print and online publications. Represented in recent editions of the Pushcart Prize, O. Henry, New Stories from the Midwest, and Best American Short Stories Anthologies. Offered for unpublished stories about family. Word count should not exceed 12,000. All shorter lengths welcome. See complete writing guidelines and submit online at website. "We are looking for stories about families of all configurations.It's fine to draw heavily on real life experiences, but the work must read like fictionand all stories accepted for publication will be presented as fiction." Deadlines: April 30 and October 31. Prize: Prizes: 1st Place: $1,500, publication in *Glimmer Train Stories*, and 20 copies of that issue; 2nd Place: $500; 3rd Place: $300. 2nd and 3rd place prizes vary if accepted for publication.

GLIMMER TRAIN'S VERY SHORT FICTION AWARD (JANUARY)

Glimmer Train Press, Inc., 4763 SW Maplewood Rd., P.O. Box 80430, Portland OR 97280. (503)221-0836. **Fax:** (503)221-0837. **E-mail:** eds@glimmertrain.org. **Website:** www.glimmertrain.org. **Contact:** Susan Burmeister-Brown. "Offered to encouragethe art of the very short story. Word count: 3,000 maximum. Submit by January 31. Submit online at www.glimmertrain.org. Winners will be called on March 31." Prize: 1st Place: $1,500, publication in *Glimmer Train Stories*, and 20 copies of that issue; 2nd Place: $500; 3rd Place: $300.

TIPS "There is no minimum word count, though it is rare for a piece under 500 words to read as a full story."

GLIMMER TRAIN'S VERY SHORT FICTION CONTEST (JULY)

Glimmer Train Press, Inc., 4763 SW Maplewood Rd., P.O. Box 80430, Portland OR 97280. (503)221-0836. **Fax:** (503)221-0837. **E-mail:** eds@glimmertrain.org. **Website:** www.glimmertrain.org. **Contact:** Susan Burmeister-Brown. "Offered to encourage the artof the very short story. Word count: 3,000 maximum. Open July 1-31. Submit online at www.glimmertrain.org." Winners are contacted by September 30 and results are officially announced one week later. Prize: 1st Place: $1,500, publication in *Glimmer Train Stories*, and 20 copies of that issue; 2nd Place: $500; 3rd Place: $300.

TIPS "There is no minimum word count, though it is rare for a piece under 500 words to read as a full story."

GOVERNOR GENERAL'S LITERARY AWARD FOR FICTION

Canada Council for the Arts, 350 Albert St., P.O. Box 1047, Ottawa ON K1P 5V8 Canada. (613)566-4414, ext. 5573. **Fax:** (613)566-4410. **Website:** www.canadacouncil.ca/prizes/ggla. Offered annually for the best English-language and the best French-language work of fiction by a Canadian. Publishers submit titles for consideration. Deadline depends on the book's publication date. Books in English: March 15, June 1 or August 7. Books in French: March 15 or July 15. Prize: Each laureate receives $25,000; non-winning finalists receive $1,000.

G. S. SHARAT CHANDRA PRIZE FOR SHORT FICTION

BkMk Press, Sharat Chandra Prize for Fiction, BkMk Press, University of Missouri-Kansas City, 5100 Rock-

hill Rd., Kansas City MO 64110-2499. (816)235-2558. **Fax:** (816)235-2611. **E-mail:** bkmk@umkc.edu. **Website:** http://cas.umkc.edu/bkmk/poetry.html. Offered annually for the best book-length ms collection (unpublished) of short fiction in English by a living author. Translations are not eligible. Initial judging is done by a network of published writers. Final judging is done by a writer of national reputation. Guidelines for SASE, by e-mail, or on website. Short fiction collections should be approximately 125 pages minimum, 300 pages maximum, double spaced. Deadline: January 15 (postmarked). Prize: $1,000, plus book publication by BkMk Press.

LYNDALL HADOW/DONALD STUART SHORT STORY COMPETITION

Fellowship of Australian Writers (WA), P.O. Box 6180, Swanbourne WA 6910 Australia. (61)(8)9384-4771. **Fax:** (61)(8)9384-4854. **E-mail:** admin@fawwa.org.au. **Website:** www.fawwa.org.au. Annual contest for unpublished short stories (maximum 3,000 words). "We reserve the right to publish entries in a FAWWA publication or on its website." Guidelines online or for SASE. Deadline: June 1. Prize: 1st Place: $400; 2nd Place; $100; Highly Commended: $50.

DRUE HEINZ LITERATURE PRIZE

University of Pittsburgh Press, Eureka Building, 5th Floor, 3400 Forbes Ave., Eureka Bldg., 5th Floor, Pittsburgh PA 15260. (412)383-2492. **Fax:** (412)383-2466. **Website:** www.upress.pitt.edu. Offered annually to writers who have published a book-length collection of fiction or a minimum of 3 short stories or novellas in commercial magazines or literary journals of national distribution. Does not return mss. Deadline: Submit May 1- June 30 only. Prize: $15,000. Judged by anonymous nationally known writers such as Robert Penn Warren, Joyce Carol Oates, and Margaret Atwood.

LORIAN HEMINGWAY SHORT STORY COMPETITION

Hemingway Days Festival, P.O. Box 993, Key West FL 33041. **E-mail:** shortstorykw@gmail.com. **Website:** www.shortstorycompetition.com. **Contact:** Eva Eliot, editorial assistant. Award to "encourage literary excellence and the efforts of writers whose voices have yet to be heard." Offered annually for unpublished short stories up to 3,500 words. Guidelines available via mail, e-mail, or online. Accepts inquiries by SASE, e-mail, or visit website. Entries must be unpublished.

"Open to all writers whose work has not appeared in a nationally distributed publication with a circulation of 5,000 or more. We look for excellence, pure and simple—no genre restrictions, no theme restrictions. We seek a writer's voice that cannot be ignored. All entrants will receive a letter from Lorian Hemingway and a list of winners, via mail or e-mail, by October 1." Deadline: May 15. Prize: 1st Place: $1,500, plus publication of his or her winning story in *Cutthroat: A Journal of the Arts*; 2nd-3rd Place: $500; honorable mentions will also be awarded. Judged by a panel of writers, editors, and literary scholars selected by author Lorian Hemingway. (Lorian Hemingway is the competition's final judge.) Results announced at the end of July during Hemingway Days festival. Winners notified by phone prior to announcement. For contest results, send e-mail or visit website.

TONY HILLERMAN PRIZE

Wordharvest, 1063 Willow Way, Santa Fe NM 87507. (505)471-1565. **E-mail:** wordharvest@wordharvest. com. **Website:** www.wordharvest.com. **Contact:** Anne Hillerman and Jean Schaumberg, co-organizers. Annual competition/award for novels. Categories: Unpublished mystery novels set in the American southwest, written by a first-time author in the mystery genre. Results announced at the Tony Hillerman Writers Conference. St. Martin's Press notifies the winner by phone or by e-mail 2-3 weeks prior to the conference. Results made available to entrants on website.All entries must be mailed to St. Martin's Press at the address below. Entry form is online at the website. For additional copies of the rules and to request an entry form, please send a SASE to: **St. Martin's Press/ Hillerman Mystery Competition Thomas Dunne Books/St. Martin's Press, 175 Fifth Ave., New York, NY 10010.** Multiple entries accepted. Accepts inquiries by e-mail, phone. Entries should be unpublished; self-published work is generally accepted. Length: no less than 220 type written pages, or approximately 60,000 words. Cover letter should include name, address, phone, e-mail, list of publishing credits. Please include SASE for response. Writers may submit their own work. "Make sure murder or another serious crime or crimes is at the heart of the story, and emphasis is on the solution rather than the details of the crime. The story's primary setting should be the southwest US, which includes CA, AZ, CO, NV, NM, OK, TX, and UT." "To honor the contributions made by Tony Hillerman to the art and craft of the mystery." Deadline: June 1. Prize: $10,000 advance and publication by St. Martin's Minotaur imprint. Nominees will be selected by judges chosen by the editorial staff of St. Martin's Press, with the assistance of independent judges selected by organizers of the Tony Hillerman Writers Conference (Wordharvest), and the winner will be chosen by St. Martin's editors.

TOM HOWARD/JOHN H. REID SHORT STORY CONTEST

c/o Winning Writers, 351 Pleasant St., PMB 222, Northampton MA 01060-3961. (866)946-9748. **Fax:** (413)280-0539. **E-mail:** adam@winningwriters.com. **Website:** www.winningwriters.com. Now in its 20th year. Open to all writers. Prizes of $3,000, $1,000, $400 and $250 will be awarded, plus 6 Most Highly Commended Awards of $150 each. Submit any type of short story, essay or other work of prose. "You may submit work that has been published or won prizes elsewhere, as long as you own the online publication rights." **Entry fee:** $15. Make checks payable to Winning Writers ("US funds only, please"). Submit on line or by mail. Early submission encouraged. Contest is sponsored by Tom Howard Books and assisted by Winning Writers. Judges: John H. Reid and Dee C. Konrad. See the complete guidelines and past winners. Guidelines available in July on website. Prefers inquiries by e-mail. **Deadline:** March 31. "Both published and unpublished works are accepted. In the case of published work, the contestant must own the online publication rights." Length: 5,000 words max per entry. Cover letter should include name, address, phone, e-mail, story title, and place(s) where story was previously published (if any). Only the title should be on the actual ms. Writers may submit own work. Read past winning entries at www.winningwriters.com/contests/tomstory/ts_pastwinners.php. Winners notified by e-mail. Results made available to entrants on website. **Contact:** Adam Cohen, President. Now in its 21st year. Open to all writers. Submit any type of short story, essay or other work of prose. "You may submit work that has been published or won prizes elsewhere, as long as you own the online publication rights. Both published and unpublished works are accepted. In the case of published work, the contestant must own the online publication rights." Contest is sponsored by Tom Howard Books and assisted by Winning Writers. Submit online or by mail. Early submission encouraged. Prefers inquiries by e-mail. Length: 5,000 words max per entry. Cover letter should include name, address, phone, e-mail, story title, and place(s) where story was previously published (if any). Only the title should be on the actual ms. Writers may submit own work. Deadline: April 30. Prize: Prizes: 1st Place: $3,000; 2nd Place: $1,000; 3rd Place: $400; 4th Place: $250; and 6 Most Highly Commended Awards of $150 each. The winners will be published on the Winning Writers website. Judged by John H. Reid; assisted by Dee C. Konrad.

L. RON HUBBARD'S WRITERS OF THE FUTURE CONTEST

P.O. Box 1630, Los Angeles CA 90078. (323)466-3310. **Fax:** (323)466-6474. **E-mail:** contests@authorservicesinc.com. **Website:** www.writersofthefuture. com. **Contact:** Joni Labaqui, contest director. Foremost competition for new and amateur writers of unpublished science fiction or fantasy short stories or novelettes. Offered "to find, reward and publicize new speculative fiction writers so they may more easily attain professional writing careers." Open to writers who have not professionally published a novel or short novel, more than 1 novelette, or more than 3 short stories. Entries must be unpublished. Limit 1 entry per quarter. Open to any writer. Results announced quarterly in e-newsletter. Winners notified by phone. Eligible entries are previously unpublished short stories or novelettes (under 17,000 words) of science fiction or fantasy. Guidelines for SASE or on website. Accepts inquiries by fax, e-mail, phone. Mss: White paper, black ink; double-spaced; typed; each page appropriately numbered with title, no author name. Include cover page with author's name, address, phone number, e-mail address (if available), as well as estimated word count and the title of the work. Deadline: December 31, March 31, June 30, September 30. Prize: Prize (awards quarterly): 1st Place: $1,000; 2nd Place: $750; and 3rd Place: $500. Annual grand prize: $5,000. "Contest has 4 quarters. There shall be 3 cash prizes in each quarter. In addition, at the end of the year, the 4 first-place, quarterly winners will have their entries rejudged, and a grand prize winner shall be determined." Judged by K.D. Wentworth (initial judge), then by a panel of 4 professional authors.

INDIANA REVIEW FICTION CONTEST

Ballantine Hall 465, Indiana University, 1020 E. Kirkwood Ave., Bloomington IN 47405-7103. (812)855-3439. **Fax:** (812)855-4253. **E-mail:** inreview@indi-ana.edu. **Website:** http://indianareview.org. **Contact:** Deborah Kim, editor. Contest for fiction in any style and on any subject. Open to any writer. Mss will not be returned. No works forthcoming elsewhere, are eligible. Simultaneous submissions accepted, but in the event of entrant withdrawal, contest fee will not be refunded. Length: 35 pages maximum, double spaced. "We look for a command of language and structure, as well as a facility with compelling and unusual subject matter. It's a good idea to obtain copies of issues featuring past winners to get a more concrete idea of what we are looking for." Deadline: Mid-October. Prize: $1,000, publication in the Indiana Review and contributor's copies. Judged by guest judges.

INTERNATIONAL 3-DAY NOVEL CONTEST

Box 2106 Station Terminal, Vancouver BC V6B 3T5 Canada. **E-mail:** info@3daynovel.com. **Website:** www.3daynovel.com. **Contact:** Melissa Edwards, managing editor. "Can you produce a masterwork of fiction in three short days? The 3-Day Novel Contest is your chance to find out. For more than 30 years, hundreds of writers step up to the challenge each Labour Day weekend, fuelled by nothing but adrenaline and the desire for spontaneous literary nirvana. It's a thrill, a grind, a 72-hour kick in the pants and an awesome creative experience. How many crazed plotlines, coffee-stained pages, pangs of doubt and moments of genius will next year's contest bring forth? And what will you think up under pressure?" Entrants write in whatever setting they wish, in whatever genre they wish, anywhere in the world. You may start writing as of midnight on Friday night, and must stop by midnight on Monday night. Then you print up your entry and mail it in to the contest for judging. Deadline: Friday before Labor Day weekend. Prize: first place receives publication; second place receives $500; third place receives $100.

THE IOWA SHORT FICTION AWARD

Iowa Writers' Workshop, 507 N. Clinton St., 102 Dey House, Iowa City IA 52242-1000. **Website:** www.uiowapress.org. **Contact:** Jim McCoy, director. Annual award "to give exposure to promising writers who have not yet published a book of prose." Open to any writer. Current University of Iowa students are not eligible. No application forms are necessary. Announcement of winners made early in year following competition. Winners notified by phone. No application forms are necessary. Do not send original ms. Include SASE for return of ms. Entries must be unpublished, but stories previously published in periodicals are eligible for inclusion. "The ms must be a collection of short stories of at least 150 word-processed, double-spaced pages." Deadline: September 30. Submission period: August 1-September 30. Packages must be postmarked by September 30. Prize: publication by University of Iowa Press Judged by senior Iowa Writers' Workshop members who screen mss; published fiction author of note makes final selections.

JERRY JAZZ MUSICIAN NEW SHORT FICTION AWARD

Jerry Jazz Musician, 2207 NE Broadway, Portland OR 97232. **E-mail:** jm@jerryjazzmusician.com. **Website:** www.jerryjazz.com. Three times a year, *Jerry Jazz Musician* awards a writer who submits, in our opinion, the best original, previously unpublished work of approximately 3,000-5,000 words. The winner will be announced via a mailing of our *Jerry Jazz* newsletter. Publishers, artists, musicians, and interested readers are among those who subscribe to the newsletter. Additionally, the work will be published on the home page of *Jerry Jazz Musician* and featured there for at least 4 weeks. The *Jerry Jazz Musician* reader tends to have interests in music, history, literature, art, film, and theater—particularly that of the counter-culture of mid-20th century America. Guidelines available online. Deadline: September, January, and May. Prize: $100. Judged by the editors of *Jerry Jazz Musician*.

JESSE JONES AWARD FOR FICTION

P.O. Box 609, Round Rock TX 78680. **E-mail:** tilsecretary@yahoo.com. **Website:** http://texasinstituteofletters.org. Offered annually by Texas Institute of Letters for work published January 1-December 31 of year before award is given to recognize the writer of the best book of fiction entered in the competition. Writers must have been born in Texas, have lived in the state for at least 2 consecutive years at some time, or the subject matter of the work should be associated with the state. President changes every 2 years. See website for guidelines. Deadline: See website for exact date. Prize: $6,000.

JAMES JONES FIRST NOVEL FELLOWSHIP

Wilkes University, Creative Writing Department, Wilkes University, 84 West South Street, Wilkes-Barre PA 18766. (570)408-4547. **Fax:** (570)408-3333. **E-mail:** Jamesjonesfirstnovel@wilkes.edu. **Website:** www.wilkes.edu/pages/1159.asp. Offered annually for unpublished novels, novellas, and closely-linked short stories (all works in progress). The competition is open to all American writers who have not previously published novels. A two-page (maximum) outline of the entire novel and the first 50 pages of the novel-in-progress are to be submitted. The manuscript must be typed and double-spaced; outline may be single-spaced. Entrants submitting via snail mail should include their name, address, telephone number and e-mail address (if available) on the title page, but nowhere else on the manuscript. For those entrants submitting online, name, address, telephone number and e-mail address should NOT appear anywhere on the manuscript. Pages should be numbered. The award is intended to honor the spirit of unblinking honesty, determination, and insight into modern culture exemplified by the late James Jones. Deadline: March 1. Prize: $10,000; 2 runners-up get $750 honorarium.

⊕ THE JAMES KNUDSEN EDITOR'S PRIZE FOR FICTION

Bayou Magazine, Dept. of English, University of New Orleans, 2000 Lakeshore Dr., New Orleans LA 70148. **Website:** cola.uno.edu/cww/bayou. Established in memory of the late James Knudsen, author, teacher and Creative Writing Workshop Director (2001-2003) at The University of New Orleans, the James Knudsen Editor's Prize for Fiction aims to encourage and celebrate the work of emerging fiction writers. Deadline: December 31. Prize: $500 and publication. All other entries will be considered for publication. Judged by Bayou editorial staff. First publishing rights are acquired for winning ms.

THE LEDGE ANNUAL FICTION AWARDS COMPETITION

The Ledge Magazine, 40 Maple Avenue, Bellport NY 11713. **E-mail:** info@theledgemagazine.com. **Website:** www.theledgemagazine.com. **Contact:** Timothy Monaghan, editor-in-chief. Stories must be unpublished and 7,500 words or less. There are no restrictions on form or content. Guidelines online or for SASE. Deadline: Feb. 28. Prize: 1st Place: $1,000 and publication; 2nd Place: $250 and publication; 3rd Place: $100 and publication.

LITERAL LATTÉ FICTION AWARD

Literal Latté, 200 E. 10th St., Suite 240, New York NY 10003. (212)260-5532. **E-mail:** litlatte@aol.com. **Website:** www.literal-latte.com. **Contact:** Edward Estlin, contributing editor. "Award to provide talented writers with 3 essential tools for continued success: money, publication, and recognition. Offered annually for unpublished fiction (maximum 10,000 words). Guidelines online. Open to any writer." Deadline: January 15. Prize: 1st Place: $1,000 and publication in *Literal Latté*; 2nd Place: $300; 3rd Place: $200; also up to seven honorable mentions.

TIPS "Winners notified by phone. Winners announced in April. All winners published in *Literal Latté*."

LITERAL LATTE SHORT SHORTS CONTEST

Literal Latte, 200 E. 10th St., Suite 240, New York NY 10003. (212)260-5532. **E-mail:** litlatte@aol.com. **Website:** www.literal-latte.com. **Contact:** Jenine Gordon Bockman, editor. Annual contest. Send unpublished shorts. 2,000 words max. All styles welcome. Postmark by June 30th. Name, address, phone number, email address (optional) on cover page only. Include SASE or email address for reply. All entries considered for publication Deadline: June 30. Prize: $500. Judged by the editors.

THE MARY MACKEY SHORT STORY PRIZE

Category in the Soul-Making Keats Literary Competition under the auspice of the National League of American Pen Women, The Webhallow House, 1544 Sweetwood Dr., Broadmoor Village CA 94015. **E-mail:** SoulKeats@aol.com. **Website:** www.soulmakingcontest.us. **Contact:** Eileen Malone. Open annually to any writer. "One story/entry, up to 5,000 words. All prose works must be typed, page numbered, and double-spaced. Identify only with 3x5 card." Deadline: November 30 (annually). Prize: Cash prizes.

☺ THE MALAHAT REVIEW NOVELLA PRIZE

The Malahat Review, University of Victoria, P.O. Box 1700 STN CSC, Victoria BC V8W 2Y2 Canada. (250)721-8524. **E-mail:** malahat@uvic.ca. **Website:** malahatreview.ca. **Contact:** John Barton, editor. "Held in alternate years with the Long Poem Prize. Offered to promote unpublished novellas. Obtains first world rights. After publication rights revert to the author. Open to any writer." Submit novellas between 10,000 and 20,000 words in length. Include separate page with author's name, address, e-mail, and novella title; no identifying information on mss. pages. No e-mail submissions. Do not include SASE for results; mss will not be returned. Guidelines available on website. Deadline: February 1 (even years). Prize: $1,500 CAD and one year's subscription. 2010 winner was Tony Tulathimutte. Winner and finalists contacted by e-mail. Winner published in summer issue of *The Malahat Review* and announced on website, Facebook page, and in quarterly e-newsletter, *Malahat Lite*.

MARY MCCARTHY PRIZE IN SHORT FICTION

Sarabande Books, P.O. Box 4456, Louisville KY 40204. (502)458-4028. **Fax:** (502)458-4065. **E-mail:** info@sarabandebooks.org. **Website:** www.sarabandebooks.org. **Contact:** Kirby Gann, managing editor. Offered annually to publish an outstanding collection of stories, novellas, or a short novel (less than 250 pages). All finalists considered for publication. Deadline: January 1-February 15. Prize: $2,000 and publication (standard royalty contract).

DAVID NATHAN MEYERSON PRIZE FOR FICTION

Southwest Review, P.O. Box 750374, Dallas TX 75275-0374. (214) 768-1037. **Fax:** (214) 768-1408. **E-mail:** swr@smu.edu. **Website:** www.smu.edu/southwestreview. **Contact:** Jennifer Cranfill, senior editor. Annual award given to a writer who has not published a first book of fiction, either a novel or collection of stories. All contest entrants will receive a copy of the issue in which the winning piece appears. Submissions must be no longer than 8,000 words. Work should be printed without the author's name. Name and address should appear only on the cover letter. Submissions will not be returned. Postmarked deadline for entry is May 1. Prize: $1,000 and publication in the *Southwest Review*.

TIPS "A cover letter with name, address, and other relevant information may accompany the piece which must be printed without any identifying information. Get guidelines for SASE or online."

NATIONAL READERS' CHOICE AWARDS

Oklahoma Romance Writers of America (OKRWA), **E-mail:** nrca@okrwa.com. **Website:** www.okrwa.com. Contest "to provide writers of romance fiction with a competition where their published novels are judged by readers." See the website for categories and descriptions. Additional award for best first book. All entries must have an original copyright date during the current contest year. Entries will be accepted from authors, editors, publishers, agents, readers, whoever wants to fill out the entry form, pay the fee and supply the books. No limit to the number of entries, but each title may be entered only in one category. Open to any writer published by an RWA approved non-vanity/non-subsidy press. For guidelines, send e-mail or visit website. Deadline: January 15. Prize: Plaques and finalist certificates awarded at the awards banquet hosted at the Annual National Romance Writers Convention.

NATIONAL WRITERS ASSOCIATION NOVEL WRITING CONTEST

The National Writers Association, 10940 S. Parker Rd. #508, Parker CO 80134. (303)841-0246. **E-mail:** natlwritersassn@hotmail.com. **Website:** www.nationalwriters.com. **Contact:** Sandy Whelchel, director. Categories: Open to any genre or category. Entry fee: $35. Opens December 1. Open to any writer. Entries must be unpublished. Length: 20,000-100,000 words. Annual contest to help develop creative skills, to recognize and reward outstanding ability, and to increase the opportunity for the marketing and subsequent publication of novel mss. Deadline: April 1. Prize: 1st Place: $500; 2nd Place: $250; 3rd Place: $150. Judged by editors and agents.

TIPS "Contest forms are available on the NWA website or an attachment will be sent if you request one through e-mail or with an SASE."

NATIONAL WRITERS ASSOCIATION SHORT STORY CONTEST

The National Writers Association, 10940 S. Parker Rd. #508, Parker CO 80134. (303)841-0246. **E-mail:** natlwritersassn@hotmail.com. **Website:** www.nationalwriters.com. **Contact:** Sandy Whelchel, director. Annual contest to encourage writers in this creative form, and to recognize those who excel in fiction writing. Deadline: July 1. Prize: 1st Place: $200; 2nd Place: $100; 3rd Place: $50.

THE NELLIGAN PRIZE FOR SHORT FICTION

Colorado Review/Center for Literary Publishing, 9105 Campus Delivery, Dept. of English, Colorado State University, Ft. Collins CO 80523-9105. (970)491-5449. **E-mail:** creview@colostate.edu. **Website:** http://nelliganprize.colostate.edu. **Contact:** Stephanie G'Schwind, editor. "The Nelligan Prize for Short Fiction was established in memory of Liza Nelligan, a writer, editor, and friend of many in Colorado State University's English Department, where she received her master's degree in literature in 1992. By giving an award to the author of an outstanding short story each

year, we hope to honor Liza Nelligan's life, her passion for writing, and her love of fiction." Annual. Competition/award for short stories. Receives approximately 900 stories. All entries are read blind by Colorado Review's editorial staff. 15 entries are selected to be sent on to a final judge. Send credit card information or make checks payable to Colorado Review. Payment also accepted via our online submission manager link from website. Deadline: March 12. Prize: $1,500 and publication of story in *Colorado Review*.

ON THE PREMISES CONTEST

On The Premises, LLC, 4323 Gingham Court, Alexandria VA 22310. (202) 262-2168. **E-mail:** questions@onthepremises.com. **Website:** www.onthepremises.com. "*On the Premises* aims to promote newer and/or relatively unknown writers who can write what we feel are creative, compelling stories told in effective, uncluttered and evocative prose. Each contest challenges writers to produce a great story based on a broad premise that our editors supply as part of the contest." Competition/award for short stories. 1st Prize: $180; 2nd Prize: $140; 3rd Prize: $100; Honorable Mentions recieve $40. All prize winners are published in *On the Premises* magazine in HTML and PDF format. Entries are judged blindly by a panel of judges with professional editing and writing experience. Open to everyone. No entry fee. Contests held every 4 months. Check website for exact dates. Submissions are accepted by e-mail only. Entries should be unpublished. Length: minimum 1,000 words; maximum 5,000. E-mail should include name, address, e-mail, and novel/story title, with ms attached. No name or contact info should be in ms. Writers may submit own work. "Write something compelling, creative, and well-crafted. Above all, clearly use the contest premise." Results announced within 2 weeks of contest deadline. Winners notified via newsletter and with publication of *On the Premises*. Results made available to entrants on website and in publication. **Contact:** Tarl Roger Kudrick or Bethany Granger, co-publishers. "*On the Premises* aims to promote newer and/or relatively unknown writers who can write what we feel are creative, compelling stories told in effective, uncluttered and evocative prose. Each contest challenges writers to produce a great story based on a broad premise that our editors supply as part of the contest." Submissions are accepted by e-mail only. Entries should be unpublished. Length: minimum 1,000 words; maximum 5,000. E-mail should include name, address, e-mail, and novel/story title, with ms attached. No name or contact info should be in ms. Writers may submit own work. Check website for details on the specific premise that writers should incorporate into their story. Deadline: Contests held every four months, check website for exact dates. Prize: 1st Prize: $180; 2nd Prize: $140; 3rd Prize: $100; Honorable Mentions recieve $40. All prize winners are published in *On the Premises* magazine in HTML and PDF format. Entries are judged blindly by a panel of judges with professional editing and writing experience.

KENNETH PATCHEN AWARD FOR THE INNOVATIVE NOVEL

Eckhard Gerdes Publishing, Civil Coping Mechanisms, 12 Simpson Street, Apt. D, Geneva IL 60134. **E-mail:** egerdes@experimentalfiction.com. **Website:** www.experimentalfiction.com. **Contact:** Eckhard Gerdes. "This award will honor the most innovative novel submitted during the previous calendar year. Kenneth Patchen is celebrated for being among the greatest innovators of American fiction, incorporating strategies of concretism, asemic writing, digression, and verbal juxtaposition into his writing long before such strategies were popularized during the height of American postmodernist experimentation in the 1970s." See guidelines and application form online at website. Deadline for entry: All submissions must be postmarked between January 1 and July 31. Prize: $1,000, 20 complimentary copies. Judged by novelist Yuriy Tarnawsky.

THE PATERSON FICTION PRIZE

The Poetry Center at Passaic Community College, One College Blvd., Paterson NJ 07505. (973)684-6555. **Fax:** (973)523-6085. **E-mail:** mgillan@pccc.edu. **Website:** www.pccc.edu/poetry. **Contact:** Maria Mazziotti Gillan, executive director. Offered annually for a novel or collection of short fiction published the previous calendar year. For more information, visit the website or send SASE. April 1. Prize: $1,000.

PEARL SHORT STORY PRIZE

3030 E. Second St., Long Beach CA 90803. (562)434-4523. **E-mail:** Pearlmag@aol.com. **Website:** www.pearlmag.com. **Contact:** Marilyn Johnson, fiction editor. Award to "provide a larger forum and help widen publishing opportunities for fiction writers in the small press and to help support the continuing publication of *Pearl*." Include a brief bio and SASE for reply or return of mss. Accepts simultaneous submissions, but asks to be notified if story is accepted elsewhere. Entries must be unpublished. "Although we are open to all types of fiction, we look most favorably on coherent, well-crafted narratives containing interesting, believable characters in meaningful situations." Length: 4,000 words maximum. Open to any writer. Guidelines for SASE or on website. Accepts queries by e-mail or fax. Results announced in September. Winners notified by mail. For contest results, send SASE, e-mail, or visit website. April 1-May 31 submission period. Prize: $250, publication in *Pearl* and 10 copies of the journal. The editors of *Pearl*: Marilyn Johnson, Joan Jobe Smith, Barbara Hauk.

EDGAR ALLAN POE AWARD

1140 Broadway, Suite 1507, New York NY 10001. (212)888-8171. **Fax:** (212)888-8107. **E-mail:** mwa@mysterywriters.org. **Website:** www.mysterywriters.org. Mystery Writers of America is the leading association for professional crime writers in the United States. Members of MWA include most major writers of crime fiction and non-fiction, as well as screenwriters, dramatists, editors, publishers, and other professionals in the field. Purpose of the award: to honor authors of distinguished works in the mystery field. Previously published submissions only. Submissions made by the author, author's agent; "normally by the publisher." Work must be published/produced the year of the contest. Deadline: November 30. Prize: Awards ceramic bust of "Edgar" for winner; scrolls for all nominees. Judged by professional members of Mystery Writers of America (writers).

THE KATHERINE ANNE PORTER PRIZE FOR FICTION

Nimrod International Journal, The University of Tulsa, 800 S. Tucker Dr., Tulsa OK 74104. (918)631-3080. **Fax:** (918)631-3033. **E-mail:** nimrod@utulsa.edu. **Website:** www.utulsa.edu/nimrod. **Contact:** Eilis O'Neal. 7,500-word maximum for short stories. Deadline: April 30. Prize: Prizes: 1st Place: $2,000 and publication; 2nd Place: $1,000 and publication. The *Nimrod* editors select the finalists and a recognized author selects the winners.

☼ THE ROGERS WRITERS' TRUST FICTION PRIZE

The Writers' Trust of Canada, 90 Richmond St. E., Suite 200, Toronto ON M5C 1P1 Canada. (416)504-

8222. **Fax:** (416)504-9090. **E-mail:** info@writerstrust. com. **Website:** www.writerstrust.com. **Contact:** Amanda Hopkins. "Awarded annually for a distinguished work of fiction—either a novel or short story collection—published within the previous year. Presented at the Writers' Trust Awards event held in Toronto each fall. Open to Canadian citizens and permanent residents only." Deadline: August. Prize: $25,000 and $2,500 to 4 finalists.

◑ SASKATCHEWAN FICTION AWARD

Saskatchewan Book Awards, Inc., P.O. Box 20025, Regina SK S4P 4J7 Canada. (306)569-1585. **E-mail:** director@bookawards.sk.ca. **Website:** www.bookawards.sk.ca. Offered annually. "This award is presented to a Saskatchewan author for the best book of fiction (novel or short fiction), judged on the quality of writing." Deadline: November 1. Prize: $2,000 (CAD).

THE SATURDAY EVENING POST GREAT AMERICAN FICTION CONTEST

The Saturday Evening Post Society, 1100 Waterway Blvd., Indianapolis IN 46202. **E-mail:** fictioncontest@saturdayeveningpost.com. **Website:** www.saturdayeveningpost.com/fiction-contest. "In its nearly 3 centuries of publication, *The Saturday Evening Post* has included fiction by a who's who of American authors, including F. Scott Fitzgerald, William Faulkner, Kurt Vonnegut, Ray Bradbury, Louis L'Amour, Sinclair Lewis, Jack London, and Edgar Allan Poe. The *Post*'s fiction has not just entertained us; it has played a vital role in defining who we are as Americans. In launching this contest, we are seeking America's next great, unpublished voices." Entries must be character- or plot-driven stories in any genre of fiction that falls within the *Post*'s broad range of interest. "We are looking for stories with universal appeal touching on shared experiences and themes that will resonate with readers from diverse backgrounds and experience." Stories must be submitted by the author and previously unpublished (excluding personal websites and blogs), and 1,500-5,000 words in length. No extreme profanity or graphic sex scenes. Submit story via the online at www.saturdayeveningpost.com/fiction-contest. All submissions must be made electronically in Microsoft Word format with the author's name, address, telephone number, and e-mail address on the first page. Do not submit hard copies via the mail; physical mss will not be read. "Due to staff limitations, we will not be able to update entrants on the status of their stories. We will inform winners or runners-up within 30 days of publication. We regret we will not be able to notify non-winning entrants." Deadline: July 1. Prize: The winning story will receive $500 and publication in the magazine and online. Five runners-up will be published online and receive $100 each.

MICHAEL SHAARA AWARD FOR EXCELLENCE IN CIVIL WAR FICTION

Civil War Institute at Gettysburg College, 300 N. Washington St., Campus Box 435, Gettysburg PA 17325. (717)337-6574. **Fax:** (717)337-6596. **E-mail:** civilwar@gettysburg.edu. **Website:** www.gettysburg.edu/cwi. Offered annually for fiction published January 1-December 31. Contest "to encourage examination of the Civil War from unique perspectives or by taking an unusual approach." All Civil War novels are eligible. Publishers should make nominations, but authors and critics can nominate as well. Prize: $5,000, which includes travel stipend. No entry fee. **Deadline: December 31.** Entries must be previously published. Judged for presentation of unique perspective, use of unusual approach, effective writing, contribution to existing body of Civil War literature. Competition open to authors of Civil War novels published for the first time in the year designated by the award (i.e. for 2008 award, only novels published in 2008 are eligible). Guidelines available on website. Accepts inquiries by fax, e-mail, and phone. Cover letter should include name, address, phone, e-mail, and title. Need 4 copies of novel. "Enter well before deadline. Results announced in July. Winners notified by phone. For contest results, visit website." **Contact:** Diane Brennan. "Offered annually for fiction published for the first time in January 1-December 31 of the year of the award to encourage examination of the Civil War from unique perspectives or by taking an unusual approach. All Civil War novels are eligible. To nominate a novel, send 4 copies of the novel to the address above with a cover letter. Nominations should be made by publishers, but authors and critics can nominate as well." Any novel about the Civil War published (for the first time) in the current calendar year to "encourage fresh approaches to Civil War fiction" is eligible. Self published books are not eligible. This includes books printed and bound by a company hired and paid by the author to publish his/her work in book form. Deadline: December 31. Prize: $5,000.

THREE CHEERS AND A TIGER

E-mail: editors@toasted-cheese.com. **Website:** www.toasted-cheese.com. **Contact:** Stephanie Lenz, editor. Purpose of contest is to write a short story (following a specific theme) within 48 hours. Contests are held first weekend in spring (mystery) and first weekend in fall (sf/f). Categories: Short stories. No entry fee. Word limit announced at the start of the contest. Contest-specific information is announced 48 hours before the contest submission deadline. Results announced in April and October. Winners notified by e-mail. List of winners on website. Entries must be unpublished. Open to any writer. Accepts inquiries by e-mail. "Follow the theme, word count and other contest rules. We have more suggestions at our website." Cover letter should include name, address, e-mail, word count and title. Information should be in the body of the e-mail. It will be removed before the judging begins. Prize: Amazon gift certificates and publication. Blind-judged by 2 *Toasted Cheese* editors. Each judge uses his or her own criteria to choose entries.

WORLD FANTASY AWARDS

P.O. Box 43, Mukilteo WA 98275. **E-mail:** sfexecsec@gmail.com. **Website:** www.worldfantasy.org. Awards "to recognize excellence in fantasy literature worldwide." Offered annually for previously published work in several categories, including life achievement, novel, novella, short story, anthology, collection, artist, special award-pro and special award-nonpro. Works are recommended by attendees of current and previous 2 years' conventions and a panel of judges. Prize: Bust of HP Lovecraft. Judged by panel. No entry fee. Guidelines available in December for SASE or on website. **Deadline: June 1.** Entries must be previously published. Published submissions from previous calendar year. Word length: 10,000-40,000 for novella, 10,000 for short story. "All fantasy is eligible, from supernatural horror to Tolkien-esque to sword and sorcery to the occult, and beyond." Cover letter should include name, address, phone, e-mail, word count, title, and publications where submission was previously published, submitted to the address above and the panel of judges when they appear on the website. Results announced November 1 at annual convention. For contest results, visit website. **Contact:** Peter Dennis Pautz, president. Awards "to recognize excellence in fantasy literature worldwide." Offered annually for previously published work in several categories, including life achievement, novel, novella, short story, anthology, collection, artist, special award-pro and special award-nonpro. Works are recommended by attendees of current and previous 2 years' conventions and a panel of judges. Judged by panel. No entry fee. Entries must be previously published. Published submissions from previous calendar year. Word length: 10,000-40,000 for novella, 10,000 for short story. "All fantasy is eligible, from supernatural horror to Tolkien-esque to sword and sorcery to the occult, and beyond." Cover letter should include name, address, phone, e-mail, word count, title, and publications where submission was previously published, submitted to the address above and the panel of judges when they appear on the website. Results announced November 1 at annual convention. For contest results, visit website. Prize: Bust of HP Lovecraft.

WOW! WOMEN ON WRITING QUARTERLY FLASH FICTION CONTEST

WOW! Women on Writing, P.O. Box 41104, Long Beach CA 90853. **E-mail:** contestinfo@wow-womenonwriting.com. **Website:** www.wow-womenonwriting.com/contest.php. **Contact:** Angela Mackintosh, editor. Contest offered quarterly. "We are open to all themes and genres, although we do encourage writers to take a close look at our literary agent guest judge for the season if you are serious about winning." Entries must be 250-750 words. Deadline: August 31, November 30, February 28, May 31. Prize: "1st place: $350 cash prize, $25 Amazon gift certificate, book from our sponsor, story published on WOW! Women On Writing, interview on blog; 2nd place: $250 cash prize, $25 Amazon gift certificate, book from our sponsor, story published on WOW! Women On Writing, interview on blog; 3rd place: $150 cash prize, $25 Amazon gift certificate, book from our sponsor, story published on WOW! Women On Writing, interview on blog; 7 runners up: $25 Amazon gift certificate, book from our sponsor, story published on WOW! Women on Writing, interview on blog;10 honorable mentions: $20 gift certificate from Amazon, book from our sponsor, story title and name published on WOW!Women On Writing."

NONFICTION

ANTHEM ESSAY CONTEST

The Ayn Rand Institute, P.O. Box 57044, Irvine CA 92619-7044. (949)222-6550. **Fax:** (949)222-6558. **E-**

mail: essay@aynrand.org. **Website:** www.aynrand. org/contests. "Offered annually to encourage analytical thinking and excellence in writing (600-1,200 word essay), and to expose students to the philosophical ideas of Ayn Rand. For information contact your English teacher or guidance counselor or visit our website. Open to 8th, 9th and 10th graders." Deadline: March 20. Prize: 1st Place: $2,000; 2nd Place (5): $500; 3rd Place (10): $200; Finalist (45): $50; Semifinalist (175): $30.

THE ASCAP DEEMS TAYLOR AWARDS

American Society of Composers, Authors & Publishers, One Lincoln Plaza, New York NY 10023. (212)621-6318. **E-mail:** jsteinblatt@ascap.com. **Website:** www. ascap.com. **Contact:** Jim Steinblatt. Written works must be published in the U.S. in English, during the calendar year of 2012. The subject matter may be biographical or critical, reportorial or historical - almost any form of nonfiction prose about music and/or its creators. However, instructional textbooks, how-to-guides, or works of fiction will not be accepted. "The ASCAP Deems Taylor Awards program recognizes books, articles, broadcasts, and websites on the subject of music selected for their excellence." Deadline: May 31. Prize: "Several categories of cash prizes are presented to writers of award-winning books and newspaper, journal, or magazine articles (includes program notes, liner notes and on-line publications). Awards are also presented to the authors and journalists as well as to their respective publishers."

ATLAS SHRUGGED ESSAY CONTEST

The Ayn Rand Institute, P.O. Box 57044, Irvine CA 92619-7044. (949)222-6550, ext. 247. **Fax:** (949)222-6558. **E-mail:** essay@aynrand.org. **Website:** www. aynrand.org/contests. Essay length: 800-1,600 words. Essays are judged both on style and content. Guidelines on the website. "The winning applicant will be judged on both style and content. Judges will look for writing that is clear, articulate and logically organized. Winning essays must demonstrate an outstanding grasp of the philosophic meaning of Atlas Shrugged. Essay submissions are evaluated in a fair and unbiased four-round judging process. Judges are individually selected by the Ayn Rand Institute based on a demonstrated knowledge and understanding of Ayn Rand's works." "Offered annually to encourage analytical thinking and excellence in writing, and to expose students to the philosophic ideas of Ayn

Rand. Open to 12th graders and college undergraduate and graduate students." Deadline: September 17. Prize: Prizes: 1st Place: $10,000; 2nd Place (3 awards): $2,000; 3rd Place (5 awards): $1,000; Finalists (25 awards): $100; Semifinalists (50 awards): $50.

⊕ BANCROFT PRIZE

Columbia University, c/o Office of the University Librarian, 517 Butter Library, Mail Code 1101, 535 W. 114th St., New York NY 10027. (212)854-7309. **Fax:** (212)854-9099. **Website:** www.columbia.edu/eguides/ amerihist/bancroft.html. **Contact:** Bancroft Prize Committee. "Offered annually for work published in previous year. Winning submissions will be chosen in either or both of the following categories: American history (including biography) and diplomacy. Open to all writers except previous recipients of the Bancroft Prize." Deadline: November 1. Prize: $10,000 for the winning entry in each category.

☯ CANADIAN LIBRARY ASSOCIATION STUDENT ARTICLE CONTEST

Canadian Library Association, 1150 Morrison Dr., Suite 400, Ottawa ON K2H 8S9 Canada. (613)232-9625, ext. 322. **Fax:** (613)563-9895. **E-mail:** info@cla. ca. **Website:** www.cla.ca. **Contact:** Judy Green. Offered annually to unpublished articles discussing, analyzing, or evaluating timely issues in librarianship or information science. Open to all students registered in or recently graduated from a Canadian library school, a library techniques program, or faculty of education library program. Submissions may be in English or French. Deadline: March 31. Prize: $200 and the winning article will be published in *Feliciter*, the magazine of the Canadian Library Association.

THE DOROTHY CHURCHILL CAPPON CREATIVE NONFICTION AWARD

New Letters, University of Missouri-Kansas City, 5101 Rockhill Rd., Kansas City MO 64110. (816)235-1168. **Fax:** (816)235-2611. **E-mail:** newletters@umkc. edu. **Website:** www.newsletters.org. **Contact:** Ashley Kaine. Contest is offered annually for unpublished work to discover and reward emerging writers and to give experienced writers a place to try new genres. Acquires first North American serial rights. Open to any writer. Guidelines by SASE or online. Deadline: May 18. Prize: 1st Place: $1,500 and publication in a volume of *New Letters*; runner-up will receive a copy of a recent book of poetry or fiction courtesy of BkMk

Press. All entries will receive consideration for publication in future editions of *New Letters*.

MORTON N. COHEN AWARD

Modern Language Association of America, 26 Broadway, 3rd Floor, New York NY 10004-1789. (646)576-5141. **Fax:** (646)458-0030. **E-mail:** awards@mla.org. **Website:** www.mla.org. **Contact:** Coordinator of Book Prizes. Awarded in odd-numbered years for a distinguished edition of letters. At least 1 volume of the edition must have been published during the previous 2 years. Editors need not be members of the MLA. Under the terms of the award, the winning collection will be one that provides readers with a clear, accurate, and readable text; necessary background information; and succinct and eloquent introductory material and annotations. The edited collection should be in itself a work of literature. Deadline: May 1. Prize: A cash award and a certificate to be presented at the Modern Language Association's annual convention in January.

○ THE SHAUGHNESSY COHEN PRIZE FOR POLITICAL WRITING

The Writers' Trust of Canada, 90 Richmond St. E., Suite 200, Toronto ON M5C 1P1 Canada. (416)504-8222. **Fax:** (416)504-9090. **E-mail:** info@writerstrust.com. **Website:** www.writerstrust.com. **Contact:** Amanda Hopkins, program coordinator. "Awarded annually for a nonfiction book of outstanding literary merit that enlarges our understanding of contemporary Canadian political and social issues. Presented at the Politics & the Pen event each spring in Ottawa. Open to Canadian citizens and permanent residents only." Prize: $25,000 and $2,500 to 4 finalists.

CARR P. COLLINS AWARD FOR NONFICTION

The Texas Institute of Letters, P.O. Box 609, Round Rock TX 78680. **E-mail:** tilsecretary@yahoo.com. **Website:** http://texasinstituteofletters.org/. Offered annually for work published January 1-December 31 of the previous year to recognize the best nonfiction book by a writer who was born in Texas, who has lived in the state for at least 2 consecutive years at one point, or a writer whose work has some notable connection with Texas. See website for guidelines. Deadline: See website for exact date. Prize: $5,000.

COWBOY UP SHORT STORY CONTEST

Moonlight Mesa Associates, Inc., 18620 Moonlight Mesa Rd., Wickenburg AZ 85390. **E-mail:** orders@moonlightmesaassociates.com. **Website:** www.moonlightmesaassociates.com. Fiction only: 3,500 words maximum. Must involve cowboy(s) or other western character(s). "You may enter as many stories as you like. Submit a separate registration form for each story. See guidelines online. Specific themes/topics for the stories vary yearly. Check website for updates." Open March 1-September 1. Prize: $75-250

○ THE DONNER PRIZE

The Award for Best Book on Public Policy by a Canadian, The Donner Canadian Foundation, 400 Logan Ave., Toronto ON M4M 2N9 Canada. (416)368-8253. **E-mail:** sherry@mdgassociates.com. **Website:** www.donnerbookprize.com. **Contact:** Sherry Naylor. "Offered annually for nonfiction published January 1-December 31 that highlights the importance of public policy and to reward excellent work in this field. Entries must be published in either English or French. Open to Canadian citizens." November 30. Prize: $50,000; other shortlisted titles get $7,500 each.

EDUCATOR'S AWARD

The Delta Kappa Gamma Society International, P.O. Box 1589, Austin TX 78767-1589. (888)762-4685. **Fax:** (512)478-3961. **Website:** www.dkg.org. **Contact:** Kathy Flynn, chair. "Offered annually for quality research and nonfiction published January-December of previous year. This award recognizes educational research and writings of female authors whose work may influence the direction of thought and action necessary to meet the needs of today's complex society. The book must be written by 1 or 2 women who are citizens of any country in which The Delta Kappa Gamma Society International is organized: Canada, Costa Rica, Denmark, Estonia, Finland, Germany, Great Britain, Guatemala, Iceland, Mexico, The Netherlands, Norway, Puerto Rico, Sweden, US, Panama. Guidelines (required) for SASE." The Educators Award Committee is charged with the responsibility of selecting an appropriate book as winner of the annual Educator's Award. Committee members read and evaluate books submitted by publishers that meet the criteria of having been written by women and whose content may influence the direction of thought and action necessary to meet the needs of today's complex society; furthermore, the content must be of more than local interest with relationship, direct or implied, to education everywhere. Deadline: February 1. Prize: $2,500. Judged by Educators Award Committee.

EVANS BIOGRAPHY & HANDCART AWARDS

Mountain West Center for Regional Studies, Room 339, Old Main, 0735 Old Main Hill, Utah State University, Logan UT 84322-0735. (435)797-0299. **Fax:** (435)797-1092. **E-mail:** mwc@usu.edu. **Website:** http://mountainwest.usu.edu/evans.aspx. **Contact:** Patricia Lambert, director. The Evans Biography and Handcart Awards encourage the best in research and writing about the Interior West through the giving of two annual prizes for excellence in biography. Send six copies of the book and one copy of the author's resume. See website for details. The Evans Biography Award is a prize given to the best biography of a person who lived a significant portion of his or her life in the Interior West, or, in the words of the awards' founders, "Mormon Country" - that region historically influenced by Mormon institutions and social practices. The Evans Handcart Award is given to a biography addressing similar subjects as the Evans Biography Award, but often by an emerging author or written as a family history. Deadline: January 1 for books published in the previous calendar years. Prize: $10,000 for the Evans Biography Award; and $2,500 for the Evans Handcart Award. All submitted books are read by a local jury of five scholars and book experts.

THE GILDER LEHRMAN LINCOLN PRIZE

Gettysburg College and Gilder Lehrman Institute of American History, 300 N. Washington St., Campus Box 435, Gettysburg PA 17325. (717)337-8255. **Fax:** (717)337-6596. **E-mail:** lincolnprize@gettysburg.edu. **Website:** www.gettysburg.edu/lincolnprize. The Gilder Lehrman Lincoln Prize, sponsored by the Gilder Lehrman Institute and Gettysburg College, is awarded annually for the finest scholarly work in English on Abraham Lincoln or the American Civil War era. Deadline: November 1. Prize: $50,000. **TIPS** "This contest is for adults writers only."

JOHN GUYON LITERARY NONFICTION PRIZE

Crab Orchard Review, Department of English, Fane Hall 2380 - Mail Code 4503, 1000 Faner Drive, Carbondale IL 62901. **E-mail:** jtribble@siu.edu. **Website:** www.craborchardreview.siu.edu. **Contact:** Jon C. Tribble, managing editor. "Offered annually for

unpublished work. This competition seeks to reward excellence in the writing of creative nonfiction. This is not a prize for academic essays. *Crab Orchard Review* acquires first North American serial rights to submitted works. Open to US citizens only." Deadline: March 1-May 4. Prize: $2,000 and publication.

IRA OUTSTANDING DISSERTATION OF THE YEAR AWARD

International Reading Association, 800 Barksdale Rd., P.O. Box 8139, Newark DE 19714-8139. (302)731-1600. **Fax:** (302)731-1057. **E-mail:** research@reading.org. **Website:** www.reading.org. **Contact:** Marcie Craig Post, Executive Director. Dissertations in reading or related fields are eligible for the competition. Studies using any research approach (ethnographic, experimental, historical, survey, etc.) are encouraged. Each study is assessed in the light of this approach, the scholarly qualification of its report, and its significant contributions to knowledge within the reading field. The application process is open to those who have completed dissertations in any aspect of the field of reading or literacy between May 15, 2011, and May 14, 2012. A routine check is made with the home university of the applicant to protect all applicants, their universities, and the International Reading Association from false claims. Studies may use any research approach (ethnographic, experimental, historical, survey, etc.). Each study will be assessed in light of its approach, its scholarship, and its significant contributions to knowledge within the reading/literacy field. Deadline: October 1. Prize: $1,000

TILIA KLEBENOV JACOBS RELIGIOUS ESSAY PRIZE

Category in the Soul Making Keats Literary Competition, The Webhallow House, 1544 Sweetwood Dr., Broadmoor Village CA 94015-2029. **E-mail:** SoulKeats@mail.com. **Website:** www.soulmakingcontest.us. **Contact:** Eileen Malone. "Call for thoughtful writings of up to 3,000 words. No preaching, no proselytizing." Open annually to any writer. Previously published material is accepted. Indicate category on cover page and on identifying 3x5 card. Up to 3,000 words, double-spaced. See website for more details. Deadline: November 30. Prize: 1st Place: $100; 2nd Place $50; 3rd Place $25.

KATHERYN KROTZER LABORDE LITERARY NONFICTION PRIZE

Category in the Soul Making Keats Literary Competition, The Webhallow House, 1544 Sweetwood Dr., Broadmoor Village CA 94015-2029. **E-mail:** Eileen-Malone@comcast.net. **Website:** www.soulmaking-contest.us. **Contact:** Eileen Malone. All prose works must be typed, page numbered, and double-spaced. Each entry up to 3,000 words. Identify only with 35 card. Open annually to any writer. "A narrative of up to 3,000 words that takes an experience or event and gives it personal meaning. Creative nonfiction is the child of fiction and journalism. Unlike fiction, the characters and events are real, not imagined. Unlike journalism, the writer is part of the story she tells, if not as a participant then as a thoughtful observer. I will be looking for a strong voice, a solid sense of the story, and a clear sense of one's writing style. One last note: think about the STORY you are trying to tell and don't be a slave to the truth, the whole truth, and nothing but. This is art, not sworn testimony!" Deadline: November 30. Prize: Prizes: First Place: $100; Second Place: $50; Third Place: $25.

◎ LITERARY NONFICTION CONTEST

PRISM International, Creative Writing Program, UBC, Buch E462—1866 Main Mall, Vancouver BC V6T 1Z1 Canada. **E-mail:** prismwritingcontest@gmail.com. **Website:** www.prismmagazine.ca. **Contact:** Andrea Hoff, Contest Manager. Offered annually for published and unpublished writers to promote and reward excellence in literary nonfiction writing. "*PRISM* buys first North American serial rights upon publication. We also buy limited Web rights for pieces selected for the website. Open to anyone except students and faculty of the Creative Writing Program at UBC or people who have taken a creative writing course at UBC in the 2 years prior to contest deadline. All entrants receive a 1-year subscription to *PRISM*. Guidelines for SASE (Canadian postage only), via e-mail, or visit our website." Deadline: November 328. Prize: $1,500 grand prize, $300 runner-up, and $200 second runner up.

RICHARD J. MARGOLIS AWARD

c/o Margolis & Bloom, LLP, 535 Boylston St., 8th Floor, Boston MA 02116. (617)267-9700, ext. 517. **Fax:** (617)267-3166. **E-mail:** hsm@margolis.com. **Website:** www.margolis.com/award. **Contact:** Harry S. Margolis. "Sponsored by the Blue Mountain Center, this an-nual award is given to a promising new journalist or essayist whose work combines warmth, humor, wisdom, and concern with social justice." "Applications should include at least two examples of the your work (published or unpublished, 30 pages maximum) and a short biographical note including a description of your current and anticipated work. Also please indicate what you will work on while attending the Blue Mountain residency. Please send three copies of these writing samples. Samples will not be returned." Deadline: July 1. Prize: $5,000.

MLA PRIZE FOR A DISTINGUISHED SCHOLARLY EDITION

Modern Language Association of America, 26 Broadway, 3rd Floor, New York NY 10004. (646)576-5141. **Fax:** (646)458-0030. **E-mail:** awards@mla.org. **Website:** www.mla.org. Offered in odd-numbered years. "To qualify for the award, an edition should be based on an examination of all available relevant textual sources; the source texts and the edited text's deviations from them should be fully described; the edition should employ editorial principles appropriate to the materials edited, and those principles should be clearly articulated in the volume; the text should be accompanied by appropriate textual and other historical contextual information; the edition should exhibit the highest standards of accuracy in the presentation of its text and apparatus; and the text and apparatus should be presented as accessibly and elegantly as possible." Editor need not be a member of the MLA. Deadline: May 1. Prize: A cash award and a certificate to be presented at the Modern Language Association's annual convention in January.

MLA PRIZE FOR INDEPENDENT SCHOLARS

Modern Language Association of America, 26 Broadway, 3rd Floor, New York NY 10004. (646)576-5141. **Fax:** (646)458-0030. **E-mail:** awards@mla.org. **Website:** www.mla.org. Offered in even-numbered years for a book in the field of English, or another modern language, or literature published in the previous year. Authors who are enrolled in a program leading to an academic degree or who hold tenured or tenure-track positions in higher education are not eligible. Authors need not be members of MLA. Guidelines and application form for SASE. Deadline: May 1. Prize: A cash award, a certificate, and a year's membership in the MLA.

Fax: (706)542-2455. **E-mail:** sdendy@uga.edu. **Website:** sha.uga.edu. **Contact:** Dr. John B. Boles, Editor. Awarded for a distinguished book in Southern history published in even-numbered years. The decision of the Award Committee will be announced at the annual meeting in odd-numbered years. The award carries a cash payment to be fixed by the Council, a certificate for the author(s), and a certificate for the publisher. Deadline: March 1.

PRESERVATION FOUNDATION CONTESTS

The Preservation Foundation, Inc., 2213 Pennington Bend, Nashville TN 37214. **E-mail:** preserve@storyhouse.org. **Website:** www.storyhouse.org. **Contact:** Richard Loller, publisher. "Two contests offered annually for unpublished nonfiction. General nonfiction category (1,500-5,000 words)—any appropriate nonfiction topic. Travel nonfiction category (1,500-5,000 words)—must be true story of trip by author or someone known personally by author. E-mail entries only (no mss). Open to any previously unpublished writer. Defined as having earned no more than $750 by creative writing in any previous year." Stories must be submitted by e-mail or as electronic files by regular mail. No paper manuscripts can be considered. No story may be entered in more than one contest. See website for details on how to submit your story. Deadline: August 31. Prize: 1st Place: $100 in each category; certificates for finalists.

EVELYN RICHARDSON NONFICTION AWARD

Writers' Federation of Nova Scotia, 1113 Marginal Rd., Halifax NS B3H 4P7 Canada. (902)423-8116. **Fax:** (902)422-0881. **E-mail:** programs@writers.ns.ca. **E-mail:** director@writers.ns.ca. **Website:** www.writers.ns.ca. **Contact:** Hillary Titley. "This annual award is named for Nova Scotia writer Evelyn Richardson, whose book *We Keep a Light* won the Governor General's Literary Award for nonfiction in 1945. There is no entry fee or form. Full-length books of nonfiction written by Nova Scotians, and published as a whole for the first time in the previous calendar year, are eligible. Publishers: Send four copies and a letter attesting to the author's status as a Nova Scotian, and the author's current mailing address and telephone number." Deadline: First Friday in December. Prize: $2,000.

SASKATCHEWAN NONFICTION AWARD

Saskatchewan Book Awards, Inc., P.O. Box 20025, Regina SK S4P 4J7 Canada. (306)569-1585. **E-mail:** director@bookawards.sk.ca. **Website:** www.bookawards.sk.ca. Offered annually for work published. "This award is presented to a Saskatchewan author for the best book of nonfiction, judged on the quality of writing." Deadline: November 1. Prize: $2,000 (CAD).

SASKATCHEWAN SCHOLARLY WRITING AWARD

Saskatchewan Book Awards, Inc., P.O. Box 20025, Regina SK S4P 4J7 Canada. (306)569-1585. **E-mail:** director@bookawards.sk.ca. **Website:** www.bookawards.sk.ca. Offered annually. "This award is presented to a Saskatchewan author for the best contribution to scholarship. The work must recognize or draw on specific theoretical work within a community of scholars, and participate in the creation and transmission of scholarly knowledge." Deadline: November 1. Prize: $2,000 (CAD).

ALDO AND JEANNE SCAGLIONE PRIZE FOR COMPARATIVE LITERATURE STUDIES

Modern Language Association of America, 26 Broadway, 3rd Floor, New York NY 10004-1789. (646)576-5141. **Fax:** (646)458-0030. **E-mail:** awards@mla.org. **Website:** www.mla.org. **Contact:** Coordinator of Book Prizes. The Committee on Honors and Awards of the Modern Language Association invites authors to compete for the twenty-first annual Aldo and Jeanne Scaglione Prize for Comparative Literary Studies, to be awarded for an outstanding scholarly work in the field of comparative literary studies involving at least two literatures. For the competition in 2013, the committee solicits entries of books written by current members of the association and published in 2012. Works of literary history, literary criticism, philology, and literary theory are eligible, as are works dealing with literature and other arts and disciplines, including cinema; books that are primarily translations will not be considered. To enter a book into the competition, authors or publishers should send four copies and a letter identifying the work and confirming the author's membership in the MLA. Deadline: May 1. Prize: A cash award and a certificate to be presented at the Modern Language Association's annual convention in January.

ALDO AND JEANNE SCAGLIONE PRIZE FOR FRENCH AND FRANCOPHONE STUDIES

Modern Language Association of America, 26 Broadway, 3rd Floor, New York NY 10004. (646)576-5141. **Fax:** (646)458-0030. **E-mail:** awards@mla.org. **Website:** www.mla.org. Offered annually for work published in the preceding year that is an outstanding scholarly work in the field of French or francophone linguistic or literary studies. *Author must be a member of the MLA.* Works of scholarship, literary history, literary criticism, and literary theory are eligible; books that are primarily translations are not eligible. Deadline: May 1. Prize: A cash award and a certificate to be presented at the Modern Language Association's annual convention in January.

ALDO AND JEANNE SCAGLIONE PRIZE FOR STUDIES IN GERMANIC LANGUAGES & LITERATURE

Modern Language Association of America, 26 Broadway, 3rd Floor, New York NY 10004. (646)576-5141. **Fax:** (646)458-0030. **E-mail:** awards@mla.org. **Website:** www.mla.org. Offered in even-numbered years for outstanding scholarly work appearing in print in the previous 2 years and written by a member of the MLA on the linguistics or literatures of the Germanic languages. Works of literary history, literary criticism, and literary theory are eligible; books that are primarily translations are not eligible. Deadline: May 1. Prize: A cash award, and a certificate to be presented at the Modern Language Association's annual convention in January.

CHARLES S. SYDNOR AWARD

Southern Historical Association, Rm. 111 A LeConte Hall, Athens GA 30602-1602. (706)542-8848. **Fax:** (706)542-2455. **E-mail:** sdendy@uga.edu. **Website:** sha.uga.edu/awards/syndor.htm. **Contact:** Southern Historical Association. Offered in even-numbered years for recognition of a distinguished book in Southern history published in odd-numbered years. Publishers usually submit books. Next award will be in 2014 for a book published during 2013. Deadline: March 1.

VFW VOICE OF DEMOCRACY

Veterans of Foreign Wars of the U.S., 406 W. 34th St., Kansas City MO 64111. (816)968-1117. **E-mail:** kharmer@vfw.org. **Website:** www.vfw.org. The Voice of Democracy Program is open to students in grades 9-12 (on the Nov. 1 deadline), who are enrolled in a public, private or parochial high school or home study program in the United States and its territories. Contact your local VFW Post to enter. Purpose is to give high school students the opportunity to voice their opinions about their responsibility to our country and to convey those opinions via the broadcast media to all of America. Deadline: November 1. Prize: Winners receive awards ranging from $1,000-30,000.

WESTERN WRITERS OF AMERICA

271CR 219, Encampment WY 82325. (307)329-8942. **Fax:** (307)327-5465 (call first). **E-mail:** wwa.moulton@gmail.com. **Website:** www.westernwriters.org. **Contact:** Candy Moulton, executive director. "17 Spur Award categories in various aspects of the American West." Send entry form with your published work. "The nonprofit Western Writers of America has promoted and honored the best in Western literature with the annual Spur Awards, selected by panels of judges. Awards, for material published last year, are given for works whose inspirations, image and literary excellence best represent the reality and spirit of the American West."

TIPS "Accepts multiple submissions, each with its own entry form."

☉ THE HILARY WESTON WRITERS' TRUST PRIZE FOR NONFICTION

The Writers' Trust of Canada, 90 Richmond St. E., Suite 200, Toronto ON M5C 1P1 Canada. (416)504-8222. **Fax:** (416)504-9090. **E-mail:** info@writerstrust.com. **Website:** www.writerstrust.com. **Contact:** Amanda Hopkins. "Offered annually for a work of nonfiction published in the previous year. Award presented at a a gala event held in Toronto each fall. Open to Canadian citizens and permanent residents only." Deadline: August. Prize: $25,000 (Canadian), and $2,500 to 4 finalists.

WRITING CONFERENCE WRITING CONTESTS

P.O. Box 664, Ottawa KS 66067-0664. (785)242-1995. **Fax:** (785)242-1995. **E-mail:** jbushman@writingconference.com. **E-mail:** support@studentq.com. **Website:** www.writingconference.com. **Contact:** John H. Bushman, contest director. Unpublished submissions only. Submissions made by the author or teacher. Purpose of contest: to further writing by students with awards for narration, exposition and poetry at the elementary, middle school and high school levels. Deadline: January 8. Prize: Awards plaque and publication of winning entry in The Writers' Slate online, April issue. Judged by a panel of teachers.

YEARBOOK EXCELLENCE CONTEST

100 Adler Journalism Building, Iowa City IA 52242-2004. (319)335-3457. **Fax:** (319)335-3989. **E-mail:** quill-scroll@uiowa.edu. **Website:** www.uiowa.edu/~quill-sc. **Contact:** Vanessa Shelton, executive director. High school students who are contributors to or staff members of a student yearbook at any public or private high school are invited to enter the competition. Awards will be made in each of the 18 divisions. There are two enrollment categories: Class A: more than 750 students; Class B: 749 or less. Winners will receive Quill and Scroll's National Award Gold Key and, if seniors, are eligible to apply for one of the Edward J. Nell Memorial or George and Ophelia Gallup scholarships. Open to students whose schools have Quill and Scroll charters. Previously published submissions only. Submissions made by the author or school yearbook adviser, Must be published in the 12-month span prior to contest deadline. Visit website for list of current and previous winners. To recognize and reward student journalists for their work in yearbooks and to provide student winners an opportunity to apply for a scholarship to be used freshman year in college for students planning to major in journalism. Deadline: November 1.

WRITING FOR CHILDREN & YOUNG ADULTS

HANS CHRISTIAN ANDERSEN AWARD

Nonnenweg 12, Postfach Ba CH-4003 Switzerland. **E-mail:** liz.page@ibby.org. **E-mail:** ibby@ibby.org. **Website:** www.ibby.org. **Contact:** Liz Page, director. The Hans Christian Andersen Award, is the highest international recognition given to an author and an illustrator of children's books. The Author's Award has been given since 1956, the Illustrator's Award since 1966. Her Majesty Queen Margrethe II of Denmark is the Patron of the Hans Christian Andersen Awards. The Hans Christian Andersen Jury judges the books submitted for medals according to literary and artistic criteria. The awards are presented at the biennial congresses of IBBY. A Hans Christian Andersen Medal shall be awarded every two years by the International Board on Books for Young People (IBBY) to an author and to an illustrator, living at the time of the nomination, who by the outstanding value of their work are judged to have made a lasting contribution to literature for children and young people. The complete works of the author and of the illustrator will be taken into consideration in awarding the medal, which will be accompanied by a diploma. Candidates are nominated by National Sections of IBBY in good standing.

JOHN AND PATRICIA BEATTY AWARD

2471 Flores St., San Mateo CA 94403. (650)376-0886. **Fax:** (650)539-2341. **E-mail:** ncole@cla-net.org. **E-mail:** Clio.Hathaway@hayward-ca.gov. **Website:** www.cla-net.org. **Contact:** Clio Hathaway. The California Library Association's John and Patricia Beatty Award, sponsored by Baker & Taylor, honors the author of a distinguished book for children or young adults that best promotes an awareness of California and its people. A committee of CLA members selects the winning title from books published in the United States during the preceding year. Prize: $500 and an engraved plaque.

THE IRMA S. AND JAMES H. BLACK AWARD

Bank Street College of Education, 610 W. 112th St., New York NY 10025-1898. (212)875-4458. **Fax:** (212)875-4558. **E-mail:** kfreda@bankstreet.edu;apryce@bankstreet.edu. **Website:** http://www.bankstreet.edu/childrenslibrary/irmasimonton-blackhome.html. **Contact:** Kristin Freda. Purpose of award: "The award is given each spring for a book for young children, published in the previous year, for excellence of both text and illustrations." Entries must have been published during the previous calendar year (between January '11 and December '11 for 2012 award). Deadline for entries: mid-December. "Publishers submit books to us by sending them here to me at the Bank Street Library. Authors may ask their publishers to submit their books. Out of these, three to five books are chosen by a committee of older children and children's literature professionals. These books are then presented to children in selected first-, second-, and third-grade classes here and at a number of other cooperating schools. These children are the final judges who pick the actual award winner. A scroll (one each for the author and illustrator, if they're different) with the recipient's name and a gold seal designed by Maurice Sendak are awarded in May."

⊙ ANN CONNOR BRIMER AWARD

The Ann Connor Brimer Award, P.O. Box 36036, Halifax NS B3J 3S9 Canada. **Website:** www.nsla.ns.ca/index.php/about/awards/ann-connor-brimer-award. **Contact:** Heather MacKenzie, award director. In 1990, the Nova Scotia Library Association established the Ann Connor Brimer Award for writers residing in Atlantic Canada who have made an outstanding contribution to children's literature. Author must be alive and residing in Atlantic Canada at time of nomination. Book intended for youth up to the age of 15. Book in print and readily available. Fiction or non-fiction (except textbooks). To recognize excellence in writing. Prize: $2,000.

⊙ THE NORMA FLECK AWARD FOR CANADIAN CHILDREN'S NONFICTION

The Canadian Children's Book Centre, 40 Orchard View Blvd., Suite 217, Toronto ON M4R 1B9 Canada. (416)975-0010 ext. 222. **Fax:** (416)975-8970. **E-mail:** info@bookcentre.ca. **Website:** www.bookcentre.ca. **Contact:** Meghan Howe, library coordinator. The Norma Fleck Award was established by the Fleck Family Foundation in May 1999 to honour the life of Norma Marie Fleck, and to recognize exceptional Canadian nonfiction books for young people. Publishers are welcome to nominate books using the online form. Offered annually for books published between January 1 and December 31 of the previous calendar year. Open to Canadian citizens or landed immigrants. The jury will always include at least 3 of the following: a teacher, a librarian, a bookseller, and a reviewer. A juror will have a deep understanding of, and some involvement with, Canadian children's books. The Canadian Children's Book Centre will select the jury members. Prize: $10,000 goes to the author (unless 40% or more of the text area is composed of original illustrations, in which case the award will be divided equally between the author and the artist). Deadline: February 8. Prize: $10,000.

GOLDEN KITE AWARDS

Society of Children's Book Writers and Illustrators (SCBWI), SCBWI Golden Kite Awards, 8271 Beverly Blvd., Los Angeles CA 90048-4515. (323)782-1010. **E-mail:** awards@scbwi.org. **Website:** www.scbwi.org. Society of Children's Book Writers and Illustrators, 8271 Beverly Blvd.Los Angeles CA 90048. (323)782-1010. **E-mail:** scbwi@scbwi.org. **Website:** www.scbwi.org. **Contact:** SCBWI Golden Kite Coordinator. Annual award. Estab. 1973. "The works chosen will be those that the judges feel exhibit excellence in writing, and in the case of the picture-illustrated books—in illustration, and genuinely appeal to the interests and concerns of children. For the fiction and nonfiction awards, original works and single-author collections of stories or poems of which at least half are new and never before published in book form are eligible—anthologies and translations are not. For the picture-illustration awards, the art or photographs must be original works (the texts—which may be fiction or nonfiction—may be original, public domain or previously published). Deadline for entries: December 15. SASE for award rules. No entry fee. Awards, in addition to statuettes and plaques, the four winners receive $2,500 cash award plus trip to LA SCBWI Conference. The panel of judges will consist of professional authors, illustrators, editors or agents." Requirements for entrants: "must be a member of SCBWI and books must be published in that year." Winning books will be displayed at national conference in August. Books to be entered, as well as further inquiries, should be submitted to: The Society of Children's Book Writers and Illustrators, above address. "The works chosen will be those that the judges feel exhibit excellence in writing and, in the case of the picture-illustrated books, in illustration, and genuinely appeal to the interests and concerns of children. For the fiction and nonfiction awards, original works and single-author collections of stories or poems of which at least half are new and never before published in book form are eligible—anthologies and translations are not. For the picture-illustration awards, the art or photographs must be original works (the texts—which may be fiction or nonfiction—may be original, public domain or previously published)." To be eligible to submit your book(s) for the Golden Kite Award, and/or the Sid Fleischman Award, you must be a current member of the SCBWI with your membership current through April 1st, 2014. You may submit your book to one category only, except in the case of Picture Book Text and Picture Book Illustration. See website for more details. Deadline: December 4. Prize: In addition to statuettes and plaques, the 4 winners receive $2,500 cash award plus trip to LA SCBWI Conference.

GOVERNOR GENERAL'S LITERARY AWARD FOR CHILDREN'S LITERATURE

Canada Council for the Arts, 350 Albert St., P.O. Box 1047, Ottawa ON K1P 5V8 Canada. (613)566-4414, ext. 5573. **Fax:** (613)566-4410. **Website:** www.canadacouncil.ca/prizes/ggla. Offered for the best English-language and the best French-language works of children's literature by a Canadian in 2 categories: text and illustration. Publishers submit titles for consideration. Deadline depends on the book's publication date. Books in English: March 15, June 1, or August 7. Books in French: March 15 or July 15. Prize: Each laureate receives $25,000; non-winning finalists receive $1,000.

EZRA JACK KEATS/KERLAN MEMORIAL FELLOWSHIP

113 Elmer L. Andersen Library, 222 21st Ave. S., University of Minnesota, Minneapolis MN 55455. **E-mail:** clrc@tc.umn.edu. **Website:** http://special.lib.umn.edu/clrc/. **Contact:** Lisa Von Drasek, curator. This fellowship from the Ezra Jack Keats Foundation will provide $1,500 to a "talented writer and/or illustrator of children's books who wishes to use the Kerlan Collection for the furtherance of his or her artistic development." Special consideration will be given to someone who would find it difficult to finance a visit to the Kerlan Collection. The Ezra Jack Keats Fellowship recipient will receive transportation costs and a per diem allotment. See website for application deadline and for digital application materials. For paper copies of the application send a large (6×9 or 9×12) SAE with 97¢ postage.

KENTUCKY BLUEGRASS AWARD

Northern Kentucky University, 405 Steely Library, Nunn Drive, Highland Heights KY 41099. (859)572-6620. **Website:** kba.nku.edu. The Kentucky Bluegrass Award is a student choice program. The KBA promotes and encourages Kentucky students in kindergarten through grade 12 to read a variety of quality literature. All Kentucky public and private schools, as well as public libraries, are welcome to participate in the program. To nominate a book, see the website for form and details. Each year, a KBA committee for each grade category chooses the books for the four Master Lists (K-2, 3-5, 6-8 and 9-12). Students read books from the appropriate Master Lists and choose their favorite which they indicate on a ballot. All the ballots are counted and the results are transferred to an online tally sheet which is submitted to the KBA by the volunteer on-site, teacher or librarian coordinator. A winner is declared for each level.

THE VICKY METCALF AWARD FOR CHILDREN'S LITERATURE

The Writers' Trust of Canada, 90 Richmond St. E., Suite 200, Toronto ON M5C 1P1 Canada. (416)504-8222. **Fax:** (416)504-9090. **E-mail:** info@writerstrust.com. **Website:** www.writerstrust.com. **Contact:** Amanda Hopkins, program coordinator. "The Metcalf Award is presented to a Canadian writer for a body of work in children's literature at The Writers' Trust Awards event held in Toronto each Fall. Open to Canadian citizens and permanent residents only."

MUNICIPAL CHAPTER OF TORONTO IODE JEAN THROOP BOOK AWARD

40 Orchard View Blvd., Suite 219, Toronto ON M4R 1B9 Canada. (416)925-5078. **Fax:** (416)925-5127. **E-mail:** ioedtoronto@bellnet.ca. **Website:** www.bookcentre.ca/awards/iode_book_award_municipal_chapter_toronto. **Contact:** Jennifer Werry, contest director. The award-winner must be a Canadian citizen, resident in Toronto or the surrounding area, and the book must be published in Canada. Since 1974 the Municipal Chapter of Toronto IODE has presented an award intended to encourage the publication of books for children between the ages of 6 and 12 years. Deadline: November 1. Prize: Award and cash prize of $2,000. Judged by a selected committee.

HELEN KEATING OTT AWARD FOR OUTSTANDING CONTRIBUTION TO CHILDREN'S LITERATURE

10157 SW Barbur Blvd. #102C, Portland OR 97219. (503)244-6919. **Fax:** (503)977-3734. **E-mail:** csla@worldaccessnet.com. **Website:** www.cslainfo.org. **Contact:** Jeri Baker, chair of committee; Judy Janzen, administrator of CSLA. Annual award. "This award is given to a person or organization that has made a significant contribution to promoting high moral and ethical values through children's literature." Recipient is honored in July during the conference. Awards certificate of recognition, the awards banquet, and one-night's stay in the hotel. "A nomination for an award may be made by anyone. An application form is available by contacting Judy Janzen. Elements of creativity and innovation will be given high priority by the judges." "A detailed description of the reasons for thenomination should be given, accompanied by-

documentary evidence of accomplishment. The nominator should give his or her name, address, telephone number, e-mail address and a brief explanation of his or her knowledge of the individual's efforts. Elements of creativity and innovation will be given high priority." "Applications should include at least two examples of the your work (published or unpublished, 30 pages maximum) and a short biographical note including a description of your current and anticipated work. Also please indicate what you will work on while attending the Blue Mountain residency. Please send three copies of these writing samples. Samples will not be returned."

PATERSON PRIZE FOR BOOKS FOR YOUNG PEOPLE

The Poetry Center at Passaic County Community College, One College Blvd., Paterson NJ 07505. (973)523-6085. **Fax:** (973)523-6085. **E-mail:** mgillan@pccc.edu. **Website:** www.pccc.edu/poetry. **Contact:** Maria Mazziotti Gillan, executive director. Award for a book published in the previous year in each age category (Pre-K-Grade 3, Grades 4-6, Grades 7-12). Postmark deadline March 15. Prize: $500.

THE KATHERINE PATERSON PRIZE FOR YOUNG ADULT AND CHILDREN'S WRITING

Hunger Mountain, Vermont College of Fine Arts, 36 College St., Montpelier VT 05602. (802)828-8517. **E-mail:** hungermtn@vcfa.edu. **Website:** www.hungermtn.org. **Contact:** Miciah Bay Gault, editor. The annual Katherine Paterson Prize for Young Adult and Children's Writing offers $1,000 and publication in *Hunger Mountain*; 3 runners-up receive $100 and are also published. Submit young adult or middle grade mss, and writing for younger children, short stories, picture books, or novel excerpts, under 10,000 words. Guidelines available on website. "An annual prize for Young Adult and Children's Literature. A chance for your YA and Children's Lit to be read by Hunger Mountain editors and guest judges." Deadline: June 30. Prize: $1,000 and publication for the first place winner; $100 each and publication for the three category winners.

PEN/PHYLLIS NAYLOR WORKING WRITER FELLOWSHIP

PEN American Center, 588 Broadway, Suite 303, New York NY 10012. **E-mail:** awards@pen.org. **Website:** www.pen.org. **Contact:** Nick Burd, awards program director. Offered annually to an author of children's or young-adult fiction. Candidates have published at least two novels for children or young adults which have been received warmly by literary critics, but have not generated suficient income to support the author. Writers must be nominated by an editor or fellow author. See website for eligibility and nomination guidelines. The Fellowship has been developed to help writers whose work is of high literary caliber but who have not yet attracted a broad readership. The Fellowship is designed to assist a writer at a crucial moment in his or her career to complete a book-length work-in-progress. Deadline: February 15. Prize: $5,000.

PLEASE TOUCH MUSEUM BOOK AWARD

Memorial Hall in Fairmount Park, 4231 Avenue of the Republic, Philadelphia PA 19131. (215)578-5153. **Fax:** (215)578-5171. **E-mail:** hboyd@pleasetouchmuseum.org. **Website:** www.pleasetouchmuseum.org. **Contact:** Heather Boyd. "To be eligible for consideration, a book must: (1) Be distinguished in text, illustration, and ability to explore and clarify an idea for young children (ages 7 and under); (2) be published within the last year by an American publisher; and (3) be by an American author and/or illustrator." Books must be published between September and August of preceeding year. This prestigious award has recognized and encouraged the publication of high quality books for young children. The award is given to books that are imaginative, exceptionally illustrated and help foster a child's life-long love of reading. Deadline: October 1. Judged by a panel of volunteer educators, artists, booksellers and librarians in conjunction with museum staff.

POCKETS FICTION-WRITING CONTEST

P.O. Box 340004, Nashville TN 37203-0004. (615)340-7333. **Fax:** (615)340-7267. **E-mail:** pockets@upperroom.org. **Website:** www.pockets.upperroom.org. **Contact:** Lynn W. Gilliam, senior editor. Designed for 6- to 12-year-olds, *Pockets* magazine offers wholesome devotional readings that teach about God's love and presence in life. The content includes fiction, scripture stories, puzzles and games, poems, recipes, colorful pictures, activities, and scripture readings. Freelance submissions of stories, poems, recipes, puzzles and games, and activities are welcome. Stories should be 750-1,000 words. Multiple submissions are permitted. Past winners are ineligible. The primary purpose of Pockets is to help children grow in their relationship with God and to claim the good news of the gospel of Jesus Christ by applying it to their daily lives. Pockets espouses respect for all human beings and for God's creation. It regards a child's faith journey as an integral part of all of life and sees prayer as undergirding that journey. Deadline: November 1. Prize: $500 and publication in magazine.

QUILL AND SCROLL INTERNATIONAL WRITING AND PHOTO CONTEST, AND BLOGGING COMPETITION

School of Journalism, Univ. of Iowa, 100 Adler Journalism Bldg., Iowa City IA 52242-2004. (319)335-3457. **Fax:** (319)335-3989. **E-mail:** quill-scroll@uiowa.edu. **E-mail:** vanessa-shelton@uiowa.edu. **Website:** quillandscroll.org. **Contact:** Vanessa Shelton, contest director. Entries must have been published in a high school or profesional newspaper or website during the previous year, and must be the work of a currently enrolled high school student. Open to students. Annual contest. Previously published submissions only. Submissions made by the author or school newspaper adviser. Deadline: February 5. Prize: Winners will receive *Quill and Scroll*'s National Award Gold Key and, if seniors, are eligible to apply for one of the scholarships offered by *Quill and Scroll*. All winning entries are automatically eligible for the International Writing and Photo Sweepstakes Awards. Engraved plaque awarded to sweepstakes winners.

TOMÁS RIVERA MEXICAN AMERICAN CHILDREN'S BOOK AWARD

Dr. Jesse Gainer, Texas State University, 601 University Drive, San Marcos TX 78666-4613. (512)245-2357. **Website:** http://www.education.txstate.edu/about/Map-Directions.html. **Contact:** Dr. Jesse Gainer, award director. Texas State University College of Education developed the Tomas Rivera Mexican American Children's Book Award to honor authors and illustrators who create literature that depicts the Mexican American experience. The award was established in 1995 and was named in honor of Dr. Tomas Rivera, a distinguished alumnus of Texas State University. The book will be written for children and young adults (0-16 years). The text and illustrations will be of highest quality. The portrayal/representations of Mexican Americans will be accurate and engaging, avoid stereotypes, and reflect rich characterization. The book may be fiction or non-fiction. See website for more details and directions. Deadline: November 1.

SCBWI MAGAZINE MERIT AWARDS

8271 Beverly Blvd., Los Angeles CA 90048. **Website:** www.scbwi.org. **Contact:** Stephanie Gordon, award coordinator. Purpose of the award: "to recognize outstanding original magazine work for young people published during that year and having been written or illustrated by members of SCBWI." Previously published submissions only. Entries must be submitted between January 1 and December 15 of the year of publication. For rules and procedures see website. No entry fee. Must be a SCBWI member. Awards plaques and honor certificates for each of 4 categories (fiction, nonfiction, illustration, poetry). Judging by a magazine editor and two "full" SCBWI members. "All magazine work for young people by an SCBWI member—writer, artist or photographer—is eligible during the year of original publication. In the case of co-authored work, both authors must be SCBWI members. Members must submit their own work." Requirements for entrants: 4 copies each of the published work and proof of publication (may be contents page) showing the name of the magazine and the date of issue. The SCBWI is a professional organization of writers and illustrators and others interested in children's literature. Membership is open to the general public at large

SYDNEY TAYLOR BOOK AWARD

Association of Jewish Libraries, P.O. Box 1118, Teaneck NJ 07666. (212)725-5359. **E-mail:** chair@sydneytaylorbookaward.org; heidi@cbiboca.org. **Website:** www.sydneytaylorbookaward.org. **Contact:** Barbara Bietz, chair. Offered annually for work published during the current year. "Given to distinguished contributions to Jewish literature for children. One award for younder readers, one for older readers, and one for teens." Publishers submit books. Guidelines on website. Awards certificate, cash award, and gold or silver seals for cover of winning book. December 31, "but we cannot guarantee that books received after December 1 will be considered.".

☺ TD CANADIAN CHILDREN'S LITERATURE AWARD

The Canadian Children's Book Centre, 40 Orchard View Blvd., Suite 217, Toronto ON M4R 1B9 Canada. (416)975-0010, ext. 222. **Fax:** (416)975-8970. **Website:** www.bookcentre.ca. **Contact:** Meghan Howe. "All books, in any genre, written and illustrated by Canadians and for children ages 1-12 are eligible. Only books first published in Canada are eligible for submission. Books must be published between January 1 and December 31 of the previous calendar year. Open to Canadian citizens and/or permanent residents of Canada." To honour the most distinguished book of the year for young people in both English and French. Submission deadline: February 8. Prize: Prizes: Two prizes of $30,000, 1 for English, 1 for French. $10,000 will be divided among the Honour Book English titles and Honour Book French titles, to a maximum of 4; $2,500 shall go to each of the publishers of the English and French grand-prize winning books for promotion and publicity.

TIPS "Please visit website for submission guidelines and eligibility criteria, as well as specific submission deadline."

VEGETARIAN ESSAY CONTEST

The Vegetarian Resource Group, P.O. Box 1463, Baltimore MD 21203. (410)366-VEGE. **Fax:** (410)366-8804. **E-mail:** vrg@vrg.org. **Website:** www.vrg.org. A 2-3 page essay on any aspect of vegetarianism. Entrants should base their paper on interviewing, research, and/or personal opinon. You need not be a vegetarian to enter. Three different entry categories: age 14-18; age 9-13; and age 8 and under. Prize: $50 savings bond.

RITA WILLIAMS YOUNG ADULT PROSE PRIZE

Soul-Making Keats Literary Competition, The Webhallow House, 1544 Sweetwood Drive, Broadmoor Village CA 94015-2029. **E-mail:** pennobhill@aol. com. **Website:** www.soulmakingcontest.us. **Contact:** Eileen Malone. The Soul-Making Keats Literary Competition was started in 1992 by Eileen Malone as a poetry contest to further enhance the outreach of The Source Center for Spiritual Development and Wholeness which was founded by Janice Farrell, Regional Coordinator for Spiritual Directors International. All prose works must be typed, double-spaced, page numbered, and paper-clipped. Please indicate word count on title page Grades 9-12 or equivalent age. Up to 3,000 words in story, essay, journal entry, creative nonfiction or memoir. Deadline: November 30 (postmarked). Prize: $100 for first place; $50 for second place; $25 for third place. Judged by Rita Wiliams, an Emmy-award winning investigative reporter with KTVU-TV in Oakland, California.

TIPS "This contest is for young adult writers, high school age writers; no adults writing for children."

PAUL A. WITTY SHORT STORY AWARD

Executive Office, International Reading Association, International Reading Association, 800 Barksdale Rd., P.O. Box 8139, Newark DE 19714-8139. (302)731-1600. **Fax:** (302)731-1057. **E-mail:** committees@reading.org. **Website:** www.reading.org. Offered to reward author of an original short story published for the first time in a periodical for children. Write for guidelines or download from website. Deadline: November 15. Prize: $1,000 stipend.

ALICE WOOD MEMORIAL OHIOANA AWARD FOR CHILDREN'S LITERATURE

Ohioana Library Association, 274 E. First Ave., Suite 300, Columbus OH 43201. (614)466-3831. **Fax:** (614)728-6974. **E-mail:** ohioana@ohioana.org. **Website:** www.ohioana.org. **Contact:** Linda R. Hengst. Offered to an author whose body of work has made, and continues to make, a significant contribution to literature for children or young adults, and through their work as a writer, teacher, administrator, and community member, interest in children's literature has been encouraged and children have become involved with reading. Nomination forms for SASE. Recipient must have been born in Ohio or lived in Ohio at least 5 years. Guidelines for SASE. Accepts inquiries by phone and e-mail. Results announced in August or September. Winners notified by letter in May. For contest results, call or e-mail Ohioana Library: Linda Hengst, executive director. Deadline: December 31. Prize: $1,000.

WORK-IN-PROGRESS GRANT

Society of Children's Book Writers and Illustrators (SCBWI), 8271 Beverly Blvd., Los Angeles CA 90048. (323)782-1010. **E-mail:** scbwi@scbwi.org. **Website:** www.scbwi.org. Four grants—one designated specifically for a contemporary novel for young people, one for nonfiction, one for an unpublished writer, one general fiction—to assist SCBWI members in the completion of a specific project. Open to SCBWI members only. Applications received only between February 15 and March 15.

☺ YOUNG ADULT CANADIAN BOOK AWARD

1150 Morrison Dr., Suite 400, Ottawa ON K2H 8S9 Canada. (613)232-9625. **Fax:** (613)563-9895. **Website:** www.cla.ca. **Contact:** Barb Janicek. This award recognizes an author of an outstanding English language Canadian book which appeals to young adults between the ages of 13 and 18. To be eligible for consideration, the following must apply; it must be a work of fiction (novel, collection of short stories, or graphic novel), the title must be a Canadian publication in either hardcover or paperback, and the author must be a Canadian citizen or landed immigrant. The award is given annually, when merited, at the Canadian Library Association's annual conference. Established in 1980 by the Young Adult Caucus of the Saskatchewan Library Association. **Deadline:** December 1. **Prize:** $1,000.

GENERAL

AUSTRALIAN CHRISTIAN BOOK OF THE YEAR AWARD

Australian Christian Literature Society, c/o SPCK-Australia, P.O. Box 198, Forest Hill Victoria 3131 Australia. **E-mail:** acls@spcka.org.au. **Website:** www.spcka.org.au. **Contact:** Book of the Year coordinator. The Australian Christian Book of the Year Award is given annually to an original book written by an Australian citizen normally resident in Australia and published by an Australian publisher. The award recognises and encourages excellence in Australian Christian writing. **Deadline:** March 31. **Prize:** $2,500 (AUD) and a framed certificate.

JAMIE CAT CALLAN HUMOR PRIZE

Category in the Soul Making Keats Literary Competition, The Webhallow House, 1544 Sweetwood Dr., Broadmoor Village CA 94015-2029. **E-mail:** EileenMalone@comcast.net. **Website:** www.soulmakingcontest.us. **Contact:** Eileen Malone. Any form, 2,500 words or less. One piece per entry. Previously published material is accepted. Open annually to any writer. "Make me laugh out loud." **Deadline:** November 30. **Prize:** First Place: $100; Second Place: $50; Third Place: $25. Judged by Jamie Cat Callan.

THE FOUNTAINHEAD ESSAY CONTEST

The Ayn Rand Institute, P.O. Box 57044, Irvine CA 92619-7044. **E-mail:** essay@aynrand.org. **Website:** www.aynrand.org/contests. "Offered annually to encourage analytical thinking and excellence in writing, and to expose students to the philosophic ideas of Ayn Rand. For information contact your English teacher or guidance counselor, or visit our website. Length: 800-1,600 words. Open to 11th and 12th graders." **Deadline:** April 26. **Prize:** 1st Place: $10,000; 2nd Place (5): $2,000; 3rd Place (10): $1,000; Finalist (45): $100; Semifinalist (175): $50.

INDEPENDENT PUBLISHER BOOK AWARDS

Jenkins Group/Independent Publisher Online, 1129 Woodmere Ave., Ste. B, Traverse City MI 49686. (231)933-4954, ext. 1011. **Fax:** (231)933-0448. **E-mail:** jimb@bookpublishing.com. **Website:** www.independentpublisher.com. **Contact:** Jim Barnes. "The Independent Publisher Book Awards were conceived as a broad-based, unaffiliated awards program open to all members of the independent publishing industry. The staff at *Independent Publisher* magazine saw the need to bring increased recognition to the thousands of exemplary independent, university, and self-published titles produced each year." The IPPY Awards reward those who exhibit the courage, innovation, and creativity to bring about change in the world of publishing. Independent spirit and expertise comes from publishers of all areas and budgets, and we judge books with that in mind. Entries will be accepted in 67 categories, visit website to see details. Open to any published writer. **Deadline:** March 16. **Prize:** Gold, silver and bronze medals for each category; foil seals available to all. Judged by a panel of experts representing the fields of design, writing, bookselling, library, and reviewing.

NACUSA YOUNG COMPOSERS' COMPETITION

Box 49256 Barrington Station, Los Angeles CA 90049 United States. (541)765-2406. **E-mail:** nacusa@music-usa.org. **Website:** www.music-usa.org/nacusa. **Contact:** Greg Steinke. Encourages the composition of new American concert hall music. **Deadline:** October 30. **Prize:** 1st Prize: $400; 2nd Prize: $100; and possible Los Angeles performances. Applications are judged by a committee of experienced NACUSA composer members.

OHIOANA WALTER RUMSEY MARVIN GRANT

Ohioana Library Association, 274 E. First Ave., Suite 300, Columbus OH 43201. (614)466-3831. **Fax:** (614)728-6974. **E-mail:** ohioana@ohioana.org. **Website:** www.ohioana.org. **Contact:** Linda Hengst. Award "to encourage young, unpublished writers 30 years of age or younger." Competition for short stories or novels in progress. Open to unpublished authors born in Ohio or who have lived in Ohio for a minimum of 5 years. Must be 30 years of age or younger. Guidelines for SASE or on website. Winner notified in May or June. Award given in October. Up to 6 pieces of prose may be submitted; maximum 60 pages, minimum 10 pages double-spaced, 12-point type. Entries must be unpublished. Deadline: January 31. Prize: $1,000.

PULITZER PRIZES

The Pulitzer Prize Board, Columbia University, 709 Pulitzer Hall, 2950 Broadway, New York NY 10027. (212)854-3841. **E-mail:** pulitzer@.pulitzer.org. **Website:** www.pulitzer.org. **Contact:** Sig Gissler, administrator. Journalism in U.S. newspapers and news websites (published daily or weekly), and in letters, drama, and music by Americans. Deadline: December 31 (music); January 25 (journalism); June 15 and October 15 (letters); December 31 (drama). Prize: $10,000.

PUSHCART PRIZE

Pushcart Press, P.O. Box 380, Wainscott NY 11975. (631)324-9300. **Website:** www.pushcartprize.com. **Contact:** Bill Henderson. Published every year since 1976, The Pushcart Prize - Best of the Small Presses series "is the most honored literary project in America. Hundreds of presses and thousands of writers of short stories, poetry and essays have been represented in the pages of our annual collections." Little magazine and small book press editors (print or online) may make up to six nominations from their year's publicatoins by the deadline. The nominations may be any combination of poetry, short fiction, essays or literary whatnot. Editors may nominate self-contained portions of books — for instance, a chapter from a novel. Deadline: December 1.

DAVID RAFFELOCK AWARD FOR PUBLISHING EXCELLENCE

National Writers Association, 10940 S. Parker Rd., #508, Parker CO 80134. (303)841-0246. **E-mail:** natlwritersassn@hotmail.com. **Website:** www.nationalwriters.com. **Contact:** Sandy Whelchel. "Contest is offered annually for books published the previous year." Published works only. Open to any writer. Guidelines for SASE, by e-mail or on website. Winners announced in June at the NWAF conference and notified by mail or phone. List of winners available for SASE or visit website. Its purpose is to assist published authors in marketing their works and to reward outstanding published works. Deadline: May 15. Prize: Publicity tour, including airfare, valued at $5,000.

TEXAS INSTITUTE OF LETTERS AWARD FOR MOST SIGNIFICANT SCHOLARLY BOOK

The Texas Institute of Letters, P.O. Box 609, Round Rock TX 78680. **E-mail:** tilsecretary@yahoo.com. **Website:** http://texasinstituteofletters.org. Offered annually for submissions published January 1-December 31 of previous year to recognize the writer of the book making the most important contribution to knowledge. Writer must have been born in Texas, have lived in the state at least 2 consecutive years at some time, or the subject matter of the book should be associated with the state. See website for guidelines. Deadline: Visit website for exact date. Prize: $2.500.

FRED WHITEHEAD AWARD FOR DESIGN OF A TRADE BOOK

Texas Institute of Letters, P.O. Box 609, Round Rock TX 78680. **E-mail:** tilsecretary@yahoo.com. **Website:** www.texasinstituteofletters.org. Offered annually for the best design for a trade book. Open to Texas residents or those who have lived in Texas for 2 consecutive years. See website for guidelines. **Deadline: early January**; see website for exact date. Prize: $750.

☺ THE WRITERS' TRUST ENGEL/FINDLEY AWARD

The Writers' Trust of Canada, 90 Richmond St. E., Suite 200, Toronto ON M5C 1P1 Canada. (416)504-8222. **Fax:** (416)504-9090. **E-mail:** info@writerstrust.com. **Website:** www.writerstrust.com. **Contact:** Amanda Hopkins. "The Writers' Trust Engel/Findley Award is presented annually at The Writers' Trust Awards Event, held in Toronto each fall, to a Canadian writer for a body of work in hope of continued contribution to the richness of Canadian literature. Open to Canadian citizens and permanent residents only." Prize: $25,000.

JOURNALISM

THE AMERICAN LEGION FOURTH ESTATE AWARD

The American Legion, The American Legion, 700 N. Pennsylvania St., Indianapolis IN 46204. (317)630-1253. **E-mail:** pr@legion.org. **Website:** www.legion.org/presscenter/fourthestate. Offered annually for journalistic works published the previous calendar year. Subject matter must deal with a topic or issue of national interest or concern. Entry must include cover letter explaining entry, and any documentation or evidence of the entry's impact on the community, state, or nation. No printed entry form. Guidelines for SASE or on website. Deadline: February 18. Prize: $2,000 stipend to defray expenses of recipient accepting the award at The American Legion National Convention in August. Members of The National Public Relations Commission of The American Legion.

AMY WRITING AWARDS

The Amy Foundation, P.O. Box 16091, Lansing MI 48901. (517)323-6233. **Fax:** (517)321-2572. **E-mail:** amyfoundtn@aol.com. **Website:** www.amyfound.org. "Offered annually to recognize creative, skillful writing that applies biblical principles. Submitted articles must be published in a secular, non-religious publication (either printed or online) and must be reinforced with at least one passage of scripture. The article must have been published between January 1 and December 31 of the current calendar year." The article must have been published in a mainstream, non-religious publication, as determined by the Awards Panel. The article must contain at least one passage of scripture. Deadline: January 31. Prize: 1st Prize: $10,000, 2nd Prize: $5,000; 3rd Prize: $4,000; 4th Prize: $3,000; 5th Prize: $2,000; and 10 prizes of $1,000.

INVESTIGATIVE JOURNALISM GRANT

Fund For Investigative Journalism, Fund for Investigative Journalism, 529 14th Street NW, 13th Floor, Washington DC 20045. (202662-7564. **Fax:** (301)576-0804. **E-mail:** fundfij@gmail.com. **Website:** www.fij.org. **Contact:** Sandy Bergo, Executive Director. Offered 3 times/year for original investigative newspaper and magazine stories, radio and TV documentaries, books and media criticism. Guidelines online or by e-mail. The fund also offers an annual $25,000 FIJ Book Prize in November for the best book chosen by the board during the year. See website for details on applying for a grant. Deadlines: March 11, and again in June, September, and December. Prize: Grants of $500-10,000. (Average $5,000.)

SCIENCE IN SOCIETY AWARDS

National Association of Science Writers, Inc., P.O. Box 7905, Berkeley CA 94707. (510)647-9500. **E-mail:** director@nasw.org. **Website:** www.nasw.org. **Contact:** Tinsley Davis. Offered annually for investigative or interpretive reporting about the sciences and their impact on society. Categories: books, commentary and opinions, science reporting, and science reporting with a local or regional focus. Material may be a single article or broadcast, or a series. Works must have been first published or broadcast in North America between June 1 and May 31 of the previous year. Deadline: February 1. Prize: $2,500, and a certificate of recognition in each category.

☼ SOVEREIGN AWARD

The Jockey Club of Canada, P.O. Box 66, Station B, Etobicoke ON M9W 5K9 Canada. (416)675-7756. **Fax:** (416)675-6378. **E-mail:** jockeyclub@bellnet.ca. **Website:** www.jockeyclubcanada.com. **Contact:** Stacie Roberts, exec. dir. The Jockey Club of Canada was founded in 1973 by E.P. Taylor to serve as the international representative of the Canadian Thoroughbred industry and to promote improvements to Thoroughbred racing and breeding, both in Canada and internationally. Submissions for these media awards must be of Canadian Thoroughbred racing or breeding content. They must have appeared in a media outlet recognized by The Jockey Club of Canada. See website for eligibility details and guidelines. Deadline: December 31.

TRANSLATION

DER-HOVANESSIAN PRIZE

New England Poetry Club, 654 Green St., No. 2, Cambridge MA 02139. **E-mail:** contests@nepoetryclub.org. **Website:** www.nepoetryclub.org. **Contact:** NEPC contest coordinator. For a translation from any language into English. Send a copy of the original. Funded by John Mahtesian. "Contest open to members and nonmembers. Poems should be typed and submitted in duplicate with author's name, address, phone, and e-mail address of writer on only 1 copy. Label poems with contest name. Entries should be sent by regular mail only. Entries should be original, unpublished poems in English. No poem should be entered in more than 1 contest, nor have won a previous contest." Deadline: May 31. Prize: $200. Judges are well-known poets and sometimes winners of previous NEPC contests.

SOEURETTE DIEHL FRASER AWARD FOR BEST TRANSLATION OF A BOOK

P.O. Box 609, Round Rock TX 78680. **E-mail:** tilsecretary@yahoo.com. **Website:** http://texasinstituteofletters.org. Offered every 2 years to recognize the best translation of a literary book into English. Translator must have been born in Texas or have lived in the state for at least 2 consecutive years at some time. Deadline: early January; see website for exact date. Prize: $1,000.

THE FRENCH-AMERICAN AND THE FLORENCE GOULD FOUNDATIONS TRANSLATION PRIZES

28 W. 44th St., Suite 1420, New York NY 10036. (646)588-6786. **E-mail:** ebriet@frenchamerican.org. **Website:** www.frenchamerican.org. French-American Foundation, 28 W. 44th St., Suite 1420, New York NY 10036. (212)829-8800. **Fax:** (212)829-8810. **E-mail:** earcher@frenchamerican.org. **Website:** www.frenchamerican.org. **Contact:** Emma Archer. Annual contest to "promote French literature in the United States, to give translators and their craft more visibility, and encouraging the American publishers who bring significant French texts to the English reading audience." Entries must have been published the year before the prizes are awarded. **Deadline:** December 31. Judged by a jury committee made up of translators, writers, and scholars in French literature and culture. **Contact:** Eugenie Briet. Annual contest to promote French literature in the United States. Entries must have been published for the first time in the United States between January 1 and December 31, of the previous year. To "give translators and their craft more visibility, and to encourage the American publishers who bring significant French texts to the English reading audience." December 31. Prize: "The foundation presents a $10,000 cash award for the best English translation of French in both fiction and nonfiction. Jury committee made up of translators, writers, and scholars in French literature and culture.

✪ GOVERNOR GENERAL'S LITERARY AWARD FOR TRANSLATION

Canada Council for the Arts, 350 Albert St., P.O. Box 1047, Ottawa ON K1P 5V8 Canada. (613)566-4414, ext. 5573. **Fax:** (613)566-4410. **Website:** www.canadacouncil.ca/prizes/ggla. Offered for the best English-language and the best French-language work of translation by a Canadian. Publishers submit titles for consideration Deadline depends on the book's publication date. Books in English: March 15, June 1, or August 7. Books in French: March 15 or July 15. Prize: Each laureate receives $25,000; non-winning finalists receive $1,000.

PEN TRANSLATION PRIZE

PEN American Center, 588 Broadway, Suite 303, New York NY 10012. (212)334-1660, ext. 108. **Fax:** (212)334-2181. **E-mail:** awards@pen.org. **Contact:** Literary Awards coordinator. Offered for a literary book-length translation into English published in the calendar year. No technical, scientific, or reference books. Publishers, agents, or translators may submit 3 copies of each eligible title. All eligible titles must have been published in the US. Self-published books are not eligible. 1) Pay the $50 entry fee online and proceed to checkout. If paying by check, skip to step 2. 2) Fill out the online submission form and click "Submit Form." 3) Mail 3 copies of the candidate's book, your printed submission form, and proof of online payment or a check. Nominations must be received between October 1 and February 1. Early submissions are strongly recommended. Prize: $3,000.

LOIS ROTH AWARD FOR A TRANSLATION OF A LITERARY WORK

Modern Language Association, 26 Broadway, 3rd Floor, New York NY 10004. (646)576-5141. **Fax:** (646)458-0030. **E-mail:** awards@mla.org. **Website:** www.mla.org. Offered every 2 years (odd years) for an outstanding translation into English of a book-length literary work published the previous year. Translators need not be members of the MLA. Deadline: April 1. Prize: A cash award and a certificate to be presented at the Modern Language Association's annual convention in January.

ALDO AND JEANNE SCAGLIONE PRIZE FOR A TRANSLATION OF A LITERARY WORK

Modern Language Association, 26 Broadway, 3rd Floor, New York NY 10004-1789. (646)576-5141. **Fax:** (646)458-0030. **E-mail:** awards@mla.org. **Website:** www.mla.org. **Contact:** Coordinator of Book Prizes. The Committee on Honors and Awards of the Modern Language Association invites translators and publishers to compete for the eleventh Aldo and Jeanne Scaglione Prize for a Translation of a Literary Work. The prize, established by the Aldo and Jeanne Scaglione Endowment Fund, is awarded each even-numbered year for an outstanding translation into English of a book-length literary work. To enter a translation into the competition, authors or publishers should send six copies along with brief biographical and professional data about translator(s); a total of 12–15 pages of the text in its original language taken from the beginning, middle, and end of the work; and a letter identifying the work to the Scaglione Prize. Deadline: April 1.

Prize: A cash award and a certificate to be presented at the Modern Language Association's annual convention in January.

POETRY

ACORN-PLANTOS AWARD FOR PEOPLES POETRY

Acorn-Plantos Award Committee, 36 Sunset Ave., Hamilton ON L8R 1V6 Canada. **E-mail:** jeffseff@allstream.net. **Contact:** Jeff Seffinga. "Annual contest for work that appeared in print in the previous calender year. This award is given to the Canadian poet who best (through the publication of a book of poems) exemplifies populist or peoples poetry in the tradition of Milton Acorn, Ted Plantos, et al. Work may be entered by the poet or the publisher; the award goes to the poet. Entrants must submit 5 copies of each title. Poet must be a citizen of Canada or a landed immigrant. Publisher need not be Canadian." Deadline: June 30. Prize: $500 (CDN) and a medal. Judged by a panel of poets in the tradition who are not entered in the current year.

THE AMERICAN POETRY JOURNAL BOOK PRIZE

P.O. Box 2080, Aptos CA 95001-2080. **E-mail:** editor@americanpoetryjournal.com. **Website:** www.americanpoetryjournal.com. The American Poetry Journal Book Prize awards $500 and book publication. Submit 50-65 paginated pages of poetry, table of contents, acknowledgments, bio, and e-mail address (for results). No SASE required; mss will be recycled. Guidelines available on website. **Entry fee:** $25. Make checks payable to Dream Horse Press, **Deadline:** February 28 (check website for updates). Winners of previous contests were Lisa Lewis, and Mark Conway, and Quinn Latimer. Both free and formal verse styles are welcome. Multiple submissions are acceptable. The American Poetry Journal Book Prize awards $500 and book publication. Deadline: February 28. Prize: $1,000 and 20 published copies. All entries will be considered for publication.

ANNUAL VENTURA COUNTY WRITERS CLUB POETRY CONTEST WITH TWO DIVISIONS FOR YOUNG POETS

Ventura County Writers Club Poetry Contest, P.O. Box 3373, Thousand Oaks CA 91362. (805)524-6970. **E-mail:** info@venturacountywriters.com. **Website:** www.venturacountywriters.com. **Contact:** Kate Sex-

ton, president. The Ventura County Writers Club announced its twelfth annual Poetry Contest, which includes an exciting Audio/Visual category to address more forms of poetry. The contest will continue its two youth categories for poets under 18: Division A is open to entrants ages 13 to 18; and, Division B is open to poets ages 12 and under. Poets 18 and older are invited to enter in the Adult category. The contest is open to poets worldwide as long as the poem is in English. For both print and electronic entries, checks should be made payable to Ventura County Writers Club or VCWC and mail to: Ventura County Writers Club Poetry Contest, P. O. Box 3373 Thousand Oaks, CA 91362. Email: VenturaCountyWriters@yahoo.com with 'Poetry Contest' in the subject line. Send one poem per attachment. Send cover sheet in separate attachment with information as shown above. Include a cover sheet copy with your entry fee(s). Deadline: February 15. Prize: The adult and A/V categories will award $100 for first place, $75 for second and $50 for third place. The two youth categories will award $50 for first place, $35 for second and $25 for third place.

ANNUAL WORLD HAIKU COMPETITION & ANNUAL WORLD TANKA CONTEST

P.O. Box 17331, Arlington VA 22216. **E-mail:** lpezinesubmissions@gmail.com. **Website:** http://lyricalpassionpoetry.yolasite.com. **Contact:** Raquel D. Bailey. Contest is open to all writers. Requires first rights for all previously unpublished works. "Promotes Japanese short form poetry." Deadline: November 30, 2012. (Dates are subject to change each year. See website for details). Prize: Monetary compensation and publication. Judged by experienced editors and award-winning writers from the contemporary writing community.

TIPS "E-mail and snail mail entries accepted."

THE PATRICIA BIBBY FIRST BOOK AWARD

Patricia Bibby Award, Tebot Bach, P.O. Box 7887, Huntington Beach CA 92615-7887. **E-mail:** mifanwy@tebotbach.org. **Website:** www.tebotbach.org. **Contact:** Mifanwy Kaiser. The Patricia Bibby First Book Award offers $1,000 and publication of a book-length poetry ms by Tebot Bach (see separate listing in Book/Chapbook Publishers). Open to "all poets writing in English who have not committed to publishing collections of poetry of 36 poems or more in editions of over 400 copies." Complete guidelines available by e-mail or on website. Deadline: October 31 (postmark). Prize: $1,000 and book will be published. Judged by Ralph Angel in 2013.

BINGHAMTON UNIVERSITY MILT KESSLER POETRY BOOK AWARD

Binghamton University Creative Writing Program, Department of English, General Literature, and Rhetoric, Library North Room 1149, Vestal Parkway East, P.O. Box 6000, Binghamton NY 13902-6000. (607)777-2713. **Fax:** (607)777-2408. **E-mail:** cwpro@binghamton.edu. **Website:** www2.binghamton.edu/english/creative-writing/binghamton-center-for-writers. **Contact:** Maria Mazziotti Gillan, creative writing program director. Offers annual award for a book of poetry judged best of those published during the previous year. Books must be 48 pages or more. Print on demand is acceptable but no self-published or vanity press work will be considered. Each book submitted must be accompanied by an application form available online. Poet or publisher may submit more than 1 book for prize consideration. Send 3 copies of each book. Deadline: March 1. Prize: $1,000.

BLUE MOUNTAIN ARTS/SPS STUDIOS POETRY CARD CONTEST

P.O. Box 1007, Boulder CO 80306. (303)449-0536. **Fax:** (303)447-0939. **E-mail:** poetrycontest@sps.com. **Website:** www.sps.com. "We're looking for original poetry that is rhyming or non-rhyming, although we find that non-rhyming poetry reads better. Poems may also be considered for possible publication on greeting cards or in book anthologies. Contest is offered biannually. Guidelines available online." Deadline: December 31 and June 30. Prize: 1st Place: $300; 2nd Place: $150; 3rd Place: $50. Blue Mountain Arts editorial staff.

THE FREDERICK BOCK PRIZE

Poetry, 61 W. Superior St., Chicago IL 60654. (312)787-7070. **Fax:** (312)787-6650. **E-mail:** editors@poetry-magazine.org. **Website:** www.poetryfoundation.org. Several prizes are awarded annually for the best work printed in *Poetry* during the preceding year. Only poems already published in the magazine are eligible for consideration, and no formal application is necessary. The winners are announced in the November issue. Upon acceptance, *Poetry* licenses exclusive worldwide first serial rights, including electronic rights, for publication, as well as non-exclusive rights to reprint, reuse, and archive the work, in any format, in perpetu-

ity. Copyright reverts to author upon first publication. Any writer may submit poems to *Poetry*. Prize: $500.

BOULEVARD EMERGING POETS CONTEST

PMB 325, 6614 Clayton Rd., Richmond Heights MO 63117. **E-mail:** kellyleavitt@boulevardmagazine.org. **Website:** www.boulevardmagazine.org. Annual Emerging Poets Contest offers $1,000 and publication in *Boulevard* (see separate listing in Magazines/Journals) for the best group of 3 poems by a poet who has not yet published a book of poetry with a nationally distributed press. "All entries will be considered for publication and payment at our regular rates." Submissions must be unpublished. Considers simultaneous submissions. Submit 3 poems, typed; may be a sequence or unrelated. On page one of first poem type poet's name, address, phone number, and titles of the 3 poems. Include ASP for notification of receipt of ms; mss will not be returned. Guidelines available on website. **Entry fee:** $15/group of 3 poems, $15 for each additional group of 3 poems; includes one-year subscription to *Boulevard*. Make checks payable to Boulevard. **Deadline:** June 1 (postmark). Judge: editors of *Boulevard* magazine. "No one editorially or financially affiliated with *Boulevard* may enter the contest." **Contact:** Kelly Leavitt, managing editor. Annual Emerging Poets Contest offers $1,000 and publication in *Boulevard* for the best group of 3 poems by a poet who has not yet published a book of poetry with a nationally distributed press. "All entries will be considered for publication and payment at our regular rates." Submissions must be unpublished. Considers simultaneous submissions. Submit 3 poems, typed; may be a sequence or unrelated. On page one of first poem type poet's name, address, phone number, and titles of the 3 poems. Deadline: June 1. Prize: $1,000 and publication.

BRICK ROAD POETRY BOOK CONTEST

Brick Road Poetry Press, Inc., P.O. Box 751, Columbus GA 31902. (706)649-3080. **Fax:** (706)649-3094. **E-mail:** editor@brickroadpoetrypress.com. **Website:** www.brickroadpoetrypress.com. **Contact:** Ron Self and Keith Badowski, co-editors/founders. Offers annual award. The 1st Prize winner will receive a publication contract with Brick Road Poetry Press, $1,000, and 25 copies of the printed book. The winning book will be published in both print and e-book formats. "We may also offer publication contracts to the top finalists." Submissions must be unpublished as a collection, but individual poems may have been previously published elsewhere. Submit 70-100 pages of poetry. Guidelines available by e-mail or online. Competition receives 150 entries/year. Judged by Ron Self and Keith Badowski. Winners notified February 15. Copies of winning books available for $15.95. "The mission of Brick Road Poetry Press is to publish and promote poetry that entertains, amuses, edifies and surprises a wide audience of appreciative readers. We are not qualified to judge who deserves to be published, so we concentrate on publishing what we enjoy. Our preference is for poetry geared toward dramatizing the human experience in a language rich with sensory image and metaphor, recognizing that poetry can be, at one and the same time, both familiar as the perspiration of daily labor and outrageous as a carnival sideshow." Deadline: November 1.

TIPS "The best way to discover all that poetry can be and to expand the limits of your own poetry is to read expansively."

BRIGHT HILL PRESS POETRY CHAPBOOK COMPETITION

Bright Press Hill & Literary Center, P.O. Box 193, 94 Church St., Treadwell NY 13846. (607)829-5055. E-mail: brighthillpress@stny.rr.com. **Website:** www.brighthillpress.org. The annual Bright Hill Press Chapbook Award offers $300, publication of a chapbook-length ms, and 25 author's copies. Guidelines available for SASE, by e-mail, or on website. Collection of original poetry, 48064 pages, single spaced, one poem to a page (no name) with table of contents. Manuscript must be submitted in Times New Roman, 12 pt. type only. No illustrations, no cover suggestions. Bio and acknowledgments of poems that have been previously published should be included in Comments Box. See website for more details, and information on submitting a hard copy. Deadline: December 15. Prize: a publication contract with Bright Hill Press and $1,000, publication in print format, and 30 copies of the printed book.

TIPS "Publish your poems in literary magazines before trying to get a whole ms published. Publishing individual poems is the best way to hone your complete ms."

GERALD CABLE BOOK AWARD

Silverfish Review Press, P.O. Box 3541, Eugene OR 97403. (541)344-5060. **E-mail:** sfrpress@earthlink.net. **Website:** www.silverfishreviewpress.com. **Con**-tact: Rodger Moody, editor. Offers annual award of $1,000, publication by Silverfish Review Press, and 25 author copies to a book-length ms of original poetry by an author who has not yet published a full-length collection. No restrictions on the kind of poetry or subject matter; no translations. Individual poems may have been previously published elsewhere, but must be acknowledged. Considers simultaneous submissions (notify immediately of acceptance elsewhere). Submit at least 48 pages of poetry, no names or identification on ms pages. Include separate title sheet with poet's name, address, and phone number. Include SASP for notification of receipt and SASE for results; no mss will be returned. Accepts e-mail submissions in Word, plain text, or rich text; send entry fee and SASE by regular mail. Guidelines available for SASE, by e-mail, or on website. **Entry fee:** $25. Make checks payable to Silverfish Review Press. **Deadline:** October 15 (postmark). Winner announced in March. Copies of winning books available through website. "All entrants who enclose a booksize envelope and $2.23 in postage will receive a free copy of a recent winner of the book award."

TIPS "Now accepting e-mail submissions (save money on postage and photocopying); use Paypal for reading fee payment, see website for instructions."

THE CENTER FOR BOOK ARTS POETRY CHAPBOOK COMPETITION

The Center for Book Arts, 28 W. 27th St., 3rd Floor, New York NY 10001. (212)481-0295. **Fax:** (866)708-8994. **E-mail:** info@centerforbookarts.org. **Website:** www.centerforbookarts.org. Contest needs poetry chapbooks. Offered annually for unpublished collections of poetry. Individual poems may have been previously published. Collection must not exceed 500 lines or 24 pages (does not include cover page, title pages, table of contents, or acknowledgements pages). Copies of winning chapbooks available through website. "The cover page should contain, on a single detachable page, the ms title and author's name, along with address, phone number, and e-mail. The author's name should not appear anywhere else. A second title page should be provided without the author's name or other identification. Please provide a table of contents and a separate acknowledgements page containing prior magazine or anthology publication of individual poems. Mss should be bound with a simple spring clip. Poems may have appeared in journals or anthologies but not as part of a book-length collection. Competition is open to all poets writing in English who have published no more than 2 full-length books. Poets may not have studied with either judge in a degree-granting program for the last 5 years. "Center for Book Arts is a nonprofit organization dedicated to the traditional crafts of bookmaking and contemporary interpretations of the book as an art object. Through the Center's Education, Exhibition, and Workspace Programs, we ensure that the ancient craft of the book remains a viable and vital part of our civilization." Deadline: December 15 (postmarked). Prize: $500 award, $500 honorarium for a reading, publication, and 10 copies of chapbook. Judged by Harryette Mullen and Sharon Dolin in 2013.

CIDER PRESS REVIEW BOOK AWARD

P.O. Box 33384, San Diego CA 92163. **E-mail:** editor@ciderpressreview.com. **Website:** http://ciderpressreview.com/bookaward. Annual award from *Cider Press Review*. Submissions must be unpublished as a collection, but individual poems may have been previously published elsewhere. Submit book-length ms of 48-80 pages. "Submissions can be made online using the submission form on the website or by mail. If sending by mail, include 2 cover sheets—1 with title, author's name, and complete contact information; and 1 with title only, all bound with a spring clip. Check website for change of address coming in the future. Include SASE for results only if no email address included; notification via email and on the website; manuscripts cannot be returned. Online submissions must be in Word for PC or PDF format, and should not include title page with author's name. The editors strongly urge contestants to use online delivery if possible." Review the complete submission guidelines and learn more online at website. Deadline: submit September 1 - November 30 (postmark). Prize: $1,500, publication, and 25 author's copies of a book length collection of poetry. Author receives a standard publishing contract. Initial print run is not less than 1,000 copies. CPR acquires first publication rights. The 2012 judge was Gray Jacobik.

CLEVELAND STATE UNIVERSITY POETRY CENTER PRIZES

Cleveland State University Poetry Center, Cleveland State University Poetry Center Prizes, Department of English, 2121 Euclid Avenue, Cleveland OH 44115-2214. (216)687-3986. **Fax:** (216)687-6943. **E-mail:** poetrycenter@csuohio.edu. **Website:** www.csuohio.

edu/poetrycenter. **Contact:** Frank Giampietro. Manuscript should contain a minimum of 48 and a maximum of 100 pages of poetry. See website for specific details and rules. Offered annually to identify, reward, and publish the best unpublished book-length poetry ms (minimum 48 pages) in 2 categories: First Book Award and Open Competition (for poets who have published at least one collection with a press run of 500). Deadline: March 13. Prize: First Book and Open Book Competitions award publication and a $1000 advance against royalties for an original manuscript of poetry in each category

CLOCKWISE CHAPBOOK COMPETITION

Tebot Bach, Tebot Bach, Clockwise, P.O. Box 7887, Huntington Beach CA 92615. (714)968-0905. **Fax:** (714)968-4677. **E-mail:** mifanwy@tebotbach.org. **Website:** www.tebotbach.org/clockwise.html. **Contact:** Gail Wronsky. Must be previously unpublished poetry for the full collection; individual poems may have been published. Purpose of award is to honor the winning entry. Deadline: April 15. Prize: Book Publication in Perfect Bound Editions. Judged by Gail Wronsky.

CLOUDBANK CONTEST

P.O. Box 610, Corvallis OR 97339. **E-mail:** michael@cloudbankbooks.com. **Website:** www.cloudbankbooks.com. **Contact:** Michael Malan, poetry and short fiction. For contest submissions, the writer's name, address, e-mail, and the titles of the poems/prose pieces being submitted should be typed on a cover sheet only, not on the pages of poems or short fiction. No electronic submissions. Send no more than 5 poems or short prose pieces (500 words or less) for the contest or for regular submissions. Prize: $200 and publication, plus an extra copy of the issue in which the winning poem appears Judged by Michael Malan (final) and Reading Board (initial).

THE COLORADO PRIZE FOR POETRY

Colorado Review/Center for Literary Publishing, Department of English, Colorado State University, 9105 Campus Delivery, Ft. Collins CO 80523. (970)491-5449. **E-mail:** creview@colostate.edu. **Website:** http://coloradoprize.colostate.edu. **Contact:** Stephanie G'Schwind, editor. Submission must be unpublished as a collection, but individual poems may have been published elsewhere. Submit mss of 48-100 pages of poetry (no set minimum or maximum) on any subject, in any form, double- or single-spaced. Include 2 titles pages: 1 with ms title only, the other with ms title and poet's name, address, and phone number. Enclosed SASP for notification of receipt and SASE for results; mss will not be returned. Guidelines available for SASE or by e-mail. "Guidelines available for SASE or online at website. Poets can also submit online via our online submission manager through our website." To connect writers and readers by publishing exceptional writing. Annual deadline is early January. Check website for exact deadline. Prize: $2,000 and publication of a book-length ms.

CONCRETE WOLF POETRY CHAPBOOK CONTEST

P.O. Box 1808, Kingston WA 98346. **E-mail:** concretewolf@yahoo.com. **Website:** http://concretewolf.com. The Concrete Wolf Poetry Chapbook award offers publication and 100 author copies of a perfectly bound chapbook. Considers simultaneous submissions if notified of acceptance elsewhere. "We prefer chapbooks that have a theme, either obvious (i.e., chapbook about a divorce) or understated (i.e., all the poems mention the color blue). We like a collection that feels more like a whole than a sampling of work. We have no preference as to formal or free verse. We probably slightly favor lyric and narrative poetry to language and concrete, but excellent examples of any style get our attention." Submit up to 26 pages of poetry, paginated. Include table of contents and acknowledgments page. Include 2 cover sheets: 1 with ms title, poet's name, address, phone number, and e-mail; 1 without poet's identification. Include SASE for results; mss will not be returned. Guidelines available on website. Deadline: November 30. Prize: 100 copies of a perfect-bound chapbook.

CPR EDITOR'S PRIZE BOOK AWARD

P.O. Box 33384, San Diego CA 92163. **E-mail:** editor@ciderpressreview.com. **Website:** http://ciderpressreview.com/bookaward. Annual award from *Cider Press Review*. Submissions must be unpublished as a collection, but individual poems may have been previously published elsewhere. Submit book-length ms of 48-80 pages. "Submissions can be made online using the submission form on the website or by mail. If sending by mail, include 2 cover sheets—1 with title, author's name, and complete contact information; and 1 with title only, all bound with a spring clip. Check website for change of address coming in the future. Include SASE for results only if no email address

included; notification via email and on the website; manuscripts cannot be returned. Online submissions must be in Word for PC or PDF format, and should not include title page with author's name. The editors strongly urge contestants to use online delivery if possible." Review the complete submission guidelines and learn more online at website. Deadline: submit April 1 - June 30 (postmark). Prize: $1,000, publication, and 25 author's copies of a book length collection of poetry. Author receives a standard publishing contract. Initial print run is not less than 1,000 copies. CPR acquires first publication rights. Judged by *Cider Press Review* editors.

CRAB ORCHARD SERIES IN POETRY FIRST BOOK AWARD

First Book Award, Dept. of English, Mail Code 4503, Southern Illinois University Carbondale, 1000 Faner Drive, Carbondale IL 62901. (618)453-6833. **E-mail:** jtribble@siu.edu. **Website:** www.craborchardreview.siu.edu. **Contact:** Jon Tribble, series editor. "A first book of poems will be selected for publication from an open competition of manuscripts, in English, by a U.S. citizen or permanent resident who has neither published, nor committed to publish, a volume of poetry 48 pages or more in length in an edition of over 500 copies* (individual poems may have been previously published; for the purposes of the Crab Orchard Series in Poetry, a manuscript which was in whole or in part submitted as a thesis or dissertation as a requirement for the completion of a degree is considered unpublished and is eligible)." See website for complete formatting instructions. Guidelines available for SASE or on website. Deadline: July 6. Prize: Offers $3,500 ($2,000 prize plus $1,500 honorarium for a reading at Southern Illinois University Carbondale) and publication.

THE ROBERT DANA ANHINGA PRIZE FOR POETRY

Anhinga Press, P.O. Box 3665, Tallahassee FL 32315. (850)577-0745. **Fax:** (850)577-0745. **E-mail:** info@anhinga.org. **Website:** www.anhinga.org. **Contact:** Rick Campbell, poetry editor. Offered annually for a book-length collection of poetry by an author who has not published more than 1 book of poetry. Guidelines for SASE or on website. Open to any writer writing in English. Manuscripts must be 48-80 pages, excluding front matter. Submissions will be accepted from February 15-May 15. Prize: $2,000, a reading tour of selected Florida colleges and uninversities, and the winning manuscript will be published. Past judges include Donald Hall, Joy Harjo, Robert Dana, Mark Jarman, and Tony Hoagland. Past winners include Frank X. Gaspar, Earl S. Braggs, Julia Levine, Keith Ratzlaff, and Lynn Aarti Chandhok, and Rhett Iseman Trull.

DANCING POETRY CONTEST

AEI Contest Chair, Judy Cheung, 704 Brigham Ave., Santa Rosa CA 95404-5245. (707)528-0912. **E-mail:** jhcheung@comcast.net. **Website:** www.dancingpoetry.com. **Contact:** Judy Cheung, contest chair. Line Limit: 40 lines maximum each poem. No limit on number of entries. Send two typed, clear copies of each entry. Show name, address, telephone number, e-mail and how you heard about the contest on one copy only. Poems must be in English or include English translation "We always look for something new and different including new twists to old themes, different looks at common situations, inovative concepts for dynamic, thought provoking entertainment." Deadline: May 15. Prize: Prizes: Three Grand Prizes wil receive $100 each plus the poems will be danced and videotaped; six First Prizes will receive $50 each; twelve Second Prizes will receive $25 each; and thirty Third Prizes will receive $10 each.

T.S. ELIOT PRIZE FOR POETRY

Truman State University Press, 100 E. Normal Ave., Kirksville MO 63501. (660)785-7336. **Fax:** (660)785-4480. **E-mail:** tsup@truman.edu. **Website:** tsup.truman.edu. **Contact:** Nancy Rediger. "The manuscript may include individual poems previously published in journals or anthologies, but may not include a significant number of poems from a published chapbook or self-published book." Submit 60-100 pages. Include 2 title pages: 1 with poet's name, address, phone number, and ms title; the other with ms title only. Include SASE for acknowledgment of ms receipt only; mss will not be returned. Guidelines available for SASE or on website. Competition receives about 500 entries/year. Deadline: October 31. Prize: $2,000 and publication. Judge announced after close of competition.

JANICE FARRELL POETRY PRIZE

Category in the Soul-Making Keats Literary Competition, under the auspice of the National League of American Pen Women, The Webhallow House, 1544 Sweetwood Dr., Broadmoor Village CA 94015. **E-mail:** SoulKeats@aol.com. **Website:** www.soulmakingcontest.us. **Contact:** Eileen Malone. "Poetry

may be double- or single-spaced. One-page poems only, and only 1 poem/page. All poems must be titled. Three poems/entry. Indicate category on each poem. Identify with 3x5 card only. Open to all writers." Judged by a local San Francisco successfully published poet. Previously published okay. November 30. Prize: Cash prizes.

FIELD POETRY PRIZE

Oberlin College Press/FIELD, 50 N. Professor St., Oberlin OH 44074-1095. (440)775-8408. **Fax:** (440)775-8124. **E-mail:** oc.press@oberlin.edu. **Website:** www.oberlin.edu/ocpress/prize.htm. The annual FIELD Poetry Prize for a book-length collection of poems offers $1,000 and publication in the FIELD Poetry Series. Mss of 50-80 pages must be submitted during May through our online submissions manager. See our website for details. Entry Fee: $28; includes one-year subscription to FIELD: Contemporary Poetry and Poetics (see separate listing in Magazines/Journals). **Deadline:** submit during May only. 2012 winner was Mary Ann Samyn (My Life in Heaven). **Contact:** Marco Wilkinson, managing editor. "Offered annually for unpublished work. Contest seeks to encourage the finest in contemporary poetry writing. Open to any writer." Deadline: Submit in May only. Prize: $1,000 and the book is published in Oberlin College Press's FIELD Poetry Series.

THE FINCH PRIZE FOR POETRY

The National Poetry Review, P.O. Box 2080, Aptos CA 95001-2080. **E-mail:** editor@nationalpoetry review.com. **Website:** www.nationalpoetryreview.com. **Contact:** C.J. Sage, editor. The Finch Prize for Poetry offers $500 plus publication in *The National Poetry Review*. All entries will be considered by the editor for publication. Submissions must be unpublished and uncommitted. Considers simultaneous submissions, "but if the work is selected by *The National Poetry Review* for the prize or for publication, it must be withdrawn from elsewhere unless you have withdrawn it from us 2 weeks before our acceptance." Submit up to 3 poems/entry (10 pages maximum per group of 3). Include cover letter with bio and contact information, including e-mail address for results. Complete guidelines available on website. Deadline: June 30 (postmark). Prize: $500 plus possible publication.

FOUR WAY BOOKS POETRY PRIZES

Four Way Books, P.O. Box 535, Village Station, New York NY 10014. **E-mail:** editors@fourwaybooks.com.

Website: www.fourwaybooks.com. Four Way Books runs different prizes annually. The Intro Prize in Poetry, The Four Way Books Levis Poetry Prize. Open to all poets, regardless of publication history. Submissions guidelines will be posted on site at the end of December. For guidelines send a SASE or download from website. Deadline: March 31. Prize: $1,000 and book publication. Judged by James Longenbach (2013).

ALLEN GINSBERG POETRY AWARDS

The Poetry Center at Passaic County Community College, One College Blvd., Paterson NJ 07505. (973)684-6555. **Fax:** (973)523-6085. **E-mail:** mgillan@pccc.edu. **Website:** www.pccc.edu/poetry. **Contact:** Maria Mazziotti Gillan, executive director. All winning poems, honorable mentions, and editor's choice poems will be published in *Paterson Literary Review*. Winners will be asked to participate in a reading that will be held in the Paterson Historic District. Submissions must be unpublished. Submit up to 5 poems (no poem more than 2 pages long). Send 4 copies of each poem entered. Include cover sheet with poet's name, address, phone number, e-mail address and poem titles. Poet's name should not appear on poems. Include SASE for results only; poems will not be returned. Guidelines available for SASE or on website. April 1 (postmark). Prize: 1st Prize: $1,000; 2nd Prize: $200; 3rd Prize: $100.

GIVAL PRESS POETRY AWARD

Gival Press, LLC, P.O. Box 3812, Arlington VA 22203. (703)351-0079. **E-mail:** givalpress@yahoo.com. **Website:** www.givalpress.com. **Contact:** Robert L. Giron, editor. "Offered annually for a previously unpublished poetry collection as a complete ms, which may include previously published poems; previously published poems must be acknowledged, and poet must hold rights. Guidelines for SASE, by e-mail, or online." Must be at least 45 typed pages of poetry, on one side only. Entrants are asked to submit their poems without any kind of identification (with the exception of the titles) and with a separate cover page with the following information: Name, address (street, city, state, and zip code), telephone number, e-mail address (if available), short bio, and a list of the poems by title. Checks drawn on American banks should be made out to Gival Press, LLC. The competition seeks to award well-written, original poetry in English on any topic, in any style. Deadline: December 15 (postmarked). Prize: $1,000, publication, and 20 copies of the publication. The editor narrows entries to the top 10; previous winner selects top 5 and chooses the winner—all done anonymously.

TIPS "Open to any writer, as long as the work is original, not a translation, and is written in English. The copyright remains in the author's name; certain rights fall to the publisher per the contract."

⟳ GOVERNOR GENERAL'S LITERARY AWARD FOR POETRY

Canada Council for the Arts, 350 Albert St., P.O. Box 1047, Ottawa ON K1P 5V8 Canada. (613)566-4414, ext. 5573. **Fax:** (613)566-4410. **Website:** www.canadacouncil.ca/prizes/ggla. Offered for the best English-language and the best French-language work of poetry by a Canadian. Publishers submit titles for consideration. Deadline depends on the book's publication date. Books in English: March 15, June 1, or August 7. Books in French: March 15 or July 15. Prize: Each laureate receives $25,000; non-winning finalists receive $1,000.

KATHRYN HANDLEY PROSE POEM PRIZE

Category in the Soul-Making Keats Literary Competition, under the auspice of the National League of American Pen Women, The Webhallow House, 1544 Sweetwood Dr., Broadmoor Village CA 94015-2029. **E-mail:** SoulKeats@aol.com. **Website:** www.soulmakingcontest.us. **Contact:** Eileen Malone. Open annually to all writers. Poetry may be double- or single-spaced. 1-page prose poems only, and only 1 prose poem/page. Three poems/entry. Indicate category on each poem. Identify only with 3x5 card. November 30. Prize: 1st Place: $100; 2nd Place: $50; 3rd Place: $25.

THE BESS HOKIN PRIZE

Poetry, 61 W. Superior St., Chicago IL 60654. (312)787-7070. **Fax:** (312)787-6650. **E-mail:** editors@poetrymagazine.org. **Website:** www.poetrymagazine.org. Offered annually for poems published in *Poetry* during the preceding year (October-September). Upon acceptance, *Poetry* licenses exclusive worldwide first serial rights, including electronic rights, for publication, as well as non-exclusive rights to reprint, reuse, and archive the work, in any format, in perpetuity. Copyright reverts to author upon first publication. "Established in 1947 through the generosity of our late friend and guarantor, Mrs. David Hokin, and is given annually in her memory." Prize: $1,000.

FIRMAN HOUGHTON PRIZE

New England Poetry Club, 654 Green St., Apt. 2, Cambridge MA 02139 . **E-mail:** contests@nepoetry-clug.org. **Website:** www.nepoetryclub.org. **Contact:** NEPC contest coordinator. For a lyric poem in honor of the former president of NEPC. Deadline: May 31. Prize: $250. Judges are well-known poets and sometimes winners of previous NEPC contests.

TOM HOWARD/JOHN H. REID POETRY CONTEST

Tom Howard Books, Tom Howard Books, c/o Winning Writers, 351 Pleasant St., PMB 222, Northampton MA 01060-3961. (866)946-9748. **Fax:** (413)280-0539. **E-mail:** johnreid@mail.qango.com. **Website:** www.winningwriters.com. **Contact:** John Reid, award director. Any type of original short story, essay or other work of prose is eligible. Competition receives about 1,000 entries/year. Winners announced in February at WinningWriters.com. Entrants who provide valid e-mail addresses will also receive notification. Submissions may be published or unpublished and may have won prizes elsewhere. Considers simultaneous submissions. Submit poems in any form, style, or genre. "There is no limit on the number of lines or poems you may submit." No name on ms pages; type or computer-print on letter-size white paper, single-sided. Submit online or by regular mail. Guidelines available for SASE or on website. Deadline: April 30. Prize: Prizes: First prize: $3,000. Second prize: $1,000. Third prize: $400. Fourth prize: $250. There will also be six Most Highly Commended Awards of $150 each. The top 10 entries will be published on the Winning Writers website (over one million page views per year) and announced in Tom Howard Contest News and the Winning Writers Newsletter.

THE LYNDA HULL MEMORIAL POETRY PRIZE

Crazyhorse, Department of English, College of Charleston, 66 George St., Charleston SC 29424. (843)953-4470. **E-mail:** crazyhorse@cofc.edu. **Website:** http://crazyhorse.cofc.edu. **Contact:** Prize Director. The annual Lynda Hull Memorial Poetry Prize offers $2,000 and publication in *Crazyhorse*. All entries will be considered for publication. Submissions must be unpublished. Submit online or by mail up to 3 original poems (no more than 10 pages). Include cover page (placed on top of ms) with poet's name, address, e-mail, and telephone number; no identifying information on mss (blind judging). Accepts multiple submissions with separate fee for each. Include SASP for notification of receipt of ms and SASE for results only; mss will not be returned. Guidelines available for SASE or on website. Deadline: January 31.

INDIANA REVIEW POETRY PRIZE

Indiana Review, Poetry Prize, Indiana Review, Ballantine Hall 465, 1020 E. Kirkwood Ave., Bloomington IN 47405-7103. (812)855-3439. **Fax:** (812)855-9535. **E-mail:** inreview@indiana.edu. **Website:** www.indianareview.org. **Contact:** Michael Mlekoday, Poetry Editor. Offered annually for unpublished work. Open to any writer. Send no more than 3 poems per entry. Guidelines on website and with SASE request. Send no more than three poems per entry, eight pages maximu. Each fee entitles entrant to a one-year subscription. Deadline: April1. Prize: $1,000 Honorarium and Publication. Judged by Nikky Finney in 2013.

IOWA POETRY PRIZES

University of Iowa Press, 119 West Park Rd., 100 Kuhl House, Iowa City IA 52242. (319)335-2000. **Fax:** (319)335-2055. **E-mail:** uipress@uiowa.edu. **Website:** www.uiowapress.org. Offered annually to encourage poets and their work. Submissions must be postmarked during the month of April; put name on title page only. This page will be removed before ms is judged. Open to writers of English (US citizens or not). Mss will not be returned. Previous winners are not eligible. Deadline: April 30. Prize: Publication under standard royalty agreement.

RANDALL JARRELL POETRY COMPETITION

North Carolina Writers' Network, Terry L. Kennedy, MFA Writing Program, 3302 MHRA Building, UNC Greensboro, Greensboro NC 27402-6170. **E-mail:** tlkenned@uncg.edu. **Website:** www.ncwriters.org. **Contact:** Terry L. Kennedy. Offered annually for unpublished work "to honor Randall Jarrell and his life at UNC-Greensboro by recognizing the best poetry submitted." Competition is open any writer who is a legal resident of North Carolina or a member of the NC Writers Network. The competition is open to any writer who is a legal resident of North Carolina or a member of the North Carolina Writers' Network. Submissions should be one poem only (40-line limit). Poem must be typed (single-spaced) and stapled in the left-hand corner. Author's name should not appear on the poem. Instead, include a separate cover sheet with author's name, address, e-mail address, phone number, and poem title. Poem will not be returned. Include a self-addressed stamped envelope for a list of winner and finalists. The winner and finalists will be announced in May. Deadline: March 1. Prize: $200, publication in the Crucible literary journal, and an invitation to read his/her poetry at UNC Greensboro's Founders Day activities.

LEVIS READING PRIZE

Virginia Commonwealth University, Department of English, Levis Reading Prize, VCU Department of English, 900 Park Avenue, Hibbs Hall, Room 306, P.O. Box 842005, Richmond VA 23284-2005. (804)828-1329. **Fax:** (804)828-8684. **E-mail:** kileyk@vcu.edu. **E-mail:** englishgrad@vcu.edu. **Website:** www.has. vcu.edu/eng/resources/levis_prize/levis_prize.htm. **Contact:** Katelyn Kiley, Levis Fellow. "Offered annually for books of poetry published in the previous year to encourage poets early in their careers. The entry must be the writer's first or second published book of poetry. Previously published books in other genres, or previously published chapbooks or self-published material, do not count as books for this purpose." Entries may be submitted by either author or publisher, and must include three copies of the book (48 pages or more), a cover letter, and a brief biography of the author including previous publications. (Entries from vanity presses are not eligible.) The book must have been published in the previous calendar year. Entrants wishing acknowledgment of receipt must include a self-addressed stamped postcard. Deadline: January 15. Prize: $2,000 and an expense-paid trip to Richmond to present a public reading.

THE RUTH LILLY POETRY PRIZE

Poetry, 61 W. Superior St., Chicago IL 60654. (312)787-7070. **Fax:** (312)787-6650. **E-mail:** editors@poetry-magazine.org. **Website:** www.poetrymagazine.org. Awarded annually, the $100,000 Ruth Lilly Poetry Prize honors a living U.S. poet whose lifetime accomplishments warrant extraordinary recognition. Established in 1986 by Ruth Lilly, the Prize is one of the most prestigious awards given to American poets and is one of the largest literary honors for work in the English language. Deadline: Varies. Prize: $100,000.

THE MACGUFFIN NATIONAL POET HUNT CONTEST

The MacGuffin, The MacGuffin, Schoolcraft College, 18600 Haggerty Rd., Livonia MI 48152. (734)462-4400, ext. 5327. **Fax:** (734)462-4679. **E-mail:** mac-guffin@schoolcraft.edu. **Website:** www.macguffin. org. **Contact:** Gordon Krupsky, managing editor. The MacGuffin, established in 1984, is a national literary magazine from Schoolcraft College in Livonia, Michigan. An entry consists of three poems. Poems must not be previously published, and must be the original work of the contestant. See website for additional details. The mission of The MacGuffin is to encourage, support, and enhance the literary arts in the Schoolcraft College community, the region, the state, and the nation. Deadline: must be postmarked between April 1 and June 3. Prize: $500.

NAOMI LONG MADGETT POETRY AWARD

Lotus Press, Inc., P.O. Box 21607, Detroit MI 48221. **E-mail:** lotuspress@comcast.net. **Website:** www.lotus-press.org. **Contact:** Constance Withers. Offered annually to recognize an unpublished book-length poetry ms by an African American. Guidelines for SASE, by e-mail, or online. Deadline: January 2-March 1. Prize: $500 and publication by Lotus Press.

◯ THE MALAHAT REVIEW LONG POEM PRIZE

The Malahat Review, Box 1700 STN CSC, Victoria BC V8W 2Y2 Canada. **E-mail:** malahat@uvic. ca (queries only). **Website:** www.malahatreview.ca. **Contact:** John Barton, editor. "Long Poem Prize offered in alternate years with the Novella Contest." Offers 2 awards of $1,000 CAD each for a long poem or cycle (10-20 printed pages). Includes publication in *The Malahat Review* and a 1-year subscription. Open to "entries from Canadian, American, and overseas authors." Submissions must be unpublished. No simultaneous submissions. Submit a single poem or cycle of poems, 10-20 published pages (a published page equals 32 lines or less, including breaks between stanzas); no restrictions on subject matter or aesthetic approach. Include separate page with poet's name, address, e-mail, and title; no identifying information on mss pages. No e-mail submissions. Do not include SASE for results; mss will not be returned. Guidelines available on website. "Preliminary reading by editorial board; final judging by 3 recognized poets. Obtains first world rights. After—publication rights revert to the author. Open to any writer." Winners published in the summer issue of *The Malahat Review*, announced in summer on website, Facebook page, and in quarterly e-newsletter *Malahat lite*. Submissions must be unpublished. No simultaneous submissions. Submit a single poem or cycle of poems, 10-20 published pages (a published page equals 32 lines or less, including breaks between stanzas); no restrictions on subject matter or aesthetic approach. Include separate page with poet's name, address, e-mail, and title; no identifying information on mss pages. No e-mail submissions. Do not include SASE for results; mss will not be returned. Guidelines available on website. February 1 of odd-numbered years. Prize: Two $1,000 prizes.

THE MORTON MARR POETRY PRIZE

Southwest Review, Southern Methodist University, P.O. Box 750374, Dallas TX 75275. (214)768-1037. **Fax:** (214)768-1408. **E-mail:** swr@mail.smu.edu. **Website:** www.smu.edu/southwestreview. **Contact:** Prize coordinator. Annual award for poem(s) by a writer who has not yet published a book of poetry. Submit no more than 6 poems in a "traditional" form (e.g., sonnet, sestine, villanelle, rhymed stanzas, blank verse, et al.). Submissions will not be returned. All entrants will receive a copy of the issue in which the winning poems appear. Postmarked deadline for entry is September 30. Prize: Prizes: $1,000 for 1st place; $500 for 2nd place; plus publication in the Southwest Review.

VASSAR MILLER PRIZE IN POETRY

University of North Texas Press, 1155 Union Circle, #311336, Denton TX 76203. (940)565-2142. **Fax:** (940)565-4590. **Website:** http://untpress.unt.edu. **Contact:** John Poch. Annual prize awarded to a collection of poetry. Deadline: November 15. Prize: Winner will receive $,1000 and publication by University of North Texas Press. Judged by a "different eminent writer selected each year. Some prefer to remain anonymous until the end of the contest."

TIPS "No limitations to entrants. In years when the judge is announced, we ask that students of the judge not enter to avoid a perceived conflict. All entries should contain identifying material only on the one cover sheet. Entries are read anonymously."

THE KATHRYN A. MORTON PRIZE IN POETRY

Sarabande Books, Inc., P.O. Box 4456, Louisville KY 40204. (502)458-4028. **E-mail:** info@sarabandebooks.org. **Website:** www.SarabandeBooks.org. **Contact:** Sarah Gorham, editor-in-chief. Member: CLMP. The Kathryn A. Morton Prize in Poetry is awarded annually to a book-length ms (at least 48 pages). All finalists are considered for publication. Competition receives approximately 1,400 entries. 2012 judge was

Cole Swensen. "To avoid conflict of interest, students in a degree-granting program or close friends of a judge are ineligible to enter the contest in the genre for which their friend or teacher is serving as judge. Sarabande, as a member of CLMP, complies with its Contest Code of Ethics." Entry form and SASE are required. Accepts simultaneous submissions, but must be notified immediately if manuscript is accepted elsewhere. Guidelines available for SASE, by e-mail, or on website. Deadline: Submit January 1-February 15 (postmark) only. Prize: $2,000, publication, and a standard royalty contract.

SHEILA MARGARET MOTTON PRIZE

New England Poetry Club, 2 Farrar St., Cambridge MA 02138. (617)744-6034. **E-mail:** info@nepoetryclub.org. **Website:** www.nepoetryclub.org. **Contact:** NEPC contest coordinator. Checks for all contests should be made to New England Poetry Club. All entries should be sent in duplicate with name, address, phone, and email of writer on only one copy. (Judges receive copies without names). Send 2 copies of book of poetry published in the last 2 years. "Contest open to members and nonmembers. Poems should be typed and submitted in duplicate with author's name, address, phone, and e-mail address of writer on only 1 copy. (Judges receive copies without names.) Copy only. Label poems with contest name. Entries should be sent by regular mail only. Special delivery or signature required mail will be returned by the post office. Entries should be original, unpublished poems in English. No poem should be entered in more than 1 contest, nor have won a previous contest. No entries will be returned. NEPC will not engage in correspondence regarding poems or contest decisions." Deadline: May 31. Prize: $500. Judges are well-known poets and sometimes winners of previous NEPC contests.

ERIKA MUMFORD PRIZE

New England Poetry Club, 654 Green St., Apt. 2, Cambridge MA 02139. **E-mail:** contests@nepoetryclub.org. **Website:** www.nepoetryclub.org/contests.htm. **Contact:** NEPC contest coordinator. Offered annually for a poem in any form about foreign culture or travel. Funded by Erika Mumford's family and friends. Contest open to members and nonmembers. Deadline: May 31. Prize: $250. Judges are well-known poets and sometimes winners of previous NEPC contests.

THE NATIONAL POETRY REVIEW BOOK PRIZE

The National Poetry Review, P.O. Box 2080, Aptos CA 95001-2080. **E-mail:** editor@nationalpoetryreview.com. **Website:** www.nationalpoetryreview.com. **Contact:** C.J. Sage, editor. Submit 45-80 pages of poetry via e-mail and PayPal (strongly preferred) or via mail. Include cover letter with bio and acknowledgments page. Include e-mail address (no SASEs; mss will be recycled). Guidelines available on website. Deadline: June 30 (postmark). Prize: $1,000 plus publication and 15 copies of the book.

NATIONAL WRITERS ASSOCIATION POETRY CONTEST

The National Writers Association, 10940 S. Parker Rd. #508, Parker CO 80134. (303)841-0246. **E-mail:** natlwritersassn@hotmail.com. **Website:** www.nationalwriters.com. **Contact:** Sandy Whelchel, director. "Annual contest to encourage the writing of poetry, an important form of individual expression but with a limited commercial market." Deadline: October 1. Prizes: 1st Place: $100; 2nd Place: $50, 3rd Place: $25.

HOWARD NEMEROV SONNET AWARD

320 Hunter Dr., Evansville IN 47711. **E-mail:** mona.3773@yahoo.com. **Website:** www.theformalist.evansville.edu/home.htm. **Contact:** Mona Baer, contest coordinator. *The Formalist* sponsors the annual Howard Nemerov Sonnet Award. 2011 winner was Robert W. Crawford. 2011 judge was A. M. Juster. Submit original, unpublished sonnets; no translations; sonnet sequences are acceptable, but each sonnet will be considered individually. Poets may enter as many sonnets as they wish. Poet's name, address, phone number, and e-mail address should be typed on the **BACK** of each entry. Enclose SASE for contest results; entries cannot be returned. Guidelines available on website or for SASE. Deadline: November 15 postmark. Prize: Offers $1,000 prize for a single sonnet. Winner and 11 finalists will be published in *Measure: A Review of Formal Poetry*.

THE PABLO NERUDA PRIZE FOR POETRY

Nimrod International Journal, 800 S. Tucker Dr., Tulsa OK 74104. (918)631-3080. **Fax:** (918)631-3033. **E-mail:** nimrod@utulsa.edu. **Website:** www.utulsa.edu/nimrod. **Contact:** Eilis O'Neal. Annual award to discover new writers of vigor and talent. Open to US residents only. Submissions must be unpublished. Work must be in English or translated by original author. Submit 3-10 pages of poetry (1 long poem or several short poems). Poet's name must not appear on ms. Include cover sheet with poem title(s), poet's name, address, phone and fax numbers, and e-mail address (poet must have a US address by October of contest year to enter). Mark "Contest Entry" on submission envelope and cover sheet. Include SASE for results only; mss will not be returned. Guidelines available for #10 SASE or on website. **Entry fee:** $20; includes 1-year subscription (2 issues) to *Nimrod*. Make checks payable to *Nimrod*. Winners will be announced on *Nimrod*'s website. Submissions must be unpublished. Work must be in English or translated by original author. Submit 3-10 pages of poetry (1 long poem or several short poems). Poet's name must not appear on ms. Include cover sheet with poem title(s), poet's name, address, phone and fax numbers, and e-mail address (poet must have a US address by October of contest year to enter). Mark "Contest Entry" on submission envelope and cover sheet. Include SASE for results only; mss will not be returned. Guidelines available for #10 SASE or on website. Deadline: April 30. Prize. Prizes: 1st Place: $2,000 and publication; 2nd Place: $1,000 and publication. Judged by the *Nimrod* editors (finalists). A recognized author selects the winners.

THE JOHN FREDERICK NIMS MEMORIAL PRIZE

Poetry, 61 W. Superior St., Chicago IL 60654. (312)787-7070. **Fax:** (312)787-6650. **E-mail:** poetry@poetrymagazine.org. **E-mail:** mail@poetryfoundation.org. **Website:** www.poetrymagazine.org. Offered annually for poems published in *Poetry* during the preceding year (October-September). Upon acceptance, *Poetry* licenses exclusive worldwide first serial rights, including electronic rights, for publication, as well as nonexclusive rights to reprint, reuse, and archive the work, in any format, in perpetuity. Copyright reverts to author upon first publication. Copyrights are returned to the authors on request. The John Frederick Nims Memorial Prize for translation work is permanently endowed through a fund established by Bonnie Larkin Nims, Trustees of The Poetry Foundation, and friends of the late poet, translator, and Editor of *Poetry*. Prize: $500.

THE PATERSON POETRY PRIZE

The Poetry Center at Passaic County Community College, One College Blvd., Paterson NJ 07505. (973)684-6555. **Fax:** (973)523-6085. **E-mail:** mgillan@pccc.

edu. **Website:** www.pccc.edu/poetry. **Contact:** Maria Mazziotti Gillan, executive director. The Paterson Poetry Prize offers an annual award of $1,000 for the strongest book of poems (48 or more pages) published in the previous year. The winner will be asked to participate in an awards ceremony and to give a reading at The Poetry Center. Minimum press run: 500 copies. Publishers may submit more than 1 title for prize consideration; 3 copies of each book must be submitted. Include SASE for results; books will not be returned (all entries will be donated to The Poetry Center Library). Guidelines and application form (required) available for SASE or on website. Deadline: February 1 (postmark). Prize: $1,000.

PAVEMENT SAW PRESS CHAPBOOK AWARD

321 Empire St., Montpelier OH 43543-1301. **E-mail:** info@pavementsaw.org. **E-mail:** editor@pavementsaw.org. **Website:** www.pavementsaw.org. **Contact:** David Baratier, editor. "Pavement Saw Press has been publishing steadily since the fall of 1993. Each year since 1999, we have published at least 4 full-length paperback poetry collections, with some printed in library edition hard covers, 1 chapbook and a yearly literary journal anthology. We specialize in finding authors who have been widely published in literary journals but have not published a chapbook or full-length book." Submit up to 32 pages of poetry. Include signed cover letter with poet's name, address, phone number, e-mail, publication credits, a brief biography, and ms title. Also include 2 cover sheets: 1 with poet's contact information and ms title, 1 with the ms title only. Do not put name on mss pages except for first title page. No mss will be returned. Deadline: December 31 (postmark). Prize: Chapbook Award offers $500, publication, and 50 author copies.

PEARL POETRY PRIZE

Pearl Editions, 3030 E. Second St., Long Beach CA 90803. (562)434-4523. **Fax:** (562)434-4523. **E-mail:** pearlmag@aol.com. **Website:** www.pearlmag.com. **Contact:** Marilyn Johnson, editor/publisher. The annual Pearl Poetry Prize awards $1,000, publication, and 25 author's copies for a book-length ms. Guidelines available for SASE or on website. "Offered annually to provide poets with further opportunity to publish their poetry in book-form and find a larger audience for their work. Mss must be original works written in English. Guidelines for SASE or online. Open to

all writers." Submit May 1-June 30 only. Prize: $1,000 and publication by Pearl Editions.

JEAN PEDRICK PRIZE

New England Poetry Club, 654 Green St., Apt. 2, Cambridge MA 02139. **E-mail:** contests@nepoetryclub.org. **Website:** www.nepoetryclub.org. **Contact:** NEPC contest coordinator. Prize for a chapbook published in the last two years. Deadline: May 31. Prize: $100. Judges are well-known poets and sometimes winners of previous NEPC contests.

PEN/JOYCE OSTERWEIL AWARD FOR POETRY

PEN American Center, 588 Broadway, Suite 303, New York NY 10012. (212)334-1660, ext. 126. **E-mail:** awards@pen.org. **Website:** www.pen.org. **Contact:** Jasmine Davey, literary awards coordinator. *Candidates may only be nominated by members of PEN.* This award recognizes the high literary character of the published work to date of a new and emerging American poet of any age, and the promise of further literary achievement. Nominated writer may not have published more than 1 book of poetry. Offered in odd-numbered years and alternates with the PEN/Voelcker Award for Poetry. Send letters of nomination to Pen American Center. See website for details. Deadline: February 1. Prize: $5,000. Judged by a panel of 3 judges selected by the PEN Awards Committee.

PEN/VOELCKER AWARD FOR POETRY

PEN American Center, 588 Broadway, Suite 303, New York NY 10012. (212)334-1600, ext. 108. **E-mail:** awards@pen.org. **Website:** www.pen.org. **Contact:** Jasmine Davey, literary awards coordinator. Deadline: See website. Prize: $5,000 stipend. Judged by a panel of 3 poets or other writers.

PERUGIA PRESS PRIZE

Perugia Press, P.O. Box 60364, Florence MA 01062. **E-mail:** info@perugiapress.com. **Website:** www.perugiapress.com. **Contact:** Susan Kan. The Perugia Press Prize is for a first or second poetry book by a woman. Poet must have no more than 1 previously published book of poems (chapbooks don't count). Submissions must be unpublished as a collection, but individual poems may have been previously published in journals, chapbooks, and anthologies. Considers simultaneous submissions if notified of acceptance elsewhere. "Follow online guidelines carefully. Electronic submissions available through our website." No translations or self-published books. Multiple submissions accepted if accompanied by separate entry fee for each. Entry fee: $25. Make checks payable to Perugia Press. "Use USPS or electronic submission, not FedEx or UPS." Winner announced by April 1 by e-mail or SASE (if included with entry). Deadline: Submit August 1-November 15 (postmark). Prize: $1,000 and publication. Judges: Panel of Perugia authors, booksellers, scholars, etc.

POETS & PATRONS ANNUAL CHICAGOLAND POETRY CONTEST

Sponsored by Poets & Patrons of Chicago, 416 Gierz St., Downers Grove IL 60515. **E-mail:** eatonb1016@aol.com. **Website:** www.poetsandpatrons.org. **Contact:** Barbara Eaton, director. Annual contest for unpublished poetry. Guidelines available for self-addressed, stamped envelope. The purpose of the contest is to encourage the crafting of poetry. Deadline: September 1. Prize: Prize is $45, $20, $10 cash. Poet retains rights. Judged by out-of-state professionals.

A. POULIN, JR. POETRY PRIZE

BOA Editions, Ltd., BOA Editions, Ltd., P.O. Box 30971, Rochester NY 14604. **E-mail:** conners@boaeditions.org. **Website:** www.boaeditions.org. BOA Editions, Ltd. sponsors the annual A. Poulin, Jr. Poetry Prize for a poet's first book. Published books in other genres do not disqualify contestants from entering this contest. Send by first class or priority mail (recommended). Entrants must be a citizen or legal resident of the US. Poets, who are at least 18 years of age, who have yet to publish a full-length book collection of poetry. Translations are not eligible. Individual poems may have been previously published in magazines, journals, anthologies, chapbooks of 32 pages or less, or self-published books of 46 pages or less, but must be submitted in ms form. Considers simultaneous submissions. Submit 48-100 pages of poetry, paginated consecutively, typed or computer-generated in 11 point font. Bind with spring clip (no paperclips). Include cover/title page with poet's name, address, and telephone number. Also include table of contents; list of acknowledgments; and entry form (available for download on website). Multiple entries accepted with separate entry fee for each. No e-mail submissions. The A. Poulin, Jr. Poetry Prize is awarded to honor a poet's first book, while also honoring the late founder of BOA Editions, Ltd., a not-for-profit publishing house of poetry and poetry in translation.

Deadline: Submit between August 1-Nov. 30. Prize: Awards $1,500 honorarium and book publication in the A. Poulin, Jr. New Poets of America Series. Judged by Dorianne Laux.

LORI RUDNITSKY FIRST BOOK PRIZE

Persea Books, P.O. Box 1388, Columbia MO 65205. **Website:** www.perseabooks.com. "This annual competition sponsors the publication of a poetry collection by an American woman poet who has yet to publish a full-length book of poems." Deadline: October 31. Prize: $1,000, plus publication of book. In addition, the winner receives the option of an all-expenses-paid residency at the Civitella Ranieri Center, a renowned artists retreat housed in a 15th-century castle in Umbertide, Italy.

ERNEST SANDEEN PRIZE IN POETRY

University of Notre Dame, Dept. of English, 356 O'Shaughnessy Hall, Notre Dame IN 46556-5639. (574)631-7526. **Fax:** (574)631-4795. **E-mail:** creative-writing@nd.edu. **Website:** http://english.nd.edu/creative-writing/publications/sandeen-sullivan-prizes. **Contact.** Director of Creative Writing. The Sandeen Prize in Poetry is awarded to the author who have published at least one volume of short fiction or one volume of poetry. Awarded biannually, but judged quadrennially. "Though the Sandeen Prize is open to any author, with the exception of graduates of the University of Notre Dame, who has published at least one book of short stories or one collection of poetry, we will pay special attention to second volumes. Please include a vita and/or a biographical statement which includes your publishing history. We will be glad to see a selection of reviews of the earlier collection." Please submit two copies of your manuscript and inform us if the manuscript is available on computer disk. Include an SASE for acknowledgment of receipt of your submission. If you would like your manuscript returned, please send an SASE. Manuscripts will not otherwise be returned. Submissions Period: May 1 - September 1. Prize: A $1,000 prize, a $500 award and a $500 advance against royalties from the Notre Dame Press.

MAY SARTON AWARD

New England Poetry Club, 654 Green St., No. 2, Cambridge MA 02139. **Website:** www.nepoetryclub.org. **Contact:** NEPC contest coordinator. "Given intermittently to a poet whose work is an inspiration to other poets. Recipients are chosen by the board."

"Contest open to members and nonmembers. Poems should be typed and submitted in duplicate with author's name, address, phone, and e-mail address of writer on only 1 copy. (Judges receive copies without names.) Copy only. Label poems with contest name. Entries should be sent by regular mail only. Special delivery or signature required mail will be returned by the post office. Entries should be original, unpublished poems in English. No poem should be entered in more than 1 contest, nor have won a previous contest. No entries will be returned. NEPC will not engage in correspondence regarding poems or contest decisions." To recognize emerging poets of exceptional promise and distinguished achievement. Established to honor the memory of longtime Academy Fellow May Sarton, a poet, novelist, and teacher who during her career encouraged the work of young poets. Deadline: May 31. Prize: $250. Judges are well-known poets and sometimes winners of previous NEPC contests.

◎ SASKATCHEWAN POETRY AWARD

Saskatchewan Book Awards, Inc., P.O. Box 20025, Regina SK S4P 4J7 Canada. (306)569-1585. **E-mail:** director@bookawards.sk.ca. **Website:** www.bookawards.sk.ca. Offered annually. "This award is presented to a Saskatchewan author for the best book of poetry, judged on the quality of writing." Deadline: November 1. Prize: $2,000 (CAD).

SLAPERING HOL PRESS CHAPBOOK COMPETITION

The Hudson Valley Writers' Center, 300 Riverside Dr., Sleepy Hollow NY 10591. (914)332-5953. **Fax:** (914)332-4825. **E-mail:** info@writerscenter.org. **Website:** www.writerscenter.org. 300 Riverside Dr., Sleepy Hollow NY 10591-1414. (914)332-5953. **Fax:** (914)332-4825. **E-mail:** info@writerscenter.org. **Website:** www.slaperingholpress.org. Established 1990. **Contact:** Margo Stever. The Slapering Hol Press Chapbook Competition offers an annual award of $1,000, publication, 10 author's copies, and a reading at The Hudson Valley Writers' Center (see separate listing in Organizations). Open only to poets who have not previously published a book or chapbook. Submit 16-20 pages of poetry (collection or one long poem), any form or style. Manuscript should be anonymous with separate cover sheet containing name, address, phone number, e-mail address, a bio, and acknowledgments. Include SASE

for results only; manuscripts will not be returned. Guidelines available for SASE, by fax, e-mail, or on website. **Entry fee:** $15. Make checks payable to The Hudson Valley Writers' Center. **Deadline:** May 15. Winner will be announced in September. Competition receives more than 300 entries. 2006 winner was Mary Kaiser (Falling Into Velázquez). Winning chapbooks available through website and www.amazon.com. **Contact:** Margo Stever, editor. The annual competition is open to poets who have not published a book or chapbook, though individual poems may have already appeared. Manuscripts may be either a collection of poems or one long poem and should be a minimum of 16 pages and a maximum of 20 pages (not including the title page or table of contents). To provide publishing opportunities for emerging poets. Deadline: May 15. Prize: $1,000, publication of chapbook, 20 copies of chapbook, and a reading at The Hudson Valley Writers' Center. Uses a blind judging system.

SLIPSTREAM ANNUAL POETRY CHAPBOOK CONTEST

Slipstream, Slipstream Poetry Contest, Dept. W-1, P.O. Box 2071, Niagara Falls NY 14301. **E-mail:** editors@slipstreampress.org. **Website:** www.slipstreampress.org. **Contact:** Dan Sicoli, co-editor. Slipstream Magazine is a yearly anthology of some of the best poetry you'll find today in the American small press. Send up to 40 pages of poetry: any style, format, or theme (or no theme). Send only copies of your poems, not originals. Manuscripts will no longer be returned. See website for specific details. Offered annually to help promote a poet whose work is often overlooked or ignored. Open to any writer. Deadline: December 1. Prize: $1,000 plus 50 professionally-printed copies of your book.

HELEN C. SMITH MEMORIAL AWARD FOR POETRY

The Texas Institute of Letters, P.O. Box 609, Round Rock TX 78680. **E-mail:** tilsecretary@yahoo.com. **Website:** http://texasinstituteofletters.org/. Offered annually for the best book of poems published January 1-December 31 of previous year. Poet must have been born in Texas, have lived in the state at some time for at least 2 consecutive years, or the subject matter must be associated with the state. See website for guidelines. Deadline: early January. Prize: $1,200.

THE RICHARD SNYDER MEMORIAL PUBLICATION PRIZE

Ashland Poetry Press, 401 College Ave., Ashland University, Ashland OH 44805. **E-mail:** app@ashland.edu. **Website:** www.ashlandpoetrypress.com. **Contact:** Sarah Wells, managing editor. Offers annual award of $1,000 plus book publication in a paper-only edition of 1,000 copies. Submissions must be unpublished in book form. Considers simultaneous submissions. Submit 50-80 pages of poetry. Competition receives 375 entries/year. Winners will be announced in *Writer's Chronicle* and *Poets & Writers*. Copies of winning books available from Small Press Distribution and directly from the Ashland University Bookstore online. The Ashland Poetry Press publishes 2-4 books of poetry/year. Deadline: April 30 (annually). 2013 judge: Alicia Ostriker.

THE SOW'S EAR CHAPBOOK COMPETITION

The Sow's Ear Review, P.O. Box 127, Millwood VA 22646. (540)955-3955. **E-mail:** rglesman@gmail.com. **Website:** www.sows-ear.kitenet.net. **Contact:** Robert G. Lesman, managing editor. *The Sow's Ear Poetry Review* sponsors an annual chapbook competition. Open to adults. Open to adults. Send 22-26 pages of poetry plus a title page and a table of contents, all without your name. On a separate sheet list chapbook title, your name, address, phone number, e-mail address if available, and publication credits for submitted poems, if any. No length limit on poems, but no more than one poem on a page. Simultaneous submission is allowed, but if your chapbook is accepted elsewhere, you must withdraw promptly from our competition. Poems previously published are acceptable if you hold publication rights. Send SASE or e-mail address for notification. Entries will not be returned. Deadline: May 1 (postmark). Prize: Offers $1,000, publication as the spring issue of the magazine, 25 author's copies, and distribution to subscribers.

SPARK QUARTERLY WRITING CONTEST

Spark: A Creative Anthology (Empire & Great Jones Creative Arts Foundation), 13024 S. 3100 W, Riverton UT 84065. **E-mail:** editor@sparkanthology.org. **Website:** www.SparkAnthology.org/contests. **Contact:** Brian Lewis, contest director. "This contest is open to any writer without restriction on age, location, genre, or previous publication credits. We encourage both established and emerging writers to participate." Submissions must be unpublished. Entries are accepted and managed online. Writers can view their work's status on the submission site, and winners will be posted at http://SparkAnthology.org/contests/winners. "Prizes are awarded for excellent poetry and excellent prose, with no regard to the entrant's previous publication experience. Prose includes both fiction and nonfiction, and poetry includes all forms and meters." Prize: "Grand Prize (one each for Poetry and Prose) always includes cash and publication." Judged by "staff of *Spark: A Creative Anthology* plus two previously-published professional writers as 'Guest Judges' who are not on Spark staff. Guest Judges change with each contest."

SPORTS FICTION AND ESSAY CONTEST

Winning Writers, 351 Pleasant St., PMB 222, Northampton MA 01060-3961. (866)946-9748. **Fax:** (413)280-0539. **E-mail:** adam@winningwriters.com. **Website:** www.winningwriters.com. Offers annual award of 1st Place: $1,500, 2 awards; 2nd Place: $500, 2 awards; Honorable Mentions (10): $100 each. All prize winners receive online publication at WinningWriters.com. Submissions must be unpublished. Considers simultaneous submissions. Submit 1-2 poems, 1 story, or 1 essay on a sports-related theme. Submit online. Guidelines available on website. **Entry fee:** $15 for 1-2 poems, 1 story, or 1 essay. Multiple entries accepted. **Deadline:** November 15-May 31. "This is a new competition for 2012." Final judge: Jendi Reiter. Winners announced on November 15 at WinningWriters.com and in free e-mail newsletter. Entrants who provided valid e-mail addresses will also receive notification. See separate listing for the Wergle Flomp Humor Poetry Contest in this section. **Contact:** Adam Cohen. "Whether you're a player or a fan, or the kid who counted the minutes till gym class was over, sports can bring out the best and the worst in human nature. In this arena, teamwork, loyalty, courage, disappointment, failure, fame (and shame), and second chances are regularly on display. Sports can reinforce bullying and social dominance, or offer personal empowerment to an underdog. Yet stories and essays about sports are too often dismissed as 'genre writing'. This contest aims to bridge the gap between the worlds of physical culture and literary culture. We'd like to see the jocks and the writers sit down at the same lunchroom table and discover that they're both on a journey of self-transformation through

CONTEST & AWARDS

disciplined risk-taking..and that they both really, really like to win." Deadline: May 31. Prize: Prizes: 1st Prize: $1,000 cash; 5 honorable mentions: $100 cash each. Prizes are available in both categories. Judged by award-winning poet Jendi Reiter.

THE ELIZABETH MATCHETT STOVER MEMORIAL AWARD

Southwest Review, Southern Methodist University, P.O. Box 750374, Dallas TX 75275-0374. (214)768-1037. **Fax:** (214)768-1408. **E-mail:** swr@mail.smu.edu. **Website:** www.smu.edu/southwestreview. **Contact:** Jennifer Cranfill, senior editor, and Willard Spiegelman, editor-in-chief. "Offered annually to the best works of poetry that have appeared in the magazine in the previous year. Please note that mss are submitted for publication, not for the prizes themselves. Guidelines for SASE and online." Prize: $300 Judged by Jennifer Cranfill and Willard Spiegelman.

TIPS "Not an open contest. Annual prize in which winners are chosen from published pieces during the preceding year."

⊗ STROKESTOWN INTERNATIONAL POETRY COMPETITION

Strokestown International Poetry Festival, Strokestown Poetry Festival Office, Strokestown, County Roscommon Ireland. (+353) 71 9633759. E-mail: director@strokestownpoetry.org. **Website:** www.strokestownpoetry.org. **Contact:** Martin Dyar, Director. Poem cannot exceed 70 lines. Ten short-listed poets will be invited to Strokestown for the 2013 festival. This annual competition was established to promote excellence in poetry and participation in the reading and writing of it. Acquires first publication rights. Deadline: January. Prize: €3,000 Judged by Iggy McGovern and Michael Schmidt.

TEXAS INSTITUTE OF LETTERS BOB BUSH MEMORIAL AWARD FOR FIRST BOOK OF POETRY

Texas Institute of Letters, P.O. Box 609, Round Rock TX 78680. **Website:** http://texasinstituteofletters.org. Offered annually for best first book of poetry published in previous year. Writer must have been born in Texas, have lived in the state at least 2 consecutive years at some time, or the subject matter should be associated with the state. See website for exact date. Prize: $1,000.

TUFTS POETRY AWARDS

Claremont Graduate University, Claremont Graduate University, School of Arts & Humanities, 831 N. Dartmouth Ave., Claremont CA 91711-6165. (909)621-8612. **Website:** www.cgu.edu/tufts. **Contact:** Wendy Martin, program director. "Unlike many literary awards, which are coronations for a successful career or body of work, the Kingsley Tufts Poetry Award was created to both honor the poet and provide the resources that allow artists to continue working towards the pinnacle of their craft." "Any poet will tell you that the only thing more rare than meaningful recognition is a meaningful payday. For two outstanding poets each year, the Kingsley and Kate Tufts awards represent both." Deadline: must be submitted between September 1 and August 31. Prize: $100,000 for the Kingsley Tufts Poetry Award and $10,000 for the Kate Tufts Discovery Award.

☺ UTMOST CHRISTIAN POETRY CONTEST

Utmost Christian Writers Foundation, 121 Morin Maze, Edmonton Alberta T6K 1V1 Canada. (780)265-4650. **E-mail:** nnharms@telusplanet.net. **Website:** www.utmostchristianwriters.com. **Contact:** Nathan Harms, executive director. Utmost is founded on — and supported by — the dreams, interests and aspirates of individual people. Contest is only open to Christians. Poems may be rhymed or free verse, up to 60 lines, but must not have been published previously or have won any prize in any previous competition of any kind. Deadline: February 28. Prize: Prizes: 1st Place: $1,000; 2nd Place: $500; 10 prizes of $100 are offered for honorable mention; $300 for best rhyming poem and $200 for an honorable mention rhyming poem. Judged by a committee of the Directors of Utmost Christian Writers Foundation (who work under the direction of Barbara Mitchell, chief judge).

TIPS "Besides providing numerous resources for Christian writers and poets, Utmost also provides a marketplace where Christian writers and poets can sell their work. Please follow our guidelines. We receive numerous unsuitable submissions from writers. We encourage writers to submit suitable material. The best way to do this is to read the guidelines specific to your project—poetry, book reviews, articles—and then take time to look at the material we have already published in that area. The final step is to evaluate your proposed submission in comparison to the material we have used previously. If you complete these steps and strongly feel that your material is appropriate for us, we encourage you to submit it. Please use the submission link on the appropriate Web page. For example, if you are submitting a poem, please click the 'Poetry Gallery' link and use the submission link 'Poetry Guidelines'. If you fail to follow these instructions, it's possible your submission will be lost."

DANIEL VARUJAN AWARD

New England Poetry Club, 654 Green St., Apt. 2, Cambridge MA 02139. **E-mail:** contests@nepoetryclub.org. **Website:** www.nepoetryclub.org. **Contact:** NEPC contest coordinator. "For a poem on any subject, worthy of poet Daniel Varujan who was executed by the Ottoman Turks in the 1915 genocide of the Armenian population. Jailed while awaiting execution he finished a manuscript of sweet pastoral poems." "Send entry in duplicate, one without name and address of writer." Deadline: May 31. Prize: $1,000. Judges are well-known poets and sometimes winners of previous NEPC contests.

WERGLE FLOMP HUMOR POETRY CONTEST

Winning Writers, 351 Pleasant St., PMB 222, Northampton MA 01060. (866)946-9748. **Fax:** (413)280-0539. **E-mail:** adam@winningwriters.com. **Website:** www.winningwriters.com. **Contact:** Adam Cohen. "This annual contest seeks today's best humor poems. One poem of any length should be submitted. The poem should be in English. Inspired gibberish is also accepted. See website for guidelines, examples, and to submit your poem. Nonexclusive right to publish submissions on WinningWriters.com, in e-mail newsletter, and in press releases." Submit one humor poem online. No length limit. April 1. Prize: $2,500 in prizes, with a top prize of $1,000. Jendi Reiter. **TIPS** "Submissions may be previously published and may be entered in other contests. Competition receives about 2,000 entries/year. Winners are announced on August 15 at WinningWriters.com. Entrants who provide a valid e-mail address will also receive notification."

WHITE PINE PRESS POETRY PRIZE

White Pine Press, P.O. Box 236, Buffalo NY 14201. **E-mail:** wpine@whitepine.org. **Website:** www.whitepine.org. **Contact:** Dennis Maloney, editor. Offered annually for previously published or unpublished poets. Manuscript: Up to 80 pages of original work; translations are not eligible. Poems may have appeared in magazines or limited-edition chapbooks. Open to any US citizen. Deadline: November 30 (postmarked). Prize: $1,000 and publication. Final Judge is a poet of national reputation. All entries are screened by the editorial staff of White Pine Press.

WICK OPEN POETRY CHAPBOOK COMPETITION

Wick Poetry Center, 301 Satterfield Hall, Kent State University, P.O. Box 5190, Kent OH 44242-0001. (330)672-2067. **Fax:** (330)672-3333. **E-mail:** wickpoety@kent.edu. **Website:** www.kent.edu/wick. **Contact:** David Hassler, director. Offered annually for a chapbook of poems (15-25 pages) by a poet currently living in Ohio. Poets currently residing in Ohio may enter the Open Competition. Poets currently enrolled in Ohio institutions of higher education may enter the Student Competition. See website for full rules and requirements. Deadline: October 31. Prize: 2 mss selected for publication in the Wick Chapbook Series, published by the Kent State University Press. The winners will also give a reading at Kent State University.

THE J. HOWARD AND BARBARA M.J. WOOD PRIZE

Poetry, 61 W. Superior St., Chicago IL 60654. (312)787-7070. **Fax:** (312)787-6650. **E-mail:** editors@poetrymagazine.org. **Website:** www.poetrymagazine.org. Offered annually for poems published in *Poetry* during the preceding year (October-September). Upon acceptance, *Poetry* licenses exclusive worldwide first serial rights, including electronic rights, for publication, as well as non-exclusive rights to reprint, reuse, and archive the work, in any format, in perpetuity. Copyright reverts to author upon first publication. Prize: $5,000.

WORKING PEOPLE'S POETRY COMPETITION

Blue Collar Review, P.O. Box 11417, Norfolk VA 23517. **E-mail:** red-ink@earthlink.net. **Website:** www.partisanpress.org. The Working People's Poetry Competition offers $100 and a 1-year subscription to *Blue Collar Review* (see separate listing in Magazines/Journals) and "1 year posting of winning poem on our website. Poetry should be typed as you would like to see it published, with your name and address on each page. Include cover letter with entry." Guidelines available on website. Deadline: May 15.

ZONE 3 POETRY AWARD

ZONE 3, Austin Peay State University, Austin Peay State University, P.O. Box 4565, Clarksville TN 37044. (931)221-7031. **Fax:** (931)221-7149. **E-mail:** wallacess@apsu.edu. **E-mail:** falconerb@apsu.edu. **Website:** www.apsu.edu/zone3/. **Contact:** Susan Wallace, managing editor. Offered annually for unpublished poetry. Zone 3 is now accepting submissions for its annual poetry award. Submit up to three poems via online submissions manager. Deadline: December 31. Prize: $250.

MULTIPLE WRITING AREAS

◉ AESTHETICA CREATIVE WORKS COMPETITION

P.O. Box 371, York YO23 1WL United Kingdom. **E-mail:** pauline@aestheticamagazine.com. **E-mail:** submissions@aestheticamagazine.com. **Website:** www.aestheticamagazine.com. The Aesthetica Creative Works Competition represents the scope of creative activity today, and provides an opportunity for both new and established artists to nurture their reputations on an international scale. There are three categories: Short Film Festival, Art Prize, and Creative Writing. Art Prize has four sub-categories, Creative writing has two. See website for guidelines and more details. The Aesthetica Creative Works Competition represents the scope of creative activity today, and provides an opportunity for both new and established artists to nurture their reputations on an international scale. There are three categories: Artwork & Photography, Fiction and Poetry. See guidelines online. The Aesthetica Creative Works Competition is looking to discover talented artists and writers. The editor of Aesthetica is a Fellow of the Royal Society of Arts. See guidelines online. Works should be done in English August 31, 2011. Prize: £500-1,000, Each winner will receive an additional prize from our competition partners. Winners will be published in the Aesthetica Creative Works Annual. Winners will receive a complimentary copy of the Aesthetica Creative Works Annual and publication of the work in their creative section (3 winners). **TIPS** "You will be notified by Oct. 31, 2011; please do not contact us beforehand. For further equeries, visit our FAQ page online at website."

THE AMERICAN GEM LITERARY FESTIVAL

Film*Makers* Magazine/Write Brothers, **Website:** www.filmmakers.com/contests/short/. Deadlines: March 1 (early bird deadline); June 1 (regular deadline); August 1 (late deadline); September (final deadline).

AMERICAS AWARD

University of Wisconsin-Milwaukee, P.O. Box 413, Milwaukee WI 53201. **Website:** http://www4.uwm.edu/clacs/aa/index.cfm. **Contact:** Claire Gonzalez. The award winners and commended titles are selected for their (1) distinctive literary quality; (2) cultural contextualization; (3) exceptional integration of text, illustration and design; and (4) potential for classroom use. The Américas Award is given in recognition of U.S. works of fiction, poetry, folklore, or selected non-fiction (from picture books to works for young adults) published in the previous year in English or Spanish that authentically and engagingly portray Latin America, the Caribbean, or Latinos in the United States. By combining both and linking the Americas, the award reaches beyond geographic borders, as well as multicultural-international boundaries, focusing instead upon cultural heritages within the hemisphere. Deadline: January 18. Prize: $500, plaque and a formal presentation at the Library of Congress, Washington DC.

ARIZONA AUTHORS' ASSOCIATION ANNUAL NATIONAL LITERARY CONTEST AND BOOK AWARDS

Arizona Authors' Association, 6145 W. Echo Ln., Glendale AZ 85302. (623)847-9343. **E-mail:** info@azauthors.com. **Website:** www.azauthors.com. Offered annually for previously unpublished poetry, short stories, essays, novels, and articles. Awards for published books in fiction, anthology, nonfiction, and children's. Winners announced at an award banquet in Glendale in November, and short pieces and excerpts published in *Arizona Literary Magazine*. Open to all writers anywhere in the world. Guidelines for unpublished and published categories vary, see website for guidelines. Deadline: July 1. Prize: First Prize: $100 and publication, and/or feature in the *Arizona Literary Magazine*. Additional prizes awarded in all categories and individual, specific categories.

ART AFFAIR ANNUAL WRITING CONTEST

Art Affair, P.O. Box 54302, Oklahoma City OK 73154. **E-mail:** artaffair@aol.com. **Website:** www.shadetreecreations.com. Purpose of contest is to encourage new and established writers and to publicly recognize them for their efforts. Open to any writer or poet. Deadline: October 1 (every year). **Contact:** Barbara Shepherd. "Fiction and poems must be unpublished. Multiple entries accepted and may be mailed in the same packet. For (general) Short Story, double-space in 12-point font (put page and word count in upper right-hand corner of first page—5,000 word limit. Include cover page with writer's name, address, phone number, and title of story. For Western Short Story, follow same directions but type 'Western' on cover page. For Poetry, submit original poems on any subject, in any style, no more than 60 lines (put line count in the upper right-hand corner of first page). Include cover page with poet's name, address, phone number, and title. Do not include SASE; mss will not be returned." To encourage new and established writers and to publicly recognize them for their efforts. Open to any writer or poet. Deadline: October 1. Prize: Prizes: Short Story: 1st Prize: $50; 2nd Prize: $25; 3rd Prize: $15. Western Short Story: 1st Prize: $50; 2nd Prize: $25; 3rd Prize: $15. Poetry: 1st Prize: $40, 2nd Prize: $25; 3rd Prize: $15. (all winners also receive certificates. Additional certificates for Honorable Mentions will be awarded at discretion of the judges). **TIPS** "Guidelines and entry forms available for SASE and on website."

ART AFFAIR SHORT STORY AND WESTERN SHORT STORY CONTESTS

Art Affair - Contest, P.O. Box 54302, Oklahoma City OK 73154. **E-mail:** artaffair@aol.com. **Website:** www.shadetreecreations.com. The annual Art Affair Writing Contests include (General) Short Story and Western Short Story categories. Open to any writer. All short stories must be unpublished. Multiple entries accepted in both categories with separate entry fees for each. Submit original stories on any subject and timeframe for general Short Story category, and submit original western stories for Western Short Story - word limit for all entries is 5,000 words. Guidelines available on website. Put word count in the upper right-hand corner of first page; mark "Western" on western short stories. All ms. must be double-spaced on 8.5x11 white paper. Type title of short story on first page and headers on following pages. Include cover page with writer's name, address, phone number, and manuscript title. Deadline: postmarked by October 1. Prize: $50, $25, $15.

ARTIST TRUST FELLOWSHIP AWARD

1835 12th Ave., Seattle WA 98122. (209)467-8734 ext. 9. **Fax:** (866)218-7878. **E-mail:** miguel@artisttrust.org. **Website:** artisttrust.org. "Artist Trust Fellowship awards practicing professional Washington State artists of exceptional talent and demonstrated ability." Annual. Prize: $7,500. "The Fellowship awards are multidisciplinary awards. The categories for 2012 are Emerging Fields & Cross-disciplinary, Folk & Traditional, Visual and Performing Art; for 2012 are Literary, Music, Media and Craft. Accepted genres for Literary are: poetry, fiction, graphic novels, experimental works, creative non-fiction, screen plays, film scripts and teleplays." Receives about 175 entries per category. Entries are judged by work samples as specified in the guidelines. Winners are selected by a multidisciplinary panel of artists and arts professionals. No entry fee. Guidelines available around December, please check website. Accepts inquiries by e-mail, phone. Submission period is December-February. Website should be consulted for the exact date. Entries can be unpublished or previously published. Washington State residents only. Length: up to 15 pages for poetry, fiction, graphic novels, experimental works and creative non-fiction, and up to 20 pages for screen plays, film scripts and teleplays. All mss must be typed with a 12-pnt font size or larger and cannot be single spaced (except for poetry). Include artist statement and resume with name, address, phone, e-mail, and novel/story title. "The Fellowship awards are highly competitive. Please follow guidelines with care." Results announced in the spring. Winners notified by mail. Results made available to entrants on website. **Contact:** Miguel Guillen, Program Manager. "The fellowship is a merit-based award of $7,500 to practicing professional Washington State artists of exceptional talent and demonstrated ability. Literature fellowships are offered every other year. The award is made on the basis of work of the past 5 years. Applicants must be individual artists; Washington State residents; not matriculated students; and generative artists. Offered every 2 years in even years. Guidelines and application online." Deadline: February 18. Prize: $7,500.

THE ART OF MUSIC BIENNIAL WRITING CONTEST

P.O. Box 85, Del Mar CA 92014. (619)884-1401. **Fax:** (858)755-1104. **E-mail:** info@theartofmusicinc.org.

E-mail: eaxford@aol.com. **Website:** www.theartof-musicinc.org; www.pianopress.com. **Contact:** Elizabeth C. Axford. Offered biannually. Categories are: Essay, short story, poetry, song lyrics, and illustrations for cover art. Acquires one-time rights. All entries must be accompanied by an entry form indicating category and age; parent signature is required of all writers under age 18. Poems may be of any length and in any style; essays and short stories should not exceed 5 double-spaced, typewritten pages. All entries shall be previously unpublished (except poems and song lyrics) and the original work of the author. Inquiries accepted by e-mail, phone. Short stories should be no longer than 5 pages typed and double spaced. Open to any writer. "Make sure all work is fresh and original. Music-related topics only." Results announced October 31. Winners notified by mail. For contest results, send SASE or visit website. All writings should be on music-related topics. "The purpose of the contest is to promote the art of music through writing." Deadline: June 30. Prize: Trophy, certificate, publication online and in the eBook, *The Art of Music: A Collection of Writings*. Judged by a panel of published poets, authors and songwriters.

◌ ATLANTIC WRITING COMPETITION FOR UNPUBLISHED MANUSCRIPTS

Writers' Federation of Nova Scotia, 1113 Marginal Rd., Halifax NS B3H 4P7. (902)423-8116. **Fax:** (902)422-0881. **E-mail:** programs@writers.ns.ca. **Website:** www.writers.ns.ca. "Annual contest for beginners to try their hand in a number of categories: novel, short story, poetry, writing for younger children, writing for juvenile/young adult. Only 1 entry/category is allowed. Established writers are also eligible, but must work in an area that's new to them. Because our aim is to help Atlantic Canadian writers grow, judges return written comments when the competition is concluded. Anyone residing in the Atlantic Provinces for at least 6 months prior to the contest deadline is eligible to enter."$35 fee for novel ($30 for WFNS members); $25 fee for all other categories ($20 for WFNS members). Needs poetry, essays, juvenile, novels, articles, short stories. **Contact:** Hillary Titley. "Annual contest for beginners to try their hand in a number of categories: adult novel, writing for children, poetry, short story, juvenile/young adult novel, creative non-fiction, and play. Because our aim is to help Atlantic Canadian writers grow, judges return written comments when

the competition is concluded." Page lengths and rules vary based on categories. See website for details. Anyone resident in the Atlantic Provinces since September 1st, 2012 is eligible to enter. Only one entry per category is allowed. Each entry requires its own entry form and registration fee. "We encourage writers in Atlantic Canada to explore and expand their talents by sending in their new, untried work." Deadline: November 9. Prize: Prizes vary based on categories. See website for details.

AUTUMN HOUSE POETRY, FICTION, AND NONFICTION PRIZES

P.O. Box 60100, Pittsburgh PA 15211. (412)381-4261. **E-mail:** msimms@autumnhouse.org. **Website:** http://autumnhouse.org. **Contact:** Michael Simms, editor. Offers annual prize of $2,500 and publication of book-length ms with national promotion. Submission must be unpublished as a collection, but individual poems, stories, and essays may have been previously published elsewhere. Considers simultaneous submissions. Submit 50-80 pages of poetry or 200-300 pages of prose ("blind judging—2 cover sheets requested"). Guidelines available for SASE, by e-mail, or on website. Competition receives 1,500 entries/year. Winners announced through mailings, website, and ads in *Poets & Writers*, *American Poetry Review*, and *Writer's Chronicle* (extensive publicity for winner). Copies of winning books available from Amazon.com, Barnes & Noble, and other retailers. "Autumn House is a non-profit corporation with the mission of publishing and promoting poetry and other fine literature. We have published books by Gerald Stern, Ruth L. Schwartz, Ed Ochester, Andrea Hollander Budy, George Bilgere, Jo McDougall, and others." June 30, annually. 2012 judges were Stephen Dunn, Stewart O'Nan, and Phillip Lopate.

TIPS "Include only your best work."

AWP AWARD SERIES

Association of Writers & Writing Programs, George Mason University, 4400 University Drive, MSN 1E3, Fairfax VA 22030. **E-mail:** supriya@awpwriter.org. **Website:** www.awpwriter.org. **Contact:** Supriya Bhatnagar, director of publications. AWP sponsors the Award Series, an annual competition for the publication of excellent new book-length works. The competition is open to all authors writing in English regardless of nationality or residence, and is available to published and unpublished authors alike. Guidelines on website. Entries must be unpublished. Open to any writer. Offered annually to foster new literary talent. Deadline: Postmarked between January 1 and February 28. Prize: AWP Prize for the Novel: $2,000; Donald Hall Prize for Poetry: $5,000; Grace Paley Prize in Short Fiction: $5,000; and AWP Prize for Creative Nonfiction: $2,000.

BOROONDARA LITERARY AWARDS

City of Boroondara, 340 Camberwell Rd., Camberwell VIC 3124 Australia. **E-mail:** bla@boroondara.vic. gov.au. **Website:** www.boroondara.vic.gov.au/libraries/boroondara-literary-awards. "Contest for unpublished work in 2 categories: Young Writers, 7th-9th grade and 10th-12th grade (prose and poetry on any theme) and Open Short Story (2,000-3,000 words)." Deadline: August 30. Prize: **Young Writers**—1st Place: $300; 2nd Place: $150; 3rd Place: $100. **Open Short Story**—1st Place: $1,500; 2nd Place: $500; 3rd Place $250.

THE BOSTON AUTHORS CLUB BOOK AWARDS

The Boston Authors Club, 15 Pine Crest Road, Newtown MA 02459. (617)244-0646. **E-mail:** sml@sarahlamstein.com. **Website:** www.bostonauthorsclub. org. **Contact:** Sarah Lamstein. Julia Ward Howe Prize offered annually in the spring for books published the previous year. Two awards are given: one for trade books of fiction, nonfiction, or poetry, and the second for children's books. Authors must live or have lived within 100 miles of Boston within the past five years. No picture books or subsidized publishers. There must be two copies of each book submitted. Authors must live within 100 miles of Boston the year their book is published. Deadline: January 15. Prize: $1,000 in each category.

BURNABY WRITERS' SOCIETY CONTEST

E-mail: info@bws.bc.ca. **Website:** www.bws.bc.ca; http:burnabywritersnews.blogspot.com. **Contact:** Eileen Kernaghan. "Offered annually for unpublished work. Open to all residents of British Columbia. Categories vary from year to year. Send SASE for current rules. For complete guidelines see website or burnabywritersnews.blogspot.com." Purpose is to encourage talented writers in all genres. Deadline: May 31. Prize: 1st Place: $200; 2nd Place: $100; 3rd Place: $50; and public reading.

CHRISTIAN BOOK AWARDS

Evangelical Christian Publishers Association, 9633 S. 48th St., Suite 140, Phoenix AZ 85044. (480)966-3998. **Fax:** (480)966-1944. **E-mail:** info@ecpa.org; mkuyper@ecpa.org. **Website:** www.ecpa.org. **Contact:** Mark W. Kuyper, president and CEO. Since 1978 the Evangelical Christian Publishers Association has recognized quality and encouraged excellence by presenting the ECPA Christian Book Awards (formerly known as Gold Medallion) each year. Categories include children, fiction, nonfiction, Bibles, Bible reference, inspiration, and new author. "All entries must be evangelical in nature and submitted through an ECPA member publisher." Submission period: September 1-30. See website for all details The Christian Book Awards recognize the highest quality in Christian books and is among the oldest and most prestigious awards program in Christian publishing. Deadline: September 30.

COLORADO BOOK AWARDS

Colorado Center for the Book, 1490 Lafayette St., Suite 101, Denver CO 80218. (303)894-7951, ext. 21. **Fax:** (303)864-9361. **E-mail:** goff@coloradohumanities.org. **Website:** www.coloradohumanities.org. **Contact:** Christine Goff. An annual program that celebrates the accomplishments of Colorado's outstanding authors, editors, illustrators, and photographers. Awards are presented in at least ten categories including anthology/collection, biography, children's, creative nonfiction, fiction, history, nonfiction, pictorial, poetry, and young adult. To be eligible for a Colorado Book Award, a primary contributor to the book must be a Colorado writer, editor, illustrator, or photographer. Current Colorado residents are eligible, as are individuals engaged in ongoing literary work in the state and authors whose personal history, identity, or literary work reflect a strong Colorado influence. Authors not currently Colorado residents who feel their work is inspired by or connected to Colorado should submit a letter with his/her entry describing the connection. To celebrate books and their creators and promote them to readers.

CORDON D 'OR - GOLD RIBBON ANNUAL INTERNATIONAL CULINARY ACADEMY AWARDS

The 'Accolade of the 21st Century', Cordon d 'Or - Gold Ribbon Inc., P.O. Box 40868, St. Petersburg FL 33743. (727)347-2437. **E-mail:** cordondor@aol.com.

Website: www.goldribboncookery.com. **Contact:** Noreen Kinney. "Contest promotes recognition of food authors, writers, and culinary magazines and websites, food stylists and food photographers and other professionals in the culinary field. See website www.cordondorcuisine.com for full details. Open to any writer. All categories can be found on the website. The only criteria is that all entries must be in the English language." Deadline: December 31. Prize: Cordon d 'Or - Gold Ribbon Crystal Globe Trophies (with stands and engraved marble bases) will be presented to winners. An outstanding winner chosen by the judges from among all entries will also win a cash award of $1,000. Judged by professionals in the fields covered in the awards program.

THE CRUCIBLE POETRY AND FICTION COMPETITION

Crucible, Barton College, College Station, Wilson NC 27893. (800)345-4973 x6450. **E-mail:** crucible@barton.edu. **Website:** www.barton.edu/SchoolofArts&Sciences/English/Crucible.htm. **Contact:** Terrence L. Grimes, editor. "Offered annually for unpublished mss. Fiction is limited to 8,000 words; poetry is limited to 5 poems. Guidelines online or by email or for SASE. All submissions should be electronic." Deadline: May 1. Prize: 1st Place: $150; 2nd Place: $100 (for both poetry and fiction). Winners are also published in *Crucible*. Judged by in-house editorial board.

CWW ANNUAL WISCONSIN WRITERS AWARDS COMPETITION

Council for Wisconsin Writers, **Website:** www.wisconsinwriters.org. **Contact:** Geoff Gilpin; Jerriane Hayslett and Karla Huston, awards co-chairs; and Carolyn Washburne, Christopher Latham Sholes Award and Major Achievement Award co-chair. Offered annually for work published by Wisconsin writers the previous calendar year. Nine awards: Major/life achievement alternate years; short fiction; short nonfiction; nonfiction book; poetry book; fiction book; children's literature; Lorine Niedecker Poetry Award; Sholes Award for Outstanding Service to Wisconsin Writers Alternate Years; Essay Award for Young Writers. Open to Wisconsin residents. Guidelines, rules, and entry form on website. Deadline: January 31 (postmark). Prize: Prizes: $500 and a week-long residency at Shake Rag Alley or Maplewood Lodge in Mineral Point. Essay Contest: $150. "This year only the Essay Award for Young Writers prize will be $250."

DANA AWARDS IN THE NOVEL, SHORT FICTION, ESSAY AND POETRY

www.danaawards.com, 200 Fosseway Dr., Greensboro NC 27445. (336)644-8028. **E-mail:** danaawards@pipeline.com. **E-mail:** danaawards@gmail.com. **Website:** www.danaawards.com. **Contact:** Mary Elizabeth Parker, chair. Four awards offered annually for unpublished work written in English. Purpose is monetary award for work that has not been previously published or received monetary award, but will accept work published simply for friends and family. Works previously published online are not eligible. No work accepted by or for persons under 16 for any of the 4 awards: **Novel**—For the first 40 pages of a novel completed or in progress; **Fiction**—short fiction (no memoirs) up to 10,000 words; **Essay**—personal essay, memoir, or creative nonfiction up to 10,000 words; **Poetry**—for best group of 5 poems based on excellence of all 5 (no light verse, no single poem over 100 lines). Deadline: October 31 (postmarked). Prize: Prizes: $1,000 for each of the 4 awards.

EATON LITERARY AGENCY'S ANNUAL AWARDS PROGRAM

Eaton Literary Agency, P.O. Box 49795, Sarasota FL 34230-6795. (941)366-6589. **Fax:** (941)365-4679. **E-mail:** eatonlit@aol.com. **Website:** www.eatonliterary.com. Offered biannually for unpublished mss. Prize: $2,500 (over 10,000 words); $500 (under 10,000 words). Judged by an independent agency in conjunction with some members of Eaton's staff. No entry fee. Guidelines available for SASE, by fax, e-mail, or on website. Accepts inquiries by fax, phone and e-mail. Deadline: **March 31** (mss under 10,000 words); **August 31** (mss over 10,000 words). Entries must be unpublished. Open to any writer. Results announced in April and September. Winners notified by mail. For contest results, send SASE, fax, e-mail, or visit website. **Contact:** Richard Lawrence, V.P. Offered biannually for unpublished mss. Entries must be unpublished. Open to any writer. Guidelines available for SASE, by fax, e-mail, or on website. Accepts inquiries by fax, phone and e-mail. Results announced in April and September. Winners notified by mail. For contest results, send SASE, fax, e-mail, or visit website. Deadline: March 31 (short story); August 31 (book-length). Prize: $2,500 (book-length); $500 (short story). Judged by an independent agency in conjunction with some members of Eaton's staff.

THE VIRGINIA FAULKNER AWARD FOR EXCELLENCE IN WRITING

Prairie Schooner, 123 Andrews Hall, University of Nebraska-Lincoln, Lincoln NE 68588-0334. (402)472-0911. **Fax:** (402)472-1817. **E-mail:** PrairieSchooner@unl.edu. **Website:** www.prairieschooner.unl.edu. **Contact:** Kwame Dawes. Offered annually for work published in *Prairie Schooner* in the previous year. Categories: short stories, essays, novel excerpts and translations. Guidelines for SASE or on website. Accepts inquiries by fax and e-mail. "We only read mss from September 1 through May 1." Winning entry must have been published in *Prairie Schooner* in the year preceeding the award. Results announced in the Spring issue. Winners notified by mail in February or March. Prize: $1,000. Judged by Editorial Board.

☺ FREEFALL SHORT PROSE AND POETRY CONTEST

Freefall Literary Society of Calgary, 922 9th Ave. SE, Calgary AB T2G 0S4 Canada. **E-mail:** freefallmagazine@yahoo.ca. **Website:** www.freefallmagazine.ca. **Contact:** Lynn C. Fraser, managing editor. Offered annually for unpublished work in the categories of poetry (5 poems/entry) and prose (3,000 words or less). The purpose of the award in both categories is to recognize writers and offer publication credits in a literary magazine format. Contest rules and entry form online. Acquires first Canadian serial rights; ownership reverts to author after one-time publication. Deadline: December 31. Prize: 1st Place: $300 (CAD); 2nd Place: $150 (CAD); 3rd Place: $75; Honourable Mention: $25. All prizes include publication in the spring edition of *FreeFall Magazine*. Winners will also be invited to read at the launch of that issue if such a launch takes place. Honorable mentions in each category will be published and may be asked to read. Travel expenses not included. Judged by current guest editor for issue (who are also published authors in Canada).

GEORGETOWN REVIEW

Georgetown Review, 400 East College St., Box 227, Georgetown KY 40324. (502) 863-8308. **Fax:** (502) 863-8888. **E-mail:** gtownreview@georgetowncollege.edu. **Website:** georgetowncolleged.edu/georgetown-review. **Contact:** Steve Carter, editor. Our magazine is a collaboration between English faculty at George-

town College and undergrads who learn the editing business as they go and who always amaze their elders with their dedication and first-rate work. "We will consider only original collections of poems written in English. (You may include individual poems that have appeared elsewhere.) Students, colleagues, and close friends of the judge, and current students and employees of Georgetown College are not eligible." See website for details on paper and online submission guidelines. Deadline: October 15. Prize: $1,000 and publication; runners-up receive publication.

HACKNEY LITERARY AWARDS

1305 2nd Ave. N, #103, Birmingham AL 35203. (205)226-4921. **E-mail:** info@hackneyliteraryawards.org. **Website:** www.hackneyliteraryawards.org. **Contact:** Myra Crawford, PhD, executive director. Offered annually for unpublished novels, short stories (maximum 5,000 words) and poetry (50 line limit). Guidelines on website. Deadline: September 30 (novels), November 30 (short stories and poetry). Prize: $5,000 in annual prizes for poetry and short fiction ($2,500 national and $2,500 state level). 1st Place: $600; 2nd Place: $400; 3rd Place: $250); plus $5,000 for an unpublished novel. Competition winners will be announced on the website each March.

THE ERIC HOFFER AWARD (BOOKS)

Best New Writing, P.O. Box 11, Titusville NJ 08560. **Fax:** (609)818-1913. **E-mail:** info@hopepubs.com. **Website:** www.hofferaward.com. **Contact:** Christopher Klim, chair. Annual contest recognizing excellence in publishing. "This contest recognizes excellence in independent publishing in many distinct categories. Honors by press type (academic, micro press, small press, and self-published) and category (art, poetry, general fiction, commercial fiction, children, young adult, culture, memoir, business, reference, home, health, self-help, spiritual, legacy fiction, and legacy (fiction and nonfiction) and eBook (fiction and nonfiction). Also awards the Montaigne Medal for most though-provoking book, the Da Vinci Eye for best cover, and the First Horizon Award for best new authors. Results published in the *US Review of Books*." Deadline: January 21. Prize: $2,000. Judged by authors, editors, agents, publishers, book producers, artists, experienced category readers, and health and business professionals.

THE ERIC HOFFER AWARD (PROSE)

Best New Writing, P.O. Box 11, Titusville NJ 08560. **Fax:** (609)964-1718. **E-mail:** info@hofferaward.com. **Website:** www.hofferaward.com. **Contact:** C. Klim, editor. "Annual contest for new and unpublished prose. Purchases first publication and one-time anthology rights for winning entries." "The Eric Hoffer Award for short prose (i.e., fiction and creative nonfiction - 10,000 words or less) was established at the start of the 21st century as a means of opening a door to writing of significant merit. It honors the memory of the great American philosopher Eric Hoffer by highlighting salient writing. The winning stories and essays are published in *Best New Writing*." Prize: $250; publication contract.

THE JULIA WARD HOWE/BOSTON AUTHORS AWARD

The Boston Authors Club, 45 Pine Crest Rd., Newton MA 02459. (617)244-0646. **E-mail:** bostonauthors@aol.com; SarahM45@aol.com. **Website:** www.bostonauthorsclub.org. **Contact:** Sarah Lamstein. This annual award honors Julia Ward Howe and her literary friends who founded the Boston Authors Club in 1900. It also honors the membership over 110 years, consisting of novelists, biographers, historians, governors, senators, philosophers, poets, playwrights, and other luminaries. There are 2 categories: trade books and books for young readers (beginning with chapter books through young adult books). Works of fiction, nonfiction, memoir, poetry, and biography published in 2010 are eligible. Authors must live or have lived (college counts) within a 100-mile radius of Boston within the last 5 years. Subsidized books, cook books and picture books are not eligible. Fee is $25 per title.

INDIANA REVIEW ½ K (SHORT-SHORT/PROSE-POEM) CONTEST

Indiana Review, Ballantine Hall 465, 1020 E. Kirkwood Ave., Indiana University, Bloomington IN 47405-7103. (812)855-3439. **Fax:** (812)855-9535. **E-mail:** inreview@indiana.edu. **Website:** http://indianareview.org. **Contact:** Jennifer Luebers, editor. Offered annually for unpublished work. Maximum story/poem length is 500 words. Guidelines available in March for SASE, by phone, e-mail, on website, or in publication. Open to any writer. Cover letter should include name, address, phone, e-mail, word count and title. No identifying information on ms. "We look for command of language and form." Results announced

in August. Winners notified by mail. For contest results, send SASE or visit website. Deadline: May 31. Prize: $1,000, plus publication, contributor's copies, and a year's subscription to *Indiana Review*.

INSIGHT WRITING CONTEST

Insight Magazine, 55 W. Oak Ridge Dr., Hagerstown MD 21740. **Fax:** (301)393-4055. **E-mail:** insight@rhpa.org. **Website:** www.insightmagazine.org. **Contact:** Dwain Esmond, editor. Annual contest for writers in the categories of student short story, general short story, and student poetry. Unpublished submissions only. General category is open to all writers; student categories must be age 22 and younger. "Your entry must be a true, unpublished work by you, with a strong spiritual message. We appreciate the use of Bible texts." Deadline: June 3. Prize: Prizes: Student Short and General Short Story: 1st Prize: $250; 2nd Prize: $200; 3rd Prize: $150. Student Poetry: 1st Prize: $100; 2nd Prize: $75; 3rd Prize: $50.

THE IOWA REVIEW AWARD IN POETRY, FICTION, AND NONFICTION

308 EPB, University of Iowa, Iowa City IA 52242. **E-mail:** iowa-review@uiowa.edu. **Website:** www.iowareview.org. *The Iowa Review* Award in Poetry, Fiction, and Nonfiction presents $1,500 to each winner in each genre, $750 to runners-up. Winners and runners-up published in *The Iowa Review*. Submissions must be unpublished. Considers simultaneous submissions (with notification of acceptance elsewhere). Submit up to 25 pages of prose, (double-spaced) or 10 pages of poetry (1 poem or several, but no more than 1 poem per page). Submit online or by mail. Include cover page with writer's name, address, e-mail and/or phone number, and title of each work submitted. Personal identification must not appear on ms pages. Label mailing envelope as a contest entry, E.G., "Contest: Fiction." One entry per envelope. Include SASP for confirmation of receipt of entry, SASE for results. Guidelines available on website. Deadline: Submit January 1-31 (postmark). 2013 Judges: Mary Jo Bang, Z.Z. Packer, Susan Orlean.

LEAGUE OF UTAH WRITERS CONTEST

The League of Utah Writers, P.O. Box 88, Logan UT 84323. (435)755-7609. **E-mail:** luwcontest@gmail.com. **Website:** www.luwriters.org. Open to any writer, the LUW Contest provides authors an opportunity to get their work read and critiqued. Contest submission period opens March 1 and closes June 1. Multiple categories are offered; see webpage for details. Entries are judged by professional authors and editors from outside the League. Entries must be the original and unpublished work of the author. Winners are announced at the Annual Writers Round-Up in September. Those not present will be notified by e-mail. Cash prizes are awarded. **Contact:** Tim Keller, Contest Chair. Open to any writer, the LUW Contest provides authors an opportunity to get their work read and critiqued. Multiple categories are offered; see webpage for details. Entries must be the original and unpublished work of the author. Winners are announced at the Annual Writers Round-Up in September. Those not present will be notified by e-mail. Submission Period: March 15 to June 15. Entries are judged by professional authors and editors from outside the League.

LET'S WRITE LITERARY CONTEST

The Gulf Coast Writers Association, P.O. Box 10294, Gulfport MS 39505. **E-mail:** writerpllevin@gmail.com. **Website:** www.gcwriters.org. **Contact:** Philip Levin. "The Gulf Coast Writers Association sponsors this nationally recognized contest, which accepts unpublished poems and short stories from authors all around the US. This is an annual event which has been held for over 20 years." Deadline: April 15. Prize: 1st Prize: $100; 2nd Prize: $60; 3rd Prize: $25. **TIPS** "See guidelines online."

MANITOBA BOOK AWARDS

c/o Manitoba Writers' Guild, 218-100 Arthur St., Winnipeg MB R3B 1H3 Canada. (204)944-8013. **E-mail:** info@mbwriter.mb.ca. **Website:** www.manitobabookawards.com. Offered annually: The McNally Robinson Book of Year Award (adult); The McNally Robinson Book for Young People Awards (8 and under and 9 and older); The John Hirsch Award for Most Promising Manitoba Writer; The Mary Scorer Award for Best Book by a Manitoba Publisher; The Carol Shields Winnipeg Book Award; The Eileen McTavish Sykes Award for Best First Book; The Margaret Laurence Award for Fiction; The Alexander Kennedy Isbister Award for Non-Fiction; The Manuela Dias Book Design of the Year Award; The Best Illustrated Book of the Year Award; and the biennial Le Prix Littéraire Rue-Deschambault. Guidelines and submission forms available online (accepted until mid-January). Open to Manitoba writers only. Prize: Several prizes up to $5,000 (Canadian).

THE MCGINNIS-RITCHIE MEMORIAL AWARD

Southwest Review, P.O. Box 750374, Dallas TX 75275-0374. (214)768-1037. **Fax:** (214)768-1408. **E-mail:** swr@mail.smu.edu. **Website:** www.smu.edu/southwestreview. **Contact:** Jennifer Cranfill, senior editor, and Willard Spiegelman, editor-in-chief. "The McGinnis-Ritchie Memorial Award is given annually to the best works of fiction and nonfiction that appeared in the magazine in the previous year. Mss are submitted for publication, not for the prizes themselves. Guidelines for SASE or online." Prize: $500. Judged by Jennifer Cranfill and Willard Spiegelman.
TIPS "Not an open contest. Annual prize in which winners are chosen from published pieces during the preceding year."

MIDLAND AUTHORS AWARD

Society of Midland Authors, Society of Midland Authors, P.O. Box 10419, Chicago IL 60610-0419. **E-mail:** loerzel@comcast.net. **Website:** www.midlandauthors.com. **Contact:** Robert Loerzel, President. Since 1957, the Society has presented annual awards for the best books written by Midwestern authors. The contest is open to any title with a recognized publisher that has been published within the year prior to the contest year. Open to authors or poets who reside in, were born in, or have strong ties to a Midland state, which includes Illinois, Indiana, Iowa, Kansas, Michigan, Minnesota, Missouri, Nebraska, North Dakota, South Dakota, Ohio and Wisconsin. Categories: children's nonfiction and fiction, adult nonfiction and fiction, adult biography, and poetry. "Established in 1915, the Society of Midland Authors Award (SMA) is presented to one title in each of six categories 'to stimulate creative effort,' one of SMA's goals, to be honored at the group's annual awards banquet in May." Deadline: February 1. Prize: cash prize of at least $300 and a plaque that is awarded at the SMA banquet.

MISSISSIPPI REVIEW PRIZE

Mississippi Review, 118 College Dr., #5144, Hattiesburg MS 39406-0001. (601)266-4321. **Fax:** (601)266-5757. **E-mail:** msreview@usm.edu; rief@mississippireview.com. **Website:** www.mississippireview.com. "Our annual contest awards prizes of $1,000 in fiction and in poetry. Winners and finalists will make up next winter's print issue of the national literary magazine *Mississippi Review*. Contest is open to all writers in English except current or former students or employees of The University of Southern Mississippi. Fiction entries should be 1,000-5,000 words, poetry entries should be three poems totaling 10 pages or less. There is no limit on the number of entries you may submit. Entry fee is $15 per entry, payable to the *Mississippi Review*. Each entrant will receive a copy of the prize issue. No manuscripts will be returned. Previously published work is ineligible. Contest opens April 2. Deadline is October 1. Winners will be announced in late January and publication is scheduled for May next year. Entries should have 'MR Prize,' author name, address, phone, e-mail and title of work on page 1."

TIPS "No mss returned."

NEW MILLENNIUM AWARDS FOR FICTION, POETRY, AND NONFICTION

New Millennium Writings, NMW, Room M2, P.O. Box 2463, Knoxville TN 37901. (423)428-0389. **Website:** www.newmillenniumwritings.com/awards. "No restrictions as to style, content or number of submissions. Previously published pieces OK if online or under 5,000 print circulation. Send any time between now and midnight, June 17, for the Summer Awards program, January 31 for the Winter Awards. Simultaneous and multiple submissions welcome. Each fiction or nonfiction piece is a separate entry and should total no more than 6,000 words, except for the Short-Short Fiction Award, which should total no more than 1,000 words. (Nonfiction includes essays, profiles, memoirs, interviews, creative nonfiction, travel, humor, etc.) Each poetry entry may include up to 3 poems, not to exceed 5 pages total. All 20 poetry finalists will be published. Include name, phone, address, e-mail, and category on cover page only." Apply online via submissions manager. "Send SASE or IRC for list of winners or await your book." Deadline: postmarked on or before January 31. Prize: $1,000 for Best Poem; $1,000 for Best Fiction; $1,000 for Best Nonfiction; $1,000 for Best Short-Short Fiction.

NEW SOUTH WRITING CONTEST

English Department, Georgia State University, P.O. Box 3970, Atlanta GA 30302-3970. **E-mail:** newsouth@gsu.edu. **Website:** newsouthjournal.com/contest. **Contact:** Matt Sailor, editor-in-chief. Offered annually to publish the most promising work of up-and-coming writers of poetry (up to 3 poems) and fiction (9,000 word limit). Rights revert to writer upon publication. Guidelines online. Deadline: March 15.

Prize: 1st Place: $1,000 in each category; 2nd Place: $250; and publication to winners. Judged by Marily Kallet in poetry and Amber Sparks in prose.

TIPS "We look for engagement with language and characters we care about."

☮ OPEN SEASON AWARDS

The Malahat Review, University of Victoria, P.O. Box 1700, Stn CSC, Victoria BC V8V 2Y2 Canada. **Fax:** (250)472-5051. **E-mail:** malahat@uvic.ca. **Website:** www.malahatreview.ca. **Contact:** John Barton, editor. The annual Open Season Awards offers $1,000 CAD and publication in *The Malahat Review*. The Open Season Awards accepts entries of poetry, fiction, and creative nonfiction. Submissions must be unpublished. No simultaneous submissions. Submit up to 3 poems per entry, each poem not to exceed 100 lines; one piece of fiction (2500 words max.), or one piece of creative nonfiction (2500 words max.), no restrictions on subject matter or aesthetic approach. Include separate page with writer's name, address, e-mail, and title(s); no identifying information on mss pages. No e-mail submissions. Do not include SASE for results; mss will not be returned. Guidelines available on website. Winner and finalists contacted by e-mail. Winners published in spring issue of *Malahat Review* announced in winter on website, facebook page, and in quarterly e-newsletter, *Malahat lite*. Submissions must be unpublished. No simultaneous submissions. Submit up to 3 poems of 100 lines or less; 1 piece of fiction 2,500 words maximum; or 1 piece of creative nonfiction, 2,500 words maximum. No restrictions on subject matter or aesthetic approach. Include separate page with writer's name, address, e-mail, and title(s); no identifying information on mss pages. No e-mail submissions. Do not include SASE for results; mss will not be returned. Guidelines available on website. November 1 of each year. Prize: Offers $1,000 CAD and publication in *The Malahat Review* in each category.

JUDITH SIEGEL PEARSON AWARD

Judith Siegel Pearson Award, c/o Department of English, Wayne State University, Attn: Rhonda Agnew, 5057 Woodward Ave, Ste. 9408, Detroit MI 48202. (313)577-2450. **Fax:** (313)577-8618. **E-mail:** ad2073@wayne.edu. Offers an annual award of up to $500 for the best creative or scholarly work on a subject concerning women. The type of work accepted rotates each year: Drama in 2012; poetry in 2013 (poetry,

20 pages maximum); essays in 2014; fiction in 2015. Open to all interested writers and scholars. Submissions must be unpublished. Guidelines available by e-mail. No late or electronic submissions accepted. Deadline: Mid-late February. Offers an annual award of up to $500 for the best creative or scholarly work on a subject concerning women. The type of work accepted rotates each year: Drama in 2012; poetry in 2013 (poetry, 20 pages maximum); essays in 2014; fiction in 2015. Open to all interested writers and scholars. Submissions must be unpublished. Guidelines available by e-mail. No late or electronic submissions accepted. Deadline: Mid-late February. **Contact:** Rhonda Agnew. No late or electronic submissions accepted. Welcome in their respective years are unpublished fiction, drama, poetry or essays on literary studies. Prose or drama entries should be limited to no more than 20 pages double-spaced. Poetry entries should consist of 4-10 poems (20 pp. limit). Subjects must concern women. Submissions are open to all interested writers and scholars. An award for poetry will be awarded in 2013, and an award for essays in 2014. Submissions should be anonymous with the author's name and address on a separate title page. There should be two copies of each entry clearly typed on one side of 8 1/2 x 11" paper, double-spaced, and proofread carefully. The award is an annual prize for the best creative or scholarly work on a subject concerning women. Deadline: February 25.

THE PINCH LITERARY AWARD IN FICTION AND POETRY

Fiction/Poetry Contest, The Pinch, Department of English, The University of Memphis, Memphis TN 38152-6176. (901)678-4591. **E-mail:** editor@thepinchjournal.com. **Website:** www.thepinchjournal.com. Offered annually for unpublished short stories of 5,000 words maximum or up to three poems. Guidelines on website. Cost: $20, which is put toward one issue of *The Pinch*. Deadline: March 15. Prize: 1st place Fiction: $1,500 and publication; 1st place Poetry: $1,000 and publication. Offered annually for unpublished short stories of 5,000 words maximum or up to three poems. Guidelines on website. Cost: $20, which is put toward one issue of *The Pinch*. Deadline: March 15. Prize: 1st place Fiction: $1,500 and publication; 1st place Poetry: $1,000 and publication. Offered annually for unpublished short stories of 5,000 words maximum or up to three poems. Guidelines on

website. Deadline: April 5. Prize: Prizes: $1,000 for 1st place in both competitions.

PNWA LITERARY CONTEST

Pacific Northwest Writers Association, PMB 2717-1420 NW Gilman Blvd., Suite 2, Issaquah WA 98027. (425)673-2665. **Fax:** (425)961-0768. **E-mail:** pnwa@pnwa.org. **Website:** www.pnwa.org. **Contact:** Kelli Liddane. **Open to students.** Annual contest. Purpose of contest: "Valuable tool for writers as contest submissions are critiqued (2 critiques)." Unpublished submissions only. Submissions made by author. Deadline: February 18. Prize: 1st: $700; 2nd: $300.

PRAIRIE SCHOONER BOOK PRIZE

Prairie Schooner and the University of Nebraska Press, Prairie Schooner Prize Series, Attn: Fiction, 123 Andrews Hall, Lincoln NE 68588-0334. (402)472-0911. **E-mail:** PSBookPrize@unl.edu. **Website:** prairieschooner.unl.edu. **Contact:** Kwame Dawes, editor. Annual competition/award for story collections. The Prairie Schooner Book Prize Series welcomes manuscripts from all living writers, including non-US citizens, writing in English. Both unpublished and published writers are welcome to submit manuscripts. Writers may enter both contests. Simultaneous submissions are accepted, but we ask that you notify us immediately if your manuscript is accepted for publication somewhere else. No past or present paid employee of Prairie Schooner or the University of Nebraska Press or current faculty or student at the University of Nebraska will be eligible for the prizes. Deadline: March 15. Prize: $3,000 and publication through the University of Nebraska Press.

THE PRESIDIO LA BAHIA AWARD

Sons of the Republic of Texas, 1717 Eighth St., Bay City TX 77414-5033. (979)245-6644. **Fax:** (979)244-3819. **E-mail:** srttexas@srttexas.org. **Website:** www.srttexas.org. **Contact:** Scott Dunbar, chairman. "Material may be submitted concerning the influence on Texas culture of our Spanish Colonial heritage in laws, customs, language, religion, architecture, art, and other related fields." Offered annually to promote suitable preservation of relics, appropriate dissemination of data, and research into Texas heritage, with particular attention to the Spanish Colonial period. Deadline: September 30. Prize: Prizes: $2,000 available annualy for winning participants; 1st Place: Minimum of $1,200; 2nd and 3rd prizes at the discretion of the judges Judged by members of the Sons of the

Republic of Texas on the Presidio La Bahia Award Committee.

PRESS 53 OPEN AWARDS

Press 53, 411 W. Fourth St., Suite 101A, Winston-Salem NC 27101. **E-mail:** kevin@press53.com. **Website:** www.press53.com. **Contact:** Kevin Morgan Watson, publisher. The Press 53 Open Awards Writing Contest is open to writers anywhere in the world who write in English (excluding Press 53 employees and family members). Previously published pieces are accepted so long as any previous publishing agreements do not prohibit Press 53 from publishing the work in the winning anthology. Deadline: March 31. Prize: 1st Place: Press 53 Open Award, publication, 2 complimentary copies of anthology; 2nd Place: Personalized certificate, complimentary copy of anthology; Honorable Mention: Personalized certificate, complimentary copy of anthology.

PRISM INTERNATIONAL ANNUAL SHORT FICTION, POETRY, AND LITERARY NONFICTION CONTESTS

Prism International, Creative Writing Program, UBC, Buch. E462, 1866 Main Mall, Vancouver BC V6T 1Z1 Canada. **E-mail:** prismwritingcontest@gmail.com. **Website:** www.prismmagazine.ca/contests/. "Offered annually for unpublished work to award the best in contemporary fiction, poetry, drama, translation, and nonfiction. Works of translation are eligible. Guidelines are available on website. Acquires first North American serial rights upon publication, and limited Web rights for pieces selected for website. Open to any writer except students and faculty in the Creative Writing Department at UBC, or people who have taken a creative writing course at UBC within 2 years of the contest deadline." **Costs:** $28 per entry; $7 each additional entry (outside Canada pay US currency); includes subscription. Deadline: January 27 (poetry, short fiction; November 30 (nonfiction). 1st Place: $1,000-2,000; runners-up (3): $200-300 each (depends on contest); winners published. "Our fiction judge this year is Jessica Grant, an award-winning fiction writer, a member of Newfoundland's Burning Rock Collective (members include Michael Winter and Lisa Moore), and the author of *Making Light of Tragedy* and *Come, Thou Tortoise*. This year's poetry judge is Jen Currin, author of three books of poetry: *The Sleep of Four Cites* (Anvil Press, 2005); *Hagiography* (Coach House, 2008); and *The Inquisition*

Yours (Coach House, 2010), which is shortlisted for the 2011 Dorothy Livesay Poetry Prize, the Lambda Literary Award in Poetry, and the Audre Lorde Poetry Award. You may pay entry fees via cheque or online through our store. Download a PDF entry form and guidelines." **Contact:** Andrea Hoff, Contest Manager. "Offered annually for unpublished work to award the best in contemporary fiction, poetry, drama, translation, and nonfiction. Works of translation are eligible. Guidelines are available on website. Acquires first North American serial rights upon publication, and limited Web rights for pieces selected for website. Open to any writer except students and faculty in the Creative Writing Department at UBC, or people who have taken a creative writing course at UBC within 2 years of the contest deadline." Deadline: January 27 (poetry, short fiction); November 30 (nonfiction). Prize: 1st Place: $1,000-2,000; runners-up (3): $200-300 each (depends on contest); winners are published.

RANDOM HOUSE, INC. CREATIVE WRITING COMPETITION

One Scholarship Way, P.O. Box 297, St. Peter MN 56082. (212)782-0316. **Fax:** (212)940-7590. **E-mail:** creativewriting@randomhouse.com. **Website:** www.randomhouse.com/creativewriting. Offered annually for unpublished work to NYC public high school seniors. Three categories: poetry and graphic novel, fiction & drama and personal memoir. Prize: 72 awards given in literary (3) and nonliterary (2) categories. Awards range from $500-10,000. Categories: short stories and poems. Judged by various city officials, executives, authors, editors. No entry fee. Guidelines available in October on website and in publication. **Deadline: February 10.** Entries must be unpublished. Word length: 2,500 words or less. Applicants must be seniors (under age 21) at a New York high school. No college essays or class assignments will be accepted. Results announced mid-May. Winners notified by mail and phone. For contest results, send SASE, fax, e-mail or visit website. **Contact:** Melanie Fallon Hauska, director. Offered annually for unpublished work to NYC public high school seniors. Four categories: poetry, fiction/drama, personal essay and graphic novel. Applicants must be seniors (under age 21) at a New York high school. No college essays or class assignments will be accepted. Deadline: February 10 for all categories. Prize: Awards range from $500-10,000. The program usually awards just under $100,000 in scholarships.

☼ THE RBC BRONWEN WALLACE AWARD FOR EMERGING WRITERS

The Writers' Trust of Canada, 90 Richmond St. East, Suite 200, Toronto, Ontario M5C 1P1 Canada. (416)504-8222. **Fax:** (416)504-9090. **E-mail:** info@writerstrust.com. **Website:** www.writerstrust.com. **Contact:** Amanda Hopkins. Presented annually to "a Canadian writer under the age of 35 who is not yet published in book form. The award, which alternates each year between poetry and short fiction, was established in memory of poet Bronwen Wallace." Deadline: January 31. Prize: $5,000 and $1,000 to 2 finalists.

☼ REGINA BOOK AWARD

Saskatchewan Book Awards, Inc., P.O. Box 20025, Regina SK S4P 4J7 Canada. (306)569-1585. **E-mail:** director@bookawards.sk.ca. **Website:** www.bookawards.sk.ca. Offered annually. "In recognition of the vitality of the literary community in Regina, this award is presented to a Regina author for the best book, judged on the quality of writing." Books from the following categories will be considered: Children's; drama; fiction (short fiction by a single author, novellas, novels); nonfiction (all categories of nonfiction writing except cookbooks, directories, how-to books, or bibliographies of minimal critical content); poetry. Deadline: November 1. Prize: $2,000 (CAD).

SUMMERFIELD G. ROBERTS AWARD

Sons of the Republic of Texas, 1717 Eighth St., Bay City TX 77414-5033. (979)245-6644. **Fax:** (979)244-3819. **E-mail:** srttexas@srttexas.org. **Website:** www.srttexas.org. **Contact:** David Hanover, chairman. The manuscripts must be written or published during the calendar year for which the award is given. No entry may be submitted more than one time. There is no word limit on the material submitted for the award. The manuscripts may be fiction, nonfiction, poems, essays, plays, short stories, novels, or biographies. The competition is open to all writers everywhere; they need not reside in Texas nor must the publishers be in Texas. Judges each year are winners of the award in the last three years. The purpose of this award is to encourage literary effort and research about historical events and personalities during the days of the Republic of Texas,1836-1846, and to stimulate interest in this period. Deadline: January 15. Prize: $2,500.

☼ SASKATCHEWAN BOOK OF THE YEAR AWARD

Saskatchewan Book Awards, Inc., P.O. Box 20025, Regina SK S4P 4J7 Canada. (306)569-1585. **E-mail:** director@bookawards.sk.ca. **Website:** www.bookawards.sk.ca. Offered annually. "This award is presented to a Saskatchewan author for the best book, judged on the quality of writing. Books from the following categories will be considered: children's; drama; fiction (short fiction by a single author, novellas, novels); nonfiction (all categories of nonfiction writing except cookbooks, directories, how-to books, or bibliographies of minimal critical content); poetry. Visit website for more details." Deadline: November 1. Prize: $3,000 (CAD).

☼ SASKATCHEWAN FIRST BOOK AWARD

Saskatchewan Book Awards, Inc., P.O. Box 20025, Regina SK S4P 4J7 Canada. (306)569-1585. **E-mail:** director@bookawards.sk.ca. **Website:** www.bookawards.sk.ca. Offered annually. "This award is presented to a Saskatchewan author for the best first book, judged on the quality of writing." Books from the following categories will be considered: Children's; drama; fiction (short fiction by a single author, novellas, novels); nonfiction (all categories of nonfiction writing except cookbooks, directories, how-to books, or bibliographies of minimal critical content); and poetry. Deadline: November 1. Prize: $2,000 (CAD).

THE SCARS EDITOR'S CHOICE AWARDS

829 Brian Court, Gurnee IL 60031-3155. **E-mail:** editor@scars.tv. **Website:** http://scars.tv. Award "to showcase good writing in an annual book." Categories: short stories, poetry. Entry fee: $19/short story, and $15/poem. Deadline: Revolves for appearing in different upcoming books as winners. Prize: Publication of story/essay and 1 copy of the book. Entries may be unpublished or previously published, "as long as you retain the rights to your work." Open to any writer. For guidelines, visit website. Accepts inquiries by e-mail. "E-mail is always preferred for inquiries and submissions. (If you have access to e-mail, we will request that you e-mail your contest submission, and we will hold it until we receive the reading fee payment for the submission.)" Length: "We appreciate shorter works. Shorter stories, more vivid and more real storylines in writing have a good chance." Results announced at book publication, online. Winners notified by mail when book is printed. For con-

test results, send SASE or e-mail or look at the contest page at website. " Award "to showcase good writing in an annual book." Categories: short stories, poetry. Entry fee: $19/short story, and $15/poem. Deadline: Revolves for appearing in different upcoming books as winners. Prize: Publication of story/essay and 1 copy of the book. Entries may be unpublished or previously published, "as long as you retain the rights to your work." Open to any writer. For guidelines, visit website. Accepts inquiries by e-mail. "E-mail is always preferred for inquiries and submissions. (If you have access to e-mail, we will request that you e-mail your contest submission, and we will hold it until we receive the reading fee payment for the submission.)" Length: "We appreciate shorter works. Shorter stories, more vivid and more real storylines in writing have a good chance." Results announced at book publication, online. Winners notified by mail when book is printed. For contest results, send SASE or e-mail or look at the contest page at website. " **Contact:** Janet Kuypers, editor/publisher (whom all reading fee checks need to be made out to). Award to showcase good writing in an annual book. Categories: short stories, poetry. Entries may be unpublished or previously published, "as long as you retain the rights to your work." Open to any writer. For guidelines, visit website. Accepts inquiries by e-mail. "E-mail is always preferred for inquiries and submissions. (If you have access to e-mail, we will request that you e-mail your contest submission, and we will hold it until we receive the reading fee payment for the submission.)" Length: "We appreciate shorter works. Shorter stories, more vivid and more real storylines in writing have a good chance." Results announced at book publication, online. Winners notified by mail when book is printed. For contest results, send SASE or e-mail or look at the contest page at website. " Deadline: Revolves for appearing in different upcoming books as winners. Prize: Publication of story/essay and 1 copy of the book.

THE MONA SCHREIBER PRIZE FOR HUMOROUS FICTION & NONFICTION

3940 Laurel Canyon Blvd., #566, Studio City CA 91604. **E-mail:** brad.schreiber@att.net. **Website:** www.bradschreiber.com. **Contact:** Brad Schreiber. "The purpose of the contest is to award the most creative humor writing, in any form less than 750 words, in either fiction or nonfiction, including but not limited to stories, articles, essays, speeches, shopping lists, diary entries, and anything else writers dream

up." Deadline: December 1. Prize: 1st Place: $500; 2nd Place: $250; 3rd Place: $100. Judge: Brad Schreiber, author, journalist, consultant, and instructor. Complete rules and previous winning entries on website.

TIPS "No SASE's, please. Non-US entries should enclose US currency or checks written in US dollars. Include email address. No previously published work."

THE BERNICE SLOTE AWARD

Prairie Schooner, 123 Andrews Hall, P.O. Box 880334, Lincoln NE 68588-0334. (402)472-0911. **Fax:** (402)472-1817. **E-mail:** PrairieSchooner@unl. edu. **Website:** www.prairieschooner.unl.edu. **Contact:** Kwame Dawes. Categories: short stories, essays and poetry. Judged by editorial staff of Prairie Schooner. No entry fee. For guidelines, send SASE or visit website. "Only work published in the journal during the previous year will be considered." Work is nominated by the editorial staff. Offered annually for the best work by a beginning writer published in Prairie Schooner in the previous year. Celebrates the best and finest writing that they have published for the year. Prize: $500.

KAY SNOW WRITING CONTEST

Willamette Writers, Willamette Writers, 2108 Buck St., West Linn OR 97068. (503)305-6729. **Fax:** (503)344-6174. **E-mail:** wilwrite@willamettewriters. com. **Website:** www.willamettewriters.com. **Contact:** Lizzy Shannon, contest director. "Willamette Writers is the largest writers' organization in Oregon and one of the largest writers' organizations in the United States. It is a non-profit, tax-exempt Oregon corporation led by volunteers. Elected officials and directors administer an active program of monthly meetings, special seminars, workshops and annual writing conference. Continuing with established programs and starting new ones is only made possible by strong volunteer support." See website for specific details and rules. There are six different categories writers can enter: Adult Fiction, Adult Non-Fiction, Poetry, Juvenile Short Story, Screenwriting and Student Writer. "The purpose of this annual writing contest, named in honor of Willamette Writer's founder, Kay Snow, is to help writers reach professional goals in writing in a broad array of categories and to encourage student writers." Deadline: April 23. Prize: One first prize of $300, one second place prize of $150, and a third place prize of $50 per winning entry in each of the six categories.

SOUL MAKING KEATS LITERARY COMPETITION

The Webhallow House, 1544 Sweetwood Dr., Broadmoor Vlg CA 94015-2029. **E-mail:** SoulKeats@mail. com. **Website:** www.soulmakingcontest.us. Annual open contest offers cash prizes in each of 13 literary categories, including poetry and prose poem. **Contact:** Eileen Malone, Award Director. Competition receives 600 entries/year. Names of winners and judges are posted on website. Winners announced in January by SASE and on website. Winners are invited to read at the Koret Auditorium, San Francisco. Event is televised. Submissions in some categories may be previously published. No names or other identifying information on mss; include 3x5 card with poet's name, address, phone, fax, e-mail, title(s) of work, and category entered. Include SASE for results only; mss will not be returned. Guidelines available on website. Deadline: November 30. Prize: Prizes: 1st Prize: $100; 2nd Prize: $50; 3rd Prize: $25.

WILLA LITERARY AWARD

Women Writing the West, 8547 East Arapaho Rd., #J-541, Greenwood Village CO 80112-1436. **E-mail:** pamtartaglio@yahoo.com. **Website:** www.womenwritingthewest.org. **Contact:** Pam Tartaglio. The WILLA Literary Award honors the best in literature featuring women's or girls' stories set in the West published each year. Women Writing the West (WWW), a nonprofit association of writers and other professionals writing and promoting the Women's West, underwrites and presents the nationally recognized award annually (for work published between January 1 and December 31). The award is named in honor of Pulitzer Prize winner Willa Cather, one of the country's foremost novelists. The award is given in 7 categories: Historical fiction, contemporary fiction, original softcover fiction, creative nonfiction, scholarly nonfiction, poetry, and children's/young adult fiction/nonfiction. Deadline: February 1. Prize: Winner receives $100 and a trophy. Finalist receives a plaque. Award announcement is in early August, and awards are presented to the winners and finalists at the annual WWW Fall Conference. Judged by professional librarians not affiliated with WWW.

WRITER'S DIGEST WRITING COMPETITION

Writer's Digest, 700 E. State St., Iola WI 54990. (715)445-4612, ext. 13430. **E-mail:** WritersDigestWritingCompetition@fwmedia.com. **Website:** www.writersdigest.com. Contest open to all writers. Categories include: Inspirational, Memoirs/Personal Essay, Magazine Feature Article, Genre Short Story, Mainstream/Literary Short Story, Rhyming Poetry, Non-rhyming Poetry, Stage Play, Television/Movie Script, Children's/Young Adult Fiction. Deadline: June 3; Early bird deadline: May 6. Grand Prize: $3,000, consultation with multiple editors, trip to NYC for Writer's Digest Conference, and more; 1st Place: $1,000, 2nd Place: $500, 3rd Place: $250; and more prizes for 4th-10th places.

WRITER'S DIGEST INTERNATIONAL SELF-PUBLISHED BOOK AWARDS

Writer's Digest, 700 E. State St., Iola WI 54990. (715)445-4612, ext. 13430. **E-mail:** WritersDigestWritingCompetition@fwmedia.com. **Website:** www.writersdigest.com. **Contact:** Nicole Florence. Contest open to all English-language self-published books for which the authors have paid the full cost of publication, or the cost of printing has been paid for by a grant or as part of a prize. Categories include: Mainstream/Literary Fiction, Genre Fiction, Nonfiction, Inspirational (spiritual/new age), Life Stories (biographies/autobiographies/family histories/memoirs), Children's Books, Reference Books (directories/encyclopedias/guide books), Poetry, Middle-Grade/Young Adult Books. Deadline: May 1; Early bird deadline: April 1. Prize: Grand Prize: $3,000, promotion in *Writer's Digest* and *Publisher's Weekly,* and 10 copies of the book will be sent to major review houses with a guaranteed review in *Midwest Book Review*; 1st Place (9 winners): $1,000, promotion in *Writer's Digest*; Honorable Mentions: promotion in *Writer's Digest*, $50 of Writer's Digest Books, and a certificate.

THE YOUTH HONOR AWARD PROGRAM

Skipping Stones Magazine, P.O. Box 3939, Eugene OR 97403. (541)342-4956. **E-mail:** info@skippingstones.org. **E-mail:** editor@skippingstones.org. **Website:** www.skippingstones.org. **Contact:** Arun N. Toke, Editor and Publisher. "Original writing and art from youth, ages 7 to 17, should be typed or neatly handwritten. The entries should be appropriate for ages 7 to 17. Prose under 1,000 words; poems under 30 lines. Non-English and bilingual writings are welcome." To promote multicultural, international and nature awareness. Deadline: June 25. Prize: An Honor Award Certificate, a subscription to Skipping Stones and five nature and/or multicultural books. They are also invited to join the Student Review Board.

PROFESSIONAL ORGANIZATIONS

AGENTS' ORGANIZATIONS

ASSOCIATION OF AUTHORS' AGENTS (AAA), 5-8 Lower John Street, Golden Square, London W1F 9HA . E-mail: anthonygoff@davidhigham.co.uk. Website: www.agentsassoc.co.uk.

ASSOCIATION OF AUTHORS' REPRESENTATIVES (AAR). E-mail: info@aar-online.org. Website: www.aar-online.org.

ASSOCIATION OF TALENT AGENTS (ATA), 9255 Sunset Blvd., Suite 930, Los Angeles CA 90069. (310)274-0628. E-mail: shellie@agentassociation.com. Website: www.agentassociation.com.

WRITERS' ORGANIZATIONS

ACADEMY OF AMERICAN POETS 584 Broadway, Suite 604, New York NY 10012-5243. (212)274-0343. Fax: (212)274-9427. E-mail: academy@poets.org. Website: www.poets.org.

AMERICAN CRIME WRITERS LEAGUE (ACWL), 17367 Hilltop Ridge Dr., Eureka MO 63205. Website: www.acwl.org.

AMERICAN INDEPENDENT WRITERS (AIW), 1001 Connecticut Ave. NW, Suite 701, Washington DC 20036. E-mail: info@aiwriters.org. Website: www.americanindependentwriters.org.

AMERICAN MEDICAL WRITERS ASSOCIATION (AMWA), 30 West Gude Drive, Suite 525, Rockville MD 20850-4347. (301)294-5303. Fax: (301)294-9006. E-mail: amwa@amwa.org. Website: www.amwa.org.

AMERICAN SCREENWRITERS ASSOCIATION (ASA), 269 S. Beverly Dr., Suite 2600, Beverly Hills CA 90212-3807. (866)265-9091. E-mail: asa@goasa.com. Website: www.asascreenwriters.com.

AMERICAN TRANSLATORS ASSOCIATION (ATA), 225 Reinekers Lane, Suite 590, Alexandria VA 22314. (703)683-6100. Fax: (703)683-6122. E-mail: ata@atanet.org. Website: www.atanet.org.

EDUCATION WRITERS ASSOCIATION (EWA), 2122 P St., NW Suite 201, Washington DC 20037. (202)452-9830. Fax: (202)452-9837. E-mail: ewa@ewa.org. Website: www.ewa.org.

HORROR WRITERS ASSOCIATION (HWA), 244 5th Ave., Suite 2767, New York NY 10001. E-mail: hwa@horror.org. Website: www.horror.org.

THE INTERNATIONAL WOMEN'S WRITING GUILD (IWWG),P.O. Box 810, Gracie Station, New York NY 10028-0082. (212)737-7536. Fax: (212)737-9469. E-mail: dirhahn@aol.org. Website: www.iwwg.com.

MYSTERY WRITERS OF AMERICA (MWA), 1140 Broadway, Suite 1507, New York NY 10001. (212)888-8171. Fax: (212)888-8107. E-mail: mwa@mysterywriters.org. Website: www.mysterywriters.org.

NATIONAL ASSOCIATION OF SCIENCE WRITERS (NASW), P.O. Box 7905, Berkeley, CA 94707. (510)647-9500. E-mail: LFriedmann@nasw.org. website: www.nasw.org.

NATIONAL ASSOCIATION OF WOMEN WRITERS (NAWW), 24165 IH-10 W., Suite 217-637, San Antonio TX 78257. Phone/Fax: (866)821-5829. Website: www.naww.org.

ORGANIZATION OF BLACK SCREENWRITERS (OBS). Golden State Mutual Life Insurance Bldg., 1999 West Adams Blvd., Rm. Mezzanine Los Angeles, CA 90018. Website: www.obswriter.com.

OUTDOOR WRITERS ASSOCIATION OF AMERICA (OWAA), 121 Hickory St., Suite 1, Missoula MT 59801. (406)728-7434. E-mail: krhoades@owaa.org. Website: www.owaa.org.

POETRY SOCIETY OF AMERICA (PSA), 15 Gramercy Park, New York NY 10003. (212)254-9628. website: www.poetrysociety.org. Poets & Writers, 90 Broad St., Suite 2100, New York NY 10004. (212)226-3586. Fax: (212)226-3963. Website: www.pw.org.

ROMANCE WRITERS OF AMERICA (RWA), 114615 Benfer Road, Houston TX 77069. (832)717-5200. Fax: (832)717-5201. E-mail: info@rwanational.org. Website: www.rwanational.org.

SCIENCE FICTION AND FANTASY WRITERS OF AMERICA (SFWA), P.O. Box 877, Chestertown MD 21620. E-mail: execdir@sfwa.org. Website: www.sfwa.org.

SOCIETY OF AMERICAN BUSINESS EDITORS & WRITERS (SABEW), University of Missouri, School of Journalism, 30 Neff Annex, Columbia MO 65211. (602) 496-7862. E-mail: sabew@sabew. org. Website: www.sabew.org.

SOCIETY OF AMERICAN TRAVEL WRITERS (SATW), 7044 S. 13 St., Oak Creek WI 53154. (414)908-4949. Fax: (414)768-8001. E-mail: satw@satw.org. Website: www.satw.org.

SOCIETY OF CHILDREN'S BOOK WRITERS & ILLUSTRATORS (SCBWI), 8271 Beverly Blvd., Los Angeles CA 90048. (323)782-1010. E-mail: scbwi@scbwi.org. Website: www.scbwi.org.

WESTERN WRITERS OF AMERICA (WWA). E-mail: spiritfire@kc.rr.com. Website: www.westernwriters.org.

INDUSTRY ORGANIZATIONS

AMERICAN BOOKSELLERS ASSOCIATION (ABA), 200 White Plains Rd., Suite 600, Tarrytown NY 10591. (914)591-2665. E-mail: info@bookweb.org. Website: www.bookweb.org.

AMERICAN SOCIETY OF JOURNALISTS & AUTHORS (ASJA), 1501 Broadway, Suite 302, New York NY 10036. (212)997-0947. E-mail: director@asja.org. Website: www.asja.org.

ASSOCIATION FOR WOMEN IN COMMUNICATIONS (AWC), 3337 Duke St., Alexandria VA 22314. (703)370-7436. E-mail: info@womcom.org. Website: www.womcom.org.

ASSOCIATION OF AMERICAN PUBLISHERS (AAP), 71 5th Ave., 2nd Floor, New York NY 10003. Or, 50 F St. NW, Suite 400, Washington DC 20001. Website: www.publishers.org.

THE ASSOCIATION OF WRITERS & WRITING PROGRAMS (AWP), Mail Stop 1E3, George Mason University, Fairfax VA 22030. (703)993-4301. Fax: (703)993-4302. E-mail: services@awpwriter. org. website: www.awpwriter.org.

THE AUTHORS GUILD, INC., 31 E. 32nd St., 7th Floor, New York NY 10016. (212)563-5904. Fax: (212)564-5363. E-mail: staff@authorsguild.org. website: www.authorsguild.org.

CANADIAN AUTHORS ASSOCIATION (CAA), P.O. Box 581, Stn. Main Orilla ON L3V 6K5 Canada. (705)653-0323. E-mail: admin@canauthors.org. Website: www.canauthors.org.

CHRISTIAN BOOKSELLERS ASSOCIATION (CBA), P.O. Box 62000, Colorado Springs CO 80962-2000. (800)252-1950. Fax: (719)272-3510. E-mail: info@cbaonline.org. website: www.cbaonline.org.

THE DRAMATISTS GUILD OF AMERICA, 1501 Broadway, Suite 701, New York NY 10036. (212)398-9366. Fax: (212)944-0420. Website: www.dramatistsguild.com.

NATIONAL LEAGUE OF AMERICAN PEN WOMEN (NLAPW), 1300 17th St. NW, Washington DC 20036-1973. (202)785-1997. E-mail: nlapw1@verizon.net. Website: www.americanpen-women.org.

NATIONAL WRITERS ASSOCIATION (NWA), 10940 S. Parker Rd., #508, Parker CO 80134. (303)841-0246. Fax: (303)841-2607. E-mail: natlwritersassn@hotmail.com. Website: www. nationalwriters.com

NATIONAL WRITERS UNION (NWU), 256 West 38th Street, Suite 703, New York, NY 10018. (212)254-0279. Fax: (212)254-0673. E-mail: nwu@nwu.org. Website: www.nwu.org.

PEN AMERICAN CENTER, 588 Broadway, Suite 303, New York NY 10012-3225. (212)334-1660. Fax: (212)334-2181. E-mail: pen@pen.org. Website: www.pen.org.

THE PLAYWRIGHTS GUILD OF CANADA (PGC), 215 Spadina Ave., Suite #210, Toronto ON M5T 2C7 Canada. (416)703-0201. Fax: (416)703-0059. E-mail: info@playwrightsguild.ca. Website: www.playwrightsguild.com.

VOLUNTEER LAWYERS FOR THE ARTS (VLA), One E. 53rd St., 6th Floor, New York NY 10022. (212)319-2787. Fax: (212)752-6575. Website: www.vlany.org.

WOMEN IN FILM (WIF), 6100 Wilshire Blvd., Suite 710, Los Angeles CA 90048. (323)935-2211. Fax: (323)935-2212. E-mail: info@wif.org. Website: www.wif.org.

WOMEN'S NATIONAL BOOK ASSOCIATION (WNBA), P.O. Box 237, FDR Station, New York NY 10150. (212)208-4629. Fax: (212)208-4629. E-mail: publicity@bookbuzz.com. Website: www. wnba-books.org.

WRITERS GUILD OF ALBERTA (WGA), 11759 Groat Rd., Edmonton AB T5M 3K6 Canada. (780)422-8174. Fax: (780)422-2663. E-mail: mail@writersguild.ab.ca. Website: writersguild.ab.ca.

WRITERS GUILD OF AMERICA-EAST (WGA), 555 W. 57th St., Suite 1230, New York NY 10019. (212)767-7800. Fax: (212)582-1909. e-mail: info@wgaeast.org. Website: www.wgaeast.org.

WRITERS GUILD OF AMERICA-WEST (WGA), 7000 W. Third St., Los Angeles CA 90048. (323)951-4000. Fax: (323)782-4800. Website: www.wga.org.

WRITERS UNION OF CANADA (TWUC), 90 Richmond St. E., Suite 200, Toronto ON M5C 1P1 Canada. (416)703-8982. E-mail: info@writersunion.ca. Website: www.writersunion.ca.

GLOSSARY

#10 ENVELOPE. A standard, business-size envelope.

ADVANCE. A sum of money a publisher pays a writer prior to the publication of a book. It is usually paid in installments, such as one-half on signing contract; one-half on delivery of complete and satisfactory manuscript.

AGENT. A liaison between a writer and editor or publisher. An agent shops a manuscript around, receiving a commission when the manuscript is accepted. Agents usually take a 10-15% fee from the advance and royalties.

ARC. Advance reader copy.

ASSIGNMENT. Editor asks a writer to produce a specific article for an agreed-upon fee.

AUCTION. Publishers sometimes bid for the acquisition of a book manuscript that has excellent sales prospects. The bids are for the amount of the author's advance, adver-

tising and promotional expenses, royalty percentage, etc. Auctions are conducted by agents.

AVANT-GARDE. Writing that is innovative in form, style, or subject.

BACKLIST. A publisher's list of its books that were not published during the current season, but that are still in print.

BIMONTHLY. Every two months.

BIO. A sentence or brief paragraph about the writer; can include education and work experience.

BIWEEKLY. Every two weeks.

BLOG. Short for weblog. Used by writers to build platform by posting regular commentary, observations, poems, tips, etc.

BLURB. The copy on paperback book covers or hard cover book dust jackets, either promoting the book and the author or featuring testimonials from book reviewers or well-known people in the book's field. Also called flap copy or jacket copy.

BOILERPLATE. A standardized contract.

BOUND GALLEYS. Prepublication edition of book, usually photocopies of final galley proofs; also known as "bound proofs."

BYLINE. Name of the author appearing with the published piece.

CATEGORY FICTION. A term used to include all types of fiction.

CHAPBOOK. A small booklet usually paperback of poetry, ballads or tales.

CIRCULATION. The number of subscribers to a magazine.

CLIPS. Samples, usually from newspapers or magazines, of a writer's published work.

COFFEE-TABLE BOOK. An heavily illustrated oversize book.

COMMERCIAL NOVELS. Novels designed to appeal to a broad audience. These are often broken down into categories such as western, mystery and romance. See also genre.

CONTRIBUTOR'S COPIES. Copies of the issues of magazines sent to the author in which the author's work appears.

CO-PUBLISHING. Arrangement where author and publisher share publications costs and profits of a book. Also known as cooperative publishing.

COPYEDITING. Editing a manuscript for grammar, punctuation, printing style and factual accuracy.

COPYRIGHT. A means to protect an author's work.

COVER LETTER. A brief letter that accompanies the manuscript being sent to and agent or editor.

CREATIVE NONFICTION. Nonfictional writing that uses an innovative approach to the subject and creative language.

CRITIQUING SERVICE. Am editing service in which writers pay a fee for comments on the salability or other qualities of their manuscript. Fees vary, as do the quality of the critiques.

CV. Curriculum vita. A brief listing of qualifications and career accomplishments.

ELECTRONIC RIGHTS. Secondary or subsidiary rights dealing with electronic/multimedia formats (i.e., the Internet, CD-ROMs, electronic magazines).

ELECTRONIC SUBMISSION. A submission made by modem or on computer disk.

EROTICA. Fiction that is sexually oriented.

EVALUATION FEES. Fees an agent may charge to evaluate material. The extent and quality of this evaluation varies, but comments usually concern salability of the manuscript.

FAIR USE. A provision of the copyright law that says short passages from copyrighted material may be used without infringing on the owner's rights.

FEATURE. An article giving the reader information of human interest rather than news.

FILLER. A short item used by an editor to "fill" out a newspaper column or magazine page. It could be a joke, an anecdote, etc.

FILM RIGHTS. Rights sold or optioned by the agent/author to a person in the film industry, enabling the book to be made into a movie.

FOREIGN RIGHTS. Translation or reprint rights to be sold abroad.

FRONTLIST. A publisher's list of books that are new to the current season.

GALLEYS. First typeset version of manuscript that has not yet been divided into pages.

GENRE. Refers either to a general classification of writing, such as the novel or the poem, or to the categories within those classifications, such as the problem novel or the sonnet.

GHOSTWRITER. Writer who puts into literary form article, speech, story or book based on another person's ideas or knowledge.

GRAPHIC NOVEL. A story in graphic form, long comic strip, or heavily illustrated story; of 40 pages or more.

HI-LO. A type of fiction that offers a high level of interest for readers at a low reading level.

HIGH CONCEPT. A story idea easily expressed in a quick, one-line description.

HONORARIUM. Token payment.

HOOK. Aspect of the work that sets it apart from others and draws in the reader/viewer.

HOW-TO. Books and magazine articles offering a combination of information and advice in describing how something can be accomplished.

IMPRINT. Name applied to a publisher's specific line of books.

JOINT CONTRACT. A legal agreement between a publisher and two or more authors, establishing provisions for the division of royalties the book generates.

KILL FEE. Fee for a complete article that was assigned and then cancelled.

LEAD TIME. The time between the acquisition of a manuscript by an editor and its actual publication.

LITERARY FICTION. The general category of serious, non-formulaic, intelligent fiction.

MAINSTREAM FICTION. Fiction that transcends popular novel categories such as mystery, romance and science fiction.

MARKETING FEE. Fee charged by some agents to cover marketing expenses. It may be used to cover postage, telephone calls, faxes, photocopying or any other expense incurred in marketing a manuscript.

MASS MARKET. Non-specialized books of wide appeal directed toward a large audience.

MEMOIR. A narrative recounting a writer's (or fictional narrator's) personal or family history; specifics may be altered, though essentially considered nonfiction.

MIDDLE GRADE OR MID-GRADE. The general classification of books written for readers approximately ages 9-11. Also called middle readers.

MIDLIST. Those titles on a publisher's list that are not expected to be big sellers, but are expected to have limited/modest sales.

MODEL RELEASE. A paper signed by the subject of a photograph giving the photographer permission to use the photograph.

MULTIPLE CONTRACT. Book contract with an agreement for a future book(s).

MULTIPLE SUBMISSIONS. Sending more than one book or article idea to a publisher at the same time.

NARRATIVE NONFICTION. A narrative presentation of actual events.

NET ROYALTY. A royalty payment based on the amount of money a book publisher receives on the sale of a book after booksellers' discounts, special sales discounts and returns.

NOVELLA. A short novel, or a long short story; approximately 7,000 to 15,000 words.

ON SPEC. An editor expresses an interest in a proposed article idea and agrees to consider the finished piece for publication "on speculation." The editor is under no obligation to buy the finished manuscript.

ONE-TIME RIGHTS. Rights allowing a manuscript to be published one time. The work can be sold again by the writer without violating the contract.

OPTION CLAUSE. A contract clause giving a publisher the right to publish an author's next book.

PAYMENT ON ACCEPTANCE. The editor sends you a check for your article, story or poem as soon as he decides to publish it.

PAYMENT ON PUBLICATION. The editor doesn't send you a check for your material until it is published.

PEN NAME. The use of a name other than your legal name on articles, stories or books. Also called a pseudonym.

PHOTO FEATURE. Feature in which the emphasis is on the photographs rather than on accompanying written material

PICTURE BOOK. A type of book aimed at preschoolers to 8-year-olds that tells a story using a combination of text and artwork, or artwork only.

PLATFORM. A writer's speaking experience, interview skills, website and other abilities which help form a following of potential buyers for that author's book.

POD. Print on demand.

PROOFREADING. Close reading and correction of a manuscript's typographical errors.

PROPOSAL. A summary of a proposed book submitted to a publisher, particularly used for nonfiction manuscripts. A proposal often contains an individualized cover letter, one-page overview of the book, marketing information, competitive books, author information, chapter-by-chapter outline, and two to three sample chapters.

QUERY. A letter that sells an idea to an editor or agent. Usually a query is brief (no more than one page) and uses attention-getting prose.

REMAINDERS. Copies of a book that are slow to sell and can be purchased from the publisher at a reduced price.

REPORTING TIME. The time it takes for an editor to report to the author on his/her query or manuscript.

REPRINT RIGHTS. The rights to republish a book after its initial printing.

ROYALTIES, STANDARD HARDCOVER BOOK. 10 percent of the retail price on the first 5,000 copies sold; 121/2 percent on the next 5,000; 15 percent thereafter.

ROYALTIES, STANDARD MASS PAPERBACK BOOK. 4-8 percent of the retail price on the first 150,000 copies sold.

ROYALTIES, STANDARD TRADE PAPERBACK BOOK. No less than 6 percent of list price on the first 20,000 copies; 7½ percent thereafter.

SASE. Self-addressed, stamped envelope; should be included with all correspondence.

SELF-PUBLISHING. In this arrangement the author pays for manufacturing, production and marketing of his book and keeps all income derived from the book sales.

SEMIMONTHLY. Twice per month.

SEMIWEEKLY. Twice per week.

SERIAL. Published periodically, such as a newspaper or magazine.

SERIAL FICTION. Fiction published in a magazine in installments, often broken off at a suspenseful spot.

SERIAL RIGHTS. The right for a newspaper or magazine to publish sections of a manuscript.

SHORT-SHORT. A complete short story of 1,500 words.

SIDEBAR. A feature presented as a companion to a straight news report (or main magazine article) giving sidelights on human-interest aspects or sometimes elucidating just one aspect of the story.

SIMULTANEOUS SUBMISSIONS. Sending the same article, story or poem to several publishers at the same time. Some publishers refuse to consider such submissions.

SLANT. The approach or style of a story or article that will appeal to readers of a specific magazine.

SLICE-OF-LIFE VIGNETTE. A short fiction piece intended to realistically depict an interesting moment of everyday living.

SLUSH PILE. The stack of unsolicited or misdirected manuscripts received by an editor or book publisher.

SOCIAL NETWORKS. Websites that connect users: sometimes generally, other times around specific interests. Four popular ones at the moment are MySpace, Facebook, Twitter and LinkedIn.

SUBAGENT. An agent handling certain subsidiary rights, usually working in conjuction with the agent who handled the book rights. The percentage paid the book agent is increased to pay the subagent.

SUBSIDIARY RIGHTS. All right other than book publishing rights included in a book publishing contract, such as paperback rights, book club rights and movie rights. Part of an agent's job is to negotiate those rights and advise you on which to sell and which to keep.

SUBSIDY PUBLISHER. A book publisher who charges the author for the cost to typeset and print his book, the jacket, etc., as opposed to a royalty publisher who pays the author.

SYNOPSIS. A brief summary of a story, novel or play. As part of a book proposal, it is a comprehensive summary condensed in a page or page and a half, single-spaced.

TABLOID. Newspaper format publication on about half the size of the regular newspaper page.

TEARSHEET. Page from a magazine or newspaper containing your printed story, article, poem or ad.

TOC. Table of Contents.

TRADE BOOK. Either a hardcover or softcover book; subject matter frequently concerns a special interest for a general audience; sold mainly in bookstores.

TRADE PAPERBACK. A soft-bound volume published and designed for the general public; available mainly in bookstores.

TRANSLATION RIGHTS. Sold to a foreign agent or foreign publisher.

UNSOLICITED MANUSCRIPT. A story, article, poem or book that an editor did not specifically ask to see.

YA. Young adult books

INDEX